GAINSBO[ ]
Stallio[ ]

CU00704229

IN *ENGLAND*

CADEAUX GENEREUX
£20,000 October 1st SLF

GREEN DESERT
£40,000 October 1st SLF

ROYAL APPLAUSE
£6,500 October 1st

ZILZAL
£10,000 October 1st SLF

IN *IRELAND*

GERMANY
IR£1,000 October 1st

KEY OF LUCK
IR£3,500 October 1st

RUSSIAN REVIVAL
IR£3,000 October 1st

IN *CANADA*

ASCOT KNIGHT
$6,500 (Canadian) Live Foal

IN *USA*
at Gainsborough Farm

ELUSIVE QUALITY
$10,000 October 1st Live Foal

LABEEB
$7,500 October 1st Live Foal

QUIET AMERICAN
$35,000 October 1st Live Foal

SHADEED
$5,000 October 1st Live Foal

TORRENTIAL
$10,000 October 1st Live Foal

at Three Chimneys Farm

RAHY
$40,000 September 1st Live Foal

IN *SOUTH AFRICA*

BAROON
BRAASHEE
DESERT TEAM
IKTAMAL
RAMBO DANCER

Enquiries to: M.H. Goodbody,
Gainsborough Stud, Woolton Hill, Newbury, RG20 9TE.
Telephone: (01635) 253273. Fax: (01635) 254690.
Website: www.gainsborough-stud.com

or Allen Kershaw, **Gainsborough Farm,**
7200, Steele Road, Versailles, Kentucky 40383, USA.
Telephone: (606) 873 8918. Fax: (606) 873 2462.
Website: www.gainsboroughfarm.com

AGE, WEIGHT & DISTANCE TABLE
Timeform's scale of weight-for-age for the flat

Dist	Age	Jan 1-16	17-31	Feb 1-16	17-28	Mar 1-16	17-31	Apr 1-16	17-30	May 1-16	17-31	June 1-16	17-30
5f	4	10-0	10-0	10-0	10-0	10-0	10-0	10-0	10-0	10-0	10-0	10-0	10-0
	3	9—5	9—5	9—6	9—7	9—7	9—8	9—8	9—9	9—9	9-10	9-10	9-11
	2						8—0	8—1	8—3	8—4	8—5	8—6	8—7
6f	4	10-0	10-0	10-0	10-0	10-0	10-0	10-0	10-0	10-0	10-0	10-0	10-0
	3	9—2	9—3	9—4	9—5	9—5	9—6	9—7	9—7	9—8	9—8	9—9	9—9
	2									8—0	8—2	8—3	8—4
7f	4	9-13	9-13	10-0	10-0	10-0	10-0	10-0	10-0	10-0	10-0	10-0	10-0
	3	9—0	9—1	9—2	9—3	9—4	9—4	9—5	9—6	9—6	9—7	9—8	9—8
	2											7-13	8—1
1m	4	9-13	9-13	9-13	9-13	10-0	10-0	10-0	10-0	10-0	10-0	10-0	10-0
	3	8-12	8-13	9—0	9—1	9—2	9—2	9—3	9—4	9—5	9—5	9—6	9—7
	2												
9f	4	9-12	9-12	9-12	9-13	9-13	9-13	9-13	10-0	10-0	10-0	10-0	10-0
	3	8-10	8-11	8-12	8-13	9—0	9—1	9—2	9—2	9—3	9—4	9—5	9—5
	2												
1¼m	4	9-11	9-12	9-12	9-12	9-13	9-13	9-13	9-13	9-13	10-0	10-0	10-0
	3	8—8	8—9	8-10	8-11	8-12	8-13	9—0	9—1	9—2	9—2	9—3	9—4
	2												
11f	4	9-10	9-11	9-11	9-12	9-12	9-12	9-13	9-13	9-13	9-13	9-13	10-0
	3	8—6	8—7	8—8	8—9	8-10	8-11	8-12	8-13	9—0	9—1	9—2	9—2
1½m	4	9-10	9-10	9-10	9-11	9-11	9-12	9-12	9-12	9-13	9-13	9-13	9-13
	3	8—4	8—5	8—6	8—7	8—8	8—9	8-10	8-11	8-12	8-13	9—0	9—1
13f	4	9—9	9—9	9-10	9-10	9-11	9-11	9-11	9-12	9-12	9-12	9-13	9-13
	3	8—2	8—3	8—4	8—5	8—7	8—8	8—9	8-10	8-11	8-12	8-13	9—0
1¾m	4	9—8	9—8	9—9	9—9	9-10	9-10	9-11	9-11	9-12	9-12	9-12	9-13
	3	8—0	8—2	8—3	8—4	8—5	8—6	8—7	8—8	8—9	8-10	8-11	8-12
15f	4	9—7	9—8	9—8	9—9	9—9	9-10	9-10	9-11	9-11	9-11	9-12	9-12
	3	7-13	8—0	8—1	8—2	8—4	8—5	8—6	8—7	8—8	8—9	8-10	8-11
2m	4	9—6	9—7	9—7	9—8	9—9	9—9	9-10	9-10	9-11	9-11	9-11	9-12
	3	7-11	7-12	7-13	8—1	8—2	8—3	8—4	8—5	8—6	8—7	8—8	8—9
2¼m	4	9—5	9—5	9—6	9—7	9—7	9—8	9—9	9—9	9-10	9-10	9-10	9-11
	3	7—8	7—9	7-11	7-12	7-13	8—0	8—2	8—3	8—4	8—5	8—6	8—7
2½m	4	9—3	9—4	9—5	9—6	9—6	9—7	9—7	9—8	9—9	9—9	9-10	9-10
	3	7—5	7—7	7—8	7—9	7-11	7-12	7-13	8—1	8—2	8—3	8—4	8—5

For 5-y-o's and older, use 10-0 in all cases
Race distances in the above tables are shown only at 1 furlong intervals.
For races over odd distances, the nearest distance shown in the table should be used:
thus for races of 1m to 1m 109 yards, use the table weights for 1m;
for 1m 110 yards to 1m 219 yards use the 9f table

**The age, weight and distance table covering July to December
appears on the end paper at the back of the book**

RACEHORSES
OF 1999

Price £68.00

A TIMEFORM PUBLICATION

CONTENTS

3	Introduction
13	Timeform Champions
14	The Timeform 'Top Hundred'
16	1999 Statistics
19	Explanatory Notes
22	The Form Summaries and Rating Symbols
23	Racehorses of 1999
1149	Promising Horses
1154	Selected Big Races 1999
1179	Timeform 'Top Horses Abroad'
1202	The 1999 Timeform Irish Handicap
1213	Index to Photographs
1220	Stallion Section

The age, weight and distance tables, for use in applying the ratings in races involving horses of different ages, appear on the end papers at the front and back of the book

Compiled and produced by

G. Greetham (Director), C. S. Williams (Managing Editor & Handicapper), P. Morrell (Editor), S. D. Rowlands (Handicapper & Editor), G. J. North, M. J. Taylor (Handicappers), R. J. C. Austen, J. Early, E. K. Wilkinson (Essays), J. Ingles (Essays & 'Top Horses Abroad'), S. Boow, R. J. O'Brien, J. A. Todd (Short Commentaries), C. J. Curry, G. J. McGibbon (Additional Essays), G. Crowther, M. Hall, D. Holdsworth, G. Johnstone, W. Muncaster, A-M. Stevens, R. Todd, C. Wright (Production)

© **Portway Press Limited 2000**   ISBN 1 901570 17 7

Racehorses of 1999

Introduction

'Advertisements contain the only truths to be relied on in a newspaper.' Thomas Jefferson's view is clearly shared by British Horseracing Board chairman Peter Savill. His address to a press conference in November, following an acrimonious outcome to the first betting levy negotiations for five years, was published in its entirety in a full page advertisement in the *Racing Post*. Savill's abrasive, presidential style of leadership—his hand was perceived to be at work with the BHB advert—has tarnished his image since he emerged, Messiah-like, to replace Lord Wakeham as chairman of the BHB in 1998. The placing of the paid-for advertisement was an unprecedented step and it drove a wedge between the sport's governing authority and the Levy Board, the sport's paymasters, whose three Government-appointed members, including chairman Rob Hughes, were effectively accused of 'stitching up' the BHB by making an agreement with the bookmakers over the levy for 2000 (which is forecast to yield £61m from punters, an increase of £8m on 1999).

*The BHB used an advertisement in the **Racing Post** to attack the Levy Board chairman*

RACING POST ADVERTISEMENT Thursday, November 4, 1999 5

Racing Calls On Hughes To Explain Imposed Levy Settlement

The British Horseracing Board unanimously agreed on 1st November to call on the Chairman of the Levy Board, Robert Hughes, to answer five questions about last week's imposed Levy settlement.

The questions were put by the BHB Chairman, Peter Savill, in a letter to Mr. Hughes and were included in his address to a press conference. The text of that address is reproduced in full below.

THE FIVE QUESTIONS FOR THE LEVY BOARD CHAIRMAN

- What was the figure that the three government-appointed members decided in September could and should be paid by the bookmakers for the Levy?
- Why did the Levy Board Chairman not honour his public promise to advise the parties to the negotiation what that figure was?
- Why did the Levy Board accept a lower figure than the three government-appointed members had agreed should be paid?
- Why did the Levy Board not refer the matter to the Home Secretary if the offer was less than the three government-appointed members believed should be paid?
- Why did the Levy Board Chairman make no attempt to get the betting industry and the racing industry to sit round the negotiating table together to agree the figure that he was looking for?

THE BHB CHAIRMAN'S ADDRESS

THE decision of the three government-appointed members of the Levy Board on Friday to accept an offer from the Bookmakers' Committee which, by their own admission, was less than all three of them would have liked, is, quite simply, unacceptable to Racing.

It is now more than two years since we began work on the Financial Plan. It argued coherently that Racing needed £105 million per year in additional funding and that £80 million per year should come from an increased

grounds that to pass judgement on the Financial Plan could be seen as interfering in the upcoming levy negotiations.

So for the last year we have been laying before the three government-appointed members of the Levy Board the merits of our case. We've gone to great effort and expense to produce in-depth analyses of the impact of prize money on the industry, on the needs of marketing and the problems of the British breeding industry - three areas that account for over 90% of the funding shortfall.

There is an inference in an article in the media this

bookmakers can and should pay for the levy. I'm not in a position, in all honesty, to tell you yet. But mark my words, when we've done that analysis, it will be open for everyone to see it - the bookmakers, Peter Savill, everyone else - and that is the figure we will be proposing". They apparently reached their decision by early September.

I wonder what the figure was ... it will be interesting to find out. Was it indeed £4.7 million plus £1.4 million if turnover goes up by 2% plus £1.9 million for marketing for one year only with strings attached? I doubt if somehow.

prizes should be maybe an extra few thousand a year when we have shown that unless we inject around £10 million a year our breeding industry will suffer a further serious decline.

And what do they think of the betting industry's capacity to pay? Their very own survey confirmed what we have been saying for a long time. That betting industry profits have risen from a claimed £100 million in 1995 to around £350 million in 1998, a rise of almost £250 million since the last Levy deal. So how much of that £250 million do the Levy Board think they should pay to the

three government-appointed members would have liked, it is therefore presumably not as much as they thought the bookmakers should have paid. And if it's not as much as they thought they should have paid, they surely had an obligation to refer it to the Home Secretary with a firm recommendation of what they thought they should pay.

The BHB is also very unhappy with the way in which the imposed settlement was conducted, and I have today written to Mike O'Brien at the Home Office to ask for an urgent meeting to discuss this and other matters pertaining

to get the betting industry and the racing industry to sit round the negotiating table together to agree the figure that he was looking for?

I feel deeply sorry for the racing industry which was depending on the Levy Board Chairman to protect it from abuse of the betting industry's monopoly position and from the flawed process which puts the power in bookmaking hands.

The racing industry, the public and the government are entitled to insist on the transparent, open and

The BHB advertisement strongly criticised the Levy Board chairman's conduct of the levy negotiations, asking five questions revolving round a perceived disparity between a target, supposedly set in September by the Government-appointed trio, of the sum the bookmakers should pay, and the figure at which the levy was eventually fixed. There was criticism that the Levy Board chairman had not honoured a pledge to advise other parties to the negotiations of the figure agreed by the 'three wise men' and that no attempt had been made to get the different parties round the table to try to settle at the figure the Government-appointed members were looking for. Hughes afterwards denied there had ever been such a figure—'we had a range [which he declined to divulge] which might have been appropriate given specific circumstances'—and claimed he had briefed

Peter Savill—there was never a dull moment with the BHB chairman

Savill 'throughout the process.' The three BHB members, he claimed, had been free 'at any stage' to hold independent talks with the chairman of the Bookmakers Committee (also a member of the Levy Board), whose revised recommendations were finally accepted by the 'three wise men' and by the chairman of the Tote, Peter Jones, in a five-three split. The BHB members, incidentally, reportedly never proferred a figure for negotiation, sticking to the BHB's much-criticised Financial Plan—to which a Government response is still awaited after two years—which claims racing needs £80m a year from the bookmakers to put the sport on a firm footing. The BHB members seemed to be angling for arbitration by the Home Secretary and, according to Hughes, 'took no further part' in the negotiating process after condemning the bookmakers' opening offer of a £5.2m increase. 'It is not good enough to walk away from the table,' said Hughes. 'People have to engage in adult and mature negotiations and not just adopt rhetorical stances.'

In the aftermath of the levy settlement Peter Savill took the decision—reportedly involving little consultation with his fellow BHB directors—to resign his seat on the Levy Board. Savill expressed 'serious and growing' concerns about the way the Levy Board operates, his frustration stemming not just from the levy negotiations but also from the Levy Board's role earlier in the year in bringing about a BHB compromise on a plan for seven-day-a-week racing for most of the summer during 2000 (there will still be more than one hundred consecutive days' racing from the end of May to early-September). A rift between the BHB and the Racecourse

Association (which, among other things, opposed the wholesale sacrificing of existing Saturday evening racing) led to the resignation of the Racecourse Association's chairman Angus Crichton-Miller as deputy chairman of the BHB after he went against Savill in the Levy Board vote to reject the BHB's plan.

The BHB's relationship with the racecourses—of which a dozen of the best known formed a 'consortium' to negotiate TV contracts collectively (a ten-year deal, maintaining existing terrestrial coverage, has been struck)—was placed under further strain when Savill campaigned for the levy system, which the Home Secretary subsequently announced is being pensioned off, to be replaced by the sale to bookmakers of rights to the pictures beamed into betting shops and of essential pre-race data. The Racecourse Association has warned the BHB about mounting a challenge to racecourses' media rights. 'Starting again without the levy might not be that easy,' warned Crichton-Miller. 'Whatever scheme is put forward, media rights for audio and pictures from the racecourses will not be part of the game . . . It would be wrong in principle and unrealistic in practice to expect any negotiations on media rights to be regarded as a levy replacement deal.' The top racecourses are involved with plans to set up a digital TV channel to include betting on live action. The battle lines are drawn for a struggle over who takes control of racing's finances when the Levy Board is eventually wound up. The BHB does not look well placed. Copyright of basic pre-race information, such as runners, riders and the draw, for the 1,200 or so fixtures is not acknowledged by everyone but is one of the few items of potential value that the BHB lays claim to.

The BHB also lost the battle over future ownership of the Tote, a key generator of funds for racing which the Government has decided to sell off, either to the private sector or to racing. Peter Savill is a member of the Tote board but Tote chairman Peter Jones was quick to issue a 'hands off' warning. 'The BHB's aim to put racing on a sounder financial footing would not be advanced by placing the Tote directly under BHB control,' he said. 'The Tote is a commercial organisation and the BHB has no experience as a body of running commercial enterprises . . . there would be numerous areas of conflict of interest . . . it would seem inequitable for a body which governs racing, and may shape conditions which affect the operations and profitability of bookmakers, simultaneously to be operating a business which competes with those bookmakers.' Present relations between the BHB and the major bookmakers could hardly be worse. Peter Savill caused a furore at the BHB's annual general meeting by revealing the findings of a report commissioned by the BHB which showed, according to Savill, that only a minority of punters thought bookmakers were honest. It also showed that the vast majority of punters backed the BHB's claim for racing to receive a bigger share of betting turnover at the bookmakers' expense. Savill claimed the survey showed 'how out of touch the betting industry is with its customers and how closely punters' views mirror those of the BHB. The survey's credibility suffered a blow, however, when it was revealed that the organisation which conducted it was a sister company to the BHB's public relations advisors. In a rare display of unity, various racing bodies, including the BHB, eventually put a joint proposal to the Government that ownership of the Tote should be transferred to a racing trust. If this is agreed, however, the Government has made it clear that the transfer will not involve merely a nominal sum. 'The Tote is a public body and it is therefore reasonable that taxpayers should obtain some benefit,' was how a Home Office minister put it to Parliament.

As well as announcing the impending sale of the Tote and the Government's withdrawal from involvement in racing's finances by scrapping the Levy Board, the Home Secretary Jack Straw has also ordered a wide-ranging review of gambling legislation. The review group will look at all forms of gambling (except the National Lottery) with a view to recommending a new structure to replace the range of bodies—including the Gaming Board, local authorities and magistrates' courts—which are involved in its regulation. Racing should be a major beneficiary of any liberalisation of the archaic gambling laws. The bookmakers currently maintain the infrastructure—including 8,500 licensed betting shops—by which the public bets on racing. Sports bars and Australian-type gaming parlours—at present banned—may challenge the bookmakers' monopoly in future, offering greater choice, as well as wider exposure for racing. The review body is also likely to make much-needed recommendations in the area of consumer protection. This is a particular concern given the burgeoning growth in offshore and internet betting; punters should always have clear information about the company with which they are betting. The review group will also look at the taxation of gambling, though the Government may be forced beforehand to review its internationally uncompetitive rate of betting tax.

Victor Chandler—started the offshore betting revolution

Victor Chandler drove a coach and horses through the betting duty provisions when switching credit betting operations in May to the offshore tax haven of Gibraltar (customers pay a 3% 'service charge' compared to the 9% deduction in Britain). Chandler's action, said to have been sparked by the decision of the Irish government to halve its off-course betting tax from 10% to 5%, caused other major bookmakers, including William Hill, Ladbroke, Coral and even the state-sponsored Tote, to take steps to limit the effects of Britain's high tax regime. Telephone betting amounts to about ten per cent of turnover, but there were growing fears that traditional betting shop cash customers might also be tempted away eventually by the lower deductions on offshore telephone betting.

Calls for a cut in the rate of betting duty (currently 6¾%, which produces a deduction of 9% when the levy is included) received short shrift. The Government seemed to be focussing its efforts on a search for ways to stem the loss of revenue caused by offshore betting (this could even involve a bizarre change in the law so that a bet is deemed to be struck where the punter lives rather than where the bookmaker has his base). The Government could, however, learn from the Irish experience. The tax changes which came into effect in Ireland in July evidently increased turnover in that country's 750 betting shops significantly enough (around 20% to 30% was one reported estimate) for informed sources to conclude that the cut in betting duty would prove to be tax revenue neutral within a fairly short time. The Government should, in any case, ask itself how British punters will tolerate being charged betting tax—at a true rate of 33% given that betting money is bet and rebet—when offshore and internet sites all over the world are, or soon will be, offering tax-free betting? The suggestion from William Hill's chief executive John Brown—'I can't sit back and see my business disappearing'—that deductions from punters should be replaced by a special flat-rate 20% tax on bookmakers' gross profits is the most radical solution offered so far. As well as undermining tax-avoidance-driven illegal betting in Britain—estimated by Brown at 'up to £1,000m' a year—such a move would (given current tax laws) encourage an influx of betting into Britain, whose bookmakers are highly respected overseas, rather than driving more of it abroad. Brown's response was a clear indication that the consequences of the revolution in the betting business in 1999 could have even more serious repercussions for Britain's bookmakers than the introduction of the National Lottery in 1994. Offshore and internet betting has, of course, been good news for punters, who also benefited during the year from better margins, mostly at the big meetings, brought about by increased competition between on-course bookmakers, whose ranks were strengthened by newcomers buying pitches under a new system of sale by auction introduced by the Levy Board towards the end of 1998.

If 1999 was a particularly eventful year off the track, it was hardly less eventful on it. Racecourse attendances in Britain topped five million for the first time in many years and racegoers witnessed some performances that rank alongside the very best achieved in the now extensive post-war era. **Daylami**'s spectacular five-length victory in the King George VI and Queen Elizabeth Stakes was a performance right out of the top drawer, and gave owners Godolphin and trainer Saeed bin Suroor their third successive win in Britain's premier middle-distance event. The wider ambitions of Godolphin did not affect their continued supremacy in Britain, where their horses won nine of the twenty-six Group 1 races. Daylami, who also won the Coronation Cup, went on to secure the inaugural Emirates World Series Racing Championship, which comprised nine Group 1 or Grade 1 races across eight countries, the King George being the British leg. Daylami, who contested races on three different continents and in five different countries, won three of the races in the World Series, adding the Irish Champion Stakes and the Breeders' Cup Turf to his success at Ascot. Daylami's victory at Gulfstream in November put the icing on an already substantial cake, setting the seal on a splendid career for Daylami and providing the Godolphin operation with its first success at the Breeders' Cup.

Godolphin will have a base in the States—with thirty or so two-year-olds—in the next season, aimed at making an impact on the American Triple Crown races in 2001. Godolphin's first major US

Frankie Dettori performs his trademark 'flying dismount' after Daylami's King George victory

experience is a subject of the essay on **Adair**. The Kentucky Derby is a major target for 2000 with **Dubai Two Thousand** and **Best of The Bests** among those being lined up for a Godolphin challenge. Apart from **City On A Hill**, the Godolphin two-year-olds made little impact in Britain, but the newly-installed squadron at Evry contained a plentiful supply of lightly-raced, promising types. **Dubai Millennium**—said by Sheikh Mohammed to be 'the best-horse Godolphin has ever had'—headed a very strong team of milers, even without **Intikhab**, which also included **Aljabr** (who started the season targeted at the Kentucky Derby), **Cape Cross**, **Fly To The Stars**, **Island Sands** and **Lend A Hand**. **Diktat**, whose essay examines the concept of the newly-introduced Shergar Cup and also the controversy over watering before the Haydock Sprint Cup, flew the flag for Godolphin in some of the top sprints. **Zahrat Dubai** was among the leading middle-distance fillies, **Mutafaweq** won the St Leger and **Kayf Tara** was again the season's leading older stayer. Kayf Tara met with a set-back before his big autumn target, the Melbourne Cup, in which stand-in **Central Park** went close. **Almutawakel** kept the Dubai World Cup at home for the first time.

Without Daylami, the French-trained three-year-old **Montjeu** would have been a worthy Horse of the Year. He was imperious in the Prix du Jockey Club and the Irish Derby before landing the Prix de l'Arc de Triomphe narrowly from Japanese challenger **El Condor Pasa**, with the rest of the field well beaten. A big bonus is available in the next season, incidentally, to the winner of the Derby, the Prix du Jockey Club and the

Montjeu and El Condor Pasa show their superiority in a vintage Prix de l'Arc de Triomphe

Kentucky Derby if success follows in the Irish Derby (this and other bonuses are discussed in the essay on Teggiano). **Royal Anthem**'s striking eight-length victory in the International at York, achieved in very fast time, put him up in the 'Daylami, Montjeu, El Condor Pasa' category, helping to ensure that 1999 will be regarded by posterity as a vintage year for racing in Europe. It is the first time since 1985 that there have been four horses rated at 135 or above in *Racehorses*. Brilliance of only a slightly lesser order was also on display at Newmarket's July meeting in the form of **Stravinsky** in the July Cup. The Irish-trained colt won in scintillating fashion, before following up in the Nunthorpe at York, and was head and shoulders above the other sprinters of his year in Europe.

Stravinsky's trainer Aidan O'Brien dominated the two-year-old scene to a remarkable extent, though whether Ballydoyle inmate **Fasliyev**, who will not race again, deserved his place at the head of the International Classification is arguable, detailed analysis appearing in his essay, which also offers some of the possible reasons behind O'Brien's dominance. Eight of the top fifteen juveniles were stabled at Ballydoyle, Fasliyev being joined by **Giant's Causeway**, **Rossini**, **Aristotle**, **Bernstein**, **Brahms**, **Lermontov** and **Mull of Kintyre**. How will their careers be viewed at the end of the next season? The Dewhurst winner **Distant Music** was Timeform's highest-rated two-year-old, though he will probably have to progress again if he is to emulate Zafonic and Pennekamp, the most recent Dewhurst winners to go on to Two Thousand Guineas success. One of the season's most refreshing stories concerned another of the top two-year-old colts, Middle Park winner **Primo Valentino**, with whom twelve members of a syndicate experienced the dream of every small owner, achieving a big return for a small outlay. As for the two-year-old fillies, they were not an outstanding collection, French-trained **Morning Pride** heading the Timeform ratings. She will be returning under the Godolphin banner, as will the Clive Brittain-trained Fillies' Mile winner **Teggiano**. Mick Channon, who had the misfortune to lose the 1998 champion two-year-old filly Bint Allayl through a gallops accident before the latest season started, has another leading One Thousand Guineas prospect in **Seazun**, the Cheveley Park winner.

The Aga Khan (pictured with Sendawar) had a memorable year as an owner and breeder

The Aga Khan, who bred Daylami, ended a ten-year drought as an owner in Group 1 races in Britain when **Enzeli**, the first Irish-trained Gold Cup winner for thirty years, and **Sendawar** (St James's Palace Stakes) gave him a double at Royal Ascot. There is more about the achievements that made the Aga Khan the season's top breeder—he also owned and bred the Derby runner-up **Daliapour**—in the essay on Sendawar and under **Daryaba**, who gave him his third successive win in the Prix de Diane. Owner-breeders won both fillies' classics in Britain, Khalid Abdulla taking the One Thousand Guineas with **Wince** and Prince Fahd Salman the Oaks with **Ramruma**, who became only the fourth filly to complete the Oaks/Irish Oaks/Yorkshire Oaks treble. Another home-bred filly **Alborada** won the Champion Stakes for the second year running after being out of the limelight for much of the year; her essay has a point to make about the cramped conditions for racegoers on Champions Day, which was transferred, because of building work, from the Rowley Mile course to the smaller July course, over which Wince and Island Sands also landed their classic victories. Wince and Ramruma were both trained by Henry Cecil and ridden by Kieren Fallon, who shared a third classic victory with **Oath** in the Derby. Oath's sale to Japan continued a trend, regrettable from a British point of view, for Derby winners and other potential sires of middle-distance horses. The physical demands placed on the Derby runners, partly because of the unusual conformation of the Epsom track, featured among worries about the Derby expressed by Andre Fabre, and backed up by Lester Piggott. The essay on Oath investigates the validity of this particular claim. Oath provided Henry Cecil with his twenty-second domestic classic victory, a twentieth-century record. But he couldn't wrest the trainers' championship from Saeed bin Suroor. Richard Hannon, who trained more winners than anyone else (including **Bold Edge** and **Lots of Magic**), finished third in the table. Kieren Fallon, who lost his job as first jockey at Warren Place halfway through the season, went on to complete his third jockeys' championship, chalking up a third consecutive double century, a feat previously achieved only by Fred Archer and Sir Gordon Richards.

Another jockey to reach a notable landmark was Pat Eddery, who completed his twenty-sixth domestic century on the all-weather at Southwell in November to create a new record for a British jockey. Eddery was once first jockey to Peter Walwyn, who announced his retirement from training in the latest season. Among other trainers to sign off were Jack Berry (who hands over to his son Alan), Geoff Lewis and Peter Calver, while Peter Chapple-Hyam (career details in **Bienamado**) went to Hong Kong, to be succeeded at Manton by John Gosden. Sadly, the training ranks were also depleted by the death of Mikie Heaton-Ellis. We also record the passing, at the age of eighty-six, of that grandee of the turf, former senior steward and notable owner-breeder Lord Howard de Walden, who won the Derby with Slip Anchor and the Champion Hurdle with Lanzarote; champion miler Kris and his brother Diesis, two others to carry the famous apricot colours with distinction, have both made names for themselves at stud.

As well as the essays on the season's top pattern-race performers (including all those highlighted in bold in this introduction), a number of extended entries appear on other horses who made their mark with significant or unusual feats. These include the much travelled pair **Fruits of Love**, who helped Mark Johnston to finish second to Saeed bin Suroor

The season's top trainers—Saeed bin Suroor, champion for the third time in four years, and Henry Cecil, who reached his twenty-second domestic classic winner with the triumphs of Wince, Ramruma and Oath

Peter Walwyn and Jack Berry were two notable retirements among the trainers

in the International Racing Bureau's table of prize-money won on foreign soil, and **Running Stag**, winner of two important handicaps in the United States. In all, British-trained horses won 119 races overseas (including ten over jumps) and earned total prize-money of £8,769,132, the bulk of it accounted for by raids on Ireland, France, the USA and Italy. **Russian Revival** recorded the finest handicap performance seen in Britain for many a year in the Tote International at Ascot in August, while horses such as **Diamond White**, **Far Cry**, **Rudi's Pet**, **Sugarfoot** and **Susu** (joint top-rated older female) all made tremendous progress to end the season rubbing shoulders with some of the best. Also subjects of essays are: the Cambridgeshire and Cesarewitch winners **She's Our Mare** and **Top Cees**, both of whom have also made a name for themselves over hurdles; **Astonished**, who won the Portland in a manner rarely seen in a valuable handicap; **Killer Instinct**, whom punters are unlikely to forget in a hurry; and, last but by no means least, one of the season's unsung heroes, the rugged **Noukari** (one of the lesser-known products of the Aga Khan's breeding operation!).

Racehorses of 1999 contains all the usual additional features, including the increasingly important global coverage of the best horses in 'Top Horses Abroad', which reviews the year in Ireland, France, Germany, Italy, the United Arab Emirates, North America, Japan, Hong Kong and Australia/ New Zealand. With the publication of the complete Timeform Irish Handicap for 1999, the Annual now contains definitive Timeform Ratings for around 11,000 horses.

February 2000

HORSE OF THE YEAR
BEST OLDER MALE
BEST MIDDLE-DISTANCE HORSE
RATED AT 138
DAYLAMI

BEST TWO-YEAR-OLD FILLY RATED AT 113p
MORNING PRIDE

BEST TWO-YEAR-OLD COLT RATED AT 121p
DISTANT MUSIC

BEST THREE-YEAR-OLD FILLY RATED AT 123
RAMRUMA

BEST THREE-YEAR-OLD COLT RATED AT 137
MONTJEU

BEST OLDER FEMALES RATED AT 122
ALBORADA
SUSU

BEST SPRINTER RATED AT 133
STRAVINSKY

BEST MILER RATED AT 132
DUBAI MILLENNIUM

BEST STAYER RATED AT 130
KAYF TARA

BEST PERFORMANCE IN A HANDICAP IN BRITAIN
RUSSIAN REVIVAL
ran to 125
when winning Tote International Stakes at Ascot

BEST PERFORMANCE ON ALL-WEATHER IN BRITAIN
SUPREME SOUND
ran to 111
when winning Mitsubishi Shogun Winter Derby at Lingfield

THE TIMEFORM 'TOP HUNDRED'

Here are listed the 'Top 100' two-year-olds, three-year-olds and older horses in the annual.

2 YEAR OLDS

121p	Distant Music
120	Fasliyev
119p	Giant's Causeway
118	Rossini
116	Primo Valentino
115p	Aristotle
115p	Fath
114	Bernstein
114	Brahms
114	City On A Hill
114	Ekraar
113p	Morning Pride
112p	King's Best
112p	Lermontov
112	Mull Of Kintyre
111p	Best of The Bests
111p	Broche
111p	Hightori
111p	Invincible Spirit
111p	Monashee Mountain
111	Auenklang
111	Jokerman
111	Race Leader
110p	Barathea Guest
110p	Ciro
110p	Preseli
110+	Manzor
110	Lord Flasheart
110	Petroselli
110	Seazun
109p	Lady of Chad
109	Royal Kingdom
109	Torgau
109	Warm Heart
109	Zentsov Street
108p	Glad Master
108p	Goldamix
108p	Scarteen Fox
108p	Tough Speed
107p	Anshaam
107p	China Visit
107p	Kier Park
107p	Millenium Moonbeam
107p	Teggiano
107	Umistim
106p	Cape Town
106p	Sakhee
106+	Khasayl
106	Bachir
106	Barrier Reef

106	Halland Park Girl
106	Hoh Dear
106	Sarafan
106	Seven No Trumps
106	Sir Nicholas
105P	Inchlonaig
105p	Ejlaal
105p	Sinndar
105	Trouble Mountain
105	Victory Day
104P	Inkling
104p	Chinatown
104p	Desert Fury
104p	Island Sound
104p	Lahan
104p	Monte Carlo
104	Elaflaak
104	Heathyardsblessing
104	Kingsclere
104	Night Style
104	Port Vila
104	Shining Hour
104	The Tatling
103p	Bach
103p	Clog Dance
103p	Mastermind
103p	River's Curtain
103p	Saintly Speech
103p	Valentino
103p	Zyz
103+	Dramatic Quest
103+	Warrior Queen
103	Compton Bolter
103	French Fellow
103	Littlefeather
103	Rowaasi
103	Watching
103	Winning Venture
102p	Akeed
102p	The Deputy
102+	Amethyst
102	Crimplene
102	Eurolink Raindance
102	Femme Fatale
102	Icicle
102	Journalist
102	Master Fay
102	Total Love
102	Trinculo
102	Whyome

3 YEAR OLDS

137	Montjeu
133	Stravinsky
132	Dubai Millennium
129	Mutafaweq
129	Sendawar
125	Aljabr
125	Bertolini
125	Dansili
125	Oath
123p	Adair
123	Fantastic Light
123	Ramruma
123	Saffron Walden
122	Daliapour
122	Island Sands
122	Lots of Magic
121	Amilynx
121	Compton Admiral
121	Daryaba
121	Enrique
121	State Shinto
120	Beat All
120	Belenus
120	Nowhere To Exit
120	Sicnee
120	Strategic
119p	Astonished
119	Bienamado
119	Ela Athena
119	Golden Snake
119	Hibiscus
119	Housemaster
119	Slickly
118	Acambaro
118	Caffe Latte
118	Flamingo Road
118	Gold Academy
118	Gracioso
118	Josr Algarhoud
118	Mujahid
118	Munjiz
118	Noushkey
118	Sampower Star
118	Slip Stream
117	All The Way
117	Etizaaz
117	First Magnitude
117	Glamis
117	Goombayland
117	Imperial Beauty
117	Little Rock

14

117 Major Force
117 Signorina Cattiva
117 Sumitas
117 Wallace
117 Wince
117 Zaajer
117 Zindabad
116 Alrassaam
116 Dazzling Park
116 Fairy Queen
116 Indian Danehill
116 Iscan
116 Kingsalsa
116 Lucido
116 Mus-If
116 Orpen
116 Salford Express
116 Touch 'N' Fly
116 Valentine Waltz
116 Val Royal
116 Wannabe Grand
116 Zarfoot
115 Balisada
115 Brancaster
115 Chelsea Manor
115 Danzigaway
115 Haafiz
115 King Adam
115 Manndar
115 Mayaro
115 Rhagaas
115 Star of Akkar
115 Tabareeh
115 Tiger Shark
115 Vision of Night
115 Way of Light
114 Cerulean Sky
114 Compton Ace
114 Katiykha
114 Marnor
114 Mary Stuart
114 Mukhalif
114 Sumati
114 Tchaikovsky
114 Tissifer
114 Zahrat Dubai
113 Azouz Pasha
113 Emma Peel
113 Fairy Godmother
113 Fragrant Oasis
113 Lavery
113 Mitcham
113 Mother of Pearl
113 Nasheed
113 Pink Cristal
113 Red Sea

OLDER HORSES

138 Daylami
136 El Condor Pasa
135 Royal Anthem
130 Kayf Tara
129 Cape Cross
127 Fruits of Love
127 Tiger Hill
126 Almutawakel
126 Croco Rouge
126 Diktat
126 Enzeli
126 Nedawi
125 Gold Away
125 Russian Revival
125 Silver Patriarch
124 Docksider
124 Fly To The Stars
124 Insatiable
124 Jim And Tonic
124 Lear Spear
124 Lend A Hand
124 Running Stag
123 Arkadian Hero
123 Bold Edge
123 Central Park
122 Alborada
122 Arctic Owl
122 Caitano
122 Dark Moondancer
122 Dream Well
122 Great Dane
122 High-Rise
122 Indigenous
122 Invermark
122 Sagamix
122 Susu
122 Xaar
121 Craigsteel
120 Agnes World
120 Borgia
120 Celeric
120 Courteous
120 Keos
120 Marcus Maximus
120 Muhtathir
119 Almushtarak
119 Chester House
119 Danish Rhapsody
119 Field of Hope
119 Greek Dance
119 Kabool
119 Public Purse
119 Sea Wave
119 Shiva
119 Trans Island
119 Ungaro
118 Burden of Proof

118 Elle Danzig
118 Epistolaire
118 Handsome Ridge
118 Intikhab
118 Rudi's Pet
118 Sugarfoot
118 Sunshine Street
118 Yavana's Pace
118 Zomaradah
117 Altibr
117 Bimbola
117 Capri
117 Dr Fong
117 Far Cry
117 Lonesome Dude
117 Maridpour
117 Rainbow High
117 Running Stag
117 Sand Falcon
117 Sayarshan
117 Sibling Rival
117 Tajoun
117 Tarry Flynn
117 Tomba
117 Tumbleweed Ridge
117 Vicious Circle
117 Warningford
116 Barbola
116 Blueprint
116 Bold Fact
116 Bomb Alaska
116 Cape Verdi
116 Dark Shell
116 Deep Space
116 Fa-Eq
116 Gaelic Storm
116 Gorse
116 Kadance Ville
116 Leggera
116 Limpid
116 Make No Mistake
116 Nuclear Debate
116 Power Flame
116 Prolix
116 Sadian
116 Sainte Marine
116 Spindrift
116 Superior Premium
116 Travelmate

15

1999 STATISTICS

The following tables show the leading owners, trainers, jockeys, sires of winners and horses on the Flat in Britain during 1999 (Jan 1–Dec 31). The prize-money statistics, compiled by *Timeform*, relate to first-three prize money and win-money. Win money was traditionally used to decide the trainers' championship, until in 1994 the BHB and the National Trainers' Federation established a championship decided by total prize-money as determined by *Racing Post*. The jockeys' championship has traditionally been decided by the number of winners ridden during the year, though since 1997 the Jockeys' Association has recognised a championship that runs for the turf season (Mar–Nov).

OWNERS (1,2,3 earnings)	Horses	Indiv'l Wnrs	Races Won	Runs	%	Stakes £
1 Godolphin	66	27	40	121	33.0	2,643,688
2 Mr Hamdan Al Maktoum	179	79	106	657	16.1	1,341,897
3 The Thoroughbred Corporation	17	8	12	55	21.8	988,581
4 Mr K. Abdulla	90	42	52	263	19.7	892,763
5 Maktoum Al Maktoum	74	35	46	293	15.6	745,145
6 H. H. Aga Khan	34	14	21	101	20.7	677,812
7 H. R. H. Prince Fahd Salman	37	17	23	129	17.8	567,972
8 Sheikh Mohammed	83	34	43	248	17.3	518,526
9 Mr M. Tabor & Mrs John Magnier	25	8	10	58	17.2	450,325
10 Sheikh Ahmed Al Maktoum	36	15	23	130	17.6	406,366
11 Mr A. E. Oppenheimer	15	6	6	49	12.2	344,286
12 Mr Saeed Suhail	9	7	9	34	26.4	297,013

OWNERS (win-money, £½m+)	Horses	Indiv'l Wnrs	Races Won	Runs	%	Stakes £
1 Godolphin	66	27	40	121	33.0	2,087,935
2 The Thoroughbred Corporation	17	8	12	55	21.8	894,656
3 Mr Hamdan Al Maktoum	179	79	106	657	16.1	846,136
4 Mr K. Abdulla	90	42	52	263	19.7	674,595
5 Maktoum Al Maktoum	74	35	46	293	15.6	523,792

TRAINERS (1,2,3 earnings)	Horses	Indiv'l Wnrs	Races Won	Runs	%	Stakes £
1 Saeed bin Suroor	66	27	40	121	33.0	2,643,688
2 H. R. A. Cecil	98	49	65	276	23.5	2,381,217
3 R. Hannon	186	86	123	1075	11.4	1,496,459
4 B. W. Hills	168	80	109	739	14.7	1,490,116
5 J. L. Dunlop	170	79	122	665	18.3	1,430,143
6 Sir Michael Stoute	136	62	81	404	20.0	1,340,881
7 J. H. M. Gosden	128	54	74	409	18.0	1,056,706
8 M. Johnston	141	66	113	765	14.7	954,275
9 I. A. Balding	94	34	50	459	10.8	755,630
10 L. M. Cumani	72	24	34	226	15.0	728,467
11 A. P. O'Brien, Ireland	30	10	11	44	25.0	712,479
12 P. F. I. Cole	97	52	76	407	18.6	699,997

TRAINERS (win-money, £1m+)	Horses	Indiv'l Wnrs	Races Won	Runs	%	Stakes £
1 Saeed bin Suroor	66	27	40	121	33.0	2,087,935
2 H. R. A. Cecil	98	49	65	276	23.5	1,814,718
3 B. W. Hills	168	80	109	739	14.7	1,095,621
4 J. L. Dunlop	170	79	122	665	18.3	1,014,683

TRAINERS (with 100+ winners)	Horses	Indiv'l Wnrs	Races Won	2nd	3rd	Runs	%
1 R. Hannon	186	86	123	136	127	1075	11.4
2 J. L. Dunlop	170	79	122	101	78	665	18.3
3 M. Johnston	141	66	113	102	69	765	14.7
4 B. W. Hills	168	80	109	104	84	739	14.7

JOCKEYS (by winners)	1st	2nd	3rd	Unpl	Total Mts	%
1 K. Fallon	202	155	124	507	988	20.4
2 T. Quinn	151	117	126	523	917	16.4
3 L. Dettori	132	94	89	312	627	21.0
4 K. Darley	119	100	95	540	854	13.9
5 T. Sprake	111	94	86	609	900	12.3
6 Pat Eddery	104	85	86	464	739	14.0
7 R. Hughes	95	90	75	443	703	13.5
8 J. Fortune	94	88	81	446	709	13.2
9 M. Hills	94	83	70	367	614	15.3
10 S. Sanders	90	54	75	538	757	11.9
11 R. Cochrane	82	86	78	475	721	11.3
12 G. Duffield	80	76	69	506	731	10.9

Note: K. Fallon was leading jockey in the turf season with 200 winners

JOCKEYS (1,2,3 earnings, £1m+)	Races Won	Rides	%	Stakes £
1 K. Fallon	202	988	20.4	3,444,878
2 L. Dettori	132	627	21.0	3,114,456
3 T. Quinn	151	917	16.4	1,785,613
4 Pat Eddery	104	739	14.0	1,555,225
5 Gary Stevens	45	210	21.4	1,378,864
6 R. Hills	77	530	14.5	1,241,668
7 M. Hills	94	614	15.3	1,206,054
8 R. Hughes	95	703	13.5	1,074,290
9 J. Fortune	94	709	13.2	1,044,914
10 K. Darley	119	854	13.9	1,001,637

JOCKEYS (win-money, £1m+)	Races Won	Rides	%	Stakes £
1 K. Fallon	202	988	20.4	2,555,976
2 L. Dettori	132	627	21.0	2,519,436
3 T. Quinn	151	917	16.4	1,222,810
4 Pat Eddery	104	739	14.0	1,057,625

APPRENTICES (by winners)	1st	2nd	3rd	Unpl	Total Mts	%
1 N. Callan	56	64	60	365	545	10.2
2 P. Doe	54	58	45	481	638	8.5
3 R. Winston	54	54	59	478	645	8.3
4 N. Pollard	52	38	24	402	516	10.0

SIRES OF WINNERS (1,2,3 earnings)	Races Won	Runs	%	Stakes £
1 Fairy King (by Northern Dancer)	22	237	9.2	1,182,894
2 Sadler's Wells (by Northern Dancer)	22	175	12.5	740,476
3 Diesis (by Sharpen Up)	26	174	14.9	685,458
4 Warning (by Known Fact)	61	432	14.1	681,051
5 Indian Ridge (by Ahonoora)	64	466	13.7	663,509
6 Alzao (by Lyphard)	35	326	10.7	561,950
7 Doyoun (by Mill Reef)	15	89	16.8	558,311
8 Silver Hawk (by Roberto)	23	117	19.6	544,711
9 Royal Academy (by Nijinsky)	44	360	12.2	517,772
10 Green Desert (by Danzig)	52	366	14.2	504,885
11 Nureyev (by Northern Dancer)	27	86	31.3	503,051
12 Shirley Heights (by Mill Reef)	41	241	17.0	476.133

SIRES OF WINNERS (win-money)	Horses	Indiv'l Wnrs	Races Won	Stakes £
1 Fairy King (by Northern Dancer)	64	16	22	923,786
2 Warning (by Known Fact)	80	41	61	544,493
3 Doyoun (by Mill Reef)	26	10	15	532,379
4 Indian Ridge (by Ahonoora)	84	37	64	464,923
5 Alzao (by Lyphard)	69	25	35	458,802
6 Diesis (by Sharpen Up)	45	21	26	453,684
7 Silver Hawk (by Roberto)	27	16	23	417,313
8 Green Desert (by Danzig)	69	33	52	397,699
9 Nureyev (by Northern Dancer)	23	16	27	392,841
10 Shirley Heights (by Mill Reef)	44	24	41	369,840
11 Nashwan (by Blushing Groom)	44	18	26	364,203
12 Turtle Island (by Fairy King)	35	17	31	354,319

LEADING HORSES (1,2,3 earnings)	Races Won	Runs	Stakes £
1 Oath 3 b.c. Fairy King – Sheer Audacity	2	4	643,105
2 Daylami 5 gr.h. Doyoun – Daltawa	2	2	460,000
3 Ramruma 3 ch.f. Diesis – Princess of Man	4	5	395,210
4 Mutafaweq 3 b.c. Silver Hawk – The Caretaker	3	4	304,253
5 Royal Anthem 4 b.c. Theatrical – In Neon	1	3	284,725
6 Daliapour 3 b.c. Sadler's Wells – Dalara	1	4	248,500
7 Alborada 4 gr.f. Alzao – Alouette	1	2	228,200
8 Dubai Millennium 3 b.c. Seeking The Gold – Colorado Dancer	3	4	222,020
9 Aljabr 3 gr.c. Storm Cat – Sierra Madre	1	2	200,210
10 Compton Admiral 3 b.c. Suave Dancer – Sumoto	2	5	194,600
11 Fantastic Light 3 b.c. Rahy – Jood	3	6	190,590
12 Stravinsky 3 b.c. Nureyev – Fire The Groom	2	3	182,475

EXPLANATORY NOTES

'Racehorses of 1999' deals individually, in alphabetical sequence, with every horse that ran on the Flat in Britain in 1999 (including on the all-weather tracks), plus many foreign-trained horses that did not race here. For each of these horses is given (1) its age, colour and sex, (2) its breeding, and, where this information has not been given in a previous Racehorses Annual, a family outline (3) a form summary giving details of its performances during the last two seasons, together, where applicable, with the horse's rating in 1998, which appears at the start of the form summary, (4) a rating of its merit in 1999 (which appears in the margin), (5) a Timeform commentary on its racing or general characteristics as a racehorse, with some suggestions, perhaps, regarding its prospects for 2000, and (6) the name of the trainer in whose charge it was on the last occasion it ran. For each two-year-old the foaling date is also given.

The book is published with a twofold purpose. Firstly, it is intended to have permanent value as a review of the exploits and achievements of the more notable of the Flat-racing thoroughbreds in 1999. Thus, while the commentaries upon the vast majority of the horses are, of necessity, in note form, the best horses are more critically examined. The text is illustrated by half-tone portraits of the most notable horses (where these are available) and photographs of the major races. Secondly, the book is designed to help the punter to analyse races, and the notes which follow contain instructions for using the data. The attention of foreign buyers of British bloodstock, and others who are concerned with Timeform Ratings as a measure of absolute racing class in terms of a standard scale, is particularly drawn to the section headed 'The Level of the Ratings'.

TIMEFORM RATINGS

The Timeform Rating of a horse is simply the merit of the horse expressed in pounds and is arrived at by careful examination of its running against other horses using a scale of weight for distance beaten which, without going into the complexities, ranges from around 3 lb a length at five furlongs and 2 lb a length at a mile and a quarter to 1 lb at two miles. Timeform maintains a 'running' handicap of all horses in training throughout the season.

THE LEVEL OF THE RATINGS

At the close of each season the rating of all the horses that have raced is re-examined. It is also necessary to adjust the general level of the handicap, so that all the ratings are kept at the same standard level from year to year. This explains why, in this book, the ratings may be different from those in the final issue of the 1999 Timeform Black Book.

RATINGS AND WEIGHT-FOR-AGE

The reader has, in the ratings in this book, a universal handicap embracing all the horses in training it is possible to weigh up, ranging from tip-top performers, with ratings from 130 to 145, down to the poorest, rated around the 20 mark. All the ratings are at weight-for-age, so that equal ratings mean horses of equal merit: perhaps it would be clearer if we said that the universal rating handicap is really not a single handicap, but four handicaps side by side: one for two-year-olds, one for three-year-olds, one for four-year-olds and one for older horses. Thus, a three-year-old rated, for argument's sake, at 117 is deemed to be identical in point of 'merit' with a four-year-old also rated at 117: but for them to have equal chances in, say, a mile race in May, the three-year-old would need to be receiving 9 lb from the four-year-old, which is the weight difference specified by the Age, Weight and Distance Tables on the end papers at the front and back of the book.

USING THE RATINGS

In using Timeform Ratings with a view to discovering which horses in any race have the best chances at the weights, we have two distinct cases, according to whether the horses taking part are of the same age or of different ages. Here is the procedure in each case:-

A. Horses of the Same Age

If the horses all carry the same weight there are no adjustments to be made, and the horses with the highest ratings have the best chances. If the horses carry different weights, jot down their ratings, and to the rating of each horse add one point for every pound the horse is set to carry less than 10 st, or subtract one point for every pound it has to carry more than 10 st. When the ratings have been adjusted in this way the highest resultant figure indicates the horse with the best chance at the weights.

Example (any distance: any week of the season)

2 Good Girl (9-6)	....	Rating 119	....	add 8	....	127
2 Paulinus (9-4)	....	Rating 113	....	add 10	....	123
2 Abilene (8-11)	....	Rating 107	....	add 17	....	124
2 Bob's Joy (8-7)	....	Rating 108	....	add 21	....	129
2 Time Warp (8-2)	....	Rating 100	....	add 26	....	126
2 Eagle Eye (7-7)	....	Rating 92	....	add 35	....	127

Bob's Joy (129) has the best chance strictly on form;
Good Girl (127) and Eagle Eye (127) are the next best

B. Horses of Different Ages

Take no notice of the weight any horse receives from any other. Instead, consult the Age, Weight and Distance Tables printed on the end papers at the front and back of the book. Treat each horse separately, and compare the weight it has to carry with the weight prescribed for it in the tables, according to the age of the horse, the distance of the race and the time of the year. Then, add one point to the rating for each pound the horse has to carry less than the weight given in the tables: or, subtract one point from the rating for every pound it has to carry more than the weight prescribed by the tables. The highest resultant figure indicates the horse most favoured by the weights.

Example (1½ miles on June 30th)

(Table Weights: 5-y-o 10-0; 4-y-o 9-13; 3-y-o 9-1)

6 Nimitz (10-2)	....	Rating 115	....	subtract 2	113
4 Red Devil (9-9)	....	Rating 114	....	add 4	118

6 Sweet Cindy (9-5)	....	Rating 115	....	add 9	....	124
3 Jailhouse (9-2)	....	Rating 120	....	subtract 1	....	119
4 Haakon (8-11)	....	Rating 101	....	add 16	....	117
3 Fine Strike (8-7)	....	Rating 108	....	add 8	....	116

Sweet Cindy (124) has the best chance at the weights,
with 5 lb in hand of Jailhouse

TURF AND ALL-WEATHER RATINGS

When a horse has raced on turf and on all-weather and its form on one is significantly different from the other, the two ratings are given, the all-weather set out below the turf preceded by 'a'.

Thus with FREE FOR ALL 47
a55

the top figure, 47, is the rating to be used in turf races, and the one below, a55, is for use in all-weather races. Where there is only one rating, that is to be used for both turf and all-weather.

NOTE ON RIDERS' ALLOWANCES

For the purposes of rating calculations it is assumed that the allowance a rider is able to claim is nullified by his or her inexperience. The adjustments to the ratings *should therefore be calculated on the weight allotted by the handicapper, or determined by the conditions of the race*. No extra 7 lb should be added to the rating when a rider claims 7 lb. This is the general routine procedure; but of course, after the usual adjustments have been made, the quality of jockeyship is still an important factor to be considered when deciding between horses with similar chances.

WEIGHING UP A RACE

The ratings tell you which horses in a particular race are most favoured by the weights; but complete analysis demands that the racing character of each horse, as set out in the commentary upon it, is also studied carefully to see if there is any reason why the horse might be expected not to run up to its rating or indeed might improve on it. It counts for little that a horse is thrown in at the weights if it has no pretensions whatever to staying the distance, or is unable to act on the prevailing going.

These two matters, suitability of distance and going, are no doubt the most important points to be considered. But there are others. For example, the ability of a horse to accommodate itself to the conformation of the track. Then there is the matter of temperament and behaviour: nobody would be in a hurry to take a short price about a horse with whom it is always an even chance whether it will give its running.

A few minutes spent checking up on these matters in the commentaries upon the horses concerned will sometimes put a very different complexion on a race from that which is put upon it by the ratings alone. We repeat, therefore, that the correct way to use Timeform, or this annual volume, in the analysis of individual races is, first to use the ratings to discover which horses are most favoured by the weights, and second, to check through the comments on the horse to discover what factors other than weight might also affect the outcome of the race.

THE FORM SUMMARIES

The form summary enclosed in the brackets shows for each individual horse the distance, the state of the going and where the horse finished in each of its races on the Flat during the last two seasons. Performances are in chronological sequence, the earliest being given first.

The distance of each race is given in furlongs, fractional distances being expressed in the decimal notation to the nearest tenth of a furlong. Races on an all-weather surface are prefixed by letter 'a'.

The going is symbolised as follows: h=hard; f=firm (turf) or fast (all-weather/dirt); m=good to firm; g=good (turf) or standard (all-weather/dirt); d=good to soft/dead; s=soft (turf) or slow, sloppy, muddy or wet (all-weather/dirt); v=heavy.

Placings are indicated, up to sixth place, by the use of superior figures, an asterisk being used to denote a win.

Thus [1998 81: 10s* 12f^3 1999 11.7g a11g^2 Sep 7] signifies that the horse was rated 81 in 1998, when winning over 10 furlongs on soft going first time out and finishing third over twelve furlongs on firm going next time out. In 1999 he finished out of the first six over 11.7 furlongs on good going, then second over eleven furlongs on standard going on an all-weather track. The date of his last run was September 7.

Included in the pedigree details are the highest Timeform Annual ratings during their racing careers of the sires, dams and sires of dams of all horses, where the information is available.

Where sale prices are considered relevant F denotes the price as a foal, Y the price as a yearling, 2-y-o as a two-year-old, and so on. These are given in guineas unless prefixed by IR (Irish guineas), $ (American dollars) or accompanied by francs (French francs). Other currencies are converted approximately into guineas or pounds sterling at the prevailing exchange rate.

THE RATING SYMBOLS

The following symbols, attached to the ratings, are to be interpreted as stated:-

p   likely to improve.

P   capable of *much* better form.

+   the horse may be better than we have rated it.

d   the horse appears to have deteriorated, and might no longer be capable of running to the rating given.

§   unreliable (for temperamental or other reasons).

§§   so temperamentally unsatisfactory as not to be worth a rating.

?   the horse's rating is suspect. If used without a rating the symbol implies that the horse can't be assessed with confidence, or, if used in the in-season Timeform publications, that the horse is out of form.

RACEHORSES OF 1999

Horse	Commentary	Rating

AA-YOUKNOWNOTHING   3 b.g. Superpower 113 – Bad Payer 72 (Tanfirion 110) [1998 74: 5d 5g² 5s* 5d* 5d⁶ 5g 5.1g² 6f 1999 a5g³ a5g² a5g a5g 5d⁵ 5d⁵ 6.1m 6g 5g 5m³ 5m 5m a5g a5g³ a5g³ a5g⁴ a5g* Dec 29] tall, angular gelding: fair handicapper: made virtually all when winning at Lingfield in December: best at 5f: acts on good to firm ground, soft and all-weather: effective blinkered/visored or not: often tongue tied: usually races prominently: has drifted left under pressure and looked none too keen. *Miss J. F. Craze*   **74**

ABAJANY   5 b.g. Akarad (FR) 130 – Miss Ivory Coast (USA) (Sir Ivor 135) [1998 96: 10.1s⁴ 10.3g² 10m 8g 10.2g⁴ 9m 10.2d* 9.9g 8.1g³ 8s* 8m² 8d 8m⁴ 9g 8s³ 8s 1999 8.3m⁴ 8m⁶ 8m⁴ 8m 8.5d 8m 8g 8f⁵ 9m⁶ 8f 10s³ 9g³ 8m⁴ 8.3m⁵ 8.5g 8s³ 7.1s³ 8d⁵ 8d² 8s⁴ Nov 6] sturdy, good-bodied gelding: fairly useful performer: mostly creditable efforts in 1999: effective at 1m to 1¼m: acts on firm and soft going, yet to race on all-weather: tends to wander in front and requires strong handling (usually held up). *M. R. Channon*   **91**

ABARIS (IRE)   2 ch.g. (Apr 10) Kris 135 – Amaranthus (Shirley Heights 130) [1999 7m Jun 24] 5,400Y: fifth foal: half-brother to 3-y-o Salsify and 7.5f winner Acidanthera (by Alzao): dam unraced daughter of smart sprinter Amaranda: 25/1, very green when last of 7 in maiden at Newcastle. *T. D. Easterby*   **–**

ABBAJABBA   3 b.g. Barrys Gamble 102 – Bo' Babbity 75 (Strong Gale 116) [1998 82: 5g⁶ 6g² 5m 6s⁵ 5g⁴ 1999 6m 6d 5m 7g⁶ 5d 6g⁶ 6.1f⁶ 6d⁶ a7g Nov 12] quite good-topped gelding: has a round action: fair maiden: stays 6f: acts on soft going, probably on firm (below form on fibresand final start). *C. W. Fairhurst*   **70**

ABBEY THEATRE (IRE)   5 b.g. Sadler's Wells (USA) 132 – Altiyna 109 (Troy 137) [1998 NR 1999 11.9f³ a16g 13.3f 12d 12g a13g 11.7m Jul 15] compact gelding: bad maiden: tried blinkered/visored. *M. Salaman*   **29**

ABBYANN   3 b.f. Nalchik (USA) – Zoomar 30 (Legend of France (USA) 124) [1998 NR 1999 8m³ 8g⁴ 8.3s 8f Sep 6] fourth foal: dam lightly-raced maiden: poor maiden: will stay beyond 1m: acts on good to firm going. *B. Palling*   **45**

ABCO BOY (IRE)   2 b.c. (Mar 5) Full Extent (USA) 113 – Double Stitch 74 (Wolver Hollow 126) [1999 8d Sep 16] half-brother to 3 winners, including 5f winner Absolutely Nuts (by Absalom) and 9.4f winner Chastleton (by Presidium): dam 1m winner: last of 15 in seller at Ayr. *Martyn Wane*   **–**

ABDERIAN (IRE)   2 b.c. (Feb 4) Machiavellian (USA) 123 – Aminata 98 (Glenstal (USA) 118) [1999 6g* 7d⁴ 7m² Oct 19] IR 150,000Y: closely related to smart Irish 7f (at 2 yrs) and 1m winner Swift Gulliver (by Gulch), later successful in USA, and half-brother to fairly useful thorough stayer Turquoise Sea (by Shirley Heights): dam, Irish 2-y-o sprint winner, later best at 1m: won maiden at Ripon in August: fairly useful form in minor events after, 2½ lengths second of 7 to Catchy Word (who got first run) at Yarmouth: should stay at least 1m: carried head rather awkwardly second start: should prove capable of better still. *J. Noseda*   **92 p**

ABERFELDY   3 b.f. Petong 126 – Klewraye (Lord Gayle (USA) 124) [1998 65: 5m⁵ 6d³ 6d⁶ 1999 6g 5v 5g⁵ 7f⁵ 5g 7.1m Sep 2] sparely-made filly: fair form at 2 yrs: well beaten in 1999. *J. Berry*   **–**

ABERKEEN   4 ch.g. Keen 116 – Miss Aboyne 64 (Lochnager 132) [1998 59: 7d 7v⁴ 9.9s 8d 6s 7d³ 7g 7d 6m 1999 7g³ 7.1m³ 7.1m⁶ 7m* 7g 7m 7.1d⁴ a7g⁵ 7f² 8.2g a6g⁶ 7v a7g³ Dec 15] workmanlike gelding: fair handicapper: won 21-runner apprentice event at Doncaster in May: best around 7f: acts on firm going, good to soft and fibresand: visored (well beaten) once at 3 yrs. *M. Dods*   **68 a64**

ABISSINIA   3 b.f. Puissance 110 – Amathus Glory 76 (Mummy's Pet 125) [1998 ?, a46: 5.1d a5g² a5g 5g³ a5g a5g⁶ a6g a5g⁵ a5g 1999 5d 5m 5.9g 5m Jun 24] good-topped filly: poor maiden: best form at 5f on fibresand. *N. Tinkler*   **–**

ABLE AYR   2 ch.c. (May 27) Formidable (USA) 125 – Ayr Classic (Local Suitor   **76**
(USA) 128) [1999 5g³ 5d⁴ 6d⁴ 5g* 5m 5m⁴ 6m⁵ 6g Aug 16] 17,000Y: small, sturdy
colt: fourth foal: half-brother to 7f to 8.5f winner People Direct (by Ron's Victory)
and 3-y-o Class Wan: dam 2-y-o 5f/6f winner: fair performer: won maiden at Carlisle
in June: below form last 3 starts: should stay 6f. *J. S. Goldie*

ABLE LASS (IRE)   5 ch.m. Classic Music (USA) – Miami Life (Miami Springs
121) [1998 –: a8g 1999 a10g Jan 9] no form. *R. W. Armstrong*

ABLE MILLENIUM (IRE)   3 ch.g. Be My Guest (USA) 126 – Miami Life   **65**
(Miami Springs 121) [1998 NR 1999 a7g³ a8.5g³ a8.5g³ a7g Dec 15] half-brother to
1½m winners Distinct Native (fairly useful) and Native Joy (in Ireland), both by Be
My Native: dam unraced: fair maiden: will stay beyond 8.5f. *R. W. Armstrong*

ABLE NATIVE (IRE)   2 b.f. (May 18) Thatching 131 – Native Joy (IRE) 76 (Be   **68**
My Native (USA) 122) [1999 7s 7v² 8d⁵ Oct 27] first foal: dam Irish 1½m and
hurdles winner: fair form in maidens: stays 1m. *R. W. Armstrong*

ABLE PETE   3 b.c. Formidable (USA) 125 – An Empress (USA) (Affirmed (USA))   **–**
[1998 64: 6.1m 7s 1999 a6g a8g 10g 8v 8.2m a10g Nov 24] neat colt: no form since
debut. *A. G. Newcombe*

ABLE PLAYER (USA)   12 b. or br.g. Solford (USA) 127 – Grecian Snow (CAN)   **–**
(Snow Knight 125) [1998 NR 1999 12m⁶ May 26] very lightly raced and poor form
at best since 1991. *K. J. Drewry, Isle of Man*

A BOB LIGHT (IRE)   2 br.f. (Mar 17) Bob's Return (IRE) 123 – Light Hand 80   **62**
(Star Appeal 133) [1999 6g⁶ 7m⁴ 7m² 7m⁴ 8d⁵ 7s Oct 5] close-coupled filly: has a
quick action: third foal: half-sister to fairly useful 1998 2-y-o 5f and 7f winner Light
Fingered (by Soviet Lad): dam 1¼m winner: modest maiden: second at Folkestone
in July: creditable efforts in nurseries next 2 starts: likely to be well suited by 1¼m+:
acts on good to firm and good to soft going, well beaten on soft. *M. H. Tompkins*

ABOO HOM   5 b.h. Sadler's Wells (USA) 132 – Maria Waleska (Filiberto (USA)   **58**
123) [1998 NR 1999 13.9d a16.2g a16.2g³ Dec 15] tall, useful-looking horse: modest
maiden: stays 2m: acts on soft going and fibresand: has worn tongue strap. *S. Dow*

ABOVE BOARD   4 b.g. Night Shift (USA) – Bundled Up (USA) (Sharpen Up   **38 +**
127) [1998 –: 8.1g 7s 6.9d 5g 7.1d 1999 a6g a6f a6f⁵ a6g⁴ a6g 6f a6g⁶ a7g 5g a8.5g⁵
a8g⁵ a6g⁶ Dec 17] small, robust gelding: poor maiden: best at 6f: acts on good to firm
going and fibresand: blinkered twice: has had tongue tied. *R. F. Marvin*

ABRAKA   2 gr.f. (Apr 4) Petong 126 – Lady Lucy Linnet (Zalazl (USA) 120)   **–**
[1999 5d⁶ 6m 6m⁶ 5m Jul 19] 1,500F, IR 7,000Y: second foal: dam, no form, half-
sister to useful sprinter Sir Harry Hardman: no sign of ability in sellers/claimer: tried
blinkered. *J. S. Wainwright*

A BREEZE   5 br.g. Precocious 126 – Wasimah 84 (Caerleon (USA) 132) [1998 48,
a–: a6g 7g 8m⁶ 8m⁵ 6m⁶ 5m 8m⁵ 7s a8g 1999 a8g Feb 16] compact gelding: poor
handicapper in 1998: reportedly finished distressed only 5-y-o start: barely stays 7f:
acts on good to firm going: blinkered/visored once each. *D. Morris*

ABSALOM'S LAD   4 gr.c. Absalom 128 – Rose Bouquet 78 (General Assembly   **–**
(USA)) [1998 74, a56+: 7.9g³ 8.1g 7.1m a8.5g* a8g 1999 a9.4g 10d Apr 28] lengthy
colt: has been freeze-fired: formerly fair performer: no show both 4-y-o starts,
reportedly lame final one: stays 8.5f: acts on fibresand (probably equitrack), best turf
form on good going. *P. W. Harris*

ABSCOND (USA)   2 b.f. (Feb 23) Unbridled (USA) 128 – Lemhi Go (USA)   **97 p**
(Lemhi Gold (USA) 123) [1999 7f² 7m² Aug 27] big, rangy, rather raw-boned filly:
fluent mover: third foal: half-sister to 4-y-o Triple Treasure: dam won 12 times in
USA, including Grade 2 1½m event: favourite, useful form when second in maidens
at Goodwood (decidedly green) and Newmarket, leading over 1f out until near finish
when beaten a head by My Hansel on latter track: will be suited by 1¼m/1½m: useful
prospect, sure to win a race or 2. *Sir Michael Stoute*

ABSENTEE   4 br.f. Slip Anchor 136 – Meliora 73 (Crowned Prince (USA) 128)   **32 §**
[1998 66: 9.9f⁴ 11.8m a12g⁴ 14.1g* 14g 16d⁵ 14.1g 1999 14.1s 14.1d 14.1s 16.2d
12d 14.1m 16m⁵ Sep 13] poor handicapper nowadays: stays 2m: acts on good to firm
going: has flashed tail/downed tools: needs treating with caution. *J. L. Harris*

ABSENT FRIENDS   2 b.c. (Apr 26) Rock City 120 – Green Supreme (Primo **70**
Dominie 121) [1999 5m 5s³ 6g 6v Oct 23] third foal: half-brother to 3-y-o Sampower
Star: dam unraced: fair maiden: best effort when third in minor event at Beverley in
September: will prove best at 5f/6f. *J. Cullinan*

ABSINTHER   2 b.c. (Feb 25) Presidium 124 – Heavenly Queen (Scottish Reel **62**
123) [1999 7.1m 7s³ 6g 6d Oct 26] 9,500F: good-bodied colt: fourth foal: brother to
modest 6f/7f winner Abstone Queen, closely related to 3-y-o Hadeqa and half-
brother to 4-y-o Heavenly Abstone: dam maiden: modest maiden: should stay 1m:
acts on soft ground. *E. J. Alston*

ABSOLUTE FANTASY   3 b.f. Beveled (USA) – Sharp Venita 84 (Sharp Edge **54**
123) [1998 NR 1999 8.3g 6d 8.3d a8g⁴ Nov 26] half-sister to 3 winners, including
1m to 11.6f winner Fern's Governor (by Governor General) and useful 7f winner
Sharpalto (by Noalto): dam sprinter: form in maidens only when blinkered and fourth
at Lingfield: stays 1m: acts on equitrack. *W. M. Wheeler*

ABSOLUTELY ABSTONE   5 gr.m. Petong 126 – Odilese 82 (Mummy's Pet
125) [1998 NR 1999 7g 7s a5g 5m 6s a5g Jun 19] tall, angular mare: bad maiden:
tried blinkered/visored. *W. M. Brisbourne*

ABSOLUTE MAJORITY   4 ch.g. Absalom 128 – Shall We Run 59 (Hotfoot
126) [1998 NR 1999 a7g a10g⁵ a9.4g* a12g⁵ a8.5g 8.3m 10d a9.4g³ a7g a7g⁴ a8g **a64**
Dec 13] 8,500Y, 3,500 2-y-o: second foal: brother to a twice-raced maiden: dam,
third at 5f at 2 yrs, sister to useful Fire Top and half-sister to very smart but unreliable
sprinter Dead Certain (by Absalom): modest performer: won maiden at Wolverhampton (final start for B. Curley) in February: mostly below form after: stays 9.4f:
acts on fibresand, little show both starts on turf. *P. Howling*

ABSOLUTE UTOPIA (USA)   6 b.g. Mr Prospector (USA) – Magic Gleam **76**
(USA) 122 (Danzig (USA)) [1998 75: 10m⁴ 10g 9g² 9d⁵ 12m* 11.5f⁴ 11.9m⁴ 1999
10m 12m³ 12m² 12m⁴ 12m² 11.5s Oct 8] tall gelding: has been hobdayed and had
soft palate operation: fair handicapper: lightly raced but at least as good as ever in
1999: probably best around 1½m: acts on firm and good to soft ground, well held
both starts on soft: held up: consistent. *N. E. Berry*

ABSTRACT (IRE)   3 b.f. Perugino (USA) 84 – Kalapa (FR) (Mouktar 129)   –
[1998 47: 6m⁵ 6g 6m⁵ 5d⁴ 6m 1999 a7g a8f⁵ a7g6 a6g⁴ a7g 10m 7g⁴ 7g 5g 5m⁶ Jul 12]
sparely-made filly: poor maiden: stays 6f: tried blinkered/visored. *J. S. Wainwright*

ABTAAL   9 b.g. Green Desert (USA) 127 – Stufida (Bustino 136) [1998 65, a62:   **60**
6m⁴ 7g 6.1g 6g³ 7g* 6.9d⁵ 7m* a7g* 8f a7g² a7g⁶ a7g a7g³ a6g 1999 a6g a7f a7f⁵   **a70**
a7g* a6g⁴ a7g* a7g a7g³ a7g² a7g⁴ a7g³ a7g* 7f a7g⁶ 7m⁵ a7g a7g Oct 13]
good-bodied gelding: fair performer, raced mainly on all-weather in 1999: won
seller at Southwell in February and claimer in March and handicap in May, both at
Wolverhampton: below form last 5 starts: probably best at 7f: acts on good to firm
ground, soft and all-weather: blinkered/visored: usually held up. *Mrs N. Macauley*

ABU CAMP   4 b.g. Indian Ridge 123 – Artistic Licence (High Top 131) [1998 66:   **51**
8f⁶ 6m 8m 7.6m³ 10d 8g 1999 8g 8s 8g 7m⁶ 7f Jul 29] close-coupled gelding: modest
maiden: stays 7.6f: acts on good to firm going: tried visored: wears tongue strap:
none too consistent. *M. J. Heaton-Ellis*

ABULJJOOD (IRE)   4 b.g. Marju (IRE) 127 – Midway Lady (USA) 126 (Alleged   **66**
(USA) 138) [1998 73: 12d 10.3g⁶ 10.5d 11.5g⁶ 12f³ 14m⁵ 1999 a12g² a12g* a16f⁶   **a69**
a12g² a12g a12g 12.1m³ Jul 9] big, lengthy gelding: fair performer: won claimer at
Wolverhampton in January: left P. Haslam after fourth start and M. Waring after
sixth: off 4 months before final one: stays 1½m: acts on firm ground and fibresand
(below best on equitrack): usually blinkered: has been bandaged: sometimes looks
none too genuine. *Ian Williams*

ABUSAMRAH (USA)   4 b.g. Riverman (USA) 131 – Azayim 111 (Be My Guest   –
(USA) 126) [1998 76d: 7g⁵ 8g³ 9s 8.2g a10g a9.4s a6g⁵ 1999 a8g a16g 10.3d
Jun 2] leggy gelding: disappointing maiden: visored once: has worn tongue strap.
A. T. Murphy

ABUZAID (USA)   2 br.c. (Feb 18) Nureyev (USA) 131 – Elle Seule (USA) 122 **88 p**
(Exclusive Native (USA)) [1999 6m⁵ 6g 6d* Oct 20] good-topped colt: good walker:
eighth foal: brother to very smart 6f (at 2 yrs) to 1m winner Mehthaaf, closely related

to 3 winners, notably high-class sprinter Elnadim (by Danzig), and half-brother to fairly useful sprinter Jawlaat (by Dayjur): dam French 1m to 10.5f winner out of outstanding broodmare Fall Aspen: green and raced keenly first 2 starts (carried head awkwardly on second one) then won maiden at Newcastle by 2 lengths from Boanerges, drifting left: should stay 7f: should make useful 3-y-o. *J. L. Dunlop*

ABYAAN (IRE) 4 b.f. Ela-Mana-Mou 132 – Anna Comnena (IRE) 71 (Shareef   **106**
Dancer (USA) 135) [1998 97: 10.2s* 10m⁵ 1999 10v³ 12s² 12m⁶ 10.1m⁵ 10s³ 14.6g
12.5v³ 12s Nov 6] strong, lengthy filly: useful performer: best efforts when third in
listed race at Deauville on fifth start and Prix de Royallieu at Longchamp (beaten a
length by Fairy Queen) on seventh: stays 12.5f well (got poor run in 14.6f Park Hill
Stakes at Doncaster): acts on heavy ground (well below best all starts on good to
firm): visored last 2 starts. *J. H. M. Gosden*

ACAMBARO (GER) 3 b.c. Goofalik (USA) 118 – Astica (GER) (Surumu   **118**
(GER)) [1998 7d⁴ 8.5v⁵ 7.5d* 8v² 1999 9v³ 10.3g⁵ 10s* 12m² Jul 4] approx 30,000Y
in Germany: third foal: half-brother to 2 winners in Germany, Alamos (7f/1m, by Big
Shuffle) and Auetaler (1m to 11f, by Niniski), latter also useful hurdler here: dam
German 7f/1m winner: smart performer: progressed well at 3 yrs, winning Grosser
Muller Brot-Preis at Munich in May by ½ length from Evening Storm before length
second of 18 to Belenus in Deutsches Derby at Hamburg: stayed 1½m: won on soft
ground, best effort on good to firm: sustained tendon injury and to stand at Gestut
Ohlerweiherhof, Germany. *P. Rau, Germany*

ACCEPTING 2 b.c. (Mar 24) Mtoto 134 – D'Azy 91 (Persian Bold 123) [1999 8g   **81 p**
9m² Sep 24] sturdy colt: sixth foal: brother to very smart middle-distance performer
Presenting and French 1¼m winner Introducing and half-brother to 1992 2-y-o 7f
winner Azilian (by Top Ville): dam, 2-y-o 7f winner, half-sister to smart middle-
distance performer Sirk: much better effort in maidens (burly on debut) when
½-length second of 10 to easy winner Miletrian at Redcar, carrying head awkwardly
and tending to hang before staying on well: will stay at least 1½m: should prove
capable of better. *J. H. M. Gosden*

ACCYSTAN 4 ch.g. Efisio 120 – Amia (CAN) (Nijinsky (CAN) 138) [1998 68:   **–**
a8s⁶ a9.4g⁴ a10g³ a8.5g³ a11g⁴ a11g⁵ 12g⁴ 12.1g³ a9.4g³ 1999 8m a12g* 13.8m Aug   **a68**
3] quite good-topped gelding: fair on all-weather, modest on turf: only form in 1999
when winning seller at Southwell in July by 9 lengths: stays 1½m: acts on fibresand,
well beaten only try on equitrack. *M. D. Hammond*

John Smith's Cup (Handicap), York—Achilles (white socks) rallies bravely to regain the advantage from Siege

ACEBO LYONS (IRE)   4 b.f. Waajib 121 – Etage (Ile de Bourbon (USA) 133)   **62**
[1998 73: 9g 10d³ 10m 10.5d* 10m 10s⁵ 1999 10.3d 11.5g⁶ 9.9m 11.6m³ 14m 10g²   **a–**
11m⁶ a12g 11.5g⁴ 12d a12g Dec 11] leggy, close-coupled filly: modest handicapper:
stays 11.6f, probably not 1¾m: acts on good to firm and good to soft going, well held
on fibresand: sometimes looks none too hearty. *A. P. Jarvis*

ACE OF PARKES   3 b.g. Teenoso (USA) 135 – Summerhill Spruce 70 (Wind-   **95**
jammer (USA)) [1998 98+: 5.1m⁴ 6g 5m* 6.1m* 6.1d* 6g³ 6v⁵ 1999 6g⁶ 5d⁶ 6.1m⁵
5.1m⁵ 6.1g 6s⁶ Sep 27] lengthy, good-topped gelding: useful performer: creditable
efforts in rated stakes and listed event at Chester third and fourth starts: well held last
2: stays 6f: acts on good to firm and good to soft going, probably on heavy: has been
bandaged: usually early to post: usually races up with pace. *J. Berry*

ACE OF TRUMPS   3 ch.g. First Trump 118 – Elle Reef (Shareef Dancer (USA)   **68**
135) [1998 61: 5.3d⁶ 5d⁵ 5.1d 7f² 7g⁶ 6m² 7m* 7.1m² 8m 8g 7d⁶ 1999 7f 8.2m*   **a–**
10.5s* 9.3g 9.1g 10m 8.5g 10m³ 12s⁵ 10.9v³ 9.1v³ 11d⁵ a12g a8g Nov 15] sturdy
gelding: fair performer: won 18-runner selling handicap at Nottingham then 5-runner
claimer at Warwick (final start for W. Haggas) in May: respectable efforts at best
after: best up to 10.5f: acts on any turf going, no show on fibresand: effective
blinkered/visored or not: tongue tied. *J. Hetherton*

A CHEF TOO FAR   6 b.g. Be My Chief (USA) 122 – Epithet 105 (Mill Reef   **53**
(USA) 141) [1998 NR 1999 9v 12d⁴ a8g Dec 13] leggy, close-coupled gelding: fair
winner at 3 yrs: modest form at best in 3 runs since: stays 1½m: acts on soft ground,
probably on firm: tongue tied last 2 starts. *R. G. Frost*

ACHILLES   4 ch.g. Deploy 131 – Vatersay (USA) (Far North (CAN) 120) [1998   **110**
96: 10.3d* 12s² 11.5m⁵ 12d 11m⁶ 12g⁶ 12d 1999 10m⁶ 10.4s² 11.9d* 10g 10.4f*
9.9f² 10.4g² 10.9d³ 12f³ 12f⁶ Dec 4] smallish gelding: smart performer: won minor
event in June and John Smith's Cup (Handicap) in July, both at York, latter by ½
length from Siege: good efforts after in handicaps at Goodwood and York (short-head
second to Algunnaas), listed race at Ayr (final start for K. Burke, 4 lengths third to
Leggera) and Grade 3 at Santa Anita (3 lengths third to Public Purse): below form
final outing: effective at 1¼m/1½m: yet to race on heavy going, acts on any other:
visored final 3-y-o appearance: often sweating/edgy: usually races prominently:
game and consistent. *D. Vienna, USA*

ACHILLES SKY   3 b.c. Hadeer 118 – Diva Madonna 85 (Chief Singer 131)   **79 p**
[1998 79: 8.2d⁴ 7.9g 8d 1999 9m 10g* 11.9m⁶ Sep 3] strong, close-coupled colt: has
scope: fair performer, lightly raced: reportedly finished distressed on reappearance,
then did well to win 16-runner maiden handicap at Nottingham in July, hampered 2f
out but squeezing through under pressure: shaped like non-stayer in Haydock
handicap on return from another short break final start: stays 1¼m: yet to race on
extremes of going: should still do better. *K. R. Burke*

ACHILLES STAR   3 ch.g. Deploy 131 – Norbella (Nordico (USA)) [1998 85+:   **109**
5d* 5g⁵ 7g 7.3m 6g² 6g* 6v 7d a8g² a7g⁴ 1999 8s 6m⁵ 7m* 7d* 7f 7f⁵ 7g² 7g 8m*
8.5d Oct 15] smallish, sturdy gelding: useful handicapper: won at Newmarket in

*Vodafone Network Stakes (Handicap), Epsom—Achilles Star (rail) holds off Song 'N Dance Man
and Susan's Pride (second right) in a close finish*

April, Epsom in June and Newbury (came from well off good pace to beat Tarawan by 3 lengths) in September: refused to settle in listed race at Newmarket final start: probably needs further than 6f, and stays 1m well: acts on equitrack and probably any turf going: refused to enter stalls fourth intended start: sent to USA. *K. R. Burke*

ACICULA (IRE) 3 b.f. Night Shift (USA) – Crystal City (Kris 135) [1998 94p: **96** 5s⁴ 5d² 5m⁵ 5m² 5g* 6g² 6m* 1999 6m⁴ 6g 7f² 6g⁵ a8g 7s⁵ 6d⁶ Oct 20] lengthy, rather unfurnished filly: unimpressive mover: useful performer: best efforts when fourth in handicap at Lingfield, second in minor event at Goodwood and fifth in listed race at Pontefract between May and August: stays easy 7f: acts on firm going, probably on good to soft. *M. Johnston*

ACID TEST 4 ch.g. Sharpo 132 – Clunk Click 72 (Star Appeal 133) [1998 74, **79** a63: 8g 7.9g 7g 7d⁵ 7m* 7m 8m a8.5g 7d 6m 8g² 7g a7g a9.4g a6g a6g* a7g 1999 a6g³ a6g* a6f a6f* a7g² a7g a7g² a6g⁴ a6g⁶ 7m* 7d* 6d 7m 7f⁴ 7d 6d Oct 9] good-bodied gelding: fair handicapper: won at Lingfield (twice) in January, Catterick in May and Chester in June: well below form last 5 starts (off 6 weeks and gelded after third of them): effective at 6f to 1m: acts on good to firm going, good to soft and equitrack (well held on fibresand): free-going sort. *M. A. Buckley*

ACQUITTAL (IRE) 7 b.g. Danehill (USA) 126 – Perfect Alibi (Law Society **58 d** (USA) 130) [1998 39: 10g⁶ 10d² 10.8g⁶ 10g 10.2m 1999 10.3m³ 10d² 10.5m⁴ 12.3m³ 10m 10m 10m 10.3s Sep 22] modest handicapper: below par after second start: needs good test at 1¼m, and stays 1½m: probably acts on any going: blinkered once, usually visored: not entirely genuine. *A. Streeter*

ACROBATIC 2 br.c. (Apr 28) Warning 136 – Ayodhya (IRE) (Astronef 116) **84 p** [1999 6m* 7.3s⁶ Oct 22] 21,000Y: third foal: half-brother to 4-y-o Ambitious and 3-y-o Astronomer: dam French 2-y-o 6f/7f winner: favourite, overcame greenness to win 15-runner maiden at Newbury in September by short head from Hilltop Warning, getting up late on: some improvement when about 9 lengths sixth of 9 to Umistim in Horris Hill Stakes on same course following month, slowly away and not given hard time when held: should make useful 3-y-o up to 1m. *J. R. Fanshawe*

ACTION JACKSON 7 ch.g. Hadeer 118 – Water Woo (USA) 102 (Tom Rolfe) **44** [1998 49, a–: 9.7s 11.9g 10m² 10g 10d 10.1m 9.7m⁴ 14.1g² 16.2m 14.1f⁴ 10.1g² 11.5d⁶ 14.1s⁵ 1999 9g a14g² a16g 10d⁴ 14.1m⁶ a11g 14.1g⁴ Jul 3] close-coupled, angular gelding: poor performer: effective at 1¼m to 1¾m: acts on firm going, soft and fibresand: races up with pace. *B. J. McMath*

ACTUALLY (IRE) 2 b.f. (Apr 9) Namaqualand (USA) – Extra Time 66 (Shadeed **39** (USA) 135) [1999 5.1s 7m 6f⁵ 8d a8g a8.5g Nov 20] 4,500Y: second foal: dam, maiden who stayed 1¾m, daughter of Ribblesdale winner Expansive: poor maiden: stays 1m: acts on firm ground and fibresand: blinkered (well beaten) final start. *Andrew Reid*

ADAIR (USA) 3 ch.c. Theatrical 128 – Amore Cielo (USA) (Conquistador **123 p** Cielo (USA)) [1998 9f* 1999 12g 14.6m³ Sep 11]
All of the sums involved have never been made public, but it is safe to say that Godolphin's transatlantic purchase of horses in training prior to the latest season was, at the end of it, firmly in the red. One estimate, not including relocation fees, would be: expenditure, more than ten million dollars; returns in prize money, little more than 100,000 dollars. Godolphin's stateside target in the spring was the Kentucky Derby for which it had eight entries, including six who had previously been trained in the United States. Worldly Manner and Comeonmom were reportedly snapped up for five million and three million dollars respectively. Worldly Manner ran in both the Kentucky Derby and Preakness Stakes but finished only seventh (after showing up prominently) and twelfth, before spending the summer in Newmarket; Comeonmom finished last of nine in the Peter Pan Stakes in May. Their fellow Kentucky Derby entries were Festive Bid and Breathtaking View, neither of whom saw action at all in the United States in 1999; Prado's Landing, who was last of eight in the Blue Grass Stakes and fifth in an allowance race; and Always Believe who won an allowance race in May. Another US purchase, reportedly for 1,100,000 dollars,

was Holy Pole, who made fourth in an allowance event, while the ex-Argentine mare Lignify came tenth in a non-graded handicap. April and May were not fruitful months for the Godolphin US raiders then, though one might also consider the quartet formerly trained in Britain—Blue Snake, Charmes, Mitchigan and Sicnee—who ran once each and between them captured second-place money in one maiden and an allowance race. A brighter spot was provided four months later by another US buy, Adair, when he brought home no less than £39,050 when finishing third in the St Leger, which was won by a more traditional Godolphin representative, Mutafaweq.

Adair was a unique acquisition for Godolphin because, unlike the others, he was purchased from the United States to race in the European classics. He duly appeared in two of them, but that was all that was seen of him. There was, however, no shortage of talk about him. Most of it was in the run-up to his first European appearance, in the Derby. Positive noises from past and present connections coincided with his promotion to the head of the ante-post market early in the year, followed by a move in the opposite direction when a series of 'psychiatric' reports following his arrival in Britain described him variously as homesick, depressed and refusing to eat. Withdrawn from the Dante Stakes at York, it took a racecourse gallop at Leicester less than two weeks before the classic to put Adair back into the Derby picture. Making the Godolphin team is some recommendation in itself, but his form meant virtually nothing to British racegoers and not much more to those in the United States, because Adair had run only in one maiden race, over nine furlongs at Belmont Park in October, winning by eleven lengths. The form of the beaten horses in that race made uninspiring reading by the time of the Derby incidentally. Nevertheless, it was a considerable anti-climax when, finally unveiled, 16/1-chance Adair pulled hard under restraint in the last two and made only minimal headway; he lost a shoe, possibly when he was checked badly before halfway. Three months later, starting at 9/1 in the St Leger, he made that biggest return on Godolphin's American investment and did so in a manner which suggested he could make a much more sizeable contribution as a four-year-old. The final classic may ultimately be remembered for Mutafaweq's game victory over Ramruma, but it was a three-way battle most of the way up the straight after Adair moved up strongly to lead rounding the home turn. Beaten four lengths in third, clear of the remainder, this was very smart form.

One good reason for believing that Adair could make the grade in Europe was the record of his sire Theatrical. Second in the Irish Derby, Theatrical went on to win seven turf starts from nine outings as a five-year-old in the United States, six of those wins Grade 1, including the Breeders' Cup Turf. As a sire, so many of his best results have been on turf, with the likes of Royal Anthem, European classic winners Zagreb and Madeleine's Dream, St Leger second Broadway Flyer, Breeders' Cup Mile second Geri, Flower Bowl Handicap winners Auntie Mame and Dahlia's Dreamer and Japanese champion Hishi Amazon. Adair's dam Amore Cielo won three of her fifteen starts on dirt and Adair is her fifth foal, following an unraced filly, the Opening Verse colts Apak and Hoxie, who both won on dirt, and Rotar (by Blushing John) who won once each on dirt and turf. Apak was placed (at four and five years) in minor stakes company. That was also the height of his dam's achievements (as a four-year-old), but her dam, Header Card, was from a very different mould, winner of the Grade 1 Oak Leaf Stakes and rated just 1 lb below the top US two-year-old filly of 1981 in the Experimental Free Handicap. The following year Header Card gained only a minor stakes win, in November. There are several European turf performers in the family. Amore Cielo is half-sister to Varsavia, a fairly useful miler enterprisingly campaigned by Lord Huntingdon to win two listed races in Germany. More notably, Header Card is related to two colts who ended their two-year-old seasons with serious classic aspirations but failed to win a race of any description at three: she was a half-sister both to the dam of Undercut, a high-class two-year-old in 1987, and to Bellotto, who that

Godolphin's "Adair"

same year was beaten a neck by *Don't Forget Me* in the Two Thousand Guineas and one and a half lengths and a short head behind *Reference Point* in the Derby. Both colts made the journey back to the United States; Bellotto did not race again, and, although Undercut won once there, his greatest achievement was when third in a Grade 3 handicap.

	Theatrical	Nureyev	Northern Dancer
	(b 1982)	(b 1977)	Special
Adair (USA)		Tree of Knowledge	Sassafras
(ch.c. 1996)		(b 1977)	Sensibility
	Amore Cielo (USA)	Conquistador Cielo	Mr Prospector
	(b 1985)	(b 1979)	K D Princess
		Header Card	Quack
		(b 1979)	Shelf Talker

It will come as a surprise if Adair has exhausted his opportunities in Europe. A tall, rather leggy, close-coupled colt, he has raced only on good going or firmer and might prove best around a mile and a half. As the winner of just a maiden, there are plenty of good races open to him. *Saeed bin Suroor*

ADAMAS (IRE)   2 b.f. (Feb 22) Fairy King (USA) – Corynida (USA) (Alleged (USA) 138) [1999 6m² Sep 24] IR 110,000Y: third foal: closely related to Irish 3-y-o 7f (at 2 yrs)/1m winner Corrientes (by Night Shift) and half-sister to 1m/9f winner in Italy by Second Set: dam unraced: 20/1, 2 lengths second of 13 to Melanzana in maiden at Redcar, keeping on well from midfield: bred to stay at least 1m: should improve. *Andrew Turnell*   **73 p**

A DAY ON THE DUB   6 b.g. Presidium 124 – Border Mouse (Border Chief 101) [1998 41: 8v⁴ 1999 a12g* 12g⁴ 9g⁶ 10.1m⁴ 6.9m 9.9s 8.3s² 8d* 11d* 8.2s² a12g⁵ Dec 21] strong gelding: modest performer: won maiden at Southwell in January and handicap at Newcastle then claimer at Redcar in October, last 2 in large fields: ran   **57**

well when in frame otherwise: suited by testing conditions at 1m, and stays 1½m: acts on good to firm going, soft (showed promise on heavy) and fibresand. *D. Eddy*

ADDITION 3 b.f. Dilum (USA) 115 – Cedar Lady (Telsmoss 91) [1998 62: 5g⁴ **65** 5.1g⁴ 5.1d³ 5.7m⁶ 6m⁶ 1999 6.1v⁶ 6m 6f 6.1g² 6.1m³ 6.8m* 7m 7.1m 7s⁶ 8s Oct 26] fair handicapper: won at Warwick in July: below form after: effective at 6f/7f: acts on good to firm and good to soft going. *R. J. Hodges*

ADELPHI BOY (IRE) 3 ch.g. Ballad Rock 122 – Toda 53 (Absalom 128) [1998 **80** 79+, a87p: 5d 7g⁵ 7g⁵ 6m⁴ a5g² a5g* a5g* a5g* 1999 a6g² a7g³ a7g⁴ 8d³ 7g 8f⁴ **a91** 10.4d 6m 6f 6.1g³ 6g 7f 8d⁵ 10d 8s² 7s⁴ Nov 2] compact, workmanlike gelding: poor mover: fairly useful handicapper: generally creditable efforts in 1999: effective at 6f to 1m: acts on all-weather and soft going, probably on firm: has given trouble at stalls. *M. C. Chapman*

ADILABAD (USA) 2 b.c. (Feb 2) Gulch (USA) – Adaiyka (IRE) 110 (Doyoun **95 p** 124) [1999 7.1d* 7d* Oct 15] first foal: dam (placed over 9f (including at 2 yrs) and 1¼m winner): successful in small fields in minor events at Sandown (by 1½ lengths from Nicobar) and Newmarket (by 3 lengths from Camberley) following month, in latter dictating slow pace and keeping on well under firm hands and heels: should stay at least 1¼m: looks a smart performer in the making, and seems sure to win more races. *Sir Michael Stoute*

ADILOV 7 b.g. Soviet Star (USA) 128 – Volida 105 (Posse (USA) 130) [1998 –: **–** a12g 1999 a13g⁵ a16g Feb 11] rangy gelding: poor maiden: lightly raced and no form since 1996: tried visored. *J. J. Bridger*

ADIRPOUR (IRE) 5 gr.g. Nishapour (FR) 125 – Adira (IRE) (Ballad Rock 122) **61** [1998 40, a49: 16v 16g 8m² 7d³ 7.8m 5g³ 5s³ a6g⁵ a7g² 1999 a8g⁵ a8g a7g⁴ a8f **a46** a9.4g⁴ a5g a8g⁶ a8g 7s* 7m* 7.1d 8g 6d⁶ 7.6m⁴ 7m⁴ 8.1d 7.5g⁴ 7m 8.5g 8s⁴ 7s 7d 8.2s a8g a8g⁶ a8.5g a11g³ a12g Dec 27] lengthy gelding: modest on turf, poor on all-weather: won seller at Leicester in April and claimer at Newcastle in May: effective at 6f (given bit of a test) to 11f: acts on good to firm ground, soft and all-weather: tried blinkered: usually held up: has looked less than keen: none too reliable. *R. Hollinshead*

ADJUTANT 4 b.g. Batshoof 122 – Indian Love Song 68 (Be My Guest (USA) **104** 126) [1998 97: 7d⁵ 8.2s⁵ 7d² 7m* 8d 7g 7.1m² 7.1m* 1999 8m 7.1g⁴ 7m 7d 7.3m² 7d³ 7s* 8.2s³ Nov 1] tall gelding: has knee action: useful performer: won minor event at Leicester in October: best effort when close third to Family Man in rated stakes at Newmarket previous start: best around 7f: acts on good to firm and soft going. *B. J. Meehan*

ADMIRAL'S CUP (IRE) 2 b.c. (Mar 20) Bluebird (USA) 125 – Flying Fairy 79 **100 p** (Bustino 136) [1999 6s* Oct 2] 300,000Y: half-brother to 2 winners, notably top-class miler Desert Prince (by Green Desert): dam, maiden who stayed 1½m, daughter of 1000 Guineas winner Fairy Footsteps: 11/8 favourite, comfortably won 19-runner maiden at the Curragh in October by length from Soorah, soon travelling strongly just off pace, leading over 1f out and staying on well: should improve and win more races. *A. P. O'Brien, Ireland*

ADMIRALS FLAME (IRE) 8 b.g. Doulab (USA) 115 – Fan The Flame 69 **65** (Grundy 137) [1998 65, a–: 7s 8d 8.2m 7g 8.3d* 8d³ 8.3g 8.1d 8g³ 8g 8.2s 1999 7m 8s* 8.3g⁴ 8.1d 8d Oct 11] leggy gelding: fair handicapper: won 20-runner event at Leicester in June: best around 1m on good going or softer: none too consistent. *C. F. Wall*

ADMIRAL'S GUEST (IRE) 7 ch.g. Be My Guest (USA) 126 – Watership **–** (USA) (Foolish Pleasure (USA)) [1998 NR 1999 14.1g Jul 3] maiden handicapper: tried visored. *W. Clay*

ADMIRALS PLACE (IRE) 3 ch.c. Perugino (USA) 84 – Royal Daughter **73** (High Top 131) [1998 –: 6m 6f 1999 a6g³ a7g³ a8g* a9.4g² 9.9g² a12g⁶ 9.9s* 10s² 10d a10g⁵ Dec 22] close-coupled colt: fair handicapper: won at Lingfield in June and Beverley in September, and ran well when placed otherwise: left R. Armstrong 25,000 gns before final start: stays 1¼m (pulled much too hard at 1½m): acts on all-weather, easily best turf efforts on good going or softer (reportedly finished lame on firm): drifted right second start. *H. J. Collingridge*

ADMIRALS SECRET (USA) 10 ch.g. Secreto (USA) 128 – Noble Mistress **63 d**
(USA) (Vaguely Noble 140) [1998 71: 11.9g* 12m² 11.6g 11.5m* 11.5g* 12.1g
11.5g 11.5f⁴ 12m⁴ 1999 12g 12.3m 11.9f 11.8g⁶ a12g Jun 19] strong gelding: carries
condition: has a round action: modest handicapper: on the downgrade: effective at
11.5f to 1¾m: acts on any turf going and on all-weather: normally held up. *C. F. Wall*

ADNAAN (IRE) 3 ch.c. Nashwan (USA) 135 – Whakilyric (USA) 113 (Miswaki **107**
(USA) 124) [1998 104p: 7m² 8.1m³ 8.2d² 10d* 10s* 1999 10m 9.9g⁵ 12m* 12f³ 14g³
14s² Sep 24] strong, lengthy colt: has a quick, fluent action: useful performer: won
6-runner minor event at Newmarket in July by 2½ lengths from Memorise: ran well
after in Gordon Stakes (behind Compton Ace) and listed race (length second to
Yavana's Pace) at Goodwood then minor event at Haydock (6 lengths second to
Generosity, racing freely in blinkers): stays 1¾m: yet to race on heavy going, acts on
any other: has wandered and idled: carries head high. *J. L. Dunlop*

ADOBE 4 b.g. Green Desert (USA) 127 – Shamshir 116 (Kris 135) [1998 –: 6d 6g **62**
6d 7m 1999 8.3v³ 10v 8.3m³ 8.3s 7.7s 7.5d 8.3m² 8g* 9.2f 8m² 8.2m* 8.5m 8.1d⁴ **a54**
8.2g 7.5g 8.1s⁵ 8.3s³ a8.5g³ 8s 8g a8.5g Nov 13] small, stocky gelding: modest
handicapper: won in large fields at Bath (maiden event, swished tail) in June and
Nottingham in July: best around 1m: acts on good to firm going, soft and fibresand:
tongue tied: usually waited with. *W. M. Brisbourne*

ADORA'S DREAM (IRE) 3 b.c. Mujtahid (USA) 118 – Shady Bank (USA) 62 **–**
(Alleged (USA) 138) [1998 –: 8s⁶ 8d 1999 a8.5g 12.5d Apr 5] lengthy colt: no form,
including in blinkers. *J. W. Hills*

ADORNMENT 3 b.f. Magic Ring (IRE) 115 – Miss Loving 89 (Northfields **68 d**
(USA) [1998 NR 1999 5.8v 6m⁶ 8m 7g⁴ 7m 6g 6g a6g a8.5g Dec 1] 9,000Y, 8,200
2-y-o: half-sister to several winners, including useful sprinter Love Returned (by
Taufan): dam 2-y-o 5f/7f winner: fair maiden: trained by J. Harley in Ireland first 7
starts: no show after fourth: stays 7f: acts on good to firm going. *K. McAuliffe*

ADRENALIN 4 ch.g. Risk Me (FR) 127 – High Cairn (FR) 74 (Ela-Mana-Mou **–**
132) [1998 53d: a6g⁵ a6g* a6g 6v a6g a7g a7g 1999 a6g Jan 25] good-topped
gelding: no form since winning maiden at Southwell early in 1998 (reportedly bled
only 4-y-o start). *T. T. Clement*

ADULATION (USA) 5 ch.g. Sheikh Albadou 128 – Pedestal (High Line 125) **80**
[1998 82: 8.1m³ 8m² 8m² 10.2d³ 1999 a8.5g² 7m 8.1g 7.7m⁴ 8m 7m 8.2s⁵ Oct 5]
unfurnished gelding: fairly useful maiden: below form after fourth start: likely to
prove best around 1m: acts on fibresand and good to firm going: joined J. J. O'Neill.
P. W. Chapple-Hyam

AEGEAN 5 b.g. Rock Hopper 124 – Sayulita 67 (Habitat 134) [1998 NR 1999 8m **–**
Jun 24] tall gelding: no form: blinkered once. *Mrs S. J. Smith*

AEGEAN DREAM (IRE) 3 b.f. Royal Academy (USA) 130 – L'Ideale (USA) **84**
(Alysheba (USA)) [1998 NR 1999 10d 10m² 10.1m² 10m² 10g⁵ 8.5m* 8m 10g⁵ Oct
11] 45,000Y: first foal: dam, lightly-raced maiden, half-sister to Loup Sauvage and
Loup Solitaire and daughter of French Oaks runner-up Louveterie: fairly useful
performer: won maiden at Epsom in September: good fifth of 20 in handicap final
start: stays 1¼m: yet to race on extremes of going. *R. Hannon*

AEGEAN FLAME 3 ch.f. Anshan 119 – Dizzydaisy 57 (Sharpo 132) [1998 82: **86 ?**
5d 5v² 5.2s³ 5m² 5g 5g* 5.2g* 5.2m³ 1999 6g 5s⁴ 6g 6.1m 7m 8.1d Sep 15] leggy,
close-coupled filly: fairly useful performer at best: well below form in 1999 except
when fourth in rated stakes at Sandown in April: should stay 6f: acts on soft going
and on good to firm. *B. J. Meehan*

AEGEAN GLORY 3 b.f. Shareef Dancer (USA) 135 – Sayulita 67 (Habitat 134) **53**
[1998 –: 8.2s 1999 7m 7f⁵ 10g 8d² 7g 9m³ 10f³ a10g³ a10g⁴ 8.9m Sep 1] rather leggy
filly: modest maiden: left R. M. Flower after eighth start: stays 1¼m: acts on firm
going, good to soft and equitrack (yet to race on fibresand): reportedly had wind
infirmity third start (tongue tied final one). *J. G. M. O'Shea*

AEGEAN WIND 2 b.c. (Feb 19) Dolphin Street (FR) 125 – Perdicula (IRE) **– p**
(Persian Heights 129) [1999 7s Nov 5] lengthy, unfurnished colt: first reported foal:
dam unraced half-sister to Derby winner High-Rise: 14/1, green and backward,
always behind in maiden at Doncaster: likely to do better. *J. L. Dunlop*

AESOPS (USA)   3 ch.c. Diesis 133 – Affirmative Fable (USA) (Affirmed (USA))   **99**
[1998 99p: 7m³ 8.1m² 1999 10g⁴ 10.1g* 10.3m⁶ 7.9g Oct 6] tall, unfurnished colt:
useful performer: very easy winner of maiden at Yarmouth in August: well held last
2 starts, virtually bolting when tailed off on first occasion: will prove best up to 1¼m:
raced only on good/good to firm going: has been bandaged in front: headstrong: sent
to UAE. *J. H. M. Gosden*

AFAAN (IRE)   6 ch.h. Cadeaux Genereux 131 – Rawaabe (USA) 87 (Nureyev   **102**
(USA) 131) [1998 103: 5d 5s 5f³ 5m* 5f* 5f² 5d⁵ 5d 5m² 1999 5m⁶ 5d 5m 5g   **a90**
5.1m⁵ 6d 5d⁵ 5d⁵ 5d a5g⁴ a6g³ a5g³ a6g Dec 22] big horse: useful on turf, fairly
useful on all-weather: best efforts in 1999 when fifth in listed race (behind Sakha) at
Newmarket and in handicap (to Superior Premium) at Ascot on seventh and eighth
starts: speedy front runner, best at 5f: acts on firm going, good to soft and all-weather:
usually blinkered/visored, but has run well when not: often bandaged (has suffered a
lot of leg problems). *R. F. Marvin*

AFARKA (IRE)   6 b.m. Kahyasi 130 – Afasara (IRE) (Shardari 134) [1998 71:   –
12g⁵ 14g⁴ 16g 12m² 1999 a16.2g Jul 23] ex-Irish mare: first foal: dam Irish 1¼m
winner: fair handicapper for S. Treacy at 4/5 yrs: well beaten at Wolverhampton
(all-weather debut) only 6-y-o start: stays 2m: acts on good to firm and good to soft
ground: blinkered (well held) once at 4 yrs. *B. Palling*

AFFIDAVIT   3 b.f. Slip Anchor 136 – Lady Barrister (Law Society (USA) 130)   **72**
[1998 65: 8.2s⁵ 8s⁶ 1999 10m 12.5m⁵ 12g² 14.1f³ 12d³ 14.1g³ Jul 2] sturdy, lengthy
filly: has a round action: fair maiden: stays 1¾m: acts on firm ground, probably
soft: has looked none too keen: sold 12,000 gns, sent to New Zealand. *M. L. W. Bell*

AFICIONADO (IRE)   5 b.g. Marju (IRE) 127 – Haneena 118 (Habitat 134)   –
[1998 59d: 8d² 8s 9.2m⁵ 8g⁶ 9.9m 9.9m 8m 8m 1999 a10g Jan 21] workmanlike
gelding: modest handicapper at best: disappointing since 4-y-o reappearance: sold
780 gns in May. *R. J. Hodges*

AFREET   3 ch.c. Kris 135 – Cambara 97 (Dancing Brave (USA) 140) [1998 NR   **– p**
1999 7m Sep 7] second foal: dam, 1m winner, half-sister to smart middle-distance
performers Pluralisme, Singletta and Classic Tale: favourite, seventh in steadily-run
maiden at Lingfield, unable to challenge having been slowly away and very free
early: should stay beyond 7f: sent to UAE: should improve. *A. C. Stewart*

AFRICA (IRE)   2 b.f. (Jan 26) Namaqualand (USA) – Tannerrun (IRE) 65 (Run-   **57**
nett 125) [1999 5d 5m 5d 6m⁵ 7m* 7f⁴ 7f² 7.1m⁶ 7s 7g³ 7g³ 8d Nov 1] IR 3,800F,
12,000Y: sturdy filly: first foal: dam, 2-y-o 5f winner, half-sister to useful performer
up to 7f Nashcash: modest performer: won seller at Catterick in July: in frame in
claimers/nurseries after: should stay 1m: acts on firm going, well held on softer than
good: blinkered (well beaten) once: has been slowly away. *T. D. Barron*

AFRICAN PETE   2 b.c. (Jan 18) Lugana Beach 116 – Highland Bonnie (Dreams   **66**
To Reality (USA) 113) [1999 6.1m 6d³ 8s⁶ Oct 26] 500Y: sturdy colt: second foal:
brother to 3-y-o Silver Mist: dam ran once: fair form at best in maidens (off course 5
months after debut): may prove best up to 7f. *G. G. Margarson*

AFRICAN SUN (IRE)   6 b.g. Mtoto 134 – Nuit d'Ete (USA) 90 (Super Con-   –
corde (USA) 128) [1998 39, a–: a12g⁵ a12g a12g 10.3g⁶ 11.9d 11.6g 10s⁴ 10g 10.3g
8m 10g⁵ 10f⁶ 10.4g 1999 13.9s 8g 10f⁶ 10g⁵ 12s Nov 2] close-coupled, workmanlike
gelding: poor maiden at best: stays 1¼m: possibly needs good going or softer: tried
blinkered: tongue tied. *M. C. Chapman*

AFRIETINO   5 b.m. Tina's Pet 121 – African Lass 47 (Skyliner 117) [1998 NR   **41**
1999 8m a7g⁵ 6g⁶ 6s 5m a5g⁶ 5f Aug 2] strong, lengthy mare: second foal: half-sister
to German 9f/1m winner Jim Figgerty (by Infantry): dam 6f and 1m winner: poor
maiden: acted on fibresand: blinkered last 2 starts: dead. *Mrs N. Macauley*

AFTER EIGHT   4 b.g. Presidium 124 – Vickenda 52 (Giacometti 130) [1998 62:   **46**
a8g⁵ a6g* a6g 5.7s 6g 5.7d 6m² 7s a7g a6g 1999 a6f a6g⁶ 8f 6m⁵ 5.1m 7.1m 7.1m⁶
6d 7g Sep 14] smallish gelding: has a quick action: poor performer: stays 7f: acts
on good to firm going (probably good to soft) and equitrack: sometimes blinkered
(including for win): inconsistent. *M. S. Saunders*

AFTERJACKO (IRE)   3 ch.g. Seattle Dancer (USA) 119 – Shilka (Soviet Star   **95**
(USA) 128) [1998 NR 1999 9m 8.1d 11.7f* 10d⁵ 11.8d³ Oct 11] 54,000F, IR

29,000Y, 5,000 2-y-o: sturdy gelding: second foal: dam once-raced half-sister to Pentire: useful performer: won maiden at Bath in September: creditable efforts in handicaps at Newmarket and Leicester after: will stay beyond 1½m: yet to race on soft/heavy going, acts on any other: has been bandaged in front. *D. R. C. Elsworth*

AFTER THE BLUE (IRE)   2 b.c. (Mar 7) Last Tycoon 131 – Sudden Interest   **63 p** (FR) (Highest Honor (FR) 124) [1999 8d⁶ Oct 27] IR 24,000Y: first foal: dam, French 9f and 10.5f winner, half-sister to very smart middle-distance performer Sudden Love: 6/1, about 8 lengths sixth of 10 to Scotty Guest in maiden at Yarmouth, bumped after 2f out then running on: will be suited by 1¼m+: should do better. *M. R. Channon*

AGAINST THE BILL (IRE)   3 b.g. Petorius 117 – Galka 98 (Deep Diver 134)   **45** [1998 NR 1999 6d 5g⁶ 7m 6g 6f⁵ 5.9g 5g 5d⁵ Jun 28] IR 13,500Y: robust, sprint type: half-brother to several winners, including 1m winner Guess Again (by Stradavinsky), the dam of useful Irish 2-y-o's Eva Luna and Cois Na Tine: dam, 2-y-o 5f winner, half-sister to top-class sprinter Double Form: poor maiden: stayed 6f: blinkered after third start: hung/carried head awkwardly: dead. *T. D. Easterby*

AGANON   4 b.g. Aragon 118 – Plain Tree 71 (Wolver Hollow 126) [1998 –: 6d   **–** 1999 5.7m 7.6f 7m Aug 6] leggy gelding: disappointing maiden: visored once. *M. R. Channon*

AGENT LE BLANC (IRE)   4 b.g. Kahyasi 130 – White Witch (USA) 79   **78** (Nureyev (USA) 131) [1998 67: 10.3g 10m² 11.5g⁵ 1999 10m⁵ 14.6m² 15.9m 12.3d Aug 14] leggy, plain gelding: fair maiden: stays 2m: acts on good to firm going, yet to race on soft/heavy. *T. J. Etherington*

AGENT MULDER   5 b.g. Kylian (USA) – Precious Caroline (IRE) 60 (The   **84** Noble Player (USA) 126) [1998 67: 10g 8d³ 8.2d² 8.3g⁴ 9m 8d 6.1s* 6.1s* 7s 1999   **a61** 6.1v⁵ 6.1s* 6d⁴ a7g⁶ 6g* 6d 7g 7s Oct 22] fairly useful handicapper on turf: won in large fields at Nottingham (third course success) in April and Salisbury in June: well held last 2 starts (off 2 months before each): effective at 6f (given testing conditions) to 1m: off nearly a year after racing on firm going, and probably best on good or softer (modest form on fibresand): usually blinkered. *P. D. Cundell*

AGIOTAGE   3 br.g. Zafonic (USA) 130 – Rakli 84 (Warning 136) [1998 85p: **80** 6.1d⁴ 7g 7d* 1999 10g 9g⁶ 9m 10.3m⁴ 10.3d Aug 20] angular gelding: fairly useful handicapper: looked none too keen in blinkers when fourth at Doncaster: disappointing otherwise in 1999: probably stays 1¼m: acts on good to soft going, probably on good to firm: sold 2,700 gns in October, joined S. Williams. *H. R. A. Cecil*

AGITANDO (IRE)   3 b.g. Tenby 125 – Crown Rose (Dara Monarch 128) [1998   **97** NR 1999 10.2g 8g⁶ 9.9m* 9.9f 12s² 11.9f² 12s⁶ Sep 26] IR 12,000F, IR 66,000Y: has a quick action: third foal: half-brother to a winner up to 1½m in Japan by Waajib: dam twice-raced half-sister to very smart Irish performer up to 1¼m Lord Bud: useful performer: won maiden at Goodwood in June: creditable efforts in handicaps last 3 starts, runner-up at Kempton and York: stays 1½m: yet to race on heavy going, acts on any other. *R. Charlton*

AGNES WORLD (USA)   4 b.c. Danzig (USA) – Mysteries (USA) 111   **120** (Seattle Slew (USA)) [1998 8d² 1999 6m⁶ 6f² 6f² 6f⁵ 8f 6f* 6f* 5v* 6f* 6f² Dec 19]

El Condor Pasa's brave attempt to make all in the Prix de l'Arc de Triomphe stole much of the limelight from his compatriot Agnes World, winner of the Prix de l'Abbaye less than an hour before. Japanese horses winning big races in France has lost some of its novelty value after the historic successes of Seeking The Pearl and Taiki Shuttle in 1998 and El Condor Pasa's successful campaign in the latest season, but that shouldn't detract from Agnes World's achievement.

For one thing, Agnes World had never raced over five furlongs before and had almost certainly never encountered conditions as testing as at Longchamp; the ground is almost always very firm in Japan. Only Sweet Revenge (in 1971) and Mr Brooks (1992) had recorded slower winning times in the Abbaye in the last thirty years and the jockeys were of the opinion that the ground was actually worse on the sprint track than on the round course. Assuming that Agnes World could handle the conditions and trip, there were still doubts about his being good enough judged on his form in Japan. Even in the absence of Stravinsky (put aside for the Breeders' Cup) and Rudi's Pet (ineligible to run, as a gelding), who'd shown some of the best five-furlong form in Europe, Agnes World still faced tough opposition, including the very speedy French filly Sainte Marine, and Bertolini, Arkadian Hero and Keos who all came into the race after good efforts over six furlongs.

Not only did Agnes World master both the conditions and his thirteen rivals, he did so in remarkable fashion. Few sprinters in Europe have managed to match strides early on with Sainte Marine in the last couple of seasons but Agnes World did just that whilst the rest of the field struggled off the bridle. After Sainte Marine gave way Agnes World still had enough in reserve to repel the challenge of Imperial Beauty in the closing stages for a short-neck win. Keos stayed on one and a half lengths back to nose out Sampower Star for third, while Sainte Marine faded into sixth, one place ahead of unlucky-in-running Timote. Favourite Bertolini beat only two home.

Agnes World had raced only four times before the latest season, winning his first two starts from three outings at two (including a Group 3 event over six furlongs) and then having a year's absence after finishing second in a Group 3 mile contest on his reappearance at three. His two attempts in Group 1 company in Japan in the latest season had yielded fifth place in the six-furlong Takamatsunomiya Kinen at Chukyo (beaten around three lengths behind the winner Masa Lucky) and eighth place in the Yasuda Kinen at Tokyo over a mile won by Air Jihad, the latter race seemingly proving too far. Stable-mate Seeking The Pearl was placed in both contests, incidentally, suggesting that Agnes World had something to find at Longchamp. Before then, however, he had two more outings in lesser company (though both races were worth considerably more than the Abbaye!), winning them both at Kokura and reportedly setting a new Japanese six-furlong record in the process. Agnes World ran twice more in Japan after the Abbaye, gaining revenge on Masa Lucky in a Group 2 event at Kokura by half a length before going down by a neck to the five-year-old Black Hawk in the Group 1 Sprinters Stakes at Nakayama.

Prix de l'Abbaye de Longchamp Majestic Barriere, Longchamp—
Agnes World (No.9) proves a fine advertisement for Japanese racing with a gritty success;
Imperial Beauty (rail) is only just touched off, while Keos (No.7) stays on for third
with Sampower Star (rail) and Antinnaz (No.12) coming next

At 1,500,000 dollars, Agnes World was the most expensive Danzig yearling of 1996 and one of the ten highest-priced yearlings worldwide that year. His appeal from a Japanese point of view was largely down to the fact that his dam had already produced the very smart Japanese sprinter/miler Hishi Akebono (by Woodman), her second winner after the American two-year-old stakes winner My Sea Castles (by Polish Navy). Fourth foal Agnes World is followed by a two-year-old by Kingmambo, a yearling by Woodman and a foal by Gone West. Their dam, Mysteries, ran four times and failed to win, showing smart form when third in the Musidora over an extended ten furlongs, but giving the impression she'd have been suited by shorter. A tendency to pull was also a trait of grandam Phydilla, though that didn't prevent her showing high-class form in France at a mile, winning the Prix Quincey and finishing fourth in the Prix du Moulin. Phydilla was a half-sister to the Irish Derby and Coronation Cup runner-up Observation Post, out of Godzilla, who won in Italy as a two-year-old before showing useful form in sprints in Britain the following season. Godzilla's own Far East connection goes no further than being a name-sake of the giant lizard of Japanese monster-movie fame, though another of her offspring is Royal Suzuka, a smart sprinter/miler in Japan in recent seasons.

		Northern Dancer (b 1961)	Nearctic
	Danzig (USA)		Natalma
	(b 1977)	Pas de Nom (b 1968)	Admiral's Voyage
Agnes World (USA)			Petitioner
(b.c. 1995)		Seattle Slew (b or br 1974)	Bold Reasoning
	Mysteries (USA)		My Charmer
	(b 1986)	Phydilla (b 1978)	Lyphard
			Godzilla

Agnes World is a strong, lengthy colt, who looked in very good shape at Longchamp where he was bandaged all round. His rider at Longchamp was Yutaka Take whose previous experience of Arc day five years earlier had been one to forget when slated in the British press for his riding of White Muzzle and suspended for careless riding after finishing first in the Prix de l'Opera. Agnes World and his veteran travelling-companion Dojima Muteki (last-but-one in the Abbaye) were based in Newmarket at Robert Armstrong's stable during their time in Europe. Agnes World could be back at Newmarket to race if plans to contest the July Cup come to fruition; both horses figured among the original entries for the contest in 1999. *H. Mori, Japan*

AGRIPPINA 2 b.f. (Feb 27) Timeless Times (USA) 99 – Boadicea's Chariot **99** (Commanche Run 133) [1999 5m² 7d* 7s* Oct 2] smallish, good-topped filly: second foal: dam Irish 1½m winner, also successful over hurdles: won maiden at Ayr in September and listed race at Newmarket (12-runner contest, by ½ length from High Walden) in October, dictating pace in former, leading final 1f in latter: may prove best at 7f/1m. *A. Bailey*

AGUA CABALLO (IRE) 2 b.g. (Mar 11) Petorius 117 – Beauty Appeal (USA) **72 d** (Shadeed (USA) 135) [1999 5f³ 5g* 5d⁶ 7f⁴ 5m* 6g 6g 6m 7s⁶ 5g⁵ 6s⁶ Nov 2] 11,000Y: close-coupled gelding: first foal: dam unraced: fair performer at best: won maiden at Carlisle in May and claimer at Beverley in July: rather disappointing after: effective at 5f to 7f: acts on firm and good to soft going. *S. E. Kettlewell*

AHDAAB (USA) 3 ch.f. Rahy (USA) 115 – Dish Dash 118 (Bustino 136) [1998 **73** –p: 7g 1999 10.1g³ 10.4m⁵ 7.5s Sep 21] sparely-made filly: fair maiden: may prove best at 1¼m/1½m: best effort on good to firm going: sent to USA. *R. W. Armstrong*

AHOUOD 3 b.f. Merdon Melody 98 – Balidilemma 77 (Balidar 133) [1998 –p: **53** a7g⁶ 1999 6m 10m 6g³ 7.7m⁶ Jul 17] modest maiden: form only in handicap at Windsor third start: should stay beyond 6f. *K. Mahdi*

AIMA (IRE) 2 b. or br.c. (Feb 25) Brief Truce (USA) 126 – Palmyra (GER) **93** (Arratos (FR)) [1999 6.1f 7f² 7m² 7m⁴ Aug 17] 18,000Y: neat colt: sixth foal:

half-brother to German 6.5f to 7.5f winner Super Shirley and to 3-y-o Grandioso (both by High Estate): dam German 2-y-o 6f winner from good family: fairly useful form: runner-up in maidens at York and Leicester before good fourth of 5, beaten over 3 lengths by King's Best, in listed race at York: will stay 1m: took good hold first 2 starts: sent to USA. *G. C. H. Chung*

AIRA FORCE (USA)   2 ch.g. (Mar 7) Dehere (USA) 121 – Cinnamon Splendor (USA) (Trempolino (USA) 135) [1999 5m 5m³ 5g³ 5m* 5s Sep 21] $50,000F, $45,000Y: second foal: dam maiden from family of Derby runner-up City Honours: fair performer: won maiden at Haydock in September, racing alone and making most: should be suited by further than 5f: raced on good/good to firm going before well beaten on soft final start. *J. Noseda*   **74 +**

AIR ATTACHE (USA)   4 b.g. Sky Classic (CAN) – Diplomatic Cover (USA) (Roberto (USA) 131) [1998 79: 8.5s³ 10.1g 9m³ 8.1g 12m² 14g⁴ 11.6f⁴ 9.7s 1999 10.2g 10d⁶ 12m² 11.5g⁶ 12m⁴ 14.1g⁴ 12m a12g³ a12g² 11.9d² Oct 21] tall, quite good-topped gelding: good walker: fair maiden handicapper: generally creditable efforts in 1999: effective at 1½m/1¾m: acts on firm going, soft and all-weather: blinkered (ran poorly) once at 3 yrs: usually tongue tied: sometimes makes running: sold 6,500 gns, joined C. Mann. *D. Sasse*   **66**

AIR DEFENCE   2 br.c. (May 11) Warning 136 – Cruising Height 112 (Shirley Heights 130) [1999 7d² Oct 12] sixth foal: half-brother to smart stayer Corradini and St Leger runner-up High And Low (both by Rainbow Quest): dam, stayed 1½m, half-sister to Park Hill winner Trampship: weak 14/1-shot, shaped well when 2½ lengths second of 15 to Ferzao in maiden at Leicester, slowly away but running on well without being given hard time: should be suited by 1¼m+: sure to improve and win a race. *B. W. Hills*   **82 p**

AIR MARSHALL (IRE)   2 ch.c. (Apr 29) In The Wings 128 – Troyanna 109 (Troy 137) [1999 7m² 8m* 8s⁴ Oct 23] lengthy colt: half-brother to several winners, including smart French 1m and 1¼m winner Break Bread (by Bering) and fairly useful 1½m winner Lucrezia (by Machiavellian): dam 7f winner at 2 yrs and fourth in Irish Oaks: landed odds in maiden at Goodwood in September, making virtually all: free to post and sweating, over 8 lengths fourth of 9 to Aristotle in Racing Post Trophy at Doncaster following month, keeping on from rear: will be very well suited by 1¼m+: type to make a more than useful 3-y-o. *Sir Michael Stoute*   **99 p**

AIR OF ESTEEM   3 b.g. Forzando 122 – Shadow Bird 70 (Martinmas 128) [1998 61+: 6s⁵ 1999 a8.5g² a8g* a8g² 8d 8.1d* 8.3g³ 8m 10m 9g² 8g⁶ 8.9d Oct 9] smallish gelding: fairly useful on turf, fair on all-weather: won maiden at Lingfield in January and (best effort) handicap at Haydock in June, latter in good style by 8 lengths: largely disappointing after: stays 9f: acts on all-weather and good to soft going. *P. C. Haslam*   **92**
a80

AISLE   2 b.c. (Feb 25) Arazi (USA) 135 – Chancel (USA) 60 (Al Nasr (FR) 126) [1999 5d 6.1g⁶ a6g³ 7.5g 5m a6g* 6.1s* a7g Dec 15] small colt: second foal: dam, maiden who should have stayed beyond 11f, half-sister to smart winner up to 10.5f Church Parade and smart middle-distance stayer Castle Rising: modest performer: trained first 3 starts by I. Balding: improved efforts in the autumn, winning nurseries at Southwell and Nottingham, carrying head awkwardly and edging left under pressure on second occasion: likely to prove best up to 7f: acts on soft ground and fibresand: usually races prominently. *S. R. Bowring*   **61**

AIWAI (IRE)   2 b.c. (Apr 14) Thatching 131 – Peach Melba 96 (So Blessed 130) [1999 7m 6d² 6g Oct 19] 14,000Y: half-brother to several winners, including useful winner up to 9.4f Reported (by Heraldiste): dam 2-y-o 5f winner: easily best effort in maidens when 1¾ lengths second of 22 to Avezzano at Ayr in September: ran poorly final start: will stay at least 7f. *G. C. H. Chung*   **81**

AIX EN PROVENCE (USA)   4 b.g. Geiger Counter (USA) – Low Hill (Rousillon (USA) 133) [1998 –: 7d⁶ 7d 10v 7m 8.5d 10m a8.5g 8m* 7g 8m⁵ 10.1d a10g a8g Nov 23] fair performer nowadays: left M. Johnston before winning selling handicap at Yarmouth in August: stays 1m: best efforts on good going or firmer (well beaten on all-weather): has had tongue tied: reportedly broke blood vessel eighth start: inconsistent. *C. A. Dwyer*   **65**
a–

AJDAR   8 b.g. Slip Anchor 136 – Loucoum (FR) 93 (Iron Duke (FR) 122) [1998   **50**
47, a58: a8s⁶ a11g² a12g* a12g⁴ a11g³ a14g⁶ 10.3d⁴ 12.3v⁵ 10v a12g⁵ 11.9g⁴ 12.3s
10.3g 12.3g 1999 a11g a12f⁴ a12g⁴ a12g a12g 12.3m a14g a12g Dec 21] angular gelding:
poor handicapper: stays 15.4f: acts on firm ground, good to soft and all-weather: tried
visored: held up. *Mrs S. Lamyman*

AJHIBA (IRE)   3 ch.f. Barathea (IRE) 127 – Welsh Love (Ela-Mana-Mou 132)   **110**
[1998 NR 1999 8m* 9.9d* 14.6g Sep 8] IR 950,000Y: rangy filly: sixth foal: closely
related to fairly useful Irish 1¼m winner (stayed 1½m) Catalyst (by Sadler's Wells)
and half-sister to 3 winners, notably 4-y-o Second Empire (by Fairy King): dam, Irish
1½m winner, half-sister to dam of Salsabil and Marju: made a most promising start
to her career, winning well-contested maiden at Newmarket in May and listed race at
Salisbury (beat Choirgirl by 1¼ lengths, despite carrying head awkwardly) in
August: slowly away and ran as though something amiss when tailed-off last in Park
Hill Stakes at Doncaster: should stay beyond 1¼m. *Saeed bin Suroor*

AJIG DANCER   4 b.f. Niniski (USA) 125 – Gloire (Thatching 131) [1998 83d: **84**
8v 6d⁴ 7m 6g³ 5g⁶ 5m 6d 6.1v 5.1v⁶ a7g a6g⁵ a6g⁴ a5f⁴ a5g² 1999 a7g³ a7f² a7g a7g³   **a68**
7s* 7s 8.1m 7f 6m² 6m⁶ 7g* 7s² 7g* 7m⁴ 7.1d 6m⁶ Sep 24] leggy, lengthy filly: has
reportedly been covered by Fraam: fairly useful on turf, fair on all-weather: won
handicap at Warwick in March and minor event at Brighton then handicap at
Yarmouth in August: stays 7f: acts on all-weather, good to firm and soft going: held
up. *M. R. Channon*

AJJAE (IRE)   3 b.g. High Estate 127 – Lake Ormond (Kings Lake (USA) 133)   **48**
[1998 –: 7s⁶ 8.3d 7s 7.1s⁴ 1999 8.3d 7.1g 7m² 8.3f⁵ 7.5g* 9.2m² 8.3s⁶ 12g a9.4g Nov
17] sturdy gelding: poor performer: won claimer at Beverley in August, making
most: effective at 7f to 9.2f: acts on heavy going, acts on any other on turf
(below form on fibresand final start): wears visor/blinkers. *I. Semple*

AJNAD (IRE)   5 b.g. Efisio 120 – Lotte Lenta (Gorytus (USA) 132) [1998 64+,   **71**
a71+: a7g⁴ a7g⁵ a6g³ a5g 7s³ 6g 6m 5f⁶ 5m² a5g 6g 5m 5g² 5m 5d⁴ a5g² a5f³ 1999   **a84 +**
a6g* a6f² a6g⁶ 6f³ 5d May 8] deep-bodied gelding: fairly useful on all-weather, fair
on turf: won maiden at Lingfield in January: good efforts after when placed in
handicaps: slowly away final start: effective at 5f/6f: unraced on heavy going, acts on
any other turf/all-weather: visored once at 4 yrs, effective blinkered or not: sometimes bandaged/tongue tied: has hung left: often ridden by S. Righton. *R. F. Marvin*

AKALIM   6 b.g. Petong 126 – Tiszta Sharok 81 (Song 132) [1998 68: a7g⁴ 6g²   **75 ?**
7m 6m 7.1g⁵ a8.5g 7.1d* 7v² 6s² 1999 7s 7.1d⁵ 7.1g² 7s 7v 7d² 7s* 7s Nov 2]
good-topped gelding: has a quick action: fair handicapper: probably flattered when
winning 25-runner apprentice event at Newbury in October, one of only 2 to race far
side: only a few creditable efforts otherwise, including when runner-up: effective at
6f/7f: acts on any turf ground and equitrack, probably fibresand: tried blinkered/
visored: often races prominently. *L. G. Cottrell*

AKBAR (IRE)   3 b. or br.c. Doyoun 124 – Akishka (Nishapour (FR) 125) [1998   **106**
95p: 7s* 7s³ 1999 8m⁵ 12d² 12d² 12g 14m³ 12.3v² 10d³ 12s Nov 6] ex-Irish colt:
sixth foal: brother to useful Irish 1m winner (including at 2 yrs) Akhiyar, closely
related to useful Irish 1½m winner Akdariya (by Shirley Heights) and half-brother to
Irish 9.6f winner Akilara (by Kahyasi): dam unraced daughter of Arc winner Akiyda:
useful performer: won maiden at Tipperary at 2 yrs: best efforts in 1999 when third in
listed race at Leopardstown (behind Yeoman's Point, final start for J. Oxx) in July
and rated stakes at Ascot (1½ lengths behind Monsajem) in October: effective at
1¼m to 1¾m: acts on good to firm going, probably on heavy. *M. Johnston*

AKEED (USA)   2 ch.c. (Feb 7) Affirmed (USA) – Victorious Lil (CAN) (Vice   **102 p**
Regent (CAN)) [1999 7m* 7g⁴ 7s⁴ Nov 5] $180,000Y: strong, lengthy colt: has
scope: second foal: half-brother to top-class American colt up to 1½m (won Belmont
Stakes) Victory Gallop (by Cryptoclearance): dam Canadian 1m stakes winner: won
maiden at York in October very easily: reportedly lame next time but showed useful
form when 1½ lengths fourth of 8 to Touch of The Blues in Criterium de
Maisons-Laffitte final start, leading 2f out until final 1f: will be suited by 1¼m/1½m:
sort to improve again. *P. F. I. Cole*

AKHIRA   2 b.f. (Jan 24) Emperor Jones (USA) 119 – Fakhira (IRE) 83 (Jareer   **90**
(USA) 115) [1999 7d⁴ 7d⁵ Oct 20] 50,000Y: first foal: dam, Irish 2-y-o 5f winner,

half-sister to smart 6f/7f winner Danehill Dancer: promising fourth of 17 to Inchlonaig in valuable sales event at Newmarket: odds on, only fifth of 10 in maiden at Newcastle following month: bred to be best up to 1m. *S. P. C. Woods*

ALAAMA (IRE) 3 ch.f. Elmaamul (USA) 125 – Rahik 103 (Wassl 125) [1998 71p: 7m⁴ 1999 7.1m² 8m⁴ 10d 7.7m 8.5s Sep 21] workmanlike filly: fair maiden: should stay 1¼m: acts on good to firm ground, probably not on softer than good: sent to USA. *R. W. Armstrong* **72**

ALABAMA WURLEY 2 b.f. (Jan 10) Environment Friend 128 – Logarithm (King of Spain 121) [1999 5v³ 5d 6m⁶ 7m² 7m⁴ a7g² 7g* 7m 8s³ Sep 16] 1,000Y: third foal: half-sister to 6-y-o General Equation: dam poor half-sister to smart sprinter Northern Goddess: modest performer: won seller at Newmarket in August: creditable third in nursery at Yarmouth: should stay beyond 1m: acts on good to firm ground, soft and fibresand. *D. Morris* **60**

ALABAQ (USA) 3 b. or br.f. Riverman (USA) 131 – Salsabil 130 (Sadler's Wells (USA) 132) [1998 94+: 6g² 7g* 8s⁴ 1999 8g² 10m* 12m³ 9.9f⁶ 10m² 9.9m⁴ 8f* Oct 17] smallish filly: smart performer: won listed race at Newmarket (by 1¾ lengths from Ela Athena) in May and Premio Bagutta at Milan (by 1¾ lengths from Euryanthe) in October: ran creditably when in frame in between, 2 lengths third to Fairy Queen in Ribblesdale Stakes at Royal Ascot and 1½ lengths second to Zindabad in Winter Hill Stakes at Windsor: effective at 1m to 1½m: acts on firm going, probably on soft: edged left/swished tail/found little fourth start: stud. *J. L. Dunlop* **111**

ALAKDAR (CAN) 5 ch.g. Green Dancer (USA) 132 – Population (General Assembly (USA)) [1998 –: 12g 11.5g 1999 11.6m 11.6d a16.2g² a16.2g⁶ Dec 15] fairly useful winner at 3 yrs: form since only when second of 4 in claimer on final start for B. Meehan: stays 2m: best effort on soft going. *Jane Southcombe* **65 ?**

Mr Hamdan Al Maktoum's "Alabaq"

ALAMEIN (USA)   6 ch.g. Roi Danzig (USA) – Pollination 100 (Pentotal) [1998   **52 §** \
71§: a7g* 8d a8g 6.9d⁶ 8m² 8.1d³ 8m³ 7.1s⁶ 6.9m 1999 a8g³ a7g* a7g* a8g⁴ a7g⁶ 7g   **a79 §** \
8d² 6.9g⁴ 8m⁴ 8.1m Jul 21] big, workmanlike gelding: fair on all-weather, modest on \
turf: won claimer and apprentice handicap at Lingfield in February: best at 7f/1m: \
acts on firm ground, good to soft and all-weather: effective blinkered or not: has been \
bandaged: carries head high, and has failed to go through with effort: not one to trust: \
sold 2,400 gns in October, joined W. Storey. *D. Nicholls*

ALANA'S CAVALIER (IRE)   3 b.c. Forest Wind (USA) 111 – Annais Nin   **50 §** \
(Dominion 123) [1998 55, a49: 7m 7g 7.1m 8m 10d³ 8.2v³ a9.4g⁴ a8g⁴ a7g⁴ a8g 1999 \
a8g a8g* a8g a11g a7g a12g⁶ 12.5d⁴ 9.9g⁶ 9.9d⁴ 10m 10f a11g⁵ 10m³ 10.5m³ 10.5m \
12m³ 12.4f² 10g³ a12g⁴ 13.8g 10d 14.1f Oct 20] small colt: modest performer: won \
seller at Southwell in January: effective at 1m to 1½m: acts on fibresand, good to \
firm (probably firm) and heavy going: visored once, effective blinkered or not: none \
too genuine: sold 4,500 gns, sent to Kuwait. *R. Hollinshead*

ALARMING MOTOWN   4 b.f. Warning 136 – Sweet Soul Dream (USA) 61   – \
(Conquistador Cielo (USA)) [1998 NR 1999 a8g Jan 12] leggy filly: well held in \
maidens 15 months apart. *M. R. Channon*

ALASAN (IRE)   2 b.c. (Mar 29) Zilzal (USA) 137 – Alasana (IRE) (Darshaan   **78 p** \
133) [1999 7g⁴ Aug 6] first living foal: dam, French 1m/9f winner, half-sister to \
high-class French 1½m performer Altayan: 3/1, promising 5½ lengths third of 8 to \
King's Best in maiden at Newmarket, becoming rather unbalanced halfway and not \
knocked about: will stay at least 1m: seems sure to do better. *L. M. Cumani*

ALASTAIR SMELLIE   3 ch.g. Sabrehill (USA) 120 – Reel Foyle (USA) 77   **84 +** \
(Irish River (FR) 131) [1998 83: 7.1d⁶ 7m 7.6f 6m³ 6s* 6g⁶ 6m³ 1999 6g³ 6.1m⁵ 7d⁴ \
6d 7d 6s⁴ Nov 6] good-topped gelding: has a quick action: fairly useful handicapper: \
creditable efforts first 4 starts in 1999 (off 4 months after fourth one): seemed to excel \
himself when fourth of 20 to Pipalong in listed event at Doncaster final outing: stays \
7f: acts on good to firm going, but goes very well on soft: flashes tail, looks awkward \
ride and best covered up for as long as possible. *B. W. Hills*

AL ATAYA (USA)   2 b.g. (Apr 12) Dayjur (USA) 137 – Sajjaya (USA) 97 (Blush-   **59 p** \
ing Groom (FR) 131) [1999 7d⁵ 7d Oct 22] smallish gelding: fifth foal: closely \
related to useful 1997 2-y-o 6f winner Shuhrah (by Danzig) and half-brother to \
7-y-o Raased: dam, 7f/1m winner, half-sister to Lahib: burly, better effort in October \
maidens when never-nearer seventh of 22 to Fame At Last at Doncaster: sold 15,000 \
gns later in October: should stay 1m: should do better. *J. L. Dunlop*

ALAWAR   2 ch.c. (Apr 15) Wolfhound (USA) 126 – Ghassanah 73 (Pas de Seul   **71** \
133) [1999 5m 6m³ 6g Oct 19] closely related to 4-y-o Sand Hawk and to 1m winner \
Willisa (both by Polar Falcon) and half-brother to several winners, including 3-y-o \
Little Amin and 5-y-o Return of Amin: dam 7f winner: fair maiden: 3 lengths third of \
15 to Acrobatic at Newbury in September, best effort: should stay 7f: tongue tied \
final start: bandaged. *C. G. Cox*

ALA WASHAK   3 b.g. Green Desert (USA) 127 – Shadha (USA) 77 (Devil's Bag   **64** \
(USA)) [1998 NR 1999 6g⁴ 6d⁵ Oct 28] 5,000 3-y-o: third foal: dam 2-y-o 6f winner \
here and 1m/9f winner in USA at 4 yrs, daughter of very smart French 1m to 1½m \
filly Treizieme: modest form in maidens at Redcar then Windsor (given vigorous \
ride): should stay 7f. *Mrs L. Stubbs*

ALAZAN   4 ch.c. Risk Me (FR) 127 – Gunnard 62 (Gunner B 126) [1998 –: 11.5g⁴   – \
1999 11.9f 10m 8g Aug 12] workmanlike colt: tailed off in varied company. *W. de \
Best-Turner*

AL AZHAR   5 b.g. Alzao (USA) 117 – Upend 120 (Main Reef 126) [1998 NR   **101** \
1999 8.1s² 10.4s⁶ 10g⁵ 12g² 12v³ 12d Oct 14] well-made gelding: has reportedly had \
knee trouble: useful performer: ran creditably most starts in 1999, though had to be \
led to post and possibly didn't put it all in on penultimate one: effective at 1m to \
1½m: acts on good to firm and heavy going: sold 21,000 gns, joined M. Dods. \
I. A. Balding

ALBAADRI   4 b.c. Cadeaux Genereux 131 – Actraphane (Shareef Dancer (USA)   – \
135) [1998 NR 1999 8.3g Oct 11] 72,000Y: second foal: half-brother to 1m winner \
Besweetome and 3-y-o Ashbourne Pat (both by Mtoto): dam French 11.8f winner

from good German family of Annus Mirabilis: 10/1 from 4/1, very slowly away and always beaten in maiden at Windsor: sent to UAE. *J. H. M. Gosden*

ALBARAHIN (USA)　4 b.c. Silver Hawk (USA) 123 – My Dear Lady (USA)　**114** (Mr Prospector (USA)) [1998 77: 10.4g³ 10v⁴ 1999 10g* 10m* 10s⁶ 9v* 8d² Oct 30] strong, deep-girthed colt: smart performer: reportedly fractured leg in spring of 1998: better than ever in 1999, winning handicaps at Leicester then Sandown in August and Newbury (beat Island House 4 lengths in rated stakes, edged left) in October: good ¾-length second to Bomb Alaska in steadily-run listed event at Newmarket final start: barely stays 1¼m when conditions are testing: yet to race on firm going, acts on any other: may do better still. *M. P. Tregoning*

ALBARDEN　2 ch.c. (Feb 5) Mujtahid (USA) 118 – Aljood 111 (Kris 135) [1999　**65 ?** 7m⁴ 6m Jul 12] 17,500Y: sixth foal: half-brother to several winners, including useful 1998 2-y-o 6f winner Society Snoop (by Warning), 1½m winner Just Grand (by Green Desert) and 8-y-o Desert Invader: dam, lightly-raced maiden, fourth in Prix Marcel Boussac: appeared to show fair form at Newcastle on first of 2 starts in maidens in the summer. *T. D. Easterby*

ALBATA　2 b.g. (Feb 4) Alhijaz 122 – Basenite (Mansingh (USA) 120) [1999 7m　**–** a8.5g Sep 8] 3,000Y: fourth foal: half-brother to a winner in Italy by Statoblest: dam poor sister to high-class sprinter Petong: no promise in maidens. *M. A. Jarvis*

ALBEMINE (USA)　10 b.g. Al Nasr (FR) 126 – Lady Be Mine (USA) 76 (Sir　**46** Ivor 135) [1998 –, a52: a12g⁵ a16.2g⁶ 1999 a14.8g⁵ a16g³ a14.8g² a14g a16.2g⁵ 13.8g a16.2g Nov 17] poor performer nowadays: stays 2m: acts on soft ground and all-weather: often leads. *A. G. Juckes*

ALBERGO (IRE)　2 b.g. (Mar 14) Deploy 131 – River Dove (USA) 86 (River-　**–** man 131) [1999 8v 7d Oct 21] 11,000Y: seventh foal: half-brother to 5-y-o Mungo Park and 7f/1m winner Square Deal (by Sharpo): dam, 2-y-o 6f winner, half-sister to 5-y-o Running Stag: well beaten in maidens. *M. Blanshard*

ALBERICH (IRE)　4 b.g. Night Shift (USA) – Tetradonna (IRE) 102 (Teenoso　**101** (USA) 135) [1998 97: 11.9g* 12g⁴ 1999 12g 10v⁵ 12m² 13.9s 13.9m 12m³ 13.3m* a12g* Nov 11] sturdy, good-bodied gelding: good mover: usually takes the eye: useful performer: gelded and off 4 months after fourth start: better than ever on last 3, winning Tote Sporting Index Autumn Cup (Handicap) at Newbury in September by ½ length from Bold Gait, and minor event at Lingfield in November easily by 4 lengths from China Castle: stays 13.3f: acts on good to firm ground (probably on soft) and equitrack: usually races prominently/leads. *M. Johnston*

ALBERKINNIE　4 b.f. Ron's Victory (USA) 129 – Trojan Desert 97 (Troy 137)　**37** [1998 45, a38: a7g⁴ 9g a8g 7g 8.3d⁶ 8m 8.3s 10v⁶ 9g⁵ a9.4g 1999 8g 9d 10m 10.1m 8g⁵ 10.5m 8g² 8.2m⁶ 10.1f⁴ 8g⁴ 11.9m 11.5m² a12g Dec 21] sturdy filly: poor maiden handicapper: effective at 1m to 11.5f: acts on good to soft, good to firm going and fibresand: has hung: carries head high. *J. L. Harris*

ALBERTINA JANE　2 b.f. (Apr 19) Beveled (USA) – Austral Jane 74 (Domin-　**39** ion 123) [1999 5.1g 5.1m 7f⁴ Jul 13] 1,000Y: second foal: dam, maiden best up to 1m, half-sister to smart middle-distance stayer Party Season: poor maiden: hung left final start. *M. D. I. Usher*

ALBERT THE BEAR　6 b.g. Puissance 110 – Florentynna Bay 61 (Aragon 118)　**73** [1998 88, a–: 8d 7.6m³ᵈⁱˢ 7g 6.1g⁵ 6.1g⁶ 7m³ 7.6g 6s 1999 7.6m 7m 7d⁵ 5.9g⁴ 5.9m*　**a–** 6d* 6f² 6m³ 7m 6.1m 6g⁴ 6.9g⁶ 6d 6d Nov 1] tall gelding: easy mover: fair performer nowadays: won seller at Carlisle in June and handicap at Pontefract in July: effective at 6f/7f: acts on any turf going, no show on fibresand: effective blinkered/visored or not: often leads. *J. Berry*

ALBOOSTAN　4 b.c. Sabrehill (USA) 120 – Russian Countess (USA) 104 (Nur-　**105** eyev (USA) 131) [1998 108: 9s² 11.5m⁴ 10s⁴ 1999 8.5g 10m² 10.1g⁴ 10g⁴ 8d³ 7.9g 8d⁵ Sep 18] good-bodied colt: useful performer: generally creditable efforts in 1999, including fourth of 20 to Moutahddee in Hong Kong Jockey Club Trophy (Handicap) at Sandown on fourth start: effective at 1m to 1¼m: has won on good to firm ground, better form on good or softer: blinkered last 2 starts: usually races prominently: sent to UAE. *B. W. Hills*

ALBORADA   4 gr.f. Alzao (USA) 117 – Alouette 105 (Darshaan 133) [1998   **122**
122: 10s* 9.9g* 10d² 10g* 1999 9.9f⁵ 10g* Oct 16]

Those who saw the Dubai Champion Stakes—which wasn't everyone
on the packed July course at Newmarket—were treated to a command performance by a filly who had been out of the limelight all year. Her victory, repeating
that of the previous season, was also a huge feather in the cap of her trainer Sir
Mark Prescott, who had had to show consummate patience and skill with the
filly in a far-from-trouble-free campaign.

As a three-year-old Alborada had shown very smart form to win three
of her four starts. The Champion Stakes, in which she defeated Insatiable and
Daylami, was her best performance, but she also notched the Pretty Polly
Stakes at the Curragh and the Nassau Stakes at Goodwood, as well as running
second to Swain in the Irish Champion Stakes at Leopardstown. As a four-
year-old she started cantering in May, with her campaign geared towards
starting off in either the Pretty Polly Stakes or the Eclipse. The Irish race was
deemed to come too soon, and a dirty throat prevented Alborada's participation
in the Eclipse. Next on the agenda was a bid for another victory in the Nassau
Stakes. Alborada started favourite, though later in the season it was revealed
that she was not one hundred percent after banging a splint bone. Held up, she
ran a bit wide on the top bend, briefly losing her footing, and was unable to
quicken in the closing stages, finishing under two lengths fifth to Zahrat Dubai.
The Irish Champion was then mooted, but further problems intervened in the
shape of what her trainer called 'a lot of hiccups' and a corn on a foot.

Alborada was, however, fully fit for the Dubai Champion Stakes, which
assumed the character of a make-or-break event for her. It can hardly be
claimed that transferring all the races usually run on the Rowley Mile course to
the July course during the construction of the new Millennium Stand affected
the outcome of any, but it did have an effect on the paying public, particularly
on Champions Day. The crowd of just over 16,300 was simply too large for
the course to cope with satisfactorily. When racing is competing with many
other activities for the leisure pound, it seemed counter-productive to subject
customers to the type of discomfort and organisational chaos evident on
this day. If a racegoer pays £30 to gain entrance to the members' enclosure, he
or she can reasonably expect to be able to see the runners in the paddock,
have a bet and watch the race. Doing any two of these three was difficult
on Champions Day, and doing the whole lot was virtually impossible as
everywhere became woefully clogged up. Having the unsaddling enclosure and
presentation podium in the paddock made for almost laughable delays and
confusion, with the result that the runners for the Cesarewitch were officially
divided between the main paddock and the pre-parade ring. Some of the
Dewhurst Stakes field—a championship event—spent a derisory amount of

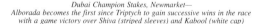

Dubai Champion Stakes, Newmarket—
Alborada becomes the first since Triptych to gain successive wins in the race
with a game victory over Shiva (striped sleeves) and Kabool (white cap)

time in the paddock, and Alborada and one of her rivals, Greek Dance, were among a number of runners through the afternoon to get a bit worked up in the pre-parade ring, possibly because of the number of people crowding in. The course knew there might be problems, and, although hoping for an even bigger crowd in 2000, clerk of the course Nick Lees added this crucial note: 'We will have the capacity in the Millennium Stand and be able to look after them properly.' This was tantamount to an admission of what everyone on the July course already knew—that racegoers were not looked after properly on Champions Day. If wishes were horses beggars could ride, but what a shame that it was not feasible to transfer the meeting lock, stock and barrel to a course—such as Ascot—capable of providing a comfortable afternoon's sport for such a sizeable crowd.

Getting a bit warm had no ill effect on Alborada. In addition to Greek Dance, sixth in the Prix de l'Arc de Triomphe two weeks earlier, she faced eleven opponents in a field not up to the usual standard of the race, in which the average Timeform rating of the winner from 1978 to 1997 was 129, with none lower than 124. The favourite was Shiva, winner of the Group 1 Tattersalls Gold Cup from Daylami in the spring but not seen out since putting in a below-par effort in the Group 2 Prince of Wales's Stakes at Royal Ascot. Lear Spear, the winner of that race and of a Group 3 at Goodwood from Kabool, was next in the market, followed by Alborada, High-Rise trying to redeem his reputation, and Greek Dance. The remainder included Kabool and smart three-year-olds Golden Snake (winner of the Prix Jean Prat) and Gold Academy. In a race that was not truly run—the tenth horse to finish was beaten just over four lengths—Kabool led for most of the way, and those queuing up to challenge him with two furlongs left were headed by Alborada, Shiva and Greek Dance. Alborada, who had taken quite a strong hold and was always well positioned, produced the best turn of foot to lead at the distance, and, kept up to her work, she beat Shiva by a length and a quarter. The runner-up, who gave the impression slight lack of fitness might have told, held off Kabool by a neck, with Gold Academy, Greek Dance and High-Rise the next to finish. Alborada became the fourth horse since the war to win the Champion Stakes twice, following Dynamiter in 1951 and 1952, Brigadier Gerard in 1971 and 1972, and Triptych in 1986 and 1987. Overall, eleven have achieved the feat, the others being Tristan (who won three in a row), Velasquez, Lemberg (including a walkover), Orpheus, Fairway, Wychwood Abbot and Hippius.

		Lyphard	Northern Dancer
	Alzao (USA)	(b 1969)	Goofed
	(b 1980)	Lady Rebecca	Sir Ivor
Alborada		(b 1971)	Pocahontas II
(gr.f. 1995)		Darshaan	Shirley Heights
	Alouette	(br 1981)	Delsy
	(gr 1990)	Alruccaba	Crystal Palace
		(gr 1983)	Allara

Her Champion Stakes victory proved Alborada was as good as in 1998, but unfortunately there were few suitable targets left for her. Bypassing the Premio Roma, she was aimed at the Japan Cup, though there was no guarantee she'd stay a mile and a half at the sort of pace at which that race is run normally. Such suspicions became irrelevant as bad luck played one final trick when she injured her off-hind heel a couple of days before the race, forcing her withdrawal. Alborada was promptly retired and is to be mated with Danzig. That sire invariably has an exceptional book of mares but Alborada, whose overall record reads six wins and three placings from ten outings for earnings of almost £600,000, will not be outshone by many of them in terms of ability. The resultant progeny will have Northern Dancer in both halves of the pedigree, a fairly common occurrence these days. There is little to add to what we said about Alborada's breeding in the wake of her first Champion Stakes victory. Her two-year-old half-brother by Hernando is named Dapper and has yet to race, and the dam Alouette has subsequently foaled fillies by Hernando again and by Alzao. The last-named, who has done much better with his fillies than his colts, is the sire of Alborada and of very smart Last Second, a half-sister to Alouette successful in the Nassau Stakes and Sun Chariot Stakes in 1996. Alborada, a smallish, quite good-topped filly, stayed a mile and a quarter well and acted on any going. She was thoroughly game and reliable. *Sir Mark Prescott*

ALCONLEIGH   4 ch.g. Pursuit of Love 124 – Serotina (IRE) 73 (Mtoto 134)   **91 d**
[1998 97: 7.9g 10.3m⁴ 10m 10m 1999 10g 8m 8m³ 8m⁵ 8.1g 7.1d⁵ a8.5g³ 8m⁵ 6.9g²
10.3m⁵ 10m 10m 10m 10m 10g 10.1d 8.2s Nov 1] strong, lengthy gelding: useful
handicapper at 3 yrs: deteriorated badly after fourth start in 1999: claimed from
M. Johnston £10,000 after ninth start: barely stays 1¼m: acts on firm and soft
ground: blinkered once: tends to wander: has had tongue tied: normally races up with
pace. *B. Ellison*

ALDBURGH   3 ch.f. Bluebird (USA) 125 – Eastern Shore (Sun Prince 128) [1998   **–**
NR 1999 8.3mᵈⁱˢ Apr 19] 85,000Y: half-sister to several winners, including useful
1¼m winner Ruscino (by Rousillon): dam, maiden who stayed 1½m, granddaughter
of very smart sprinter Lucasland: disqualified after failing dope test when well beaten
in maiden at Windsor: sold 12,000 gns in December. *J. H. M. Gosden*

AL DESIMA   2 b.f. (Apr 12) Emperor Jones (USA) 119 – Miss Up N Go (Gorytus   **93**
(USA) 132) [1999 7m³ 7f* 7.1m⁴ 8g³ 7s⁴ 7g Oct 16] 11,500F, 8,000Y, 11,000 2-y-o:
close-coupled filly: third foal: half-sister to 3-y-o Mishor and a winner in Turkey
by Damister: dam unraced half-sister to dam of Derby winner Oath: fairly useful
performer: won maiden at Folkestone in July: good fourth of 12 to Agrippina in listed
race at Newmarket in October, best work at finish: wintry, ran poorly final start:
should stay 1m: acts on firm and soft going: reared stalls and off bridle throughout
fourth start: tail swisher: sold 25,000 gns in December. *K. McAuliffe*

ALDWYCH ARROW (IRE)   4 ch.g. Rainbows For Life (CAN) – Shygate (Shy   **69**
Groom (USA)) [1998 69, a63: a12g³ a12g² a11g² a12g⁴ 11.6g 12d² 14.1d² 13.1g*   **a54**
14s* 16.2g² 16m 16.4f³ 16.1m 16.1g³ 16s⁵ a14.8g⁴ 1999 a16g⁵ a11g a11f⁴ a11g²
a12g 13.8g² 12.3m³ 12s* 14g² 13.8m 12g 13.9d 13.8s Nov 2] fair handicapper on
turf, modest on all-weather: won at Catterick in April: below form last 4 starts, off 4
months before penultimate one: effective at 1½m to 2m: has form on firm going, but
all wins on good or softer (also acts on fibresand): blinkered (below form) once:
usually races up with pace: game. *M. A. Buckley*

ALEANBH (IRE)   4 ch.g. Classic Secret (USA) 91 – Highdrive (Ballymore 123)   **35**
[1998 –: 7d 1999 8s a8.5g⁶ a12g a8.5g Dec 27] poor maiden: stays 8.5f. *R. A. Fahey*

ALEGRIA   3 b.f. Night Shift (USA) – High Habit 79 (Slip Anchor 136) [1998 80p: **94 +**
6g⁵ 6g* 1999 6f² 6d 6m³ 6m⁶ 5g⁴ 5.2g⁵ 6.1g³ 6d Oct 9] good-topped, attractive filly:
useful handicapper: generally in good form in 1999: stays 6f: acts on firm ground,
below form on good to soft: free-going sort. *J. M. P. Eustace*

AL EURO (FR)   2 ch.f. (Apr 29) Mujtahid (USA) 118 – Ibtisamm (USA) 71   **57**
(Caucasus (USA) 127) [1999 6g 6s⁴ 6s³ 6d Oct 14] unfurnished filly: half-sister to
several winners, including high-class miler Air Express (by Salse) and useful 1¼m/
1½m winner Aljazzaf (by Mtoto): dam, 1m winner, half-sister to dam of Breeders'
Cup Juvenile winner Success Express: modest maiden: well beaten in nursery final
start: should stay 1m: sold 23,000 gns in November. *C. E. Brittain*

ALEXANDER   3 b.g. Be My Chief (USA) 122 – Arminda (Blakeney 126) [1998   **53**
–: 7d 1999 a12s⁴ 13.4m⁴ 18m⁴ Jul 3] modest maiden: trained by C. Thornton
on reappearance: stays 2¼m: acts on good to firm going, probably on heavy.
B. P. J. Baugh

ALEXANDRINE (IRE)   2 b.f. (Mar 19) Nashwan (USA) 135 – Alruccaba 83   **– p**
(Crystal Palace (FR) 132) [1999 7d 7d⁶ 8.3d Oct 28] big, rangy filly: half-sister to
several winners, including very smart 1¼m filly Last Second (by Alzao), 6f/7f
winner at 2 yrs, smart Irish performer up to 1¾m Arrikala (by Darshaan) and useful
Irish 1½m winner Alouette, herself the dam of Alborada: dam 2-y-o 6f winner:
always in rear in maidens: bred to do much better at 1¼m+. *Sir Mark Prescott*

ALEXIS (IRE)   3 b.f. Alzao (USA) 117 – Sister Golden Hair (IRE) (Glint of Gold   **107**
128) [1998 98+: 6s³ 7g* 7d⁴ 6s³ 7s⁴ 1999 8g³ 8d* 8m 8.5f⁴ 8f² 8f³ 8.5f* 8f* a7f Nov
21] smallish, sturdy filly: useful performer: trained at 2 yrs by D. Weld in Ireland: 3¾
lengths third to Claxon in listed race at Kempton before making all in 5-runner
similar event at Chantilly later in April (beat Ares Vallis by length): helped set strong
pace when well held in Poule d'Essai des Pouliches at Longchamp, final start for
J. Noseda: successful in optional claimer and a conditions event, both at Woodbine
in October: will probably stay 1¼m: acts on firm and soft going. *B. MacDonald,
Canada*

ALFAHAAL (IRE)   6 b.g. Green Desert (USA) 127 – Fair of The Furze 112   **59**
(Ela-Mana-Mou 132) [1998 60: a7g a8g³ a8g 7s 1999 6.1v 8.3m 8g 10m⁵ 8g² 7m*
8s⁵ 8f 8g⁶ 7m⁶ 7m 6s⁶ 7g 7s 7d⁴ 8.2s Nov 1] robust gelding: modest handicapper:
won at Yarmouth in May: best at 7f/1m: acts on good to firm going, soft and
equitrack: has been bandaged: best held up in well-run race: none too consistent.
C. A. Dwyer

AL FAHDA   3 b.f. Be My Chief (USA) 122 – Fleetwood Fancy (Taufan (USA)   **93**
119) [1998 93: 5m 6g* 6g² 7d* 7g³ 7.1m⁵ 7m³ 1999 8d 10s⁵ 8s³ 8m* 9.9d Aug 11]
leggy, useful-looking filly: fairly useful performer: won minor event at Salisbury in
August by ¾ length from King Midas, dictating pace: last of 9 in listed race there 5
days later: stays 1¼m: acts on soft going and on good to firm: decidedly on toes (ran
creditably) second start: joined C. Clement in USA. *R. Hannon*

ALFAILAK   2 b.c. (Mar 1) Green Desert (USA) 127 – Great Inquest 80 (Shernazar   **95**
131) [1999 5g* 6d⁴ 5.1m⁴ 5f³ 5g² 5m 5d Oct 9] 52,000Y: well-made colt: good
walker: first foal: dam, 7f winner, half-sister to very smart sprinter Owington (by
Green Desert): useful performer: won maiden at Newmarket in April: best efforts
when placed in Molecomb Stakes at Goodwood and listed race (head second to Buy
Or Sell) at York: likely to prove best at 5f/6f: yet to race on very soft ground.
M. R. Channon

ALFATH (USA)   3 ch.c. Diesis 133 – Lady Express (IRE) (Soviet Star (USA)   **79**
128) [1998 NR 1999 7f⁵ 6g² 5s⁵ 6d² 8.5m² 7m⁴ Sep 24] 280,000Y: strong, lengthy
colt: second foal: dam, 7f winner in France, daughter of Phoenix Champion winner
Park Express and half-sister to a Group 1 winner in Japan: fair maiden: ran creditably
when runner-up: barely stays 8.5f: acts on good to firm and good to soft going,
possibly not soft: sent to UAE. *A. C. Stewart*

ALFIE BOY (IRE)   3 b.g. Forest Wind (USA) 111 – Ballinlee (IRE) (Skyliner   **105**
117) [1998 NR 1999 7s* 8g³ 8f⁴ Jul 31] IR 10,000Y: first foal: dam unraced sister to
smart sprinter Blyton Lad: won 5-runner maiden at Goodwood in June: useful form
in listed race at same course after, under a length third to Ramooz then over 6 lengths
last of 4 to Slip Stream: unlikely to stay beyond 1m. *A. P. Jarvis*

ALFIE LEE (IRE)   2 ch.c. (Feb 17) Case Law 113 – Nordic Living (IRE) 53   **82**
(Nordico (USA)) [1999 5g⁵ 5g⁴ 5g* 5m 5m Jun 17] 50,000Y: compact, well-made
colt: unimpressive mover: second foal: brother to 3-y-o Lively Jacq: dam ran 4 times
in Ireland: fairly useful form: won maiden at Goodwood in May: best effort when
ninth of 13 in Norfolk Stakes at Royal Ascot on final start, though never a threat:
should stay 6f. *C. N. Allen*

ALFINI   2 ch.c. (Feb 24) Selkirk (USA) 129 – Vivre En Paix (Nureyev (USA) 131)   **101 p**
[1999 7s² 6d* Oct 14] 22,000Y: tall, rather shallow-girthed colt: half-brother to 3
winners, including fairly useful 1m/1¼m winner Treaty of Peace (by Alleged): dam
French 1m winner from very good family: favourite, bandaged behind and still green
to post, confirmed considerable promise when winning maiden at Newmarket by 3½
lengths from Free Rider, travelling strongly behind leaders and quickening clear up
hill: bred to stay 1m, but has good deal of speed: potentially a smart performer, sure
to win more races. *D. R. C. Elsworth*

AL GHABRAA   2 ch.f. (Apr 10) Pursuit of Love 124 – Tenderetta (Tender King   **86 p**
123) [1999 8g* Oct 15] 20,000Y: fourth foal: sister to fair 1998 2-y-o 5.7f winner
Pursuit of Gold: dam fairly useful Irish 6f and 1m winner: 8/1, won maiden at
Redcar by head from Riddlesdown, travelling smoothly to lead under 2f out then
green: should stay bit beyond 1m: likely to make useful 3-y-o. *J. W. Hills*

Motability Rated Stakes (Handicap), York—a good battle between Algunnaas (visor) and Achilles; the Lincoln winner Right Wing (partly hidden) is third

ALGUNNAAS 4 b.c. Red Ransom (USA) – Swame (USA) (Jade Hunter (USA)) **109**
[1998 NR 1999 8.2s² 10g* 10m⁴ 10.3g⁵ 10g³ 10g* 10.4g* 11.9m* 12m² Sep 10]
100,000Y: lengthy colt: first foal: dam, won up to 9f in USA, granddaughter of
top-class 1m/1¼m filly Rose Bowl: useful performer: won maiden at Leicester in
April, minor event at Newmarket and rated stakes at York (by short head from
Achilles) in August and Haydock in September: creditable 2½ lengths second of 5 to
Azouz Pasha in listed race at Doncaster final start: effective at 1¼m/1½m: raced only
on good/good to firm ground after debut: visored after fourth start: sent to UAE.
J. H. M. Gosden

ALHASAD (USA) 3 b.c. Sheikh Albadou 128 – Valley Prospector (USA) (North- **96**
ern Prospect (USA)) [1998 77: 6m² 6f⁵ 5m³ 6m 1999 8.2f* 10m² 9.9f 10g² Sep 25]
sturdy, compact colt: useful performer: won maiden at Nottingham in June:
runner-up after in handicap at Newmarket then minor event at Nottingham (beaten 2
lengths by Badaayer): stays 1¼m: raced only on good going or firmer: sent to UAE.
A. C. Stewart

ALHAWA (USA) 6 ch.g. Mt Livermore (USA) – Petrava (NZ) (Imposing (AUS)) **87**
[1998 74: 7d 8g 8f⁵ 9d 10f⁵ 7.9g 8s 10.4g⁵ 10v³ 12s⁶ 1999 11.9d⁵ 13.3f 12g⁴
12m³ 11.4m³ 12m* 14.8m* 14.8m* 16.1m* 14.8m 13.3m 17.3g⁶ Oct 16] leggy,
sparely-made gelding: fairly useful handicapper: better than ever in 1999, winning at
Doncaster and Newmarket (twice) in July and Newmarket in August: back to best
(race not run to suit previous 2 starts) when sixth of 32 to Top Cees in Cesarewitch at
Newmarket final outing: stays 17f well: acts on any ground: blinkered (below form)
once at 3 yrs: usually held up. *N. P. Littmoden*

ALHESN (USA) 4 b. or br.g. Woodman (USA) 126 – Deceit Princess (CAN) **54**
(Vice Regent (CAN)) [1998 60: 12m 12m³ 10.1f² 14.1m² 16.1m⁵ 12d⁴ 1999 11.9f **a78**
12.3m 11.5g 14.1m* 16f* 14.1m⁶ 12m a16g* 16m⁶ a16.2g* a14.8g² a14g⁵ a16g
a16.2g* a16.2g⁵ Dec 4] angular gelding: fair handicapper on all-weather, modest on
turf: won at Yarmouth (twice) in July, Lingfield in August and Wolverhampton in
September and December: should stay beyond 2m: acts on all-weather and firm
going (yet to race on soft/heavy): has been visored/tongue tied. *C. N. Allen*

ALHEYRAH 3 b.f. Ezzoud (IRE) 126 – Hamama (USA) (Majestic Light (USA)) **64 ?**
[1998 NR 1999 10.5g⁵ 12d² 8g² 10.2m 10v Sep 24] angular filly: third foal: dam,
third at 7f in Ireland, half-sister to Quick As Lightning: modest maiden: seems to stay
1½m: tongue tied final start: sent to USA. *B. Hanbury*

ALHUFOOF (USA) 2 b.f. (Jan 30) Dayjur (USA) 137 – Cheval Volant (USA) **90 p**
(Kris S (USA)) [1999 6f³ 6f* Jul 27] long-backed filly: fifth foal: closely related to
3-y-o Habub and half-sister to 1m winners Amanah (useful) and Alrayyih (in UAE),
both by Mr Prospector: dam 5.5f to 8.5f winner in USA, twice in Grade 1 events:

favourite, improved to win 6-runner maiden at Goodwood in July easily by 6 lengths (had 2 handlers in preliminaries): probably a useful prospect at least. *M. P. Tregoning*

ALHUWBILL 4 b.g. Full Extent (USA) 113 – Hale Lane 59 (Comedy Star (USA) 121) [1998 NR 1999 a10g a7g 7m 6g 6g 7f⁵ 8m 10f 9.9m 7d 9s Oct 8] brother/half-brother to poor maidens (one a winning pointer): dam third at 6f at 2 yrs: poor maiden at best. *J. J. Bridger* —

ALIABAD (IRE) 4 b. or br.g. Doyoun 124 – Alannya (FR) (Relko 136) [1998 79: 8g 11.9f² 11.5m² 12.3g 16g⁵ 1999 17.2s Sep 27] smallish, leggy gelding: fair maiden for Sir Michael Stoute at 3 yrs: no show only start in 1999: stays 1½m: acts on firm going: visored (found nothing) penultimate 3-y-o start. *P. G. Murphy* —

ALIGN 3 gr.f. Petong 126 – Affirmation 75 (Tina's Pet 121) [1998 –p: 7d 1999 a8g* 8m⁶ 10g 10g 10d a8.5g a10g Oct 25] lengthy filly: fair performer at best: won maiden at Southwell in April: generally well beaten after: stays 1m, possibly not 1¼m: acts on good to firm going and fibresand. *J. W. Hills* 69 d

ALI YA YA 3 b.f. Puissance 110 – Manor Adventure 75 (Smackover 107) [1998 NR 1999 7g 6g Sep 20] 4,600Y: first foal: dam, 5f winner, half-sister to useful sprinter Bunty Boo: well beaten in claimers at Leicester. *B. Smart* —

ALIZEE (IRE) 3 b.f. College Chapel 122 – Richly Deserved (IRE) (Kings Lake (USA) 133) [1998 NR 1999 8g 8g 10m Jun 23] IR 19,000Y: fifth foal: half-sister to 2 winners, including French 11f/1½m winner Kastelorizo (by Alzao): dam unraced half-sister to high-class Star Pastures: best effort in maidens on debut: should stay beyond 1m: sold 3,000 gns in July. *P. W. Chapple-Hyam* 66

ALJABR (USA) 3 gr.c. Storm Cat (USA) – Sierra Madre (FR) 119 (Baillamont (USA) 124) [1998 121p: 7.1g* 7d* 7s* 1999 8m² 8f* 8m⁴ Sep 5] 125

Fortune did not deal kindly with the bold decision to aim Aljabr at the Kentucky Derby, since the colt failed to make the line-up, by which time he had effectively missed the possibility of gaining classic glory in Europe. Equally, Godolphin won the Two Thousand Guineas with Island Sands, and on his return from the States Aljabr proved himself one of the best milers in training by winning the Sussex Stakes, so perhaps the Churchill Downs venture can be viewed as nothing more than a temporary inconvenience. It is a racing certainty that further attempts will be made on the Run for the Roses, because Sheikh Mohammed is on record as saying: 'My aim is to win the race in the next four years.' It pays not to underestimate anything the Godolphin operation does, but setting out to win races of the calibre of the Kentucky Derby is no easy task. Godolphin is to set up a satellite two-year-old base in the States for around thirty horses, the most promising being trained for the big three-year-old events with the Kentucky Derby the number-one target. It is just as tough a race to win as the Derby, and although members of the Maktoum family have won the Epsom classic with Nashwan, Erhaab, Lammtarra, who spent the winter in

Champagne Lanson Sussex Stakes, Goodwood—Aljabr puts up a gutsy display under a superb ride; the game Docksider has to settle for second but is clear of the rest

Godolphin's "Aljabr"

Dubai before scoring in 1995, and High-Rise, no horse carrying the colours of Sheikh Mohammed or Godolphin has triumphed. This is from twenty-one attempts for Sheikh Mohammed starting with Jalmood's pathfinding performance in 1982, and six for Godolphin.

Aljabr, successful in all three of his starts as a juvenile, culminating in a defeat of Stravinsky in the Prix de la Salamandre, pleased his connections when finishing second to Worldly Manner in a private nine-furlong trial in Dubai in March, and it was next stop Kentucky. He faced a stiff task in taking on the American colts on their home ground. Apart from having to cope with acclimatisation and a different, track-based, training regime, his form at two left him with a bit to find to win a classic, as was noted in *Racehorses of 1998*. His somewhat nervy disposition, with a tendency to sweat and be on his toes, did not help him in·Kentucky, where he looked headstrong once on the gallops in his preparation. He was freely available at 33/1 by the time he was reportedly hanging in a canter the day before the big race and was withdrawn because his connections feared something might be hurting him. He was later found to be lame in a hind leg and was returned to Newmarket, with the aim of contesting the St James's Palace Stakes at Royal Ascot. Press reports indicated Aljabr was working superbly in the run-up to the Royal meeting, and he started a well-backed second favourite behind Sendawar. He got a bit warm beforehand but settled well in the race, was shaken up to lead halfway up the straight and kept on well without being able to cope with the favourite's powerful late turn of foot. At the line he was one and a quarter lengths down, five lengths clear of the third horse, Gold Academy. This was the best performance to that point by a British-trained miler among the three-year-olds, better than that of Island Sands in the Guineas, and Aljabr confirmed his status in the Champagne Lanson Sussex Stakes at Goodwood.

The Sussex did not boast a vintage field and Aljabr started at 11/10 to beat seven opponents. The classic crop was also represented by Enrique, runner-up in the Two Thousand Guineas and the Irish equivalent; Coronation Stakes victress Balisada; Gold Academy again; and Raise A Grand, fifth in the St James's Palace Stakes before chasing home Diktat in the Van Geest Criterion Stakes. The older brigade consisted of Queen Anne Stakes runner-up Docksider, lately a Group 2 winner at Hoppegarten, much travelled French gelding Jim And Tonic, and miling stalwart Almushtarak. Aljabr set off in front at only a fair gallop from Docksider, then quickened the tempo markedly rounding the home turn, catching out some of those who were being held up. Running on well, the leader had enough in reserve to hold Docksider's determined challenge by a length, with third-placed Almushtarak five lengths adrift. Aljabr was a worthy winner, and a return clash with Sendawar was something to look forward to. The rematch came in the Prix du Moulin de Longchamp in September, after Aljabr had bypassed the Prix Jacques le Marois won by his stable-companion Dubai Millennium. Sendawar was an odds-on shot, but when Aljabr smoothly took up the running two furlongs out he looked for all the world as though he would give the favourite a real fight. In the event he found nothing as the French colt surged past, and he ended up in fourth place, beaten about three and a half lengths. This was not his form—Gold Away and Dansili also beat him—and the day after the race he was found to be lame in one of his forelegs. The Queen Elizabeth II Stakes and Breeders' Cup Mile were mentioned as targets, but Aljabr was not seen out again.

		Storm Bird	Northern Dancer
	Storm Cat (USA)	(b 1978)	South Ocean
	(b or br 1983)	Terlingua	Secretariat
Aljabr (USA)		(ch 1976)	Crimson Saint
(gr.c. 1996)		Baillamont	Blushing Groom
	Sierra Madre (FR)	(b 1982)	Lodeve
	(ro 1991)	Marie d'Irlande	Kalamoun
		(gr 1980)	La Ferte Milon

A tall, lengthy colt who acts on any going, Aljabr stays in training. Providing he stays sound he should prove a very able deputy to Dubai Millennium over a mile or a mile and a quarter, a trip he can be expected to stay. Though he runs for Godolphin, Aljabr was bred by Sheikh Hamdan's Shadwell Farm and is proof of the regard the Sheikh, along with everyone else, has for Storm Cat. In 1999 the mares sent to that stallion from Shadwell included top performers and/or producers Elle Seule, Height of Fashion, Histoire, Shadayid and Sierra Madre. Aljabr is the first foal out of Sierra Madre, who was purchased privately at the end of her racing career, the highlights of which were victories in the Prix Marcel Boussac and Prix Vermeille. Ideally suited by a mile and a half, she is also dam of the two-year-old Makaarem (by Danzig), successful over six furlongs at Maisons-Laffitte in June on his only start, and of a yearling colt by Silver Hawk. The grandam Marie d'Irlande was a minor winner and a sister to very smart colt Dom Racine, winner of the Prix Jean Prat. *Saeed bin Suroor*

ALJA LAD 2 br.g. (Apr 17) Forzando 122 – Cactus Road (FR) (Iron Duke (FR) **56** 122) [1999 5.1g⁵ 6m Sep 7] 9,000Y: ninth foal: half-brother to 3-y-o Danielle's Lad and a 7f winner in Austria by Petardia: dam French 1¼m to 13.5f winner: modest form in maidens at Nottingham (green and slowly away) and Lingfield. *B. Palling*

ALJAWF (USA) 2 gr. or ro.c. (Feb 27) Dehere (USA) 121 – Careless Kitten (USA) **80 p** (Caro 133) [1999 6g⁵ 6.1m* Sep 13] $300,000F: half-brother to several winners, including 4-y-o Arkadian Hero and winner up to 1¼m (useful as a sprinter) Masnun (by Nureyev): dam, successful up to 9f in USA, from family of US Grade 1 winners, including Belmont Stakes winner Editor's Note: better effort in maidens (unnerved in stalls on debut) when justifying favouritism in 12-runner event at Nottingham by 3 lengths from Nuts In May, disputing lead travelling comfortably and eased close home: should stay 1m: likely to make useful 3-y-o. *E. A. L. Dunlop*

ALJAZ 9 b.g. Al Nasr (FR) 126 – Santa Linda (USA) (Sir Ivor 135) [1998 –, a76: a5g² a5g* a5g* a5g² a5g³ a6g a5g² a5g² 5m a5g² a5g⁴ a5g² a6g* a6g² 1999 a6g a5g a6g³ a6f⁶ a6g a5g a6g⁴ a5g³ a6g a6g* a5g a8g a6g² a7g a6g² a6g² a6g³ Dec 11] fair handicapper: won at Southwell in May: best at 5f/6f: acts on all-weather (no form in only 4 races on turf since 1995): blinkered once at 5 yrs. *Miss Gay Kelleway* — **a72**

ALJAZIR 2 b.g. (Jan 25) Alhijaz 122 – Duxyana (IRE) (Cyrano de Bergerac 120) [1999 5.1d³ 5m 5.1m⁶ 6m 5g 6s⁵ 6v⁴ Oct 11] third foal: half-brother to 4-y-o Vista Alegre: dam unraced half-sister to dam of smart sprinter Indian Rocket: fair maiden: got poor run when creditable fourth in nursery at Ayr: stays 6f: best efforts on ground softer than good: raced too freely only try in blinkers. *E. J. Alston* — **68 ?**

ALLEGRESSE (IRE) 2 b.f. (Mar 15) Alzao (USA) 117 – Millie Musique (Miller's Mate 116) [1999 7s³ 7m⁶ Sep 7] 52,000Y: fourth foal: half-sister to 3 winners, including fairly useful Irish 1997 2-y-o 5f/6f winner Sideman (by Brief Truce): dam once-raced daughter of top-class French filly Luth Enchantee: slowly away and soon off bridle in maidens, better effort when third of 13 to Naval Affair at Kempton in August: should be suited by 1¼m/1½m. *J. L. Dunlop* — **76**

ALLEZ CYRANO (IRE) 8 b.g. Alzao (USA) 117 – Miss Bergerac (Bold Lad (IRE) 133) [1998 –: a8.5g⁶ 1999 a9.4g⁶ Jan 6] leggy gelding: formerly useful: lightly raced and little form on Flat since 1996: tried visored. *D. Burchell* — **–**

ALL GOOD THINGS (IRE) 2 b.c. (Mar 20) Marju (IRE) 127 – Garah 107 (Ajdal (USA) 130) [1999 7d 7d Oct 22] second foal: half-brother to 6f winner in USA by Midyan: dam sprinter out of smart sprinter Abha: better effort in October maidens when eighth of 22 to Fame At Last at Doncaster on second start: should improve further. *J. L. Dunlop* — **56 p**

ALLIED IMPERIAL 3 b.f. Morpeth § – Super Sarena (IRE) 87 (Taufan (USA) 119) [1998 NR 1999 10v Sep 24] first foal: dam maiden on Flat (stayed 1¾m) and over jumps: well beaten in maiden at Lingfield. *R. J. O'Sullivan* — **–**

ALLINSON'S MATE (IRE) 11 b.g. Fayruz 116 – Piney Pass (Persian Bold 123) [1998 56: a7s³ a7g a7g⁵ a7g a8g a8g⁶ 6.9d² 7.1g 6.9s⁶ 7g² 8d 7g 7.1s 7g* 8m 7g 8v 1999 6.9m⁴ 7s 7.1m⁴ 7m 7.1g Jun 14] small, robust gelding: unimpressive mover: poor nowadays: effective at 7f to 8.5f: acts on firm ground, good to soft and all-weather: usually blinkered/visored: held up: often apprentice ridden: none too consistent. *T. D. Barron* — **40**

ALLMAITES 4 b.g. Komaite (USA) – Darling Miss Daisy 77 (Tina's Pet 121) [1998 71§: a5g³ a6g⁵ 5.1g³ 5m⁶ 5g² 6s 5d² 5.1m 5g⁴ 5s 1999 5s Apr 13] sturdy gelding: fair maiden at best but is temperamentally unsatisfactory: started slowly last 3 starts in 1998 and refused to race only 4-y-o outing: tried blinkered. *A. J. McNae* — **§§**

ALL NIGHT LONG (IRE) 2 b.f. (Mar 5) Night Shift (USA) – Shakey (IRE) (Caerleon (USA) 132) [1999 5m⁶ 5m⁶ 6f³ 6m⁶ 5.3g³ 5d² 6m 5v 5.3d⁴ 5.1g Oct 21] 17,000F, 12,000Y: neat filly: first foal: dam, unraced, from family of Missionary Ridge, smart here and in USA (seemed best at 1¼m): modest maiden: below form after second at Windsor: stays 6f: acts on firm and good to soft ground: sold 12,500 gns in December. *R. Guest* — **64**

ALLOTROPE (IRE) 4 b.g. Nashwan (USA) 135 – Graphite (USA) 80 (Mr Prospector (USA)) [1998 77: 9v² 12g⁵ 14g* 16s 1999 16s 16f⁴ 16f⁶ 13.9m Sep 1] angular, workmanlike gelding: sixth foal: half-brother to fairly useful 7f winner Clovis Point (by Kris) and to 11f winner in UAE by Old Vic: dam 9f winner out of half-sister to dam of Swain (by Nashwan): fair handicapper: sold from J. Oxx, Ireland, 42,000 gns after final 3-y-o start: form in 1999 only on second start (first since being gelded): stays 2m: probably acts on any going: blinkered penultimate outing. *Mrs M. Reveley* — **70**

ALL OUR HOPE (USA) 3 b.f. Gulch (USA) – Knoosh (USA) 113 (Storm Bird (CAN) 134) [1998 87p: 7m³ 1999 11.4m a8.5g* 10s³ 12d Oct 9] tall, lengthy, rather unfurnished filly: fairly useful performer: easily won maiden at Wolverhampton (after 4-month break) in September: good 9 lengths third to Lady In Waiting in SunChariot Stakes at Newmarket next time, finding her stride late on: got no sort of run in Princess Royal at Ascot final start: should be suited by 1½m: acts on fibresand and soft going, showed promise first try on good to firm. *Sir Michael Stoute* — **96**

ALLRIGHTHEN   3 b.g. Sizzling Melody 117 – Luckifosome 45 (Smackover — 107) [1998 50: 6g 6g 7m 5d 6m 6m⁶ 1999 a7g 8d 7.5d 7.1g⁶ 8m a6g Jun 28] tall, unfurnished gelding: modest maiden at best: no show in 1999. *T. Wall*

ALL ROSES (IRE)   2 b.f. (Apr 10) River Falls 113 – All Laughter (Vision (USA)   **54** [1999 6f 7d² 7m a7g a7g Nov 22] small, leggy filly: fourth foal: half-sister to Irish   **a–** 3-y-o 9.5f winner Gabby Hayes (by Tirol): dam placed at 7f/1m in Ireland at 2 yrs: modest maiden: likely to stay 1m: well beaten on fibresand. *Noel T. Chance*

ALLSPICE   2 b.f. (Apr 27) Alzao (USA) 117 – Allegra 73 (Niniski (USA) 125)   — [1999 7d 7m 7f³ 8s Sep 16] IR 200,000Y: strong filly: sixth foal: half-sister to 2 winners by Selkirk, including 1996 2-y-o 6f winner All Is Fair: dam, 1½m winner, half-sister to Last Second and to dam of Alborada, both very smart 1¼m fillies by Alzao: little form in maidens/nursery: bred to do much better at 1¼m+. *Sir Mark Prescott*

ALLSTARS DANCER   6 b.m. Primo Dominie 121 – Danzig Harbour (USA)   — (Private Account (USA)) [1998 40, a44: a6s³ a7g² a6g⁵ a6g³ a7g⁵ a6g 6s 7f⁵ 5g* 1999 a6f⁶ a6g⁶ a6g 5m 6g Jun 30] poor handicapper: well beaten in 1999: stays 7f: acts on all-weather, best turf effort on good ground: often blinkered. *T. J. Naughton*

ALL THE GEARS (USA)   2 b.c. (Feb 8) Gone West (USA) – Buckeye Gal   **82** (USA) (Good Counsel (USA)) [1999 7d 7d² 7d³ Nov 1] $450,000Y: close-coupled, quite attractive colt: half-brother to 3 winners abroad, including very smart French/US winner up to 1½m River Bay (by Irish River): dam, stakes winner up to 9f in USA, out of sister to dam of Oh So Sharp: fairly useful form: placed in maidens at Doncaster (1½ lengths second of 22 to Fame At Last) and Redcar, never travelling well when odds on in latter: should stay at least 1m: coltish on debut, edgy at Doncaster. *Sir Michael Stoute*

ALL THE WAY (IRE)   3 b.c. Shirley Heights 130 – Future Past (USA) (Super   **117** Concorde 128) [1998 77p: 8.2m³ 1999 12g² 12m* 12g⁵ 14.6m⁴ Sep 11] leggy, angular colt: has a quick action: smart performer: won minor event at Newmarket in May by 1¼ lengths from Rhagaas: best efforts after in Derby at Epsom (made running when 4½ lengths fifth to Oath) and St Leger at Doncaster (11 lengths fourth to Mutafaweq), reportedly suffering heel infection in between: should stay 2m+: raced only on good/good to firm going: sometimes bandaged behind: races up with pace: genuine: joined Godolphin. *T. G. Mills*

ALLZI (USA)   3 ch.f. Zilzal (USA) 137 – All For Hope (USA) (Sensitive Prince   **83** (USA)) [1998 NR 1999 8s 8g 8m³ 10m⁴ Jul 16] big, rangy filly: has plenty of scope: sixth reported foal: closely related to French 11f winner Sahalik (by Theatrical) and half-sister to 2 winners by Trempolino, including 14.8f winner Elpida: dam unraced half-sister to Prix de Diane winner Lacovia: fairly useful maiden: better at 1¼m than 1m: acts on good to firm going: races up with pace. *Lady Herries*

AL MABROOK (IRE)   4 b.c. Rainbows For Life (CAN) – Sky Lover (Ela-   **68** Mana-Mou 132) [1998 76: 6d 8g⁶ 7g³ 7g 10d 8m a6g* a6g⁶ 1999 a7g⁴ 6f 7v⁵ 6g a7g⁵ a8g a7g Dec 21] leggy colt: fair handicapper: stays 7f: acts on equitrack (well beaten on fibresand), very best turf runs on good going: has had tongue tied. *K. Mahdi*

ALMAMZAR (USA)   9 b.g. Theatrical (USA) – Promising Risk (USA) (Exclusive   **42** Native (USA)) [1998 NR 1999 12g 16.2s⁵ 16d 17.1g⁶ 14.1m⁴ 12s 17.1s a14g a14g⁵ Nov 22] poor nowadays: left N. Tinkler after reappearance (first run for 5 years): probably stays 17f: acts on soft and good to firm going, no form on fibresand: has had tongue tied: held up. *Don Enrico Incisa*

ALMASHROUK (IRE)   2 b.c. (Mar 14) Common Grounds 118 – Red Note   **73** (Rusticaro (FR) 124) [1999 7d 6d⁴ 6s Nov 5] 26,000Y: compact colt: half-brother to several winners, including 3-y-o Kuwait Dawn and 4-y-o Selkirk Rose: dam lightly raced in Ireland: easily best effort in maidens when fourth of 19 to Pax at Newmarket, making running: faltered markedly final start: may prove best up to 7f. *K. Mahdi*

ALMASI (IRE)   7 b.m. Petorius 117 – Best Niece 84 (Vaigly Great 127) [1998 86:   **83** 6g⁵ 6g⁵ 6d 6m 6m 6m⁴ 6s 1999 6f 6m 6g* 6m³ 6m 6f² 6m 6.1m⁶ 6m 6s³ 6d Oct 9] sparely-made mare: fairly useful handicapper: won at Doncaster in June: mostly creditable efforts after: best at 6f: yet to race on heavy going, acts on any other: sometimes slowly away, and comes from behind: has won for apprentice. *C. F. Wall*

Mr Hamad Al-Mutawa's "Almushtarak"

ALMATY (IRE) 6 b.h. Dancing Dissident (USA) 119 – Almaaseh (IRE) 63 **108**
(Dancing Brave (USA) 140) [1998 113: 5m² 5m³ 5g 5f 5.1m² 5d 5m* 5g² 5m* 1999
5m⁴ 5m² 5m 5g⁶ 5.1m⁴ 5m⁶ 5d 5d³ Oct 14] well-made horse: useful performer:
creditable efforts most starts in 1999, including when head second to Proud Native in
listed race at Kempton, over 5 lengths sixth to Stravinsky in Nunthorpe Stakes at
York (fourth start) and third to Ellens Lad in rated stakes at Newmarket: best at 5f:
acts on firm and good to soft going: visored (ran poorly) twice: has worn tongue
strap: effective from front or held up: sold 40,000 gns. *W. R. Muir*

ALMAZHAR (IRE) 4 b.g. Last Tycoon 131 – Mosaique Bleue (Shirley Heights **59**
130) [1998 –: 7.5d⁴ 8s 8g 1999 a8.5g⁵ a8g a7g² a8g² 8g a8g⁴ 8m⁶ 9f⁵ 9.9v⁶ 8m* **a87**
a8g* a7g* 7.5m 7f 8.1d a6g² a8.5g⁶ a7g³ a7g* a6g² a7g* a6g² a7g⁶ Dec 21] strong
gelding: fairly useful handicapper on all-weather, modest on turf: won at Redcar
(amateur maiden) and Southwell in June, Southwell in July and Wolverhampton in
November and December: effective at 6f to 9f: acts on firm going and fibresand, well
beaten on soft/heavy: blinkered/visored (well held). *J. L. Eyre*

ALMERINA (IRE) 4 b.f. Erins Isle 121 – Pennine Music (IRE) (Pennine Walk **86 d**
120) [1998 89: 8g⁵ 9d⁶ 8d⁶ 7.5d⁷ 8d* 9s⁴ 8s⁶ 1999 8s 10g⁵ 9g² 8.3f⁴ 7m 8m 10.5s⁶
10.4g Oct 6] tall, lengthy, angular filly: second foal: half-sister to Irish 1996 2-y-o
7f winner Adua (by Kenmare): dam Irish 6f (at 2 yrs) to 1m winner: fairly useful
handicapper in Ireland: sold out of J. Bolger's stable 23,000 gns after fifth start: well
beaten in handicaps in Britain: stays 9f: yet to race on heavy going, acts on any other.
J. Mackie

ALMINSTAR 3 b.f. Minshaanshu Amad (USA) 91§ – Joytime (John de Coombe **41**
122) [1998 –: 7d 1999 8.3m 10f⁶ 10g a14.8g 10m⁵ 16m⁵ 11.9d Aug 17] close-
coupled, sparely-made filly: poor maiden: stays 1¼m, possibly not 2m: acts on firm
ground. *C. A. Cyzer*

ALMOHAD   4 ch.g. Belmez (USA) 131 – Anna Paola (GER) (Prince Ippi (GER))   **57**
[1998 54: 10.3s² 9.3v 9.3g* 8d⁵ 8s⁵ 9m a10g a16g 1999 a11f a16g 12g 10.9s³   **a–**
a14g 11.6s* 11.5g⁶ 9.9v Sep 29] tall, quite good-topped gelding: modest
handicapper: best effort in 1999 when winning at Windsor in August, making
virtually all: stays 11.6f: acts on soft going, little show on all-weather: tried
blinkered/visored. *Dr J. D. Scargill*

ALMOST AMBER (USA)   3 ch.f. Mt Livermore (USA) – Kelly Amber (USA)   **– §**
(Highland Park (USA)) [1998 88: 5d⁵ 5m* 5f² 5g 1999 6m 6.1m Aug 28]
useful-looking filly: has quick, fluent action: fairly useful at 2 yrs: well held both
3-y-o starts, giving temperamental display (led to post, refused to race) on second:
sold 6,000 gns in December: one to treat with caution. *J. H. M. Gosden*

ALMOST GOT IT   4 ch.f. St Ninian 104 – Star Leader (Kafu 120) [1998 44:   **–**
9.9m² 10.1m⁶ 1999 a11g 10d a12g Jul 24] poor maiden at best. *J. Parkes*

AL MUALLIM (USA)   5 b.g. Theatrical 128 – Gerri N Jo Go (USA) (Top   **102**
Command (USA)) [1998 105: 7m 7d² 7g³ 7d² 1999 7g⁵ 7g 7m² 6m Jun 18] compact
gelding: useful performer: best effort in 1999 when 2 lengths second of 6 to easy
winner Fa-Eq in minor event at Doncaster in May: not discredited when eighth in
Wokingham Handicap at Royal Ascot final start: best at 7f: yet to race on soft/heavy
going, acts on any other: free-going sort: best held up: gelded. *J. W. Payne*

ALMUSHTARAK (IRE)   6 b.h. Fairy King (USA) – Exciting (Mill Reef (USA)   **119**
141) [1998 122: 9s² 8.1s* 8m⁵ 8.5m³ 8d⁴ 8d² 10.4f 8m² 8s⁶ 8g⁶ 10g 9m³ 1999 8.1s³
8d³ 8m³ 8f³ 10.4m⁴ 8g³ 8s² 10g Oct 16] good-quartered, attractive horse: takes the
eye: smart performer: invariably acquits himself with credit in the top races: third in
Sandown Mile (beaten 2 necks behind Handsome Ridge), Lockinge Stakes at
Newbury (beaten nearly 2 lengths by Fly To The Stars), Queen Anne Stakes at Royal
Ascot (beaten 1½ lengths by Cape Cross) and Sussex Stakes at Goodwood on first 4
starts, and 6 lengths second of 4 to Dubai Millennium in Queen Elizabeth II Stakes at
Ascot in September: effective at 1m to 10.4f: acts on firm and soft ground: has been
attended by 2 handlers in preliminaries: usually held up, and suited by strongly-run
race: tough and remarkably dependable. *K. Mahdi*

ALMUTAWAKEL   4 b.c. Machiavellian (USA) 123 – Elfaslah (IRE) 107   **–**
(Green Desert (USA) 127) [1998 118: 8d 9g* 10m² 9.8d 1999 a10f* 10.4m a9f²   **a126**
a10s³ a10f⁵ Nov 6]
      Like its inaugural winner Cigar, the latest winner of the Dubai World
Cup showed marked improvement for a change in racing surface. But while
Cigar had already proved himself a top-class performer on dirt in America by
the time he was taken to Dubai, Almutawakel's transformation was more or
less instant given that the Dubai World Cup was his debut (in public, at any
rate) on such a surface. Almutawakel had last been seen trailing in in eighth in
the Prix Dollar at Longchamp the previous October, and even on his best piece
of turf form (second in the Grand Prix de Paris) he looked to face a stiff task in
Dubai. Almutawakel did have a Group 1 win to his name but that had been
achieved by scrambling home in a blanket finish to the Prix Jean Prat.
      The North American challenge for the Dubai World Cup looked a
strong one, comprising the first and fourth from the previous year's race, Silver
Charm and Malek, plus Belmont Stakes winner Victory Gallop. Godolphin's
defence was four-strong in total, and like Almutawakel, their three other
representatives had raced only on turf before. They were: Derby winner
High-Rise, their most notable acquisition since the previous season; Daylami,
who'd shown high-class form as a four-year-old; and Italian Derby winner
Central Park. Running Stag, who had himself proved at least as good on dirt in
America the previous autumn as on turf, completed the field as the only
European-based runner. Almutawakel was reckoned to be only third choice
among Godolphin's team alone and was offered as long as 14/1 with British
bookmakers; the price returned on him in America was 44/1. Wrongly, as it
turned out, the leaked outcome of a private trial held between Godolphin's
contenders wasn't taken at face value. In the trial, Almutawakel had reportedly

Dubai World Cup, Nad Al Sheba—Almutawakel improves to give Dubai its first home-trained winner; Malek runs a fine race to make the frame for the second successive year

beaten Central Park by half a length with High-Rise only third. Dettori stuck by High-Rise, however, whilst Almutawakel was partnered by Richard Hills in the colours of Sheikh Hamdan.

That finishing order was replicated in the race itself. After Central Park made the running until over a furlong out, Almutawakel, racing handily as usual, was sent into the lead and kept on gamely to fend off the challenges of Malek, beaten three quarters of a length in second, and Victory Gallop, the same distance away third. Fourth-placed Central Park was followed home by Daylami who'd been squeezed out at the first turn, a disappointing Silver Charm who was found to have bled quite badly, Running Stag and then High-Rise a distant last.

The Dubai World Cup regained its status as the world's richest race in 1999, worth five million dollars in total, three million (over £1.8m) of it going to the winner. The Maktoums were winning back their own money, of course, but despite that and Godolphin's almost routine big-race successes worldwide, there was little concealing how much Almutawakel's 'home win' meant to connections whose post-race celebrations are usually left to their stable jockey. 'We will party for a week' declared Sheikh Mohammed.

It was more than a week—over three months in fact—before it was decided that Almutawakel's win had after all constituted the first round of the inaugural Emirates World Series Racing Championship, of which more details can be found in the essay on Daylami. Having proved himself on dirt (the Nad Al Sheba track is apparently a copy of the surface at Churchill Downs), the remainder of Almutawakel's campaign was geared to the other race on dirt in the World Series, the Breeders' Cup Classic. His next appearance, however, was back on turf, when, although looking fit and well after a five-month break, Almutawakel could finish only seventh in the Juddmonte International at York, running as if the outing was needed. His autumn campaign in America got off to a good start when he lost by a nose to River Keen in the Woodward Stakes at Belmont, the winner another who'd shown much better form on the all-weather than on turf in Britain and had improved for racing on dirt in America. In sloppy going on the same track three weeks later, Almutawakel was beaten a fair bit further by River Keen when third in the Jockey Club Gold Cup, the pair split by Behrens, but Almutawakel finished ahead of both those rivals when a respectable fifth to Cat Thief in the Breeders' Cup Classic at Gulfstream.

Almutawakel's successful switch from turf to dirt had a couple of precedents in the form of his elder half-brothers Mawjud (by Mujtahid) and Fayik (by Arazi). Mawjud won at Yarmouth as a two-year-old but has done most of his racing on dirt in Dubai, winning three ten-furlong handicaps and showing fairly useful form. Fayik did even better for the switch to the all-weather in Britain, winning four races in a row (at all three of the all-weather tracks) in 1998 before finishing third to Running Stag in the inaugural Winter Derby at Lingfield. An interesting spin-off from Almutawakel's success is that Fayik is to be promoted as Europe's first 'all-weather stallion', with the incentive of thirty free nominations to owners of mares which have won at up to a mile on the all-weather in Britain. Almutawakel's three-year-old half-sister Thurayya (by Nashwan) doesn't look as if she's going to see a racecourse but it will be interesting to see how his future half-brothers and -sisters are campaigned; the two-year-old filly Inaaq (by Lammtarra) was in training with David Loder but hasn't raced. All three mares on the bottom line of Almutawakel's pedigree enjoyed their best moments at the Curragh; the useful Elfaslah won a listed race there (one of three successes at around ten furlongs), smart grandam Fair of The Furze won the Tattersalls Rogers Gold Cup, and it was the location of great grandam Autocratic's only success, over five furlongs as a two-year-old. The family could already boast a high-class colt on turf in Italian Derby winner and Arc/King George runner-up White Muzzle, a half-brother to Almutawakel's dam.

Almutawakel (b.c. 1995)	Machiavellian (USA) (b or br 1987)	Mr Prospector (b 1970)	Raise A Native Gold Digger
		Coup de Folie (b 1982)	Halo Raise The Standard
	Elfaslah (IRE) (b 1988)	Green Desert (b 1983)	Danzig Foreign Courier
		Fair of The Furze (b 1982)	Ela-Mana-Mou Autocratic

Godolphin's "Almutawakel"

Evidently, Almutawakel's name is no easier to translate than it is to pronouce—'in the hand of God' and 'keeping faith' were two of the offerings that came to light. He's a tall, angular colt with a quick, fluent action. He has never raced on extremes of ground on turf (his best run on it was on good to firm, though he won on good to soft on his debut) and nor is he likely to, as his future lies on dirt in Florida with Mark Hennig, with the aim of finding a Grade 1 race for him before he is retired to stud. Almutawakel, a genuine colt, stays a mile and a quarter. *Saeed bin Suroor*

AL NABA (USA) 3 ch.c. Mr Prospector (USA) – Forest Flower (USA) 127 (Green **102** Forest (USA) 134) [1998 9p: 6g² 6m* 1999 6d⁵ 7m² 7m* 7d Oct 1] sturdy, well-made colt: good walker: has a quick action: useful performer: best effort when winning minor event at Goodwood (after 4-month break) in September by 1¼ lengths from Mutamayyaz, dropped out last and running on to lead inside final 1f: bandaged behind, tailed off in handicap at Newmarket final start: should stay 1m: yet to race on extremes of going: sent to USA. *E. A. L. Dunlop*

ALNAJASHEE 3 b.g. Generous (IRE) 139 – Tahdid 91 (Mtoto 134) [1998 63: 8s **63** 8.2s⁶ 1999 11.7f² 16.2m⁵ 12m⁵ 14.1m⁶ Aug 23] sturdy gelding: modest maiden: should stay beyond 1½m: yet to race on heavy going, seems to act on any other: reportedly had breathing problems last 2 starts (tongue tied final one): sold 8,500 gns, joined M. Bosley. *P. T. Walwyn*

AL NAKHLAH (USA) 3 b.f. Sheikh Albadou 128 – Magic Slipper 97 (Habitat **66** 134) [1998 –p: 7d 1999 7.1m⁵ 10m² 11.8g⁵ 10.3s Sep 22] big, rangy filly: fair maiden: best effort at 7f: acts on good to firm going: swished tail second start: sent to USA *P T Walwyn*

ALONSA (IRE) 3 b.f. Trempolino (USA) 135 – Alimana 74 (Akarad (FR) 130) **69** [1998 55p: 6g 6g 1999 9m⁵ 11.5g 10m⁵ 12m 11.8g⁴ 12g 11.9s⁶ Sep 29] smallish filly: has stringhalt: fair maiden: stays 1¼m, probably not 1½m: raced mainly on good/good to firm going: sold 12,000 gns in December. *C. E. Brittain*

ALOYSIA (USA) 3 ch.f. Diesis 133 – Alyanaabi (USA) 74 (Roberto (USA) 131) **59 ?** [1998 –: 7m 1999 9f³ Aug 4] rather unfurnished filly: has a round action: modest form at best in maidens: sold 4,200 gns in December. *J. H. M. Gosden*

ALPATHAR (IRE) 2 ch.f. (Mar 16) Simply Great (FR) 122 – Royal Language **65** (USA) 56 (Conquistador Cielo (USA)) [1999 6d⁵ 5g⁵ 5m⁶ a6g⁴ 7.5g 7s² 7s⁵ Oct 5] IR 7,800Y: rather sparely-made filly: sixth living foal: dam stayed 1m: fair maiden: short-headed at Newcastle penultimate start: should stay at least 1m: acts on soft going, probably on fibresand. *M. Dods*

ALPENGLOW 3 b.f. Ezzoud (IRE) 126 – Aquaglow 84 (Caerleon (USA) 132) **106 p** [1998 NR 1999 7m* 7s⁶ 8d* 8d³ Oct 30] 26,000F, 400,000 francs Y: deep-girthed, attractive filly: has a quick action: sixth foal: half-sister to several winners, including useful middle-distance performer Attitre (by Mtoto), 8.2f winner at 2 yrs, and useful 6f and (at 2 yrs) 7f winner Please Suzanne (by Cadeaux Genereux): dam 7f and 1m winner: useful form: won maiden at Newmarket in April and minor event at Leicester in October: further improvement when 2 lengths third to Bomb Alaska in steadily-run listed event at Newmarket final start, held up and running on well: should stay beyond 1m: capable of better still. *J. H. M. Gosden*

ALPEN WOLF (IRE) 4 ch.g. Wolfhound (USA) 126 – Oatfield 69 (Great **83** Nephew 126) [1998 73: 6s 6m⁴ 6m³ 6g⁵ 5.3m 5m⁴ 5m 6f* 6m* 6f* 7m* 7g 1999 6g 6f* 7m³ 7.1g⁶ 6f³ 6m² 6f 5.7m* 6g 5.7f⁵ Sep 6] sturdy, rather dipped-backed gelding: fairly useful handicapper: won at Brighton (fourth course success) in April and Bath in August: generally respectable efforts otherwise: unlikely to stay beyond 7f: raced mainly on good going or firmer (acts on firm): tried visored: usually races prominently. *W. R. Muir*

ALPHA 3 b.g. Primo Dominie 121 – Preening 62 (Persian Bold 123) [1998 74: 5d* **—** 5m⁴ 6g⁶ 6g 7v 1999 5.9m 5.9m Jun 23] good-bodied gelding: lost form at 2 yrs after winning debut and no promise only start in 1999: should stay at least 6f: sold 6,000 gns in August, sent to Macau. *C. W. Thornton*

ALPHA HEIGHTS (IRE)   2 b.f. (Jan 20) Namaqualand (USA) – Mnaafa (IRE)   **68 +**
70 (Darshaan 133) [1999 5m³ 5g 6.3m⁵ 7m 7.9f Sep 2] IR 15,000Y: leggy filly:
second foal: half-sister to fairly useful 1998 2-y-o 6f winner Island Hero (by Polar
Falcon): dam, 1¼m winner who stayed 1½m well, from family of Alderbrook: fair
maiden: possibly flattered (could be rated 78) when fifth in valuable sales race at the
Curragh: well beaten after: should stay at least 7f. *Mrs P. N. Dutfield*

ALPHA ROSE   2 ch.f. (Feb 27) Inchinor 119 – Philgwyn 66 (Milford 119) [1999   **54**
7v⁶ Sep 20] 32,000Y: half-sister to several winners, including useful 7f to 1¼m
winner here and in Scandinavia Philidor (by Forzando) and 6-y-o Philistar: dam,
maiden who stayed 7f, half-sister to very smart sprinter Primo Dominie: 7½ lengths
sixth of 9 in maiden at Kempton, starting slowly but briefly getting back in touch:
joined M. Bell: may do better. *R. J. R. Williams*

ALPHILDA   2 gr.f. (Jan 23) Ezzoud (IRE) 126 – Desert Delight (IRE) (Green   **83**
Desert (USA) 127) [1999 5m³ 5m⁴ 6g² 6m⁴ 6g* 6f 6g² 6m² 6d² 7d Sep 28] 37,000F,
35,000Y: smallish, lengthy filly: second foal: half-sister to a winner in South Africa
by Pursuit of Love: dam unraced half-sister to smart but untrustworthy winner up to
1m Intimate Guest: fairly useful performer: won nursery at Ayr in July: good second
in similar events after: should stay 7f: acts on good to firm and good to soft ground:
carries head high under pressure, and hung left penultimate start. *B. W. Hills*

ALPINE FUGUE (IRE)   5 b.g. Classic Music (USA) – Val Gardena (Ahonoora   **63 ?**
122) [1998 NR 1999 14.1m⁵ Jul 10] second foal: dam once on Flat and placed
over hurdles: poor form in bumpers in Ireland at 4 yrs for M. Halford: some promise
in maiden at Salisbury on Flat debut. *J. W. Mullins*

ALPINE HIDEAWAY (IRE)   6 b.g. Tirol 127 – Arbour (USA) 76 (Graustark)   **70 d**
[1998 74: 8d a8g 8d² 8m⁴ 1999 8v⁶ 8m 7.5v 7g 8f 8.5g* 8m⁶ 8m³ Aug 31] useful-
looking gelding: has a round action: fair performer: below best after reappearance,
including when winning claimer at Beverley in August: stays 8.5f (probably not
1½m): acts on any turf ground and fibresand: races freely: blinkered twice.
M. W. Easterby

ALPINE PARK (IRE)   2 ch.f. (Feb 21) Barathea (IRE) 127 – Park Charger 105   **87**
(Tirol 127) [1999 6f* 6.1f² 6s* 6d⁶ 7d Aug 14] 48,000Y: smallish, lengthy filly: first
foal: dam 1m/1¼m winner: fairly useful performer: made all in maiden at Kempton
in May and minor event at Pontefract in June: not discredited in listed race at
Newmarket final start: likely to stay 1m: acts on firm and soft ground: sold 25,000
gns in December. *J. Noseda*

ALPINE RED   3 b.g. Tirol 127 – Rohita (IRE) 94 (Waajib 121) [1998 NR 1999 8s   **–**
8d 10v Apr 24] 66,000Y: first foal: dam, 2-y-o 5f/6f winner, bred to stay 1m: behind
in maidens: sold 1,000 gns in July: dead. *M. L. W. Bell*

ALQAWAASER (USA)   2 b. or br.c. (May 29) Dayjur (USA) 137 – Alghuzaylah   **66**
90 (Habitat 134) [1999 7d³ 6d Oct 14] good-bodied colt: half-brother to several
winners, including very smart miler Zaahi (by Slew O'Gold) and fairly useful Irish
sprinter Aljjawarih (by Nureyev): dam, 2-y-o 5f winner who stayed 1m, half-sister to
very smart French winner up to 10.5f Pitasia: very green when third of 9 to Decarchy
in maiden at Yarmouth: again half-reared leaving stalls when well held in similar
event at Newmarket: sold 26,000 gns later in October. *E. A. L. Dunlop*

ALRABYAH (IRE)   4 br.g. Brief Truce (USA) 126 – Bean Siamsa (Solinus 130)   **–**
[1998 64d: 8m⁵ 10.1g 12.3g⁶ 8f 8m 1999 8.2m 8s 8m Jun 16] compact gelding:
disappointing maiden: blinkered final start. *K. A. Morgan*

ALRASSAAM   3 b.c. Zafonic (USA) 130 – Lady Blackfoot 108 (Prince Tender-   **116**
foot (USA) 126) [1998 71p: 7g 7mm 8m* 8m 8.1g* 8m⁶ 9m* 10v² Aug 14] rangy,
angular colt: usually impresses in appearance: fluent mover: smart performer: won
maiden at Newbury (33/1, by 2 lengths from Killer Instinct) in April, minor event at
Haydock (by ½ length from Teapot Row) in May and Prix Daphnis at Chantilly (beat
Val Royal ¾ length) in July: good head second to Val Royal in Prix Guillaume
d'Ornano at Deauville final start: well held in 2000 Guineas at Newmarket and St
James's Palace Stakes at Royal Ascot other starts: stays 1¼m: yet to race on firm
going, acts on any other. *M. A. Jarvis*

Godolphin's "Altibr"

ALSAHIB (USA) 6 b.g. Slew O'Gold (USA) – Khwlah (USA) 99 (Best Turn **48**
(USA)) [1998 56, a84: a12g³ a11g* a12g a11g⁵ 8.1g 9d 11.7m⁴ 10.4g 10.4g 10s **a74**
a12g* a12g⁴ 1999 a12g² a12g⁴ a12g³ a12g* a12g³ a12g* 11.9f⁵ 12g⁵ 11.6d³ a11g⁴
11.8m³ 11.6m⁵ 11.9d⁴ 14.1m⁴ Aug 28] big, robust gelding: fair on all-weather, poor
on turf: won claimers at Southwell in February and April: needs further than 1m,
and stays 1¾m: acts on firm ground, soft and all-weather: tried
blinkered: held up, and suited by strongly-run race: joined O. Sherwood. *W. R. Muir*

AL SAQIYA (USA) 3 b.f. Woodman (USA) 126 – Augusta Springs (USA) **–**
(Nijinsky (CAN) 138) [1998 68: 7m 7.5m⁴ 7v 1999 8.3m 8m May 13] strong,
useful-looking filly: fair maiden at best: little show in handicaps in 1999, blinkered
final start: should stay 1¼m: well beaten on heavy going: sent to USA. *J. L. Dunlop*

AL'S FELLA (IRE) 4 br.g. Alzao (USA) 117 – Crystal Cross (USA) 88 (Roberto **74**
(USA) 131) [1998 81, a70: a9.4g³ a10g⁴ a8g² a8.5g² a8.5g 8.9g 11d* 1999
12s⁶ 12.3m⁵ 14.1m 14d⁴ 11.8m* 14.1m⁴ 11.6s* Aug 9] sparely-made gelding: fair
performer: didn't need to be at best to win claimer at Leicester (made all) in July and
seller at Windsor (by easy 8 lengths) in August: effective at 11f, probably 1¾m: acts
on soft going, good to firm and fibresand (probably on equitrack): sometimes
blinkered, but is as effective without: has looked a difficult ride and carried head
awkwardly. *P. F. I. Cole*

ALSHAKR 2 b.f. (Apr 26) Bahri (USA) 125 – Give Thanks 123 (Relko 136) **72 p**
[1999 7m⁶ 6.1d⁴ Oct 5] closely related to 6-y-o Shahrur and half-sister to 2 winners,
including 1½m winner Saffaanh (by Shareef Dancer), dam of 1000 Guineas winner
Harayir: dam 9f to 1½m winner (including Irish Oaks) and second in Park Hill: better
effort in maidens (slowly away and green on debut) when never-nearer fourth of
15 to Resounding at Nottingham: bred to be suited by 1m+: should do better still.
P. T. Walwyn

ALTAY 2 b.g. (Feb 17) Erins Isle 121 – Aliuska (IRE) 70 (Fijar Tango (FR) 127) **59** [1999 6f⁵ 5g 7m⁶ Sep 19] has scope: first foal: has gelding: dam Irish 5f winner at 2 yrs (only season to race): modest form at best in maidens. *R. A. Fahey*

ALTIBR (USA) 4 ch.c. Diesis 133 – Love's Reward (Nonoalco (USA) 131) [1998 **117** –: 8f 1999 a8f² a9f* a10f² a10f* 8.5g⁴ 9g² Jun 27] big, strong colt: carries condition: fluent mover, though shows knee action: smart performer: ran only once each at 2 and 3 yrs: won listed race and Dubai Duty Free (by 3½ lengths from Spindrift) at Nad Al Sheba in February/March: just as good on turf, best effort when 2 lengths second of 5 to Great Dane in International Stakes at the Curragh: stays 1¼m: acts on dirt, most turf runs on good going: usually makes running: joined K. McLaughlin in USA/ UAE. *Saeed bin Suroor*

ALTICHIERO 3 b.g. Polish Precedent (USA) 131 – Anna Matrushka (Mill Reef **102 p** (USA) 141) [1998 68p: 7.1m⁶ 8d 1999 9.9m² a12f* Oct 2] smallish, well-made gelding: progressive form, useful already: favourite, easily won 6-runner handicap at Wolverhampton in October by 5 lengths from High Tatra, soon clear when shaken up: likely to prove best at 1¼m/1½m: yet to race on extremes of going on turf: sent to UAE: open to further improvement. *Sir Michael Stoute*

ALTIZAF 3 b.f. Zafonic (USA) 130 – Altiyna 109 (Troy 137) [1998 NR 1999 **66** 10m⁵ 10.4m Sep 1] 30,000Y: tall, angular filly: seventh foal: half-sister to 3 winners, including Irish 1½m winner Altishar (by Darshaan): dam, 2-y-o 7f winner and third in Park Hill, half-sister to disqualified Oaks winner Aliysa: much better effort in maidens on debut. *W. R. Muir*

AL TOWD (USA) 2 b.c. (Apr 21) Kingmambo (USA) 125 – Toujours Elle (USA) **94 p** (Lyphard (USA) 132) [1999 7m³ 7m* 7d² 8d³ Oct 29] 80,000Y: rangy, rather unfurnished colt: has a rather rounded action: fourth foal: half-brother to useful Italian 1¼m and 11f winner Toto Le Heros (by Saumarez) and French 10.5f winner Horse Man (by Exit To Nowhere): dam, French maiden, closely related to Elnadim and Mehthaaf and granddaughter of Fall Aspen: useful form: won maiden at Newcastle in September: placed after in minor events at York (½-length second of 6 to Zoning, rallying well) and Newmarket (2¾ lengths third behind Autonomy): remains likely to do better at 1¼m/1½m. *J. L. Dunlop*

ALUSTAR 2 b.f. (Feb 8) Emarati (USA) 74 – Chiming Melody 71 (Cure The **71** Blues (USA)) [1999 5d a5g³ 5g³ 5d* 5m² 5m 6s 5s Oct 13] 4,400Y: sturdy, lengthy filly: fourth foal: sister to a 5f and 7.5f winner in Spain and half-sister to 1992 2-y-o 5f winner Polity Prince and 8-y-o Ocean Park (both by Dominion): dam 1m winner: fair performer: won maiden at Pontefract (broke loose before start) in June: well below form last 3 starts: raced mainly at 5f: acts on fibresand, good to firm and good to soft going. *M. W. Easterby*

ALVA GLEN (USA) 2 b.c. (Apr 19) Gulch (USA) – Domludge (USA) (Lyphard **94 p** (USA) 132) [1999 6m⁴ 7s² 8.2d* Oct 21] $625,000Y: good-topped colt: has plenty of scope: closely related to useful French winner up to 7f Vassia (by Machiavellian) and half-brother to 3 winners, notably smart performer up to 15.5f Shrewd Idea (by Alleged): dam lightly-raced sister to dam of Hatoof and half-sister to high-class Mrs Penny: progressive form in maidens, landing odds in 11-runner event at Nottingham (by 1½ lengths from Hidden Brave) despite tending to hang right: will be well suited by 1¼m: useful prospect. *Sir Michael Stoute*

AL WAFFI 3 b.c. Fairy King (USA) – Darrery 98 (Darshaan 133) [1998 102: 7g² **102** 7m* 8g⁴ 7m* 8s³ 1999 10.5m⁴ 8g² 8g² a7.5f Dec 23] good-bodied colt: useful performer: off 3 months after reappearance, then runner-up to Touch'N' Fly in minor event at Salisbury (visored and tongue tied, beaten 7 lengths) and Miami Blues (final start for S. bin Suroor, beaten a neck) in listed race at Baden-Baden: should stay 1¼m: acts on soft and good to firm going. *S. Seemar, UAE*

ALWAYS ALIGHT 5 ch.g. Never So Bold 135 – Fire Sprite 83 (Mummy's Game **98** 120) [1998 102: 6d⁵ 6d⁴ 6g⁵ 6d 6g 7f 6g 6s* 7.1m⁴ 6s* 6g⁵ 6m 6v³ 6d 1999 6d³ 6g⁶ 6g 6m 6s 6d⁴ 6m 6m³ 6d⁶ 6s³ Sep 27] good-bodied gelding: useful performer: ran at least respectably on several occasions in 1999, including when third to Tedburrow in listed race at Doncaster on reappearance and sixth to Grangeville in Ayr Gold Cup penultimate start: best at 6f: acts on any going: occasionally blinkered/visored: usually early to post: sometimes soon off bridle. *K. R. Burke*

ALWENA 4 ch.f. Henbit (USA) 130 – Brenig 68 (Horage 124) [1998 33: 8m a8.5g –
a12g a11g⁵ 1999 a11g⁵ a12f Jan 14] poor maiden at best: visored in 1999:
headstrong. *S. C. Williams*

ALYPORTENT 5 b.g. Warning 136 – Alilisa (USA) (Alydar (USA)) [1998 NR –
1999 6s 6g 8m 5.9g 7f Jul 24] angular gelding: little form: tried visored.
Mrs J. Jordan

ALYSKA (IRE) 2 b.f. (Apr 10) Owington 123 – Simouna (Ela-Mana-Mou 132) –
[1999 5m Jun 18] IR 13,000F, IR 28,000Y: third foal: half-sister to useful 1998 Irish
2-y-o 7f/1m winner Athlumney Lady (by Lycius) and fairly useful 1996 Irish 2-y-o
7f winner Red Castle (by Common Grounds): dam unraced daughter of half-sister to
Seymour Hicks and Princess Pati: well beaten in maiden at Redcar. *J. Berry*

ALZAO STORM (IRE) 2 ch.f. (Apr 27) Mukaddamah (USA) 125 – Brockley –
Hill Lass (IRE) (Alzao (USA) 117) [1999 6.1g 7f Jul 14] 500Y: second foal: sister to
3-y-o Hill Storm: dam ran once at 2 yrs: last in maidens. *J. W. Payne*

ALZITA (IRE) 2 b.f. (Jan 29) Alzao (USA) 117 – Tiavanita (USA) (J O Tobin –
(USA) 130) [1999 7v Sep 20] IR 30,000Y: fifth foal: half-sister to 3 winners, notably
2000 Guineas winner Island Sands (by Turtle Island): dam, French maiden, half-
sister to very smart middle-distance colt Corrupt: slowly away and always behind in
maiden at Kempton: may do better. *J. A. R. Toller*

ALZOLA (IRE) 2 b.f. (Mar 31) Alzao (USA) 117 – Polistatic 53 (Free State 125) **63 p**
[1999 6g Aug 13] small, compact filly: fourth foal: half-sister to 3-y-o Purple Flame
and 5-y-o Regal Academy: dam, 11f and 1½m winner, sister to useful middle-
distance winner Mango Express and Ebor winner Western Dancer: 66/1 and burly,
over 11 lengths eleventh of 16 to Teggiano in maiden at Newbury, never dangerous
after slow start: likely to be suited by 1¼m+: should do better. *C. A. Horgan*

ALZOOMO (IRE) 7 b.g. Alzao (USA) 117 – Fandangerina (USA) (Grey Dawn –
II 132) [1998 NR 1999 12g Mar 25] strong gelding: fair maiden at 4 yrs: tongue tied
and visored, well beaten only start since: sold 2,800 gns in June. *J. A. Glover*

AMADOUR (IRE) 6 b.g. Contract Law (USA) 108 – Truly Flattering (Hard –
Fought 125) [1998 –, a79: a12g*ᵈⁱˢ a12g a12g² 1999 12m May 3] workmanlike
gelding: one-time fair performer: reportedly lame only 6-y-o start: should stay
beyond 1½m: best form on equitrack (well held only run on fibresand). *P. Mitchell*

AMAD'S PRINCESS 3 b.f. Minshaanshu Amad (USA) 91§ – Cleeveland Lady –
(Turn Back The Time (USA)) [1998 –: 8d 8g⁶ 7s 1999 12v⁶ 11.9f May 12] second
foal: dam 2m hurdler: trained by G. O'Neill in Ireland at 2 yrs: no form in maidens/
handicap. *W. G. M. Turner*

AMALIA (IRE) 3 b.f. Danehill (USA) 126 – Cheviot Amble (IRE) 105 (Pennine **103**
Walk 120) [1998 75p: 6g⁶ 8.2s³ 1999 8g² 8m* 8f³ 8f² 7.6d* 9m⁴ 10.3m* 10d Oct 14]
small filly: has a quick action: useful performer: won maiden at Redcar (made all) in
June and handicaps at Chester in August and Doncaster (got up final 75 yds to beat
Robin Lane by 1¼ lengths despite drifting left) in September: eased once beaten and
well held in listed event at Newmarket final start: seems better at 1¼m or shorter,
and will probably stay 1½m: acts on firm and good to soft going: has worn bandages
behind: usually held up. *P. W. Harris*

AMAL JUMAIRAH 3 b.c. Barathea (IRE) 127 – Fair Shirley (IRE) 75 (Shirley **69**
Heights 130) [1998 69p: 7m 8s⁵ 1999 10g⁶ 8m⁴ 10m⁴ 10.2g³ 9.7f Jul 14] quite
attractive colt: fair maiden: stays 1¼m: acts on soft going, possibly not on firm: sent
to UAE. *M. A. Jarvis*

AMARANTH (IRE) 3 b.g. Mujadil (USA) 119 – Zoes Delight (IRE) (Hatim **88**
(USA) 121) [1998 68: 6d² 5s* 1999 7d 5d 5d² 5g³ 6m* 6d 6s⁶ 5m 5m 5m* 5m⁶ Sep
19] angular, quite good-topped gelding: fairly useful handicapper: won at Newcastle
in June and Newmarket (ladies race) in August: stays 6f: acts on good to firm and soft
ground: usually tongue tied: may do better still. *J. L. Eyre*

AMARETTO FLAME (IRE) 3 ch.f. First Trump 118 – Vestal Flame 45 **69**
(Habitat 134) [1998 60p: 7d 1999 10m 10v² 11.6g 16m³ 11.6m* 12f³ Jul 30] tall,
rather leggy filly: fair performer: not at best when winning seller at Windsor in July:
probably stays 1½m: has form on firm going, best effort on heavy. *B. J. Meehan*

AMARICE   3 b.f. Suave Dancer (USA) 136 – Almitra (Targowice (USA) 130)   **85**
[1998 75: 6m³ 6d⁵ 7s* 7s 1999 8m 9.1g² 9.9g² 10.2m⁵ 8f³ Jul 31] leggy filly: fairly
useful handicapper: placed at Ayr, Beverley and Thirsk in June/July: stays 1¼m: yet
to race on heavy going, acts on any other: has been bandaged. *M. Johnston*

AMARO   3 b.f. Emarati (USA) 74 – Redcross Miss 64 (Tower Walk 130) [1998 NR   **59**
1999 6s⁵ a5g⁴ a6g⁵ 5m² 5m² 5g 5g⁴ 5v 5d a6g⁵ Dec 27] seventh living foal: half-sister   **a44 +**
to several winners, including 1993 2-y-o 5f winner Valiant Man (by Valiyar) and 11f
winner Manoy (by Precocious): dam middle-distance maiden: modest maiden:
raced mainly at 5f: acts on good to firm going (below form on heavy), probably on
fibresand: races up with pace. *J. Wharton*

AMAZED   2 ch.f. (Apr 7) Clantime 101 – Indigo 86 (Primo Dominie 121) [1999   **51 P**
5d⁶ Oct 26] fifth foal: sister to sprinters Bishops Court (smart) and Surprise Mission
(useful), and half-sister to 3-y-o Astonished and 4-y-o Surprised: dam 2-y-o 5f
winner: second favourite, too green to do herself justice when under 5 lengths sixth
of 16 to Footprints in maiden at Redcar, carrying head awkwardly and edging left in
latter stages but not given hard time: sure to leave form well behind and win races at
3 yrs. *I. A. Balding*

AMAZING DREAM (IRE)   3 b.f. Thatching 131 – Aunty Eileen (Ahonoora   **98**
122) [1998 94+: 5.2m⁵ 5d⁴ 5d 5g* 5g² 5.2m* 6g* 1999 7g 7m 5.1m 6m 6f 5m 5m⁶
Sep 7] good-quartered filly: has a round action: useful performer: best efforts in 1999
on fourth and final starts: best at 5f/6f: acts on good to firm ground, yet to race on
soft/heavy: has worn tongue strap. *R. Hannon*

AMAZING FACT (USA)   4 b.g. Known Fact (USA) 135 – Itsamazing (USA)   **–**
85 (The Minstrel (CAN) 135) [1998 69d: 7m³ 7.1s 8.5m⁶ 7f 10g 9.7s 1999 8m 6g a7g
8d a8.5g Dec 1] disappointing maiden: no show in 1999: should stay 1m.
J. M. Bradley

AMBER BAY   2 b.c. (Feb 27) Petong 126 – Dependable (Formidable (USA) 125)   **–**
[1999 7g 7g 7d Aug 26] 6,500Y: fifth foal: half-brother to 6f (at 2 yrs) to 14.8f winner
Certain Magic and 4-y-o Elba Magic (both by Faustus): dam (unraced) from family
of Chilibang: no show in maiden and sellers. *C. A. Dwyer*

AMBER BROWN   3 b.f. Thowra (FR) – High Velocity 53 (Frimley Park 109)   **62**
[1998 NR 1999 5s⁶ 6g 6m⁶ 5g⁶ 5.3f 6d⁵ 5g Jul 2] workmanlike filly: sixth foal:
half-sister to 3 winners, including fairly useful 1997 2-y-o 5f winner Banningham
Blade (by Sure Blade) and 5-y-o Anokato: dam 5f performer: modest maiden: will
probably stay 7f: acts on good to firm and good to soft ground: has been bandaged in
front: seemed unsuited by track at Brighton fifth start. *K. T. Ivory*

AMBER FORT   6 gr.g. Indian Ridge 123 – Lammastide 93 (Martinmas 128)   **84**
[1998 87: 8g 8m 8f⁴ 8.3d⁵ 7g* 7d* 7m 8m 7g³ 7.1g³ 8m³ 7g⁵ 7g 1999 7m 7m⁵ 7m⁵
7.1g³ 7m³ 7m 7g⁴ 7m 7g 7g³ 7.1m² 7.3m 8v 7d Oct 9] tall gelding: fairly useful
handicapper: effective at 7f/1m: acts on equitrack, firm and soft going: usually
blinkered/visored: not an easy ride (flashes tail and tends to wander), and best held
up. *J. M. Bradley*

AMBER GO GO   2 ch.f. (Apr 17) Rudimentary (USA) 118 – Plaything 69 (High   **–**
Top 131) [1999 5.1s 5m 5g 5m 5f³ 5g 8d Sep 23] 500Y: sixth foal: half-sister to fairly
useful 1½m and 2m winner Little Acorn (by Unfuwain) and 3-y-o Slip of The
Tongue: dam awarded 1m race: little form. *K. W. Hogg, Isle of Man*

AMBER JASMINE (IRE)   3 b.g. Petardia 113 – Hollyberry (IRE) (Runnett   **56**
125) [1998 57: 5m⁵ 5g³ 6g 5d 1999 a5g² a6g⁵ a5g³ Apr 6] modest maiden: likely to
prove best at 5f/6f: acts on fibresand, yet to race on extremes of going on turf:
may be untrustworthy (carried head high/flashed tail final start): sent to Spain.
P. C. Haslam

AMBER MUSIC   2 ch.f. (Apr 5) Interrex (CAN) – Silly Sally (Music Boy 124)   **28**
[1999 a6g³ May 17] second foal: half-sister to 4-y-o Amber Regent (by King's
Signet): dam, no form, looked temperamental final start: third of 7 in seller at
Southwell: fatally injured when rearing in stalls following month. *W. G. M. Turner*

AMBER REGENT   4 ch.g. King's Signet (USA) 110 – Silly Sally (Music Boy   **–**
124) [1998 61: a6s⁵ a7g³ a7g⁴ a7g* a7g⁴ a8g⁵ 7.5m² 9.1m a9.4g 8.3s⁴ a9.4g² 10.8m
a11g a8.5g 1999 a7g⁶ a9.4g a8g a8g a14.8g Nov 27] strong, workmanlike gelding:

61

modest performer at best: no show in 1999: effective at 7f, probably 9.4f: acts on good to firm ground and fibresand, probably on equitrack: tried blinkered/visored: tends to carry head awkwardly. *Miss S. J. Wilton*

AMBIDEXTROUS (IRE) 7 b.h. Shareef Dancer (USA) 135 – Amber Fizz (USA) (Effervescing (USA)) [1998 58, a49: a12g⁵ a12g⁶ a12g³ 11v⁶ 12.3m⁴ 12m⁵ 10.3g 12s³ 12d 10.5m² 10.3g⁵ 11.1d³ 11.9d 11m³ 10.4g² 12d⁶ 9.9m 11.9g⁴ 10.1v 12s a10f 1999 a11g⁵ a11g³ a12g⁶ a12g 12m² 12.3m 12m⁵ 12g 12m 10.3m³ 10m⁵ 12.1m² 11.9d 10g 12.3d* 12g* 10.3s⁵ 14.1g⁵ 12d⁶ 10.1d² 12g a12g a12g² Dec 27] good-bodied horse: modest on turf, poor on all-weather: won amateur handicap at Chester and claimer at Carlisle in August: effective at 1¼m/1½m: acts on firm going, soft and fibresand: tried visored/blinkered: has worn net muzzle (tried to bite an opponent fifth start): has been slowly away/hung/found little, and usually held up: untrustworthy. *E. J. Alston* **54 §** **a46 §**

AMBITIOUS 4 b.f. Ardkinglass 114 – Ayodhya (IRE) (Astronef 116) [1998 49: 5d a6g² a6g⁴ 1999 a7g⁶ a6f² a6g* a6g⁵ 7s⁵ 5d² 6.1s 6g² 6f 5m⁵ 6m 6m 5m² 5d* 5g³ 6g 5f⁶ 5d⁶ 5g* 5g* 5d² 5d Oct 28] lengthy filly: fairly useful performer: had a good year, recapturing 2-y-o form and improving again late on: successful in handicap at Southwell in February, claimer at Sandown in June, handicap at Sandown in August then minor event at Redcar and handicap at York in October: good effort penultimate start: best at 5f/easy 6f: acts on good to firm going, good to soft and all-weather: visored/blinkered second to seventh 4-y-o starts: has been bandaged in front: best held up: trained by J. Fanshawe until after eighth outing. *K. T. Ivory* **85 +**

AMBUSHED (IRE) 3 b.g. Indian Ridge 123 – Surprise Move (IRE) (Simply Great (FR) 122) [1998 NR 1999 a7g a10g Dec 29] IR 21,000Y: third foal: half-brother to Irish 1996 2-y-o 7f winner Trapped (by River Falls): dam unraced half-sister to dam of very smart miler Pennine Walk: well held in maidens at Lingfield. *M. Johnston* **–**

AMEENA (USA) 4 b.f. Irish River (FR) 131 – London Pride (USA) 106 (Lear Fan (USA) 130) [1998 72: 8d³ 9m 6g⁴ 7.1g⁶ 7m⁵ 7d 1999 7d³ 6.1s² 7s 6d 6m a7g 6g a7g 9s Oct 8] useful-looking, unfurnished filly: fair maiden handicapper at best: below form after second start: should stay 7f: acts on soft ground. *R. A. Fahey* **69 d**

AMELIA JESS (IRE) 2 ch.f. (Apr 14) Mac's Imp (USA) 116 – Vieux Carre (Pas de Seul 133) [1999 6d 6d 6.1d 5g Oct 14] 4,400Y: tall, close-coupled filly: poor mover: sixth foal: half-sister to 3 winners, including 1996 2-y-o 6f and 7f winner Contravene (by Contract Law) and 1998 2-y-o 6f winner Vintage Pride (by Pips Pride): dam, poor maiden, sometimes appeared reluctant: well held in maidens: has had tongue tied. *B. S. Rothwell* **–**

AMERCIUS 7 ch.g. Old Vic 136 – Elarrih (USA) (Sharpen Up 127) [1998 NR 1999 18m Jun 29] sparely-made gelding: poor staying maiden in 1996: well held only Flat start since, but successful over fences in July: sometimes blinkered. *R. Simpson* **–**

AMERICAN COUSIN 4 b.g. Distant Relative 128 – Zelda (USA) (Sharpen Up 127) [1998 63: 7d 6g 5g² 5m⁵ 5m 5d 1999 5g 5m 6m 6f 5g² 6m* 5g⁴ 5m² 5m* 5.7m⁵ 6m² 5.3s⁴ 5g Oct 6] fair handicapper: won apprentice events at Doncaster in June and July: stays 6f: acts on good to firm and soft ground: blinkered twice (very slowly away second time). *D. Nicholls* **68**

AMETHYST (IRE) 2 b.f. (Mar 23) Sadler's Wells (USA) 132 – Zummerudd (Habitat 134) [1999 6m* 7g² 7m⁴ 6s³ Oct 23] smallish, rather angular filly: sister to 2000 Guineas winner King of Kings and closely related to useful sprinters Furajet (by The Minstrel) and General Monash (by Thorn Dance): dam (ran twice) from family of several good sprinters, sister to dam of very smart 1¼m performer Batshoof: useful performer: won maiden at Naas in May: in frame after in listed races at Leopardstown and Doncaster and Moyglare Stud Stakes (fourth to Preseli) at the Curragh in between: will probably stay 1m: acts on good to firm and soft ground. *A. P. O'Brien, Ireland* **102 +**

AMEZOLA 3 gr.g. Northern Park (USA) 107 – Yamamah 54 (Siberian Express (USA) 125) [1998 83p: 7g 8v* 1999 9.9g⁴ 13m³ 14d² 14.8d 16s⁶ Oct 22] quite good-topped gelding: fairly useful handicapper, lightly raced: good second at Sandown in September, clear of rest: well beaten both starts after, though paid price for **94**

forcing strong pace (tongue tied) final one: should stay 2m: acts on heavy going. *Mrs A. J. Perrett*

AMIARGE   9 b.g. Reference Point 139 – Scotia Rose (Tap On Wood 130) [1998 –: **42** 16m 16g 16v 16d 15.9g 1999 16.2d 16m 14.1m 16.1m 16.4d Aug 12] small gelding: poor handicapper: stays 2¼m: acts on firm and soft going: effective visored/blinkered or not: inconsistent. *M. Brittain*

AMICO D'ORO   2 b.c. (Jan 25) Mistertopogigo (IRE) 118 – Don't Jump (IRE)   **–** 71 (Entitled 126) [1999 5m 6v a6g Oct 16] 9,500F, 9,000Y: first foal: dam won up to 1m: well beaten in maiden/claimers: sold 500 gns. *J. Berry*

AMILYNX (FR)   3 gr.c. Linamix (FR) 127 – Amen (USA) (Alydar (USA)) [1998 **121** 7v³ 1999 12s* 12d 15s² 15m³ 15v* 15.5v* Oct 24] third foal: brother to fair 1m winner (probably stays 1½m) Amenixa: dam won 5 races in USA and second in Grade 3 6f event: very smart performer: won minor event at Saint-Cloud in March then off course nearly 4 months after next start: revelled in heavy ground at Longchamp in October, winning Prix Hubert de Chaudenay Casino Menton Barriere by 8 lengths from Northerntown and Prix Royal-Oak (leading inside final 1f, by 1½ lengths from Tajoun) 3 weeks later: will stay beyond 2m. *A. Fabre, France*

AMINGTON GIRL   4 b.f. Tragic Role (USA) – Millfields House 70 (Record   **42** Token 128) [1998 48: 6.1s 8m² 8f⁶ 7.1s³ 6.1g³ a6g² 8.2g* 8g⁴ 8m 8m 9.1s a6g 1999 a8g a8.5g⁴ a7g³ a7g a7g a8.5g a7g³ a7g⁵ a6g⁵ a8.5g³ 8d⁴ a7g a8.5g 7.7s May 29] poor performer: ran twice at same meeting on twelfth/thirteenth starts: effective at to 1m: acts on fibresand, best efforts on turf on good/good to firm going: usually visored/blinkered: often bandaged. *P. D. Evans*

AMIRANTES   3 b.c. Elmaamul (USA) 125 – Angel Drummer 59 (Dance In Time   **–** (CAN)) [1998 NR 1999 a7g⁶ a7f 6g 5.1s 5g 8.2m 5m Aug 4] tall, angular colt: seventh foal: half-brother to 1993 2-y-o 6f winner Wandering Angel (by Sharrood), 5-y-o Danka and a 7f/1m winner in Italy by Dilum: dam, 2-y-o 7f winner, later successful over hurdles: no form: tried blinkered: dead. *M. J. Polglase*

AMONG ISLANDS   8 b.m. Jupiter Island 126 – Queen of The Nile (Hittite Glory   **–** 125) [1998 NR 1999 a12g⁶ Feb 25] lightly raced and little sign of ability on Flat: modest winning hurdler. *G. F. H. Charles-Jones*

AMORAS (IRE)   2 b.f. (Apr 8) Hamas (IRE) 125§ – Red Lory 87 (Bay Express   **73** 132) [1999 5g 5m⁶ 6.1m² 6s⁵ 6.1m³ 8f* 8d⁵ 7.3v⁴ Oct 23] IR 19,000F, IR 20,000Y: good-bodied filly: half-sister to several winners, including useful French/US sprinter Cyrano Storme (by Cyrano de Bergerac) and 7f/1m winner King Parrot (by King of Spain): dam 2-y-o 5f winner: fair performer: won nursery at Bath in September: stays 1m: acts on any going. *J. W. Hills*

Prix Royal-Oak, Longchamp—
Amilynx denies the Aga Khan a hat-trick of victories in the race as he beats Tajoun comfortably;
Leggera is disqualified due to a weight discrepancy after finishing third in her final race

AMRAK AJEEB (IRE)   7 b.h. Danehill (USA) 126 – Noble Dust (USA) (Dust   **81 §**
Commander (USA)) [1998 a10f 8f a8f⁴ 1999 7m⁴ 8m* 8f⁴ a8f⁶ 8m⁶ 10m 10m 9m⁴
13.3m 12s 10s Oct 22] leggy, good-topped horse: usually takes the eye: useful for
B. Hanbury at 5 yrs: joined D. Selvaratnam in UAE and won handicap at Abu Dhabi
in January: fairly useful form at best on return to Britain: effective at 1m to 10.5f: acts
on good to firm and soft going: sometimes taken early/last to post: usually held up:
none too genuine: sold 7,500 gns, joined R. Baker. *M. R. Channon*

AMRON   12 b.g. Bold Owl 101 – Sweet Minuet (Setay 105) [1998 54: 5g 5.9d 6g   **68**
7.1m⁴ 6g 6d 8s³ 7s³ 7.1g 8s* 8s 1999 8g⁴ 8.3m⁵ 8d* 8d 8.3d 8m 8g 9.2f⁶ 8m 10m*
9g² 10m 10.9d 8g 10v Oct 11] sparely-made gelding: fair handicapper: won at
Redcar in May and Ayr in August: stays 1¼m: acts on any going: usually held up:
inconsistent. *J. Berry*

AMSARA (IRE)   3 b.f. Taufan (USA) 119 – Legend of Spain (USA) (Alleged   **46**
(USA) 138) [1998 –: 8.1m 7m 1999 12.5d⁶ 12d* a12g 12d a14.8g⁴ a12g a12g⁵ a12g²
16d⁵ 16.2g 14.1m a14g Sep 28] tall filly: poor performer: won seller at Pontefract
(final start for M. Channon) in April: generally well held after: stays 1½m, not 2m:
acts on good to soft going and fibresand: reportedly had wind infirmity when pulled
up fourth outing. *D. W. Chapman*

ANAAM   3 b.f. Caerleon (USA) 132 – Narwala 120 (Darshaan 133) [1998 NR   **81 p**
1999 10f* Oct 20] fifth foal: half-sister to 1¼m/1½m winner Altamura (by El Gran
Senor) and French 1½m and 15f winner Affidavit (by Affirmed), both smart: dam
won 1½m Princess Royal Stakes: landed odds in 14-runner maiden at Nottingham by
1¾ lengths from Wood Pound, tracking leaders, running green on leading 2f out then
staying on well: will stay 1½m+: potentially useful. *Saeed bin Suroor*

ANAK-KU   6 ch.g. Efisio 120 – City Link Lass 92 (Double Jump 131) [1998 87:   **64**
9.9d* 10.4f 9.9g 10f³ 10.1s⁶ 10.1s⁵ 1999 a12g a10g⁵ 9.9m 10.2m 10m 10.2g 10m
9.9v³ 11.5s 11.5g⁶ Oct 19] leggy gelding: fair handicapper nowadays: best forcing
pace around 1¼m: acts on equitrack and any turf going: tried blinkered/visored: none
too inconsistent. *Miss Gay Kelleway*

ANALYTICAL   3 b.g. Pursuit of Love 124 – Risha Flower 85 (Kris 135) [1998   **84**
NR 1999 8m³ 8.2m* 8d³ 8m 7d Oct 30] 35,000Y: fourth foal: half-brother to 7f/1m
winners in Italy by Persian Bold and Persian Heights: dam, 1m winner, half-sister to
useful winner at up to 1m Tatsfield: fairly useful form: comfortably won maiden at
Nottingham in July by 5 lengths: easily best effort in handicaps after when third at
Thirsk (poorly drawn final start): likely to prove best up to 1m: yet to race on
extremes of going. *R. Charlton*

ANAMORE   3 b. or br.g. Sanglamore (USA) 126 – Ancara 109 (Dancing Brave   **92**
(USA) 140) [1998 NR 1999 11.7f² 10s* Oct 2] first foal: dam French 1¼m and 1½m
winner out of half-sister to very smart middle-distance performers Princess Pati and
Seymour Hicks: favourite, confirmed debut promise when winning maiden at
Sandown (reluctant stalls) by 2 lengths from Variety Shop, racing freely in front and
battling on well: will stay 1½m: sold 60,000 gns, joined C. Mann. *R. Charlton*

ANBARI   2 b.c. (Mar 19) Muhtarram (USA) 125 – Mashair (USA) 100 (Diesis   **75**
133) [1999 7m* 7f³ 8m⁵ 8d 7.9d Oct 7] useful-looking colt: first foal: half-brother to
2 winners abroad, including 3-y-o El Tina (by Unfuwain), 7f winner in Italy at 2 yrs:
dam 1¼m winner out of high-class US 7f to 9f winner Lucky Lucky Lucky: fair
performer: won maiden at Lingfield in July: may prove best up to 1m: acts on good to
firm ground, seemingly not at best on good to soft: sold 11,000 gns, sent to Sweden.
J. L. Dunlop

ANCHOR VENTURE   6 b.g. Slip Anchor 136 – Ski Michaela (USA) (Devil's   **–**
Bag (USA)) [1998 44d, a64d: a8g² a8.5g 10v 8m 8m⁶ 12.1g 9.9g 8m 10m 9.9m a14g
a8g⁶ a12g a8.5g 1999 a10g a8g a6g Dec 17] rangy gelding: poor handicapper: no
form in 1999, including in blinkers. *D. W. Chapman*

ANCIENT CITY (USA)   2 b.g. (Mar 19) Dehere (USA) 121 – Lilian Bayliss   **69**
(IRE) 100 (Sadler's Wells (USA) 132) [1999 5.1m⁵ 6g⁵ 5.2f⁶ 6d⁴ Aug 6] strong,
lengthy gelding: has scope: fifth foal: half-brother to 2 winners, including 3-y-o
Strike A Blow (by Red Ransom), useful 6f to (in Italy) 1m winner at 2 yrs: dam, 7f
(at 2 yrs) and 9f winner, sister to smart French sprinter Ernani and half-sister to

high-class French miler Phydilla, from family of Agnes World: fair maiden: stays 6f: sold 8,500 gns, sent to USA. *P. W. Chapple-Hyam*

ANDAMAN 5 b.g. Riverman (USA) 131 – Balleta (USA) 87 (Lyphard (USA) 132) **64 d**
[1998 77, a69: a9.4g⁶ a10g⁴ a12g² 12.5s² 10s 12.5s² 12d 12.3m⁶ 12.5d 11.8s 1999
a12g a12g⁶ 12.5s⁴ a16.2g 14.1s 11.8g May 31] one-time useful maiden: reportedly
had breathing problem final 4-y-o start, and little sign of retaining ability in 1999
after third outing: blinkered last 2 starts, tongue tied final one. *D. J. G. Murray Smith*

ANDREYEV (IRE) 5 ch.g. Presidium 124 – Missish (Mummy's Pet 125) [1998 **111**
116: 6v* 6g 6s³ 6v* 6g³ 6m⁴ 6g* 6m⁴ 7.3g⁶ 7v⁶ 1999 6d⁴ 7d 5g³ 6m 6g² 6m
5.2d 5d² 5d⁴ 6d⁴ 6s Nov 6] tall gelding: impresses in appearance: smart performer:
best efforts in 1999 in Prix de Ris-Orangis at Deauville (½-length second to Keos) on
fifth start and listed races at Newmarket (including fourth of 20 to Gaelic Storm) and
rated stakes at Ascot on ninth to eleventh: effective at 5f (given a test) to 7f: has form
on good to firm ground, very best form on good or softer: blinkered last 4 starts: held
up. *R. Hannon*

ANDROMEDES (USA) 2 b.c. (Mar 10) Sadler's Wells (USA) 132 – Utr (USA) **84 p**
(Mr Prospector (USA)) [1999 7s³ Nov 5] IR 260,000Y: sturdy, lengthy colt: first foal:
dam, probably of unsatisfactory temperament, daughter of smart 7f/1m performer
Hasbah: 13/2, green and burly when 2½ lengths third of 20 to Golovin in maiden at
Doncaster, staying on well: will stay at least 1¼m: sure to improve. *H. R. A. Cecil*

ANDY'S ELECTIVE 2 b.c. (Mar 22) Democratic (USA) 101 – English Mint **55**
66 (Jalmood (USA) 126) [1999 5m 6m⁵ 6s⁴ Oct 1] seventh foal: brother to 3-y-o
Franklin-D: dam (disappointing maiden) stayed 1m: modest maiden: will probably
stay 1m. *J. R. Jenkins*

ANEED (USA) 3 ch.c. Woodman (USA) 126 – Crockadore (USA) 102 (Nijinsky **69**
(CAN) 138) [1998 NR 1999 7g⁴ Jun 8] 400,000Y: fourth foal: brother to fairly useful
Irish 6f winner Shunaire (should have stayed at least 1m) and closely related to
fairly useful Irish 1996 2-y-o 6f winner Mynador (by Forty Niner) and disappointing
4-y-o Golden Hawk (by Silver Hawk): dam, Irish 1m/US Grade 2 1½m winner,
half-sister to smart sprinter Flowing: shaped well when fourth of 16 in maiden
at Salisbury, staying on well from 2f out: should stay at least 1m: sent to UAE.
J. H. M. Gosden

ANEMOS (IRE) 4 ch.g. Be My Guest (USA) 126 – Frendly Persuasion (General **80**
Assembly (USA)) [1998 80: 10s³ 8m³ 8g 10.2d² 10v³ 1999 10g 8.3m 10g³ 9f 10g*
10m 9m 10g⁶ 10d² 10d a10g* Dec 8] tall gelding: type to carry condition: fair
performer: won minor event at Nottingham in August and handicap at Lingfield in
December: best around 1¼m: acts on equitrack and soft going, probably on firm:
usually blinkered, not for final win. *M. A. Jarvis*

AN EXECUTIVE DO 3 ch.g. Executive Man 119 – Annacando 48 (Derrylin **69 §**
115) [1998 63: 5g⁴ 7g* 1999 a8g⁵ a10g² a10g³ a10g* a12g³ Feb 26] fair performer:
won claimer at Lingfield in February, attempting to pull himself up when clear in
straight: found nothing and wandered final start: stays 1¼m: acts on equitrack, raced
only on good going on turf: one to treat with caution: sold 4,000 gns, sent to Macau
P. C. Haslam

ANGE D'HONOR (FR) 4 b.g. Hero's Honor (USA) – Surfing Angel (FR) **71**
(Monseigneur (USA) 127) [1998 84p: 12m² 1999 14g⁵ 14.1m³ 12m 11.9d Oct 7]
sturdy, close-coupled gelding: fair maiden: ran as though something amiss final
start: stays 1¾m: yet to race on extremes of going: sold 7,000 gns, joined E. James.
S. E. H. Sherwood

ANGELA'S PET (IRE) 2 ch.f. (May 17) Ridgewood Ben 113 – Centenary Year **–**
(Malinowski (USA) 123) [1999 6d 5m 7.1m⁶ 6g 7m 5v 7s a6g⁶ Dec 22]
IR 7,400Y: tall, leggy filly: half-sister to fairly useful Irish 6f/7f winner Hint-of-
Romance (by Treasure Kay) and 1½m to 2m winner Asian Punter (by M Double M):
dam race twice: no form. *J. C. Fox*

ANGEL BORNE (USA) 3 b.f. Exbourne (USA) 125 – Secret Angel (Halo **57**
(USA)) [1998 69p: 8.1g⁵ 1999 10g⁴ 10v⁶ 10g Oct 14] small, compact filly: has a
quick action: showed promise only 2-y-o start: disappointing in 1999. *B. W. Hills*

ANGEL HILL 4 ch.f. King's Signet (USA) 110 – Tawny 81 (Grey Ghost 98) **80**
[1998 78: 5g³ 6s⁶ 6g² 6g 5m 1999 5d 6s³ 5f³ 5d 6m 6m* 6f⁶ 6m 6d⁴ 5g 6d 6d Nov 1]
strong filly: fairly useful handicapper at best: won 4-runner event at Newcastle in
July: below form after: effective at 5f/6f: acts on firm and soft going: blinkered 5 of
last 7 starts, including when successful: often claimer ridden, and tends to hang right.
R. A. Fahey

ANGEL LANE 2 b.f. (Apr 23) Merdon Melody 98 – Young Whip (Bold Owl 101) **–**
[1999 6m 6m 6s 6d 8.3d Nov 4] 17,000F, 3,200Y and 500Y: unfurnished filly:
seventh foal: sister to 3 winners, including fair 7f/1m winner Mountgate and 3-y-o
Elmhurst Boy, both unreliable: dam unraced: no form: should stay 7f: has worn
tongue strap. *A. W. Carroll*

ANGELLO 2 ch.g. (Jan 10) Selkirk (USA) 129 – Pomorie (IRE) 67§ (Be My
Guest (USA) 126) [1999 8s 7s a8g Nov 24] big, strong, close-coupled gelding: first
foal: dam, 1¼m winner from good family, became untrustworthy: tailed off in
maidens, very green and mulish to post on debut. *M. L. W. Bell*

ANGELS VENTURE 3 ch.c. Unfuwain (USA) 131 – City of Angels (Woodman **91**
(USA) 126) [1998 85p: 8m⁴ 1999 8m³ 12g³ 10m⁴ 8.5d³ 8m³ 10.1g³ 11.5m* 11.9d²
12.3g 12.4m³ 11.5s² 11.9d* Oct 21] close-coupled colt: fairly useful performer: won
maiden at Yarmouth in July and handicap at Brighton (did well to come from off slow
pace) in October: stays 1½m: acts on good to firm and soft going: consistent: sold
44,000 gns, joined J. Jenkins. *S. P. C. Woods*

ANGHARAD LYN 3 b.f. Perpendicular 119 – Champers Galore (Governor **67 d**
General 116) [1999 NR 1999 8.1g⁴ 8g 7m 10.2m 11.7m⁶ 10.3s 10d Oct 11] first foal:
dam lightly-raced maiden: fair maiden: disappointing after debut: tongue tied on fifth
start, slowly away second and third. *D. Burchell*

ANGIE BABY 3 b.f. Puissance 110 – Hyde Princess 75 (Touch Paper 113) [1998 **81**
89: 5s² 5s* 5.1m* 5m⁴ 5m* 5.1g⁶ 5f* 1999 5d* 6.1m 6d⁵ 5s⁶ 5.1g 6f 5.1m 5f² 6f² 5g⁵
5g² 5f 5d⁶ 5d 5.1s Oct 26] heavy-topped filly: fairly useful performer: won claimer at
Ripon in April: left Jack Berry after seventh start: generally creditable efforts for new
trainer: effective at 5f/6f: yet to race on heavy going, acts on any other: wears
bandages: often a front runner. *R. Ingram*

ANGIE MARINIE 3 b.f. Sabrehill (USA) 120 – Lambast 70 (Relkino 131) **71**
[1998 48p: 6m⁶ 1999 a8f a7g a6g 8.2s* 8.2s³ 10m² 10.5s³ a9.4g 10.3m⁵ Jul 9] fair **a–**
performer: won seller at Nottingham (final start for R. Fahey) in April: good efforts
when placed afterwards: should stay 1½m: acts on good to firm and soft ground: has
raced freely: successful over hurdles 5 times after final Flat start. *M. C. Pipe*

ANGIES QUEST 2 b.f. (Mar 31) Inchinor 119 – Chanson d'Avril 54 (Chief **74**
Singer 131) [1999 7m⁶ 7.7g³ 6g Sep 8] 10,000Y: second foal: dam, maiden who
stayed 1¼m, out of half-sister to top-class 7f (at 2 yrs) to 10.5f winner Beldale
Flutter: fair maiden: will prove suited by 1m+: joined D. Sasse. *K. R. Burke*

ANGLESEY SEA VIEW 10 gr.m. Seymour Hicks (FR) 125 – Lexham View 72 **53**
(Abwah 118) [1998 NR 1999 16.1s 15.8g² 15.8s Oct 5] leggy, angular mare: modest
handicapper: stays 2m: acts on good to firm going, soft and fibresand: ran well only
try in blinkers. *Mrs M. Reveley*

ANGUS-G 7 br.g. Chief Singer 131 – Horton Line 89 (High Line 125) [1998 –: **96 d**
12d 1999 11.9d 10d² 12f³ 11.9f 12m⁵ Aug 4] big, useful-looking gelding: impresses
in appearance: good mover: useful handicapper at best: well below par in 1999,
other than when short-head second at Ayr in May: effective at 1¼m/1½m: acts on
firm and good to soft going: held up and tends to idle in front: has been bandaged.
Mrs M. Reveley

ANGUS THE BOLD 3 b.g. Puissance 110 – Floral Spark 69 (Forzando 122) **–**
[1998 61+: 5d² 1999 5.9g a5g Jun 19] leggy gelding: well beaten in seller/claimer in
1999. *J. L. Eyre*

ANITA AT DAWN (IRE) 4 br.f. Anita's Prince 126 – Dawn Is Breaking (Import **60**
127) [1998 77: 7v 6.1m a7g⁴ a7g² a7g a9.4g a7g⁶ 8.2m a7g Jul 9]
sparely-made filly: fair handicapper at 3 yrs: below form in 1999: stays 7f: acts on
all-weather, best efforts on turf on good to soft/soft going. *B. Palling*

AN JOLIEN 2 b.f. (Apr 7) Aragon 118 – Joli's Girl 79 (Mansingh (USA) 120) **61**
[1999 5g 5m 6m⁵ 6d Oct 28] closely related to 13f and 1¾m seller winner Side Bar
(by Mummy's Game) and half-sister to 4-y-o Imperial Prince and useful 6f (at 2 yrs)
to 1m winner Joli's Princess (both by Prince Sabo): dam, 9f winner, stayed 1½m:
modest maiden: acts on good to firm ground, blinkered when well held on
good to soft. *M. J. Ryan*

AN LU ABU (IRE) 3 b.g. Distinctly North (USA) 115 – Dunbally 57 (Dunphy **59**
124) [1998 –: 6m 5d 6.3s 7.8m 1999 8.3v 7.8m² 7g 7m⁶ 8g 7g⁵ 7.8m 7.8f³ 9f 9s a7g **a–**
a8.5g Dec 27] IR 6,500F, IR 10,000Y: seventh foal: half-brother to 1993 2-y-o 5f
winner Mr B Reasonable (by Reasonable): dam third at 6f at 2 yrs: modest maiden
handicapper: placed twice at Dundalk in 1999: left M. Halford, Ireland, and well held
both starts in Britain: stays 1m: form only on going firmer than good: blinkered (well
beaten) twice. *K. R. Burke*

ANNADAWI 4 b.g. Sadler's Wells (USA) 132 – Prayers'n Promises (USA) **43**
(Foolish Pleasure (USA)) [1998 NR 1999 12d 12m⁶ 8m 6g a7g⁴ a8.5g⁴ Dec 27] 8,000
3-y-o: quite good-topped gelding: closely related to several winners, including very
smart sprinter Nabeel Dancer (by Northern Dancer) and useful 1990 2-y-o 6f winner
Anjiz (by Nureyev), later successful in USA: dam Grade 1 winner at 6f and 7f at 2
yrs: sold out of J. Hassett's stable 24,000 gns in May after finishing in frame both
starts in Irish bumpers early in 1999: poor maiden: best effort at Wolverhampton final
start: should stay beyond 8.5f. *C. N. Kellett*

ANNANDALE (IRE) 3 ch.f. Balla Cove 119 – Gruinard Bay (Doyoun 124) **43**
[1998 54: 5d⁶ 5m³ 5d⁶ 6m 1999 8.2s 8d 8f⁶ a8g 9.3g 9.9m⁵ Jul 2] angular, close-
coupled filly: poor maiden handicapper: probably stays 9f: acts on good to firm
going, well beaten on fibresand: blinkered (seemingly best 3-y-o effort) penultimate
start: joined D. Nicholls. *K. A. Ryan*

ANNAPURNA (IRE) 3 b.f. Brief Truce (USA) 126 – National Ballet (Shareef **100**
Dancer (USA) 135) [1998 90: 7m 7g² 7d* 7g 1999 9.9g² 10g² 8s Aug 22] leggy filly:
useful performer: easily best effort in 1999 when neck second to Ipledgeallegiance in
handicap at Newbury penultimate start: last of 9 in listed race at Deauville 9 days
later: unlikely to stay beyond 1¼m: acts on good to soft going. *B. J. Meehan*

ANNELIINA 3 b.f. Cadeaux Genereux 131 – Blasted Heath 105 (Thatching 131) **57**
[1998 80?: 6m 7m⁴ 7d⁵ 7g 1999 8m 7m 6g² 6.1g⁵ 7d Oct 4] unfurnished filly: modest
maiden: may prove best up to 7f: yet to race on extremes of going: sometimes slowly
away: has carried head awkwardly. *C. N. Allen*

ANNESPRIDE 2 b.f. (Apr 15) Komaite (USA) – Lindrake's Pride (Mandrake **–**
Major 122) [1999 6m Sep 24] ninth foal: half-sister to useful 6f (at 2 yrs) to 9.3f winner
Superpride (by Superpower) and 1990 2-y-o 7.5f winner Darika Lad (by Belfort):
dam unraced: tailed off in maiden at Redcar. *Mrs M. Reveley*

ANNIE APPLE (IRE) 3 ch.f. Petardia 113 – Art Duo 86 (Artaius (USA) 129) **60**
[1998 57: 6m 7f 6m⁵ 7f* a8g 1999 a10g a7g³ a8f* a7g⁴ a8g⁴ 10m 8m 8.2m 6d 6m⁴
7m² 8f² 7d⁴ 7s² 7g³ 8s a8g Dec 6] leggy, quite good-topped filly: modest performer:
won seller at Lingfield (final start for R. Hannon) in January: left D. Nicholls after
eighth start and G. Lewis after twelfth: stays 1m: acts on firm going, soft and all-
weather: visored (well below form) penultimate start. *N. Hamilton*

ANNIJAZ 2 b.f. (Apr 9) Alhijaz 122 – Figment 75 (Posse (USA) 130) [1999 6g⁴ **66**
6.8m² 6f³ 7d² Oct 14] 3,800Y: fourth foal: dam winning sprinter: fair maiden: off
nearly 3 months before ¾-length second of 20 to Castle Sempill in Newmarket seller
final start: should stay 1m: acts on firm and good to soft ground: joined G. McCourt.
A. P. Jarvis

ANNIVERSARY DAY 3 ch.g. Lion Cavern (USA) 117 – Doyce 75 (Formidable **–**
(USA) 125) [1998 73?: 8.3d 6v² 7d 1999 9.1m 8.3g⁶ 9.2s⁶ 7g Oct 15] fair maiden at
best: little show in 1999: blinkered final start. *W. S. Cunningham*

ANN'S MILL 2 b.f. (May 16) Pelder (IRE) 125 – Honey Mill 67 (Milford 119) **57**
[1999 6f 6g 7m* 7m 10d Oct 30] leggy, unfurnished filly: fourth foal: half-sister to
3-y-o Erinvale and 4-y-o Minjara: dam maiden who should have stayed 1m: modest
performer: best effort to win seller at Thirsk in August: left M. Blanshard before well
out of depth final start: stays 7f. *Derrick Morris*

ANNUS MIRABILIS (FR) 7 b.h. Warning 136 – Anna Petrovna (FR) 90 [1998 118: a9f² a9f² a10f* 10m² 10d³ 10m* 10g⁴ 1999 9.9d May 8] tall horse: very smart performer, widely travelled: won 3 consecutive runnings of Winter Hill Stakes at Windsor (1996-8) and was also successful in Group 2 race at Tokyo (in 1996) and Dubai Duty Free at Nad Al Sheba (in 1998): last of 10 in valuable contest at Goodwood only outing in 1999: stayed 1½m (close third in 1995 Irish Derby) but raced mainly at 9f/1¼m in recent years: acted on firm ground, soft and on dirt: usually visored: often made running (was a lead horse for Godolphin at home) and tended to wander under pressure: tough and consistent: had been due to stand at stud in Japan but died from pneumonia in November. *Saeed bin Suroor* –

ANOKATO 5 b.g. Tina's Pet 121 – High Velocity 53 (Frimley Park 109) [1998 66, a73: a5g* a5g⁶ a5g* a6g³ 5.1g 6f² 6f 6g 5g a5g³ 5.1d⁴ 5d 6m a5g⁴ a5g* 1999 a6g² a5g² a6g* a6g² a6g⁶ a6g⁶ a6g³ a7g* a7g⁵ a7g⁴ 7f 6g 6m a8g³ 6g a10g* 10.1m⁵ 10d² Aug 17] good-topped gelding: has a round action: fair on all-weather, modest on turf: won claimers in January (final start for T. Mills) and March and seller in July (final one for Mrs N. Macauley), all at Lingfield: effective at 5f to easy 1¼m: acts on firm going, good to soft and equitrack, probably on fibresand: blinkered/visored: not the easiest of rides and often gets behind: joined R. Baker. *R. J. Hodges* — **64 a79**

ANONYM (IRE) 7 b.g. Nashamaa 113 – Bonny Bertha (Capistrano 120) [1998 –, a67d: a9.4g* a8.5g* a8g² a8g² a10g⁴ a7g a8.5g⁶ a8.5g³ 6.9m 7s a8.5g a8.5g a8g 1999 a8f² a8g* a8g⁵ a8g³ 9g² 8.5m⁵ 9f Jun 1] leggy, lengthy gelding: has a quick action: modest performer: won handicap at Southwell in February: stays 9.4f: acts on firm going and all-weather: usually blinkered before 1999. *G. M. Moore* — **49 a56**

ANOTHER ARTHUR 3 b.g. Puissance 110 – Traumatic Laura (Pragmatic 115) [1998 –: a7g 1999 a11g a11g Feb 5] no show in maidens. *W. McKeown* —

ANOTHERBAMBO (IRE) 4 b.g. Conquering Hero (USA) 116 – Twilight In Paris (Kampala 120) [1998 NR 1999 10.2g⁴ 8m 11.7g³ 11.7m⁵ 8.1m 10g Aug 14] 3,000 2-y-o: third foal: half-brother to Irish 7f to 1¼m winner Bailiwick Frontier (by Imperial Frontier): dam unraced: poor maiden: should stay 1½m+: blinkered (gave impression something amiss) second start: joined G. Ham. *R. J. Baker* — **46**

ANOTHER CENTURY 4 gr.g. Belfort (FR) 89 – Miss Cuddles 83 (Mummy's Game 120) [1998 NR 1999 a7g Feb 12] tall gelding: fourth reported foal: dam 1m winner: well beaten in maiden at Southwell. *D. Nicholls* —

ANOTHER LAURA 4 b.f. Puissance 110 – Traumatic Laura (Pragmatic 115) [1998 57: 7g⁵ 1999 10.1m 10d⁴ May 21] tall filly: first live foal: dam of little account on Flat: modest form on debut at 3 yrs: well beaten in 1999. *W. McKeown* —

ANOTHER LOVER 3 ch.f. Then Again 126 – Love Street 62 (Mummy's Pet 125) [1998 –: 5d⁴ 6m⁶ 1999 a5g⁶ 6v Apr 20] fourth foal: half-sister to 4-y-o Contrary Mary and 5f winner La Belle Dominique (by Dominion): dam sprint maiden out of smart 2-y-o Crime of Passion: no show in minor event/maidens. *S. G. Knight* —

ANOTHER MONK (IRE) 8 br.g. Supreme Leader 123 – Royal Demon (Tarboosh (USA)) [1998 NR 1999 a16.2g² 14d 11.5g³ a12g³ a16g² a16.2g Dec 4] modest handicapper: generally sound efforts in 1999: stays 2m: acts on all-weather, best turf effort on good going. *B. R. Johnson* — **50 a60**

ANOTHER NIGHT (IRE) 5 ch.g. Waajib 121 – Little Me (Connaught 130) [1998 73d: 13.3g⁵ 14s⁶ 14m 12g 14.1m 1999 18d⁶ May 19] leggy gelding: fluent mover: fairly useful at 3 yrs: disappointing since: should stay beyond 1¼m: yet to race on heavy going, acts on any other: has been bandaged near-hind: has hinted at temperament. *P. G. Murphy* —

ANOTHER NIGHTMARE (IRE) 7 b.m. Treasure Kay 114 – Carange (Known Fact (USA) 135) [1998 46§: a7g 6v 5g⁵ 6d 6v 6g 5s² 5g⁵ 6m 5g³ 6m³ 6m⁶ 6g 5g 5d⁶ 6d 5d³ 6v a5g a6g³ a6g a6g 1999 a6g* a6f* a5g a6g 6d 5m² 5m* 5m 5g⁶ 5g⁶ 5m 5f* 5m² 5d a5g a5g* a5g a6g³ Dec 6] leggy, sparely-made mare: modest handicapper: won at Wolverhampton (amateurs) and Lingfield in January and Hamilton in May and August: best at 5f/6f: acts on firm going, soft and all-weather: blinkered once at 6 yrs: often hangs right/forces pace: none too consistent. *D. W. Barker* — **57**

ANOTHER PEARL 2 br.f. (Apr 29) Ezzoud (IRE) 126 – Pearly River 72 (Elegant Air 119) [1999 6v* Oct 23] workmanlike filly: second foal: half-sister to 3-y-o **73 p**

Dashing: dam, 7f (at 2 yrs) and 1½m winner, out of half-sister to Roseate Tern and Ibn Bey: 33/1, won maiden at Newbury by ¾ length from Star Princess, niggled along some way out but staying on to get up near finish: will be suited by 1m+: should improve. *L. G. Cottrell*

ANOTHER QUESTION (USA) 3 b.c. Quest For Fame 127 – Another Notch (USA) (Cox's Ridge (USA)) [1998 NR 1999 10.2s⁶ Sep 27] 78,000Y: third foal: half-brother to a winner in USA by Mari's Book: dam won up to 9f in USA: 8/1, seemed in need of experience when sixth of 12 in maiden at Bath, not given hard time: sold 24,000 gns: should do better. *R. Charlton* **– p**

ANOTHER RAINBOW (IRE) 3 br.f. Rainbows For Life (CAN) – Phylella (Persian Bold 123) [1998 65: 5.2m⁴ 6f⁵ 6g² 1999 8m⁵ 9g 10g² 10m⁴ 11.9f⁵ 12m³ 11.8m⁶ 11.5m² a13g⁵ a10g Dec 22] fair maiden: below form last 4 starts: stays 1½m: raced only on good going or firmer on turf (no form on all-weather): has been slowly away/reluctant early/found little: one to treat with caution. *Miss Gay Kelleway* **72 §**
a– §

ANOTHER TIME 7 ch.g. Clantime 101 – Another Move 69 (Farm Walk 111) [1998 100: 10.1s 10d 10.4g⁵ 9.7m⁴ 10.1m⁴ 10g* 10d 9.9g³ 10m⁶ 9.9g 10f* 10m 10g 9g 1999 a8.5g⁵ 10m⁵ 9.7m³ 10m⁶ 10m 10g 10m⁴ 9.9m* 10.1m² 10.1d 10d 10.1m Oct 19] neat gelding: poor mover: fairly useful handicapper: won at Leicester in August: best around 1¼m: acts on any turf going except heavy, well beaten only run on fibresand: usually held up, and suited by strong pace: consistent. *S. P. C. Woods* **91**

ANSARI (IRE) 2 b.c. (Jan 31) Selkirk (USA) 129 – Anaza 100 (Darshaan 133) [1999 7s⁵ 7g⁵ 7s² 8d* Oct 29] well-made, quite attractive colt: fluent mover: seventh foal: closely related to fairly useful Irish 1m winner Anazara (by Trempolino) and half-brother to several winners, notably very smart French performer up to 1½m Astarabad (by Alleged): dam, French 1m and 8.5f winner, ran only at 2 yrs: displayed more temperament than ability first 2 starts, but showed fairly useful form after, winning nursery at Brighton in October by ½ length from Kookaburra (pair clear): will be suited by 1¼m/1½m: raced only on good going or softer: type to do better still. *L. M. Cumani* **90 p**

ANSCHLUSS 3 gr.c. Alzao (USA) 117 – Avice Caro (USA) 85 (Caro 133) [1998 75p: 7.1s³ 1999 8g⁶ 10m⁶ 10d³ 10.3f³ 8m 10.1g⁴ 10.1m* 9.9f Jul 30] good-topped colt: fairly useful performer: highly tried first 2 starts in 1999: didn't have to be at best to win maiden at Newcastle in July: well beaten in valuable handicap at Goodwood final start: stays 1¼m: acts on firm and good to soft going, showed promise on soft: blinkered third, fifth and sixth outings: has worn tongue strap: tends to race freely: has hung/found little and is one to treat with caution. *C. E. Brittain* **92 §**

ANSELLAD (IRE) 2 b.g. (May 2) Dancing Dissident (USA) 119 – Dutch Queen (Ahonoora 122) [1999 6d³ 5.1g* 5.7g² 5.2m 5f³ 5m³ 6g Sep 8] IR 6,400F, 11,000Y: leggy gelding: half-brother to a 6f winner in Hong Kong by Unblest and 2 winners in Italy, including one at 1m by Magical Wonder: dam of little account: fairly useful performer: won minor event at Bath in June: best effort when third in nursery at Goodwood on fifth start: will prove best at 5f: acts on firm ground. *J. Berry* **88**

ANSELLMAN 9 gr.g. Absalom 128 – Grace Poole (Sallust 134) [1998 93: a5g 5d⁵ 5s⁴ 6g⁴ 6d* 5d² 5f³ 5d² 6d 6g² 5g² 5.6g³ 6s 5s 1999 5d 5d⁴ 6g 6d 5m 5.7g⁴ 6m⁴ 5.1m 5m 5m 6f 5.1h* 6d 5.7m 5m 5s 5s³ 5.1s 5s Nov 5] sturdy gelding: carries condition: has a round action: fair handicapper nowadays: won at Bath in August: generally creditable efforts otherwise: effective at 5f/6f: acts on any turf/all-weather: blinkered/visored. *J. Berry* **79**

ANSHAAM (IRE) 2 b.c. (Mar 11) Alzao (USA) 117 – Anna of Saxony 111 (Ela-Mana-Mou 132) [1999 8s* 8s² Aug 21] second foal: half-brother to French 1997 2-y-o 1m (Prix d'Aumale) winner Anna Palariva (by Caerleon): dam 11.5f to 14.6f (Park Hill) winner, half-sister to very smart middle-distance filly Annaba: comfortably won 6-runner newcomers event at Deauville in August before ¾-length second of 7 to Barathea Guest in listed race there later in month, headed inside final 1f after leading entering straight: will stay at least 1¼m: will improve again. *D. R. Loder, France* **107 p**

AN SMEARDUBH (IRE) 3 b.f. Dolphin Street (FR) 125 – Forest Berries (IRE) (Thatching 131) [1998 NR 1999 8.3m 8.3d 8m 10.1g 8.2m Jun 16] 6,000Y: half-sister to 1996 2-y-o 6f winner Tycoon Girl (by Last Tycoon) and 1998 3-y-o 5f **–**

winner (including at 2 yrs) Arjan (by Paris House): dam unraced half-sister to smart middle-distance colt Pencader: little form: slowly away last 2 starts. *M. J. Ryan*

ANSOMAR 3 b.f. Never So Bold 135 – Lorlanne (Bustino 136) [1998 NR 1999 10s[6] 10g 12g 12s Oct 5] lengthy, sparely-made filly: first foal: dam no form: little sign of ability. *D. Moffatt*   –

ANSTAND 4 b.g. Anshan 119 – Pussy Foot 83 (Red Sunset 120) [1998 82: 7s 8g[5] 6g* 6v 6g[3] 7f 6g 5m[4] 6m 6g[4] 6g* 1999 5s 5d 6g[5] 5.7g 5.7f Jun 26] tall, useful-looking gelding: good walker: fair handicapper: easily best effort in 1999 when fifth of 11 at Goodwood: poorly drawn both starts either side: best at 6f on good/good to firm going: has given trouble at stalls and drifted left: blinkered twice, running well first time: usually held up. *M. S. Saunders*   **74**

ANSTAR 2 ch.g. (Apr 2) Anshan 119 – Star Arrangement (Star Appeal 133) [1999 5m[2] 5f[5] 6m 6m* 7f[5] 7m[6] Aug 29] 7,000Y: leggy, lengthy gelding: sixth foal: half-brother to 3 winners, including 4-y-o Ellway Prince and 1m winner in Germany (both by Prince Sabo): dam, poor maiden, half-sister to Bold Arrangement: fair performer: won nursery at Leicester in July: not discredited final start: should stay 1m: raced only on ground firmer than good: visored last 3 starts: sold 14,000 gns in October, sent to USA. *I. A. Balding*   **69**

ANTARCTIC STORM 6 b.g. Emarati (USA) 74 – Katie Scarlett 70 (Lochnager 132) [1998 72, a69: 7.6m[3] 8g 7.6f 8.3d[4] 8s 8s a6g[4] a8g[5] a7g 1999 a8g 7m* 7s[2] 8d* 7.1m[2] 8g 8m 8m[4] 8.3m[2] 8.5g[3] 8s Sep 29] strong, close-coupled gelding: fair performer: won claimer at Newcastle and seller (20-runner race) at Ripon in May: ran creditably when placed otherwise: effective at 7f/1m: acts on good to firm going, soft and firesand: tried blinkered/visored: usually edgy/has rope halter in preliminaries: sometimes early to post (got loose on way to post third start): usually leads: sold 2,700 gns. *R. A. Fahey*   **65** **a–**

ANTHEM 3 b.c. Saddlers' Hall (IRE) 126 – Full Orchestra 83 (Shirley Heights 130) [1998 75p: 8.2d[5] 7.9g[4] 1999 12d[3] 12m* 13.9s[5] May 11] good-topped colt: has scope: has a round action: half-brother to useful 6f (at 2 yrs) and 9f winner Rudimental (by Rudimentary): dam 1¼m winner: fairly useful performer: easily best effort when winning maiden at Thirsk in April by 14 lengths: disappointing on soft ground in minor event at York only start after: should stay beyond 1½m: hung on reappearance: sent to UAE. *M. A. Jarvis*   **89**

ANTHEM FLIGHT (USA) 3 b.f. Fly So Free (USA) 118 – Anthem (USA) (Deputy Minister (CAN)) [1998 NR 1999 8.2m 10m 10m Jun 11] $47,000F, $48,000Y: third foal: half-sister to winners in Japan (by Key To The Mint) and USA (by Corporate Report): dam winning sprinter in USA: well beaten in maidens/minor event: pulled up lame second start: sold 1,000 gns. *P. W. Harris*   –

ANTHEMION (IRE) 2 ch.g. (Feb 14) Night Shift (USA) – New Sensitive (Wattlefield 117) [1999 5g 5m[3] 6m 6m Jul 31] IR 36,000F, 65,000Y: good-topped gelding: third foal: half-brother to a winner up to 11f in Belgium by Tom Boat: dam, won 9 times in Belgium, half-sister to Hever Golf Rose: modest maiden: probably stays 6f: raced only on good going or firmer: sweating and on toes final start: has gone freely to post. *P. C. Haslam*   **63 +**

ANTHONY MON AMOUR (USA) 4 b.g. Nicholas (USA) 111 – Reine de La Ciel (USA) (Conquistador Cielo (USA)) [1998 69: a6g 7d[3] a8g[4] 7g[4] 6.1g* 6g[3] a6g* 6g[5] 1999 a6g[2] 6d[2] 6s[3] 5m 6g a6g[4] 5.2s Oct 22] strong gelding: fair handicapper: best efforts in 1999 when in frame: ran as though something amiss final start: will prove best at 5f/6f: acts on firesand and soft going: has worn tongue strap: usually races prominently: edged right third start: sold 12,000 gns, joined D. Nicholls: may well make more of a mark in 2000. *W. J. Haggas*   **73**

ANTIGONEL (IRE) 2 b.f. (Mar 4) Fairy King (USA) – Euromill (Shirley Heights 130) [1999 7v 6s Nov 5] IR 50,000Y: seventh foal: sister to useful 6.3f (at 2 yrs) and 1m winner Tadwiga and useful 6f (at 2 yrs) to 1¼m winner in Ireland/Italy Bartok, and half-sister to fairly useful Irish 3-y-o 7f/1m winner Delray (by Wolfhound): dam Irish middle-distance stayer from family of Old Vic: signs of ability though well held in maidens at Lingfield and Doncaster: may do better. *R. Hannon*   –

ANTINNAZ (IRE)   3 ch.f. Thatching 131 – Tootling (IRE) (Pennine Walk 120)   **111**
[1998 90: 6d² 5g* 6d² 6s⁵ 1999 6d³ 6d* 6m⁵ 5d³ 5v⁵ Oct 3] IR 18,000Y: tall,
sparely-made filly: fourth living foal: half-sister to 11f winner in Belgium by Tirol:
dam, lightly-raced maiden, daughter of very smart winner up to 1¼m Tootens: smart
performer: won maiden at the Curragh at 2 yrs and listed race at Haydock in June:
good efforts last 2 starts, third to Tedburrow in Flying Five at Leopardstown
(sweating and early to post) then 2½ lengths fifth to Agnes World in Prix de l'Abbaye
de Longchamp: effective at 5f/6f: raced mainly on good going or softer (acts on
heavy): on toes/led by 2 handlers in preliminaries third start. *T. Stack, Ireland*

ANTONIA'S DOUBLE   4 ch.f. Primo Dominie 121 – Mainly Sunset (Red   **84**
Sunset 120) [1998 69: 5d⁵ 5g 5g* 5.7m⁵ 5d 1999 a5g² 5d a5g² 5g 5f* a5g² 5m* 5m²
5m² 5f* 5g Aug 30] strong, lengthy filly: easy mover: fairly useful handicapper: won
at Redcar and Salisbury in June then Newcastle in July: run best forgiven (lost ground
at start and switched across to stand side) final outing: best making running at 5f on
good going or firmer/all-weather: often bandaged behind. *J. Berry*

ANTONIA'S DREAM   2 ch.f. (Mar 26) Clantime 101 – Militia Girl (Rarity 129)   **70 d**
[1999 5m⁶ 5m³ 5d⁴ 5.1g⁶ 5f⁴ 5g⁵ 5f⁴ Sep 13] 25,000Y: close-coupled filly: has a
quick action: half-sister to several winners, including 4-y-o Dancing Em and 6-y-o
Jo Mell: dam once-raced half-sister to Royal Lodge winner Bengal Fire and US
Grade 1 winner Kings Island: maiden: fair form second start, but only modest at best
subsequently and hung right in first-time visor final start: raced only at 5f, mainly on
good going or firmer. *J. Berry*

ANTONIO CANOVA   3 ch.g. Komaite (USA) – Joan's Venture (Beldale Flutter   **78 p**
(USA) 130) [1998 NR 1999 6g⁶ 6g² 5g² 6d³ Oct 9] stocky gelding: second reported
foal: dam unraced half-sister to useful sprinter Marbella Silks: fair maiden: best
effort when third of 23 in minor event at York, faring easily best of those on stand
side: may stay 7f: raced only on good/good to soft going: may well do better at 4 yrs.
Bob Jones

ANUSHKA (IRE)   3 ch.f. Indian Ridge 123 – Shaping Up (USA) 89 (Storm Bird   **62**
(CAN) 134) [1998 NR 1999 8.3g 7f⁴ 6d⁵ Aug 14] IR 60,000F, 45,000Y: lengthy filly:
has a round action: second foal: half-sister to Irish 9f winner Islamorada (by Persian
Bold): dam 2-y-o 5.7f winner who stayed 7f: best effort in maidens when fifth of 8 at
Newmarket: sold 1,800 gns in December. *H. R. A. Cecil*

ANYHOW (IRE)   2 b.f. (Apr 12) Distant Relative 128 – Fast Chick 93 (Henbit   **58 +**
(USA) 130) [1999 a7g³ Aug 14] 11,500Y: fifth foal: half-sister to 3-y-o Catch Me
and smart 6f (at 2 yrs) to 1m winner Missile (by Rock City): dam 9f to 1½m winner:
33/1, 3½ lengths third of 9 to Dance In Tune in maiden at Wolverhampton, wandering
under pressure. *Andrew Reid*

AOIFE (IRE)   4 ch.f. Thatching 131 – Aunt Hester (IRE) 68 (Caerleon (USA)   **83**
132) [1998 78+: 7m² 7d² 7v⁴ a6g* a6g⁴ 1999 a6g* Feb 2] angular filly: fairly useful
performer: won handicap at Lingfield only 4-y-o start: stays 7f: acts on equitrack,
good to firm and good to soft going: refused to enter stalls second intended 3-y-o
start: covered by Entrepreneur. *G. Wragg*

APADI (USA)   3 ch.g. Diesis 133 – Ixtapa (USA) (Chief's Crown (USA)) [1998   **?**
5.5d² 5.5g* 7g⁶ 1999 10.5d 6g 6d 8g 8g⁶ a12g⁶ a10g a10g Dec 8] ex-French gelding:
fourth foal: half-brother to smart French 7.5f (at 2 yrs) and 10.5f winner Dark Nile
(by Riverman): dam, French 1½m winner, closely related to smart performer up to
1m Tertian and half-sister to very smart 1¼m performer Kefaah: fairly useful
performer at best: won minor event at Maisons-Laffitte at 2 yrs: little show in listed
race and handicaps in France in 1999: left Mme C. Head for 19,000 gns in October,
then well held in 3 minor events at Lingfield: bred to be suited by at least 1m.
W. R. Muir

APLOY   2 b.f. (Mar 4) Deploy 131 – Amidst 86 (Midyan (USA) 124) [1999 6g²   **69**
6m⁵ 6.1m³ 7s Oct 8] first foal: dam 6f (at 2 yrs) and 1m winner: fair maiden: likely to
stay 1m: acts on good to firm going, poorly drawn and not knocked about on soft.
R. F. Johnson Houghton

APOLLO RED   10 ch.g. Dominion 123 – Woolpack (Golden Fleece (USA) 133)   **63**
[1998 78, a86: a7g a6g 7d 6g⁵ 6g 7g* 7.6m³ 6m 6m⁵ 6m 5.3g a8f⁴ a6g 1999 5g 6g   **a79 +**

7.6m⁵ 7f 8.1m⁴ 7s³ 8m² 8d³ 6g 7d² a8g a7g⁶ a7g* a7g³ Dec 29] sturdy gelding: fair on all-weather, modest on turf: made virtually all in seller at Lingfield in December: probably best at 7f/easy 1m nowadays: acts on firm going, good to soft and equitrack: effective visored (not tried since early 1995): usually races up with pace. *G. L. Moore*

APPLE GREEN   2 b.f. (Apr 11) Superlative 118 – Green Divot (Green Desert (USA) 127) [1999 5.7f⁶ 7f³ 7g⁶ Aug 12] 500Y resold 800Y: first foal: dam lightly-raced half-sister to Ebor winner Far Ahead: gambled on, easily best effort in maidens when third of 10 at Folkestone: should stay 1m. *R. Charlton*   **60**

APPLE OF KENT (USA)   3 b. or br.f. Kris S (USA) – Proflare (USA) 101 (Mr Prospector (USA)) [1998 NR 1999 7m² 8g* 10.5d 10.1g⁶ Sep 14] tall, good-topped filly: sixth foal: closely related to French 11f winner Profluent (by Sunshine Forever) and half-sister to 3 winners, including useful French/US 5.5f (at 2 yrs) to 8.5f (Grade 2) winner True Flare (by Capote): dam French 1m (at 2 yrs) and 9f winner: fairly useful form when heavily backed first 2 starts, winning maiden at Newmarket in May: well beaten after in Prix de Diane at Chantilly and listed race at Yarmouth: should be suited by further than 1m: sent to J. Kimmel in USA. *J. H. M. Gosden*   **88**

APPLE PEELER (IRE)   2 ch.f. (Apr 15) Rainbows For Life (CAN) – Golden Pleasure 82 (Glint of Gold 128) [1999 5m a5g 5d* 6m 5g 5g² 5m⁶ 5f 6g 6m³ 6m 7.5g⁵ Sep 15] 4,000 2-y-o: unfurnished filly: half-sister to several winners abroad: dam maiden who stayed 1½m: modest performer: won claimer at Thirsk in May: stays 7.5f: acts on good to firm and good to soft going: usually blinkered: slowly away several times. *K. A. Ryan*   **56**

APPLES AND PEARS (IRE)   3 b.f. High Estate 127 – Tiempo 50 (King of Spain 121) [1998 57: 5g⁵ 5m 6g 1999 5s a5g⁴ 5m⁵ 5g² 6s 5g⁴ 5.3g³ 5.2s⁶ 5.1s Oct 26] modest maiden handicapper: likely to prove best at 5f/easy 6f: acts on good to firm and soft going: off course 4 months before penultimate start. *M. H. Tompkins*   **59 +**

APPLE SAUCE   4 b.f. Prince Sabo 123 – Mrs Bacon 82 (Balliol 125) [1998 70p: 7m 6m⁵ 5.7d² 5.1g* 5m² 5g 5m 1999 6g 5.7g 5.1m⁴ 5.1h⁶ 8m Sep 2] strong, good-bodied filly: fair handicapper at 3 yrs: largely disappointing in 1999: best at 5f/6f: acts on good to firm and good to soft ground: sold 10,000 gns. *L. G. Cottrell*   **60**

APPROACHABLE (USA)   4 b. or br.c. Known Fact (USA) 135 – Western Approach (USA) 115 (Gone West (USA)) [1998 –: 8g 8g 7d 1999 a10g³ a10g⁵ a7g² a7g a8.3m a8.5g³ a9.4g* a8.5g* a8.5g⁶ a9.4f⁶ a8g² a8.5g⁴ a8g Dec 17] leggy, unfurnished colt: has been freeze-fired: fair performer: won maiden handicap in March (left R. Phillips 2 starts later) and 2 claimers in July (for K. Morgan), all at Wolverhampton: probably best at 7f to 9.4f: acts on all-weather, no form on turf: well held in blinkers/visor. *Miss S. J. Wilton*   **–**   **a72**

APPROBATION (USA)   2 ch.c. (Apr 16) With Approval (CAN) – Exotic Beauty (USA) (Java Gold (USA)) [1999 7m 7g⁴ 7s Nov 5] $50,000Y: workmanlike colt: first foal: dam won at up to 9f in USA: best effort in maidens when never-nearer fourth of 12 to Francesco Guardi at Catterick: well beaten on much softer going final start: should stay at least 1m: may still do better. *P. W. Harris*   **67 +**

APPROVED QUALITY (IRE)   6 b.m. Persian Heights 129 – Greatest Pleasure (Be My Guest (USA) 126) [1998 52: 6m 4g 7g³ 5d 8m 8.5g⁶ 6s⁴ 9m 12m⁵ 1999 a12g² a12g Mar 27] 5,500Y: half-sister to 3 winners, including fairly useful 1998 2-y-o 5f winner Choto Mate (by Brief Truce): dam unraced half-sister to Lancashire Oaks winner Sing Softly (the dam of Top Cees): poor maiden: trained in Ireland by J. Coogan in Ireland: better effort in handicaps in 1999 when second at Southwell: barely stays 1½m: acts on soft going (probably good to firm) and sand: blinkered twice as a 4-y-o. *F. Murphy*   **44**

APPYABO   4 ch.g. Never So Bold 135 – Cardinal Palace 85 (Royal Palace 131) [1998 69d: a8g² a10g² a10g³ 9.9s 12.5g 8g 8.1m 9.9m a13g⁴ 13.8s a10g⁶ 1999 a12g³ a16g a12g⁶ a12g⁴ 12.4m a14g 11.9f⁶ a10g a10g a13g Dec 10] unfurnished gelding: poor maiden: stays 13f: acts on good to firm going and all-weather: visored (finished last) once: has tried to run out: untrustworthy. *M. Quinn*   **– §**   **a43 §**

APRIL ACE   3 ch.g. First Trump 118 – Champ d'Avril 89 (Northfields (USA)) [1998 72, a?: 6s 6.1d⁴ 5.7s* 7m⁵ 7m⁶ 6m⁴ a6g⁴ 6g 6.1v⁶ 1999 a6g 7s⁶ 7s⁵ 6m 6d 8m³ 7g⁶ 7.1g² 8.1m³ 8.2m* 7g 9m² 8g* 8d⁴ 9g³ 7.6g² 8.5m³ Sep 4] big, lengthy gelding: **63**

modest performer: in good form in summer, winning handicaps at Nottingham and Brighton: stays 9f: acts on soft and good to firm going (below form on fibresand): visored (ran poorly) once: usually leads. *M. Quinn*

APRIL'S COMAIT   2 br.f. (Apr 3) Komaite (USA) – Sweet Caroline 62 (Squill (USA) 122) [1999 5m 5m⁴ a5g⁴ 5m 6g a5g 5g a5g³ Dec 21] 1,300Y: workmanlike filly: poor walker: first foal: dam little worthwhile form: poor maiden: should stay 6f: acts on good to firm going and fibresand. *Miss J. F. Craze*   **43**

APRIL SPIRIT   4 b.f. Nomination 125 – Seraphim (FR) 48 (Lashkari 128) [1998 –: 10.5m⁴ 11.9s a12g a14.8g⁶ 1999 a16g⁶ a16.2g⁶ Feb 6] of no account. *R. Hollinshead*   **–**

APRIL STOCK   4 ch.f. Beveled (USA) – Stockline (Capricorn Line 111) [1998 84: 11.9g² 14d⁴ 12g² 11.9m² 16v³ 16.5d³ 1999 12v* 14.1m 18d 12g⁴ 11.6g* 12d Oct 29] leggy, unfurnished filly: fair performer: won maiden in April at Folkestone and minor event at Windsor (first outing for 4 months and since leaving Miss G. Kelleway) in October: below form final start: effective at 1½m (given good pace) to 2m: raced mainly on good going or softer (well held both starts on good to firm): tongue tied last 2 starts. *G. A. Butler*   **80**

APRIL TREASURE   4 b.f. Stani (USA) 84 – Eleri (Rolfe (USA) 77) [1998 –: 11.7s⁶ 12g 10.5g 13.1m 10.8m 1999 a14.8g Sep 18] angular filly: no form: blinkered once. *Mrs P. Ford*   **–**

A PROPER CHARLIE   3 b.g. Cashwyn – Kate's Girl (Lighter 111) [1998 NR 1999 11.8m⁶ 10m 8.3m a11g Sep 28] first foal: dam winning pointer/steeplechaser: no form: blinkered final start. *J. L. Spearing*   **–**

AQRABA   3 b.f. Polish Precedent (USA) 131 – Aquaba (USA) (Damascus (USA)) [1998 NR 1999 8m² 10g⁴ May 18] sturdy filly: fifth foal: closely related to sprinter Millstream (by Dayjur) and 1995 2-y-o 6f winner Polska (by Danzig) who stayed 7f, and half-sister to Irish 1m and 1¼m winner Woodsia (by Woodman), all useful fillies: dam 7f to 9f winner in USA: fair form in maidens at Warwick and Pontefract: likely to prove better at 1¼m than 1m. *L. M. Cumani*   **69**

AQUARIUM (IRE)   2 b.c. (Mar 26) Dolphin Street (FR) 125 – Mo Pheata (Petorius 117) [1999 6d 6m* 6m³ 7f² 8f⁶ Aug 30] 16,000Y: smallish colt: fifth foal: half-brother to Irish 1993 2-y-o 7f winner Newport Madam (by Al Hareb) and French 1¼m winner Halle Aux Grains (by Shardari): dam, Irish 2-y-o 6f winner, half-sister to Middle Park winner Mister Majestic and smart French 1¼m performer Homme de Loi: fairly useful performer: won maiden at Windsor in June: best effort when ½-length second to Carousing in nursery at Goodwood on final start for J. Dunlop: well held in allowance race on only outing in USA: better at 7f than shorter, and should stay 1m: acts on firm going. *Kathy Walsh, USA*   **93**

AQUATIC KING (IRE)   4 b.g. In The Wings 128 – Sea Ballad (USA) (Bering 136) [1998 NR 1999 8.2s 10v³ 10g⁵ 13g 14.1v 11.9d a14.8g⁶ 11.5m a12g Nov 19] well-made gelding: poor mover: first foal: dam once-raced daughter of useful 1½m winner Ocean Ballad: modest maiden: should stay 1½m+: best effort on heavy going, twice well held on fibresand: looks moody. *K. R. Burke*   **58 §** **a– §**

ARABELLA GIRL   2 ch.f. (Mar 14) Aragon 118 – Bella Helena (Balidar 133) [1999 6.1f 5g 6m Jul 21] workmanlike filly: second foal: half-sister to 3-y-o Bevelena: dam, winning sprinter in Italy, tailed off only start in Britain: well beaten in maidens: has been bandaged behind. *P. D. Evans*   **–**

ARABESQUE   2 b.f. (Feb 4) Zafonic (USA) 130 – Prophecy (IRE) 109 (Warning 136) [1999 6s³ 7d² Oct 30] well-made, attractive filly: second foal: sister to 3-y-o Threat: dam, best at 2 yrs when Cheveley Park winner, stayed 1m: fairly useful form in Newmarket maidens: ½-length second of 16 to Premier Prize in steadily-run event on second start, racing freely early and leading briefly final 1f having had to wait for a run: should stay 1m: remains open to improvement. *H. R. A. Cecil*   **84 p**

ARAB GOLD   4 b.g. Presidium 124 – Parklands Belle 73 (Stanford 121§) [1998 –: 7s 6d 1999 a8g a6g a7g a6g³ 7m⁶ 10f a7g⁵ a10g a10g a7g Dec 8] tall, leggy gelding: poor maiden: stays 7f: acts on good to firm going and equitrack. *M. Quinn*   **42**

ARABIAN HEIGHTS 6 ch.g. Persian Heights 129 – Arabian Rose (USA) –
(Lyphard (USA) 132) [1998 NR 1999 a9.4g May 14] modest, headstrong and
inconsistent handicapper in 1996: ran poorly only start since. *J. Mackie*

ARABIAN MOON (IRE) 3 ch.c. Barathea (IRE) 127 – Excellent Alibi (USA) **98**
(Exceller (USA) 129) [1998 72p: 7s 6g 1999 7g 7m 8g 9.9g⁴ 9.9g² 12.3m* 11.6m*
16.2m³ 13.9g 12s Sep 26] leggy, quite good-topped colt: easy mover: useful
handicapper: won at Ripon in June and Windsor in July: good third of 7 to First Ballot
at Ascot in August: below form last 2 starts, stiffish task on penultimate: effective at
1½m to 2m: acts on good to firm ground, possibly not soft. *C. E. Brittain*

ARABIS 3 ch.f. Arazi (USA) 135 – Mill On The Floss 117 (Mill Reef (USA) 141) **88**
[1998 NR 1999 10d* 10.1m³ 13.3m 11.9d⁴ Oct 7] sparely-made, plain filly: good
walker: half-sister to several winners, including useful middle-distance performers
Hatta's Mill (by Green Desert), Milly Ha Ha (by Dancing Brave) and Yeltsin (by
Soviet Star): dam 7f (at 2 yrs) and 1½m winner from very good family: fairly useful
form: overcame greenness and slow start to win maiden at Newmarket in June: ran
creditably in minor events/handicap after: stays 13.3f: yet to race on extremes of
going. *H. R. A. Cecil*

ARAGANT (FR) 3 b. or br.g. Aragon 118 – Soolaimon (IRE) 71 (Shareef Dancer **77**
(USA) 135) [1998 NR 1999 7m⁴ 10.2g⁴ 9.9m⁵ 10m³ 8g³ 8s Oct 4] first reported foal:
dam maiden who should have stayed 1½m: fair maiden: left P. Chapple-Hyam before
final start: stays 1¼m: acts on good to firm going, well held on soft. *R. J. Hodges*

ARAGROVE 9 b.g. Aragon 118 – Grovehurst (Homing 130) [1998 46: 5.7f 6g –
5.7d 6m 5m 5.1g⁵ 5g⁶ 5.7g 5m 5m 1999 a6g a6f⁵ a8g Jan 28] compact gelding: poor
mover: poor handicapper nowadays: no form in 1999: stays 6f: acts on firm going,
soft and equitrack: effective blinkered or not. *M. D. I. Usher*

ARAMIL 2 ch.f. (May 6) First Trump 118 – Ever So Artful (Never So Bold 135) **47**
[1999 6m a6g Aug 14] 3,200 2-y-o: second foal: half-sister to Italian 5f and 6f winner
Mister Mirco (by Polish Patriot): dam unraced: poor form at best in maiden and
minor event. *D. W. P. Arbuthnot*

ARANA 4 b.f. Noble Patriarch 115 – Pod's Daughter (IRE) 43 (Tender King 123) –
[1998 NR 1999 8.1m 8g 7.1g 8g 8d 8.3d a10g a10g Dec 10] small filly: no form.
W. de Best-Turner

ARANUI (IRE) 2 b.c. (Mar 7) Pursuit of Love 124 – Petite Rosanna 89 (Ile de –
Bourbon (USA) 133) [1999 a5g Nov 12] 600F, IR 10,000Y: fourth reported foal:
half-sister to 1998 2-y-o 7f winner Rose Hill (by Sabrehill) and to a minor winner
abroad: dam 1¼m winner: 20/1, slowly away in maiden at Southwell. *R. Hollinshead*

ARANYI (USA) 2 gr.c. (Mar 10) El Gran Senor (USA) 136 – Heather's It (USA) **82**
(Believe It (USA)) [1999 7m⁶ 7d⁴ 8.2d⁴ Oct 21] $130,000Y, resold 190,000Y: well-
made, stocky colt: fluent mover: third foal: half-brother to a winner in USA by Lively
One: dam once-raced half-sister to US Grade 1 winners Bull Inthe Heather (9f) and
Heatherten (8.5f to 1¼m): fairly useful form when fourth in maidens won by Zentsov
Street at Newmarket and Western Summer at Nottingham, beaten about 4 lengths on
each occasion: will probably stay 1¼m. *J. L. Dunlop*

ARAWAK PRINCE (IRE) 3 ch.g. College Chapel 122 – Alpine Symphony **87**
(Northern Dancer) [1998 NR 1999 7.1d⁵ 10d* 12v⁶ Sep 20] 34,000F, 35,000Y:
lengthy gelding: ninth foal: half-brother to smart 1m to 1½m winner High Baroque
and 1¼m winner Dancing Heights (both by High Estate): dam unraced half-sister to
smart miler Captain James: fairly useful form: improved considerably to win maiden
at Windsor in August: stiffer task when last of 6 in minor event at Kempton, carrying
head awkwardly under pressure and again swishing tail: should prove better at 1¼m
than 1½m: raced only on ground softer than good. *J. Noseda*

ARBENIG (IRE) 4 b.f. Anita's Prince 126 – Out On Her Own (Superlative 118) **62**
[1998 61, a63: 6.1s 6.9v⁵ 7f* a7g³ 7.1d² a7g⁶ 7m⁵ 7d³ 7m 7m 7.1d 7m 7s⁴ a7g³
a8.5g 1999 8.3m³ 8f⁶ 7.1d² 8s³ 8.3m 8.3g 7.1m² 8.1m⁶ 7s⁶ 7.1m 7g Sep 18] neat
filly: modest handicapper: stays easy 1m: acts on firm going, soft and fibresand:
often blinkered, probably as effective when not: often races up with pace: none too
consistent. *B. Palling*

ARBOR EALIS (IRE)   3 b.f. Woods of Windsor (USA) – North Lady (North- **40**
fields (USA)) [1998 62: 5g 6g a5g* 6s a6g³ 5g 5.7m³ a6g 7d 1999 a6g a8g 10.2g⁵
11.8m 8.1m 5.1m 5.7h⁶ 8m⁴ Sep 1] sparely-made filly: poor performer: stays 6f: acts
on hard going and fibresand: blinkered last 3 starts: has had tongue tied. *R. J. Baker*

ARCADIAN CHIEF   2 b.g. (May 2) Be My Chief (USA) 122 – May Hinton 82 **38**
(Main Reef 126) [1999 5g 6f⁶ 5f⁴ 6d 5f⁴ Jul 24] 4,000Y: angular, workmanlike
gelding: half-brother to 4-y-o Sharp Hint, fairly useful 1994 2-y-o 5f winner Hinton
Rock (by Ballad Rock), and 1m winner Hint of Victory (by Ron's Victory): dam
2-y-o 6f winner: poor form at best in maiden/sellers. *K. T. Ivory*

ARCANE STAR (IRE)   4 b.g. Arcane (USA) – Chatsworth Bay (IRE) (Fairy **–**
King (USA)) [1998 55d: a6g² a6g⁴ a7g³ a6g³ 6d² 5m 6.1g 6d⁴ 6m⁶ a5g a6g 6d 1999
a6g 6v 8m a6g Sep 28] modest maiden at best: no form in 1999: tried visored.
B. P. J. Baugh

ARCETTA (USA)   3 b.f. Woodman (USA) 126 – Dawn Deal (USA) (Grey Dawn **60**
II 132) [1998 –: 6g 7d 1999 8.3m⁴ 8g 14.1f 10.1g Jun 10] small, strong filly: modest
maiden: well beaten in handicaps after reappearance: should have stayed beyond
8.3f: dead. *C. E. Brittain*

ARCHELLO (IRE)   5 b.m. Archway (IRE) 115 – Golden Room (African Sky **47**
124) [1998 54: 6g 5g⁵ 6.1g 7d⁵ 7m 7m⁶ 7.9g 7m 1999 6d 7.1m 8d 7m 6g 6g 7m 6.9m
7d⁴ 8m 7g a8g Nov 22] robust mare: poor handicapper: best at 7f: acts on firm and
soft going: visored twice: inconsistent. *M. Brittain*

ARCHIE BABE (IRE)   3 ch.g. Archway (IRE) 115 – Frensham Manor (Le **75**
Johnstan 123) [1998 63: 5g³ 5g⁶ 6m 7g* 7m 7.9g 8d⁶ 7d 1999 8.2d 8.2s⁵ 10s* 10g*
12v³ 12.3m² 12g⁵ 10m⁴ 12g² 10g⁵ 11.6d³ 11d* Nov 1] workmanlike gelding: fair
handicapper: won at Redcar and Pontefract in May then Redcar in November:
effective at 1¼m/1½m: yet to race on firm going, acts on any other: has worn dropped
noseband: game and consistent. *J. J. Quinn*

ARCHITECT (IRE)   3 b.g. Grand Lodge (USA) 125 – Olean (Sadler's Wells **104**
(USA) 132) [1998 92p: 8m⁴ 8s³ 1999 10.5d* 11.9m² 12s Sep 26] tall, useful-looking
gelding: type to make a better 4-y-o: useful form: easily won maiden at Haydock in
August by 5 lengths: very good ½-length second of 18 to Dee Pee Tee Cee in quite
valuable handicap at York later in month, seeming green when first under pressure
but knuckling down really well: rather edgy in preliminaries and failed to see race
out when bit below par in Ritz Club Handicap at Ascot final start: will stay beyond
1½m: acts on good to firm and good to soft going: joined N. Henderson. *Sir Michael
Stoute*

ARCH RIVAL (IRE)   2 ch.g. (May 5) Archway (IRE) 115 – Abbessingh (Man- **–**
singh (USA) 120) [1999 5f 6m 7f Jul 30] 500Y: leggy, sparely-made gelding: sixth
foal: half-brother to several winners, including 1993 French 2-y-o 7f winner Fasil
(by Diamond Prospect): dam French maiden half-sister to useful sprinter Roaring
Riva: well held in minor event, seller and claimer. *J. R. Turner*

ARC (IRE)   5 b.g. Archway (IRE) 115 – Columbian Sand (IRE) (Salmon Leap **67**
(USA) 131) [1998 58, a71: 5m 6m⁶ 7.5m a6g⁶ a6g⁶ a8.5g² a8.5g² 1999 a8g a7g³ **a71**
a8.5g² a7g* a8.5s a8g a9.4g⁴ a9.4g a7g 10m² 9m² 10m⁶ 10g² 8m² 8g* 8f a8.5g²
a9.4g⁴ Nov 27] tall gelding: fair performer: won maiden handicap at Wolverhampton
in February and minor event at Carlisle (held up) in July: effective at 7f to 1¼m: acts
on soft going, good to firm and fibresand: blinkered twice (below form) at 3 yrs:
usually races up with pace: genuine and consistent. *F. Jordan*

ARCTIC CHAR   3 br.f. Polar Falcon (USA) 126 – Breadcrumb 111 (Final Straw **102**
127) [1998 NR 1999 7s* 6g* 7g² 7d³ 7m 6d⁵ 7g² Oct 18] 40,000Y: small, lengthy,
unfurnished filly: seventh foal: sister to fair 1997 2-y-o 7f winner Arctic Air and
half-sister to 3 winners, including useful 1990 2-y-o 5f/6f winner Heard A Whisper
(by Bellypha): dam 6f/7f winner from good sprinting family: useful performer: won
maiden at Leicester in April and minor event at Kempton in May: some good efforts
after, including when runner-up in listed races at Newmarket (beaten short head by
Fragrant Oasis) and Deauville (¾ length behind Capistrano Day): effective at 6f/7f:
acts on soft going, moved short to post and ran poorly on good to firm (off over 2
months after). *B. J. Meehan*

ARCTIC FANCY (USA)   6 ch.g. Arctic Tern (USA) 126 – Fit And Fancy (USA)   **85**
(Vaguely Noble 140) [1998 81: 14d³ 14s³ 16.2g 14.1m² 14.1m 12g* 11.9s* 12v³ 10s⁶
1999 11.9d⁶ 12m² 11.9f² Jul 12] big, good-topped gelding: fairly useful handicapper:
better effort in 1999 at Epsom on second start: stays 1¾m: acts on any going: has
been bandaged behind: tends to carry head high and hang fire: has won for
inexperienced rider. *J. G. Smyth-Osbourne*

ARCTIC OWL   5 b.g. Most Welcome 131 – Short Rations (Lorenzaccio 130)   **122**
[1998 122: 12g* 13.9s* 16.1v³ 15d* 16g* 1999 13.9s³ 16.4g* 12m² 15.9m²
16.1s² 15.5v⁶ Oct 24]
      For a gelding of Arctic Owl's ability, one pattern-race victory was a
rather disappointing haul in 1999. He did, though, perform creditably when
runner-up in similar contests on three other occasions, each time conceding
weight to the winner and in the process confirming himself a very smart
performer. Arctic Owl should continue to make his presence felt in top races in
2000—and not necessarily just in staying events.
      Arctic Owl's campaign began with a creditable third in the Yorkshire
Cup at York in May, which put him spot on for the Bonusprint (Henry II) Stakes
at Sandown later in the month. The race produced Arctic Owl's sole victory, as
he defeated Rainbow High by a short head in a thrilling race, quickening well
to lead on the post after being checked and forced to switch when hampered
about a furlong out. Arctic Owl's next intended outing was the Gold Cup—for
which he had been installed the 5/1 ante-post second favourite—but trainer
James Fanshawe chose to take him out at the overnight stage on account of the
good to firm ground. 'There is only one Gold Cup—but there is only one Arctic
Owl, too!' said Fanshawe, so the gelding had to wait until the Princess of
Wales's Stakes at Newmarket in July. Racing over a shorter trip than usual
mattered little, as he was beaten only a length into second by Craigsteel in an
eight-runner race, travelling sweetly before making good ground over two
furlongs out and staying on strongly. It is interesting to note that the ground at
Newmarket was, by our reckoning, on the firm side of good, suggesting that
connections may well be mistaken in their belief that Arctic Owl requires good
going or softer; whether or not Arctic Owl will have to bypass big races on
account of firmish ground in the future remains to be seen, but he wouldn't if
he were ours. Arctic Owl also finished a length second in the Lonsdale Stakes

*Bonusprint Stakes (Henry II), Sandown—Arctic Owl (right) uses his turn of foot to good effect,
catching Rainbow High on the line; Maridpour is clear of the others in third*

at York in August (again on going probably a shade firmer than the official 'good'). He was beaten by Celeric on this occasion in another smallish field, giving the impression he might have fared better had he been held up longer. Arctic Owl's other second came in a three-runner tactical affair for the Jockey Club Cup at Newmarket in October, when Rainbow High beat him a neck. He was possibly not over that race when putting in a tame effort, last of seven (promoted to sixth), behind Amilynx in the Prix Royal-Oak at Longchamp three weeks later.

		Be My Guest	Northern Dancer
Arctic Owl (b.g. 1994)	Most Welcome (ch 1984)	(ch 1974)	What A Treat
		Topsy (ch 1976)	Habitat
			Furioso
	Short Rations (br 1975)	Lorenzaccio (ch 1965)	Klairon
			Phoenissa
		Short Commons (b 1962)	Hard Tack
			Padus

Arctic Owl's pedigree was covered fully in *Racehorses of 1998*. There is nothing new to add. A rangy, raw-boned gelding who shows pronounced knee action, Arctic Owl acts on good to firm and heavy ground. He is effective at a mile and a half to two miles, and is usually held up. His style of racing should help his prospects of staying the Gold Cup trip should he be tried in the race another year. *J. R. Fanshawe*

ARCTIC PATCH   2 ch.c. (Feb 19) Inchinor 119 – Arctic Poppy (USA) 67 (Arctic   **51** Tern (USA) 126) [1999 5.3f 7m 7d 8g³ 7d Oct 14] leggy colt: first foal: dam, maiden best at 2 yrs, should have stayed at least 1¼m: modest maiden: only form when blinkered last 2 starts: sold 6,000 gns. *I. A. Balding*

ARCTIC STAR   4 b.g. Polar Falcon (USA) 126 – Three Stars 93 (Star Appeal   **–** 133) [1998 –, a61d: a10g⁴ a12g³ 9.7d⁵ 9.9s a9.4g⁴ 12.1d³ 12s 17.2d 1999 a12g 9g Apr 1] leggy, unfurnished gelding: modest maiden: no form in 5 starts for current stable: races freely and possibly doesn't quite stay 1½m: acts on good to firm going, good to soft and all-weather. *V. Thompson*

ARCTIC THUNDER (USA)   8 b.g. Far North (CAN) 120 – Flying Cloud   **–** (USA) (Roberto (USA) 131) [1998 70: a12g a12g⁵ a12g⁴ 16.1v 14m 13.8d⁴ 12f 14g a12g⁵ a14.8g a14.8g* 1999 a14.8g⁶ Jan 13] leggy, workmanlike gelding: shows knee action: fair handicapper: below form only 8-y-o start: effective at 1½m/1¾m: acts on good to firm going, good to soft and fibresand: sometimes tongue tied/bandaged: inconsistent. *B. Palling*

ARDENT   5 b.g. Aragon 118 – Forest of Arden (Tap On Wood 130) [1998 56: a8g⁶   **60** a8g⁵ a10g² 8d* 8g 10m 8f 9m 8.1m 8.3m 8d² 8g³ 8s⁵ a8g² 1999 8f² 9m* 9d 8.3m 8.3m* 8.5m³ 8m 8.3m⁶ 10.1m⁶ 8d² 7s a10g² a10g² a10g a10g⁶ Dec 18] well-made gelding: modest handicapper: won at Kempton (apprentices) in May and Windsor in June: effective at 1m to 1¼m: acts on equitrack, firm and good to soft going: blinkered (sweating and too free) once at 4 yrs, wore hood final start: none too consistent. *Miss B. Sanders*

ARDLEIGH CHARMER   4 ch.g. Theatrical Charmer 114 – Miss Adventure 69   **75** (Adonijah 126) [1998 79: a8.5g⁶ 12d⁶ 9.7v² 9v* 10d* 11.5m⁵ 11.4d* 12.3s* 13.9f 11.9m 14.6m 14.1d⁵ 11.8d 14m 1999 11.8s² 13v* 12s 13g³ 12s⁴ 14m 13.1g⁴ Jul 26] smallish, lengthy gelding: poor mover: fair handicapper: won 17-runner race at Hamilton in April: didn't have ideal circumstances last 2 starts, off track 8 weeks before final one: needs good test around 1¼m, and stays 1¾m: best on good going or softer: held up, and best in truly-run race: game. *C. A. Dwyer*

ARDUINE   2 ch.f. (Apr 17) Diesis 133 – Ardisia (USA) 87 (Affirmed (USA))   **60 p** [1999 7d⁶ Oct 22] 90,000Y: unfurnished filly: third foal: half-sister to 3-y-o Ashgar (by Bien Bien): dam, winner around 1¼m, half-sister to Ramruma (by Diesis): weak 14/1-shot, stayed on under hands and heels when sixth of 22 to Fame At Last in maiden at Doncaster: flicked tail constantly in paddock: will do better at 1m+. *J. H. M. Gosden*

AREEN ALASAD 3 b.c. Cadeaux Genereux 131 – Pass The Peace 116 (Alzao **61**
(USA) 117) [1998 NR 1999 7.1s⁴ 7m 6m⁴ 7g⁴ 8g 7m Dec 17] quite good-topped colt:
sixth foal: brother to 1997 Cheveley Park winner Embassy and half-brother to 1994
2-y-o 1m winner Puck's Castle (by Shirley Heights) and a winner in Belgium by
Reference Point: dam won Cheveley Park Stakes and second in Poule d'Essai des
Pouliches: modest maiden: trained by M. Jarvis until final outing: should be suited
by further than 7f: seems to act on good to firm and soft going. *D. J. Selvaratnam,
UAE*

AREISH (IRE) 6 b.m. Keen 116 – Cool Combination 76 (Indian King (USA) **63**
128) [1998 –, a46: a13g⁴ a11g* a12g⁵ a11g³ a12g⁶ a12g⁵ a12g* a12g⁴ a11g³ a12g
1999 a11g² a9.4g* a9.4g² a9.4g² a8g* a9.4g³ a8.5g² a9.4g³ a12g a9.4g² a11g Nov
30] good-topped mare: modest performer: won seller at Wolverhampton in January
and handicap at Southwell in February: not at best after 5-month break final 4 starts:
effective at 1m to 1½m: raced mainly on all-weather: tried blinkered/visored: usually
held up: consistent. *J. Balding*

ARETHA (IRE) 2 ch.f. (May 12) Indian Ridge 123 – Smaoineamh (Tap On Wood **95**
130) [1999 7g⁴ 7m 7s³ 6d* 7.3s³ 8d⁵ Oct 30] strong filly: good walker: half-sister to
3 winners, including useful miler Dathuil (by Royal Academy): dam, Irish 2-y-o 6f
winner and useful up to 1¾m, half-sister to champion sprinter Double Form and Lupe
winner Scimitarra: useful performer: won maiden at Naas in October: also creditable
third in C. L. Weld Park Stakes at the Curragh and listed race at Newbury (beaten 2½
lengths by Corinium): bred to stay 1m: acts on good to firm and soft going.
J. S. Bolger, Ireland

ARETINO (IRE) 2 ch.c. (Mar 2) Common Grounds 118 – Inonder 31 (Belfort **88**
(FR) 89) [1999 6m* 7s² 6f² 7s 7m³ Oct 19] 20,000Y: useful-looking colt: third foal:
brother to 4-y-o Chips and 3-y-o Democracy: dam poor maiden from family of smart
French sprinter Three For Fantasy (by Common Grounds): fairly useful performer:
won maiden at Pontefract (bandaged in front) in July: best efforts in minor events
after when runner-up, beaten 1½ lengths by Dashing Duke at York on third start:
stays 7f: acts on firm and soft going. *P. W. Harris*

AREYDHA 2 b.f. (Feb 17) Cadeaux Genereux 131 – Elaine's Honor (USA) **94**
(Chief's Crown (USA)) [1999 5s* 6m 6m Jul 6] 150,000Y: sturdy, lengthy filly with
scope: has a powerful, round action: second foal: half-sister to a 1m winner in Japan
by Indian Ridge: dam, French winner around 8.5f, half-sister to useful French 2-y-o
6.5f/7f winner Savannah's Honor, later winner up to 1½m in USA: favourite, made
impressive winning debut in minor event at York in May: failed to progress as
anticipated on much firmer ground when seventh of 18 in Coventry Stakes at Royal
Ascot (upset in stalls) and ninth of 12 in Cherry Hinton Stakes at Newmarket (raced
on unfavoured far side): may prove best at 5f/6f. *M. R. Channon*

ARGENTAN (USA) 2 b.c. (Feb 18) Gulch (USA) – Honfleur (IRE) 100 (Sadler's **85 p**
Wells (USA) 132) [1999 7d³ 7d³ Oct 27] tall, good-topped colt, rather unfurnished:
first foal: dam, 1¼m and 13.5f winner, sister to Arc winner Carnegie and daughter of
Arc winner Detroit: fairly useful form when third in maidens at Newmarket (behind
Zentsov Street, when trained by P. Chapple-Hyam) and Yarmouth (odds on, drifted
left and carried head awkwardly under pressure) in the autumn: should stay at least
1¼m: blanketed for stalls entry: remains likely to improve. *A. G. Foster*

ARGENT FACILE (IRE) 2 b.c. (Apr 29) Midhish 109 – Rosinish (IRE) **75**
(Lomond (USA) 128) [1999 5g⁵ 5.3f⁶ 5s⁶ 5d² 5.1m 5m⁴ 5m* 5g Aug 20] IR 6,000Y:
first foal: dam once-raced maiden: fair performer: ridden more patiently than
previously when winning nursery at Leicester in August, hanging left under pressure
close home: raced only at 5f: acts on good to firm and good to soft going: well held
only try in blinkers: usually tongue tied: has been bandaged (reportedly returned with
sore shins third start and found to be lame final outing). *D. J. S. Cosgrove*

ARIAS (IRE) 2 b.g. (May 9) Dancing Dissident (USA) 119 – Nollia (IRE) (Belmez **–**
(USA) 131) [1999 6g Aug 21] IR 10,500F: second foal: dam unraced half-sister to
smart middle-distance stayer Top Class: well beaten in maiden at Ripon: sold 800
gns in October. *P. Calver*

ARIF (IRE) 7 b. or br.g. Try My Best (USA) 130 – Sable Royale (USA) (Real **37**
Value (USA)) [1998 NR 1999 16f⁶ 18m⁴ 16.2s⁶ 16.2m⁵ Jul 13] strong gelding: poor

handicapper: stays 2¼m: acts on firm and soft ground: tried blinkered (not since 4 yrs): tongue tied. *Mrs H. L. Walton*

ARISTOCRAT   2 b.c. (Feb 8) Bin Ajwaad (IRE) 119 – Bereeka (Main Reef 126)   **69**
[1999 6m 7d³ Oct 12] 16,000F, 16,000Y: close-coupled, good-bodied colt: seventh foal: half-brother to 2m winner Dawn Summit (by Salse): dam unraced half-sister to Wollow: fair form in maidens at Newbury and Leicester: should stay 1m. *R. Hannon*

ARISTOTLE (IRE)   2 b.c. (Feb 18) Sadler's Wells (USA) 132 – Flamenco   **115 p**
Wave (USA) 103 (Desert Wine (USA)) [1999 7g* 8s* Oct 23]
          Aristotle—the philosopher, not the horse—believed wisdom and temperance were two essential characteristics of human goodness, and, in that light, it would be interesting to hear his views on trainer Aidan O'Brien's so-called 'scattergun' technique when entering his hugely powerful team of juveniles in top races. The three British Group 1 events for two-year-old colts—the Middle Park Stakes, Dewhurst Stakes and Racing Post Trophy—drew a total of seventy-five O'Brien entries, compared with thirty-six from Sir Michael Stoute, twenty-nine from Peter Chapple-Hyam, twenty-two from John Gosden and fifteen from Henry Cecil. When the five-day declarations for the Dewhurst were made, O'Brien had eight of the twelve, and in the Racing Post Trophy he had seven out of seventeen. Critics claim that this is far from temperate, since the cost to owners is considerable, and the confusion which results until the runners are known is unhelpful to the race, to racegoers and to the betting public.
          These views are questionable, and for our money O'Brien's policy is quite wise enough to satisfy Aristotle. Making initial entries in bulk almost certainly avoids the necessity of supplementing a runner, which is a pricey business. Supplementing two runners to the Dewhurst, for instance, would have cost £30,000, whereas entering twenty-eight colts and running two, Brahms and Zentsov Street, cost around £4,000 less. Assuming all the horses are equally well prepared to contest the race, making mass declarations enables O'Brien to identify opponents and calculate which of his team has the best chance of landing the spoils and earning place money. Presumably his owners are not complaining at this tactic, which leads to the question, who exactly is

Racing Post Trophy, Doncaster—Ballydoyle's domination of the European two-year-old races continues as Aristotle belies his inexperience to beat his stable-companion Lermontov (centre) and Ekraar (rail)

inconvenienced by mass declarations at the five-day stage? Not the race or the sponsors, since one or more of O'Brien's horses is bound to line up on the day and add to the contest's significance, a crucial point when a number of leading trainers seem to be treating the best juvenile events with suspicion. There is no real inconvenience to racegoers, as the attendance of very few of them depends purely on the presence of one particular two-year-old. There is only marginal inconvenience to punters, since there's little evidence that top two-year-old events generate much ante-post business, compared with three-year-old or all-aged Group 1 events and major handicaps at any rate. To claim, as one national newspaper did, that O'Brien's methods were wrecking ante-post betting is laughable, but at least those who make a virtue out of sucking lemons will have a small sweetener in 2000, when forty-eight-hour declarations will apply for all Group 1 races in an attempt to promote them, particularly overseas. A voluntary scheme was already in operation for most of the classics and the King George VI and Queen Elizabeth Diamond Stakes.

The Racing Post Trophy worked out well-nigh perfectly for trainer O'Brien as he landed a one-two with Aristotle and Lermontov, while the shortest-priced of his trio, Zentsov Street, finished fifth of the nine runners. From a fairly early stage during the week Aristotle reportedly was the trainer's only certain runner, but his form, while marking him down as a decidedly promising colt, was of no help in assessing his prospects for a championship race. He had run just once, landing the odds easily in an eight-runner maiden at Galway in July. His eight rivals at Doncaster were headed by the favourite Scarteen Fox, a decisive winner of the Somerville Tattersall Stakes. Also in attendance were the Coventry Stakes third Cornelius, smooth Goodwood maiden race winner Air Marshall, Ekraar, an impressive winner of the Lanson Champage Stakes at Goodwood but disappointing behind Distant Music in the Champagne Stakes at Doncaster, and Aristotle's two stable companions.

Mrs John Magnier's "Aristotle"

Zentsov Street had finished third to Distant Music in the Dewhurst Stakes a week earlier and Lermontov had landed the Beresford Stakes narrowly at the Curragh.

Close up initially as Lermontov and the outsider Optimaite set a strong gallop, Aristotle was caught flat-footed three furlongs out, where Ekraar was eased into the lead, and he dropped back to sixth place. With a furlong to travel Lermontov, who had refused to give in, was having a battle royal with Ekraar, and Aristotle was making ground, though still the best part of four lengths off the lead. Urged on vigorously by his rider, the veteran George Duffield, Aristotle relentlessly reduced the gap, led fifty yards out and ran on strongly for a one-and-a-quarter-length victory over his stable companion, who saw the trip out better than third-placed Ekraar. The first three were seven lengths clear of the remainder, and Aristotle was immediately quoted at 16/1 for the Derby.

Aristotle was the fourth and final Group 1 winner in Britain and Ireland sired by Sadler's Wells in a season that saw progeny of the Coolmore-based sire earn more than £1.8m in those two countries to give him his eighth championship in a row and his ninth overall. He was also champion in France, due principally to Montjeu. Most of the sire's runners are suited by middle distances, and Aristotle will be no exception. His dam was a useful two-year-old, successful on both her starts over six furlongs on soft going, notably the Moyglare Stud Stakes. She failed to train on, finishing last on both her outings at three, and initially her stud career was ordinary, with two minor winners from her first three foals. By the time her fourth produce, the Belmez filly Spanish Falls, had shown her talent by landing the Group 3 Prix de Royaumont, Flamenco Wave had been sold for 45,000 guineas to John Magnier at the 1995 December Sales. She was barren at the time, but looked a bargain when Spanish Falls did her stuff, and an even bigger one when her 1994 foal, the Soviet Star colt Starborough, showed himself a high-class miler in winning the Prix Jean Prat and St James's Palace Stakes. Aristotle has put icing on the cake, and Flamenco Wave has a yearling filly and colt foal by Sadler's Wells. The grandam, Armada Way, was one of the leading juvenile fillies in Canada in 1978.

Aristotle (IRE) (b.c. Feb 18, 1997)	Sadler's Wells (USA) (b 1981)	Northern Dancer (b 1961)	Nearctic
			Natalma
		Fairy Bridge (b 1975)	Bold Reason
			Special
	Flamenco Wave (USA) (ch 1986)	Desert Wine (b 1980)	Damascus
			Anne Campbell
		Armada Way (ch 1976)	Sadair
			Hurry Call

Aristotle, quite a good-topped colt, has a round action and acts well on soft going. However, it would be premature to say he requires such a surface—at Doncaster the underfoot conditions assisted him by putting a premium on stamina rather than anything else. The million-pound bonus open to the winner of the Racing Post Trophy, Derby and St Leger will be an added incentive to make the Derby his main target in the first part of the season. The trip will not pose a problem, but will he be good enough? At this stage he is some way adrift of Reference Point, Armiger, King's Theatre and Celtic Swing, the last four colts to make their presence felt in the classics after winning the Racing Post Trophy. He should train on though, and has just about the best form of those Derby candidates who have been exposed so far to serious racecourse competition. Whether he can cope with the numerous unexposed colts who must be waiting in the wings remains to be seen. *A. P. O'Brien, Ireland*

ARIUS 3 ch.c. Royal Academy (USA) 130 – Ville Eternelle (USA) (Slew O' Gold **68** (USA)) [1998 6.5d⁴ 6g 1999 9s 8.8s* 8m* 8.3m² 8g 9g⁴ 12v Oct 23] fourth foal: half-brother to French 1m winner Arme Fatale (by Trempolino) and French 1¼m winner Villafranca (by In The Wings): dam, French 9.5f to 1½m winner, half-sister to Arlington Million winner Mill Native and high-class 1m/9f winner French Stress:

trained until after reappearance by A. Fabre: won minor events at La Guerche-de-Bretagne and Loudeac (for G. Henrot) in the spring: out of depth and tailed off in St Simon Stakes at Newbury on British debut: stays 8.8f: acts on soft and good to firm going: blinkered third to fifth starts. *P. J. Hobbs*

ARIZONA LADY   2 ch.f. (Mar 21) Lion Cavern (USA) 117 – Unfuwaanah 74   **54**
(Unfuwain (USA) 131) [1999 6f⁴ 7f³ 7s 7g⁴ 8d Nov 1] IR 1,600Y: first foal: dam 7f winner: modest maiden: should stay 1m. *I. Semple*

ARKADIAN HERO (USA)   4 ch.c. Trempolino (USA) 135 – Careless   **123**
Kitten (USA) (Caro 133) [1998 119: 7s⁴ 8d 6g² 6f⁴ 5f 6m 1999 6m⁶ 6f⁴ 6m*
6m* 6m³ 5v Oct 3]
      Punters confronted with Arkadian Hero in the top sprints in 2000 will have a choice. Will they believe the talk of connections, who maintain that Arkadian Hero is top class but has not had his fair share of luck? Or will they rely on the bare facts, which state that, good though he undoubtedly is, he has been placed only once in eight attempts in Group 1 company? Perhaps such a statistic is unnecessarily damning, but it does suggest that it is probably wisest to opt for the more cautious choice. Arkadian Hero will probably need to show further improvement as a five-year-old if he is finally to grab the Group 1 prize his connections feel he is up to.
      Arkadian Hero's latest campaign began in the Cork and Orrery Stakes at Royal Ascot, where lack of fitness told as he finished over three lengths behind Bold Edge. That the outing put Arkadian Hero spot on for his next race, the July Cup at Newmarket, mattered not a jot as the field was annihilated by Stravinsky. In occupying fourth place for the second consecutive year Arkadian Hero finished over four and a half lengths behind the winner from what trainer Luca Cumani felt, justifiably, was a poor draw. Arkadian Hero was always in touch and stayed on willingly, despite flashing his tail under pressure and briefly appearing to try to bite Stravinsky's quarters. The drop to listed company on his next two starts brought Arkadian Hero his first wins since victory in the Mill Reef Stakes as a two-year-old. The first came at the scene of that triumph, Newbury, and was completed with the minimum of fuss, Arkadian Hero showing a fine turn of foot, after a troubled run, to storm clear in the final furlong, beating Night Shot by four lengths. An even better effort came back at Newmarket, where he was always going strongly and asserted inside the final two furlongs under no more than firm hands and heels to beat Ho Leng by three lengths. These two victories confirmed Arkadian Hero as a leading contender for a Group 1 sprint, this time the Stanley Leisure Sprint Cup at Haydock. When the chips were down, however, he was simply not good enough, coming under two lengths third behind Diktat. Both the then co-owner, Michael Tabor, and the trainer were furious with Haydock for what they believed was an excessive watering policy fashioned to produce going softer

Hopeful Stakes, Newmarket—
Arkadian Hero looks a class above his rivals as he wins his second successive listed race by a wide margin;
Ho Leng (blaze), Grangeville (white colours) and Maghaarb (striped cap) fill the frame

Mr M. Tabor and Mrs John Magnier's "Arkadian Hero"

than good to attract the Godolphin-trained winner. But race times on the day suggest that the ground was not slow, so it's difficult to justify that as an excuse for Arkadian Hero's failure. Arkadian Hero's final start of the year, the Prix de l'Abbaye de Longchamp, saw him below form under genuinely muddy conditions over five furlongs when eighth behind Agnes World; he was off the bit from an early stage.

Arkadian Hero (USA) (ch.c. 1995)	Trempolino (USA) (ch 1984)	Sharpen Up (ch 1969)	Atan
			Rocchetta
		Trephine (b 1977)	Vice Regal
			Quiriquina
	Careless Kitten (USA) (gr 1980)	Caro (gr 1967)	Fortino II
			Chambord
		T. C. Kitten (ch 1969)	Tom Cat
			Needlebug

Arkadian Hero's Arc-winning sire Trempolino is, unsurprisingly, largely an influence for stamina, but Arkadian Hero, a sprinter pure and simple, is his best performer. Since Arkadian Hero's pedigree was last detailed in *Racehorses of 1997*, Trempolino has been represented by a number of other smart performers in Europe, including For Valour, French-trained Juvenia, ex-French and now UAE-trained Makaruka, German-trained Saugerties and the runaway 1998 Cesarewitch winner Spirit of Love. Arkadian Hero's dam, Careless Kitten, has produced a full sister to Arkadian Hero, the year-younger Carefree Cheetah, who showed only fair form at best before being exported to the USA. Careless Kitten's two-year-old in 1999, Aljawf, cost 300,000 dollars as a foal and is a promising type who could make into a useful three-year-old. The very smart Arkadian Hero, a strong, rangy, full-quartered colt with a fluent action, has shown his best form around six furlongs on good going or firmer. Expect to see Arkadian Hero racing in new colours in 2000. For the last two seasons he has been leased to Tabor and Mrs John Magnier, but ownership is reverting to Sean Kelly and Geoff Howard Spink; the horse will eventually retire to Kelly's Raffin Stud in Berkshire. *L. M. Cumani*

ARMEN (FR)   2 b.c. (Apr 15) Kaldoun (FR) 122 – Anna Edes (FR) (Fabulous Dancer (USA) 124) [1999 8d Oct 12] 350,000 francs Y: fifth foal: brother to useful French 3-y-o 10.5f and 1½m winner Aubergade and smart French 10.5f winner Abbatiale: dam, French maiden, bred to stay middle distances: always towards rear in maiden at Leicester. *M. C. Pipe*   **–**

ARMENIA (IRE)   2 ch.f. (Apr 2) Arazi (USA) 135 – Atlantic Flyer (USA) 98 (Storm Bird (CAN) 134) [1999 7g⁵ 7.7d⁴ 7d 7v³ Oct 25] smallish ex-Irish filly: fourth foal: half-sister to 3-y-o Treasury and 6-y-o Van Gurp (both by Generous) and a winner in Germany by Suave Dancer: dam, 2-y-o 6f winner and third in Fillies' Mile, should have stayed further: fair maiden: trained by N. Meade on debut: should be suited by at least 1m: raced only on good going or softer. *R. Hannon*   **67**

AROB PETE   2 b.c. (Jan 20) Robellino (USA) 127 – An Empress (USA) (Affirmed (USA)) [1999 6s Aug 18] 15,000Y: fourth live foal: half-brother to 3-y-o Able Pete and to 1991 2-y-o 7f winner Alto Jane (by The Minstrel) and 7f/1m winner Aerleon Jane (by Caerleon), both fairly useful and later successful abroad: dam US Grade 3 8.5f winner: well beaten in maiden at Kempton. *A. J. McNae*   **–**

AROGANT PRINCE   2 ch.c. (Apr 12) Aragon 118 – Versaillesprincess (Legend of France (USA) 124) [1999 5.3f³ 5s 5m⁴ 5f⁶ 5g Aug 14] third reported foal: dam, ran once on Flat and twice over hurdles, no form: modest maiden: below form last 3 starts, carrying head awkwardly under pressure on penultimate one. *J. J. Bridger*   **55**

AROUND THE WORLD (IRE)   3 b.f. Thatching 131 – Wild Applause (IRE) 71 (Sadler's Wells (USA) 132) [1998 69: 5m⁵ 7v⁴ 7d⁴ 1999 8g* 7f⁴ 8.1f⁵ 8f 8m⁶ 9g 10.4f 12g 8s 8d 8d Oct 29] leggy, quite good-topped filly: fairly useful handicapper at best: won at Pontefract in May: disappointing after, including in blinkers: best effort at 1m on good going: sold 5,800 gns in December. *M. Johnston*   **83 d**

ARPEGGIO   4 b.g. Polar Falcon (USA) 126 – Hilly 96 (Town Crier 119) [1998 81+: 7d³ 8.1s 7.6m 8g⁴ 7g 1999 6s* 6f 7m 7d Sep 17] good-topped gelding: has a quick action: fairly useful performer: won 18-runner maiden at Thirsk in May: much stiffer tasks when below form in handicaps since, off 3½ months before penultimate start: effective at 6f/7f: acts on good to firm and soft ground. *D. Nicholls*   **81**

ARPELLO   2 b.f. (May 21) Unfuwain (USA) 131 – Arpero 107 (Persian Bold 123) [1999 a5g a6g a7g Dec 10] third foal: half-sister to useful 7f winner Master Boots (by Warning): dam 7f/1m winner: behind in maidens: not at all knocked about final start: should do better at 1m+. *Sir Mark Prescott*   **– p**

ARROGANT   2 b.g. (May 15) Aragon 118 – Miss Ark Royal (Broadsword (USA) 104) [1999 7.1m 7m 6d 5.3s⁴ 7m 7d a7g Nov 23] second foal: dam winning selling hurdler: signs of only a little ability. *R. M. Flower*   **31**

ARRY MARTIN   4 b.g. Aragon 118 – Bells of St Martin 89 (Martinmas 128) [1998 61: a6g⁴ 6v 6m⁵ 5d 6g 5m 7m³ a8.5g 6g³ 6.1s³ 7d 1999 6.1f 5.7g 7m⁶ 7g⁴ 6g 6g² 6g* 6s Sep 16] quite attractive gelding: modest handicapper: won seller at Lingfield in August: best up to 7f: acts on good to firm and soft going: blinkered twice. *W. R. Muir*   **52**

ARTERXERXES   6 b.g. Anshan 119 – Hanglands (Bustino 136) [1998 82, a85: a7g² a8g 7m 7g 7m 6.9m* 8.3m⁶ 8m 1999 7g⁶ 7g 7m⁴ 7.7m 8m* 8h 7.9m² 8d a8g Nov 15] lengthy gelding: fairly useful handicapper: trained first 6 starts by M. Heaton-Ellis, winning at Kempton in July: best effort after when second of 23 at York: stays 1m: acts on equitrack, firm and good to soft going: visored once: front runner. *C. G. Cox*   **83**

ARTFUL DANE (IRE)   7 b.g. Danehill (USA) 126 – Art Age (Artaius (USA) 129) [1998 –§: 8d 10s 8g 8.1g 8.1g 8.3g 8s 8s 1999 8.3m⁵ 8g⁴ 8d 9f 8.2m² 8.3m 8m 8m 8m⁴ Sep 10] strong, good-quartered gelding: formerly fairly useful, just modest   **56 §**

nowadays: trained until after penultimate start by M. Heaton-Ellis: best around 1m: acts on firm and soft going: blinkered/visored: unreliable: sold 2,200 gns. *C. G. Cox*

ARTHURS KINGDOM (IRE)   3 b.g. Roi Danzig (USA) – Merrie Moment   **70** (IRE) (Taufan (USA) 119) [1998 63+: 7d 7f 7g⁵ 7g³ 1999 a11g² a12g 10m³ 12g 12g 12.3d⁶ Jul 5] fair maiden: best effort when third of 19 in handicap at Leicester in May: should stay beyond 1½m: acts on fibresand and good to firm ground: visored final start. *A. P. Jarvis*

ARTIC BAY   7 b.g. Arctic Lord 114 – Galley Bay 55 (Welsh Saint 126) [1998 NR   **68 ?** 1999 12m⁴ 12s⁵ 11.9d⁶ Oct 4] fair at 4 yrs: sign of retaining ability in 1999 only on reappearance (possibly flattered): sold out of D. Smith's stable 720 gns before final start. *C. L. Popham*

ARTIC COURIER   8 gr.g. Siberian Express (USA) 125 – La Reine de France   **57 §** (Queen's Hussar 124) [1998 66, a72: a12g⁴ a12g⁴ 12s 12d⁶ 14.4m⁵ 12m³ 12m³ 14.9g⁶ 12s⁴ 12d 1999 a12g³ a13g³ a16g³ a12g² a16g⁵ a13g 12g² 11.7m² 12m 12m³ 12g Aug 30] good-topped gelding: modest performer: hasn't won since 1996: probably stays 2m: acts on firm going, soft and all-weather: effective blinkered/visored or not: usually held up: sometimes wanders/carries head awkwardly: none too genuine. *D. J. S. Cosgrove*

ART SOCIETY (IRE)   3 ch.c. Perugino (USA) 84 – Nisha Society (IRE) (Law   **–** Society (USA) 130) [1998 –: 8m 8s 7v 1999 a12g a8g⁶ Jun 4] workmanlike colt: no form. *J. J. Sheehan*

ARTS PROJECT (IRE)   5 b.m. Project Manager 111 – Amparo (IRE) (Taufan   **57** (USA) 119) [1998 57: 8s 8.5d 9m⁶ 12m* 9g⁵ 12d² 1999 13m⁵ 12g 12m⁴ 12f* 12m³ 12m⁶ 12m² 11g⁶ 8.2d 8s Oct 25] first living foal: dam, Irish 2-y-o 5f/6f winner, out of half-sister to dam of top-class sprinter Lake Coniston: modest handicapper: won at Dundalk in July: left C. Roche, Ireland, before penultimate start: possibly finds 1m on sharp side, and stays 1½m: acts on firm going. *P. D. Evans*

ARZILLO   3 b.g. Forzando 122 – Titania's Dance (IRE) 61 (Fairy King (USA))   **63** [1998 –: 6s 6g 6m 1999 6m 6m⁴ 7m 6m 8m³ 7.6g Aug 24] small gelding: modest maiden: will prove best up to 1m: acts on good to firm going: looked none too keen final 2-y-o start: sold 1,900 gns. *S. Dow*

ASAAL   2 b.c. (Apr 22) Machiavellian (USA) 123 – Rawaabe (USA) 87 (Nureyev   **97** (USA) 131) [1999 6m³ 6m* 6v* 7.3s Oct 22] rangy, good sort: fifth foal: half-brother to several winners, including 3-y-o Dahshah, 6-y-o Afaan and useful 7f/1m performer La-Faah (by Lahib): dam, 5f winner, closely related to smart sprinter Doulab: useful form: won maiden at Pontefract in August and minor event at Salisbury (by 2½ lengths, making all, from Launfal) in September: last of 9 in Group 3 at Newbury final start, possibly failing to stay longer trip in testing conditions: acts on good to firm and heavy going. *B. W. Hills*

ASAALA (USA)   3 ch.f. Slew O'Gold (USA) – Alghuzaylah 90 (Habitat 134)   **63** [1998 67: 7d³ 7d 1999 8g 9.7f³ 11.5f⁴ 10s Sep 29] quite good-topped filly: sister to very smart miler Zaahi: dam 2-y-o 5f winner who stayed 1m: modest maiden: stays 1¼m: acts on firm and good to soft going: sent to USA. *M. P. Tregoning*

ASANOVO (USA)   2 ch.c. (Feb 27) Nureyev (USA) 131 – Golden Darling (USA)   **96** 55 (Slew O'Gold (USA)) [1999 5d* 5m³ Jun 17] strong-quartered, heavy-topped colt: half-brother to several winners in USA: dam, ran twice in Britain then winning sprinter in USA, half-sister to dam of smart filly up to 1m Dancing Tribute (by Nureyev): landed odds in 3-runner maiden at the Curragh in April: useful form when 1¾ lengths third of 13 to Warm Heart in Norfolk Stakes at Royal Ascot, but not seen after: very much a sprinter on looks. *A. P. O'Brien, Ireland*

ASCARI   3 br.g. Presidium 124 – Ping Pong 65 (Petong 126) [1998 69d: 6m⁴ 7.5m⁶   **69** 7g⁴ 7m a6g⁶ a7g⁴ a7g 1999 8.3m 8g 7m⁵ 10m² 10f² 10.1m 9.9s⁶ 10d³ 10d* Oct 21] neat gelding: fair handicapper: won at Nottingham in October, making most: ran creditably when placed otherwise: will prove best around 1¼m: acts on firm going, good to soft and fibresand (well beaten on equitrack): visored once at 2 yrs: sold 22,000 gns, joined M. Banks. *P. W. Harris*

ASCOT MASCOT (USA)   3 b. or br.c. Storm Bird (CAN) 134 – Croquetallie   **82 +** (USA) (Alydar (USA)) [1998 NR 1999 10g⁴ 10.1m* 11.9v⁶ 12s⁵ Oct 23] $200,000F,

IR 300,000Y: finely-made colt: third foal: dam, sprint winner at 4 yrs in USA, daughter of Grade 1-placed Croquis, a half-sister to good American colt Linkage: fairly useful form: confirmed promise when winning maiden at Newcastle in May: stiff tasks both starts 5 months later: should stay beyond 1¼m: has been bandaged in front: sold 25,000 gns, sent to France. *J. L. Dunlop*

ASEF ALHIND 5 ch.g. Indian Ridge 123 – Willowbed 66 (Wollow 132) [1998 **93** 83: 8d 8m⁶ 8g² 7.1d³ 1999 7m² 7m⁴ 8m³ 8.1m* 8f² 8d Aug 8] close-coupled, good-bodied gelding: fairly useful performer: didn't need to be at best to win claimer at Sandown (final start for B. Hanbury) in June: good second of 17 to Naviasky in handicap at Goodwood next start, didn't get run of race final one: best at 7f/1m: acts on firm and good to soft ground: tongue tied last 2 starts: has been bandaged in front: has raced freely: reliable: sent to USA. *G. A. Butler*

ASH BOLD (IRE) 2 ch.g. (May 26) Persian Bold 123 – Pasadena Lady (Captain **53** James 123) [1999 7d 7s a7g Dec 10] IR 24,000F, IR 20,000Y: compact gelding: brother to 3-y-o Karisal, and half-brother to several winning sprinters, including smart Palacegate Episode (by Drumalis): dam unraced: best effort in maidens when mid-division on debut: slowly away next time. *R. M. Whitaker*

ASHBOURNE PAT 3 b.f. Mtoto 134 – Actraphane (Shareef Dancer (USA) 135) **99** [1998 82+: 8g* 10d⁴ 1999 11.5g 10s* 12d² 11g² 11.5d* 12d³ Oct 25] leggy, un-furnished filly: tailed off in listed race at Lingfield on reappearance (final outing for J. Pearce): won minor events at Pompadour in June and Angers in October and ran well when length third to Turbotiere in listed race at Toulouse final start: stays 1½m: acts on soft going. *H-A. Pantall, France*

ASHBRITTLE LADY 3 ch.f. King's Signet (USA) 110 – Lady Longmead **41** (Crimson Beau 124) [1998 –: 6.1g 6d 5.7g a6g 1999 a7g⁴ a8.5g⁴ Feb 20] plain filly: poor maiden: may prove best up to 7f: acts on equitrack, probably on fibresand: covered by Spectrum, sent to USA. *L. G. Cottrell*

ASHGAR (USA) 3 ch.c. Bien Bien (USA) 125 – Ardisia (USA) 87 (Affirmed **112** (USA)) [1998 NR 1999 10.2s⁴ 11.8m² 14.1m* 14.8m² 15.9m⁴ 15m Sep 7] $28,000F, 37,000Y: quite good-topped colt: second foal: dam, winner at around 1¼m, half-sister to Ramruma and useful middle-distance pair Ausherra and Royal Scimitar: smart performer: won maiden at Redcar in June: very good efforts in listed races at Newmarket and York (40/1, 4½ lengths fourth to Celeric) next 2 starts: tailed off in Prix de Lutece at Longchamp final one: will prove best at 2m+: acts on good to firm ground, showed promise on soft: carried head high second start. *C. E. Brittain*

ASHJAAN (USA) 2 gr.f. (Feb 10) Silver Hawk (USA) 123 – Shadayid (USA) **77** 122 (Shadeed (USA) 135) [1999 7m² 7f² 7d² 7.5g² 7d* 8d Oct 30] close-coupled filly: fourth foal: half-sister to 1995 2-y-o 6f/7f winner Bint Shadayid (by Nashwan), also third in 1000 Guineas and 1¼m Group 3, and useful 7f winner (including in USA) Shawaf (by Mr Prospector): dam, won 1000 Guineas and non-staying third in the Oaks, half-sister to Irish Oaks winner Alydaress: runner-up first 4 starts in maidens, flashing tail on 3 of them: won similar event at Newcastle in October: last of 10 in listed race at Newmarket final start: should stay 1m: acts on firm and good to soft going: consistent, but looks difficult ride. *J. L. Dunlop*

ASHLEIGH BAKER (IRE) 4 b. or br.f. Don't Forget Me 127 – Gayla Orchestra **60** (Lord Gayle (USA) 124) [1998 68: a9.4g 7.5d⁵ 8.2g⁶ 8.5g 10.9s* 9.2d 10.5g 10.3g⁶ **a–** 10s 13.1s 15.8d 8d 1999 8g³ 9.9g⁴ a9.4g 9g 10s⁵ 12g³ Nov 3] modest handicapper: should stay beyond 1½m: acts on soft going (yet to race on firmer than good), well held both starts on fibresand: tried blinkered: tended to run in snatches penultimate start. *M. Johnston*

ASH MILLSHAW (IRE) 3 gr.g. Archway (IRE) 115 – Yalciyna 92 (Nishapour **43** (FR) 125) [1998 58, a55: 7g 6g 6m a7g⁴ 5.7v* a7g⁵ a6g⁴ 1999 a7g⁴ 7s 8d 6d⁶ 6.1d 8.2f a6g Jun 28] leggy, plain gelding: poor performer: effective at 6f (given test)/7f: acts on heavy going and fibresand: visored last 2 starts: joined F. Murtagh. *R. Hollinshead*

ASHOVER AMBER 3 b.f. Green Desert (USA) 127 – Zafaaf 105 (Kris 135) **81** [1998 59: 5g³ 6.1m³ 6m 1999 a6g* a6g² 6.1v a6g⁶ 5d⁶ 5f⁶ 5m* a6g³ 5m* 5m³ Jul 22] sturdy, good-quartered filly: poor mover: fairly useful performer: won at Southwell (maiden) in February and Carlisle in June (handicap) and July (minor event):

AST

effective at 5f/6f: acts on fibresand, firm and good to soft ground: consistent. *T. D. Barron*

ASILANA (IRE) 3 b.g. College Chapel 122 – Uninvited Guest 57 (Be My Guest **41** (USA) 126) [1998 –: 5s⁵ 1999 a8f⁴ a7g⁶ a7g 7m May 3] lengthy gelding: poor maiden: stayed 1m: acted on fibresand: dead. *T. D. Easterby*

AS-IS 5 b.g. Lomond (USA) 128 – Capriati (USA) 83 (Diesis 133) [1998 –: a12g **–** a13g a16.2g a11g 1999 a12g⁵ Feb 18] sturdy gelding: shows knee action: modest in 1997: no form since, reportedly finishing distressed final 4-y-o start. *J. J. Bridger*

ASPIRANT DANCER 4 b.g. Marju (IRE) 127 – Fairy Ballerina (Fairy King **77** (USA)) [1998 76, a71+: 9.7d² a11g* 9.7v* 10.5g* 10.1g a9.4g² 10.5g⁴ 11.9m 10.4g 1999 a10g 10.8d⁴ 12s² 10d* 12g³ 10.2g³ a12g² 10d* 12m³ 12g 10d* 10d⁶ Oct 4] rather leggy, good-topped gelding: fair performer: won handicap in May and minor events in July and September, all at Pontefract: effective at 1¼m/1½m: has form on good to firm going, goes very well on softer than good/fibresand: normally races prominently: often claimer ridden: tough and reliable: won over hurdles in December for Mrs L. Wadham. *M. L. W. Bell*

ASPRILLA (IRE) 4 b.g. Sharp Victor (USA) 114 – Aspire (Nebbiolo 125) [1998 **–** NR 1999 8d Oct 20] no sign of ability. *B. Ellison*

ASSURED GAMBLE 5 b.g. Rock Hopper 124 – Willowbank 66 (Gay Fandango **52** (USA) 132) [1998 84: 12s* 12g 10g 12m 12s³ 10.3m 1999 10.2g³ 16f Jun 21] lengthy, good-bodied gelding: fairly useful handicapper in 1998 for C. Brittain: just modest at best in 1999: needs further than 1¼m, and stays 2m: acts on good to firm and soft ground: joined R. Baker. *R. J. Hodges*

ASSURED MOVEMENTS (USA) 3 b.c. Northern Flagship (USA) 96 – Love **76 d** At Dawn (USA) (Grey Dawn II 132) [1998 76+: 5g 6m⁵ 6d 1999 10f⁵ 10g² 12g 10.1d 11.6m 9f 11.5g⁵ 10g⁴ 10d Oct 18] good-topped colt: fair maiden at best: disappointing after second start in 1999: likely to prove best around 1¼m: sold 6,000 gns, joined B. Llewellyn. *C. E. Brittain*

ASSURED PHYSIQUE 2 b.c. (Apr 14) Salse (USA) 128 – Metaphysique (FR) **?** (Law Society (USA) 130) [1999 8.5m 8s⁶ 8d 8d Oct 29] 14,000Y: tall, attractive colt: fifth foal: brother to a disappointing maiden and half-brother to 3-y-o Sergeant York and 5-y-o Philosophic (both by Be My Chief): dam, French 1¼m winner, out of sister to Try My Best and El Gran Senor: appeared to show fair form (could be rated 75) in slowly-run Newmarket maiden third outing: well beaten in nursery final start: will stay beyond 1m. *C. E. Brittain*

ASTON EYRE 3 ch.f. Pharly (FR) 130 – Lady Keyser 68 (Le Johnstan 123) **–** [1998 –: 5.7d 6g 5.1m 1999 5.1s⁵ 6m a6g 5d 6s 7g Oct 19] little form: left A. Juckes after third start: tried blinkered. *J. Pearce*

ASTONISHED 3 ch.g. Weldnaas (USA) 112 – Indigo 86 (Primo Dominie **119 p** 121) [1998 90p: 5m³ 5d* 6m* 5d³ 6v⁶ 1999 5.5m² 6g⁵ 6g* 5.6g* 6d Sep 18]
     Followers of the questionable maxim that jockeys are the worst judges would have found comfort in Kieren Fallon's column 'The Inside Line' in the *Daily Mail* on Ayr Gold Cup day. Under the headline 'Astonished? I will be if he's beaten', Fallon told readers that had he not been bound by a retainer to ride Grangeville for trainer Ian Balding, he would much rather have ridden Astonished. 'I think Astonished is a good thing', he said. Fallon had partnered Astonished to a most impressive victory under 9-6—a record weight for a three-year-old winner of the race—in the Tote Trifecta Portland Handicap at Doncaster ten days earlier, on the horse's first start in Britain since his two-year-old days, when he had been trained by Lynda Ramsden. Owner-breeder David Brotherton had plenty of success with the Ramsdens with Astonished's sprinting half-brothers, the smart Bishops Court and the useful Surprise Mission, and Astonished himself landed a huge gamble from a big field in a nursery on Doncaster's St Leger day programme in Mrs Ramsden's final season. Astonished looked a good prospect that day, very much the type to train on, and when Mrs Ramsden handed in her licence he was transferred, reportedly on the Ramsdens' advice, to John Hammond in France. Astonished

87

Tote Trifecta Portland (Handicap), Doncaster—
Kieren Fallon has time to look over his shoulder as Astonished lands a gamble in remarkable style;
Cretan Gift (visored) squeezes through for second place with Ocker (noseband) in third

left the form of his first three races for Hammond (including a victory in a
minor event at Deauville in July) behind at Doncaster, where he quickened
clear under hands and heels after being held up to win in a manner rarely seen
in a valuable handicap, his four-length margin of victory over Cretan Gift a
considerable understatement of his superiority on the day. Astonished started
favourite at Doncaster and was immediately a very warm order for the Ayr Gold
Cup, for which he incurred a 7-lb penalty. His running at Ayr—under pressure
over two furlongs out when only thirteenth of twenty-eight behind Grangeville
on good to soft going—should be ignored.

The big, good-topped Astonished will have no difficulty making the
transition from handicaps to pattern sprints in the next season, judged on his
Portland performance. Still quite lightly raced, Astonished acts on good to firm
going and is possibly unsuited by softer than good. He has joined Richard
Fahey, at whose yard he lodged between Doncaster and Ayr. *J. E. Hammond,
France*

ASTON MARA   2 b.g. (Feb 8) Bering 136 – Coigach 110 (Niniski (USA) 125)   **80**
[1999 7m* 8m⁵ 8.1v⁴ Oct 13] 18,000Y: first foal: dam 1m (at 2 yrs) to 14.6f (Park
Hill) winner from good staying family: won maiden at Newcastle in June, leading
after halfway and staying on well: failed to repeat that form in listed race/minor
event: should be suited by 1m+. *M. Johnston*

ASTRAC (IRE)   8 b.g. Nordico (USA) – Shirleen (Daring Display (USA) 129)   **93**
[1998 104: 6v 6d 6g* 6s⁵ 6d 6.1g 5m³ 6s* 7d⁶ 1999 a7g 6g 7g 5.1m 6g⁶ 6m⁵ 6g³ 6m
6g 7.3m 5s³ 6s* 6d⁶ 6d⁴ 5d 8d a7g³ a6g³ a6g⁵ Dec 13] sturdy gelding: impresses
in appearance: fairly useful performer: won apprentice minor event at Catterick in
October: ran well penultimate start: better at 6f than 7f: winner on firm ground, best
on soft/fibresand: well beaten only try in blinkers. *A. J. McNae*

ASTRAL INVADER (IRE)   7 ch.g. Astronef 116 – Numidia (Sallust 134) [1998   **–**
–, a46d: a7g² a6g⁴ a6g⁶ a7g 1999 a6g⁶ a7f Jan 14] leggy gelding: poor performer: **a33**
stays 7.6f: acts on any turf/all-weather: tried visored (including when successful)/
blinkered: sold 700 gns in July. *M. S. Saunders*

ASTRAL RHYTHM   4 b.c. Scorpio (FR) 127 – Suzannah's Song (Song 132)   **–**
[1998 NR 1999 10m 10.1g 8m a7g Nov 19] brother to fair 6f (at 2 yrs) and 1¼m
winner Just Flamenco and half-brother to 2 winners: dam unraced: well beaten in
maidens/handicap. *G. G. Margarson*

ASTROLFELL (IRE)   4 ch.f. River Falls 113 – Indian Starlight (Kafu 120)   **–**
[1998 24: 8f³ 1999 7m 8g 7f 9.9m 8m Sep 1] bad maiden. *J. S. Moore*

ASTRONOMER 3 br.g. Ardkinglass 114 – Ayodhya (IRE) (Astronef 116) [1998 **81**
79p: 6.1m 6g³ 7g⁴ 1999 7m⁴ 7m³ 7.5v* 8f 7.1s⁶ 7g 8d³ Oct 21] leggy, sparely-made
gelding: fairly useful performer: won maiden at Beverley in June by 5 lengths: off
nearly 3 months after next start (on firm ground), back to best when third in minor
event at Brighton final one: stays 1m: acts on good to firm and heavy going: sold
6,500 gns. *J. R. Fanshawe*

ASTURIAN LADY (IRE) 2 b.f. (Apr 22) Zieten (USA) 118 – Thubut (USA) **88**
(Tank's Prospect (USA)) [1999 5g⁵ 6.1m* 6g⁵ 6d⁵ Sep 18] IR 14,000Y: sturdy,
attractive filly: third foal: half-sister to 6-y-o Waasef and a 7.5f winner in Italy by
Kahyasi: dam unraced half-sister to 2000 Guineas runner-up and US Grade 1 1¼m
winner Exbourne: fairly useful performer: won minor event at Nottingham in
August: good fifth of 9 in Lowther Stakes at York, but well held after helping force
early pace in listed race at Ayr final start: bred to stay further, but may prove best as a
sprinter. *A. P. Jarvis*

ASYAAD (USA) 4 br.g. Zilzal (USA) 137 – Shihama (USA) 88 (Shadeed (USA) **–**
135) [1998 –: 7d 8.2m 5.7m 7s a6g 1999 a6g⁵ 6m May 2] rather unfurnished gelding:
fair maiden at 2 yrs: disappointing since: sold 700 gns. *Mrs L. Stubbs*

ATALYA 2 ch.g. (Mar 8) Afzal 83 – Sandy Looks 69 (Music Boy 124) [1999 8.2d⁶ **60**
a6g⁶ a8.5g Dec 11] 1,750F: seventh reported foal: half-brother to 7f winner Forget **a47**
To Remindme (by Forzando): dam, winning hurdler (lightly raced on Flat), daughter
of Irish 1000 Guineas second Hannah Darling: some ability in maidens/minor event:
bred to need further than 6f. *F. Jordan*

ATAVUS 2 b.c. (Apr 9) Distant Relative 128 – Elysian 94 (Northfields (USA)) **77 p**
[1999 6.8d⁵ 6d³ 7g* Oct 19] 5,800Y: sturdy colt: half-brother to several winners,
including 1991 2-y-o 1m winner Anchorite (later best at 1½m) and 13f to 2m
winner Arcady (both by Slip Anchor): dam 2-y-o 6f winner who seemed to stay
1½m: fair form: strong-finishing third of 20 (beaten ¾ length) to Magic of Love in
valuable sales race at Newmarket: justified favouritism in maiden at Lingfield
following week by 3 lengths from Soller Bay: likely to prove suited by 1m+: slowly
away first 2 starts: remains open to improvement. *W. R. Muir*

ATHENIAN HEIGHTS 4 b.f. Timeless Times (USA) 99 – Woodbegood 47 **–**
(Athens Wood 126) [1998 –: a6g a6g⁶ 1999 a7g a11g Feb 5] no form. *M. Waring*

ATHENRY 6 gr.h. Siberian Express (USA) 125 – Heresheis 69 (Free State 125) **88**
[1998 NR 1999 14.1s⁶ 14d 18g⁴ 16.4g 20m 14.8m⁶ Jul 17] tall, leggy horse: has a
long, round action: useful and thoroughly genuine at 3 yrs (subsequently tore tendon
sheath): just some fairly useful form in 1999: should prove best at 2m+: best form on
good/good to firm ground, yet to race on firm: heavily bandaged nowadays: took
strong hold to post fourth start (also raced too freely previous 2). *J. Pearce*

ATIENZA (USA) 6 ch.m. Chief's Crown (USA) – Hattab Voladora (USA) **–**
(Dewan (USA)) [1998 NR 1999 a14.8g 14.1d Oct 27] modest staying maiden at best.
Dr J. D. Scargill

ATLANTA 4 b.f. Rock City 120 – Olympic Run 56 (Salse (USA) 128) [1998 59: **–**
7g 6m 5g 5m⁴ 6.1g⁴ 6.1d 6.1g⁵ a6g 1999 a6f 6g Aug 20] lengthy, unfurnished filly:
modest maiden at best: last both starts in 1999: stays 6f: acts on fibresand, yet to race
on extremes of going on turf: blinkered on reappearance. *G. Woodward*

ATLANTIC ACE 2 b.c. (Apr 6) First Trump 118 – Risalah (Marju (IRE) 127) **54**
[1999 5g Aug 24] 15,000Y: first foal: dam ran once: 12/1, seventh of 8 in maiden at
Lingfield, not unduly punished once fading. *B. Smart*

ATLANTIC CHARTER (USA) 3 b.c. Gone West (USA) – Silk Slippers (USA) **78**
104 (Nureyev (USA) 131) [1998 NR 1999 8s 7.1m⁶ 7g 7.1f³ a8.5g 10.2m 10g* 10d
Oct 12] $475,000Y: good-topped colt: third foal: closely related to fairly useful 6f (at
2 yrs) and 1m (in USA) winner Silk Masque (by Woodman): dam won Fillies' Mile:
fair performer: won handicap at Redcar (final start for P. Chapple-Hyam) in October,
getting up on line: will stay beyond 1¼m: no form on ground softer than good.
A. G. Foster

ATLANTIC DESTINY (IRE) 3 b.f. Royal Academy (USA) 130 – Respect- **98**
fully (USA) (The Minstrel (CAN) 135) [1998 99+: 6g³ 6g² 5d 5d³ 6d* 6g⁵ 7g⁴ 1999
7g⁵ 8m 6g⁴ 6m 6m⁵ 8m⁶ 6g* 8.5g⁶ Nov 20] big, useful-looking filly: did well

physically from 2 to 3 yrs: useful performer: ran creditably when eleventh of 22 to Wince in 1000 Guineas at Newmarket and fifth to Halmahera in listed event at Newcastle on second and fifth outings: left M. Johnston after next start: won conditions event at Laurel in October: effective at 6f, probably 1m: yet to race on extremes of going: early to post on reappearance, on toes fourth start: has flashed tail. *H. G. Motion, USA*

ATLANTIC PRINCE (IRE)   3 b.g. Fairy King (USA) – Idle Chat (USA) 93   **86 d**
(Assert 134) [1998 NR 1999 7.5d* 8m 10.1m⁴ 7.9f 6d 7m 7.1d Sep 26] IR 40,000Y: quite good-topped gelding: second living foal: half-brother to fairly useful 7.5f and 10.8f winner Central Committee (by Royal Academy): dam, 2-y-o 1m winner who stayed 11.5f (later successful in Australia), half-sister to useful 1991 2-y-o Musicale out of half-sister to Committed: fairly useful performer: won maiden at Beverley in June: largely disappointing after: may prove best at 1m: tongue tied final start: has gone early to post: sold 800 gns, joined Mrs K. Lamb. *M. Johnston*

ATLANTIC RHAPSODY (FR)   2 b.c. (May 7) Machiavellian (USA) 123 –   **88**
First Waltz (FR) 117 (Green Dancer (USA) 132) [1999 6m² 6g² 7g³ 8s² Oct 25] IR 50,000Y: tall, rather leggy, attractive colt: half-brother to 4 winners, including a winner in Macau by Arazi and useful 1m winner Gaitero (by Groom Dancer) and winner up to 1½m Tenet (by Reference Point), both in France: dam won Prix Morny: fairly useful maiden: should stay beyond 1m: acts on good to firm and soft ground: found little second start and hung under pressure third one. *M. Johnston*

ATLANTIC VIKING (IRE)   4 b.g. Danehill (USA) 126 – Hi Bettina 96 (Henbit   **94**
(USA) 130) [1998 90: 5m 6s 7.1d 7g³ 5g 6g⁵ 7m 7g 7g 1999 5m² 5s 5f² 6d 6m⁶ 5m 5m* 5f⁴ 6f* Aug 2] well-made gelding: fairly useful handicapper: won at Pontefract in July and Ripon (made most in 6-runner race) in August: ran well when in frame otherwise: best at 5f/6f: acts on firm and good to soft ground: effective blinkered or not. *D. Nicholls*

AT LARGE (IRE)   5 b.g. Night Shift (USA) – Lady Donna 92 (Dominion 123)   **80**
[1998 84: 5.1f² 5g³ 1999 5s⁴ 6m 6m 6m 6m⁴ 5d² 5g 6s Sep 20] small, stocky gelding: fairly useful handicapper: mostly respectable efforts in 1999 (not well drawn last 2 starts): has form at 7f, but raced mainly at 5f/6f: acts on firm and soft ground: blinkered last 3 starts: sold 12,500 gns, joined W. Musson. *J. A. R. Toller*

AT LIBERTY (IRE)   7 b.g. Danehill (USA) 126 – Music of The Night (USA)   **–**
(Blushing Groom (FR) 131) [1998 NR 1999 11.7m 12.1m 8.1m Aug 5] sturdy gelding: has a quick action: fairly useful at best: no show in 1999: stays 1½m: acts on good to firm going, soft and equitrack: blinkered once. *J. C. Tuck*

AT MY COMMAND (IRE)   3 ch.f. Barathea (IRE) 127 – Fly Dont Run (USA)   **46**
59 (Lear Fan (USA) 130) [1998 60: 7g⁵ 7g 7.1s³ 1999 7s 6m 6g 5.9m 5m 8m⁵ 9.9g Aug 28] poor maiden: stays 1m: acts on good to firm and soft going: carried head awkwardly penultimate start, looked none too keen (in visor) final one. *M. W. Easterby*

A TOUCH OF FROST   4 gr.f. Distant Relative 128 – Pharland (FR) (Bellypha   **97**
130) [1998 74: 7s 8m* 8.3m 10g 1999 8g 10m 7g* 7.1d² 7f* 8.3s 7m* 7d⁵ 8g Oct 16] workmanlike filly: useful handicapper: won at Salisbury (claiming event) in June, York in July and Salisbury again (by 4 lengths from Gracious Gift) in September: far from disgraced last 2 starts: effective at 7f/1m: acts on firm and good to soft going: blinkered after second start: races prominently. *G. G. Margarson*

ATTARIKH (IRE)   6 b.g. Mujtahid (USA) 118 – Silly Tune (IRE) (Coquelin   **–**
(USA) 121) [1998 46d: 8g 8g⁶ 8m a7g 6g 1999 a8g⁵ a8.5g Jan 13] lengthy gelding: has been hobdayed: disappointing maiden: reportedly lost his action final start: tried visored/blinkered. *Mrs A. L. M. King*

ATWAAR (USA)   2 ch.c. (Feb 19) Woodman (USA) 126 – Haniya (IRE) 92 (Caer-   **92**
leon (USA) 132) [1999 7m² 7f* 8g³ 10d² Oct 11] strong, compact colt: has a rounded action: first foal: dam, 1½mile winner (stayed 1¾m), half-sister to very smart horse up to 1½m Volochine: fairly useful performer: odds on, won maiden at Redcar in July: good efforts in minor events both subsequent starts: stays 1¼m: acts on firm and good to soft ground: took good hold to post third start: reared leaving stalls first 2 outings: sold 46,000 gns, sent to USA. *J. L. Dunlop*

ATYLAN BOY (IRE)   2 b.g. (Mar 13) Efisio 120 – Gold Flair 93 (Tap On Wood   **66**
130) [1999 5g 5s⁶ 5.7g⁵ 7s Oct 1] 22,000F, 35,000Y: leggy, close-coupled gelding:
sixth foal: half-brother to 1993 2-y-o 7f winner Duball Remy (by Roi Danzig),
French 3-y-o 12f winner Harlem Swing (by Night Shift) and a winner in Norway by
Distant Relative: dam, middle-distance maiden, sister to very smart middle-distance
performer Nisnas: fair maiden: should stay 7f. *B. J. Meehan*

AUBRIETA (USA)   3 b.f. Dayjur (USA) 137 – Fennel 97 (Slew O' Gold (USA))   **67**
[1998 73+: 5.2m⁶ 5d 6g³ 6.1g³ 6.5g 5m³ 5s 1999 6m 7d 7m⁶ 8.2g 6m³ 6f 7d 6m
6.1d⁶ 5.2s a6g² Nov 11] tall filly: fair performer: won maiden on all-weather debut at
Lingfield in November: stays 7f: acts on good to firm going and equitrack, probably
on good to soft: sometimes blinkered (including for win)/visored. *D. Haydn Jones*

AUCHONVILLERS   2 b.c. (Apr 5) Deploy 131 – Forbearance 77 (Bairn (USA)   **65 p**
126) [1999 7.9g⁶ Oct 6] 2,500F: third foal: dam, 1m winner at 2 yrs, also won
over hurdles: 33/1 and green, 8½ lengths sixth of 26 to Miss Lorilaw in maiden at
York, never nearer: shapes as though well suited by 1¼m+: should do better.
B. A. McMahon

AUCTION HOUSE (USA)   3 b.c. Exbourne (USA) 125 – Fast Flow (USA)   **102**
(Riverman (USA) 131) [1998 120: 7s⁴ 7m* 7f* 7g* 7g² 1999 8m 7.3g⁴ 8m 7g Oct
16] smallish, well-made colt: fluent mover: smart at 2 yrs, winning 3 races (notably
Champagne Stakes at Doncaster): looked a shadow of his former self in pattern races
in 1999: stays 7f: acts on firm going, showed promise on soft: joined R. Frankel in
USA. *B. W. Hills*

AUDACITY   3 b.g. Minshaanshu Amad (USA) 91§ – Glory Isle 60 (Hittite Glory   **–**
125) [1998 –: 6s 6m 6m 1999 7.6m 8.1m 10f⁵ a12g a13g Oct 1] tall gelding: little
sign of ability. *N. Hamilton*

AUDIOSTREETDOTCOM   2 ch.g. (Feb 16) Risk Me (FR) 127 – Ballagarrow   **–**
Girl 66 (North Stoke 130) [1999 6d 5.1m 5v 6s 7.3v Oct 23] 3,000F, 15,500Y: brother
to a winner in Poland and half-brother to 1990 2-y-o 5f winner Northern Nation (by
Nomination) and a winner abroad: little form, including in a claimer: dam, maiden,
suited by 1¼m: visored last 3 starts. *G. B. Balding*

AUDITION   3 b.f. Machiavellian (USA) 123 – Dance To The Top 107 (Sadler's   **81**
Wells (USA) 132) [1998 NR 1999 8f² 7.1m³ 8.1m² 8m³ 9g 10v* 10d Oct 4] close-
coupled, rather unfurnished filly: first foal: dam, 2-y-o 7f winner and stayed 1¼m,
from good family: fairly useful performer: won maiden at Lingfield in September:
raced freely when below form in handicap final start: stays 1¼m: seems to act on any
going. *Sir Michael Stoute*

AUENKLANG (GER)   2 ch.c. (Feb 10) Big Shuffle (USA) 122 – Auenglocke   **111**
(GER) (Surumu (GER)) [1999 5s² 5g* 5.5g² 6g* Sep 3] approx. 26,000Y in
Germany: third foal: half-brother to German 1m winner Auenlowe (by Shirley
Heights): dam German 7f and 7.8f winner: won listed race at Hamburg (by ¾ length
from Chagall) in July and 5-runner Raab Karcher Baustoffe-Cup at Baden-Baden (by
4½ lengths from Arc Royal) in September: disputed lead until 2f out when 5 lengths
second of 5 to Rossini in Prix Robert Papin at Maisons-Laffitte in between: stays 6f:
blinkered all starts: joined Godolphin. *H. W. Hiller, Germany*

AUGUSTAN   8 b.g. Shareef Dancer (USA) 135 – Krishnagar (Kris 135) [1998 60:   **–**
12m 12s⁴ 9.9m⁴ 10.3g⁴ 12d⁴ 11.5g⁶ 11.6m⁶ 12.3g² 12m² 14.1f⁶ 12m⁵ 12d 9.9m⁵ 1999
11.5m 12d Jun 5] heavy-bodied gelding: has a markedly round action: modest
handicapper at 7 yrs: well beaten both starts in 1999: effective at 1¼m/1½m: acts on
firm and soft going: tried visored (not since 1996): has started slowly, and usually
held up. *S. Gollings*

AUNT DORIS   2 b.f. (Apr 24) Distant Relative 128 – Nevis 61 (Connaught 130)   **60 +**
[1999 6m 5g* 6m³ 6m Sep 6] 1,000Y: fourth foal: half-sister to 4-y-o Mountain
Magic and 6f (seller at 2 yrs) and 8.3f winner Naivasha (by Petong): dam
lightly-raced half-sister to Paris House: modest form: won seller at Leicester in
August: stays 6f: raced only on good/good to firm going. *J. Berry*

AUNT FLO (IRE)   3 b.f. Royal Academy (USA) 130 – Quinsigimond 71 (Form-   **99**
idable (USA) 125) [1998 85+: 6s² 6g² 6f 5.1m* 5g⁶ 6g⁴ 1999 6g² 7m⁵ 6d⁴ 6m³ 6m
6m* 6g 6d Oct 1] tall filly: useful performer: didn't have things go her way on several

occasions before winning 5-runner minor event at Newmarket in July by neck from Ellway Star: ran poorly both starts after: stays 6f: best efforts on good to firm ground: tends to idle in front and probably best with exaggerated waiting tactics: sold 34,000 gns in December. *M. L. W. Bell*

AUNTY ROSE (IRE)   2 b.f. (Apr 15) Caerleon (USA) 132 – Come On Rosi 77   **96 p** (Valiyar 129) [1999 7m* 8m³ 7g Oct 16] unfurnished filly: closely related to 5-y-o Generous Libra and 4-y-o Generous Rosi (both by Generous) and half-sister to very smart 7f/1m performer Bin Rosie and useful sprinter Shanghai Girl (both by Distant Relative): dam 6f winner: fairly useful form: won maiden at Newmarket in July: good efforts both subsequent starts, still green when third of 12 to Teggiano in May Hill Stakes at Doncaster and wintry in coat when seventh of 12 to Lahan in Rockfel Stakes (unruly stalls) at Newmarket: stays 1m: slowly away all 3 outings: should do better still. *J. L. Dunlop*

AURAMINE (IRE)   4 ch.g. Rainbows For Life (CAN) – Les Saintes (Kris 135)   **70 d** [1998 NR 1999 7f 8s 8m³ 8m⁵ 10.5s⁵ 9.9m 7.1m⁶ 10m Sep 16] IR 12,000Y, 44,000 2-y-o: workmanlike gelding: half-brother to several winners, including 1994 2-y-o 6f winner Santa Fan (by Taufan), later minor stakes winner in USA, and 1¼m winner Muntgiak (by Ela-Mana-Mou): dam French winner up to 11f from good family: fair maiden: well below par after third and fourth starts: stays 1m: acts on good to firm going. *J. L. Eyre*

AURA OF GRACE (USA)   2 b. or br.f. (Jan 22) Southern Halo (USA) – Avarice   **59** (USA) (Manila (USA)) [1999 6g Jun 22] $95,000F: fourth foal: half-sister to a winner in USA by Proper Reality: dam unraced half-sister to top-class 1½m performer Law Society: green and slowly away when seventh of 11 in maiden at Lingfield. *R. W. Armstrong*

AURATUM (USA)   2 ch.f. (Feb 13) Carson City (USA) – Gilded Lilly (USA)   **90 p** (What A Pleasure (USA)) [1999 6g* Jul 10] $230,000F, $700,000Y: half-sister to numerous winners in USA, notably 1992 champion 2-y-o colt Gilded Time (by Timeless Moment), winner of Breeders' Cup Juvenile: dam minor winner in USA: won minor event at Deauville in July in very good style by 2½ lengths from Fonage, making all and quickening clear from over 1f out: sure to improve, and likely to win more races. *D. R. Loder, France*

AURIGNY   4 b.f. Timeless Times (USA) 99 – Dear Glenda 66 (Gold Song 112)   **95** [1998 92: 6m 5m⁶ 5.1d 5.2g 5f 5g⁶ 1999 5m 5m 5g⁴ 5m⁵ 5m⁶ 5m³ 5m⁵ 5f* 5g 5d 5d   **a87** a5g⁵ a6g⁵ Dec 22] close-coupled filly: useful performer: below form after winning 3-runner minor event at Goodwood in July: seems to stay easy 6f: acts on firm and good to soft going, probably on all-weather: sometimes slowly away: effective from front or held up: often claimer ridden. *S. Dow*

AUSPICIOUS   3 b.f. Shirley Heights 130 – Blessed Event 117 (Kings Lake (USA)   **103** 133) [1998 92+: 7.5m² 8s⁵ 1999 10.2g* 11.9g⁴ 10d² 8m² 7.1d² a7g* Oct 16] angular filly: has a quick action: useful performer, lightly raced: landed odds in maiden at Bath (very reluctant stalls) in May: much better form in listed races next 2 starts when fourth at York (behind Innuendo) and Newmarket (sweating, 2 lengths behind Khibrah), off bridle long way out both times: effective at 1¼m/1½m: best effort on good to soft going. *Sir Michael Stoute*

AUSTIN POWERS (IRE)   3 b.c. Sadler's Wells (USA) 132 – Guess Again   **–** (GER) (Stradavinsky 121) [1998 NR 1999 10f⁶ Jul 8] 310,000Y: close-coupled, quite attractive colt: closely related to 2 winners in Ireland, including 1m winner Heike (by Glenstal), and half-brother to 3 winners in Ireland, including useful 2-y-o winners Cois Na Tine (at 5f to 1m in 1993) and Eva Luna (6f in 1994), both by Double Schwartz: dam, 1m winner, half-sister to top-class sprinter Double Form: 4/1, tailed-off last of 6 in maiden at Newmarket. *J. Noseda*

AUTOMATIC   3 b.g. Clantime 101 – Gentle Gypsy 94 (Junius (USA) 124) [1998   **76** 66p: 6g⁴ 1999 a8g³ a9.4g³ 7m 7m³ 7g² 7m² 8.5m³ 8d² 8m² 7.1d² a7g* Oct 16] fair performer: visored, won maiden at Wolverhampton in October, hanging right once asserting: likely to prove best at 7f/1m: acts on fibresand, yet to race on extremes of going on turf: consistent: sold 21,000 gns, sent to Singapore. *M. L. W. Bell*

AUTONOMY (IRE)   2 b.c. (May 16) Doyoun 124 – Debbie's Next (USA) 82   **100 p** (Arctic Tern (USA) 126) [1999 7.1d* 7.1g⁵ 8d* Oct 29] sixth foal: half-brother to several winners, including 7-y-o Nordinex, smart French/American 3-y-o 1m/1¼m winner Caffe Latte (by Seattle Dancer) and French middle-distance winner Debbie's Law (by Law Society): dam, maiden, stayed 1m: progressive form: won maiden at Sandown in August and minor event at Newmarket in October, settling well and asserting final 1f when beating Francesco Guardi by 1¼ lengths in 6-runner race on second occasion: will probably stay beyond 1m: likely to improve further. *M. L. W. Bell*

AUTUMN COVER   7 gr.g. Nomination 125 – Respray 64 (Rusticaro (FR) 124) **76** [1998 77, a–: 8g* 8.5m 8.3m 10.1s⁵ 10g 10g⁴ a10g 1999 8g³ 8g May 18] strong, **a–** lengthy gelding: fair performer on turf: better effort in handicaps in 1999 when close third of 29 to Scene at Ascot: stays 1¼m: has form on firm going, but best recent form on good ground: tried blinkered: sometimes flashes tail: often makes running: not one to trust implicitly. *P. R. Hedger*

AUTUMN LEAVES   3 b.f. Warning 136 – Misty Goddess (IRE) 63 (Godswalk **35** (USA) 130) [1998 NR 1999 8.2d 8.3d a8.5g a8.5g⁶ Dec 27] first foal: dam 7f (at 2 yrs) to 10.8f winner: poor maiden: form only on final start: should stay beyond 8.5f. *N. P. Littmoden*

AUTUMN RAIN (USA)   2 br.c. (Mar 15) Dynaformer (USA) – Edda (USA) **72 p** (Ogygian (USA)) [1999 7m⁵ 7.1s⁵ Sep 25] $85,000Y: rather leggy colt: first foal: dam won at up to 9f in USA at 4 yrs: encouraging fifth in maidens at York and Haydock, in steadily-run race on latter course: will be suited by 1m+: bandaged off-hind on debut: should improve. *E. A. L. Dunlop*

AUTUM ROUGE (IRE)   5 ch.m. Phardante (FR) 123 – Red Leaf (Carry Off 92) **–** [1998 NR 1999 8.1m Sep 9] 800 3-y-o: half-sister to 3 winners, including fairly useful Irish 6f to 1m winner Nordic Oak (by Nordico): dam unplaced on 5 starts in Ireland: well beaten in seller at Chepstow. *Mrs P. Ford*

AVANTI   3 gr.c. Reprimand 122 – Dolly Bevan 53 (Another Realm 118) [1998 –: **78** 6m 1999 8m 8g⁴ 7.1g* 8.1m² 7.6g Aug 24] half-brother to sprinter Oggi and 6f (at 2 yrs) and 7-y-o Pengamon (both fairly useful performers by Efisio): dam, 2-y-o 6f winner, half-sister to smart sprinter Pips Pride: fair performer: won handicap at Sandown in May: not disgraced in similar events after, found to be lame after final start: may prove best short of 1m: raced only on good/good to firm ground: sold 8,500 gns, joined Dr J. Naylor. *P. J. Makin*

AVARITIOUS   3 br.f. Avarice – Captain Bonnie 60 (Captain James 123) [1998 NR **–** 1999 6.1s Apr 27] half-sister to modest sprint winners Doesyoudoes (by Bay Express) and Check The Gate (by Blushing Scribe): dam, ran only at 2 yrs, placed over 5f: behind in Nottingham seller. *Miss J. F. Craze*

AVEIRO (IRE)   3 b.c. Darshaan 133 – Avila 76 (Ajdal (USA) 130) [1998 NR **–** 1999 8g 11.5g⁵ 12d³ 8m 10m Sep 16] big, good-topped colt: third foal: closely related to a winner in Austria by Shirley Heights and half-brother to 4-y-o Mama-San: dam, third once from 2 starts at 7f, half-sister to smart middle-distance colts Nomrood, Alleging and Monastery: little sign of ability: blinkered last 2 starts: sold 3,000 gns, joined Mrs D. Haine. *C. E. Brittain*

AVENGING ANGEL (IRE)   3 b.f. College Chapel 122 – Dromacomer Lady **84** (IRE) (Taufan (USA) 119) [1998 61: 5g⁶ 6m a7g a6s² 1999 a6g* Jan 13] best effort in maidens when winning at Wolverhampton by 8 lengths, making all: stayed 6f: acted on fibresand: dead. *N. P. Littmoden*

AVERHAM STAR   4 ch.g. Absalom 128 – Upper Sister (Upper Case (USA)) **–** [1998 –, a33: a8s⁴ a8g⁵ a8g⁴ a11g⁶ a8g⁴ a12g³ 8m a12g⁵ 6g a8.5g 1999 a7g⁶ a8g a12g a12g⁶ 5g a6g⁶ a7g 8f 10m 12.3d⁵ 10.5m Sep 3] bad maiden: had several trainers in 1999: tried blinkered/visored. *W. Clay*

AVERTI (IRE)   8 b.h. Warning 136 – Imperial Jade 105 (Lochnager 132) [1998 **104** 115: 5d 5m³ 5d 6f 5g 5f 6g³ 6m³ 5d² 1999 5f 5g 5v Oct 3] robust, attractive horse: smart performer at best: looking in good shape on return from stallion duties, useful form when seventh to Rudi's Pet in King George Stakes at Goodwood on reappearance: well held after in Nunthorpe Stakes at York and Prix de l'Abbaye de Longchamp: effective at 5f/6f: acts on firm and good to soft ground, probably on soft: usually held up. *W. R. Muir*

AVEZZANO   2 b.g. (May 10) Most Welcome 131 – Moushka (Song 132) [1999 **100 p**
5g⁶ 5m⁶ 6d* 6g* 7s* Oct 23] 1,000Y: leggy, workmanlike gelding: has a quick
action: fifth foal: half-brother to 3 winners, including useful but temperamental 5f
performer Mr Oscar (by Belfort) and fairly useful 5f (at 2 yrs) to 7f winner One
Singer (by Anshan): dam unraced: progressive form: won maiden at Ayr in
September and nurseries at York and Doncaster (came from some way off pace to
beat Eastways by 3 lengths) in October: will stay at least 1m: acts on soft ground:
sold to race in USA: already useful, and may well do better still. *W. McKeown*

AVONDALE GIRL (IRE)   3 ch.f. Case Law 113 – Battle Queen 85 (Kind of **73 +**
Hush 118) [1998 65: 5d³ 5.2g* 5f³ a5g⁶ 1999 a5g⁶ a6g⁴ a5g³ a6g² a5g* 5d³ 5s 6m⁶ **a67**
6m* 5m a5g Dec 21] small filly: fair performer: won seller at Wolverhampton in
March and ladies handicap at Thirsk (only second start since leaving C. Dwyer) in
June: off 6 months before well beaten final start: stays 6f, at least when conditions
aren't testing: acts on firm and good to soft ground, better form on fibresand than
equitrack. *M. Dods*

AVRO ANSON   11 b.g. Ardross 134 – Tremellick 87 (Mummy's Pet 125) [1998 **–**
61: 18d⁴ 1999 18d⁶ 16.2d May 8] big gelding: one-time very smart hurdler/smart
chaser: lightly raced on Flat (fair staying handicapper at best), well held both starts in
1999. *Miss J. A. Camacho*

AWAKE   2 ch.c. (Mar 22) First Trump 118 – Pluvial 90 (Habat 127) [1999 5g² 6m* **97 p**
6v* 6s⁴ Nov 22] half-brother to several winners, including sprinter Monaassib (by
Cadeaux Genereux) and 7f/1m performer Rain Burst (by Tolomeo), both smart: dam,
sprinting half-sister to very smart 1973 2-y-o Splashing, herself dam of Middle Park
winner Bassenthwaite: useful form: won maiden at Epsom in August and nursery at
Newbury (by 3½ lengths from First Blood) in October: 1½ lengths second to Zeiting
in listed race at Maisons-Laffitte final start, demoted to fourth after edging left: likely
to prove best at 6f/7f: acts on good to firm and heavy ground: seems sure to improve
further. *M. Johnston*

AWESOME VENTURE   9 b.g. Formidable (USA) 125 – Pine Ridge 80 (High **–**
Top 131) [1998 –, a41+: a7s⁴ a7g⁵ a7g³ a8g⁴ a8g⁶ a11g⁶ a8g⁴ a8g⁴ a8g⁵ a6g³ **a55**
a8g⁴ a6g⁵ a7g³ 6d a7g a7g⁴ 1999 a8g a6g⁵ a7g³ a8g³ a6g a8f⁴ a6g³ a7g a7g⁴
a6g⁶ a6g³ a7g² a8g⁴ a8g⁵ a7g⁵ 7s a8g a8g a11g⁶ 8g 8g a7g a7g 8m a11g⁵ Sep 28]
poor performer: effective at 6f to 1m: raced mainly on fibresand nowadays: tried
blinkered, effective visored or not: sold 500 gns. *M. C. Chapman*

AWTAAN (USA)   2 b.f. (Mar 3) Arazi (USA) 135 – Bashayer (USA) 103 (Mr **77**
Prospector (USA)) [1999 8.1d⁴ 8.2d³ Oct 21] second foal: sister to 3-y-o Rahayeb:
dam, 1m winner (including at 2 yrs) and second in Cheshire Oaks, half-sister to
Nashwan and Unfuwain: in frame in maidens at Sandown and Nottingham: will be
suited by 1¼m+: may still do better. *M. P. Tregoning*

AWWALIYA   3 b.f. Distant Relative 128 – El Rabab (USA) 70 (Roberto (USA) **66**
131) [1998 79: 6g² 7d² 1999 7v 9m 7m 6.8m⁵ 7m 6s² Oct 5] well-made filly: fair
maiden: stays 7f: acts on good to firm and good to soft going: visored third and final
(wandered) starts: sent to USA. *P. T. Walwyn*

AYEM (IRE)   4 ch.g. Sharp Victor (USA) 114 – Morning Crown (USA) (Chief's **69**
Crown (USA)) [1998 71: 7g⁵ 7s 8s⁶ 1999 20m 16.4m⁴ a16g⁴ Jul 31] IR 4,800Y:
close-coupled gelding: first foal: dam winning sprinter in USA: fair maiden: trained
by L. Browne in Ireland in 1998 (sold IR 3,000 gns): probably stays 2½m: acts on
good to firm and soft going, below form on equitrack final start: has been tongue tied:
successful over hurdles in September. *C. Weedon*

AYE READY   6 ch.g. Music Boy 124 – Cindy's Princess (Electric 126) [1998 NR **–**
1999 8.3g 5m May 6] of little account. *D. A. Nolan*

AYIDA (IRE)   3 b.f. Shernazar 131 – Flower Dell 72 (Wolver Hollow 126) [1998 **–**
NR 1999 11.5m 10d Oct 28] seventh reported foal: half-sister to poor plater here/
Swiss 1¼m winner Noble Tenor (by The Noble Player): dam (unraced) out of half-
sister to an Italian Oaks winner: well held in maiden (slowly away, pulled hard) and
seller. *G. L. Moore*

AZIHAAM (USA)   3 ch.f. Cozzene (USA) – Tatwij (USA) 94 (Topsider (USA)) **70**
[1998 –: 7.3g 8.2g a8g⁵ a8g⁶ 1999 a10g a10g* a10g* 10.8d² 9g⁵ 10.1g⁵ 10m²

10g Oct 11] fair handicapper: won twice at Lingfield in February: ran well when runner-up after: effective at 1¼m/11f: acts on good to firm going, good to soft and equitrack: blinkered after reappearance: ran in snatches final start: sold 11,000 gns. *N. A. Graham*

AZIMAH 3 b.f. Unfuwain (USA) 131 – Rafif (USA) 68 (Riverman (USA) 131) **75** [1998 NR 1999 10.2s 10.3m² 12m³ 10.5s² 10.4g⁴ 10d Nov 4] smallish, sturdy filly: second foal: sister to 4-y-o Kadir: dam 1¼m winner out of close relative of Ribblesdale winner Thawakib and half-sister to Celestial Storm: fair maiden: best efforts when placed: stays 1½m: acts on good to firm and soft going: sent to USA. *A. C. Stewart*

AZIRA 2 ch.f. (May 3) Arazi (USA) 135 – Free City (USA) (Danzig (USA)) [1999 **45** 6d⁵ a6g⁶ Nov 8] fourth foal: half-sister to a winner in Belgium by Suave Dancer: dam French 1m winner from family of Chief's Crown: poor form in maidens at Brighton and Lingfield. *P. R. Chamings*

AZIZZI 7 ch.g. Indian Ridge 123 – Princess Silca Key 61 (Grundy 137) [1998 –: **99** 5.6g 6s 1999 7d⁵ 7m⁴ 6v⁵ 5d³ 5d* 5s³ 5d* Oct 28] stocky gelding: useful performer: won in large fields at Newmarket (claimer) in August and Pontefract and Windsor (both handicaps) in October, last-named under well-judged ride by 1½ lengths from Classy Cleo, racing alone in centre from halfway: has form at 7.6f, but best at 5f: acts on any going: usually races up with pace. *C. R. Egerton*

AZOUZ PASHA (USA) 3 b.c. Lyphard (USA) 132 – Empress Club (ARG) **113** (Farnesio (ARG)) [1998 68p: 7.3g 1999 10m* 8m⁴ 9.9f* 11.6m² 12m* Sep 10] small, quite attractive colt: smart performer: successful in maiden at Lingfield in June, 17-runner £38,000 handicap at Goodwood (from West Escape) in July and 5-runner listed race at Doncaster (visored, readily beat Algunnaas by 2½ lengths) in September: good second to New Abbey in minor event at Windsor penultimate start: stays 1½m: raced only on good ground or firmer: hung left penultimate start: held up: may still do better, and well worth his place in pattern company. *H. R. A. Cecil*

AZULA 3 b.f. Bluebird (USA) 125 – Dimant Rose (USA) (Tromos 134) [1998 NR **80** 1999 8.3g 10g* 10.1m⁴ 10s 10d Nov 4] 25,000F: half-sister to 1¼m winner Major Yaasi (by Arctic Tern) and a winner in Italy by Rahy: dam unraced half-sister to Rainbow Quest: fairly useful performer: comfortable winner of maiden at Lingfield (penultimate run for P. Chapple-Hyam) in June: not sure to stay beyond 1¼m: acts on good to firm and good to soft going. *H. Morrison*

AZUR (IRE) 2 b.f. (May 3) Brief Truce (USA) 126 – Bayadere (USA) 61 (Green **76 p** Dancer (USA) 132) [1999 7g 7g* Oct 19] 18,000Y: fourth foal: half-sister to 3-y-o Petal and 4-y-o Bryony Brind: dam staying maiden: won maiden at Lingfield in October by 2½ lengths from Cracow, forging clear final 1f: will stay at least 1¼m+: type to progress further with racing, and should make a fairly useful handicapper at least. *J. R. Fanshawe*

Volvo Contracts Globetrotter Stakes (Handicap), Goodwood—
Azouz Pasha (right) continues on the upgrade as he comes out on top in a strongly-contested affair,
beating West Escape (No.15) and Prairie Wolf (closest to winner)

AZZAN (USA) 3 b. or br.g. Gulch (USA) – Dixieland Dream (USA) (Dixieland **75 §**
Band (USA)) [1998 79P: 6s 6m 6d⁵ 1999 8d⁴ 8m 8.2m⁴ 8m 8m a9.4g⁶ Dec 15] **a57 §**
unfurnished gelding: reportedly fractured cannon-bone prior to debut: fair maiden:
failed by long way to confirm abundant 2-y-o promise, sold from J. Dunlop 3,800
gns before final start: stays 1m: best efforts on good to soft going: tried blinkered: has
worn tongue strap: moody and needs treating with caution. *T. Keddy*

B

BAAJIL 4 b.g. Marju (IRE) 127 – Arctic River (FR) (Arctic Tern (USA) 126) **–**
[1998 73, a–: 7m³ 7d⁵ a8g⁴ 1999 a10g² a10g² a10g⁴ 10v 8.2f a10g* a10g⁴ a10g⁶ Dec **a65**
22] small gelding: fair performer: off over 5 months before winning minor event at
Lingfield in November: stays easy 1¼m: acts on equitrack, no form on turf since
second 3-y-o start: often races prominently. *D. J. S. Cosgrove*

BAALBEK 3 b.f. Barathea (IRE) 127 – Temple Row (Ardross 134) [1998 NR 1999 **76**
8g⁵ 10.5m 8m⁵ 7m⁴ 8.3m² 8m 8s* 8.1d³ 8d³ 10d⁶ Nov 4] good-topped, attractive
filly: half-sister to several winners including fairly useful 10.5f and 1½m winner
Mount Row (by Alzao) and 13f winner Back Row (by In The Wings): dam unraced
half-sister to smart sprinter Colmore Row out of Irish 1000 Guineas winner Front
Row: fair performer: won maiden at Brighton in August: creditable efforts after,
including in handicaps: stays 1¼m: acts on soft and good to firm going: joined
E. James. *L. M. Cumani*

BABY BARRY 2 b.c. (Mar 29) Komaite (USA) – Malcesine (IRE) 46 (Auction **78**
Ring (USA) 123) [1999 5.1s a5g² 5s² a5g³ 5d⁶ 5.1m² 5m³ 5m³ 6d⁴ 6g 5g* 6d² Oct
22] 3,000Y: good-topped colt: third foal: brother to 4-y-o Piccolo Cativo and a 5.5f
to 1m winner in Austria/Germany: dam 1m seller winner: fair performer: generally
progressive form: won 22-runner maiden at Redcar in October: very good second
of 18 to Chagall in sales race at Doncaster final outing: effective at 5f and 6f: acts
on fibresand, good to firm and soft ground: tried visored, blinkered last 3 starts:
sometimes hangs and looks awkward ride: usually races prominently. *Mrs G. S. Rees*

BABY ROCKET (IRE) 2 ch.f. (May 25) Imperial Frontier (USA) 112 – Boher- **–**
bawn (IRE) 43 (Shernazar 131) [1999 5.7h 6v 7g a5g⁴ Nov 27] 2,100 2-y-o: first
foal: dam, Irish maiden, stayed 1¼m: no sign of ability. *R. Hannon*

BABY SPICE 4 ch.f. Then Again 126 – Starawak 68 (Star Appeal 133) [1998 –, **48**
a51: 7v 8.2s 6m 8m a8g⁵ 10.2d a7g* a7g a7g 1999 a8.5g 8.3d⁵ 8.3g³ 9.2d
10.3m 7.7m 8.3m⁴ 8.3s 8.1m⁴ Sep 9] plain filly: poor performer: stays 1m: acts on
fibresand, good to soft and good to firm going: blinkered (no form) twice:
inconsistent. *R. F. Johnson Houghton*

BACCHUS 5 b.g. Prince Sabo 123 – Bonica 56 (Rousillon (USA) 133) [1998 –: **73**
6g 6g 1999 8d 7.5v 7.5m* 7.5m⁵ 8.1d 7.5g* 7g⁵ Oct 14] workmanlike gelding: fair
handicapper: won at Beverley in July (seller) and August (gambled on): stays 7.5f:
best form on good going or firmer: carries head high: sometimes slowly away:
inconsistent. *Miss J. A. Camacho*

BACHELOR 3 b.c. In The Wings 128 – So Romantic (IRE) 97 (Teenoso (USA) **79 p**
135) [1998 NR 1999 10d 10d⁶ 14.1m³ 14.1g² 14.1v* Sep 29] fourth foal: half-brother
to 4-y-o Ireland's Eye: dam, 7f to 9f winner, half-sister to Lowther and Nassau
winner Ela Romara: progressive form: favourite, won handicap at Salisbury in good
style by 4 lengths: should stay 2m: acts on heavy ground: capable of better still.
M. A. Jarvis

BACHELORS PAD 5 b.g. Pursuit of Love 124 – Note Book 94 (Mummy's Pet **67**
125) [1998 82: 7s 7d 7m⁵ 8.3d³ 8m 8g 7m⁴ 7f² 7g 1999 7g 8d⁶ 8d³ 10.3m² 10d⁴ 8.5d
10m 8m 8m⁵ 8g 7.5g² 8.3m⁵ 9.1d² 10.4d Oct 7] leggy gelding: has plenty of knee
action: fair nowadays: runner-up in handicaps/claimer at 5 yrs: effective at 7.5f to
1¼m: acts on good to firm and good to soft going: has run creditably blinkered:
sometimes looks none too keen: inconsistent. *D. Nicholls*

Richmond Stakes, Goodwood—Bachir gives Sheikh Mohammed his first winner in the race, defeating Hunting Lion (striped sleeves) and Ginola's Magic in course-record time

BACH (IRE)   2 b.c. (Mar 15) Caerleon (USA) 132 – Producer (USA) 130 (Nashua)   **103 p**
[1999 7g* 7m* Jun 17] IR 200,000Y: strong, good-quartered colt: brother to fairly useful maiden Shalimar Garden, closely related to 2 winners, including useful Irish 6f and 1¼m winner Dancing Goddess (by Nijinsky) and half-brother to 3 winners, including Oaks d'Italia third Las Flores (by Sadler's Wells): dam second in Irish Oaks but better at shorter (won 7f Prix de la Foret and 9f Prix de l'Opera): won maiden at Gowran in May and listed Chesham Stakes (by ½ length from Hastenby, edging right) at Royal Ascot, useful form in latter, but not seen again: should stay at least 1¼m: sent to USA: should make a smart colt. *A. P. O'Brien, Ireland*

BACHIR (IRE)   2 b.c. (Mar 8) Desert Style (IRE) 121 – Morning Welcome (IRE)   **106**
(Be My Guest (USA) 126) [1999 6.1m* 6f* 6s³ 7d³ Sep 18] IR 31,000F, IR 50,000Y: strong, good-topped colt: has plenty of scope: fluent mover: fourth foal: half-brother to a 6f seller winner by Mac's Imp and an Italian 1m winner by Statoblest: dam, Irish maiden who probably stayed 1½m, half-sister to useful Italian performers Sotabrasciet (sprinter) and Sole Che Sorgi (miler): useful form: won maiden at Chepstow and Richmond Stakes at Goodwood (beat Hunting Lion 1½ lengths) in July: progressed again when third to Fasliyev in Prix Morny at Deauville (beaten 6½ lengths) and to Giant's Causeway in Prix de la Salamandre at Longchamp (took good hold, beaten 4 lengths) last 2 starts, blanketed for stalls entry both times: likely to prove best up to 1m: acts on firm and soft ground: joined Godolphin. *J. H. M. Gosden*

BACKCLOTH (IRE)   3 b.g. Scenic 128 – Traumerei (GER) 70 (Surumu (GER))   **103 p**
[1998 70p: 7d 8d³ 1999 10g³ 11.8v* 11.6g³ 10.2m² 10d* 10d* 10d² Oct 9] angular gelding: useful handicapper: won at Leicester in April, Sandown in August and Pontefract in September (last 2 comfortably): good second to Monsajem in rated stakes at Ascot final start, though seemed to hang fire initially: probably best around 1¼m: goes well on ground softer than good: sold 110,000 gns, sent to Saudi Arabia: open to further improvement. *J. L. Dunlop*

BACKEND CHARLIE   5 b.g. Sylvan Express 117 – Red Eska (Smackover 107)   –
[1998 NR 1999 12m⁶ 13.8g⁵ Jun 4] first foal: dam unraced: poor form in bumpers: no promise on Flat. *B. W. Murray*

BACKHANDER (IRE)   7 b.g. Cadeaux Genereux 131 – Chevrefeuille 87 (Ile de Bourbon (USA) 133) [1998 45d: a6g² a7g 6g⁶ a7g a7g 6g⁶ 6.9d⁴ 7.1g 7.5d 6m a8.5g 7m 8.1d 1999 a6g a6g⁴ a8.5g Jan 20] no longer of any account. *M. Waring*

BACKSCRATCHER   5 b.g. Backchat (USA) 98 – Tiernee Quintana (Artaius   **36**
(USA) 129) [1998 –: 15.8d⁴ 1999 15.8m⁵ 12s⁶ 12g Oct 16] poor form in bumpers and in sellers/claimer on Flat. *S. Gollings*

97

BADAAYER (USA) 3 b. or br.f. Silver Hawk (USA) 123 – Katiba (USA) 99 **105** (Gulch (USA)) [1998 NR 1999 8m* 10.2m⁴ 10g* 10d³ 12s² Nov 6] tall, rather angular filly: second foal: half-sister to useful 1m winner Kariyh (by Shadeed): dam 6f (at 2 yrs) and 7f winner who stayed 1¼m: useful performer: won maiden at Salisbury in August, and minor event at Nottingham in September: good efforts in listed races at Newmarket (2 lengths third to Khibrah) and Doncaster (2 lengths second to Maylane) last 2 starts: stayed 1½m: acted on soft going and on good to firm: stud. *J. L. Dunlop*

BADAGARA 3 b.g. Warning 136 – Badawi (USA) 103 (Diesis 133) [1998 81: 7g² **97** 7g³ 7d⁵ 1999 8m* 8.1s³ 10m Jul 23] leggy, angular gelding: useful handicapper: won rated stakes at Newbury in April: below best both starts after: stays 1m, possibly not 1¼m: acts on good to firm going. *C. E. Brittain*

BADRINATH (IRE) 5 b.g. Imperial Frontier (USA) 112 – Badedra (Kings Lake **66 §** (USA) 133) [1998 58: a10g* a10g² a10g a8g³ a7g 8g* 7g 10m 10m* 11.5d² a12g **a– §** 1999 a12g a10g 10.1g 10m⁴ 10d² 11.9d 10f³ 10d⁵ a10g Nov 24] fair performer: trained first 2 starts by J. Pearce: placed in handicap/minor event afterwards: effective at 1¼m, probably at 11.5f: acts on all-weather, firm and good to soft going: sometimes races freely and finds little. *H. J. Collingridge*

BADR RAINBOW 2 b.c. (Mar 14) Rainbow Quest (USA) 134 – Baaderah (IRE) **85** 102 (Cadeaux Genereux 131) [1999 7.1m 7.1m 7s⁴ 8d² Oct 22] has a free, round action: first foal: dam 6f winner (including at 2 yrs) who stayed 1m: fairly useful maiden: best efforts last 2 starts, ½-length second of 12 to Lonely Place in nursery at Doncaster on final one: should stay 1¼m: acts on soft ground. *M. A. Jarvis*

BAFFIN BAY 4 b.c. Bustino 136 – Surf Bird (Shareef Dancer (USA) 135) [1998 **87** 100: 12d⁴ 14g⁵ 12g⁵ 13.9f 12g 12g 1999 11.9d 10f 12m 15.9d 12f² 12d Sep 28] strong colt: carries condition: fairly useful handicapper: short-head second at Thirsk in September: ran poorly final start (subsequently sold 22,000 gns): probably best at 1½m to 1¾m: acts on firm and good to soft going: blinkered last 3 starts: wore tongue strap once at 3 yrs. *H. R. A. Cecil*

BAHAMAS (IRE) 2 b.g. (Jan 26) Barathea (IRE) 127 – Rum Cay (USA) 75 (Our **– p** Native (USA)) [1999 7.1m 7.1s 6s 7d Oct 21] 110,000Y: good-topped gelding: has scope: sixth foal: half-brother to several winners, notably 6-y-o Persian Punch: dam 14.6f and bumper winner: weak in betting and always behind in maidens and nursery: sort to do much better over 1¼m+ at 3 yrs. *Sir Mark Prescott*

BAHAMIAN BANDIT 3 b.c. First Trump 118 – Sound of The Sea 91 (Wind- **111** jammer (USA)) [1998 99p: 6f⁵ 6g* 1999 7g² 8m⁶ 8g 8f² 10m Aug 28] close-coupled, quite attractive colt: smart performer: won minor event at Newmarket in April: best efforts when 4 lengths sixth to Island Sands in 2000 Guineas at Newmarket and 3 lengths second of 4 to Slip Stream in listed race at Goodwood: stays 1m, probably not 1¼m: raced only on good going or firmer: sold to race in Dubai. *R. Hannon*

BAHAMIAN PIRATE (USA) 4 ch.g. Housebuster (USA) – Shining Through **75 p** (USA) (Deputy Minister (CAN)) [1998 63p: 7d⁵ 8m 5m 6g² 5m⁶ 1999 a6f⁴ a7g³ a6g² 5d* Aug 14] sturdy gelding: fair performer: improved on return from 6-month break (gelded and bone chips removed from knees) to win maiden at Ripon, making most and hanging right: likely to prove best at 5f/6f: acts on fibresand, yet to race on extremes of going on turf: probably capable of better still. *D. Nicholls*

BAHAMIAN PRINCE (IRE) 2 b.g. (Apr 26) Night Shift (USA) – Fairy Water **–** 88 (Warning 136) [1999 7.1d a6g Dec 22] 32,000F, IR 130,000Y: second foal: dam Irish 1m winner: well beaten in maidens at Sandown (for H. Cecil) and Lingfield (got worst of kickback), slowly away each time. *J. Noseda*

BAHIA BLANCA SUN (IRE) 4 b.g. Tirol 127 – Wild Applause (IRE) 71 **55** (Sadler's Wells (USA) 132) [1998 –: 12g⁴ 10v⁵ 1999 a14g² Mar 10] modest maiden, lightly raced: stays 1¾m: acts on fibresand. *J. L. Eyre*

BAHRAIN (IRE) 3 ch.c. Lahib (USA) 129 – Twin Island (IRE) (Standaan (FR) **69** 118) [1998 –: 6v 1999 8s⁵ 7m May 22] stocky colt: lightly-raced maiden: form only when fifth at Newbury. *A. P. Jarvis*

BAILEYS BLACK TIE 3 b.g. Suave Dancer (USA) 136 – Three Stars 93 (Star **67** Appeal 133) [1998 NR 1999 10f⁶ 10d 10d* 10.9s 13m 10g* 10.4f Sep 2] 26,000F,

8,000Y: leggy, sparely-made gelding: has a round action: half-brother to several winners at 1¼m+, notably Irish Oaks winner Bolas (by Unfuwain): dam 1½m winner from staying family: fair performer: won sellers at Ripon in July and August (handicap): ran poorly final start: should stay at least 1½m. *M. Johnston*

BAILEYS FIRECAT   2 b.f. (Feb 12) Catrail (USA) 123 – Dazzling Fire (IRE)   **67** 78 (Bluebird (USA) 125) [1999 5g 5m³ May 24] IR 19,000Y: third foal: half-sister to 3-y-o 6f winner Mohawk (5.5f winner in Norway, by Indian Ridge): dam 1½m winner: better effort in maidens when third of 9 at Leicester: will be well suited by 6f+: looked open to further improvement. *M. Johnston*

BAILEYS PRIZE (USA)   2 ch.c. (May 25) Mister Baileys 123 – Mar Mar (USA)   **67** (Forever Casting (USA)) [1999 6g⁴ 7g⁵ Oct 16] $30,000F: half-brother to several minor winners in USA: dam US Grade 3 8.5f winner: fair form in maidens at York and Catterick in October: should stay 1m. *M. Johnston*

BAILEY'S WHIRLWIND (USA)   2 b.f. (Jan 28) Mister Baileys 123 – Tornado   **88 +** Cat (USA) (Storm Cat (USA)) [1999 6.1m 6m* 6s* 6d Sep 28] $20,000Y: first foal: dam, winning sprinter in USA, out of half-sister to very smart Asteroid Field: fairly useful form: easy winner of minor events at Windsor (from Out of Africa) in August and Yarmouth (beat Distinctly East by 1¾ lengths) in September: bandaged near-hind, twelfth of 14 in Cheveley Park Stakes at Newmarket final start: likely to prove best at 6f/7f: acts on soft going and on good to firm. *M. L. W. Bell*

BAILIWICK FRONTIER (IRE)   8 b.g. Imperial Frontier (USA) 112 – Twilight   **65** In Paris (Kampala 120) [1998 –: 9m 10s 1999 8m⁴ 8g 10g 7.8f⁶ 9g⁶ a8g 10d Nov 1] first foal: dam unraced: fair handicapper: left J. Geoghegan in Ireland after fifth start: well beaten for new stable: stays 1¼m: acts on firm and soft ground: blinkered once at 4 yrs. *D. Carroll*

BAISSE D'ARGENT (IRE)   3 b.g. Common Grounds 118 – Fabulous Pet (Some-   **–** thingfabulous (USA)) [1998 73p: 7m 6m⁴ 8d* 9999 10g 11.8v 12m⁶ 14.1g 10m Aug 23] leggy, useful-looking gelding: fair winner at 2 yrs: well held in handicaps in 1999, though successful over hurdles in September and November: should stay 1¼m: blinkered final start. *D. J. S. Cosgrove*

BAJAN BELLE (IRE)   2 b.f. (Apr 25) Efisio 120 – With Love (Be My Guest   **72** (USA) 126) [1999 5f³ 5m* Jul 16] IR 6,600F, 5,000Y: third foal: half-sister to fairly useful 1998 2-y-o 7f/1m winner Maybe Special (later won in USA, by Then Again): dam once-raced half-sister to smart 1986 2-y-o 6f/7f winner Genghiz: made all in 6-runner maiden at Carlisle in July by 2½ lengths from Shalarise despite carrying head awkwardly and drifting left: looked likely to improve again. *M. Johnston*

BAJAN BROKER (IRE)   2 br.f. (Apr 5) Turtle Island (IRE) 123 – Foxrock   **66** (Ribero 126) [1999 6.8d⁴ 7g³ Oct 19] IR 12,000Y: tall filly: closely related to 3 winners by Fairy King, including an Irish 1m/9f winner: dam Irish middle-distance staying maiden: modest form in maidens at Warwick and Lingfield: should stay at least 1m. *J. E. Banks*

BAJAN SUNSET (IRE)   2 ch.c. (Apr 13) Mujtahid (USA) 118 – Dubai Lady 78   **–** (Kris 135) [1999 8d Oct 15] 18,000Y: strong, long-backed, angular colt: seventh foal: half-brother to 3-y-o Descant and smart 1m (at 2 yrs) and 1¼m winner Ela-Aristokrati (by Danehill): dam, middle-distance maiden, half-sister to smart Bluegrass Prince: backward and green, always behind in maiden at Newmarket. *J. D. Bethell*

BAKKAR (IRE)   5 b.g. Darshaan 133 – Bayyasa (IRE) (Caerleon (USA) 132)   **82 ?** [1998 NR 1999 18.7m 16.1m Jun 26] compact gelding: first foal: dam Irish 1½m winner: useful form on Flat at 3 yrs for J. Oxx in Ireland: fairly useful over hurdles in 1998/9 (reportedly had breathing operation): fair seventh in Chester Cup, better effort back on Flat: may prove best around 1¾m/2m: visored and wore tongue strap in 1999: returned to Ireland with M. Vaughan. *T. D. Easterby*

BALA   4 ch.f. Casteddu 111 – Baladee (Mummy's Pet 125) [1998 –: 6.1g 6.1s 1999   **–** 5d 6m 6m Jun 24] lengthy filly: disappointing maiden: tends to hang. *N. E. Berry*

BALA HASAD   2 b.c. (Jan 29) Elmaamul (USA) 125 – Astern (USA) 67 (Polish   **71** Navy (USA)) [1999 8v⁴ 8d 7v Oct 25] first foal: dam, 1m winner, closely related to useful 7f winner Dawson Place: twice failed to confirm promise of debut in maiden at Salisbury: should stay 1¼m: raced only on ground softer than good. *M. P. Tregoning*

BALANAK (USA) 8 b.g. Shahrastani (USA) 135 – Banque Privee (USA) 78 (Private Account (USA)) [1998 NR 1999 16.4d⁴ 16.4g² 18.2s³ 17.2s Sep 27] second foal: dam 1½m winner: won maiden from 3 starts for J. Oxx in Ireland at 3 yrs: fair handicapper in 1999: stays 2¼m: acts on soft going: visored last 2 starts, running poorly final one. *D. R. Gandolfo* **66**

BALANITA (IRE) 4 b.g. Anita's Prince 126 – Ballybannon 76 (Ballymore 123) [1998 82, a53: 6g 6g* 7m 6s a7g⁴ a6g⁶ 1999 7m² 7g 7m a7g Nov 11] fairly useful handicapper, modest on all-weather: stays 7f: acts on good to firm ground (probably on soft) and all-weather: races prominently: inconsistent. *B. Palling* **81 a55**

BALFOUR (IRE) 2 b.c. (Mar 22) Green Desert (USA) 127 – Badawi (USA) 103 (Diesis 133) [1999 6d⁶ 7.1m 7s Sep 29] third foal: brother to 5-y-o Saguaro and half-brother to 3-y-o Badagara: dam 1m/9f winner: modest maiden: failed to see race out and carried head to one side final start: may prove best short of 7f. *C. E. Brittain* **59**

BALI BATIK (IRE) 2 b.g. (Apr 14) Barathea (IRE) 127 – Miss Garuda 94 (Persian Bold 123) [1999 6f Jul 28] quite attractive gelding: sixth foal: half-brother to 8.5f winner Pampered Guest (by Be My Guest) and 1¼m winner Indonesian (by Alzao): dam, 2-y-o 7f winner, stayed 1¼m: burly, well beaten in maiden at Goodwood: should do better. *G. Wragg* **– p**

BALI DANCE 4 br.f. Rambo Dancer (CAN) 107 – Baliana 75 (Midyan (USA) 124) [1998 66: a7g a8g⁶ 7d 7g⁴ 8d* 8.1g³ 8m⁵ 8m⁴ 8d⁶ 8d⁵ 1999 7m 8g 8s 8d 10s Nov 1] close-coupled filly: poor performer: stays 1m: acts on firm going, soft and equitrack: tried blinkered at 2 yrs. *C. B. B. Booth* **–**

BALIDARE 2 b.f. (Jan 3) King's Signet (USA) 110 – Baligay 84 (Balidar 133) [1999 6m 5v Sep 24] robust, lengthy filly: third foal: half-sister to 1m (seller at 2 yrs) and 8.7f (in Sweden) winner Bali-Pet (by Tina's Pet): dam effective at 5f to 7f: well beaten in maidens. *M. J. Weeden* **–**

BALISADA 3 ch.f. Kris 135 – Balnaha 67 (Lomond (USA) 128) [1998 85p: 6g² 6g³ 7v* 1999 8g² 8m* 8m² 8f⁴ 8s⁴ Sep 26] **115**

Balisada's victory in the Coronation Stakes at Royal Ascot had many similarities with that of Rebecca Sharp for the same connections in 1997. Both had won just one race, in maiden company, both started at a big price, Rebecca Sharp at 25/1 and Balisada at 16/1, both showed a splendid turn of foot to triumph, and neither managed to win again during the season.

Balisada ran three times as a two-year-old, being placed in maidens before winning one decisively at Lingfield. Always held in high regard by her trainer, Balisada was prevented from tackling the One Thousand Guineas because of a set-back and she made her reappearance in a listed race at Goodwood towards the end of May. Showing improved form there, she finished two lengths second to Hawriyah, taking a strong hold and keeping on without being given an unduly hard time. Rebecca Sharp had made the Guineas line-up, finishing thirteenth of fifteen, and in the Coronation she took on the winner of that classic, Sleepytime, and the Irish One Thousand Guineas winner Classic Park. The latest Guineas winner, Wince, was an absentee from the Coronation Stakes, but the nine-runner field included the filly who had chased her home at Newmarket, Wannabe Grand, who started favourite. There were also two classic winners in Hula Angel (Irish One Thousand Guineas) and Valentine Waltz (third in the Guineas before collecting the Poule d'Essai des Pouliches), as well as Golden Silca, who had finished second to Hula Angel, and Hawriyah. In a race run at a muddling pace, Balisada made them all look leaden footed. Dropped out and still with just one behind her entering the straight, she was moved to the outside while some of her rivals were getting in each other's way and produced sparkling acceleration to cut down Golden Silca and win going away by a length and three quarters. Wannabe Grand and Valentine Waltz dead-heated for third, just behind the runner-up, with Hula Angel only eighth. There were some hard-luck stories—the stewards found that Golden Silca had

Coronation Stakes, Royal Ascot—a repeat of 1997 as trainer Geoff Wragg wins with an outsider; in a muddling race, Balisada (No.1) produces a splendid turn of speed; it's tight for the places with Golden Silca (blaze), Valentine Waltz (hidden), Wannabe Grand (white sleeves) and Pescara (rail) all in the hunt

interfered with Valentine Waltz—but Balisada scored so emphatically that few observers questioned her right to be seen as a worthy winner.

Few would have expected Balisada to fail to win again, but that's how it turned out. She ran well under a penalty in the Falmouth Stakes at Newmarket, failing to cope with the late burst of French filly Ronda, who beat her by just over a length receiving 6 lb, but her displays in the Sussex Stakes at Goodwood and Queen Elizabeth II Stakes at Ascot were lacklustre. At Goodwood she flashed her tail repeatedly at the start and never threatened to take a hand, ending up around seven lengths fourth of eight to Aljabr, and in the Queen Elizabeth II Stakes—a race in which Rebecca Sharp had been an unlucky runner-up to Air Express—she was routine dope tested after finishing nearly thirty lengths last of four to Dubai Millennium, having again been fractious beforehand. The soft ground was probably a factor here, as, although her maiden win had come on heavy, both her best runs had been on good to firm. Balisada, whose form was some way behind Rebecca Sharp's, has been retired to stud, where she will visit Sadler's Wells—the same stallion Rebecca Sharp was covered by in 1999.

	Kris (ch 1976)	Sharpen Up (ch 1969)	Atan
			Rocchetta
		Doubly Sure (b 1971)	Reliance II
Balisada (ch.f. 1996)			Soft Angels
	Balnaha (ch 1990)	Lomond (b 1980)	Northern Dancer
			My Charmer
		On Show (br 1978)	Welsh Pageant
			African Dancer

Balisada, a sturdy filly with a quick action who tended to take a strong hold, is the eleventh Group 1 or Grade 1 winner for her veteran sire Kris. She is not the first member of her family to contest the Coronation Stakes. Her dam's smart sister Inchmurrin, winner of the Child Stakes, ran second in 1988 and a half-sister, Guest Artiste, finished third the following year. Balisada's dam,

Balnaha, sold in foal to Deploy for 42,000 guineas the year Balisada was foaled and for 400,000 guineas in foal to Kris in December, was a moderate performer on the course, winning a one-mile maiden race at Carlisle from four starts. Balisada is her only winner from three foals of racing age; her foal by Kris fetched 220,000 guineas in December. The grandam On Show, a daughter of Cheshire Oaks and Park Hill Stakes winner African Dancer, was suited by middle distances, putting up her best effort when second in the November Handicap. On Show has excelled at stud and is responsible for eight winners overall, including Mill Reef winner Welney, a colt of similar merit to Inchmurrin, who has herself done well at stud, producing two stakes performers. The better of that pair was Inchinor, who won the Greenham and the Hungerford Stakes and was placed in the Dewhurst and Sussex Stakes. Inchmurrin's very promising two year-old Inchlonaig won the valuable Tattersalls Houghton Sales Stakes in the autumn and has been bought by Godolphin. *G. Wragg*

BALI-STAR   4 b.g. Alnasr Alwasheek 117 – Baligay 84 (Balidar 133) [1998 NR 1999 7s 6m 6g Jun 12] second foal: half-brother to 1m (seller at 2 yrs) and 8.7f (in Sweden) winner Bali-Pet (by Tina's Pet): dam won at 5f to 7f: no form in maidens. *M. J. Weeden*   **–**

BALLA D'AIRE (IRE)   4 b. or br.g. Balla Cove 119 – Silius (Junius (USA) 124) [1998 59d, a48?: 8.3g 10g⁴ 12f 14.1f 10m 8d a10g a16g⁴ 1999 a16g⁴ a16g May 29] leggy gelding: disappointing maiden: blinkered final start. *B. R. Johnson*   **–**

BALLADONIA   3 b.f. Primo Dominie 121 – Susquehanna Days (USA) 68 (Chief's Crown (USA)) [1998 79p: 7d² 7d² 1999 8.3m² 9g* 10d⁴ 10.1m³ 10.2m⁴ 10s 12v² 12d⁴ Oct 14] smallish, leggy filly: useful performer: won maiden at Goodwood in May: in frame in varied events (placed in listed races): creditable fourth to Katiykha in rated stakes at Newmarket final start: stays 1½m: very best form on going softer than good. *Lady Herries*   **101**

BALLASILLA   4 b.f. Puissance 110 – Darussalam 78 (Tina's Pet 121) [1998 –, a50: 8f 6g a7g⁶ a6g⁵ a5g a5g a6g⁴ a5g 1999 a5g⁵ a5g 5.1s Apr 27] poor maiden handicapper: stays 6f: acts on all-weather: tried blinkered. *B. Palling*   **– a45**

BALLET HIGH (IRE)   6 b.g. Sadler's Wells (USA) 132 – Marie d'Argonne (FR) 104 (Jefferson 129) [1998 NR 1999 16m³ Apr 16] tall, sparely-made gelding: fair maiden: first run on Flat since 3 yrs (though winning hurdler in interim), third in handicap at Newbury: stays 2m: raced only on good/good to firm going on Flat (has form on heavy over hurdles). *R. Dickin*   **76**

BALLET-K   5 ch.m. Gunner B 126 – Nicolene 91 (Nice Music 115) [1998 NR 1999 9.9m 10.2d³ 10g⁴ 17.2g* 16.1m Jun 26] sixth foal: half-sister to winners over jumps/in points: dam 1¼m/1½m winner: useful bumper winner: fairly useful on Flat: won handicap at Bath in June by short head: below form in Northumberland Plate final start: stays 17f. *J. Neville*   **80**

BALLET MASTER (USA)   3 ch.c. Kingmambo (USA) 125 – Danse Royale (IRE) 112 (Caerleon (USA) 132) [1998 92P: 7s* 1999 8.1s⁴ Apr 23] impressive winner of maiden at Yarmouth in 1998: again odds on, only fourth of 5 in minor event at Sandown only outing in 1999, beaten 4 lengths by Little Rock: should stay at least 1m: sold 17,000 gns in October, joined M. W. Easterby. *H. R. A. Cecil*   **84**

BALLETS RUSSES (IRE)   2 b.f. (Apr 12) Marju (IRE) 127 – Elminya (IRE) (Sure Blade (USA) 130) [1999 6d⁵ 7d 8.3d Oct 28] 30,000Y: workmanlike filly: fourth foal: half-sister to fairly useful 1997 2-y-o 6f/7f winner Belle de Nuit (by Statoblest), a 7f (at 2 yrs) to 1½m winner (by Mujadil and winning staying hurdler Pleasureland (by Don't Forget Me): dam unraced half-sister to Ruby Tiger: poor form in maidens. *H. J. Collingridge*   **43**

BALLINA LAD (IRE)   3 b.g. Mac's Imp (USA) 116 – Nationalartgallery (IRE) (Tate Gallery (USA) 117) [1998 65d: 5d⁴ 5g 5d⁵ 6g⁴ 6m 6m 7m 1999 6m* 6m³ 5g 7g 6m 6g Oct 14] angular gelding: fair handicapper at best: won at Ripon in May: ran poorly after next start: stays 6f: acts on good to firm and good to soft going: blinkered final 2-y-o start: carries head awkwardly: doesn't hold his form for long. *J. G. FitzGerald*   **71 d**

BALLISTIC BOY 2 ch.c. (Feb 27) First Trump 118 – Be Discreet (Junius (USA) 124) [1999 7m 7.1m 7d Oct 9] 34,000F, 38,000Y: half-brother to several winners, notably smart 7f/1m performer Gothenberg (by Polish Patriot) and 5-y-o Omaha City: dam won up to 7f in France: well held in maidens and minor event: gave trouble at stalls and withdrawn third intended start. *A. T. Murphy* –

BALLSBRIDGE (IRE) 2 b.c. (May 6) Sadler's Wells (USA) 132 – Future Treasure 88 (Habitat 134) [1999 8v Sep 29] 140,000F, 320,000Y: fifth foal: closely related to a winner in Italy by Be My Guest: dam, 7f winner (her only start), out of half-sister to very smart 7f/1m performer Brocade, herself dam of Barathea: weak in market, well-held seventh of 11 in maiden at Salisbury, not given hard time: sold 14,000 gns: likely to improve. *Sir Michael Stoute* – p

BALLY CYRANO 2 b.c. (Feb 19) Cyrano de Bergerac 120 – Iolite 85 (Forzando 122) [1999 5g³ 5.1m 6.1m 5g Aug 5] 8,800Y: first foal: dam, 5f/6f winner at 2 yrs, out of sister to Petong: well beaten after showing modest form on debut: possibly none too genuine. *B. A. McMahon* 62 d

BALLYKISSANGEL 6 ro.g. Hadeer 118 – April Wind 91 (Windjammer (USA)) [1998 –, a24: a11g a12g a11g³ a12g 8.3v a11g 1999 a14g 13.8m 16.2g Aug 12] bad maiden. *N. Bycroft* –

BALLYMORRIS BOY (IRE) 3 b.c. Dolphin Street (FR) 125 – Solas Abu (IRE) 82 (Red Sunset 120) [1998 64: 7m⁶ a7g⁴ a8g³ a8g a8g 1999 10m 8.3m 6f³ 6m 7f² 7d⁶ 8m 7m 8s 7s a10g a7g a7g⁵ a7g³ a7g⁴ Dec 22] modest maiden handicapper: stays 1m: acts on all-weather and firm ground. *J. Pearce* 61 a52

BALLY PRIDE (IRE) 2 ch.g. (Mar 3) Pips Pride 117 – Ballysnip (Ballymore 123) [1999 6s³ 5m⁵ 6m² 6.3m* 6f⁵ 6g³ 6m 6g⁶ 6d² Oct 9] 13,500F, IR 15,000Y: smallish, sturdy gelding: fluent mover: half-brother to several winners, including Ballyloop (up to 1m, by Petorius) and a 1¼m/1½m winner in France by Dancing Dissident: dam ran once in Ireland: useful form: won 16-runner Goffs £100,000 Challenge (sales race) at the Curragh in June: very good efforts at York afterwards when 4¼ lengths third to Mull of Kintyre in Gimcrack Stakes and when short-head second to Out of Africa in listed event, blinkered in latter: will stay 7f: acts on good to firm and good to soft ground: ruined winning chance by getting very upset in stalls second start and usually blanketed for entry afterwards: has been bandaged near-fore: genuine: gelded after final outing. *T. D. Easterby* 99

Goffs £100,000 Challenge, the Curragh—
a British-trained first and third with Bally Pride and Imperialist;
Yara (noseband) finishes well to separate the pair

BALSOX   3 b.g. Alzao (USA) 117 – Bobbysoxer 79 (Valiyar 129) [1998 71p: 6m **88 §** 7d⁴ 1999 8.2s* 8.1s² 9g 10m⁶ 10.3m⁵ 11.6d⁴ 14s Sep 25] strong gelding: fairly useful performer: won maiden at Nottingham in March: some creditable efforts in handicaps after, but looked ungenuine in visor/blinkers final 3 starts: stays 1¼m: acts on soft and good to firm going: flashes tail: not to be trusted: sold 14,000 gns in October, joined S. Dow. *J. L. Dunlop*

BAMBOO GARDEN (USA)   3 b.g. Desert Secret (IRE) 106 – Miss Mischievous **60** (USA) (Brazen Brother (USA)) [1998 –: 7g⁶ 7.9g 7d⁶ 1999 a10g⁶ a8f* a8g³ a8g⁵ a8.5g Mar 6] quite attractive gelding: modest performer: won selling handicap at Southwell in February: stays 1m: acts on fibresand: usually blinkered/visored: none too reliable. *G. C. H. Chung*

BANAFSAJYH (IRE)   2 b.f. (Jan 16) Lion Cavern (USA) 117 – Arylh (USA) 87 **70** (Lyphard (USA) 132) [1999 6m⁶ 6.1m² 6m³ Sep 24] tall, rather unfurnished filly: has scope: fourth foal: half-sister to Irish 1m/9f winner Iftatah (by Cadeaux Genereux): dam, 6f winner, out of half-sister to smart French miler Lypheor: fair form in maidens, third of 13 to Melanzana at Redcar on final start: takes good hold, and not sure to stay much beyond 6f. *A. C. Stewart*

BANBURY (USA)   5 b.g. Silver Hawk (USA) 123 – Sugar Hollow (USA) (Val de **100** L'Orne (FR) 133) [1998 –: 11.9m 12m 1999 a10g² a12f* a16f a12g* a12g² 12s⁴ 12m³ 11.9d² 12m² 13.9f² Jul 10] small gelding: useful performer: won claimer, apprentice handicap and minor event early in year, all at Lingfield: good placed efforts in handicaps last 4 starts, second in Duke of Edinburgh at Royal Ascot (behind Blueprint) and listed rated stakes at York (finished lame when beaten neck by Rainbow Ways) final 2: stays 1¾m: acts on equitrack, firm and soft going: tongue tied last 4 starts. *C. A. Dwyer*

BANCO SUIVI (IRE)   2 b.f. (Feb 3) Nashwan (USA) 135 – Pay The Bank 81 **81 p** (High Top 131) [1999 7d⁵ Oct 30] fifth foal: half-sister to smart 5f (at 2 yrs) to 7f winner My Branch and fairly useful 7f/1m winner Guaranteed (both by Distant Relative): dam, 2-y-o 1m winner, stayed 1¼m: promising 1¾ lengths fifth of 16 to Premier Prize in steadily-run maiden at Newmarket, doing well considering set plenty to do: will stay at least 1m: will improve, and sure to win races. *B. W. Hills*

BANDANNA   2 gr.f. (Mar 28) Bandmaster (USA) 97 – Gratclo 65 (Belfort (FR) **91** 89) [1999 6.1g* 6m⁴ 5g² 6m³ 6v⁵ 6d Oct 22] 4,800Y: big, close-coupled filly: fifth foal: half-sister to 3 winners, including useful 1996 2-y-o 6f winner Rich Ground (by Common Grounds), who stayed 7f: dam seemed best at 7f: fairly useful performer: won seller at Chepstow in May by 6 lengths: much improved next 3 starts, 3 lengths third to Saintly Speech in Princess Margaret Stakes at Ascot in July: well below form final start: stays 6f: acts on good to firm ground. *R. J. Hodges*

BANDAR PERAK   8 b.g. Aragon 118 – Noire Small (USA) (Elocutionist (USA)) **–** [1998 NR 1999 a14g 14.1g 16.2m Jul 13] of no account nowadays. *R. C. Spicer*

BANDBOX (IRE)   4 ch.g. Imperial Frontier (USA) 112 – Dublah (USA) (Private **74** Account (USA)) [1998 76: 6v 6g 7m 5g 6f² 6.1m 6m 6g³ 5g 5g² 6.1g⁶ 5g 1999 5.1d 6f 5.7g 6m⁶ 6d 6m³ 5.1m² 5m³ 6.1m³ 6g* 5.7m 5.1m³ 6d 5s Oct 2] small gelding: fair performer: won minor event at Leicester in August: effective at 5f/6f: acts on firm and good to soft ground: best in blinkers nowadays, has been visored: has worn tongue strap. *M. Salaman*

BANDLER CHING (IRE)   2 b.c. (Apr 28) Sri Pekan (USA) 117 – Stanerra's **72** Wish (IRE) (Caerleon (USA) 132) [1999 7m³ 7g² 8g⁵ 7.9f³ 8.3g³ Oct 11] IR 24,000Y: angular colt: tubed: second foal: half-brother to high-class Irish middle-distance performer Stanerra: fair maiden: trained by C. Allen first 2 starts: good third in nurseries at York and Windsor last 2 outings: should stay 1¼m: raced only on good going or firmer. *Pat Mitchell*

BANDOLERA BOY   2 b.c. (Apr 6) Casteddu 111 – Explosiva (USA) 88§ **–** (Explodent (USA)) [1999 5f⁵ 6m 5m 7f 8.2d a8g a7g Nov 16] 2,800Y: closely related to 2 winners by Efisio, including fairly useful 1994 2-y-o 5f winner Quiz Time, and half-brother to several winners, including useful 1992 2-y-o 1m winner Brockette (by Bustino): dam 2-y-o 5f winner: no form, including in blinkers. *T. J. Naughton*

BANGALORE 3 ch.c. Sanglamore (USA) 126 – Ajuga (USA) 102 (The Minstrel **89**
(CAN) 135) [1998 57p: 7g 7s 1999 10v* 12.3m² 11.9d⁵ 10m 12.3d³ 15d³ 10d⁶ Oct 1]
big, lengthy colt: unimpressive mover: fairly useful performer: won maiden at Pontefract in April: mostly creditable efforts in handicaps after: stays 1½m: has form on
good to firm going, though gives impression may prove best on good or softer (acts
on heavy): sold 35,000 gns, joined Mrs A. Perrett. *B. W. Hills*

BAN GARDAI (IRE) 4 b.f. Mukaddamah (USA) 125 – Femme Gendarme (USA) **61 ?**
(Policeman (FR) 124) [1998 NR 1999 a8.5g a7f⁶ a9.4g 5.9m³ 8d 6m 7f 6.9g⁴ 8m Sep
2] tall, workmanlike filly: fifth foal: half-sister to Joseph's Wine (winner up to 11f):
dam won up to 9f in USA: modest maiden at best: bred to stay beyond 7f:
inconsistent. *E. J. Alston*

BANGLED 2 ch.c. (Apr 22) Beveled (USA) – Bangles 83 (Chilibang 120) [1999 **60**
5.1g³ 5.7g 5.1g⁴ 6m⁵ 6.1m Sep 13] first foal: dam 5f winner: modest maiden: will
prove best at 5f/6f. *D. J. Coakley*

BANIYAR (IRE) 2 ch.c. (Apr 7) Alzao (USA) 117 – Banaja (IRE) (Sadler's **62 p**
Wells (USA) 132) [1999 7d Sep 30] strong, rangy colt: fluent mover: fourth foal:
half-brother to a fairly useful Irish 1¼m winner by Doyoun and an Irish 2m winner
by Kahyasi: dam unraced half-sister to Arc second Behera: green, never dangerous
in maiden at Newmarket: likely to do much better over 1¼m+. *Sir Michael Stoute*

BANK HOUSE (IRE) 4 ch.g. Zafonic (USA) 130 – Shebasis (USA) (General **60**
Holme (USA) 128) [1998 48: 8m 6g 5m³ 5v a8g 1999 5m 6m* Jul 17] lengthy
gelding: modest handicapper: blinkered, improved to win 17-runner maiden event at
Ripon easily by 5 lengths in July: stays 6f: acts on good to firm ground: reared and
unseated rider stalls on reappearance: has had tongue tied. *G. P. Kelly*

BANK ON HER (USA) 3 ch.f. Rahy (USA) 115 – Bank On Love (USA) (Gallant **76 +**
Romeo (USA)) [1998 71p: 7v³ 1999 7g* 7g Oct 14] big, good-topped filly: carries
condition: rare form: still green (swished tail in paddock) and short to post, won
maiden at Goodwood in May: behind in handicap at Redcar nearly 5 months after:
will stay 1m. *J. H. M. Gosden*

BANK ON HIM 4 b.g. Elmaamul (USA) 125 – Feather Flower 74 (Relkino 131) **53**
[1998 39, a73: a8g³ a7g² 9.7d⁴ a8g³ a8g² 10d⁴ a8.5g* a10g² a10g² a10g⁵ a10g³ 1999 **a81**
a10f* a10g* a10g a10g⁴ 9d 9m⁴ Jun 19] unfurnished gelding: fairly useful handicapper on all-weather, modest on turf: won twice at Lingfield in January and February:
good fourth at same course final start: stays easy 1¼m: acts on all-weather and good
to firm going: has hung left: reliable. *G. L. Moore*

BANK ON MEE 3 b.f. Weldnaas (USA) 112 – Heemee 81 (On Your Mark 125) **–**
[1998 50: 7m 5m² 1999 6d 6m 7m 5v Jun 9] leggy, unfurnished filly: poor maiden at
2 yrs: showed nothing in 1999: tried visored. *J. J. Quinn*

BANNERET (USA) 6 b.g. Imperial Falcon (CAN) – Dashing Partner 71 (Formid- **– ,**
able (USA) 125) [1998 –, a74d: a9.4g* a9.4g⁶ 10.3g a12g² a12g* a12g³ a12g⁵ **a69**
1999 a12g² 10m a11g* a12g² a12g⁵ a12g³ a12g⁴ Dec 27] good-bodied gelding: fair
performer: won claimer at Southwell in September and handicap at Wolverhampton
in October: stays 1½m: acts on fibresand (yet to race on equitrack), no recent form on
turf: blinkered (out of form) twice in 1997. *Miss S. J. Wilton*

BANNINGHAM BELLE 4 gr.f. Touch of Grey 90 – Fire Gold 48 (Never So **–**
Bold 135) [1998 NR 1999 6s 6g⁶ a7g 5g⁶ a6g 6m 5g 5g Aug 18] workmanlike filly:
tried blinkered/visored. *D. Shaw*

BANNINGHAM BREEZE 3 br.g. Cyrano de Bergerac 120 – Strapped 57 **53**
(Reprimand 122) [1998 69d: 5d 5m⁶ 6f⁶ 6g² 6g⁶ 6g⁴ a6g 6g 6f a6g 6m* 8m 7d⁵
8g 6s 1999 a6g a6g⁶ a6g⁶ 6m 6.1d⁵ 5.9m 5f 7.1m 6m 8m Sep 16] sparely-made
gelding: poor handicapper: stays 6f: acts on good to firm going, good to soft and
fibresand: effective blinkered/visored or not: seems none too keen. *D. Nicholls*

BAPSFORD 5 b.g. Shalford (IRE) 124§ – Bap's Miracle (Track Spare 125) [1998 **– §**
–§, a64§: 10g 8g 9.4g a8g³ a8.5g⁴ a8g² a7g a10g² a10g⁶ a8.5g³ a12g a12g² 1999 **a60 d**
a12g* a12g⁵ a12g² a9.4g⁵ a12g a12g⁵ a11g⁶ a11g Jun 11] neat gelding: has suffered
from lameness: modest performer: won seller at Wolverhampton in January: below
form last 5 starts: stays easy 1½m: acts on all-weather, no recent form on turf: some-

times blinkered/visored: has hung left/found little, and best held up: unreliable: sold 500 gns in June. *M. Waring*

BAPTISMAL ROCK (IRE) 5 ch.g. Ballad Rock 122 – Flower From Heaven **58**
(Baptism 119) [1998 40: 5m 5m^{4dis} 1999 a6g2 a6g* a6f* a6g* a5g3 a5g4 5.1s6 5m2 **a62**
6g3 5m5 5m2 5f3 5m2 5d2 5.3s6 5m3 5g6 a6g6 a6g3 a6g a5g Nov 13] good-bodied
gelding: poor mover: modest handicapper: won at Wolverhampton (amateurs), Lingfield and Southwell in January: mostly creditable efforts after: best at 5f/6f: acts on
all-weather, firm and good to soft going: usually races prominently. *A. G. Newcombe*

BARABASCHI 3 b.g. Elmaamul (USA) 125 – Hills' Presidium (Presidium 124) **77 §**
[1998 79p: 7m3 7.9g5 1999 7s2 6v 7m2 5.9m4 8f 7m3 7d2 7d2 Oct 22] angular,
unfurnished gelding: fair maiden: trained by P. Chapple-Hyam first 6 starts: stays 7f:
acts on good to firm and soft ground: raced too freely in blinkers sixth start: has
flashed tail and tends to hang: needs treating with caution. *A. G. Foster*

BARAFAMY (IRE) 3 gr.f. Barathea (IRE) 127 – Infamy 123 (Shirley Heights **103**
130) [1998 103p: 7g2 7m2 7g* 8d3 8s* 1999 10.4d3 11m4 8.1m5 10s6 Oct 2]
workmanlike filly: shows knee action: useful performer: good 1½ lengths fourth to
Nagoya in Oaks d'Italia at Milan in May: well below form after 3-month break final
2 starts: needed further than 1m, and stayed 11f well: acted on soft and good to firm
going: stud. *J. L. Dunlop*

BARAKULA 2 b.f. (Jan 23) Barathea (IRE) 127 – Bright Generation (IRE) 111 **89 p**
(Rainbow Quest (USA) 134) [1999 6m* 8s5 Sep 26] sturdy, lengthy filly: third foal:
half-sister to 3-y-o Celebrate and a winner in USA by Gone West: dam 6f (at 2 yrs) to
1½m (Oaks d'Italia) winner: won minor event at Windsor in June: shade edgy, plenty
of improvement despite seeming all-at-sea under conditions when 6½ lengths fifth of
6 to Teggiano in Fillies' Mile at Ascot 3 months later: had sore shins in between: will
be suited by 1¼m+: will improve again. *P. F. I. Cole*

BARANN 3 ch.g. Henbit (USA) 130 – Opalkino 36 (Relkino 131) [1998 NR 1999 **–**
10f a8.5g a8.5g a12g Dec 21] first reported foal: dam, maiden, stayed 1m: well
beaten in maidens/handicap. *J. M. Bradley*

BARATHEA GUEST 2 b.c. (Mar 30) Barathea (IRE) 127 – Western Heights **110 p**
(Shirley Heights 130) [1999 6g* 6m 7d* 8s* 8s2 Oct 10] 70,000Y: close-coupled,
good-topped colt: has round action: fourth foal: half-brother to 3 winners, including
3-y-o Dollar Law and 5-y-o Pinchincha: dam unraced half-sister to smart middle-
distance filly Startino: progressed really well, making into a smart performer: won
maiden at Yarmouth in June then minor event at Salisbury and listed race at Deauville
(by ¾ length from Ansham) in August: first past post in 3-runner Grand Criterium
at Longchamp on final start, beating Ciro a neck, but demoted after hampering
runner-up: will stay 1¼m: acts on soft going: capable of better still. *G. G. Margarson*

BARBADOS 2 b.c. (Jan 29) Muhtarram (USA) 125 – Brisighella (IRE) (Al Hareb **60**
(USA) 123) [1999 5m 6d5 5.1m 5.9g5 7d2 7.1m2 8g 8d 8.2d Oct 21] 4,000Y: first foal:
dam Italian 5f (at 2 yrs) to 1m winner: modest maiden: below form last 3 starts:
should stay at least 1m: yet to race on extremes of going: has worn tongue strap: sold
2,200 gns, sent to Kuwait. *M. H. Tompkins*

BARBASON 7 ch.g. Polish Precedent (USA) 131 – Barada (USA) (Damascus **75**
(USA)) [1998 83: a7s2 a8g* a7g6 a8g2 a8g3 a8g5 a8g 8g* 8m6 9g 8g2 8m2 8.5m5 8m
8s6 a8g3 a8g2 a8g2 1999 a8g3 a10g6 a8g* a8g 8f 10d* 9m6 8f 8.1m* 8m4 8m* 9v 8d6
10d a8g3 a10g* a8g3 a10g Dec 22] compact gelding: fair performer: had a good year
in 1999, winning claimers at Lingfield, Sandown and Brighton, amateur handicap at
Newbury and minor event at Lingfield: effective at 1m/1¼m: acts on firm ground,
good to soft and equitrack: successful in blinkers, at least as effective without:
usually bandaged in front: usually held up. *G. L. Moore*

BARBOLA (USA) 4 ch.c. Diesis 133 – Barboukh 95 (Night Shift (USA)) [1998 **116**
110: 10.5g2 10g3 10s3 10s* 10s2 1999 10s* 10d2 10m3 10d3 9.8v4 8v4 Nov 6]
250,000Y: first foal: dam, 1m winner who stayed 1¼m, out of half-sister to Old Vic:
smart performer: unraced at 2 yrs: won listed race at Chantilly at 3 yrs and Prix
Exbury at Saint-Cloud (by 1½ lengths from Borgia) in March: at least creditable
efforts in pattern races afterwards, running well when 1½ lengths second of 4 to Dark
Moondancer in Prix d'Harcourt at Longchamp and when length third to Chelsea

Manor in La Coupe de Maisons-Laffitte fourth start: stays 1¼m: acts on good to firm and heavy ground. *J. de Roualle, France*

BARCELONA 2 b.c. (Mar 17) Barathea (IRE) 127 – Pipitina 91 (Bustino 136) **70** [1999 8d 8d 8d³ Oct 27] 20,000F, IR 40,000Y: smallish, sturdy colt: fifth foal: half-brother to 3-y-o Pipa and German 1m winner Larissa (by Soviet Star): dam 2m winner from very good family: progressive form in maidens, best effort when 6 lengths third of 10 to Scotty Guest at Yarmouth: will stay 1½m. *J. Noseda*

BARDEN LADY 2 b.f. (May 2) Presidium 124 – Pugilistic (Hard Fought 125) **–** [1999 6s 7s Nov 5] 2,000Y: close-coupled filly: sixth foal: half-brother to a bumper winner by Gunner B: dam unraced: well held in maidens. *B. C. Morgan*

BARITONE 5 b.g. Midyan (USA) 124 – Zinzi (Song 132) [1998 52, a57: a7s⁴ a7g³ a7g⁵ a7g⁵ 7s 9v 8m⁶ 7.5d 8g³ 6.9d 8g⁴ a8g³ 7.5m 6m 7.1d³ a6g² 1999 a7g a6f a6f² a5g⁴ a6f* a6g a6g⁵ a6g 6g 5m⁵ a6g a7g a6g Dec 27] close-coupled gelding: modest handicapper: won at Southwell in February: generally below form after: effective at 6f to 1m: acts on good to firm going (probably soft) and all-weather: tried blinkered, usually visored: inconsistent. *S. E. Kettlewell* **a57 d**

BARLEY MEADOW (IRE) 7 ch.g. Phardante (FR) 123 – Foredefine (Bonne **42** Noel 115) [1998 NR 1999 16g³ 12.4f 12g 15.8d Sep 21] sparely-made ex-Irish gelding: second foal: brother to winning jumper Jimmy's Cross: dam unraced: poor performer at best: stays 2m: usually visored: tongue tied. *R. Ford*

BARNABY 2 b.g. (Mar 22) Theatrical Charmer 114 – Fruitful Affair (IRE) 71 **–** (Taufan (USA) 119) [1999 7m Jul 8] 4,000Y: first foal: dam 6f (at 2 yrs) and 1½m winner (stayed 2m): always behind in maiden at Lingfield. *J. R. Arnold*

BARNACLA (IRE) 3 ch.f. Bluebird (USA) 125 – Reticent Bride (IRE) 71 (Shy **83 +** Groom (USA)) [1998 –: 6g 1999 6m 6s² 6d* 6m 6g⁶ Jul 5] angular, unfurnished filly: poor mover: fairly useful handicapper: won at Windsor in June: creditable efforts after: stays 6f: acts on good to soft ground, probably good to firm: has worn tongue strap/bandages. *C. F. Wall*

Mr John Guest's "Barathea Guest"

BARNEY KNOWS (IRE)   4 b.g. In The Wings 128 – Afeefa (Lyphard (USA) –
132) [1998 NR 1999 14.1m May 21] half-brother to several winners, including useful
1¼m winners Afriyd (by Darshaan) and Afkar (by Mouktar): dam unraced daughter
of half-sister to Val de Loir and Valoris: fairly useful bumper winner: well held in
maiden only Flat run. *M. A. Peill*

BARNIE RUBBLE   3 ch.g. Pharly (FR) 130 – Sharp Fairy (Sharpo 132) [1998
NR 1999 6g Oct 14] first live foal: dam lightly-raced half-sister to top-class miler
Desert Prince: behind in claimer. *A. Bailey*

BARN OWL   3 ch.f. Sabrehill (USA) 120 – Ever Welcome 58 (Be My Guest
(USA) 126) [1998 –: 7g 7.5m 7.9g 1999 13.8g 12s Sep 21] sturdy filly: has a round
action: little sign of ability in maidens/sellers. *K. W. Hogg, Isle of Man*

BARON DE PICHON (IRE)   3 b.c. Perugino (USA) 84 – Ariadne 79 (Bustino –
136) [1998 63: 5d 6g 5.1v a7g a8g² 1999 a7g² a8.5g* a7g* a8.5g* a7f* a8.5g² a8g* **a89**
a9.4g 7.9s a8g⁴ 8m⁶ a8.5g² 7.1g a8.5g⁶ Aug 6] workmanlike colt: fairly useful
handicapper: won at Wolverhampton (3 times), Southwell and Lingfield in January/
February: rare poor effort final start: effective at 7f to 8.5f: acts on all-weather, little
form on turf: visored (carried head awkwardly) second 2-y-o outing: genuine: sent to
USA. *N. P. Littmoden*

BARON FERDINAND   9 ch.g. Ferdinand (USA) – In Perpetuity 90 (Great –
Nephew 126) [1998 NR 1999 10f May 29] strong, lengthy gelding: smart at best:
only twice raced since 1995 and well below form. *R. Charlton*

BAROSSA VALLEY (IRE)   8 b.g. Alzao (USA) 117 – Night of Wind 101 –
(Tumble Wind (USA)) [1998 –: 6.9v 8m 7g a8g 1999 a8g a14g Nov 30] no longer of
much account. *P. Butler*

BARR BEACON   3 br.g. Puissance 110 – Lominda (IRE) 80 (Lomond (USA) **43**
128) [1998 66: 5g a5g⁶ a5g² 1999 a5g⁵ a5g Mar 13] modest maiden at 2 yrs: well
below form in 1999: acts on all-weather: blinkered on reappearance. *T. G. Mills*

BARREN LANDS   4 b.g. Green Desert (USA) 127 – Current Raiser 108 (Fili- –
berto (USA) 123) [1998 67: 7s 7d 7m⁵ 6d² 5g⁴ 6d* 7g 5g 6v 10.3d⁶ 1999 8g Apr 28]
robust, deep-bodied gelding: fair performer at best: well beaten since winning
maiden in 1998: best at 6f: blinkered once: won over hurdles in December. *K. Bishop*

BARRETTSTOWN   4 ch.g. Cadeaux Genereux 131 – Sagar 74 (Habitat 134) **59**
[1998 NR 1999 11.9d³ 10.2g² a11g a12g⁴ Jul 9] big, lengthy gelding: closely related
to 1988 2-y-o 5f winner Gold Ducat (by Young Generation) and half-brother to
several winners, including smart 7f to 1¼m performer Tarawa (by Caerleon) and
8-y-o Be Warned: dam French 10.5f winner: poor form in 2 bumpers: modest form
when placed in claimers: joined P. Chamings. *M. C. Pipe*

BARRIER REEF (IRE)   2 b.c. (Feb 18) Perugino (USA) 84 – Singing Millie **106**
(Millfontaine 114) [1999 5.8f* 5.2m 6g⁴ 8.5v* 6s⁵ 8s² Oct 16] IR 19,000Y: closely
related to an Irish 13f winner by Posen: dam, Irish 7f/1m winner, half-sister to dam
of Seattle Rhyme: useful performer: wide-margin winner of maiden at Navan in June
and minor event at Galway in September: best effort when short-head second of 6 to
stable-mate Lermontov in Beresford Stakes at the Curragh: stays 8.5f: acts on any
going: forces pace. *A. P. O'Brien, Ireland*

BARRIER RIDGE   5 ch.g. Lycius (USA) 124 – Star Ridge (USA) (Storm Bird **58**
(CAN) 134) [1998 –, a45: a8g a9.4g⁵ a8.5g⁶ a7g 7d 8d 7g 7g 6s a7g a8g³ a7g **a49**
a10g 1999 10f* 10f a8g² 8m 10.5d 10d⁴ a8g⁶ a10g Nov 24] good-topped gelding:
unimpressive mover: modest on turf, poor on all-weather: won seller at Brighton in
May: barely stays 1¼m: acts on firm and good to soft going and equitrack: blinkered
twice (ran creditably) in 1998. *G. L. Moore*

BARRINGER (IRE)   2 b.g. (Apr 10) Nicolotte 118 – Prosaic Star (IRE) 81 **92**
(Common Grounds 118) [1999 5d² 5v* 5g² 5.1s* 5.1m⁶ 5g* 5m 6v 6v Oct 23] IR
13,000Y: leggy, unfurnished gelding: first foal: dam, Irish 2-y-o 1m winner, stayed
1¼m: fairly useful performer: won minor events at Hamilton, Nottingham and
Windsor in April/May: off course over 3 months before running respectably last 2
starts: should be at least as effective over 6f as at 5f: acts on heavy going, well below
best on good to firm: sold 10,000 gns. *M. R. Channon*

BARRISTER (IRE)   3 ch.g. Barathea (IRE) 127 – Silver Hut (USA) 80 (Silver   **102**
Hawk (USA) 123) [1998 NR 1999 8.2s³ 8.3d* 10.2d⁵ 8.1d* 8m⁵ 8.1m⁵ Jul 3] IR
65,000Y: rangy, rather unfurnished gelding: has a round action: first foal: dam, 1m
winner from 3 starts at 2 yrs: useful performer: won maiden at Windsor in May and
handicap at Haydock in June: easily better subsequent effort when good fifth to
Pythios in Britannia Handicap at Royal Ascot penultimate start: stays 1m well: acts
on good to firm and good to soft going: sent to USA. *R. Charlton*

BARROW (SWI)   2 br.c. (Jan 27) Caerleon (USA) 132 – Bestow 76 (Shirley   **70 p**
Heights 130) [1999 7.1d 8.2m³ 7.7d⁴ Sep 21] 85,000Y: lengthy, rather unfurnished
colt: fourth foal: closely related to 1¼m winner Prize Pupil (by Royal Academy) and
half-brother to 5-y-o Tonight's Prize: dam 1¾m and 2m winner from family of
Seattle Slew and Lomond: fair maiden: best effort when third of 5 in steadily-run
event at Nottingham: not given hard time final start: will stay at least 1½m: likely to
do better. *J. L. Dunlop*

BARRYS DOUBLE   2 br.c. (Mar 3) Barrys Gamble 102 – Pennine Star (IRE) 68   **55**
(Pennine Walk 120) [1999 5m⁴ 5f 5g a6g³ 5g a6g a6g⁴ a8g Dec 21] close-coupled
colt: third foal: dam 1½m winner: modest maiden: well below form 3 of last 4 starts,
including in visor: may prove best around 6f: acts on fibresand: often soon off bridle.
C. W. Fairhurst

BARTEX (FR)   5 b.h. Groom Dancer (USA) 128 – Belisonde (FR) (Gay Mecene   **101**
(USA) 128) [1998 8v 7s* 7s⁴ 1999 8v³ 8d² 8.5s* 7m⁴ 9.5s³ 10s 7m 8v² 8v* 8s⁴ Nov
22] 42,000 francs F: small horse: fourth reported foal: half-brother to French 11f and
11.5f winner Mayerville (by Sky Lawyer): dam lightly-raced French maiden: useful
performer: successful in 1999 at Longchamp in April (minor event) and October
(18-runner handicap): well held in Tote International Handicap at Ascot seventh start
(trained before then by Mme C. Barbe): effective at 7f, stays 9.5f: acts on good to
firm and heavy ground: effective blinkered or not. *T. Clout, France*

BARTHOLOMEW (IRE)   3 b.c. Second Set (IRE) 127 – Why Not Glow (IRE)   **100**
(Glow (USA)) [1998 79p: 5v⁵ 6d² 7s⁵ 6s² a6g* 1999 a6g* a7g* a6g* 6s* 8s⁵
6m⁶ 6m³ 6d 6d Jun 12] quite attractive colt: useful performer: won 3 handicaps at
Lingfield and minor event at Saint-Cloud between January and March: good third in
handicap at Lingfield in May: stays easy 7f: acts on equitrack, soft and good to firm
going: drifted markedly left under pressure on sixth outing. *T. J. Naughton*

BARTON LEA (IRE)   2 b.f. (Apr 29) Distinctly North (USA) 115 – La Mazya   **–**
(IRE) (Mazaad 106) [1999 a8g a8g Dec 17] IR 3,000Y: first foal: dam unraced
daughter of a winner in Sweden: well beaten in Southwell maidens. *R. A. Fahey*

BARTON MISS   2 ch.f. (Mar 15) Whittingham (IRE) 104 – Miss Derby (USA)   **–**
(Master Derby (USA)) [1999 5g 8.3d Oct 28] 10,000Y: sister to 3-y-o Oo Ee Be and
half-sister to several winners, including a 7f winner by Gold Crest: dam, winner up
to 9f in USA, from very good family: behind in maidens. *G. L. Moore*

BASHER JACK   3 b.c. Suave Dancer (USA) 136 – Possessive Lady 62 (Dara   **51**
Monarch 128) [1998 –: 8m 1999 10g 10m 10s⁵ a14.8g⁵ 10s⁴ a12g* 11.9d⁶
a16g⁴ Aug 25] leggy, shallow-girthed colt: modest performer: won maiden handicap
at Wolverhampton in August: stays 1½m, probably not 1¾m: acts on good to firm
going, soft and fibresand: wears tongue strap. *C. N. Allen*

BASHFUL BRAVE   8 ch.g. Indian Ridge 123 – Shy Dolly 74 (Cajun 120) [1998   **44 d**
49, a45: a6g⁵ 5m 6m 5g 5d 5g 5g³ 5.1g 5m 6f² 6m 6d 1999 a6g 5s 5m³ a6g 5g 5m 5f⁵   **a–**
5m 5m Aug 26] smallish gelding: poor handicapper: stays 6f: acts on all-weather,
possibly needs good going or firmer on turf: tried visored/blinkered. *J. L. Eyre*

BASIC INSTINCT   2 ch.f. (Apr 21) Prince Sabo 123 – Constant Delight 80 (Never   **43**
So Bold 135) [1999 6g a7g³ a7g⁵ a6g a7g Dec 15] 4,400Y: leggy filly: fourth foal:
sister to 5-y-o Princess of Hearts and half-sister to 1994 2-y-o 6f winner Corio (by
Sharpo): dam 9f winner: poor maiden: left M. Tompkins 1,900 gns after third start
(drifted left): likely to stay 1m: acts on fibresand. *R. Brotherton*

BASMAN (IRE)   5 b.h. Persian Heights 129 – Gepares (IRE) (Mashhor Dancer
(USA)) [1998 99?: 9.9g 10s 10s⁴ 12d 1999 11.8s⁵ Oct 25] big horse: useful at 3 yrs:
little solid form on Flat since (though fairly useful form over hurdles): probably stays

1½m: raced only on good going or softer: takes strong hold (net muzzle to post final start). *B. Smart*

BASSINELLO (USA) 3 ch.f. Nureyev (USA) 131 – Feminine Wiles (IRE) 110 **82** (Ahonoora 122) [1998 69p: 7g⁶ 1999 8m* 9.7d 8d⁶ Oct 12] rather sparely-made filly: won steadily-run maiden at Pontefract in August: below form subsequently: trained until after second start by P. Chapple-Hyam: should stay 1¼m. *A. G. Foster*

BATAAN (USA) 8 b.h. Manila (USA) – Comtesse de Loir (FR) 131 (Val de Loir **47** 133) [1998 49: a7g³ a8g³ 9s a8g* 8g² 9m⁴ 8g 8f² 8s 9d³ 8.3d⁶ 10v a10g 1999 a8g³ a7.5g* 9s² 8s⁶ a7.5g 7g 9m* 8g 9d² 9d 8s⁶ Nov 5] poor performer nowadays: third in handicap at Lingfield on reappearance: won handicap at Boitsfort in March and amateur claimer at Dieppe in July: stays 1¼m: acts on good to soft ground, firm and dirt/equitrack. *Alex Vanderhaeghen, Belgium*

BATALEUR 6 b.g. Midyan (USA) 124 – Tinkerbird 76 (Music Boy 124) [1998 **69 ?** 54, a–: a6g 6v⁵ 7.1g 6s 6.1g 6m⁵ 7g 6v* a7g a6g a6g 1999 6g 6m 6g 6d² 5s* Nov 2] **a–** angular, good-quartered gelding: modest performer: seemed to excel himself when winning claimer at Catterick: effective at 5f and 6f: acts on heavy going, probably on good to firm, no form on fibresand: tried blinkered. *G. Woodward*

BATANTA 3 br.f. Bob's Return (IRE) 123 – Atlantic Air (Air Trooper 115) [1998 **53** NR 1999 10g May 10] 10,200Y: half-sister to several winners, including Italian 4-y-o Plan Maison (by Thowra), 7f to 1¼m winner (including at 2 yrs), and fairly useful 7f (including at 2 yrs) and 1m winner Mullitover (by Interrex): dam Italian 1¼m winner at 4 yrs: tenth in Windsor maiden: dead. *K. R. Burke*

BATCHWORTH BELLE 4 b.f. Interrex (CAN) – Treasurebound 63 (Beldale **100** Flutter (USA) 130) [1998 94: 6v³ 6g 5.3f² 6g 5d³ 5d⁵ 5.1d³ 5m² 5m³ 6m 5.3m* 5d* 5.2g⁶ 5m 5m 1999 a5g* 5.2m³ 5s⁵ 5.1m 6m⁶ 5m³ 5m³ 5m³ 5m* 5m³ 5d 5m 5g³ 5d² Oct 9] lengthy, good-topped filly: useful handicapper: won at Lingfield in April and Newmarket in July: generally in good form otherwise, good second to Superior Premium at Ascot final start: has won over easy 6f, best around 5f: acts on equitrack and probably any turf ground: tried blinkered: seems best produced late. *E. A. Wheeler*

BATHWICK BABE (IRE) 2 b.f. (Apr 24) Sri Pekan (USA) 117 – Olean **–** (Sadler's Wells (USA) 132) [1999 8.2g 8.3d Oct 28] IR 15,500F, 17,000Y: seventh foal: half-sister to several winners, including 3-y-o Architect and fairly useful Irish 1¼m and 11f winner Two Shonas (by Persian Heights): dam ran twice: well held in maidens. *B. Smart*

BATHWICK (IRE) 3 b.c. Midyan (USA) 124 – Dancing Heights (IRE) 80 (High **105** Estate 127) [1998 88+: 7d² 7g* 7g² 7g 7.3m a6g⁶ 8m* 8.1g* 8s⁶ 1999 8s⁵ 8.3m* 10m 9g* 8m 10m⁶ 9.9f 8m* Aug 22] small, quite attractive colt: useful performer: won minor event at Windsor in April, valuable handicap at Goodwood in May and 5-runner minor event at Bath (best effort, beat Sir Effendi by a head): best at 1m/9f: acts on good to firm and good to soft going: visored once as 2-y-o and on penultimate 3-y-o start: usually front runner: sent to UAE. *B. Smart*

BATOUTOFTHEBLUE 6 br.g. Batshoof 122 – Action Belle (Auction Ring **49** (USA) 123) [1998 49, a71: a14g² 16g⁴ 14s³ 16.1d a14.8g⁴ 16.1g⁶ 17.1m* 17.1d⁶ 1999 16.1d 16g* 16.2d 16m² 18g⁴ 16m⁴ 14.1m⁴ 16f⁴ 17.1g³ Aug 22] big, strong gelding: poor walker: fair handicapper when last seen on all-weather, poor on turf: won at Musselburgh (carried head high) in April: mostly creditable efforts after: suited by thorough test of stamina: acts on fibresand, firm and soft going: blinkered seventh and eighth starts: often gets behind, and not the easiest of rides. *W. W. Haigh*

BATSMAN 5 b.g. Batshoof 122 – Lady Bequick 81 (Sharpen Up 127) [1998 53, **55** a60: a7g⁴ a7g* a8g² a8g⁶ a7g⁴ 7g 7m² 7g 7g⁶ 8m 8m 1999 a7g³ a7g **a60** a8g 7g 8.5m³ 8.3m 7s³ 7.1m⁴ 7f² 8m 8g 6.9m 7.5m⁶ 7g⁶ 8d⁶ 10g⁴ a12g⁵ 8m Sep 16] strong, close-coupled gelding: modest performer: stays 1¼m, not 1½m: acts on all-weather, firm and soft going: effective blinkered/visored or not: has had tongue tied: usually held up. *M. Dods*

BATSWING 4 b.g. Batshoof 122 – Magic Milly 60 (Simply Great (FR) 122) [1998 **77** –: 7.1d 10m 10.1s 1999 12s 13.3f³ 12m 14m⁴ 12s 12m⁶ Sep 10] fair handicapper:

stays 13f: acts on any going: sometimes blinkered at 2 yrs: has been bandaged off-hind: sold 13,000 gns. *B. R. Millman*

BATTLE GLEN (FR)   4 ch.g. Green Forest (USA) 134 – Battle Quest (FR) (Noblequest (FR) 124) [1998 54: 8m³ 8g 8.2v a8.5g³ 1999 a7g 8m Aug 4] ex-French gelding: modest maiden at best: probably stayed 8.5f: blinkered final start: carried head high/hung: joined M. W. Easterby: dead. *A. Bailey*

BATTLE WARNING   4 b.g. Warning 136 – Royal Ballet (IRE) (Sadler's Wells **67** (USA) 132) [1998 –: 11.7s 1999 10m 10.2m⁵ 11.6m 10s Oct 5] very lightly-raced gelding: fair form and easily best effort when fifth in handicap at Bath in July: stays 1¼m: sold 6,500 gns. *H. Candy*

BAUGET JOUETTE   2 gr.f. (Feb 20) Son Pardo 107 – Petite Louie 45 (Chili- **51 d** bang 120) [1999 5d 5.3f⁵ 6f⁵ 6s³ 6m⁵ 6m 6f 7m 8s 8.3d a7g Dec 8] second foal: half-sister to 3-y-o Crash Call Lady: dam, poor maiden, daughter of half-sister to Environment Friend: poor maiden: best run on soft ground: blinkered once: has shown reluctance at stalls. *Jamie Poulton*

BAVARIO (USA)   6 ch.g. Theatrical 128 – Hawaiian Miss (USA) (Hawaii) [1998 –: 10s⁶ 1999 10s Apr 19] tall, short-backed ex-Irish gelding: fairly useful 1¼m/1½m handicapper at 3 and 4 yrs for D. Weld: soundly beaten both Flat outings in Britain. *D. L. Williams*

BAWSIAN   4 b.g. Persian Bold 123 – Bawaeth (USA) 72 (Blushing Groom (FR) **94** 131) [1998 98: a8.5g* a8.5g* 10.3d* 12.3m⁴ 10.4d* 10.4s⁵ 10.3g 10.4f⁶ 10.3m 10s⁴ 12v 1999 a12g² 12d⁴ 10v⁴ 10m 10.4s⁴ 10f³ 11.9s 10.4f⁴ 10m Jul 24] small, close-coupled gelding: fairly useful handicapper: mostly creditable efforts when in frame, notably strong-finishing fourth in John Smith's Cup at York on penultimate start: brought down before halfway final one: effective at 1¼m/1½m: acts on fibresand, probably on any turf going: tends to get behind, and suited by well-run race. *J. L. Eyre*

BAYANIYA (IRE)   3 b.f. Barathea (IRE) 127 – Bayrika (IRE) 109 (Kahyasi 130) **82** [1998 NR 1999 8m² 8m⁴ 8.3d² Nov 4] strong, lengthy filly: first foal: dam, won 15.5f Prix Berteux, daughter of Arc runner-up Behera: fairly useful maiden: best effort when second at Doncaster on debut in July: bred to be well suited by further than 1m: edgy penultimate start, tended to wander final 2: sent to France. *L. M. Cumani*

BAYARD LADY   3 b.f. Robellino (USA) 127 – Lurking 69 (Formidable (USA) **47** 125) [1998 61: 5v³ 5s 5d* 5.9m⁵ 5d³ 6m 6s 6.1v⁵ 1999 8.3v⁴ 8d 8m⁴ 12m⁴ 12g 8f⁴ 8.1d 10g 7g⁵ 8d⁵ a8g Nov 15] small filly: poor handicapper: stays 1½m: acts on good to firm and heavy going. *L. R. Lloyd-James*

BAYCHESTER   2 ch.g. (Apr 22) Chaddleworth (IRE) 103 – Runabay (Run The Gantlet (USA)) [1999 7.9g 7d 8s Nov 6] 500Y: sparely-made gelding: seventh foal: closely related to a winner in Italy by Indian Ridge: dam French maiden: well beaten in maidens. *G. Woodward*

BAYFORD GREEN (IRE)   3 b.f. Distinctly North (USA) 115 – Paddys Cocktail **50** (IRE) (Tremblant 112) [1998 60: 6m 5d 5d² 5g 1999 6g 5d⁴ Jun 28] modest maiden: best at 5f: blinkered second start: sold 700 gns. *J. Berry*

BAY OF BENGAL (IRE)   3 ch.f. Persian Bold 123 – Adjamiya (USA) (Shah- **55** rastani (USA) 135) [1998 42: 7.5d 6g 7m³ 5m 8g 1999 10f* 12g* 9.9m 11f⁴ 13.8g Sep 18] leggy filly: modest handicapper: won selling events at Nottingham in May and Pontefract in June: ran poorly final 3 starts: stays 1½m: acts on firm going. *J. S. Wainwright*

BAY OF ISLANDS   7 b.g. Jupiter Island 126 – Lawyer's Wave (USA) (Advocator) **98** [1998 94: 10.3g 12g* 11.9m² 12m³ 13.9f 13.3g 12m 12d 1999 12m 14.1m* 16.2d² 16.1m³ Jun 26] strong gelding: fluent mover: useful handicapper: won at Nottingham in May: good efforts last 2 starts, third of 20 to Far Cry in Northumberland Plate at Newcastle final one: effective at 1½m to 2m: acts on firm going, and good to soft: has been visored, including last 3 starts. *D. Morris*

BAYONET   3 b.f. Then Again 126 – Lambay 88 (Lorenzaccio 130) [1998 72: 5g⁴ **64** 5m² 5.3d² 1999 6m 7m 6m 6m 6.1m⁴ 8m 7.1m a6g Sep 28] deep-girthed filly: modest maiden handicapper: left R. F. Johnson Houghton after fifth start: will prove best at 5f/6f: raced mainly on good to firm going: blinkered second and third starts. *Jane Southcombe*

BAY PRINCE (IRE)   4 b.c. Mujadil (USA) 119 – Kingston Rose (Tudor Music 131) [1998 –: 6m 6s 1999 5.2m 6v Sep 29] lengthy colt: no form since 2 yrs: left Mrs L. Stubbs before final start (blinkered): sold 800 gns. *Miss Gay Kelleway*   –

BAYT ALASAD (IRE)   3 b.f. Lion Cavern (USA) 117 – Safa 109 (Shirley Heights 130) [1998 NR 1999 10.2m³ 10m² 10g³ 11.7f 10f³ a8.5g* Oct 30] angular, quite attractive filly: third foal: half-sister to smart 1m to 10.5f winner Saafeya (by Sadler's Wells): dam, 6f winner at 2 yrs, stayed 1½m: fair performer: won maiden at Wolverhampton: stays 1¼m: acts on fibresand, raced only on good going or firmer on turf: sold 18,000 gns. *M. P. Tregoning*   77

BAYTOWN HARMONY   2 ch.f. (Feb 15) Muhtarram (USA) 125 – Merryhill Maid (IRE) 71 (M Double M (USA)) [1999 5d 5v⁵ a6g⁵ 7g 6g² 6.8s⁶ a5.5g³ 8d 10v⁵ 9d⁴ Nov 28] 800Y: sparely-made filly: third foal: half-sister to 4-y-o Haunt The Zoo: dam winning sprinter: trained by P. McEntee first 4 starts: in frame for new stable in minor events at Ovrevoll: probably stays 9f. *Mrs W. B. Allen, Norway*   ?

BAYTOWN MELODY   2 b.f. (Mar 25) Alhijaz 122 – Wendy's Way 53 (Merdon Melody 98) [1999 5d⁵ 5.1s⁴ a5g 5g⁴ 6g² 6d⁴ 6f³ 6g⁴ 5g² 5m² a6g⁵ 5.3s Sep 29] 1,300F, 500Y: plain filly: second foal: half-sister to 3-y-o Mummy Nose Best: dam 2-y-o 5f winner: won seller at Yarmouth in July: mostly creditable efforts after: stays 6f: acts on firm and good to soft going, poor on all-weather (blinkered third start): sold 1,000 gns in October, sent to Sweden. *P. S. McEntee*   52 a39

BAYTOWN RHAPSODY   2 b.f. (May 5) Emperor Jones (USA) 119 – Sing A Rainbow (IRE) 68 (Rainbow Quest (USA) 134) [1999 6d² 6.8m⁶ 7f⁵ 7g⁵ 7.1m 7s Sep 29] 800Y: third foal: half-sister to winner up to 1½m in Holland by Batshoof: dam maiden stayed 1¼m: modest maiden: should stay 1m. *P. S. McEntee*   51

BAY VIEW   4 b.f. Slip Anchor 136 – Carmita (Caerleon (USA) 132) [1998 –: a7g 1999 8s² Sep 29] third foal: half-sister to 1m and 1½m winner Golden Thunderbolt (by Persian Bold): dam French 1½m listed winner: much better effort in maidens when head second at Brighton: will stay beyond 1m: sold 4,500 gns. *K. Mahdi*   78

BEACH BABY   2 ch.f. (Apr 6) Mizoram (USA) 105 – Kina (USA) (Bering 136) [1999 a7g a10g Dec 18] fifth reported foal: half-sister to 1m (at 2 yrs)/1¼m winner Respond (by Reprimand) and a winner in Scandinavia by Prince Daniel: dam unraced: well held in maidens at Lingfield. *J. J. Bridger*   –

BEACON SILVER   5 b.m. Belmez (USA) 131 – Nettle 106 (Kris 135) [1998 NR 1999 11.7s 10g a9.4g Sep 8] tailed off all starts on Flat since 3 yrs. *Ian Williams*   –

BEACON VALE (IRE)   3 ch.g. Forest Wind (USA) 111 – Pam Story (Sallust 134) [1998 NR 1999 11.1v³ 12d a11g Jun 17] IR 9,200F, 7,000Y: half-brother to several winners, including 1992 2-y-o 6f seller winner Stroika (by Shy Groom) and 1989 2-y-o 5f winner Midsummer Breeze (by Tumble Wind): dam placed in Ireland/France: modest maiden at best: tailed off in seller/claimer final 2 starts: sold 1,000 gns in June. *M. G. Meagher*   55 ?

BEADING   2 b.f. (Mar 6) Polish Precedent (USA) 131 – Silver Braid (USA) 101 (Miswaki (USA) 124) [1999 7d Oct 11] sturdy filly: fourth foal: half-sister to 6-y-o Kass Alhawa: dam, 2-y-o 7f winner, later best at 1m: well beaten in Leicester maiden. *J. W. Hills*   –

BE ADMONISHED   2 b.f. (Apr 2) Warning 136 – La Sorrela (IRE) (Cadeaux Genereux 131) [1999 5d 7.5g Sep 15] 4,500Y: small filly: first foal: dam unraced half-sister to smart sprinter Central City: tailed off in maidens: sold 650 gns. *Mrs P. N. Dutfield*   –

BEAT ALL (USA)   3 b. or br.c. Dynaformer (USA) – Spirited Missus (USA) (Distinctive (USA)) [1998 103p: 7m² 7.1d* 1999 10m* 12g³ 12g⁴ Jun 27]   120
    The arrival in Britain of top American jockey Gary Stevens at the beginning of June lent itself to a photo opportunity for the Derby organisers. Stevens had been booked to ride leading Derby contender Beat All some weeks earlier after the papers carried stories of his plans for an extended stay in

Mr Saeed Suhail's "Beat All"

Beat All (USA) (b. or br.c. 1996)	Dynaformer (USA) (b or br 1985)	Roberto (b 1969)	Hail To Reason Bramalea
		Andover Way (b or br 1978)	His Majesty On The Trail
	Spirited Missus (USA) (b or br 1976)	Distinctive (b or br 1966)	Never Bend Precious Lady
		Missus Beau (ch 1957)	Bolero Gal In Calico

Britain. Stevens was pictured in Derby week walking the Epsom course with nine-times Derby winner Lester Piggott whom he described afterwards as 'a man of few words.' Piggott's message for Stevens, who had never ridden at the course before, was, apparently, short and sweet—'If you're on the best horse you'll win.' Lester presumably thought it a waste of breath to follow up with practical advice on how to ensure that came about—scour the form-book then reach for the phone to persuade the trainer to put you up! As it was, Stevens was on a colt who had shown plenty of promise, putting himself in the Derby picture in a very open year with an emphatic three-length victory under Pat Eddery in the Green Ridge Stables Newmarket Stakes over a mile and a quarter at the Guineas meeting. Beat All drew away readily that day from the Godolphin representative Mukhalif, staying on very strongly, and reports of the sparkling home work that followed resulted in his heading the Derby betting for a time at around 6/1. Beat All wasn't seen out again before Epsom—plans to run him in the Dante were shelved when the going changed to soft—and after news of a training set-back with a bruised foot he was overtaken in the betting by Godolphin's number-one Dubai Millennium, the Dee Stakes winner Oath and the Lingfield Derby Trial winner Lucido. Beat All came a good third, running

113

on strongly in the straight to be beaten a length and three quarters and a length and a half by Oath and Lingfield Derby Trial runner-up Daliapour. Lacking the experience of the first two and nothing like so well placed as them early on in the race, Beat All looked sure to go on to win good races. In the event, he was seen out only once more, when a below-form fourth behind Montjeu in the Irish Derby, pushed along from some way out and challenging only briefly on the home turn. The decision to keep Beat All in training as a four-year-old provides a belated opportunity for him to justify his trainer's very high opinion of him.

The tall, rather leggy Beat All, who looked in fine shape on Derby Day, has an all-American pedigree. His sire Dynaformer is a son of Derby winner Roberto and stayed a mile and a half well enough himself, while his dam Spirited Missus won at up to a mile. Easily the best of several winners bred by Spirited Missus is the 1988 Breeders' Cup Juvenile Fillies runner-up Darby Shuffle (by Darby Creek Road, another Roberto stallion). Beat All stays a mile and a half well and has yet to race on extremes of going. *Sir Michael Stoute*

BEAT HOLLOW   2 b.c. (Mar 22) Sadler's Wells (USA) 132 – Wemyss Bight   **97 P**
121 (Dancing Brave (USA) 140) [1999 8s* Sep 16]
Warren Place, which went on to win three of the five classics, started the latest season with the biggest Flat string in Britain. The one hundred and ninety-one inmates listed in *Horses In Training* included no fewer than eighty-eight two-year-olds, but the stable had a relatively quiet time with its juveniles, winning only eleven races and having only one runner in a two-year-old pattern race, Rowa in the May Hill. One who did make a big impression was the impeccably-bred Beat Hollow, successful in a twelve-runner maiden at Yarmouth in mid-September on his only start. Beat Hollow, sent off at 5/2-on, looked to the manner born as he readily drew clear for a three-length win, with his rider looking round after leading on the bridle two furlongs out. Newcomers filled the first four places as the field finished strung out, and the race worked out well, runner-up Peacock Jewel winning in good style at Newmarket next time and the third and fifth also scoring before the end of the turf season. As

EBF Custom Kitchens Maiden Stakes, Yarmouth—Beat Hollow lives up to his breeding and home reputation, beating Peacock Jewel in the style of a very promising performer

for Beat Hollow, he was taken out of the Racing Post Trophy before he ran at Yarmouth, the plan clearly being that he should not be tried too highly in his first season. He is capable of much better than he showed at Yarmouth and should really come into his own at a mile and a quarter plus as a three-year-old.

Beat Hollow (b.c. Mar 22, 1997)	Sadler's Wells (USA) (b 1981)	Northern Dancer (b 1961)	Nearctic
			Natalma
		Fairy Bridge (b 1975)	Bold Reason
			Special
	Wemyss Bight (b 1990)	Dancing Brave (b 1983)	Lyphard
			Navajo Princess
		Bahamian (ch 1985)	Mill Reef
			Sorbus

Beat Hollow is the third foal of Irish Oaks winner Wemyss Bight and a half-brother to Yaralino (by Caerleon), who began the latest season as one of Warren Place's classic hopes, Henry Cecil advising readers in a two-page feature on the Warren Place horses in the *Racing Post* in mid-April that he was 'one to keep an eye on with the Derby in mind.' Yaralino landed a maiden at Lingfield impressively on his racecourse debut in May but didn't make the Derby line-up and after only two more runs (including the King Edward VII Stakes at Royal Ascot) was sold for 45,000 guineas at the Newmarket Autumn Sales. Cecil's summary of Yaralino's prospects would serve ideally to describe Beat Hollow's—if he fulfils his potential, he could be the horse to provide his outstanding sire Sadler's Wells with that elusive Epsom Derby winner. He is available in some lists at 33/1 for the race at the time of writing. *H. R. A. Cecil*

BEAUCHAMP KING   6 gr.h. Nishapour (FR) 125 – Afariya (FR) (Silver Shark   –
129) [1998 113d: 7.1d* 8m 8.5m 7.9m⁴ 10s 1998 8d 7.1g May 1] good-bodied horse: had a rather round action: smart performer at best, successful in Racing Post Trophy at Doncaster and Craven Stakes at Newmarket: well below form after reappearance in 1998: stayed 1m: acted on any going: sometimes edgy: usually held up: to stand at Scarvagh House Stud, Co Down, Ireland. *G. A. Butler*

BEAUCHAMP MAGIC   4 b.g. Northern Park (USA) 107 – Beauchamp Buzz   **46 §**
85 (High Top 131) [1998 73: 8.2s 12m³ 16m² 16.2m⁶ 14.1g⁵ 16s 1999 15.4v 11.9f⁶ 16d 16m 12m 16d a12g a16.2g* a16.2g⁶ Dec 15] good-bodied gelding: poor handicapper: trained first 3 starts by G. Butler: won at Wolverhampton in December: stays 2m: acts on all-weather and good to firm going: tried blinkered/visored: often tongue tied: temperamental. *M. D. I. Usher*

BEAUCHAMP NOBLE   3 b.g. Northern Park (USA) 107 – Beauchamp Cactus   **76**
86 (Niniski (USA) 125) [1998 62p: 8.2s⁵ 8s⁶ 1999 10.3d⁴ 12.3d⁵ 14.6f⁴ 14.1m⁴ 11.5d⁴ 11.6m⁶ Jun 21] tall, unfurnished gelding: fair maiden: disappointing final 2 starts, and possibly becoming less than enthusiastic: stays 14.6f: acts on firm and soft ground: has had tongue tied: has taken strong hold: successful over hurdles in August: sold 6,000 gns in October, sent to Italy. *G. A. Butler*

BEAUCHAMP NYX   3 b.f. Northern Park (USA) 107 – Beauchamp Image 79   –
(Midyan (USA) 124) [1998 –: 8d 1999 10s 11.9v a12g⁶ Nov 22] good-bodied filly: well beaten in maidens. *G. A. Butler*

BEAU CHEVALIER   3 b.g. Up And At 'em 109 – Exceptional Beauty 94 (Sallust   **68 d**
134) [1998 NR 1999 5d⁵ 6g 7.5v 6f 5v Oct 11] 14,000F, 15,000Y: small gelding: half-brother to 2-y-o 5f winners Winterbound (in 1994) and Good Fetch (in 1993), both by Siberian Express: dam 1½m winner: well beaten after showing fair form on debut. *J. L. Eyre*

BEAUMONT (IRE)   9 br.g. Be My Native (USA) 122 – Say Yes (Junius (USA)   **71**
124) [1998 –: a16s 1999 12g⁶ 13.9s 14m⁴ 16.1m⁴ 14.8m 17.3g Oct 16] compact gelding: fair handicapper on Flat, fairly useful winning hurdler: should stay beyond 2m: acts on fibresand and any turf going: below form in blinkers earlier in career: normally held up: joined N. Callaghan. *J. E. Banks*

BEAU REGARDE   8 b.m. Clantime 101 – Noor Jehan (Taj Dewan 128) [1998   –
NR 1999 8m Sep 19] fifth foal: dam unraced: tailed-off last in maiden on debut. *J. S. Wainwright*

BEAU ROBERTO 5 b.g. Robellino (USA) 127 – Night Jar 102 (Night Shift **66** (USA)) [1998 57: a8g³ a8g³ a11g⁴ 11.1v⁶ 8.3d 8d³ 6g 8s⁴ 8.3d³ 10.1s² 11.1m* 9.1d⁴ 8m⁴ 11.1d* 10s³ 12.1s⁴ 11m⁶ 12.1d 1999 9.2v 10v⁴ 12m 12m³ 12g² 12g⁶ 12m 12g 13f* 11.1f⁴ 11.1m⁴ 16m³ 13m* 14m³ 12.1m⁴ 12f² 13s⁴ 14.1g 13.1v⁵ 12g² Nov 3] small, strong gelding: shows knee action: fair handicapper: won at Hamilton (all 4 wins there) in July and August: mostly creditable efforts after: effective at 11f to 2m: acts on fibresand and probably any turf going: tried blinkered, not since 1997. *J. S. Goldie*

BEAU VIENNA 4 b.f. Superpower 113 – Waltz On Air 86 (Doc Marten 104) **–** [1998 –: a7g a8g⁶ 8g⁶ 8m 9.2s⁵ 10.9m 8s a8g 1999 a7g 9.2v Mar 29] no longer of any account. *A. R. Dicken*

BEBE COSMONAUT 3 ch.f. Cosmonaut – Bebe Altesse (GER) (Alpenkonig **–** (GER)) [1998 –p: 7m 6m a7g⁴ 1999 a7g³ a10g a8g⁵ a8g 8m 7m 8f 10s Sep 29] **a50** unfurnished filly: modest maiden: stays 1m, possibly not 1¼m: acts on all-weather. *A. G. Newcombe*

BEBE DE CHAM 2 b.f. (Feb 18) Tragic Role (USA) – Champenoise 64 (Forzando **75** 122) [1999 5g 5d* 5f 6.8m a5g⁵ 7m 7f² 6m⁶ 6m* 6.5g 6g Oct 2] 2,000Y: unfurnished filly: second foal: sister to 3-y-o Drowned In Bubbly: dam 1m winner at 4 yrs: fair performer: won minor event in April and nursery in August, both at Thirsk: stays 7f: acts on firm and good to soft going: races prominently/leads: tended to hang sixth start, edged right next time: blinkered (stiff task, well beaten) final start: none too consistent. *J. L. Eyre*

BE BRAVE 9 b.g. Never So Bold 135 – Boo 77 (Bustino 136) [1998 51?: a16g⁶ **–** a14g⁴ a11g⁶ a14g 1999 a16g Jan 8] poor maiden on Flat: modest winning hurdler: should stay 2m+: raced only on fibresand: blinkered (well held) only start in 1999. *T. J. Etherington*

BECKON 3 ch.f. Beveled (USA) – Carolynchristensen 58 (Sweet Revenge 129) **61** [1998 45: 5g 5m 5d 1999 a7g⁴ 8.2m⁵ a8g⁶ 7m³ 8.5m 7g a7g a10g* a10g³ Dec 18] leggy, lengthy filly: modest performer: trained first 3 starts by T. D. Barron: won seller at Lingfield in December by 10 lengths: stays 1¼m: acts on good to firm going and equitrack: has hung right. *B. R. Johnson*

BEDARA 2 b.f. (Jan 12) Barathea (IRE) 127 – Cutting Reef (IRE) 105 (Kris 135) **91 p** [1999 7d 8d² Oct 30] 75,000F, 80,000Y: strong, lengthy filly: has scope: second foal: half-sister to German 1¼m winner Sampa Coeur (by Caerleon): dam French stayer: burly and green on debut, then marked improvement when 1¼ lengths second of 10 to Silver Colours in steadily-run listed event at Newmarket, disputing lead from 3f out: will stay at least 1¼m: useful prospect. *B. W. Hills*

BEDAZZLE 8 b.g. Formidable (USA) 125 – Wasimah 84 (Caerleon (USA) 132) **–** [1998 –: 11.6g 9.2s 12m⁶ a12g 1999 a11g Feb 5] no longer of any account. *M. Brittain*

BEDAZZLING (IRE) 2 gr.f. (Mar 9) Darshaan 133 – Dazzlingly Radiant 81 (Try **96** My Best (USA) 130) [1999 6d 7m³ 7v* 7d² 7.3s Oct 23] 88,000F, 96,000Y: leggy, useful-looking filly: sixth foal: half-sister to 3 winners, including 3-y-o Bound For Pleasure and useful Irish 6f winner Alarme Belle (by Warning): dam, 6f winner, from family of Poule d'Essai des Pouliches winner Danseuse du Soir: useful performer: won maiden at Kempton in September: best effort when ½-length second of 17 to Inchlonaig in sales event at Newmarket later in month: ran poorly final start: will probably stay 1¼m: acts on good to firm and heavy ground. *J. R. Fanshawe*

BEDEVILLED 4 ch.g. Beveled (USA) – Putout 69 (Dowsing (USA) 124) [1998 **70** 76: 5s⁴ 6d⁴ 6m⁵ 7.1g 1999 6g 6v 6m⁶ 6m² 6f⁶ 5d 5g* a6g Sep 4] close-coupled gelding: fair performer: trained by M. Heaton-Ellis first 3 starts: won maiden at Beverley in August: effective at 5f/6f: acts on good and good to soft going: visored second start: reportedly bled final outing. *T. D. Barron*

BEDOUIN QUEEN 2 ch.f. (Feb 14) Aragon 118 – Petra's Star 61 (Rock City **55** 120) [1999 5m 6g 6.1f³ a6g a8g a7g⁵ Dec 10] 500Y: first foal: dam ran 3 times: modest maiden: should stay 7f, unlikely to get much further: blinkered final start. *R. F. Johnson Houghton*

BEECHCROFT BAY   5 b.g. Teamster 114 – Galley Bay 55 (Welsh Saint 126)   –
[1998 NR 1999 14.1m Jul 10] second foal: half-brother to 7-y-o Artic Bay: dam 1¾m
winner in Ireland: little form in bumpers or over hurdles and well beaten in maiden
on Flat debut: sold 600 gns in September, joined J. de Giles. *Mrs P. N. Dutfield*

BEE EIGHT   2 b.c. (Feb 5) Mujtahid (USA) 118 – Creme de Menthe (IRE) (Green   **95**
Desert (USA) 127) [1999 5m 5g² 6s³ 6d² 6m 6m³ 5.2m⁴ 6f⁴ Jul 28] 30,000Y: strong,
lengthy colt: good walker: first foal: dam unraced half-sister to In The Groove: useful
maiden: in frame in varied company, including listed race at Epsom and Richmond
Stakes at Goodwood: should stay 7f: acts on firm and good to soft ground: sold
85,000 gns, sent to USA. *D. R. C. Elsworth*

BEE GEE   2 b.f. (Mar 13) Beveled (USA) – Bunny Gee (Last Tycoon 131) [1999   –
7m 7m 8.1g 6g Sep 20] second foal: half-sister to 3-y-o Tomasean: dam no worthwhile form: always behind in maidens/nursery. *M. Blanshard*

BEE HEALTH BOY   6 b.g. Superpower 113 – Rekindle 70 (Relkino 131) [1998   **54**
76, a–: 6v⁶ 6v² 5s² 5d⁵ 6s⁶ 6g² 6s 6d* 6g⁴ 6f 6m 6m 6m 6s 6v 1999 6d 6s 6g⁶ 6.1f 6d   **a–**
6f³ 7m² 6m Sep 3] lengthy, good-topped gelding: modest handicapper nowadays:
stays 7f: has won on good to firm going, but best efforts on good or softer (unsuited
by fibresand): usually blinkered: has run well sweating: usually races prominently.
G. Holmes

BEGGARS BELIEF (IRE)   3 b.f. Common Grounds 118 – Perfect Alibi (Law   **86**
Society (USA) 130) [1998 NR 1999 7m 8m³ 8g³ 9.9d³ 9f 10d 7.7d* 8d* 10d Nov 4]
angular, useful-looking filly: half-sister to several winners, including fairly useful 6f
winner (including at 2 yrs) Likely Story (by Night Shift) and 7-y-o Acquittal: dam,
unraced half-sister to Phoenix Stakes winner Aviance and Prix du Cadran winner
Chief Contender, from excellent family: fairly useful performer: won maiden at
Warwick in September and handicap at Leicester (comfortably) in October: effective
at 1m to 1¼m: acts on good to firm and good to soft going: has been bandaged.
J. L. Dunlop

BE GONE   4 ch.g. Be My Chief (USA) 122 – Hence (USA) (Mr Prospector (USA))   **100**
[1998 95p: 8f⁵ 9g* 1999 10m³ 12g³ 12m 11.9s 8m⁵ 7.9g a12g³ a12g Dec 17]   **a89**
good-topped gelding: not a good walker: useful performer on turf, fairly useful on
all-weather: reportedly suffered fractured pelvis in 1998: best efforts when third in
minor events at Newmarket and Goodwood in May: left H. Cecil 10,000 gns after
sixth start: ran in snatches (bad moover: stays 1½m: acts on good to firm going and
equitrack: tried blinkered/visored (ran poorly). *C. A. Dwyer*

BEGORRAT (IRE)   5 ch.g. Ballad Rock 122 – Hada Rani (Jaazeiro (USA) 127)   **68**
[1998 71: 11.1v 12.4d⁶ 11.9d⁴ 10d² 12d 13.1d⁴ 10.1g⁴ 11.9f 10.9d⁴ 10s* 12v⁴ 1999
11.1v 11d 11.9d 10.1m² 8.9d 10m Jun 19] rangy, angular gelding: fair handicapper:
does not stay 1½m when conditions are testing: acts on good to firm and soft going:
effective blinkered or not, also tried visored: sometimes makes running. *J. S. Goldie*

BEGUILE   5 b.g. More Welcome 131 – Captivate 79 (Mansingh (USA) 120) [1998   **50**
54: a6g a6g a12g a7g⁵ a8f³ a7g³ 1999 a10g⁴ a6f⁶ a8g Feb 25] modest maiden
handicapper: likely to prove best at 7f/1m: raced almost exclusively on equitrack:
tends to start slowly. *B. R. Johnson*

BEHARI (IRE)   5 b.g. Kahyasi 130 – Berhala (IRE) (Doyoun 124) [1998 NR   –
1999 11.9v Oct 13] IR 4,400 3-y-o: first foal: dam unraced half-sister to Arc
runner-up Behera: poor maiden hurdler: sold 6,100 gns in August, no show in maiden
on Flat debut. *R. Hollinshead*

BEHIND THE SCENES   5 ch.g. Kris 135 – Free Guest 125 (Be My Guest   **55**
(USA) 126) [1998 –, a68d: a16.2g³ 11.9g a12g a10g⁵ 12m 11.7d a16g³ a16m⁴ a14.8g
a12g 1999 a16f³ a16g a16g² a16g* a16.2g⁴ 17.2g⁴ Jun 30] strong, angular gelding:
modest performer: won claimer at Lingfield in May: stays 17f: acts on good to soft
ground and all-weather: blinkered (well beaten) final 4-y-o start: inconsistent: sold
14,000 gns in July. *C. A. Cyzer*

BELEAGUER   4 ch.f. Rainbow Quest (USA) 134 – Armeria (USA) 79 (Northern   **88**
Dancer) [1998 NR 1999 10.5f³ 10.1g⁵ 8.3d* 8s Nov 22] leggy, angular filly: fourth
living foal: sister to useful 1997 2-y-o 1m winner Besiege, useful 1¼m winner Quota
and top-class 1992 2-y-o 1m winner Armiger, also second in St Leger: dam, best at

1¼m, half-sister to Park Hill winner I Want To Be, from good family: first form in maidens when winning 17-runner event at Windsor in November easily by 5 lengths from Bayaniya: only seventh in listed race at Maisons-Laffitte later in month: bred to have been suited by at least 1¼m: stud. *H. R. A. Cecil*

BELENUS (GER)   3 ch.c. Lomitas 129 – Beaute (GER) (Lord Udo (GER)) [1998 NR 1999 10.5s* 8.5s³ 10s² 11g* 12m* 12g* 12g³ 12d* Sep 26] third foal: half-brother to German winners Berlanga (7f, by Executive Pride) and Bellinda (1m, by Peking Opera): dam German 7f/1m winner: very smart performer: won maiden at Bremen in April, national listed event there in June, 18-runner BMW Deutsches Derby at Hamburg (by length from Acambaro) in July, BMW-Europachampionat at Hoppegarten (by 5 lengths) in August and Post Express-Europa-Preis (by head from Hibiscus) at Cologne in September: also good 3 lengths third to Tiger Hill in Grosser Preis von Baden penultimate start: stays 1½m: acts on good to firm and good to soft going, probably on soft: stays in training. *A. Wohler, Germany*   **120**

BELIEVING   2 b.f. (Feb 2) Belmez (USA) 131 – Australia Fair (AUS) (Without Fear (FR) 128) [1999 6m⁴ 5.3f* 5.2m⁵ a6g Oct 8] half-sister to 3-y-o Ozzie and 2 winners by Town And Country, notably smart sprinter Double Blue: dam ran once: fair form: won maiden at Brighton in July, and ran well in nursery at Newbury next time: stays 6f: sweating final start. *R. Hannon*   **74**

BELISARIO (IRE)   5 b. or br.g. Distinctly North (USA) 115 – Bold Kate (Bold Lad (IRE) 133) [1998 NR 1999 a12g⁶ Jan 11] IR 10,500F: half-brother to numerous winners, including 1985 2-y-o 6f and 1m winner Bohea Destroyer (by Crofter): dam second at 8.5f at 2 yrs in Ireland: fairly useful bumper winner/fair novice hurdler: behind in maiden at Southwell on Flat debut. *N. A. Graham*   **–**

BELLA   3 ch.f. Inchinor 119 – Indian Jubilee 81 (Indian King (USA) 128) [1998 –: 7d 1999 a8f a7f⁵ Jan 30] tall, lengthy, rather unfurnished filly: no form in maidens: blinkered on reappearance: sold 3,000 gns in July. *I. A. Balding*   **–**

BELLA BELLISIMO (IRE)   2 b.f. (Mar 4) Alzao (USA) 117 – Bella Vitessa (IRE) (Thatching 131) [1999 6d⁵ 7f² 7.1m⁵ 8g⁵ 8d³ 7d⁵ Oct 7] IR 70,000Y: close-coupled, quite good-topped filly: first foal: dam, no worthwhile form, half-sister to smart 1½m performer Wind In Her Hair (by Alzao) from excellent family: fairly useful performer: won maiden at York in June: mostly creditable efforts after: will stay 1¼m: acts on firm and good to soft going: has been bandaged in front: blinkered (ran well) penultimate start. *T. D. Easterby*   **84**

BELLA PUPA   3 ch.f. Theatrical Charmer 114 – Louisa Anne 73 (Mummy's Pet 125) [1998 NR 1999 a9.4g 7m Aug 22] 1,000Y: half-sister to 2 winners abroad, including Nite Nite Louisa (by Night Shift): dam 5f/7f winner here at 2 yrs: dam sprint maiden: well held in maiden/seller: visored both starts. *Mrs N. Macauley*   **–**

BELLAS GATE BOY   7 b.g. Doulab (USA) 115 – Celestial Air 96 (Rheingold 137) [1998 54, a–: 8m 7g* 11.5m⁴ 10.1m⁶ 10m 10.9d⁴ 1999 7m⁶ 7.7s* a8.5g* 8d Oct 4] leggy gelding: fair handicapper on turf, poor on all-weather: usually runs in amateurs/ladies races: clear-cut winner at Warwick in May and Wolverhampton in June: finds 7f a minimum, barely stays 1½m: acts on soft ground, good to firm and fibresand: blinkered once earlier in career: often slowly away: inconsistent. *J. Pearce*   **65 a51**

BELLE DE JOUR   2 b.f. (Mar 10) Exit To Nowhere (USA) 122 – Nikiya (IRE) (Lead On Time (USA) 123) [1999 6.8d⁶ 7d⁶ 8.2d⁴ Oct 21] 500Y: small filly: first foal: dam placed around 9f in France: modest form in maidens/seller: may prove best at 7f/1m: sold 5,500 gns, sent to Sweden. *D. R. C. Elsworth*   **54**

BELLEFONTE (IRE)   3 b.c. Scenic 128 – La Bella Fontana (Lafontaine (USA) 117) [1998 NR 1999 9f⁵ 10d² 12m² 10m⁵ Jul 23] 70,000F, 32,000Y: tall, work-manlike colt: sixth foal: half-brother to 2 winners by Fairy King, notably very smart miler Revoque: dam once-raced half-sister to useful 5f and 7f winner Abuzz: fairly useful maiden: best effort at Pontefract second start: looked most reluctant final 2 starts: stays 1¼m: sent to UAE: must be treated with caution. *C. E. Brittain*   **84 §**

BELLEME (IRE)   3 b.f. Fairy King (USA) – Belle Passe (Be My Guest (USA) 126) [1998 NR 1999 7m Apr 30] IR 160,000Y: fifth foal: sister to smart Irish 6f to 1m performer Burden of Proof and half-sister to Italian colt Revenger (by Persian

Heights), winner up to 1¼m, including a listed race: dam ran once: 40/1 and green, always tailed off in maiden at Newmarket. *J. H. M. Gosden*

BELLE OF HEARTS   3 gr.f. Belfort (FR) 89 – Three of Hearts 62 (Governor —
General 116) [1998 52: 5g 6s² 5d³ 6g³ 6.1m 5m³ 6.1d 5s 6s 1999 a6g 6f 5g 6m 6g Oct
14] leggy, plain filly: disappointing sprint maiden: left A. Mulholland after second
start. *C. B. B. Booth*

BELLE REGARD   2 ch.f. (Apr 25) Alhijaz 122 – Imagery (Vision (USA)) [1999 —
6m 7m Sep 3] 1,000Y: third foal: sister to a poor maiden: dam, no worthwhile
form, daughter of smart 5f to 7f winner Petty Purse: well beaten in maidens: dead.
T. M. Jones

BELLES RIVES   2 ch.f. (Feb 11) Alflora (IRE) 120 – Dorazine 77 (Kalaglow   **60**
132) [1999 5v 7d⁴ 8d Oct 30] leggy, angular, plain filly: third foal: dam, 7f to 10.5f
winner, out of half-sister to St Leger winner Bruni: modest maiden: best effort when
fourth of 20 in Newmarket seller: bred to be suited by 1¼m+. *M. R. Channon*

BELMARITA (IRE)   6 ch.m. Belmez (USA) 131 – Congress Lady 93 (General —
Assembly (USA)) [1998 64+: 15.4m 1999 a12f⁶ Jan 23] good-bodied mare: fluent
mover: modest maiden on Flat, very lightly raced nowadays: will stay 2m+: raced
almost solely on good going or firmer: fairly useful winning hurdler. *G. A. Hubbard*

BELONG IN LOVE (AUS)   2 ch.f. (Apr 10) Marscay (AUS) – I'm Alert (AUS)   **54 §**
(Red Alert 127) [1999 5m⁵ 6m⁵ 6m⁶ 6s Sep 29] half-sister to numerous winners in
Australia, notably Group 1-winning sprinter With Me (by Covetous): dam 2-y-o
sprint winner: modest maiden at best: jinked badly left stalls on debut and final start,
refusing to race on latter occasion: returned to Australia: one to treat with caution.
J. A. R. Toller

BELTESHAZZAR (IRE)   4 b.g. Un Desperado (FR) 125 – Annalena (IRE) (Ela- —
Mana-Mou 132) [1998 –: 7g 8g a10g 1999 a8g 11.7g a10g Jul 7] of little account.
Mrs L. C. Jewell

BELVEDERE   2 ch.f. (Feb 10) Dilum (USA) 115 – Belle's A Singer (Chief Singer   **47**
131) [1999 6m 6f 8g⁴ 8d a8.5g Oct 16] unfurnished filly: first foal: dam unraced:
poor maiden: tried blinkered: sold 1,500 gns, sent to Holland. *T. J. Etherington*

BE MY PAL   2 b.f. (Mar 21) Be My Chief (USA) 122 – White Domino 67 (Sharpen   **54**
Up 127) [1999 6s Oct 2] 7,000Y: deep-girthed filly: half-sister to 3 winners, includ-
ing useful 1993 2-y-o 6f winner Pinkerton's Pal (by Dominion) and useful sprinter
Macrobian (by Bay Express): dam 1m winner: in need of run, last of 11 in maiden at
Newmarket. *W. Jarvis*

BE MY WISH   4 b.f. Be My Chief (USA) 122 – Spinner 59 (Blue Cashmere 129)   **56**
[1998 76, a80: 7d 7g³ 7m* 7.3m⁵ 7g⁶ 7m⁵ 8d a7g a7g² a7g³ a8g⁶ 1999 10s 10m 8.2m⁴   **a76**
10m 11.5g a8g⁴ a8.5g⁵ Nov 20] sturdy filly: good mover: fair on all-weather, modest
on turf: left S. Woods after fifth start: should prove best at 7f/1m: acts on equitrack,
possibly needs good going or firmer on turf: seems effective blinkered or not: has
been bandaged behind. *W. A. O'Gorman*

BENATOM (USA)   6 gr.g. Hawkster (USA) – Dance Til Two (USA) (Sovereign   **103**
Dancer (USA)) [1998 100: 14m³ 12m 13.9f⁶ 1999 16g⁶ 16m⁵ 14g⁴ 16f² 20m⁴ 16.1m⁶
16.1m* 16f² 14f 14g⁴ 14.1m⁵ Sep 2] well-made gelding: has a quick action: useful
handicapper: generally in good form in 1999, winning at Newmarket in July: good
fourth of 5 to Yavana's Pace in listed race at Goodwood on penultimate start: finds
1¾m a bare minimum, and stays 2½m: acts on firm and good to soft going: visored
once at 4 yrs (raced too freely). *D. R. C. Elsworth*

BENBYAS   2 b.g. (Feb 28) Rambo Dancer (CAN) 107 – Light The Way 72   **66**
(Nicholas Bill 125) [1999 6f 6g 8.5g⁴ 8d 8d Sep 26] smallish, sturdy gelding: brother
to 4-y-o Carambo and to 1995 2-y-o 5f winner Rambo Delight: dam won 1m seller:
easily best effort in maidens when fourth of 8 to Windsor Boy at Beverley: below
form in nurseries on softer ground after: stays 8.5f. *J. L. Eyre*

BEN EWAR   5 b.h. Old Vic 136 – Sunset Reef (Mill Reef (USA) 141) [1998 111:   **111**
12g 10.5v³ 10s 10g 12m 16g 12.5m* 13s* 10.5s* 9.8v* 1999 9.8d² 12d⁴ 12d²
12.5g⁴ 12g⁴ 10.5s² 12s Oct 24] smart performer: won last 4 starts at 4 yrs, including
listed races at Strasbourg and Longchamp: creditable efforts second to fourth starts

in 1999 when in frame in valuable handicap at Goodwood, listed race at Lyon Parilly (short-headed by Copeland) and Prix Maurice de Nieuil at Maisons-Laffitte (beaten just over a length by Lucky Dream): pulled up (bled) final start: stays 13f: acts on good to firm and heavy ground. *F. Doumen, France*

BEN GUNN 7 b.g. Faustus (USA) 118 – Pirate Maid (Auction Ring (USA) 123) [1998 86: 8d³ 8s 8.5m² 8m⁶ 8f* 7m² 8m* 8f 7m³ 8m⁶ 8.3m³ 8g 8g 1999 a8g 8g⁵ 8d⁵ 8m⁴ 8m 8m⁶ 8.1m* 8g 8d Oct 4] good-bodied gelding: takes the eye: fair handicapper: won ladies event at Chepstow in August: effective at 7f (given good test) to easy 1¼m: well beaten on heavy going, acts on any other turf and all-weather: well beaten in visor earlier in career: best held up in strongly-run race. *P. T. Walwyn* **77 a–**

BENHABEEBI (IRE) 2 b.g. (Apr 29) Bin Ajwaad (IRE) 119 – Alfaaselah (GER) 97 (Dancing Brave (USA) 140) [1999 6g⁴ 7m³ 7g³ 7d³ 8m Sep 7] first foal: dam 7f (at 2 yrs) to 9.5f (in Germany) winner from family of Arc winner Urban Sea: modest maiden: beaten favourite last 3 outings, finding little and flicking tail first and third occasions: should stay 1m: not one to trust: sold 3,400 gns, sent to France. *B. Hanbury* **66 §**

BENNOCHY 2 ch.g. (Feb 21) Factual (USA) 108 – Agreloui 59 (Tower Walk 130) [1999 6g 5m⁶ 5m⁶ 5s 5g 5g Nov 3] 5,000F: half-brother to several winners, including 2-y-o winners Absaloui (5f, by Absalom) and Lindas Delight (6f, by Batshoof) and 1½m winner Absolute Folly (also by Absalom): dam lightly-raced maiden: poor maiden: stays 6f: acts on good to firm ground. *J. Berry* **49**

BENOUI SPRINGS (IRE) 2 br.c. (Jan 9) Caerleon (USA) 132 – Afrique Bleu Azur (USA) (Sagace (FR) 135) [1999 7d Sep 30] angular, quite attractive colt: fourth living foal: brother to 4-y-o Cape Verdi and half-brother to useful 1½m winner L'Africain Bleu (by Saint Cyrien): dam, French 11.5f winner, sister to Breeders' Cup Classic winner Arcangues: looked green when 7 lengths eighth of 14 to Qamous in maiden at Newmarket: will stay at least 1m: capable of better. *P. W. Chapple-Hyam* **71 p**

BEN SAMSON 3 ch.g. Bold Arrangement 127 – Mr Chris Cakemaker 49 (Hotfoot 126) [1998 NR 1999 13.4m⁶ 10m⁶ Jul 16] good-topped gelding: second reported foal: dam 1m and 1¼m winner: in need of race, soundly beaten in maidens. *E. J. Alston* **–**

BENS GIFT 4 ch.f. Keen 116 – Monstrosa 70 (Monsanto (FR) 121) [1998 54: 8.3m⁶ 8.3g 10m³ 8.3m 8d 1999 9m 10m* 10f² 10.1g 10.2g Aug 30] modest handicapper: won at Windsor in July: well below form last 2 starts, reportedly finishing lame in latter: stays 1¼m: acts on firm going. *Mrs Merrita Jones* **62**

BENTYHEATH LANE 2 b.g. (Mar 30) Puissance 110 – Eye Sight 67 (Roscoe Blake 120) [1999 7d 8s Nov 6] angular, workmanlike gelding: fifth foal: half-brother to 3-y-o Sailor Ahoy, a 2-y-o 7.5f seller winner by Absalom and a 1½m winner by Handsome Sailor: dam middle-distance maiden: behind in maidens at Doncaster: has worn severe noseband. *M. Mullineaux* **–**

BENZOE (IRE) 9 b.g. Taufan (USA) 119 – Saintly Guest (What A Guest 119) [1998 81: 6d 6v 5s 6g⁴ 6g* 5g⁵ 5g 5s³ 6s⁶ 6g 6f 6m² 6g² 7g 5d 6m* 5g⁵ 6s³ 6d 1999 6m 6v 6s 6d⁶ 5m 6d 7m 6m* 6f 6f 7f 6m 6.1d 6g Oct 14] tall gelding: has a round action: fair handicapper: won at Leicester in July: well below that form afterwards: ideally suited by 6f: acts on any going: has worn blinkers/visor, not for long time: sometimes slowly away: difficult ride. *Andrew Turnell* **70**

BERBERIS 3 b.c. Green Desert (USA) 127 – Babita 107 (Habitat 134) [1998 NR 1999 7m 8.2s 7m Oct 19] sixth foal: half-brother to 1½m winner Bambara and 1995 2-y-o 7f winner (later won in USA) Babinda (both by Old Vic): dam best at 6f at 2 yrs: well beaten in maidens, off course 4 months after debut: sold 2,200 gns. *C. E. Brittain* **–**

BERGAMO 3 b.c. Robellino (USA) 127 – Pretty Thing 83 (Star Appeal 133) [1998 77: 7m⁵ 7.5m⁵ 8.1m³ 8g⁵ 10.2d* 10d 1999 10.3d 10d⁶ 12.5m 12g* 14.4g⁵ 12m⁶ 12m⁶ 14.1g* 16.2m³ 14m⁴ 14d⁴ 12m⁴ 12f³ 16m⁵ Sep 11] small, compact colt: fluent mover: fairly useful handicapper: won at Beverley in May and Yarmouth in June: generally in good form otherwise: stays 1¾m: acts on firm and good to soft going: has been bandaged behind: usually blinkered/visored and held up: sold 13,000 gns. *J. Noseda* **87**

BERGEN (IRE)   4 b.c. Ballad Rock 122 – Local Custom (IRE) (Be My Native   **80**
(USA) 122) [1998 87: 7g 8.9s 7.9g³ 8s 8.1m² 1999 7.6m 8.1g⁶ 8.5m 8m 8.5g² 8.2d
Oct 21] quite good-topped colt: fairly useful handicapper: creditable second at
Epsom in August: best around 1m: acts on good to firm going, shaped quite well first
occasion on soft: pulled hard final start. *B. W. Hills*

BERING GIFTS (IRE)   4 b.g. Bering 136 – Bobbysoxer 79 (Valiyar 129) [1998   **84 §**
87§: 8.1s² 10m⁵ 11.8m 8.3m² 8m* 9.7f* 12m⁴ 10g⁴ 8s⁴ 1999 8m 12m 9.7m* 9m⁵
10g² 9g 8.9m⁵ 12s Sep 22] tall, good sort: fairly useful handicapper: made all at
Folkestone in May: best at 1¼m: acts on firm going: tried visored/blinkered: swishes
tail: not one to trust: sold 15,000 gns, joined C. Mann. *P. F. I. Cole*

BERKELEY DIDO (IRE)   2 b.f. (Feb 4) Foxhound (USA) 103 – Dignified Air   **50**
(FR) 70 (Wolver Hollow 126) [1999 5g 5s 6f³ 7m 6s⁶ Aug 9] IR 16,500F: half-
sister to several winners, notably Proud Titania (by Fairy King), useful 7f winner in
Ireland: dam 6f winner: modest maiden: likely to prove best at 6f/7f: acts on firm
going. *M. L. W. Bell*

BERKELEY HALL   2 b.f. (Mar 13) Saddlers' Hall (IRE) 126 – Serious Affair   **58**
(Valiyar 129) [1999 6m 8.2g 6d³ Oct 18] 7,500F, 5,500Y: stocky filly: fifth foal: sister
to Italian 7f/1m winner Sadler's Affair, and half-sister to 7f winner Into Debt (by
Cigar) and a winner in Macau: dam unraced: best effort in maidens when third of 12
to Ravishing at Pontefract: should stay 1m. *B. Palling*

BERLIOZ   3 b.c. Dolphin Street (FR) 125 – Biraya (Valiyar 129) [1998 104p: 7g*   **105**
7g² 1999 8g⁶ 8g Jun 27] strong, close-coupled colt: has a quick action: useful
performer: creditable sixth to Sumitas in Mehl-Muhlens-Rennen at Cologne on reappearance: last in listed race at Goodwood next time, reportedly returning with
swollen girth: stays 1m: joined J. Gosden. *Saeed bin Suroor*

BERL'S GIFT   4 b.f. Prince Sabo 123 – Primitive Gift 38 (Primitive Rising (USA)   **–**
113) [1998 44: 7s³ 8m⁵ 10s³ 8.2g⁴ 8s 1999 10m Sep 24] poor maiden: stays 1m: acts
on good to firm going. *Mrs M. Reveley*

BERMUDA TRIANGLE (IRE)   4 b.f. Conquering Hero (USA) 116 –   **30**
Bermuda Princess (Lord Gayle (USA) 124) [1998 –, a39: a8g⁴ a8g⁴ a10g⁵ 7g 11.6d
11.6g⁵ 1999 11.6m Jul 12] leggy, short-backed filly: poor performer: stays 1¼m.
M. J. Haynes

BERNARDO BELLOTTO (IRE)   4 b.g. High Estate 127 – Naivity (IRE) 72   **65**
(Auction Ring (USA) 123) [1998 60+: 7m 7.1m 9.1s 7g 7d 1999 7g 6s³ 7m 5.9m
7.1m 7f* 7.1g* 6m Jun 24] smallish, workmanlike gelding: unimpressive mover: fair
performer: won seller at Redcar in May and claimer at Musselburgh in June: stays 7f,
should prove effective at 6f: acts on firm going, soft and fibresand: blinkered last 3
starts. *D. Nicholls*

BERNIE'S STAR (IRE)   5 b. or br.g. Arcane (USA) – Abaca (USA) (Manila   **–**
(USA)) [1998 –: 11s a14g 1999 a16g 12.1v⁵ Mar 29] of little account. *N. Bycroft*

BERNSTEIN (USA)   2 b.c. (Mar 17) Storm Cat (USA) – La Affirmed (USA)   **114**
(Affirmed (USA)) [1999 6g* 6g* 8s⁵ Sep 19]

    Same story, different horse. As with King of Kings and Stravinsky in
the two previous years, a Ballydoyle inmate with a towering home reputation
was the talk of the town after his first public appearance. The horse this time
was Bernstein, a 925,000-dollar foal who saw off five rivals with ease in a
maiden at the Curragh on Irish One Thousand Guineas day. King of Kings was
spoken of as the next Nijinsky; could Bernstein be the next King of Kings?
Trainer Aidan O'Brien waxed lyrical about the horse named after the West Side
Story composer. 'This is a very special horse. Even to get horses to lead him in
a canter at home is a big problem. We have to use a four-year-old.' O'Brien
ruled out Royal Ascot, saying that he would be 'going slowly' with the tall,
close-coupled colt who clearly needed time to fill to his frame. Both King of
Kings and Stravinsky had been installed as short-priced ante-post favourites for
the Two Thousand Guineas immediately after their debut. Similar status befell
Bernstein after his second victory, in the Arthur Guinness Railway Stakes at
the Curragh on Irish Derby day, a race King of Kings won on his second start.

Arthur Guinness Railway Stakes, the Curragh—Bernstein emulates King of Kings with an impressive display; Desert Sky and Appalachia follow him home

The long odds-on Bernstein was again impressive, as on his debut making virtually all and drawing effortlessly away in the final furlong, winning by four and a half lengths from the fairly useful filly Desert Sky. Bernstein was clear favourite with most bookmakers—as short as 7/1 in places—for the Two Thousand Guineas immediately after the Railway Stakes, Ladbrokes being out of line in making him joint favourite with Fasliyev. 'This is a serious colt and the sky is the limit' was Aidan O'Brien's post-race comment. Plans to run Bernstein in the Anglesey Stakes a fortnight later were shelved—'he needs more time'—and he was reserved for the National Stakes over a mile at the Curragh in September. Starting at 11/4-on, Bernstein ran much too freely,

Mr M. Tabor, Mrs J. Magnier and Mrs J. Maxwell Moran's "Bernstein"

bowling along with the eventual runner-up Murawwi, asserting early in the straight and looking sure to win until fading dramatically in the closing stages, managing only fifth of eight behind Sinndar. Bernstein had looked a rather highly-strung type on his debut, incidentally, when he was attended by two handlers and proved a little difficult before being mounted. He was fitted with a crossed noseband in the National Stakes and taken very quietly to post. Following a veterinary examination, a 'respiratory abnormality' was given by his stable as the cause of his disappointing run. He wasn't seen out again, unsatisfactory results from a blood test ruling him out of the Middle Park Stakes at Newmarket for which he was declared at the five-day stage.

			Northern Dancer
		Storm Bird	
	Storm Cat (USA)	(b 1978)	South Ocean
	(b or br 1983)		Secretariat
		Terlingua	
Bernstein (USA)		(ch 1976)	Crimson Saint
(b.c. Mar 17, 1997)			Exclusive Native
		Affirmed	
	La Affirmed (USA)	(ch 1975)	Won't Tell You
	(b 1983)		Round Table
		La Mesa	
		(b or br 1970)	Finance

Bernstein should have little difficulty staying a mile, judged on pedigree, though he may well have to be taught to race more tractably if he is to do himself justice at the trip as a three-year-old. Even with Fasliyev now retired, Bernstein is on offer at 14/1 for the Guineas at the time of writing. Bernstein is from the ninth crop of the top North American stallion Storm Cat. Milers Mistle Cat and Aljabr are among his offspring to have done well in pattern races in Europe, and Bernstein's dam La Affirmed gained her only racecourse success at a mile. La Affirmed is a full sister to Grade 3 juvenile winner Lovelier and three-parts sister to the Breeders' Cup Juvenile Fillies and Hollywood Starlet Stakes winner Outstandingly, who stayed a mile and a quarter and is herself the dam of smart French miler Sensation. Bernstein's full sisters Caress and Country Cat both won in graded company at up to nine furlongs. *A. P. O'Brien, Ireland*

BERSAGLIO 4 ch.c. Rainbow Quest (USA) 134 – Escrime (USA) 92 (Sharpen **75 §** Up 127) [1998 80: 12d 10d⁶ 12g⁴ 14m³ 14m⁴ 16.5g 14m³ 13.9g 1999 14.4m 14.1f² 14m 14.1g 18.2s⁵ Sep 16] big, rangy colt: fair maiden handicapper: trained first 4 starts by W. Jarvis: second at Redcar in May, only form in 1999: stays 1¾m: acts on firm and good to soft ground: not to be trusted. *K. A. Morgan*

BERTOLINI (USA) 3 b.c. Danzig (USA) – Aquilegia (USA) (Alydar (USA)) **125** [1998 106: 6g² 6d⁵ 6f* 5.5g² 6f⁴ 7g 6g² 1999 7g* 8m 7m³ 6f³ 6.5s⁵ 6m² 5v Oct 3]

Impressive or wide-margin victories grab the headlines, and headlines influence the way horses are perceived by the racing public. Nowhere was this more in evidence in 1999 than in the sprinting division. There can be little argument about Stravinsky's place at the top after his runaway victory in the July Cup, but many will have failed to notice the progress made during the season by the July Cup third Bertolini, who, through several placed efforts, ended the season ranked as the third-best sprinter of the season, behind only Stravinsky and Diktat.

The seventeen-runner July Cup was viewed by some to be lacking quality, even though the field contained thirteen pattern-race winners, three at the highest level. Bertolini, wearing a visor for the first time since his second to Lujain in the Middle Park Stakes as a two-year-old, was at 9/1 and held a slight lead from halfway before finding no answer to Stravinsky's turn of foot, also losing second to Bold Edge by a neck. Third was a smart effort, nonetheless.

Bertolini had made his reappearance in the European Free Handicap (a race which had to be reopened), belying not only his weakness in the betting, but also his trainer's doubts over his ability to stay the seven furlongs. Bertolini

Victor Chandler European Free Handicap, Newmarket—Bertolini makes a good start to the season, galloping on strongly to beat Indiana Legend, Kalidasa and Undeterred

was not hard pressed to beat an ordinary field by two and a half lengths, giving weight all round, but an unsuccessful foray to Longchamp for the Poule d'Essai des Poulains exposed seven furlongs as the limit of Bertolini's stamina. A good third at that distance in the Jersey Stakes at Royal Ascot came before he reverted to sprinting in the July Cup.

After the July Cup, Bertolini did not have to face Stravinsky again, Diktat proving the major stumbling block to a pattern-race victory. Encountering very soft ground for the first time in the six-and-a-half-furlong Prix Maurice de Gheest at Deauville in August, Bertolini ran his usual game race, making most and just losing second place to Gold Away, the pair behind Diktat. The French stewards viewed Gary Stevens' use of the whip on Bertolini to be excessive and duly fined him. However, Bertolini showed no ill-effects in the Haydock Park Sprint Cup a month later, running the best race of his career, again thwarted by Diktat. In a record field of sixteen, Bertolini drifted in the

Sheikh Mohammed's "Bertolini"

betting, but was caught only close home, beaten a neck by Diktat's late run with Arkadian Hero a length and three quarters back in third.

At 750,000 dollars, Bertolini was the fourth-most-expensive Danzig yearling sold at public auction in 1997; the three who cost more, incidentally, managed to muster only one maiden win between them. Bertolini follows on from the likes of Dayjur, Anabaa, Danehill and his relative Green Desert, as being a high-class sprinting representative for his sire, who commands one of the highest stud fees in the world. The distaff side of Bertolini's pedigree is also extremely strong, his grandam being the remarkable broodmare Courtly Dee, whose eighteen foals include nine stakes performers, three (Althea, Ali Oop and Ketoh) at the highest level. Bertolini's dam Aquilegia won the Grade 2 New York Handicap over ten furlongs as a four-year-old, and won at Grade 3 level at five. As Bertolini is her first foal, Aquilegia has quickly followed in the family tradition of producing pattern-race performers, her sisters already being responsible for the likes of Green Desert and the smart filly Aldiza, a Grade 1 winner in the USA. Bertolini's full sister Agarita was unraced as a two-year-old in 1999, but there are two more half-sisters waiting in the wings, a yearling by Dixieland Band and a Deputy Minister foal.

Bertolini (USA) (b.c. 1996)	Danzig (USA) (b 1977)	Northern Dancer (b 1961)	Nearctic
			Natalma
		Pas de Nom (b or br 1968)	Admiral's Voyage
			Petitioner
	Aquilegia (USA) (ch 1989)	Alydar (ch 1975)	Raise A Native
			Sweet Tooth
		Courtly Dee (b or br 1968)	Never Bend
			Tulle

The strong, sturdy Bertolini has a powerful, round action. Although equipped with a visor three times in 1999 and blinkers on his final start, he shows no sign of being ungenuine. He stays seven furlongs and acts on firm and soft going. He sweated up when beating only two home when favourite for the Prix de l'Abbaye de Longchamp on his final start. Bertolini will race for Godolphin in 2000 and looks well up to winning another pattern race (he won the July Stakes at two), something which his consistency deserves. *J. H. M. Gosden*

BERTY BOY 3 ch.g. Alhijaz 122 – Bridge Player 52 (The Noble Player (USA) 126) [1998 NR 1999 10.5m 8.1d⁶ 10m⁴ 12s Oct 5] first foal: dam all-weather 1¾m winner and 3m winner over hurdles: well beaten in maidens. *Mrs G. S. Rees* –

BERYL 3 ch.f. Bering 136 – Fayrooz (USA) 74 (Gulch (USA)) [1998 72: 7m 7g² 8.2g² 8v⁴ 1999 10d² 12d* 12g 11.5m³ 14.8m⁵ 14.1m 14s Sep 25] lengthy filly: fair performer: won maiden at Thirsk in April: easily best effort in handicaps after when third at Lingfield: likely to prove best at 1¼m/1½m: acts on good to firm and good to soft ground. *J. L. Dunlop* **77**

BERYL THE PERIL 3 b.f. Presidium 124 – Vague Reply (Vaigly Great 127) [1998 –: 5v⁵ 5m⁶ 1999 a7g Feb 19] no form, including in seller. *N. Bycroft* –

BESCABY BLUE (IRE) 2 b.f. (Mar 27) Blues Traveller (IRE) 119 – Nurse Tyra (USA) (Dr Blum (USA)) [1999 a5g* 5d² a6g⁵ 5v⁵ 7m 7g⁶ 6d 7s⁶ a8g a6g² Dec 27] 5,000 2-y-o: quite good-topped filly: fourth reported foal: half-sister to winners in Italy by Shalford (7f to 8.5f) and Petardia (6f): dam unraced: modest performer: won maiden at Southwell in May and claimer at Redcar in October: stays 7f: acts on fibresand and soft ground, probably on heavy. *J. Wharton* **60**

BESEECHING (IRE) 4 b. or br.f. Hamas (IRE) 125§ – Na-Ammah (IRE) 90 (Ela-Mana-Mou 132) [1998 –: 6m 7.1m⁴ 7d⁵ 1999 8d 9.9m 14.1m Jul 30] lengthy filly: modest form. *J. A. R. Toller* **50**

BEST BOND 2 ch.c. (Jan 13) Cadeaux Genereux 131 – My Darlingdaughter (Night Shift (USA)) [1999 6m 7g⁵ 7.7d⁵ Sep 21] lengthy colt: first foal: dam, once-raced sister to smart miler Nicolotte: best effort in maidens (fair form) when fifth of 7 to **71**

Nothing Daunted at Goodwood on second start: likely to prove best at 6f/7f: raced freely first 2 starts: sold 10,000 gns. *J. L. Dunlop*

BEST EVER   2 ch.c. (Mar 29) Rock City 120 – Better Still (IRE) (Glenstal (USA)   **65**
118) [1999 5m 5d 5v 7m³ 7m² 7f⁵ 7.9f² 7m 7g 7s Oct 25] 1,000Y: workmanlike colt:
third foal: dam little form: fair maiden: ridden by 7-lb claimer, best effort when
second of 14 to The Wife in nursery at York in September on seventh outing: should
stay beyond 1m: acts on firm going: none too consistent. *M. W. Easterby*

BEST KEPT SECRET   8 b.g. Petong 126 – Glenfield Portion 86 (Mummy's Pet   **– §**
125) [1998 –§: 5s 6g 5g 6m 6m 1999 5g 8.3v⁵ 5m 5s 6d 7.1g 6m 6f 9.2m 12.1m 6s
Sep 27] of little account and temperamental. *D. A. Nolan*

BEST MUSIC METROFM   2 b.g. (Apr 5) Governor General 116 – Dancing   **61**
May 31 (Tina's Pet 121) [1999 5g³ Jun 5] second reported foal: dam poor maiden:
33/1, 8 lengths third in minor event at Newcastle: joined E. Alston. *D. Eddy*

BEST OF ALL (IRE)   7 b.m. Try My Best (USA) 130 – Skisette (Malinowski   **82**
(USA) 123) [1998 84: 8d 8.3v 10d 8d 9g* 9.1d 9d* 10m* 10.1m 10s 8g³ 1999 8m⁴
10g⁴ 9f 10d⁵ 10m 8f² 10d⁶ 8d* 8s 8s Nov 6] deep-girthed mare: fairly useful
handicapper: won minor event at Musselburgh in September: hampered and fell final
start: barely stays 1¼m: acts on firm ground, soft and fibresand: blinkered/visored:
best held up: inconsistent. *J. Berry*

BEST OF OUR DAYS   4 b.c. Clantime 101 – Uptown Girl 65 (Caruso 112)   **60**
[1998 66: a5g* a5g* a5g⁶ 5g⁵ 5d 5.1m⁵ 7.1g a7g 1999 a6g³ a5g⁶ a7g a6g³ a6g⁵ a6g
5f 5f 5f 7g 5g³ 6g⁵ 6d⁶ 7g Nov 11] modest performer: ran at Lingfield first 3 starts,
third in claimer on first of them: stays 6f: acts on all-weather, best turf run on good
going. *Alex Vanderhaeghen, Belgium*

BEST OF THE BESTS (IRE)   2 ch.c. (Mar 5) Machiavellian (USA) 123 –   **111 p**
Sueboog (IRE) 109 (Darshaan 133) [1999 7m³ 7.1g* 8s² Sep 26]
 The Group 3 Solario Stakes, traditionally run on the Friday of Sandown's two-day August fixture, is to take place on the Saturday in 2000 when it
will be the feature event at the popular Variety Club meeting. Not that the
switch is likely to raise by much the profile of a race which once had the
reputation of throwing up potential classic winners, but which nowadays
is usually won by no-more-than-useful performers. True, the 1995 winner
Alhaarth went on to be that year's champion two-year-old, but you have to go
back as far as Oh So Sharp in 1984 for the last winner of the Solario Stakes to
go on to classic success. The next one to try will be Best of The Bests,
considered by his trainer at two years to be a Derby prospect. Best of The Best's
form is a long way short of that required to win a Derby, but he's a lightly-raced
imposing colt with plenty of scope for improvement who could well develop
into a leading contender for good middle-distances races, provided he proves to
have the necessary stamina. Best of The Bests will, from now on, be racing in
the Godolphin colours. His first target will be the new UAE Derby over nine
furlongs on dirt in March, followed, if he comes through that, by a tilt at the
Kentucky Derby.
 Best of The Bests did spring something of a surprise at Sandown.
Having only his second race and the one maiden in the seven-runner field, he
was sent off at 20/1 despite having shaped promisingly when third to Distant
Music at Doncaster over three weeks beforehand. The hot favourite was French
challenger Consonant, an easy winner at Chantilly on his sole appearance,
while next in the betting came Sarafan and Kingsclere, who had finished
second and fourth respectively behind Ekraar in another Group 3 event, at
Goodwood, on their previous starts. Consonant proved most disappointing,
setting a strong pace but already dropping away when Sarafan quickened to
lead over two furlongs out. At this point Best of The Bests, who'd been waited
with, was beginning to make headway widest of all, and he came through to
take a narrow advantage one and a half furlongs out. He still looked a bit green
as he did so, but kept on strongly and soon put the issue beyond doubt, drawing
two lengths clear of Sarafan, who just held on to second place from the

strong-finishing Kingsclere. Two lengths separated Best of The Bests and Kingsclere when they met again in the Royal Lodge Stakes at Ascot a month later, the pair finishing second and third respectively behind the favourite, Royal Kingdom. Best of The Bests, who'd still seemed immature both physically and mentally in the paddock (he was on his toes and looking about him), ran right up to his Sandown form on softer ground. Again held up, he quickened to take a narrow lead around a furlong out and kept on gamely, but a rallying Royal Kingdom proved just too strong for him close home.

Best of The Bests (IRE) (ch.c. Mar 5, 1997)	Machiavellian (USA) (b 1987)	Mr Prospector (b 1970)	Raise A Native / Gold Digger
		Coup de Folie (b 1982)	Halo / Raise The Standard
	Sueboog (IRE) (b 1990)	Darshaan (br 1981)	Shirley Heights / Delsy
		Nordica (ch 1983)	Northfields / Princess Arabella

Best of The Bests saw the mile out well in the testing ground and will get a mile and a quarter, probably a mile and a half. His sire Machiavellian only just got a mile, but is responsible for plenty who stay much further. Best of The Bests's dam, Sueboog, also trained by Clive Brittain, probably stayed a mile and a half, finishing a respectable fourth in the Oaks, but both her wins were over seven furlongs, including in the Fred Darling Stakes. She's a daughter of the useful Nordica. While Nordica stayed a mile and a quarter, she showed better form and gained all her victories at shorter distances, winning three races at a mile in England and over six furlongs after being moved to Ireland. The next dam Princess Arabella, a half-sister to the Oaks winner Fair Salinia, raced only at seven furlongs, over which distance she won a maiden. Best of The Bests, a big, rangy individual, unfurnished at present, is Sueboog's second foal. Her first, Sena Desert, showed fairly useful form for Brittain in the latest season. *C. E. Brittain*

Mr Mohamed Obaida's "Best of The Bests"

BEST PORT (IRE)   3 b.g. Be My Guest (USA) 126 – Portree 82 (Slip Anchor   **28**
136) [1998 –: 8g 7d 1999 10f 10g 8f 13.8g⁶ a11g 10d 14.1f⁶ Oct 20] bad maiden:
stays 1¾m: acts on firm and good to soft going. *J. Parkes*

BEST QUEST   4 b.c. Salse (USA) 128 – Quest For The Best (Rainbow Quest   **–**
(USA) 134) [1998 64, a80: a7g² 7.1g³ 8m 7.1g a7g² 7g 7d* a8g⁵ a7g³ a8f⁶ a7g* 1999   **a78**
a7g a6g⁴ a6g a6g a6g a7g⁴ a7g a7g³ a7g a7g a7g Dec 21] small colt: poor mover:
fair handicapper: effective at 6f, barely stays 1m: acts on all-weather, not raced on
turf of late: visored fourth start: has worn tongue strap: usually held up: carries head
awkwardly: none too consistent. *K. R. Burke*

BETCHWORTH SAND   3 ch.g. Aragon 118 – Gay Patricia 63 (Gay Fandango   **–**
(USA) 132) [1998 NR 1999 a7g Nov 8] third reported foal: dam maiden who stayed
7f: very slowly away when tailed off in Lingfield maiden. *T. E. Powell*

BE THANKFULL (IRE)   3 gr.f. Linamix (FR) 127 – Thank One's Stars (Alzao   **95 p**
(USA) 117) [1998 –p: 6s 1999 8m* 8d⁶ 9m² 10d* Oct 1] lengthy, unfurnished filly:
useful performer: won maiden at Ascot in July and (improved effort) handicap at
Newmarket (gamely) in October: stays 1¼m: acts on good to firm and good to soft
going: should do better still. *Major D. N. Chappell*

BE THE CHIEF   3 ch.c. Be My Chief (USA) 122 – Blink Naskra (USA) (Naskra   **58**
(USA)) [1998 102+: 6g* 6d² 1999 8m 7.3g 7m⁵ Aug 27] close-coupled colt: useful
at 2 yrs, but reported to have split a pastern after final start: modest form at best in
1999, including in claimer: should stay at least 1m: has been bandaged: sold 3,800
gns in September. *T. G. Mills*

BETHESDA   2 gr.f. (Feb 20) Distant Relative 128 – Anneli Rose 56 (Superlative   **91**
118) [1999 6d² 6d⁶ 6d⁵ Oct 9] rangy filly: fourth foal: half-sister to 1994 Middle
Park winner Fard (by Reprimand) and 7f winner Double-O-Seven (by Tirol): dam, 6f
winner, half-sister to Gallic League: made encouraging debut, then showed fairly
useful form when dead-heating for sixth behind Seazun in Cheveley Park Stakes at
Newmarket: didn't give her running in listed event at York final start: stays 6f: raced
only on good to soft ground. *J. M. P. Eustace*

BETTINA BLUE (IRE)   2 b.f. (Mar 17) Paris House 123 – Born To Fly (IRE) 57   **65**
(Last Tycoon 131) [1999 5s⁵ 5g 5v⁶ a6g⁵ Nov 8] IR 1,700F, 3,500Y: fourth foal:
half-sister to unreliable (fairly useful at best) 7f/1m winner Blue Flyer (by Bluebird):
dam suited by 6f: fair form in maidens first 2 starts, well held after (pulled much too
hard final start): will stay 6f. *R. Ingram*

BETTRON   4 b.g. Alnasr Alwasheek 117 – Aigua Blava (USA) (Solford (USA)   **54 §**
127) [1998 84§: a9.4g⁴ 8s³ 9v⁵ 7m⁴ 10g⁴ 10d* 8.1g 1999 7s² a7g May 10] leggy,
lengthy gelding: fairly useful at 3 yrs: well below form in 1999, leaving R. Hannon
after reappearance: effective at 7f to 1¼m: acts on firm and soft going: edgy sort,
and no easy ride: virtually refused to race final 1998 start: best treated with caution.
D. J. Wintle

BETTY BATHWICK (IRE)   2 b.f. (Apr 28) Common Grounds 118 – Tynagh-   **49**
mile (IRE) (Lyphard's Special (USA) 122) [1999 5m 5.7g 7.5g 6f² Aug 6] 10,000
2-y-o: third living foal: half-sister to Italian 11f winner Bella Elisa (by Seattle
Dancer): dam lightly raced in Ireland: only sign of ability when 6 lengths second of
12 to It's Allowed in seller at Lingfield: should stay at least 7f. *B. Smart*

BETTYJOE   2 ch.f. (Apr 15) Inchinor 119 – Jay Gee Ell 78 (Vaigly Great 127)   **60**
[1999 5m³ 6g⁶ 5g⁵ 6g² 6g³ 6m 6v 7s Nov 6] 25,000Y: lengthy filly: seventh foal:
sister to 4-y-o Friar Tuck, closely related to 5f/6f winner We're Joken (by Statoblest)
and half-sister to 2 winners, including 3-y-o Kaibo: dam, 2-y-o sprint winner, later
best at 1¼m: modest maiden: best efforts when placed in nurseries on fourth/fifth
starts: should stay 7f: below form on soft/heavy ground. *J. S. Goldie*

BE VALIANT   5 gr.g. Petong 126 – Fetlar (Pharly (FR) 130) [1998 54: 8.2s 8.3m   **44**
8m⁶ 10g* 10m² 10.1g⁴ 8.2s 8s⁶ a11g 1999 a8g⁴ a10g⁴ 10g May 31] rather leggy
gelding: poor performer: should stay beyond 1¼m: acts on all-weather and good to
firm going, possibly not soft: tried visored. *Mrs N. Macauley*

BEVELED CRYSTAL   5 ro.m. Beveled (USA) – Countess Mariga (Amboise   **?**
113) [1998 NR 1999 7f 10d 8m 5s⁶ a6g a6g Dec 6] sparely-made mare: poor maiden:

possibly worth a rating of 43 on fourth start: may prove best at 5f/6f: blinkered final start. *M. Madgwick*

BEVELED HAWTHORN   4 b.f. Beveled (USA) – Sideloader Special 66 (Song **40 p**
132) [1998 –: 7s 6d 1999 7g⁶ 5f* Sep 4] well supported on only second start for present stable, first form when winning 18-runner maiden handicap at Thirsk: likely to prove best at 5f/6f (took strong hold over 7f on reappearance): probably capable of further improvement. *D. Nicholls*

BEVELENA   3 ch.f. Beveled (USA) – Bella Helena (Balidar 133) [1998 69: 5.1g⁶   **84**
a5g² 5.2m² 5g* 5.3m² 1999 6m³ 5d* 5.1m⁵ 5g 5g Aug 18] rather leggy filly: poor mover: fairly useful handicapper: won at Catterick in April: ran poorly final 2 starts: effective at 5f/6f: acts on good to soft and good to firm ground, showed promise only try on fibresand. *P. D. Evans*

BEVERLEY MONKEY (IRE)   3 b.f. Fayruz 116 – Godly Light (FR) 47 (Vay- **47**
rann 133) [1998 69d: 5v⁴ 6m* 5g* 5g 7.1m² 7g² 7d⁶ a6g⁶ 6m 6s³ 6f* 6.5g 1999 6v a6g 6m 5.9m³ 8g 5.9m 7m⁵ 6g⁵ Sep 20] angular, deep-girthed filly: poor performer: stays 7f: acts on firm going: sometimes blinkered: has shown signs of temperament (reared and unseated rider leaving stalls fifth start): joined J. M. Bradley. *J. Berry*

BEVIER   5 b.g. Nashwan (USA) 135 – Bevel (USA) (Mr Prospector (USA)) [1998   **56**
–: 10m 1999 8.3m⁶ 10m³ 10g May 31] leggy gelding: modest handicapper now-adays: will probably stay 1½m: blinkered (raced freely) final start. *W. Jarvis*

BEWARE   4 br.g. Warning 136 – Dancing Spirit (IRE) 72 (Ahonoora 122) [1998   **82**
80: 6v 6m 6s 7m² 5g³ 7s 1999 5s³ 5g⁵ 6d 5.7f 6d² 5d 7d a6g³ a6g Dec 1] smallish   **a58**
gelding: fair handicapper on turf, modest on all-weather: best at 5f/6f: acts on firm going, soft and fibresand. *D. Nicholls*

BE WARNED   8 b.g. Warning 136 – Sagar 74 (Habitat 134) [1998 71, a90: a8g²   **72**
a7g* a6g³ a9.4g* a10g a9.4g* a8g* a8g⁵ a9.4g 7.5m 7.1m³ a8.5g⁵ 8g⁴ a7g² 7v* 7s⁵   **a85**
a8.5g⁴ a8.5g² a9.4g² 1999 a12g³ a9.4g² a9.4g a11g a12g² 7s³ 7g a8.5g⁵ 7d 8m 9.1d 8d⁴ a12g* Oct 30] good-topped gelding: unimpressive mover: fairly useful on all-weather, fair on turf: didn't have to be anywhere near best to win claimer at Wolverhampton on final start: effective at testing 7f to easy 1½m: acts on good to firm going, heavy and all-weather: has won in blinkers, wears visor nowadays: tends to get behind. *J. Pearce*

BEWILDERED (IRE)   2 br.f. (Jan 12) Prince Sabo 123 – Collage 69 (Ela- **52**
Mana-Mou 132) [1999 5g 6g⁶ 5f⁴ Jun 26] IR 13,500Y: sixth foal: half-sister to 1993 2-y-o 6f winner Fromage (by Formidable), fairly useful 1m winner Strachin (by Salse) and top-class hurdler/promising chaser Decoupage (by Bustino): dam maiden stayed 1m: modest maiden: disappointed on final start: joined D. Chapman. *G. Lewis*

BEYOND CALCULATION (USA)   5 ch.g. Geiger Counter (USA) – Placer **76**
Queen (Habitat 134) [1998 73: 7f 6g⁶ 5.7d³ 5.7s⁴ 6m 5.7d⁵ 6m 5.7m 6m 6v 1999 6.1v 6s 5.9m⁵ 6f 5g⁵ 6m⁶ 6m² 6m* 6d³ 6f² 5.7m* 6f* 6f* 5.7m 5.7f⁴ 5.2g 5g 6g Oct 11] rather unfurnished gelding: fair handicapper: won at Windsor in June, Bath and Thirsk in July, and Brighton in August: best around 6f: acts on fibresand, firm going and probably on soft: has been bandaged: often races up with pace: seems best with strong handling. *J. M. Bradley*

BEYOND THE CLOUDS (IRE)   3 b.g. Midhish 109 – Tongabezi (IRE) 75 **59**
(Shernazar 131) [1998 NR 1999 8g 6v⁶ a8g 6g 5.9m³ 6d 6m⁶ 5m⁵ Jul 28] IR 6,100Y: first foal: dam 7f winner at 2 yrs in Ireland: modest maiden handicapper: effective at 5f/6f: acts on good to firm going: visored (ran well) final start. *J. S. Wainwright*

B GRADE THE SECOND   3 b.f. Lugana Beach 116 – B Grade 59 (Lucky **–**
Wednesday 124) [1998 –: a6g a7g 1999 6m⁶ a6g 8f 10g Aug 21] leggy, workmanlike filly: no form. *Miss J. F. Craze*

BHAVNAGAR (IRE)   8 br.g. Darshaan 133 – Banana Peel (Green Dancer (USA) **–**
132) [1998 –: 15s 16v⁵ 1999 17.1s 13.8g Oct 16] winning hurdler/chaser: of little account on Flat nowadays. *B. Ellison*

BHUTAN (IRE)   4 b.g. Polish Patriot (USA) 128 – Bustinetta 89 (Bustino 136) **74**
[1998 71: 9v 9d* 11g* 12s⁵ 9f³ 12m⁶ 8s* 1999 12m³ 9.9s³ 12.4m* 12.3m³ 9.9m³ 11.8g³ 9g 10.9d 13.8g* 10f⁴ 16g⁴ Nov 3] IR 58,000Y: lengthy gelding: first foal:

dam, 11f winner who stayed 2m, out of half-sister to Terimon (by Bustino): fair performer: won handicap at Newcastle in July and minor event (in good style) at Catterick in October: effective at 1¼m to 2m: acts on firm and soft ground: sometimes finds little: fair hurdler. *Mrs M. Reveley*

BHUTAN PRINCE 2 b.c. (Apr 4) Robellino (USA) 127 – Seal Indigo (IRE) 93 **78** (Glenstal (USA) 118) [1999 7m⁴ 7m² 7d² 8.5g² 8.1m⁵ 7.7d³ 7s² 7g² a6g* Nov 8] 36,000F, 28,000Y: angular colt: fourth foal: half-brother to 3-y-o Neptune: dam, best at 1½m, out of half-sister to Irish Oaks winner Give Thanks: fair performer: made all in maiden at Lingfield in November: effective at 6f to 8.5f: acts on equitrack, good to firm and soft going: has worn crossed noseband: consistent. *J. Noseda*

BIANCONI (USA) 4 b.c. Danzig (USA) – Fall Aspen (USA) (Pretense) [1998 **113** 123: 5.8v* 8m⁴ 7d⁵ 6m* 6m² 6m* 5d 1999 6g⁴ 6m 6f 6.5s Aug 8] big, strong, good-bodied colt: very smart in 1998, winner of Diadem Stakes at Ascot: not so good at 4 yrs, best efforts when fourth (2¼ lengths behind Eastern Purple) in Greenlands Stakes at the Curragh and ninth (on third start) in July Cup at Newmarket: best at 6f: had form on heavy going, best effort on good to firm: bandaged/visored final start: to stand at Ashford Stud, Kentucky, fee $10,000. *A. P. O'Brien, Ireland*

BICTON PARK 5 b.g. Distant Relative 128 – Merton Mill 68 (Dominion 123) **–** [1998 –: 5s a5g 5.1g 5m 6m 6g a6g a6g 1999 a5g a7g² a7g a7g a6g a8.5g 7m⁶ 8.3d **a40** a7g a8g a8g Dec 17] poor maiden: should stay 1m: acts on fibresand: tried blinkered/visored/tongue tied: inconsistent. *K. C. Comerford*

BID ME WELCOME 3 b.g. Alzao (USA) 117 – Blushing Barada (USA) 53 **88** (Blushing Groom (FR) 131) [1998 62: 6d⁴ 1999 8s⁶ 10g 12.5m* 12g⁵ 14.1f⁵ 12.3s⁴ 12g 11.5g² 12m³ 14.1g² 14.1m* 14.1g⁵ 14.8d* Oct 15] angular gelding: fluent mover: fairly useful handicapper: won at Warwick in May, Nottingham in August and Newmarket in October: will stay 2m: acts on firm and soft ground: tends to carry head high: has raced prominently/led of late. *H. J. Collingridge*

BIENAMADO (USA) 3 ch.c. Bien Bien (USA) 125 – Nakterjal (Vitiges (FR) **119** 132) [1998 111p: 8.1m* 9d⁴ 10v² 1999 12m⁵ 11.9m² 12m² 12g⁵ Oct 17]

Bienamado's late withdrawal from the Arc de Triomphe took away any lingering chance of a gloss being put on trainer Peter Chapple-Hyam's impending departure from Manton. It was announced in August by Manton's owner Robert Sangster that Chapple-Hyam would be replaced in 2000 by John Gosden, and Chapple-Hyam followed that by announcing he would train instead in Hong Kong. Sweet had turned sour! Chapple-Hyam, who is married to Sangster's step-daughter Jane, won the Derby with Dr Devious in 1992, little over a year after receiving a licence, and in the same season won the English and Irish Two Thousand Guineas with Sangster's Rodrigo de Triano. Turtle Island, Spectrum and Victory Note also won Chapple-Hyam major European classics, but, despite some close calls, his efforts to add further classic successes at home proved fruitless and were undermined by the sale to Godolphin at the end of their two-year-old careers of Sangster's Balanchine and Cape Verdi. City Honours was also sold out of the yard by Sangster before finishing a close second to High-Rise in the Derby. Numerically, Chapple-Hyam never came close to matching the best seasonal tally of his immediate predecessor at Manton, Barry Hills, who saddled a hundred and one winners there in 1987 (seventy-three of them for Sangster) while leasing the stable; fifty-two was Chapple-Hyam's best total. Chapple-Hyam did win a string of other big races, including the Champion Stakes at home and in Ireland, the Juddmonte International, the Prix de l'Abbaye and the Prix du Cadran, and major two-year-old prizes such as the Middle Park, the Dewhurst and the Racing Post Trophy, the last-named in 1998 with Commander Collins, winter favourite for the 1999 Derby.

Chapple-Hyam's record in the Derby stands comparison with that of most trainers in the 'nineties, despite the occasional drain on his resources. Having a horse run well at Epsom isn't an annual occurrence, even among some of the more successful trainers, yet, apart from Dr Devious, Chapple-Hyam had Colonel Collins and Romanov placed, while Cairo Prince also reached the frame, like the latter two placed horses doing so in Sangster's colours. Bien-amado perhaps wasn't so sorely missed from the latest renewal as Sangster's Commander Collins, the original intention having been to send him for the Prix du Jockey Club in France, where he'd won the Prix de Conde at Longchamp on the second of his three starts as a two-year-old, but he'd have put up a bold show had he been ready all the same. Instead, Bienamado made his reappear-ance against older horses in the Princess of Wales's Stakes at Newmarket in July, travelling strongly for a long way before finishing fifth of eight behind Craigsteel. Bienamado's only two subsequent runs in Europe were against three-year-olds and he showed himself firmly among the upper echelons of his age group each time, finishing second of seven to Fantastic Light in the Great Voltigeur Stakes at York in August, beaten a length and a quarter, and filling the same position behind a confidently-ridden Montjeu in the Prix Niel at Longchamp in September, flattered to be beaten only a head after his rider tried to poach the race from the front in a small field. Having bypassed the Arc, Bienamado, now trained by Chapple-Hyam's assistant George Foster, then ran in Canada, where he put up a creditable effort to be beaten four lengths into fifth behind the home-trained Thornfield in the Grade 1 Canadian International at Woodbine.

Bienamado (USA) (ch.c. 1996)	Bien Bien (USA) (ch 1989)	Manila (b 1983)	Lyphard / Dona Ysidra
		Stark Winter (ch 1973)	Graustark / Winter Wren
	Nakterjal (b 1980)	Vitiges (ch 1973)	Vale / Phaeton
		Kilavea (b 1974)	Hawaii / Special

It was presumably Bienamado's performances in Europe which encouraged the decision to move his sire Bien Bien from Kentucky to the Kirtlington Stud in Oxfordshire in October. Bien Bien is unusual among North

J. Toffan, T. McCaffery and Mr R. Sangster's "Bienamado"

American-raced stallions in that he had one of his biggest successes on the track over a mile and three quarters, in the Grade 1 San Juan Capistrano Handicap as a five-year-old. Bien Bien was also responsible in the latest season for the smart three-year-old stayer Ashgar as well as Bienamado's two-year-old brother Troilus. Troilus is the ninth foal of Bienamado's dam Nakterjal, a poor daughter of a half-sister to Nureyev and the dam of Sadler's Wells. Bien Bien was runner-up in the Breeders' Cup Turf as a four-year-old and it's possible the lightly-raced Bienamado will bid to go one better as he's to be trained in America by J. Paco Gonzalez in 2000. The tall, angular Bienamado shows no lack of speed for a middle-distance colt and has given the impression a return to a mile and a quarter will suit him as well as the mile and a half he tackled exclusively as a three-year-old. He acts on good to firm ground and was below par when runner-up on heavy once as a two-year-old. *A. G. Foster*

BIENCARN (USA) 3 ch.f. Bien Bien (USA) 125 – Newdaydawning (USA) – (Gone West (USA)) [1998 NR 1999 8m 10.2m⁶ Jun 29] $30,000F: second foal: dam unraced daughter of sister to US Grade 1 9f winner and Preakness runner-up Brian's Time: seventh in maiden at Ripon on debut: tailed off next time: sent to USA. *P. W. Chapple-Hyam*

BIENNALE (IRE) 3 b.c. Caerleon (USA) 132 – Malvern Beauty 100 (Shirley Heights 130) [1998 93p: 8.1g² 8g² 8m² 1999 11.1g* 12m³ Jun 17] lengthy colt: not a good walker: useful performer: landed odds in maiden at Hamilton in May: very good third of 19 to Elmutabaki in King George V Handicap at Royal Ascot next time: likely to prove suited by further than 1½m: yet to race on ground softer than good: stays in training. *Sir Michael Stoute* **102**

BIFF-EM (IRE) 5 ch.g. Durgam (USA) – Flash The Gold (Ahonoora 122) [1998 51: 6v³ 5.9d 5v³ 5d 8d 5s³ 6d⁵ 5g³ 6m⁴ 6m* 7g⁴ 6g 7d 6d⁵ 5s⁵ 5d 6m 6v 1999 5s⁴ 6d³ 5g² 6g² 5m 6f³ 6m 5f 6v Oct 12] rather leggy gelding: modest handicapper: mostly creditable efforts until well below form last 3 starts: needs thorough test at 5f, barely stays 7f: probably acts on any going: has run well when sweating. *Miss L. A. Perratt* **51**

BIG AL (IRE) 3 b.g. Shalford (IRE) 124§ – Our Pet 64 (Mummy's Pet 125) [1998 68+: 7m 6g* 6d⁶ 1999 7.5m⁶ 8m 10m 8m⁶ 8s 8d 11d Nov 1] quite attractive gelding: has a quick, fluent action: fair handicapper at best: generally on downgrade in 1999: had wind operation before sixth start: stays 1¼m: acts on good to firm ground, below form on softer than good. *R. A. Fahey* **67 d**

BIG BEN 5 ch.h. Timeless Times (USA) 99 – Belltina 41 (Belfort (FR) 89) [1998 74, a77: 6.9d* 6.9v³ 6g 7m* 6m 7m 7g 7m 7m⁵ 7m² 7d 7g a6g³ a7g a7g* a6g⁵ a7g⁶ 1999 a7g³ 6g³ 7.1g 8m⁵ 7m³ 8.3m⁵ 7d⁶ 7g 7m a7g³ a7g⁵ a8g* a8g Dec 10] small, leggy horse: poor mover: fair performer: won claimer at Lingfield in November: stays 1m: acts on any turf going/all-weather. *R. Hannon* **71**
a74

BIG CHIEF 3 ch.g. Be My Chief (USA) 122 – Grove Daffodil (IRE) 83 (Salt Dome (USA)) [1998 –: 6g⁶ 6m 7m 1999 11.6m 8d 8.3d⁵ 7g 6.9g⁵ 7g⁶ 7.1d 10s 10m Aug 30] rather leggy, good-topped gelding: poor maiden: left M. Tompkins before final start: stays 1m: sometimes visored: none too consistent. *M. E. Sowersby* **48**

BIG ISSUE 2 b.c. (May 14) First Trump 118 – Hollow Heart 89 (Wolver Hollow 126) [1999 7.3f 6g 5.7s* 7s Nov 6] 5,800Y: half-brother to 3-y-o Carpetsmade-indevon and 3 winners, including useful 7f to 8.5f winner Aradu (by Posse): dam 2-y-o 5f winner: modest form: trained by K. McAuliffe on debut: dropped in class, won seller at Bath in October: ran poorly in nursery final start: stays 5.7f: acts on soft going. *B. Smart* **61**

BIG MOVIE STAR 2 ch.f. (Mar 13) Risk Me (FR) 127 – Bocas Rose 106 (Jalmood (USA) 126) [1999 5s⁶ 5g³ 5m⁶ 6s 6d⁵ a5.5g³ a7.5g² a7.5g* Dec 18] 14,500Y: big, leggy, workmanlike filly: sixth foal: sister to several winners, including 4-y-o Redswan and useful German 1998 2-y-o 5f/6f winner Scrapper: dam best when sprint winner at 2 yrs: fair form at best in Britain (sold from B. Meehan 1,000 gns after fifth start): won maiden at Neuss (Germany) in December: stays 7.5f: blinkered/hooded last 2 starts in Britain. *J. Pubben, Holland* **76**

BIG TARGET (IRE) 5 b.g. Suave Dancer (USA) 136 – Prima Domina (FR) 89 **46** (Dominion 123) [1998 –: 11.1v 12d⁶ 1999 11.1m⁶ 9.2f² 11.1m 8.3m⁴ Aug 11] only poor nowadays: visored/blinkered final 4 starts. *R. Allan*

BIG WHEEL 4 ch.g. Mujtahid (USA) 118 – Numuthej (USA) 50 (Nureyev **67** (USA) 131) [1998 67: 10s 10.5g 10.5g* 10.3g² 8.2g⁵ 9m³ 8.2s 1999 10.2s 10s* Nov 1] fair performer: won seller at Nottingham in November: stays 1¼m: acts on good to firm and soft ground: has been bandaged: effective blinkered or not. *M. C. Pipe*

BIGWIG (IRE) 6 ch.g. Thatching 131 – Sabaah (USA) 65 (Nureyev (USA) 131) **53** [1998 NR 1999 a16f⁴ a12g⁶ a13g* a13g* a14g⁴ a13g⁵ Dec 22] modest handicapper: won amateur events at Lingfield in February and March: off course 9½ months (had been hurdling, ran out once) before running poorly (found little) final start: stays 13f: acts on all-weather: blinkered all 6-y-o starts. *G. L. Moore*

BIJA 4 b.g. Librate 91 – Guilty Sparkle (Roc Imp) [1998 NR 1999 a8.5g a8.5g 10f **33** 7f 8m⁴ 9.2m⁶ 10d 10m⁴ Aug 23] fourth foal: dam no sign of ability in bumpers: bad maiden. *J. M. Bradley*

BILKO 5 gr.g. Risk Me (FR) 127 – Princess Tara 85 (Prince Sabo 123) [1998 84: **74** 5g 6g 5m* 6m 6m³ 5d* 5.1m³ 5m² 5g² 1999 a5g 6d 5m 5d 5.9g³ 5m³ 5g² 5.1d⁶ 5g 5m Sep 4] big, lengthy gelding: fair performer: left D. Nicholls after fifth start, creditable efforts next 3 outings: stays 6f: yet to race on extremes of going on turf: often sweating and edgy: sold 700 gns in October. *E. J. Alston*

BILLADDIE 6 b.g. Touch of Grey 90 – Young Lady (Young Generation 129) **74** [1998 79: a10g* a10g³ a10g³ a10g³ a10g 8m 10g⁴ 12s² 12g* 11.4g³ 14m 12g⁶ 11.5f² 12m² 12d* 12m² 12s³ 10v* 10s⁵ 1999 12m 12s 12s Aug 18] leggy, angular gelding: fair handicapper: below form after reappearance: stays 1½m: acts on equitrack and any turf going: has run well sweating: tends to idle in front and is held up: tough. *R. M. Flower*

BILLICHANG 3 b.c. Chilibang 120 – Swing O'The Kilt (Hotfoot 126) [1998 –: **61** 6g a6g 7m⁴ a8g 1999 a7g⁴ a8f⁴ a8g⁵ a10g² 8.2s a9.4g² a9.4g⁴ 8.2f 8m⁵ a10g³ 10m a9.4g³ a10g a10g* Dec 29] strong colt: modest performer: won maiden at Lingfield in December: effective at 1m (given test)/1¼m: acts on all-weather and good to firm ground: visored (ran creditably) once: game. *P. Howling*

BILLY BATHWICK (IRE) 2 ch.c. (Jan 24) Fayruz 116 – Cut It Fine (USA) **67** (Big Spruce (USA)) [1999 6.1m⁴ 6m⁴ 6m 7s⁴ 8.3g 8s⁶ Nov 6] 15.0 months: smallish, close-coupled colt: brother to fairly useful 1m (at 2 yrs) to 1¼m winner Dead-line Time and half-brother to 3 winners, including 5-y-o Ciro's Pearl: dam staying maiden: fair maiden: creditable efforts most starts: stays 1m: acts on good to firm and soft ground. *B. Smart*

BILLY BOX 7 gr.g. Lord Bud 121 – Counter Coup (Busted 134) [1998 –: 14m **51** 22.2d 11.7s 7.1g 1999 a12f² a16g a14g Mar 16] modest maiden handicapper: form only when second in amateur event at Southwell in January: stays 1½m: acts on fibresand: has had tongue tied: blinkered in 1999. *I. A. Balding*

BILLY BUSHWACKER 8 b.g. Most Welcome 131 – Secret Valentine 71 **–** (Wollow 132) [1998 NR 1999 10.4d Oct 7] workmanlike gelding: fairly useful performer in 1997: seventh in claimer at York, only start since: stays 1½m: acts on good to firm and good soft ground: tried blinkered: held up. *Mrs M. Reveley*

BILLY MCCAW 3 b.c. Efisio 120 – Thakhayr (Sadler's Wells (USA) 132) [1998 **93** 84: 7g⁴ 7.1m³ 7m³ 6m* 1999 7g* 6m⁵ 7.9s³ 8.1m 8m Jun 15] quite attractive colt: has a scratchy action: fairly useful handicapper: won at Newmarket in April: credi-table third at York in May: may prove best at 7f/1m with waiting tactics: acts on good to firm and soft going: sold 22,000 gns in October, sent to Saudi Arabia. *P. F. I. Cole*

BILLY MOONSHINE 7 ch.g. Nicholas Bill 125 – Indian Moonshine 60 **–** (Warpath 113) [1998 –, a57: 11.7m 10.2d⁵ 8g 12s a13g³ a16g 1999 a9g a16g⁶ 17.2m Aug 22] maiden handicapper on Flat: below form in 1999, leaving G. Moore after reappearance. *P. Bowen*

BILLY'S BLUNDER (IRE) 2 b.f. (May 1) Hamas (IRE) 125§ – Open Date **–** (IRE) (Thatching 131) [1999 a5g a5g Dec 21] IR 2,500Y: fourth foal: half-sister to 2 winners, including 1m winner Rocky Dance (by Rock Hopper): dam unraced half-sister to useful sprinter Peace Girl: tongue tied, no form at Southwell in maiden (hung left) then seller (visored). *P. D. Evans*

BIMBOLA (FR) 5 br.m. Bikala 134 – Agnes Lily 66 (Raise A Cup (USA)) [1998 112: 12d* 12s* 12.5d³ 15.5v⁶ 1999 10s 11d⁶ 12m* 13.5g* 12.5g² 12.5v⁵ 12m² Dec 12] leggy, lengthy mare: third foal: half-sister to a 1m to 1¼m winner by Goldneyev: dam maiden from family of Enrique: smart performer: better than ever in 1999, winning Premio Legnano at Milan in June and Prix de Pomone at Deauville (by 3 lengths from Innuendo) in August: best efforts (beaten head both times) when second to Courteous in Grand Prix de Deauville and Borgia in Hong Kong Vase at Sha Tin: will stay beyond 13.5f: acts on good to firm and soft ground: usually held up, though made virtually all at Milan: stays in training. *J. Bertran de Balanda, France* **117**

BIN ALMOOJID 3 b.g. Almoojid 69 – Stella Royale (Astronef 116) [1998 –: a5g 1999 11.7s Oct 26] no sign of ability. *A. D. Smith* **–**

BINT ALJOOD 2 b.f. (Mar 21) Bin Ajwaad (IRE) 119 – Shareehan (Dancing Brave (USA) 140) [1999 a7g 6g 5m 6.1m⁵ 6s⁴ 6.1s⁵ Nov 1] second foal: half-sister to 3-y-o Goodbye Goldstone: dam unraced, from family of Ardross: modest maiden: creditable efforts in nurseries last 3 starts: stays 6f: acts on good to firm and soft going. *B. A. McMahon* **56**

BINTALREEF (USA) 2 ch.f. (Jan 29) Diesis 133 – Solar Star (USA) 93 (Lear Fan (USA) 130) [1999 7g* Oct 20] 90,000F: fourth foal: half-sister to fairly useful 1m winner Irish Light (by Irish River) and a winner in USA by Boundary: dam, 2-y-o 6f winner, half-sister to smart US 6f/7f performer Gold Land: impressive winner of 5-runner minor event at Deauville in October by 6 lengths from Tencarola, making all and drawing clear final 1f: likely to stay 1m: an interesting prospect. *D. R. Loder, France* **99 p**

BINTANG TIMOR (USA) 5 ch.g. Mt Livermore (USA) – Frisky Kitten (USA) (Isopach (USA)) [1998 79: 7v 6g² 7m⁴ 6m² 6d 6g 6m* 6m⁴ 6m 6g² 7g⁶ 6m 7g 7g 7s 1999 6.1s³ 7m* 7g 7m² 7f² 7f³ 7m 6m³ 7d 7f 7.3m 7s 7g 7d* 7d³ Oct 30] close-coupled gelding: unimpressive mover: fair handicapper: won apprentice event at Newmarket in May and 20-runner race at Yarmouth in October: stays 7f: acts on firm and soft going: held up. *W. J. Musson* **79**

BINT HABIBI 2 b.f. (Feb 11) Bin Ajwaad (IRE) 119 – High Stepping (IRE) (Taufan (USA) 119) [1999 7m⁴ 7f² 7g 8.3g Oct 11] first reported foal: dam never ran: modest form in maidens first 2 starts, but well beaten after: should stay 1m. *M. R. Channon* **59**

BINT ST JAMES 4 b.f. Shareef Dancer (USA) 135 – St James's Antigua (IRE) 79 (Law Society (USA) 130) [1998 62: a7g a8g⁴ 12g⁴ 12g³ 12.3g⁴ 12m a12g³ 16.1m⁴ a14g a14.8s³ a12g 1999 a12g⁴ a16g Feb 19] modest maiden handicapper at 3 yrs: below form in 1999, leaving J. Bethell after reappearance: stays 2m: acts on good to firm and fibresand: won over hurdles in November. *W. Clay* **–**

BIRCH GROVE (IRE) 3 b.f. Forest Wind (USA) 111 – Volkova 60 (Green Desert (USA) 127) [1998 NR 1999 8.2s 7s 8.3g 12g Jun 28] IR 3,700Y: first foal: dam, modest maiden, half-sister to useful stayer Red Guitars: bad maiden: sold 1,450 gns in July, sent to Bahrain. *W. J. Musson* **21**

BIRCHWOOD SUN 9 b.g. Bluebird (USA) 125 – Shapely Test (USA) (Elocutionist (USA)) [1998 63: 7s² 6d² 5.9d* 7s* 7d* 5.9s 8d⁶ 5.9g³ 5.9d* 6.9m 6d 6m 9.2d 7g 1999 7s 6v* 7d³ 7m² 5.9m 5.9g 5.9m 6f³ Jul 9] compact gelding: poor mover: modest performer: won seller at Pontefract in April: effective at 6f to 1m: acts on any going: used to be blinkered, visored nowadays: comes from behind, and well ridden by J. Weaver. *M. Dods* **57**

BIRD OF PREY (IRE) 4 b.f. Last Tycoon 131 – Red Partridge (Solinus 130) [1998 69: 10d⁵ 8g³ 8g⁴ 7.8d 8d 1999 a10g⁵ a8g⁴ 8.3d² 8g 8.3d* 9m 9.2m⁶ 8.3s 10d⁴ a9.4g 8.1s Sep 24] half-sister to several winners, including smart 9f to 1½m winner Firing Line (by Slip Anchor): dam Irish 2-y-o 1m winner: fair performer: trained by T. Stack in 1998: won minor event at Hamilton in May: below form in handicaps after: stays 1¼m: acts on good to soft going and equitrack (below form twice on fibresand): tends to hang. *A. G. Newcombe* **65**

BIRDSAND   2 ch.f. (Jan 13) Bluebird (USA) 125 – Nottash (IRE) 74 (Royal   **– p** Academy (USA) 130) [1999 6m Aug 27] lengthy filly: first foal: dam, 7f winner, half-sister to Lake Coniston (by Bluebird): midfield in Thirsk maiden, slowly away and not given hard time: should stay 1m: will probably do better. *J. R. Fanshawe*

BIRTHDAY VENTURE   4 b.f. Soviet Star (USA) 128 – Maestrale (Top Ville   **65** 129) [1998 65p: 7v³ a7g* 1999 a7g* 8d a8g² a8g* a10g* a9.4g³ a12g³ Jun 16] fair performer: won handicap at Southwell and minor event at Lingfield in May: stays 1½m: raced mainly on all-weather. *S. P. C. Woods*

BIRTH OF THE BLUES   3 ch.c. Efisio 120 – Great Steps 88 (Vaigly Great 127)   **72** [1998 66p: 7.1m 7.6f⁵ 8s 1999 8.2d 8v* 8d 9.7d 11.9m Sep 3] lengthy, angular colt: fair handicapper: won at Leicester in April: sold from J. Dunlop 7,500 gns after next start: probably acts on any going. *N. P. Littmoden*

BIRTHPLACE (IRE)   9 b. or br.g. Top Ville 129 – Birthday Party (FR)   **–** (Windwurf (GER)) [1998 NR 1999 a16g Feb 12] formerly fairly useful winner in Ireland: tailed off only run on Flat since 1994. *J. L. Eyre*

BISHOPSTONE MAN   2 b.g. (Apr 27) Piccolo 121 – Auntie Gladys 49 (Great   **66** Nephew 126) [1999 6.8m 7.1m 6.8d 6s³ 6g Oct 11] 10,000Y: well-made gelding: third foal: half-brother to 6-y-o Family Man: dam placed up to 2m: fair maiden: best effort when third of 11 at Lingfield: should stay 7f: acts on soft going. *S. Mellor*

BISHOPSTONE POND (IRE)   3 b.f. Persian Bold 123 – Swift And Early   **43** (IRE) (Alzao (USA) 117) [1998 –: a5g 6.1g a5g⁶ 6m 1999 10m 9.7v³ a12g 12d 10.5s⁵ 9.9m Jul 2] small filly: poor maiden handicapper: stays 1½m: acts on heavy ground. *S. Mellor*

BISQUET-DE-BOUCHE   5 ch.m. Most Welcome 131 – Larive 80 (Blakeney   **38** 126) [1998 NR 1999 14.1g 16d Oct 21] shallow-girthed mare: poor maiden handicapper: should stay 2m+. *A. W. Carroll*

BITTER SWEET   3 gr.f. Deploy 131 – Julia Flyte 91 (Drone) [1998 67: 6g⁵ 7d⁵   **64** 7m⁵ 7m⁴ 7.6f³ 8m 8v 1999 10.2s 10g 13.1f 9s² 10g Oct 19] modest maiden: should stay beyond 1¼m: acts on firm and soft going: sold 13,000 gns, joined J. Spearing. *D. R. C. Elsworth*

BITTY MARY   2 ch.f. (Apr 12) Be My Chief (USA) 122 – Souadah (USA)   **49** (General Holme (USA) 128) [1999 7.5g 6m 6.1m⁵ 8d Sep 23] 10,000Y: leggy filly: seventh foal: half-sister to 3 winners, including 4-y-o Theme Tune and fairly useful 1996 2-y-o 5f winner Blue Ridge (later won in USA, by Indian Ridge): dam unraced: poor maiden: should stay 1m. *J. D. Bethell*

BLACK AMBER (IRE)   3 b.g. College Chapel 122 – Flying Diva 100 (Chief   **108** Singer 131) [1998 108: 6g* 6f³ 5.5g* 6m⁴ 1999 5g 6m⁵ 6d 6g⁶ 6s 7g² 6d Oct 15] strong, well-made gelding: useful performer: in-and-out form in 1999, good second to Kumait in minor event at Redcar on penultimate start: stays 7f: acts on firm ground, possibly not on softer than good: blinkered (below form) 3 times: joined D. Nicholls for 45,000 gns, then gelded. *N. A. Callaghan*

BLACK ARMY   4 b.g. Aragon 118 – Morgannwg (IRE) 86 (Simply Great (FR)   **79** 122) [1998 75: 6d 6d⁴ 6g 1999 6.1v⁴ 6.1s 5d* 6d 5g 5m⁵ a5g³ 5d a6g³ a6g Nov 30] good-topped gelding: fair handicapper: well drawn, won 19-runner event at Beverley in May: effective at 5f/6f: acts on fibresand, good to firm and heavy going: blinkered twice, running well first occasion. *J. M. P. Eustace*

BLACK EMPEROR   2 br.c. (Apr 28) Emperor Jones (USA) 119 – Hush Baby   **–** (IRE) 49 (Ballacashtal (CAN)) [1999 8s Nov 6] lengthy colt: third foal: half-brother to 1998 French 2-y-o 7f winner El Matar (by Cosmonaut): dam 1½m winner: bandaged, tailed off in maiden at Doncaster. *P. L. Gilligan*

BLACKEYED BOY (IRE)   3 ch.g. Forest Wind (USA) 111 – Blackeye (Busted   **–** 134) [1998 –: 6g 7g 7.5m 10d⁶ 1999 a12g 14.1f a14.8g a12g 10g Aug 21] of no account. *A. Bailey*

BLACKFOOT (IRE)   3 br.g. River Falls 113 – Northern Amber (Shack (USA)   **61** 118) [1998 NR 1999 a5g² 5m 5g² 5g a5g Dec 1] 10,500Y: small gelding: half-brother   **a64** to winning sprinters Minizen Music (by Anita's Prince) and Karseam (by Mon

Tresor): dam lightly raced: modest maiden: form only when second: raced only at 5f: blinkered: pulled very hard second outing. *J. Balding*

BLACKHEATH (IRE) 3 ch.c. Common Grounds 118 – Queen Caroline (USA) **103 p** 67 (Chief's Crown (USA)) [1998 NR 1999 6m² 6d³ 6g* 7m 6m 6m³ 6m³ 6.1g Sep 25] 24,000F, IR 19,000Y: strong, round-barrelled colt: type to carry condition: third foal: half-brother to 1997 2-y-o 5f winner Third Cousin (by Distant Relative) and 1¼m winner Regal Reprimand (by Reprimand): dam maiden (stayed 10.5f) half-sister to smart 1986 2-y-o Glory Forever, later third in Poule d'Essai des Poulains: useful performer: won maiden at Lingfield in June: good third after in handicaps at Leicester and York (to Ho Leng in rated stakes): likely to prove best at 6f/7f: acts on good to firm going, probably on good to soft: likely to do better still. *J. A. R. Toller*

BLACK ICE BOY (IRE) 8 b.g. Law Society (USA) 130 – Hogan's Sister **50** (USA) (Speak John) [1998 50: 16.1d⁴ 21.6s* 16.2m 18s³ 18s³ 18s³ 1999 a16g⁶ 16.1d **a–** a14g 17.1s* 18d a16.2g Dec 4] tall, workmanlike gelding: modest handicapper: won at Pontefract in October by 5 lengths: pulled up final start: suited by thorough test of stamina: has won on good to firm ground, much better form on soft/heavy: blinkered/visored: normally front runner. *R. Bastiman*

BLACK JACK GIRL (IRE) 2 br.f. (Mar 18) Ridgewood Ben 113 – Shiyra **–** (Darshaan 133) [1999 6f Jun 1] 500Y: half-sister to an Italian 5f/6f winner by Mac's Imp: dam Irish 1m and 1¼m winner: behind in maiden at Redcar. *J. S. Wainwright*

BLACK MAGIC 5 b.m. Cigar 68 – Mossage 75 (Ballymoss 136) [1998 NR 1999 **–** a11g Jun 17] half-sister to a 6f winner by Night Shift and a 5f winner by Tower Walk: dam stayed 1½m: tailed off in bumpers in 1998: behind in claimer at Southwell, only Flat run: sold 850 gns in July. *P. Howling*

BLACK ORPHEUS (IRE) 4 b.g. Astronef 116 – Cri Basque (Gay Fandango **51** (USA) 132) [1998 61: 7d⁴ 6g 6g⁵ 7d⁶ 6.1g 5m a6g 1999 6d 5.1m 6f² Jun 1] close-coupled, workmanlike gelding: modest maiden: stays 7f: acts on firm going and on good to soft: has had tongue tied: headstrong: joined D. Nicholls. *P. S. Felgate*

BLACKPOOL MAMMA'S 2 b.f. (Apr 3) Merdon Melody 98 – Woodland **73** Steps 86 (Bold Owl 101) [1999 5g* 5m⁵ 5.1m² 6f* 5g³ 6m³ 6.1m* 6d⁵ 5m² a6g² 6m⁴ Jul 31] 1,500Y, resold 1,000Y: leggy, workmanlike filly: fourth foal: sister to 3-y-o Red Symphony and a 5f to 1m winner in Denmark: dam, 2-y-o 7f winner, sister to one-time useful sprinter Amron: fair performer: won maiden at Musselburgh in April and claimers at Newcastle in May and Chepstow in June: likely to prove best at 5f/6f: acts on firm going, good to soft and fibresand: consistent. *J. Berry*

BLACK ROCK DESERT (USA) 3 b.c. Danzig (USA) – City Dance (USA) **112** (Seattle Slew (USA)) [1998 94p: 6s* 1999 7d⁶ 5m* 5g⁶ 5v Oct 3] robust, attractive colt: smart form when winning Prix de Saint-Georges at Longchamp in May by 2½ lengths from Imperfect World: well beaten other starts, reportedly suffering from respiratory distress on reappearance and pulled muscles in hind-quarters third outing: likely to prove best at 5f/6f. *A. P. O'Brien, Ireland*

BLACK ROCKET (IRE) 3 br.f. Perugino (USA) 84 – Betelgeuse 86 (Kalaglow **60** 132) [1998 66: 6m⁶ 5d 5d 6f 5.2m 1999 6m a8g 7m⁶ a7g a10g⁶ a12g a8.5g* a8.5g Dec 27] lengthy filly: has a quick action: modest performer: won maiden at Wolverhampton in December: may prove best up to 8.5f: acts on fibresand and good to firm going. *K. Mahdi*

BLACK SILK 3 b.g. Zafonic (USA) 130 – Mademoiselle Chloe 106 (Night Shift **94 §** (USA)) [1998 79: 6g² 6m³ 6m⁴ 7g 1999 7g² 7m² 8m² 7.7m* 8m⁵ 7m³ 7m 7.3m⁵ 7d 8d³ Oct 14] smallish, strong gelding: has a quick action: fairly useful performer: won maiden at Thirsk in July: mostly creditable efforts after: stays 1m: yet to race on extremes of going: usually held up: no battler, and one to treat with caution. *C. F. Wall*

BLACKWATCH (IRE) 2 b.g. (Apr 2) Night Shift (USA) – Hollybank Lady **61 d** (USA) (Sir Ivor 135) [1999 5d 5m⁴ 6g⁵ 5m 7m a7g a8d³ Dec 12] third foal: half-brother to 4-y-o Katie-Jane: dam, second over 12.5f in Ireland, daughter of good US winner up to 11f Lady Norcliffe: modest form in maidens first 3 starts: disappointing after, looking difficult ride: sold 5,500 gns from N. Callaghan before final start. *Camilla Nilsson, Sweden*

BLACK WEASEL (IRE) 4 br.c. Lahib (USA) 129 – Glowlamp (IRE) 93 (Glow **65** (USA)) [1998 72: 8.2s 9m 8m⁴ 9s 10g* 9m 9m 10s 1999 a11f a6g 7.7s a8.5g 12.3f a9.4g⁵ a14g² a16.2g⁴ Dec 4] strong, quite attractive colt: fair handicapper: stays 1¾m: acts on good to firm going and fibresand: tried blinkered/visored: has had tongue tied. *A. Bailey*

BLAIR (IRE) 2 b.g. (Mar 23) Persian Bold 123 – Zara's Birthday (IRE) 71 **–** (Waajib 121) [1999 7s Nov 2] IR 9,000F, 8,200Y: first foal: dam Irish maiden who stayed 1½m: well held in maiden at Catterick. *W. W. Haigh*

BLAKENMOR 6 b.g. No Evil 98 – Kinz (Great Nephew 126) [1998 NR 1999 **–** 10g a16g 14.1g⁶ 12m Jul 26] little form. *J. R. Best*

BLAKESET 4 ch.c. Midyan (USA) 124 – Penset (Red Sunset 120) [1998 92: **83** 7.6m 7m 7.1m 7g⁴ 7.3m² 7m² 1999 8d 7.6m² 7g 6m⁵ 8m 7.1d 7m² 7.3m⁶ **a88 +** 7s a7g* a6g² a6g Dec 22] sturdy colt: fairly useful handicapper: left R. Hannon for 11,500 gns before making all at Lingfield in November: ran well next time, poorly drawn final start: effective at 6f/7f: acts on all-weather and good to firm going, possibly not soft: blinkered last 6 starts: has been bandaged behind/tongue tied. *T. G. Mills*

BLAKEY (IRE) 3 b.g. Maledetto (IRE) 103 – Villars 84 (Home Guard (USA) **59 d** 129) [1998 –: 6g 5m 5d⁵ 1999 6f² 6s³ 5g² a5g⁵ 6f⁵ 5f 5g 5g 6f⁴ 7.1f Sep 13] tall, leggy gelding: modest maiden at best: didn't progress: stays 6f: acts on firm going (probably on soft), well beaten only outing on fibresand. *J. Berry*

BLANKENBERGE (IRE) 3 ch.g. Pips Pride 117 – Renata's Ring (IRE) **77** (Auction Ring (USA) 123) [1998 NR 1999 8m⁶ 8g² 10.1f² a9.4g⁴ 7.7d⁵ 8.3g⁴ Oct 11] 42,000Y: good-topped gelding: third foal: brother to fairly useful 7f and 7.6f winner Bodfari Pride and half-brother to fairly useful 1996 2-y-o 5f winner Joint Venture (by Common Grounds): dam placed at 7f in Ireland: fair maiden, trained until after penultimate start by P. Chapple-Hyam: stays 1¼m: acts on firm going: sold 9,000 gns, sent to Macau. *A. G. Foster*

BLAYNEY DANCER 2 b.c. (May 2) Contract Law (USA) 108 – Lady Poly **–** (Dunbeath (USA) 127) [1999 6v 6d⁶ a8g Dec 6] first foal: dam, little worthwhile form on Flat, winning selling hurdler: no sign of ability. *Jamie Poulton*

BLAZER'S BABY 5 ch.m. Norton Challenger 111 – Qualitair Blazer 55 **–** (Blazing Saddles (AUS)) [1998 –: a8g a12g 11.9m 1999 a14g⁵ 10.5m 12s Sep 21] no form since 1997. *K. S. Bridgwater*

BLAZING BILLY 4 ch.g. Anshan 119 – Worthy Venture 76 (Northfields (USA)) **–** [1998 –: a6g⁴ a8.5g⁶ 6.1s 5m 8f 5g 1999 6g 6m 8m 5g Aug 18] leggy, lightly-made gelding: little sign of ability: tried visored. *C. A. Dwyer*

BLAZING FLAME 3 br.g. Chaddleworth (IRE) 103 – Blazing Sunset 55 **–** (Blazing Saddles (AUS)) [1998 –: a5g⁵ a5g 5g 7g 7d 8v 1999 7f 5.9g a9.4g Aug 14] of little account. *Mrs N. Macauley*

BLAZING IMP (USA) 6 ch.g. Imp Society (USA) – Marital (USA) (Marine **–** Patrol (USA)) [1998 57: 6g 5d 5m* 5m⁴ 5g 5d⁵ 5m⁴ 5g 1999 5m 6d 5m 5g 5m 5f 5m Sep 6] modest performer at best, little worthwhile form in 1999. *Mrs J. Jordan*

BLAZING PEBBLES 2 ch.f. (May 29) Pebble Powder – Wrightway Blues 75 **–** (Majority Blue 126) [1999 6d 6m 8d a6g a5g a7g Dec 15] 650Y: fourth reported foal: dam 2-y-o 5f winner: no form. *P. S. McEntee*

BLAZING ROCK 2 b.g. (Mar 15) Rock Hopper 124 – Blazing Pearl 57 (Blazing **–** Saddles (AUS)) [1999 a6g a8g Dec 6] first reported foal: dam best at 2 yrs when 6f seller winner, later stayed 11.8f: well beaten in sellers. *P. S. McEntee*

BLESS 2 ch.f. (Mar 18) Beveled (USA) – Ballystate 71 (Ballacashtal (CAN)) [1999 **58 ?** 5s⁴ 6g 7m 6s 6m⁶ Aug 23] first foal: dam, maiden on Flat, fair hurdler (stayed 2¾m): modest form at best in maidens/nursery: well beaten in blinkers. *M. Madgwick*

BLESSINGINDISGUISE 6 b.g. Kala Shikari 125 – Blowing Bubbles 72 **90** (Native Admiral (USA)) [1998 105: 5g⁶ 5d 5m* 5g* 6f 5.6g 5s 1999 5d 6d 5d 5f 5m 5m⁴ 5f 6m 5m 5m* 5g Oct 16] strong gelding: fairly useful handicapper: made all at Newcastle in September: best at 5f on good going or firmer nowadays: best in blinkers: often gives trouble at stalls (unseated rider once, and has been blanketed for entry). *M. W. Easterby*

BLESS THE BRIDE (IRE) 2 b.f. (Feb 13) Darshaan 133 – Feather Bride (IRE) **65 p** (Groom Dancer (USA) 128) [1999 8v⁴ 7.1v⁶ 8.3d⁶ Oct 28] 20,000Y: first foal: dam French 10.5f winner from family of Breeders' Cup Turf winner Kotashaan (by Darshaan): clear promise in maidens, best effort when sixth to impressive Kalypso Katie at Windsor on final start: likely to prove very well suited by 1¼m+: sure to do better stepped up in trip. *J. L. Dunlop*

BLINDING MISSION (IRE) 2 b.f. (Feb 5) Marju (IRE) 127 – Blinding (IRE) **67 p** (High Top 131) [1999 7m⁵ 8d Oct 15] 105,000F, 140,000Y: lengthy, good-bodied filly: fluent mover: fourth foal: sister to 6-y-o High Priority and half-sister to a 1m winner in Denmark by Caerleon: dam twice-raced half-sister to smart 7f/1m performer Hadeer, from very good family: considerably handled in maidens at Salisbury and Newmarket, swishing tail in paddock and taking good hold on latter course: should stay 1¼m: capable of better. *J. Noseda*

BLIND TRUST (IRE) 3 b.c. Mtoto 134 – Ancestry (Persepolis (FR) 127) [1998 **–** 78p: 7m 1999 8m May 2] rather leggy, angular colt: fair form only start at 2 yrs: hampered and broke leg in Newmarket maiden on reappearance: dead. *C. F. Wall*

BLISS (IRE) 4 b.f. Statoblest 120 – Moira My Girl (Henbit (USA) 130) [1998 71: **57** 6v a5g 5m 5m⁶ 5.1m 5.1d 6m² 5m 6m 5g 1999 5m 5.1m 5.3f⁴ 6m Jul 26] work-manlike, close-coupled filly: only modest handicapper at best in 1999: best form on good/good to firm going: has had tongue tied: sometimes slowly away. *Mrs P. N. Dutfield*

BLIZZARD 3 gr.f. Petong 126 – Tempesta Rossa (IRE) (Persian Heights 129) **–** [1998 –: 6s a6g a8g 1999 8.3g May 10] no form, including in claimer. *B. Smart*

BLOCKADE (USA) 10 b.g. Imperial Falcon (CAN) – Stolen Date (USA) **49** (Sadair) [1998 56: 8m 10.1f³ 10.1m³ 10.2d⁵ 8m⁶ 10.1g² 10m 9.9m⁴ 9.9m 1999 10.1m³ 10.1g* 10.1m 10.1d 10.5m 10.1m 10m Aug 28] close-coupled gelding: tubed: poor handicapper: won apprentice race at Yarmouth in June: stays 1¼m, probably not 11.5f: acts on firm and good to soft going: sometimes sweats: none too consistent. *M. L. W. Bell*

BLOOD ORANGE 5 ch.h. Ron's Victory (USA) 129 – Little Bittern (USA) 73 **–** (Riva Ridge (USA)) [1998 –: a12g a7g 5s 6g 1999 8g May 15] good-topped horse: little form, including in handicaps. *G. G. Margarson*

BLOODY MARY (IRE) 2 ch.f. (Apr 26) Prince of Birds (USA) 121 – Royaltess **65** (Royal And Regal (USA)) [1999 5g 6g² 6m³ 7f 6.8m² 7m³ 8.3g⁴ Oct 11] IR 8,000Y: leggy, quite good-topped filly: eighth foal: closely related to a winner in USA by Bluebird and half-sister to 3-y-o Havana, useful 1989 2-y-o 6f winner Makbul (by Fairy King) and 1m and 1¼m winner Hunt Hill (by High Estate): dam unraced: fair maiden: stays 8.3f: raced only on good ground or firmer. *R. Hannon*

BLOOMING AMAZING 5 b.g. Mazilier (USA) 107 – Cornflower Blue **83** (Tyrnavos 129) [1998 86, a66: a7g³ a8g⁵ a12g² a12g² 12d⁴ a9.4g³ 7.5m* 8m 8.5d² **a62** a8.5g⁴ 7.5m* 8m* 7.9g⁶ 8s 10.4g⁶ 1999 a8g⁵ a11g 8.5m 8m³ 7m 8.5g² 8g 8m 7.9m 8d⁵ a8g³ a7g Dec 21] tall, plain gelding: has stringhalt: fairly useful handicapper on turf, modest on all-weather: trained by J. L. Eyre first 10 starts: effective at 1m to 1½m: acts on good to firm ground, good to soft and fibresand: effective visored or not: usually races prominently. *G. Woodward*

BLOT 5 b.g. Warning 136 – Rattle Along 80 (Tap On Wood 130) [1998 NR 1999 **–** 8d Oct 14] leggy, sparely-made gelding: fairly useful maiden at 3 yrs: tongue tied, last in handicap only start since: raced only at 1m: often bandaged behind. *C. R. Egerton*

BLOWING AWAY (IRE) 5 b. or br.m. Last Tycoon 131 – Taken By Force **40** (Persian Bold 123) [1998 54: 8.3g⁴ 9g³ 10.1m² 10.8s⁵ 10g² 9m⁴ 11.5g 10.1m³ 12f³ 10.9d⁶ 12d³ 10s 1999 10m a14g Sep 28] leggy mare: poor handicapper: stays 1¾m: acts on fibresand, firm and good to soft going (well beaten on soft): ran poorly in visor once at 3 yrs. *J. Pearce*

BLOW ME A KISS 4 ch.f. Kris 135 – Lassoo 87 (Caerleon (USA) 132) [1998 72: 7.5d³ 8g 8d² 10.1g² 10g² 10.4g³ 10v² 11.8s a14g 1999 a12g 11m a11g Nov 30] rather sparely-made filly: fair maiden at 3 yrs: well beaten in 1999: stays 1¼m: acts on good to soft going. *C. W. Thornton*

BLUE ANCHOR   4 b.g. Robellino (USA) 127 – Fair Seas 72 (General Assembly (USA)) [1998 41: a6g⁴ a7g a11g* a11g⁶ 11.1d 14.1s³ a12g a14.8g⁶ 1999 a13g Jan 5] small gelding: poor handicapper at 3 yrs: stays 1¾m: acts on fibresand and soft going. *A. W. Carroll* –

BLUEBELLE   4 b.f. Generous (IRE) 139 – Hi Lass 106 (Shirley Heights 130) [1998 80p: 8g⁴ 10d³ 12.3d* 1999 14m 14d 15.9d Aug 21] leggy filly: fairly useful at 3 yrs: no form in handicaps in 1999, reportedly lost shoe on reappearance, then saddle slipped next time: should stay beyond 1½m. *Sir Mark Prescott* –

BLUEBELL WOOD (IRE)   2 ch.f. (Feb 17) Bluebird (USA) 125 – Jungle Jezebel 107 (Thatching 131) [1999 7s Oct 8] 15,000Y, 24,000 2-y-o: half-sister to 1997 2-y-o 7f winner Jungle Story (by Alzao) and a 5f winner in Japan by Fairy King: dam, 2-y-o 7f winner who stayed 1m, granddaughter of Irish 1000 Guineas winner Lady Capulet: signs of ability though never dangerous in maiden at Lingfield: likely to do better. *A. J. McNae* – p

BLUE BOLIVAR (IRE)   2 b.c. (Apr 21) Blues Traveller (IRE) 119 – Cappuchino (IRE) 59 (Roi Danzig (USA)) [1999 7.1m* 6g² 8s⁵ Sep 26] 25,000Y: tall, rather unfurnished, close-coupled colt: second foal: dam 7f winner: won maiden at Sandown in June: off course 3 months, then showed useful form when short-head second of 21 to Sheer Hamas in sales race at Doncaster and over 5 lengths fifth of 6 to Royal Kingdom in Royal Lodge Stakes at Ascot (finished tired): likely to be suited by 7f/1m: may still do better. *R. Hannon* 99

BLUE CAVALIER (IRE)   2 b.c. (Apr 23) Blues Traveller (IRE) 119 – Age of Elegance (Troy 137) [1999 a8g⁶ a8.5g Dec 11] 12,000Y: half-brother to several winners, including useful 6f (at 2 yrs) to 1¼m (in Italy) winner Sheer Precocity (by Precocious) and 4-y-o Netta Rufina: dam French 1½m winner: little show in maiden and minor event on fibresand. *S. Dow* –

BLUE DAWN (IRE)   4 ch.f. Bluebird (USA) 125 – Spring Carnival (USA) (Riverman (USA) 131) [1998 73, a49: 7.3m 8.5d⁵ 8g 8.9g a7g⁵ a8.5g⁵ a10g 1999 a10g⁵ a7g Jan 7] leggy filly: fair maiden at 3 yrs: stays easy 8.5f: acts on good to soft going and fibresand: blinkered final start: has been bandaged behind. *B. R. Johnson* –

BLUE DIAMOND   3 b.f. First Trump 118 – Lammastide 93 (Martinmas 128) [1998 –: 6g 7d 1999 9.9m 10f May 28] little sign of ability, including in selling handicap: blinkered final start. *J. S. Moore* –

BLUE DOVE (IRE)   2 b.f. (Jan 20) Bluebird (USA) 125 – Paradise Forum 78 (Prince Sabo 123) [1999 6m Sep 18] sparely-made filly: third foal: half-sister to 3-y-o Tyrolean Love: dam 2-y-o 5f winner: always behind in Newbury maiden. *C. A. Horgan* 52

BLUE GLASS   3 b.f. Ardkinglass 114 – Kajetana (FR) (Caro 133) [1998 52: 7.9g a8.5g⁴ a8.5g* 1999 a8.5g⁴ Mar 6] modest form: fourth in minor event only start in 1999: should stay 1¼m: acts on fibresand: sold 1,100 gns in October. *N. P. Littmoden* 58

BLUE GOLD   2 b.c. (Feb 15) Rainbow Quest (USA) 134 – Relatively Special 112 (Alzao (USA) 117) [1999 6m⁵ 7.1m* 8.1m³ 7d³ Oct 12] 410,000Y: close-coupled, attractive colt: has a quick action: second foal: half-brother to 3-y-o Ring The Relatives: dam, 2-y-o 6f/7f (Rockfel) winner who was later best at 1¼m, half-sister to One So Wonderful, a very good family: fairly useful form: made all in maiden at Sandown in July: good third in minor events at Haydock and Leicester afterwards: bred to be suited by 1¼m+: may do better still. *R. Hannon* 91

BLUEGRASS MOUNTAIN   2 b.c. (Jan 21) Primo Dominie 121 – Florentynna Bay 61 (Aragon 118) [1999 5d³ 6d⁶ 5g May 28] 12,000Y: brother to 4-y-o Sunstreak and half-brother to 3 winners, including 6-y-o 5f winner The Bear: dam, 2-y-o 5f winner, half-sister to smart sprinter Superpower: well backed, best effort in maidens when third at Warwick on debut: well held after. *T. D. Easterby* 72

BLUE HAWAII (IRE)   2 ch.c. (Mar 21) Up And At 'em 109 – Astral Way (Hotfoot 126) [1999 6g³ 7.5g⁶ 6m 7g 8d Nov 1] 5,000F, 10,500Y: quite good-topped colt: half-brother to 3-y-o Gowiththeflow and several winners, including useful 1991 64 d

2-y-o 7f winner Ruhr (by Flash of Steel) and stayer Arian Spirit (by High Estate): dam French 2-y-o 1m winner: modest form when third in maiden at Ayr, but well beaten after: sold 1,000 gns, joined S. R. Bowring. *B. S. Rothwell*

BLUE HAWK (IRE)   2 ch.g. (Mar 18) Prince of Birds (USA) 121 – Classic   **61**
Queen (IRE) (Classic Secret (USA) 91) [1999 6s 7m⁵ 7m 7m³ 10s 7g Oct 16] first reported foal: dam well beaten at 2 yrs in Ireland: modest maiden: probably stays 1¼m: acts on good to firm and soft ground. *R. Hollinshead*

BLUE HOLLY (IRE)   2 b.f. (Apr 29) Blues Traveller (IRE) 119 – Holly Bird   **76**
(Runnett 125) [1999 5g 5m 5.1m 5v² 5s² 5s³ 5g* 5.2d² 5s³ Nov 5] IR 6,100Y, 13,000 2-y-o: half-sister to 3 winning sprinters, including 5-y-o Mangus (by Mac's Imp): dam Irish 7f and 1½m winner: fair performer: won maiden at Lingfield in October: good efforts in nurseries at Yarmouth and Doncaster last 2 starts: likely to prove best at 5f: acts on heavy going. *J. S. Moore*

BLUE HOPPER   5 b.m. Rock Hopper 124 – Kimble Blue 56 (Blue Refrain 121)   **41**
[1998 43: a12g⁴ a12g⁶ a9.4g⁴ a12g² a12g 11.8s 9.9s 9v 8.3m³ 10g a12g⁶ a8.5g 8g⁶ 8.1g³ 10.2d 8m 9.2s 1999 a11g² a12g³ a12g⁶ Jan 18] workmanlike mare: poor maiden: effective at 1m to 1½m: acts on good to firm going and fibresand: has run well in blinkers and visor: sometimes pulls hard. *M. Quinn*

BLUE KITE   4 ch.g. Silver Kite (USA) 111 – Gold And Blue (IRE) (Bluebird   **68**
(USA) 125) [1998 77: a5g⁵ a5g⁴ 6.1m⁵ 6m 6f 6s² a7g² 6m 6.1g⁴ 6g a6g a6g a6g a6g⁵   **a80 +**
a6g 1999 a5g⁵ a7g 6m⁴ 6m² 5d 6.1f⁴ 7d 6g 5g a6g⁵ 7d a6g* a6f² a6g² a7g³ a6g³ a7g² a7g⁶ a6g* Dec 21] stocky gelding: unimpressive mover: fair handicapper: trained by P. D. Evans third to eighth starts: rejoined previous trainer, won at Wolverhampton in September and Southwell in December: stays 7f: acts on all-weather, firm and soft going: tried blinkered/visored/tongue tied, rarely in 1999: sometimes slowly away, usually races prominently otherwise. *N. P. Littmoden*

BLUE LASER (IRE)   3 b.g. Mujtahid (USA) 118 – Dazzling Fire (IRE) 78   **–**
(Bluebird (USA) 125) [1998 63: 5m 6d 1999 8.5s 8m 8.3m 6.1d Jun 2] rather unfurnished gelding: poor form at best in 1999: blinkered final 2 starts. *B. J. Meehan*

BLUE LEGEND (IRE)   2 b.f. (Apr 4) Blues Traveller (IRE) 119 – Swoon Along   **49**
(Dunphy 124) [1999 6g 5.7f 7.5s² 7f* a7g⁶ 7d 7m 8.2d Oct 21] IR 2,200Y: seventh foal: half-sister to winners abroad by Entitled and Pips Pride: dam ran twice in Ireland: modest performer: won claimer at Brighton in July: well below form after: should stay beyond 7.5f: acts on soft and firm going. *J. S. Moore*

BLUE LINE ANGEL   3 b.g. Cyrano de Bergerac 120 – Northern Line 92   **56**
(Camden Town 125) [1998 –: 5g 6d 5s 1999 8f 9.3g³ 8m⁴ 8.2g⁴ 7m 7.1m⁴ 8.5s 7g a8g Nov 22] modest maiden handicapper at best: creditable efforts only when in frame: should prove best at 7f (given test) to 9f: acts on good to firm going, possibly not on soft: often claimer ridden. *R. A. Fahey*

BLUE LINE LADY (IRE)   2 b.f. (Mar 2) Common Grounds 118 – Best   **68**
Academy (USA) (Roberto (USA) 131) [1999 6f² 6g 6m² 5m 5m⁶ 6g 7g 7s Nov 6] 9,000Y: fourth foal: half-sister to Italian 3-y-o Legem Dicere (by Lycius), 7.5f and 9f winner at 2 yrs, and 2 winners abroad: dam Irish 8.5f winner: fair maiden at best: well below form last 3 starts: should stay 7f: acts on firm going. *R. A. Fahey*

BLUE MELODY (USA)   3 b. or br.f. Dayjur (USA) 137 – Blue Note (FR) 122   **93**
(Habitat 134) [1998 103: 5m* 6f 6f² 6g² 6.5g² 6s⁴ 1999 6g 5m 6d² 6s Nov 6] sparely-made filly: unimpressive mover: only fairly useful performer at 3 yrs: left Saeed bin Suroor after disappointing in valuable event at Goodwood on reappearance: best effort after when second in minor event at Newmarket: stays 6.5f: acts on firm and good to soft going, possibly not on soft. *J. H. M. Gosden*

BLUE MONK (IRE)   4 ch.g. Bluebird (USA) 125 – High Habit 79 (Slip Anchor   **35**
136) [1998 NR 1999 a11g a12g a12g 8.1m 10.2g⁶ 14.1g 14.1m Jul 17] big, strong gelding: bad maiden: sold 660 gns in August. *A. G. Newcombe*

BLUE MOUNTAIN   2 ch.c. (May 12) Elmaamul (USA) 125 – Glenfinlass   **80**
(Lomond (USA) 128) [1999 5g² 6f³ 6f⁵ Sep 2] 20,000Y: strong, lengthy colt: fourth reported foal: half-brother to French 9f winner Bolder Still (by Never So Bold): dam unraced sister to 10-y-o Inchcailloch and half-sister to smart middle-distance performer Prize Giving: fairly-useful form in maidens at Windsor and Goodwood

first 2 starts: bandaged in front, short to post and sweating when last of 5 in York minor event final outing: bred to stay at least 7f. *R. F. Johnson Houghton*

BLUE MUSIC (IRE) 4 ch.g. Keen 116 – Coast Wind (USA) (Chief's Crown (USA)) [1998 66: 6v 5.8v 10m* 8.5d 9g 12s* 12s 1999 12m Sep 8] IR 3,000Y: first foal: dam, placed at 2 yrs in Ireland, out of Blue Wind: fair handicapper when trained at 3 yrs by D. Gillespie in Ireland, winning at Clonmel and Roscommon: successful 3 times over hurdles in the summer but well beaten only outing on Flat in 1999: stays 1½m: acts on soft going and on good to firm. *P. J. Hobbs* –

BLUE OF THE NIGHT 3 b.f. Runnett 125 – Upping The Tempo (Dunbeath (USA) 127) [1998 NR 1999 6f⁶ 6m Jul 16] lengthy filly: first foal: dam unraced half-sister to useful sprinter Up And At'Em: slowly away and last in maidens at Lingfield and Newmarket (far too free to post). *C. F. Wall* –

BLUE PERU (IRE) 3 b.f. Perugino (USA) 84 – Blue Czarina (Sandhurst Prince 128) [1998 48+: 6m 7f⁴ 7.5m a9.4g a7g 1999 7f May 4] small, leggy filly: form only when fourth in seller at 2 yrs: stays 7f. *B. Smart* –

BLUEPRINT (IRE) 4 b.c. Generous (IRE) 139 – Highbrow 112§ (Shirley Heights 130) [1998 103: a12g⁴ a12g* a12g* 12s³ 11.9m² 14g³ 13.9f* 15d 16g⁵ 1999 12m* 12m* 12m* 13.3g⁴ 12m² Sep 4] **116**

By Royal Appointment ... Sir Michael Stoute celebrated his first season as one of the Queen's trainers with a highly appropriate winner at Royal Ascot. Blueprint, whom Stoute took over as a useful handicapper on the retirement of Lord Huntingdon, was earmarked for the Royal meeting after showing improved form when gaining a smooth success on his reappearance at Newmarket on One Thousand Guineas day. Blueprint had come third in the mile-and-a-half King George V Stakes at Royal Ascot as a three-year-old and

Duke of Edinburgh Stakes (Handicap), Royal Ascot—the first name change to a race at the meeting in twenty-six years; Blueprint is a very apt winner for The Queen; Banbury (right), Just In Time (rail) and Carry The Flag make the frame

The Queen's "Blueprint"

the target in the latest season was the inaugural running, over the same distance, of the Duke of Edinburgh Stakes, a race formerly run in honour of the 5th Earl of Bessborough, a nineteenth-century dignitary at Ascot. The first change of a race name at Royal Ascot for more than a quarter of a century was prompted by the loss of the Duke of Edinburgh Stakes for two-year-olds at the track's truncated October fixture. Blueprint, who started favourite, was always handily placed in the eighteen-runner field and asserted himself approaching the final furlong to win by a length and a half from Banbury. The traditional raising of hats in recognition of a winner in the Royal colours was in evidence for a third successive Blueprint victory eleven days later in the Fred Archer Stakes, a listed event at Newmarket, also over a mile and a half, in which Blueprint dished out an emphatic beating to Yavana's Pace, Memorise and Strategic Choice. There was talk afterwards of a tilt at the Melbourne Cup before two subsequent defeats in pattern company (last of four behind Silver Patriarch in the Geoffrey Freer at Newbury and a half-length reverse at odds on to Yavana's Pace in the September Stakes at Epsom).

Blueprint showed that he stays a mile and three quarters when winning the Melrose Stakes at York as a three-year-old and he should get the Melbourne Cup trip of two miles. The big, rangy Blueprint, who shows knee action, has also proven himself fairly versatile so far as ground requirements are concerned, showing form on going ranging from firm to soft on turf, as well as scoring two wins on the all-weather as a three-year-old (visored on both occasions, as he was in the King George V Stakes and on his next start as a three-year-old). *Sir Michael Stoute*

BLUE ROCK LADY   3 br.f. Rock City 120 – Blues Player 70 (Jaazeiro (USA) – 127) [1998 –: 6s 7s 1999 8g 8m Jun 26] sparely-made filly: no sign of ability in maidens/claimer: sold 1,200 gns in July. *C. F. Wall*

BLUE SAPPHIRE (IRE)   2 b.f. (Apr 29) Blues Traveller (IRE) 119 – Era 70   **37** (Dalsaan 125) [1999 5d 5g 5m³ 5g⁶ 7f 6d a5f 5g a5g Nov 12] 1,200 2-y-o: small filly: **a–** fourth living foal: half-sister to 3 winners, including fairly useful 1992 2-y-o 6f/7f winner After The Last (by Infantry): dam second at 5f at 2 yrs: poor maiden: form only at 5f: sold 700 gns in October. *D. W. Barker*

BLUE SNAKE (USA)   3 br.c. Gone West (USA) – Dabaweyaa 118 (Shareef   **96** Dancer (USA) 135) [1998 89p: 6m⁴ 8g³ 8s 1999 a8f² 8m* Jul 15] close-coupled colt: useful form: placed in maidens at 2 yrs (at Newmarket) and on reappearance (in USA) prior to winning similar event at Doncaster, making all and pushed clear to beat Bayaniya by 3½ lengths: unlikely to stay beyond 1m: acts on good to firm going: early to post at Doncaster: looked open to further improvement. *Saeed bin Suroor*

BLUES OF THE NIGHT   3 bl.f. Petong 126 – Candane 73 (Danehill (USA)   **39** 126) [1998 –: 6d 7g 1999 7.5m 12m⁴ 12.4f³ 10g⁵ 10m Aug 30] sturdy filly: poor maiden: stays 1½m: acts on firm going: joined Mrs E. Moscrop. *N. Tinkler*

BLUE STAR   3 b.g. Whittingham (IRE) 104 – Gold And Blue (IRE) (Bluebird   **75** (USA) 125) [1998 ?, a87: a5g² a6g³ 6m a6g* 7g a6g² 1999 7g 6.1m 6m 6m 6g 7m⁴ 6s³ 6m⁴ 6f³ 6.1g 7m⁵ 8m Sep 8] rangy gelding: fair handicapper: barely stays 7f: acts on firm and soft going, and fibresand: visored nowadays. *N. P. Littmoden*

BLUE SUGAR (USA)   2 ch.c. (Feb 7) Shuailaan (USA) 122 – Chelsea My Love   **90 p** (USA) (Opening Verse (USA) 126) [1999 7.6g* Aug 25] 10,000Y: first foal: dam tailed off only start: won 16-runner maiden at Lingfield in August by 3 lengths from First Manassas, travelling strongly and asserting under hands and heels from over 1f out: will stay at least 1m: should make a useful performer. *J. R. Fanshawe*

BLUES WHISPERER (IRE)   2 b.c. (May 3) Blues Traveller (IRE) 119 –   **–** Princess Roxanne 68 (Prince Tenderfoot (USA) 126) [1999 7m Aug 22] 7,300Y: third foal: half-brother to 4-y-o Carolines Pet: dam effective from 1m to 1½m: tailed off in maiden at Leicester: wore tongue strap. *B. R. Millman*

BLUE VELVET   2 gr.f. (May 30) Formidable (USA) 125 – Sweet Whisper 63   **88** (Petong 126) [1999 5d⁴ a5g⁴ 5.3f² 5m³ 5g⁴ 5.1g² a5g* 5m² 5.2m 5f 5.2m⁶ 5d* 6g 6d² 6v⁴ Oct 23] 5,600Y: well-made filly: poor mover: second foal: half-sister to 3-y-o So Willing: dam 2-y-o 5f/6f winner: fairly useful performer: generally progressive form: won maiden at Southwell in June and nursery at Newmarket in September: creditable efforts in valuable contests at Redcar and Newmarket and nursery at Newbury last 3 starts: effective at 5f/6f: acts on any turf going and all-weather: often bandaged: used to front-run, better efforts held up: tough. *K. T. Ivory*

BLUEWAIN LADY   4 b.f. Unfuwain (USA) 131 – Blue Guitar 88 (Cure The   **70** Blues (USA)) [1998 73: 10.3m 10f⁵ 11.9m 14m³ 11.9s* 1999 14.1s⁵ 16.2d 13.8m² 14m⁵ 14.1g⁵ Jun 30] tall filly: fair handicapper: stays 1¾m: acts on good to firm and soft ground: has hung and found little: blinkered last 2 starts in 1998. *P. W. Harris*

BLUEWATER BAY   3 b.f. Lugana Beach 116 – Dominion Blue 66 (Dominion   **60** 123) [1998 60p: a6g³ 1999 a6g³ a7g⁴ 8m⁴ 10.1g a8.5g² a9.4g* 10g⁴ 8m Sep 2] modest performer: won seller at Wolverhampton (final outing for J. Eustace) in August: good fourth in handicap at Lingfield next time: stays 1¼m: acts on all-weather, raced only on good/good to firm going on turf. *Andrew Reid*

BLUNDELL LANE (IRE)   4 ch.g. Shalford (IRE) 124§ – Rathbawn Realm   **81** (Doulab (USA) 115) [1998 87d: a6g³ 7d 6.1m* 6f 6g 5.1m 6m 5.7m 1999 6g   **a75** 6s a5g⁴ 6m* 6f 6g³ 5m⁶ 6f 6m 5m a6g a6g a6g Dec 27] fairly useful performer: won minor event at Warwick in May: below form last 6 starts: effective at 5f/6f: acts on firm and fibresand: tried visored/blinkered: usually races prominently. *A. P. Jarvis*

BLURRED IMAGE (IRE)   8 ch.g. Exactly Sharp (USA) 121 – Bear's Affair   **36** (Gay Fandango (USA) 132) [1998 NR 1999 7.1m 10g 10m Aug 28] leggy, good-topped gelding: good mover: poor performer nowadays: probably stays 1¼m: acts on firm and soft ground, ran poorly both starts on all-weather: joined Mrs A. Price 800 gns in October. *Julian Poulton*

BLURRED (IRE)   6 ch.g. Al Hareb (USA) 123 – I'll Take Paris (USA) 103   **–** (Vaguely Noble 140) [1998 NR 1999 10.8d 12g 10g 11.9f Jul 13] big, heavy-topped gelding: fairly useful handicapper around 1¼m at 3 yrs: well beaten since: visored/tongue tied final start: joined Dr J. Naylor 3,100 gns in August. *M. H. Tompkins*

BLUSHING GRENADIER (IRE)   7 ch.g. Salt Dome (USA) – La Duse 66 (Junius (USA) 124) [1998 65, a60: a7g² a6g* a7g³ a6g³ a6g 6g* 6.1g 5d² a5g³ 5d⁴ a6g 6m* 5g 5s³ 6v* 6s 5d a5g a7g 1999 a7g⁴ a7g 6.1v 6.1s⁶ 6s² 6d* a5g⁴ 6g 5.9g* a6g² a7g³ 6d⁵ 5d a6g a8.5g³ a8.5g⁴ a7g Dec 15] leggy gelding: fair on turf, modest on all-weather: won claimers at Redcar in May and Carlisle in June: effective at 5f (given good test) to 8.5f: acts on good to firm ground, heavy and all-weather: usually blinkered/visored: usually races prominently. *S. R. Bowring* **69 a57**

BLUSHING VICTORIA   4 b.f. Weldnaas (USA) 112 – Bollin Victoria 51 (Jalmood (USA) 126) [1998 NR 1999 a7g 6d 6.1s 6s Jun 12] leggy filly: won 5f maiden at 2 yrs: little form since: blinkered penultimate start. *J. A. Glover* **–**

BLUSIENKA (IRE)   2 b.f. (May 24) Blues Traveller (IRE) 119 – Pudgy Poppet (Danehill (USA) 126) [1999 8s* Nov 6] unfurnished filly: first reported foal: dam tailed off only start: 16/1 from 25/1, showed fairly useful form despite seeming green to win 16-runner maiden at Doncaster by ½ length from Grand Oro, leading near finish: will stay 1¼m: should make a useful 3-y-o. *G. A. Butler* **89 p**

BOADICEA THE RED (IRE)   2 gr.f. (Feb 23) Inchinor 119 – Kanika §§ (Be My Chief (USA) 122) [1999 5g² 6d⁵ 6d⁶ 6d² 7s a6g³ Dec 22] 1,400F, 800Y: first foal: dam, all but refused to race only outing, out of half-sister to Dewhurst winner Kala Dancer: fair maiden: likely to prove best at 6f/7f: acts on equitrack, raced only on good ground or softer on turf. *B. S. Rothwell* **72**

BOANERGES (IRE)   2 br.c. (Feb 19) Caerleon (USA) 132 – Sea Siren 68 (Slip Anchor 136) [1999 6.1g⁴ 7s³ 6d² Oct 20] 35,000F, 110,000Y: second foal: dam, maiden who should have been suited by further than 1m, closely related to very smart middle-distance filly Infamy, from family of High-Rise and In The Wings: fairly useful maiden: visored, best effort (despite hanging left) when 2 lengths second of 12 to Abuzaid at Newcastle on final start: bred to be suited by 1m+, but free-going sort, and not certain to be so: sold 17,500 gns, joined R. Guest. *J. Noseda* **82**

BOAST   2 ch.f. (Apr 15) Most Welcome 131 – Bay Bay 101 (Bay Express 132) [1999 5.1f* 5d⁶ 6.1g² 6m⁴ 6m* 7g⁶ Oct 16] tall, workmanlike filly: poor mover: seventh foal: half-sister to 5-y-o Butrinto, 1993 2-y-o 5f winner Baskerville (by Night Shift) and 5f (at 2 yrs) and 1m winner Great Bear (by Dominion): dam 7.6f winner: useful performer: won minor events at Nottingham in May and Newmarket in July: off course 3½ months before creditable sixth of 12 to Lahan in Rockfel Stakes on latter course final start: stays 7f, not sure to get much further: acts on firm going. *R. F. Johnson Houghton* **96**

BOATER   5 b.g. Batshoof 122 – Velvet Beret (IRE) (Dominion 123) [1998 75§: 7s² 7d³ 8g 9g³ 10.2s⁴ 8.1g 8.1m 8m a7g 1999 10.2g⁴ 10d² 12d Oct 9] well-made gelding: winning hurdler, fair handicapper on Flat: stays 1¼m (not sure to get further): acts on firm ground, soft and equitrack: blinkered once: usually races up with pace: carries head high under pressure: none too genuine. *A. T. Murphy* **65 §**

BOATING SONG (IRE)   2 b.f. (Mar 10) College Chapel 122 – Flower From Heaven (Baptism 119) [1999 5.2f³ 6g³ 5m⁵ 6s* 6.5g 6d 6v Oct 23] IR 15,000Y: half-sister to 3 winners, including 5-y-o Baptismal Rock and fairly useful Irish 9f/1¼m winner Angel From Heaven (by Bob Back): dam Irish sprinter: fair performer: won nursery at Windsor in August: well below form in similar events after: should stay 7f: acts on firm and soft going: sold 3,500 gns, sent to Kuwait. *R. Hannon* **74**

BOATMAN (USA)   3 ch.c. Irish River (FR) 131 – Peplum (USA) 108 (Nijinsky (CAN) 138) [1998 99p: 8g* 8s² 1999 10d⁴ 10m³ 10.3m 10d⁵ 10s⁶ Oct 22] big, good-topped colt: useful handicapper: good third at Newmarket in August: respectable efforts final 2 starts: should stay at least 1½m: acts on good to firm going, probably on soft: blinkered last 3 starts: sent to R. Frankel in USA. *R. Charlton* **97**

BOB-BOY   7 ch.g. Executive Man 119 – Quay Seat (Quayside 124) [1998 NR 1999 12m Aug 3] tailed off in claimer on Flat debut. *P. D. Evans* **–**

BOBBYDAZZLE   4 ch.f. Rock Hopper 124 – Billie Blue 63 (Ballad Rock 122) [1998 81: 8.1s 10m⁶ 8s* 10.1v⁴ 8f 8.1g 8d 1999 8.5m⁵ 8g⁵ 8.1g³ 8m 8d 8d 8s a8.5g³ Nov 20] angular, workmanlike filly: fairly useful at best on turf: well below form **80 d**

after second start: stays 1m well: acts on firm and soft going, placed only outing on fibresand: blinkered penultimate start: has sweated and got on edge. *Dr J. D. Scargill*

BOBONA   3 b.c. Interrex (CAN) – Puella Bona 60 (Handsome Sailor 125) [1998   **32** NR 1999 6m a7g a5g 6s⁵ a7g 11.6s a12g³ 10g⁴ 14.1f a11g* Dec 13] first foal: dam,   **a44** half-sister to several winners, placed at 6f/7f: poor handicapper: won apprentice claimer at Southwell in December: may prove best at 1¼m/1½m: acts on fibresand: blinkered fifth start: possibly none too genuine. *M. D. I. Usher*

BOB'S BUSTER   3 b.g. Bob's Return (IRE) 123 – Saltina (Bustino 136) [1998 ?:   **57** 5.1d⁶ 5s² 6m 6f 8g 1999 8.2s⁴ 8d 10.5s³ 8.2m 8.2g a8g⁵ Jul 10] tall gelding: modest maiden: somewhat headstrong: best at 1m: acts on soft going and on good to firm: somewhat headstrong. *J. Wharton*

BOB'S PRINCESS   3 b.f. Bob's Return (IRE) 123 – Princess Rosananti (IRE)   **57** (Shareef Dancer (USA) 135) [1998 69p: 7m* 7m³ 1999 9g 8.3m 11.5g⁴ 10m 12m⁴ 10.2s Oct 26] just modest at best in handicaps in 1999: stays 1½m: acts on good to firm going: visored last 2 starts: has looked less than keen. *P. R. Chamings*

BOCA CHICA   2 gr.f. (May 24) Environment Friend 128 – Scoffera 63 (Scottish   **–** Reel 123) [1999 6f 7.5s 7m 8d Sep 16] 1,000 2-y-o: second foal: dam won up to 1¼m and also over hurdles: well beaten in claimer and sellers. *N. Tinkler*

BODFARI ANNA   3 br.f. Casteddu 111 – Lowrianna (IRE) 50 (Cyrano de   **52** Bergerac 120) [1998 61, a49: 5d 5s⁵ a5g⁵ a5g² 5g⁴ 6g² 7g 6m² 6.1g* 6m⁶ 6s² 6m⁴ 6m⁴ 7g⁵ a5g 1999 a6g 6g 6g 6m a5g⁴ 6g³ 6f⁵ 6f⁴ 6f² 7.1d⁴ 6m* 6m 6m 6v 7g Oct 15] leggy, unfurnished filly: has a round action: modest handicapper: won seller at Haydock in September: stays 6f, probably not 7f: acts on firm and soft going and fibresand: blinkered/visored: sometimes slowly away: has looked none too hearty. *J. L. Eyre*

BODFARI JET (IRE)   2 b.f. (Apr 9) Grand Lodge (USA) 125 – River Jet (USA)   **54** (Lear Fan (USA) 130) [1999 5g⁴ 6g 6d Oct 20] unfurnished filly: third foal: half-sister to 1¼m winner Step N Go (by Alzao): dam, French 1m (at 2 yrs) and 10.5f winner, half-sister to useful French stayer River Test: no form after fourth of 17 in maiden at Beverley on debut: should stay at least 6f. *M. W. Easterby*

BODFARI KOMAITE   3 b.g. Komaite (USA) – Gypsy's Barn Rat 55 (Balliol   **69 p** 125) [1998 65: 5v 5s⁶ 5m⁶ 5d³ 5m* 5d 6s 5d 1999 5d 7m⁶ 7.1d 5g* 6g⁴ 5m* 5d⁴ 5g 5m⁶ 5s⁶ Sep 29] workmanlike gelding: fair handicapper: won at Musselburgh in June and Doncaster in July: better than results suggest after, and almost certainly did well having raced virtually alone when sixth to Daawe at Newcastle on final outing: best form at 5f: acts on good to firm and good to soft going: reportedly injured in stalls fifth outing: likely to improve further at 4 yrs. *M. W. Easterby*

BODFARI QUARRY   3 b.f. Efisio 120 – Last Quarry 52 (Handsome Sailor 125)   **80** [1998 78*: 5m* 5m³ 6s 7d³ 1999 7g⁶ 7.6m 8g⁴ 9.1g* 8.5s 10g³ 9f⁵ 10.2m 10d a9.4f*   **a92** 10d 10.2s a12g* a12g* a12g⁶ Dec 29] strong filly: fairly useful handicapper: won at Ayr in June, Wolverhampton in October and November and Southwell in December: well beaten on equitrack debut at Lingfield final start: stays 1½m: acts on firm going, good to soft and fibresand: has been bandaged behind/tongue tied: tried blinkered, better form without. *B. W. Hills*

BODFARI SIGNET   3 ch.g. King's Signet (USA) 110 – Darakah 78 (Doulab   **63** (USA) 115) [1998 61: 5s 5d 5g 5g⁵ 6f 6g⁶ 6m⁵ 5d 7m² 7m⁵ 7g 7s² 1999 10m 10v 8m   **a–** 9.9g a8g 8.3m* 9.2m⁵ 9.9m⁵ a8.5g Dec 1] leggy, lengthy gelding: modest handicapper: won maiden event at Hamilton in June: left M. W. Easterby 4,500 gns before final start: may prove best around 1m: acts on good to firm and soft going: usually blinkered: tends to find little: inconsistent. *B. P. J. Baugh*

BODFARI TIMES   3 ch.f. Clantime 101 – Tendency 77 (Ballad Rock 122) [1998   **–** 72d: 5.1g⁶ 5m² 5d 5g 5s⁵ 5.2s⁶ a5g 1999 5g 5v Oct 11] sparely-made filly: fair maiden at best: little form since fifth 2-y-o start: likely to prove best at 5f: acts on good to firm going, probably on soft. *L. J. Barratt*

BODFARI VISTA   3 b.f. Scenic 128 – Tomard (Thatching 131) [1998 NR 1999   **–** 7.1m 7.5v⁶ 7.6m 8.1d Aug 5] 15,000Y: good-topped filly: poor mover: half-sister to several winners, including useful sprinter Tourandot (by Emarati) and 15f winner

Tophard (by Lyphard's Special): dam Irish 2-y-o 5f winner: well beaten in maidens/seller: sold 1,200 gns, sent to Belgium. *B. W. Hills*

BOFFY (IRE)   6 ch.h. Mac's Imp (USA) 116 – No Dowry (Shy Groom (USA))   –
[1998 –, a37: a5g a5g a5g⁴ a5g a7g a6g a5g a5g⁶ a5g⁵ a5g a5g⁶ a6g⁴ a6g 5m a6g a6g a6g a6g a5g⁵ 1999 a5g a6g a6f Feb 8] poor performer: showed nothing in 1999: best at 5f: acts on all-weather, rarely raced on turf nowadays: sometimes blinkered/visored. *B. P. J. Baugh*

BOGUS DREAMS (IRE)   2 ch.c. (Feb 12) Lahib (USA) 129 – Dreams Are Free   **94**
(IRE) 71 (Caerleon (USA) 132) [1999 7f* 7s* 8d³ Oct 18] 6,000Y: angular colt: third foal: half-brother to 1997 2-y-o 6f winner Truth Teller (by Statoblest) and 3-y-o Live To Tell: dam 1¼m winner from family of Seattle Slew and Lomond: fairly useful form: won maiden at Thirsk and minor event at Ascot in September: conceding weight all round, good third of 6 to Hataab in listed race at Pontefract final start: should stay at least 1¼m: acts on firm and soft ground. *S. P. C. Woods*

BOHEMIA   3 b.f. Polish Precedent (USA) 131 – Horseshoe Reef 88 (Mill Reef   **63**
(USA) 141) [1998 70p: 6f 7m⁴ 8g⁵ 1999 9.9g⁶ 8.2m 10d⁴ Jul 6] quite attractive filly: modest maiden: well below form after reappearance: should stay at least 1¼m: sold 7,000 gns in October. *J. R. Fanshawe*

BOLD AMUSEMENT   9 ch.g. Never So Bold 135 – Hysterical 68 (High Top   **74**
131) [1998 65: 9m 12.1s 10.1v⁵ 10d* 1999 8d⁵ 11d⁵ 10.1m* 10.1m* 12.4m² 10.1f² 10.3m⁵ 8.9d Oct 9] strong gelding: fair handicapper: won twice at Newcastle in June: at least creditable efforts after: effective at 1¼m/1½m: acts on firm and soft going: tried blinkered earlier in career: edged right final start. *W. S. Cunningham*

BOLD ARISTOCRAT (IRE)   8 b.g. Bold Arrangement 127 – Wyn Mipet (Welsh   –
Saint 126) [1998 –, a67: a7s³ a7g⁶ a6g² a6g* a6g⁴ a6g* a6g* a6g² a7g⁶ a7g³ a7g⁵ a7g   **a69**
a7g a6g⁵ 1999 a7g⁴ a6g a6f⁶ a6f² a6g² a6g* a6g* a6g³ Mar 10] fair performer, raced exclusively on all-weather since 1996: successful 11 times at Southwell, including in claimer and seller in February: best at 6f/7f: acts on fibresand, raced only once (well held in blinkers) on equitrack: has worn pricker near side: usually held up: tends to carry head high. *R. Hollinshead*

BOLD BAHAMIAN (IRE)   2 b.g. (Mar 18) Persian Bold 123 – Nordic Pride   **68 p**
(Horage 124) [1999 8.1m⁵ 8s⁴ 8d Oct 27] seventh foal: brother to useful Irish 7f (at 2 yrs) to 1¼m winner Identify (stayed 1½m) and closely related to winning 2m hurdler Dignified (by Pennine Walk): dam Irish 2-y-o 6f winner: fair form in maidens: pulled hard first 2 starts, upset in stalls final one: bred to stay at least 1¼m, but needs to settle: remains capable of better. *J. Noseda*

BOLD BECKY   5 b.m. Never So Bold 135 – Princess Silca Key 61 (Grundy 137)   **41**
[1998 ?: a10g⁴ a8.5g⁵ 1999 a10f⁶ a13g a8g Feb 12] lightly-raced maiden: poor form: stays 1¼m: acts on equitrack. *A. P. Jones*

BOLDBIRD   2 b.g. (May 21) Puissance 110 – Plum Bold 83 (Be My Guest (USA)   –
126) [1999 6g Oct 11] 17,000Y: brother to 1m winner Pomona, later smart up to 1¼m in USA, and half-brother to 5 winners, including useful Italian sprinter Plumbird (by Statoblest): dam 6f winner from family of top-class Breton: well beaten in Windsor maiden. *D. J. Coakley*

BOLD BLUE (IRE)   3 b.g. Bluebird (USA) 125 – Evangola (Persian Bold 123)   **49**
[1998 NR 1999 8.1d 8m 8m⁶ 5.9g 7m 7.1f Sep 13] 72,000Y: sixth foal: half-brother to 3 winners, including useful Irish performer at up to 7f Persian Creek (by Treasure Kay): dam unraced: poor maiden handicapper: well held all starts: likely to prove best at 7f/1m: tried blinkered/visored: sold 800 gns, sent to Spain. *M. Johnston*

BOLD BOUNTY   2 ch.f. (Mar 8) Absalom 128 – Daring Gift (Never So Bold   –
135) [1999 5d 5.1s 5g May 28] 900Y: small, compact filly: first foal: dam, no worthwhile form, out of half-sister to smart performers up to 7f So Factual and Bold Fact: no sign of ability in sellers. *M. Brittain*

BOLD BUSTER   6 b.g. Bustino 136 – Truly Bold 76 (Bold Lad (IRE) 133) [1998   **69**
–: 12v 11.9g 1999 12g³ 12.3m⁴ 12m Sep 17] good-topped gelding: fair handicapper: creditable eforts in amateur/ladies events first 2 starts only: stays 2m: acts on good to firm and heavy going. *I. A. Balding*

BOLD CARDOWAN (IRE)   3 br.g. Persian Bold 123 – Moving Trend (IRE)   **56**
(Be My Guest (USA) 126) [1998 –: 6m 7d 1999 7m 9.3g⁶ 12.1m 10.9s³ 14.1m³ 16v*
16s⁴ 18d⁶ 16g Nov 3] angular, sparely-made gelding: modest handicapper: below
form after winning at Lingfield in September: will prove best at 2m+: acts on good to
firm ground, goes well on heavy: tended to wander fifth start. *John Berry*

BOLD CONQUEROR   3 br.f. Anshan 119 – Freudenau (Wassl 125) [1998 –:   **–**
5g 6.1m 7.1s 1999 6.1v 7f 8.1m Jun 29] no sign of ability, including in seller.
J. M. Bradley

BOLD EDGE   4 ch.c. Beveled (USA) – Daring Ditty (Daring March 116)   **123**
[1998 113: 6s* 6m* 7d² 6m² 8g⁵ 6m² 6m⁵ 6m* 1999 6g* 6s 6m* 6f² 5f 6m⁴ 6s*
Sep 26]
          With no other suitable races open to him before the end of the season,
the very smart six-furlong performer Bold Edge was allowed to take his chance
in the Gardner Merchant Diadem Stakes at Ascot in September, even though
Richard Hannon considered the soft going to be against the horse. Not only did
Hannon's fears prove unfounded, but he was also left with some egg on his face
after Bold Edge had won this Group 2 event. The horse coped perfectly well
with conditions far worse than those he'd encountered at Haydock three weeks
earlier when fourth to Diktat in the Sprint Cup, following which Hannon was
one of three trainers to lodge an official complaint about the ground, described
as good to firm. We agreed with that description, but Messrs Hannon, Cumani
and Noseda were of the opinion that it had been made loose and softer due to
excessive watering. Events at Ascot were to prove that Bold Edge's defeat in
the Sprint Cup had little to do with the state of the ground. Indeed, in going
down by a couple of lengths to Diktat at Haydock, the pair split by Bertolini
and Arkadian Hero, Bold Edge ran very close to his best. None of the three
who'd finished in front of Bold Edge were in the field at Ascot, and in what
looked just an average renewal of the Diadem it was the three-year-old Munjiz
who gave him most to do. Able to make the running without needing to set a
strong pace, Bold Edge wandered when coming under pressure after the
two-furlong marker but found plenty to hold the strong late challenge of Munjiz
by a short head.
          This was Bold Edge's seventh success overall and his third in a season
in which he'd shown himself an improved performer as early as his reappearance. As in the two previous seasons Bold Edge's first outing was a winning

Cork And Orrery Stakes, Royal Ascot—a game performance from Bold Edge,
who beats Russian Revival (white cap) and the fast-finishing Vision of Night (No.19)

Gardner Merchant Diadem Stakes, Ascot—another very smart performance from Bold Edge at the course, but this time the winning margin is narrower, with only a short head to spare over Munjiz (striped cap); Show Me The Money (extreme left) takes third

one. It came in a listed event, the NGK Spark Plugs Abernant Stakes at Newmarket, where he had things sewn up entering the final furlong and won by four lengths from Cretan Gift, eased the best part of a length close home. Next time out, Bold Edge finished last of fourteen at York with his trainer blaming the softer ground for the horse's dismal performance, a point he underlined when Bold Edge bounced back to form to win the Group 2 Cork And Orrery Stakes at Royal Ascot, which was run on good to firm. One of nineteen runners in an open-looking Cork And Orrery, Bold Edge showed excellent speed from the off, leading or disputing the lead until taking a definite advantage two furlongs out and running on gamely after briefly hanging left inside the final furlong. At the line he had a length and a quarter to spare over his nearest pursuer Russian Revival, with Vision of Night half a length further back in third. Bold Edge had two more races before Haydock. He acquitted himself well in the first of them when four lengths second to Stravinsky in the July Cup, finishing just ahead of Bertolini and Arkadian Hero; but he was unable to dominate and finished well held in the King George Stakes at Goodwood when tried over five for the first time since his two-year-old days.

		Sharpen Up (ch 1969)	Atan
	Beveled (USA) (ch 1982)		Rocchetta
		Sans Arc (gr 1974)	High Echelon
Bold Edge (ch.c. 1995)			Salmon Lake
		Daring March (br 1974)	Derring-Do
	Daring Ditty (br 1985)		March Spray
		Dawn Ditty (ch 1979)	Song
			Chick

Apparently Bold Edge will eventually take the place of his late sire Beveled at the Benham Stud, but he'll have plenty of opportunities to boost his reputation still further before then. Beveled himself had only limited success as a stallion. Among the best known of his representatives still in training are the very smart hurdler Master Beveled and the useful veteran handicappers Chewit and Brave Edge. The last-named is a full brother to Bold Edge, and also his stable companion. Their dam Daring Ditty, who also produced the modest twelve-furlong winner Sparky's Song (by Electric), showed nothing in her only two starts, but their grandam Dawn Ditty and great grandam Chick were both useful two-year-olds. Bold Edge, a rangy, good sort with a round action, invariably impresses in the preliminaries, though he is sometimes edgy and on his toes and sweated up at the start when running poorly at York. Tried over seven furlongs and a mile as a three-year-old, he ran as well as he did all that season over the former trip when second to Diktat in the Jersey Stakes at Royal Ascot.

Lady Whent and Friends' "Bold Edge"

Bold Edge, who acts on firm and soft going, has had his tongue tied. He usually helps force the pace and, though he does tend to hang under pressure, is very game. *R. Hannon*

BOLD EFFORT (FR) 7 b.g. Bold Arrangement 127 – Malham Tarn (Riverman (USA) 131) [1998 101, a90: a5g⁶ 6d³ 6d 5.1g³ 6m* 6m⁶ 6d 5d* 6g 6f 5.6g 5s⁵ 6v a7g a6g 1999 a6g* a7g⁴ a6g⁵ 6g 6m 6.1m⁶ 5m⁴ 5.6g 6v a6g Dec 22] good-quartered, dipped-backed gelding: poor mover: useful handicapper on all-weather: beat Mukarrab 4 lengths at Lingfield in February: fairly useful on turf, creditable effort in 1999 only when fourth at Sandown in August: has won at 1m, best form at 5f/6f: acts on firm ground, soft and all-weather: wears blinkers, has been visored: usually held up. *K. O. Cunningham-Brown* **87 a104**

BOLD EMMA 2 b.f. (Mar 21) Emarati (USA) 74 – Nevita (Never So Bold 135) [1999 a5g Nov 30] first reported foal: dam unraced daughter of sister to smart sprinter Jester: 20/1, well beaten in maiden at Southwell. *D. J. S. ffrench Davis* **–**

BOLDER ALEXANDER (IRE) 2 b.c. (May 20) Persian Bold 123 – Be Yourself (USA) (Noalcoholic (FR) 128) [1999 6g 6g a6g⁶ 7g* 7f⁶ 5m² 7f³ 7.1m 7d 7m³ 7s 8.3d Nov 4] 15,000Y: half-brother to winners in Australia: dam, successful twice in USA, daughter of very smart Irish 2-y-o filly Welsh Garden and half-sister to smart stayer Molesnes: modest performer: won seller at Brighton in June, then left P. Cole: should stay 1m: acts on firm ground: effective blinkered or not: none too consistent. *G. L. Moore* **53**

BOLD EWAR (IRE) 2 ch.c. (Apr 26) Persian Bold 123 – Hot Curry (USA) (Sharpen Up 127) [1999 7.1m 7m² 7m 7m⁵ 7g³ 8g 8d a8g⁴ a8g* Nov 30] 7,000Y: tall, workmanlike colt: sixth foal: brother to modest 11.5f winner Marchant Ming and half-brother to 1996 2-y-o 6f seller winner Jingoist (by Polish Patriot) and **78**

149

3-y-o Mujkari: dam 1m winner in USA: fair performer: won nursery at Southwell in November: stays 1m: acts on good to firm going and fibresand: blinkered 4 of last 5 starts. *C. E. Brittain*

BOLD FACT (USA) 4 b.c. Known Fact (USA) 135 – Sookera (USA) 117 (Roberto (USA) 131) [1998 113: 7m* 7d 6f 7f* 7m³ 1999 6g 6m* 6m 6f Jul 8] strong, attractive colt: impresses in appearance: has a quick action: smart performer: won listed race at Lingfield (beat Tipsy Creek by ¾ length) in May: well held after in Cork And Orrery Stakes at Royal Ascot (damaged hoof when spreading front plate) and July Cup at Newmarket: likely to prove best at 6f/7f on good going or firmer: sometimes hung markedly right/wandered earlier in career: sent to USA. *H. R. A. Cecil* **116**

BOLD FELICITER 3 ch.f. Bold Arrangement 127 – Jersey Maid 82 (On Your Mark 125) [1998 45: 5s⁶ 5g 7s 7g 7g⁶ 8.1m 8d⁶ 8.3s 1999 12m⁶ 12d⁴ 12.1m 14.1f 12.1m⁵ Jun 29] sparely-made filly: poor maiden at best: stays 1½m: acts on soft and good to firm going. *D. Moffatt* **39**

BOLD FRONTIER 7 gr.g. Chief Singer 131 – Mumtaz Flyer (USA) (Al Hattab (USA)) [1998 61, a75: 6.1s 5m 5m a5g* a5g⁴ 5m 5m³ 5m* 5g 5m 1999 a5g* a5g Feb 3] fair on all-weather, modest on turf: didn't need to be anywhere near best to win claimer at Wolverhampton in January: best at 5f/6f: acts on good to firm going and all-weather: usually blinkered/visored. *K. T. Ivory* **– a56 +**

BOLD GAIT 8 ch.g. Persian Bold 123 – Miller's Gait 74§ (Mill Reef (USA) 141) [1998 93: 14.6d 13.3g⁶ 18g 1999 13.3g* 14.6m 13.3m² Sep 18] good-topped gelding: smart handicapper at best: lightly raced nowadays: useful form when winning at Newbury in August: unlucky when good second to Alberich in Autumn Cup there final start, switched and finishing strongly: should stay beyond 2m: acts on firm and good to soft going: held up. *J. R. Fanshawe* **102**

BOLD HUNTER 5 b.g. Polish Precedent (USA) 131 – Pumpona (USA) (Sharpen Up 127) [1998 76: 8g 8m 8.5g⁶ 7g² 6m 7m 7m³ 6m⁵ 6g 10g 10s 1999 8.5d 6g 6.8m Jul 17] strong gelding: formerly fairly useful but on the downgrade: stays 1m, should prove as effective around 6f: acts on soft and good to firm going: usually blinkered: sold 5,200 gns in November. *Mrs P. N. Dutfield* **–**

BOLD KING 4 br.g. Anshan 119 – Spanish Heart 86 (King of Spain 121) [1998 82: a8g* 7g⁴ 8d⁶ 8.1m⁴ 7.9g⁵ 9.9m³ 10g 1999 8g² 8.1g³ 7d² 7m 7g* 7g⁵ 7s² 7g⁴ Oct 16] rangy gelding: fairly useful handicapper: improved to win competitive event at Newbury in August: good efforts at Goodwood, Newcastle and Newmarket after: best at 7f: acts on soft going, probably on good to firm. *J. W. Hills* **93**

BOLDLY CLIFF (BEL) 5 br.h. Never So Bold 135 – Miami Beach (Miami Springs 121) [1998 5v³ 7.8m³ 8.3d* 5g² 6g 5g 6d⁴ 6d 5m² 6.8s⁴ 6s 1999 a6g⁴ a6g 5d* 5m⁵ 5f² 5d*ᵈⁱˢ 5g⁵ 5f⁶ 5s 5s 5s⁴ 5s⁴ a8g a5g* Dec 10] Belgian-bred horse: dam won 3 times in Belgium: fair performer: won twice in Belgium for C. Dondi at 3 yrs and minor event in French Provinces for G. Henrot at 4 yrs: successful in 1999 in handicaps at Ostend in April, Chantilly (disqualifed after failing dope test) in June and Lingfield (in fine style) in December: has won around 1m, though probably at least as effective at sharp 5f: probably acts on good to firm ground, heavy and dirt/equitrack: often blinkered. *Andre Hermans, Belgium* **67**

BOLDLY GOES 3 b.c. Bold Arrangement 127 – Reine de Thebes (FR) 67 (Darshaan 133) [1998 76: 5s* a6g* 7m* 7f 6g* 1999 8d⁶ 7m³ Jul 10] rather leggy colt: useful at 2 yrs: below form in minor events in 1999: should stay 1m. *C. W. Fairhurst* **–**

BOLD ORIENTAL (IRE) 5 b.g. Tirol 127 – Miss Java 78 (Persian Bold 123) [1998 78: 9m 12m 14m a8f* 1999 a10f a10g³ 8f 8.3m 8m* 8f⁴ 10m* 9f 9g² Aug 28] fairly useful performer: won claimer at Salisbury in June and amateur handicap at Nottingham in July: stays 1¼m: acts on firm going, soft and equitrack: tried blinkered: has found little/looked none too keen: sold 7,000 gns in October. *J. W. Hills* **81**

BOLD PRECEDENT 2 b.c. (May 8) Polish Precedent (USA) 131 – Shining Water (USA) (Riverman (USA) 131) [1999 8d Oct 27] 22,000Y: fifth foal: half-brother to useful French performers up to around 1½m Blue Water and Norton Sound (both by Bering): dam French 1¼m winner: tailed off in maiden at Yarmouth. *P. W. Harris* **–**

BOLD RAIDER 2 b.g. (Apr 16) Rudimentary (USA) 118 – Spanish Heart 86 **56** (King of Spain 121) [1999 7g 7.1m 7s Sep 29] fifth foal: half-brother to 1995 2-y-o 7f winner Spanish Luck (by Mazilier) and 4-y-o Bold King: dam effective at 7f to 9f: green, modest form in maidens: may do better. *I. A. Balding*

BOLD SABOTEUR 2 b.g. (Apr 30) Prince Sabo 123 – Latest Flame (IRE) 66 **– p** (Last Tycoon 131) [1999 7d 7s 6v Oct 23] 2,000Y: tall, workmanlike gelding: second foal: dam 2-y-o 7.5f winner who stayed 1¼m: signs of ability in maidens at Newbury (2) and Lingfield: looks sort to do better at 3 yrs. *D. R. C. Elsworth*

BOLD SARAH 5 ch.m. Bold Arrangement 127 – Miss Sarajane 74 (Skyliner 117) **–** [1998 –: 5s 6g 8.2g 6.9m 8.1d 8m 9.9m a11g 1999 a11g a12g Jan 18] of little account. *R. Hollinshead*

BOLD STATE 2 b.g. (Apr 8) Never So Bold 135 – Multi-Sofft 30 (Northern State **76** (USA) 91) [1999 5g² 6.1m⁵ 7g³ 5.9m⁶ 7g² 7g⁵ 7.1g² 7.9m* 7.7d 8d Oct 15] 9,700Y: leggy, quite good-topped gelding: second foal: half-brother to a winner in Turkey by Magic Ring: dam, probably stayed 13.8f, out of Cheshire/Lancashire Oaks winner One Over Parr, herself sister to Oaks winner Polygamy: fair performer: won maiden at York in September: stays 1m: acts on good to firm going, possibly not on good to soft: tried visored (ran well) and blinkered: has looked none too keen: best forcing pace. *M. H. Tompkins*

BOLD WILLY 2 b.c. (Mar 3) Never So Bold 135 – Indian Star 58 (Indian King **–** (USA) 128) [1999 6d 6f⁶ 7.5s Jul 3] 5,900Y: third reported foal: half-brother to a 5.5f winner in Slovakia: dam 5f/6f winner: little form. *C. W. Fairhurst*

BOLEYN CASTLE (USA) 2 ch.c. (Feb 12) River Special (USA) – Dance Skirt **92** (CAN) (Caucasus (USA) 127) [1999 5d* 5m⁶ 5.1m⁵ Jul 9] $37,000F, 36,000Y: strong, compact colt: fourth foal: half-brother to a winner in USA by High Brite: dam ran 3 times in North America: won maiden at Windsor in April: clearly best effort when sixth of 13 to Warm Heart in Norfolk Stakes at Royal Ascot, speed over 3f then appearing to lose action: failed to handle track at Chester final start: should stay 6f. *T. G. Mills*

BOLLIN ANN 4 b.f. Anshan 119 – Bollin Zola 90 (Alzao (USA) 117) [1998 59: **71** 7s 6d 6g⁵ 5.9g³ 5.9d 6g² 5g² 5m* 6g 6.1d⁵ 5g 1999 5d⁶ 5m⁴ 5d 6m 5d⁴ 5m* 6f 5g³ 5g 5m 6.1m² 5d⁴ 5g Oct 6] good-quartered filly: fair handicapper: won at Beverley in July: very good second at Nottingham in September: best at stiff 5f/6f: acts on good to firm and good to soft going. *T. D. Easterby*

BOLLIN ETHOS 4 b.g. Precocious 126 – Bollin Harriet (Lochnager 132) [1998 **63** 64: 6d 6s 5s⁶ 6g 7.1g² 7s⁴ 7g* 7f 7.1g 1999 7g 6f 7.5d³ 7.5v³ 6.9m⁶ 7.1d a7g² 7g⁶ 6g² a6g 6.1d Oct 5] good-topped gelding: modest handicapper: stays 7.5f: acts on fibre-sand and heavy ground, not on firm: usually races prominently/leads. *T. D. Easterby*

BOLLIN FRANK 7 b.g. Rambo Dancer (CAN) 107 – Bollin Emily 82 (Loch- **72** nager 132) [1998 72: 8d 8.5m⁵ 8.2m* 8g⁴ 8.1g² 8g 7.6g² 7.6d 8g² 8s 1999 7.6m 8.2m³ 8.1g 8.2m 8.5m² 7.5m 8.5m² 8.1d⁶ 8g⁴ 8m⁴ 8.5g⁴ 8.1s⁴ Sep 24] good-topped gelding: fair handicapper: best around 1m: acts on firm and soft ground, well below form on heavy: blinkered once at 3 yrs: sometimes hangs: usually races prominently/leads. *T. D. Easterby*

BOLLIN NELLIE 2 ch.f. (Apr 24) Rock Hopper 124 – Bollin Magdalene 55 **60** (Teenoso (USA) 135) [1999 7m⁴ 7f³ 7m⁵ 8d⁴ Sep 23] sparely-made, plain filly: second foal: dam, staying maiden on Flat, fairly useful winning stayer over hurdles: modest maiden: best effort when fourth of 16 in nursery at Pontefract final start: will prove suited by 1¼m+. *T. D. Easterby*

BOLLIN RITA 3 b.f. Rambo Dancer (CAN) 107 – Bollin Harriet (Lochnager **82** 132) [1998 69: 5d² 5d² 6m³ 6f⁴ 6m² 7.5m⁴ 1999 6d* 6.1m⁴ 6m² 6d 5m⁶ 6f⁶ 6m³ 5m 6d Oct 9] rather leggy, close-coupled filly: fairly useful performer: won maiden at Thirsk in April: ran creditably when in frame in handicaps after: likely to prove best at 5f/6f: acts on firm and good to soft ground: blinkered (below form) sixth start. *T. D. Easterby*

BOLLIN ROBERTA 3 b.f. Bob's Return (IRE) 123 – Bollin Emily 82 (Loch- **68** nager 132) [1998 67: 6g³ 5g⁵ 7.5d² 7m⁴ 6m 6.1d² 1999 7.1s⁵ 5d 7m³ 7m⁵ 7.1d⁴ 7m² 6.9m² 7f⁴ 6.1g 7.1m* 8.5s 6g Oct 14] strong filly: fair performer: won maiden at

Musselburgh in September: below form in handicaps after: needs further than 6f, and should stay 1m: acts on firm and good to soft ground: has hung and swished tail: races prominently/leads. *T. D. Easterby*

BOLLIN ROLAND　3 b.c. Reprimand 122 – Bollin Zola 90 (Alzao (USA) 117) [1998 NR 1999 6d 7d 6s 8f 8.1d Jun 4] good-topped colt: half-brother to several winners, including smart sprinter Bollin Joanne (by Damister) and 5-y-o Bollin Terry: dam 5f (at 2 yrs) and 7.6f winner: signs of only a little ability in maidens/handicaps: likely to prove best up to 7f. *T. D. Easterby*　–

BOLLIN TERRY　5 b.h. Terimon 124 – Bollin Zola 90 (Alzao (USA) 117) [1998 88: 8d 8.1g 7g³ 7f³ 8g* 9.3g⁶ 8m⁴ 8m³ 8m² 8g 1999 8v 9g Aug 21] tall, good-topped horse: fairly useful handicapper at 4 yrs: well held both starts in 1999: probably best at 7f/1m: acts on firm and good to soft going: usually held up. *T. D. Easterby*　–

BOLSHAYA　4 gr.f. Cadeaux Genereux 131 – Mainly Dry (The Brianstan 128) [1998 74: 5.9g⁴ 6d* 6m 6g* 6g⁶ 6g 1999 7s 6.1f 6g² 6g⁴ 6m* 6m⁴ 6m⁶ 6f⁵ 6g³ 5g³ 5d² 5d Oct 20] lengthy filly: fair handicapper: won at Salisbury in June: good second at Pontefract on penultimate outing: raced mainly at 6f, effective at 5f given a test: acts on good to firm and good to soft going. *J. Berry*　71

BOLT FROM THE BLUE　3 b.g. Grand Lodge (USA) 125 – Lightning Legacy (USA) 78 (Super Concorde (USA) 128) [1998 54: 5g 5g 5m⁴ 6g 1999 6.1s 7s 9.9d³ 8f 9.9g⁶ 14.1m⁵ 16.1s 10.9v² 11d² 11d⁴ a12g Nov 19] close-coupled gelding: modest maiden handicapper: left N. Tinkler after fourth start: stays 11f: acts on good to firm and heavy going (poor effort on fibresand): blinkered (unruly to post) fourth start. *Don Enrico Incisa*　58

BOMB ALASKA　4 br.g. Polar Falcon (USA) 126 – So True 116 (So Blessed 130) [1998 77p: 7m⁶ 8d 7m⁴ 8m² 8m² 8d⁶ 8g* 8s 8s² 1999 8d* 8m* 8m³ 8g* 8d² 10s² 8d* Oct 30]　116

　　　'Surfing the net' became a new pastime for some in the latest season as the band of racing websites continued to grow. Visitors to one of the newest, www.tobybalding.co.uk, which includes a horse-by-horse guide to the stable's runners, will find plenty about Bomb Alaska. He has easily the largest entry of any of the stable's Flat horses, and rightly so since he enjoyed a splendid campaign in 1999. Bomb Alaska 'will be ready to run in the first week of the turf season and could go for the Lincoln', according to his trainer. The horse didn't make the field for a good-quality renewal of the Lincoln in 1999, his BHB assessment of 73 consigning him to the consolation event, the Worthington Spring Mile, the day before—which he won narrowly. There won't be any danger of Bomb Alaska 'missing the cut' if connections do target the Lincoln again. After Doncaster, he won three more races, culminating in a listed success in the Ben Marshall Stakes at Newmarket in late-October, when he beat Albarahin by three quarters of a length. On his penultimate start, running off a mark 22 lb higher than when gaining his first win of the season, Bomb Alaska started favourite for the thirty-three runner Tote Cambridgeshire

Ladbrokes Spring Cup (Handicap), Newbury—
Bomb Alaska shows himself to be a step ahead of the handicapper with a comfortable win over Topatori,
Radar (No.17) runs on for third with Pantar (No.2) fourth

and ran the winner She's Our Mare (who received 17 lb) to a neck. Competitive handicaps at Newbury (the Ladbrokes Spring Cup) and Goodwood had provided Bomb Alaska with two further victories in the first half of the season before a damaged knee, sustained while being prepared for the Royal Hunt Cup, kept him off the course for four months.

The big, rangy Bomb Alaska, who is often bandaged in front, was still progressing at the end of the season and may well prove capable of making his mark in pattern company as a five-year-old. He stays a mile and a quarter, acts on good to firm and soft going and is usually held up. One piece of information for the uninitiated not to be found on the stable's website, incidentally, is the origin of the horse's provocative-sounding name: a quick phone call to the trainer, however, established that it has only a metaphorical connection with munitions or rocketry, being a heated dessert comprising mainly meringue, ice cream and raspberries! Delicious! *G. B. Balding*

BOMBARD (USA) 3 ch.c. Lord At War (ARG) – Mama Hawk (USA) (Silver Hawk (USA) 123) [1998 94p: 7.1d² 7g* 1999 10s⁴ 10.3m³ 12m 10.1g⁴ Aug 30] rather leggy, lengthy colt: useful performer: in frame in Thresher Classic Trial at Sandown (to Fantastic Light) and listed race at Chester (behind Oath) first 2 starts: well below best after: stays 1¼m: acts on soft and good to firm ground: blinkered penultimate start: races freely: sent to USA. *P. F. I. Cole* **103**

BOMBAY MIX (IRE) 4 b.g. Shalford (IRE) 124§ – Some Spice (Horage 124) [1998 69: 8d* 9s⁵ 8m⁶ 7d⁵ 1999 8m a8.5g 9.9v Sep 29] IR 1,500F, 5,000Y: half-brother to a 9f winner in Italy by Conquering Hero: dam, lightly-raced maiden, half-sister to very smart Irish performer Burslem: fair performer for D. Wachman in Ireland at 3 yrs: little show in Britain: stays 1m: acts on soft ground: blinkered. *J. G. Portman* **–**

BOMBELLINA (IRE) 2 b.f. (Mar 30) Robellino (USA) 127 – Beetwentysix (USA) (Buckaroo (USA)) [1999 5m 5m 6m² 6s² 6.1m⁵ 7g⁶ 6s a6g⁴ a8g Dec 29] 6,200Y: leggy filly: closely related to 3 winners, including 1995 2-y-o 5f winner Red Stream (by Red Ransom), and half-sister to a winner in USA by Green Forest: dam, French 9f and 1¼m winner, from family of Lear Fan: modest maiden: runner-up in seller and nursery third and fourth starts: should stay at least 7f: acts on good to firm and soft going: reared leaving stalls final start. *J. M. P. Eustace* **55** **a46 +**

BONAGUIL (USA) 2 b.g. (Apr 17) Septieme Ciel (USA) 123 – Chateaubrook (USA) (Alleged (USA) 138) [1999 7g 7d⁴ Oct 12] $40,000F, 28,000Y: second foal: half-brother to 3-y-o Sailor Jack: dam, American maiden, half-sister to smart miler Fantastic Fellow out of half-sister to Derby winner Henbit: better effort in maidens when fourth of 15 to easy winner Misraah at Leicester, still looking green: will be suited by 1¼m+: should improve further. *C. F. Wall* **65 p**

BON AMI (IRE) 3 b.c. Paris House 123 – Felin Special (Lyphard's Special (USA) 122) [1998 91: 5s* 6m³ 6s⁴ 6s² 5.1g² 5d² 5.1g³ 5f² 6g* 6m* 6m² 6d 1999 5s⁴ 6m 6g 6m 6d 6m³ 6m² 7f⁴ 6d² 6m² 6d Sep 18] rather leggy colt: fluent mover: useful handicapper: without a win, but generally progressive in 1999, beaten short head by Pipalong in Great St Wilfrid Handicap at Ripon on ninth start: has form at 7f, very best efforts at 6f: acts on firm and soft ground: sometimes edges left and carries head high. *J. Berry* **105**

BOND BOY 2 b.c. (Mar 1) Piccolo 121 – Arabellajill 97 (Aragon 118) [1999 6g⁴ 6m³ 6g⁶ 5v² Sep 24] 10,000F, 44,000Y: second foal: half-brother to Italian 7f (at 2 yrs) to 1m winner Aramaic (by Pursuit of Love): dam sprinter: fairly useful form: best efforts when sixth of 21 in sales race at Doncaster and head second of 17 in maiden at Lingfield final 2 starts: stays 6f: acts on good to firm and heavy ground: should win a race. *B. Smart* **86**

BOND DIAMOND 2 gr.g. (Apr 3) Prince Sabo 123 – Alsiba 68 (Northfields (USA)) [1999 6d 5.7g 6d⁵ 8f⁴ Sep 4] 5,400F, 35,000Y: ninth foal: half-brother to 3-y-o Dashiba and fairly useful 1¼m/1½m winner Smart Blade (by Elegant Air): dam staying half-sister to dam of Oscar Schindler: modest maiden: takes good hold, but stays 1m: acts on firm ground. *B. Smart* **55**

BOND GIRL   3 b.f. Magic Ring (IRE) 115 – Whirling Words 75 (Sparkler 130)   –
[1998 –p: 6d 1999 8m 7m 7m a8.5g Sep 18] strong filly: poor maiden at best: tongue
tied final start. *B. Smart*

BONDI BAY (IRE)   2 b.f. (Apr 18) Catrail (USA) 123 – Sodium's Niece (North-   **53**
fields (USA)) [1999 5m⁵ 5g 5.1g 6.1g a7g 6g a7g³ a8g⁵ Nov 24] IR 11,000F,
11,000Y: half-sister to 3 winners, including useful 7f winner Rickenbacker (by
Bluebird) and fairly useful 6f (at 2 yrs) and 9f winner Danzarin (by Kings Lake):
dam, lightly raced, third at 8.5f in Ireland at 2 yrs: modest maiden: stays 1m: tried
visored/tongue tied. *A. T. Murphy*

BONDOSAN   3 b.g. Barathea (IRE) 127 – Fern 100 (Shirley Heights 130) [1998   **75**
NR 1999 11m⁵ 12g⁵ May 15] 140,000Y: well-made gelding: third foal: half-brother
to 1997 2-y-o 7f winner Frond (by Alzao) and German 1m/9.5f winner Flying
Heights (by Kris): dam, 1½m winner, half-sister to Oaks second Shamshir: fair form
in maidens at Newbury (bandaged behind, unimpressive to post and hung badly left)
and Newmarket: sold 2,000 gns, joined J. Coupland. *H. R. A. Cecil*

BONDS GULLY (IRE)   3 b.c. Pips Pride 117 – Classic Ring (IRE) 50 (Auction   **66**
Ring (USA) 123) [1998 NR 1999 8f 7d⁴ 8.3m 7.6g 7.7d Sep 21] IR 32,000Y:
third foal: half-brother to a winner in Denmark: dam, 2-y-o 7f seller winner, stayed
1m: fair maiden: well below form last 2 starts: blinkered/tongue tied fourth start.
R. W. Armstrong

BONELLI   3 ch.c. Casteddu 111 – Tawnais 80 (Artaius (USA) 129) [1998 64: 6g⁵   **49**
7m 1999 7s 8v⁴ 8.3m⁶ 10.2s Oct 26] angular colt: poor maiden: ran badly in handicap
final start: should stay 1¼m. *J. R. Arnold*

BONNES NOUVELLES   3 b.f. Shirley Heights 130 – La Belle Creole (Rainbow   **81**
Quest (USA) 134) [1998 74p: 7d⁵ 7v⁵ 1999 11.9v³ 12d a12g⁵ Nov 22] fairly useful   **a–**
maiden: best effort when third at Haydock in October: will stay beyond 1½m: raced
only on ground softer than good on turf. *J. L. Dunlop*

BONNE VILLE   5 gr.m. Good Times (ITY) – Ville Air 85 (Town Crier 119) [1998   –
–, a59: 10.8g a12g 14.9g a12g² a14g a12g² a14.8g³ a12g⁶ a12g* 1999 a11g⁵ a12g³   **a42**
a14.8g⁶ a16f⁶ a9.4g⁵ a11g⁵ 14.1g Jul 3] poor performer: mostly disappointing in
1999: stays 14.8f: acts on fibresand, no form on turf: blinkered (poor effort) once at 3
yrs. *Miss S. J. Wilton*

BONNIE DUNDEE   3 b.f. Rock City 120 – Shy Dolly 74 (Cajun 120) [1998 57+:   **55**
6m⁶ 5g⁴ 5m 5s 1999 7m* 8.1d 7m⁵ 7m 7g 8d⁵ 8f⁶ 8.2g² 8s Oct 26] sparely-made
filly: modest performer: won claimer at Salisbury in May: well below form final 2
starts: stays 1m: acts on good to firm and good to soft going, possibly not on soft:
tongue tied first 5 starts: visored/blinkered 6 of last 7 starts. *M. Kettle*

BONNIE FLORA   3 b.f. Then Again 126 – My Minnie 67 (Kind of Hush 118)   –
[1998 NR 1999 9.9m 8g Jun 9] first foal: dam 1m to 11f winner: only signs of ability
in maidens at Salisbury: claimer ridden. *D. R. C. Elsworth*

BOOGY WOOGY   3 ch.g. Rock Hopper 124 – Primulette 82 (Mummy's Pet   **69**
125) [1998 71: 6m⁴ 6g⁶ 7s 7.9g 8d⁵ 7d⁴ 7s 7v* 7d⁴ 1999 8d⁶ 8m 10g 9m³ 11f² 12f*
12m³ 11m⁴ 12.3g³ 11.9m 12g³ 14.1g³ 14.1g³ Oct 15] lengthy, unfurnished gelding:
fair handicapper: won at Thirsk in July: creditable efforts most other starts: stays
1¾m: acts on any ground: blinkered: usually held up: has found little and looked
none too keen: fairly useful form over hurdles after final Flat outing. *T. D. Easterby*

BOOMERANG BLADE   3 b.f. Sure Blade (USA) 130 – Opuntia (Rousillon   **100**
(USA) 133) [1998 98: 6.1g² 6f* 6m³ 6d* 7g⁶ 1999 7m⁴ 8m 7g 10d⁶ 8m⁵ 6m³ 6.1g⁵
6s² 6d 6s Oct 22] neat filly: useful performer: in frame in DDF (Fred Darling) Stakes
at Newbury and minor events at Doncaster and Hamilton (2½ lengths second to
Tajasur): below form last 2 starts: probably best at 6f/7f: acts on firm and soft going.
B. Smart

BOOMSHADOW   2 ch.g. (May 29) Imperial Frontier (USA) 112 – Marie de   –
Sologne (Lashkari 128) [1999 7g 7d Nov 1] 4,000Y: third foal: half-brother to useful
French 1¼m and 1½m winner Minervitta (by Warrshan) and 8.5f winner Two To
To Tango (by Anshan): dam unraced half-sister to smart winner up to 1½m Coeur
de Lion: 100/1, signs of a little ability when well held in maidens at Catterick

(hampered) and Redcar, slowly away both times: has had tongue tied: should stay at least 1m. *J. L. Eyre*

BORANI 4 b.g. Shirley Heights 130 – Ower (IRE) 71 (Lomond (USA) 128) [1998 **86** 86: 10.2s⁴ 8.1m 9d 9.9m² 8d⁴ 1999 10m 8m 8.1m² 8.3s⁶ 8m³ 8m* 7.3m³ Sep 17] strong, lengthy gelding: fairly useful handicapper: won 22-runner event at Goodwood in September, making all: effective at 7f to 1¼m: acts on good to firm and soft going: tongue tied (ran as though something amiss) second start: withdrawn after getting loose intended fourth start: sold 23,000 gns. *I. A. Balding*

BORDER ARROW 4 ch.c. Selkirk (USA) 129 – Nibbs Point (IRE) 107 (Sure **114** Blade (USA) 130) [1998 120: 9s* 8d³ 10.4g³ 12m³ 1999 9.9d³ May 8] big, lengthy colt: has a markedly round action: very smart performer in 1998, winner of listed race at Newmarket and third in 2000 Guineas and Derby: off nearly a year (reportedly pin-fired in the interim) before 2½ lengths third to Handsome Ridge in valuable contest at Goodwood only run in 1999 (reportedly had recurrence of leg problem): stays 1½m: has form on good to firm and soft going, though may not take much racing on former: tends to sweat and has taken strong hold. *I. A. Balding*

BORDER GLEN 3 b.g. Selkirk (USA) 129 – Sulitelma (USA) 63 (The Minstrel **63** (CAN) 135) [1998 –p: 6.1m 5m 5s 5d 5g 1999 6m 8f 8ag* 8m* 8m 8m 8.1s 8d⁵ 8s⁴ **a68** a8g³ a8g³ a8.5g⁴ Dec 27] big, good-topped gelding: poor mover: fair handicapper: won at Southwell and Musselburgh (made all, penultimate start for Sir Mark Prescott) in June: ended year in decent heart: best form around 1m: acts on good to firm going, soft and all-weather: effective blinkered/visored or not: has raced freely/ wandered markedly/carried head high/found little. *D. Haydn Jones*

BORDER PRINCE 3 ch.g. Selkirk (USA) 129 – Princess Oberon (IRE) 91 **82** (Fairy King (USA)) [1998 81p: 7g 8m⁶ 1999 7g² 8.5s² 8m 6g³ 6.8m² Jul 10] leggy, unfurnished gelding: has a quick action: fairly useful maiden: creditable efforts when second: finds 7f bare minimum and stays 8.5f: acts on good to firm and soft ground: joined I. Wood for 16,500 gns in October. *I. A. Balding*

BORDER RUN 2 b.g. (Apr 22) Missed Flight 123 – Edraianthus 78 **61 ?** (Windjammer (USA)) [1999 7g 8.5m⁵ 8d⁶ Sep 28] 9,500F, 19,000Y: rather leggy, unfurnished gelding: eighth foal: half-brother to Esquire (by Safawan), useful 1m winner in France at 2 yrs and later successful in USA, and fairly useful 1993 2-y-o 6f winner Close To Reality (by Dreams To Reality): dam (maiden) best at 6f: modest form in maidens: appeared to run best race in slowly-run event final start: should stay further than 1m. *B. J. Meehan*

BORDERS 3 b.g. Selkirk (USA) 129 – Pretty Poppy 67 (Song 132) [1998 74p: 6g **109 p** 6s 1999 6m² 6g³ 5g* 5g⁴ 5g² 5s* 5s² Oct 3] big, well-made gelding: useful performer: won maiden at Doncaster (easily) in June and minor event at Beverley (dictated pace, easily best effort) in September: not discredited when second in listed race at Dortmund final start: has deal of speed, and best at 5f: acts on soft and good to firm going: has worn dropped noseband: likely to improve further at 4 yrs. *H. Candy*

BORDER STARLETTE (IRE) 4 b.f. Ela-Mana-Mou 132 – Fillette Lalo (FR) **–** (Huntercombe 133) [1998 –: 7g 8v 8.2s 14.1g 11.1d 16.2m⁶ 1999 12.4m 10g Jul 3] bad maiden handicapper. *Mrs M. Reveley*

BORDER TRADER (IRE) 4 ch.g. Sharp Victor (USA) 114 – Hi Dad (USA) **–** (Verbatim (USA)) [1998 55: 10d 10.2g⁴ 10m 11.6f 10s 10v 1999 a12g Jan 1] modest maiden handicapper at 3 yrs: stays 1¼m: acts on heavy going, well beaten on all-weather debut, only outing in 1999. *J. S. Moore*

BOREHILL JOKER 3 ch.g. Pure Melody (USA) 77 – Queen Matilda 44 (Castle **39** Keep 121) [1998 36: a5g² 5v⁵ a5g⁴ 6.1m⁴ a6g⁶ 1999 a9.4g 7.1m Aug 5] bad maiden: tried blinkered/visored. *W. G. M. Turner*

BORGIA 4 ch.f. Machiavellian (USA) 123 – Cut Ahead 85 (Kalaglow 132) **91** [1998 78p: 10.5g³ 10m⁵ 10g 10g 11.8d* 1999 12m² 12s⁵ 12.1g³ 12g² 14m³ 13.3m* 14f 14m⁴ 13.9m* 13.3m⁵ 16.1d⁶ Oct 29] rangy filly: fairly useful handicapper: won at Newbury in July and York in September: should stay beyond 1¾m: acts on good to firm and good to soft going, below form on extremes: usually visored/ blinkered: usually held up, and has found little: consistent: sold 20,000 gns in December. *R. Charlton*

Hong Kong Vase, Sha Tin—French-trained mares Borgia (left) and Bimbola fight out the finish

BORGIA (GER)   5 b.m. Acatenango (GER) 127 – Britannia (GER) (Tarim)   **120**
[1998 106+: a10f 10.5s² 1999 10s² 12m⁴ 12d⁵ 12g⁵ 12m² 12v 11g⁵ 12f 12m* Dec 12]
rangy mare: very smart performer: won German Derby and placed in Arc and
Breeders' Cup Turf at 3 yrs: back to near best and first win since when successful in
Hong Kong Vase at Sha Tin in December by head from Bimbola: had run at least
respectably on several occasions beforehand, including when short-neck second to
El Condor Pasa in 3-runner Prix Foy at Longchamp on fifth start: below form in Prix
de l'Arc de Triomphe next time and Japan Cup at Tokyo on eighth outing but looked
unlucky in between when length fifth to Soaring Softly in Breeders' Cup Filly &
Mare Turf at Gulfstream, hampered before far turn then finishing strongly: better at
1½m than shorter and would have stayed further: acted on any going: tough: visits
Sadler's Wells. *A. Fabre, France*

BORN A LADY   6 ch.m. Komaite (USA) – Lucky Candy 61 (Lucky Wednesday   **36**
124) [1998 41: 5g² a5g⁴ 5m a11g⁶ 1999 a8g a8g a7g a8g⁶ a8.5g Feb 20] poor
handicapper: best up to 1m: acts on firm ground and fibresand: has been visored,
usually blinkered: sometimes reluctant at stalls. *N. P. Littmoden*

BORN FREE   3 ch.f. Caerleon (USA) 132 – Culture Vulture (USA) 118 (Timeless   **77**
Moment (USA)) [1998 77: 6g⁵ 7d² 1999 8g 10m² 10d³ a8.5g Dec 1] fair maiden: **a–**
placed in handicaps at Windsor in June and November: stays 1¼m: yet to race on
extremes of going on turf, ran poorly on fibresand debut. *P. F. I. Cole*

BORN TO RULE   2 ch.c. (Apr 6) Mujtahid (USA) 118 – Born To Glamour (Ajdal   **62**
(USA) 130) [1999 5.1g 5g⁴ 6m⁴ Sep 10] IR 14,000F: third foal: half-brother to 3-y-o
Sailing Shoes and fairly useful Irish 1¼m winner Tarbaan (by Nashwan): dam Irish
2-y-o 6f winner: modest maiden: fourth at Lingfield and Goodwood last 2 starts: may
prove best at 5f/6f. *M. S. Saunders*

BOSSCAT   2 b.c. (Jan 16) Presidium 124 – Belltina 41 (Belfort (FR) 89) [1999 5m   **59**
5.1s⁶ 6.1m 7.6g Aug 25] 17,000Y: fourth foal: half-brother to 3-y-o Little Cinnamon,
5-y-o Big Ben and 6-y-o Ticka Ticka Timing: dam stayed 7f: modest form at best in
maidens: may prove best up to 7f. *K. McAuliffe*

BOSS TWEED (IRE)   2 b.g. (Apr 30) Persian Bold 123 – Betty Kenwood 39   **51**
(Dominion 123) [1999 5g 6g⁶ a6g⁵ a7g Nov 12] 5,500Y: second foal: dam, staying
maiden on Flat, won over hurdles: signs of a little ability. *G. C. Bravery*

Gestut Ammerland's "Borgia"

BOSSY SPICE 2 br.f. (Jan 27) Emperor Jones (USA) 119 – Million Heiress –
(Auction Ring (USA) 123) [1999 5d⁶ 5.1s a8.5g 8.2d Oct 21] 6,000Y: compact filly:
fifth foal: half-sister to 4-y-o Elhabub, 5-y-o Colway Ritz and 1994 2-y-o 5f winner
Stato One (by Statoblest), later useful up to 9f in Scandinavia: dam poor maiden:
little sign of ability in maidens/sellers: trained first 2 starts by M. Channon: tried
visored. *N. M. Babbage*

BOSTING PRIDE (FR) 7 b.h. Hero's Honor (USA) – Palanges (FR) (Gay **59**
Mecene (USA) 128) [1998 a8.5g 8.5v 1999 a8f a9g* 8.5s 8v⁵ 7.5g⁴ 8g* 8g Jul 24]
28,000 francs Y: has done most of his racing in Germany for current stable, winning
5 times prior to 1998: well held in Lingfield claimer on reappearance: won amateur
race at Dortmund in February and handicap at Dusseldorf in June: stays 9f: acts on
heavy ground and sand. *C. Dondi, Belgium*

BOTTELINO JOE (IRE) 2 b. or br.c. (Mar 18) Bluebird (USA) 125 – My-O- **59**
My (IRE) 105 (Waajib 121) [1999 5.1g 7.1m 5.7d⁴ 6s⁵ Oct 1] IR 20,000Y: second
foal: dam Irish 5f performer: modest maiden: will be suited by return to 7f+.
M. S. Saunders

BOULEVARD ROUGE (USA) 4 b.f. Red Ransom (USA) – Beetwentysix –
(USA) (Buckaroo (USA)) [1998 71: a8.5g³ a8g² 8.1g 11m² 10m³ 10.5s 10.3v 1999
8d 7d 9f Jun 1] smallish, good-topped filly: fair maiden handicapper in 1998: well
beaten in 1999: barely stays 11f: acts on all-weather and good to firm going (poor
efforts on soft/heavy): has been early to post. *M. W. Easterby*

BOUNDARY EXPRESS 7 b.g. Sylvan Express 117 – Addison's Jubilee 73 –
(Sparkler 130) [1998 NR 1999 14.1g 16.2m Jul 13] workmanlike gelding: one-time
modest handicapper: pulled up lame final start: dead. *S. Gollings*

BOUND FOR PLEASURE (IRE) 3 gr.c. Barathea (IRE) 127 – Dazzlingly **81**
Radiant 81 (Try My Best (USA) 130) [1998 83p: 7g 7m² 7v* 1999 7s 7m⁶ 9g 10.1d
Jun 4] big, strong colt: not a good walker/mover: fairly useful performer: form in
1999 (reportedly had breathing problem on reappearance) only when creditable sixth
in handicap at Newmarket: should be suited by further than 7f: acts on good to firm
and heavy going: blinkered final start: joined J. Gosden. *G. L. Moore*

BOUND TO PLEASE 4 b.g. Warrshan (USA) 117 – Hong Kong Girl 94 (Petong **66**
126) [1998 NR 1999 6m⁶ 5.7g 6g 7s⁵ a6g a7g* a8g³ Dec 13] neat gelding: fair
handicapper: won at Southwell in November: may prove best up to 7f: acts on soft
ground, good to firm and fibresand. *P. J. Makin*

BOUNTIFUL LADY (USA) 3 ch.f. Irish River (FR) 131 – Bounding Away **88**
(CAN) (Vice Regent (CAN)) [1998 83p: 7v* 1999 8m 10.4d⁴ May 11] close-
coupled, attractive filly: fluent mover: fairly useful form in 1000 Guineas at
Newmarket (slowly away, never dangerous seventeenth) and Musidora Stakes at
York (13½ lengths fourth of 6 to Zahrat Dubai): should prove better at 1¼m than
shorter: sent to Australia. *Sir Michael Stoute*

BOWCLIFFE 8 b.g. Petoski 135 – Gwiffina 87 (Welsh Saint 126) [1998 77: **66**
a9.4g* a9.4g⁴ a8.5g² a8g 8s 9.3s⁴ 8.1g⁵ 8.9s⁶ 8d 8g² 8f 8g⁵ 9.3g³ 9m² 8m* 8s 8g 1999
a9.4g 8m* 8m 8.1g 8m 8m 8d 10m² 10m² 8g² 10m 10m⁶ 8g 8.2d Oct 21] good-
topped gelding: fair handicapper: won minor event at Musselburgh in April: below
form final 4 starts: stays 1¼m: acts on fibresand, firm and soft going: tried blinkered/
visored: held up. *E. J. Alston*

BOWCLIFFE GRANGE (IRE) 7 b.g. Dominion Royale 112 – Cala-Vadella **47**
110 (Mummy's Pet 125) [1998 52: a5g a5g² 5d³ 5d² 5f 5m 5m⁵ 5d 5g⁴ 1999 a5g⁶ **a50**
a5g⁶ a5g* a5g 5g⁶ 5m 5g³ 5m 5f⁴ 5m 5m 5m* a5g² a5g a5g a5g Dec 10] good-topped
gelding: modest handicapper: on all-weather, poor on turf: won at Lingfield in March
and Hamilton (apprentice event) in September: best at 5f: acts on firm ground, good
to soft and all-weather (though hasn't run up to best at Wolverhampton): tried blinkered (not since 1997): has run well sweating: trail-blazer, sometimes finds little.
D. W. Chapman

BOWLERS BOY 6 ch.g. Risk Me (FR) 127 – Snow Wonder (Music Boy 124) **70 d**
[1998 81: 5d 6g 5d 6s⁶ 6s* 6d³ 6v 6g 6g 6d⁴ 5m 6v⁶ 5d* 5.1v² 5d* 1999 6m 5d 6d 5d⁵
5d⁵ 6f 6d 6g 5m 6g 5d 6v³ 5.1s⁵ Oct 26] workmanlike gelding: fair handicapper at 5
yrs: deteriorated after fifth start in 1999 (blinkered last 2): effective at 5f (on stiff
track) to 7f: acts on good to firm and heavy ground: carries head high: winner 4 times
at Pontefract. *J. J. Quinn*

BOW PEEP (IRE) 4 b. or br.f. Shalford (IRE) 124§ – Gale Force Seven (Strong **51**
Gale 116) [1998 74: 6s 6g⁵ 6g* 5.1m* 5m 6m⁴ 5m 1999 6d 5m 5m 6g 5m 5g Aug 28]
leggy, useful-looking filly: only modest performer nowadays: effective at 5f/6f:
acts on good to firm going: blinkered once as 2-y-o (ran creditably) and on final start
(found nothing). *M. W. Easterby*

BOW STRADA 2 ch.c. (Apr 26) Rainbow Quest (USA) 134 – La Strada (Niniski **92 p**
(USA) 125) [1999 8g* 10d* Oct 11] 13,000Y: leggy, quite attractive colt: second
foal: half-brother to 3-y-o Vie Indienne: dam, champion 2-y-o filly in Spain, half-
sister to smart German/New Zealand middle-distance horse Vialli: fairly useful form:
won maiden at Yarmouth in August and minor event at Leicester in October, staying
on well to lead close home when beating Atwaar by length on second occasion: will
be suited by 1½m+: capable of further improvement, and likely to make a useful
performer. *P. W. Harris*

BOXBERRY 2 b.f. (Jan 13) Owington 123 – Chatterberry 67 (Aragon 118) [1999 **–**
5m 5g 6.1m 5f 5.3d Oct 4] 7,500Y: third foal: half-sister to 2-y-o 5f winners Inkberry
(in 1998, by Cadeaux Genereux) and Cloudberry (in 1997, by Night Shift), latter
fairly useful: dam, lightly-raced 2-y-o 5f winner, sister to smart sprinter Argentum:
little form: tried blinkered: sold 2,300 gns in December. *N. A. Callaghan*

BOX CAR (IRE) 2 b.c. (Mar 20) Blues Traveller (IRE) 119 – Racey Naskra **56**
(USA) 75 (Star de Naskra (USA)) [1999 7m 7m 7.6g 8.3d⁶ a8g⁶ a10g² Dec 18]
7,000Y, 9,500 2-y-o: fifth foal: half-brother to a winner in Sweden by Contract Law:

dam 7.5f winner: modest maiden: best effort when 10 lengths second of 13 to Double Banger at Lingfield final start: stays 1¼m: acts on equitrack. *G. L. Moore*

BRAHMS (USA)　2 br.c. (Mar 31) Danzig (USA) – Queena (USA) (Mr Prospector (USA)) [1999 6g² 6g* 7g² 6d³ 7g² a8.5f Nov 6]　**114**
　　　A million-dollar yearling, placed in the Middle Park and the Dewhurst, would be a rare asset for most stables. With the right blend of breeding and performance, such an animal would offer much for connections to look forward to, both in the short and the long term. In the circumstances it is perhaps unfortunate for Brahms that he is trained at Ballydoyle, where expensively-bought yearlings—whilst not exactly ten-a-penny—are in fairly plentiful supply. For example, Brahms counts among his neighbours Monashee Mountain and Mull of Kintyre, two other million-dollar Danzig colts with smart form, as well as the likes of Bernstein and Giant's Causeway, not to mention the two-million-dollar purchase Hardy, an unraced close relative to Bosra Sham. With such an embarrassment of riches at trainer Aidan O'Brien's disposal, Brahms, through no fault of his own, may well have a fight on to represent his stable in the top races as a three-year-old, which may in turn limit his claims to a high-ranking position on the Coolmore stallion roster when his racing days are over. From what he showed as a two-year-old, however, Brahms looks as if he could be up to the challenge.
　　　Brahms made a relatively inauspicious start to his racing career, being among that small group of Aidan O'Brien-trained juveniles not to make a winning debut. Brahms went down by a short head over six furlongs at Leopardstown in July when 4/1-on. He landed the odds next time, fitted with blinkers, in a Fairyhouse maiden, and improved again, stepped up to seven furlongs, when very much second best to his odds-on stable-companion Giant's Causeway in the Futurity Stakes at the Curragh at the end of August.
　　　Blinkers were replaced by a visor at Newmarket in the Middle Park Stakes, another race in which Brahms was originally expected to play second fiddle to one of his stable-mates. The defection of Bernstein, however, after an unsatisfactory blood test, left Brahms to fly the Ballydoyle flag alone. Four of his five opponents started at shorter odds, but Brahms put up a smart effort, despite being first off the bridle over a trip arguably on the short side for him by that stage of his career, to finish third, beaten a length and a half by the winner Primo Valentino. O'Brien was responsible for eight of the twelve five-day entries in the Dewhurst Stakes at Newmarket a month later, Brahms once again finding himself overshadowed by a stable-mate in the run up to the race, this time by Fasliyev. In the latter's absence, Brahms again proved himself an able deputy, chasing home the favourite Distant Music, getting closer to him at the finish than any other horse all season, beaten a length with another Ballydoyle inmate Zentsov Street two lengths further away in third. Brahms stayed on after being headed a furlong out, giving the impression that a stiffer test of stamina could bring about further improvement. Unfortunately, the Breeders' Cup Juvenile did not provide a valid opportunity to test this theory, Brahms' outside draw seemingly putting him at a distinct disadvantage; forced widest of all into the first turn, he never got into the race, managing only seventh of fourteen to Anees, three places behind the Ballydoyle first string Mull of Kintyre.

		Danzig (USA) (b 1977)	Northern Dancer (b 1961)	Nearctic
Brahms (USA) (br.c. Mar 31, 1997)				Natalma
			Pas de Nom (b or br 1968)	Admiral's Voyage
				Petitioner
		Queena (USA) (b 1986)	Mr Prospector (b 1970)	Raise A Native
				Gold Digger
			Too Chic (b or br 1979)	Blushing Groom
				Remedia

　　　The price fetched by Brahms as a yearling reflected his pedigree. His sire Danzig needs little introduction whilst his dam Queena's race record and pedigree can hardly be bettered. Queena, a daughter of Mr Prospector, was champion older mare in the USA in 1991 (at five years), with three Grade 1 victories between seven and eight and a half furlongs. Queena's elder sister Chic Shirine was also a Grade 1 winner at around a mile (taking the Ashland Stakes at three), as was Queena's dam, the Maskette Stakes winner Too Chic. This is also the family of two horses more familiar to followers of racing in Britain—Oaks winner Monade and dual Gold Cup winner Sadeem. Queena had had a somewhat disappointing stud record before Brahms came along, producing only a winner in South Africa from two visits apiece to Storm Cat and Danzig. Brahms' unraced three-year-old brother Mendelssohn made only 8,500 guineas at the latest Newmarket July Sales (he had cost 775,000 dollars as a yearling). Queena's 1998 foal died but she has since produced a colt foal by A P Indy.

The strong, compact, deep-bodied Brahms—a real bull of a colt, who has a quick, fluent action—should stay a mile on pedigree and he should do well at up to that distance as a three-year-old. He may yet outshine some of his more widely-touted stable companions even. He was blinkered or visored in all his races after his debut and has been raced so far only on good/good to soft going on turf. *A. P. O'Brien, Ireland*

BRAMBLE BEAR   5 b.m. Beveled (USA) – Supreme Rose 95 (Frimley Park   **66 d**
109) [1998 72: 5s³ 5.1s⁵ 5m* 5m⁴ 5.1g⁵ 5m² 5m³ 5.7d 5.1m² 5.3m 5g 5m 1999 5.1s 5.1d³ 5m 5f⁴ 5m³ 5.7m 5.1m³ 5m⁵ 5.3s³ 5f⁵ 5.3d⁶ 5.2s⁵ 5.1s³ Oct 26] leggy mare: modest handicapper: best at 5f: acts on firm and soft going: usually held up: consistent: sold 7,200 gns in December. *M. Blanshard*

BRAMBLES WAY   10 ch.g. Clantime 101 – Streets Ahead 67 (Ovid 95) [1998   **–**
47: 8d 9g 10.5m 12d⁶ 10m² 9.2d⁵ 10.1v 1999 a11g Jun 11] strong, lengthy gelding: poor performer: may be best around 1¼m: acts on firm ground, probably on good to soft, well held on fibresand (including only run in 1999): tried blinkered/visored. *F. Jordan*

BRANCASTER (USA)   3 br.c. Riverman (USA) 131 – Aseltine's Angels (USA)   **115**
(Fappiano (USA)) [1998 107p: 7.1m* 7.3v* 1999 8g² 8m⁴ 12g 10g Jun 27] leggy, quite attractive colt: smart performer: in frame at Newmarket in Craven Stakes (length second to Compton Admiral) and 2000 Guineas (best effort when staying-on fourth of 16 to Island Sands): never going well when tenth of 16 to Oath in Derby at Epsom then pulled hard in visor when tailed-off last in Grand Prix de Paris at Longchamp: should be suited by further than 1m: yet to race on very firm going, acts on any other: bandaged near-fore on reappearance: tended to wander at 2 yrs: joined Sir Michael Stoute. *P. W. Chapple-Hyam*

BRANDON COURT (IRE)   8 b.g. Law Society (USA) 130 – Dance Date (IRE)   **64**
(Sadler's Wells (USA) 132) [1998 NR 1999 14.1s⁴ 13v 12m 12m⁶ 10d² 9g 10.9d* Sep 16] modest handicapper nowadays: won strongly-run 20-runner amateur event at Ayr final start: stays 1¾m: acts on any turf going, except possibly heavy: fair hurdler. *I. A. Balding*

BRANDON MAGIC   6 ch.g. Primo Dominie 121 – Silk Stocking 109 (Pardao   **54 +**
120) [1998 NR 1999 a7g a8g* Feb 5] good-topped, lengthy gelding: one-time fairly useful performer for I. Balding: better effort in 1999 (modest form) when winning apprentice claimer easily at Southwell: barely stays 1¾m: acts on fibresand and soft ground, probably on firm: blinkered (refused to settle) once. *D. Nicholls*

BRANDON ROCK   2 b.g. (Apr 15) Robellino (USA) 127 – The Kings Daughter   **79**
79 (Indian King (USA) 128) [1999 7m 5d* 5s 6d Oct 14] 25,000F, IR 16,000Y, 15,000 2-y-o: good-topped gelding: fifth foal: half-brother to 3 winners, including fairly useful 5f/6f winner The Kings Ransom (by Cadeaux Genereux) and 5-y-o King Uno: dam 5f/6f winner: confirmed promise when narrowly winning maiden at Sandown in September: badly hampered next time, wintry and something possibly amiss final start: should prove at least as effective at 6f as 5f. *I. A. Balding*

BRANDONVILLE   6 b.g. Never So Bold 135 – Enduring (Sadler's Wells (USA)   **–**
132) [1998 –: 8.2s 1999 a8g a7g a8g Nov 22] big gelding: one-time fair handicapper: well held since 1997. *N. Tinkler*

BRANDY N PORT (IRE)   2 ch.g. (May 6) Forest Wind (USA) 111 – Achtung   –
Lady (IRE) 53 (Warning 136) [1999 8.3d Nov 4] second foal: half-brother to 3-y-o
Pretty Fly Guy: dam, ran 3 times in Ireland at 2 yrs, daughter of half-sister to dis-
qualified Oaks winner Aliysa: tailed off in seller at Windsor. *John A. Harris*

BRANSTON BERRY (IRE)   4 ch.f. Mukaddamah (USA) 125 – Food of Love   57
109 (Music Boy 124) [1998 78, a86: a8.5g⁵ a8.5g² a6g² 7d 5s⁵ 6.1m 6s 5s* 7d⁴ 1999
a6g 6d 6.1s Apr 27] close-coupled filly: formerly fairly useful winner: only a little
sign of retaining ability in 1999: stays easy 8.5f: acts on good to firm going, soft and
fibresand: has been bandaged behind: sold 4,200 gns in July. *J. L. Eyre*

BRANSTON FIZZ   2 b.f. (Apr 15) Efisio 120 – Tuxford Hideaway 102 (Caws-   80
ton's Clown 113) [1999 6g² 6s² a6g³ Nov 8] small, sparely-made filly: half-sister to
several winners, notably smart 6f/7f performer Branston Abby (by Risk Me): dam
sprinter: fair form in maidens first 2 starts: ran poorly on equitrack final outing.
M. Johnston

BRANSTON LUCY   2 b.f. (Apr 1) Prince Sabo 123 – Softly Spoken 87 (Mummy's   57
Pet 125) [1999 5m⁴ a5g 5g⁵ 5f³ 5m* Sep 24] half-sister to three 2-y-o sprint winners,
including fairly useful Here Comes Risky (by Risk Me), later successful up to 9f
abroad: dam sprinter: modest performer: best effort when winning 21-runner nursery
at Redcar in September, always well there: should stay 6f: raced only on good going
or firmer on turf, ran poorly on fibresand. *T. J. Etherington*

BRANSTON PICKLE   2 ch.g. (Apr 28) Piccolo 121 – Indefinite Article (IRE)   77
(Indian Ridge 123) [1999 5m⁶ 6d⁶ 5g a5g³ 5g⁶ a5g* 6d⁴ 6s* 5s a6g* Nov 17]   a73
17,000Y: smallish gelding: first foal: dam unraced sister to very smart Definite
Article and half-sister to 3-y-o Salford Express: fair performer: won seller at
Wolverhampton in October and nursery at Catterick (by 5 lengths) and claimer at
Wolverhampton in November: better at 6f than 5f: acts on fibresand and soft going,
shaped well on good to firm: genuine. *T. J. Etherington*

The Royal Ascot Racing Club's "Brancaster"

BRATBY (IRE)   3 b.g. Distinctly North (USA) 115 – Aridje 79 (Mummy's Pet **40**
125) [1998 –: 7g 5s 6s 1999 a8f* a7g⁵ a8g⁶ 10f 8.2f⁵ 7g⁴ 10m 7g Oct 19] quite **a51**
attractive gelding: modest handicapper on all-weather, poor on turf: won at Lingfield
(apprentices) in January: left M. Bell after sixth start, little show after: headstrong but
stays sharp 1m: acts on equitrack: sometimes slowly away. *D. R. C. Elsworth*

BRATHAY MAJIC   5 ch.m. Totem (USA) 118 – Roches Roost (Pauper) [1998   **–**
NR 1999 a8g Nov 15] 500 4-y-o: third foal: dam winning hurdler: 50/1, well beaten
in seller at Southwell. *D. Eddy*

BRAVACCIO (IRE)   3 b.c. Petorius 117 – So Stylish 77 (Great Nephew 126)   **75**
[1998 67: 5m 8g 7s⁵ 1999 a8g a12g⁶ 10d* 10g* 12g² 8.5f 11f a10f⁶ 7.5f Dec 18]
strong, lengthy colt: only a little sign of ability in varied events for P. McEntee (left
stable after second start): fair form for N. Clement in claimers in France, winning at
Le Lion-d'Angers in May and Chantilly in June: well held in similar events in USA
last 4 outings, leaving P. Aguirre before final one: stays 1½m: acts on good to soft
going: visored/blinkered second and final 3-y-o starts. *L. J. Jones, USA*

BRAVE BURT (IRE)   2 ch.c. (Feb 20) Pips Pride 117 – Friendly Song 48 (Song   **86**
132) [1999 5m* 5.1g* 5m³ 5g Jul 2] 21,000Y: good-topped colt: fifth foal: brother to
4-y-o Pip's Song and 3-y-o Charlene Lacy, and half-brother to a 2-y-o 5f winner by
Timeless Times: dam, poor maiden, sister to smart sprinter Fayruz: fairly useful
form: won maiden at Carlisle and minor event at Bath in May: creditable third of 16
to Kalindi in Windsor Castle Stakes at Royal Ascot: reportedly returned with cut on
off-hind when well held final start: will prove best at 5f/6f: joined J. Noseda. *J. Berry*

BRAVE EDGE   8 b.g. Beveled (USA) – Daring Ditty (Daring March 116)   **101**
[1998 108§: 6d⁶ 6d⁴ 5g² 5m 6d 5d⁶ 6g* 5g 6g 5.6g⁶ 6s³ 5m 6v⁴ 1999 6g² 5.2m 6m
6s³ 6d⁶ 6m 6m² 6m 6f⁶ 6m 5.6g 6d 6v⁴ 6s⁴ 6d Nov 1] good-topped gelding: useful
handicapper: several creditable efforts in 1999, including when neck second to
Central Coast at Newbury on seventh start: effective at 5f (given bit of a test)/6f:
probably acts on any turf going (unraced on all-weather): usually races just off pace.
R. Hannon

BRAVE ENVOY   5 b.g. High Estate 127 – Restless Anna (Thatching 131) [1998   **61**
67: 10m 8g⁶ 10.2s³ 8.1g⁵ 8.2m² 8.1d⁴ 7.9g 8m⁴ 8.2s* 10v⁴ 1999 10v 10m 8g³
8m⁴ 10m⁵ 10.5m⁵ 10m 9g Oct 15] sturdy gelding: modest performer: trained by
M. Heaton-Ellis until fourth start: well beaten after next outing: effective at 1m/1¼m:
acts on firm and soft ground: effective visored or not: needs plenty of driving: sold
2,000 gns. *C. G. Cox*

BRAVE KNIGHT   2 b.c. (Mar 11) Presidium 124 – Agnes Jane (Sweet Monday   **–**
122) [1999 7.9g Oct 6] 1,000Y: fifth foal: dam unraced: signs of ability though well
held in maiden at York. *N. Bycroft*

BRAVE REWARD (USA)   4 b.c. Lear Fan (USA) 130 – A Tad Better (USA)   **113**
(Northern Prospect (USA)) [1998 104: 7g⁵ 7g³ 8d 8.1g⁶ 8d 10.3g* 1999 10.1g² 10g
9.9f³ 10.4g Aug 18] leggy colt: smart handicapper: better than ever in 1999: placed
in valuable events at Epsom in June and Goodwood (close third under topweight to
Ormelie) in July: never going with any fluency when well held at York final start:
should stay beyond 1¼m: acts on firm and good to soft going (yet to race on softer):
held up: sold 125,000 gns, sent to Saudi Arabia. *Sir Michael Stoute*

BRAVE VISION   3 b.g. Clantime 101 – Kinlet Vision (IRE) 56 (Vision (USA))   **60 d**
[1998 –: 6.1m 7m 7d 1999 9.7s⁴ 10.2s³ 10m 11.8m⁴ 11.4m 10s 10d⁵ 8.2s a7g Nov 11]
disappointing maiden: below form after first 2 starts in 1999: stays 1¼m: acts on soft
going: blinkered last 2 starts: has looked none too keen. *J. R. Arnold*

BRAVO TWO ZERO (IRE)   2 b.f. (Mar 14) Desert Style (IRE) 121 – Nozet   **–**
(Nishapour (FR) 125) [1999 5d Apr 5] 10,000F, 13,000Y: half-sister to 4 winners,
notably 6-y-o Sorbie Tower: dam French 9f winner: well-held eighth of 10 in maiden
at Warwick: dead. *M. L. W. Bell*

BRAZILIAN MOOD (IRE)   3 b.c. Doyoun 124 – Sea Mistress (Habitat 134)   **70**
[1998 NR 1999 8.2d 8.3d² a10g* a8.5g Dec 1] 65,000Y: half-brother to several
winners, including smart Irish 6f/7f winner Nautical Pet (by Petorius), also successful at 1m at 2 yrs, and 9f and 1¾m winner Touching Moment (by Pennine Walk): dam

unraced: fair form: changed hands 2,200 gns after debut: won maiden at Lingfield in November: may stay beyond 1¼m: acts on equitrack. *C. E. Brittain*

BREAD WINNER   3 b.g. Reprimand 122 – Khubza 86 (Green Desert (USA)   **68** 127) [1998 68+: 5.2m⁴ 5.7d⁶ 1999 6s⁴ 7d³ 6m² 7g⁵ 7g 7m³ 7.6f² 7m² 8.5m⁴ 9.9m⁴ 13.1f 8s⁵ Sep 27] fair maiden handicapper: stays 1¼m: acts on firm going, not soft: blinkered second to fifth starts. *I. A. Balding*

BREAKIN EVEN   4 ch.g. Chilibang 120 – Bee Dee Dancer (Ballacashtal (CAN))   **–** [1998 60, a40: a6g⁶ 5.9s 6g⁸ 7d 6m a8g 1999 a6g* 7g 6f 5.9m 7m a7g 5.9g 7m Jul   **a50** 21] lengthy gelding: modest handicapper: landed gamble at Southwell in March: no form after: possibly best at 6f: acts on fibresand, best turf effort on good going: has been tongue tied: wears blinkers: unreliable. *J. L. Eyre*

BREAK THE CODE (USA)   2 b.c. (Feb 28) Red Ransom (USA) – Kissogram   **81** Girl (USA) 100 (Danzig (USA)) [1999 5f 6f² 6f* 8m 7s⁵ 6s⁶ Oct 2] stocky colt: fifth foal: half-brother to 3-y-o Precocious Miss: dam, 5f (at 2 yrs) and 8.5f (in USA) winner, sister to Green Desert: fairly useful form: won minor event at Hamilton in August: below best in nurseries after, finding little in blinkers final start: should stay 7f: acts on firm going: sold 6,000 gns, sent to Spain. *M. Johnston*

BREAK THE GLASS (USA)   2 b. or br.g. (Jan 16) Dynaformer (USA) – Greek   **61 p** Wedding (USA) (Blushing Groom (FR) 131) [1999 7.5m⁴ 8.2m⁴ Aug 28] $50,000Y: third foal: half-brother to useful 4-y-o Smart Squall: dam, French 9f (including at 2 yrs) to 11.5f winner, out of Washington International runner-up Persian Tiara: modest form when fourth of 5 in steadily-run maidens at Beverley and Nottingham: likely to be well suited by 1¼m/1½m. *E. A. L. Dunlop*

BREAK THE RULES   7 b.g. Dominion 123 – Surf Bird (Shareef Dancer (USA)   **–** 135) [1998 76, a71: a12g⁴ a11g a12g 10.3d³ 11.1v 10v⁶ 10s³ 10.3g* 10m 10.3g³ 10.3g⁴ 1999 10.5m Aug 30] neat gelding: fair handicapper for D. Nicholls in 1998: well beaten only outing in 1999: effective at 1¼m to 1½m: acts on any turf going, probably on fibresand: blinkered once, at least as effective when not: has carried head high under pressure, and not a straightforward ride. *A. G. Juckes*

BREAKWATER (USA)   2 b.f. (Apr 4) Boundary (USA) 117 – Flippers (USA)   **78 +** (Coastal (USA)) [1999 7g⁴ 7d Oct 30] half-sister to several winners in USA, including Grade 1 9f winner Hail Atlantis (by Seattle Slew): dam, minor stakes winner and second in Grade 2 9f event, half-sister to Observer Gold Cup winner Apalachee from excellent family: similar form in maidens at Redcar (fourth of 15 to Lahan) and Newmarket (seventh of 16 to Premier Prize): will stay 1m. *L. M. Cumani*

BREATHLESS DREAMS (IRE)   2 ch.c. (Mar 19) College Chapel 122 – Foston   **90** Bridge 68 (Relkino 131) [1999 6s² 7m* Jun 24] 17,000Y, 22,000 2-y-o: half-brother to several winners, including 1995 2-y-o 7f winner More Than You Know (by Kefaah), who stayed 13f: dam placed at 7f at 2 yrs: favourite, confirmed promise when winning 16-runner maiden at Salisbury in June by length from Clonmany despite still seeming green: seemed likely to progress, but not seen again: joined G. Brown. *M. L. W. Bell*

BRECONGILL LAD   7 b.g. Clantime 101 – Chikala 81 (Pitskelly 122) [1998   **80 +** 75§: 6g² 5g² 6s 5g³ 6s⁴ 5d 1999 5m⁶ 5g 5m⁶ 6g 6g⁶ 6m 5m* 5g* 5.2g* 5f² 6m* 5m³ 5g³ Oct 6] tall gelding: fairly useful handicapper: left M. Hammond after sixth start: revitalised subsequently, winning at Catterick, Pontefract, Yarmouth and Goodwood in August/September: effective at 5f/6f: acts on firm and good to soft going: tried blinkered/visored earlier in career: has hung and often carries head high. *D. Nicholls*

BREEDS HILL   3 b.f. Chaddleworth (IRE) 103 – Breed Reference (Reference   **–** Point 139) [1998 53: 7g 7m⁶ 7m⁶ 1999 6m 7g 6f 7m 7g Sep 18] poor performer at best: well beaten in 1999: has worn tongue strap: sold 2,000 gns, sent to Kuwait. *C. F. Wall*

BREEZED WELL   13 b.g. Wolverlife 115 – Precious Baby (African Sky 124)   **43** [1998 –: 7.5m 7g⁵ 10.5m 11.5m 9.9d 10m⁶ 8.1m 1999 a6g 7.5d 7m 10.5d⁵ a8.5g 10m³ 9.9m 8.1m Aug 5] smallish, sparely-made gelding: poor mover: poor handicapper: inconsistent in amateur events in 1999: probably needs further than 7f and stays 1¼m: acts on any going: blinkered once at 3 yrs. *B. R. Cambidge*

BREEZY LOUISE 2 b.f. (Feb 27) Dilum (USA) 115 – Louise Moillon 79 (Mansingh (USA) 120) [1999 5m 5g⁴ 5.3f⁴ 5.1g 5m* 5m⁶ a6g² a6g⁵ 7d Aug 26] 2,000Y, 8,400 2-y-o: half-sister to several winners abroad, including French 11f winner Vajjia (by Nishapour): dam, 2-y-o 5f winner, also successful over jumps in France, half-sister to very smart Whip It Quick: modest performer: won seller at Windsor in June: stays 6f: acts on good to firm going and fibresand. *R. J. Hodges*   **55 a59**

BREEZY MELODY 3 b.f. Sizzling Melody 117 – Breezy Day 85 (Day Is Done 115) [1998 –: a5g 1999 a6g a6g a6g⁶ 6g 6s 5f Aug 2] no sign of ability. *J. G. Given*   **–**

BREEZY TIME 3 ch.c. Timeless Times (USA) 99 – Miss Merlin 79 (Manacle 123) [1998 NR 1999 6g 5m a6g³ Jul 9] 5,000Y, 5,700 2-y-o: brother to 5f seller winner Dande Times and half-brother to several winners, including fairly useful 5f performer Lyndseylee (by Swing Easy): dam 6f winner, including at 2 yrs: modest form in claimers and maiden: acts on fibresand: stays 6f. *V. Soane*   **64**

BREMRIDGE (IRE) 2 ch.g. (Apr 17) Ridgewood Ben 113 – Eimkar (Junius (USA) 124) [1999 6.1m 6.1g⁵ 7m 7.6g 8.3g² Oct 11] IR 16,000F, IR 23,000Y: eighth foal: half-brother to untrustworthy 1997 2-y-o 6f winner Shannon (by Mujadil) and 1m winner Ladybower (by Pennine Walk): dam unraced half-sister to high-class French miler Daring Display: fair maiden: trained first 4 starts by P. Chapple-Hyam: easily best effort when second of 16 to Polar Red in nursery at Windsor final start: stays 1m well: yet to race on ground softer than good: sold 20,000 gns. *A. G. Foster*   **78**

BRENDA DEE (IRE) 3 br.f. Perugino (USA) 84 – Children's Hour (Mummy's Pet 125) [1998 65: 6g² 6.1g⁴ 7m⁵ 7.9g² 10s⁵ 1999 a8f³ a11g³ a10g a11g⁴ 8.3d³ 8m 8g a8.5g⁴ Sep 4] leggy, sparely-made filly: fair maiden on turf, modest on all-weather: effective at 1m and probably stays 11f: acts on soft going and all-weather: has carried head high: inconsistent. *A. P. Jarvis*   **65 a54**

BRENNER'S PARK (IRE) 2 b.g. (Mar 24) Night Shift (USA) – Brentwood (IRE) 92 (Waajib 121) [1999 5g⁶ 7d⁵ a7g³ 7m 7f 8m 8d Sep 26] 32,000Y: sturdy, close-coupled gelding: first foal: dam, 1½m winner, later 1m/9f winner in Italy: fair form on all-weather, poor on turf: probably stays 1m: acts on fibresand: blinkered last 2 starts: sold 5,000 gns. *M. Johnston*   **44 a67**

BRETECHE (FR) 4 b.f. Fijar Tango (FR) 127 – Foinery 66 (Reference Point 139) [1998 12d⁶ 13s 12g 12.5m 10.5g² 1999 a12g³ Apr 6] 6,000 francs and 22,000 francs Y: first foal: dam, maiden here, 12.5f winner in France at 4 yrs: trained by G. Brillet in France at 3 yrs, second in claimer at Saint-Cloud (claimed 110,000 francs): poor form in apprentice seller at Southwell on British Flat debut: stays 10.5f: tried blinkered/visored/tongue tied: sold 4,200 gns, joined N. Hawke. *M. C. Pipe*   **35 §**

BREVITY 4 b.g. Tenby 125 – Rive (USA) (Riverman (USA) 131) [1998 74: 8s 10s² 1999 10v 12m 8g 10f 8d 7m⁵ a7g⁴ 6g* 5g² 6m² a6g⁵ 6s a6f⁶ 6d Oct 20] strong gelding: fair handicapper on turf, modest on all-weather: landed gamble in apprentice race at Newbury in August: had excuses on 3 of final 4 outings: likely to prove best at 6f/stiff 5f: acts on good to firm going (probably on soft) and fibresand (yet to race on equitrack): has worn crossed noseband/tongue strap/bandages in front: has been early to post: retained 10,000 gns. *D. Sasse*   **73 a63 +**

BREW 3 b.c. Primo Dominie 121 – Boozy 111 (Absalom 128) [1998 75: 6s 5g² 6v 1999 5.3f² 6f 5.7g 5m 5m⁶ 5s Sep 22] well-made colt: fair maiden handicapper at best: below form after reappearance: likely to prove best at 5f: acts on firm ground: has been bandaged. *R. Hannon*   **76 d**

BREYDON 6 ch.g. Be My Guest (USA) 126 – Palmella (USA) 89 (Grundy 137) [1998 39: 8s⁶ 12.1v* 11.1d³ 12d⁵ 12.1d⁵ 16s³ 16g³ 10.9d² 12.4g² 16d 1999 16m⁶ 11.1s 11.1f⁶ 10.9g⁵ 11.1m 12.1m 16d] angular, plain gelding: poor performer: effective at 11f, barely stays 2m: acts on firm and heavy ground. *P. Monteith*   **39**

BRIAN'S BLUE (IRE) 4 ch.c. Statoblest 120 – Lamya 73 (Hittite Glory 125) [1998 –: a9.4g a6g 1999 6d a6g 6d May 10] unfurnished colt: no sign of ability. *B. P. J. Baugh*   **–**

BRIDAL WHITE 3 b.f. Robellino (USA) 127 – Alwatar (USA) 64 (Caerleon (USA) 132) [1998 66: 7m⁴ 6.1m³ 7d⁶ 6m³ 7g 1999 a8.5g 7s⁵ 7m 8m a7g 6.1m 8d 10d Nov 1] tall, quite good-topped filly: modest maiden handicapper: lost her form after   **64 d**

second start: stays 7f: acts on good to firm and soft going, below form both starts on fibresand. *M. J. Ryan*

BRIDE'S ANSWER   4 ch.f. Anshan 119 – Ivory Bride 86 (Domynsky 110)   – [1998 81: 8s 8d* 8m³ 10m³ 8d³ 1999 10.3m 10d 12.3g 8.5g 10d 10d Oct 26] big, workmanlike filly: fairly useful form at 3 yrs for M. Channon: no form in 1999: tried blinkered final start. *C. Grant*

BRIDGEND BLUE (IRE)   3 b.g. Up And At 'em 109 – Sperrin Mist 83 (Camden   **43** Town 125) [1998 62d: 5d 6.1g⁶ 6g⁵ 5.2g a6g⁶ a8g 1999 6m 5m 7m³ 10m 7m Jul 12] quite good-topped gelding: poor maiden: stays 7f: acts on good to firm going and fibresand: looked temperamental in visor fourth 2-y-o start: joined N. Waggott 1,000 gns in July. *M. L. W. Bell*

BRIDGE POOL   3 ch.f. First Trump 118 – Treble Hook (IRE) (Ballad Rock 122)   **74 d** [1998 68: 6m⁴ 5g 7s³ 7s⁴ 6d 1999 6m² 5m² 5g² 5m* 6f³ 5d 6s³ 7g 6.1d 7d Oct 27] 10,000Y: lengthy filly: fourth foal: half-sister to Italian sprint winner Ninfa of Cisterna (by Polish Patriot): dam Irish 2-y-o 6f/7f winner: fair performer at best: trained by P. Flynn in Ireland at 2 yrs: runner-up first 3 starts in maidens in 1999 for J. Noseda: won similar event at Leicester in July: ran poorly last 3 starts: effective at 5f to 7f: acts on good to firm going: tried blinkered/visored: sold 5,000 gns. *Dr J. D. Scargill*

BRIDIE'S PRIDE   8 b.g. Alleging (USA) 120 – Miss Monte Carlo 75 (Reform   **71** 132) [1998 71, a–: a16.2g⁶ 16.2g* 18s² 16.4g² 16.2g 16.2s³ 18g⁶ 16.5d² 1999 16g³   **a–** 16.4s² 18d 20m Jun 15] sparely-made gelding: fair handicapper: good placed efforts first 2 starts: reportedly finished lame final outing: stays 2¼m: raced mostly on good ground or softer (well beaten both starts on all-weather): has been bandaged: front runner: game in his prime. *G. A. Ham*

BRIEF CALL (IRE)   2 ch.f. (Mar 28) Case Law 113 – Collected (IRE) (Taufan   **55** (USA) 119) [1999 5.1f³ 5.1g 6.1g 5.3f⁵ 5.7h⁵ 5g 5m a5g³ a6g⁵ Oct 30] IR 1,000F, IR 1,100Y: second foal: dam Irish maiden on Flat and over hurdles: modest maiden: may prove best at 5f: acts on fibresand, raced only on good going or firmer on turf: visored (ran poorly) once: usually makes running. *B. Palling*

BRIEF ENCOUNTA (FR)   3 ch.g. Brief Truce (USA) 126 – Villa Blanca (SPA)   **73** (Rheffissimo (FR) 120) [1998 83+: 5f⁵ 6d* 7g⁴ 7g⁴ 8g 1999 8.5g 7.5m⁴ 8.3m 10s* 10.5g⁶ 10.5d Nov 3] fairly useful at 2 yrs: won claimer at Deauville in August under enterprising ride from R. Hughes (final start for B. Meehan): stays 1¼m: acts on soft going: effective blinkered or not. *W. J. S. Cargeeg, France*

BRIERY MEC   4 b.g. Ron's Victory (USA) 129 – Briery Fille 81 (Sayyaf 121)   **52** [1998 –: 8.2s 10d 11.8g 1999 10.1g 10.5m 8.2m 9.9m² 10.1d³ 10s³ Nov 1] tall gelding: modest maiden handicapper: best efforts last 3 starts: stays 1¼m: acts on soft going and on good to firm. *H. J. Collingridge*

BRIGHSTONE   6 ch.h. Cadeaux Genereux 131 – High Fountain 102 (High Line   **– §** 125) [1998 58§: 11.6d⁵ 10.2d² 10.8d² 8.1g 11.7d⁴ 10m 1999 10m 10.5d Sep 21] sturdy horse: formerly tubed: modest at best in 1998 for M. Pipe, no show in 1999: best efforts up to 1¼m: acts on firm and soft going: front runner: none too resolute. *Mrs A. L. M. King*

BRIGHT BLADE   3 b.c. Sure Blade (USA) 130 – Gay Gem (Sparkler 130) [1998   – NR 1999 8.2d 8.3d a8g Nov 26] first reported foal: dam of little account over hurdles: behind in maidens. *P. Mitchell*

BRIGHTER (USA)   3 ch.f. Gone West (USA) – Top Trestle (USA) (Nijinsky   **69** (CAN) 138) [1998 86p: 7m⁴ 1999 10m 12.3d⁵ 11.9m Sep 3] fairly useful form in maiden on only start at 2 yrs: disappointing in similar events and a handicap (blinkered) in 1999: should stay at least 1m: sold 42,000 gns. *H. R. A. Cecil*

BRIGHTEST STAR   3 b.f. Unfuwain (USA) 131 – Shirley Superstar 94 (Shirley   **77** Heights 130) [1998 NR 1999 10d³ 12m² 11.5m³ Jul 20] 280,000Y: quite attractive filly: seventh foal: half-sister to Oaks winner Lady Carla (by Caerleon) and 9f winner Azores (by Polish Precedent): dam lightly-raced 7f winner (at 2 yrs) out of smart filly at up to 1¾m Odeon: fair maiden: will be suited by 1¾m+: tail swisher. *H. R. A. Cecil*

Kingston Rated Stakes (Handicap), Sandown—front-running Brilliant Red (left) keeps himself out of trouble; the unlucky Lonesome Dude (dark sleeves) and Therhea finish strongly

BRIGHT HOPE (IRE) 3 b.f. Danehill (USA) 126 – Crystal Cross (USA) 88 **84** (Roberto (USA) 131) [1998 62p: 8d 1999 10f³ 10m* Sep 16] useful-looking filly: good walker: progressive in maidens, fairly useful form when winning at Pontefract in September by 1¼ lengths from Zariliya: will stay 1½m: may improve again. *P. W. Harris*

BRIGHT QUESTION 2 ch.c. (Jan 21) Nashwan (USA) 135 – Ozone Friendly **72 p** (USA) 107 (Green Forest (USA) 134) [1999 7g⁵ 8m Sep 17] rangy, good sort: has scope: superb mover: fifth foal: half-brother to 3 winners by Sadler's Wells, including smart 1m winner (including at 2 yrs) Musalsal, who stayed 1¼m, and useful French 1¼m winner Amusing Time: dam won Prix Robert Papin: 2/1, encouraging debut when fifth of 6 to Mana-Mou Bay in listed race at Newbury: only seventh of 8 to Ethmaar in minor event there following month: will be suited by 1¼m+: likely to do better. *B. W. Hills*

BRIG O'TURK 2 ch.g. (Mar 5) Inchinor 119 – Sharmood (USA) (Sharpen Up **62 p** 127) [1999 8s Oct 26] 23,000Y: eighth foal: half-brother to 3 winners, including 6-y-o King Kato: dam maiden in USA: signs of ability though never dangerous in maiden at Bath: should stay 1¼m: probably capable of better. *Mrs A. J. Perrett*

BRILLIANCE DAWNS 2 ch.f. (Feb 13) Chilibang 120 – Mrs Dawson 52 **–** (Sharrood (USA) 124) [1999 5d a5g Apr 26] lengthy filly: third foal: dam 1m winner: tailed off in minor event/seller. *D. Nicholls*

BRILLIANT RED 6 b.g. Royal Academy (USA) 130 – Red Comes Up (USA) **113** (Blushing Groom (FR) 131) [1998 100: a8g³ a10g* a10g* a10g 8d 10f³ 10m² 10g* 9g 8s 1999 8g 8.1g² 10m* 8.1m* 10m³ 10m 10s 8g 8d² a10g* Nov 16] tall, lengthy gelding: has a long stride: smart performer: won handicaps at Ascot (quite valuable event) and Sandown (rated stakes by neck from Lonesome Dude) in the summer and minor event at Lingfield (beat Running Stag by neck) in November, able to dominate on first 2-named: very good neck second of 19 to Tayseer in Autumn Handicap at Newmarket penultimate start: effective at 1m/1¼m: acts on firm going, soft and all-weather: wears tongue strap: usually races up with pace: didn't look entirely keen and edged right seventh start. *Mrs L. Richards*

BRIMSTONE (IRE) 4 ch.g. Ballad Rock 122 – Blazing Glory (IRE) (Glow **60** (USA)) [1998 83: 5g² 6.1g⁴ 5g 1999 5d 5s a6g a7g a8g⁶ Dec 18] tall, good-topped gelding: fairly useful handicapper at 3 yrs: modest at best in 1999: probably amiss second start: probably stays 1m: acts on good to firm going, probably on equitrack. *H. J. Collingridge*

BRING SWEETS 3 b.g. Sabrehill (USA) 120 – Che Gambe (USA) (Lyphard **95** (USA) 132) [1998 94p: 7g 7.9g 8v* 8d* 8v² 1999 9m³ 10.2s³ 9g May 18] quite attractive gelding: has a quick action: useful form: better effort in minor events first 2 starts when third at Bath penultimate outing: first-time blinkers, last of 16 in Goodwood handicap final outing: stays 1¼m, not sure to get further: acts well on going softer than good: joined M. Pipe for 38,000 gns in July, and fairly useful form when winning 3 juvenile hurdles in autumn. *B. W. Hills*

BRISBANE ROAD (IRE) 2 b.g. (Feb 6) Blues Traveller (IRE) 119 – Eva Fay **– p** (IRE) (Fayruz 116) [1999 7.9g 8s Oct 26] IR 35,000F, 28,000Y: second foal: dam unraced half-sister to smart Italian miler Teach Dha Mhile and top-class chaser Remittance Man: signs of ability in maidens at York and Bath: likely to do better. *I. A. Balding*

BRISTOL BEAUFORT 2 b.g. (Apr 12) Forzando 122 – Fairey Firefly 64 (Hall- **–** gate 127) [1999 7d Nov 1] first foal: dam, 6f winner (including on all-weather), half-sister to very smart jumper Avro Anson: tailed off in Redcar maiden. *Miss J. A. Camacho*

BRITANNIA (USA) 2 b.f. (Apr 15) Sea Hero (USA) 124 – Brave And True **100** (USA) (Fappiano (USA)) [1999 7m³ 8.1g³ 8.1d² 8s² Sep 26] big, leggy filly: third reported foal: half-sister to 3-y-o Sankaty Light and 4-y-o Fields of Omagh: dam, sprint winner at 2 yrs in USA, out of half-sister to Washington International winner Run The Gantlet: placed in maidens prior to showing improved form (useful effort) when ¾-length second of 6 to Teggiano in Fillies' Mile at Ascot on final start, making most and battling on gamely: will be well suited by 1¼m/1½m: easily best effort on soft ground. *I. A. Balding*

BROADSTAIRS BEAUTY (IRE) 9 ch.g. Dominion Royale 112 – Holy Water **–** (Monseigneur (USA) 127) [1998 92, a89: a7g⁴ a6g* a6g² 6v⁵ 5m 5g* 5g* 6s 5s 5g* 5f 5.6g 6s 5m 1999 6d 6m Apr 7] workmanlike gelding: has a quick action: fairly useful handicapper in 1998: gave impression something amiss in 1999: effective at 5f to 7f: acts on good to firm going, heavy and fibresand: blinkered/visored: usually bandaged. *D. Shaw*

BROADWAY LEGEND (IRE) 2 b.f. (Feb 21) Caerleon (USA) 132 – Tetra- **69 p** donna (IRE) 102 (Teenoso (USA) 135) [1999 7v³ 7g Oct 16] 100,000F and Y: tall, angular filly: second living foal: half-sister to 4-y-o Alberich: dam, second in Nell Gwyn Stakes but disappointing after, stayed 1½m: shaped well when third of 10 to Bedazzling in maiden at Kempton, unable to sustain promising effort only in final 1f: tailed off in Rockfel Stakes at Newmarket (bit reportedly slipped) month later: will be suited by 1¼m+: worth another chance to confirm debut promise. *J. W. Hills*

BROCATELLE 3 b.f. Green Desert (USA) 127 – Brocade 121 (Habitat 134) [1998 **65** NR 1999 7m³ 8.1m 6.8v² 7v Dec 1] half-sister to several winners, including high-class miler Barathea (by Sadler's Wells) and smart French 1m/1¼m performer Zabar (by Dancing Brave): dam 7f and 1m winner: 2¾ lengths third in maiden at Newmarket in July: gave impression something amiss next time (final start for L. Cumani), then better effort for new trainer when second in minor event at Lyon Parilly: very stiff task final outing: best around 7f. *J. E. Pease, France*

BROCHE (USA) 2 b.c. (Mar 20) Summer Squall (USA) – Ribbonwood (USA) **111 p** 100 (Diesis 133) [1999 7g* Jun 27] second foal: half-brother to useful 1998 2-y-o 7f winner Crown of Trees (by Chief's Crown): dam, 2-y-o 6f winner and second in Fred Darling Stakes, half-sister to Preakness and Belmont winner Risen Star: 4/1, won maiden at the Curragh in June by 2½ lengths from Ciro, making virtually all and merely pushed out: joined Godolphin: should go on to better things. *J. Oxx, Ireland*

BROCTUNE GOLD 8 b.g. Superpower 113 – Golden Sunlight (Ile de Bourbon **50** (USA) 133) [1998 65: 7s 8.5m 7d 8s* 8s² 9g 7.5m 7d* 7m 8m 7.5m 7s⁶ 8s 1999 8m 8d 6.9m 7.5m 7m⁶ 8d Aug 9] leggy, workmanlike gelding: easy mover: only modest handicapper nowadays: effective at 7f to 8.5f: acts on firm and soft ground, below form on all-weather: has had tongue tied: often races prominently: has looked less than willing on occasions. *Mrs M. Reveley*

BROCTUNE LINE 5 ch.g. Safawan 118 – Ra Ra (Lord Gayle (USA) 124) [1998 **–** 44, a60: a11g a11g² 11v 12.4d 8m⁴ 8g² 1999 a8g a11g³ a8g³ a8g 9g a11g⁵ May 17] **a56**

close-coupled gelding: modest on all-weather, poor on turf: below form after second start: effective at 1m to 11f: acts on fibresand, best turf runs on good going or firmer: effective blinkered or not: joined T. Keddy 1,000 gns in June. *Mrs M. Reveley*

BRODESSA   13 gr.g. Scallywag 127 – Jeanne du Barry 74 (Dubassoff (USA))   **60** [1998 67: a16g⁵ 13.8d² 13.8g² 16g² 16g* 16.5g⁵ 14.1m² 16.2m* 14.1m* 16d* 14.1d 16s⁶ 1999 13.8g* 13.8g* 16f² 16g* 14.1f* 14.1m² Aug 28] big gelding: tough veteran, still capable of modest form: won seller/claimers at Catterick in May and June, Musselburgh in July and Redcar in August: ideally needs further than 1½m, and stays 2m: acts on firm ground, soft and fibresand: suitable mount for inexperienced rider. *Mrs M. Reveley*

BROKENBOROUGH   2 ch.g. (May 3) Beveled (USA) – Swilly Express   **55** (Ballacashtal (CAN)) [1999 5d 6m 7m⁶ 7m Jul 8] second reported foal: brother to 3-y-o Lady Lazarus: dam staying hurdler: modest maiden: stays 7f. *M. Blanshard*

BROKE ROAD (IRE)   3 b.g. Deploy 131 – Shamaka 53 (Kris 135) [1998 –: a7g   **61** 1999 a7g a7f⁴ a8g² 9.3g 8f³ 7f⁴ 10g³ 9.9g³ 9.9g³ 9.9s⁶ 8.3s* 12s⁴ Oct 5] angular gelding: modest handicapper: won at Hamilton in September by 5 lengths: effective at 1m, barely stays lasting 1½m: acts on firm going, soft and fibresand: very best form in blinkers: joined Mrs V. Ward for 16,000 gns. *T. D. Barron*

BROMPTON BARRAGE   2 b.c. (Mar 3) Rudimentary (USA) 118 – Song of   **73** Hope 103 (Chief Singer 131) [1999 6m 7g⁶ 6s⁴ 7.7d Sep 21] 24,000Y: sturdy colt: fifth living foal: half-brother to several winners, including 5-y-o Song of Skye and 7f/1m winner Kingdom Princess (by Forzando): dam, 2-y-o 5f winner, from family of Mummy's Pet: fair maiden: ran poorly on nursery debut final start: should stay 1m: acts on soft going. *R. Hannon*

BRON HILDA (IRE)   2 b.f. (Apr 6) Namaqualand (USA) – Maura's Guest (IRE)   **50** (Be My Guest (USA) 126) [1999 6g³ 5m² 5f³ 7g⁴ 6g⁴ 7g 7d Oct 21] IR 3,000F, IR 4,700Y: workmanlike filly: fifth foal: half-sister to fairly useful 6f/7f winner Ray of Sunshine (by Rainbows For Life) and a 6f winner in Slovakia by Bob Back: dam unraced half-sister to 2 smart French sprinters: modest maiden: left R. Guest after third start: well beaten in nurseries final 2 outings: probably better at 7f than shorter: raced mainly on good going or firmer: acts on good to firm going: edgy sort: refused to enter stalls on intended debut: sometimes slowly away. *R. C. Spicer*

BRONZE LASS   2 b.f. (Apr 28) Formidable (USA) 125 – Bronzess (Magic   **–** Mirror 105) [1999 5f⁴ 5m Aug 11] first reported foal: dam unraced: well beaten in maiden and seller. *W. T. Kemp*

BRONZINO   4 ch.g. Midyan (USA) 124 – Indubitable 87 (Sharpo 132) [1998 65:   **65** 9.9m³ 9m 10.2d⁶ 12g 11.9g 11d³ 1999 10v⁵ 10d³ 12m 10.5d 10g 9.9d* 9.9v⁴ 11.9d 10s Nov 1] close-coupled, sparely-made gelding: fair handicapper: gained first win at Salisbury in August: stays 1¼m: acts on good to firm and heavy going: visored last 4 starts: held up: none too consistent. *G. B. Balding*

BROOKFURLONG   3 br.f. Rock City 120 – Call of The Night (IRE) 72 (Night   **–** Shift (USA)) [1998 NR 1999 5d 6g Sep 14] first foal: dam, 1m winner, should have been suited by at least 1¼m: well held in maidens. *J. R. Fanshawe*

BROOKHOUSE LADY (IRE)   4 b.f. Polish Patriot (USA) 128 – Honagh Lee   **–** (Main Reef 126) [1998 61, a–: 10g 8m⁵ 8m⁵ a9.4g 10.8m² 10g* 11.9g 10.5s⁴ 10.3d 1999 10s 8d 10d 8s Oct 25] leggy, angular filly: modest handicapper at best: no form in 1999: blinkered final start: sold 500 gns. *Ian Williams*

BROOKSEES DREAM   5 ch.m. Glacial Storm (USA) 127 – Good Holidays 60   **–** (Good Times (ITY)) [1998 NR 1999 10.2d 10.2g 7f 10.2m Jul 15] of little account. *B. J. Llewellyn*

BROTHER BEACON   8 ch.g. High Line 125 – Flaming Peace 104 (Queen's   **–** Hussar 124) [1998 NR 1999 a16f Jan 14] lightly raced and no form. *P. R. Chamings*

BROTHER TOM   2 b.c. (Apr 7) Prince Sabo 123 – Danseuse Davis (FR) (Glow   **–** (USA)) [1999 5d 6d 5m 5m⁴ 5.1h Aug 3] 500F: smallish, unfurnished colt: second foal: half-brother to 3-y-o Polly Mills: dam, no form, half-sister to useful stayer Top of The World: little form: tried visored: has worn tongue strap. *P. D. Evans*

BROUGHTON BELLE   3 b.f. Chaddleworth (IRE) 103 – Broughtons Pet (IRE) – (Cyrano de Bergerac 120) [1998 –: 6.1s 1999 7m 12d Sep 30] lengthy, plain filly: has shown nothing in maiden/claimers. *W. J. Musson*

BROUGHTONS ERROR   5 ch.g. Most Welcome 131 – Eloquent Charm (USA)   **73** (Private Account (USA)) [1998 NR 1999 a8g a10g⁴ 10m* 8g 10m 10g* 10m² 10m*   **a52** Jul 31] workmanlike gelding: fair handicapper on turf, modest on all-weather: won at Newmarket in April and at Windsor and Newmarket again in July: stays 1¼m: acts on equitrack, best turf form on good/good to firm ground: tends to carry head awkwardly: usually held up. *W. J. Musson*

BROUGHTON SIREN   4 b.f. Most Welcome 131 – Royal Form (Formidable – (USA) 125) [1998 –: 8m 7m 7d 1999 a8g a11g³ 12.3m a11g³ a16g May 29]   **a37** workmanlike filly: poor maiden: stays 11f, probably not 2m: acts on fibresand. *W. J. Musson*

BROUGHTONS LURE (IRE)   5 ch.m. Archway (IRE) 115 – Vaal Salmon   **46** (IRE) (Salmon Leap (USA) 131) [1998 55: 12.5d² 12.5g*ᵈⁱˢ a12g⁶ 12.3g⁶ 11.1m 11.9g² 14.6d 1999 10d 11.9d 12d a16.2g⁵ a12g² Dec 21] poor handicapper: good second of 16 at Southwell final start: stays 1½m well: acts on fibresand and good to soft ground, probably on good to firm. *W. J. Musson*

BROUGHTONS MILL   4 ch.g. Ron's Victory (USA) 129 – Sandra's Desire   **55** (Grey Desire 115) [1998 NR 1999 a7g⁵ a7g 9.9s 10.1d³ Oct 20] modest maiden, lightly raced: easily best effort in 1999 in handicap at Newcastle final start: stays 1¼m: acts on good to soft going, probably good to firm: sold 7,000 gns. *W. J. Musson*

BROUGHTONS TURMOIL   10 b.g. Petorius 117 – Rustic Stile (Rusticaro   **72** (FR) 124) [1998 81: 6d 6m³ 7m² 7.1d⁵ a8g* 8g 6g⁴ 8m³ 6d 8s⁶ 6g⁵ 7s⁴ 1999 7g 8g 6g* 5m⁴ 7m⁵ 6m 6m⁶ 5.7h 7d a7g* a7g³ a6g Dec 17] lengthy, workmanlike gelding: fair performer: won claimer at Windsor in May and seller at Wolverhampton in November: best form at 6f to 1m: acts on firm ground, good to soft and all-weather: takes good hold, and usually held up: inconsistent. *B. R. Millman*

BROWNING   4 b.g. Warrshan (USA) 117 – Mossy Rose 78 (King of Spain 121)   **64** [1998 64, a70+: a8g² a8.5g² a10g² 8.3m 10g⁶ 8m⁴ 11.6f* a10g⁴ 1999 14.1d 11.9f 12m² 12m² 12g 11.4m Jul 3] modest handicapper: good second at Salisbury and Kempton: stays 1½m: acts on firm going and all-weather: takes good hold and races prominently. *D. J. Coakley*

BROWNS DELIGHT   2 b.f. (Mar 28) Runnett 125 – Fearless Princess (Tyrnavos   **59** 129) [1999 6f 6m 6d a6g² a7g Nov 26] seventh reported thoroughbred foal: half-sister to 3-y-o Brown's Flight: dam unraced: modest maiden: best effort when second to Illusive in nursery at Lingfield: should stay at least 7f. *S. Dow*

BROWN'S FLIGHT   3 b.f. Jupiter Island 126 – Fearless Princess (Tyrnavos   **61** 129) [1998 72: 6g⁵ 6g³ 7g⁴ 7g 6m² 7g 1999 6m 6m⁵ 10.1d 9.9g⁶ 10m⁶ a12g 10f 8.5m 7d⁴ 7g Aug 29] close-coupled filly: has a quick action: modest maiden handicapper: below form last 5 starts: needs further than 7f, and stays easy 1¼m: acts on good to firm and good to soft going: blinkered (ran as if something amiss) seventh start, visored (slowly away) final outing: sometimes races freely: sold 900 gns. *S. Dow*

BRUFF STREAM (IRE)   5 b.g. Accordion – Littlepace (Indian King (USA)   **62** 128) [1998 NR 1999 a8.5g³ a8.5g³ a12g a10g⁶ Feb 11] first foal: dam won at 5f in Ireland as 5-y-o and 7-y-o: similar form (modest) in maidens at Wolverhampton first 2 starts: well beaten after: not sure to stay much beyond 8.5f: joined J. Geoghegan in Ireland. *M. Johnston*

BRUMON (IRE)   8 b.g. Sadler's Wells (USA) 132 – Loveliest (USA) (Tibaldo) – [1998 NR 1999 17.1s Oct 4] one-time fair winner: no form since 1995. *M. Mullineaux*

BRUTAL FANTASY (IRE)   5 b.g. Distinctly North (USA) 115 – Flash Donna   **76** (USA) 70 (Well Decorated (USA)) [1998 80, a75: a7g a8.5g⁶ a6g⁴ a5g⁴ a6g⁵ 6d 5s 6g   **a73** 5s 5m⁵ a6g⁴ 1999 5s 5m² 5.7g 5g* 5g 5m 5f⁵ 5m 5f 5d* 5g⁶ 5.2g² 5m⁶ 5.2g 5s 5g a6g a6g a5g² a5g⁵ Dec 29] good-quartered gelding: fair handicapper: won at Lingfield in May (left P. Murphy after seventh start) and Ascot in August: effective at 5f/6f: acts on all-weather, firm and good to soft ground, not soft: tried blinkered/visored at 4 yrs. *P. Howling*

BRYNKIR 5 b.g. Batshoof 122 – Felinwen (White Mill 76) [1998 45, a52: a12s **48**
a16g⁴ a16.2g* a16g⁵ 16m⁵ 16d⁶ 17.1d 1999 12.1m 17.2m³ Aug 22] sturdy gelding:
poor handicapper: third at Bath final outing: stays 17f: acts on fibresand, and on good
to firm ground. *B. J. Llewellyn*

BRYONY BRIND (IRE) 4 ch.f. Kris 135 – Bayadere (USA) 61 (Green Dancer **105**
(USA) 132) [1998 102: 8.2m* 10.8d³ 12d² 11.9g* 12.5m* 14.6d⁵ 12s⁴ 1999 13.4m⁵
12m³ 13.5g 14.1m² 12d³ 16.1d⁵ Oct 29] tall filly: useful performer: good efforts
when third in listed race at Newmarket (to Suhaad) and in handicap (to Rada's
Daughter) at same course: stays 14.6f: acts on good to firm and soft ground: has run
creditably when sweating. *J. R. Fanshawe*

BUCENTAURE 4 ch.f. Ron's Victory (USA) 129 – Gecko Rouge (Rousillon **–**
(USA) 133) [1998 –: 8m⁶ 7m 1999 10.1m 9f 11.1m 8.3s 10.1d Oct 20] leggy, angular
filly: probably of little account. *Martyn Wane*

BUCKLE (IRE) 3 b.f. Common Grounds 118 – Maratona (Be My Guest (USA) **77**
126) [1998 72p: 7m³ 7v 1999 8d* 8m 8d² 9d 8s* Nov 17] tall, lengthy, rather unfurnished filly: fair form: won 5-runner maiden at Goodwood in May (left W. Jarvis
after next start) and minor event at Nantes in November: not sure to stay beyond 1m:
acts on soft going. *H.-A. Pantall, France*

BUCKMINSTER (USA) 2 br.c. (May 11) Silver Hawk (USA) 123 – Buckarina **77 p**
(USA) (Buckaroo (USA)) [1999 7s⁴ Nov 5] $170,000Y: big, close-coupled,
good-topped colt: has scope: ninth foal: half-brother to 3 winners in North America,
including 1991 champion Canadian 2-y-o filly Buckys Solution (by Tiffany Ice):
dam won twice in USA: particularly burly and green when promising fourth of 20 to
Hopeful Light in maiden at Doncaster, travelling strongly before edging left when
pushed along: type to do fair bit better over 1m+ at 3 yrs. *J. H. M. Gosden*

BUCKSTONES ROAD (IRE) 2 ch.g. (May 9) Shalford (IRE) 124§ – Grave **41**
Error (Northern Treat (USA)) [1999 5g a5g³ a6g⁵ 6g Aug 11] IR 1,300Y: half-brother
to several winners, including 3-y-o Miss Take and 4-y-o Muja's Magic: dam Irish
1½m winner: poor maiden. *N. Tinkler*

BUDELLI (IRE) 2 b.c. (Feb 9) Elbio 125 – Eves Temptation (IRE) (Glenstal **68 p**
(USA) 118) [1999 6d⁵ Nov 4] second foal: dam unraced: weak in market and con-
siderately handled when never-nearer fifth of 17 to Scarlett Ribbon in maiden at
Windsor: should improve. *M. R. Channon*

BUGGY RIDE (IRE) 2 b.c. (Apr 26) Blues Traveller (IRE) 119 – Tambora 75 **64**
(Darshaan 133) [1999 6m 7m³ 7d⁵ 7m 8.3g a7g² a7g⁴ a6g² Dec 22] 11,000Y: **a74**
unfurnished colt: third foal: half-brother to a sprint winner in Sweden by Mac's Imp:
dam 1¼m winner: fair maiden: left R. Charlton 8,000 gns after fifth start: in frame
on all-weather last 3 outings: races keenly, but should stay 1m: acts on equitrack:
visored fourth/fifth outings: unseated rider leaving paddock and awkward at stalls
third one. *Miss Gay Kelleway*

BULAWAYO 2 b.c. (Apr 3) Prince Sabo 123 – Ra Ra Girl 77 (Shack (USA) 118) **46 p**
[1999 6s a6g⁶ Nov 15] strong, good-topped colt: half-brother to 3-y-o Hot Legs,
4-y-o Ra Ra Rasputin and 5f winner Sing With The Band (by Chief Singer): dam 6f
winner: showed some ability when sixth of 10 in maiden at Southwell on second
start: should do better. *B. A. McMahon*

BULLET 4 b.g. Alhijaz 122 – Beacon (High Top 131) [1998 74: 10m³ 11.7m² **78**
11.9s³ 1999 11.1v² 14.1m⁴ a14.8g⁵ 12m⁶ 12g* 12g² 12m* 12m² 13.9m Sep 1] quite
attractive gelding: fair performer: won claimer at Beverley in June (final start for
W. Haggas) and minor event at Carlisle in July: stays 1¾m: acts on good to firm and
heavy ground, below form only start on fibresand: races prominently/leads. *Martin
Todhunter*

BULLETIN 2 b.f. (Jan 30) Prince Sabo 123 – Storm Warning 117 (Tumble Wind **71**
(USA)) [1999 5d³ 6m* 6d 5d Sep 30] strong, lengthy filly: has a short, quick action:
half-sister to 1m winner Dust (by Green Desert) and 7f to 8.5f winner Present
Situation (by Cadeaux Genereux): dam sprinter: confirmed promise when winning
maiden at Brighton in August: ran poorly in nurseries at Ayr and Newmarket after:
stays 6f: acts on good to firm going: sold 6,500 gns in December. *M. L. W. Bell*

BUMBLE BE 4 b.g. Precocious 126 – Lingering 96 (Kind of Hush 118) [1998 –: –
6m 8.3m 7.6m 11.5m⁵ 1999 5g 6m Jun 18] of little account. *S. Dow*

BUN ALLEY 3 b.g. Be My Guest (USA) 126 – Neptunalia 70 (Slip Anchor 136) 86
[1998 66P: 7m 6g 1999 7f³ 7m² 7d 7.1m² 8s⁴ 7m⁴ 6g⁶ Oct 15] strong, good-topped
gelding: fluent mover: fairly useful maiden: at least creditable efforts when placed,
including in handicap at Sandown on fourth start: below form after: free-going sort,
but bred to stay at least 1m: acts on firm going, possibly not on softer than good: sold
13,000 gns: sent to Macau. *J. A. R. Toller*

BUNDY 3 b.g. Ezzoud (IRE) 126 – Sanctuary Cove (Habitat 134) [1998 71, a?: 74 d
5.1g⁶ 5d³ 6.3s 7g 6m⁴ 6g* 6m³ 6m* 6s 6d a7g 1999 6.1v³ 6.1s⁴ 6m³ 6m⁶ 7s⁴ 5.9m⁴
8.2g 7m 7.1m Aug 26] smallish, leggy gelding: fair handicapper at best: generally
regressed in 1999: probably stays 7f, not 1m: acts on good to firm going and heavy,
below form on fibresand: blinkered penultimate start. *M. Dods*

BUNNIES OWN 4 b.f. Flockton's Own 98 – Walsham Witch 61 (Music Maestro 48
119) [1998 –, a55d: a11g⁵ a9.4g⁴ a8g⁶ a8g² a7g* a7g⁴ a9.4g 7g⁵ a8g 9g a8.5g⁶ a7g a42
a8g⁶ 1999 a11g³ a12g³ a11g a8g⁵ 8g³ 9.9g² 10m a8g⁶ 10g 8m Jul 16] small, leggy
filly: poor performer: probably stays 1½m: acts on fibresand (untried on equitrack),
best turf efforts on good going. *J. L. Harris*

BUNTY 3 b.f. Presidium 124 – Shirlstar Investor (Some Hand 119) [1998 57d: 5d⁴ 57
5s³ 5s 5d⁴ 7m 5.1g⁴ 6f⁶ 6m 6d⁵ 6m 1999 a7g a7g a7g 8f 6f⁶ 6s 8f 8.5m² 10f⁴ 8.5m* a–
8d⁶ 7d 8d 8.2s* a7g⁶ Nov 16] workmanlike filly: modest handicapper: won at Epsom
(maiden event) in July and Nottingham in November: best form around 1m: acts on
firm and soft going, no form on all-weather. *C. A. Dwyer*

BUONA SERA 3 b.c. Marju (IRE) 127 – Blueberry Walk (Green Desert (USA) 69
127) [1998 82: 6g³ 6m⁴ 8d a7g² a7g* a7g⁵ 1999 6m 7m⁴ 7f 7d 7m Sep 7] good-
bodied colt: fair handicapper: good fourth at Kempton, always behind after: should
stay 1m (needed race when tried): acts on equitrack and good to firm going: sent to
Macau. *W. R. Muir*

BURCOT GIRL (IRE) 2 b.f. (Apr 7) Petardia 113 – Phoenix Forli (USA) (Forli –
(ARG)) [1999 5.7d 8d 7s Nov 2] 3,200 2-y-o: sixth foal: dam Irish 1½m winner: well
beaten in maidens. *J. L. Spearing*

BURDEN OF PROOF (IRE) 7 b.h. Fairy King (USA) – Belle Passe (Be My 118
Guest (USA) 126) [1998 118: 7v⁴ 8g* 6m⁴ 7s⁴ 8v* 8d* 8m³ 6s* 1999 8g* 8m⁶
7s Sep 18] tall horse: smart performer: successful in 12 races, most of them listed/
Group 3 or 2: easily best effort in 1999 when winning listed event at Leopardstown
in May (for third year running) by head from Access All Areas: effective at 6f to 1m:
acts on good to firm and heavy ground: often leads: genuine. *A. P. O'Brien, Ireland*

BURES (IRE) 8 b.g. Bold Arrangement 127 – Grid (FR) (Grundy 137) [1998 NR 50
1999 15.8g 13.8m³ 16d Aug 9] lengthy gelding: modest handicapper: only second
run on Flat since 1995 when creditable third at Catterick: probably stays 1¾m: acts
on firm and good to soft ground: normally visored prior to 1999: often a front runner.
Mrs J. Brown

BURGUNDIAN RED (USA) 2 b.c. (Jan 24) Red Ransom (USA) – Chesa Plana 78
(Niniski (USA) 125) [1999 6.1g⁵ 7d 7d⁴ Oct 27] IR 28,000Y: first foal: dam, useful
German 6f (at 2 yrs) to 1¼m winner who stayed 1¾m, half-sister to Oaks runner-up
Noushkey and smart Irish stayer San Sebastian: fair form in maidens, best effort
when fourth of 12 to Fast Track at Yarmouth final start: bred to be suited by 1¼m+:
joined A. Berry. *R. W. Armstrong*

BURMA BABY (USA) 3 ch.c. Woodman (USA) 126 – Rangoon Ruby 110 68
(Sallust 134) [1998 66p: 6v 6d 1999 8m 12g² 11.6m⁵ 14.6m* 15.8m³ 16m² 16.2g⁶
Aug 29] strong, good-bodied colt: has a quick action: fair handicapper: won at
Warwick in July: possibly something amiss final start: stays 2m: acts on good to firm
and heavy going: sold 10,000 gns, sent to Macau. *B. W. Hills*

BURNING LOVE 4 b.f. Forzando 122 – Latest Flame (IRE) 66 (Last Tycoon –
131) [1998 –: 8s 6s 5m 5s 1999 6f 5m 5f 9.1v Oct 12] close-coupled filly: seems of
little account. *B. W. Murray*

BURNING SUNSET 2 ch.f. (May 12) Caerleon (USA) 132 – Lingerie (Shirley **78 p**
Heights 130) [1999 7m⁶ 7g³ Oct 2] tall, quite attractive filly: has scope: fourth foal:
half-sister to 4-y-o Shiva and French 10.5f to 1½m winner Limnos, both very smart
performers by Hector Protector: dam, French maiden, daughter of top-class middle-
distance filly Northern Trick: favourite both starts, better effort when 3½ lengths
third of 15 to Lahan in Redcar maiden: will be very well suited by 1¼m+: should
make a better 3-y-o. *H. R. A. Cecil*

BURNING TRUTH (USA) 5 ch.g. Known Fact (USA) 135 – Galega (Sure **72**
Blade (USA) 130) [1998 74: 8.5d 8d 9.2g 9m² 10m² 10s 8s⁵ 1999 9.2v 8f³ 8m³ 8.1s
a8g⁴ 10d⁴ Oct 26] angular gelding: fluent mover: fair maiden: effective at 1m to
1¼m: acts on firm and soft going and fibresand. *Mrs A. Duffield*

BURNING (USA) 7 b.g. Bering 136 – Larnica (USA) (Alydar (USA)) [1998 63: **58**
a12g⁴ a12g⁶ 10.3g³ a10g 14g 10m³* 8m² 10d 9d a8.5g* a9.4g⁵ 1999 a9.4g² a8.5g* **a62**
a8.5g⁵ a8g⁴ a10g a8.5g⁵ 10f a8.5g 10.3m* 10.5m 10.1g³ 10m² 10m 10d Aug 14]
big, rangy gelding: modest performer: won seller at Wolverhampton in January and
amateur handicap at Doncaster in June (final start for N. Littmoden): ran creditably
after only when placed: effective at 1m to 1½m: acts on fibresand and firm ground,
seemingly not on softer than good: blinkered (below form) 3 times: usually held up.
C. N. Kellett

BURN PARK 2 ch.f. (Apr 23) Fraam 114 – Dewberry 68 (Bay Express 132) [1999 **54**
5.1s* 5m⁶ 6m 7s Oct 1] 1,400Y: half-sister to several winners, including 1994 2-y-o
5f winner Loganberry (by Lugana Beach) and 9f and 1¼m winner Bobby On The
Bank (by Monsanto): dam 6f winner: modest performer: won seller at Nottingham in
April: best effort when sixth in minor event at Salisbury next time: off course 3 then
2 months before well held last 2 starts: should stay at least 7f. *B. R. Millman*

BURTONS FOLLY 3 b.c. Casteddu 111 – Nelliellamay (Super Splash (USA) **38**
106) [1998 41: 7.6f 7d⁶ 8m a8g³ 1999 a10g⁶ a8g³ a12g⁵ a12g⁶ Feb 23] smallish,
sturdy colt: poor maiden: stays 1¼m: acts on all-weather: blinkered (raced too freely)
final start: hurdling with J. O'Connor in Ireland. *R. Ingram*

BURUNDI (IRE) 5 b.g. Danehill (USA) 126 – Sofala 103 (Home Guard (USA) **70**
129) [1998 74: 10g² 14s² 14m⁴ 14.4d⁵ 15.9g 14.6d² 1999 11.9s⁴ 12d³ Oct 9] tall
gelding: fair handicapper: respectable efforts over barely adequate trip in 1999, reportedly lame second one: stays 2m: acts on firm ground, soft and fibresand: visored
once in 1997. *A. W. Carroll*

BUSHWHACKER 5 b.g. Green Desert (USA) 127 – Missed Again 84 (High **–**
Top 131) [1998 80: 7v² 6g 1999 7s 8v 10.2g 11.8g May 31] good-topped geld-
ing: lightly raced: little form in 1999: should stay 1m: blinkered last 2 starts.
C. R. Egerton

BUSINESS WOMAN 3 b.f. Primo Dominie 121 – Golden Cay (Habitat 134) **–**
[1998 –: a6g 5g 6g 1999 a5g⁶ 5d Apr 21] good-topped filly: little sign of ability.
M. W. Easterby

BUSTLING RIO (IRE) 3 b.g. Up And At 'em 109 – Une Venitienne (FR) **73**
(Green Dancer (USA) 132) [1998 –: a7g 6m a5g 1999 a8g⁴ a8.5g³ a11g* a11g* 12g*
14.1f⁴ a14.8g³ a12g⁴ a14g² a16g* Nov 15] good-topped gelding: fair handicapper:
won at Southwell in February and November and at Pontefract in May: stays 2m: acts
on fibresand, best turf effort on good going: has wandered, and not the easiest of
rides: consistent. *P. C. Haslam*

BUSTOPHER JONES 5 b.g. Robellino (USA) 127 – Catkin (USA) (Sir Ivor **57**
135) [1998 51: a11g* 1999 14.1g³ Aug 12] big, strong gelding: modest handicapper:
lightly raced: good third at Salisbury, only outing in 1999: stays 1¾m. *C. R. Egerton*

BUSY BUSY BEE 2 gr.f. (May 11) Batshoof 122 – Rectitude 99 (Runnymede **–**
123) [1999 6.8m 7m a7g² Aug 14] 7,500Y: half-sister to numerous winners, includ- **a59 ?**
ing 1993 2-y-o sprinter Nightitude (by Night Shift), who became untrustworthy, and
middle-distance stayer Farmer's Pet (by Sharrood), both fairly useful: dam 7f (at 2
yrs) to 8.5f winner: 66/1, form in maidens only when second of 9 in Dance In Tune
at Wolverhampton, staying on past beaten rivals in strongly-run contest and almost
certainly flattered: will stay at least 1m. *N. P. Littmoden*

BUSY GUNNER   2 ch.f. (Feb 28) Gunner B 126 – Bustle'em (IRE) 63 (Burslem   –
123) [1999 7d⁶ 6m Sep 3] first foal: dam 1m winner: well beaten in maiden and
claimer. *D. McCain*

BUSY JACQ (IRE)   2 b.f. (Feb 17) Petardia 113 – Saga's Humour 61 (Bustino   –
136) [1999 a6g 7g Jun 10] 3,600Y: half-sister to several winners, including fairly
useful 1991 2-y-o 5f winner Atmospheric Blues (by Double Schwartz), later successful in Italy, and 1m (at 2 yrs) and 1¼m winner First Bite (by Be My Native): dam best
at 6f: last in sellers. *C. N. Allen*

BUSY LIZZIE (IRE)   2 b.f. (Mar 23) Sadler's Wells (USA) 132 – Impatiente   **– p**
(USA) (Vaguely Noble 140) [1999 7d 8d Oct 22] 60,000Y: rangy filly: fifth
foal: sister to 4-y-o Eminence Grise and half-sister to winners abroad by Storm Cat
and Theatrical: dam, French maiden, daughter of US Grade 1 9f and 1¼m winner
Sangue: well held in maidens at Leicester and Doncaster: should stay at least 1½m:
sort to do much better. *J. L. Dunlop*

BUTRINTO   5 ch.g. Anshan 119 – Bay Bay 101 (Bay Express 132) [1998 79: 6d   **a76**
5v 6m* 6g 7f 6m⁵ 6f 7f 6g 6.1v⁶ a7g² a6g⁵ a7g* a7g 1999 a7g a7g a8f² a7g⁵ a8g 6.1s
6g 6s 8g 6g 7d a8g Nov 8] tall, stocky gelding: good mover: fair handicapper on
all-weather, no form in 1999 on turf: tried blinkered/visored: often races up with
pace. *J. Pearce*

BUTTERSCOTCH   3 b.g. Aragon 118 – Gwiffina 87 (Welsh Saint 126) [1998   **66**
60: 7m 6m 7.5m³ 7.9g 6v 1999 8g 7.5m⁴ 9.9g⁴ 9.9g 10g⁴ 11m³ 10f³ 12m⁶ 8.3m 9.9g²
10.4f 10.9d Sep 16] close-coupled, sparely-made gelding: fair maiden: may prove
best around 1¼m: acts on any going: none too consistent. *J. L. Eyre*

BUXTED'S FIRST   2 gr.f. (Mar 14) Mystiko (USA) 124 – Sea Fairy 64 (Wollow   **– p**
132) [1999 6g 6d Nov 4] 3,000Y: half-sister to several winners, including 3-y-o Ones
Enough and 7f/1m winner Leviathan Mystery (by Elegant Air): dam, 2-y-o 6f
winner, later successful in Spain: signs of ability in maidens at Lingfield (travelled
well to halfway) and Windsor (not given hard time): will probably stay 1m: probably
capable of better. *G. L. Moore*

BUYERS DREAM (IRE)   9 b.g. Adonijah 126 – Twist And Shout (Cure The   –
Blues (USA)) [1998 NR 1999 10.1m⁶ 13.8m⁴ Jul 21] first foal: dam no promise:
modest winning handicap chaser: well beaten in maidens on Flat. *B. Ellison*

BUYING A DREAM (IRE)   2 ch.g. (Apr 7) Prince of Birds (USA) 121 – Carta-   **74 +**
gena Lady (IRE) (Prince Rupert (FR) 121) [1999 5m 7m* 6m² 7f⁴ Jul 23] IR 13,000F,
IR 11,000Y: lengthy, quite good-topped gelding: third foal: dam (unraced) from
family of Sonic Lady: fair form: won maiden at Thirsk in June: improved again when
second of 4 in minor event at Pontefract: gave impression something amiss final start:
stays 7f. *Andrew Turnell*

BUY OR SELL (IRE)   2 b.c. (Apr 15) Brief Truce (USA) 126 – Repetitious 103   **95**
(Northfields (USA)) [1999 6.1m² 5m* 7f² 6m² 6d⁴ 5g* 5m⁶ Sep 11] 30,000F,
14,000Y, 26,000 2-y-o: lengthy colt: brother to useful 1m winner Brief Escapade and
half-brother to several winners, including 3-y-o Indian Lodge and very smart French
middle-distance performer Sarhoob (by Alydar): dam won Stewards' Cup and later
stakes-placed winner in USA: useful performer: won maiden at Pontefract, minor
event at Ripon (made all) and listed race at York (turned out quickly, by head from
Alfailak, unable to make running but responding gamely to lead near finish), all in
the summer: creditable sixth to Mrs P in Flying Childers at Doncaster final start:
effective at 5f/6f: acts on good to firm and good to soft going: sent to UAE.
T. D. Easterby

BUZZ   4 b.g. Anshan 119 – Ryewater Dream 72 (Touching Wood (USA) 127) [1998   –
89: 6s⁶ 6d² 7g 6g⁵ 6d⁵ 7s³ 9.2d² 9g* 11.9g 10g 11.9g² 1999 8.1s 10.4g Oct 6] leggy
gelding: fairly useful handicapper at 3 yrs for C. Thornton: no show in 1999: should
stay beyond 9f: raced almost entirely on good going or softer. *J. J. O'Neill*

BUZZING (IRE)   4 ch.g. Ballad Rock 122 – Buzzing Around (Prince Bee 128)   –
[1998 62: 7d⁶ 7v⁵ 6g⁴ 6s⁵ 1999 6g 5.3f Apr 29] workmanlike gelding: modest maiden
at 3 yrs: no show in 1999, including in claimer: stays 7f: acts on good to soft ground.
R. Hannon

BUZZ THE AGENT 4 b.g. Prince Sabo 123 – Chess Mistress (USA) 59 (Run **43**
The Gantlet (USA)) [1998 62: 10v 6g 6g 8.5g² 9.9g³ 12.3g 12m² 9.9m 12m* 12g
11.9g 10s 1999 12g 12.3m⁵ 10g⁶ 12.4m⁴ 12m 12g⁴ 11m⁵ 9.9s³ Sep 21] good-topped
gelding: poor handicapper: stays 1½m: acts on good to firm and soft going: blinkered: tongue tied final 3 starts: possibly best forcing pace. *M. W. Easterby*

B W LEADER 2 b.g. (Mar 28) Owington 123 – Showery 76 (Rainbow Quest **51**
(USA) 134) [1999 5d Apr 27] first foal: dam 6f winner out of useful sprinter
Anodyne: weak in market and green when tenth of 16 in maiden at Windsor: sold 650
gns in November, joined H. Collingridge. *P. F. I. Cole*

BY THE GLASS 3 b.g. Ardkinglass 114 – Mia Fillia 65 (Formidable (USA) 125) **–**
[1998 72: a5g⁵ 5g* 6d⁴ 6m³ 6g⁵ 7m⁶ 8m 7d 1999 7d 6.1s 7s 8m 7.1d 8.2f⁶ 8g 8f 8m
7m⁶ 10g 6s Oct 4] close-coupled gelding: little form in 1999, leaving N. Tinkler after
seventh start: tried blinkered/visored. *Don Enrico Incisa*

BYZANTIUM 5 b.g. Shirley Heights 130 – Dulceata (IRE) (Rousillon (USA) **75**
133) [1998 –, a81: 8m 10m 12m 12g 8s a10g³ a10g* a10g* a9.4g² 1999 a10f³ 10.8m⁴
10s 10m⁵ 8.3m³ 8.3m² 9m⁴ 8.3m* 8g² 7.9m³ 8v⁵ 8.2d Oct 21] good-bodied gelding:
fair handicapper: won at Windsor in August: good efforts next 2 starts only: effective
at 1m to 1¼m: acts on good to firm going (possibly not on softer than good) and
all-weather: effective visored or not: takes good hold. *M. J. Fetherston-Godley*

C

CABALLERO 3 b.c. Cadeaux Genereux 131 – On Tiptoes 107 (Shareef Dancer **109**
(USA) 135) [1998 98: 6g⁴ 6m² 6d 6f* 6d 5m⁴ 1999 7g⁶ 5m 6g³ 6m 7d² 7d* 7.3m² 7m
7g² 7.3d Sep 19] strong, good-topped colt: useful performer: won minor event at
Yarmouth in July: good second in listed race at Epsom (beaten neck length behind Cybinka),
minor event at Newbury (to Teapot Row) and rated stakes at Goodwood (beaten neck
by Granny's Pet): stays 7.3f: acts on firm and good to soft going. *C. E. Brittain*

CABALLE (USA) 2 ch.f. (Apr 21) Opening Verse (USA) 126 – Attirance (FR) **84 p**
(Crowned Prince (USA) 128) [1999 8d² Oct 22] 35,000Y: rangy, good sort: has
plenty of scope: useful good walker: half-sister to several winners, including useful Irish 6f
(at 2 yrs) and 1m winner Attractive Crown (by Chief's Crown): dam French listed
1m winner: well-backed 13/2-shot, shaped well when ¾-length second of 18 to
Interlude in maiden at Doncaster, staying on strongly after racing freely early on: will
stay at least 1¼m: sure to improve and win a race. *S. P. C. Woods*

CABARET QUEST 3 ch.g. Pursuit of Love 124 – Cabaret Artiste (Shareef **69**
Dancer (USA) 135) [1998 66p: 7.3g 7m 6m 1999 8.3m 10.2s 8m* 8.1m³ 10m⁶ Jun
14] fair performer: won claimer at Leicester in May: should stay 1¼m: acts on good
to firm ground, well beaten on soft: sold 6,000 gns in August. *R. Hannon*

CABBAGE CRUSADER 3 b.f. Mon Tresor 113 – Edith Piaf 70 (Thatch (USA) **–**
136) [1998 –: 5g 5.7v 1999 7v Apr 20] no form in maidens/seller. *P. L. Gilligan*

CABCHARGE BLUE 7 b.m. Midyan (USA) 124 – Mashobra 75 (Vision **52**
(USA)) [1998 52, a33: a8g³ a12g 9.9s² 8.3d² 8.3d⁶ 10.1f⁶ 8m 8.3m⁶ 8d 11.1m² 10g **a–**
a13g 1999 9.7v⁴ 11.7s⁵ 11.9f* 10.2g⁵ 11.8m² 14m 14m 10f⁴ 12g 11.9m 14.1v Sep
29] angular mare: modest handicapper on turf, poor on all-weather: won at Brighton
in May: below form after next 2 starts: stays 1½m: acts on firm ground, soft and
fibresand: tends to hang and get behind: inconsistent. *T. J. Naughton*

CABCHARGE GLORY 5 ch.m. Executive Man 119 – Clipsall 57 (Petitioner **–**
83) [1998 45: a13g³ a12g⁴ a16g a16g a14g 1999 a12g⁵ a13g⁶ Feb 6] poor maiden at
best: stays 13f: acts on equitrack: visored once. *T. T. Clement*

CABLE MEDIA GIRL (IRE) 3 b.f. River Falls 113 – Brass Button (IRE) (Fools **–**
Holme (USA)) [1998 –: 6m 7v 7d 1999 a10g Feb 27] unfurnished filly: little sign of
ability. *S. E. Kettlewell*

CABRIAC 2 b. or br.c. (Jan 19) Machiavellian (USA) 123 – Chief Bee 89 (Chief's **86 p**
Crown (USA)) [1999 7m² 7d Sep 28] 70,000Y: first foal: dam, 9f to 14.6f winner,
sister to very smart 1989 2-y-o Be My Chief, from very good family: well-backed

favourite, short-headed by Merry Merlin (pair clear) in 16-runner maiden at Newmarket, making most: only ninth of 17 in valuable sales event there month later: will be suited by 1¼m+: should still do better. *J. L. Dunlop*

CACHUCHA (USA) 3 ch.f. Diesis 133 – Baffling Ballerina (USA) (Northern Dancer) [1998 NR 1999 9.9m⁵ 10m 10m⁴ 10d³ Jul 6] $20,000Y: tall, sparely-made filly: fourth foal: half-sister to French 9f (at 2 yrs) to 11.5f winner Truth Or Die (by Proud Truth): dam, won twice in USA, out of 1000 Guineas and Oaks winner Mysterious: fair maiden: stays 1¼m. *P. W. Harris* **72**

CACOPHONY 2 b.g. (Apr 21) Son Pardo 107 – Ansellady 67 (Absalom 128) [1999 5g 5m a6g 6m⁴ 6.1m⁶ 5m a7g³ a7g a6g³ a6g³ Dec 27] 5,000F, 6,200Y: second foal: half-brother to 3-y-o Melody Lady: dam 6f winner: modest maiden: effective at 6f/7f: acts on all-weather: tried blinkered: sometimes slowly away. *S. Dow* **54**

CADEAUX CHER 5 ch.g. Cadeaux Genereux 131 – Home Truth 98 (Known Fact (USA) 135) [1998 101: 6d 6d 6m⁵ 6m⁵ 5.1g 7d 6m⁶ 6g* 6m* 6m* 6f 6g 5.6g* 6s 6g 5m 1999 6m 6s 6m⁶ 6s 6f 6d 6g 6.1g 6d 6.1f¹⁴ 6d Nov 1] lengthy gelding: unimpressive mover: only fairly useful handicapper in 1999: generally below form last 6 starts: best around 6f: acts on good to firm going: tried blinkered in 1998: wears bandages: sometimes hangs left, including penultimate start: held up. *B. W. Hills* **91 d**

CADIE 3 b.f. St Ninian 104 – Lucky Lena (Leander 119) [1998 NR 1999 10d Oct 11] third foal: dam of little account: tailed off in seller. *B. D. Leavy* **–**

CADILLA 2 ch.f. (Apr 27) Cadeaux Genereux 131 – Tahilla 112 (Moorestyle 137) [1999 6.1m 7g⁶ 7d 7s Oct 25] smallish, leggy filly: half-sister to several winners, including sprinter Pluck and 7f winner Self Reliance (both by Never So Bold): dam, best at 1m, half-sister to very smart sprinter Piccolo: modest maiden: likely to prove best at 6f/7f. *E. A. L. Dunlop* **58**

CADMAX (IRE) 4 b.g. Second Set (IRE) 127 – Stella Ann (Ahonoora 122) [1998 48: 11.1v³ 8g 8.1m 8m 12d 12d² 12.4v³ 1999 11.8s 10.1m May 26] leggy, workmanlike gelding: poor maiden handicapper: no form in 1999. *K. R. Burke* **–**

CADMUS (IRE) 3 ch.g. Shalford (IRE) 124§ – Candle Hill (Sallust 134) [1998 NR 1999 a6g a7f a6g 6v⁶ 8d 6m 6m 6g a6g 8m 10g Aug 21] IR 10,500F, 18,500Y: half-brother to winners in Belgium (by Indian King) and Hong Kong (by Bob Back): dam Irish 6f winner: of little account: joined S. Clark. *D. W. Chapman* **–**

CA'D'ORO 6 ch.g. Cadeaux Genereux 131 – Palace Street (USA) 103 (Secreto (USA) 128) [1998 72: 6v³ 8g³ 7g 8m 8.3m 8.1g 8d 7d² 7.1d³ 7.1g² 7g 8d² 8.2v* 8d 1999 8v² 8g 7.1d 6g 7s² 7g 8v⁶ 7.1s 7s² 7d 8s Nov 6] small gelding: fair handicapper: won at Kempton in August: good second of 25 at Newbury, best effort after: effective at 6f (given a thorough test) to 1m: probably best on good going or softer: usually comes from off pace: none too consistent. *G. B. Balding* **78**

CADW (IRE) 4 b.g. Cadeaux Genereux 131 – Night Jar 102 (Night Shift (USA)) [1998 75: 6d 8g⁴ 8.2v⁴ 8d 1999 7v 7m 7m⁷ 8.2m Jun 16] fair maiden: third in handicap at Newbury, only creditable run in 1999: stays 1m: acts on any going: sold 10,500 gns in October. *I. A. Balding* **69**

CAERAU 3 ch.f. Nashwan (USA) 135 – Charming Life 88 (Habitat 134) [1998 NR 1999 10.2m⁵ 10.4g* 10.1d* 10.5d Nov 11] 45,000F, 110,000Y: half-sister to smart French 5f (at 2 yrs) to 1m winner Run And Gun (by Lomond), 8.2f winner Saddle Bow (by Sadler's Wells) and winners in Japan by Green Desert and Lomond: dam 7f winner from very good family: progressive form: won 5-runner maiden at York and 7-runner minor event at Yarmouth in October: ran well when 5 lengths eighth of 12 to Neptune's Bride in Prix Fille de l'Air at Toulouse final start: will stay 1½m: already useful and may do better yet. *H. R. A. Cecil* **99**

CAERDYDD FACH 3 b.f. Bluebird (USA) 125 – Waitingformargaret 78 (Kris 135) [1998 53?: 5.7g 6m³ 6.1g⁵ 7f 8g⁶ 8g 7.1s a7g 1999 a11g⁵ a9.4g⁶ a10g 8g 8d⁵ 8.2f 8d⁴ 10.1g⁴ 11f⁶ 8.1d⁵ 10.1g Aug 19] small filly: good mover: poor maiden: probably stays 1¼m: acts on soft going, probably on firm (no form on all-weather). *J. A. Gilbert* **40**

CAERLESS (IRE) 3 b.f. Caerleon (USA) 132 – Barger (USA) (Riverman (USA) 131) [1998 NR 1999 10.2d⁵ 10d⁵ 11.7f* 12.3d⁵ 11.8d⁴ 12d⁴ Oct 29] fifth live foal: **77**

half-sister to Baya (by Nureyev), smart performer around 1¼m in France: dam, sister to Triptych, smart winner around 1¼m in France: fair performer: won 4-runner maiden at Bath in June: not discredited in handicaps after: stays 1½m: acts on firm going and good to soft: flashed tail under pressure on fourth start. *L. M. Cumani*

CAERNARFON BAY (IRE)   4 ch.g. Royal Academy (USA) 130 – Bay Shade (USA) 90 (Sharpen Up 127) [1998 68d: a9.4g² 11.1d 12s a8g⁵ 8g 10g⁵ 12d³ 8v 1999 a10g⁴ a10g* a12g³ a12g⁵ a12g³ 11.9f* 10f² 12d 11.5m² 12g⁶ a10g² a10g Dec 18] tall, leggy gelding: modest handicapper: won at Lingfield (amateurs) in January and Brighton in April: stays 1½m: acts on firm ground, good to soft and all-weather: blinkered twice in 1998: consistent. *G. L. Moore*   **55 a60**

CAEROSA   4 b.f. Caerleon (USA) 132 – Famosa (Dancing Brave (USA) 140) [1998 70d: 7.5m⁴ 8g⁵ 7.5d 10m 6.9d 8.5m 7d 1999 12.3m⁵ 9.9g a10g⁵ 10g² 12g² 10s 12g⁵ 13.1g² 12.3m³ 10.5m a12g³ 14.1m⁴ 11.5f³ 11.1m* 11m³ 11.9m⁶ 10m² 9.9s⁵ 11.9d* 10v² 11.7s* 12g⁵ a12g⁴ a12g a16.2g Dec 4] angular filly: fair handicapper on turf, poor on all-weather: won at Hamilton in August then at York (apprentices) and Bath in October: effective at 1¼m to 13f: acts on any turf going: visored/blinkered: sometimes slowly away. *M. Johnston*   **70 a47**

CAFE OPERA (USA)   2 b.f. (Jan 17) Sadler's Wells (USA) 132 – Takreem (USA) 77 (Mr Prospector (USA)) [1999 7s⁴ 7m² Sep 2] $90,000F, 40,000Y: first foal: dam, disappointing maiden who stayed 7f, from family of Singspiel: fair form in maidens at Kempton and Salisbury, second of 10 to Dancing Mirage on second occasion: will stay at least 1m. *J. W. Hills*   **76**

CAFFE LATTE (IRE)   3 b.f. Seattle Dancer (USA) 119 – Debbie's Next (USA) 82 (Arctic Tern (USA) 126) [1998 NR 1999 9s² 8g* 10d* 8f² 9f 10f² 11g⁴ Nov 6] ex-French-trained filly: fifth foal: half-sister to 3 winners, including 1m winner Nordinex (by Nordico) and French middle-distance winner Debbie's Law (by Law Society): dam minor winner who stayed 1m: won minor event at Chantilly in May and listed race at Maisons-Laffitte (final start for N. Clement) in June: smart form in USA after, in frame in Grade 2 at Del Mar in July, Yellow Ribbon at Santa Anita (1¼ lengths second to Spanish Fern) in October and Breeders' Cup Filly & Mare Turf at Gulfstream (length fourth to Soaring Softly): stays 11f: acts on firm and good to soft going: comes from well off pace. *J. C. Canani, USA*   **118**

CAIRN DHU   5 ch.g. Presidium 124 – My Precious Daisy (Sharpo 132) [1998 –: a6g⁵ 5g 6m 7m 1999 6d a7g² a6g Dec 17] robust gelding: poor performer nowadays: stays 7f: acts on equitrack: tried blinkered. *D. W. Barker*   **37**

CAIR PARAVEL (IRE)   2 b. or br.c. (Mar 2) Dolphin Street (FR) 125 – Queen's Ransom (IRE) 70 (Last Tycoon 131) [1999 5m⁵ 6s* Jun 27] IR 65,000F, IR 70,000Y: first foal: dam 2-y-o 7f winner from very good family: won 16-runner maiden at Leicester (beat Commonwood by ½ length) and 2-runner minor event at Doncaster (beat Cautionary by same margin, though appeared to idle in front and probably value 3 lengths) in June, drifting left each time: looked open to improvement, but not seen out again. *R. Hannon*   **83**

CAITANO   5 b.h. Niniski (USA) 125 – Eversince (USA) (Foolish Pleasure (USA)) [1998 125: 12m 12g³ 12s² 12d⁵ 12f 12f 12m⁴ 1999 12m³ 11s* 11m* Jun 27] tall, angular horse: high-class performer at best: won 5-runner Grosser Preis der Baden-Airpark at Baden-Baden (by ½ length from Tiger Hill, who gave 6lb) and Idee Hansa-Preis (easy task, by 8 lengths from Prince of Denial) at Hamburg in June: suffered foot injury and not seen out again: stays 1½m: acts on good to firm and heavy going: blinkered last 4 starts: has been slowly away: has found little, including when 6 lengths third to Fruits of Love in Dubai Turf Classic at Nad Al Sheba on reappearance: reportedly stays in training. *A. Schutz, Germany*   **122**

CAJOLE (IRE)   3 ch.f. Barathea (IRE) 127 – Frendly Persuasion (General Assembly (USA)) [1998 NR 1999 8.3m⁶ 8s 10m 10g 8m 7m² Sep 7] 80,000Y, 8,000 2-y-o: tall, useful-looking filly: has a quick action: third foal: half-sister to fairly useful 1¼m winner Anemos (by Be My Guest) and Irish 1½m winner Friendly Bird (by Bluebird): dam fairly useful up to 1½m in Ireland: fair maiden: best effort on final start, carrying head awkwardly: bred to stay beyond 7f: acts on good to firm going. *R. F. Johnson Houghton*   **72**

CAKEBREAD CELLAR   2 b.g. (Mar 3) Piccolo 121 – Little Bittern (USA) 73   –
(Riva Ridge (USA)) [1999 6m Sep 18] 12,000Y: tall, sturdy gelding: half-brother to
3 winners abroad, including Italian 3-y-o My Pretty Love (by Batshoof), 7f winner at
2 yrs: dam maiden who should have stayed 1m, from family of Miswaki: very green
when soundly beaten in Newbury maiden: sold 2,500 gns. *J. M. P. Eustace*

CALAMA (IRE)   2 b.f. (Apr 10) Desert Style (IRE) 121 – Popcorn (Pharly (FR)   **43**
130) [1999 5.7d 6g 5.7s⁴ Oct 26] IR 1,100F, IR 4,000Y: second foal: dam ran twice:
poor form in maidens/seller: carried head awkwardly final start: dead. *P. G. Murphy*

CALANDO (USA)   3 b.f. Storm Cat (USA) – Diminuendo (USA) 126 (Diesis 133)   **110**
[1998 110: 5s⁵ 7m* 8d* 8s² 1999 8m³ 10.5d 10m³ 11.9g 10g² Sep 25] small, leggy,
close-coupled filly: smart performer: made creditably all starts in 1999, including when
2½ lengths third to Valentine Waltz in Poule d'Essai des Pouliches at Longchamp,
close third to Polaire in Pretty Polly Stakes at the Curragh and 2¾ lengths second
behind Zomaradah in Premio Lydia Tesio at Rome: barely stays 1½m: acts on soft
going and on good to firm: races close to pace. *Saeed bin Suroor*

CALANDRELLA   6 b.m. Sizzling Melody 117 – Maravilla 73 (Mandrake Major   **49**
122) [1998 39, a–: a7g a6g 6s 5.1v³ 5.1s⁴ 6g⁶ 5m 5.3m a5g 5.1d⁵ 1999 a6g 5m³   **a–**
5g² 6.8m⁴ 5f 6m² 5d 5g* 5g⁵ 5.1m 6.1m Sep 13] modest handicapper: won maiden
event at Musselburgh in August: best at 5f/6f: acts on heavy and good to firm going:
often claimer ridden: none too consistent. *A. G. Newcombe*

CALCAVELLA   3 b.f. Pursuit of Love 124 – Brightside (IRE) 99 (Last Tycoon   **70**
131) [1998 75+: 6m³ 6d 5g² 6g² 1999 6d 6g 7s Oct 22] workmanlike filly: fair
maiden: form in 1999 only on second start: should be suited by 7f/1m. *M. Kettle*

CALCUTTA   3 b.c. Indian Ridge 123 – Echoing 93 (Formidable (USA) 125) [1998   **108**
80: 5d³ 6g³ 6d* 1999 7g³ 7d⁴ 7g 8m 8f* 8m² 7.9g² 8m* 10s 8d⁶ Oct 30] smallish,
sturdy colt: useful handicapper: improved greatly at 3 yrs and won at Newmarket in
July and Doncaster (heavily-backed favourite, easily best effort when beating Indian
Lodge by 2 lengths) in September: below form last 2 starts: effective at 7f/1m (when
conditions aren't testing): acts on firm and good to soft ground: held up, and has good
turn of foot: reliable. *B. W. Hills*

CALCUTTA KING   3 ch.g. Democratic (USA) 101 – Calcutta Queen 51 (Night   –
Shift (USA)) [1998 –: 5g 7.1d 7m 1999 7.5m 7m 6f 5f Aug 2] small, stocky gelding:
no form, including in sellers: tried visored. *W. Storey*

CALDEY ISLAND (IRE)   2 b.c. (Apr 9) Turtle Island (IRE) 123 – Lady Taufan   **68**
(IRE) (Taufan (USA) 119) [1999 5v 6.1m⁴ 6m⁶ 6.1m³ 7m 6m³ 7m⁵ 6m⁶ 6s a6g
Oct 18] 30,000Y: rather leggy colt: fourth foal: half-brother to useful 1996 2-y-o
6f winner Speedball (by Waajib) and 1997 2-y-o 5f winner Golden Strategy (by
Statoblest): dam, Irish maiden: fair maiden: consistent until well beaten
last 2 starts, visored second occasion: stays 7f: acts on good to firm ground: sold
5,600 gns. *D. W. P. Arbuthnot*

CALEB'S BOY   2 b.c. (May 11) Son Pardo 107 – Lon Isa 80 (Grey Desire 115)   –
[1999 7.7d 7.9g Oct 6] good-bodied colt: second foal: half-brother to 3-y-o Lemon
Strip: dam, maiden who stayed 1½m, half-sister to useful middle-distance performer
Naked Welcome: well beaten in maidens. *B. Palling*

CALEDONIAN EXPRESS   4 b.f. Northern Park (USA) 107 – New Edition 72   –
(Great Nephew 126) [1998 66: 9d 9.7m³ 10g 1999 a12g⁶ 10s Nov 1] rangy filly: fair
maiden handicapper for J. Dunlop at 3 yrs: well held in 1999: stays 1¼m: acts on
good to firm going, probably on good to soft. *J. R. Best*

CALICO   2 b.f. (Apr 26) Barathea (IRE) 127 – Craigmill 85 (Slip Anchor 136)   **65**
[1999 7m 7m* 7.7g⁵ 8d Sep 23] 27,000Y: smallish, leggy, close-coupled filly: first
foal: dam, 2-y-o 7f winner (bred to stay well), half-sister to smart middle-distance
stayers Applecross (dam of Invermark and Craigsteel) and Coigach: fair maiden, best
effort penultimate start: will be suited by 1¼m+. *J. G. Smyth-Osbourne*

CALICO LADY   3 ch.f. First Trump 118 – Cottonwood 80 (Teenoso (USA) 135)   **58 ?**
[1998 64d: 5d⁶ 5g⁴ 5s² 5v⁶ 6g 6g 6d 7d 6d⁵ 7.1g 1999 7d³ 8g 12.1s⁶ 9.2d 8g 9.2f
12.5s⁶ Oct 28] small filly: modest maiden on Flat: left W. Kemp after sixth start:
seems to stay 1½m: acts on soft going: ran poorly in blinkers fifth outing: fair form
over hurdles late in year. *M. Hourigan, Ireland*

CALIFORNIA SON (IRE) 3 ch.g. Lycius (USA) 124 – Madame Nureyev **40** (USA) (Nureyev (USA) 131) [1998 NR 1999 8m 9.9m⁵ 10g² 10d Oct 11] sixth foal: brother to Miss Universal, useful maiden here and later Grade 3 11f winner in USA, and half-brother to 3 winners, including fairly useful 1¼m winner Cloak of Darkness (by Thatching): dam French 2-y-o 6f winner: trained by P. Cole, reportedly unsound after debut: poor form at best in maiden/claimer/seller after: sold 500 gns, joined Miss A. Stokell. *M. Quinn*

CALIWAG (IRE) 3 b.g. Lahib (USA) 129 – Mitsubishi Style (Try My Best (USA) **76** 130) [1998 NR 1999 6m⁴ 7m⁶ 8f⁵ 7g Jun 8] IR 16,000Y: sixth living foal: half-brother to Italian 5f to 7f winner (including at 2 yrs) Golden Center (by Brief Truce) and fairly useful Irish 1992 2-y-o 5f winner Preponderance (by Cyrano de Bergerac): dam third at 1m in Ireland: fair maiden: stays 1m. *D. R. C. Elsworth*

CALKO 2 ch.g. (Mar 24) Timeless Times (USA) 99 – Jeethgaya (USA) 61 (Critique **59** (USA) 126) [1999 6g 5m³ 5g 6s 6d⁶ 5g³ a6g* a6g⁵ Dec 10] 1,200Y: sturdy gelding: fourth reported foal: half-brother to 3-y-o Kocal: dam, maiden, best around 1¼m, from very good family: modest performer: won seller at Southwell in November: effective at 5f/6f: acts on good to firm going and fibresand: blinkered last 3 starts. *T. D. Barron*

CALLAS 2 b.f. (Apr 2) Mtoto 134 – Ower (IRE) 71 (Lomond (USA) 128) [1999 **72 p** 7d 8d⁴ Oct 21] 5,000Y: angular filly: fifth foal: closely related to 3-y-o Ruby Laser and half-sister to 4-y-o Borani: dam, 7f winner, half-sister to smart middle-distance colts Weigh Anchor and Dr Massini: fair form in maidens at Newbury (behind Scarteen Fox) and Brighton (travelled well long way) in the autumn: likely to prove suited by 1¼m+: open to further improvement. *R. F. Johnson Houghton*

CALLDAT SEVENTEEN 3 b.g. Komaite (USA) – Westminster Waltz (Dance **84** In Time (CAN)) [1998 –p: 7.9g 1999 a8g* 9g 8.5s* 7m 8.2m 7.1g³ 9m 7.1g 8.5m* 9.7d⁶ 10d³ 8.9d 10d⁴ a10g Nov 16] good-bodied gelding: fairly useful performer: won maiden at Lingfield in February, minor event at Epsom in April and handicap at Epsom in August: creditable efforts when in frame in handicaps otherwise: stays 1¼m: acts on good to firm going, soft and equitrack. *P. W. D'Arcy*

CALLING THE SHOTS 2 b.c. (May 6) Democratic (USA) 101 – Two Shots **46** (Dom Racine (FR) 121) [1999 7m 6s 6g Oct 14] half-brother to 1989 2-y-o 5f winner Two Toffs (by Another Realm): dam ran twice at 2 yrs: poor maiden. *W. Storey*

CALLITWHATYOUWANT 3 b.g. Weldnaas (USA) 112 – Alcassa (FR) **– §** (Satingo 129) [1998 60: 5d 5d² 5m² 5s⁵ 5g⁵ a6g⁶ 1999 a7g Jan 12] modest form at best: should stay 6f: looked none too keen both starts on all-weather: best treated with caution. *Jamie Poulton*

CALL ME LUCKY 3 b.f. Magic Ring (IRE) 115 – Lucky Message (USA) 71 **53** (Phone Trick (USA)) [1998 65: 5d⁵ 5g 5g 5g² 5g³ 6f* 6g 6m 6.1d 6m 1999 6.1s⁵ 6.1f⁴ 6g 6g Oct 14] small, leggy filly: modest performer: better at 5f than 7f: acts on firm going: inconsistent: sold 500 gns. *M. Brittain*

CALL MY GUEST (IRE) 9 b.g. Be My Guest (USA) 126 – Overcall (Bustino **26** 136) [1998 –: a12g a12g a16g 12.1g 1999 a12g a12f²¹ 11.9d⁶ Aug 6] fairly useful hurdler/poor at best on Flat nowadays: stays at least 1½m: acts on heavy going: tried blinkered at 2 yrs. *R. E. Peacock*

CALYS HALO 4 ch.g. Cigar 68 – My-Ninon (Grand Conde (FR) 90) [1998 NR **–** 1999 a8g⁵ 8.5s Apr 21] fifth foal: dam unraced half-sister to a useful 5f/6f winner: no form in maidens. *J. G. Smyth-Osbourne*

CAMAIR CRUSADER (IRE) 5 br.g. Jolly Jake (NZ) – Sigrid's Dream (USA) **–** (Triple Bend (USA)) [1998 NR 1999 11.1g³ 12.1s 10f 8.3m 12m 10.1d Oct 20] IR 2,400 4-y-o, resold 5,800 4-y-o: tall gelding: half-brother to 3 winners in USA: dam, won 3 races in USA, half-sister to US Grade 1 winner up to 1½m Interco: little sign of ability in maidens/handicaps. *W. McKeown*

CAMANOE (USA) 3 br.f. Gone West (USA) – Prodigious (FR) (Pharly (FR) **63** 130) [1998 NR 1999 8.3g⁶ 8.1m Jul 22] half-sister to several winners abroad, including very smart French 1¼m to 12.5f winner Public Purse (by Private Account) and US Grade 1 1¼m winner Super Staff (by Secretariat): dam French 1m and 1¼m winner: promising sixth in maiden at Windsor: reportedly found to have irregular heartbeat next time: stud. *H. R. A. Cecil*

CAMARADERIE 3 b.g. Most Welcome 131 – Secret Valentine 71 (Wollow 132) **60** [1998 NR 1999 7.1d⁶ 8m⁶ a6g⁵ 8m 9.9g 7.1f 12s³ 10.1d⁴ Oct 20] 5,000Y: leggy, workmanlike gelding: seventh foal: brother to useful 8-y-o Billy Bushwacker and half-brother to winning sprinters Gondo (by Mansingh) and 4-y-o Ithadtobeyou: dam 6f to 1m winner: modest maiden: creditable efforts in frame in handicaps: stays 1½m: acts on soft going: has been blanketed for stalls entry. *Mrs M. Reveley*

CAMBERLEY (IRE) 2 b.c. (Apr 16) Sri Pekan (USA) 117 – Nsx 74 (Roi Danzig **80 p** (USA)) [1999 7d⁶ 7d² Oct 15] rangy colt: has scope: good mover: second foal: dam 2-y-o 5f winner: shaped quite well at Newmarket in maiden and minor event (raced freely and travelled better than winner for long way when 3 lengths second of 4 to Adilabad) in the autumn: likely to prove best up to 1m: joined P. Cole: type to progress. *Miss Gay Kelleway*

CAMBRAI (IRE) 3 b.g. Indian Ridge 123 – Cambrel (IRE) 91 (Soviet Star **67** (USA) 128) [1998 74p: 8s 1999 8.3m 8.3s 7.1m Sep 4] fair maiden: below form after reappearance, in handicap final start: should stay beyond 1m: sent to UAE. *M. P. Tregoning*

CAMEO (IRE) 4 b.g. Statoblest 120 – Centella (IRE) (Thatching 131) [1998 56: **–** 5s 7v 6s 6g 5s⁴ 5d a6g² a6g⁵ a5g 5s 6m a5g 1999 a6g⁵ a6f⁵ a5g a6g⁴ a6g a5g* a5g **a54** a5g⁶ 5d 6s Apr 13] smallish, good-bodied gelding: poor mover: modest performer: won seller at Wolverhampton in March: effective at 5f/6f: acts on all-weather, best turf efforts on soft going: visored last 5 outings: often claimer ridden. *M. R. Channon*

CAMERON JACK 4 b.g. Elmaamul 125 – Ile de Reine 64 (Ile de Bour- **58 d** bon (USA) 133) [1998 61: 10.3d⁶ 10.1d 10g⁴ 9.9m⁴ 12m³ 11.9g 10.3d⁵ 1999 12.4m² 12g³ 12g 12m 10d 12m⁵ 10f⁵ Aug 7] tall, leggy, sparely-made gelding: modest maiden: below form after first 2 starts: should stay beyond 1½m: acts on good to firm going: visored last 2 starts: sold 6,600 gns. *J. D. Bethell*

CAMEROSA 3 b.c. Risk Me (FR) 127 – High Heather (Shirley Heights 130) **–** [1998 NR 1999 8s 8s a8.5g a7g Dec 4] 5,800 2-y-o: third foal: half-brother to 7f winner Arawa (by Doulab) and Swedish winner at up to 1m (including at 2 yrs) Watchman (by Mazaad): dam unraced: no show in maidens/claimers: tried blinkered. *A. G. Newcombe*

CAMPAIGN 8 b.g. Sure Blade (USA) 130 – Just Cause (Law Society (USA) 130) **51** [1998 NR 1999 16.1d⁶ 21.6d⁵ Apr 28] sturdy gelding: has markedly round action: useful staying hurdler: very lightly-raced on Flat, modest at best nowadays: probably stays 21f. *M. D. Hammond*

CAMPARI (IRE) 4 b.f. Distinctly North (USA) 115 – Foolish Flight (IRE) 57 **–** (Fools Holme (USA)) [1998 –: 10f 8d 8s⁴ a10g a7g 1999 9g 9.2v 9.9g Apr 22] sparely-made filly: fair maiden at 2 yrs, no form after: dead. *Mrs A. M. Naughton*

CAMP FIRE (IRE) 2 ch.f. (Mar 24) Lahib (USA) 129 – Smouldering (IRE) **81** (Caerleon (USA) 132) [1999 6.1f* 6.8m³ Jun 23] 12,000Y: third foal: half-sister to a 5f/6f winner in Italy by Cadeaux Genereux: dam once-raced half-sister to Irish 2000 Guineas winner Flash of Steel: won minor event at Nottingham in May: still green, better effort when third of 9 in similar event at Warwick following month, hanging under pressure. *R. Charlton*

CAMPIONE (IRE) 4 b.g. Common Grounds 118 – Kyrenia 75 (Zino 127) [1998 **–** –: 9.7d 7f 5.9d 6d 5g 9g a10f 1999 a7g 5.3f⁶ a6g a5g 7f Jul 22] tall, leggy gelding: little form: tried visored. *M. H. Tompkins*

CANADIAN APPROVAL (USA) 3 ch.f. With Approval (CAN) – A Taste For **79** Lace (USA) (Laomedonte (USA) 116) [1998 78: 7m⁵ 7.6f* 7g³ 8m³ 1999 8m 8g³ 8g 8m⁴ 8m⁴ 7g Aug 19] tall, sparely-made filly: fair handicapper: creditable efforts when in frame: will stay 1¼m: acts on firm ground, yet to race on softer than good: sold 11,000 gns in October. *P. W. Harris*

CANDELLINO 3 b.f. Robellino (USA) 127 – By Candlelight (IRE) 84 (Roi **45** Danzig (USA)) [1998 59?: 5f 6.1m 5g 7s 1999 6g⁶ 8.2s 7m 8.2m 10f May 28] leggy, sparely-made filly: poor maiden: carries head awkwardly: probably stays 1m: blinkered (well held) third start. *T. R. Watson*

CANDLERIGGS (IRE) 3 ch.g. Indian Ridge 123 – Ridge Pool (IRE) 74 (Blue- **90** bird (USA) 125) [1998 78p: 7g 6g⁵ 6g² 1999 6g* 6g⁶ 6d² 6d 6f⁵ Jul 11] smallish, sturdy, lengthy gelding: impresses in appearance: poor mover: fairly useful handicapper: won at Kempton in April: good second at Newbury in May: stays 6f: acts on good to soft ground. *E. A. L. Dunlop*

CANDLE SMILE (USA) 7 b.g. Pleasant Colony (USA) – Silent Turn (USA) **90** (Silent Cal (USA)) [1998 90: 18.7m 18d⁶ 1999 16m² 18.7m May 5] very big gelding: shows knee action: fairly useful handicapper, lightly raced nowadays: creditable second at Newbury on reappearance, reportedly struck into when well held in Chester Cup next time (bandaged front): stays 2½m: acts on firm and good to soft ground, yet to race on softer: probably best with strong handling and front-running tactics. *G. Barnett*

CANFORD (IRE) 2 b.c. (May 7) Caerleon (USA) 132 – Veronica (Persian Bold **80 p** 123) [1999 7d⁴ Oct 27] 45,000Y: fifth foal: closely related to 3-y-o Venetian Pearl and to 1m winner Dawam Allail (by Night Shift) and 1993 2-y-o 1m winner Truck-haven Secret (by Secreto): dam won at around 1m in USA: weak in market, 2 lengths fourth of 11 to Shaibani in maiden at Yarmouth, tracking leaders throughout: should stay at least 1¼m: looks sure to improve. *W. Jarvis*

CANNY 2 b.f. (Jan 23) Piccolo 121 – Shady Deed (USA) 80 (Shadeed (USA) 135) **49** [1999 6m 7.5g 6.8m 7m 6g 6s Sep 29] 5,000Y: first foal: dam 1m winner who stayed 1¼m: poor maiden: blinkered (slowly away and looked reluctant) final start: sold 600 gns. *C. E. Brittain*

CANNY CHIFTANE 3 b.g. Be My Chief (USA) 122 – Prudence 68 (Grundy **69** 137) [1998 NR 1999 11.5g⁴ 10d⁶ a9.4g⁶ 14.1m⁶ a12g³ a12g* 14s Sep 25] 6,000F, IR 32,000Y: close-coupled gelding: brother to a winner in Hong Kong and half-brother to several winners, including useful 8.5f and 1½m winner Heathyards Rock (by Rock City): dam middle-distance maiden: fair handicapper: won at Wolverhampton in September: probably stays 1¾m: acts on good to firm going and fibresand: joined J. I. A. Charlton. *M. A. Jarvis*

CANNY HILL 2 ch.g. (Mar 19) Bold Arrangement 127 – Jersey Maid 82 (On **63 ?** Your Mark 125) [1999 5d 7.1g⁶ a8g⁴ Dec 17] 1,200Y: brother to 3-y-o Bold Feliciter, and half-brother to 1996 2-y-o 5f winner Tazibari (by Barrys Gamble) and 1m winner Mai Pen Rai (by All Systems Go): dam 2-y-o 5f winner who stayed 7f: best effort in maidens (set pace, possibly flattered) when fourth of 14 to Elegant Escort at South-well: stays 1m: acts on fibresand. *D. Moffatt*

CANON CAN (USA) 6 ch.g. Green Dancer (USA) 132 – Lady Argyle (USA) **109** (Don B (USA)) [1998 117: 16.4g 20s⁵ 16d² 15.9f⁴ 18d³ 20d⁶ 1999 16.2d³ 16.4g⁶ 22.2m³ 16f⁵ 15.9m⁶ Aug 17] tall, good-topped gelding: fluent mover: smart performer at best: not quite so good in 1999, best effort when 3 lengths third to Celeric in Sagaro Stakes at Ascot on reappearance: below form after: stays 2¾m: acts on firm and good to soft going, probably on soft: visored final start: sold 34,000 gns, joined N. Meade in Ireland. *H. R. A. Cecil*

CANOVAS HEART 10 b.g. Balidar 133 – Worthy Venture 76 (Northfields **92** (USA)) [1998 92, a–: 5g⁵ 5f 5.2g⁵ 6.1g* 6g 5s 1999 6f⁴ 6g 6m⁶ 6m⁵ 6d 7d* Oct 9] **a–** neat gelding: has a quick action: fairly useful handicapper: best effort in 1999 when winning 24-runner race at York final start: stays 7f: acts on firm ground, soft and fibresand: usually races prominently: genuine. *Bob Jones*

CANTABELLA 4 b.f. Tragic Role (USA) – Bella Travaille 82 (Workboy 123) **–** [1998 NR 1999 a7g 8m May 3] half-sister to several winners, including 1m winner Buzzards Bellbuoy (by Buzzards Bay): dam, best at 2 yrs, won 3 times at 5f: no sign of ability in maidens. *H. J. Collingridge*

CANTA KE BRAVE (USA) 3 ch.g. River Special (USA) – Stubborn Star **101** (USA) (Star Choice (USA)) [1998 90p: 8.1m² 8m* 8s⁴ 1999 9m⁵ 8.5g⁶ 10.4d 8m 8f 9f* a9.4g³ 12m* 12d² 12d Oct 14] big, lengthy gelding: has a powerful, round action: useful handicapper: made all at Ripon and Goodwood in August: good second to Rada's Daughter at Newmarket penultimate start: free-going sort, but stays 1½m:

acts on firm going, soft and fibresand: front runner: sometimes early to post: sold 100,000 gns, joined J. Old and gelded. *S. P. C. Woods*

CANTGETYOURBREATH (IRE) 3 ch.g. College Chapel 122 – Cathy Garcia (IRE) (Be My Guest (USA) 126) [1998 65, a68+: 6m 6m³ 6m⁶ 6s² a6g³ a6g* a7g⁴ a6g⁶ a6f² 1999 a6g⁴ a6g a6g³ a6g⁴ a6g 6g a6g 7m a7g 7m 7m a6f a8.5g a7g⁵ a6g* Dec 17] lengthy, unfurnished gelding: fair performer at best: left B. Meehan after reappearance and Mrs N. Macauley after eleventh outing: won seller at Southwell in December: barely stays 7f: acts on all-weather, best turf effort (at 2 yrs) on soft ground: blinkered/visored: often races prominently. *B. P. J. Baugh* – **a66**

CANTINA 5 b.m. Tina's Pet 121 – Real Claire (Dreams To Reality (USA) 113) [1998 84: 7.6m*ᵈⁱˢ 7g 6g 7.6m* 6g³ 7.6g 7.6f* 7.6d³ 8g 6s 1999 7.6m⁶ 7d 7m 7m⁵ 6m⁶ 7f* 7.6m³ 7m 7.6d⁴ 7g⁵ 7.1m a7g² a7g Dec 29] leggy, good-topped mare: fairly useful performer: won amateur minor event at Redcar in July: needs further than 6f and stays 7.6f: acts on equitrack, firm and good to soft going: front runner: inconsistent. *A. Bailey* – **81**

CANTON VENTURE 7 ch.g. Arctic Tern (USA) 126 – Ski Michaela (USA) (Devil's Bag (USA)) [1998 –, a79: a12g³ 12g⁵ 1999 a14.8g⁶ 14.1g 16f 14.1m a16g⁴ a12g Oct 1] lengthy, angular gelding: formerly fairly useful handicapper: little form in 1999: probably stays 15f: acts on firm going (unraced on softer than good) and all-weather: tried blinkered and visored: races prominently/leads: joined A. Carroll. *S. P. C. Woods* –

CANYOUHEARME 3 b.f. Sabrehill (USA) 120 – Fiveofive (IRE) 61 (Fairy King (USA)) [1998 44: 7f⁶ 7m⁵ 7f 8g⁵ 6m⁵ a6f⁶ 1999 a8g Jan 1] poor maiden: seems to stay 1m: acts on firm going and equitrack. *N. A. Callaghan* –

CAPA 2 gr.c. (May 10) Salse (USA) 128 – Pippas Song 75 (Reference Point 139) [1999 8g² 8d² Sep 28] 70,000F, 85,000Y: lengthy, angular colt: third foal: half-brother to 3-y-o Piaf and useful 5f to 7f performer Nightbird (by Night Shift): dam, 1½m winner, daughter of Nassau Stakes winner Dancing Rocks: runner-up in September in maidens at Doncaster (beaten 3½ lengths by Shamrock City) and Newmarket (went down by 1¾ lengths to Peacock Jewel), caught flat-footed in steadily-run race on latter course: will be suited by 1¼m/1½m: likely to improve, and sure to win a race. *B. W. Hills* – **85 p**

CAPACOOSTIC 2 ch.f. (Mar 26) Savahra Sound 111 – Cocked Hat Girl 47 (Ballacashtal (CAN)) [1999 5g 6m a8g Dec 17] second foal: half-sister to 3-y-o Rex Is Okay: dam placed up to 12.5f: well held in maidens, awkward leaving stalls and taking strong hold second start. *S. R. Bowring* –

CAPE CLEAR 3 b.f. Slip Anchor 136 – Wise Speculation (USA) (Mr Prospector (USA)) [1998 NR 1999 12.3m 12m⁴ 13.8m² Jul 21] IR 4,000Y: rather leggy, workmanlike filly: half-sister to several winners, including smart middle-distance stayer Always Friendly (by High Line) and 1½m winner Minnisam (by Niniski): dam ran 3 times: fair maiden: stays 1¾m. *R. A. Fahey* – **71**

CAPE COAST (IRE) 2 b.c. (Jan 25) Common Grounds 118 – Strike It Rich (FR) (Rheingold 137) [1999 6.1m² 6m⁶ Sep 7] IR 12,000Y: brother to 1m winner here and in UAE Brigand and half-brother to several winners, including useful 1m to 1½m winner Lady Bentley (by Bellypha): dam, Irish 1¼m winner, half-sister to smart stayer Yawa: better effort in maidens when short-head second of 12 to Pedro Jack at Nottingham in August: made running both starts: will probably stay 7f: joined J. Osborne. *D. Marks* – **74**

CAPE CROSS (IRE) 5 b.h. Green Desert (USA) 127 – Park Appeal 122 (Ahonoora 122) [1998 123: a9f² a8f⁵ 8m* 8d⁵ 8d³ 8g⁴ 8f 1999 a8f³ 8m* 8g* 8f⁶ Sep 19] – **129**

Those who think that England's sporting woes, most notably in cricket and football, will be solved if the old guard are replaced with young blood, might reflect on the racing record of Cape Cross in 1999. Twice he was expected to defer to younger, more fancied stable-mates but on both occasions it was Cape Cross who stood in the winner's enclosure, taking the plaudits, especially after a career-best effort in the Celebration Mile at Goodwood.

Queen Anne Stakes, Royal Ascot—Cape Cross provides Godolphin with their fourth consecutive win in the race, putting up a good performance to beat Docksider (right) with Almushtarak third

Cape Cross went off at 5/2 in the Group 2 contest, a race in which he was disqualified after passing the post first as a three-year-old. John Reid was in the saddle, Frankie Dettori riding odds-on stable-companion Josr Algarhoud. Cape Cross, conceding more than weight-for-age all round, showed that proven ability was more than a match for expected potential on this occasion with a length-and-a-half beating of his younger stable-mate. In a race run at a steady pace, Cape Cross was allowed to dictate affairs and never looked like being caught by Josr Algarhoud. The result should not have been a big surprise to anyone who had seen the performance of Cape Cross in the Queen Anne Stakes at Royal Ascot two months earlier.

Godolphin was aiming for its fourth consecutive victory in the Queen Anne and the betting, added to the booking of Frankie Dettori, seemed to suggest that, of Godolphin's trio in the race, Fa-Eq was the most fancied, followed by Fly To The Stars, the winner of the Lockinge Stakes, the race Cape

Celebration Mile, Goodwood—
another high-class effort from Cape Cross, who gives more than weight-for-age all round;
odds-on stable-mate Josr Algarhoud is second with Almushtarak again back in third

Cross had won as a four-year-old. Despite being the longest-priced of the three, Cape Cross was proven on good to firm ground, had the assistance of Gary Stevens and had shown that he retained his ability with a very smart run behind Lend A Hand and Muhtathir at Nad Al Sheba in March. In the race itself, Cape Cross put up a very game performance. Allowed to dictate, he battled hard to regain the lead in the last twenty yards after Docksider passed him around two furlongs out. By the end of the season, giving Docksider 5 lb and a short-head beating would look to be high-class form indeed.

Cape Cross was sent to Canada in September for what turned out to be his final appearance—in the Grade 1 Atto Mile at Woodbine. He finished only sixth of the fifteen runners behind the subsequently-demoted Hawksley Hill. Possible engagements in the Breeders' Cup Mile and the Hong Kong Mile were never fulfilled and Cape Cross was retired to Sheikh Mohammed's Kildangan Stud in Ireland where he will stand at a fee of IR £8,000.

			Danzig	Northern Dancer
	Green Desert (USA)		(b 1977)	Pas de Nom
	(b 1983)		Foreign Courier	Sir Ivor
Cape Cross (IRE)			(b 1979)	Courtly Dee
(b.h. 1994)			Ahonoora	Lorenzaccio
	Park Appeal		(ch 1975)	Helen Nichols
	(br 1982)		Balidaress	Balidar
			(gr 1973)	Innocence

Cape Cross should have appeal as a stallion, not least because he is a member of a most consistent pattern-winning family. His dam Park Appeal won the Cheveley Park, as did her half-sister Desirable, the latter going on to find further fame as the dam of Shadayid. Another half-sister, Alydaress, added

Godolphin's "Cape Cross"

the Irish Oaks to the family's Group 1 tally, improving the remarkable record of their dam Balidaress. Park Appeal herself is also proving to be a good broodmare, producing not only Cape Cross, but also Pastorale and Arvola, the dams of Kareymah and dual Group 1 winner Diktat respectively. Park Appeal's 1999 two-year-old colt Samood (by Caerleon) was unraced when with David Loder, but she also has a colt foal by Sadler's Wells and visited Cape Cross's sire Green Desert in 1999.

Cape Cross is a big horse who carried condition and had a somewhat lethargic disposition. He won on firm ground as a two-year-old but showed his best form between good to firm and good to soft going and he probably stayed nine furlongs, the longest distance he tackled. All in all he was not only a high-class performer but a game and reliable one, who performed with credit at the highest level for three seasons—in a stable full of stars his presence will still be missed. *Saeed bin Suroor*

CAPE GRACE (IRE) 3 b.f. Priolo (USA) 127 – Saffron (FR) (Fabulous Dancer **96** (USA) 124) [1998 95p: 6g* 6g² 7g⁶ 1999 8g⁴ 10m⁴ Apr 17] strong, good-bodied filly: useful performer: creditable fourth in listed race at Kempton and in minor event at Newbury: stays 1¼m: raced only on good/good to firm ground. *R. Hannon*

CAPE HOPE 4 b.c. Risk Me (FR) 127 – Bernstein Bette 76 (Petong 126) [1998 – 56d: a7g⁵ a6g⁴ 6s* 6d⁵ 6.1s a7g a7g a6g a8g 1999 6.1v a5g Apr 10] small colt: has a round action: modest performer at best: little form since only win at 3 yrs. *S. R. Bowring*

CAPERCAILLIE 4 ch.g. Deploy 131 – Tee Gee Jay 63 (Northern Tempest **39** (USA) 125) [1998 43: a10s¹ a8g¹ a8g⁶ 8.3g 10d 8g 10.1g⁵ 14.1g³ a16g³ a14g³ 14.1v⁴ a12g⁶ a12g⁴ 1999 11.9f 10.1m⁷ 10.1g² Jun 3] poor maiden handicapper: stays easy 2m: acts on all-weather and good to firm going, probably on heavy: visored twice (ran creditably on first occasion), blinkered once. *J. E. Banks*

CAPE TOWN (IRE) 2 gr.c. (Apr 14) Desert Style (IRE) 121 – Rossaldene 79 **106 p** (Mummy's Pet 125) [1999 7s* 7.3s² Oct 22] IR 12,500F, IR 21,000Y: half-brother to several winners, including useful 6f (at 2 yrs) and 1m winner Regiment (by Shaadi) and fairly useful 1998 2-y-o 5f winner Mujadene (by Mujadil): dam 2-y-o 5f winner: impressive winner of 18-runner maiden at Lingfield in October by 2½ lengths from Alva Glen, quickening well despite drifting left: favourite, would have gone close with a clearer run when 1¼ lengths second of 9 to stable-mate Umistim in Horris Hill Stakes at Newbury later in month: will stay 1m: should make a smart 3-y-o. *R. Hannon*

CAPE VERDI (IRE) 4 b.f. Caerleon (USA) 132 – Afrique Bleu Azur (USA) **116** (Sagace (FR) 135) [1998 126: 8g* 12m 19m 8m³ 9.9f Jul 31] leggy filly: brilliant winner of 1000 Guineas at Newmarket in 1998, probably failed to stay when favourite for Derby at Epsom: suffered hairline fracture of hind pastern shortly after: better effort at 4 yrs when 2 lengths third to Ronda in Falmouth Stakes at Newmarket: last in Nassau Stakes at Goodwood later in month: probably best around 1m: raced only on good going or firmer: retired. *Saeed bin Suroor*

CAPILANO PRINCESS 6 b.m. Tragic Role (USA) – Lady Capilano 87 **84** (Nebbiolo 125) [1998 NR 1999 10.3m⁶ 10m 11.6g³ Jul 5] workmanlike mare: fairly useful performer: creditable efforts in handicaps/minor event: stays 1½m: acts on good to firm and soft going, modest form on fibresand at 2 yrs. *D. Haydn Jones*

CAPISTRANO DAY (USA) 3 b.f. Diesis 133 – Alcando 113 (Alzao (USA) **110** 117) [1998 89p: 6g 7v* 1999 7m³ 8m⁴ 8g 7f⁵ 8.1m 7m³ 7g* 8.5g Nov 20] strong, useful-looking filly: smart performer: very good 3 lengths fourth of 22 to Wince in 1000 Guineas at Newmarket in May and back to form in listed races at Doncaster (1½ lengths third to Susu) and Deauville (beat Arctic Char ¾ length) in the autumn: well below best when 2 lengths third at Churchill Downs final start: stays 1m: won on heavy ground at 2 yrs, raced only on good or firmer otherwise. *J. H. M. Gosden*

CAPITALIST 3 br.g. Bigstone (IRE) 126 – Pinkie Rose (FR) (Kenmare (FR) 125) **63 d** [1998 66§: 6g⁵ 5s⁴ 5d⁴ 7m³ 7m 8m 8d 8d⁵ 1999 8m 9.1m⁶ 11f⁶ 9.3m⁶ 8m a8.5g 12g

9.9s 10.4d Oct 7] close-coupled gelding: largely disappointing: visored final start: seems temperamental. *R. M. Whitaker*

CAPLAW SKEEN 4 b.g. Sure Blade (USA) 130 – Mary From Dunlow 49 – (Nicholas Bill 125) [1998 45: 9.1v^2 1999 17.2m Jun 23] poor maiden, lightly raced: stayed 9f: dead. *J. J. O'Neill*

CAPPELLA (IRE) 3 br.f. College Chapel 122 – Mavahra 93 (Mummy's Pet 125) **72** [1998 75+: 6m^3 6m^2 5g* 5d^4 6m 5m* 6.5g 5.2g^6 1999 6g^6 5.1m 6g 6d^3 6s 5g 6m 6m^4 6g Sep 20] quite attractive filly: fair handicapper: stays 6f: acts on good to firm and good to soft going: blinkered final 2 starts: has swished tail: inconsistent: sold 5,400 gns. *R. Hannon*

CAPPELLINA (IRE) 2 b.f. (Mar 30) College Chapel 122 – Santa Ana Wind **51** (Busted 134) [1999 6.8m 7g Aug 12] IR 4,100Y, resold IR 6,000Y: half-sister to several winners abroad, including Irish 13f and 2¼m winner Slaney Glow (by Glow): dam lightly raced in Ireland: showed ability in maidens at Warwick and Salisbury: will stay at least 1m. *P. G. Murphy*

CAPPUCINO LADY 2 b.f. (Apr 1) Prince Sabo 123 – Cubist (IRE) 71 (Tate **46 ?** Gallery (USA) 117) [1999 6f 6g 6f^3 7g 5g^6 a6g Dec 22] 500Y: third foal: half-sister to 3-y-o Square Dancer: dam 7f winner, including at 2 yrs: form only when third in claimer at Lingfield: has shown signs of temperament. *J. J. Bridger*

CAPRI 4 ch.c. Generous (IRE) 139 – Island Jamboree (USA) (Explodent (USA)) **117** [1998 117: 12d* 12d* 10.4g^2 16.2d^3 14.8f^2 12m* 1999 12m 12d* 12m Jul 6] rangy colt: smart performer: won 4-runner Grand Prix de Chantilly in June by 2½ lengths from Epistolaire: has form at 2m but seems best around 1½m: acts on firm and good to soft going: sweating (well beaten in Princess of Wales's Stakes at Newmarket having forced strong pace) final start: often forces pace/races prominently: genuine. *H. R. A. Cecil*

CAPRICE 2 gr.f. (Feb 18) Mystiko (USA) 124 – Tebre (USA) 70 (Sir Ivor 135) – [1999 8.3d Nov 4] 2,000Y: third foal: half-sister to 3-y-o Tiger Talk: dam Irish 1½m winner: always behind in seller at Windsor. *S. C. Williams*

Godolphin's "Cape Verdi"

Ed Weetman Haulage And Storage Lincoln Trial Stakes (Handicap), Wolverhampton—
Captain Scott forges ahead to take the most valuable handicap on the all-weather,
beating Welville (right) and Nomore Mr Niceguy

CAPRIOLO (IRE)   3 ch.g. Priolo (USA) 127 – Carroll's Canyon (IRE) (Hatim **80**
(USA) 121) [1998 82d: 6f³ 6g⁴ 7m³ 7.9g 1999 10g 9m 10f² 11.4m³ 9.9m* 12g²
11.6m 12m⁶ 12m² 12m 12s 10d* Oct 12] rather leggy gelding: fairly useful handicapper: won at Salisbury in June and Leicester in October: stays 1½m: acts on firm
and good to soft going: usually blinkered, visored second start: has carried head high:
usually races prominently. *R. Hannon*

CAPTAIN BLIGH   3 b.c. Green Desert (USA) 127 – Hyabella 111 (Shirley **70**
Heights 130) [1998 NR 1999 8g⁴ 8m 9f Nov 20] 250,000Y: good-bodied, attractive
colt: fourth foal: half-brother to fairly useful 1m winner Summer Dance (by Sadler's
Wells) and 10.2f winner Hyperspectra (by Rainbow Quest): dam, 1m winner, half-
sister to high-class 1¼m performer Stagecraft from family of Opera House and Kayf
Tara: burly, 4¼ lengths fourth in newcomers race at Newmarket in April: in rear in
maidens at Kempton (final start for Sir Michael Stoute) and Hollywood (blinkered)
6½ months apart. *T. Pinfield, USA*

CAPTAIN BRADY (IRE)   4 ch.g. Soviet Lad (USA) – Eight Mile Rock 76 **62**
(Dominion 123) [1998 NR 1999 9.2v³ 8.3g 8.3s* 8.3g⁵ 9.2g² 9.2m³ 9.2f 9.9m² 9g*
10.9d 8.3s 10v³ 10d Oct 18] lengthy, workmanlike gelding: modest handicapper:
won at Hamilton in May and Ripon in August: barely stays 1¼m when conditions are
testing: acts on good to firm going, heavy and fibresand: blinkered (ran creditably)
final 2-y-o start: front runner. *J. S. Goldie*

CAPTAIN CARAT   8 gr.g. Handsome Sailor 125 – Gem of Gold 52 (Jellaby 124) **37**
[1998 43: a5g 5.9d a6g a6g⁶ 6m 6m³ 6m 6m⁴ 5s⁴ 5m 5d a6g 1999 5m 5m⁵ 6f⁴ 6m 7g
6f 5m Sep 6] tall gelding: poor handicapper: effective at 5f/6f: acts on any going:
effective blinkered or not, well held in visor final start. *D. W. Chapman*

CAPTAIN FLINT   5 b. or br.g. Bedford (USA) 109 – Sun Yat Chen (Chou Chin **–**
Chow 99) [1998 NR 1999 a11g a14g Jul 8] leggy gelding: won selling handicap in
1997: well beaten both starts since. *A. Smith*

CAPTAIN LOGAN (IRE)   4 b.c. Fairy King (USA) – Heaven High (High Line **–**
125) [1998 90: 7.1g² 7g* 8g² 7.1m 1999 8.1s 8d 7s a8g Nov 23] good sort: fairly
useful performer at 3 yrs for D. Loder: no show in 1999, leaving J. Noseda after third

start: should stay beyond 1m: acts on good to firm going: tried visored: has carried head high and found little. *A. Kelleway*

CAPTAIN MARMALADE 10 ch.g. Myjinski (USA) – Lady Seville 64 (Orange Bay 131) [1998 –: a12g 1999 a16g Feb 11] workmanlike gelding: no form in only 2 races since 1997. *D. T. Thom*

CAPTAIN MCCLOY (USA) 4 ch.g. Lively One (USA) – Fly Me First (USA) **51** (Herbager 136) [1998 40, a43: 11.4d 9.9m 11.5m a10g³ 11.6m 9m 10g 1999 10v 10f³ 10g⁴ 10.5m⁴ 10.5m* 11.6m⁶ 9.9m³ 10s² 10d⁶ 10m⁴ 10.5d 10s a10g⁵ a10g Dec 18] lengthy gelding: modest handicapper: won seller at Warwick in July: stays 10.5f, probably not 1½m: acts on firm and soft going (poor form at best on equitrack): often visored/blinkered: often races prominently. *N. E. Berry*

CAPTAIN MILLER 3 b.g. Batshoof 122 – Miller's Gait 74§ (Mill Reef (USA) **74** 141) [1998 70d: 5.1d 5.1s⁶ 5.1g⁵ 6f² 7d* 7m 7m⁶ 7d⁵ 7.3g⁶ 6g⁵ 7s⁶ 7s⁴ 1999 7s* 8.3v* 8.3m 8.3g² 8m* 8.1m Jun 11] quite attractive gelding: fair performer: won handicap at Leicester and minor event at Hamilton in April then claimer at Ripon in May: should stay 1¼m: acts on any going: joined N. Henderson and won over hurdles. *M. R. Channon*

CAPTAIN SCOTT (IRE) 5 b.g. Polar Falcon (USA) 126 – Camera Girl (Kala- **100** glow 132) [1998 92: 8d⁶ 8d³ 10g³ 10g² 10.4f⁶ 1999 a8.5g* 8d² 10f⁴ 8m 10.4f Jul 10] tall, lengthy gelding: useful handicapper: off 8 months, won valuable event at Wolverhampton in March: in frame in Lincoln at Doncaster (½ length second to Right Wing) and Zetland Gold Cup at Redcar: ran poorly last 2 starts: effective at 1m and stays 10.4f: acts on fibresand, firm and good to soft going (ran poorly on soft): probably best with patient tactics. *J. A. Glover*

CAPTAIN'S LOG 4 b.g. Slip Anchor 136 – Cradle of Love (USA) 87 (Roberto **83** (USA) 131) [1998 88: 8.2s⁶ 10d 8g* 8.5m 8s⁵ 9s* 10f⁶ 10.1g² 10m⁴ 10m 8s 10v 1999 10g⁴ 10.3m⁵ 10.5d² 10m⁴ 10m 11.9m⁶ 10d⁶ 8s Oct 25] leggy, rather lightly-made gelding: fairly useful handicapper: mostly in good form in 1999: stays 1½m: acts on firm and soft ground: usually held up: has run well when sweating. *M. L. W. Bell*

CARABINE (USA) 3 gr.f. Dehere (USA) 121 – Caracciola (FR) (Zeddaan 130) – [1998 –p: 6g 6m⁶ 6.1s 1999 6.9m Aug 22] leggy, lengthy filly: never a threat in maidens at 2 yrs, and minor event (never going well): sold 32,000 gns in December. *Sir Mark Prescott*

CARADOC 4 ch.g. Bustino 136 – Hathaway (Connaught 130) [1998 53, a–: 12d – 14.1g 14.1d⁴ 1999 12m Sep 17] modest maiden handicapper: tailed-off last only run in 1999: stays 1¾m: acts on good to soft going. *Mrs L. C. Jewell*

CARAMBO 4 b.f. Rambo Dancer (CAN) 107 – Light The Way 72 (Nicholas Bill **72** 125) [1998 82, a88: 7d³ 8s⁶ 6.1m 7.9g² 7d² 7m⁶ 6s 7.5m⁴ 8g 7s 6g a6g⁵ a7g 1999 7s 7m 7g 8m 7.1d³ 8m⁶ 6.9m³ 7g 7.5g⁵ 6.1m* 7g³ 7.1d 6g⁴ 8d a8.5g a6g a7g Dec 29] unfurnished filly: fair handicapper: won at Nottingham in September: left J. L. Eyre after thirteenth start: no form for new stable: effective at 6f to 1m: acts on fibresand, good to firm and good to soft going: blinkered at Nottingham and on next 3 starts. *T. D. Barron*

CARAMBOLA (IRE) 3 b.f. Danehill (USA) 126 – Purchasepaperchase 104 **100** (Young Generation 129) [1998 –p: 7d⁵ 1999 8s* 7m⁴ 8g* 8g⁶ 12m 8m² 10d Sep 11] 330,000Y: rangy, angular filly: sister to fair 7f/1m winner Purchasing Power and half-sister to several winners, notably Irish 1000 Guineas winner Matiya (by Alzao): dam 1m/1¼m performer: useful performer: won maiden at Cork in April and listed race at Leopardstown in May: 5½ lengths second of 6 to Dazzling Park in Matron Stakes at the Curragh: behind in Ribblesdale Stakes at Royal Ascot fifth start: stays 1m, possibly not 1¼m: acts on soft and good to firm going: usually races prominently: sent to USA. *A. P. O'Brien, Ireland*

CARBON 4 b.g. Batshoof 122 – Reyah 83 (Young Generation 129) [1998 73: 6m – 7.1m⁶ 6m 5.7d 7m 6d⁴ 7m 1999 7.1g 7.1d 10m 7m a7g Aug 25] close-coupled gelding: fair handicapper at best: well held in 1999: stays 1m, probably not 1¼m: acts on good to firm and good to soft going: carries head high: blinkered final start: sold 3,200 gns, sent to Italy. *Lady Herries*

CARD GAMES 2 b.f. (Mar 11) First Trump 118 – Pericardia 60 (Petong 126) **87** [1999 5m³ 5.1m⁴ 5.1m 6m* 6m³ 6g* 6.5g⁴ 7s² 6s Oct 2] 4,000F, 4,200Y: lengthy filly: second foal: half-sister to a 1½m winner in Italy by Deploy: dam lightly-raced half-sister to smart 6f/7f performer Prince Ferdinand: fairly useful performer: won minor event at Salisbury and nursery at Pontefract (idled markedly) in the summer: stays 7f: acts on good to firm and soft going: visored 2 of last 3 starts, running well first time: sold 11,000 gns. *I. A. Balding*

CARDIFF ARMS (NZ)   5 b.g. Lowell (USA) 114 – Shuzohra (NZ) (Tom's Shu   **100** (USA)) [1998 8g⁵ 7g³ 8g² 8g* 8g 8g 7d 8g 10g* 10.5g 10.5g⁵ 1999 11g⁴ 10.5d³ 11g³ 10.5g³ 10g* 12.5g³ 12d Oct 1] workmanlike New Zealand-bred gelding: dam won 15 races in Australasia from 6f to 2m, including Group 1 event at latter trip: useful form: won St Leger Trial at Otaki in February: very close third of 15 in Group 3 New Zealand St Leger at Trentham in March, final start for T. Cole: better for race, below best when 14 lengths ninth of 11 in listed race at Newmarket on only outing in Britain (drifted left): probably better suited by around 1½m than shorter and should stay further: raced only on good/good to soft going: joined Miss V. Williams. *M. Johnston*

CARDINAL FAIR (IRE)   2 b.f. (Apr 19) Namaqualand (USA) – Irish Affaire   **42** (IRE) (Fairy King (USA)) [1999 a6g a7g⁵ Dec 15] IR 1,000Y, 4,600 2-y-o: third foal: half-sister to 4-y-o Sara Moon Classic: dam Belgian 2-y-o 7f winner: better effort in sellers at Wolverhampton second start. *B. P. J. Baugh*

CAREFREE CHEETAH (USA) 3 gr.f. Trempolino (USA) 135 – Careless Kitten   **66** (USA) (Caro 133) [1998 NR 1999 10s² 9.9g⁶ 10m Jun 11] sister to 4-y-o Arkadian Hero and half-sister to several winners, including winner up to 1¼m (useful as a sprinter) Masnun (by Nureyev): dam won up to 9f in USA: fair maiden: best effort on debut: sent to USA. *J. Noseda*

CARELESS   2 b.f. (Mar 17) Robellino (USA) 127 – Life's Too Short (IRE) 49   **60 +** (Astronef 116) [1999 6m⁴ 7g 6.8d Sep 21] 11,000F, 4,500Y: smallish, sturdy filly: first foal: dam, maiden who stayed 1¼m, half-sister to St Leger winner Bob's Return: shaped quite well when fourth of 18 in maiden at Lingfield: first home on stand side at Salisbury next time: should be well suited by 1m+: may still do better. *J. E. Banks*

CARENS HERO (IRE)   2 ch.g. (Apr 9) Petardia 113 – Clear Glade (Vitiges (FR)   **62 p** 132) [1999 8s Nov 6] 6,000Y: strong gelding: has scope: sixth foal: brother to Italian 1m winner Sevanbra and half-brother to winners abroad by Heraldiste and Contract Law: dam French maiden: burly when eighth of 18 to Summoner in maiden at Doncaster, chasing winner 5f: should improve. *Mrs A. J. Perrett*

CAREQUICK   3 ch.f. Risk Me (FR) 127 – Miss Serlby 65 (Runnett 125) [1998   **48** 55: 5d 6g 6g 5m⁵ 5m 1999 7m a7g 5m 6.1d a11g a8g⁵ a8.5g³ Dec 27] leggy, unfurnished filly: poor maiden: ran creditably in claimer/handicap final 2 starts: stays 8.5f: acts on fibresand: tried blinkered. *A. Bailey*

CARHUE LASS (IRE)   5 b.m. Common Grounds 118 – Return Journey (IRE)   **104** 68 (Pennine Walk 120) [1998 100: 5s² 5m 5d² 5d 5d⁴ 5s 1999 5s⁵ 5.1s* 5g² 5d 5d Sep 30] lengthy, sparely-made mare: first foal: dam Irish 6.5f and 1m winner: useful performer: won 5-runner listed event at Bath in April by 3 lengths from Inya Lake: good ½-length second to Proud Native in Ballyogan Stakes at Leopardstown, best effort after: best at 5f on good going or softer: usually races up with pace. *Patrick O'Leary, Ireland*

CARIBBEAN MONARCH (IRE)   4 b.g. Fairy King (USA) – Whos The Blonde   **88 +** (Cure The Blues (USA)) [1998 105p: 6d* 6g* 8d⁴ 1999 7g 7s⁴ 6s Nov 6] rangy, good sort: useful performer in 1998: shaped better than result on return in handicap at Newmarket, minor event at Leicester (unlucky not to be involved in finish), both in October, and listed race at Doncaster (eased once held): races quite freely, but stays 1m well: raced only on good going or softer. *Sir Michael Stoute*

CARIBBEAN SURFER (USA)   10 b.g. Summing (USA) – Caribbean Surfing   **–** (USA) (Northjet 136) [1998 NR 1999 a16g May 29] winning hurdler in 1994/5: very lightly raced and no form on Flat. *P. Eccles*

CARINTHIA (IRE)   4 br.f. Tirol 127 – Hot Lavender (CAN) 67 (Shadeed (USA)   **69** 135) [1998 82: 6m³ 7m⁵ 6m* 7m 7m⁴ 8d³ 8v⁴ 1999 7m 8.3m 10d Sep 23] fair performer: generally disappointing in 1999: stays 1m well: acts on good to firm and heavy going: has shown tendency to hang. *C. F. Wall*

CARISBROOKE 5 b.h. Kahyasi 130 – Dayanata (Shirley Heights 130) [1998 NR – 1999 16.4s Apr 23] lightly-raced horse (has chipped bone in knee): useful form in 1997 for H. Cecil: tailed off in handicap at Sandown (reportedly suffered from a breathing problem), only run since: should stay 2m+. *D. R. C. Elsworth*

CARLISLE BAY (IRE) 5 b.g. Darshaan 133 – My Potters (USA) (Irish River – (FR) 131) [1998 –: 8s⁶ 10m 7g⁶ 1999 7s 10.9g Jul 26] ex-Irish gelding: second foal: half-brother to Irish Oaks winner Winona (by Alzao) and 1995 Irish 2-y-o 1m winner Western Seas (by Caerleon): dam, Irish 1m winner, is half-sister to champion US sprinter My Juliet and to very smart middle-distance colt Lyphard's Special: fairly useful at best for J. Oxx in Ireland at 2 yrs: well beaten since, including in seller final start. *J. S. Goldie*

CARL'S BOY 3 ch.g. Itsu (USA) – Adelbaran (FR) (No Pass No Sale 120) [1998 – NR 1999 12.1g⁴ 12g 8.2f Jun 21] second foal: dam awarded 1m race in France at 2 yrs: no form in minor event/maidens. *D. Burchell*

CARLTON (IRE) 5 ch.g. Thatching 131 – Hooray Lady 92 (Ahonoora 122) [1998 **82** 73, a62: 6.9d 6.1v² 8g⁵ 8m 7g² 6m* 7d⁵ 7m* 7.6m² 7m³ 6d² a6g³ 7g⁶ 6s 1999 6g 6s 7f 7g³ 6m⁵ 6m* 8m³ 6f³ 7m 6d³ 6g* 6g² 7s³ 6d* a6g* a7g² a6g* Nov 20] sturdy gelding: fairly useful performer: first past post in handicaps at Doncaster (disqualified for interference), Epsom, Windsor (twice, former on first run after leaving G. Lewis) and Southwell and minor event at Wolverhampton, all between June and November: effective at 6f to 1m: acts on fibresand, good to firm and heavy going: usually blinkered, but is as effective when not. *D. R. C. Elsworth*

CARLYS QUEST 5 ch.g. Primo Dominie 121 – Tuppy (USA) (Sharpen Up 127) **90** [1998 90: 10d* 10m³ 10m³ 10.8m* 10.1m⁵ 11.9m 10g² 12.5d² 12s³ 12v² 12d² 1999 10m⁴ 11.9d 16.1m 12m³ 12m³ 11.9s³ 12s 12s² Nov 6] leggy gelding: fairly useful handicapper: creditable efforts when in frame, second (for second year running) in November Handicap at Doncaster final start, beaten a head by Flossy: effective at 1¼m (given good gallop) to 12.5f (failed to stay 2m): acts on good to firm and heavy going: often off bridle early on, and comes from behind: visored/blinkered: tongue tied final start. *J. Neville*

CARMARTHEN BAY 6 ch.h. Prionsaa 76 – Pattie's Grey 71 (Valiyar 129) [1998 – –: 10s 8d 7g 10g a7g 9.9s a14g 1999 a12f Jan 14] workmanlike horse: fairly useful handicapper on all-weather/fair on turf in 1996: little show since. *B. J. Llewellyn*

CARMARTHEN (IRE) 3 ch.g. Hamas (IRE) 125§ – Solar Attraction (IRE) 60 **58** (Salt Dome (USA)) [1998 68: 5f² 5g⁶ 5g⁵ 5m 1999 5g 5d 5.1g³ 6.1d 5d³ 5.1m² 5.1m **a53** 6f 5g 5f³ a6g a6g⁴ a5g⁴ a5g⁴ Dec 29] modest maiden: left N. Tinkler after fifth start, D. Williams after seventh: effective at 5f/easy 6f: acts on firm going, good to soft and equitrack: none too consistent. *K. R. Burke*

CARNAGE (IRE) 2 b.c. (May 20) Catrail (USA) 123 – Caranina (USA) 85 (Caro **51** 133) [1999 6m 6m 10.2s Sep 27] IR 5,000Y: half-brother to several winners, including Irish 3-y-o 1m winner Misniuil (by Unblest) and useful 1¼m winner Star of Persia (by Persian Bold): dam Irish 6f winner: led to post early, seventh of 22 in maiden at Windsor on debut: well held after: likely to prove best up to 1m. *Mrs P. N. Dutfield*

CAROL AGAIN 7 b.m. Kind of Hush 118 – Lady Carol 42 (Lord Gayle (USA) – 124) [1998 –, a48: a11g a11g a11g* a12g⁴ a14g* a12g 1999 a12g⁶ a16g a14g a12g a11g Jun 11] close-coupled mare: poor handicapper: no form in 1999. *N. Bycroft*

CAROLE'S DOVE 3 b.f. Manhal – Nimble Dove 62 (Starch Reduced 112) – [1998 NR 1999 5s Mar 27] half-sister to a winning hurdler by Celtic Cone and a bumper winner by Riberetto: dam, soft-ground stayer, also won over hurdles: behind in maiden at Warwick. *C. J. Price*

CAROLINE'S PET (IRE) 4 b.f. Contract Law (USA) 108 – Princess Roxanne – 68 (Prince Tenderfoot (USA) 126) [1998 –: 5.9d 10d⁴ 10.5d 1999 a9.4g a8f Feb 1] leggy filly: poor mover: no form: tried blinkered/visored. *P. D. Evans*

CAROLS CHOICE 2 ch.f. (Mar 5) Emarati (USA) 74 – Lucky Song 91 (Lucky **61** Wednesday 124) [1999 5m 5m 6.1d⁵ 5.1m³ 5m⁶ Jun 28] 8,500Y: half-sister to 3 winners, including 1990 2-y-o 5f/6f winner Level Xing (by Stanford) and 1991 2-y-o

6f/7f winner X My Heart (by Aragon): dam 5f (at 2 yrs) and 7f winner: modest maiden: best effort when third of 18 at Nottingham: should stay 6f. *D. Haydn Jones*

CAROL'S DREAM (USA)   7 ch.g. Risen Star (USA) – Merle Halton (USA) (Rattle Dancer) [1998 NR 1999 a12g Jan 16] fair 1¼m winner on equitrack in 1997: well beaten only run on Flat since. *M. Pitman* —

CAROUSAL (IRE)   3 b.f. Distinctly North (USA) 115 – Mountain Hop (IRE) (Tirol 127) [1998 39+: 6g 5m⁶ 6m 6m⁴ 8g 1999 a7g May 10] lengthy, unfurnished filly: poor maiden: sold 800 gns in August. *J. P. Leigh* —

CAROUSING   2 b.c. (Feb 16) Selkirk (USA) 129 – Moon Carnival 94 (Be My Guest (USA) 126) [1999 5m⁶ 7g* 7f* Jul 31] 10,000Y: good-bodied colt: third foal: half-brother to fairly useful 1998 2-y-o 7f winner Distant Moon (by Distant Relative): dam, won around 1½m, half-sister to Moon Madness and Sheriff's Star: progressive form: won maiden at Lingfield in June and nursery at Goodwood in July, set plenty to do in race run at strong pace on second occasion: will stay at least 1¼m: has raced only on good ground or firmer: probably capable of better still. *M. Johnston*   **94 p**

CARPETSMADEINDEVON   3 ch.g. Elmaamul (USA) 125 – Hollow Heart 89 (Wolver Hollow 126) [1998 NR 1999 6g 7g 7g 10s Nov 1] 4,400Y: half-brother to 3 winners, including useful 7f to 8.5f winner Aradu (by Posse): dam 2-y-o 5f winner: well beaten, including in seller. *Mrs P. N. Dutfield* —

CARRIE POOTER   3 b.f. Tragic Role (USA) – Ginny Binny 113 (Ahonoora 122) [1998 68: 5s 5d⁵ 6g* 6m⁴ 6m 1999 a6g⁴ a8g³ a7g² a7g² a7g* a7g² 6s³ a6g² 7s² 6m 7f 6f 6m* 7m 6.8g² 6.1m⁴ a7g⁵ Sep 4] workmanlike filly: fair handicapper: won at Southwell in March and Hamilton in July: stays 7f: acts on fibresand, good to firm and heavy going: usually blinkered: sometimes slowly away. *T. D. Barron*   **78**

CARROLLS MARC (IRE)   11 b.g. Horage 124 – Rare Find (Rarity 129) [1998 41: a12g a12g a14g³ a16.2g* 15.4s a16.2g⁵ a12g⁶ a16g⁴ a11g² a16g⁴ a12g⁶ a14g 1999 a14g a12g Apr 26] angular gelding: poor mover: poor performer: well held in claimers in 1999: effective at 1½m to 2m: acts on all-weather. *Pat Mitchell* —

CARRY THE FLAG   4 b.c. Tenby 125 – Tamassos 67 (Dance In Time (CAN)) [1998 99: 10.4d³ 12m 12s⁶ 10m² 1999 10g* 12d* 12g⁴ 12m⁴ 10.9d² 11g* Oct 24] leggy colt: smart performer: better than ever in 1999, winning Coral Rosebery Stakes at Kempton in April and Coolmore Stud Shergar Cup at Goodwood in May, both handicaps: good 1½ lengths second to Leggera in listed race at Ayr penultimate start, then (after sold from P. Cole for reported £160,000) won very valuable Singapore Gold Cup by head from Ouzo: stays 1½m: acts on good to firm and good to soft going: genuine and consistent. *M. Kent, Singapore*   **114**

CARTESIAN   3 b.f. Shirley Heights 130 – Danilova (USA) (Lyphard (USA) 132) [1998 NR 1999 11.9d 9s⁴ 11.7s³ Oct 26] second foal: half-sister to 9.4f winner Danakil (by Warning): dam unraced half-sister to Sanglamore: fair maiden: stayed at least 1½m: raced only on ground softer than good: raced freely first 2 starts: stud. *R. Charlton*   **78**

CARTMEL PARK   3 ch.g. Skyliner 117 – Oh My Oh My (Ballacashtal (CAN)) [1998 78: 5d 5m² 5g² 5d² 5g* 5m² 5g³ 5m* 5d 1999 5d a5g 5m 5s³ 5m² 5g* 5.1m⁶ 5g 5d⁵ 5d 5s 5g* Oct 16] fairly useful handicapper: won at Sandown in July and Catterick (raced alone against stand rail, possibly flattered) in October: raced only at 5f: acts on soft and good to firm going: visored 3 times, running well only on first occasion: usually races prominently: swerved violently right tenth start and not to be trusted. *J. Berry*   **89 §**

CASATI (IRE)   4 b.f. Silver Kite (USA) 111 – Inishmot (IRE) 67 (Glenstal (USA) 118) [1998 –: 7m 8g⁶ 9g 9d 9s 7d 1999 a6g a6g a8.5g³ a11g Feb 5] ex-Irish filly: first foal: dam fourth from 5f to 1½m in Ireland: fair maiden at 2 yrs: no form since: stays 7f: best efforts on good going. *P. S. Felgate* —

CASHAPLENTY   6 ch.g. Ballacashtal (CAN) – Storm of Plenty (Billion (USA) 120) [1998 –, a44+: a12g⁶ a12g² 1999 a11g⁶ Jan 15] poor performer, lightly raced on Flat: stays 1½m: acts on fibresand (unraced on equitrack). *N. P. Littmoden* —

CASHIKI (IRE)   3 ch.f. Case Law 113 – Nishiki (USA) (Brogan (USA) 110) [1998 69: a5g 5.1s a5g⁶ 6.1m² 6m* 6.1d* 7m² 6m² 6m* 7d³ 7g⁵ 6d⁴ 1999 6m 7m   **69 d**

8.3m⁴ 8.2m 8m 7g 8.2g a7f⁴ 10d² 10f 10s a10g a9.4g Nov 17] small, sparely-made filly: fair performer: disappointing in 1999 after third start: probably stays 1¼m: acts on good to soft ground, probably on firm. *B. Palling*

CASHMERE LADY   7 b.m. Hubbly Bubbly (USA) – Choir (High Top 131)   **71**
[1998 82, a94: a9.4g⁴ a12g* 8s* 10.3g 9.9m 8.9s 10m⁵ 10m 9.9m² 12g² 10s 13.9g   **a80**
10.1v⁴ 8d⁵ a12g⁴ a9.4g⁴ 1999 8m 12m 12f⁴ 10m³ 10d⁶ 10.5m* 10d 10g 9g 8d⁶ a12g⁵
Nov 11] tall mare: fairly useful handicapper on all-weather, fair on turf: won amateur
event at Haydock in September: needs true test at 1m, stays 1½m: acts on any going
and fibresand: inconsistent. *J. L. Eyre*

CASIMIR (IRE)   3 b.c. Roi Danzig (USA) – Have A Cut (IRE) (Al Hareb (USA)   **99**
123) [1998 70: 5d⁵ 5g* 6m² 6g 7d⁶ 1999 7g 8m⁴ 8.1m* 8m* 8m² 8s Sep 26] leggy
colt: useful handicapper: improved and won comfortably at Chepstow and Ascot in
July: good second of 20 to Naviasky at Leicester: stays 1m: acts on good to firm
going, seemingly not on soft: may still be capable of better. *A. C. Stewart*

CASINO ROYALE (IRE)   3 b.c. Royal Academy (USA) 130 – Sharata (IRE)   **83**
(Darshaan 133) [1998 74p: 7d³ 1999 8.1s³ 7.9d⁴ 10.3m³ 10g⁵ 10.4m⁶ 10s³ 10v³ Oct
23] big, rangy colt: fairly useful maiden: mainly creditable efforts in 1999: barely
stays 1¼m when conditions are testing: acts on good to firm going, probably on
heavy: refused to enter stalls intended second start, looked difficult ride on third: sold
23,000 gns, sent to USA. *J. W. Hills*

CASSANDRA   3 b.f. Catrail (USA) 123 – Circo 77 (High Top 131) [1998 NR   **66 ?**
1999 7m⁶ 6m⁴ 8d 9.9m⁵ 10.4f 8s Sep 16] 3,000Y: half-sister to several winners,
including useful Circus (1¼m, by Caerleon) and 5-y-o Topton: dam placed up to
1¼m, including in France: fair maiden: easily best effort at Ripon third start: may
prove best at 1m: acts on good to soft going: has looked a bit wayward. *M. Brittain*

CASSANDRA GO (IRE)   3 gr.f. Indian Ridge 123 – Rahaam (USA) 91 (Secreto   **104**
(USA) 128) [1998 70p: 7g 1999 7g* 8d³ 8g 6m* 6m⁴ 6d⁶ 6d Oct 15] lengthy, angular
filly: useful performer: won maiden at Newmarket in April and minor event on same
course in June: creditable efforts in listed races/minor event after: effective at 6f/7f:
acts on good to firm and good to soft ground: has worn crossed noseband and tongue
strap. *G. Wragg*

CASSINI (IRE)   3 b.c. Exit To Nowhere (USA) 122 – Venerate (IRE) (Ahonoora   **–**
122) [1998 NR 1999 10m 11.9d Aug 7] 15,000Y: lengthy colt: second foal: half-
brother to a winner in Germany by Elmaamul: dam, French 11f winner, out of sister
to dam of Mt Livermore and Magical Wonder: well held in maidens at Ripon (burly
and slowly away) and Haydock (tailed off). *M. Brittain*

CASTANEA SATIVA (IRE)   2 b.f. (Mar 19) In The Wings 128 – Chesnut Tree   **58**
(USA) 97 (Shadeed (USA) 135) [1999 7.5g⁶ 8.3m⁴ 7s² 7.9d Oct 7] lengthy,
unfurnished filly: fifth foal: half-sister to 3-y-o Lucky Rascal: dam, 1½m winner,
half-sister to dam of smart Phantom Gold, out of Ribblesdale winner Expansive:
modest form in maidens: had gone in coat when well beaten on nursery debut final
start: will be suited by 1½m+. *T. D. Easterby*

CASTARA BEACH (IRE)   3 b.f. Danehill (USA) 126 – Sea Harrier (Grundy   **–**
137) [1998 74p: 5m⁵ 6.9f 7g⁴ 1999 7.6g 8.5m⁵ Sep 3] quite attractive filly: fair form
at best in 2-y-o maidens: well below that level both starts in 1999, looking difficult
ride on final one: should stay 1m+. *N. A. Callaghan*

CASTAWAY PRINCESS   3 b.f. Casteddu 111 – Princess Dina 87 (Huntercombe   **–**
133) [1998 –: 6d 6s 7g 7m 1999 12d 8g Jun 14] small filly: little form. *D. W. Barker*

CASTEL ROSSELO   9 br.h. Rousillon (USA) 133 – On The House (FR) 125   **–**
(Be My Guest (USA) 126) [1998 NR 1999 8.3m 8.3s Aug 9] smallish horse: fair
handicapper at 7 yrs: well beaten both starts since. *D. Haydn Jones*

CASTLE ASHBY JACK   5 gr.g. Chilibang 120 – Carly-B (IRE) 42 (Commanche   **–**
Run 133) [1998 45, a62d: a10g a6g³ a7g² a7g² a8g² a7g* a7g³ a7g⁵ a7g a7g a7g   **a48**
8.3g 6f 6.9m⁵ 6g a7g³ 7f⁵ 7.6g a8g² 6g a8.5g a7g a10g a7g³ a8f³ 1999 a7g a8g
a10g⁵ a11g a8g² a8g⁵ a7g a8g a7g Jun 5] strong, lengthy gelding: poor performer:
stays 1m: acts on firm going (yet to race on softer than good) and all-weather:
visored/blinkered earlier in career: usually races prominently: sometimes wanders:
inconsistent. *P. Howling*

CASTLE BELLE   3 ch.f. King's Signet (USA) 110 – Castle Maid 38 (Castle Keep 121) [1998 NR 1999 7.1m 5.1m 6g Aug 24] second foal: dam 5f winner: never a danger in maidens/claimer. *R. J. Hodges* –

CASTLEBRIDGE   2 b.g. (Apr 22) Batshoof 122 – Super Sisters (AUS) (Call Report (USA)) [1999 a8g a8g a8g Dec 29] 1,200Y: half-brother to several winners, including 1995 2-y-o 1m winner Red Rusty (by The Carpenter): dam, won twice at 7f in Australia, half-sister to a Group 2 winner there: no sign of ability. *D. Morris* –

CASTLES BURNING (USA)   5 b. or br.g. Minshaanshu Amad (USA) 91§ – Major Overhaul (Known Fact (USA) 135) [1998 60, a70: a10g⁴ 11.9g⁶ 11.6m 10m* 11.9m² 11.5f a12g⁵ a7g⁴ a10g⁵ a10g³ a10f* a10g* 1999 a10g⁴ a8g* a10g³ a8g⁵ a9.4g² a10g² a8g³ a8g* 11.9g⁴ a10g² a16g⁵ a7g⁴ Aug 25] compact gelding: fair on all-weather, modest at best on turf: won minor events at Lingfield in March and June: effective at 1m to 1½m: acts on all-weather, good to firm and to good to soft going: effective blinkered or not: carries head awkwardly and tends to edge right under pressure: consistent. *C. A. Cyzer*   **a74**

CASTLE SECRET   13 b.g. Castle Keep 121 – Baffle 87 (Petingo 135) [1998 –: a16.2g 1999 a14.8g a14g Nov 12] one-time fairly useful winner on Flat/useful hurdler: lightly raced of late. *D. Burchell* –

CASTLE SEMPILL   2 b.c. (Mar 5) Presidium 124 – La Suquet 72 (Puissance 110) [1999 5s² 5.1g⁴ 5m³ 5m 6m⁴ 7.7d³ 7s³ 7d* 7s a8g⁴ a7g³ a6g* Dec 22] 6,500Y: smallish colt: first foal: dam 5f winner: fair performer: won 20-runner seller at Newmarket (sold from J. Fanshawe 12,500 gns) in October and nursery at Lingfield in December: best form short of 1m: acts on good to firm going, soft and equitrack: visored last 2 starts: consistent. *R. M. H. Cowell*   **70**

CATALONIA (IRE)   2 ch.f. (May 6) Catrail (USA) 123 – Shakanda (IRE) (Shernazar 131) [1999 7.5g⁶ 7d⁵ Oct 22] 18,000F, 52,000Y: strong, quite good-topped filly: fourth foal: half-sister to 5-y-o Shadiann and 4-y-o The Glow-Worm: dam Irish 1½m winner: wintry, much better of efforts in maidens when fifth of 22 to Fame At Last at Doncaster: should be suited by 1m+: will do better still. *J. A. Glover*   **72 p**

CATAMARAN   4 ch.g. Rainbow Quest (USA) 134 – Cattermole (USA) (Roberto (USA) 131) [1998 NR 1999 10m³ 10.2s Sep 27] second foal: brother to useful 1½m winner Scattergun: dam, French 8.5f winner, half-sister to very smart 7f performer Condrillac: 7¼ lengths third of 11 to Bright Hope in Pontefract maiden, slowly away, running green and not knocked about once held: ran poorly on soft ground at Bath later in September: sold 25,000 gns, joined Lady Herries. *J. H. M. Gosden*   **74**

CATAPULT (IRE)   3 ch.g. Catrail (USA) 123 – Flimmering (Dancing Brave (USA) 140) [1998 –: 6d 1999 7m⁴ 5m⁶ 7.1g 5m⁶ 6m 6.9m³ 8.3m 7.5g⁶ 6f⁶ 7.1f⁵ 9.2s⁵ 7g Oct 15] close-coupled gelding: modest maiden: pulls hard, but stays 7f: acts on good to firm ground, probably soft: blinkered (below form) ninth start: not the easiest of rides: sold 3,400 gns, sent to Spain. *I. Semple*   **64 d**

CATCH BALL   3 ch.f. Prince Sabo 123 – Canoodle 66 (Warpath 113) [1998 –: 6.1g 7g 7f 1999 9.7s 12m⁶ 10m May 24] little form on Flat. *T. R. Watson* –

CATCH ME   3 b.f. Rudimentary (USA) 118 – Fast Chick 93 (Henbit (USA) 130) [1998 75: 6s 7.5m* 7m* 7g² 7g 7f 7.9g 1999 8d 8g⁵ 8m Jun 15] sturdy filly: fair winner at 2 yrs: form only on second start in 1999: stays 1m: sold 2,500 gns in December. *T. D. Easterby*   **63**

CATCHMENT   5 ch.g. Persian Bold 123 – Cachou (USA) 74 (Roberto (USA) 131) [1998 –, a40: 12.5d 11.6m 11.6f a12g a14g² a14.8g a16g⁴ 1999 a16g a13g² a16g Mar 8] poor maiden handicapper: stays 2m: acts on all-weather: has run well for amateur. *Mrs A. J. Perrett*   **40**

CATCHTHEBATCH   3 b.g. Beveled (USA) – Batchworth Dancer 67 (Ballacashtal (CAN)) [1998 53: 6d a5g a5g⁴ 1999 a5g⁴ a6g* a6g⁵ 6m⁶ 5d⁵ 6g 5.1m 5m³ 5.2s a6g Dec 11] fair performer on all-weather, modest on turf: made all in maiden at Lingfield in January: best effort after when third in handicap at Goodwood: effective at 5f/easy 6f: acts on equitrack (little form on fibresand) and good to firm going. *E. A. Wheeler*   **59 a66**

CATCHY WORD 2 ch.c. (Feb 18) Cadeaux Genereux 131 – Lora's Guest 99 (Be **99**
My Guest (USA) 126) [1999 6d* 7d³ 7d⁶ 7m* Oct 19] 110,000Y: close-coupled,
good-topped colt: sixth foal: half-brother to smart miler Centre Stalls (by In The
Wings) and fairly useful 1¾m winner Nawahil (by Shirley Heights): dam, 7f winner,
sister to 1000 Guineas winner On The House: useful performer: won maiden at
Haydock (veered left under pressure) in June and minor event at Yarmouth in
October, making all by 2½ lengths from Abderian on second occasion: will prove
best up to 7f: yet to race on extremes of going. *E. A. L. Dunlop*

CATERINA SFORZA 4 ch.f. Machiavellian (USA) 123 – Symeterie (USA) **–**
(Seattle Song (USA) 130) [1998 9g²* 9s 10m³ 11s 10g³ 10m² 10s 1999 10.4s⁶ May
12] rangy, angular filly: second foal: closely related to Italian 9f and 11f winner
Mount Taurus (by Lycius): dam, ran twice in France, half-sister to high-class
sprinter/miler Proskona and smart performer up to 9f Korveya (dam of Hector
Protector and Bosra Sham): useful performer (rated 95) at 3 yrs for G. Botti in Italy,
winning minor event at Milan and finishing creditable seventh in Oaks d'Italia on
same course (blinkered) fourth start: last of 6 in listed event at York on only outing in
Britain: stays 11f: acts on soft and good to firm going: returned to Italy. *J. L. Dunlop*

CATRIONA 3 b.f. Bustino 136 – Nadia Nerina (CAN) (Northern Dancer) [1998 **75**
69p: 7d⁴ 1999 8g³ 8.3m 8g³ 8f² 7.5v³ 8g 7f* 7g⁵ Aug 5] angular filly: fair form: made
all in maiden at Catterick in July: bred to stay beyond 1m: acts on firm going: front
runner: visored final 2 starts: sold 13,500 gns in December. *J. Noseda*

CATULLUS 3 b.g. Prince Sabo 123 – Rive-Jumelle (IRE) 78 (M Double M **75**
(USA)) [1998 63: 6m⁴ 7m⁴ 7m⁶ 8m 7s 1999 a13g² 12d⁴ 10f* a9.4g⁴ 10.2m⁴ 10.5m⁵ **a55**
10m³ 12m⁴ 14.1g* 14.1m 14.1g Oct 2] angular gelding: fair handicapper on turf,
modest on all-weather: won at Nottingham in May and August: stays 1¾m: acts on
fibresand and firm going, well beaten on soft: sold 16,000 gns, joined M. Pipe.
M. L. W. Bell

CAUDA EQUINA 5 gr.g. Statoblest 120 – Sea Fret 96 (Habat 127) [1998 83: 5d **93**
5v⁵ 6s⁵ 6g⁶ 5.1g 6m 6m 6d⁵ 6m³ 6g² 6m² 6m⁵ 5.9m³ 5g⁵ 5.7d³ 6g 5.7g* 6g⁶ 6m² 5g*
5.7m* 6d 5m⁶ 6g² 5s² 6v³ 1999 5g⁶ 5d⁵ 6m³ 5s 5.1g* 6m² 6d 5.7g⁶ 6.1m⁴ 6g 5.1g*
6m 6f 6f⁴ 5.2g³ 5d* 5.7m² 5.6g 6d 6v 6s³ 5d 5s Oct 23] good-topped gelding:
unimpressive mover: fairly useful performer: won minor events at Bath in May
(dead-heat) and Lingfield in August (sixth win there): then Lingfield in August: acts on
good to firm and heavy going: twice visored (ran respectably) in 1998: usually held
up: tough: winner 5 times for T. Quinn. *M. R. Channon*

CAUDILLO (IRE) 6 b.m. Nordico (USA) – Over Swing (FR) (Saint Cyrien (FR) **–**
128) [1998 57, a62: a7g² a7g⁴ a8.5g² a7g 6.9m⁴ 7g² 8m⁴ 8.3g³ 7m⁵ 1999 a8g Jan 11]
small, strong mare: modest handicapper: well beaten only start in 1999: effective at
6f to 1¼m: acts on firm ground, soft and fibresand. *Miss Gay Kelleway*

CAUNTON 2 b.f. (Mar 16) Suave Dancer (USA) 136 – Arminda (Blakeney 126) **59**
[1999 7m 8m⁴ 8.2s Oct 5] half-sister to 3-y-o Alexander and several winners,
including 1997 2-y-o 7f winner Optimistic (by Reprimand) and fairly useful 7f (at 2
yrs) to 12.5f winner Carburton (by Rock City): dam unraced half-sister to Prix de
Diane winner Madam Gay: probably best effort in maidens when over 10 lengths
fourth of 5 to High Walden at Leicester: gave trouble at stalls final start: will stay at
least 1½m: sold 1,700 gns. *M. L. W. Bell*

CAUSED CONFUSION (USA) 4 b.g. Miswaki (USA) 124 – Reassert (USA) **–**
(Assert 134) [1998 NR 1999 11.8g⁶ 10.2s⁵ Sep 27] $140,000Y: angular gelding:
half-brother to a winner in USA by Spend A Buck: dam, won 5 times in USA,
including 8.5f minor stakes, out of half-sister to top-class 1972 French 2-y-o
Targowice: signs of a little ability: bandaged front/pulled hard on debut. *G. Barnett*

CAUTION 5 b.m. Warning 136 – Fairy Flax (IRE) 97 (Dancing Brave (USA) 140) **75**
[1998 69: 7g 5g⁵ 5g² 5g 5s⁴ 6g 6g⁶ 6g² 6m³ 6m 7m 5m 5v* 1999 6g 5m² 5m 6m²
5.1s³ 5g 5d⁵ Oct 18] small, unfurnished mare: fair handicapper: creditable efforts
when placed and on final start: winner over 7.5f, best at 5f (given strong pace)/6f:
acts on good to firm and heavy going: blinkered (below form) once in 1998:
sometimes slowly away, and usually comes from behind. *S. Gollings*

CAUTIONARY (IRE) 2 b.f. (Feb 3) Warning 136 – Iltimas (USA) 95 (Dayjur **78**
(USA) 137) [1999 5v² 5g* 6s² 6s² 7g Jul 26] IR 13,000Y: first foal: dam, 5f/6f

winner, half-sister to Queen Mary winner Nadwah: fair performer: won maiden at Hamilton in May, and ran creditably next 2 starts: stays 6f (possibly didn't stay 7f final outing): raced only on good ground or softer. *J. Berry*

CAUTIOUS JOE 2 b.f. (Mar 3) First Trump 118 – Jomel Amou (IRE) (Ela-Mana-Mou 132) [1999 5m* 5d a5g Dec 17] 6,500F, 6,200Y: neat filly: second foal: dam Irish 1¼m and 1½m winner who stayed 1¾m: fair form: won 19-runner maiden at Newcastle in May: poorly drawn next time, off 6 months before showing up well long way in Southwell nursery final start: should be suited by fair bit further than 5f. *R. A. Fahey* **70**

CAVALIER 2 b.c. (Mar 15) Bigstone (IRE) 126 – Belle Arrivee 87 (Bustino 136) [1999 7.1d⁶ 8s⁵ 7.1v* Oct 13] 45,000Y: sixth foal: dam 1¼m winner Berenice (by Groom Dancer) and fair 7f winner Kafani Al Widd (by Royal Academy): dam, 1¼m winner, closely related to Mtoto: easily best effort in maidens when winning at Haydock by short head from Nooshman, challenging from 2f out: should stay 1m: raced only on ground softer than good: sold 30,000 gns, sent to Norway. *W. J. Haggas* **81**

CAVALLINA (USA) 4 b.f. Theatrical 128 – Sedulous 107 (Tap On Wood 130) [1998 85, a?: 8g³ 9s³ 9g⁵ 8v⁴ 1999 a8g a8g Feb 15] half-sister to several winners, including useful miler So Sedulous (by The Minstrel): dam winner from 5f to 1m at 2 yrs in Ireland and later won in USA: fairly useful maiden at best for D. Weld in Ireland: well beaten both starts on all-weather early in 1999: stays 1m: blinkered (below form) final start at 3 yrs. *K. R. Burke* **–**

CAVERNISTA 3 b.f. Lion Cavern (USA) 117 – Princess Genista 108 (Ile de Bourbon (USA) 133) [1998 68p: 7g 7.1s⁵ 1999 8g⁴ 9f⁴ Jun 26] leggy filly: fair maiden: best effort at Salisbury on reappearance: should stay 1¼m: sold 4,500 gns in December. *J. L. Dunlop* **75**

CAVERSFIELD 4 ch.c. Tina's Pet 121 – Canoodle 66 (Warpath 113) [1998 70, a65: 7.1g 7g 7d⁴ 10.2s 8m³ 7f⁶ 7m 7.6m² 7m 7s³ 8.2s 7d 7s³ a7g³ a9.4g⁶ 1999 a8g⁶ 7f² 8f⁴ 8s⁴ 7m³ 8.3g⁵ 7f³ 7.1m³ 8.3m 8m 8m Sep 2] workmanlike colt: modest handicapper: stays 1m: acts on firm going, soft and equitrack: blinkered/visored (below form) once each: inconsistent: joined Miss E. Lavelle. *R. Hannon* **64**

CAXTON LAD 2 b.c. (Jan 16) Cyrano de Bergerac 120 – Urania 66 (Most Welcome 131) [1999 6d³ 5.1m⁶ 6d 5s* 5.2d⁶ a5g* Dec 17] 9,500Y: first foal: dam, lightly raced, placed at 1m/1¼m: easily best efforts when winning nurseries at Haydock in October (by 5 lengths) and Southwell in December (comfortably by 3½ lengths from Sirene): ran as though something amiss in between: speedy, but likely to stay 6f: acts on soft going and fibresand: useful performer in the making, and should win more races. *P. J. Makin* **93 p**

CD FLYER (IRE) 2 ch.g. (Mar 12) Grand Lodge (USA) 125 – Pretext (Polish Precedent (USA) 131) [1999 5.2m⁶ 5d³ 5g⁴ 5d* 5d³ 5m⁴ 7m 6s* 6d 7.3v⁵ Oct 23] 17,000F, 13,000Y: lengthy, angular gelding: good walker: second foal: half-brother to 3-y-o Why Worry Now: dam twice-raced half-sister to smart French 1m to 1½m performer Bon Point: fair performer: won minor event at Thirsk in May and nursery at Newmarket in October: stays 7f: acts on good to firm and heavy going: held up: consistent. *M. R. Channon* **79**

CEDAR BOSS 2 gr.g. (Mar 7) Mystiko (USA) 124 – Strapless 84 (Bustino 136) [1999 a6g Dec 6] 5,800Y: half-brother to several winners, including useful 6f (at 2 yrs)/7f winner Polish Admiral (by Roi Danzig), fairly useful 5f to 7f (at 2 yrs) winner Faith Alone (by Safawan) and 4-y-o Uplifting: dam, 6f winner, daughter of very smart 2-y-o Dame Foolish: showed nothing in maiden at Lingfield. *R. J. O'Sullivan* **–**

CEDAR CHIEF 2 b.c. (May 18) Saddlers' Hall (IRE) 126 – Dame Ashfield 90 (Grundy 137) [1999 7g 7m 7.6g 10.2s Sep 27] 10,000Y: half-brother to 3-y-o Pancake Wood, a 7-y-o Select Equiname and several winners, including stayers Rosina Mae (by Rousillon) and Shirley Sue (by Shirley Heights): dam 1½m winner out of Park Hill winner African Dancer: well held in maidens. *R. J. O'Sullivan* **–**

CEDAR FLAG (IRE) 5 br.g. Jareer (USA) 115 – Sasha Lea (Cawston's Clown 113) [1998 NR 1999 a10g a12g⁶ a7g Dec 8] half-brother to a winner over hurdles: dam unraced: poor form, including in seller, at Lingfield. *R. J. O'Sullivan* **29**

CEDAR GUV'NOR (IRE)   2 b.g. (Apr 13) Perugino (USA) 84 – Start Again **54**
(IRE) (Cyrano de Bergerac 120) [1999 5g 5.3f⁴ 6g 5m³ 6f⁶ 5g 6s a6g⁶ a6g⁶ a8g Nov **a50**
16] IR 5,000F, 5,800Y: leggy gelding: first foal: dam unraced: modest maiden: stays
6f: acts on firm ground and equitrack: inconsistent. *R. J. O'Sullivan*

CEDAR LIGHT (IRE)   2 b.c. (Apr 30) Dolphin Street (FR) 125 – Maxencia   **–**
(FR) (Tennyson (FR) 124) [1999 5d Apr 27] 6,500Y: half-brother to numerous
winners, including smart French middle-distance colt Magistros (by Carwhite) and
fairly useful 1¾m winner Eelious (by Nureyev): dam French 2-y-o 1m winner: well
beaten in maiden at Windsor. *R. J. O'Sullivan*

CEDAR LORD   2 b.c. (Apr 26) Emperor Jones (USA) 119 – Bint Damascus   **–**
(USA) (Damascus (USA)) [1999 5m May 22] 1,000Y: fifth living foal: half-brother
to fairly useful 1¼m/1½m winner Serendipity (by Mtoto): dam, placed once in USA,
closely related to Grade 1 9f winner Moment To Buy: dwelt and always behind in
minor event at Lingfield: bred to need further than 5f. *R. J. O'Sullivan*

CEDAR MASTER (IRE)   2 b.c. (Apr 25) Soviet Lad (USA) – Samriah (IRE)   **89**
(Wassl 125) [1999 5m⁵ 5.3f³ 6.1d* 6m 6m³ 5.2m³ 6m³ 6g 7g² 8s⁴ Oct 22] 15,000F,
15,500Y: quite attractive colt, shade unfurnished: third foal: half-brother to a 5f
winner in Hong Kong and fairly useful 1997 2-y-o 5f winner Baby Grand (both by
Mukaddamah): dam unraced: fairly useful performer: won maiden at Chepstow in
May: creditable efforts after when placed in minor events and Super Sprint at
Newbury (66/1, third of 25 to Don Puccini): stays 7f: acts on firm and good to soft
ground: best efforts in blinkers: often soon off bridle. *R. J. O'Sullivan*

CEDAR PRINCE (IRE)   2 b.c. (Apr 7) Namaqualand (USA) – Supreme Crown   **77**
(USA) (Chief's Crown (USA)) [1999 6g 6d² 6m 6m 7f³ 7m* 7m² 7s Sep 22] 7,500Y:
leggy, unfurnished colt: sixth foal: brother to 3-y-o Tough Guy and half-brother to 2
winners, including fairly useful 1993 2-y-o 1m winner Violet Crown (by Kefaah):
dam unraced daughter of US Grade 1 2-y-o 6f winner Share The Fantasy: fair
performer: improved efforts in nurseries when blinkered and ridden from front sixth
and seventh starts, winning at Ascot (stayed against favoured far rail) and runner-up
at Goodwood: stays 7f: acts on good to firm and good to soft going: blinkered last 3
starts. *R. J. O'Sullivan*

CEDAR WELLS (USA)   3 b.g. Desert Secret (IRE) 106 – Sans Sorrow (USA)   **65**
(Barachois (CAN)) [1998 61+: 6d⁴ 5m⁴ 6.1g 7s a7g³ a7g* 1999 7m 6m⁵ 8.1m 8f⁵
8.5g² 8f² 8f 8m Sep 10] fair performer: good second in claimer at Epsom and
handicap at Brighton in June/July: stays 1m: acts on equitrack and firm going: has
carried head high: has reportedly broken blood vessels: front runner. *G. Lewis*

CEEDEBEE   3 b.f. Cyrano de Bergerac 120 – Bonita Bee 50 (King of Spain 121)   **–**
[1998 NR 1999 6d Oct 28] first foal: dam, maiden, best effort at 6f: showed nothing
in Windsor maiden (tongue tied, went freely to post). *J. C. McConnochie*

CEE-N-K (IRE)   5 b.g. Thatching 131 – Valois (Lyphard (USA) 132) [1998 52:   **31**
a9.4g² a8g 7d 8.5m 7g 7.6m 10.1g³ 8.1d 8.3s 8m 10m 1999 10s 8m 8d 8g 11.1m
12.1f 11m Aug 28] poor handicapper nowadays: left D. Nicholls after fourth start:
probably stays 1½m: acts on firm going and all-weather: sometimes blinkered/
visored: sold 1,800 gns, joined D. McCain. *Mrs G. S. Rees*

CELANDINE   6 b.m. Warning 136 – Silly Bold (Rousillon (USA) 133) [1998 67:   **68 d**
6.1s 7g² 7g 7m* 7m 7g⁴ 7m* 7g⁵ 7v 1999 7g⁴ 7.5d 7.1m⁵ 7m 7m 7m⁶ 7f 7m 7.5g 7g
7.5s Sep 21] leggy mare: has a quick action: fair handicapper: disappointing after
reappearance: best around 7f: acts on firm and good to soft going: blinkered/visored
once each: none too consistent, and has hinted at temperament. *Andrew Turnell*

CELEBES   2 b.g. (Mar 6) Weldnaas (USA) 112 – Shift Over (USA) 62 (Night Shift   **69**
(USA)) [1999 6d⁵ 6s⁶ 7m⁴ Jul 7] 5,500F, 32,000Y: well-grown, good-topped gelding:
brother to 7-y-o Night Dance and half-brother to 4-y-o Sharp Steel: dam, third at 6f
at 2 yrs, from family of April Run: fair form in maidens at Newbury, Leicester and
Epsom: should stay 1m. *I. A. Balding*

CELEBRATE (IRE)   3 ch.f. Generous (IRE) 139 – Bright Generation (IRE) 111   **77**
(Rainbow Quest (USA) 134) [1998 64: 6m⁶ 7m⁴ 1999 9.9m³ 7.6m⁵ 8.3m³ 8g 8f³
a8.5g Sep 18] workmanlike filly: fair maiden handicapper: should stay beyond 1m:
raced only on good going or firmer on turf. *S. P. C. Woods*

CELEBRATION CAKE (IRE)   7 b.g. Mister Majestic 122 – My Louise 54   **31**
(Manado 130) [1998 60: 8d³ 9g⁵ 10.9d⁴ 8m 9.2d* 9.2s⁴ 9.2d 9.1s 9.1v⁶ 8v 1999 9.2m
9.2f 9.2f 10.9g 12.1m⁶ 8m 9.2m³ 9.2m Sep 6] workmanlike gelding: has reportedly
had wind operation: poor performer nowadays: stays 9f: used to act on firm and soft
going: tried blinkered/visored: reportedly finished lame third start. *Miss L. A. Perratt*

CELEBRATION TOWN (IRE)   2 b. or br.g. (Apr 1) Case Law 113 – Battle   **67 ?**
Queen 85 (Kind of Hush 118) [1999 5d⁵ 5g 5g⁵ Aug 25] 30,000Y: brother to 3-y-o
Avondale Girl and half-brother to 2 winners, including 1994 2-y-o 5f winner C-Yer-
Simmie (by Prince Rupert): dam best at 6f/7f: fifth of 8 to Pipadash in Pontefract
minor event on debut: disappointing after, very reluctant to leave stalls next start and
needed to be led to post final one. *J. J. O'Neill*

CELERIC   7 b.g. Mtoto 134 – Hot Spice (Hotfoot 126) [1998 122: 12d 13.9g⁶   **120**
20s 16d³ 15.9f² 16g² 1999 16.2d* 16.4g⁵ 20m⁴ 16f⁶ 15.9m* 18m³ 16.1s³ Oct 2]
        What a difference a year makes. That grand servant Celeric didn't win a
race in 1998 when he had to carry a Group 1 penalty in most of his races, the
result of his Gold Cup victory the year before. Unburdened of the penalty in the
latest season, Celeric added the Insulpak Sagaro Stakes at Ascot in April and
the Weatherbys Insurance Lonsdale Stakes (his second win in the race) at York
in August to his list of triumphs in the principal staying events. He took both
races in typical fashion, working his way through the field after being held up
and being produced late to lead. Celeric's victory in the Lonsdale from Arctic
Owl and Rainbow High was his sixth at York—a course where he usually goes
well—but he has won at seven different tracks during his career. A good fourth
in the Gold Cup to Enzeli and a somewhat-unlucky third to Far Cry on his
penultimate outing, in the Doncaster Cup, in which he was hemmed against the
rail when trying to launch his finishing run, were the pick of Celeric's other
efforts. The tall, close-coupled Celeric, who usually takes the eye in the
paddock, is less consistent nowadays—he was reportedly worked in blinkers at
home after a below-form run in the Goodwood Cup—but he is still capable of
very smart form and should continue to pay his way. Stayers with his turn of
foot aren't usually kept out of the winner's enclosure for long. He acts on firm
going and on good to soft. *J. L. Dunlop*

Weatherbys Insurance Lonsdale Stakes, York—
Celeric shows he's still one of the best stayers around with his sixth course success;
Arctic Owl (left) loses nothing in defeat while Rainbow High (white sleeves) runs on again for third

Letheby & Christopher Old Newton Cup (Handicap), Haydock—
Celestial Welcome, Hill Farm Blues (right) and She's Our Mare (behind runner-up) make it a female 1–2–3

CELESTIAL BAY (IRE)   4 b.f. Star de Naskra (USA) – Kandara (FR) 88 (Dalsaan 125) [1998 50: 5s 5.1g 6m 8m 8m 6m³ 7m⁵ a6g 7d⁴ 1999 7s⁵ 6f⁴ 6f² 8f 6g² 6.1g 6m Jun 24] modest maiden handicapper: creditable efforts when in frame: best at 6f/7f: acts on firm and good to soft going: has reared leaving stalls/tended to hang, and possibly temperamental. *E. A. Wheeler* **60**

CELESTIAL CHOIR   9 b.m. Celestial Storm (USA) 132 – Choir (High Top 131) [1998 –: 11.9d 1999 12m Jun 15] angular mare: fairly useful at best: well beaten both starts on Flat since 7 yrs: fair hurdler/chaser. *J. L. Eyre* **–**

CELESTIAL KEY (USA)   9 br.g. Star de Naskra (USA) – Casa Key (USA) (Cormorant (USA)) [1998 95, a86+: a9g³ a8g⁶ a9g 8s² 7.1g⁶ 7m 8g² 9g* 8g 8s a8.5g a9.4g 1999 a8.5g 8v³ Apr 25] close-coupled, good-topped gelding: has a quick action: useful at best: well below par in 1999: best at 1m/9f: acts on good to firm, soft ground and fibresand: soundly beaten in blinkers: none too consistent. *M. Johnston* **79**

CELESTIAL WELCOME   4 b.f. Most Welcome 131 – Choral Sundown 81 (Night Shift (USA)) [1998 78: 8.3v* 9.3d* 8d* 7d* 8d 8s 11d⁶ 1999 8g* 10s² 10m² 10.5d* 8.9d 11.9s* 11.9f⁶ 12g⁶ 10d 12s 12s⁶ Oct 23] strong, workmanlike filly: useful handicapper: won at Newcastle in April and Haydock in June and July (Letheby & Christopher Old Newton Cup by ½ length from Hill Farm Blues): also creditable efforts eighth and tenth starts: seems best at 1¼m/1½m on ground softer than good. *Mrs M. Reveley* **96**

CELESTRIA   3 b.f. Cosmonaut – Celestial Air 96 (Rheingold 137) [1998 NR 1999 7m 7g⁴ Jun 3] half-sister to several winners, including fairly useful Deer Hunt (by Hadeer), best at 9f/1¼m, and 1½m winner Bellton (by Bellypha): dam 1½m winner: signs of a little ability in maidens at Kempton and Yarmouth: bred to need further. *W. Jarvis* **–**

CELTIC CROSS   4 b.f. Selkirk (USA) 129 – Abbey Strand (USA) 78 (Shadeed (USA) 135) [1998 NR 1999 7.1m* 8m² Jun 24] tall, useful-looking filly: good mover: second foal: dam, 1m winner, half-sister to smart 6f to 10.5f winner Church Parade and smart middle-distance stayer Castle Rising: useful form: lightly raced: won maiden at Haydock by 5 lengths: best effort when length second of 5 to Risque Lady in minor event at Newcastle following month: stayed 1m: raced only on good to firm ground: stud. *Sir Michael Stoute* **100**

CELTIC FLING   3 b.f. Lion Cavern (USA) 117 – Celtic Ring 93 (Welsh Pageant 132) [1998 NR 1999 7.1d² 8.3d* Nov 4] rather unfurnished filly: fourth foal: closely related to Celtic Swing (by Damister) and half-sister to 1992 2-y-o 7f winner Cissbury Ring (by Jalmood): dam 1¼m and 1½m winner from very good staying **77 p**

family: promising efforts in maidens 4 months apart, winning 17-runner event at Windsor by 5 lengths from Brazilian Mood: will stay 1¼m: slowly away on debut: capable of further improvement. *Lady Herries*

CELTIC SEAL 3 br.f. Lugana Beach 116 – Celtic Bird 77 (Celtic Cone 116) **54** [1998 61: 5m 5d⁵ 5g a5g* a5g 1999 a5g⁴ 5g a6g Sep 28] tall, leggy filly: modest performer: form in 1999 only on reappearance: likely to prove best at 5f: acts on fibresand, some promise on turf: looks a tricky ride. *J. Balding*

CELTIC VENTURE 4 ch.g. Risk Me (FR) 127 – Celtic River (IRE) (Caerleon **58** (USA) 132) [1998 NR 1999 5.3f* 5g 5m a5g a5g Nov 23] modest performer: won **a47 +** claimer at Brighton in April on return from 20-month break, making most: not discredited on equitrack fourth start: bred to stay at least 1m. *Julian Poulton*

CENSOR 6 b.g. Kris 135 – Mixed Applause (USA) 101 (Nijinsky (CAN) 138) **54** [1998 –: a11g 8g 7.5m a6g 9.1v 1999 10m 10g 10.3m⁴ 11.7m³ Jul 15] big gelding: one-time useful performer, only modest nowadays: ran creditably in claimer/seller last 2 starts: stays 11.7f, at least when conditions aren't testing: raced mainly on good/good to firm going (below form in 3 runs on fibresand): blinkered (out of form) final start at 5 yrs. *B. J. Llewellyn*

CENTAUR SPIRIT 2 b.g. (Mar 4) Distant Relative 128 – Winnie Reckless **–** (Local Suitor (USA) 128) [1999 8d Oct 30] 500Y: fourth foal: dam, tailed off both starts, out of unraced half-sister to top-class Wollow: seemed very green but ran on past beaten horses when ninth of 18 in Newmarket seller: may do better. *A. Streeter*

CENTER STAGE (IRE) 2 ch.c. (Feb 3) In The Wings 128 – Secret Feeling **72 p** (USA) (Riverman (USA) 131) [1999 7v⁴ 7s⁶ Nov 5] IR 12,000Y, 10,000 2-y-o: useful-looking colt: eighth foal: half-brother to 3 winners, including 6f to 1m winner Secret Always (by Always Fair): dam, Irish 2-y-o 1m winner, from family of Mysterious and J O Tobin: fair form in maidens at Lingfield and Doncaster (sixth of 20 to Golovin): likely to prove suited by 1¼m/1½m: open to improvement. *R. Hannon*

CENTRAL COAST (IRE) 3 b.c. Hamas (IRE) 125§ – Clairification (IRE) 57 **90 +** (Shernazar 131) [1998 89p: 6m² 6.1m* 6v 1999 8m 7m 6g⁵ 6m⁴ 5g⁴ 6m* 6m² 6m Aug 17] fairly useful handicapper: won at Newbury in July, and good second in rated stakes at Ascot 9 days later: ran poorly final start: may prove best at 6f/7f: acts on good to firm going, stiff task on heavy: may well do better. *J. M. P. Eustace*

CENTRAL PARK (IRE) 4 ch.c. In The Wings 128 – Park Special (Relkino **123** 131) [1998 115: 8d 12m* 12d⁴ 10g³ 12g* 12s⁵ 1999 a10f⁴ 10m* 12d 10.4m 16m² Nov 2]

Whether or not Godolphin's principal hope Kayf Tara would have won the Melbourne Cup, had he been able to participate, is open to question, but his stand-in Central Park ran a tremendous race to achieve the highest ever position by a British-trained horse when runner-up to Rogan Josh. Central Park was re-routed from the Mackinnon Stakes (a race also won by Rogan Josh) to the Melbourne Cup following the injury to Kayf Tara a week before. With doubts about his effectiveness over the two miles at Flemington, Central Park started at 50/1, longer odds than either of the two other runners from Britain, Yavana's Pace and Travelmate. Watched by a crowd of over one hundred thousand Central Park made most of the running, Frankie Dettori being allowed to dictate a steady pace, and although he held off several challenges inside the final two furlongs, Rogan Josh was just too strong at the finish. The winner, who received 17 lb from Central Park and was giving trainer Bart Cummings his eleventh win in the race, won by half a length, with Travelmate beaten less than a length in fifth despite suffering interference.

The Melbourne Cup ended Central Park's season on an unexpectedly high note—he had finished down the field in the Coronation Cup and the Juddmonte International when viewed largely as a pacemaker on his last two appearances in Europe—and he had gained his only victory during the year in May when returned to the scene of his Italian Derby triumph of the previous year. Central Park put up a very smart performance to beat the German filly

Premio Presidente della Repubblica, Rome—
an international flavour as Central Park returns to the scene of his Derby Italiano win;
the German filly Elle Danzig and French-trained Barbola (No.2) chase him home

Elle Danzig by two and a half lengths in the Group 1 Premio Presidente della Repubblica at Rome over a mile and a quarter. Central Park's first objective had been the Dubai World Cup in March when he put up a creditable performance on his first start on dirt, beaten three lengths into fourth behind stable-companion Almutawakel.

		Sadler's Wells	Northern Dancer
	In The Wings	(b 1981)	Fairy Bridge
	(b 1986)	High Hawk	Shirley Heights
Central Park (IRE)		(b 1980)	Sunbittern
(ch.c. 1995)		Relkino	Relko
	Park Special	(b 1973)	Pugnacity
	(b 1984)	Balilla	Balidar
		(b 1976)	Fighting

Central Park, who cost only 42,000 guineas as a yearling, is by In The Wings who, though primarily known as the sire of Singspiel, has the Irish Derby winner Winged Love and the very smart filly Annaba among his other notable progeny. Central Park's dam Park Special, who won a mile and a quarter maiden in Ireland, is also responsible for the Lowther winner Velvet Moon (by Shaadi) who won over a mile and a quarter as a three-year-old. The family is, in general, a speedy one with Park Special's half-brothers including the useful miler Careafolie and the Horris Hill winner Gouriev, and her dam Balilla winning over five furlongs at two. However, Central Park is not alone in showing stamina in excess of speed, as Balilla's half-sister Krakow produced the Prix Royal-Oak winner Braashee (who is by In The Wings' sire, Sadler's Wells). Park Special's 1996 foal Haaris (by Bigstone) is, not surprisingly, owned by Godolphin but he failed to see the racecourse whilst under the care of David Loder as a two-year-old. In 1999 she produced a full sister to Central Park and visited Entrepreneur, another son of Sadler's Wells.

The strong, lengthy Central Park acts on firm and good to soft going and on dirt, and stays two miles, at least when conditions aren't testing. He often takes a good hold and is a front runner. Although Central Park is several pounds below the best he should be able to add to his four pattern wins when found suitable opportunities, possibly abroad. Whatever the future holds though, with his gallant run in Australia Central Park has already made his own contribution to the 'internationalisation' of racing. *Saeed bin Suroor*

CEPHALONIA   2 b.f. (Mar 12) Slip Anchor 136 – Cephira (FR) (Abdos 134) **71 p** [1999 7v 8.2s 8.3d⁴ Oct 28] sister to 1¼m winner Set Adrift and half-sister to numerous winners, including 3-y-o Gevity, useful 1¼m winner Fast Manouvre (by Fast Topaze) and useful French 5f (at 2 yrs) to 7f winner Shaindy (by American Stress): dam ran 3 times in France: easily best effort in maidens when fourth of 13 to impressive Kalypso Katie at Windsor: slowly away first 2 starts: will be suited by 1¼m+: likely to do better still, and should make a fairly useful handicapper. *J. L. Dunlop*

CERIAD   3 b.f. Merdon Melody 98 – Teanarco (IRE) 94 (Kafu 120) [1998 NR — 1999 7.1m 7m Aug 22] first foal: dam 5.8f (at 2 yrs) to 7f winner: little sign of ability in maiden/seller. *J. Neville*

CERULEAN SKY (IRE)   3 b.f. Darshaan 133 – Solo de Lune (IRE) (Law **114** Society (USA) 130) [1998 104?: 8m* 8s⁶ 8d⁶ 8d⁶ 1999 8s* 9.3g⁶ 10d* 10.5d⁶ 11.9g 12m³ 12v 10g² 9f⁶ Nov 28] neat filly: second foal: half-sister to useful French 1997 2-y-o 7f/1m winner Diner de Lune (by Be My Guest): dam, French 11f winner, half-sister to smart French middle-distance filly Truly A Dream, from very good family: smart performer: successful in 1999 in listed race at Saint-Cloud in March and Prix Saint-Alary at Longchamp (by 2 lengths from Juvenia) in May: ran creditably when 4 lengths third to Daryaba in Prix Vermeille at Longchamp and when 1½ lengths second to Insight in E. P. Taylor Stakes at Woodbine: not discredited in Prix de Diane at Chantilly and Yorkshire Oaks fourth/fifth starts, stiff task when eighth in Prix de l'Arc de Triomphe on seventh one: stays 1½m: acts on good to firm and soft ground. *R. Collet, France*

CHABROL (CAN)   6 b.g. El Gran Senor (USA) 136 – Off The Record (USA) — (Chas Conerly (USA)) [1998 59, a66: a16g² 14.1d 14.8f⁵ 16m 16g⁴ 1999 a16g³ **a63** a14.8g⁵ a12g⁵ a16g 12d 16f⁵ 12d Sep 30] leggy gelding: modest handicapper: has had a variety of trainers: below form after second start, left P. Gilligan after fourth: stays 2m: acts on all-weather and any turf going: said to have had wind infirmity on fourth outing. *J. A. Gilbert*

CHAGALL   2 b.c. (Apr 11) Fraam 114 – Pooka 65 (Dominion 123) [1999 5d* **88** 5g² 5g* 5.5g 6.5s³ 6d* Oct 22] 750Y, resold 550Y: smallish, strong colt: fifth foal: half-brother to a winner in Greece by Emarati: dam placed at 5f at 2 yrs: fairly useful performer: won maiden at Baden-Baden in June, national listed race at Dusseldorf in July and 18-runner £18,000 sales race at Doncaster (by 1½ lengths from Baby Barry) in October: stays 6.5f: yet to race on ground firmer than good: blinkered final start. *Bruce Hellier, Germany*

CHAHAYA TIMOR (IRE)   7 b.g. Slip Anchor 136 – Roxy Hart (High Top 131) — [1998 –, a71: a16g⁴ a14.8g* a16.2g* a16g⁶ a14.8g⁴ 1999 a14.8g⁴ Dec 11] sturdy **a49** gelding: fair performer at 6 yrs: off course 21 months before only start at 7 yrs: stays 2m: best efforts on all-weather. *Miss S. J. Wilton*

CHAKA ZULU   2 b.g. (Mar 28) Muhtarram (USA) 125 – African Dance (USA) — (El Gran Senor (USA) 136) [1999 6g 6d 6d Nov 4] sixth foal: half-brother to fairly useful 1996 2-y-o 6f winner Telemania (by Mujtahid) and 1¼m winner Congo Man (by Rainbow Quest): dam, Irish maiden, daughter of Oaks runner-up Fleur Royale: always behind in maidens. *W. J. Haggas*

CHAKRA   5 gr.g. Mystiko (USA) 124 – Maracuja (USA) (Riverman (USA) 131) **51** [1998 61: a6g 5.1m³ 5g 5.1g 5g* 5d 5m* 5.3m⁶ 5g 5.1d 6g⁵ 5m³ 5.3g⁶ 1999 5d 5m 5g 5g⁴ 5g² 5.3g 5m 5.7m 5.1m⁶ 5m⁴ 5g 5.3m³ 5g 5m⁴ 5.1m Sep 9] big gelding: modest handicapper: stays 6f: acts on good to firm ground, probably not on softer than good: has been slowly away: usually held up. *J. M. Bradley*

CHALCEDONY   3 ch.g. Highest Honor (FR) 124 – Sweet Holland (USA) **64** (Alydar (USA)) [1998 64: 5s⁴ 6g 5.9d a7g³ a8g⁴ 1999 a10g* a11g* 14.6f³ 14.1m⁵ **a74** 12.1m Jun 23] tall, quite good-topped gelding: fair handicapper on all-weather, modest on turf: made all at Lingfield in January and Southwell in April, drifting right under pressure both times: stays 1¾m: acts on all-weather and firm going, probably on soft: reliable, though ran poorly in blinkers final start. *T. D. Barron*

Prix Saint-Alary, Longchamp—Cerulean Sky springs a 30/1 surprise, beating Juvenia, Visionnaire (rail) and Louve (No.10)

CHALIAPIN 4 b.g. Tragic Role (USA) – Last Note (Welsh Pageant 132) [1998 **55** NR 1999 a11g⁴ a12g² 11.8g Apr 8] 6,200Y: lengthy gelding: fourth foal: dam, ran once, out of half-sister to very useful stayer Fortissimo: modest form at best in maidens: in frame twice at Southwell: will stay beyond 1½m. *Bob Jones*

CHALLENGES (FR) 3 b.g. Zieten (USA) 118 – La Toscanella (FR) (Riverton **77 §** (FR) 124) [1998 91: 6s³ 6g² 7s⁵ 7g³ 8g³ 1999 10.3d³ 11.1g 12g 11.6g 10f³ 10.5s² 11.9d 8d 8s 12s 10v Nov 8] rather leggy, useful-looking gelding: fairly useful maiden at 2 yrs: inconsistent and only fair form at best in 1999, leaving B. Meehan after seventh start and J. Hammond after ninth: stays 11f: acts on soft going: tried blinkered, no improvement: has run in snatches and found little: one to treat with caution. *Mme E. Holmey, France*

Mr R. C. Strauss's "Cerulean Sky"

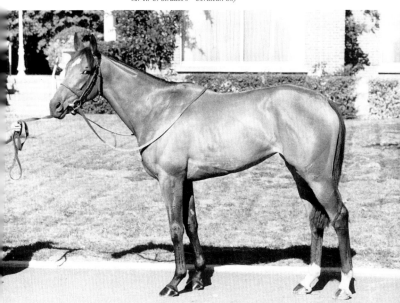

CHALOUPE 3 b.f. College Chapel 122 – Shallop 55 (Salse (USA) 128) [1998 **57** 58: 6m 6d 5s⁶ 1999 19m 6m 6.1m⁵ 7m⁶ 6m 6g² 7s 6d Oct 28] neat filly: modest maiden handicapper: should stay 7f: below form on ground softer than good. *H. Candy*

CHALUZ 5 b.g. Night Shift (USA) – Laluche (USA) 100 (Alleged (USA) 138) **–** [1998 –, a65: a8g* a8g² a7g* a6g a8g⁴ a7g⁴ a8g a7g 8f a7g 1999 a6g⁵ a8f a8g a6s* **a59** a6g³ a5g² a6g⁴ a6g a6g⁵ a7g⁶ a6g⁴ a7f⁵ a7g² a7g² a7g⁵ a6g⁵ Dec 27] small, close-coupled gelding: fluent mover: modest performer on all-weather: left K. Burke after winning claimer at Wolverhampton in February: ran at least respectably most starts afterwards: best up to 1m: acts on all-weather, lightly raced and little recent form on turf: tongue tied: has hung right: usually races prominently/leads. *N. P. Littmoden*

CHAMBOLLE MUSIGNY (USA) 3 b.f. Majestic Light (USA) – Bridal Up **59 §** (USA) (Sharpen Up 127) [1998 NR 1999 9.9m 10m 8g 11.5f⁴ 12f⁵ 7f 10g Sep 20] $75,000Y: fifth foal: sister to a winner in USA and half-sister to another by Leo Castelli: dam, won at up to 1m in USA, closely related to Rothmans International winner Husband: modest maiden at best: needs further than 7f and stays 11.5f: blinkered final start: temperamental, and needs treating with caution. *P. F. I. Cole*

CHAMBRE SEPAREE (USA) 3 ro.f. Cozzene (USA) – Ice House 89 (North- **83** fields (USA)) [1998 74p: 7d 7d⁴ 1999 7g 8.2s⁵ 9m³ 8g 8.3g² 8m* 8s 7m 10.1d Sep 15] tall, lengthy filly: fairly useful performer: won 6-runner maiden at Ascot in July, making all: not discredited in handicap at Salisbury penultimate start: should stay 1¼m: acts on good to firm ground, seemingly not on softer than good. *G. Wragg*

CHAMELI 4 b.f. Nordico (USA) – Try Vickers (USA) 72 (Fuzzbuster (USA)) **–** [1998 –, a58: a12g³ a10g³ a8g³ 7s 12m 8.3s a9.4g 1999 12m a11g Dec 13] modest maiden handicapper at best: no form at 4 yrs: stays 1½m: acts on good to firm ground and equitrack: blinkered (well held) once. *C. N. Kellett*

CHAMPAGNE 3 b.g. Efisio 120 – Success Story 60 (Sharrood (USA) 124) [1998 **70** NR 1999 7g 10.2m⁴ 10g* 12m Sep 2] first foal: dam 1¼m winner out of smart 1¼m performer Starlet: modest form in maidens prior to winning claimer at Leicester in August (final start for R. Charlton): not given hard race when last in minor event at Musselburgh final start: stays 1¼m, not certain to get further. *Andrew Reid*

CHAMPAGNE LADY (IRE) 2 b.f. (Feb 7) Turtle Island (IRE) 123 – Lucky **65** Fountain (IRE) (Lafontaine (USA) 117) [1999 5g⁶ 5.1g 7m⁴ 7m³ 7m⁶ 7g Oct 19] IR 11,000Y: smallish, sturdy filly: fourth living foal: half-sister to Irish 1995 2-y-o 6f winner Classic Fountain (by Classic Music), later 1m winner in Hong Kong, and a winner in Germany by Satco: dam unraced half-sister to smart middle-distance stayer Shambo: fair maiden: below form last 2 starts, final one after 2½-month absence: stays 7f. *R. Hannon*

CHAMPAGNE N DREAMS 7 b.m. Rambo Dancer (CAN) 107 – Pink Sensation **67** 69 (Sagaro 133) [1998 60: 8m² 10.1m² 8.1m* 10.4g 7m³ a7g 1999 8m³ 9f⁴ 5m 7.5g 10m⁴ 7g* 8g Oct 2] sturdy mare: fair handicapper: shaped encouragingly (horse banned 40 days, trainer fined and jockey banned under non-triers' rule on third outing) before winning at Catterick in September: probably best at 7f to 9f: acts on firm ground, below form only outing on soft: blinkered (below form) once at 4 yrs: ridden by 7-lb claimer Jenny Benson. *W. W. Haigh*

CHAMPAGNE RIDER 3 b.c. Presidium 124 – Petitesse 55 (Petong 126) [1998 **96** 90: 5v* 5.1g³ 6g* 6d 5d⁴ 5.2m⁶ 5d⁵ 1999 7g 7.6m⁴ 7d 6m⁵ 6g 6d³ 6m³ 7.1g 6m⁵ 6f 6m 6m* 6g 6.1g Sep 25] leggy, angular colt: good walker: useful handicapper: won at Leicester in August: well beaten both starts after: should prove as effective at 7f as 6f: acts on good to firm and heavy ground. *K. McAuliffe*

CHAMPFIS 2 b.c. (Apr 15) Efisio 120 – Champ d'Avril 89 (Northfields (USA)) **66 p** [1999 6s 5s³ Oct 5] 16,500 2-y-o: closely related to 1990 2-y-o 5f winner Zandril (by Forzando) and half-brother to several winners, including 3-y-o April Ace and smart sprinter Superpower (by Superlative): dam, 5f winner, seemed to stay 7f: much better effort in maidens when close third (first home on far side of course) of 14 to Poppy's Song at Catterick: likely to prove best at 5f: slowly away both starts: should do better still. *M. Johnston*

CHAPEL ROYALE (IRE) 2 gr.c. (Apr 25) College Chapel 122 – Merci Royale **78** (Fairy King (USA)) [1999 6d 6d 7s* Sep 29] IR 12,000Y, 12,000 2-y-o: tall colt:

second foal: dam ran once in Irish bumper: improved considerably to win 11-runner maiden at Newcastle in September by 1¼ lengths from Infotec, staying on strongly to lead final 1f: will stay 1m: raced only on good to soft/soft going. *Andrew Turnell*

CHARALAMBOUS (USA) 2 b.c. (Mar 14) Hermitage (USA) – Hula Lei (USA) **54 p** (State Dinner (USA)) [1999 7d⁴ Sep 15] $10,000F, IR 9,500Y: third foal: half-brother to a winner in USA by Sir Naskra: dam maiden in USA: weak 16/1-shot, some promise when never-nearer 13 lengths fourth of 9 to Decarchy in maiden at Yarmouth: will improve. *W. J. Haggas*

CHARGE 3 gr.g. Petong 126 – Madam Petoski 61 (Petoski 135) [1998 76: 5.7s³ **72** 5.7g⁴ 5g³ 1999 6v 5g⁴ 6d³ 5.7f⁴ a6g² a6g⁶ Dec 22] fair performer: won maiden at Lingfield in November: will prove best at 5f/6f: acts on equitrack and soft going, below form on firm: usually tongue tied. *B. Smart*

CHARITY CRUSADER 8 b.g. Rousillon (USA) 133 – Height of Folly 81 **59** (Shirley Heights 130) [1998 55: 16.1d⁶ 16s 16d⁴ 14s⁴ 14s² 14.1m³ 16m² 16g* 16v⁴ 16d 1999 14.1m² 14d⁶ 14.1m 12m² 14.1f⁴ 12g 16m Sep 2] modest performer: creditable efforts only when in frame, including in claimers: stays 2m: acts on any ground: has run in snatches: usually blinkered. *Mrs M. Reveley*

CHARLEIGH KEARY 2 b.f. (Apr 22) Sulaafah (USA) 119 – Woolcana 71 **55** (Some Hand 119) [1999 5v* a6g⁴ 5.3s 5.7s Oct 26] half-sister to several winners, including fairly useful 1990 2-y-o 6f winner Ageetee (by Tina's Pet) and 7f winner Pullover (by Windjammer): dam 5f winner: won claimer at Folkestone in April: well below that form in sellers after (off course 4½ months after second start): should stay 6f. *J. S. Moore*

CHARLEM 2 br.f. (Apr 28) Petardia 113 – La Neva (FR) (Arctic Tern (USA) 126) **–** [1999 7d 7s Nov 5] 4,000Y: tall, angular filly: seventh foal: half-sister to 1¾m winner Great Tern (by Simply Great): dam French 12.5f winner: well beaten in maidens at Doncaster. *D. Shaw*

CHARLENE LACY (IRE) 3 ch.f. Pips Pride 117 – Friendly Song 48 (Song **66** 132) [1998 77+: 5d* 5s 5m⁴ 5.2m 1999 6g 6g a6g 5g Aug 18] sparely-made filly: fair form at 2 yrs: below that level in 1999, best effort after 4-month break in handicap at York final start: likely to prove best at 5f. *A. P. Jarvis*

CHARLIE CHANG (IRE) 6 b.g. Don't Forget Me 127 – East River (FR) **41** (Arctic Tern (USA) 126) [1998 –, a45: a11g⁶ a9.4g² 10s 1999 a9.4g 15.8d⁵ 14.1v Sep 29] close-coupled gelding: poor handicapper on Flat and over hurdles: form in 1999 only in apprentice event second start: probably stays 2m: acts on firm going, good to soft and all-weather: effective blinkered or not. *B. J. Llewellyn*

CHARLIE GIRL 3 b.f. Puissance 110 – Charolles 82 (Ajdal (USA) 130) [1998 **68** 70: 5.1d 5m* 5.9m² 5d³ 5m³ 5g⁴ 5d² 5m² 5s³ 1999 5d⁶ 5d 5f 5g 5m 5m Jun 30] tall, leggy filly: fair performer: not so consistent as at 2 yrs: will prove best at 5f/6f: free-going sort, sometimes makes running. *J. Berry*

CHARLIE K (IRE) 2 ch.c. (Apr 26) River Falls 113 – So Ladylike (Malinowski **–** (USA) 123) [1999 5d³ May 24] 9,000 2-y-o: half-brother to a 6f winner in Italy by Scenic: dam lightly-raced maiden: always behind in 3-runner claimer at Hamilton: sold 500 gns, sent to Holland. *J. G. Given*

CHARLIES BRIDE (IRE) 4 b. or br.f. Rich Charlie 117 – Nordic Bride (IRE) **66** (Nordico (USA)) [1998 70: 6d* 5s² 6d⁵ 8.3d⁴ 5.9d 7.1g 8.3s 6.9d* 7.5m⁴ 7d 1999 7s 8d³ 8g 7.1d 8d Jul 6] small filly: fair handicapper: below form after second start: better at 7f/1m than shorter: acts on good to soft going: blinkered. *J. J. O'Neill*

CHARLIE'S DESTINY (HUN) 3 ch.c. Try Star – Masolat (HUN) (Andor **–** (HUN)) [1998 NR 1999 10d 12d Jun 4] angular, workmanlike, Hungarian-bred colt: soundly beaten in maidens at Newbury and Goodwood. *G. P. Enright*

CHARLIE'S GOLD 4 b.g. Shalford (IRE) 124§ – Ballet 61 (Sharrood (USA) **46** 124) [1998 54: 7s a6g 6.1m a14.8g* a16m 1999 a16g 12d 12g³ 14.1m² 14.1m² 12m⁵ 15.9d 14.1s 12g⁵ Nov 3] poor handicapper: creditable efforts when placed, and on final start: stays 14.8f: acts on fibresand and good to firm going: effective blinkered or not: has been slowly away: had saddle slip after racing freely final 2 starts: none too consistent. *A. Bailey*

CHARLIE SILLETT 7 ch.g. Handsome Sailor 125 – Bystrouska (Gorytus 78 (USA) 132) [1998 NR 1999 6v 6f 6g 6g Aug 21] tall gelding: fairly useful but unreliable handicapper in 1997: fair form on reappearance at 7 yrs, no show after: effective at testing 6f and stays 7f: used to go well in the mud: usually slowly away and has carried head high: nervy sort, usually early to post. *B. W. Hills*

CHARLIE'S QUEST 3 b.g. Kylian (USA) – Pleasure Quest (Efisio 120) [1998 – NR 1999 8.1d 8m 10v⁶ Oct 23] first foal: dam no worthwhile form: no show in maidens. *D. W. P. Arbuthnot*

CHARLOTTE RUSSE 2 b.f. (Jan 29) Rudimentary (USA) 118 – Do Run Run – 75 (Commanche Run 133) [1999 6.1m 7d a8g Nov 15] 4,700F: medium-sized, good-topped filly: fourth foal: sister to 4-y-o Deeceebee, and half-sister to 3-y-o Laylee: dam 1m winner: well beaten in maidens: tried visored. *Mrs N. Macauley*

CHARLOTTE'S CHOICE 2 b.f. (Apr 16) Noble Patriarch 115 – Covent Garden – Girl 67 (Sizzling Melody 117) [1999 5g 5d a5g⁵ Apr 26] sparely-made filly: first foal: dam 5f winner: well beaten in minor event, claimer and seller: has been tongue tied and bandaged: sent to Holland. *M. W. Easterby*

CHARLOTTEVALENTINA (IRE) 2 ch.f. (Apr 14) Perugino (USA) 84 – 78 The Top Diesis (USA) (Diesis 133) [1999 5g⁴ 5m⁶ 5m 6m* 6m 6.1d⁶ Aug 20] IR 8,500Y, 25,000 2-y-o: workmanlike filly: sixth foal: half-sister to 7-y-o San Michel: dam Italian 6.5f and 7.5f winner: fair performer: won maiden at Catterick in June: pulled too hard in visor final start: may prove better at 6f than 5f. *P. D. Evans*

CHARMANOVA 3 ch.f. Theatrical Charmer 114 – Mazurkanova 63 (Song 132) 56 d [1998 NR 1999 8.3d 9.9m 8.1g⁶ 7m 8g⁶ Aug 4] half-sister to winning sprinters by Indian Forest and Touchanova: dam, 2-y-o 6f winner, stayed 7.5f: modest form at best in maidens: ran poorly in claimer final start. *B. R. Millman*

CHARMING ADMIRAL (IRE) 6 b.g. Shareef Dancer (USA) 135 – Lilac 56 Charm 87 (Bustino 136) [1998 59d: a14g³ 16.2m a14g a12g 1999 a16.2g⁴ 21.6d² 13s³ 18g³ 16.1s⁴ 18g⁵ Jun 14] workmanlike gelding: modest maiden handicapper: at least respectable efforts most starts in 1999: stays 2¾m: acts on fibresand and soft ground, probably on good to firm: tried blinkered. *Mrs A. Duffield*

CHARMING LOTTE 2 b.f. (Mar 31) Nicolotte 118 – Courtisane (Persepolis 80 (FR) 127) [1999 5g³ 5s² 5.1m 6.5g 6m 7s³ 6v* 6v⁵ Oct 23] 3,000Y: leggy, angular filly: half-sister to 2 winners in Germany, including 11f winner Cicciolina (by Caerleon): dam French 2-y-o 7f winner from family of Seattle Slew and Lomond: fairly useful performer: best efforts last 2 starts, winning nursery at Ayr (eased) in October then creditable fifth of 17 in similar event at Newbury: stays 7f: goes well on soft/heavy ground: visored last 3 starts: sold 10,000 gns. *P. Shakespeare*

C-HARRY (IRE) 5 ch.h. Imperial Frontier (USA) 112 – Desert Gale (Taufan 69 (USA) 119) [1998 57, a63: a6g a7g⁵ a6g³ a6g⁵ a7g⁶ a7g² a7g³ a7g⁵ 6g³ 7d⁵ 5.9g 5.9d² a74 7g a7g³ a8.5g³ 7d a7g³ a7g⁴ a6g⁴ a7g a7g* a7g* 1999 a7g* a7g² a7g* a7g³ a7g⁴ a7g² a7g³ 7g a7g 6m* a6g* a7g² a8.5g⁴ 6g 7f² a7g* a7f⁶ a7g a7g⁵ a7g a7g⁴ a7g* a7g³ a7g a6g³ Dec 27] small, workmanlike horse: bad mover: fair performer: won claimers at Southwell and Wolverhampton in January, selling handicap at Leicester in May, handicap at Wolverhampton in June and claimer there in September, and seller at Southwell in November: effective at 6f/7f: acts on firm going, good to soft and fibresand (yet to race on equitrack): won in visor at 2 yrs, not tried since: has been bandaged: held up: tough and reliable. *R. Hollinshead*

CHARTER FLIGHT 3 b.g. Cosmonaut – Irene's Charter 72 (Persian Bold 123) 69 [1998 67p: 7s a9.4g² 1999 a8g³ 8m a8.5g* Sep 4] tall, rangy gelding: fair performer: won maiden handicap at Wolverhampton in September: stays 8.5f: acts on fibresand. *A. G. Newcombe*

CHASE THE PENNANT (USA) 2 ch.c. (Feb 7) Miswaki (USA) 124 – Ruth 72 Pitcher (USA) (Ack Ack (USA)) [1999 5m⁶ 5g⁵ 5d² Jun 5] $160,000Y: smallish, well-made colt: brother to fairly useful 1m winner Romantic Past and a winner in USA, closely related to 2 winners in USA by Forty Niner and half-brother to 2 minor stakes winners in USA: dam won at up to 9f in USA: fair form in maidens: should have stayed at least 7f: dead. *B. W. Hills*

CHASETOWN CAILIN 4 b.f. Suave Dancer (USA) 136 – Kilvarnet 78 (Furry **45**
Glen 121) [1998 –: 8d⁵ 10.3g 10.8m⁴ 8m 1999 9.9g 9.3m 10g a8g⁴ 8m 8.3m 8d² 8m⁵
8.1d 6f 10m 8d³ 8d Oct 26] leggy filly: poor maiden handicapper: stays 1¼m: acts on
good to firm going and good to soft: inconsistent. *Don Enrico Incisa*

CHASKA 4 b.f. Reprimand 122 – Royal Passion 78 (Ahonoora 122) [1998 –: **46**
a8.5g 8.5m 1999 a6g a8.5g 7g⁵ 8.3s 9.1v⁵ 11.5m³ 16g a16.2g Nov 17] unfurnished
filly: poor performer: stays 11.5f, unlikely to get 2m: acts on good to firm and heavy
going, little show on fibresand: tried visored: none too consistent. *A. Bailey*

CHATER FLAIR 2 b.g. (May 7) Efisio 120 – Native Flair 87 (Be My Native **–**
(USA) 122) [1999 7.1m 7m Jul 21] 8,000Y: rather leggy gelding: fifth foal: half-
brother to 4-y-o Holy Smoke and 6-y-o Nosey Native: dam 1¼m and 1½m winner:
well beaten in maidens at Sandown (missed break and flashed tail) and Leicester.
A. P. Jarvis

CHATER JADE (USA) 2 ch.g. (Apr 15) Miswaki (USA) 124 – Hispanola (FR) **77**
(Kris 135) [1999 6g 6g⁶ 7.1m³ 7.1m² Jul 3] IR 34,000Y: workmanlike gelding: sixth
foal: half-brother to 4-y-o Darwell's Folly and a winner in USA by Sovereign
Dancer: dam, French 1m/9f winner, half-sister to Derby winner Erhaab: fair form in
maidens: stays 7f: sent to Hong Kong. *A. P. Jarvis*

CHATTING (USA) 3 b.c. Exbourne (USA) 125 – Non Stop Talker (USA) (Arctic **99**
Tern (USA) 126) [1998 105p: 7m⁵ 7.1d* 8.1s* 1999 10.3s³ 8m⁵ 9f Dec 2] angular,
quite attractive colt: useful form: won minor event at Haydock by 10 lengths on final
start in 1998: best effort at 3 yrs when third to Zomaradah in similar race at Doncaster
on reappearance: reportedly suffered from bruised foot and off course 2½ months
before next outing (final one for Sir Michael Stoute): best effort at 1m: acts on soft
going. *A. Hassinger, USA*

CHAYANEE'S ARENA (IRE) 4 b.f. High Estate 127 – Arena 86 (Sallust 134) **–**
[1998 –: 8m 9.9m 1999 9.9g 9.9v a12g Dec 21] close-coupled filly: probably of little
account. *A. G. Newcombe*

CHEEK TO CHEEK 5 b.m. Shavian 125 – Intoxication 73 (Great Nephew 126) **71**
[1998 71: a12g* 13.1f* 12.1m 14.1g* 14m 12m 1999 a14.8g⁵ 11.9f⁴ 13.1g⁶ a12g⁶ **a62**
14.1g² 14.8m³ 16f² a16g⁵ Aug 20] workmanlike mare: unimpressive mover: fair
handicapper: creditable placed efforts in June/July: stays 2m: acts on fibresand (well
beaten on equitrack final start) and firm ground: flashes tail. *C. A. Cyzer*

CHEEKY MONKEY (USA) 3 ch.f. Beau Genius (CAN) – Crystal Lake (IRE) **61**
95 (Shirley Heights 130) [1998 60: 6f 6m 8g⁵ 10s 1999 11.6g 10m 10m² 10.5m*
11.7g² a12g Oct 1] leggy filly: modest performer: won seller at Warwick in June:
stays 11.7f: acts on good to firm going (well beaten on equitrack final start): tongue
tied: sold 2,000 gns. *R. T. Phillips*

CHEERFUL GROOM (IRE) 8 ch.g. Shy Groom (USA) – Carange (Known **37**
Fact (USA) 135) [1998 32, a64: a7g³ a6g⁴ a7g⁴ a6g⁶ a8g³ a7g² a8g² a8g⁶ a8.5g² a7g⁶ **a–**
8d⁴ 8m a8.5g* a7g a9.4g⁴ a8.5g* a8g³ a8.5g* a9.4g 1999 a8g⁴ a9.4g a8f a8g a8g 7s
a7g⁵ a8g a8.5g⁶ 7m⁶ a8.5g 7g 10m Sep 7] sturdy gelding: poor performer nowadays:
stays 9.4f: acts on fibresand and good to firm ground: tried visored. *D. Shaw*

CHELONIA (IRE) 2 g.f. (Feb 22) Turtle Island 123 – Whirl 79 (Bellypha **71**
130) [1999 7m³ Jul 16] IR 10,500F, 30,000Y: useful-looking filly, unfurnished: third
reported foal: half-sister to 1½m winner Top (by Shirley Heights) and a winner in
Italy (8.5f to 1½m) by Alhijaz: dam, 10.5f winner, half-sister to smart miler Dance
Turn: 2½ lengths third of 8 to Solaia in steadily-run maiden at Newmarket, leading
halfway until over 1f out: took eye to post: looked type to improve. *B. W. Hills*

CHELSEA BARRACKS 3 b.g. Deploy 131 – Hymne d'Amour (USA) 58 **98**
(Dixieland Band (USA)) [1998 84p: 8s⁴ 8.2s² 8d* 1999 8m⁶ 10.4d 10.4d² 12.3d* 12s
12d⁶ᵈⁱˢ Oct 14] smallish, sturdy gelding: useful handicapper: dead-heated with
Flossy but awarded race outright at Ripon in August: respectable sixth at Newmarket
final start (rider failed to weigh in): free-going sort, but stays 1½m: acts on good to
firm and good to soft going: often edgy: sold 45,000 gns, sent to USA. *J. L. Dunlop*

CHELSEA MANOR 3 b.c. Grand Lodge (USA) 125 – Docklands (USA) (Theat- **115**
rical 128) [1998 8g⁴ 8s⁵ 1999 10d² 10d* 10d* 10.5g² 9m⁴ 10d* Sep 22] second foal:
dam, ran once in Britain at 2 yrs and winner at 1m and 1¼m in France at 4 yrs,

half-sister to smart performer at up to 9f Wharf from family of Dahlia: smart performer: won minor events at Longchamp in April and May and La Coupe de Maisons-Laffitte (beat Agol Lack a length) in September: stays 1¼m: acts on good to firm and good to soft ground: stays in training. *P. Bary, France*

CHEMCAST 6 ch.g. Chilibang 120 – Golden October 62 (Young Generation 129) [1998 61, a65: a6g⁶ a5g³ a5g⁵ a5g³ a5g³ a5g 5s³ 5s⁴ 5g⁴ 5s 5f 5g a5g⁵ 6g 5v a5s a5g 1999 5m⁵ 5g 5f 5m 5m 5m² 5m a5g* a5g a6g Dec 6] lengthy gelding: modest handicapper: won strongly-run race at Lingfield in November: best at 5f: acts on firm going, soft and all-weather: effective blinkered or not: has worn tongue strap. *J. L. Eyre* **52**

CHEMIN-DE-FER 7 b.g. Darshaan 133 – Whitehaven 116 (Top Ville 129) [1998 NR 1999 14g Aug 14] 4,200 3-y-o: first foal: half-brother to 3 younger winners in France, notably smart middle-distance stayer Copeland (by Generous): dam French 1m (at 2 yrs) to 13.5f winner: behind in maiden at Lingfield. *B. A. Pearce* **–**

CHEM'S TRUCE (IRE) 2 b.c. (Mar 4) Brief Truce (USA) 126 – In The Rigging (USA) 78 (Topsider (USA)) [1999 5g⁵ 6m² 7s* Nov 2] 25,000F, 14,000Y: sixth foal: half-brother to German 1¼m winner Lambaran (by Law Society) and useful 1997 2-y-o 6f to 1m winner Wren (by Bob Back): dam 1m winner from family of Light Cavalry, Fairy Footsteps and Desert Prince: off course 5 months, confirmed previous promise when winning maiden at Catterick in November by 3½ lengths from Sea Squirt, travelling well and asserting over 1f out: will stay 1m: should improve further, and could be a useful performer in the making. *W. R. Muir* **83 p**

CHENNELL'S HILL 4 ch.f. Hubbly Bubbly (USA) – Oakhurst § (Mandrake Major 122) [1998 –: 10.1g⁴ 8m 1999 12.3m 10.4f Sep 2] seems of little account. *J. Norton* **–**

CHERISH ME 3 b.f. Polar Falcon (USA) 126 – Princess Zepoli 61 (Persepolis (FR) 127) [1998 NR 1999 7m⁵ 6.1g² 6g³ 7d a6g* a6g* Dec 11] fifth foal: sister to 6-y-o Polar Eclipse and half-sister to fairly useful 1994 2-y-o 5f winner Princess Sadie (by Shavian): dam 9f winner: fair form on turf: much improved on all-weather final 2 starts, winning maiden in November and handicap in December, both at Wolverhampton: better form at 6f than 7f: acts on fibresand and good to soft going: races prominently. *J. G. Given* **68 a88 +**

CHEROKEE CHARLIE 4 ch.g. Interrex (CAN) – Valentine Song 63 (Pas de Seul 133) [1998 –: a8g a11g 13.8m 10m 1999 16m 9.9s Sep 21] no sign of ability. *R. Craggs* **–**

CHEROKEE FLIGHT 5 b.g. Green Desert (USA) 127 – Totham 84 (Shernazar 131) [1998 69, a62: 10d 10g⁶ 10g 8g 10m 10m² 10m⁵ 10.2m* 1999 10d 10.3m 10m 10m⁴ 10g 10m 10.2g³ a12g Sep 18] strong gelding: modest handicapper: best at 1m to 1¼m: acts on fibresand and good to firm going: tried visored/blinkered, at least as effective without: inconsistent, and possibly temperamental. *S. Mellor* **59**

CHERRY PICKINGS (USA) 2 b.c. (Apr 11) Miner's Mark (USA) 120 – Cherry d'Or (USA) (Cassaleria (USA)) [1999 6m⁶ 6d 6g 6f⁴ 8f³ 8d Sep 26] $155,000Y: strong, quite attractive colt: sixth foal: half-brother to 2 winners in USA by Eastern Echo, notably 1994 2-y-o Grade 3 8.5f winner Western Echo: dam, winning sprinter in USA, half-sister to US Grade 1 9f winner Back Bay Barrister: modest maiden: likely to prove best up to 1m: acts on firm going: raced too freely in visor final start: sent to UAE. *J. H. M. Gosden* **60 +**

CHESHIRE CAT (IRE) 3 b.f. Ezzoud (IRE) 126 – Riyda 101 (Be My Guest (USA) 126) [1998 77: 6.1d³ 7s² 7d⁴ 1999 10.4d 10m⁶ 10.2m² 10s* 8.5f⁴ Dec 17] lengthy, angular filly: has a round action: fair performer: won maiden at Ayr in July, despite wandering, on final start for B. Hills: off 5 months subsequently: should stay 1½m: acts on good to firm and soft going: blinkered last 2 outings: has been bandaged: has carried head high under pressure. *B. L. Jackson, USA* **77**

CHESTER HOUSE (USA) 4 b.c. Mr Prospector (USA) – Toussaud (USA) 120 (El Gran Senor (USA) 136) [1998 123: 8v⁴ 10.3m* 10d² 10m* 10.4f³ 9.9m² 10g⁶ 1999 10.3m* 10m* 10m⁴ 10m⁴ 10.4m³ a10f⁴ Nov 6] tall, attractive colt: easy mover: smart performer: won listed race at Chester (idled) in May and Brigadier Gerard Stakes at Sandown (by 4 lengths from Generous Rosi) following month: in frame **119**

afterwards in Prince of Wales's Stakes at Royal Ascot (seemed less than resolute under pressure), Eclipse Stakes at Sandown, Juddmonte International at York (final start for H. Cecil, 9¾ lengths third of 12 to Royal Anthem) and Breeders' Cup Classic at Gulfstream (stumbled start and tailed off early but finished strongly when 3½ lengths fourth to Cat Thief): stays 1¼m: acts on firm going, good to soft and dirt: has become upset in preliminaries and not the easiest of rides. *R. Frankel, USA*

CHEWIT   7 gr.g. Beveled (USA) – Sylvan Song (Song 132) [1998 99, a112: a7g*   **79 +**
a10g⁴ 7.6m 7m* 6d⁴ 7f⁵ 7m² 7m 7g 7g 7s⁶ 1999 8d 8d a8.5g³ a8g⁵ Dec 18] tall   **a108**
gelding: useful performer, better on all-weather than turf: not disgraced when seventh in Lincoln Handicap at Doncaster on reappearance: withdrawn after proving mulish and bolting to post next intended outing (Victoria Cup in April): off 6 months after: creditable third to King Priam at Wolverhampton penultimate outing: very best form at 6f/7f: acts on all-weather, firm and good to soft ground (probably on soft): tried visored: has pulled hard, and best held up in strongly-run race. *G. L. Moore*

CHEZ CHERIE   2 ch.f. (Mar 12) Wolfhound (USA) 126 – Gerante (USA)   **97**
(Private Account (USA)) [1999 7f* 7m⁴ 8v⁵ Oct 3] quite attractive filly: second foal: dam, ran once in France, out of half-sister to smart French 1¼m winner Glity: useful form: overcame greenness when 20/1-winner of strongly-run maiden at Goodwood in July, leading 1f out: good efforts after when ½-length fourth of 9 to Icicle in Prestige Stakes on same course and 5½ lengths fifth of 11 to Lady of Chad in Prix Marcel Boussac at Longchamp, in latter staying on having been off bit in rear early on: will stay 1¼m: seems acts on any going. *P. W. Chapple-Hyam*

CHIANG MAI (IRE)   2 b.f. (Mar 30) Sadler's Wells (USA) 132 – Eljazzi 92   **98 p**
(Artaius (USA) 129) [1999 8d* 9s* Nov 7] IR 80,000Y: half-sister to several winners, including Prix de Diane winner Rafha (by Kris), herself dam of 4-y-o Sadian and fairly useful 1½m and 1¾m winner Sarawat (by Slip Anchor): dam, 2-y-o 7f winner, stayed 1¼m from family of very smart stayer Assessor: won 18-runner maiden at Navan by 2½ lengths in October and 9-runner listed race at Leopardstown (by ¾-length from Homer) following month: will be suited by 1¼m+: will improve further and should make a smart filly. *A. P. O'Brien, Ireland*

Davenport Hotel Eyrefield Stakes, Leopardstown—Chiang Mai upsets the odds laid on stable-mate Homer

CHICADEE (FR) 2 ch.f. (Jan 29) In A Tiff (IRE) 114 – Cos I Do (IRE) (Double **65 ?**
Schwartz 128) [1999 5g⁶ 6g 6.1m⁶ 5d Sep 30] strong, close-coupled filly: unimpressive mover: third reported foal: dam unraced half-sister to South African Grade 1 11f
and 2m winner Devon Air: modest maiden: bandaged behind final outing: should
stay 1m: sold 1,600 gns, sent to Slovakia. *D. Sasse*

CHICAGO BEAR (IRE) 3 ch.g. Night Shift (USA) – Last Drama (IRE) (Last **61**
Tycoon 131) [1998 –p: 6s 7d 7v⁶ 1999 11.4m 10m* 11.6m 10d 10s Oct 5] strong
gelding: good mover: modest performer: won claimer at Sandown in June: left
P. Cole after next start, well beaten final 2: best form at 1¼m: acts on good to firm
ground, well held on softer than good: blinkered (including at Sandown)/visored last
4 starts. *J. Mackie*

CHICAGO BLUES (IRE) 2 b.f. (Feb 13) Blues Traveller (IRE) 119 – Flight of **48**
Pleasure (USA) 74 (Roberto (USA) 131) [1999 5d 5.1s 6d 6g 7m 7g⁵ 8m 5.7s⁶ a8.5g⁴ **a45**
a8g⁶ Nov 30] 2,000Y: workmanlike filly: has a quick action: fifth foal: half-sister to
3 winners abroad, including Italian 1¼m winner Mama Vocasi (by Be My Chief):
dam, 2-y-o 6f/7f winner, later stayed 1¾m: poor maiden: stays 8.5f: acts on good to
firm going, soft and fibresand. *A. G. Newcombe*

CHICODOVE 3 b.f. In The Wings 128 – Chicobin (USA) (J O Tobin (USA) 130) **91**
[1998 75p: 7m⁴ a7g³ 8.1m⁴ 1999 9.1m² 11f* 14.4g² 16.2m³ 11.9d⁵ 14m² 12m* 12g*
14.8d Oct 15] big, lengthy filly: fairly useful handicapper: won at Redcar in May
then Goodwood (amateurs) and Catterick in September: very best form around 1½m:
acts on firm going, below form on good to soft/only run on fibresand: flashes tail/
carries head high. *Sir Mark Prescott*

CHIEF ABBA 3 ch.c. Be My Chief (USA) 122 – Themeda 69 (Sure Blade (USA) **53**
130) [1998 –: 6s 7g 7m⁵ 7g 1999 10f⁶ 10f⁴ 10.5m Jul 2] good-topped colt: had a
fluent, round action: modest maiden: left R. Hannon after second start: stayed 1¼m:
acted on firm ground: dead. *G. Woodward*

CHIEF CASHIER 4 b.g. Persian Bold 123 – Kentfield (Busted 134) [1998 82: **85**
8.1m² 9s 8m⁴ 10.1m* 11.5f⁶ 9.7f⁴ 10.1s* 9.9m⁴ 11.8d⁶ 1999 12.5s² 10.1s* 10.3m⁴
10.1g Jun 5] close-coupled gelding: fairly useful handicapper: has won 3 of his 4
starts at Epsom, including in April: not discredited after: ran creditably at 12.5f,
very best efforts around 1¼m: acts on firm and soft going: often makes running.
G. B. Balding

CHIEF JUSTICE 2 b.g. (Jan 23) Be My Chief (USA) 122 – Supreme Kingdom **–**
85 (Take A Reef 127) [1999 6g May 19] leggy, useful-looking gelding: half-brother
to 5-y-o Indian Brave, 7f to 9f winner Equerry (by Midyan) and 6f to 1¼m winner
Sakharov (by Bay Express): dam 2-y-o 7f winner who became temperamental:
attended by 2 handlers in paddock and unseated rider to post prior to finishing last of
10 in maiden at Goodwood. *N. P. Littmoden*

CHIEF MONARCH 5 b.g. Be My Chief (USA) 122 – American Beauty 74 **–**
(Mill Reef (USA) 141) [1998 89: 7d 10g⁶ 8.5g⁴ 8d 1999 8g 7g Oct 14] tall gelding:
fairly useful handicapper at 4 yrs, soundly beaten in 1999: effective at 1m to 1¼m:
acts on good to firm and good to soft going, possibly not on soft: fair form over
hurdles late in year. *R. A. Fahey*

CHIEF MOUSE 6 b.g. Be My Chief (USA) 122 – Top Mouse (High Top 131) **–**
[1998 NR 1999 15.8d Sep 21] sturdy gelding: winning hurdler/chaser: one-time fair
8.5f winner: well beaten only Flat start since 1997: sent to France. *Ian Williams*

CHIEF OF JUSTICE 2 b.c. (Apr 4) Be My Chief (USA) 122 – Clare Court **–**
89 (Glint of Gold 128) [1999 7m 7.1s 7d Oct 12] 12,000F, 16,000Y: close-coupled,
good-bodied colt: fourth foal: half-brother to smart Italian 9f and 1¼m winner Snake
Snap (by Shareef Dancer): dam 1m (at 2 yrs) to 1¾m winner from family of Silver
Patriarch: well held in maidens. *D. Shaw*

CHIEF PREDATOR (USA) 5 ch.g. Chief's Crown (USA) – Tsavorite (USA) **–**
(Halo (USA)) [1998 NR 1999 17.2m Aug 22] close-coupled gelding: modest maiden
at 3 yrs, well held in handicap only Flat run since: stays 1½m: acts on firm and soft
ground and equitrack (unraced on fibresand): tried blinkered/visored. *D. L. Williams*

CHIEF REBEL (USA) 3 b.c. Chief's Crown (USA) – Robellino Miss (USA) **98**
(Robellino (USA) 127) [1998 97: 6m* 7g² 6g 1999 8f³ 8m³ 7g 7.1g 8d² Oct 1] strong,

attractive colt: good mover, with a long stride: useful performer: creditable efforts when placed in minor events, second to impressive Tillerman at Newmarket: stays 1m: acts on firm and good to soft going: takes good hold: sold 43,000 gns, sent to Saudi Arabia. *G. Wragg*

CHIEF RESPONSE   2 b.c. (Mar 12) Be My Chief (USA) 122 – Red Rosein 97 (Red Sunset 120) [1999 5m² 5.1g² 6f⁴ 5d* 5g⁵ 6.1d² 6g 8d Oct 9] 15,000Y, 24,000 2-y-o: compact colt: third foal: half-brother to 3-y-o Young Rosein: dam, tough sprinter, won Wokingham: fair performer: won maiden at Thirsk in August: acts on good to firm and good to soft going, reportedly finished with sore shins after running on firm: sent to Denmark. *Miss Gay Kelleway*   **78**

CHIEF'S SONG   9 b.g. Chief Singer 131 – Tizzy 79 (Formidable (USA) 125) [1998 35: 16.4m⁴ 1999 16.4g Aug 20] tall gelding: useful hurdler/chaser, successful in October: still a maiden handicapper on Flat, lightly raced and only poor form since 1995: stays 2m: acts on good to firm and heavy going: tried visored. *S. Dow*   **36**

CHIEF WALLAH   3 b.c. Be My Chief (USA) 122 – Arusha (IRE) 84 (Dance of Life (USA)) [1998 NR 1999 10f⁶ Oct 20] second foal: dam, 2-y-o 1m winner, half-sister to 2000 Guineas winner Don't Forget Me: 20/1, needed experience in maiden at Nottingham, some late progress: should improve. *D. R. C. Elsworth*   **– p**

CHIKAL   4 b.g. Nalchik (USA) – Ty-With-Belle 67 (Pamroy 99) [1998 44: 10s³ 9.7v⁵ a9.4g 10d 10g 1999 a16.2g Apr 10] poor maiden handicapper: was best up to 1¼m: acted on good to firm and heavy going, well held both starts on fibresand: dead. *B. Palling*

CHIKO   2 b.g. (Apr 30) Afif 92 – Walsham Witch 61 (Music Maestro 119) [1999 5d* 5g 5d 6.1m a7g 6d⁵ 6.1s⁴ 7s a7g Nov 12] 1,200Y: angular, unfurnished gelding: second foal: half-brother to 4-y-o Bunnies Own: dam, 2-y-o 6f winner, probably stayed 2m: fair performer: won seller at Doncaster in March: clearly best efforts on sixth (possibly worth a rating of 71) and seventh outings: should stay 7f: acts on soft ground: visored last 4 starts: very slowly away both starts on fibresand: inconsistent, and possibly has some temperament. *J. L. Harris*   **65 + a?**

CHILDREN'S CHOICE (IRE)   8 b.m. Taufan (USA) 119 – Alice Brackloon (USA) (Melyno 130) [1998 60: 14.8f 12g 16g² 14.1f 16d 12m 14.1d⁴ 12g* 1999 a11g a16.2g⁶ 11.8s 15.4v⁴ 16m⁶ 13d a16g³ 17.2f² 14.1g³ 14.1m² 11.9g* 16.2g³ 17.1g 14.1m* 16m³ 15.8s⁵ 16d a16.2g² a16.2g⁶ Dec 4] workmanlike mare: modest performer: left D. Morris after second start: won sellers at Brighton (handicap) and Redcar in August: effective at 1½m to 17f: acts on all-weather and any turf going: blinkered (ran creditably) once at 5 yrs, effective visored or not: usually held up: not the easiest of rides, but is consistent. *J. Pearce*   **55**

CHI-LIN   4 b.f. Precocious 126 – Cool Combination 76 (Indian King (USA) 128) [1998 53, a–: a7g⁴ a7g 6.1v² 6.1s⁴ 8.3g 6s a6g a6g 1999 a6g 6d Oct 29] modest maiden: well beaten both starts in 1999: stays 7f: acts on heavy ground and equitrack. *P. Butler*   **–**

CHILI PEPPER   2 b.f. (Apr 22) Chilibang 120 – Game Germaine (Mummy's Game 120) [1999 5g² 5v 6m⁴ 6d⁴ 7.5s⁴ 5m⁵ 7.5g Sep 15] 500Y: leggy filly: third foal: half-sister to 4-y-o The Woodcock (by Handsome Sailor) and a 6.5f and 1m winner in Denmark by Cyrano de Bergerac: dam ran twice: poor maiden: should stay 7f: blinkered last 3 starts: has been bandaged: has carried head awkwardly. *A. Smith*   **48**

CHILLI   2 br.g. (Jan 28) Most Welcome 131 – So Saucy 59 (Teenoso (USA) 135) [1999 6g 7g 7g⁴ 8d Oct 18] 2,800Y: quite attractive gelding: second foal: brother to 3-y-o Most-Saucy: dam 1¼m and 17f winner: poor maiden: tailed off in nursery final start. *C. E. Brittain*   **51**

CHILLIAN   3 b.g. Chilibang 120 – Five Islands 62 (Bairn (USA) 126) [1998 49?: 5s 5d⁵ 5d⁵ 5d 5m 1999 5g 5g 7m Jul 12] little sign of ability: has shown signs of waywardness. *M. Brittain*   **–**

CHILWORTH (IRE)   2 ch.c. (Apr 13) Shalford (IRE) 124§ – Close The Till (Formidable (USA) 125) [1999 5g 6d⁶ 7g⁴ Jul 24] IR 2,600F, IR 4,800Y: second foal: dam, Irish 2-y-o 6f winner, also successful over hurdles: steady improvement in maidens, fourth of 16 to Carousing at Lingfield: should stay 1m. *T. M. Jones*   **65**

CHIMES OF PEACE   4 b.f. Magic Ring (IRE) 115 – Leprechaun Lady 57 (Royal Blend 117) [1998 60: 8s 8g* 8m⁵ 10s⁵ 10g³ 9.9m² 12m 10.4g⁴ 9.9m⁴ 1999 10v 9.3m 11.8g 10s³ 10m⁵ 10g 9.2m⁴ Aug 11] small filly: modest handicapper: creditable effort in 1999 only when third in apprentice event at Pontefract: probably stays 1½m: acts on good to firm and soft going: sold 850 gns in November. *J. L. Eyre*   **60 d**

CHIMNEY DUST   2 b.c. (May 7) Pelder (IRE) 125 – Evening Falls 82 (Beveled (USA)) [1999 6g 6.8m* 7m² 7s 7s⁴ Nov 6] 4,400Y: second foal: dam sprinter: fairly useful maiden: won maiden at Warwick in August: good fourth of 22 in Doncaster nursery final start: likely to prove best at 7f/1m: has veered (at stalls on debut)/ hung/ducked left on various occasions, and may prove best with waiting tactics. *G. C. H. Chung*   **84 +**

CHINABERRY   5 b.m. Soviet Star (USA) 128 – Crimson Conquest (USA) 85 (Diesis 133) [1998 –, a56: 8s 6g 7d a8g⁶ a8g² 8.3g 7g 7m 7.1d a6g³ a8.5g⁴ 1999 a8g* a8f a8g a8g a8g³ 8d³ a7g a8g⁴ a8g 8f² 8g 8.2g² 9g 8.9m⁶ 7g⁴ Sep 18] sturdy mare: modest handicapper: won at Southwell in January: mostly creditable efforts when in frame after: stays 1m: acts on firm ground, good to soft and fibresand: has looked less than keen: unpredictable. *M. Brittain*   **52 §**

CHINA CASTLE   6 b.g. Sayf El Arab (USA) 127 – Honey Plum 57 (Kind of Hush 118) [1998 –, a90: a11g² a12g* a12g* a12g⁴ a12g³ a9.4g² a8.5g⁴ a9.4g a12g a8.5g 1999 a11g* a12g* a11g* a12g* a9.4g³ a12g* a12g* a9.4g³ a12g* 11.9s 13v 14.1f⁵ 10.9s 11.1f* 11.1m a12g² a8.5g⁵ a10g⁴ Dec 8] good-topped gelding: useful on all-weather, modest on turf: won 6 handicaps and a minor event at Southwell and Wolverhampton from January to March, and a handicap at Hamilton in July: needs further than 9.4f and probably stays 1¾m: acts on all-weather (slightly better form on fibresand than equitrack) and firm ground: gets behind: tough. *P. C. Haslam*   **63 a107**

CHINAIDER (IRE)   4 b.f. Mujadil (USA) 119 – We Two (Glenstal (USA) 118) [1998 70: 7d 8m 7.5m 7.1g⁵ 8m 6g⁶ 6m² 6.1d a7g³ 6d⁶ 1999 a8g⁵ a6f 7m 6g 8f⁵ Sep 4] lengthy filly: just modest form in 1999: effective at 6f, probably at 1m: acts on fibresand, good to firm and good to soft ground: blinkered second start: sold 1,800 gns. *D. Nicholls*   **56**

CHINA MAIL (IRE)   7 b.g. Slip Anchor 136 – Fenney Mill 99 (Levmoss 133) [1998 NR 1999 a16f a16f a16g Feb 11] ungenuine winning staying hurdler: still a maiden, and no sign of retaining ability on Flat. *M. Quinn*   **–**

CHINA RED (USA)   5 br.g. Red Ransom (USA) – Akamare (FR) (Akarad (FR) 130) [1998 91: a8g⁵ 8m* 8m² 8.1m 8g* 8g⁶ 7.9g² 1999 8d a8g* 8g³ a8g* 8m 8g Jun 27] tall gelding: has a fluent, round action: useful handicapper on all-weather, fairly useful on turf: won twice at Lingfield in May: unable to dominate final 2 starts: stays 1m: acts on good to firm ground and equitrack (untried on fibresand): seems best making running on a turning track: game. *J. W. Hills*   **93 a104**

CHINATOWN (IRE)   2 br.c. (Feb 14) Marju (IRE) 127 – Sunley Saint 79 (Artaius (USA) 129) [1999 7.1d³ 7g* 8s⁴ Sep 26] IR 60,000F, IR 33,000Y: good-topped colt: good walker: has a quick action: eighth foal: half-brother to useful Italian winner up to 1½m Toaff (by Nordico) and fairly useful Irish 6f (at 2 yrs) and 1m winner Guided Tour (by Doubletour): dam, maiden, suited by 1½m: progressive form: won maiden at Newcastle in August: clearly best effort when under 3 lengths fourth of 6 to Royal Kingdom in Royal Lodge Stakes at Ascot, keeping on well: will prove suited by 1¼m/1½m: raced only on good ground or softer: joined Sir Michael Stoute: looks a smart 3-y-o in the making, sure to win more races. *P. W. Chapple-Hyam*   **104 p**

CHINA VISIT (USA)   2 b.c. (Mar 18) Red Ransom (USA) – Furajet (USA) 101 (The Minstrel (CAN) 135) [1999 6.5v* Aug 14] fourth foal: dam, best at 5f, closely related to 2000 Guineas winner King of Kings: made good impression when winning 4-runner newcomers event at Deauville in August, leading throughout and drawing right away in final 1f to beat Deep Sleep 8 lengths: looks a smart performer in the making. *D. R. Loder, France*   **107 p**

CHIN UP (IRE)   2 b.f. (May 15) Port Lucaya 118 – Tiempo 50 (King of Spain 121) [1999 5g 6f 6m⁵ Jul 26] close-coupled filly: fifth foal: half-sister to 3-y-o Apples And Pears and fairly useful 1997 2-y-o 1m winner Ten Bob (by Bob's   **58**

Return): dam, sprint maiden, half-sister to smart sprinter Grey Desire: modest maiden: should stay 7f. *M. H. Tompkins*

CHIPS (IRE) 4 ch.g. Common Grounds 118 – Inonder 31 (Belfort (FR) 89) [1998 **80 d** –: 6f 7g 7f 1999 6g 6m 8.1m⁵ 5.7h 7d³ 5m² Aug 30] big, good-topped gelding: only fair form at best in 1999: stays 7.5f: acts on good to firm and heavy going: visored (well below) once: has been bandaged: has high head carriage and sometimes finds little: sold 10,600 gns, to race in Saudi Arabia. *D. R. C. Elsworth*

CHIQUITA (IRE) 2 ch.f. (Feb 17) College Chapel 122 – Council Rock 74 **77 +** (General Assembly (USA)) [1999 5g⁵ 5.2g³ 6f² a5g* 5s* Oct 2] rather unfurnished filly: half-sister to 3-y-o 7f winner Royal Artist (by Royal Academy) and 3 winners abroad: dam, maiden best at 1¼m, daughter of Nassau winner Dancing Rocks: fair performer: won nurseries at Wolverhampton in September and Sandown in October: likely to prove best at 5f/6f: acts on firm going, soft and fibresand: has been bandaged behind: usually held up: sold 23,000 gns. *W. J. Haggas*

CHIST (USA) 4 b. or br.c. Lear Fan (USA) 130 – Morna 82 (Blakeney 126) [1998 **105** 109p: 10s* 11.8s² 12d³ 1999 12m⁵ 13.9s⁶ May 13] lengthy, angular colt: useful performer, lightly raced: respectable efforts in Jockey Club Stakes at Newmarket (4½ lengths fifth to Silver Patriarch) and Yorkshire Cup at York: probably stays 1¾m: acts on good to firm and soft ground. *M. H. Tompkins*

CHIT CHAT (IRE) 3 b.g. Mujadil (USA) 119 – Rhoman Ruby (IRE) (Rhoman **–** Rule (USA)) [1998 NR 1999 a9.4g Aug 6] IR 15,000F, 21,000Y, 700 2-y-o: second foal: dam Irish 7f to 8.5f winner: well beaten in maiden at Wolverhampton. *D. Burchell*

CHLOANNA (IRE) 3 b. or br.f. Up And At 'em 109 – Exclusive Lass (IRE) **54 d** (Doulab (USA) 115) [1998 –: 5m 6s 6.5v 1999 6g 7g 5f a6g Oct 18] third living foal: dam Irish 5f to 7f winner: form for J. Coogan in Ireland only when eighth in handicap at the Curragh on reappearance: no show only start in Britain. *D. Carroll*

CHOIRGIRL 3 b.f. Unfuwain (USA) 131 – Choir Mistress (Chief Singer 131) **106** [1998 99: 6g⁵ 6f⁴ 7m* 7m² 8s 1999 7m 8d² 8g⁴ 8m⁶ 8m 9.9d² 10.1g⁴ Sep 14] lengthy filly: has a long, round action: useful performer: best efforts when second in valuable event at Goodwood (to Mythical Girl) in May and in listed race at Salisbury (beaten 1¼ lengths by Ajhiba) in August and when close sixth to Balisada in Coronation Stakes at Royal Ascot in between: stays 1¼m: acts on firm and good to soft going: nervy type, sometimes has blanket for stalls entry and takes good hold: hung right third start: inconsistent and can't be relied upon implicitly: sent to USA. *J. H. M. Gosden*

CHOK-DI 3 b.g. Beveled (USA) – Pendona 72 (Blue Cashmere 129) [1998 47: **40** 5d⁶ 5d 5s⁵ 5d 5m 1999 6.1v 5d 6f⁵ 6f 5f 5f Sep 4] poor maiden handicapper: may prove best at 5f. *Mrs M. Reveley*

CHORUS 2 b.f. (Mar 17) Bandmaster (USA) 97 – Name That Tune 40 (Fayruz **71 +** 116) [1999 5s 5m⁶ 5g² 6m⁴ 5g⁴ 5d⁵ 5.1g⁵ 5.1f² 5d⁵ 6d⁴ 5s⁴ Nov 5] 2,000Y: neat filly: first foal: dam poor sprint maiden: fair maiden: best efforts when fourth in sales race at Doncaster and nursery on same course final 2 starts, meeting trouble in latter: stays 6f: acts on firm and soft going. *B. R. Millman*

CHORUS OF APPROVAL 3 b.g. Clantime 101 – Fyas 52 (Sayf El Arab (USA) **–** 127) [1998 58?: 6g 5m⁵ 6d⁶ 5g 6s 1999 5g 5.9g 5g 6f³ 7g 7g Jul 26] probably of little account nowadays. *Miss L. A. Perratt*

CHRISMAS CAROL (IRE) 3 b.f. Common Grounds 118 – Stockrose (Horage **–** 124) [1998 72: 6.1g³ 6.1s 1999 6g 7d 7m 6g 7m 7g a7g Nov 16] small, angular filly: modest maiden at best at 3 yrs: probably stays 7f: visored (no show) third start: has looked difficult ride: inconsistent. *P. W. Harris*

CHRIS'S LITTLE LAD (IRE) 2 ch.g. (Apr 5) Hamas (IRE) 125§ – Jeema **59** 102 (Thatch (USA) 136) [1999 7m 7.6g⁴ 6m 5g⁷] half-brother to several winners, including 3-y-o Sir Effendi and useful Irish 1997 2-y-o 6f winner Wish Me Luck (by Lycius): dam, best at 2 yrs, won 3 times at 5f: modest form in maidens, best effort when fourth of 16 at Lingfield (not well drawn in big field there final start): may prove best up to 7f. *W. R. Muir*

CHRISTIANSTED (IRE)   4 ch.g. Soviet Lad (USA) – How True (Known Fact   **85**
(USA) 135) [1998 77: 9v³ 9v³ 10s⁶ 12s* 12s 1999 12.3m* 14.4m⁴ 14.1m* 16.1m⁵
16g² Jul 26] leggy gelding: fifth foal: dam unraced: fairly useful handicapper: trained
in 1998 by Ms J. Morgan in Ireland: improved in 1999, winning 20-runner race at
Ripon in April and 15-runner apprentice event at Nottingham in June: good efforts
after, fifth in Northumberland Plate at Newcastle and runner-up at Galway: stays 2m:
successful on soft going, best form on good/good to firm. *F. Murphy*

CHRISTOPHERSSISTER   2 br.f. (Apr 20) Timeless Times (USA) 99 – Petite   **60**
Elite 47 (Anfield 117) [1999 5f⁶ 5d⁶ 5m⁴ 6m⁵ a5g² a5g Dec 13] 2,500Y: plain filly: **a55**
sixth foal: sister to 3-y-o E B Pearl and half-sister to 3 winners, including fairly useful
7f winner Effervescence (by Efisio): dam (maiden) stayed 7f: modest maiden:
effective at 5f/6f: acts on fibresand and good to firm ground. *N. Bycroft*

CHRYSOLITE (IRE)   4 ch.g. Kris 135 – Alamiya (IRE) (Doyoun 124) [1998   **64**
81: 9v 9m* 8g 9.9g⁴ 10.3f 1999 8g⁶ 10d⁵ 10m a8.5g 10d Nov 1] well-made, attractive
gelding: modest performer: below form after second start: stays 1¼m: acts on good
to firm and good to soft going: sold 4,000 gns, joined M. Sowersby. *B. W. Hills*

CHURCH FARM FLYER (IRE)   2 b.f. (May 1) College Chapel 122 – Young   **64**
Isabel (IRE) (Last Tycoon 131) [1999 7g 7m 8d⁶ a8g⁶ a7g³ a8g* a7g* Dec 15] IR
5,200Y: first foal: dam placed in Italy: modest performer: won seller at Lingfield and
nursery at Wolverhampton in December: stays 1m: acts on all-weather, best turf
effort on good to soft ground. *C. N. Allen*

CHURCHILL'S SHADOW (IRE)   5 b.h. Polish Precedent (USA) 131 – Shy   **59**
Princess (USA) 117 (Irish River (FR) 131) [1998 54, a58: a8g⁶ 7g* a7g⁵ a7g a6g a8f
1999 8m⁵ 7m⁴ 7g 7.7m 8.1m* 7m² 7.1m⁴ 7m⁵ a7g³ Dec 15] strong horse: easy
mover: modest handicapper: won seller at Chepstow in July: best at 7f/1m: acts on
firm going and equitrack (shaped well on fibresand final start): has been slowly
away/headstrong/wandered/flashed tail: usually held up. *B. A. Pearce*

CHURCHSTANTON (IRE)   7 b.g. Celio Rufo – Bailieboro (Bonne Noel 115)   **–**
[1998 NR 1999 22.2m Jun 18] IR 7,000 4-y-o: third foal: dam unraced: fairly useful
bumper winner: tailed off in Queen Alexandra Stakes at Royal Ascot on Flat debut.
Paddy Farrell

CHURLISH CHARM   4 b.c. Niniski (USA) 125 – Blushing Storm (USA) 102   **111**
(Blushing Groom (FR) 131) [1998 107: 12d² 12m* 16.2d⁵ 12g* 16g* 14s 1999 12d³
13.9s* 20m Jun 17] good-bodied colt: smart performer: 25/1-winner of 9-runner
Merewood Homes Yorkshire Cup at York in May by neck from Largesse, off bridle
long way out but responding to lead final 50 yds: creditable third to Carry The Flag
in handicap at Goodwood previous outing: stays 2m (seemed not to stay 2½m in
Gold Cup at Royal Ascot): acts on soft going and on good to firm: tends to wander.
R. Hannon

Merewood Homes Yorkshire Cup, York—a shock result
as 25/1-shots Churlish Charm (left) and Largesse (rail) finish ahead of the favourite Arctic Owl (second left);
Yavana's Pace is fourth

CIBENZE   2 b.f. (Jan 30) Owington 123 – Maria Cappuccini 70 (Siberian Express **68**
(USA) 125) [1999 6m⁵ 5g² 5g⁶ 5s⁵ 5.2d³ Oct 27] 15,000F, 37,000 2-y-o: leggy,
angular filly: fourth foal: half-sister to 4-y-o Mariana, 7f winner Agent (by Anshan)
and a winner in South Africa by Polar Falcon: dam, 5f winner who stayed 7f, half-
sister to smart performer up to 7f Marina Park: fair maiden: good staying-on third of
6 in nursery at Yarmouth: effective at 5f/6f: acts on good to firm and good to soft
going (ran poorly on soft). *M. R. Channon*

CICERONE   9 br.g. Tina's Pet 121 – Emma Royale 69 (Royal And Regal (USA))   **–**
[1998 NR 1999 9.2g May 2] leggy gelding: modest handicapper in 1996, well beaten
only start since: tried blinkered, won in a visor. *Miss Lucinda V. Russell*

CIEL DE REVE (USA)   5 b.g. Septieme Ciel (USA) 123 – Reve de Reine (USA)   **– §**
97 (Lyphard (USA) 132) [1998 60: 8s 8.5d 8d 8d 10g² 12s 8.5s³ 10m⁴ 8.5g⁴ a12g
a10g⁶ a8f a16g⁶ 1999 a16.2g 14.1s 8.3m 10m a8g Nov 22] poor and temperamental
handicapper nowadays: tried blinkered earlier in career. *K. C. Comerford*

CILANTRO   2 b.c. (Mar 23) Minshaanshu Amad (USA) 91§ – Laquette (Bairn   **41**
(USA) 126) [1999 6.1g⁵ 5.1m 7m 6.8d a6g Oct 16] 2,000Y: first foal: dam, half-sister
to dam of high-class French colt Highest Honor, showed little: poor maiden.
Miss A. Stokell

CINDER HILLS   4 ch.f. Deploy 131 – Dame du Moulin 81 (Shiny Tenth 120)   **–**
[1998 72: a6g a7g⁶ a11g² 10v* 12.3s* 12.3m³ 14m² 12.3s⁴ 15.8d 1999 16.1d 13.8s
Nov 2] workmanlike filly: has a round action: fair handicapper in 1998: well beaten
at 4 yrs, changing hands 4,000 gns in May: stays 1¾m: acts on good to firm ground,
heavy and fibresand. *M. W. Easterby*

CINDESTI (IRE)   3 b.c. Barathea (IRE) 127 – Niamh Cinn Oir (IRE) (King of   **65**
Clubs 124) [1998 –: 7m 8d 1999 10.3m⁴ 11.9m 10g a12g* a14.8g* Sep 18] good-   **a76**
bodied colt: fair performer: won handicap then minor event at Wolverhampton in
September: stays 14.8f: acts on fibresand, turf form only on good to firm going: tends
to edge right: may be capable of better still on all-weather. *B. A. McMahon*

CINEMA POINT (IRE)   2 b.g. (Mar 16) Doyoun 124 – Airport (Warpath 113)   **–**
[1999 7.5g 8d 8s Nov 6] IR 11,000Y: strong, lengthy gelding: seventh foal: closely
related to fairly useful Irish 1989 2-y-o 7f winner Hero's Welcome (by Simply
Great), later successful in USA, and half-brother to 2 winners, including Irish 9f
winner Final Contract (by Shaadi): dam, maiden, sister to Derby fourth Shotgun:
well held in maidens and a seller, slowly away each time. *M. H. Tompkins*

CINNAMON COURT (IRE)   2 b.f. (Mar 30) College Chapel 122 – Henrietta   **56**
Street (IRE) 83 (Royal Academy (USA) 130) [1999 6.1d 7g Oct 19] 10,000Y: first
foal: dam, Irish 1m winner, closely related to smart Irish sprinter Bradawn Breever:
some promise when seventh of 15 to Resounding in Nottingham maiden, but well
held in similar event at Lingfield later in October: should stay 7f. *J. R. Arnold*

CINNAMON LADY   3 ch.f. Emarati (USA) 74 – Nice Lady 65 (Connaught 130)   **77**
[1998 65: 7g 7g⁶ 6s 7s² 1999 7v² 7d³ 7d* 7d 7s³ a7g 8s Oct 4] angular, quite good-
topped filly: fair performer: won 24-runner handicap at Newbury in May: should
prove best up to easy 1m: yet to race on going firmer than good, hampered only
outing on fibresand: races prominently. *D. Morris*

CINNAMON STICK (IRE)   6 ch.g. Don't Forget Me 127 – Gothic Lady   **–**
(Godswalk (USA) 130) [1998 –: 12m 1999 12g 16.2g 17.2g a16.2g Sep 8] close-
coupled gelding: fair winning hurdler at best/no form on Flat: tried blinkered.
Mrs S. Lamyman

CIRCLE OF GOLD (IRE)   3 ch.f. Royal Academy (USA) 130 – Never So Fair   **110**
65 (Never So Bold 135) [1998 101+: 6g² 6m* 7m* 6g⁶ 1999 7g³ 8m 8.5f² 9g² 9f*
8.5f⁵ 8.5g³ Nov 20] leggy, quite attractive filly: easy mover: smart form: creditable
3¾ lengths third to Valentine Waltz in Nell Gwyn Stakes at Newmarket on reappearance: blinkered, well held in 1000 Guineas there next time and left P. Chapple-Hyam:
won allowance race at Belmont in October and good third in Grade 2 at Churchill
Downs final start: stays 9f: acts on firm going. *P. Byrne, USA*

CIRCLE OF LIGHT   2 b.f. (Feb 22) Anshan 119 – Cockatoo Island 99 (High   **87 p**
Top 131) [1999 7.6g* 8m Sep 9] half-sister to 4-y-o Treasure Island, fairly useful 7f
winner Coachella (by Warning) and useful 1¾m and Champion Hurdle winner

Collier Bay (by Green Desert): dam 1½m to 14.8f winner: well-backed favourite, won 16-runner maiden at Lingfield in August by 4 lengths from Water Jump, making all: similar form when eighth of 12 to Teggiano in Group 3 at Doncaster following month, racing freely in lead until over 3f out: should prove suited by 1¼m/1½m: probably capable of better still. *P. W. D'Arcy*

CIRCUITEER (IRE)   4 ch.g. Pips Pride 117 – Day Dress (Ashmore (FR) 125)   **48**
[1998 84: a6g² 7s⁵ 7.1d* 8m* 8s³ a7g* 8.5d⁶ 7g⁵ 8m 8m 1999 8v 8.1g a8.5g⁴ 8m   **a73**
7.6m 8m 7.1m³ 8.5g⁶ 8.3f a7g² 8m Sep 16] tall, lengthy gelding: fairly useful performer at 3 yrs: not so good in 1999, easily best efforts on all-weather: stays 1m: acts on fibresand, firm and good to soft going, probably on soft: blinkered once at 2 yrs: sent to UAE. *J. Berry*

CIRO'S PEARL (IRE)   5 b.m. Petorius 117 – Cut It Fine (USA) (Big Spruce   –
(USA)) [1998 75d: 12s 12m³ 14.4m⁶ 10g 10.1g 10g 10s⁴ 11.9s 1999 11.6m 12.1m 12.3g 15.8s a12g Oct 16] fair handicapper at best in 1998: on the downgrade. *A. W. Carroll*

CIRO (USA)   2 ch.c. (Apr 18) Woodman (USA) 126 – Gioconda (USA)   **110 p**
(Nijinsky (CAN) 138) [1999 7g² 8.5d* 8s* Oct 10]

    The recent domination of the best French two-year-old races for colts by raiders from Britain or Ireland might well be giving the authorities in that country cause for concern. The figures are staggering, as in the last five years fifty-four of the one hundred and two horses to have contested the Prix Morny, Prix de la Salamandre and Grand Criterium have been trained outside France, and they have won eleven of the fifteen races. In the latest season, ten of the fifteen runners in these events—a derisory overall total, given the prize-money on offer—were visitors. They occupied the first three places in the Morny, the first four places in the Salamandre and the first two places in the Grand Criterium, which with only three contestants had its smallest and worst field in our experience. Virus problems at Chantilly did nothing to help the French cause—champion Andre Fabre had only Grigorovich represent him in the three races—and in the interests of competitive racing it is to be hoped some improvement in the situation ensues in 2000 and beyond.

    Ciro, a well-bred individual of great promise, was awarded the Grand Criterium at Longchamp in October on the demotion of first-past-the-post Barathea Guest, a more experienced colt with a listed victory to his name. Ciro had run twice, finishing second at odds on when green in a maiden race won by Broche at the Curragh in June and scooting home by seven lengths in a similar event at Galway in September. The only rival for Ciro and Barathea Guest was Ocean of Wisdom, a brother to Machiavellian who had won the three-runner

Grand Criterium, Longchamp—only three runners for France's most prestigious two-year-old race but the first two manage to get in each other's way; Ciro finishes a neck behind Barathea Guest but is awarded the race, giving trainer Aidan O'Brien his third French two-year-old Group 1 winner of the year

Prix La Rochette comfortably three weeks earlier. Looking decidedly green again, Ciro, a 5/4-on shot, made the running. As they turned into the straight he was niggled at before moving out towards the centre of the track, followed by the two others. Barathea Guest quickly launched an attack and took it up, and although he moved across Ciro towards the rail he seemed clear at the time. While Barathea Guest made the best of his way home, Ciro, switched outside without appearing to lose momentum, found hidden reserves in the final hundred yards and finished to such purpose that he went down by only a neck, in the process wandering quite markedly under pressure. Ocean of Wisdom played no part in the finish and was eased. Presumably the winning margin had some bearing on the decision of the Longchamp stewards to demote Barathea Guest, and on the decision of the authorities to turn down an appeal by that colt's trainer.

		Mr Prospector		Raise A Native
	Woodman (USA)	(b 1970)		Gold Digger
	(ch 1983)	Playmate		Buckpasser
Ciro (USA)		(ch 1975)		Intriguing
(ch.c. Apr 18, 1997)		Nijinsky		Northern Dancer
	Gioconda (USA)	(b 1967)		Flaming Page
	(ch 1990)	Korveya		Riverman
		(ch 1982)		Konafa

Ciro, a brother to stakes-placed American 1998 two-year-old winner Woodyousmileforme and closely related to a winner in Japan by Forty Niner, comes from a spectacularly successful distaff family. He is closely related to

Mr M. Tabor, Mrs J. Magnier and Mr R. Santulli's "Ciro"

two first-class performers by his sire Woodman, who was also responsible for Irish One Thousand Guineas winner Hula Angel in the latest season. The two are Hector Protector, the top two-year-old colt of 1990 and a dual Group 1 winner the following year, and Bosra Sham, whose tally included the Fillies' Mile, One Thousand Guineas and Champion Stakes. Hector Protector and Bosra Sham are both out of Ciro's grandam Korveya, also dam of Shanghai (Poule d'Essai des Poulains). The third dam Konafa, runner-up in the One Thousand Guineas, foaled a pattern-winning brother to Korveya in the smart sprinter Keos, plus another speed merchant, Proskona. This is also the family of Oaks winner Snow Bride and her son Lammtarra, and it is hardly surprising that horses from this source have been highly prized, and highly priced, at the sales. Bosra Sham was the top-priced yearling in Britain in 1994 and Korveya's son by Woodman's sire Mr Prospector fetched the top price of 2,100,000 dollars at the Keeneland September Sale in 1998—named Hardy, he is a stable-mate of Ciro but has yet to race. Korveya herself equalled the world-record price for a broodmare when sold for 7,000,000 dollars in foal to Woodman two months later. Ciro, out of a mare who won one of her four starts in France, over a mile at Deauville, ostensibly fetched 500,000 dollars at the same sale as Hardy, though his breeders are still part-owners. Gioconda's next foal, a colt by Woodman again, was led out unsold at Keeneland in September, the bidding having reached 175,000 dollars. Ciro, who acts on soft going and has yet to encounter firmer than good, will stay at least a mile and a quarter. The experience gained at Longchamp is sure to stand him in good stead and he should improve, but it has to be said he'll need to if he's to make a mark in classic company. *A. P. O'Brien, Ireland*

CITIZEN KANE (IRE)   5 b.g. Sadler's Wells (USA) 132 – Princess Tiara 111   – (Crowned Prince (USA) 128) [1998 NR 1999 11.9g⁵ 12m Jul 10] IR 75,000Y: brother to fairly useful 1½m to 16.5f winner Royal Standard, closely related to 3 winners, including very smart 10.4f winner Infantry (by Northfields), later stakes winner in USA, and half-brother to several winners: dam, 2-y-o 7f winner, appeared to stay 1¼m: fairly useful in Ireland at 3 yrs for A. O'Brien: modest winning hurdler for new stable: little encouragement on return to Flat: should stay at least 1½m: acts on soft going and on good to firm: effective blinkered or not. *O. Sherwood*

CITY FLYER   2 br.c. (Apr 2) Night Shift (USA) – Al Guswa 98 (Shernazar 131)   **66** [1999 6s 5.9m⁴ 6m⁵ 8d 8d⁴ Oct 18] 15,000Y: fourth foal: half-brother to 5-y-o Tough Leader, 3-y-o King Flyer and a winner in Turkey by Salse: dam Irish 1m (at 2 yrs) and 1¼m winner: fair maiden: not disgraced in nursery final start: probably stays 1m. *J. D. Bethell*

CITY GAMBLER   5 b.m. Rock City 120 – Sun Street 73 (Ile de Bourbon (USA)   **67 d** 133) [1998 74: 7g⁶ 8.3g a8g⁴ 10g 10m* 11.8m² 12m⁵ 12g 11.1m³ 10s⁴ 10d² 10.1d³ 12g⁵ 1999 8g 10g 10g³ 12m⁵ 11.5m² 10.1f⁵ 10g 8g 11.9m⁵ 12m⁴ 10.3s Sep 22] rangy mare: fair handicapper at best: below form after third start: stays easy 1½m: acts on firm and good to soft going: held up. *G. C. Bravery*

CITY GOLF BAR (IRE)   2 b.c. (Mar 20) Namaqualand (USA) – Zalamera 45   **61** (Rambo Dancer (CAN) 107) [1999 5g 6.8m 7m⁶ 7m 8.3g Oct 11] IR 20,000F, 22,000Y: second foal: brother to a 1m winner in Sweden: dam, poor maiden, half-sister to dam of very smart Irish middle-distance performer Definite Article: modest maiden: stays 7f: sold 3,000 gns. *W. Jarvis*

CITY GUILD   3 b.g. Saddlers' Hall (IRE) 126 – Indubitable 87 (Sharpo 132)   – [1998 –p: 7d⁴ 8m 7d 1999 11.4m Jun 11] sturdy gelding: signs of a little ability at 2 yrs, behind only start in 1999: bred to stay well. *G. B. Balding*

CITY OF GOLD (IRE)   3 b.f. Sadler's Wells (USA) 132 – Northern Script   **91** (USA) 95 (Arts And Letters (USA)) [1998 76p: 7v* 1999 12g* 15v⁶ Oct 2] long-backed, angular filly: won maiden at 2 yrs for D. Loder: off 10 months, won minor event at Beverley in August by short head from Minivet, still green and leading close home: very stiff task, tailed off in Group 2 event at Longchamp: should stay beyond 1½m: may still be capable of better. *J. H. M. Gosden*

TNT International Aviation July Stakes, Newmarket—
City On A Hill maintains his unbeaten record ahead of Mull of Kintyre and Sir Nicholas (white cap)

CITY ON A HILL (USA)   2 ch.c. (Jan 20) Rahy (USA) 115 – Ville d'Amore   **114**
(USA) (Irish River (FR) 131) [1999 5.5g* 5.5g* 6m* 6s Aug 22]

In 1999 French racing braced itself for an invasion. A team of blue-blooded two-year-olds was expected to arrive and dominate the juvenile scene. Godolphin SNC came, but could only sit and watch as Ballydoyle did the conquering, plundering three Group 1 victories. On the face of it, a disappointing season for the beige arm of the 'boys in blue', or so their critics would have people believe. However, most of the two-year-olds under David Loder's care at Evry weren't trained to be precocious two-year-olds. Over half of Godolphin's runners ended the season rated 90 or more, a respectable performance; one of those, City On A Hill, the operation's first runner and winner, put up one of the best performances by a two-year-old at the time when winning the July Stakes at Newmarket.

May 25th at Chantilly produced a good start for Godolphin as City On A Hill had little trouble in winning his first race, justifying odds-on favouritism easily by a length and a half in a newcomers race. The Coventry Stakes at Royal Ascot was mooted as a possible target for City On A Hill, but on the day that Fasliyev was stamping his authority in that race, City On A Hill found himself back at Chantilly making all to win the listed Prix La Fleche in good style, once again needing only to be shaken up in the closing stages to beat the subsequent Prix de Cabourg winner Harbour Island by a length and a half.

The July Stakes at Newmarket signalled the first clash between the juvenile battalions of Loder and O'Brien. Few at the time would have expected this to have been Loder's only victory in Britain. City On A Hill, markedly weak in the betting, and racing on good to firm ground for the first time, gave 3 lb and a beating to Aidan O'Brien's Mull of Kintyre and Sir Nicholas, who had been Fasliyev's closest pursuer in the Coventry. City On A Hill made the running to win by a length and a quarter and three quarters of a length and, although he arguably had the run of the race, he still produced a smart performance, quickening over two furlongs out and finding plenty when meeting the rising ground. The form was boosted by Mull of Kintyre's Gimcrack victory, something which made City On A Hill's eclipse in the Prix Morny the following month even more disappointing.

Coupled with the Sheikh Mohammed-owned duo of Bachir and Warm Heart, City On A Hill started at 5/2-on, but finished last of the seven runners, beaten around nine lengths by the winner Fasliyev. Restrained after breaking well, City On A Hill was close enough to challenge two furlongs out, but he was unable to quicken and Frankie Dettori did not give him a hard time once his chance had gone. The fact that the Morny was run on soft ground could explain City On A Hill's defeat because, although he would have had trouble coping with Fasliyev, there seems to be no other reason why Harbour Island and Grigorovich should have overturned the Prix La Fleche form so resoundingly. The Middle Park Stakes at Newmarket in late-September was considered as an option but, in the end, City On A Hill wasn't seen out again.

City On A Hill is by Rahy, an American-based half-brother to Singspiel, who was also represented by the Great Voltigeur winner and Eclipse third Fantastic Light in 1999. However, the average winning distance of Rahy's three-year-old runners is just under nine furlongs so Fantastic Light is the exception rather than the rule. There is some stamina on the distaff side of City On A Hill's pedigree; although Ville d'Amore (by Irish River) didn't win beyond a mile (at which trip she won two listed races), her grandam is the high-class middle-distance filly Little Bonny, and City On A Hill's Hansel half-sister Loving Claim was second in the 1998 Prix Saint-Alary over ten furlongs after winning the Prix Marcel Boussac the previous year. Incidentally, Loving Claim was also below her best on her only attempt on ground softer than good, though she reportedly bled on that occasion. Ville d'Amore produced a full sister to Loving Claim in 1999.

		Rahy (USA) (ch 1985)	Blushing Groom (ch 1974)	Red God Runaway Bride
City On A Hill (USA) (ch.c. Jan 20, 1997)			Glorious Song (b 1976)	Halo Ballade
		Ville d'Amore (USA) (ch 1988)	Irish River (ch 1976)	Riverman Irish Star
			Hanoof (b 1983)	Northern Dancer Little Bonny

The robust, strong-quartered, attractive City On A Hill has a fluent action and has worn a crossed noseband. On pedigree he is likely to stay at least a mile and should be able to put his Morny running behind him when he encounters more suitable conditions. *D. R. Loder, France*

CITY PRINCESS 2 b.f. (May 7) Rock City 120 – Nordico Princess 71 (Nordico (USA)) [1999 5d⁶ 5s⁴ 5d 6f* 5m* 7.1m 5m³ 6m 6m² 6v a6g⁶ a7g Nov 12] 8,200Y: small, workmanlike filly: first foal: dam 5f/6f winner out of close relative to Dewhurst winner/2000 Guineas second Wind And Wuthering: modest performer: won sellers at Redcar and Hamilton within 4 days in August: good second in nursery at Hamilton in September: stays 6f: acts on firm and soft ground: often early to post: has given trouble at stalls and twice virtually refused to race: inconsistent, temperamental, and needs treating with caution. *M. Dods* — **62 §** **a– §**

CITY PURSUIT 3 b.c. Pursuit of Love 124 – Diabaig 76 (Precocious 126) [1998 60: 7s⁴ 8d 1999 10g Apr 8] angular colt: well beaten in maidens. *J. Pearce* — **–**

CITY REACH 3 b.g. Petong 126 – Azola (IRE) 63 (Alzao (USA) 117) [1998 73p: 6v⁴ 1999 8s 8f 7.7d⁶ a6g⁵ a7g³ a7g² Dec 15] strong, useful-looking gelding: fair maiden: probably stays 1m: acts on heavy going, and all-weather: has been blanketed for stalls entry/edged left. *P. J. Makin* — **64**

CITY STANDARD (IRE) 3 b.g. Rainbow Quest (USA) 134 – City Fortress (Troy 137) [1998 NR 1999 10m⁴ 11.5g³ 12d³ 11.9d 14d Sep 15] rather leggy, lengthy gelding: has a quick action: half-brother to several winners, including high-class French/US 1m/1¼m performer Fastness (by Rousillon) and smart colt up to 1½m Desert Boy (by Green Desert), later a leading performer in Hong Kong under the name of Oriental Express: dam French 1¼m and 12.5f winner: fair maiden: below form in handicaps last 2 starts, visored and running in snatches on final one: should be suited by 1¾m+: sold 15,000 gns, joined S. Dow. *Sir Michael Stoute* — **75**

CIVIL LIBERTY 6 b.g. Warning 136 – Libertine 114 (Hello Gorgeous (USA) 128) [1998 NR 1999 10g⁶ 10.1m 10m⁶ 8.1d² 8.5g a9.4g* 9v² a9.4f⁴ 10.1d⁶ Oct 20] well-made gelding: fair handicapper: won at Wolverhampton in September in good style: good second of 20 in amateur race at Kempton next time: effective at 9f to 11.5f: acts on any turf going and fibresand: well beaten in blinkers: usually wears tongue strap: sometimes edges left: retained 8,000 gns after final start. *D. Sasse* — **76**

CLADANTOM (IRE) 3 b.f. High Estate 127 – Riflebird (IRE) 60 (Runnett 125) [1998 64p: 7.5m⁴ 6.1g⁵ 1999 7m 7f² 7f* 7.1d 7d a8.5g a7g⁶ Dec 8] sturdy filly: fair performer on turf, poor on all-weather: left W. Jarvis after reappearance: won maiden at Thirsk in July: well below form final 4 starts (retained 3,000 gns before penultimate outing): should stay 1m: acts on firm going. *D. W. Barker* — **70** **a37 +**

CLAIM GEBAL CLAIM 3 b.g. Ardkinglass 114 – Infra Blue (IRE) (Bluebird **53**
(USA) 125) [1998 63: 5m 6g³ 5m⁴ 5m³ 6g⁶ 5d³ 5m a7g 1999 7g² 6v⁵ 7f 5.9g 5.9m 5f⁵
7m⁴ 10g⁶ Aug 21] small gelding: poor maiden: probably stays 1¼m: acts on firm
going, ran badly on fibresand: blinkered fifth and sixth starts: usually races prominently. *Mrs A. Duffield*

CLAIRESWAN (IRE) 7 ch.g. Rhoman Rule (USA) – Choclate Baby (Kashiwa **–**
115) [1998 NR 1999 a16.2g⁵ 21.6d Apr 28] workmanlike gelding: fair handicapper
at 3 yrs, lightly raced and no form on Flat since. *Mrs N. Macauley*

CLANBLUE CHICK 4 b.f. Clantime 101 – Lavenham Blue (Streetfighter 120) **–**
[1998 –: a5g 5g 1999 6.1f Jun 21] poor form at 2 yrs: soundly beaten since.
P. D. Evans

CLANDESTINE 3 b.f. Saddlers' Hall (IRE) 126 – Fleeting Affair 98 (Hotfoot **95**
126) [1998 NR 1999 11.9g⁴ 11.9d* 11.9g⁶ 14.6g Sep 8] well-made filly: half-sister to
several winners, including 6-y-o Infatuation and 1¼m winner Harmony Hall (by
Music Boy): dam, 1¼m/1½m winner, stayed 2m: won maiden at Haydock in August
by 4 lengths: stiffer tasks after, creditable sixth of 8 to Innuendo in listed race at York:
should be suited by further than 1½m: joined N. Henderson and won over hurdles in
November. *J. H. M. Gosden*

CLANSMAN 2 ch.g. (Mar 23) Clantime 101 – Chili Lass (Chilibang 120) [1999 **66 ?**
5.7m⁵ 5m 5g⁴ 5.3m⁵ Sep 1] first reported foal: dam of little account: fair maiden at
best: possibly flattered when fourth of 7 to Performing Magic at Leicester third start:
likely to prove best at 5f/6f. *T. R. Watson*

CLANTYRE 3 b.c. Clantime 101 – Tyrian Belle 77 (Enchantment 115) [1998 –: **45**
5g 5s a6g 1999 6v⁴ 5d 5m 5.9g Jun 10] poor maiden handicapper: below form after
reappearance, leaving M. Johnston after penultimate start: stays 6f: acts on heavy
going. *Miss J. F. Craze*

CLARA BLUE 3 gr.f. Alhijaz 122 – Hazy Kay (IRE) 77 (Treasure Kay 114) **–**
[1998 76: 5.1s 5f 6m 5.3f⁶ 6m⁵ 5m 5s* 1999 5d 5m 5m 5s 5.3d 6g 5.2s a5g Nov 16]
fair 5f winner at 2 yrs: no show in 1999, leaving T. McCarthy after second start.
R. Ingram

CLARANET 2 ch.f. (May 14) Arazi (USA) 135 – Carmita (Caerleon (USA) 132) **72**
[1999 8d³ 8.3d⁴ Oct 28] fifth foal: half-sister to 4-y-o Bay View and 1m and 1½m
winner Golden Thunderbolt (by Persian Bold): dam French 1½m listed winner: fair
form in frame in maidens at Brighton and Windsor: will stay 1¼m, probably 1½m.
K. Mahdi

CLARANNA 3 b.f. Local Suitor (USA) 128 – Zolica 60 (Beveled (USA)) [1998 **48**
54: a5g 5g² 6d² 6s³ 6s* 7g 1999 6g⁵ 6v 6.1s Apr 27] small, angular filly: poor
performer: well below form after reappearance: should stay 7f: raced only on good
ground or softer on turf. *R. A. Fahey*

CLARENDON (IRE) 3 ch.c. Forest Wind (USA) 111 – Sparkish (IRE) (Persian **85 p**
Bold 123) [1998 66: 6g⁴ 7d⁴ 6g⁶ 7f 7.9g⁶ 8.3s⁴ 8d 8d 1999 10m⁴ 10.2m* 10m* 10d³
9m 10s Oct 22] tall, good-topped colt: fairly useful handicapper: won at Chepstow in
June and Ascot in July: good third at Sandown (none too clear run) next time and not
knocked about final start: should stay 1½m: acts on firm and soft going: blinkered
(poor effort) final 2-y-o start: probably capable of better still. *V. Soane*

CLARINCH CLAYMORE 3 b.g. Sabrehill (USA) 120 – Salu 65 (Ardross 134) **59**
[1998 –: 6s 8.1m 7.5m⁵ 7.9g 1999 10s 12m 9.3g 8g³ 9.3m⁴ 8.5g* 10.5m⁴ 10.9d² a11g
Nov 30] smallish gelding: modest handicapper: won amateur event at Beverley in
August: stays 11f: acts on good to firm and good to soft going, probably on fibresand.
J. M. Jefferson

CLASSIC COLOURS (USA) 6 ch.g. Blushing John (USA) 120 – All Agleam **55 §**
(USA) (Gleaming (USA)) [1998 50§, a–§: 8.2s⁶ 10.8g³ 8.2m⁶ 10d⁵ 9.9m a7g 1999
a9.4g⁴ a12g⁶ 10.8d² 10v³ 10.8m 10.2g 10.5m 9.2s Nov 1] strong gelding: modest
maiden: creditable efforts in 1999 only when placed in handicaps in April: stays 11f:
acts on heavy ground, probably on good to firm: usually tongue tied: tends to carry
head awkwardly/wander under pressure: unreliable. *G. H. Yardley*

CLASSIC CONKERS (IRE) 5 b.g. Conquering Hero (USA) 116 – Erck (Sun **52 §**
Prince 128) [1998 59: 8m 10m⁵ 8.1m 8f 6f⁶ 8m⁶ 10.8m⁵ 11.5d* 14.1s² 12s 1999

14.1d 11.9f 11.5m⁴ 12d 10.1d⁶ 14.1g 11.6m 16f⁵ 10.1g⁴ 14.1g⁶ 14.1d Oct 27] modest performer: stays 1¾m: acts on soft going, probably on good to firm: has carried head awkwardly: sometimes slowly away: not to be trusted. *Pat Mitchell*

CLASSIC EAGLE 6 b.g. Unfuwain (USA) 131 – La Lutine 95 (My Swallow 134) [1998 NR 1999 8d 10d 11.9d⁴ Oct 29] workmanlike gelding: fairly useful hurdler nowadays: no form on Flat since 1996. *Pat Mitchell* –

CLASSIC FIGHTER (IRE) 3 ch.g. Up And At 'em 109 – Classic Choice (Patch 129) [1998 –: 6d 8m⁶ 1999 a8.5g⁶ 10g a8g 7g 8m Jun 24] workmanlike gelding: no form: blinkered final start. *J. J. Sheehan* –

CLASSIC IMPACT (IRE) 4 gr.g. Generous (IRE) 139 – Vaison La Romaine 100 (Arctic Tern (USA) 126) [1998 86: 8s 11.4d⁵ 12s* 12g² 12d 11.9m 11.8d² 1999 16s Oct 22] tall, unfurnished gelding: fairly useful handicapper for P. Chapple-Hyam at 3 yrs: no show only run on Flat in 1999: should stay further than 1½m: acts on soft going. *P. G. Murphy* –

CLASSIC LORD 2 b.g. (May 20) Wolfhound (USA) 126 – Janaat 74 (Kris 135) [1999 7d² 7m⁵ 7m⁵ 8d 8v Oct 12] good-topped gelding: fluent mover: third foal: closely related to 4-y-o Lend A Hand: dam 1½m winner: failed to progress after encouraging second in maiden at Ayr on debut: beaten at odds on next time, blinkered final start: should be suited by further than 7f. *M. Johnston* **62**

CLASSIC MANOEUVRE (USA) 4 ch.g. Sky Classic (CAN) – Maid of Honor (USA) (Blushing Groom (FR) 131) [1998 78: 10.5d⁴ 9.9d³ 10.1g³ 10.2d³ 9.9m² 12m 10g a10g³ 1999 12g Jun 8] leggy gelding: good mover: fair maiden: below form in handicap only start in 1999: stays 10.5f: acts on good to soft ground and equitrack: below form in visor twice as 3-y-o: none too consistent: joined C. Mann, and won over hurdles in August. *M. C. Pipe* –

CLASSIC MASQUERADE (CAN) 4 b.g. Regal Classic (CAN) – Muskoka Command (USA) (Top Command (USA)) [1998 62d: 10g⁴ 11.9f⁴ 12m⁵ 12g⁶ 11.9g⁴ 17.2g⁴ 1999 12m May 13] modest but disappointing maiden at 3 yrs: well held only outing on Flat in 1999, though won 4 times over hurdles in the summer: stays 1½m: acts on firm going. *M. C. Pipe* –

CLASSIC REFERENDUM (IRE) 5 ch.g. Classic Music (USA) – My Alanna (Dalsaan 125) [1998 NR 1999 14g* 13g* 14g² 12m² 12m 14d 14s 13.9d 13.8s a16.2g a16.2g Dec 15] fourth foal: half-brother to fair 1m/1¼m winner Classic Defence (by Cyrano de Bergerac): dam Irish stayer: fair performer for L. Browne in Ireland, winning maiden at Leopardstown and handicap at Wexford in June: long way below form all 7 starts in Britain: stays 1¾m: acts on good to firm and good to soft ground: blinkered (ran poorly) once at 3 yrs: possibly temperamental. *B. J. Curley* **79 d**

CLASS WAN 3 ch.f. Safawan 118 – Ayr Classic (Local Suitor (USA) 128) [1998 74: 5d 5m 6d⁵ 6m⁵ 5d⁴ 5g* 6s⁶ 6s* 5d 1999 7d 6d Apr 16] angular filly: fair performer at 2 yrs: well beaten in handicaps both starts in 1999: stays 6f: acts on soft going and on good to firm: held up. *J. S. Goldie* –

CLASSY CLEO (IRE) 4 b.f. Mujadil (USA) 119 – Sybaris 91 (Crowned Prince (USA) 128) [1998 100: a6g³ a5g⁵ a7g² a5g 6d 6s⁴ 6s⁵ 5.1g* 5g 6d 5s 5.1m* 6m⁵ 5g 5f 5m 5.1m² 6g² 5m⁵ 5s² 6d* a7g⁵ 1999 a5g² a7g⁴ a6g³ a7g⁴ a5g⁵ a7g⁶ a6g⁶ 6d 6m 5.1m⁵ 6d 6m² 5m 6g³ 6m⁴ 6.1m³ 5m 5.1m 6m 6.1m³ 6m² 6.1g 7d⁵ 6g 5m 5m⁵ 5.1s⁵ 5s⁵ 6s² 5d³ 5d² 6d* a5g³ a6g² Dec 22] neat filly: unimpressive mover: useful handicapper: held her form extremely well through another very busy season and won 22-runner event at Redcar (won same race in 1998) in November: effective at 5f to easy 7f: acts on firm and soft going, goes well on all-weather: often sweats/gets on toes: has been bandaged: suitable mount for 7-lb claimer: often makes running (did at Redcar): very tough and consistent. *P. D. Evans* **91 a104**

CLAUDIUS 3 b.g. Clantime 101 – Pokey's Pet 56 (Uncle Pokey 116) [1998 52: 5g 5g 5m⁴ 5m 1999 6m 8f 6f Aug 7] sturdy gelding: modest maiden handicapper at best: well beaten in 1999: sometimes pulls hard, and may prove best at 5f. *K. A. Ryan* –

CLAUDIUS TERTIUS 2 b.g. (Apr 30) Rudimentary (USA) 118 – Sanctuary Cove (Habitat 134) [1999 7m 7.1d 7.7d 7s 8d Nov 1] 17,000F, IR 35,000Y: sturdy, good-quartered gelding: has a round action: sixth foal: half-brother to 3 winners, including 3-y-o Bundy and 1997 2-y-o 1¼m seller winner Hiding Place (by Saddlers' **?**

Hall): dam Irish maiden from family of Quiet Fling and Peacetime: seemed to show modest form (possibly worth a rating of 60) second start: should stay at least 1m. *M. A. Jarvis*

CLAXON 3 b.f. Caerleon (USA) 132 – Bulaxie 110 (Bustino 136) [1998 87p: 7m² 7g³ 8v* 1999 8g* 9.9g* 12d⁵ Jun 4] big, good-topped filly: useful performer: won listed races at Kempton in April and Goodwood (changed legs and drifted left under pressure, beat Musical Treat 2½ lengths) in May: third favourite, only 13 lengths fifth of 10 to Ramruma in Oaks final start at Epsom: should have stayed 1½m: best efforts on good ground: stud. *J. L. Dunlop* **108**

CLEAR CRYSTAL 2 b.f. (Apr 9) Zilzal (USA) 137 – Shoot Clear 111 (Bay Express 132) [1999 7d⁵ 7m⁶ 7d Aug 26] half-sister to several winners, including 1996 2-y-o 5f winner Jhazi (by Arazi) and middle-distance performer Shoot Ahead (by Shirley Heights), both useful: dam, 5f to 7f winner at 2 yrs and fourth in 1000 Guineas, half-sister to Yorkshire Oaks winners Sally Brown and Untold: modest form in maidens: should stay 1m. *R. M. H. Cowell* **62**

CLEAR MOON (IRE) 2 b.c. (Mar 21) Lake Coniston (IRE) 131 – Tenea (Reform 132) [1999 5m 5g 6g 6d⁶ 6s³ Nov 2] IR 14,000Y: half-brother to several winners, including useful 1992 2-y-o 1m winner Taos (by Sadler's Wells): dam once-raced half-sister to several smart or better performers, including Irish Derby winner Tyrnavos: modest maiden: creditable efforts in nurseries last 2 outings: will be suited by 7f+: acts on soft going: edged right penultimate start. *Miss L. A. Perratt* **54**

CLEAR NIGHT 3 b.c. Night Shift (USA) – Clarista (USA) 67 (Riva Ridge (USA)) [1998 84: 5d⁴ 6d⁵ 6g³ 7g⁶ 1999 7d 6g 7m 6f 7.1g 8.1m* 7m 8g⁶ 9s a8.5g a8g² Nov 22] strong, well-made colt: fair at best in 1999: won seller (left R. Hannon) at Chepstow in June: mostly well below that form after: stays 1m: acts on good to firm going and fibresand: tried blinkered: has had tongue tied: sometimes looks none too keen. *J. J. Sheehan* **68 §**
a60 §

CLEAR PROSPECT (USA) 2 b.c. (Jan 4) Virginia Rapids (USA) 122 – Cameo Performance (USA) 104 (Be My Guest (USA) 126) [1999 7.3f⁶ 8d⁴ 10d³ Oct 11] $115,000Y: strong, lengthy, good sort: has plenty of scope: fifth foal: half-brother to fairly useful 1995 2-y-o 7f winner Friendly Forester (by Woodman) and to a winner in USA by Housebuster: dam, 1¼m to 1½m winner, half successful in USA: fairly useful maiden: trained first 2 starts by P. Chapple-Hyam: best effort when 1½ lengths third of 8 to Bow Strada in minor event at Leicester final outing: should stay 1½m: sold 40,000 gns, joined M. Buckley. *A. G. Foster* **87**

CLEF OF SILVER 4 b.c. Indian Ridge 123 – Susquehanna Days (USA) 68 (Chief's Crown (USA)) [1998 95: 6f 6m⁵ 6d 6g* 1999 6s Apr 21] close-coupled colt: has reportedly suffered split pastern: fairly useful performer at 3 yrs: reportedly finished lame only start in 1999: effective at 5f/6f: acts on good to firm going, below form on softer than good: has reared start: has tended to wander. *W. Jarvis* **–**

CLEVER CITATION (USA) 2 b.c. (May 2) Chief's Crown (USA) – Besha (USA) (Turkoman (USA)) [1999 6.1g³ 7m⁵ Oct 24] $190,000Y: second foal: dam twice-raced sister to US Grade 3 8.5f and 11f winner Young Daniel and half-sister to US Grade 1 2-y-o 8.5f winner Script Ohio: encouraging debut when third of 12 to Shannon Dore in maiden at Nottingham: possibly still green when well held in minor event at Yarmouth following month: should stay at least 1m. *Sir Michael Stoute* **79 +**

CLEVER GIRL (IRE) 2 b.f. (Jan 29) College Chapel 122 – Damezao (Alzao (USA) 117) [1999 5m⁶ 5m⁵ 6g³ 6g* 7m⁶ 7g* 7m² 8v* 8s⁵ Nov 5] 5,000Y: tall, good-topped filly: has scope: sixth foal: half-sister to 1993 2-y-o 6f winner Salvezza (by Superpower) and 1995 2-y-o 8.5f winner Nose No Bounds (by Cyrano de Bergerac): dam unraced: fairly useful performer: won maiden at Pontefract in June and nurseries at Ayr in July and October: gave impression something amiss final start: should stay bit beyond 1m: acts on good to firm and heavy going. *T. D. Easterby* **88**

CLIPPER 2 b.f. (May 11) Salse (USA) 128 – Yawl 112 (Rainbow Quest (USA) 134) [1999 7d 8v* Oct 12] big, useful-looking filly: third foal: half-sister to useful 11.5f winner Genoa (by Zafonic): dam, 7f (Rockfel) winner at 2 yrs but mostly disappointing afterwards, daughter of Oaks winner Bireme: still green when winning 6-runner maiden at Ayr in October by 1¼ lengths from Sabreon, nudged along from **88 p**

before halfway but responding well for strong pressure: will stay at least 1½m: likely to improve fair bit further, and should make a useful performer. *B. W. Hills*

CLOAK OF DARKNESS (IRE)   4 b.g. Thatching 131 – Madame Nureyev   **91** (USA) (Nureyev (USA) 131) [1998 86: 10g* 8d 10f⁵ 10m³ 10.3d⁵ 12m³ 1999 10m 12m⁶ 10d* 10f⁴ 10m⁴ 10m² 11.9m Aug 17] smallish, good-topped gelding: fairly useful handicapper: made all at Windsor (only previous success also there) in June: rare poor effort final start: stays 1½m: acts on firm and good to soft going: often makes running: sold 12,000 gns in October, joined M. Pipe. *R. Hannon*

CLODION (IRE)   3 b.c. Nikos 124 – Didia Clara (FR) (Sea Break 129) [1998 6d³   **103** 7.5d³ 8d* 1999 9.9g³ May 18] leggy, attractive ex-French colt: brother to 2 winners in France, including smart 1m and 1¼m winner La Favorita, and half-brother to several winners, including useful French stayer El Shitane (by Fabulous Dancer): dam French 6.5f to 1½m winner: useful form at 2 yrs for E. Lellouche, winning minor event at Deauville: creditable 8½ lengths third of 6 to stable-companion Dubai Millennium in listed event at Goodwood only outing in 1999, making most of running: bred to stay at least 1¼m. *Saeed bin Suroor*

CLOG DANCE   2 b.f. (May 6) Pursuit of Love 124 – Discomatic (USA) (Roberto   **103 p** (USA) 131) [1999 8.1d³ 7g² Oct 16] rangy filly with scope: sixth living foal: half-sister to 3 winners, including smart 1¾m winner Tuning and fairly useful French 1½m winner Raincloud (both by Rainbow Quest): dam, French 9f winner, half-sister to Phoenix Stakes winner Digamist: shaped well on debut, then useful form when neck second of 12 to Lahan in Rockfel Stakes at Newmarket: very much on toes, tended to edge left and carry head awkwardly whilst running on strongly in latter: bred to stay at least 1¼m: sure to improve further, and will win races. *B. W. Hills*

CLOHAMON   4 b.g. Aragon 118 – Almadaniyah (Dunbeath (USA) 127) [1998   **–** 60, a–: 5m 5g⁴ 6d⁵ 5d a7g a7g a6g 1999 5g 6g 5m 6f Jul 9] disappointing 5f/6f maiden: trained on reappearance (visored) by S. Kettlewell. *M. A. Peill*

CLONMANY (IRE)   2 ch.c. (Mar 1) Petardia 113 – Romangoddess (IRE)   **90** (Rhoman Rule (USA)) [1999 5.2f 7m² 7m² 7f* 8m⁴ 7g³ 7d⁴ Oct 7] 15,500Y: quite good-topped colt: fourth foal: brother to 4-y-o Petara and half-brother to 3-y-o Kuwait Thunder: dam Irish 2-y-o 7f winner: fairly useful performer: won maiden at Goodwood in July: good fourth in minor event at York final start: stays 7f: acts on firm and good to soft going: troublesome and edgy in stalls on third start: carries head high: sold 72,000 gns, reportedly to join W. Dollase in USA. *R. Hannon*

CLONOE   5 b.g. Syrtos 106 – Anytime Anywhere 77 (Daring March 116) [1998   **52** 52, a42: a12g a6g⁴ a7g² a6g³ a7g³ a7g⁴ 6.9d² 6s* 7d 6m² 6d 6m 7m⁴ 7m³ 7m 8m*   **a43** 8.1m⁵ 7f³ 7d 8s a7g 1999 a8g² a7f a10g* a10g² a8g⁵ a8g a8g 8f³ 6.1f 7f 8f 7m 7.7m 7m* 7m 8.1m 7m⁶ 7s Oct 23] strong, plain gelding: modest handicapper: won at Lingfield in January and Folkestone in July: below form after: effective at 6f to easy 1¼m: unraced on heavy going, acts on any other turf/all-weather: blinkered once at 3 yrs: has hung and looked none too keen: often races up with pace. *R. Ingram*

CLOPTON GREEN   2 b.g. (Feb 19) Presidium 124 – Silkstone Lady (Puissance   **53** 110) [1999 a6g³ a6g a5g⁶ Dec 4] 4,000Y, 11,000 2-y-o: first foal: dam unraced: modest form in maiden at Southwell on debut: well held after, including in seller: has had tongue tied. *J. W. Payne*

CLOSER NOW (USA)   2 b.c. (Mar 24) Distant View (USA) 126 – Stageira   **54** (CAN) (Halo (USA)) [1999 7.1d 8v Sep 20] $77,000Y: fourth foal: dam, placed in USA, half-sister to useful 1¼m performer Geisway and to dam of Irish Oaks winner Knight's Baroness: showed a little ability in maidens at Sandown and Kempton: sold 5,500 gns, sent to Sweden. *P. W. Chapple-Hyam*

CLOTH OF GOLD   2 b.c. (Mar 3) Barathea (IRE) 127 – Bustinetta 89 (Bustino   **– p** 136) [1999 7s Nov 5] 52,000Y: leggy, quite attractive colt: second foal: half-brother to 4-y-o Bhutan: dam, 11f winner who stayed 2m, out of half-sister to Terimon: well held in maiden at Doncaster: will be suited by 1½m+: should do better. *Lady Herries*

CLOTTED CREAM (USA)   2 gr.f. (Mar 12) Eagle Eyed (USA) 111 – Seattle   **76 p** Victory (USA) (Seattle Song (USA) 130) [1999 6g 5v³ Sep 24] $21,000F: sturdy, compact filly: has a quick action: first foal: dam, French 1m (listed race) and 1¼m winner, later successful in USA: better effort in maidens when close third of 17 to

Inventive at Lingfield, always prominent: bred to stay at least 7f: capable of better still. *P. J. Makin*

CLOUD INSPECTOR (IRE)   8 b.g. Persian Bold 123 – Timbale d'Argent   **38** (Petingo 135) [1998 87: 12.4s² 18.7m 20d 16.1v 14m⁶ 15g 1999 16m 14m 16m⁶ a14g 14.1m 14.1g 18d⁵ Oct 18] big, useful-looking gelding: one-time fairly useful performer: has deteriorated considerably: stays 2½m: acts on good to firm ground, probably on heavy: tried blinkered/visored. *M. Johnston*

CLOUDS OF GLORY   4 b.f. Lycius (USA) 124 – Dance A Jig (Dance In Time   – (CAN)) [1998 64, a–: 6v 6g 8m⁴ 8.2d a8g⁴ 1999 a8g a11g a7g 8d 12.3m 8m Jun 18] sturdy, angular filly: modest maiden in 1998: no form for new stable. *J. Norton*

CLOUDY SKY (IRE)   3 b.c. Sadler's Wells (USA) 132 – Dancing Shadow 117   **103** (Dancer's Image (USA)) [1998 NR 1999 8g² 10m* 10.3m⁴ 12d Oct 1] strong, good-bodied colt: brother to smart middle-distance filly Dancing Bloom, 6f winner at 2 yrs, and half-brother to 3 winners, including smart French filly at up to 1m River Dancer (by Irish River), herself dam of Spectrum: dam, 1m and 1¼m winner, half-sister to Saddlers' Hall (by Sadler's Wells) and Sun Princess: useful performer: won maiden at Sandown in June: best effort when 5 lengths fourth of 6 to Timahs in well-contested minor event at Doncaster in September: should be well suited by 1½m (sweated and below form when tried at trip, on good to soft going): acts on good to firm ground. *Sir Michael Stoute*

CLOVERWAY MAGIC (IRE)   3 ch.g. Magical Strike (USA) 114 – A New   – Rose (IRE) (Saher 115) [1998 NR 1999 10f 10m⁵ 10g 7f 10g 8m 10d Oct 28] fifth foal: half-brother to a winner in Singapore by Imperial Frontier: dam unraced: little form in claimers/sellers: tried visored. *R. P. C. Hoad*

CLUED UP   6 b.m. Beveled (USA) – Scharade 74 (Lombard (GER) 126) [1998   **63 §** 63§, a–§: 10.3g² 10.5m 12.3g* 10g 11.9g* 10.2g⁶ 12.3m⁴ 12g 10.5m⁶ 15.9g⁵ 12d   **a–** 12d 10d⁵ 1999 10.3d⁶ 12.1v² 12.3m 13v 10s* 12.3m 13.1d⁶ 10.3s 12s 10s Nov 1] tall, workmanlike mare: modest handicapper: won 5-runner contest at Nottingham in April: below form after: effective at 1¼m to 2m: acts on good to firm and heavy going, no form on all-weather: blinkered/visored: not to be trusted. *P. D. Evans*

CLUNIE   3 ch.f. Inchinor 119 – Bonita 57 (Primo Dominie 121) [1998 69: 6m 6m*   **84** 6.1d* 6m 6m* 6m 1999 6d⁴ 6g* 5m 5g³ 6m Jul 20] sparely-made filly: fairly useful handicapper: won at Goodwood in June: ran well despite not getting clear run when third at Sandown penultimate start: finished lame next time: stays 6f: yet to race on extremes of going: may prove best covered up. *W. J. Haggas*

CLYTHA HILL LAD   8 b.g. Domitor (USA) 98 – Quae Supra 79 (On Your Mark   **50** 125) [1998 51: 8f 9g 1999 7.1d 7m 8f 7.7m² 8.1m 7.1m 8.1m³ 8d³ 9.2m 10m³ 10m 8m⁵ 10.5d Sep 21] big, lengthy gelding: modest handicapper: stays 1¼m: acts on good to firm and good to soft going: effective blinkered or not: usually bandaged: takes good hold and races prominently. *J. M. Bradley*

COACH (FR)   4 ch.c. Bering 136 – Charara (USA) (Top Command (USA)) [1998   **106** 10.5d² 11g* 10m* 10g* 12m* 12s⁴ 10s 15v² 12v⁴ 1999 12s³ 10s* 14d⁶ 12d 12m² 12g⁵ 10g³ Oct 11] 120,000 francs 2-y-o: fourth foal: half-brother to French 8.5f winner Foreman Davis (by Al Nasr) and French 1½m winner Zoulou Boy (by Danehill): dam French 1m winner: useful performer: has won 6 times in French Provinces, including listed race at Toulouse in March: below-par sixth to Opera King in valuable handicap at Goodwood next time: creditable efforts last 3 starts, around 1½ lengths third to Kadance Ville in Prix Andre Baboin at Marseille Borely on final outing: effective at 1¼m, stays 15f: acts on good to firm and heavy ground: held up. *Francois Rohaut, France*

COASTAL BLUFF   7 gr.g. Standaan (FR) 118 – Combattente (Reform 132)   **93 d** [1998 108: 5d 5d 1999 6g 6d 5m⁶ 6f 6m 5.6g 5d 6d 5d Oct 28] tall, angular gelding: one-time smart performer: well held in 1999, undergoing third wind operation before third start: effective at 5f/6f: acts on soft going and on good to firm: usually heavily bandaged behind: tried blinkered: has been tongue tied. *N. P. Littmoden*

COASTGUARDS HERO   6 ch.g. Chilibang 120 – Aldwick Colonnade 62   **22** (Kind of Hush 118) [1998 34, a39: a13g³ a13g* a16g³ a13g⁴ a16g* a16g⁶ a16g a14g 11.9d⁵ a16g a16g³ 16.4m a13g* 14.1g⁵ 11.9g² a16g⁵ 11.9m⁶ a16g 1999 a13g a12f⁵ a13g⁶ a13g a16g 11.9f 11.9f⁶ a13g⁶ a10g 12m⁶ Jul 26] sturdy gelding: bad handicapper: stays 2m: acts on all-weather, best turf form on good going or firmer. *B. A. Pearce*

COCHISE   3 ch.g. Cosmonaut – Paircullis (Tower Walk 130) [1998 –: 6g 7.5m 7g   –
1999 10s 13.8g Oct 16] workmanlike gelding: no form: sold 700 gns in November. *J. Cullinan*

COCHITI   5 b.m. Kris 135 – Sweet Jaffa 73§ (Never So Bold 135) [1998 23: a16g   30
a12g⁵ 1999 a12g 12m⁵ 12.3m⁶ 11.9f Jul 22] unfurnished mare: bad maiden handicapper: stays 1½m: acts on good to firm ground and fibresand: tried blinkered/tongue tied: has been reluctant to post. *P. W. Hiatt*

COCKATRICE   3 b.f. Petong 126 – Noble Peregrine (Lomond (USA) 128) [1998   –
61: 6f 6m 6.9f 7s⁴ 7d 1999 8v 6g May 18] lengthy, rather sparely-made filly: modest maiden: no show either start in 1999, visored, mulish and led to post final one: should stay 1m. *D. Morris*

COCOBAY   3 b.f. Runnett 125 – Romantic Melody 56 (Battle Hymn 103) [1998   –
–: 7g 1999 10m 6s 5.3g 5.1m Jul 15] of little account. *G. M. McCourt*

COCO DE MER   2 ch.c. (Apr 1) Prince Sabo 123 – Musica 82 (Primo Dominie   87
121) [1999 5g² 5g⁴ 5.3f⁵ 5.1m² 5.1m* 5.2m 5f² 5g 5d Sep 16] 8,500Y: useful-looking colt: has a quick action: first foal: dam won at around 5f, including at 2 yrs: fairly useful performer: won maiden at Chester in July: good second in nurseries at Goodwood and Lingfield after: something seemingly amiss final start: will prove best at 5f: acts on firm going: edgy sort, and has shown signs of temperament. *A. P. Jarvis*

COCO GIRL   3 ch.f. Mystiko (USA) 124 – Cantico 58 (Green Dancer (USA) 132)   58 d
[1998 71p: 7g 7m⁵ 1999 10m⁴ 9m 8f 11.5g⁴ a12g⁶ a14.8g a13g⁴ Dec 22] tall filly: modest maiden: well below form after reappearance, leaving I. Balding after third start: stays 1¼m: well held on all-weather, raced only on good going or firmer on turf: tends to race freely. *Mrs A. E. Johnson*

COCO LOCO   2 b.f. (Mar 17) Bin Ajwaad (IRE) 119 – Mainly Me 76 (Hunting-   –
dale 132) [1999 7d Oct 27] second foal: half-sister to 3-y-o Harquebusier: dam maiden who stayed 1m: very green, well beaten in maiden at Yarmouth. *J. Pearce*

COCONUT   3 b.g. Shirley Heights 130 – Magical Retreat (USA) 115 (Sir Ivor   –
135) [1998 NR 1999 7m⁴ 10m 11.5g⁶ Jun 30] first foal: dam, 1¼m winner who stayed 14.8f, second in Yorkshire Oaks at 4 yrs: no show in minor event/maidens: sold 700 gns in August. *C. A. Cyzer*

COCO (USA)   2 ch.f. (Apr 11) Storm Bird (CAN) 134 – Fond Romance (USA)   – p
(Fappiano (USA)) [1999 7v Oct 25] $145,000Y: fourth foal: dam, won at up to 1¼m in USA, out of half-sister to smart 1¼m filly Optimistic Lass: weak 3/1-shot, over 11 lengths seventh of 11 to Decision Maid in maiden at Lingfield, considerably handled having got worked up in stalls and started slowly: likely to do fair bit better. *Sir Michael Stoute*

CODICIL   3 ch.f. Then Again 126 – Own Free Will 87 (Nicholas Bill 125) [1998   58
66: 6g⁵ 6s³ 5d* 7g⁴ 8m 8s⁶ 6s 7s⁵ 6s⁵ 1999 8.2d 8.3d 10g³ 10.9s⁵ Jul 19] workmanlike filly: modest performer: stays 1¼m: acts on soft going and on good to firm: sometimes gives trouble stalls/starts slowly. *M. Dods*

COEUR DE LA MER (IRE)   2 b.f. (May 18) Caerleon (USA) 132 – Cochineal   87 p
(USA) 52 (Vaguely Noble 140) [1999 8v³ 8.3d* Oct 28] IR 14,000Y: fourth foal: closely related to fairly useful 1995 2-y-o 1m winner Ski Academy (by Royal Academy): dam, maiden, stayed at least 11.7f: confirmed debut promise when winning 13-runner maiden at Windsor in October easing up by 4 lengths from Original Spin: will stay 1¼m: looks a useful prospect. *A. G. Foster*

COEUR DU LION   3 b.f. Whittingham (IRE) 104 – The Fernhill Flyer (IRE) 71   –
(Red Sunset 120) [1998 51?: 5s⁵ 5g 5m 1999 a7g 7f 5f Sep 4] sturdy, compact filly: little form: blinkered final start. *D. Nicholls*

COFFEE CREAM   3 b.f. Common Grounds 118 – Sugar Town (IRE) 72 (Tate   83
Gallery (USA) 117) [1998 87: 6d⁵ 7m* 7g 1999 7.5g³ 7d 7m² 8.3m* 9f 8.1g⁵ 7m
Aug 28] unfurnished filly: fairly useful handicapper: dead-heated with Gaily Mill in

6-runner event at Windsor in July: stays 8.3f: acts on good to firm going: has raced freely: none too consistent. *B. J. Meehan*

COHAN   2 b.c. (Mar 10) Petong 126 – Katie Jo 80 (Taufan (USA) 119) [1999 5m **54** 5v 5m⁴ 6.1d May 19] 3,600Y: leggy colt: fourth foal: dam won from 9f to 1½m: modest form in maidens first 3 starts: dead. *B. Palling*

COHIBA   6 b.g. Old Vic 136 – Circus Ring 122 (High Top 131) [1998 51: 11.9g* **51** 11.6g 12s² 16g 12f 16d 15.8d 1999 10g² 14.1m* 12.1g⁶ Aug 30] angular gelding: modest handicapper: favourite, won selling race at Nottingham (also won same event in 1997) in July: left B. Curley after: stays 1¾m: acts on soft going and on good to firm: idled markedly on reappearance: none too consistent. *A. G. Juckes*

COLD CLIMATE   4 b.g. Pursuit of Love 124 – Sharpthorne (USA) 91 (Sharpen **67** Up 127) [1998 77d: 6d 6d³ 6m 7m 8.1m 6m 1999 6.1v 5s⁶ 5d² 5m 5s⁵ 5g 6m² 5m⁴ 6m 6m³ 6g* 6g³ 7m 6s Sep 20] lengthy gelding: shows a quick action: fair handi-capper: won at Newmarket in August: poorly drawn in big fields final 2 starts: best at 5f/6f: acts on good going and on good to firm: visored third to sixth starts. *Bob Jones*

COLD FRONT   4 br.c. Polar Falcon (USA) 126 – Chandni (IRE) (Ahonoora 122) **–** [1998 57: 8s 6d 8m⁵ 10.8m⁶ 8m⁴ a8.5g² 1999 8m 8.3m a12g⁵ Aug 14] leggy colt: **a51** modest maiden: form in handicaps in 1999 only at Wolverhampton (apprentices) final start: races freely, but seems to stay 1½m: acts on fibresand, good to firm going and good to soft: a difficult ride. *N. P. Littmoden*

COLDHARBOUR LASS   3 ch.f. Aragon 118 – Don't Loiter (Town And **–** Country 124) [1998 NR 1999 8.3d Nov 1] sixth reported foal: closely related to 7f winner Feather Face (by Tina's Pet): dam maiden: slowly away and tailed off in maiden. *E. L. James*

COLERIDGE   11 gr.g. Bellypha 130 – Quay Line 117 (High Line 125) [1998 42§, **38 §** a61§: a16g² 17.2g² 17.2m⁵ 17.2d a16.2g 16.4m⁶ 16.1m⁴ a14.8g a16.2g⁵ a14.8g⁵ **a57 §** a16g* 1999 a16g² a16f⁴ a16f a16g* a16g³ a16.2g³ a16.2g a16g⁴ 16d² 18m⁶ a16.2g 16.4d Aug 12] tall gelding: unimpressive mover: modest handicapper on all-weather, poor on turf: won at Southwell in February: best around 2m: acts on all-weather, firm and good to soft going: won in visor earlier in career, wears blinkers nowadays: very slowly away/reluctant to race on occasions, and invariably soon off bridle: usually claimer ridden: not one to trust. *J. J. Sheehan*

COLETTE (IRE)   2 b.f. (Mar 17) Nicolotte 118 – Ascensiontide (Ela-Mana-Mou **67 p** 132) [1999 8.3d Oct 28] 6,000Y: half-sister to several winners, including fairly useful 1m winner Elmi Elmak (by Fairy King) and 6f (at 2 yrs) and 1m winner Sharp Cracker (by Hamas): dam Irish 1½m winner out of Child Stakes winner Rose Above: looked green after much of 13 in Windsor maiden, not handling home turn well: should stay 1¼m: should improve. *Major D. N. Chappell*

COLEY   2 ch.f. (Jan 31) Pursuit of Love 124 – Cole Slaw (Absalom 128) [1999 6g **53** 6v* 7d 8.3d Nov 4] useful-looking filly: second foal: sister to 1998 2-y-o 5f winner Ivory's Promise: dam unraced: 25/1, best effort when dead-heating in 19-runner claimer at Lingfield (left H. Candy £4,000) in September: below form in sellers for new stable: should stay 7f. *L. Montague Hall*

COLINS CHOICE   5 ch.m. Risk Me (FR) 127 – Give Me A Day (Lucky **–** Wednesday 124) [1998 49: a9.4g⁶ a9.4g⁵ a9.4g a8.5g a9.4g⁴ 10v³ 11.7s⁴ a8.5g a9.4g⁴ 1999 a11g Jan 15] poor handicapper: always behind only outing in 1999: stays 11.7f: acts on heavy ground and fibresand: joined T. Cuthbert. *J. L. Spearing*

COLLEGE BLUE (IRE)   3 b.f. College Chapel 122 – Mitsubishi Centre (IRE) **56** (Thatching 131) [1998 73: 5m² 5g² 5d a6g⁵ a6g a5g³ 1999 a5g² Feb 13] fair maiden: below form only outing in 1999: seems best at 5f: visored last 3 starts. *T. G. Mills*

COLLEGE CHOIR (IRE)   3 b.g. College Chapel 122 – Lypharden (IRE) **?** (Lyphard's Special (USA) 122) [1998 NR 1999 a6g 8.2s Apr 19] 26,000F, 15,500Y: fourth foal: dam poor Irish maiden out of half-sister to Irish 1000 Guineas and Yorkshire Oaks winner Sarah Siddons: well beaten in maiden and seller (reportedly suffered a breathing problem): sold 1,000 gns in May and subsequently won over 7.5f in Spain. *G. L. Moore*

COLLEGE DEAN (IRE) 3 ch.g. College Chapel 122 – Phyllode (Pharly (FR) **67 d**
130) [1998 70: 6g⁴ 5m⁶ 6g³ 7f 6d* 6s 6s⁶ 1999 7g⁵ 7.5m 6d 7d 6d 6m 9.3g 8m a6g
7.5g Aug 29] leggy, close-coupled gelding: fair performer at best: should stay 7f: acts
on soft going: often visored: has had tongue tied. *J. J. O'Neill*

COLLEGE GALLERY 2 b.g. (Apr 4) College Chapel 122 – Gallarus (IRE) **52**
(Standaan (FR) 118) [1999 6m 6d a5g a7g Nov 23] 5,500F, 3,800Y, 9,000 2-y-o: **a–**
angular gelding: first foal: dam unraced: some ability in maidens first 2 starts: trained
by M. Heaton-Ellis on debut, C. Cox for second outing. *B. I. Case*

COLLEGE KING (IRE) 3 b.c. College Chapel 122 – Genetta (Green Desert
(USA) 127) [1998 NR 1999 7m 8m⁴ 7.5d⁵ Jun 2] first foal: dam unraced daughter of
half-sister to Kalaglow: no form. *M. Brittain*

COLLEGE MAID (IRE) 2 b.f. (May 5) College Chapel 122 – Maid of Mourne **63**
(Fairy King (USA)) [1999 5d 5v⁴ 5d² 5m² 5m* 5g² 5d³ 5f⁴ 5m³ 6d⁴ 6s 6g 6d⁵ 5s⁶ Nov
5] 7,000Y: sturdy filly: fifth foal: half-sister to a 6f/7f winner in Hong Kong by Pips
Pride: dam Irish 2-y-o 6f winner: modest performer: won maiden at Musselburgh in
May: held her form well, including in nurseries: stays 6f: acts on any going:
consistent. *J. S. Goldie*

COLLEGE MUSIC (IRE) 3 b. or br.f. College Chapel 122 – Lute And Lyre **60 d**
(IRE) 96 (The Noble Player (USA) 126) [1998 64: 5v² 5s² 5s⁴ 5d* 6g 6f³ 6m⁴ 6s 6m
6m 1999 6v 6m⁵ 5f 6m 6s 6g a6g⁵ 7.1d 6.1g Aug 13] leggy, close-coupled filly:
modest handicapper: disappointing in 1999 after second start: stays 6f: acts on any
ground: has been bandaged off-hind: tail flasher: none too reliable. *M. Brittain*

COLLEGE PRINCESS 5 b.m. Anshan 119 – Tinkers Fairy (Myjinski (USA)) **46**
[1998 53: 5m³ 5m 5.1g 5m 5m 1999 5m⁴ 5m 5.3g⁵ 5m⁴ 6f Jul 31] unfurnished mare:
poor handicapper: should stay 6f: acts on firm and good to soft ground. *S. C. Williams*

COLLEGE ROCK 2 ch.c. (Apr 8) Rock Hopper 124 – Sea Aura 89 (Roi Soleil **53**
125) [1999 5.1s 7g 6m² 7g² 7m 7.5g 6s³ 7d³ Oct 15] small, sturdy colt: half-brother
to several winners, including 1990 2-y-o 6f winner Caspian Grey (by Absalom) and
middle-distance performer Charlie Bigtime (by Norwick): dam 2-y-o 6f winner:
modest maiden: form only when runner-up in sellers and third in claimer/private
race: stays 7f: acts on good to firm and soft going: visored seventh start, then left
S. Williams: has given trouble in preliminaries. *Mrs A. E. Johnson*

COLLEGE ROSE 4 b.f. Prince Sabo 123 – Tinkers Fairy (Myjinski (USA)) **–**
[1998 –: 7g⁴ 6f 1999 6g 5f 5g Aug 18] no form: blinkered final start. *S. C. Williams*

COLLISION TIME 2 b.f. (May 27) Timeless Times (USA) 99 – Kaleidophone **57**
73 (Kalaglow 132) [1999 5m³ 5d³ 5g⁴ 5m⁴ 6d³ 5m Jul 10] neat filly: sixth foal:
half-brother to a winner in Norway by Music Boy: dam 1m winner: modest maiden:
may prove best at 5f: visored twice, running creditably. *P. D. Evans*

COLNE VALLEY AMY 2 b.f. (May 6) Mizoram (USA) 105 – Panchellita **52**
(USA) 78 (Pancho Villa (USA)) [1999 6m 5g 8s Nov 6] 1,300Y: second foal: dam 6f
(at 2 yrs) and 7f winner: modest form in maiden at Newbury on debut, but well held
after. *G. L. Moore*

COLOMBE D'OR 2 gr.g. (Jan 19) Petong 126 – Deep Divide 74 (Nashwan **55**
(USA) 135) [1999 5m 7d 6d a8g⁶ Dec 21] 17,000F, 19,000Y: first foal: dam, third
over 1m at 2 yrs, out of close relative to top-class French 1m/9f winner Thrill Show:
modest maiden: best effort when eighth of 17 at Haydock penultimate start: should
stay at least 1m: tends to carry head awkwardly. *P. C. Haslam*

COLONEL CUSTER 4 ch.g. Komaite (USA) – Mohican 75 (Great Nephew **–**
126) [1998 53, a65: a7g³ a8g⁵ a7g² 7g⁵ a7g 1999 a11g⁵ a8g a11g* a12g⁵ a12g⁶ 10s **a65**
a10g⁵ a11g a12g a12g* Dec 27] tall, angular gelding: fair performer on all-weather:
won Southwell handicap in February and Wolverhampton seller (comfortably) in
December: stays 1½m: best form on fibresand (below form on equitrack and lightly
raced on turf): tends to wander/carry head awkwardly under pressure. *J. Pearce*

COLONEL MUSTARD 3 ch.c. Keen 116 – Juliet Bravo 61 (Glow (USA)) **79**
[1998 79: 6f⁶ 7m 7.6f* 8d 1999 7g 9m 10m⁶ 10m* 9m 11.6m Jul 12] unfurnished
colt: has long stride: fair handicapper: won at Windsor in June: well below form after:
stays 1¼m (too free over 11.6f): acts on firm going, possibly not on good to soft:
races prominently/leads. *J. R. Fanshawe*

COLONEL NORTH (IRE) 3 b.g. Distinctly North (USA) 115 – Tricky 66 **80** (Song 132) [1998 –: 7s 1999 8m⁶ 10g 11.4m 8f* 8m* 8.5s⁶ a10g⁶ a10g⁴ a10g Dec **a71** 10] fair performer: won claimer at Newmarket (final start for W. Muir) and handicap at Carlisle in June: best around 1m: acts on firm ground and equitrack, possibly not on soft. *Andrew Reid*

COLONEL SAM 3 b.g. Puissance 110 – Indian Summer 78 (Young Generation **61** 129) [1998 72: 5g³ 5g⁵ 5.1g⁵ 6m 1999 a6g⁵ 5d 6g⁶ a5g a6g⁶ 7m⁶ 8.2m 6.1g 5f² 5g 5g 5d Sep 30] strong, good-quartered gelding: modest maiden: stays 7f: acts on firm going and fibresand: blinkered last 5 starts. *J. A. Glover*

COLONIAL RULE (USA) 2 b.c. (Jan 21) Pleasant Colony (USA) – Musicale **91** (USA) 109 (The Minstrel (CAN) 135) [1999 7m 8.1g² 7d³ 8d* Oct 21] close-coupled, quite attractive colt: fourth foal: half-brother to 1998 Mill Reef Stakes third Belasco (by Gone West): dam, unbeaten in 5 starts at 2 yrs and in Fred Darling Stakes, should have been well suited by 1m+: progressive form in maidens (trained first 3 starts by P. Chapple-Hyam), winning at Brighton in October by 4 lengths from Makasseb, galloping on strongly despite carrying head rather high: will stay beyond 1m. *A. G. Foster*

COLONIAL STATE (USA) 3 b.c. Pleasant Colony (USA) – Star Pastures 124 **74** (Northfields (USA)) [1998 NR 1999 12d⁵ 10g³ 10.5m 12m 11.9d 10.3d Oct 22] tall, unfurnished colt: brother to a Canadian stakes winner and half-brother to several winners, including 4-y-o Marcus Maximus and useful 7f to 1½m performer Monza (both by Woodman): dam, 6f to 8.5f winner, stayed 1¼m: fair form in maidens in May on second and third starts: well below par in handicaps last 3 outings (trained by P. Chapple-Hyam until after penultimate one): should have stayed 1½m: acted on good to firm and good to soft going: visored (much too free and ran poorly) fourth appearance: sold 17,000 gns, joined G. M. Moore: dead. *A. G. Foster*

COLORFUL AMBITION 9 b.g. Slip Anchor 136 – Reprocolor 114 (Jimmy **33 §** Reppin 131) [1998 NR 1999 16.2g 12g⁶ Aug 25] lengthy gelding: winning hurdler (sold cheaply out of Mrs M. Jones' stable in May): poor form on Flat subsequently: has twice refused to race. *W. W. Haigh*

COLOURS TO GOLD (IRE) 4 ch.f. Rainbows For Life (CAN) – Brave Ivy 68 **–** (Decoy Boy 129) [1998 50: 6.1m 6m 8s a8g 8m³ 9.2d 8m 1999 9.2v 7d Apr 29] unfurnished filly: modest maiden handicapper: well beaten in 1999, including in seller: stays 1m: acts on good to firm going, probably on soft: visored (pulled hard) once at 3 yrs. *J. L. Eyre*

COLUMNA 3 gr.f. Deploy 131 – Copper Trader 53 (Faustus (USA) 118) [1998 –: **–** 6.9f 1999 10.2d 12.1g 16v⁶ 11.5m Oct 19] only a little sign of ability: left H. Candy after second start: blinkered once. *M. D. I. Usher*

COLWAY RITZ 5 b.g. Rudimentary (USA) 118 – Million Heiress (Auction Ring **90** (USA) 123) [1998 82: 7d 10m⁵ 10d⁶ 8d² 8.5d* 8g⁴ 8g 10.1g³ 12.3m² 11.9f⁵ 12g 11.9m³ 10v 1999 8g 12s 12m³ 11.9d 10d* 10f* 8.9d 10m* 8.5m³ 11.9f⁴ 10m⁵ 8f 9.2f³ 10m⁶ 10.1m⁵ 7g 7d Oct 26] big, strong gelding: good mover: fairly useful handicapper: won at Ripon and Redcar (Zetland Gold Cup by neck from Farmost) in May and Redcar again in June: several creditable efforts after: effective at 8.5f, barely stays 1½m: acts on firm and good to soft going (possibly not on soft): tried blinkered: held up, and best in truly-run race. *W. Storey*

COL-WOODY 3 ch.g. Safawan 118 – Sky Fighter 43 (Hard Fought 125) [1998 **73 §** 66: 7.1d⁴ 7m⁴ 7m 7.9g⁴ 8s a7g 1999 8g² 8d 8.1d² 8.1m 10m³ 11.9d² 14.1g 14.1m⁶ Aug 28] leggy, close-coupled gelding: fair maiden: creditable efforts in 1999 only when placed: stays 1½m: acts on good to firm and good to soft going: visored 2 of last 3 starts: carries head high and far from genuine (not run on sixth start): joined G. McCourt, poor form over hurdles after. *A. P. Jarvis*

COMANCHE QUEEN 2 ch.f. (Jan 24) Totem (USA) 118 – Chess Mistress **62 ?** (USA) 59 (Run The Gantlet (USA)) [1999 6g 6s 7m 8d Sep 23] 500Y: fourth foal: half-sister to 4-y-o Buzz The Agent: dam 1½m winner in France: form in maidens only on second outing. *K. W. Hogg, Isle of Man*

COMBINED VENTURE (IRE) 3 b.c. Dolphin Street (FR) 125 – Centinela 67 **41** (Caerleon (USA) 132) [1998 57: 6g⁵ 5g³ 5g² 5g 7.1g³ 8s 1999 8g 8m 7g 7.5m⁵ 11f⁴

10f 10f 10.1g³ 9.9g⁶ 10.1d⁶ Sep 15] leggy colt: poor maiden: left E. Weymes after seventh start: stays 11f: has worn tongue strap: inconsistent. *K. A. Morgan*

COME FLY WITH ME   2 b.f. (May 11) Bluebird (USA) 125 – Waffle On 89 (Chief Singer 131) [1999 7d Oct 20] 52,000Y: second foal: half-sister to French 3-y-o 9.5f winner La Frou Frou (by Night Shift): dam, 6f winner at 2 yrs, daughter of half-sister to high-class sprinter College Chapel: well-held seventh of 10 to Ashjaan in maiden at Newcastle: joined M. Bell: should do better. *J. H. M. Gosden* – **p**

COME ON GEORGE (IRE)   3 b.g. Barathea (IRE) 127 – Lacovia (USA) 128 (Majestic Light (USA)) [1998 NR 1999 10.4m 10m⁴ 11.9v Oct 13] 150,000Y: good-topped gelding: half-brother to several winners in France, including useful 1m to 1¼m winner Cirino (by Gone West) and useful miler Otavalo (by Diesis): dam won Prix de Diane: fair maiden: sold 15,000 gns, joined H. Daly. *J. L. Dunlop* **72**

COME ON MURGY   2 b.f. (Mar 16) Weldnaas (USA) 112 – Forest Song 60 (Forzando 122) [1999 5.1m 6d⁶ 6f 5m 5m 5s a5g⁶ 5g a7g* a8g³ Dec 29] 1,100Y: leggy filly: second foal: dam third at 7f as 2-y-o: modest performer: won seller at Wolverhampton in December: stays 1m: acts on good to firm going and all-weather: tried blinkered, better form without. *A. Bailey* **52**

COMEOUTOFTHEFOG (IRE)   4 b.g. Mujadil (USA) 119 – Local Belle (Ballymore 123) [1998 58, a68: a8g³ a8g⁴ a8g² a7g* a8g* a7g⁴ a7g 8.1g 8.2g² 9.7m⁵ 8m 8.5s 7g³ a9.4g a7g² a7g⁶ a8g³ a8g³ a8f⁴ 1999 a6g⁵ a7f a7g⁴ a8g 7s⁶ 8.3m⁴ 8m⁶ a7g* 7m 7.6f³ a7g a7g² Dec 29] small gelding: fair handicapper on all-weather, modest on turf: won apprentice seller at Lingfield in June: left A. McNae and off course 4 months, ran well there final start: effective at 7f/1m: acts on all-weather, best turf form on good going or firmer: blinkered (well beaten) once at 2 yrs. *S. Dow* **54 a67**

COMET DUST   2 b.f. (May 19) Ezzoud (IRE) 126 – Galaxie Dust (USA) 86 (Blushing Groom (FR) 131) [1999 7s 8.3d Oct 28] half-sister to several winners, including 3-y-o Elm Dust, very smart middle-distance performer Zimzalabim (by Damister), smart 7f to 1½m winner Dust Dancer (by Suave Dancer) and useful 7f (at 2 yrs) to 1¼m winner Bulaxie: dam 2-y-o 6f winner: tailed-off last in maidens. *T. D. McCarthy* –

COMEX FLYER (IRE)   2 ch.g. (Apr 9) Prince of Birds (USA) 121 – Smashing Pet (Mummy's Pet 125) [1999 5m 6m⁶ 7f⁴ 7.5g⁶ Sep 15] IR 12,500Y: close-coupled, useful-looking gelding: half-brother to 3-y-o Red Charger: dam lightly-raced half-sister to very smart 1m/1¼m performer Broken Hearted: modest maiden: probably stays 7.5f: raced only on good going or firmer. *J. Berry* **52**

COMIC (IRE)   3 b.f. Be My Chief (USA) 122 – Circus Act (Shirley Heights 130) [1998 69p: 8g⁴ 8.1m⁵ 1999 10g* 11.5g* 12m 11.8g⁵ Aug 18] tall, leggy filly: easy mover: fairly useful performer: won maiden at Windsor in May and handicap at Yarmouth in June (made all): stiff task in Ribblesdale Stakes at Royal Ascot penultimate start, below par in handicap final outing: should stay beyond 11.5f: raced only on good ground or firmer. *J. H. M. Gosden* **87**

COMING UP ROSES   2 b.f. (Feb 18) Sabrehill (USA) 120 – Peaches Polly 76 (Slip Anchor 136) [1999 6f Jun 18] first foal: dam, middle-distance maiden, sister to User Friendly: last of 10 in maiden at Newmarket: sold 3,500 gns in July, joined D. Shaw. *B. W. Hills* –

COMMANCHE RIDGE   2 b.g. (Apr 18) Bonny Scot (IRE) 119 – Cleeveland Lady (Turn Back The Time (USA)) [1999 10.2s 10d Oct 11] strong, workmanlike gelding: third foal: half-brother to 3-y-o Amad's Princess: dam winning hurdler: well beaten in maiden and minor event. *W. G. M. Turner* –

COMMANDER   3 b.c. Puissance 110 – Tarkhana (IRE) (Dancing Brave (USA) 140) [1998 NR 1999 8m 8.2d⁵ Oct 21] 13,000F, 72,000Y: fifth foal: dam Irish 4-y-o 13f winner out of Princess Royal winner Tashtiya: better effort in maidens (over 5 months apart) when fifth at Nottingham: sold 15,000 gns, joined M. Kettle. *H. R. A. Cecil* **68**

COMMANDER COLLINS (IRE)   3 b.c. Sadler's Wells (USA) 132 – Kanmary (FR) 117 (Kenmare (FR) 125) [1998 120p: 7f* 7g² 8v* 1999 8m 10v⁴ Aug 14] tall, rangy, rather unfurnished colt: one of the best 2-y-o's of 1998, winner of listed event at Newmarket and Racing Post Trophy at Doncaster: well below form in 1999, only eleventh in 2000 Guineas at Newmarket (wandered and reportedly returned **103**

bit sore) in May, then fourth of 5 to Val Royal in Prix Guillaume d'Ornano at Deauville 3½ months later: should prove suited by further than 1m: has won on firm and (best effort) heavy ground: tends to be edgy and somewhat wilful in preliminaries (swished tail on reappearance): carries head awkwardly and has drifted left. *P. W. Chapple-Hyam*

COMMENDATORE   4 b.g. Magic Ring (IRE) 115 – Miss Hocroft (Dominion   –
123) [1998 –: 8.2v a6g⁶ a7g 1999 7v⁶ a14g⁶ Jun 11] little sign of ability, including in seller: trained on reappearance by D. Elsworth. *Miss A. Stokell*

COMMONBIRD   2 b.f. (Jan 4) Common Grounds 118 – Queenbird 90 (Warning   **46 d**
136) [1999 5s 5.1s 5s³ 6g⁵ 6.1m 5.2m⁵ 7.5s a7g 5.3g⁵ 6g 7m Sep 1] 30,000F: first foal: dam, 2-y-o 5f to 7f winner, became untrustworthy: poor maiden: seems to stay 7f: no improvement in blinkers. *Andrew Reid*

COMMON CAUSE   3 b.f. Polish Patriot (USA) 128 – Alongside 58 (Slip Anchor   **87**
136) [1998 6s 6.1m 10g 11.5d³ 11.5m* 11.6m² 11.6m³ 11.8g* 11.9m Sep 3] 4,000 2-y-o: small, lightly-made filly: first foal: dam, Irish 9f winner, half-sister to smart French 1m to 1¼m winner Kirkwall from family of 2-y-o Distant Music and top-class middle-distance performers Vanlandingham and Temperence Hill: fairly useful handicapper: won at Lingfield in June and Leicester in August: well held final start: stays 1½m: acts on good to firm and good to soft ground. *C. F. Wall*

COMMON CONSENT (IRE)   3 b.f. Common Grounds 118 – Santella Bell   **62**
(Ballad Rock 122) [1998 –: 5g 7v 1999 10g 11.5m² 16.2m⁴ 12d 9.9m 11.5m³ 11.5g 11.9d³ Oct 29] modest maiden: should be suited by 1½m+: acts on good to firm going. *S. Woodman*

COMMON PLACE   2 b.g. (Mar 6) Common Grounds 118 – One Wild Oat 63   **75 +**
(Shareef Dancer (USA) 135) [1999 6s⁴ 6.1m⁴ 6m⁴ 7f 7m* 7m 8d Oct 15] 34,000Y: rather leggy gelding: fluent mover: second foal: dam, 1½m winner in France, half-sister to Arctic Owl: fair performer: won nursery at Goodwood in August: well below form in similar events after: stays 7f: acts on good to firm and soft going: has shown plenty of temperament (sweating and reluctant in preliminaries before win, has started slowly and usually races freely), and may improve for having been gelded: sold 20,000 gns. *C. F. Wall*

COMMONWEALTH (IRE)   3 b.c. Common Grounds 118 – Silver Slipper 67   **80**
(Indian Ridge 123) [1998 62+: 7m⁶ 7.6f⁶ 1999 8m² 8.3m* 7.1d 8.3m³ 10d 7g Oct 14] reported to have fractured a pastern on final 2-y-o start and had 4 screws inserted: fairly useful performer: won maiden at Windsor in July: left G. Lewis after fourth outing, below form last 2 starts: stays 1m (raced too freely over 1¼m): acts on good to firm going, possibly not on good to soft: sold twice after final start, on latter occasion for 6,400 gns. *M. L. W. Bell*

COMMONWOOD   2 b.g. (Mar 12) Rudimentary (USA) 118 – Mira Lady   **70**
(Henbit (USA) 130) [1999 5m³ 5d 5m² 5.1m 5.7m⁴ 6m⁴ 6m 7s⁶ Oct 25] 4,000F, 9,400Y, resold 9,000Y: fifth foal: half-brother to 3 winners, including 1995 2-y-o 8.3f winner Eric's Bett (by Chilibang) and 1m winner Nuin-Tara (by Petoski): dam won in Germany: fair maiden: best effort when second at Leicester in June (only occasion tongue tied): stays 6f: acts on good to firm going: edgy sort. *J. G. Smyth-Osbourne*

COMPATIBLE (IRE)   3 b.c. Ela-Mana-Mou 132 – Good Enough (IRE) (Simply   **87**
Great (FR) 122) [1998 NR 1999 10m* 11.6g Jul 5] IR 45,000Y: first foal: dam won 7 times in Scandinavia, including Norwegian 1000 Guineas: won maiden at Windsor in May: broke down only other start: dead. *J. H. M. Gosden*

COMPATRIOT (IRE)   3 b.g. Bigstone (IRE) 126 – Campestral (USA) 97   **82 d**
(Alleged (USA) 138) [1998 87: 6g 6f⁴ 6m² 7m⁴ 1999 7.1s² 8.3d³ 7d 5g³ 5m⁴ 6m⁴ 5d³ 6.1g 7m⁴ Oct 19] tall gelding: poor mover: fairly useful maiden: below form after reappearance: stays 7f: acts on firm and soft going: blinkered fifth to seventh starts: has looked none too genuine. *N. A. Callaghan*

COMPENSATION (IRE)   3 gr.g. Turtle Island (IRE) 123 – Fontenoy (USA) 63   **72 §**
(Lyphard's Wish (FR) 124) [1998 72: 7m 6s⁴ 7.1m² 7s⁴ 7d⁶ 1999 7v² 8.2m⁶ 7.1m³ 7.7m⁴ 7m² 7s⁴ 7m 7d³ 7d a8s⁴ Dec 28] close-coupled, rather unfurnished gelding: fair maiden: sold 5,400 gns from M. Jarvis before final start: stays 1m: acts on heavy and good to firm going: blinkered (below form) sixth start: carries head high: ungenuine. *M. Kahn, Sweden*

Peugeot Gordon Stakes, Goodwood—
Compton Ace puts up a smart performance, beating Time Zone (centre) and Adnaan

COMPLIMENTARY 3 b.g. Superpower 113 – Syke Lane 44 (Clantime 101) **60**
[1998 45: 7m a7g 6s a7g⁴ 1999 a6g² a6g² a7s⁴ a7g⁵ 7g⁶ 8.2f* 10.2g* Jun 30] small, **a48**
close-coupled gelding: unimpressive mover: modest on turf, poor on all-weather:
improved form to win handicaps at Nottingham (seller) and Bath in June, taking
while to get going both times: better at 1¼m than shorter: acts on firm going and
all-weather: tried blinkered/visored: sold 8,000 gns, sent to Kuwait. *W. J. Haggas*

COMPLIMENTARY PASS 3 b.f. Danehill (USA) 126 – Capo di Monte 118 **80**
(Final Straw 127) [1998 NR 1999 8m² 9.2s⁴ Sep 27] 39,000 3-y-o: seventh foal:
closely related to 3 winners by Danzig, including 8-y-o Daawe and fair 1m winner
Dafrah: dam, 6f (at 2 yrs) to 11f (Grade 3 event at 4 yrs in USA) winner, half-sister to
smart middle-distance filly Wind In Her Hair: much better effort in maidens when
second at Newmarket on debut: easy to back and travelled well for long way next
time: should stay 1¼m: sold 37,000 gns in December. *G. C. Bravery*

COMPRADORE 4 b.f. Mujtahid (USA) 118 – Keswa 94 (Kings Lake (USA) **73**
133) [1998 78: 6m 5g 5g⁴ 5d 5.2g 7m 5.7m⁴ 5g 5.1m 6g⁶ 6s* 1999 6g 6v⁴ 7m³ 7f⁵
6g⁵ 7m 6m 7m² 8m⁶ 8g⁴ 8.3m⁵ 8v 8d³ 7s Oct 22] leggy, good-quartered filly: fair
handicapper: mostly creditable efforts in 1999: stays 1m: acts on any going: held up.
M. Blanshard

COMPREHENSION (USA) 3 b.f. Diesis 133 – Je Comprend (USA) (Caerleon **87 §**
(USA) 132) [1998 77p: 6m⁶ 1999 8m* 7g³ 8d Aug 8] angular, quite attractive filly:
fairly useful form: off over 10 months, won maiden at Yarmouth in June: below form
next time and refused to race final start: stays 1m: has raced freely: one to be wary of.
C. E. Brittain

COMPTON ACE 3 ch.c. Pharly (FR) 130 – Mountain Lodge 120 (Blakeney 126) **114**
[1998 60p: 7m 7m 10.2d⁴ 1999 12g² 13.9s² 13.3f* 16.2m³ 12f⁵ Jul 27] good-topped
colt: has a moderate, quick action: progressed into a smart performer, winning
handicap at Newbury in May and (after meeting trouble when third in Queen's Vase
at Royal Ascot) Peugeot Gordon Stakes at Goodwood (led inside final 1f when
beating Time Zone by 1½ lengths in 6-runner race but reportedly found to have
cracked a bone in a knee) in July: effective at 1½m, and stays 2m: acts on firm and
soft going: flashes tail: tongue tied final 3 starts: has gained both successes under
K. Fallon. *G. A. Butler*

COMPTON ADMIRAL 3 b.c. Suave Dancer (USA) 136 – Sumoto 101 **121**
(Mtoto 134) [1998 104+: 6m² 7s² 7g* 7.1m² 1999 8g* 8m 12g 10m* 10.4m⁵
Aug 17]

    If the first word of a horse's name is either Beauchamp or Compton then
it's more than likely to be owned by Erik Penser, who uses part of the title of the
village in which he lives, Compton Beauchamp, in the naming of all of his

230

string, Beauchamp for the home-breds and Compton for those purchased at auction. Penser, who in December became a member of the Jockey Club, takes the naming procedure a stage further by giving an identical first letter to the second name for those of the same age, moving on through the alphabet year by year. So, the first of the Beauchamps to reach the racecourse back in 1985 had a second name beginning with the letter 'A', while those who appeared for the first time in 1999 had the letter 'O'. The Comptons are very much the newcomers in this game, with the letter 'A' being used for the first time in 1998, yet they've already matched the Beauchamps by picking up a Group 1 race. While it was eleven years before the home-breds achieved that feat through Beauchamp King, who won the Racing Post Trophy, Compton Admiral got the new team off to a flying start when winning the Coral-Eclipse Stakes at Sandown in July.

Compton Admiral was the first three-year-old to win the Coral-Eclipse since Environment Friend sprang a surprise at odds of 28/1 in a field of seven in 1991, and he's also the longest-priced winner of the race since then, the outsider of eight at 20/1. Compton Admiral had run well below his best in his two most recent races, namely the Two Thousand Guineas and the Derby, whereas most of his opponents arrived at Sandown with good recent performances to their name. Three of them had been successful on their most recent starts, the favourite Croco Rouge in the Prix d'Ispahan at Longchamp, Running Stag in the Brooklyn Handicap at Belmont and Lear Spear in the Prince of Wales's Stakes at Royal Ascot; and the three who followed home Lear Spear, namely Fantastic Light, Xaar and Chester House, were also in the line-up, which was completed by Insatiable, who had finished fourth to Daylami in the 1998 Eclipse. Daylami appeared in the entries at the five-day stage but was kept for the King George VI and Queen Elizabeth Diamond Stakes, leaving Xaar, who like Running Stag was supplemented for £15,000, as the sole representative of the Godolphin team, which had won three of the previous four runnings of the Eclipse. With no confirmed front runners in the field the pace, as had been widely anticipated, was a steady one, at least until the turn where Xaar, who had led from the start, quickened it appreciably. Compton Admiral, who had been settled at the rear, was kept to the rail as the race developed in the straight, a brave decision by his rider Darryll Holland which paid off handsomely as Compton Admiral enjoyed a clear run through to deliver his challenge approaching the final furlong. It was then that Holland almost undid all of his good work, dropping the near rein, but fortunately for him he was able to recover it quickly and his mount responded splendidly when gathered for his final effort. Indeed, Compton Admiral quickened so well between Xaar and Fantastic Light that, after hitting the front near the finish, Holland was able to take things a shade easily on him, Compton Admiral value for a touch more

Coral-Eclipse Stakes, Sandown—a steadily-run affair as 20/1-chance Compton Admiral provides trainer Gerard Butler with his first Group 1 win; Xaar (rail) and Fantastic Light (right) are placed

than the neck he had to spare over Xaar. Fantastic Light took third, a further half a length away, followed by Chester House. It was by no means a vintage Eclipse, but there's no doubt that Compton Admiral was a worthy winner of it.

This was Compton Admiral's third success. He'd got off the mark in a two-year-old maiden at Ascot, where he'd become the first of many to dent the reputation of Killer Instinct; and on his reappearance in the latest season he had the ante-post favourite for the Two Thousand Guineas, Mujahid, well behind when winning the City Index Craven Stakes at Newmarket. Compton Admiral stepped up on his two-year-old form to win the Craven in workmanlike style by a length from Brancaster, who went on to finish fourth in the Guineas, one place behind Mujahid. Unfortunately Compton Admiral jarred a knee in the Guineas and was unable to do himself justice, but he did give a much better account of himself in the Derby, finishing eighth of sixteen to Oath. Compton Admiral, who was bumped at the top of the hill at Epsom, made progress to get to within hailing distance of the leaders in the straight but then tired. While seeming not to stay a mile and a half that day, Compton Admiral's performance on his final start, over an extended mile and a quarter in the Juddmonte International at York, left the impression that he's probably worth another chance at the former trip. Though never able to reach a challenging position Compton Admiral, held up as usual, did stay on all the way to the line to finish fifth behind the most impressive winner Royal Anthem, running only a little below his Eclipse form. Sadly, he fractured a bone in his off-fore knee in the race and the likelihood is that it will be mid-season at least before he'll be ready for action in 2000. Mr Penser and his trainer Gerard Butler therefore had the misfortune to have their two best horses suffer similar injuries within the space of three weeks, Compton Ace having returned lame after winning the Gordon Stakes at Goodwood.

Compton Admiral (b.c. 1996)	Suave Dancer (USA) (b 1988)	Green Dancer (b 1972)	Nijinsky
			Green Valley
		Suavite (b 1981)	Alleged
			Guinevere's Folly
	Sumoto (b 1990)	Mtoto (b 1983)	Busted
			Amazer
		Soemba (b 1983)	General Assembly
			Seven Seas

A figure of around £25,000 is normally the maximum Penser is prepared to lay out when buying a horse, and he's to be applauded for purchasing both Compton Ace and Compton Admiral as yearlings for under that sum. Compton Admiral, who cost 21,000 guineas, is from the third crop of the Arc de Triomphe winner Suave Dancer out of the useful Sumoto. Sumoto won over six furlongs at Ascot on her only start at two years, beating the subsequent One Thousand Guineas winner Sayyedati, and returned from several set-backs to win a seven-furlong minor event at Lingfield from five outings at three. Judged on her pedigree, Sumoto should have stayed a fair bit further. Her sire Mtoto was effective at up to a mile and a half, while her dam Soemba won over nine furlongs and is a daughter of the seven-furlong and eleven-furlong winner Seven Seas, a half-sister to the smart seven-furlong to mile-and-a-quarter winner Fluellen. Compton Admiral is the second foal and second winner produced by Sumoto; her two-year-old colt by Inchinor, the promising Summoner, won a maiden over a mile at Doncaster in November. Apart from when an unlucky second in the Chesham Stakes, which was run on soft going, Compton Admiral has done all of his racing on good or good to firm going. A smallish, sturdy colt with a fluent, quick action, he usually takes the eye before his races and races most genuinely during them. It's to be hoped he makes a full recovery and there are plenty of opportunities to see him again. *G. A. Butler*

COMPTON AJAX (IRE) 3 gr.g. Paris House 123 – Fear Naught 99 (Connaught – § 130) [1998 –p: 7s 1999 8d Apr 15] leggy, rather lightly-made gelding: looked temperamental both starts on Flat: dead. *G. A. Butler*

COMPTON AKKA (IRE)   3 b.f. Balla Cove 119 – Adjanada 108 (Nishapour   – §
(FR) 125) [1998 56§: 5m 6m 6m² 6.1d³ 6m a6g a6g⁶ 1999 a7g² a8f² a7g* a7g* a8g⁵   **a64** §
a7g² 6m 6f a8.5g 6g Aug 24] rather leggy, good-quartered filly: modest performer:
won maiden and minor event at Lingfield in February: stayed 1m: acted on good to
firm going, good to soft and equitrack: blinkered twice: showed temperament: dead.
G. A. Butler

COMPTON AMBER   3 b.f. Puissance 110 – Amber Mill 96 (Doulab (USA)   **65 d**
115) [1998 78: 6m 6m⁴ 6g⁴ 7m³ 6d⁶ 5s 5s² 5d 1999 a6g³ 5.1s a6g 8f⁶ 8m a8g 8.5m⁶
a10g a6g a6g a7g Dec 15] sparely-made filly: fair maiden at 2 yrs: well below form
in 1999, refusing to race sixth start: left G. Butler after ninth start: tried blinkered: has
worn tongue strap: best left alone. *J. Berry*

COMPTON AMICA (IRE)   3 gr.f. High Estate 127 – Nephrite 106 (Godswalk   **87**
(USA) 130) [1998 55: 6m 6g 7m 7s⁵ 1999 9.7s* 12m³ 11.6g* 11.4m* 12m 12m⁴
10.5g³ 12m 15d⁴ Sep 16] tall, close-coupled filly: fairly useful handicapper: won at
Folkestone in March, Windsor in May and Sandown in June: should stay beyond
1½m (raced bit freely over 15f): acts on soft and good to firm ground: sold 19,000
gns in October. *G. A. Butler*

COMPTON ANGEL (IRE)   3 b.f. Fairy King (USA) – Embla 121 (Dominion   **82**
123) [1998 68p: 6g 6.1s⁴ 1999 7m 7d⁶ 10g⁴ 10.1g a10g² 10d⁴ 8s⁴ 10.5v⁶ a10g* 8s
a10g⁵ Dec 8] smallish, rather dipped-backed filly: fairly useful performer: won
handicap at Lingfield in October: flattered when seventh of 10 in listed race at
Saint-Cloud penultimate start: stays 1¼m: acts on equitrack, may prove best on good
going or softer on turf (moved poorly on good to firm): tongue tied third and fourth
starts: has wandered and looked less than keen. *G. A. Butler*

COMPTON ARROW (IRE)   3 b.c. Petardia 113 – Impressive Lady 98 (Mr   **104**
Fluorocarbon 126) [1998 95p: 7.3g⁵ 6g* 6g 7s³ 6s* 6d⁴ 1999 8g³ 7m⁶ 7d 8m 8.1g³
7.3m³ 7.9g Aug 19] big, rangy colt: has a quick action: useful performer: good third
in listed race at Kempton (2 lengths behind Dehoush) and minor events at Sandown
and Newbury (beaten 3¼ lengths by Teapot Row): ran poorly in valuable handicap at
York final start: not sure to stay beyond 1m: acts on soft going and on good to firm.
G. A. Butler

COMPTON AVIATOR   3 ch.c. First Trump 118 – Rifada 103 (Ela-Mana-Mou   **80**
132) [1998 NR 1999 10m⁴ 10m³ 7m³ Aug 29] 16,000Y: third reported foal: half-
brother to smart French 10.5f and 1½m winner Rifapour (by Shahrastani): dam, 1½m
winner, would have stayed further: fairly useful form in maidens: stays 1¼m: tongue
tied on first and final starts. *G. A. Butler*

COMPTON BANKER (IRE)   2 br.c. (Feb 6) Distinctly North (USA) 115 –   **82 p**
Mary Hinge 100 (Dowsing (USA) 124) [1999 6f⁶ 6g 6d⁵ Nov 4] 52,000Y: strong,
good-topped colt: second foal: half-brother to 3-y-o Night Adventure: dam sprinter:
fairly useful form in 2 maidens, not knocked about final outing: best effort when 10½
lengths seventh of 10 in Gimcrack Stakes at York (bandaged in front, raced freely)
second start: should stay 7f: probably still capable of better. *G. A. Butler*

COMPTON BOLTER (IRE)   2 b.c. (Apr 25) Red Sunset 120 – Milk And Honey   **103**
102 (So Blessed 130) [1999 7m³ 7f² 8.1m* 7d² 7s³ Nov 5] IR 17,000Y: brother to a
winner abroad and half-brother to several winners, including useful but ungenerous
sprinter Hana Marie (by Formidable): dam, sprint winner at 2 yrs (didn't train on),
half-sister to smart 1½m performer Beeshi (by Red Sunset): useful form: won
maiden at Chepstow in September, racing freely and leading on line despite drifting
left: good placed efforts after in minor event at Ascot and Criterium de Maisons-
Laffitte (length third of 8 to Touch of The Blues): stays 1m: acts on soft going and on
good to firm. *G. A. Butler*

CONCER ARALL   5 ch.g. Ron's Victory (USA) 129 – Drudwen (Sayf El Arab   –
(USA) 127) [1998 52d: a7g² a7g a8g a7g a8g 1999 a8g a7g Jan 7] modest handicapper on all-weather, unraced on turf: no form since 4-y-o reappearance. *P. D. Evans*

CONCER UN   7 ch.g. Lord Bud 121 – Drudwen (Sayf El Arab (USA) 127) [1998   **84**
91: 7m³ 8.5g 8d 8.1g 8d 1999 7m 7g 7.6d⁶ 7.9m⁵ 9m⁵ 8v⁴ 8.9d Oct 9] smallish,
lengthy gelding: tough, genuine and useful handicapper at his best: steadily on
the downgrade: needs good test at 7f, and stays 9f: acts on any going: sometimes
bandaged: often slowly away. *S. C. Williams*

CONCINO (FR) 2 b.g. (Apr 16) Zafonic (USA) 130 – Petronella (USA) (Nureyev –
(USA) 131) [1999 6g 6.1m 7s Sep 29] 40,000Y: second foal: half-brother to 3-y-o
Indian Dance: dam unraced sister to useful winner up to 1½m Mellaby: well beaten
in maidens, unruly in stalls and slowly away penultimate start. *P. W. Harris*

CONCLUSION 2 ch.c. (Apr 29) Prince Sabo 123 – High Finish 58 (High Line   **58**
125) [1999 6.1d⁶ 6m³ 6.1m 6m⁶ 6g* 6m 6v a6g³ a6g a6s⁴ Dec 21] 9,500Y: first foal:
dam, lightly-raced maiden, half-sister to smart performers Munwar (up to 1½m) and
Hateel (up to 1¾m): modest performer: won selling nursery at Leicester in August:
sold from M. Blanshard 1,500 gns before final start: should stay 7f: acts on equitrack,
best turf effort on good ground. *M. Kahn, Sweden*

CONFIDENTIAL 3 ch.f. Generous (IRE) 139 – Just You Wait (Nonoalco (USA)   **60**
131) [1998 NR 1999 12g⁶ 12s⁴ Jun 27] big, leggy filly: half-sister to several winners,
notably very smart pair Reprimand (miler, by Mummy's Pet) and Wiorno (up to
1½m, by Wassl): dam unraced daughter of smart 1¼m winner Sleat: favourite,
promising sixth in maiden at Kempton, seeming very green early on: well beaten in
similar event next time: sold 23,000 gns in December. *H. R. A. Cecil*

CONFLICT (FR) 3 b.c. Warning 136 – La Dama Bonita (USA) 87 (El Gran Senor   **105**
(USA) 136) [1998 89p: 6.1g 7d* 1999 8g⁶ 10s⁶ 9.9g⁴ 10d⁵ 12.4m⁶ 10.5d* 10.4g⁶
Aug 18] close-coupled, angular colt: useful performer: best effort when allowed to
dictate and winning handicap at Haydock in August by ½ length from Ex Gratia: ran
respectably in listed/Group 3 company first 4 starts: stays 10.5f: acts on good to soft
going, well below form only outing on good to firm. *C. E. Brittain*

CONFRONTER 10 ch.g. Bluebird (USA) 125 – Grace Darling (USA) (Vaguely
Noble (USA)) [1998 61: 10d⁶ 9.5g 8g a10g⁴ 9.7s⁴ 8d³ 8g 8f⁵ 10.2g 8g⁶ 10m⁵ 8f⁶ 8m³   **a68**
a8g² a10f³ 1999 a10g² a10g* 10g 8g⁵ a10g⁴ a10g* 8f⁵ 10f⁵ 9d a10g⁶ a10g⁴ a10g⁵
Dec 18] tall gelding: fair on all-weather, modest on turf: won handicaps at Lingfield
in January and April: effective at 1m to 1¼m: acts on any going: has run well in
blinkers/visor, not tried since 1994: none too consistent. *S. Dow*

CONNECT 2 b.c. (Apr 15) Petong 126 – Natchez Trace 52 (Commanche Run 133)   **94**
[1999 5d² 5m* 5d³ 5d⁶ Oct 9] 14,000F, 19,000Y: workmanlike colt: unimpressive
mover: fourth foal: half-brother to 1½m winner Be True (by Robellino): dam,
maiden, should have been well suited by further than 1m, from family of Paris House
(by Petong): fairly useful form: won maiden at Pontefract in September: narrowly-
beaten third of 16 in nursery at Newmarket next time, and not disgraced in Group 3
at Ascot final start: speedy, but should stay 6f. *M. H. Tompkins*

CONORA (NZ) 6 b.g. Conquistarose (USA) – Soundora (NZ) (Sound Reason   –
(CAN)) [1998 6d⁵ 7v³ 7s* 7s³ 8v 8g² 8d 1999 8.2s a7g Dec 4] New Zealand-bred
gelding: dam won at 1¼m and 11f in New Zealand: won maiden at Hastings in 1998,
before leaving K. Marshment in New Zealand: no form in Britain. *O. O'Neill*

CONSIDERATION (IRE) 2 ch.f. (Apr 7) Perugino (USA) 84 – Reflection   **47**
Time (IRE) (Fayruz 116) [1999 5g⁶ 5v² a7g⁴ a6g⁴ Jul 10] quite good-topped filly: **a–**
second foal: sister to 3-y-o Red Venus: dam unraced: poor maiden: well beaten on
all-weather last 2 starts: should stay at least 6f. *J. Berry*

CONSONANT (IRE) 2 ch.c. (Jan 27) Barathea (IRE) 127 – Dinalina (FR) (Top   **95**
Ville 129) [1999 7g* 7.1g Aug 20] 200,000Y: eighth foal: closely related to 2 winners
in France by Sadler's Wells, including useful 1m and 1¼m winner Swalina, and half-
brother to several winners, including Prix de Diane winner Caerlina (by Caerleon):
dam French 2-y-o 1¼m winner: made all in minor event at Chantilly in July:
favourite, gave impression something amiss when tailed-off last in Solario Stakes at
Sandown following month: bred to stay at least 1m. *D. R. Loder, France*

CONSORT 6 b.h. Groom Dancer (USA) 128 – Darnelle 83 (Shirley Heights 130)   **90**
[1998 100: 8d 8m⁶ 8d 7f² 7.6f² 7d 7g 9g² 8s 1999 7g 7m 8m 7.6m⁶ 8d 7d⁴ 8.3m⁴ 9m⁶   **a79**
10s 8d 8s a10g a8g³ a7g Dec 29] good-topped horse: has a quick action: fairly useful
handicapper on turf, just fair on all-weather: mainly below form from seventh start:
sold 12,000 gns and left Mrs A. Perrett after eleventh one: best at 1m/9f: has form on
good to soft going, best efforts on good or firmer: best held up in strongly-run race.
A. J. McNae

Bollinger Champagne Challenge Series Final Handicap (Gentleman Amateurs), Ascot—
Les Jefford seals the Bollinger Champagne title on nine-year-old Conspicuous (right)
as they win their second race of the season together; Protocol rallies well and Burundi is third

CONSPICUOUS (IRE) 9 b.g. Alzao (USA) 117 – Mystery Lady (USA) (Vaguely **91**
Noble 140) [1998 97: 8g⁵ 8m² 10.1m⁶ 10g⁶ 9.9g⁴ 9.9g⁴ 9d 8s⁵ 10v 10s* 1999 10.2d⁶
10.1g⁶ 10m⁶ 10m⁶ 9.9f 9g 9v* 12d* Oct 9] close-coupled gelding: has a quick action:
fairly useful handicapper: won amateur races at Kempton in September and Ascot
(well ridden by Mr L. Jefford) in October: effective at 1m to 1½m: acts on any turf
going and all-weather: visored (ran poorly) once as 6-y-o: takes good hold and is
waited with. *L. G. Cottrell*

CONSTANT 2 b.c. (Feb 1) Deploy 131 – Avowal (Kris 135) [1999 7.1m 8d 8d⁵ **73**
Oct 12] smallish, well-made colt: has a round action: third foal: closely related to 9.7f
winner Vellum (by Warning): dam unraced half-sister to very smart French/US miler
Rainbow Corner out of Lowther winner Kingscote: best effort in maidens (fair form)
when fifth of 19 to Imperial Rocket at Leicester: should stay at least 1¼m: sold
17,000 gns. *B. W. Hills*

CONSULTANT 3 b.g. Man of May – Avenita Lady 57 (Free State 125) [1998 64, **–**
a76: a5g³ a5g* 5.1f² 5g a6g⁴ a6g* 5m⁴ 6m 1999 a5g⁶ a5g⁶ a5g² a6g⁴ 6m a5g⁶ 5.1m **a74**
5d a7g a5g a6g a6g Dec 27] good-bodied gelding: fair handicapper on all-weather,
modest at best on turf: creditable efforts in 1999 only on third and fourth starts: left
N. Littmoden after penultimate outing: stays 6f: acts on fibresand and firm going:
usually races up with pace. *C. N. Kellett*

CONTENTMENT (IRE) 5 b.h. Fairy King (USA) – Quality of Life (Auction **52**
Ring (USA) 123) [1998 70, a54: 10s a10g⁴ 10m² 10.5d 10.4g 7g⁶ a8g⁶ a7g a10f 1999
a8g 10m 10d 8g 10m 10.5d 9.9v⁴ 11.8d Oct 12] small horse: modest handicapper:
left Miss G. Kelleway after fourth start: finds 7f on sharp side, and stays 1¼m: acts
on good to firm ground, heavy and equitrack: tongue tied: sometimes bandaged/starts
slowly: tail swisher, and often a weak finisher: sent to Italy. *B. R. Millman*

CONTINUOUS TIME (USA) 3 b.f. Shadeed (USA) 135 – Trattoria (USA) 62 **62**
(Alphabatim (USA) 126) [1998 56+: 6m⁶ 7m 7s 1999 7d 7m 8g 7d Oct 12] useful-
looking filly: well held in handicaps 1999: blinkered final start. *J. R. Jenkins*

CONTRACT GIRL (IRE) 5 b.m. Contract Law (USA) 108 – Paradise Regained **–**
41 (North Stoke 130) [1998 NR 1999 a12g⁶ a9.4g Feb 20] half-sister to 3 winners,
including 1½m winner Al Shany (by Burslem): dam placed up to 15f: well held in
bumpers, over hurdles and in sellers on Flat (trained on debut by P. Bevan).
B. D. Leavy

CONTRARIE   6 b.m. Floose 99 – Chanita (Averof 123) [1998 NR 1999 16.2g   –
10.5d Sep 21] tall mare: well beaten on return from 2-year absence: dead. *M. J. Ryan*

CONTRARY MARY   4 b.f. Mujadil (USA) 119 – Love Street 62 (Mummy's Pet   **66**
125) [1998 75, a60+: a7g 7d 7g² 5.7s³ 6m³ 7m 7m* 7g 7.1m⁴ 6d a6g 7s 1999 6g 7v*   **a–**
6m 6m 6.1g⁴ 7f⁴ 6m 6m³ 7m⁴ 6d⁵ Nov 4] smallish, lightly-made filly: fair performer:
won falsely-run minor event at Folkestone in April: creditable efforts final 3 starts:
effective at 6f/7f: acts on good to firm and heavy going: has got upset in preliminaries, and sometimes looks difficult ride. *J. Akehurst*

COOGAN (ITY)   3 ch.c. Caerleon (USA) 132 – Tapage Nocturne (USA) (Irish   **72**
River (FR) 131) [1998 –p: 7s⁴ 1999 11.1g⁵ 7.5m⁵ 9d 9d Oct 17] leggy colt: fifth in
maiden at Kempton on reappearance in April (final start for P. Cole): probably stays
11f. *L. Camici, Italy*

COOGEE BAY   3 gr.f. Petong 126 – Dark Eyed Lady (IRE) 82 (Exhibitioner   **36**
111) [1998 NR 1999 7.1m 6d 6d a7g a7g Oct 16] IR 5,000Y: first foal: dam
winning sprinter, including at 2 yrs: poor maiden: blinkered/visored final 2 starts.
D. W. P. Arbuthnot

COOKIE   2 ch.g. (Mar 7) Then Again 126 – Baking (King of Spain 121) [1999   **74**
5.1s 5.1g² a5g* 5m Dec 31] 2,500Y, resold IR 6,400Y: first foal: dam unraced half-
sister to useful sprinter Bay Bay: fair form: won maiden at Wolverhampton in May
on final start for R. Hannon: renamed Projectstar, behind in handicap on Hong Kong
debut 7 months later: will stay 6f. *D. Hill, Hong Kong*

COOL AFFAIR (IRE)   4 ch.g. Statoblest 120 – Ukraine's Affair (USA) (The
Minstrel (CAN) 135) [1998 NR 1999 10m 6m Jun 19] little sign of ability.
K. W. Hogg, Isle of Man

COOL EDGE (IRE)   8 ch.g. Nashamaa 113 – Mochara (Last Fandango 125)   **102**
[1998 113: 7.1g⁴ 7g³ 7.3m³ 8.9g⁴ 8d⁵ 7s³ 7g 1999 7m* 7m⁵ 7m 7d 7.1g⁶ 7d 8g 7s
8.2s⁵ Nov 1] rangy gelding: only useful performer nowadays: won 4-runner minor
event at Leicester in June by a head from Cretan Gift: creditable efforts after only on
fifth and sixth outings: effective at 7f, probably 9f: yet to race on heavy, acts on
any other going: visored (ran well) twice at 4 yrs: early to post: free-going sort.
M. H. Tompkins

COOLING CASTLE (FR)   3 ch.g. Sanglamore (USA) 126 – Syphaly (USA)   **70 d**
(Lyphard (USA) 132) [1998 70: 6m³ 7g 7g 1999 11.6m 9.9g* 14.6f 12v⁵ 9g⁶ 10g⁵
12.4g 10s Sep 29] useful-looking gelding: fluent mover: fair performer: won claimer
at Beverley in April (left B. Meehan): below form after, and shaped as though all
wasn't well penultimate start: possibly doesn't stay 1½m when conditions are very
testing: acts on good to firm going. *Ronald Thompson*

COOL INVESTMENT (IRE)   2 b.c. (May 15) Prince of Birds (USA) 121 –   **76 p**
Superb Investment (IRE) (Hatim (USA) 121) [1999 8f* Sep 13] IR 14,000Y: second
live foal: half-brother to 1998 2-y-o 7f seller winner Investment Hero (by Imperial
Frontier): dam champion 2-y-o filly in Czechoslovakia: 5/2, won 5-runner maiden at
Musselburgh in September by 3 lengths from Principle, drawing clear final 1f: will
stay 1¼m: should improve. *M. Johnston*

COOL JUDGE (IRE)   2 b.g. (Mar 5) Superpower 113 – Carlton Glory (Blakeney   **48**
126) [1999 5d 5d 5m⁶ 6f² 6m³ 6f 7f 7g a6g Dec 13] IR 3,000F, IR 6,000Y: close-
coupled gelding: eighth foal: half-brother to 3 winners, including 5-y-o Molly Music
and stayer Reach For Glory (by Reach): dam modest maiden: poor maiden: placed in
claimer and seller: stays 7f: form only on going firmer than good. *W. W. Haigh*

COOL KATIE   3 b.f. Komaite (USA) – Pomade 79 (Luthier 126) [1998 55: 5g²   **53 d**
5g⁴ 5m⁴ 5g² 5d⁵ 5m 1999 a6g 5g⁴ 6g 7g 5.9m 5f 5g 5m 5f Sep 4] small, workmanlike
filly: modest maiden at 2 yrs: no form in 1999 after second start: blinkered seventh
outing. *K. A. Ryan*

COOL LOCATION   2 b.f. (Apr 25) Pelder (IRE) 125 – Hello Lady (Wolverlife   **–**
115) [1999 5.7g a7g 8.2d a8g Nov 12] second foal: dam maiden hurdler: no promise
in maidens/sellers: tried blinkered. *M. Quinn*

COOL PROSPECT   4 b.g. Mon Tresor 113 – I Ran Lovely (Persian Bold 123)   **55**
[1998 70: 6s 6d² 7.5g⁴ 6g² 6d 6g a6g³ a6g² 7s 1999 a6g³ a8.5g 7g 7g 9d 12.4m⁶ 9.3m   **a73**

12m 8m⁴ 6f* 6.9m 7.6m a7g 6g a6f Oct 2] neat gelding: fluent mover: fair handicapper on all-weather, modest on turf: convincing winner of 26-runner amateur
maiden event at Redcar in June: below form after: best form at 6f, sometimes tackles
much further: acts on firm going, good to soft and fibresand: effective blinkered or
not: none too consistent. *K. A. Ryan*

COOL SECRET   4 gr.g. Petong 126 – Cool Run 87 (Deep Run 119) [1998 61, **68**
a70: 7d 8g a6g³ 6g 6m 7.1g⁴ 6v 1999 a6f* a7g a7g⁶ a6g* a8g² a7g* 6d a8g⁶ a8.5g* **a100**
8g² 9g⁵ 8f Jul 27] strong, compact gelding: shows knee action: useful on all-weather,
fair on turf: winner in 1999 at Southwell (claimer and 2 handicaps, left K. Ryan after
first one) and at Wolverhampton (best effort, beat Baron de Pichon 2½ lengths in
handicap in June): good second in handicap at Goodwood (wandered) later in month:
needs good test at 6f, and stays 1m: acts on good to firm going and fibresand, and
probably unsuited by softer than good: sent to USA. *K. R. Burke*

COOL TEMPER   3 b.g. Magic Ring (IRE) 115 – Ovideo 58 (Domynsky 110) **81**
[1998 NR 1999 6v² 6.1f² 6g² 7m² 6m² 6m² Jul 16] 18,500 2-y-o: sturdy gelding:
second foal: dam, 2-y-o 7f winner, half-sister to smart middle-distance horse Captain
Horatius: fairly useful maiden: runner-up on all 6 starts: stays 7f: usually tongue tied:
bandaged off-hind final start. *J. E. Banks*

COOL VIBES   4 br.g. Rock City 120 – Meet Again (Lomond (USA) 128) [1998 **81**
83: 8m* 10.3g⁵ 8s³ 1999 10m 10g 10g⁵ Jun 30] neat gelding: fairly useful performer,
lightly raced: ran creditably in handicap on reappearance, but disappointing after:
stays 1¼m: best efforts on good to firm ground: sold 1,800 gns in August, joined
D. Bridgewater. *J. Pearce*

COOL WATERS   4 b.f. Puissance 110 – Keep Cool (FR) 42 (Northern Treat **–**
(USA)) [1998 –: 7v 12.1g 8.3m 1999 8.3g May 10] seems of little account. *R. Dickin*

COOPER ISLAND   3 ch.c. Generous (IRE) 139 – Colza (USA) 89 (Alleged **67**
(USA) 138) [1998 75p: 8g⁶ 8g⁶ 1999 8s 12.3m⁴ 12.3d³ 14m³ 12.3f³ 14.1m Aug 23]
strong, sturdy colt: has a quick action: fair maiden handicapper: creditable efforts
when in frame: well worth a try beyond 1¾m: acts on firm and good to soft going:
moved poorly to post penultimate start: sold 14,000 gns in October. *B. W. Hills*

COPERNICUS   4 b.g. Polish Precedent (USA) 131 – Oxslip 106 (Owen Dudley **82**
121) [1998 79: 10f² 1999 a12g⁵ 10m³ 10d² 14g⁵ 16.4m⁶ 14.1m² 12m* 14d* 14s 12g*
Oct 16] leggy gelding: fairly useful performer: won claimer at Catterick in August,
handicap at Sandown in September and an apprentice claimer at Catterick in
October: effective at 1¼m, doesn't quite stay 2m: acts on fibresand, firm and good
to soft going: blinkered/visored last 8 starts: usually leads/races prominently, and
sometimes wanders. *P. F. I. Cole*

COPPER COOKIE   4 ch.f. Selkirk (USA) 129 – Festival Fanfare (Ile de Bour- **37**
bon (USA) 133) [1998 –, a30: 8m 8.3m 11.5m⁴ 7m 10d 8.2v a7g a12g³ 1999 a12g **a–**
a12g a12f a16f a12g 7.5d⁴ a8g 8.2f a12g 10d 9.9g 8.2s⁶ Oct 5] tall, angular filly:
poor maiden handicapper: stays 1½m: acts on fibresand and good to soft ground.
M. J. Polglase

COPPER SHELL   5 ch.g. Beveled (USA) – Luly My Love (Hello Gorgeous **–**
(USA) 128) [1998 –: 16d 1999 a12g* a16g⁵ a11g* a12f* a11f² a12g* 12m **a74**
a12g Dec 29] fair handicapper on all-weather: won 3 times at Southwell (maiden
event and 2 amateur races) in January and once at Wolverhampton (apprentices) in
February: off course 7½ months before well beaten final 2 starts: stays 1¾m,
seemingly not 2m: acts on fibresand: has worn tongue strap. *Mrs L. C. Jewell*

COPPLESTONE (IRE)   3 b.g. Second Set (IRE) 127 – Queen of The Brush **73**
(Averof 123) [1998 80: 6m 7.5m³ 7.1d⁴ 7f³ 8m⁴ a8.5g³ 1999 9.7m⁴ May 26] tall
gelding: fair maiden: pulled hard when fourth in handicap on only outing in 1999:
should stay 1¼m: acts on firm, good to soft and fibresand: forces pace: visored
twice (ran creditably) at 2 yrs. *P. W. Harris*

COPYFORCE BOY   3 ch.g. Mystiko (USA) 124 – Surpassing 79 (Superlative **–**
118) [1998 –: 6m 7m 7g 1999 7m May 16] strong, lengthy gelding: well held in
maidens. *Miss B. Sanders*

COPYFORCE GIRL   3 b.f. Elmaamul (USA) 125 – Sabaya (USA) 92 (Seattle **70**
Dancer (USA) 119) [1998 70, a?: 6m 7m 7m³ a8g⁶ 1999 11.5m⁶ 10m 11.5f² 16.4d **a–**

a13g 11.9d⁴ 10d Nov 4] angular filly: fair maiden handicapper: creditable efforts only when in frame: stays 11.5f: acts on firm and good to soft going: reportedly bled from nose second 2-y-o start. *Miss B. Sanders*

COQUELLES (FR) 3 b.f. In The Wings 128 – La Toja (FR) (Gift Card (FR) 124) **78** [1998 NR 1999 10.5m² 11.5d³ 12.5m* 11d⁵ 11.6m 14.1m Sep 2] ex-French filly: fourth foal: half-sister to 2 winners abroad, including French 7f (at 2 yrs) to 10.5f winner Mayence (by Mondrian): dam French 2-y-o 7.5f winner on only start: won maiden at Nort-sur-Erdre in May: left H-A. Pantall after next start: stiff tasks, well held in minor events both British starts: stays 12.5f. *P. Eccles*

CORAL BEACH 3 gr.f. Lugana Beach 116 – Thames Glow 69 (Kalaglow 132) **–** [1998 NR 1999 6g Jun 12] 2,100Y: second foal: half-sister to Italian 5f (including at 2 yrs) and 6f winner Reve Indien (by Indian Ridge): dam 7f winner who should have stayed beyond 1m: 50/1, showed little in maiden at Lingfield. *M. J. Haynes*

CORAL ISLAND 5 b.g. Charmer 123 – Misowni (Niniski (USA) 125) [1998 NR **–** 1999 12g Jun 22] leggy gelding: modest form when winning handicap on reappearance in 1997: below par since: joined R. Stronge 1,400 gns in August and won twice over hurdles subsequently, showing fairly useful form: should stay 1¼m: acts on firm going: tried blinkered/visored. *J. G. FitzGerald*

CORAL REEF (IRE) 3 ch.f. Karinga Bay 116 – Mamara Reef 71 (Salse (USA) **51** 128) [1998 47: 6g 7.5m 7g² a7g³ 7m⁶ 1999 a10g⁵ a8g⁶ 12.5d³ 12m⁵ Apr 14] modest maiden on turf, poor on all-weather: stays 12.5f: acts on good to soft, good to firm ground and fibresand: blinkered/visored. *W. G. M. Turner*

CORAL SHELLS 2 b.f. (Apr 4) Formidable (USA) 125 – Elle Reef (Shareef **53** Dancer (USA) 135) [1999 6.1m 7f⁶ 7s 7s² 8d⁵ Oct 18] 3,000F, 7,500Y: sturdy filly: third foal: half-sister to 3-y-o Ace of Trumps and a winner in Italy by Aragon: dam unraced: modest maiden: second in nursery at Catterick in October: will probably stay beyond 1m: sold 5,000 gns. *P. T. Walwyn*

CORAL WATERS (IRE) 3 b.f. College Chapel 122 – Premier Leap (IRE) 56 **46** (Salmon Leap (USA) 131) [1998 67: 6m 7g 6s 1999 8m 11.6g 8.1m a8g⁵ a7g⁴ 7g³ 7m a10g Jul 31] unfurnished, rather dipped-backed filly: poor maiden: left C. Cyzer after sixth start, and well held in handicaps after: probably best at 6f/7f: acts on equitrack and soft going: has hung. *R. Curtis*

CORBLETS 2 b.f. (May 15) Timeless Times (USA) 99 – Dear Glenda 66 (Gold **69** Song 112) [1999 5m⁴ 5g² 6m⁵ 5g Oct 19] seventh living foal: sister to 3 winning sprinters, including 4-y-o Aurigny and 3-y-o Giffoine, and half-sister to 5f winner Jade City (by Belfort): dam sprinter: best effort in maidens at Lingfield (yet to race elsewhere) when short-head second of 8 to Nantucket in August: not ideally drawn final start: likely to prove best at 5f/6f. *S. Dow*

CORDIAL KNIGHT (USA) 6 b.g. Night Shift (USA) – Temperence Cordial **–** (USA) (Temperence Hill (USA)) [1998 –: 11.6m 1999 8.1m Aug 5] fairly useful maiden handicapper up to 1¼m for D. Weld in Ireland at 4 yrs: soundly beaten both starts on Flat since: usually blinkered. *C. P. Morlock*

CORINIUM (IRE) 2 br.f. (Apr 23) Turtle Island (IRE) 123 – Searching Star 63 **101 p** (Rainbow Quest (USA) 134) [1999 7.5g³ 7.7d* 7.3s* Oct 23] IR 115,000Y: good-topped, attractive filly: fourth foal: half-sister to 3 winners, including 3-y-o Ellway Star and 4-y-o Fa-Eq: dam, maiden, half-sister to smart performer around 1½m Beldale Star: progressive form: won maiden at Warwick (by 7 lengths) in September and listed event at Newbury (beat Iftiraas by short head, switched having been unable to obtain clear run then quickening well to lead close home) in October: will stay 1¼m: acts on soft going: smart performer in the making. *H. R. A. Cecil*

CORK HARBOUR (FR) 3 ch.g. Grand Lodge (USA) 125 – Irish Sea 66 (Irish **75** River (FR) 131) [1998 NR 1999 10.2s⁶ 10v³ Oct 12] 1,600,000 francs Y: half-brother to several winners abroad, including US Grade 2 8.5f winner Shir Dar (by Lead On Time), earlier successful in France: dam French 9f winner at 4 yrs from family of Hellenic and Greek Dance: better effort in maidens when third at Ayr: sold 7,500 gns. *B. W. Hills*

CORNDAVON (USA) 3 b.f. Sheikh Albadou 128 – Ferber's Follies (USA) **79** (Saratoga Six (USA)) [1998 80: 5g⁵ 5d⁵ 5g² 5.1m³ 5.2g² 6m⁴ 1999 5.1g⁵ 6d 6m* 6m⁶

5d³ 6m 7.3m 7.1s Oct 2] angular, unfurnished filly: fair performer: didn't need to be at best to win maiden at Warwick in July: good seventh in handicap at Newbury penultimate start: run best ignored (raced wide) final outing: probably finds 5f on sharp side, and stays 7f: acts on good to firm and good to soft going: has been bandaged off-hind: consistent. *M. J. Fetherston-Godley*

CORN DOLLY (IRE)   3 ch.f. Thatching 131 – Keepers Lock (USA) (Sunny's   **60** Halo (CAN)) [1998 NR 1999 6.1g 6g 8.3d a6g⁴ a7g* Dec 22] third foal: sister to fairly useful 6f winner Latching and half-sister to 1995 2-y-o 6f winner Keepers Dawn (later stayed 7.3f, by Alzao): dam unraced: modest form: won maiden at Lingfield in December: will prove best up to 1m: acts on equitrack. *R. F. Johnson Houghton*

CORNELIUS   2 b.c. (Mar 25) Barathea (IRE) 127 – Rainbow Mountain 71   **100** (Rainbow Quest (USA) 134) [1999 6s* 6m³ 8s⁶ Oct 23] 65,000Y: tall, good-topped colt: has an unimpressive, rather rounded action: second foal: half-brother to 3-y-o Saddle Mountain: dam 11.5f winner out of useful sister to Italian Derby winner My Top: won maiden at York in May: useful form when 5 lengths third of 18 to Fasliyev in Coventry Stakes at Royal Ascot following month (reportedly finished sore): only sixth of 9, beaten 12 lengths, to Aristotle in Racing Post Trophy at Doncaster over 4 months later: should be well suited by 7f+: slowly away all outings. *P. F. I. Cole*

CORNISH ECLIPSE   2 b.c. (Apr 25) Formidable (USA) 125 – Julie's Star (IRE)   **–** 45 (Thatching 131) [1999 5m 6v 6d Nov 4] 5,000Y: rangy colt: fourth foal: half-brother to 6-y-o King of Peru and 3-y-o Peruvian Star: dam, placed twice at 3 yrs, from family of Kooyonga: well held in maidens. *M. D. I. Usher*

CORRIDOR CREEPER (FR)   2 ch.c. (Apr 3) Polish Precedent (USA) 131 –   **85** Sonia Rose (USA) (Superbity (USA)) [1999 7m 6g² 6m² 6d* Oct 29] 600,000 francs Y: useful-looking colt: sixth foal: brother to French 1997 2-y-o 6f/1m winner Polish Lancer and half-brother to a winner in USA by Broad Brush: dam, won at up to 1m in USA, half-sister to Breeders' Cup Sprint winner Smile: fairly useful form in maidens, best effort when second at Newbury third start: didn't have to reproduce that form to win at Brighton in October, making all: should stay 7f: yet to race on extremes of going. *P. W. Harris*

CORTACHY CASTLE (IRE)   4 ch.g. Pips Pride 117 – Maricica (Ahonoora   **108** 122) [1998 102: 6m³ 5m² 5s* 5d 5m* 5d⁶ 5m 1999 5.2m² 5m³ 5m³ 5g⁶ 5m 5m* 5f 6m³ 5g 5.2d Sep 19] well-made gelding: good walker: had a rather round action: useful performer: won listed race at Sandown in July under good ride, beating Flanders 3½ lengths: also ran creditably when placed in handicap at Newbury, Palace

Porcelanosa Sprint Stakes, Sandown—
the game Cortachy Castle makes all to beat Flanders and Dashing Blue (on rail, mostly hidden)

House Stakes at Newmarket (1½ lengths third to Rambling Bear) and Prix de Saint-Georges at Longchamp (third behind Black Rock Desert) on first 3 starts: below form last 4 outings: was probably best at 5f: acted on soft going and on good to firm: usually raced prominently/led: was game: dead. *B. J. Meehan*

CORUNNA   2 b.g. (Jan 25) Puissance 110 – Kind of Hush (Kind of Hush 118)   **72**
[1999 5m 5g² 5m² 5.7m² 6m³ 6f⁶ 5.1m² 5m⁴ 6m 5s⁶ Sep 21] 25,000Y: good-bodied, workmanlike gelding: has a quick action: fifth foal: brother to 2 winning sprinters, including 1997 2-y-o 5f winner Miss Puci, and half-brother to a winning sprinter by Mon Tresor: dam maiden who stayed 1m: fair maiden: creditable efforts most starts, but well below form final one (first outing on ground softer than good): effective at 5f/6f. *J. Berry*

CORUSCATING   2 gr.g. (Feb 11) Highest Honor (FR) 124 – Mytilene (IRE) 103   **65 p**
(Soviet Star (USA) 128) [1999 7s 8.2d 8d⁵ Oct 27] 35,000Y: first foal: dam 2-y-o 7f winner out of smart performer up to 1½m Dancing Meg: clearly best effort in maidens (fair form) when fifth of 10 to Scotty Guest at Yarmouth, keeping on after taking fierce hold: unlikely to stay much beyond 1m: raced only on good to soft/soft going: remains likely to do better. *Sir Mark Prescott*

CORVINO   3 b.c. Tragic Role (USA) – Clare Island 108 (Connaught 130) [1998   **76**
NR 1999 10m⁵ 10g⁶ 10m² 11g 11.7s² 16g² Nov 3] 11,000Y: half-brother to several winners, including useful stayer Clare Heights (by Shirley Heights) and fairly useful 1½m winner Island Lake (by Kalaglow): dam, 7f/8.5f winner, half-sister to Coronation Cup winner Caliban: fair maiden: best efforts when runner-up, including in handicaps final 2 starts: stays 2m: acts on good to firm and soft going. *M. Kettle*

COSCOROBA (IRE)   5 ch.m. Shalford (IRE) 124§ – Tameeza (USA) (Shah-   **39**
rastani (USA) 135) [1998 61: 8d³ 9.2s* 8g² 9.2g 8v 12s 1999 9.2g³ 11.1m⁵ 12g 10.9g² 10m⁶ 9.1v Oct 12] poor performer: stays 11f: acts on soft going. *P. Monteith*

COSMENA   2 b.f. (Jan 29) Cosmonaut – Royal Deed (USA) 76 (Shadeed (USA)   **58**
135) [1999 5.1s² 5d⁴ 5f⁴ 5g³ 5m⁴ 5m⁴ 6g 5m² Aug 26] 11,000Y: rather unfurnished filly: second foal: sister to 3-y-o Lightning Blaze: dam, 2-y-o 5f winner, became one to avoid: modest maiden: second in seller at Musselburgh final start: will prove best at 5f: acts on firm and soft ground: unseated rider and galloped loose before start (still ran well) third outing: has hung left: consistent. *R. M. Whitaker*

COSMIC ALTITUDE   3 b.c. Cosmonaut – Elaine Ann 66 (Garda's Revenge   **–**
(USA) 119) [1998 –: a5g⁶ 5.1g a5g 1999 a5g a5g Mar 22] little sign of ability. *A. G. Newcombe*

COSMIC BUZZ   2 ch.g. (Mar 26) Cosmonaut – G'Ime A Buzz (Electric 126)   **67**
[1999 5g a6g 7m 7d* 8f⁵ a8g⁵ 8d 8.3d Nov 4] first foal: dam won bumper and over   **a–**
hurdles: fair performer: won claimer at Salisbury in August by 9 lengths: well beaten most other starts: should stay at least 1m: acts on good to soft going. *A. T. Murphy*

COSMIC CASE   4 b.f. Casteddu 111 – La Fontainova (IRE) (Lafontaine (USA)   **51**
117) [1998 59: 5d⁶ 7.1g 8d³ 8m* 8g⁵ 9.1g³ 9s 9g 7g 8m⁴ 1999 7.1m 9g 11.1m⁵ 12.1f 10.4f 12f Sep 13] angular filly: modest handicapper: form only on third start: stays 11f: acts on good to firm going, probably on good to soft: ran poorly in visor once at 2 yrs. *J. S. Goldie*

COSMIC SONG   2 b.f. (Apr 29) Cosmonaut – Hotaria 68 (Sizzling Melody 117)   **42**
[1999 5g 6s a8g⁵ Nov 22] 1,400Y, resold 500Y: big, strong, lengthy filly: third foal: dam 6f winner, including at 2 yrs: poor maiden. *R. M. Whitaker*

COSMO JACK (IRE)   3 b.g. Balla Cove 119 – Foolish Law (IRE) (Law Society   **64**
(USA) 130) [1998 64: 5m³ 5.1d³ 5.7s 5.1g* 5m* 7.1m* 6g⁵ 7.1m* 8m 7s 1999 7m 10.2m⁶ 11.9f 8.1d* 11.6s⁴ 10g⁵ 8.9m 8.1m* Sep 9] leggy gelding: modest performer: won sellers at Haydock in August and Chepstow in September: barely stays 1¼m: acts on good to firm going and good to soft: blinkered (both recent wins)/visored last 5 starts: often races prominently: won twice over hurdles late in year. *M. C. Pipe*

COSSACK COUNT   6 ch.h. Nashwan (USA) 135 – Russian Countess (USA)   **–**
104 (Nureyev (USA) 131) [1998 92+: a7g⁵ 1999 6m 6f May 26] good mover: one-time useful handicapper: well held (prominent long way) both starts in 1999: stays 7f: acts on good to firm going, good to soft and equitrack. *S. Dow*

COST AUDITING   2 ch.f. (Apr 1) Bluebird (USA) 125 – Elabella (Ela-Mana-Mou 132) [1999 5m⁶ 5.2g⁴ 5.2m⁴ a5g² 5f 5m a6g Oct 18] 46,000Y: sixth foal: half-sister to 3-y-o Sovereign Abbey, useful sprinter Espartero (by Ballad Rock), later 1m winner in USA, and 1½m winner Typographer (by Never So Bold): dam unraced, from family of high-class 2-y-o Sovereign: modest maiden: below form last 3 starts: should stay at least 6f: acts on good to firm going and fibresand: joined Andrew Reid. *Sir Mark Prescott* **59 a62**

COTE SOLEIL   2 ch.c. (Jan 21) Inchinor 119 – Sunshine Coast 86 (Posse (USA) 130) [1999 5.1s* 6g² 6m 7f³ 7m⁶ 6s⁴ 6m 8.1m⁴ Sep 4] 57,000Y: rather leggy, useful-looking colt: seventh foal: half-brother to 3 winners abroad, including Italian winner up to 1¼m Athena Bird (by Sharpo): dam suited by 7f: fairly useful performer: won maiden at Nottingham in April: several creditable efforts, including fourth of 5 in listed race at Newmarket fourth start: probably stays 1m: has won on soft going, best form on good or firmer: ran poorly only try in a visor. *M. R. Channon* **90**

COTTAGE MAID   3 ch.f. Inchinor 119 – Mossy Rose 78 (King of Spain 121) [1998 –: 8d⁶ a8g 1999 8g a12g 10.2g⁵ Jun 30] leggy filly: little worthwhile form in maidens/handicaps: may prove best short of 1½m. *D. J. Coakley* **–**

COTTAGE PRINCE (IRE)   6 b.g. Classic Secret (USA) 91 – Susan's Blues (Cure The Blues (USA)) [1998 50: 9.3s 9g 12d⁵ 11.5g³ 12g² 1999 11d 12g⁶ 12.3m³ 12m 13.8m⁵ Aug 3] sturdy, sharp-bodied gelding: poor handicapper: visored final outing: acts on firm and good to soft ground: has hung. *J. J. Quinn* **42**

COTTAM LILLY   2 b.f. (Mar 22) Sabrehill (USA) 120 – Karminski 70 (Pitskelly 122) [1999 5g Oct 14] 1,100Y: half-sister to a winner abroad by Blazing Saddles: dam middle-distance stayer: 100/1, tailed off in maiden at Redcar. *M. W. Easterby* **–**

COTTEIR CHIEF (IRE)   8 b.g. Chief Singer 131 – Hasty Key (USA) (Key To The Mint (USA)) [1998 NR 1999 9v Sep 20] close-coupled gelding: one-time useful performer: very lightly raced on Flat these days, and well beaten on only Flat outing of 1999: stays 12.5f: acts on fibresand: usually wears near-side pricker: held up: returned to M. Pipe and fairly useful form over hurdles. *J. Neville* **–**

COTTON HOUSE (IRE)   2 b.f. (Apr 29) Mujadil (USA) 119 – Romanovna (Mummy's Pet 125) [1999 5d* 5m² 5d⁴ Jun 22] IR 18,000Y: lengthy, useful-looking filly: sixth foal: sister to Italian 3-y-o Re Burleone, 6f winner at 2 yrs: dam poor maiden out of half-sister to Eclipse winner Connaught: fair form: won maiden at Warwick in April: failed to improve, but unfavoured by run of race (had to be switched wide) in minor event final start: will stay 6f. *M. R. Channon* **77**

COUCHANT (IRE)   8 b.g. Petoski 135 – Be Easy 110 (Be Friendly 130) [1998 NR 1999 15.8d² Sep 21] small gelding: formerly useful hurdler: poor maiden handicapper on Flat: stays 2m: acts on soft going and on good to firm: blinkered only outing in 1999. *P. J. Hobbs* **45**

COUGHLAN'S GIFT   3 ch.f. Alnasr Alwasheek 117 – Superfrost 49 (Tickled Pink 114) [1998 56: 7d 6s⁶ 6s³ 1999 6m 7d 7.1g 7g² 8.2m 6g⁵ 7d² 7.5g 7v 7s 8s* 8.2s² a8g⁵ Dec 18] fair handicapper: won at Bath in October: stays 1m: acts on soft going and equitrack: often claimer ridden: has hung under pressure: none too consistent. *J. C. Fox* **70**

COUL BANK   3 b.g. Robellino (USA) 127 – Future Options 71 (Lomond (USA) 128) [1998 –: 6d 7g 6d 1999 8g Sep 20] leggy gelding: no form. *J. G. Smyth-Osbourne* **–**

COULD BE EXPENSIVE   2 b.g. (Mar 27) Pursuit of Love 124 – High Typha 61 (Dowsing (USA) 124) [1999 8d 7d 7s Nov 5] 16,000Y: angular, good-topped gelding: first foal: dam, 7f winner, stayed 8.5f: burly and green, well beaten in maidens. *M. H. Tompkins* **–**

COULTHARD (IRE)   6 ch.g. Glenstal (USA) 118 – Royal Aunt (Martinmas 128) [1998 90: 10m² 10g⁴ 10d* 10.3g⁶ 9g 1999 11.9s* 11.9d 12m 12d Oct 14] smallish, sturdy gelding: unimpressive mover: useful handicapper: won at Haydock in April: below form after, off 4 months before final start: stays 1½m: goes well on ground softer than good (well held on good to firm): blinkered once in Ireland: usually held up: fairly useful hurdler. *Mrs P. Sly* **95**

COUNSEL 4 ch.g. Most Welcome 131 – My Polished Corner (IRE) 53 (Tate –
Gallery (USA) 117) [1998 58d, a65d: a10g² 10.3d⁶ 11.6m 10g⁶ 10g 8g⁵ 8m² 9.9m⁶
10g 10.4g 8d 8.5m 7d a8g a10g 1999 a8f a9.4g a11f 9m May 22] strong gelding:
formerly fair maiden: has lost his form: blinkered once: sold 500 gns in June.
D. W. Chapman

COUNT BASIE 6 b.g. Batshoof 122 – Quiet Harbour (Mill Reef (USA) 141) –
[1998 NR 1999 a11g Jan 18] deep-girthed gelding: fairly useful 1¼m winner (should
stay further) on good to firm going for H. Cecil in 1996: tailed off in handicap at
Southwell only outing since: sold 1,400 gns in March. *J. L. Eyre*

COUNT DE MONEY (IRE) 4 b.g. Last Tycoon 131 – Menominee (Soviet Star **46**
(USA) 128) [1998 46, a66p: 12s⁵ 11.8m 11.9d⁶ a14g³ 17.2d 12g a14g³ a12g* **a78**
a12g³ 1999 a11g³ a12g* a12g⁵ 11.8s a12g² a12g* 10f⁵ 12d a11g* a11g* 10d 12.3m²
10m⁵ 10m⁴ a12g⁵ a12g* a12g² a12g⁵ a11g² a14g² a12g* Dec 21] smallish, sturdy
gelding: fair on all-weather, poor on turf: had a good year, winning 2 handicaps, 2
claimers and a minor event at Southwell and another claimer at Wolverhampton from
February onwards: finds 1¼m a bare minimum, and stays 1¾m: acts on fibresand
(probably equitrack) and good to firm going (no recent form on softer than good):
reportedly had a wind infirmity on fourth start: often soon niggled along: tough.
S. R. Bowring

COUNTERFEIT (IRE) 3 b.g. In The Wings 128 – Bogus John (CAN) (Blush- –
ing John (USA) 120) [1998 NR 1999 10v⁴ Apr 20] 110,000Y: strong, close-coupled
gelding: first foal: dam (unraced) from family of dual Breeders' Cup Mile winner
Lure: 10/1, well-beaten fourth in maiden at Pontefract, carrying head high off bridle:
sold 4,000 gns in October. *M. Johnston*

COUNTESS PARKER 3 ch.f. First Trump 118 – Hoist (IRE) 75 (Bluebird **78**
(USA) 125) [1998 NR 1999 8g² 8.3m 8s⁴ Sep 29] 22,000Y: first foal: dam, 6f winner
at 4 yrs, daughter of half-sister to Sun Princess and Saddlers' Hall: fair form when
second in maiden at Yarmouth: disappointing both starts after (lost off-fore plate first
occasion): sold only 1,100 gns in December. *H. R. A. Cecil*

COUNT FREDERICK 3 b.g. Anshan 119 – Minteen (Teenoso (USA) 135) [1998 **54**
–: 8m 1999 7s 7v³ 8.3m 8g⁴ 8.5m³ 12m⁶ 9s 10s² 10g² 10.2s Oct 26] quite good-
topped gelding: modest maiden handicapper: stays 1¼m: acts on heavy going:
inconsistent. *J. R. Jenkins*

COUNT ON THUNDER (USA) 2 ch.c. (Mar 31) Thunder Gulch (USA) 129 – **58 p**
Count On A Change (USA) (Time For A Change (USA)) [1999 7d 7d 8s Oct 25]
$180,000Y: big, angular colt with scope: has quick action: fourth foal: dam, minor 7f
stakes winner in Canada, half-sister to dam of champion US 1997 2-y-o filly
Countess Diana: modest form in maidens: caught the eye not knocked about final
start: will be suited by 1¼m+: likely to do better as a 3-y-o. *E. A. L. Dunlop*

COUNTRY BUMPKIN 3 ch.g. Village Star (FR) 131 – Malham Tarn (River- –
man (USA) 131) [1998 NR 1999 10.2m 8.3m Aug 2] half-brother to several winners,
notably useful performer up to 1m Bold Effort (by Bold Arrangement): dam
(unraced) out of smart miler Mary Mitsu: easy to back and well beaten in maidens.
K. O. Cunningham-Brown

COUNTRY ORCHID 8 b.m. Town And Country 124 – Star Flower (Star **73**
Appeal 133) [1998 –p: 8m⁴ 7m⁶ 1999 a12g³ 12g⁴ 12m* Jul 16] lengthy mare: fairly
useful hurdler: lightly raced on Flat: caught eye 2 starts before improved effort to win
handicap at Pontefract in July without coming under maximum pressure: will stay
further than 1½m. *Mrs M. Reveley*

COUNT TIROL (IRE) 2 b.g. (Mar 30) Tirol 127 – Bid High (IRE) (High Estate **63**
127) [1999 5.1g 6d 5.7m³ Jul 15] 5,500F, 9,000Y: sturdy, close-coupled gelding: first
foal: dam, unraced, from good middle-distance staying family: easily best effort in
maidens (lost action and collided with rail second start) when fourth (promoted a
place) of 11 at Bath: will stay at least 1m. *M. J. Heaton-Ellis*

COUPLED 4 ch.f. Wolfhound (USA) 126 – Twice A Fool (USA) (Foolish Plea- **55**
sure (USA)) [1998 64: a7g⁵ 7d⁴ 7s² 7g 8d 1999 7s 7m 7m 7f⁶ 7f 8m Sep 2] modest
maiden at best: should stay 1m: blinkered (too free) final start: has been slowly away.
S. C. Williams

Grand Prix de Deauville—
Courteous overcomes a near eleven-month absence to finish ahead of Bimbola (rail), Public Purse and Sadian

COURAGE UNDER FIRE 4 b.g. Risk Me (FR) 127 – Dreamtime Quest (Blakeney 126) [1998 61: a9.4g⁶ 9.7v³ 8d a12g* a12g⁴ 10m² 12.1m³ 10.9d 10v² 1999 9.9s⁴ a12g⁵ Oct 13] modest handicapper: stays 1½m: acts on fibresand, good to firm and heavy going: reared leaving stalls penultimate start at 3 yrs. *D. W. P. Arbuthnot* **54**

COURTEOUS 4 b.c. Generous (IRE) 139 – Dayanata (Shirley Heights 130) [1998 117: 10s* 12m 12d⁶ 11.9m² 12d 1999 12.5g* 12g³ 12g Nov 6] tall, leggy colt: very smart performer: won Thresher Classic Trial at Sandown early in 1998: off course nearly 11 months, won Grand Prix de Deauville in August by head from Bimbola, rallying: ran well when 2 lengths third to Thornfield and Fruits of Love in Canadian International at Woodbine in October, clear turning for home: respectable seventh to Daylami in Breeders' Cup Turf at Gulfstream final start: will stay beyond 12.5f: acts on soft going and on good to firm: seemed very much unsuited by track at Epsom in Derby at 3 yrs: races up with pace. *P. F. I. Cole* **120**

COURT EXPRESS 5 b.g. Then Again 126 – Moon Risk 62 (Risk Me (FR) 127) [1998 64: 5.9d 5.9s 6.1m⁴ 7g 5.9m 8.2m³ 8.5g⁴ 7g 9m 8.5m 9d⁵ 1999 a8g 8d 8.3g* 8.3m² 8g* 8m³ 9.2f* 9.9m* 8f* 9.2f⁵ 7.9m 8g Oct 2] leggy gelding: fairly useful handicapper: had a good season, and won at Hamilton (twice), Carlisle, Beverley and Redcar between May and August: stays 1¼m: acts on firm ground, probably on soft: blinkered once (below form) at 4 yrs: held up: consistent. *W. W. Haigh* **82**

COURT FLIRT 2 b.f. (May 31) Charmer 123 – Willow Court (USA) (Little Current (USA)) [1999 7g Oct 15] 1,000Y: half-sister to 9f winner Media Messenger (by Hadeer) and several winners abroad: dam unplaced in USA: behind throughout in claimer at Redcar. *C. W. Fairhurst* **–**

COURT HOUSE 5 b.g. Reprimand 122 – Chalet Girl (Double Form 130) [1998 –: a8g 8m 8m 12m⁵ 8.5m⁶ 10.1g 10s 1999 7g⁶ a12g⁵ Aug 13] leggy, sparely-made gelding: formerly modest winner: no form since 1997: has shown signs of temperament: sold 425 gns in September. *B. R. Johnson* **–**

COURTING 2 gr.f. (Mar 3) Pursuit of Love 124 – Doctor's Glory (USA) 91 (Elmaamul (USA) 125) [1999 7m* 7f* 7f* 7m* 7d 8m Sep 9] tall, good-bodied filly: first foal: dam, 5f (at 2 yrs) and 6f winner, half-sister to useful 1½m to 2m winner On Call: fairly useful performer: won maiden at Catterick in June and minor events on same course, Thirsk (impressively, by 7 lengths from Buy Or Sell) and Newmarket in July, all in small fields: not disgraced, though never dangerous, when seventh of 12 to Teggiano in May Hill Stakes at Doncaster final outing: probably stays 1m: acts on firm going: raced too freely fifth start. *Sir Mark Prescott* **93**

COURTLEDGE 4 b.g. Unfuwain (USA) 131 – Tremellick 87 (Mummy's Pet 125) [1998 –: 10.1d 10g 7.5d a12g⁶ 1999 12.4m⁴ 16m 16.1m 15.8g Aug 13] big, good-topped gelding: modest form only when fourth in handicap on reappearance (gave trouble before start): should stay beyond 1½m. *Miss J. A. Camacho* **56 d**

COURTNEY GYM (IRE) 4 ch.g. Shalford (IRE) 124§ – Fair Or Foul (Patch **43**
129) [1998 –: 7d 6.1g 8g 6g 10m 9m 7.6m 8g 7s 1999 a8g a8g a7g⁶ 7m 8g a7g 6m
6g⁵ 6f² 5.1m 5m 6d Aug 17] poor maiden handicapper: best efforts at 6f: acts on firm
going, probably on equitrack: usually blinkered/visored. *P. Burgoyne*

COURT OF APPEAL 2 ch.c. (Feb 12) Bering 136 – Hiawatha's Song (USA) **66 p**
(Chief's Crown (USA)) [1999 8d Oct 27] 52,000Y: second foal: half-brother to 4-y-o
Robin Lane: dam French 1½m winner out of Criterium des Pouliches winner
Hippodamia: green, well-held ninth of 10 to King Spinner in maiden at Yarmouth,
not knocked about: likely to do better. *J. R. Fanshawe*

COURT OF JUSTICE (USA) 3 b.g. Alleged (USA) 138 – Captive Island 116 **–**
(Northfields (USA)) [1998 NR 1999 12g Apr 13] closely related to smart middle-
distance stayer Court of Honour (by Law Society) and half-brother to several
winners, including Derby Italiano winner Single Empire (by Kris): dam French 6f
and 1m winner: 10/1, well held in Newmarket maiden (bandaged behind, slowly
away): sold 11,000 gns in August. *P. W. Chapple-Hyam*

COURT SHAREEF 4 b.g. Shareef Dancer (USA) 135 – Fairfields Cone (Celtic **66**
Cone 116) [1998 77: 11.8s⁴ 10d⁶ 11.6g* 11.8g* 12m³ 12d³ 11.9g⁵ 14g 1999 11.8g⁴
13.3g⁵ 14.8m 14.4m⁴ 15.9s⁴ 13.9d 11.7s⁵ Oct 26] fair handicapper: stays 2m: acts on
soft going and on good to firm: consistent, but tends to find little. *R. Dickin*

COVER UP (IRE) 2 b.g. (Apr 19) Machiavellian (USA) 123 – Sought Out (IRE) **84 p**
119 (Rainbow Quest (USA) 134) [1999 8d³ 8.1v² Oct 13] close-coupled, quite
good-topped gelding: third foal: half-brother to 4-y-o Treasure Chest: dam won Prix
du Cadran, from very good family: fairly useful form in maiden at Newmarket
(swished tail repeatedly in paddock) and minor event at Haydock, never really on
bridle when 6 lengths second of 4 to Holding Court on second occasion: will stay at
least 1½m: likely to do better. *Sir Michael Stoute*

COWBOYS AND ANGELS 2 b.c. (Apr 18) Bin Ajwaad (IRE) 119 – Halimah **64**
56 (Be My Guest (USA) 126) [1999 5s³ 5m² 5.3f Apr 29] 9,000Y: fifth foal: half-
brother to 3-y-o True Love Ways and 5f winner Impish (by Imp Society): dam, Irish
9f winner, out of sister to speedy Bitty Girl and Hot Spark: modest form in maidens
early in year. *W. G. M. Turner*

COY DEBUTANTE (IRE) 5 ch.m. Archway (IRE) 115 – Presentable 60 **58**
(Sharpen Up 127) [1998 NR 1999 10v 8m 8.3g 9f 8g 9.9g⁵ 10.5m³ Sep 3] 3,100Y:
tall, workmanlike mare: half-sister to several winners, including fairly useful 6f (at 2
yrs) to 1m winner in Italy Spaghetti Western (by Chilibang): dam, placed over 1½m,
half-sister to Gimcrack winner Wishing Star: placed in bumper for M. Pipe in 1998:
modest maiden on Flat: good third in amateur handicap at Haydock: stays 10.5f: acts
on good to firm going. *W. J. Musson*

CRACK DANCER (IRE) 2 b.f. (Apr 25) Dancing Dissident (USA) 119 – **53**
Polish Crack (IRE) (Polish Patriot (USA) 128) [1999 5.7g 5m 6.3m 6m a5g 6s 7s
6.1f⁶ 6.1s a7g Nov 12] IR 5,000Y: first foal: dam unraced half-sister to useful performer up to 7f Fast Crack: modest maiden: flattered in sales race at the Curragh third
start: stays 6f: acts on good to firm and soft going, no form on all-weather: none too
consistent: sold 1,600 gns. *Mrs P. N. Dutfield*

CRACKER 5 br.g. Lugana Beach 116 – Greta's Song (Faraway Times (USA) **–**
123) [1998 43: 5m 7m 10v 1999 a8g a6g Jun 17] poor maiden: form only on 4-y-o
reappearance: blinkered final start. *A. Senior*

CRACKLE 3 gr.f. Anshan 119 – Crackling 57 (Electric 126) [1998 82+: 5g³ 6.1m² **85**
5.7d* 7m² 8m 7.3g⁴ 7s⁴ 8d* 7d 1999 10g⁵ 9.9g* 14.1g⁴ 10.3m³ 9.9g 10.3d³ 11d³
a12g⁴ Nov 11] angular filly: fairly useful handicapper: won at Beverley in May:
mostly creditable efforts after: stays 1½m: acts on equitrack, good to firm and soft
going: sometimes early to post/edges left/runs in snatches. *B. W. Hills*

CRACK SHOT 5 ch.m. Gunner B 126 – Lucky Angel 68 (Lucky Wednesday **–**
124) [1998 NR 1999 a12g 10.2d 8.1g⁵ 14m Jun 12] fifth foal: half-sister to 6f winner
Angelic Dancer (by Komaite) and 7f winner Chickcharnie (by Stanford): dam 2-y-o
5f winner: dual bumper winner: probably flattered in steadily-run maiden third start:
little other form. *J. Neville*

CRACOW (IRE) 2 b.c. (Apr 29) Polish Precedent (USA) 131 – Height of Secrecy **81**
(Shirley Heights 130) [1999 7g 7d⁵ 7g² Oct 19] IR 14,000Y: useful-looking colt, still
unfurnished: first foal: dam (unraced) from family of Seattle Slew and Lomond: best
effort in maidens (fairly useful form) when fifth of 14 to Qamous at Newmarket: bred
to stay beyond 7f, but pulls hard and not sure to do so. *J. W. Hills*

CRAGGY MOUNTAIN 3 ch.c. Cadeaux Genereux 131 – Jet Ski Lady (USA) **61**
122 (Vaguely Noble 140) [1998 NR 1999 6g 8.3d 7m May 16] robust colt: third foal:
half-brother to fairly useful Irish 1½m winner Legaya (by Shirley Heights): dam won
Oaks: modest maiden: best effort second start: will stay 1¼m: sold 6,500 gns, sent to
Kuwait. *B. W. Hills*

CRAIGARY 8 b.g. Dunbeath (USA) 127 – Velvet Pearl 52 (Record Token 128) **34**
[1998 –: a11g 1999 11.1m 13m⁵ 12.1f⁶ Aug 24] poor handicapper: stays 1½m:
acts on good to soft going, probably firm: effective blinkered/visored or not.
Mrs A. Duffield

CRAIGSTEEL 4 b.c. Suave Dancer (USA) 136 – Applecross 117 (Glint of **121**
Gold 128) [1998 111p: 12g* 16g⁴ 14.6d* 1999 12m* 13.3g² 12v Oct 23]
It was the same for Craigsteel in 1999 as in the previous year; he
reached the racecourse only three times. Quarter cracks in Craigsteel's feet are
apparently the ongoing reason for his being so lightly raced, yet he improved
again as a four-year-old and established himself as a very smart performer. If
Craigsteel's connections can continue to manage his problems successfully
there is no reason to doubt that the colt will achieve further pattern success
again in 2000.
For the second successive year Craigsteel made a winning reappearance, taking the eight-runner Princess of Wales's Greene King Stakes at
Newmarket in July by a length from Arctic Owl. Travelling strongly in behind
as his stable-companion, Capri, set a good pace Craigsteel struck the front well
over two furlongs out before staying on strongly under pressure to score with a
little in hand; he broke Desert Team's course record, set in the same race in
1993, by an official margin of 1.41 seconds. Allowing for the usual adjustments
between hand and electric times, we made the winning time about 0.3 seconds
slower than that given officially, but Craigsteel's timefigure was still a smart
one. The mile-and-a-half time on the Newmarket July course was not the
toughest of course records to break, by the way, seeing that the Princess of
Wales's Stakes in a typical year is the best race run over course and distance.
A four-runner field lacking a confirmed front runner made things less
straightforward for Craigsteel in his next race, the Geoffrey Freer Stakes at
Newbury in August. He came a creditable half-length second to Silver Patriarch in a steadily-run affair, making the running himself and being headed only

Princess of Wales's Greene King Stakes, Newmarket—Craigsteel overcomes his problems
to make a belated winning reappearance from Arctic Owl (right), Silver Rhapsody and Sea Wave (rail)

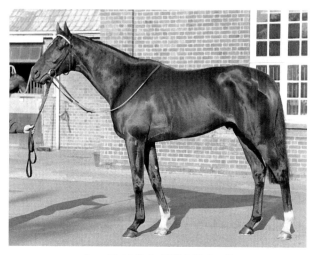

Exors of the late Sir David Wills's "Craigsteel"

in the final furlong. Lack of a strong pace was not to blame for Craigsteel's defeat on his final outing, in the Perpetual Stakes (St Simon) back at Newbury in October. He came a distant seventh behind Signorina Cattiva in a ten-runner field, clearly failing to act at all on the barely raceable going.

	Suave Dancer (USA)	Green Dancer	Nijinsky
	(b 1988)	(b 1972)	Green Valley
Craigsteel		Suavite	Alleged
(b.c. 1995)		(b 1981)	Guinevere's Folly
	Applecross	Glint of Gold	Mill Reef
	(b 1987)	(b 1978)	Crown Treasure
		Rynechra	Blakeney
		(b 1981)	Marypark

Craigsteel, a strong, close-coupled colt and a good mover, is by the 1991 Prix de l'Arc de Triomphe winner Suave Dancer who died when struck by lightning in Australia in December 1998. Suave Dancer has failed to sire anything nearly so good as himself, though he did have a 1999 Group 1 winner in Eclipse victor Compton Admiral. Craigsteel's dam, Applecross, has a good record at stud. Smart when trained by Henry Cecil, finishing second in the Park Hill and the Princess Royal Stakes, Applecross has now produced three pattern winners from five foals to race, namely Craigsteel, very smart stayer Invermark (by Machiavellian), and smart Norwegian middle-distance stayer Inchrory (by Midyan), the last-named a useful two-year-old for Cecil. Two daughters of Applecross are also in training with Cecil. Three-year-old Pennygown (by Rainbow Quest) won a maiden in good style on her one appearance in 1999 and there is also an unraced two-year-old by Warning, called Apple Town. Applecross was herself unraced at two, as was her dam, and she would have stayed beyond a mile and three quarters given the chance. The family as a whole have

246

tended to improve with age and are evidently suited by a test of stamina. Craigsteel, who acts on good to firm and good to soft going, may prove best at a mile and a half to a mile and three quarters; he may have found two miles just beyond him on his only attempt at the trip, as a three-year-old. He has given trouble to post. *H. R. A. Cecil*

CRASH CALL LADY   3 b.f. Batshoof 122 – Petite Louie 45 (Chilibang 120)   –
[1998 36: a5g 5.1m a6g⁴ 7d⁴ 7d³ 7d a7g⁴ 10d 8d a7g³ a8g a7g 1999 a11g⁴ a11g⁵   **a46**
a12s* a12g² 12s⁶ a11g a12g a12g a14.8g² 16m⁵ a14g⁴ a14.8g³ a16.2g² Dec 15]
sturdy, plain filly: poor performer: won maiden at Wolverhampton in February: stays
2m: acts on good to soft going (possibly not on good to firm) and fibresand: tried
visored/blinkered, only once in 1999. *C. N. Allen*

CREAM TEASE   2 b.f. (Mar 5) Pursuit of Love 124 – Contralto 100 (Busted 134)   **85**
[1999 7.3f⁴ 7m* 7m⁶ 8m 7.3s Oct 23] 8,200Y: sturdy filly: half-sister to numerous
winners, including smart performers around 1m Soprano (by Kris) and Enharmonic
(by Diesis): dam 2-y-o 6f/7f winner: fairly useful form: won maiden at Salisbury in
August: creditable efforts in Group 3 events at Goodwood (sixth of 9 to Icicle) and
Doncaster (tenth of 12 to Teggiano) next 2 starts: stays 1m: acts on good to firm
ground, very edgy when tailed off on soft final start. *D. J. S. ffrench Davis*

CREDENZA   3 ch.f. Superlative 118 – Carousel Music 56 (On Your Mark 125)   –
[1998 42: 5d⁴ 5v² 6f⁴ 6g⁵ 7g 5m³ 5.1g 6m⁴ 1999 a5g a6g⁵ a6g a7g 5s 6g Jun 30] poor
maiden at 2 yrs: no form in 1999. *R. C. Spicer*

CREDIT-A-PLENTY   3 ch.f. Generous (IRE) 139 – On Credit (FR) (No Pass No   **111**
Sale 120) [1998 78p: 7.1s* 1999 11.5g² 12m 11.9g² 14.6g² 12d Oct 9] leggy, angular
filly: smart performer: runner-up in listed races at Lingfield (1½ lengths behind
Ramruma) and York (beaten neck by Innuendo, losing place completely 4f out and

Hesmonds Stud's "Credit-A-Plenty"

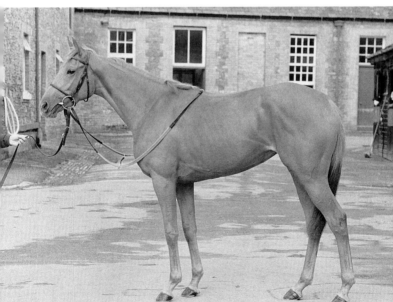

finishing strongly) and in Park Hill Stakes (beaten ½ length by Mistle Song) at Doncaster: broke blood vessel when well beaten in Ribblesdale Stakes and Group 3 event also at Ascot other 2 starts: stayed 14.6f: best efforts on good going, won on soft on only start at 2 yrs: stud. *J. L. Dunlop*

CREME CARAMEL (USA) 3 b.f. Septieme Ciel (USA) 123 – Vexation (USA) **85**
(Vice Regent (CAN)) [1998 88: 6g⁵ 7.1m⁴ 7m² 7g* 1999 8m 7.6m³ 8.1d⁶ Sep 15] fairly useful performer: ran respectably final 2 starts: should be suited by 1m/1¼m: yet to race on extremes of going: sent to USA. *P. W. Chapple-Hyam*

CREME DE CASSIS 3 ch.f. Alhijaz 122 – Lucky Flinders 77 (Free State 125) **49 §**
[1998 –: 7s a7g 1999 8.3m 7m 10f 10m 9s 8f 10s 14.1f³ a14.8g⁵ Dec 11] poor maiden: may prove best up to 1¾m: acts on firm going and fibresand: refused to race fifth start: not to be trusted implicitly. *P. J. Makin*

CRESSET 3 ch.c. Arazi (USA) 135 – Mixed Applause (USA) 101 (Nijinsky (CAN) **48**
138) [1998 NR 1999 8.2m 8.2m 8f a10g⁶ Dec 29] half-brother to several winners, notably high-class miler Shavian (by Kris) and Gold Cup winner Paean (by Bustino): dam won up to 7f at 2 yrs: poor form in maidens, sixth of 12 at Lingfield (after 7 months off) final start: should stay 1½m. *W. Jarvis*

CRESTED KNIGHT (IRE) 7 gr.g. Night Shift (USA) – Casual (USA) (Caro **45**
133) [1998 NR 1999 7m 8m⁵ Aug 4] leggy, good-topped gelding: modest handicapper: only poor form in 2 outings since 1996: may prove best up to 1m: acts on firm ground, shaped well on soft: has worn net muzzle: inconsistent. *C. A. Horgan*

CRETAN GIFT 8 ch.g. Cadeaux Genereux 131 – Caro's Niece (USA) 86 (Caro **109**
133) [1998 116: a5g* 6d² 6d² 5d⁶ 6g⁵ 6g² 5m 6s⁴ 6v² 6.8s 6m⁶ 6m 6m 7d³ 6m 1999 6d⁵ 7d⁴ 6g² 7d 6s 7m² 6g² 6m 7f⁶ 6m* 7m 6d 6m⁵ 6g* 5.6g² 6d 6.1g⁴ 6d 6s³ 6s Nov 6] lengthy gelding: useful performer: won rated stakes at Ascot (by 1½ lengths from Central Coast) in July and minor event at Yarmouth (beat Deep Space ½ length) in August: creditable efforts when in frame in handicaps (including second to Astonished in Portland at Doncaster) after: best at 5.6f to 7f: acts on firm ground, soft and fibresand: wears blinkers/visor and crossed/dropped noseband: often gets behind: tough. *N. P. Littmoden*

CRICKET'S SONG (IRE) 3 b.f. College Chapel 122 – The Multiyorker (IRE) **–**
72 (Digamist (USA) 110) [1998 –: 5m 5.7m 6g 6m 1999 5m 5g 5g⁶ Aug 18] little form: tried blinkered: probably temperamental: dead. *Miss Gay Kelleway*

CRIMPLENE (IRE) 2 ch.f. (Jan 11) Lion Cavern (USA) 117 – Crimson Conquest **102**
(USA) 85 (Diesis 133) [1999 6g² 6f* 6m³ 6g 6m* 6d³ Sep 28] rangy, quite attractive, rather unfurnished filly: fifth foal: half-sister to 3-y-o Crimson Glory, 5-y-o Chinaberry and fairly useful 1997 2-y-o 7f winner Cerisette (by Polar Falcon): dam, 2-y-o 6f winner, stayed 1¼m: useful performer: won maiden at Redcar in June and minor event at Salisbury in September: best effort when third of 14 to Seazun in Cheveley Park Stakes at Newmarket final start: should stay 1m, but races freely: acts on firm and good to soft going: has flashed tail under pressure. *C. E. Brittain*

CRIMSON GLORY 3 ch.f. Lycius (USA) 124 – Crimson Conquest (USA) 85 **75**
(Diesis 133) [1998 66p: 6.9f⁴ 8.1g⁶ 1999 7.5d 8g² 7f³ 7.6m⁵ 8f⁴ 10.2m Sep 9] fair maiden handicapper: creditable efforts in 1999 only when placed: ran badly final outing: may stay further than 1m: acts on firm ground: sold 16,000 gns in December. *C. E. Brittain*

CRIOLLO (IRE) 3 ch.f. Dolphin Street (FR) 125 – Phantom Row 37 (Adonijah **76**
126) [1998 64: 6g 8g 6s 1999 6d* 6m 6g⁴ 6.8m 6d² 7g Aug 19] 20,000F: fifth foal: half-sister to 1¼m seller winner Kentavrus Way (by Thatching) and a winner in Hong Kong by Waajib: dam lightly-raced half-sister to smart 1987 2-y-o 5f winner Colmore Row: fair handicapper: won at Ballinrobe in May: below form final 3 starts (first of them at Warwick): stays 6f: acts on good to firm and good to soft ground: sold 6,500 gns in October. *T. Stack, Ireland*

CRISIS (IRE) 3 b.g. Second Set (IRE) 127 – Special Offer (IRE) 64 (Shy Groom **66**
(USA)) [1998 ?: 10s 1999 7g 8m 10.2g May 21] good-bodied gelding: showed ability in maidens without being unduly knocked about: sold 12,000 gns in July, joined P. Dalton. *L. M. Cumani*

CRISS CROSS (IRE) 2 b.c. (Feb 1) Lahib (USA) 129 – La Belle Katherine **71 p**
(USA) (Lyphard (USA) 132) [1999 6d⁶ Aug 11] IR 15,000Y: first foal: dam, ran
twice in France, from family of 6-y-o Russian Revival: green, clear promise when
sixth of 14 to Millenium Moonbeam in maiden at Salisbury, always chasing leaders:
should improve. *R. Hannon*

CRITICAL AIR 4 b.g. Reprimand 122 – Area Girl 76 (Jareer (USA) 115) [1998 **58**
58, a64: 7g⁴ a5g³ a6g⁴ a7g 8m 7.1g* 7g³ 7d a7g a10g⁴ a10f³ 1999 a10g⁴ a8g* a8g **a62**
a7g⁴ 8.5d 8f 8.3g² 8m³ 10m 8.3s⁴ 8.5g³ 8m a8.5g⁵ 7s³ a8g³ a8d⁵ a8g⁴ Dec 2] useful-
looking gelding: modest handicapper: won at Lingfield in January: mostly creditable
efforts after (sold from A. McNae 10,000 gns before final start): best at testing 7f to
easy 1¼m: acts on all-weather, soft and good to firm going: blinkered (too free) once
at 3 yrs: sold 10,000 gns. *R. Haugen, Norway*

CROAGH PATRICK 7 b.g. Faustus (USA) 118 – Pink Pumpkin 52 (Tickled **–**
Pink 114) [1998 –: a8g 1999 7g Jun 8] little sign of ability on Flat. *J. C. Fox*

CROCO ROUGE (IRE) 4 b.c. Rainbow Quest (USA) 134 – Alligatrix **126**
(USA) 111 (Alleged (USA) 138) [1998 126: 10.5v* 10.5f* 12g² 10m³ 12s²
12d⁴ 1999 10.5g³ 9.3d* 10m 12m³ 12v³ Oct 3]
Of the three best French middle-distance colts of 1998, all of whom
stayed in training, Croco Rouge had the least to lose and the most to gain from
another season on the track. On three-year-old form there was little to choose
between the three, but while Dream Well could boast the French/Irish Derby
double (the first leg of which was gained at Croco Rouge's expense) and
Sagamix the Arc (in which Croco Rouge was a close fourth), Croco Rouge's
achievements looked a little light by comparison, his most important win
coming in the Prix Lupin.
It was, however, Croco Rouge who enjoyed the most successful campaign of the trio at four. Just three weeks after his reappearance, his record was
looking a lot better thanks to his win in the Prix d'Ispahan at Longchamp over
an extended nine furlongs. The pick of his form previously had been at a mile
and a half, and after finishing third to the race-fit Dark Moondancer in the
Prix Ganay (in which Dream Well and Sagamix finished second and fourth
respectively) it was something of a surprise to see Croco Rouge dropped back

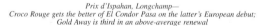

Prix d'Ispahan, Longchamp—
Croco Rouge gets the better of El Condor Pasa on the latter's European debut;
Gold Away is third in an above-average renewal

in distance rather than stepped up. However, he ran right up to his best to defeat El Condor Pasa, making his debut in Europe, and some in-form rivals with proven form at a mile or nine furlongs, including Prix du Muguet winner Gold Away and Sandown Mile winner Handsome Ridge. After looking trapped on the rail at one stage, Croco Rouge produced a good turn of foot once in the clear for a three quarter length win from El Condor Pasa.

One of the reasons given for Croco Rouge not contesting the Derby the year before had been the concern about how he'd cope with travelling abroad. Those fears were realised on his next outing when sent over for the Eclipse at Sandown. Sweating, light in condition and generally failing to impress in the preliminaries, Croco Rouge started an uneasy favourite and never gave his backers much hope after coming off the bridle in rear three furlongs out, in the end beating only one home in the field of eight. Croco Rouge's flop was the subject of a Jockey Club inquiry after his trainer had given no indication of anything untoward in a television interview before the race, but under instruction H14, requiring trainers to make known anything which may have affected a horse's performance, Pascal Bary stated that Croco Rouge was 'sweating more than usual on account of the humid weather and the effects of travelling abroad for the first time'.

With further foreign ventures off the agenda from then on, the remainder of Croco Rouge's season was directed towards a second crack at the Arc. Looking in much better shape than at Sandown, he returned from a two-month break in the Prix Foy at Longchamp in September. As an Arc trial, the steadily-run three-runner contest was an unsatisfactory test for the big race itself and, after being settled in last place, Croco Rouge finished with a flourish to be beaten less than two lengths by El Condor Pasa and Borgia. Considerably softer conditions at Longchamp three weeks later suited Croco Rouge much better. He improved a place on his effort twelve months earlier but was beaten further (six and a half lengths) in a much stronger field. Having entered the straight in a similar position to Montjeu, Croco Rouge was left behind as the favourite went in pursuit of El Condor Pasa but still managed to finish clear of the remainder, putting five lengths between himself and the placed horses from the previous year, Leggera and Tiger Hill.

			Blushing Groom	Red God
	Rainbow Quest (USA)		(ch 1974)	Runaway Bride
	(b 1981)		I Will Follow	Herbager
Croco Rouge (IRE)			(b 1975)	Where You Lead
(b.c. 1995)			Alleged	Hoist The Flag
	Alligatrix (USA)		(b 1974)	Princess Pout
	(b 1980)		Shore	Round Table
			(b 1964)	Delta

A lot has happened in Croco Rouge's immediate family in the three years since he was sold as a yearling for 205,000 guineas at the Houghton Sales. At that stage his useful half-sister Alidiva (by Chief Singer) was in the catalogue as the dam of just a couple of listed winners, but within a year both of them, Taipan and Ali-Royal, had won Group 1 events and a third foal, Sleepytime, had won the One Thousand Guineas. Another of Croco Rouge's half-sisters, the unraced Itching (by Thatching) is now the dam of the very smart mile to mile and a quarter performer Great Dane. Croco Rouge is much the best of six winners out of the largely disappointing Alligatrix, who failed to build on a win over seven furlongs and a third place in the Fillies' Mile at two. His year-younger half-sister Whispering (by Royal Academy) failed to get her head in front in four starts for Henry Cecil in the latest season. There are numerous good horses further back in Croco Rouge's pedigree. Grandam Shore, a stakes winner in the USA as a two-year-old and the winner of six races in all, was a sister to the North American stakes winners Canal and Cabildo and to the dam of Prix de l'Abbaye winner Polonia. Shore's half-brothers Dike and Okavango were also noteworthy stakes winners, Dike finishing third in both the Kentucky Derby and Belmont Stakes. Great grandam Delta was by no means outshone by her offspring as she won sixteen races herself, including the six-furlong Arlington Lassie Stakes at two and the one mile Arlington Matron Handicap at four. Delta's half-sisters Bayou (grandam of American champion Slew O'Gold) and Levee (ancestress of Nicholas and Strategic Choice) also won numerous good stakes races between them.

The leggy, quite good-topped Croco Rouge, who possessed a powerful, round action, has been retired to the Irish National Stud at a fee of IR £12,500 (October 1st). He was effective at around nine furlongs and while he never won at a mile and a half, his efforts in two Arcs, as well as second places in the Prix du Jockey Club and Prix Niel, rated among his best performances. Although Croco Rouge won the Prix Lupin on very firm ground, his best efforts came on softer than good and he acted on heavy. He was held up and had a fine turn of foot. *P. Bary, France*

CROESO ADREF 2 ch.f. (May 5) Most Welcome 131 – Grugiar (Red Sunset 120) [1999 a5f a5g 8d a7g³ Dec 8] small, sparely-made filly: third reported foal: half-sister to 11f to 15f winner Barti-Ddu (by Mister Majestic): dam ran 3 times at 2 yrs: poor maiden: stays 7f: acts on equitrack. *S. C. Williams* — **39**

CROESO CARIAD 2 b.f. (Apr 18) Most Welcome 131 – Colorsnap (Shirley Heights 130) [1999 6m⁵ 5.1m* 7d⁵ 7m² 7g* 7d Sep 28] 200,000Y: good-topped filly: fifth foal: half-sister to fairly useful 1997 Irish 2-y-o 6f/7f winner Photogenic (by Midyan) and 1996 2-y-o 1m winner General's Star (by Night Shift): dam unraced half-sister to Bella Colora (dam of Stagecraft), Colorspin (dam of Opera House and Kayf Tara) and Cezanne: useful performer: won maiden at Chepstow in August and (after being short-headed by Icicle in Prestige Stakes at Goodwood) listed race at Milan in September: well below par in sales event at Newmarket final start: stays 7f: acts on good to firm going. *M. L. W. Bell* — **98**

CROFTERS EDGE 4 ch.g. Beveled (USA) – Zamindara (Crofter (USA) 124) [1998 50: a6g⁶ a6g a8.5g 6m 7s 7f² 8f² 8f³ 8m⁶ 10g 8v³ 1999 a10f⁶ a9.4g³ a8g 9g⁶ 8m 10m May 7] close-coupled, workmanlike gelding: poor maiden: well beaten after second start: stays 9.4f: acts on any turf/all-weather. *A. P. Jarvis* — **49**

CROFT SANDS 6 ch.g. Crofthall 110 – Sannavally (Sagaro 133) [1998 –: 7g 6m 7m 8d 1999 a8g a13g Dec 10] poor maiden at best: no form in 1999. *J. Akehurst* — **–**

CROMABOO COUNTESS 2 b.f. (May 15) Makbul 104 – La Belle Epoque (Tachypous 128) [1999 6g 5g a7g a7g Nov 13] half-sister to a winning selling hurdler: dam ran once: no sign of ability. *B. D. Leavy* — **–**

CROMER PIER 4 b.g. Reprimand 122 – Fleur du Val (Valiyar 129) [1998 63d: 7s 8.2m 11.6m⁴ 14.1g³ 11.1d 12d² 11.5g⁵ 13.8m⁴ a11g 11.8d³ 1999 14.1d 11.8g 10v 12s 13.8g May 21] leggy gelding: poor maiden: barely stays 1¾m: probably acts on good to firm and good to soft going: often blinkered/visored. *G. Fierro* — **–**

CROOKFORD WATER 2 b.g. (Feb 7) Rock City 120 – Blue Nile (IRE) 70 (Bluebird (USA) 125) [1999 6.1m 7.9m 7g Oct 16] 6,800Y: tall, workmanlike gelding: first foal: dam, 1¼m winner, half-sister to smart 1¼m performer Revelation: modest form at best in maidens. *J. A. Glover* — **53**

CROSBY DONJOHN 2 ch.c. (Apr 16) Magic Ring (IRE) 115 – Ovideo 58 (Domynsky 110) [1999 7m⁵ 7m⁴ 6m⁵ 7f 7.1m⁵ 8d a8g a7g² Dec 15] 17,500F, 14,500Y: good-bodied colt: third foal: brother to 3-y-o Cool Temper: dam, 2-y-o 7f winner, half-sister to smart 1¼m to 1½m winner Captain Horatius, also successful at 7f/1m at 2 yrs: modest maiden: will stay 1m: acts on good to firm ground and fibresand: blinkered both starts on all-weather. *E. Weymes* — **63**

CROSS DALL (IRE) 2 b.f. (Apr 19) Blues Traveller (IRE) 119 – Faapette 56 (Runnett 125) [1999 7d 7d 8.3d a7g³ Nov 16] IR 5,000Y, 7,200 2-y-o: useful-looking a49 filly: half-sister to 5-y-o Wagga Moon and 3 winners, including 1990 2-y-o 5f winner Bellerofonte (by Tate Gallery) and Irish 11f winner Premier Leap (by Salmon Leap): dam Irish 2-y-o 1m winner: modest maiden: stays 1m: tried blinkered/visored: looked reluctant on debut. *R. Ingram*

Joe Jennings Bookmakers Stakes (Handicap), Newmarket—
the much improved Cruinn A Bhord does well to win a competitive event,
beating Family Man (No.8) and Grangeville

CROSS TALK (IRE) 7 b.g. Darshaan 133 – Liaison (USA) (Blushing Groom (FR) 131) [1998 NR 1999 10v² 10.8m 12g 14.1m 11.6s Aug 9] close-coupled gelding: modest handicapper: below form after reappearance (first start for 2 years): stays 1¾m: acts on any turf/all-weather: looks none too keen. *E. A. Wheeler*   **56 §**

CROWDED AVENUE 7 b.g. Sizzling Melody 117 – Lady Bequick 81 (Sharpen Up 127) [1998 96: 5d⁴ 5.2g⁵ 5m³ 5f⁴ 5m³ 1999 5f² 5g 5d⁴ a7g Nov 24] compact gelding: lightly raced and only fairly useful performer nowadays: creditable efforts when in frame at 7 yrs: best at 5f: acts on firm and good to soft going: has worn tongue strap: edgy sort, and tends to sweat: usually held up. *P. J. Makin*   **92**

CROWN MINT (USA) 2 gr.c. (May 16) Chief's Crown (USA) – Add Mint (USA) (Vigors (USA)) [1999 7d 6d a8g Nov 24] 15,000Y: brother to Irish 1998 2-y-o 7f winner Filitosa, and half-brother to minor US winners by Cox's Ridge and Northern Baby: dam minor US stakes winner: well held in maidens. *R. T. Phillips*   **–**

CROWN SECRET 3 b.g. Zafonic (USA) 130 – Free City (USA) (Danzig (USA)) [1998 69: 7m⁴ 7m 7.1m⁶ 8g 1999 8.1d 7g Jun 14] useful-looking, unfurnished gelding: fair form at best at 2 yrs: well held in handicaps in 1999: has looked headstrong, and will need to settle to stay 1m. *P. W. Harris*   **–**

CRUINN A BHORD 4 b.f. Inchinor 119 – Selection Board 75 (Welsh Pageant 132) [1998 69: 7m² 7m* 8.1g² 1999 8m 8m² 7m* 7d* 7m 8g 8d Oct 30] leggy, unfurnished filly: made into useful performer at 4 yrs: won quite valuable handicaps at Newmarket in July and August (best effort to beat Family Man by length): didn't go on in expected manner, twice well beaten in listed company: effective at 7f/1m: best effort on good to soft ground, yet to race on extremes. *A. C. Stewart*   **107**

CRUISE 2 ch.c. (Apr 22) Prince Sabo 123 – Mistral's Dancer (Shareef Dancer (USA) 135) [1999 a7g⁵ a6g* Dec 6] half-brother to fairly useful 7f/1m performer Queen's Pageant and 1¼m/1½m winner Kristal Breeze (both by Risk Me): dam maiden best at 7f: won maiden at Lingfield in December by 5 lengths: should stay at least 7f: capable of better still. *R. Hannon*   **70 p**

CRUISE AHEAD 3 b.g. Arazi (USA) 135 – Cut Clear 82 (Kris 135) [1998 NR 1999 8.3m 10m 11.5m⁵ 8s a10g Nov 26] first reported foal: dam, second over 6f at 2 yrs on only start, daughter of 1000 Guineas fourth Shoot Clear, herself half-sister to Yorkshire Oaks winners Sally Brown and Untold: little form: visored (slowly away/pulled hard) third start. *R. M. H. Cowell*   **–**

CRUISING 2 ch.g. (Apr 24) Superpower 113 – Petitesse 55 (Petong 126) [1999 5.3f 6.1d a7g⁴ a6g² a6g 6g Aug 16] 8,500F, 16,000Y: fifth foal: half-brother to 3-y-o Champagne Rider and 1997 2-y-o 5f/6f winner Always Lucky (by Absalom): dam,   **? a71**

5f/6f winner (including at 2 yrs), sister to Paris House: form only when in frame in maidens at Southwell in June/July: should stay 7f: acts on fibresand: blinkered last 4 starts: sent to Hong Kong. *K. McAuliffe*

CRUMPTON HILL (IRE) 7 b.g. Thatching 131 – Senane 86 (Vitiges (FR) 132) [1998 102: 7s 8d³ 7m* 8d 7m 7.9f⁴ 7g⁵ 7g 8s 1999 7f 8m 7m Sep 7] workmanlike gelding: useful performer: won 4 races, including Bunbury Cup in 1996: well beaten in 1999: probably best at 7f/1m: acted on firm and good to soft going: ran well sweating: blinkered last 6 starts: took good hold (carried head high), and usually held up: retired, reportedly due to knee problems. *N. A. Graham* —

CRUSTY LILY 3 gr.f. Whittingham (IRE) 104 – Miss Crusty 45 (Belfort (FR) 89) [1998 –: 6d 1999 a7g⁶ 8g 6m 6.8m² 7f⁵ 6g* 6.1m a6g Oct 8] poor handicapper: won 16-runner event at Yarmouth in August: probably stays 7f: yet to race on very soft going, no form on all-weather. *N. P. Littmoden* **49** **a–**

CRUZ SANTA 6 b.m. Lord Bud 121 – Linpac Mapleleaf 69 (Dominion 123) [1998 42, a24: a11s a11s* a11g a11g a11g a12g⁴ a12g⁶ 7g³ 10.1f 8m 8m 8.5m 1999 15.8g 16.2m 16d⁴ Aug 9] poor performer: stays 2m: acts on fibresand, firm and soft going. *Mrs M. Reveley* **42**

CRY FOR FREEDOM 4 b.f. Komaite (USA) – Heresheis 69 (Free State 125) [1998 58, a54: 8.3m⁶ 8f⁴ 8m² 8g 10g⁶ 10.8g⁵ 10m⁶ 10s* a12g⁵ a14.8s 1999 a13g⁴ a13g⁴ a16g* Feb 11] workmanlike filly: won selling handicap at Lingfield in February: barely stays 2m: acts on soft going and all-weather: has worn severe noseband: sold twice after final start, on latter occasion 1,000 gns in November. *J. Pearce* **47**

CRYHAVOC 5 b.g. Polar Falcon (USA) 126 – Sarabah (IRE) 83 (Ela-Mana-Mou 132) [1998 –: 6g⁶ 6d 7g 7.3m 7g a6g 1999 5d 5m 6g* 6m* 6m* 7m⁴ 6m³ 7m* 5s* 6m² 7f² 5m⁵ 6m⁶ 5.6g⁵ 6d Sep 18] sturdy gelding: useful handicapper: had excellent year, winning at Yarmouth, Goodwood (apprentice race), Windsor and Catterick in June and Beverley in July: badly short of room when fifth of 21 in Portland at Doncaster penultimate start (would almost certainly have been placed): effective at 5f (given test) to easy 7f: acts on firm going and soft: sometimes carries head awkwardly: blinkered (out of form) twice in 1998: much tougher and more reliable nowadays. *D. Nicholls* **98**

CRYSTAL CANYON 2 ch.f. (Mar 3) Efisio 120 – Manor Adventure 75 (Smack-over 107) [1999 6g⁶ 6.1m Aug 28] 15,000Y: second foal: half-sister to 3-y-o Ali Ya Ya: dam, 5f winner, half-sister to useful sprinter Bunty Boo: modest form when sixth of 16 in maiden at Lingfield on debut: well held only subsequent outing: may prove best at 5f. *B. Smart* **59**

CRYSTAL CRAZE 4 b.f. Warrshan (USA) 117 – Single Gal 97 (Mansingh (USA) 120) [1998 a8g² 8d⁶ 11.9f 8m 5g 1999 a8g a8g Mar 22] sturdy filly: poor maiden: has lost her form. *P. Bowen* —

CRYSTAL CREEK (IRE) 3 b.g. River Falls 113 – Dazzling Maid (IRE) 64 (Tate Gallery (USA) 117) [1998 –p: 7m 7d 1999 8m* 7g 7d 8f* 8f³ 8m³ 10.3d² 9m⁵ 8m Sep 18] good-bodied gelding: fairly useful performer: won maiden at Kempton in May and handicap at Bath in June, both steadily run: remained in good form in handicaps until final start: stays 1¼m: acts on firm going and good to soft: usually races prominently/leads. *Mrs A. J. Perrett* **93**

CRYSTAL DOWNS (USA) 3 b.f. Alleged (USA) 138 – Gazayil (USA) 80 (Irish River (FR) 131) [1998 105p: 7m⁴ 7d³ 8d² 7s* 1999 7v² 8g⁴ 12d 8m² 8d² 8f Oct 17] leggy, quite attractive filly: good mover: fourth foal: half-sister to 3 winners in Australia, including ones up to 7f by Polish Patriot and Damister: dam, 2-y-o 7f winner later successful in Australia, half-sister to smart 1¼m winner Husyan (by Alleged): useful performer: runner-up in listed races at the Curragh, Leopardstown and Naas and fourth in Irish 1000 Guineas (easily best effort of 1999, under 3 lengths behind Hula Angel) at the Curragh: bred to stay further than 1m (well beaten in the Oaks at Epsom only try): best efforts on good and good to soft going. *A. P. O'Brien, Ireland* **105**

CRYSTAL FALLS (IRE) 6 b.g. Alzao (USA) 117 – Honourable Sheba (USA) (Roberto (USA) 131) [1998 80: 13.8d³ 10.3g² 11.9d² 12g² 11.9s⁴ 12d⁵ 11.9m⁵ 12.3g* 12.4g⁶ 12g² 12.3m 12.3m³ 13.9g 10.3m 12m³ 1999 12s³ Apr 21] small, strong **70**

gelding: fair handicapper: respectable third at Catterick, only start in 1999: effective at 1½m/1¾m: acts on soft and good to firm going: blinkered final 5-y-o start: has been bandaged behind: tends to hang under pressure, and wears brush pricker near-side. *T. D. Easterby*

CRYSTAL FLITE (IRE) 2 b.f. (Feb 1) Darshaan 133 – Crystal City (Kris 135) **73 +**
[1999 7.3f 7f⁵ 7d 7d⁶ 7.3v³ Oct 23] 34,000F, IR 30,000Y: medium-sized, quite attractive filly: half-sister to 3-y-o Acicula: dam French 10.5f winner out of Fillies' Mile and Yorkshire Oaks winner Untold: ran creditably in nurseries last 2 starts: will stay at least 1¼m: seems to act on any ground. *W. R. Muir*

CRYSTAL LASS 3 b.f. Ardkinglass 114 – That's Rich (Hot Spark 126) [1998 58: **–**
a5g⁵ a5g⁵ 6.1g a6g² 6m a6g³ a6g³ a6g⁴ a6g⁴ 1999 a7g² a7g⁵ 8f a8g* a8.5g a7g⁴ 7d **a85**
a7g⁴ Nov 12] fairly useful handicapper on all-weather, modest on turf: won maiden event at Southwell in June by 6 lengths: mostly below form after: stays 1m: acts on good to firm going and fibresand: effective blinkered or not. *J. Balding*

CRYSTAL LOUGH (IRE) 4 b.f. Maelstrom Lake 118 – Holy Water (Monseigneur (USA) 127) [1998 –: 5s 5m 1999 a5g 6f May 3] behind in maidens/claimers. **–**
N. Tinkler

CRYSTAL ROSIE 3 gr.f. Ardkinglass 114 – Indian Crystal 66 (Petong 126) [1998 **–**
59+, a?: 6g³ 6.1g a7g 1999 7g 8m Jun 16] well beaten after debut, including in sellers. *Mrs A. Duffield*

CUBISM (USA) 3 b.c. Miswaki (USA) 124 – Seattle Kat (USA) (Seattle Song **110 ?**
(USA) 130) [1998 86+: 6g⁵ 6m⁴ 6f* 6m 5g⁵ 1999 6g 6m* 6m² 6m* 6m⁶ 6g⁶ 7m 6m⁶ 5m⁴ Sep 9] smallish, well-made colt: smart performer: won rated stakes at Salisbury and listed rated stakes at Haydock (by head from Munjiz), both in May: stiff tasks, appeared to run very well in listed races at Newmarket and Doncaster (never-nearer length fourth of 7 to Flanders) last 2 starts: stays 6f: acts on firm going, yet to race on softer than good. *J. W. Hills*

CUGINA 5 b.m. Distant Relative 128 – Indubitable 87 (Sharpo 132) [1998 99: **96**
10v⁶ 10d⁵ 10.4g 10d* 9g⁴ 12s 10s 1999 11.9s³ 10v* 10.4s³ 11.9d³ Jun 11] sturdy mare: useful performer: won minor event at Pontefract in April: ran at least creditably after: stays 1½m: raced mostly on good going or softer (acts well on heavy): often held up: game. *G. B. Balding*

CUIGIU (IRE) 2 b.c. (Jan 28) Persian Bold 123 – Homosassa 82 (Burslem 123) **71**
[1999 5m 6g 5m⁵ 8.5d 7.8d² 7.5g⁵ a6g⁴ a8.5g Dec 11] ex-Irish colt: fourth foal: dam, **a55**
maiden, best at 5f: fair form in nurseries at Dundalk (second) and Punchestown last 2 starts for C. Collins in Ireland: modest at best on all-weather here: stays 7.8f: acts on good to soft ground. *Noel T. Chance*

CULTURED PEARL (IRE) 2 ch.f. (Mar 20) Lammtarra (USA) 134 – Culture **72 p**
Vulture (USA) 118 (Timeless Moment (USA)) [1999 8.3d⁵ Oct 28] second foal: half-sister to 3-y-o Born Free: dam, won Prix Marcel Boussac and Poule d'Essai des Pouliches, out of half-sister to dams of Zilzal and Polish Precedent: encouraging fifth of 13 to Coeur de la Mer in Windsor maiden, not knocked about when unable to quicken: will stay at least 1¼m: sure to do fair bit better. *P. F. I. Cole*

CULZEAN (IRE) 3 b.g. Machiavellian (USA) 123 – Eileen Jenny (IRE) 112 (Kris **94**
135) [1998 94p: 7g* 8.1g 1999 10.2s² 10.3m 12m 11.9s 10.1m⁴ 10m⁵ 10.5d⁵ 10g³ 11.9f 10g³ Sep 25] leggy gelding: fairly useful performer: mostly creditable efforts in 1999: better form over 1¼m than 1½m: acts on good to firm and soft ground. *R. Hannon*

CUMBRIAN BLUE 3 b.g. Weldnaas (USA) 112 – Baroness Gymcrak 53§ **73**
(Pharly (FR) 130) [1998 NR 1999 a8.5g 6g a7g* 8m⁵ 7d 8m⁴ a7g 7g Jul 26] 15,000Y: rangy, unfurnished gelding: fourth foal: dam, ungenerous sprint maiden, half-sister to smart 1982 2-y-o sprinter Domynsky (later middle-distance stakes winner in USA) and smart 1¼m performer Petrullo: fair performer: won maiden at Southwell in April: creditable efforts in handicaps next 3 starts: stays 1m: acts on good to firm going, good to soft and fibresand: has wandered and given flash of tail: sold 2,200 gns: sent to Kuwait. *T. D. Easterby*

CUMBRIAN CARUSO 4 b.g. Primo Dominie 121 – Conquista 87 (Aragon **55**
118) [1998 70: 7.5s 7d 5g 5d⁴ 6f 6s 5g 5m³ 5d³ 5d 6s 1999 7g 7g 8d 8m 7f³ 5.9g⁶ Jun

10] shallow-girthed gelding: poor mover: just a modest handicapper in 1999: stays 7f, not 1m: acts on firm and soft going: sometimes blinkered, including 4 of last 5 outings. *T. D. Easterby*

CUMBRIAN CONCERTO 2 br.f. (Feb 25) Petong 126 – Peperonata (IRE) 91 **44** (Cyrano de Bergerac 120) [1999 6m 6d 5g⁵ 6g Aug 21] 26,000Y: smallish, deep-girthed filly: poor mover: second foal: dam, 2-y-o 5f winner who became one to treat with caution, sister to very smart middle-distance colt Millkom: poor form at best in maidens: tried blinkered. *T. D. Easterby*

CUMBRIAN PRINCESS 2 gr.f. (Apr 13) Mtoto 134 – Cumbrian Melody 83 **57** (Petong 126) [1999 6g⁶ 7m 7s 6s* 6d Oct 28] 8,000Y: seventh foal: half-sister to 3 winners, including 7f winner Titanium Honda (by Doulab): dam 2-y-o 5f/6f winner: modest form: best effort when winning nursery at Pontefract in October, making all (wandered): ran badly in similar event at Windsor final outing: stays 6f. *M. Blanshard*

CUPBOARD LOVER 3 ch.g. Risk Me (FR) 127 – Galejade 58 (Sharrood **75** (USA) 124) [1998 59?, a?: 7m a7g⁵ 7.1d⁵ a8g 1999 11.6g⁵ 10m 12.1m⁴ 11.6m 14.1m³ 11.9m 14.1g* 14.1g Oct 15] fair handicapper: won at Hamilton in June and Nottingham in September: stays 1¾m: acts on good to firm going: tried blinkered at 2 yrs: has given trouble in preliminaries: tends to pull hard: none too consistent. *D. Haydn Jones*

CUPIDS CHARM 2 b.f. (Apr 30) Cadeaux Genereux 131 – Chapka (IRE) 68 **69 p** (Green Desert (USA) 127) [1999 6m⁴ Sep 24] third foal: dam, maiden who stayed 8.3f, half-sister to Old Vic: 11/4 from 4/1, shaped promisingly when fourth of 13 to Melanzana in maiden at Redcar, always chasing leaders: should stay 1m: joined R. Guest: should improve. *P. W. Chapple-Hyam*

CUPID'S DART 2 ch.g. (Feb 22) Pursuit of Love 124 – Tisza (Kris 135) [1999 **85 d** 6g 6d⁴ 7m³ 6m² 7g 6m⁶ 7m⁶ a6g³ 8d a8.5g³ a8g⁶ Dec 17] strong, useful-looking gelding: fluent mover: third foal: half-brother to 3-y-o Dancin' Doll: dam, twice-raced half-sister to smart middle-distance performer Twist And Turn, out of sister to smart sprinter Defecting Dancer: disappointing maiden: left B. Meehan before final start: best efforts up to 7f: acts on good to firm ground and fibresand: tried blinkered: none too consistent, and possibly temperamental. *P. Howling*

CUSIN 3 ch.g. Arazi (USA) 135 – Fairy Tern 109 (Mill Reef (USA) 141) [1998 83: **83** 6m² 6f² 7m 1999 7g 7m⁴ 8g 8g 8m* 8v 10.1m Oct 19] close-coupled, angular gelding: has a short action: fairly useful handicapper: won at Salisbury in September: below form both starts after: should stay beyond 1m: raced mainly on good going or firmer: sold 18,000 gns, joined D. Nicholls. *J. R. Fanshawe*

CUTE CAROLINE 3 ch.f. First Trump 118 – Hissma 84 (Midyan (USA) 124) **56** [1998 –: 7g 1999 7m 7.5d³ 6.9g 8.5g Sep 15] modest maiden: tailed off final start: will stay 1m+. *C. W. Thornton*

CUT THE SPICE 3 b.g. Suave Dancer (USA) 136 – No Chili 86 (Glint of Gold **85** 128) [1998 58: 7d⁴ 7m 1999 8d 12g⁶ 14.1f³ 13.1g⁵ 12m* 12f⁶ 14m⁵ 12s* 10.3d² 11d⁵ Nov 1] unfurnished gelding: fairly useful handicapper: won at Beverley in July and Catterick in July and October: disappointing final start: stays 1½m: acts on firm going and soft: sometimes takes good hold: usually races prominently: genuine. *T. D. Easterby*

CUTTING ANSHAKE 4 gr.g. Anshan 119 – Golden Scissors 76 (Kalaglow 132) **50** [1998 50: 9.9s⁴ 14.6g⁵ 8m⁴ 8m⁶ 9.3m³ 10.1v 1999 14g⁴ 15.8g Jul 1] tall gelding: modest handicapper: stays 1¾m, not sure to get much further: acts on fibresand and good to firm ground: successful over hurdles in September. *Martin Todhunter*

CYBER BABE (IRE) 2 b.f. (Apr 5) Persian Bold 123 – Ervedya (IRE) (Doyoun **54** 124) [1999 a5g⁵ a5g⁶ 6m⁴ 6f² 7g² 7.5s 7d 8g a7g a8.5g a7g a8.5g Nov 20] IR **a43** 2,200F, IR 4,000Y: first foal: dam ran once: modest maiden on turf, poor at best on all-weather: stays 1m: acts on firm ground: often visored: none too consistent. *Andrew Reid*

CYBERTECHNOLOGY 5 b.g. Environment Friend 128 – Verchinina 99 (Star **74** Appeal 133) [1998 87: 7g 7d* 7.9m 10m⁵ 8.1g⁶ 7.5m² 7.1m⁵ 7.1g 7.3g 7g² 7g 8v 1999 8v 8m 8m 8s⁶ 6.9m³ 8.1m² 8m* 8f 8m⁵ 8m 8m 8d Oct 26] workmanlike gelding: fair handicapper: won at Doncaster in July: below form final 3 starts: best form at 7f/1m: acts on firm and good to soft ground: blinkered/visored (no form) once each: has been bandaged in front. *M. Dods*

CYBINKA 3 ch.f. Selkirk (USA) 129 – Sarmatia (USA) (Danzig (USA)) [1998 88: 6m⁶ 7g* 7g 1999 7.6m 6m 7d* 6m 7m 6d Oct 1] unfurnished filly: useful performer: best effort when winning 6-runner listed race at Epsom in June by length from Caballero, dictating steady pace: not disgraced next start, well beaten last 2: stays 7f: acts on good to soft going. *R. Hannon* **107**

CYCLONE FLYER 3 br.f. College Chapel 122 – Mainly Dry (The Brianstan 128) [1998 66: 5m⁶ 5m 5g³ 1999 5.1s² 6s³ 5m⁴ 5m² 5s² 5m* 5m Jul 28] leggy, close-coupled filly: has a short action: fair performer: won maiden at Newcastle in July: should prove best at 5f/6f: acts on good to firm and soft ground: has been bandaged behind. *J. Berry* **67**

CYMBAL MELODY 3 b.f. Merdon Melody 98 – Cymbal 80 (Ribero 126) [1998 –: 5d 7m 7m 8d 1999 9.7s 11.6g 11.8m 14.1g a11g 12g a12g Oct 30] little form. *R. Hollinshead* **–**

CYPRESS CREEK (IRE) 2 b.f. (Apr 19) College Chapel 122 – Akayid 79 (Old Vic 136) [1999 7m 7g 8.2g 7g Oct 19] 4,500Y: first foal: dam, 1¼m winner from 3 starts, well held in maidens. *J. S. Moore* **–**

CYRAN PARK 3 b.g. Cyrano de Bergerac 120 – Kimberley Park 72 (Try My Best (USA) 130) [1998 70: 6g 6m⁶ 6s 1999 5g 6g a7g⁶ a6g Jul 10] workmanlike gelding: modest maiden on turf: best effort in 1999 in handicap on reappearance: may be best at 5f: no form on all-weather: sold 1,000 gns, joined W. Storey. *W. Jarvis* **64 a–**

CYRO 3 b.g. Cyrano de Bergerac 120 – Odile (Green Dancer (USA) 132) [1998 66: a5g 5.1d* 5d⁶ 5f⁶ 7m⁶ 7m⁵ 8g 7s a5g 1999 a8g³ a7g* a8g³ a8f 6.1v 7s Apr 21] sturdy, close-coupled gelding: modest performer: won seller at Southwell in January: well beaten in handicaps final 3 starts: stays 1m: acts on good to firm going, good to soft and fibresand: very slowly away final outing: sent to Spain. *D. Nicholls* **59**

CZARINA'S SISTER 3 b.f. Soviet Lad (USA) – Tallow Hill (Dunphy 124) [1998 NR 1999 7m 7.1m 8.3s 9.9m 10v Oct 23] sixth living foal: sister to fairly useful winner around 1¼m Grinkov and half-sister to 2-y-o winners Talberno Boy (at 6f/7f in 1991) and Lowrianna (at 5f in 1992), both by Cyrano de Bergerac: dam unraced half-sister to Cheveley Park winner Pass The Peace: little form in maidens/handicap: sold 4,000 gns in November. *V. Soane* **–**

CZAR WARS 4 b.g. Warrshan (USA) 117 – Dutch Czarina 45 (Prince Sabo 123) [1998 62: 8.2s 7g 6g 7d² 7d⁴ 6g 6g⁴ 6m 7d 8.2s² 8d a12g 1999 a8g a8g⁵ a9.4g⁴ a8g⁵ a11g⁵ a12g 10.8d 8d 8.2m 7.7m 7.7m 6g 7d 5s³ a5g⁵ a5g a6g⁴ a6g⁴ Dec 21] sturdy gelding: modest performer: effective at 5f, and probably stays 11f: acts on soft going and fibresand: often blinkered: often races freely: sometimes looks less than keen under pressure: none too reliable. *P. T. Dalton* **54**

D

DAAWE (USA) 8 b.h. Danzig (USA) – Capo di Monte 118 (Final Straw 127) [1998 85: 5s* a5g³ 5m 6g* 5.1g 6v 6m 6m² 5m⁵ 5m 5g 1999 a6g⁵ a5g⁶ a5g⁵ 6d 7g⁴ 6f⁵ 6f 6m⁶ 7g 6d 6m 5f 6g 5d* 5s* 5g⁶ 7d 5d⁶ 5s Nov 5] big, robust horse: fair handicapper: won at Pontefract (first run after leaving J. Glover) and Newcastle in September: suited by easy 6f/stiff 5f: acts on fibresand, firm and soft going: sometimes visored/blinkered. *D. Nicholls* **75 a80**

DABUS 4 b.g. Kris 135 – Licorne 93 (Sadler's Wells (USA) 132) [1998 96: 10f³ 10m* 11.6m³ 1999 10.3g³ 8.2s⁶ Nov 1] useful-looking gelding: has a short, round action: useful form at best: flattered when just over 5 lengths last of 3 to Prolix in minor event at Doncaster on reappearance (final start for H. Cecil): well beaten next time after proving reluctant at stalls: stays 11.6f: tends to race freely: needs treating with some caution. *M. C. Chapman* **?**

D'ACCORD   2 ch.g. (Mar 15) Beveled (USA) – National Time (USA) (Lord Avie   **80** (USA)) [1999 6m 5v⁴ 5s⁴ 5g³ a6g* a5g* Dec 29] half-brother to 3 winning sprinters, including Kildee Lad (by Presidium) and 7-y-o Malibu Man, both fairly useful: dam ran twice at 2 yrs: fairly useful form: gained comfortable successes in maiden and nursery at Lingfield in December: speedy, and will prove best at 5f/easy 6f: acts on equitrack and heavy ground. *E. A. Wheeler*

DACOIT (USA)   5 b.h. Red Ransom (USA) – Krishka (CAN) (Drone) [1998 NR   **–** 1999 10.3s⁵ 10g⁵ 10.1f⁵ Jul 24] medium-sized, good-topped horse: fairly useful for M. Stoute at 2 yrs: little form on Flat in 1999 (bandaged in front, trained by K. Morgan on reappearance). *A. R. Dicken*

DADDY'S POLLY (IRE)   5 b.m. Waajib 121 – Pollys Glow (IRE) 91 (Glow   **–** (USA)) [1998 38: 11v 16g⁴ 17g 1999 a16f⁶ a16g Feb 11] first foal: sister to 4-y-o My Pledge: dam, Irish 1m and 1½m winner, half-sister to Irish 1000 Guineas winner Prince's Polly: poor maiden handicapper/winning hurdler in Ireland for S. Treacy: poor efforts over hurdles and on all-weather in Britain. *B. J. Llewellyn*

DAFA   3 b.g. Deploy 131 – Linpac North Moor 69 (Moorestyle 137) [1998 NR   **42** 1999 a9.4g 10m 8m 12g a12g⁵ Jun 17] 15,000Y: stocky gelding: sixth foal: half-brother to fairly useful 1995 2-y-o 5f/6f winner Benny Glow (by Presidium) and a winner in Germany by Elmaamul: dam won at 7f/1m: poor form in maidens/handicaps. *B. J. Curley*

DAHIYAH (USA)   8 b.g. Ogygian (USA) – Sticky Prospect (USA) (Mr Prospector   **42** (USA)) [1998 –: a7g 1999 8.3g 12.1m 11.6m Aug 2] rangy gelding: one-time fair performer, only poor nowadays: seems to stay 1½m: acts on firm ground and all-weather: tried blinkered/visored: sold 1,100 gns in October, joined Katie Thory. *D. L. Williams*

DAHLIDYA   4 b.f. Midyan (USA) 124 – Dahlawise (IRE) 76 (Caerleon (USA)   **–** 132) [1998 31, a61: a7g a6g⁴ a5g* a6g 5.3d³ 5.7f 6.1g⁵ a7g 8g 6m a8.5g 7s a6g⁴ a6g*   **a67** 1999 a6g³ a6g⁴ a7f⁴ a7g³ a7g⁶ a6g⁴ a7g a6g² 6m a7g 7.1g a6g a8.5g a6g⁵ a6g³ a6g* a7g Dec 21] angular filly: fair performer: best effort in 1999 when winning handicap at Southwell in December: barely stays 7f: acts on fibresand, no recent form on turf: tried blinkered: sometimes slowly away (including final start). *M. J. Polglase*

DAHSHAH   3 ch.f. Mujtahid (USA) 118 – Rawaabe (USA) 87 (Nureyev (USA)   **77** 131) [1998 77: 5.1m⁶ 6m² 6g³ 1999 7m⁴ 8g* 8.3d⁵ 8m⁵ 8s Oct 4] sturdy, lengthy filly: has a quick, fluent action: fair performer: won maiden at Bath in May: below form in minor event and handicaps after: stays 1m: acts on good to firm going: sent to USA. *B. W. Hills*

DAINTREE (IRE)   5 b.m. Tirol 127 – Aunty Eileen (Ahonoora 122) [1998 64,   **64** a–: 6.1s⁶ 7g 7f² 8s⁴ 7g 8g² 8.3m* 8.3f² 8.3m² 7.1g 8m³ 8d a10g 1999 8g⁶ 8s³ 8.3m²   **a–** 7.7m² 8.3m³ 8.3m⁵ 9f³ 7.5s 8d Oct 11] leggy, angular mare: modest handicapper on turf, poor on all-weather: best at 7f/1m: acts on firm ground, soft and all-weather: tried visored, not since early 1998: races freely. *H. J. Collingridge*

DAINTY DISH (IRE)   3 ch.f. Nucleon (USA) 94 – Thornhaven (IRE) (Doulab   **42** (USA) 115) [1998 –: 7s 7v 8g a8.5g 8d a6g 1999 7g 5m 5g³ 5f³ 7s a6g⁵ Nov 12]   **a30** unfurnished filly: poor maiden: left M. Peill after fourth start: may prove best at 5f: acts on good going: visored (well held) on reappearance. *K. A. Ryan*

DAJAN BOY   2 b.g. (Apr 26) Mistertopogigo (IRE) 118 – Joseno 52 (Siberian   **–** Express (USA) 125) [1999 6d Oct 18] 2,000Y: angular gelding: first foal: dam disappointing maiden: hampered leaving stalls and well held in maiden at Pontefract. *S. R. Bowring*

DAKISI ROYALE   2 ch.f. (Mar 14) King's Signet (USA) 110 – Marcroft 91   **52** (Crofthall 110) [1999 5m 5d 5m 7m² 7f 7m³ 7.9m 7.5g 7s 6d⁶ a6g⁵ a8.5g Nov 20] 1,200Y: sturdy filly: fourth foal: half-sister to 5-y-o Martine and fairly useful 5f (at 2 yrs) to 7f winner Safio (by Efisio): dam best at 7f/1m: poor maiden: placed in sellers at Catterick and Thirsk in the summer: stays 7f: acts on good to firm and good to soft going: tried visored: none too consistent: joined L. Barratt. *R. M. Whitaker*

DAKOTA SIOUX (IRE)   2 ch.f. (May 4) College Chapel 122 – Batilde (IRE)   **62 p** (Victory Piper (USA) 100) [1999 5f³ Sep 13] IR 2,200F, IR 8,000Y: first foal: dam placed in Italy: length third of 7 to Desert Safari in maiden at Musselburgh, staying on once switched: should stay at least 6f: should improve. *R. A. Fahey*

DALAAUNA   3 ch.f. Cadeaux Genereux 131 – Gunner's Belle 69 (Gunner B 126)   **58**
[1998 62p: 6g⁶ 1999 6g⁶ 6v⁶ 5g⁶ 6m a8.5g⁶ Sep 18] sturdy filly: modest maiden: well beaten in handicaps final 2 starts: best form at 5f/6f on good going. *J. H. M. Gosden*

DALBY OF YORK   3 ch.g. Polar Falcon (USA) 126 – Miller's Creek (USA) 62   **67**
(Star de Naskra (USA)) [1998 54: 6m 6m 6m 8m⁴ 10s 1999 11.6m* 11.6d³ 14f* 14.1m⁵ 15.4m² 17.2h³ a12g 14.1d 10d Nov 4] strong gelding: has a round action: fair performer: won handicap at Windsor in April and minor event at Musselburgh in May: below form final 4 starts: needs further than 1¼m, and stays 15.4f: possibly best on going firmer than good: blinkered (all-weather debut, poor form) seventh outing. *P. F. I. Cole*

DALI   4 b.g. Rock City 120 – Supreme Kingdom 85 (Take A Reef 127) [1998 63p: **–**
7.1m³ 7s⁴ 1999 7v Apr 13] some promise at 3 yrs: last in maiden, only run of 1999. *B. J. Meehan*

DALIAPOUR (IRE)   3 b.c. Sadler's Wells (USA) 132 – Dalara (IRE) 114   **122**
(Doyoun 124) [1998 108p: 7g⁶ 8.1m* 8g³ 8s* 1999 10.1s* 11.5g² 12g² 12g² 12m Jul 24]
    The Aga Khan/Luca Cumani partnership was terminated in the aftermath of the disqualification of Zalal, who tested positive after winning at Goodwood in June, the second of the owner's horses in Cumani's stable to fail a dope test within twelve months. The Aga Khan was said to be dissatisfied with the trainer's failure—though Cumani took issue with that—to introduce safeguards to ensure 'there could be no repeat of the situation' and he removed his thirty horses from the yard. Up to ten two-year-olds due to be trained by

H.H. Aga Khan's "Daliapour"

Cumani are to go elsewhere. Cumani had been one of the chief sufferers when the Aga Khan boycotted British racing for four years until 1996 following the disqualification (after a positive test for camphor) of the 1989 Oaks winner Aliysa, who was trained by Michael Stoute. Among those the Aga Khan had with Cumani was the Derby runner-up Daliapour, whose season was cut short by injury but who will be back in action in 2000 under the care of Stoute. Daliapour has his limitations, but there's no doubt that he's up to winning good races at four kept away from the best.

Cumani was responsible for one of the three Derby winners owned by the Aga Khan, Kahyasi in 1988, and approaching the two-furlong marker in the latest edition it looked as if he might provide him with another. At that point Daliapour, who had taken a handy position at the top of the hill and turned for home in third, was in front and running on strongly, but, when the crunch came, he couldn't quicken with Oath when that horse came at him soon after and went down by a length and three quarters. Daliapour had put himself in the Derby picture on his final start as a two-year-old, winning a listed race run over a mile on soft going at Ascot by eight lengths. He gave a satisfactory performance on similar ground when landing the odds in the Schroder Unit Trusts Blue Riband Trial Stakes at Epsom on his reappearance, but then failed to step up on that when second to Lucido in the Derby Trial at Lingfield, which was run on good ground. However, Daliapour went on to show that he didn't require ground softer than good to show his form, not only in the Derby but in the Irish Derby at the Curragh. In the latter Daliapour was beaten five lengths by Montjeu, swept aside in the final furlong having taken it up turning into the straight, but keeping on gamely under pressure and finishing well clear of the remainder. Daliapour and Oath were the only representatives of their generation in the King George VI and Queen Elizabeth Diamond Stakes at Ascot, and the first two home in the Derby provided an unusual sight as they trailed home last and second-last respectively, both having suffered injuries during the race. Daliapour's occurred when he stumbled as the stalls opened, sustaining a nasty cut to his near-fore heel, and he was quickly done with after the home turn.

Daliapour (IRE) (b.c. 1996)	Sadler's Wells (USA) (b 1981)	Northern Dancer (b 1961)	Nearctic
			Natalma
		Fairy Bridge (b 1975)	Bold Reason
			Special
	Dalara (IRE) (br 1991)	Doyoun (b 1985)	Mill Reef
			Dumka
		Delsy (b 1972)	Abdos
			Kelty

Daliapour has yet to race beyond a mile and a half, but, judged on his pedigree, he'll stay further and the St Leger, run over an extended mile and three quarters, would have been just the race for him had he been able to continue his three-year-old career. Sadler's Wells is one of the strongest influences for stamina among the leading sires, while Daliapour's dam Dalara was successful twice at a mile and a half at Longchamp, including in the Prix de Royallieu, and also showed smart form when third behind Moonax in the Prix Royal-Oak over fifteen and a half furlongs there. Dalara is closely related to the Prix du Jockey Club winner Darshaan, another strong influence for stamina at stud, and a half-sister to several other winners, including Darara, successful in the Prix Vermeille. The next dam, Delsy, was also a winner at a mile and a half and stayed further. Daliapour is Dalara's first foal. Her second Dalampour, by Shernazar, has yet to race. Daliapour, a small, quite attractive colt, is a good walker and has a short, fluent action. The going was good to firm when he won a maiden at Chepstow, but he may prove best on good ground or softer. *L. M. Cumani*

DALLACHIO (IRE) 8 ch.g. Shernazar 131 – Mafiosa 69 (Miami Springs 121) – [1998 NR 1999 11.7s a16.2g Nov 17] stocky gelding: fair performer in Ireland at 3 yrs: very lightly raced on Flat since: has had tongue tied. *A. G. Newcombe*

DALLIMORE BANKES   3 b.g. Keen 116 – Run For Love 70 (Runnett 125)   –
[1998 –: a5g 5g 5m 1999 5f a6g Aug 6] of little account. *W. G. M. Turner*

DALLY BOY   7 b.g. Efisio 120 – Gay Hostess (FR) (Direct Flight) [1998 51: 16.1d⁵   **51**
16s⁴ 21.6s⁵ 16d* a14g² 16d⁶ 14s* 16.1d⁴ 15.9m a14g² 1999 12g² 17.1g Aug 22]
close-coupled gelding: modest handicapper: stays 2m (not disgraced at 21.6f): acts
on good to firm ground, soft and fibresand: blinkered (no show) once at 6 yrs.
T. D. Easterby

DALWHINNIE   6 b.m. Persian Bold 123 – Land Line (High Line 125) [1998 61,   **44**
a49: a12s² a12g* a11g a16g 11.8d 14.1s* 12g² a14g a12g 1999 a16g 14.1s 13d   **a–**
14.1m⁵ 14.1m a14g a16.2g⁴ Dec 15] leggy mare: poor mover: poor handicapper at
best nowadays: left J. Wharton after recent start: stays 1¾m: acts on good to firm
ground, soft and fibresand: effective blinkered or not. *J. G. Given*

DALYAN (IRE)   2 b.g. (May 26) Turtle Island (IRE) 123 – Salette 110 (Sallust   **68**
134) [1999 7.1d 7.5g⁴ 7.9m⁴ 7.5g⁵ Sep 15] IR 15,000F, IR 9,000Y: tall, workmanlike
gelding, unfurnished: half-brother to several winners, including Irish 3-y-o 1½m
winner Ciel d'Or (by Tenby), Irish 7f and 9f winner Steelette (by Flash of Steel) and
dam of smart Italian sprinter Late Parade: dam 5f (at 2 yrs) and 1m winner: fair form:
good fourth of 20 to Bold State in maiden at York on penultimate start: will prove best
at 7f/1m: acts on good to firm going: ran wide on bend final outing. *T. D. Easterby*

DAMALIS (IRE)   3 b.f. Mukaddamah (USA) 125 – Art Age (Artaius (USA) 129)   **98**
[1998 89: 5d³ 5s² 5.1m* 5d⁴ 6.1m³ 5m⁴ 5d* 5m⁶ 5d⁶ 1999 5s³ 5s* 5.1m⁴ 5d⁶ 5m⁴
6m⁶ 5s⁴ 5s⁴ 6d Oct 1] lengthy, sturdy filly: useful handicapper: won at Sandown in
April: mainly in good form after: best at 5f/easy 6f: acts on good to firm and soft
ground: sometimes edgy/on toes: has run poorly when sweating. *E. J. Alston*

DAMASQUINER   2 b.f. (Feb 4) Casteddu 111 – Hymn Book (IRE) 65 (Darshaan   –
133) [1999 5g 5g 5g 6m 5.3d⁶ a6g⁶ Dec 6] smallish filly: second foal: dam, maiden
who shaped like a stayer on Flat, temperamental over hurdles: little form: probably a
short runner. *T. E. Powell*

DAME FONTEYN   2 b.f. (Apr 16) Suave Dancer (USA) 136 – Her Honour 94   **48**
(Teenoso (USA) 135) [1999 8.2s 8d 8.3d Oct 28] plain filly: has scarred near-
fore: first foal: dam, won all 3 starts at 1¼m/1½m, also a smart but ultimately
temperamental staying hurdler, from family of One In A Million: poor form in
maidens: likely to be suited by 1½m+. *M. L. W. Bell*

DAME JUDE   3 ch.f. Dilum (USA) 115 – Three Lucky (IRE) 46 (Final Straw 127)   **69**
[1998 76: 5.1d⁵ 5.3d* 5.1d⁴ 6g⁵ 6m 6g⁴ 5m* 5.3f⁴ 6.5g 6v 1999 6m 6g⁶ 6m⁶ 6g³
7m 7m⁴ 7g 6.1m 7g Sep 14] unfurnished filly: fair performer: below form final 3
starts: stays easy 7f: acts on good to firm/good to soft ground: none too consistent.
W. R. Muir

DAMIEN'S LAW   2 b.g. (Mar 22) Contract Law (USA) 108 – Cinderella Derek   –
61 (Hittite Glory 125) [1999 7g Aug 12] 2,800Y: fifth foal: half-brother to a winner in
Norway by Almoojid: dam winning sprinter/hurdler: tailed off in Salisbury maiden.
A. D. Smith

DANAKIL   4 b.g. Warning 136 – Danilova (USA) (Lyphard (USA) 132) [1998   **71**
NR 1999 a6g⁵ a6g a9.4g* 10m 8.1g 8.3m³ 8.3g⁶ Jul 5] small ex-French gelding:
unimpressive mover: first foal: dam unraced half-sister to Sanglamore: third in minor
events at Chantilly and Deauville at 2 yrs for A. Fabre, subsequently sold for 18,000
gns: fair performer: won maiden at Wolverhampton in March: will stay at least 1¼m:
acts on fibresand, soft and good to firm going: joined K. Burke. *J. E. Banks*

DANAKIM   2 b.g. (Jan 29) Emarati (USA) 74 – Kangra Valley 56 (Indian Ridge   **74**
123) [1999 5d⁶ 5.1m⁴ 5m² 6g 6m⁴ 6m Sep 10] 25,000Y: lengthy, good-quartered
gelding: first foal: dam 2-y-o 5f winner: fair maiden: trained by R. Hannon first 3
starts: stays 6f. *E. Weymes*

DANAMALA   3 b.f. Danehill (USA) 126 – Carmelized (CAN) (Key To The Mint   **70**
(USA)) [1998 NR 1999 7m 7.1m³ 7g³ 6m Jun 28] 90,000Y: big, strong, lengthy filly:
second foal: closely related to fairly useful 1¼m winner Abi (by Chief's Crown):
dam, won up to 9f in North America, from family of Chief's Crown: fair form in
maidens/handicap: will prove best up to 1m. *R. Hannon*

DANA POINT (IRE) 7 br.g. Phardante (FR) 123 – Wallpark Princess (Balidar **57**
133) [1998 NR 1999 13.8g⁶ Mar 31] close-coupled gelding: fair in 1996 for
T. D. Barron and useful hurdler since: ran respectably in handicap, only Flat run of
1999: should stay 1¾m: acts on good to firm ground, possibly not on softer than
good. *Mrs S. J. Smith*

DANARI (IRE) 2 b.f. (Mar 14) Petorius 117 – Base Camp 80 (Derring-Do 131) **–**
[1999 a5g 6.1g 6d 5g 7m 6g Sep 20] IR 1,100Y: neat filly: half-sister to several
winners, including fairly useful stayer Revisit (by Busted) and useful performer up
to 1¼m Crampon (by Shirley Heights): dam won 3 times up to 1¼m: little sign of
ability. *N. P. Littmoden*

DANCE IN TUNE 2 ch.g. (Mar 1) Mujtahid (USA) 118 – Dancing Prize (IRE) **87**
99 (Sadler's Wells (USA) 132) [1999 7.5m³ 7m² a7g* 7.1m* 7.9f⁴ 7.6s³ 7d Oct 12]
good-topped individual: third foal: half-brother to Italian 3-y-o 6f (at 2 yrs) to 1¼m
winner Special War (by Warning) and 4-y-o Dancing Phantom: dam, lightly-raced
maiden (third in Lingfield Oaks Trial), out of smart performer up to 1m Aim For The
Top: fairly useful form: won maiden at Wolverhampton and nursery at Musselburgh,
both in August: well below form last 2 starts: not sure to stay much beyond 1m: acts
on firm going and fibresand, possibly unsuited by ground softer than good: gelded
after final start. *Sir Mark Prescott*

DANCE LADY 3 b.f. Cosmonaut – Lady Lustre 70 (On Your Mark 125) [1998 **–**
NR 1999 6f⁶ May 31] 5,000Y: workmanlike filly: second foal: dam 1m winner: last
of 6 in maiden at Redcar: bandaged in front. *J. A. Gilbert*

DANCE LITTLE LADY (IRE) 2 b.f. (Jan 28) Common Grounds 118 – **56**
Kentucky Tears (USA) (Cougar (CHI)) [1999 6m 5m 5g⁶ 5s 5s a5g⁶ a5g⁴ Dec 4]
14,000Y: seventh foal: half-sister to 2-y-o seller winners Kentucky Dreams (7f, by
Dreams To Reality) and En-Cee-Tee (5f, by Risk Me), and to fairly useful winning
hurdler Noble Colours (by Distinctly North): dam, unraced, out of half-sister to
Eclipse winner Solford: modest maiden: may prove best at 5f: acts on good to firm
going, soft and fibresand. *J. Berry*

DANCEMMA 2 ch.f. (Apr 25) Emarati (USA) 74 – Hanglands (Bustino 136) **76 +**
[1999 5g⁴ 5g 5m 6d³ 5.1g² 6m⁶ 5.2m 6.1d² Oct 5] big, lengthy filly: sister to a winner
in Denmark and half-sister to 3 winners, including useful 1992 2-y-o 5f/6f winner
Zuno Warrior (later successful in USA, by Dominion) and 6-y-o Arterxerxes (by
Anshan): dam lightly raced: fair maiden: best effort final start: should stay 7f: acts on
good to soft ground, below form on good to firm. *M. Blanshard*

DANCE TO THE BEAT 4 b.f. Batshoof 122 – Woodleys (Tyrnavos 129) [1998 **51**
51: a7g 7g 7f² 6.9m 7d⁶ 6d 1999 8.1g 8s 8.2m 10d⁶ a12g⁴ 11.8m Aug 22]
modest performer: probably stays 1½m: acts on firm ground and all-weather:
effective blinkered or not, visored (stiff task) final start: inconsistent. *P. Shakespeare*

DANCE TRIBUNE (USA) 3 ch.f. Nureyev (USA) 131 – Sam's Diary (USA) **67**
(Private Account (USA)) [1998 NR 1999 8g 10m 7.1m Jul 3] first foal: dam, won up
to 9f in USA, daughter of Grade 2 1½m winner Dancing All Night, herself sister to
Breeders' Cup Sprint winner Dancing Spree: fair form in maidens first 2 starts: stays
1¼m: sold 45,000 gns in December. *P. W. Chapple-Hyam*

DANCIN' DOLL 3 ch.f. Grand Lodge (USA) 125 – Tisza (Kris 135) [1998 –p: **–**
8.3d⁶ 7m 8.2s 1999 10.3d 12g 11.8m 12g 16f⁶ Sep 13] no form: tongue tied final
start. *J. J. O'Neill*

DANCING-ALONE 7 ch.g. Adbass (USA) 102 – Lady Alone 59 (Mr Fluorocar- **50**
bon 126) [1998 56: a12g³ a10g a11g* 1999 a12g Jan 21] modest handicapper,
very lightly raced: stays 1½m: raced only on all-weather: has worn bandages/tongue
strap. *D. Morris*

DANCING BAY 2 b.g. (Feb 14) Suave Dancer (USA) 136 – Kabayil 75 (Dancing **64 p**
Brave (USA) 140) [1999 7m⁵ 7g Oct 16] first foal: dam 1¼m winner and fairly useful
hurdler: better effort in maidens when seventh of 12 at Catterick on second start: will
stay at least 1½m: should do better when stepped up in trip. *Miss J. A. Camacho*

DANCING DERVISH 4 b.g. Shareef Dancer (USA) 135 – Taj Victory 68 (Final **–**
Straw 127) [1998 63: 7s² 7.5s 7g 8.2m 11.7d² 9.9m 10g⁵ 9.7f³ 8m* 8m 1999 10.8m
8g May 15] smallish, good-bodied gelding: modest handicapper: well beaten both

starts in 1999: stays 9.7f: acts on firm and soft ground: blinkered/visored 5 of last 6 starts. *S. Mellor*

DANCING EM   4 b.f. Rambo Dancer (CAN) 107 – Militia Girl (Rarity 129) **58**
[1998 60: 8s 6g⁴ a8g⁴ 8d³ 7g 7.5d² 8.5g⁵ 8m* 6.9d* 8m² 8d 8g 7m 1999 7s 9f 8.2m³ 8d* 8d³ 6.9m³ 7f 8m³ 7g² 8g³ 7.5g 7g Sep 18] tall, sparely-made filly: modest handicapper: won at Musselburgh in June: best at 7f/1m: acts on good to firm and good to soft going: probably effective blinkered or not. *T. D. Easterby*

DANCING EMPRESS   2 b.f. (Mar 22) Emperor Jones (USA) 119 – Music Khan **73**
(Music Boy 124) [1999 5g 5g 5m² 6s³ 5.1m² 5.1f³ 6d a5g² a5g* Dec 13] 14,000Y: smallish filly: second foal: dam French 6f and 1m winner: fair performer: won maiden at Southwell in December: stays 6f: acts on soft and good to firm ground: sometimes finishes weakly. *M. A. Jarvis*

DANCING GISELLE (IRE)   3 b.f. Dancing Dissident (USA) 119 – Lady Bidder **–**
(Auction Ring (USA) 123) [1998 –: 5.7m 6m 6f a5g 1999 8d 6g 8m 8m Aug 4] little sign of ability, including in sellers: sold 900 gns. *P. Howling*

DANCING JACK   6 ch.g. Clantime 101 – Sun Follower (Relkino 131) [1998 39: **42**
a8g 5g 5g⁶ 5m 5f 5m⁶ a7g a6g² 1999 a6g⁰ a6g⁶ a6f⁵ a5f² a5g⁵ a5g⁶ a5g⁵ a5g **a36**
a6g 5m 7m 6s⁴ 6m 6m 5d 5s³ 5.3d a5g a7g a7g a5g⁶ Dec 29] workmanlike gelding: poor handicapper: best at 5f/6f: acts on firm going, soft and equitrack: tried blinkered: often needs plenty of driving: inconsistent. *J. J. Bridger*

DANCING KING (IRE)   3 b.c. Fairy King (USA) – Zariysha (IRE) (Darshaan
133) [1998 –p: 7d 1999 7f May 3] good-bodied colt: first foal: dam unraced sister to Greenham winner Zayyani: well beaten in maidens: fitted with severe noseband and looked none too tractable only outing in 1999: joined J. Bethell. *L. M. Cumani*

DANCING KRIS   6 b.g. Kris 135 – Liska's Dance (USA) (Riverman (USA) 131) **107**
[1998 8d⁴ 7.6g² 8s 8.5m* 1999 9.8d* 8.5s³ 10g² 8v³ 8s* 9.9s Sep 22] ex-French gelding: third reported foal: half-brother to several winners abroad, including 5-y-o French 11f winner L'Antillaise (by Generous): dam, French 1m and 1¼m winner, from family of top-class miler Irish River: useful performer, quite lightly raced: won minor event at Longchamp in April: left Mme C. Head after next start and generally in good form, winning 18-runner £17,000 handicap at Deauville in August: ran poorly in listed event at Goodwood final start (fractured a splint bone): stays 1¼m: acts on good to firm and heavy ground. *Ian Williams*

DANCING LAWYER   8 b.g. Thowra (FR) – Miss Lawsuit (Neltino 97) [1998 **51**
58: a8g 8g* 8g* 6.9s² 8f 8.3d⁴ 8.5g 8m⁴ 8m 8v³ 1999 10.3d³ 8g⁶ 9.2g⁴ 8d 10.5d² 9g⁴ 10.1m 8g 8m 8d Oct 20] sturdy gelding: modest handicapper: well below best final 4 starts: effective from 7f to 1¼m: acts on any turf going and equitrack: tried blinkered/visored: takes good hold and normally races prominently. *B. Ellison*

DANCING LILY   2 ch.f. (May 5) Clantime 101 – Sun Follower (Relkino 131) **44**
[1999 5m 6m 5m 5f⁵ 6s 6m 5d Sep 15] 6,200Y: fourth foal: sister to 6-y-o Dancing Jack and half-sister to 6f winner Durable George (by Durandal): dam showed little over hurdles: poor form in maidens. *J. J. Bridger*

DANCING MARY   2 gr.f. (Mar 8) Sri Pekan (USA) 117 – Fontenoy (USA) 63 **59**
(Lyphard's Wish (FR) 124) [1999 7.5g⁵ 7.5g⁵ 8d⁵ 8.2d Oct 21] 9,500Y: leggy, unfurnished filly: second foal: half-sister to 3-y-o Compensation: dam lightly raced in Ireland: modest maiden: stays 1m. *B. Smart*

DANCING MIRAGE (IRE)   2 ch.f. (Apr 7) Machiavellian (USA) 123 – Krae- **83**
mer (USA) (Lyphard (USA) 132) [1999 5m 6f² 7m² 6g³ 7m* 7d Sep 28] 100,000F, 110,000Y: smallish, quite attractive filly: eighth foal: half-sister to 3-y-o Silver Gyre, 17f winner Kriva (by Reference Point) and French 1m winner Glenarff (by Irish River): dam, 7.5f winner in France at 2 yrs and later successful up to 9f in USA, half-sister to very smart French miler Shaanxi: fairly useful form: won maiden at Salisbury in September: well beaten (good to soft ground) in valuable sales event at Newmarket final start: should stay 1m: acts on firm going. *R. Hannon*

DANCING MYSTERY   5 b.g. Beveled (USA) – Batchworth Dancer 67 (Balla- **78**
cashtal (CAN)) [1998 67+, a79: 5.1s⁶ 6g 5.1m 6m⁶ 5.3m³ 5.1g² 5g* 5m 5d 5m 5f⁴ **a87**
a6g³ a6g² 5m* a6g³ 1999 5d⁶ 5d³ 5m* 5g² 5.1m³ a5g* 5m 5m⁵ 5m* 5m³ 5m⁵ 5f⁴ 6f² 5d⁴ 5.3s 5f 5d* a5g Nov 17] close-coupled gelding: fairly useful performer on

all-weather, fair on turf: won handicaps at Lingfield in May, Southwell in June and Warwick in July, and minor event at Redcar in November: stays easy 6f (below form both times tried in 1999): acts on firm going, good to soft and all-weather: has won in blinkers: takes strong hold and usually tracks pace: has spoilt chance by rearing stalls, consistent otherwise. *E. A. Wheeler*

DANCING PHANTOM 4 b.g. Darshaan 133 – Dancing Prize (IRE) 99 (Sadler's **105** Wells (USA) 132) [1998 99: 10.3g² 10d* 12d 1999 10.1s 10.4s 8.5g⁴ 10.1g 10.4f 9.9g² 7.9g 12m 12s* Oct 23] quite attractive gelding: has a quick action: useful performer: benefited from shrewd ride (taken to race on wide outside) when making all in handicap at Doncaster final start by 5 lengths: stays 1½m: acts on soft ground: sometimes edgy/on toes in preliminaries: free-going sort, and usually races prominently: none too consistent: won over hurdles in November. *M. W. Easterby*

DANCING RIDGE (IRE) 2 b.c. (Apr 17) Ridgewood Ben 113 – May We Dance **56** (IRE) 57 (Dance of Life (USA)) [1999 5.1h⁶ 7d⁶ 6m² 6s 5s⁶ 5s Oct 13] IR 8,500Y: first foal: dam, Irish maiden, best at 1¼m: trained on debut by S. Woodman: easily best effort when second of 14 in claimer at Haydock in September: subsequently left G. Lewis £5,000: went with little zest last 2 starts: stays 6f: form only on good to firm ground. *P. D. Evans*

DANCING RIO (IRE) 4 ch.g. Roi Danzig (USA) – Tameen (FR) (Pharly (FR) **83** 130) [1998 86: a8s* a9.4g² a10g² a8g* a10g* a12g* a12g⁵ 9.9s* 14.6g⁶ 12.3m* 12.3g² 12m a8g 11.9m a12g a14g⁵ 1999 a12g* a12g³ a12g³ a11g⁵ a12g² a11g⁴ 16s⁴ 20m 16.1m 13f⁶ 16f⁵ 12.3g Aug 21] strong gelding: fairly useful handicapper: won at Lingfield in January: mostly creditable efforts after: probably stayed 2½m: acted on all-weather, good to firm and soft ground: flashed tail/wandered under pressure: dead. *P. C. Haslam*

DANCING SEA (USA) 3 b.f. Storm Cat (USA) – Coral Dance (FR) 111 (Green **80** Dancer (USA) 132) [1998 NR 1999 8s⁵ 7d³ 7g² 7m³ 7m² 7s⁵ 8s a8g⁴ Nov 26] half-sister to several winners, notably 2000 Guineas winner Pennekamp (by Bering) and high-class French/US 1¼m to 1¾m winner Nasr El Arab (by Al Nasr): dam, 1m winner, later successful in USA: fairly useful maiden: well below form on last 2 starts (disputing lead until 3f out on British debut at Lingfield final one): unproven beyond 7f: acts on good to firm and soft ground: blinkered fourth start. *J. S. Bolger, Ireland*

DANDANNA (IRE) 2 gr.f. (Apr 22) Linamix (FR) 127 – Dayanata (Shirley **97 p** Heights 130) [1999 6d⁵ Aug 8] unfurnished filly: sixth foal: half-sister to several winners, including 4-y-o Courteous and 5-y-o Carisbrooke: dam unraced sister to Darshaan: well-backed favourite, overcame greenness to win 4-runner maiden at Ascot, swerving markedly left leaving stalls and in rear before staying on to lead final 1f: will be suited by at least 1m: seems well regarded (was entered in Fillies' Mile), and sure to do better. *P. F. I. Cole*

DANDE'S RAMBO 2 gr.g. (Mar 28) Rambo Dancer (CAN) 107 – Kajetana (FR) **–** (Caro 133) [1999 8g 8s Nov 6] 17,000Y: big, strong, lengthy gelding: half-brother to several winners, including 3-y-o Blue Glass and useful 7f to 1¼m winner K-Battery (by Gunner B): dam unraced: burly, well held in maidens. *D. W. P. Arbuthnot*

DANDE TIMES 4 ch.g. Timeless Times (USA) 99 – Miss Merlin 79 (Manacle **52** 123) [1998 53: a5s² a5g² a5g² a5g⁵ a5g* 5s⁵ a5g⁶ a5g a5g a5g 1999 a5g³ a5f³ a5f³ a5g a5g a5g³ a5g³ a5g⁴ a5g⁶ 5d⁶ 5m⁵ 5g⁵ 5g May 29] modest performer: generally ran creditably in 1999: stays easy 6f: acts on all-weather, good to firm and good to soft going: has been visored, blinkered nowadays: sold 4,000 gns in July. *K. T. Ivory*

DANDILUM 2 b.c. (Feb 26) Dilum (USA) 115 – Renira 60 (Relkino 131) [1999 **78** 6.1d² 5m³ 5m 6g² 6.1f² Oct 20] 7,000Y: leggy, quite attractive colt: brother to a winner in Austria and half-brother to several winners, including Hotsocks (1m, by Hotfoot): dam, lightly raced, from family of Definite Article and Salford Express: fair maiden: runner-up 3 times: will stay at least 7f. *V. Soane*

DANDY NIGHT 2 b.f. (Feb 15) Lion Cavern (USA) 117 – Desert Venus 74 (Green **89** Desert (USA) 127) [1999 5m* 5.2d⁴ 5m 5m² Jul 2] 5,500Y: angular filly: first foal: dam, maiden who should have stayed 1m, out of half-sister to Poule d'Essai des Pouliches winner Dumka (dam of Doyoun): fairly useful form: won maiden at Newmarket in May: similar form in better company after, seventh of 13 in Queen Mary Stakes at Royal Ascot: will stay at least 6f. *B. Hanbury*

DANDY REGENT   5 b.g. Green Desert (USA) 127 – Tahilla 112 (Moorestyle   **51**
137) [1998 74d: a7g² 7d* 8g³ 8d 7m 7g⁶ 7g 7f a8g⁴ᵈⁱˢ a7g a8g⁵ 1999 a8f⁶ a8g a7f a6g   **a–**
6v² 7d⁵ 6d⁴ 6m⁴ 6m⁵ 7.7m Jul 2] angular gelding: modest performer nowadays: stays
1m: acts on good to firm going, heavy and equitrack. *J. L. Harris*

DANE   3 b.f. Doyoun 124 – Iviza (IRE) 105§ (Sadler's Wells (USA) 132) [1998 NR   **96**
1999 10f* 10m⁴ 12s Sep 26] smallish, well-made filly: first foal: dam, 2-y-o 7f
winner and second in Ribblesdale, probably ungenuine: won maiden at Newmarket
in July, despite flashing tail and carrying head awkwardly: similar form in minor
event at Ascot later in month, but looked temperamental in listed race there final
start: should stay further than 1¼m: one to treat with some caution. *A. C. Stewart*

DANE FRIENDLY   3 b.c. Danehill (USA) 126 – Always Friendly 111 (High Line   **–**
125) [1998 NR 1999 7g 10g May 8] 130,000Y: smallish, sturdy, attractive colt: first
foal: dam, smart middle-distance stayer, won Princess Royal Stakes: short-priced
favourite, found little and well held in maidens at Kempton and Lingfield: bandaged
behind on debut: sent to Italy. *P. W. Chapple-Hyam*

DANEGOLD (IRE)   7 b.g. Danehill (USA) 126 – Cistus 123 (Sun Prince 128)   **77**
[1998 75, a–: 12v 11.9g³ 16m⁴ 16m* 16.1m 17.2m⁴ 16m* 15.8d* 16.2s* 16s⁶ 16v
1999 18d* 16g 16m⁶ 21.6d³ 18d 15.9m⁵ 16.2m* 20f³ 14d² 16.4g 14.6m⁶ 13.9d 17.3g
16s 16g Nov 3] sturdy, close-coupled gelding: fair handicapper: won at Doncaster in
March and Ascot in July: unlucky when second at Sandown, far from discredited in
Cesarewitch at Newmarket thirteenth start: effective at 1¾m to 2¼m, possibly not
quite 2½m: acts on firm and soft ground, below form on all-weather earlier in career:
usually visored before 1998: usually comes from behind. *M. R. Channon*

DANEHILL FLAME (IRE)   4 b.f. Danehill (USA) 126 – Hillbrow 100 (Swing   **64 §**
Easy (USA) 126) [1998 NR 1999 7m 8.3g 7.1m 10g 8m 8s a8.5g⁴ a9g a9.8g⁶ Dec 29]
IR 20,000Y: sturdy, angular filly: half-sister to several winners, notably very smart
winner up to 7f Indian Ridge (by Ahonoora): dam 2-y-o 6f winner: modest maiden:
left P. Harris 15,000 gns after sixth start (looked reluctant): will prove best up to 1m:
one to treat with caution. *M. Hofer, Germany*

DANESTAR   4 b.f. Danehill (USA) 126 – Ministra (USA) (Deputy Minister   **44**
(CAN)) [1998 64: 10d⁶ 9d 10s 1999 10g⁵ 10g 10.9d a8.5g Dec 27] third foal: half-
sister to 5-y-o Hibernate and 6-y-o Strazo: dam, French 12.5f winner, daughter of
Irish 1000 Guineas and Irish Oaks winner Godetia: modest maiden for D. Kelly in
Ireland at 3 yrs: well below best in handicaps in 1999: raced only on good going or
softer on turf. *K. R. Burke*

DANGER BABY   9 ch.g. Bairn (USA) 126 – Swordstown Miss (USA) (Apala-   **58**
chee (USA) 137) [1998 NR 1999 15.8g³ 17.2s* 18d⁴ a16.2g Dec 15] better known as
useful but thoroughly ungenuine chaser (often refuses to race) nowadays: modest
handicapper on Flat: only second outing since 1993, won at Bath in September:
looked none too keen under pressure next time: best at 2m+: acts on good to firm and
soft going: well beaten in blinkers/visor. *P. Bowen*

DANGEROUS DANCER   3 b.f. Warning 136 – Silabteni (USA) (Nureyev   **67**
(USA) 131) [1998 79: 5m² 5m² 5f² 6d 1999 5.1s 5m⁴ 5m³ 5m³ a6g* 8m Sep 8] small,
quite attractive filly: fair performer: won seller at Wolverhampton in August:
reportedly lame when tailed off in handicap final start (slowly away): stayed 6f: acted
on fibresand, possibly unsuited by ground softer than good: dead. *B. W. Hills*

DANGEROUS FORTUNE (USA)   3 b.c. Barathea (IRE) 127 – Miss Demure   **87**
106 (Shy Groom (USA)) [1998 NR 1999 7m⁵ 7s² 8m³ a8.5g² 7m* 8.2d⁵ Oct 21]
$40,000Y: half-brother to 3 useful performers, namely 6-y-o Steamroller Stanly,
1994 6f 2-y-o winner Missel (by Storm Bird) and 1997 Cheveley Park Stakes third
Royal Shyness (by Royal Academy): later won in USA: dam won Lowther Stakes:
fairly useful performer: best effort in maidens when winning at Redcar in September:
creditable fifth in handicap final start: likely to stay beyond 1m: acts on good to firm
going, soft and fibresand. *J. W. Hills*

DANIEL DERONDA   5 b.h. Danehill (USA) 126 – Kilvarnet 78 (Furry Glen   **72**
121) [1998 72, a–: 10d 10g⁶ 10g 10.5d² 12m a14g 1999 14.1s 10s 11.6m⁵ 10g⁶
11.5g² 10m* Jul 17] big, good-topped horse: fair handicapper: gained first win at
Nottingham in July: best around 1¼m: acts on heavy and good to firm ground: often
takes strong hold: sometimes bandaged. *J. Cullinan*

Theo Fennell Glorious Rated Stakes (Handicap), Goodwood—
Danish Rhapsody defies top weight in beating Mardani (rail), Muhib (right) and Generous Rosi

DANIELLA RIDGE (IRE)   3 b.f. Indian Ridge 123 – Daniella Drive (USA)   **73**
(Shelter Half (USA)) [1998 85: 6m³ 6g⁵ 1999 8f³ 8g⁶ 8.1m³ 10m³ 10d Sep 19]
angular, unfurnished filly: easy mover: fair maiden: well behind in handicap final
start: barely stays 1¼m: acts on firm going. *R. Hannon*

DANIELLE'S LAD   3 b.g. Emarati (USA) 74 – Cactus Road (FR) (Iron Duke   **95**
(FR) 122) [1998 87: 5m⁴ 5m³ 5m* 6d 5v³ 5d* a5g 1999 6g 6g² 5m 5.1m³ 5f⁶ 6m 6.1g   **a?**
6v² 5d⁵ 6s a5g Nov 17] strong, rangy gelding: useful handicapper: good second
at Kempton in June and Salisbury in September: stays 6f: acts on good to firm and
heavy going (not knocked about on all-weather): has run poorly when sweating:
often a front runner. *B. Palling*

DANISH RHAPSODY (IRE)   6 b.g. Danehill (USA) 126 – Ardmelody (Law   **119**
Society (USA) 130) [1998 115: 10.5g* 9.8s 10d 9.9g³ 7.3m² 8g 7.3g⁵ 9.9m* 8g⁶ 9m
1999 9.9d⁵ 9.9g⁵ 10m³ 10f* 12f* Jul 30] tall, good-topped gelding: smart performer:
better than ever at 6 yrs, successful in 4-runner minor event at Newbury (by 1½
lengths from Redbridge) then listed rated stakes at Goodwood (eased close home
when beating Mardani by 1½ lengths for fifth course success), both in July: effective
at 7f to easy 1½m: acts on firm and soft ground: races prominently/leads: tough,
game and versatile. *Lady Herries*

DANIYSHA (IRE)   2 b.f. (Feb 14) Doyoun 124 – Danishara (IRE) (Slew O'Gold   **73 p**
(USA)) [1999 6s⁴ Oct 25] workmanlike filly: first foal: dam unraced daughter of
Grand Criterium winner Danishkada: green, stayed on well when length fourth of 13
to Picot in maiden at Leicester: will stay at least 1m: sure to improve. *Sir Michael
Stoute*

DANKA   5 gr.g. Petong 126 – Angel Drummer 59 (Dance In Time (CAN)) [1998   **55 d**
55d: a12g a12g³ 14.1d a8.5g a12g a11g³ 1999 a8g a11g* a8g a9.4g a12g 15.8s 16d⁴
a9.4g a14g a16.2g⁵ Dec 15] good-bodied gelding: modest performer at best: won
seller at Southwell in March: below form after: stays 2m: acts on firm going, good to
soft and all-weather: often visored earlier in career, but effective when not:
sometimes tail swisher/slowly away. *K. C. Comerford*

DANNY DEEVER   3 b.g. Deploy 131 – Yes 72 (Blakeney 126) [1998 –: 7m 6d   **43**
7g⁴ 8m 7g 1999 10m 11.6m a12g⁵ a16g 12d⁶ 12.1m² 11.5m⁵ 10m 12g⁴ 14.1m 14.1f
a16g Nov 15] smallish, strong gelding: poor maiden handicapper: should stay 1¾m:
acts on good to firm and good to soft going: tried blinkered (little form): has looked a
hard ride. *D. T. Thom*

DANNY POWER (IRE)   3 gr.g. Priolo (USA) 127 – Fillette Lalo (FR) (Hunter-   **62**
combe 133) [1998 –: 8m 7d 7v 1999 a6g⁶ 6s 6f⁴ 7.3g³ 5m 6g⁵ 5g* 5f 5m² 5d 5m 5m⁶
Sep 2] 4,800Y, 27,000 2-y-o: ex-Irish gelding: fifth foal: half-brother to a winner
in Japan by Persian Bold: dam French 7f winner: modest handicapper: won at
Musselburgh in July: will prove as effective at 6f as 5f: acts on good to firm going,
probably on good to soft: tried blinkered, including last 4 starts: has looked difficult
ride (unseated rider and bolted to post second outing): sold 1,600 gns. *T. D. Barron*

DANSEUSE ARGENTINE (FR)   4 b.f. Fijar Tango (FR) 127 – Danseuse   **–**
Etoile (FR) (Green Dancer (USA) 132) [1998 10.5s⁴ 9g 10.5s² 10.5d 12m³ 10.5g⁴

12.5s 1999 13.8g a11g 10.3m Jun 23] closely related to French 1¼m winner In The Star (by In Fijar) and half-sister to 3 winners abroad: dam French 1½m winner: maiden, fair form in 1998 for B. Secly in France: little show in 3 starts in Britain: stays 1½m: acts on good to firm and soft ground. *F. Jordan*

DANSILI   3 b.c. Danehill (USA) 126 – Hasili (IRE) (Kahyasi 130) [1998 8v* **125** 1999 8g* 8m² 9s⁴ 8g* 8v³ 8m³ Sep 5]

As the betting suggested, joint-favourite Dansili proved the best of the four Andre Fabre-trained runners in the Poule d'Essai des Poulains at Longchamp in May. Though unable to get to grips with the one and a half length winner Sendawar, he ran on strongly through the last two furlongs to pull clear of the remainder. It represented further significant improvement from Dansili, who had won minor events at Longchamp, at two years, and Chantilly on his only previous starts. Given his inexperience, there was a chance that if Sendawar and Dansili were to meet again Dansili would make an even closer race of it with the winner. Yet, when eventually they did, in the Prix du Moulin run over the same course and distance and on similar ground in September, the margin between the pair was almost the same. Dansili finished third to Sendawar this time, the pair split by Gold Away. Dansili had three races in between and won one of them, the Group 3 Prix Messidor at Deauville in July. He and Kabool occupied the first two places in the betting and in the race itself, but whereas Dansili had just shaded favouritism his superiority on the track was much more clear cut. Dansili took the lead around two furlongs out and drew four lengths clear in the final furlong, with Kabool holding on to second by half a length from Miss Berbere. Although the ground was heavy when Dansili made a winning debut, it would seem that good or good to firm ground suits him best judged on his performances in his two other races. Long odds-on for the Prix Jean Prat at Chantilly, which was run on soft ground, Dansili could finish only

Mr K. Abdulla's "Dansili"

fourth to Golden Snake; on heavy ground in the Prix Jacques le Marois at Deauville, Dansili was again below form in finishing third of five to Dubai Millennium.

		Danzig	Northern Dancer
Danehill (USA)		(b 1977)	Pas de Nom
(b 1986)		Razyana	His Majesty
Dansili		(b 1981)	Spring Adieu
(b.c. 1996)		Kahyasi	Ile de Bourbon
	Hasili (IRE)	(b 1985)	Kadissya
	(b 1991)	Kerali	High Line
		(ch 1984)	Sookera

Dansili is the first foal of Hasili, who also raced in France for Khalid Abdulla, showing useful form and winning four races from five furlongs to eight and a half furlongs as a two-year-old. The next dam Kerali, successful over seven furlongs, has produced several other winners including the smart hurdler Kerawi. Dansili's great grandam Sookera, who won the 1977 Cheveley Park Stakes, is the dam of a couple of horses who have done very well for Mr Abdulla in good races at up to seven furlongs, the smart Bold Fact and very smart So Factual. Dansili, a good-topped colt, has done all his racing at a mile, apart from in the nine-furlong Prix Jean Prat, and that will probably prove his optimum trip. *A. Fabre, France*

DANSKER (IRE) 3 b.g. Darshaan 133 – Nassma (IRE) 95 (Sadler's Wells (USA) **83** 132) [1998 76P: 7d⁶ a7g² 8s 8s⁵ 1999 10g² 9d* 10.2m 13s 10d² 10v Oct 11] fairly useful performer: won 3-runner minor event at Musselburgh in June: good second in handicap penultimate start: should stay 1½m: acts on good to soft going, possibly unsuited by soft/heavy: often makes running: sent to UAE. *Sir Mark Prescott*

DANZAS 5 b.g. Polish Precedent (USA) 131 – Dancing Rocks 118 (Green Dancer **48** (USA) 132) [1998 55: 10v 8g 8g 8.3d 8.1g⁴ 7g 9.9m 1999 10s 9d 8m⁴ 7f 8.2f* 8g² 8g⁶ 8f² 8.3m 8.1m 8f 7f 7m 8d⁴ 9.2m 8.1m² a7g⁵ Oct 13] well-made gelding: poor handicapper: won at Nottingham (apprentice maiden event) in May: some creditable efforts after: best at 1m/1¼m: acts on firm going, soft and fibresand: usually blinkered nowadays: has had tongue tied. *J. M. Bradley*

DANZIGAWAY (USA) 3 b.f. Danehill (USA) 126 – Blushing Away (USA) **115** (Blushing Groom (FR) 131) [1998 98+: 6d* 6d² 5d³ 5.5s⁵ 1999 8g⁴ 8s 8m* 8s* 7d⁴ 8v* Nov 6] fifth foal: closely related to French winner up to 7.5f Posen Tune (by Polish Precedent) and half-sister to smart French 7f winner Blushing Gleam (by Caerleon) and very smart French 5f (at 2 yrs) to 9.3f winner Gold Away (by Goldneyev): dam French 6.5f winner: smart performer: won newcomers race at Chantilly at 2 yrs: successful in 1999 in minor event at Longchamp and listed race at Saint-Cloud in September and Prix Perth (by 3 lengths from Sossus Vlei, tended to flash tail) at Saint-Cloud in November: also ran well when length fourth to Field of Hope in Prix de la Foret at Longchamp penultimate start: stays 1m: acts on heavy ground, has won on good to firm: held up: stays in training. *Mme C. Head, France*

DANZIGEUSE (IRE) 2 b.f. (Mar 11) Zieten (USA) 118 – Baliana 75 (Midyan **58** (USA) 124) [1999 5.1g⁵ 5.1m 6m 6m Sep 18] 4,500F, 23,000Y: unfurnished filly: second foal: half-sister to 4-y-o Bali Dance: dam unreliable sprinter: modest maiden: best effort final start: should stay 7f. *R. Charlton*

DANZIG FLYER (IRE) 4 b.c. Roi Danzig (USA) – Fenland Express (IRE) **–** (Reasonable (FR) 119) [1998 –: 8.5m 8m 8g 12m 11.9g a12g a12g 1999 a11g a12g 10.3m 7g 10.1d Sep 15] sturdy colt: seems of little account nowadays. *B. P. J. Baugh*

DAPHNE'S DOLL (IRE) 4 b.f. Polish Patriot (USA) 128 – Helietta 78 **61** (Tyrnavos 129) [1998 72, a63: 7m⁴ 8.3m⁵ 9.9g 8.2v³ a8.5g⁴ a7g* 1999 a7g 8g 6m⁴ 5m 7m³ 7.1m² 8d 8.2s a8g⁴ a10g* Dec 18] big filly: modest handicapper: left Miss G. Kelleway after eighth start: won at Lingfield in December: stays 1¼m: acts on good to firm going, heavy and equitrack. *Dr J. R. J. Naylor*

DARA DANCER 3 b.f. Batshoof 122 – Dara Dee 87 (Dara Monarch 128) [1998 **–** NR 1999 7m 8m⁵ a8g⁴ 8m 7m Sep 7] 2,500Y: quite attractive filly: third foal:

half-sister to fairly useful 1¼m winner Beneventus (by Most Welcome): dam 7f/1m winner: little show in maidens/claimer: sold 1,000 gns, sent to Belgium. *P. Howling*

DARAJAT (IRE) 4 b.g. Imperial Frontier (USA) 112 – Fantasy To Reality (IRE) (Jester 119) [1998 –: 8m 6m 8.2g 8m 7.1m 1999 a8g Jan 11] no form. *J. G. Portman*

DARAK (IRE) 3 b.c. Doyoun 124 – Dararita (IRE) (Halo (USA)) [1998 NR 1999 10m 12g⁵ Jun 9] small, well-made colt: first foal: dam, French 12.5f winner, half-sister to several at least useful middle-distance performers out of Prix Vermeille winner Darara, herself half-sister to Darshaan: better effort in maidens (8 days apart) when fifth of 12 to Rain In Spain at Kempton: should be suited by 1¾m+: sold 26,000 gns in July. *Sir Michael Stoute* **73**

DARAYDAN (IRE) 7 b.g. Kahyasi 130 – Delsy (FR) (Abdos 134) [1998 NR 1999 20m Jun 15] close-coupled gelding: useful on Flat in 1996 but no form in 3 runs since: useful hurdler, won in June and October. *M. C. Pipe* **–**

DARCY DANCER 2 b.c. (May 8) Be My Chief (USA) 122 – Little White Star (Mill Reef (USA) 141) [1999 7f³ 8g⁵ 9m Sep 24] 12,000Y: half-brother to several winners, including useful sprinter Moon Drop (by Dominion) and smart winner up to 1½m Beldale Star (by Beldale Flutter): dam poor maiden: modest form when third of 5 in maiden at Newcastle in July: last both outings after: should stay at least 1¼m. *Martyn Wane* **55**

DARE 4 b.g. Beveled (USA) – Run Amber Run (Run The Gantlet (USA)) [1998 63?: 6d 7m⁴ 7m 8m 7m 9.9m 1999 8.3g 10m 8f 8g 8.3s* 9.9v* a8g* 8s* 10.2s⁵ a12g³ a9.4g a8g* a11g a8g a10g Dec 22] fair handicapper: left E. James after fourth start, then won at Hamilton and Salisbury (apprentice race) in September, Southwell (another apprentice race) and Leicester in October, and Southwell (amateurs) in November: effective at 1m and stays 1¼m well: acts on fibresand (not at best on equitrack) and heavy ground, probably on good to firm: effective visored or not: tough. *P. D. Evans* **72**

DARE HUNTER (USA) 2 ch.g. (Apr 9) Gulch (USA) – Dabawyaa 118 (Shareef Dancer (USA) 135) [1999 7.1m* 7m⁵ 7d⁶ Oct 7] sturdy, well-made gelding: good walker: half-brother to several winners, including 3-y-o Blue Snake, smart 6.5f to 1¼m winner (including in UAE/USA) Magellan (by Hansel) and earlier performers up to 7f Alanees (by Cadeaux Genereux) and Bin Nashwan (by Nashwan): dam 7f/1m winner and second in 1000 Guineas: overcame greenness to win maiden at Sandown in July: no improvement in 2 starts after, though didn't get run of race on first occasion and sweating and edgy after 2½-month break on second one: should stay 1m. *B. W. Hills* **83 +**

DARGO 5 b.g. Formidable (USA) 125 – Mountain Memory 109 (High Top 131) [1998 58, a51: a9.4g a7g 8.3d 8.3g² 12d 13d⁴ 12.1d 10.9d a11g² 10.1v³ 12s⁴ a12g² 19mm a16.2g* a16.2g³ Mar 13] has a round action: fair handicapper: won at Wolverhampton in February by a distance: respectable third there next time: stays 2m: acts on fibresand and heavy ground, showed promise only outing on good to firm: won maiden hurdle in June. *D. G. Bridgwater* **74**

DARING NEWS 4 b.g. Risk Me (FR) 127 – Hot Sunday Sport 42 (Star Appeal 133) [1998 –, a33: a8.5g⁵ 11.6g 10d a9.4g⁵ 1999 a8g a12f a7g a9.4g Feb 20] rangy gelding: poor maiden: no form on Flat in 1999, though awarded selling hurdle in March: blinkered last 2 starts: possibly ungenuine. *O. O'Neill* **–**

DARK AGE (IRE) 6 b.g. Darshaan 133 – Sarela (USA) (Danzig (USA)) [1998 41: 8d 10g 7g⁶ 7m 1999 8f 8.1m⁵ 8.2m² 10.1m* Jul 28] poor handicapper: unlucky second at Nottingham, then won apprentice event at Epsom, dictating pace under good ride: stays 1¼m: acts on good to firm going: inconsistent. *J. Akehurst* **46**

DARK ALBATROSS (USA) 3 b.f. Sheikh Albadou 128 – Rossard (DEN) (Glacial (DEN)) [1998 89+: 6m* 6s² 6m³ 7.3m⁴ 7.3g³ 8m 1999 8m 10g² 9m³ 12m 10m⁶ 9.7d⁵ 10.2m⁴ 10d³ 10.3d⁶ 10d² a8.5g Nov 20] leggy, quite attractive filly: good walker: has a round action: fairly useful handicapper: mostly creditable efforts in 1999 without winning: should prove at least as effective at 1½m as 1¼m: acts on good to firm and good to soft going, probably on soft: visored eighth and ninth starts: sold 20,000 gns in December. *J. L. Dunlop* **89**

DARK MENACE   7 br.g. Beveled (USA) – Sweet And Sure (Known Fact (USA)   **58**
135) [1998 42§, a45§: a6g a7g 8.3m² 7g⁵ a7g* a8g⁵ 7f⁶ 7.6g 1999 a7g³ a7g⁵ a7g⁶
a8g³ a7g⁵ a8g² 7f* 7f⁴ a6g³ 7m⁵ a7g² a7g² 7.7m 8f² 7f⁴ 7.1m² a8g³ a7g⁶ 5m a8g²
a7g³ a7g a7g* Dec 8] workmanlike gelding: modest performer: won handicap at
Brighton in May and seller at Lingfield in December: effective at stiff 6f, and stays
1m well: best on good to firm/firm going or all-weather: wears blinkers: consistent.
E. A. Wheeler

DARK MOONDANCER   4 b.c. Anshan 119 – Oh So Well (IRE) (Sadler's   **122**
Wells (USA) 132) [1998 115: 9s³ 12g* 12.5d* 12.5g⁴ 14.6m⁶ 12s* 1999 10s⁴
10d* 10.5g* 12m* 12g Nov 6]
        Dark Moondancer, trained by Peter Chapple-Hyam as a three-year-old,
began his four-year-old career with a new owner in the care of Alain de Royer-
Dupre. Brazilian Benjamino Arbib, so the story goes, had been holidaying at
Deauville with his cousin Martyn, the owner of Strategic Choice, when Dark
Moondancer first caught his eye as a three-year-old by finishing fourth in the
Grand Prix de Deauville, one place behind his cousin's horse. The rest of the
story about Dark Moondancer's acquisition is best left to Mr Arbib himself.
        'He was for sale' he told *Paris Turf* in an interview. 'I wanted to buy
him, but my cousin's son convinced me he was too expensive. So I forgot
about the horse until October; the day Dark Moondancer won a Group 3 at
Newmarket. The next day, at 6.45 in the morning, my cousin Martyn called me;
he was going mad on the phone because he thought I'd bought the horse and
couldn't understand why it wasn't me who'd collected the trophy for the St
Simon Stakes. The funny thing was, his company sponsored the race and he'd
chosen a nicer cup in the belief that I was the winning owner! A few days later I
jumped on a plane to buy the horse: on November 13th I signed the cheque.'
        It proved money well spent. A big, useful-looking colt with scope, Dark
Moondancer had looked the sort to do well from three to four but judged on his
efforts at Deauville and Newmarket, and when sixth in the St Leger in between,
it had seemed most likely that Dark Moondancer would need at least a mile and

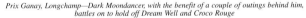

*Prix Ganay, Longchamp—Dark Moondancer, with the benefit of a couple of outings behind him,
battles on to hold off Dream Well and Croco Rouge*

Charles J. Cella's "Dark Moondancer"

a half to progress further at four. His first three starts over a mile and a quarter in France the following spring quickly proved otherwise. Following a fourth place in the Prix Exbury at Saint-Cloud on his reappearance, he beat the Exbury winner Barbola by one and a half lengths on better terms in the four-runner Prix d'Harcourt at Longchamp in April, making most of the running. Lining up for the Prix Ganay at the same course over an extra half furlong in early-May, Dark Moondancer had a fitness advantage over his three main rivals, Sagamix, Dream Well and Croco Rouge who were all making their reappearances in the Group 1 contest. Dark Moondancer had no easy task at level weights against the high-class trio but in a steadily-run race (the only other runner Northern Quest didn't do much of a job as Sagamix's pacemaker) Dark Moondancer stepped up a little on his previous form, battling on well when joining issue in the straight to hold off Dream Well by a head, with Croco Rouge a length back in third and Sagamix a well-held fourth. Dark Moondancer was the third horse trained by Alain de Royer-Dupre to complete the Harcourt-Ganay double in four years, following Valanour in 1996 and Astarabad in 1998, and Dark Moondancer completed another notable treble for the stable on his next outing at Milan. The Gran Premio was a third Group 1 for the stable in eight days after Daryaba had won the Prix de Diane and Sendawar the St James's Palace Stakes. Although intended as an easier alternative to the Coronation Cup, the Gran Premio looked like eluding Dark Moondancer for a time as he was boxed in behind the front-running Ungaro for much of the straight. Once clear, however, Dark Moondancer led close home to beat his German-trained rival by a nose.

The second half of Dark Moondancer's season went far less smoothly; a minor set-back prevented him taking his chance in the Prix Foy and a disappointing workout caused him to be taken out of the Arc. By the time he did make it back to the track, Dark Moondancer had changed stables and owners again, finishing ninth to Daylami in the Breeders' Cup Turf at Gulfstream on his debut for Ron McAnally. He was never a factor after being checked and losing his place after two furlongs.

Dark Moondancer is a long way from being fashionably bred. For a start, he's much the best product of his sire Anshan, the Free Handicap winner and Two Thousand Guineas third who has since had his attentions turned to National Hunt mares. On the distaff side, Dark Moondancer is the latest chapter in his family's remarkable rags-to-riches story. Great grandam Mild Wind, a twin bought for 360 guineas as a yearling, showed little in poor company on the Flat and was tailed off in a seller on her only outing over hurdles. Her daughter Soba looked little better herself ('only plating class' was her *Timeform* comment at two) until improving out of all recognition at three and developing into one of Europe's best sprinters at four. Soba's mating with Sadler's Wells resulted in Dark Moondancer's unraced dam Oh So Well. Dark Moondancer is her third foal, following the twice-raced Dance of The Moon (by High Estate) and the useful filly Dances With Dreams (by Be My Chief), the latter's best effort coming when a close fourth in the Poule d'Essai des Pouliches. Dances With Dreams' full brother was sold for 100,000 guineas at the latest Houghton Yearling Sales.

	Anshan (ch 1987)	Persian Bold (br 1975)	Bold Lad
			Relkarunner
Dark Moondancer		Lady Zi (b 1980)	Manado
(b.c. 1995)			Exbury Grace
	Oh So Well (IRE) (b 1988)	Sadler's Wells (b 1981)	Northern Dancer
			Fairy Bridge
		Soba (ch 1979)	Most Secret
			Mild Wind

Dark Moondancer is effective at a mile and a quarter and stays a mile and a half well; at the time, his sixth place in the St Leger was at least as good as anything he'd achieved previously. He acts on good to firm and soft ground. In his early days Dark Moondancer looked something of a hard ride but there was little wrong with his demeanour in the latest season. *R. McAnally, USA*

DARK SHELL (IRE) 4 b.c. Darshaan 133 – Grecian Urn 123 (Ela-Mana-Mou 132) [1998 108: 10d* 11.9m⁶ 12g⁴ 10.3g² 11g⁴ 1999 10s³ 13.3d* 12m³ Jul 25] rather leggy, quite good-topped colt: smart performer: improved to win steadily-run 6-runner listed race at Newbury in May by 7 lengths from Kadaka: creditable 1½ lengths third of 5 to Ungaro in WGZ Bank-Deutschlandpreis at Dusseldorf over 2 months later: stays 13f: acts on good to firm and good to soft ground: took fierce hold and carried head awkwardly under pressure on reappearance. *Sir Michael Stoute* **116**

DARK TROJAN (IRE) 3 b.c. Darshaan 133 – Trojan Miss 104 (Troy 137) [1998 NR 1999 11.9d² 12d² 10.4m³ 12v² 11.9d² 11.9v⁵ Oct 13] leggy, close-coupled colt: on the weak side at 3 yrs: brother to French 1m and 11f winner Dart Board and half-brother to several winners in France, notably smart miler Trojan Sea (by Bering): dam 2-y-o 7f winner who stayed 1½m: fairly useful maiden: good second to Fair Warning in minor event at York penultimate start: odds on when running poorly next time: stays 1½m: acts on heavy ground, probably on good to firm: tends to wander under pressure: sold 60,000 gns. *Sir Michael Stoute* **94**

DARLING COREY 3 b.f. Caerleon (USA) 132 – Tass (Soviet Star (USA) 128) [1998 NR 1999 8s⁶ 10m² 10.2s⁴ Sep 27] quite attractive filly: second foal: dam unraced half-sister to good middle-distance performers Alleging, Nomrood and Monastery: off nearly 4 months before best effort in maidens second start: below form on soft ground next time: should stay beyond 1¼m. *R. Charlton* **75**

DARRAS SKY 3 ch.g. Clantime 101 – Sky Music 85 (Absalom 128) [1998 62d: 5d³ 5g⁶ 5d 6d 1999 7f 6g Aug 16] good-bodied gelding: modest maiden: visored (ran poorly) final 2-y-o start. *Miss S. E. Hall* **–**

DARU (USA) 10 gr.g. Caro 133 – Frau Daruma (ARG) (Frari (ARG)) [1998 NR 1999 a14g Mar 10] one-time useful stayer: lightly raced on Flat since 1993: has become most temperamental (including over hurdles): often blinkered/visored: best left alone. *R. Hollinshead* **§§**

DARVAN 2 b.g. (Mar 23) Efisio 120 – Do You Miss Me (CAN) (El Gran Senor (USA) 136) [1999 7f⁴ 5f⁵ 6g 8g⁶ 7g Oct 16] 33,000Y: lengthy gelding: fourth foal: half-brother to a winner in Italy by Arctic Tern: dam twice-raced half-sister to dam of Mind Games: modest maiden: has worn crossed noseband and had tongue tied. *M. W. Easterby* **50**

DARWELL'S FOLLY (USA) 4 ch.g. Blushing John (USA) 120 – Hispanola (FR) (Kris 135) [1998 –, a88: a6g* a7g* 12.4d 8.9g 8.2v 1999 9g 7m* 7m 7.5s² 8s 7d a7g* 7d Oct 27] sturdy, good-topped gelding: fair performer: won handicap at Leicester in September: mostly below form after, not having to be anywhere near best to win claimer at Wolverhampton in October: stays 7.5f: acts on soft going, good to firm and fibresand: blinkered/visored: wears tongue strap: has looked moody, and one to treat with caution. *M. Johnston* **73 §**

DARYABAD (IRE) 7 b.g. Thatching 131 – Dayanata (Shirley Heights 130) [1998 72, a56: a7g 7s 8s 7g* 7m² 8m³ 7g⁴ 7m⁶ 7s a7g⁴ a7g² 1999 7g 8d 8g a7g* a7g* a7g⁶ Dec 8] big, strong gelding: fair performer: won minor event at Lingfield in October and handicap there in November: badly hampered and finished strongly final start: best at 7f/1m: acts on firm ground, soft and all-weather: often blinkered, including when successful. *R. McGhin* **77**

DARYABA (IRE) 3 b.f. Night Shift (USA) – Darata (IRE) (Vayrann 133) [1998 NR 1999 10d² 10m* 10.5d* 12m* 12v Oct 3] **121**

1999 saw the fiftieth 'Gala des Courses', the awards ceremony held on the eve of the Prix de Diane at which the previous year's French champion jockeys on the Flat and over jumps are honoured. The 1999 event also honoured the top owner, trainer and jockey of the last half of the century as chosen by readers of two French racing publications and a panel of judges. The trainer and jockey awards went to Francois Mathet and Yves Saint-Martin respectively while the vote for the top owner went to the Aga Khan. In a particularly successful year all round as a breeder, as well as owner, it was therefore appropriate that the next day His Highness won the Prix de Diane for the third year running, Daryaba following on from the successes of Vereva in 1997 and Zainta in 1998.

Daryaba made her debut at Chantilly in April in the same race that Vereva had won two years earlier. Daryaba went down to Shabby Chic (who ended the year with smart form in America) but made amends in another minor event at the same course three weeks later with a four-length win considered impressive enough to make her second choice in an open-looking Prix de Diane. The supplemented Prix Vanteaux winner Star of Akkar was sent off favourite and others prominent in the betting in the fourteen-strong field included the first four from the Prix Saint-Alary, Cerulean Sky, Juvenia, Visionnaire and Louve, and the placed horses from the Poule d'Essai des Pouliches, Karmifira and Calando.

In one of the slowest runnings of the Prix de Diane in the last thirty years, Daryaba took the big step up in class in her stride under a good ride from

Prix de Diane Hermes, Chantilly—
Daryaba (noseband) provides her owner, trainer and jockey with their third consecutive success in the race;
Star of Akkar (rail) is second with Visionnaire (second right) third

Prix Vermeille Normandy Barriere, Longchamp—
Daryaba becomes only the third filly in the last fifteen years to complete the Diane/Vermeille double;
she has something to spare over Etizaaz and Cerulean Sky

Gerald Mosse. Leading the tightly-grouped field wide of the inside rail into the straight, Daryaba ran on well despite flashing her tail under the whip to hold off the only serious threat, delivered by Star of Akkar, by a length. Visionnaire fared best of those who'd contested the Saint-Alary, beaten a further length and a half in third, just ahead of Louve. Daryaba's success was the fourth in all in the Prix de Diane for the Aga Khan and trainer Alain de Royer-Dupre (they'd also been successful with Shemaka in 1993), while Mosse was winning the Diane for the fifth time, having been on board Resless Kara in 1988 as well as the Aga Khan's quartet.

Winning the Prix de Diane in early-June is one thing, but winning the Prix Vermeille, over a longer trip, and three months further into the season when later-developing fillies have had the chance to appear on the scene, is quite another. Fortunately for Daryaba, no worthy challengers had come to the fore in France over the summer, while the best British-trained middle-distance filly, Ramruma, contested the St Leger the day before the Vermeille instead. Daryaba herself had been kept off the track since the Diane, a bout of coughing causing her to miss the Prix de la Nonette at Deauville in August.

Daryaba was much the most emphatic winner on the day of Longchamp's three Arc trials in the Vermeille, tracking the Sandown listed winner Etizaaz until cutting her down impressively for a two and a half length win. Cerulean Sky improved on her running in the Diane to finish third, but the Vermeille also represented further progress for Daryaba. With more improvement expected in the Arc, Daryaba lined up as fourth choice behind the coupled pairing of Montjeu and Genghis Khan, as well as El Condor Pasa and Daylami. However, in marked contrast to the situation in the 'eighties, the Arc has proved a graveyard for most of the French-trained three-year-old fillies who have taken their chance in the race in the last decade. In finishing out at the back, Daryaba met with the same fate as her owner's two other Diane winners to have contested the Arc, Shemaka and Zainta. Daryaba was reported to have bled a little subsequently and returned with mucus in her lungs. There was briefly the possibility of her running at the Breeders' Cup or in the Japan Cup but in the event she was retired to stud.

The choice of Night Shift as a mate for Daryaba's dam Darata represented a departure from the middle-distance types responsible for her first three foals, all successful in Ireland. Daryaba was preceded by bumper winner Darsarak (by Shirley Heights), the useful mile and a half and two mile winner Darbela (by Doyoun), also successful over hurdles, and Darsannda (by Kahyasi), who won over an extended mile and a half. Their dam Darata won a listed race over a mile and a half at Longchamp before being placed in the Prix de Royaumont and Prix Minerve and finishing fourth in the Prix de

H.H. Aga Khan's "Daryaba"

Royallieu—coincidentally her pacemaker on that last occasion was Zaila, the dam of Zainta. Out of Darazina, who won over an extended mile and a quarter, Darata is a half-sister to the smart Prix Minerve winner Daralinsha as well as to Darabaka, the dam of the Northumberland Plate and Doncaster Cup winner Far Cry. Another more distant family member successful in 1999 was Running Stag, a great grandson of Daryaba's fourth dam Dalama.

	Night Shift (USA) (b 1980)	Northern Dancer (b 1961)	Nearctic Natalma
		Ciboulette (b 1961)	Chop Chop Windy Answer
Daryaba (IRE) (b.f. 1996)		Vayrann (br 1978)	Brigadier Gerard Val Divine
	Darata (IRE) (b 1988)	Darazina (b 1979)	Labus Djebellina

Although her career stretched to only five races, the smallish, good-bodied Daryaba proved herself one of the two best three-year-old fillies in Europe in 1999 along with Ramruma. She stayed a mile and a half and acted on good to firm and good to soft ground. *A. de Royer Dupre, France*

DASHARAN (IRE) 6 b.g. Shahrastani (USA) 135 – Delsy (FR) (Abdos 134) [1998 NR 1999 14m May 29] workmanlike gelding: half-brother to numerous winners, notably French classic winners Darshaan (by Shirley Heights) and Darara (by Top Ville): dam 1½m winner: fairly useful handicapper for J. Oxx in Ireland in 1997: well beaten only Flat run since: should stay further than 1¾m: acts on good to soft going: successful over hurdles in June/July. *Ian Williams* –

DASHIBA 3 ch.f. Dashing Blade 117 – Alsiba 68 (Northfields (USA)) [1998 90: 5.2m³ 7s³ 7.1d⁴ 6m³ 6f 6d³ 7m² 1999 6m³ 7m² 7m² 8.3g³ 9.9f 10g* 9m* 10s Oct 2] **102**

big, good-topped filly: has a quick, fluent action: useful performer: won maiden at Sandown and £14,800 handicap at Goodwood (improved form, by 3½ lengths from Be Thankfull) in August: wintry and bandaged behind, in rear in Group 2 at Newmarket final start: will prove best up to 1¼m: acts on firm and soft going: sometimes hangs: has flashed tail and looked a weak finisher, but did nothing wrong under well-judged rides from K. Fallon for both successes. *D. R. C. Elsworth*

DASHING 3 b.g. Suave Dancer (USA) 136 – Pearly River 72 (Elegant Air 119) [1998 –: a8g 1999 10.2s a9.4g⁴ 10.2g 10.2m Jul 5] little form, including in claimers: dead. *L. G. Cottrell* —

DASHING BLUE 6 ch.g. Dashing Blade 117 – Blubella 86 (Balidar 133) [1998 114: 6d⁵ 5d 6g⁴ 5m 5.1m³ 5g 6m⁵ 5f³ 5d³ 5.2g 5g³ 1999 6g 5g² 5m* 5m³ 5.1m⁴ 5f³ 5g⁵ 5m³ 5.2d⁶ 5d 5d Oct 9] big, good-bodied gelding: smart performer: easily landed odds in minor event at Sandown in June: good third in King George Stakes at Goodwood (2½ lengths behind Rudi's Pet) on fifth start and in listed race at Doncaster (2 short heads behind Flanders): also ran well when fifth in Nunthorpe Stakes at York (had little luck in running when 4½ lengths behind Stravinsky) in between: barely stays 6f: acts on firm and good to soft going: has been bandaged off-hind: sometimes slowly away: held up, and best coming off strong pace. *I. A. Balding* — 112

DASHING CHIEF (IRE) 4 b.g. Darshaan 133 – Calaloo Sioux (USA) 100 (Our Native (USA)) [1998 101: 12s³ 11.5m³ 12m 11.9m 10.1m⁵ 1999 10m 8.5g³ 8.1m⁶ 10s⁵ Aug 9] compact gelding: useful performer at best at 3 yrs: well beaten over hurdles for R. Frost, and only fair form on return to Flat: stays 11.5f: acts on good to firm ground (probably on soft): has worn crossed noseband. *W. J. Musson* — 76

DASHING DENISE 2 b.f. (Apr 18) Noble Patriarch 115 – Maid O'Cannie 72 (Efisio 120) [1999 5v⁵ 5d Apr 17] 1,100Y: first foal: dam 6f winner: well held in maiden and claimer: subsequently won in Belgium. *M. W. Easterby* — ?

DASHING DUKE (IRE) 2 b.c. (Feb 18) Mujadil (USA) 119 – Alzeam (IRE) 61 (Alzao (USA) 117) [1999 6f* Sep 2] 28,000F, 72,000Y: rangy, shade unfurnished colt: has plenty of scope: has a short, scratchy action: second foal: half-brother to a winner in Italy by Case Law: dam, lightly-raced maiden, from family of Flame of Tara, Salsabil and Marju: 11/10, but unimpressive to post and green, won 5-runner minor event at York by 1½ lengths from Aretino, given plenty of time to find stride before leading over 1f out: held several big-race entries, but not seen again: will stay 7f, probably 1m: should make a useful performer at least. *J. Noseda* — 89 p

DASHING INVADER (USA) 6 ch.g. Pirate Army (USA) 118 – Cherie's Hope (USA) (Flying Paster (USA)) [1998 NR 1999 a13g Mar 2] heavy-topped gelding: had a powerful, round action: modest handicapper on all-weather in 1997, poor on turf: well beaten only start in 1999: stayed 2m: acted on good to firm and good to soft ground: blinkered: often front runner: dead. *D. L. Williams* —

DATE 3 b.c. Cadeaux Genereux 131 – Faribole (IRE) 106 (Esprit du Nord (USA) 126) [1998 80: 7f³ 1999 7g* 8d² 8.1m* May 29] small, good-bodied colt: has a long, — 105

Tote Credit Club Silver Bowl (Handicap), Haydock—Date has poached a decisive advantage as Riverblue (third right) and Swallow Flight (No.8) try to close the gap; Hoh Steamer (rail) is fourth

round action: made into useful performer: successful in maiden at Newmarket in April and 17-runner valuable handicap at Haydock (by length from Riverblue, poaching a decisive advantage 2f out) in May: stays 1m: acts on good to firm going: sent to UAE. *E. A. L. Dunlop*

DATURA 2 b.f. (Jan 22) Darshaan 133 – Realize 84 (Al Nasr (FR) 126) [1999 6d 6g³ 7.5g² 7d⁴ 7s a8g Nov 16] well-made filly: second foal: dam, 7f (at 2 yrs)/1m winner, half-sister to useful middle-distance filly Shemozzle: fair form when placed in maidens at Leicester and Beverley, making running: well below best final 3 starts: should stay at least 1¼m. *J. H. M. Gosden*   **74**

DAUNTED (IRE) 3 b.g. Priolo (USA) 127 – Dauntess (Formidable (USA) 125) [1998 61, a82: 6m 7d 5g 7s 8d² a8g* a7g³ a8.5g² a8f* 1999 a8g* a7f² a10g² a12g³ 8.3m⁵ 9m a8g³ 9.9g a7g³ a8.5g⁴ 8.5m⁵ 8.1s 10g⁶ 8d⁴ 10d a10g Dec 8] quite good-topped gelding: fairly useful on all-weather, fair on turf: won claimer at Lingfield in January: generally creditable efforts after: races mainly around 1m (may prove best short of 1½m): acts on all-weather, good to soft and good to firm going: blinkered: sometimes slowly away. *G. L. Moore*   **75** **a87**

DAUNTING (IRE) 4 br.f. Formidable (USA) 125 – Durun 89 (Run The Gantlet (USA)) [1998 –: 8.3g 10m 10m 11.5g 10.4g 1999 a12g Jul 7] little form. *G. L. Moore*   **–**

DAUNTING LADY (IRE) 4 b.f. Mujadil (USA) 119 – Dauntess (Formidable (USA) 125) [1998 107: 7.3s* 8g⁶ 7m 8d 6.8s 6m 7d 6s 1999 7g⁶ 7m³ 7g 6d³ 6.8g a6g* a8g² a6g⁵ a8.8g² a5.5g* Nov 4] lengthy, angular filly: useful performer: left R. Hannon after third start: won minor event at Jagersro in August and handicap at Ovrevoll in November: stays 8.8f: acts on good to firm going, soft and dirt: blinkered (below form) final start in 1998. *W. Neuroth, Norway*   **101**

DAUPHIN (IRE) 6 b. or br.g. Astronef 116 – Va Toujours 109 (Alzao (USA) 117) [1998 44: 14.1s 11.5m 11.6m⁶ 10m⁴ 11.6m³ᵈⁱˢ 16.4m 12.1d 14.1s 11.5d 1999 a11g Jan 2] workmanlike gelding: poor handicapper: well beaten only outing in 1999: stays 1½m: acts on any going: flashes tail and carries head high. *H. S. Howe*   **–**

DAVID 3 ch.g. Risk Me (FR) 127 – Capriati (USA) 83 (Diesis 133) [1998 63, a54: a5g⁵ a5g³ 6g* 6.1d⁴ 6m 8s a6g a7g² 1999 a8f² a7g⁵ a5g Mar 3] only poor performer in 1999: stays 7f: headstrong: has given trouble at stalls and hung: sold 900 gns in May, sent to Spain. *Miss Gay Kelleway*   **a46**

DAVIS ROCK 5 ch.m. Rock City 120 – Sunny Davis (USA) 71 (Alydar (USA)) [1998 63, a71: a7g* a7g³ a7g³ a7g² a7g² 7s² 7m 6d 6.9d 7d 7d a7g* a6g 1999 a7g 6m² 6.8m⁶ 7f² 7g a7g³ 7s⁵ 8.2s* a8.5g⁵ a8g⁵ Dec 13] modest performer: won 17-runner handicap at Nottingham in November: best at 7f/1m: acts on firm ground, soft and all-weather. *W. R. Muir*   **54** **a60**

DAWN 2 b.f. (Feb 28) Owington 123 – Realisatrice (USA) (Raja Baba (USA)) [1999 5g⁶ 5m³ 6m⁴ Jun 30] small, lengthy filly: eighth foal: half-sister to 3-y-o Hibaat and French 1992 2-y-o 5f winner Infant Protege (by Theatrical): dam, French maiden, daughter of high-class sprinter Realty and half-sister to dam of 1000 Guineas winner Ravinella: fair form in maidens in first half of year: stays 6f: sold 800 gns in November. *N. A. Graham*   **65**

DAWN ALARM 2 b.f. (Feb 9) Warning 136 – Throw Away Line (USA) (Assert 134) [1999 5m 7m 7d Oct 11] 60,000Y: sister to a winner in USA and half-sister to 3 winners abroad, including useful French winner up to 1½m Rebuff (by Kris): dam, minor winner at 4 yrs in USA, half-sister to champion US filly Go For Wand: well beaten in maidens, trained by P. Chapple-Hyam first 2 starts: blinkered final outing. *A. G. Foster*   **47**

DAWN PATROL 4 ch.f. Weldnaas (USA) 112 – Silverdale Rose (Nomination 125) [1998 52: 5d⁵ 6d 5g² 5s* 6g⁵ 6g 1999 6.1s 5d Apr 29] leggy filly: modest handicapper at 3 yrs: stumbled and unseated rider at start on reappearance, then slowly away when tailed off only other run in 1999: stays 6f: acts on soft going and on good to firm. *K. W. Hogg, Isle of Man*   **–**

DAWN'S DANCER (IRE) 2 b.f. (Feb 22) Petardia 113 – Cree's Figurine 63 (Creetown 123) [1999 5f³ 5m⁴ 5.3f² Jul 12] 9,500Y: quite attractive filly: sister to 3-y-o Langans Figurine and half-sister to 2 winners, including useful sprinter Royale   **64**

Figurine (by Dominion Royale): dam, 2-y-o 5f winner, from family of Persian Heights: modest form in minor event and maidens: should stay 6f. *G. C. H. Chung*

DAWN TREADER (USA)   4 gr.g. El Prado (IRE) 119 – Marie de La Ferte   – (Amber Rama (USA) 133) [1998 –: 9.7v 11.6g 10m² a11g 10s⁶ 1999 a12g⁵ a13g⁶ a14.8g Jan 27] poor maiden: little form since 2 yrs: blinkered second start. *J. S. Moore*

DAY-BOY   3 b.g. Prince Sabo 123 – Lady Day (FR) (Lightning (FR) 129) [1998   **76** 79: 6g* 6m⁴ 6s 1999 7d 8f⁴ 8d 7.1g⁴ 7.1m³ 7d Sep 17] fair performer: stays 7f: best efforts on good ground or firmer: sold 12,000 gns in October. *Denys Smith*

DAY JOURNEY (USA)   2 b.c. (Feb 13) Dayjur (USA) 137 – Dayflower (USA)   **98** 108 (Majestic Light (USA)) [1999 6m² 6m 6m* 6d* 6g⁴ Aug 18] sturdy, lengthy colt with a powerful, rounded action: second foal: dam, 7f (at 2 yrs) and 1¼m winner, from family of Woodman: useful performer: made all when winning minor events at Newmarket and Haydock in the summer: ridden more patiently when good fourth of 10 to Mull of Kintyre in Gimcrack Stakes at York final start: should stay 7f: yet to race on extremes of going. *E. A. L. Dunlop*

DAYLAMI (IRE)   5 gr.h. Doyoun 124 – Daltawa (IRE) (Miswaki (USA) 124)   **138** [1998 126: 10m* 10d³ 10g* 12m⁴ 11m* 10g³ 1999 a10f⁵ 10.5g² 12d* 12m* 10d* 12v 12g* Nov 6]

In Daylami, the inaugural Emirates World Series Racing Championship found a horse worthy of its ambition. The concept of a world champion in racing, which had seemed decidedly grandiose, not to say remote, when the series was announced, does not now seem so unrealistic. Daylami ran on three continents and in five different countries in 1999, taking part in four World Series races and winning three of them. He left one of the season's most striking images with the unrestrained zest with which he sprinted clear in the King George VI And Queen Elizabeth Stakes at Ascot—then he did it again in the Irish Champion Stakes and the Breeders' Cup Turf.

Last year's essay on Daylami discussed the strength of the latest Godolphin team and asked the question 'What odds Godolphin having the first "World Champion"?' If odds were available, those who snapped them up would have been delighted at the Maktoum family's efforts, as, in addition to the best that they could muster from Europe, the latest Godolphin team was supplemented by arrivals from Argentina and the United States. Godolphin have now bought horses from Khalid Abdulla, Messrs Sangster, Magnier and Tabor, Fahd Salman, Jean-Luc Lagardere and Allen Paulson. As the millennium ended, horses to race in the royal blue appeared to dominate Maktoum thinking.

Vodafone Coronation Cup, Epsom—Daylami triumphs in a steadily-run race,
beating Royal Anthem, Dream Well (white cap), the other grey Silver Patriarch and Borgia

Daylami himself had been a most conspicuous acquisition after the 1997 season, from the Aga Khan. In his colours, Daylami had won the Poule d'Essai des Poulains and registered three other Group 1 placings over a mile as a three-year-old. At four he added victories in the Tattersalls Gold Cup, the Eclipse and the Man o'War Stakes, along with fourth place in the King George and third in the Champion Stakes. This was hardly a record to cavil at, but Daylami was one of half a dozen horses, at the very least, in his stable who might conceivably have emerged as challengers for the World Series title. His is no ordinary stable, of course, but Daylami arguably lacked a certain amount of 'star quality'. Consistency and willingness were his hallmarks, admirable in themselves but not nearly enough to make a world champion. In *Racehorses of 1998*, Daylami was rated 126, joint-fourth best among the European older horses, with eight from that season's batch of three-year-olds ahead of him as well. Over the winter, High-Rise, Saratoga Springs, Xaar, Diktat, Limpid, Lend A Hand, Mutamam and Muhtathir all took up the Godolphin banner, under which high-class performers already serving included Intikhab, Kayf Tara, Cape Verdi, City Honours, Nedawi, Sea Wave, Almutawakel, Central Park, Cape Cross and Kahal.

In the Dubai World Cup at Nad Al Sheba in March, Saeed bin Suroor fielded four of the eight runners; from a choice of Daylami, High-Rise, Almuta-wakel (racing in Sheikh Hamdan's colours) and Central Park, stable-jockey Dettori took the ride on High-Rise. He got a remote and receding view of the finish. Daylami's jockey John Velazquez had looked set for a similar fate when the grey was a detached last on the turn into the straight, partly due to trouble in running, but Daylami stayed on gamely on the alien surface to finish fifth, beaten four and a quarter lengths behind the winner Almutawakel. Although no-one knew it at the time, this turned out to be the first leg of the World Series Championship. The nine-race series had been due to get under way with the King George in July and end with the Dubai World Cup in March 2000, but this scheme was fine-tuned shortly before the King George so that the competition would now bear some resemblance to a conventional calendar season and end with the Hong Kong Cup in December. Points for the Dubai World Cup were therefore awarded retrospectively. The Emirates World Series, framed around the structure of the world's top middle-distance races, required that a horse would necessarily have to travel outside its own country to win the champion-ship and thereby earn a bonus of 1,000,000 dollars. In between Dubai and Hong Kong, the series took in top events in Britain (for the King George), Ireland (Irish Champion Stakes), Canada (Canadian International), Australia (Cox Plate), the United States (Breeders' Cup Classic and Breeders' Cup Turf) and Japan (Japan Cup).

Inevitably, given the scope of such a championship, there were going to be criticisms of its format. Races on turf outnumber those on dirt by seven to two; sprinters, milers and stayers are not catered for at all and Australasian connections could no doubt point to the fact that the Cox Plate is the only contest in the Series in their part of the world. The intended addition of the Prix de l'Arc de Triomphe, Grosser Preis von Baden and Arlington Million to the

King George VI And Queen Elizabeth Diamond Stakes, Ascot—
Daylami beats his stable-mate Nedawi in tremendous style with Fruits of Love staying on well in third

Series in 2000 only serves to reinforce the image of essentially a northern hemisphere middle-distance turf championship. The organisers could also be criticised for taking the easy option when it came to the issue of medication, deciding that each country's local rules should apply to the individual races rather than adopting a blanket drug-free policy. Few will be surprised to see a Godolphin horse top of the Series rankings but connections with considerably fewer resources deserve credit for taking up foreign challenges, notably those concerned with Fruits of Love and the Hong Kong-trained Indigenous. Encouraging the best horses to be campaigned against each other worldwide is the most important benefit the Series has brought. The individual races, aided by the enhanced competition for them which the world series should bring, remain more important than the rankings which cannot, in all honesty, fairly represent the relative merits of the horses concerned, and more important also than conferring the title of 'world champion'.

Quite how many people were keeping count in the series was open to question. Not that many one suspects, given the complete lack of comment provoked by that change in the rules once the competition had already begun. Saeed bin Suroor now enjoyed a comfortable lead in the trainers' prize, while there were also points on offer for the owners and jockeys. The Godolphin team's willingness to travel and their commitment to the series was never in any question. The enthusiasm of others would be tested first in the King George VI and Queen Elizabeth Diamond Stakes. For Godolphin, who were going for a third consecutive King George victory, Daylami was joined by Nedawi. Dettori was Daylami's partner this time, as he had been earlier in the season in both the Tattersalls Gold Cup at the Curragh and the Coronation Cup at Epsom. Henry Cecil and Kieren Fallon had got the better of a ring-rusty Daylami at the Curragh, with Shiva, and were widely expected to do so again at Epsom where they were responsible for the 2/1 favourite Royal Anthem, firing a first salvo in a campaign that many expected would result in his being crowned Britain's top older horse over middle distances. That Royal Anthem failed to enhance his claims at this first attempt was widely attributed to a masterful piece of planning by Godolphin. Daylami, the 9/2 co-third-favourite whose only previous run at the trip had been when three lengths fourth to Swain in the 1998 King George, was thought by some to be more vulnerable at a mile and a half than at a mile and a quarter, while the opposite appeared true of most of the non-Godolphin contenders, in betting order Royal Anthem, Dream Well, Silver Patriarch, Fruits of Love and Borgia. The one remaining runner played what was perceived as a key role at the time: Godolphin second-string Central Park set the pace but was in no hurry about it. The Coronation Cup was not a test of stamina. Royal Anthem went on early in the straight, with Daylami soon emerging as his nearest pursuer and finally wearing him down in the last half furlong to win by three quarters of a length; Dream Well and Silver Patriarch finished in fairly close attendance, never nearer.

The connections of Silver Patriarch and Fruits of Love took Daylami on again in the King George, sent off at 10/1 and 4/1 respectively, Fruits of Love looking a rather stronger contender now that he had himself beaten Royal Anthem in the Hardwicke Stakes at Royal Ascot; Royal Anthem, whose connections preferred the revised opinion that he would prove best at a mile and a quarter, was put aside for the International at York. Daylami was at 3/1 and Nedawi 8/1, with the only three-year-olds, the Derby first and second Oath and Daliapour, at 9/4 and 8/1. Like the three-year-olds, challengers from abroad were very thin on the ground. Eye-catchingly, there was the first Hong Kong-trained runner in Britain, Ivan Allan's six-year-old Indigenous, the racehorse formerly known (in Ireland) as Qualtron. The 1998 International Vase had been among his twelve victories in Hong Kong, and his career earnings thus far apparently totalled £2,000,219, but at Ascot his trainer stated that 'If he's back to his best, I'd say he has a place chance. If he's not, then he'll have problems.' He started at 20/1. To observers inclined to wariness over a horse escorted

by two handlers in the parade ring, it cannot have looked a good sign that Indigenous, sweating profusely, required four! Less conspicuously, the 1998 Derby fourth and St Leger third Sunshine Street had been sent from Ireland. He started at 25/1, and that was the extent of the foreign challenge. World Series or no World Series, there is an obvious gulf in the attractiveness of the Dubai World Cup, the world's richest race, and the King George, which ranked forty-first.

At the time, it was considered a disappointing turnout for the King George, Ramruma and Montjeu being notable absentees. Nevertheless the 1999 King George produced a vintage performance. Much of the race was conducted in a two by two—Daliapour and Nedawi ahead of Daylami and Oath, Silver Patriarch and Indigenous, Sunshine Street and Fruits of Love—but two furlongs out was where Daylami first revealed that he possessed a touch of brilliance. Forfeiting a couple of lengths as he manoeuvred for a run off the rails on the final turn, at which point, strange to relate, Silver Patriarch overtook him, Daylami soon got back on an even keel and found his stride as the three-year-olds weakened; shooting past Nedawi, Daylami passed the furlong marker with a lead of three lengths, which he extended with the utmost enthusiasm to five at the line. Fruits of Love kept on for third, beaten another half length, with a further two and a half back to Silver Patriarch in fourth, Sunshine Street fifth and the three-year-olds in rear. Daylami's spectacular performance was one of those which demands to be put in a wider context. Generous won the King George by seven lengths; Mill Reef, Dahlia and St Jovite by six. In terms of form, only Generous and St Jovite among King George winners can be compared to Daylami in the 'nineties. Before that, Daylami is worth a higher annual rating than all winners of the race except Reference Point, Dancing Brave, Shergar, Brigadier Gerard, Mill Reef, Nijinsky and Ribot. In short, in winning as he did, Daylami joined a list of racing greats. He also proved beyond doubt that he stayed a mile and a half!

1999 was an unusual but satisfying season for having several deeply impressive wide-margin wins in the top races. Though few would have believed it after the King George, there was once again a very real possibility that Daylami was not the best middle-distance horse in Britain after Royal Anthem had registered a record eight-length triumph in the International. In the ESAT Digifone Champion Stakes over a mile and a quarter on rain-softened ground at Leopardstown in September, Daylami was sent off at 6/4 with Royal Anthem 11/8. Some still had faith in Dream Well at 7/2, but Sunspangled, Dazzling Park, Lord of Men (the Godolphin pacemaker) and Sunshine Street seemed accurately assessed at 33/1 or longer. Tantalisingly, Montjeu had been declared to run, but was always far more likely to take his place in the Prix Niel. However, there was still Daylami and Royal Anthem. Something nearly always contrives to spoil these keenly anticipated 'showdowns', and did so again here, but this was nevertheless one of the races of the season. Harried up front by Lord of Men for much of the way, Royal Anthem retained the lead entering the

280

straight but Daylami, following closely, slipped through on the inside and joined him. A convivial interlude followed in which Dettori twice turned and spoke to Gary Stevens on Royal Anthem. 'I asked Gary how much he had left. I got no reply,' said Dettori afterwards. Well perhaps he did get a reply but just couldn't hear it, because when Dettori then moved low into the saddle and started pushing, Daylami almost immediately put daylight between himself and the rest; there was no-one for Dettori to chat with, or even within hailing distance, when the jockey turned round again a hundred yards from home, and he made the rest of his way to the post in celebration, having to do nothing from the saddle except raise his right arm and point his forefinger in a victorious salute. Daylami won by an incredible nine lengths, eased close home. It goes almost without saying that this was one of the best performances seen in the Irish Champion in its fifteen-year history. Daylami did not have to improve on the form he showed in the King George, but, for a top race, the manner of his win, particularly considering the very short straight at Leopardstown, was singularly dominant. For whatever reason, and ultra-efficient pacemaking by the Godolphin team may have been one, the rain-softened ground another, Royal Anthem was a big disappointment. He was back in fifth, with Dazzling Park, Dream Well and Sunshine Street ahead of him among the also-rans. Dettori reflected that 'We've met Royal Anthem three times and the score is 2-1 for Daylami. I'm sure we'll meet again.' Perhaps Royal Anthem's connections had other ideas, because he was transferred to the United States.

As befits Europe's top race and Godolphin's top horse, Daylami was aimed at the Prix de l'Arc de Triomphe. On the day it was only Sheikh Mohammed's refusal to duck the challenge which resulted in his taking part. Heavy rain made conditions exceptionally testing, and most in the Godolphin team believed that Daylami's chance had probably been washed away. On the final turn, the fears were confirmed and the one-time Arc favourite was put under pressure for only a furlong or so before Dettori very wisely decided that further efforts were pointless. The target now was the Breeders' Cup Turf, and, in handling his mount so tenderly at Longchamp, Dettori arguably gave Daylami as good a ride in defeat as any that he gave him in 1999's stunning victories.

The proof came when Daylami stepped out at Gulfstream Park four weeks later. In years to come, there is a danger that his triumph here will be

Breeders' Cup Turf, Gulfstream—Daylami's crowning moment as he becomes the first European-trained winner of a Breeders' Cup race in Florida with a third victory over Royal Anthem; the previous year's first and second Buck's Boy (rail) and Yagli follow them home

regarded as something of a formality, the year's outstanding racehorse simply taking a last well-earned victory bow before retirement. The truth is very different, as hinted at by the fact that, before 1999, thirty-two European horses had taken part in two previous stagings of the Breeders' Cup at Gulfstream and none had won. Another thirteen chanced their arm unsuccessfully on November 6th before the Turf, Docksider, Lend A Hand, Zomaradah and Mull of Kintyre making the frame. Remember also that, in addition to only one previous placing at Gulfstream, thanks to Most Welcome in 1989, victories for British-based runners in the entire Breeders' Cup series could still be counted on the fingers of one hand. Daylami was made 16/10 favourite to emulate Pebbles (Turf, 1985), Sheikh Albadou (Sprint, 1991) Barathea (Mile, 1994) and Pilsudski (Turf, 1996). Prices available with the major bookmakers at home that morning were a good deal longer, ranging from 5/2 to 7/2. Easily Daylami's most dangerous rivals were Man o'War and Turf Classic winner Val's Prince (52/10), 1998 Breeders' Cup Turf winner Buck's Boy (64/10), multiple Grade 1 winner Yagli (73/10) and, trained now by Bill Mott, Royal Anthem (87/10) again. Among the outsiders, Dream Well, Courteous and First Magnitude completed the European challenge, with other familiar names in Dark Moondancer and Fahris now stabled in the US. Commencing the turn for home, about three furlongs out, pacesetter Buck's Boy was still in front from a weakening Courteous, with Royal Anthem soon to go second and Daylami and Yagli moving into the chase in fourth and fifth. Buck's Boy was still there entering the straight, but on the outside Royal Anthem was just about to tackle him and Daylami, in turn, was about to tackle Royal Anthem. Royal Anthem was playing his part this time, but Daylami quickly took his measure, and soon it was just a question of 'by how far ?'. The answer on this occasion was by two and a half lengths, as Daylami took over about a furlong out and raced clear, increasing his superiority with every stride at the finish.

Godolphin's "Daylami"

The Breeders' Cup Turf was Daylami's seventh Group or Grade 1 win, taking him level with Acatenango and Irish River, two behind Triptych and three behind Miesque. In the Emirates World Series, it took Daylami's points tally to 38 and an unassailable lead. Almutawakel eventually finished second on 14, with Saeed bin Suroor, Frankie Dettori and Godolphin duly taking their prizes as leading trainer, jockey and owner.

By the time, therefore, that the last two legs of the World Series were run in Japan and Hong Kong, Daylami was resting on his laurels back at his birthplace, the Aga Khan's Gilltown Stud in Ireland. His sire Doyoun meanwhile had just completed his first covering season at the Turkish Jockey Club National Stud at Izmit. Doyoun had the 1993 National Stakes winner in Manntari, while other pattern successes came via Dalara, Adaiyka and Takarian, but as so often seems to be the case with stallions, the year after his export gave Doyoun his best results. Without Daylami, the smart three-year-olds Kalanisi and Manndar would be considered two of his best colts, while he also had promising two-year-olds in Autonomy and Manntari's brother Fast Track. In marked contrast to that of her son, the racecourse career of Daylami's dam Daltawa ended in April as a three-year-old, with second place in the ten and a half furlong Prix Penelope. Most of the celebrities in her family are somewhat removed, her grandam Denia being a half-sister to St James's Palace runner-up Raykour and three-parts sister to Prix de Diane winner Crepellana. Daltawa's second foal Daymarti (by Caerleon) was second in the 1998 Lupin and belatedly got off the mark as a four-year-old in the latest season when he also won a listed race in the Provinces. Her third is the 1999 two-year-old Daltabad (by Priolo) and he is followed by a sister to Daylami.

		Mill Reef	Never Bend
	Doyoun	(b 1968)	Milan Mill
	(b 1985)	Dumka	Kashmir II
Daylami (IRE)		(br 1971)	Faizebad
(gr.h. 1994)		Miswaki	Mr Prospector
	Daltawa (IRE)	(ch 1978)	Hopespringseternal
	(gr 1989)	Damana	Crystal Palace
		(gr 1981)	Denia

A well-made horse with a powerful, round action, Daylami will be covering at a fee of IR £20,000. A classic winner over a mile, it was over middle distances as a five-year-old that he really flourished. He acquitted himself with credit on soft ground as a two-year-old and on the fast dirt track at Nad Al Sheba, but went on to record his three best efforts on good to firm, good to soft and good. Even more striking than his versatility were his toughness, consistency, enthusiasm and, ultimately, his quality. Instead of the Emirates World Series finding a horse worthy of it, it is much nearer the truth to say that Daylami found a title which was worthy of him. Whether this series can regularly come up with truly international champions of similar credibility remains to be seen, but Daylami was a racehorse who deserved almost any plaudit. *Saeed bin Suroor*

DAYLIGHT IN DUBAI (USA) 5 ch.h. Twilight Agenda (USA) 126 – Lady **103** Godolphin (USA) (Son Ange (USA)) [1998 8d* 10d⁴ 10m 10s 1999 7g 5d 7m⁵ 6m 6m* 7d⁶ 7m 6m 7g Aug 28] tall, useful-looking horse: fluent mover: useful performer: trained at 2 yrs by P. Chapple-Hyam (won Railway Stakes at the Curragh), at 3 yrs by J. Noseda in USA and at 4 yrs by Mme C. Head in France: won minor event at Yarmouth in June: not discredited next 2 starts: effective at 6f, probably at 1¼m: acts on firm ground and good to soft: blinkered final outing: has been bandaged in front: sold 28,000 gns in October. *D. Nicholls*

DAYNABEE 4 b.f. Common Grounds 118 – Don't Wary (FR) (Lomond (USA) **55** 128) [1998 60, a55: 6.1s 6d 6d 6d 6m² 6g² 7m⁵ 6m* 6m⁵ 7m⁶ 6.1m a7g⁶ a7g⁵ a7g³ 1999 5d 5.7g 6m 6m⁶ 6m³ 6m 7s² 7m 6.1m a7g 5.2s a7g⁵ a7g⁴ a7g² a6g⁵ a6g² Dec 27] smallish, good-quartered filly: unimpressive mover: modest handicapper: effective at 6f/7f: acts on good to firm going, soft and all-weather: none too consistent. *A. J. McNae*

DAYRAVEN   3 ch.g. Midyan (USA) 124 – Aunt Judy (Great Nephew 126) [1998 **45** –: 8s 7d 7v 1999 10m 11.6m 12d 10m 10f⁶ Jul 12] close-coupled gelding: has a quick action: poor maiden: visored 4 of last 5 starts. *I. A. Balding*

DAYS OF GRACE   4 gr.f. Wolfhound (USA) 126 – Inshirah (USA) 90 (Caro **63** 133) [1998 58: 6g 5.3g⁵ 5m⁴ 6d 1999 5s³ 5m 5m 6m³ 5g⁴ 5g 5.7f³ 6s⁴ a6g* 6g³ **a69** a6g* a7g² a6g⁴ Dec 13] lengthy filly: fair handicapper: returned to 2-y-o form when winning at Southwell in September and Wolverhampton in October: stays 7f: acts on firm and soft going and fibresand: tends to carry head high. *L. Montague Hall*

DAYS OF THUNDER   11 ch.g. Vaigly Great 127 – Silent Prayer 58 (Queen's **–** Hussar 124) [1998 NR 1999 10.5m Aug 30] sturdy gelding: poor maiden in 1995: winning hurdler/chaser, lost his form and well beaten on return to Flat. *Mrs P. Ford*

DAY STAR   3 b.f. Dayjur (USA) 137 – Krisalya 98 (Kris 135) [1998 58p: 7d 1999 **77** 5d 6d⁴ 6.1g 6g* 6d Nov 4] smallish, sturdy filly: fair performer: best effort when winning 21-runner handicap at Redcar in October, making virtually all: should stay 7f, at least when conditions aren't testing: raced only on good/good to soft going: refused to enter stalls on intended reappearance. *C. F. Wall*

DAYTIME   3 b.c. Danehill (USA) 126 – Zenith 88 (Shirley Heights 130) [1998 –: **94** 7m 1999 8s² 7.1d² 8.3m² 7.1g* 7f 8.5f² 9f² 9f* 9f* 9f⁴ Dec 27] close-coupled colt: fairly useful performer: won handicap at Sandown in July: left R. Hannon after next start and successful in allowances races at Santa Anita and Hollywood in November/ December: stays 9f: acts on firm going. *Kathy Walsh, USA*

DAZILYN LADY (USA)   4 ch.f. Zilzal (USA) 137 – Jetbeeah (IRE) 95 (Lomond **105** (USA) 128) [1998 100: 8v² 8g⁶ 8g 7g² 7.9f 8d⁶ 8s² 8s⁴ 8s³ 7v² 1999 8m 8d⁵ 7m⁴ 7.1m 7d⁴ 7g Oct 16] good-topped filly: has a round action: useful performer: sweating on return from 4-month break, best effort when fourth to Family Man in rated stakes at Newmarket on penultimate start: effective at 7f/1m: seems unsuited by firm going, acts on any other: tends to get on toes: sold 42,000 gns in December to join J. Hammond in France. *P. W. Harris*

DAZZLING PARK (IRE)   3 br.f. Warning 136 – Park Express 123 (Ahonoora **116** 122) [1998 100: 8d* 7s² 8s 1999 8g⁴ 8g³ 10s³ 9g* 8m* 10d² 9.3v⁶ 10m Dec 12] rather sparely-made filly: good walker: half-sister to 3 winners, including a stakes winner in Japan by Green Desert and French winner up to 1m Tycoon King (by Last Tycoon): dam won Phoenix Park Champion Stakes: smart performer: successful in maiden at the Curragh at 2 yrs: creditable third to Hula Angel in Irish 1000 Guineas at the Curragh before winning listed race at Cork in August and Matron Stakes at the Curragh (by 5½ lengths from Carambola) in September: ran well when 9 lengths second of 7 to Daylami in Champion Stakes at Leopardstown next time: well held in Hong Kong Cup at Sha Tin final outing: stays 1¼m: acts on soft going and on good to firm, below par on heavy. *J. S. Bolger, Ireland*

DAZZLING QUINTET   3 ch.f. Superlative 118 – Miss Display 47 (Touch Paper **59 ?** 113) [1998 73: 5d 5m 5g 5g⁴ 5g* 6.1g³ 5m⁴ 5m³ 5s⁵ 1999 5.1m 5.3f 6m 5m 6.1m 6s² 5.2s Oct 22] sturdy filly: modest performer: form in 1999 only when second of 17 in claimer at Pontefract: barely stays 6f: acts on good to firm going, probably on soft: races prominently/leads. *C. Smith*

DAZZLING STONE   5 b.g. Mujtahid (USA) 118 – Lady In Green (Shareef **41** Dancer (USA) 135) [1998 49: 5g⁵ 6g³ 7d⁶ 5m² 6d⁴ 1999 a6g³ a7g 6g 7.1m 6.9m⁵ Jul **a44** 16] poor maiden: stays 7f: acts on good to firm going, good to soft and fibresand: visored final start. *C. W. Fairhurst*

DEAD AIM (IRE)   5 b.g. Sadler's Wells (USA) 132 – Dead Certain 123§ (Absalom **–** 128) [1998 81: 12s 12d³ 12f³ 13.3g² 14.8f 12.4g 10.5m 10m 1999 12m Jul 2] strong, lengthy gelding: fairly useful handicapper at best: has lost his form: stays 13f: acts on firm and soft going: visored final 4-y-o start/tongue tied only run of 1999. *Mrs J. Brown*

DEADLY NIGHTSHADE (IRE)   3 b.f. Night Shift (USA) – Dead Certain 123§ **105 p** (Absalom 128) [1998 105p: 5.1m* 6m* 5s² 1999 5m 6d Oct 15] strong, good-quartered filly: useful performer, lightly raced: managed just 2 runs in 1999 but shaped as if retaining all her ability, in King's Stand Stakes at Royal Ascot on first occasion, then doing best work at finish when seventh of 20 to Gaelic Storm in listed race at Newmarket when next seen out: likely to be best at 5f/6f: acts on good to firm and soft ground: held up: still has potential if all remains well. *D. R. C. Elsworth*

DEAL FAIR 3 b.c. Grand Lodge (USA) 125 – Darshay (FR) 87 (Darshaan 133) **101** [1998 9op: 7g³ 8s* 1999 10.2s* 10.4s³ 10d³ 12m Jun 17] good-topped colt: useful performer: won minor event at Bath in April: put up good efforts in listed events at York and Newmarket prior to running poorly in King George V Handicap at Royal Ascot: should stay 1½m: raced mainly on good going or softer (acts on soft): sent to Germany. *H. R. A. Cecil*

DEAR PRUDENCE 3 b.f. Puissance 110 – Coir 'a' Ghaill 38 (Jalmood (USA) – 126) [1998 NR 1999 10s 10v 8.3d Nov 4] fourth foal: dam staying maiden: little form in maidens, though signs of ability at Windsor final start. *J. G. Portman*

DE BALLIOL 3 b.c. Sadler's Wells (USA) 132 – Khalafiya 104 (Darshaan 133) **83 §** [1998 83p: 7s⁶ 8s 1999 10.2s⁶ 10g⁵ 10.1g² 10.1m³ 11.9d⁵ Aug 7] smallish, rather leggy colt: fairly useful maiden: best effort at Epsom third start: should stay 1½m: blinkered final start: has carried head awkwardly and not one to trust: sent to UAE. *B. W. Hills*

DEBBIE'S HOPE 3 ch.f. Be My Chief (USA) 122 – Appleton Heights (Shirley **70 §** Heights 130) [1998 60p: 5d a6g⁵ a6g³ 1999 7m² 8f³ 7g 7f³ 7.6f³ 6d³ 7.6g 7.7d 8s 7d Oct 22] lengthy filly: fair maiden at best: well below form final 4 starts: should stay at least 1m: acts on good to firm and good to soft going, probably on all-weather: has been slowly away: tail flasher: has hung left/found little: sold 4,500 gns in October: none too genuine, and best left alone. *K. Mahdi*

DEBBIE'S WARNING 3 b.c. Warning 136 – Lomond Blossom 98 (Lomond **111 d** (USA) 128) [1998 NR 1999 8d² 8g³ 8m 8f* 7d⁵ 8m 8g⁵ 7m³ 7.3d Sep 19] 10,000Y, 32,000 2-y-o: big, useful-looking colt: half-brother to 3 winners, including Irish 1½m winner Ptarmigan Lodge (by Reference Point) and German 1996 2-y-o 6f winner La Jara (by Selkirk): dam, Irish 2-y-o 6f and 1m winner who probably stayed 1½m, out of half-sister to Le Moss and Levmoss: smart form when third to Compton Admiral in Craven Stakes and seventh to Island Sands in 2000 Guineas, both at Newmarket: nowhere near that level after, making hard work of landing odds in maiden at Kempton in May: last of 8 in listed race at Newbury final start: will probably stay beyond 1m: acts on firm going: wore tongue strap seventh/eighth starts (said to have had breathing problems second occasion): usually bandaged. *K. Mahdi*

DEB'S DELIGHT 4 ch.f. Most Welcome 131 – Adana (FR) (Green Dancer (USA) – 132) [1998 –: 8v 8g 8m⁶ 9.1v 1999 8.3m 10d 8g⁵ 11.9d 9g⁶ Aug 18] tall, workman-like filly: disappointing maiden: bred to stay further than 1m: probably unsuited by heavy going. *D. A. Nolan*

DEB'S SON 2 b.g. (Apr 15) Minster Son 130 – Deb's Ball 70 (Glenstal (USA) **55 ?** 118) [1999 8g⁴ 8.3m⁵ 10s⁴ Oct 4] 7,600Y: second foal: dam winner up to 13f and useful hurdler: appeared to show modest form in maidens first and final starts, remote fourth of 7 at Pontefract final one: will be suited by 1½m+. *D. Moffatt*

DECARCHY (USA) 2 b.c. (Apr 26) Distant View (USA) 126 – Toussaud (USA) **91 p** 120 (El Gran Senor (USA) 136) [1999 7d* Sep 15] third foal: closely related to 4-y-o Chester House and half-brother to US Grade 2 7f winner Honest Lady (by Seattle Slew): dam, 6f/7f winner in Britain, later Grade 1 9f winner in USA: favourite, created very good impression when winning steadily-run 9-runner maiden at Yarmouth by 7 lengths from Infotec, soon handy, leading halfway and running on strongly under no more than hand riding: sure to stay 1m: sure to progress and may well be a smart performer in the making. *H. R. A. Cecil*

DECISION MAID (USA) 2 b.f. (Feb 25) Diesis 133 – Robellino Miss (USA) **81 p** (Robellino (USA) 127) [1999 6.1d⁵ 7v* Oct 25] third foal: half-sister to 3-y-o Chief Rebel and French 1997 2-y-o 7f winner Fille Formidable (by Trempolino): dam, won up to 9f in USA, out of close relative of high-class sprinter Silver Fling: made expected improvement to win 11-runner maiden at Lingfield by 4 lengths from Eljariha, quickening to lead about 2f out (initially tended to wander once in front): should stay 1m: probably a useful filly in the making. *G. Wragg*

Cadogan Silver Salver Handicap, York—
one of five wins during the season for the much improved Dee Pee Tee Cee (right); Tom Dougal is second

DECISIVE ACTION (USA) 4 br.g. Alleged (USA) 138 – Maria Balastiere **83** (USA) (Majestic Light (USA)) [1998 –: 11g 1999 a9.4g² 10m 11.6d* a12g⁵ 11d 16g² 16s Oct 2] angular gelding: fairly useful performer: won claimer at Windsor in June: left P. Cole after next outing: good second in handicap at Tipperary on penultimate outing: stays 2m at least when conditions aren't testing: seems suited by good ground or softer on turf, acts on fibresand. *A. Slattery, Ireland*

DECODED 3 ch.g. Deploy 131 – Golden Panda 77 (Music Boy 124) [1998 54: 7s **–** 8.5m 8.3d⁴ 7.1g⁵ 10s 8d 8d 1999 16.1s Sep 29] close-coupled gelding: modest maiden at 2 yrs: well beaten in handicap, only run of 1999: should stay at least 1½m: tried blinkered/visored (no form). *G. M. Moore*

DEECEEBEE 4 b.g. Rudimentary (USA) 118 – Do Run Run 75 (Commanche **–** Run 133) [1998 –: 9.3d 9s 8m⁶ 12.3m 1999 10d 7m May 29] angular gelding: no form in handicaps since 2 yrs. *J. L. Eyre*

DEE DIAMOND (USA) 2 b.f. (Apr 3) Eagle Eyed (USA) 111 – Noumea (USA) **59** (Plugged Nickle (USA)) [1999 7.5g⁴ 8.1s Sep 25] $52,000F, IR 55,000Y: quite good-topped filly: has scope: third foal: half-sister to a winner in USA by Allen's Prospect: dam, won up to 9f in USA, half-sister to smart US Grade 1 8.5f and 1¼m winner Urbane, from family of Lyphard: in need of race, fourth of 8 to Via Camp in Beverley maiden: well beaten on soft going only subsequent outing: will stay 1¼m. *Andrew Turnell*

DEEP BLUE 2 b.c. (Jan 15) Lake Coniston (IRE) 131 – Billie Blue 63 (Ballad **77** Rock 122) [1999 5g⁵ 5m³ 5s² 5.1g² 5g Sep 15] well-made colt: half-brother to several winners, including 4-y-o Bobbydazzle and 6-y-o Tumbleweed Ridge: dam second over 7f on only start: fair maiden: beaten favourite last 3 outings, well below form at Beverley (after 3-month absence) on final one: should stay 6f. *Dr J. D. Scargill*

DEE PEE TEE CEE (IRE) 5 b.g. Tidaro (USA) – Silver Glimpse 108 (Petingo **92** 135) [1998 –: 9m 7.9g 8g 1999 8d⁶ 10.3d* 10s* 8.9d* 9.2g* 10.4f⁶ 11.9m* 12s 10s Oct 2] tall gelding: has a round action: fairly useful handicapper: had excellent year, winning at Chester, Pontefract (apprentices), York and Hamilton in June and York again in August: rare poor efforts final 2 starts: effective at 9f to 1½m: acts on good to firm and soft going: has been bandaged in front: races prominently, and goes with lots of enthusiasm. *M. W. Easterby*

DEEP SPACE (IRE) 4 br.g. Green Desert (USA) 127 – Dream Season (USA) **116** (Mr Prospector (USA)) [1998 88p: 6g² 6m⁴ 6s 5g* 5m⁴ 6m* 6f⁶ 6m 6.1g 1999 6g 7m* 7g⁶ 7m² 6m* 7f 6f 6.1g* 6g² 6d Oct 15] good-topped gelding: smart performer:

Wokingham Stakes (Handicap), Royal Ascot—
the judge takes fifteen minutes to separate Deep Space and Halmahera (near side);
Young Josh, making his reappearance, is third with Doctor Spin fourth;
Tussle, first home on the far side, finishes fifth overall

much improved at 4 yrs, and won handicaps at Lingfield in May and Royal Ascot (30-runner Wokingham Stakes, by short head from Halmahera) in June and minor event at Nottingham (beat Harmonic Way) in August: very good second to Cretan Gift in minor event at Yarmouth penultimate start: got no sort of run on final appearance: effective at 6f/7f: acts on firm going: has been taken early to post/reared stalls: usually held up. *E. A. L. Dunlop*

DEFIANCE 4 b.g. Warning 136 – Princess Athena 119 (Ahonoora 122) [1998 71: **43**
7.9g 1999 8v 7.6m 7.7s 8.1d 6g 5f⁵ 5.1m Sep 9] tall gelding: fair maiden at best: only a little form in 1999: usually blinkered. *A. P. James*

DEHOUSH (USA) 3 ch.c. Diesis 133 – Dream Play (USA) (Blushing Groom **109**
(FR) 131) [1998 102: 6g* 7f³ 7g 1999 8g* 10s² 12m 10s⁴ Jul 19] rangy, angular colt: has fluent, round action: useful performer: overcame trouble to win listed race at Kempton in April by length from Wallace: good short-head second to Fantastic Light in Classic Trial at Sandown: ran poorly in Scottish Classic at Ayr on final start: likely to prove best around 1¼m: acts on soft going, probably on firm: edgy, free-going sort, has had 2 handlers in preliminaries. *A. C. Stewart*

DEKELSMARY 4 b.f. Komaite (USA) – Final Call 79 (Town Crier 119) [1998 **53**
46, a56: 7d 5g 5.9g 6g⁶ a6g³ 6g a6g 6g a6g⁵ a8.5g³ a7g* a7s⁶ 1999 a8g a7f⁶ a7g² a7g⁵ 6g 5v⁶ 5m³ a5g³ 5m⁴ a5g 5g 5m* 5g a6g 6.1d a6g Dec 21] lengthy, good-topped filly: modest handicapper: won apprentice event at Thirsk in August: below form after: effective at 5f to 7f: acts on good to firm ground and fibresand: blinkered once at 3 yrs (well beaten): usually tongue tied. *J. Balding*

DELAMERE (USA) 2 b.f. (Mar 17) Brocco (USA) – Shelia Dacre (USA) **56 p**
(Nureyev (USA) 131) [1999 6g Oct 11] fifth foal: half-sister to winners in Japan by Slew O'Gold and Halo: dam, French 9f winner, closely related to smart 1993 2-y-o Stonehatch and half-sister to US Grade 1 1¼m winner Danger's Hour: green, eighth of 21 to Toleration in maiden at Windsor, off bridle halfway and keeping on: will stay at least 1m: should do better. *A. G. Foster*

DELCIANA (IRE) 4 b.f. Danehill (USA) 126 – Delvecchia (Glint of Gold 128) **44**
[1998 51: 6g 6g 8m 7m³ 7g 8d 8d 1999 6s 6f 7f 7m 8m 10g 8f 10.1d³ a11g²
11.5m⁴ a12g a14.8g a11g Dec 13] small, sturdy filly: poor maiden: stays 11f: acts
on good to firm going, good to soft and fibresand: blinkered (no form) third start.
G. G. Margarson

DELEGATE 6 ch.g. Polish Precedent (USA) 131 – Dangora (USA) 98 (Sovereign **102 +**
Dancer (USA)) [1998 98: 5g⁴ 1999 5m⁴ 6d³ 5s⁶ 6d³ 6s Oct 22] lengthy gelding: poor
mover: useful performer: won in France in 1995: appeared to run very well (possibly
worth a rating of 111) when 1¾ lengths third of 20 to Gaelic Storm in listed race at
Newmarket on penultimate start: in rear in handicap next time: stays 6.5f: acts on
good to soft and good to firm going: has been bandaged: slowly away (ran poorly)
final start. *J. E. Banks*

DELIGHT OF DAWN 7 b.m. Never So Bold 135 – Vogos Angel 54 (Song 132) **63**
[1998 60: 7s* 7s 8f 8.3m 8g⁴ 7m 7m⁴ 7m 8d³ 7m⁶ 8g⁴ 8d* 7s a7g a8.5g³ 1999 a8g* **a54**
a8g a8g⁵ a7g a7g⁵ 7s⁴ 8.3m* 8d 9m 7m 8.3g 7m 7.6f⁶ 8.3m 8.1d⁴ 7s⁶ a7g⁶ a8g² Dec
6] angular mare: modest handicapper: won at Lingfield in January and Windsor in
April: effective at 7f/1m: acts on firm and soft going, better form on equitrack than
fibresand: sometimes slowly away: held up: blinkered. *E. A. Wheeler*

DELIUS (USA) 2 b. or br.c. (Mar 2) A P Indy (USA) 131 – Hot Novel (USA) **89 P**
(Mari's Book (USA)) [1999 8s* Oct 25] $500,000Y: good-topped colt: sixth foal:
half-brother to 3 winners in USA, notably top-class 9f/1¼m performer Behrens (by
Pleasant Colony): dam, sprinter/miler, Grade 3 winner and second in Grade 1 event:
favourite (looked well and moved fluently to post), won 19-runner maiden at Leicester by ½ length from Atlantic Rhapsody, set plenty to do but running on strongly to
lead final 1f despite drifting left: will stay at least 1¼m: most likeable type with
plenty of scope, and looks sure to go on to much better things. *Sir Michael Stoute*

DELLUA (IRE) 5 b.m. Suave Dancer (USA) 136 – Joma Kaanem (Double Form **68**
130) [1998 65: 10d 10m 10.2m⁴ 11.1m⁶ 10s a12g 1999 a10g³ a12g² 11.6m* 12.3m⁶ **a63**
11.8m 12.4m⁴ 12g a12g⁵ 12m⁵ 12m Sep 10] strong mare: fair performer: won
handicap at Windsor in April and 5-runner minor event at Newcastle in June: barely
stays 13f: acts on good to firm going, soft and equitrack: none too consistent: sold
5,000 gns. *J. W. Hills*

DELMO 4 ch.g. Democratic (USA) 101 – Charlotte Piaf (Morston (FR) 125) **–**
[1998 –: 7g 8.1g⁶ 1999 a12f a14.8g Jan 27] little sign of ability: reared stalls,
unseating rider, on reappearance. *R. Simpson*

DELPHINI (IRE) 3 b.f. Seattle Dancer (USA) 119 – Breyani 101 (Commanche **–**
Run 133) [1998 NR 1999 10m a8g² a8g* a8g* a10g³ 7.5s Sep 21] third foal: half- **a69**
sister to Moyglare Stud Stakes/Irish 1000 Guineas winner Tarascon (by Tirol): dam
Irish 11f/2m winner: fair performer: won maiden at Southwell and minor event at
Lingfield in July: stays easy 1¼m: acts on all-weather, no form on turf. *J. Noseda*

DELPHINIUS (IRE) 2 br.c. (Feb 22) Dolphin Street (FR) 125 – Stellar Empress **97**
(USA) (Star de Naskra (USA)) [1999 6m* 6d² Aug 14] 130,000Y: lengthy, quite
attractive colt: third foal: half-brother to fairly useful Irish 7f winner Welsh Queen
(by Caerleon): dam Irish 2-y-o 5f/6f winner: useful form: won maiden at Windsor in
July, and improved when head second of 4 to Buy Or Sell in minor event at Ripon:
reportedly fractured a cannon-bone later in August: dead. *G. Wragg*

DELTA GEORGIA 3 ch.f. Tina's Pet 121 – Bacolet (Dominion 123) [1998 NR **50**
1999 a6g⁵ a7g⁵ 7.1m 8.1m² Jun 29] 1,000Y: closely related to a winner in Singapore
by Precocious: dam ran twice: modest form in sellers/maiden: stays 1m: acts on good
to firm going. *A. Bailey*

DELTA SOLEIL (USA) 7 b.h. Riverman (USA) 131 – Sunny Roberta (USA) **82 §**
(Robellino (USA) 127) [1998 82: a7g a8g 7s 6s 7f⁶ 6g 6g* 6m 6m* 6g² 6f 6m 6d
1999 6g 5s 6f* 6f 6g 6m 6.1m³ 6m 6f 6g 6.1f Oct 20] good-bodied horse: fairly useful
handicapper: won 19-runner event at Kempton in May: generally well below form
after: best at 6f on good going or firmer: sometimes takes last and steadily to post:
usually races prominently/leads: untrustworthy. *V. Soane*

DEMERARA 2 br.f. (Feb 28) Dilum (USA) 115 – Springtime Sugar (USA) (Halo **–**
(USA)) [1999 7m Jun 15] 1,000Y: fifth foal: dam, placed once from 5 starts in USA,

half-sister to dam of high-class French miler Priolo: last of 12 in Thirsk maiden: sold 600 gns in October, sent to Denmark. *C. E. Brittain*

DEMETER (USA) 2 b.f. (Mar 30) Diesis 133 – Nicer (IRE) 113 (Pennine Walk 120) [1999 8.3d³ Oct 28] second foal: dam, 6f (at 2 yrs) and Irish 1,000 Guineas winner, out of Musidora winner Everything Nice: weak in market, promising third of 13 to impressive Kalypso Katie in Windsor maiden, travelling well behind leaders and not knocked about once held: should stay 1¼m: sure to improve. *H. R. A. Cecil*   **79 p**

DEMI-MONDAINE 2 b.f. (Apr 10) Democratic (USA) 101 – Alo Ez 100 (Alzao (USA) 117) [1999 6d⁶ 7m Jul 20] fifth living foal: half-sister to 3-y-o Pleasant Mount and winning sprinters Alamode and 7-y-o Mousehole (both by Stateblest): dam sprinter: showed little in sellers: played up in stalls second start. *J. G. Smyth-Osbourne*   **–**

DEMOCRACY (IRE) 3 ch.g. Common Grounds 118 – Inonder 31 (Belfort (FR) 89) [1998 78: 5.2m³ 1999 7v⁶ 7m³ 8g⁶ 7s³ 9f² 8.1m³ 8f³ 8g⁴ 7m² 6d² 5.7f* a7g Dec 8] fairly useful performer: won maiden at Bath in September: left R. Hannon 17,000 gns following month: effective at 5.7f, and probably stays 9f: acts on firm and soft going: visored/blinkered last 7 starts: consistent, but ungenuine. *P. G. Murphy*   **84 §**

DEMOLITION JO 4 gr.f. Petong 126 – Fire Sprite 83 (Mummy's Game 120) [1998 89, a72: a6g⁵ 7.6g 6.1m 6g² 6f 6s 7g* 6g 7f⁵ 6g² 6.1g² 6m⁶ 7g 6s 6g a6g 6d 5d² 6d⁶ a6g 1999 a5g⁶ 5d 6d 6v⁶ 5s 7.6m 5d² 6d 6m 5m 5d⁵ 6d⁵ 6.1s³ 6v 5g a6g 5d 5d³ 6d³ 5s² a6g Nov 15] small, sparely-made filly: fairly useful handicapper on turf, fair on all-weather: several creditable efforts in 1999, including last 3 starts on turf: effective at 5f (given test) to 7f: acts on good to firm ground, soft and fibresand: visored: tough. *P. D. Evans*   **85 a69**

DENA 2 b.f. (Feb 21) Deploy 131 – Isabena (Star Appeal 133) [1999 7s⁵ Nov 5] quite attractive filly: fourth reported foal: half-sister to 1996 2-y-o 7f winner Priena (by Priolo), later fairly useful at 1¼m: dam won 5 times in Spain from 2 to 4 yrs: in need of race, shaped well when 5 lengths fifth of 20 to Golovin in maiden at Doncaster, chasing leading group and not punished once fading: should stay 1¼m: will improve. *W. Jarvis*   **75 p**

DENBRAE (IRE) 7 b.g. Sure Blade (USA) 130 – Fencing (Viking (USA)) [1998 62: a8.5g³ a8g⁴ a7g⁵ 7s a7g⁵ a7g 7g⁴ 6.1g 7g³ 8.1g⁶ 7m 7g 7.1d⁵ 7m⁶ 7d 1999 a8g³ a7g* a8g² a8g 6d* a7g² 6f*ᵈⁱˢ 5g³ 5m 6d Nov 4] lengthy gelding: modest handicapper: first past post in amateur events at Southwell in March and Hamilton in May and July, disqualified for interference on final occasion: needs test at 5f and stays 1m: acts on firm ground, good to soft and all-weather: often beaten off bridle. *J. Pearce*   **61 a55**

DENNIS BERGKAMP (IRE) 2 b.g. (Apr 3) Night Shift (USA) – Indian Express 61 (Indian Ridge 123) [1999 5d 5m 7.3f 5m³ 6g 7s Oct 25] IR 25,000Y: quite good-topped gelding: second foal: half-brother to 3-y-o Smoke Signal: dam, 8.5f and 1¼m winner, sister to useful 6f/7f performer Cheyenne Spirit: modest maiden: easily best efforts at 5f: sold out of M. Channon's stable 3,200 gns after fifth start: tried visored. *W. Clay*   **50**

DENOUEMENT 3 b. or br.f. Lapierre 119 – Star Attention 91 (Northfields (USA)) [1998 NR 1999 7f Jul 31] half-sister to Irish 6f/7f winner One Man Band (by Chief Singer): dam best at sprint distances: 50/1, tailed off in maiden. *C. W. Fairhurst*   **–**

DEN'S-JOY 3 b.f. Archway (IRE) 115 – Bonvin (Taufan (USA) 119) [1998 NR 1999 7m³ a9.4g⁵ Dec 15] closely related to 1997 2-y-o 7f winner Miss Main Street (by Shalford) and half-sister to 1992 2-y-o 1m winner Bonarme (by Vacarme): dam Irish 5f (at 2 yrs) and 1m winner: slightly better effort in maidens (fair form) when third at Yarmouth (slowly away) in October. *H. J. Collingridge*   **65**

DENTARDIA (IRE) 4 br.g. Petardia 113 – Modena (Sassafras (FR) 135) [1998 47, a70: a8.5g³ 9.7d a12g³ 14m² 14.1d 14d 12g a12g 1999 a10f⁶ a13g a13g 11.5m⁶ 12d 16f Jun 21] leggy, workmanlike gelding: poor maiden: out of sorts in 1999: stays 1¾m: acts on fibresand, easily best turf efforts on good to firm going. *J. M. P. Eustace*   **–**

DENTON LADY 2 br.f. (Feb 28) Inchinor 119 – Lammastide 93 (Martinmas 128) [1999 5m 6g⁴ 6g 6m⁵ 7f⁵ 7f 8d⁴ 8.1s⁵ 7s Oct 5] 5,400F, 11,000Y: leggy, sparely-made filly: half-sister to 3-y-o Blue Diamond and several winners up to 1m, including 6-y-o Amber Fort: dam 2-y-o 5f winner: poor maiden on balance: may prove best up to 1m: blinkered last 3 starts: inconsistent. *W. T. Kemp*   **49**

DEPLOY VENTURE 3 ch.g. Deploy 131 – Tasseled (USA) (Tate Gallery (USA) **105**
117) [1998 81: 7.1d³ 7g² 7.1d² 7.6f³ a8.5g* 8m⁴ 1999 9g² 9.9g⁵ 12s* 12s² 12m⁵ 11.9s
12m* 13.9g⁵ 11.9f⁴ 12s 13.1v³ Oct 12] leggy, angular gelding: useful handicapper:
won at Newbury in May and Ascot (in good style) in July: creditable fifth in Ebor at
York, best effort afterwards: effective at 1½m/1¾m: acts on good to firm going, soft
and fibresand: sometimes races freely/wanders under pressure, and likely to prove
best held up: sold 92,000 gns, to join D. Vienna in USA. *S. P. C. Woods*

DEPUTISE (IRE) 3 b.c. Caerleon (USA) 132 – Depaze (USA) (Deputy Minister **77**
(CAN)) [1998 –p: 7d 1999 10.5m⁵ 10v² Oct 12] rangy, good sort: fair form in
maidens at Haydock and Ayr (no match for 7-length winner Laiyl after 4-month
absence): wore rope halter for stalls entry on debut: sent to UAE. *J. H. M. Gosden*

DERBY AFFAIR 3 b.f. Teenoso (USA) 135 – Formal Affair 78 (Rousillon **62 d**
(USA) 133) [1998 NR 1999 10.1s² 10.2m 11.6m 10g Aug 18] first foal: dam, 7f
(at 2 yrs) to 1¼m and hurdles winner, half-sister to high-class hurdlers Anzum
(stayer) and Jazilah: modest form in maiden on debut: well below that level after, in
claimer final start: pulled hard last 2 starts. *D. Nicholson*

DERRYQUIN 4 b.g. Lion Cavern (USA) 117 – Top Berry 87 (High Top 131) [1998 **62**
–: 10.2s⁴ 7.3m 8m⁵ 8m 7.1g 7v 1999 10m 8m⁵ 7d⁶ 6g⁴ 6d 6d Nov 4] good-bodied
gelding: modest handicapper nowadays: probably finds 6f bare minimum, and
stays 1m: acts on good to firm and good to soft going: blinkered 4 of last 5 starts:
sometimes sweating/edgy. *P. L. Gilligan*

DESARU (USA) 3 br.c. Chief's Crown (USA) – Team Colors (USA) (Mr Prospec- **108**
tor (USA)) [1998 103p: 7m² 7g* 8s³ 1999 8m 7m Jun 16] angular, quite attractive
colt: has a sharp, quick action: useful performer: bandaged, best effort when over 5
lengths ninth to Island Sands in 2000 Guineas at Newmarket on reappearance:
heavily bandaged, ran as though all wasn't well at Royal Ascot next time: likely to
stay 1¼m: seemed ill at ease on soft going at 2 yrs. *J. Noseda*

DESCANT (IRE) 3 b.f. Bluebird (USA) 125 – Dubai Lady 78 (Kris 135) [1998 **66**
66: 5m⁴ 1999 7d Jun 10] fair form (swerved left start) in minor event on only 2-y-o
start: well beaten at Newbury over year later: sold 5,000 gns in December. *R. Hannon*

DESDEMONA (IRE) 3 b.f. Lahib (USA) 129 – Tragic Point (IRE) 89 (Tragic **89**
Role (USA)) [1998 72p: 6m² 8.2s 1999 7g 7m² 7g* 8m⁶ 7m 9f² 11m² 8.5f Dec 17]
tall, leggy, unfurnished filly: fairly useful performer: won maiden at Yarmouth in
June: good second in handicaps later in summer: left G. Wragg before final start:
stays 11f: acts on firm ground, possibly not on soft: blinkered (well below form) fifth
outing. *I. P. D. Jory, USA*

DESERT CAT (IRE) 6 b.g. Green Desert (USA) 127 – Mahabba (USA) 74 **53**
(Elocutionist (USA)) [1998 53: 8.2m³ 8d⁶ 8d⁵ 8.3d 8g³ 8g⁴ 8.2m 6.9d⁴ 8.3d⁴ 9m
7.1d* 8v⁶ 1999 8.5m 7m 7.1g⁴ 8m 8g* 7g 8d 8m 8d Oct 20] big, strong gelding:
carries condition: modest performer: won selling handicap at Musselburgh in July:
below form after: effective at 7f to 9f: acts on any ground: no form blinkered/visored
once each: usually held up, though raced more prominently for his wins: none too
consistent. *Martyn Wane*

DESERT CHARM 2 b.f. (Apr 10) Desert Style (IRE) 121 – Autumn Fall (USA) **–**
(Sanglamore (USA) 126) [1999 8g 8d 7g Oct 2] 12,000Y: leggy, unfurnished filly:
first foal: dam (unraced) from family of Luso and Common Grounds: well beaten in
maidens and seller. *N. Tinkler*

DESERT DARLING 3 b.f. Green Desert (USA) 127 – Habibti 136 (Habitat 134) **65**
[1998 69: 5m³ 5g 5m⁶ 1999 5g 6m 5g⁴ a5g⁵ Jul 9] fair maiden handicapper: creditable efforts in blinkers final 2 starts: will prove best at 5f: acts on fibresand: sent to
Australia. *J. Berry*

DESERT DUKE 3 b.c. Green Desert (USA) 127 – Guilty Secret (IRE) 109 (Kris **85**
135) [1998 87p: 6g³ 6m³ 1999 7v 7.6m³ May 4] sturdy, well-made colt: fluent
mover: fairly useful maiden: creditable third in handicap final start: stays 1m: sent to
Bahrain. *Sir Michael Stoute*

DESERT FIGHTER 8 b.g. Green Desert (USA) 127 – Jungle Rose 90 (Shirley **74**
Heights 130) [1998 76: 10s 12g³ 10.1s² 12s 10.1s³ 10g² 9m⁵ 12d⁴ 12.3g⁴ 1999
12d³ 12s* 11.9d* 11.11f* 12f² 12f⁴ Sep 4] good-topped gelding: fair performer: won
claimers at Thirsk in May then at Haydock, Hamilton and Catterick in July: credit-

able effort in handicap on final start: stays 1½m: acts on firm and soft ground: probably best held up. *Mrs M. Reveley*

DESERT FURY 2 b.c. (Apr 9) Warning 136 – Number One Spot 71 (Reference **104 p** Point 139) [1999 5.1m* 6m³ Sep 11] 50,000Y: smallish, deep-girthed colt: third foal: half-brother to 3-y-o Trafford and 4-y-o Royal Axminster: dam, 7f winner, closely related to top-class miler Milligram out of 1000 Guineas winner One In A Million: backward and unimpressive to post, won maiden at Chester in May: much improved when narrowly-beaten third of 7 to Tabheej in minor event at Doncaster over 4 months later, travelling well and keeping on willingly: should stay 7f: seems sure to improve further. *B. Hanbury*

DESERT INVADER (IRE) 8 br.g. Lead On Time (USA) 123 – Aljood 111 (Kris **–** 135) [1998 32, a68: a7s⁶ a6g⁴ a6g a7g⁴ 5s a6g² 5d⁴ a6g³ a7g a7g* a7g⁴ a6g* a8.5g⁵ **a56** a7g⁵ a6g a6g a6g⁶ 1999 a7g⁶ a7g⁵ a6f a6g⁶ a7g⁶ a8g a6g² a8g a7g a6g⁵ a7g³ Jun 17] strong, lengthy gelding: good mover: poor handicapper: best at 6f/7f nowadays: acts on fibresand (rarely tried on equitrack), good to firm and soft ground: tried blinkered: none too consistent. *D. W. Chapman*

DESERT ISLAND DISC 2 b.f. (Feb 24) Turtle Island (IRE) 123 – Distant Music **64** (Darshaan 133) [1999 7s 7v⁵ 8s Nov 6] 6,800Y: first foal: dam unraced grand-daughter of high-class French 1m to 1½m filly Dancing Maid: modest form in maidens: will be suited by 1¼m+: raced only on soft/heavy ground. *N. A. Graham*

DESERT KNIGHT 3 b.c. Green Desert (USA) 127 – Green Leaf (USA) 97 **103 p** (Alydar (USA)) [1998 NR 1999 8g* 8m² Sep 10] tall, good sort: brother to useful 6f (at 2 yrs) and 1m winner Desert Green and to useful though irresolute miler/very smart 2m chaser Green Green Desert, and half-brother to 2 winners by Sadler's Wells, including useful middle-distance performer Double Leaf: dam, 2-y-o 6f winner, stayed 1¼m well: well-backed favourite when easy winner of maiden at Pontefract in August, beating Tarawan by 4 lengths: 3½ lengths second of 5 to Swallow Flight in minor event at Doncaster on only other run, travelling well but no extra final 1f: likely to prove best around 1m: bandaged in front both starts: remains open to improvement. *J. Noseda*

DESERT LORE 8 b.g. Green Desert (USA) 127 – Chinese Justice (USA) (Diesis **–** 133) [1998 –: 6d 6m⁴ 1999 5m 6f Jul 9] no form since 1996. *D. A. Nolan*

DESERT RECRUIT 3 b.g. Marju (IRE) 127 – Storm Gayle (IRE) (Sadler's **49 §** Wells (USA) 132) [1998 –: 7s 1999 7m⁶ 9d⁴ 5.9g 8.3g 8.3m 9.1g⁵ 11.1m* 11.1m⁴ Aug 11] poor handicapper: won apprentice event at Hamilton in July: stays 11f: acts on good to firm going: reportedly had wind infirmity second start: slowly away and found little final outing: needs treating with caution. *I. Semple*

DESERT ROSE 2 b.f. (Feb 14) Green Desert (USA) 127 – Splice 114 (Sharpo **–** 132) [1999 7d Oct 20] second foal: half-sister to 3-y-o Entwine: dam sprinter: 5/1, tailed off in maiden at Newcastle: sold 14,000 gns. *Sir Michael Stoute*

DESERT SAFARI (IRE) 2 b.f. (Feb 20) Desert Style (IRE) 121 – Dublah (USA) **65** (Private Account (USA)) [1999 5g 5g³ 5m³ 5.1m 6m⁴ 5g² 6g⁵ 5m⁴ 6g a5g⁴ 5f* Sep 13] IR 6,000Y: sturdy, lengthy filly: fifth foal: half-sister to 3 winning sprinters, including 3-y-o Perugino Bay and 4-y-o Bandbox: dam unraced: fair performer: won maiden at Musselburgh in September: effective at 5f/6f: acts on firm going (yet to race on softer than good) and fibresand: blinkered last 3 starts. *E. J. Alston*

DESERT SAND 4 b.f. Tragic Role (USA) – Miss Suntan (Bruni 132) [1998 80: **45** 8m 8g⁵ 9.1s* 10m 1999 9.2g⁶ 10.2g 12.3m⁶ 10s 11.5m⁵ Oct 19] leggy filly: fair performer at 3 yrs: poor form in 1999, seeming reluctant to start on third outing: should stay 1¼m: probably needs good ground or softer. *K. A. Morgan*

DESERT SONG 4 ch.f. Desert Dirham (USA) 108 – Affaire de Coeur 55 (Imperial **–** Fling (USA) 116) [1998 51: 7g³ 7m³ 7m³ 9.9m 8g 1999 8f 7g Sep 14] modest maiden at 3 yrs: well beaten over hurdles and on Flat since. *R. G. Frost*

DESERT SPA (USA) 4 b.g. Sheikh Albadou 128 – Healing Waters (USA) (Tem- **64** perence Hill (USA)) [1998 64: 10.2s³ 10.5g 10m⁶ 9m 10g 8m a12g* 12s a12g³ 1999 a12g a12g² Dec 11] workmanlike gelding: has a round action: modest handicapper: better effort in 1999 when second at Wolverhampton: stays 1½m: acts on soft going and fibresand, probably on firm: below form blinkered. *P. J. Makin*

DESERT VALENTINE   4 b.g. Midyan (USA) 124 – Mo Ceri 63 (Kampala 120)   **56**
[1998 65: 6d 9m⁶ 8m 8d* 8d⁶ 8v 1999 8l.m 8m 9.9v⁵ 10.2s Oct 26] tall, lengthy
gelding: has high knee action: only modest handicapper now: barely stays 1¼m: acts
on heavy ground: tends to race freely. *L. G. Cottrell*

DESERT WARRIOR (IRE)   5 b.g. Fairy King (USA) – Highland Girl (USA)   **74 ?**
(Sir Ivor 135) [1998 –: 6v 6g a8g 7g 1999 7g² 8.3m² 7m 8f May 27] well-made
gelding: fair maiden at best: runner-up at Kempton (appeared to run really well in
steadily-run race) and Windsor (handicap): well beaten after: probably stays 1m:
joined D. Nicholls. *K. Mahdi*

DESILU   2 b.f. (Apr 30) Skyliner 117 – Munequita (Marching On 101) [1999 6m   **48**
6g⁵ Sep 18] sister to winning 2-y-o sprinters Monkey's Wedding (in 1993, later
successful in Scandinavia) and Monkey Adel (in 1994) and half-sister to winning
sprinter Beckyhannah (by Rambling River): dam ran once at 2 yrs: poor form in
maidens. *W. W. Haigh*

DESIRE'S GOLD   4 br.g. Grey Desire 115 – Glory Gold 59 (Hittite Glory 125)   **49 ?**
[1998 –: 10v 8m 9.1m 11.1d 1999 10v 10v 12g 12g⁵ a12g Nov 13] close-coupled
gelding: poor maiden at best. *M. Brittain*

DESRAYA (IRE)   2 b.g. (Apr 15) Desert Style (IRE) 121 – Madaraya (USA)   **61**
(Shahrastani (USA) 135) [1999 5.1s 6d⁴ 6g 5.9m 8d Sep 17] IR 11,000F, 8,200Y:
fourth foal: dam (unraced) closely related to dam of 4-y-o Maridpour, out of half-
sister to Poule d'Essai des Pouliches winner Masarika: modest maiden at best: off
course 3 months, well beaten in nursery at Ayr final start: stays 6f: acts on good to
firm and good to soft ground. *K. A. Ryan*

DESTINATION   2 ch.g. (Mar 22) Deploy 131 – Veuve (Tirol 127) [1999 8s Oct   **–**
26] second foal: half-brother to Swedish 3-y-o winner Suzie-Q (by Batshoof):
dam unraced half-sister to useful German sprinter Premiere Cuvee: green, well
beaten in maiden at Bath. *C. A. Cyzer*

DETECTIVE   3 ch.g. Wolfhound (USA) 126 – Ivoronica 89 (Targowice (USA)   **73**
130) [1998 –p: 7g 1999 8m 8m 7g⁵ 6f² 6.8g 6g Oct 14] strong gelding: fair maiden:
left J. Gosden after third start: soundly beaten last 2 starts: may prove best short of
1m: raced only on good going or firmer. *Dr J. D. Scargill*

DE TRAMUNTANA   2 b.f. (Feb 9) Alzao (USA) 117 – Glamour Game 80   **71 p**
(Nashwan (USA) 135) [1999 7d 8.3d Oct 28] workmanlike filly: first foal: dam, Irish
1¼m winner, also successful over hurdles (2½m) in Britain: better effort in maidens
(fair form) when seventh of 13 at Windsor final start, giving impression still in need
of race: will be well suited by 1¼m+: likely to do better still. *W. Jarvis*

DETROIT CITY (IRE)   4 b.g. Distinctly North (USA) 115 – Moyhora (IRE)   **64**
(Nashamaa 113) [1998 64: 7s a6g 9.9m 7.1s* 7.5g* 7.5m 6.9d⁴ 7.1g⁵ 8d⁵ 6d² 7s 1999   **a48**
a6g⁶ a7g⁶ a8f a7g⁶ 7g 8.5m 7.1m* 6.9m³ 7.1m⁶ 7.5v⁵ 7.1g² 6.9m⁵ 6.9g 6g 8f 8g Nov
3] leggy gelding: modest on turf, poor on all-weather: won handicap at Musselburgh
in April: mostly below form after: best around 7f: acts on any turf going and fibresand: visored (well below form) fifth start: leads/races prominently. *B. S. Rothwell*

DEVASTATING   2 b.f. (May 3) Bluebird (USA) 125 – Winning Appeal (FR) 62   **70**
(Law Society (USA) 130) [1999 6g⁵ 7m⁴ 8.1m Sep 15] third foal: half-sister to 3-y-o
Meteorite: dam, maiden, stayed 1¼m, sister to useful Irish/US middle-distance colt
Olympic Majesty and half-sister to smart French winner around 1¼m D'Arros, out
of sister to El Gran Senor: best effort in maidens when fourth of 11 to Miss Orah at
Salisbury: gave impression something amiss final start: will stay 1¼m. *R. Hannon*

DEVILETTA (USA)   3 ch.f. Trempolino (USA) 135 – Polish Devil (USA) (Devil's   **60 +**
Bag (USA)) [1998 78: 6g² 5m² 6g 6v⁴ 1999 a6g* 6g 6m Aug 30] close-coupled,
rather unfurnished filly: fair form as 2-y-o: won maiden at Lingfield in February:
well held in handicaps after, looking none too keen final start: likely to stay
beyond 6f: acts on good to firm going and equitrack: sold 5,000 gns in December.
J. H. M. Gosden

DEVIL'S IMP (IRE)   3 ch.f. Cadeaux Genereux 131 – High Spirited 80 (Shirley   **76**
Heights 130) [1998 84p: 7m* 1999 7g² 6f* 6.1f³ Oct 20] angular, quite attractive
filly: fair performer: won private sweepstakes at Newmarket only 2-y-o start and
maiden at Thirsk in September: stays 7f: raced only on good going or firmer.
E. A. L. Dunlop

DEVILS NIGHT 4 b.g. Faustus (USA) 118 – Up All Night 56 (Green Desert – (USA) 127) [1998 –: a6g 1999 a8.5g 10g a11g Dec 17] well beaten, including in seller. *K. Bell*

DEVON DREAM (IRE) 3 b.g. Paris House 123 – Share The Vision (Vision 61 (USA)) [1998 –: 6.1g 5.7g 6d 1999 6m 5.3f* 6g³ 5.1m⁶ 5.3f³ 6f 7m⁴ 5m Sep 11] leggy gelding: modest performer: won handicap at Brighton in May: mostly respectable efforts after: effective at 5f, and seems to stay 7f: acts on firm ground. *M. J. Weeden*

DEVON REEF 4 ch.f. Bandmaster (USA) 97 – Reef Bay (IRE) (Phardante (FR) – 123) [1998 NR 1999 10m May 22] first foal: dam unraced: tailed off in bumper and seller. *R. C. Spicer*

DEWI SANT 5 ch.g. Nalchik (USA) – Secret Ingredient (Most Secret 119) [1998 – NR 1999 10.2g Jun 12] tailed off in maidens/claimer. *D. Burchell*

DE-WOLF 4 gr.f. Petong 126 – Doppio 62 (Dublin Taxi) [1998 62d: 7g⁴ 6g 6.1d – 6.1s a6g⁴ a6g 1999 a7g a7g⁶ Feb 3] leggy filly: disappointing maiden: tried visored. *P. J. Makin*

DIABLO DANCER (IRE) 3 b.c. Deploy 131 – Scharade 74 (Lombard (GER) 97 d 126) [1998 89: 5.1d* 5d³ 6g³ 7m² 7m* 7m⁴ 7.3m⁵ 8m⁴ 10d³ 10s⁵ 1999 10.1s⁴ 9.9m² 12d⁶ 11.9f 13.3m 9.9f 10d 12m Aug 29] well-made colt: useful handicapper: deteriorated after finishing second at Salisbury: should stay beyond 1¼m: acts on good to firm and soft going: blinkered (well beaten) sixth start: usually races up with pace. *B. R. Millman*

DIAGHILEF (IRE) 7 b.g. Royal Academy (USA) 130 – Miss Audimar (USA) 99 (Mr Leader (USA)) [1998 90: 11.8d⁶ 14.1m⁴ 13.3m⁴ 12d 1999 13.9s 12f* 11.9s 11.8m* 13.9g Aug 18] tall, good-topped gelding: good mover: smart performer in 1995, when winner of King George V Handicap at Royal Ascot: useful handicapper in 1999, successful at Doncaster in May and Leicester in July: stayed 1¾m: acted on firm ground, seemed unsuited by soft: reported in September as having been put down after suffering an attack of grass sickness. *M. A. Buckley*

DIAMOND BEACH 6 b.g. Lugana Beach 116 – Cannon Boy (USA) (Canonero 57 § (USA)) [1998 NR 1999 9g⁶ 10.1m⁴ 10.4g 11g 13.8s Nov 2] tall gelding: modest maiden: stays 11f: acts on firm and good to soft going: probably ungenuine. *G. M. Moore*

DIAMOND BLUSH 3 ch.f. Sure Blade (USA) 130 – Dawn Ditty 100 (Song 132) 47 [1998 –: 5.1m a7g 1999 a8g⁵ a9.4g³ a6g³ a6g² a7g a7g Apr 6] tall filly: poor maiden: should stay beyond 6f: acts on fibresand: sometimes troublesome at start: joined A. Hobbs. *N. P. Littmoden*

DIAMOND CONCORDE (IRE) 2 b. or br.f. (Feb 17) Blues Traveller (IRE) 53 d 119 – Petova (IRE) (Petorius 117) [1999 5g⁵ 5g³ a6g² a7g³ a7g⁵ 6f Aug 6] IR 4,500Y: first foal: dam poor maiden, from family of smart sprinter Governor General: only poor form after debut: probably stays 7f: tried blinkered/visored: tongue-tied first 2 starts: very slowly away penultimate outing. *P. D. Evans*

DIAMOND CROWN (IRE) 8 ch.g. Kris 135 – State Treasure (USA) (Secre- 48 § tariat (USA)) [1998 51: 10m 10g³ 10d³ 8m 10g² 10.9d* 8g 12.4g* 10m 10m³ 16d³ 12m⁵ 14.1g⁶ 15.8d² 14.1v 16v⁶ 1999 16m 13.8g⁴ 13g³ 14d² 12.4m 13f* 13.8m⁴ 13m² 12.3g⁵ 14m⁴ 16m 14.1g 10.1d Oct 20] leggy gelding: poor handicapper: won at Hamilton in July: poor efforts final 3 starts: stays 2m: acts on firm and soft going, tailed off on fibresand: visored once at 7 yrs: often set plenty to do and looks far from keen. *Martyn Wane*

DIAMOND DECORUM (IRE) 3 ch.g. Fayruz 116 – Astra Adastra (Mount 89 Hagen (FR) 127) [1998 73: 7m 7m 6g⁴ 5m* 6m⁶ 7m⁵ 7d⁴ 1999 a8g 7d 7m⁵ 7d 7m⁵ a69 6m* 5g 7f² 6f⁴ a7g 7m 7.1s⁴ 5d 5g 8d 8s Nov 6] workmanlike gelding: fluent mover: fairly useful handicapper: won at Lingfield in June: best effort when runner-up at Goodwood: best at 6f/easy 7f: acts on firm and soft going, well beaten on all-weather: races freely: has been bandaged: has worn tongue strap. *P. D. Evans*

DIAMOND DIANA 3 ch.f. Selkirk (USA) 129 – Lady Vivienne (Golden Fleece – (USA) 133) [1998 NR 1999 10s⁴ 7m Jun 15] 7,500Y: half-sister to several winners here and abroad, including fairly useful 1994 2-y-o 7f winner Gaylord (by Tirol), later successful up to 11f in Hong Kong: dam, Irish 1½m winner, half-sister to very smart middle-distance performer Erin's Isle: only a little sign of ability in maidens: pulled hard second start: sold 1,000 gns in December. *J. L. Eyre*

DIAMOND FLAME 5 b.g. Suave Dancer (USA) 136 – Eternal Flame 73 (Primo Dominie 121) [1998 88, a91: a10g* a9.4g* a10g 12s 10.4g 12g⁵ 10g 10v⁵ 10.3v³ 10s a12g 1999 a12g a9.4g⁵ a9.4g 10s⁴ 10m 10d⁵ 10f 12g 11.5f 10m⁴ 9.9v 10f² 10.2s Oct 26] quite attractive gelding: has reportedly had knee trouble: fairly useful on all-weather, fair on turf: effective at 9.4f, probably at 1½m: acts on any all-weather/turf: usually held up and sometimes hangs. *P. W. Harris*
67 a84

DIAMOND GEEZER (IRE) 3 br.c. Tenby 125 – Unaria (Prince Tenderfoot (USA) 126) [1998 63: 6m 6g 6f⁶ 7g 5g* 6s 7m⁵ 7v a8g a6g 1999 a6g a7f⁵ a6g* a7g² a7g⁵ 6g 6m⁴ 6f² 7g³ 6m 6g* 6m* 6f⁵ 6s a6g² 6d⁵ 6d a6g² a6g* a6g² a6g³ Dec 22] sturdy, good-quartered colt: fair handicapper: won at Lingfield in January and November and twice at Windsor in July: stays easy 7f: acts on firm going, good to soft (possibly not on soft) and all-weather: blinkered (well beaten) on reappearance: usually races prominently. *R. Hannon*
77

DIAMOND GEORGIA (IRE) 2 ch.f. (Feb 3) Soviet Lad (USA) – Secret Assignment 71 (Vitiges (FR) 132) [1999 5d⁶ 7g⁶ a5g Dec 13] IR 5,400Y: angular filly: poor walker and mover: half-sister to Irish 1995 2-y-o 1m winner Secret Magic (by Magical Strike) and 2 winners abroad by Simply Great: dam, 1m winner from 3 starts, half-sister to smart 7f to 1½m winner Sheer Grit: modest form at best in minor event/maidens on turf: should stay 1m: soundly beaten on fibresand. *John Berry*
54 a–

DIAMOND ISLE 2 b.f. (May 10) Clantime 101 – Five Islands 62 (Bairn (USA) 126) [1999 5g⁵ 5m 5m 5m² 5g 5g⁶ 5m³ 6f 6.1m 6d a5g⁶ Nov 13] 1,400Y: leggy, angular filly: second foal: half-sister to 3-y-o Chillian: dam 2-y-o 5f winner: poor maiden: effective at 5f/6f: acts on good to firm ground. *M. Brittain*
44

DIAMOND KISS (IRE) 2 b.f. (Apr 7) Perugino (USA) 84 – Kunuz (Ela-Mana-Mou 132) [1999 6g May 18] IR 10,000Y: half-sister to several winners, including fairly useful sprinter Kunucu (by Bluebird) and useful Italian performer up to 1m Difesa Indiana (by High Estate): dam ran twice: burly, always behind in maiden at Pontefract. *Mrs P. N. Dutfield*
–

DIAMOND LAD (IRE) 3 b.g. Namaqualand (USA) – Eight Mile Rock 76 (Dominion 123) [1998 –: 5s 7m 7d 6d⁶ 7.9g 1999 12d² 14f³ 13.1d* 12v⁶ 14.1m 15d 15.8s Oct 5] angular, workmanlike gelding: modest performer: won minor event at Ayr in May: well beaten last 3 starts: stays 13f: acts on good to soft going: usually blinkered: reportedly lame when virtually pulled up second start: sold 500 gns, sent to Holland. *W. T. Kemp*
56

DIAMOND LILLY (IRE) 2 b.f. (Apr 11) Namaqualand (USA) – Mousseux (IRE) (Jareer (USA) 115) [1999 6g 7m⁶ 7m³ 7g 7m 7.1m⁶ a8.5g⁵ 8d⁶ a8.5g 8.3d⁶ Nov 4] third foal: half-sister to 3-y-o 7f (at 2 yrs) to 11f winner Irish Archer (by Archway): dam unraced: modest maiden: best efforts on first 4 starts: should stay 1m: yet to race on extremes of going on turf, well held on all-weather: tried blinkered: sold 1,500 gns, sent to Holland. *J. G. Portman*
63 d a–

DIAMOND LOOK (USA) 2 b.c. (Apr 30) Dayjur (USA) 137 – Pedestal (High Line 125) [1999 6d² Jun 10] 40,000Y: sixth foal: half-brother to 3-y-o Worship, 5-y-o Adulation, useful 7f to 8.5f winner Lionize (by Storm Cat) and 1¼m winner Plinth (by Dowsing): dam once-raced half-sister to Precocious and Jupiter Island: promising ¾-length second of 14 to With Iris in maiden at Newbury: looked sure to do better. *E. A. L. Dunlop*
81

DIAMOND OLIVIA 2 b.f. (Apr 20) Beveled (USA) – Queen of The Quorn 53 (Governor General 116) [1999 a5g³ 5m⁶ a5g⁴ a5f Oct 2] 2,600Y: workmanlike filly: third foal: half-sister to 3-y-o Tony Tie: dam 6f/7f winner: modest form when third in maiden at Wolverhampton in April: well beaten after: should stay 6f. *W. G. M. Turner*
60 d

DIAMOND PROMISE (IRE) 2 b.f. (Mar 19) Fayruz 116 – Cupid Miss (Anita's Prince 126) [1999 5d² 5d⁵ 5d* 5d² 5g* 5d² 5.1m 5f⁶ 5g a6g² 6v* 6s² 5.3d³ a6g⁵ Dec 27] IR 5,800Y: small filly: fourth reported foal: sister to Italian sprint winner Italian Force and half-sister to 2 winners, including 4-y-o Perecapa: dam Irish 6f (at 2 yrs)
72 d a56

and 1m winner: modest performer: won claimers at Thirsk in April, Leicester in May and Lingfield (dead-heat) in September: off 2½ months before final start: effective at 5f/6f: acts on heavy ground and fibresand, below form both starts on going firmer than good: usually races prominently. *P. D. Evans*

DIAMOND RACHAEL (IRE)   2 b.f. (Feb 28) Shalford (IRE) 124§ – Brown   **60**
Foam (Horage 124) [1999 7d a5g³ a5g⁴ Dec 13] IR 4,200Y: strong, plain filly: fourth foal: sister to 4-y-o Pass The Rest: dam ran twice: modest maiden: visored, similar efforts in frame at Southwell, showing good speed: form only at 5f: moved poorly to post on debut. *Mrs N. Macauley*

DIAMOND ROAD (IRE)   2 b.c. (Mar 20) Dolphin Street (FR) 125 – Tiffany's   **–**
Case (IRE) 65 (Thatching 131) [1999 7d Sep 19] good-bodied colt: second foal: half-brother to 3-y-o Legal Set: dam 1m winner: burly and green, well held in 22-runner maiden at Newbury. *C. A. Horgan*

DIAMOND ROUGE   3 b.f. Puissance 110 – Maravilla 73 (Mandrake Major 122)   **–**
[1998 53: a5g 5m⁵ 5d³ 1999 a6g⁶ a6g⁶ Feb 17] poor maiden: should stay 6f: no form on all-weather: has had tongue tied. *A. Bailey*

DIAMOND STEALTH   3 b.f. Ardkinglass 114 – Alumia (Great Nephew 126)   **–**
[1998 62p: 7v⁵ 1999 6d a6g 8.3d 10m Jun 16] leggy, angular filly: has round action: no form since debut, including in selling handicap. *J. L. Eyre*

DIAMOND VANESSA (IRE)   2 b.f. (Apr 30) Distinctly North (USA) 115 –   **–**
Elegant Act (USA) (Shecky Greene (USA)) [1999 7d a6g a5g Dec 13] 3,000Y: half-sister to a winner in Hungary by Tenby: dam won 5 races in USA: little form. *J. Hetherton*

DIAMOND WHITE   4 b.f. Robellino (USA) 127 – Diamond Wedding (USA)   **113**
65 (Diamond Shoal 130) [1998 100, a105: 10g 8.1g 10m⁴ 8g⁵ 7m* 7f 8m 8m⁶ 7.6f 9d³ 8s⁶ 10g* 8s 10s⁵ 10m³ 8s³ 10.3d* a8.5g⁶ a9.4g² 1999 a7g⁵ a9.4g⁶ a10g 10g⁴ 8.5g 10s 10m 10.4s³ 9.9g² 10m³ 11.8s⁵ 10m 11.9s⁴ 10m³ 9.9f³ 8d² 10m 8.9f² 9.9m³ 9m² 9.9s* 9.3v* 10d Oct 14]

When Diamond White comes to be sold at the end of the 2000 season, her entry in the catalogue could take up most of the page by itself. In many sale catalogues, even the great grandam and the accomplishments of her offspring can get a prominent billing, but there will not be much room for that with Diamond White. Her owner has horses for racing rather than breeding, hence Diamond White's reported visit to the sales ultimately, and he could not have found a better vehicle for that interest than this filly. A win or placing in any race can be mentioned in the catalogue for a horse (and its dam) being sold at

Prix de l'Opera Hotel du Lac Barriere, Longchamp—
Diamond White wins her biggest prize on her twenty-second outing of the season;
Miss Berbere and Juvenia finish in the places

the Tattersalls Horses In Training Sales—vendors do not often skimp on the details—and to date Diamond White has won six and been placed in another sixteen, three of those wins and ten of the places carrying the much sought after 'black type' status denoting a pattern or listed race.

One is spoilt for choice when searching for statistics to illustrate the scale of Diamond White's endeavours in 1999, but the starting point has to be that she ran in twenty-three races. This number in one season is an assignment which most sprint handicappers would baulk at. It is virtually unheard of for a European pattern-race performer, and that latest schedule was following on from seven races as a two-year-old in 1997 and nineteen in 1998. In a campaign stretching from March 3rd to October 14th, her longest break in 1999 was one of twenty days. Last of eight in the Winter Hill Stakes on her return from that August vacation, perhaps the inactivity did not suit her. Diamond White unquestionably thrived on hard work. 1998 had finished off with a fine second in a listed race on the all-weather in late-November, and in 1999 she was at least as good at the end of the season as she had been at any time during it.

The finales were all a far cry from the start of her two latest campaigns when Diamond White struggled in vain to make an impact. In 1998, Diamond White was well below form for her first three outings after her return from winter quarters, and in 1999 seven races had already gone in 1999 before she managed even a place. There was a suspicion at the time that that performance, on soft ground at York in May, may have flattered her given the way the race was run, but it turned out to be just the first of six occasions in listed company in 1999 that her characteristic late flourish was rewarded with a finish in the first three. Listed races were by no means the height of connections' ambition for her, and she managed to force herself into the shake-up in pattern races as

Mr Peter P. Scott's "Diamond White"

well, notably on her fifteenth start when going down by just half a length and a head at 50/1 in the Group 1 Nassau Stakes at Glorious Goodwood. But there remained the question of whether place money would be the limit of her accomplishments as a four-year-old. Diamond White had won a listed race at two, at 25/1 in the Sweet Solera Stakes at Newmarket, but her three wins the following season had come at a less exalted level via a handicap, a classified stakes and a conditions stakes. After twenty races and ten different jockeys in 1999, the closest she had come was when short-headed, on that twentieth start, in a conditions stakes at Newbury. For the twenty-first race, a listed event at Goodwood, there was an eleventh jockey, Tim Sprake. It did the trick. Ridden closer to the pace than usual, Diamond White came to the front over one and a half furlongs out and went on to beat Prolix by four lengths. To prove that the feat was not so difficult, the combination clicked again with very similar tactics eleven days later; this time Diamond White beat Miss Berbere a length and registered her first pattern win in the Group 2 Prix de l'Opera Hotel du Lac Barriere at Longchamp on Arc day.

Both of those races were on very soft ground, the Nassau was on firm, and Diamond White has no problems with either of them, nor the fibresand at Wolverhampton. Her very best efforts have been over nine furlongs or a mile and a quarter, but she has also performed creditably over a mile when the ground is on the soft side. A new test for her was planned in the Breeders' Cup Filly And Mare Turf at Gulfstream Park but had to be scrapped when she put in a below-par performance in a Newmarket listed race and returned with a minor blood disorder. She would, of course, have had to improve on her previous form to feature prominently at the Breeders' Cup, but for all that she is some way off the best in her division, she has set new standards in toughness. A US campaign is being planned for Diamond White as a five-year-old after another crack at the Nassau Stakes, but it seems safe to say that racegoers here will still be seeing plenty of her.

			Roberto		Hail To Reason
	Robellino (USA)		(b 1969)		Bramalea
	(b 1978)		Isobelline		Pronto
Diamond White			(b 1971)		Isobella
(b.f. 1995)			Diamond Shoal		Mill Reef
	Diamond Wedding (USA)		(b 1979)		Crown Treasure
	(b 1989)		Wedding		Noholme II
			(ch 1973)		Charming Alibi

A workmanlike filly, Diamond White is the only winner so far from her dam's four offspring of racing age. Of the others, Wedding Music (by Music Boy) and Diamond Diaz (by Cyrano de Bergerac) have been poor but First Venture (by Formidable) showed fair form in the latest season. A colt by Be My Chief made 9,200 guineas as a foal at the 1998 Tattersalls December Sales, when his was one of those aforementioned catalogue entries which relied heavily on exploits listed under the third dam. Diamond White's dam, Diamond Wedding, ended up a modest middle-distance maiden with a question mark over her temperament, while grandam Wedding won a newcomers race over a mile and a quarter at Longchamp in April as a three-year-old and was not seen out again. Where their entries in the catalogue are necessarily concise, those of third dam Charming Alibi are extensive indeed. Having won sixteen of her own seventy-one races, she produced seven winners and one of those was Dahlia, outstanding on the racecourse and scarcely less so at stud, the dam of four winners at Grade 1 level and another two at Group/Grade 2. These family entries show that there is still plenty for Diamond White to aspire to. *M. J. Ryan*

DIBOLA 4 ch.g. Dilum (USA) 115 – Bella Bambola (IRE) 42 (Tate Gallery (USA) –
117) [1998 –: 5g 1999 a7g a8g⁶ a10g Feb 4] of little account. *J. S. Wainwright*

DICK TURPIN (USA) 5 br.g. Red Ransom (USA) – Turn To Money (USA) **65**
(Turn To Mars (USA)) [1998 73: a11g² a12g³ a10g* a10g⁶ a10g 1999 a12g⁴ a11g* **a81**

a11f* a11g³ a11g³ 12.5s⁵ 10m⁵ 10m 11.9d 11.9g³ 11.9f⁶ 10m 12d Aug 26] strong, lengthy gelding: fluent mover: fairly useful handicapper on all-weather, fair on turf: won at Southwell in January and February: below form final 3 starts: barely stays 1½m: acts on all-weather, good to firm and good to soft going. *B. Smart*

DIDIFON 4 b.c. Zafonic (USA) 130 – Didicoy (USA) 104 (Danzig (USA)) [1998 **89** 89: 8s 10d⁴ 10g³ 11.5g² 1999 9m 10.5d³ 10g* 10m⁴ 10d⁵ Oct 4] strong, good sort: fairly useful performer: won maiden at Ripon in August by 8 lengths, dictating pace: creditable effort in handicap at Brighton final start: stays 11.5f: acts on good to soft going: sold 22,000 gns. *B. W. Hills*

DIFFERENTIAL (USA) 2 b. or br.c. (Mar 12) Known Fact (USA) 135 – Talk **91** About Home (USA) (Elocutionist (USA)) [1999 5m* 5m³ 6m⁴ 5m Sep 11] $18,000Y, resold 19,000Y, 26,000 2-y-o: small, sturdy, quite attractive colt: half-brother to numerous winners in USA: dam minor winner in USA: fairly useful form: won maiden at Windsor in July: not disgraced in stronger company after, in frame at Ascot and Ripon, twelfth of 14 in Flying Childers at Doncaster final start: may prove best at 5f: raced only on good to firm ground: wore net muzzle second start. *B. Smart*

DIG FOR GOLD 6 ch.g. Digamist (USA) 110 – Formidable Task 61 (Formidable **–** (USA) 125) [1998 NR 1999 8.5m 12s 14.1m Jun 19] robust gelding: modest winning hurdler: little sign of ability on Flat: has had tongue tied. *R. D. E. Woodhouse*

DIGITAL IMAGE 2 b.c. (Feb 19) Presidium 124 – Sally Tadpole 44 (Jester 119) **88 +** [1999 5.1m* 6m 6m⁶ 5.2m Jul 17] 14,000Y: useful-looking colt: has a quick action: fourth foal: brother to 3-y-o Podium and half-brother to Italian 6f and 1¼m winner Bodolino (by Timeless Times): dam, ran 3 times, second at 5f at 2 yrs: won minor event at Chester in May: stiff tasks after, clearly best effort despite hanging left when sixth of 7 to City On A Hill in July Stakes at Newmarket: well below that form only subsequent start: stays 6f: raced only on good to firm ground. *R. Hannon*

DIGITAL OPTION (IRE) 5 b.g. Alzao (USA) 117 – Elevated (Shirley Heights **–** 130) [1998 NR 1999 a16g a12g Mar 10] robust gelding: poor maiden on Flat: visored (no form) in 1999. *Mrs N. Macauley*

DIGNIFY (IRE) 2 b.f. (Apr 28) Rainbow Quest (USA) 134 – Her Ladyship 119 **101** (Polish Precedent (USA) 131) [1999 7g* 7d³ 8g* 8v Oct 3] small, well-made filly: second foal: dam, French 10.5f winner (second in Prix de Diane), half-sister to smart middle-distance horse Lord of Men: useful form: won minor event at Chantilly in July and 7-runner Prix d'Aumale there in September, in latter leading over 1f out and holding rather unlucky Well Minded by short neck: 1½ lengths third to Princess Ellen in listed race at Newmarket in between: only seventh of 11 in Prix Marcel Boussac at Longchamp final start: will stay 1¼m. *D. R. Loder, France*

DIGON DA 3 ch.g. Sparky Lad 89 – Fleur Power (IRE) 54 (The Noble Player **77** (USA) 126) [1998 NR 1999 10m 8.3m³ 8.3m 7.7m⁴ 8m 10.2s Sep 27] second foal: brother to poor maiden: dam, third over 6f/7f, ran only at 2 yrs: fair maiden: ran creditably when in frame at Windsor and Warwick: stays 8.3f: acts on good to firm going: has looked wayward/headstrong: none too consistent. *B. Palling*

DIHATJUM 2 b.g. (Feb 27) Mujtahid (USA) 118 – Rosie Potts 83 (Shareef Dancer **60** (USA) 135) [1999 5m 6m 6m³ 7f³ 6g 6m⁵ 7g 7g² 8d⁶ Nov 1] 16,500Y: rather leggy, workmanlike gelding: fifth foal: half-brother to 3 winners, including 4-y-o Secret Style and fairly useful 1995 2-y-o 6f winner Greek Icon (by Thatching): dam, 6f (at 2 yrs) and 1m winner, half-sister to smart middle-distance performer Trakady: modest maiden: creditable efforts most starts, head second of 23 in claimer at Redcar penultimate start: changed hands 10,000 gns before final outing: should stay 1m: acts on firm going: visored (raced freely) once. *T. D. Easterby*

DIKTAT 4 br.c. Warning 136 – Arvola 75 (Sadler's Wells (USA) 132) [1998 **126** 121p: 7s* 7g* 7d* 7g² 1999 7d* 7m* 7m* 6.5s* 6m* 7d⁵ Oct 17]
Until meeting his Waterloo in the Prix de la Foret at Longchamp in October, Diktat laid down the law in four successive races, two of them Group 1. A very smart colt at the start of his campaign, he finished it as one of the very best sprinters around, second only to Stravinsky in Europe's pecking order. Not that Diktat can be regarded as a specialist sprinter—although his best runs have

come at around six furlongs, he gives the impression he may well be worth trying at a mile, even allowing for the fact that Godolphin already has great strength in depth at that distance.

Diktat had been trained by David Loder as a three-year-old, winning the Jersey Stakes at Royal Ascot in great style and losing narrowly to Decorated Hero in the Beeswing Stakes at Newcastle. His reappearance came in the Dubai Sports Shergar Cup Seven at Goodwood in May, part of a new event involving six well-endowed races, in each of which two teams of a maximum of five horses took each other on. The Shergar Cup teams represented the Middle East and Europe and were captained respectively by Sheikh Mohammed and Robert Sangster. There was sponsorship and television coverage, with an audience of 2.6 million tuning in, and the card was a good one, among the runners such pattern performers as Handsome Ridge and Running Stag in the mile and a quarter Classic, and Diktat, Russian Revival, Keos, Tomba and Ramooz in the Seven, the other race on the card worth £50,000. It was, however, stretching a point to claim, as the publicity did, that this represented 'the stars of the desert taking on the pride of Europe.' It was also stretching a point to imagine that, with the intention of boosting racing's appeal, the sport could ever be turned into an event along the lines of golf's Ryder Cup in a minor key, with partisanship through affinity for a team firing the imagination of a mass of people. Such a notion denies one of racing's essential characteristics. In any race, fans and punters give interest and loyalty to individual horses, and most of the time it matters not one iota where they come from or who owns them. If value is there in the market, it will be irrelevant to the logical punter whether the horse concerned belongs to a saint or a serial killer. Partisan support of the type the Shergar Cup hopes to engender seldom occurs in horseracing, and when it does, such as on occasions in the Arc and the Breeders' Cup, it does so precisely because it hasn't been stage managed. The kind of edge that exists in football or even (judged on the latest renewal!) the Ryder Cup, in which each side is distinct and supporters identify with their chosen side fiercely to the point of feeling distaste for the opposition, just doesn't happen in racing. Especially when each member of a team is trying to defeat not only the opposition but other members of the same team, and no special team tactics are allowed in the way they are in Formula One motor racing.

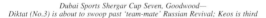

Dubai Sports Shergar Cup Seven, Goodwood—
Diktat (No.3) is about to swoop past 'team-mate' Russian Revival; Keos is third

Prix Maurice de Gheest, Deauville—Diktat continues Godolphin's tremendous Group 1 record; Gold Away finishes best of all in second place with Bertolini (visored) third

Shergar Cup day's final eccentricity consisted of the prices charged for admission. The fee for the Richmond Enclosure was £35, twice the price of most meetings and only £5 less than admission for Glorious Goodwood in July. Those going into the Gordon Enclosure paid £20, the same as at Glorious Goodwood and twice the usual rate. Such palpably exaggerated prices, set not by the course but by the marketing company which was running the day, were hardly likely to attract new racegoers or enthuse existing fans, even when half-price tickets were available up until three weeks beforehand. Whereas the Shergar Cup attracted 5,515 paying customers, the same day's Lingfield Derby Trial card—which took place on an equally dull afternoon—drew around 6,000. Beverley, with a tenth of the Goodwood prize money on offer, though admittedly in a completely different catchment area, had a crowd of 6,500. One thing is certain. If the Shergar Cup is to go even part way towards achieving its organisers' aims, they will need to spend a lot more time at the drawing board. In the event, Diktat put up an impressive display in his race, producing an excellent turn of foot to get out of trouble in the closing stages and beat Russian Revival a shade cosily by half a length.

Diktat's supposed inability to cope with firm ground has been a recurring theme in his career—after being supplemented for the July Cup as a three-year-old he was withdrawn because of the underfoot conditions—and it led to some trouble in the summer. The going at Goodwood was on the soft side, but when Diktat next faced the starter, in the Van Geest Criterion Stakes at Newmarket at the end of June, it was good to firm. In the interim he had had a slight set-back, which kept him out of calculations for Royal Ascot. Only five took him on, none of them in the same league, and after travelling strongly throughout Diktat breezed to the front a furlong from home. Despite idling a bit in front, something he had been noted as doing once or twice previously, he scored by a length and a half from Raise A Grand. The ground appeared not to inconvenience him in the slightest, but his connections had nothing to worry about on his next start, in the Prix Maurice de Gheest at Deauville in August, since it took place on soft going. This was Diktat's first, and fully deserved, crack at a Group 1 prize and he took the upgrade in his stride after starting at odds on, coupled with July Cup third Bertolini. Three others from that event were in the Deauville race—Vision of Night (fifth), Sampower Star (eighth) and Bianconi (ninth), as was Irish 2,000 Guineas third Orpen. There were also two of the horses beaten by Diktat in the Shergar Cup, Tomba and Keos, who had recently won the Prix de Ris-Orangis on the course, and the very smart

300

four-year-old miler Gold Away, potentially the best of the French if he could cope with the short trip. Diktat was drawn against the stand rail and, after being held up as usual, he quickened to challenge widest of all one and a half furlongs out as Bertolini made the running. In no danger inside the last furlong, Diktat won by a length from the strong-finishing Gold Away with Bertolini half a length back in third and Vision of Night fourth.

The Maurice de Gheest is over six and a half furlongs but Diktat's next target was over six, the Stanley Leisure Sprint Cup at Haydock on the first Saturday in September, which came at the end of a relatively dry couple of months. The executive watered the course during the week, putting on ten millimetres (nearly half an inch), with everything completed by lunchtime two days before the race. This provoked a furore and a complaint to the Jockey Club by three trainers, who believed that the watering had changed the going and was designed to ensure that certain horses, including by implication Diktat, ran. The Jockey Club decided no rules had been broken and exonerated the course's staff, who had made no secret of their intentions when general manager Lisa Rowe stated: 'We'll water to keep the ground good to firm if necessary, but we'll only have good ground if it rains.' Haydock at least has a modern, efficient watering system, one which produces uniform coverage, and in that respect it is ahead of a number of courses. The going on Friday and Saturday was officially good to firm, an assessment with which we concurred. One can debate the rights and wrongs of watering until blue in the face, but, in this instance, the watering was not excessive, the ground was not false, the eventual going was not dramatically different from what it would have been without being watered, and trainers and the public were kept fully and accurately informed. Moreover, the best horse in the race won, though it definitely was not a cakewalk for Diktat—he, and his rider Frankie Dettori, needed a full measure of determination to triumph.

In a record field of sixteen, Bertolini, Sampower Star and Tomba tried their luck again. Other tough opponents for the favourite at Haydock included

Stanley Leisure Sprint Cup, Haydock—fourth win in a row for Diktat, who is made to work harder this time by Bertolini

in-form Arkadian Hero, successful in listed races on his last two starts, Cork And Orrery Stakes winner Bold Edge and three-year-olds Imperial Beauty and Wannabe Grand. As Imperial Beauty led with Bertolini close up, all the runners moved across towards the stand side. This meant that Diktat, drawn on the rail and dropped out in a race where the pace wasn't strong, faced a wall of horses when Dettori started to push him along at halfway. He was tenth there and still only seventh over a furlong out, where the whip was produced. Thwarted in his attempt to get a run up the rail, Dettori switched the colt to challenge Bertolini, who wasn't stopping, and in a thrilling finale Diktat mustered the necessary pace to catch the leader twenty yards out. The winning margin was a neck, with Arkadian Hero one and three quarter lengths behind Bertolini in third and Bold Edge fourth. A memorable victory, and one of the most exciting races of the season.

Unfortunately, after the Lord Mayor's Show came the dustcart, in a manner of speaking. Diktat was an intended runner in the Queen Elizabeth II Stakes, which would have been his first race at a mile, but when the ground came up heavy at Ascot he was re-routed to the Prix de la Foret at Longchamp. The ground was slightly better than at Ascot, but Diktat singularly failed to run up to his best, running on without posing a threat in the straight to be fifth to Field of Hope. A challenge for the Breeders' Cup Mile was discounted and Diktat went back to Dubai for the winter.

		Known Fact	In Reality
	Warning	(b 1977)	Tamerett
	(b 1985)	Slightly Dangerous	Roberto
Diktat		(b 1979)	Where You Lead
(br.c. 1995)		Sadler's Wells	Northern Dancer
	Arvola	(b 1981)	Fairy Bridge
	(b or br 1990)	Park Appeal	Ahonoora
		(br 1982)	Balidaress

Godolphin's "Diktat"

There is little to add to the details carried in *Racehorses of 1998* regarding Diktat's breeding. Just as Warning was the best son of Known Fact, so Diktat is the best son of Warning, who has sired some good runners, including Charnwood Forest, Decorated Hero, Piccolo and Prophecy, but no outstanding ones. Warning is now based in Japan, as is Diktat's dam Arvola, who won over a mile and comes from a splendid family which boasts a number of Group 1 scorers, including her champion juvenile dam Park Appeal. Arvola, a half-sister to the high-class five-year-old Cape Cross, has had one other runner, the Nashwan three-year-old filly Shoei Mizuki, who has won in Japan, and her two-year-old is a colt by Hector Protector. Diktat, a good-topped, angular colt, is as game and consistent as they come and is altogether an admirable type. If he follows the example of a couple of other recent Godolphin five-year-olds, Swain and Daylami, who showed better form at that age than at three or four, he could be in for a cracking season. Let's hope so. *Saeed bin Suroor*

DIL 4 b.g. Primo Dominie 121 – Swellegant 84 (Midyan (USA) 124) [1998 88: 6d³ 6s 5m⁴ 5g* 6g⁴ 6g* 6f 6m 5.2g 5m* 5g 1999 a5g* 5d 5.2m a5g* 5d 6m 5d 5.2g 5.2g 5g 6.1s a5g⁵ a8.5g a7g³ Dec 21] lengthy, good-topped gelding: useful handicapper on all-weather, fairly useful on turf: improved form in former sphere in 1999, winning at Southwell in March and Wolverhampton (top weight, beat Consultant a length) in April: at least respectable efforts final 3 starts: effective at 5f and seems to stay 7f: acts on good to firm going, good to soft and fibresand: has worn net muzzle to post: visored tenth and eleventh starts: usually races prominently/leads. *Mrs N. Macauley* **85 a101**

DILETIA 2 b.f. (Feb 9) Dilum (USA) 115 – Miss Laetitia (IRE) (Entitled 126) [1999 7d⁶ 7m Sep 7] second foal: dam of little account: better effort in maidens (modest form) when sixth of 11 at Folkestone: slowly away next time: should stay 1m. *N. A. Graham* **64**

DILETTO (IRE) 3 b.f. Mujadil (USA) 119 – Avidal Park 68 (Horage 124) [1998 63: a5g⁶ 5d a5g³ 5.1g² 5.1g⁶ 5f³ 6m⁴ 6m⁴ 6s 6d⁴ 7g² 8m 1999 a6g 8g³ 7.5m 7.6m 8m⁵ 8m³ 7m 7g⁶ 10.9s 8m⁵ 9.2m³ 8d⁶ 7m 10m³ 9.9s 10.9v⁶ Oct 11] smallish, lengthy filly: fair maiden at best: stays 1¼m: acts on fibresand and firm going, probably on good to soft: blinkered thirteenth start: probably ungenuine. *E. J. Alston* **70 d**

DILIGENCE (IRE) 4 b.g. Dilum (USA) 115 – Florinda (CAN) (Vice Regent (CAN)) [1998 –: 5g 1999 6g 5s Oct 2] smallish, strong gelding: useful form at 2 yrs: well held since, in claimers in 1999. *G. B. Balding* **–**

DILKUSHA (IRE) 4 b.g. Indian Ridge 123 – Crimson Glen 70 (Glenstal (USA) 118) [1998 78: 8m 7g⁴ 8.1s 8s 7m⁵ 7.1m⁶ 7.1g³ 7m⁶ 7m* 7m⁵ 7m² 7.1g 1999 7m* 8m 7m* 7.6f⁵ 7m 7m³ 7m 7.1d⁶ a8g⁶ Nov 8] rather leggy gelding: has a quick action: fairly useful handicapper: better than ever at 4 yrs, well ridden by T. Quinn when winning at Kempton in June and Newbury in July: stays 7f: possibly best on good going or firmer, below form on equitrack: blinkered (not discredited) once at 3 yrs: has looked less than genuine in the past: usually held up. *B. J. Meehan* **84**

DILLUS 3 b.f. Dilum (USA) 115 – Lismore 61 (Relkino 131) [1998 58: 6g 5g² 6s⁴ 7.5d⁶ 6g² 6m⁶ 7m⁴ 7g 1999 8d 7m 8.2m 6g⁶ 6f⁶ Jul 14] leggy filly: modest form at 2 yrs, little in 1999: stays 6f: visored final 2 starts. *B. S. Rothwell* **–**

DILSAA 2 ch.c. (Feb 10) Night Shift (USA) – Llia 94 (Shirley Heights 130) [1999 7m⁵ 7.1m⁵ 7.1s² 7g⁵ Oct 16] 50,000Y: lengthy colt: first foal: dam, 2-y-o 7f winner who stayed 1½m, daughter of smart performer up to 9f Llyn Gwynant: fair maiden: well backed, best effort when fifth of 15 to It's Allowed in nursery at Catterick final start: will be suited by 1m+: raced freely on second start. *P. W. Harris* **77**

DIMINUTIVE (USA) 6 b.g. Diesis 133 – Graceful Darby (USA) (Darby Creek Road (USA)) [1998 82: 10g⁴ 10g 9.9m² 10.2g* 10m 10m³ 10m⁴ 10.1d 1999 10g³ 9.9m 10.2m 9f³ 10.1m³ 11.8m* 12d 12d a12g⁶ Oct 25] leggy gelding: has a round action: fair performer in 1999: won minor event at Leicester in August: below form final 3 starts: stays 1½m: acts on firm and good to soft going: joined Miss M. Rowland. *J. W. Hills* **76**

DIMMING OF THE DAY 2 ch.f. (Jan 22) Muhtarram (USA) 125 – Darkness At Noon (USA) (Night Shift (USA)) [1999 a5g 5.1m 5m³ 5f² 5.1h² 5g 5m⁴ a5f² a5g* **51 a64 ?**

a5g³ a5g³ Dec 4] good-topped filly: first foal: dam unraced, from family of Zilzal, Polish Precedent and Culture Vulture: modest performer: ran in sellers all starts, winning one at Wolverhampton in November (left B. Meehan 5,600 gns): raced at 5f: acts on fibresand, raced only on good going or firmer on turf: usually blinkered, not final 2 starts: races prominently/leads. *A. T. Murphy*

DIM OFAN   3 b.f. Petong 126 – Wilsonic 78 (Damister (USA) 123) [1998 80: 6g⁶   **73**
6.1g⁵ 6m⁵ 6.1g* 6m² 6m² 6s⁵ 6.1v* 1999 10.2g³ 8g 6m 6g 6.1g 6.1m 7s a7g⁴ a8g⁶ Dec 6] only fair performer in 1999: stays 7f: has form on good to firm ground, goes well on heavy and probably acts on all-weather. *B. Palling*

DIM OTS   4 b.f. Alhijaz 122 – Placid Pet 65 (Mummy's Pet 125) [1998 92: 6v* 6m   **–**
7m⁴ 6m⁵ 6m² 6m 6s 7g 1999 a7g a7g Feb 26] leggy filly: has a fluent, round action: fairly useful handicapper at 3 yrs: stays 6f: acts on good to firm going and heavy, well beaten on fibresand: blinkered final start. *B. Palling*

DINAR (USA)   4 b.c. Dixieland Band (USA) – Bold Jessie (Never So Bold 135)   **51**
[1998 NR 1999 7.1m 5g 7.5v 12.1m³ 11.1g 9.9g⁴ 12m* 12m² 11.9d 10s Nov 1] rangy colt: third foal: half-brother to useful sprinter Abou Zouz (by Miswaki): dam, won ff Tattersalls Breeders Stakes at 2 yrs, half-sister to good sprinters Prince Sabo and Millyant: modest performer: won handicap at Kempton in September: below form after next start: should prove best around 1½m: acts on good to firm going, below best on softer than good. *P. Bowen*

DING DONG   3 b.f. Librate 91 – Dawn Bell 55 (Belfort (FR) 89) [1998 –: 5g⁶ 5.1g   **–**
1999 a5g 6g a5g Apr 24] no sign of ability: has had tongue tied. *J. M. Bradley*

DINKY   2 ch.f. (May 14) Floose 99 – Marinsky (USA) 63 (Diesis 133) [1999 6s   **–**
8.2d 6d a6g a7g Nov 16] second reported foal: dam twice-raced daughter of smart French 10.5f winner Indoor: soundly beaten, including in seller. *M. J. Ryan*

DINKY-WINKY   2 gr.f. (Feb 14) Petong 126 – Just Julia (Natroun (FR) 128)   **–**
[1999 5m⁵ 5f⁶ 5g 6d 5g Nov 3] 7,000Y: third foal: half-sister to 4-y-o Facsimile and fairly useful 1996 2-y-o 5f/6f winner Just Visiting (by Superlative): dam no worth-while form: little sign of ability. *Miss L. A. Perratt*

DINO'S GIRL   2 ch.f. (Mar 2) Sabrehill (USA) 120 – Nashya (Rousillon (USA)   **–**
133) [1999 6g⁵ 7d 6d Oct 18] 4,000Y: third foal: half-sister to 3-y-o Ocean View and 5f winner General Sir Peter (by Last Tycoon): dam unraced daughter of smart 2-y-o Nashia: well beaten in maidens. *W. T. Kemp*

DION DEE   3 ch.f. Anshan 119 – Jade Mistress 51 (Damister (USA) 123) [1998   **–**
68: 7m³ 8g 7m 1999 10.2d May 17] tall, unfurnished filly: headstrong, and has failed to go on from debut: sold 1,500 gns in September. *A. P. Jarvis*

DIONYS (GER)   5 ch.h. Acatenango (GER) 127 – Desmona (Rainbow Quest   **52**
(USA) 134) [1998 48: 9.3v⁴ 9g 9d 10f⁵ 9.5s⁴ 10g 8.3d 8g a10g³ 1999 a12g³ a8f a10f⁴ a11.5g 9f 10s Aug 18] Belgian-trained horse: poor form at Lingfield first 3 starts in 1999: stays 10.3f: acts on heavy ground and equitrack: tried blinkered/visored. *C. Dondi, Belgium*

DIPLOMAT   3 b.g. Deploy 131 – Affair of State (IRE) 99 (Tate Gallery (USA)   **90**
117) [1998 78: 7.1m⁵ 7g⁴ 6m² 6m² 1999 6s* 6m 7g⁴ 8m² 8f 8m³ 8.1s* 7d⁶ a8g Nov 15] fairly useful performer: won maiden at Folkestone in March: mostly creditable efforts in handicaps after: races freely, and will prove best at 7f/1m: acts on soft and good to firm going: has carried head high: sent to USA. *D. W. P. Arbuthnot*

DIRECT DEAL   3 b.c. Rainbow Quest (USA) 134 – Al Najah (USA) 96 (Top-   **88**
sider (USA)) [1998 66: 7d³ 1999 11.1g 10g 10m 9m⁴ 10.2m* 10g³ Aug 11] rather leggy colt: fairly useful performer: won maiden at Bath in July: creditable third in handicap final start: should stay 1½m: acts on good to firm and good to soft going: sometimes tongue tied: sold 16,000 gns in October. *E. A. L. Dunlop*

DIRECT REACTION (IRE)   2 b.g. (Feb 5) College Chapel 122 – Mary's Way   **72**
(GR) 78 (Night Shift (USA)) [1999 5g⁴ a5g² 6g 5m⁵ 7s a7g⁵ a8g³ Dec 17] IR 12,500F, 36,000Y: lengthy, quite attractive gelding: first foal: dam lightly-raced 1m winner from family of In The Groove: fair maiden: stays 1m: acts on all-weather: blinkered (below form) fourth start. *Miss Gay Kelleway*

DISCERNING AIR   3 b.f. Ezzoud (IRE) 126 – Jhansi Ki Rani (USA) 94 (Far   **58 ?**
North (CAN) 120) [1998 68: 9m⁴ 8v² 8v³ 1999 12d⁴ 14.1m 14d Jul 1] leggy, sparely-
made filly: modest maiden: probably stays 1½m: acts on heavy going: sold 3,200 gns
in August. *E. Weymes*

DISCO TEX   4 b.g. Rambo Dancer (CAN) 107 – Andbracket (Import 127) [1998   **–**
52: 9.3d a12g⁶ 12m⁶ 12d 11s³ 13m* 12m³ 12g⁶ 9.9m⁶ 14.1m⁵ 15.8m³ 15.8d 1999
16.2m Jul 13] workmanlike gelding: modest handicapper: well below form only Flat
run of 1999: stays 2m: acts on soft and good to firm going: usually blinkered at 3 yrs:
successful twice over hurdles in July. *M. W. Easterby*

DISCRETION (IRE)   4 b.f. Alzao (USA) 117 – Sawaki 71 (Song 132) [1998 –:   **41**
7m⁴ 7d⁵ 8g 7g 6.1d 6.1s 1999 12.3m 9.9g 8.5d 6f 5g 6g Oct 15] smallish filly: poor
handicapper. *S. Gollings*

DISHABILLE   3 b.f. Dilum (USA) 115 – Swagger Lady 54 (Tate Gallery (USA)   **35**
117) [1998 38: 5m⁶ 6g⁶ 7d a6g⁵ 6m 1999 7m 7s⁴ 6g 7f May 31] tall, workmanlike
filly: modest maiden: stays 7f: acts on soft going and fibresand: blinkered final 3 starts.
J. D. Bethell

DISPOL AQUA (IRE)   2 b.f. (Feb 22) Namaqualand (USA) – Easter Morning   **38**
(FR) (Nice Havrais (USA) 124) [1999 6m⁶ 6d⁵ 7m Jul 21] IR 1,000F, 1,900Y: leggy,
angular filly: fourth foal: half-sister to 3-y-o Renaissance Lady: dam won over jumps
in France: form in sellers only on second start: has worn severe noseband. *P. Calver*

DISPOL CLAN   3 ch.f. Clantime 101 – She's A Breeze 35 (Crofthall 110) [1998   **53**
63: 5.1s* 5d² 5g² 5g⁴ 5d² a5g³ 5g a5g* a5g⁴ a5g* 1999 a5g a5s² a5g⁶ a5g Mar 13]
modest performer: best at 5f: acts on fibresand, raced only on good going or softer on
turf: sold 1,000 gns in June. *D. J. G. Murray Smith*

DISPOL DIAMOND   6 b.m. Sharpo 132 – Fabulous Rina (FR) (Fabulous Dancer   **59**
(USA) 124) [1998 72: 8.2s* 8d* 8.5m 8g³ 8.9s² 8g⁶ 7.9m⁶ 8m 8.9g 8.2v 1999 10.3f⁶
10d⁶ 9.2d⁴ 10g⁵ 8s 8d⁴ 8m 10.4f 8d⁴ Oct 26] leggy mare: modest handicapper: left
N. Tinkler after fifth start: creditable effort after only on final outing: stays 1¼m: acts
on firm and soft ground: usually comes from off pace. *J. S. Wainwright*

DISPOL EMMA   2 b.f. (Apr 12) Emarati (USA) 74 – Swift Pursuit 57 (Posse   **–**
(USA) 130) [1999 5d 5g 5f 5g Jul 1] 500Y: leggy, lightly-made filly: closely related
to a winner in Austria by Danehill and half-sister to 3-y-o Strip Search and 1994
2-y-o 5f winner Singing Rock (by Ballad Rock): dam second at 1m at 4 yrs: little sign
of ability, including in seller. *P. Calver*

DISPOL JAZZ   2 ch.f. (Feb 26) Alhijaz 122 – Foxtrot Pie 77 (Shernazar 131)   **70**
[1999 5.1f 6m* 5v³ 5g³ 6m² 5.9g* 7f⁶ 6m⁵ 7g² 6s⁴ 7s* 6d Oct 22] 500Y: leggy filly:
fifth foal: dam (maiden) should have been suited by 1½m+: fair performer: won
seller at Thirsk in May, minor event at Carlisle in July and nursery at Catterick in
October: should stay 1m: acts on soft and good to firm going: has tended to hang and
worn pricker: sometimes slowly away. *S. E. Kettlewell*

DISPOL MAGIC (IRE)   2 br.g. (Feb 28) Magic Ring (IRE) 115 – Miss Doody   **60**
63 (Gorytus (USA) 132) [1999 5m 5m 5d 6m* 7g⁴ 6g⁴ 7.1m 7.5g* 8d⁵ 7g Oct 15]
6,500Y: leggy, close-coupled, lightly-made gelding: third foal: half-brother to 3-y-o
Miss Doodybusiness: dam 6f (at 2 yrs) and 1¼m winner: modest performer: won
sellers at Hamilton in June and Beverley (nursery) in September: should stay 1m:
acts on good to firm going: has been bandaged in front: sold 2,500 gns, sent to
Denmark. *P. Calver*

DISPOL MISS CHIEF   2 ch.f. (Apr 3) Be My Chief (USA) 122 – Tino-Ella 73   **–**
(Bustino 136) [1999 7f⁵ 7.9m 7.9g Oct 6] 900Y: tall, unfurnished filly: seventh foal:
half-sister to 3-y-o Tikotino and 3 winners, including fairly useful 1997 2-y-o 7f
winner Absolutly Sparklin (by Midyan) and 1¾m winner Doddington Flyer (by
Distant Relative): dam 1¼m winner out of half-sister to Teenoso: well beaten in
maidens. *P. Calver*

DISPOL PRESIDENT   3 b.g. Presidium 124 – Sister Hannah 70 (Monseigneur   **–**
(USA) 127) [1998 59: 5s 5g⁶ 5m 1999 5d 5m⁶ 5g 8m Jun 18] close-coupled gelding:
no form since second 2-y-o outing: blinkered penultimate start: sold 1,200 gns.
P. Calver

DISPOL ROCK (IRE) 3 b.g. Ballad Rock 122 – Havana Moon (Ela-Mana-Mou **86**
132) [1998 69: 7g³ 7g 7g* 1999 8d 8m 8f³ 10m² 9f² 10m* 10.1m⁶ 10.3d Oct 22]
leggy, angular gelding: fairly useful handicapper: best effort when winning easily at
Ripon in August: stays 1¼m: acts on firm going, not at best on softer than good.
P. Calver

DISPOL TRUMP 3 ch.f. Chilibang 120 – Broken Silence 63 (Busted 134) [1998 **48**
48?: 5s 5d⁴ 6g 6m 1999 a7g 10m 12m² a12g 12g 12m 12g Aug 29] lengthy filly: poor
maiden: left P. Calver after fifth start: probably stays 1½m: no form on all-weather.
J. Norton

DISTANT BELLE 3 b.f. Distant Relative 128 – Moments Joy 56 (Adonijah 126) **–**
[1998 –: a6s 1999 a8.5g a7g⁵ a7s⁶ Feb 10] well beaten in maidens/handicap on
all-weather. *N. P. Littmoden*

DISTANT FLAME 2 b.f. (Apr 15) Distant Relative 128 – Brockton Flame 72 **–**
(Emarati (USA) 74) [1999 6.1g Jul 3] 10,000Y: first foal: dam 6f winner, including at
2 yrs: second favourite but well held in maiden at Nottingham. *N. A. Graham*

DISTANT GUEST 2 b.c. (Feb 26) Distant Relative 128 – Teacher's Game 64 **?**
(Mummy's Game 120) [1999 6.1m 8s 8d Oct 27] 11,500F, 24,000Y: seventh foal:
half-brother to 1994 2-y-o 7f winner Pleasure Beach (by Pharly) and 1¼m winner
Ludo (by Petong): dam sprint maiden: modest maiden: probably flattered (could be
worth a rating of 67) when seventh of 10 to King Spinner in steadily-run race at
Yarmouth on final start: likely to prove best up to 1m. *G. G. Margarson*

DISTANT KING 6 b.g. Distant Relative 128 – Lindfield Belle (IRE) 78 (Fairy **–**
King (USA)) [1998 60: a7g 5s 8s⁶ 9v 6v 7d 10s 5s³ 5m* 5g⁴ 5m* 5g* 7g 6m 5m 6m
5m 6m 5m 5v 1999 5d 5m 5g 5m 5g 5m 5m⁶ 6f 6m 5g⁶ 6v 5d a6g Nov 20] sturdy
gelding: poor mover: modest performer at best: little form in 1999, flattered tenth
start: stays 6f: tried blinkered. *G. P. Kelly*

DISTANT MUSIC (USA) 2 b.c. (Feb 3) Distant View (USA) 126 – Musicanti **121 p**
(USA) (Nijinsky (CAN) 138) [1999 7m* 7m* 7g* Oct 16]
The death of Mr Prospector, who was put down on June 1st at Claiborne
Farm in Kentucky because of acute peritonitis, ended a long and supremely
successful chapter in the history of bloodstock. The twenty-nine-year-old, who
had 1,049 foals with more to come from the forty-seven mares he covered in
the spring, boasts a running total, at the time of writing, of one hundred and
sixty-five stakes winners, making him the world leader ahead of Nijinsky.
In the States, where he was twice champion sire, Mr Prospector has been
responsible for a host of top-flight performers, including Horse of the Year
Conquistador Cielo, champions Eillo, Forty Niner, Gold Beauty, Golden
Attraction, Gulch, It's In The Air, Queena and Rhythm, plus such Grade 1
scorers as Fappiano, Gone West, Seeking The Gold and Tank's Prospect. At
one stage there was a preconception that his progeny were not 'natural' turf
performers, so could not be expected to shine in Europe, but that theory has
been undermined to a large degree by Coup de Genie, Distant View, Kingmambo, Machiavellian, Miswaki, Ravinella and Woodman among others.
A mighty impressive list, but, while one chapter may be over, the story
is a long way from finished. A number of Mr Prospector's sons, grandsons and
daughters have been having a major impact at stud, a fact confirmed by a glance
at the best horses in training in Europe in the latest season. Dubai Millennium,
El Condor Pasa, Almutawakel, Fruits of Love, Ciro and Rossini are all by sons
of the old stallion, as is the best two-year-old, Distant Music, who comes from
the first crop of high-class miler Distant View. Fasliyev, one of his rivals for the
title of top juvenile, is out of a mare by Mr Prospector, as are Brahms, whom
Distant Music beat in the Dewhurst Stakes, and Lermontov, runner-up in the
Racing Post Trophy.
Distant Music is unbeaten and a clear favourite for the Two Thousand
Guineas, a position he occupied even before Fasliyev's injury. The race looks
tailor-made for him, though as usual with ante-post prices on the classics these
days the odds hardly encourage one to rush to make an investment. But to begin

at the beginning. Distant Music made his debut in the maiden race at Doncaster in July which Auction House had won easily the previous year, and he emulated his stable-companion by putting seven rivals firmly in their place, landing the odds easily by four lengths from Eternal Spring with Best of The Bests in third. Auction House had contested the Acomb Stakes before winning the Champagne Stakes at Doncaster; Distant Music went straight to the latter course for the Champagne, sponsored by Frigidaire. Although only five took him on, there wasn't a duffer among them. Rossini, from the immensely powerful Aidan O'Brien yard, had won all his three starts, including two pattern races, the Anglesey Stakes and the Prix Robert Papin, the latter of which he had inflicted a five-length defeat on the German colt Auenklang, easy winner next time out of a Group 2 race at Baden-Baden. Ekraar had made all to win the Champagne Lanson Vintage Stakes, Dramatic Quest and Winning Venture had collected useful races at Ascot and Kempton respectively, and Tioga had been runner-up in listed company at Newbury. Distant Music, receiving 4 lb from the pattern winners, started favourite and put up a tremendously impressive display, the best of the season by a juvenile. He settled really well in the rear as Ekraar led, made ground effortlessly as the race took shape two and a half furlongs out and quickened readily to assert his authority over Rossini, staying on strongly with just one crack of the whip to beat the Irish colt by two and a half lengths. Winning Venture was five lengths back in third with Ekraar, who dropped out rather tamely and didn't give his running, fourth. Despite the style of Distant Music's victory, he was only third favourite for the Guineas with most firms at a best price of 10/1 behind O'Brien's Bernstein and Fasliyev immediately after the race, though his odds had contracted considerably by early-October in the run-up to the Dewhurst Stakes, the race in which Auction House had run second after his Champagne victory.

The Dewhurst lacked a sponsor, and for bizarre reasons that owed more to a Dick Francis thriller than real life. The Thoroughbred Corporation, which had put up the money in 1997 and 1998, was going to do so again, but reportedly 'gave' the event to their partners Saudi Arabian Airlines. However, as Emirates Airlines were sponsoring the Dubai Champion Stakes—without, be it noted, having their name in the title—it was decided, for no logical reason that we saw, that different airlines should not sponsor on the same card. The Thoroughbred Corporation was then going to re-enter the fray, but at a late stage decided not to, and Newmarket was left to find the money to ensure the race retained its value. It would have been highly instructive to see a fit Fasliyev taking on Distant Music in the Dewhurst, but he was taken out a few days beforehand, ostensibly because he had already proved himself at Group 1 level, whereas Brahms and Zentsov Street had not. The bookmakers had no doubts about which colt had the better chance, having made Distant Music 5/4 favourite with Fasliyev at 2/1, though that obviously had no bearing on Fasliyev's withdrawal. In the event Fasliyev fractured a pastern and couldn't have run anyway. Distant Music started at odds on, with King's Best, successful in the Acomb Stakes, second favourite ahead of Port Vila, a winner at Newbury and Kempton. The O'Brien hopes, Middle Park Stakes third Brahms and

Frigidaire Champagne Stakes, Doncaster—Distant Music puts up the best performance of the season by a two-year-old, Rossini having no answer to the winner's turn of foot

Dewhurst Stakes, Newmarket—Distant Music maintains his unbeaten record with an authoritative performance from Brahms (visor) and Zentsov Street (star on cap)

Newmarket maiden winner Zentsov Street, were the outsiders of the party, but they were the ones who gave Distant Music most to do. Zentsov Street made the running at a modest pace as King's Best pulled hard for his head, ruining whatever chance he had, while Distant Music was waited with. Cruising through to challenge from halfway, Distant Music quickened decisively when shaken up over a furlong out and went more than two lengths clear. However, instead of running away with the race he idled noticeably on meeting the rising ground and had only a length to spare over Brahms, who put in a renewed though never-threatening effort. Zentsov Street was two lengths away third. Taken at face value, Distant Music's Dewhurst form falls some way short of Guineas-winning standard in a normal year, but, in all probability, Distant Music, who has a splendid turn of foot, will be suited by being waited with for longer. The Guineas looks ideal for Distant Music, as it is almost certain to attract a larger field than the Dewhurst and his jockey should be able to hold him up for as long as necessary before unleashing him.

Distant Music (USA) (b.c. Feb 3, 1997)	Distant View (USA) (ch 1991)	Mr Prospector (b 1970)	Raise A Native / Gold Digger
		Seven Springs (ch 1982)	Irish River / La Trinite
	Musicanti (USA) (b 1991)	Nijinsky (b 1967)	Northern Dancer / Flaming Page
		Populi (b or br 1975)	Star Envoy / Sister Shannon

Distant Music contributed the lion's share of the earnings that enabled Distant View to land the first-season sires' title, though promising Decarchy, useful Observatory and Kelso Magic also won for him. Distant View did not get the chance to race beyond a mile and he did not race beyond the age of three either, due to training troubles. He showed his mettle in his classic season by running fifth in the Guineas as a once-raced maiden, finishing second in the St James's Palace Stakes and beating six Group 1 scorers in the Sussex Stakes. He did not run up to his best in the Queen Elizabeth II Stakes and Breeders' Cup Mile and eventually was retired to Juddmonte Farm in Kentucky at a modest fee of 10,000 dollars. One of the seventy-eight mares he covered in his initial season was Musicanti, who had run five times in France, showing only useful form and winning over fourteen and a half furlongs at Saint-Cloud. Distant Music is her first foal and she produced a sister to him in January before being covered by Quest For Fame. Musicanti stayed well and comes from a family

with some top-notch middle-distance performers close up. Her first two dams were only minor winners, but Populi produced Vanlandingham, successful in the Washington DC International and Jockey Club Gold Cup over a mile and a half and the Suburban Handicap over a mile and a quarter. Sister Shannon produced Temperence Hill, who won the Belmont Stakes, Jockey Club Gold Cup, Travers Stakes and Suburban Handicap. Looking at this pedigree, and paying due attention to the way he races, the Guineas trip should suit Distant Music at least as well as seven furlongs and he should stay a mile and a quarter in due course. A tall, attractive individual, who has raced only on good ground or firmer, Distant Music has every chance of making the progress that will probably be necessary for him to emulate Zafonic and Pennekamp, the most recent winners of the Dewhurst Stakes to add the Guineas to their tally. *B. W. Hills*

DISTANT PROSPECT (IRE) 2 b.c. (Mar 24) Namaqualand (USA) – Ukraine's **64** Affair (USA) (The Minstrel (CAN) 135) [1999 6d 6.1m 6.8m³ 7.9f Sep 2] IR 9,000F, 11,000Y: unfurnished colt: fifth foal: half-brother to 4-y-o Cool Affair and 3 winners, including 5-y-o Protocol and Irish 1994 2-y-o 5f winner Aliuska (by Fijar Tango): dam, unraced, from family of Poule d'Essai des Pouliches winner Ukraine Girl: 33/1, best effort in maidens when third of 9 to Ecstasy at Warwick: well held in nursery at York final start: should stay 1m. *J. R. Arnold*

DISTANT STORM 6 ch.g. Pharly (FR) 130 – Candle In The Wind 90 (Thatching **60 §** 131) [1998 54: a16.2g³ a16g² a16g³ a16g⁵ 14.1v² 14.1s³ 1999 a16.2g 18d² 16.1s² 18g² Jun 14] robust gelding: modest handicapper: good efforts on form last 3 starts, but found little final one: stays 2¼m: acts on all-weather, probably on any turf: blinkered/visored: one to treat with caution: fair hurdler. *B. J. Llewellyn*

DISTINCTIVE DREAM (IRE)   5 b.g. Distinctly North (USA) 115 – Green   **82 §**
Side (USA) 37 (Green Dancer (USA) 132) [1998 91§: 6g 6g² 6g² 6g 6g 7g 7d 1999
6f⁶ 7.1m⁶ 7m² 7.1f* 7.6f⁴ 7f Jul 26] strong, lengthy gelding: fairly useful performer:
won minor event at Haydock in July: stays 7f: acts on any turf going and on fibresand: visored last 3 starts, usually blinkered previously: sometimes slowly away, and
is held up: moody: sold 1,500 gns in October, joined A. Bailey. *Lady Herries*

DISTINCTLY BLU (IRE)   2 b.f. (Apr 3) Distinctly North (USA) 115 – Stifen   **–**
(Burslem 123) [1999 5g 5m May 26] 750Y: leggy filly: half-sister to 4-y-o Ruzen,
3-y-o Reason Why and 3 winners abroad: dam unraced: well held in maidens.
K. A. Ryan

DISTINCTLY EAST (IRE)   2 b.g. (Apr 8) Distinctly North (USA) 115 – Raggy   **77**
(Smoggy 115) [1999 5m* 6m⁴ 5d⁵ 6g⁶ 8m 6s² 6d Oct 15] IR 6,000F, 6,200Y:
smallish, useful-looking gelding: fluent mover: half-brother to a winner in Holland
by Shalford: dam French 9f winner: fair performer: won maiden at Ripon in April:
easily best efforts when in frame in small-field minor events at Yarmouth: stays
6f: acts on soft and good to firm going: none too consistent. *M. H. Tompkins*

DISTINCTLY WELL (IRE)   2 b.g. (Apr 29) Distinctly North (USA) 115 –   **75**
Brandywell (Skyliner 117) [1999 5g⁴ 5.1s² 5.1m² a6g² 6d 5.1d⁴ 5.1m⁴ 6.8m⁴ 5.1m⁶
6m⁵ 6g⁵ 7d* 7.9f⁶ 7m 7.9d 7g Oct 16] 2,800Y: angular gelding: eighth foal: half-
brother to 3-y-o Yakareem and 1996 2-y-o 6f winner Parijazz (by Astronef): dam,
poor Irish maiden, granddaughter of Irish 1,000 Guineas winner Princess Trudy: fair
performer: made all in nursery at Chester in August: well held last 3 starts: probably
stays 1m: acts on firm going, soft and fibresand: visored (well beaten) once: often on
toes, and tends to sweat. *P. D. Evans*

DIVA D'ARGENT   3 gr.f. Petong 126 – Duxyana (IRE) (Cyrano de Bergerac   **–**
120) [1998 –: a5g a6g 1999 a5g a6g⁵ Jan 16] no form. *W. R. Muir*

DIVE   2 b.g. (Jan 28) Slip Anchor 136 – Delightful Chime (IRE) 79 (Alzao (USA)   **– p**
117) [1999 8.1m 7d 7s⁶ Sep 22] 52,000Y: first foal: dam, Irish 2-y-o 1m winner,
sister to Cheveley Park and Moyglare Stud Stakes winner Capricciosa: well beaten
in maidens at Chepstow (slowly away and hampered early), Yarmouth and Chester:
should do better over 1¼m+. *Sir Mark Prescott*

DIVER'S PEARL (FR)   2 b.f. (Apr 28) Prince Sabo 123 – Seek The Pearl 91   **74 p**
(Rainbow Quest (USA) 134) [1999 6d⁶ 6m³ Sep 7] third foal: half-sister to 3-y-o
Enlighten and 1997 2-y-o 7f winner Opposition Leader (by Be My Chief): dam 1¼m
winner: length third of 19 to Iftiraas in maiden at Lingfield, keeping on without
being given hard time: should stay 7f, probably 1m: likely to improve again.
J. R. Fanshawe

DIVIDE AND RULE   5 b.h. Puissance 110 – Indivisible 56 (Remainder Man   **33**
126§) [1998 –: a5g a7g 5g 5m 5.1d a6g a5g³ 1999 a6s 5f 6d 5m 6m 5.1m a5g a6g Dec
1] smallish horse: poor performer nowadays. *R. Hollinshead*

DIVIDED HONOURS (IRE)   2 b.c. (Apr 22) Sri Pekan (USA) 117 – It's All   **–**
Academic (IRE) 91 (Mazaad 106) [1999 5f 5.1m⁶ 6s⁴ 7m Jul 21] 17,000F, 20,000Y:
small colt: second living foal: half-brother to 5-y-o Warrior King: dam, 2-y-o 5f
winner: well beaten in varied company. *D. Shaw*

DIVINE HOSTESS   2 br.f. (Feb 9) Batshoof 122 – Divina Mia 66 (Dowsing   **–**
(USA) 124) [1999 6m 6f⁴ 7f Jul 30] 3,000F: leggy, lengthy filly: first foal: dam, 2-y-o
6f winner who stayed 11f, out of useful half-sister to Shirley Heights: always behind,
looking hard ride, in maidens and claimer. *M. W. Easterby*

DIVINE MISS-P   6 ch.m. Safawan 118 – Faw (Absalom 128) [1998 90: a6g*   **85 d**
a6g³ a6g⁵ a5g² a5g* 5d* a5g⁶ 5.3d² 6g² 5.1g* 5m³ 6m 5.7d⁵ 5.1d* 5d² 5g³ 5g
5.6g 5.2g 5s 1999 5s 5.1g* 5m 5g³ 5.1m⁶ 5m 6.1s 5s² 5d 5.1s 5d a5g a5g Nov 19]
lengthy mare: fairly useful performer at best: dead-heated with Cauda Equina in
minor event at Bath in May: lost her form in second half of year: barely stays 6f: acts
on good to firm going, soft and all-weather: has been bandaged in front: used to race
prominently, but ridden with more restraint of late. *J. Cullinan*

DIVINE PROSPECT (IRE)   2 b. or br.f. (Apr 14) Namaqualand (USA) – Kayu   **75**
(Tap On Wood 130) [1999 5s³ 6f 6g⁵ 7m⁶ 7g* 7.3g⁵ 7.9f 8d⁶ Oct 15] IR 12,000Y: tall,
close-coupled filly: half-sister to several winners, including Irish 7f (at 2 yrs) and
1½m winner Vincitore (by Petorius) and 1994 2-y-o 6f winner Rich Victim (by

Lapierre), later useful up to 1½m in Hong Kong under name of Mazal: dam, unraced, from family of 3-y-o Fairy Queen and Irish St Leger winner M-Lolshan: fair performer: won nursery at Newmarket in August: creditable efforts in similar events last 2 starts: should stay 1¼m: acts on firm and good to soft going: held up. *A. P. Jarvis*

DIVORCE ACTION (IRE) 3 b.g. Common Grounds 118 – Overdue Reaction **75** (Be My Guest (USA) 126) [1998 63: 6m⁵ 7d³ 7m 8d 1999 8g⁵ 10.5m⁵ 11.6m 9m* 10d⁵ 9.7d Aug 26] fair performer: won claimer at Kempton (final start for P. Cole) in August: found little final start: stays 10.5f: yet to race on extremes of going: has carried head high. *P. R. Hedger*

DIXIE FLYER (IRE) 2 b.f. (Apr 26) Blues Traveller (IRE) 119 – African Cousin **34** (Kampala 120) [1999 5d 5d 7m 7f a5g Oct 13] IR 2,500Y: rangy filly: half-sister to 5f winner Nordoora (by Fayruz): dam Irish 2-y-o 5f/6f winner: little form. *E. J. Alston*

DIXIE JAZZ 3 br.f. Mtoto 134 – Dixie Favor (USA) 82 (Dixieland Band (USA)) **51** [1998 –p: 8m⁶ 7v 1999 8g⁵ Apr 7] workmanlike filly: signs of ability in maidens: likely to stay 1¼m. *Miss J. A. Camacho*

DIXIELAKE (IRE) 2 b.f. (Feb 9) Lake Coniston (IRE) 131 – Rathvindon 93 **59 p** (Realm 129) [1999 7s Nov 5] 11,500F, 28,000Y: angular filly: half-sister to 4-y-o Soneva and several winners, notably dual 1m winner Lady Fairfax (by Sharrood) and fairly useful 1¼m/1½m winner Andrath (by Commanche Run): dam 5f winner: travelled strongly 5f when eighth of 20 to Golovin in maiden at Doncaster: should do better. *H. Candy*

DIXXY DANCER (IRE) 2 b.c. (May 19) Dancing Dissident (USA) 119 – Biddy **?** Mulligan (Ballad Rock 122) [1999 5m 5m⁵ 5.1m⁶ 6s 6d 8s 6v Nov 24] 17,500 2-y-o: brother to useful Irish 5f winner Miss Potter and half-brother to 3 winners abroad: dam, placed up to 1m in Ireland, half-sister to high-class sprinter The Blues: appeared to show modest form (could be rated 60) on second start: left M. Channon after next outing and showed little for 3 different trainers in France: tried blinkered. *B. Goudot, France*

DIZZY KNIGHT 2 b.f. (May 4) Distant Relative 128 – Top Treat (USA) 101 **61** (Topsider (USA)) [1999 6m Sep 18] rather angular filly: eighth foal: half-sister to 3 winners, including 3-y-o Oscietra and middle-distance stayer Ela Man Howa (by Mtoto): dam, 6f winner, probably stayed 1m: showed ability when eighth of 15 in Newbury maiden, though never a threat: may do better. *M. J. Fetherston-Godley*

DIZZY TILLY 5 b.m. Anshan 119 – Nadema (Artaius (USA) 129) [1998 64d: **59** 10g 10d³ 9.9m 10g 10g 14.1m 10.8m⁵ 11.5m⁵ 12g 10v⁶ 1999 11.6m 10g 11.5g⁵ 9m⁵ 11.6m* 10g² 11.6m⁴ 12m⁵ 12s³ 11.6m⁶ 12m² 14.1g³ 11.6g Oct 11] tall mare: modest handicapper: won at Windsor (all 3 successes there) in June: several creditable efforts after: stays 1¾m: acts on soft and good to firm going: usually races prominently: sold 12,000 gns. *A. J. McNae*

DJAIS (FR) 10 ch.g. Vacarme (USA) 121 – Dame de Carreau (FR) (Targowice **–** (USA) 130) [1998 NR 1999 18g⁶ May 18] good-topped gelding: one-time smart middle-distance stayer in France, just fairly useful form at best at 7 yrs and better known nowadays as a modest and unreliable hurdler, successful in October. *J. R. Jenkins*

D'MARTI 4 b.f. Emarati (USA) 74 – Hellene (Dominion 123) [1998 80: 6d 5s³ 5s³ **68 d** 5m 6s⁵ 5g⁴ 5d² 5d* 5.1d 5d 5g 5d³ 1999 5g 5d³ 5d 5g⁵ 6g 6g 5d 6.1d 6g Oct 14] useful-looking filly: fair handicapper at best: below form after second start: probably best at 5f: acts on soft going, well held on fibresand: sold 1,000 gns, sent to Israel. *C. B. B. Booth*

DOBAANDI SECRET 3 b.g. Reprimand 122 – Secret Dance (Sadler's Wells **–** (USA) 132) [1998 –: 7m 8d a9.4g 1999 10.3d 14.1m May 7] strong gelding: no sign of ability: ran as if something amiss final start. *A. Bailey*

DOBERMAN (IRE) 4 br.g. Dilum (USA) 115 – Switch Blade (IRE) 60 (Robel- **60 §** lino (USA) 127) [1998 71, a53: 5f² 6f² 7m⁵ 5.7m⁴ a6g⁴ a7g a8g 1999 a10g⁵ a8.5g² **a53 §** a8g a10g⁶ 10s⁶ 8m 10.5d 6.1g a8.5g⁴ a8.5g² 7f 8.1m² a8.5g³ 10m 8.1m³ 9.1d⁶ a8.5g⁴ a12g a10g⁴ Nov 26] rangy gelding: modest maiden: left B. Meehan after fourth outing and S. Brookshaw after ninth: barely stays 1¼m: acts on firm and soft going and all-weather: seems effective blinkered/visored or not: has tongue tied: has wandered under pressure: inconsistent and none too genuine. *P. D. Evans*

DOCKLANDS MERC (IRE)   3 b.f. Common Grounds 118 – Chouette 54 (Try   –
My Best (USA) 130) [1998 –: 5.1m 1999 a7g⁵ a10g⁵ 7s Apr 1] angular, close-
coupled filly: no sign of ability in maidens/seller. *R. T. Phillips*

DOCKSIDER (USA)   4 ch.c. Diesis 133 – Pump (USA) (Forli (ARG)) [1998   **124**
109: 7s 8g² 8g 8.1m* 8m 1999 10m* 9.9g³ 8g* 8m² 8m* 8f² 10f⁶ 8g³ 8m*
Dec 12]

Following Docksider's emphatic victory in the Hong Kong Mile at Sha
Tin in December his trainer John Hills was still clinging to the faint hope that a
decision to retire the colt might be reversed. 'He's a very sound horse and is
getting better and better—we would know exactly what we've got to go to war
with next season', said Hills. Unfortunately for him the best horse he has ever
trained is set to take up stallion duties at the Airlie Stud at a fee of IR £6,000.
Docksider couldn't have ended his racing career in a better fashion. The short-
priced favourite in a twelve-runner field for this Group 2 contest worth over
£326,000 to the winner, Docksider dominated the majority of the race under a
fine ride from Olivier Peslier. The early pace was steady and after a couple of
furlongs or so Peslier sent Docksider to the front, kicking on turning for home.
Docksider responded immediately to go clear and was in no danger from
thereon, passing the post a length and three quarters ahead of Field of Hope,
who just got the best of Resfa and Muhtathir in the battle for the minor placings.

Docksider might well have shown further improvement had he been
kept in training, as he made remarkable progress in his third and final season.
He'd begun it as a no more than useful performer with just a couple of wins to
his name, one in a maiden at Salisbury at two years and the other in a minor
event at Sandown at three. Within the space of a month at the start of his

Hong Kong Mile, Sha Tin—British-trained Docksider makes most of the running

four-year-old campaign, Docksider had doubled that total. Stepped up to a mile and a quarter, Docksider easily won a minor event at Newmarket on his reappearance; and two outings later he was even more impressive when winning the Group 3 Laurent-Perrier-Meile at Baden-Baden by six lengths. German racegoers were treated to a similar performance from Docksider when he won the Group 2 Berlin Brandenburg-Trophy at Hoppegarten in July by seven lengths, breaking the course record in the process, but if anything his reputation was enhanced more by a couple of defeats which he suffered around the same time. The Queen Anne Stakes at Royal Ascot saw Docksider making his first appearance for his new owner Gary Tanaka, and he did him proud in finishing a short-head second to Cape Cross, holding a slight advantage from over two furlongs out until well inside the last. It was another Godolphin runner, the three-year-old Aljabr, who came between Docksider and a Group 1 victory in the Sussex Stakes at Goodwood. The pair had a great battle through the last three furlongs as they pulled clear of the remainder, but hard though Docksider tried he was forced to give best near the finish, going down by a length. Docksider wasn't seen out again in Britain, his two races prior to Hong Kong both taking place in the USA. After missing a race at Woodbine in mid-September because of a bruised foot, Docksider then failed to do himself justice in the Oak Tree Turf Championship at Santa Anita, finishing last of the six runners. However, he more than made up for that in the Breeders' Cup Mile at Gulfstream. Docksider didn't get the best of starts and was therefore unable to take up his usual prominent position, but he stayed on well to finish third behind Silic and Tuzla, beaten only a neck and a head.

Docksider (USA) (ch.c. 1995)	Diesis (ch 1980)	Sharpen Up (ch 1969)	Atan
			Rocchetta
		Doubly Sure (b 1971)	Reliance II
			Soft Angels
	Pump (USA) (ch 1982)	Forli (ch 1963)	Aristophanes
			Trevisa
		Espadrille (b 1977)	Damascus
			Thong

Mr Gary A. Tanaka's "Docksider"

As a very smart and thoroughly genuine and consistent racehorse with a good pedigree, Docksider should prove popular at stud. His dam, the unraced Pump, comes from a very good family, out of a stakes-winning daughter of the excellent broodmare Thong. Among Thong's ten winning produce were the top-class sprinter Thatch, the Coronation Stakes winner Lisadell and the Irish Derby and St Leger runner-up King Pellinore, who trained on into an even better horse in the States; while Thong is also the grandam of Nureyev and great grandam of Sadler's Wells. Docksider, whose yearling sister was sold for 600,000 guineas at the Houghton Sales in October, is himself a half-brother to several winners, three of them by Nijinsky, including the useful middle-distance performer Classic Sport. The useful-looking Docksider, a free-running sort with a fluent, round action who often sweated, was effective at a mile and a mile and a quarter. He did virtually all of his racing on, and almost certainly needed, good ground or firmer. *J. W. Hills*

DOC RYAN'S 5 b.h. Damister (USA) 123 – Jolimo 92 (Fortissimo 111) [1998 **64** 73§, a66§: 11.8s⁵ 12s⁶ 11v 12.5s⁵ 12s* 12d 12d 14.1g 12s² a14g² a14g⁴ a14g⁴ 1999 **a82** 15.4v⁵ a14g* a16g* a16g³ a14g* a16.2g* a12g* 11.9d³ 16g² 12m⁶ 12d Sep 30] small horse: poor mover: fairly useful on all-weather, modest on turf: won 2 handicaps at Southwell in May and claimers at same course and Wolverhampton (2) in June: effective at 1½m to 2m: acts on fibresand, possibly best on ground softer than good on turf: blinkered: sometimes finds little: fair novice hurdler, won in October. *M. J. Ryan*

DOCTOR BRAVIOUS (IRE) 6 b.g. Priolo (USA) 127 – Sharp Slipper (Sharpo **47** 132) [1998 45: 9.3s 8g 7.5g³ 8s 6.9d⁶ 8g² 8g 1999 12v² 13.3f⁵ 12d Jun 5] rangy gelding: poor handicapper: stays 13f: acts on any turf going and fibresand: visored/blinkered: has found little, and sometimes hangs left and swishes tail. *Jamie Poulton*

DOCTOR DENNIS (IRE) 2 b.g. (Mar 21) Last Tycoon 131 – Noble Lustre **67** (USA) 71 (Lyphard's Wish (FR) 124) [1999 6g 7.1m⁵ 7.1m 8f⁶ 10.2s 8.3g 7d² Oct 21] 17,000F, IR 24,000Y: good-bodied gelding: fifth foal: half-brother to useful 7f and (in USA) 1m winner Royal Rebuke (by Reprimand): dam, 6f winner who stayed 1m, from family of US Grade 1 winner Buckhar: fair maiden: blinkered last 3 starts, returning to best when length second of 16 in nursery at Brighton on final one: best at 7f: acts on good to firm and good to soft going. *B. J. Meehan*

DOCTOR KOOL 3 ch.g. Local Suitor (USA) 128 – Hasty Sarah 56 (Gone **70** Native) [1998 67: 5g⁴ 5m 6m⁴ 7.9g 8v⁴ 1999 8d⁵ 12m Jun 24] workmanlike gelding: has a round action: fair maiden: ran creditably first of only 2 starts in 1999: stays 1m, not 1½m: acts on good to firm and heavy going: tends to wander. *T. P. Tate*

DOCTOR SPIN (IRE) 3 b.c. Namaqualand (USA) – Madam Loving 99 (Vaigly **103** Great 127) [1998 96: 5.1s⁵ 5m* 5g* 1999 6g⁴ 5s 6m⁶ 7g³ 6m⁴ 6m Jul 17] tall, leggy colt: developed into a useful handicapper: ran a fine race when fourth of 30 to Deep Space in the Wokingham at Royal Ascot: well held in listed race at Newbury month later: not seen out again: stays 7f: best on good going or firmer: edgy sort, often sweats. *R. F. Johnson Houghton*

DODO (IRE) 4 b.f. Alzao (USA) 117 – Dead Certain 123§ (Absalom 128) [1998 **90** 90: 6d 7m³ 7m³ 8f³ 6m 8m 7m³ 5.7m³ 6m* 6g³ 6g³ 6d⁶ 1999 7.1g³ 7d³ 5m 6m Jul 25] neat filly: fluent mover: fairly useful handicapper: good third at Sandown and Newbury: well held over shorter trips both starts after: should stay 1m: acts on firm and good to soft going: below form when blinkered twice at 3 yrs: reportedly in foal to Cadeaux Genereux. *D. R. C. Elsworth*

DOLFINESSE (IRE) 2 ch.f. (Apr 24) Dolphin Street (FR) 125 – Gortadoo **52 +** (USA) (Sharpen Up 127) [1999 6.1g⁶ 6m 7f⁵ 6g 6.8m⁵ 7.5g Sep 15] IR 3,400F, 3,000Y: small filly: fifth foal: half-sister to 6f (at 2 yrs) and 1m winner Gladys Althorpe (by Posen) and a winner in Italy by Mukaddamah: dam once-raced daughter of smart 5f to 7f winner Fenny Rough: modest maiden at best: should stay 7f. *M. Brittain*

DOLLAR BIRD (IRE) 2 b.f. (Apr 23) Kris 135 – High Spirited 80 (Shirley **93 p** Heights 130) [1999 7m⁶ 8.2g* 8d Oct 30] sixth foal: half-sister to several winners, including 3-y-o Devil's Imp, French 10.5f and 1½m winner Legend Maker (by Sadler's Wells) and 1½m winner Amfortas (by Caerleon), last 2 both smart: dam, 1¾m and 2m winner, sister to High Hawk (dam of In The Wings) and half-sister to dam of Derby winner High-Rise: still noticeably green, won maiden at Nottingham in September by short head from Purple Heather, strong run to lead post after handling bend none too well: only seventh of 10 in steadily-run listed event at Newmarket final outing: will need at least 1¼m at 3 yrs, and may well stay beyond 1½m: almost certainly capable of better still. *J. L. Dunlop*

DOLLAR LAW   3 ch.g. Selkirk (USA) 129 – Western Heights (Shirley Heights 130) [1998 89: 7g² 7m⁴ 8d* 1999 8.3m 10.3g 12d 10.4d Oct 7] leggy, short-backed gelding: fairly useful performer: ran creditably in 1999 only on second start: may prove best around 1m: yet to race on extremes of going: has been taken steadily/alone to post (unseated rider third start). *P. F. I. Cole*   **81**

DOLLY DAY DREAM (IRE)   3 ch.f. Magic Ring (IRE) 115 – Lariston Gale 81 (Pas de Seul 133) [1998 64: a5g⁴ a5g⁴ 5.3d³ 5d⁴ a5g⁵ 5g 6g² 6s⁶ 6m* 5m⁵ a6g² 6f² 1999 a6g a5g a6g⁶ a5s³ a6g⁴ a6g⁶ a5g⁵ a5g 5s⁶ 5.3f⁴ 6m 6d a7g⁵ 6g Jul 5] small, good-bodied filly: modest performer: mostly below form in 1999: stays 6f: acts on fibresand (probably on equitrack), firm and good to soft going (well below form on soft): has been bandaged behind: effective blinkered/visored or not: inconsistent: sold 4,200 gns, sent to Kuwait. *K. T. Ivory*   **52**

DOLPHINELLE (IRE)   3 b.c. Dolphin Street (FR) 125 – Mamie's Joy (Prince Tenderfoot (USA) 126) [1998 68: 6m⁶ 6m 6m 6g 5.3m³ 6m⁴ 5d 1999 5s⁵ 8f 7m³ 8g 6g* 6m 7.1f² 7m 6.1m 6s² 6s⁵ 7s⁴ 6g a7g⁴ a6g⁶ a7g⁵ a7g⁴ Dec 15] sturdy colt: fair handicapper: won at Brighton in June: stays 7f: acts on firm going, soft and equitrack, probably on fibresand: sometimes blinkered/visored: sometimes makes running. *R. Hannon*   **75**

DOLPHIN FRIENDLY (IRE)   3 b.f. Dolphin Street (FR) 125 – Sound Performance (IRE) 63 (Ahonoora 122) [1998 58: 6.1g 7f² 7m⁵ 8d 1999 8.3m 10.1g⁴ 12m⁵ 11.9d 14.1m 10.1d² 10g⁵ 10d⁶ 8s Oct 25] sparely-made filly: poor maiden: probably stays 1½m: acts on firm going: sold 3,200 gns, sent to Germany. *J. W. Payne*   **48**

DOMAPPEL   7 b.g. Domynsky 110 – Appelinda 63 (Star Appeal 133) [1998 83: 12.3m* 12m² 15.9m² 14.8f² 12m² 13.3m⁴ 13.9g⁴ 1999 12s 12.3m² 14.1m² 12f³ 12g Jun 5] strong, lengthy gelding: fairly useful handicapper: creditable efforts when placed: effective at 1½m, barely stays 2m: acts on firm and good to soft going (unraced on all-weather): has run well when sweating: usually races prominently/leads: consistent: joined M. Banks. *W. Jarvis*   **83**

DOMINANT DANCER   3 ch.f. Primo Dominie 121 – Footlight Fantasy (USA) 68 (Nureyev (USA) 131) [1998 87+: 5f⁴ 6m 6d² 6m* 6v 1999 6g² 6g 6m⁵ 7m³ 7f 7.1d⁴ 6d⁶ 7s³ Oct 25] rangy, rather unfurnished filly: good mover: useful performer: best effort in handicap at Newmarket fourth start: likely to prove best at 6f/7f: acts on good to firm and heavy ground: often sweating/edgy. *J. W. Hills*   **97**

DOMINANT DUCHESS   5 b.m. Old Vic 136 – Andy's Find (USA) (Buckfinder (USA)) [1998 83: 13.3m⁶ 14.8g⁴ 13.3g 17.2d⁴ 18g 1999 14.4m* 16f⁵ 20m⁶ 16.1m 16f⁴ 20f 12d² 17.3g² Oct 16] lengthy mare: has a long, round action: fairly useful performer: won handicap at Kempton in May: lost her way mid-season (bled when pulled up sixth start) but strong-finishing second in 32-runner Tote Cesarewitch final start, beaten 1¼ lengths by Top Cees: best at 1¾m+: acts on firm and good to soft going, ran poorly on soft: held up. *J. W. Hills*   **90**

DOMINELLE   7 b.m. Domynsky 110 – Gymcrak Lovebird 84 (Taufan (USA) 119) [1998 74: 5m 5m⁵ 5m² 6g* 5g 6d 6g³ 5m⁴ 5g³ 7g⁶ 5m* 6m* 5m 6m* 6.1m⁶ 5g 6m⁶ 5g 1999 6d 5d² 5d 6s 5f 6g 6m 6m² 5s² 6d 5m³ 5m⁴ 6g 5g² 5g⁴ 7f 6m⁶ 5s 6.1f Oct 20] small mare: shows knee action: fair handicapper: generally respectable efforts in at least in 1999: effective at 5f/6f: acts on firm and soft going: blinkered once as 2-y-o: often sweating/edgy: tends to wander/flash tail. *T. D. Easterby*   **69**

DOMINO FLYER   6 b.g. Warrshan (USA) 117 – Great Dilemma 77 (Vaigly Great 127) [1998 62, a66: a7g² 8s⁵ 8.3d⁴ a8g a8g* a11g⁴ 11.9g 1999 a11f a11g a8g² 9.2v⁴ a8g⁵ a11g Nov 30] leggy, angular gelding: modest performer: effective at 1m to 11f, possibly not 1½m: acts on fibresand and soft ground: has worn near-side pricker and tongue tie. *Mrs A. Duffield*   **62**

DOM MIGUEL (FR)   2 b.g. (May 4) Fairy King (USA) – Damasquine (USA)   **57**
(Damascus (USA)) [1999 7m 7d⁵ Aug 21] 450,000 francs Y: half-brother to 7f
winner Galibis (by Groom Dancer) and several winners abroad: dam French 9f
winner: better effort in maidens in August on debut: should stay 1m. *P. W. Harris*

DOM SHADEED   4 b.g. Shadeed (USA) 135 – Fair Dominion 107 (Dominion   **–**
123) [1998 73: 8m 7s⁵ 8.2m⁵ a8.5g* 1999 a9.4g 8.5s 10s 12g 11.5f Jun 25] tall,
unfurnished gelding: fair performer at 3 yrs, well below form in 1999: stays 8.5f:
blinkered final start: sold 7,000 gns. *R. Charlton*

DONA FILIPA   6 ch.m. Precocious 126 – Quissisanno 76 (Be My Guest (USA)   **46**
126) [1998 46: 5.1m 5m 5s³ 5g 5d³ 5d⁵ a5g² a5g³ a6g 5d² 6g* 6v 6v 1999 a6f a6s⁶
a5g² 6d 5m 7s a5g a6g³ a6g a6g a7g 6g Oct 14] good-topped mare: poor performer:
effective at 5f/6f: acts on good to firm going, heavy and fibresand: inconsistent.
Miss L. C. Siddall

DONATUS (IRE)   3 b.c. Royal Academy (USA) 130 – La Dame du Lac (USA)   **78**
(Round Table) [1998 82: 6g³ 6d 7s⁵ 1999 10m 9f² 8d 9m 8.1s² 8.2f⁶ 10d Nov 4] IR
85,000Y: brother to useful Irish 1997 2-y-o 6f winner Heeremandi and closely related
to 4 winners by Nijinsky, including dam of top USA filly Flawlessly, and half-brother
to 3 winners: dam, unraced, from very good family: fairly useful maiden handicapper: trained in Ireland at 2 yrs by C. O'Brien: best efforts here when runner-up at
Goodwood in July and Sandown (beaten by Tarawan) in October: stays 9f: acts on
firm and soft going: none too consistent. *S. Dow*

DON BOSCO (IRE)   3 ch.g. Grand Lodge (USA) 125 – Suyayeb (USA) (The   **77 +**
Minstrel (CAN) 135) [1998 64p: 7g 6g 1999 8.2m⁶ 6m* 7m Jul 17] strong gelding:
easy mover: fair performer: best effort when winning handicap at Ripon in June:
free-going sort, likely to prove best at 6f/7f. *J. E. Banks*

DONE AND DUSTED (IRE)   3 ch.f. Up And At 'em 109 – Florentink (USA)   **73**
(The Minstrel (CAN) 135) [1998 62, a64: 5.1m⁵ 5g 6m³ 5d² 6g⁶ 6.1g a5g⁴ a6g³ a6g⁴
a7g* a7g* a7g⁴ 1999 a6g⁶ a7g* a8g⁴ a6g³ a7g³ 6m* 6g⁵ 7d 6m a6g a7g a7g⁶ a6g
a6g* Dec 27] good-topped filly: fair handicapper: won at Lingfield in February,
Windsor in April and Wolverhampton in December: effective at 6f/7f (raced freely in
slowly-run race at 1m): acts on good to firm going, good to soft and all-weather:
inconsistent. *R. Brotherton*

DONE WELL (USA)   7 b.g. Storm Bird (CAN) 134 – Suspicious Toosome (USA)   **–**
(Secretariat (USA)) [1998 –: 10s 12d 9.1v 1999 12g Nov 3] big, lengthy gelding:
lightly raced and no form since 1995. *P. Monteith*

DON FAYRUZ (IRE)   7 b.g. Fayruz 116 – Gobolino (Don 128) [1998 NR 1999   **–**
a8.5g Dec 1] half-brother to 2 winners, including fairly useful Irish 1m to 2m performer Bolino Star (by Stalker): dam Irish 2-y-o 7f winner: fairly useful winner at 2
yrs in Italy for F. Brogi, winning 6 times, including 7.5f listed race: also won once in
USA at 4 yrs: lightly-raced winner since over hurdles in Britain (sold cheaply out of
H. Daly's stable in October): well held in seller on return to Flat. *D. Burchell*

DONNA'S DOUBLE   4 ch.g. Weldnaas (USA) 112 – Shadha 57 (Shirley Heights   **75**
130) [1998 62: 8s³ 12m 12d³ 9.3d³ 12g⁴ 10.9s² 8.3s⁴ 10g 7.1d* 8.3s* 7d³ 8.2s 1999   **a54**
a7g a11f 7.1m² 8.3s⁶ 9f 8m⁴ 9.2f² 8f⁶ 7g 9g² 7g² 7d 8s⁶ 8.9d 7g* 8d* 8s Nov 6] rather
leggy gelding: fair handicapper on turf, modest on all-weather: best efforts to win at
Catterick and Redcar in October: best at 7f to 9f: acts on firm going, soft and
fibresand: none too consistent, and has looked less than keen. *D. Eddy*

DON PEPE   8 br.g. Dowsing (USA) 124 – Unique Treasure (Young Generation   **65**
129) [1998 66, a53: a7g a7g⁵ a6g⁵ a7g 5.9d 7d³ 6.9d⁵ 7g³ 7m* 7d⁴ 7m⁴ 7f⁴ 6m 1999   **a–**
8m⁵ 7m⁵ 7d 6m² 7f 6.9m⁴ 7m 7m³ 7g Aug 19] leggy gelding: has a round action: fair
on turf, modest when last ran on all-weather: effective at 6f to 1m: acts on firm
ground, soft and all-weather: blinkered once (well beaten) at 6 yrs: has worn crossed
noseband: inconsistent. *D. Nicholls*

DON PUCCINI   2 ch.c. (Mar 21) Piccolo 121 – Baileys By Name 66 (Nomination   **101**
125) [1999 5g³ 6f* 6m⁶ 5.2m* Jul 17] 18,000Y: lengthy, workmanlike colt: fourth
living foal: half-brother to 1m seller winner Prime Partner (by Formidable): dam
2-y-o 6f winner: useful form: won minor event at Kempton in May and Weatherbys
Super Sprint at Newbury in July, always close up when beating Halland Park Girl by

½ length in latter: creditable sixth to Fasliyev in Coventry Stakes at Royal Ascot in between: reported in August to have sustained a stress fracture of off-fore cannon bone: likely to prove best at 5f/6f: quite highly-strung, and trouble-some at stalls all starts: races prominently. *B. Smart*

DON QUIXOTE (IRE)   3 b.c. Waajib 121 – Maimiti (Goldhill 125) [1998 –p: 7d   **53** 1999 8d 7d 6m³ 5m Jul 14] close-coupled colt: modest maiden: should be suited by further than 6f: form only on good to firm going. *L. M. Cumani*

DON'T ASK   3 b.g. Paris House 123 – Glenfield Portion 86 (Mummy's Pet 125)   **41** [1998 69: 5m⁴ 5s 1999 a5g⁵ 5g 5.3d a6g Oct 18] poor maiden: left D. Murray Smith after second start: sold 500 gns. *Mrs L. C. Jewell*

DONTBESOBOLD (IRE)   2 b.g. (Apr 25) River Falls 113 – Jarmar Moon (Unfu-   **62** wain (USA) 131) [1999 5m⁴ 6g 6m⁶ 7m 7f 6.8d⁴ 8d Oct 18] 5,500Y: workmanlike gelding: second foal: half-brother to 3-y-o Moon Glow: dam, well beaten, daughter of useful winner up to 9f Shark Song: modest maiden: stays 6.8f, unlikely to get much further: acts on good to soft going. *B. S. Rothwell*

DON'T DROP BOMBS (USA)   10 ch.g. Fighting Fit (USA) – Promised Star   **35** (USA) (Star de Naskra (USA)) [1998 35, a43: a8s³ a12g² a10g² a8g² a13g a7g³ a8g 8m a8.5g⁴ a7g⁵ a8.5g 10g³ 8.1m 10m⁵ 1999 a8g a12g⁴ a10g a13g⁵ 12d 11.5m Jun 19] angular gelding: poor handicapper, mainly runs in amateurs/ladies events: stays 13f: acts on firm going and all-weather: usually visored: often front runner: mostly ridden by Miss J. Feilden. *H. J. Collingridge*

DONT GO MAD (USA)   2 b. or br.c. (Jan 21) Blush Rambler (USA) 119 –   **79** Flaming Reason (USA) (Limit To Reason (USA)) [1999 5g⁴ 6g* May 15] $35,000F, 82,000Y: tall, leggy colt: has scope: eighth foal: half-brother to 3 winners, notably smart 1990 2-y-o sprinter Mac's Imp (by Imp Society): dam won at up to 7f in USA: won maiden at Newmarket in May: should have stayed 7f: dead. *K. R. Burke*

DON'T SURRENDER (IRE)   2 b.c. (Mar 4) St Clair Star   **93 p** (Sallust 134) [1999 6m² 6d² 6g* 6d* Oct 29] IR 17,000F, IR 43,000Y: small colt: half-brother to several winners, including useful Irish 1998 2-y-o 7f winner St Clair Ridge (later won in USA, by Indian Ridge) and 1½m winner Bold Saint (by Persian Bold): dam, winner in Canada, half-sister to Superlative: fairly useful form: won maiden at Lingfield and all-aged minor event at Newmarket in October, battling on most gamely when holding Blue Melody by ½ length in latter: raced only at 6f: acts on good to firm and good to soft going: unimpressive to post on second start: type to do better still at 3 yrs. *J. L. Dunlop*

DONT WORRY BOUT ME (IRE)   2 b.g. (Jan 29) Brief Truce (USA) 126 –   **75 d** Coggle 60 (Kind of Hush 118) [1999 5g³ 6g² 6m⁶ a6g³ 6s 8d a8g Dec 8] 13,000F, 14,000Y: first foal: dam, 1½m winner, closely related to smart middle-distance stayer Capstan, from family of Bireme: fair form first 2 starts in maidens: seemed to go the wrong way: bred to stay at least 1m. *T. G. Mills*

DON'T WORRY MIKE   5 ch.g. Forzando 122 – Hat Hill (Roan Rocket 128)   **–** [1998 43: a9.4g⁶ a8.5g⁶ 10m a8.5g⁴ a11g 1999 a8.5g Jan 6] leggy, workmanlike gelding: poor maiden: stays 8.5f: acts on good to firm going and fibresand: effective blinkered or not. *K. S. Bridgwater*

DOODLE BUG   2 b.f. (Mar 1) Missed Flight 123 – Kaiserlinde (GER) (Frontal   **68 ?** 122) [1999 7g³ 8.1g Aug 30] 3,000Y: half-sister to 4-y-o Marlene and 3 winners in Germany at 1¼m/1½m: dam unraced from good German family: 100/1, probably flattered when third of 11 in steadily-run maiden at Leicester: still green, behind in similar race at Chepstow later in August: should stay at least 1m. *T. R. Watson*

DOONAREE (IRE)   3 b.c. Sadler's Wells (USA) 132 – Rosananti 107 (Blushing   **102** Groom (FR) 131) [1998 NR 1999 12.4g* 12s* 12.3m 11.8s² 12g³ 10.1m⁴ 10d Oct 1] IR 200,000Y: angular, good-topped colt: has a quick action: half-brother to several winners, including smart stayer Rubicund and useful French 8.3f (at 2 yrs) to 11.5f winner Rosabella (both by Niniski): dam, 6f to 1m (Italian 1000 Guineas) winner, stayed 1½m: useful performer: won maiden at Newcastle and minor event at Catterick in April: creditable third in handicap at Pontefract in August: will stay 1¾m: acts on soft going: tongue tied last 3 starts, running poorly final one (sweating profusely and raced freely): sold 70,000 gns. *M. Johnston*

DOOWALEY (IRE) 3 b.c. Sadler's Wells (USA) 132 – Dwell (USA) 96 (Habitat 134) [1998 NR 1999 10g* 8d⁶ 10d* Nov 9] 100,000Y, 47,000 3-y-o: angular colt: fifth foal: closely related to German 11f winner Dwings (by In The Wings) and half-brother to 2 winners abroad, including useful Hong Kong sprinter Quick Action (by Alzao): dam 1m winner: won minor events at Milan in September and Rome in November: ran well when keeping-on 5 lengths sixth to Indian Lodge in listed race at Newmarket in between: likely to prove better at 1¼m+ than 1m: should improve further. *M. R. Channon* **98 p**

DORCHESTER 2 b.g. (Feb 8) Primo Dominie 121 – Penthouse Lady (Last Tycoon 131) [1999 5g 5.9m 5.1g* a5g* 5m* 5.2f² 6g³ 5m 6m⁴ Oct 19] 50,000Y: good-topped gelding: good walker: first foal: dam unraced half-sister to very smart French/US middle-distance performer Louis Cyphre and smart French performer up to 1m Psychobabble: fairly useful performer: won maiden at Nottingham, nursery at Southwell and minor event at Doncaster, all in July: ran well next 3 starts, including when third in listed race at La Teste and seventh of 14 to Mrs P in Flying Childers at Doncaster: effective at 5f/6f: acts on firm going and fibresand: tends to edge right and idle in front. *Sir Mark Prescott* **93**

DORISSIO (IRE) 3 b.f. Efisio 120 – Floralia 81 (Auction Ring (USA) 123) [1998 –: 5v⁶ 1999 7v⁴ 6m 7g 6m⁶ 6g 6g 8f* 8s* Oct 4] rather leggy, unfurnished filly: fair handicapper: won in large fields at Bath (seller) in September and Pontefract (by 5 lengths) in October: stays 1m: acts on firm and soft going: slowly away both starts prior to final one: capable of further progress. *I. A. Balding* **75 p**

DOROTHEA SHARP (IRE) 2 b. or br.f. (May 15) Foxhound (USA) 103 – Captain's Niece 84 (Vitiges (FR) 132) [1999 6f 6m 8.2s Oct 5] IR 2,000F, IR 4,500Y, 15,000 2-y-o: plain filly: half-sister to a winner in Switzerland by Local Suitor: dam 1m to 1¼m winner: form in maidens only when eighth of 12 at Kempton (slowly away, not given hard time) second start: tailed off on soft ground. *N. P. Littmoden* **50**

DOROTHY ALLEN 3 b.f. Mon Tresor 113 – Anytime Anywhere 77 (Daring March 116) [1998 61: 5m 5s³ 5.7v 1999 a7g a7g a8g Dec 6] form only when third in maiden at 2 yrs: left M. Channon after reappearance. *R. Ingram* **–**

DORRINGTON 4 b.g. Puissance 110 – Prydwen (Hard Fought 125) [1998 –: 6.9m⁶ 7.5g 8f 1999 a9.4g Jan 6] little sign of ability. *B. P. J. Baugh* **–**

DORTON GRANGE 4 ch.f. Absalom 128 – Stranger To Fear (Never So Bold 135) [1998 48: 6m 6g³ 5m 6.1g 6m 1999 8g 7v a6g⁵ 6m May 24] leggy filly: little form. *H. J. Manners* **–**

DOUBLE ACTION 5 br.g. Reprimand 122 – Final Shot 91 (Dalsaan 125) [1998 102d: 6s⁵ 6d³ 6g⁵ 6s² 6d 6g 6m 6g 6s 7g 7s 1999 6m 7m⁴ 6d 7m⁴ 6d 7m 7f 6g³ 7m³ 7d² 6d 8s 7d⁶ Oct 9] well-made gelding: has a quick action: formerly smart handicapper: fairly useful form third start, but below even that level after: stays 7f: acts on good to firm and soft going: sometimes hangs left: below form both outings in blinkers. *T. D. Easterby* **83 d**

DOUBLE BAILEYS 3 b.g. Robellino (USA) 127 – Thimblerigger 62 (Sharpen Up 127) [1998 74p: 9m³ 1999 12g⁵ 11.1g² 13.9s 17.2m² 11.9f³ 16.2m a13g⁵ 14.8d Oct 15] tall gelding: fair maiden: stays 17f: acts on firm going, possibly not on softer than good/equitrack: visored fifth and sixth outings: has run in snatches: sold 13,000 gns. *M. Johnston* **74**

DOUBLE BANGER (IRE) 2 b.c. (Apr 3) Ela-Mana-Mou 132 – Penny Banger (IRE) 74 (Pennine Walk 120) [1999 10s³ 10d⁴ a10g* Dec 18] big, strong, lengthy colt: third foal: half-brother to 3-y-o Roman Candle: dam fairly useful form: won maiden at Lingfield in December eased by 10 lengths: shapes as though will stay at least 1½m: has worn crossed noseband: should do better still. *M. Johnston* **80 p**

DOUBLE BLADE 4 b.g. Kris 135 – Sesame 117 (Derrylin 115) [1998 80§: 9m³ 14m² 14.1d³ 14.8g 12d³ 12m 16.1g⁵ 13.1v⁶ 1999 12m 16m⁴ 14.1m Aug 28] big, angular gelding: fairly useful maiden at 3 yrs: only fair form at best in handicaps in 1999: probably stays 2m: acts on good to firm and good to soft going: blinkered (ran poorly) once at 3 yrs: ungenuine: successful 4 times over hurdles after final Flat outing, showing fairly useful form. *Mrs M. Reveley* **68 §**

DOUBLE BOUNCE 9 b.g. Interrex (CAN) – Double Gift 68 (Cragador 110) **77**
[1998 91?: 6d 6v⁵ 6d 1999 6g 6m⁶ 6f Jul 31] good-quartered gelding: fairly useful
handicapper at best, lightly raced in last 2 seasons: shaped quite encouragingly at
Newbury second start, not well drawn when behind in Stewards' Cup at Goodwood
next time: best at 6f: acts on firm and good to soft ground, probably on heavy:
blinkered once in 1997: usually bandaged: successful when sweating: normally held
up. *H. Morrison*

DOUBLE BRANDY 4 ch.g. Elmaamul (USA) 125 – Brand (Shareef Dancer **86**
(USA) 135) [1998 81: 7d⁵ 6v⁵ 6m* 7g 6g 7s 1999 7g 7.6m 8.3m* 8m* 8f 8f⁶ 7.9m
Sep 1] lengthy gelding: fairly useful handicapper: won at Windsor and Doncaster in
June: at least respectable efforts final 2 starts: stays 8.3f: probably acts on firm going,
probably unsuited by heavy. *I. A. Balding*

DOUBLE CHOICE (IRE) 3 b.f. Doubletour (USA) – Virginia Cottage 45 **64**
(Lomond (USA) 128) [1998 78: 5v⁴ 5g⁴ 6g⁶ 5f* 5d* 1999 5s 5d 5g 5g⁵ 5m⁵ 6m Aug
6] tall, quite attractive filly: fair performer at 2 yrs: form in handicaps in 1999 only
on fourth and fifth starts: best at 5f: acts on firm and good to soft going: sold 7,000
gns in December. *R. Hannon*

DOUBLE DESTINY 3 b.g. Anshan 119 – Double Gift 68 (Cragador 110) [1998 **69**
NR 1999 7.1m⁶ 6d 7m Sep 7] fourth reported foal: half-brother to winning sprinters
Double Bounce (9-y-o) and Double March (6-y-o): dam winning sprinter: fair
maiden: easily best effort at Chepstow on debut, tending to run in snatches: still
seemed rather green final start. *H. Candy*

DOUBLE ECHO (IRE) 11 br.g. Glow (USA) – Piculet 69 (Morston (FR) 125) **34**
[1998 51d: a12g³ a11g* a12g* a11g* a12g³ a11g² a12g a12g⁴ a12g 12g⁵ 10g 12g
a12g a12g⁵ a11g a12g⁴ 1999 a11g² a12f³ a12g a14g⁵ a12g Mar 19] sturdy, compact
gelding: poor handicapper: effective at 11f to 2m: acts on firm ground, good to soft
and all-weather: blinkered once early in career: usually held up. *J. D. Bethell*

DOUBLE ENTRY 2 b.g. (Mar 22) Rambo Dancer (CAN) 107 – Andbracket **–**
(Import 127) [1999 6m 8d 6d Oct 18] 7,000Y: strong, workmanlike gelding: fourth
foal: brother to 4-y-o Disco Tex and fair 1m/9f winner Dispol Gem: dam unraced:
backward, well held in maidens. *D. Nicholls*

DOUBLE FAULT (IRE) 2 br.f. (Apr 2) Zieten (USA) 118 – Kashapour 81 **53**
(Nishapour (FR) 125) [1999 5d 6f 5m² 5m 7d⁴ 7.9f Sep 2] IR 12,500Y: angular filly:
sixth foal: half-sister to 1993 2-y-o 7f winner Kezio Rufo (by Persian Heights) and a
winner in Sweden by Auction Ring: dam, placed at 6f and 7f at 2 yrs, half-sister to
2000 Guineas winner Roland Gardens and to dam of Kooyonga: modest maiden: best
effort when fourth of 9 in nursery at Chester: should stay 1m. *T. D. Easterby*

DOUBLE FLIGHT 5 b.m. Mtoto 134 – Sariah (Kris 135) [1998 66: a10g³ 1999 **57**
a13g⁴ a12g 9m⁶ 12m 9v Sep 20] big, angular mare: modest handicapper: effective at
1¼m (granted decent test) to 13f: acts on firm ground, good to soft and equitrack: has
reportedly bled from nose over hurdles: wears tongue strap. *Miss B. Sanders*

DOUBLE GUN 2 b.c. (Mar 7) Puissance 110 – Star of Jupiter (Jupiter Island 126) **70**
[1999 6m 6m⁴ 6g³ Oct 19] leggy, quite good-topped colt: fourth foal: dam unraced
half-sister to useful sprinter Boozy: steady improvement in maidens, third of 18 at
Lingfield final start: raced only at 6f on good/good to firm going. *R. Hannon*

DOUBLE IDENTITY 4 b.f. Rudimentary (USA) 118 – Frivolous Fancy 63 **–**
(Piaffer (USA) 113) [1998 NR 1999 12v 8.3g 6g 10d 8.3g Oct 11] first reported foal:
dam, maiden, best effort at 5f at 2 yrs: probably of little account. *T. D. McCarthy*

DOUBLE-J (IRE) 5 b.g. Fayruz 116 – Farriers Slipper (Prince Tenderfoot (USA) **44**
126) [1998 –: 8d 7v⁴ 6s 8g 8m 8.5m 8m 1999 7d 8d 8g⁵ 8m⁵ 9.9s Sep 21] close-
coupled gelding: fairly useful handicapper at 3 yrs: poor form in 1999: stays 7f: acts
on firm and soft ground: tried visored/blinkered. *M. Brittain*

DOUBLE M 2 ch.c. (Feb 11) First Trump 118 – Girton Degree 41 (Balliol 125) **76 +**
[1999 5m⁶ a5g² 5m⁴ 5.1m* 5.3g⁴ 6.1m 5m⁴ Aug 31] third foal: dam, maiden
(stayed 1m), sister to smart sprinter Singing Steven: fair performer: made all in
maiden at Nottingham in July: speedy, and best at 5f: blinkered/visored after debut.
J. L. Spearing

DOUBLE MARCH   6 b.g. Weldnaas (USA) 112 – Double Gift 68 (Cragador   **73**
110) [1998 74: 6.1m* 6.1m 6g³ 6d* 6m⁴ 5d³ 6m² 6g⁴ 6m⁴ 6s 6.1v* 1999 6f 6f 6g⁵
5.7m 6g 6s⁴ 6g Oct 11] sturdy gelding: fair handicapper: left K. Ivory after second
start: best effort in 1999 on next appearance: stays 6f well: acts on good to firm going,
heavy and all-weather: often bandaged of late. *H. Candy*

DOUBLE-O   5 b.g. Sharpo 132 – Ktolo 80 (Tolomeo 127) [1998 –, a86: a6g a6g*   **80**
a5g* a5g 5d a6g a5g⁵ 1999 a6g a6g a6g³ 5d⁶ 6g² 5g 6s 5.3d* 5d 5s a5g³ a6g Nov 30]
leggy, lengthy gelding: fairly useful handicapper: won at Brighton in October by 4
lengths, only one to race on stand side in straight: effective at 5f/easy 6f: acts on good
to soft going and all-weather: usually blinkered. *W. Jarvis*

DOUBLE OSCAR (IRE)   6 ch.g. Royal Academy (USA) 130 – Broadway   **90**
Rosie 101 (Absalom 128) [1998 92, a95: a6g* a6g² a5g² a5g³ 6d 5s³ a5g* 5m⁴ 5g 6g
5g⁵ 5g⁶ 5d* 5m* 6m³ 6f 5f 6s 5g 5d 1999 6d 6g 5d² 5.1m 5.1g⁶ 5m 5g* 6g² 5.1m⁴ 5m
5f² 6f 6d 6m 6s⁴ 6d 5d 5s Nov 5] good-bodied gelding: fairly useful performer: won
handicap at Ayr in June: best at 5f/6f: acts on firm going, soft and all-weather: visored
once, usually blinkered (ran poorly all starts without in 1999, including final 4): has
had tongue tied and been bandaged: sometimes slowly away: usually waited with,
and best in strongly-run race. *D. Nicholls*

DOUBLE PLATINUM   2 ch.f. (Mar 8) Seeking The Gold (USA) – Band (USA)   **88**
(Northern Dancer) [1999 6s² 7g Oct 16] unfurnished filly: third foal: half-sister to
1998 2-y-o 7f winner Houston Time and 1995 2-y-o 5f/6f (Cherry Hinton) winner
Applaud (both useful performers by Rahy): dam, maiden daughter of high-class
sprinter Swingtime, later successful in graded stakes up to 9f in USA: similar form
when ½-length second of 11 in maiden at Newmarket (trained by P. Chapple-Hyam)
and when eighth of 12 in Rockfel Stakes there later in October: not bred to stay much
beyond 7f. *A. G. Foster*

DOUBLE RED (IRE)   2 b.f. (Apr 17) Thatching 131 – Local Custom (IRE) (Be   **70**
My Native (USA) 122) [1999 6m 6.1m 5m 10s² 8d² Oct 18] IR 38,000Y: fourth foal:
half-sister to 3-y-o Moonlight, 4-y-o Bergen and Irish 1m winner Calamander (by
Alzao): dam, Irish maiden, half-sister to Middle Park winner Balla Cove: fair
performer: improved efforts when second in nurseries at Nottingham and Pontefract
(beaten neck by Fashion) last 2 starts: stays 1¼m: acts on soft going. *L. W. Bell*

DOUBLE RUSH (IRE)   7 b.g. Doulab (USA) 115 – Stanza Dancer (Stanford   **56 d**
121§) [1998 51, a65: a10g² a10g⁶ 8f⁶ 12s⁵ 12m 10m⁴ 9.7m² 10.8g³ 11.7d* 11.9g⁵
10g 10.8m 11.9g⁴ 10s 1999 14.6s³ 12d² a12g 14.6m³ 12m⁴ 12.1m⁵ 12.1m⁴ 14.1m³
16m 14.1v⁶ a14g Dec 13] rangy gelding: modest handicapper: below form after
second start: stays 1¾m, though not under very testing conditions: acts on firm going,
soft and equitrack: blinkered (out of form) once: none too consistent. *T. Keddy*

DOUBLE SPLENDOUR (IRE)   9 b.g. Double Schwartz 128 – Princess   **93**
Pamela 70 (Dragonara Palace (USA) 115) [1998 105d: 6g* 6g⁴ 6g⁵ 6g² 6m⁴ 6f 6g 6s
6.1g 7g 6d 1999 6d 6m 6m² 6m³ 6m* 6g 6m⁵ 6m 6.1g 6d 6d Nov 1] good-topped
gelding: has been hobdayed: useful handicapper: won at Newmarket in July: mostly
below form after: stays 6f: acts on firm ground, soft and equitrack: held up.
P. S. Felgate

DOUBLE STAR   8 b.g. Soviet Star (USA) 128 – Startino 111 (Bustino 136) [1998   **50**
NR 1999 14.1g⁵ 14.1m 16.2g² 17.2g 12s³ 14.1g Sep 25] tall gelding: modest maiden:
stays 2m: acts on soft going: sold 500 gns in October. *J. L. Harris*

DOUBLE STYLE   2 b.c. (Feb 5) Presidium 124 – Sorrowful (Moorestyle 137)   **–**
[1999 6m 8f⁶ Sep 4] 2,500Y: rather unfurnished colt: eighth foal: half-brother to 3
winners, including 6-y-o Meranti and Sorridar (both 6f/7f winners by Puissance):
dam ran twice: well held in maidens at Thirsk. *J. L. Eyre*

DOUBLE TWO (IRE)   3 br.g. Petardia 113 – Reasonably French (Reasonable   **–**
(FR) 119) [1998 58: 5m⁴ 5s 5s³ 5d⁴ 6d³ 7d 6s 7g 1999 8d 7g Jun 4] leggy gelding:
modest maiden: no form since fifth start at 2 yrs: often blinkered: sold 4,800 gns, sent
to Spain. *T. D. Easterby*

DOUBLE VISION   2 ch.c. (Apr 17) Most Welcome 131 – Two Moons (Bold Lad   **–**
(IRE) 133) [1999 6d 7d a8.5g⁶ a8g Nov 30] sturdy colt: carries condition: fourth

reported foal: half-brother to 3-y-o New Moon: dam no sign of ability: no form, including in seller. *C. W. Thornton*

DOUBTLESS RISK   2 b.c. (Apr 6) Risk Me (FR) 127 – Doubtfire 71 (Jalmood (USA) 126) [1999 5m⁶ 6d⁵ 6g⁴ 7g 8d 8v 7.1g Nov 3] third reported foal: dam, 2-y-o 6f seller winner, probably stayed 1¼m: modest form in maidens first 3 starts: well beaten last 4 outings, blinkered last 2: should stay beyond 6f: acts on good to soft going: carries head awkwardly. *Miss L. A. Perratt*   **56 d**

DOUX DELICE   3 b.f. Deploy 131 – Springs Welcome 86 (Blakeney 126) [1998 NR 1999 10s 9.9m 11.7m Aug 22] fourth foal: sister to 4-y-o Jonas Nightingale and half-sister to winning stayers Sipowitz (by Warrshan) and Duncombe Hall (by Salse): dam stayed 2m: well beaten in maidens: sold 800 gns in October. *C. A. Cyzer*   **–**

DOVEBRACE   6 b.g. Dowsing (USA) 124 – Naufrage (Main Reef 126) [1998 66d, a–: a7g⁶ a7g⁶ a7g 7s 5.9d 7.1m² 7g 7m⁵ 7m 7m 7.6d 7.1g 8g⁶ 7s 1999 7.1m 7.1m³ 8d 8f⁶ 6.9m 7.6m³ 7.1m 7m 10.3s⁶ Sep 22] leggy gelding: unimpressive mover: poor handicapper nowadays: probably stays 1m, not 10.3f: acts on soft and good to firm going, probably on equitrack: tried blinkered/visored at 3 yrs: tends to be slowly away: none too consistent. *A. Bailey*   **47**

DOVEDON TIMES   3 ch.g. Timeless Times (USA) 99 – La Pepper 63 (Workboy 123) [1998 53: a6g a7g⁵ 1999 a8.5g a6g³ a7g² a6g⁵ a8g 7.7m 8f a8g Aug 20] lengthy gelding: poor maiden: well beaten in selling handicaps last 3 starts: may prove best up to 1m: form only on fibresand: visored penultimate start. *H. Akbary*   **–**
a47

DOVE'S DOMINION   2 b.g. (Apr 3) Primo Dominie 121 – Dame Helene (USA) (Sir Ivor 135) [1999 6g 6v 6d Nov 4] lengthy, unfurnished gelding: third foal: half-brother to fairly useful 1998 2-y-o 7f winner Autocrat (by Polar Falcon): dam, no form, out of half-sister to very smart French middle-distance colt Sarhoob: eighth of 22 to Spencers Wood in maiden at Windsor on debut, but failed to confirm the promise: should be suited by 7f+. *M. R. Channon*   **56**

DOVIRI (USA)   3 ch.f. Irish River (FR) 131 – Storm Dove (USA) 108 (Storm Bird (CAN) 134) [1998 NR 1999 9s³ 10f⁴ Oct 20] second foal: dam, 6f/7f winner, out of smart French winner up to 1¼m Daeltown: fair form in maidens at Lingfield (slowly away) and Nottingham (drifted left), flashing tail both times: sold 13,000 gns in December. *R. Charlton*   **72**

DOWER HOUSE   4 ch.c. Groom Dancer (USA) 128 – Rose Noble (USA) 62 (Vaguely Noble 140) [1998 101+: 8g² 12f³ 10.1g* 10.3g³ 10.4f 1999 10g 8.5g⁴ 10.1s⁵ 10.1g Jun 5] lengthy, rather leggy colt: has a fluent, round action: useful performer: seemingly best effort (probably flattered) when fourth to Shiva in Earl of Sefton Stakes at Newmarket: well held in £32,000 handicap at Epsom final start: form at 8.5f to 1¼m: acts on firm going, probably soft: stirrup broke and unseated rider on reappearance: takes good hold. *W. Jarvis*   **107 ?**

DOWNLAND (IRE)   3 b.c. Common Grounds 118 – Boldabsa 96 (Persian Bold 123) [1998 69p: 6g 1999 6g² 6m* 6d 6m⁶ 8m² 10.1d Oct 27] tall, good sort: fairly useful performer: won 4-runner maiden at Lingfield in July: back to form when good second in handicap at Newcastle: best effort at 1m (tailed off at 1¼m): yet to race on extremes of going. *G. Wragg*   **89**

DRAGON STAR   2 b.f. (Feb 8) Rudimentary (USA) 118 – Nazakat 68 (Known Fact (USA) 135) [1999 5m³ 6m⁶ a5g⁶ a6g⁵ Nov 24] 900Y: sparely-made filly: half-sister to 7f and 8.5f winner Dragonjoy (by Warrshan) and a winner in Hong Kong by Petong: dam 2-y-o 5f winner: modest maiden: below form in Lingfield nursery final start: moved poorly to post on debut: should stay 7f. *J. W. Payne*   **54**

DRAGON TRIUMPH (IRE)   4 b.c. Alzao (USA) 117 – Tir-An-Oir (IRE) (Law Society (USA) 130) [1998 107: 10v* 10s⁶ 12d² 12m⁴ 12.3m* 12g⁵ 14d⁶ 16v 1999 10v⁵ 14d 14m 12.3g 12m Jul 30] IR 23,000Y: fourth foal: half-brother to a winner up to 1¼m in Italy by Magical Strike: dam unraced half-sister to high-class 7f to 1¼m performer Kilijaro: useful performer: won Ulster Harp Derby at Down Royal in 1998: form at 4 yrs only when seventh in valuable handicap at Goodwood on second start: lame then broke blood vessel next 2 appearances: stays 1½m: acts on good to firm and heavy ground. *J. T. Gorman, Ireland*   **95**

DRAKENSBERG   4 b.g. Bering 136 – Theme (IRE) (Sadler's Wells (USA) 132)   **80 d**
[1998 –p: 8g 1999 10v* 10m 11.4m 14s 10d Oct 12] robust gelding: fairly useful
performer at best: won maiden at Leicester in April: little show in handicaps after
(reportedly gurgled on fourth start): stays 1¼m: acts on heavy ground: sometimes
pulls hard: tongue tied last 2 starts: one to treat with caution. *Lady Herries*

DRAMATIC QUEST   2 b.c. (Apr 19) Zafonic (USA) 130 – Ultra Finesse (USA)   **103 +**
107 (Rahy (USA) 115) [1999 6s 6g* 7m* 7m⁵ Sep 10] strong, good-topped colt: has
plenty of scope: good mover: first foal: dam, French 8.5f and 1¼m winner who
stayed 12.5f, half-sister to Arc winner Suave Dancer: useful form: won minor events
at Pontefract in May and Ascot (beat Meadaaar by a neck, pair clear) in July:
looked in need of step up in trip when only fifth of 6 to Distant Music in Champagne Stakes
at Doncaster final start, off bridle from early stage: will stay at least 1¼m: may still
do better. *M. Johnston*

DRAMATIC SCENES   3 b.f. Deploy 131 – Dramatic Mood (Jalmood (USA)   –
126) [1998 –: 8v⁶ 1999 11.1g 12v 11.8m Jun 1] little form. *J. S. Moore*

DRAM TIME   3 b.g. Clantime 101 – Chablisse 69 (Radetzky 123) [1998 60?: 5g⁴   –
5g⁶ 5g 7g 1999 8g 7d⁶ Apr 17] tall gelding: little show since debut. *T. D. Easterby*

DRAWING ROOM (IRE)   3 b.f. Grand Lodge (USA) 125 – Wild Abandon   –
(USA) (Graustark) [1998 –: 7d 7d 1999 8m 10m 7m Jun 26] tall filly: little form: sold
9,000 gns in July. *R. F. Johnson Houghton*

DR COOL   2 b.c. (Mar 14) Ezzoud (IRE) 126 – Vayavaig 78 (Damister (USA)   **66 p**
123) [1999 7s a8g³ Nov 24] 21,000Y: medium-sized, quite good-topped colt: third
foal: half-brother to 6f winners Green Pursuit (Irish, by Green Desert) and Wolfhunt
(by Wolfhound), latter later 1m winner in USA: dam, 2-y-o 6f winner, half-sister to
smart sprinter Vaigly Great: not knocked about on debut, then 10-length third in
maiden at Lingfield, getting hang of things late on: should do better. *W. Jarvis*

DR DUKE (IRE)   2 b.g. (Feb 9) Dolphin Street (FR) 125 – Diamond Lake (Kings   **54**
Lake (USA) 133) [1999 5v⁴ 5.1g 5g³ 7m⁶ 5.1h³ 7.1m³ 7m² 6.1m a6f 8g a8.5g⁵ a8g⁵
a10g⁵ Dec 18] 11,500F, 8,200Y: good-bodied gelding: seventh foal: brother to 3-y-o
Royal Dolphin and half-brother to 3 winners, including 5-y-o Smart Kid and 1½m
seller winner Bunker (by Scenic): dam Irish 2-y-o 7f winner from very good family:
modest maiden: left R. Hodges after second in seller at Brighton: below form after:
should stay at least 1m: seems to act on any turf going: visored (well beaten) ninth
start. *Mrs N. Macauley*

DREAM CARRIER (IRE)   11 b.g. Doulab (USA) 115 – Dream Trader (Auction   –
Ring (USA) 123) [1998 –, a38: a8s a7g⁴ a7g⁶ a8g a8.5g a7g a8.5g 1999 a7g a8g⁵   **a37**
a7g⁵ a8.5g a7g⁶ Jul 8] strong gelding: poor performer nowadays: stays 1m: acts on
firm ground, good to soft and all-weather: tried blinkered/visored: sometimes starts
slowly. *R. E. Peacock*

DREAM ON ME   3 b.f. Prince Sabo 123 – Helens Dreamgirl 95 (Caerleon (USA)   **56**
132) [1998 55, a58: 5d³ 5.2g² 7f² 8.2v⁴ a7g a8g* 1999 a7g* a7g⁶ a6g⁵ a8g² a8g² a7g⁵   **a60**
a7g 7f 8m* 8g³ 7g a7g⁴ a8.5g³ a9.4g⁵ a8.5g Dec 27] modest performer: won
handicap at Lingfield in January and seller (left G. L. Moore) at Leicester in July:
stays 9.4f: acts on all-weather and probably any turf going: none too consistent.
H. J. Manners

DREAM WELL (FR)   4 b.c. Sadler's Wells (USA) 132 – Soul Dream (USA)   **122**
78 (Alleged (USA) 138) [1998 127: 10v² 12s² 12g* 12g* 12v* 12s³ 12d 1999
10.5g² 12d³ 12g³ 10v* 10d³ 12g² 12g⁵ Nov 6]
    For Dream Well, 1999 was a far cry from the previous season in which
he became only the third horse to complete the Prix du Jockey Club and Irish
Derby double. He was placed in all but one of his races as a four-year-old, and
fifth in the Breeders' Cup Turf was an honourable exception, but his only win
of the campaign came when he was dropped in class. In terms of form, the
difference between Group 1 winner in 1998 and Group 1 placed in 1999 was
perhaps not that great. Bear in mind also that, although Dream Well was
undeniably somewhat below the form he showed as a three-year-old, he did not
have ideal conditions in which to reproduce his best. His finest performance

remains his four and a half length victory over City Honours on heavy ground in the Irish Derby, and he never faced anything like the same test of stamina in the latest season.

In fact, the only occasion in which Dream Well ran at a mile and a half on going softer than good as a four-year-old was in the Coronation Cup, but that race was rendered meaningless as a stamina test by the guarded pacemaking efforts of Central Park. The usual tactics employed on Dream Well—coming from well off the pace—also put him at an immediate disadvantage that day, but it was still on a par with his best performances of the season. In staying on strongly in the final furlong, despite hanging left in the straight when the pace quickened, to be beaten just one and a quarter lengths in third to Daylami, Dream Well could be said to have run promisingly at the time. However, he failed to build on that effort in three subsequent appearances at a mile and a half on good ground, in the Grand Prix de Saint-Cloud, the Turf Classic Invitational at Belmont, where he was a length second to Val's Prince, and the Breeders' Cup Turf at Gulfstream. His form was also no better over shorter trips in the Prix Ganay at Longchamp on his reappearance and the Champion Stakes at Leopardstown in September, although, in going down by only a head to Dark Moondancer, his Ganay effort was another one which at the time promised better. All of those aforementioned races were Group or Grade 1. For his sole win of 1999, Dream Well lined up in the Group 3 Prix Gontaut-Biron at Deauville in August. That was over a mile and a quarter, but the heavy ground and quality of his four 'rivals'—the runner-up was the useful seven-year-old Trait de Genie—meant that Dream Well was not at all pressed to score by two and a half lengths.

While conceding that Dream Well's four-year-old season was not as bad as it appears at first glance, it should also be said that there is, and possibly always has been, something of the reluctant hero about Dream Well. A son of Sadler's Wells carrying his head awkwardly is not an unusual sight, but there is something in his usually wearing blinkers (though he has run well without

Niarchos Family's "Dream Well"

them, including in the Coronation Cup) and the exaggerated come-from-behind tactics which suggests that Dream Well might have more quirks than the average offspring of his champion sire. This is largely circumstantial evidence, but there is more. His sideways progress up the straight at Epsom was only the most extreme example of the difficulties in keeping Dream Well on the straight and narrow. Cash Asmussen, who has ridden Dream Well virtually throughout his career, can take the art of race description into new dimensions. After the King George, for instance, he reported that his mount Indigenous 'all the way was going left and right like a snake.' We suspect that Asmussen could also come up with a few ripe similes in description of Dream Well. Sylvain Guillot incidentally rode him at Deauville when Asmussen was injured.

				Nearctic
Dream Well (FR) (b.c. 1995)	Sadler's Wells (USA) (b 1981)		Northern Dancer (b 1961)	Natalma
			Fairy Bridge (b 1975)	Bold Reason
				Special
	Soul Dream (USA) (b 1990)		Alleged (b 1974)	Hoist The Flag
				Princess Pout
			Normia (gr 1981)	Northfields
				Mia Pola

A sturdy, quite attractive colt, Dream Well has a round action and raced only on good ground or softer. His pedigree was described in detail in *Racehorses of 1998*, but a mention should be given to his year-younger half-brother Archipelago (by Caerleon), who won over fifteen furlongs in France in the latest season. Dream Well would probably have stayed that far but never raced beyond a mile and a half, at which trip he was ideally suited by a good stamina test. Conditions in the latest Arc would have been very much in his favour, but, even at his best, there is no chance that he could have finished better than third in that race. By that stage he was already being sent in search of easier opportunities. Dream Well has been retired to stand at Teruya Yoshida's Shadai Farm in Japan. *P. Bary, France*

DR EDGAR 7 b.g. Most Welcome 131 – African Dancer 116 (Nijinsky (CAN) – 138) [1998 55, a66: a11g³ a11g² a9.4g² a12g² 10.3d² 1999 a12g Dec 11] strong gelding: fair handicapper on all-weather, modest to soft turf: reportedly bled from nose on only outing of 1999: stays 1½m: acts on good to soft going, firm and all-weather: visored (ran creditably) in 1998, blinkered once: has wandered under pressure. *J. L. Eyre*

DR FONG (USA) 4 ch.c. Kris S (USA) – Spring Flight (USA) (Miswaki (USA) 117 124) [1998 128: 10d* 10.4g⁴ 9g³ 8d* 10d* 8g² 9f² 9d⁵ 1999 a9f² a10f⁴ a9s⁴ 9f⁴ 8.5s Aug 28] quite good-topped, attractive colt: high-class performer in 1998, successful in St James's Palace Stakes at Royal Ascot and Prix Eugene Adam at Maisons-Laffitte: ½-length second to Desert Prince in Queen Elizabeth II Stakes at Ascot: left H. Cecil after and never recaptured his form in USA: second in Grade 2 at Santa Anita in February, 4 lengths fourth to Free House in Santa Anita Handicap next time and close fourth in Grade 2 at Hollywood on penultimate outing (final one for N. Drysdale): stayed 1¼m: probably acted on any going: blinkered final 3-y-o start: sometimes sweated up and got on edge: game: to stand at Side Hill Stud, nr Newmarket, fee £10,000, Oct 1st. *J. C. Kimmel, USA*

DRIVE ASSURED 5 gr.g. Mystiko (USA) 124 – Black Ivor (USA) (Sir Ivor 135) – [1998 77, a?: a10g 10.1s 10g a8g⁵ 7.5m² 7m² 7.6g 7f⁵ 7.5m³ 8.1m 8g* 8m 1999 8m Jul 17] workmanlike gelding: fair handicapper in 1998: well held in seller, only Flat run of 1999: best form at 7f/1m: acts on good to firm and good to soft going: successful over hurdles in October. *K. A. Morgan*

DR MARTENS (IRE) 5 b.g. Mtoto 134 – Suyayeb (USA) (The Minstrel (CAN) 55 135) [1998 –: 8d a8g 1999 8.3m 8.3m 10g 12d⁶ Aug 26] strong, compact gelding: has a quick action: fairly useful at 3 yrs: modest form (well held) in handicaps in 1999: may prove best around 1m/1¼m: has tended to sweat/get on edge. *W. J. Musson*

DROMINEER (IRE) 8 b.g. Conquering Hero (USA) 116 – Glenamara (Furry 74 Glen 121) [1998 70: 16g⁴ 16m⁶ 1999 16g 14g** 17f 16g⁵ 16f³ 15m² 16s 14d Oct 13] winning jumper: fair handicapper: won at Tipperary in July: creditable placed efforts at Galway and Ayr after: stays 2m: acts on good to soft and firm ground. *T. Hogan, Ireland*

DROWNED IN BUBBLY 3 b.g. Tragic Role (USA) – Champenoise 64 (Forzando 122) [1998 –: 5s 6.1m 1999 8d 12d 8m 13.8g⁴ 16.2m 16d 15.8g 13.8g a16g Nov 15] workmanlike gelding: no form: tried blinkered/tongue tied. *J. L. Eyre*   –

DRURIDGE BAY (IRE) 3 b.g. Turtle Island (IRE) 123 – Lady of Shalott 61 (Kings Lake (USA) 133) [1998 65d: 5d⁴ 6m⁵ 5.2m 7m⁴ 7g 6f⁶ 8g 5.3g 7m 8.2v³ 8s a8g⁶ a8.5g² a7g² a8g⁴ a7g 1999 8v 7f⁶ 7m⁶ 8.2m 10m Aug 23] useful-looking gelding: poor maiden: left M. Channon and off 3 months before final start: stays 8.5f: acts on any turf/all-weather: often finds little. *K. S. Bridgwater*   46

DR WILLIE CARSON (USA) 2 ch.c. (Mar 4) Carson City (USA) – Always Nettie (USA) (Vice Regent (CAN)) [1999 6.1g Sep 25] $300,000Y: first foal: dam won 8 races in USA, including minor 1m stakes: green and never a threat when seventh of 12 to Shannon Dore in maiden at Nottingham: sent to USA: should improve, particularly over 1m+. *H. R. A. Cecil*   60 p

DR WOODSTOCK 5 br.g. Rock City 120 – Go Tally-Ho 66 (Gorytus (USA) 132) [1998 42: 8d 8d⁴ 8m³ 6.9m⁴ 8m⁵ 7m⁵ 11m 9.9m² 10m⁵ 8v 1999 a7f a11g 9g³ 12.3m² 11d³ 12.1m² 11.1s² 12g 10s⁶ 10m² 12g⁶ Jun 22] tall gelding: poor maiden: left W. Storey after seventh start: stays 1½m: acts on good to firm and heavy ground (no form on all-weather): sometimes hangs: finds little, and one to be wary of. *M. E. Sowersby*   47 § a– §

DRYAD 4 ch.g. Risk Me (FR) 127 – Lizzy Cantle 52 (Homing 130) [1998 –, a65: a7g⁶ a6g⁴ a6g³ 6g 6g a7g² 6.1d a6g⁵ a6g² 5.9d a7g² a6g² 1999 a7g⁴ a6g* a6g⁵ a7g² a6g² 6s³ a5g a6g⁵ a6g* a6g⁴ 6g⁵ a6g³ Sep 4] angular gelding: fair performer on all-weather, modest on turf: won maiden at Wolverhampton in January and minor event at Southwell in June: best form at 6f/7f: acts on soft going and fibresand (untried on equitrack): usually blinkered in 1999, visored tenth start: doesn't look easiest of rides, but is consistent. *N. P. Littmoden*   53 a66

DRYING GRASS MOON 3 b.f. Be My Chief (USA) 122 – Sickle Moon (Shirley Heights 130) [1998 NR 1999 9.9g⁴ 9.9m⁶ Jun 25] 3,800Y: third foal: half-sister to German 1m winner Misty Moon (by Polar Falcon): dam unraced daughter of useful 7f and 8.5f winner Clare Island: fourth in maiden at Beverley, not knocked about after hampered under 2f out: last of 6 in similar event at Goodwood, though not given particularly hard time (reportedly injured a knee). *J. R. Fanshawe*   66

DUBAI DOLLY (IRE) 6 b.m. Law Society (USA) 130 – Lola Sharp (Sharpen Up 127) [1998 NR 1999 a14.8g³ May 14] poor winning hurdler: form on Flat only when third in seller at Wolverhampton, only run of 1999: acts on fibresand: tried blinkered. *J. W. Mullins*   44

DUBAI MILLENNIUM 3 b.c. Seeking The Gold (USA) – Colorado Dancer 122 (Shareef Dancer (USA) 135) [1998 108p: 8s* 1999 8f* 9.9g* 12g 10g* 8v* 8s* Sep 26]   132

Without supreme optimism, racing would be unsustainable. Owners and punters in particular, but also breeders, trainers and jockeys, all believe their horses can win, defeating rivals whose connections feel exactly the same way, and they back their conviction with hard cash. Moralists might argue that while optimism is fine, tempting providence isn't, but this line of thinking appears not to weigh heavily with Sheikh Mohammed when changing the names of his horses. Reportedly after the two-year-old Yaazer had shown himself the best of the Sheikh's juveniles on the Newmarket gallops in 1998 his name was changed to Dubai Millennium in the belief that he might turn out to be good enough to win the 2000 Dubai World Cup at four. On what we've seen so far, Dubai Millennium could easily live up to this exalted expectation, since his ability matches his undoubted good looks and has already enabled him to become Europe's top miler. He is likely to be in most lists of horses to follow, and, following the same principle, Dubai Two Thousand would doubtless be a popular choice as well.

Dubai Millennium trounced a good field of maidens at Yarmouth on his debut, a victory, which along with his reputation, resulted in quotes of 25/1 for the Two Thousand Guineas and 16/1 for the Derby. By March the Derby price was down to 12/1, much to the astonishment of Sheikh Mohammed, who called it 'ridiculous'. As a point of interest, at the same stage Iftitah was quoted at 10/1 for the Guineas and Etizaaz at 8/1 for the fillies' equivalent. Neither raced before August. Dubai Millennium failed to sparkle in the Godolphin trial for colts in Dubai towards the end of March, finishing unplaced behind Island Sands, Adair and Mukhalif, but apparently he had been held up in his preparation. He reappeared in a minor conditions race at Doncaster in May, when he made all and routed his three opponents headed by Ettrick, scoring by nine lengths. We were taken with this performance as well as with Dubai Millennium's appearance—he is a tall, good-looking colt who progressed physically as the season went on—and our enthusiasm did not lessen after his victory in the Predominate Stakes at Goodwood later in the month. He took the step up in distance in his stride, dropped in behind before being eased out early in the straight and cruising to the front with a quarter of a mile to go. Dubai Millennium drifted right as he went clear and tended to idle but still won by three and half lengths, pushed out with hands and heels, from Red Sea.

Dubai Millennium was a best-priced 7/1 for the Vodafone Derby after this race, and once Frankie Dettori had selected him in preference to Adair in the week leading up to the classic he shortened and was 5/1 favourite on the day. Godolphin runners frequently outshine their opponents in the paddock with their well-being but regrettably Dubai Millennium tried to outshine them in another, unhelpful, respect by behaving coltishly. By the time the runners had gone through the protracted Derby preliminaries he was undoubtedly keyed up and once they got going he fought for his head through the first half mile. He didn't look comfortable coming down the hill either, and after being checked in the straight he had nothing left to offer, finishing only ninth of sixteen behind Oath. Dubai Millennium, whose connections described him as 'babyish' after the Derby, evidently needed to become less excitable if he was to fulfil his potential, and fortunately he did, maturing and putting up three striking displays. However, he still tends to get stirred up before his races and takes a good hold once in action, and for that reason it's hard to imagine his being tried over a mile and a half again in the foreseeable future.

The first step on the road to restoring Dubai Millennium's reputation was over a mile and a quarter in the Prix Eugene Adam at Maisons-Laffitte in July. He faced four opponents, including British challengers Manndar and Salford Express and smart French colt State Shinto, and treated them with something approaching disdain, making the running and being in no danger after quickening early in the straight. At the finish he had three lengths to spare over State Shinto. A return to Group 1 company beckoned and Dubai

Millennium received his chance when reverting to a mile in the Prix du Haras de Fresnay-le-Buffard Jacques le Marois at Deauville in August. Torrential rain played havoc with the plans of various trainers in the run-up to the race—Sendawar was a late withdrawal—and in the event only five faced the starter on the heavy going. There were no older runners but it was still a good field, with two Andre Fabre-trained contenders in Slickly, successful in the Prix Noailles and Grand Prix de Paris, and Dansili, who had won the Prix Messidor and run second in the Poule d'Essai des Poulains. The other two were Grand Criterium victor Way of Light and the smart filly Venize. Dubai Millennium made them look a bunch of plodders, going straight off in front in dismal conditions and facing no challengers in the closing stages, eventually scoring by two and a half lengths from Slickly with Dansili a length back in third. The ground clearly did not inconvenience Dubai Millennium and nor did it for his final start in the Queen Elizabeth II Stakes at Ascot in September.

It was a miracle the Queen Elizabeth II Stakes took place at all, since the Saturday card on which it and the Fillies' Mile were supposed to be run had to be called off due to waterlogging. Both races were transferred to the Sunday, making for a nine-race card with two Group 1 races, two Group 2, one listed and a couple of well-contested, valuable handicaps. A cracking day, yet the crowd of 13,691 was almost a thousand down on the same day the previous year which had lacked the Group 1 events. Admittedly the weather was not reliable, but it was not raining cats and dogs either, and it's a cause for concern that racing cannot act as a greater magnet for the public. There were, for instance, fifteen English soccer matches that weekend which attracted bigger crowds than Ascot. Perhaps a new BHB initiative aimed at impressing youngsters with the delights of racing will help change things—the pilot scheme, which begins in the spring, will include educational visits to studs, training stables and racecourses, and a teaching pack for primary schoolchildren linked to the National Curriculum. Anything is worth a try, though as regards the race, Alain de Royer-Dupre decided a couple of days beforehand that it was not worth a try with Sendawar. This was a pity, as the clash between the French colt and Dubai Millennium could have settled the debate once and for all over which was the better miler. We side with Dubai Millennium, and we side with him largely on the basis of his triumph at Ascot. Only three took him on—regular pattern-race runner Almushtarak, St James's Palace Stakes third Gold Academy, recently an easy winner of the Strensall Stakes at York, and Coronation Stakes winner Balisada. Gold Academy made the running, with Dubai Millennium, a 9/4-on shot, tucked in behind moving sweetly. Once the

Queen Elizabeth II Stakes, Ascot—a small field but a top-class performance from Dubai Millennium who quickens away strikingly from Almushtarak (right), Gold Academy and Balisada

favourite hit the front under two furlongs out he swiftly put distance between himself and the rest, and he passed the post, with his rider Dettori posing for the cameramen, six lengths clear of Almushtarak. Gold Academy was third with Balisada running a stinker in last place. Allowing for the limitations of his opponents, this was still a stunning display, one in which Dubai Millennium put up a good timefigure of 1.16 fast, equivalent to a rating of 129.

Dubai Millennium (b.c. 1996)	Seeking The Gold (USA) (b 1985)	Mr Prospector (b 1970)	Raise A Native / Gold Digger
		Con Game (br 1974)	Buckpasser / Broadway
	Colorado Dancer (b 1986)	Shareef Dancer (b 1980)	Northern Dancer / Sweet Alliance
		Fall Aspen (ch 1976)	Pretense / Change Water

When Dubai Millennium comes to be retired to stud he is guaranteed to be highly sought after, not only on account of his proven merit but because he has a superb pedigree. His grandsire is Mr Prospector, one of the most commercial stallions of the 'eighties and 'nineties, who was put down in 1999. Dubai Millennium's sire Seeking The Gold, who stood at 125,000 dollars in the latest season, was a top performer and he is making a significant mark with his progeny. Seeking The Gold won the Dwyer Stakes over nine furlongs and the Super Derby over ten, and finished second in the Metropolitan Mile and Breeders' Cup Classic. His big winners in Europe also include Lujain (Middle Park Stakes) and top Japanese filly Seeking The Pearl (Prix Maurice de Gheest), while in the States he is responsible for champion fillies Heavenly Prize and Flanders plus Florida Derby winner Cape Town. None of his best progeny has scored over as far as a mile and a half. On the female side, Dubai

Godolphin's "Dubai Millennium"

Millennium hails from one of the most fashionable families around, one which has gained its status within the last twenty years. This is thanks almost entirely to Dubai Millennium's grandam Fall Aspen, who has been mentioned regularly in these Annuals, most recently in the essay on Bianconi in 1998. Fall Aspen's achievements—she died in 1998—bear repeating. A Grade 1 winner in the seven-furlong Matron Stakes as a juvenile, to date as a broodmare she has twelve winners from the same number of runners, nine of them in stakes company, including Grade 1 performers Northern Aspen (Gamely Handicap) and Timber Country (Champagne Stakes, Breeders' Cup Juvenile and Preakness Stakes) and Group 1 performers Hamas (July Cup) and Fort Wood (Grand Prix de Paris), the last-named finding fame as the sire of the outstanding South African performer Horse Chestnut. One of her Group 2 scorers, Elle Seule, is dam of Mehthaaf (Irish One Thousand Guineas) and champion sprinter Elnadim and grandam of Occupandiste (Maurice de Gheest and Foret), and her unraced daughter Dance of Leaves has produced good miler Charnwood Forest and Racing Post Trophy victor Medaaly. A phenomenal record!

Dubai Millennium's dam Colorado Dancer was a very smart middle-distance filly, successful in two pattern events, notably the Group 2 Prix de Pomone over thirteen and a half furlongs. She was also placed in the Prix Vermeille and Yellow Ribbon Handicap. Dubai Millennium is her fourth foal and third winner—she has since produced the unraced two-year-old colt Hobb Alwahtan and a yearling colt called Breckenridge (both by Machiavellian), then a colt foal by Highest Honor. She visited Groom Dancer in 1999. Her two other winners were both suited by middle distances and were both stakes-placed, Denver County (by Mr Prospector and thus closely related to Dubai Millennium) in the Group 2 Prix Greffulhe and Fort Morgan (by Pleasant Colony) in the listed Mooresbridge Stakes. At distances of a mile to a mile and a quarter Dubai Millennium will be worth following as a four-year-old whatever the company. He has a short, unimpressive action but acts on any going. Sheikh Mohammed believes the colt is the best horse to have carried the Godolphin colours, which is praise indeed considering it places him ahead of Mark of Esteem, Daylami, Intikhab, Swain, Halling and Balanchine. Dubai Millennium's form doesn't yet justify the claim, but he's not far behind, and it would take a brave person indeed to bet against his scaling that pinnacle in due course. *Saeed bin Suroor*

DUBAI NURSE 5 ch.m. Handsome Sailor 125 – Lady Eccentric (IRE) (Magical Wonder (USA) 125) [1998 54: a7g a6g 6d 5d² 5g 5d6 5g² 5d 6d 5s² 5g 5g 5v 5d² 1999 6s 5d Oct 20] modest maiden at best: tailed off both starts in 1999. *A. R. Dicken*   –

DUBAI TWO THOUSAND 2 b.c. (Feb 25) Nashwan (USA) 135 – Queen's View (FR) 103 (Lomond (USA) 128) [1999 8s* Oct 10]   **94 P**

A record of eight British classic victories in five years for trainer Saeed bin Suroor should merit keen interest in the composition of his select British-based string for the next season. The performances of Godolphin's two-year-olds, following the establishment of David Loder at Evry in the latest season, hardly set the pulse racing. However, there were a large number of once- or twice-raced individuals who could make into classic contenders. Potentially top of this list of Loder graduates transferred to spend the winter in Dubai is once-raced Dubai Two Thousand. His narrow victory in a four-runner minor event at Longchamp in October caused only a ripple in the ante-post betting on the Guineas—his price was unaltered at 33/1 in one book—but there is no doubt that he is held in the highest regard by those who have worked closely with him and by the end of the year his odds had shortened to 20/1. Connections went to the trouble of registering a change of name—he was originally called Parterre of Latona—a little over a fortnight before he made his debut and Loder's post-race eulogy is worth repeating. 'At this stage of his career, Dubai Two Thousand is a better horse than Dubai Millennium . . .

Prix de Blaison, Longchamp—
the well-regarded Dubai Two Thousand makes all to beat Alyzig (No.4) and Negociateur

ideally he needs to be held up and race on better ground. He didn't really race today, cocking his ears and changing his legs. Racing in front doesn't suit him and he was too relaxed.' Dubai Two Thousand may well not be in the line-up for the Guineas after all. He is one of four horses—the others being Best of The Bests, Broche and Sun Charm—which Godolphin will prepare for the newly instigated nine-furlong UAE Derby run on dirt at Nad Al Sheba on March 25th, with a view to assessing their potential for the Kentucky Derby.

Dubai Two Thousand (b.c. Feb 25, 1997)	Nashwan (USA) (ch 1986)	Blushing Groom (ch 1974)	Red God Runaway Bride
		Height of Fashion (b 1979)	Bustino Highclere
	Queen's View (FR) (b 1990)	Lomond (b 1980)	Northern Dancer My Charmer
		Mill Path (b 1985)	Mill Reef Parthica

Dubai Two Thousand is by Nashwan—average distance of all races won by his progeny just under a mile and a quarter—out of the useful Queen's View who stayed a mile. Neither of the two previous foals out of Queen's View provided a clue about her likely influence as a broodmare, and her own dam Mill Path ran only once, but the most illustrious member of the immediate family, Mill Path's half-sister Give Thanks, had a string of high-class performances to her name at a mile and a half, including a victory in the Irish Oaks, and stayed a mile and three quarters. The dam of Mill Path and Give Thanks, the quite useful mile winner Parthica, is a daughter of Violetta III, whose offspring in an illustrious career at stud included Oaks runner-up Furioso, the dam of Derby and King George winner Teenoso. *D. R. Loder, France*

DUBELLE 9 b.m. Dubassoff (USA) – Flopsy Mopsy (Full of Hope 125) [1998 –: 8g 14.1g 12m 1999 9.9m May 13] winning chaser: no form on Flat. *J. S. King*   —

DUBERRA (USA) 2 b.f. (Feb 22) Defensive Play (USA) 118 – Coffee Ice 92 (Primo Dominie 121) [1999 6f 7g⁵ 7g³ 7m⁵ 6g Aug 11] $2,500Y: second foal: dam 2-y-o 5f winner, later sprint winner in USA, from family of 6-y-o Insatiable: poor maiden: stays 7f: raced only on good going or firmer: sold 700 gns. *M. L. W. Bell*   **42 +**

DUBLIN RIVER (USA) 6 b.g. Irish River (FR) 131 – Vivre Libre (USA) **43**
(Honest Pleasure (USA)) [1998 NR 1999 a12f a11g⁶ 12f⁵ a12g⁴ a12g Oct 13] fairly
useful winner at 2 yrs: only poor form in varied company in 1999: probably stays 11f:
visored 4 of last 5 starts: sold 500 gns in December, joined M. Evans. *J. G. M. O'Shea*

DUBLINTWOTHOUSAND (IRE) 2 ch.f. (Apr 29) Port Lucaya 118 – Dublin **–**
Millennium (Dalsaan 125) [1999 7g a7g a6g a10s Dec 21] leggy, sparely-made filly:
seventh foal: half-sister to 6f (at 2 yrs) to 2m winner Cliburnel News (by Horage):
dam Irish 1½m winner: little sign of ability: sold from M. Tompkins 1,300 gns before
final start. *Patrick Wahl, Sweden*

DUCHAMP (USA) 2 b.c. (Feb 14) Pine Bluff (USA) – Higher Learning (USA) **84 p**
(Fappiano (USA)) [1999 7.1m⁶ 8.1g⁶ 8.2m² 10.2s² 7.9d* Oct 7] tall, quite attractive
colt: has scope: third foal: dam unraced daughter of US Grade 3 11f winner High
Browser from family of Iktamal and Rose Bowl: fairly useful form: looked in
splendid shape when winning 20-runner nursery at York by neck from William
Barraud, battling back tenaciously having been tapped for speed 2f out: will stay at
least 1½m, and likely to develop into a useful handicapper. *I. A. Balding*

DUCIE 2 b.f. (Mar 18) Distant Relative 128 – Ellebanna 69 (Tina's Pet 121) [1999 **70**
5d² 5f² 5.1g 5g² 5d Sep 30] 25,000Y: lengthy, unfurnished filly: fourth foal:
half-sister to 4-y-o Gift of Gold and 3-y-o King Midas: dam sprinting half-sister to
very smart sprinter Bolshoi: fair maiden: should stay 6f: acts on good to soft ground.
I. A. Balding

DUCK OVER 3 b.f. Warning 136 – Waterfowl Creek (IRE) 88 (Be My Guest **72**
(USA) 126) [1998 NR 1999 8s 8f⁴ 9.9m 8.3g³ 8.2d⁴ a10g Nov 16] angular filly: third **a–**
foal: half-sister to useful 1¼m winner Maid of Camelot (by Caerleon) and a winner
in Sweden: dam 1m winner from family of smart performers Guest Artiste,
Inchmurrin and Welney: fair maiden: should stay 1¼m: best effort on good going
(faded tamely only run on all-weather). *R. Charlton*

DUCK ROW (USA) 4 ch.g. Diesis 133 – Sunny Moment (USA) (Roberto (USA) **113**
131) [1998 113: 8d⁶ 7g³ 8d³ 10g 8s³ 1999 8.5g 8d* 8d⁶ 10m Jun 23] sturdy,
close-coupled gelding: smart performer on his day: benefited from change of tactics
when winning 5-runner minor event at Ascot in April, dictating pace and beating
Right Wing by 1¾ lengths (easily best effort of 1999): better at 1m than 7f, seems not
to stay 1¼m: acts on good to soft ground, below form on soft (after 3-month absence)
and good to firm. *J. A. R. Toller*

DUDEEN (IRE) 4 br.f. Anshan 119 – Pipers Pool (IRE) 94 (Mtoto 134) [1998 –: **62**
10g 10g⁶ 1999 12v⁴ 12.3m Jun 23] leggy, sparely-made filly: modest maiden: ran
poorly final start: stays 1½m: acts on heavy going. *T. P. McGovern*

DUDLEY ALLEN 4 ch.g. Superlative 118 – Smooth Flight 78 (Sandhurst Prince **39**
128) [1998 –, a43: 10.8s 9g 8m 9.7f 7m⁵ 7.1d 7m a7g a11g² 1999 a12g⁵ a12g⁴ a12g⁵
Jan 25] poor maiden: reportedly finished lame final start: stays 12f: acts on fibresand:
inconsistent. *T. T. Clement*

DUEL ISLAND 4 b.g. Jupiter Island 126 – Duellist (Town Crier 119) [1998 66: **–**
10.2g² 10m⁴ 10m⁴ 12.3m 11.7m 1999 8.1d 10.2g Aug 30] smallish gelding: fair
maiden at 3 yrs: well held in handicaps in 1999: should stay beyond 1¼m: blinkered
reappearance: tongue tied final start. *J. L. Spearing*

DUELLING GIRL (USA) 3 b.f. Dayjur (USA) 137 – Carduel (USA) (Buck- **89 §**
passer) [1998 74p: 6g⁵ 1999 7m³ 8.1g² 7g* 8m 7.6m Jul 25] big, close-coupled filly:
fairly useful performer: won maiden at Yarmouth in June, making all: well held after
in listed rated stakes and handicap: stays 7f: has raced only on good/good to firm
ground: has been attended by 2 handlers and mulish at stalls: ungenuine: sent to
Japan. *Sir Michael Stoute*

DUELLO 8 b.g. Sure Blade (USA) 130 – Royal Loft 105 (Homing 130) [1998 64: **64**
8.2m 8g 8.3d 10g⁴ 9m 11.6m⁴ 12m³ 9.9m⁵ 12m² 9.9m 12d² 14.1g* 13.9g⁶ 12s⁶ 1999
14.1s 11.6d² 14.1m 12g⁵ 14m 12g⁵ 14.4m 14.1g⁵ 11.9d² 11.8d* Oct 12] leggy
gelding: has a round action: modest performer: won claimer at Leicester in October:
stays 1¾m when conditions aren't testing: acts on good to firm ground, heavy and
fibresand: blinkered once at 3 yrs: usually held up: has high head carriage: tough.
M. Blanshard

DUE RISK (IRE)   2 b.g. (Feb 10) Kris 135 – Dukrame 76 (Top Ville 129) [1999   **63**
7.1m 7d⁴ 7m a8s* Dec 28] 20,000Y: quite attractive gelding: second foal: half-
brother to a winner abroad by Slip Anchor: dam 1¼m winner: failed to repeat form
of debut and sold from J. Noseda 4,200 gns after third start: won maiden at Taby in
December: will stay further than 1m. *Alex McLaren, Sweden*

DUKE OF ASTON (IRE)   2 ch.c. (Feb 10) Shalford (IRE) 124§ – Glenstal   **89**
Priory 53 (Glenstal (USA) 118) [1999 5s* 6d³ 6m 7f⁵ 7m² 7d³ 8.1v³ Oct 13] 32,000Y:
second reported foal: half-brother to 1997 2-y-o 6f winner Edna's Gift (later won in
Denmark, by Cyrano de Bergerac): dam stayed 2¼m: fairly useful performer: won
maiden at Goodwood in June despite wandering: several good efforts after, close
third of 5 to Shablam in minor event at Ayr penultimate start: stays 7f, failed to last
home over 1m on heavy ground: acts on soft going and on good to firm: has tended to
sweat: takes strong hold. *A. P. Jarvis*

DUKE OF MODENA   2 ch.g. (Apr 16) Salse (USA) 128 – Palace Street (USA)   **78 p**
103 (Secreto (USA) 128) [1999 7.1m⁶ 6g 6v³ Oct 23] sturdy gelding: fourth foal:
half-brother to 6-y-o Ca'd'Oro: dam won at 6f/7f: easily best effort in maidens when
8 lengths third of 14 to Out of Reach at Newbury: should stay at least 1m: acts on
heavy going (several relatives go particularly well in the mud): should make a fairly
useful handicapper. *G. B. Balding*

DUKHAN (USA)   5 b.h. Silver Hawk (USA) 123 – Azayim 111 (Be My Guest   **–**
(USA) 126) [1998 78, a74: a11g⁶ a8.5g⁶ a12g* a12g³ 12s 11.9d³ 12m 12.3m⁵ 10.5d
11.9f 16s a9.4g 1999 a11g 10d Oct 18] big, good-topped horse: fair performer at best:
has lost his form: stays 1½m: acts on fibresand and good to soft going. *E. J. Alston*

DULFORD   3 b.g. Never So Bold 135 – Cabra (Red Sunset 120) [1998 67: 6.1d³   **55**
6m⁴ 1999 a9.4g 8.2d 8g⁵ 11.4m 10.2s Sep 27] modest form at best in 1999, tailed off
last 2 starts: stays 1m: sold 800 gns. *B. R. Millman*

DULZIE   2 b.f. (Apr 28) Safawan 118 – Dulzura (Daring March 116) [1999 7g⁶ 7d   **56**
Oct 11] small filly: first foal: dam, no form on Flat, winning hurdler: better effort
(modest form) in Leicester maidens on debut: free to post next time: should stay at
least 1m. *A. P. Jarvis*

DUN DISTINCTLY (IRE)   2 b.g. (May 2) Distinctly North (USA) 115 –   **38**
Dunbally 57 (Dunphy 124) [1999 6m⁴ 6d 5m 6d a7g Dec 15] IR 7,800F, 9,700Y:
half-brother to 1993 2-y-o 5f winner Mr B Reasonable (by Reasonable): dam third at
6f at 2 yrs: first form when seventh in nursery final start. *P. C. Haslam*

DUNKELD CHAMP   2 br.g. (Mar 4) Be My Chief (USA) 122 – Callipoli (USA)   **–**
81 (Green Dancer (USA) 132) [1999 6g 7.1g Aug 18] 3,000Y: fourth foal: brother to
German 3-y-o 8.5f winner Barg Alail and half-brother to 5-y-o Noirie: dam, 1m/9f
winner, from family of Faithful Son: well held in maidens. *A. R. Dicken*

DUNKELLIN HOUSE (IRE)   2 gr.g. (Apr 4) Petorius 117 – More Magnani-   **55**
mous (King Persian 107) [1999 5m⁶ 5g 5d Oct 26] IR 3,400Y, IR 11,000Y: fifth foal:
brother to a 3-y-o 8.5f winner and half-brother to a winner by Shy Groom, both in
Italy: dam unraced: modest form when sixth of 11 in maiden at Pontefract on debut:
well beaten at Redcar both starts after. *R. A. Fahey*

DUNSTON DURGAM (IRE)   5 b.g. Durgam (USA) – Blazing Sunset 55   **–**
(Blazing Saddles (AUS)) [1998 27: a11s³ a12g⁶ a12g a12g⁵ a16.2g a14g 8m a8.5g
10.5m 11.5m a14g a12g⁵ a14g a14g a12g 1999 a12g Jan 11] bad maiden handicapper. *N. P. Littmoden*

DURAID (IRE)   7 ch.g. Irish River (FR) 131 – Fateful Princess (USA) 95   **87**
(Vaguely Noble 140) [1998 80: 8d 8d 8.5m⁴ 8g⁶ 8s⁵ 7.9m 7g⁵ 8m 8m 1999 7m⁶ 8m²
8.5m* 8m 8.5m⁶ 7g 8m* 8g 7d⁴ 7g 7s* Nov 2] workmanlike gelding: has a round
action: fairly useful handicapper: won at Beverley in July, Ripon in August and
Catterick (best form since 1997) in November: effective at 7f when conditions are
testing, stays 9f: acts on soft and good to firm going: visored once in 1998: has rather
a high head carriage: held up and best in truly-run race. *Denys Smith*

DURGAMS DELIGHT (IRE)   4 b.f. Durgam (USA) – Miromaid (Simply   **–**
Great (FR) 122) [1998 44, a47: a8g a11g⁴ a11g⁵ 9.9m³ 14.1g² 12d⁴ 11.1d⁵ 14.1g
1999 16m Sep 2] poor maiden handicapper: stays 1¾m: acts on good to firm ground,
good to soft and fibresand: effective blinkered or not. *J. L. Eyre*

DURGAMS FIRST (IRE)   7 ch.g. Durgam (USA) – Miromaid (Simply Great   **56**
(FR) 122) [1998 51: 12.3v⁵ a11g⁵ 12d² a11g 11.1g² 1999 a8.5g 10g* 10m⁶ Aug
28] small gelding: has been fired: modest performer: won seller at Pontefract in
August: stays 1¾m (pulled hard over 2m): acts on firm going, soft and fibresand.
Mrs M. Reveley

DURHAM   8 ch.g. Caerleon (USA) 132 – Sanctuary (Welsh Pageant 132) [1998   **69 §**
73, a–: 11.5m³ 14g⁶ 14.1m² 14m* 14m³ 13.9g 14g⁴ 12m³ 1999 15.4v² 14.1s 14.4m⁵
14.6s⁴ 14g* 14m⁶ 14m³ 14m² 16.5f² 16g 14d Sep 15] sparely-made gelding: fair
handicapper: won at Goodwood (hung left) in June: stays 2m: acts on equitrack, firm
and soft going: usually blinkered/visored: usually held up and not easiest of rides
(seemed uncooperative penultimate start, something seemingly amiss final one).
G. L. Moore

DURHAM DANCER   3 b.f. Magic Ring (IRE) 115 – Final Shot 91 (Dalsaan   **59**
125) [1998 NR 1999 6d 5s³ 5m⁴ 6f 5d 6f Sep 4] 15,000Y: rather leggy filly: has a
round action: sister to 4-y-o Magical Shot and half-sister to 2 winners, notably 5-y-o
Double Action: dam won Ayr Gold Cup: modest maiden: below form final 2 starts:
raced only at 5f/6f: acts on firm going: sold 6,200 gns in November. *T. D. Easterby*

DURHAM DANDY   3 b.g. Inchinor 119 – Disco Girl (FR) (Green Dancer (USA)   **51**
132) [1998 56?: 5g⁶ 6g 6f 6g 1999 9.9g 9m⁶ 9.3m² 10f 12.4g 14.1m Aug 28] leggy,
quite attractive gelding: modest maiden: best effort when second in handicap at
Carlisle: stays 9f, not 1½m: acts on good to firm going. *T. D. Easterby*

DURHAM FLYER   4 b.g. Deploy 131 – Hyde Princess 75 (Touch Paper 113)   **–**
[1998 64: 10v 6d⁵ 6g 6d³ 5.9g⁶ 7d* 7d 7.5g² 7g 6.9d* 8.5m⁵ 10g 8.5m 8v⁴ 1999 8.3m
7f 7g 7s 9.9s a8g a10g Nov 11] sturdy gelding: little form in 1999: sold 1,500 gns.
J. Cullinan

DURLSTON BAY   2 b.c. (May 6) Welsh Captain 113 – Nelliellamay (Super   **–**
Splash (USA) 106) [1999 8.3d Nov 4] brother to 7f/1m winner Tuigamala: dam
unraced: soundly beaten in seller at Windsor. *R. Ingram*

DUSHANBE (IRE)   4 b.g. Alzao (USA) 117 – Atyaaf (USA) 48 (Irish River (FR)   **–**
131) [1998 91: 7.5d* 7.6m³ 7g 1999 8d 7g 10.3m May 4] leggy, useful-looking
gelding: fairly useful form at 3 yrs: little form in 1999: stayed 7.6f: dead.
N. A. Callaghan

DUSKY VIRGIN   2 b.f. (May 5) Missed Flight 123 – Rosy Sunset (IRE) (Red   **57**
Sunset 120) [1999 5g 6g 5.7g⁶ 6g⁵ 7f* Aug 4] 1,000F, IR 6,200Y: fourth foal:
half-sister to 3-y-o Evening Promise: dam lightly-raced half-sister to smart middle-
distance 7-y-o Diaghilef: modest maiden: dropped in class and upped in trip, won seller
at Brighton in August, racing freely and going clear final 1f (subsequently joined
S. Woodman 13,500 gns): stays 7f: acts on firm ground. *M. Quinn*

DUSTY DANCER   3 ch.g. Risk Me (FR) 127 – Eternal Triangle (USA) 76   **–**
(Barachois (CAN)) [1998 68: 5f 5d⁵ 5m 5g 1999 a6g⁶ a8f 7.1d 6s 7.1m Aug 5] fair
maiden at 2 yrs, no form in 1999: left Gay Kelleway after fourth start: best at 5f.
W. G. M. Turner

DUTCH DYANE   6 b.m. Midyan (USA) 124 – Double Dutch 100 (Nicholas Bill   **41**
125) [1998 41, a–: 15.4s 16.2g 12.5m³ 16v² 1999 15.4v 16.1s³ Jun 7] poor maiden   **a–**
handicapper: stays 2m: acts on good to firm and heavy going, no form on all-weather:
won handicap hurdle in November. *G. P. Enright*

DUTCH LAD   4 b.g. Alnasr Alwasheek 117 – Double Dutch 100 (Nicholas Bill   **83**
125) [1998 83: 11.8s² 12s* 9.9s³ 12.3m² 12s 11.6g² 11.8f⁵ 1999 10m 12g⁵ 12m Jun
16] sturdy, angular gelding: unimpressive mover: fairly useful performer: easily best
effort in 1999 (saddle slipped on reappearance) when fifth at Doncaster: stays 1½m:
acts on good to firm and soft ground: usually held up: reportedly had breathing
problem final 3-y-o start. *M. H. Tompkins*

DUTCH NIGHTINGALE   5 b.m. Warrshan (USA) 117 – Double Dutch 100   **47**
(Nicholas Bill 125) [1998 –: 10m 11.5g 1999 9.9m⁶ 9.9d 9v⁶ 10s 10s Nov 1] modest
maiden: should be suited by 1½m+: acts on heavy going. *G. P. Enright*

DUTY SQUADRON (IRE)   3 b.g. Mac's Imp (USA) 116 – Guess Who 76 (Be   **–**
My Guest (USA) 126) [1998 NR 1999 a8f Jan 23] 5,000Y: brother to a winner up to

7f in Sweden and half-brother to several winners, including 9-y-o Hazard A Guess: dam, disqualified 10.4f winner, from family of Derby second Cavo Doro: tailed off in Lingfield maiden. *P. Mitchell*

DUVET 7 b.m. Squill (USA) 122 – Embroideress 80 (Stanford 121§) [1998 NR 1999 7.7m a13g 8.3g 8.3d Nov 4] 1,500 6-y-o: half-sister to 3 winners, including fairly useful sprinter Sacque (by Elegant Air) and 1m and 1¼m seller winner Tom Clapton (by Daring March): dam 5f to 7f winner: of little account over hurdles and on Flat. *Miss K. M. George*   –

D W MCCEE 3 b.g. Keen 116 – Miss Coco (Swing Easy (USA) 126) [1998 NR 1999 9f⁶ 10.2m 8s⁵ 8s Oct 25] 8,500Y: second foal: brother to fair 1m winner Keen Alert: dam unraced: little sign of ability. *Miss Gay Kelleway*   –

DYCE 5 b.m. Green Ruby (USA) 104 – Miss Display 47 (Touch Paper 113) [1998 39: 6g 5g⁵ 5g a5g⁵ 5d a5g⁵ 1999 a6g a5g a5g a5g⁵ a5g⁵ Mar 27] tall mare: poor performer: best at 5f: acts on fibresand: usually blinkered. *J. Balding*   **33**

DYHIM DIAMOND (IRE) 5 ch.h. Night Shift (USA) – Happy Landing (FR) (Homing 130) [1998 117: 6g* 5g⁴ 6s² 6g² 6.5m⁴ 6g⁴ 1999 6d² 6f 6s⁵ 6s* Sep 27] robust, good sort: smart performer: won minor event at Bordeaux in September: earlier ¾-length second to Auenadler in Benazet-Rennen at Baden-Baden and 1½ lengths fifth to Seltitude in Prix de Seine-et-Oise at Chantilly: well beaten in July Cup at Newmarket: seems best around 6f: acts on good to firm and soft ground: usually races prominently/forces pace: joined W. Mott in USA. *C. Laffon-Parias, France*   **112**

DYNAMIC DREAM (USA) 2 b.f. (Mar 10) Dynaformer (USA) – Hip Hip Hur Rahy (USA) (Rahy (USA) 115) [1999 7d* Aug 26] $32,000Y: first foal: dam, successful up to 1m in USA, including at 2 yrs: won maiden at Folkestone by head from Ghuffran, seeming to idle off bridle: will stay at least 1m: should do better. *P. W. Harris*   **81 p**

DYNAMISM (FR) 4 b.g. Caerleon (USA) 132 – Fextal (USA) (Alleged (USA) 138) [1998 92: 10m⁶ 10g* 1999 10g³ 10s 10m 10f⁴ 10g⁵ 10d 10s a10g a12g⁶ Dec 17] lengthy, good-topped gelding: useful on his day: easily best effort in 1999 when third in listed race at Kempton: pulled up lame next start, and generally well held after: stays 1¼m: tried blinkered/visored. *Mrs L. Stubbs*   **104 d**

E

EAGLESHAM (IRE) 3 b.c. Barathea (IRE) 127 – High Hawk 124 (Shirley Heights 130) [1998 NR 1999 8d⁵ 8g⁶ 8m* Jun 16] sturdy colt: closely related to 3 middle-distance winners by Sadler's Wells, all useful or better, notably Breeders' Cup Turf winner In The Wings, and half-brother to 2 winners, including useful winner around 1¼m Mohawk River (by Polish Precedent): dam, middle-distance stayer, half-sister to dam of Derby winner High-Rise: progressive form in maidens, winning at Ripon by length from Manicure: will stay 1¼m: sent to race in Dubai. *B. W. Hills*   **85**

EARLEY SESSION (IRE) 2 b.c. (Mar 15) Puissance 110 – Shabby Doll 69 (Northfields (USA)) [1999 6g 6g a7g Nov 13] half-brother to several winners, including useful 6f/7f winner Chickawicka (by Dance of Life) and a winner up to 1¼m in Italy by Elmaamul: dam, 1¼m/11f winner, out of half-sister to smart middle-distance colt Beauvallon: form in maidens well on debut. *J. C. Tuck*   **40**

EARLY DAISY 4 ch.f. Crofthall 110 – Heldigvis 63 (Hot Grove 128) [1998 NR 1999 7.1m⁵ May 22] 2,200Y: half-sister to 2 Flat winners, including Grouse-N-Heather (up to 13.8f, by Grey Desire), also successful over jumps: dam 2-y-o 7f/1m winner: poor form at best in bumpers: 40/1, fifth in claimer at Musselburgh on Flat debut. *R. Allan*   **52**

EARP (IRE) 7 b.g. Anita's Prince 126 – Ottavia Abu (Octavo (USA) 115) [1998 64: 7v² 7s 5v⁴ 5.8s 1999 8d 12g Nov 13] fifth foal: half-brother to a winner abroad by Mummy's Treasure: dam Irish maiden: fairly useful performer at best: just modest form in handicaps for N. Meade in Ireland in 1998: modest winning hurdler: –

well held on return to Flat: stays 1m: acts on good to firm and heavy ground: tried blinkered. *F. P. Murtagh*

EASAAR 3 b.c. Machiavellian (USA) 123 – Matila (IRE) 98 (Persian Bold 123) **104** [1998 105p: 7g² 7g* 1999 8m May 1] sturdy colt: has a quick action: useful performer: won maiden at Newmarket at 2 yrs: only run of 1999 when 7 lengths tenth to Island Sands in 2000 Guineas on same course, soon beaten once race began in earnest: stays 1m: raced only on good/good to firm going. *Saeed bin Suroor*

EAST ARRAN STREET 2 b.f. (Apr 25) Balla Cove 119 – Spy Girl (Tanfirion – 110) [1999 5f Aug 6] half-sister to several winners, including 5f to 1m winner Pearl Dawn (by Jareer) and 7-y-o Witney-de-Bergerac: dam unraced: very slowly away and soon tailed off in maiden at Lingfield: got loose before start and withdrawn later in August. *Noel T. Chance*

EASTERN CHAMP (USA) 3 ch.c. Star de Naskra (USA) – Dance Troupe (USA) **78** (Native Charger) [1998 NR 1999 8g 8m 8s 8.2m² 8.5m² 9m* 10g⁴ 8.5m² 8m a8.5g² a8g Nov 8] tall, unfurnished colt: has a quick action: brother to US Grade 2 8.5f winner and Kentucky Derby third Dance Floor and half-brother to several winners in USA: dam won 10 races in USA: fair performer: won maiden at Redcar in August: good efforts after when second in handicaps at Epsom and Wolverhampton: stays 9f, possibly not 1¼m: acts on good to firm going and fibresand: has reportedly had soft palate operation: tongue tied since debut. *S. P. C. Woods*

EASTERN LYRIC 4 gr.f. Petong 126 – Songlines 78 (Night Shift (USA)) [1998 **– §** 93: 5.1g 5g 5s⁴ 5m* 5.1m 5.1d* 5g* 5f 6m² 1999 6g 5.1s⁵ 5m 8m 7f 7m⁵ 6m 6m Sep 16] lengthy, quite good-topped filly: fairly useful at 3 yrs: no form in 1999, leaving C. Brittain after sixth start: stays 6f: acts on good to firm and good to soft going: blinkered fifth start: refused to race final outing. *D. Nicholls*

EASTERN PROJECT (IRE) 5 b.g. Project Manager 111 – Diandra (Shardari – **–** 134) [1998 NR 1999 11.9d Jun 12] rather leggy gelding: fair maiden for J. Bolger in Ireland for most of 1997: no show either start on Flat in Britain, though has shown fair form over jumps: stays 9.6f: acts on good to soft ground. *M. D. Hammond*

EASTERN PROPHETS 6 b.g. Emarati (USA) 74 – Four Love (Pas de Seul 133) **70** [1998 75, a72: a6g⁴ a6g³ a6g³ a6g³ a6g⁶ 6v 6s⁶ 6g* 6d⁴ 6f⁵ 6d 6g³ 5g 5d⁴ 5m 5m⁴ 5.3m² 5.2g² 5m a6g 6s⁶ 1999 5g⁴ 6.1s 6.1f* 5.7g 6.1f 5g 6m 5g² 5m 5m² 6m² 5.1m³ 6f 7f³ 6.9g² a6f 7g Oct 16] good-quartered gelding: fair performer: won apprentice handicap at Nottingham in May: effective at 5f to 7f: acts on firm going, good to soft and all-weather: sometimes on toes/sweating: often blinkered/visored, but is as effective without: none too consistent. *M. Dods*

EASTERN PURPLE (IRE) 4 b.c. Petorius 117 – Broadway Rosie 101 (Absalom **113** 128) [1998 109: 5.1g 6d* 6s 5d 6g⁵ 6g³ 7f⁵ 6m 6s⁶ 6d 1999 6d² 6s 6g* 6m⁵ 7f⁵ 6d³ 7g

Weatherbys Ireland Greenlands Stakes, the Curragh—
Eastern Purple (No.2) just gets the better of Gaelic Storm after a rare battle;
One Won One (partly hidden) is third with Bianconi fourth

6m 6d Sep 18] robust, strong-quartered colt: carries condition: smart performer: won Weatherbys Ireland Greenlands Stakes at the Curragh in May by short head from Gaelic Storm: ran well when 3 lengths fifth to Bold Edge in Cork And Orrery Stakes at Royal Ascot next time and when 2 lengths third to Gorse in Phoenix Sprint Stakes at Leopardstown in August: below form after, including in visor: best at 6f: acts on firm and good to soft ground, probably on soft: effective blinkered or not: game. *K. A. Ryan*

EASTERN RAINBOW (IRE)   3 b.c. Bluebird (USA) 125 – Insaf (USA) (Raise   –
A Native) [1998 NR 1999 7m⁶ 8s 10m 12.1m Jun 23] 16,000Y, 12,000 2-y-o: lengthy colt: fifth reported foal: dam unraced daughter of Coronation Stakes winner Kesar Queen: little form: looked reluctant in blinkers final start. *K. A. Ryan*

EASTERN SPICE   2 b.c. (May 21) Polish Precedent (USA) 131 – Mithl Al Hawa   **76**
99 (Salse (USA) 128) [1999 6g 7.1m⁶ 7m² 7g 7m³ 8d⁵ Oct 21] lengthy, quite good-topped colt: third foal: half-brother to fairly useful 7f/1m winner Cornflower Fields (by Cadeaux Genereux): dam, 2-y-o 6f winner, stayed 7f: fair maiden: best effort when third of 17 in nursery at Doncaster penultimate start: stays 7f: acts on good to firm ground. *R. Hannon*

EASTERN TRUMPETER   3 b.c. First Trump 118 – Oriental Air (IRE) 56   **72**
(Taufan (USA) 119) [1998 64: 5s⁵ 5.1g² 1999 a5g² 5s* 6m 5g⁴ 6g³ 5s* 6g 5.1m⁵ 5.1m³ 5g 5.1d 5.1s 5s a6g³ 5.2s³ 5d 5s⁵ Nov 5] compact colt: fair performer: won claimer at Folkestone in April and handicap at Ayr in June: effective at 5f/easy 6f: acts on good to firm going, soft and fibresand: tough and consistent. *J. M. Bradley*

EASTERN VENTURE   2 b.c. (Apr 25) Last Tycoon 131 – Imperial Jade 105   **56**
(Lochnager 132) [1999 6g 8s Oct 25] brother to 6f winner Taalif and fairly useful 7f winner Royal Jade and half-brother to several winners, notably 8-y-o Averti: dam sprinting sister to smart sprinter Reesh: green, seventh of 22 to Spencers Wood in maiden at Windsor on debut: bandaged in front and moved poorly to post, well beaten only subsequent outing. *W. R. Muir*

EASTER OGIL (IRE)   4 ch.g. Pips Pride 117 – Piney Pass (Persian Bold 123)   **90**
[1998 87: 5s* 5.1g 6f 6m² 5.1d⁴ 6g⁴ 6f² 7m³ 7.1g* 7.1m 1999 6d 6g³ 6v 7m⁶ 7g 6f 6g⁶ 6d² 7m³ 6f 7.1d⁴ 5.7f* 7.1d⁵ 6v 8d 9v Oct 23] lengthy gelding: unimpressive mover: fairly useful handicapper: won at Bath in September: not at best after: probably stays 1m, not 9f: acts on firm and soft ground: usually visored (not last 2 starts): often soon off bridle: usually comes from off pace. *I. A. Balding*

EASTLEIGH   10 b.g. Efisio 120 – Blue Jane 81 (Blue Cashmere 129) [1998 –,   **43**
a27: a8g a8g a8g a8g⁵ a8.5g⁶ a8g⁶ a9.4g⁵ a11g⁶ a7g a9.4g a10g 1999 a8.5g⁶ a8g² a8g 8.5m a9.4g⁶ a8.5g May 22] lengthy, workmanlike gelding: poor performer: stays 1¼m: acts on all-weather, no recent form on turf: tried visored/blinkered (not since 1996): sometimes flashes tail. *R. Hollinshead*

EASTWAYS   2 ch.c. (May 11) Efisio 120 – Helens Dreamgirl 95 (Caerleon (USA)   **93 p**
132) [1999 5d³ 5m² 5d* 6d⁵ 7s² Oct 23] close-coupled colt: has a round action: fifth foal: half-brother to 4 winners, including 3-y-o Dream On Me and 7-y-o House of Dreams: dam 1¼m winner: fairly useful performer: won minor event at Beverley in June: off course over 4 months: ran very well in nurseries at Newmarket and Doncaster (still clear entering final 1f, beaten 3 lengths by Avezzano) on return: stays 7f: acts on good to firm and soft ground: capable of better still. *M. Johnston*

EASTWELL HALL   4 b.g. Saddlers' Hall (IRE) 126 – Kinchenjunga 67 (Dar-   **89**
shaan 133) [1998 82: 9.7d⁴ 10.2s* 12.5g* 11.8g² 12g² 12m⁶ 16g 17.2d³ 1999 14d 17.2s⁵ 17.3g⁴ Oct 16] tall, close-coupled gelding: fairly useful handicapper: better than ever when 2¼ lengths fourth of 32 to Top Cees in Tote Cesarewitch at Newmarket, getting unbalanced and bumped when leading briefly over 1f out: stays 17f: acts on soft going: held up: won over hurdles in December. *T. P. McGovern*

EASTWELL STAR   3 b.f. Saddlers' Hall (IRE) 126 – Kinchenjunga 67 (Darshaan   –
133) [1998 –: 7s 1999 12v Sep 20] tailed off in maidens: bred to stay well. *Miss Gay Kelleway*

EASTWOOD DRIFTER (USA)   2 ch.c. (Mar 6) Woodman (USA) 126 – Man-   **56**
darina (USA) 105 (El Gran Senor (USA) 136) [1999 7m⁶ 8v 8.2d Oct 21] 450,000 francs Y: angular, unfurnished colt: first foal: dam 7f winner, including at 2 yrs, from

family of City Honours: modest form in maidens at Ascot, Kempton and Nottingham (raced very freely): likely to prove best up to 1m. *W. R. Muir*

EASYCALL 5 b.h. Forzando 122 – Up And Going (FR) (Never So Bold 135) [1998 115: 5d³ 5d⁶ 5d³ 6f 5m² 5g 5f 5g* 5d* 5d⁵ 5v² 1999 5.2d Sep 19] good-quartered horse: good walker: smart performer: winner of 7 races, including Richmond Stakes at Goodwood, Flying Childers Stakes at Doncaster and Cornwallis Stakes at Ascot at 2 yrs and listed race at Doncaster in 1998, when trained by B. Meehan: behind only outing of 1999: effective at 5f/easy 6f: acted on any going: tried blinkered (ran creditably)/visored: raced prominently: to stand at Fares Stables, nr Royston, Hertfordshire, fee £2,500 Oct 1st, no foal free return. *J. Noseda* —

EASY DOLLAR 7 ch.g. Gabitat 119 – Burglars Girl 63 (Burglar 128) [1998 –: 6m 6d 1999 6g⁵ 6m⁶ 7d 6m 5m⁵ 7.3m⁵ 6m⁵ 7f⁴ 7g⁶ 6g 6m² 6.1g* 6d 6s⁶ Oct 22] tall, plain gelding: does not impress in appearance: useful performer: first win since 1995 at Nottingham (handicap) in September: mostly at least respectable efforts otherwise, including in listed events: effective at 5f (on stiff track) to 7f: acts on firm going, probably on soft: blinkered/visored. *B. Gubby* **100**

EASY TO LOVE (USA) 3 b.f. Diesis 133 – La Sky (IRE) 107 (Law Society (USA) 130) [1998 NR 1999 10g⁵ Apr 13] useful-looking filly: third foal: half-sister to French 1½m winner Laurentine and a winner in USA (both by Private Account): dam 1¼m winner (probably stayed 1¾m), closely related to Champion Stakes winner Legal Case: promising debut when under 3 lengths fifth to Mirjan in Newmarket maiden but not seen out again: will stay 1½m. *H. R. A. Cecil* **77**

EATON SQUARE (USA) 4 b.c. Nureyev (USA) 131 – Jolypha (USA) 123 (Lyphard (USA) 132) [1998 108p: 8m* 9.5g* 12f 1999 8.1g⁵ 10.3s⁴ Jun 27] smallish, robust colt: shows a quick action: useful performer at 3 yrs: well below form in minor events in 1999: should stay 1½m: sold to stud in Cyprus. *H. R. A. Cecil* **90**

EBBA 2 ch.f. (Mar 12) Elmaamul (USA) 125 – Strawberry Song 87 (Final Straw 127) [1999 5g* 6g* 7m 5.2f* 5.2g⁵ 6g 5g⁵ Sep 19] 8,000Y: leggy, sparely-made filly: eighth foal: sister to 4-y-o Sans Rivale: dam 1¼m winner: fairly useful performer: won maiden at Catterick in May and minor events at Yarmouth in June and July: fifth in listed races at Newbury (ran creditably) and Rome (below form) after: best form at 5f: raced only on good ground or firmer. *M. L. W. Bell* **88**

EBEN AL HABEEB (IRE) 8 ch.g. Nashwan (USA) 135 – Family Style (USA) (State Dinner (USA)) [1998 NR 1999 a16.2g 11.9d Jun 3] big, lengthy gelding: has had soft palate operation and been hobdayed: fair maiden handicapper for R. Hern in 1995: winning hurdler/chaser for current stable, successful in August: soundly beaten on first Flat starts for nearly 4 years. *D. McCain* —

EBINZAYD (IRE) 3 b.g. Tenby 125 – Sharakawa (IRE) (Darshaan 133) [1998 87p: 8.2m⁴ 8.2d 8g* 8d 1999 11.9d³ 12.3d⁵ 12m³ 10.3g⁴ 11.9d⁵ Oct 7] sturdy gelding: fluent mover: fairly useful performer: creditable efforts when in frame: stays 1½m: yet to race on extremes of going: found little second and final starts: sold 44,000 gns. *E. A. L. Dunlop* **91**

EBONY 3 b.f. Mujtahid (USA) 118 – Sharia (USA) (Irish River (FR) 131) [1998 51?, a–: 6m 5.3g² 7m a8g a8g 1999 8.2f 10.1g a6g Aug 6] small filly: no form after second 2-y-o start: should stay beyond 5f: blinkered final outing. *B. J. McMath* —

EBONY HEIGHTS 3 br.c. Polar Falcon (USA) 126 – Maestrale (Top Ville 129) [1998 60: 7g 1999 8s² 8.1g³ 8m 8m* 8.1m 8m 7.9g Oct 6] leggy, useful-looking colt: reportedly fractured pelvis leaving stalls only 2-y-o start: useful performer: won steadily-run handicap at Newmarket in July: below form after: stays 1m, should be at least as effective at 7f: acts on good to firm and soft going: often races freely: sold 25,000 gns, sent to Saudi Arabia. *W. R. Muir* **95**

E B PEARL 3 ch.f. Timeless Times (USA) 99 – Petite Elite 47 (Anfield 117) [1998 –: 5g 6g 5g 6s a5g⁵ a6g 6m 7g 7m a7g 1999 a8g⁶ a7g³ a8g⁶ a7f a7g⁴ a7g³ a5g* a7g⁵ 6g⁶ 5g⁴ 6m² a6g 5f* 5m 5m⁴ 5g 5f 5m 6.1m Sep 13] rather sparely-made filly: modest performer: won maiden claimer at Southwell in April and selling handicap at Redcar in July: below form last 4 starts: effective at 5f, probably at 7f: acts on fibresand and firm going: sometimes blinkered. *N. Bycroft* **51**

E B TREASURE   4 b.f. Precocious 126 – Petite Elite 47 (Anfield 117) [1998 NR   –
1999 a7g a11g a8g Jan 11] of little account. *N. Bycroft*

ECLECTIC   3 b.f. Emarati (USA) 74 – Great Aim (Great Nephew 126) [1998 –:   –
6m 7m 1999 7g 8.3m Apr 19] tall, angular filly: little sign of ability. *S. Dow*

ECO FRIENDLY   4 ch.c. Sabrehill (USA) 120 – Flower Girl 108 (Pharly (FR)   **89**
130) [1998 114: 10s² 10m 14.6m 9.8d³ 10g 1999 10g 10.5d⁵ 8m⁴ 8s⁴ 9v⁵ Oct 23]
strong, lengthy colt: smart in 1998: well below form in 1999 after reappearance:
seems to stay 14.6f: acts on good to firm and heavy going: blinkered third start: has
been bandaged behind: sold 50,000 gns. *B. W. Hills*

ECSTASY   2 b.f. (Apr 28) Pursuit of Love 124 – Gong 84 (Bustino 136) [1999   **77**
5.1m⁶ 6.1g² 6.8m* 6s⁴ 6.5g 7d³ 6d Oct 15] 1,400Y: unfurnished filly: third foal: dam,
1½m winner who stayed 1½m, half-sister to smart middle-distance stayer Waterfield:
fair performer: won maiden at Warwick in July: best effort when close third of 19 in
nursery at Newmarket penultimate start: needs further than 6f, and likely to stay
1¼m+: acts on good to firm and good to soft going. *P. T. Walwyn*

ECUDAMAH (IRE)   3 ch.g. Mukaddamah (USA) 125 – Great Land (USA)   **75**
(Friend's Choice (USA)) [1998 76: 5m 7.1g⁵ 5.1m² 5m⁵ 5m³ 6d 5m⁴ 6d² 5s² 5g 1999
5s³ 5.1s⁵ 5f 5f 5d 6g 5.1s⁴ a5g* a5g² a5g⁴ a5g⁶ Dec 18] useful-looking gelding: fair
handicapper: left K. Bell after fifth start: won at Wolverhampton in November:
effective at 5f (given test)/6f: acts on all-weather, goes well on soft going on turf:
sometimes rears stalls/slowly away. *Miss Jacqueline S. Doyle*

EDABIYA (IRE)   3 ch.f. Rainbow Quest (USA) 134 – Ebaziya (IRE) 111 (Dar-   **110**
shaan 133) [1998 111p: 7d⁷ 7d* 8s³ 1999 8g 12m⁵ 15v⁴ Oct 2] rangy, unfurnished
filly: has short, unimpressive action: smart performer: one of the top 2-y-o fillies of
1998, winner of Moyglare Stud Stakes at the Curragh: easily best effort in 1999 when
6½ lengths fifth to Daryaba in Prix Vermeille at Longchamp: should stay further than
1½m: acts on soft going and good to firm: blinkered final 2 starts. *J. Oxx, Ireland*

EDE'IFF   2 b.f. (Mar 1) Tragic Role (USA) – Flying Amy 40 (Norwick (USA)   **64**
125) [1999 7d⁶ a8.5g 8.3d* Nov 4] 500Y: third foal: dam poor maiden: 50/1, first
form when winning 17-runner seller at Windsor in November by 1½ lengths from
Momentous Jones: should stay 1¼m. *W. G. M. Turner*

EDEN DANCER   7 b.g. Shareef Dancer (USA) 135 – Dash (Connaught 130)   –
[1998 NR 1999 9.9d⁶ Aug 11] sturdy gelding: fairly useful front-running hurdler,
successful 4 times between May and October: poor form at best on Flat since 1995:
stays 1½m. *M. C. Pipe*

EDEN (IRE)   3 b.f. Polish Precedent (USA) 131 – Isle of Flame (Shirley Heights   **88**
130) [1998 80p: 7d* 1999 8d⁴ 9.9g⁶ 8m³ 8.3m Aug 28] smallish, good-topped filly:
fairly useful performer: good efforts 3 of 4 starts, not getting best of runs in rated
stakes at Windsor final one (bandages came loose): should stay 1¼m: acts on good to
firm and good to soft going. *L. M. Cumani*

EDEN MELODY   3 b.f. Noble Patriarch 115 – Edensong (Lochnager 132) [1998   –
NR 1999 10d⁶ 10m 13.8g⁶ Jul 1] first foal: dam unraced: no form in maidens.
J. J. O'Neill

EDIFICE (JPN)   3 ch.c. Carroll House 132 – Moon Tosho (JPN) (Steel Heart 128)   **76**
[1998 –p: 8g 1999 7g 8.3m⁵ 10g 10m⁴ 10d 11.6d Oct 28] smallish, sturdy colt: fair
maiden: stays 1¼m: well held on good to soft going: has looked none too keen.
A. C. Stewart

EDMO HEIGHTS   3 ch.g. Keen 116 – Bodham 88 (Bustino 136) [1998 68: 6g⁶   **76 d**
6g⁵ 7.5m² 7.5m² 7.9g⁶ 7.5m* 8m 1999 9.9g 8.2m 8.5d 9m* 12.3d 9.9m* 12m 9.9g⁵
10m 10m 10g Oct 2] leggy, angular gelding: fair performer: won handicap at Redcar
in June and dead-heated in minor event at Beverley in July: well below form final 3
starts: stays 1¼m: acts on good to firm going, yet to race on extremes. *T. D. Easterby*

EDRAAK (IRE)   3 b.c. Shirley Heights 130 – Sahara Star 95 (Green Desert (USA)   **101**
127) [1998 94p: 8g³ 1999 12d⁴ 16.2m Jun 16] lengthy, useful-looking colt: has a
short, round action: useful performer: won maiden at Goodwood in June: better form
when 7½ lengths seventh to Endorsement in Queen's Vase at Royal Ascot: probably
stays 2m: sent to race in Dubai. *Saeed bin Suroor*

ED'S FOLLY (IRE)   6 b.g. Fayruz 116 – Tabriya 61 (Nishapour (FR) 125) [1998 – –: 8d 8m 10g 12m 11.9g 11.9g 10m⁵ 1999 a8g a7g⁵ a7g 7f⁶ a16g⁵ May 25] good-quartered gelding: poor mover: formerly modest maiden: no form since 1997: tried blinkered: has worn tongue strap. *L. A. Dace*

EDWARDIAN   4 ch.g. Sanglamore (USA) 126 – Woodwardia (USA) 93 (El Gran – Senor (USA) 136) [1998 98p: 10d² 10d⁵ 9.9d* 12m* 12d 1999 11.9d May 11] good-topped gelding: useful performer at 3 yrs: below form only run of 1999: stays 1½m: acts on good to soft and good to firm going: sold 3,000 gns in October, sent to Kuwait. *Mrs A. J. Perrett*

EFFANDEMM (IRE)   3 ch.g. Up And At 'em 109 – Bermuda Princess (Lord – Gayle (USA) 124) [1998 –: 5d 7.1m 1999 a6g a7g⁶ Feb 24] no form in maidens. *A. Bailey*

EFHARISTO   10 b.g. Dominion 123 – Excellent Alibi (USA) (Exceller (USA)   **44** 129) [1998 NR 1999 11.6g 14.1d⁶ Oct 27] angular gelding: formerly fairly useful: just poor form both starts since 1996: stays 1¼m: acts on good to firm and good to soft going: sometimes blinkered/visored before this year. *J. Cullinan*

EHTEFAAL (USA)   8 b.g. Alysheba (USA) – Bolt From The Blue (USA) (Blue   **50** Times (USA)) [1998 NR 1999 17.2s⁶ Sep 27] useful-looking gelding: fairly useful performer at 3 yrs: twice raced on Flat since (modest staying hurdler): stays 2m+: acts on firm ground, probably on soft: effective in visor, tried blinkered. *J. S. King*

EI EI   4 b.g. North Briton 67 – Branitska (Mummy's Pet 125) [1998 80: 7v* 8g 7g⁶ 8d 8f 7.5m³ 8s 8m 1999 8.5s 7m 7d 7m 7s a10g Dec 22] angular gelding: fairly useful performer for B. Hills at 3 yrs: little form in 1999. *G. L. Moore*

EIFFEL TIGER (IRE)   4 b. or br.g. Paris House 123 – Rosa Bengala (Balidar – 133) [1998 47: 8f 6g 7g 9m 8m⁴ 8d⁵ 8.2g a8f 1999 a8.5g a11g Mar 10] poor maiden at best: stays 1m: acts on good to firm and good to soft going (well beaten on all-weather): visored once at 3 yrs. *Bob Jones*

EIGHTEENTH MSF   2 b.f. (Apr 2) Presidium 124 – Peters Pet Girl (Norwick   **49** (USA) 125) [1999 6d 5m⁴ 6f⁵ 6f⁴ 5g 6m Aug 30] 2,300Y: leggy filly: half-sister to untrustworthy 7f winner Lancashire Legend and 1m winner A Million Watts (both by Belfort): dam unraced: poor form in sellers: stayed 6f: tried blinkered: dead. *N. Tinkler*

EIGHT (IRE)   3 ch.g. Thatching 131 – Up To You (Sallust 134) [1998 62: 6g   **75** 1999 7g⁶ 7.7m³ 8.2m³ 8g 8m Sep 8] workmanlike gelding: fair maiden: trained by M. Heaton-Ellis first 3 starts: ran poorly after: stays 1m: acts on good to firm going. *C. G. Cox*

EILEAN SHONA   3 b.f. Suave Dancer (USA) 136 – Moidart 90 (Electric 126)   **102 p** [1998 75p: 7m 9m* 10s⁶ 1999 12g² 12.3m⁴ 14d³ 14.1m* 16.1d* Oct 29] smallish, close-coupled filly: made into a useful handicapper, winning at Redcar in September and Newmarket (listed rated stakes by 2 lengths from Trellis Bay) in October: stays 2m well: acts on good to firm and good to soft going: capable of better still. *J. R. Fanshawe*

EIN TRESOR   5 b.g. Mon Tresor 113 – Play The Game 70 (Mummy's Game 120)   – [1998 56, a–: 9d⁴ 11s² 12s 16m 12m⁶ 1999 a12f Jan 14] 7,400Y: third foal: half-brother to 6-y-o Power Game and fairly useful 1997 2-y-o 5f winner Lets Be Fair (by Efisio): dam 2-y-o 5f winner: modest maiden handicapper in Ireland for J. Hayden: broke down only Flat outing in Britain: stayed 11f: acted on soft and good to firm going: blinkered once in 1997: dead. *B. J. Llewellyn*

EJLAAL (IRE)   2 br.f. (Feb 24) Caerleon (USA) 132 – Genovefa (USA) 107   **105 p** (Woodman (USA) 126) [1999 8s* Aug 17] first foal: dam, won 1½m Prix de Royaumont, closely related to smart French 1m/1¼m winner Grafin: won maiden at Clairefontaine in August by 7 lengths from subsequent listed race winner Zeiting: bred to be suited by at least 1¼m: sure to improve. *D. R. Loder, France*

EJTITHAAB (IRE)   2 ch.c. (Mar 26) Arazi (USA) 135 – Cunning 118 (Bustino   **60 p** 136) [1999 7d⁶ Oct 12] third foal: dam won Princess Royal Stakes and second in Prix Vermeille: weak in market, some promise when sixth of 15 to Ferzao in maiden at Leicester: will stay at least 1¼m: should do better. *P. T. Walwyn*

EKRAAR (USA)   2 b.c. (Feb 13) Red Ransom (USA) – Sacahuista (USA)   **114**
(Raja Baba (USA)) [1999 7m² 7f* 7m⁴ 8s³ Oct 23]

In the 'nineties, the Champagne Lanson Vintage Stakes at Goodwood
has had one of the best records among the two-year-old races for producing
Group 1-scoring horses from its winners, six in all, including the English
classic victors Dr Devious and Mister Baileys. Whether the 1999 winner,
Ekraar, can boost the statistics is open to some doubt, but he certainly proved
himself to be a smart two-year-old, and a good advertisement for his trainer,
Marcus Tregoning, who, in only his second season, was also responsible for
another of the leading two-year-olds in Fath.

Ekraar started second favourite for the Goodwood race, on the strength
of a promising debut at the Newmarket July meeting, where, although favourite
and carrying plenty of stable confidence, he was beaten two and a half lengths
by the highly-regarded Race Leader, looking very much as if he would strip
fitter for the race (four years earlier, incidentally, Alhaarth defeated Mark
of Esteem in the same maiden). The field of five in the Vintage Stakes was
the smallest for ten years, and Ekraar made all, running on with plenty of
enthusiasm to beat Sarafan by two lengths in what had become virtually a
two-horse race early in the straight, the favourite Kingsclere proving
disappointing. The contest may have taken more out of Ekraar than had first
appeared, for this was the only explanation Tregoning could come up with for
his colt's disappointing effort in the Champagne Stakes at Doncaster six weeks
later—Ekraar's fourth to Distant Music there was well below the level he
attained in the Goodwood race, form which had been upheld by Sarafan in the
Stardom Stakes that very day. The Racing Post Trophy six weeks later gave
Ekraar the opportunity to prove the form on his last visit to Doncaster all
wrong. The step up to a mile was expected to suit him, and he was also fitted
with blinkers for the first time (following laziness on the gallops at home).
Ekraar moved like the best horse for a long way, leading three furlongs out but

Hamdan Al Maktoum's "Ekraar"

was edged out well inside the final furlong by a couple of stouter stayers in Aristotle and Lermontov in a race run on very soft ground.

Ekraar (USA) (b.c. Feb 13, 1997)	Red Ransom (USA) (b 1987)	Roberto (b 1969)	Hail To Reason Bramalea
		Arabia (b 1977)	Damascus Christmas Wind
	Sacahuista (USA) (b 1984)	Raja Baba (b 1968)	Bold Ruler Missy Baba
		Nalees Flying Flag (b 1975)	Hoist The Flag Nalee

Ekraar, who cost 200,000 dollars as a foal, is by the Kentucky-based stallion Red Ransom, best known as the sire of Intikhab. However, with horses like Sri Pekan, and the latest Queen Mary winner Shining Hour, Red Ransom has also shown himself capable of producing smart two-year-olds. Ekraar's dam Sacahuista won the Grade 1 Oak Leaf Stakes at two. She was even better at three, being named champion three-year-old filly in the States after wins in the Grade 1 Breeders' Cup Distaff and Spinster Stakes, both over nine furlongs. Sacahuista has had a fair record at stud, producing three winners from five previous foals, her best runner before Ekraar being the Mr Prospector colt Hussonet, stakes placed in North America. Ekraar's family includes the Breeders' Cup Mile runner-up Geri and Stormin Fever, twice runner-up in the Vosburgh Stakes, who are both grandsons of his unraced grandam Nalees Flying Flag. There is also some stamina in the family with the Belmont Stakes second Johns Treasure and the Irish St Leger winner Meneval being half-brothers to Ekraar's dam and grandam respectively. The well-made Ekraar is a good walker, who acts on both firm and soft ground and stays a mile. He should train on and perhaps achieve more success in pattern company. *M. P. Tregoning*

ELA AGAPI MOU (USA) 6 b.g. Storm Bird (CAN) 134 – Vaguar (USA) **64** (Vaguely Noble 140) [1998 64, a–: 15.4v* 17.2g 1999 15.4v⁴ 18d May 19] rather leggy gelding: has a round action: modest handicapper: better effort in 1999 at Folkestone on reappearance: should stay 2m+: acts on any ground (no form on all-weather): blinkered both starts at 6 yrs: joined M. Coombe. *G. L. Moore*

ELAANDO 4 b.c. Darshaan 133 – Evocatrice 91 (Persepolis (FR) 127) [1998 – 10m⁴ 9s* 12d⁴ 11g⁶ 10.8s* 11.5s³ 1999 10.1m Jul 7] third foal: closely related/half-brother to French 1¼m winners by Slip Anchor and Seattle Dancer: dam French 2-y-o 7f winner: trained by J. Pease in France at 3 yrs, winning maiden at Dieppe and minor event at Segre: fit from hurdling (fair winner), tailed off in minor event at Epsom on British Flat debut: stays 10.8f: gained both Flat wins on soft ground, goes well on firm over hurdles: blinkered once. *Mrs Merrita Jones*

ELA ATHENA 3 gr.f. Ezzoud (IRE) 126 – Crodelle (IRE) (Formidable (USA) **119** 125) [1998 NR 1999 10m* 10m² 10.2m* 11.9g² Aug 18]
Ela Athena was unraced as a two-year-old but quickly made into a smart performer at three, and distinguished herself by finishing the closest of any filly all season to Ramruma when runner-up in the Yorkshire Oaks. Unfortunately, a rematch with the winner in the St Leger had to be shelved, Ela Athena having injured her right knee after her fine effort at York. She was still progressing at the time and, provided she makes a full recovery from an operation to remove a bone chip, she should make her presence felt in the top races for fillies and mares as a four-year-old.
Ela Athena began her career by winning a fillies maiden at Newbury in April and was quickly stepped up in class. She acquitted herself very well when second to Alabaq in the Pretty Polly Stakes at Newmarket in May, performing in a manner that suggested even better was to come, losing out to a more experienced rival. Off the course for twelve weeks afterwards, Ela Athena came back to win the Fawley Stud Golden Daffodil Stakes at Chepstow in July in good style by two and a half lengths from Keld, leading over three furlongs out and being comfortably on top at the finish, her performance again hinting

strongly that further progress was on the cards. Ela Athena still went into the Yorkshire Oaks as one of those with the weakest prospects on form, reflected by her starting price of 33/1, but she improved significantly once again, running Ramruma to one and a quarter lengths and finishing six places ahead of her much shorter-priced stable-mate Noushkey. Ela Athena had given the impression thus far that a mile and a quarter might well turn out to be her trip, but she thrived on the step up to a mile and a half, rallying and staying on strongly after dropping back to last place early in the straight.

Ela Athena (gr.f. 1996)	Ezzoud (IRE) (b 1989)	Last Tycoon (b 1983)	Try My Best
			Mill Princess
		Royal Sister II (b 1977)	Claude
			Ribasha
	Crodelle (IRE) (gr 1988)	Formidable (b 1975)	Forli
			Native Partner
		Pizziri (gr 1981)	Artaius
			Croda Alta

Ela Athena, who cost 29,000 guineas as a yearling, is by far the best performer produced by either her sire or dam. She is from the first crop of Ezzoud, who, after making an inauspicious start at stud, died in August 1998 following complications arising from a series of operations to cure laminitis. The sometimes wayward Ezzoud had his best season as a five-year-old, winning the Eclipse, the Juddmonte International (for the second year running) and coming a close fourth in the Prix de l'Arc de Triomphe. Ela Athena's dam Crodelle, by contrast, was successful only once, in a minor event over nine and a half furlongs at three in France. Her two other racecourse representatives so far (by Pursuit of Love and Indian Ridge) are of no great consequence. Ela Athena's grandam, Pizziri, won three times up to a mile and was listed placed in Italy, herself producing pattern-placed French performer Femme Grise. Ela Athena is her family's best performer since great grandam Croda Alta, champion three-year-old filly in Italy in 1978. A tall, lengthy, quite good-topped filly, Ela Athena stays a mile and a half and has raced only on good to firm and good going. *M. A. Jarvis*

ELAFLAAK (USA) 2 b.f. (May 15) Gulch (USA) – Catnip (USA) (Flying Paster (USA)) [1999 5m* 6m* 5.2g* 6d Sep 28] $150,000Y: rangy, attractive filly: second foal: dam, won 8.5f minor stakes in USA, half-sister to Belmont Stakes winner Editor's Note, an excellent American family: useful form: won maiden at Beverley and minor event and listed race at Newbury (by 2½ lengths from Kalindi, travelling comfortably and leading over 1f out) in July/August: second favourite, too free to post and in race, found nothing when last of 14 in Cheveley Park Stakes at Newmarket final start: effective at 5f/6f: carried tail awkwardly last 2 outings. *M. P. Tregoning* **104**

ELA-YIE-MOU (IRE) 6 ch.g. Kris 135 – Green Lucia 116 (Green Dancer (USA) 132) [1998 –: 11.9d a12g 1999 a16f Jan 14] tall gelding: one-time fairly useful 1¾m winner: lightly raced on Flat and no form since 1997. *L. A. Dace* **–**

ELBA MAGIC (IRE) 4 b.f. Faustus (USA) 118 – Dependable (Formidable (USA) 125) [1998 72, a65: a7g* a8g⁴ 8.3g² 10.1d³ 8.2d³ 10.1m* 9m⁵ 10.1f³ 10g* 9.9m 10g 8d² 9.7s a10g 1999 8g⁴ 8.5s 8g 10.2g³ 10d² 10m⁵ 8g³ 10.1f³ 10f³ 10d 10m⁵ 8.3m² 8.5g* a9.4f 8d Oct 11] robust filly: fair handicapper: placed 6 times before winning at Beverley in September: well below form final 2 starts: effective at 1m (given a test) to 1¼m: acts on fibresand, firm and good to soft going (probably not on soft): has hung/looked less than keen of late, and usually held up. *C. A. Dwyer* **67**

EL CONDOR PASA (USA) 4 b.c. Kingmambo (USA) 125 – Saddlers Gal (IRE) (Sadler's Wells (USA) 132) [1998 128: a9s* a8s* 7s* 8g* 9f² 12f* 1999 9.3d² 12g* 12m* 12v² Oct 3] **136**

Given the considerable success in Europe recently of such Japanese-trained runners as Seeking The Pearl, Taiki Shuttle and Agnes World, all Group 1 winners, it's a shade ironic that easily the best performance by a horse from that country should have come in defeat, when another Group 1 victor, El Condor Pasa, just lost out to Montjeu in the Prix de l'Arc de Triomphe. In most years, the four-year-old's battling display, and the rating he received on the strength of it, would have been sufficient to gain him the spoils, but he was unlucky to come up against one of the best winners of the race in the 'nineties. El Condor Pasa will not be trying to go one better in 2000, since he has been retired to stud at Shadai Farm in Hokkaido, alongside perennial champion Sunday Silence, Japan Cup winner Special Week and Arc winners Carnegie and Helissio, among others, after reportedly being syndicated for around 21,600,000 dollars.

Even before he arrived in Europe in mid-April, El Condor Pasa was better known than his Group 1-winning compatriots, since his success in the Japan Cup as a three-year-old had been well publicised. That win, gained decisively from a field containing Special Week and high-class raiders Chief Bearhart, Faithful Son and Caitano, was the sixth in seven starts for the colt and earned him a rating of 128 in *Racehorses of 1998*, only 2 lb behind the joint-top three-year-olds Desert Prince and High-Rise. The Japan Cup was also El Condor Pasa's first race at a distance beyond nine furlongs—his earlier victories had included a Grade 2 over seven furlongs and the NHK Mile Cup—and the fact that he combined stamina with pace gave his connections plenty of options once it was decided to send him to France for a full campaign rather than just a flying visit. Stabled with Tony Clout at Lamorlaye, though still officially in the care of his Japanese trainer Yoshitaka Ninomiya, El Condor Pasa occupied the box Taiki Shuttle had been in for his 1998 visit. Perhaps Clout will consider charging extra for occupancy of this one in future! The colt, only workmanlike in appearance and certainly no oil painting, made his European debut in the Group 1 Prix d'Ispahan at Longchamp towards the end of May, attended by sixty Japanese journalists. The race was broadcast live on Japanese television and the viewers would have seen El Condor Pasa run creditably, leading a furlong out until close home, beaten three quarters of a length by Croco Rouge. This was form not quite up to the level El Condor Pasa had shown in the Japan Cup, since Kabool and Handsome Ridge were close up, but it boded well for the rest of his campaign, which tentatively included the Prince of Wales's Stakes and Eclipse Stakes. El Condor Pasa missed those in favour of the Grand Prix de Saint-Cloud, in part because his connections believed at the time that he was better suited by a left-handed track.

The Grand Prix de Saint-Cloud has an impressive roll of honour and the latest running was no exception. There were no Maktoum/Godolphin hopes, a rare event indeed, but the nine other runners included Dream Well, Sagamix, Tiger Hill and Borgia, who between them had won a Prix du Jockey Club, Irish Derby, Prix de l'Arc de Triomphe, two Grosser Preis von Badens and a Deutsches Derby, with places gained in two Arcs and the Breeders' Cup Turf. Those achievements were in previous seasons, and arguably the form of three

Grand Prix de Saint-Cloud—a good quality event which goes largely to form with El Condor Pasa beating Tiger Hill and the blinkered Dream Well

of the quartet in the run-up to the Grand Prix had not been up to their best. Dream Well had been placed in the Prix Ganay (Sagamix fourth) and Coronation Cup (Borgia fifth), and Tiger Hill had won the Gerling-Preis before finishing second to Caitano in another German Group 2. The remainder included Prix Jean de Chaudenay winner Public Purse and British hope Greek Dance. El Condor Pasa travelled easily throughout the race, followed Tiger Hill through when that colt took it up from the pacemakers two furlongs out, swept past him and ran on strongly to win by two and a half lengths, with Dream Well the same distance away third. A mighty impressive performance, and one which suggested Montjeu might not have things all his own way come the Arc in October.

By mid-August El Condor Pasa was 4/1 second favourite in ante-post lists for the Arc, and the game of guessing where he would next run was in full flow. The Irish Champion Stakes and Grosser Preis von Baden were mooted and rejected, and he lined up instead in a three-horse field for a race regarded as a classic Arc trial, the Prix Foy Gray d'Albion Barriere over the same course and distance in September. Like Montjeu later in the afternoon, El Condor Pasa did not win by far, having a short neck to spare over Borgia after making all at a less-than-breakneck pace, but his trainer admitted he had left something to work on and the expectation was that El Condor Pasa would show to better advantage in the Arc. The enthusiasm of the Japanese for their challengers on Arc day resulted in two thousand racegoers from that country turning up, which equated to eight per cent of the crowd, with one hundred and fifty or so media representatives also in attendance. Agnes World and El Condor Pasa gave them plenty to cheer about.

In the week before the race El Condor Pasa was reported to have worked superbly, and he was a firm second choice in the market behind the coupled pairing of Montjeu and his pacemaker Genghis Khan. The heavy ground was unlike any El Condor Pasa had encountered—although he had won on soft in Japan, his best form was on firmer, including the Japan Cup on firm. Over a mile and a half in such conditions front-running tactics require courage, confidence in the stamina of one's own mount and considerable judgement of pace. El Condor Pasa's jockey Masayoshi Ebina was not inexperienced, having partnered over seven hundred and fifty winners, but the way he went about his business once the stalls opened left most observers bemused. Genghis Khan couldn't get to the front as El Condor Pasa soon took a three-length advantage and maintained a scorching gallop, having no trouble with the ground and racing with plenty of zest. If the other jockeys thought El Condor Pasa would come back to them, they were in for a major disappointment. Tiger Hill had a futile crack at him half a mile out, and with two furlongs left El Condor Pasa, extending his lead to some four lengths, had seen off just about all his rivals, who were under severe pressure and getting nowhere. The one he hadn't broken was Montjeu, who had got clear of the pack and was bearing down relentlessly on the leader. El Condor Pasa didn't stop at all, and increased his margin over the rest of the field in the closing stages, but for all his courage he simply had no answer to Montjeu, surrendering the lead in the final fifty yards and going down by half a length. It takes two to make a cracking race—Grundy and Bustino in the 1975 King George VI and Queen Elizabeth Stakes, for example —and the part El Condor Pasa, and his jockey, played in making the Arc the race of the season can easily be underestimated. They were magnificent, and it was astonishing that Ebina's front-running ride came in for some criticism after the race from the colt's connections, one of whom said: 'I can't say I'm happy —we did not plan to do that.' Some people are never satisfied, because to our eyes Ebina's ride was one of the best of the season in Europe. His tactics enabled his mount to come closer to beating an outstanding colt than anyone could have predicted.

The Japanese bloodstock industry has been making great strides thanks to stallions and broodmares imported in the last couple of decades, and with

Mr Takashi Watanabe's "El Condor Pasa"

El Condor Pasa (USA) (b.c. 1995)	Kingmambo (USA) (b 1990)	Mr Prospector (b 1970)	Raise A Native
			Gold Digger
		Miesque (b 1984)	Nureyev
			Pasadoble
	Saddlers Gal (IRE) (b 1989)	Sadler's Wells (b 1981)	Northern Dancer
			Fairy Bridge
		Glenveagh (b 1986)	Seattle Slew
			Lisadell

horses such as El Condor Pasa retiring to stud there the progress should be maintained. Interestingly, though, all four of the Japanese-raced Group 1 scorers in Europe in the last two seasons have been by stallions based in the United States and have been foaled in that country as well. El Condor Pasa, who was owner-bred, is by a horse who is making a name for himself a second time round. Kingmambo, a son of Mr Prospector and brilliant miler Miesque, lived up to his breeding by landing three important races as a three-year-old, the Poule d'Essai des Poulains, St James's Palace Stakes and Prix du Moulin. Kingmambo did not race beyond a mile but he is not getting just milers at stud. El Condor Pasa stays a mile and a half really well, and another of his sire's sons, Lemon Drop Kid, was one of the best of the classic crop in the States in the latest season, winning the Belmont Stakes over that trip. The dam Saddlers Gal has had four other foals—an unnamed colt by A P Indy in 1994, an unraced filly called Gal From Seattle by the same sire in 1996, a filly by Gulch in 1997 and a colt by Silver Hawk in 1998. She was the cheapest yearling by Sadler's Wells sold in 1990 and did nothing on the track to show that her IR 22,000 guineas price tag was a bargain, running nine times without making the frame. She was one of two non-winners foaled by her unraced dam, who came from a fine family, as the third dam Lisadell won the Coronation Stakes and was a half-sister out of Thong to top sprinter-miler Thatch, top sprinter Marinsky and high-class middle-distance stayer King Pellinore. Another half-sister, Special, about whom more can be found in the essay on Inkling, died in December 1999. She produced Nureyev and is grandam of Sadler's Wells, so Thong appears three times in El Condor Pasa's pedigree. How much, if at all, that, plus a double dose of Northern Dancer, contributed to the colt's merit is a matter for debate. Suffice it to say whatever the source of his ability, he was exceptional. *Y. Ninomiya, Japan*

EL CURIOSO (USA) 2 b.c. (May 12) El Gran Senor (USA) 136 – Curious (USA) (Rare Performer (USA)) [1999 6f² 7m*dis 7m⁵ 7.3g 7.7d* 8d⁴ Oct 15] $20,000Y: rangy, angular colt: half-brother to a minor winner in USA by Academy Award: dam minor winner in USA and half-sister to a stakes winner there: useful performer: first past post in maiden at Salisbury (disqualified after failing dope test) in July and nursery at Warwick in September: met good deal of trouble in running in 20-runner nursery at Newmarket on final start and did very well to finish fourth: will stay beyond 1m: acts on good to soft going: still open to improvement, and should win more races. *P. W. Harris* **96 p**

ELDERBERRY 2 gr.f. (Mar 7) Bin Ajwaad (IRE) 119 – Silver Berry (Lorenzaccio 130) [1999 6m Jul 12] 11,000Y: half-sister to numerous winners, notably smart sprinter Argentum (by Aragon): dam poor maiden: well beaten in maiden at Windsor. *B. J. Meehan* **–**

EL DOLOR (IRE) 2 br.g. (Feb 24) Elbio 125 – Payne's Grey (Godswalk (USA) 130) [1999 6m² 6d⁵ 6d 6s Oct 4] IR 7,000Y: sturdy, good-bodied gelding: easy mover: fourth reported foal: brother to 4-y-o Maas and half-brother to Italian 3-y-o 5.5f (at 2 yrs) to 1m winner Gold Windsor (by Woods of Windsor): dam unraced: modest form in maidens first 2 starts: well beaten after. *R. A. Fahey* **62**

ELEANOR RIGBY (IRE) 3 b.f. Turtle Island (IRE) 123 – Eleanor Antoinette (IRE) (Double Schwartz 128) [1998 –: 7s⁵ 1999 a7g a7g⁶ a8g Feb 22] little sign of ability, including in handicap. *M. Johnston* **–**

ELEGANT DANCE 5 ch.m. Statoblest 120 – Furry Dance (USA) (Nureyev (USA) 131) [1998 71: 8s 6.1m² 6m⁶ 6m* 7m 7m 6m 1999 a7g 6m³ 6g 6m 7f 7m a7g a7g Nov 24] rather leggy mare: fair handicapper: below form after second outing: stays 6f: acts on good to firm going: reared leaving stalls fifth start: inconsistent. *J. J. Sheehan* **69 a–**

ELEGANT ESCORT (USA) 2 b.c. (Mar 21) Take Me Out (USA) – Get With It (USA) (King Pellinore (USA) 127) [1999 a6f² a8g* Dec 17] $10,000Y: half-brother to numerous minor winners in USA: dam, won in USA, from family of champion US older mare Hidden Lake: confirmed debut promise when winning 14-runner maiden at Southwell in December by 3½ lengths from Sea Squirt, leading over 1f out: should stay beyond 1m: should improve further. *Mrs G. S. Rees* **80 p**

ELEGANT FAN (USA) 4 b. or br.g. Lear Fan (USA) 130 – Elegance (USA) (Providential 118) [1998 –: 8s 10.5m⁵ 8.2s⁶ 11.9s 1999 9f 10s 8m Jun 16] smallish gelding: little sign of ability: blinkered final start: has worn tongue strap: sold 750 gns in November. *W. Storey* **–**

ELEGANT FELLOW 2 b.c. (Jan 20) Green Desert (USA) 127 – Lailati (USA) 66 (Mr Prospector (USA)) [1999 6d³ 7s⁵ Oct 8] good-topped colt: third foal: half-brother to French 8.5f and 1½m winner Look And Learn (by Rock Hopper) and French 1m winner Copper Carnival (by Petit Loup): dam, lightly-raced maiden, half-sister to very smart 1m to 1½m performer Faithful Son: better effort in maidens when third of 14 to Lagoon at Pontefract, slowly away: still green next time: should stay 1m. *Sir Michael Stoute* **73**

ELEGANT LADY 3 ch.f. Selkirk (USA) 129 – Prompting 76 (Primo Dominie 121) [1998 78p: 6g⁶ 7g 6m⁴ 5g² 1999 6.1m* 5g³ 5m 5d 5s Oct 23] lengthy, good-topped filly: good walker/mover: fairly useful handicapper: idled when winning at Chester in May: below form final 3 starts, off track 4 months after first of them: stays easy 6f: acts on good to firm going: has been slowly away and looked headstrong. *J. H. M. Gosden* **89**

ELEGIA PRIMA 2 ch.f. (Apr 20) Mon Tresor 113 – Miss Milton (Young Chris- 66
topher 119) [1999 7m* 7m⁶ 8m 7m Sep 7] half-sister to winning sprinter Poets Cove
(by Bay Express), useful at 2 yrs: dam lightly raced on Flat: 20/1-winner of maiden at
Salisbury in June: soundly beaten after, including in blinkers. *Major D. N. Chappell*

EL EMPERADOR 2 b.c. (Feb 27) Emperor Jones (USA) 119 – Car Stop (USA) 69 p
(Stop The Music (USA)) [1999 6.1g⁶ Sep 25] 38,000Y: second foal: half-brother to
Italian 3-y-o Grigio Perla (by Highest Honor), 7f to 9f winner at 2 yrs: dam French 9f
to 10.5f winner: sixth of 12 to Shannon Dore in maiden at Nottingham, keeping on
from rear: likely to stay 1m: should do better at 3 yrs. *J. R. Fanshawe*

ELENII 3 b.f. Risk Me (FR) 127 – Sunday Sport's Pet 58 (Mummy's Pet 125) –
[1998 NR 1999 7s a6g⁵ 8.2s a11g Dec 7] 3,200Y: third reported foal: sister to 9f
winner Sporting Risk, later winning sprinter in Scandinavia: dam should have stayed
7f: no sign of ability: left Miss G. Kelleway 500 gns after third start. *T. T. Clement*

ELFLAND (IRE) 8 b.g. Fairy King (USA) – Ridge The Times (USA) 78 (Riva 82
Ridge (USA)) [1998 89: 7d⁴ 7s³ 8g 1999 8f⁶ 8f 7.3m Sep 17] lengthy gelding: carries
plenty of condition: has a high knee action: fairly useful handicapper: ran creditably
in 1999 only on reappearance: best form at 6f/7f: probably acts on any going: usually
held up: reportedly broke blood vessel on second start at 7 yrs. *Lady Herries*

EL FUERTE 4 b.g. Perpendicular 119 – Sleekit 78 (Blakeney 126) [1998 –: 10g –
10d 10.2s⁵ a14g 10.8m 1999 11.8m a16.2g Jul 23] poor form over hurdles: little show
on Flat. *W. Clay*

EL GRAN LOVE (USA) 3 b.f. El Gran Senor (USA) 136 – Where Is She (USA) 40
(Cure The Blues (USA)) [1998 NR 1999 8s 11.9g 12.3m 12m Jul 16] $125,000Y:
small filly: second foal: dam, won up to 1m in USA, daughter of Grade 2 9f winner
Fashionably Late: poor maiden: stays 1½m: ran creditably in blinkers final start: sold
1,650 gns in August. *T. D. Easterby*

EL GRAN PAPA (USA) 2 b.c. (Apr 20) El Gran Senor (USA) 136 – Banner 77 p
Hit (USA) (Oh Say (USA)) [1999 7g⁵ 7d³ Oct 12] $72,000F, $220,000Y: fifth foal:
half-brother to a winner in USA by Thirty Six Red: dam 6.5f/8.5f minor stakes
winner in USA at 2 yrs: similar form in maidens at Newmarket and Leicester
(third to Ferzao) over 2 months apart: should stay 1m: remains likely to do better.
J. H. M. Gosden

ELHABUB 4 b.g. Lion Cavern (USA) 117 – Million Heiress (Auction Ring (USA) 77
123) [1998 82: 7d⁵ 8g⁵ 6m 8g⁴ 10v² 9g² a10g² a10g* a12g6 1999 a10f a8.5g² 10m
10.2g² 10f⁶ Jun 21] well-made gelding: fairly useful handicapper at 3 yrs: fair form
in 1999, leaving Miss G. Kelleway after reappearance: stayed 1¼m (pulled too hard
at 1½m): acted on good to firm going, heavy and equitrack: dead. *D. Burchell*

ELHAYQ (IRE) 4 b.c. Nashwan (USA) 135 – Mahasin (USA) 90 (Danzig (USA)) 113
[1998 101: 10s² 12s* 13.9d² 12d 13.9f⁶ 14.6d⁴ 12s² 1999 11.9s² 10m* 10f* 10m⁶
10.3m³ Sep 10] tall, lengthy colt: has a round action: smart performer: better than
ever at 4 yrs, winning rated stakes at Newmarket and minor event at Newbury (by
neck from Pegnitz) in May: off course nearly 3 months, good third of 6 to Timahs in
well-contested minor event at Doncaster: effective at 1¼m to 1¾m: acts on firm and
soft going: flashed tail on reappearance, but seems genuine enough: sent to USA.
J. L. Dunlop

ELHIDA (IRE) 3 ch.f. Mujtahid (USA) 118 – Nouvelle Star (AUS) (Luskin Star 99
(AUS)) [1998 98+: 6f² 6g* 5m 1999 6g⁴ 6m⁵ 6g 5m³ 5d Sep 30] smallish, strong
filly: good mover: useful performer: good efforts in minor events third and fourth
starts: may prove best at 5f: raced only on good going or firmer until final outing
(stiffish task, well held): has worn crossed noseband. *M. P. Tregoning*

EL HIDALGO (IRE) 2 br.g. (Jan 16) Namaqualand (USA) – Dancing Sensation 67
(USA) 72 (Faliraki 125) [1999 5s* 6m 7.5g³ 6m* 9d⁴ 7.5m² 7.5m⁵ 6d⁴ 7.5d* 7.5d⁴
Dec 28] 20,000F, 8,500Y: first foal: dam 7f to 1½m winner: won minor events at
Livorno in June and (having left M. Quinlan after third start) Florence in September:
also successful in claimer at Livorno in December: stays 7.5f. *R. Pecoraro, Italy*

ELHILMEYA (IRE) 3 b.f. Unfuwain (USA) 131 – Awayed (USA) 108 (Sir Ivor 94
135) [1998 NR 1999 10.5g* 10s³ May 14] good-topped filly: fifth foal: closely
related to 6-y-o Raed and a winner at 6f to 8.5f in Sweden (both by Nashwan): dam

Irish 1m/9f winner from good family: overcame greenness to win 7-runner maiden at Haydock in May by 1¾ lengths from Zariliya: better form when 6¾ lengths third of 10 to Nasheed in listed race at Newbury: stayed 10.5f: stud. *M. P. Tregoning*

ELITE HOPE (USA) 7 ch.m. Moment of Hope (USA) – Chervil (USA) (Greenough (USA)) [1998 –, a74: a6g² a7g* a6g⁴ a7g⁶ a7g* a6g² a7g* 7.6m a7g² a7s⁴ a6g⁵ a6g⁴ 1999 a6g⁴ a7g a7g³ a7f* a7g* a7g² a7g³ a7g⁴ a7g³ a7g² a7g³ a8g⁴ a6g² a7g⁴ Dec 4] heavy-topped mare: fair performer: won handicap and claimer at Southwell in February: stays 7f, not 1m: acts on fibresand (below form only start on equitrack), lightly raced and no recent form on turf: blinkered (well beaten) once at 4 yrs: has won 7 times at Wolverhampton: usually races prominently. *N. Tinkler* **a76**

ELJARIHA 2 b.f. (Feb 28) Unfuwain (USA) 131 – Hiwaya 106 (Doyoun 124) [1999 7v² Oct 25] first foal: dam 6f to 1m winner (including at 2 yrs) from very good American family: 4 lengths second of 11 to Decision Maid in maiden at Lingfield, racing freely and never far away: should stay at least 1m: sure to improve. *M. P. Tregoning* **71 p**

EL KARIM (USA) 3 ch.c. Storm Cat (USA) – Gmaasha (IRE) (Kris 135) [1998 7p²: 6g 7g³ 1999 7m 5s Jun 12] fair maiden at best: reportedly had wind infirmity final outing: stays 7f: sold 2,700 gns, joined R. Ford. *J. L. Dunlop* **64**

ELKEYVOR 4 b.g. Elmaamul (USA) 125 – Petonica (IRE) 77 (Petoski 135) [1998 –: 11.9s 10.3g 1999 12d Jul 6] tall, lengthy sort: last in maidens. *S. Gollings* **–**

ELLE DANZIG (GER) 4 b.f. Roi Danzig (USA) – Elegie (GER) (Teotepec) [1998 115: 9v* 8d* 11d* 11s* 10s* 12s⁴ 10s* 1999 10v* 10m² 11s⁴ 10g* 9.3v⁴ 10s* Nov 7] smart performer: landed odds in Group 3 events at Gelsenkirchen in April and Baden-Baden in August before beating Handsome Ridge 1½ lengths in Premio Roma in November: below best when fourth in Prix de l'Opera at Longchamp penultimate start: stays 1½m, though seems ideally suited by 1¼m: acts on good to firm and heavy going: stays in training. *A. Schutz, Germany* **118**

ELLEN BE CHIC 3 gr.f. Touch of Grey 90 – Lingfield Lass (USA) 60 (Advocator) [1998 NR 1999 8m 7g 6g 7g Oct 19] third foal: sister to a poor maiden: dam 1¼m winner: no sign of ability in maidens/seller. *R. M. Flower* **–**

ELLENS ACADEMY (IRE) 4 b.c. Royal Academy (USA) 130 – Lady Ellen 67 (Horage 124) [1998 59: 10g⁴ 8g³ 7m 8m² 8d 1999 6.1s⁴ 5.9m² 6f* 6m 7f⁴ 6m* 6m 7.1m 6d Sep 18] big, useful-looking colt: developed into fairly useful handicapper at 4 yrs: won at Newbury in May and Newmarket in July: not best of runs when respectable eighth of 29 in Ayr Silver Cup final start: likely to prove best at 6f/7f: acts on firm going, probably on soft: tried blinkered at 3 yrs: may still do better. *E. J. Alston* **90 +**

ELLENS LAD (IRE) 5 b.g. Polish Patriot (USA) 128 – Lady Ellen 67 (Horage 124) [1998 92: 6g⁴ 5.1g² 6v 5f* 5g⁶ 5g⁶ 6f 6s 5g⁶ 5s³ 6f⁶ 5.7g² 5m³ 5m 5m 6g 5.2g²* 5m* 5m⁴ 5d* 5s² Oct 23] close-coupled, good-quartered gelding: useful handicapper: better than ever at 5 yrs, winning at Newbury in August, Haydock in September and at Newmarket (beat Light The Rocket a head) in October: stays 6f when conditions aren't testing: acts on firm and soft ground: blinkered (poorly drawn) once at 4 yrs: held up. *W. J. Musson* **103**

ELLE QUESTRO 3 b.f. Rainbow Quest (USA) 134 – Lady Be Mine (USA) 76 (Sir Ivor 135) [1998 –: 7m 8.2s 8s 1999 11.6m³ 14.1m 12f* 14.1m² 16.1s Sep 29] small filly: modest handicapper: won at Thirsk in July: will stay at least 2m: acts on firm going: visored for win and final start (ran poorly). *J. L. Dunlop* **61**

ELLERBECK 4 b.f. Priolo (USA) 127 – Cadisa 82 (Top Ville 129) [1998 63d: 10.5d 10m 16.2m⁴ 16.5g⁴ 16m 17.5s 1999 14.1g Sep 25] modest maiden handicapper at 3 yrs: no show only run of 1999. *J. M. Jefferson* **–**

ELLIS 3 br.f. Terimon 124 – Singing Reflection (Chief Singer 131) [1998 NR 1999 7g⁴ 9.1d 10.5s⁴ 10v Oct 11] 2,000Y: second foal: dam, 13f winner at 4 yrs in France, also successful here over hurdles, half-sister to smart 5f to 7f winner Blue Siren: easily best effort when fourth in maiden at Haydock penultimate start. *J. J. O'Neill* **71**

ELLIS ISLAND 3 ch.c. Most Welcome 131 – Dry Land 84 (Nonoalco (USA) 131) [1998 NR 1999 8.1d⁵ 10g⁵ 7.5m⁶ 12m Jul 27] 5,500Y, resold 9,500Y: leggy colt: half-brother to several winners, including 7f winner Trojan Desert (by Troy) and 1m winner River's Rising (by Mendez), both fairly useful: dam 5f winner: little form, including in handicap. *T. D. Easterby*

ELLOPASSOFF   7 b.m. Librate 91 – Elena Patino (Dubassoff (USA)) [1998 66: a9.4g 8g⁶ 9.9f⁶ 8m* 10.2s* 8s 9g 1999 8m* 8m⁵ 10m⁴ 10.2m* 8g⁵ 8f 8.2g 8g 10.2g Aug 30] workmanlike mare: fair handicapper: won at Nottingham (apprentices) in May and Chepstow in July: mostly below form after: stays 1¼m: acts on good to firm and soft ground: races prominently: has been bandaged. *J. M. Bradley*   **69**

ELLPEEDEE   2 b.g. (May 14) Wolfhound (USA) 126 – Kilvarnet 78 (Furry Glen 121) [1999 5m 5.1g³ 5g 5m 6g 6d Oct 18] 3,800Y: quite attractive gelding: half-brother to several winners, including 3-y-o McGillycuddy Reeks and 5-y-o Daniel Deronda: dam 5f (at 2 yrs) to 7.6f winner: third of 9 in maiden at Nottingham in August: poor form otherwise: should stay at least 6f. *N. Tinkler*   **67 ?**

ELLWAY DANCER (IRE)   3 b.f. Mujadil (USA) 119 – Moonlight Partner (IRE) 81 (Red Sunset 120) [1998 56p: 6s 6s⁶ 1999 6m Jun 24] signs of ability in maidens, slowly away only run of 1999: sold 15,000 gns in October. *I. A. Balding*   **–**

ELLWAY PRINCE   4 b.g. Prince Sabo 123 – Star Arrangement (Star Appeal 133) [1998 58, a80: 7v 7.1g⁶ 7g 8.5m 6f⁴ 6m² a6g⁴ a6g² a6g* a6g² a6g² a6g³ a7g² 1999 a6g⁵ a6g a6g⁶ a6g a6g² 6s 7m⁵ 6g 6m⁶ 6g 6m⁶ 7m 6g a7g a7g a6g a5g⁴ a5g Dec 18] close-coupled gelding: fair handicapper on all-weather, poor on turf: stays easy 7f: acts on good to firm going, good to soft and all-weather: blinkered/visored: often races prominently: inconsistent. *Mrs N. Macauley*   **47 a72**

ELLWAY STAR (IRE)   3 ch.f. Night Shift (USA) – Searching Star 63 (Rainbow Quest (USA) 134) [1998 90p: 5m* 1999 7g 5.1s³ 6g 7m³ 6m² 5m 6m² 6g⁵ 5m* 5d 5d Oct 14] strong, lengthy filly: useful performer: best effort when winning minor event at Leicester in September by 1½ lengths from Repertory: mostly creditable efforts on other starts, third in listed race at Bath on second one: best at 5f/6f: acts on soft and good to firm going. *B. Hanbury*   **104**

ELM DUST   3 ch.f. Elmaamul (USA) 125 – Galaxie Dust (USA) 86 (Blushing Groom (FR) 131) [1998 86: 7m⁵ 7d² 7d² 1999 7m 6m May 24] rather unfurnished filly: fairly useful at 2 yrs: soundly beaten on return: stays 7f: wore blanket for stalls on reappearance: races freely. *J. L. Dunlop*   **–**

ELMHURST BOY   3 b.c. Merdon Melody 98 – Young Whip (Bold Owl 101) [1998 77: 6m³ 6v 1999 6s² 6v³ 8m² 8g⁴ 8g⁵ 7f³ 6m² 7f³ 7m* 7m 7.1s a8g² a7g* Dec 29] good-topped colt: fairly useful performer: won maiden at Epsom in August and handicap at Lingfield in December: best efforts at 7f/1m: acts on firm going and equitrack: visored/blinkered of late: has found little and carried head high. *S. Dow*   **86 a92**

EL MOBASHERR (USA)   3 b.c. Machiavellian (USA) 123 – Sheroog (USA) 77 (Shareef Dancer (USA) 135) [1998 NR 1999 12g 10d⁵ 10m² 10f² 10m* 8g a10f⁶ Dec 16] tall, good-topped colt: fourth foal: brother to smart winner up to 1¾m Sharaf Kabeer and half-brother to 2 winners, notably 4-y-o Kabool: dam, 7f winner who probably stayed 1¼m, daughter of outstanding broodmare Fall Aspen: useful form: runner-up in maidens at Sandown and Newmarket before landing odds in similar 5-runner contest at Ascot in July: well below best in handicaps after, leaving M. Jarvis before final start: stays 1¼m. *D. J. Selvaratnam, UAE*   **96**

EL MONICA (IRE)   2 b.f. (May 15) Kahyasi 130 – Parnala (USA) 89 (Assert 134) [1999 5m³ 7g 7.5g² 6.8m⁴ 7.5d² 7.5m* 10v³ Nov 21] IR 7,000Y: second foal: dam Irish 11f winner who stayed 2m: modest form in Britain: left M. Quinlan and won minor event at Florence in October: bred to be suited by 1¼m+. *A. Renzoni, Italy*   **62**

ELMS SCHOOLGIRL   3 ch.f. Emarati (USA) 74 – Ascend (IRE) (Glint of Gold 128) [1998 67: 5g 6m³ a6g⁶ 1999 6m 8m⁶ 8g 10g* 10g 10f* 11.9g* 11.9d⁵ 11.9m³ Sep 1] unfurnished filly: fair performer: won minor event at Brighton in June and handicaps at same course in July and August: stays 1½m: acts on firm ground (well below form only outing on softer than good). *J. M. P. Eustace*   **79**

ELMS SCHOOLPREFECT   2 b.f. (Mar 22) Emarati (USA) 74 – Ascend (IRE) (Glint of Gold 128) [1999 7f 6g 8g 8s Sep 16] 4,000Y: second foal: sister to 3-y-o Elms Schoolgirl: dam unraced granddaughter of smart French miler Arosa: form only when seventh of 12 in maiden at Yarmouth, third start. *J. M. P. Eustace*   **42**

King George V Stakes (Handicap), Royal Ascot—Elmutabaki wins impressively; chasing him home are, from right to left, Tier Worker, Biennale and Mirjan

ELMUTABAKI   3 b.c. Unfuwain (USA) 131 – Bawaeth (USA) 72 (Blushing **112** Groom (FR) 131) [1998 71p: 7d⁵ 1999 12g⁴ 10.3m² 10.5m² 12m* 11.9s* 11.9m⁵ 14.6m Sep 11] sturdy colt: unimpressive mover: smart performer: won 19-runner King George V Stakes (Handicap) at Royal Ascot (beat Tier Worker by 3½ lengths) in June and listed race at Haydock (by 3 lengths from Flaming Quest) in July: well held in pattern races last 2 outings, kicked by rival at start of St Leger on final one: should stay beyond 1½m: acts on soft going and on good to firm: sweating penultimate start. *B. W. Hills*

EL NAFIS (USA)   3 b.f. Kingmambo (USA) 125 – Ghashtah (USA) (Nijinsky   **–** (CAN) 138) [1998 73+: 7m 8.1m* 7g 1999 7.1g 10m 8g Aug 12] rather leggy, attractive filly: fair form at 2 yrs: behind in handicaps in 1999: should stay beyond 1m: sent to USA. *P. T. Walwyn*

EL NAHRAWAN (USA)   3 br.c. Red Ransom (USA) – Woodja (USA) (Wood-   **87** man (USA) 126) [1998 87p: 7m⁴ 7m² 1999 8g³ 8.5g² 10f⁴ 7.1m* 8.5g Aug 30] quite attractive colt: fairly useful performer: won maiden at Chepstow in August: said to have lost action in handicap at Epsom final start: will prove best at short of 1¼m: raced only on good going or firmer: sent to UAE. *M. P. Tregoning*

EL PICADOR   3 b.g. Aragon 118 – Hawaiian Bloom (USA) 87 (Hawaii) [1998   **65 d** 61: 5.2m 5g 1999 7g⁵ 7f 7m 10f May 28] angular gelding: best effort in maidens on reappearance: well beaten in claimers/seller after: sold 500 gns in July. *B. J. Meehan*

EL RACHA   3 b.f. Midyan (USA) 124 – Lady Anfield (Anfield 117) [1998 NR   **–** 1999 6m 7.1m 8.5g Jun 30] 1,000Y: half-sister to a winner in Italy by Jalmood: dam Italian 5f winner: last all 3 starts. *T. J. Naughton*

ELSA DAWN   4 ch.f. Weldnaas (USA) 112 – Agnes Jane (Sweet Monday 122)   –
[1998 –: a8g 7.5m 6g 10s⁶ 1999 a8g Jun 4] lengthy, angular filly: no form. *N. Bycroft*

EL SALIDA (IRE)   3 b.g. Second Set (IRE) 127 – Tradescantia (GER) (Wind-   77
wurf (GER)) [1998 NR 1999 8g⁴ 8m³ 8s⁴ a7g⁴ Nov 19] IR 10,000Y: half-brother to 2
winners in Germany by Konigsstuhl: dam German 1m winner: fair maiden: will stay
beyond 1m: acts on soft going and on good to firm: successful over hurdles in
December. *J. G. FitzGerald*

ELSIE BAMFORD   3 b.f. Tragic Role (USA) – Sara Sprint (Formidable (USA)   55
125) [1998 51: 5g⁶ 5.9d 5g 5d 1999 7s⁴ a7g 8f 7g⁵ 8.3g³ 8m 7m⁵ 8.5m⁶ 8.3m⁶ 12s
a12g³ a10g a12g a12g⁶ Dec 21] leggy, close-coupled filly: modest maiden: left Jack
Berry after ninth start: stays 1½m: acts on good to firm going, soft and fibresand:
inconsistent. *M. Johnston*

ELTARS   2 ch.g. (Apr 18) Elmaamul (USA) 125 – Iradah (USA) 66 (Topsider   53
(USA)) [1999 5.7m Jul 15] first living foal: dam, 7f winner, from family of Coronation Stakes winner Magic of Life: slowly away when seventh in maiden at Bath: sold
5,000 gns in October. *P. T. Walwyn*

ELTAWAASUL (USA)   3 ch.c. Nureyev (USA) 131 – Grand Falls (USA) (Ogy-   108
gian (USA)) [1998 99: 6m* 6g* 7g³ 7g³ 1999 8d⁴ 8d³ 8d* 10d⁴ Jun 5] lengthy colt:
has a quick action: useful performer: best effort when winning 3-runner minor event
at Thirsk in May by short head from Date: stays 1m, possibly not 1¼m: acts on good
to firm and good to soft going: sent to USA. *J. L. Dunlop*

ELTON LEDGER (IRE)   10 b.g. Cyrano de Bergerac 120 – Princess of Nashua   – §
(Crowned Prince (USA) 128) [1998 55, a74: a8s⁴ a7g a7g⁴ a6g⁴ a6g² a6g⁶ a6g³ a6g*   a66 §
a6g⁴ a6g² a6g² 6.1s² 5.1v² 5.1s 6g³ a7g² 6m a7g⁶ 6d a6g* 6.1g a7g⁴ a7g⁴ a5g a6g²
5.1d 6m 7g³ 6g² 7d³ 6.1s a8g⁶ a7g² a5g* a6g* a6g* a5g* 1999 a6g⁴ a7g³ a6g* a6f⁴
a6g a7g⁶ Nov 12] good-topped gelding: fair on all-weather, modest on turf: winner
15 times at Southwell, including seller in January: best at 5f to 7f: acts on any turf
going, and on fibresand: effective blinkered/visored or not: has increasingly given
trouble to post/at stalls, withdrawn on 2 of last 3 intended starts. *Mrs N. Macauley*

ELVINGTON BOY   2 ch.c. (Apr 5) Emarati (USA) 74 – Catherines Well 99   77
(Junius (USA) 124) [1999 5g⁴ 5m² 5m² 5m* 6g 5s Nov 5] 2,400Y: half-brother
to 5-y-o William's Well and a winner abroad at up to 1m by Sadler's Wells: dam
sprinter: fair performer: won maiden at Ripon in August: soundly beaten in nurseries
final 2 starts: will prove best at 5f/6f: acts on good to firm going: tongue tied third
outing. *M. W. Easterby*

EL ZITO (IRE)   2 b.g. (Apr 13) Mukaddamah (USA) 125 – Samite (FR) (Tenny-   59 +
son (FR) 124) [1999 8.5s² a8g³ Nov 22] IR 10,000Y: half-brother to several winners
abroad, including French 1½m winner Concur (by Rousillon): dam French 1½m
winner at 4 yrs: placed in newcomers race at Milan and maiden at Southwell.
B. J. Meehan

EMALI   2 b.g. (Mar 14) Emarati (USA) 74 – Princess Poquito (Hard Fought 125)   57
[1999 7.5g 7s⁶ Oct 8] 13,000F: quite good-topped gelding: fifth foal: half-brother to
6-y-o Eurobox Boy and 6f to 1m winner Phoenix Princess (by Nomination): dam
unraced half-sister to smart 1¼m to 1¾m filly Senorita Poquito: better effort in
maidens when sixth of 18 to Cape Town at Lingfield, racing prominently: should stay
1m. *C. E. Brittain*

EMARINA   3 b.f. Emarati (USA) 74 – Cushina 61 (Sparkler 130) [1998 50: 5.7s   –
a5g a6s⁴ 1999 a7g⁴ a5g⁶ 6.1m⁶ 5g 6.1m a8.5g⁵ a7g Oct 16] tall, leggy filly: poor maiden: a48
stays 8.5f: form only on fibresand: tongue tied final 4 starts. *J. L. Spearing*

EMBATTLE   3 ch.g. Rock City 120 – Sleepline Princess 86 (Royal Palace 131)   61
[1998 57p: 7.9g 1999 7s 7s⁶ 8.3m³ 8g 8.3g⁵ 9.1g⁶ Jun 18] small gelding: modest
maiden handicapper: stays 1m: acts on good to firm going, possibly not on soft:
visored final start. *M. R. Channon*

EMBEZL   2 b.f. (Apr 6) Belmez (USA) 131 – Kiya (USA) 85 (Dominion 123)   72
[1999 5s 5m² 6m² 5.1m² 7v 6d Oct 28] fifth foal: half-sister to a winner in Sweden by
Sharrood and a winner in USA by Night Shift: dam, best at 1m, half-sister to smart
1993 2-y-o Lemon Souffle: fair maiden: runner-up 3 times: should stay 7f (raced
freely when tried): acts on good to firm going, below form on softer than good.
R. Hannon

EMBRACED   2 b.f. (Apr 14) Pursuit of Love 124 – Tromond 94 (Lomond (USA) **77 P**
128) [1999 8.2s* Oct 5] second foal: half-sister to 3-y-o Nowhere To Exit: dam, 9f
winner who stayed 1½m, out of half-sister to Yorkshire Oaks winner and St Leger
second Hellenic: short-priced favourite, created most favourable impression when
winning 14-runner maiden at Nottingham by 1¼ lengths from Skimra, held up on
outside, quickening to challenge 2f out and asked to do no more than necessary to
assert: should stay at least 1¼m: will improve considerably and looks a useful filly in
the making at least. *J. R. Fanshawe*

EMBRYONIC (IRE)   7 b.g. Prince Rupert (FR) 121 – Belle Viking (FR) (River- **70**
man (USA) 131) [1998 80: 12g 16g 16g⁵ 1999 16m⁶ 12g Jun 14] leggy gelding: fair
handicapper, lightly raced of late: respectable sixth on reappearance: best at 1¾m+:
acts on firm and good to soft ground. *Martin Todhunter*

EMERALD HEIGHTS   4 b.g. Shirley Heights 130 – Lady In Green (Shareef **–**
Dancer (USA) 135) [1998 98: 8.2s⁴ 12d³ 12m* 10.5g* 12s² 10.4f 13.4d 11.9g 1999
10g 16.2d Jun 3] tall, leggy gelding: useful handicapper: lost his form at 4 yrs: stays
1½m: acts on soft and good to firm going: sold 8,000 gns in October. *J. R. Fanshawe*

EMERALD HUNTER (USA)   4 b. or br.g. Quest For Fame 127 – In Jubilation **53**
(USA) (Isgala) [1998 68: 10m⁵ 10m⁵ 1999 10g 12v 12m a14.8g* a16g 14g Jun 14]
tall gelding: won seller at Wolverhampton in May: tailed off both starts after:
blinkered final start: joined P. Ritchens for 725 gns. *P. S. McEntee*

EMERALD IMP (IRE)   2 ch.f. (Mar 26) Mac's Imp (USA) 116 – Lady Montekin **52**
(Montekin 125) [1999 6s 7v⁴ Oct 11] IR 15,000Y: fourth foal: sister to fairly useful
1998 2-y-o 5f winner Open Secret and half-sister to winners abroad by Contract Law
and Classic Secret: dam third at 7f in Ireland: 33/1, better effort in maidens when
fourth of 6 to Marvel at Ayr, going in snatches: will probably stay 1m. *M. S. Saunders*

EMERALD PEACE (IRE)   2 b.f. (May 11) Green Desert (USA) 127 – Puck's **96**
Castle 92 (Shirley Heights 130) [1999 5.1g⁵ 5.2g² 5f* 5g* 5m² Sep 11] 81,000F, IR
70,000Y: first foal: dam, 1m winner who ran only at 2 yrs (would have been suited by
middle distances), half-sister to Cheveley Park winner Embassy out of Cheveley
Park winner Pass The Peace: useful form: won maiden and minor event at Lingfield
in August: best effort when head second of 14 to Mrs P in Flying Childers Stakes at
Doncaster final start: raced only at 5f on good going or firmer: races up with pace:
may do better still. *M. A. Jarvis*

EMERGING MARKET   7 b.g. Emarati (USA) 74 – Flitteriss Park 62§ (Beldale **99**
Flutter (USA) 130) [1998 100: 6g 7m 6m² 5.6g 7g 1999 7g 6m⁶ 6m 6m⁴ 6m³ 6m⁶
6.1g⁶ Sep 25] smallish, lengthy gelding: has a round action: useful handicapper:
mostly respectable efforts in 1999: effective at 6f/7f: acts on firm going, below form
only run on softer than good: best held up, and suited by strongly-run race.
J. L. Dunlop

EMILY'S LUCK CHARM (USA)   3 b. or br.c. Lear Fan (USA) 130 – Emily's **106**
Charm (CAN) (Dom Alaric (FR) 126) [1998 101+: 6f² 6d⁶ 6m* 6f 7.6g* 1999 7.1g³
7.3d⁶ 8s² 7d⁶ Oct 7] quite attractive colt: useful performer: good efforts in rated
stakes at Haydock (2 lengths third to Late Night Out in listed event) in May and York
(sixth of 8 to Omaha City) final start: should stay 1m (hung badly right when tried):
acts on good to firm and good to soft going: tongue tied: sent to UAE. *Sir Michael
Stoute*

EMINENCE GRISE (IRE)   4 b.g. Sadler's Wells (USA) 132 – Impatiente **97**
(USA) (Vaguely Noble 140) [1998 74: 12d⁵ 12m³ 12m 12f² 1999 13.9s³ 16f* 20m
22.2m⁴ 16.1m² 14f⁴ 13.9g⁴ 14.1m⁶ 14.6s⁴ Nov 5] deep-girthed, attractive gelding:
useful performer: easily won handicap at Kempton in May: generally remained in
good heart, including when fourth in Queen Alexandra Stakes at Royal Ascot and
Ebor Handicap at York: effective at 1¾m to 2¾m: acts on firm and soft ground:
effective blinkered or not: gelded after final start. *H. R. A. Cecil*

EMINENT BLAZE   3 b.g. Presidium 124 – Fair Madame 88 (Monseigneur **–**
(USA) 127) [1998 –: 6f 6g 5m 1999 a7g a8g 8d May 16] close-coupled gelding: no
sign of ability, including in sellers. *D. Nicholls*

EMLEY   3 b.f. Safawan 118 – Bit of A State 68 (Free State 125) [1998 NR 1999 7f⁵ **61 p**
7f⁶ 5d³ Aug 14] unfurnished filly: half-sister to fairly useful 1991 2-y-o 6f winner

Greetland Folly (by Crofthall): dam ideally suited by 1m: modest form: easily best effort in maidens when 3 lengths third to Bahamian Pirate at Ripon, staying on without being given a hard time: should improve again. *D. Nicholls*

EMMA AMOUR   2 b. or br.f. (Feb 26) Emarati (USA) 74 – Ella Mon Amour 65 **67** (Ela-Mana-Mou 132) [1999 6m² 6s a6g⁵ Nov 17] 3,000F, 2,600Y: heavy-topped filly: half-sister to 6-y-o Khabar and 3 winners, including 3-y-o Pulau Tioman (by Robellino) and 1½m winner Myosotis (by Don't Forget Me): dam, maiden, stayed 9f: easily best effort (fair form) when second in maiden at Lingfield in August: left J. Fanshawe 5,500 gns after. *M. W. Easterby*

EMMACAN (IRE)   5 b.m. Mazaad 106 – Minerstown (IRE) (Miner's Lamp 114) **–** [1998 NR 1999 11.5m⁶ Jul 20] fourth foal: sister to a fair middle-distance maiden: dam unraced: lightly raced in bumpers/novice hurdles: tailed off in Yarmouth maiden on Flat debut. *G. A. Hubbard*

EMMAJOUN   4 b.f. Emarati (USA) 74 – Parijoun (Manado 130) [1998 67: 5m⁵ **60 d** 5m 5m⁴ 6d² 6.1g³ 5.7m 1999 a5g* a5g 6d 5.3f⁴ 6g² 7.1g 5.3g 5m a6g³ a6g⁶ a7g² a6g⁵ Dec 17] strong filly: modest nowadays: won maiden at Lingfield in March: barely stays 7f: acts on good to firm, good to soft going and all-weather. *W. G. M. Turner*

EMMA-LYNE   3 b.f. Emarati (USA) 74 – Moreton's Martha (Derrylin 115) [1998 **59 d** 65: 6g² 7m² 6m³ 1999 8.2d 6.1m⁶ 6m⁶ 7g⁶ 9s⁶ 7g⁵ 7g Oct 15] angular filly: modest performer: deteriorated in 1999: stays 7f: acts on good to firm going: visored fifth/sixth starts: has hung left/looked none too keen: joined D. Morris. *A. P. Jarvis*

EMMA PEEL   3 b.f. Emarati (USA) 74 – Trigamy 112 (Tribal Chief 125) [1998 **113** 87: 6.1s* 6d² 1999 6g² 6g⁴ 5g² 6g* 6m⁴ 5m² 5d³ 5g* 5g* 5m² 5.2d⁵ Sep 19] small, sturdy filly: smart filly: had excellent season, winning listed race at Baden-Baden (awarded race) in May and competitive handicaps at York and Epsom (beat Angie Baby 1¾ lengths) in August: creditable short-head second to Flanders back in listed company at Doncaster penultimate start: effective at 5f/6f: acts on soft going and on good to firm: usually waited with: genuine and consistent. *B. J. Meehan*

EMMAS HOPE   2 b.f. (Apr 2) Emarati (USA) 74 – Ray of Hope 53 (Rainbow **33** Quest (USA) 134) [1999 6g 5m⁴ 5g 5g 5m a5g² 6g⁵ Dec 18] first foal: dam lightly-raced maiden: poor maiden: left B. Baugh after seventh outing: tried visored/blinkered. *P. D. Evans*

EMMINNI   2 b.g. (Apr 25) Emarati (USA) 74 – Sheesha (USA) (Shadeed (USA) **–** 135) [1999 6.1g 7m 6.1m Jul 3] third reported foal: dam once-raced close relative of smart stayer Samraan: well held, including in seller. *S. G. Knight*

EMPEROR NAHEEM (IRE)   4 b.g. Imperial Frontier (USA) 112 – Desert **89** Gale (Taufan (USA) 119) [1998 89: 6s⁴ 5.1g⁴ 6g 5m 5.1m² 5g 5d³ 5g⁵ 5d 7m⁶ 5m* **a84** 6g³ 5m* 5.2g⁶ 5f³ 5m* 5d⁴ 1999 5.1m² 5m² 5m 5d 5.2g 5m⁵ 5m⁴ 5m 5d 5d⁶ 5s a6g² a6g³ a6g Dec 22] fairly useful handicapper: barely stays 6f: acts on firm going, soft and equitrack: sometimes blinkered: best held up: finds little. *B. J. Meehan*

EMPEROR'S GOLD   4 gr.g. Petong 126 – Tarnside Rosal 68 (Mummy's Game **42** 120) [1998 –, a66d: a8g* a10g³ a10g² a8g³ a8.5g a8.5g a9.4g a8.5g 9g 1999 a6g a11g Dec 13] poor performer: stays 1¼m: acts on all-weather, probably on good to firm going: visored once at 2 yrs. *M. G. Quinlan*

EMPIRE GOLD (USA)   4 ch.g. Strike The Gold (USA) – Careless Halo (USA) **–** (Sunny's Halo (CAN)) [1998 69: 7d 6m⁵ 8s 8g 10.3g 8m⁶ 8m* 1999 8d 10d Oct 18] useful-looking gelding: has a quick action: fair handicapper: well held both starts (6 months apart) in 1999: should stay beyond 1m: acts on good to firm ground: blinkered final start. *Andrew Turnell*

EMPIRE PARK   4 b.g. Tragic Role (USA) – Millaine 69 (Formidable (USA) 125) **72** [1998 NR 1999 9.9m 10d 13.9s 12f⁶ 8g 9.9m³ 10.5d* Aug 6] leggy, workmanlike gelding: fair performer: won handicap at Haydock in August: probably stays 1¾m: acts on good to firm going, probably on soft: blinkered (well below form, too free on first occasion) twice: joined C. Egerton. *T. D. Easterby*

EMPIRE STATE (IRE)   4 b.g. High Estate 127 – Palm Dove (USA) (Storm Bird **53** (CAN) 134) [1998 74: 8s³ 8g 10g⁴ 7d 5.9d* 6d⁴ 6g* 5.9m⁵ 6g 7g 6v 7d 1999 6m 5.9m 7m 6.9m 5.9g 6g 8f 8m⁴ 10m² 11.5g² 11.7s Oct 26] strong, workmanlike gelding: modest handicapper: left P. Felgate after sixth start: stays 11.5f (at least when conditions aren't testing): acts on soft and good to firm going: tried visored/blinkered: won over hurdles in December. *R. A. Fahey*

EMPRESS OF LIGHT 2 b.f. (May 4) Emperor Jones (USA) 119 – Lovely Noor (USA) (Fappiano (USA)) [1999 7g 8.1g 7d Sep 28] 56,000Y: tall, leggy filly: seventh foal: half-sister to 3 winners, notably smart 1m to 1½m winner Medaille Militaire (by Highest Honor) and useful 7f (at 2 yrs) to 13f winner Wahiba Sands (by Pharly), both winning hurdlers: dam, won around 1m in USA, out of half-sister to Light Cavalry and Fairy Footsteps: showed a little ability in maidens and in valuable sales event at Newmarket. *M. P. Tregoning* — 47

EMWILLGEO (IRE) 3 b.f. Petardia 113 – Lhotse (IRE) 67 (Shernazar 131) [1998 –: 6g 5d⁵ 5g 1999 a7g Jan 9] no sign of ability. *P. C. Haslam* — –

ENAAQ (USA) 2 b.f. (Jan 13) Bahri (USA) 125 – Elhasna (USA) 88 (Danzig (USA)) [1999 5m² 5.7m² 5.1m³ 5.1g* 5.2m Sep 17] well-made filly: third foal: dam, 6f winner, sister to Dayjur and closely related to US Grade 1 9f and 1¼m winner Maplejinsky: fair performer: best effort when making all in nursery at Chepstow in August: last of 11 in similar event at Newbury next time: raced only around 5f on good/good to firm going: visored last 2 outings. *P. T. Walwyn* — 79

ENBORNE 4 b.c. Slip Anchor 136 – Pris (Priamos (GER) 123) [1998 NR 1999 12.4g⁴ 12m⁵ 10.1m⁵ 12m 14m³ 12d⁶ 11.9d⁵ 15s* 14d³ Jul 2] 2,600 3-y-o: tall, useful-looking colt: closely related to smart 1¼m performer Perpendicular (by Shirley Heights) and half-brother to 2 winners, including Lockinge winner Prismatic (by Manado): dam unraced half-sister to Kris, Diesis and Presidium: bumper winner in January: fair handicapper: won at Ayr in June: stayed 15f: went well on soft going: had started slowly/edged left/flashed tail: forced pace final 2 starts: reportedly had operation on small intestine early in July: dead. *D. W. Barker* — 74

ENCHANTED ISLE 3 b.f. Mujtahid (USA) 118 – Belle Ile (USA) 67 (Diesis 133) [1998 47: 5d⁴ 6g 6g⁵ 6.9m 7g 8g 1999 a7g Apr 1] small filly: poor maiden: visored once at 2 yrs: sold 1,000 gns in December. *C. A. Dwyer* — –

ENCOUNTER 3 br.g. Primo Dominie 121 – Dancing Spirit (IRE) 72 (Ahonoora 122) [1998 68d: 5d 7.1d³ 7.5m 6g 7s a6g⁶ a8g 1999 8.3v⁵ 8.3v² 7.1m⁶ a7g 7m 6m 5.9m 6.9m³ 7g 6.9m⁴ 7m* 6m* 7.1m² 6m⁶ 7m 8.3s 6s 6v 7g a7g Nov 30] unfurnished gelding: moderate performer: won seller at Ayr and handicap at Hamilton on successive days in August: mostly below form after: effective at 6f/7f: acts on good to firm going, probably on heavy (poor form at best on all-weather): pulls hard. *J. Hetherton* — 63 a–

ENDLESS JOURNEY (IRE) 2 b.f. (Apr 25) Blues Traveller (IRE) 119 – Spinelle 88§ (Great Nephew 126) [1999 6g⁶ 7m* 7m⁵ 7f⁵ 7.1m 8m Sep 7] 4,000 2-y-o: rather angular filly: half-sister to 4-y-o Thatoldblackmagic, fairly useful 1996 2-y-o 5f winner Snap Crackle Pop (by Statoblest) and untrustworthy 7f winner Sweet Jaffa (by Never So Bold): dam 1½m winner: poor maiden: won seller at Redcar in June: well beaten last 3 starts: will stay 1m: raced only on good going or firmer: sold 1,100 gns, sent to Holland. *N. P. Littmoden* — 47

END OF STORY (IRE) 3 b.c. Doubletour (USA) – Baliana (CAN) (Riverman (USA) 131) [1998 71p: 7d 1999 7g⁴ 8.3d 8.1m⁶ 7.1m⁵ 7m 7d a10g Nov 26] leggy, lengthy colt: has pronounced knee action: fair maiden: well beaten last 3 starts, leaving R. Hannon 900 gns before final one: stays 1m: yet to race on extremes of going: has been bandaged: has looked difficult ride. *P. Butler* — 67 d

ENDORSEMENT 3 b.f. Warning 136 – Overdrive 99 (Shirley Heights 130) [1998 NR 1999 10s³ 12d* 16.2m* 13.5g⁶ Aug 1] tall, leggy, quite attractive filly: fourth reported foal: half-sister to 1992 2-y-o 1m winner Dakar Rally (by Green Desert) and useful 6f winner (including at 2 yrs) Zugudi (by Night Shift): dam stayer from good staying family: useful form: easily landed odds in maiden at Thirsk in May and followed up in Queen's Vase at Royal Ascot following month by ½ length from Time Zone: beaten around 8 lengths in Prix de Pomone won by Bimbola at Deauville (reportedly found to have mucus in larynx) final start: better at 2m than shorter and will stay further: acts on firm and good to soft ground. *H. R. A. Cecil* — 107

ENDYMION (IRE) 2 ch.f. (Apr 21) Paris House 123 – Vaguely Jade (Corvaro (USA) 124) [1999 5m 5.1g⁵ 5m⁴ 5m³ 6m 6g 5.2m³ 5s Oct 2] IR 4,800Y: sparely- — 73 +

made filly: half-sister to several winners, including fairly useful performers up to 1¼m Lord Oberon (by Fairy King) and Shining Jewel (by Exhibitioner): dam unraced: fair maiden: still in front when saddle slipped and unseated rider over 1f out in nursery at Kempton on fifth start: very good third in similar event at Newbury penultimate outing: should stay 6f: acts on good to firm ground, well beaten on soft. *Mrs P. N. Dutfield*

ENEMY ACTION (USA)   3 b.f. Forty Niner (USA) – Sun And Shade 93 (Ajdal   **99** (USA) 130) [1998 105+: 6g* 6f* 6f⁴ 7d 1999 7g⁴ 6g³ a7f 7.5f² 8.5f³ Dec 19] well-made filly: useful performer: respectable efforts when in frame at 3 yrs in Nell Gwyn Stakes at Newmarket (to Valentine Waltz), minor event at Kempton (subsequently left H. Cecil) and allowance race then minor stakes, both at Calder: stays 8.5f: acts on firm ground. *C. Clement, USA*

ENFILADE   3 b.g. Deploy 131 – Bargouzine 67 (Hotfoot 126) [1998 64: 6m 7s³   **82** 7m⁵ 7g⁵ 8m 1999 7s⁴ 9.9g³ 12.3m* 11.4m³ 14d* 12.3m⁴ 14f⁴ 14.1m⁴ Aug 23] sturdy gelding: fairly useful handicapper: won at Chester in May and Haydock in July: probably finds 1½m a bare minimum, and will stay 2m: acts on soft and good to firm going: blinkered twice (ran creditably) at 2 yrs. *B. Hanbury*

ENGLAND'S ROSE (IRE)   3 b.f. Alzao (USA) 117 – Gold Tear (USA) (Tejano   **73** (USA)) [1998 NR 1999 10g² 9.9g May 25] IR 120,000Y: second foal: half-sister to a winner in Japan by Caerleon: dam, won twice around 11f in France, closely related to French winners up to around 1¼m Gabina and Galetto, both at least smart: second in maiden at Lingfield on debut: odds on, ran no sort of race when last in similar event at Beverley: sent to A. Hassinger in USA. *H. R. A. Cecil*

ENGLISH LADY (IRE)   4 b.f. Fayruz 116 – Paradise Regained 41 (North Stoke   **–** 130) [1998 54d: 6d⁵ 5m⁵ 6g⁵ 5m 5m 6s a5g a6g⁶ 1999 a6g a8g 6s Apr 21] modest sprint maiden: well beaten since third 3-y-o start: blinkered on reappearance: has worn tongue strap. *M. J. Haynes*

EN GRISAILLE   3 gr.f. Mystiko (USA) 124 – Hickleton Lady (IRE) 64 (Kala   **53** Shikari 125) [1998 53: 7g a7g⁴ 6f* 7m⁴ 7.1m 8g 1999 9m 8.2m⁶ 8m⁵ 10.1g* 9.9s Sep 21] lengthy filly: modest performer: won claimer at Yarmouth in August: stays 1¼m: acts on firm going, well beaten on fibresand. *John Berry*

ENLIGHTEN   3 br.g. Zafonic (USA) 130 – Seek The Pearl 91 (Rainbow Quest   **–** (USA) 134) [1998 NR 1999 10d 10f Oct 20] second foal: half-brother to 1997 2-y-o 7f winner Opposition Leader (by Be My Chief): dam 1¼m winner: behind in maidens at Sandown then Nottingham, never on terms and not knocked about on latter course. *J. R. Fanshawe*

ENNOBLE   3 b.g. Highest Honor (FR) 124 – Villella (Sadler's Wells (USA) 132)   **64** [1998 63: 7g 7.3g 7.1m 1999 12.5m² 12g 11.8m a9.4g 12.3g Aug 13] neat gelding: modest handicapper: below form after finishing good second at Warwick (drifted markedly left): stays 1½m: sold 3,000 gns in October. *H. Morrison*

Queen's Vase, Royal Ascot—Endorsement holds the rallying Time Zone (left) to give trainer Henry Cecil his eighth success in the race; Compton Ace is clear of the others

ENRIQUE 3 b.c. Barathea (IRE) 127 – Gwydion (USA) 118 (Raise A Cup **121**
(USA)) [1998 116p: 7g* 7g* 7g⁴ 1999 7m* 8m² 8g² 7m² 8f⁵ Jul 28]

For almost three months, it seemed that the worst thing Henry Cecil and
Kieren Fallon would have to reflect on in the latest season was Enrique's
second place in the Two Thousand Guineas. The trainer and his stable jockey
registered their third, fourth and fifth classic successes in just two seasons
together with Wince in the One Thousand, Ramruma in the Oaks and Oath
in the Derby, but Enrique had narrowly failed to overhaul Island Sands.
Reviewing the Two Thousand, it is not hard to imagine a slightly different
scenario. Despite sixteen runners, the Guineas was not run at a strong pace,
and, when the action really started three furlongs out, Island Sands was at the
front of the field and Enrique at the back. Checked at that point, Enrique had
about five lengths to make up; emerging from the pack, a sustained, head-down
effort from horse and jockey over the last furlong and a half saw them past
Mujahid but they succeeded only in whittling down Island Sands's advantage
from two lengths to a neck. 'It's a pity I didn't get the gaps on Enrique that I
got with the filly,' rued Fallon after Wince's triumph twenty-four hours later,
'Enrique still had more to give.'

Enrique was sent off the 7/1 second favourite for the Guineas, drifting
on course from 11/2. In marked contrast to most of the supposed leading
contenders, he had appeared in a trial and won it, but the Tripleprint Stakes at
Newbury had still left many observers scratching their heads. For a start, what
had happened to the course's ninety-three-year-old Guineas trial, the Greenham
Stakes? In an attempt by the sponsors to promote their name more for their
monetary outlay, the old race title was relegated to a position in brackets,
causing a fair amount of ruffled feathers amongst the traditionalists, the full
race title being The Tripleprint Stakes (registered as the Greenham Stakes).

Tripleprint Stakes (Greenham), Newbury—Enrique is pressed strongly by Exeat (right) and Perugino Bay

That issue aside, Enrique's performance in the race did not make his Guineas prospects an awful lot clearer. He was fully entitled to win on his two-year-old form, and entitled to do so by more than half a length and three quarters. Taking up the running two furlongs out, it appeared that the 5/4 favourite's superiority over Exeat and Perugino Bay would be a great deal more than that, but Fallon had to ask Enrique some serious questions in the last half furlong and did not receive much of an answer. It looked to us as if Enrique was taking things easily in front, but one had also to consider his rather over-exuberant manner in the early stages and on the way to post, along with the possible influence of his dam Gwydion, whose stamina had given out at the same meeting thirteen years earlier when she ran in the Fred Darling; Enrique also blew more than his rivals afterwards in the winner's enclosure. For his part, Cecil confidently predicted that Enrique would stay the extra furlong and observed that if Fallon had held on to the colt longer then Enrique would have won by further. As he has trained Guineas candidates for the best part of thirty years, perhaps one should have taken his word for it. The sight of Enrique still gaining on the winner at the post in the Guineas provided an indisputable vindication for Cecil's prediction, but also showed that the tactical issue had not made Fallon's task any easier.

Enrique's connections had to wait only three weeks for a first chance to gain compensation, in the Irish Two Thousand Guineas. Sent off at 5/2 after a scare when he bruised a foot earlier in the week, Enrique duly turned the tables on Island Sands (the 2/1 favourite) but again had to settle for the runner-up spot himself, ridden much closer to the pace this time and getting his nose in front only to have Saffron Walden sail past half a furlong from home. Given Saffron Walden's form before and after that classic, one could suggest that Enrique was unlucky on this occasion as well, an argument that is even more applicable to his third second placing of the season, to a barely recognisable Lots of Magic over seven furlongs in the Jersey Stakes at Royal Ascot. 12/1-chance Saffron Walden and 33/1-chance Lots of Magic both beat Enrique by three lengths. Cecil and Fallon might have begun to feel a little out of sorts after this series of reverses. That, however, was as nothing compared to Enrique's next appearance, at Goodwood in the Sussex Stakes on the day dominated by Cecil's announcement that Fallon would cease to be employed by him at the end of the week. Catching the prevailing mood, this was Enrique's nadir for the season and he finished well below his best in fifth, over seven lengths behind the winner Aljabr, beaten as soon as he was ridden along early in the straight. He was not seen out again.

	Barathea (IRE) (b 1990)	Sadler's Wells (b 1981)	Northern Dancer Fairy Bridge
Enrique (b.c. 1996)		Brocade (b 1981)	Habitat Canton Silk
	Gwydion (USA) (b 1983)	Raise A Cup (b 1971)	Raise A Native Spring Sunshine
		Papamiento (ch 1973)	Blade Commemoration

A strong, well-made, attractive colt, Enrique usually takes the eye in appearance. He used to get excited in the preliminaries but calmed down a good deal on his last four starts. He is unlikely to stay beyond a mile and has not yet raced on ground softer than good. He remains the best progeny of his sire Barathea, who was also represented in 1999 by the Prix Penelope winner La Sylphide, by listed winner Ajhiba and by Barathea Guest, demoted winner of a substandard Grand Criterium. Enrique is also the best of Gwydion's first seven foals, but Piperi (by Machiavellian) showed smart five-furlong form in 1998. Her eighth foal, Silk Glove (by Hernando), also in training with Cecil, has not yet seen a racecourse, but Enrique remains in training. *H. R. A. Cecil*

EN SILENCE (USA) 3 b.f. Rahy (USA) 115 – No More Ironing (USA) (Slew O'Gold (USA)) [1998 NR 1999 7g 7m 6s⁴ 6.8s³ a7g² 6m⁵ a6g* a7g Jul 24] 85,000Y: **78**

lengthy, quite attractive filly: has a quick action: fifth foal: half-sister to US 8.5f stakes winner Sneaky Quiet (by Seeking The Gold): dam 2-y-o sprint winner in USA from family of Glint of Gold and Diamond Shoal: fair performer: won maiden at Wolverhampton in July: well held next time: probably better at 6f than 7f: acts on fibresand, below form on good to firm going (found nothing): visored last 5 starts: has been bandaged behind. *J. Noseda*

ENTAIL (USA)   2 b. or br.f. (Apr 3) Riverman (USA) 131 – Estala (Be My Guest (USA) 126) [1999 8d³ Oct 22] neat filly: second foal: dam, French 2-y-o 9f winner, half-sister to smart French stayer Erudite: better for race and equipped with rope halter for stalls, led over 1f out when 1¼ lengths third of 18 to Interlude in maiden at Doncaster: should stay beyond 1m: useful prospect, sure to improve and win races. *J. H. M. Gosden*   **83 p**

ENTERTAINER (IRE)   3 b.g. Be My Guest (USA) 126 – Green Wings (General Assembly (USA)) [1998 95: 7.1m² 8g² 7.1s 1999 10g² 11.5g⁵ 10.5f² Jul 11] strong, useful-looking gelding: fair maiden: ran poorly on soft going: stays 11.5f: sold 40,000 gns, joined P. Nicholls. *P. W. Chapple-Hyam*   **78**

ENTIKAA (IRE)   3 b.c. Sadler's Wells (USA) 132 – Miranisa (Habitat 134) [1998 NR 1999 10g 8s 12.3m³ Jun 16] IR 340,000Y: smallish, sturdy colt: sixth foal: half-brother to fairly useful French 5f (at 2 yrs) and 1¼m winner Marishaan (by Darshaan) and a winner in Turkey by Royal Academy: dam twice-raced half-sister to Poule d'Essai des Pouliches winner Masarika: best effort in maidens when 7 lengths third of 17 to Raaqi at Ripon, keeping on without being unduly punished: has been bandaged behind: sold 9,000 gns in October. *Sir Michael Stoute*   **80**

ENTITY   2 ch.g. (Mar 22) Rudimentary (USA) 118 – Desert Ditty 67 (Green Desert (USA) 127) [1999 6m 6m⁵ 6m⁴ 6g⁴ 8d Oct 22] 31,000Y: big, lengthy gelding: has scope: third foal: brother to fairly useful French 1996 2-y-o 6f winner Aberelle: dam 6f winner out of useful 6f/7f winner Royal Loft: fair maiden: creditable fourth in nursery at York penultimate start: should move best at 7f/1m. *T. D. Barron*   **69**

ENTROPY   3 b.f. Brief Truce (USA) 126 – Distant Isle (IRE) (Bluebird (USA) 125) [1998 72: 5d³ 5.1g² 5.1g³ 6g³ 6m⁵ 5.7m* 6.1g⁶ 6.5g 1999 6.1m 7d 7.1d 6g⁵ 6g 5m 6m 6g a7g a8g⁵ a7g Dec 15] close-coupled filly: has a quick, fluent action: fair performer: left R. Hannon 3,600 gns after eighth start: should stay 7f: yet to race on extremes of going on turf. *B. A. Pearce*   **69 d**

ENTWINE   3 b.f. Primo Dominie 121 – Splice 114 (Sharpo 132) [1998 86p: 5m⁴ 5m* 5g* 5s 1999 6g³ 6m³ 6d 6m 6m⁶ Jul 23] small, sturdy filly: shows a quick action: fairly useful handicapper: good third of 15 to Munjiz at Newmarket on reappearance: better than result suggests all starts after: stays 6f: acts on good to firm ground: usually held up: slowly away second to fourth starts. *J. R. Fanshawe*   **92**

ENVY (IRE)   3 gr.f. Paris House 123 – Rhett's Choice 67 (Beveled (USA)) [1998 NR 1999 a8.5g Dec 27] second foal: dam 2-y-o 5f winner: showed little in Wolverhampton maiden. *J. G. Given*   **–**

ENZELI (IRE)   4 b.c. Kahyasi 130 – Ebaziya (IRE) 111 (Darshaan 133) [1998 112: 10m⁵ 14m* 12s* 12v³ 14d⁴ 16v* 1999 14m* 20m* 14s⁴ Sep 18]   **126**

Twelve months back, Enzeli was the apparent under-achiever of his family. Putting up one of the best handicap performances of the season—in the two-mile Leopardstown November Handicap—was all very well, but it did not look so good alongside the Group 1 victories of his year-older and year-younger half-sisters, Ebadiyla and Edabiya. Now Enzeli has a Group 1 win of his own to boast of in the Aga Khan's silks, and is rated superior to both of them.

Enzeli's less-exalted place in the pecking order looked clear enough in September as a three-year-old when he was assigned pacemaking duties for Ebadiyla in the Irish St Leger. From that point on, however, his path took a different course. Ebadiyla's bid for a repeat success in the Irish classic ended with a nosebleed down at the start, and, ridden with his own interests in mind, Enzeli made the frame, beaten twelve lengths in fourth of seven to Kayf Tara. The Leopardstown November Handicap was his next start and confirmed that

Gold Cup, Royal Ascot—Enzeli leads home the largest field in the history of this famous race, chased by Invermark and Kayf Tara

the merit of his classic performance could be taken at face value. This was markedly superior form to his odds-on wins in a maiden and a minor event and to his third of six in one listed race.

Enzeli's first two starts of 1999 spectacularly extended this upward curve. First came a listed win, registered in impressive fashion over a mile and three quarters at Leopardstown in May. The bare form he showed to justify favouritism that day did not pose a threat to the established stayers, but when Enzeli lined up in the Gold Cup at Royal Ascot, the eighth race of his career, he had to be considered a challenger with potential. Starting at 20/1, he was soon positioned halfway down the field on the inside by jockey John Murtagh. No nearer to the action as they began the final turn, he made his move as they completed the sweep into the straight, getting a clear run between the weakening outsiders Solo Mio and Laurentide and emerging alongside Kayf Tara as the two of them went in pursuit of Spirit of Love. They surged past the Cesarewitch winner at the two-furlong pole and Enzeli rapidly gained the upper hand from Kayf Tara, two lengths in front by the time Invermark challenged in the final furlong, which was comfortably enough to hold on. In fact, holding on does not do Enzeli justice; Enzeli was running on so strongly that Invermark managed to reduce his advantage to only a length and a half, despite the winner being eased close home. This was a win to rank alongside the decade's best in the Gold Cup, up there with Classic Cliche's one and a half length defeat of Double Trigger in 1996. As well as the 1998 winner Kayf Tara, Enzeli also had 1997 winner Celeric behind him, the pair beaten four lengths and five and three quarter lengths respectively in third and fourth. 1998 St Leger winner Nedawi was fifth with the 1998 Gold Cup third, Three Cheers, in sixth. Some way removed from the first six, apart from Spirit of Love, the other also-rans included Chester Cup winner Rainbow High (tenth), who put up a bold show in his four other pattern appearances in 1999, Yorkshire Cup winner Churlish Charm (eleventh), that stalwart of the staying division Persian Punch (twelfth) and France's top older-horse stayer Tajoun (who wore the Aga Khan's first colours but finished last of seventeen). To summarise, although Arctic Owl was absent, this was a strong renewal of the Gold Cup, with the strength in depth to confirm the rude health of Flat racing's greatest staying race which had already been suggested by the largest field in the event's one hundred and ninety two year history, one more than the record set twelve months earlier. The previous record, incidentally, had been thirteen, set in 1910, 1929, 1950, 1988 and 1997 after the total had reached double figures only three times in the eighteen hundreds.

The Gold Cup remains easily the highlight of Enzeli's career because he made only one appearance afterwards and ran poorly. In finishing fourth in the Irish St Leger, he filled the same position as in 1998 but was beaten twelve lengths further. He should, however, be back in action as a five-year-old. A

359

neat colt, Enzeli was on his toes in the preliminaries at Royal Ascot. That race demonstrated clearly enough that he is high class at two and a half miles on good to firm ground; his Irish November Handicap triumph indicates that he acts on heavy.

		Ile de Bourbon (br 1975)	Nijinsky Roseliere
Enzeli (IRE) (b.c. 1995)	Kahyasi (b 1985)	Kadissya (b 1979)	Blushing Groom Kalkeen
	Ebaziya (IRE) (b 1989)	Darshaan (br 1981)	Shirley Heights Delsy
		Ezana (ch 1983)	Ela-Mana-Mou Evisa

The racecourse record of Enzeli's dam, the smart mile and a half filly Ebaziya, and of the next three generations of her family were detailed in the last two editions of this Annual and they now look pretty meagre set alongside her producing record. The three-year-old career of Edabiya (by Rainbow Quest) is the only major disappointment in the careers of her first three foals, but she had already won the Moyglare Stud Stakes. In producing three Group 1 winners with her first three foals, Ebaziya emulated the achievements of Alidiva earlier in the decade; in doing so with the offspring of three different sires (first foal Ebadiyla is by Sadler's Wells), she is out on her own. After a relatively lean spell, the Aga Khan Studs have been enjoying plenty of success again in recent years and Enzeli's sire Kahyasi has played a major part. Enzeli is his best offspring, but he also had Group 1 successes in 1998 with Zainta (Prix de Diane and Prix Saint-Alary) and in 1997 with Vereva (Prix de Diane). Without the Aga Khan's support, Kahyasi would have had a negligible impact: Kahyasi's eight pattern winners have all been bred by his owner. Thanks to him, there has been some quality in Kahyasi's consorts. There has not been much cause to

H.H. Aga Khan's "Enzeli"

thank other breeders, and the 1999 Flat season in Britain and Ireland saw only six Kahyasi three-year-olds on the racecourse and four two-year-olds. Enzeli's maternal grandsire Darshaan, contrastingly, has never suffered for popularity or results. Interestingly, Darshaan and Ebaziya are from the same family; Albanilla is the fourth dam of Darshaan and third dam of Ebaziya. *J. Oxx, Ireland*

EPCOT BOY (IRE)   2 b.g. (Apr 24) Mukaddamah (USA) 125 – Lightning Laser 68 (Monseigneur (USA) 127) [1999 6d⁶ 7.1m⁵ 7m 8.3f Aug 24] 6,200F, 12,000Y: leggy gelding: seventh foal: half-brother to several winners, including 7f/1m performers Mozambique (by Fayruz) and Morocco (by Cyrano de Bergerac): dam, 7f winner, ran only at 2 yrs: well held after debut. *J. J. O'Neill*   **50 d**

EPERNAY   3 b.f. Lion Cavern (USA) 117 – Decant 68 (Rousillon (USA) 133) [1998 NR 1999 7.7d² 7m⁵ Oct 19] first foal: dam, 1m winner, out of half-sister to dam of Hector Protector and Bosra Sham: well backed, better effort in maidens when neck second to Beggars Belief at Warwick on debut. *J. R. Fanshawe*   **69**

EPISTOLAIRE (IRE)   4 b.c. Alzao (USA) 117 – Epistolienne (Law Society (USA) 130) [1998 118: 12g² 13g* 12.5d³ 12.5g* 12s⁴ 1999 10d³ 12d³ 12d² 12.5g⁵ Jul 24] close-coupled colt: smart performer: creditable efforts when placed in small fields in Prix d'Harcourt at Longchamp (1¾ lengths third to Dark Moondancer), Prix Jean de Chaudenay at Saint-Cloud (length third to Public Purse) and Grand Prix de Chantilly (short of room when 2½ lengths second to Capri): stays 13f: raced mainly on good/good to soft ground: sent to USA. *A. Fabre, France*   **118**

EPONA   2 ch.f. (May 3) Inchinor 119 – Zelda (USA) (Sharpen Up 127) [1999 6g a5g a6g⁶ Dec 13] half-sister to 3 winning sprinters, including fairly useful Irish 3-y-o 6f winner Robzelda (by Robellino) and 1996 2-y-o 6f winner Spaniards Inn (by Dominion), later 9f winner in Hong Kong: dam once-raced half-sister to Moorestyle: well held in maidens/seller. *T. D. Easterby*   **–**

EPSOM CYCLONE (USA)   4 ch.c. Rahy (USA) 115 – Aneesati 85 (Kris 135) [1998 95: 6d* 6s² 6m 5.6g 6s* 5s 1999 7g 6g 6v Sep 29] robust colt: useful at 3 yrs (had wind operation after third start): no show in handicaps in 1999: sold only 1,000 gns, sent to Italy. *B. W. Hills*   **–**

EPWORTH   5 b.m. Unfuwain (USA) 131 – Positive Attitude 82 (Red Sunset 120) [1998 –§: 10.3g 8m⁵ 10.8m a8.5g 7m 11.9s 10v 1999 a9.4g⁴ a12g² 12.3m a12g5 17.2m³ 18m Jul 3] tall, useful-looking mare: modest maiden nowadays: stays 17.2f: acts on soft going, good to firm and fibresand: tried blinkered/visored earlier in career: ungenuine. *L. J. Barratt*   **53 §**

EQUERRY   8 b.g. Midyan (USA) 124 – Supreme Kingdom 85 (Take A Reef 127) [1998 –: 8m 6.9d 8s a8.5g 1999 a8g 9g* 10m 9m 8g⁴ 8g⁵ 8g³ Jun 18] quite attractive gelding: poor selling handicapper nowadays: won at Musselburgh in April: effective at 1m/9f: acts on fibresand, best turf form on good going or firmer: effective in blinkers earlier in career: none too consistent. *M. Dods*   **48 §**

ERIN ANAM CARA (IRE)   2 ch.f. (Jan 25) Exit To Nowhere (USA) 122 – Honey Heather (IRE) 56 (Kris 135) [1999 5g a5g⁶ 6.1g 6m⁵ 6m⁴ 6.8m⁴ 8m³ Sep 7] 6,500Y: robust filly: fourth foal: half-sister to 2 winners in France, a 7f and (at 2 yrs) 1m winner by Highest Honor and a 7.5f winner by Thatching: dam, maiden, out of half-sister to Irish 2000 Guineas winner Flash of Steel: modest maiden: stays 1m: raced only on good/good to firm going on turf, below form on fibresand: consistent. *D. J. S. Cosgrove*   **56**

ERINVALE   3 ch.g. Mon Tresor 113 – Honey Mill 67 (Milford 119) [1998 68?, a57: a5g³ 5m 5g⁴ a6g a6g 1999 a6g² a5g* a7g² a6g³ a7f³ a7g* a6g⁴ a8g³ 6.1d⁶ 6g 7.5m 5.9m Aug 2] fair on all-weather, modest on turf: won minor event in January and claimer in February, both at Lingfield: stays 7f: acts on all-weather, best turf effort on good going: visored (well held) final start: sold 4,000 gns. *P. C. Haslam*   **51 a66**

ERITH'S CHILL WIND   3 b.f. Be My Chief (USA) 122 – William's Bird (USA) 104 (Master Willie 129) [1998 48+: 6f 7m 6m⁶ 6f³ 7g 1999 9.7s 8g 10f² 10f² 9s³ 10m* 10s a10g⁴ a10g⁴ Nov 24] modest handicapper: won at Brighton (flashed tail) in August: stays 1¼m: acts on good to firm going and equitrack. *G. L. Moore*   **61**

ERMINE (IRE)   3 ch.f. Cadeaux Genereux 131 – Nibbs Point (IRE) 107 (Sure   **86**
Blade (USA) 130) [1998 63p: 7m 7v⁶ 1999 8g² 9m 10.3m² 10d³ 7.9f² 8m* 10g
10d Oct 29] sparely-made filly: fairly useful performer: won maiden at Newcastle
in September, making most: ran as if something amiss final start: better around
1¼m than shorter: acts on good to firm and good to soft going, probably on firm.
L. M. Cumani

ERRO CODIGO   4 b.g. Formidable (USA) 125 – Home Wrecker (DEN) (Affilia-   **63**
tion Order (USA) 89) [1998 66: a6g⁶ a6g* a6g³ a6g⁶ 7v⁵ 6d 6g 7.1g³ 5.9d⁴ 7g² 7d³   **a57**
7g⁵ 5m⁵ 1999 7m 7m 9g 6m 6m⁴ 6g* 6d a7g a5g a6g³ a6g⁴ Dec 27] strong, good-
topped gelding: modest handicapper nowadays: won at Lingfield in October: best at
6f/7f: acts on fibresand, good to firm and good to soft going: visored final 3-y-o start.
S. E. Kettlewell

ERTLON   9 b.g. Shareef Dancer (USA) 135 – Sharpina (Sharpen Up 127) [1998   **70**
71: a8g³ a8g 7m⁴ 1999 a7g³ a10f³ a10g⁵ a10g³ a8g⁶ Feb 25] close-coupled gelding:
fair performer: below form after reappearance: effective at 7f, probably stays easy
1¼m: acts on all-weather and probably any going on turf: blinkered (ran creditably)
once at 4 yrs: has been bandaged/tongue tied. *C. E. Brittain*

ERUPT   6 b.g. Beveled (USA) – Sparklingsovereign 53 (Sparkler 130) [1998 64,   **59**
a–: a7g 6.1s 7.1g* 7.6m 7s⁵ 6.9d 7.6m 7g 6m⁶ a7g 1999 a8f² a7f a7g a8g 7g 8d 7.1m⁶
a7g⁴ 7s⁴ 8.2m a8g 8m² 8s* 8d 8g a9.4g a7g⁶ Nov 19] plain, leggy gelding: modest
handicapper: won at Newcastle in September: effective at 6f to 1m: acts on good to
firm going, heavy and fibresand: blinkered (below form) seventh start, effective
visored: has been tongue tied: none too consistent. *M. Brittain*

ESCALADE   2 b.g. (Feb 28) Green Desert (USA) 127 – Sans Escale (USA)   **62**
(Diesis 133) [1999 6m 7m 8.5m⁶ 7d³ 8d Oct 29] small, compact gelding: third
reported foal: half-brother to 3-y-o West Escape: dam, French 11f winner, out of Prix
de Diane winner Escaline: modest maiden: best effort when third of 16 in nursery at
Brighton: should stay 1m. *M. A. Jarvis*

ESCORT   3 b.g. Most Welcome 131 – Benazir 91 (High Top 131) [1998 83p: 6m   **83**
6s 8d* 1999 8.1m⁴ 8.1g⁴ 10d 10g 11.6d⁶ Oct 28] strong, sturdy gelding: fairly useful
handicapper: well below form after first 2 starts: should stay 1¼m: acts on good to
soft and good to firm going: joined J. Leigh. *W. J. Haggas*

ES GO   6 ch.g. Dunbeath (USA) 127 – Track Angel 43 (Ardoon 124) [1998 54:   **–**
16.2m 13m³ 14.1m 15.8m² 12d⁴ 10.1v* 10.1v² 1999 10v 12.4m 12s 10.1d Oct 20]
robust gelding: modest handicapper at 5 yrs: well held in 1999: was effective at 1¼m,
probably stayed 2m: best efforts on heavy going: visored (well beaten) third 5-y-o
start: dead. *R. Bastiman*

ESHTIAAL (USA)   5 b. or br.h. Riverman (USA) 131 – Lady Cutlass (USA)   **67 §**
(Cutlass (USA)) [1998 –: 10g 1999 10.1s 12m 11.9d³ a12g³ a12g² a13g⁴ Dec 10]
useful at 3 yrs: just fair at best in 1999: stays 1½m: acts on good to firm going, good
to soft and equitrack: wears blinkers: tends to carry head high: not an easy ride, and
one to treat with caution. *G. L. Moore*

ESPADA (IRE)   3 b.c. Mukaddamah (USA) 125 – Folk Song (CAN) (The   **95**
Minstrel (CAN) 135) [1998 74: 5s⁵ 5.9d⁴ 6d² 6g² 6m* 1999 7d⁵ 7m* 8f⁵ 8m 8m² 7d*
7s⁵ 7g Oct 16] smallish, quite attractive colt: improved into useful performer at 3 yrs:
won minor event at Thirsk in May and handicap at Ayr in September: effective at 7f/
1m: acts on firm and soft going: drifted badly left fifth start: consistent. *P. Calver*

ESPERE D'OR   2 b.c. (Apr 23) Golden Heights 82 – Drummer's Dream (IRE) 48   **–**
(Drumalis 125) [1999 a8.5g Dec 11] first foal: dam 5f winner: 50/1, tailed off in
minor event at Wolverhampton. *T. Wall*

ESPOIR D'ETE (BEL)   2 ch.c. (Apr 28) Last Hope 80 – Summer Moss 56   **– §**
(Ballymoss 136) [1999 7.1m 6g 7d Oct 14] strong, lengthy colt: first reported foal:
dam 1½m winner: last in maidens/seller, slowly away and looking reluctant in
blinkers final start. *G. L. Moore*

ESSANDESS (IRE)   4 b.f. Casteddu 111 – Ra Ra (Lord Gayle (USA) 124) [1998   **43**
50: a7g a8g⁵ a8g 7s 7g 10g 8g a6g⁶ 7d a7g⁴ 1999 a12g a11g⁴ a12g³ a12f a8g Jul
8] sparely-made filly: poor maiden handicapper: stays 1½m: acts on soft going and
fibresand, probably on good to firm. *J. L. Eyre*

ESSE   4 ch.f. Rudimentary (USA) 118 – School Concert 80 (Music Boy 124) [1998   –
–: a11g 1999 a7g 5g 7d 6g May 18] good-topped filly: no longer of much account.
A. Smith

ESSIE   2 b.f. (Mar 11) Ezzoud (IRE) 126 – Safari Park 43 (Absalom 128) [1999   47
5g 5.1m 7f⁵ 6.1m² a6g Sep 8] 6,000Y: first foal: dam maiden on Flat and poor
winning hurdler: poor maiden: stays 6f: raced only on good going or firmer on turf,
well beaten on fibresand: blinkered last 2 starts: sold only 800 gns in October.
C. E. Brittain

ESTABELLA (IRE)   2 ch.f. (Apr 11) Mujtahid (USA) 118 – Lady In Green   52
(Shareef Dancer (USA) 135) [1999 6g 6.1g 7g 7g⁵ Sep 14] 3,500F, IR 17,000Y: fifth
foal: sister to US winner around 1m Shady Link and half-sister to 4-y-o Emerald
Heights and 1994 2-y-o 6f winner Green Seed (by Lead On Time): dam unraced:
modest maiden: respectable fifth in nursery at Yarmouth final start: should stay 1m.
S. P. C. Woods

ESTABLISHED   2 b.g. (Feb 4) Not In Doubt (USA) 101 – Copper Trader 53   39
(Faustus (USA) 118) [1999 6m⁶ 6d 7f 7m 7m 8s 10s Oct 5] neat gelding: third foal:
half-brother to 3-y-o Columna and 5-y-o Mary Culi: dam third at 1¼m: poor maiden
on balance: trained by H. Candy first 3 starts: should stay at least 1m. *J. R. Best*

ESTABLISHMENT   2 b.g. (Feb 24) Muhtarram (USA) 125 – Uncharted Waters   60
68 (Celestial Storm (USA) 132) [1999 7m⁶ 7.1m 7m Jul 28] workmanlike gelding:
first foal: dam 1¼m and 1½m winner: modest form in maidens: should stay 1¼m+.
C. A. Cyzer

ESTACADO (IRE)   3 b.f. Dolphin Street (FR) 125 – Raubritter (Levmoss 133)   –
[1998 –: 6m 7m 5g 7m⁶ 1999 10m 8.3g Jul 5] useful-looking filly: little form on
Flat: visored final two 2-y-o starts: sold 1,300 gns and won 3 times over hurdles for
J. W. Mullins, showing fairly useful form. *B. Gubby*

ESTERAAD (IRE)   3 ch.f. Cadeaux Genereux 131 – Eclipsing (IRE) 93 (Bailla-   89
mont (USA) 124) [1998 90p: 6g⁵ 6.1g* 7.1g³ 1999 7m 8m 10m⁴ 12s 10.3s² Nov 5]
leggy, angular filly: fairly useful performer: creditable efforts when in frame in
handicap at Ascot and minor event at Doncaster: stays 1¼m: acts on good to firm and
soft going: none too consistent. *J. L. Dunlop*

ESTERELLE (USA)   4 ch.f. Trempolino (USA) 135 – Duck Flighting (USA)   – §
(Far North (CAN) 120) [1998 –§: 8.3m 16f 10g 11.8m⁴ 1999 a12g Apr 24] rather
leggy, close-coupled filly: no sign of ability on Flat: temperamental. *H. J. Manners*

ESTOPPED (IRE)   4 b.g. Case Law 113 – Action Belle (Auction Ring (USA)   –
123) [1998 –, a55d: a10s³ a9.4g a10g⁴ a11g a7g⁶ a8g⁴ a8.5g a10g⁴ 9.9s 8g 14.1m
11.6m 7s 1999 a10g a12g Nov 24] poor maiden: tried visored. *M. Quinn*

ETERNAL SPRING (IRE)   2 b.c. (Mar 12) Persian Bold 123 – Emerald Waters   91
(Kings Lake (USA) 133) [1999 7m² 7.5g* 7m³ 8d² Sep 18] quite good-topped colt:
second foal: brother to 3-y-o Persian Waters: dam Irish 11f winner: fairly useful
performer: won maiden at Beverley in August: beaten favourite (but creditable
efforts) both subsequent starts, second of 9 to Modish in minor event at Ayr on final
one: will stay at least 1¼m. *E. A. L. Dunlop*

ETHMAAR (USA)   2 b.c. (May 17) Silver Hawk (USA) 123 – Minifah (USA) 69   100 p
(Nureyev (USA) 131) [1999 8m* 8s³ Oct 22] tall, rather unfurnished colt: half-
brother to several winners, including 7f winner Jinsiyah (by Housebuster) and 1m
winner Bintalshaati (by Kris), both useful, and 5-y-o Zibak: dam, maiden who stayed
1½m, half-sister to Kentucky Derby winner Winning Colors: promising debut when
winning minor event at Newbury by 2½ lengths from Paradise Garden, powering
clear late on despite looking green: well-beaten third of 5 to Island Sound in similar
event on same course month later: will stay at least 1¼m: has scope to make a smart
3-y-o, and worth another chance. *M. P. Tregoning*

ETISALAT (IRE)   4 b.g. Lahib (USA) 129 – Sweet Repose (High Top 131) [1998   54
–: 8g 7m⁵ 8.2s 1999 9g 8d 7m² 8g* 8s 7m 7d⁶ 8d 8.2s a10g* a8g Dec 13]
quite good-topped gelding: modest handicapper: won at Yarmouth (seller) in June
and Lingfield (given enterprising ride) in November: stays easy 1¼m: acts on good
to firm going and equitrack. *J. Pearce*

Godolphin's "Etizaaz"

ETIZAAZ (USA) 3 b.f. Diesis 133 – Alamosa (Alydar (USA)) [1998 110p: 7m* **117**
7f² 1999 8.1m* 12m² 10s⁵ Oct 2] lengthy, unfurnished filly: has a round action: smart
performer: bandaged in front, won listed event at Sandown in August by 3½ lengths
from Selfish, making all: good 2½ lengths second of 11 to Daryaba in Prix Vermeille
at Longchamp following month: odds on, well below form in Sun Chariot Stakes at
Newmarket final outing: stays 1½m: acts on firm going, possibly not on soft: races
up with pace: sent to USA. *Saeed bin Suroor*

ETMA ROSE (IRE) 3 b.f. Fairy King (USA) – Lassalia (Sallust 134) [1998 –: **–**
6.1g 5g 7m 7d 1999 a6g Jan 13] little form. *R. Hollinshead*

ETTERBY PARK (USA) 6 b.g. Silver Hawk (USA) 123 – Bonita Francita (CAN) **89**
(Devil's Bag (USA)) [1998 99: a14.8g⁵ 20d² 16.1m³ 16.1m⁴ 18.2g*16.2d² 18g² 16g*
16.5d⁵ 1999 18.7m 16.2d⁶ 18.7m⁵ 16d* 17.3g Oct 16] small, sturdy gelding: fairly
useful handicapper nowadays: returned to form when winning at Musselburgh in
September: respectable eighth of 32 in Tote Cesarewitch at Newmarket final start:
best at 2m+: unraced on heavy going, acts on any other turf and on fibresand: races
prominently/leads: genuine. *M. Johnston*

ETTRICK 3 b.c. Selkirk (USA) 129 – Lucia Tarditi (FR) (Crystal Glitters (USA) **105**
127) [1998 91p: 7d 7d* 1999 7g⁴ 8f² 8m⁴ 7m 8f Oct 30] good-topped, attractive colt:
has scope: useful performer: best effort when close fourth to River Times in rated
stakes at Newmarket in July: below form last 2 starts in Tote International Handicap
at Ascot (final outing for A. Stewart) and allowance race at Aqueduct: stays 1m: acts
on firm and good to soft ground: free-going sort. *C. Clement, USA*

ETTY B 3 b.f. Clantime 101 – Paquerette 35 (Crofthall 110) [1998 NR 1999 10.5d **–**
7m Aug 22] first foal: dam, maiden who stayed 1¾m, winning pointer: no sign of
ability in maiden/seller. *Andrew Turnell*

EUROBOX BOY 6 ch.g. Savahra Sound 111 – Princess Poquito (Hard Fought **73**
125) [1998 76, a58: a10g⁶ a8g⁴ a11g³ a9.4g³ a9.4g⁴ 8d 8.1m³ 8f 8s³ 8.3d 8g² 1999
7g 7m 7.6m⁴ 8.2m² May 22] compact gelding: fair performer on turf, modest on
all-weather: effective at 1m to 11f: acts on good to firm going, soft and all-weather:
tried visored: has been bandaged near-hind: often apprentice ridden. *B. A. McMahon*

EURO DANDY 2 b.g. (Feb 17) Rambo Dancer (CAN) 107 – Kagram Queen 64 –
(Prince Ragusa 96) [1999 5d 5m 6d 8d Nov 1] 4,000Y, 4,000 2-y-o: first foal: dam,
7f (at 2 yrs) to 11f winner, also successful over hurdles: well beaten in maidens/
nursery. *D. Nicholls*

EUROLINK MAYFLY 2 b.f. (May 20) Night Shift (USA) – North Kildare 55
(USA) (Northjet 136) [1999 7m 6m Sep 18] 10,500Y: compact filly: fifth foal: half-
sister to 6f (at 2 yrs) to 1¼m winner Flying North (by Distinctly North): dam unraced
half-sister to 3-y-o Alrassaam, very smart miler Labeeb and high-class performer up
to 1¼m Fanmore: better effort in maidens when seventh of 15 to Acrobatic at
Newbury: very green on debut: will probably stay 1m. *J. L. Dunlop*

EUROLINK MOUSSAKA 4 b.g. Superlative 118 – Albiflora (USA) (Manila –
(USA)) [1998 66p: 6.1g⁵ 7g⁵ a7g* 1999 a8g a8g* 7m 10d May 16] fairly useful a85
handicapper on all-weather: won at Southwell in February: stays 1m: acts on fibresand, little form on turf. *J. L. Eyre*

EUROLINK RAINDANCE (IRE) 2 b.f. (Feb 28) Alzao (USA) 117 – Euro- 102
link Mischief 84 (Be My Chief (USA) 122) [1999 6f² 6.1g* 7m* 7d² 7m⁵ Sep 5]
first foal: dam 1½m winner: useful performer: won minor events at Chepstow and
Salisbury in June: creditable ¾-length second of 11 to Princess Ellen in listed race at
Newmarket (hung right and flashed tail) in August: not discredited in Moyglare Stud
Stakes at the Curragh final start: bred to stay at least 1m: acts on good to firm and
good to soft going. *J. L. Dunlop*

EUROLINK WINDSONG (IRE) 5 ch.m. Polish Patriot (USA) 128 – Delvec- 31
chia (Glint of Gold 128) [1998 NR 1999 15.8g⁴ 17.2g Aug 25] sturdy mare: poor
maiden handicapper: stays 2m. *Martyn Wane*

EURO VENTURE 4 b.g. Prince Sabo 123 – Brave Advance (USA) 98 (Bold 84 +
Laddie (USA)) [1998 70: a6g* a6g 5g 6g⁴ 5.9d 1999 a6g⁴ a6g² a6g* a6g⁵ 6f² 6s* 6g²
6.9m* 6m² 6m 6f³ Jul 23] sturdy gelding: fairly useful handicapper: had a good
season, winning at Southwell in February, Thirsk in May and Carlisle in June: very
good second of 19 at Newcastle ninth start: effective at 6f/7f: unraced on heavy
going, acts on any other turf and on fibresand: usually races prominently. *D. Nicholls*

EVANDER (IRE) 4 ch.g. Indian Ridge 123 – Heavenly Hope (Glenstal (USA) 91
118) [1998 87: 10d⁶ 8g³ 8m* 9g³ 12s 1999 10m⁶ 10s 12d⁵ 10.1d² 12s⁴ Nov 6] strong,
close-coupled gelding: fairly useful performer: ran at least creditably all starts, fourth
of 16 in November Handicap at Doncaster, making most: rather headstrong and best
at 1¼m/1½m: acts on soft and good to firm going. *P. F. I. Cole*

EVASIVE STEP 3 b.f. Batshoof 122 – Tread Carefully 51 (Sharpo 132) [1998 70
70: 6s³ 7m⁵ a7g⁵ 7.5m⁶ 7m 8d² 7.1s³ 1999 10g 8.2m⁵ 9.9m 12f Jul 30] leggy, plain
filly: has a round action: fair maiden: form in 1999 only in modest form on second start:
stays 1m: acts on soft and good to firm going: carries head high and possibly not
entirely genuine. *T. D. Easterby*

EVENING PROMISE 3 b.f. Aragon 118 – Rosy Sunset (IRE) (Red Sunset 120) 108
[1998 99: 6m² 6g⁴ 6.1g* 6f⁵ 6m⁴ 6s* 1999 7m 8m 6g³ 8.1m 6.1g* 6g⁴ 6d² 6.5f⁵ 5.5f
Nov 25] leggy, sparely-made filly: useful performer: best efforts on sixth/seventh
starts when fourth in listed race at Pontefract then fast-finishing head second of
28 to Grangeville in Ayr Gold Cup: left B. McMahon before final start: may prove
best at 5f/6f: acts on firm going, best efforts on good ground or softer: game. *Kathy
Walsh, USA*

EVENING SCENT 3 b.f. Ardkinglass 114 – Fresh Line 60 (High Line 125) 55
[1998 NR 1999 a8.5g a8g a9.4g⁴ 14.1f 13.8g⁴ 15.8s³ 18d Oct 18] half-sister to
winning stayer All On (by Dunbeath): dam, middle-distance maiden, sister to
Yorkshire Cup winner Line Slinger: modest performer: won seller at Catterick in
September: creditable third in handicap next time: stays 2m, probably not 2¼m: acts
on soft going. *J. Hetherton*

EVENING WORLD (FR) 4 ch.c. Bering 136 – Pivoine (USA) (Nureyev (USA) 111
131) [1998 105: 10s² 7.9g⁴ 10g* 10.4s* 10s⁶ 9m 1999 10s² 9.9g 10.5d⁴ 10.3m⁵
11.9v⁵ Oct 13] tall, quite attractive colt: has badly scarred foreleg: smart performer:
improved effort on reappearance when short-head second to Generous Rosi in
Gordon Richards Stakes at Sandown, making most: well below form after: stays

10.4f, probably not 1½m: ideally suited by soft ground: often wears crossed noseband: races freely and not the easiest of rides. *M. C. Pipe*

EVENTUALITY 3 b.f. Petoski 135 – Queen's Tickle 57 (Tickled Pink 114) [1998 77
63: 8v³ 8d⁴ 1999 7m⁶ 9m 10m 7m* 7f⁴ 7m* 6m⁴ 7s⁶ Oct 2] leggy, lengthy filly:
fair handicapper: won at Salisbury in July and Epsom in September: ran well
penultimate start: effective at 6f/easy 7f: acts on firm and soft going: takes good hold.
R. F. Johnson Houghton

EVEREST (IRE) 2 ch.c. (Feb 19) Indian Ridge 123 – Reine d'Beaute 97 (Caer- 87 p
leon (USA) 132) [1999 7.1m² Sep 4] 120,000Y: fifth foal: half-brother to 3 winners,
including 3-y-o Miss Universe and useful German 7f (at 2 yrs) to 11f winner Silver
Sign (by Shirley Heights): dam 1m/9f winner at 4 yrs on only starts: evens, stayed on
well when head second of 14 to Hunting Tiger in maiden at Haydock: will stay at
least 1m: sure to improve and win races. *P. F. I. Cole*

EVERGREEN (IRE) 2 ch.f. (Mar 26) Lammtarra (USA) 134 – Nettle 106 (Kris 74
135) [1999 5.7g³ 6d⁴ 6.1f 5.7m 8.3d³ 7s Nov 6] eighth foal: half-sister to 3-y-o Holly
Blue and 1m winner Stinging Reply (by Belmez): dam 2-y-o 6f/7f winner who
seemed to stay 1½m: fair maiden: off course nearly 4 months before penultimate
start: poorly drawn final one: should stay beyond 1m: acts on good to soft ground,
ran poorly both starts on firmer than good. *R. Hannon*

EVERGREEN VENTURE 3 b.c. Pursuit of Love 124 – Georgica (USA) (Raise 84
A Native) [1998 72: 6f 1999 8.5s⁶ 10g* 10g⁴ 10.1d 8g³ 8m³ 10g 8g* 8m⁶ Sep 16]
rather leggy, useful-looking colt: fairly useful performer: won maiden at Lingfield in
May and handicap at Pontefract in August: effective at 1m/1¼m: acts on good to
firm going, possibly not on softer than good: sold 16,000 gns, sent to Switzerland.
S. P. C. Woods

EVERLASTING LOVE 2 b.f. (Jan 21) Pursuit of Love 124 – Now And Forever 99
(IRE) (Kris 135) [1999 7m 7g⁴ 7m* 8m² 7s Oct 2] good-bodied filly: first foal: dam
unraced half-sister to smart stayer Witness Box out of close relative to Dahlia: useful
form: won minor event at Redcar in August: easily best effort when 3 lengths second
of 12 to Teggiano in May Hill Stakes at Doncaster following month: better at 1m
than 7f, and will stay further: acts on good to firm going, well below form on soft.
M. L. W. Bell

EVER PUNCTUAL 2 b.f. (May 9) Timeless Times (USA) 99 – Vital Witness –
(Garda's Revenge (USA) 119) [1999 a7g 8eg 500Y: third reported foal: dam ran
once on Flat at 2 yrs: well beaten in seller at Southwell. *J. S. Moore*

EVER REVIE (IRE) 2 b.f. (Feb 7) Hamas (IRE) 125§ – Lucy Limelight 98 (Hot 51
Spark 126) [1999 6g⁶ 7.5g 7.5s* 7m 8d Sep 23] IR 5,000Y: leggy filly: sister to 1997
Italian 2-y-o winner (including 5.5f listed race) Primas Agere and half-sister to
several winners, including 5-y-o Meilleur and useful 5f/6f performer Lucedeo (by
Godswalk): dam 2-y-o 5f winner: modest performer: won seller at Beverley in July:
stays 7.5f: acts on soft going: blinkered third and fourth starts. *T. D. Easterby*

EVERY PENNY 4 b.f. Interrex (CAN) – Shiny Penny 70 (Glint of Gold 128) –
[1998 –: 8m a13g 1999 a8g⁴ Mar 22] leggy filly: lightly-raced maiden: poor form at
best. *R. T. Phillips*

EVESHAM (USA) 3 b.g. Septieme Ciel (USA) 123 – Evening Air (USA) (J O 64
Tobin (USA) 130) [1998 NR 1999 10v⁴ 12m⁴ 12.1s⁴ 9.9g 13.8g* 13f⁵ 12m Jul 27]
tall, leggy gelding: eighth foal: half-brother to 3 winners, including 1991 May Hill
winner Midnight Air (dam of Oaks third Midnight Line) and useful 1¼m winner
Greenstead (both by Green Dancer): dam, unraced, from good American family:
modest performer: won maiden at Catterick in July: well held on firmer going both
starts after: stays 1¾m: raced freely in blinkers final outing: sent to UAE.
M. Johnston

EVEZIO RUFO 7 b.g. Blakeney 126 – Empress Corina 74 (Free State 125) [1998 53 §
48, a63d: a16g a12g³ a11g² a13g* a12g* a12g* a12g² a13g² a12g⁵ a12g² a12g²
a12g* a14.8g⁶ a12g⁴ 12g⁵ 11.6g a11g³ a12g⁴ a12g³ a14g⁵ 12.3g⁶ a12g a11g⁴ 11.8d⁵
a14g³ a12g³ a14g⁶ a12g⁶ a14.8g² a12g⁵ 1999 a13g³ a11g⁴ a14.8g³ a11g⁶ a14.8g*
a12f a13g a14.8g⁶ a12g* a11g⁶ a14g⁴ 14g⁵ a12g⁵ Dec 21] neat gelding:
modest performer: won seller in January and handicap in March, both at Wolverhampton: mostly below form otherwise, off course 6 months before final start: stays

15f: acts on all-weather and soft going: usually blinkered/visored: usually held up (though has won from front): has hung: not one to trust. *N. P. Littmoden*

EVIE HONE (IRE) 3 ch.f. Royal Academy (USA) 130 – Tochar Ban (USA) 83 **61 §**
(Assert 134) [1998 69: 7g 7g 8d⁴ 1999 9.1m⁵ 14.1m Jun 18] leggy, quite good-topped filly: fair maiden at 2 yrs: temperamental and virtually refused to race final start in 1999 and is one to leave alone: sold 6,000 gns in October. *B. W. Hills*

EWENNY 3 b.f. Warrshan (USA) 117 – Laleston 73 (Junius (USA) 124) [1998 71: **49**
5g* 5g³ 6f³ 1999 a7f³ a6f⁴ Feb 8] fair form at 2 yrs: poor form in sellers at Southwell in 1999: likely to prove best at 5f/6f. *J. M. P. Eustace*

EXALT 3 b.g. Puissance 110 – Gild The Lily 83 (Ile de Bourbon (USA) 133) [1998 **43**
–: a6g 1999 8d a7g⁴ 8.2s Apr 27] unfurnished gelding: poor maiden: form only at Southwell penultimate start: should stay at least 1m. *A. W. Carroll*

EXALTED (IRE) 6 b.g. High Estate 127 – Heavenward (USA) (Conquistador **64**
Cielo (USA)) [1998 –: 16.2g 1999 10.3d⁴ 13g May 2] good-topped gelding: has round action: fair but untrustworthy winning hurdler: modest handicapper nowadays on Flat: should stay 1½m: acts on good to firm and good to soft ground. *T. A. K. Cuthbert*

EXEAT (USA) 3 b. or br.c. Dayjur (USA) 137 – By Your Leave (USA) (Private **111**
Account (USA)) [1998 110: 6g² 6g* 6d² 7s⁴ 1999 7m² 8m 8m 8.1g² 7.3g³ 7s⁵ 7g³ Oct 2] good-topped colt: smart performer: good efforts on first 2 starts, ½ length second to Enrique in Tripleprint (Greenham) Stakes at Newbury and 3¾ lengths eighth to Island Sands in 2000 Guineas at Newmarket: easily best effort after when 1¼ lengths second of 5 to Triple Dash in minor event at Sandown in July: stays 1m: acts on good to firm and soft going: visored (well below form) final start. *J. H. M. Gosden*

EXECUTIVE CHOICE (IRE) 5 b.g. Don't Forget Me 127 – Shadia (USA) 53 **36**
(Naskra (USA)) [1998 46: 10v 9d a8g 7g³ 10d⁶ 8g⁴ 10m 8.3s⁴ 9.1v 1999 9d 12.1m⁵ 10d 8m Jun 18] ex-Irish gelding: poor maiden handicapper: probably stays 1½m: acts on soft going: effective blinkered or not: has been tongue tied: successful over hurdles in July/August. *B. Ellison*

EX GRATIA (USA) 3 b.g. Exbourne (USA) 125 – Populi (USA) (Star Envoy **95 p**
(USA)) [1998 NR 1999 8m 8s⁴ 8.1d* 7.9f 10.5d² 10.3g* 12d⁴ Sep 28] rangy gelding: has scope: fluent mover: half-brother to numerous winners, including top-class American middle-distance performer Vanlandingham and 1½m winner Polyphony (both by Cox's Ridge) and to dam of Distant Music: dam, US 2-y-o 7f winner, half-sister to Belmont Stakes winner Temperence Hill: useful performer: won maiden at Haydock in June and minor event at Doncaster in September: should prove best around 1¼m: acts on good to soft going (well below form only start on firm): held up: has given trouble start (withdrawn intended debut) and been free to post: probably open to further progress. *B. W. Hills*

EXILE 2 b.g. (Feb 4) Emperor Jones (USA) 119 – Silver Venture (USA) (Silver **72**
Hawk (USA) 123) [1999 5g⁴ 6g⁴ 7m⁶ 6m 5g⁴ 7.9f 7s Oct 1] 21,000Y: close-coupled gelding: third foal: half-brother to 3-y-o Little John and a 7f winner in Sweden by Al Nasr: dam placed at 1½m in France: fair maiden: trained until after fifth start by G. Lewis: never dangerous in nurseries for new yard: should stay at least 7f: best efforts on good ground: blinkered fifth and final outings: sold 6,800 gns. *W. J. Haggas*

EXIT 3 b.f. Exbourne (USA) 125 – Meteoric 102 (High Line 125) [1998 67: 7m⁶ **82**
1999 8.5g* 7.6m 10.2m⁶ Jul 23] fair form to win 4-runner maiden at Beverley in June by short head: stiff tasks and well held last 2 starts: should stay beyond 1m. *B. Smart*

EXORCET (FR) 2 b.f. (Apr 24) Selkirk (USA) 129 – Stack Rock 111 (Ballad **60 p**
Rock 122) [1999 6v 7d Oct 30] 18,000F: angular filly: second foal: half-sister to 3-y-o Polish Girl: dam sprinter: better effort in maidens in October (backward and green on debut) when twelfth of 16 at Newmarket: bred to prove best short of 1m: likely to do better still. *I. A. Balding*

EXPEDIENT 2 ch.g. (Jan 16) Polish Precedent (USA) 131 – Widows Walk **–**
(Habitat 134) [1999 7s 6v Oct 23] 42,000Y: strong, lengthy gelding with scope: half-brother to several winners, including 1¼m winner Sadler's Walk (by Sadler's Wells) and 1¼m/1½m winner Rainbow Walk (by Rainbow Quest), both fairly useful, and

3-y-o Swagger: dam once-raced daughter of On The House: backward, well held in maidens at Lingfield and Newbury: may do better at 3 yrs. *J. L. Dunlop*

EXPRESS GIFT 10 br.g. Bay Express 132 – Annes Gift (Ballymoss 136) [1998 – NR 1999 14.1s⁵ Nov 1] angular gelding: useful hurdler at best: modest performer on Flat: signs of retaining some ability only run of 1999: stays 1¾m well: goes well on ground softer than good. *M. Pitman*

EXUDE (IRE) 2 br.f. (Mar 30) Namaqualand (USA) – Betelgeuse 86 (Kalaglow 132) [1999 7d a8g⁶ a7g⁵ a8g Dec 29] 1,200Y: fourth foal: half-sister to 3-y-o 8.5f winner Black Rocket (by Perugino) and 2 winners abroad, including Italian winner up to 1¼m Emergency Crisis (by Mujadil): dam 1¾m winner: poor form in maidens/sellers: slowly away final start. *D. J. S. Cosgrove* **42**

EYEBALLS OUT 3 b.c. Polar Falcon (USA) 126 – Jacquelina (USA) 66 (Private Account (USA)) [1998 70: 6d 6m 6s⁵ a7g 1999 a8.5g 11.9s 10s* 10g⁶ Oct 14] tall colt: has been freeze-fired: fair handicapper: won at Nottingham in October: ran respectably final start: stays 1¼m: acts on soft ground: usually races prominently: sold 28,000 gns. *Sir Mark Prescott* **79 a–**

EYELETS ECHO 2 b.c. (Mar 21) Inchinor 119 – Kinkajoo 53 (Precocious 126) [1999 7d⁶ Sep 15] 17,000Y: sixth foal: brother to 3-y-o Sharoura: dam lightly raced: well-held sixth of 9 to Decarchy in maiden at Yarmouth. *D. Morris* **50**

F

FABILLION 7 ch.g. Deploy 131 – Kai (Kalamoun 129) [1998 75: 18d² 16v² 20d⁶ 16.4g⁶ 1999 16.2g³ Aug 11] workmanlike gelding: fair handicapper: not far below best only outing of 1999: probably needs good test at 2m nowadays, and stays 2½m: acts on good to firm and heavy going: has been bandaged. *D. Nicholson* **70**

FABRICE 4 b.g. Pursuit of Love 124 – Parfum d'Automne (FR) (Sharpen Up 127) [1998 70: 6m⁴ 7m² 8m 1999 7m 8g⁵ 10.2g 8d 10.2s 10s Nov 1] modest maiden handicapper: well held final 4 starts: probably stays 1m: acts on good to firm and good to soft going. *H. Candy* **56**

FACE THE CLASS (IRE) 3 ch.f. Up And At 'em 109 – Siva (FR) (Bellypha 130) [1998 59: 8s 1999 7s⁶ 7v⁵ a8g² a12g⁶ 10g 10f a8g 10g³ 10s 10d* Oct 11] modest performer: won 18-runner seller at Leicester in October (sold 7,500 gns), despite again flashing tail: stays 1¼m: acts on soft going and fibresand: successful twice over hurdles for M. Pipe, showing fair form. *A. Kelleway* **52 a59**

FACILE TIGRE 4 gr.g. Efisio 120 – Dancing Diana 82 (Raga Navarro (ITY) 119) [1998 73: 7s 5.3d⁴ 5m² 5m² 5m² 5.3g* 5g⁴ 5m⁶ 5g 5.1m 5f 5.3m 5d⁶ 5m 5.3g 6s* 1999 a6g a5g⁵ 5s 6s 6f 5m 5g 6f⁵ 6s 5f 5s 5.3d² 6g 6d a5g⁴ a6g⁴ a6g⁶ a6g⁶ Dec 27] leggy, close-coupled gelding: modest handicapper: best at 5f/6f: acts on firm going, soft and all-weather: sometimes slowly away: unreliable. *S. Dow* **63 §**

FACSIMILE 4 b.f. Superlative 118 – Just Julia (Natroun (FR) 128) [1998 67, a44: 7m⁴ 7m² 8d⁴ a6g³ a8.5g 1999 6f Jul 12] leggy filly: fair maiden on turf, poor on all-weather at best: probably finds 6f on sharp side, and stays 1m: has been edgy/given trouble start. *John Berry* **–**

FADHEL (USA) 3 b.g. Zilzal (USA) 137 – Nice Life (USA) (Sportin' Life (USA)) [1998 –: 7g 1999 8m 9.5m² 7m⁵ 9.2m⁵ 10d Nov 4] $28,000Y, resold IR 130,000Y: ex-Irish gelding: second foal: half-brother to a winner in Italy by Eastern Echo: dam, won up to 9f in USA, half-sister to US Grade 3 2-y-o 5.5f winner Eternal Flight: best effort (fair form) when head second in maiden at Gowran in June: left D. Weld after next outing: tailed off in handicaps in Britain: stays 9.5f: blinkered second and third starts. *D. Haydn Jones* **75**

FA-EQ (IRE) 3 ch.c. Indian Ridge 123 – Searching Star 63 (Rainbow Quest (USA) 134) [1998 116: 8g* 8m² 8d⁵ 1999 7m⁴ 8m⁴ 6f 7g* Aug 19] sturdy, attractive colt: had a quick action: smart performer: 3 lengths second to Desert Prince in Irish 2,000 Guineas at the Curragh in 1998: won minor event at Kempton in May and listed race at York (beat Tumbleweed Ridge by ½ length despite hanging) in August: creditable 2¼ lengths fourth of 8 to Cape Cross in Queen Anne Stakes at Royal Ascot **116**

in between: best at 7f/1m: acted on good to firm going: put down after reportedly fracturing off-fore sesamoid on gallops in September. *Saeed bin Suroor*

FAFESTA (IRE)   3 b.f. Rainbow Quest (USA) 134 – Dancing Berry (Sadler's Wells (USA) 132) [1998 ?: 9s 1999 10m⁴ 12m Jul 28] fair maiden: best effort when fourth at Windsor in July: should be suited by 1½m+: sent to Italy. *L. M. Cumani*   **66**

FAGIN   2 b.g. (Apr 23) Formidable (USA) 125 – Rich Pickings 44 (Dominion 123) [1999 6m⁶ 7s³ 8d⁶ Oct 21] 7,800Y, resold 15,000Y: third foal: half-brother to 3-y-o Mrs Bossy Boots: dam 2¼m winner at 4 yrs, also successful over hurdles: easily best effort in maidens (green and slowly away on debut) when third of 11 to Lady Upstage at Brighton: well held on same course final outing: should stay at least 1m: joined M. Tompkins. *B. J. Meehan*   **77**

FAHAN (IRE)   2 b.f. (Feb 21) Sri Pekan (USA) 117 – Damemill (IRE) 83 (Danehill (USA) 126) [1999 6g 6.1m⁴ 7.5g³ 8m Oct 19] IR 22,000F, IR 42,000Y: smallish, unfurnished filly: first foal: dam Irish 7f winner out of half-sister to disqualified Oaks winner Aliysa: easily best effort (fair form) when third of 9 to Kind Regards in maiden at Beverley: should be suited by 1m+. *B. W. Hills*   **71**

FAHS (USA)   7 b. or br.g. Riverman (USA) 131 – Tanwi 101 (Vision (USA)) [1998 86, a93p: 8g³ 10.1m³ 12g³ 10d⁶ 10m³ 14g⁵ 12m⁴ 12m⁴ 12s 10.1g³ 11.9m 12s 10.1d² 10s⁴ a12g⁴ 1999 10.1s 10g⁵ 12m³ 10g⁴ 10.1m* 10.1d² 10m² 12m³ 10.1d⁶ 10.1m a10g³ a13g* Dec 22] strong, good sort: impresses in appearance: fairly useful handicapper: won at Yarmouth in June and Lingfield (apprentices) in December: effective at 1¼m to 1¾m: acts on firm going, good to soft and equitrack: waited with: consistent. *N. Hamilton*   **82** **a88**

FAILED TO HIT   6 b.g. Warrshan (USA) 117 – Missed Again 84 (High Top 131) [1998 42, a74: a8.5g⁴ a12g³ a8g* a8g⁴ a8.5g* a10g* a9.4g a8g⁴ a9.4g* a8.5g³ a8.5g⁴ a8.5g³ 9.9m 10m⁴ a12g* a12g a12g⁵ a9.4s⁴ a9.4g* a9.4g³ 1999 a12g* a12g a12g⁵ a12g² a12g⁶ a10g 12d a12f³ a10g⁵ a12g* a16.2g⁵ a10g² a10g2 Dec 22] lengthy gelding: fair performer: won handicap at Wolverhampton in January and claimer at Lingfield in November: stays easy 1½m: acts on all-weather, lightly raced and little recent form on turf: blinkered/visored: often forces pace. *N. P. Littmoden*   **–** **a77**

FAIR CESTRIAN (IRE)   3 b.g. Petardia 113 – Fair Chance (Young Emperor 133) [1998 –: 6m 5s 7.5m 6m 1999 10.5m 17.2m 10g 7.1m 8d Oct 20] leggy gelding: little form: blinkered final start. *A. Bailey*   **–**

FAIR FLIGHT   3 b.g. Green Desert (USA) 127 – Barari (USA) (Blushing Groom (FR) 131) [1998 98p: 6s 7m⁴ 6f⁴ 7g* 8m² 8d 8m* 1999 8g 8.5g 8.5g³ 8s* 8m 7.9f³ 8f 8m Aug 30] good-topped gelding: useful performer: won 3-runner minor event at Goodwood in June: creditable efforts in handicaps next 2 starts only: stays 1m well: acts on firm and soft ground: sent to Singapore. *E. A. L. Dunlop*   **97**

FAIR IMPRESSION (IRE)   2 ch.f. (Mar 29) Arazi (USA) 135 – Al Najah (USA) 96 (Topsider (USA)) [1999 6s 7d² Oct 27] angular filly: has a round action: sixth foal: closely related to 3-y-o Direct Deal and half-sister to useful sprinter Tabook (by Cadeaux Genereux) and a winner in Sweden by Mujtahid: dam 8.5f winner: better effort in maidens when 1½ lengths second of 11 to Shaibani at Yarmouth: should stay 1m: may improve further. *E. A. L. Dunlop*   **76**

FAIR LADY 2 b.f. (Mar 1) Machiavellian (USA) 123 – Just Cause (Law Society **76** (USA) 130) [1999 7s 7m² 8d⁶ Oct 22] leggy, quite attractive filly: sixth foal: closely related to 6f to 1m winner Committal (useful in Britain, later won in France/USA at 6f to 1½m, by Lycius) and half-sister to 3 winners, including useful 1994 2-y-o 7f/1m winner Jural (by Kris) who stayed 11f: dam unraced: fair maiden: creditable efforts at Salisbury (second of 11) and Doncaster (sixth of 18) final 2 starts: should stay beyond 1m. *B. W. Hills*

FAIRLY SURE (IRE) 6 b.m. Red Sunset 120 – Mirabiliary (USA) 74 (Crow **38** (FR) 134) [1998 –: a6g a8.5g 7m 8m⁵ 1999 a8g⁵ a7g a8g a10g 10f 10.2m* 10.1f⁶ 9.9v Sep 29] poor handicapper: 66/1, easily best effort for some time when dead-heating with Twin Time at Bath in July: stays 1¼m: acts on firm going and equitrack, tailed off on heavy. *N. E. Berry*

FAIRTOTO 3 b.g. Mtoto 134 – Fairy Feet 78 (Sadler's Wells (USA) 132) [1998 **55** –p: 8g 8.2d 8g 1999 a12g 10s a14.8g³ Oct 13] leggy, plain gelding: modest maiden: likely to stay 2m+: acts on fibresand, best turf run on good going. *D. J. Wintle*

FAIR VERONA (USA) 3 b.f. Alleged (USA) 138 – Just Juliet (USA) (What A **–** Pleasure (USA)) [1998 NR 1999 8g 8g Aug 30] half-sister to 1996 2-y-o 7f winner Julietta Mia (by Woodman) and several winners abroad: dam, 2-y-o sprint winner in USA, half-sister to US Grade 1 winners Tis Juliet and Stella Madrid: well held in maidens. *B. W. Hills*

FAIR WARNING (GER) 3 b.c. Warning 136 – Fairy Bluebird 66 (Be My Guest **102** (USA) 126) [1998 85: 6f³ 1999 8m³ 8g³ 8g* 8m³ 8m 9m 8m 10g⁴ 11.9d* 12d² Oct 14] angular, workmanlike colt: useful performer: won maiden at Yarmouth in June and minor event at York (best effort to beat Dark Trojan by 3½ lengths) in October: creditable second to Katiykha in rated stakes at Newmarket final start: stays 11½m: acts on good to soft going. *J. W. Hills*

FAIRY CONTESSA (IRE) 3 b.f. Fairy King (USA) – More Fizz (Morston (FR) **63** 125) [1998 NR 1999 7m 6f² 7g⁴ 6f³ Oct 30] IR 110,000Y: closely related to Australian 6.5f winner Rock Point (by Sadler's Wells) and half-sister to several winners, including useful 1m (at 2 yrs) and 10.2f winner Success And Glory (by Alzao) and 1991 Gimcrack winner River Falls (by Aragon), later successful at 1m: dam French 9f winner from good family: modest maiden: below form final 2 starts, including on all-weather debut at Wolverhampton: stays 7f: raced only on good going or firmer on turf: usually tongue tied: has taken good hold. *N. P. Littmoden*

FAIRY FLAME 3 b.f. Fairy King (USA) – Favoridge (USA) 122 (Riva Ridge **73** (USA)) [1998 NR 1999 7m⁴ 6m⁶ May 26] eighth living foal: half-sister to 3 winners, including fairly useful 1992 2-y-o 5f to 6.5f winner Falsoola (by Kris) and 1m winner Vote In Favour (by General Assembly): dam, very smart sprinting 2-y-o who later stayed 1m, from excellent family: much better effort in maidens when 3 lengths fourth of 16 at Kempton: dead. *Sir Michael Stoute*

FAIRY GEM (IRE) 2 b.f. (Mar 21) Fairy King (USA) – Cajo (IRE) (Tirol 127) **95** [1999 5m* 5m² 5m 6m⁶ 7.1g⁴ 7m⁶ 7s Oct 2] IR 36,000Y: compact, quite attractive filly: first foal: dam unraced: useful performer: won minor event at Salisbury in May: best efforts when 3½ lengths fourth of 7 in Solario Stakes at Sandown and sixth of 12 in Moyglare Stud Stakes at the Curragh following start: should stay 1m: acts on good to firm ground, never going well on soft: attended by 2 handlers at Sandown. *R. Hannon*

FAIRY GODMOTHER 3 b.f. Fairy King (USA) – Highbrow 112§ (Shirley **113** Heights 130) [1998 NR 1999 10d* 10d* Jun 10] sixth foal: half-sister to 3 winners at 1¼m or more, including 4-y-o Blueprint: dam, 2-y-o 1m winner later second in Ribblesdale Stakes, from family of Height of Fashion (dam of Nashwan and Unfuwain): smart form: won maiden at Newbury in May (swished tail) and 6-runner listed event there following month, in latter beating Ras Shaikh comfortably by 1¼ lengths: will stay 1½m: has worn blanket for stalls/crossed noseband. *R. Charlton*

FAIRY PRINCE (IRE) 6 b.g. Fairy King (USA) – Danger Ahead (Mill Reef **69** (USA) 141) [1998 76: 5.1g 6g² 6m 6g⁵ 6m 5g* 5m² 6m 5m⁴ 5.7m⁶ 6m² 6g 1999 6m 6m 6s 7m 7m⁵ 7.1d⁵ 7m² 7.6f² 7f² 6.9m⁶ 6g² 5.7f a6g Oct 16] leggy gelding: fair performer: stays 7.6f: acts on firm going (probably on soft), well beaten on fibresand final start: visored (ran well) eleventh outing. *Mrs A. L. M. King*

Ribblesdale Stakes, Royal Ascot—
Fairy Queen proves well suited by the step up in trip in winning from Samoa (left) and Alabaq

FAIRY QUEEN (IRE)   3 b.f. Fairy King (USA) – Dedicated Lady (IRE) 101   **116**
(Pennine Walk 120) [1998 102p: 7g* 7.1m* 1999 8m 8.5d* 12m* 12m⁴ 12.5v*
10s⁴ Nov 7]

     The reliability of Godolphin's private pre-season trials in Dubai was
shown again in 1999 when Almutawakel and Island Sands followed up their
'wins' with immediate Group 1 victories. Although Fairy Queen did not reach
those heights, initially being aimed at the One Thousand Guineas after her own
Dubai trial victory, she did prove herself a smart filly over middle distances
later in the season, winning the Ribblesdale Stakes at Royal Ascot and the Prix
de Royallieu Hotel du Golf Barriere on Arc weekend.
     After the Prix de Royallieu, the main headlines were made by Thierry
Jarnet's twenty-day ban for easing prematurely after the first winning post. In
truth, Fairy Queen was a lucky winner, getting up close home to beat Jarnet's
mount Daring Miss and another British-trained challenger Abyaan by three

Prix de Royallieu Hotel du Golf Barriere, Longchamp—
confusion as two riders ease up at the wrong winning post; Fairy Queen (second right) takes full advantage
and goes on to beat Daring Miss (No.5) and the blinkered Abyaan

Godolphin's "Fairy Queen"

quarters of a length and a neck. Fairy Queen had already achieved smart form when running on gamely under a patient ride to beat Samoa by a length in the Ribblesdale Stakes, but she was not able to secure a Group 1 win, missing the Irish Oaks (which came too soon after Royal Ascot) and coming fourth in both the Prix Vermeille and, when below form, in the Premio Roma. Fairy Queen showed better form over a mile and a half than shorter, but she did win the Vodafone Victress Stakes over an extended mile at Epsom after her unplaced effort in the Guineas (her first race since leaving David Loder).

	Fairy King (USA) (b 1982)	Northern Dancer (b 1961)	Nearctic
			Natalma
		Fairy Bridge (b 1975)	Bold Reason
Fairy Queen (IRE) (b.f. 1996)			Special
	Dedicated Lady (IRE) (b 1989)	Pennine Walk (b 1982)	Persian Bold
			Tifrums
		Salabella (b 1979)	Sallust
			Supreme Lady

Fairy Queen emulated Helissio and Oath in excelling well beyond the average winning distance (just short of a mile) of the progeny of their sire Fairy King, who died in 1999. Fairy Queen is the second living foal of Dedicated Lady, who won three times in Ireland at two over five and six furlongs; she is also the dam of the fair winning two-year-old Speedfit Free, successful over six furlongs. Further back in the pedigree the Irish St Leger winner M-Lolshan was a half-brother to Fairy Queen's grandam, the modest maiden Salabella. Fairy Queen's achievements were no doubt the main reason that Dedicated Lady made 145,000 guineas at the December Sales in foal to Entrepreneur (who is by Fairy King's brother, Sadler's Wells). The quite attractive, quick-actioned Fairy Queen, who was sometimes bandaged behind, acted on good to firm and heavy going. A most game and genuine filly, Fairy Queen will be at stud in 2000. *Saeed bin Suroor*

FAIRYTIME   3 b.f. Efisio 120 – Fairy Flax (IRE) 97 (Dancing Brave (USA) 140)   – [1998 57p: 6d³ 1999 5s 6d 7d 7d 5m Sep 11] sparely-made filly: no show since debut. *J. R. Arnold*

FAITH AGAIN (IRE)   3 b.f. Namaqualand (USA) – Intricacy 65 (Formidable   **54** (USA) 125) [1998 61: 5m⁵ 6s⁵ 7m⁶ 8g 1999 7m 10m 8m² 8.2m⁵ 9m³ 10g⁴ Aug 18] neat filly: modest maiden: probably stays 9f, not 1¼m: acts on good to firm going, probably on soft: blinkered last 4 starts (looked none too keen penultimate one): joined A. Streeter and successful 3 times over hurdles in the autumn. *C. F. Wall*

FAIT LE JOJO (FR)   2 b.g. (May 20) Pistolet Bleu (IRE) 133 – Pretty Davis   **78 +** (USA) (Trempolino (USA) 135) [1999 a8.5g³ a8.5g* Sep 28] 80,000 francs F, 11,500Y: rather unfurnished gelding: has scope: first foal: dam 1¼m winner in France: fairly useful form: best effort when easy winner of maiden at Wolverhampton in September: third outing in as many weeks when beaten at odds on in minor event at Southwell final start: will stay 1¼m+: raced only on fibresand: slowly away first 2 starts. *S. P. C. Woods*

FALCONIDAE   2 ch.c. (Apr 22) Polar Falcon (USA) 126 – Barbary Court (Grundy   **74** 137) [1999 6v⁶ 6d⁴ Nov 4] good-topped colt: seventh foal: half-brother to 3-y-o Turnofacard, 7f winner Noble Pet (by Petong) and fairly useful 1m winner Mazcobar (by Mazilier): dam poor maiden: much better effort in maidens when fourth of 18 to Free Rider at Windsor, keeping on well: will probably stay 1m: may do better still. *P. J. Makin*

FALCON PARTNER (USA)   2 ch.c. (Apr 3) Silver Hawk (USA) 123 – L'Esqui-   – mau (USA) (Arctic Tern (USA) 126) [1999 7m Jul 6] $150,000Y: rather unfurnished colt: first foal: dam, won at up to 9f in USA, half-sister to US Grade 1 1¼m winner Thunder Rumble: weak in market and bandaged behind, last of 9 in maiden at Newmarket: sent to USA. *H. R. A. Cecil*

FALCON SPIRIT   3 b.g. Polar Falcon (USA) 126 – Amina 80 (Brigadier Gerard   **69** 144) [1998 NR 1999 7.6m 7g³ 9f² 10d⁵ 10m⁵ a8.5g³ a12g² 11g Oct 14] 35,000Y: big, lengthy gelding: half-brother to several winners, including 8-y-o Jayannpee and 7f/1m winner Salmino (by Salmon Leap): dam, 1¼m performer, sister to Lancashire Oaks winner Princess Eboli: fair maiden: stays 1½m: acts on firm going and all-weather: has been bandaged behind: blinkered last 4 starts: looked reluctant for long way sixth outing: sold 14,000 gns, joined G. M. Moore. *W. J. Haggas*

FALKENBERG (FR)   4 ch.g. Polish Precedent (USA) 131 – Mithi Al Gamar   – (USA) 68 (Blushing Groom (FR) 131) [1998 65d: a7g⁴ a8s⁶ a7g⁶ a8g⁴ a10g⁵ a7g 6.9d a7g 6d 6.9m³ 7g a7g a8g³ 10m a10g 8m a7g a10g⁵ a10g a10g 1999 a7g a7g⁴ a12g Feb 25] smallish, sturdy gelding: disappointing maiden handicapper: tried blinkered: has looked none too keen. *B. A. Pearce*

FALLACHAN (USA)   3 ch.g. Diesis 133 – Afaff (USA) (Nijinsky (CAN) 138)   **90** [1998 61: 8g 8s a8g⁴ 1999 8g* 8.2d* 8m² 8m⁵ 8f 7m² 7m² 8s Sep 26] angular, good-topped gelding: fairly useful handicapper: won at Musselburgh (maiden event, landed gamble) and Nottingham in April: best efforts when runner-up at Kempton and Doncaster sixth/seventh starts: stays 8.2f: acts on good to soft and good to firm ground, possibly not on soft. *M. A. Jarvis*

FALLS O'MONESS (IRE)   5 b.m. River Falls 113 – Sevens Are Wild 40 (Pet-   **61** orius 117) [1998 61, a42: a10g a9.4g a8g 10s 8s⁴ 10s 8m 8m 9.2s³ 9.1d⁵ 8d⁶ 8m*   **a–** 9.2s³ 8d⁵ 9.1s⁴ 8.1m⁵ 8.3s* 9d³ 8d 1999 9.3m³ 8.3s 8.3g 8m⁶ 10.5s⁴ 8m⁴ 8.1d 8d* 9g 8g 8f⁴ 9.1d³ 8d 8.3s⁵ 8d Oct 20] modest handicapper on turf, poor on all-weather: won seller at Thirsk in August: below best after: best at 1m to 1¼m: acts on firm going, soft and all-weather: tried blinkered/visored earlier in career: often rather headstrong, and usually held up. *E. J. Alston*

FAL 'N' ME   2 b.f. (Feb 27) Cyrano de Bergerac 120 – Azola (IRE) 63 (Alzao   – (USA) 117) [1999 5m a5f a5g Nov 13] 3,000Y: small, sparely-made filly: second foal: half-sister to 3-y-o City Reach: dam, 1m winner, half-sister to very smart miler Sarab: no sign of ability. *J. L. Eyre*

FALSE DAWN 4 b.f. Reprimand 122 – Mardessa 74 (Ardross 134) [1998 –: 7.9g 7.1m 8d 1999 8m 12m 14.1g Jul 3] leggy filly: of little account. *M. Mullineaux*

FAME AT LAST (USA) 2 b.f. (Jan 31) Quest For Fame 127 – Ranales (USA)   **87 p**
(Majestic Light (USA)) [1999 7d* Oct 22] lengthy filly: second foal: half-sister to 3-y-o Theme Tune: dam 2-y-o 1m winner from 2 starts in USA: well-backed second favourite, though green and unimpressive to post, made winning debut in 22-runner maiden at Doncaster, racing in touch after sluggish start and staying on strongly to lead final 1f and beat All The Gears by 1½ lengths: will be suited by 1¼m+: sure to improve and looks a useful performer in the making at least. *B. W. Hills*

FAMILY MAN 6 ch.g. Indian Ridge 123 – Auntie Gladys 49 (Great Nephew 126)   **105**
[1998 88: 8.5m 8f⁵ 9.9d³ 10.1g² 10m 9m⁴ 7g* 8g 7g* 8g 1999 6g 7g⁴ 7m² 7m⁴ 8m 7d² 8m* 7d* 7g² 7s² Oct 23] workmanlike gelding: useful performer: better than ever, winning minor event at Thirsk in August and rated stakes at Newmarket (by neck from Holly Blue) in October: good second final 2 starts: better at 7f than further (needs emphasis to be on speed at 1m): acts on good to firm going and soft: visored second 5-y-o start: travels strongly, has turn of foot and best held up: tough, genuine and consistent: sold 44,000 gns, sent to Saudi Arabia. *J. R. Fanshawe*

FAMILY TREE (IRE) 3 ch.f. Soviet Lad (USA) – The Woman In Red 68 (Red   **–**
Regent 123) [1998 63, a–: 6g⁶ 7d⁴ 6g 7d 8m³ 8d* 8d a7g a8g 1999 a10g a8f a7g 6s 8d a8g 8f May 27] quite attractive filly: modest at best: no form in 1999: tried blinkered: sold 1,800 gns in June, sent to Holland. *D. W. Chapman*

FAMOUS (FR) 6 b.g. Tropular – Famous Horse (FR) (Labus (FR)) [1998 54: 10g   **54**
8.3m 8.1d⁶ 7g⁴ 8d 8m 8g⁵ 8.1m 8m⁶ 9.9m³ 8d 10g² 9.9s a12g⁶ a10g² a10g a10f 1999 a10g a8g² a8g a8g⁶ 8.3m⁶ 8f⁴ 7.7s 9d 10m 10m 8.1m 11.6s⁵ 10d* 12m² 14.1v 10s* 12d 11.9d a10g⁴ a10g⁵ a10g a10g² Dec 22] quite attractive gelding: poor mover: modest handicapper: won apprentice races at Brighton in August and Sandown in October: stays 1½m: acts on firm going, soft and equitrack: rarely blinkered/visored nowadays: none too consistent. *J. J. Bridger*

FANADIYR (IRE) 7 b.g. Kahyasi 130 – Fair Fight 84 (Fine Blade (USA) 121)   **39**
[1998 NR 1999 16m* 12.1m 16m 16d Jun 28] poor performer: won claimer at Musselburgh in April: well beaten in handicaps after: acts on good to firm ground: probably stays 2m: tried blinkered. *J. S. Goldie*

FANCY A FORTUNE (IRE) 5 b.g. Fools Holme (USA) – Fancy's Girl (FR)   **61**
(Nadjar (FR) 128) [1998 63: 7d⁵ 8s 8g 7g* 6.9m³ 8s 7.5d* 8g 8g³ 7g⁴ 7g² 7f 7.5m⁴ 1999 7s⁶ 8d² 8m 8g⁵ 6.9m⁶ 7.5m² 8m 8f⁵ 8d² 8m⁶ 8f² 9.1v Oct 12] lengthy gelding: modest performer: below form final 3 starts: effective at 7f to easy 9f: acts on any going: has won for apprentice: often blinkered, twice visored at 2 yrs: often races prominently/leads. *D. Nicholls*

FANCY DESIGN (IRE) 6 b.m. Cyrano de Bergerac 120 – Crimson Robes 48   **–**
(Artaius (USA) 129) [1998 44, a55d: a7g³ a10g⁵ a8g² a8g a8g a8g⁶ 8g⁶ a10g⁵ 8.3m⁶ 9g 8.3m² 8m 8.3g³ 8.3g 10m 8.3m 1999 8m 10f 12.3m 8f 10f 10m⁶ Aug 23] of little account now. *J. M. Bradley*

FANCY MY CHANCE 3 b.c. Rainbow Quest (USA) 134 – Yazeanhaa (USA)   **85**
68 (Zilzal (USA) 137) [1998 84p: 7m 7m 8g⁴ 7.9g 8d* 1999 10.3d³ 10g 10m 12m⁵ Jul 7] smallish, sparely-made colt: has a round action: fairly useful performer: good third in handicap at Doncaster on reappearance: disappointing after: stays 1¼m: acts on good to soft going: blinkered final start: has hung and possibly not easiest of rides: sold 11,500 gns, sent to Macau. *E. A. L. Dunlop*

FANDANGO DREAM (IRE) 3 ch.c. Magical Wonder (USA) 125 – Fandikos   **68 d**
(IRE) (Taufan (USA) 119) [1998 –: 6g 1999 8m 8s 8.1g⁴ 9.9d⁶ 9m 8m 9.9d⁴ 10.4f 10.3s 10s 10g 10d Oct 21] smallish, angular colt: fair maiden handicapper: ran poorly final 5 starts: stays 1¼m: seems suited by good going or soft: tried blinkered/visored: none too reliable and probably less than genuine. *M. D. I. Usher*

FANETTA (IRE) 3 b.f. Taufan (USA) 119 – Bold Fille (IRE) (Bold Arrangement   **43**
127) [1998 52: 7.5m⁴ 7g 6g⁶ 6m a7g⁶ 1999 a10g 10g 11.6d⁶ 10.5m 10.9g Jul 26] poor maiden: probably stays 11.6f: acts on good to firm going (probably on good to soft): tongue tied final 3 starts. *M. H. Tompkins*

374

FANFARE 2 b.f. (Mar 14) Deploy 131 – Tashinsky (USA) (Nijinsky (CAN) 138) **64**
[1999 8s⁵ 8s Nov 6] angular filly: sixth foal: half-sister to 3 winners, namely 7-y-o
Ten Past Six, useful 7f (at 2 yrs) and 1m winner Harry Wolton (by Distant Relative)
and fairly useful 1¼m and 11f winner Sovereign Page (by Caro): dam, showed
some ability in France, half-sister to very smart miler Mukaddamah: better effort in
maidens when never-nearer fifth of 12 to Top Hand at Bath: never going well at
Doncaster next time: will stay at least 1¼m. *G. A. Butler*

FANNY PARNELL 3 b.f. Local Suitor (USA) 128 – Heart Broken 78 (Bustino **–**
136) [1998 NR 1999 a8g Nov 15] first foal: dam 6f/7f winner: well beaten in seller at
Southwell. *J. G. FitzGerald*

FANTASTIC BELLE (IRE) 3 b.f. Night Shift (USA) – Gay Fantastic (Ela- **79**
Mana-Mou 132) [1998 63p: 6d 5.7g⁶ 1999 7g⁵ 7m² 6.8s² 7m 7.6m² 6m* 6m Sep 16]
close-coupled filly: fluent mover: fair performer: won 6-runner maiden at Salisbury
in July: well held in handicap 7 weeks later: will stay 1m: acts on good to firm
ground: sold 45,000 gns in December. *P. J. Makin*

FANTASTIC DANCE (USA) 3 br.f. Imperial Ballet (IRE) 110 – Fantastic Bid **76**
(USA) (Auction Ring (USA) 123) [1998 54p: 6s⁴ 1999 7g* 8.3m⁴ a7g 7d Oct 22] fair
performer: won maiden at Salisbury in August: form after in handicaps only on next
outing: stays 1m: acts on good to firm going: sweating/edgy final start. *P. J. Makin*

FANTASTIC FANTASY (IRE) 2 b.f. (Feb 28) Lahib (USA) 129 – Gay **64 p**
Fantasy (Troy 137) [1999 8m³ 8.2g 8d Oct 12] half-sister to several winners,
including 3-y-o Fantasy Hill, 4-y-o Fantasy Night and useful winners Son of Sharp
Shot (at 1m to 1½m, by Sharp Shot) and Lucky Guest (1m to 1¼m, by Be My Guest):
dam unraced half-sister to Miss Petard: clear signs of ability in Midlands maidens,
though rather disappointing final start: bred to do much better over 1¼m+ at 3 yrs.
J. L. Dunlop

FANTASTIC LIGHT (USA) 3 b.c. Rahy (USA) 115 – Jood (USA) 87 **123**
(Nijinsky (CAN) 138) [1998 103p: 7.1g* 8.1m* 8d³ 1999 10s* 11.5g⁴ 10m²
10m³ 11.9m* 11d* 12v Oct 3]
     There is a good and bad side to Fantastic Light and, after three pattern
victories in 1999, it seems fair to say that the bad side is largely superficial. The
disconcerting thing about him is that he is so often among the first, if not *the*
first, to come off the bridle. After his debut win in August as a two-year-old, he
was niggled along even when the pace was steady and *Timeform Perspective*
observed that this was down to greenness. Now, with another nine outings to
consider, we can probably conclude that it wasn't. He may require some riding
to find his rhythm, but from ten career outings Fantastic Light has won five.
In this case, being the first pushed along does not equate to being the first
beaten. Dehoush by a short head, Bienamado by a length and a quarter and
High-Rise by three quarters of a length—Fantastic Light made hard work of all

Stakis Casinos Great Voltigeur Stakes, York—
Fantastic Light runs on strongly ahead of Bienamado (left), Glamis (right) and Mutafaweq

Dubai Arc Trial, Newbury—Fantastic Light and High-Rise (right) pull clear of Pegnitz

those victories in the latest season, but the names of the runners-up suggest that he made impressive progress. That impression is not misleading.

Fantastic Light's season began in underwhelming fashion, even in victory. It was an exciting race, but the Thresher Classic Trial at Sandown can seldom have had less of a bearing on classic calculations, not least because the first two did not have an Epsom entry. At that stage, connections seemed firmly of the belief that Fantastic Light would not stay a mile and a half. Prior to the race, there had also been a strong body of opinion that he would not act on soft ground—his only defeat as a two-year-old had come on good to soft—but this victory at the first time of asking as a three-year-old appeared to scotch that. With the Easter Stakes winner Dehoush setting just a fair pace, Darryll Holland sensibly kept Fantastic Light in close attendance, but, less sensibly, when Fantastic Light had only just got the better of a protracted battle, dropped his hands a few strides before the post so that the issue required the judge's magnifying glass. Fantastic Light had been sent off at 13/2 in a seven-runner field, looking rather burly beforehand. The 11/10 favourite was Glamis, who finished one and a quarter lengths back in third on his first outing in a visor.

Soon it was suggested that Fantastic Light, too, should be sporting headgear. The Lingfield Derby Trial was his next appearance, a fact-finding mission to see whether he should be supplemented into the Derby field. Joe Mercer, the owner's racing manager, now observed: 'Michael [Stoute] thinks the colt will get a mile and a half. We would like to lead, but he travelled so well at Sandown it's not too much of a worry. We're looking for a big run.' None of which bore much relation to what happened at Lingfield; getting rather warm in the preliminaries, Fantastic Light was on and off the bridle from halfway, and, having posed a brief threat, he hung to his left and was beaten off over a furlong out, finishing only fourth of five. He was not supplemented for the Derby.

Sweating in the preliminaries, running in snatches and tending to hang were all seen again from him later in the season, but the disappointing Fantastic Light of Lingfield was not, and in his next four races he proved himself one of Britain's very best middle-distance three-year-olds. First, back at a mile and a quarter, he played a big part in wholehearted finishes to the Prince of Wales's Stakes and the Eclipse Stakes: a head was his margin of defeat by Lear Spear at Royal Ascot; he came a neck and half a length behind Compton Admiral and Xaar at Sandown. Fantastic Light's next two performances showed that he did after all stay beyond a mile and a quarter. The steadily-run Great Voltigeur

Stakes at York did not represent a stiff examination at a mile and a half, but Fantastic Light had clearly the best answers to the test that was provided. Hitting the front three furlongs out—too soon according to his jockey Gary Stevens—he went a length and a half clear soon afterwards and then had the stamina and resolution to maintain his effort ahead of Bienamado, Glamis and Mutafaweq. Having seen the way in which Fantastic Light stuck to his guns here, and indeed at Royal Ascot and Sandown before that, it was not a great surprise to see him find too much for a ring-rusty High-Rise when battle was joined over the last three furlongs in the listed Dubai Arc Trial (over eleven furlongs) at Newbury the following month. The Arc itself proved much too stiff a task for him, but by then Fantastic Light had already had a highly successful season.

	Rahy (USA) (ch 1985)	Blushing Groom (ch 1974)	Red God Runaway Bride
Fantastic Light (USA) (b.c. 1996)		Glorious Song (b 1976)	Halo Ballade
	Jood (USA) (b 1989)	Nijinsky (b 1967)	Northern Dancer Flaming Page
		Kamar (b 1976)	Key To The Mint Square Angel

Fantastic Light returned his sire to prominence in Britain for the first time since Rahy was a smart two-year-old in 1987. After fracturing a pastern, he won just a Brighton minor event from three more starts as a three-year-old before he was packed off to the United States. As a sire, Rahy enjoyed similarly fleeting two-year-old glory in Britain with Applaud and Raphane, and the smart handicap wins of Hawksley Hill. As both racehorse and sire, however, Rahy has enjoyed far greater success in the United States. In the former role, he won the Grade 2 Bel Air Handicap over a mile by ten lengths; in the latter he has had

Maktoum Al Maktoum's "Fantastic Light"

a champion in Serena's Song, another Grade 1 winning filly in Exotic Wood, and the multiple wins and Breeders' Cup Mile second of the aforementioned Hawksley Hill.

Fantastic Light, his sire and the broodmare Jood have all carried the colours of Maktoum Al Maktoum; Fantastic Light is home bred, the other two both cost him 2,000,000 dollars as yearlings. For Jood, Fantastic Light (her third foal) represents the first major return on that investment. The princely sum of £1,215 came back when she finished third in two maiden races, a 2/1 favourite on both occasions. Jood's first two foals, the Mr Prospector pair Madraar and Wanice, did rather better when winning in Dubai and France respectively, but this is a pedigree peppered with major earners. Most immediately, Jood is a half-sister to Canadian champion Key To The Moon, a triple US Grade 1 winner in Gorgeous, a Kentucky Oaks winner in Seaside Attraction and, in Britain, the Princess Margaret Stakes winner Hiaam. Their dam Kamar and grandam Square Angel were both champion three-year-olds in Canada. Of more recent fame, both sides of Fantastic Light's pedigree have provided outstanding older-horse flag-bearers for Sheikh Mohammed; Rahy is a half-brother to Singspiel and Kamar is a sister to Love Smitten, the Grade 1 winning dam of Swain. It may be too much to ask of Fantastic Light for him to emulate that pair's achievements, but it is not too hard to imagine that he too will improve his racecourse record. A strong, lengthy colt and a fluent mover, he stays a mile and a half and acts on soft and good to firm ground; the going was heavy when he was well beaten in the Arc. He often sweats and runs in snatches, and it would not be a surprise to see him in blinkers or a visor, but, to reiterate, none of these supposedly worrying traits seem to have affected his reliability greatly. *Sir Michael Stoute*

FANTASY 2 ch.f. (Feb 22) Cadeaux Genereux 131 – Elfin Laughter 76 (Alzao (USA) 117) [1999 5m⁴ 7m² Jun 26] leggy, lengthy filly: first foal: dam 2-y-o 7.5f and 1m winner: ½-length second of 4 in maiden at Doncaster in June, flashing tail under pressure: stays 7f: sent to USA. *R. Hannon* **80**

FANTASY ADVENTURER 2 b.g. (Feb 15) Magic Ring (IRE) 115 – Delicious 51 (Dominion 123) [1999 6g 5m⁴ a6f Oct 2] 7,000Y: first foal: dam, lightly-raced maiden, half-sister to useful 2-y-o 5f/6f winner (later stayed 1¼m) Anthelia: easily best effort in maidens when fourth of 14 to Elvington Boy at Ripon in August, still seeming green: well held on all-weather: should stay at least 6f. *J. J. Quinn* **60**

FANTASY HILL (IRE) 3 b.g. Danehill (USA) 126 – Gay Fantasy (Troy 137) [1998 75+: 7g³ 7g⁵ 8.2m⁵ 1999 12.3d⁴ 14.1f* 14.1g³ 14.8d 16.5s² Nov 6] useful handicapper: won 5-runner event at Nottingham in May: good second of 15 to Il Principe at Doncaster final start, staying on well despite wandering: gelded afterwards: likely to stay beyond 2m: acts on firm and soft going: lightly raced, and should do better still. *J. L. Dunlop* **101 p**

FANTASY NIGHT (IRE) 4 b.g. Night Shift (USA) – Gay Fantasy (Troy 137) [1998 78: 10.2s² 11g² 12m⁴ 12m* 14.1g⁴ 14.1g³ 11.9f⁴ 9.9m 1999 10s² 10m 12m⁵ 14g⁴ 15.8m* 15.9m³ 16f² 15.9d* 16d³ Sep 19] smallish gelding: useful handicapper: won at Warwick in June and Chester (despite trying to bite a rival) in August: better at 2m than shorter: acts on firm and soft going: held up. *J. L. Dunlop* **95**

FANTAZIA 3 b.f. Zafonic (USA) 130 – Trescalini (IRE) (Sadler's Wells (USA) 132) [1998 71: 8g³ 7.5m⁶ 8v⁶ 1999 8.2m³ 8m 9.9s⁵ 10f* 11m* 10m* Aug 28] leggy, close-coupled filly: fairly useful handicapper: won at Redcar in July and August, and Newmarket final start: stays 11f: acts on firm going, below form both starts on going softer than good: should be capable of better still. *J. R. Fanshawe* **89 p**

FAN-TC GEM 3 b.f. Lugana Beach 116 – Florac (IRE) 59 (Sayf El Arab (USA) 127) [1998 49: 5m a5g a5g⁴ 1999 a6g Nov 17] poor maiden: well beaten only 3-y-o start. *J. Balding* **–**

FARAJ 2 ch.c. (Mar 14) Mizoram (USA) 105 – Petite Butterfly 67 (Absalom 128) [1999 7v⁶ 7.1g Nov 3] third foal: brother to fairly useful 1998 2-y-o 6f winner **68**

378

Laabed: dam 6f/7f winner: sixth in maiden at Lingfield: sustained fatal injury at Musselburgh. *M. Johnston*

FARAWAY LASS 6 b.m. Distant Relative 128 – Vague Lass 85 (Vaigly Great **86** 127) [1998 94: 6m 5.2g 6m² 6m* 6g² 5m⁴ 6d a7g 1999 6g 6m 6m² 6m Sep 11] rangy mare: fluent mover: fairly useful performer: creditable efforts final 2 starts, though looked none too keen on penultimate outing: effective at 5f/6f: acts on firm going (stiff task on good to soft). *D. J. Coakley*

FARAWAY MOON 3 gr.f. Distant Relative 128 – Moon Magic 62 (Polish **61** Precedent (USA) 131) [1998 61p: 6s⁶ 1999 8m⁵ 7f³ 9.7d 8m 6.1g³ a7g a6g a8g² Nov 26] lengthy, sparely-made filly: modest maiden: stays 1m: acts on firm going and equitrack. *Lady Herries*

FARCEUR DU MESNIL (FR) 6 b.g. Pharly (FR) 130 – Grundygold (FR) **47** (Grundy 137) [1998 NR 1999 a11g Jun 28] sixth foal: half-brother to 3 winners in France: dam French 1¼m to 11.5f winner: useful performer at around 1½m for R. Litt in France, winning 4 times including listed race at Dax at 3 yrs: ran only once at 4 yrs and joined present stable for 10,500 gns in August 1998: blinkered, poor form only outing on Flat in Britain. *K. A. Morgan*

FAR CRY (IRE) 4 b.g. Pharly (FR) 130 – Darabaka (IRE) (Doyoun 124) **117** [1998 81p: a6g 7.6g 6.1g⁵ a8.5g a12g* a14g* a12g* 1999 a16f* a16g³ a16.2g* 16g* 20m² 16.1m* 18m* 17.3g⁵ Oct 16]

It's a far cry from defeat off a mark of 62 under the floodlights at Wolverhampton to success in the Doncaster Cup, but Far Cry managed the transition in less than ten months. What's more, for good measure, he won the Northumberland Plate in between and went on to establish himself as a Champion Hurdle contender by the end of the year.

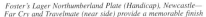

Foster's Lager Northumberland Plate (Handicap), Newcastle—
Far Cry and Travelmate (near side) provide a memorable finish

Great North Eastern Railway Doncaster Cup, Doncaster—Far Cry (rail) shows further improvement, gamely holding off Rainbow High and Celeric (left)

The ignominy of that Wolverhampton run, in November 1998, was soon forgotten when Far Cry rattled up a hat-trick of successes at longer trips by the year's end. Wins in handicaps at Southwell and back at Wolverhampton followed in February and March, but, in between, Far Cry was beaten at odds on at Lingfield, the horse's only run on equitrack, and few eyebrows were raised when connections parted with him for 35,000 guineas at the end of March. The first return came when Far Cry took the Milcars Queen's Prize at Kempton five days after his sale, with new trainer Martin Pipe giving credit to previous handler Sir Mark Prescott for the success. No such modesty was required from Pipe when Far Cry won a thrilling race for the Foster's Lager Northumberland Plate at Newcastle in June by a short head from Travelmate, having run second to High And Mighty in the Ascot Stakes shortly before. Far Cry's victory in Europe's most valuable two-mile handicap took his win and place prize money in this first three months with Pipe to over £90,000.

Far Cry reappeared ten weeks later facing a stiffer task in the GNER Doncaster Cup. Far Cry again rose to the occasion, kicked into the lead four furlongs out following a steady early pace and responding to his rider's every call to hold Rainbow High by a head, with Celeric a length and a quarter back in third. The win prize money was just £23,650 but the prestige was worth more, even though Far Cry was a gelding. Far Cry reverted to handicap company for his only subsequent start on the Flat in the Tote Cesarewitch at Newmarket. He lost little caste in defeat in finishing under four lengths fifth to Top Cees off a mark of 103, actually doing best of those who raced prominently from some way out in a race run at a good pace.

When Far Cry's attentions were turned to hurdling—connections evidently regarded his successes on the Flat as 'just a bonus'—he quickly made his mark, winning at Newbury in November most impressively and putting up a high-class effort when a neck second to Relkeel in the BonusPrint Bula Hurdle at Cheltenham.

Far Cry (IRE) (b.g. 1995)	Pharly (FR) (ch 1974)	Lyphard (b 1969)	Northern Dancer
			Goofed
		Comely (ch 1966)	Boran
			Princesse Comnene
	Darabaka (IRE) (b 1990)	Doyoun (b or br 1985)	Mill Reef
			Dumka
		Darazina (b 1979)	Labus
			Djebellina

Far Cry, who cost 5,000 guineas as a foal and 26,000 Irish guineas as a yearling, is the second foal of the unraced Darabaka, following the French mile and a quarter winner Dariyba (by Kahyasi). Darabaka herself is a half-sister to the smart French middle-distance filly (winner of the Prix Minerve) Daralinsha and also to Darata, the dam of the latest Prix de Diane and Prix Vermeille winner Daryaba. Far Cry's sire, Pharly, has been largely an influence for stamina, despite being best up to a mile and a quarter himself. In 1999 he was also responsible for the Queen's Vase third and Gordon Stakes winner Compton Ace, as well as the high-class hurdler Wahiba Sands. Far Cry, who has raced only on good and good to firm going on turf, stays two and a quarter miles but is by no means a one-paced plodder. He needs to improve further to get to the top of the staying division in 2000, but that is not out of the question. *M. C. Pipe*

FARFIELDS PRINCE 7 b.g. Weldnaas (USA) 112 – Coca (Levmoss 133) [1998 – NR 1999 a11g 10.1d Oct 20] leggy gelding: poor maiden handicapper, lightly raced: has looked difficult ride. *G. M. Moore*

FARHAN (USA) 5 b.g. Lear Fan (USA) 130 – Mafatin (IRE) 74 (Sadler's Wells – (USA) 132) [1998 NR 1999 a12g Jul 24] big, lengthy gelding: fairly useful performer at best: well beaten in seller, only run since 1997. *K. A. Morgan*

FARMOST 6 ch.g. Pharly (FR) 130 – Dancing Meg (USA) 113 (Marshua's Dancer **85** (USA)) [1998 –: a10g 1999 8.1s 8m 8.5d 10d 9m³ 10f² 10.2g* 10.3m* 9f* 10.1m **a94** a10g* Nov 23] big, good-topped gelding: fairly useful performer: won handicaps at Chepstow and Chester and minor event at Redcar in the summer and handicap at Lingfield in November: best at 9f/1¼m: acts on all-weather, firm and good to soft going: twice refused to enter stalls in 1999: usually races up with pace. *Sir Mark Prescott*

FAR MOUNT 2 ch.c. (Apr 1) Bluebird (USA) 125 – One False Move (IRE) 99 **99** (Don't Forget Me 127) [1999 a6g* 5m* 6m* 6f 6s³ Sep 16] smallish, workmanlike colt: has a quick action: first foal: dam Irish 7f and 9f winner: useful performer: won maiden at Wolverhampton in June and small-field minor events at Beverley and Doncaster in July: well beaten when second favourite for Richmond Stakes at Goodwood and again when blinkered on final start: should stay 7f: acts on good to firm going and fibresand: sold 23,000 gns, sent to Saudi Arabia. *Sir Mark Prescott*

FAR REMOVED (IRE) 4 b.g. Distant Relative 128 – Cormorant Creek 73 **80** (Gorytus (USA) 132) [1998 80: 6s 8m 8g 8g³ 7m² 8m* 7d 7.1m³ 7g 8.2v⁴ 1999 8d 7f⁴ 8m 7m³ 7m⁴ 8m 8m* 8m⁴ 10g 8d⁵ Oct 21] tall, strong gelding: fairly useful handicapper: won at Redcar in August: effective at 7f/1m: acts on any going: effective visored or not: usually held up. *Mrs V. C. Ward*

FARRFESHEENA (USA) 2 ch.f. (Mar 17) Rahy (USA) 115 – Bevel (USA) **70 +** (Mr Prospector (USA)) [1999 6m⁵ Jun 19] well-made, attractive filly: fourth foal: closely related to 5-y-o 1m winner Bevier (by Nashwan): dam French 1m winner out of half-sister to Ajdal, Formidable and the dam of Arazi: weak 5/4-shot, green and burly, well-held fifth of 9 to Red Letter in minor event at Ascot, slowly away and unable to improve: seemed likely to do better. *D. R. Loder, France*

FARRIER'S GAMBLE 3 ch.f. Belmez (USA) 131 – Chrisanthy 81 (So Blessed – 130) [1998 NR 1999 8.3d Nov 4] half-sister to several winners, including 7f (at 2 yrs) to 1¼m winners Ivan The Terrible (by Siberian Express) and Satis Dancer (by Mashhor Dancer): dam 2-y-o 5f winner who failed to train on: slowly away when tailed off in maiden. *R. M. Flower*

FARRINGDON HILL 8 b.g. Minster Son 130 – Firgrove 73 (Relkino 131) **64 d**
[1998 71: 9.9m⁵ 12d³ 1999 11.5m 12g 12m 12.3m 11.6m³ 12.3g⁵ 14.1m 10m a11g Sep 28] rangy gelding: good mover: modest handicapper: well below form final 3 starts: stays 1¾m: acts on firm and soft going: has been bandaged behind: has won for amateur and often owner-ridden: best blinkered/visored and ridden up with pace: has worn tongue strap: sometimes slowly away: sold 1,500 gns. *D. Sasse*

FAR-SO-LA 4 b.g. Absalom 128 – Fara 66 (Castle Keep 121) [1998 54, a–: 7f* **37**
7m 8m² 7m⁴ 8d a7g a7g a10g⁴ 1999 a8g a7g* a8g 9.7v a8.5g 7m a7g⁵ 7.7m 8f⁶ 8m⁶ **a44**
a8g⁶ Aug 20] poor performer: won seller at Southwell in January: effective at 7f/1m: acts on fibresand, raced mainly on good ground or firmer on turf: blinkered once at 2 yrs: often races up with pace. *Mrs L. C. Jewell*

FAS 3 ch.g. Weldnaas (USA) 112 – Polly's Teahouse 68 (Shack (USA) 118) [1998 **–**
NR 1999 a6g⁵ 6g 6d⁶ 6m a8g 6m 7m 6s Oct 5] lengthy gelding: seventh foal: brother to 5f performer Polly Golightly, 7f winner Seven and a winner in Hong Kong: dam sprint maiden: little form: blinkered final 2 starts. *J. D. Bethell*

FASHION 2 b.f. (Apr 2) Bin Ajwaad (IRE) 119 – New Generation 91 (Young **74 p**
Generation 129) [1999 a8.5g⁴ a8.5g³ 8.3s³ 8d* Oct 18] angular filly: sixth living foal: closely related to Oaks d'Italia winner Bright Generation (won at 6f at 2 yrs, by Rainbow Quest) and half-sister to 3 winners, including fairly useful 1m (at 2 yrs) to 2m winner Moving Out (by Slip Anchor): dam 6f (at 2 yrs) to 1m winner: progressive form: best effort when winning 19-runner nursery at Pontefract in October by neck from Double Red, getting up close home after being checked entering straight: will stay at least 1¼m: should develop into a fairly useful 3-y-o at least. *Sir Mark Prescott*

FASHION VICTIM 4 b.g. High Estate 127 – Kirkby Belle 44 (Bay Express 132) **40**
[1998 –: 12g 1999 10.3f 8.2m 7.5v 7m 10d 9g⁶ 8.3m 10m 9v Sep 20] close-coupled gelding: poor handicapper at best nowadays: stays 9f: acts on good to firm and soft ground: sold 800 gns in November, joined M. Tate. *T. H. Caldwell*

FASLIYEV (USA) 2 b.c. (Feb 9) Nureyev (USA) 131 – Mr P'S Princess **120**
(USA) (Mr Prospector (USA)) [1999 5m* 5g* 6m* 6d* 6s* Aug 22]
      Now you see him, now you don't! After five starts and five wins involving 5m 41.69sec of action, Fasliyev has been retired to Coolmore Stud in County Tipperary at a fee of IR 25,000 guineas (October 1st). For the purposes of comparison, Daylami retires to Gilltown Stud at a fee of IR £20,000 (October 1st) after twenty-one starts, eleven wins and just under forty-four minutes of action. The comparison is not strictly fair, since it is hardly Fasliyev's fault that injury curtailed his career before he had the opportunity to contest the classics—at the time of the accident he was 6/1 second favourite for the Two Thousand Guineas. But it can be seen as a comment on the commercial reality of bloodstock breeding in Europe, where having a stone in hand in ability counts for little if a horse doesn't also have a stone in hand in pedigree. The injury Fasliyev sustained was a fracture to a pastern when he was cantering in a paddock reportedly just a day after being announced a non-runner in the Dewhurst Stakes and retired for the season. He was operated on successfully at the Troytown Equine Hospital at the Curragh, having five pins inserted into his fetlock, and with no problems developing he is expected to be covering in the spring. He will doubtless be well patronised in his new home, which is at the leading edge of commercial stallion management and gives its sires plenty to do. In 1999 two of the stud's freshmen, Peintre Celebre and Victory Note, covered 120 and 137 mares respectively, while Sadler's Wells covered 162, Grand Lodge 167, Entrepreneur 152, Danehill 147 and Spectrum 146.
      Fasliyev can also be advertised as a racetrack champion, since he topped the International Classification for two-year-olds by the considerable margin of 5 lb on the basis of his victory in the seven-runner Prix Morny at

Deauville in late-August. It is rare to have a champion who did not contest either the Dewhurst Stakes, Racing Post Trophy or Grand Criterium—Warning, who won the Champagne Stakes, and Machiavellian, successful in the Prix de la Salamandre, are the only other examples since the Classifications commenced in 1977. This doesn't mean that the top two-year-old has to run in one of the late-season events. Indeed, there's no reason why a Prix Morny-winning performance shouldn't head the table, but, in our opinion, the 1999 Morny was not quite the best juvenile race of the year and for winning it, even in the style he did, Fasliyev isn't rated so highly as Distant Music. Though unbeaten, Fasliyev did not start favourite at Deauville, partly because Sheikh Mohammed/Godolphin had three runners who were coupled in the race, but also because Fasliyev's victory in the Heinz 57 Phoenix Stakes at Leopardstown a fortnight earlier had been less than impressive. He had hung across the course in beating perennial runner-up Yara by a length and a half at odds of 7/2-on, prompting trainer Aidan O'Brien to admit some time later that the colt was not fully fit for what he described a shade dismissively as 'his comeback race'. O'Brien also said on the Racing Channel, presumably tongue in cheek, that the Phoenix was 'just a bit of work' in preparation for the Morny. Food for thought for the Pattern Committee when they next look at a race which is categorised as one of the finest in Europe for juveniles.

The coupled market leaders for the Morny were the unbeaten pattern-winning trio Warm Heart, successful in the Norfolk Stakes at Royal Ascot, Bachir, who had recently landed the Richmond Stakes, and City On A Hill, whose three victories included a listed race at Chantilly and the July Stakes. Fasliyev was coupled with Grigorovich, runner-up in a listed event at Deauville, and the other contenders were Harbour Island and Mount Abu, first and second in the Prix de Cabourg. Fasliyev lay close up racing freely—he wore a crossed noseband—as Harbour Island and Warm Heart made the running. Hitting the front with less than two furlongs to go, he was pushed clear before being eased near the finish and won by four lengths from Warm Heart, with Bachir two and a half lengths away third and Grigorovich fourth. City On A Hill, probably unsuited by the soft going, ran poorly in last. An impressive display, one which led the BHB's two-year-old handicapper to say: 'I was absolutely thrilled with Fasliyev—even if he never raced again he could be worthy of champion status.' Prophetic words, but prophets are not usually noted for forecasting their own behaviour, and handicappers might be wise to apply the same principle. The remarks quoted above left little room for manoeuvre, hinting as they did that the remainder of the year's top juvenile races, including a stack of Group 1 contests, might be discounted. In the event,

Coventry Stakes, Royal Ascot—
Fasliyev is already being eased; Sir Nicholas and Cornelius follow him home

Prix Morny, Deauville—Fasliyev takes his unbeaten run to five with an impressive display; the Gosden-trained pair Warm Heart and Bachir take the minor placings

none of the horses that finished behind Fasliyev did much racing afterwards and none of them won, though Warm Heart ran respectably to be fourth in the Middle Park Stakes and Bachir finished third to Fasliyev's stable-companion Giant's Causeway in the Prix de la Salamandre. The bias shown towards Fasliyev sadly undermines the work by those responsible for drawing up the International Classification. The assessments of the Prix Morny second and fourth, for example, look more than a little suspect. Warm Heart was beaten as far by the winner of the Middle Park, Primo Valentino, as he was by Fasliyev and seems flattered considerably by his Classification mark of 117. By placing Warm Heart on the same mark as the Middle Park second and third, Fath and Brahms, the Classification certainly does not reflect the result of that race (Warm Heart is also rated only 1 lb inferior to Primo Valentino). The Prix Morny fourth Grigorovich finished last in the Prix de la Salamandre and his merit too is exaggerated by his Classification figure of 112. Those that chased Fasliyev home at Deauville are not top-class horses by any stretch of the imagination, and however good Fasliyev might ultimately have been, he did not, in our view, show himself the champion which the Classification makes him out to be.

The Prix Morny provided Fasliyev's third win in a pattern race, following the Coventry Stakes at Royal Ascot as well as the Phoenix Stakes. Favourite at 15/8 for the eighteen-runner Coventry on the strength of successes gained in a maiden race at Leopardstown in April and the listed Victor Chandler Marble Hill Stakes at the Curragh in May, he trounced his rivals, quickening at will a quarter of a mile out and winning with his ears pricked by two and a half lengths from Sir Nicholas. Filling a gap left by rivals is usually a sensible policy for a jockey, and O'Brien's juveniles are living proof that it's a sensible policy for trainers as well. By the end of the season, when Chiang Mai landed a listed event at Leopardstown, his two-year-olds had won sixty-five races in Europe, including fourteen pattern events, five of them Group 1, putting him well clear in that department. Fasliyev was the leading contributor to both totals.

It is not just a matter of using precocious, fit horses for a series of 'quick-fix' strikes of the sort that suit the financial commitments and expectations of O'Brien's main owners. There is a distinct lack of competition in many two-year-old races in Ireland, and in some respects in Britain and France as well. It helped the O'Brien cause that for various reasons the Godolphin two-year-olds with David Loder had little impact, gaining just two pattern victories, but that was only part of the story. In the last two seasons put together Henry Cecil has garnered fewer wins with his two-year-olds, twenty-three, than in any one of the preceding five years. John Gosden had significantly fewer runners in the latest season than in 1997 or 1998, and between them, Cecil (one) and Gosden ran just eight different horses in the twenty-six British pattern events for two-year-olds in 1999. Barry Hills, John Dunlop and Sir Michael Stoute have maintained their number of active juveniles in recent years, but they were not well represented in these pattern events either, notching a total of nineteen different contestants. For the record, in *Horses In Training* three hundred and sixty-seven two-year-olds were listed under these five trainers. It is difficult to identify any single reason for the shortfall of runners. Prize money for two-year-old pattern races is excellent, and even in maidens, where fit contestants can often profit handsomely from lack of fitness among some of their opponents, the funding is satisfactory.

There is no serious suggestion that the thoroughbred is more fragile than formerly, and few people would claim that training two-year-olds impairs their prospects at three. Indeed, racing at two must be beneficial for a horse with classic pretensions, particularly in the Guineas. That's O'Brien's philosophy, as he said during the season: 'It's good for [two-year-olds] to race as it educates them for their three-year-old careers.' One reason for not having a go may be fear of how the handicapper will rate winning horses, something about which leading trainers have complained on a number of occasions, but this does not really apply to pattern performers. Handicapping is certainly not a problem for O'Brien in Britain, and he has another advantage not possessed by every trainer. He knows that if members of his stable show promise at two, they are in little danger of being purchased by, or transferred to, Godolphin, which has the will and the resources to strengthen its team, and does so regularly. To the list mentioned in our notes on Aljabr last year, which was headed by Cape Verdi, Central Park, Classic Cliche, Moonshell and Mark of Esteem, can now be added Best of The Bests, Fath, Teggiano and Inchlonaig, who left their British trainers at the end of the season to go to Dubai. Whether fear of losing good horses is making some trainers cautious about running juveniles is impossible to prove, and it can hardly explain the full extent of the current situation anyway, but common sense says it may well be a factor. It will be fascinating to see what happens in 2000, when O'Brien is guaranteed to have another powerful team of youngsters.

Fasliyev will not be the first good two-year-old to cover at three after succumbing to injury, and if he does half as well as American champion juveniles Hail To Reason and Raise A Native he will be a success. The former got two first-rate performers, Belmont Stakes winner Hail To All and champion Straight Deal, in his small initial crop, and followed them with around forty more led by Bold Reason, Halo, Priceless Gem, Roberto, Stop The Music and Trillion. Raise A Native produced seventy-eight stakes winners, including twice leading sire Exclusive Native in his first crop, Alydar, Majestic Prince and Mr Prospector. It is in Fasliyev's favour that he's an imposing individual, tall and good-topped—John Gosden, trainer of the second and third in the Morny, jokingly asked 'Are you sure he's not a three-year-old?'—and that he

Mr M. Tabor and Mrs John Magnier's "Fasliyev"

		Northern Dancer (b 1961)	Nearctic
	Nureyev (USA) (b 1977)		Natalma
		Special (b 1969)	Forli
Fasliyev (USA) (b.c. Feb 9, 1997)			Thong
		Mr Prospector (b 1970)	Raise A Native
	Mr P'S Princess (USA) (b 1993)		Gold Digger
		Anne Campbell (b 1973)	Never Bend
			Repercussion

boasts an impressive pedigree. He fetched 450,000 dollars as a yearling at the Keeneland September Sale, where his year-younger half-brother by Kris S, the second foal out of unraced Mr P'S Princess, topped the latest sale at 3,900,000 dollars. Nureyev has been one of the best sires of the last couple of decades, responsible for more than twenty Group 1 or Grade 1 winners, including Theatrical, Miesque, Zilzal, Peintre Celebre and Stravinsky. Although horses like Soviet Star and Zilzal have had their moments as stallions, apart from Theatrical Nureyev's record as a sire of sires has been disappointing up until now. Fasliyev's dam is out of a useful stakes winner who has produced two Grade 1 scorers among seven successful progeny. Anne Campbell's three-year-old Menifee won the Blue Grass Stakes and the Haskell Invitational and was second in the Kentucky Derby and Preakness Stakes, and Desert Wine—maternal grandsire of Aristotle—earned over 1,600,000 dollars, winning eight races including the Hollywood Gold Cup, Charles H. Strub Stakes and Californian Stakes. Another of Anne Campbell's progeny, the English listed winner Arsaan, was by Nureyev. *A. P. O'Brien, Ireland*

FAST AND NEAT (IRE)   3 ch.g. Soviet Lad (USA) – Stop The Cavalry (Relko 136) [1998 –: 6m 6s^6 6.1g 7g 8g 10s 1999 9.9m 11.5m^2 16f^3 12m* 11.9d^3 12m^3 Sep   **60**

8] quite attractive gelding: modest handicapper: won at Salisbury in August: stays 1½m: acts on good to firm going, probably on good to soft: joined R. Guest. *G. Lewis*

FASTBEAT RACING   2 b.f. (Feb 12) Safawan 118 – Little Vixen (Aragon 118)   –
[1999 7.1d Aug 6] 1,200Y: leggy, plain filly: first foal: dam unraced: gave trouble at start before tailed off in Haydock maiden. *A. Senior*

FASTESTBARBERALIVE   4 b.g. Full Extent (USA) 113 – Please Please Me   –
(IRE) 45 (Tender King 123) [1998 NR 1999 6d Oct 28] first live foal: dam poor winning hurdler: 33/1, very edgy and unseated rider leaving stalls in Windsor maiden. *J. J. Bridger*

FAST FORWARD FRED   8 gr.g. Sharrood (USA) 124 – Sun Street 73 (Ile de   –
Bourbon (USA) 133) [1998 63: a12g⁵ 16.4m² 18g* 17.2d² 17.2m* 16.4m* 16m 1999 16.4s Apr 23] big, lengthy gelding: shows knee action: modest handicapper: shaped as though in need of run only start of 1999: stays 2¼m: acts on firm ground. *L. Montague Hall*

FAST FRANC (IRE)   4 ch.g. Paris House 123 – Elle Va Bon (Tanfirion 110)   –
[1998 76d: a6g* a6g* a6g³ a7g* a6g* 7d⁵ 6.1m 6m 6g 6g 7m 7s a7g 1999 a6g a6f a7g 6s 7m Sep 3] workmanlike gelding: fair performer early in 1998: has lost his form. *T. J. Naughton*

FASTRACK TIME   2 ch.g. (Apr 16) Clantime 101 – Bitch 53 (Risk Me (FR)   **59**
127) [1999 5m 5.1g 6m 6.8d 5g Oct 14] 9,500Y: angular gelding: first foal: dam 2-y-o 6f seller winner: modest maiden: best efforts at 5f. *S. Mellor*

FAST TO LIGHT   3 ch.f. Pharly (FR) 130 – Khadino (Relkino 131) [1998 –:   –
7.5m 6g 1999 12s Nov 2] behind in maidens and over hurdles. *N. Tinkler*

FAST TRACK (IRE)   2 b.c. (Mar 20) Doyoun 124 – Manntika 77 (Kalamoun   **93 p**
129) [1999 7d* Oct 27] ninth foal: brother to Irish 7f (National Stakes) and 1m winner Manntari and half-brother to several winners, including 1½m winner Madiyla (by Darshaan): dam 1¼m winner: 6/1, made most encouraging debut when winning 12-runner maiden at Yarmouth by 1½ lengths from Tantalus, settled in rear before coming with strong run to lead final 100 yds: will stay at least 1m: a useful prospect at the very least. *Sir Michael Stoute*

FAST TRICK   2 b.f. (Feb 18) First Trump 118 – Alacrity 62 (Alzao (USA) 117)   **76 ?**
[1999 5d³ 5g⁴ 6f 6g⁴ 8d* 8v³ 8v Oct 26] 1,500Y: second foal: dam 11f winner out of sister to smart 1¼m performer Perpendicular: modest form in 4 starts for R. Whitaker, in valuable seller at York on last of them: seemingly best effort when winning 19-runner claimer at Maisons-Laffitte in September: stays 1m: acts on heavy ground, below form on firm. *J. de Roualle, France*

FASTWAN   3 ch.g. Nashwan (USA) 135 – Jammaayil (IRE) 80 (Lomond (USA)   **35**
128) [1998 –: 8s² 7g 8v⁶ 1999 10m 10.9m 13.1g 12.1m⁴ 10.9s 10.9g⁴ 9.2m⁵ 9m⁶ 9.2m 9.1d Sep 17] poor maiden: stays 11f: acts on good to firm going: usually tongue tied: has been bandaged in front. *J. S. Goldie*

FATEHALKHAIR (IRE)   7 ch.g. Kris 135 – Midway Lady (USA) 126 (Alleged   **70**
(USA) 138) [1998 42: 10.1s⁴ 12.1d² 1999 a12g² 11d* 12m 12g* 12g³ 12m* 13f² 12m⁴ 12f* 12g³ 10.4g Oct 6] leggy, angular gelding: poor mover: useful hurdler: fair handicapper on Flat: had a good season, winning at Redcar in April, Catterick (twice) in June and Thirsk in September: stays 13f: acts on fibresand, firm and good to soft ground: visored once at 4 yrs: all wins on left-handed tracks. *B. Ellison*

FATHER JUNINHO (IRE)   2 b.c. (Mar 18) Distinctly North (USA) 115 –   **91**
Shane's Girl (IRE) (Marktingo) [1999 6d 6m 7m² 7f⁵ 8g 7m* 8.3d² Nov 4] IR 16,000F, 28,000Y: first foal: dam unraced from family of Environment Friend: fairly useful performer: won nurseries at Redcar in July and Doncaster in September: best effort when beaten neck by Imperial Rocket in similar event at Windsor final start: should stay 1¼m: acts on firm and good to soft going. *A. P. Jarvis*

FATHER SKY   8 b.g. Dancing Brave (USA) 140 – Flamenco Wave (USA) 103   **65**
(Desert Wine) [1998 73: a16.2g³ 18d 1999 a16f a16g⁴ a16g 20m 14.8m⁵ 16.2m 14.1m* 14.1g 12m Sep 17] strong, lengthy gelding: fair handicapper: left O. Sherwood after third start: won ladies event at Yarmouth in August: effective at 1¾m/2m: acts on good to firm ground and all-weather: has been blinkered/visored: usually held up: successful over fences in September. *D. L. Williams*

FATH (USA)   2 b.c. (May 2) Danzig (USA) – Desirable 119 (Lord Gayle   **115 p**
(USA) 124) [1999 6g* 6d² Sep 30]

The last two champion sprinters, Elnadim and Stravinsky, both made
their debuts in the Moorestyle Convivial Maiden Stakes at York's August
meeting, and it would be no great surprise if the next one turns out to have done
the same. There are two candidates from the five Convivial runners, but the one
with probably the better credentials is the winner Fath. As with Stravinsky,
Fath will no doubt start off his three-year-old season, when he'll be racing for
Godolphin, being prepared for the Two Thousand Guineas. While Fath's
pedigree suggests that he should stay a mile, his performances in his two races
to date suggest he'll prove more effective at shorter distances, and that he'll end
up being campaigned as a sprinter.

Around half an hour after Stravinsky had captured the Nunthorpe
Stakes, his stable-companion Van Dantzig was sent off favourite for the
Convivial, just ahead of Fath, with the other newcomers Tough Speed and Kier
Park next in the betting and the well-exposed Garth Pool the rank outsider.
Fath, a smallish, good-topped individual, was rather overshadowed in the
paddock, but it was very much the reverse in the race itself. He travelled
strongly from the start, moved easily into the lead two furlongs out and, despite
running green and hanging left off the bridle, readily quickened clear. At the
line Fath, who was eased a little close home, had two lengths to spare over
Tough Speed, who finished well to snatch second place from Van Dantzig,
while Kier Park was four lengths behind the winner in fourth. Tough Speed
went on to win a minor event at Doncaster and Van Dantzig a maiden at Naas
(though he didn't have to reproduce the York form), while Kier Park was
successful twice, including in the Cornwallis Stakes at Ascot. Fath also did his
bit for the form, even though he didn't manage to win. Taking on five much
more experienced rivals in the Middle Park Stakes at Newmarket, Fath ran a
cracking race to finish second, beaten a neck by Primo Valentino, who was
completing a five-timer. As at York, Fath raced freely early on, tracking Primo
Valentino, who was able to dictate the pace. Responding well when asked to
challenge, Fath went upsides the leader going into the final furlong but couldn't
quite sustain his effort near the finish. If Fath is to stay further he'll need to
become more amenable to restraint.

Moorestyle Convivial Maiden Stakes, York—
Fath quickens clear of (from left to right) Tough Speed, Van Dantzig and Kier Park

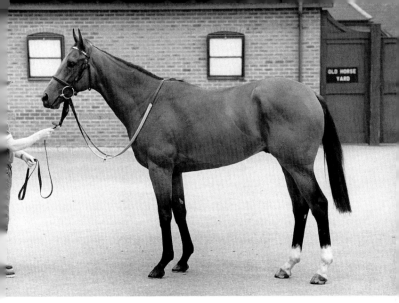

Hamdan Al Maktoum's "Fath"

Fath (USA) (b.c. May 2, 1997)	Danzig (USA) (b 1977)	Northern Dancer (b 1961)	Nearctic
			Natalma
		Pas de Nom (b or br 1968)	Admiral's Voyage
			Petitioner
	Desirable (gr 1981)	Lord Gayle (b 1965)	Sir Gaylord
			Sticky Case
		Balidaress (gr 1973)	Balidar
			Innocence

By Elnadim's sire Danzig out of the Cheveley Park winner and One Thousand Guineas third Desirable, Fath is a brother to the smart Dumaani. Dumaani finished twelfth of twenty-three in the 1994 Two Thousand Guineas then went on to show better form over seven furlongs before leaving Britain, subsequently winning pattern races in Japan and the USA. Fath, who is Desirable's ninth foal, is a half-brother to three winners, notably the 1991 One Thousand Guineas winner Shadayid (by Shadeed). Desirable is a half-sister to the Irish Oaks winner Alydaress and to another Cheveley Park winner Park Appeal, as well as the latter's brother, the smart Irish middle-distance colt Nashamaa. Success for this excellent family has spread still wider in recent years, with Shadayid producing the One Thousand Guineas third Bint Shadayid, Park Appeal the high-class miler Cape Cross (she's also the grandam of Diktat) and Alydaress the 1997 Prix Cleopatre winner Allurement. Fath's grandam Balidaress won from seven to ten furlongs as well as being placed over hurdles. Fath looks sure to continue to play his part in the family's success story. Shortly before the Middle Park his trainer said of Fath that 'He'll be a much nicer colt next season. He's growing and developing all the time—he's not big at the moment—but you can see where he will fill out.' Further improvement from Fath would seem to be very much on the cards.
M. P. Tregoning

FATINA 3 ch.f. Nashwan (USA) 135 – Gharam (USA) 108 (Green Dancer (USA) **98**
132) [1998 79p: 8d* 1999 10g⁴ Jul 2] strong, well-made filly: good mover: won
maiden at Doncaster in 1998: only outing at 3 yrs when 3 lengths fourth of 6 to
Victory Cry in listed race at Chantilly, running on again: will stay beyond 1¼m:
tended to edge left both starts: sent to USA. *Saeed bin Suroor*

FATOOMAH 3 b.f. Skyliner 117 – Phantom Singer 58 (Relkino 131) [1998 NR **60 d**
1999 7g 8m² 8.3g 12m⁵ 8.2m 7.6f² 8g 10g 7m 7g 10s 9s Oct 8] 550Y, resold 4,000Y,
10,500 2-y-o: second foal: dam 11f winner: modest maiden: should stay beyond 1m:
acts on firm ground: blinkered final start: sold 2,000 gns. *K. Mahdi*

FAUTE DE MIEUX 4 ch.g. Beveled (USA) – Supreme Rose 95 (Frimley Park **81**
109) [1998 72: 5s⁵ 6v² 5m² 6g 6f 6g⁶ 1999 5d⁴ 5d 5d* 6m 5m² 5m² 5f 5f 5d 5g a5g **a–**
Dec 18] useful-looking gelding: fairly useful performer: left J. Smyth-Osbourne after
second start: won minor event at Windsor in June: best efforts after when second in
handicaps: left Derrick Morris before final start: stays 6f: acts on heavy going,
probably on firm: has had tongue tied: has been early to post. *E. A. Wheeler*

FAVORISIO 2 br.g. (Feb 17) Efisio 120 – Dixie Favor (USA) 82 (Dixieland Band **55**
(USA)) [1999 6m 6g Oct 14] good-bodied gelding: third foal: half-brother to 3-y-o
Dixie Jazz and 4-y-o Stately Favour: dam Irish 6f (at 2 yrs) to 1m winner: no better
than modest form in maidens at Thirsk and Redcar, keeping on late on second
occasion: may still do better. *Miss J. A. Camacho*

FAVOURED 3 ch.f. Chief's Crown (USA) – Barboukh 95 (Night Shift (USA)) **76**
[1998 78p: 7d³ 1999 7m⁶ 8.3g⁵ May 17] big, strong, lengthy filly: fair form in
maidens (bolted and withdrawn before second intended start at 2 yrs): fifth to Hawala
at Windsor in May, making most: will be suited by 1¼m+. *J. H. M. Gosden*

FAYEZ 4 ch.g. Interrex (CAN) – Forest Nymph (Native Bazaar 122) [1998 –: a10g⁵ **44**
a14.8g 15.8d 1999 a12g² Jul 9] poor maiden: second in seller at Wolverhampton,
only run on Flat of 1999: stays 1½m: tried visored. *K. McAuliffe*

FAYM (IRE) 5 b.m. Fayruz 116 – Lorme (Glenstal (USA) 118) [1998 –, a60: a7g³ **–**
a7g² a6g⁴ a8.5g a7g 6g a8g⁵ a8g a7g⁴ a7g a7s* a7g³ 1999 a7g⁵ a7g* a7g² a7f a8.5g **a58**
a7g a7g⁶ a7g a7f Oct 2] modest performer: won seller at Wolverhampton in January:
left J. Wharton after next start and showed little: seems best at 7f: acts on fibresand,
rarely tried on turf: sometimes visored/blinkered at 4 yrs. *Miss S. J. Wilton*

FAYRWAY RHYTHM (IRE) 2 b.c. (Apr 17) Fayruz 116 – The Way She Moves **79**
(North Stoke 130) [1999 5.1g 7g² 8d² 7.9g⁴ 8s⁴ Nov 6] IR 14,000F, IR 19,000Y:
strong, workmanlike colt: brother to modest 1¼m winner Zuryaf and a 1998 2-y-o 5f
winner in Italy, and half-brother to 2 winners: dam no form: fair maiden: in frame last
4 starts, fourth of 18 to Summoner at Doncaster on final one: stays 1m: raced only on
good going or softer. *M. A. Jarvis*

FEAR AND GREED (IRE) 3 b.f. Brief Truce (USA) 126 – Zing Ping (IRE) 80 **95**
(Thatching 131) [1998 106: 6s* 6m⁶ 7d² 8d^{dis} 1999 8m 8g 7d⁴ 6s⁵ Oct 16] good-
topped filly: first foal: dam Irish maiden from family of Alysheba: useful performer:
stiff tasks in 1999, seeming to run creditably when thirteenth in 1000 Guineas at
Newmarket and fifth in listed race at the Curragh (blinkered) first and final starts:
probably stays 1m: acts on soft going, probably on firm: sold 75,000 gns in
December. *T. Stack, Ireland*

FEARBY CROSS (IRE) 3 b.g. Unblest 117 – Two Magpies 43 (Doulab (USA) **90 d**
115) [1998 87+: 5d³ 6d* 6v 6s⁵ 1999 7d 6m 6d⁴ 6m 7f 7g 7d 6d⁶ Oct 9] strong, quite
attractive gelding: poor mover: fairly useful handicapper: good strong-finishing
fourth of 23 to Pepperdine in William Hill Trophy at York in June: well below form
after: should stay 7f: acts on good to firm and good to soft going (withdrawn lame on
firm on intended debut): blinkered final start: has swished tail/raced freely: sold
15,000 gns, joined W. Musson. *J. D. Bethell*

FEARSOME FACTOR (USA) 4 b.g. Alleged (USA) 138 – Spark of Success **87**
(USA) 84 (Topsider (USA)) [1998 85: 10s⁶ 10g 12g 8s⁴ 10v* 1999 9s³ 9m 10m a9.4g
Dec 11] ex-Irish gelding: third foal: half-brother to Irish 1¼m/1½m winner Party Poll
(by Bering): dam 2-y-o 6f winner in Ireland: fairly useful performer: won maiden at
Leopardstown at 2 yrs: best effort in handicaps in 1999 when third at Cork: sold out

of D. Weld's stable only 3,000 gns before final outing: stays 1¼m: form only on soft/heavy going: sometimes blinkered. *B. J. Curley*

FEAST OF ROMANCE   2 b.c. (Mar 11) Pursuit of Love 124 – June Fayre **82** (Sagaro 133) [1999 5v 5s 5v⁵ a6g* a5g³ Dec 17] 6,300Y, 5,500 2-y-o: half-brother to several winners, including 6f winner who stayed 11f Absolutely Fayre (by Absalom) and 5f (including at 2 yrs) winner Hay Yuen (by Primo Dominie): dam ran twice: modest form on turf: much improved (fairly useful form) when winning maiden at Southwell (all-weather debut) in November: will stay 7f: acts on fibresand, raced only on soft/heavy going on turf. *Miss Gay Kelleway*

FEATHER 'N LACE (IRE)   3 b.f. Green Desert (USA) 127 – Report 'em (USA) **70** 51 (Staff Writer (USA)) [1998 73: 6m³ 5g³ 1999 7g³ 6g³ 6g 6m 8g 7m 7g⁴ 7m* 8m³ 10g Oct 11] leggy, angular filly: fluent mover: fair performer: didn't need to show best form when winning claimer at Newmarket in August: stays 1m, probably not 1¼m: raced only on good/good to firm going: blinkered sixth start. *C. A. Cyzer*

FEATHERSTONE LANE   8 b.g. Siberian Express (USA) 125 – Try Gloria (Try **46** My Best (USA) 130) [1998 52, a71: a5g² a5g³ a5g² a5g* a5g² a6g³ a6g³ a5g* **a61 d** a5g⁵ a5g⁴ a5g* a5g* a5g 5.1m 5.1g³ 5g a5g⁵ a5g6 a5g 1999 a5g a5g⁶ a5g a5g⁵ a5g⁶ a5g a5g 5m⁶ a5g³ a6g² 5.9g 5m⁶ 5f a5g⁴ 5f⁶ a6g a6g⁴ a6g⁵ a6g Dec 27] workmanlike gelding: modest on all-weather, poor on turf: effective at 5f/easy 6f: acts on firm going, good to soft and all-weather: formerly visored: often gets behind. *Miss L. C. Siddall*

FEATHERTIME   3 b.f. Puissance 110 – Midnight Owl (FR) (Ardross 134) [1998 **62** NR 1999 a10g 5.9m⁵ 7.1d a9.4g 6m³ 7.1f⁶ 8.2g⁵ 8d* 8.2s⁴ Nov 1] 1,800Y: leggy, angular filly: fourth foal: half-sister to 1½m winner Regency Rake (by Ti King): dam lightly raced: modest handicapper: left P. Shakespeare after debut: best efforts last 2 starts, winning claiming event at Newcastle in October: stays 1m: acts on good to firm and soft going. *Mrs G. S. Rees*

FEBRUARY   6 b.m. Full Extent (USA) 113 – Foligno (Crofter (USA) 124) [1998 **–** –: a5g 1999 a6g⁶ a5g 5g 5g Jul 3] of little account nowadays. *J. P. Smith*

FEEL A LINE   5 b.g. Petong 126 – Cat's Claw (USA) (Sharpen Up 127) [1998 **55** 55: 8g³ 8d 8d 1999 a8g a8g a8.5g³ 9g Apr 1] lengthy gelding: modest performer: form in 1999 only when third: left M. Bielby after: stays 8.5f: yet to race on heavy going, acts on any other on turf and on fibresand: usually blinkered/visored: has looked difficult ride. *J. G. Given*

FEEL NO FEAR   6 b.m. Fearless Action (USA) 116 – Charm Bird 60 (Daring **59** March 116) [1998 64: 10.8g 10g 12m 8d⁶ 7g² 7.1g⁵ 8m* 7m⁶ 8m² 8g 8d 1999 7g 8g 8m 8.5g⁴ 8f⁵ 7d² a8g* 7m a7g a8g* a10g² a8g⁶ Nov 23] modest performer: left R. Simpson after fifth start: won selling handicap at Lingfield in August and seller there in October: best form at 1m: acts on good to firm going and equitrack (some promise on fibresand ninth start): pulled hard in blinkers third start. *B. J. Meehan*

FEE MAIL   3 b.f. Danehill (USA) 126 – Wizardry 83 (Shirley Heights 130) [1998 **73** 66p: 7g 7m³ 1999 8m 7.7m⁶ 8m 7s 11g² 11.6d* Oct 28] tall, quite good-topped filly: fair performer: returned to form final 2 starts, winning handicap at Windsor, dictating pace: stays 11.6f: acts on good to firm and good to soft going. *I. A. Balding*

FEITICEIRA (USA)   3 b.f. Deposit Ticket (USA) – Dogwood Lane (USA) **79** (Alydar (USA)) [1998 NR 1999 8g² 8m⁵ 8.2s Oct 5] $87,000Y: second foal: sister to a winner in USA: dam unraced daughter of US Grade 2 7f winner and Breeders' Cup Sprint runner-up Pine Tree Lane: encouraging second in maiden at Salisbury on debut: well below that form in similar events at Ascot (sweating and edgy) and Nottingham (first start for over 2 months, reportedly lost action) after. *J. Noseda*

FELONA   3 b.f. Caerleon (USA) 132 – Felawnah (USA) 111 (Mr Prospector **92** (USA)) [1998 NR 1999 9m* 10.2m* 10d Oct 14] unfurnished filly: first foal: dam, winner at 1¼m and fourth in 1000 Guineas and Irish 1000 Guineas, daughter of champion mare in USA Ambassador of Luck: won maiden at Kempton (landed odds) in May and 4-runner minor event at Chepstow (still green) in September: not discredited in listed event at Newmarket final start: stays 1¼m. *Saeed bin Suroor*

Faucets First For Faucets Firth of Clyde Stakes, Ayr—
an all-the-way win for Femme Fatale, who beats Roo and Misty Miss (rail)

FELONY (IRE)   4 ch.c. Pharly (FR) 130 – Scales of Justice 85 (Final Straw 127)   **37**
[1998 37: a10s⁵ a9.4g a12g³ a11g³ a12g³ a11g⁴ a16.2g⁶ a14g a12g 1999 a11g a16g²
a16.2g⁵ a14.8g Aug 6] successful over hurdles in May, but poor at best on Flat:
probably stays 2m: form only on all-weather: usually tongue tied. *R. Brotherton*

FEMME FATALE   2 b.f. (Feb 26) Fairy King (USA) – Red Rita (IRE) 97§   **102**
(Kefaah (USA) 124) [1999 5.2d⁴ 6g² 6m³ 6d* Sep 18] 53,000Y: rather leggy, lengthy
filly: first foal: dam, best at 2/3 yrs at 6f/7f, didn't win until 4 yrs and not one to
trust, from family of Samraan: generally progressive form: won listed race at Ayr in
September by 5 lengths from Roo, making all under positive ride from K. Fallon: will
stay 7f: on toes first 3 starts, and attended by 2 handlers on debut: useful. *W. Jarvis*

FENCER'S QUEST (IRE)   6 ch.g. Bluebird (USA) 125 – Fighting Run (Runnett   **44**
125) [1998 NR 1999 5.1m 10m 6g 8s⁴ a7g Nov 17] poor winning hurdler: poor
maiden on Flat, lightly raced: stays 1m: acts on soft going: hung left penultimate
start. *J. C. Tuck*

FERNY FACTORS   3 ch.g. King Among Kings 60 – Market Blues (Porto Bello   **63**
118) [1998 57: 5d 6g 7.5m⁶ 7.5d* 7m⁶ 7.5m⁵ 10s 1999 10m 9.9g⁴ 9.9d* 12d* 12.1m
a12g Jul 10] lengthy gelding: modest performer: won at Beverley in May (seller)
and June (handicap, made all): poor efforts after: stays 1½m: acts on soft going:
blinkered/visored 3 of final 4 starts at 2 yrs. *Ronald Thompson*

FERNY HILL (IRE)   5 b.g. Danehill (USA) 126 – Miss Allowed (USA) (Alleged   **93**
(USA) 138) [1998 104: 13.3m² 16.4g 11.6m* 12s³ 12g 1999 12m 12d⁶ 12d a12g Dec
17] lengthy gelding: useful performer at 4 yrs: has reportedly had breathing problem/
leg injury, and not at best on belated return in 1999: should stay beyond 1¾m: acts on
good to firm and soft going: often used to be a front runner. *W. R. Muir*

FEROCITY   3 ch.f. Superlative 118 – Tantalizing Song (CAN) (The Minstrel   **–**
(CAN) 135) [1998 –: a6g a8g 1999 6v 10f⁶ 7m May 26] well held in maidens/
claimers: sold 800 gns. *M. A. Jarvis*

FERRET EDDIE (IRE)   3 ch.g. Be My Guest (USA) 126 – Musical Essence 65   **50 ?**
(Song 132) [1998 –: 5g 1999 8d 9d³ 8f May 27] short-backed gelding: has a quick
action: signs of ability in maiden/handicap final 2 starts. *T. P. Tate*

FERZAO (IRE)   2 b.c. (Mar 17) Alzao (USA) 117 – Fer de Lance (IRE) (Diesis   **88 p**
133) [1999 7d 7d* Oct 12] IR 40,000F, IR 50,000Y: strong, attractive colt: first foal:
dam unraced daughter of 5f/6f-winning sister to smart sprinter Rustic Amber:
showed considerable improvement and fairly useful form when winning 15-runner
maiden at Leicester by 2½ lengths from Air Defence, making most despite edging
left: should stay 1m: has the scope to make a useful 3-y-o. *Mrs A. J. Perrett*

FESTIVAL FLYER   4 b.g. Alhijaz 122 – Odilese 82 (Mummy's Pet 125) [1998   **–**
66: 10g⁴ 10d 1999 a8g a10f a12g Feb 6] tall, close-coupled gelding: fair maiden at

2 and 3 yrs: no show at Lingfield in 1999: stays 1¼m: acts on good to soft going, probably on firm. *Miss Gay Kelleway*

FESTIVAL HALL (IRE) 3 b.c. Sadler's Wells (USA) 132 – Handsewn (USA) **97** (Sir Ivor 135) [1998 101p: 8d³ 9d³ 8s* 1999 10s⁵ 12g Jun 27] quite good-topped colt: useful performer: won Beresford Stakes at the Curragh at 2 yrs: fifth of 7 to Fantastic Light in Thresher Classic Trial at Sandown, much better effort in 1999: last of 10 in Irish Derby at the Curragh 2 months later: should be well suited by 1½m: looks a lazy sort: sent to Australia. *A. P. O'Brien, Ireland*

FESTIVE 3 b.f. Rudimentary (USA) 118 – Champagne Season (USA) 54 (Vaguely **82** Noble 140) [1998 59p: a5g⁴ 1999 a7g* 7.1g 7m* 7d* 7.5m⁴ 7.1s³ 6s³ Oct 4] unimpressive mover: fairly useful performer: won maiden at Wolverhampton in January and handicaps at Redcar in June and Yarmouth in July: creditable third in handicap at Haydock penultimate start: needs further than 6f, and will stay 1m: has won on good to firm going, possibly suited by more testing conditions and acts on soft ground (also on fibresand): sold 9,400 gns. *W. J. Haggas*

FEZ 2 ch.f. (Apr 7) Mujtahid (USA) 118 – Velvet Beret (IRE) (Dominion 123) **94** [1999 5g⁵ 5m² 5s⁵ 5m* 5m* 5m* 5f² 5m⁴ Sep 11] small filly: has quick action: second foal: half-sister to 5-y-o Boater: dam unraced half-sister to smart 7f/1m performer Luzum: fairly useful performer: improved with racing, winning maiden at Redcar, minor event at Doncaster and nursery at York in June/July: good efforts when length second of 10 to Misty Miss in Molecomb Stakes at Goodwood and close fourth of 14 to Mrs P in Flying Childers Stakes at Doncaster final 2 starts: raced only at 5f: acts on firm ground. *M. Johnston*

FHULAAD (USA) 2 b.c. (Apr 24) Blush Rambler (USA) 119 – Now That's Funny **58** (USA) (Saratoga Six (USA)) [1999 8.3s⁵ 7.9g Oct 6] $60,000Y: fifth foal: half-brother to 4 winners, including very smart performer up to 1m in Britain/USA Lucayan Prince (by Fast Play) and to Comic Strip (by Red Ransom) and Silver Comic (by Silver Hawk), both US graded winners around 9f: dam, won at 4 yrs in USA, half-sister to Marcel Boussac winner Tropicaro: modest form in maidens: sold 6,200 gns: dead. *M. Johnston*

FICKLE 3 b.f. Danehill (USA) 126 – Fade (Persepolis (FR) 127) [1998 NR 1999 **95** 8g³ 8g 8g* 8g³ 10.1g* Aug 30] fourth foal: half-sister to useful French winner at up to 13.5f Faru (by Mtoto) and French 7.5f and 10.5f winner Flip Fantasia (by Batshoof): dam, daughter of Cheshire Oaks winner One Over Parr, herself sister to Polygamy: useful performer: won maiden at Brighton in June and listed handicap at Newcastle (quickened clear around 2f out when beating Robin Lane 1¾ lengths) in August: stays 1¼m, will prove at least as effective returned to 1m: seems suited by waiting tactics: may improve again. *M. L. W. Bell*

FICTITIOUS 3 ch.f. Machiavellian (USA) 123 – Trying For Gold (USA) 103 **100 +** (Northern Baby (CAN) 127) [1998 81p: 7g⁵ 7g³ 1999 9.9m* 12m⁶ 10.1m* 10.2m⁵ 8.5f* Dec 24] angular, quite attractive filly: useful performer: won maiden at Salisbury in May and listed race at Newcastle (by 3 lengths from Maria Isabella, settling well and showing turn of foot) in June: pulled too hard in Ribblesdale Stakes at Royal Ascot in between and when favourite for listed event at Chepstow in July (final start for Sir Michael Stoute, found little from front): won allowance race at Calder in December: stays 1¼m: acts on firm going: gave trouble to post on reappearance: sweating, edgy and walked to start third outing: has some temperament. *C. Clement, USA*

FIELDGATE FLYER (IRE) 4 b.f. Sabrehill (USA) 120 – Orba Gold (USA) 67 **–** (Gold Crest (USA) 120) [1998 –: 8.1g⁶ 12d⁶ 1999 10.5m a14.8g Dec 11] leggy filly: of little account: left R. Hollinshead after reappearance. *M. Mullineaux*

FIELD MASTER (IRE) 2 ch.c. (Mar 14) Foxhound (USA) 103 – Bold Avril **71** (IRE) (Persian Bold 123) [1999 7m 6m⁴ 6d⁴ 7g⁴ 7.3v Oct 23] IR 14,500F, IR 21,000Y: strong colt: fourth living foal: half-brother to a 7f/1m winner in Italy by Shalford: dam unraced daughter of sister to Middle Park winner and 2000 Guineas runner-up Mattaboy: fair maiden: good fourth of 15 in nursery at Catterick penultimate start: should stay 1m: acts on good to firm and good to soft going, well beaten on heavy: sold 18,000 gns, joined S. Dow. *A. C. Stewart*

Prix de la Foret, Longchamp—Field of Hope is almost home as the blinkered Keos finishes strongly; Trans Island, Danzigaway (partly hidden) and odds-on Diktat are close up behind

FIELD OF HOPE (IRE)   4 ch.f. Selkirk (USA) 129 – Fracci (Raise A Cup **119** (USA)) [1998 110: 8m² 8s³ 8m² 8g* 8s* 8v² 1999 8v⁵ 8d* 8g* 8m⁶ 7d* 8m² Dec 12] second foal: half-sister to Italian 7f to 1¼m winner Stage Set (by Old Vic): dam Italian 5f (at 2 yrs) to 7f winner, Group 3 placed at 1m: smart performer: successful in minor event at Milan at 2 yrs and listed races at Milan (final start for G. Botti in Italy) and Saint-Cloud at 3 yrs: won Prix du Chemin de Fer du Nord at Chantilly (by neck from Alliteration) in June, 4-runner Prix d'Astarte at Deauville (by 1½ lengths from Miss Berbere) in August and Prix de la Foret at Longchamp (by ¾ length from Keos) in October: good 1¾ lengths second to Docksider in Hong Kong Mile at Sha Tin final start: stayed 1m: probably acted on any going: held up and had good turn of foot: visits Sadler's Wells. *P. Bary, France*

FIELD OF VISION (IRE)   9 b.g. Vision (USA) – Bold Meadows 80 (Persian **50** Bold 123) [1998 74, a69: a12g⁴ a11g⁶ a12g³ a11g a12g² a12g⁴ 13d* 12m* a14g⁴ 13s⁵ 11.9s 16m⁵ 1999 12g⁴ 11d Oct 26] neat gelding: has a quick action: fair handicapper at 8 yrs: probably in need of both outings on belated return: stays 2m: acts on any turf/all-weather: effective in blinkers (not tried since 6-y-o reappearance). *Mrs A. Duffield*

FIELDS OF OMAGH (USA)   4 b.g. Pleasant Tap (USA) – Brave And True **89** (USA) (Fappiano (USA)) [1998 78: 8d 9.9m⁵ 12s⁵ 11.7s 12g⁴ 10.2g³ 9.7f⁶ 13.1m* 14g⁶ 1999 a12g* a12g* a12g² Jan 28] big, good-topped gelding: fairly useful handicapper: won twice at Lingfield in January: good second there later in month: should stay 1¾m: acts on good to firm going and equitrack: held up: sold 15,000 gns, sent to USA. *I. A. Balding*

FIERY WATERS   3 b.g. Rudimentary (USA) 118 – Idle Waters 116 (Mill Reef **68** (USA) 141) [1998 NR 1999 10m 10m³ 10m 10d 14.1m Aug 23] unfurnished gelding: half-brother to several winners, including 4-y-o Phantom Waters and smart stayer Shining Water (by Kalaglow), the dam of Tenby: dam won Park Hill Stakes: fair maiden: may prove best at 1¼m/1½m: acts on good to firm and good to soft going. *D. W. P. Arbuthnot*

FIFE AND DRUM (USA)   2 b. or br.g. (Apr 26) Rahy (USA) 115 – Fife (IRE) **63** 95 (Lomond (USA) 128) [1999 7m 8s 7s Oct 8] smallish, well-made gelding: fifth foal: half-brother to 1995 2-y-o 6f/7f winner Witch of Fife (by Lear Fan), 3-y-o Pay The Pied Piper and useful French/UAE 1m winner Hudood (by Gone West): dam, 1m winner who stayed 1½m, half-sister to smart stayer El Conquistador: easily best effort in maidens when seventh of 10 to Akeed at York on debut: well beaten on soft ground both starts after: will be suited by 1¼m+. *E. A. L. Dunlop*

Grundy Bloodstock Limited's "Field of Hope"

FIFTEEN REDS   4 b.g. Jumbo Hirt (USA) 90§ – Dominance (Dominion 123)   –
[1998 NR 1999 a12g a9.4g⁵ 10g 11d 14.1g a14g Oct 18] close-coupled gelding:
fourth foal: brother to fair stayer Onefourseven and half-brother to winner up to 2m
Can She Can Can (by Sulaafah): dam unraced daughter of Oaks/Irish Oaks winner
Juliette Marny: only a little sign of ability: visored final 2 starts. *D. Shaw*

FIFTH EDITION   3 b.f. Rock Hopper 124 – Glossary (Reference Point 139)   **66**
[1998 NR 1999 8.3g 8.3m 7.1m⁴ 8g 8.5s⁵ Sep 21] 2,500Y: second foal: half-sister
to 1m winner Fifth Emerald (by Formidable): dam unraced close relative of smart
middle-distance filly Valley of Gold: fair maiden: best effort when fourth at Chepstow, despite tending to carry head a little high (reportedly lost both hind plates): well
beaten in handicaps after: best effort at 7f: raced only on good/good to firm going
prior to final start. *C. F. Wall*

FIGAWIN   4 b.g. Rudimentary (USA) 118 – Dear Person (Rainbow Quest (USA)   –
134) [1998 48: a7g² a7g⁵ a8g³ a10g⁶ a8g⁴ a8g a7g 6.1v 8.2s 8.2g⁴ 10g 8m 1999 a8g
Feb 2] poor performer: stays 1m, probably not 1¼m: acts on good to firm going and
all-weather: effective blinkered or not. *Mrs H. L. Walton*

FIGHTER SQUADRON   10 ch.g. Primo Dominie 121 – Formidable Dancer 70   –
(Formidable (USA) 125) [1998 –: a6g 7g a6g a6g 1999 a10g a8.5g a7g⁶ a6g a7g Jul
8] leggy gelding: no longer of much account. *R. E. Peacock*

FIGURE IT OUT   4 ch.g. Dilum (USA) 115 – Count On Me 77 (No Mercy 126)   –
[1998 –: 7.1d 6m 1999 5m 8.1m 11.6m Jul 19] well held in claimers/selling
handicaps. *R. J. Hodges*

FILEY BRIGG   4 b.f. Weldnaas (USA) 112 – Dusty's Darling (Doyoun 124) [1998   –
–: 8s⁶ 7.5g 8g 6s⁵ 8.3s 6g⁵ 6g 8.2v 6v 1999 7g 7g 8.3m 13s⁶ 10g 9g Jun 14] one-time
fairly useful winner: no form in 1999. *W. T. Kemp*

FILIAL (IRE)   6 b.g. Danehill (USA) 126 – Sephira (Luthier 126) [1998 76: a12s²   **54**
a12g² a12g³ a12g* 12d² 12.3v* 12s 12g⁴ 13d³ 13d* 11.9g² 13s 10.4g⁴ 12s² 11s* a12g

1999 12s 13g 12g³ 13.8g⁵ Oct 16] smallish gelding: only modest at best in 1999: stays 13f: acts on good to firm going, heavy and all-weather: blinkered (well beaten) once at 4 yrs. *Mrs A. Duffield*

FINAL DIVIDEND (IRE)   3 b.g. Second Set (IRE) 127 – Prime Interest (IRE)   **81** (Kings Lake (USA) 133) [1998 73?: 5f 6s⁵ 5.7g³ 6g 6m⁵ 7.3g 1999 7v⁴ 7m³ 8m* 8.2m 8m 7.6g⁶ 8m⁶ 8.5s* 8.9d a8g Nov 15] close-coupled gelding: fairly useful handicapper: won 17-runner event at Salisbury in May and 16-runner event at Beverley in September: should stay beyond 8.5f: acts on good to firm and soft going: sold out of M. Featherston-Godley's stable 14,000 gns before running poorly (all-weather debut) final start. *J. M. P. Eustace*

FINAL KISS (IRE)   2 b.c. (Mar 2) Dolphin Street (FR) 125 – Mystery Train (Bay Express 132) [1999 6m 6g 6m 6g Oct 11] IR 9,000Y, 13,500 2-y-o: half-brother to a winner in Sweden by Hatim: dam, won twice in Scandinavia and third in Norwegian 1000 Guineas, half-sister to useful middle-distance filly Frustration: well held in maidens/minor event, including in tongue strap. *J. R. Jenkins*

FINAL LAP   3 b.g. Batshoof 122 – Lap of Honour 100 (Final Straw 127) [1998   **76** NR 1999 8m 7.7d⁴ 8.2d² 8.3d⁴ a10g⁵ Nov 16] half-brother to several winners, including useful miler Lap of Luxury (by Sharrood): dam won over 6f and 7f: fair maiden: best effort when second at Nottingham: stays 8.2f: yet to race on extremes of going. *W. Jarvis*

FINAL ROW   2 b.c. (Mar 20) Indian Ridge 123 – The Jotter 99 (Night Shift   **95** (USA)) [1999 6.1f² 6m* 6s² 6m 5s² 5d⁴ 6m² Oct 19] small colt: good mover with a quick action: first foal: dam, 2-y-o 5f and 6.5f winner, granddaughter of Irish 1,000 Guineas winner Front Row: useful performer: won maiden at Catterick in July: good efforts last 2 starts: stays 6f: acts on soft and good to firm going: sold 27,000 gns, sent to USA. *W. Jarvis*

FINAL SETTLEMENT (IRE)   4 b.g. Soviet Lad (USA) – Tender Time (Tender   **70** King 123) [1998 66: 8.3g³ 8.3m* 11.5m* 1999 10m 12m⁴ 10s³ 11.7s³ Oct 26] angular gelding: good mover: fair handicapper: stays 1½m: acts on good to firm and soft going: carried head bit high final start. *J. R. Jenkins*

FINAL STAB (IRE)   6 b.g. Kris 135 – Premier Rose 117 (Sharp Edge 123) [1998   **–** –, a53: a12g³ 8g 10m a7g⁵ a9.4g 1999 a9.4g* a8g* a8.5g⁶ a8.5g⁶ 8.2g a9.4g⁴ Sep 8]   **a63** rangy, angular gelding: showed knee action: reportedly had a stress fracture of hind leg at 3 yrs: modest handicapper: won at Wolverhampton in May and Southwell in June: probably stayed 1½m: acted on fibresand: blinkered final start: successful over hurdles in October, fell fatally following month. *Miss S. J. Wilton*

FINAL TRIAL (IRE)   5 b.g. Last Tycoon 131 – Perfect Alibi (Law Society   **68** (USA) 130) [1998 –: 10.1d⁴ 12.3g 10.3m 10.2d 1999 9.7v 10.3m³ 12m 12m 12m 10m* 10d⁴ 10.1d⁶ Oct 20] sturdy gelding: fair handicapper: won at Pontefract in September: stays 1¼m: acts on good to firm and good to soft ground: sold 18,000 gns. *G. Wragg*

FINAL TRICK   2 b.f. (Mar 20) Primo Dominie 121 – Tricky Note 97 (Song 132)   **–** [1999 5f⁶ 5m Aug 13] half-sister to several winners, including 3-y-o Full Pitch and Irish 1¼m winner Ros Castle (by Reference Point): dam sprinting sister to smart sprinter Jester: always outpaced in maidens at Lingfield. *W. J. Haggas*

FINCH   2 b.f. (May 8) Inchinor 119 – Wryneck 89 (Niniski (USA) 125) [1999 7d   **–** 6v 6d Nov 4] smallish, good-topped filly: half-sister to 3-y-o Wry Ardour and several winners, including useful 7f/1m performer Wrybill (by Sharpo) and 1½m winner Strategic Ploy (by Deploy): dam 2-y-o 7f winner on only start: well beaten in maidens. *R. Charlton*

FINE AND ROSY   4 b.f. Petoski 135 – Vaigly Fine (Vaigly Great 127) [1998 NR   **–** 1999 a9.4g 7d 8g⁶ 6.1s 5.9m 6d 6.9m 8g 7g 7f 5g 5f Sep 4] compact filly: second foal: dam no sign of ability over hurdles: no form: tried blinkered/visored. *M. Dods*

FINGALS COVE   2 b.f. (Apr 21) Puissance 110 – Polar Cove (Polar Falcon   **–** (USA) 126) [1999 6f Jun 1] 1,600Y: first foal: dam unraced: well held in maiden at Redcar. *J. Berry*

FINGERS HENRY (IRE)   2 b.c. (Feb 7) Shalford (IRE) 124§ – Running For   **51** You (FR) (Pampabird 124) [1999 5d 5d a6g² a5g⁶ a7g² a6g² a6g a8s³ Dec 28] 8,200F, 4,200Y: quite good-topped colt: third foal: half-brother to 4-y-o Sing For Me and a

1½m winner in Russia by Kahyasi: dam French 1m winner: modest maiden: form in Britain only in sellers on fibresand: sold 800 gns from Ronald Thompson before final start: stays 1m: blinkered final outing. *Alex McLaren, Sweden*

FINISHED ARTICLE (IRE)   2 b.c. (May 9) Indian Ridge 123 – Summer Fashion 84 (Moorestyle 137) [1999 8v⁵ 7s Nov 5] IR 45,000Y: small colt: fifth foal: brother to very smart Irish 7f (at 2 yrs) to 1¼m winner and Irish Derby runner-up Definite Article and half-brother to 3-y-o Salford Express: dam 1m and 1¼m winner: similar form in maidens at Salisbury (green) and Doncaster, mid-division behind Golovin on latter course: will stay at least 1¼m: likely to do better. *D. R. C. Elsworth*   **66 p**

FINISTERRE (IRE)   6 b.g. Salt Dome (USA) – Inisfail (Persian Bold 123) [1998 56: 7.1g 7d* 6s 7g² 5.9m⁶ 7f³ 7g² 7g 7s⁵ 8.2v⁶ a7g³ a8g⁵ 1999 7g³ 8v Apr 20] leggy gelding: fair handicapper on turf, modest on all-weather: good third of 18 at Catterick, much better effort in 1999: best at 7f/1m: acts on any turf going and fibresand: blinkered once at 2 yrs: usually held up. *J. J. O'Neill*   **72 a–**

FIONA'S DREAM (IRE)   3 b. or br.f. Soviet Lad (USA) – Woody's Colours (USA) (Caro 133) [1998 –: 6g 7m 1999 7.6f 7m⁴ a13g Oct 1] rather leggy filly: little sign of ability in maidens: sold 800 gns. *Miss Gay Kelleway*   **–**

FIONN DE COOL (IRE)   8 b.g. Mazaad 106 – Pink Fondant (Northfields (USA)) [1998 72: 8.2s⁶ 8g 8.3d 8.1g* 8d³ 8d⁶ 8g 8s 7s 1999 8d 8.5m 8m 8.1d⁵ 8m³ Aug 23] small, sturdy gelding: poor mover: modest handicapper: stays 8.5f: acts on firm and good to soft going, probably not on soft: none too consistent. *J. Akehurst*   **58**

FIORI   3 b.g. Anshan 119 – Fen Princess (IRE) 72 (Trojan Fen 118) [1998 93, a67: 6m⁶ 6g³ a6g² 7m⁴ 7.9g² 8d² 7.9g² 7s³ a8g³ 1999 8d 9.2m* 11f³ 12v* 10.4d* 10.3d⁵ 12m⁵ 13s Sep 27] close-coupled gelding: has a round action: useful on turf, fair on all-weather: won maiden at Hamilton in May and handicaps at Beverley and York in June: well beaten form of last 3 starts: stays 1½m: acts on any turf going: tends to drift left under pressure (has worn near-side pricker). *P. C. Haslam*   **99 a–**

FIRECREST (IRE)   2 b.f. (May 11) Darshaan 133 – Trefoil (FR) (Blakeney 126) [1999 7d 8s Oct 25] IR 50,000Y: angular filly: sixth foal: closely related to Irish 1996 2-y-o 7f winner Celtic Slip (by Slip Anchor) and half-sister to French 9.5f to 11.8f winner Trois Etoiles (by Alysheba): dam French 10.5f to 1½m winner: behind in 2 maidens at Leicester: type to do better over 1¼m and beyond at 3 yrs. *J. L. Dunlop*   **– p**

FIRE DOME (IRE)   7 ch.g. Salt Dome (USA) – Penny Habit (Habitat 134) [1998 112: a6g⁶ a5g⁶ 5d 6s* 6g 7.1g 6v⁵ 5d* 6g 6m 6g 1999 6g³ 6s 5g⁵ 6g⁶ 6m 5d² 5s³ 5s* 6d 6g* 5s 6d 5s⁴ Nov 2] smart performer in prime: on downgrade in 1999: didn't have to be at best to win claimers at Sandown and Redcar in October: best at 5f/6f: has form on good to firm going, but best on good or softer: blinkered twice, no improvement: has had tongue tied: best waited with: none too consistent. *D. Nicholls*   **101 d**

FIREPOWER (IRE)   2 br.c. (May 19) Hamas (IRE) 125§ – Winchester Queen (IRE) (Persian Bold 123) [1999 6g 5m³ 5m³ 6m 5m 6d⁵ 5m² 5v⁵ 5.3s* 5s⁶ Oct 13] 12,000F, IR 9,000Y: quite attractive colt: first living foal: dam, unraced, from family of 1000 Guineas third Joking Apart: fair performer: landed odds in seller at Brighton in September: raced mainly at 5f: blinkered fifth start: has swished tail, carried head awkwardly: sold 6,400 gns in October, sent to Macau. *B. J. Meehan*   **77**

FIRST BACK (IRE)   2 b.g. (Mar 13) Fourstars Allstar (USA) 122 – Par Un Nez (IRE) (Cyrano de Bergerac 120) [1999 7.5g 9m 10s⁶ Oct 4] 21,000F, 15,000Y: lengthy, rather dipped-backed gelding: second foal: half-brother to useful 1997 2-y-o 5f/6f (Gimcrack) winner Carrowkeel (by Waajib): dam unraced: signs of only a little ability in maidens. *C. W. Fairhurst*   **–**

FIRST BALLOT (IRE)   3 b.g. Perugino (USA) 84 – Election Special 78 (Chief Singer 131) [1998 –: 7s 1999 9.9m⁴ 12f* 10m⁶ 16.2m* 15m Sep 7] tall, leggy gelding: useful performer: won maiden at Newbury in July and handicap at Ascot (by short head from Son of Snurge) in August: stiff task and well beaten in Prix de Lutece at Longchamp final start: stays 2m well: acts on firm going. *D. R. C. Elsworth*   **100**

FIRST BLOOD   2 b.c. (Mar 14) Rambo Dancer (CAN) 107 – Bollin Victoria 51 (Jalmood (USA) 126) [1999 5s* 5g* 5g³ 7s⁵ 7d⁶ 6d 6v² Oct 23] 15,000Y: smallish, angular colt: third foal: half-brother to 4-y-o Blushing Victoria: dam, ran only at 2 yrs, third over 7f: fairly useful performer: won maiden at Folkestone in March and   **91**

minor event at Newmarket in April: improved subsequently: best effort when second of 17 to Awake in nursery at Newbury on final start: probably suited by testing conditions at 6f, and should stay 1m: acts on heavy ground, yet to race on firmer than good: sold 48,000 gns, sent to USA. *T. G. Mills*

FIRST CUT (USA)   3 b.f. Diesis 133 – Super Jamie (USA) (Nijinsky (CAN) 138)   **75**
[1998 NR 1999 8.1g 9m 12m² 12m⁴ 12g³ 9.9m⁴ 10.2s⁵ a10g Nov 16] $44,000F, IR 30,000Y: tall, useful-looking filly: half-sister to several winners in USA, including Grade 3 7f to 8.5f winner Nijinsky's Gold (by Lot O'Gold): dam unraced: fair maiden: best form at 1½m: acts on good to firm going, below form on equitrack: none too consistent and has looked less than keen: sold 30,000 gns. *J. W. Hills*

FIRST DANCE   4 b.f. Primo Dominie 121 – Soviet Swan (USA) (Nureyev (USA) 131) [1998 –: 8f 1999 7d 6m Jul 16] leggy filly: lightly raced and no form since 2 yrs. *Dr J. D. Scargill*

FIRST FANTASY   3 b.f. Be My Chief (USA) 122 – Dreams 88 (Rainbow Quest   **91 p**
(USA) 134) [1998 –p: 7s 1999 7s 8m 10.1g² 10m³ 10.5m* 10.1f* 10.5d⁴ 9.7d* 10.1d* Sep 15] fairly useful handicapper: won at Warwick and Yarmouth in July, Folkestone in August and Yarmouth again in September: stays 10.5f: acts on firm and good to soft going: likely to prove best with exaggerated waiting tactics (has flicked tail, and twice found little/carried head awkwardly): open to further improvement if temperament holds. *J. R. Fanshawe*

FIRST FRAME   4 b.g. Mukaddamah (USA) 125 – Point of Law (Law Society   **64**
(USA) 130) [1998 64: 6d³ 8s 6d 8g² 6d 8m 10g 1999 a7g* a7g⁵ a7g⁶ a6g 7d a8g 7s Oct 23] leggy gelding: modest performer: won claimer at Southwell in January: well beaten after 9-month absence final 3 starts: stays 1m: acts on fibresand and good to soft ground: visored once/blinkered in 1999: sold 800 gns, sent to Italy. *D. Shaw*

FIRST GOLD   10 gr.g. Absalom 128 – Cindys Gold 69 (Sonnen Gold 121) [1998   **–**
NR 1999 7d 8d a7g Jul 8] lengthy gelding: poor at best nowadays: sometimes blinkered/visored. *A. Smith*

FIRST HUSSAR   3 b.c. Primo Dominie 121 – Third Movement 75 (Music Boy   **66 d**
124) [1998 66: 6m⁴ 6.1m 7g 1999 7m 9m³ 9m 9.7m⁵ 10.1g 11.5g 8.2g 7d Oct 12] fair handicapper: below form after second start, including in selling events: stays 9f: acts on good to firm going: has been bandaged in front: blinkered sixth start: sold 2,800 gns, sent to Italy. *P. Howling*

FIRST IMPRESSION   4 b.g. Saddlers' Hall (IRE) 126 – First Sapphire (Simply   **74**
Great (FR) 122) [1998 66p: 8g⁶ 8d 10v 1999 10v² 12m⁴ 13.3m⁵ Jul 17] workmanlike gelding: fair maiden: stays 13f: acts on good to firm and heavy going: edgy sort. *Lady Herries*

FIRST LEGACY   3 ch.f. First Trump 118 – Loving Legacy 82 (Caerleon (USA)   **–**
132) [1998 –: 5g⁶ 5m 5f 1999 5g Apr 22] smallish, rather sparely-made filly: no signs of ability since debut: visored final start at 2 yrs. *M. Brittain*

FIRST MAGNITUDE (IRE)   3 ch.c. Arazi (USA) 135 – Crystal Cup (USA)   **117**
(Nijinsky (CAN) 138) [1998 8v³ 1999 12s* 10.5s⁴ 12v² 12.5s* 12m³ 12d* 12g Nov 6] 85,000F, 115,000Y: close-coupled colt: half-brother to several winners, including very smart 6f/7f performer Iktamal (by Danzig Connection) and fairly useful middle-distance stayer Crystal Cross (by Roberto): dam twice-raced daughter of top-class Rose Bowl: smart performer: won minor event at Saint-Cloud in April, listed race at Deauville in August and steadily-run Prix du Conseil de Paris at Longchamp (beat Zarfoot a short neck) in October: 2 lengths third of 4 to Montjeu in Prix Niel at Longchamp on fifth outing: behind in Breeders' Cup Turf at Gulfstream final start: stays 12.5f well: acts on good to firm and heavy ground. *A. Fabre, France*

FIRST MAITE   6 b.g. Komaite (USA) – Marina Plata (Julio Mariner 127) [1998   **109**
99, a90: a6g³ a6g³ a8g² a6g⁶ a8g² 7d³ a8g³ 6s⁴ 6g² 5m* a6g² 5s³ 5g⁵ a7g* 6m⁴ 5.6g   **a97**
6s 5s* 7s 7d a6g⁴ a7g⁴ 1999 a5g 6s* 5m 6m 6f 5d* 6d 6m 5.6g 5s² 5s* 5d 6s 6s a7g* a8g⁵ a6g⁴ a7g Dec 21] tall, lengthy gelding: has a round action: useful handicapper: won at York in May, Haydock in August, Ascot (by 2½ lengths from Monkston Point) in September and Southwell in November: has form up to 1m, best efforts at 5f/6f: acts on good to firm going, soft and fibresand: usually wears blinkers, visored once: has been tongue tied: often makes running, and sometimes hangs (goes well for K. Fallon): tough. *S. R. Bowring*

FIRST MANASSAS (USA) 2 b. or br.c. (Feb 25) Sea Hero (USA) 124 – Ispahan (USA) (Majestic Light (USA)) [1999 7f⁵ 7.6g² 8.1m* 8d³ Sep 17] first foal: dam, unraced half-sister to Red Ransom, from family of high-class American middle-distance performer Winter's Tale: fairly useful form: won maiden at Haydock in September, finding plenty for pressure despite tending to carry head high: good third of 20 in nursery at Ayr final start, faring best of those who raced prominently: bred to stay at least 1½m: acts on good to firm and good to soft going: remains open to improvement. *I. A. Balding* **87 p**

FIRST MASTER 4 ch.g. Primo Dominie 121 – Bodham 88 (Bustino 136) [1998 82: 8m 10.8m² 10g³ 11.6f 10g² 10.3d² 11d² a12g² a10g* a10g³ 1999 a12g a11g 12g 12s 12f⁵ 12.3s⁵ 10m Jun 22] unfurnished gelding: fair handicapper at best in 1999: well below form final 4 starts: stays 1½m: acts on good to firm, good to soft going and equitrack (moved poorly to post on soft fourth start): often bandaged: joined B. R. Millman. *Miss Gay Kelleway* **75 d**

FIRST MUSICAL 3 ch.f. First Trump 118 – Musical Sally (USA) (The Minstrel (CAN) 135) [1998 92: 5.1d² 5d² 5m² 5s* 5m* 6g* 6g* 6m⁴ 6s² 6g 6v 1999 6d² 5m 6.1g⁶ 6m 6d 6d 5s⁴ Oct 23] workmanlike filly: useful handicapper: ½-length second of 23 to Pepperdine in William Hill Trophy at York on reappearance: seemingly somewhat flattered by that effort, though not disgraced when fourth at Doncaster final start: stays 6f: acts on good to firm and soft going: has worn near-side pricker: usually apprentice ridden: often front runner. *M. Brittain* **107 d**

FIRST NIGHT (IRE) 3 b.f. Sadler's Wells (USA) 132 – Morning Devotion (USA) 102 (Affirmed (USA)) [1998 NR 1999 10m⁴ 8g* 8s² Aug 5] rather unfurnished filly: closely related to several winners, including Oaks and Irish Derby winner Balanchine (by Storm Bird) and smart winner up to 1½m Romanov (by Nureyev): dam, 2-y-o 6f winner, stayed 1½m: won maiden at Salisbury in June: improved again when length second to Choice Spirit in listed race at Deauville: bred to be well suited by further than 1m: tended to edge left final 2 starts: sent to USA: likely to improve further. *P. W. Chapple-Hyam* **102 p**

FIRST TRUTH 2 b.c. (Mar 5) Rudimentary (USA) 118 – Pursuit of Truth (USA) 69 (Irish River (FR) 131) [1999 5.1m 6s⁴ 6m 8d² 8d* 8d⁵ Oct 18] 14,500F, 31,000Y: workmanlike colt: brother to 3 winners, including 3-y-o Spring Pursuit, and half-brother to 1995 2-y-o 7f winner Truth (by Prince Sabo): dam, 2-y-o 7f winner on only start, out of half-sister to Sun Princess and Saddlers' Hall: fairly useful performer: won maiden at Pontefract in September: good fifth of 6 to Hataab in listed race there final start: will stay at least 1¼m: acts on good to soft going: has been bandaged in front. *A. Bailey* **86**

FIRST VENTURE 2 b.c. (Feb 18) Formidable (USA) 125 – Diamond Wedding (USA) 65 (Diamond Shoal 130) [1999 6g 6d a6g² a7g² a7g³ a7g⁵ Aug 14] lengthy, useful-looking colt: fourth foal: half-brother to 4-y-o Diamond White: dam (maiden) should have stayed beyond 1½m: fair maiden: stays 7f: acts on fibresand: blinkered (respectable effort) final start. *C. N. Allen* **62 a72**

FISHER ISLAND (IRE) 2 b. or br.f. (Jan 30) Sri Pekan (USA) 117 – Liberty Song (IRE) (Last Tycoon 131) [1999 6d⁴ 7.1g⁵ 6.8m 6g⁵ 6s³ 8v⁴ 7s⁵ 8d Nov 1] IR 7,500Y: first foal: dam, French 1m and 11f winner, granddaughter of Oaks winner Lupe: modest maiden: should stay 1¼m: acts on heavy going: carries head awkwardly: sold only 700 gns. *R. Hollinshead* **59**

FISHERMAN'S COVE (USA) 4 b.g. Caerleon (USA) 132 – Free At Last 115 (Shirley Heights 130) [1998 67: 14m³ 1999 12.3m 14.1m 12d⁴ 10.4f 17.1s² 18d Oct 18] second foal: brother to smart US winner up to 1½m Coretta: dam, 7f winner at 2 yrs and fourth in 1000 Guineas (later stakes winner up to 1½m in USA), half-sister to Barathea: fair maiden: trained by A. O'Brien only start at 3 yrs: good second in handicap on penultimate outing: reportedly choked next time: stays 17f well: acts on soft going: tongue tied final 2 starts. *L. Lungo* **69**

FITZWILLIAM (USA) 6 b.g. Rahy (USA) 115 – Early Lunch (USA) (Noble Table (USA)) [1998 NR 1999 a11g⁶ Jan 18] tall, lengthy gelding: fairly useful at 3 yrs: well held first Flat outing since: stays 1½m: yet to race on ground softer than good: sold 8,000 gns in May, sent to USA. *I. A. Balding* **–**

FIVE OF WANDS 2 b.f. (Mar 24) Caerleon (USA) 132 – Overact (IRE) 92 (Law **64 p**
Society (USA) 130) [1999 7d Oct 30] second foal: half-sister to 3-y-o Woodcote
Warrior: dam, 2-y-o 7f winner, stayed 12.5f, half-sister to dam of Vintage Crop:
eleventh of 16 in Newmarket maiden, slowly away: bred to be suited by at least 1¼m:
will do better. *J. L. Dunlop*

FIZZYGIG 3 br.f. Efisio 120 – Buzzbomb 98 (Bustino 136) [1998 61, a49: 6d **71**
a5g a6s 1999 7s³ 10.2s⁴ 10g 7.1g 7g* 8.2m⁴ 8.3g³ 8v² Sep 20] smallish, unfurnished **a–**
filly: fair handicapper: won at Salisbury in June: ran well all 3 starts after: stays 1m:
acts on good to firm and heavy going, below best on fibresand at 2 yrs. *R. F. Johnson
Houghton*

FLAG FEN (USA) 8 b. or br.g. Riverman (USA) 131 – Damascus Flag (USA) **76**
(Damascus (USA)) [1998 73, a?: a11g⁵ a12g a11g 10g* 9m⁵ 10g⁴ 10g* 8g 12d 1999
10m 8g 12d³ 10m³ 10.1d* 10m 10m 9.9f⁵ Jul 27] rangy gelding: fair handicapper:
won ladies event at Yarmouth in July: best around 1¼m: acts on fibresand, firm and
good to soft going: blinkered once as 5-y-o: has tended to hang right: often apprentice
ridden: often makes running. *H. J. Collingridge*

FLAK JACKET 4 b.g. Magic Ring (IRE) 115 – Vaula 49 (Henbit (USA) 130) **88 +**
[1998 89+: 6d 6.1m 5g³ 6s* 6m* 1999 6f 6g 6m 7g 6g² 6d⁶ 5s 5g Oct 6] strong,
good-bodied gelding: impresses in appearance: fairly useful handicapper: good neck
second of 27 to Royal Result at Goodwood in August: just respectable efforts after:
stays 6f: acts on firm and soft ground: blinkered third start: probably best held up:
joined D. Nicholls for 14,500 gns: may well be capable of better. *B. J. Meehan*

FLAME CUTTER (USA) 3 ch.f. Miswaki (USA) 124 – Flaming Torch 92 **79**
(Rousillon (USA) 133) [1998 NR 1999 8m³ 8s* Sep 29] second foal: closely related
to 1996 2-y-o 7f winner Flaming West (by Gone West): dam, 2-y-o 1m winner in
France and Grade 3 11f winner in USA at 4 yrs, out of close relative to Coronation
Cup winner Quiet Fling: landed odds in Brighton maiden in September: stud.
H. R. A. Cecil

FLAMENCO RED 2 b.f. (Feb 8) Warning 136 – Spanish Wells (IRE) (Sadler's **86 +**
Wells (USA) 132) [1999 5g³ 6.1f* 6m² 7s³ 6m⁵ Aug 28] quite good-topped filly: first
foal: dam, French 12.5f winner, half-sister to Irish Oaks winner Wemyss Bight: fairly
useful form: won maiden at Nottingham in June: will stay 1m, probably 1¼m: acts
on firm going (raced alone on soft): visored (ran in snatches but performed creditably) final start. *R. Charlton*

FLAME OF FORTUNE (IRE) 3 ch.f. Nucleon (USA) 94 – Lovely Leitrim **–**
(IRE) (Erin's Hope 117) [1998 NR 1999 8.5m Sep 3] first foal: dam, poor maiden, at
best in Irish bumpers/hurdles: 40/1, last of 9 in maiden at Epsom. *S. Dow*

FLAME OF GLORY 5 ch.g. Polish Precedent (USA) 131 – Danishkada 119 **–**
(Thatch (USA) 136) [1998 –: 8g 1999 10m 7.7m 7s 7d 9s Oct 8] tall gelding: well
beaten in maidens/handicaps. *Miss Z. C. Davison*

FLAME TOWER (IRE) 4 ch.g. Archway (IRE) 115 – Guantanamera (USA) **60**
(El Gran Senor (USA) 136) [1998 60: a6g⁴ a8g³ 6d⁶ 8f² 7d³ 7g⁴ 9.9m 7m⁵ 7m⁴
a10g⁴ a8.5g* a8f 1999 a7g³ 7s a8.5g a12g Nov 20] strong, angular gelding: modest
performer: left R. Hannon after third in Southwell claimer on reappearance: no form
after: stays 1m, probably not 1¼m: acts on all-weather, firm and good to soft going:
has had tongue tied: none too consistent. *Miss A. Stokell*

FLAMINGO ROAD (GER) 3 b.f. Acatenango (GER) 127 – Fabula Dancer **118**
(USA) (Northern Dancer) [1998 NR 1999 10.5v* 11g* 11d* 12m³ 12s³ 12g² 12v Oct
3] big, workmanlike filly: half-sister to several winners in Germany, including useful
performers at 1½m or further Flamingo Paradise and Flamingo Garden (both by
Rainbow Quest) and Flamingo Queen (by Surumu): dam unraced half-sister to 2
graded stakes winners in USA: smart performer, the top 3-y-o filly in Germany: won
maiden, listed race and Preis der Diana, all at Mulheim in April/May, beating Rose of
Zollern 2 lengths in last-named event: placed in Group 1 events next 3 starts (2¾
lengths third to Belenus in Deutsches Derby at Hamburg on first occasion), best
effort when 3 lengths second of 6 to Tiger Hill in Grosser Preis von Baden penultimate outing: always behind in Prix de l'Arc de Triomphe at Longchamp final start:
stays 1½m: won on heavy going, best effort on good ground. *A. Schutz, Germany*

Scarbrough Stakes, Doncaster—
a finish of short heads concerning Flanders (second left), Emma Peel and Dashing Blue (noseband)

FLAMING QUEST 3 b.c. Rainbow Quest (USA) 134 – Nearctic Flame 111 **106**
(Sadler's Wells (USA) 132) [1998 NR 1999 10d² 11.8m* 12.1g* 12m² 11.9s² 11.9m
Aug 17] leggy, good-topped colt: brother to smart winner up to 1½m Happy
Valentine and closely related to useful 1¼m to 1¾m winner Blushing Flame (by
Blushing Groom): dam, 1¼m winner, sister to Salsabil and half-sister to Marju:
useful performer: landed odds in maiden at Leicester and minor event at Chepstow
in May: second in 4-runner listed races at Ascot and Haydock (beaten 3 lengths by
Elmutabaki): last of 7 in Great Voltigeur Stakes at York final start: stays 1½m: acts
on good to firm and soft ground: sold 85,000 gns, sent to USA. *Sir Michael Stoute*

FLANDERS (IRE) 3 b.f. Common Grounds 118 – Family At War (USA) 71 **110**
(Explodent (USA)) [1998 103: 5m* 5d* 5d* 5.2m* 6f³ 6d² 6g 1999 6g 5m² 5m² 5m²
5f⁵ 5g 5m* 5d⁶ Sep 30] smallish, angular, good-quartered filly: good walker: has a
powerful, round action: smart performer: won listed race at Doncaster in September,
rallying to beat Emma Peel a short head: best effort on second start when short-
headed by Mitcham in King's Stand Stakes at Royal Ascot: best at 5f: acts on firm
and good to soft going: sometimes on toes: front runner: genuine. *T. D. Easterby*

FLASHFEET 9 b.g. Rousillon (USA) 133 – Miellita 98 (King Emperor (USA)) **–**
[1998 –: a7g a7g 1999 a7g a8g a7g a8.5g 7m a8.5g Dec 1] lightly raced and no form
since 1995: tried blinkered. *P. D. Purdy*

FLAVIAN 3 b.f. Catrail (USA) 123 – Fatah Flare (USA) 121 (Alydar (USA)) **–**
[1998 90p: 6g² 6g* 1999 6g May 15] tall, unfurnished filly: fairly useful form at 2
yrs: last of 8 in listed event at Newmarket, only run of 1999: should stay 7f/1m.
H. Candy

FLAXEN PRIDE (IRE) 4 ch.f. Pips Pride 117 – Fair Chance (Young Emperor **50**
133) [1998 44: 7d 7.1s 9.3m 7g 6m 5g⁴ 1999 6d 8d 8m 8g* 9g⁵ 8g⁶ Aug 25]
unfurnished filly: modest handicapper: won at Leicester in August: bit below form
after: best up to 1m: acts on good to firm going. *Mrs M. Reveley*

FLEETING FANCY 2 b.f. (Apr 12) Thatching 131 – Fleetwood Fancy (Taufan **55**
(USA) 119) [1999 7g 6d Oct 29] 18,000 2-y-o: half-sister to several winners,
including 3-y-o Al Fahda and 1¼m and 1.6f winner Elly Fleetfoot (by Elmaamul):
dam, Irish 2-y-o 5f winner, later won up to 9f in USA: well held in maidens at
Lingfield and Newmarket. *S. Dow*

FLETCHER 5 b.g. Salse (USA) 128 – Ballet Classique (USA) 84 (Sadler's Wells **79 §**
(USA) 132) [1998 84: 16g² 20d 14g³ 10m² 11.6m⁶ 11.7m² 12m⁶ 10g⁵ 12g² 12s* 10s
1999 10m 12m⁶ 11.9m 12s² 12d³ 13.1v 11.7s a14g Dec 13] useful-looking gelding:
easy mover: fair performer: well below form last 3 starts: finds 1¼m a bare minimum
and stays 2m: acts on firm and soft going: visored once at 3 yrs: carries head
awkwardly: unreliable. *H. Morrison*

FLEUR D'OR   3 b.f. Alhijaz 122 – Forever Shineing 62 (Glint of Gold 128) [1998   –
–: 5g a6g⁶ a6g 7f 6m 10.2d 1999 a11g Feb 5] neat filly: no sign of ability.
M. J. Polglase

FLICKER   4 b.f. Unfuwain (USA) 131 – Lovers Light (Grundy 137) [1998 52:   –
12.3s 10.2s⁵ 11.6g 10.8s³ a8g 8v⁴ 1999 10m 7.7m Jul 2] modest maiden: well beaten
in 1999: stays 1¼m: acts on heavy going: visored last 5 starts in 1998. *W. Clay*

FLIGHT ETERNAL (IRE)   2 ch.g. (Apr 19) Prince of Birds (USA) 121 –   –
Timeless Classic (Ahonoora 122) [1999 5d 6m 6m 5m⁵ 7g a8g Nov 15] IR 7,500Y,
4,400 2-y-o: leggy gelding: half-brother to a winner in Macau by Digamist: dam Irish
maiden: well beaten, including in sellers: usually blinkered/visored. *J. L. Eyre*

FLIGHT FOR FREEDOM   4 b.f. Saddlers' Hall (IRE) 126 – Anatroccolo 47   –
(Ile de Bourbon (USA) 133) [1998 58: 10.1d⁶ 9.9m 11.1d⁶ 10g² a9.4g 10g 1999 10d
Jun 7] sparely-made filly: modest maiden: fit from successful spell over hurdles, well
held only Flat run of 1999: stays 1¼m: acts on soft ground. *F. Murphy*

FLIGHT OF DREAMS (IRE)   2 b.f. (May 16) College Chapel 122 – Lady   –
Portobello (Porto Bello 118) [1999 5m 8.2g 6.1d Oct 5] IR 6,000Y: half-sister to 3
winners, including fairly useful Irish 1995 2-y-o 6f winner Archobello (by Archway)
and 13f winner Missed The Boat (by Cyrano de Bergerac): dam (maiden) best effort
at 7f: little sign of ability in maidens, off nearly 5 months after debut. *B. S. Rothwell*

FLIGHT REFUND   2 ch.g. (May 8) Missed Flight 123 – Settlement (USA) 75   –
(Irish River (FR) 131) [1999 7d 7s a8g Dec 17] angular, workmanlike gelding: fifth
foal: half-brother to 3-y-o Pretty Obvious and winners abroad by High Estate and
Alzao: dam 1¼m winner: well beaten in maidens. *R. Hollinshead*

FLIGHT SEQUENCE   3 b.f. Polar Falcon (USA) 126 – Doubles 85 (Damister   **79**
(USA) 123) [1998 NR 1999 8g² 8.3g⁴ 8.3m² 10g⁴ Aug 16] 6,000 2-y-o: unfurnished
filly: unimpressive mover: third foal: half-sister to French 1¼m winner Trebles (by
Kenmare): dam, 1¼m to 1¾m winner here and in France, daughter of useful stayer
Obertura: fair maiden: best around 1m. *Lady Herries*

FLINT KNAPPER   5 ch.g. Kris 135 – Cyro's Isle (Be My Guest (USA) 126)   –
[1998 97: 10.3g 10g* 10g 1999 9m 8m Aug 6] quite attractive gelding: useful
performer, lightly raced: well beaten both starts in 1999: stays 1¼m: acts on firm and
good to soft ground: sold 8,000 gns in October. *G. Wragg*

FLINTSTONE   2 b.g. (Mar 12) First Trump 118 – South Rock 102 (Rock City   **64**
120) [1999 6m 7m³ Jun 15] 27,000Y: unfurnished gelding: first foal: dam, won at 7f
(including listed race)/1m, from good middle-distance staying family: better effort in
maidens when third of 12 to Buying A Dream at Thirsk: will stay 1m. *J. A. Glover*

FLIQUET BAY (IRE)   2 b.g. (Feb 20) Namaqualand (USA) – Thatcherite (Final   **62**
Straw 127) [1999 7g⁶ 7.6g 8v Sep 29] 15,000Y, 12,500 2-y-o: seventh foal: half-
brother to several winners, including useful 5f (at 2 yrs) and 1¼m winner Uncondi-
tional Love (by Polish Patriot): dam unraced half-sister to very smart 7f performer
Kampala: form in maidens only on debut: should stay 1m. *Mrs A. J. Perrett*

FLITE OF ARABY   2 b.c. (Mar 12) Green Desert (USA) 127 – Allegedly Blue   **59**
(USA) 106 (Alleged (USA) 138) [1999 7d 7d 8.2d Oct 21] 75,000F, 40,000Y: leggy,
close-coupled colt: eighth foal: brother to useful winner up to 2m Hawait Al Barr and
half-brother to 2 winners at 1½m+: dam 1½m winner and third in Park Hill Stakes:
modest form when considerately handled in maiden at Newbury on debut: stiff task
next time, played up in stalls and raced too freely final start: should prove suited by
1¼m+. *W. R. Muir*

FLITE OF LIFE   3 gr.g. Forzando 122 – Frighten The Life (Kings Lake (USA)   **75**
133) [1998 75: 6s⁴ 5.7g 6f⁴ 6m⁴ 6m² 5.2g 1999 6m 6g 5.1s a7g a8g⁵ a8g* Dec 13]
rangy gelding: fair handicapper: won (for first time) at Southwell in December: stays
1m: acts on firm going and fibresand: sometimes slowly away: inconsistent.
W. R. Muir

FLIT 'N' FLIRT   2 gr.g. (Apr 30) Most Welcome 131 – David's Dream (HOL)   –
(Superlative 118) [1999 5.1m 6g 8.2d a6g⁶ Oct 30] 1,200Y, resold 500Y: second foal:
dam ran once at 2 yrs: no sign of ability: tried blinkered. *R. Brotherton*

FLOATING CHARGE   5 b.g. Sharpo 132 – Poyle Fizz (Damister (USA) 123)   **84**
[1998 70: 6s⁵ 7.6m⁵ 10s⁵ 9m* 9m 8.1m⁶ 7g 1999 8.3m* 8g 8.5d 8m² 8f⁴ 8.3s³ 8g⁶

8v* Sep 20] very tall gelding: fairly useful handicapper: won at Windsor in April and at Kempton (ridden more positively than usual, dictated pace) in September: twice found little after travelling strongly in between: stays 1m: acts on any going: no improvement visored/blinkered. *J. R. Fanshawe*

FLOATING EMBER 2 b.f. (Apr 14) Rambo Dancer (CAN) 107 – Spark (IRE) – 79 (Flash of Steel 120) [1999 5g 6d 6g⁶ 8d 6v Oct 11] 6,600Y: second foal: half-sister to a 6f (including at 2 yrs) to 1m winner in Sweden by Superpower: dam 2-y-o 6f winner, later stayed 10.4f: little sign of ability. *J. L. Eyre*

FLOORSO'THEFOREST (IRE) 3 ch.g. Forest Wind (USA) 111 – Ravens- 72 dale Rose (IRE) (Henbit (USA) 130) [1998 NR 1999 7d⁴ 7d⁶ 8s⁶ 10d³ 9.3g 9.1g³ 9m 9d² 10.9s 9.2m* 10m⁴ Aug 10] IR 6,500F, 8,000Y: angular gelding: third foal: half-brother to a winner abroad by Balla Cove: dam ran twice at 2 yrs in Ireland: fair performer: won handicap at Hamilton in July: stays 1¼m: acts on soft and good to firm going. *Miss L. A. Perratt*

FLORA DREAMBIRD 5 b.m. Mandalus 110 – Dame Flora (Celtic Cone 116) 41 [1998 NR 1999 a12g⁶ a12g⁵ 15.8m² 17.2g⁶ a14.8g⁶ Dec 11] second reported foal: dam, lightly raced on Flat, winning staying hurdler: poor maiden on Flat: stays 2m: blinkered when winning over hurdles in October. *P. W. Hiatt*

FLORAL RAJ (IRE) 3 ch.c. Indian Ridge 123 – Spring Daffodil 97 (Pharly 90 (FR) 130) [1998 77p: 7m 6.1d⁴ 1999 7g* 8.1s 8g⁴ 8.5f Dec 1] leggy, useful-looking colt: won maiden at Catterick in September: good fourth of 20 in handicap at Newmarket in October: sold from Sir Michael Stoute for 60,000 gns: well held in allowance race at Laurel: stays 1m: possibly unsuited by soft ground. *Ann W. Merryman, USA*

FLORIDA BORGHESE (ITY) 2 gr.f. (Apr 25) Lomond (USA) 128 – Filicaia – 79 (Sallust 134) [1999 7g 8g Oct 15] third foal: dam 5f/6f winner: soundly beaten in Redcar maidens. *Don Enrico Incisa*

FLORISMART 7 b.g. Never So Bold 135 – Spoilt Again 91 (Mummy's Pet 125) – [1998 –: 12.3v 12.1v 8m 1999 12.3m Apr 7] of no account nowadays. *B. P. J. Baugh*

FLOSSY 3 b.f. Efisio 120 – Sirene Bleu Marine (USA) (Secreto (USA) 128) [1998 94 NR 1999 a7f⁵ a7g⁴ a8.5g⁵ 10m 9.9m* 12g* 10m* 12m² 12.3d² 12.4g* 11.9m* 13.1d⁶ 10s² 12s* Nov 6] leggy filly: fourth foal: half-sister to winner up to 1¼m Society Girl (by Shavian): dam unraced: fairly useful handicapper: progressed with almost every

Tote Scoop6 November Stakes (Handicap), Doncaster—
Flossy crowns a fine season, shading Carlys Quest (blinkers) and the grey Lord Lamb

race and enjoyed a good season: won at Beverley, Musselburgh and Newbury in July, Newcastle in August, Haydock in September and Doncaster (16-runner Tote Scoop6 November Handicap by head from Carlys Quest, left with bit to do 3f out, led close home): demoted after dead-heating at Ripon ninth outing: effective at 1¼m/1½m: acts on soft and good to firm going: often held up (has taken strong hold and wandered): tough and game. *C. W. Thornton*

FLOTSAM 3 ch.c. Beveled (USA) – Parrot Fashion 86 (Pieces of Eight 128) –
[1998 NR 1999 8m Sep 17] plain colt: brother to fair 7.6f winner Designer Lines: dam best at 1¼m: 66/1 and bandaged in front, well beaten in maiden at Newbury. *M. D. I. Usher*

FLOWERING 2 b.f. (Apr 14) Deploy 131 – Ajuga (USA) 102 (The Minstrel – p
(CAN) 135) [1999 7s Nov 5] medium-sized, quite good-topped filly: seventh living foal: half-sister to 3-y-o Bangalore and several winners, notably smart German middle-distance performer Bad Bertrich Again (by Dowsing) and 4-y-o Prolix: dam 6f (at 2 yrs) and 7f winner out of Irish 1000 Guineas and Champion Stakes winner Cairn Rouge: 11/2 favourite, not knocked about when mid-division in maiden at Doncaster (bandaged near-hind): will stay at least 1¼m: open to plenty of improvement. *B. W. Hills*

FLOWER O'CANNIE (IRE) 4 b.f. Mujadil (USA) 119 – Baby's Smile 68 84
(Shirley Heights 130) [1998 87: 8s 7.9g 8s² 10s² 10m⁵ 13.9g 10s³ 12.4v* 12s* 12d 1999 11.1v³ 13v⁶ 12.3m 12m 11.9d* 12.3m⁴ 12m 14d⁵ 12.3d⁴ 12.3g² 10d 11.9d Oct 7] workmanlike filly: fairly useful handicapper: won Queen Mother's Cup at York in June: mostly at least respectable efforts otherwise: stays 1½m: best on good going or softer (acts on heavy): sometimes edgy. *M. W. Easterby*

FLOWERS COVE 4 ch.f. Then Again 126 – Lady St Lawrence (USA) 65 (Bering –
136) [1998 45d: 8.3m 8g 11.6g² 9.7m⁴ 10m⁶ 10.8m 8.1d 10m⁶ 11.8d 14.1v 1999 a12g Feb 22] quite good-topped filly: poor maiden at best: well held on all-weather debut, only run of 1999: stays 11.6f. *K. S. Bridgwater*

FLOWER STATE 3 b.c. Sabrehill (USA) 120 – Flower Arrangement (Lomond 64
(USA) 128) [1998 NR 1999 7.1m 7d⁵ 7s⁵ Aug 8] 100,000Y: good-topped colt: fourth foal: half-brother to 2 winners in Italy by Shavian, including fairly useful 1994 2-y-o 5f and 7.5f winner Armenian Dancer: dam unraced half-sister to Kentucky Derby runner-up Bold Arrangement: form only when fifth in maiden at Newbury on second start: may prove best up to 7f: sent to UAE. *J. H. M. Gosden*

Queen Mother's Cup (Ladies) Handicap, York—
Flower O'Cannie wins the most valuable lady riders' race in Europe from Lancer, Minivet and Totem Dancer

FLOWINGTON (IRE) 2 b.f. (Apr 14) Owington 123 – Persian Flower (Persian **94**
Heights 129) [1999 5.1m a5g* 6.8m* 6m³ 6m 7s Oct 2] 2,000F, IR 2,100Y: leggy,
angular filly: first foal: dam lightly-raced maiden: fairly useful form: won seller at
Wolverhampton and minor event at Warwick, both in June: easily best effort when
staying-on third of 12 to Torgau in Cherry Hinton Stakes at Newmarket: reportedly
lost action next time, and off track 10 weeks before final start: should stay at least 7f.
N. P. Littmoden

FLUME 2 br.f. (Mar 15) Zafonic (USA) 130 – Rainy Sky (Rainbow Quest (USA) **81**
134) [1999 6g⁴ 7m⁴ Sep 17] tall, leggy filly: second foal: dam, French 1½m winner,
sister to smart French winner up to 1½m Bonash: promising fourth of 16 to Teggiano
in maiden at Newbury: similar form when fourth of 7 to Veil of Avalon in minor
event there following month: bred to stay at least 1m. *B. W. Hills*

FLUSH (FR) 4 b. or br.f. Warning 136 – Garden Pink (FR) (Bellypha 130) [1998 **–**
69: 8g³ 9.9m 8m 8m⁶ 7m 8.1g³ 7g 8s* 8d 1999 a7g a7g a10g Dec 8] close-coupled
filly: fair performer at best: well beaten on Flat in 1999, though modest winning
hurdler for M. Pipe early in year. *R. E. Peacock*

FLY HOME 4 br.f. Skyliner 117 – Fille de Phaeton (Sun Prince 128) [1998 59, a–: **–**
7m³ 9m a7g a7g a8.5g 1999 11.6s 10.5m a14g Nov 30] no form since debut in 1998.
H. E. Haynes

FLYING BEAN (IRE) 2 b.f. (Apr 11) Mujadil (USA) 119 – Coffee Bean (Doulab **69**
(USA) 115) [1999 5g² 5m⁵ Aug 31] 5,000Y: sixth foal: sister to a winner in Austria
and half-sister to 3 winners by Red Sunset, including 7.5f to 1¼m winner Java Red:
dam poor Irish maiden: better effort in maidens when second at Tipperary: prominent
long way at Ripon 12 days later. *P. M. J. Doyle, Ireland*

FLYING BOLD (IRE) 4 ch.g. Persian Bold 123 – Princess Reema (USA) (Affirm- **54**
ed (USA)) [1998 70: 8g 7.9g 9.9m⁴ 10g⁵ 12m 11.6f² 11.5f* 12m³ 12g⁶ 10g 12g⁵ 1999
10.9s⁶ 12m 12f³ 15.8s Oct 5] rather sparely-made gelding: fair handicapper at 3 yrs:
only modest in 1999, though won selling hurdle in October: stays 11.6f: acts on firm
going and fibresand. *L. Lungo*

FLYING CARPET 2 b.f. (Apr 11) Barathea (IRE) 127 – Flying Squaw 102 (Be **–**
My Chief (USA) 122) [1999 5s May 11] leggy, angular filly: first foal: dam, 2-y-o
5f/6f winner, from family of Bireme: bandaged behind, not right in coat and green
throughout when last of 7 in minor event at York. *T. D. Easterby*

FLYING EAGLE 8 b.g. Shaadi (USA) 126 – Fly Me (FR) 116 (Luthier 126) **82**
[1998 86: 10m* 9.7m 10.2d* 10.8d* 10m* 12m² 10g³ 10m* 12m* 12m⁶ 12s 12m
18g 10m a10g a13g⁵ 12m 12m 12g² 12m 11.9f⁵ 10g³ 11.9s⁴ 12g* 12m⁵ 11.6g³ Oct
11] fairly useful performer: left R. Simpson after second start: easily won amateur
handicap at Epsom in August: stays 1½m: acts on good to firm and good to soft going
(possibly not on soft): best held up: inconsistent. *G. L. Moore*

FLYING FLIP 5 b.m. Rolfe (USA) 77 – Needwood Sprite 58 (Joshua 129) [1998 **67**
61: 10s* 12m⁵ 11.8g² 11.8m³ 14.1d⁴ 12g⁴ 13.9g⁵ 16v 1999 11.8s⁵ 14.1s* 13g⁵ 13d*
13g⁴ 15.9d 14s 13.9d Oct 9] unfurnished mare: has a round action: fair handicapper:
won at Nottingham in April and Hamilton in May: below form final 3 starts: should
stay 2m: acts on soft and good to firm going: tongue tied. *B. C. Morgan*

FLYING HIGH (IRE) 4 b.g. Fayruz 116 – Shayista 63 (Tap On Wood 130) **–**
[1998 NR 1999 10m 12s 8d 8d a7g Nov 17] no worthwhile form: tried blinkered.
B. Ellison

FLYING HOME 4 b.g. Flying Tyke 90 – Bellinote (FR) 71 (Noir Et Or 125) [1998 **–**
–: 13.8g⁶ 1999 12m 12g May 21] no sign of ability in maidens. *Mrs M. Reveley*

FLYING MEMORY 3 b.f. Greensmith 121 – Flying 82 (Head For Heights 125) **–**
[1998 –: a5g a6g⁶ 5d 1999 a6g⁶ a5g 6g Sep 20] little sign of ability, including in
sellers. *N. P. Littmoden*

FLYING OFFICER 3 ch.g. Efisio 120 – Area Girl 76 (Jareer (USA) 115) [1998 **109**
91+: a5g² a5g² a6g* a8f⁴ 1999 a7g* a6g* a8g² a7g* a5g⁵ 6s Jun 27] useful
performer: winner at Wolverhampton of handicap in January and minor events later
in month and in March: best effort on last occasion to beat Weetman's Weigh by 5

lengths: well below form in listed races in Scandinavia last 2 starts: best at 6f/7f: raced only on all-weather until final start. *Sir Mark Prescott*

FLYING PENNANT (IRE) 6 gr.g. Waajib 121 – Flying Beckee (IRE) 60 (Godswalk (USA) 130) [1998 60: 7g² 7g⁶ 7g³ 7.1d* 6.9d³ 7.1g 7m 7m⁶ 7.5m³ 7.1d 7g 1999 7.1m 7f 7.1d 7.5d⁴ 7.1g⁴ 7.7m 7.6m 7f⁵ 7.1m 7f³ 7m⁵ 7m Sep 3] strong, good-bodied gelding: has a quick action: modest handicapper: stays 1m: acts on good to firm and good to soft going: blinkered/visored: usually comes off pace, and suited by strongly-run race: often claimer ridden. *J. M. Bradley* **52**

FLYING RUN (IRE) 2 b.f. (Apr 8) Lake Coniston (IRE) 131 – Kaskazi (Dancing Brave (USA) 140) [1999 5.7g⁴ 6g⁵ 6.1f 6m Sep 10] 19,000Y: third foal: half-sister to 3-y-o Trinity: dam, Irish 9f/1¼m winner, out of smart French middle-distance filly Fly Me: modest maiden: best efforts at Bath and Kempton on first 2 starts: should stay at least 7f. *J. R. Arnold* **56**

FLYING THE FLAG (IRE) 3 b.f. Thatching 131 – Flagpole (IRE) (Be My Guest (USA) 126) [1998 75: 5m⁶ 6m⁵ 5m² 5.7g³ 1999 6.1m 5d 6m⁵ 6m 6m⁵ 8.1f³ 8m 8g 7.5g⁵ 7.1f 8.2g 10.9v Oct 11] sturdy, lengthy filly: disappointing maiden: tried blinkered: sold 800 gns. *J. J. Quinn* **66 d**

FLYING TOUCH 4 ch.f. Greensmith 121 – Flying 82 (Head For Heights 125) [1998 –: a6g a5g a5g⁶ 1999 a6g a7g a7g⁵ a8.5g Feb 24] little sign of ability: sold 950 gns in May. *N. P. Littmoden* **–**

FLY LIKE A BIRD 3 ch.f. Keen 116 – Turtle Dove (Gyr (USA) 131) [1998 67: 7g 7g⁶ 8.2g 10s³ 1999 12g⁶ 12m Apr 14] small, sparely-made filly: fair maiden: should stay at least 1½m: acts on soft and good to firm going. *S. P. C. Woods* **57**

FLY LIKE THE WIND 2 br.f. (Mar 2) Cyrano de Bergerac 120 – Thulium (Mansingh (USA) 120) [1999 5m⁵ May 22] 4,200F, 4,000Y: half-sister to 4-y-o Zilva and several winners, including fairly useful 2-y-o winners Iolite (5f/6f, by Forzando) and Crystal Magic (5f, by Mazilier): dam lightly-raced sister to Petong: green, modest form when fifth of 12 to Halland Park Girl in minor event at Lingfield: bred for sprinting: looked sure to improve. *M. A. Jarvis* **58**

FLYNN 3 b.g. My Generation 111 – Sky Mariner 59 (Julio Mariner 127) [1998 NR 1999 6g 6.1s 8.1g May 31] sixth reported foal: half-brother to 8-y-o Lochon: dam, 2-y-o 7f winner, stayed 1m: well beaten in sellers/maiden. *N. M. Babbage* **–**

FLYOVER 2 b.f. (Apr 28) Presidium 124 – Flash-By (Ilium 121) [1999 5v² 5.1m 6g⁴ 6m³ 7f 6d 7s Oct 1] 1,200Y: third foal: dam unraced half-sister to smart US performer at around 1m Mighty Forum (by Presidium): modest performer: won maiden at Salisbury in June: well held in nurseries last 3 starts: should stay 7f. *B. R. Millman* **63**

FLY TO THE STARS 5 b.h. Bluebird (USA) 125 – Rise And Fall (Mill Reef (USA) 141) [1998 123: a8f² a9f³ a10f³ 8d² 8d* 8d* 8f⁵ 1999 8d* 8m 8m Sep 5] Godolphin had a very strong team for the top mile races in the latest season. Three-year-olds Dubai Millennium, Aljabr and Island Sands all won at Group 1 level over the trip, as did the five-year-old Fly To The Stars. Fly To The Stars wasn't the best older miler in the Godolphin camp—that honour went to the Queen Anne and Celebration Mile winner Cape Cross—but he recorded the best performance of his career when making a winning reappearance in the Juddmonte Lockinge Stakes at Newbury in May. As on all his starts in the latest season, Fly To The Stars wasn't the number-one Godolphin representative. The Lockinge saw the eagerly-awaited return of the previous season's top miler Intikhab, side-lined since a striking victory in the Queen Anne Stakes at Royal Ascot the previous year. Intikhab, minus the suspended Dettori, started 7/4-on and Fly To The Stars at 9/1 in the field of six, which also included the well travelled French five-year-old Jim And Tonic, successful in the Queen Elizabeth II Cup in Hong Kong on his most recent appearance in April. Front-running Fly To The Stars turned in a typically game performance to hold off Jim And Tonic by a length and a half under jockey Willie Supple with Almushtarak and Intikhab (subsequently found to have gone lame) close behind. The going at Newbury was good to soft—Fly To The Stars had **124**

Juddmonte Lockinge Stakes, Newbury—Fly To The Stars upstages stable-companion Intikhab, the pair split by Jim And Tonic (striped sleeves) and Almushtarak (far side)

encountered similar conditions when putting up his best performances the previous year—and he didn't reproduce his Lockinge form in two subsequent outings on good to firm. He came off worst of the three Godolphin runners in the Queen Anne Stakes, dropping away to finish seventh of eight to Cape Cross (Fa-Eq was fourth), and again beat only one home when next seen out, behind Sendawar in the Prix du Moulin de Longchamp in September when he was coupled in the betting with second favourite Aljabr (Dettori).

Fly To The Stars (b.h. 1994)	Bluebird (USA) (b 1984)	Storm Bird (b 1978)	Northern Dancer South Ocean
		Ivory Dawn (b 1978)	Sir Ivor Dusky Evening
	Rise And Fall (b 1984)	Mill Reef (b 1968)	Never Bend Milan Mill
		Light Duty (b 1972)	Queen's Hussar Highlight

The tall, angular Fly To The Stars, a powerful galloper with a round action, has yet to show that he stays beyond a mile, but three of his half-brothers have won over further, German-raced Royal Rarity (by Formidable) and the smart Danseur Landais (by Damister) at up to a mile and a quarter, and, in the latest season, Warring Kingdom, successful at up to seventeen furlongs. The dam Rise And Fall showed little but is a product of the Highlight family from the Royal Studs, and made 90,000 guineas at the December Sales in 1987. She is a daughter of Ribblesdale and Yorkshire Oaks runner-up Light Duty, who is a full sister to the Queen's One Thousand Guineas and Prix de Diane winner Highclere, the grandam of Nashwan. Fly To The Stars has form on good to firm going but goes particularly well on good to soft (he hasn't raced on softer since his debut). He stays in training. *Saeed bin Suroor*

FNAN   3 b.c. Generous (IRE) 139 – Rafha 123 (Kris 135) [1998 75p: 7m 8.2m 8d³ 8d³ 1999 10.3d 12.4g² 14.6f* 14d* 15s² 16m* 16.1m² 16.1g* 17.3g Oct 16] smallish, well-made colt: useful handicapper: had a good season, justifying favouritism at Doncaster, Haydock, Newbury and Newcastle (beat Murghem 1¾ lengths) between May/August: respectable ninth of 32 in Cesarewitch at Newmarket final start: should be suited by further than 2m: acts on firm going and soft: genuine and consistent: sold 74,000 gns. *J. L. Dunlop*   **105**

FOE (IRE)   2 b.c. (Mar 7) Fayruz 116 – Paryiana (IRE) (Shernazar 131) [1999 6g 5m* 6.3m 5g⁶ 6g⁵ 6f⁴ 5m Sep 11] IR 21,000F, IR 27,000Y: big, strong, good sort: has plenty of scope: third foal: brother to fair 1997 2-y-o 7f winner Fayrana, later 1m   **88**

winner in USA, and half-brother to 3-y-o Forest King: dam (unraced) from good French family: fairly useful performer: won minor event at Windsor in May: generally ran creditably afterwards, usually in useful company: stays 6f: raced only on good going or firmer: sold 18,000 gns in October. *R. Hannon*

FOIST   7 b.g. Efisio 120 – When The Saints (Bay Express 132) [1998 68: 5.9d 6d* 6g* 6.1m⁵ 6s 6m 5d 7s 6v 6f 1999 6g 6g 6g 6g⁵ 6g Aug 21] small, good-topped gelding: modest handicapper: creditable effort in 1999 only on penultimate start: effective at 6f/7f: has form on good to firm going and fibresand, probably best on good or softer: blinkered (too free) once at 4 yrs: sometimes gives trouble start. *M. W. Easterby*   **59**

FOLEY BIGTIME   2 ch.g. (Apr 9) Timeless Times (USA) 99 – Trachelium 65 (Formidable (USA) 125) [1999 5g 5v 7m Jun 24] 14,000Y: quite good-topped gelding: third foal: half-brother to 3-y-o Innes and 4-y-o Uniform: dam, maiden who should have stayed 1m, daughter of smart 2-y-o 5f winner Penny Blessing: well beaten in maidens, off course 2 months before final start. *M. Quinn*   **–**

FOLLOW ME   3 ch.g. Keen 116 – Fairlead 57 (Slip Anchor 136) [1998 –: 6g 6f 6m 1999 11.1s* May 14] modest performer: won selling handicap at Hamilton: should stay 1½m: sold 11,000 gns later in month, joined J. J. O'Neill. *C. W. Thornton*   **51**

FOLLOW SUIT   2 ch.c. (Mar 6) First Trump 118 – Indian Lament 52§ (Indian Ridge 123) [1999 6m* 7v⁵ Sep 29] 18,000Y: small colt: first foal: dam, one to avoid, daughter of sister to very smart sprinter Prince Sabo: green, won maiden at York in July, getting up close home: off course nearly 3 months, floundered off bridle on heavy ground when well-held fifth of 6 in minor event at Salisbury: not sure to stay further than 6f. *J. L. Dunlop*   **74**

FOLLOW THAT DREAM   3 b.f. Darshaan 133 – Try To Catch Me (USA) (Shareef Dancer (USA) 135) [1998 NR 1999 8.2m⁵ 10g⁵ 10.5m⁶ 12g⁵ 12.3m* 14m² 14d⁴ 13.3g³ 13.9m² 14.6g⁵ 14.1m⁵ Sep 24] smallish, good-topped filly: fourth foal: half-sister to useful 11f to 13f winner Desert Frolic (by Persian Bold) and 1993 2-y-o 7f winner Nawafell (by Kris): dam French miler out of high-class North American 6f to 1¼m winner It's In The Air: fairly useful handicapper: won at Chester in June: probably flattered in Park Hill Stakes at Doncaster penultimate start: stays 1¾m when conditions aren't testing: acts on good to firm ground: has got edgy in paddock. *E. A. L. Dunlop*   **90 +**

FONZY   5 b.g. Phountzi (USA) 104 – Diavalezza (Connaught 130) [1998 –: 6m 10m a6g 1999 a7g Jan 4] no form since 2 yrs: sent to Holland. *M. Brittain*   **–**

FOOL ON THE HILL   2 b.g. (Apr 1) Reprimand 122 – Stock Hill Lass 87 (Air Trooper 115) [1999 6g 7s⁶ Nov 5] workmanlike gelding: brother to 5-y-o In The Stocks and half-brother to 4-y-o Hill Magic: dam won up to 1m: better effort in maidens (green on debut) when well-held sixth of 20 to Hopeful Light at Doncaster: should stay at least 1m. *L. G. Cottrell*   **62**

FOOLS PARADISE (IRE)   2 ch.g. (Jan 12) Barathea (IRE) 127 – Sadly Sober (IRE) 70 (Roi Danzig (USA)) [1999 a8g Nov 11] 12,000Y: first foal: dam, maiden who stayed 1¼m well, half-sister to smart winner up to 11f Overbury: tailed off in maiden at Lingfield. *C. A. Cyzer*   **–**

FOOTPRINTS (IRE)   2 b.f. (May 3) College Chapel 122 – Near Miracle (Be My Guest (USA) 126) [1999 5s 5g² 5d* Oct 26] IR 6,500Y: half-sister to several winners, including Italian winner up to 1¼m Persona Gradita (by Shahrastani): dam Irish 7f winner: fair form: got up final 50 yds to win maiden at Redcar by ½ length from Marshall St Cyr: will stay at least 6f: raced only on good going or softer: remains capable of better. *M. Johnston*   **73 p**

FORBEARING (IRE)   2 b.c. (Feb 20) Bering 136 – For Example (USA) 66 (Northern Baby (CAN) 127) [1999 7d⁵ 6s⁶ a8g* a8.5g* Dec 11] 85,000Y: tall colt: has scope: first foal: dam, third from 2 starts at 1¼m in Ireland, from family of Zilzal, Polish Precedent and Culture Vulture: raced freely and showed only modest form first 2 starts: much improved on all-weather, winning maiden at Lingfield in November and minor event at Wolverhampton (beat You're Special by 4 lengths) in December: stays 8.5f: already useful, and open to further improvement. *Sir Mark Prescott*   **95 p**

FORCING BID   5 b.g. Forzando 122 – Cox's Pippin (USA) (Cox's Ridge (USA))   –
[1998 NR 1999 a6g a7g 10d 7m May 26] fairly useful in 1997, winner 3 times at 6f
on fibresand: no promise on return: twice blinkered, winning once. *John Berry*

FOREIGN EDITOR   3 ch.g. Magic Ring (IRE) 115 – True Precision 84 (Pre-   **85**
sidium 124) [1998 61: 5d³ 5m 5s⁵ 1999 5d 6g 5.9g a6g⁶ 7g⁶ 8s⁵ a7g⁴ a7g* a6g* Dec
27] fairly useful handicapper: much improved in winning twice at Wolverhampton in
December, by 9 lengths on second occasion: better form at 6f than 7f: acts on
fibresand and good to soft going: tried blinkered. *R. A. Fahey*

FOREIGN RULE (IRE)   5 b.g. Danehill (USA) 126 – Guida Centrale (Teenoso   –
(USA) 135) [1998 –: 16v 1999 16m 14m Jun 12] lengthy gelding: fairly useful
handicapper (won at 1¾m) at 3 yrs: well held since: visored final start. *J. R. Jenkins*

FOREIGN SECRETARY (USA)   2 b.c. (May 1) Kingmambo (USA) 125 –   **78 P**
Misinskie (USA) 84 (Nijinsky (CAN) 138) [1999 7m⁴ Sep 8] $385,000Y: closely
related to 3 winners, including smart miler Ajfan (by Woodman) and useful 1¼m
winner Turning Wheel (by Seeking The Gold), and half-brother to St Leger second
Minds Music (by Silver Hawk): dam, best at 2 yrs, half-sister to Clever Trick: weak
in market, encouraging fourth of 6 to Port Vila in well-contested minor event at
Kempton on debut, slowly away, travelling well for much of way and given easy time
once unable to quicken: will stay at least 1¼m: held entry in Racing Post Trophy:
open to plenty of improvement, and should prove at least useful. *Sir Michael Stoute*

FOREON   2 b.f. (Feb 27) Formidable (USA) 125 – Honey Vision 55 (Vision (USA))   –
[1999 a8g Nov 24] first foal: dam maiden who stayed 1m: showed nothing in maiden
at Lingfield. *G. L. Moore*

FOREST BOY   6 b.g. Komaite (USA) – Khadine 79 (Astec 128) [1998 –: 8.5s⁶   –
1999 a8.5g 8.3d⁶ 10.5s Jun 7] sturdy, workmanlike gelding: fair handicapper in 1997:
well beaten since: stays 9.4f: acts on fibresand and soft ground: sometimes visored/
blinkered, including when successful: has looked a difficult ride. *M. R. Bosley*

FOREST CALL   4 ch.f. Wolfhound (USA) 126 – Balnaha 67 (Lomond (USA)   **66 +**
128) [1998 67: 7s 7m⁴ 8d² 8.2v⁵ 7s 1999 7d⁴ 7m 8.3m a5g² Jul 9] strong, lengthy
filly: fair maiden: blinkered first time and gambled on, neck second in handicap at
Wolverhampton final start, stumbling stalls and finishing strongly: stays 1m: acts on
heavy going and fibresand: sold 40,000 gns in December. *Lady Herries*

FOREST DREAM   4 b.f. Warrshan (USA) 117 – Sirenivo (USA) 113 (Sir Ivor   **71**
135) [1998 62: 8.3m⁵ 8g 8.5m³ 8.1g⁶ 8m 8g a8.5g⁴ 1999 8g⁵ 8g⁶ 9.9m² 10.2m 10f*
12m 12m a12g² 10.2s² a12g² a12g⁴ a10g Dec 18] fair handicapper: won at Lingfield
in August: ran well when second after: left Lady Herries before final outing: stays
easy 1½m: acts on firm going, soft and fibresand. *L. A. Dace*

FOREST FIRE (SWE)   4 b.f. Never So Bold 135 – Mango Sampaquita (SWE)   **88**
(Colombian Friend (USA)) [1998 74+: 8.2s 8g³ 12d³ 11.6m⁵ 11.5m² 12f⁶ 9m* 8.1g*
10d⁶ 1999 8.3d⁴ 10s⁴ 8.9d⁶ 10m* 12m* 10m 12m⁵ 12s⁶ 12d Oct 9] useful-looking
filly: fairly useful handicapper: won twice at Newmarket in July: out of depth final 2
starts: stays 1½m: acts on good to firm and soft ground: held up. *B. Hanbury*

FOREST FRIENDLY   2 b.f. (Mar 29) Unfuwain (USA) 131 – Butsova 93 (Form-   **81 p**
idable (USA) 125) [1999 7d⁴ Oct 30] eighth foal: half-sister to 4-y-o Sabre Butt and 2
winners by Bustino, including 11f winner Bustinetta who stayed 2m: dam, 6f winner,
half-sister to Terimon: shaped well when fourth of 16 to Garota Do Leblon in
Newmarket maiden, staying on from mid-division: likely to prove suited by 1¼m+:
open to plenty of improvement. *B. W. Hills*

FOREST GREEN FLYER   3 b.f. Syrtos 106 – Bolton Flyer (Aragon 118) [1998   –
NR 1999 7.1g 7m 7.1m Jul 3] second reported foal: dam, Irish 7f winner, stayed
1¼m: soundly beaten in claimer/maidens. *O. O'Neill*

FOREST GREY   3 gr.g. Petong 126 – Holyrood Park (Sharrood (USA) 124) [1998   **27**
–: 5.1g 6m 6g 1999 a12g 8m 10m 12g⁶ 10.5m Aug 30] leggy gelding: bad maiden:
visored once at 2 yrs. *K. McAuliffe*

FOREST HEATH (IRE)   2 gr.g. (Mar 22) Common Grounds 118 – Caroline Lady   **71**
(JPN) (Caro 133) [1999 6d 7d Oct 27] 15,000F, IR 11,000Y, 6,500 2-y-o: quite
good-topped gelding: not a good walker: fourth foal: half-brother to Irish 3-y-o 1¼m

winner Sandholes (by Tirol) and a winner in Japan by Generous: dam French 1½m winner: fair form in maidens, seventh of 11 to Shaibani at Yarmouth on second start: should stay 1m+: needs to settle better. *J. E. Banks*

FOREST KING (IRE) 3 b.g. Forest Wind (USA) 111 – Paryiana (IRE) (Shernazar 131) [1998 –: 7f 7m 1999 10g a10g⁴ 11.4m 10.2g⁴ a12g² a16g³ 11.7s Oct 26] fair maiden on all-weather, poor on turf: stays 1½m: acts on all-weather, seemingly best turf effort on soft going: has had tongue tied: has given trouble at start/reared stalls: sold 6,000 gns, sent to Spain. *G. A. Butler* **43 +**
a68

FOREST QUEEN 2 b.f. (Mar 18) Risk Me (FR) 127 – Grey Cree 64 (Creetown 123) [1999 5g 5d⁴ 5g² 6m 5g 5g³ 6m 6d⁵ 6d Oct 26] leggy, shallow-girthed filly: poor walker: sister to German 3-y-o 7.5f winner Broadmeadows and 5-y-o Misconduct: dam 2-y-o 5f/6f winner: modest maiden: well held after 2-month absence last 2 starts: best at 5f. *K. W. Hogg, Isle of Man* **57**

FOREST ROBIN 6 ch.g. Formidable (USA) 125 – Blush Rambler (IRE) (Blushing Groom (FR) 131) [1998 67, a57: a7g² 8m³ 6g* 6g 9.9d⁴ 8m* 8m² 7g 8f* 8m 9m 7.5m 8g a10g a10f 1999 a8g² a8f a8g⁴ a8g* 7m⁶ 9m 7m 8f⁵ 7m² 8f⁵ 8f⁶ 7.6f⁴ 7m⁴ 7d 8.3s a8g⁶ a10g⁴ a9.4g a11g Dec 13] good-quartered gelding: modest handicapper: best at 6f to 1m: acts on firm going, good to soft and all-weather: tried visored/ blinkered: usually comes from behind: usually contests amateur/apprentice events. *Mrs L. Stubbs* **59**

FORESTRY 5 b.g. Highest Honor (FR) 124 – Arboretum (IRE) 83 (Green Desert (USA) 127) [1998 NR 1999 10f⁴ a8g Jun 17] bad maiden. *M. J. Wilkinson* **27**

FOREST SHADOW (IRE) 3 b.c. Sadler's Wells (USA) 132 – Bay Shade (USA) 90 (Sharpen Up 127) [1998 98: 7g 7m* 8.1s² 10s² 9d 1999 10m⁵ 10f³ 12d⁵ 12g⁵ 10d⁶ 9d 9d Oct 24] small, sparely-made colt: useful performer: best 3-y-o effort on reappearance: left P. Chapple-Hyam after third start: probably stays 1½m. *S. Porcu, Italy* **95**

FOREVER MIDNIGHT (IRE) 2 b.f. (Mar 31) Night Shift (USA) – Timeless 58 (Royal Academy (USA) 130) [1999 6g* 6m² 6m⁵ 6m² 6d⁴ 6d 7.3s Oct 23] IR 21,000F, IR 42,000Y: angular, quite attractive filly: first foal: dam, maiden, half-sister to very smart Glory of Dancer, winner at up to 1¼m: useful performer: won maiden at Goodwood in June: easily best efforts after when second in listed event at Newmarket (beaten length by Hoh Dear) and in minor event at Salisbury (went down by a head to Crimplene): seems not to stay 7f in testing conditions: acts on good to firm going: started very slowly last 2 starts: sold 26,000 gns in December. *B. W. Hills* **99**

FORGIE (IRE) 6 b.g. Don't Forget Me 127 – Damia (Vision (USA)) [1998 88: 14.1v* 18.7m 16.2g⁴ 15m³ 15.9m 14g³ 15.9g⁴ 14.6d³ 1999 14.1s⁵ 13.9s 15s⁶ 15.9m Jul 10] lengthy gelding: has a round action: fair handicapper: disappointing after reappearance in 1999: best at 1¾m to 2m: acts on any going: usually held up: sold 9,500 gns, joined K. Morgan. *P. Calver* **77**

FORGLORI 4 b.g. Formidable (USA) 125 – Glorietta (USA) (Shadeed (USA) 135) [1998 –: 7g 7s 7g 8g 1999 10m 10.5m Jul 2] big, strong, good-topped gelding: no form: sold 3,200 gns in August. *Miss B. Sanders* **–**

FORGOTTEN TIMES (USA) 5 ch.m. Nabeel Dancer (USA) 120 – Etoile d'Amore (USA) 81 (The Minstrel (CAN) 135) [1998 54, a76: a7g⁵ a6g a6g a6g* a6g a6g⁵ 6m 5m 5m³ᵈⁱˢ 6m 5m 5m 5m 5.3g⁵ 1999 5d 5.1s⁴ 5m 5g* 5m* 6m⁵ 5m⁵ 5g* 5m⁴ 5f 5d* 5.3m* 5f⁴ 5.2g 5s* 5.3d 5g 5.1s⁶ 5s Nov 5] good-quartered mare: fair handicapper: had a good year, winning at Goodwood and Folkestone in May, Salisbury in July, Windsor and Brighton in August, and back at Goodwood in September: effective at 5f/6f: acts on equitrack, firm and soft going: usually blinkered/visored: often claimer ridden (including for first 5 wins in 1999): usually held up. *K. T. Ivory* **73**

FOR HEAVENS SAKE 2 b.c. (Feb 13) Rambo Dancer (CAN) 107 – Angel Fire (Nashwan (USA) 135) [1999 5d a6g⁴ a5g⁶ a7g⁶ Dec 15] second foal: brother to 3-y-o Shall We Dance: dam unraced granddaughter of Arc winner All Along: modest form in maidens/nursery: probably stays 7f: acts on fibresand. *C. W. Thornton* **53 +**

FORLORN HOPE 2 b.c. (May 8) Tragic Role (USA) – Rum N Raisin (Rakaposhi King 119) [1999 5g 5.1s 6d 8.2d Oct 21] tall, rather unfurnished colt: first foal: dam refused to race in 2 of 3 starts in bumpers: little form, including in sellers. *B. D. Leavy* **–**

FORMAL BID (USA)   2 b. or br.c. (Mar 24) Dynaformer (USA) – Fantastic Bid   **80**
(USA) (Auction Ring (USA) 123) [1999 7g³ 8g⁵ Sep 8] good-topped colt: fourth
foal: half-brother to 3-y-o Fantastic Dance: dam, French 1m winner, half-sister to
smart middle-distance performer Germano: promising third of 13 to Port Vila in
maiden at Newbury: only fifth of 12 to Shamrock City in similar event at Doncaster
following month: should stay at least 1m: joined P. Makin: good type physically, and
may still do better. *P. W. Chapple-Hyam*

FORMERIC   3 ch.g. Formidable (USA) 125 – Irish Limerick 89 (Try My Best   **–**
(USA) 130) [1998 NR 1999 a6g 6d Oct 28] 5,500Y: half-brother to 3 winners,
including fairly useful sprinter Kira (by Starry Night): dam 2-y-o 6f winner: well
beaten in maidens at Southwell and Windsor. *Miss L. C. Siddall*

FORMER LOVE (USA)   4 b.f. Dynaformer (USA) – Love And Legend (USA)   **–**
84 (Lyphard's Wish (FR) 124) [1998 –: 10m 8m 12.5m⁴ 1999 a8g 10.3d 8g 9.9g 8.2m
10f May 28] well-made filly: poor maiden handicapper: stays 1m. *T. W. Donnelly*

FORMIDABLE FLAME   6 ch.g. Formidable (USA) 125 – Madiyla 73 (Dar-   **35**
shaan 133) [1998 48: a7g⁶ 9.4g³ 10.5m a12g 10.1s²ᵈⁱˢ 10.8g³ 11.6g 10s 1999 a12g⁴
a13g a16.2g³ a16.2g 17.2m Aug 22] lengthy gelding: poor maiden: tailed off final
2 starts: probably stays 2m: acts on soft ground and fibresand: held up: blinkered
penultimate outing. *G. A. Ham*

FORMIDABLE SPIRIT   5 ch.g. Formidable (USA) 125 – Hicklam Millie 49   **42**
(Absalom 128) [1998 –: 8v 1999 5.9g 8d² 9g³ 8m 11.1m⁶ 6.9g Aug 25] poor
maiden: stays 9f: acts on good to soft going: often blinkered/visored earlier in career.
B. Mactaggart

FORSAKEN (IRE)   2 b.f. (Apr 29) Lake Coniston (IRE) 131 – Faakirah (Dragon-   **?**
ara Palace (USA) 115) [1999 6s² 6g³ 6.8g⁴ 5.8g⁵ 6.8s⁵ Sep 26] 16,000Y: unfurnished
filly: half-sister to several winners, including fairly useful Irish 1996 2-y-o 5f winner
Klinsman (by Danehill) and 7f to 1¼m winner Upper Grosvenor (by Alzao): dam,
ran twice in Ireland, sister to Crime of Passion: neck second (rated 64) in minor event
at Haydock on debut in July: sold out of G. Lewis' stable 32,000 gns afterwards: in
frame in minor events at Ovrevoll next 2 starts. *J. Bjordal, Norway*

FORSIO   3 b.g. Efisio 120 – Foreseen (Reform 132) [1998 NR 1999 7m 10m 9.9m   **–**
12s 8d Oct 11] closely related to 1¼m winner Fengari (by Formidable) and a winner
in Hong Kong by Forzando and half-brother to a winner in Germany by Never So
Bold: dam unraced half-sister to Derby Italiano winner My Top: well held all starts:
raced freely in visor final 2: sold 6,200 gns. *Lady Herries*

FOR SWAN   3 ch.f. Forzando 122 – My Precious Daisy (Sharpo 132) [1998 –:   **–**
a5g⁶ a5s 1999 5m 5g 6.9g 9.3m 8f Jul 23] small, sturdy filly: signs of ability but no
form, including in sellers. *R. A. Fahey*

FORTHECHOP   2 b.g. (Apr 18) Minshaanshu Amad (USA) 91§ – Cousin Jenny   **–**
(Midyan (USA) 124) [1999 a8.5g⁶ 10s a8g a7g⁶ Nov 22] 1,000Y: sturdy gelding:
second foal: dam well beaten only start: no form in maidens/sellers. *Mrs H. L. Walton*

FORT KNOX (IRE)   8 b.g. Treasure Kay 114 – Single Viking (Viking (USA))   **33**
[1998 42, a–: 11.9g 8f⁵ 8.3m 7g² 7.6g 1999 8f 7f 7f May 12] poor handicapper: stays   **a–**
1m: acts on all-weather: wears blinkers: joined Jamie Poulton. *R. M. Flower*

FORT SUMTER (USA)   3 b.c. Sea Hero (USA) 124 – Gray And Red (USA)   **72**
(Wolf Power (SAF)) [1998 75: 7g 8.5s² 8m² 1999 12d⁶ 8m 12g⁶ 9.9d³ 9.9m 11.9s
Sep 28] tall, quite attractive colt: fair maiden handicapper: creditable effort in 1999
only on fourth start: stays 1¼m: acts on soft and good to firm ground. *P. R. Hedger*

FORTUNE COOKIE   3 ch.f. Selkirk (USA) 129 – Lucky Round 82 (Auction   **–**
Ring (USA) 123) [1998 NR 1999 8g 10m 14g 7m 7g a12g a10g Nov 16] big,
strong, good-topped filly: sixth foal: half-sister to 3 winners, including 1¼m winner
Missfortuna (by Priolo) and French 11f winner Harmonie du Soir (by Top Ville): dam
1¼m winner: no form (trained by J. Fanshawe on debut), including in a seller: tried
visored. *R. M. H. Cowell*

FORTUNE HOPPER   5 gr.g. Rock Hopper 124 – Lots of Luck 73 (Neltino 97)   **41**
[1998 NR 1999 17.2m Jun 23] close-coupled, workmanlike gelding: poor maiden
handicapper: should stay beyond 13f: tried visored. *Martin Todhunter*

FORTY FORTE   3 b.g. Pursuit of Love 124 – Cominna (Dominion 123) [1998   **81**
NR 1999 a7g² a8g² a8.5g³ 8.2s* 8.3m² 7.5g* 6m 7g 7d 7s a10g* a9.4g³ a8g² a7g Dec
4] fifth foal: half-brother to 1994 2-y-o 6f winner Prima Cominna and 6-y-o Go With
The Wind: dam unraced sister to Primo Dominie: fairly useful performer: won seller
at Nottingham (by 15 lengths on final outing for M. Channon) in March, rated stakes
at Beverley in April and handicap at Lingfield in November: best form at 1m/1¼m:
acts on soft ground, good to firm and all-weather: free-going front runner: none too
consistent. *K. R. Burke*

FORUM   4 b.f. Lion Cavern (USA) 117 – Top Society (High Top 131) [1998 –: 8v⁶   **84**
8g 9.9m⁶ 7d 10.1g⁵ 8d⁴ 1999 8m 7g⁵ 8m³ 8m³ 8g 8.5m* 7m⁶ Jul 28] tall, good-topped
filly: easy mover: fairly useful handicapper: won at Epsom in July: stays 8.5f: acts on
firm ground: has high head carriage: not easy ride: reportedly in foal to Amfortas.
C. E. Brittain

FORUM GIRL (USA)   3 b.f. Sheikh Albadou 128 – Brava (GER) (Arratos (FR)   **79**
[1998 NR 1999 7d⁵ 7g* 8m⁵ 8f⁵ 8g² Aug 22] 25,000Y: tall, quite good-topped filly:
half-sister to several winners, including 2-y-o 8.5f stakes winner in USA by El Baba:
dam, winner in Germany, from useful German family: fair performer: won maiden at
Ayr in June: best effort in handicaps after final start: stays 1m. *M. Johnston*

FOR VALOUR (USA)   6 b.h. Trempolino (USA) 135 – Glitter (FR) 70 (Reliance   –
II 137) [1998 113: 10.5d 12f² 12g³ 12g⁴ 12m 10s² 10m a12g 1999 12d⁵ 10g⁵ 10m⁵
14g 10m 10d Oct 4] sparely-made horse: smart when trained by A. Fabre in France:
little show in 7 runs for new trainer, often looking difficult ride and running as though
something amiss when tailed off final start: stays 1½m: acts on firm and soft ground:
sometimes blinkered/visored. *K. O. Cunningham-Brown*

FOR YOUR EYES ONLY   5 b.g. Pursuit of Love 124 – Rivers Rhapsody 104   **104**
(Dominion 123) [1998 113: 7d³ 10.4g² 8.1g* 8d 8.1g* 8d* 8.9g 9g⁶ 1999 a8f⁴ a9f
10f³ a8f* a8f⁵ 8f 7.9g 8m⁶ Sep 11] small gelding: unimpressive mover: smart handicapper for T. Easterby at 4 yrs: trained by P. Rudkin in UAE first 5 starts in 1999,
winning at Jebel Ali in March: respectable efforts on return to Britain: effective at 1m
to 10.4f: acts on firm and soft going: usually blinkered: has wandered. *C. E. Brittain*

FORZARA   6 ch.m. Risk Me (FR) 127 – Valldemosa 81 (Music Boy 124) [1998   –
NR 1999 5.1m⁵ 5m Aug 3] modest 5f handicapper at best: well beaten since 1996.
R. Hollinshead

FOSTON FOX   2 b.f. (Apr 8) Foxhound (USA) 103 – Enaam 65§ (Shirley   –
Heights 130) [1999 6s 7g 6s a7g⁶ a10g⁴ Dec 18] 12,000Y: small, sturdy filly: fifth
foal: half-sister to 3-y-o Leave It To Me, useful 1997 2-y-o 6f winner Linden Heights
(by Distinctly North) and ungenuine 1m seller winner Linda's Joy (by Classic
Secret): dam should have stayed beyond 1¼m: little form. *C. B. B. Booth*

FOSTON SECOND (IRE)   2 ch.f. (Mar 26) Lycius (USA) 124 – Gentle Guest   –
(IRE) (Be My Guest (USA) 126) [1999 7s 6d Oct 18] 3,000Y: good-topped filly:
sixth foal: half-sister to 3-y-o Cops and 1m winner Freedom Chance (by Lahib): dam,
unraced, from very good family: burly, well beaten in maidens at Newcastle (very
green) and Pontefract (swished tail throughout preliminaries). *C. B. B. Booth*

FOUND AT LAST   3 b.g. Aragon 118 – Girton 68 (Balidar 133) [1998 51: 6g   **55**
1999 6s 8m⁵ 7g 6m 6s⁵ Oct 5] leggy, close-coupled gelding: dam 5f/6f winner:
modest maiden: left Miss S. Hall 720 gns after penultimate start: may prove best
short of 1m: acts on soft and good to firm going. *G. Woodward*

FOUND AT SEA   4 ch.f. Handsome Sailor 125 – Close Call (Nearly A Hand 115)   –
[1998 –: 10s⁶ 1999 10v⁶ Oct 12] well beaten in maidens. *Miss L. A. Perratt*

FOUNDRY LANE   8 b.g. Mtoto 134 – Eider 80 (Niniski (USA) 125) [1998 81:   **81**
13.9g* 14.6d 1999 13.9s⁵ 16.2d³ 13.9m⁴ 14.1m⁴ 17.3g Oct 16] rangy gelding: has
a fluent, round action: fairly useful handicapper: creditable efforts in frame at
Haydock, York and Redcar: should stay beyond 2m: acts on any going: winning
novice chaser/useful hurdler. *Mrs M. Reveley*

FOUR COUNTIES   2 ch.c. (Apr 17) Elmaamul (USA) 125 – Joyce's Best 58   –
(Tolomeo 127) [1999 5m 7f 6m Aug 13] 2,000Y: leggy colt: sixth foal: half-brother
to 3 winning sprinters, including fairly useful 1993 2-y-o 6f winner Sixpees (by

Efisio), later successful up to 7f in Hong Kong: dam lightly-raced half-sister to very smart middle-distance stayer Band: tailed off in maidens. *T. J. Naughton*

FOURDANED (IRE)   6 b.g. Danehill (USA) 126 – Pro Patria 86 (Petingo 135)   **28 §** [1998 53, a59: 12v 11.9g⁶ 12m 11.5m² 12m 10m 15.4m a12g⁴ 1999 a12g⁶ a10g⁵ a13g a16g a13g 12m⁵ 16d 11.5m⁵ 12g 12m 7m 10m a12g⁵ Nov 16] small gelding: poor maiden handicapper: stays 1½m, probably not 2m: acts on soft going, good to firm and equitrack: blinkered twice: carries head awkwardly: often lady ridden: inconsistent. *B. R. Johnson*

FOURGREYS   3 gr.g. Paris House 123 – Wild Moon (USA) (Arctic Tern (USA)   **61** 126) [1998 –: 6g 5m 6g 1999 a7g 9.3g⁵ 10g 8.5m* 8m Aug 4] modest handicapper: won apprentice event at Beverley in July, making all: stays 9f: has raced only on good going or firmer on turf, well held only run on fibresand: has been bandaged in front: raced too freely third start: sold 4,000 gns, sent to Kuwait. *Miss J. A. Camacho*

FOUR MEN (IRE)   2 b.g. (Apr 15) Nicolotte 118 – Sound Pet (Runnett 125)   **41** [1999 6d 5m 7f⁴ 7.5g Aug 12] IR 16,000F, IR 9,500Y: tall gelding: half-brother to 3 winners, including unreliable 5f to 7f winner Rockville Pike (by Glenstal): dam placed in Germany: well held in maidens, minor event and nursery. *J. Berry*

FOUR OF SPADES   8 ch.g. Faustus (USA) 118 – Fall To Pieces (USA) 101 (Forli   **–** (ARG)) [1998 –, a45: a10g² a10g⁶ a10g⁶ a10g 1999 a10g a12g Feb 6] tall, lengthy gelding: has a quick action: poor handicapper up to 1¼m: no form since very early in 1998: usually blinkered/visored: has been tongue tied. *R. J. Hodges*

FOURTH TIME LUCKY   3 b.g. Timeless Times 99 – Wych Willow   **36** (Hard Fought 125) [1998 60d: 5d⁴ 6f 6m 5m 7d 5s a6g a7g 1999 a8g⁵ a7f⁵ a8f² a8g a7g 8f 7.5g⁶ a8g Dec 17] good-topped gelding: poor maiden: stays 1m: acts on fibresand, no form on turf since debut: blinkered once (looked irresolute) at 2 yrs. *B. W. Murray*

FOXDALE (FR)   2 ch.f. (Jan 15) Emarati (USA) 74 – Fox Croft (FR) (Bustino   **46** 136) [1999 6m Jun 21] first reported foal: dam French 1m winner: nearest finish after slow start when eighth of 22 in maiden at Windsor. *H. Morrison*

FOXES TAIL   5 gr.g. Batshoof 122 – Secret Gill 88 (Most Secret 119) [1998 58:   **56** 10m 9g 8s⁶ 10.3g⁵ 10g² 10.5d⁴ 12.3m⁵ 10.4g 10.9d 1999 9.7v* 10d 10m 10g May 31] tall gelding: modest handicapper: won at Folkestone in April: below form after: probably stays 1½m: acts on good to firm and heavy going: tried visored as 4-y-o: usually bandaged: tends to look none too keen: joined S. Gollings. *R. J. Hodges*

FOXIE LADY   4 ch.f. Wolfhound (USA) 126 – Final Thought (Final Straw 127)   **–** [1998 77: 7g² 7.5m² 7m² 8.5m⁵ 10g 7d⁶ 1999 a7g⁶ 7s 11.7s 8.3g May 10] smallish, angular filly: fair form first 3 starts at 3 yrs: well beaten since: stays 7.5f: acts on good to firm going. *P. G. Murphy*

FOXKEY   2 ch.f. (Apr 3) Foxhound (USA) 103 – Latch Key Lady (USA) 48   **61 d** (Tejano (USA)) [1999 5d² 5d* a5g* 5v 6s a5g⁶ Dec 29] workmanlike filly: first foal: dam well beaten after debut: modest performer: trained on debut by B. Rothwell: won sellers at Catterick and Southwell in April for E. Alston: off 5 months, no form subsequently: blinkered final start. *Miss Gay Kelleway*

FOX'S IDEA   2 b.f. (Feb 27) Magic Ring (IRE) 115 – Lindy Belle 32 (Alleging   **66** (USA) 120) [1999 5.7g 5.1g³ 6m³ 5m⁴ 6.8d Sep 21] 5,400F, 5,000Y: neat filly: second foal: half-sister to 3-y-o Trina's Pet: dam, poor maiden, half-sister to Italian Oaks winner Maria Waleska, herself dam of high-class sprinter Polish Patriot: fair maiden: should stay at least 6f: acts on good to firm ground: has been slowly away. *D. Haydn Jones*

FOX STAR (IRE)   2 b.f. (Apr 1) Foxhound (USA) 103 – Our Pet 64 (Mummy's   **61** Pet 125) [1999 5s 6f⁵ 5.3f³ 6f 7g⁴ 7g 6s⁶ a8g a7g Nov 23] 33,000Y: leggy, sparely-   **a–** made filly: eighth reported foal: half-sister to 3-y-o Big Al, 2-y-o seller winners by Shalford (at 6f) and Don't Forget Me (5f) and to 6f (at 2 yrs) and 1m winner Southern Memories (also by Don't Forget Me): dam 2-y-o 1m winner: modest maiden: left R. Hannon before well beaten (blinkered on all-weather) last 2 starts: should stay 7f: acts on firm going. *Julian Poulton*

FOXY ALPHA (IRE) 2 ch.f. (Apr 18) Foxhound (USA) 103 – Ice Baby (Grundy 137) [1999 6g Oct 15] IR 2,500F: half-sister to 3 winners, including Irish 7.5f and (at 2 yrs) 1m winner Kentucky Baby (by Shy Groom): dam Irish maiden: soundly beaten in Redcar maiden. *A. B. Mulholland*   –

FOXY BROWN 2 b.f. (Apr 2) Factual (USA) 108 – Miltak 43 (Risk Me (FR) 127) [1999 a5g² 5d a5g² a5g³ Dec 13] 500Y: leggy filly: first foal: dam maiden who stayed 13f: modest maiden: raced only at 5f: acts on fibresand. *Miss I. Foustok*   **60**

FRAGRANT OASIS (USA) 3 ch.f. Rahy (USA) 115 – Raahia (CAN) 92 (Vice Regent (CAN)) [1998 96+: 7m⁴ 7g* 7g² 7g 1999 8m 7g* 6m 6m³ 7f³ 6d² 6d⁶ Oct 15] sturdy, lengthy filly: has a quick action: smart performer: won slowly-run listed race at Newmarket in May by short head from Arctic Char: better efforts in similar races at York (third to Imperial Beauty) and Goodwood (½ length third to Selfish) and handicap at Newmarket (went down by a neck to Two Clubs): effective at 6f/7f, possibly not quite 1m: acts on firm and good to soft going: usually held up. *E. A. L. Dunlop*   **113**

FRAME OF MIND (FR) 4 b.g. Unfuwain (USA) 131 – Namatanga (USA) (Foolish Pleasure (USA)) [1998 12d⁶ 12d 10d 15g⁵ 12m⁶ 15d² 12.5s* 12d⁵ 1999 a12g Jan 20] closely related to winning sprinter Tate Dancer (by Tate Gallery) and half-brother to 2 winners abroad, including French 1m/9f winner Lili d'Aubuis (by Lycius): dam, French maiden, daughter of Poule d'Essai des Pouliches second Nonoalca: won maiden at Le Croise-Laroche at 2 yrs and claimer at Deauville in 1998 for C. Laffon-Parias: well beaten only start in Britain: probably stays 15f: acts on heavy going: raced mainly on good ground or softer: blinkered last 4 starts: returned to France. *F. Jordan*   –

FRAMPANT 2 ch.f. (Feb 12) Fraam 114 – Potent (IRE) (Posen (USA)) [1999 6d 6.8m 5.7h 5d* 5g⁴ 6.5g 5v⁴ 5s⁴ 6v 6.1s² Nov 1] 7,200Y: workmanlike filly: second foal: dam never ran: fair performer: 50/1-winner of maiden at Windsor in August: good second of 13 in nursery at Nottingham final start: not certain to stay much beyond 6f: acts on heavy ground. *M. Quinn*   **68**

FRANCE LAMBERT (ITY) 3 g.r.f. Tirol 127 – Filicaia 79 (Sallust 134) [1998 –: 6g 6m⁶ 6g 6s 8d 1999 7d 6m 7m 7d 6m 7m Jul 12] no sign of ability: visored final start: sent to Italy. *Don Enrico Incisa*   –

FRANCESCA'S FOLLY 4 b.f. Efisio 120 – Nashville Blues (IRE) 94 (Try My Best (USA) 130) [1998 51, a–: 10g⁵ 10d³ 11.9g⁵ 10.1m⁶ 10m² 10.1g* 10.8m⁴ 12g a14.8g 1999 a9.4g 10.2g 11.6d 17.2f 11.9f³ 11.9g⁶ Aug 5] small, angular filly: poor performer: stays 1½m: acts on good to firm and good to soft ground: blinkered (no form) second to fourth starts: has flashed tail: sold 500 gns. *C. L. Popham*   **30**

FRANCESCO GUARDI (IRE) 2 b.c. (Mar 10) Robellino (USA) 127 – Lamees (USA) (Lomond (USA) 128) [1999 7g* 8d² Oct 29] 45,000Y: sixth foal: brother to useful 7f (at 2 yrs) and 1¼m winner Lomberto and half-brother to 2 winners, including 6f winner Ella Lamees (by Statoblest): dam unraced: made winning debut in maiden at Catterick in October: much better form when 1¼ lengths second of 6 to Autonomy in minor event at Newmarket later in month: should stay 1¼m: already useful, and likely to continue to progress. *P. F. I. Cole*   **95 p**

FRANCO MINA (IRE) 3 b.g. Lahib (USA) 129 – Play The Queen (IRE) (King of Clubs 124) [1998 88: 5d 5f* 5m 1999 7d⁴ 7g 5g 5m 5g⁵ 5.1m⁴ 6m⁵ 5f 5g 5m 6m⁶ a6.5f Dec 16] close-coupled, workmanlike gelding: fairly useful handicapper: some creditable efforts in 1999 but well below form last 4 outings, leaving M. Channon before final 2: stays 7f: acts on firm and good to soft going: has been early to post: may not be one to trust implicitly. *P. L. Rudkin, UAE*   **81 d**

FRANCPORT 3 b.c. Efisio 120 – Elkie Brooks 82 (Relkino 131) [1998 NR 1999 6d⁵ 5d* 6s 5.1m² 5g 5d Sep 30] big, lengthy colt: has plenty of scope: brother to 3 winners, including smart sprinter Pips Pride and half-brother to 2 winners: dam, second over 6f at 2 yrs, didn't train on: fair form: won maiden at Beverley in May: well held in handicaps final 2 starts: will prove best at 5f. *J. Berry*   **79**

FRANKIE FAIR (IRE) 4 b.f. Red Sunset 120 – Animate (IRE) 62 (Tate Gallery (USA) 117) [1998 73, a52: 6.1s 6m 6.9m* 8g* 7m* 8g³ 7m a7g⁶ 1999 a7g² Jan 7]   **– a56**

fair on turf, modest on all-weather: head second in seller at Lingfield, only run of 1999: stays easy 1m: acts on good to firm ground and equitrack: usually front runner: joined Andrew Reid. *G. L. Moore*

FRANKINCENSE (IRE)   3 gr.c. Paris House 123 – Mistral Wood (USA) (Far   **57**
North (CAN) 120) [1998 –: 6g 1999 5d⁵ 6d⁴ 6g⁴ Sep 14] modest form in maidens:
blinkered final start: sold 3,700 gns, sent to Germany. *J. A. R. Toller*

FRANKLIN-D   3 ch.g. Democratic (USA) 101 – English Mint 66 (Jalmood (USA)   **56**
126) [1998 60: 5.1g⁵ 6f 5m 1999 6g 6m 7s a7g³ Nov 16] modest maiden at best:
stays 7f: acts on firm ground and equitrack: visored final 2-y-o start: inconsistent.
J. R. Jenkins

FRANKLIN LAKES   4 ch.g. Sanglamore (USA) 126 – Eclipsing (IRE) 93   **45**
(Baillamont (USA) 124) [1998 –: 9m⁵ 11.4d 11.6m 12g 16m⁴ 16.4f 1999 12.5s
10.8d 6.1f⁵ 7m⁵ 7.7s 6.1g⁶ 8.1m 6.8m 7.6f⁵ 7m a8g⁵ a7g a7g Dec 22] poor maiden
handicapper: has run tubed: may prove best around 1m: acts on equitrack, firm going
and good to soft: visored/blinkered. *M. R. Bosley*

FRAPPE (IRE)   3 b.f. Inchinor 119 – Glatisant 104 (Rainbow Quest (USA) 134)   **92**
[1998 93p: 6d* 7g 1999 7g 7g⁴ 8d 10.1g⁴ Aug 29] compact filly: fairly useful
performer: creditable seventh of 11 in steadily-run Nell Gwyn Stakes at Newmarket
in April: below that form final 3 starts: should stay 1m+: blinkered penultimate start:
gave trouble at stalls/raced freely final outing. *G. Wragg*

FRATERNITY   2 b.c. (Mar 3) Grand Lodge (USA) 125 – Catawba 98 (Mill Reef   **81 p**
(USA) 141) [1999 7m 8d² Oct 27] brother to 3-y-o Tyler's Toast and half-brother to
several middle-distance winners, notably very smart 1½m winner Catchascatchcan
(by Pursuit of Love): dam 1¼m winner out of Ribblesdale winner Catalpa: better
effort in maidens at Yarmouth when head second of 10 to King Spinner, soon close
up and running on determinedly: should prove suited by 1¼m/1½m: seems sure to
improve further. *W. Jarvis*

FRECKLES   4 b.f. High Kicker (USA) – Ship of Gold 78 (Glint of Gold 128)   **–**
[1998 47: 7v⁵ 8f a8g 8d⁴ 7g⁴ 8s 8g 7g 10g 8m 8d 10g 1999 8.5m Apr 14] poor
handicapper: well beaten only run of 1999: stays 7f: probably acts on good to soft
going: tried blinkered/visored: inconsistent: sent to Holland. *M. J. Ryan*

FREDDY FLINTSTONE   2 b.c. (Feb 8) Bigstone (IRE) 126 – Daring Ditty   **71 p**
(Daring March 116) [1999 7d 6v⁵ Oct 23] good-topped, attractive colt: sixth foal:
half-brother to 3 winners, notably 4-y-o Bold Edge and 8-y-o Brave Edge: dam
twice-raced daughter of useful sprinter Dawn Ditty: similar form in Newbury
maidens, still not fully wound up when fifth of 14 to Another Pearl: may prove best
up to 7f: should do better at 3 yrs. *R. Hannon*

FREDERICK JAMES   5 b.g. Efisio 120 – Rare Roberta (USA) 118 (Roberto   **72**
(USA) 131) [1998 –: a7g⁴ 1999 a6g⁴ a6f⁵ a6f³ a6f³ a7g³ a6g⁴ 6.1v* 6.1s 6m³   **a62**
5.7g⁴ 6g² 6g 6.1m² 7.7m⁴ 6m 6g³ 6m 6g Oct 11] fair handicapper on turf, modest
on all-weather: won at Nottingham in March: creditable efforts when in frame
after: effective at 6f to 7.7f: acts on all-weather, good to firm and heavy going.
H. E. Haynes

FREDORA   4 ch.f. Inchinor 119 – Ophrys 90 (Nonoalco (USA) 131) [1998 93:   **91**
8m⁶ 7g⁴ 7m 7.1d² 7.1m² 7m* 7.9f 8g 1999 8.3m 7.6m 10f³ 9.9g* 10m⁴ 10m³ 10m
10.3g² 10m 11.9d Oct 7] tall, lengthy filly: reportedly split a pastern at 2 yrs: fairly
useful performer: won minor event at Salisbury in June: creditable efforts after until
running poorly final 2 outings: stays 1¼m: acts on firm and good to soft going: edgy
(ran well) fourth 3-y-o start. *M. Blanshard*

FREE   4 ch.g. Gone West (USA) – Bemissed (USA) (Nijinsky (CAN) 138) [1998   **67**
57: 10s⁵ 12m⁶ 12m⁴ 14.1g 17.2d 1999 12s⁶ 14.1f³ 14.1m⁵ 17.2m² 16.2m³ 16.1f*
16g² 16m² 16f³ Sep 13] angular gelding: good mover: fair handicapper: won
3-runner race at Newcastle in August: creditable placed efforts otherwise: stays 17f:
acts on firm ground: has sweated and got on edge (seems better nowadays): won
novice chases in October and November. *Mrs M. Reveley*

FREEDOM QUEST (IRE)   4 b.g. Polish Patriot (USA) 128 – Recherchee (Rain-   **67**
bow Quest (USA) 134) [1998 76: 7m⁴ 9g⁴ 7.9g 7d 1999 a7f² a9.4g⁴ 7g 7.1m⁴ 10d
9m³ 8m 9g² 8m² 9.9s* 10m³ 10.1f³ 12f² 12g⁴ 12f* 10.4g Oct 6] tall, close-coupled

gelding: fair handicapper: won at Beverley in July and Musselburgh in September: stays easy 1½m: acts on firm ground, soft and fibresand: visored (well held) final 3-y-o start: has been bandaged behind: generally reliable. *B. S. Rothwell*

FREE FINISH (IRE) 3 b.f. Distinctly North (USA) 115 – Brave Louise 76 – (Brave Shot) [1998 –: 5d 6g 1999 7d 5.1s 6d a7g 6g 6f Jun 1] sturdy, lengthy filly: no form: blinkered (very slowly away) final start: has had tongue tied. *N. Tinkler*

FREE OPTION (IRE) 4 ch.g. Indian Ridge 123 – Saneena 80 (Kris 135) [1998 **102** 102: 8d⁴ a10g³ 8g⁴ 8s 7.6m* 7g² 7m³ 8.1m⁵ 7.3g* 10m² 1999 7g 8m⁵ 8m* 8.1g 7.1m 8.1m 7m* 7m 7f⁶ 8g* 8d Oct 30] strong, lengthy gelding: useful performer: won handicap at Kempton in May, minor event at Chester in July and another handicap at Newmarket (beat Mayaro Bay by ¾ length in 20-runner event) in October: best form at 7f/1m: acts on good to firm and good to soft ground (tailed off on soft): tends to carry head awkwardly and edge left (has run poorly for lady rider): rather inconsistent. *B. Hanbury*

FREE RIDER 2 b.c. (Feb 16) Inchinor 119 – Forever Roses 70 (Forzando 122) **97 p** [1999 6d² 6v² 6d* Nov 4] 9,800F: good-topped colt: first foal: dam, third at 5f on only start, half-sister to smart sprinter Gallic League: runner-up in maidens at Newmarket (won by Alfini) and Newbury (won by Out of Reach) prior to beating Kathology in emphatic style by 4 lengths in similar event at Windsor: has lots of speed, and likely to prove best at 5f/6f: looks a smart sprinter in the making, sure to win more races. *I. A. Balding*

FREE TO SPEAK (IRE) 7 ch.h. Be My Guest (USA) 126 – Love For Poetry **113** (Lord Gayle (USA) 124) [1998 104: 9s⁶ 8s² 9m³ 9m 8.5d* 8m⁶ 8d 9d³ 10s³ 7v* 1999 8s 8m 8g* 8.5m 8g* 7d Sep 11] smallish horse: smart performer: won £26,000 handicap at the Curragh in June and listed race at Tralee (by 2 lengths from Danse Classique) in August: not discredited other starts, though only tenth in Hunt Cup at Royal Ascot second one: stays 1¼m: acts on good to firm and heavy ground: blinkered: genuine and consistent. *D. K. Weld, Ireland*

FREETOWN (IRE) 3 b.g. Shirley Heights 130 – Pageantry 83 (Welsh Pageant **74 p** 132) [1998 NR 1999 12d⁴ 10.9v* Oct 11] IR 120,000Y: tall, leggy gelding: seventh foal: closely related to smart winner up to 1½m Up Anchor (by Slip Anchor) and half-brother to 3 winners, including smart stayer Generosity (by Generous): dam, ran only at 2 yrs when placed at 5f/6f, sister to Italian Derby winner Welnor: fair form in claimers, winning 7-runner event at Ayr (claimed to join L. Lungo for £20,000), running green inside final 1f: stoutly bred: capable of better. *P. F. I. Cole*

FREE-VALLEY-MOU (IRE) 3 b.g. Ela-Mana-Mou 132 – Kilcoy (USA) – (Secreto (USA) 128) [1998 NR 1999 10g 12g 10.2s Sep 27] 14,000Y: strong, robust gelding: third foal: half-brother to 1996 2-y-o 1m winner Double Espresso (by Taufan) and a middle-distance winner abroad by Anshan: dam unraced: well held in maidens at Pontefract (backward, took strong hold), Kempton (awkward round final bend) and Bath. *P. W. Harris*

FRENCH CONNECTION 4 b.g. Tirol 127 – Heaven-Liegh-Grey 90 (Grey **71** Desire 115) [1998 87: 9.2v* 8.1d* 10.1v² 8f⁴ 10.3g⁵ 10.3m 8s 1999 8m 10d 8.1d 6g 8d⁴ 7.5m⁴ 8.5g⁵ 9g⁵ 7.5s⁶ 8s⁵ Oct 11] smallish, sturdy gelding: has a round action: fair handicapper: left Jack Berry after sixth start, and just modest form for new stable: effective at 1m/1¼m: acts on any going: blinkered (below form) third, fourth and final starts: retained 3,500 gns in November. *D. Nicholls*

FRENCH FANCY (IRE) 2 gr.f. (Apr 28) Paris House 123 – Clipping 76 (Kris **47 d** 135) [1999 5d 5.1s³ 5g 6m⁴ 7g 5.2m⁴ 6d³ 7m 6f⁴ 6g 6g⁵ 6v 6s⁴ Oct 1] 500Y: leggy, plain filly: fourth reported foal: dam 1m winner: poor maiden: mainly below form after fourth start: stays 6f: acts on any going: tried visored: sold 800 gns, joined B. Pearce. *C. A. Dwyer*

FRENCH FELLOW (IRE) 2 b.c. (Apr 4) Suave Dancer (USA) 136 – Madem- **103** oiselle Chloe 106 (Night Shift (USA)) [1999 5f⁵ 6g* 6m* 7g* 8g² 8m* 8d* Oct 9] 13,000Y: strong, good-bodied colt: has scope: has a quick action: sixth foal: half-brother to 7f all-weather winner Cloette (by Damister) and 3-y-o Black Silk: dam 2-y-o 5f winner: useful performer: won maiden at Ayr in June, nurseries at Redcar and York in August and Doncaster in September, and listed race at Ascot (beat One

Tom McGee Autumn Stakes, Ascot—
French Fellow (left) rallies splendidly as One Step At A Time puts in a strong challenge;
Total Love (No.11) finishes well for third place

Step At A Time by neck) in October: stays 1m: acts on good to firm and good to soft going: genuine: may do better still. *T. D. Easterby*

FRENCH GINGER 8 ch.m. Most Welcome 131 – French Plait (Thatching 131) [1998 36, a–: 8g 8s⁶ 7g 7.5d 8m 8.5m 8s⁴ 12m a11g 1999 8g 7.1m⁵ 7.1m 10m 7m a8g Nov 15] lengthy mare: poor performer: stays 1m: acts on equitrack: tried visored/ blinkered: has worn tongue strap: none too consistent. *L. R. Lloyd-James* **36 a–**

FRENCH GRIT (IRE) 7 b.g. Common Grounds 118 – Charbatte (FR) 93 (In Fijar (USA) 121) [1998 64d: 6s 6g⁵ 6d 6g 5m³ 6m 5m 1999 a6g a6g⁵ a6f 5d⁴ 5.9m 5m⁵ 6g⁵ 6.1f² 6m⁴ 6f² 6f³ 5m 6s a5g² a5g⁵ Dec 18] workmanlike gelding: modest handicapper: left D. Barker after thirteenth start: has form at 7f, but races mostly over shorter: acts on all-weather, raced mainly on good ground or firmer on turf: tends to hang and look less than keen: sometimes early to post: not one to trust. *K. A. Ryan* **60 § a55 §**

FRENCH HILL 4 br.g. Dromod Hill – Dear France (USA) (Affirmed (USA)) [1998 NR 1999 a16g May 25] eighth reported foal: dam never ran: 66/1, soundly beaten in claimer at Lingfield. *G. M. McCourt* **–**

FRENCH HORN 2 b.g. (Feb 9) Fraam 114 – Runcina (Runnett 125) [1999 7m 6m 7m 7m⁶ 7s⁵ 7s* Oct 25] 2,000Y: workmanlike gelding: fifth reported foal: dam unraced: fair performer: best effort when winning 20-runner nursery at Leicester on final start by short head from Safarando, leading on line: will stay at least 1m: seems well suited by soft ground. *M. J. Ryan* **68**

FRENCH LIEUTENANT 2 b.c. (Mar 3) Cadeaux Genereux 131 – Madame Crecy (USA) (Al Nasr (FR) 126) [1999 7.1m 7d³ 8s² Nov 5] angular, workmanlike colt: third foal: half-brother to French 1m winner Which Hand (by Indian Ridge): dam, third at 1m in France, half-sister to Polar Falcon: fairly useful form: best effort when 2 lengths second of 5 to Shouf Al Badou in minor event at Doncaster: unlikely to stay much further than 1m: should do better still. *G. A. Butler* **83 p**

FRENCH MASTER (IRE) 2 b.g. (Mar 14) Petardia 113 – Reasonably French (Reasonable (FR) 119) [1999 6m 6m⁴ 7m⁶ 6f³ 7f³ 7g⁶ a8g⁴ Nov 12] IR 6,000F, 5,200Y: close-coupled gelding: sixth foal: brother to 3-y-o Double Two and half-brother to a German 8.5f winner by Classic Secret: dam Irish 2-y-o 7f winner: modest maiden: below form after second start: raced only on good going or firmer on turf: tried visored: has tended to sweat. *P. C. Haslam* **64 d**

FRENCH MYSTERY 2 b.f. (Feb 18) Mystiko (USA) 124 – La Reine de France (Queen's Hussar 124) [1999 5d 5d² a5g⁴ May 10] 1,000Y: half-sister to several winners, including 1987 2-y-o 6f winner Rectory Maid (by Tina's Pet) and 8-y-o Artic Courier: dam unraced: poor form in frame in sellers: will stay 6f: visored last 2 starts. *P. D. Evans* **45**

FRENCH SPICE 3 b.f. Cadeaux Genereux 131 – Hot Spice (Hotfoot 126) [1998 NR 1999 a6g⁶ a7g a6g⁶ a8.5g* Dec 27] leggy, sparely-made filly: half-sister to several winners, notably Celeric and smart middle-distance stayer Sesame (by Derry- **63 p**

417

lin): dam poor maiden: much improved on handicap debut to win 13-runner event at Wolverhampton in December: races freely, but should stay well beyond 8.5f: capable of better. *Sir Mark Prescott*

FRIAR TUCK 4 ch.g. Inchinor 119 – Jay Gee Ell 78 (Vaigly Great 127) [1998 **92 d** 103: 5.1g² 5g 6s* 6s 6s³ 6v 1999 6s 5m 6d 6m 6s 5g² 6f⁴ 5d⁵ 6d 9.2f 6d 7.1d 6d Oct 9] leggy, lengthy gelding: useful handicapper at best: lost his way completely after sixth start: unlikely to stay beyond 6f: acts on good to firm and soft going: reluctant to race final start. *Miss L. A. Perratt*

FRIEND FOR LIFE 3 b.f. Lahib (USA) 129 – Hardihostess 104 (Be My Guest **64** (USA) 126) [1998 NR 1999 8g 8g⁴ 10.2m⁶ 10d Aug 14] 25,000Y: lengthy, angular filly: closely related to 1994 2-y-o 6f winner Divina Mia (by Dowsing) who stayed 11f, and half-sister to 7f (at 2 yrs) and 1½m winner Impetuous Air (by Warning): dam, 2-y-o 7f winner who stayed 1½m, half-sister to Shirley Heights: modest maiden: below form final 2 starts: should stay 1¼m. *W. R. Muir*

FRIENDLY ALLIANCE 3 b.g. Shareef Dancer (USA) 135 – Snow Huntress 80 **50** (Shirley Heights 130) [1998 –: 8d 7g 7v 1999 7m 10g 8g² 10m⁶ Aug 23] tall, workmanlike gelding: modest performer: form only in apprentice handicap at Salisbury on penultimate start (unruly stalls). *R. M. Flower*

FRIENDLY BRAVE (USA) 9 b.g. Well Decorated (USA) – Companionship **–** (USA) (Princely Native (USA)) [1998 48, a61: a6s³ a5g⁴ a5g² a5g⁴ 5s⁴ 5m 5m⁵ 6m⁵ **a61** 5m 5.3m a5g⁴ 5m⁵ 5f⁶ 6m² 6d a6g⁴ a5g⁴ a6g³ a5g⁵ a5f² 1999 a6g³ a6g⁴ a6f⁶ a5f⁵ a6g⁴ a7g⁵ a6g³ a5g³ a5g² 5s⁵ a5g Apr 24] strong, good-quartered gelding: modest on all-weather, poor on turf: stayed 7f: acted on any turf/all-weather: effective with blinkers or not: was consistent: fell fatally in April. *Miss Gay Kelleway*

FRILLY FRONT 3 ch.f. Aragon 118 – So So 84 (Then Again 126) [1998 80: **73** 5s* 5d³ 5g⁴ 5g³ 5g⁴ 5s 5g³ 5d 1999 5d 5d 5s 5m³ 5f 6m 5m 5s⁴ 5d³ **a64** 5v⁶ 6g² 5d³ 5.2s 5s³ a6g⁴ a5g* a5g Dec 15] compact filly: fair handicapper: won at Wolverhampton in November: effective at 5f/6f: acts on good to firm and heavy going: blinkered (ran poorly) tenth start: sometimes slowly away: usually forces pace. *T. D. Barron*

FRIPPET (IRE) 3 b. or br.f. Ela-Mana-Mou 132 – Happy Tidings (Hello Gorgeous **87** (USA) 128) [1998 NR 1999 11.1g* 11.5g⁴ 12d Jun 14] IR 24,000F, 24,000 2-y-o: leggy, angular filly: seventh reported foal: sister to 2-y-o 1¼m winners Trigger Happy (in 1997) and Eldorado (in 1996) and half-sister to 2 winners, including Irish 1½m to 2¼m winner Fleeting Vision (by Vision): dam unraced half-sister to Snurge (by Ela-Mana-Mou): fairly useful form: won maiden at Kempton in April: 15½ lengths fourth of 7 in listed race at Lingfield following month: tailed off in the Oaks at Epsom final start, giving impression something amiss: should be suited by 1½m+: sold 21,000 gns in October. *S. Dow*

FRISKY FOX 5 b.m. Risk Me (FR) 127 – Hill Vixen 69 (Goldhill 125) [1998 –: **58 d** 12.3d³ 1999 8.2s⁴ 10g 10v a12g 11.9d⁴ 8d 10s a16.2g Nov 17] unfurnished mare: modest maiden: well below form final 6 starts: stays 1¼m. *R. Hollinshead*

FRISKY SILK 5 b.m. Risk Me (FR) 127 – Power And Red (Skyliner 117) [1998 **–** NR 1999 a8.5g Mar 3] 2,000Y: fourth foal: half-sister to modest 5f (at 2 yrs) and 6f winner Abbey House (by Efisio): dam Irish 5f winner: 50/1, well beaten in maiden at Wolverhampton. *R. Guest*

FRONTIER 2 b.c. (Apr 18) Indian Ridge 123 – Adatiya (IRE) (Shardari 134) **93 p** [1999 6m⁴ 7m² 7s* Oct 8] 27,000Y: well-made, attractive colt: has scope: good walker: third foal: dam, French 9.5f winner, half-sister to smart French 9f and 1¼m winner Adaiyka: fairly useful form: justified favouritism in 18-runner maiden at Lingfield by 1¼ lengths from Ansari, leading from before halfway: will stay at least 1m: remains capable of better. *R. Hannon*

FRONTIER FLIGHT (USA) 9 b.g. Flying Paster (USA) – Sly Charmer (USA) **–** (Valdez (USA)) [1998 NR 1999 a16g a16f 16g⁵ a12g⁶ 18v a16.2g Dec 15] rangy gelding: formerly fairly useful winner: lightly raced and no form on Flat since 1993: winning jumper. *P. W. Hiatt*

FRONTLINER (IRE) 4 b. or br.g. Last Tycoon 131 – Eyeliner (USA) (Raise A **59** Native) [1998 55: 7d 8s 8m 9d² 8g⁴ 9m³ 12m 1999 7m 8.5f 12g² 12m* 11g 14m a14g

Oct 18] tall gelding: half-brother to fairly useful 5f/6f winner Don't Care (by Nordico) and 1¾m winner Glowing Lines (by Glow): dam unraced half-sister to Irish Derby winner Malacate: modest handicapper: won at Tramore in August: ran poorly after (including at Southwell): stays 1½m: acts on good to firm and good to soft ground: sometimes blinkered (only on reappearance in 1999). *T. Doyle, Ireland*

FROSTED AIRE 3 ch.g. Chilibang 120 – Suzannah's Song (Song 132) [1998 NR 1999 7.6m 6m 8.3s 6m Aug 30] workmanlike gelding: has a quick action: half-brother to 3 winners, including 1992 2-y-o 5f winner Meadmore Magic (by Mansingh) and 6f (at 2 yrs) and 1¼m winner Just Flamenco (by Scorpio): dam unraced: signs of a little ability in maidens: broke blood vessel and pulled up in handicap final start. *G. G. Margarson* —

FROSTY (IRE) 3 ch.g. Lahib (USA) 129 – Chilblains 83 (Hotfoot 126) [1998 –: 8.1m 1999 10.5s 8s Oct 4] short-backed gelding: no show in maidens. *T. D. Easterby* —

FROZEN SEA (USA) 8 ch.g. Diesis 133 – Ocean Ballad 104 (Grundy 137) [1998 NR 1999 a13g 11.6m 11.9g² a12g² Aug 13] strong gelding: poor performer: probably stays 2m: raced mainly on good ground or firmer on turf, acts on equitrack. *G. L. Moore* 48

FRUITS OF LOVE (USA) 4 b.c. Hansel (USA) – Vallee Secrete (USA) (Secretariat (USA)) [1998 116: 10.4g³ 10g⁵ 12d 10d² 12f* 10g³ 12.5g⁵ 12m 12v⁴ 12m⁵ 1999 12m* 12d⁶ 12m* 12m³ 12g² 12f Nov 28] 127

Occasional success, but mostly heartache—that is one summary of the last three years regarding Fruits of Love. Through press interviews and his column in the *Racing Post*, Mark Johnston has provided a lucid account of some of the frustrations involved in training racehorses, and of those with Fruits of Love in particular. The starting point is that this was a horse for whom

Dubai Turf Classic, Nad Al Sheba—the angle is deceiving as Fruits of Love (No.7) gains a narrow victory over Nedawi

he had long held high hopes. 'I've always thought he was an absolutely top-class horse. As a two-year-old his gallops with Lend A Hand were absolutely top-notch,' Johnston said in June. Until the latest season Fruits of Love had not revealed as much on the racecourse and his trainer had not seen fit to run him in a Group 1. His sole win as a three-year-old, in the Princess of Wales's Stakes at Newmarket in July, had come in a poor renewal of the race and the promise of that performance was followed by his being placed only once from five starts later in the year. Strictly on form, Fruits of Love was performing with some consistency, but his connections clearly believed him capable of much better.

It had not helped his cause that Fruits of Love had suffered injuries, starting with the fractured pelvis which confined him to three runs in August as a two-year-old. In December the following year, his bid for the Hong Kong International Vase was prejudiced when he went lame in the week beforehand. Most dramatic of all, however, was the attack of road rage on the M25 in April 1999 during which Fruits of Love became trapped upside down in his horsebox, having to be driven to an equine hospital in Hertfordshire where he was given a general anaesthetic (vet Dr Sarah Freeman was later named Lanson Lady of The Year for her contribution to the racing industry) and then freed from his box by rescuers from the Potters Bar and Hatfield fire stations. Johnston later reported that 'My thought at the time was that there was little chance of him surviving, then of his chances of having a stud career knowing the race in Dubai had no Group status. It never entered my head that he would race again and it also occurred to me that he was desperately under-insured.' The race which had necessitated this journey, and which would have paid for a few higher premiums, was the £154,652 Dubai Turf Classic six days earlier in which Fruits of Love (a 20/1-shot) had responded with grim determination to a powerful ride from Kieren Fallon to catch Nedawi in the dying strides at Nad Al Sheba.

Amazingly, Fruits of Love's injuries necessitated only a few days at the hospital and he was back in action for the Coronation Cup at Epsom in the first

Hardwicke Stakes, Royal Ascot—Fruits of Love cuts down his rivals in the straight for an impressive success; Royal Anthem is second, ahead of Sea Wave (right) and Sunshine Street (left)

week in June. In this race, however, it became clear that, even if his trainer did get Fruits of Love to the racecourse fit and well, there was still a lot more that could conspire against him. Fruits of Love is a mile and a half performer best with a strong pace, who has put up his best efforts on good to firm ground. He got neither in the Coronation Cup and never got in a blow in finishing sixth of seven. For the King George in July, Johnston felt cause to criticise the Ascot authorities (for watering the course) before the race and to bemoan his bad luck in running (for the early pace being too slow, and then for interference in the straight) after it. An erroneous weather forecast predicting soft ground contributed to Fruits of Love missing the International Stakes at York and he was not seen out again until mid-October, at Woodbine for the Canadian International in which he had to be switched before staying on well in the final furlong, beaten a length into second by Thornfield. It was the first time that Fruits of Love had started a short-priced favourite since his two-year-old days and easily his best chance to gain that precious Group 1 victory, as his trainer reflected pointedly the following week in an article headlined 'Fruits of Love defeat a bitter pill to swallow.' The Japan Cup was next on Fruits of Love's itinerary but on this occasion he performed disappointingly and finished ninth of fourteen. At first, his trainer was inclined to blame revised riding tactics, keeping him closer to the pace than at Woodbine, but the following month it emerged that Fruits of Love had a suspensory ligament injury to his near-fore, a problem which led to his withdrawal from the Hong Kong International Vase.

In that Woodbine article, Johnston wrote that 'Fruits of Love is now recognised by most people as a good Group 1 performer. . . He needs, and I believe he deserves, a Group 1 win.' Three races in the latest season no doubt gave the grounds for his belief. First there was the Dubai Turf Classic. Then in the summer there was that King George, in which he was beaten five and a half lengths in third, giving the impression he might have pipped Nedawi again behind the runaway winner with a clearer run from the rear, and before that the Hardwicke Stakes at Royal Ascot. The last-named race was as good as we have seen from Fruits of Love so far. To the casual observer, it may have looked discouraging when 12/1-shot Fruits of Love was off the bridle in last place as they began the turn for home; to his trainer, it was exactly what he wanted to see as the eight-runner field proceeded at a good pace before Fruits of Love made dramatic progress, throwing down his challenge to 6/5-favourite Royal Anthem one and a half furlongs out and passing him at the furlong marker. Welcoming his three-length winner afterwards, Johnston asked 'Royal Anthem is supposed to be the best horse in Europe, so who's the best in Europe now?' Fruits of Love was a 4/1 chance when Daylami made his much more persuasive claim in the King George.

Fruits of Love is a quite good-topped, attractive colt and an easy mover. He will prove best with an end-to-end gallop over a mile and a half and would stay further if given the opportunity. He wore blinkers on his penultimate outing in 1998, a visor for all his starts since. Mark Johnston was one of the few trainers who rose to the challenge of the Emirates World Series in the latest season and he is again likely to target Fruits of Love at the rich rewards available from those races. With his latest injury, the Dubai World Cup will come too soon for the horse, but he should be in action again for the King George.

Fruits of Love passed through the sale-ring for 70,000 dollars as a foal and IR75,000 guineas as a yearling. He is a son of the 1991 Belmont and Preakness winner Hansel and his best offspring so far, in front of 1997 Marcel Boussac winner Loving Claim and the former Clive Brittain-trained Magellan, a Grade 2 winner in the United States. Four previous winners out of Fruits of Love's dam Vallee Secrete include the smart two-year-old sprinter Mujadil (by Storm Bird) and the smart Irish miler Sagamore (by Simply Great). Further back, the family is famous for its feats on behalf of the Wertheimer family and their trainers Alec and Criquette Head. Vallee Secrete won a minor event over a mile, while her dam Midou was smart at that distance and is both a half-sister

Mr M. Doyle's "Fruits of Love"

		Woodman	Mr Prospector
	Hansel (USA)	(ch 1983)	Playmate
	(b 1988)	Count On Ronnie	Dancing Count
Fruits of Love (USA)		(b 1981)	Buena Notte
(b.c. 1995)		Secretariat	Bold Ruler
	Vallee Secrete (USA)	(ch 1970)	Somethingroyal
	(b 1977)	Midou	Saint Crespin III
		(br 1970)	Midget II

and daughter of Cheveley Park winners, in Mige and Midget II. Midget II, the grandam of another celebrity in Ma Biche, also counted the Coronation Stakes, the Queen Elizabeth II, the Foret and Maurice de Gheest among her victories, but was nevertheless regarded as a rather unlucky filly in some quarters. This was largely due to the 1956 One Thousand Guineas, about which one observer wrote: 'Unfortunately she was racing alone on the far side of the course and Poincelet, deceived by the angle, thought he had won quite comfortably; his satisfaction was soon punctured by the deeply chagrined Alec Head, who pointed out, with some asperity, that Honeylight, on the stand side, had in fact won the race by two lengths.' Hopefully, this is one calamity that Fruits of Love will manage to avoid. *M. Johnston*

FUDGE BROWNIE 3 b.g. Deploy 131 – Carte Blanche 67 (Cadeaux Genereux **58** 131) [1998 NR 1999 10m 8m May 3] first foal: dam 1m winner: modest form in maidens: probably needs further than 1m: sold 6,500 gns, joined G. M. Moore. *C. A. Cyzer.*

FUEGIAN 4 ch.g. Arazi (USA) 135 – Well Beyond (IRE) 101 (Don't Forget Me **69** 127) [1998 –: 10d 8.3m 8d a7g a7g⁴ 1999 a10f 8.3m 8.3g⁵ 8.1m⁵ 7g 8m² 8.3g* 8.3m² 8.1d⁶ 8m⁶ 7s Oct 22] rangy gelding: fair handicapper: won 18-runner event at Windsor in July: good second on same course following month, easily best effort after: stays 1m: acts on good to firm going, little form on equitrack: usually visored: often a front runner. *M. Madgwick*

FUERO REAL (FR) 4 b.g. Highest Honor (FR) 124 – Highest Pleasure (USA) **45** (Foolish Pleasure (USA)) [1998 10s 10d⁴ 12g³ 12s 12g* 11d 1999 8.3g 11.9d⁶ 11.6d 10m² 11.5f² 12.1m⁴ a10g Dec 18] 340,000 francs Y: lengthy gelding: fourth foal: brother to useful French winner up to 1½m Honor Kenmare: dam French 1¼m winner: poor handicapper: won 4-runner event at Toulouse when trained by R. Litt in 1998: stays 1½m: acts on firm ground, well beaten on equitrack. *R. J. Hodges*

FUJIYAMA CREST (IRE) 7 b.g. Roi Danzig (USA) – Snoozy Time 65 (Cavo **78** Doro 124) [1998 NR 1999 20m 14m⁴ 16g³ Aug 13] tall gelding: one-time fairly useful handicapper: winner over hurdles for N. Henderson in 1998: sold 8,200 gns in May: just fair form when in frame in 1999: best around 2m: acts on firm and good to soft ground: effective visored or not: often bandaged: sometimes wanders closing stages. *R. Curtis*

FULHAM 3 ch.c. Safawan 118 – Sister Sal 74 (Bairn (USA) 126) [1998 NR 1999 **–** 7m 10m 9f 7d Aug 20] 3,800Y, resold 2,200Y: fourth foal: half-brother to 2-y-o 5f winners Exosal (by Exodal) and Northern Sal (by Aragon): dam 2-y-o 6f winner who later stayed 1¼m: no sign of ability in maidens/handicap on Flat. *M. J. Haynes*

FULL AHEAD (IRE) 2 b.c. (Mar 17) Slip Anchor 136 – Foulard (IRE) (Sadler's **76** Wells (USA) 132) [1999 7m⁴ 8.1g⁵ Aug 30] 65,000F, IR 85,000Y: smallish, robust colt: second foal: half-brother to French 3-y-o 11.5f winner Gazar (by Kris): dam unraced sister to high-class miler Barathea: burly, promising fourth of 9 to Race Leader in maiden at Newmarket: no improvement when only fifth of 9 to Unaware in similar event at Chepstow following month, off bridle by halfway: should stay 1½m+. *M. H. Tompkins*

FULL EGALITE 3 gr.g. Ezzoud (IRE) 126 – Milva 56 (Jellaby 124) [1998 68: **62** 6.1g 6d⁶ 6s* 1999 8.5s⁴ 7m 8d⁶ 10.5s 9m 10.1g Aug 19] smallish, sturdy gelding: modest performer: well below form final 3 starts: stays 1m: acts on soft going, probably on good to firm: visored penultimate start: joined Miss B. Sanders. *W. J. Haggas*

FULL FLOW (USA) 2 b.c. (Apr 2) Eagle Eyed (USA) 111 – Fast Flow (USA) **99** (Riverman (USA) 131) [1999 6m* 7f² 6g Aug 18] smallish, strong, close-coupled colt: second foal: half-brother to 3-y-o Auction House: dam unraced daughter of useful 6f/7f performer Meteoric: won maiden at Newcastle in June: best effort (useful form) when short-head second of 5 to Thady Quill in listed race at Newmarket following month, edged out in tremendous duel: well-held eighth of 10 in Gimcrack Stakes at York final start: stays 7f: raced only on good ground or firmer. *B. W. Hills*

FULL MOON 4 b.g. Almoojid 69 – High Time (FR) (Adonijah 126) [1998 –: **36** a6g⁵ a8.5g 1999 a12g a16.2g⁴ a14.8g 9.2v⁶ 11.1v Apr 10] close-coupled gelding: poor maiden: tried blinkered/visored. *W. M. Brisbourne*

FULL OF MISCHIEF 2 b.f. (Mar 21) Be My Chief (USA) 122 – Hafhafah **–** (Shirley Heights 130) [1999 a5g Jun 17] 500Y: fourth foal: half-sister to an Italian 1¼m and 1¾m winner by Taufan: dam 1m winner: broke down 2f out in Southwell maiden: dead. *M. J. Polglase*

FULLOPEP 5 b.g. Dunbeath (USA) 127 – Suggia (Alzao (USA) 117) [1998 61: **69** 9.9d⁶ 12s³ 12m⁴ 1999 15.8g² Sep 18] sturdy gelding: fair handicapper: short-head second at Catterick only Flat run of 1999: should stay beyond 2m: acts on good to firm going: promising jumper, won over fences in October. *Mrs M. Reveley*

FULL PITCH 3 ch.g. Cadeaux Genereux 131 – Tricky Note 97 (Song 132) [1998 **93** NR 1999 5s* Jul 3] 49,000Y: sixth foal: half-brother to 3 winners, including 1997 2-y-o 6f winner Composition (by Wolfhound) and Irish 1¼m winner Ros Castle (by Reference Point): dam sprinting sister to smart sprinter Jester: most taking debut when winning 6-runner maiden at Beverley by 9 lengths, despite pulling hard early: seemed sure to improve. *W. J. Haggas*

FULL SPATE   4 ch.c. Unfuwain (USA) 131 – Double River (USA) (Irish River (FR) 131) [1998 82: 8d² 7g³ 8s⁴ 1999 8.2s⁵ 7s³ 7m* 6d⁵ 7g 7d 7m⁶ 7f 6m 6g 7.1m 7m Sep 9] leggy, quite good-topped colt: fairly useful handicapper: recorded first success at Thirsk in May: ran poorly final 5 starts: may well prove best up to 7f: acts on good to firm going: sometimes slowly away. *J. M. Bradley*   **82 d**

FUN LOVER   2 b.f. (Jan 22) Lahib (USA) 129 – Funun (USA) 84 (Fappiano (USA)) [1999 6g 6s⁵ Oct 25] 20,000F: half-sister to smart performer up to 7f in Britain and UAE Hattab (by Marju) and fairly useful 7f/1m performer Marjaana and 7-y-o Intiaash (both by Shaadi): dam 5f to 7f winner: wintry, much better effort in maidens when staying-on fifth of 13 to Picot at Leicester: likely to prove suited by 7f/1m: sold 7,500 gns, sent to Sweden. *D. R. C. Elsworth*   **64**

FUNNY GIRL (IRE)   2 b.f. (Mar 28) Darshaan 133 – Just For Fun (FR) (Lead On Time (USA) 123) [1999 8.1g⁴ 8.2g⁵ Sep 25] IR 140,000Y: first foal: dam, German 9.5f winner, from family of White Muzzle and Almutawakel: fair form in maidens at Chepstow and Nottingham, tiring and caught final 1f having been sent for home 4f out on second occasion: bred to be suited by 1¼m/1½m. *W. R. Muir*   **74**

FURNESS   2 b.g. (Apr 15) Emarati (USA) 74 – Thelma (Blakeney 126) [1999 7.9g 8s 8s Nov 6] 15,000Y: leggy, workmanlike gelding: third foal: dam unraced: modest form in maidens at York, Leicester and Doncaster. *J. G. Smyth-Osbourne*   **52**

FURSAN (USA)   6 b.g. Fred Astaire (USA) – Ancient Art (USA) (Tell (USA)) [1998 NR 1999 12m a14.8g Oct 13] lengthy, attractive gelding: fair maiden for N. Graham at 3 yrs: well below that form both Flat starts since (visored final one): stays 1½m. *R. T. Phillips*   **57**

FURTHER OUTLOOK (USA)   5 gr.g. Zilzal (USA) 137 – Future Bright (USA) (Lyphard's Wish (FR) 124) [1998 89: 8g 8.1g 7m 7.3g³ 7g 8m 8s² 1999 8d 10g 6d* 6g² 6d* 6m 5m* 5d 6d⁶ 6m Aug 17] tall, useful-looking gelding: useful handicapper: won at Pontefract in April and Epsom (£25,000 race by ½ length from The Fugative) and Doncaster in June: good effort penultimate start: best at 5f to 7f: acts on firm and soft going: has had tongue tied: has worn crossed noseband: takes strong hold, and usually races prominently. *D. Nicholls*   **106**

Timeform Sprint Rated Stakes (Handicap), Doncaster—
third win of the season for Further Outlook (left);
in close pursuit are Ziggy's Dancer (stars on cap), Ellens Lad (noseband),
Pipalong (white cap) and Indian Spark (right)

FUSUL (USA) 3 ch.c. Miswaki (USA) 124 – Silent Turn (USA) (Silent Cal (USA)) **62**
[1998 70p: 7.1m⁵ 6g 1999 7m⁴ 8m 7m 7m a7g a8g a10g⁴ Dec 18] tall, useful-looking
colt: fair maiden: left B. Hanbury 1,800 gns after third start: stays 1¼m: acts on
equitrack: has been tongue tied. *G. L. Moore*

FUTURE COUP (USA) 3 b.g. Lord At War (ARG) – Holy Moly (USA) (Halo **66**
(USA)) [1998 NR 1999 8d³ 7.5m* 10m² 9m⁶ 10.1g⁴ 7.5g² 8m⁵ 8.2g* Sep 25]
$37,000Y: lengthy, quite attractive gelding: sixth foal: brother to 2 winners in USA
and half-brother to 2 winners there: dam, winning sprinter in USA, half-sister to US
Grade 1 2-y-o 6.5f winner Papal Power: fair performer: won claimer at Beverley in
July and selling handicap (comfortably) at Nottingham in September: stays 1¼m:
acts on good to firm going: joined Lord Tyrone. *W. J. Haggas*

FUTURE PROSPECT (IRE) 5 b.g. Marju (IRE) 127 – Phazania (Tap On Wood **75**
130) [1998 75: 8m* 8.5g 8g 6.9m² 7.1g⁴ a8.5g* 8.5m a9.4g 8.3d³ 7.5m 12s a8g 1999 **a53**
a8.5g⁴ a7g a8g⁵ a8g² 8d⁶ 8.3m* 8m 9f* 8s 9.2m 9.2f⁴ 10m 8m⁴ a8.5g 8.9m² 8m 8.5g
8g Oct 2] leggy gelding: has a round action: fair on turf, modest on all-weather: won
handicaps at Hamilton in May and Redcar in June: stays 9f when conditions aren't
testing: acts on firm ground, good to soft (possibly not on soft) and all-weather:
blinkered (well beaten) second start. *M. A. Buckley*

F-ZERO 2 b.g. (Feb 15) Bin Ajwaad (IRE) 119 – Saluti Tutti 77 (Trojan Fen 118) **70**
[1999 7.1m 7m² 7.1m Sep 4] lengthy gelding: sixth foal: half-brother to winner up to
1m (5f/6f at 2 yrs) Mazeeka (by Glow): dam sprint maiden: fair maiden: well held
final start: may prove best up to 7f. *C. F. Wall*

G

GABIDIA 2 br.f. (Mar 8) Bin Ajwaad (IRE) 119 – Diabaig 76 (Precocious 126) **73 p**
[1999 7m³ Sep 8] second foal: half-sister to 3-y-o City Pursuit: dam 1m winner:
favourite, third of 7 to Silent Night in steadily-run maiden at Kempton, keeping on
after winner got first run: should stay at least 1m: likely to improve. *M. A. Jarvis*

GABLESEA 5 b.g. Beveled (USA) – Me Spede (Valiyar 129) [1998 62: a7g⁶ a8g³ **66**
a8g 7g³ 7.5d⁵ a6g⁵ 7.1g² 7.6m³ 7.1g* 8.1d⁵ 7.9g 7.5m 8g² a8.5g³ a8g² 1999 a8.5g
8d² 8.3g³ 8d³ 7m³ 8s 8m⁶ 7.1d 7.6m⁶ 7.1m 7m 8d 8s a8.5g Oct 16] tall gelding: fair
handicapper: below form after fifth start: effective at 7f to easy 9.4f: acts on good to
firm going, good to soft and fibresand: tough. *B. P. J. Baugh*

GABRIEL (IRE) 3 b.f. River Falls 113 – Los Angeles (IRE) 69 (Double Schwartz **56**
128) [1998 NR 1999 8m⁶ 8g⁴ 8.3s⁶ 9g⁵ 10s Sep 29] IR 3,000Y: first foal: dam,
maiden who stayed 1m, half-sister to useful Irish 7f winners Tantum Ergo and Bene-
diction, latter dam of Melbourne Cup winner Might And Power: modest maiden: ran
poorly final 2 starts: stays 1m: has raced freely. *M. H. Tompkins*

GADGE 8 br.g. Nomination 125 – Queenstyle 58 (Moorestyle 137) [1998 75, a62: **– §**
a6g² a6g a8g² a7g⁴ 5d 5g 6v 6s 7.5m² 6g⁴ 5m 7.1d 7g 7g* 6v 6v a7g⁴ a6g 1999 a8g² **a63 §**
a7g³ a7g⁴ a8g⁴ 6m 6.9g 6v a8.5g a6g⁶ 6d a8g³ a7g⁴ a7g a8.5g Dec 27] sturdy, lengthy
gelding: formerly fairly useful: just modest handicapper at best in 1999: effective at
6f to 1m: acts on good to firm going, soft and all-weather: tried visored/blinkered,
not since 1996: sometimes bandaged in front: sometimes runs in snatches: needs
treating with caution. *A. Bailey*

GAD YAKOUN 6 ch.g. Cadeaux Genereux 131 – Summer Impressions (USA) 70 **–**
(Lyphard (USA) 132) [1998 –: a5s a6g 1999 a9.4g Jan 6] fair winner at 3 yrs: lightly
raced and well beaten since. *M. G. Meagher*

GAELIC FORAY (IRE) 3 b.f. Unblest 117 – Rich Heiress (IRE) 49 (Last Tycoon **–**
131) [1998 NR 1999 7g Oct 19] second foal: dam maiden who stayed 1m: behind in
seller at Lingfield. *R. P. C. Hoad*

GAELIC STORM 5 b.g. Shavian 125 – Shannon Princess (Connaught 130) [1998 **116**
115: 7m 6s³ 6s* 6v* 6g 7m² 6m 6s 7g 7g* 6v* 6d⁶ 1999 7d² 6d³ 7v⁵ 6s⁶ 6g* 6g²
7.1d⁶ 6m 6m 6d* 6.8g²* a6g³ 7g⁴ 6m 6d 6d* 6s² 6s⁶ Nov 6] small, sturdy gelding:
smart performer: won minor event at Goodwood in May, similar contest then listed
race at Ovrevoll in July and 20-runner listed race (by 1¼ lengths from Pipalong)
at Newmarket in October: possibly unlucky when neck second of 14 to Superior

Bedford Lodge Hotel Bentinck Stakes, Newmarket—
Gaelic Storm takes an ultra-competitive event from Pipalong (left) and Delegate (white socks)

Premium in rated stakes at Newbury penultimate outing: best at 6f (given good test)/ 7f: seems to act on any turf going, below form on fibresand/dirt: sometimes sweats/ gets on edge: usually bandaged behind: usually comes with late run. *M. Johnston*

GAILY MILL 4 b.f. Keen 116 – Island Mill 79 (Mill Reef (USA) 141) [1998 86p: 6d³ 6d⁴ 6m³ 7m² 7d* 7m⁵ 8m⁵ 7g⁵ 8m* 8.5m* 8g² 8g⁶ 1999 8g² 8m 8m⁶ 8.5d⁵ 8.3m* 9f⁵ 8g Aug 12] leggy, angular filly: has a round action: fairly useful handicapper: dead-heated at Windsor in July: well below form final start: probably stays 9f: acts on firm and good to soft going (yet to race on softer): tends to be slowly away (has been blanketed in stalls) and usually held up (made running and hung left at Windsor). *I. A. Balding* **88**

GAIN LINE (USA) 6 b.g. Dayjur (USA) 137 – Safe Play (USA) (Sham (USA)) [1998 54: 6.9d⁵ 10d 8m⁵ 7f 8f 7g 7f⁴ 7m³ 8d⁵ 1999 a8g* a8f⁵ a8g² a8g⁶ a8.5g⁴ 8f 7m a7g a8.5g Jul 23] big, strong gelding: modest handicapper on all-weather, poor on turf: won apprentice event at Southwell in January: below form final 4 starts: best at 7f/1m: acts on fibresand, firm and good to soft going (unraced on softer): tried visored/tongue tied: usually takes strong hold and races prominently. *K. Bell* **39 a57**

GAIN TIME 2 b.g. (Jan 30) Timeless Times (USA) 99 – Axed Again (Then Again 126) [1999 5v³ 5m³ 5g² 6g 6d² 6m² 6m 6m 6g 6s 6v a6g⁶ 6d² 6.1s³ a7g Nov 12] 11,000Y: compact gelding: first foal: dam, no sign of ability, sister to Stewards' Cup winner For The Present: fair maiden: best efforts fifth and sixth outings: stays 6f well: acts on good to firm and soft going, probably on fibresand: blinkered final 5 starts: unseated rider and bolted before start twelfth outing: too free/wandered penultimate outing: may prove best held up. *T. D. Barron* **76 d**

GALANTY SHOW 3 b.f. Danehill (USA) 126 – Sacristy 54 (Godswalk (USA) 130) [1998 NR 1999 6m³ 5.7f² 6.1g* Sep 25] strong, good-topped filly: fifth living foal: sister to useful 7f to 9f winner Holtye and half-sister to Irish 1992 2-y-o 1m winner Laatansa (by Don't Forget Me), later successful up to 9.5f in Hong Kong: dam lightly-raced half-sister to Desirable and Park Appeal: fair form: won 20-runner maiden at Nottingham in September: should have stayed 7f: stud in USA. *J. H. M. Gosden* **76**

GALAPINO 6 b.g. Charmer 123 – Carousella 62 (Rousillon (USA) 133) [1998 77, a66+: a13g³ a13g² 12d 16.4s 20d⁴ 16.4g⁴ 16g 20d 12.3m 9.9m* 10.2m 12s² 12d 14.1v² 16s 1999 a12g 12s 13.3f⁶ 20m 16m³ 14.1m³ 16.4d* 16.4g³ 18.2s⁴ 17.2s 16.5s Nov 6] smallish gelding: modest handicapper: won at Sandown in August: stays 2½m: acts on any turf/all-weather: blinkered once, effective visored or not: has been bandaged in front: none too consistent. *Jamie Poulton* **64**

GALETTE 3 b.f. Caerleon (USA) 132 – Madame Dubois 121 (Legend of France (USA) 124) [1998 NR 1999 10f² 12d* Aug 14] leggy, angular filly: fifth foal: half-sister to fairly useful winners at around 1½m Place de l'Opera (by Sadler's Wells) and Richelieu (by Kris): dam won Park Hill Stakes: better effort in maidens when winning 3-runner event at Newmarket in August by 7 lengths from eased Dark Trojan: will stay beyond 1½m: should improve further. *H. R. A. Cecil* **94 p**

GALI 3 gr.c. Petong 126 – Wasimah 84 (Caerleon (USA) 132) [1998 66: 5m 7s⁴ **44**
1999 6s³ 6g 8.3m 8.1m Jun 11] modest maiden at 2 yrs, poor in 1999. *C. A. Horgan*

GALLANT 2 b.c. (Feb 10) Rainbow Quest (USA) 134 – Gay Gallanta (USA) 112 **– p**
(Woodman (USA) 126) [1999 6d Oct 29] first foal: dam, won Queen Mary and
Cheveley Park and later stayed 1m, half-sister to very smart Irish 7f and 1¼m winner
Sportsworld: green, got hang of things late on when fifteenth of 19 to maiden at
Newmarket won by Pax: will be suited by 1m+: sure to do better. *Sir Michael Stoute*

GALLANT FELLOW (FR) 4 ch.g. Cadeaux Genereux 131 – Hiwaayati (Sha- **42**
deed (USA) 135) [1998 –: 8.1m 5.7m 5m a7g a6g a8g a10g 1999 6g⁵ 6f 6.8s⁴ 7g 6g **a36**
5.1m 7f 6m⁵ 6g⁵ 6d a7g 8m³ 5d a6g a10g⁵ a7g Dec 8] poor maiden: stays 1m: acts
on good to firm going, good to soft and equitrack: has carried head awkwardly.
J. J. Bridger

GALLANT GLORY (USA) 3 b.c. Dynaformer (USA) – Triomphe (CHI) **–**
(Nobloys (FR) 103) [1998 72p: 8g 8g 1999 8d 10m 11.6m a10f Dec 23] strong colt:
has a markedly round action: fair form at 2 yrs: no show in 1999, leaving J. Gosden
before final start: should be suited by at least 1¼m. *W. D. Mather, UAE*

GALLEON BEACH 2 b.c. (Feb 16) Shirley Heights 130 – Music In My Life **99**
(IRE) 59 (Law Society (USA) 130) [1999 7m³ 8.3m* 8.1s³ 10d² Oct 30] 50,000F,
35,000Y: fourth foal: half-brother to 5-y-o Mutahadeth, 4-y-o Premium Pursuit and
3-y-o Teyaar: dam (maiden) stayed 1m: progressive form: won maiden at Hamilton
in September: very good second of 10 to Monte Carlo in listed event at Newmarket
final start: will be well suited by 1½m+: acts on soft and good to firm going: has good
attitude, and should win more races when conditions place emphasis on stamina.
J. W. Hills

GALLERY GOD (FR) 3 ch.c. In The Wings 128 – El Fabulous (FR) 111 (Fab- **89**
ulous Dancer (USA) 124) [1998 74p: 6m 7s⁴ 1999 10g 10v³ 10m³ 10d 10m³ 12.4m*
11.9d⁶ Oct 7] rangy colt: has a quick action: fairly useful performer: improved to win
minor event at Newcastle in September: sweating, edgy and early to post when well
beaten final start: should stay beyond 1½m: acts on good to firm and heavy going.
G. Wragg

GALLOWAY BOY (IRE) 2 ch.c. (Mar 17) Mujtahid (USA) 118 – Supportive **100**
(IRE) (Nashamaa 113) [1999 5d* 6g⁴ 6.3m⁶ 5g* 5f 6d⁴ 5d Sep 11] IR 32,000Y:
third foal: brother to 3-y-o Grand Lad (useful 5f/6f winner at 2/3 yrs) and half-
brother to German 6f/7f winner Porcellina (by Last Tycoon): dam fairly useful Irish
5f performer: useful performer: won maiden at Navan in May and minor event at
Tipperary in July: respectable 2½ lengths fourth of 6 to Fasliyev in Heinz 57 Phoenix
Stakes at Leopardstown on penultimate start: best at 5f: best efforts on good/good to
soft going (ran poorly on firm in Molecomb Stakes at Goodwood): often leads
(ridden too forcefully final start). *S. J. Mahon, Ireland*

GAMBADER (USA) 2 b.f. (May 14) Holy Bull (USA) 134 – Now Dance (USA) **73 p**
(Sovereign Dancer (USA)) [1999 8.2d⁵ Oct 21] $300,000Y: half-sister to winners
in USA by Time For A Change (including stakes at 2 yrs) and Housebuster (minor
sprints): dam stakes winner in USA from family of Breeders' Cup Classic second
Turkoman: reluctant at stalls (equipped with rope halter and blanket), fifth of 11 to
Western Summer in maiden at Nottingham, keeping on despite looking green: will
stay 1¼m: should do better. *J. H. M. Gosden*

GAME JOHN 3 b.g. Sirgame – Raffles Virginia 73 (Whistling Deer 117) [1998 **–**
NR 1999 8g 10m 8f 7g Jun 30] third foal: brother to a poor maiden: dam best at 6f: of
little account. *J. Pearce*

GAMEKEEPER 3 ch.c. Mujtahid (USA) 118 – High Tern 93 (High Line 125) **68**
[1998 71p: 8.2s⁴ 1999 12g 8m⁴ 11.9d Aug 17] angular, unfurnished colt: fair maiden:
ran poorly final start: sold 7,000 gns in October. *C. E. Brittain*

GAME TUFTY 3 b.g. Sirgame – Melancolia 77 (Legend of France (USA) 124) **68**
[1998 66: 7g 7m³ 8g 8d⁵ 1999 7m 11.5g⁵ 10.5m⁴ 10g² 10f 9.9m a12g 8s³ 8s 10d³ **a–**
10d* 10d Nov 4] workmanlike gelding: has a quick action: fair performer: won seller
at Windsor in October: stays 11.5f: acts on soft and good to firm going (no show only
run on fibresand): none too reliable. *J. Pearce*

GARBO 4 b.f. Superlative 118 – Valence (BEL) (Sarajevo (FR)) [1998 49: 6d 7m   –
7d⁶ 6d* 8m 8f a6g 1999 7.1m 8d a12g Nov 19] strong, workmanlike filly: poor
performer: should stay 7f: acts on good to soft going. *D. W. P. Arbuthnot*

GARGOYLE GIRL 2 b.f. (Mar 4) Be My Chief (USA) 122 – May Hills Legacy   **?**
(IRE) 68 (Be My Guest (USA) 126) [1999 6d 6g⁵ 7d⁶ 6g³ 7g 6m 8d Sep 17] 15,500Y:
second foal: half-sister to 3-y-o Legacy of Love: dam 6f (at 2 yrs) and 1¼m winner
out of Yorkshire Oaks/Park Hill winner May Hill: poor maiden on balance of form,
probably flattered (could be worth a rating of 66) when third of 7 to Howard's Lad
at Ayr: well beaten in nurseries last 3 starts: stays 6f: tends to be slowly away.
J. S. Goldie

GARNOCK VALLEY 9 b.g. Dowsing (USA) 124 – Sunley Sinner 93 (Try My   **62**
Best (USA) 130) [1998 69, a63: 5s* 5d³ 5f 5g⁶ 5g 5d² 5d 5d 6.1s² 6v a5g³ a7g⁴ a6g³   **a77**
1999 a6g⁴ a6g² a6s* a7g* a7g² a8g a7g* 7.1m 7.1m 8g 7g 6f 6v² 5.2s* a6g* a6g⁵
a6g² Dec 21] neat gelding: fair on all-weather, modest on turf: won claimers at
Wolverhampton and Lingfield in February, minor event at Southwell in April, and
handicaps at Newbury in October and Southwell in November: effective at testing 5f
to easy 7f: acts on all-weather, best on ground softer than good on turf: sometimes
blinkered/visored (former for third win in 1999): sometimes slowly away. *J. Berry*

GAROTA DO LEBLON (USA) 2 b.f. (May 11) Thunder Gulch (USA) 129   **85**
– Smart Angle (USA) (Quadrangle) [1999 6d² 6m⁵ 7d* Oct 30] $320,000Y: quite
good-topped filly: half-sister to numerous winners, including fairly useful 5f to (in
UAE) 1m winner Three Stops (by Nureyev) and US Grade 2 7f winner Houston (by
Seattle Slew): dam champion 2-y-o filly in USA: confirmed debut promise when
making all in 16-runner maiden at Newmarket by 1¼ lengths from Papabile: free-
going sort who may prove best up to 7f: acts on good to soft ground, disappointing
(off course more than 2 months after) on good to firm. *J. Noseda*

GARTH POOL (IRE) 2 b.g. (Feb 8) Sri Pekan (USA) 117 – Millionetta (IRE)   **71**
75 (Danehill (USA) 126) [1999 5g⁴ 6d⁵ 5m⁵ 5.1m³ 5f³ 6g⁵ 5f² 6s⁵ 6v Oct 11] 39,000F,
IR 28,000Y: good-bodied gelding: second foal: half-brother to 4-y-o Tiebreaker:
dam, Irish 6.5f winner, granddaughter of Irish 1000 Guineas winner Favoletta: fair
maiden: creditable efforts most starts, in blinkers seventh and eighth starts: effective
at 5f/6f: acts on firm and soft going, well held on heavy: effective blinkered or not:
has wandered: often makes running. *J. Berry*

GATECRASHER 4 b.g. Suave Dancer (USA) 136 – Benazir 91 (High Top 131)   **90**
[1998 90: 8s⁶ 8d* 10.5g² 1999 11.9s 10m⁴ 10.4s 10.5d⁵ Jun 3] lengthy gelding: fairly
useful handicapper: ran well second start: stayed 1¼m: acted on good to firm and
good to soft ground: dead. *J. R. Fanshawe*

GATEMAN 2 b.c. (Apr 1) Owington 123 – Scandalette (Niniski (USA) 125) [1999   **99 +**
5.2f⁵ 6m⁴ 6d* 6m⁵ 7.3g³ 7g* 7.6s* 8.5f* Oct 29] smallish, well-made colt: third
foal: half-brother to 3-y-o Surprise Venture and 4-y-o Night Flyer: dam unraced
half-sister to high-class sprinter Polish Patriot: progressed with virtually every
outing, winning maiden at Haydock in July and minor events at Epsom in August and
Chester (final start for B. Meehan) in September then non-graded race at Keeneland:
stays 8.5f: acts on firm and soft going. *W. E. Walden, USA*

GATHERING CLOUD (IRE) 3 b.f. Mukaddamah (USA) 125 – Adocentyn   **–**
(USA) (Upper Nile (USA)) [1998 –: a6g 1999 7.6f⁵ 7m 8s a8g Nov 15] signs of just
a little ability: trained until after reappearance by M. Heaton-Ellis. *C. G. Cox*

GAUNTLET (IRE) 3 ch.c. Suave Dancer (USA) 136 – Be My Everything (IRE)   **75**
67 (Be My Guest (USA) 126) [1998 83p: 6m⁵ 7m³ 7m² 1999 7d² 7g⁴ Apr 13] leggy
colt: fair maiden: should stay 1m: yet to race on extremes of going: has worn crossed
noseband. *J. Noseda*

GAVEL (IRE) 2 b.g. (Feb 10) Rhoman Rule (USA) – Fall of The Hammer (IRE)   **59**
(Auction Ring (USA) 123) [1999 6s 5m⁶ 7.6g³ 8s Sep 16] IR 3,000F, IR 10,000Y:
third foal: half-brother to 4-y-o I Cried For You: dam third over 7f at 2 yrs in Ireland:
modest maiden: will stay 1m: reluctant at stalls final start. *M. H. Tompkins*

GAY BREEZE 6 b.g. Dominion 123 – Judy's Dowry 80 (Dragonara Palace   **90**
(USA) 115) [1998 85: 6.1v* 6g* 5g* 5g² 5g 5.2g 5m⁵ 1999 5d⁶ 5d³ 6d 5d³ 5m 5g⁵
5.1d² 5.2g² 5s⁴ 5g⁴ 5g⁵ Oct 16] compact gelding: fairly useful handicapper: left
P. Felgate after fifth start: best effort when neck second at Yarmouth on eighth outing:

not discredited after: has won over 6f, much better form at 5f: acts on any going: usually races prominently: sold 13,500 gns, rejoined P. Felgate. *D. Nicholls*

GAY LASS (IRE) 2 ch.f. (Feb 7) Mujtahid (USA) 118 – Maracuja (USA) (Riverman (USA) 131) [1999 6.8m⁴ 6.8m³ 7s⁴ 8m Oct 19] 6,200Y: fifth foal: half-sister to German 1995 2-y-o 7f/1m winner Massada (by Most Welcome), 5-y-o Chakra and 4-y-o Royal Story: dam French 2-y-o 1m winner from very good family: fair maiden: should stay 1m: sold 6,500 gns, sent to Sweden. *J. R. Fanshawe* **68**

GDANSK (IRE) 2 b.g. (Mar 22) Pips Pride 117 – Merry Twinkle (Martinmas 128) [1999 6d 6g⁵ 7s⁵ Nov 2] IR 6,400F, 16,000Y: eighth foal: half-brother to Irish 1993 2-y-o 1m winner Miss Nutwood (by Prince Rupert) and Irish 7f winner Sparkling Harmony (by Common Grounds): dam ran twice in Ireland: modest form when fifth in maidens at Redcar and Catterick: likely to prove best at 7f/1m: has shown reluctance at stalls. *J. Berry* **63**

GEE BEE BOY 5 ch.g. Beveled (USA) – Blue And White (Busted 134) [1998 68: 11.6g² 14.1d 11.6m² 11.6m³ 11.5g⁶ 16.4m 11.9s² 1999 a12g a10g⁴ a12g a13g⁶ Mar 2] strong, close-coupled gelding: poor handicapper: stays 13f, probably not 2m: acts on good to firm going, soft and equitrack. *G. M. McCourt* **45**

GEEFORCE (IRE) 3 ch.f. Soviet Lad (USA) – Great Pleasure (GER) (Star Appeal 133) [1998 NR 1999 7g³ 7m⁶ 7.9g 7m 6s 1999 a7g 9.9g a9.4g* a8.5g Dec 27] poor performer: won maiden handicap at Wolverhampton in June: tailed off 6 months later: stays 9.3f: acts on fibresand: headstrong. *M. Brittain* **43**

GEEGEE EMMARR 6 b.m. Rakaposhi King 119 – Fair Sara 65 (McIndoe 97) [1998 48: 8.5m 5m 6g⁵ 7.1d 7s³ 1999 7m a7g⁴ a8g 7.5m 10m⁵ 10m 8.5g 6g a12g Dec 21] poor maiden handicapper: left S. Gollings and off 4 months before final start: stays 1¼m: acts on soft and good to firm going. *M. J. Polglase* **40**

GEMINI GUEST (IRE) 3 ch.c. Waajib 121 – Aldhabyih 86 (General Assembly (USA)) [1998 NR 1999 7g³ 7m* 8.2m³ 8m 7s Oct 2] 16,500F, 65,000Y: strong, close-coupled colt: half-brother to several winners, including smart German miler Jashin (by Soviet Star) and fairly useful 6f (at 2 yrs) to 9.4f winner Duke Valentino (by Machiavellian): dam, 2-y-o 5f winner, stayed 7f: landed odds in maiden at Thirsk in May: no form after: not certain to stay 1m: sweating final start. *G. G. Margarson* **78**

GEM OF WISDOM 2 gr.c. (Apr 5) Factual (USA) 108 – Indian Crystal 66 (Petong 126) [1999 a5g⁵ 5g⁵ a6g³ 5g⁴ 5.2m² a5g* a5g* 5f⁵ 5g³ a5g⁶ 5m a5g a5g Dec 17] 7,000Y: second foal: half-brother to 3-y-o Crystal Rosie: dam, 5f winner, became unreliable: modest performer: won sellers at Southwell in June/July: well below form final 3 starts: may prove best at 5f: acts on firm going, best form on fibresand: usually visored, blinkered twice. *J. Berry* **48** **a55**

GENERAL ACADEMY (IRE) 6 b.g. Royal Academy (USA) 130 – Hastening (Shirley Heights 130) [1998 NR 1999 7.5m 8m⁶ 7m 10.4f Sep 2] big, lengthy gelding: useful in 1997: no form since (fell final start): stays 10.5f: acts on good to firm ground: blinkered/visored once each. *M. W. Easterby* **–**

GENERAL ASSEMBLY (IRE) 7 b.g. Pharly (FR) 130 – Hastening (Shirley Heights 130) [1998 87d: 12s 18.7m⁶ 16g 13.9s⁶ 15.9m⁶ 16.2g 1999 a16g a16g 12g Apr 14] rangy gelding: poor mover: formerly fairly useful staying handicapper: little show in 1999: blinkered penultimate start. *G. G. Margarson* **–**

GENERAL EQUATION 6 b.g. Governor General 116 – Logarithm (King of Spain 121) [1998 –§, a50§: a5g⁶ a5g* a5g⁴ a5g³ a5g a5g⁶ a5g³ 5v a5g⁴ a5g a5g³ a5g a5g a5g⁴ 1999 a5g a5g a5g Jan 23] modest handicapper at best on all-weather, rarely tried on turf: best at 5f: acts on fibresand and soft ground: blinkered/visored nowadays: front runner: unreliable. *J. Balding* **– §**

GENERAL KLAIRE 4 b. or br.f. Presidium 124 – Klairover 50 (Smackover 107) [1998 53, a74: 7s 7v⁶ 6.1v 8g 6g⁶ a6g* 7.1g⁶ a6g⁶ a6g a6g² 1999 a6g² a7g⁵ a6g a6g² 7s 6d⁶ 6.1s³ 6g 6g a7g³ 7g a6g² 6.1m⁵ a6g² a7g* a6g⁵ a7g⁶ a6g⁵ a6g³ Dec 13] fairly useful handicapper on all-weather, modest on turf: won 16-runner race at Southwell in September: stays 7f: acts on fibresand, soft and good to firm going: held up, and possibly not easiest of rides. *B. A. McMahon* **58** **a82**

GENERIC (IRE) 2 b.c. (Feb 12) Fairy King (USA) – Wannabe 84 (Shirley Heights 130) [1999 6s⁶ 7d³ Oct 22] IR 150,000Y: good-topped colt: has scope: second foal: half-brother to 3-y-o Wannabe Grand: dam 1m winner here, later successful over **81 p**

1¼m in France: trained on debut by P. Chapple-Hyam: improved greatly when 2 lengths third of 22 to Fame At Last in maiden at Doncaster, making most: should stay 1m: wears tongue strap: type to do better still. *A. G. Foster*

GENEROSITY   4 ch.c. Generous (IRE) 139 – Pageantry 83 (Welsh Pageant 132)   **111**
[1998 109: 11.4d* 12g³ 12m⁴ 14g* 13.9f³ 15s* 14g² 1999 18.7m² 22.2m⁵ 16.1m 16f³ 18.7m² 15.9m⁵ 14.1m⁴ 14s* 17.3g 16.1d⁴ Oct 29] tall, leggy colt: smart performer: runner-up in 2 handicaps at Chester (including Chester Cup behind Rainbow High) prior to winning minor event at Haydock by 6 lengths from Adnaan in September: probably stays 2¾m: acts on firm and soft going: usually held up, though made running at Haydock. *P. F. I. Cole*

GENEROUS DIANA   3 ch.f. Generous (IRE) 139 – Lypharitissima (FR) (Light-   **75**
ning (FR) 129) [1998 NR 1999 7m⁴ 7g² 7g² 9s* Oct 8] sister to 4-y-o One Dinar and half-sister to French 1m and 10.5f winner Silver Phantom (by Fast Topaze): dam unraced sister to Prix de Diane winner Lypharita: fair form: won maiden at Lingfield in October: stays 9f: acts on soft going. *K. Mahdi*

GENEROUS LIBRA   5 b.g. Generous (IRE) 139 – Come On Rosi 77 (Valiyar   **111**
129) [1998 111: 10d² 10.4g² 12d 10d 10m⁴ 10.4f⁵ 10.1m* 10.1d* 10g 8d² 8s* 1999 8d² 10.3m³ 8f³ 10.1g³ 9m⁴ 8.5d⁵ 10d⁶ Oct 29] tall, angular gelding: smart performer: placed in listed races/minor contests first 4 starts, including when second to White Heart at Doncaster on reappearance: below form after: stays 1¼m: acts on firm and soft going: sometimes starts slowly/pulls hard/carries head high: best in well-run race: sent to France. *J. L. Dunlop*

GENEROUS PRESENT   6 ch.g. Cadeaux Genereux 131 – Dance Move (Shareef   –
Dancer (USA) 135) [1998 –: 10.1f 1999 8m 6g⁶ 7f 7d Aug 14] tall gelding: no form since 3 yrs: tried blinkered. *J. W. Payne*

GENEROUS ROSI   4 b.c. Generous (IRE) 139 – Come On Rosi 77 (Valiyar 129)   **112**
[1998 110: 10m² 11.8m² 10g² 10f* 9.9g² 7.9f² 8g² 8s² 1999 10g* 10s* 10m² 10m 12f⁴ 9.9s⁵ 8.5d 10d Oct 29] big, good-bodied colt: smart performer: won listed race at Kempton then Marriott Hotels (Gordon Richards) Stakes at Sandown in April,

Mr Wafic Said's "Generous Rosi"

latter by short head from Evening World: creditable efforts after only when in frame in Brigadier Gerard Stakes at Sandown (4 lengths second to Chester House) and listed rated stakes at Goodwood (fourth to Danish Rhapsody): barely stays 1½m: acts on firm and soft ground: usually races prominently: blinkered final start: sent to B. Cecil in USA. *J. L. Dunlop*

GENEROUS TERMS 4 ch.c. Generous (IRE) 139 – Time Charter 131 (Saritamer (USA) 130) [1998 104: 11.8m* 14.1m* 14m² 1999 13.3d⁴ 16.4g 14.1m³ Jun 24] **104** close-coupled, quite attractive colt: useful performer: creditable fourth of 6 to Dark Shell in listed race at Newbury: disappointing both starts after: should stay 2m: acts on good to firm and good to soft ground: tongue tied/tended to hang final start: sold 11,000 gns in October. *H. Candy*

GENEROUS WAYS 4 ch.g. Generous (IRE) 139 – Clara Bow (USA) (Coastal (USA)) [1998 77: 10d 8.1g⁵ 9m³ 11.6f⁵ 14.1m* 16.1m³ 12.3m 14.1s **74 §** 12.4m³ 13.1d⁵ 14m 16.2m* 16.4m 16.2m³ 16g⁵ 14.8m⁵ 17.3g Oct 16] leggy, quite good-topped gelding: fair handicapper: won at Ascot in June: only form after when third on same course: stays 2m: acts on good to firm going, possibly not on softer than good: blinkered fifth start: has found little, and probably less than genuine. *E. J. Alston*

GENGHIS KHAN (IRE) 3 b.c. Sadler's Wells (USA) 132 – Doff The Derby **105** (USA) (Master Derby (USA)) [1998 NR 1999 10g⁴ 12s* 12g 12d⁴ 13.9g 14s⁵ 12v Oct 3] 360,000F: small, well-made colt: brother to smart Irish 1m/9f winner Strawberry Roan and half-brother to several winners, notably Generous (by Caerleon): dam unraced half-sister to Arc runner-up Trillion, the dam of Triptych: useful performer: won maiden at the Curragh in June and minor event at Leopardstown in August: well beaten in Ebor at York on fifth start: acted as pacemaker in Arc final start: should stay further than 1½m: sold 70,000 gns, reportedly to go hurdling. *A. P. O'Brien, Ireland*

GENIUS (IRE) 4 b.g. Lycius (USA) 124 – Once In My Life (IRE) 114 (Lomond **–** (USA) 128) [1998 63, a74: a7g a10g² a8g* a8g* 7d 6.9v⁴ 7g a8g⁵ 8d³ 12g 8.2g 8m⁵ **a74 d** 8m⁶ 7m 8.5s 8d 10g a8g a8g³ 1999 a10g a8g a8g⁶ a8g⁶ a7g 7m a8.5g 8m a8g a7g a8g a6g⁴ a8.5g Dec 27] big, good-bodied gelding: fair handicapper: won at Lingfield in February on final start for S. Dow: little form after, other than penultimate start: effective at 7f/1m: acts on equitrack, no recent form on turf: blinkered once at 2 yrs. *D. W. Chapman*

GENSCHER 3 b.g. Cadeaux Genereux 131 – Marienbad (FR) (Darshaan 133) **61** [1998 –: 8s 7d 1999 8g³ 9.2m⁴ 12.1m* 12.1f² 12s⁶ 10.1d Oct 20] lengthy, workmanlike gelding: modest handicapper: won at Hamilton in September: below best after next start: stays 1½m: acts on firm going, possibly not on softer than good: won on hurdling debut in November. *R. Allan*

GENTLE ANNE 2 b.f. (Mar 4) Faustus (USA) 118 – Gentle Stream 55 (Sandy **46** Creek 123) [1999 7m⁴ 6g 7g⁵ 7.5g 9m⁶ 7g⁶ 8.2d⁶ a8g³ a7g⁴ a8g⁵ Dec 17] 2,900Y: workmanlike filly: half-sister to 3-y-o Lady of Aragon and 3 winners, including Irish 1m/9f winner Zoe Baird (by Aragon) and Irish 1½m winner Three Rivers (by Warrshan): dam Irish 1½m winner: poor maiden: will be suited by 1¼m+: acts on good to firm going and fibresand: has looked less than keen. *Ronald Thompson*

GENTLE DAME 3 ch.f. Kris 135 – Cascassi (USA) 91 (Nijinsky (CAN) 138) **75** [1998 NR 1999 7m⁶ 8m⁵ 9.9g³ 12m³ 10f* 10d Aug 14] small, useful-looking filly: first foal: dam, 1¼m and (in France at 4 yrs) 12.5f winner, half-sister to Oaks and Irish Oaks winner Diminuendo (dam of Calando): fair performer: best effort when winning maiden at Ripon in August: well below form in handicap next time: effective at 1¼m: form only on good going or firmer. *B. W. Hills*

GENTLEMAN VENTURE 3 b.c. Polar Falcon (USA) 126 – Our Shirley 84 **93** (Shirley Heights 130) [1998 NR 1999 8d³ 10s* 10.5g 10m³ 12f⁴ 11.9m 10.3g 12s 10g Oct 11] tall, quite attractive colt: half-brother to several winners, including fairly useful stayer Peart Venture (by Salse) and ungenuine 6f (at 2 yrs) to 1m winner Soviet Express (by Siberian Express): dam 1¼m winner: fairly useful performer: won maiden at Redcar in May: best efforts when in frame in quite valuable handicaps at Newmarket and Goodwood in July: rather disappointing after (found little final start): stays 1½m: acts on firm and soft going: headstrong and twice failed to handle left-handed turns: sold 20,000 gns, joined J. Akehurst. *S. P. C. Woods*

GENUINE JOHN (IRE)   6 b.g. High Estate 127 – Fiscal Folly (USA) (Foolish   **61**
Pleasure (USA)) [1998 61, a48: a8g³ a8g³ a8g² a7g³ a8.5g⁴ 8d* 8.3d* 9g⁵ 8g⁵ a8g²   **a45**
9.2m 8g* 8.5g⁵ a8g 8d³ 8.5m⁵ 7.5m a11g⁵ 8v 1999 a8g a8g 9g⁴ 8.5m* 8d 9m 8.5d⁵
8d 8m 8.3f 8d³ 10s a8g a11g⁶ a12g³ Dec 21] sturdy gelding: modest on turf, poor on
all-weather: won seller at Beverley in April: mainly below form after: has form at
1½m, best recent efforts on turf around 1m: acts on firm going, soft and fibresand:
effective blinkered or not: has had tongue tied: inconsistent. *J. Parkes*

GEORDIE LAD   5 ch.g. Tina's Pet 121 – Edraianthus 78 (Windjammer (USA))   **–**
[1998 –: a6s a7g 1999 6m 7f Jul 14] of little account. *M. Bradstock*

GEORGE (IRE)   4 b.g. Distinctly North (USA) 115 – Heather Lark (Red Alert 127)   **60**
[1998 78: 5.8v 7m⁵ 5d² 6g* 5s 6g 7.1m 8d 1999 6.1v 6.1s 7.1d a7g 10.5d 7m² 6s⁵
6.1d 7g Oct 16] good-topped gelding: modest handicapper: left P. Felgate after second start and B. Hanbury before final one: stays 7f: acts on good to firm going: tried
blinkered: has started slowly and looked less than keen under pressure. *S. Gollings*

GEORGETTE (USA)   3 ch.f. Geiger Counter (USA) – Odori (USA) (The   **88**
Minstrel (CAN) 135) [1998 92p: 7g 6g* 6d* 1999 8d⁶ 6m⁶ Jun 21] big, lengthy filly:
fairly useful performer: better effort at 3 yrs on reappearance: stays 1m: acts on good
to soft ground. *J. H. M. Gosden*

GERONIMO   2 b.c. (Apr 1) Efisio 120 – Apache Squaw 54 (Be My Guest (USA)   **56 p**
126) [1999 a5g Nov 20] third foal: dam, middle-distance maiden, half-sister to very
smart middle-distance colt Apache: slowly away when seventh of 10 behind Waffles
of Amin in maiden at Wolverhampton: should improve. *C. W. Thornton*

GET A LIFE   6 gr.m. Old Vic 136 – Sandstream 72 (Sandford Lad 133) [1998 32:   **–**
a12g 10s 8.3d 10m 8g 13.1g⁵ 13m 8d² 8.3d² 9.9m 9.9m 1999 a8g⁶ 10d 7.5d 7m 8f 8g
8m Aug 31] no longer of much account. *G. Woodward*

GET ON GEORGE   5 b.g. Rudimentary (USA) 118 – Glint of Victory 96 (Glint   **–**
of Gold 128) [1998 NR 1999 8d a10g a12g Aug 13] fifth foal: half-brother to 1¼m
winner Nelly's Cousin (by Distant Relative): dam, 1¼m winner, stayed 1½m: no
form in sellers. *Mrs L. C. Jewell*

GET STUCK IN (IRE)   3 b.g. Up And At 'em 109 – Shoka (FR) 86 (Kaldoun   **92 §**
(FR) 122) [1998 81: 6g⁵ 5m² 5g³ 5g² 5g⁵ 6g 6d² 5g² 6g² 5s² 5.1v² 1999 6d³ 5.1m 5m
6f⁴ 5g⁴ 6m* 6g² 5.1m⁶ 5m⁵ 6g* 6m² 6d 5s 6d* 8v⁴ 6d Oct 20] leggy, quite attractive
gelding: fairly useful performer on his day: won amateur event at Hamilton in June
and handicaps at Ripon in August and York (beat Pepperdine by a length in Coral
Sprint Trophy, hanging right towards runner-up) in October: stays 6f: acts on good
to firm and heavy going: blinkered fourth start: sometimes slowly away, races
prominently otherwise: carries head high (often finds little) and not an easy ride.
Miss L. A. Perratt

Coral Sprint Trophy (Handicap), York—
despite hanging across the course, Get Stuck In keeps the race from Pepperdine

GET THE POINT   5 b.h. Sadler's Wells (USA) 132 – Tolmi 122 (Great Nephew   **63**
126) [1998 –: 8d 1999 14.1s³ Apr 27] sturdy, close-coupled horse: fair maiden,
lightly raced since 3 yrs: third in handicap at Nottingham, only run of 1999: may
prove best short of 1¾m: acts on soft and good to firm going: often wanders under
pressure. *S. Gollings*

GEVITY   3 b.f. Kris 135 – Cephira (FR) (Abdos 134) [1998 61p: 7s⁵ 1999 a8.5g³   **76**
a8.5g* 8s⁴ 8.5s 8g* 7.1g⁴ 8.2m² a8.5g Oct 13] leggy, plain filly: fair performer: won
maiden at Wolverhampton in March and handicap at Bath in May: off course 4
months before final start: stays 8.5f: acts on good to firm going and fibresand: pulled
too hard fourth outing. *W. Jarvis*

GHAAZI   3 ch.g. Lahib (USA) 129 – Shurooq (USA) 94 (Affirmed (USA)) [1998   **67**
67+: 7.1m 7.6f⁴ 7.1m³ 8m 1999 8f⁶ 9.9d 10g a7g⁴ a7g³ a8g* a8.5g⁴ Dec 27] tall
gelding: has scope: fluent mover: fair performer: left E. Dunlop after second start:
won maiden at Lingfield in November: stays 8.5f: acts on all-weather and firm going:
blinkered (ran creditably) final outing: has worn tongue strap. *Miss Gay Kelleway*

GHALIB (IRE)   5 ch.h. Soviet Star (USA) 128 – Nafhaat (USA) 91 (Roberto   **–**
(USA) 131) [1998 101: 7.1d⁵ 10g⁵ 8s² 7s* 1999 7d⁶ 8s⁶ Sep 27] strong horse: useful
performer, lightly raced: well below form in 1999: stays 1¼m: acts on good to firm
and heavy going: has been bandaged: sent to Italy. *M. P. Tregoning*

GHOST PATH   4 gr.f. Absalom 128 – Glide Path 91 (Sovereign Path 125) [1998   **–**
–: 7d 8g 11.5g² 1999 a12g⁵ Feb 23] tailed off in maidens. *R. J. O'Sullivan*

GHUFFRAN (USA)   2 b.f. (May 1) Wild Again (USA) – Halholah (USA) 65   **80**
(Secreto (USA) 128) [1999 6m⁴ 7m² 7d² 7m² 7.7d³ Sep 21] leggy, quite good-topped
filly: seventh foal: half-sister to smart 6f (at 2 yrs) to 10.5f winner Murajja and fairly
useful 1m and 15f winner Yanabi (both by Silver Hawk): dam daughter of 9f Grade-1
winning half-sister to Alydar: fairly useful form in maidens second to fourth starts:
should stay 1m. *P. T. Walwyn*

GHUROOB (IRE)   3 ch.f. Arazi (USA) 135 – Tablah (USA) 86 (Silver Hawk   **–**
(USA) 123) [1998 –: 8s 1999 8.3m Apr 19] well held in maidens: sent to USA.
P. T. Walwyn

GHUTAH   5 ch.g. Lycius (USA) 124 – Barada (USA) (Damascus (USA)) [1998   **–**
a7f 8m 1999 5.9g 8.2f⁵ 6.9g 9.2f⁴ 9.1v 8d Oct 20] sixth foal: related to several
winners, including 12.5f winner Pica (by Diesis): fairly useful form in 2 runs over 6f
at 2 yrs for A. Fabre in France: no form for K. McLaughlin in UAE at 3 and 4 yrs, and
well held in varied company in Britain in 1999: tried blinkered/visored: has been
bandaged. *Martyn Wane*

GIANT'S CAUSEWAY (USA)   2 ch.c. (Feb 14) Storm Cat (USA) – Mariah's   **119 p**
Storm (USA) 116 (Rahy (USA) 115) [1999 6m* 7g* 7d* Sep 18]

  Still best-priced at 20/1 for the Two Thousand Guineas after his win in
the Prix de la Salamandre in mid-September, Giant's Causeway was as low as
7/2 after the Dewhurst just a month later, and that was without leaving his box.
Following the defeat of the highly regarded Bernstein in the National Stakes
the day after Giant's Causeway won at Longchamp, and then the career-ending
injury sustained by the stable's top two-year-old Fasliyev, Giant's Causeway
is now at the head of the queue as Ballydoyle's main Two Thousand Guineas
contender and looks a serious threat to Dewhurst winner Distant Music.
  Along with most first appearances by his stable's two-year-olds in
the latest season, Giant's Causeway's debut was less a question of whether he
would win, more a question of by how far. His seven-length demolition of eight
rivals at Naas in July was as impressive a debut as any by an O'Brien two-year-
old all year, and, after having to miss the Acomb Stakes at York the following
month because of a slight knock, Giant's Causeway started at long odds on
again for the four-runner King of Kings EBF Futurity Stakes at the Curragh at
the end of August. He won easily once more, just needing to be pushed out after
leading approaching the final furlong to beat his stable-mate Brahms by two
and a half lengths. Brahms was sent off the 14/1 outsider of the quartet on that
occasion but some smart placed efforts in the Middle Park and Dewhurst later

on entitled him to be considered Giant's Causeway's most notable victim by the end of the season.

Giant's Causeway's rivals in the Prix de la Salamandre, none of whom raced again afterwards, were some way removed from the best of their generation; both Bachir and Grigorovich had been put firmly in their place when reaching the frame behind Fasliyev in the Prix Morny, Race Leader had finished only third to King's Best in the Acomb and Valentino had won a newcomers race at Ascot on his only outing. Having tracked the pace in his first two races, Giant's Causeway was sent on at Longchamp and was ridden out firmly in the straight to account for Race Leader by two lengths, followed by Bachir the same distance back in third. None of his rivals was able to land a serious blow. 'I was going to keep his mind on the job but I threw my stick away at the two-furlong marker' admitted Michael Kinane afterwards. 'Giant's Causeway stays well and is very laid-back. He was doing nothing in front and looking around during the long run up the straight. He's never been in the lead for so long before.'

Like the previous year's Salamandre winner Aljabr, Giant's Causeway is by currently the most sought-after North American sire Storm Cat. On the same weekend as the Salamandre, two of Storm Cat's daughters, Catinca and Finder's Fee, took Grade 1 events in the States, which, together with Storm Cat's success at the September Yearling Sales, prompted an increase in Storm Cat's fee for 2000 to 300,000 dollars from the 250,000 dollars originally announced earlier in the year. Giant's Causeway and Bernstein are two of the small number of runners Storm Cat had in the British Isles in the latest season, but news that Coolmore has purchased a number of breeding rights to him should ensure wider representation in years to come. More immediately, the Magnier/Tabor team purchased a 3,000,000-dollar Storm Cat colt at the latest Keeneland July Sales. The same buyers had had to go to 2,600,000 dollars to secure Mariah's Storm at Keeneland in November 1996 (they were the under-bidders for Bernstein's dam at the same sale), making her the top-priced broodmare in North America that year. In foal to Storm Cat, the result was her first foal, Giant's Causeway. Mariah's Storm compiled a fine record of ten wins from sixteen starts, six of them in graded stakes at a mile to nine furlongs. A Grade 1 race eluded her, but she took the Grade 2 Arlington-Washington Lassie Stakes at two and the Turfway Park Budweiser Breeders' Cup Handicap at four. Mariah's Storm's close relative Panoramic (by Rainbow Quest) showed very smart form over middle distances for Andre Fabre, winning the Prix d'Harcourt at four when also runner-up in the Rothmans International at Woodbine. Their dam Immense won the Grade 3 Little Silver Handicap over eight and a half

Prix de la Salamandre, Longchamp—
Giant's Causeway maintains his unbeaten record with an efficient display of front-running;
Race Leader is unable to threaten the winner

Mrs John Magnier & Mr M. Tabor's "Giant's Causeway"

furlongs and was a half-sister to the joint-top North American two-year-old filly of 1975, Dearly Precious.

		Storm Bird	Northern Dancer
	Storm Cat (USA)	(b 1978)	South Ocean
	(b or br 1983)	Terlingua	Secretariat
Giant's Causeway (USA)		(ch 1976)	Crimson Saint
(ch.c. Feb 14, 1997)		Rahy	Blushing Groom
	Mariah's Storm (USA)	(ch 1985)	Glorious Song
	(b 1991)	Immense	Roberto
		(b 1979)	Imsodear

The strong, good-topped Giant's Causeway will stay a mile, possibly a mile and a quarter. His rider had no doubts about the latter. 'He's more of a staying sort and ten furlongs will be within his range.' Kinane was, however, speaking while the stable still had other live Guineas candidates in Fasliyev and Bernstein, and in any case there are plenty of promising colts in the O'Brien yard more obviously bred to do duty over ten furlongs or more. Giant's Causeway is yet to race on extremes of ground and, even before missing the Acomb with a vet's certificate, connections had warned they would consider withdrawing him if the ground deteriorated. *A. P. O'Brien, Ireland*

GIFFOINE 3 b.f. Timeless Times (USA) 99 – Dear Glenda 66 (Gold Song 112) **52**
[1998 79: 5m⁴ 5f* 5.2m⁵ 6d 5m⁶ 1999 6g 6g 5m 5m a5g⁵ 6f 6m Jul 28] close-coupled filly: only modest form in 1999: should stay 6f: has given trouble at stalls/been slowly away. *S. Dow*

GIFT OF GOLD 4 ch.c. Statoblest 120 – Ellebanna 69 (Tina's Pet 121) [1998 **89**
83: 7.6g² 7g 6g³ 7g⁴ 7.1d 7m* 7g³ 7f⁵ 7g 7s⁴ a7g⁶ 1999 a8.5s⁶ a7g 7g 7g² 7m 7d* **a68**

435

7.1m⁵ 8m 7s 6d³ 7d 7d⁴ a7g Dec 21] good-topped, close-coupled colt: fairly useful handicapper on turf, fair on all-weather: won at Goodwood in June: effective at 6f/7f: acts on all-weather, soft and good to firm going: game. *A. Bailey*

GIGETTA (IRE)   3 ch.f. Brief Truce (USA) 126 – Mrs Fisher (IRE) 94 (Salmon   – Leap (USA) 131) [1998 NR 1999 a7g Jun 5] IR 17,000Y, 3,600 2-y-o: third foal: sister to fairly useful 1m and (at 2 yrs) 8.5f winner Pedro: dam 7f winner, including at 2 yrs: last in maiden at Wolverhampton. *N. P. Littmoden*

GIKO   5 b.g. Arazi (USA) 135 – Gayane 125 (Nureyev (USA) 131) [1998 76: 7.3g³   – 7g⁴ 7.1d⁶ 9g* 8.1g³ 8.1m* 8g 8s⁴ 8g² 1999 7m 8g 8m Jun 18] leggy gelding: has a round action: fair handicapper at 4 yrs: below form in 1999 (reportedly struck into second start): effective at 7f to 9f: acts on soft going, good to firm and fibresand. *Jamie Poulton*

GILDERSLEVE   4 ch.f. Gildoran 123 – Fragrant Hackette 32 (Simply Great   – (FR) 122) [1998 –, a52d: a8g³ 8f a7g 7d 8g 7.6g 7m 7m a8g a10f 1999 a7g Jan 4] disappointing maiden. *N. E. Berry*

GILFOOT BREEZE (IRE)   2 b.g. (Mar 23) Forest Wind (USA) 111 – Ma Bella   – Luna 76 (Jalmood (USA) 126) [1999 6g a7g 7.5g 8.5g 7.5g⁶ a8g Nov 15] IR 3,400F, 2,300 2-y-o: first foal: dam 1m winner: little form. *J. Norton*

GILGAMESH (USA)   4 br.c. Mr Prospector (USA) – Danzante (USA) 107 (Dan-   **73** zig (USA)) [1998 5.5s⁴ 1999 8g⁴ 10m Sep 7] second foal: brother to useful French 1996 2-y-o 7f winner Alpha Plus: dam, winning sprinter in France/USA, half-sister to Breeders' Cup Classic winner Skywalker: ran once (blinkered) for A. Fabre in 1998: fourth in maiden at Pontefract in August: well tailed off next time: sent to J. Kimmel in USA. *J. H. M. Gosden*

GILLY WEET   3 b.f. Almoojid 69 – Sindos 89 (Busted 134) [1998 –: 8.1m 7.9g   – 8d 1999 12m 10s⁶ 16m⁶ 10m Sep 7] big, lengthy filly: bad maiden: has raced freely. *R. Hollinshead*

GILOU   3 b.f. Midyan (USA) 124 – Lunagraphe (USA) (Time For A Change (USA))   **60 d** [1998 62, a?: 5g⁴ a6g 7.5d⁴ 6.1d 8m⁵ 1999 10m⁴ 9d 8m 12g 14.1f⁴ 17.2m⁴ 16.2m⁶ 16.2m⁶ 12f⁵ Jul 30] leggy, plain filly: modest maiden handicapper: below form after reappearance: seems not quite to stay 2m: acts on good to firm and good to soft going, well beaten on fibresand. *C. W. Fairhurst*

GIMCO   2 b.c. (Apr 12) Pelder (IRE) 125 – Valetta (Faustus (USA) 118) [1999   **67** 7.1m⁵ Jun 11] 9,000Y: first foal: dam well beaten: fifth of 11 to Blue Bolivar in maiden at Sandown: joined G. Chung. *A. Kelleway*

GINGER FLOWER   10 ch.m. Niniski (USA) 125 – Monterana 99 (Sallust 134)   **35** [1998 –: a7g 1999 11.9d 17.1g 14.1m⁶ a14g 11d Oct 26] poor nowadays. *B. W. Murray*

GINGER ROGERS   5 ch.m. Gildoran 123 – Axe Valley 89 (Royben 125) [1998   **54** NR 1999 14.1g⁴ 14m 16g⁴ 17.1s³ 16d Oct 21] lengthy mare: modest handicapper nowadays: stays 17f: acts on soft going and on good to firm: has been bandaged in front: joined N. Henderson. *D. W. P. Arbuthnot*

GINISKI PARK   3 b.f. Risk Me (FR) 127 – Georgina Park 88 (Silly Season 127)   – [1998 –: 5.1v 6d a6g a5g 1999 a8g Dec 17] no form: tried blinkered. *Mrs N. Macauley*

GINNER MORRIS   4 b.g. Emarati (USA) 74 – Just Run (IRE) 45 (Runnett 125)   **44** [1998 56: 7g 8d 7.1d 8.1m 7m 6d 8v⁴ 8v² 10d⁴ a8g⁴ a10f² a10g 1999 a8g a8g 9d⁴ 10m⁵ May 7] modest maiden handicapper: stays easy 1¼m: acts on heavy ground and all-weather: joined J. Hetherton. *C. B. B. Booth*

GIN OCLOCK (IRE)   2 b.f. (Jan 9) Bin Ajwaad (IRE) 119 – Suspiria (IRE) 87   **75** (Glenstal (USA) 118) [1999 6g 7m* 7g² 7m⁴ 7.3g Aug 14] 18,500Y: second foal: dam, fairly useful Italian 2-y-o 5f winner, half-sister to smart miler Ventiquattrofogli: fair form: won maiden at Thirsk in June: below form last 2 starts: should stay 1m: front runner. *M. R. Channon*

GINOLA'S MAGIC (IRE)   2 b.c. (Apr 20) Perugino (USA) 84 – Simple Annie   **97** (Simply Great (FR) 122) [1999 6g* 7g* 6m⁶ 6f³ 6g 6m⁵ Sep 8] IR 26,000Y: rather leggy colt: third foal: closely related to 1995 2-y-o 6f winner Beas River (by Classic Music) and half-brother to 1997 Irish 2-y-o 7f winner Hermitage Bay (by Waajib), both later successful in Hong Kong: dam lightly-raced half-sister to Annie Edge, the dam of Selkirk: won maiden at Kempton and minor event at Epsom in June: useful form when third of 7 to Bachir in Richmond Stakes at Goodwood in July: below form last 2 starts: stays 7f: raced only on good ground or firmer: has been bandaged: reportedly suffered an overreach on third outing: sold 42,000 gns, sent to Germany. *R. Hannon*

GINO'S SPIRITS 3 ch.f. Perugino (USA) 84 – Rising Spirits 77 (Cure The Blues (USA)) [1998 77: 5.1g 5m⁴ 7m* 7.5m³ 8m 7g² 7g⁵ 8m⁵ 1999 10.3d⁵ 10g³ 9g² 10.5g³ 8m 8m³ 9f 9g²* 9m⁶ 10.1g* 10s² 10d Oct 14] leggy, lightly-made filly: useful performer: won handicap at Lingfield in August and listed race at Yarmouth (by short head from Kittiwake) in September: creditable second to Lady In Waiting in Sun Chariot Stakes at Newmarket penultimate start: stays 1¼m: acts on soft and good to firm going, well held on firm: sometimes sweating/on toes: sold 66,000 gns, sent to USA. *C. E. Brittain* **98**

GINZBOURG 5 b.g. Ferdinand (USA) – Last Request 92 (Dancer's Image (USA)) [1998 76d: 8d⁶ 10v 10.1s 8m 9.9m 7m 7g 10.1m 10.8m³ a12g³ a13g⁴ 1999 a12g⁵ a12f⁶ Jan 19] modest form at 4 yrs: little show in 1999, said to have been lame on final start: stays 1½m: acts on good to firm ground, good to soft and equitrack: well beaten in blinkers: unreliable. *R. J. O'Sullivan* **–**

GIPSY ANNA (IRE) 2 b.f. (Jan 30) Marju (IRE) 127 – Anna Comnena (IRE) 71 (Shareef Dancer (USA) 135) [1999 5g⁵ 5.2d* May 14] 22,000Y: strong, good-topped filly: fourth foal: half-sister to 4-y-o Abyaan and Italian winner up to 15f Archipova (both by Ela-Mana-Mou): dam, should have stayed 1½m, half-sister to dams of Annus Mirabilis and Annaba: fairly useful form: won maiden at Haydock and minor event at Newbury in May, improving considerably when making all in latter by ½ length from Rowaasi: bred to stay at least 1m. *B. J. Meehan* **94 +**

GIPSY ROSE LEE (IRE) 3 b.f. Marju (IRE) 127 – Rainstone 57 (Rainbow Quest (USA) 134) [1998 100: 5d* 6m* 6m² 1999 7m 8d³ 7m 6d⁴ 8d⁶ 8d³ Oct 12] leggy, close-coupled filly: has a round action: useful performer: good fourth in rated stakes at Newmarket in October: involved in scrimmaging and far from discredited in listed race at Ascot next time: probably stays 1m: acts on good to firm and good to soft going: sometimes flashes tail under pressure. *B. J. Meehan* **98**

GIPSY SPIRIT 3 b.f. Alhijaz 122 – What A Pet (Mummy's Pet 125) [1998 –: 6.1m 1999 8m Jul 21] well beaten in maiden/seller. *P. G. Murphy* **–**

GIRLIE SET (IRE) 4 b.f. Second Set (IRE) 127 – Heavenward (USA) (Conquistador Cielo (USA)) [1998 NR 1999 11d⁴ a9.4g⁴ 12g a8g³ 9m* a8g² 9g* 9m* 8g* 7m Jul 20] big, close-coupled filly: fairly useful handicapper: made all at Lingfield in June and Musselburgh, Lingfield and Yarmouth (by 10 lengths) in July: will prove best at 1m to 1¼m: acts on fibresand, yet to race on extremes of going on turf: races freely: looked none too keen once: joined A. Streeter. *Sir Mark Prescott* **86**

GIRL'S BEST FRIEND 2 b.f. (Apr 28) Nicolotte 118 – Diamond Princess 69 (Horage 124) [1999 7g a8.5g² 6s* 8g 8d⁴ 6s Nov 22] fifth foal: half-sister to 3 winners, including stayers Princess Topaz (5-y-o) and Cut Diamond (ungenuine, by Keen): dam 1½m winner: fairly useful form: won maiden at Lingfield in October by 9 lengths: easily best effort after (though pulled hard) when good fourth of 10 to Silver Colours in steadily-run listed event at Newmarket penultimate start: bred to stay at least 1¼m: acts on soft going, yet to race on firmer than good. *D. W. P. Arbuthnot* **89**

GIVE AN INCH (IRE) 4 b.f. Inchinor 119 – Top Heights (High Top 131) [1998 70: 7d⁶ 7d⁵ 8m 6g 8s 8d³ 9.3m 11m* 12d² 15s* 14g 16.1m² 17.5s* 16.1g 14.1d 1999 16.1d⁴ 14g⁴ 16s² 16m³ 18g* 16.1g* 17.5d* 14s Sep 25] leggy, sparely-made filly: fairly useful handicapper: won at Pontefract in June and Ayr (third course success, repeating 1998 win in same race) in September: stays 2¼m, and needs good test at shorter: acts on soft and good to firm going: usually held up: has given trouble stalls/flashed tail, but is game. *W. Storey* **81**

GIVEN 3 b.f. Minshaanshu Amad (USA) 91§ – Little Morston (Morston (FR) 125) [1998 NR 1999 8f May 27] 400Y: first live foal: dam unraced: slowly away and always behind in maiden at Brighton. *G. L. Moore* **–**

GIVE NOTICE 2 b.c. (May 18) Warning 136 – Princess Genista 108 (Ile de **54** Bourbon (USA) 133) [1999 7d⁶ 7d Oct 27] eighth foal: half-brother to 3-y-o Cavernista and useful performers Tsarnista and Sovinista (both best up to 1m, by Soviet Star) and Tomos (up to 1½m, by Sure Blade): dam, 1m (including at 2 yrs) winner, stayed 15f: modest form in maidens at Leicester and Yarmouth: should stay 1¼m. *J. L. Dunlop*

GIVE THE SLIP 2 b.c. (Jan 18) Slip Anchor 136 – Falafil (FR) (Fabulous Dancer **87** (USA) 124) [1999 7d³ 8d⁴ Oct 15] 43,000F, 42,000Y: rather leggy, good-topped colt: has a round action: sixth foal: half-brother to 3 winners in France, including 1m winner (including at 2 yrs) Rebenac (by Highest Honor): dam, French 1¼m and 11.5f winner, half-sister to dam of very smart middle-distance performer Stowaway (by Slip Anchor): edgy and wearing crossed noseband, fairly useful form in frame in maidens at Newmarket won by Qamous and by Pawn Broker, racing freely and beaten less than a length both times: bred to stay 1½m+. *Mrs A. J. Perrett*

GLAD MASTER (GER) 2 b.c. (Feb 14) Big Shuffle (USA) 122 – Glady Star **108 p** (GER) (Star Appeal 133) [1999 8g* 7g*dis 8s* 8s* Nov 1] approx. 9,600Y in Germany: brother to German 6f/7f winner Glad Shuffle and half-brother to several winners in Germany, including 1m (at 2 yrs) to 11f winner Glady Sum (by Surumu): dam German 6f to 1m winner: first past post all 4 starts, maiden at Hoppegarten in August, 5-runner minor event there in September (disqualified after rider weighed in light), Preis der Winterfavoriten (by ¾ length from Global Dancer after leading close home) at Cologne in October and national listed race at Munich in November: stays 1m: joined Godolphin: likely to do better still. *H. W. Hiller, Germany*

GLAMIS (USA) 3 b.c. Silver Hawk (USA) 123 – Glaze (USA) (Mr Prospector **117** (USA)) [1998 110: 7m³ 7m* 8d² 8s² 8v³ 1999 10g* 10s³ 10.4s 12g⁶ 11.9m³ Aug 17] strong, good-topped colt: has a powerful, round action: smart performer: won minor event at Kempton in April: bit disappointing next 2 starts, but ran well when 4¾ lengths sixth to Oath in Derby at Epsom and when 2½ lengths third to Fantastic Light in Great Voltigeur Stakes at York final 2 outings: stays 1½m: acts on good to firm and heavy ground: visored (better form without) second and third starts: tends to sweat: has been bandaged behind: has gone in snatches, wandered and flashed tail: fractured a cannon bone in September when being prepared for St Leger: joined Godolphin. *J. H. M. Gosden*

GLANCE (IRE) 4 b.c. Ela-Mana-Mou 132 – Cursory Look (USA) (Nijinsky **84** (CAN) 138) [1998 90p: 12g⁴ 12g* 1999 10v⁶ 12m Jun 16] rangy, rather unfurnished colt: has free round action: fairly useful performer: sixth of 8 in minor event at Pontefract (first start for 10 months) in April: never a threat in valuable handicap at Royal Ascot next time: will stay 1¾m+: sent to UAE. *L. M. Cumani*

GLANWYDDEN (IRE) 3 ch.c. Grand Lodge (USA) 125 – Brush Away **86** (Ahonoora 122) [1998 86: 5g⁶ 7.5d* 7f⁴ 7m³ 7.5m 7s³ 7.1g³ 7s³ 1999 8d⁵ 7.6m⁶ 7.9s² 8m⁶ 7.5m³ 7d 8m 7.1s Sep 25] tall, rather unfurnished colt: fairly useful performer: good second in handicap at York, making most: stays 1m: acts on firm and soft going: free-going sort: none too consistent. *J. Berry*

GLASHEDY ROSE 3 br.f. Hamas (IRE) 125§ – Arabian Rose (USA) (Lyphard **–** (USA) 132) [1998 NR 1999 7d 8.3g 10.1f⁵ May 27] 7,200F, 11,000Y: half-sister to several winners, including fairly useful stayer Moonlight Quest (by Nishapour): dam ran once in France: little promise in maidens. *H. J. Collingridge*

GLASTONBURY (IRE) 3 b.g. Common Grounds 118 – Harmonious 69 (Shar- **60 d** rood (USA) 124) [1998 68: 5g 6s⁴ 5g³ 7g 7m⁶ 6s 7s² 7s³ a6g a7g* a7g⁶ a8g³ 1999 a7g⁶ a6g a7g* a7f a7g a7g⁴ a6g³ a5g 6.1v 6m 7f 7d 8g 8f a6g Jul 8] workmanlike gelding: unimpressive mover: modest performer at best: won seller at Lingfield in January: lost his form after seventh start: best at 6f/7f: acts on soft ground and equitrack: none too reliable. *P. Howling*

GLENDAMAH (IRE) 2 b.g. (Mar 25) Mukaddamah (USA) 125 – Sea Glen **77** (IRE) (Glenstal (USA) 118) [1999 5g⁵ 5.9m³ 6m⁴ 7g 6f* 6m³ 8g 6s² 6g 6v³ 7d³ Oct 26] 24,000Y: good-bodied gelding: second foal: dam unraced half-sister to useful sprinter Crofter's Cline: fair performer: won maiden at Newcastle in August: placed in 3 nurseries and a minor event after: may prove best around 6f: acts on any going: effective visored or not. *E. Weymes*

GLENMEAD   4 ch.c. Polish Precedent (USA) 131 – Fair Country 89 (Town And   **96**
Country 124) [1998 85: 10g 10g³ 12m³ 12m* 1999 11.9d 12m* 12m² 12s³
Oct 23] tall, sparely-made colt: useful handicapper on his day: won at Pontefract in
August: second of 4 at Haydock, only other form at 4 yrs: should stay 1¾m: acts on
soft and good to firm going: none too consistent: sold 70,000 gns. *A. C. Stewart*

GLEN PARKER (IRE)   6 ch.g. Bluebird (USA) 125 – Trina's Girl (Nonoalco   **45**
(USA) 131) [1998 75: 7.6m⁵ 9.7m 10d⁴ 9.9m⁶ 10.4g 1999 8.3g 8d 10d⁶ 12.3m
11.1m⁵ 9.2f⁵ Jul 16] sturdy, good-bodied gelding: good mover: one-time fairly useful
performer: just poor form in 1999: seems to stay 11f: acts on good to firm going:
visored (looked irresolute) once, blinkered final start at 6 yrs. *D. A. Lamb*

GLENROCK   2 ch.c. (Apr 3) Muhtarram (USA) 125 – Elkie Brooks 82 (Relkino   **89**
131) [1999 5m² 5f² 5.9m 5m⁴ 5m³ 6m* 6.1d* 6m 7s³ Sep 22] 22,000Y: half-brother
to several winners, including 3-y-o Francport, smart sprinter Pips Pride and fairly
useful 7f/1m performer Sunday's Hill, all by Efisio: dam, second over 6f at 2 yrs,
didn't train on: fairly useful performer: won maiden at Lingfield and minor event at
Chester in August: stays 7f: acts on firm and soft going. *J. Berry*

GLEN ROSIE (IRE)   2 ch.f. (Mar 2) Mujtahid (USA) 118 – Silver Echo (Caer-   **90**
leon (USA) 132) [1999 5.2m* 5.2f³ 7d⁶ 6.5g⁶ 7d³ Oct 9] IR 58,000Y: leggy, lengthy
filly: sixth foal: sister to 6-y-o Mutadarra and half-sister to 3 winners, including smart
French 3-y-o Hello Soso (by Alzao), 7f winner at 2 yrs: dam unraced: fairly useful
form: won maiden at Newbury in July: best effort when sixth of 20 in valuable
nursery at Doncaster penultimate start: should stay 1m: acts on firm and good to soft
going: edgy type: tail flasher. *B. W. Hills*

GLEN VALE WALK (IRE)   2 ch.g. (May 5) Balla Cove 119 – Winter Harvest   **60**
(Grundy 137) [1999 7f 8.3s 8.2d³ Oct 21] IR 1,800F, IR 3,500Y: half-brother to 2
winners, including 8-y-o Murphy's Gold: dam second at 1½m in Ireland: dropped in
class, third of 18 in seller at Nottingham: will stay 1¼m. *Mrs G. S. Rees*

GLENWHARGEN (IRE)   2 b.f. (Apr 15) Polar Falcon (USA) 126 – La Veine   **63**
(USA) (Diesis 133) [1999 5g⁴ 5g⁶ a6g⁴ 6s² 7s a6g⁵ a8.5g³ 7s a8g⁴ a8g⁵ Dec 29]   **a55**
2,500F, 6,700Y: second foal: dam once-raced granddaughter of top-class French
sprinter/miler Lianga: modest maiden: stays 8.5f: acts on soft ground and fibresand:
blinkered (well below form) eighth start. *M. Johnston*

GLIDER (IRE)   4 b.f. Silver Kite (USA) 111 – Song of The Glens (Horage 124)   **–**
[1998 65: a7g² a7g⁴ a8g* a10g³ a8g⁴ 8.2d 1999 a7g 10f 8s Jun 12] fair handicapper
at best: last all starts in 1999: probably stays 1¼m: best form on equitrack.
R. Brotherton

GLIM TRAIL (IRE)   3 b.f. Catrail (USA) 123 – Glim (USA) (Damascus (USA))   **–**
[1998 NR 1999 7m 6s May 14] IR 5,500Y: leggy, unfurnished filly: half-sister to
several winners, including fairly useful Irish 1995 2-y-o 5f winner Ribot's Secret
(by Danehill), later successful in USA, and French 1m/1¼m winner Cotton Kisser
(by Suave Dancer): dam unraced, from family of Caerleon: last in maidens.
A. B. Mulholland

GLINT IN HER EYE (USA)   3 b.f. Arazi (USA) 135 – Wind In Her Hair (IRE)   **76**
114 (Alzao (USA) 117) [1998 NR 1999 10m 11.7f⁴ 10m⁴ 11.6d 13.1f⁴ a13g⁴ 11.7s⁵
Oct 26] angular filly: first foal: dam 1¼m/1½m winner from family of Unfuwain and
Nashwan: fair maiden: should stay beyond 13f: acts on firm and soft going, well
below form only all-weather outing: failed to handle bends at Windsor. *J. W. Hills*

GLOBAL CONCEPT (USA) 3 b.c. Warning 136 – Sweet Snow (USA) (Lyphard   **78**
(USA) 132) [1998 NR 1999 7.6m³ 7m 8s² 8.5m³ 8v a8.5g* Oct 13] 74,000Y: **a93**
half-brother to several winners, notably smart 1994 2-y-o 6f winner (Gimcrack
Stakes) Chilly Billy, later 1m winner in USA, and fairly useful 6f (at 2 yrs) and 1m
winner Weaver Bird (both by Master Willie): dam won at 1¼m in France and is
daughter of Kentucky Oaks winner Sun And Snow: fairly useful performer: much
improved when winning handicap on all-weather debut at Wolverhampton: stays
8.5f: acts on soft going, good to firm and fibresand: sold 42,000 gns, sent to USA.
P. W. Harris

GLOBAL DRAW (IRE)   3 ch.g. Be My Guest (USA) 126 – Almost A Lady (IRE)   **37**
70 (Entitled 126) [1998 – : 7s⁵ 6d 1999 8m 7.1g 10m³ 8m 9.9g 12s Sep 21] tall gelding: poor form since debut: left M. Jarvis after fourth start: tried blinkered. *J. Parkes*

GLOBE QUEEN (IRE) 2 ch.f. (Mar 1) River Falls 113 – Kristar (Kris 135) [1999 **40**
6m 6m⁵ a7g Jul 23] IR 1,000Y, 1,200 2-y-o: half-sister to 1997 2-y-o 7f seller winner
Impulse (by Imp Society), later successful abroad: dam Italian 1m winner: showed
some ability in sellers. *J. J. O'Neill*

GLOBE RAIDER 4 b.g. Safawan 118 – Polola 42 (Aragon 118) [1998 –: 7d⁴ 8d **–**
5d⁵ 1999 6v 8g Jul 5] good-topped gelding: no form: tried blinkered. *J. J. O'Neill*

GLOROSIA (FR) 4 ch.f. Bering 136 – Golden Sea (FR) (Saint Cyrien (FR) 128) **102**
[1998 103: 12m³ 12d⁵ 10.2d² 1999 8.5d⁴ 10m* 10m⁴ 9.9d⁵ 8.9f⁵ Sep 2] rangy,
good-topped filly: useful performer: made all in 3-runner minor event at Windsor in
June: ran creditably in listed events after: probably stays 1½m: acts on firm and good
to soft ground: sent to Germany. *L. M. Cumani*

GLORY OF GROSVENOR (IRE) 4 ch.g. Caerleon (USA) 132 – Abury (IRE) **–**
104 (Law Society (USA) 130) [1998 –: 8.5s⁶ 12.3m 12m 1999 12g Apr 14] strong,
lengthy gelding: fairly useful at 2 yrs: well beaten since, including in blinkers: joined
J. J. O'Neill. *P. W. Chapple-Hyam*

GLORY OF LOVE 4 b.g. Belmez (USA) 131 – Princess Lieven (Royal Palace **–**
131) [1998 NR 1999 13.1d 12m⁶ 14.1f⁵ 14m Aug 26] modest maiden at 2 yrs: well
beaten in 1999: should stay beyond 1m: visored final 2 starts. *J. Hetherton*

GLORY QUEST (USA) 2 b.c. (Mar 18) Quest For Fame 127 – Sonseri 95 **86 p**
(Prince Tenderfoot (USA) 126) [1999 6f³ 6d³ Sep 16] 22,000Y: good-topped colt:
half-brother to 7f winner Star Goddess (by Northern Jove) and 2 winners abroad by
Fighting Fit: dam, 5f and 6f winner who stayed 1m, half-sister to useful 6f to 1m
winner Apres Demain: shaped quite well, showing fairly useful form, in minor event
at York (burly and very green) and maiden at Ayr: will stay at least 1m: should still
do better. *Miss Gay Kelleway*

GLOW 3 br.f. Alzao (USA) 117 – Shimmer 55 (Bustino 136) [1998 65, a?: 8m a8g **55**
1999 10.2g 11.7g⁴ 18m⁶ Jul 3] angular, plain filly: modest maiden: stays 1½m, not
2¼m: sold 2,000 gns in December. *I. A. Balding*

GLOWING 4 b.f. Chilibang 120 – Juliet Bravo 61 (Glow (USA)) [1998 68: 6v **81**
6m³ 6m² 6g⁴ 6g³ 6.1g² 6f* 1999 6d⁴ 6g⁴ 6g 6.1m* 5m* 5g Oct 6] fairly useful
handicapper: won at Nottingham in August and Doncaster in September: effective at
5f/6f: acts on firm and good to soft going: has worn tongue strap (not final 3 outings):
consistent. *J. R. Fanshawe*

GO BRITANNIA 6 b.g. Machiavellian (USA) 123 – Chief Celebrity (USA) 85 **–**
(Chief's Crown (USA)) [1998 NR 1999 20f Jul 28] tall gelding: has round action:
fairly useful handicapper at 4 yrs: tailed off on only Flat run since. *F. Jordan*

GOCHINOS 3 b.g. Wolfhound (USA) 126 – Reflection 111 (Mill Reef (USA) **66**
141) [1998 59: 5g⁵ 5g⁵ 5.1m³ 5m⁶ 7.1g 5d 1999 a6g a5g⁴ a5s 5g³ a5g² 5.3f* 5.3f⁴ 5g
5d* 5.1m⁵ 5m⁵ Aug 4] sturdy gelding: fair performer: won handicaps at Brighton in
May and Musselburgh (seller) in June: best form around 5f: acts on firm and good to
soft going (poor form on fibresand): visored final start: usually front runs: tends to
carry head high: sold 2,800 gns, sent to Italy. *S. C. Williams*

GODLEY (IRE) 3 b.g. Fayruz 116 – Divine Apsara (Godswalk (USA) 130) **56**
[1998 75: 6g 7m² 7m⁴ 7m⁴ 7.3m⁶ 8m² 7.9g⁴ 1999 8g 8.1g⁶ 8f⁶ 8.1m⁶ 12m 9.9d 9.9m
13.1f² 12m 14.1v Sep 29] sturdy, close-coupled gelding: unimpressive mover:
modest maiden handicapper: effective at 1m to 13f: raced mainly on good going or
firmer (tailed off on heavy final start): often visored: inconsistent: sold 3,500 gns,
sent to Germany. *M. J. Fetherston-Godley*

GODMERSHAM PARK 7 b.g. Warrshan (USA) 117 – Brown Velvet 68 (Man- **–**
singh (USA) 120) [1998 –, a79: a7g* a8g* a8g* a7g³ a8.5g* a7g a8g 7s 8d 10g 7.6g **a74 d**
8.3f a9.4g a7g⁴ a8.5g⁴ a9.4g 1999 a8g a7g² a8g a9.4g⁴ a8f⁴ a7g a8g a8.5g⁶ a10g⁵
11d a7g a6g⁴ a7g³ a7g³ a8g³ a8.5g⁴ a7g a8g a8.5g³ a8g a8.5g⁵ Dec 27] lengthy,
good-topped gelding: fair handicapper: in frame on all-weather in 1999: effective at
7f to 9f: acts on firm ground and fibresand: blinkered/visored (below best) once each:
refused to enter stalls once. *P. S. Felgate*

GOES A TREAT (IRE) 3 b.f. Common Grounds 118 – Just A Treat (IRE) 47 **82**
(Glenstal (USA) 118) [1998 NR 1999 6s 7m³ 6.8m* 7m² 7m⁶ 7s Nov 2] 15,000Y:

smallish, angular filly: fourth foal: half-sister to useful 1997 2-y-o 6f winner Special Treat (by Wolfhound): dam, 2-y-o 5f winner, from family of Golden Fleece and Be My Guest: fairly useful performer (trained by P. Chapple-Hyam until final start): made all in maiden at Warwick in July: stays 7f: acts on good to firm going: has edged left: sold 14,000 gns. *A. G. Foster*

GOING GLOBAL (IRE) 2 ch.c. (Apr 1) Bob Back (USA) 124 – Ukraine Girl **84 p** 121 (Targowice (USA) 130) [1999 8g³ 8s* Sep 22] 76,000Y: angular colt: half-brother to several winners, including Irish 1½m winner Sadler's Lad and 1991 2-y-o 7f winner Well Saddled (both by Sadler's Wells): dam won Poule d'Essai des Pouliches: encouraging third at Doncaster in September before overcoming trouble to win maiden at Goodwood in September readily by ¾ length from Malleus: should prove suited by 1¼m/1½m: should make a useful colt. *S. P. C. Woods*

GOING HOME (IRE) 2 b.g. (Mar 2) Thatching 131 – Princess of Dance (IRE) **58 ?** (Dancing Dissident (USA) 119) [1999 5m 5g⁵ 5g⁴ 5g 6s Sep 27] IR 19,500Y: first foal: dam unraced: modest form at best: probably flattered third start, well beaten last 2: tried visored and blinkered. *J. L. Eyre*

GOING PLACES 4 b.f. Risk Me (FR) 127 – Spring High 74 (Miami Springs **39** 121) [1998 46: 6g 6m 5m a5g² 7m⁶ a7g 5.1d 5m a5g² 1999 a6g a5g a5g 5s 5d Apr 5] rather leggy, workmanlike filly: poor performer nowadays: best at 5f: acts on fibresand and good to soft ground: usually blinkered/visored: has found little/carried head high: sold 1,200 gns in July. *K. T. Ivory*

GOLCONDA (IRE) 3 br.f. Lahib (USA) 129 – David's Star (Welsh Saint 126) **92** [1998 68p: 5g³ 7g 1999 a7g² a7g* 10s² 9m* 10g* 9.9g² 10.4f³ 12f⁶ 10.1g Aug 30] good-bodied filly: fairly useful performer: won maiden at Wolverhampton in February and handicaps at Kempton and Lingfield in May: very good third to Achilles in John Smith's Cup at York: probably stays 1½m: acts on all-weather, firm and soft going: usually held up: dwelt final start: genuine. *M. L. W. Bell*

GOLD ACADEMY (IRE) 3 b.c. Royal Academy (USA) 130 – Soha (USA) 58 **118** (Dancing Brave (USA) 140) [1998 100: 6g⁴ 7d³ 7g⁵ 1999 8d² 8.5g² 8m⁵ 8.1g* 8m³ 8f 8.9f* 8s³ 10g⁴ Oct 16] big, close-coupled, good sort: usually takes the eye: smart performer: won maiden at Chepstow in May and listed contest at York (by 3½ lengths

Strensall Stakes, York—Gold Academy settles the issue with a fine turn of speed two furlongs out; Diamond White (noseband) snatches second place off Spindrift (third left)

Mr George E. K. Teo's "Gold Academy"

from Diamond White, showing good turn of foot) in September: also ran creditably in listed race at Newmarket (½-length second to Golden Snake) on second start, 2000 Guineas on same course (3½ lengths fifth to Island Sands), St James's Palace Stakes at Royal Ascot (third behind Sendawar) on fifth outing and Champion Stakes at Newmarket (2 lengths fourth to Alborada): stays 1¼m: acts on firm and good to soft going: type to make a better 4-y-o. *R. Hannon*

GOLDAMIX (IRE) 2 gr.f. (Feb 9) Linamix (FR) 127 – Gold's Dance (FR) **108 p** (Goldneyev (USA) 114) [1999 9s* 10v* Oct 31]

      Fillies tend not to contest the majority of open Group 1 events for two-year-olds, notably the Prix de la Salamandre, Dewhurst Stakes, Grand Criterium and Racing Post Trophy, because alternatives are usually available for them and the colts' races are generally too tough anyway. Only three have had a crack at the Racing Post Trophy in the last thirteen years and two, Ivanka and Fairy Heights, acquitted themselves with credit in second. By contrast, the Criterium de Saint-Cloud, Europe's longest pattern race for juveniles, which was made Group 1 in 1987, has drawn eleven fillies in the same period. Goldamix, successful in the latest running at the end of October, is the first to win, emulating Escaline, who landed the spoils in 1982. Escaline went on to land the Prix de Diane, and since her several other contestants have emerged to make a name for themselves at three or four, including classic scorers Darshaan, Mouktar, Fast Topaze, Hours After, Snurge, Ragmar and Daylami (second in 1996), plus top performers The Wonder, Bon Sang, Pistolet Bleu, Sunshack, Tikkanen and Croco Rouge. Goldamix clearly has quite a lot to live up to, but she is lightly raced and open to improvement.

      The odds-on favourite for the seven-runner Criterium was Royal King-dom, workmanlike winner of the Royal Lodge Stakes at Ascot the previous month and attempting to secure a fourth French Group 1 juvenile race for trainer Aidan O'Brien. The second favourite was Cosmographe while Goldamix was third in the market—both were winners of minor events on soft ground at Maisons-Laffitte earlier the same month. The other runners included the Prix de Conde runner-up Crystal d'Ass and third, Petroselli, blinkered for the first time. Goldamix set off in front, pulling hard initially, and nothing else got a look in as she galloped on powerfully despite running green to beat Petroselli by a length with Cosmographe four lengths away third. Royal Kingdom ran below form in fifth, soon ridden along and unable to make any headway in the straight. The form is not outstanding but Goldamix still looks a filly to follow over a mile and a quarter and a mile and a half as a three-year-old.

		Mendez	Bellypha
	Linamix (FR)	(gr 1981)	Miss Carina
	(gr 1987)	Lunadix	Breton
Goldamix (IRE)		(gr 1972)	Lutine
(gr.f. Feb 9, 1997)		Goldneyev	Nureyev
	Gold's Dance (FR)	(b or br 1986)	Gold River
	(b 1991)	Anitra's Dance	Green Dancer
		(b 1978)	Azurella

Goldamix is by Linamix, the leading French-based sire and champion there in 1998. He did not stay a mile and a half and was best at around a mile but has got his share of performers effective over further. Arc winner Sagamix, Grand Prix de Saint-Cloud winner Fragrant Mix and Amilynx, successful in the Prix Royal-Oak a week before Goldamix's victory, are cases in point. Goldamix is the first foal of her dam, who won at up to a mile and a half and was sold in foal to Darshaan for 32,000 guineas in 1997. The resultant progeny was a filly. The grandam Anitra's Dance was a pattern winner, in the Prix de Minerve over a mile and a half, and foaled six successful foals, notably the

Criterium de Saint-Cloud—a rare success for a filly in this race
as Goldamix makes all to beat the blinkered Petroselli; odds-on Royal Kingdom (left) is only fifth

stakes performers Solveig, who landed the Prix Fille de l'Air, and Vaguely Gay. The third dam Azurella was also a smart middle-distance filly, landing the Prix de Malleret and Prix de Royaumont. *C. Laffon-Parias, France*

GOLD ANGEL   3 ch.f. Machiavellian (USA) 123 – Dafrah (USA) 78 (Danzig (USA)) [1998 NR 1999 7g 7g⁵ Jun 10] tall, leggy filly: fourth foal: half-sister to useful 1¼m winner Bold Demand (by Rainbow Quest): dam 1m winner from family of Nashwan and Unfuwain: fair form in maiden at Newmarket on debut: reportedly had a breathing problem only other start: wears tongue strap: sold 8,700 gns in July. *E. A. L. Dunlop*   **74**

GOLD AWAY (IRE)   4 ch.c. Goldneyev (USA) 114 – Blushing Away (USA) (Blushing Groom (FR) 131) [1998 122: 9.3g* 9g² 8s² 8d² 8v³ 1999 8s* 8v* 9.3d³ 6.5s² 8m² Sep 5]   **125**

Gold Away's four-year-old campaign followed a similar pattern to his three-year-old season, beginning with a successful spring but yielding only place money from good efforts in the best company thereafter. He made the most of a couple of fairly straightforward tasks at Saint-Cloud in April before the competition got too hot, starting with a one-and-a-half-length defeat of Sand Falcon in the five-runner Prix Edmond Blanc. Seventeen days later over the same trip, and this time accompanied by a pacemaker, Gold Away followed up in the Prix du Muguet by the same margin from another smart rival, Lone Bid. The rest finished six lengths or more behind in the heavy ground, among them Insight and Field of Hope who were to gain notable wins in the autumn in the E.P. Taylor Stakes and Prix de la Foret respectively.

Gold Away's remaining tasks were much tougher but he emerged with plenty of credit each time, starting with third place, beaten less than two lengths, behind Croco Rouge and El Condor Pasa in the Prix d'Ispahan at Longchamp. At Deauville in August he avoided a clash with Dubai Millennium in the Prix Jacques le Marois only to run into another Godolphin ace in Diktat in the Prix Maurice de Gheest. The much shorter trip (six and a half furlongs) looked barely enough of a test for Gold Away who finished strongly to get within a length of Diktat at the line with several good sprinters behind. Gold Away's meeting with some of the best milers around was only delayed, however, as what turned out to be his final start (and career-best effort) came in the Prix du Moulin at Longchamp in September. For the second year running, Gold Away had to settle for second place, staying on well to split the Poule d'Essai des Poulains one-two Sendawar and Dansili, beaten one and a half lengths. Gold Away was to have contested the Breeders' Cup Mile, and was sent to Florida in plenty of time to acclimatise, but suffered a knee-ligament injury during a workout. He has been retired to the Haras de Quesnay at a fee of 20,000 francs (October 1st).

Prix du Muguet, Saint-Cloud—testing conditions for Gold Away and Lone Bid as they draw clear

Gold Away's sire Goldneyev faced a tall order to live up to his parentage (by Nureyev out of Arc winner Gold River) on the track, and although second in the Poule d'Essai des Poulains, showed no better than smart form in just six outings. Gold Away is easily his best representative to date, and his only pattern winner. Blushing Away, Gold Away's dam, on the other hand had taken her tally of pattern winners to three by the end of the season from just five runners. Three-year-old Danzigaway (by Danehill), who won the Prix Perth in November, was her latest scorer at that level and Blushing Gleam (by Caerleon), the 1996 Prix du Calvados winner, was her first. Her other winner, first foal Posen Tune (by Polish Precedent), has won several minor races in France at short of a mile. Her two-year-old Runaway Gold (by Nureyev) was in training with Criquette Head but is yet to race. Blushing Away herself won just once, in a six and a half furlong amateur event at Evry, though she also finished second in listed company at Deauville over five furlongs. Her dam Sweet Revenge won several graded events in the USA as a two-year-old, including the Grade 2 Alcibiades Stakes, and was placed at Grade 1 level in both the Frizette and Matron Stakes.

		Nureyev	Northern Dancer
	Goldneyev (USA)	(b 1977)	Special
	(b or br 1986)	Gold River	Riverman
Gold Away (IRE)		(ch 1977)	Glaneuse
(ch.c. 1995)		Blushing Groom	Red God
	Blushing Away (USA)	(ch 1974)	Runaway Bride
	(ch 1987)	Sweet Revenge	Raja Baba
		(ch 1978)	Away

The sturdy Gold Away retires with an admirably consistent record. After finishing fourth on his debut at Compiegne, he made the first three in all fifteen of his remaining outings. Highlight of his two-year-old campaign was a victory in the Prix Thomas Bryon at Saint-Cloud, and after winning the Prix de Guiche at Longchamp on his reappearance at three he was placed in the Prix Jean Prat, Prix du Moulin, Prix du Rond-Point and Prix Perth. He also showed plenty of versatility, proving himself effective at six and a half furlongs to around nine, and on ground ranging from good to firm to heavy. He wore blinkers on his final three-year-old outing and, unlike many horses to race in the Wertheimers' colours, was held up. *Mme C. Head, France*

GOLD BLADE 10 ch.g. Rousillon (USA) 133 – Sharp Girl (FR) 114 (Sharpman) **59**
[1998 –: 9.9g a12g 1999 a12g³ a12f³ a16f 12d 11.5m* 10d* 11.1f² 10.9d⁵ Sep 16] big, good-topped gelding: poor mover: modest handicapper: won amateur events at Lingfield (awarded race) in June and Pontefract in July: stays 13f, possibly not 2m: acts on any turf/all-weather: sometimes blinkered earlier in career: held up: usually ridden by Mrs L. Pearce. *J. Pearce*

GOLD CAMP (USA) 3 b.c. Mr Prospector (USA) – Dance Colony (USA) (Plea- **73 p**
sant Colony (USA)) [1998 NR 1999 9.9m⁶ Sep 11] $300,000Y: third foal: closely related to a stakes-placed winner in USA by Forty Niner: dam, US Grade 2 2-y-o 6f/ 7f winner, half-sister to two Grade 1 winners from family of Lyphard: 6/1, sixth in maiden at Goodwood, slowly away and travelling well in rear, then running green and not knocked about: sent to UAE: should improve. *J. H. M. Gosden*

GOLD CHANCE (IRE) 3 ch.g. Fayruz 116 – Maura Paul (Bonne Noel 115) **45**
[1998 63: 6g 5g⁴ 6m³ 6.1m 7m 1999 a6g a5g a5g⁴ 5s⁵ 8f Jul 23] smallish geld-ing: disappointing maiden: stays 6f: tried blinkered/visored: sold 1,500 gns. *G. C. H. Chung*

GOLD COAST 3 b.g. Alhijaz 122 – Odilese 82 (Mummy's Pet 125) [1998 –: 5m **–**
6m⁶ 7g 6g a7g 1999 a8g Jan 1] no form. *S. Dow*

GOLD DESIRE 9 b.g. Grey Desire 115 – Glory Gold 59 (Hittite Glory 125) [1998 **–**
NR 1999 12s Oct 4] sparely-made, plain gelding: poor mover: fair handicapper in 1997: well held only run since: stays 13f: acts on any going: sometimes bandaged: visored (ran poorly) once at 3 yrs. *M. Brittain*

GOLD EDGE   5 ch.m. Beveled (USA) – Golden October 62 (Young Generation **44 d**
129) [1998 54, a–: 6.1s 5.9d 5s² 5s³ 5m 6g 5g⁴ 6d⁴ 5d⁴ 5d⁴ 5.1g 6m 5g 5d a5g a6g
1999 5d⁵ 5m 5s 5m 5v 5m a5g 5f 5g⁵ a6g a6g Dec 21] sturdy mare: poor performer
nowadays: left Don Enrico Incisa after fifth start, N. Tinkler after ninth: stays 6f: acts
on firm and soft going: visored ninth outing. *A. G. Newcombe*

GOLDEN ACE (IRE)   6 ch.g. Archway (IRE) 115 – Gobolino (Don 128) [1998 **48**
57, a–: a8g a11g 10s² 10s³ 10s³ 11v³ 12m 10.1s³ 12s⁵ a12g 10g 10g⁶ 10.5d² 10.4g⁵ **a–**
12d⁴ 12d 11.9g 1999 14.1s³ 12.3m⁶ 12v⁷ 14.1s⁴ a14g 12.3s² 12g 9.9s 10s⁵ 11.8d Oct
12] big, strong, lengthy gelding: poor mover: poor handicapper: won apprentice race
at Folkestone in April: barely stays 1¾m: may need good going or softer (no form on
fibresand): usually blinkered: tongue tied: held up and tends to hang (has worn
near-side pricker): sometimes appears none too genuine. *R. C. Spicer*

GOLDEN BIFF (IRE)   3 ch.g. Shalford (IRE) 124§ – Capable Kate (IRE) **65**
(Alzao (USA) 117) [1998 65: 5m 6d³ 5d² 6s² 5d a6g a6g³ a5g 1999 5m 5g³ 7g 5d
7.1m⁶ 7.1m² 7.1f 6s* 6v a6g⁶ Nov 20] good-bodied gelding: fair performer: won
maiden at Catterick in October: below form after: best at 6f: acts on soft going and
fibresand: looked reluctant in blinkers once, visored fourth 3-y-o start: has been early
to post. *I. Semple*

GOLDEN CHARM (IRE)   3 b.f. Common Grounds 118 – Credit Crunch (IRE) **48**
51 (Caerleon (USA) 132) [1998 63: 5g⁶ 6.1m* 6g⁵ 6m⁴ 6m 6.1d⁴ 7g² 7s 1999 7v 8m
9.9g a6g 7m 6g⁶ 7g 7g Oct 19] compact filly: poor form in 1999: stays 7f: acts on
good to firm and good to soft going, possibly not on soft/heavy: visored 2 of final 3
starts: sold 7,200 gns in November. *J. E. Banks*

GOLDEN CHIMES (USA)   4 ch.g. Woodman (USA) 126 – Russian Ballet **88 d**
(USA) (Nijinsky (CAN) 138) [1998 95: 10d* 10s⁵ 1999 12m 12s 10.5g⁶ 10m 12m
11.5s³ 16s Oct 22] close-coupled gelding: fourth foal: brother to 2 winners in Ireland,
notably Irish Derby runner-up Dr Johnson: dam in frame both starts in Ireland at 2
yrs: fairly useful handicapper: trained at 2/3 yrs by C. O'Brien in Ireland: deteriorated in 1999: stays 1½m: acts on soft going: tongue tied third start, blinkered last
2: sold 18,000 gns, joined E. Tuer. *Major D. N. Chappell*

GOLDEN FAWN   6 ch.m. Crowning Honors (CAN) – Hill of Fare (Brigadier **–**
Gerard 144) [1998 –: a10g 1999 a12g 11.9f May 12] modest maiden at 3 yrs, lightly
raced. *M. J. Haynes*

GOLDEN FORCE   3 b.g. Forzando 122 – Silverlocks 88 (Sharrood (USA) 124) **–**
[1998 74: 6m 6m³ 6g³ 1999 6d 6g a7g* 8d Jun 5] well-made gelding: fairly useful **a81**
handicapper: form in 1999 only when winning at Wolverhampton in May: should
stay 1m: acts on fibresand, well below form on good to soft going. *R. Hannon*

GOLDENGIRLMICHELLE (IRE)   4 b.f. Project Manager 111 – Arbour Day **41**
(Artaius (USA) 129) [1998 37, a–: a11g⁵ 10.8d⁴ 12m⁵ a12g 12m a11g 1999 12.3m
12g 12f⁴ Jul 14] poor maiden: left F. Murphy after reappearance: stays 1½m: acts on
firm and good to firm going: tried blinkered: has had tongue tied. *J. J. O'Neill*

GOLDEN GLORY   6 b.g. Grey Desire 115 – Glory Gold 59 (Hittite Glory 125) **–**
[1998 NR 1999 12s Oct 4] no sign of ability. *M. Brittain*

GOLDEN HADEER   8 ch.g. Hadeer 118 – Verchinina 99 (Star Appeal 133) **–**
[1998 –, a73: a16s a16g³ a16g 14.1v a14g* 14.9d 14.1g⁴ 17.2d 16g³ 16d 14.1s 12g
a14.8s 1999 15.4v 14.1s a16.2g May 8] close-coupled gelding: formerly fair winner
up to 2m: has lost his form: tried blinkered/tongue tied. *M. J. Ryan*

GOLDEN HARVEST (IRE)   2 ch.g. (Apr 28) Vettori (IRE) 119 – Dissidence **73**
(IRE) (Dancing Dissident (USA) 119) [1999 6m⁴ 6m 6d³ 6d⁴ 6m² 6m 6v Oct 23] IR
20,000F, 30,000Y: close-coupled gelding: second foal: dam second at 1m in France
at 2 yrs: fair maiden: well below form last 2 starts: should stay 7f: acts on good to
firm and good to soft ground: often front runner: sold 10,000 gns. *B. J. Meehan*

GOLDEN HAWK (USA)   4 ch.g. Silver Hawk (USA) 123 – Crockadore (USA) **62**
102 (Nijinsky (CAN) 138) [1998 69: 7s 9m⁵ 16s² 15.8d⁶ 1999 12m 14d⁶ 14m⁵ 14.1g
Aug 29] close-coupled gelding: has a markedly round action: fair maiden at best at 3
yrs: below form in 1999: stays 2m: acts on soft ground, possibly not on good to firm:
takes good hold: successful over hurdles in September. *S. Dow*

GOLDEN LEGEND (IRE) 2 b.c. (Apr 19) Last Tycoon 131 – Adjalisa (IRE) – p
65 (Darshaan 133) [1999 6m 6g Aug 19] IR 80,000Y: smallish, useful-looking colt:
second foal: half-brother to useful Irish 3-y-o Access All Areas (by Approach The
Bench), 5f/6f winner at 2 yrs: dam, Irish maiden who stayed 1m, half-sister to Irish
2000 Guineas second Adjareli: green, signs of ability in maidens at Newmarket and
Yarmouth: should do better with experience. *G. Wragg*

GOLDEN LOCKET 2 ch.f. (Apr 19) Beveled (USA) – Rekindled Flame (IRE) 65
(Kings Lake (USA) 133) [1999 7v⁵ 7d 7v Oct 25] workmanlike filly: fourth foal:
sister to 3-y-o Goodenough Mover: dam unraced daughter of half-sister to very smart
7f to 1¼m performer Motavato: fair form in maidens at Kempton (trained by P.
Chapple-Hyam) and Leicester: likely to prove best at 7f/1m: slowly away on debut
and when tailed off final start: joined M. Kettle. *A. G. Foster*

GOLDEN LYRIC (IRE) 4 ch.g. Lycius (USA) 124 – Adjala 89 (Northfields – §
(USA)) [1998 49, a41: 8s⁶ 7g 10m 8d 8.2g 8m⁴ 8m⁴ 10g⁴ 10.4g a13g⁶ a12g² 1999 **a47** §
a10g a8g³ a8f³ a8g³ a8g² a11g* a8g⁶ 8f 11.5f 10.5m a12g a9.4g³ a10g a11g Nov 30]
big, good-topped gelding: poor handicapper: won maiden at Southwell in March:
barely stays 1½m: acts on good to firm going and all-weather: blinkered once at 3
yrs: has worn tongue strap: tends to hang: not one to trust. *J. Pearce*

GOLDEN MIRACLE (FR) 2 b.c. (Mar 31) Cadeaux Genereux 131 – Cheeky 81
Charm (USA) 56 (Nureyev (USA) 131) [1999 6d⁴ 5.9m⁵ 5m⁴ 6g⁵ 6m* 7g³ 6s* 6v⁵
Oct 11] sturdy, lengthy colt: first foal: dam, twice-raced close relative of smart
middle-distance colts Mohaajir and Theatrical Charmer, out of sister to Dahlia: fairly
useful performer: won 2 nurseries at Hamilton in September: likely to prove best up
to 7f: acts on good to firm and soft ground: found little final start. *M. Johnston*

GOLDEN NOTE 2 ch.c. (Mar 19) Efisio 120 – Triple Tricks (IRE) 70 (Royal 71
Academy (USA) 130) [1999 7g 6m 7.1v⁴ Oct 13] first foal: dam, maiden who stayed
1m, out of sister to smart sprinter Jester: easily best effort (fair form) when fourth of
9 to Cavalier in maiden at Haydock final start: unlikely to stay beyond 7f: sold 4,600
gns, sent to Sweden. *B. J. Meehan*

GOLDEN POUND (USA) 7 b.g. Seeking The Gold (USA) – Coesse Express 63 d
(USA) (Dewan (USA)) [1998 85: 6d 6v 6g* 6g 6g⁴ 5m⁵ 5g 6f⁴ 6m⁴ 7g 5m 6s 5.1v 6s
1999 6g 5.7g⁶ 6f 6g⁴ 6m⁴ 6f⁴ 6f⁵ 6s 6g⁵ 6d⁶ Oct 29] lengthy gelding: modest
handicapper nowadays: left Mrs L. Stubbs after third start: best at 6f/stiff 5f: acts on
all-weather, firm and soft going: best blinkered/visored: has worn tongue strap: has
run well sweating. *Miss Gay Kelleway*

GOLDEN PRINCE (IRE) 3 b.c. Polish Patriot (USA) 128 – Cathryn's Song 78 p
(Prince Tenderfoot (USA) 126) [1998 NR 1999 8m 8m 7m⁴ 8s* 8.2f* Oct 20] IR
20,000F, 55,000Y: rather leggy colt: half-brother to several winners, including 7f to
10.5f winner Wentbridge Lad (by Coquelin): dam unraced: improved when winning
minor event at Brighton in September and handicap at Nottingham (set plenty to do,
led last 100 yds) following month: stays 1m: likely to do better still. *R. Hannon*

GOLDEN RAINBOW (IRE) 3 b.g. Rainbows For Life (CAN) – Nawadder 73 42
(Kris 135) [1998 58: 5s⁵ 7m 7m⁶ 6d² 6g 7s 1999 9.7v 7g 8.1m⁶ 8.1m 14.1f⁵ Oct 20]
poor maiden: stays 1¾m: acts on firm and good to soft going: blinkered third start
(then left B. R. Millman): sold 500 gns in November. *Mrs P. N. Dutfield*

GOLDEN REEF 3 b.g. Puissance 110 – Cloudy Reef 57 (Cragador 110) [1998 66
65d: 5d 5s² 5.1s² 6d⁵ 5.9d 6g 5f⁵ 1999 6.1v⁵ 6.1s 8.2s 6g³ 7.1d⁶ 7m 6.1m Jul 3] sturdy
gelding: fair maiden: stays 6f: raced mainly on good going or softer (acts on heavy):
usually misses break: sold 3,200 gns in October, sent to Germany. *R. Hollinshead*

GOLDEN RETRIEVER (USA) 2 b. or br.c. (Jan 16) Red Ransom (USA) – 60 p
Golden Rhyme 87 (Dom Racine (FR) 121) [1999 6d Oct 29] IR 95,000Y: half-
brother to several winners, notably 1991 Racing Post Trophy winner Seattle Rhyme
(by Seattle Dancer) and useful winner up to 1m Rapid Success (by Sort): dam 7f
winner: 9/1 from 6/1, shaped promisingly when thirteenth of 19 to Pax in maiden
at Newmarket, running green (tended to hang) when pushed along and soon
considerably handled: should stay 1m: should be all the better for the experience.
D. R. C. Elsworth

GOLDEN ROD 2 ch.g. (May 17) Rainbows For Life (CAN) – Noble Form **64**
(Double Form 130) [1999 7.6g⁴ 7g 8s Nov 6] 5,000Y, 8,500 2-y-o: small gelding:
fifth living foal: half-brother to 3-y-o Italian 6f (at 2 yrs) and 1m winner Polish Form
and 4-y-o Noble Patriot (both by Polish Patriot): dam, French 1m and 10.5f winner,
half-sister to smart French middle-distance mare Darine: modest form in maidens:
should stay 1¼m. *P. W. Harris*

GOLDEN SHOT 3 ch.f. Pharly (FR) 130 – Hoop La (Final Straw 127) [1998 NR **–**
1999 10m a9.4g 10m 11.7s Oct 26] second living foal: dam, lightly-raced maiden,
half-sister to smart 6f (at 2 yrs) and 7f winner Mojave: no form. *J. L. Spearing*

GOLDEN SILCA 3 ch.f. Inchinor 119 – Silca-Cisa 93 (Hallgate 127) [1998 104: **110**
5.2s* 5.1g² 5.2m* 6m* 6m⁶ 6d³ 6d* 6g* 6g 1999 7m² 8m 8g² 8m² Jun 16] lengthy,
sparely-made filly: smart performer: fine efforts when runner-up in Irish 1,000
Guineas at the Curragh (checked entering final 1f, beaten a neck by Hula Angel) and
Coronation Stakes at Ascot (beaten 1¾ lengths by Balisada) final 2 starts: stays 1m:
acts on soft and good to firm going: has won when edgy: tough, game and genuine.
M. R. Channon

GOLDEN SKY (IRE) 3 b.f. Petardia 113 – Oriental Splendour 85 (Runnett 125) **–**
[1998 –: 5d 5s 6m 7d 1999 7m 10s 8g 8m Jun 24] tall, close-coupled filly: little form:
usually wears tongue strap. *Don Enrico Incisa*

GOLDEN SNAKE (USA) 3 b.c. Danzig (USA) – Dubian 120 (High Line 125) **119**
[1998 88p: 7m⁵ 8g* 1999 8.5g* 10.4s² 9s* 10.4m⁶ 10g Oct 16] rangy, rather unfurnished colt: fluent mover: smart performer: won listed race at Newmarket in April
by ½ length from Gold Academy and Prix Jean Prat Emirates Airlines at Chantilly in
June by neck from Slip Stream: set strong pace and better than result suggests when
15 lengths sixth to Royal Anthem in Juddmonte International at York, then bit below

Mr Mohamed Obaida's "Golden Snake"

best when tenth of 13 to Alborada in Champion Stakes at Newmarket: stayed 1¼m: acted on soft ground: to stand at National Stud, Newmarket, fee £6,500, Oct 1st. *B. W. Hills*

GOLDEN SYRUP (IRE) 3 b.f. Dolphin Street (FR) 125 – Sprint For Gold (USA) **59**
85 (Slew O'Gold (USA)) [1998 62: 6g⁵ 6m 6m⁴ 7.3m 6m⁴ 1999 a8g* a8g² a8f²
a7f² a8g⁴ a7g⁴ 6g* 8.2s 7m 7m⁵ 8.2m May 21] leggy, unfurnished filly: modest
performer: won sellers at Southwell in January and Leicester in April: below form
after: stays 1m: acts on fibresand and good to firm ground: sold 3,600 gns in July.
P. Howling

GOLDEN WAY (IRE) 2 ch.f. (Jan 10) Cadeaux Genereux 131 – Diavolina (USA) **60 p**
(Lear Fan (USA) 130) [1999 6s Oct 2] 120,000Y: big, lengthy filly: has scope: half-
sister to several winners, including 1997 2-y-o 6f/7f winner The Rich Man (by Last
Tycoon), useful 6f (at 2 yrs) and 7f winner Polish Spring (by Polish Precedent), later
successful in USA, and useful French 1¼m winner Go Boldly (by Sadler's Wells):
dam French 1¼m winner: unimpressive to post, shaped as though in need of run
when tenth of 11 to Philantha in maiden at Newmarket, not given hard time: will stay
1m: should improve. *E. A. L. Dunlop*

GOLDFAW 2 ch.c. (May 18) Wing Park 104 – Sailors Moon 38 (Indian Ridge –
123) [1999 6m 5v Oct 25] first foal: dam maiden who stayed 7f: always behind in
minor events at Windsor and Lingfield. *A. T. Murphy*

GOLDFINCH 2 b.f. (Mar 22) Zilzal (USA) 137 – Garconniere (Gay Mecene – p
(USA) 128) [1999 6g Oct 11] 33,000F: half-sister to several winners abroad,
including Italian 7f (at 2 yrs, listed race) and 1m winner Giselle Penn
(by Cozzene): dam ran twice in France: considerably handled when twelfth of 21
to Toleration in maiden at Windsor: should stay 1m: seems sure to do better.
J. R. Fanshawe

GOLD HALO (IRE) 3 b.f. Strike The Gold (USA) – Halo's Charm (USA) (Halo –
(USA)) [1998 NR 1999 7f⁶ 10v a13g Oct 1] 12,000Y: second foal: half-sister to US
sprint winner Kermitthecomedian (by Hermitage): dam sprint winner in USA: well
held in maidens. *A. Kelleway*

GOLD HONOR (FR) 3 gr.g. Highest Honor (FR) 124 – Golden Sea (FR) (Saint **77**
Cyrien (FR) 128) [1998 67, a58: 6m a6g³ 7m 7g⁴ 7.3m 8d 8d* a8g a8g a8.5g³
1999 12s⁴ 12d³ 10f² 8m⁵ 10g⁴ 10.5g⁴ 10.5g⁵ 10g⁴ 10d⁴ 10g* 12g* 10s 10v³ 10s 10g*
15m⁴ 10.5s 11.8v 10.5v Nov 24] strong, well-made gelding: fair performer: left
B. Meehan after third start: won handicap at Vichy in July and 2 claimers at Deauville
in August: claimed out of C. Boutin's stable before penultimate outing: stays 1½m:
acts on fibresand and probably any turf going: usually blinkered in Britain. *J. Arnou,
France*

GOLD KRIEK 2 b.g. (May 22) High Kicker (USA) – Ship of Gold 78 (Glint of –
Gold 128) [1999 8s a7g a7g Dec 18] plain gelding: fifth foal: brother to 4-y-o
Freckles and 1m winner Gold Clipper: dam, disappointing maiden, stayed 1½m: no
sign of ability. *N. A. Callaghan*

GOLD LANCE (USA) 6 ch.g. Seeking The Gold (USA) – Lucky State (USA) **60**
(State Dinner (USA)) [1998 –: 10m 10f⁶ a8g 1999 10m 11.9f³ 10g 9m² 8.3m 10.1m
11.6m⁶ 10d Oct 21] angular gelding: modest handicapper: poor efforts final 4 starts:
barely stays 1½m: acts on firm going, good to soft and all-weather: tried blinkered.
R. J. O'Sullivan

GOLDLINER GOSSIP (IRE) 4 b.f. Pips Pride 117 – Swift And Early (IRE) –
(Alzao (USA) 117) [1998 34: 8.2s⁵ 8m 7g 1999 7s a7g a11g May 17] angular filly:
little form: blinkered final start. *Miss M. E. Rowland*

GOLD LODGE 3 ch.g. Grand Lodge (USA) 125 – Glimmering Girl (USA) 67 **75**
(Spectacular Bid (USA)) [1998 80p: 7f 8.5m⁴ 9m² 1999 12d² 12.3m 14.1m³ 14.1m³
17.2m³ 11.7s⁶ Oct 26] leggy, quite good-topped gelding: fair maiden: stays 17f: acts
on good to firm and good to soft ground: sold 3,800 gns. *S. C. Williams*

GOLD MILLENIUM (IRE) 5 gr.g. Kenmare (FR) 125 – Gold Necklace 86 **53**
(Golden Fleece (USA) 133) [1998 NR 1999 7g 7m 8g 8m 12m 14.1g⁴ 11g Oct 14]
tall gelding: fifth foal: half-brother to useful French 1¼m winner Melina Mou

(by Persian Bold): dam Irish 2-y-o 7f winner: modest maiden: should stay 2m. *C. A. Horgan*

GOLD QUEST (IRE)   2 ch.c. (Mar 18) Rainbow Quest (USA) 134 – My Potters   **– p**
(USA) (Irish River (FR) 131) [1999 8g Sep 8] rangy colt: has scope: fifth foal:
half-brother to 3 winners in Ireland, including 1998 Irish Oaks winner Winona (also
fairly useful 7f winner at 2 yrs, by Alzao) and 1m (at 2 yrs) and 1¾m winner Western
Seas (by Caerleon): dam, Irish 1m winner, half-sister to champion US sprinter My
Juliet and very smart middle-distance colt Lyphard's Special: burly and tongue tied,
soon chased along when never dangerous in maiden at Doncaster: swished tail
repeatedly in paddock: bred to do better. *Sir Michael Stoute*

GOLD SEEKER   2 ch.f. (Apr 7) Superlative 118 – Goldsearch (IRE) 58 (Fayruz   **55**
116) [1999 5d⁵ 5d 5g⁴ 5m Sep 24] 1,400Y: smallish, sturdy filly: first foal: dam, ran
only at 2 yrs, maiden best at 6f, half-sister to 4-y-o Sprindrift: modest maiden: easily
best effort on third start: sold 1,000 gns in October. *D. W. Barker*

GOLDSTAR (IRE)   4 b.g. Fayruz 116 – Scarlet Red (Pas de Seul 133) [1998 –:   **–**
7g 7v 7.5d 1999 a9.4g a11g³ 11.9d⁶ 11.6m Jul 19] neat ex-Irish gelding: first reported
foal: dam Irish 1m winner: little sign of ability: tried blinkered/tongue tied. *P. Eccles*

GOLLACCIA   5 gr.m. Mystiko (USA) 124 – Millie Grey 52 (Grey Ghost 98)   **–**
[1998 NR 1999 12s Sep 21] of little account on Flat. *B. Ellison*

GOLOVIN (GER)   2 b.c. (Feb 8) Bering 136 – Guilinn (IRE) (Last Tycoon 131)   **89 p**
[1999 7s* Nov 5] leggy colt: first known foal: dam, German 7f and 11f winner, half-
sister to St Leger winner Snurge: 6/1, won 20-runner maiden at Doncaster by 2
lengths from Orangeville, going well before leading over 1f out, then wandering:
showed fluent, round action to post: will be suited by 1¼m/1½m: useful prospect.
M. J. Grassick, Ireland

GO MAN (IRE)   5 b.g. Mandalus 110 – Cherry Park (Netherkelly 112) [1998 NR   **–**
1999 a12g⁶ Apr 24] fourth foal: brother to winning staying hurdler/chaser Sam-
morello and bumper winner My Blackbird: dam unraced: little promise in bumpers
and maiden at Wolverhampton on Flat debut. *P. D. Evans*

GONE FOR A BURTON (IRE)   9 ch.g. Bustino 136 – Crimbourne 83   **61**
(Mummy's Pet 125) [1998 76: 10d 10d 10.5m³ 12g⁵ 10.4g⁵ 1999 10.8d 12g⁶ 11.6s
Aug 9] workmanlike gelding: modest handicapper, lightly raced nowadays: stays
1½m: acts on soft and good to firm going: blinkered once. *P. J. Makin*

GONE IN THE WIND (FR)   3 ch.c. Sanglamore (USA) 126 – Miss Silca Key   **42**
102 (Welsh Saint 126) [1998 NR 1999 7m 8.1m⁶ 10v Oct 23] 55,000Y: half-brother
to several at least useful winners, including smart Central City (by Midyan), best up
to 7f, and useful 6f (at 2 yrs) and 7f (in France) winner Miss Zafonic (by Zafonic):
dam won Jersey Stakes: poor maiden: best effort at 1m on good to firm ground (raced
too freely at 1¼m): sold 1,400 gns, sent to Spain. *R. Hannon*

GONE SAVAGE   11 b.g. Nomination 125 – Trwyn Cilan 89 (Import 127) [1998   **–**
NR 1999 5m 6m Jun 28] strong, good-bodied gelding: fairly useful performer at 9
yrs: well beaten in 1999: races mostly at 5f: acts on firm and soft ground and on
equitrack: blinkered (below form) twice: held up. *W. J. Musson*

GOODBYE GATEMEN (IRE)   5 gr.g. Soviet Lad (USA) – Simple Love   **49**
(Simply Great (FR) 122) [1998 60: a5g⁶ a6g² a7g³ a6g⁵ a5g⁴ a7g⁵ a5g⁵ a6g³ a5g⁴ 6g
1999 7v 5m May 7] poor handicapper: effective at 5f to easy 7f: acts on equitrack,
firm and soft going: blinkered once: front runner: has hung left. *A. J. McNae*

GOODBYE GOLDSTONE   3 b.c. Mtoto 134 – Shareehan (Dancing Brave   **80**
(USA) 140) [1998 70: 7v³ 1999 a8f³ a8.5g a11g⁶ 9.7v* 12.3m⁴ 10.1d² 8.9d Jun 12]   **a52**
sparely-made colt: fairly useful handicapper on turf, modest on all-weather: won at
Folkestone in April: ran well penultimate start but slowly away and found little final
outing: stays 1½m: goes well on ground softer than good. *T. J. Naughton*

GOODENOUGH MOVER   3 ch.g. Beveled (USA) – Rekindled Flame (IRE)   **65 d**
(Kings Lake (USA) 133) [1998 NR 1999 8.3m⁶ 7g 6d⁶ 8m 8s Sep 29] third foal: dam
unraced: fair form only on debut. *G. F. H. Charles-Jones*

GOOD EVANS ABOVE   2 br.f. (Apr 28) Tragic Role (USA) – Dark Amber 68   **–**
(Formidable (USA) 125) [1999 5m a5g⁴ 5.1m a5g⁴ 6m May 24] 500Y: seventh foal: **a55**

half-sister to fairly useful Italian middle-distance stayer Di Giacomo (by Bustino): dam, 1m winner at 4 yrs, half-sister to smart middle-distance stayer Rakaposhi King: modest maiden: no form on turf: should stay at least 7f: acts on fibresand: has carried head high. *P. D. Evans*

GOOD FRIDAY (IRE)   2 b.f. (Mar 6) Tenby 125 – Sign of Peace (IRE) 78 (Posen (USA)) [1999 6g⁶ 7.5g⁶ 6.8m⁵ 7g³ 7.9m Sep 1] IR 3,800F, IR 5,500Y: lengthy filly: first foal: dam Irish 13f and hurdles winner: modest form in maidens, best effort when third of 18 to Noble Pursuit at Salisbury: should be well suited by 1¼m+: raced only on good/good to firm going. *Mrs P. N. Dutfield*   **61**

GOOD WHIT SON   3 b.c. Whittingham (IRE) 104 – Davemma 81 (Tachypous 128) [1998 NR 1999 a6g a6g Nov 23] sixth live foal: half-brother to 1990 2-y-o 7f winner Melting Tears (by Noalto) and 1991 2-y-o 8.3f winner Brilliant Disguise (by Ballacashtal): dam, disappointing maiden, stayed 1½m: well beaten in maidens at Lingfield. *G. F. H. Charles-Jones*   **–**

GOODWOOD BLIZZARD   2 ch.f. (Mar 29) Inchinor 119 – Icecapped 91 (Caerleon (USA) 132) [1999 6g⁴ 6g* 7g² 7m* 7m³ 8m² Oct 10] 12,000Y: useful-looking filly: closely related to a winner in Hungary by Don't Forget Me and half-sister to several winners, including fairly useful Irish 1997 2-y-o 7f winner Have Merci (by High Estate) who stays 1½m: dam 1½m and 16.5f winner: useful performer: won maiden at Salisbury in June and minor event at Ascot (drifted markedly right) in July: good placed efforts in Prestige Stakes at Goodwood and Premio Dormello at Milan (beaten head by Sonda) last 2 starts: should stay 1¼m: raced only on good ground or firmer. *J. L. Dunlop*   **97**

GOODWOOD JAZZ (IRE)   3 b.f. Night Shift (USA) – Wood Violet (USA) (Riverman (USA) 131) [1998 74: 6g 6g³ 7f² 7m³ 7d 7s 1999 8v³ 8g 7m Jun 19] well-made filly: unimpressive mover: fair maiden handicapper: disappointing after reappearance: stays 1m: acts on any going: blinkered final start: sold 9,000 gns in July, sent to New Zealand. *J. L. Dunlop*   **69**

GOOMBAYLAND (IRE)   3 ch.g. Common Grounds 118 – House of Fame (USA) (Trempolino (USA) 135) [1998 NR 1999 8s⁴ 10.1g* 10d* 10.3m² Sep 10] 45,000F: lengthy, rather unfurnished gelding: first foal: dam (unraced) from family of Oh So Sharp: smart performer: banned for 30 days under 'non-triers' rule (jockey and trainer fined) on debut: successful in maiden at Epsom in June and minor event at Windsor in August: very good neck second of 6 to Timahs (who rec 6 lb) in minor event at Doncaster final start: stays 1¼m well: acts on good to firm and good to soft ground: sold privately and joined Godolphin. *J. Noseda*   **117**

GO ON GRACE   2 b.f. (May 3) Minshaanshu Amad (USA) 91§ – Peach Brandy 46 (Pharly (FR) 130) [1999 6g 7g 7.5s Jul 3] 500Y: second foal: dam 2m winner at 5 yrs: well beaten in maiden/sellers: joined R. Cowell. *D. Morris*   **32**

GORECKI (USA)   2 b.c. (Feb 11) Hermitage (USA) – Leading Candidate (USA) (Allen's Prospect (USA)) [1999 5m⁴ 6g⁴ 6f* 6d* 7f⁵ 7g Aug 17] $16,000Y, resold IR 57,000Y: lengthy, rather unfurnished colt: fifth foal: half-brother to winners in USA by Alwuhush and Hickman Creek: dam unraced: fairly useful performer: won minor event at Brighton in May and listed race at Epsom in June: well held in listed race at Newmarket and nursery at York last 2 starts: stays 6f: acts on firm and good to soft ground: edgy type: sold 29,000 gns in October. *N. A. Callaghan*   **92**

GORETSKI (IRE)   6 b.g. Polish Patriot (USA) 128 – Celestial Path 101 (Godswalk (USA) 130) [1998 80, a85: 6d 6v 5s 5d 5d 5s* 5s 5d⁵ a5g* a5g⁵ 5m² 5m* 5m 5g⁵ 5d 5m 5g 5d 5d³ 1999 5d 5g 5d 6v 6g 5m* 5m 5m⁵ 5m* 5g* 5.1d³ 5m 5d 5s 5s 5g² 5s Nov 5] tall gelding: unimpressive mover: fairly useful handicapper: won at Hamilton in June and at Pontefract and Beverley in August: has won at 6f, but races mainly at 5f: acts on fibresand, soft and good to firm going: blinkered once at 3 yrs: usually races prominently: tough and genuine, though usually takes a few runs to strike form. *N. Tinkler*   **82**

GORMIRE   6 ro.m. Superlative 118 – Lady of The Lodge 60 (Absalom 128) [1998 –§: a6g a5g 1999 a6g Feb 19] temperamental, and of no account now. *B. W. Murray*   **– §**

GORSE   4 b.c. Sharpo 132 – Pervenche (Latest Model 115) [1998 106p: 6d* 6m² 6g⁴ 6m 6d* 6d* 1999 6g³ 6d³ 6m* 6d* 6g² 6s⁵ Sep 26] big, strong, lengthy colt: **116**

Girsonfield Ltd's "Gorse"

didn't race at 2 yrs due to stress fracture of near-fore fetlock: smart performer: better than ever at 4 yrs, winning Holsten-Trophy at Hamburg (by 2 lengths from Night Shot) in July and Phoenix Sprint Stakes at Leopardstown (by ½ length from Grazia) in August: ran creditably last 2 starts, beaten neck by Keos in Goldene Peitsche at Baden-Baden and 2 lengths when fifth to Bold Edge in Diadem Stakes at Ascot: stays 6f: acts on soft and good to firm going. *H. Candy*

GO SALLY GO (IRE) 3 b.f. Elbio 125 – Pollette (Stanford 121§) [1998 46, a–: – a5g a5g 5d a5g 5g³ 5m 1999 8m 7s⁵ 6g 8d a6g a7g Nov 19] smallish, close-coupled filly: poor maiden. *F. Murphy*

GOTHIC REVIVAL (IRE) 2 b.c. (Feb 17) Indian Ridge 123 – Gothic Dream **70** (IRE) 113 (Nashwan (USA) 135) [1999 7s⁴ 8d Oct 12] smallish, stocky, angular colt: second foal: half-brother to Irish 3-y-o 2m winner Gothic Theme (by Zafonic): dam, Irish 2-y-o 7f winner (later best at 1½m), out of Irish St Leger winner Dark Lomond: very green when fourth of 5 to Bogus Dreams in steadily-run minor event at Ascot: well held in maiden at Leicester following month: will stay at least 1¼m. *J. L. Dunlop*

GO THUNDER (IRE) 5 b.g. Nordico (USA) – Moving Off (Henbit (USA) 130) **51** [1998 62: 9s⁶ 10d 11g 14g³ 12g 1999 13.1d 8.3s 10v Oct 11] IR 3,000Y, 12,500 2-y-o: fourth foal: half-brother to winners abroad by Nordance and Archway: dam Irish maiden: fairly useful at 2 yrs, winning nursery at Tralee: left W. Mullins in Ireland after final start in 1998: tongue tied, well beaten in 1999: stays 1¾m: acts on soft ground. *D. A. Nolan*

GOT ONE TOO (FR) 2 ch.g. (May 8) Green Tune (USA) 125 – Gloria Mundi **61** (FR) (Saint Cyrien (FR) 128) [1999 a7g 7m 7m⁵ 7.7d 8d 8d Oct 22] tall gelding:

third foal: half-brother to 1997 2-y-o 7.6f winner Holy Wine (by Thorn Dance): dam, useful French middle-distance performer, also won over jumps: modest maiden: well held in nurseries last 2 outings: stays 7f: blinkered on debut: retained 3,000 gns after final start. *D. Sasse*

GO TOO MOOR (IRE) 6 b.g. Posen (USA) – Gulistan (Sharpen Up 127) [1998 – NR 1999 10s a14g Nov 30] poor maiden: left P. McEntee after reappearance. *C. A. Dwyer*

GOWITHTHEFLOW (IRE) 3 b.g. River Falls 113 – Astral Way (Hotfoot 126) – [1998 64: 5g⁵ 5s³ 5s⁴ 6g 6d 1999 8.2s 5d May 8] good-topped gelding: modest form at 2 yrs: no show in 1999: has had tongue tied. *B. S. Rothwell*

GO WITH THE WIND 6 b.g. Unfuwain (USA) 131 – Cominna (Dominion 123) 57 § [1998 –§: 13.1d³ 15m⁴ 16.1d 1999 14m 15s 16f⁶ 12m* 13.8m² 11.1m² 12g 12f³ Sep 13] lengthy gelding: unimpressive mover: modest handicapper: won at Beverley in July: stays 2m: acts on firm and good to soft ground: tried visored/blinkered: swishes tail: often finds little and needs treating with caution. *J. S. Goldie*

GRACE 5 b. or br.m. Buzzards Bay 128§ – Bingo Bongo 60 (Petong 126) [1998 61 66, a–: 6.1v⁴ 6.1s² 6g 6.1m 5g⁶ 6.1d* 6m² 6g a6g 6s⁶ 6v 6s⁵ 1999 6.1v 5d 6.1f² 6s a– 7.1d⁴ 6.1g 6s⁶ 7m⁶ 6m 8d ¯7m 7f³ 7m⁶ 6.1m 6.1m⁴ 5d 5.2s² Oct 22] modest handicapper: creditable efforts when in frame, unlucky second of 27 at Newbury final start: effective at testing 5f to easy 7f: acts on any turf going except possibly heavy, well beaten only run on fibresand: blinkered 4 of last 6 starts. *J. M. Bradley*

GRACE AND POWER (IRE) 2 b.f. (Feb 25) Brief Truce (USA) 126 – Tantum 74 Ergo 106 (Tanfirion 110) [1999 6g² 6f⁴ 7g² Aug 11] IR 46,000Y: third living foal: half-sister to Irish 6f winner Sacrementum (by Night Shift): dam Irish 2-y-o 6f/7f (CL Weld Park Stakes) winner: fair maiden: not sure to stay much beyond 7f: raced only on good going or firmer. *J. L. Dunlop*

GRACE PARK 2 gr.f. (Apr 18) Absalom 128 – Aspark (Sparkler 130) [1999 5m – Sep 3] 6,000Y: half-sister to 6f (at 2 yrs) to 8.2f winner Amidst (by Midyan) and unreliable 6f performer Arturian (by Vaigly Great), both fairly useful: dam little form: 9/4, last of 13 in maiden at Haydock, very slowly away. *R. F. Johnson Houghton*

GRACIOSO (USA) 3 ch.c. Nureyev (USA) 131 – Don't Sulk (USA) 115 (Grau- 118 stark) [1998 8v* 1999 10.5s³ 10.5m* 12s⁶ 10g⁴ Jun 27] good-topped colt: brother to several winners, including smart French/US winner up to 9f Caesour and useful 1½m performer Professional Girl, and closely related/half-brother to 3 winners in France/USA: dam won 1½m Prix de Royallieu: smart performer: won 4-runner Prix Lupin at Longchamp in May, kicking on early in straight and running on strongly to beat below-par Montjeu a length: failed to repeat that form in Prix du Jockey Club at

Prix Lupin, Longchamp—
Gracioso floors the 10/1-on pairing of Montjeu (No.4) and pacemaker Obviously Fun

Sheikh Mohammed's "Gracioso"

Chantilly and Grand Prix de Paris at Longchamp: stays 10.5f: has won on heavy going, best effort on good to firm: joined Godolphin. *A. Fabre, France*

GRACIOUS GIFT 3 ch.f. Cadeaux Genereux 131 – Gentle Persuasion 95 **96** (Bustino 136) [1998 76: 6g⁶ 6.1s² 1999 7m⁵ 7m* 7m⁴ 6m* 7m² 6d³ 6d Oct 9] leggy filly: good walker: useful performer: won maiden at Salisbury in June and handicap at Windsor in July: ran well when placed in handicaps after: effective at 6f/7f: acts on soft going and on good to firm: held up. *R. Hannon*

GRACIOUS PLENTY (IRE) 3 ch.f. Generous (IRE) 139 – Formide (USA) **105** (Trempolino (USA) 135) [1998 88: 7m³ 7d² 7g⁵ 1999 a10g* 12m⁵ a12f⁶ 9f⁶ a9f⁶ 10s Oct 15] small, sparely-made filly: fluent mover: useful performer: landed odds in maiden at Lingfield: ran very well when 5 lengths fifth to Fairy Queen in Ribblesdale Stakes at Royal Ascot 2½ months later: left B. Hills and well held in varied company in USA: stays 1½m: acts on good to firm going and equitrack. *M. Hennig, USA*

GRALMANO (IRE) 4 b.g. Scenic 128 – Llangollen (IRE) 87 (Caerleon (USA) **78** 132) [1998 85§, a95§: a8g* a10g³ a9.4g² 9d 9m⁴ 11.4d³ 12s 10.3f⁵ 10g³ 10g⁵ 1999 **a95** a8g⁴ a10g⁴ a9.4g⁴ a10g 10g 10m 12m⁶ 14m⁶ 10.1m² 10g⁴ 8m* 8g* 8m² 8d Sep 18] strong, good-topped gelding: useful on all-weather, fair on turf: won minor event at Redcar (first run after leaving N. Littmoden) and handicap at Pontefract in August: has form at 1½m, at least as effective around 1m: acts on good to firm going, soft and all-weather: usually visored/blinkered for previous stable: edgy sort: races prominently/leads. *K. A. Ryan*

GRANBY BELL 8 b.g. Ballacashtal (CAN) – Betbellof 65 (Averof 123) [1998 **–** NR 1999 13.3f May 26] tall gelding: modest winning hurdler: well held both starts on Flat since 1996. *P. Hayward*

GRAND CHAPEAU (IRE)   7 b.g. Ballad Rock 122 – All Hat (Double Form 130) [1998 72, a68: a5g 6g⁵ 5g 6s 5m 6f⁴ a6g* 6m 5m⁴ 6m 1999 a6g a6g a6g a6f a6f⁶ 6g 5s Nov 2] good-topped gelding: takes the eye: fair handicapper at 6 yrs: generally below best in 1999, including in seller/claimers: off course 8 months after fifth outing: stays 6f when conditions aren't testing: acts on fibresand, firm and good to soft going: usually races prominently. *D. Nicholls*   **64 d**

GRAND CORONET   3 b.f. Grand Lodge (USA) 125 – Coronati (IRE) (Bluebird (USA) 125) [1998 –: 7d 1999 a8g³ a7g* a7g⁴ 7m 7m² Sep 1] fair performer: won maiden at Lingfield in January: off 4 months, best effort on turf when second in minor event at Brighton final start: acts on equitrack. *T. G. Mills*   **59 a66**

GRAND CRU   8 ch.g. Kabour 80 – Hydrangea 73 (Warpath 113) [1998 55, a44: a14.8g 12g 14.1s 11.8d⁴ a12g a14g⁴ a14g 1999 14.1s 12m a12g 11.8d 16d 14.1s³ a14g⁴ a14g* Nov 30] angular gelding: modest performer: won amateur minor event at Southwell in November: stays 2m well: acts on soft ground and fibresand: visored final 6 starts. *J. Cullinan*   **62**

GRAND ESTATE   4 b.g. Prince Sabo 123 – Ultimate Dream 74 (Kafu 120) [1998 82: 6s² 5s⁵ 5m³ 6d 6g⁶ 6g 1999 5d a6g² 6g⁵ 6s a7g 6m* 6f* a5g 5g⁴ 6g a7g⁵ Sep 4] neat gelding: fair on turf, modest on all-weather: left T. Easterby after reappearance: won minor event in June and amateur handicap (awarded race) in July, both at Hamilton: probably best at 5f/6f: yet to race on heavy going but acts on any other turf, and on fibresand: blinkered fourth 3-y-o start: possibly none too genuine. *D. W. Chapman*   **72 a60**

GRANDIOSO (IRE)   3 b.g. High Estate 127 – Palmyra (GER) (Arratos (FR)) [1998 56: 6v⁵ 8s⁶ 1999 a8g⁶ 10s⁶ 12g⁵ 12d² 13.1g⁴ 12.1m³ 14d⁶ 12m 11.9d⁵ Aug 6] workmanlike gelding: modest maiden handicapper: stays 1½m: acts on good to firm and good to soft going, some promise on fibresand: a difficult ride, and none too consistent: joined M. Hammond. *C. W. Thornton*   **60**

GRAND LAD (IRE)   5 ch.h. Mujtahid (USA) 118 – Supportive (IRE) (Nashamaa 113) [1998 NR 1999 6g Jun 10] lengthy horse: one-time useful performer: tailed off only run of 1999: stays 6f: acts on firm and good to soft going. *R. W. Armstrong*   **–**

GRAND MAITRE (USA)   3 gr. or ro.c. Gone West (USA) – La Grande Epoque (USA) 120 (Lyphard (USA) 132) [1998 76p: 7m 7.1m³ 7m⁵ 1999 8.2s* 8g² 8.5f⁶ 8.5g 8.5f³ 8.5d² 8.5d⁵ 8.5f Nov 17] leggy, angular colt: shows knee action: useful performer: won maiden at Nottingham in March easily: left J. Dunlop then placed in 3 allowance races in USA: stays 8.5f: acts on firm and good to soft going: blinkered last 3 starts. *A. E. Goldberg, USA*   **97**

GRANDMA ULLA (IRE)   2 b.f. (Jan 30) Muhtarram (USA) 125 – Trojan Lady (USA) (Irish River (FR) 131) [1999 7m⁵ 6m* 5f 6.5g 6v Oct 23] 3,400Y, 6,300Y: fourth foal: half-sister to unreliable 6f winner Zain Dancer (by Nabeel Dancer), 4-y-o Trojan Wolf and 5-y-o Nubile: dam, placed in France, out of half-sister to Sun Princess and Saddlers' Hall: fair form: won maiden at Kempton in July: well held in nurseries last 2 starts: bred to stay at least 1m: blanketed for stalls entry. *R. J. O'Sullivan*   **77**

GRAND ORO   2 ch.c. (Mar 3) Suave Dancer (USA) 136 – Hence (USA) (Mr Prospector (USA)) [1999 8s² Nov 6] 6,500Y: rather leggy, lengthy colt: half-brother to several winners, including 3-y-o Be Gone and 1¼m winner Ruby Heights (by Shirley Heights): dam 7f winner in USA from good family: weak in market, fit but green, plenty of promise when ½-length second of 18 to Blusienka in maiden at Doncaster: should stay at least 1¼m/1½m: should make a useful 3-y-o, and looks sure to win races. *G. C. H. Chung*   **93 p**

GRAND RUN (IRE)   3 ch.g. Grand Lodge (USA) 125 – Entracte 109 (Henbit (USA) 130) [1998 NR 1999 7d Mar 26] IR 16,000Y: angular, good-topped gelding: sixth foal: half-brother to 1¼m winners Maeterlinck (fairly useful, by Bluebird) and Soralena (by Persian Bold): dam, 2-y-o 7f winner, out of half-sister to Sun Princess and Saddlers' Hall: well held in maiden at Doncaster. *J. W. Hills*   **–**

GRAND SLAM (IRE)   4 b.g. Second Set (IRE) 127 – Lady In The Park (IRE) (Last Tycoon 131) [1998 79: 7m² 7.1m⁴ 7g² 8m² 7.1g⁴ 8m* 8m 1999 8d 8f³ 8f 8.3m⁵ 8m⁶ 8m² 8f 8m⁴ 8m² Sep 10] smallish, useful-looking gelding: fair handicapper: stays 1m: acts on good to firm going, well beaten on good to soft: blinkered fourth and fifth starts: sold 14,000 gns, joined L. Lungo. *R. Hannon*   **74**

Ladbroke Bunbury Cup (Handicap), Newmarket—
Grangeville lands an ante-post gamble from Salty Jack (left) and the blinkered Teofilio

GRAND SONNET (IRE) 3 b.c. Second Set (IRE) 127 – Mali (USA) (Storm **88**
Bird (CAN) 134) [1998 –p: 7s 1999 7g^4 8.1s^2 8m^4 10m^3 8.1d^4 9.9m^5 8m Sep 17]
strong, stocky colt: carries condition: fairly useful maiden: best efforts when second
at Sandown (minor event) in April and fourth at Kempton in May: well below form
last 2 starts: stays 1m: acts on soft going and on good to firm: has been bandaged
behind: sold 19,000 gns, joined N. Gaselee. *D. R. C. Elsworth*

GRAND VIEW 3 ch.g. Grand Lodge (USA) 125 – Hemline 77 (Sharpo 132) **74**
[1998 –p: 6d^5 6g 5.1v^6 1999 6.1s^2 6m^4 6d 6m 6m* 6g 5g^3 6g 6g Oct 19] unfurnished
gelding: fair performer: won handicap at Salisbury in July: well held after good third
in minor event at Redcar: should stay 7f: acts on soft and good to firm going: none
too consistent: sold 9,400 gns. *R. Hannon*

GRANGEVILLE (USA) 4 b.g. Gulch (USA) – Cor Anglais (USA) 78 **109**
(Nijinsky (CAN) 138) [1998 95p: 8s 8f^4 8.3m^3 8m^5 7m^2 7.1g* 8.1m 7g^4 1999
7.5m^3 7g 7.1m^2 7f* 7m 7d^3 6m^3 6d* Sep 18]
'Type to improve and win a good handicap or two in 1999', was how
Racehorses of 1998 summed up Grangeville's prospects. The assessment
proved spot-on as the progressive Grangeville landed the Ladbroke Bunbury
Cup at Newmarket in July and the Ladbroke (Ayr) Gold Cup in September.

Ladbroke (Ayr) Gold Cup (Handicap)—a second major handicap falls to Grangeville and Kieren Fallon,
who hold on from Evening Promise (No.12) and Royal Result (hidden by winner)

He shaped well on his three outings prior to the Bunbury Cup and was backed from 14/1 to 13/2 favourite ante-post. The gamble was landed in style, Grangeville travelling sweetly just behind the leader in a nineteen-runner field before quickening ahead two furlongs out to win decisively by a length and a quarter from Salty Jack, with Teofilio and Peartree House filling the frame. Grangeville's free-running style suggested that a drop back to six furlongs wouldn't inconvenience him, and so it proved. A good third of ten to Arkadian Hero, beaten over three lengths, in listed company at Newmarket preceded Grangeville's narrow victory at Ayr, where he won, keeping on gamely, by a head and a short head from Evening Promise and Royal Result in a twenty-eight runner field. Grangeville looked capable of making his mark in listed or minor pattern company in 2000, but he will be racing in the USA, his owner George Strawbridge reportedly preferring not to race horses in Britain if he peceives they are below pattern-race class. A big, rather leggy gelding, with a tendency to carry his head high, Grangeville is nonetheless a genuine sort, and he responded well to Kieren Fallon's strong handling in his victories at Newmarket and Ayr. He acts on firm and good to soft going. *I. A. Balding*

GRANITE CITY 2 ro.g. (May 29) Clantime 101 – Alhargah (Be My Guest (USA) 126) [1999 5m⁴ 5m⁵ 5g 5f³ 5g⁵ 6m 5f⁵ 6v⁶ 5g Nov 3] 15,000Y: half-brother to several winners, including fairly useful 1990 2-y-o 6f winner Moy River (by Dominion) and 2m winner Guest Alliance (by Zaffaran): dam no form: poor maiden: stays 6f: acts on any going. *J. S. Goldie*   **46**

GRANNY RICH 5 ch.m. Ardross 134 – Weareagrandmother 65 (Prince Tenderfoot (USA) 126) [1998 NR 1999 10m⁶ 8.1m 11.6d⁴ 11.9d⁵ 15.8m⁶ 14.1m⁴ Jul 17] unfurnished mare: first foal: dam 1m (at 2 yrs) and 12.5f winner, also successful over hurdles: poor maiden: stays 2m: much improved over hurdles late in year, winning all 3 starts. *P. M. Rich*   **46 +**

GRANNY'S PET 5 ch.g. Selkirk (USA) 129 – Patsy Western 81 (Precocious 126) [1998 105: 8s 6g⁶ 7m⁵ 7.1m* 7g 7g² 6v 1999 7d² 7.1g 6m 7.1d² 7d* 7g* 7.1g³ 7m* 7d² 7s* Oct 23] angular, close-coupled gelding: has a quick action: smart performer: in very good form, winning rated stakes at Chester and Goodwood in August, Goodwood (by 1¾ lengths from Kumait) again in September and minor event at Doncaster in October: best at 7f: acts on soft going and on good to firm: usually waited with: tried blinkered earlier in career: much more consistent nowadays. *P. F. I. Cole*   **112**

GRANNYS RELUCTANCE (IRE) 3 b. or br.f. Anita's Prince 126 – Dawn Is Breaking (Import 127) [1998 61: 5f⁶ 6.1d³ 6.1g 5s 1999 5.7g 6.1f a6g⁶ a9.4g⁵ 7.7d³ a7g⁶ 8s² a8.5g⁶ a7g Nov 19] workmanlike filly: modest maiden: stays 1m: acts on soft going and fibresand. *B. Palling*   **63 a53**

GRANTED (FR) 2 b.f. (Apr 23) Cadeaux Genereux 131 – Germane 100 (Distant Relative 128) [1999 6s⁵ 7d⁴ Oct 20] 77,000Y: tall, unfurnished filly: has scope: first foal: dam 2-y-o 7f (Rockfel Stakes) winner out of half-sister to Running Stag: green, shaped well when fifth of 11 to Philantha in maiden at Newmarket: below that form in similar event at Newcastle later in October: should stay at least 1m. *M. L. W. Bell*   **76**

GRANTLEY 2 b.g. (May 7) Deploy 131 – Matisse 65 (Shareef Dancer (USA) 135) [1999 6d 6d Sep 16] 5,400Y: first foal: dam, maiden, stayed 1m: well held in maidens. *J. D. Bethell*

GRASSLANDIK 3 b.c. Ardkinglass 114 – Sophisticated Baby 39 (Bairn (USA) 126) [1998 64f: a5g* 1999 a5g³ a5g² a5g⁵ 5d 5.7g 5g⁴ 5g² 5g a6g a6f a6g⁵ a6g a6g² Dec 27] fair handicapper: stays easy 6f: acts on all-weather, raced mostly on good going on turf: held up. *A. G. Newcombe*   **66**

GRATE SPARK (IRE) 3 b.g. Posen (USA) – Linda's Fantasy 108 (Raga Navarro (ITY) 119) [1998 –: 7.9g 7d 8d 1999 15.8g³ 17.2g Aug 25] sturdy gelding: form only when third in maiden handicap at Catterick: reportedly had breathing problem final start: stays 2m: visored final 2-y-o outing: sold 6,400 gns in November, joined J. Coupland. *E. Weymes*   **39**

GRAY PASTEL (IRE)   5 gr.g. Al Nasr (FR) 126 – Gay Pastel (FR) (No Pass No   –
Sale 120) [1998 55: 11.8m* 11.8d 1999 11.8m⁶ Jul 15] tall, angular gelding: lightly
raced and modest form at best in Britain: stays 2m: acts on good to firm ground.
M. C. Pipe

GRAZIA   4 b.f. Sharpo 132 – Dance Machine 111 (Green Dancer) (USA) 132) [1998   **108**
111: 6m* 6.5m 1999 7v⁶ 6m³ 6d² 6m Sep 4] tall filly: lightly raced: useful performer:
easily best effort in 1999 when ½-length second of 10 to Gorse in Phoenix Sprint
Stakes at Leopardstown, running on strongly: last of 16 in Sprint Cup at Haydock
final start: should stay 7f: acts on good to firm and good to soft going, probably
unsuited by heavy. *Sir Mark Prescott*

GREAT CRUSADER   7 ch.g. Deploy 131 – Shannon Princess (Connaught 130)   – §
[1998 NR 1999 14m 20m Jun 15] smallish, strong gelding: useful handicapper at 3
yrs: fit from hurdling, well held both starts in 1999: stays 16.2f: acts on soft and good
to firm going: blinkered last 2 starts at 3 yrs: difficult ride (has looked reluctant) and
one to be wary of. *R. Rowe*

GREAT DANE (IRE)   4 b.c. Danehill (USA) 126 – Itching (IRE) (Thatching   **122**
131) [1998 117: 8.1g* 8.1g* 8d 10.3g³ 8g* 8.9g* 10s* 1999 9.9g* 9g* Jun 27]
Great Dane reached the racecourse only twice in the latest season,
extending his winning sequence to five before being retired to the National
Stud, Newmarket, at a fee for 2000 of £4,500 (October 1st). Great Dane's last
three victories as a three-year-old (when he chalked up five in all) established
him as a smart performer, the last of them when a very rare runner for his stable
in the French Provinces. That victory, in a weak Group 3 event at Lyon-Parilly,
was over a mile and a quarter, a distance which seemed to stretch Great Dane's
stamina to its limits as a three-year-old. He was, however, entered for the
Eclipse in the latest season and made his reappearance over a mile and a quarter
at Goodwood in May when he won a very competitive-looking listed event in
good style from Diamond White and Docksider. Great Dane—described by his
regular rider Fallon as 'twice the horse this year'—looked set for a rewarding
season but his next appearance, at the Curragh on Irish Derby day in the
Budweiser International Stakes, proved to be his last. He went out on a high
note, making all in the nine furlong event and winning from the keeping-on
Altibr by two lengths, the pair dominating throughout.

Great Dane (IRE) (b.c. 1995)	Danehill (USA) (b 1986)	Danzig (b 1977)	Northern Dancer Pas de Nom
		Razyana (b 1981)	His Majesty Spring Adieu
	Itching (IRE) (b or br 1989)	Thatching (b 1975)	Thatch Abella
		Alligatrix (b 1980)	Alleged Shore

The rather leggy Great Dane is by the shuttle stallion Danehill, who has
built up a fine record in recent seasons in both Britain and Australia. Danehill

Budweiser International Stakes, the Curragh—
Great Dane wins his fifth race in a row, stretched over two seasons;
Altibr and Access All Areas chase home the all-the-way winner

himself was best at sprint distances, but his sprinters are in a minority and, despite his success with Danetime, his best European-trained winners, Desert King and Tiger Hill, both enjoyed their biggest wins at a mile and a half. Danehill, incidentally, had no two-year-old runners in Europe in the latest season after spending the 1996 northern hemisphere covering season in Japan. Great Dane's dam Itching, also responsible for the fairly useful miler Witching Hour, is an unraced half-sister to the useful Alidiva, the dam of Group 1 pattern winners Sleepytime, Ali-Royal and Taipan. Alidiva and Itching are half-sisters to the high-class French middle-distance performer Croco Rouge, in whose essay further details of this superb family can be found. Great Dane, who was effective at a mile to a mile and a quarter, acted on soft ground and probably on firm. He displayed a high head carriage at times but was genuine. *H. R. A. Cecil*

GREAT HOPPER   4 b.f. Rock Hopper 124 – Spun Gold 106 (Thatch (USA) 136)   – [1998 NR 1999 11.1g 12g 12s Nov 2] 600F, 1,600Y: sixth foal: half-sister to several winning stayers, including Record Lover (by Alzao) and Great Oration (by Simply Great): dam 7f (at 2 yrs) and 12.2f winner: no form. *F. Watson*

GREAT MELODY (IRE)   4 ch.g. Pips Pride 117 – Unbidden Melody (USA)   **66** (Chieftain II) [1998 75d: a8g² a8g* 8s⁶ 8g² 7m 8.1s 8.5s 8g⁶ 10g 1999 8.3m⁴ 10d 8g⁵ a8g 8m⁶ 8m⁵ 7.1m* 7m Aug 22] workmanlike gelding: fair performer: won seller at Chepstow in August: stays 1m: acts on equitrack and good to firm going: usually visored/blinkered: temperament under suspicion: sold twice after final start (reportedly finished lame), for 1,000 gns on second occasion and joined D. Shaw. *D. J. S. Cosgrove*

GREAT NEWS   4 b.g. Elmaamul (USA) 125 – Amina 80 (Brigadier Gerard 144)   **93** [1998 79p: 7s³ 6m² 7g² 7.6g³ 7m² 7s* 1999 7g² 7g* 7d³ 7m 8.3m* 8d³ 7d Oct 1] tall, angular gelding: fairly useful handicapper: won Insulpak Victoria Cup at Ascot (ridden by 5-lb claimer, beat Gift of Gold by ½ length) in April and 12-runner rated stakes at Windsor in August: not discredited last 2 starts: stays 1m: acts on soft going and on good to firm: sold 40,000 gns. *I. A. Balding*

GREAT ORATION (IRE)   10 b. or br.g. Simply Great (FR) 122 – Spun Gold   – 106 (Thatch (USA) 136) [1998 67: 16.1d 15.9m⁵ 16m³ 16m⁵ 17.1m 1999 18g 16.1m Jun 24] angular gelding: has round action: fair handicapper: little show in 1999: best at 2m+: acts on any turf going and on fibresand: sometimes visored earlier in career: usually held up. *F. Watson*

GREAT RICHES   2 b.g. (Mar 21) Mon Tresor 113 – Glitter of Gold 68 (Glint of   – Gold 128) [1999 7.9g 8g 5d Oct 26] first foal: dam, disappointing maiden, half-sister to smart 6f (at 2 yrs) to 1¼m winner Starstreak: well beaten in maidens. *Mrs M. Reveley*

GREAT WHITE   2 gr.g. (Apr 8) Marju (IRE) 127 – Galava (CAN) (Graustark)   **74 d** [1999 5g³ 5g⁵ 5.1m³ 6m 5.1g 5s a5g Nov 19] 41,000Y: strong, well-made gelding: has a quick action: fifth foal: closely related to fairly useful 1997 2-y-o 1m winner Merciless (by Last Tycoon) and half-brother to 2 winners, including 13.8f winner Grey Galava (by Generous): dam placed at 7f/1m in France: fair maiden: lost his form last 3 starts: should stay beyond 6f: acts on good to firm ground. *R. Hannon*

GRECIAN TALE (IRE)   3 b.g. Catrail (USA) 123 – Athens Belle (IRE) 101   **59** (Groom Dancer (USA) 128) [1998 73: 5v⁶ 6m³ 6f 6s 6m² 6g³ 6m 1999 a6g 7d 6.1s 5s 6f⁵ 5.3f³ 6d Nov 4] tall, quite good-topped gelding: fair maiden at 2 yrs, modest at best in 1999: stays 6f: acts on firm going, probably on fibresand: has worn tongue strap: usually forces pace. *A. P. Jarvis*

GREEK DANCE (IRE)   4 b.c. Sadler's Wells (USA) 132 – Hellenic 125 (Darshaan 133) [1998 119p: 10d* 10.4g* 12m⁵ 1999 10m⁵ 12g 10.5d* 10.4m² 12v⁶ 10g⁵   **119** Oct 16] strong, compact colt: has a short, round action: smart performer: injured near-hind in Derby at Epsom in 1998: returned to form when beating Prolix by easy 2 lengths in Petros Rose of Lancaster Stakes at Haydock before creditable 8 lengths second to Royal Anthem in Juddmonte International at York, both in August:

Petros Rose of Lancaster Stakes, Haydock—Greek Dance toys with runner-up Prolix

ran respectably in Prix de l'Arc de Triomphe at Longchamp (sixth to Montjeu) and Champion Stakes at Newmarket (sweating, fifth to Alborada) last 2 starts: stays 1½m: acts on good to firm and heavy ground. *Sir Michael Stoute*

GREEK FAYR (IRE)   2 b.f. (May 7) Fayruz 116 – Greek Music (Tachypous 128)   **39** [1999 5v⁴ a5g⁴ 5m⁵ 7g⁶ 7m⁵ 7m 7f 7g a8.5g⁶ Oct 16] 3,000Y: rather unfurnished filly: unimpressive mover: half-sister to 2-y-o sprint winners Angels Answer (in 1991, by Stalker) and Leap of Faith (in 1993, by Northiam): dam ran twice: poor maiden: stays 7f: usually visored/blinkered. *P. D. Evans*

GREEK MYTH (IRE)   3 b.f. Sadler's Wells (USA) 132 – Greektown (Ela-   **58** Mana-Mou 132) [1998 NR 1999 9.9m⁴ 11.9g⁶ May 28] fifth living foal: half-sister to useful 7f (at 2 yrs) and 1¼m winner Athens Belle (by Groom Dancer) and smart 1¼m and 13f winner Multicoloured (by Rainbow Quest): dam, French 1¼m/1½m winner, half-sister to Prix du Cadran winner Sought Out: modest form when fourth in maiden at Salisbury in May: well held in similar event at Haydock: likely to stay beyond 1¼m: sold 140,000 gns in December. *R. Charlton*

GREENAWAY BAY (USA)   5 ch.g. Green Dancer (USA) 132 – Raise 'n Dance   **65** (USA) (Raise A Native) [1998 69+: a8.5g⁴ 10g 10s³ 10g 10f³ 9m 10g⁴ 10g 8.9g⁴ 8.2v³ 1999 10d⁵ 8m 10m 8m* 8.3m⁶ 8.9d⁴ 9g⁶ 10d³ Nov 1] quite good-topped gelding: fair handicapper: left W. Musson prior to winning at Brighton in August: mostly ran creditably after: effective at 1m (given good test) to 1¼m: acts on any going. *K. R. Burke*

GREEN BOPPER (USA)   6 b.g. Green Dancer (USA) 132 – Wayage (USA) (Mr   **81** Prospector (USA)) [1998 67: a7g² a8g* a8.5g* a8.5g* 8m a9.4g⁵ a8g⁴ a8.5g⁶ 1999 a8g⁵ a9.4g⁵ a11g* a12g² a11g* a12g⁴ 11.9d 10.5s* 10.5d³ 12.3d⁶ 10d² 10d Nov 1] close-coupled gelding: fairly useful handicapper: won at Southwell in February and March and Haydock (apprentices) in July: ran well penultimate start: effective at 1¼m/1½m: acts on soft ground and fibresand: visored once at 3 yrs. *G. Woodward*

GREEN CARD (USA)   5 b.h. Green Dancer (USA) 132 – Dunkellin (USA) (Irish   **107** River (FR) 131) [1998 110: 9s⁵ 8g 8.2g* 8g² 8m* 8d⁵ 8g³ 8d⁴ 8g⁴ 8s⁶ 1999 8.5g³

8.5g⁵ 8g⁵ 8g⁵ 8f⁴ 8m³ 11.9m³ Sep 4] quite attractive horse: one-time smart performer: useful in 1999: third to Shiva in falsely-run Earl of Sefton Stakes at Newmarket on reappearance in April: below par most other starts: barely stays 1¼m: acts on good to firm and good to soft going: visored (poor effort) final 4-y-o start: often held up: sold 45,000 gns in December. *S. P. C. Woods*

GREEN CASKET (IRE)   2 b.c. (Feb 15) Green Desert (USA) 127 – Grecian   **71 P**
Urn 123 (Ela-Mana-Mou 132) [1999 8d⁶ Oct 27] fifth living foal: half-brother to several winners, including 4-y-o Dark Shell and useful French middle-distance performer Grecian Dart (both by Darshaan): dam French 6.5f (at 2 yrs) to 9f winner: weak 4/1-shot and green, sixth of 10 to King Spinner in maiden at Yarmouth, jumping path early on and generally shaping as though experience would do him power of good: will probably stay at least 1¼m: should do good deal better at 3 yrs. *Sir Michael Stoute*

GREEN GINGER   3 ch.g. Ardkinglass 114 – Bella Maggio (Rakaposhi King   **81**
119) [1998 77: 6f 6m 6.1g⁴ 1999 6.1f⁴ 6m⁴ 7.1d⁴ 6.8m³ 6.1m* 6m 6.1f Oct 20] fairly useful performer: won maiden at Nottingham in August, making all: stays 6f, possibly not 7f: acts on good to firm going: often races up with pace. *A. Streeter*

GREEN GOD (IRE)   3 b.c. Common Grounds 118 – Inanna 105 (Persian Bold   **74**
123) [1998 –: 6g 1999 8d 7s² 7m⁶ 7s² 8s Oct 4] angular colt: fair maiden: best effort when second in handicap (final run for M. Heaton-Ellis) penultimate start: shaped as though in need of run 4 months later: should stay further than 7f: acts on soft going and on good to firm. *C. G. Cox*

GREEN JACKET   4 b.g. Green Desert (USA) 127 – Select Sale (Auction Ring   **–**
(USA) 123) [1998 78d: 9v 9m⁶ 10m 9g 7.6m⁵ a7g a8f 1999 a10g a10g a8g a13g⁵ a13g Mar 2] workmanlike gelding: fair maiden at best: has lost his form: usually blinkered of late: probably ungenuine. *R. J. O'Sullivan*

GREENSAND   3 b.f. Green Desert (USA) 127 – Totham 84 (Shernazar 131)   **96 ?**
[1998 96p: 6g 6m³ 6m* 6d⁶ 1999 8m 6d⁶ 6m² 6.1g Aug 13] tall, good-topped filly: useful performer: second in minor event at Newmarket, only form of 1999, though dictated steady pace and possibly flattered: best efforts at 6f: acts on good to firm going. *R. Hannon*

GREEN SNAKE   3 ch.f. Royal Academy (USA) 130 – Tigwa 68 (Cadeaux Gene-
reux 131) [1998 80p: 7.5m* 6s 1999 8m Jul 28] fair performer: last of 7 in handicap on only run of 1999: should stay 1m: sold 7,000 gns. *C. E. Brittain*

GREENSPAN (IRE)   7 b.g. Be My Guest (USA) 126 – Prima Ballerina (FR)
(Nonoalco (USA) 131) [1998 77: a12g* a12g* a12g² a12g* a12g² a12g² a12g³ a12g³ a12g* 1999 a16.2g Jan 9] useful-looking gelding: bad mover: fair performer: tailed off when pulled up, only run of 1999: effective at 1½m to 2m: acts well on fibresand, raced only once on turf since 1995: blinkered once (fell) as 3-y-o. *Miss S. J. Wilton*

GREENSTONE (IRE)   3 b.f. Green Desert (USA) 127 – Mahabba (USA) 74   **81**
(Elocutionist (USA)) [1998 84: 6m 7g² 7g⁴ 8v⁴ 1999 8m* 9g 8m 10m³ 8f⁴ 8.3m 10d⁵ a12g Nov 16] smallish, sturdy filly: fairly useful performer: won maiden at Warwick in May: mostly creditable efforts after: stays 1¼m: acts on good to firm and good to soft ground, probably unsuited by heavy. *J. W. Hills*

GREEN TURTLE CAY (IRE)   3 b.g. Turtle Island (IRE) 123 – Pinta (IRE)   **57**
(Ahonoora 122) [1998 NR 1999 7d 7.1d 6d⁶ Aug 14] smallish, sturdy gelding: first foal: dam 2-y-o 5f (in Ireland) and 7.5f (Italian listed) winner, also 7f winner in Italy at 3 yrs: modest maiden: has been bandaged behind: sold 1,900 gns. *J. Noseda*

GRENADIER (IRE)   2 b.c. (Feb 9) Sadler's Wells (USA) 132 – Sandhurst God-   **67 p**
dess 103 (Sandhurst Prince 128) [1999 8s⁴ Oct 25] 170,000Y: brother to useful Irish 1996 2-y-o 6f winner Star Profile, closely related to 4-y-o Lady Alexander and half-brother to 1994 5f to 7f winner Lady Davenport (by Contract Law): dam Irish 5f to 7f winner: 9 lengths fourth of 19 to Delius in maiden at Leicester, keeping on steadily: showed short, quick action to post: not sure to stay much beyond 1m: likely to improve. *W. R. Muir*

GREY BIRD (IRE)   2 ro.f. (Apr 12) Prince of Birds (USA) 121 – Ganador 67   **–**
(Weldnaas (USA) 112) [1999 7m 7m Aug 3] 700Y: first foal: dam, maiden, stayed 1¼m: well beaten in seller and maiden. *Martyn Wane*

GREY BUTTONS 4 gr.f. Norton Challenger 111 – Albury Grey (Petong 126) – [1998 –: 8m 9g^6 8.3g 1999 12d 10.1d Jul 1] poor maiden at best. *D. G. Bridgwater*

GREYCOAT BOY 7 gr.g. Pragmatic 115 – Sirdar Girl 69 (Milford 119) [1998 – NR 1999 21.6d^6 Apr 28] tall, angular gelding: fair handicapper at 4 yrs: well held only Flat run of 1999: should stay extreme distances: acts on soft going and on good to firm: normally blinkered. *J. S. King*

GREY COSSACK 2 gr.g. (Apr 29) Kasakov – Royal Rebeka (Grey Desire 115) **65 p** [1999 5s^4 Oct 5] 1,200Y: second foal: dam no sign of ability: well backed and beaten less than a length when fourth of 14 to Poppy's Song in maiden at Catterick, making much of running: should do better. *M. Brittain*

GREY EMINENCE (FR) 2 gr.c. (Apr 19) Indian Ridge 123 – Rahaam (USA) **71 +** 91 (Secreto (USA) 128) [1999 7m^5 Jul 6] 160,000F: tall, sturdy colt: has scope: fifth foal: brother to 3-y-o Cassandra Go and half-brother to 3 winners, including smart 6f (Coventry Stakes) and 1m (in USA) winner Verglas (by Highest Honor) and useful 6f (at 2 yrs) and 1m (in France) winner Persian Secret (by Persian Heights): dam 7f winner who stayed 1¼m: better for race, considerably handled when fifth of 9 to Race Leader in maiden at Newmarket: looked sure to improve. *R. Hannon*

GREYFIELD (IRE) 3 b.g. Persian Bold 123 – Noble Dust (USA) (Dust Com- **82** mander (USA)) [1998 58: 6m 7.3g 7m 8.1m^5 8m^4 7.9g 8d^4 1999 10g^2 9.3g^2 11.7g^2 11.6m^3 11.5f^2 9.7f* 9.9m* 9.7m^2 10.5d^3 10d 10.3d* 9m^3 10.2m^3 10d 10g^6 Oct 11] leggy gelding: fairly useful performer: won minor events at Folkestone and Beverley in July and handicap at Chester in August: stays 1½m: acts on firm and good to soft going: consistent. *M. R. Channon*

GREY FLYER 2 gr.g. (Apr 20) Factual (USA) 108 – Faraway Grey 99 (Absalom **56 +** 128) [1999 a5g^6 5m* 5s 5g^6 a6g^4 a6g^2 Dec 18] half-brother to fairly useful 5f/6f (including at 2 yrs) winner Royal Dream (by Ardkinglass) and 1m winner Mrs Dawson (by Sharrood): dam, 2-y-o 5f winner, stayed 1m: modest performer: won Musselburgh claimer in September: will prove best at 5f/6f: acts on good to firm ground and equitrack. *Mrs L. Stubbs*

GREY KINGDOM 8 gr.g. Grey Desire 115 – Miss Realm 86 (Realm 129) [1998 **85** 86: 8d 6v^4 7s^3 7d^6 8.5m 6s* 7g 6v^3 6g 7f^5 7s* 7g 7g^6 7m^4 7.9g 8m 7s 6s^2 6g 6v 1999 6d 5d 6m 6d* 7f 6m 7.1d^6 7f 7.1d 7f 7d^6 6d* 6d Oct 9] angular, leggy gelding: fairly useful handicapper: won at York in June (same race for third year running) and Ayr (Ladbroke Silver Cup, having been runner-up in 1998) in September: battled on typically gamely to lead final 75 yds when beating Princely Dream by 1½ lengths in 29-runner race at Ayr: effective at 6f to 7.5f: acts on any turf going (though best efforts in 1999 on going softer than good), lightly raced on fibresand: has been heavily bandaged in front: usually ridden by claimer D. Mernagh: usually races up with pace: tough and game. *M. Brittain*

Charles Henry Memorial Handicap, York—Grey Kingdom (third left) completes a hat-trick in the race; Pigeon (spots on cap) is caught in the last stride with Miss Fit (diamond on cap) battling on to dead-heat for third place with Present Chance (blinkers, just behind winner)

Ladbroke (Ayr) Silver Cup (Handicap)—Grey Kingdom goes one better in the race than in 1998; Princely Dream (No.6), Tom Tun (No.7) and Lady Boxer (No.25) fill the frame

GREY MATTER 3 gr.f. Tina's Pet 121 – Phar Lapa 59 (Grundy 137) [1998 –: 5d⁵ 5g 5g 6m 1999 a7g 6.1s⁴ 8d 5.9g a7g Jun 17] quite good-topped filly: poor maiden. *T. H. Caldwell* **36**

GREY PRINCESS (IRE) 3 gr.f. Common Grounds 118 – Miss Goodbody (Castle Keep 121) [1998 88+: 6m* 6m* 6g² 6f 5.3m* 5m² 5.3g* 1999 5.1m 6g³ 6d 5m 5.1m 5f 5.2g Aug 14] lengthy filly: fairly useful handicapper: mostly disappointing after second outing: likely to prove best at 5f/6f: acts on good to firm going: reared stalls fifth start: usually races prominently. *P. W. Harris* **92 d**

GREY PROSPECT 5 b.g. Grey Desire 115 – Nicky Mygirl 46 (Chief Singer 131) [1998 46: 7g 10s² 8s 8g⁵ 8m 1999 a8g 7d 8d⁶ 10g 10d Jul 5] poor maiden: stays 1¼m: acts on soft ground: has hung/found nothing. *M. Brittain* **43**

GREY STRIKE (IRE) 3 gr.g. Magical Strike (USA) 114 – Narrow Band (IRE) (Standaan (FR) 118) [1998 51: 6g 7.5m a6g² a5g⁴ 6m a7g 6d⁶ a6g 1999 a6g a5g⁶ a6g Mar 10] modest maiden: little form in 1999: best at 5f/6f: acts on fibresand and good to soft going: blinkered 3 times. *J. Berry* **–**

GRIEF (IRE) 6 ch.g. Broken Hearted 124 – Crecora (Royal Captive 116) [1998 85: 10v 10d 12m⁵ 1999 12v⁴ 12d 11.9d* 11.8d³ Oct 12] big, strong gelding: fair performer nowadays: first win for 2 years in claimer at Brighton in October: effective at 1¼m/1½m: acts on soft going and on good to firm: wears bandages: usually held up (raced prominently and drifted markedly right final start): successful twice over hurdles in December. *D. R. C. Elsworth* **75**

GRINKOV (IRE) 4 b. or br.g. Soviet Lad (USA) – Tallow Hill (Dunphy 124) [1998 84p: 7d⁴ 8.3m 10g* 10g* 10d⁵ 9.7s* 10s² 1999 10m* 11.9d³ 12m⁴ 10d⁵ 10s⁴ Oct 2] tall gelding: fairly useful handicapper: won 22-runner event at Newbury in April: good fourth of 33 to She's Our Mare in Cambridgeshire at Newmarket final start: effective at 1¼m/1½m: acts on soft and good to firm going: tends to sweat/take good hold: sold 62,000 gns, joined P. Hughes in Ireland. *H. Morrison* **94**

GRINLING GIBBONS 3 ch.c. Woodman (USA) 126 – Saddle Bow 87 (Sadler's Wells (USA) 132) [1998 –: 6m 7g 7d 1999 10m 11.9s Sep 29] close-coupled colt: little form: sold 5,000 gns in October. *J. L. Dunlop* **–**

GRIP FAST 3 b.g. Saddlers' Hall (IRE) 126 – Comic Talent 105 (Pharly (FR) 130) **73**
[1998 49: 8.2s 8s⁵ a8g 1999 11.6m² 14.1m* 14d² Jun 4] good-bodied gelding: fair
form: won handicap at Nottingham in May, despite hanging right: good second of 4
in similar contest at Haydock final outing: subsequently found to have broken a bone
in off-fore but reportedly recovered: should stay 2m: acts on good to firm and good
to soft going: visored first 2 starts in 1999. *I. A. Balding*

GRIZELDA (IRE) 3 ro.f. Bluebird (USA) 125 – Phazania (Tap On Wood 130) **57 d**
[1998 57: 5g 6d 5.1v⁴ 1999 7s² 8f a8g 8.2m 7g 7.1m 10g Sep 20] leggy, sparely-made
filly: modest maiden: no form after reappearance: should stay 1m: form only on
ground softer than good: blinkered fifth/sixth starts: sold 800 gns. *J. D. Bethell*

GROESFAEN LAD 2 b.c. (Mar 28) Casteddu 111 – Curious Feeling (Nishapour **78**
(FR) 125) [1999 5v⁴ 5m² 5.1g⁵ 5.1m⁵ 5.1m⁴ 6.8m² 7f² 7.7d 6g 6d Oct 22] 5,500Y:
workmanlike colt: third foal: half-brother to 4-y-o Tui: dam winning hurdler: fair
maiden: stays 7f: acts on firm ground, possibly not on softer than good: blinkered last
2 starts: often forces pace. *B. Palling*

GROESFAEN LADY (IRE) 3 b.f. Anita's Prince 126 – Out On Her Own **52**
(Superlative 118) [1998 54: 5.1m 6s a5g³ a6g⁴ a5g⁶ 1999 6.1f 5m⁴ a6g³ a5g⁶ 5g
5d⁶ a6f⁴ a6g² a6g⁴ a5g a5g Nov 27] modest maiden: barely stayed 6f: acted on firm
going and fibresand, probably on equitrack: tried visored/blinkered: dead. *B. Palling*

GROOMS GOLD (IRE) 7 ch.g. Groom Dancer (USA) 128 – Gortynia (FR) (My **43**
Swallow 134) [1998 61: a8g² a8g a8g³ 8m² 7.6g 9.9m⁶ 10m⁶ a8.5g 1999 a11g⁴ a10g³ **a52**
a8g⁵ a8.5g 10.5d⁴ 10.1d 11.5g 16f⁶ 10f⁶ a12g³ a12g⁴ a11g³ a12g³ a12g Nov 19]
lengthy gelding: modest on all-weather, poor on turf: stays 1½m: acts on all-weather,
firm and good to soft going: blinkered (ran respectably) ninth outing. *J. Pearce*

GROSVENOR FLYER (IRE) 3 ch.g. Dolphin Street (FR) 125 – Kilcsem Eile **83**
(IRE) (Commanche Run 133) [1998 74: 8g 7s 1999 10g 10.2s³ 12.3m³ 10g⁵ 11.5d²
12m⁶ 11.9d 9g³ 11.6g² 14.6d² 16.5s Nov 6] big, close-coupled gelding: good mover:
fairly useful maiden: several creditable efforts in 1999, leaving A. G. Foster after
penultimate start: stays 14.6f (raced too freely over 2m final outing): acts on soft and
good to firm going: tends to take good hold: often races prominently. *T. D. McCarthy*

GROVEFAIR LAD (IRE) 5 b.g. Silver Kite (USA) 111 – Cienaga (Tarboosh **33**
(USA)) [1998 33, a53: a12s⁶ a12g* a12g* 14.1s a11g⁶ 8.2d 10g⁴ 1999 12.3m⁶ a8g⁶ **a53**
a16.2g a11g* 11.8g³ 12d⁵ 12.3m⁴ a14g Jul 8] close-coupled gelding: has a quick
action: modest performer on all-weather, poor on turf: won claimer at Southwell
in May: needs further than 1m and stays 1½m (well held over 2m): acts on firm
ground and fibresand, probably on soft: tried blinkered/visored: has been bandaged.
S. R. Bowring

GROVE LODGE 2 b.c. (Mar 3) Donna's Red – Shanuke (IRE) 56 (Contract Law **–**
(USA) 108) [1999 6v 6d 6d Nov 4] first foal: dam 1½m winner: well beaten in
claimer/maidens. *S. Woodman*

GRUB STREET 3 b.c. Barathea (IRE) 127 – Broadmara (IRE) 91 (Thatching 131) **–**
[1998 NR 1999 8g⁵ 8.2d Oct 21] 74,000Y: first foal: dam, Irish 2-y-o 1m winner,
out of half-sister to top-class 6f/7f performer Salieri: signs of ability in maiden at
Newcastle on debut: shaped as though all not well next time: sold 4,800 gns.
J. H. M. Gosden

GRUINART (IRE) 2 br.g. (Mar 14) Elbio 125 – Doppio Filo (Vision (USA)) **–**
[1999 6.8m Aug 30] IR 4,400F, 7,000Y: fifth foal: brother to 4-y-o Saligo and
half-brother to 7f (at 2 yrs) and 1m winner Iron Man (by Conquering Hero): dam
unraced: tailed off in maiden at Warwick. *H. Morrison*

GUARD DUTY 2 b.g. (Mar 24) Deploy 131 – Hymne d'Amour (USA) 58 (Dixie- **89**
land Band (USA)) [1999 8s³ 8s³ Nov 6] small gelding: third foal: brother to 3-y-o
Chelsea Barracks: dam, lightly raced on Flat, winning hurdler out of half-sister to
Alzao: fairly useful form in maidens at Bath and Doncaster, taking good hold to post
when third of 18 to Blusienka on latter course: will stay 1½m. *M. P. Tregoning*

GUARDED SECRET 2 ch.c. (Feb 13) Mystiko (USA) 124 – Fen Dance (IRE) **76 p**
82 (Trojan Fen 118) [1999 8.2m³ Sep 13] second foal: dam 7f winner, should have
stayed further: very green, 8 lengths third of 6 to easy winner Sakhee in maiden
at Nottingham, pulling hard and not knocked about once held: should improve.
P. J. Makin

GUDLAGE (USA)   3 b.g. Gulch (USA) – Triple Kiss 106 (Shareef Dancer (USA)   **100**
135) [1998 100p: 7m² 7m* 8s⁵ 1999 7m 10.4d³ 10g⁵ May 22] strong, lengthy
gelding: useful handicapper: ran creditably when third in £17,000 rated stakes won
by Tier Worker at York (tongue tied) and fifth at Lingfield later in month: will
probably prove more effective over 1½m than 1¼m: acts on good to firm and good to
soft going, below best on soft (sweating and edgy). *B. Hanbury*

GUESSTIMATION (USA)   10 b.g. Known Fact (USA) 135 – Best Guess   **60 d**
(USA) (Apalachee (USA) 137) [1998 69, a47+: a12g⁴ a11g 10g³ 10g⁵ 9.2m⁶ 10.1g*
8m³ 10f² 10m* 10.8m⁴ 10g³ 10g 9.1v 1999 8m⁴ 11.1m 10d 10.1g⁵ 10g⁴ 10.5m⁶ 10.5d
10d 12s 10d⁵ Oct 21] good-topped gelding: poor form after reappearance: stays 11f:
acts on any turf going and all-weather: has been blinkered/visored (not for long time):
tends to wander, and is usually held up. *J. Pearce*

GUEST ENVOY (IRE)   4 b.f. Paris House 123 – Peace Mission (Dunbeath (USA)   **38**
127) [1998 52§: 11.8s⁵ 10d 7.5m 7g⁶ a7g 7f 7g 5.9d² 6d* 7m 6m 6g 6v 7s 6s⁵ 1999 6f   **a53**
6.1f 6m 7m⁴ 8g a6g⁴ a7g⁴ a6g³ a8.5g* a7g 7g⁴ a7g a7g⁵ a9.4f Oct 2] sparely-made
filly: modest handicapper on all-weather, poor on turf: won at Wolverhampton in
August: generally below form after: effective at 6f to 8.5f: acts on firm going, good
to soft and fibresand: tried visored: has worn tongue strap: usually held up, and
sometimes looks none too keen: none too consistent. *C. N. Allen*

GUEST ISLAND (IRE)   3 ch.g. Grand Lodge (USA) 125 – Guest Room (IRE)   **87 §**
(Be My Guest (USA) 126) [1998 NR 1999 10.5d⁵ 10d³ 10g⁶ 9.9m* 10d Oct 1] IR
310,000Y: second foal: dam unraced close relative of Saddlers' Hall and half-sister
to Sun Princess: fairly useful performer: won maiden at Goodwood in September:
very slowly away when last of 12 in handicap final outing: bred to stay beyond 1¼m:
yet to race on extremes of going: visored first 3 starts, blinkered last 2: sent to UAE:
has some temperament, and one to treat with caution. *J. H. M. Gosden*

GUEST OF HONOUR   3 gr.f. Petong 126 – Special Guest 67 (Be My Guest   **61**
(USA) 126) [1998 –: 6g 6g 6m 1999 5g* 7s a6g² 6d 6m⁵ Jun 22] rather leggy, angular   **a75**
filly: fair on all-weather, modest on turf: won minor event at Catterick in March: only
all-weather start when head second in handicap at Wolverhampton: effective at 5f/6f:
acts on fibresand, best turf efforts on good ground or firmer. *B. W. Hills*

GUILSBOROUGH   4 br.g. Northern Score (USA) – Super Sisters (AUS) (Call   **58**
Report (USA)) [1998 62: 6m⁶ 7f 6g 7.6m⁵ 7d⁴ 8s 1999 7d² a7g² a7g* 7.1d⁶ a7g² 7g⁶   **a81**
7d a8g⁶ a7g Dec 4] close-coupled, workmanlike gelding: fairly useful on all-weather,
modest on turf: won amateur handicap at Southwell in June: stays 7f: acts on good to
firm going, good to soft and fibresand: visored third 3-y-o start. *D. Morris*

GUILTY SUSPECT   2 b.f. (Apr 30) Reprimand 122 – Island Desert (IRE) 55   **–**
(Green Desert (USA) 127) [1999 5d May 10] 2,000F: third foal: half-sister to 1997
2-y-o 5.8f winner Brandon Frank (by Beveled), later won in Macau: dam placed over
11f and 1½m: last of 10 in minor event at Redcar. *D. Shaw*

GUINEA HUNTER (IRE)   3 b.g. Pips Pride 117 – Preponderance (IRE) 85   **109**
(Cyrano de Bergerac 120) [1998 98+: 6g² 5.9d* 6.1m² 1999 6g⁵ 6g* 6s⁶ 6m³ᵈⁱˢ 6d
6d³ Jul 2] big, lengthy, good sort: usually takes the eye: useful performer: won minor
event at Haydock in May: best effort when third of 15 (placed last due to interference)
to Cubism in listed rated stakes there later in month: only fair third of 5 in minor
event at Haydock final start: subsequently gelded: will prove best up to 7f: acts on
good to firm ground, probably on soft. *T. D. Easterby*

GULF SHAADI   7 b.g. Shaadi (USA) 126 – Ela Meem (USA) (Kris 135) [1998   **90 §**
101: a8.5g⁶ a9.4g* a8.5g 8d 7s² 8.1s 7.9g² 8.1g 8d 8.1g⁴ 8d 7f⁶ 7.9f 8d 8m 9g 8g 8s
a9.4g 1999 8.1g 8m 8m³ 10m⁴ 8f² 7.7m³ 8f² 8f 8m 8s 7g⁶ 7d a8g a8g Dec 10] lengthy
gelding: has a quick action: fairly useful handicapper: well below form final 3 starts:
best at 7f (given test) to 9f: acts on any all-weather/turf: visored once: has had tongue
tied: usually early to post and held up (sometimes starts slowly): unreliable. *Miss
Gay Kelleway*

GULLAND   4 b.c. Unfuwain (USA) 131 – Spin (High Top 131) [1998 113: 8s²   **–**
12.3g* 12m 1999 8m 8d Sep 30] strong, lengthy colt: easy mover: smart performer at
best, winner of Chester Vase in 1998: suffered strain on off-fore suspensory final
3-y-o start, little sign of retaining ability in 1999: stayed 1½m: acted on soft going: to

stand at Forth Mountain Stud, Co. Wexford, Ireland, fee IR£1,000 (Oct 1st, no foal, free return). *G. Wragg*

GUNBOAT DIPLOMACY   4 b. or br.g. Mtoto 134 – Pepper Star (IRE) (Salt   **43** Dome (USA)) [1998 –: 7f 6.9m 6g 1999 12.4m 12m 12g Jun 4] lightly-raced maiden: poor form: will be suited by 1¾m+. *Mrs M. Reveley*

GUNNER SAM   3 ch.g. Emarati (USA) 74 – Minne Love 67 (Homeric 133) [1998   **65** 72: 6g 6g⁶ 6s³ 1999 6g² 7s* 7m 7m 7g a6g⁶ a6g a7g⁶ a6g⁵ Dec 17] strong, lengthy   **a59** gelding: fluent mover: fair on turf, modest on all-weather: won maiden at Catterick in April: left B. Hills for 3,500 gns after running poorly next 3 starts: stays 7f: acts on fibresand and soft going, possibly unsuited by firmer than good: blinkered (ran creditably) final start: has looked a difficult ride. *J. L. Harris*

GUTTERIDGE (IRE)   9 b.g. Roselier (FR) – Buck's Fairy (Master Buck) [1998   **–** NR 1999 a12g⁴ Nov 22] eighth foal: dam, half-sister to 2 winning jumpers, never ran: fair winning jumper: well beaten only start on Flat: dead. *P. D. Evans*

GYMCRAK FIREBIRD (IRE)   2 ch.f. (Jan 24) Petardia 113 – Fiery Song   **53** (Ballad Rock 122) [1999 7.5g 5g 7f⁶ 5m a7g² a7g⁴ a8.5g⁶ Dec 11] 10,000Y: fifth foal: half-sister to 5-y-o Jay-Owe-Two and 8.5f to 1½m winner Contrafire (by Contract Law): dam lightly raced: modest maiden: stays 8.5f: acts on fibresand, raced only on good going or firmer on turf. *G. Holmes*

GYMCRAK FLYER   8 b.m. Aragon 118 – Intellect (Frimley Park 109) [1998   **61** 70: 7d⁶ 8g 7.5g 8d² 7g⁴ 8g⁵ 8.5g⁶ 8m³ 7.5m*ᵈⁱˢ 7.5m 7g² 7.5m 7s 1999 8d 7s 7.7s⁵ 8d 6.9m 8.5m 8.5g 8g* 8m* 8.5g 8s Sep 29] small mare: modest maiden: won at Carlisle in August and Musselburgh in September: effective at 7f/1m: acts on firm and good to soft going, below form only run on fibresand: effective blinkered, visored last 4 starts: usually bandaged behind. *G. Holmes*

GYMCRAK MYSTERY   4 br.f. Ballacashtal (CAN) – Little Unknown (Known   **–** Fact (USA) 135) [1998 –, a50d: a9.4g a6g⁴ 6.9d 7m a6g a6g a7g a11g a11g 1999 a7g a7f⁵ Feb 1] modest performer at best on all-weather: blinkered final start. *G. Holmes*

GYPSY HILL   4 ch.f. Theatrical Charmer 114 – Mirkan Honey 83 (Ballymore   **72** 123) [1998 72: 10d 8s⁴ 8.1g⁵ 8g 9.7f 10.2d 1999 10.8m⁶ 10m* 10d² 10.2g⁴ 10m⁴ 12.1m² 10.2g⁶ Aug 30] rather unfurnished filly: fair handicapper: won 20-runner event at Windsor in May: mostly creditable efforts otherwise: stays 1½m: acts on good to firm and soft ground: sent to USA. *D. Haydn Jones*

GYPSY (IRE)   3 b.g. Distinctly North (USA) 115 – Winscarlet North (Garland   **76** Knight 92) [1998 66: 6g 7d³ 7m⁵ 7d⁴ 7m* 7.5m 8g⁵ 8d⁶ 1999 9.9g² 9g* 11.5g⁴ 10.1m⁵ 10.1m⁶ Jun 26] leggy, sparely-made gelding: fair handicapper: won 6-runner race at Lingfield in May: below par final start: effective at 9f to 11.5f: acts on good to firm and good to soft going. *M. H. Tompkins*

GYPSY MUSIC (IRE)   3 b.f. Treasure Kay 114 – Mighty Special (IRE) (Head   **–** For Heights 125) [1998 55d: 5d 5s³ 5m⁴ 5s⁶ 5g 6m 6m² 7.1m 7g⁶ 7.5m 7g⁶ 1999 6.1s a7g Apr 26] poor maiden: probably stays 7f: acts on soft going and on good to firm: has run creditably visored: has given trouble stalls. *M. Brittain*

GYPSY SINGER (USA)   2 b.f. (Feb 13) Kingmambo (USA) 125 – Zakota (IRE)   **–** (Polish Precedent (USA) 131) [1999 7m 8.1d Sep 15] 90,000F, 180,000Y: strong, lengthy filly: second foal: sister to 3-y-o Nimello: dam, French 9.5f winner, half-sister to Irish 1000 Guineas winner Ensconse: well held in maidens at Newmarket (flashed tail throughout) and Sandown. *P. F. I. Cole*

H

HAAFIZ (IRE)   3 b.c. Green Desert (USA) 127 – Midway Lady (USA) 126   **115** (Alleged (USA) 138) [1998 97p: 6f³ 6m* 6m* 6g⁴ 1999 7g⁴ 8.1m 6m* 6m* 7g⁶ 6m⁵ 6d Oct 15] quite attractive colt: smart performer: won 17-runner handicap at Newmarket (fine effort to beat Munjiz by ½ length) in July and minor event at Yarmouth in August: respectable fifth to Ho Leng in rated stakes at York in

September, best effort after: may well prove best at 6f: acts on good to firm going, possibly not on good to soft: often sweats: usually held up: sent to USA. *B. Hanbury*

HAAMI (USA) 4 b.c. Nashwan (USA) 135 – Oumaldaaya (USA) 111 (Nureyev (USA) 131) [1998 117: 8d^5 12m 8.1m^2 9g^2 9m* 1999 8.5g^2 8.1s 9.9g^4 8m^2 7f^2 8m* 8g^3 Aug 31] well-made colt: fluent mover: smart performer: made all to win Ridgewood Pearl Desmond Stakes at the Curragh in August by 3½ lengths from Castle Quest: good efforts otherwise in 1999 when second in Earl of Sefton Stakes at Newmarket (to Shiva), listed race at Ascot (beaten short head by Wallace) and Beeswing Stakes at Newcastle (to Josr Algarhoud): best at 7f to 9f: acts on firm and good to soft going, probably not soft: has reportedly suffered from wind trouble, and usually tongue tied: blinkered last 3 starts: sent to USA. *J. L. Dunlop* **114**

HABIBI 3 b.f. Alhijaz 122 – Balearica 90 (Bustino 136) [1998 50: a6g^2 6d* a6g^5 a6g^5 5m^6 a5g 1999 a8g a7g^6 a5g Mar 3] lightly-made filly: poor performer: no form in 1999: visored final start: sold 1,100 gns. *Mrs N. Macauley* **–**

HABUB (USA) 3 b. or br.c. Danzig (USA) – Cheval Volant (USA) (Kris S (USA)) [1998 90p: 6.1d^2 6.1g* 1999 6d^5 6g 6g^5 7m Sep 11] strong, good-bodied colt: carries condition: useful performer: best effort when seventh of 9 to Lavery in valuable event at Goodwood second start: off 4 months before final outing: best at 6f: yet to race on extremes of going: races freely: sent to UAE. *J. H. M. Gosden* **98**

HADATH (IRE) 2 br.c. (May 12) Mujtahid (USA) 118 – Al Sylah 118 (Nureyev (USA) 131) [1999 6m^6 7.1m^4 7v^2 7d^5 Oct 12] small, quite attractive colt: has a quick action: eighth foal: half-brother to 3-y-o Mukayed, fairly useful 7f winner Yaqthan (by Kris), later successful around 1m/9f in UAE/USA, and useful 6f/7f winner in Britain and in UAE/1m in USA Laafee (by Machiavellian): dam sprinter: fairly useful maiden: neck second of 6 to Kingsdon in minor event at Salisbury: should stay 1m: had 2 handlers in paddock on debut: joined M. Buckley. *M. P. Tregoning* **81**

HADEQA 3 ch.g. Hadeer 118 – Heavenly Queen (Scottish Reel 123) [1998 67: 5d^5 5v^5 a6g 6m* 6f^3 7d 6m^2 6m^5 7v^3 6s 6m 7v^5 1999 7d^5 7s* 8.2s^6 7.6m^5 8d^4 10m 10.5g^6 8g* 6.9g* 10s 10d Oct 18] small gelding: good mover: fair performer: won at Catterick (handicap) in April, Pontefract (seller) in June and Carlisle (claimer, left P. D. Evans) in July: best at 7f/1m: acts on any going: usually blinkered/visored (not when well held final 2 starts): runs in snatches. *F. Jordan* **78**

HADITOVSKI 3 b.g. Hatim (USA) 121 – Grand Occasion 63 (Great Nephew 126) [1998 –: 7.5m 1999 7d 7.5v Jun 9] stocky gelding: well beaten in minor event and maidens: has given trouble at stalls: won over hurdles in November: sold 10,000 gns later in month and joined J. Mackie. *T. P. Tate* **–**

HADLEIGH (IRE) 3 b.c. Perugino (USA) 84 – Risacca (ITY) (Sir Gaylord) [1998 82: 6g^5 7f^3 6m* 6m 7d^4 1999 7g 6m 8m 7.1s^5 7d Oct 30] leggy, quite attractive colt: fair handicapper: stays 7f: acts on soft and good to firm going: joined H. Collingridge. *R. W. Armstrong* **77**

HAIFAA (IRE) 3 b. or br.f. Doyoun 124 – Mayaasa (USA) 70 (Lyphard (USA) 132) [1998 NR 1999 8m 10s^5 Oct 2] rather leggy, unfurnished filly: third foal: half-sister to useful 6f (at 2 yrs) and 1m winner Hirasah and 4-y-o Zaha (both by Lahib): dam 1¼m winner: well beaten in maidens, pulling hard second start. *R. W. Armstrong* **–**

HAIKAL 2 b.c. (Apr 14) Owington 123 – Magic Milly 60 (Simply Great (FR) 122) [1999 6.1m Sep 13] 70,000Y: fifth foal: closely related to 1998 2-y-o 6f winner Hidden Magic (by Magic Ring), and half-brother to several winners, including 6-y-o Westcourt Magic, 4-y-o Batswing and 6f (at 2 yrs) to 10.8f winner Folly Finesse (by Joligeneration): dam 2-y-o 1m winner: shaped better than position suggests when seventh of 12 in maiden at Nottingham, unable to quicken 2f out and not knocked about: should do better. *N. A. Graham* **– p**

HAIL SHEEVA 2 ch.f. (May 12) Democratic (USA) 101 – Sun Storm (Sunyboy 110) [1999 6f Aug 6] first reported foal: dam tailed off in bumper: well beaten in seller at Lingfield. *Miss K. M. George* **–**

HAIL THE CHIEF 2 b.c. (May 11) Be My Chief (USA) 122 – Jade Pet 90 (Petong 126) [1999 7m Jun 24] second foal: half-brother to 3-y-o Just Wiz (by Efisio): dam, 5f winner, stayed 6f: green, tenth of 15 in maiden at Salisbury: looked likely to improve. *R. Hannon* **–**

HAITHEM (IRE) 2 b.c. (Feb 24) Mtoto 134 – Wukk (IRE) (Glow (USA)) [1999 **72**
6m⁴ 7m² 7d Nov 1] close-coupled colt: first reported foal: dam 5f winner in Dubai:
fair maiden: still looked green when second of 10 to Al Towd at Newcastle: should
stay 1m: well held on good to soft ground: possibly temperamental. *M. Johnston*

HAJR (IRE) 5 b.g. Rainbow Quest (USA) 134 – Dance By Night 84 (Northfields **104**
(USA)) [1998 104: 8d 10.1s 10d⁴ 12m* 12m* 12d 1999 11.9s⁴ 12g³ 12m⁴ May 2]
small, good-bodied gelding: unimpressive mover: useful handicapper: in frame at
Haydock and Newmarket (twice, to Blueprint on second occasion) in 1999: stays
1½m: has form on soft going, but best efforts on good/good to firm: held up: hung
right final start: sold only 1,500 gns, sent to Kuwait. *E. A. L. Dunlop*

HAKEEM (IRE) 4 ch.g. Kefaah (USA) 124 – Masarrah 91 (Formidable (USA) **69**
125) [1998 72: 6s 7d 7g 7g 7.1d 8g 8d 1999 a8f a8g 6.1v 7g 8m* 7.5d 7g 7m² 6m Jun **a–**
19] sturdy, lengthy gelding: fair handicapper: won at Thirsk in May, and good second
there penultimate start: probably needs further than 6f, and stays 1m: acts on soft and
good to firm going. *M. Brittain*

HALBERD (IRE) 3 b.c. Barathea (IRE) 127 – Hanzala (FR) (Akarad (FR) 130) **81**
[1998 NR 1999 7.1d³ 7m* 7m 7s Oct 2] IR 120,000Y: well-made colt: half-brother
to several winners, including 1997 2-y-o 7.5f winner Hanzanar (by Alzao) and 1¼m
winner Hasainiya (by Top Ville), both useful in Ireland: dam French listed 1¼m and
12.5f winner: won maiden at Newmarket in July: disappointing in handicaps last 2
starts: bred to stay beyond 7f: sent to UAE. *J. H. M. Gosden*

HALBERT 10 b.g. Song 132 – Stoneydale 83 (Tickled Pink 114) [1998 –: 6g 5d **–**
5.3m 5.1g 6f 1999 a6g a6g⁵ a6f a6g Jan 28] formerly fair sprint winner: no form since
1996: tried blinkered, visored nowadays. *P. Burgoyne*

HALF MOON BAY 2 b.g. (Feb 25) Cyrano de Bergerac 120 – Tarnside Rosal 68 **90**
(Mummy's Game 120) [1999 5m* 5d⁵ 5g⁵ 5m* 5f* Jul 30] tall, rather unfurnished
gelding: has a quick action: third foal: brother to 3-y-o Pisces Lad and half-brother to
4-y-o Emperor's Gold: dam 2-y-o 5f/6f winner who stayed 7.6f: fairly useful
performer: won minor event at Thirsk in May and nurseries at Doncaster (first run
after being gelded) and Thirsk in July: will prove best at 5f: best efforts on good to
firm/firm going: has been early to post: takes good hold. *T. D. Barron*

HALF TIDE 5 ch.h. Nashwan (USA) 135 – Double River (USA) (Irish River (FR) **55**
131) [1998 52: 6m 7m⁶ 7.1m 8d a10g⁶ a10f² 1999 a10g² a10g² a12g* a12g³ a10g³
Dec 22] modest handicapper: won at Lingfield in February: off 10 months before
final start: stays 1½m: acts on equitrack, probably on fibresand, little form on turf.
P. Mitchell

*Tattersalls Breeders Stakes, the Curragh—Halland Park Girl provides trainer Richard Hannon with his fourth
consecutive win in the race; The Tatling (No.11) and Trinculo (left) make it a British-trained 1–2–3*

HALF TONE 7 gr.h. Touch of Grey 90 – Demilinga (Nishapour (FR) 125) [1998 **62**
68, a71: a6g^2 a7s^5 a5g^3 a6g^2 a6g^3 a5g^2 a5g^6 a5g a5g^3 5m 5m^5 5g 5m^4 5m 5m^4 5g^3 **a71**
5m^3 5d 5m 5m 5m* 5m 5m 5m 5.3g 5.1v* 6s^2 a5g^6 a6g a5g^6 a5f 1999 a6g^4 a5g^3 a6f^2
a5f* a5g^3 a5g^2 a5g^2 a5g^2 a5g^2 6m 5m 5d 5d^4 5g 5m 5.7f 5s^5 5.3d Oct 4] leggy horse:
fair handicapper on all-weather, modest on turf: winner at Lingfield in January, then
good efforts placed there in February/March: below form last 5 starts: effective at 5f/
6f: acts on any turf/all-weather: usually blinkered, visored once: usually gets behind,
and needs strong pace: sometimes edges left: tough. *R. M. Flower*

HALHOO LAMMTARRA 2 ch.c. (May 16) Lammtarra (USA) 134 – Shadha **89 p**
(USA) 77 (Devil's Bag (USA)) [1999 8m^2 Sep 11] fourth foal: half-brother to 3-y-o
Ala Washak: dam, 2-y-o 6f winner in Britain and 1m/9f winner in USA at 4 yrs,
daughter of very smart French 1m to 1½m filly Treizieme: promising 4 lengths
second of 7 to Air Marshall (pair clear) in maiden at Goodwood, looking to be going
best 2f out and not unduly knocked about once clearly held: will stay 1¼m, probably
1½m: sure to improve and win races. *M. R. Channon*

HAL HOO YAROOM 6 b.h. Belmez (USA) 131 – Princess Nawaal (USA) 86 **66**
(Seattle Slew (USA)) [1998 –, a68: a13g^2 a16g^2 a16g^3 a16g^6 16g^3 14m 1999
a16g^4 15.8m^5 17.2g^2 15.8m* 20f^4 17.2m^5 Aug 22] angular horse: good mover: fair
handicapper: won at Bath in June and Warwick (by 6 lengths) in July: probably stays
2½m: acts on firm going and all-weather. *J. R. Jenkins*

HALLAND PARK GIRL (IRE) 2 b.f. (Apr 27) Primo Dominie 121 – Katsina **106**
(USA) 98 (Cox's Ridge (USA)) [1999 6f^4 5m* 6m^2 6m* 5.2m^2 6m* 6g* 6s* Oct 23]
IR 5,000Y: sturdy filly: sixth foal: half-sister to Irish 5f winner Keiko (by Generous)
and 4-y-o Rainstorm: dam 2-y-o 7f winner: useful performer: won minor event at
Lingfield in May, nursery at Ascot and minor event at Salisbury in July, 24-runner
sales race at the Curragh (by 1½ lengths from The Tatling) in August and listed race
at Doncaster (by ¾ length from Seven No Trumps, idling after leading entering final
1f) in October: better at 6f than 5f: acts on soft and good to firm going: genuine and
reliable. *R. Hannon*

Mrs B. Burchett's "Halland Park Girl"

HALLOA 3 ch.f. Wolfhound (USA) 126 – Fairy Fortune 78 (Rainbow Quest – (USA) 134) [1998 88: 6.1g* 6m³ 7f³ 7m⁶ 6g 1999 6g⁶ May 15] quite good-topped, attractive filly: fairly useful performer at 2 yrs: stiff task, well held in listed event, only run of 1999: stays 7f: acts on firm going. *J. R. Fanshawe*

HALMAHERA (IRE) 4 b.g. Petardia 113 – Champagne Girl 67 (Robellino 115 (USA) 127) [1998 104: 5s⁵ 5g 6v⁴ 5d⁴ 6m⁵ 5.1m⁵ 5s 5s⁵ 5m 1999 5s² 6m² 6d² 6m² 6m* 6f² 6g⁴ 6m 6s⁶ Sep 26] rather leggy, good-topped gelding: has a round action: smart performer: had an excellent season, winning listed race at Newcastle in June: runner-up on all starts in handicaps, notably in Wokingham at Royal Ascot (beaten short head by Deep Space) and Stewards' Cup (beaten 1½ lengths by Harmonic Way) at Goodwood: ran creditably in pattern races last 3 starts: best at 6f/stiff 5f: acts on any going: visored (ran poorly) once at 3 yrs: tends to carry head awkwardly, but genuine. *I. A. Balding*

HALMANERROR 9 gr.g. Lochnager 132 – Counter Coup (Busted 134) [1998 71 63, a52: 6g* 6f 6.9m² a7g³ 7g* 8m⁶ 8s⁴ 7g 6g⁴ 6m³ 1999 7s² 6s⁴ 7.1d* 7g⁵ 7.1g* a8.5g 7.1m 7d 7d Oct 29] good-topped gelding: fair handicapper: won at Chepstow in May and June: no form last 4 starts: effective at 6f to 1m: acts on any turf ground and fibresand: sometimes gives trouble at stalls: best covered up in truly-run race. *G. M. McCourt*

HAMARATARA 3 b.f. Sheikh Albadou 128 – Low Hill (Rousillon (USA) 133) 59 [1998 NR 1999 6m⁶ 8.1m 7g⁴ Aug 30] sparely-made filly: fourth foal: half-sister to 4-y-o Aix En Provence and a winner in USA by Ela-Mana-Mou: dam, Italian 2-y-o 5f winner, half-sister to smart winner up to 1½m Beldale Star: form in maidens only at Newmarket on debut: sold 3,000 gns. *A. J. McNae*

HAMBLEDEN 2 b.g. (Mar 2) Vettori (IRE) 119 – Dalu (IRE) 72 (Dancing Brave 65 (USA) 140) [1999 7g 6d Oct 29] 14,000Y: first foal: dam 1m winner: still green, better effort in maidens when ninth of 19 to Pax at Newmarket second start: likely to be suited by 1m+: may do better still. *M. A. Jarvis*

HAMERKOP 4 br.f. Damister (USA) 123 – Royal Scene (NZ) (Sovereign Edition 38 109) [1998 –: 6v 6.1m a8g 9.9d 10f 14.1v 1999 a12g 8d⁵ 10.1g⁶ 14.1m 10.1d⁵ Sep 15] poor maiden: seems to stay 1¼m: tried blinkered. *John Berry*

John Smith's Extra Smooth Chipchase Stakes, Newcastle—a deserved win for Halmahera (left) over Nigrasine

HAMLYN (IRE) 2 gr.c. (Apr 21) Lure (USA) 131 – Passamaquoddy (USA) **68 p**
(Drone) [1999 7s⁵ 6d Oct 29] 60,000F, 55,000Y: good-bodied, attractive colt:
half-brother to several winners, including useful 2-y-o sprinters Tamim (by Topsider)
and Humam (by Nijinsky) and smart French middle-distance filly Papago (by
Sadler's Wells): dam, won up to 9f in USA, sister to dam of Dancing Brave: easily
better effort (fair form) when eighth of 19 to Pax in maiden at Newmarket, though
never a threat: should stay 7f: likely to improve further. *D. R. C. Elsworth*

HAMMER AND SICKLE (IRE) 2 b.c. (Apr 22) Soviet Lad (USA) – Pre- **92**
ponderance (IRE) 85 (Cyrano de Bergerac 120) [1999 5d* 5f*ᵈⁱˢ 5m² 5f* 5m Jun 17]
11,000Y: good-topped, quite attractive colt: has scope: third foal: half-brother to
3-y-o Guinea Hunter and 1997 2-y-o 5f winner Three Star Rated (both by Pips Pride):
dam Irish 2-y-o 5f winner: fairly useful form: first past post in maiden at Ripon in
April and minor events at Doncaster (disqualified for early interference) and Redcar
in May: well below best in Norfolk Stakes at Royal Ascot final start: will stay 6f: acts
on firm and good to soft ground: races prominently. *M. Johnston*

HAMMER AND TONGS (IRE) 3 ch.g. Hamas (IRE) 125§ – Bag Lady 86 (Be **55**
My Guest (USA) 126) [1998 NR 1999 7.6m a7g³ 7m Oct 19] 8,500Y: half-brother to
several winners, including Fresh Look (11f, by Alzao) and Bag of Tricks (1¼m/1½m,
by Chief Singer): dam, ungenuine maiden, stayed 1m: modest maiden: bred to stay
beyond 7f: sold 5,500 gns, sent to Germany. *M. Johnston*

HANA'S PRIDE (IRE) 3 gr.f. Pips Pride 117 – Singhana (IRE) (Mouktar 129) **–**
[1998 –: 5g⁶ 1999 a5g⁶ 5m Jul 21] no form in maidens/claimer. *Mrs A. Duffield*

HAND CRAFT (IRE) 7 b.g. Dancing Dissident (USA) 119 – Fair Flutter (Beldale **66 §**
Flutter (USA) 130) [1998 NR 1999 a8.5g* 8m⁴ 10g* 9.2f* 10.1m⁴ 10m⁵ 8m a8.5g
Oct 16] fair performer: won claimers at Wolverhampton and Brighton in June, and at
Hamilton in July: temperamental displays last 3 starts, rearing stalls final one: stays
1¼m: acts on fibresand, and firm ground: tongue tied: needs treating with caution.
W. G. M. Turner

HANDSOME BEAU 4 ch.g. Handsome Sailor 125 – Chester Belle 42 (Balla- **–**
cashtal (CAN)) [1998 –: 7.1m⁶ 7m⁶ 1999 8.1m a8g Nov 15] little sign of ability,
including in blinkers. *A. Bailey*

HANDSOME DUKE 2 ch.g. (Apr 8) Handsome Sailor 125 – Dutch Girl 78 (Work- **–**
boy 123) [1999 5d a5g 6m 5g May 25] 1,000Y: half-brother to winning sprinter
Golden Flats (by Sonnen Gold): dam 5f winner: no sign of ability. *M. W. Easterby*

HANDSOME RIDGE 5 ch.h. Indian Ridge 123 – Red Rose Garden 87 (Electric **118**
126) [1998 121: 8.1s³ 10d⁵ 8g² 10m⁴ 8d* 9.8d² 8v* 9m 1999 8.5g⁶ 8.1s* 9.9d* 9.3d⁵

Dubai City of Gold Shergar Cup Classic, Goodwood—
an exciting finale to the inaugural running of this day's team event, the Europeans grabbing victory from the
Middle East with Handsome Ridge, Running Stag and Border Arrow (not on picture) providing a 1–2–3

Platt Promotions Ltd's "Handsome Ridge"

10m[5] 8m 9.8v[6] 10g 10s[2] Nov 7] good-bodied, workmanlike horse: smart performer: won Credit Suisse Private Banking Mile at Sandown (by neck from On The Ridge) in April and valuable Dubai City of Gold Shergar Cup Classic at Goodwood (by ½ length from Running Stag) in May: several creditable efforts in pattern company otherwise, including when 1½ lengths second to Elle Danzig in Premio Roma final outing: effective at 1m to 1¼m: acts on good to firm and heavy going: tough and genuine. *J. H. M. Gosden*

HANNAH PARK (IRE)   3 b.f. Lycius (USA) 124 – Wassl This Then (IRE) 74   **67**
(Wassl 125) [1998 –: 7d 1999 8m[4] 8.2s[4] 10.9m[2] 10g 11m[4] 10g[4] 7m 10g 10m[2] 11.5g[3] 11g[6] Oct 14] workmanlike filly: fair maiden: stays 11f: acts on good to firm going, probably on soft: visored final 2 starts (looked none too keen second occasion): inconsistent: sold 10,000 gns, sent to Germany. *M. L. W. Bell*

HANNIBAL LAD   3 ch.g. Rock City 120 – Appealing 49 (Star Appeal 133)   **71**
[1998 64: a6g[5] a7g* 7m[3] 7s[5] 7d 1999 a9.4g* 12.3m 8.1d a8.5g[4] a8.5g[2] Dec 27] leggy gelding: fair performer: won seller at Wolverhampton in April: left P. D. Evans after fourth start: first race for 6 months, ran well in handicap final outing: stays 9.4f: acts on good to firm going and fibresand. *W. M. Brisbourne*

HAPPY CHANGE (GER)   5 ch.h. Surumu (GER) – Happy Gini (USA) (Ginistrelli (USA) 117) [1998 111: 12s 11g[6] 10.5g* 10.5g* 10d* 12d[5] 1999 10d[2] 10.1g*   **113**
Aug 30] ex-German horse: smart performer: better effort in minor events when winning 4-runner race at Epsom, making all by 2½ lengths from Muhib: stays 1½m: acts on soft ground: rejoined Venetia Williams. *M. Johnston*

HAPPY DAYS   4 b.g. Primitive Rising (USA) 113 – Miami Dolphin 85 (Derrylin   **52**
115) [1998 56: 7g 5s 8s 10d[4] 10d[4] 9.3d[6] 7.1g 8.3s 1999 12.3m 17.1v[5] 16m* 14m 17.5d 17.1s Oct 4] smallish, sturdy gelding: modest handicapper: won at Ripon in May: no form after: stays 2m: acts on good to firm and good to soft ground, probably on heavy: blinkered final start at 3 yrs: inconsistent. *D. Moffatt*

472

HAPPY DAYS AGAIN (IRE)   4 b.f. Elbio 125 – Tacheo 64 (Tachypous 128)   **55**
[1998 76: 5g 5f 5.1g 5s 5g⁶ 5.1m⁴ 5m 5g 5g 5d 1999 5s⁴ a5g a5g 5f 5v 5m⁶ 5m 5.2s   **a–**
Oct 22] close-coupled filly: modest handicapper: mostly disappointing in 1999: best
forcing pace at 5f: acts on good to firm, probably on heavy (no form on all-weather):
sometimes blinkered/visored: sold 2,000 gns, sent to Italy. *J. Wharton*

HAPPY DIAMOND (USA)   2 b.c. (Feb 18) Diesis 133 – Urus (USA) (Kris S   **80 +**
(USA)) [1999 5m² 5f* Jul 31] $11,000Y: sturdy, quite attractive colt: first foal: dam
won up to 1¼m in USA, including minor stakes: fairly useful form: landed odds in
maiden at Thirsk in July by 2½ lengths from Scafell, despite still looking green: bred
to be suited by much further than 5f: looked sure to improve further. *M. Johnston*

HAPPY HOOLIGAN   2 b.c. (May 14) Ezzoud (IRE) 126 – Continual (USA)   **74**
(Damascus (USA)) [1999 6d² May 21] half-brother to 3 winners, notably 2000
Guineas winner Shadeed (by Nijinsky): dam, 6f/7f winner in USA, from very good
family: weak in market, shaped well when 1¾ lengths second of 10 to Niagara in
maiden at Ayr, running on well, but not seen again. *M. Johnston*

HAPPY LADY (FR)   3 b.f. Cadeaux Genereux 131 – Siwaayid 97 (Green Desert   **72**
(USA) 127) [1998 –p: 6d 1999 9g 8g³ 7.6m 6m⁵ 6g⁵ Oct 15] angular, unfurnished
filly: fair maiden: sold 5,500 gns in December. *B. W. Hills*

HAPPY LANDING   3 b.f. Minshaanshu Amad (USA) 91§ – Cee Beat § (Bairn   **60 ?**
(USA) 126) [1998 NR 1999 8.3m⁵ 8.3d 7m May 7] second foal: dam temperamental
half-sister to useful winner around 7f Sharpalto: probably flattered in maiden at
Windsor on debut: well held after. *E. A. Wheeler*

HAPPY MEDIUM (IRE)   6 b.g. Fairy King (USA) – Belle Origine (USA)   **–**
(Exclusive Native (USA)) [1998 37: 11.5m 12m a14g* 1999 a16g⁶ a16g Feb 25]
strong gelding: poor handicapper: stays 1¾m: acts on all-weather: has carried head
awkwardly. *G. P. Enright*

HAPPY OMEN   2 b.f. (Apr 3) Warning 136 – Valika 75 (Valiyar 129) [1999 7s   **– p**
Nov 5] compact filly: half-sister to several winners, including 3-y-o Lighthouse and
notably 1993 Middle Park winner First Trump (by Primo Dominie) who stayed 1m:
dam, placed at up to 1½m, half-sister to high-class sprinter Mr Brooks: backward and
green, mid-division behind Golovin in maiden at Doncaster, travelling well to past
halfway and not at all knocked about: sure to do better. *L. M. Cumani*

HAPPY TIMES   2 b.g. (Apr 21) Timeless Times (USA) 99 – Penny Hasset 73   **85 +**
(Lochnager 132) [1999 5d⁵ 6g⁶ 5g* 5m³ 5f⁴ 5g² 6m* Aug 31] 1,300Y: sturdy, lengthy
gelding: third foal: half-brother to 3-y-o Silvano's Express: dam winning sprinter:
won maiden at Musselburgh in July (tended to hang) and nursery at Ripon in August:
stays 6f: acts on firm ground: sent to Macau. *M. W. Easterby*

HAPPY VALENTINE   5 b.h. Rainbow Quest (USA) 134 – Nearctic Flame 111   **108**
(Sadler's Wells (USA) 132) [1998 114: 12f⁸ 12d⁵ 13.3m 10d* 12m 10d 12d 10g
1999 9.9d⁴ May 8] rangy, attractive horse: smart performer at best: 5 lengths fourth
to Handsome Ridge in valuable contest at Goodwood, only run of 1999: likely to
prove best at 1¼m/1½m: acts on firm and good to soft going: has been bandaged
behind: often takes strong hold. *Saeed bin Suroor*

HARD DAYS NIGHT (IRE)   2 b.g. (Apr 10) Mujtahid (USA) 118 – Oiche   **62 d**
Mhaith 74 (Night Shift (USA)) [1999 6d 6m⁵ 6d 6m 7.1m 8d⁶ 7d Oct 21] 18,000Y:
neat gelding: has a quick action: second foal: half-brother to a 5f to 7.5f winner in
Italy by Thatching: dam 6f winner in Ireland: modest maiden: below form last 3
starts, including in nurseries: may prove best at 6f/7f. *M. Blanshard*

HARD LINES (USA)   3 b.g. Silver Hawk (USA) 123 – Arctic Eclipse (USA)   **–**
(Northern Dancer) [1998 87: 6m* 1999 7s Oct 23] rangy gelding: fairly useful form
when winning Newbury maiden at 2 yrs: bandaged, long way below that form in
claimer, only outing in 1999. *I. A. Balding*

HARD TO FIGURE   13 gr.g. Telsmoss 91 – Count On Me 77 (No Mercy 126)   **78**
[1998 88: 6v³ 5.1s³ 6m 7g³ 6g 6g³ 6.1g⁵ 5.7g² 6m 6m 5.7m² 6s³ 6s⁶ 6g⁴ 6.1v 1999
5.7g 5.7f³ 5.7m³ 6f² 6.1m² 5.7m 5.7f Sep 6] workmanlike gelding: grand old
campaigner, winner of Ayr Gold Cup (1993) and 2 listed races: still capable of fair
form in 1999: stayed 7f: acted on any going: usually held up, and was suited by strong
gallop: game and consistent: reportedly retired. *R. J. Hodges*

Vodafone Stewards' Cup (Handicap), Goodwood—Harmonic Way displays a sparkling turn of foot to beat Halmahera (No.2), Literary Society (far side) and Twice As Sharp

HARDWICK LODGE   3 ch.f. Grand Lodge (USA) 125 – Mrs Musgrove (Jal-   –
mood (USA) 126) [1998 –: 7s 1999 8.3m 10d⁶ 12g Sep 15] good-topped filly: well
held in maidens/handicap. *M. J. Ryan*

HARIK   5 ch.g. Persian Bold 123 – Yaqut (USA) 77 (Northern Dancer) [1998 –,
a76: a12g* a12g² a13g* 12s 12d 1999 a12g⁶ a16f³ a16f⁴ a16g* a16g² a16g² 11.6g   **a78**
16s Oct 22] rather leggy gelding: fair handicapper: won at Lingfield in February:
stays 2m: acts on equitrack, no recent form on turf. *G. L. Moore*

HARIYANA (IRE)   3 gr.f. Kahyasi 130 – Harouniya (Siberian Express (USA)   –
125) [1998 66p: 7g 8.2s³ 1999 8.2s⁶ 10.5v Oct 13] rangy, unfurnished filly: good
mover: fair performer at 2 yrs: no form in 1999: will stay beyond 1m: flashes tail:
sold 10,000 gns in December. *L. M. Cumani*

HARKNESS WARRIOR (USA)   5 b.g. Geiger Counter (USA) – Judaire's   **44**
Mint (USA) (Key To The Mint (USA)) [1998 56, a45: 9v 8m 8v⁵ 1999 a12g⁴ a16f
Feb 1] raced in France in 1997, Ireland in 1998: poor form in Britain: probably stays
1½m: tried blinkered/tongue tied: joined H. Alexander. *B. S. Rothwell*

HARLEQUIN DANCER   3 b.g. Distant Relative 128 – Proudfoot (IRE) (Shareef   **92**
Dancer (USA) 135) [1998 NR 1999 8g⁴ 8m⁵ 8g⁴ 8g* 8m³ 8m⁵ 10s 8.2d Oct 21]
40,000Y: strong, good-topped gelding: fourth foal: half-brother to useful 1996
2-y-o 5f winner Head Over Heels (by Pursuit of Love), Italian 7.5f/1m winner
Second Barrage (by Royal Academy) and French 1¼m winner Tiriana (by Common
Grounds): dam Irish 1¾m winner: fairly useful performer: won maiden at Leicester
in May: easily best effort in handicaps after when 2½ lengths third of 32 to Pythios in
Britannia at Royal Ascot: may prove best around 1m: acts on good to firm going, ran
poorly on softer than good: visored final 4 outings: has hung. *J. H. M. Gosden*

HARMONIC (USA)   2 b.f. (Feb 5) Shadeed (USA) 135 – Running Melody 86   **77**
(Rheingold 137) [1999 6m⁶ 7m⁶ 6m² 6g⁴ Oct 11] 32,000Y: quite attractive filly:
half-sister to several winners, including one-time useful 8-y-o Waikiki Beach: dam
1m/1¼m winner: best effort in maidens (fair form) when short-head second of 12 to
Princess Louise at Kempton: stays 7f. *D. R. C. Elsworth*

HARMONIC WAY   4 ch.c. Lion Cavern (USA) 117 – Pineapple 77 (Superlative   **109**
118) [1998 102: 6m⁶ 6f² 6v⁴ 7f³ 6g⁵ 7m 7m⁴ 7g³ 1999 7g 6s² 6f⁴ 6d³ 6m⁵ 6f² 6f*
6.1g² 6m² 6d 6d Oct 15] angular colt: useful handicapper: several creditable efforts
before winning Vodafone Stewards' Cup at Goodwood in August by 1½ lengths from
Halmahera, coming from long way back: good second to Ho Leng in rated stakes at
York on ninth start, best effort after: effective at 6f/7f: acts on any going: has run well
sweating: has worn net muzzle: tongue tied last 5 outings: best held up in strongly-
run race: reliable. *R. Charlton*

HARMONIZE   2 b.f. (Apr 15) Emperor Jones (USA) 119 – Hemline 77 (Sharpo   **45**
132) [1999 6g 5f⁶ 5m⁶ Jul 27] 3,000Y: sixth foal: half-sister to 3-y-o Grand View, 6f

winner Pirates Gold (by Vaigly Great) and fairly useful 11.6f winner Heart of Armor (by Tirol): dam, 7f winner, out of Galtres winner Ma Femme: poor maiden: should stay 6f: raced only on good going or firmer. *Martyn Wane*

HARMONY HALL   5 ch.g. Music Boy 124 – Fleeting Affair 98 (Hotfoot 126)   **73**
[1998 73: 10d² 12f⁴ 10g⁵ 10g* 10m⁵ 10g³ 10.5d⁶ 1999 10.8d 10s 8g² 8.3m 9m² 8.5d²
8g² 8m⁵ 8.1m⁶ 8m 9g⁵ 8m³ 9v 10g⁴ 8d Oct 4] big, lengthy gelding: fair handicapper:
effective at 1m, barely stays 1¾m: acts on firm and good to soft going: visored once
at 4 yrs: has been bandaged: fairly useful novice hurdler. *J. M. Bradley*

HARNAGE (IRE)   4 b.g. Mujadil (USA) 119 – Wilderness 88 (Martinmas 128)   **37**
[1998 –: 8d 8d 7s 1999 10v⁵ 10g 10f 8g Jun 3] close-coupled gelding: poor maiden
handicapper: should stay 1½m. *P. Burgoyne*

HAROLDON (IRE)   10 ch.g. Heraldiste (USA) 121 – Cordon 89 (Morston (FR)   **48**
125) [1998 56, a–: 10g⁶ 10m⁴ 10m* 10g⁶ 11.9f⁵ 10d⁵ 10.8d 9.7m⁶ 10.8g 11.9g
10.2m³ a10g 1999 10d 10m⁴ 10m 11.6m 10g 10.5m 11.7m⁶ 10m³ 8.3m³ 10s⁶ 8.2g⁵
10m 10m² 10.5d³ 12g³ 10.2s 10s⁵ Nov 1] good-bodied gelding: poor performer: ran
more consistently than usual in second half of season: effective at 1¼m to easy 1½m:
acts on firm ground and soft: visored (below form) twice: not an easy ride. *B. Palling*

HARPER'S FERRY (USA)   2 b.c. (Mar 28) Eastern Echo (USA) – Gray And   **57**
Red (USA) (Wolf Power (SAF)) [1999 8m⁴ 8s 10s⁵ Oct 4] fourth foal: half-brother to
3-y-o Fort Sumter: dam won up to 7f in USA: fourth of 7 in maiden at Goodwood on
debut, best effort: visored final start: sold 11,000 gns, sent to USA. *I. A. Balding*

HARPOON LOUIE (USA)   9 b.g. Eskimo (USA) – Twelfth Pleasure (USA)   **61**
(Fappiano (USA)) [1998 68: a9.3g* a9.3g* 8d 8f a10g⁴ 1999 a8g⁴ a8g* a8g a7g*
a7g² a8g⁴ a7g² a8g⁴ Nov 23] big, lengthy gelding: modest nowadays: won claimers
at Lingfield in January and Boitsfort in March: stays 9.3f: acts on good to firm ground
(very likely firm), soft and all-weather. *Alex Vanderhaeghen, Belgium*

HARP PLAYER (IRE)   3 ch.g. Pips Pride 117 – Angelic Sounds (IRE) (The   **60**
Noble Player (USA) 126) [1998 –: 6m 6g 6m 1999 10.8d* 11.6m⁵ a11g 12g 10.5s²   **a–**
11.4m² a12g Jun 17] good-topped gelding: modest handicapper: won at Warwick in
April: mostly creditable efforts on turf after: stays 1½m: acts on good and good to
firm going, well held both starts on fibresand: sold 17,000 gns, joined M. Sowersby.
M. L. W. Bell

HARQUEBUSIER   3 ch.f. Keen 116 – Mainly Me 76 (Huntingdale 132) [1998   **36**
48, a38: 5m⁴ 6f⁶ 5m³ 5m 5.3g³ a6g a5s a7g³ 1999 7g⁶ 6d 6g 7g Sep 14] poor maiden:
stays 7f: acts on good to firm going and fibresand. *J. Pearce*

HARRYANA   2 b.f. (Jan 17) Efisio 120 – Allyana (IRE) 83 (Thatching 131) [1999   **79**
5v² 5.1m* 5g⁵ 5m* 5m 6g 6d 5.2d⁴ 5s² Nov 5] 6,200Y: small, strong filly: good
walker: first foal: dam 5f winner: fair performer: won maiden at Chester in May and
minor event at Redcar in August: creditable efforts in nurseries last 2 starts: likely to
prove best at 5f: acts on soft and good to firm going, probably on heavy: has been
bandaged behind. *M. Johnston*

HARRY TASTERS   2 ch.c. (Apr 8) Efisio 120 – Laugharne (Known Fact (USA)   **66**
135) [1999 6m⁵ 7s Oct 8] good-topped colt: has scope: shows a quick action: closely
related to useful sprinter Power Lake (by Formidable) and half-brother to 3-y-o Top
Tarn and 3 winners, including fairly useful 6f winner Lough Erne (by Never So
Bold): dam, ran once, from family of Bireme and Buoy: burly and green, fifth of 15
in steadily-run maiden at Newbury: well held on soft ground only subsequent outing:
may still do better. *D. R. C. Elsworth*

HARTSTOWN GIRL (IRE)   4 ch.f. Common Grounds 118 – Very Sophis-   **75**
ticated (USA) (Affirmed (USA)) [1998 87: 5.8v 8v³ 8s⁵ 6s* 8.5s 7g² 7d 7s³ 7v⁴ 1999
6m 7g 7m 6d* 7m⁵ 7g Sep 14] IR 18,000Y: sister to a winner in USA and half-sister
to Irish 1m to 1¼m winner Sir True Blue (by Bluebird): dam unraced: fair performer:
won maiden at 3 yrs and claimer in July, both at Ballinrobe: left E. Lynam in Ireland
and ran poorly only outing in Britain: stays 7f: acts on good to firm and heavy
ground: blinkered final 3-y-o start. *J. C. Fox*

HARVEY'S FUTURE   5 b.g. Never So Bold 135 – Orba Gold (USA) 67 (Gold   **48**
Crest (USA) 120) [1998 43, a50: 5.1s² 5v a5g⁵ 6g 5.1g⁴ a5g² 5g⁴ 6d⁶ 6s³ 1999 5.1s*

a5g 6g² 6g Jun 30] rather sparely-made gelding: poor handicapper: won at Bath in April: stays 6f: acts on soft going and fibresand. *P. L. Gilligan*

HARVEY WHITE (IRE)   7 b. or br.g. Petorius 117 – Walkyria (Lord Gayle (USA) 124) [1998 58, a49: 10g³ 8.9g⁶ a9.4g³ a10g 1999 a12g² a13g² a10g³ a12g³ a16g⁵ a16.2g² 9m 10g 10m 10m 10d 10m 10m 10d⁶ Oct 21] rather leggy gelding: poor handicapper: best form at 1¼m to 13f: acts on firm going, soft and all-weather: has hung under pressure. *J. Pearce*   **43 a46**

HASTA LA VISTA   9 b.g. Superlative 118 – Falcon Berry (FR) (Bustino 136) [1998 64, a–: 13.8d⁵ 14.1s 12m⁴ 12m* 13.8d* 16.2g 12g* 14g³ 12g³ 12d³ 15.8m 11.9g 14.1v⁵ 1999 13.8g 12s 12.4m a11g 13.8m⁵ 12g⁶ 12m⁶ 12m⁴ 12g² 12.1m² 14.1g Sep 25] compact gelding: has a round action: modest handicapper: effective at 1½m to 2m: acts on good to firm and heavy going, won on fibresand earlier in career: nearly always blinkered/visored: usually races prominently/leads. *M. W. Easterby*   **50 a–**

HASTATE   4 b.g. Persian Bold 123 – Gisarne (USA) 104 (Diesis 133) [1998 61, a–: 8.3d 9.3m 12m³ 12.5m² a12g 16.4f* 1999 14.1d 15.4v 11.9f 11.8g⁵ 14.1v Sep 29] heavy-bodied gelding: poor handicapper: well below form in 1999, leaving W. Jarvis before final start: stays 2m: acts on firm going, well held on softer than good and all-weather. *J. W. Mullins*   **49**

HASTENBY (IRE)   2 b.f. (Jan 18) Tenby 125 – Dahsala (Top Ville 129) [1999 5.7g² 6g² 7m² 8f* 8f³ 8f⁴ Nov 26] IR 3,000Y: smallish, angular filly: half-sister to several winners, including French 1¼m winner Dhaka (by Lashkari) and German 1½m winner Top Wings (by In The Wings): dam French 11.5f winner: second in maidens at Bath and Salisbury and in Chesham Stakes at Royal Ascot (final start for Mrs P. N. Dutfield, beaten ½ length by Bach): won maiden at Del Mar in September and ran creditably after, including when 2¼ lengths fourth in Grade 3 event at Hollywood in November: will stay beyond 1m: acts on firm going. *R. Frankel, USA*   **97**

HASTY WORDS (IRE)   3 b.f. Polish Patriot (USA) 128 – Park Elect (Ahonoora 122) [1998 98: 5.1m² 5g* 6f 7m 7g³ 7g³ 1999 8m 8m⁶ Jul 7] tall filly: useful performer: in rear in 1000 Guineas at Newmarket on reappearance: creditable sixth of 8 to Ronda in steadily-run Falmouth Stakes there 2 months later: stays 1m: acts on firm going, yet to race on softer than good: bandaged behind final start. *B. W. Hills*   **102**

HATAAB (USA)   2 ch.c. (Jan 30) Woodman (USA) 126 – Miss Mistletoes (IRE) 89 (The Minstrel (CAN) 135) [1999 7m* 7g² 8d* Oct 18] $275,000F: rangy, good-topped colt: has scope: has a fluent, round action: third foal: half-brother to fairly useful Irish 1998 2-y-o 1m winner Faddad (by Irish River): dam, Irish 7f to 9f winner, out of half-sister to Le Moss and Levmoss: useful form: won maiden at Ascot in July and listed event at Pontefract in October, beating Paradise Garden a neck in latter: sweating freely and attended by 2 handlers, 4-length second of 4 to impressive Tough Speed in minor event at Doncaster in between: will stay at least 1¼m: yet to race on extremes of going: free-going sort: should do better still. *E. A. L. Dunlop*   **99 p**

Tote Bookmakers Silver Tankard Stakes, Pontefract—
Hataab (striped cap) keeps on bravely to catch the front-running Paradise Garden, with Bogus Dreams third

HATHNI KHOUND   3 b.f. Reprimand 122 – Rattle Along 80 (Tap On Wood   **53** 130) [1998 –: a7g 1999 a6g a8f 10.8d³ 11.6m 10.2s² a12g a10g Dec 29] modest   **a–** maiden handicapper: stays 10.8f: acts on soft going, well beaten on all-weather. *D. Marks*

HAUNT THE ZOO   4 b.f. Komaite (USA) – Merryhill Maid (IRE) 71 (M Double   **48** M (USA)) [1998 NR 1999 7m³ a6g 7f⁴ 6g 8.3m⁵ 6f⁴ 7g⁶ a6g* a6g* a7g Dec 15]   **a62** tall filly: modest handicapper on all-weather, poor on turf: won at Southwell in November and Lingfield in December: best at 6f: acts on all-weather, raced only on good going or firmer on turf: has been bandaged: reared leaving stalls and pulled hard seventh start. *J. L. Harris*

HAVANA (IRE)   3 b.f. Dolphin Street (FR) 125 – Royaltess (Royal And Regal   **66** (USA)) [1998 NR 1999 8g³ 9m³ Jul 17] IR 28,000Y: quite attractive filly: seventh foal: half-sister to 3 winners, including useful 1989 2-y-o 6f winner Makbul (by Fairy King) and 1m and 1¼m winner Hunt Hill (by High Estate): dam unraced: better effort in maidens when third at Brighton on debut: raced freely next time: changed hands 24,000 gns in between. *J. E. Banks*

HAVEN SUNRISE   3 b.f. Chaddleworth (IRE) 103 – Gaynor Goodman (IRE) 43   **–** (Fayruz 116) [1998 –: 6s 6s 1999 8.3g 6f Jul 24] tailed off in maidens/handicap. *P. R. Hedger*

HAVENT MADE IT YET   2 ch.f. (Feb 15) Be My Guest (USA) 126 – Onika 54   **–** (Great Nephew 126) [1999 6m 8.2s 8.3d Oct 28] sixth living foal: dam 1m winner: soundly beaten in maidens. *J. R. Jenkins*

HAWA AL NASAMAAT (USA)   7 b.g. Houston (USA) – Barrera Miss (USA)   **61 d** (Barrera (USA)) [1998 73d: 6d⁶ 6g 5m 6g 7g 6s 6s a6g⁵ a7g⁶ 1999 a7f³ a7g a6g 6.1s a7g⁶ a6g 8d Oct 20] modest at best nowadays: below form after reappearance: stays 7f: acts on firm going (probably good to soft) and fibresand. *M. Brittain*

HAWAII STORM (FR)   11 b.g. Plugged Nickle (USA) – Slewvindaloo (USA)   **–** (Seattle Slew (USA)) [1998 41, a53d: a8g a7g a8g* a7g⁵ a8g⁵ a8g a8g² a8g⁵ 8d a8g⁵   **a37** 7.1m a8g⁴ 8m a8g⁴ a7g 1999 a8g a8g² a8g⁵ Feb 13] leggy gelding: poor mover: poor performer: blinkered final 2 starts. *D. J. S. ffrench Davis*

HAWALA (IRE)   3 b.f. Warning 136 – Halawa (IRE) (Dancing Brave (USA) 140)   **97** [1998 77p: 6d³ 1999 8.3g* 8.5d⁶ 8f⁴ 9f 7.9g Aug 19] unfurnished filly: useful performer: won maiden at Windsor in May: best effort when strong-finishing fourth in handicap at Newmarket 2 months later: should stay beyond 1m: acts on firm ground: has found little. *Sir Michael Stoute*

HAWKSBILL HENRY (USA)   5 ch.g. Known Fact (USA) 135 – Novel   **53 §** Approach (USA) (Codex (USA)) [1998 53, a64: 10m³ 10m⁶ 9m² 9m² 9.9m⁵ a10g*   **a64 §** 10m⁴ 8.1m³ a10g² 1999 a10g⁴ a10g² a10g² a10g a10g⁴ a10g² 10g⁵ 9m⁵ 11.5f³ 12m a10g a10g Dec 18] angular, useful-looking gelding: modest handicapper: stays 11.5f: acts on equitrack, raced only on good going or firmer on turf: visored/blinkered seventh/eighth outings: has idled, and difficult to win with. *Mrs A. J. Perrett*

HAWKSBURY (IRE)   4 b.g. Simply Great (FR) 122 – Hawksbill Special (IRE)   **75** (Taufan (USA) 119) [1998 77: 7g⁵ 6m² 7m² 6d⁴ 5d 1999 6g⁵ 6m 5m* 5d 5g 5.3m⁵ 6d 6g Oct 11] smallish, strong gelding: first foal: dam unraced daughter of half-sister to high-class sprinter Sayf El Arab: fair handicapper: trained by J. Harley in Ireland at 3 yrs: won strongly-run handicap at Sandown in July: below that form after: effective at 5f/6f: acts on good to firm and good to soft going: blinkered (ran creditably) final 3-y-o start. *N. Hamilton*

HAWRIYAH (USA)   3 b. or br.f. Dayjur (USA) 137 – Lady Cutlass (USA)   **103** (Cutlass (USA)) [1998 82p: 6.1g² 7d⁴ 1999 7g² 7m² 8g* 8m 7m 8d Oct 9] sturdy filly: has a round action: useful performer: won listed race at Goodwood in May by 2 lengths from Balisada: second earlier in Nell Gwyn Stakes (beaten 3 lengths by Valentine Waltz) and minor event, both at Newmarket: well beaten final 3 starts: stayed 1m: best efforts on good ground: usually raced prominently: stud. *J. L. Dunlop*

HAYAAIN   6 b.h. Shirley Heights 130 – Littlefield 100 (Bay Express 132) [1998   **66** NR 1999 12s 15.8m³ Aug 30] fairly useful performer in 1996: better effort on return when third in handicap at Warwick: will stay further than 2m: acts on firm going: useful hurdler. *K. C. Bailey*

HAYDN JAMES (USA)   5 ch.g. Danzig Connection (USA) – Royal Fi Fi (USA)   **57 §**
94 (Conquistador Cielo (USA)) [1998 65: 10m⁴ 10m* 11.6g⁴ 10s⁴ 10g 8.3m 10f*   **a68 §**
10.4g 9.9s a9.4g* a10g 1999 a12g² a12g² a12g³ 10s 10d 9.3m² 10m 10.1d³ 10d
a9.4g² a9.4f³ a12g² a10g⁶ Nov 8] modest handicapper: effective at 9.4f to easy 1½m:
acts on all-weather, firm and good to soft going: occasionally blinkered/visored:
unreliable. *P. W. Harris*

HAYELAH   2 b.f. (Feb 19) Polish Precedent (USA) 131 – Mesaafi (IRE) 85 (Slip   **62**
Anchor 136) [1999 8.3f³ 8.1s⁴ 7.1v Oct 13] second foal: half-sister to a 6f (in
Germany) and 1m (in Italy) winner by Fairy King: dam, 2-y-o 6f winner, bred to stay
1m: modest form when third in maiden at Hamilton on debut: well beaten in the mud
both subsequent outings (edgy and early to post on first of them). *M. Johnston*

HAYMAKER (IRE)   3 b.g. Thatching 131 – Susie Sunshine (IRE) 81 (Waajib   **81**
121) [1998 –: 8d 1999 7v³ 8.3d 8d 8.1g⁶ 7m³ 7.1s² 7g 7s² a8.5g³ a7g* a6g³ Dec 21]   **a76**
quite good-topped gelding: has a round action: fairly useful performer: left I. Balding
after seventh start: won maiden at Southwell in November: best efforts at 6f/7f: acts
on good to firm going, heavy and fibresand. *B. S. Rothwell*

HAYSTACKS (IRE)   3 b.g. Contract Law (USA) 108 – Florissa (FR) (Persepolis   **66**
(FR) 127) [1998 66: 5g⁶ 6v³ 6d⁶ 6g 5d 7m⁴ 7g 6d⁵ 7.1s² 1999 10m⁶ 9.2m³ 10.9m³
12.3m⁶ 10.9s² 10.5d 12.4g⁵ 12g⁶ Sep 15] strong, close-coupled gelding: fair maiden
handicapper: stays 1½m: acts on good to firm and heavy ground: effective visored or
not: has pulled hard: sometimes carries head high and wanders. *D. Moffatt*

HAZARD A GUESS (IRE)   9 ch.g. Digamist (USA) 110 – Guess Who 76 (Be   **–**
My Guest (USA) 126) [1998 –: 10.3g 1999 10m 8.5m Jul 27] tall, leggy gelding:
fairly useful handicapper in 1997: lightly raced and well below that form since: best
at 1¼m to 1½m: acts on any going: usually held up. *D. Nicholls*

HEART   6 ch.m. Cadeaux Genereux 131 – Recipe 66 (Bustino 136) [1998 –:   **87**
12d 1999 11.7s* 12.3m⁴ 12d⁶ 9.9g² 10d* 12d Oct 9] angular mare: fairly useful
handicapper: won at Bath in April and Ayr (well ridden by 7-lb claimer A. Beech) in
September: stiff task final start: stays 1½m: acts on soft and good to firm going: has
had tongue tied: has worn crossed noseband: held up: returned to Miss H. Knight and
won over hurdles in November. *G. A. Butler*

HEARTS ABLAZE   4 b.g. Excelsis 78 – Qualitair Blazer 55 (Blazing Saddles   **–**
(AUS)) [1998 –: a6g a8g a5g⁶ 1999 a7g Jan 18] no form. *K. T. Ivory*

HEARTWOOD (USA)   3 ch.f. Woodman (USA) 126 – Good Example (FR) 110   **77**
(Crystal Glitters (USA) 127) [1998 77: 6m⁴ 7d³ 7v² 1999 8m⁶ 8.3g⁶ 9.9g* 12m 10m
10d⁵ 9.9g⁵ Aug 29] smallish, sturdy filly: good mover: fair performer: won maiden at
Beverley in May: below form after: stays 1¼m: possibly best on good going or softer:
sold 86,000 gns in December. *G. C. Bravery*

HEATHER VALLEY   3 ch.f. Clantime 101 – Sannavally (Sagaro 133) [1998 NR   **–**
1999 6g 6.1g 7d Oct 11] 8,000Y: half-sister to useful 6f to 8.5f winner Croft Valley
(by Crofthall): dam ran once on Flat and over hurdles: well beaten in maidens, racing
too freely final start. *C. F. Wall*

HEATHYARDSBLESSING (IRE)   2 b.c. (Mar 14) Unblest 117 – Noble Nadia   **104**
(Thatching 131) [1999 5.1m 5g* 6.1m⁴ 5.1m³ 5.1m² 5.1m* 6g 5m⁵ 6g² 6.1f* Oct
20] IR 4,300F, IR 9,000Y: quite good-topped colt: first foal: dam unraced: useful
performer: won maiden at Haydock in May, nursery at Chester in July and minor
event at Nottingham (carried head awkwardly and edged left) in October: excellent
neck second of 26 to Khasayl in Two-Year-Old Trophy at Redcar penultimate start:
likely to prove best at 5f/6f: raced only on good going or firmer. *R. Hollinshead*

HEATHYARDS JAKE   3 b.c. Nomination 125 – Safe Bid 44 (Sure Blade (USA)   **53**
130) [1998 72: 5d⁴ 5g² 6.1d³ 5d 5g³ a6g² a7g² a6g a6g⁴ 6v a7g⁵ a8g³ a8.5g⁵ 1999   **a65**
a6f³ a7g² a12g³ a8g⁶ a8g² 8.2d a8g⁴ 8d 8m⁵ 7s⁵ a9.4g² 8m 8m⁴ 8.1d² 8g³ a9.4g² a8.5g
7d a8.5g² a9.4g⁶ a8.5g² a9.4g² a8.5g* Dec 27] small colt: fair on all-weather, modest
on turf: won maiden at Wolverhampton in December: stays 9.4f, probably not 1½m:
acts on good to firm going, good to soft and fibresand: often starts slowly/gets
behind. *R. Hollinshead*

HEATHYARDS LAD (IRE)   2 b.c. (Mar 16) Petardia 113 – Maiden's Dance 65   **63**
(Hotfoot 126) [1999 5g 5s³ 5m⁴ a5g⁵ a6g⁴ 6.1f⁶ 6d³ 6m⁵ 5f⁴ a7g⁴ 6g⁵ 6m⁴ a8.5g* 8d⁶   **a76 +**
8d⁴ Oct 22] 6,500Y: leggy colt: sixth foal: half-brother to 3 winners, including useful

1m/9f winner Dancing Monarch (by Dara Monarch): dam, maiden who stayed 1m, possibly temperamental: fair performer on all-weather, modest on turf: won maiden at Wolverhampton in September: better at 8.5f than shorter: acts on fibresand, firm and soft going: usually comes from behind. *R. Hollinshead*

HEATHYARDS MATE 2 b.g. (Feb 25) Timeless Times (USA) 99 – Quenlyn **76** (Welsh Pageant 132) [1999 5d⁶ 7m 7.5m⁵ 5g⁴ 6.1m¹³ 5m 6m a5g⁵ a7g⁴ a8.5g² a8g² a8g* a8g* a8.5g⁴ a8g³ Dec 21] 8,200Y: fair sort: half-brother to several winners, including 1997 2-y-o 5f winner Tamerin Bay (by Lugana Beach) and 5f (at 2 yrs) to 7f winner Chilibang Bang (by Chilibang): dam ran 3 times at 2 yrs: fair performer: won maiden and nursery at Southwell in November: stays 8.5f: acts on good to firm going, good to soft and fibresand. *R. Hollinshead*

HEATHYARDS TIPPLE (IRE) 3 b.f. Marju (IRE) 127 – Nikki's Groom (Shy **58** Groom (USA)) [1998 59, a49: 5g a6g³ 7g⁴ 7f a7g 7.6g⁴ a8.5g⁶ 1999 6g³ 8d⁶ a6g⁴ a8g⁵ a7g³ 8.2f³ a9.4g⁶ 8m³ 8.1f⁴ 7m⁴ 8.3m⁵ Aug 11] rather leggy filly: modest maiden: stays 1m: acts on fibresand and firm going: blinkered final 2 starts: held up: successful over hurdles in August/September. *D. McCain*

HEAVENLY ABSTONE 4 b.f. Interrex (CAN) – Heavenly Queen (Scottish **42** Reel 123) [1998 65: a6g⁵ a7g² a6g a7g⁶ a5g⁴ a5g³ 5s⁵ a6g³ 6.1m 6.1m 6.1g³ 5g 6s 5d³ 6g⁴ 5m 5d 1999 6f 6.9m 6d 6g 6d⁶ 6g 6m Sep 3] sturdy filly: poor performer nowadays: stays 7f: acts on soft going (ran poorly on firm), good to firm and all-weather: has been bandaged near-fore: usually visored. *P. D. Evans*

HEAVENLY MISS (IRE) 5 b.m. Anita's Prince 126 – Heavenly Blessed (Mon- **59** seigneur (USA) 127) [1998 55§: 5m 5g 5d 6m² 6m 6g⁶ 6m 6m³ 5m³ 6m 5m 5g³ 6s 7d 1999 a6g⁶ a6g⁴ a6g² a5g a6g 6d* a5g* a5g³ 5.1m⁴ 5f 5d⁶ a6g⁵ 6v 5d² 5.1s* 6d a5g⁵ a6g⁴ a5g⁵ a6g Dec 21] modest handicapper: won at Thirsk and Wolverhampton in April and Bath in October: best at 5f/6f: acts on soft and good to firm going and all-weather: blinkered nowadays: usually held up. *D. Shaw*

HEIGHT OF FANTASY (IRE) 3 b.f. Shirley Heights 130 – Persian Fantasy **101** 94 (Persian Bold 123) [1998 72p: 7g 7v² 1999 11.8g³ 14d¹* 16.2m² 16.2m* 16.2m⁶ 16.2g* 18.2s² 17.3g Oct 16] good-bodied filly: useful performer: won maiden at Haydock in June and handicaps at Chepstow in July and Beverley in August: good second of 5 to Little Brave in handicap at Yarmouth penultimate start, though looked less than keen: appeared to break down final outing: stays 2¼m: acts on good to firm and heavy ground: has flashed tail. *J. L. Dunlop*

HELENA JOHN (IRE) 2 b.f. (Apr 27) Perugino (USA) 84 – Deirdre's Music **–** (Advocator) [1999 7.5g 7m Sep 7] tall, unfurnished filly: half-sister to fairly useful Irish 1m winner Trigger Happy John (by Martin John): dam unplaced: last in maidens. *J. L. Eyre*

HELEN ALBADOU (USA) 2 b.f. (Feb 25) Sheikh Albadou 128 – Sister Troy **72 +** (USA) (Far North (CAN) 120) [1999 5g³ Jul 5] 15,000F: sixth foal: close up to a winner in USA and half-sister to 2 others by Fit To Fight and Rahy: dam, sprint winner in USA at 4 yrs, half-sister to smart 1980 2-y-o filly Exclusively Raised: shaped well when 2 lengths third of 15 to Passion Flower in maiden at Windsor, short of room: looked sure to do better. *J. M. P. Eustace*

HELEN'S STARDUST 3 br.f. Ballacashtal (CAN) – Legendary Lady (Repri- **43** mand 122) [1998 52, a44: 6d 6m* 7s a6g⁶ a7g⁴ 1999 8.2m 7.1g 7f⁶ 6d 6g⁶ Aug 24] poor performer: probably stays 7f (raced too freely at 1m): acts on good to firm going and equitrack: has carried head awkwardly. *W. R. Muir*

HELEN'S WEDDING 3 b.f. Minshaanshu Amad (USA) 91§ – Doris Doors 61 **–** (Beveled (USA)) [1998 NR 1999 a6g a9.4g a6g⁴ Feb 2] first foal: dam 5f/6f winner: no sign of ability in maidens/seller. *J. Berry*

HELLO HOLLY 2 b.f. (Feb 18) Lake Coniston (IRE) 131 – Amandine (IRE) **–** (Darshaan 133) [1999 7d 7.7d 8.2s Oct 5] 17,000F, 19,000Y: lengthy filly: second foal: half-sister to 3-y-o Waabl: dam, French 1m winner, out of smart French 5.5f and 1m winner Libertine: well held in maidens. *Mrs A. L. M. King*

HELLO SAILOR 2 ch.f. (Apr 7) Handsome Sailor 125 – Miss Marjorie 50 **–** (Swing Easy (USA) 126) [1999 5g 5m Aug 2] 1,500Y: second foal: dam, 5f (at 2 yrs)/ 6f winner, became unreliable: soundly beaten in northern maidens. *Mrs D. Thomson*

HELLO VEGAS   2 b.c. (Feb 12) First Trump 118 – Meet Again (Lomond (USA) **– p** 128) [1999 8.2d⁶ Oct 21] 18,000Y: fourth foal: half-brother to 4-y-o Cool Vibes and 1¼m seller winner Today Tonite (by Adbass): dam ran once: never-dangerous sixth of 11 in maiden at Nottingham: should do better. *J. H. M. Gosden*

HELVETIUS   3 b.c. In The Wings 128 – Hejraan (USA) 73 (Alydar (USA)) [1998 **101** 74p: 7.6g² 1999 10g⁴ 10.1s³ 10.4s⁵ 11.9f* 12m³ 11.9s³ 12f⁵ 12.5g⁶ 12d Oct 1] tall, leggy colt: useful performer: landed odds in 3-runner maiden at Brighton in May: creditable efforts next 3 starts in listed races at Ascot and Haydock and valuable handicap at Goodwood: stays 1½m: acts on firm and soft ground: blinkered sixth outing: sold 20,000 gns. *C. E. Brittain*

HENBIRD   3 b.f. Henbit (USA) 130 – View Halloa (Al Sirat (USA)) [1998 NR **–** 1999 10d 10f a12g Oct 30] fifth reported foal: dam unraced: no sign of ability, including in seller: blinkered final start. *A. Senior*

HENBURY DANCER   3 br.f. Teamster 114 – Record Flight (Record Token 128) **–** [1998 NR 1999 12v 11.7s Oct 26] second foal: dam, maiden on Flat, winning jumper: well held in maidens. *B. R. Millman*

HENRIETTA HOLMES (IRE)   3 gr.f. Persian Bold 123 – Faakirah (Dragon- **61** ara Palace (USA) 115) [1998 –p: 7m 7m⁵ 6m 1999 8m 8d⁶ 8f 8m³ 10.1g² 10.5m² 11.5g* a10g⁴ a12g⁶ a13g⁵ Dec 10] leggy filly: modest performer: won claimer at Yarmouth (final start for J. Fanshawe) in September: stays easy 13f: acts on good to firm going and equitrack: visored third/fourth starts. *Mrs L. Richards*

HENRY HALL (IRE)   3 b.c. Common Grounds 118 – Sovereign Grace (IRE) **107** 101 (Standaan (FR) 118) [1998 90: 5g* 5f² 5m³ 5d* 5m* 5g⁵ 5f⁴ 5s 1999 5s² 5m 5d² 6m 5m² 5m⁶ 6f 5g 5g 5.6g 5m² 5d 5s Oct 23] leggy colt: has a round action: useful performer: very good second of 15 to Pips Magic in handicap at Ascot fifth start: generally respectable efforts but well held last 2 outings: best form at 5f: acts on firm and soft going: usually held up/tracks pace. *N. Tinkler*

HENRY ISLAND (IRE)   6 ch.g. Sharp Victor (USA) 114 – Monterana 99 (Sallust **84 §** 134) [1998 97: 12s 14m* 12d 14g 12g 16g⁴ 1999 18d³ 16m a12g Nov 24] **a– §** workmanlike gelding: good mover: fairly useful handicapper nowadays: probably stays 2¼m: acts on good to firm and good to soft ground: tends to sweat: seemed to down tools final start, and has been reluctant over hurdles: untrustworthy: joined Mrs A. Bowlby. *M. Pitman*

HENRY THE HAWK   8 b.g. Doulab (USA) 115 – Plum Blossom (USA) (Gallant **51** Romeo (USA)) [1998 53, a39: 5g⁴ a6g a6g 5d³ 5v* 6m² 5f² 5d² a6g 5g 6m⁶ 5m⁵ 6d **a–** 5s⁶ 5d⁵ 1999 5m² 5s⁵ 5m⁵ 6m⁶ 5g 6f⁵ 6f² 6d 6g⁴ Aug 24] small gelding: modest on turf, poor on all-weather: effective at 5f/6f: acts on any turf/all-weather: effective visored/blinkered or not: usually bandaged. *M. Dods*

HERECOMESCHARLIE   3 b.g. Theatrical Charmer 114 – Excavator Lady 65 **–** (Most Secret 119) [1998 NR 1999 12d⁶ 10s⁵ 10m 8m Aug 4] 6,000Y: half-brother to several winners, including fairly useful 5f performer Tuscan Dawn (by Clantime) and 1¼m winner Glenugie (by Insan): dam, 9.4f and 13f winner, also successful over hurdles: well beaten in maidens/handicap: visored final start. *M. G. Meagher*

HERE COMES HERBIE   7 ch.g. Golden Lahab (USA) – Megan's Move 66 **69** (Move Off 112) [1998 –: 18d 1999 21.6d 16s 11.9d 15s³ 16.1m* Jun 24] lengthy gelding: fair handicapper: reportedly finished lame after winning at Newcastle in June: stayed 2m well: probably acted on any going: held up: dead. *W. Storey*

HERE'S TO HOWIE (USA)   5 b.g. Hermitage (USA) – Choice Comment **–** (USA) (Rich Cream (USA)) [1998 NR 1999 a12g Feb 2] tall gelding: modest handicapper in 1997: well held only outing since: stays 1½m: acts on firm ground, good to soft and equitrack. *M. R. Bosley*

HERITAGE PARK (IRE)   2 gr.g. (Apr 22) Paris House 123 – Caradene (IRE) **77** 64 (Ballad Rock 122) [1999 6g³ 7g³ 6m² 5m* 5d⁵ 6m⁶ Sep 10] IR 7,400F, 6,000Y: tall, lengthy gelding: first foal: dam, maiden, half-sister to useful performer up to 1m Regiment: fair performer: won maiden at Sandown in July: not discredited last 2 starts: stays 6f: acts on good to firm going. *R. Hannon*

HERMINIUS (IRE)   4 b.g. Ballad Rock 122 – Scotia Rose (Tap On Wood 130) **–** [1998 78: 8g 7.9g 9s⁴ 1999 10s Mar 29] workmanlike gelding: fair handicapper in

1998: little show only Flat run of 1999: should stay 1¼m: acts on soft going. *G. B. Balding*

HEROIC BLUE (USA) 3 ch.c. Known Fact (USA) 135 – To Act (USA) (Roberto (USA) 131) [1998 NR 1999 6g³ 7m⁵ 6g* 8.5f³ 8.5f⁴ 8f⁴ Oct 1] $52,000Y: compact colt: third foal: half-brother to winners in USA by Broad Brush and Wild Again: dam maiden daughter of US Grade 1 1¼m winner Comedy Act: fairly useful performer: won maiden at Lingfield in June, last outing for J. Noseda: ran well when 1¾ lengths fourth in non-graded race at Santa Anita final start: stays 8.5f: visored/blinkered last 3 appearances: has tended to wander under pressure. *V. Cerin, USA* **80 +**

HEROS FATAL (FR) 5 ch.h. Hero's Honor (USA) – Femme Fatale (FR) (Garde Royale 120) [1998 12.5s⁴ 15.5v 12v³ 12f³ 11.5d³ 12.5g 12.5m* 13s² 12d* 1999 8f⁵ 6m⁴ 10g⁵ 17.3g³ Oct 16] smallish, deep-bodied horse: first foal: dam won up to 2½m in France: useful in France for H. Pantall in 1998, winner of listed race at Toulouse on final start: later sold 520,000 francs: back to somewhere near best on final 5-y-o start (qualified for a mark over much shorter trips) when 1¼ lengths third of 32 to Top Cees in Tote Cesarewitch at Newmarket, staying on from off pace: will stay beyond 17f: probably acts on any turf going: effective in blinkers, though hasn't worn them in Britain: useful hurdler, successful 3 times in November/December. *M. C. Pipe* **89 +**

HER OWN WAY (USA) 2 b.f. (Mar 21) Danzig (USA) – Formidable Lady (USA) (Silver Hawk (USA) 123) [1999 8s⁴ Nov 5] $325,000Y: strong, lengthy filly: fifth foal: sister to a winner in Japan and closely related to useful Irish 6f (at 2 yrs) and 1m winner Sheffield (by Dayjur): dam minor stakes winner at around 1m in USA: weak in market and gone in coat, well-held fourth of 5 to Shouf Al Badou in minor event at Doncaster, travelling well 5f: not sure to stay beyond 1m: will almost certainly prove capable of fair bit better. *J. H. M. Gosden* **64 p**

HERR TRIGGER 8 gr.g. Sharrood (USA) 124 – Four-Legged Friend 101 (Aragon 118) [1998 68, a91: a10g³ a10g* a10g³ a12g⁵ 10g 10f⁴ 10.1f⁶ 12d 10g 1999 a10g a10g a10g⁶ 10m⁵ a10g* 10.3m³ a10g⁴ 10d a10g⁵ Nov 11] leggy gelding: fair on all-weather, modest on turf: won minor event at Lingfield in May: stays 1½m: acts on firm going and equitrack (yet to race on fibresand): wears blinkers/visor: carries head high: has won when sweating/edgy. *Dr J. D. Scargill* **61 a75**

HE'S GOT WINGS (IRE) 6 b.g. In The Wings 128 – Mariella 123 (Sir Gaylord) [1998 NR 1999 a16g* a16g³ a16g 14.1d* 14.1s 16.2d May 8] smallish gelding: has a quick action: modest handicapper: won at Southwell in February and Nottingham in April: below form after: should stay beyond 2m: acts on fibresand, good to firm and good to soft going: blinkered once, effective visored or not. *M. A. Peill* **62**

HETRA HAWK 3 ch.g. Be My Guest (USA) 126 – Silver Ore (FR) 94 (Silver Hawk (USA) 123) [1998 –p: 7m 8d 1999 a8.5g 12d Sep 30] quite good-topped gelding: unimpressive mover: little form. *W. J. Musson* **–**

HETRA HEIGHTS (USA) 4 b.f. Cox's Ridge (USA) – Top Hope 115 (High Top 131) [1998 52: 8.2s 12m² 12g 12g 1999 13.1g 12d 14.1m⁵ Jul 20] strong, leggy filly: modest maiden handicapper: well beaten in 1999: stays 1½m: none too consistent. *W. J. Musson* **–**

HEVER FEVER 4 br.f. Machiavellian (USA) 123 – Wanisa (USA) (Topsider (USA)) [1998 –, a51: a7g⁴ a10g⁵ a8.5g³ a8g⁵ a9.4g² 9.7v a10g⁴ a9.4g 10g 14.1v 1999 10f May 4] modest maiden handicapper: stays 1¼m: acts on all-weather, no form on turf: sent to USA. *T. J. Naughton* **–**

HEVER GOLF GLORY 5 b.g. Efisio 120 – Zaius 94 (Artaius (USA) 129) [1998 87d: a10g⁴ a8.5g⁵ a10g a8g⁶ 8m 8.1d² 8s 8s 8f 8d 8.1d⁶ 7m⁴ 7.9g 8.5m 7s a7g 1999 a7g a8f⁶ a8.5g* a8g a8g⁵ 7g⁶ 8.3m 8.5d a8.5g* a9.4g 8m 9f⁶ a8.5g 8m 8m⁴ a7g a9.4g a8g Dec 18] leggy gelding: fairly useful handicapper on all-weather, modest on turf: won at Wolverhampton in February and May, latter by 12 lengths: mostly well below form after: stays 9f: acts on firm ground, good to soft and all-weather: none too consistent. *C. N. Kellett* **52 d a83 d**

HEVERGOLF PRINCESS (IRE) 4 ch.f. Petardia 113 – High Profile (High Top 131) [1998 58: a7g² a7g* 9.7d³ 8.5m⁵ 8f⁵ 8m 1999 a7g a10g a8g⁶ a8f Feb 1] leggy filly: modest performer at 3 yrs: no show in 1999: unlikely to stay beyond 9.7f: acts on good to soft going and equitrack: blinkered final 2 starts. *T. J. Naughton* **–**

UCB Films Cumberland Plate (Handicap), Carlisle—
a 1–2 for owner Nigel Shields as Hibernate (left) gets the better of Over To You

HEVER GOLF RANGER   4 b.c. Efisio 120 – Bold Green (FR) (Green Dancer   –
(USA) 132) [1998 89: a7g² a7g* 7m⁵ 8s⁴ 7.1d 7m 1999 a7g a6f a7g Feb 15]
close-coupled colt: fairly useful performer in first half of 1998: little form since: best
at 7f/1m: acts on soft ground and equitrack. *T. J. Naughton*

HEVER ROSINA   3 b.f. Efisio 120 – Truly Bold 76 (Bold Lad (IRE) 133) [1998   **63 ?**
62p: 6s⁴ 1999 5m⁵ 5g⁵ 6m* 6g 6m 6.1m 6g Oct 14] modest performer: won maiden
at Redcar in June: below form in handicaps after: likely to prove best at 5f/6f: sold
1,200 gns in December. *J. Berry*

HIBAAT   3 ch.c. Zafonic (USA) 130 – Realisatrice (USA) (Raja Baba (USA))   –
[1998 77p: 7g 1999 8g 7.1d⁵ 7m a6g Dec 13] strong colt: little show in 1999, leaving
little show in 1999, leaving P. Walwyn 2,000 gns after third start. *M. C. Chapman*

HIBERNATE (IRE)   5 ch.g. Lahib (USA) 129 – Ministra (USA) (Deputy Minister   **87**
(CAN)) [1998 NR 1999 a10g² a12g* a12g⁵ 12g⁵ 10.8m² 12s² 11.5m² 12g* 12m*
11.9s 11.9f* 10m⁴ 11.9m 12g² 12m⁴ 12d Oct 14] big, lengthy gelding: fairly useful
performer: won maiden at Lingfield in February and handicaps at Musselburgh and
Carlisle in June and Brighton in July: stays 1½m: acts on equitrack and firm going,
not on softer: genuine front runner. *K. R. Burke*

HIBISCUS (GER)   3 b.c. Law Society (USA) 130 – Hold On (Surumu (GER))   **119**
[1998 8.5v² 7v² 7.8v* 1999 9v* 10.3g² 10s* 11d* 12m⁶ 11g* 12d² Sep 26] first foal:
dam, German 1m and 11f winner, half-sister to smart German middle-distance horse
Hondo Mondo: smart performer: won minor event at Gelsenkirchen in April, listed
races at Dortmund in May and Dresden in June, and Furstenberg-Rennen (by 1¼
lengths from Universus) at Baden-Baden in August: only sixth to Belenus in
Deutsches Derby at Hamburg fifth start but improved effort when running him to a
head in Europa-Preis at Cologne final outing: stays 1½m: raced mainly on good
ground or softer: stays in training. *A. Schutz, Germany*

HI BUDDY   2 br.g. (Apr 26) High Kicker (USA) – Star Thyme (Point North 73)   **61**
[1999 7.1g⁶ 8.3f 8f³ 8v 8d⁴ 7.1g² a8g Nov 30] 2,000Y: first foal: dam poor novice
hurdler: modest maiden: should stay beyond 1m: acts on good to soft ground:
blinkered last 3 starts. *Miss L. A. Perratt*

HICKLETON MELODY   5 b.g. Sizzling Melody 117 – Honest Opinion 68 (Free   –
State 125) [1998 NR 1999 a12g⁵ Jul 9] half-brother to several minor winners,
including 7f/1m winner Hickleton Lady (by Kala Shikari): dam 5f winner at 2 yrs:
poor form in 2 bumpers in June: soundly beaten in seller on Flat debut. *J. Pearce*

HICKORY (IRE)   4 b.g. Fayruz 116 – La Mortola (Bold Lad (IRE) 133) [1998 –:   –
7d 1999 a8g a10g⁶ Mar 2] leggy, useful-looking gelding: fair form first 2 starts at 2
yrs: lightly raced and little show since. *M. J. Haynes*

HIDDEN BRAVE   2 b.c. (Feb 22) Bin Ajwaad (IRE) 119 – Fire Lily (Unfuwain   **90 p**
(USA) 131) [1999 8.2d² Oct 21] 42,000Y: second foal: half-brother to 3-y-o Sari:

dam no form: weak in market, promising 1½ lengths second of 11 to Alva Glen in maiden at Nottingham, never far away: should stay beyond 1m: useful prospect, and looks a sure-fire winner of a similar contest. *M. Johnston*

HIDDEN ENEMY 3 b.c. Meqdaam (USA) – Orchard Bay 47 (Formidable (USA) 125) [1998 NR 1999 8.2d 8.3d⁴ a7g⁶ Nov 19] first foal: dam, 2-y-o 5f winner, daughter of half-sister to Rich Charlie: easily best effort in maidens when fourth at Windsor, slowly away and staying on. *R. Hollinshead* **66**

HIDDEN FORT 2 ch.c. (Feb 7) Mujtahid (USA) 118 – Temple Fortune (USA) 74 (Ziggy's Boy (USA)) [1999 5s⁵ 5m* 5g 5f⁶ 7m 5d Sep 30] 21,000F: robust, stocky colt: second foal: half-brother to a winner abroad by Midyan: dam 5f/6f winner: fairly useful performer: won minor event at Windsor in June: raced mainly at 5f (failed to stay 7f): best efforts on good to firm/firm ground: has been early to post (bolted prior to running poorly third start): races freely. *S. Dow* **82**

HIDDNAH (USA) 2 ch.f. (Mar 5) Affirmed (USA) – L'Extra Honor (USA) (Hero's Honor (USA)) [1999 6g² 7m³ 7f* 8m⁵ Sep 9] $45,000Y: lengthy, unfurnished filly: fifth foal: half-sister to a Grade 3-placed winner at 2 yrs in USA by Gone West: dam, won at 1½m in France at 4 yrs (including listed race), half-sister to very smart 1¼m winner Montelimar: fairly useful form: won maiden at Newcastle in July: creditable fifth of 12 to Teggiano in May Hill Stakes at Doncaster final start, never landing blow: will be well suited by 1¼m/1½m. *M. Johnston* **90**

HI-FALUTIN 3 b.f. Lugana Beach 116 – Hitravelscene (Mansingh (USA) 120) [1998 NR 1999 a8.5g Oct 30] sister to fair winner up to 9.4f Tropical Beach and half-sister to winning sprinter B Grade (by Lucky Wednesday): dam poor plater: well beaten in maiden at Wolverhampton. *A. T. Murphy* **–**

HIGH AND MIGHTY 4 b.g. Shirley Heights 130 – Air Distingue (USA) 120 (Sir Ivor 135) [1998 84: 12d 12.3m* 12.3m² 11.5m³ 14.1g³ 14m* 1999 10m² 12d⁶ 13.9s⁴ 20m* 20f* Jul 28] **106**

Bringing back the success of his colours in major handicaps such as the Chester Cup (in which they have been successful twice), the Royal Hunt Cup, the Cambridgeshire and the Cesarewitch, and restoring former glories in the betting ring, might not have been at the top of the agenda when Robert Sangster took the decision to install John Gosden at Manton in 2000. Nevertheless, if the victories in those respective races of Arapahos, Top Cees, Imperial Ballet, Risen Moon and Nomadic Way are to be repeated, there aren't many trainers better equipped to do it than Gosden, who has few peers at preparing a horse

Ascot Stakes (Handicap), Royal Ascot—useful performances from the first two, Frankie Dettori riding a confident race on High And Mighty to beat Far Cry; 66/1-shot Western Chief (dark cap) is third

Marriott Hotels Goodwood Stakes (Handicap), Goodwood—
High And Mighty completes a staying handicap double, holding off a determined Mutanassib

with a specific target in mind. The Sheikh Mohammed-owned High And Mighty's victory in the Ascot Stakes was Gosden's fifth in a handicap at the Royal meeting since he came from America to train, and left him second only to John Dunlop in handicaps won there in the 'nineties. High And Mighty had been only fourth on his previous outing in a handicap at York in May, but, like his stable-companion Plan-B, who failed to reach a place at the same York meeting then went on to finish second in the Royal Hunt Cup, High And Mighty showed improved form at Ascot. Starting at 10/1 in a traditionally large field, he won very much in the style of a horse that had been primed especially for the big day, confidently ridden and soon on top once taking the lead under two furlongs out, beating Far Cry by a length and a half with Western Chief two and a half lengths further back in third. High And Mighty's Ascot penalty would have left him 8 lb worse off with Far Cry had the pair renewed rivalry in the Northumberland Plate at Newcastle later in the month, but injury ruled him out. The reason for High And Mighty's overnight-stage withdrawal evidently stemmed from Ascot, though he had been prominent in ante-post lists all week. 'After Ascot he came back with a little bit of filling in a joint,' his trainer told the *Racing Post* belatedly. Ante-post backers were given little prior warning either when High And Mighty was withdrawn from the Ebor at York in August. He'd been second favourite with some bookmakers at the time after winning the Marriott Hotels Goodwood Stakes by a length from Mutanassib. Trainers aren't bound to keep the betting public informed, of course, and some are more forthcoming than others, but Gosden's quote about High And Mighty when pressed ('he came back after his last run with a bit of a pulled muscle. It was never the intention to run him at York') did little for the stable's public relations. High And Mighty is the ninth foal of Prix de Diane third Air Distingue and a half-brother to Godolphin's Poule d'Essai des Poulains winner Vettori (by Machiavellian) among several winners. He missed the Cesarewitch due to another injury and is likely to be out of action for some time. He acts on firm and soft going, and was visored on his final four outings, although he seems perfectly genuine. *J. H. M. Gosden*

HIGH BEAUTY   2 br.f. (Apr 9) High Kicker (USA) – Tendresse (IRE) 60 (Tender King 123) [1999 6m 8s 7.7d Sep 21] angular, unfurnished filly: first reported foal: dam 6f (at 2 yrs) to 1¼m winner: little sign of ability. *M. J. Ryan*   –

HIGHBORN (IRE)   10 b. or br.g. Double Schwartz 128 – High State 72 (Free State 125) [1998 96d: 7s 7.1d 10.4g⁶ 10.5g 10.3g 7.9m⁴ 9.3g a8g 8g 8s 9g 8.9g 7s 8d 1999 a8g 9.3m 8m* 8m 8d 7.6m⁶ 8g⁵ 9g 7.9m 8s 8d³ 8.2s⁶ Nov 1] sturdy gelding: **77 d**

only fair handicapper at best in 1999: won at Ripon (well drawn) in May: below form after: stays 1¼m: acts on firm and soft going: has run well sweating/for apprentice. *P. S. Felgate*

HIGHCAL 2 gr.g. (Apr 17) King's Signet (USA) 110 – Guarded Expression 51 **53** (Siberian Express (USA) 125) [1999 6d 7m 7m Aug 4] 7,400Y, resold 12,000Y: second foal: half-brother to 3-y-o Jackie's Baby: dam lightly raced at 2 yrs: modest form in maidens: bred to prove best up to 7f: sold 2,500 gns in November. *D. R. C. Elsworth*

HIGH CAPACITY (IRE) 2 b.f. (Mar 5) Dolphin Street (FR) 125 – Foresta **55 d** Verde (USA) 46 (Green Forest (USA) 134) [1999 5m⁶ 5g³ 6g 7m 7m 6s 8d Nov 1] 18,000F, 13,500Y: second foal: dam maiden: modest maiden at best: well below form last 4 starts, including in blinkers: should stay 7f. *T. D. Easterby*

HIGH CARRY 4 b.f. Forzando 122 – Carn Maire 83 (Northern Prospect (USA)) **62** [1998 84: 6v 5.1g⁶ 5g 7d 5.1g 5g 5.1m 5m 5g⁴ 5m² 5f⁵ 6g 5g 5m² 5g 5s³ 1999 5m 5f 5d 5g 6m⁵ 5s 5m³ 5m³ 5g² 5g⁴ 5d 5g 5g Oct 6] lengthy, good-topped filly: has a rather round action: modest handicapper: effective at 5f/sharp 6f: acts on firm and soft going: reluctant stalls final outing: usually races prominently. *N. Tinkler*

HIGH CHEVIOT 2 b.c. (May 28) Shirley Heights 130 – Cutleaf 81 (Kris 135) **82 +** [1999 7.5m² 8.3f² 8s* 10d Oct 30] 26,000Y: fourth foal: half-brother to 3-y-o Oh So Grand, 7f (at 2 yrs) and 1½m winner Goodwood Lass (by Alzao) and German 11f winner Cheba (by Royal Academy): dam, 10.5f winner, sister to useful middle-distance winners Kenanga and Knifeboard: progressive form in maidens, winning one at Newcastle in September: ran poorly in listed event at Newmarket final outing: should stay at least 1¼m: acts on firm and soft ground. *M. Johnston*

HIGH COURT 2 ch.f. (Feb 15) Unfuwain (USA) 131 – Lady Barrister (Law – Society (USA) 130) [1999 7s 7m Sep 2] seventh foal: half-sister to 3-y-o Affidavit and several winners, including 1994 2-y-o 1m winner Edipo Re (by Slip Anchor) and 1997 2-y-o 6f winner Eloquent (by Polar Falcon), both fairly useful: dam, unraced, from family of Kings Lake and Salmon Leap: well beaten in maidens: sold 4,000 gns. *M. L. W. Bell*

HIGH DOMAIN (IRE) 8 b.g. Dominion Royale 112 – Recline 70 (Wollow 132) – [1998 53d: 5g 5m³ 5g 5g 5g 5.1g⁶ 5m 5.1d 1999 5s 5d 8.2m 6m⁵ 6m 6d 6g Oct 14] sturdy, strong-quartered gelding: good mover: one-time fairly useful sprinter: very much on the downgrade: tried blinkered. *J. L. Spearing*

HIGH ESTEEM 3 b.g. Common Grounds 118 – Whittle Woods Girl 80 (Emarati **61** (USA) 74) [1998 –: 5g.1g⁶ 6g 1999 6.1f⁶ 6g 6m 5f 5d⁴ 5v⁴ 5d Oct 20] big gelding: modest maiden: raced only at 5f/6f: acts on firm and heavy going: sweating and edgy before fifth start. *M. A. Buckley*

HIGH FASHION 3 b.f. Puissance 110 – Superb Fashion (USA) (Topsider – (USA)) [1998 –: 7v 1999 5.9g 5.9m 6.9m 11d Oct 26] no sign of ability. *J. S. Haldane*

HIGHFIELDER (IRE) 3 br.g. Unblest 117 – River Low (IRE) (Lafontaine **52** (USA) 117) [1998 –: 7.6f 6.1d 6g 1999 5g 8d⁴ a8g³ 8g 7f⁶ a8.5g a7g 7g³ a7g a12g⁴ a8g a12g³ a13g a10g⁶ Dec 22] leggy, workmanlike gelding: modest maiden: effective at 7f, probably at 1½m: acts on equitrack (possibly not fibresand), firm and good to soft going: tried blinkered and visored: races prominently. *J. S. Moore*

HIGHFIELD FIZZ 7 b.m. Efisio 120 – Jendor 82 (Condorcet (FR)) [1998 58, **47** a–: 16.1d 16s⁵ 17.1d* 21.6s 16.2m 14.1g² 18s² 16m* 16m 16.1g³ 15.9g⁵ **a–** 16v⁶ 1999 16.1d 17.1v 14g⁶ 16.2d³ 16m* 16m May 26] good-topped mare: has a round action: poor handicapper: won at Musselburgh in May: stays 2¼m: acts on any ground: tends to carry head high, and has reportedly had breathing problems: has been bandaged off-hind. *C. W. Fairhurst*

HIGH HOYLAND 3 b.c. High Estate 127 – Waffling 68 (Lomond (USA) 128) **79** [1998 NR 1999 8g³ 8.5s³ 7f³ 10.1d 8m 8m² 7m² 8.5m⁴ 8s⁵ 8s a7g² 9v Oct 23] 12,000Y: tall, quite good-topped colt: fourth foal: brother to 15f winner High Jinks: dam, maiden who probably stayed 1¼m, granddaughter of 1000 Guineas winner Night Off: fair maiden: mostly creditable efforts, including fifth of 21 in £32,000 handicap at Ascot: below form last 3 starts: effective at 7f to 1¼m: acts on firm and soft going: has carried head high: blinkered final outing: sold 18,500 gns. *R. Hannon*

HIGH KING (IRE)   3 b.c. Fairy King (USA) – Ploy 87 (Posse (USA) 130) [1998   **109**
85p: 8s⁵ 1999 10m* 10g³ 12m 12.3g³ 10m⁴ 9d* 10m⁵ Aug 14] IR 650,000Y: strong,
good-bodied colt: not a good walker: sixth foal: half-brother to smart Italian miler
Poliuto (by Last Tycoon) and 7f to 11f winner Sir Norman Holt (by Ela-Mana-Mou):
dam maiden half-sister to Sun Princess and Saddlers' Hall: useful performer: won
maiden at Leopardstown in April and handicap on same course in August: behind at
Royal Ascot third start: stays 1¼m: acts on good to firm and good to soft ground:
blinkered/tongue tied and made running last 3 starts: reportedly joined M. Kent in
Singapore. *A. P. O'Brien, Ireland*

HIGHLAND BLUE   3 b.f. Never So Bold 135 – Highland Rowena 59 (Royben   **55**
125) [1998 NR 1999 5.1s⁶ 6.1f a7g Jun 5] 5,200, 20,000 2-y-o: first foal: half-
sister to 3 winning sprinters, including useful pair Lord Kintyre (by Makbul) and
Crofters Ceilidh (by Scottish Reel): dam sprinter: form in maidens only on debut at
Nottingham: may prove best up to 7f. *N. P. Littmoden*

HIGHLAND GOLD (IRE)   2 ch.c. (Mar 30) Indian Ridge 123 – Anjuli (North-   **64 p**
fields (USA)) [1999 7d⁶ 7s⁵ Nov 5] IR 32,000Y: big, close-coupled colt: has plenty
of scope: half-brother to several winners, notably high-class 1m/1¼m filly Kooyonga (by Persian Bold): dam unraced half-sister to 2000 Guineas winner Roland
Gardens: still in need of race, better effort when well-held fifth of 20 to Hopeful
Light in maiden at Doncaster: will stay 1m, probably 1¼m: will improve further.
Miss L. A. Perratt

HIGHLAND SPICE (IRE)   3 b.f. Fayruz 116 – Gaelic Song (Mansingh (USA)   **–**
120) [1998 NR 1999 a5g 7s Apr 21] IR 7,500Y: fourth foal: half-sister to 3 winners
abroad, including Swedish sprinter Impelino (by Mac's Imp): dam Irish 7f winner:
showed little in maidens at Southwell (claimer) and Catterick. *Miss L. A. Perratt*

HIGHLY FANCIED   3 b.f. High Kicker (USA) – Angie's Darling (Milford 119)   **51**
[1998 70: 6g³ 5.9m² 6f 6d² 7.1g⁶ 7g² 6s³ 6s⁴ 6s⁴ 1999 12g 7.9s 8.2m 7g⁶ 5.9g⁵ 7g 6m
Sep 24] leggy filly: modest maiden: left S. Kettlewell after sixth start and rejoined
former trainer: effective at 6f (given test) and 7f: acts on soft going, possibly not on
firm. *Miss L. A. Perratt*

HIGHLY PLEASED (USA)   4 b.g. Hansel (USA) – Bint Alfalla (USA) (Nureyev   **70**
(USA) 131) [1998 73: 7m² 8m³ 1999 10m 7m 7m 7d 8d 8.3m⁶ Jun 23] quite
good-topped gelding: fair maiden handicapper: stays 1m: acts on firm ground.
P. Burgoyne

HIGHLY PRIZED   5 b.g. Shirley Heights 130 – On The Tiles (Thatch (USA)   **76**
136) [1998 82: 14.1s² 14m³ 14d 17.2g⁶ 14.1g³ 14.1m* 14m⁴ 16d⁶ 17.2d 1999 14.1m⁵
14m 12m⁴ 14.8m⁴ 14.1m² a16g⁵ a12g⁴ a13g³ Dec 10] strong, deep-girthed gelding:
fair handicapper: should stay 2m: acts on equitrack and good to firm ground,
probably on soft: often races prominently: consistent. *J. S. King*

HIGHLY SOCIABLE   2 b.f. (May 31) Puissance 110 – Come To Tea (IRE) (Be   **56**
My Guest (USA) 126) [1999 6.8m⁵ 6d³ 6.8m 6s Sep 24] 8,000Y: fourth foal: dam,
Irish 2-y-o 7f winner, half-sister to smart filly up to 1¼m in Europe/USA Danish and
high-class chaser Sybillin: modest maiden: should stay 7f: well held on good to firm
ground. *S. A. Brookshaw*

HIGH NOON   4 b.c. Shirley Heights 130 – Hocus 88 (High Top 131) [1998 73d: **–**
9.9m⁴ 12.3s⁶ 10.2g a12g 11.8d 8s² 9g a8.5g a9.4g⁶ a10g⁴ a8.5g* 1999 a8g³ a8g⁴   **a68**
a9.4g* a9.4g* a8g² a9.4g* a9.4g⁴ a8g 9g 9.9v 10d Oct 18] good-bodied colt: fair
handicapper: won 3 times at Wolverhampton in January/February: reportedly lost
action eighth start: left N. Littmoden cheaply and no further action after: seems best at 1m to
1¼m: better form on fibresand than equitrack (best turf form on good to firm going):
held up. *B. J. Llewellyn*

HIGH ON LIFE   5 b.g. Mazilier (USA) 107 – Tina Rosa (Bustino 136) [1998 58d,   **§§**
a–§: 12s 12f 17.2m⁶ 11.9m 11.5f⁵ 13.1m 11.9s³ a12g⁶ a12g 1999 11.5m Jun 19] quite
good-topped gelding: very temperamental maiden: best avoided. *J. Akehurst*

HIGH POLICY (IRE)   3 ch.g. Machiavellian (USA) 123 – Road To The Top 84   **79**
(Shirley Heights 130) [1998 –p: 7d 1999 10m⁶ 12g³ May 21] well-made, good sort:
easily best effort in maidens when third at Catterick final start: stays 1½m: sold
10,000 gns, joined D. Murray Smith. *Sir Michael Stoute*

HIGH PRIORITY (IRE)   6 b.g. Marju (IRE) 127 – Blinding (IRE) (High Top   –
131) [1998 –: 6m 1999 6g 6m Jun 14] fairly useful 2-y-o: lightly raced and no form
after: dead. *J. J. Sheehan*

HIGH PYRENEES   7 b.g. Shirley Heights 130 – Twyla 101 (Habitat 134) [1998   65
NR 1999 13v³ 17.1v Apr 20] sturdy gelding: fair handicapper: very lightly raced on
Flat: stayed 13f: acted on heavy going: dead. *F. Murphy*

HIGH REGARD (JPN)   3 b.c. Nashwan (USA) 135 – Hebba (USA) 80 (Nure-   72
yev (USA) 131) [1998 72: 7m² 7.5d³ 7d² 8m⁶ 7.9g 1999 9.9g a9f⁵ a10f Dec 23]
leggy, sparely-made colt: good mover: fair maiden: trained on reappearance by
M. Johnston: off 7 months and well held after: bred to stay at least 1¼m: acts on good
to firm and good to soft going. *W. D. Mather, UAE*

HIGH-RISE (IRE)   4 b.c. High Estate 127 – High Tern 93 (High Line 125)   122
[1998 130: 10d* 11.5m* 12m* 12m² 12d 1999 a10f 11d² 10g⁶ 12f³ Nov 28]
'Godolphin have shown how they can improve older horses like Swain
and Daylami. Let's hope it can be the same with High-Rise.' Frankie Dettori's
upbeat assessment after High-Rise's good third in the Japan Cup at Tokyo in
November provided relief in a year of almost unmitigated gloom for those
associated with the 1998 Derby winner. High-Rise was the first Derby winner
kept in training as a four-year-old since 1990 winner Quest For Fame (who also
raced as a five-year-old in North America), and only the ninth to race on in
thirty years. We predicted in *Racehorses of 1998* that the enterprise shown
by High-Rise's connections—he was returned to Europe under the Godolphin
banner—would be well rewarded. High-Rise had progressed well as a three-
year-old, winning the Derby on only his fourth racecourse appearance and
finishing a very good second to Swain in the King George VI and Queen
Elizabeth Stakes; the King George was his first defeat, and on his only
subsequent outing he was a close-up seventh in the Prix de l'Arc de Triomphe,
despite being unable to get a clear run in the straight. The first major target
for High-Rise as a four-year-old was the Dubai World Cup over a mile and a
quarter on dirt at Nad Al Sheba in March. He trailed in last after dropping right
out from the home turn and wasn't seen out again until September. High-Rise
had a set-back after the Dubai World Cup but was reported back in full training
for the King George at Ascot in July, only to be side-lined again before that race
with a bruised foot. He clearly wasn't back to his old self when beaten at odds
on by Fantastic Light in the Dubai Arc Trial at Newbury (he reportedly missed
the Arc itself because of the heavy ground) and managed only sixth of thirteen,
pulling hard early on, in the Dubai Champion Stakes at Newmarket in mid-
October. When the Breeders' Cup panel controversially nominated High-Rise
as only third reserve for the Breeders' Cup Turf, High-Rise was re-routed to the
Japan Cup, in which he ran his best race of the year, finishing one and a half
lengths behind the winner Special Week. In that form he should be up to
winning a good contest or two in 2000.

		Shirley Heights	Mill Reef
	High Estate	(b 1975)	Hardiemma
	(b 1986)	Regal Beauty	Princely Native
High-Rise (IRE)		(b or br 1981)	Dennis Belle
(b.c. 1995)		High Line	High Hat
	High Tern	(b 1966)	Time Call
	(gr 1982)	Sunbittern	Sea Hawk II
		(gr 1970)	Pantoufle

The lengthy, good-topped High-Rise, who would get further than a mile
and a half if required, acts on good to soft and firm going. There is only a little
to add to the pedigree details provided in last year's Annual. Zomaradah, who
is a daughter of a half-sister to High-Rise, had another successful season in
1999, winning two more pattern races and finishing third in the Breeders' Cup
Filly & Mare Turf at Gulfstream. High-Rise's year-younger half-brother Gamekeeper (by Mujtahid) failed to live up to the promise of his only two-year-old

start, eventually changing hands for only 7,000 guineas at the Newmarket Autumn Sales. *Saeed bin Suroor*

HIGH SHOT   9 b.g. Darshaan 133 – Nollet (High Top 131) [1998 74: 10g⁵ 9.9m   **67**
10g² 10g 1999 10d a10g² a10g² Dec 18] big gelding: fair handicapper, lightly raced: good second at Lingfield final start: unlikely to stay beyond 1¼m: acts on equitrack: reportedly had breathing problem second start in 1998. *G. L. Moore*

HIGHSPEED (IRE)   7 ch.g. Double Schwartz 128 – High State 72 (Free State   **28**
125) [1998 47d: 8.2d 8g⁵ 7.5m 11.6f 8s 10.8m a11g 1999 a8g a8g a11g⁵ a12f a16f a8g Feb 12] small, lightly-made gelding: bad handicapper: stays 1¼m: acts on firm ground, good to soft and fibresand: tried blinkered. *P. S. Felgate*

HIGH SUN   3 b.c. High Estate 127 – Clyde Goddess (IRE) 92 (Scottish Reel 123)   **68**
[1998 62: 10d⁵ 8v⁵ 8s 1999 10g 8m 8.5m 11f 12m 8g* 7m 7.5g³ 8.5s 7g⁴ 7d* 8d*
Oct 29] heavy-topped colt: fair performer: won claimer at Leicester in August and large-field apprentice handicaps at Doncaster and Newmarket in October: best at 7f/1m: best efforts on good/good to soft going: blinkered (below form) third and fourth starts: tends to be slowly away. *S. Gollings*

HIGH TATRA (IRE)   3 b.g. Polish Patriot (USA) 128 – Bouffant (High Top 131)   **91**
[1998 –p: 7.6f 7g 8g 1999 12g* 12.3d* 12d* 10s* 12.3d³ 12m* 11.9d⁶ 12m 9.9g
10.3g 10m a12f² 11.8d* Oct 11] tall, leggy gelding: fairly useful performer: successful in minor events at Musselburgh, Thirsk and Nottingham and handicaps at Ripon and Thirsk in April/May: returned to form last 2 starts, winning handicap at Leicester on final one: effective at 1¼m/1½m: acts on soft going, good to firm and fibresand: sometimes on edge/pulls hard: sent to USA. *S. P. C. Woods*

HIGH TOPPER (FR)   2 b.c. (May 10) Wolfhound (USA) 126 – Blushing Barada   **56 p**
(USA) 53 (Blushing Groom (FR) 131) [1999 8d Oct 27] second foal: half-brother to 3-y-o Bid Me Welcome: dam, maiden, half-sister to Irish St Leger winner Authaal: weak in market, well-held seventh of 10 to Scotty Guest in maiden at Yarmouth: will be well suited by 1¼m+: should improve. *M. Johnston*

HIGHTORI (FR)   2 b.c. (Mar 21) Vettori (IRE) 119 – High Mecene (Highest   **111 p**
Honor (FR) 124) [1999 7.5s³ 8g* 9v⁵ 9v* 8s* Nov 13] second foal: dam unraced close relation to very smart French miler Kendor: smart performer: won minor events at Longchamp in August and October and Prix Thomas Bryon at Saint-Cloud (held up before leading 1f out) in November, showing much improved form in scoring by 2½ lengths from Crystal d'Ass in last named: should stay beyond 9f: should continue to progress. *P. H. Demercastel, France*

HIGH WALDEN (USA)   2 b.f. (Apr 28) El Gran Senor (USA) 136 – Modena   **98 p**
(USA) (Roberto (USA) 131) [1999 7m⁴ 8m* 7s² Oct 2] good-topped, attractive filly: closely related to Fillies' Mile and Oaks winner Reams of Verse (by Nureyev) and half-sister to several winners, notably high-class middle-distance colt Elmaamul (by Diesis): dam unraced half-sister to smart miler Zaizafon (dam of Zafonic): useful form: landed odds in maiden at Leicester in September: best effort when ½-length second of 12 to Agrippina in listed race at Newmarket (equipped with rope halter), held up after tardy start and staying on strongly: should stay at least 1¼m: fitted with blanket for stalls all starts (refused to enter on intended debut): open to further progress, and should make into a smart filly. *H. R. A. Cecil*

HIGHWAY   5 gr.g. Salse (USA) 128 – Ivory Lane (USA) (Sir Ivor 135) [1998 –:   **38**
8v 9.1d 11.1d⁵ 15s 17.2d 1999 a7g⁵ a8f Jan 29] poor form in 1999: dead. *Denys Smith*

HI GUYS (IRE)   2 ch.f. (Mar 22) Imp Society (USA) – Gorgeous Annie (Hello   **–**
Gorgeous (USA) 128) [1999 7g Aug 12] IR 6,000Y: fourth foal: closely related to a winner in Macau by Mac's Imp and half-sister to 4-y-o Lady of Guadalope and a winner in Italy by Mazaad: dam, second over 7f at 2 yrs in Ireland, half-sister to smart performers up to 1m Darcy's Thatcher and Rasa Penang: well beaten in maiden at Salisbury. *Mrs P. N. Dutfield*

HI-JENNY (IRE)   3 b.f. High Estate 127 – Dream of Jenny 73 (Caerleon (USA)   **56**
132) [1998 37, a42: 5d⁶ a6g³ 7m³ a6g 7m⁵ 6m⁶ 7g 1999 12m* 12g⁴ 11f⁵ 12m² 9.9m⁴
12f 12.4g 10m Aug 30] smallish, quite attractive filly: modest handicapper: made all at Beverley in April: below form final 3 starts: stays 1½m: acts on firm ground: blinkered once: tail flasher, and has wandered: often makes running. *W. Storey*

HILL FARM BLUES   6 b.m. Mon Tresor 113 – Loadplan Lass 63 (Nicholas Bill   **83**
125) [1998 63: 15.9g⁶ 12.1s 16s* 16s 1999 14.1d⁴ 11.7s³ 14.1m³ 14m* 16.2d* 11.9s²
16f⁵ 18.7m⁴ 14d 13.9g 14.6m⁴ 12s 17.3g Oct 16] lengthy, sparely-made mare: fairly
useful handicapper: won at Haydock in May and June: mostly creditable efforts
after, including second in Old Newton Cup on same course: effective at 1½m (given
testing conditions) to 2m: acts on good to firm and soft ground, poor efforts on
fibresand: sometimes slowly away, but has raced genuinely enough of late: joined
Miss S. Baxter. *W. M. Brisbourne*

HILL FARM DANCER   8 ch.m. Gunner B 126 – Loadplan Lass 63 (Nicholas   **37 §**
Bill 125) [1998 53, a–: 12g² 11.8m⁵ 13s² 12d 12g* 12.3m² 12g 12g⁴ 11.7m⁵ a9.4g   **a58 §**
10.8m⁶ a12g 14.1v a12g 1999 a12g⁴ a12g 12.1v a12g* a12g⁴ 12.1m a12g³ a11g²
11.8g⁴ a9.4g 14g³ 12g a14.8g 12.1f a12g⁶ a14g a12g⁵ 12g⁴ a12g a14.8g⁴ a12g a12g³
Dec 27] sparely-made mare: fluent mover: modest performer: won minor event at
Southwell in April: mostly below form after, looking increasingly temperamental:
stays 15f: acts on fibresand, firm and soft going: held up: often slowly away, and has
refused to race: not one to trust. *W. M. Brisbourne*

HILLINSKI (IRE)   5 b.g. Danehill (USA) 126 – Llangollen (IRE) 87 (Caerleon   **–**
(USA) 132) [1998 –: 6g 7.1d 7.5d 5g 11.9d 6.9d 1999 a7g a8.5g 10.8m 16m May 22]
of little account. *M. Mullineaux*

HILL MAGIC   4 br.g. Magic Ring (IRE) 115 – Stock Hill Lass 87 (Air Trooper   **102 d**
115) [1998 96: 6v⁵ 6d² 6m* 6m* 6f 6d 6f⁶ 8f 1999 6g* 6g 6s 6m 5s⁵ Oct 2] close-coupled,
useful-looking gelding: useful performer: won minor event at Kempton in April by
1¾ lengths from Brave Edge: well below this form after: best at 6f: acts on firm and
good to soft ground: has run well sweating: sold 29,000 gns. *D. R. C. Elsworth*

HILLSIDE ROSE (IRE)   4 b.f. Danehill (USA) 126 – Miss Belgravia (USA)   **–**
(Smarten (USA)) [1998 68: 8m 8d³ 7.8d 7v² 1999 10.2d a12g Oct 13] 32,000Y:
close-coupled, rather leggy filly: fifth foal: half-sister to French 1m winner Non
Mais (by High Estate) and French 1994 2-y-o 1¼m winner Tirolean Belle (by Tirol):
dam lightly-raced sister to champion Canadian filly Street Ballet: fair maiden for
C. O'Brien in Ireland at 3 yrs: well beaten both starts in Britain (left R. Frost after
reappearance): stays 1m: acts on good to firm and heavy ground. *A. T. Murphy*

HILL STORM (IRE)   3 b.g. Mukaddamah (USA) 125 – Brockley Hill Lass   **57**
(IRE) (Alzao (USA) 117) [1998 57: 6m 6m 6m⁶ 7g 1999 a10g⁶ a12g⁴ a12g Sep 4]
modest maiden: seems to stay 1½m. *K. McAuliffe*

HILLSWICK   8 ch.g. Norwick (USA) 125 – Quite Lucky 69 (Precipice Wood   **43**
123) [1998 43: 17.2m² 1999 16d 18m² 17.2m² 16g³ Aug 9] angular gelding: poor
handicapper: stays 2¼m: acts on firm and soft going: successful over hurdles in
August. *J. S. King*

HILLTOP   3 b.f. Absalom 128 – Just Irene 50 (Sagaro 133) [1998 NR 1999 6m 5d⁶   **45**
5g 6s⁴ 5.2s Oct 22] small, sturdy filly: half-sister to fairly useful 1990 2-y-o 5f winner
Dale Hill Daisy (by Mummy's Game): dam 1¼m seller winner: poor maiden: may
prove best at 5f. *R. Guest*

HILLTOP WARNING   2 b.c. (Apr 26) Reprimand 122 – Just Irene 50 (Sagaro   **79**
133) [1999 6m² 6s² 6d³ Oct 20] smallish, useful-looking colt: closely related to fairly
useful 1990 2-y-o 5f winner Dale Hill Daisy (by Mummy's Game): dam 1¼m seller
winner: fair maiden: placed all starts, bit below form of first 2 efforts when third at
Newcastle on final one: will be well suited by 7f+. *S. P. C. Woods*

HILLZAH (USA)   11 ch.g. Blushing Groom (FR) 131 – Glamour Girl (ARG)   **49**
(Mysolo 120) [1998 53, a56: a16g a16g* a16.2g⁵ 21.6s 13.8d³ a14g⁴ 14.1g
13.8s⁵ 16v⁴ a14g a14.8s⁴ a14.8g³ 1999 a16g a14.8g³ a16g⁵ a14g² 12.3m⁵ 12.1m May
6] workmanlike gelding: poor mover: poor performer: creditable fifth in selling
handicap at Ripon penultimate start: best at 1½m to around 2m: acts on any turf going
and fibresand (unraced on equitrack): sometimes hangs markedly. *R. Bastiman*

HILTONS EXECUTIVE (IRE)   5 b.m. Petorius 117 – Theatral (Orchestra   **51**
118) [1998 58: a5g³ a5g³ a5g² a5g² a5g* 5s⁵ 5s 5f* 5g² 5g² 5d⁵ 5m 5m 5v a6g* a6g⁶
a6g* 1999 a6g a5g 6d 7s⁶ 5m⁶ 6g 5m 7g⁴ 5m a5g⁵ 6.1m a7f Oct 2] leggy mare:
modest handicapper: effective at 5f and probably stays 7f: acts on firm ground, soft
and fibresand (unraced on equitrack): seems effective blinkered/visored or not: has
pulled hard and hung off bridle. *E. J. Alston*

HI MUJTAHID (IRE) 5 ch.g. Mujtahid (USA) 118 – High Tern 93 (High Line   **38**
125) [1998 43: a6g a8g 5.9s 5g 7g 7g 6g 10.3g 9.9m 8.3s 8.2s a6g a7g a8.5g*
1999 a9.4g⁶ a8g a7g a6g a8.5g⁵ a8.5g a8.5g³ 10.1d 10m 8.1m Aug 5] lengthy,
good-quartered gelding: poor handicapper: stays 8.5f: acts on good to firm going,
soft and fibresand: used to be effective in blinkers: inconsistent. *Mrs H. L. Walton*

HINDI 3 b.g. Indian Ridge 123 – Tootsiepop (USA) (Robellino (USA) 127) [1998   **74 ?**
NR 1999 8.2s 8.3d 8m⁴ 10.4g⁵ 8.3d⁶ Nov 4] 35,000Y: sixth foal: half-brother to
champion 1997 German 2-y-o El Maimoun (by Royal Academy), winner at 5f to 1m:
dam, won once in USA, half-sister to Gimcrack winner Splendent: form only when
fourth in maiden at Newcastle (probably flattered): stays 1m: retained 12,000 gns
after penultimate start. *N. A. Graham*

HI NICKY 3 ch.f. High Kicker (USA) – Sharp Top 62 (Sharpo 132) [1998 72:   **84 ?**
6m* 1999 6m⁴ 8d⁶ 7d 7m³ 7.1g Jul 2] tall filly: fairly useful performer: appeared to
run well in minor event and listed race (probably flattered) first 2 starts: should prove
better at 1m than shorter. *M. J. Ryan*

HINT OF MAGIC 2 b.c. (Apr 2) Magic Ring (IRE) 115 – Thames Glow 69   **73**
(Kalaglow 132) [1999 8s⁵ 10s² Oct 4] 8,500F, 7,000Y: third foal: half-brother to
3-y-o Coral Beach and Italian sprint winner Reve Indien (by Indian Ridge): dam 7f
winner who should have stayed beyond 1m: fair form in maidens at Goodwood and
Pontefract, carrying head awkwardly both times: will stay 1½m. *J. G. Portman*

HISHMAH 3 b.f. Nashwan (USA) 135 – Na-Ayim (IRE) 68 (Shirley Heights 130)   **79**
[1998 79: 6f⁴ 7s⁶ 7.5m² 1999 10.5s 8g⁴ 7d² 7m 7.6m* Jul 9] tall, lengthy filly: fair
performer: won maiden at Chester in July: races freely, and may prove best around
1m: acts on soft and good to firm going: flashes tail: sent to USA. *E. A. L. Dunlop*

HISTORIC (IRE) 3 b.c. Sadler's Wells (USA) 132 – Urjwan (USA) 98 (Seattle   **90**
Slew (USA)) [1998 NR 1999 12v⁴ 11.9v² 12s² Nov 2] IR 62,000Y: sixth foal:
half-brother to 3 winners, including stayer Jiyush (by Generous) and fairly
useful 1996 2-y-o 7f winner Bareeq (by Nashwan), later successful in USA: dam, 1m
winner from 2 starts, daughter of Kentucky Oaks winner White Star Line: fairly
useful maiden: second at Haydock and Catterick (short-headed after tough tussle):
will stay at least 1¾m: capable of winning a race. *W. J. Haggas*

HOH DEAR (IRE) 2 b.f. (Feb 8) Sri Pekan (USA) 117 – Miss Kristin (IRE) 89   **106**
(Alzao (USA) 117) [1999 5g* 5.2d³ 6m* 6m² 8f* 8.5f⁶ 8f* Nov 18] IR 30,000Y:
smallish, good-topped filly: first foal: dam Irish 7f winner, including at 2 yrs:
progressive form: won maiden at Newmarket in April and listed race there in June:
ran well when 1¼ lengths second of 12 to Torgau in Cherry Hinton Stakes on same
course (final outing for M. Bell): won Canadian Grade 3 event (2nd division) at
Woodbine in September and allowance race at Churchill Downs in November: stays
1m: acts on firm going. *T. Amoss, USA*

HOH DISCOVERY (IRE) 2 ch.g. (Mar 2) Emarati (USA) 74 – Sabonis (USA)   **83**
68 (The Minstrel (CAN) 135) [1999 5.2m² 5v*ᵈⁱˢ 5g² May 10] 27,000Y: strong,
well-made gelding: fifth foal: half-brother to 4-y-o Premium Quest: dam 2-y-o 6f
winner: fairly useful form: first past post in maiden at Leicester in April (later
disqualified after failing dope test): good second in Windsor minor event only
subsequent outing: dead. *I. A. Balding*

HOH EXPLORER (IRE) 5 ch.g. Shahrastani (USA) 135 – Heart's Harmony   **–**
(Blushing Groom (FR) 131) [1998 –: 12.1v 13.8d 16v 1999 15.8s Oct 5] modest
hurdler but no form on Flat: tried blinkered. *D. W. Barker*

HOH GEM 3 b.c. Be My Chief (USA) 122 – Jennies' Gem (Sayf El Arab (USA)   **–**
127) [1998 NR 1999 6g 6d 7m 10s Sep 29] 4,200Y: fourth foal: brother to 5f winner
(at 2 yrs here, and in Denmark) Hit Or Miss and half-brother to 5f winner Miss Hit
(by Efisio): dam won 3 times at 5f at 2 yrs: well held in maidens/handicap: left Gay
Kelleway after debut. *B. R. Millman*

HOH HOH SEVEN (IRE) 3 b.g. College Chapel 122 – Fighting Run (Runnett   **75 §**
125) [1998 NR 1999 6d⁶ 7f⁴ 6.8s⁵ 8f³ 7.6m 8m⁵ 8.1d⁶ 9g⁵ 8m 10s Oct 2] 35,000Y:
lengthy, workmanlike gelding: eighth foal: half-brother to 3 winners, including 7.6f
winner Croire (by Lomond) and a winner up to 9f in Germany by Royal Academy:
dam, lightly raced, from family of Braashee, Bassenthwaite and Hadeer: fair maiden:

left I. Balding after fourth start: stays 1m: acts on firm going: visored final start: has an awkward head carriage and looks none too resolute. *N. E. Berry*

HOH NAVIGATOR (IRE)   4 ch.g. Common Grounds 118 – Flying Diva 100   **58 d**
(Chief Singer 131) [1998 77: 6m² 6m 6m³ 8m⁴ 7.1g⁴ 6.1g 7s² 7s a7g² a7g 1999 a8g⁶
a7g³ 7v 8m 7.1d 8g⁶ 8m⁶ 8.1m Jul 9] strong, lengthy gelding: modest maiden at best
in 1999: below form after second start: best form at 6f/7f: acts on fibresand and good
to firm going, possibly on soft: seems effective visored/blinkered or not: none too
reliable. *D. J. S. ffrench Davis*

HOH NO   3 b.g. Efisio 120 – Primetta (Precocious 126) [1998 78: 6m 6g 6m 7.9g³   **88**
8m* 7.9g³ 1999 10g² 10m* 12m 10m 9.9f⁴ 9m 10.3m 10.1m Oct 19] tall gelding:
fairly useful performer: justified favouritism in minor event at Nottingham in May:
at least respectable efforts in competitive handicaps next 4 starts: best around 1¼m:
acts on firm going: usually held up: sold 26,000 gns, joined P. Nicholls. *M. L. W. Bell*

HOH STEAMER (IRE)   3 gr.g. Perugino (USA) 84 – Dane's Lane (IRE) (Dane-   **94**
hill (USA) 126) [1998 94p: 5d 5s⁶ 6d⁴ 7g 7.3m* 7f* 8m* 7.3g² 1999 8.1m⁴ 8m* 8m
7f⁵ 9g Oct 17] good-topped gelding: fairly useful performer: won minor event at
Ascot in June: at least respectable efforts otherwise in Britain: left M. Bell, then last
of 8 in Grade 2 race at Belmont in October: stays 1m well: acts on firm going.
C. Clement, USA

HOLDING COURT   2 b.c. (Feb 17) Hernando (FR) 127 – Indian Love Song 68   **98**
(Be My Guest (USA) 126) [1999 7.1m⁶ 7d² 8.1v* 8s Oct 23] tall colt: has scope:
shows knee action: seventh foal: half-brother to 3 winners, notably 5-y-o Tomba and
4-y-o Adjutant: dam maiden who stayed 1½m: useful form: best effort when making
all in 4-runner minor event at Haydock in October by 6 lengths from Cover Up,
carrying head rather high: well-held eighth of 9 in Racing Post Trophy at Doncaster
later in month: will stay 1¼m: acts on heavy ground. *B. J. Meehan*

HO LENG (IRE)   4 ch.g. Statoblest 120 – Indigo Blue (IRE) 56 (Bluebird (USA)   **112**
125) [1998 112: 7g⁴ 7d 7f* 6s 6m⁴ 7v 1999 7.9d 7m⁴ 7f 7m² 7m 6m² 6m* 6d 6.1g
6s⁵ 8g³ Oct 16] leggy, lengthy gelding: smart performer on his day: won 11-runner
rated stakes at York in September by a head from Harmonic Way: also ran well when
placed at Newmarket in handicaps in July and October and in listed race (3 lengths
second to Arkadian Hero) in between: effective at 6f to 1m: acts on firm going, below
form on softer than good: none too consistent. *Miss L. A. Perratt*

HOLLOWAY MELODY   6 ch.m. Cree Song 99 – Holloway Wonder 93 (Swing   **49**
Easy (USA) 126) [1998 53, a46: a9.4g⁶ a8g³ a7g² a8g a7g⁵ a9.4g⁵ a8g 7s 6d⁶ a8g³   **a–**
10g a7g³ 8s a8g³ 8g* 8.1g* a8.5g⁴ 8m⁶ a7g⁴ 8d⁴ a7g 1999 7s³ Apr 1] workmanlike
mare: poor performer: third in seller at Leicester, only run of 1999: stays 1m: acts on
fibresand, firm and soft going: effective blinkered or not. *B. A. McMahon*

HOLLY BLUE   3 ch.f. Bluebird (USA) 125 – Nettle 106 (Kris 135) [1998 74: 7g⁴   **107**
7m⁵ 7d⁶ 1999 10m 8g* 8m* 8m⁶ 8.1d⁴ 7m² 7d² 8g Oct 16] rangy, useful-looking
filly: useful handicapper: well ridden by R. Hughes to win at Bath and Ascot (listed
rated stakes by head from Ma-Arif) in June: good efforts when runner-up at
Newmarket after, beaten neck by Family Man on second occasion: finds 7f barely
sufficient test, and stays 1m: yet to race on extremes of going: wears crossed
noseband: held up. *R. Charlton*

HOLME FARM BOY (IRE)   3 b.g. River Falls 113 – Lady Conchita (IRE)   **–**
(Whistling Deer 117) [1998 NR 1999 8m 10g⁴ 13.8m³ 12.4g 14.1m Aug 28] 3,500
2-y-o: first foal: dam well beaten in 2 Irish bumpers: well beaten in maidens/
handicaps. *G. M. Moore*

HOLY SMOKE   4 b.f. Statoblest 120 – Native Flair 87 (Be My Native (USA)   **72**
122) [1998 71: a7g² 8.3v³ a8g² 8m 8d* 8.5m 8d⁵ 8.2s 8s* a8g* 1999 a8g* a9.4g   **a83**
10.3d⁴ 8v⁴ 8.5d a8g 8s Nov 6] leggy filly: fairly useful handicapper on all-weather,
fair on turf: won amateur event at Southwell in January and ladies race at Doncaster
in March: well below form on return from 5-month absence last 2 starts: stays 1¼m:
acts on fibresand, probably on good firm and heavy ground. *J. L. Eyre*

HOME COUNTIES (IRE)   10 ch.g. Ela-Mana-Mou 132 – Safe Home 94   **61**
(Home Guard (USA) 129) [1998 NR 1999 12g⁵ 17.5d² 14s³ 13.9d² Oct 9] lengthy
gelding: modest handicapper now: creditable efforts last 3 starts: stays 17.5f: acts on

good to firm and soft ground: used to be visored on occasions, including for only win on Flat: tongue tied. *J. Hetherton*

HOME FORCE 2 b.g. (Feb 18) Chaddleworth (IRE) 103 – Breed Reference (Reference Point 139) [1999 8s⁴ 7s Sep 29] 4,000F, 5,500Y: third foal: brother to 3-y-o Breeds Hill and half-brother to 4-y-o Jocasta: dam placed in France from 1¼m to 14.5f: much better effort in maidens (modest form) when fourth of 12 to Beat Hollow at Yarmouth: should stay 1¼m. *C. F. Wall* **64**

HOME OFFICE 3 b.c. Danehill (USA) 126 – Liaison (USA) (Blushing Groom (FR) 131) [1998 75: 8d³ 8m² 8m 1999 10.2s³ 11.9v⁴ Oct 13] strong, well-made colt: has scope: fairly useful maiden: best effort at Bath on belated reappearance: stays 1¼m, probably not 1½m: carried head high final start: sold 82,000 gns. *Mrs A. J. Perrett* **85**

HOMESTEAD 5 ch.g. Indian Ridge 123 – Bertrade 75 (Homeboy 114) [1998 49: a8g³ a10g⁴ a8g⁵ a10g⁴ a10g 1999 a8g² a10g⁵ a8g⁴ a8g² a7g⁶ 8.3m² 10v* 10v* 10d⁴ a9.4g* a9.4g³ 10g⁵ 10m⁵ 10.1m² 10s⁴ 10.2g 9v 10d⁶ a12g* Nov 19] close-coupled gelding: unimpressive mover: fair handicapper on turf, modest on all-weather: successful at Pontefract and Leicester in April, Wolverhampton in May and South-well in November: stays 1½m: probably acts on any turf ground/all-weather: blinkered penultimate start. *R. Hannon* **77 a59 +**

HONEST BORDERER 4 b.g. Selkirk (USA) 129 – Tell No Lies 96 (High Line 125) [1998 87: 8.2s² 9.9d³ 8f 8m⁴ 9m* 10.1g 1999 10m³ 10m⁵ 10m 8m 8m³ 8d⁶ Oct 14] tall, leggy, rather sparely-made gelding: fairly useful performer at best: good efforts in handicap on reappearance and in minor event and handicap final 2 starts: stays 1¼m: acts on soft and good to firm going: blinkered final 2 starts: has been bandaged in front. *J. L. Dunlop* **86**

HONEST VILLAIN (USA) 2 b.g. (Mar 1) St Jovite (USA) 135 – Villandry (USA) 113 (Lyphard's Wish (FR) 124) [1999 5m³ 6s 6m May 29] leggy, unfurnished gelding: third foal: dam smart French 1¼m/1½m performer, later successful in USA: failed to improve on encouraging third of 11 in maiden at Carlisle on debut: bred to be well suited by 1m+. *P. D. Evans* **62**

HONESTY FAIR 2 b.f. (Jan 31) Reprimand 122 – Truthful Image 90 (Reesh 117) [1999 5g³ 5m⁶ 6m 6d Oct 15] 13,000Y: sparely-made filly: unimpressive mover: first foal: dam 5f (including at 2 yrs)/6f winner: fair maiden: easily best effort when close eighth of 20 to Magic of Love in sales race at Newmarket on final start: not bred to stay much beyond 6f: acts on good to soft going. *J. A. Glover* **70**

HONEY DANCE (FR) 4 b.f. Fabulous Dancer (USA) 124 – Honey River (GER) (River River (FR) 117) [1998 8g 10m 11.5v⁶ 9s 8v 1999 8f Jul 12] fourth reported foal: half-sister to French 1992 2-y-o 7f winner Honey Flutter (by Beldale Flutter): dam French 9.5f winner: well beaten in France at 3 yrs for F. Bellenger: soundly beaten in Brighton seller (blinkered, slowly away). *M. C. Pipe* **–**

HONEY GUEST (IRE) 3 ch.f. Roi Danzig (USA) – Kuwah (IRE) 77 (Be My Guest (USA) 126) [1998 NR 1999 8g 10.2m 10m 7.7d Sep 21] 28,000Y: workman-like filly: first foal: dam Irish 1½m winner: no show in maidens: blinkered second start: sent to Italy. *G. G. Margarson* **–**

HONEY HOUSE (IRE) 3 gr.f. Paris House 123 – Heather Honey (Insan (USA) 119) [1998 NR 1999 8.3d a7g Nov 19] first foal: dam unraced: well beaten in maidens. *A. W. Carroll* **–**

HONG KONG 2 b.g. (Feb 25) Sri Pekan (USA) 117 – Sheryl Lynn (Miller's Mate 116) [1999 5m⁴ 5m 5f 7.5g 7m 8m² Sep 7] 12,500Y: workmanlike gelding: second foal: half-brother to a 1¼m winner in Italy by Be My Guest: dam, German 1m winner, daughter of half-sister to smart winner up to 1¼m Satin Wood: poor maiden: blinkered, good second of 18 in selling nursery at Leicester final start: will stay at least 1¼m: raced only on good going or firmer: has had tongue tied. *M. W. Easterby* **47**

HONOURABLE CHIEF 2 b.c. (Mar 8) Be My Chief (USA) 122 – Magic Orb 81 (Primo Dominie 121) [1999 6.1g Sep 25] 2,000Y: second foal: dam, 5f winner (including at 2 yrs), out of sister to smart sprinter Jester: 50/1, soon off bridle when ninth of 12 in maiden at Nottingham: should do better. *K. Mahdi* **54 p**

HOPEFUL HENRY 3 ch.g. Cadeaux Genereux 131 – Fernlea (USA) (Sir Ivor 135) [1998 NR 1999 a6g Nov 23] 48,000Y, 3,000 2-y-o: second foal: dam, lightly-raced Irish sprint maiden, second in listed race: weak 10/1-shot, tailed off in maiden at Lingfield. *G. L. Moore* –

HOPEFUL LIGHT 2 b.c. (Feb 3) Warning 136 – Hope (IRE) (Dancing Brave (USA) 140) [1999 7s* Nov 5] smallish, stocky colt: first foal: dam once-raced sister to Irish Oaks winner Wemyss Bight: coltish and very green, won 20-runner maiden at Doncaster by 2½ lengths from Love Divine, good headway to lead 1f out and kept up to his work: wore rope halter and blanket for stalls entry: should stay 1¼m: almost certainly a useful colt in the making. *J. H. M. Gosden* 90 p

HOPEFUL STAR (IRE) 4 ch.g. Pips Pride 117 – Mijouter (IRE) (Coquelin (USA) 121) [1998 57: a7g³ a9.4g a6g* a7g⁵ 6m 7m⁶ 7m 7s 10v a10g 1999 a7g 7f 7f 6m 6m⁶ 7m 6d 5.3m⁶ 8m⁶ Sep 1] leggy, sparely-made gelding: poor mover: plater: well held in 1999, leaving Gay Kelleway after fourth start: stays 7f: acts on equitrack (well held on fibresand) and good to firm ground: blinkered (stiff tasks) last 2 outings: has had tongue tied: inconsistent. *Jamie Poulton* 43

HOPE SPRINGS 2 b.f. (Apr 12) Makbul 104 – Sorcha (IRE) (Shernazar 131) [1999 6.8m⁶ 7d a8.5g 5g Oct 14] 4,000Y: leggy, workmanlike filly: fourth foal: half-sister to 6f and (in Denmark) 7f winner Castle Governor (by Governor General): dam, lightly raced in 2 bumpers, half-sister to smart sprinter Fire Dome: no sign of ability. *R. Hollinshead* –

HOPPIT 4 b.f. Rock Hopper 124 – Pellinora (USA) (King Pellinore (USA) 127) [1998 –: 8g a8g⁶ 8.2g 12m 9m 11.9m a10g 1999 a12g a13g a11g a16g Feb 11] smallish filly: no form, including in sellers. *P. Howling* –

HORATIA (IRE) 3 b.f. Machiavellian (USA) 123 – Ahead 113 (Shirley Heights 130) [1998 NR 1999 9g³ 10g² 10.4m² 10.2s* 10d² 12f³ Nov 13] well-made filly: fourth foal: half-sister to smart 1m/9f performer Smart Alec (by Diesis) and French winner around 11f Winsome (by Kris): dam, 1½m winner, half-sister to top-class miler Markofdistinction: useful form: won maiden at Bath in September: improved efforts last 2 starts, neck second to Khibrah in listed event at Newmarket and ¾-length third to Midnight Line in Grade 2 handicap at Aqueduct: stays 1½m: acts on firm and soft going: stayed in USA, joining C. Clement. *L. M. Cumani* 106

HORMUZ (IRE) 3 b.g. Hamas (IRE) 125§ – Balqis (USA) 93 (Advocator) [1998 –: a8g⁵ 1999 a10g* a10g² a10g* 10.3d 8m 10m* 10m² 8.5s* 10m 11m⁵ 10.1m Oct 19] well-made gelding: fairly useful performer: won maiden then handicap at Lingfield in January and March, minor event at Ripon in June and handicap at Beverley in July: well below form final 3 starts: stays 1¼m: acts on good to firm going, soft and equitrack: races prominently/leads: none too consistent: sold only 4,200 gns. *M. Johnston* 89

HORNBEAM 5 b.h. Rich Charlie 117 – Thinkluckybelucky (Maystreak 118) [1998 107: 8d* 8m 8d 8.9g⁶ 8d³ 7g 7v⁵ 9m 8m 7.9f⁵ 8m 7.9g⁴ 7.9g 8g⁵ 9v 8d⁵ Oct 30] strong, workmanlike horse: poor mover: useful handicapper: best efforts in 1999 at York on fourth and sixth starts and at Newmarket on eighth outing: best at 7f/1m: acts on any going: pulls hard, and best patiently ridden in strongly-run race: usually tongue tied: none too consistent, and not one to trust. *J. R. Jenkins* 98 §

HORTA (IRE) 2 b.c. (Mar 24) Distinctly North (USA) 115 – Roouan Girl (IRE) (Tremblant 112) [1999 5s 6.1m⁶ 7.9m 7g⁶ 6s Sep 27] IR 10,000Y: first foal: dam lightly raced in bumpers/over hurdles: modest maiden: stays 1m: acts on good to firm and soft ground: sold 6,000 gns. *G. C. Bravery* 58

HORTON DANCER 2 b.g. (May 18) Rambo Dancer (CAN) 107 – Horton Lady 46 (Midyan (USA) 124) [1999 7m⁴ Jun 15] 1,100Y: first foal: dam ran once: 100/1, 3½ lengths fourth of 12 in maiden at Thirsk: not seen out again. *M. Brittain* 59

HORTON LIGHTS 3 b.g. Clantime 101 – Blue Rhythm 72 (Blue Cashmere 129) [1998 –: 5m 5m 9m⁶ 5m Jun 29] strong gelding: no form. *Mrs A. Duffield* –

HOTELIERS PRIDE 2 b.g. (Mar 13) Lugana Beach 116 – Pride of Britain (CAN) 67 (Linkage (USA)) [1999 6g 7s Nov 5] workmanlike gelding: first foal: dam 1½m and 2m winner: well beaten in maidens. *L. G. Cottrell* –

HOT ICE (IRE)   2 b.f. (Apr 9) Petardia 113 – Blackpool Belle 70 (The Brianstan **53**
128) [1999 5m 5g 5d 5.3m³ 5f* 5m Sep 24] 12,500Y: half-sister to several winners,
notably smart sprinter Croft Pool (by Crofthall): dam sprinter: modest performer:
won nursery at Musselburgh in September: raced only at 5f: acts on firm going: sold
6,000 gns, joined P. D'Arcy. *H. Morrison*

HOT LEGS   3 b.f. Sizzling Melody 117 – Ra Ra Girl 77 (Shack (USA) 118) [1998 **44**
47: a5g 5.1v a5g 1999 5s 6d 6s a6g⁶ 5g 5g⁶ 6.1m a6g a7g Nov 27] leggy, angular
filly: poor maiden. *B. A. McMahon*

HOT PASSION   3 b.g. Keen 116 – Love You Madly (IRE) (Bob Back (USA) 124)   **–**
[1998 48: 6f 7d 6m⁴ 1999 10f 12m Jul 27] poor maiden. *M. L. W. Bell*

HOT POTATO   3 b.c. Roman Warrior 132 – My Song of Songs (Norwick (USA)   **–**
125) [1998 –: 5d⁵ 5g 5.1v a5g a8.5g⁶ 1999 a6g⁵ a6g⁵ a7f⁶ 5.9g 5v 8d a7g⁵ Nov 19] **a44**
poor maiden: left C. Smith after third start: stays 6f: acts on fibresand, little show on
turf: visored (no form) fourth and fifth outings. *J. S. Wainwright*

HOT TIN ROOF (IRE)   3 b.f. Thatching 131 – No Reservations (IRE) 87 (Com- **105**
manche Run 133) [1998 NR 1999 7g³ 6m* 7g² 6g³ 7m Sep 9] 16,000Y: close-
coupled filly: second foal: dam, 6f (at 2 yrs) and 7f winner, half-sister to smart
sprinters Hanu and Sanu: useful performer: won maiden at Newcastle in June:
much better form when placed after in minor event at Yarmouth and listed race at
Pontefract (beaten 2¼ lengths by Wannabe Grand): last of 11 at Doncaster final start:
may prove best up to 7f. *J. E. Banks*

HOUDINI'S HONEY (USA)   3 ch.f. Mr Prospector (USA) – Coup de Folie **84**
(USA) 112 (Halo (USA)) [1998 78p: 6g⁵ 1999 7m⁴ 9m² 10m* 10.1g Aug 30] leggy,
close-coupled filly: fairly useful performer: won maiden at Windsor in August:
creditable seventh in listed handicap at Newcastle next time: stays 1¼m: acts on good
to firm going: sent to USA. *Sir Michael Stoute*

HOUGOUMONT   3 b.g. Formidable (USA) 125 – Sure Victory (IRE) 75 (Stalker   **–**
121) [1998 –: 7m² 1999 8m 8m² 11.5d⁶ Jun 2] strong, good-topped gelding: no form.
P. T. Walwyn

HOUNDS OF LOVE (IRE)   2 b.f. (May 10) Foxhound (USA) 103 – Foolish   **– p**
Lady (USA) (Foolish Pleasure (USA)) [1999 7s Nov 5] IR 9,000F, 10,000Y: strong,
compact filly: half-sister to 3 winners, including 9f winner Scottish Jester (by
Northern Baby) and useful 11.4f winner Fire On Ice (by Sadler's Wells): dam maiden
half-sister to Dancing Brave: in need of race when mid-division in maiden at
Doncaster: will stay at least 1m: should improve. *R. Guest*

HOUND VENTURE   3 ch.g. Wolfhound (USA) 126 – Relatively Sharp 86 **70**
(Sharpen Up 127) [1998 70: 5m 6d³ 6m 1999 8s 8.5s 7f³ 7g a7g² 7g* 8f³ 7m⁶ 7g⁵
7m² 7m* 7d⁴ Oct 4] smallish, useful-looking gelding: fair performer: won seller at
Yarmouth in June and minor event at Brighton in September: stays 7f: acts on firm
and good to soft going (possibly not on soft) and equitrack: sold 11,500 gns.
S. P. C. Woods

HOUSEMASTER (IRE)   3 b.g. Rudimentary (USA) 118 – Glenarff (USA) **119**
(Irish River (FR) 131) [1998 100: 6m* 7s⁵ 6g⁵ 7g⁶ 8v³ 1999 8.5g³ 12.3m⁴ 12g⁴ 12m⁶
10s² 7m⁶ 8m⁵ Dec 12] tall, good-topped gelding: usually takes the eye: smart
performer: first past post in Victor Chandler Chester Vase in May (beat Peshtigo by
length but demoted to fourth having barged through) then ran well when 3¼ lengths
fourth of 16 to Oath in Derby at Epsom: sold out of M. Bell's stable after fifth start
and gelded: easily better of 2 outings at Sha Tin when 3½ lengths fifth to Docksider
in Hong Kong Mile: seems effective over 1m and stays 1½m: acts on good to firm
going, probably on soft: held up. *I. W. Allan, Hong Kong*

HOUSE OF DREAMS   7 b.g. Darshaan 133 – Helens Dreamgirl 95 (Caerleon **66**
(USA) 132) [1998 75: 12g* 12d³ 14.1m* 12m⁴ 14g⁶ 12g* 12m 14.1d 1999 12s⁵
12.4m 13.8m 12g⁶ 12f⁶ 12s² 13.8g⁴ Oct 16] small gelding: very poor mover: fairly
useful hurdler: fair handicapper on Flat: stays 1¾m: acts on firm and soft going: has
been bandaged: held up: joined Mrs M. Reveley. *G. M. Moore*

HOUT BAY   2 ch.c. (Mar 16) Komaite (USA) – Maiden Pool 85 (Sharpen Up 127) **63**
[1999 5g⁶ 5g⁴ 6g⁴ 6m Sep 10] 3,200F, 10,000Y: half-brother to several winners,
including 4-y-o Torrent and smart sprinter Rich Charlie (by Young Generation): dam
5f winner: modest maiden: stays 6f. *S. E. Kettlewell*

HOWABOYS QUEST (USA) 2 b.g. (May 15) Quest For Fame 127 – Doctor **59**
Black (USA) (Family Doctor (USA)) [1999 8.2m⁴ 7m⁴ 6s Sep 29] $6,000Y,
25,000 2-y-o: sixth foal: half-brother to 3 winners in USA/Puerto Rico: dam won
13 sprints in USA: modest maiden: best effort when staying-on fourth of 10 at
Newcastle on second start (reportedly finished sore on debut): should stay 1m.
F. Murphy

HOWARD'S LAD (IRE) 2 b.g. (Jan 26) Reprimand 122 – Port Isaac (USA) 64 **80**
(Seattle Song (USA) 130) [1999 6g 6g* 6m³ 6m⁴ 6s 7s Oct 23] IR 20,000F, 16,000Y:
rangy gelding: third foal: brother to Italian winner up to 1m Ambra Luciani: dam
lightly-raced maiden from very good US family: fairly useful performer: 50/1-
winner of maiden at Ayr in July: good efforts in nurseries third and fourth starts: left
Miss L. Perratt afterwards: should stay at least 7f: acts on good to firm going, well
beaten on soft (in visor final start). *I. Semple*

HOW HIGH 4 b.g. Puissance 110 – Lucky Starkist 57 (Lucky Wednesday 124) **–**
[1998 50: 8g³ 8.1d 8f 1999 10g 8.2s Nov 1] little sign of ability in varied company:
tried blinkered. *J. Neville*

HOWQUA RIVER 7 b.g. Petong 126 – Deep Blue Sea (Gulf Pearl 117) [1998 **–**
NR 1999 12g 12.1m 14.1g Aug 12] quite good-topped gelding: modest handicapper
at 4 yrs: well held on belated return. *J. S. King*

HOXTON SQUARE (IRE) 2 ch.f. (Feb 28) Case Law 113 – Guv's Joy (IRE) **64**
72 (Thatching 131) [1999 5g a5g² 5m² 6.8m³ Aug 30] IR 3,000Y, 6,800 2-y-o:
second living foal: dam, 2-y-o 6f winner, later stayed 1m: modest maiden: may prove
best at 5f/6f: acts on good to firm going and fibresand. *N. P. Littmoden*

HUG ME ROB 3 b.f. Robellino (USA) 127 – Hug Me 96 (Shareef Dancer (USA) **42**
135) [1998 NR 1999 10f 10m⁴ 10m⁶ 10.5d 11.8d Oct 12] 11,000Y: big filly:
half-sister to several winners, including 1997 2-y-o 6f winner Generous Embrace (by
Cadeaux Genereux) and fairly useful 1½m/1¾m winner Embracing (by Reference
Point): dam 7f (at 2 yrs) and 1½m winner: poor form in claimers: sold 1,500 gns, sent
to Spain. *W. R. Muir*

HUGWITY 7 ch.g. Cadeaux Genereux 131 – Nuit d'Ete (USA) 90 (Super **88**
Concorde (USA) 128) [1998 84: 10d 10m 8m² 7g⁴ 8g* 8f 8.1m² 8g⁶ 8m 8d² 8g 8g
a10g a7g⁶ a8g⁴ a8.5g⁵ a10g⁴ a8g* a8g* 1999 a8g² a8.5g² a7f* a8g⁶ Dec 18] big,
good-bodied gelding: fairly useful performer: won handicap at Lingfield in January:
off 10½ months before final start: effective at 7f to 1¼m: acts on firm going and
all-weather: often bandaged/apprentice ridden: often leads. *G. C. Bravery*

HULA ANGEL (USA) 3 b.f. Woodman (USA) 126 – Jode (USA) 72 (Danzig **111**
(USA)) [1998 102: 7.1g 7d³ 7m* 7d 7g³ 7g* 1999 8m⁶ 8g* 8m 8m Jul 7]
    For the third successive year the winner of the Irish One Thousand
Guineas failed to reach the first three on any of her subsequent starts. Like
Classic Park (20/1) and Tarascon (12/1) before her, 16/1-shot Hula Angel
pulled off a surprise at the Curragh but she failed signally to reproduce her
classic-winning form, beating one home in both the Coronation Stakes at Royal

Entenmann's Irish 1,000 Guineas, the Curragh—Hula Angel provides trainer Barry Hills and his son Michael
with a second victory in the race; Golden Silca (broad white face), Dazzling Park (centre)
and Crystal Downs follow her home; favourite Wince (light cap) is only fifth

Ascot and the Falmouth Stakes at Newmarket on her only other appearances before being retired to stud. Such an anti-climax could scarcely have been predicted after Hula Angel held off Golden Silca and Dazzling Park by a neck and a head in the Entenmann's-sponsored Irish Guineas. The field looked well up to standard, with seven of the runners having won pattern races and six having contested the English equivalent three weeks earlier. Hula Angel was one of those to whom both remarks applied. She had won the Rockfel Stakes at Newmarket on the last of six outings as a two-year-old, and, doing well physically from two to three, she finished a creditable sixth in the One Thousand Guineas on her reappearance. Hula Angel turned the tables on both the winner at Newmarket, Wince—a short-priced favourite to follow up at the Curragh—and the fourth Capistrano Day, neither of whom made the frame (second, third and the fourth Crystal Downs started at 25/1, 40/1 and 25/1 respectively). The lack of a true gallop, and a strong feeling that those held up in the group racing towards the far rail (which included Wince) had been caught out when the centre group quickened the tempo, left a question mark over the form. For the record, second and third both repeated the form in Group 1 company afterwards while the fourth failed in four later outings to run within a stone of what she appeared to achieve at the Curragh. Wince herself didn't run again.

Hula Angel (USA) (b.f. 1996)	Woodman (USA) (ch 1983)	Mr Prospector (b 1970)	Raise A Native
			Gold Digger
		Playmate (ch 1975)	Buckpasser
			Intriguing
	Jode (USA) (b 1989)	Danzig (b 1977)	Northern Dancer
			Pas de Nom
		Belle de Jour (b 1973)	Speak John
			Battle Dress

Mr J. R. Fleming's "Hula Angel"

The strong, close-coupled Hula Angel was bred to stay beyond the Guineas trip. Her sire Woodman wasn't bred to get further than a mile—over which distance he won as a two-year-old—but he has sired winners over a range of distances, the average distance of races won by his offspring in Europe being around nine and a half furlongs. Hula Angel's dam Jode, a half-sister to Kentucky Derby winner Spend A Buck, won at six furlongs on her only start at two and was later successful at a mile in the States. Jode is now in Japan, her only other runner in Britain and Ireland being the Seattle Slew filly Jaunting, a winner at nine furlongs. Hula Angel, who was usually held up, acted on good to firm and good to soft ground. She is to be covered by Sadler's Wells. *B. W. Hills*

HULLBANK   9 b.g. Uncle Pokey 116 – Dubavarna 72 (Dubassoff (USA)) [1998 76, a66: a14g* 16m⁶ 16.1m⁶ 18m³ 14.1m⁶ 14.1d a14g⁶ 1999 a14g⁶ 14.1f* 13.8g² 16.1m⁵ 15.8g⁵ Jul 1] tall gelding: shows knee action: fair performer: won handicap at Redcar in May: stays 2¼m: acts on firm going (possibly not on soft) and fibresand: blinkered once at 6 yrs: has been bandaged: held up: sometimes finds little. *W. W. Haigh*   **73 a–**

HUNAN SCHOLAR (IRE)   4 b.g. Royal Academy (USA) 130 – Decadence (Vaigly Great 127) [1998 66?: 6g 7g 6s⁶ 6s 6m 5g⁴ 5d⁶ 1999 5v 5m 5f 7f⁵ 6g a7g Dec 22] IR 18,000Y: ex-Irish gelding: half-brother to several winners, notably smart Mistertopogigo (by Thatching) and useful Fairy Wind (by Fairy King), both 5f performers: dam lightly-raced sister to smart sprinter Hallgate: modest maiden handicapper: left K. Prendergast, Ireland, then well beaten final start: probably stays 7f: acts on firm going, possibly not softer than good. *P. Burgoyne*   **53**

HUNTERS TWEED   3 ch.c. Nashwan (USA) 135 – Zorette (USA) 66 (Zilzal (USA) 137) [1998 –: 8s 1999 10.3d 12d⁴ 12g³ 12m* 14f⁵ 14.1m 15d⁵ Sep 16] big, rather plain, unfurnished colt: fairly useful performer: won maiden at Doncaster in July: stiffish tasks in handicaps final 3 starts: may prove best at 1½m: acts on good to firm going. *J. D. Bethell*   **81**

HUNTERS WISH   2 ch.f. (Mar 1) Wolfhound (USA) 126 – Pravolo (Fools Holme (USA)) [1999 5.7d Sep 27] 6,500F, 12,000Y: fourth foal: half-sister to 2 winners abroad, including 3-y-o Lionardo: dam, Irish maiden, half-sister to very smart sprinter Sayyaf: wearing tongue strap, no promise in maiden at Bath: sold 1,200 gns, sent to Belgium. *I. A. Balding*   **–**

HUNTING GROUND   11 b.g. Dancing Brave (USA) 140 – Ack's Secret (USA) (Ack Ack (USA)) [1998 36?: 16.2g 16m⁵ 16m⁶ 15.9g 15.8d 1999 17.2f 16f³ 16.2g 16m⁵ Sep 2] good-bodied gelding: poor handicapper: stays 17.5f: acts on firm going: usually blinkered: inconsistent. *M. Mullineaux*   **35**

HUNTING LION (IRE)   2 b.c. (Apr 30) Piccolo 121 – Jalopy 71 (Jalmood (USA) 126) [1999 5.2f⁴ 5.7m* 6f² 6g³ Sep 3] 7,000F, 34,000Y: leggy colt: has a quick action: half-brother to several winners, including fair 1998 2-y-o 5f winner Anno Domini (by Primo Dominie) and 13f winner Classy Chief (by Be My Chief): dam, 5f winner, half-sister to smart sprinter Point of Light: useful form: won maiden at Bath in July: best efforts when placed after in Richmond Stakes at Goodwood (1½ lengths second of 7 to Bachir) and Group 2 Baustoffe-Cup at Baden-Baden: will probably prove best at 5f/6f: raced only on good going or firmer. *M. R. Channon*   **98**

HUNTING TIGER   2 ch.g. (Feb 26) Pursuit of Love 124 – Pernilla (IRE) 104 (Tate Gallery (USA) 117) [1999 7d⁵ 7.6g 7.1m* 7m⁵ 6d² Oct 14] 26,000Y: workmanlike gelding: third foal: half-brother to fairly useful 1998 2-y-o 5f winner Paula's Joy (by Danehill): dam Irish 6f/7f performer: fairly useful performer: won maiden at Haydock in September: very good second of 16 in Newmarket nursery final start: likely to prove best up to 7f: acts on good to firm and good to soft going: reportedly bolted before second start, and subsequently taken early to post: front runner/races prominently. *M. R. Channon*   **87**

HURGILL DANCER   5 b.g. Rambo Dancer (CAN) 107 – Try Vickers (USA) 72 (Fuzzbuster (USA)) [1998 54, a43: 11.9g 12m⁵ 17.2d 11.9m³ 16m 14.1s a12g a8f 1999 a10g⁶ a12g⁵ a12g* a16g⁵ 10.8d 11.9f⁴ a10g³ a13g⁴ Dec 10] poor handicapper: won at Lingfield in February: effective at 1¼m to 1½m: acts on firm going and all-weather. *R. J. O'Sullivan*   **47**

HURGILL LADY 5 ch.m. Emarati (USA) 74 – Gitee (FR) (Carwhite 127) [1998 **41**
47, a54: a6s a6g² a5g² a6g² a6g 5s 5m 6g 1999 a6g⁶ a6g⁶ a5f⁴ Jan 30] well-grown
mare: poor maiden handicapper: needs further than 5f, and should stay 7f: acts on
good to firm going and fibresand: blinkered (last of 4 in claimer on equitrack debut)
final start. *D. Nicholls*

HURRICANE LOUIS (IRE) 3 b. or br.c. Fabulous Dancer (USA) 124 – **87**
Lobmille (Mill Reef (USA) 141) [1998 NR 1999 7.5v* 10.2g⁴ 8m* 8f 8g* 8d* 8d⁵
Nov 7] half-brother to several winners in France, including smart 1m winner Lone
Bid (by Priolo) and 1m to 1½m winner Lobbyist (by Mtoto): dam unraced daughter
of sister to Highclere: fairly useful performer: won maiden at Milan in March and
minor event there in June: left J. Noseda after next start and successful in minor
events at Varese and Milan in September: best at 1m (well held only outing in Britain
over further): acts on good to firm and heavy ground. *B. Grizzetti, Italy*

HURRICANE STORM 2 b.g. (Feb 18) Runnett 125 – Polar Storm (IRE) 76 **–**
(Law Society (USA) 130) [1999 7d 7v⁶ Sep 29] tall gelding: has scope: second foal:
brother to Irish 3-y-o 9f winner Lawnett: dam, 6f (at 2 yrs) to 1m winner, half-sister
to smart sprinter Polar Bird, herself dam of smart filly up to 1m Ocean Ridge: well
held in maiden at Newbury and minor event at Salisbury. *B. J. Meehan*

HURTLE 2 ch.f. (Mar 31) Prince Sabo 123 – Hurricane Dancer (IRE) 58 (Nabeel **–**
Dancer (USA) 120) [1999 5v⁶ 5m 5d Apr 21] 2,000Y: small, plain filly: first foal:
dam, 7f winner, ran only at 2 yrs: soundly beaten, including in selling company.
Martyn Wane

HUSH 4 b.f. Barrys Gamble 102 – Keep Mum 63 (Mummy's Pet 125) [1998 –: 6m **–**
1999 8d May 16] smallish, plain filly: tailed off in maiden/seller. *L. R. Lloyd-James*

HUSH MONEY 3 b.g. Aragon 118 – Penny Blessing 112 (So Blessed 130) [1998 **73**
63: 5.1m⁴ 5m⁶ 5g 7s 1999 7d* 7.1g 8.3m 7g⁴ 8.2m* 6.9m* 7d⁵ 7.5g² Aug 29]
close-coupled gelding: fair performer: won maiden at Thirsk in April and claimers at
Nottingham in July and Carlisle in August: below form final 2 starts: stays 1m: acts
on good to firm and good to soft going: has been bandaged. *B. W. Hills*

HUTCHIES LADY 7 b.m. Efisio 120 – Keep Mum 63 (Mummy's Pet 125) **46**
[1998 –: 12.1v⁴ 8.3v⁶ 13d 12.1v⁵ 11.1d 16d 1999 10g² 12g⁵ 12m⁴ 12m 12.1f Aug 24]
small, sparely-made mare: poor handicapper: probably stays 1½m: acts on good to
firm and soft going: tried blinkered/visored. *M. A. Peill*

HUTOON 2 b.c. (May 11) Mizoram (USA) 105 – Mey Madam (Song 132) [1999 **74**
7.6g 8.1m⁴ 9m³ Sep 24] sixth reported foal: dam ran 3 times: fair form in maidens:
third of 10 to Miletrian at Redcar final start: will stay 1¼m, probably 1½m. *J. W. Hills*

HUYTON HILL 2 b.c. (Mar 2) Presidium 124 – Valerle 66 (Never So Bold 135) **47**
[1999 5.1m 6m 5m⁴ 6f 5m⁴ Aug 11] 6,200Y: sturdy colt: first foal: dam 2-y-o 5f
winner: poor maiden: sold 900 gns, sent to Denmark. *K. A. Ryan*

HYDE PARK (IRE) 5 b.g. Alzao (USA) 117 – Park Elect (Ahonoora 122) [1998 **78**
78: 6g 5.1g 5m 6g⁶ 8g* 7.6g* 8.5m² 8s 8g* 8.2s a7g² a8g⁵ 1999 a7f a7g² a8g⁵ a7g
a8.5g³ 7m⁴ 7.6m 8m 7f³ 8f³ 9g³ 9g⁴ 8d Oct 26] robust gelding: fair handicapper: left
Sir Mark Prescott after fifth start: tailed off final outing: effective at 7f, barely stays
9f: acts on good to firm going and all-weather: blinkered (well beaten) fourth start:
usually races prominently. *D. Nicholls*

HYPERACTIVE (IRE) 3 b.c. Perugino (USA) 84 – Hyannis (FR) (Esprit du **77**
Nord (USA) 126) [1998 66: 6m⁴ 5d² 5g 1999 7m* Oct 19] rather dipped-backed colt:
won maiden at Yarmouth in October only outing of 1999: not sure to be suited by
further than 7f: yet to race on extremes of going. *A. C. Stewart*

HYPERICO (IRE) 5 b.g. Nordico (USA) – Hype (USA) (Hyperborean (USA)) **–**
[1998 58: a8.5g² a9.4g⁴ a8g 1999 a9.4g³ a8f a11g⁵ a5g⁴ a6g⁶ a5g 6v a6g⁶ 7.7m a7g³ **a49**
a8.5g⁴ a9.4g⁶ Aug 14] poor maiden: seems effective at 6f to 11f: acts on fibresand,
best turf run on good going: has tongue tied: tried visored/blinkered. *Miss S. J. Wilton*

HYPERSONIC 2 b.c. (Feb 21) Marju (IRE) 127 – Hi-Li (High Top 131) [1999 **78**
6.1m⁵ 6g⁴ 7v² 7s³ Nov 22] 20,000 2-y-o: sixth foal: dam unraced daughter of useful
6f/1m winner Leipzig: fair maiden: will be well suited by 1¼m+: acts on heavy going
(reportedly suffered sore shins on good to firm). *G. Wragg*

HYPNOTIZE 2 b.f. (Mar 25) Machiavellian (USA) 123 – Belle Et Deluree **95**
(USA) (The Minstrel (CAN) 135) [1999 6d⁶ 7d* 7.1m* 7m⁵ Aug 29] well-made,
attractive filly: closely related to several winners, notably smart 5f (at 2 yrs) to 7f
winner Dazzle (by Gone West), and half-sister to a winner in USA by Cozzene:
dam French 1m (at 2 yrs) and 1¼m winner: useful form: won maiden at Yarmouth
and listed race at Sandown (led by 2 handlers in preliminaries) in July: creditable
fifth of 9 to Icicle in Link Prestige Stakes at Goodwood final start: will stay 1m.
Sir Michael Stoute

HYPOTHESIS (IRE) 2 b.c. (May 25) Sadler's Wells (USA) 132 – Surmise **–**
(USA) 75 (Alleged (USA) 138) [1999 7d Oct 26] IR 130,000Y: seventh foal: brother
to 3-y-o Shaftesbury, closely related to a winner in Italy by Be My Guest and
half-brother to a winner in Macau by Royal Academy: dam, 7f winner, half-sister to
smart 7f/1m performer Aim For The Top: tailed off in minor event at Redcar.
A. Bailey

I

I CAN'T REMEMBER 5 br. or gr.g. Petong 126 – Glenfield Portion 86 **71**
(Mummy's Pet 125) [1998 68, a59: 7d⁶ 8s⁴ 10.3g 7.6m 8m⁴ 9g⁶ 8m 7g⁵ 10.3g* 8m²
8d 10.3v⁵ a10g³ 1999 10m* 8g⁶ 8s* 10m⁶ 9.9s⁶ 12m⁵ 12.3f* 12g⁵ 14.1m* a16.2g 10s
Nov 1] small, close-coupled gelding: fair performer: won seller at Nottingham in
May (final start for M. Pipe) and handicaps at Pontefract in June and Ripon and
Nottingham in August: well below form final 2 starts: effective at 1m (given test)
to 1¾m: acts on firm going, soft and equitrack: visored twice at 3 yrs: has been
bandaged: sometimes races too freely. *S. R. Bowring*

ICE 3 b.g. Polar Falcon (USA) 126 – Sarabah (IRE) 83 (Ela-Mana-Mou 132) [1998 **100**
97: 6v² 6d⁴ 7s³ 7.1g* 7.9g* 8s² 7.9g* 1999 9m⁴ 8v* 7.9s* 9g 8.1m 8m 7d 9g⁴
8d Sep 18] deep-bodied gelding: useful performer: won Swiss 2000 Guineas at
Dielsdorf in April and handicap at York in May: mostly disappointing after: should
stay 1¼m: acts on heavy going: usually visored: carries head high, and tends to
wander. *M. Johnston*

ICE AGE 5 gr.h. Chilibang 120 – Mazarine Blue 65 (Bellypha 130) [1998 52, a66: **40 +**
a6g* a6g a6g⁴ a5g³ a6g* 6m a6g⁶ 6.1g⁴ 6m* 6m 1999 a6g² a6g⁶ a6f³ a6s⁵ a6g⁴ a6g² **a60**
a6g* 5s a6g⁴ 5.1m 6g⁶ a6g a6g Dec 21] workmanlike horse: modest performer: won
seller at Southwell in March: mostly below form after, leaving R. Williams and off 6
months before final start: best at 5f/6f: acts on fibresand, best on good going or firmer
on turf: wears blinkers: races prominently: often hangs right, and isn't one to trust
implicitly. *M. J. Polglase*

ICENIC (IRE) 3 b.g. Scenic 128 – Resiusa (ITY) (Niniski (USA) 125) [1998 60: **64 d**
a8g⁴ 1999 a8f² a8g⁴ 11.6m 12m a9.4g⁵ Aug 14] quite attractive gelding: modest
maiden at best: well below form after reappearance: should stay beyond 1m:
blinkered final 2 starts: sold 4,500 gns in October. *J. M. P. Eustace*

ICE PACK 3 gr.f. Mukaddamah (USA) 125 – Mrs Gray 61 (Red Sunset 120) **63**
[1998 –: 7m 8v 1999 a7g³ a9.4g² 10f 10.2g⁶ 11.9d a12g² a11g² a12g Oct 18] modest
maiden: left J. Hills before disappointing final start: will stay beyond 1½m: acts on
fibresand, best turf effort on heavy going. *N. Tinkler*

ICICLE 2 br.f. (Mar 13) Polar Falcon (USA) 126 – Blessed Honour 77 (Ahonoora **102**
122) [1999 6m* 6m⁶ 6d² 7m* 7g⁴ Oct 16] rather sparely-made filly: first reported
foal: dam, 2-y-o 7f winner on only start, half-sister to smart middle-distance stayer
Sacrament: useful performer: won maiden at Folkestone in May and 9-runner Link
Prestige Stakes at Goodwood in August, latter by short head from Croeso Cariad:
good fourth of 12 to Lahan in Rockfel Stakes at Newmarket on final start: likely to be
suited by at least 1m at 3 yrs: yet to race on extremes of going. *J. R. Fanshawe*

ICICLE QUEEN 2 ch.f. (Mar 28) Aragon 118 – Kristal Diva 60 (Kris 135) [1999 **–**
7d 8d Oct 30] 500Y: plain filly: first foal: dam lightly-raced maiden: soundly beaten
in Newmarket sellers. *S. C. Williams*

I CRIED FOR YOU (IRE) 4 b.g. Statoblest 120 – Fall of The Hammer (IRE) **86** (Auction Ring (USA) 123) [1998 73: 6v⁶ 6g³ 5.3f* 6f³ 6g 5d 5m⁶ 6.1m 6m⁵ 5g 5.3g **a–** 6s 1999 a8f a6g 6g⁴ 6.1f* 6m* 6m² 6m 5m 5s 7d 6.1f Oct 20] angular gelding: fairly useful performer: won minor event at Nottingham in May and handicap at Windsor in June: ran very well next time but slightly disappointing after: stays 6f: probably acts on any turf going, well held both starts on fibresand: has been bandaged in front: sometimes visored/blinkered, not on turf in 1999. *J. G. Given*

IDA'S COTTAGE (IRE) 3 b.g. Fayruz 116 – Coral Pink (Miramar Reef 100§) **–** [1998 –: 7s a7g a7g⁴ 1999 a6g a7f 9m a8g Aug 20] signs of only a little ability. *P. R. Chamings*

IDOLIZE 2 ch.f. (Apr 27) Polish Precedent (USA) 131 – Knight's Baroness 116 **83 +** (Rainbow Quest (USA) 134) [1999 7f 7.7g² 8.1g* Aug 30] quite attractive filly: sixth foal: sister to very smart 9f to 1½m winner Riyadian and half-sister to 3-y-o Mischief and 4-y-o Wales: dam won Irish Oaks: progressive form in maidens, comfortably winning at Chepstow in August by 2 lengths from Sabreon: will stay at least 1½m. *P. F. I. Cole*

IFTIRAAS 2 b.f. (Jan 23) Distant Relative 128 – Ideal Home 104 (Home Guard **97** (USA) 129) [1999 6m² 6m* 6v⁴ 7.3s² Oct 23] 30,000Y: leggy, lengthy filly: half-sister to 3 winners, including 3-y-o Peaceful and smart Irish 5f/7f performer Bezelle (by Dominion), latter later 1m winner in USA: dam 2-y-o 5f winner: useful form: won maiden at Lingfield in September: easily best effort when short-head second of 12 to Corinium in listed event at Newbury final start: will stay 1m: acts on good to firm and soft ground. *J. L. Dunlop*

IFTITAH (USA) 3 ch.c. Gone West (USA) – Mur Taasha (USA) 108 (Riverman **80 +** (USA) 131) [1998 102P: 7m* 1999 7s⁵ Oct 23] strong, robust colt: has plenty of scope: impressive winner of 5-runner minor event at Newmarket, only run at 2 yrs: weak in market, only fifth in minor event at Doncaster over a year later: may prove best up to 1m: slightly reluctant at stalls at Newmarket (reportedly showed dislike of them at home). *Saeed bin Suroor*

IGNITE (IRE) 2 b.g. (Mar 29) Bluebird (USA) 125 – Save Me The Waltz 86 **76** (Kings Lake (USA) 133) [1999 5g⁶ 5m³ 5.3f 6d³ 6f³ 6m 6m⁴ 6s³ 5s⁴ 7.3v Oct 23] IR 40,000Y: strong, well-made gelding: good mover: sixth foal: half-brother to 3 winners, notably 3-y-o Valentine Waltz: dam, French 2-y-o 6.5f winner, half-sister to top-class sprinter/miler Last Tycoon: fair maiden: left G. Lewis after sixth start: stays 6f: acts on firm and soft going: tried blinkered: sold 9,500 gns. *M. L. W. Bell*

IHTIMAAM (FR) 7 b.g. Polish Precedent (USA) 131 – Haebeh (USA) 88 **– §** (Alydar (USA)) [1998 37§: 10.8g² 11.7d⁵ 8.1m 10.8m 1999 a12g Oct 13] compact gelding: poor handicapper nowadays: stays 11f: acts on fibresand: tried blinkered/ visored: temperamental. *H. E. Haynes*

IJAB (CAN) 9 b.g. Ascot Knight (CAN) 130 – Renounce (USA) (Buckpasser) **29** [1998 NR 1999 a14g⁴ Mar 16] bad performer nowadays: stays 2m: acts on good to firm going and fibresand: usually blinkered. *J. Parkes*

IKRAM BOY (USA) 5 b.g. Salem Drive (USA) – Vast Domain (CAN) (Vice **–** Regent (CAN)) [1998 –, a54: 7d 10.5m⁵ 10.9d 9.1v a9.4g³ a10g² a8.5g³ 1999 a8g³ **a48** a7g⁵ a11g⁵ a12g⁴ Mar 19] poor maiden handicapper: below form after reappearance: seems best at 1m/1¼m: acts on all-weather, little recent form on turf: blinkered (well held) once at 4 yrs. *A. Bailey*

ILAHABAD (IRE) 4 b.g. Kahyasi 130 – Ilmiyya (FR) (Kenmare (FR) 125) [1998 **–** 10.5m³ 12s³ 13.5m² 12g² 12g⁵ 12m³ 12.3m* 10.5s⁴ 1999 14s⁴ Sep 24] second foal: dam French 1m winner: fairly useful performer: won minor event at Cluny at 3 yrs: left A. de Royer-Dupre in France for 300,000 francs in October 1998: stiff task only Flat run in Britain: stays 13.5f: acts on soft and good to firm ground: useful hurdler, won in October. *J. G. FitzGerald*

IL CAPITANO 2 ch.c. (Feb 20) Be My Chief (USA) 122 – Taza (Persian Bold **95** 123) [1999 6d² 7s* 7.1g⁶ 8d⁶ 8s² Oct 22] rangy colt: good walker: second foal: dam (no form) half-sister to very smart middle-distance performer Apache: useful performer: won maiden at Ayr in July by 9 lengths: good second of 5 to Island Sound in minor event at Newbury on final start, off bridle by halfway but pulling clear of rest: will be well suited by 1¼m+: raced only on good going or softer: has been edgy in preliminaries and raced freely. *B. W. Hills*

IL DESTINO 4 b.g. Casteddu 111 – At First Sight (He Loves Me 120) [1998 63, a75: 8m 8.2g 7.6m⁶ 8g⁶ a7g a10g³ a10g⁴ 1999 a10g² 8g 9m³ 10.2m* 10m² 10m⁶ 10m² Sep 13] fair handicapper: won at Bath in July: mostly creditable efforts otherwise: stays 1¼m: acts on good to firm ground and equitrack: sold 18,500 gns. *P. J. Makin* **69 a77**

ILE DE LIBRATE 5 b.g. Librate 91 – Little Missile (Ile de Bourbon (USA) 133) [1998 64: 16g² 17.2g⁵ 16.2g 1999 a16f a16g⁶ Feb 25] unfurnished gelding: modest maiden handicapper: well held at Lingfield both starts in 1999: stays 17f: yet to race on extremes of going. *R. J. O'Sullivan* **–**

ILE DISTINCT (IRE) 5 b.g. Dancing Dissident (USA) 119 – Golden Sunlight (Ile de Bourbon (USA) 133) [1998 72: 8g⁶ 8.9g 1999 9.9g⁶ 9.2m² 9f⁴ 8m 12m³ Sep 2] leggy gelding: fair performer, lightly raced: ran creditably 3 of final 4 starts: probably stays 1½m: raced only on good going or firmer: has sweated. *Mrs A. Duffield* **70**

ILE MICHEL 2 b.c. (Feb 20) Machiavellian (USA) 123 – Circe's Isle (Be My Guest (USA) 126) [1999 6m² 6g* 6m⁵ Oct 19] 110,000Y: fifth foal: brother to smart 7f (at 2 yrs) and 1¼m winner Don Micheletto and half-brother to 3-y-o Moly and 2 winners, including 5-y-o Flint Knapper: dam unraced close relative to very smart 1¼m performer Sasuru: confirmed debut promise when easily landing odds in maiden at Catterick in September: something seemingly amiss only subsequent start: bred to stay 1m+, but doesn't look short of speed: may still do better. *G. Wragg* **88 +**

ILEWIN JANINE (IRE) 8 b.m. Soughaan (USA) 111 – Mystery Queen (Martinmas 128) [1999 NR 1999 11d⁶ Oct 26] fourth foal: dam unraced: modest winning hurdler: sixth in claimer at Redcar on Flat debut. *P. D. Evans* **50**

ILISSUS (USA) 3 b.g. Alleged (USA) 138 – Reine Des Iles (USA) (Nureyev (USA) 131) [1998 NR 1999 7.1s³ 8d² 10g a10g Dec 29] $135,000F: smallish, quite attractive gelding: fifth foal: half-brother to French 9f winner Reve de Fee (by Mr Prospector): dam French 8.5f winner: fairly useful form in maidens at Haydock and Ripon (made running): clipped heels and unseated rider early penultimate start (subsequently left M. Tregoning) and soundly beaten (after 7-month absence) final one: should stay 1¼m: has worn crossed noseband. *P. Mitchell* **82**

ILJASOOR (USA) 2 b.c. (Feb 12) Rainbow Quest (USA) 134 – Jasoorah (IRE) 98 (Sadler's Wells (USA) 132) [1999 7s Nov 5] leggy, lightly-made colt: has a quick action: fourth foal: brother to winning German middle-distance stayer Aljaarif and half-brother to 3-y-o Shamsat Mtoto: dam, 1m (at 2 yrs) to 1½m winner, granddaughter of Irish 1000 Guineas and Irish St Leger winner Pidget: soon niggled along when eighth of 20 to Hopeful Light in maiden at Doncaster in November: will stay at least 1¼m: should do better. *M. P. Tregoning* **60 p**

ILLUMINATE 6 b.g. Marju (IRE) 127 – Light Bee (USA) 86 (Majestic Light (USA)) [1998 60: 12f 14d² 16.4m 14g 1999 15.4v⁶ a14g May 10] leggy, quite attractive gelding: modest handicapper at 5 yrs: no form in 1999: stays 1¾m: acts on equitrack, good to firm and good to soft ground: reportedly bled from nose final start. *D. C. O'Brien* **–**

ILLUSIVE (IRE) 2 b.c. (Apr 26) Night Shift (USA) – Mirage 60 (Red Sunset 120) [1999 6g 5m 6.1g 6s⁵ a6g* a6g a6g² a5g* Nov 19] IR 23,000F, 22,000Y: fifth foal: half-brother to 3-y-o Swallow Flight and a winner in Germany by Thatching: dam, modest maiden here, later won listed sprints in Germany: fair performer: won nurseries at Lingfield in October and Southwell (bit slowly away) in November: sold out of W. Jarvis' stable 5,200 gns after sixth start: likely to prove best at 5f/easy 6f: acts on all-weather, well held on turf: blinkered last 4 starts. *H. J. Collingridge* **69**

IL PRINCIPE (IRE) 5 b.g. Ela-Mana-Mou 132 – Seattle Siren 101 (Seattle Slew (USA)) [1998 72: 8g 9.9m 12f 16d 17.2d⁵ 14.1d* 18g 16s³ a14.8g³ a14g³ a14.8g² a16g³ 1999 a16g⁵ 11.9g⁶ 11.9f⁴ 16f⁵ 14d* 16g² 16g* 14m³ a16.2g⁵ 17.5d³ 14s⁴ 13.9d* 17.3g 16.5s* a14g² a14g⁴ Nov 30] neat gelding: fairly useful handicapper on turf, fair on all-weather: won at Haydock and Musselburgh in August, York in October and at Doncaster in November: best at 1¾m to 2¼m: acts **86 a72**

on soft ground, good to firm and all-weather: visored (below form) twice in 1998: races prominently: tough and reliable. *John Berry*

IMAD (USA)   9 b. or br.g. Al Nasr (FR) 126 – Blue Grass Field 81 (Top Ville 129)   **54** [1998 54§: a16.2g² 16d 1999 a16.2g 21.6d* Apr 28] modest handicapper, lightly raced nowadays: won at Pontefract in April: stays 2¾m: acts on firm ground, good to soft and fibresand: looked reluctant in blinkers once at 6 yrs: has worn tongue strap. *K. C. Comerford*

IMANI   4 b.f. Danehill (USA) 126 – Santarem (USA) 71 (El Gran Senor (USA)   **83** 136) [1998 69: 8g 9g 7.1s⁶ 10.8g⁵ 10m* 10m⁵ 10m 8.5s⁴ 10g⁵ 1999 9.9g* 10.8m* 13.1g⁵ 12g* 11.9d² 11.9f 12m² 9.9g* 10.5s³ 10.1m Oct 19] good-bodied filly: fairly useful handicapper: had a good season, winning at Beverley in April, Warwick in May, Salisbury in June and Beverley in August: effective at 1¼m/1½m: acts on soft and good to firm going (finished lame on firm): usually held up: stud. *J. L. Dunlop*

IMARI   2 b.f. (Mar 3) Rock City 120 – Misty Goddess (IRE) 63 (Godswalk (USA)   **59** 130) [1999 6d⁴ 6m⁴ 6s⁴ 6g⁶ 8.3d⁴ a7g Dec 15] second foal: half-sister to 3-y-o Autumn Leaves: dam 7f (at 2 yrs) to 10.8f winner: modest maiden: should stay beyond 6f: acts on soft and good to firm ground. *J. G. Given*

IMBACKAGAIN (IRE)   4 b.g. Mujadil (USA) 119 – Ballinclogher (IRE) (Crea-   **56** tive Plan (USA)) [1998 61: a6g* a7g⁶ 7g 8.3g⁵ 7g a7g⁶ a7g a9.4g⁴ 9m² 10g 1999 a8.5g a10g a7g³ a7g² a7g³ a7g⁶ a8g a8g a8.5g a7g Dec 15] strong, close-coupled gelding: modest performer: effective at 6f to 9f: acts on fibresand and good to firm ground: tongue tied final 2 starts. *N. P. Littmoden*

IMPALDI (IRE)   4 b.f. Imp Society (USA) – Jaldi (IRE) 75 (Nordico (USA))   **48** [1998 58: 5v 7.8d⁵ 5g⁶ 6d⁶ 7v 5g 1999 5m 6m⁶ 5m⁴ 6m⁴ᵈⁱˢ 5m⁴ 5v 6f² 6m⁴ 7m 6m 5g⁵ 5f Aug 24] second foal: dam 7f winner: modest maiden in Ireland in 1998: only poor form in Britain: effective at 5f, probably 7.8f: acts on firm and good to soft going, possibly not on heavy: blinkered (below form) final start. *B. Ellison*

IMPELLING (IRE)   4 ch.g. Imp Society (USA) – Real Stunner 78 (Chief Singer   **60** 131) [1998 58: 8m 8.3m 10f 1999 a8g⁵ a10g a8g* a8g 8.3m Apr 12] workmanlike gelding: modest performer: won apprentice maiden handicap at Southwell in February: well held final 2 starts: likely to prove best short of 1¼m: acts on fibresand, raced only on firm/good to firm going on turf: often tongue tied. *K. R. Burke*

IMPERATOR (IRE)   4 b.g. Mac's Imp (USA) 116 – Secret Hideaway (USA)   **–** (Key To The Mint (USA)) [1998 50, a46: 8g 7s 7m² 6.9d 6f⁴ 6m 7d a7g⁶ a7g 1999 a10g Jan 21] tall gelding: modest maiden: stays 7f: acts on firm going and equitrack: wears crossed noseband: tail swisher. *G. L. Moore*

IMPERIAL BEAUTY (USA)   3 b.f. Imperial Ballet (IRE) 110 – Multimara   **117** (USA) (Arctic Tern (USA) 126) [1998 103p: 6m² 6g* 6g² 1999 8m 6m* 5f² 6m 5.2d* 5v² Oct 3]

A four-year-old campaign similar to the one he'd followed with Elbio in 1991 has been mapped out by trainer Peter Makin for his smart filly Imperial Beauty. It may be asking a lot for Imperial Beauty to do so well as Elbio, who developed into a high-class sprinter at four years and won the Palace House, Temple and King's Stand Stakes, but she must have good prospects of gaining a first pattern-race success. Should it happen then it will have been well deserved, Imperial Beauty having already finished second three times in such events.

The first occasion was on the last of her three starts at two years, in the Cheveley Park Stakes at Newmarket, where she was beaten half a length by Wannabe Grand. When the pair were next seen out it was in the One Thousand Guineas in May, but whereas Wannabe Grand ran an excellent race to take second, Imperial Beauty finished well down the field. After a two-month break it was back to sprinting for Imperial Beauty. A comfortable victory over Pipalong and five others in a six-furlong listed event at York on her return was followed by second place in the Group 3 King George Stakes over five furlongs at Goodwood, where she was beaten a length and three quarters by the much improved Rudi's Pet. Though far from disgraced back over six furlongs next time, when eighth to Diktat in the Sprint Cup at Haydock, Imperial Beauty's two subsequent performances, both of which were over five furlongs, suggest that she's ideally suited by the latter trip. She gave a most convincing performance when winning a listed race, the Dubai Airport World Trophy, at Newbury in September. Still travelling strongly when switched to join the group in the centre around halfway, Imperial Beauty challenged on the bridle going into the final furlong and needed only to be shaken up to edge ahead, winning by half a length from Repertory with a good deal to spare. This was Imperial Beauty's first run on ground softer than good, and she was to encounter conditions that were much more testing still on her final start in the Group 1 Prix de l'Abbaye de Longchamp. Her sire Imperial Ballet, who has been moved from Kentucky to the Ballyhane Stud in Ireland at a fee of IR £4,500 for 2000, had put up easily his best performance when winning the Royal Hunt Cup on soft ground. Imperial Beauty showed improved form in finishing a short-neck second to the Japanese challenger Agnes World on heavy ground at Longchamp. Prominent from the start, Imperial Beauty briefly looked likely to win when drawing upsides Agnes World around a furlong and a half out, but she couldn't quite get the better of him, edging right under pressure. Imperial Beauty did have a very hard race, and it is to be hoped that it hasn't left its mark.

Imperial Beauty (USA) (b.f. 1996)	Imperial Ballet (IRE) (b 1989)	Sadler's Wells (b 1981)	Northern Dancer
			Fairy Bridge
		Amaranda (b 1975)	Bold Lad
			Favoletta
	Multimara (USA) (b 1990)	Arctic Tern (ch 1973)	Sea-Bird II
			Bubbling Beauty
		Evening Air (br 1982)	J O Tobin
			Nellie Forbes

Imperial Beauty is the first reported foal of Multimara, who was placed twice from four starts in the USA. Multimara is a half-sister to the May Hill Stakes winner Midnight Air, herself the dam of the May Hill winner and Oaks

Stanley Racing Summer Stakes, York—the first of two listed-race successes for Imperial Beauty, who wins with authority from Pipalong (left)

third Midnight Line, who was successful in the Grade 2 Long Island Handicap at Aqueduct in the latest season. Imperial Beauty's grandam, the unraced Evening Air, is a daughter of Nellie Forbes, who won at a mile in Ireland on her only start at two, and granddaughter of Comely Nell, dam of the Kentucky Derby and Belmont Stakes winner Bold Forbes. Imperial Beauty, a lengthy, rather unfurnished filly and a good mover, acts on any going. *P. J. Makin*

IMPERIAL COURT (IRE)   4 b.g. Imperial Frontier (USA) 112 – Fandikos (IRE) (Taufan (USA) 119) [1998 –: a7g 6m 7.1d 1999 7.7m 8g Sep 20] little sign of ability: tried visored/tongue tied. *A. W. Carroll*   –

IMPERIAL ENVOY   4 b.g. Zafonic (USA) 130 – Imperial Jade 105 (Lochnager 132) [1998 NR 1999 a6g a6g a8g⁴ Feb 20] half-brother to several winners, notably smart 5f/6f performer Averti (by Warning): dam sprinting sister to smart sprinter Reesh: signs of a little ability in maidens. *W. R. Muir*   –

IMPERIAL HONEY (IRE)   4 b.f. Imperial Frontier (USA) 112 – Indian Honey (Indian King (USA) 128) [1998 54: 6d 5.1m 5g 5d 5m⁵ 5g⁵ 6m a6g 1999 5m a6g 5m² 6f 5m³ 5f³ 5g⁴ a6g Nov 12] poor maiden handicapper: probably stays 6f: acts on firm and good to soft going, no form in 3 starts on fibresand. *Mrs A. Duffield*   49 a–

IMPERIALIST (IRE)   2 b.f. (May 14) Imperial Frontier (USA) 112 – Petrine (IRE) (Petorius 117) [1999 5.1m⁵ 5g* 5g* 6.3m³ 5.2m⁴ 6m³ 6d⁶ 5d Oct 9] IR 6,400Y: close-coupled filly: fifth foal: half-sister to 2 winners abroad, including Italian winner up to 1¼m Simpless (by Simply Great): dam ran 4 times in Ireland: fairly useful performer: won maiden at Sandown in May and minor event at Salisbury in June: ran creditably sixth start and when sixth in Cheveley Park Stakes at Newmarket penultimate outing: likely to prove best at 5f/6f: yet to race on extremes of going: usually races prominently/leads. *R. Hannon*   93

IMPERIAL PRINCE   4 b.g. Prince Sabo 123 – Joli's Girl 79 (Mansingh (USA) 120) [1998 67, a62: a8.5g³ a9.4g² 8d² 10g⁵ a10g³ 8d⁵ 7m⁶ a10g a12g² a11g a14.8g³ 1999 12.3m² 12v 11.9f⁵ 13.1d⁴ 9g⁵ 10g⁵ 10f 10g⁶ 8m³ 10m Sep 7] fair maiden handicapper: well below form after reappearance: effective at 9f to 15f: acts on good to firm going, good to soft and all-weather: effective visored/blinkered or not: often makes running: not one to trust implicitly: sold 3,500 gns, joined A. Carroll. *S. P. C. Woods*   67 d

IMPERIAL ROCKET (USA)   2 b. or br.c. (Mar 27) Northern Flagship (USA) 96 – Starsawhirl (USA) (Star de Naskra (USA)) [1999 7d 7.9g 8d* 8.3d* Nov 4] IR 44,000Y: third foal: brother to minor winner in USA and half-brother to stakes-placed winner in USA by Alwuhush: dam stakes-placed winner at up to 9f in USA: progressive form: won maiden at Leicester (made virtually all) in October and nursery at Windsor in November, rallying well on second occasion and scoring by neck from Father Juninho (pair clear): should stay beyond 1m: raced only on good/ good to soft going: should improve further. *R. Hannon*   90 p

IMPETUS   5 b.g. Puissance 110 – Cold Line 74 (Exdirectory 129) [1998 60, a–: a12s 12s³ 10s² 9v 10g 12g⁶ 9.9m⁶ 1999 11g 10d Oct 18] leggy gelding: modest maiden handicapper, lightly raced: should stay 1½m: acts on soft ground, probably on good to firm: inconsistent. *J. Hetherton*   –

IMPORTUNE (USA)   2 b.c. (Mar 22) Defensive Play (USA) 118 – Molly Moon (FR) (Kalamoun 129) [1999 a8g Nov 22] 14,500 2-y-o: half-brother to several winners, including 1¼m winner Princess Borghese (by Nijinsky) and French 11f listed winner Moonfish (by Northern Baby): dam, lightly raced in USA, from family of Sanglamore: 33/1, last of 12 in maiden at Southwell. *N. Tinkler*   –

IMPREVUE (IRE)   5 ch.m. Priolo (USA) 127 – Las Bela 75 (Welsh Pageant 132) [1998 80: 10g³ 12m 16d 12g⁴ 12d 12.3s 1999 12g 15.4v 11.9f² 11.9f⁵ 14m 11.5g a12g² a10g* 10m* 9v³ 10f* a10g* a10g⁴ Dec 8] IR 12,500Y: lengthy mare: fourth reported foal: half-sister to 2 winners, including French winner up to 9.5f Magical Dust (by Magical Wonder): dam best at 1m: fair performer: trained before 1999 by D. Kelly in Ireland: won handicaps at Lingfield in July and Brighton (amateurs) in September and minor events at Nottingham in October and Lingfield in November: 71 has form at 2m, possibly best at 1¼m/1½m: acts on firm ground, soft and equitrack: usually blinkered nowadays: sometimes slowly away. *R. J. O'Sullivan*

I'M PROPOSIN (IRE)   4 b.c. Posen (USA) – Kitterland (Rheingold 137) [1998 –
113p: 8s* 8.1s* 8g* 1999 12m⁵ Sep 10] tall, rangy colt: smart and unbeaten at 3 yrs:
tailed off only start of 1999: has broken blood vessel on gallops: retired. *J. L. Dunlop*

IMPULSIVE AIR (IRE)   7 b.g. Try My Best (USA) 130 – Tracy's Sundown   56 §
(Red Sunset 120) [1998 69: 8d² 8g* 8d* 8g 9g 8g 7g³ 8s⁵ 6.9d 8g 8g 9d 1999 8g
8d 9m 9.2m* 9.2f 9.1g² 8.5m 10m³ 8m⁴ 8m 9.1d⁴ 10v 8d⁵ Oct 20] strong gelding:
unimpressive mover: modest performer: won handicap at Hamilton in June: effective
at 1m/1¼m: acts on firm and good to soft ground: tried visored: moody, and one to
treat with caution. *E. Weymes*

IMSHISHWAY (IRE)   4 b.c. Royal Academy (USA) 130 – Mama Lucia (Work-   75
boy 123) [1998 75: 8s 9.9s 10.2s⁵ 10f 10g 10m 9.7f 7s 10s 1999 12.3m* 12m Jul
24] tall, lengthy, good sort: good mover: fair handicapper: won amateur event at
Warwick in July: well beaten next time: stays 1½m: acts on firm and soft going: tried
blinkered. *M. C. Pipe*

I'M SOPHIE (IRE)   2 ch.f. (May 4) Shalford (IRE) 124§ – Caisson 67 (Shaadi   62
(USA) 126) [1999 5g² Jun 14] 2,000F, 4,200Y: first foal: dam lightly-raced maiden
from family of Barathea: favourite, neck second of 10 to Lady-Love in maiden at
Musselburgh on debut: looked sure to improve. *T. D. Barron*

I'M TEF   4 b.g. Noble Patriarch 115 – Who's That Lady 60 (Nordance (USA))   –
[1998 –, a71d: a7s² a6g³ a7g* a7g² a6g 8s 9m 8s a6g 1999 a7g a8f a8g⁶ a7g Feb 12]
compact gelding: fair performer at best: has lost his form: stays 7f: acts on fibresand,
little form on turf: sometimes blinkered. *T. D. Easterby*

IN A TWINKLING (IRE)   2 b.f. (Apr 21) Brief Truce (USA) 126 – Glim (USA)   74 d
(Damascus (USA)) [1999 6g³ 5g⁶ 6g⁴ 6g⁴ 6g⁶ 5s 6s Oct 25] IR 16,000Y: leggy,
angular filly: half-sister to several winners, including fairly useful Irish 1995 2-y-o
5f winner Ribot's Secret (by Danehill), later successful in USA, and French 1m to
1¼m winner Cotton Kisser (by Suave Dancer): dam (unraced) from family of
Caerleon: modest maiden: best run on debut: stays 6f: ran poorly final start, and sold
11,000 gns after. *W. M. Roper, Ireland*

IN CAHOOTS   6 gr.g. Kalaglow 132 – Royal Celerity (USA) (Riverman (USA)   –
131) [1998 NR 1999 17.2f Jun 26] leggy gelding: poor performer: better at 1¼m than
shorter: acts on firm ground: blinkered once. *A. G. Newcombe*

INCA STAR (USA)   2 b.c. (Apr 20) Trempolino (USA) 135 – Inca Empress   78 p
(USA) (Sovereign Dancer (USA)) [1999 8d³ Oct 27] 400,000 francs Y: first foal:
dam, won at up to 9f in USA, half-sister to very smart German middle-distance horse
Germany (by Trempolino): weak in market and green, shaped well when third of 10
to King Spinner in maiden at Yarmouth, finishing very strongly after starting slowly:
likely to prove suited by 1¼m/1½m: sure to improve a fair bit and should develop
into a useful performer. *M. Johnston*

INCEPTA   4 b.g. Selkirk (USA) 129 – Ringlet (USA) 58 (Secreto (USA) 128)   58
[1998 65: 8d⁶ 8g³ 9s 9.7f⁴ 10m a8f² a8.5g* 10m a8f² a7g⁴ a8f a8g⁵ Nov 23]
strong, rangy gelding: modest handicapper: well beaten final 3 starts: stays 9.7f: acts
on firm ground (probably unsuited by soft) and all-weather: visored (probably
flattered) second start: has worn tongue strap. *P. S. McEntee*

INCHALONG   4 b.f. Inchinor 119 – Reshift 94 (Night Shift (USA)) [1998 80: 7d   76
6.1m 7.3m⁴ 7g³ 7m⁴ 6s⁴ 6g 6g* 6g² 6d⁵ 5f 6g* 7g 6.1g 7g 7s 1999 a6g 7g 6d 6v   a–
7s 6.1f 6m 6.1m² 7f 6.1m⁶ 6m* 7.1d 7g² a6g a8g⁶ Nov 23] small, leggy filly:
unimpressive mover: fair handicapper: won at Pontefract in September: effective at
6f/7f: acts on soft and good to firm going (no form on all-weather): usually visored:
usually races prominently. *M. Brittain*

INCHCAILLOCH (IRE)   10 b.g. Lomond (USA) 128 – Glowing With Pride   50
114 (Ile de Bourbon (USA) 133) [1998 NR 1999 17.2m⁶ 15.8m 16m 17.2s Sep 27]
big, strong, lengthy gelding: useful hurdler/chaser: fairly useful handicapper on Flat
in 1997: modest at best in 1999: stays 2¼m: acts on firm going (won on soft at 3 yrs):
held up. *J. S. King*

INCHING CLOSER 2 b.g. (Apr 3) Inchinor 119 – Maiyaasah 75 (Kris 135) [1999 **80**
6m⁵ 6g² 8g⁴ Aug 29] 8,200F, 10,500Y: sturdy gelding: seventh foal: half-brother to
3-y-o Passions Plaything and 3 winners, including useful 6f (at 2 yrs) and 1m winner
Lead The Dance (by Lead On Time) and fairly useful 9.4f winner Serious Sensation
(by Be My Chief): dam lightly-raced maiden, who ran only at 1m: easily best effort
in maidens when 1½ lengths second of 10 to Zoning at Yarmouth, finishing well: ran
poorly final start: should stay at least 7f. *N. A. Callaghan*

INCHINNAN 2 b.f. (Apr 22) Inchinor 119 – Westering 54 (Auction Ring (USA) **69**
123) [1999 7f³ 7g⁵ 7d⁵ 7m² 7g² 7.9d⁵ 8m⁵ 8d² Oct 30] 850Y: small filly: second foal:
half-sister to 3-y-o Lake Mehra: dam maiden who should have stayed 1m: fair
maiden: second of 18 in Newmarket seller final start: stays 1m: acts on firm and good
to soft going. *D. Morris*

INCHLONAIG 2 ch.c. (Mar 22) Nashwan (USA) 135 – Inchmurrin 114 **105 P**
(Lomond (USA) 128) [1999 7d* Sep 28]

    Roger Charlton, having missed out on a Derby winner when Oath was
transferred to Henry Cecil's yard after just one run, had the misfortune to lose a
potential classic winner in the latest season. Inchlonaig, winner of the Tattersalls Houghton Sales Stakes at Newmarket in September on his debut, was sold
privately the following month, and when he returns from a winter in Dubai he'll
be racing for Godolphin. With the latest Two Thousand Guineas winner Island
Sands having been purchased by Godolphin after showing a lot of promise as a
juvenile, it must be tempting for trainers who find themselves with a classic
prospect, and who fear losing it, to keep the horse under wraps until it is a three-
year-old. Easier said than done, of course, as racecourse experience gained as a
two-year-old is probably essential for a Guineas contender.

    Inchlonaig became the first debutant to win the Houghton Sales Stakes,
a race restricted to horses catalogued in that particular sale the previous year.
Two of its seven previous winners, namely Don Corleone in 1994 and Tamarisk
in 1997, were also trained by Charlton, who beforehand was of the opinion that
Inchlonaig hadn't shown enough at home to suggest he could win. Inchlonaig's
starting price of 16/1 in what wasn't a vintage renewal reflected that lack of
confidence. Favourite at 3/1 was the sole Irish challenger Pissaro, an impressive winner of a maiden on his only start. The seventeen runners split into
two groups, Inchlonaig joining those who raced down the centre and who
appeared to have an advantage. For a long way that looked unlikely to be of any
relevance where Inchlonaig was concerned. He started slowly and ran green
early on, and, as a result, was still in last place at halfway in a race run at a
good pace, Nicobar leading the far-side group and Dancing Mirage those in the
centre. It wasn't until over two furlongs from home that Inchlonaig began to
make any significant headway, keeping on so well that just six of his rivals
remained ahead of him approaching the final furlong. Maintaining his effort as
stronger pressure was applied, Inchlonaig picked them off one by one, catching

£300000 Tattersalls Houghton Sales Stakes, Newmarket—
Inchlonaig looks a fine prospect in becoming the first debutant to win in eight runnings of the race;
Bedazzling (right) is second with Teodora (in between them) third

the leader Bedazzling in the last twenty-five yards to win by half a length. Discussing Inchlonaig immediately after the race Charlton remarked that 'He looks like a Derby horse rather than a Guineas horse to me', yet at the time the sale was announced he was quoted as saying that 'I've always thought he was a lovely horse, and he could easily make up into a Guineas horse'. Inchlonaig also provided the most valuable win of the season for his jockey Tim Sprake who went on to finish fifth in the jockeys' championship; severe injuries, sustained in a car accident in December, may well keep him out of the saddle for the whole of 2000.

	Nashwan (USA) (ch 1986)	Blushing Groom (ch 1974)	Red God Runaway Bride
Inchlonaig (ch.c. Mar 22, 1997)		Height of Fashion (b 1979)	Bustino Highclere
	Inchmurrin (b 1985)	Lomond (b 1980)	Northern Dancer My Charmer
		On Show (br 1978)	Welsh Pageant African Dancer

From what we saw of Inchlonaig over seven furlongs, albeit a testing one, we feel he wouldn't be found wanting for speed in the Guineas, and his breeding suggests that he could well have the stamina necessary for the Derby. While his half-brother Inchinor (by Ahonoora) and half-sister Ingozi (by Warning) were best at seven furlongs and a mile, his winning half-sisters by sires who are more of an influence for stamina, namely Inchkeith (by Reference Point) and Inchyre (by Shirley Heights), both stayed a mile and a half. Inchinor is the best of the crop so far, a very smart performer who won the Greenham, Criterion and Hungerford Stakes, though Inchyre showed useful form and Ingozi was fairly useful. Their dam Inchmurrin lacked size but not ability or courage. The small, light-framed Inchmurrin was a smart performer, winner of the Child Stakes and second in the Coronation Stakes over a mile and also showing her form at a mile and a quarter. There is a fair amount of stamina further back in Inchlonaig's pedigree. His grandam On Show (also the grandam of Balisada, incidentally) won at a mile and a quarter and finished second in the November Handicap, and his great grandam African Dancer won the Park Hill Stakes. There's a great deal of improvement to come from Inchlonaig, and even if he should fall short of classic-winning standard there will be good races to be won with him. *R. Charlton*

INCH PERFECT   4 b.g. Inchinor 119 – Scarlet Veil 75 (Tyrnavos 129) [1998 73: **73 +** 10.1g⁴ 11.9m³ 1999 a8g* 8d a8g a7g⁴ 10.9g³ a12g³ 10m* 10d* 10.1d* 10.2s* 8s³ a12g* Nov 13] tall, good-topped gelding: fair performer: won sellers at Southwell in March and Redcar (handicap, left J. Hetherton) in September: proved a revelation for new connections, winning handicaps at Pontefract, Newcastle (despite being badly hampered) and Bath in space of 8 days in October and at Wolverhampton in November: stays easy 1½m: acts on soft going, good to firm and fibresand: tongue tied sixth start: usually held up. *R. A. Fahey*

INCH PINCHER   2 ch.c. (Jan 25) Inchinor 119 – Cutpurse Moll 76 (Green Desert **62** (USA) 127) [1999 5.2f 5s 6.1m² 7f² 7m 7f⁴ 7d⁴ 7.1m* 7m³ 7s 8.3g⁶ 6d a7g a7g² a8g⁵ **a57** Dec 6] 12,000F, 22,000Y: lengthy colt: first foal: dam 7f winner: modest performer: won selling nursery at Sandown in August: left M. Channon for 4,000 gns after thirteenth start: stays 7f: acts on firm going and equitrack: tried visored: carries head high and sometimes looks none too keen. *P. Howling*

INCHTINA   4 b.f. Inchinor 119 – Nikitina 106 (Nijinsky (CAN) 138) [1998 85: **71** 8.2s* 10.2g⁶ 10m 10v 1999 8.3d⁶ 8g 8m 12.3m² a12g³ 12m* 12g² 14.1m 12m Sep 8] angular, good-quartered filly: fair handicapper: won apprentice events at Kempton in August: below form final 2 starts: stays 1½m: acts on soft going, good to firm and fibresand. *M. A. Jarvis*

INCLUDE ME OUT   5 ch.g. Old Vic 136 – Tafila 101 (Adonijah 126) [1998 71: **–** 9g 14.1d 10g² 10g² 10m* 10.1f⁵ 1999 8.2m 15.8m Jul 10] fair handicapper: little form in 1999: stays 1¼m: acts on good to firm going. *J. A. Pickering*

INCREDULOUS (FR)   2 ch.f. (Apr 22) Indian Ridge 123 – Fetlar (Pharly (FR)   **– p**
130) [1999 6d Oct 29] half-sister to 3 winners, including fairly useful 1995 2-y-o
7f winner Staffin (by Salse) and useful 1994 2-y-o 6f/7f winner Be Mindful (by
Warning) who stayed 1¼m: dam unraced half-sister to Jersey Stakes winner Ardkinglass: weak in market and green, clear signs of ability when fourteenth of 19 to Pax
in maiden at Newmarket: will be suited by 7f+: sure to do better. *J. R. Fanshawe*

INDEEDYEDO   2 b.f. (Apr 4) Efisio 120 – Bonita 57 (Primo Dominie 121) [1999   **87**
5g⁶ 5g³ 6f⁵ 6d³ 6m* 6m 7s³ 7s 7m⁶ Oct 19] 10,000Y: sturdy, close-coupled filly:
second foal: half-sister to 3-y-o Clunie: dam 6f/7f winner: fairly useful performer:
won maiden at Hamilton in June: off 2 months after next start, running creditably
first 2 on return (latter of them listed event): stays 7f: acts on soft and good to firm
going. *J. Pearce*

INDIA (IRE)   4 b.f. Indian Ridge 123 – Athens Belle (IRE) 101 (Groom Dancer   **54**
(USA) 128) [1998 54: 10d⁴ 7g³ 1999 8.1m⁵ 10m 8d Oct 11] quite attractive filly:
modest maiden: well held last 2 starts: stays 1m. *L. M. Cumani*

INDIANA LEGEND (IRE)   3 ch.c. Indian Ridge 123 – Mardi Gras Belle (USA)   **108**
65§ (Masked Dancer (USA)) [1998 104: 6m² 6m* 6d⁴ 6g² 6g² 1999 7g² 8m 7m⁶ Jun
16] rangy colt: useful performer: creditable efforts when 2½ lengths second of 6 to
Bertolini in European Free Handicap at Newmarket and when sixth to Lots of Magic
in Jersey Stakes at Royal Ascot: stayed 7f: acted on good to firm and good to soft
going: sent to USA: dead. *B. J. Meehan*

INDIANA PRINCESS   6 b.m. Warrshan (USA) 117 – Lovely Greek Lady   **72**
(Ela-Mana-Mou 132) [1998 63: 12m* 13g⁴ 12g* 12m⁶ 14g⁵ 1999 16m³ 16.2d⁴ 14g*
16d⁴ 13f³ 16m* 12g³ 16m³ Aug 31] workmanlike mare: fair handicapper: won twice
(apprentice events) at Musselburgh in June, and at Redcar in August: below form
final 2 starts: needs further than 13f, and stays 2m: acts on good to firm and good to
soft going. *Mrs M. Reveley*

INDIANA SPRINGS (IRE)   2 b.g. (May 3) Foxhound (USA) 103 – Moss Agate   **–**
(Alias Smith (USA)) [1999 7m 7.6g 6.8d Sep 21] IR 7,000F, 11,000Y, 10,500
2-y-o: fifth foal: half-brother to 7.5f to y-1¼m winner Scottish Park (by Scottish Reel)
and a winner in Singapore by Gallic League: dam unraced: well held in maidens.
N. P. Littmoden

INDIAN BAZAAR (IRE)   3 ch.g. Indian Ridge 123 – Bazaar Promise 58 (Native   **47**
Bazaar 122) [1998 –: 5s 5.1v 6d 1999 a12g 5.9m² 8.3m³ 9.9s Sep 21] big, good-
topped gelding: poor maiden: stays 1m: acts on good to firm going: sold 4,500 gns.
Sir Mark Prescott

INDIAN BLAZE   5 ch.g. Indian Ridge 123 – Odile (Green Dancer (USA) 132)   **91**
[1998 70+: a9.4g² a9.4g⁶ 8s 7m 7m 5.7g 6s⁴ 6s* a5g a6g³ a6g⁴ a7g* 1999 a7g a6g   **a79**
a6g 7s* 5s² 7v² 8g 6m³ 6m² 7m* 7m 8m* 7.1d 7g⁶ 7m⁴ 7.3m 8d* 8d a7g³ a7g⁴
Dec 21] workmanlike gelding: fairly useful handicapper on turf, fair on all-weather:
won at Folkestone in March, Kempton in July and August then at Newmarket in
October: effective at 6f to 1m: acts on good to firm ground, heavy and fibresand:
blinkered once at 3 yrs: has been bandaged: takes good hold: often hangs right.
D. R. C. Elsworth

INDIAN BRAVE   5 b.g. Indian Ridge 123 – Supreme Kingdom 85 (Take A Reef   **70**
127) [1998 83: 6d² 7s⁵ 6d 6g⁵ 6g 6m 6m⁵ 6g² 6m³ 1999 6s⁶ 6m⁴ 6m 6f³ 6d³ 6.9g⁵
8.1s⁶ 7d³ 7s 6d Nov 4] lengthy gelding: fair maiden: left B. Meehan after reappearance and N. Littmoden after penultimate start: stays 7f: acts on firm ground, probably
on soft: blinkered once at 4 yrs: has carried head awkwardly/hung. *John A. Harris*

INDIAN CITY   3 ch.f. Lahib (USA) 129 – Alencon (Northfields (USA)) [1998   **54**
57: 7m² 6m* 7m 1999 a7g 5.9m 5.9m⁵ 7d 7g² Oct 19] modest performer: stays 7f:
acts on good to firm going: sold 6,200 gns. *R. Guest*

INDIAN DANCE   3 ch.c. Indian Ridge 123 – Petronella (USA) (Nureyev (USA)   **63**
131) [1998 NR 1999 7m⁶ 7g⁵ 7.7m⁶ 6m 8g 7g³ 7v Sep 24] 75,000Y: big, lengthy colt:
first foal: dam unraced sister to useful winner up to 1½m Mellaby: modest maiden:
tailed off in handicap final start: should stay 1m: has had tongue tied: inconsistent:
sold 3,200 gns. *J. W. Hills*

Joel Stakes, Newmarket—
Indian Lodge (right) makes a successful transition into listed company, winning the first of two such races;
Ras Shaikh, Sunstreak (left) and Little Rock (hidden by winner) fill the frame

INDIAN DANEHILL (IRE) 3 b.c. Danehill (USA) 126 – Danse Indienne (USA) **116** (Green Dancer (USA) 132) [1998 100p: 8s* 7g 1999 8s* 8m⁵ 9s³ 10g² Jun 27] big, useful-looking colt: smart performer: won Prix de Fontainebleau at Longchamp in April by neck from Le Roi Chic before respectable fifth to Sendawar there in Poule d'Essai des Poulains: ran well last 2 starts when length third to Golden Snake in Prix Jean Prat at Chantilly (despite hitting rail and rider losing whip when short of room closing stages) and when 2 lengths second to Slickly in Grand Prix de Paris at Longchamp: stays 1¼m: acts on soft ground, ran respectably on good to firm: has pulled hard/been free to post. *A. Fabre, France*

INDIAN FLAG (IRE) 4 ch.f. Indian Ridge 123 – Flagpole (IRE) (Be My Guest **39** (USA) 126) [1998 –: 6d 8m 7d³ 6.1g 1999 7m 8.2m⁶ 7.7s a8g⁵ 10.5s 10m³ a12g⁶ Jul 7] lengthy, angular filly: poor maiden handicapper: stays 1¼m: acts on good to firm ground. *M. D. I. Usher*

INDIAN LODGE (IRE) 3 b.c. Grand Lodge (USA) 125 – Repetitious 103 **112** (Northfields (USA)) [1998 90: 7g³ 7g 8s⁶ 1999 8s* 8m* 8m⁶ 8f³ 7m 8m² 8d* 8.5d* Oct 15] sturdy colt: smart performer: had a good season, winning maiden at Newbury and minor event at Yarmouth in May and listed races at Newmarket in September (by ½ length from Ras Shaikh) and October (by head from Maidaan): stays 1m well: acts on firm and soft ground: swished tail in preliminaries (ran creditably fourth start: game: capable of making his mark in minor pattern company. *Mrs A. J. Perrett*

INDIAN MUSIC 2 b.g. (Mar 6) Indian Ridge 123 – Dagny Juel (USA) 75 (Danzig **74** (USA)) [1999 6g 6d 5g⁴ 6v 6s 5s* Nov 5] IR 28,000Y, 19,000 2-y-o: third foal: half-brother to 3-y-o Strinberg and a winner in Japan by Selkirk: dam lightly-raced 7f winner from family of Nureyev: fair performer: won nursery at Doncaster in November by neck from Harryana: well beaten previous 2 starts: should prove as effective at 6f as 5f: acts on soft going, yet to race on firmer than good. *J. Berry*

INDIAN NECTAR 6 b.m. Indian Ridge 123 – Sheer Nectar 72 (Piaffer (USA) **62** 113) [1998 –: 8.5m 1999 12.3m⁴ 10.5m³ 10.2m⁴ 10g* 12.3g³ 10g* 10.2g* 10m⁶ 9.9v Sep 29] sparely-made mare: modest handicapper: won at Nottingham, Lingfield and Chepstow in August: effective at 1¼m/1½m: acts on good to firm going, possibly not on heavy: visored once at 4 yrs: usually held up: consistent. *R. Brotherton*

INDIAN PLUME 3 b.c. Efisio 120 – Boo Hoo 68 (Mummy's Pet 125) [1998 89: **85** 6d⁵ 6m* 7s⁴ 1999 8d³ 7.1d⁴ 8m 8g Aug 16] smallish, sturdy colt: fairly useful handicapper: not discredited first and third starts: stays 1m: acts on good to firm and good to soft ground, ran poorly on soft: free-going front runner. *C. W. Thornton*

INDIAN PROSPECTOR (FR) 2 b.c. (May 11) Machiavellian (USA) 123 – **95 P** Danse Indienne (USA) (Green Dancer (USA) 132) [1999 7v* Nov 8] half-brother to smart French 1994 2-y-o winner Indian Jones and 3-y-o Indian Danehill (both by Danehill) and to 1½m winner Dancing Law (by Law Society): dam, placed up to 10.5f, half-sister to high-class middle-distance performer Antheus: impressive winner of 11-runner minor event at Maisons-Laffitte in November by 2½ lengths from Golani (pair clear), disputing lead long way until easily quickening clear final 1f: looks well up to making his mark in better company at 3 yrs. *A. Fabre, France*

INDIAN ROPE TRICK   3 ch.g. Kris 135 – Lassoo 87 (Caerleon (USA) 132)   – [1998 NR 1999 7.1d 10s 8s Oct 4] big, plain gelding: brother to 5-y-o Sioux and half-brother to 6-y-o Mustang: dam, maiden placed from 7f (at 2 yrs) to 11f, half-sister to very smart middle-distance colt Apache: little promise in maidens: has been bandaged in front. *C. W. Thornton*

INDIAN SPARK   5 ch.g. Indian Ridge 123 – Annes Gift (Ballymoss 136) [1998   **96 d** 92: 6d 6g 5m 7m⁶ 6s 5g² 5s⁵ 5d⁴ 6s² 6m* 6m⁶ 6s⁴ 6m 5g* 6s 5m 5g 5s* 6d 1999 5d 5d 6g⁵ 5s⁵ 6d³ 5m⁴ 6d* 6m 5m⁵ 6s³ 6f 6d 6m 5.6g 6d 6d 5s 5s Nov 5] close-coupled gelding: poor mover (reportedly fractured off-fore joint before 3-y-o debut): useful handicapper at best: won at York in June: lost his form after tenth start: effective at 5f/ 6f: unraced on heavy going, acts on any other: usually races prominently. *J. S. Goldie*

INDIAN SPLENDOUR (IRE)   4 b.f. Second Set (IRE) 127 – Clover Honey   – (King of Clubs 124) [1998 45: a5g⁴ a5g² a5g⁶ a6g a5s 1999 a6g Feb 19] poor maiden: no form after second 3-y-o start. *R. F. Marvin*

INDIAN STUNNER (IRE)   2 ch.c. (Apr 18) Indian Ridge 123 – Bazaar Promise   – 58 (Native Bazaar 122) [1999 6v Oct 23] IR 45,000Y: sixth foal (all by Indian Ridge): brother to 3-y-o Indian Bazaar and 3 winners, including useful sprinter Cheyenne Spirit and 8.5f and 1¼m winner Indian Express: dam temperamental sister to smart sprinter Crofthall: bandaged behind, always in rear in maiden at Newbury: sold 5,200 gns later in October. *D. R. C. Elsworth*

INDIAN SUN   2 ch.g. (Jan 29) Indian Ridge 123 – Star Tulip 99 (Night Shift   **80** (USA)) [1999 6d 6m⁶ 6s* 6v Oct 23] 35,000Y: good-bodied gelding: first foal: dam 6f winner, including at 2 yrs: progressive form in maidens, winning at Lingfield in October by 5 lengths: well beaten in nursery at Newbury final start: should stay 7f: acts on soft and good to firm going. *J. L. Dunlop*

INDIAN SWINGER (IRE)   3 ch.c. Up And At 'em 109 – Seanee Squaw (Indian   – Ridge 123) [1998 60, a69: 5m⁴ 5m 6s a6g* a7g⁶ 1999 a6g² a7g³ a8g³ 6g a8.5g⁵ Aug   **a67** 14] fair on all-weather, modest at best on turf: stays 1m: acts on all-weather, ran poorly on soft going. *J. M. P. Eustace*

INDIAN WARRIOR   3 b.g. Be My Chief (USA) 122 – Wanton 106 (Kris 135)   **81 d** [1998 87: 6m² 6f² 6m³ 7m* 7d 1999 7.1m⁶ 7m 7g 7.9m 7g* 8s Nov 6] small, quite attractive gelding: fairly useful at 2 yrs: nowhere near so good after reappearance in 1999, disappointing in handicaps prior to winning seller at Lingfield in October (left J. Noseda): races freely, and not sure to stay much beyond 7f: acts on firm going: visored third/fourth starts: usually bandaged behind: has been taken steadily to post. *W. J. Musson*

INDIGENOUS (IRE)   6 br.g. Marju (IRE) 127 – Sea Port (Averof 123) [1998   **122** 118: 8m* 11m* 5m³ 10m* 10m⁴ 8d* 12m* 8d* 9f* 8f⁴ 12m* 1999 5g 10m* 10m² 12m² 12m⁶ 5m 12f² 12m⁴ Dec 12] useful winner of 3 races for K. Prendergast in Ireland at 2/3 yrs, when named Qualtron: very smart performer nowadays: won 8 times at Sha Tin in 1998, notably Hong Kong International Vase, and successful in Hong Kong Gold Cup there in March for second year running: ran creditably when sixth to Daylami in King George VI And Queen Elizabeth Diamond Stakes at Ascot fifth start, despite sweating profusely (had four handlers in paddock) and taking good hold: had knee operation afterwards and returned in good heart, excellent 1½ lengths second to Special Week in Japan Cup at Tokyo before creditable ¾-length fourth to Borgia in Hong Kong Vase at Sha Tin final start: stays 1½m: acts on firm and good to soft going, usually held up: has worn tongue strap: tough. *I. W. Allan, Hong Kong*

INDIGO BAY (IRE)   3 b.g. Royal Academy (USA) 130 – Cape Heights (Shirley   **77** Heights 130) [1998 –p: 7m 7m 8.2s 1999 a10g 10f³ 11.9f* 14.1g 11.5m³ 12.1m² 11.5f* 11.9g² 11.5g 10.1m 11.5s a12g² a12g a13g Dec 10] leggy, useful-looking gelding: fair handicapper: won at Brighton (seller) in May and Lingfield in July: probably best around 1½m: acts on equitrack and firm going: blinkered second to fourth starts: normally leads: sometimes hangs. *S. Dow*

Mail On Sunday Millennium Mile Final (Handicap), Ascot—
a stiff test of stamina at the trip suits those coming from behind;
a career-best effort from Indium (far side), who beats The Whistling Teal and Abajany

INDIGO BEACH (IRE)   3 b.g. Rainbows For Life (CAN) – Sandy Maid (Sandy   –
Creek 123) [1998 –: 7.5m 6m a6g⁶ 7s 8d 1999 11.6g May 10] sturdy gelding: little
form: sold 3,000 gns in July. *Sir Mark Prescott*

INDIRECT   2 ch.f. (Mar 22) Interrex (CAN) – To The Point 96 (Sharpen Up 127)   **39**
[1999 5m a5g a6g⁶ 7.5s 5m⁵ 6f Aug 7] 3,000Y: sister to a modest/temperamental
maiden and half-sister to 3-y-o Kildee Gem, fairly useful 6f (at 2 yrs) and 1¼m
winner Kings Assembly (by Presidium) and several winners in USA: dam 2-y-o 5f
winner: poor form at best, mainly in sellers: tried blinkered. *K. A. Ryan*

INDIUM   5 b.g. Groom Dancer (USA) 128 – Gold Bracelet § (Golden Fleece   **87**
(USA) 133) [1998 84: a10g a10g⁵ 10d 8.5m³ 10g 8d² 8g 8f 8m*ᵈⁱˢ 8.3f 8m⁴ 8g* 7g
8g 8s 1999 8v⁵ 8g 8d² 8m⁴ 8m 7m 8m² 8m⁶ 7.9m 7.3m⁴ 8s* 8d 8d Oct 30] rangy
gelding: fairly useful handicapper: generally ran creditably in 1999, and put up
career-best effort to win 22-runner Mail On Sunday Millennium Mile Final at Ascot
in September by short head from The Whistling Teal, pair clear: given deal to do/not
well drawn final 2 starts: effective at 7f to 1¼m: acts on any turf going, well beaten
both times on equitrack: has run well when sweating: has worn crossed noseband:
usually held up. *W. J. Musson*

INDUCEMENT   3 ch.g. Sabrehill (USA) 120 – Verchinina 99 (Star Appeal 133)   **94**
[1998 85: 6s³ 7.5m³ 8.5m* 8d⁴ 7.9g⁶ 1999 9g⁵ 10.4d⁵ 9m* 8.1m⁶ 10g⁴ 10.3m 10d
Sep 23] tall, quite good-topped gelding: has a fluent, round action: fairly useful
handicapper: won at Sandown in June: left B. Hills after next outing, below form
final 2 starts: probably stays 1¼m: acts on good to firm and good to soft going: has
been bandaged: equipped with rope halter: found little fifth start. *Mrs A. J. Perrett*

INDUNA   3 ch.f. Grand Lodge (USA) 125 – Kerkura (USA) 83 (Riverman (USA)   –
131) [1998 NR 1999 12v 12m 12g May 15] 7,000 2-y-o: first foal: dam, 1½m winner,
from family of Ribblesdale winners Strigida and Catalpa: well held in maidens,
pulling hard final 2 starts. *S. Dow*

INDY CARR   2 b.f. (May 17) Pyramus (USA) 78 – Miss Adventure 69 (Adonijah   **78**
126) [1999 8d* Oct 30] 2,000Y: fourth foal: half-sister to 4-y-o Ardleigh Charmer:
dam 1½m winner: 12/1, won 18-runner seller at Newmarket most decisively by 4
lengths from Inchinnan, improving from rear over 1f after slow start: subsequently
sold 12,500 gns and joined M. Dods: will stay at least 1¼m. *H. J. Collingridge*

INDY KNIGHT (IRE)   4 ch.f. Indian Ridge 123 – Bag Lady 86 (Be My Guest   –
(USA) 126) [1998 –: 8.1m 10.8m 8d 1999 a12g 10v 8g Jun 30] big, unfurnished filly:
little sign of ability. *R. E. Peacock*

INFAMOUS (USA)   6 ch.g. Diesis 133 – Name And Fame (USA) (Arts And   **49**
Letters (USA)) [1998 77, a–: 12m⁶ 12m² 12m⁴ 12m 1999 a11g a12g² a14.8g² a16.2g²
a14.8g⁵ a16.2g³ Feb 20] angular gelding: poor form in 1999: stays 2m: acts on firm
going, soft and fibresand: blinkered (well beaten) twice: has worn tongue strap.
B. J. Llewellyn

INFATUATION   6 b.g. Music Boy 124 – Fleeting Affair 98 (Hotfoot 126) [1998   **92**
95: 12m⁴ 10m⁶ 10m 10m² 10m* 10.1g⁶ 12g⁵ 10s³ 10s⁶ 1999 10g 10m 10f 10m* 10m³
10.4g 10m⁶ 10.3m 11.5s⁴ Oct 8] tall, lengthy gelding: fairly useful handicapper: won
at Newmarket in June: in-and-out form after: best at 1¼m/easy 1½m: acts on soft and
good to firm going: often sweats: has flashed tail/carried head high: held up: has been
taken last to post. *Lady Herries*

INFOTEC (IRE)   2 b. or br.c. (Apr 13) Shalford (IRE) 124§ – Tomona (Linacre   **69**
133) [1999 6s 7d² 7s² Sep 29] IR 1,000Y, 2,000 2-y-o: half-brother to 3 winners,
including useful 1993 2-y-o 7f winner Full of Pluck (by Try My Best) and Irish 1¼m
winner Hegemonic (by Godswalk): dam Irish 1½m and hurdles winner: fair form in
maidens, runner-up at Yarmouth and Newcastle last 2 starts: should stay 1m: raced
only on good to soft/soft going. *H. Akbary*

IN GOOD FAITH   7 b.g. Beveled (USA) – Dulcidene 71 (Behistoun 131) [1998   –
–: a9.4g 1999 10s⁵ 9f⁶ Jul 17] neat gelding: no form on Flat since 1997: barely stays
1¼m: acts on fibresand: tried visored: improved over hurdles late in year, winning 3
times. *R. E. Barr*

IN GOOD ORDER (IRE)   4 b.f. Ajraas (USA) 88 – Ponstinia (Yashgan 126)   –
[1998 NR 1999 a10g a10g a12g Feb 6] IR 1,600Y: second foal: dam disqualified
1¼m winner in Ireland at 2 yrs: well beaten in maidens at Lingfield. *G. L. Moore*

INIGO JONES (IRE)   3 b.g. Alzao (USA) 117 – Kindjal 84 (Kris 135) [1998 NR   **93**
1999 10g² 10.5m³ 12g² 12s² 14.1m* 14.6m³ 14.1m³ Sep 24] rather leggy, angular
gelding: sixth living foal: closely related/half-brother to fairly useful 1¼m winners
Unforgiving Minute (by Bellypha) and Vallance (by Top Ville): dam, 1m winner
from 3 starts, out of Yorkshire Oaks and Nassau winner Connaught Bridge: fairly
useful performer: won maiden at Nottingham in August: creditable third in handicaps
after: stays 1¾m: acts on soft and good to firm going: has tended to hang: has been
bandaged in front. *P. W. Harris*

INITIATIVE   3 ch.c. Arazi (USA) 135 – Dance Quest (FR) 117 (Green Dancer   **89**
(USA) 132) [1998 89p: 7m³ 1999 8m* 8m⁵ Aug 22] smallish, quite attractive colt:
won 6-runner maiden at Thirsk in May: last of 5 in minor event at Bath next time:
may prove best around 1m: sold 22,000 gns, joined B. Murray. *H. R. A. Cecil*

INKLING (USA)   2 b.f. (Apr 5) Seeking The Gold (USA) – Number (USA)   **104 P**
(Nijinsky (CAN) 138) [1999 6s* Sep 19]
    The Ballydoyle colts carried virtually all before them in Europe's
pattern races for two-year-olds, but what of the Ballydoyle fillies? Chiang Mai,
a Sadler's Wells half-sister to Prix de Diane winner Rafha, beat much shorter-
priced stable-companions on both her starts, the second of them in a listed race
over a mile and a furlong at Leopardstown in November, and she should do
well at three. But the filly that really took the eye was the even more choicely-
bred Inkling, who trounced sixteen rivals when 6/4 favourite in a six-furlong
maiden at the Curragh in September on her only outing. It was no ordinary
maiden and several in the field showed quite useful form, yet Inkling was out
on her own, winning by five lengths from Berenica. The Anglesey Stakes
runner-up, Still Going On, was only fifth. Plans to run Inkling in one of the
big end-of-season races—she held entries in the Cheveley Park and Marcel
Boussac—came to nothing, but she won in the style of a filly who should prove
up to tackling top company, soon going well behind the pace and just pushed
clear after leading over a furlong out. With few obvious types for the One

Thousand Guineas having come to light in the latest season, even after just one run Inkling looks as good a candidate as any for the first fillies' classic.

Inkling (USA) (b.f. Apr 5, 1997)	Seeking The Gold (USA) (b 1985)	Mr Prospector (b 1970)	Raise A Native
			Gold Digger
		Con Game (b or br 1974)	Buckpasser
			Broadway
	Number (USA) (b 1979)	Nijinsky (b 1967)	Northern Dancer
			Flaming Page
		Special (b 1969)	Forli
			Thong

The medium-sized, close-coupled, deep-girthed Inkling, who looked in really good shape at the Curragh, is closely related to several winners abroad by Mr Prospector (the sire of Inkling's sire Seeking The Gold), notably the 1989 Grand Criterium winner Jade Robbery and a Grade 2 nine-furlong winner in the States called Chequer. Inkling's dam Number, a very smart racemare who won graded races at up to nine furlongs, is herself closely related to Nureyev and a half-sister to Fairy Bridge, the dam of Sadler's Wells and Fairy King. The link between all these horses is the outstanding broodmare Special, who was put down at the end of the year at Claiborne Farm in Kentucky. A half-sister to Thatch amongst others, Special ran only once, but at stud she has left a legacy which will last well into the twenty-first century. John Magnier paid over 8,000,000 dollars for six descendents of Special in 1998—the most expensive being the yearling Inkling at 3,400,000 dollars. *A. P. O'Brien, Ireland*

Mr M. Tabor & Mrs John Magnier's "Inkling"

INKWELL   5 b.g. Relief Pitcher 120 – Fragrant Hackette 32 (Simply Great (FR)   **52 §**
122) [1998 52: a10g 8g* 8m 10g⁴ 8d 8s³ 7.6g³ 8g* 8.3f 10m 8d⁵ 7s* 1999 7s 8f
8.1d 10d 8m 10.5d² 9.9v² 10.2s a10g⁴ Dec 22] smallish, robust gelding: modest
handicapper: left R. Hoad after reappearance: effective at 7f (given a test) to 1¼m:
acts on equitrack, heavy and good to firm going: tried visored, usually blinkered:
very slowly away fifth start: inconsistent. *G. L. Moore*

INNER LIGHT   4 b.g. Slip Anchor 136 – Radiance (FR) 115 (Blakeney 126)   **–**
[1998 64, a–: 8d⁵ 10v a10g a11g 15.8m⁶ Jun 23] modest maiden at 3 yrs: well
held in 1999: should stay 1½m+: acts on heavy going. *B. A. Pearce*

INNES   3 b.f. Inchinor 119 – Trachelium 65 (Formidable (USA) 125) [1998 –: 7s   **60**
1999 12m⁶ 12m³ 12.1f Aug 24] modest performer: good seventh in apprentice handicap at Hamilton final start: stays 1½m: acts on firm going: successful over hurdles in
October and December. *Miss S. E. Hall*

INNKEEPER   2 b.c. (Feb 27) Night Shift (USA) – Riyoom (USA) 83 (Vaguely   **77**
Noble 140) [1999 6g⁴ 6m⁴ 6g² 6f⁴ 6m 7g Aug 30] 52,000Y: good-topped, quite
attractive colt: third foal: half-brother to 3-y-o Shining Desert and an Italian/French
1m/1¼m winner by Alzao: dam Irish 2-y-o 1m winner: fair maiden: well below best
in nurseries last 2 starts: should stay at least 7f: raced only on good going or firmer:
sold 22,000 gns in October, joined Gay Kelleway. *Sir Michael Stoute*

INN ON THE PARK   4 b.g. Northern Park (USA) 107 – Hotel California (IRE)   **–**
58 (Last Tycoon 131) [1998 –: 12d a13g⁶ 1999 a16g Jan 9] leggy, unfurnished gelding: no form on Flat. *S. Dow*

INNUENDO (IRE)   4 b.f. Caerleon (USA) 132 – Infamy 123 (Shirley Heights   **110**
130) [1998 110p: 10g* 9.9g* 9.9m² 10.1g² 12g* 1999 12m² 13.5g² 11.9g* 14.6g⁴
Sep 8] quite well-made filly: smart performer: won listed race at York in August by a
neck from Credit-A-Plenty: in frame on other starts, listed race at Newmarket (beaten
a head by Suhaad), Prix de Pomone at Deauville (went down by 3 lengths to Bimbola) and Park Hill Stakes at Doncaster (favourite and sweating, respectable fourth
to Mistle Song): probably stays 14.6f: raced only on good/good to firm going: joined
C. Clement in USA. *L. M. Cumani*

*EBF Galtres Stakes, York—a remarkable eighth winner in the last ten runnings of the race for trainer
Luca Cumani as Innuendo holds off strong-finishing Credit-A-Plenty; Sweet Sorrow (far left) is third*

Mr Gerald Leigh's "Innuendo"

INSATIABLE (IRE) 6 b.h. Don't Forget Me 127 – Petit Eclair 94 (Major **124**
Portion 129) [1998 124: 10d* 10d* 10d 10g⁴ 9.8d* 10g² 12f 1999 10.5g⁴ 10m⁶
11s* Sep 19]
    The 1998 Champion Stakes runner-up Insatiable ran only three times
in his final season, and, though foiled by injury during his preparation to go
one better in the 1999 renewal, he managed to confirm himself a very smart
performer. At the third time of asking—after below-form efforts in the Tattersalls Gold Cup at the Curragh and the Coral-Eclipse at Sandown—Insatiable
was provided with ideal conditions for a return to his best in the Aga Khan
Studs Blandford Stakes back at the Curragh in September. With soft ground and
a sound gallop Insatiable beat the smart Theatreworld by eight lengths, settling
in behind the leaders before cutting down the runner-up in the straight to win
easily. The victory should have been the perfect stepping stone for another tilt
at the Champion Stakes, but, alas, it was to prove Insatiable's swansong.

		Ahonoora	Lorenzaccio
	Don't Forget Me	(ch 1975)	Helen Nichols
	(b 1984)	African Doll	African Sky
Insatiable (IRE)		(b 1978)	Mithril
(b.h. 1993)		Major Portion	Court Martial
	Petit Eclair	(b 1955)	Better Half
	(ch 1973)	Cafe Au Lait	Espresso
		(ch 1968)	Blue Sash

    A leggy, workmanlike horse, Insatiable stayed eleven furlongs. He
produced his best efforts on good going or softer although he had form on firm,
and he tended to carry his head high. There is nothing to add to the breeding
details that appeared in Insatiable's essay in *Racehorses of 1998*, except that

another of Don't Forget Me's progeny, Rudi's Pet, developed into a smart performer in 1999. Coincidentally, Rudi's Pet emerged as a racehorse of some significance as a five-year-old, the same age at which Insatiable first rose to prominence, winning the Brigadier Gerard Stakes and the Prix Dollar among three victories. Insatiable's connections should be applauded for giving their horse plenty of time to show his worth; their patience was justly rewarded. *Sir Michael Stoute*

IN SEQUENCE (USA) 2 gr.f. (Mar 16) Robyn Dancer (USA) – What Option **60** (USA) (Star de Naskra (USA)) [1999 5.7m4 6m Sep 7] second foal: dam sprint winner in USA: modest form in maidens at Bath (well backed) and Lingfield (slowly away and never nearer): bred to prove best up to 7f. *J. A. R. Toller*

INSIGHT (FR) 4 b.f. Sadler's Wells (USA) 132 – Or Vision (USA) 108 (Irish **115** River (FR) 131) [1998 115: 8f 8g3 10.5d3 9d2 10g2 10g2 9.3d* 1999 8v4 9.3d6 10s2 10f5 10g* 11g Nov 6] quite good-topped filly: smart performer: won E. P. Taylor Stakes at Woodbine in October by 1½ lengths from Cerulean Sky: creditable efforts otherwise when sixth to Croco Rouge in Prix d'Ispahan at Longchamp in May and fifth to Soaring Softly in Flower Bowl Invitational Handicap at Belmont in October: behind in Breeders' Cup Filly & Mare Turf at Gulfstream final start: stays 10.5f: acts on firm and good to soft ground: blinkered nowadays. *J. E. Hammond, France*

INSIGHTFUL (IRE) 2 b.g. (Mar 25) Desert Style (IRE) 121 – Insight (Ballad **89** Rock 122) [1999 6.1f5 7m* 7.9d 8d2 8d5 7s3 a7g* a7g2 Dec 18] IR 7,400F, 8,000Y: sturdy, useful-looking gelding: poor mover: fifth living foal: dam unraced: fairly useful performer: won seller at Newmarket (bought from B. Meehan 21,000 gns) in July and 4-runner minor event at Lingfield in November: best effort in minor event on latter course final start: stays 1m well: acts on good to firm going, soft and equitrack. *R. Hannon*

INSINUATE (USA) 3 ch.f. Mr Prospector (USA) – All At Sea (USA) 124 (River- **99** man (USA) 131) [1998 NR 1999 7g3 8d* 9.9g5 8m3 Jun 19] tall, quite good-topped filly: second living foal: half-sister to useful 6f and 7f winner (including at 2 yrs) Imroz (by Nureyev): dam won Prix du Moulin and Musidora and second in Oaks: useful performer: won listed race at Ascot in May all out by a head from Sweet Emotion: good third to Holly Blue in listed rated stakes there final start: seemed not to stay 1¼m: stud. *H. R. A. Cecil*

INTEABADUN 7 ch.g. Hubbly Bubbly (USA) – Madam Taylor 81 (Free State **–** 125) [1998 NR 1999 16f4 16g4 Jul 5] of little account. *M. Mullineaux*

INTENSITY 3 b.g. Bigstone (IRE) 126 – Brillante (FR) 118 (Green Dancer **90** (USA) 132) [1998 53: 7d5 1999 9f* 10m5 8m 10.1m 10.3d* Oct 22] leggy, useful-looking gelding: fairly useful performer: won maiden at Newcastle in August: left K. Burke after fourth start: improved to win handicap at Doncaster final outing: stays 1¼m: acts on firm and good to soft going. *M. H. Tompkins*

INTERDREAM 5 b.g. Interrex (CAN) – Dreamtime Quest (Blakeney 126) [1998 **–** 57: 8d 8g 8m 9m 8.3d 10.1m4 1999 12d 10m Sep 1] close-coupled gelding: fairly useful handicapper at 3 yrs: nowhere near so good since: likely to stay 1½m: acts on firm and good to soft going: tends to hang: fair hurdler. *C. J. Mann*

INTERLUDE 2 b.f. (Jan 28) Sadler's Wells (USA) 132 – Starlet 119 (Teenoso **91 P** (USA) 135) [1999 8d* Oct 22] angular, useful-looking filly: fifth foal: closely related to 7-y-o Renown and 8.5f winner Stage Whisper (by Alzao) and half-sister to a 1¼m winner by Sharrood: dam, best at 1¼m/1½m as 4-y-o, runner-up in Nassau and Sun Chariot: green, overcame slow start and good deal of trouble to win 18-runner maiden at Doncaster in taking style, weaving through to get up close home and beat Caballe by ¾ length: will prove suited by 1¼m/1½m: sure to improve considerably and win races in better company. *Sir Michael Stoute*

INTERNAL AFFAIR (USA) 4 b.g. Nicholas (USA) 111 – Gdynia (USA) (Sir **63** Ivor 135) [1998 54+, a68: 7s a5g* 5m 6g 5g 6.1s 7d5 1999 9.2v2 8g 8.3s 8s2 a8.5g5 **a72** 7.5m 7f 8d 7.5g6 a8.5g* 8d5 8.2s4 a9.4g6 a8g2 a9.4g Dec 27] sturdy gelding: fair handicapper: left W. Haggas after fifth start: won at Wolverhampton in October:

stays 9f: acts on fibresand and heavy ground, probably on good to firm: sometimes slowly away/looks none too keen. *T. D. Barron*

IN THE ARENA (USA)   2 ch.c. (Mar 18) Cadeaux Genereux 131 – Tajfah (USA)   **– p**
(Shadeed (USA) 135) [1999 6m 6g Oct 11] big, strong colt: has plenty of scope: fifth foal: dam unraced half-sister to very smart colts at 6f/7f Lead On Time and Great Commotion: very green on debut: showed promise without being knocked about when tenth of 22 to Spencers Wood in maiden at Windsor following month: bred to prove best up to 1m: should do better. *B. W. Hills*

IN THE NICK (IRE)   2 b.g. (Apr 22) Case Law 113 – Bridewell Belle (Saulingo   **65 d**
122) [1999 5m⁴ 5.1m⁶ 5m 5g Oct 14] IR 4,300Y, resold IR 7,700Y: leggy gelding: half-brother to a winner in Italy by Exactly Sharp: dam Irish 1m winner: modest form in maidens at Beverley and Chester early in year: well beaten after, and sold only 800 gns in October. *J. Berry*

IN THE STOCKS   5 b.m. Reprimand 122 – Stock Hill Lass 87 (Air Trooper 115)   **59**
[1998 59: 8g⁶ 8.3m 7g 8.3g 10m 8m 8m* 8m⁴ 8d 1999 8g⁴ 8g⁴ 8.3m⁶ 10.2m 10m⁵ 10.5d⁶ 11.5g* Oct 19] small mare: modest handicapper: won at Lingfield in October: had poor run on several earlier occasions: stays 11.5f: acts on good to firm and good to soft going, yet to race on extremes: usually held up. *L. G. Cottrell*

INTIAASH (IRE)   7 br.m. Shaadi (USA) 126 – Funun (USA) 84 (Fappiano   **63 d**
(USA)) [1998 65, a53: a6g a7g 5.7f² a6g 5.7s 5.1m⁴ 5m⁴ a7g³ 5.7m 7.1d a6g⁵ 1999 a6g³ a6g* a6f a6g² a6g a6s⁵ a5g⁴ 5.7g 6f 5.7g³ 6m a6g 5.1m⁴ 6g 6g Aug 24] tall, lengthy mare: modest handicapper: won at Southwell in January: effective at 5f to 7f: acts on any all-weather/turf: tried visored (not since 1996): sometimes slowly away/hangs left, and usually held up: inconsistent, and not one to trust. *D. Haydn Jones*

INTIKHAB (USA)   5 b.h. Red Ransom (USA) – Crafty Example (USA)   **118**
(Crafty Prospector (USA)) [1998 135: a9f* a10f² 8.5m* 8d* 1999 8d⁴ May 15]
Hopes that racegoers might witness a display from Intikhab as stunning as the one he'd given in the 1998 Queen Anne Stakes at Royal Ascot were dashed almost straight away. In winning the Queen Anne by eight lengths from the subsequent Sussex Stakes winner Among Men, showing exceptional acceleration in the last furlong, Intikhab put up the best performance by any horse that year, but, unfortunately, he had to miss the rest of the season due to a recurring splint. Subsequently fired below his off-fore knee, Intikhab didn't return to action until May in the Lockinge Stakes at Newbury. Looking in fine shape and sent off at 7/4-on, Intikhab managed only fourth of six behind his stable-companion Fly To The Stars. The latter made the running, and Intikhab had to be niggled along to try to close over two furlongs out. Although almost getting on terms, the effort took its toll and the tiring Intikhab also had to give best to Jim And Tonic and Almushtarak. Afterwards came the discovery that Intikhab had fractured his pelvis during the race. He has been retired to the Derrinstown Stud in Ireland at a fee of IR 12,000 guineas.

		Red Ransom (USA) (b 1987)	Roberto (b 1969)	Hail To Reason
Intikhab (USA) (b.h. 1994)				Bramalea
			Arabia (b 1977)	Damascus
				Christmas Wind
		Crafty Example (USA) (b 1987)	Crafty Prospector (ch 1979)	Mr Prospector
				Real Crafty Lady
			Zienelle (b 1983)	Danzig
				Past Example

Intikhab's pedigree was discussed fully in *Racehorses of 1998*. Suffice to say here that he's the second foal and second winner of the once-raced Crafty Example, a daughter of a sister to another top-class miler in Polish Precedent, and from a family which has made a big impact in the last decade. Intikhab, a sturdy, attractive horse who carried condition and usually moved short to post, was clearly best at around a mile. He put up easily his best performance on good to soft going, but he acted on good to firm and ran respectably on soft, winning on dirt as well. *Saeed bin Suroor*

INTIMAA (IRE) 3 b.f. Caerleon (USA) 132 – Nahilah 78 (Habitat 134) [1998 **104**
92: 6f* 6g³ 7g² 1999 7g³ 7m³ 8m 7m³ 8d⁵ Sep 30] small filly: useful performer:
ran at least creditably in listed events at Epsom (best effort, very close third of 7 to
Tumbleweed Ridge) and Newmarket final 2 starts: stays 1m: acts on firm and good
to soft ground: consistent. *P. T. Walwyn*

IN TIME 3 ch.f. Generous (IRE) 139 – Affection Affirmed (USA) (Affirmed (USA)) –
[1998 64: 6m⁶ 6g⁴ 6d 8m³ 1999 11.9f⁶ May 12] leggy, close-coupled filly: has a quick
action: modest maiden: well beaten only run of 1999: should stay at least 1½m: acts
on good to firm ground: sold 15,000 gns in December. *P. F. I. Cole*

INTIZAA (USA) 3 b. or br.f. Mr Prospector (USA) – Oumaldaaya (USA) 111 **77**
(Nureyev (USA) 131) [1998 75+: 6g⁴ 7g³ 1999 8.2m² 8.2m⁵ 9m 8.2d³ 8.3d⁶ Nov 4]
smallish, quite attractive filly: good mover: fair maiden: stays 1m: acts on good to
firm going, possibly not softer than good. *J. L. Dunlop*

INTRICATE WEB (IRE) 3 b.g. Warning 136 – In Anticipation (IRE) 93 **79 p**
(Sadler's Wells (USA) 132) [1998 NR 1999 7s⁵ 7g 7.9f⁵ 10m⁶ 7.1s³ 8.9d 7g* Oct 15]
sturdy, angular ex-Irish-trained gelding: first foal: dam, Irish 1½m and 1¾m winner,
out of US Grade 1 1m winner Aptostar: fairly useful performer: left D. Weld after
second start: much improved when winning 30-runner handicap at Redcar on final
outing, comfortably by 2 lengths: may prove best at 7f/1m: acts on firm and soft
going: blinkered debut: probably capable of better still. *E. J. Alston*

INTRUM MORSHAAN (IRE) 2 b. or br.f. (Apr 6) Darshaan 133 – Auntie **70 p**
Maureen (IRE) 73 (Roi Danzig (USA)) [1999 7m 8.1d⁶ 8.2s³ Oct 5] 380,000 francs
Y: first foal: dam Irish 9f/1¼m winner from family of Halling: easily best effort in
maidens when third of 14 to easy winner Embraced at Nottingham, staying on
from rear: favourite on debut: will be well suited by 1¼m+: should still do better.
J. L. Dunlop

INVADER 3 b.c. Danehill (USA) 126 – Donya 74 (Mill Reef (USA) 141) [1998 **94 ?**
82: 7m 7m 7g⁴ 7d⁴ 1999 9g⁴ 7m⁵ Apr 17] strong, good-topped colt: fairly useful
maiden: possibly flattered when fifth of 7 in Greenham Stakes at Newbury second
outing: should be suited by 1¼m: sold 52,000 gns in October. *C. E. Brittain*

INVENTIVE 2 b.f. (Feb 12) Sheikh Albadou 128 – Ingenuity 68 (Clever Trick **84**
(USA)) [1999 6m⁵ 6m² 5v* 6g⁵ 5v* Oct 25] second foal: dam, 6f winner, bred to stay
at least 1m: fairly useful performer: easily best efforts to win maiden in September
and minor event in October, both at Lingfield: will prove best at 5f/6f: clearly goes
well on heavy ground. *R. Hannon*

INVER GOLD 2 ch.c. (Apr 23) Arazi (USA) 135 – Mary Martin (Be My Guest **69**
(USA) 126) [1999 7d⁶ a8g² a8g⁴ Nov 24] closely related to 1m and 1¼m winner
Touch'N'Go and 1m winner Robbies Rainbow (both by Rainbow Quest) as well as
smart performer up to 7f Marina Park (by Local Suitor), later successful over further
in USA: dam unraced: fair form in maidens at Redcar and Lingfield first 2 starts: left
M. Johnson for 8,600 gns before final one: shapes as though will stay beyond 1m.
A. G. Newcombe

INVERMARK 5 b.g. Machiavellian (USA) 123 – Applecross 117 (Glint of **122**
Gold 128) [1998 114: 12s⁶ 16.4s⁶ 12g² 14g* 13.4d* 15.5s⁴ 20d* 15.5v 1999
18.7m³ 20m² 15s² 20v⁴ Oct 2]
    Five-year-olds enjoyed plenty of success in the 'nineties. Opera House,
Halling, Pilsudski, Singspiel and Swain (who carried on the good work at six)
won a total of thirteen Group/Grade 1 races at that age, and in 1999 Daylami
and Kayf Tara added five more between them. Although Invermark is not in the
class of any of the aforementioned, his very smart effort in the Gold Cup made
him a worthy standard bearer for the senior ranks among the stayers.
    The 1999 Gold Cup attracted the largest field in the history of the race,
and with ten pattern winners and two former winners, Celeric and Kayf Tara,
amongst the seventeen runners, Invermark ran the race of his life to finish
second, beaten a length and a half by Enzeli. Waiting tactics resulted in Invermark weaving his way through from the rear whilst Enzeli was being kicked for
home, a similar story to Invermark's seasonal reappearance in the Chester Cup

where, under top weight and conceding upwards of 10 lb all round, he ran a cracker to finish third behind Rainbow High and Generosity. Invermark's final two races of 1999 were in France, where, in the Prix Kergorlay at Deauville, he was beaten five lengths by Kayf Tara, who easily reversed the Gold Cup form; trainer James Fanshawe reportedly suggested that Invermark might have been bitten by an insect. Another, less speculative, reason was in evidence for Invermark's disappointing run when trying to win the Group 1 Prix du Cadran at Longchamp for the second year in succession. Invermark refused to settle in the first half of the race, which was very slowly run, and, after improving to have every chance turning for home, he was unable to make any further impression, finishing just over four lengths fourth to Tajoun.

Invermark (b.g. 1994)	Machiavellian (USA) (b 1987)	Mr Prospector (b 1970)	Raise A Native
			Gold Digger
		Coup de Folie (b 1982)	Halo
			Raise The Standard
	Applecross (b 1987)	Glint of Gold (b 1978)	Mill Reef
			Crown Treasure
		Rynechra (b 1981)	Blakeney
			Marypark

Invermark's pedigree was covered in detail in *Racehorses of 1998*, though since then his family's name has been upheld by his year-younger half-brother Craigsteel (by Suave Dancer), who won the Princess of Wales's Stakes at Newmarket, and by the smart Inchrory (by Midyan), who had another successful season in Scandinavia. Their dam, the Park Hill runner-up Applecross, also maintained her one-hundred-percent record with winners to runners as her three-year-old Pennygown (by Rainbow Quest) won her only start in 1999. The tall, workmanlike Invermark stays two and a half miles and

Exors of the late Sir David Wills's "Invermark"

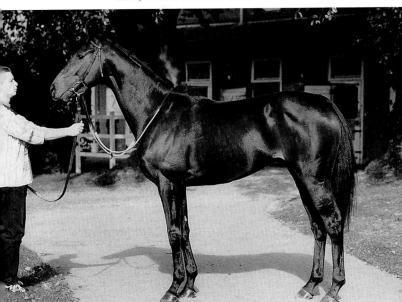

acts on soft and good to firm ground. Although he flashes his tail under pressure he's certainly game and should continue to run well. The fact that he won't have to carry a Group 1 penalty in lesser pattern races in the next season makes races such as the Sagaro Stakes at Ascot and the Henry II Stakes at Sandown particularly attractive targets before another crack at the Gold Cup. *J. R. Fanshawe*

INVINCIBLE SPIRIT (IRE) 2 b.c. (Feb 17) Green Desert (USA) 127 – Rafha **111 p** 123 (Kris 135) [1999 6f³ 6f* 6m* 6d⁶ Sep 30] strong, well-made colt: has a powerful, round action: fifth live foal: half-brother to 4-y-o Sadian, useful 1m (at 2 yrs) and 1½m winner Al Widyan (by Slip Anchor) and 3-y-o Fnan: dam won Prix de Diane and at 11.5f: progressive form first 3 starts, winning maiden at Goodwood in July and listed race at Ripon (readily by 1½ lengths from Khasayl, smart effort) in August: favourite and steadily to post, pulled too hard in rear and unable to make any headway when last of 6 in Middle Park Stakes at Newmarket final start: bred to stay beyond 6f: should still be capable of better. *J. L. Dunlop*

INVIRAMENTAL 3 b.c. Pursuit of Love 124 – Corn Futures 78 (Nomination **48** 125) [1998 NR 1999 10d a7g⁵ a8.5g a7g⁴ Dec 15] 56,000Y: good-topped colt: third foal: half-brother to useful Crazee Mental (by Magic Ring), 2-y-o 6f winner in 1997, and 6f/7f winner Trading Aces (by Be My Chief): dam, 2-y-o 6f winner, out of close relative of Wassl: poor maiden: ran creditably in blinkers final start: bred to prove best up to 7f (pulled hard over 1¼m). *D. Haydn Jones*

INVISIBLE FORCE (IRE) 2 b.c. (May 5) Imperial Frontier (USA) 112 – **–** Virginia Cottage 45 (Lomond (USA) 128) [1999 7m⁴ 7.1m Sep 4] lengthy colt: third foal: half-brother to 3-y-o Double Choice: dam poor maiden half-sister to Irish sprinter Tropical and French miler Shake The Yoke, both very smart: well held in minor event at Redcar and maiden at Haydock. *B. S. Rothwell*

Prince A. A. Faisal's "Invincible Spirit"

INYA LAKE 3 b.f. Whittingham (IRE) 104 – Special One 66 (Aragon 118) [1998 **101**
95: 5d* 5v* 5g* 5s 5g⁴ 5.2g³ 5g* 5m 5s 1999 5s* 5.1s² 5g 5m 5m⁴ 5f Jul 27] smallish,
close-coupled filly: useful performer: won 7-runner listed race at Haydock in April
by a head from Henry Hall: mostly highly tried after: raced only at 5f: acts on good to
firm and soft ground (won on heavy early at 2 yrs): has been bandaged behind:
usually held up: game. *M. R. Channon*

IONIAN SECRET 3 b.f. Mystiko (USA) 124 – Hearten (Hittite Glory 125) **43**
[1998 56: 5m⁶ 1999 6g 6f⁵ 5m 10g³ Aug 5] smallish, workmanlike filly: well held in
maidens: raced freely over 1¼m. *M. P. Tregoning*

IPANEMA BEACH 2 ch.f. (Feb 3) Lion Cavern (USA) 117 – Girl From Ipanema **58 p**
106 (Salse (USA) 128) [1999 6s⁶ Oct 25] leggy, lengthy, angular filly: first foal: dam
7f (at 2 yrs) and 1m winner who stayed 10.5f: weak in market, faded after chasing
pace over 4f (flashed tail when hit with whip) when sixth of 13 to Picot in maiden at
Leicester: should stay 1m: will probably improve. *J. W. Hills*

IPCRESS FILLY 3 b.f. Puissance 110 – Daymer Bay (Lomond (USA) 128) [1998 **–**
60: 5g⁵ 6m⁶ 7m³ 6.1d 7g⁶ a7g² a7g⁶ 1999 a7g⁶ a8g 7s 8.2m May 21] leggy filly:
modest maiden: well below form in 1999: stays 7f: acts on fibresand (ran poorly on
equitrack) and good to firm going: inconsistent. *J. M. P. Eustace*

IPLEDGEALLEGIANCE (USA) 3 b.g. Alleged (USA) 138 – Yafill (USA) **100**
80 (Nureyev (USA) 131) [1998 89p: 7g⁵ 8m⁵ 1999 10.3d² 12g⁶ 9g⁶ 10m 10g*
10m* 10m³ 10g* 10m 12d⁵ Sep 28] leggy gelding: useful performer: won maiden at
Pontefract in June and handicaps at Sandown in July and Newbury in August: should
prove best around 1¼m: yet to race on extremes of going: usually held up: consistent.
E. A. L. Dunlop

I PROMISE YOU 2 b.g. (Feb 6) Shareef Dancer (USA) 135 – Abuzz 101 (Absa- **68**
lom 128) [1999 5g 7g⁶ 7m⁴ 8s 8m³ 8.3d⁵ Nov 4] small, sturdy gelding: sixth foal:
brother to useful 5f/6f (including at 2 yrs) winner World Premier and half-brother to
5-y-o Puzzlement and 4-y-o Mysticism (both by Mystiko): dam, won at 5f (at 2 yrs)
and 7f, half-sister to dam of Grand Criterium winner Revoque: fair maiden: best
effort when third of 14 in nursery at Yarmouth in October: should stay 1¼m: acts on
good to firm going, well held on softer than good. *C. E. Brittain*

IRANOO (IRE) 2 b.c. (Mar 30) Persian Bold 123 – Rose of Summer (IRE) (Taufan **48 +**
(USA) 119) [1999 5d 5d⁶ 7g 7.1d⁴ 6m 6g 8g² Aug 30] 5,000Y: close-coupled colt:
third foal: half-brother to 3-y-o The Fossick and a winner in Belgium by River Falls:
dam once-raced half-sister to very smart Irish performer up to 1¼m Lord Bud: poor
maiden: stays 1m: acts on good to soft going: tried blinkered and tongue-tied: none
too consistent: sold 5,000 gns in October. *S. C. Williams*

I RECALL (IRE) 8 b.g. Don't Forget Me 127 – Sable Lake (Thatching 131) **49**
[1998 45: 8g 8.3d³ 9.9m 1999 10.5s² 10.5s 10.5m Jul 2] workmanlike gelding: poor
maiden handicapper: below form after reappearance: stays 10.5f: acts on soft and
good to firm going: visored. *P. Hayward*

IRELAND'S EYE (IRE) 4 b.g. Shareef Dancer (USA) 135 – So Romantic (IRE) **63**
97 (Teenoso (USA) 135) [1998 NR 1999 12g⁴ 12.3m 14.1m 14s 15.8s² 13.8g³ 13.8s⁶
a16g Nov 15] 600 3-y-o: third foal: dam, 7f to 9f winner, half-sister to Lowther and
Nassau winner Ela Romara: useful dual bumper winner on soft going: modest
maiden: ran creditably last 3 starts on turf: stays 2m: acts on soft going. *J. Norton*

IRISH CREAM (IRE) 3 b.f. Petong 126 – Another Baileys 60 (Deploy 131) **72 d**
[1998 64: 5v* 5.1g a6g⁵ 6s³ 7.1m³ a6g* 6d⁵ 6m 6s 7g⁴ a6g⁶ a6g 1999 a7g³ a7g* a7g*
a8g* a6g⁶ 7s 8s a8g 8m 6g⁵ a6g a8.5g 7g 6d⁶ a7g a12g a8g 14.1d³ Oct 27] small,
workmanlike filly: fair performer at best: left P. D. Evans after winning 2 sellers and
claimer at Southwell in February/March: well below form subsequently: stays 1m:
acts on all-weather and heavy going: usually visored (has won when not), tried
blinkered. *Andrew Reid*

IRISH DANCER (IRE) 2 ch.f. (Feb 17) Lahib (USA) 129 – Mazarine Blue **56**
(USA) (Chief's Crown (USA)) [1999 6f 7g⁵ 7f⁴ 7s⁶ 7g 8.3d a8.5g⁴ Nov 20] IR
11,000Y: second foal: half-sister to 4-y-o Poly Blue: dam, ran twice in France,
half-sister to dual Gold Cup winner Sadeem: modest maiden: should stay at least 1m:

acts on firm and soft ground: blinkered (well below form in seller on all-weather debut at Wolverhampton) final start. *Miss Gay Kelleway*

IRISH MELODY (IRE) 3 ch.f. Mac's Imp (USA) 116 – Musical Gem (USA) – (The Minstrel (CAN) 135) [1998 35: 5.7m 6g 6.1d⁵ 7g 1999 7m 8g 6m 7f 8.1m a7g a7g⁶ a10g Dec 29] poor maiden: no form in 1999: tried blinkered. *A. J. McNae*

IRISH SEA (USA) 6 b.g. Zilzal (USA) 137 – Dunkellin (USA) (Irish River (FR) 131) [1998 NR 1999 17.2f³ 18m³ Jul 3] leggy, close-coupled gelding: fair maiden at 3 yrs: poor form in 1999: stays 2¼m: raced only on good going or firmer on turf, well held only try on fibresand: blinkered once earlier in career: winning hurdler. *B. J. Llewellyn* **44**

IRIS MAY 4 b.f. Brief Truce (USA) 126 – Choire Mhor 100 (Dominion 123) **87 d** [1998 84: 5.1g⁵ 5m* 5g³ 5.1m² 5g³ 5f⁶ 6d 1999 5s² 5m 5d⁴ 5m³ 5f 6f 5.3s⁵ 5g 5m 5g Oct 2] good-topped filly: fairly useful handicapper: below form after fourth start: has form at 6f, best efforts at 5f: acts on firm and soft going: sometimes blinkered at 2 yrs: often races prominently/leads. *J. Berry*

IRON MOUNTAIN (IRE) 4 b.g. Scenic 128 – Merlannah (IRE) (Shy Groom **86** (USA)) [1998 80: 9.7d 10s 10d 8m⁵ 10g² 10.1g* 11.5g² 10.1m³ 10d* 9.7f⁵ 9.9g* 10f² 8f 10.1g⁵ 10g 8.9g 10d* 9.7s⁶ 10s 1999 10.3d⁵ 8f⁵ 8g⁴ 10m⁴ 9d* 10d⁴ 10f² 8m² 10m⁶ 8g Aug 16] good-topped gelding: fairly useful handicapper: won amateur event at Goodwood in June by 7 lengths: tailed off final start: effective at 1m to 11.5f: acts on firm and good to soft ground: blinkered once at 2 yrs: held up: tough: joined Mrs L. Jewell. *N. A. Callaghan*

IRREPRESSIBLE (IRE) 8 b.g. Don't Forget Me 127 – Lady of Shalott 61 – (Kings Lake (USA) 133) [1998 57: 8g 6.9m* 7.1d⁴ 7g 1999 7g 6g 7f 7d Oct 4] strong, lengthy gelding: modest performer: no form in 1999: tried visored. *R. J. Hodges*

IRSAL 5 ch.g. Nashwan (USA) 135 – Amwag (USA) 106 (El Gran Senor (USA) **44** 136) [1998 NR 1999 11.8m² a8.5g 12m⁵ 12g 12f⁶ a14g 13.8s a12g⁵ a16.2g Dec 15] **a–** poor performer: stays 1½m: acts on firm and soft ground. *D. W. Chapman*

ISABELLA GONZAGA 5 b.m. Rock Hopper 124 – Lawful 76 (Law Society **75** (USA) 130) [1998 69: 9.7m³ 11s 10.1m* 10m³ 11.5f⁵ 11.1m 10g a12g* a12g² a14.8g² a12g⁴ 1999 a12g³ a12f* a12g³ a12g* 10m³ 12.3m 11.8m a12g* 10.2m³ 10.1f² 10g Aug 24] lengthy, good-topped mare: fair handicapper: won at Lingfield in January and Wolverhampton in February and June: well beaten final start: effective at 1¼m to 15f: acts on all-weather and firm going: sold only 2,000 gns in December. *R. M. H. Cowell*

ISABELLA R (IRE) 2 ch.f. (Feb 5) Indian Ridge 123 – Sun Screen (Caerleon **65** (USA) 132) [1999 5s² 6g⁵ 6d³ a7g² a7g Dec 15] second reported foal: half-sister to **a57** fairly useful Irish 7f and 1¼m winner Hill Society (by Law Society), smart chaser: dam maiden half-sister to 1000 Guineas and Oaks winner Mysterious: fair maiden on turf, modest on all-weather: well beaten final start: should stay 1m: acts on soft going and fibresand. *Sir Mark Prescott*

ISCAN (IRE) 3 b.c. Caerleon (USA) 132 – Idraak (Kris 135) [1998 92: 7g³ 7f³ **116** 7m* 1999 10m³ 12.3m³ 12m² 12m² 14g² 14.6m 15v⁵ Oct 2] smallish, quite attractive colt: smart performer: runner-up in Derby Italiano at Rome (beaten 1½ lengths by Mukhalif), King Edward VII Stakes at Royal Ascot (went down by 2 lengths to Mutafaweq) and listed race at Goodwood (very unlucky when beaten ½ length by Yavana's Pace): well beaten in St Leger at Doncaster (took fierce hold to post) and Prix Hubert de Chaudenay at Longchamp final 2 starts: should stay beyond 1¾m: acts on good to firm ground: edgy type, and has given trouble at start (including final 2 starts in Britain): quirky: joined Godolphin. *Sir Michael Stoute*

ISLA (IRE) 2 b.f. (Mar 10) Turtle Island (IRE) 123 – State Treasure (USA) (Secre- – tariat (USA)) [1999 6.1m Aug 23] 18,000Y: half-sister to several winners, including fairly useful 7f (at 2 yrs) and 1m winner Double Diamond (by Last Tycoon) and 8-y-o Diamond Crown: dam minor winner in USA: tailed off in maiden at Nottingham. *T. R. Watson*

ISLAND HOUSE (IRE) 3 ch.c. Grand Lodge (USA) 125 – Fortitude (IRE) **108** (Last Tycoon 131) [1998 79p: 7m 7g⁴ 1999 8g 7.1m⁴ 7.9d² 7.9f⁴ 8m* 8v* 9v² Oct 23] tall, quite good-topped colt: has scope: useful performer: won minor events at

Pontefract (very free early) in September and Ayr (much improved) in October: good second to Albarahin in handicap at Newbury final start: will stay 1¼m+: acts on good to firm going, goes very well in the mud. *G. Wragg*

ISLAND PRINCESS (IRE) 2 b.f. (Apr 16) Turtle Island (IRE) 123 – Classic **79** Dilemma (Sandhurst Prince 128) [1999 5d⁵ 5.2m 7f 7s² 7d Aug 26] IR 7,000F, IR 5,800Y: good-bodied filly: sixth foal: half-sister to 2 winners abroad, including Italian 7f (at 2 yrs) and 7.5f winner Semper (by Soviet Lad): dam Irish 2-y-o 6f winner: easily best effort (fair form) when length second of 13 to Naval Affair in maiden at Kempton: should stay 1m: acts on soft ground. *D. R. C. Elsworth*

ISLAND SANDS (IRE) 3 b. or br.c. Turtle Island (IRE) 123 – Tiavanita **122** (USA) (J O Tobin (USA) 130) [1998 106p: 6m* 6s* 1999 8m* 8g⁵ May 22]

In the wake of Island Sands's victory in the Sagitta Two Thousand Guineas one humorist suggested that the Newmarket Craven meeting should perhaps be relocated to Dubai in 2000. Certainly the Godolphin trials in that country—private, but fortunately well reported back in Britain, albeit no longer pictured on TV—have a major bearing on the participants in the big races in the first part of the season, and the absence of any Godolphin challenger for the recognised Guineas trials in Europe makes these events less significant than formerly.

One of the stars of the Godolphin 'try-outs' in early-April, which are run as true mile contests on turf, at racing pace with each horse carrying the same weight, was Island Sands, who had been purchased out of David Elsworth's stable for an undisclosed sum at the end of a short but impressive unbeaten two-year-old campaign comprising a maiden race and minor event at Salisbury. He beat Mukhalif and Adair in the trial, with Iftitah and Dubai Millennium among those behind, and having been a 33/1-shot for the Two Thousand Guineas he was promptly cut to 16/1. Within ten days Island Sands was announced as Godolphin's main contender for the classic, and his odds were cut to 8/1. On the day he was 10/1, as a plunge on the Aidan O'Brien-trained Orpen took him to 7/2 favourite of the sixteen runners, ahead of the Henry Cecil contender Enrique, successful in the Greenham Stakes (7/1), Dewhurst Stakes runner-up Auction House (15/2), runaway Racing Post Trophy winner Commander Collins (8/1) and Mujahid, the best two-year-old of 1998 when successful in the Dewhurst but only fifth in the Craven Stakes on his reappearance (9/1). The Craven winner Compton Admiral was also 10/1, with the runner-up Brancaster at 20/1. The Guineas takes little describing. Island Sands set off in front and, when things hotted up three furlongs out, he

Sagitta 2000 Guineas Stakes, Newmarket—run on the July course because of development work; Island Sands dictates matters under Frankie Dettori and holds the late challenge of Enrique; Mujahid (in between them), the leading two-year-old of 1998, is third with Brancaster (armlets) fourth

kept finding enough to see off all challengers, first Gold Academy, then, more dangerously, Mujahid and finally the running-on Enrique, who had threaded his way through from off the pace. Island Sands won by a neck, with Mujahid just over a length further away third, Brancaster fourth and Gold Academy fifth. Orpen, who refused to settle, finished next to last.

The subsequent record of Guineas winners in their classic season has not been impressive during the 'nineties, either numerically or in terms of achievements. The six winners following Rodrigo de Triano in 1992 included a champion in Mark of Esteem, who ran another four times, but Zafonic, Mister Baileys, Pennekamp, Entrepreneur and King of Kings (the last three all injured in the Derby) had only eight runs between them, with three of them running just once. In the previous thirty years only one colt, Mon Fils in 1973, had run just once after the Guineas and four had run twice. The highest figure, seven, came from Sir Ivor in 1968 and To-Agori-Mou in 1981. Injury and illness are the acknowledged culprits for the recent shortfall, though it seems odd that such a fragile bunch of colts should all come so close together. One is tempted to wonder whether the prevailing view nowadays that the Guineas is the pinnacle for a certain type of horse, and that type of horse can be marketed purely for winning that age-restricted race rather than for showing form against older runners and over different distances, sometimes acts as a disincentive even for trying to get them back on the track. Island Sands ran just once after his triumph, when seven lengths fifth of ten to Saffron Waldon in the Entenmann's Irish Two Thousand Guineas at the Curragh later in May. Heavily bandaged behind, Island Sands didn't look right in his coat, came off the bit a long way out and was already labouring when having to be switched under two furlongs out. This clearly wasn't his form—Enrique finished second—and it was reported he had a foot problem. The foot did not respond to treatment quickly

Godolphin's "Island Sands"

enough for him to return to action, but he will be back as a four-year-old, which puts him in a distinct minority among post-war Guineas winners. He has plenty to prove, because the 1999 Two Thousand Guineas was not a good renewal. In the history of *Racehorses* his rating is the equal second-lowest with Roland Gardens (1978), ahead of the 1961 victor Rockavon on 120.

Island Sands (IRE) (b. or br.c. 1996)	Turtle Island (IRE) (b 1991)	Fairy King (b 1982)	Northern Dancer
			Fairy Bridge
		Sisania (b 1983)	High Top
			Targo's Delight
	Tiavanita (USA) (b or br 1986)	J O Tobin (b or br 1974)	Never Bend
			Hill Shade
		Nirvanita (b 1971)	Right Royal V
			Nuclea

Island Sands is the first and only pattern winner from two crops totalling one hundred and twenty-six foals sired by Turtle Island, a Group 1 winner at two and three. The promising Corinium, a listed-race winner, and Island Sound are the best so far of his second crop. The juvenile highlight for Turtle Island came in the Phoenix Stakes but that was some way behind the form he showed when landing the Irish Two Thousand Guineas by a record fifteen lengths in exceptionally testing conditions. After starting his Coolmore-based stud career at IR 9,000 guineas his fee had dropped to IR 5,000 guineas, raised to IR 6,000 guineas for 2000. Island Sands's dam Tiavanita was a poor performer, failing to make the frame in twelve starts as a three- and four-year-old, including in plating company. Island Sands, her fourth foal, is a half-brother to two minor winners, a colt by Groom Dancer and a filly by Polish Patriot, the latter in Sweden. Although the mare showed little ability on the track she is a half-sister to eight winners, notably the very smart colt Corrupt, successful in the Lingfield Derby Trial and Great Voltigeur Stakes in 1991 when he also finished sixth in the Derby as joint-favourite. The unraced grandam Nirvanita was a half-sister to two fine performers, high-class miler Nadjar, successful in the Prix d'Ispahan and Prix Jacques le Marois, and the smart No No Nanette, whose career highlight came in the Prix de la Nonette. The third dam, Nuclea, was a three-parts sister to top German runner and sire Neckar and to classic winner Naxos, grandam of another high-class German middle-distance colt in Nebos. There is enough stamina in the pedigree to suggest that Island Sands, a big, lengthy colt with plenty of scope who has won on soft and good to firm going, may stay a mile and a quarter. With only four races behind him, he may be capable of further improvement, which is just as well, as he will need to progress to register another major Group 1 victory, always assuming the foot problem can be ironed out. The penalty he will have to carry in a number of lesser pattern races for his Guineas win will not help his cause either, and all things considered a policy of 'wait and see' is advisable. *Saeed bin Suroor*

ISLAND SONG (IRE)   3 b.g. Saddlers' Hall (IRE) 126 – Island Lake 97 (Kala-   **73**
glow 132) [1998 57: 8s 8s⁴ 1999 11.1v⁴ 14.6f⁵ 13.1d 14m* 17.2m* 15.4m* 16.2m 16.4d⁵ 16.2g⁴ Aug 29] sturdy gelding: fair handicapper: gelded before winning at Lingfield, Bath and Folkestone (didn't handle bends well) in July: below form after: suited by 2m+: acts on good to firm going: has carried head awkwardly: sold only 8,000 gns in October. *M. Johnston*

ISLAND SOUND   2 b.g. (Feb 4) Turtle Island (IRE) 123 – Ballet 61 (Sharrood   **104 p**
(USA) 124) [1999 7.1d⁴ 8v* 8s* Oct 22] 35,000Y: third foal: half-brother to 4-y-o Charlie's Gold and German 7f winner Batanga (by Primo Dominie): dam, maiden, half-sister to 1983 May Hill winner Satinette: most progressive juvenile: won maiden at Salisbury in September by 12 lengths from Master George and minor event at Newbury in October by 1¼ lengths (value extra 3) from Il Capitano, making all both times and receiving only a few slaps with whip (tended to edge right) before being eased on latter course: will be well suited by 1¼m/1½m: raced only on ground softer

than good: reluctant at stalls first 2 starts: smart performer in the making, well worth his place in listed/pattern company. *D. R. C. Elsworth*

ISLAND THYMES   2 br.g. (Apr 16) Alhijaz 122 – Harmonious Sound (Auction **71**
Ring (USA) 123) [1999 6d⁴ 6d a7g⁶ Jun 28] 4,800Y, resold 9,000Y: half-brother to
several winners, including 7f/1m winner Nellie's Gamble (by Mummy's Game) and
1½m to 2m winner Puff Puff (by All Systems Go): dam unraced: fair form when
fourth of 16 in maiden at Newbury: well held after, looking none too keen final start.
B. J. Meehan

ISLAY MIST   2 b.f. (Mar 17) Distant Relative 128 – Finlaggan 83 (Be My Chief **86**
(USA) 122) [1999 a6g* 7.1m* 5.9g² 7.5m* 7m³ a7g² a8.5f⁴ Sep 22] 5,000Y: leggy,
useful-looking filly: first foal: dam 11f to 2m winner: won 2-y-o winner: won
minor events at Wolverhampton, Musselburgh and Beverley in June/July: left Sir
Mark Prescott before final outing (blinkered): should stay at least 1m: acts on fibresand and good to firm ground: lazy sort, and needs plenty of driving. *Kathy Walsh,
USA*

ISLE AU HAUT (IRE)   3 b.f. Indian Ridge 123 – Monterana 99 (Sallust 134) **80**
[1998 NR 1999 8m⁴ 7.6m² 7.7m⁵ 8d² 8.2f² 7s Nov 2] half-sister to 6-y-o Henry
Island (by Sharp Victor) and 1992 2-y-o 7f winner Ginger Flower (by Niniski): dam
6f and 7f winner at 2 yrs: fairly useful maiden: very good second in handicap at
Nottingham on penultimate start: will probably stay beyond 1m: acts on firm and
good to soft going: sold 14,000 gns in December. *G. Wragg*

ISLE OF SODOR   3 b.f. Cyrano de Bergerac 120 – Costa Verde 77 (King of Spain **–**
121) [1998 63: 5v⁶ 5d³ 5s 5d 7m³ 6m* 6m 1999 7d 6v a7g 6m May 3] workmanlike
filly: modest at 2 yrs: well held in handicaps in 1999: stays 6f: acts on good to firm
and good to soft going: slowly away final 2 starts. *K. W. Hogg, Isle of Man*

I SPY   3 b.g. Distant Relative 128 – Singing Nelly 56 (Pharly (FR) 130) [1998 NR
1999 a8.5g a9.4g⁵ May 14] 5,400Y: fourth foal: half-brother to 1996 2-y-o 5f winner
Daylight Dreams (by Indian Ridge) and a winner in Germany: dam, lightly-raced
maiden, closely related to Further Flight: little sign of ability. *K. McAuliffe*

ISSARA (IRE)   2 b.g. (Apr 25) Puissance 110 – Hollia 72 (Touch Boy 109) [1999 **–**
5m 5f⁶ 6m 5g 5m 5.3s Sep 29] 8,500Y, 4,500 2-y-o: brother to fairly useful 1996
2-y-o 5f winner Fredrik The Fierce and half-brother to several winning sprinters,
including 3-y-o Shirley Not: dam 2-y-o 5f winner: no sign of ability: tried visored.
B. A. Pearce

ISSEY ROSE (IRE)   2 b.f. (Feb 28) Bigstone (IRE) 126 – Aneeda (Rainbow **98 ?**
Quest (USA) 134) [1999 7m² 7m³ 7m* 8s⁴ 8v Oct 3] 7,000F, 30,000Y: unfurnished
filly: keen walker: fourth foal: half-sister to 3-y-o Pride of Dingle: dam unraced
daughter of half-sister to very smart sprinter Ballad Rock: won maiden at Folkestone
in July, making all: off course 2 months, apparently best effort when 1½ lengths
fourth of 5 to Teggiano in Fillies' Mile at Ascot: tailed off in Prix Marcel Boussac at
Longchamp week later: stays 1m, not sure to get much further: acts on soft and good
to firm going. *T. G. Mills*

ISTIKBAL (USA)   3 b.f. Kingmambo (USA) 125 – Tafrah (IRE) 71 (Sadler's **–**
Wells (USA) 132) [1998 NR 1999 10.2s Sep 27] third foal: half-sister to winner 7f (at
2 yrs) to 1½m winner Falak (by Diesis): dam, 1¼m winner, sister to Prix du Cadran
winner Chief Contender and closely related to grandam of Spinning World, from a
very good family: weak 6/1, seemed badly in need of experience when well beaten in
maiden at Bath, slowly away and never a threat: may do better. *M. P. Tregoning*

ISTINTAJ (USA)   3 b. or br.c. Nureyev (USA) 131 – Mathkurh (USA) 97 (River- **87 p**
man (USA) 131) [1998 NR 1999 6g⁴ 6g² 5g³ 6g* Oct 15] small, sturdy colt: fluent
mover: fourth foal: closely related to fairly useful 5f/6f winner Alumisiyah (by
Danzig) and half-brother to useful 1997 2-y-o 5f/6f (Cherry Hinton) winner Asfurah
(by Dayjur) and UAE 1¼m winner Mutamanni (by Caerleon): dam sprinter: in frame
in maidens prior to winning one at Redcar by 3½ lengths from Mukayed, always to
the fore travelling comfortably and going clear final 1f: slowly away penultimate
start: sent to USA: capable of better still. *M. P. Tregoning*

ITALIAN ROSE   4 ch.f. Aragon 118 – Cayla (Tumble Wind (USA)) [1998 58, **42**
a43+: 7.1s² 7g 7.1d 6g² 6.1v a7g a7s a7g⁵ 1999 a6g⁵ a8g a7g a8g 6m 5.7h 10s⁶ Nov **a33**

1] good-bodied, close-coupled filly: poor maiden handicapper: stays 1¼m: acts on good to firm going, soft and fibresand: blinkered once at 3 yrs. *A. W. Carroll*

ITALIAN SYMPHONY (IRE) 5 b.g. Royal Academy (USA) 130 – Terracotta **66** Hut 99 (Habitat 134) [1998 39, a95: a6g² a6g* a7g* a7g³ a7g* a7g* a7g² a6g* a7g* **a102** 7.1m 7g a8.5g³ a7g⁴ 7.1g³ a7g* 7m a8.5g³ 8d⁴ a7g² a8.5g² a6g* a7g* a6g² 8s³ a8.5g⁵ a7g³ a7g* a8.5g a8f² a7g³ 1999 a9.4g⁴ a7g⁶ a9.4g⁶ a8g* a8.5s² a7g* a8g⁴ a7g³ a8.5g⁵ a8g³ 8d 8d 7m² 7m⁴ 6g⁴ 6.9m³ 7m* 5.9g⁴ 7.6m⁵ 7f⁴ 6.8m* 7m⁴ 7m⁴ 7m* 7g⁴ 6m 8m⁵ 7m⁵ 7g² 7d⁵ 7d² 8g* 8s a8g a10g⁵ a8.5g⁴ a10g³ a9.4g⁴ a8g⁴ a8g⁴ a7g* a9.4g⁵ Dec 27] close-coupled gelding: useful performer on all-weather, fair on turf: had a very busy year, winning 7 of his 41 races: successful in minor event at Lingfield and handicap at Wolverhampton in February and handicaps at Newmarket (apprentices) in June, Warwick (another apprentices) in July, Catterick in August, Musselburgh in November and Southwell (by 3 lengths from Topton) in December: has form from 6f (given good test) to 1¼m, best efforts around 7f/1m: acts on good to firm going, soft and all-weather: has been blinkered, usually visored: extremely tough. *P. D. Evans*

IT CAN BE DONE (IRE) 2 ch.g. (May 6) Case Law 113 – Breeze Away 60 **56** (Prince Sabo 123) [1999 5.1m 5g 6d 6f⁶ Aug 2] 10,000Y: lengthy, rather unfurnished gelding: second living foal: brother to a 5f winner in Italy: dam 6f winner: modest maiden: stiff task final start: likely to prove best at 5f/6f. *R. Hollinshead*

ITCH 4 b.c. Puissance 110 – Panienka (POL) 70 (Dom Racine (FR) 121) [1998 –: **–** 5.9g 7g 1999 8.3m 7m 7.5m 5m 6v Oct 12] good-bodied colt: fair winner at 2 yrs: little form since: stays 6f: acts on good to soft going: visored final start. *R. Bastiman*

ITHADTOBEYOU 4 b.c. Prince Sabo 123 – Secret Valentine 71 (Wollow 132) **75 d** [1998 –, a80: a5g* a7g⁴ 6v⁶ 6d 1999 6f 6f 5m⁶ 6m a5g⁶ 7m³ 6g⁶ 7.1m 5s Oct 2] leggy colt: fair performer at best, but seems on the downgrade: stays 6f: acts on all-weather, probably on firm ground: usually blinkered now. *G. L. Moore*

I TINA 3 b.f. Lycius (USA) 124 – Tintomara (IRE) (Niniski (USA) 125) [1998 NR **76** 1999 11.7m² 10.2s³ 11.9v⁶ 11.7s⁴ Oct 26] third foal: dam twice-raced close relative of smart middle-distance winner Hajade: fair maiden: stays 1½m: acts on soft and good to firm going. *M. P. Tregoning*

ITSALLHAPPENING (IRE) 3 b.f. Second Set (IRE) 127 – Primo Stampari 78 **46 §** (Primo Dominie 121) [1998 57: 6m 6g 5m 6f² 6d a6g 1999 a8g⁴ a7g a7g a8f a8g⁵ 7f 8.2m 7m 17.2m⁶ a13g 11.9f⁶ a16g⁴ Aug 13] poor maiden: appears to stay 17.2f: acts on firm ground and all-weather: blinkered third start: has worn tongue strap: carries head high/hangs, and probably ungenuine. *T. J. Naughton*

IT'S ALLOWED 2 b.f. (Mar 16) Piccolo 121 – Double Flutter 92 (Beldale Flutter **81** (USA) 130) [1999 6f 6g⁵ 6g⁴ 7.5g³ 6.8m³ 6m⁴ 7f³ 7f* 6f* 6g³ 6m² 6.5g² 7d 7g* 7s 6s² Nov 2] 7,000F, 7,000Y: leggy filly: first foal: dam 7f to 1¼m winner: fairly useful performer: won claimer at Thirsk in July and seller at Lingfield in August: claimed out of M. Channon's stable 10,000 gns after tenth start: won nursery at Catterick in October: effective at 6f/7f: acts on firm and soft going: usually races prominently: consistent. *T. D. Easterby*

ITS ALL RELATIVE 4 gr.f. Distant Relative 128 – Sharp Anne 74§ (Belfort **82** (FR) 89) [1998 90: 5s³ 5.1s 5m 5g 5.1m⁵ 5f 5.6g 5m 1999 5.1g³ 5d 5m⁵ Jun 17] leggy, lengthy filly: fairly useful performer: creditable efforts 2 of 3 starts in 1999: speedy, and raced only around 5f: acts on firm and soft ground: blinkered (well beaten) once at 3 yrs: often front runner. *J. Berry*

ITS ANOTHER GIFT 2 b.f. (Jan 29) Primo Dominie 121 – Margaret's Gift 101 **64** (Beveled (USA)) [1999 6f⁵ 5g⁴ 5m³ 6f² 5g Oct 19] compact filly: second foal: half-sister to 3-y-o Margarets First: dam 5f (at 2 yrs) and 6f winner who stayed 7f: modest maiden: well below form last 2 starts: speedy, and likely to prove best over sharp 5f: raced mainly on good going or firmer. *J. Berry*

ITSANOTHERGIRL 3 b.f. Reprimand 122 – Tasmim 63 (Be My Guest (USA) **77** 126) [1998 70: 5m⁶ 5m³ 6m⁵ 8m⁴ 8.3s³ 7s* 7v⁴ 1999 6.1d⁴ 9m² 7.9m 10.3s³ 10.5v⁵ Oct 13] leggy filly: fair handicapper: creditable efforts final 2 starts: barely stays 1¼m, at least when conditions are testing: acts on good to firm and heavy going: has hung left. *M. W. Easterby*

ITSGOTTABDUN (IRE)   2 b.g. (May 5) Foxhound (USA) 103 – Lady Ingrid   **54**
(Taufan (USA) 119) [1999 6g 5g⁶ 5m⁶ 5g⁵ 6m⁵ 5d 5.3s² 5.3d a5g³ Dec 29] IR 9,200Y:
half-brother to 6f winner Amoeba (by Distinctly North): dam unraced daughter of
sister to Sparkler: modest maiden on balance: should stay at least 6f: acts on good
to firm going, soft and equitrack: blinkered (no improvement) fifth and sixth starts.
K. T. Ivory

IT'S MAGIC   3 b.g. Magic Ring (IRE) 115 – Ryewater Dream 72 (Touching   **78**
Wood (USA) 127) [1998 58: 7.6f⁵ 8.2d 7s 1999 10.8d 11.6m 8g⁶ 8f* 10g⁵ 7m 8g*
8g* 8d⁶ Oct 1] leggy, shallow-girthed gelding: fair handicapper: won at Newcastle in
May and Leicester (twice) in August: stiff task final outing: best at 1m: acts on firm
going: blinkered final 7 starts. *B. Hanbury*

ITS MY PLEASURE   5 b.m. Rock Hopper 124 – The Fink Sisters 75 (Tap On   **–**
Wood 130) [1998 –: 9m³ 1999 a14g Jun 11] little form in 3 starts. *W. S. Cunningham*

IT'S NORMAN   3 b.g. Vantastic – Arrogant Daughter (Aragon 118) [1998 NR   **–**
1999 11.6m Jul 12] first foal: dam ran twice: no show in seller. *T. R. Watson*

IT'S OUR SECRET (IRE)   3 ch.g. Be My Guest (USA) 126 – Lady Dulcinea   **73**
(ARG) (General (FR)) [1998 61: 5.1g 6m⁵ 7s 1999 8.2d² 7.5m 8m⁵ 8.2m* 8g⁶ 8f 8d
7s 7g 7d Oct 22] lengthy, sturdy gelding: fair handicapper: gained first victory in
minor event at Nottingham in May: long way below form after: stays 1m: acts on
good to firm and good to soft ground: visored final start. *M. H. Tompkins*

IVOR'S DEED   6 b.g. Shadeed (USA) 135 – Gena Ivor (USA) (Sir Ivor 135)   **– §**
[1998 53§, a65§: a7g⁵ a7g a6g⁴ a6g⁵ a7g* a7g⁴ a7g⁶ a8g 7g 8.5g 8g 8d⁶ 7m 7.6g⁶   **a55 §**
a9.4g 9.1v a8.5g a7g* a7g 1999 a8g⁵ a6f³ a7g⁶ a6g³ a7g a7g⁵ a8g⁴ a6g³ a7g 7.7s
7.6m Jul 25] sturdy gelding: modest performer: stayed 1m: acted on firm ground and
equitrack: was effective blinkered/visored or not: was unreliable: dead. *P. D. Evans*

IVOR'S FLUTTER   10 b.g. Beldale Flutter (USA) 130 – Rich Line (High Line   **81**
125) [1998 93: 16v* 14.4s* 18.7m 16g 20d 16.2d 18g 1999 17.2s⁴ 17.3g 16.1d Oct
29] workmanlike gelding: fairly useful handicapper: respectable efforts first and final
starts in 1999: stays 2¼m: acts on any going: often ridden by claimer: usually comes
from off pace. *D. R. C. Elsworth*

IVOR'S INVESTMENT   3 ch.f. Forzando 122 – Abbotswood (Ahonoora 122)   **73 d**
[1998 64: 5.1s⁶ 5.1g⁴ 6m⁴ 5f⁴ 6s³ 6.5g 1999 7m² 7.1g⁶ 7.1g* 7m² 8m² 8.5g*
6m² 8.1m⁴ 8g 7.5g⁴ᵈⁱˢ 6.1m 8g⁵ 10d Oct 21] lengthy filly: has a quick action: fair
performer: won claimers at Chepstow and Epsom in June: left D. Elsworth after
eighth start, and well below form subsequently: stays 1m, not 1¼m: acts on firm and
soft going. *B. D. Leavy*

IVORY DAWN   5 b.m. Batshoof 122 – Cradle of Love (USA) 87 (Roberto (USA)   **81**
131) [1998 80: 6.1s⁵ 6v 5.1g⁵ 6g 6d⁶ 6g⁵ 6m* 6m* 6m³ 6m⁴ 6m 6m² 6.1m⁵ 6d⁴
6m 1999 6g 6s 6f⁶ 6s 6g⁴ 6.1f⁵ 6g 6m³ 6m 6g* 6m* 6m³ 6f³ 5g 6g 6m³ 6d 6g 6.1f Oct
20] leggy, workmanlike mare: fairly useful handicapper: won at Brighton in June and
Lingfield in July, both for second year running: generally ran at least respectably
after: has form at easy 7f, races mostly at 6f now: well beaten on heavy going, acts on
any other turf: tried visored, better form without: sometimes bandaged/wears crossed
noseband: usually held up. *K. T. Ivory*

IVORY'S GRAB HIRE   6 b.g. Shavian 125 – Knees Up (USA) (Dancing Champ   **65 d**
(USA)) [1998 66, a60: a6g a6g⁴ a5g⁴ a5g⁴ a5g a5g⁵ a7g a5g³ a5g* a5g 6g 6f 6g⁴ 7g⁶
6g 5.3m⁵ 6g⁵ 5d³ 5m 5m 5.3m 5.1d 6d⁵ 5.3g² 6.1s a5g⁶ 1999 a6g⁶ a5g⁶ a5f a5g² a6g
5d² 6f⁵ 5m 5g 7g 5m 5.3g⁴ 5.1m⁴ 5m⁵ 6f⁴ 8.3m Aug 2] shallow-girthed gelding:
fair handicapper at best: below form after sixth start in 1999: best at 5f/6f: acts on
all-weather, firm and good to soft going: usually visored/blinkered: has run well for
apprentice and when sweating profusely: sometimes slowly away: tough. *K. T. Ivory*

IVORY'S GUEST (IRE)   2 gr.g. (Apr 29) Be My Guest (USA) 126 – Irish Hope   **–**
(Nishapour (FR) 125) [1999 6d 5m 7g a8g Dec 29] 6,500Y: fourth reported foal:
half-brother to 3-y-o Perchancer and Italian winner up to 1m Grey Hope (by Double
Schwartz): dam Italian 1m to 11.5f winner: no form, including in sellers: tried
blinkered/visored. *K. T. Ivory*

IVORY'S JOY   4 b.f. Tina's Pet 121 – Jacqui Joy 63 (Music Boy 124) [1998 82:   **92**
6g 5m⁴ 6f 6g² 6g³ 5g 5d³ 5.1m³ 5.1d² 5g⁶ 6f 5f 5g 5g⁵ 5v⁴ 5.1v⁵ 1999 5s³ 5d² 5d 5s*

528

6f⁶ 5g² 5m 6g 5f⁵ 5.3s 5d³ 5.2g³ 5f³ 5.2g 5s* 5g² 5d 5d a5g* a6g Nov 30] leggy filly: fairly useful handicapper: won at Thirsk in May, Haydock in September and Wolverhampton in November: stays easy 6f: acts on fibresand and probably any turf going (untried on equitrack): has won in blinkers, tried only once since 2 yrs: usually bandaged: tends to get on toes: tough. *K. T. Ivory*

IYAVAYA (USA) 2 b.f. (Apr 2) Valiant Nature (USA) 118 – Odori (USA) (The **85** Minstrel (CAN) 135) [1999 5s* 6m 5.1m* 5s⁴ 6.5g 5d⁵ 5s⁵ Oct 1] $30,000Y: leggy, angular filly: has a rounded action: second foal: half-sister to 3-y-o Georgette: dam, lightly raced in USA, granddaughter of Pretty Polly Stakes and Grade 1 9f winner Miss Toshiba: fairly useful performer: won maiden at Warwick in June and minor event at Chepstow in July: likely to prove best at 5f: acts on soft and good to firm going. *M. R. Channon*

J

JACK DAWSON (IRE) 2 b.g. (May 8) Persian Bold 123 – Dream of Jenny 73 **63** (Caerleon (USA) 132) [1999 7.1s 7.9g 8d Oct 21] neat gelding: fourth reported foal: half-brother to 3-y-o Hi-Jenny and 4-y-o Miss Money Spider: dam placed around 1m at 2 yrs (only season to race): modest form when seventh of 11 in maiden at Haydock on debut: well held after: should stay 1¼m: sold 6,000 gns, joined John Berry. *J. Noseda*

JACKERIN (IRE) 4 b.g. Don't Forget Me 127 – Meanz Beanz (High Top 131) **59 §** [1998 71§: 5g 6g 6g 5s² 5m² 5d 5g⁴ 5m 5m³ 5m⁴ 5m² 6m⁵ 5m⁴ 5g⁴ 5s* 5s 1999 5s 5d 5d 5g 5g⁵ 5m 5m⁵ 5f 5m Aug 4] strong, workmanlike gelding: modest handicapper: reportedly bled internally final start: modest at 5f: acts on soft and good to firm ground: wears visor/blinkers: sometimes slowly away: often fails to go through with effort. *B. S. Rothwell*

JACK FLUSH (IRE) 5 b.g. Broken Hearted 124 – Clubhouse Turn (IRE) (King **–** of Clubs 124) [1998 52: 8s 8.5m a8g 8.1d⁵ 8.3s 8m 9m 1999 a8g Jan 18] leggy gelding: one-time fair handicapper: generally well beaten since 1997: tried visored/ blinkered. *B. S. Rothwell*

JACK GOODMAN (IRE) 3 ch.g. Simply Great (FR) 122 – Donna Katrina **54** (Kings Lake (USA) 133) [1998 70: 6m 7d² 6m⁶ 7f* 7m⁴ 7g a7g* 1999 a8g⁶ 7.6m 7m 8m⁴ 8f 7f Jul 14] workmanlike gelding: fair performer at 2 yrs: best effort in 1999 in claimer on fourth start: unlikely to stay beyond 1m: acts on firm going, good to soft and equitrack: sold 4,200 gns, sent to Macau. *J. S. Moore*

JACKIE'S BABY 3 b.g. Then Again 126 – Guarded Expression 51 (Siberian **90** Express (USA) 125) [1998 85+, a79: 5.3d⁴ a5g³ a5g* 5.1d³ a5g* 5g⁵ 5f³ 5m* a6g² 1999 a5g 5d 5.1m² 5g 5g 5.7g 5m² 5.1m³ 5.1m* 5f Jul 30] big, good-topped gelding: fairly useful handicapper: won at Bath in July: below par final start: best at 5f: best efforts on fibresand and going firmer than good: has been bandaged behind: front runner: sometimes wanders. *W. G. M. Turner*

JACK JACKSON 3 b.c. Sizzling Melody 117 – Millfields House 70 (Record **–** Token 128) [1998 NR 1999 7m 8.3m 7.6m Jul 8] fifth foal: half-brother to 4-y-o Amington Girl and 1995 2-y-o 5f winner Amington Lass (by Cree Song): dam maiden who appeared to stay 1¼m: tailed-off last in 3 maidens. *T. D. McCarthy*

JACK THE LAD (IRE) 5 b.g. Shalford (IRE) 124§ – Indian Honey (Indian **56** King (USA) 128) [1998 –: a12g a12g⁶ 8d 11.9d 10m 1999 a12g 9.2v⁵ a12g⁵ a9.4g⁵ **a–** 12.1m* 10g Aug 16] tall gelding: has a round action: formerly fairly useful: first form in long time when winning seller at Hamilton in July: stays 1½m: acts on fibresand, firm and good to soft going: blinkered once. *J. Hetherton*

JACK TO A KING 4 b.g. Nawwar 76 – Rudda Flash (General David) [1998 –: **54** 8m⁶ 6g 7m 1999 a7g 6v a6g⁵ a5g a5g⁶ Dec 21] modest maiden: may prove best at 5f: acts on fibresand: tried blinkered. *J. Balding*

JACK TO A QUEEN 3 ch.f. Nawwar 76 – Merry Marion (Goldengazer 94) **–** [1998 NR 1999 10.5m Aug 30] sixth reported foal: dam of little account: last of 17 in seller. *J. Balding*

JACMAR (IRE)   4 br.g. High Estate 127 – Inseyab 65 (Persian Bold 123) [1998   **67 d**
67: 8d⁴ 7d 7.9g 9.2s³ 8d 8.3d 6s 6g 8s² 8s 8s 1999 8g 6v 6m³ 6s 8.3d⁴ 5g* 6g⁴ 6m³ 6f⁵
6f⁵ 5g 6.9m 6m⁶ 6g 5f 5m 5d 6m 8.3s 6v 5d Oct 20] smallish, good-bodied gelding:
has a short, round action: fair performer: won amateur handicap at Hamilton in June:
lost his form soon after: effective at 5f to 1m: below form on heavy going, acts on any
other. *Miss L. A. Perratt*

JACOBINA   4 b.f. Magic Ring (IRE) 115 – Mistitled (USA) 54 (Miswaki (USA)   **54 +**
124) [1998 71p: 8s 8.2d⁴ 7g 8g 7m² 7g² 7.1g* 7m 7.5m 1999 7m 7m 8d⁶ 7m 6g
Aug 21] workmanlike filly: fair handicapper at 3 yrs: modest form in 1999, leaving
B. Rothwell after penultimate start: effective at 7f/1m: acts on firm and good to soft
going: usually patiently ridden. *D. Nicholls*

JACQUES REPLY   2 b.c. (Mar 8) Paris House 123 – Question Ali 83 (Petoski   **75**
135) [1999 5.1s 5d³ 5g⁴ 5m³ 5.1m⁶ 5g⁶ 7g 6m³ 5g⁶ Oct 14] 9,500Y: lengthy colt: has
a round action: first foal: dam 2-y-o 6f winner: fair maiden: beaten third after third
start: good third of 22 to Kilbrannan Sound in sales race at Doncaster on penultimate
one: stays 6f: acts on good to firm going: has run well when sweating: sold 11,000
gns, sent to Sweden. *K. A. Ryan*

JADE CHEQUER   3 b.f. Green Desert (USA) 127 – Draft Board 78 (Rainbow   **56**
Quest (USA) 134) [1998 71: 5m³ 1999 5d⁴ 6g Aug 24] leggy, quite attractive filly:
injured and underwent surgery after debut: little promise on return. *J. H. M. Gosden*

JADE TIGER   3 ch.g. Lion Cavern (USA) 117 – Precious Jade 72 (Northfields   **78 §**
(USA)) [1998 77: 6m⁶ 6m² 7d⁶ 8g³ 8d 1999 7s 8.3m 8d³ 8m* 10m² 8.1m 8m³ 8m²
8g 7.6g⁴ 9.9v⁶ 10d Oct 18] smallish, workmanlike gelding: has a quick action: fair
performer: won claimer at Leicester in June (left B. Meehan): some creditable efforts
after: stays 1¼m: acts on good to firm and heavy ground: blinkered final 2-y-o start:
tends to hang: irresolute, and not one to trust. *F. Jordan*

JADIE   2 ch.f. (Apr 26) Safawan 118 – Another Jade 79 (Beveled (USA)) [1999   **42**
a6g³ a7g⁴ a6g Oct 16] close-coupled filly: first foal: dam 5f (at 2 yrs)/6f winner: poor
maiden: in frame in sellers at Wolverhampton first 2 outings. *A. P. Jarvis*

JAGUAR   3 b.g. Barathea (IRE) 127 – Oasis (Valiyar 129) [1998 76: 6d 7m 7g⁵ 8.1s³   **75**
1999 10m 8s³ 8g May 31] strong, deep-girthed gelding: good mover: fair maiden:
easily best effort in 1999 at Newbury on penultimate outing: well beaten in handicaps
otherwise: stays 1m, possibly not 1¼m: acts on soft and good to firm going: has worn
dropped noseband: won over hurdles in September. *N. A. Twiston-Davies*

JAILHOUSE ROCKET   2 gr.g. (May 17) Petong 126 – Selvi (Mummy's Pet   **89**
125) [1999 5m 5g* 5m 5s* 6g 5g³ 5v³ Oct 25] 14,000Y: fifth foal: half-brother to 3
winners, including smart sprinter Indian Rocket (by Indian Ridge) and French 1m to
13f winner Capodinegro (by Cyrano de Bergerac): dam sprint maiden: fairly useful
performer: won maiden at Carlisle in August and minor event at Beverley in
September: bit below form last 3 starts: may prove best at 5f: acts on soft and good to
firm going: sold 31,000 gns. *Sir Mark Prescott*

JALAD (IRE)   2 b.c. (Feb 5) Marju (IRE) 127 – Hamsaat (IRE) 80 (Sadler's Wells   **99**
(USA) 132) [1999 7g² 7m* 8s⁶ Sep 26] tall, good-topped colt: first foal: dam, 1m
winner on only start (would have stayed further), sister to very smart 1¼m performer
Batshoof, from family of King of Kings: useful form: 2 lengths second of 8 to
impressive King's Best in maiden at Newmarket on debut, then beat Air Marshall
short head in similar event at Leicester later in August: much stiffer task, appeared to
run best race when last of 6 to Royal Kingdom in Royal Lodge Stakes at Ascot
(attended by 2 handlers) final start, beaten around 5 lengths: should stay 1¼m.
B. Hanbury

JALB (IRE)   5 b.g. Robellino (USA) 127 – Adjacent (IRE) 82 (Doulab (USA) 115)   **68**
[1998 72: 10.8g 10g 12.5d* 12d* 12m⁴ 14.4d³ 13.3g 10d⁴ 1999 a12g² 12.5s³
14.4m⁶ 14m 14.1g Aug 12] strong, well-made gelding: fair handicapper: below form
after third start: effective from 1¼m to 1¾m: acts on soft ground, good to firm and
fibresand: has raced lazily. *P. G. Murphy*

JAMADYAN (IRE)   2 b.c. (Apr 25) Mujadil (USA) 119 – Truly Flattering (Hard   **82 p**
Fought 125) [1999 8f* Oct 16] IR 11,500F, 4,200Y, 10,000 2-y-o: fifth foal: half-
brother to 3-y-o Teen Idol and 1½m winner Amadour (by Contract Law): dam Irish

7f winner: won 5-runner minor event at Milan in October by neck from Holly Hock: should improve. *H. Akbary*

JAMAICAN FLIGHT (USA)   6 b.h. Sunshine Forever (USA) – Kalamona   **84**
(USA) (Hawaii) [1998 79, a86: a11g³ a12g² a14.8g² 18d⁵ a12g² 17.1d² 12m² 20d   **a74**
14.6g³ 15.9m³ 18.7g³ 15.9g³ 18m* 16g 15.9g 18g 1999 a12g a12g 18d⁵ 17.1v²
21.6d⁴ 18g* 16f⁴ 20m 16.1m 14.1m* 16.5f* 16.2g² 12g⁵ 18m⁶ a12f⁵ 17.3g a14g⁵
Nov 12] leggy horse: fairly useful on turf, fair on all-weather: won Phil Bull Trophy
(for second year in succession) at Pontefract in May and amateur handicaps at
Carlisle and Doncaster in July: finds 1½m a minimum, and stays 2½m: acts on any
turf going and fibresand: has been too free to post and given trouble start: best form
making running: game. *Mrs S. Lamyman*

JAMAIEL (IRE)   2 b.f. (Mar 5) Polish Precedent (USA) 131 – Avice Caro (USA)   –
85 (Caro 133) [1999 7m Sep 7] third foal: half-sister to useful French 1m winner
Actoris (by Diesis) and 3-y-o Anschluss (by Alzao): dam, 1¼m winner, half-sister to
smart miler Sensation out of Breeders' Cup Juvenile Fillies winner Outstandingly:
saddle slipped when last of 11 in Lingfield maiden (played up in stalls). *C. E. Brittain*

JAMES DEE (IRE)   3 b.g. Shalford (IRE) 124§ – Glendale Joy (IRE) (Glenstal   **69**
(USA) 118) [1998 72: a5g 5.3d² 5.1m⁵ 6m² 5d³ 5g 1999 a8g² a7s a8g⁴ a6g⁴ 7f* 7m⁴   **a83**
7.1d 6m³ 6m 6m² 6g⁴ 6g⁴ 5g a7g* Sep 4] fairly useful performer on all-weather,
fair on turf: won claimer at Brighton in May and handicap at Wolverhampton (much
improved effort) in September: effective at 5f to 1m: acts on firm going and fibresand: carries head awkwardly and sometimes looks less than keen: inconsistent.
A. P. Jarvis

JAMES STARK (IRE)   2 b.c. (Apr 14) Up And At 'em 109 – June Maid 56   **83**
(Junius (USA) 124) [1999 6.8d 7d⁵ a5g* a6g* a5g⁶ Dec 17] IR 10,000F, IR 10,000Y,
15,000 2-y-o: rather unfurnished, workmanlike colt: half-brother to several winners,
including useful sprinter Harvest Girl (by Thatching): dam second over 7f: fairly
useful performer: won maiden at Southwell (tended to wander) and nursery at
Lingfield (made virtually all) in November: effective at 5f/6f: best efforts on all-
weather: blinkered after debut. *N. P. Littmoden*

JAMESTOWN   2 b.c. (Apr 30) Merdon Melody 98 – Thabeh 57 (Shareef Dancer   **76**
(USA) 135) [1999 5m a5g⁵ 5d² 6m 6f⁵ 6.8d* 8d⁶ Oct 18] 3,700Y: workmanlike,
close-coupled colt: sixth foal: brother to 3-y-o Melody Queen: dam poor maiden: fair
performer: won maiden at Warwick in September: edgy and took good hold to post
when tailed off in listed race at Pontefract final start: stays 6.8f: acts on good to soft
going, probably on fibresand: slowly away first 2 starts. *C. Smith*

JAMIE ANN   2 b.f. (Mar 26) Son Pardo 107 – Taine Sands (Record Run 127)   –
[1999 7g 7m Jul 8] first reported foal: dam winning hurdler: well beaten in minor
event at Epsom and maiden at Lingfield. *Julian Poulton*

JAMMIE DODGER   3 b.g. Ardkinglass 114 – Ling Lane (Slip Anchor 136)   **52**
[1998 NR 1999 8g 8g⁴ 6.9g⁶ 8d 7.5g⁵ 8.2g⁴ 10g Oct 14] unfurnished gelding: first
foal: dam unraced daughter of half-sister to Irish Oaks winner Bolas: modest maiden:
should stay 1¼m: raced only on good/good to soft going. *R. M. Whitaker*

JAMORIN DANCER   4 b.g. Charmer 123 – Geryea (USA) (Desert Wine (USA))   **58**
[1998 75: 11.8s³ 10g⁵ 10g⁶ 11.9s⁴ 9g* 9.9m 8.9g 1999 9m 9.9m 9.7f⁶ 11.6s 14.1g³   **a–**
15.8g⁵ a12g a11g Nov 30] leggy gelding: modest performer: left W. Jarvis after sixth
start: probably stays 1¾m, not 2m: acts on soft ground, probably on good to firm,
well held on all-weather: tried blinkered: has been walked to post. *D. Nicholls*

JAMPET   3 b.g. No Big Deal – Jealous Lover 56 (Alias Smith (USA)) [1998 –:   –
5.1g 6.1m⁶ a6g 6.1g 1999 8.2s 8.2s 8g 10.2g 17.2f Jun 26] of no account: tried
blinkered. *A. Barrow*

JAMRR (IRE)   3 b.c. Barathea (IRE) 127 – Ela Romara 124 (Ela-Mana-Mou 132)   **82**
[1998 NR 1999 10m³ 10m³ Jun 14] lengthy, angular colt: fifth foal: closely related to
smart 10.4f and 1½m (King Edward VII Stakes) winner Foyer (by Sadler's Wells):
dam won Lowther and Nassau Stakes: third in maidens at Sandown (promising) and
Windsor (odds on, no improvement): stays 1¼m. *Saeed bin Suroor*

JANE ANN (IRE)   3 ch.f. Perugino (USA) 84 – Height of Elegance 82 (Shirley   **55**
Heights 130) [1998 56?: 7.5m 7g 7g 7f³ a8.5g⁴ 8d 1999 a11g⁴ a13g* a12g⁴ 12g⁵

a12g³ 11.8m 11.6d 14.1g⁶ 12m 10g² a12g a12g Sep 8] close-coupled filly: modest performer: won maiden at Lingfield in March: mostly below form after fifth start: stays 13f: acts on all-weather and firm going. *A. P. Jarvis*

JANEFER JOHN (IRE)   2 ch.f. (May 24) Magical Wonder (USA) 125 – John's   **69**
Vision (IRE) (Vision (USA)) [1999 6g⁵ 6f⁴ 5g 7m 6g 5s⁶ 6s Oct 2] IR 3,000Y, resold
IR 2,500Y: third foal: half-sister to an Italian 1m winner by Magical Strike: dam ran
twice in Ireland: fair maiden: trained by J. L. Eyre first 3 starts: stays 6f: acts on soft
going, probably on firm. *K. F. O'Brien, Ireland*

JANE GREY   3 br.f. Tragic Role (USA) – Kind of Shy 61 (Kind of Hush 118)   **64**
[1998 64: 5g⁴ 6.1s⁵ 6v 1999 6m 8.1m⁵ 6m⁵ 8d³ 8m 8s² 8.1s 8d Oct 11] unfurnished
filly: modest maiden: stays 1m: acts on soft and good to firm going: reared leaving
stalls final outing. *M. Salaman*

JANET   2 b.f. (Jan 26) Emperor Jones (USA) 119 – Bid Dancer (Spectacular Bid   **73**
(USA)) [1999 6g⁵ 6m² May 26] 6,500Y: fifth foal: half-sister to 3 winners in France
by Highest Honor, including 1m to 11f winner Bel Amour: dam French 1m winner:
better effort (fair form) when staying-on head second of 6 to Speedfit Free in minor
event at Yarmouth: will stay 1m: joined G. Chung. *A. Kelleway*

JANICELAND (IRE)   2 b.f. (Mar 26) Nashwan (USA) 103 – Rebecca's Girl   **65**
(IRE) (Nashamaa 113) [1999 5g⁵ 5m² 5g² 5f 6g⁶ 5g 5g³ 6m⁵ 5m a6g² a6g² a5g⁵ a6g⁴
a5g* Nov 27] IR 3,200F, 11,000Y: strong, close-coupled filly: fifth foal: half-sister
to 3-y-o Waterford Spirit and 1m seller winner (including at 2 yrs) Head Girl (by
Masterclass): dam unraced: fair performer: won seller at Wolverhampton in November: stays 6f: raced only on good going or firmer on turf, acts on fibresand: has been
bandaged behind. *S. E. Kettlewell*

JARAAB   8 b.g. Sure Blade (USA) 130 – Ostora (USA) 83 (Blushing Groom (FR)   **–**
131) [1998 –, a83: a14.8g² a14g* a14.8g⁴ a14.8g² a16g a16.2g⁵ a14.8s* 1999 a16g*   **a83**
Jan 15] stocky gelding: fairly useful on all-weather, winner of 13 races, including
weak claimer at Southwell by wide margin on only outing in 1999: no form in just
2 races on turf since 1995: stays 2m: blinkered once, visored nowadays: joined
D. Smith and successful over hurdles in March. *Miss S. J. Wilton*

JARN   2 b.c. (Apr 4) Green Desert (USA) 127 – Alkariyh (USA) 79 (Alydar (USA))   **100 p**
[1999 6m* 6s Oct 23] strong, attractive, good-topped colt: has scope: fluent mover:
fourth foal: closely related to 6f winner Al Wujud (by Polish Precedent) and
half-brother to 6f (at 2 yrs) and 7f (in UAE) winner Kabil (by Doyoun): dam 2-y-o
6f winner out of half-sister to Dunbeath and Saratoga Six: looked potentially smart
performer when making winning debut in 15-runner maiden at Newbury in
September by 5 lengths from Corridor Creeper, leading well over 1f out: possibly
unsuited by soft ground when last of 8 in listed race at Doncaster following month:
should stay 7f: worth another chance. *B. Hanbury*

JASEUR (USA)   6 b.g. Lear Fan (USA) 130 – Spur Wing (USA) (Storm Bird   **108 §**
(CAN) 134) [1998 101: 12g 16.1v 16.1f² 13.9f⁴ 1999 14g² 16.2d⁴ 22.2m² 16.1m 16f³
13.9g 15.5m⁶ Sep 5] strong gelding: useful performer: ran well on several occasions,
including when second in handicap at Goodwood in May and Queen Alexandra
Stakes at Royal Ascot (beaten head by San Sebastian) and when third in Goodwood
Cup (4¾ lengths behind Kayf Tara) in July: stays 2¾m: acts on any going: wears
visor: found little penultimate start: not one to trust implicitly. *J. H. M. Gosden*

JATHAABEH   2 ch.f. (May 12) Nashwan (USA) 135 – Pastorale 91 (Nureyev   **55 p**
(USA) 131) [1999 7s Nov 5] smallish, sturdy filly: fourth foal: half-sister to 3
winners, including smart 1998 2-y-o 7f winner Kareymah (by Zafonic) and 1m and
11.5f winner Krosno (by Kris): dam, 7f winner from 3 starts, half-sister to high-class
miler Cape Cross and closely related to dam of Diktat: mid-division in maiden at
Doncaster, slowly away and never on terms: will stay 1m, probably 1¼m: should
improve. *M. A. Jarvis*

JATHAAB (USA)   2 b. or br.c. (Feb 28) Silver Hawk (USA) 123 – Best of   **76 +**
Memories (USA) (Halo (USA)) [1999 7.1m⁴ 7.1s* 8d 8d³ Oct 29] $185,000Y, resold
400,000Y: rather sparely-made colt: second foal: dam, won up to 9f in USA,
half-sister to very smart US Grade 1 9f/9.5f winner Memories of Silver (by Silver
Hawk): fair form: won maiden at Haydock in September: raced too freely in nurseries

last 2 starts, though not disgraced second occasion: bred to stay at least 1¼m: acts on soft going. *J. L. Dunlop*

JATO DANCER (IRE) 4 b.f. Mukaddamah (USA) 125 – Que Tranquila 65 – (Dominion 123) [1998 48d: a7g³ a8g a8g a10g 8.3m* 8m 8.5g² 7g 8m 11.1m a8g a8.5g 1999 8.3g 7m 8m 8.5g a7g a7g a11g Dec 13] tall filly: no recent form: left J. R. Arnold after fourth start: tried blinkered. *R. Hollinshead*

JAVA SHRINE (USA) 8 b.g. Java Gold (USA) – Ivory Idol (USA) (Alydar – (USA)) [1998 10.0d⁵ 10.8g* 12.5m² 11.7m⁴ᵈⁱˢ 14.1m 10.8m³ a10g* 10.8m **a80** a12g³ 1999 a10g* a10g* a10f* a10g⁶ a12g³ 10.8m 10.2g 10g a10g³ a10g² a10g⁶ a9.4g Dec 27] strong, lengthy gelding: fair performer: trained by P. Eccles on reappearance, A. Reid until after fifth start and then P. Eccles again until after eighth outing: won 2 claimers and a minor event at Lingfield in January: ran well there on ninth/tenth starts: stays 1½m: acts on all-weather, no form on turf in 1999: blinkered: held up. *D. J. Wintle*

JAWAH (IRE) 5 br.g. In The Wings 128 – Saving Mercy 101 (Lord Gayle (USA) **85** 124) [1998 77: 12s 12m 20d 16.1v 11.6g⁴ 14m⁵ 16.2g 16.1m 14g² 14.1d³ 1999 14s² 13.9d 14.1g 14.6d* 16.5s Nov 6] lengthy, sparely-made gelding: fairly useful handicapper: won decisively at Doncaster in October: left K. Mahdi 24,000 gns, then soundly beaten next time: best at 1¾m to 2m: acts on soft going, probably on good to firm: sometimes blinkered/visored (mostly creditable efforts) at 4 yrs: has been bandaged behind: tends to hang: best held up. *J. R. Jenkins*

JAWHARI 5 b.g. Lahib (USA) 129 – Lady of The Land 75 (Wollow 132) [1998 **74** 72: 8d 6s 6g 7d 5.9m² 5.9m² 6d 5d 6v 1999 5m* 5f 6g⁶ 5.2g 5d Sep 16] small, sturdy gelding: has a quick action: fair handicapper: won at Catterick in July, landing a gamble: well below form after: effective at 5f to 7.6f: acts on good to firm ground, probably on soft: blinkered (raced freely) final start: usually races handily. *D. Nicholls*

JAWLA 2 ch.f. (May 14) Wolfhound (USA) 126 – Majmu (USA) 105 (Al Nasr **– p** (FR) 126) [1999 7s Nov 5] strong, compact filly: third foal: half-sister to 4-y-o Muhtathir and fairly useful 1m winner here and in UAE Maftool (by Machiavellian): dam won May Hill Stakes and stayed 1¼m: well beaten in maiden at Doncaster, eased fair bit after tracking leader over 5f: will stay at least 1m: seems sure to improve. *J. H. M. Gosden*

JAYANNPEE 8 ch.g. Doulab (USA) 115 – Amina 80 (Brigadier Gerard 144) **73** [1998 94: 6s 6d 5g 6g 6m³ 6g 6g 5.2g³ 5m⁵ 6m 6.1g 1999 6d 6m 6s 7m May 8] good-topped gelding: useful performer in his prime: well below best in 1999: effective at 5f/6f: acts on firm and good to soft ground: has worn tongue strap: usually comes from off pace. *I. A. Balding*

JAYBIRD 2 ch.f. (Feb 16) Common Grounds 118 – Flight Soundly (IRE) 78 (Caer- **72** leon (USA) 132) [1999 6g⁴ 6m² 5g* a6g Oct 8] sparely-made filly: first foal: dam 2-y-o 6f winner out of Queen Mary winner Night of Wind: fair form: won maiden at Musselburgh in September: well bred on nursery/all-weather debut at Lingfield final start: stays 6f: sold 9,000 gns in October. *Sir Michael Stoute*

JAYDOOM (IRE) 2 b.c. (Mar 11) Darshaan 133 – Truly Special 116 (Caerleon **100 p** (USA) 132) [1999 7.5s* Aug 3] seventh foal: brother to smart French middle-distance filly Truly A Dream and half-brother to 11f winners True Glory (fairly useful, by In The Wings) and Solo de Lune (in France, by Law Society): dam, won 10.5f Prix de Royaumont, from very good family: won 6-runner minor event at Deauville in August by 2½ lengths from Petroselli, making all and galloping on well: will be suited by at least 1¼m: sure to improve. *D. R. Loder, France*

JAYESAY (IRE) 3 gr.g. Mystiko (USA) 124 – Scravels Saran (IRE) 57 (Indian **–** King (USA) 128) [1998 NR 1999 8g 8.3m a8g a10g Jul 24] third foal: dam, form only at 7f at 2 yrs, became ungenuine: well held in maidens/handicap: sold 800 gns in October. *Dr J. D. Scargill*

JAY GEE (IRE) 4 b.f. Second Set (IRE) 127 – Polynesian Goddess (IRE) (Salmon **–** Leap (USA) 131) [1998 92d: 8g 6d 7m³ 5g² 5d 5g 5f 5.1m 7m 6g 5f 5m Jul 6] sturdy filly: one-time fairly useful performer: has lost her form: best at 5f/6f: acts on good to firm going: often blinkered/visored: unreliable. *G. G. Margarson*

JAYNE'S PRINCESS (IRE)   2 b.f. (Apr 21) College Chapel 122 – Water Spirit   –
(USA) (Riverman (USA) 131) [1999 6s Oct 25] 19,000Y: half-sister to 3-y-o White
Waters and several winners, including 6f (at 2yrs) to 9f winner Daytona Beach (by
Bluebird): dam unraced: tailed off in maiden at Leicester. *B. Palling*

JAY-OWE-TWO (IRE)   5 b.g. Distinctly North (USA) 115 – Fiery Song (Ballad   **83**
Rock 122) [1998 86+: 7s³ 7v 8d 8.1g 8d⁶ 6.9d 8g 8m⁶ 8m⁵ 7.5m⁶ 7.9g⁴ 8m³ 7s* 8s²
8g a8.5g* a9.4g 1999 a8g⁴ a8.5g 8d 8v 8m² 8.5d⁴ 7m 8.1g⁵ May 28] strong, lengthy
gelding: fairly useful handicapper: good second of 17 to Latalomne in Thirsk Hunt
Cup in April: needs further than 7f when ground is on firm side, and stays 8.5f: acts
on fibresand, soft and good to firm going: blinkered once, effective visored or not:
tough: sold 8,500 gns in November. *R. M. Whitaker*

JAYPEECEE   3 b.g. Never So Bold 135 – Treeline 59 (High Top 131) [1998 NR   **69**
1999 5g* 6m 6m 6g Jul 1] 7,000Y: half-brother to 1985 2-y-o 7f winner Wryneck (by
Niniski) and a winner in Scandinavia by Sharpo: dam sprint maiden: won 17-runner
maiden at Beverley in April: stiff tasks and well held in minor event and handicaps
after: should stay 6f. *J. L. Eyre*

JAZIL   4 b.c. Nashwan (USA) 135 – Gracious Beauty (USA) 67 (Nijinsky (CAN)   –
138) [1998 108p: 10.3g⁶ 10.5g² 10g* 11m³ 12g* 12g³ 1999 12d May 8] big, strong,
rangy colt: useful performer at 3 yrs: well beaten in valuable handicap at Goodwood,
only run of 1999: will stay 1¾m: acts on good to firm going: tail swisher: visored last
3 starts: sold 31,000 gns in November, joined K. Morgan. *J. H. M. Gosden*

JAZZNIC   3 b.f. Alhijaz 122 – Irenic 64 (Mummy's Pet 125) [1998 58, a64: 5m 6g   –
7m 6s⁴ a6g² a7g² 1999 a7g⁵ Dec 11] modest maiden: well beaten only 3-y-o start:
stays 7f: acts on soft going and equitrack. *P. J. Makin*

JAZZ NIGHT   2 b.g. (Feb 27) Alhijaz 122 – Hen Night (Mummy's Game 120)   –
[1999 7m Sep 19] 2,600Y, resold 2,000Y: third foal: dam unraced: well held in
maiden at Newcastle. *G. Woodward*

JAZZ TIME   2 ch.c. (Apr 3) Clantime 101 – Real Popcorn (IRE) 52 (Jareer (USA)   **77 +**
115) [1999 5d 5.1m² 5s³ 5.1g⁶ 5m³ 7m⁴ 8f⁴ 8d Oct 15] 7,600F, 18,000Y: sturdy,
lengthy colt: first foal: dam 1½m winner: fair maiden: stays 1m: acts on firm ground,
well below form on softer than good: sold 12,000 gns in October. *A. P. Jarvis*

JAZZ TRACK (IRE)   5 b.g. Sadler's Wells (USA) 132 – Minnie Hauk (USA)   –
100 (Sir Ivor 135) [1998 –: 20d 1999 18.7m May 5] workmanlike gelding: has a short
action: fairly useful at 3 yrs: well beaten on Flat since: acts on soft and good to firm
going: blinkered last 2 starts: sold 1,500 gns in July. *M. C. Pipe*

JAZZY   4 b.f. Alhijaz 122 – Irenic 64 (Mummy's Pet 125) [1998 –: 8s 10.5m a7g   –
1999 a8g a8g a7f 8d 7f May 31] close-coupled filly: little form. *J. Norton*

JAZZY MILLENNIUM   2 ch.c. (Feb 25) Lion Cavern (USA) 117 – Woodcrest   **80**
82 (Niniski (USA) 125) [1999 6m⁴ 7g² 7g² 6d Nov 4] 4,500F, 11,000Y: quite
attractive colt: first foal: dam 1½m winner: fair form in newcomers race and maidens
first 3 starts: well beaten final one: likely to stay 1¼m. *Miss Gay Kelleway*

JEAN PIERRE   6 b.g. Anshan 119 – Astolat (Rusticaro (FR) 124) [1998 40§:   **– §**
9.7f 10g⁶ a11g 1999 10.2g Jun 12] poor maiden handicapper: temperamental.
C. L. Popham

JEDI KNIGHT   5 b.g. Emarati (USA) 74 – Hannie Caulder (Workboy 123) [1998   **96**
77: 8d 8d 8.5m⁶ 8.1g³ 8.9s 8g⁴ 9.9m² 11.9f⁴ 11m² 8m⁴ 8s 8g⁵ 10.1v⁶ 1999 9.9m 8m
8.5d* 10d⁵ 8.5d² 8g⁶ 7.9f* 8f 9.2f* 8m⁴ 7.9g Oct 6] tall, good-topped gelding: useful
handicapper: won at Beverley in May, York in July and Hamilton in August: below
par last 2 starts: has form at 1½m, but seems best at 1m/9f nowadays: acts on firm
ground, probably on heavy: blinkered (well held) once at 4 yrs: has high head
carriage: often makes running nowadays: tough. *M. W. Easterby*

JEED (IRE)   2 b.f. (Feb 27) Mujtahid (USA) 118 – Secretary Bird (IRE) (Kris 135)   **86**
[1999 6m* Jun 25] IR 180,000Y: tall, rather unfurnished filly: has scope: fourth foal:
half-sister to French 3-y-o 1¼m winner Joie de Vivre (by Be My Guest): dam
unraced half-sister to Prix du Jockey Club winners Bikala and Assert and Irish St
Leger winner Eurobird: made impressive winning debut in 6-runner maiden at
Newmarket, taking strong hold, leading well over 1f out and beating Mother Molly

by 3 lengths: moved well to post: bred to stay 1m: looked a useful performer in the making, but not seen out again. *E. A. L. Dunlop*

JEFFREY ANOTHERRED 5 b.g. Emarati (USA) 74 – First Pleasure 73 (Dominion 123) [1998 87, a–: 6d 6v 8d 7d 6s² 6d³ 6d⁵ 5.9m* 6f 6s* 6m⁴ 7g² 7m⁶ 6s 5d 6v⁴ 6d a6g 1999 6d³ 6v⁵ 7m 6d 6d 6g⁶ 7d* 7m⁵ 7s* 7.6m⁴ 7.1d⁶ 7g 7d³ Sep 17] small gelding: fairly useful handicapper: won at Ayr in June and July: effective at 6f to 7.6f: has won on good to firm going, but best efforts on good or softer (well beaten both starts on fibresand): tried visored: usually held up. *M. Dods* **85 a–**

JELLYBEEN (IRE) 3 ch.f. Petardia 113 – Lux Aeterna (Sandhurst Prince 128) [1998 57+, a72+: 7.9g 7m 8s a9.4g* a8g 1999 10g 11.4m 14.1m² 14.1g⁶ 15.4m³ a16g⁵ a12g Sep 8] workmanlike filly: fair handicapper on all-weather at best, modest on turf: stays 1¾m: acts on fibresand and good to firm ground: blinkered fifth and sixth starts: has worn tongue strap: carries head awkwardly and looks less than keen. *Miss Gay Kelleway* **57 §**

JEMALINA (USA) 2 b.f. (Apr 25) Trempolino (USA) 135 – Cachondina 100 (Runnett 125) [1999 7m 7g 6s Oct 25] $70,000Y: fourth foal: closely related to a winner in USA by Pencil Point and half-sister to a winner there by Strawberry Road: dam 8.5f winner: showed some ability in maidens at Newmarket and Redcar first 2 starts: well beaten final one: should stay at least 1m: looks a tricky ride. *J. Noseda* **52**

JEMIMA 2 b.f. (May 8) Owington 123 – Poyle Fizz (Damister (USA) 123) [1999 5d⁵ 5m² 5d* 5m² 6f* 6g* 6g 6d⁵ Sep 28] 17,500Y: neat filly: has a quick action: third foal: half-sister to 5-y-o Floating Charge and 3-y-o Lost In Lucca: dam unraced daughter of half-sister to high-class sprinter Runnett: useful form: won maiden at York in June and minor event at Ripon and Peugeot Lowther Stakes at York (beat Seraphina a neck) in August: creditable fifth of 14 to Seazun in Cheveley Park Stakes at Newmarket final start: will probably stay 7f: acts on firm and good to soft going: has been blanketed for stalls entry: genuine. *T. D. Easterby* **100**

JEMINAR 2 b.f. (May 5) Clantime 101 – Bad Payer 72 (Tanfirion 110) [1999 5g 5d⁶ 5d⁴ May 15] unfurnished filly: half-sister to 3 winning sprinters, including 3-y-o AA-Youknownothing: dam 2-y-o 5f winner: poor sprint maiden. *M. W. Easterby* **46**

JENIN 2 b.f. (Apr 12) Rambo Dancer (CAN) 107 – Rich Lass (Broxted 120) [1999 5g 5m Jul 27] 1,000Y: half-sister to several winners, including 3-y-o Tayif and useful 1987 2-y-o 6f winner Fortinbras (by Junius), latter also successful in Hong Kong (where stayed 1m): dam poor maiden: behind in maidens. *J. W. Payne* **–**

JENKO (IRE) 2 b.g. (Mar 24) College Chapel 122 – Flicker of Hope (IRE) 53 (Baillamont (USA) 124) [1999 5m 6.1m⁴ 7s⁶ 6d Oct 18] IR 10,000F, 7,000Y, 3,800 2-y-o: small, good-topped gelding: second foal: half-brother to Italian 3-y-o 7f winner Heaven's Angel (by Scenic): dam Irish maiden out of sister to Alzao: easily best effort in maidens (modest form) when fourth of 11 to Loch Inch at Nottingham: may prove best up to 7f. *H. J. Collingridge* **55**

Peugeot Lowther Stakes, York—
Jemima shows improvement to beat 66/1-chance Seraphina (left) and Tabheej (far right)

JENNELLE   5 b.m. Nomination 125 – Its A Romp (Hotfoot 126) [1998 95: 5g⁴ **82**
5s² 5s* 5f⁵ 5d⁴ 6m 6g³ 5.6g 1999 6g⁵ 6s 6m 6m 5d 5.2g 5d² 5s⁴ 6d 5d 5d³ a6g⁶ Nov
15] smallish, good-quartered mare: fairly useful performer: below form last 4 starts:
effective at 5f and 6f: has form on firm ground, very best efforts on good or softer
(acts on heavy): sometimes slowly away: has been bandaged near-fore. *C. A. Dwyer*

JENNY WEST   2 ch.f. (May 6) Handsome Sailor 125 – Malindi (Mansingh (USA)   –
120) [1999 a6g a5g Nov 30] half-sister to 1992 2-y-o 6f winner Palacegate Prince
(by King of Spain) and 10.5f winner Lindi's Gold (by Sonnen Gold): dam unraced:
well beaten in seller and maiden at Southwell. *M. E. Sowersby*

JENSENS TALE (IRE)   2 b.c. (Mar 15) Mukaddamah (USA) 125 – Miss Tagalie   **57 d**
(IRE) (Cyrano de Bergerac 120) [1999 5.1s⁵ 5m 5.1s 5s⁶ 6d² 7f³ 6f⁶ 6f⁵ 6g⁶ 7.1m⁵
10s a7g Oct 18] IR 3,200F, 10,000Y: small colt: first foal: dam unraced: modest
maiden: well below form last 6 starts: stays 7f: acts on firm and good to soft going:
tried visored. *Mrs A. L. M. King*

JENUIN   4 b.f. High Kicker (USA) – Absonant (Absalom 128) [1998 NR 1999 10f   –
12.3m Jun 16] second reported foal: dam won at 1m and later over jumps: well held
in maidens: has carried head awkwardly. *G. M. Moore*

JEPAJE   2 b.g. (Apr 7) Rambo Dancer (CAN) 107 – Hi-Hunsley 82 (Swing Easy   **61**
(USA) 126) [1999 6m 6d 7s⁴ 5.3d² 6v a6g⁴ a6g Nov 27] 7,200Y: brother to 3 winners,   **a53**
including 6-y-o Myttons Mistake and 1998 2-y-o 7f seller winner Fizzy Whizzy, and
half-brother to a winner in Italy by Nicholas Bill: dam sprinter: modest maiden: best
effort when second of 10 in nursery at Brighton: may prove best around 6f. *A. Bailey*

JEREBOAM   2 b.c. (Feb 6) Grand Lodge (USA) 125 – Premiere Cuvee 109 (Form-   –
idable (USA) 125) [1999 5g 6d 5s Oct 1] 130,000Y: big colt with scope: closely
related to useful 7f/1m winner Cask (by Be My Chief) and half-brother to 3 winners,
including useful Italian miler She Bat (by Batshoof): dam sprinter: never a threat in
maidens: should stay at least 6f. *Sir Mark Prescott*

JESSINCA   3 b.f. Minshaanshu Amad (USA) 91§ – Noble Soul 67 (Sayf El Arab   –
(USA) 127) [1998 39, a47: 5g 6m 5d⁵ 5m 5.1g⁶ 6m⁴ 7m 7.9g 8d⁶ a8g⁴ a7g 1999 a8g⁴   **a48**
10f Jul 22] leggy filly: poor maiden: stays 1m: acts on good to firm going, good to
soft and fibresand. *R. T. Phillips*

JESS REBEC'S PET (IRE)   2 b.f. (Mar 16) Petorius 117 – Jess Rebec 63 (Kala   –
Shikari 125) [1999 5g 7m 6v 6d Nov 4] smallish, stocky filly: first foal: dam 5f
winner from speedy family: well held in maidens/minor event: has been bandaged.
Derrick Morris

JET AGE   3 b.g. Danehill (USA) 126 – Fawaayid (USA) 92 (Vaguely Noble 140)   **77**
[1998 9d 1999 8s⁴ 8d⁶ 12g³ 13.4m³ᵈⁱˢ 14.1m Jul 10] ex-French gelding: third foal:
closely related to useful French miler Green Lady (by Green Desert): dam won 3
races up to 1¼m at 2 yrs: trained for only race at 2 yrs by A. Fabre: fair form in
maidens: third at Goodwood and Chester (disqualified after failing dope test): pulled
up lame final start: stays 13.4f. *E. A. L. Dunlop*

JEUNE PREMIER (FR)   2 ch.g. (Mar 21) Jeune Homme (USA) 120 – Misaine   **– p**
(FR) (Saint Cyrien (FR) 128) [1999 7d Sep 19] 360,000 francs Y: first foal: dam won
10 races (including listed race) up to 1½m in France: 33/1, sixteenth of 22 to Scarteen
Fox in maiden at Newbury, weakening final 2f: should improve. *B. J. Meehan*

JEWEL FIGHTER   5 br.m. Good Times (ITY) – Duellist (Town Crier 119) [1998   **50**
–: 8.2s 8v 1999 8.2s³ 9.1v⁴ a8.5g Oct 16] unfurnished mare: modest performer:
should stay beyond 1¼m: acts on heavy going. *P. D. Evans*

JIBEREEN   7 b.g. Lugana Beach 116 – Fashion Lover 70 (Shiny Tenth 120) [1998   **57**
57, a84: a8s* a8.5g³ 8m⁶ 9g 8g⁶ 7g⁵ 8g a8g 8d 8m 7s⁴ a6g a8g² 1999 a8g* a9.4g² a6g   **a84**
a9.4g⁴ a8g³ a8g⁵ 8g² 8g a8g Dec 17] big, strong gelding: fairly useful on all-weather,
modest on turf: won claimer at Southwell in January: well below form after 8-month
absence final start: effective at 7f to 9.4f: acts on fibresand, soft and good to firm
going: has been bandaged. *P. Howling*

JIBE (USA)   4 b.f. Danzig (USA) – Slightly Dangerous (USA) 122 (Roberto   **105**
(USA) 131) [1998 105: 7d³ 8g 10m* 12s⁴ 1999 10.4s⁴ 10f³ May 26] small, sturdy
filly: has a quick, fluent action: useful performer: creditable efforts in small-field

listed/minor events in 1999: barely stayed 1½m: acted on soft and firm going: was rather nervy in preliminaries and showed a dislike of stalls: stud. *H. R. A. Cecil*

JIG (IRE)   3 b.f. Catrail (USA) 123 – River Jig (USA) 98 (Irish River (FR) 131)   **86**
[1998 89: 5s* 7.1m 1999 8d⁵ 10s 8d² 10.3s³ Nov 5] leggy, plain, close-coupled filly: fluent mover: fairly useful performer on her day: creditable efforts in listed/minor events on first and third starts: stays 1m, possibly not 1¼m: acts on soft going: bandaged off-hind on reappearance: sent to USA. *P. F. I. Cole*

JILLYS FLYER (IRE)   2 ch.f. (Apr 4) College Chapel 122 – Idle Gossip (Runnett   –
125) [1999 6g Jun 14] IR 4,000Y: half-sister to winning sprinters Heathyards Magic (by Magical Strike) and Metal Boys (by Krayyan), latter fairly useful: dam unraced: last of 10 in seller at Brighton. *J. S. Moore*

JILLY WOO   5 gr.m. Environment Friend 128 – William's Bird (USA) 104 (Master   **36**
Willie 129) [1998 41: 6.9d 10s⁴ 10.8g⁵ 10g 10m 12s 10g⁶ 10.2d 10.1m 10v 1999 a12g a12g⁵ a12f⁵ Jan 23] lightly-made mare: poor maiden handicapper: stays 1½m: acts on soft and good to firm going and all-weather: sometimes blinkered at 2 yrs. *P. Hayward*

JIM AND TONIC (FR)   5 ch.g. Double Bed (FR) 121 – Jimka (FR) (Jim   **124**
French (USA)) [1998 123: 10s² 8s⁵ 8s² 9.5f* 8g* 8d² 6.5m² 8f² 7m* 1999 10s³ 10m* 8d² 8f⁶ 8f³ 8g 10m* Dec 12]

Hong Kong has quickly become a lucrative destination for the tremendously consistent French-trained gelding Jim And Tonic. Three wins there from as many visits within twelve months have netted his owners the equivalent of over a million pounds worth of prize money. The most valuable of Jim And Tonic's wins at Sha Tin came in December, in the Hong Kong Cup, a Group 1 event and the final round of the Emirates World Series. His opponents were an international bunch without any of them being high-class animals, but the manner in which Jim And Tonic left his eleven rivals for dead was particularly impressive. Still eight to ten lengths off the pace set by the free-running New Zealand filly Sunline, and with only one behind him entering the straight, Jim And Tonic produced a remarkable burst from the two-furlong marker on the outside of the field to hit the front inside the last furlong. Still full of running, he surged clear to beat Running Stag three and three quarter lengths, with two more British-trained runners, Lear Spear and Kabool, third and fourth. Favourite Sunline dropped out to finish seventh, while among those further back were two of the leading locally-trained horses, Oriental Express and Johan Cruyff, who'd both received a beating from Jim And Tonic on his visit earlier in the year in the Audemars Piguet Queen Elizabeth II Cup in April. On that occasion Jim And Tonic had beaten Hong Kong's best middle-distance horse Indigenous by two and a half lengths, breaking the track record in the process.

Jim And Tonic appeared just once on his home turf in the latest season, and that was only as a warm-up for the Queen Elizabeth II Cup when third to Barbola and Borgia (also successful in Hong Kong in December) in the Prix Exbury at Saint-Cloud in March. Jim And Tonic's other trips abroad took him twice each to Britain and North America. At Newbury in May Jim And Tonic ran creditably when going down by one and a half lengths to Fly To The Stars in the Lockinge Stakes, but then turned in a rare lacklustre effort when only sixth in the Sussex Stakes at Goodwood next time. On both his outings in North America in the autumn Jim And Tonic met trouble in running. Giving weight to the three who finished ahead of him, he was beaten a head and two necks in the Atto Mile at Woodbine, but having been struck twice across the face by the winner's whip in the tight finish, Jim And Tonic was promoted to third on the disqualification of first-past-the-post Hawksley Hill. Starting second favourite to the same rival in the Breeders' Cup Mile at Gulfstream next time, Jim And Tonic was hampered when well placed on the far turn and then failed to get a clear run in the home straight before finishing ninth behind Silic.

Successful at Lyon Parilly on his only outing at two, it took Jim And Tonic until the summer of his four-year-old campaign to reach his current very

Mr J. D. Martin's "Jim And Tonic"

smart level of form. En route, he gained the most notable of his wins in the Prix Perth at Saint-Cloud in the autumn as a three-year-old and the Prix du Chemin de Fer du Nord at Maisons-Laffitte the following June. Hitherto best at a mile to a mile and a quarter (he'd been well beaten on his only outing at a mile and a half), Jim And Tonic's form took a leap forward when second to Seeking The Pearl in the Prix Maurice de Gheest at Deauville over six and a half furlongs. It was repeated when he was beaten a head by Labeeb in the Woodbine Mile and when he won his first race at Sha Tin, the Hong Kong International Bowl over seven furlongs on his final start as a four-year-old.

Francois Doumen also trained Jim And Tonic's sire Double Bed, whose two visits to Britain—for the Champion Stakes at three and the Prince of Wales's Stakes at four—gave little cause for him to be remembered. He was a very smart horse though, losing his maiden tag when winning the Group 2 Prix de la Cote Normande at Deauville by six lengths before finishing second to Park Express in the Phoenix Champion Stakes; as a five-year-old he also won the Grade 1 Hialeah Turf Cup in Florida over a mile and a half. Doumen has supported Double Bed in a major way (almost a quarter of the stable's eighty-odd horses are by him according to *Horses In Training*) and Double Bed's three other pattern winners, Top Shape, L'Annee Folle and Rajpoute, were all trained by Doumen, who also has some good jumpers by the same sire. Already with twenty-six runs under his belt, Jim And Tonic has some way to go to match his dam Jimka (another from the Doumen stable), who ran more than

538

seventy times on the Flat and a few more times over hurdles, winning seven races at up to ten and a half furlongs from two to six. Jim And Tonic is her eighth foal and seventh winner in total, the earlier ones having been successful either on the Flat, over jumps, or both. Among them are three other winners by Double Bed, namely eight-year-old Jimble, who has won numerous races under both codes (including at up to fifteen furlongs on the Flat in the latest season), Jimkana, who won at around eleven furlongs in the Provinces, and Gigawatt, a six-furlong winner as a two-year-old. Jimkana, incidentally, was sold in foal to Entrepreneur for 85,000 guineas at the December Sales just days before Jim And Tonic's latest win. Jimka's dam Kastueuse was a maiden daughter of Vertueuse, who was beaten a head in the 1964 Poule d'Essai des Pouliches and also finished second as a two-year-old in both the Prix de l'Abbaye and the Prix de la Foret. Vertueuse's half-brothers included the Grand Prix de Saint-Cloud winner Taneb and a very good chaser and successful sire of jumpers Kashtan.

		Be My Guest	Northern Dancer
	Double Bed (FR)	(ch 1974)	What A Treat
	(b 1983)	Claire's Slipper	Welsh Saint
Jim And Tonic (FR)		(b 1974)	Semislipper
(ch.g. 1994)		Jim French	Graustark
	Jimka (FR)	(br 1968)	Dinner Partner
	(b 1978)	Kastueuse	Kashmir II
		(b or br 1970)	Vertueuse

The leggy, sparely-made Jim And Tonic has proved as versatile as he is consistent, having shown form on firm and soft ground and over distances from six and a half furlongs to a mile and a quarter. It may well be that firmer conditions suit him ideally though, because he has a fine turn of foot. Further good prizes look sure to come his way, and it would be no surprise if he were to win more races in the Far East. *F. Doumen, France*

JIMGAREEN (IRE) 2 b. or br.f. (Mar 10) Lahib (USA) 129 – Sharp Circle (IRE) **66** 83 (Sure Blade (USA) 130) [1999 6g^2 6d 7g^4 7d 8d Sep 26] 22,000Y: fourth foal: half-sister to 3-y-o-Turntable and 1996 2-y-o 7f seller winner Compact Disc (by Royal Academy): dam, 1m winner better at 11.5f, half-sister to very smart sprinters Greenland Park and Red Sunset: fair form in frame in maidens at Ayr and Newcastle: will stay 1m: yet to show her form on ground softer than good. *Miss L. A. Perratt*

JIMMY TOO 4 b. or br.c. Nomination 125 – Cutlass Princess (USA) 41 (Cutlass **90** (USA)) [1998 103: 8d 6m^4 6d^2 5g 6g^3 6m^4 6m 6g^4 6s^5 5s 6v^2 6d^5 1999 5d 7v 6m 6s 6.1m^6 7.1d^5 6d 7.6d 6d Sep 18] smallish, lengthy colt: unimpressive mover: fairly useful handicapper, not so good in 1999 as at 3 yrs: was best at 6f: possibly needed good going or softer: tried visored, effective blinkered or not: was none too consistent: dead. *B. A. McMahon*

JIVING 3 ch.f. Generous (IRE) 139 – Kerali 88 (High Line 125) [1998 69p: 6d^3 – 1999 8g Jun 30] fair form on debut: got worked up in stalls when running badly on reappearance: should stay at least 1m: sold 17,000 gns in December. *R. Charlton*

JOB RAGE (IRE) 5 b. or br.g. Yashgan 126 – Snatchingly (Thatch (USA) 136) – [1998 –: a11g 1999 11.9d^5 Jul 2] tall gelding: well beaten in maidens/claimer: winning hurdler. *R. Ford*

JOCASTA 4 b.f. Warning 136 – Breed Reference (Reference Point 139) [1998 **92** 87: 7d 6d^2 6m* 7m^2 6.1m* 7g 7g 1999 7m^5 7f^4 6d^5 6m 7g* 7m 7s^4 7g Oct 16] leggy, quite good-topped filly: fairly useful handicapper: won at Yarmouth in August: below form after: stays 7f: acts on firm and good to soft going: ran poorly twice after giving trouble at stalls: tends to carry head awkwardly: has been bandaged behind: sold 35,000 gns, sent to Saudi Arabia. *C. F. Wall*

JOCKO GLASSES 2 ch.g. (May 5) Inchinor 119 – Corinthia (USA) (Empery – (USA) 128) [1999 6.1m^5 Aug 9] 9,000Y: eighth foal: closely related to a winner in Italy by Statoblest and half-brother to 3 winners, including 7f winner Barlogan (by Dunbeath): dam lightly raced in France: green, well-beaten last of 5 in minor event at Nottingham. *C. F. Wall*

JOCK'S DREAM 4 b.f. Noble Patriarch 115 – Bold Sophie (Bold Owl 101) – [1998 –: a10s⁶ 1999 10.5m a12g Oct 18] of little account. *K. Bell*

JOCKWEILER (IRE) 4 b.g. Night Shift (USA) – Johara (USA) 92 (Exclusive – Native (USA)) [1998 35: a8s³ a8g a6g a8g 6g 8s 8g 5m 5m a6g 1999 a6f a7f Feb 8] smallish, strong gelding: poor maiden handicapper: stays 1m: acts on good to firm going and fibresand: tried blinkered: inconsistent. *D. W. Chapman*

JOEBERTEDY (IRE) 2 b.c. (Mar 15) Tirol 127 – Hinari Disk Deck 75 (Indian – King (USA) 128) [1999 5m Apr 7] 7,000Y: fifth reported foal: half-brother to 3-y-o Shalari and a 9f winner in Holland by Common Grounds: dam, 2-y-o 5f winner, half-sister to dam of Compton Place: behind in maiden at Ripon. *Ronald Thompson*

JOEL ASH 4 b.g. Crofthall 110 – Lady Carol 42 (Lord Gayle (USA) 124) [1998 – –: 5d 8m 1999 8m 5g a6g Jun 28] poor maiden at best: sometimes tongue tied. *S. R. Bowring*

JOELY GREEN 2 b.c. (May 15) Binary Star (USA) – Comedy Lady 46 (Comedy **62** Star (USA) 121) [1999 5m a5g² a5g⁶ a6g³ a6g a6f⁶ a7g* a8g Nov 30] half-brother to 1987 2-y-o 5f winner Only In Gest (by Aragon) and 1997 2-y-o 7f winner Green-brook (by Greensmith), latter also successful in Sweden: dam won 1m seller at 4 yrs: modest performer: sold out of W. G. M. Turner's stable 5,000 gns after second start: won maiden at Wolverhampton in November: stays 7f: acts on fibresand: tried visored: has looked difficult ride: none too consistent. *N. P. Littmoden*

JOEY THE JOLLY 3 b.g. Belfort (FR) 89 – Divine Penny 65 (Divine Gift 127) – [1998 NR 1999 7d 8g 10v 7m May 22] unfurnished gelding: half-brother to 1¼m/1½m winner Divine Charger (by Treboro) and 1¾m winner Pour Encourager (by Kind of Hush): dam, placed in sellers up to 1¼m, later won in Hong Kong: no sign of ability in maidens: blinkered final start. *G. Woodward*

JOEY TRIBBIANI (IRE) 2 b.c. (Apr 19) Foxhound (USA) 103 – Mardi Gras **72** Belle (USA) 65§ (Masked Dancer (USA)) [1999 7m 6s⁶ 6d³ 6m 6m⁶ a8g⁴ Sep 28] IR 4,200F, 19,000Y: tall, rather leggy colt: seventh foal: half-brother to 3-y-o Indiana Legend: dam highly-strung maiden who stayed 1¼m: fair maiden: probably stays 1m: acts on soft going and fibresand. *C. N. Allen*

JOHAYRO 6 ch.g. Clantime 101 – Arroganza 62 (Crofthall 110) [1998 73: 7d 5g **80** 6g³ 5g⁵ 6g⁴ 5g² 6m² 5d* 5g⁴ 6g⁴ 6m 6m 5g 5d⁴ 6m 5g 6v 5d 1999 5g⁵ 5d 5m⁶ 7.1m* 5m* 5m* 5f⁵ 6g⁴ 5g⁵ 5g² 6m⁵ 6d 6f* 5g⁶ 6f⁴ 5g⁴ 6d 7.1d 6v 7d Oct 26] close-coupled gelding: has a quick action: fair handicapper: won at Musselburgh (twice) and Ayr within 5 days in May and at Thirsk in July: well held final 4 starts: effective at 5f to sharp 7f: acts on firm and good to soft going: occasionally blinkered/visored earlier in career: races prominently/leads: tough and consistent. *J. S. Goldie*

JOHN BOWDLER MUSIC 4 b.g. Soviet Star (USA) 128 – Arianna Aldini **64** (Habitat 134) [1998 73: 8.5d² 7m⁴ 8d 6v 6s⁶ 1999 a6g* a6g³ a7f a6g⁶ a6g⁴ a6g² a6g⁶ **a73** a6g 7g⁵ a6g² a8.5g² 7.1m³ a6g* 6g³ a7g³ a6g² Dec 17] angular, workmanlike gelding: fair performer: won handicap at Lingfield in January and seller at Southwell (left M. Johnston) in May: off course over 6 months, ran creditably final start: effective at 6f to 8.5f: acts on good to firm ground, good to soft and all-weather: tried blinkered/visored: has been bandaged behind: found little twice at 3 yrs: often races prominently. *Miss S. J. Wilton*

JOHN COMPANY (IRE) 2 ch.c. (Jan 29) Indian Ridge 123 – Good Policy **64** (IRE) 80 (Thatching 131) [1999 6.1m⁴ 6d⁶ 7d² a6g⁵ Nov 27] IR 42,000Y: strong colt: brother to 1m winner Seyaasi and half-brother to 1995 2-y-o 7f winner Honest Guest (by Be My Guest), latter useful up to 1¼m: dam 1m winner at 2 yrs: modest form in maidens/private race: stays 7f. *R. M. Beckett*

JOHN FERNELEY 4 b.g. Polar Falcon (USA) 126 – I'll Try 71 (Try My Best **101** (USA) 130) [1998 87p: 7v* 7g* 7.1m* 7g² 1999 8g⁴ 7d⁴ 7.9g* 9v³ 8d³ Oct 30] tall, unfurnished gelding: has a long stride: useful handicapper: 4-month break, won rated stakes by a short head from Weet-A-Minute at York in October: very good close third of 19 to Tayseer at Newmarket final start: races freely and will prove best at 7f/1m: acts on good to firm and heavy going: effective blinkered or not: probably suited by waiting tactics. *P. F. I. Cole*

JOHNNIE THE JOKER   8 gr.g. Absalom 128 – Magic Tower 76 (Tower Walk 130) [1998 –, a64: a7g a7g⁶ a11g⁵ a8g⁶ a8g³ 10g a9.4g⁴ a12g⁴ a8g⁶ a11g⁵ a12g* 1999 a12g³ a12g⁴ a12g³ 10v² a8g a11g 12.3g⁶ a9.4g⁵ 9.9s a12g a12g Nov 19] big, good-topped gelding: has a round action: modest handicapper: lost his form after fourth start: stays 1½m: acts on firm going (lightly raced on turf nowadays), heavy and fibresand: usually blinkered, has won in visor: races prominently/leads. *J. P. Leigh*   **52 d**
a64 d

JOHNNY STACCATO   5 b.g. Statoblest 120 – Frasquita (Song 132) [1998 91d, a–: 6d 6v² 5v 6d 7m 6f⁵ 6m 6g 6s 7s⁵ a7g a7g 1999 a6g a8g 7s⁴ 5.1s 5.3f² 5.7g⁵ 6m 7m 5m 6.1f 6m 6d³ 6d Oct 29] leggy gelding: has a quick action: fairly useful in his prime: only poor form in 1999: probably best at 5f/6f: acts on firm and heavy ground: sometimes slowly away, and gets behind: carries head awkwardly: unreliable. *M. Quinn*   **47**
a–

JOHN STEED (IRE)   2 b.g. (Apr 25) Thatching 131 – Trinity Hall 67 (Hallgate 127) [1999 6s⁶ 7d 8d Oct 30] smallish gelding: first foal: dam, 6f winner who stayed 7f, half-sister to 3-y-o Emma Peel: modest form in claimer and sellers: bred to prove best up to 1m: has been bandaged behind. *C. A. Horgan*   **54**

JOH'S BROTHER   3 ch.c. Clantime 101 – Arroganza 62 (Crofthall 110) [1998 –: 5d 5v 5m 5m 5d 1999 5g 5f Jul 17] no form. *J. S. Goldie*   **–**

JOIN THE PARADE   3 b.f. Elmaamul (USA) 125 – Summer Pageant 81 (Chief's Crown (USA)) [1998 NR 1999 8m 14.1m⁵ 11.5d⁵ 14.1m 10.1m² 10.1g³ 10m* 10d a12g Nov 26] leggy, plain filly: second foal: sister to Echalar, a winner in France and Spain around 11f: dam, 1½m winner, out of unraced half-sister to Sun Princess and Saddlers' Hall: fair performer: won handicap at Leicester in September: stays 1¼m: acts on good to firm going, possibly not on softer than good: has pulled hard: none too consistent. *H. J. Collingridge*   **65**

JOINT REGENT (CAN)   4 br.c. St Jovite (USA) 135 – Ice Fantasy (USA) (It's Freezing (USA) 122) [1998 88: 12d³ 1999 10m 12m 14m² 15s⁴ 14.8m² 14f⁶ 13.3g² 16.1g⁵ a13g³ 17.3g Oct 16] rangy colt: has a round action: fairly useful maiden handicapper: creditable efforts when runner-up: below form final 3 outings: should stay beyond 15f: acts on firm going, below form on soft/equitrack: usually blinkered: slowly away final start: possibly less than genuine: sold 33,000 gns, sent to Sweden. *B. W. Hills*   **88**

JOKERMAN (USA)   2 b.c. (May 19) Septieme Ciel (USA) 123 – Falcon Dancer (USA) (Imperial Falcon (CAN)) [1999 5g* 5.5m* 6g⁵ 8m* 8f* Nov 27] $26,000Y: strong, close-coupled colt: third foal: half-brother to winners by Salt Lake and Fly So Free: dam, winning sprinter in USA, ran only at 2 yrs: progressive form: won minor events at Bordeaux in May and Toulouse in June then Prix des Chenes Royal Thalasso Barriere at Longchamp (final start for J-C Rouget, beat Whyome 1½ lengths) in September and Grade 3 event at Hollywood (by a head) in November: stays 1m: acts on firm going. *N. Drysdale*   **111**

JOLI FLYERS   5 gr.h. Joli Wasfi (USA) 48 – Hagen's Bargain 62§ (Mount Hagen (FR) 127) [1998 55: 9.7s⁵ 12v⁴ 12f 12s* 12g⁵ 11.9d⁵ 14.4d⁶ 14.1d² 16v³ 1999 12d 11.9d 12s⁴ 15.8m 14.1v⁵ 11.9d² a12g Oct 18] big horse: modest handicapper: best effort in 1999 in apprentice event at York on penultimate start: should stay 2m: races mostly on good ground or softer (hung right on firm, well beaten both starts on all-weather): usually makes running/races prominently. *V. Soane*   **55**
a–

JOLI SADDLERS   3 b.f. Saddlers' Hall (IRE) 126 – Vitality 98 (Young Genera-tion 129) [1998 NR 1999 11.1g 10s⁵ 12g⁴ 12d⁶ 11.6d⁵ 10s⁶ 11.6g 12d Oct 29] 4,000 2-y-o: tall, unfurnished filly: fourth foal: half-sister to 3 winners abroad, including Italian 1m/1½m winner Rainbow Flash (by Rainbow Quest): dam, 2-y-o 6f winner who later stayed 9f, out of sister to 1000 Guineas and Prix de Diane winner High-clere: modest maiden: below form final 5 starts: stays 1½m. *M. J. Haynes*   **64**

JOLI'S SON   6 gr.h. Joli Wasfi (USA) 48 – Hagen's Bargain 62§ (Mount Hagen (FR) 127) [1998 72: 12d 10m⁵ 11.5g* 12d⁵ 16.2d 12s 1999 10s 10g 9.9m³ 10g² 10m³ 9f 9.9v Sep 29] strong, workmanlike horse: fair handicapper: creditable efforts in 1999 when placed: shaped as though something amiss penultimate start: stays 11.5f: acts on good to firm ground. *V. Soane*   **70**

JOLLY SHARP (USA) 2 ch.c. (Feb 14) Diesis 133 – Milly Ha Ha 106 (Dancing Brave (USA) 140) [1999 8.2d⁴ Oct 21] second foal: half-brother to 3-y-o No Reserve: dam, 1¼m winner who should have stayed 1¾m, daughter of smart middle-distance performer Mill On The Floss from very good family: shaped well when fourth of 11 to Alva Glen in maiden at Nottingham, smooth headway 3f out but unable to quicken: will be well suited by 1¼m/1½m: useful prospect, well up to winning races. *H. R. A. Cecil* **82 p**

JO MAXIMUS 7 b.g. Prince Sabo 123 – Final Call 79 (Town Crier 119) [1998 61: 7d a7g 7.1g³ 7g 7.1d 1999 8d 7f⁵ Jul 14] workmanlike gelding: only poor form in 1999: stays 7f: acts on equitrack, firm and soft going: blinkered once at 6 yrs, visored final start: has had tongue tied: races prominently: all 3 wins at Brighton. *J. G. Smyth-Osbourne* **42**

JO MELL 6 b.g. Efisio 120 – Militia Girl (Rarity 129) [1998 111: 7s 7.1d⁴ 7.9g 7.1g² 6v³ 7f 7m* 7f² 1999 7d⁵ 7.1g 7.9d 8.1g 8.1m 7m 7.9g 8d 7s* 7d⁵ 6d Oct 20] lengthy gelding: has a round action: smart performer in 1998, only useful at best in 1999 won 6-runner minor event at Newcastle in September: unable to dominate in handicaps after: effective at 7f/1m: acts on any going: takes good hold and usually races up with pace. *T. D. Easterby* **99**

JONA HOLLEY 6 b.g. Sharpo 132 – Spurned (USA) 91 (Robellino (USA) 127) [1998 60: 11.1v 8.3d² 9.2g² 8s⁶ 1999 9.2v⁵ 8.3g⁴ 8m 9.2g⁶ a8g⁵ 10.5d 9.9v⁶ 9.1v* 10s⁴ Nov 1] big gelding: modest performer: left M. Hammond after fifth start: won seller at Ayr in October, despite hanging left: barely stays 1¼m when conditions are testing: acts on good to firm ground, heavy and fibresand: visored/blinkered third to eighth starts. *A. Streeter* **64**

JONAS NIGHTENGALE 4 b.g. Deploy 131 – Springs Welcome 86 (Blakeney 126) [1998 81: a12g* 12.5g² 12m² 14m 1999 14g 14m³ 20m⁵ Jun 15] workmanlike gelding: fairly useful performer: ran well final 2 starts, fifth of 29 in Ascot Stakes, getting poor run before finishing well: stays 2½m well: acts on fibresand, yet to race on extremes of going on turf: has been bandaged in front. *C. A. Cyzer* **83 +**

JONATHAN'S GIRL 4 b.f. Thowra (FR) – Sicilian Vespers 44 (Mummy's Game 120) [1998 –: a10g a8g⁴ a7g³ 1999 a6g⁵ a7f³ a5g⁴ a8g a6g² 6f⁶ 5g a7g 5.3g Jun 30] poor maiden: probably stays 7f: raced mainly on equitrack, probably acts on firm going. *J. J. Bridger* **37 a43**

JONLOZ 2 ch.c. (Apr 16) Presidium 124 – Stratford Lady 48 (Touching Wood (USA) 127) [1999 5m⁶ 5g 7.7d 8g a8g⁴ a8g Dec 17] sparely-made colt: third foal: dam, untrustworthy maiden, stayed 1½m: poor form at best in maidens/nursery: edgy and sweating profusely third start. *G. Woodward* **40**

JOONAYH 2 b.f. (Feb 22) Warning 136 – Jumairah Sun (IRE) 98 (Scenic 128) [1999 6m² 6f* 7d Aug 14] angular filly: first foal: dam 1¼m winner who stayed 1½m: fairly useful form: won maiden at Thirsk in July: well held in listed race at Newmarket following month: should stay 1m. *M. R. Channon* **81**

JORROCKS (USA) 5 b.g. Rubiano (USA) – Perla Fina (USA) (Gallant Man) [1998 97d: 7s⁴ 7.1d³ 8.1g 7s⁶ 7f 7g³ 8.5m 7m 7.3g 8d³ 1999 7g 8v 8.5d 7.5d 7m 8g⁵ 8.2m 7.5s* 7g Oct 14] sturdy gelding: has a short, round action: formerly useful performer: form in 1999 only when winning 16-runner handicap at Beverley in September by 9 lengths: stays 7.5f: acts on soft and good to firm going: blinkered once at 4 yrs: has hung left and tends to carry head awkwardly when ridden. *M. W. Easterby* **80**

JOSEPH'S WINE (IRE) 10 b.g. Smile (USA) – Femme Gendarme (USA) (Policeman (FR) 124) [1998 48, a68: a8s³ a10g² a8g³ a8g 10m⁵ 8m 1999 a11g² a8g* a8.5g² Feb 24] lengthy gelding: fair on all-weather, very lightly raced and poor on turf nowadays: won seller at Lingfield in February: stays 11f: acts on all-weather and any turf going: wears blinkers: best held up. *J. Wharton* **– a68**

JOSEPH VERNET (IRE) 2 b. or br.g. (Mar 16) Owington 123 – Pizziri (Artaius (USA) 129) [1999 8.2m⁵ 7m⁶ Sep 7] IR 28,000Y: eighth foal: closely related to French/US winner up to 1½m Ianomami (by Green Desert) and half-brother to several winners, including useful French 1¼m performer Danish Field (by Danehill): dam Italian 6f/1m winner: showed little in maidens: sold 2,200 gns. *P. F. I. Cole* **–**

JO'S PRINCESS   3 b.f. Emarati (USA) 74 – Daima (Dominion 123) [1998 –: 6m   –
1999 a5g a5g Mar 22] no show in maiden/sellers. *J. R. Jenkins*

JOSR ALGARHOUD (IRE)   3 b.c. Darshaan 133 – Pont-Aven 113 (Try My   **118**
Best (USA) 130) [1998 112p: 6m³ 6f* 1999 7f* 8g² 7g³ Oct 16]
    July 21st saw the thirtieth anniversary of Neil Armstrong's 'giant leap
for mankind.' Expectations of advances in the human condition that might flow
from the moon landing—still seen today as one of the crowning achievements
of the twentieth century—were sky-high. There were, however, those at the
time who made the point that 'If you can put a man on the moon, why can't we
have a decent bus service?' A racing variant might have been 'Why can't we
have a decent timing system on all our racecourses?' While commuters wait in
vain for a smooth transport system, punters and racegoers are no closer to
having a reliable set of times. Inconsistency plagues the time-keeping at some
courses, even those equipped with electrical systems. Take the official times
returned at Newcastle on Saturday July 24th, for example. On a six-race card,
times for half the races were questionable, for which slipshod hand-timed starts
were probably responsible (though there was no indication on the judge's return
that the clock had been started by hand). There should be a difference of around
0.40 sec, allowing for reaction times, between a good hand time and an electric
time, and our research—all races are independently hand-timed by Timeform
—shows that inaccuracy in the official returns is at an unacceptably high level.
Even more astonishing, however, is the fact that 'time' has virtually stood still
over the past thirty years or so, the majority of racecourses that stage Flat racing
in Britain still lacking even basic electrical timing, while some of those that do
possess a system clearly need to keep up with maintenance.
    The official time for the principal race at Newcastle on July 24th, the
Reed Print Beeswing Stakes, was one of those which were questionable, but
there was no quibbling about the performance of the winner, Josr Algarhoud,
making his first appearance since winning the Gimcrack Stakes at York eleven
months before. Transferred from Mick Channon to Godolphin in the interim,
Josr Algarhoud beat the smart four-year-old Haami by two lengths in the Bees-

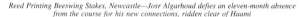

*Reed Printing Beeswing Stakes, Newcastle—Josr Algarhoud defies an eleven-month absence
from the course for his new connections, ridden clear of Haami*

Godolphin's "Josr Algarhoud"

wing, shaping as though he was going to be up to tackling the best at around a mile. In the event, Josr Algarhoud did not manage to add to his laurels, going down to his stable-companion Cape Cross when odds on for the Celebration Mile at Goodwood in August (hanging right in the closing stages after his bit reportedly slipped) and finishing third behind Susu and Lend A Hand in a good renewal of the Challenge Stakes at Newmarket in October (running on well after meeting interference when trying to challenge approaching the final furlong but beaten over four lengths, nevertheless).

		Shirley Heights (b 1975)	Mill Reef
	Darshaan (br 1981)		Hardiemma
		Delsy (br 1972)	Abdos
Josr Algarhoud (IRE) (b.c. 1996)			Kelty
		Try My Best (b 1975)	Northern Dancer
	Pont-Aven (b 1987)		Sex Appeal
		Basilea (b or br 1981)	Frere Basile
			Gay Appeal

The good-topped Josr Algarhoud has had only five races and has the scope to progress again from three to four. His pedigree was discussed in *Racehorses of 1998*—he is a half-brother to the tremendously speedy French four-year-old Sainte Marine (by Kenmare)—and the only thing to add is that the latest foal out of French Guineas runner-up Pont-Aven to reach the race-course, Cap Coz (by Indian Ridge), became her dam's fourth winner, showing useful form in France, winning a seven-furlong listed race at Deauville and finishing runner-up in the Prix du Calvados over the same course and distance. The yearling by Lycius sold for 120,000 guineas at the 1999 Houghton Sales. Josr Algarhoud stays a mile; he has so far encountered only good ground or firmer. *Saeed bin Suroor*

JOUET 3 b.f. Reprimand 122 – Babycham Sparkle 80 (So Blessed 130) [1998 NR 1999 8.3m³ 7g² 7m⁶ 7m⁶ Sep 7] sister to useful sprinter Deep Finesse and half-sister to 3 winning sprinters: dam 2-y-o 5f/6f winner: fair form in maidens first 2 starts: found little in similar events after: should prove best short of 1m: edged right second outing. *Miss Gay Kelleway* **71**

JOURNALIST (IRE) 2 b.f. (May 17) Night Shift (USA) – Schlefalora (Mas Media) [1999 6f* 6m² 6g Aug 19] 90,000Y: strong, lengthy filly: good mover, with a quick action: second foal: half-sister to 3-y-o Sheer Victory: dam, won up to 1m in Sweden, half-sister to 1000 Guineas winner Las Meninas: heavily backed, made winning debut convincingly in maiden at Newmarket in July: 6/4, good ½-length second of 8 to Saintly Speech in Princess Margaret Stakes at Ascot later in month: last of 9 in Lowther Stakes at York final start: stays 6f: joined Godolphin. *B. W. Hills* **102**

JOYEUX PLAYER (USA) 3 b.c. St Jovite (USA) 135 – Play On And On (USA) (Stop The Music (USA)) [1998 75p: 7.1d* 7.1d* 8m² 8s* 8s 1999 9m⁶ 9.9g⁶ 10m⁴ 9f³ Aug 2] strong, good-bodied colt: fluent mover: fairly useful handicapper: creditable efforts final 3 starts: stays 1¼m: acts on firm and soft going: free-going sort: sold 3,700 gns, sent to Holland. *J. L. Dunlop* **91**

JOYFUL WELD 3 ch.f. Weld 122 – Joyfulness (FR) 78 (Cure The Blues (USA)) [1998 –: a7g a8g a7g 1999 a8f Feb 1] seems of little account. *B. P. J. Baugh* **–**

JOYRENA 2 ch.f. (Mar 4) Inchinor 119 – Depeche (FR) (Kings Lake (USA) 133) [1999 a5g 6.1f 8s a8.5g Nov 20] 3,800F, 800Y: sturdy filly: fourth foal: closely related to Italian 5f to 11f winner Miss Statoblest (by Statoblest) and half-sister to 3-y-o Sharh: dam, French maiden, half-sister to smart French middle-distance performer Dastaan: no sign of ability. *P. W. D'Arcy* **–**

J R STEVENSON (USA) 3 ch.g. Lyphard (USA) 132 – While It Lasts (USA) (Foolish Pleasure (USA)) [1998 79p: 7g* 1999 10g³ 12.3m⁵ 12m⁵ 9.9s* 10m⁵ 8.9f Sep 2] sparely-made gelding: good walker: has a quick action: useful performer: won 3-runner minor event at Goodwood in June by 3 lengths from Mirjan: creditable fifth to King Adam in listed race at Kempton next start: should be suited by 1½m: acts on soft ground, probably on firm: visored last 3 outings: has been bandaged off-hind: sold 18,000 gns. *P. W. Chapple-Hyam* **105**

JUBILEE SCHOLAR (IRE) 6 b.g. Royal Academy (USA) 130 – Jaljuli 107 (Jalmood (USA) 126) [1998 34, a66: a10g³ a12g³ a12g³ a12g³ a10g⁴ a8g* 8f 10.1m 10m 8f⁵ a10g⁴ a10g* a10g⁴ a10f⁵ 1999 a10g a8g² a10g³ a8g⁵ a10g² 10f⁴ 11.9f⁵ 10g 10m a8g⁵ a10g a10g Dec 18] modest on all-weather at best, poor on turf: appeared to break down final start: best at 1m/1¼m: acts on all-weather, firm and soft going: tried visored, usually blinkered: has hung badly left: usually held up. *G. L. Moore* **34 a63 d**

JUDIAM 2 b.f. (Apr 6) Primo Dominie 121 – Hoist (IRE) 75 (Bluebird (USA) 125) [1999 6.1g 5m⁵ 5.3m³ 6m 5v³ 5d 5s² 5.2d* Oct 27] 5,500Y: rather unfurnished filly: second foal: half-sister to 3-y-o Countess Parker: dam, 6f winner at 4 yrs, from family of Sun Princess and Saddlers' Hall: fair performer: best effort when winning nursery at Yarmouth on final start: suited by 5f: acts on heavy going. *C. A. Dwyer* **74**

JUDICIOUS (IRE) 2 b.c. (Mar 5) Fairy King (USA) – Kama Tashoof 72 (Mtoto 134) [1999 7d 7s Nov 5] 180,000Y: big, good-topped colt: has plenty of scope: second foal: dam, middle-distance maiden, out of useful winner up to 1m Leipzig: better effort in maidens when eighth of 12 to Fast Track at Yarmouth on debut, very green and not punished: well beaten in similar event at Doncaster 9 days later: type to do better at 3 yrs. *G. Wragg* **57 p**

JUINEVERA (IRE) 4 b.f. Tenby 125 – Atlantic Dream (USA) (Muscovite (USA) 105) [1998 80: 8g 8m⁴ 8g³ 10s⁶ 7m 7g 12m⁶ 8d 1999 6.9m⁶ 7.1m 10m⁶ 10.1m⁶ 11.1f Jul 9] IR 9,000Y: lengthy filly: fifth foal: half-sister to 2 winners, notably useful sprinter Storiths (by Double Schwartz), later successful up to 1m in USA: dam Irish 2-y-o 6f winner: fairly useful maiden in Ireland in 1998: no form in 1999: stays 1m: tried blinkered. *J. S. Haldane* **–**

JULIA TITUS (IRE) 2 ch.f. (Feb 6) Perugino (USA) 84 – Blue Vista (IRE) (Pennine Walk 120) [1999 7v 8d Oct 22] strong, lengthy filly: fourth foal: sister to Irish 3-y-o 1m winner Sarraaf and half-sister to 1996 2-y-o 7f winner Smugurs (by **53**

Masterclass): dam unraced half-sister to smart sprinter Polykratis: well held in maidens at Kempton (hampered) and Doncaster. *W. R. Muir*

JULIES JEWEL (IRE)   4 ch.g. Simply Great (FR) 122 – Melungeon (Ardoon   **57**
124) [1998 78d: a6s* a5g a6g a7g⁴ a6g⁴ a6g⁵ 7d* 9v² 7d⁴ 7.5s² 8g 7g 6s² 8s⁴ 6f 6m
6g 6g 7f 7g 7d 9g⁴ 8d a6g 1999 a8g a8g a11g⁴ a12g² a8g Dec 13] angular gelding:
has a short, round action: modest handicapper: off 10 months before pulled up lame
final start: stays 1½m: acts on fibresand, best turf form on good ground or softer:
often tongue tied. *M. C. Chapman*

JUMBO'S FLYER   2 ch.c. (Apr 15) Jumbo Hirt (USA) 90§ – Fragrant Princess   **?**
(Germont) [1999 9m⁵ 7d 8g Nov 3] sturdy colt: second foal: dam unraced: reluctant
stalls, possibly flattered (could be worth a rating of 66) when fifth of 10 in steadily-
run maiden at Redcar: well beaten in similar events after. *J. L. Eyre*

JUMP (USA)   2 b.c. (Mar 26) Trempolino (USA) 135 – Professional Dance (USA)   **55**
(Nijinsky (CAN) 138) [1999 8.1m 6g⁵ Oct 19] $20,000Y, 28,000 2-y-o: half-brother
to several winners, including useful 1991 2-y-o 7f/1m winner Ninja Dancer (by
Miswaki) and stayer Tartique Twist (by Arctic Tern): dam (unraced) from very good
US family: modest form in maidens: will stay at least 1¼m: joined J. Osborne.
D. Marks

JUNIKAY (IRE)   5 b.g. Treasure Kay 114 – Junijo (Junius (USA) 124) [1998 59:   **64**
9.7s 8d 7g* 7f 8f 8.5g 10g⁶ 8.3g⁶ 10m 9d⁶ 10.1m⁵ 9m⁶ 8d³ 8g² 8m 1999 8.3m 8f⁵
10m* 11.6m 10g 10g² 8.5m⁶ 10.1m⁶ 8m³ 10.1m² 12g⁵ 10s⁵ 10d 10d⁴ 10.2s⁴ Oct
26] workmanlike gelding: modest handicapper: won at Nottingham in May: mostly
creditable efforts after: stays 1¼m: acts on soft and good to firm going: tried
blinkered, not since 1997: usually comes from off pace. *R. Ingram*

JUNO MARLOWE (IRE)   3 b.f. Danehill (USA) 126 – Why So Silent (Mill   **98**
Reef (USA) 141) [1998 94: 7g³ 7m* 7.1m⁴ 8d 6s⁵ 1999 8.1m 8m 7m* 7f Jul 30]
leggy, quite attractive filly: useful handicapper: won at Newmarket in July: creditable
effort in valuable race at Goodwood final start: somewhat headstrong, and better
form at 7f than 1m: acts on firm going: flashes tail. *P. W. Harris*

JUST A SNACK (IRE)   3 b.g. Tenby 125 – Opening Day (Day Is Done 115)   **–**
[1998 51: 7.1s⁴ 7s 8s 1999 12g 8.5m 7m 8f Sep 4] signs of ability only on debut.
M. A. Buckley

JUST A STROLL   4 ch.g. Clantime 101 – Willow Walk 74 (Farm Walk 111) [1998   **–**
NR 1999 a8.5g Oct 30] no form since second in seller on debut. *D. Burchell*

JUST BOB   10 b.g. Alleging (USA) 120 – Diami 81 (Swing Easy (USA) 126) [1998   **59**
69, a–: 5g 5v³ 5v 5m 5d 5f 5g⁶ 5s⁴ 5g⁴ 6d* 6g³ 6m⁶ 5.1m² 5m 5m 5d 5d 5g 5s
1999 5d 6s 5m 5m 5s³ 5m² 6d⁴ 5g⁴ 5g 5m 5f 5g⁶ 6g² 6m⁴ 6s* 5g 5d 6v⁴ 5d
Oct 20] smallish gelding: unimpressive mover: has pronounced stringhalt: modest
handicapper nowadays: won at Yarmouth in September: effective at 5f/6f: acts on
any turf going (below form on all-weather): blinkered earlier in career: tends to be
slowly away and get behind. *S. E. Kettlewell*

JUST BREMNER   2 b.c. (Mar 15) Rudimentary (USA) 118 – Legal Precedent   **63**
(Star Appeal 133) [1999 6d 7m⁴ 7f³ 7.5g 8g* 8s 8d a8g⁴ Nov 30] 7,200F: leggy colt:
shows knee action: fifth foal: brother to 3-y-o Netherhall: dam unraced sister to smart
miler Star Way: modest performer: won claimer at Newcastle in August: should stay
1¼m: acts on fibresand, best turf efforts on good going or firmer. *T. D. Easterby*

JUST DISSIDENT (IRE)   7 b.g. Dancing Dissident (USA) 119 – Betty Bun (St   **37**
Chad 120) [1998 57, a62: a5g³ a5g² a6g⁴ 5m 5m⁴ 5d 5m 5m 5m 5m a6g 5v 5d a5g   **a62**
1999 5m 5m 5m 5.1m 5g 5m 7g 5g 5m a7g* a7g a5g⁴ a7g⁴ a6g⁴ a5g⁵ Dec 10]
good-topped gelding: has reportedly had back problems: modest handicapper on
all-weather, poor on turf: made all at Lingfield in August: stays 7f: acts on equitrack
and firm going: occasionally visored: usually races prominently. *R. M. Whitaker*

JUST DREAMS   3 ch.f. Salse (USA) 128 – Pato 90 (High Top 131) [1998 NR   **85**
1999 10d² 12d⁵ 11.9v 10d 12s* Nov 2] sister to high-class 1½m to 2½m performer
Classic Cliche and half-sister to several winners, notably smart 1½m performer
My Emma (by Marju): dam, 7f (at 2 yrs) and 1¼m winner, sister to smart sprinter
Crews Hill: fairly useful performer: much improved to win maiden at Catterick in

November by short head: suited by testing conditions at 1½m, and will stay at least 1¾m: raced only on ground softer than good. *R. Guest*

JUST FOR YOU   3 b.c. Hamas (IRE) 125§ – Millie's Lady (IRE) (Common Grounds 118) [1998 NR 1999 a8.5g Nov 13] 12,000Y, 800 3-y-o: second foal: dam unraced: well held in maiden at Wolverhampton. *K. Mahdi*   –

JUST FOR YOU JANE (IRE)   3 b.f. Petardia 113 – Steffi 67 (Precocious 126) [1998 63: 6m 7m³ 7m⁵ 7.1g⁴ 6m² 7g³ 6d³ 6s 6s a7g 1999 a6g³ a6f⁴ a6g² a7g³ Feb 19] unfurnished filly: modest maiden: stays 7f: acts on good to firm going, good to soft and fibresand (hampered on equitrack): usually blinkered, but seems as effective without: has looked ungenuine. *T. J. Naughton*   56

JUST GIFTED   3 b.g. Rudimentary (USA) 118 – Parfait Amour 73 (Clantime 101) [1998 67p: 5m³ 6g⁵ 1999 8s 10g³ 7.9f 9.9g⁴ 12.4g³ 10g⁶ 10.4g 11g⁵ Oct 14] tall, quite good-topped gelding: has scope: fair maiden: mostly creditable efforts in handicaps in 1999: stays 1½m: raced mainly on good going: gelded after final start: may do better. *R. M. Whitaker*   72

JUSTINIANUS (IRE)   7 ch.h. Try My Best (USA) 130 – Justitia (Dunbeath (USA) 127) [1998 51, a40: a8g⁵ a6g⁵ 7d 6g* 5m 6f⁴ 6f⁴ 6g 6d⁴ 6m 6m⁵ 5.3d⁵ 6m a7g 7s a7g a6g⁵ 1999 a6g a7g⁵ a8f a8g a7g 5.3f⁵ 7f⁵ 6g 6f⁶ a7g⁶ 6g 5f⁶ 5m 5g 5m Aug 30] poor performer: left J. Bridger 1,600 gns after twelfth start: effective at 5f to easy 1m: acts on all-weather, firm and soft going: tried blinkered earlier in career, visored fifth start. *D. L. Williams*   43

JUST IN TIME   4 b.g. Night Shift (USA) – Future Past (USA) (Super Concorde (USA) 128) [1998 86: 8d 9m² 10m² 9.9m* 12s 1999 12g⁴ 12m³ 12m³ 16.1m 14f 12m⁶ 13.9g Aug 18] well-made gelding: useful handicapper: several good efforts in 1999, including when third in Duke of Edinburgh Stakes at Royal Ascot on third outing: well beaten in Ebor at York final start: stays 1¾m, not 2m: acts on firm going: usually makes running: genuine. *T. G. Mills*   97

JUST LOUI   5 gr.g. Lugana Beach 116 – Absaloui 64 (Absalom 128) [1998 –, a90: a7g⁴ a5g⁶ a6g² a7g* a6g* a8.5g a7g* a7g 1999 a7g⁶ a7g Dec 4] sturdy gelding: fairly useful handicapper: not seen out in 1999 until November, and some way below best: effective at 6f/easy 7f: acts on good to firm going, soft and all-weather: tried visored: usually races prominently. *K. R. Burke*   a77

JUST MAC (USA)   2 br.c. (Jan 24) Dayjur (USA) 137 – Play On And On (USA) (Stop The Music (USA)) [1999 6g⁶ a6g³ Dec 22] $30,000Y: fifth foal: half-brother to 3 winners, including 3-y-o Joyeux Player and 7f winner Neverending (by Sabona), both fairly useful: dam won in USA: modest form in maidens at Redcar (subsequently sold out of J. Noseda's stable 5,000 gns) and Lingfield: should stay 7f. *Mrs L. Stubbs*   63

JUST NICK   5 b.g. Nicholas (USA) 111 – Just Never Know (USA) (Riverman (USA) 131) [1998 NR 1999 7f 7.1m³ 8f⁴ 7s 7d 8m 8m Sep 2] smallish, good-topped gelding: fairly useful handicapper in 1997: just fair form on return, and poor efforts final 4 starts: stays 1m: acts on good to firm and heavy ground: usually races prominently. *W. R. Muir*   77

JUST NOBBY   4 b.g. Totem (USA) 118 – Loving Doll 72 (Godswalk (USA) 130) [1998 –: 8m 7d 8.3d 9.3m 11m 7m⁴ 6d 7v⁶ a7g 1999 7f 8m 10d 12f Jul 14] close-coupled, good-bodied gelding: little form: tried blinkered/tongue tied. *Don Enrico Incisa*   –

JUST SUNDAY   3 ch.f. Then Again 126 – Striking Image (IRE) 69 (Flash of Steel 120) [1998 47: 5d⁵ 5.1s 5m⁵ a5g⁴ a5g³ a7g⁶ 1999 10.2g Jun 12] tall filly: poor maiden: well beaten only outing of 1999. *J. W. Mullins*   –

JUST THE BLUES   2 b.c. (Mar 31) Merdon Melody 98 – Tripolitaine (FR) (Nonoalco (USA) 131) [1999 a6g a7g a6g a8.5g a8.5g Sep 8] 4,500Y, 16,000 2-y-o: small colt: brother to 3-y-o Tunnel Bridge and half-brother to several winners, including fairly useful sprinter Walk In The Park (by Valiyar): dam won around 11f in France: little sign of ability: sold 2,000 gns, sent to Holland. *N. P. Littmoden*   –

JUST THE JOB TOO (IRE)   2 b. or br.g. (May 20) Prince of Birds (USA) 121 – Bold Encounter (IRE) 69 (Persian Bold 123) [1999 a5g a8g Dec 17] 10,000Y: –

second foal: dam Irish 6.5f winner out of smart sprinter Welshwyn: well beaten in maidens at Southwell. *P. C. Haslam*

JUSTUPYOURSTREET (IRE)   3 b.g. Dolphin Street (FR) 125 – Sure Flyer   **78**
(IRE) (Sure Blade (USA) 130) [1998 71: 6d³ 7m 5m 7.9g³ 8s 7g⁵ 7.9g⁴ 1999 8d²
9.9g 8m³ 9.1g⁴ 8m 10s⁵ Jul 19] good-topped gelding: has a round action: fair maiden
handicapper: well below form final start: should stay at least 1¼m: acts on good to
firm and good to soft going, possibly not on soft. *J. J. O'Neill*

JUST WARNING   2 br.f. (Apr 6) Warning 136 – Stardyn (Star Appeal 133) [1999   **–**
7d Oct 30] sixth foal: half-sister to several winners, including very smart 6f to 1m
performer Young Ern and 4-y-o Young-Un (both by Efisio): dam maiden suited by
1½m: last of 16 in Newmarket maiden. *M. J. Ryan*

JUST WIZ   3 b.g. Efisio 120 – Jade Pet 90 (Petong 126) [1998 69: 6g⁵ 5m 6.1g 7s   **69**
5d⁵ a6g³ a6g⁴ a6g⁵ 1999 a7g* 7f⁵ 6m² 7m 9.7f⁴ 10g² 10d 9s 8m² 8g³ a10g* a9.4g³   **a90**
a10g* Dec 8] small gelding: fairly useful handicapper on all-weather, fair on turf:
won at Southwell (final start for Lord Huntingdon) in January and at Lingfield in
November and December: stays 1¼m: acts on all-weather, best turf form on good
going or firmer: sometimes visored/blinkered, including last 5 starts. *R. Hannon*

JUVENIA (USA)   3 b.f. Trempolino (USA) 135 – Vintage (CAN) (Foolish   **112**
Pleasure (USA)) [1998 106p: 8d* 8d² 8s² 8d³ 1999 8s³ 10d² 10.5d⁵ 9.9f 12m⁶ 9.3v³
8.5f Nov 7] leggy, close-coupled filly: good mover: smart performer: won Prix
Marcel Boussac at Longchamp on final outing at 2 yrs: placed in 1999 in Prix de la
Grotte and Prix Saint-Alary (2 lengths second to Cerulean Sky) first 2 starts and in
Prix de l'Opera (best effort, 1½ lengths third to Diamond White) on penultimate
outing, all at Longchamp: ran at least respectably in Prix de Diane at Chantilly,
Nassau Stakes at Goodwood and Prix Vermeille at Longchamp in between but poorly
in USA final start: stays 1½m: acts on any ground: consistent. *Mme C. Head, France*

JUWWI   5 ch.g. Mujtahid (USA) 118 – Nouvelle Star (AUS) (Luskin Star (AUS))   **84**
[1998 76, a83: a5g* a5g* 6s a5g 5.1g 5m 6g 7.1d⁶ 7d 7g³ 7m⁵ 6.1m³ 6m 6m⁶ 6s² 6v   **a94**
6s² 5d⁴ a6g⁶ a5g³ a6g⁵ 1999 a6g 6g 5d⁵ 6.1s 6m⁴ 5.9m⁵ 5.1d⁶ 6f³ 6g² 6s⁶ 6g 6g⁶ 5m²
5.1m* 6s 5s² 6d 6d 5d 6d² 5s⁶ a5g² a6g* a6g⁵ a7g⁵ Dec 21] robust gelding: fairly
useful handicapper: won at Carlisle in May, Chepstow in September and Southwell
in November: best at 5f/6f: acts on all-weather, firm and soft going: often ridden by
inexperienced rider: often starts slowly: tends to wander under pressure: comes from
off pace. *J. M. Bradley*

K

KAAMEN (IRE)   3 ch.c. Mujtahid (USA) 118 – Zumurrudah (USA) 82 (Spec-   **98**
tacular Bid (USA)) [1998 92+: 5m³ 5.2m* 5s⁶ 1999 6g³ 7.6m 7g 6m³ 5m⁴ 6s⁴ Jul 3]
strong, sturdy colt: useful performer: ran well when in frame in minor events/
handicap in 1999: stays 6f: acts on soft and good to firm going: blinkered (below
form) third start: has given trouble at stalls: sent to UAE. *B. Hanbury*

KABOOL   4 b.c. Groom Dancer (USA) 128 – Sheroog (USA) 77 (Shareef Dancer   **119**
(USA) 135) [1998 114p: 8g* 9g* 10d³ 1999 a10f⁶ 9.3d⁴ 8g² 9.9m² 9.8v³ 10g³ 10m⁴
Dec 12] quite attractive ex-French-trained colt: smart performer: best efforts in
1999 when in frame in Prix d'Ispahan at Longchamp (3¼ lengths fourth to Croco
Rouge), Select Stakes at Goodwood (beaten ½ length by Lear Spear) fourth start and
Champion Stakes at Newmarket (1½ lengths third to Alborada) penultimate outing:
stays 1¼m: acts on good to firm and heavy going, well beaten only start on dirt.
Saeed bin Suroor

K-ACE THE JOINT   2 ch.g. (Apr 28) Savahra Sound 111 – Be My Sweet 78   **–**
(Galivanter 131) [1999 a7g a8g a7g Dec 15] brother to 3-y-o Sounds Sweet and half-
brother to several winners, including 6f/7f winner Sweet Mate (by Komaite): dam,
1m and 1¼m winner, half-sister to Eclipse winner Gunner B: no promise in sellers on
fibresand, including in blinkers. *S. R. Bowring*

KADAKA (IRE)   4 b.f. Sadler's Wells (USA) 132 – Kadissya (USA) 107 (Blush-   **110**
ing Groom (FR) 131) [1998 110: 10g⁴ 11.5g* 12f² 11.9f³ 14.6d² 1999 12m⁶ 13.3d²

11.8s² 13.9f⁴ 13.4d² 15g* Oct 2] strong, quite attractive filly: smart performer: won listed race at Milan in October by 6 lengths: in frame earlier in similar events at Newbury and Leicester and listed rated stakes at York and Chester (beaten 3½ lengths by Salmon Ladder): stays 15f: acts on firm and soft going: genuine. *L. M. Cumani*

KADANCE VILLE (FR)   4 b.f. Fabulous Dancer (USA) 124 – Kadouville (FR)   **116** (Kaldoun (FR) 122) [1998 10m* 11g* 10d* 10d³ 9.5d³ 10.5s 9.5s* 1999 8g³ 9.5s² 10g³ 8d* 10s* 10g* 10.5d Nov 11] fourth reported foal: half-sister to French middle-distance winners Queen Ville (by King of Macedon) and Akadouville (by Akarad): dam French 8.5f to 1¼m winner: smart performer: unraced at 2 yrs: much improved in 1999, winning minor events at Bordeaux in May and La Teste in July, valuable listed race at Deauville (best effort, by 4 lengths from Insight) in August and Prix Andre Baboin at Marseilles Borely (by 1½ lengths from Milord Fontenaille) in October: stays 11f: acts on soft and good to firm going. *J-C. Rouget, France*

KADIR   4 b. or br.c. Unfuwain (USA) 131 – Rafif (USA) 68 (Riverman (USA) 131)   **96 ?** [1998 91+: 12.3s² 11.7s² 14g² 13.9f 1999 14g² 13.9g 14s³ 12s Oct 23] strong, angular colt: has a fluent, round action: useful performer on pick of form: made all in maiden at Sandown in July: easily best effort after when third of 5 in minor event at Haydock: will stay 2m: acts on soft going, disappointing on firm: has shown signs of temperament (sweating and edgy when running poorly in blinkers second start) and not one to trust implicitly: joined D. McArdle in Ireland. *M. P. Tregoning*

KAFHANEE (USA)   3 ch.f. Seeking The Gold (USA) – Baya (USA) 116   **85** (Nureyev (USA) 131) [1998 70p: 7d³ 1999 7m² 7g* Aug 30] leggy, quite attractive filly: has a quick action: trained on only 2-y-o start by D. Loder: fairly useful form in maidens, not having to be at best to land odds in 4-runner event at Epsom in August: will stay 1m+. *Saeed bin Suroor*

Godolphin's "Kabool"

KAFIL (USA) 5 b. or br.g. Housebuster (USA) – Alchaasibiyeh (USA) 85 (Seattle **47**
Slew (USA)) [1998 –, a64: a12g⁶ a8g⁵ a8g a13g a8g³ a8g² 8.5s a10g⁶ 8m a8g² a8g⁶ **a62**
9m a12g 8.2s a7g* a7g a8g a10g a8f 1999 a8g⁶ a8g³ a8g a10g 7m 9d a8g² a8g⁴ 8.3m
a10g 8.3m a9.4f² a8.5g² a7g⁵ a10g³ a10g⁶ a8g⁵ a10g⁶ a10g Dec 22] leggy gelding:
modest on all-weather, poor on turf: best at 7f to 1¼m: acts on firm ground and
all-weather. *J. J. Bridger*

KAFI (USA) 3 b.c. Gulch (USA) – Nonoalca (FR) 120 (Nonoalco (USA) 131) **69**
[1998 –p: 8g 1999 10.2s 7m 8.1m 9.9g Jun 22] strong, lengthy, good sort: good
mover: form only in maiden on second start: stays 7f, not 1¼m: headstrong, and
looks a difficult ride: sold 16,000 gns, joined A. Streeter. *M. P. Tregoning*

KAGOSHIMA (IRE) 4 b.g. Shirley Heights 130 – Kashteh (IRE) 79 (Green **–**
Desert (USA) 127) [1998 82p: 12m⁶ 1999 12g⁶ 12s⁵ Nov 2] fairly useful form on
debut: sold from L. Cumani 1,700 gns in July: well held on belated return. *J. Norton*

KAHTAN 4 b.c. Nashwan (USA) 135 – Harmless Albatross 115 (Pas de Seul 133) **112**
[1998 106: 12f² 12g³ 14.8f* 15g³ 16g⁶ 1999 14.1s³ 11.8s⁴ 13.9f³ 18.7m* 15.9m 12d*
Oct 1] good-topped colt: good walker/easy mover: smart performer: won rated stakes
at Chester in July by head from Generosity and listed event at Newmarket in October
by ¾ length from Migration: behind in Lonsdale Stakes at York in between: effective
at 1½m given testing conditions and stays 19f: acts on firm and soft ground.
J. L. Dunlop

KAHYASI MOLL (IRE) 2 b.f. (Feb 21) Brief Truce (USA) 126 – Deydarika **35**
(IRE) (Kahyasi 130) [1999 5m 6m 7g⁴ 8m⁵ 10.2s a8.5g a10g⁶ Dec 18] IR 5,000F:
second foal: dam unraced: poor form. *J. S. Moore*

KAIAPOI 2 ch.c. (Feb 7) Elmaamul (USA) 125 – Salanka (IRE) 68 (Persian **70**
Heights 129) [1999 7.1d⁵ 7.9m 7s* 7.9d 8d 7s Nov 6] 3,500F, 9,200Y: leggy, rather
plain colt: second foal: half-brother to 3-y-o Penmayne: dam, 1¼m winner, from
family of Reprimand: fair performer: won maiden at Chester in September: well
beaten in nurseries last 2 starts: will stay 1¼m: acts on soft going: has tended to hang.
R. Hollinshead

KAIBO 3 ch.c. Safawan 118 – Jay Gee Ell 78 (Vaigly Great 127) [1998 86p: 7m³ **100**
7m² 7g⁶ 6d* 6d 1999 8m 7g² 8.1m⁵ 8m 8f* a8f⁴ Sep 3] good-topped colt: useful
performer: neck second to Mayaro Bay in handicap at Goodwood in May: left
R. Hannon after fourth start: best effort to win non-graded stakes at Del Mar in
August: stays 1m: acts on firm going. *C. Dollase, USA*

KAID (IRE) 4 b.g. Alzao (USA) 117 – Very Charming (USA) (Vaguely Noble **45**
140) [1998 64: 8g 10g⁴ 10g³ 10g 1999 10.8m 14.1m⁶ 14g 14d 16.4d a16.2g⁵ Dec 15]
good-topped gelding: poor maiden at 4 yrs: left Mrs. B. Waring after fifth start:
probably stays 2m: unraced on extremes of going: tried blinkered. *N. P. Littmoden*

KALA 4 b.f. Alhijaz 122 – Flushing Meadow (USA) 103 (Raise A Native) [1998 –: **–**
9m⁵ 8.3g⁴ 8.3m 10d 8v 1999 10m 8.1m 7m⁶ Jul 30] little sign of ability. *V. Soane*

KALAHARI FERRARI 3 ch.g. Clantime 101 – Royal Agnes 71 (Royal Palace **58**
131) [1998 63d: 5v⁴ 5d⁴ 6s⁴ 6g 6g 6s⁶ 1999 7d⁵ 9.2g³ a8g⁵ 8.2m³ 8m² 8m³ 8m⁵
8g³ 7.5m³ 9v Sep 20] close-coupled gelding: modest maiden: placed 7 times in 1999:
left Jack Berry, then ran poorly final start: stays 1m: acts on soft and good to firm
going. *A. G. Hobbs*

KALANISI (IRE) 3 b.c. Doyoun 124 – Kalamba (IRE) (Green Dancer (USA) **112 p**
132) [1998 NR 1999 7v* 7m* 8f* May 29]
    A set-back following a victory gained on very firm ground at Kempton
in May brought Kalanisi's first season to a premature close, but all being well
he'll be in action again in 2000 and could well make his mark in pattern
company. Kalanisi remains unbeaten after three races. First time out he landed
the odds impressively in a maiden run on heavy going at Folkestone, and he
quickly followed up in a useful four-runner minor event at Newmarket, beating
Hawriyah by three lengths. The opposition was stronger still at Kempton,
where Kalanisi was stepped up from seven furlongs to a mile in a listed event.
He shared favouritism with the much-vaunted Killer Instinct, who'd broken his
duck on his previous start, with 10/1 bar the pair in the six-runner field. It's

unlikely that anyone would have wanted to take short odds about either with two furlongs to run, particularly Kalanisi who still had several lengths to make up on the leaders having been unable to quicken and trapped on the rail early in the straight. Kalanisi's chance looked even more remote when Mensa quickened to the front soon after, but he responded gamely to pressure and finished to such effect that he caught the leader in the last strides to win by a head. At this stage Kalanisi still held an entry in the St James's Palace Stakes, but the Poule d'Essai des Poulains winner Sendawar not surprisingly did duty for their owner the Aga Khan at Royal Ascot. Kalanisi still has a long way to go before he reaches Sendawar's level, but he is a most genuine individual who should go on improving for some time yet. Like Daliapour, he'll be trained by Sir Michael Stoute at four.

		Mill Reef	Never Bend
	Doyoun	(b 1968)	Milan Mill
	(br 1985)	Dumka	Kashmir II
Kalanisi (IRE)		(br 1971)	Faizebad
(b.c. 1996)		Green Dancer	Nijinsky
	Kalamba (IRE)	(b 1972)	Green Valley
	(b 1991)	Kareena	Riverman
		(b 1979)	Kermiya

The smallish, good-topped Kalanisi is the first foal of Kalamba, a lightly-raced mare who was third in France over nine furlongs at two years and a mile and a quarter at three. Her second foal Kalimanta (by Lake Coniston) was also in training with Luca Cumani in 1999 but has yet to race. Kalamba is out of the smart miler Kareena, a thoroughly genuine performer who was successful four times for Fulke Johnson Houghton in 1982. The next dam Kermiya won over nine furlongs and a mile and a quarter in France. Judging from the bottom half of his pedigree there's every reason for thinking that Kalanisi will stay a mile and a quarter; that he's by the Two Thousand Guineas winner and Derby third Doyoun, a fair influence for stamina and the sire of Daylami, only adds strength to that view. *L. M. Cumani*

KALAR 10 b.g. Kabour 80 – Wind And Reign 55 (Tumble Wind (USA)) [1998 –: 5d a5g6 5m 5m 1999 a5f a5g4 a5g3 a6g2 a5g 5d4 5m4 5s2 5m 5g6 a6g4 5d3 5m a5g 6f6 5f* 5m 6m 5.2s Oct 22] good-bodied gelding: modest handicapper: raced on **50 a46**

favoured side when winning 23-runner seller at Ripon in August: well below form after: effective at 5f/6f: acts on any turf/all-weather: has been visored, wears blinkers nowadays: usually a front runner. *D. W. Chapman*

KALARRAM 2 ch.f. (Mar 2) Muhtarram (USA) 125 – Kalandariya 78 (Kris 135) – [1999 7d⁵ Oct 26] 8,400Y: seventh foal: half-sister to a winner in Italy by Pursuit of Love: dam, maiden who stayed 1m, half-sister to smart 7f/1m fillies Kerita and Kareena: 100/1, signs of ability in minor event at Redcar: may do better. *C. B. B. Booth*

KALA SUNRISE 6 ch.h. Kalaglow 132 – Belle of The Dawn (Bellypha 130) **88** [1998 84: 8d 8.5m⁶ 8.1g⁵ 8g 1999 8d 7g* 8m 8m 8.5d⁵ 8.1g 7f 7.9f 8g⁶ 7.9m⁴ 8m² 8g⁴ 8d Oct 14] tall, workmanlike horse: fairly useful handicapper: won 20-runner event at Leicester in April: held his form well after: effective at 7f/1m: probably acts on any going: held up. *C. Smith*

KALIDASA (USA) 3 b.f. Nureyev (USA) 131 – Aunt Pearl (USA) (Seattle Slew **98** (USA)) [1998 98: 5.1m² 6f⁶ 6g² 7m² 8d² 7m* 1999 8g 7g³ 8d 8.5f a8f Sep 22] leggy, angular filly: useful performer: creditable 4¼ lengths third of 6 to Bertolini in European Free Handicap at Newmarket in April: well held subsequently, leaving P. Chapple-Hyam after third start: stays 1m: acts on good to soft going, probably on firm. *P. Byrne, USA*

KALINDI 2 ch.f. (Jan 27) Efisio 120 – Rohita (IRE) 94 (Waajib 121) [1999 5s⁵ 5g² **93** 5m* 6m⁵ 5.2g² 5m 6d Sep 28] sturdy, quite attractive filly: second foal: half-sister to 3-y-o Alpine Red: dam, 2-y-o 5f/6f winner, bred to stay 1m: fairly useful performer: won Windsor Castle Stakes at Royal Ascot by ½ length from Master Fay: best effort after when second to Elaflaak in listed race at Newbury in August: should stay 6f: acts on good to firm going (stiff task on good to soft). *M. R. Channon*

KALUANA COURT 3 b.f. Batshoof 122 – Fairfields Cone (Celtic Cone 116) – [1998 –: 6d 1999 10s 11.9v 8d Oct 29] no form. *R. Dickin*

KALYPSO KATIE (IRE) 2 gr.f. (Mar 7) Fairy King (USA) – Miss Toot 72 **97 p** (Ardross 134) [1999 8.3d* Oct 28] fifth living foal: sister to very smart 7f/1¼m winner Kool Kat Katie: dam 1¼m and 15f winner on only starts: most impressive when landing odds in maiden at Windsor by 6 lengths from Scarletta, travelling well, striding clear from 2f out and eased (value at least 8 lengths): bred to stay 1¼m, but clearly isn't short of speed: looks a smart filly in the making. *J. Noseda*

KAMARAZI (IRE) 2 ch.c. (Feb 16) Arazi (USA) 135 – Marie d'Argonne (FR) – 104 (Jefferson 129) [1999 8.1g 5.7s Oct 26] half-brother to several winners, including high-class 6f to 1m performer Polar Falcon (by Nureyev) and 1m/1¼m winners Mokuti and Sahara (both by Green Desert): dam won up to 1¼m in France/USA: well held in maiden at Chepstow and (blinkered) seller at Bath: sold 7,000 gns, joined S. Dow. *P. F. I. Cole*

KAMAREYAH (IRE) 2 b.f. (Feb 13) Hamas (IRE) 125§ – Nur (USA) 74 (Diesis **75** 133) [1999 6f⁴ 6m³ 6d* 7d Sep 28] small, good-topped filly: fourth foal: sister to fairly useful 1998 Irish 2-y-o 7f winner Hamouse (later successful in USA) and half-sister to 5f winners Kawafil (at 2 yrs, fairly useful but became temperamental, by Warning) and Hajat (by Mujtahid): dam, 5f/6f winner at 2 yrs, half-sister to useful 5f/ 6f winner Ra'a: fair form in maidens, making all when landing odds at Yarmouth in September: beaten long way out in nursery at Newmarket final start: should stay 7f: acts on firm and good to soft ground. *R. W. Armstrong*

KANAKA CREEK (USA) 2 ch.f. (Feb 4) Thunder Gulch (USA) 129 – Book **70** Collector (USA) 80 (Irish River (FR) 131) [1999 5m⁴ 6m 6m³ 7f⁴ 7g³ 8.1s² 7.1v³ 8g⁵ Nov 3] compact filly: sixth foal: half-sister to 3 winners, including 1m winners Bibliotheque and Literary (both by Woodman): dam 2-y-o 6f winner, later successful up to 1m in USA, half-sister to Lycius: fair maiden: mostly creditable efforts: stays 1m: acts on good to firm and heavy going: has become upset in stalls/raced freely. *J. Berry*

KANAWA 5 b.m. Beveled (USA) – Kiri Te (Liboi (USA) 76) [1998 35: 10m⁴ 10f – 10.2m 11.5g a7g⁵ a8.5g³ 1999 a10g a8g⁶ a7g⁵ a8g⁴ a7g* a8g² a8g a8g² a8g* a8g³ **a56** a9.4g⁴ 9m Jul 8] angular mare: modest handicapper: won at Southwell in February and (first run after leaving A. Jones) in May: slipped up final start: best form at 7f/ 1m: acted on good to firm going and all-weather: dead. *Derrick Morris*

KANISTARI (IRE)   2 b.c. (Mar 4) Sri Pekan (USA) 117 – Aster Aweke (IRE) 87   **81** (Alzao (USA) 117) [1999 6g⁴ 6.1m⁶ m4² 7g 7.7d² 7.9d Oct 7] 12,500Y: sturdy colt: first foal: dam dual 9f winner at 4 yrs in Ireland: fairly useful maiden: best effort when clear second of 14 in nursery at Warwick in September: should stay 1m+: acts on good to soft going: has hung left. *S. Dow*

KANZ WOOD (USA)   3 ch.g. Woodman (USA) 126 – Kanz (USA) 115 (The   **62** Minstrel (CAN) 135) [1998 68: 6s⁵ 7g³ 7m 8m 8d 1999 8g 10m⁵ 11.6m Jul 12] strong gelding: modest maiden: creditable effort in 1999 only on second start: probably stays 1¼m: has carried head high: reportedly had breathing problem final outing. *W. R. Muir*

KARAJAN (IRE)   2 b.c. (Apr 26) Fairy King (USA) – Dernier Cri 63 (Slip Anchor   **88 p** 136) [1999 8d³ Oct 15] 70,000Y: rather leggy colt: first foal: dam, French 11f/12.5f winner, half-sister to Mtoto: ½-length third of 13 to Pawn Broker in slowly-run maiden at Newmarket, green early on but finishing well: showed quick, fluent action: will stay 1½m: sure to do better. *J. W. Hills*

KARAKUL (IRE)   3 ch.f. Persian Bold 123 – Cindy's Baby 36 (Bairn (USA)   **78** 126) [1998 56: 5g 5.7m 5m 6.1d³ 7g* 7g⁶ 7m 8g 1999 7d 8f⁵ 10m* 10m² 10g* 9.9g* 9.7d 10g 10g a9.4g Dec 11] unfurnished filly: fair handicapper: won at Windsor in June and Leicester and Beverley in August: below form last 4 starts, leaving M. Fetherston-Godley 13,000 gns before final one: may stay beyond 1¼m: acts on good to firm going. *R. Brotherton*

KARALIYFA (IRE)   2 b. or br.f. (Feb 4) Kahyasi 130 – Karliyka (IRE) (Last   **86 P** Tycoon 131) [1999 7m³ Sep 17] lengthy filly: first foal: dam 8.5f to 11f winner in France: better for race and green, very encouraging third of 7 to Veil of Avalon in steadily-run minor event at Newbury, soon travelling strongly after slow start, switched over 1f out and staying on well: will be suited by 1¼m+: sure to improve good deal, and looks bound to win races. *Sir Michael Stoute*

KARAMEG (IRE)   3 b.f. Danehill (USA) 126 – House of Queens (IRE) (King of   **87** Clubs 124) [1998 65: 6.1d 6d⁴ 7v 1999 8m⁴ 8g 8.2m 7m* 7m³ 7m⁵ 6g² 6.1m³ 6m⁵ 7s* 7d⁵ Oct 30] useful-looking filly: fairly useful handicapper: won at Doncaster in June and 19-runner event at Newmarket in October: stays 7f: acts on soft and good to firm going. *P. W. Harris*

KAREEB (FR)   2 b.c. (Feb 23) Green Desert (USA) 127 – Braari (USA) 97 (Gulch   **79** (USA)) [1999 5m² 6g² 5.7m³ 6g² 6s⁴ Nov 2] second foal: dam 2-y-o 6f winner: fair maiden: sold out of B. Hills's stable 30,000 gns before final start: raced only at 5f/6f: acts on good to firm going, probably on soft: hasn't impressed with attitude, though did nothing noticeably wrong on fourth outing. *W. R. Muir*

KAREFREE KATIE (USA)   4 b.f. Lac Ouimet (USA) – Dame Cecilia (USA)   **–** (Vaguely Noble 140) [1998 68, a–: 10v² 10.3d⁶ a8.5g⁴ a8g 1999 a9.4g a12g a12s⁵ 10d Jul 5] close-coupled filly: fair maiden at 3 yrs: no form in 1999: probably stays 1¼m: blinkered final start. *J. G. Given*

KARINGA PRINCE   3 gr.g. Karinga Bay 116 – Silent Sister 78 (Kind of Hush   **–** 118) [1998 NR 1999 8g Apr 14] 7,600Y: big, rangy gelding: second reported foal: half-brother to 1995 2-y-o 7.3f winner Proud Monk (by Aragon): dam, 2-y-o 6f winner, half-sister to useful performer up to 1m Knight of Mercy: 50/1, backward and green, behind in newcomers race at Newmarket. *G. L. Moore*

KARINSKA   9 b.m. Master Willie 129 – Kaiserchronik (GER) (Cortez (GER))   **42** [1998 –: 7m 10.1m 8s 10g 7g 10.1g 12d 1999 a8f a8g⁵ a12g³ a12g⁶ a8g³ 12g⁴ 12.3m 18g 10g 12f 10m Jul 30] angular mare: fair performer in her prime: poor form in 1999: stayed 1½m: acted on fibresand, firm and soft going: dead. *M. C. Chapman*

KARISAL (IRE)   3 b.f. Persian Bold 123 – Pasadena Lady (Captain James 123)   **–** [1998 80: 5.1m⁴ 5d* 5d 1999 6m 6m 7.1d 5m⁶ Jul 16] tall, leggy filly: fair form at 2 yrs: well held on return: blinkered final start. *J. Berry*

KARIYADAN (IRE)   3 b.c. Akarad (FR) 130 – Kadissya (USA) 107 (Blushing   **63** Groom (FR) 131) [1998 –p: 8s 1999 10v 12s⁵ 12m⁴ 12g³ 12d Aug 16] smallish, sturdy colt: modest maiden: trained first 2 starts by L. Cumani: should stay beyond 1½m: acts on good to firm going. *S. Donohoe, Ireland*

KARIYFI (IRE) 2 b. or br.c. (Mar 29) Doyoun 124 – Karamiyna (IRE) (Shernazar 131) [1999 8d 7d Nov 1] smallish, sturdy colt: first foal: dam, French 1m to 11f (listed race) winner, sister to very smart 1¼m filly Kartajana: showed ability in maidens at Newmarket (burly and green) and Redcar in the autumn: will stay 1¼m: may still do better. *L. M. Cumani* — **66**

KARLAYA (IRE) 3 b.f. Darshaan 133 – Kalata (Assert 134) [1998 NR 1999 12g⁶ 12s Nov 2] fifth foal: sister to smart 1½m winner Kithana (stayed 14.6f): dam, from family of Kahyasi, ran once: some promise when sixth in maiden at Newmarket, but well beaten in similar event at Catterick 5½ months later. *H. R. A. Cecil* — **62**

KAROWNA 3 ch.f. Karinga Bay 116 – Misowni (Niniski (USA) 125) [1998 59: 7g⁵ 7.1m 7.5m 1999 7s³ 7m⁵ 6m⁴ 7m³ 7.1f⁴ 7m⁵ a8.5g Aug 6] rather leggy, useful-looking filly: fair maiden handicapper: likely to stay 1m+: acts on good to firm going: sold 3,400 gns, joined S. Brookshaw. *B. A. McMahon* — **76**

KASHRA (IRE) 2 b.f. (Mar 21) Dancing Dissident (USA) 119 – Tudor Loom (Sallust 134) [1999 5d² 5d⁶ 5g⁶ 6d* 6m² 6f* 6m* 6m⁴ 6d⁶ Sep 18] IR 16,000Y: close-coupled filly: fourth foal: half-sister to 3-y-o Midhish Two and smart US 9f winner Rainbow Blues (by Bluebird), latter also 5f/6f winner in Ireland at 2 yrs and second in Irish 2000 Guineas: dam third at 7f: fairly useful performer: won nurseries at Pontefract and Goodwood in July and Newmarket in August: last of 6 in listed race at Ayr final start: should prove best at 5f/6f: acts on firm and good to soft ground: has raced freely. *M. Johnston* — **91 +**

KASS ALHAWA 6 b.g. Shirley Heights 130 – Silver Braid (USA) 101 (Miswaki (USA) 124) [1998 76, a55: a6g* a8g² a8g⁴ a6g⁵ 7s 7.1g⁴ a7g 7.5d* a8g² 6d³ 9g⁶ 8g⁶ 8m 7.5m* 7g 7.5m² 8g³ 8.9g a7g² a8g² 1999 a8f⁴ a7f² a8g³ a7g a7g² 7g² a6g⁵ 8.5d² 7.5d 6m² a8.5g 7.5m 8.5m* 8f⁵ 9.9g³ 9g⁴ 8m 7f 7.5s 8g⁶ 7g⁴ 10d³ a8.5g* a8g Dec 13] good-topped gelding: fair on turf, modest on all-weather: won handicaps at Beverley in July and Wolverhampton in November: effective at 7f to 1¼m (when conditions aren't very testing): acts on soft going, firm and all-weather: tried blinkered. *D. W. Chapman* — **76 a61**

KASTAWAY 3 b.f. Distant Relative 128 – Flourishing (IRE) 85 (Trojan Fen 118) [1998 90: a5g* 5s* 5g* 5.2m² 5d² 5d* 5.2g⁴ 5g 1999 5.1s⁴ Apr 27] leggy, useful-looking filly: fairly useful performer at 2 yrs: well below form in 5-runner listed event at Bath only run of 1999: raced only around 5f: acts on good to firm going, soft and equitrack: races prominently. *D. R. C. Elsworth* — **74**

KATHAKALI (IRE) 2 b.c. (Apr 1) Dancing Dissident (USA) 119 – Shes A Dancer (IRE) (Alzao (USA) 117) [1999 6d 5.1g 6g⁶ 6m⁵ 6.1m⁴ 7.9m 7d Oct 12] IR 4,000Y: angular colt: fourth living foal: half-brother to 3-y-o Magique Etoile: dam unraced: modest maiden: tried visored: sold 3,200 gns in October. *V. Soane* — **60**

KATHIES PET 4 b.f. Tina's Pet 121 – Unveiled 76 (Sayf El Arab (USA) 127) [1998 67d: 7s⁶ 6s 6.1v³ 6g* 6g⁵ 6f 6g* 6m 5g 5g 6m 8g 5.1v 5.7g* 6f 6.1g 8g⁴ 8.3m⁵ 8.3m⁴ 7.1m⁵ 8.1m a7f Oct 2] rather leggy filly: fair handicapper: won at Bath in May: better at 6f than 5f, barely stays 1m: acts on good to firm and good to soft going, probably on soft. *R. J. Hodges* — **65**

KATHIR (USA) 2 ch.c. (Mar 23) Woodman (USA) 126 – Alcando 113 (Alzao (USA) 117) [1999 7.5g² 8.2m* Aug 28] $130,000Y: sturdy colt: second foal: half-brother to 3-y-o Capistrano Day: dam, 5f (at 2 yrs) to 1¼m winner, also Grade 1 9f winner in USA at 5 yrs: followed promising debut by landing odds in maiden at Nottingham later in August: should stay 1¼m: remains open to improvement. *A. C. Stewart* — **87 p**

KATHOLOGY (IRE) 2 b.c. (Feb 13) College Chapel 122 – Wicken Wonder (IRE) 71 (Distant Relative 128) [1999 5s 7d⁴ 6d² 6d² a6g² a5g³ Nov 20] 23,000Y: second foal: dam 2-y-o 6f winner: fairly useful maiden: stays 7f: acts on fibresand, raced only on good to soft/soft going on turf. *D. R. C. Elsworth* — **82**

KATHRYN'S PET 6 b.m. Blakeney 126 – Starky's Pet (Mummy's Pet 125) [1998 66: 13.8d* 12.3v 10m⁴ 12s 1999 13.8g* 12s 10d 11.9d⁴ 12d* Oct 29] good-topped mare: fairly useful handicapper: won at Catterick in March and 19-runner — **85**

race at Newmarket (produced good turn of foot) in October: stays 1¾m: acts on soft and good to firm going: often held up. *Mrs M. Reveley*

KATIE HAWK   5 b.m. Buzzards Bay 128§ – Rayne Park (Julio Mariner 127) [1998 –: 8m 11.7d 1999 10.2g 12.1m Jul 23] no sign of ability. *J. M. Bradley*   –

KATIE-JANE (IRE)   4 b.f. Midyan (USA) 124 – Hollybank Lady (USA) (Sir Ivor 135) [1998 NR 1999 a8.5g a12g a12g Dec 4] first foal: dam second at 12.5f in Ireland: modest form in bumpers: little form in maidens on Flat. *D. Shaw*   –

KATIE KOMAITE   6 b.m. Komaite (USA) – City To City 55 (Windjammer (USA)) [1998 53: 8.2s 8.3d 8.3d 8s* 9.2d⁶ 9.2g⁴ 9.2m 8.3s² 8s³ 8s⁶ 1999 8.3m⁴ 8s⁵ 8.2m 9.2f⁵ 8m 10m 9.9s 8.3s 10.1d* 10d Nov 1] angular mare: poor handicapper: won 18-runner race at Newcastle in October: stays 1¼m: acts on soft and good to firm going: tried blinkered, usually visored nowadays: has been difficult at stalls and not easiest of rides. *Mrs G. S. Rees*   46

KATIE'S CRACKER   4 b.f. Rambo Dancer (CAN) 107 – Tea-Pot 77 (Ragstone 128) [1998 53: a8s⁴ a8g⁶ a10g³ a12g³ a11g* a12g⁴ a11g a9.4g 11.6g³ 14.1m² 14m⁶ a16g 12.1d a11g 12d 14.1v* a12g a14.8s⁶ a14.8g³ 1999 a16g a16f³ a12f⁴ a13g² a13g* a16g a14g⁶ a14g* 14.1s⁶ 15.4v a14g 13.1g a16g⁴ a12g⁴ a13g² a12g 14.1m 14.1s a16g⁶ a12g a13g a12g Dec 27] smallish filly: poor performer: won selling handicap at Lingfield in February and claimer at Southwell in March: mostly below form after: stays 1¾m: acts on all-weather, good to firm and heavy ground. *M. Quinn*   35 a48

KATIE'S VALENTINE   2 b.f. (Feb 14) Balnibarbi 95 – Ring Side (IRE) (Alzao (USA) 117) [1999 5s a6g⁴ a7g⁵ Nov 13] first foal: dam unraced: poor form in maidens. *R. A. Fahey*   49 a40

KATINO   3 ch.f. Superpower 113 – Nikatino 63 (Bustino 136) [1998 NR 1999 6.1s⁶ 6s⁴ 8g Jun 14] half-sister to 1996 2-y-o 6f winner Perfect Bliss (by Superlative): dam won around 1½m and stayed well: bad maiden: sold 1,350 gns, joined M. Hourigan in Ireland. *B. D. Leavy*   28

KATIYKHA (IRE)   3 b.f. Darshaan 133 – Katiyfa (Auction Ring (USA) 123) [1998 NR 1999 12g* 11.8s* 11.9s⁶ 10.1g⁵ 12g 12s⁵ 12d* 12s² Oct 31] strong, rangy, attractive filly with plenty of scope: sixth foal: half-sister to 3 winners, fairly useful performers up to 1½m Kariniyd (by Blushing Groom) and Katiniyd (by Kahyasi) and 7-y-o Katiymann: dam French 1m and 1¼m winner: smart performer on her day: won maiden at Newmarket in May and 2-runner minor event at Leicester in June: improved form when winning rated stakes at Newmarket in October eased by 2 lengths from Fair Warning, sprinting clear from under 2f out: ran poorly several times: stays 1½m: raced only on good ground or softer. *L. M. Cumani*   114

KATIYMANN (IRE)   7 ch.g. Persian Bold 123 – Katiyfa (Auction Ring (USA) 123) [1998 NR 1999 10.3d 8.3m 10d 10g* May 31] third foal: half-brother to Irish 1992 2-y-o 7f winner Kariniyd (by Blushing Groom) and Irish 1m winner Katiniyd (by Kahyasi), both of whom stayed 1½m, and to 3-y-o Katiykha: dam French 1m and 1¼m winner: fair performer on Flat in Ireland at 3 and 5 yrs: easily best effort in Britain when winning 19-runner selling handicap at Leicester in May: stays 1¼m: yet to race on extremes of going: has worn tongue strap. *B. Ellison*   50

KATTEGAT   3 b.g. Slip Anchor 136 – Kirsten 77 (Kris 135) [1998 75p: 8g 8.2s* 1999 12.3d² 13.9s³ 13.1v* Oct 12] tall, unfurnished gelding: progressive performer: off 5 months, won 7-runner handicap at Ayr in October: will be suited by 2m: yet to race on ground firmer than good, clearly goes well in the mud: sold 105,000 gns, joined J. Old: already useful, and capable of better still. *W. Jarvis*   97 p

KATUN (FR)   6 b.h. Saumarez 132 – All Found (USA) (Alleged (USA) 138) [1998 12s³ 12m³ 12d 12m 12s* 12.5m 12d⁶ 12s 13.5s* 15s* 15.5v* 15v⁴ 15v⁴ 1999 15.5d* 15.5g* 15.5d³ 20m Jun 17] tall horse: half-brother to 3 winners in France, including stayers Roli Abi (by Bering) and Strike Oil (by Fabulous Dancer), both smart at best: dam French 10.5f winner: smart performer: improved in 1999, winning handicap and Prix de Barbeville (by head from Tajoun, who rec 7 lb) before good 3½ lengths third to Kayf Tara in Prix Vicomtesse Vigier, all at Longchamp in April/May: bandaged in front, never able to challenge when ninth of 17 in Gold Cup at Royal Ascot final start: stays 15.5f: acts on heavy ground. *X. Nakkachdji, France*   110

KATY IVORY (IRE)   2 b.f. (Feb 5) Night Shift (USA) – Echo Cove (Slip Anchor **68**
136) [1999 5m 6.1m 7g 8d² 8.3g 8d Oct 18] 11,000Y: fourth foal: closely related to
French 1¼m winner Matterhorn (by Sadler's Wells) and half-sister to Italian winner
up to 1m Dangerous Affair (by Zafonic): dam French 11f winner: fair maiden: easily
best effort when neck second of 16 in nursery at Pontefract in September: well beaten
in similar events after: should stay 1¼m. *P. W. Harris*

KATY NOWAITEE   3 b.f. Komaite (USA) – Cold Blow 67 (Posse (USA) 130) **92 p**
[1998 NR 1999 8m* 8m⁵ 8g* 8.2d² Oct 21] 6,000Y: second foal: half-sister to a
winner in Holland by Tina's Pet: dam, second at 7f at 2 yrs, from family of Yorkshire
Oaks winners Sally Brown and Untold: fairly useful form: won maiden at Newmarket in August and 22-runner handicap at Redcar in October: short-head second in
another handicap at Nottingham final start, racing freely early: should stay beyond
1m: yet to race on extremes of going: slowly away first 2 starts, markedly so second
time: game: capable of better still. *P. W. Harris*

KAY EFF ESS (IRE)   3 b.f. Nucleon (USA) 94 – My Silversmith (IRE) (Cyrano **–**
de Bergerac 120) [1998 NR 1999 6f Sep 4] first foal: dam of no account: tailed off in
maiden. *J. L. Eyre*

KAYF TARA   5 b.h. Sadler's Wells (USA) 132 – Colorspin (FR) 118 (High **130**
Top 131) [1998 126: 11.9g* 16.4g³ 20s* 16d⁵ 15d⁴ 14d* 1999 15.5d* 20m³
16f* 15s* 14s* Sep 18]

For most of the year everything went like clockwork for the Godolphin
operation, but the mechanism still underwent a few serious failures. The signal
failure of expensive buys Worldly Manner and Comeonmom to make a mark in
the States was one, the retirement of the best horse in Europe in 1998, Intikhab,
through injury after just one start, was another, and the injury sustained by Kayf
Tara a week before the Foster's Melbourne Cup was a third. It is one thing
aiming a horse at a race virtually all season, having bypassed a challenge the
previous year because of perceived immaturity; it is quite another to have the
individual clearly in top form and a worthy favourite for the race only to miss
it, and then see his lead horse get within half a length of triumphing.

It was known at the start of the season that Kayf Tara was a high-class
performer. He had proved as much in winning three of his six starts as a four-
year-old, notably the Gold Cup from Double Trigger and the Irish St Leger
from Silver Patriarch, after which he had been named as Timeform's champion
stayer. His campaign at five didn't get under way in a hurry, and he missed the
Yorkshire Cup because he wasn't ready, but his performance in the nine-runner
Prix Vicomtesse Vigier at Longchamp towards the end of May indicated he
would take all the beating in the Gold Cup. Opposed by the first four in the
Prix de Barbeville and giving weight all round, he scored emphatically by a
length and a half from the runner-up in that race, Tajoun, with the winner Katun
third. This race, like the two important ones Kayf Tara had won in 1998, was
run on softish ground, but it came up good to firm at Royal Ascot and was
perceived to be unsuitable for the horse, with the result that Frankie Dettori
decided to ride Nedawi instead. Nedawi could finish only fifth, with Kayf Tara

*Goodwood Cup—Kayf Tara dominates in most impressive fashion,
eased before beating the Sheikh Mohammed pair Three Cheers and Jaseur (rail)*

*Prix Kergorlay, Deauville—only one French-trained runner in the field of five
as Kayf Tara makes all from Invermark (left) and Largesse*

also a bit below his best in third. Kayf Tara ran his heart out though, battling on
in the straight to finish four lengths behind the winner Enzeli, with Invermark
taking second. Kayf Tara got back on the winning trail in the Goodwood Cup, a
race in which he had finished fifth the previous year. He obliterated one myth

*Jefferson Smurfit Memorial Irish St Leger, the Curragh—
Kayf Tara follows up his win in the race the previous year with another towering performance*

Godolphin's "Kayf Tara"

here, since the ground was firmer than at Ascot. Admittedly, Kayf Tara didn't move well to post, but he came back in tremendous fashion, edging closer to the pace, set by Seignorial, a mile out and sprinting clear once asked to quicken under three furlongs from home. Having gone eight lengths ahead, Kayf Tara was eased before winning by an official margin of four lengths over Three Cheers. With the intention of going for a repeat success in the Irish St Leger, Kayf Tara was aimed at the Prix Kergorlay rather than the Doncaster Cup; the Deauville race comes a couple of weeks earlier. Opposed by four rivals on soft going, including Invermark and Yorkshire Cup second Largesse—there was only one French contender—Kayf Tara had new tactics applied, making all and quickening away once shaken up in the straight to beat Invermark easily by five lengths.

    Since being opened to older horses in 1983 the Jefferson Smurfit Memorial Irish St Leger has been won by five three-year-olds, with none successful in the 'nineties. Not that many have even contested the race lately, with twenty-four runners out of a total of seventy-seven from 1990 to 1998, and only two have started favourite, Patricia in 1991 and Key Change in 1996. Just one from the classic crop, rank outsider Genghis Khan, took on Kayf Tara and three other older horses in the latest renewal. The other older horses were: Silver Patriarch, the 1997 St Leger victor recently successful in the Geoffrey Freer Stakes; Enzeli, who hadn't run since the Gold Cup; and Yavana's Pace, winner of two listed races and the September Stakes in the current season. Kayf Tara started at 2/1-on and never gave his backers a moment's worry, travelling easily as Genghis Khan made the running, going on half a mile out and galloping on much too strongly for Yavana's Pace. He won by eight lengths, with Silver Patriarch and Enzeli running below form in third and fourth. This was the best performance by Kayf Tara all year and one which placed him in a select band of three horses to have won the race twice—Vintage Crop did so in

1993 and 1994, and Oscar Schindler in 1996 and 1997. At four Kayf Tara had been allotted 9-0 in the Melbourne Cup; this time he had 9-3, making him joint top weight with Nedawi. Kayf Tara was favourite in British bookmakers' lists as soon as they appeared, at around 7/1, and by mid-October he was down to 7/2 and was also joint-favourite with the Australian bookies. Then, after working at his training base in Australia, he was found to have damaged a suspensory ligament in his near-fore, which became inflamed. A vet from Dubai was flown out but the horse was withdrawn.

Kayf Tara (b.h. 1994)	Sadler's Wells (USA) (b 1981)	Northern Dancer (b 1961)	Nearctic
			Natalma
		Fairy Bridge (b 1975)	Bold Reason
			Special
	Colorspin (FR) (b 1983)	High Top (b 1969)	Derring-Do
			Camenae
		Reprocolor (ch 1976)	Jimmy Reppin
			Blue Queen

The lightly-raced Kayf Tara—he has only thirteen runs on the scoresheet—stays in training. His admirable pedigree was discussed in some detail in *Racehorses of 1998*. Additional details are that his two-year-old half-brother Mafnood, by Rainbow Quest, was unraced with David Loder in 1999 and his dam foaled a filly by Zafonic in the spring, and was covered by Singspiel. A 210,000-guineas yearling, who has repaid the investment with interest, Kayf Tara is a well-made, attractive horse, with a quick action. He acts on any going but has put up his very best efforts on good to soft and soft. Although he stays long distances, he does not need further than a mile and three quarters to show his form, and he also has a bright turn of foot. *Saeed bin Suroor*

KAYO 4 b.g. Superpower 113 – Shiny Kay 65 (Star Appeal 133) [1998 99, a83: a6g* a7g* 7g² 6f 7s* 7v² a7g⁶ a8g 6g 8m⁵ 8s⁵ 8d* 7g 7s 1999 6m⁴ 8.1s⁶ 7.1g⁶ 6s 7.1d³ 7d 7.1d 7s³ a7g 6d⁵ 7g* 7g* 6d* 7s a8g³ a8g Nov 15] salt, leggy gelding: useful handicapper on turf, fairly useful on all-weather: left T. Etherington after ninth start: better than ever after, winning large-field handicaps at Redcar, Newmarket and Newcastle within 7 days in October, on last-named course beating Pips Song by ½ length: ran poorly final outing (reportedly had breathing problem): effective at 6f to 1m: acts on good to firm going, heavy and all-weather: blinkered (below form) sixth start: has sweated, got on toes and swished tail in preliminaries: races prominently. *M. Johnston* **103 a88**

KAYO GEE 3 b.f. Komaite (USA) – Darling Miss Daisy 77 (Tina's Pet 121) [1998 63: 6s 6s⁵ a7g a6g a5g⁴ 1999 a5g* a5g* 5g 5m 5f a6g a5g Dec 4] sturdy, lengthy filly: fair handicapper: won at Lingfield in January and February: below form after: best at 5f: acts on equitrack: blinkered: carried head high on firm ground: joined L. Montague Hall. *A. J. McNae* **– a79 d**

KAZZOUD (IRE) 3 b.f. Ezzoud (IRE) 126 – Kates Cabin 96 (Habitat 134) [1998 –: 7g 1999 10m 10f a10g a12g Dec 4] no form. *S. Dow* **–**

KEEBAAR 3 b.c. Shirley Heights 130 – Historiette (Chief's Crown (USA)) [1998 NR 1999 10v³ 10g² 12g² 11.5g* 12m⁴ 13.9g³ Aug 19] 145,000Y: sturdy, round-barrelled colt: poor mover: third foal: dam unraced close relative of high-class sprinter Polish Patriot: useful performer: landed odds in maiden at Yarmouth in June: good third in rated stakes at York final start: stays 1¾m: acts on good to firm going: sent to UAE. *M. A. Jarvis* **95**

KEEN COMPANION 6 b.m. Keen 116 – Constant Companion 84 (Pas de Seul 133) [1998 –: 7m a10g 1999 a11f a11g a14g⁵ 12.3m Jun 23] poor maiden: stays 1¾m: acts on fibresand, best turf effort on soft ground: blinkered final start. *T. J. Naughton* **30**

KEEN DANCER 5 ch.g. Keen 116 – Royal Shoe (Hotfoot 126) [1998 62: 16v⁶ 12.5s⁴ 10.8g⁶ 10.2g 1999 12.1m⁶ a12g Aug 13] heavy-topped gelding: modest maiden handicapper: reportedly lame final start: should stay beyond 12.5f: best form on good to soft/soft going: fair winning hurdler. *M. C. Pipe* **59 a–**

KEEN HANDS 3 ch.g. Keen 116 – Broken Vow (IRE) (Local Suitor (USA) 128) [1998 60: 7g a8g a5g⁶ a6g a5g² 1999 a6g² a5g* a6g⁵ a6g a5g² a7g* a5g* a6g* 6m **– a76**

a6g[6] a7g a7g a6g[3] a6g[6] a7g[4] a7g a6g[2] a6g[4] Dec 21] compact gelding: fair performer: won seller at Wolverhampton in January and 2 sellers and a handicap at Southwell in March/April: effective at 5f to 7f: acts on all-weather, well beaten both turf starts: visored. *Mrs N. Macauley*

KEEP IKIS   5 ch.m. Anshan 119 – Santee Sioux (Dancing Brave (USA) 140)   **53** [1998 NR 1999 14.1m[6] 14d[6] 12.3m 16.2s 12m 16d 16m[2] 18d[3] Oct 18] leggy, short-backed mare: first foal: dam unraced daughter of Lupe Stakes winner Scimitarra: modest maiden handicapper: left S. Gollings, then creditable effort final start (despite tending to hang right): stays 2¼m: acts on good to firm and good to soft going. *Mrs M. Reveley*

KEEPSAKE (IRE)   5 b.m. Distinctly North (USA) 115 – Souveniers (Relko 136)   **31** [1998 50: 14.1s[5] 11.7s[5] 13.1f[4] 11.8m 12d[5] 16.2g 14.9g[6] 12g 12m[4] 14.1m[4] 14.1m[6] 15.8m[5] 16.1m[3] 1999 a12f a13g[3] a16g[2] a16g[2] a16g[4] 11.9g[4] 14.1g 16m Sep 13] tall mare: poor handicapper: well below form final 2 starts: needs good test at 1½m, and stays 2m: acts on soft going, firm and all-weather: tried visored/blinkered: usually gets behind. *M. D. I. Usher*

KEEP TAPPING (IRE)   2 b.c. (Feb 14) Mac's Imp (USA) 116 – Mystery Bid   **79** (Auction Ring (USA) 123) [1999 5g[5] 5m[4] 5g[2] 6d 5m[*] 5m 5.1m[3] 5.2m 6f 7g 6m Aug 28] 16,000Y: useful-looking colt: has a quick action: seventh foal: brother to 3-y-o Spy and half-brother to 2 winners, including 1½m winner Secret Service (by Classic Secret): dam Irish maiden who stayed 1½m: fair performer: won maiden at Sandown in June: likely to prove best at 5f/6f: acts on good to firm and good to soft ground: tried visored. *A. P. Jarvis*

KEE RING   3 ch.g. Keen 116 – Rose And The Ring (Welsh Pageant 132) [1998   **62** 73p: 6m[2] 7s 1999 7m[6] 6g 6g 7.7m[5] 8m 7g[3] 6d[5] Aug 26] leggy gelding: modest maiden: stays 1m: acts on good to firm going: tends to hang and carry head awkwardly. *P. R. Chamings*

KELD (IRE)   4 b.f. Lion Cavern (USA) 117 – Society Ball 72 (Law Society (USA)   **106** 130) [1998 95p: 8d 8.1m[*] 8g[*] 1999 8.5m[3] 7.6m[5] 10.2m[2] 10.1g[4] 10s[4] 10d[5] Oct 29] rather leggy filly: useful performer: running at Lingfield second start referred to Portman Square: best efforts in listed events when second to Ela Athena at Chepstow, fourth to Fickle at Newcastle (rated stakes) fourth start and fifth to Little Rock at Newmarket final outing: stays 1¼m: acts on good to firm and good to soft going: sold to race in USA. *J. R. Fanshawe*

KELLING HALL   2 b.c. (Jan 19) Distant Relative 128 – Naulakha (Bustino 136)   **–** [1999 8.2d 8d Oct 30] 9,800F, 5,200Y: second foal: dam lightly-raced sister to N C Owen, smart winner up to 11.5f: well held in maiden and seller. *D. J. S. ffrench Davis*

KELSO MAGIC (USA)   2 ch.f. (Apr 23) Distant View (USA) 126 – Bowl of   **98** Honey (USA) (Lyphard (USA) 132) [1999 5m[2] 5m[5] 5m[*] 6m[4] 5g[2] 5.3m[*] 6.5g 5d[5] 5d[4] 6d[6] Oct 23] 23,000Y: sturdy, quite attractive filly: sixth foal: half-sister to 1½m to 2m winner Urgent Reply (by Green Dancer) and a winner in USA by Affirmed: dam unraced granddaughter of top-class Rose Bowl: useful performer: won maiden at Salisbury in June and nursery at Brighton in September: easily best effort when fourth of 13 to Kier Park in Cornwallis Stakes at Ascot, faring best of those drawn low: races freely, and likely to prove best at 5f: acts on good to firm and good to soft ground: has been bandaged in front. *B. J. Meehan*

KELTECH GOLD (IRE)   2 b.c. (Mar 10) Petorius 117 – Creggan Vale Lass   **65** (Simply Great (FR) 122) [1999 8s[5] 8s Nov 6] IR 8,000F, IR 14,500Y: heavy-topped colt: third foal: half-brother to a winner in Turkey by Ile de Chypre: dam poor Irish maiden: fair form in maidens at Bath and Doncaster. *B. Palling*

KELTIC BARD   2 b.g. (Apr 28) Emperor Jones (USA) 119 – Broughton Singer   **81** (IRE) 61 (Common Grounds 118) [1999 7f[2] 8.2m[2] a8.5g[*] 8d Oct 15] 16,500F, IR   **a90** 8,000Y: rangy gelding: has a fluent, round action: first foal: dam 9f winner: fairly useful form: won minor event at Wolverhampton in September by 5 lengths: will stay 1¼m. *S. P. C. Woods*

KENNET   4 b.g. Kylian (USA) – Marwell Mitzi 50 (Interrex (CAN)) [1998 77, a?:   **77** 6d[2] 6g[6] 7g[3] 8.1g[2] 8m[2] 8d[2] a7g 9g 1999 a10g[*] a10g 10s[3] 10m 8g 10g[*] 10m[3] 10d[3] 11.4m[4] 10d[6] 10d[3] 11.9d[*] 8s Nov 6] leggy, plain gelding: fair performer: won maiden at Lingfield in February and minor events at Windsor in May and Brighton in

October: mostly creditable efforts otherwise: probably needs further than 1m, barely stays 1½m: acts on good to firm ground, soft and all-weather. *P. D. Cundell*

KENSINGTON PRINCE 2 ch.g. (Mar 30) Prince Sabo 123 – Future Options – 71 (Lomond (USA) 128) [1999 a6g 5g 6f 5g Aug 18] 8,000Y: second foal: half-brother to 3-y-o Coul Bank: dam maiden who stayed 1m: well beaten in minor event and sellers: tried blinkered. *J. Berry*

KENT 4 b.g. Kylian (USA) – Precious Caroline (IRE) 60 (The Noble Player (USA) **53** 126) [1998 NR 1999 a12g 8.2s³ 10g a8g 8g 11.6m 12d a12g⁵ Nov 19] very big gelding: second reported foal: brother to 5-y-o Agent Mulder: dam 1¼m winner: modest maiden: stays 1m: acts on soft going: blinkered once. *P. D. Cundell*

KENTISH LAD (IRE) 3 ch.g. Caerleon (USA) 132 – Jaljuli 107 (Jalmood – (USA) 126) [1998 NR 1999 8.1d⁴ Jun 5] IR 150,000Y: rather angular gelding: fifth foal: closely related to 1m/1¼m winner Jubilee Scholar (by Royal Academy) and half-brother to a 1m winner in Japan by Persian Bold: dam, best at 2 yrs when 5f/6f winner, half-sister to Kooyonga: remote fourth of 7 in maiden at Haydock: sold 2,500 gns. *Sir Michael Stoute*

KENTUCKY BULLET (USA) 3 b.g. Housebuster (USA) – Exactly So (Caro **69 d** 133) [1998 NR 1999 a8g⁶ a10g⁵ a7g* a8g⁵ 7d* 7.5m a7g⁶ 6m 6g 5.9m 8d 7.5m⁶ a7g⁶ 8m 8.2g 7g 7d Oct 22] $15,000Y: leggy, angular gelding: half-brother to several winners, notably Prix Lupin winner Exactly Sharp (by Sharpen Up): dam won in France at 3 yrs (at 10.5f) and later Grade 3 winner in USA: fair performer: won maiden at Southwell in February and handicap at Doncaster in March: well below that form after: stays 7f: acts on good to soft going and fibresand: often blinkered: has hung, flashed tail: has worn tongue strap: sold 3,000 gns. *M. Johnston*

KEOS (USA) 5 b. or br.h. Riverman (USA) 131 – Konafa (CAN) 118 (Damascus **120** (USA)) [1998 118: 8s² 8s³ 6g* 6.5m 6g* 7v³ 1999 7d³ 6m 6g* 6.5s⁶ 6g* 5v³ 7d² Oct 17] medium-sized, attractive horse: very smart performer: won Prix de Ris-Orangis

Niarchos Family's "Keos"

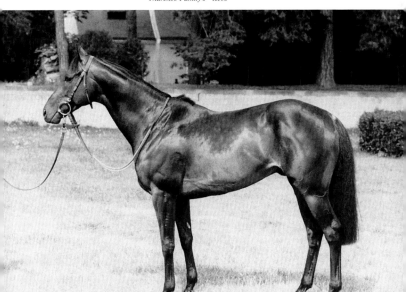

at Deauville (for second year running, by ½ length from Andreyev) in July and Jacobs Goldene Peitsche at Baden-Baden (by neck from Gorse) in September: placed in valuable event at Goodwood (3 lengths third to Diktat), Prix de l'Abbaye de Longchamp (staying-on 1¾ lengths third behind Agnes World) and Prix de la Foret on latter course (strong-finishing ¾-length second to Field of Hope): best at 6f/7f: acted on heavy ground, below form on good to firm: blinkered last 5 starts: held up: to stand at Hermitage Farm, Kentucky, fee $5,000. *J. E. Hammond, France*

KEPHREN (USA) 10 ch.g. Kenmare (FR) 125 – Marie de Russy (FR) (Sassafras (FR) 135) [1998 –: 16v 16g⁵ a12g 1999 16.1d 14.1d 17.2g Jun 12] modest handicapper in Ireland in 1997: no form after: dead. *P. Burgoyne*

KERALBA (USA) 3 b.f. Sheikh Albadou 128 – Sookera (USA) 117 (Roberto (USA) 131) [1998 NR 1999 8g Apr 14] big, strong filly: half-sister to several winners, including smart 6f/7f winner Bold Fact and very smart performer up to 7f So Factual (both by Known Fact): dam won Cheveley Park Stakes: last of 12 in newcomers race at Newmarket, only start: sold 13,500 gns in December. *B. W. Hills*

KERALIA (IRE) 3 b.f. Doyoun 124 – Keraka (USA) 104 (Storm Bird (CAN) 134) [1998 69p: 7m⁶ 7m 1999 8m² 8g² 8.5m³ 8.5m 9s⁵ Oct 8] unfurnished filly: fairly useful maiden: ran poorly final 2 starts: stays 1m: acts on good to firm going: sold 20,000 gns. *Sir Michael Stoute*   **81**

KERRIDGE CHAPEL (IRE) 2 b.f. (Feb 11) College Chapel 122 – Crimson Ring (Persian Bold 123) [1999 5d 6g a5g⁶ 5.1m 5g 5.1m⁵ a5f a8.5g a5g Nov 20] 3,000Y: small, sturdy filly: half-sister to 1m winner Fistful of Bucks (by Lochnager) and a winner up to 7f in Austria by Dowsing: dam lightly raced: little form: tried blinkered. *A. Senior*

KERRY 2 b.g. (Mar 19) Magic Ring (IRE) 115 – Sideloader Special 66 (Song 132) [1999 6d May 16] 1,400Y: fifth foal: half-brother to several winning sprinters, including Harpo's Special (by Superlative) and Jessica's Song (by Colmore Row), and to unreliable 12.4f seller winner Trumble (by Tragic Role): dam 6f winner: thirteenth of 21 in maiden at Ripon only start. *M. W. Easterby*

KESTON POND (IRE) 9 b.g. Taufan (USA) 119 – Maria Renata (Jaazeiro (USA) 127) [1998 NR 1999 7m⁵ Jul 15] tall, good-topped gelding: poor performer, lightly raced nowadays: stays 1m: acts on firm going and fibresand: blinkered (tailed off) once. *R. A. Fahey*   **40**

KESTRAL 3 ch.g. Ardkinglass 114 – Shiny Kay 65 (Star Appeal 133) [1998 55: 6g 8.1m 7.9g 7d 5.9g⁴ 6.9m⁵ 6g 7.1m 7.1m⁴ 7.1f⁴ a6g 8d 8d 8g Nov 3] leggy, angular gelding: modest maiden: creditable efforts in 1999 only when fourth: stays 7f: acts on firm going. *T. J. Etherington*   **55**

KEWARRA 5 b.g. Distant Relative 128 – Shalati (FR) (High Line 125) [1998 98: 10.1s* 10.1m 10g 10g² 9.9g 10.2m³ 12m³ 12g 10v 1999 10.1s³ 10.3m 10.1g 12m⁵ 10m Aug 21] angular gelding: fairly useful handicapper: well below form in 1999: stays 1¼m: acts on soft and good to firm going: blinkered third start. *B. R. Millman*   **82**

KEW GARDENS 2 ch.c. (Jan 27) Arazi (USA) 135 – Hatton Gardens 96 (Auction Ring (USA) 123) [1999 7m 8s⁴ 10s* 10d⁶ Oct 30] 400,000 francs Y: half-brother to several winners, including useful 7f (at 2 yrs) to 10.4f winner Ludgate (by Lyphard): dam, Irish 6f to 1m winner, half-sister to Kooyonga: fairly useful form: won maiden at Pontefract (by 6 lengths) in October: creditable sixth of 10 in listed event at Newmarket final start: will stay 1½m. *Mrs A. J. Perrett*   **86**

KEY 3 b.f. Midyan (USA) 124 – Diamond Park (IRE) 91 (Alzao (USA) 117) [1998 70: 6m⁵ 5d² 5.1m³ 7m 5.3m* 6m 6g 7s 5v⁴ 1999 6m⁵ 7.1g² 6g⁴ 7m⁵ 7m⁴ 7m⁵ 5d 6d Oct 29] sturdy, workmanlike filly: fair performer: left R. Hannon after sixth start: poor efforts after: stays 7f: acts on good to firm and heavy going. *C. E. Brittain*   **70**

KEY ACADEMY 4 b.f. Royal Academy (USA) 130 – Santa Linda (USA) (Sir Ivor 135) [1998 87: 10m² 10m² 11.7m* 12g³ 1999 11.8g² 12g² Sep 13] leggy, angular filly: useful performer: better than ever only 2 starts in 1999, 2 lengths second of 13 to Farfala in listed race at Chantilly final one: stays 1½m: raced only on good/good to firm going: sent to USA. *C. A. Horgan*   **103**

KEY TO THE CITY (IRE) 5 b.g. Shalford (IRE) 124§ – Green Wings (General **65**
Assembly (USA)) [1998 68: 7s² 7m³ 7g a6g⁴ 8g 8.5s 8d⁴ 8s 1999 a10g² a9.4g a8g⁴
a12g² 9.2v* 9g a12g² May 8] IR 22,000Y: half-brother to 1995 2-y-o 1m seller
winner Addie Pray (by Great Commotion) and winners abroad by Salt Dome and
Doulab: dam Irish 4-y-o 1½m winner: fair performer: trained in Ireland by D. Weld
in 1998: won claimer at Hamilton in March: good second in similar event at Wolverhampton final start: stays easy 1½m: acts on good to firm and heavy ground and
all-weather: effective with/without blinkers: has found little: joined D. Bridgwater.
P. Eccles

KEZ 3 b.g. Polar Falcon (USA) 126 – Briggsmaid 70 (Elegant Air 119) [1998 NR **75**
1999 8g 8.2m³ 10m³ 8.2f³ 10.1m² 11.9f* 9.7d 10.4g 10.3d Oct 22] 32,000Y: lengthy
gelding: has a quick action: second foal: half-brother to French 1m/9f winner Goldfill
(by Marju): dam 1½m to 2m winner: fair performer: won maiden at Brighton in
August: no impact in handicaps after: stays 1½m: acts on firm going. *S. P. C. Woods*

KHABAR 6 b.g. Forzando 122 – Ella Mon Amour 65 (Ela-Mana-Mou 132) [1998 **63**
NR 1999 7d 10.1m⁴ 9f³ 8m⁶ 8.3m³ 9g² 8m² 8.5m³ 8.3m 8d² 8.1s 10.1d Oct 20]
well-made gelding: modest maiden handicapper: mostly creditable efforts in 1999,
though well below form final 2 outings: stays easy 1¼m: acts on firm and good to
soft going: reportedly bled from nose second start. *R. Bastiman*

KHALED (IRE) 4 b.g. Petorius 117 – Felin Special (Lyphard's Special (USA) **–**
122) [1998 78: 8d 7d³ 8m* 1999 a9.4g⁵ 8d Mar 26] tall, quite good-topped gelding:
fair performer at 3 yrs: well beaten both starts in 1999: stays 1m: acts on good to firm
going: has had tongue tied. *K. Mahdi*

KHALIK (IRE) 5 br.g. Lear Fan (USA) 130 – Silver Dollar 106 (Shirley Heights **73**
130) [1998 73d: 6d 7g³ 6m⁴ 5.9d³ 6f 6f 6.1m 5g 1999 6g* 6g* 5.3s 5d 6g² 5.2s
a6g Nov 15] smallish, sturdy gelding: unimpressive mover: fair handicapper: won at
Salisbury (apprentices) and Lingfield in August: good second of 22 at Windsor 2
months later: has form at 5f/6f: acts on good to firm going: blinkered twice at 4 yrs
(ran creditably first time): nearly brought down fourth outing (would have run well):
often tongue tied. *Miss Gay Kelleway*

KHALIL 2 b.g. (Apr 17) Tragic Role (USA) – T O O Mamma's (IRE) 50 (Classic **51 d**
Secret (USA) 91) [1999 7.1m³ 7.1d 6d 6m⁶ a6g⁴ Sep 8] 6,000Y: leggy gelding: first
foal: dam, 9.4f and 11f winner (also successful over hurdles), half-sister to useful
sprinter Whittingham: poor form after debut. *J. Berry*

KHASAYL (IRE) 2 b.f. (Mar 11) Lycius (USA) 124 – Maraatib (IRE) 93 (Green **106 +**
Desert (USA) 127) [1999 5g² 5.1g* 6m* 7d⁴ 6m² 5d* 6g* Oct 2] tall, quite attractive
filly: has scope: fourth foal: sister to 6-y-o Mazeed and half-sister to 1m (at 2 yrs) and
1¼m winner Nebl (by Persian Bold): dam sprinter: useful performer: won maiden at
Bath and minor event at Doncaster in June/July: best efforts when winning listed
event at Ayr (by 4 lengths from Tara's Girl) in September and valuable 26-runner
ntl Two-Year-Old Trophy at Redcar (by neck from Heathyardsblessing, soon clear
over 1f out then hanging left) in October: effective at 5f to 7f: has swished tail under
whip: may do better still. *P. T. Walwyn*

ntl Two-Year-Old Trophy, Redcar—
Khasayl (rail) provides trainer Peter Walwyn with what turns out to be his final winner before retirement;
Heathyardsblessing (noseband) is beaten only a neck in second place

KHATTAFF (IRE) 4 ch.g. Hamas (IRE) 125§ – Coven (Sassafras (FR) 135) [1998 **37**
–: 8.2m⁶ 8.5d 8m 9.2d 10.4g 9m 1999 a8g 8g 8g 8d⁶ a8.5g⁵ Dec 27] smallish, strong
gelding: poor maiden handicapper: tried visored/blinkered. *M. Brittain*

KHIBRAH (IRE) 3 br.f. Lahib (USA) 129 – Sabayik (IRE) 93 (Unfuwain (USA) **107**
131) [1998 69p: 6.1s³ 6s³ 1999 7s 6.1f 8g² 8g* 8g⁴ 8f* 8f* 8.5m* 8.1d* 10d⁴
10d* Oct 14] rather sparely-made filly: fluent mover: useful performer: progressed
tremendously well at 3 yrs, winning handicaps at Brighton (3 times), Epsom and
Sandown between June and September, and improving again to win listed event at
Newmarket in October by neck from Horatia: stays 1¼m: acts on firm and good to
soft going, showed promise on soft: sent to USA. *E. A. L. Dunlop*

KHUCHN (IRE) 3 b.c. Unfuwain (USA) 131 – Stay Sharpe (USA) (Sharpen Up **67**
127) [1998 NR 1999 8.2m⁵ 10m 12g 10g* 11.8m Aug 22] half-brother to several
winners, including 1m/1¼m winner Manazil (by Generous) and 5-y-o Jalaab, both
useful: dam unraced: fair form: won minor event at Nottingham in July: found to be
lame after final outing: stays 1¼m: hasn't looked tractable on occasions: sold only
1,000 gns in October. *R. W. Armstrong*

KIBA (IRE) 3 b.f. Tirol 127 – Ornette (IRE) (Bluebird (USA) 125) [1998 NR **–**
1999 8g⁴ Apr 5] IR 3,600F, IR 1,500Y: first foal: dam unraced daughter of Oaks
runner-up Bonnie Isle: remote fourth of 6 in maiden at Newcastle. *J. J. O'Neill*

KI CHI SAGA (USA) 7 ch.g. Miswaki (USA) 124 – Cedilla (USA) 111 (Caro **44 §**
133) [1998 33, a65: a8g⁵ a8g* a8g³ a8g⁴ a8g⁴ a8g a8g* a10g⁴ 8g a10g⁴ a10g² a9.4g³ **a61 §**
a11g a10g a12g² 10s⁴ a12g³ 1999 a10g⁵ a10f² a9.4g³ a12g⁶ a8g³ a10g³ a10g⁶ 11.6d⁵
10.9s 11.1m³ 10g 11.6m 11.9d a12g* a9.4g a12g a12g a12g⁴ a12g⁴ a13g a13g² a12g
Dec 27] stocky gelding: modest on all-weather, poor on turf: won seller at Lingfield
in August: stays easy 13f: acts on good to firm and all-weather: usually
blinkered/visored: unreliable. *P. Burgoyne*

KICK ON KATOUCHE (IRE) 2 ch.g. (May 5) Forest Wind (USA) 111 – Lap- **64**
land Lights (USA) 85 (Northern Prospect (USA)) [1999 5v³ a5g³ 5g⁵ May 31] IR
5,000F, 1,200Y: rather leggy colt: second foal: brother to 3-y-o Nathan's Hero:
dam 6f winner: modest form when fourth (promoted to third) of 11 in maiden at
Leicester on debut: played up in stalls and disappointing both starts after, finding
little final one. *K. R. Burke*

KIDNAPPED 3 b.g. Emarati (USA) 74 – Haddon Anna (Dragonara Palace (USA) **–**
115) [1998 –: 5.7d 6m 1999 6.1f 5.9g 8.3d a7g a8.5g Dec 1] little form: left Mrs
A. King after second start. *A. J. McNae*

KIDOLOGY (IRE) 3 b.g. Petardia 113 – Loveville (USA) (Assert 134) [1998 **–**
NR 1999 8m 8s 12s Nov 2] 8,500Y: half-brother to 2 winners on Flat, notably smart
1m and 1¼m winner Hitman (by Contract Law): dam, lightly raced, from family of
Leap Lively and Forest Flower: well held in maidens: tongue tied. *W. Storey*

KID ORY 8 ch.g. Rich Charlie 117 – Woomargama 69 (Creetown 123) [1998 47d: **–**
a6g* a7g a7g 5v a6g a6g 5g 6g⁶ a6g a6g a6g⁶ 1999 6f 6f Aug 7] close-coupled
gelding: little form since reappearance in 1998: usually blinkered. *D. W. Chapman*

KID'Z'PLAY (IRE) 3 b.g. Rudimentary (USA) 118 – Saka Saka (Camden Town **59**
125) [1998 62: 5m 5g 1999 9.2g⁴ 5.9m 7g 8.3m* 7.1m 8m² 10.9d⁴ Sep 16] modest
handicapper: won at Hamilton in August: stays 11f: acts on good to firm and good to
soft going: hung markedly final start. *J. S. Goldie*

KIERANS BRIDGE (IRE) 4 ch.f. Arcane (USA) – Rhein Valley (IRE) (Kings **62**
Lake (USA) 133) [1998 66, a76: a12g* a12g² a12g* a14.8g³ 12s⁵ 12m⁵ 12.1m 16.1g **a68**
1999 a12s⁴ a12g⁴ 16g² 16.4s 16.2d 14.4m Sep 8] sturdy filly: fair handicapper: well
beaten after first 3 starts: stays 2m: acts on good to firm going, soft and fibresand:
reportedly gurgled penultimate outing. *A. P. Jarvis*

KIER PARK (IRE) 2 b.c. (Feb 20) Foxhound (USA) 103 – Merlannah (IRE) **107 p**
(Shy Groom (USA)) [1999 6g⁴ 6m² 5s* 5d* Oct 9]
    Recent winners of the Willmott Dixon Cornwallis Stakes at Ascot in
October have hardly gone on to set the world alight as three-year-olds. Indeed,
since the race's abandonment in 1993 due to waterlogging, its winners have
mustered only two successes between them in their second seasons. It could

well be a different matter where the latest winner is concerned. While it was no more than an average renewal and Kier Park showed form probably no better than previous winners Millstream, Mubhij, Easycall, Halmahera and Show Me The Money, there's every reason to think that he'll develop into a smart sprinter at least in the next season, one sure to gain further successes.

Kier Park went to Ascot with three runs under his belt, a promising debut at York followed by a narrow defeat in a minor event at Doncaster and a very easy win when odds on for a maiden at Lingfield. In a thirteen-runner field for the Cornwallis, Kier Park was sent off the second favourite at 4/1, the favourite at 9/4 the Moyglare Stud Stakes third Littlefeather who was dropping back to five furlongs from seven. The latter, under pressure, took a narrow advantage just inside the final two furlongs at which point Kier Park, who had been held up just off the pace, was looking for room. By the time he'd found it, after being switched outside approaching the final furlong, Littlefeather had been passed by The Tatling, who looked the likely winner at this stage. Kier Park, however, was now in full flight and, finding plenty for pressure, he caught The Tatling in the last hundred yards to win by a length and a quarter. The well-made Kier Park was progressing well at this time, and he looks the sort who will go on improving for some time to come.

A 42,000-guinea foal and 75,000-guinea yearling, Kier Park is the third foal of the Irish maiden Merlannah, a half-sister to the high-class sprinter Anita's Prince. Merlannah's first foal Perla Nera (by Distinctly North) has won several races in Italy; her second Iron Mountain (by Scenic) is a fairly useful handicapper who stays eleven and a half furlongs. The grandam Get Ready and

Willmott Dixon Cornwallis Stakes, Ascot—Kier Park confirms himself a smart sprinter in the making with a game victory over The Tatling (checked cap) and Watching (light cap)

H.R.H. Sultan Ahmad Shah's "Kier Park"

Kier Park (IRE) (b.c. Feb 20, 1997)	Foxhound (USA) (b 1991)	Danzig (b 1977)	Northern Dancer Pas de Nom
		Lassie Dear (b 1974)	Buckpasser Gay Missile
	Merlannah (IRE) (b 1989)	Shy Groom (ch 1979)	Blushing Groom Apsara
		Get Ready (b 1973)	On Your Mark La Corsaire

great grandam La Corsaire were both fairly useful winners at five furlongs. Kier Park is from the first crop of the extremely well-bred Foxhound, who showed useful form at up to seven furlongs. Distances of five and six furlongs will be where Kier Park will make his mark, though. He acts on soft and good to firm going. *M. A. Jarvis*

KIGEMA (IRE) 2 ch.f. (Apr 25) Case Law 113 – Grace de Bois (Tap On Wood 130) [1999 a5g⁵ 5s 6g⁴ 6f⁴ 6g* 6m⁵ a7g⁵ a7g a7g⁶ Dec 15] IR 6,000Y: small filly: has a short action: sister to winning sprinter in Sweden and half-sister to several minor winners: dam French 9f winner: modest performer: won seller at Brighton in June: stays 7f: acts on all-weather and good to firm going, probably on soft. *C. N. Allen* — **58** **a52**

KIKA 6 gr.m. Niniski (USA) 125 – Goeswell (Roan Rocket 128) [1998 46d, a37§: a13g² a12g⁵ a16g 11.9d* 11.9g⁴ 11.9g⁵ 12d⁶ 11.5g 12m⁴ 11.6g⁵ 11.9g 11.6f 9.9m 11.9m⁶ 11.1m 14.1s⁶ 11.9s⁶ a12g a12g a13g² a16g 1999 a13g⁴ a12g⁵ 11.9f 11.9f 11.9g 12d a12g 11.9d a12g Oct 25] no recent form: blinkered once: has looked unenthusiastic, and is unreliable. *J. J. Bridger* — **– §**

KILBOWIE HILL 3 b.f. Never So Bold 135 – Out of Hours (Lochnager 132) [1998 58, a65: 5d a5g 6g⁴ 5m* a6g* 5g⁶ a6g³ 6.1d 6m 5s 1999 6m 5g 6m a6g Jul 8] — **50**

smallish, lengthy filly: modest handicapper: best at 5f/6f: acts on fibresand and good to firm going, possibly not on softer than good. *J. L. Eyre*

KILBRANNAN SOUND 2 b.f. (Mar 3) Makbul 104 – Highland Rowena 59 **76** (Royben 125) [1999 5d² 5.1m⁵ 5.2m 5m² 6d³ 6.1m² 6m* 6s Oct 2] 7,500Y: rather leggy, useful-looking filly: fifth foal: sister to useful sprinter Lord Kintyre and half-sister to 3-y-o Highland Blue and 2 winning sprinters, including useful Crofters Ceilidh (by Scottish Reel): dam sprinter: fair performer: placed 4 times in maidens before winning 22-runner sales race at Doncaster (swished tail repeatedly before-hand) in September: likely to prove best at 5f/6f: acts on good to firm and good to soft going. *B. A. McMahon*

KILCREGGAN 5 b.g. Landyap (USA) 112 – Lehmans Lot (Oats 126) [1998 NR **68** 1999 12g⁶ 10f⁵ 8m⁴ 12m 9f⁵ 10.3m³ 10f⁶ 11m⁴ 14.1g⁶ 14.1g* 14.1g Oct 15] rangy gelding: second foal: dam, second in bumper, is half-sister to Mellottie (smart around 9f): modest form in bumpers: fair handicapper on Flat: caught eye on occasions before winning at Redcar in October: stays 1¾m: raced only on good going or firmer: has worn crossed noseband. *Mrs M. Reveley*

KILCULLEN LAD (IRE) 5 b.g. Fayruz 116 – Royal Home 69 (Royal Palace **82** 131) [1998 93, a73+: 5.1g 5g* 5m 5s 5g 5f² 6g 5m⁴ 5f⁵ 5.2g 5s⁴ a5g⁵ a7g⁴ 1999 6m **a–** 6m 6g⁶ 5m 5.3s* 5m 5g⁵ 5.7f² 5d³dⁱˢ 6d 5d⁶ 5d Oct 28] smallish, workmanlike gelding: fairly useful handicapper on turf, fair on all-weather: won at Brighton in August: generally remained in form: effective at 5f/6f: acts on firm and soft going and equitrack: usually visored, blinkered once at 2 yrs: has been bandaged: takes hold, and tends to hang right: usually held up. *R. Ingram*

KILDEE GEM 3 b.g. Minshaanshu Amad (USA) 91§ – To The Point 96 (Sharpen **–** Up 127) [1998 55: 6g 8v 1999 7g 5g a6f Oct 2] small, leggy gelding: modest form in maidens at 2 yrs: no show since. *R. G. Frost*

KILKEE BAY (IRE) 2 ch.f. (Apr 8) Case Law 113 – Persian Polly 99 (Persian **61** Bold 123) [1999 5g 5.7m⁶ 7m³ 6m³ 5.1g³ 6m⁴ 5.2m 5v Sep 24] 24,000Y: lengthy filly: half-sister to several winners, notably top-class sprinter Lake Coniston (by Bluebird): dam Irish 2-y-o 7f winner: modest maiden: may prove best at 5f/6f: acts on good to firm going, ran poorly on heavy. *M. R. Channon*

KILLARNEY JAZZ 4 b.g. Alhijaz 122 – Killarney Belle (USA) (Irish Castle **53** (USA)) [1998 –, a68: a6g⁴ a6g⁶ a8g* a8g* a8g⁴ 8f a8g⁴ 1999 a8g⁵ a8g⁴ a8.5g³ a7g⁴ **a68** a8g³ a9.4g⁴ a8g⁴ a8g² 8d a7g⁴ a9.4g⁴ Nov 17] angular gelding: fair on all-weather, modest on turf: mostly creditable efforts in 1999, leaving N. Littmoden after fifth start: off 6 months before final one: stays 9.4f: acts on fibresand and good to soft going: usually blinkered/visored: tough and consistent. *G. C. H. Chung*

KILLEEN FOX (IRE) 2 b.g. (Mar 24) Foxhound (USA) 103 – Charrua 55 **61** (Sharpo 132) [1999 5.1m³ 5.1m⁴ 5.1g⁴ 6.1m⁶ 5m a5g a5f⁵ Oct 2] IR 11,000Y: tall, workmanlike gelding: second foal: dam lightly-raced maiden: modest maiden: should prove best at 5f: acts on fibresand, raced only on good/good to firm going on turf: blinkered (found little) final start. *J. A. Glover*

KILLER INSTINCT 3 b.c. Zafonic (USA) 130 – Rappa Tap Tap (FR) 111 **111** (Tap On Wood 130) [1998 96p: 7g² 1999 8m² 8.2m* 8f⁴ 8m⁴ 10.4f⁵ Jul 10]

Depending on who you were, it either proved supremely ironic or simply inspired when the owners of a colt by Zafonic out of Rappa Tap Tap decided to call him Killer Instinct. Purely as a racehorse, the killer instinct was something which this colt most conspicuously lacked. As a betting medium, his lethal qualities were hard to exaggerate. Put another way, Killer Instinct found winning an almost insuperable problem, managing to lose on all but one occasion as a heavily-backed favourite or joint favourite; furthermore, he was also the subject of a major gamble, not once but twice, for another race he never ran in.

That race for which Killer Instinct didn't make the line-up was the Two Thousand Guineas. Killer Instinct was favourite, as low as 8/1, for the classic before he had even had his first outing as a two-year-old, in a maiden at Ascot in July. Additional gory details are that the bookmakers had been fielding bets on him since the start of May, that bets of £1,000 or more had been raining in since the start of July, and that he was beaten on that racecourse debut at 9/4-on. 'Once bitten twice shy' was alas not applied so often as it might have been with this horse, and Killer Instinct was again the big market mover for the Guineas in the spring, this time from 25/1 into as short as 4/1 favourite. He had not been seen on the racecourse since Ascot but the gallops watchers were once again singing his praises. His Ascot conqueror Compton Admiral had just won the Craven, but Killer Instinct had been as low as 6/1 even before that. When Killer Instinct himself reappeared it was in a maiden at Newbury on the same card for which stable-mate Enrique (available at 7/1 for the Guineas) would normally have been the centre of attention in the Greenham. Enrique won and ninety minutes later Killer Instinct, beaten two lengths by Alrassaam at 5/2-on, was removed from the classic betting.

Using one's eyes rather than one's ears represents a sound foundation for an education in racing, and the exploits of Killer Instinct should have brought many more around to that way of thinking. For racecourse achievement in this case, there is not a great deal more to write about. The Irish Guineas was mentioned as the next suitable target after Newbury, but Killer Instinct went to Nottingham instead for another maiden race. He won in good style, but, although there were £25,650 in recorded bets on him, at odds of 7/1-on he did not really offer much of an opportunity for recompense to punters. Without an excuse, he was beaten into fourth of six when 11/8 joint-favourite in a listed race at Kempton. With a plausible excuse, he was fourth of eleven in the St James's Palace Stakes; putting up his best effort, Killer Instinct (at 9/1 from 14/1) finished seven and a quarter lengths behind the winner Sendawar at Royal Ascot, staying on strongly after clipping the heels of the horse in front of him and stumbling quite badly entering the straight. That conspicuous mishap encouraged a surge of enthusiasm for his prospects off a handicap mark of 98 in the John Smith's Cup over an extended mile and a quarter at York in July. It also, however, helped to gloss over the fact that Killer Instinct had been off the bridle virtually throughout in the St James's Palace, and sadly this, rather than his being 12-lb well in (the York weights came out before the St James's Palace), was the overriding feature of his performance in the John Smith's. Backed heavily (ante-post and on the day) into favouritism at 7/4, Killer Instinct stayed on into fifth late on. He was despatched to the United States shortly afterwards and bookmakers showed that they had a sense of humour by quoting him at 40/1 for the Breeders' Cup Classic. Not all British punters will have shared the joke.

Killer Instinct (b.c. 1996)	Zafonic (USA) (b 1990)	Gone West (b 1984)	Mr Prospector
			Secrettame
		Zaizafon (ch 1982)	The Minstrel
			Mofida
	Rappa Tap Tap (FR) (ch 1981)	Tap On Wood (ch 1976)	Sallust
			Cat O' Mountaine
		Reprocolor (ch 1976)	Jimmy Reppin
			Blue Queen

A big, close-coupled, good-topped colt, Killer Instinct is impressive when he walks around the parade ring. He looked in outstanding condition at York, incidentally. In his faster paces, his long stride makes a striking sight and one can sympathise with the Newmarket touts, one of whom wrote on John Smith's day that 'Those who have criticised Killer Instinct all season will have their words rammed down their throats this afternoon when the horse wins the 40th John Smith's Cup at York ... Don't listen to the doom merchants, few of whom have seen him use his raking stride to good effect on the Limekilns gallops.' Perhaps there was a physical excuse for his failure to reproduce the same effect on the racecourse. He didn't race after Ascot as a two-year-old due to what was described as 'teething problems', and he wasn't seen in action again once sent to the United States. His career there will be watched with great interest, as, thirty years earlier, was that of another 'bookies' friend' Ribofilio, who left Britain with the distinction of having been the beaten favourite in four classics. For the record, Ribofilio ran eleven times in the United States as a four-year-old and was successful twice, notably when setting a track record over nine furlongs at Monmouth in the (now Grade 3) Longfellow Handicap. Killer Instinct was a 260,000-guinea yearling and comes from a famous family—his grandam is Reprocolor. Godolphin paid 250,000 guineas at the Houghton Sales for Killer Instinct's half-brother by Polish Precedent and his dam Rappa Tap Tap also had a two-year-old colt by Indian Ridge (named Indian Beat) in training with Sir Michael Stoute in 1999 but he never ran. The more unforgiving punters may wish the same could have been said of Killer Instinct. *H. R. A. Cecil*

KILMEENA LAD   3 b.g. Minshaanshu Amad (USA) 91§ – Kilmeena Glen (Beveled (USA)) [1998 78: 8s 7d 6v* 5d 1999 6g 6g 6g³ 5.1d 6g 6g 6m* 6s a6g* 7s a6g a6g⁴ Dec 22] good-quartered gelding: fairly useful handicapper: won at Newmarket (apprentice race) in August and Lingfield in October: stays 6f: acts on good to firm going, heavy and equitrack: usually held up. *E. A. Wheeler*   **81**   **a86**

KILTING   3 ch.f. Nashwan (USA) 135 – Balliasta (USA) (Lyphard (USA) 132) [1998 87P: 7d* 1999 10m³ 12d 12g 8v* Nov 4] angular, good-bodied filly: failed to confirm fully 2-y-o promise in 1999 and soundly beaten in Oaks at Epsom (still wrong in coat) and Prix de Malleret at Longchamp (final start for Saeed bin Suroor) after third in listed race at Newmarket on reappearance: won minor event at Nantes in November after 4-month break: stays 1¼m: acts on good to firm and heavy ground. *N. Clement, France*   **96**

KIMBERLEY   4 b.g. Shareef Dancer (USA) 135 – Willowbank 66 (Gay Fandango (USA) 132) [1998 90: 10d 12m² 12g⁶ 12m⁴ 16.2m⁴ 14.8g⁶ 10.4g* 10v* 1999 10.5d 10.3g 10m 10.1m 11.6g 10.1m Oct 19] heavy-topped gelding: has a round action: fairly useful performer at 3 yrs: little form in 1999: should stay beyond 1½m: acts on heavy and good to firm going: blinkered twice, including final start: sold 35,000 gns. *G. Wragg*   **–**

KINAN (USA)   3 b.c. Dixieland Band (USA) – Alsharta (USA) (Mr Prospector (USA)) [1998 89p: 6g⁶ 6m² 6m⁶ 6.1d* 1999 6g 6m 7g⁵ 8.1m May 29] quite attractive colt: fairly useful form: creditable efforts in handicaps on first and third starts in 1999: should prove best at 6f/7f: acts on good to soft going: possibly not an easy ride: sold 5,500 gns in October. *R. W. Armstrong*   **88**

KIND EMPEROR   2 br.g. (Apr 5) Emperor Jones (USA) 119 – Kind Lady 56 (Kind of Hush 118) [1999 5d³ 5m² 5f² 6s² 6g⁵ 6m a6g⁴ 5d² 5g 6g 5g 5.1d² 6d a5g³ Nov 12] 9,200F, 10,000Y: leggy, sparely-made gelding: fifth foal: half-brother to fairly useful 7f winner Amadeus Aes (by Dublin Lad) and 1½m winner Hush Baby (by Ballacashtal): dam 2-y-o 6f seller winner who probably stayed 1½m: fair maiden: will prove best at 5f/6f: acts on fibresand, best turf efforts on good ground or softer: often forces pace. *M. J. Polglase*   **76**   **a66**

KIND PRINCE   7 b.g. Kind of Hush 118 – Silent Princess (King of Spain 121) [1998 NR 1999 a8g Mar 19] leggy gelding: poor maiden in 1994: behind only Flat run since, though has won over hurdles. *R. M. Whitaker*   **–**

KIND REGARDS (IRE)   2 b.f. (Apr 22) Unfuwain (USA) 131 – Barari (USA) (Blushing Groom (FR) 131) [1999 7f 6g⁵ 8.3m² 7.5g* 7d⁴ Sep 28] tall, attractive filly: seventh living foal: half-sister to several winners, including 3-y-o Fair Flight and 4-y-o White Heart (both by Green Desert) and fairly useful 1½m winner Generous Gift (later successful in USA, by Generous): dam unraced half-sister to very smart French 1m/1¼m performer Colour Chart: fairly useful form: won maiden at Beverley in September by 5 lengths, edged left: sweating, edgy and early to post, creditable fourth of 19 in nursery at Newmarket final start, finishing best, despite tending to carry head awkwardly, having been short of room: should stay 1¼m: acts on good to soft going: probably capable of better still. *M. Johnston*   **88 p**

KIND SIR   3 b.g. Generous (IRE) 139 – Noble Conquest (USA) (Vaguely Noble 140) [1998 71p: 8m 8d⁵ 1999 a10g* a10g⁴ Mar 4] quite attractive gelding: has a   **78**

round action: fair performer: comfortable winner of 6-runner maiden at Lingfield in February: will stay beyond 1¼m: joined R. Dickin. *B. W. Hills*

KING ADAM (IRE) 3 b.c. Fairy King (USA) – Sailor's Mate 114 (Shirley **115** Heights 130) [1998 108p: 7.1m² 7g² 8d* 1999 10m* 12f⁶ Jul 27] sturdy, attractive colt: smart performer: won 8-runner listed race at Kempton on belated reappearance in June by 1¾ lengths from Prolix, responding well for pressure: last of 6 when odds on for Gordon Stakes at Goodwood and later found to be lame behind: should stay 1½m: acts on good to firm and good to soft ground: seemed unsuited by course at Chester second 2-y-o start. *Sir Michael Stoute*

KINGCHIP BOY 10 b.g. Petong 126 – Silk St James (Pas de Seul 133) [1998 52, **–** a76d: a8s a8g a8g* a7g* a8g a7g* a7g⁴ a7g⁶ a7g³ 6.9d⁴ 9.7s 8s 8d⁴ a8g 8g⁴ 7g 8d 8m **a69** 8m a8.5g 7m⁵ a7g a8g 7s a8g⁵ 1999 a8g⁵ a8g a8g* a8f a7f* a8g⁴ a7g⁵ a8.5g* a8g* a8g⁵ 8f a7g⁴ a9.4g* 7d a7g a9.4g a8g Dec 13] compact gelding: unimpressive mover: fair performer on all-weather: won handicaps and claimer at Southwell and seller and claimer at Wolverhampton from January to May: well below form last 4 starts: effective at 7f to 9.7f: acts on all-weather, lightly raced and no form on turf in 1999: effective in blinkers/visor or not (wore neither for all 1999 wins): often forces pace, and sometimes wanders. *M. J. Ryan*

KING CURAN (USA) 8 b.g. Lear Fan (USA) 130 – Runaway Lady (USA) **–** (Caucasus (USA) 127) [1998 –: 10g 12.1g 11.7d⁶ 1999 10s Apr 19] sturdy, good-bodied gelding: one-time fair handicapper: little show since 1996. *A. G. Juckes*

KING DARIUS (IRE) 4 ch.g. Persian Bold 123 – Valiant Friend (USA) (Shah- **102** rastani (USA) 135) [1998 86: 9d* 12m³ 10.1g 10g 11.6f* 10.3m⁵ 10g 10v 1999 12.5s⁶ 10g 10m³ 10.3m* 10f* 8m 10g² 11g³ 10m³ 10s Oct 2] strong gelding: useful handicapper: better than ever in 1999, well ridden by R. Hughes to win at Chester and Kempton in May: good efforts when placed after in Hong Kong Jockey Club Trophy at Sandown (second to Mouhtahdee) then rated stakes and Courage Handicap (third to Komistar) at Newbury: effective at 1¼m/easy 1½m: acts on firm and soft going: held up: reliable: sent to USA. *R. Hannon*

KINGDOM EMPEROR 5 b.g. Forzando 122 – Wrangbrook (Shirley Heights **37** 130) [1998 NR 1999 14.6m Jul 2] good-topped gelding: has a round action: modest maiden at 3 yrs: well held in handicap at Warwick only Flat run of 1999: stays 1¾m: acts on good to firm ground: has shown temperament, pulling too hard only try in visor: fair handicap hurdler (though far from easy ride). *W. Clay*

KINGDOM OF GOLD (USA) 2 b.c. (Apr 21) Gone West (USA) – Aviara **79** (USA) (Cox's Ridge (USA)) [1999 7.5g⁴ 8.3f* 8d⁶ Sep 17] tall, quite attractive colt: has scope: third foal: half-brother to 3-y-o Prokofiev: dam, French 9f winner, out of close relative to Ajdal and half-sister to Formidable and grandam of Arazi: fair form: won maiden at Hamilton in August: respectable sixth of 20 in nursery at Ayr only subsequent outing: should stay beyond 1m: acts on firm going. *Sir Mark Prescott*

KINGDOM RUBY (IRE) 4 ch.f. Bluebird (USA) 125 – Tapestry (Tap On **69** Wood 130) [1998 70: 7d⁶ 6g⁵ 6d² 6v⁶ 7v* a7g³ a8.5g⁶ 1999 6d² 7s 6m Jun 24] fair handicapper: below form after reappearance: barely stays 8.5f: acts on fibresand, raced only on good going or softer on turf. *Miss J. A. Camacho*

KINGFISHER GOLD (IRE) 3 b.g. Perugino (USA) 84 – Cerosia (Pitskelly **–** 122) [1998 60+: 5m 6d 1999 8s 6m 7.5v 5.9g 10.4d 10.1d Oct 20] tall, angular gelding: modest maiden: little form in 1999: headstrong: sometimes slowly away. *T. P. Tate*

KINGFISHERS BONNET 3 b.f. Hamas (IRE) 125§ – Mainmast 63 (Bustino **51** 136) [1998 64d: 5v³ 6.1m³ 7.1m 6g 6s⁴ 7d 6s 1999 6m 9.7v⁵ 8.3g 11.8m⁶ 11.7g⁶ 10.2g² a12g 12.1m 10g² 10s⁶ 10d² 10d⁴ Oct 28] modest maiden handicapper: seems not to stay 1½m: acts on good to soft going, probably on good to firm: inconsistent. *S. G. Knight*

KING FLYER (IRE) 3 b.g. Ezzoud (IRE) 126 – Al Guswa 98 (Shernazar 131) **79** [1998 63d: 6g⁵ 7.5g⁴ a7g 10s 1999 a8g³ a10g² a10g³ a10g* 10m* 12f² 12m³ 14.1m² **a67** 14.8d Oct 15] leggy gelding: fair performer: won claimer at Newmarket in June: good second in handicaps at Folkestone and Nottingham after: stays 1¾m: acts on equitrack (well beaten both starts on fibresand), possibly needs good going or firmer on turf: blinkered once at 2 yrs: tongue tied final 2 starts. *H. J. Collingridge*

KING FOR A DAY 3 b.g. Machiavellian (USA) 123 – Dizzy Heights (USA) **67 d**
(Danzig (USA)) [1998 72: 7m 7d⁶ 6v³ 1999 9m⁶ 11.6g 11.4m 8m 8g 14.1g Sep 25]
quite good-topped gelding: fair maiden handicapper: below form after reappearance:
left B. Hills before final start: stays 9f: acts on heavy and good to firm going:
blinkered third and fifth outings. *Bob Jones*

KING KATO 6 b.g. Unfuwain (USA) 131 – Sharmood (USA) (Sharpen Up 127) **87**
[1998 NR 1999 10s³ Oct 22] big gelding: has a long stride: fairly useful performer:
first run for 2 years when encouraging third of 16 in handicap at Newbury, though
put head in air when first ridden: stays 1½m: has won on good to firm ground, may
prove best on good or softer: has clearly had his problems. *Mrs A. J. Perrett*

KING MIDAS 3 b.c. Bluebird (USA) 125 – Ellebanna 69 (Tina's Pet 121) [1998 **100**
NR 1999 8.1d² 7.1d* 8m² 7g 7.1s Sep 25] 90,000Y: leggy, useful-looking colt: third
foal: half-brother to fairly useful 7f winner (including at 2 yrs) Gift of Gold (by
Statoblest): dam sprinting half-sister to 3 useful/smart sprinters: useful performer:
won maiden at Haydock in July, and ran well when second to Al Fahda in minor
event at Salisbury: disappointing in handicaps after, sweating and edgy on penultimate start (also hung away from rail): may prove best up to 1m: has been bandaged:
sent to UAE. *E. A. L. Dunlop*

KING OF BABYLON (IRE) 7 b.g. Persian Heights 129 – My My Marie –
(Artaius (USA) 129) [1998 NR 1999 a14.8g Jan 27] useful-looking gelding: little
form on Flat: poor winning hurdler (has refused to race): one to avoid. *F. Jordan*

KING OF MOMMUR (IRE) 4 b.g. Fairy King (USA) – Monoglow (Kalaglow **72 d**
132) [1998 75: 8s 10m 12.1m³ 14d⁶ 12g³ 12m 1999 16g 14.1s 12g³ 16.2m⁵ 16.4m
11.6m 10f 10m⁶ 12m Sep 8] lengthy, angular gelding: fair maiden handicapper: ran
poorly final 5 starts: stays 2m: acts on good to firm going: no form in blinkers: has
worn tongue strap. *B. J. Meehan*

KING OF PERU 6 br.g. Inca Chief (USA) – Julie's Star (IRE) 45 (Thatching **79**
131) [1998 83, a99: 6s a5g² 6g a6g³ 6d 5m⁴ 5f⁵ 6g 7d 1999 a6g 5d 6g 6v a5g 6s 6g² **a89**
6f* 6g³ 6m 6g⁵ 5m³ 5.7m⁶ 6f 5.1h³ 5d³ 5.2g² 5g 6g 6d 5s² 5g² Oct 2] tall, leggy
gelding: has a quick action: fairly useful handicapper: won at Brighton in May:
generally ran at least respectably otherwise: effective at 5f to 7f: acts on fibresand,
soft and hard going: effective blinkered/visored or not. *N. P. Littmoden*

KING OF TUNES (FR) 7 b.h. Chief Singer 131 – Marcotte (Nebos (GER) 129) **76 §**
[1998 93: 8d² 8.1g⁵ 8d 9d 8m⁴ 9g 1999 8m 8g 10s³ 8g 8m⁶ 10m 8d 10m 10s a10g⁴ **a61 §**
a8g⁶ Dec 13] angular horse: fair handicapper on turf, modest on all-weather: easily
best effort in 1999 at Newbury third start: effective at 1m to 1¼m: acts on equitrack,
firm and soft going: blinkered twice in 1998: often early to post: usually held up:
looked moody final start: none too consistent. *J. J. Sheehan*

KING O' THE MANA (IRE) 2 b.c. (Feb 2) Turtle Island (IRE) 123 – Olivia **100 +**
Jane (IRE) (Ela-Mana-Mou 132) [1999 6d⁶ 6.8m* 7.3g² 8g* 8d⁶ Oct 9] IR 25,000Y:
sturdy, quite attractive colt: third foal: closely related to 4-y-o Santone and half-
brother to 13.8f seller winner Ziggy's Viola (by Roi Danzig): dam unraced half-sister

*Hennessy Cognac Blaydon Race (Nursery Handicap), Newcastle—King o' The Mana interrupts the winning
sequence of the unlucky-in-running French Fellow, as he scores a comfortable success under John Reid*

to smart middle-distance stayer Luchiroverte from family of Old Vic: useful performer: won maiden at Warwick in July and valuable nursery at Newcastle in August: bit below form in listed race at Ascot final start: likely to be well suited by 1¼m/1½m: acts on good to firm going: may do better yet. *R. Hannon*

KING PERI (IRE) 3 b.g. Fairy King (USA) – Maria Roberta (USA) (Roberto (USA) 131) [1998 49: 5d 5s 7.1m⁴ 7m⁴ 7g 7.9g 1999 12d Apr 28] tall, dipped-backed gelding: has a round action: poor maiden: stays 7f: pulls hard and is a difficult ride. *N. Tinkler* — —

KING PRIAM (IRE) 4 b.g. Priolo (USA) 127 – Barinia (Corvaro (USA) 124) [1998 75: 8g⁴ 8g⁵ 10g⁵ 10g² 12f³ 9m 12.1m³ 12g* 9.7s² 12v⁶ 11d⁵ a12g 1999 a11g² a12g³ a11g² a12g⁴ a11f⁶ a9.4g³ a9.4g⁵ a8g* 10.3d² a8.5g³ 10m⁴ 10.3m 10.4s 8.9d 10f 10.3g 10d² 7.9f 12m⁵ 10.1m⁴ 10m 7.5g 12g 8g* 8.1s* 10.4g* 8.9d³ 10d⁵ 8s²ᵈⁱˢ a8g* a8.5g* a9.4g* a12g⁵ a9.4g² Dec 27] sturdy gelding: useful performer: had an excellent campaign in 1999, winning handicaps at Southwell (2), Haydock, York and Wolverhampton (2) and minor event at Leicester between March and December: good second to Weet-A-Minute in another handicap at Wolverhampton final start: best at 1m/1¼m: acts on good to firm going, soft and fibresand: usually blinkered: very tough. *M. J. Polglase* 100

KINGRHUMBA (USA) 3 b.c. Kingmambo (USA) 125 – Lady Ice (CAN) (Vice Regent (CAN)) [1998 64: 7g 8m 1999 8s 9.9g 11m* 12m⁵ 9.9m⁴ 11.5f³ 14.1g a16g* a16g² Aug 20] smallish, useful-looking colt: has a quick action: fairly useful on all-weather, fair on turf: won maiden at Redcar in June and handicap at Lingfield (by a distance) in August: stays 2m: acts on good to firm going and equitrack: visored/blinkered second to seventh starts: has been bandaged behind: sold 18,000 gns, sent to Macau. *J. Noseda* 74 a80

KINGSALSA (USA) 3 br.c. Kingmambo (USA) 125 – Caretta (Caro 133) [1998 111: 7g² 7.5d² 8s⁴ 7s² 1999 8d* 8m³ 10g⁵ Jun 27] tall, rather leggy colt: smart performer: trained by P. Demercastel at 2 yrs: won minor event at Longchamp in April: good 4½ lengths third to Sendawar in Poule d'Essai des Poulains there following month: should stay 1¼m (disappointing in Grand Prix de Paris when tried): has form on soft and good to firm going, though gives impression may not take much racing on latter (not a good walker/mover and has been bandaged behind). *A. Fabre, France* 116

KINGS ARROW (IRE) 4 b.c. Mujadil (USA) 119 – Great Leighs 87 (Vaigly Great 127) [1998 69: 7d 8v⁵ 7m 8m 6g² 6.1g 6m a10g³ a10g⁵ a10g* 1999 a10g* a10g³ a10g² a10g² a10g a10g⁶ a10g 10s a10g⁴ May 29] leggy, useful-looking colt: fair performer: won minor event at Lingfield in January: stayed 1¼m: acted on equitrack and good to soft going: dead. *P. Howling* — a69

KING'S BEST (USA) 2 b.c. (Jan 24) Kingmambo (USA) 125 – Allegretta 101 (Lombard (GER) 126) [1999 7g* 7m* 7g⁵ Oct 16] 112 p

In the space of a month King's Best went from being described by his owner's racing manager as 'a very relaxed individual with a marvellous attitude' to a 'head-case'. The reappraisal was caused by the colt's headstrong performance in the Dewhurst Stakes, in which he completely failed to live up to the good impression he had made on his first two starts, when his performances put him near the top of the ante-post lists for the Two Thousand Guineas.

King's Best's tall home reputation preceded him to the racecourse and he was sent off a short-priced favourite on his debut in August in an eight-runner Newmarket maiden. King's Best was in front all the way and needed only to be shaken up to stretch clear for an easy two-length win over Jalad, with the well-regarded Alasan three and a half lengths further back in third. King's Best was odds-on for the Breckenbrough Racing Acomb Stakes at York later in the month when once again marking himself down as a fine prospect. Again soon in front, King's Best set a good pace and forged ahead through the last two furlongs to beat Shamrock City and the subsequent Prix de la Salamandre runner-up Race Leader by two lengths and a neck.

Kieren Fallon took over from Gary Stevens on King's Best for the first time in the Dewhurst and tried to restrain him, but, in a slowly-run affair, the

colt fought hard for his head in the early stages and managed only a short-lived challenge before finishing last of the five runners, beaten over five and a half lengths by Distant Music. A disappointing end to a promising season.

		Mr Prospector	Raise A Native
	Kingmambo (USA)	(b 1970)	Gold Digger
	(b 1990)	Miesque	Nureyev
King's Best (USA)		(b 1984)	Pasadoble
(b.c. Jan 24, 1997)		Lombard	Agio
	Allegretta	(ch 1967)	Promised Lady
	(ch 1978)	Anatevka	Espresso
		(ch 1969)	Almyra

King's Best cost 2,300,000 francs as a yearling and is by El Condor Pasa's sire Kingmambo. King's Best's dam, Allegretta, a sister to the German St Leger winner Anno from a highly successful Germany family, was also trained by Sir Michael Stoute, for whom she came second in the Lingfield Oaks Trial. Allegretta was sold for 24,000 guineas to race in America and has subsequently found fame as a broodmare through the exploits of her Prix de l'Arc winning daughter Urban Sea (by Miswaki), as well as the ten and a half furlong Prix de Flore winner Allez Les Trois (by Riverman). Allegretta's daughters are also proving their worth as broodmares, Urban Sea producing the Gallinule Stakes winner Urban Ocean and her listed-placed half-sister Turbaine (by Trempolino) being responsible for the four-year-old Tertullian, a smart six and seven furlong performer, as well as Terek, a useful mile and a quarter performer in Germany, both successful in Group 3 company in the latest season. The rangy, handsome King's Best is a fine mover with plenty of scope. He will have to be taught to settle or perhaps revert to front-running tactics if he is to reach his full potential, but, on pedigree at least, he should stay at least a mile. He could still take a hand in good races provided his Dewhurst performance was an aberration. *Sir Michael Stoute*

KINGS CAY (IRE)   8 b.g. Taufan (USA) 119 – Provocation 66 (Kings Lake (USA) 133) [1998 64: 10s 11.9g 13g² 12.3s⁶ 12d³ 14.1m² 12.1g 13.9g 1999 14m 12d 12.3m 12m 12g 12.1f 12.1m Sep 6] useful-looking gelding: formerly fair performer: little form in 1999: changed hands 700 gns in November. *T. H. Caldwell*   – §

KING'S CHAMBERS   3 ch.g. Sabrehill (USA) 120 – Flower Girl 108 (Pharly (FR) 130) [1998 –: 6.1d 1999 a6g a11g Dec 17] blinkered, well held in maidens. *R. F. Marvin*   –

KINGSCLERE   2 b.c. (Mar 9) Fairy King (USA) – Spurned (USA) 91 (Robellino (USA) 127) [1999 6d* 7f* 7f⁴ 7.1g³ 8m² 8s³ Sep 26] tall, attractive colt: good walker: has a quick action: sixth foal: half-brother to several winners, including 6-y-o Jona Holley and smart pair by Selkirk 7f/1m performer Hidden Meadow and 7f/1½m winner Scorned: dam stayed 1¼m: useful performer: won minor events at Newbury in June and York in July: good efforts last 3 starts, making running when 2½ lengths   **104**

third of 6 to Royal Kingdom in Royal Lodge Stakes at Ascot final one: stays 1m: acts on firm and soft going: reluctant stalls and well below form third start: briefly planted himself in paddock at Ascot: has worn fulmar bridle over Australian noseband. *I. A. Balding*

KINGSDON (IRE)   2 b.c. (Feb 25) Brief Truce (USA) 126 – Richly Deserved (IRE) (Kings Lake (USA) 133) [1999 6d² 6s* 7g² 7.1d³ 7v* Sep 29] 67,000F, 75,000Y: sixth foal: half-brother to 3-y-o Alizee and 2 winners abroad, including French 10.5f/1½m winner Kastelorizo (by Alzao): dam unraced half-sister to high-class winner up to 1¼m here and in USA Star Pastures: fairly useful performer: won maiden at Kempton in August and minor event at Salisbury in September: will stay 1m: raced only on good ground or softer (acts on heavy): consistent. *R. Hannon*   **93**

KING'S DRAGOON (IRE)   3 ch.c. College Chapel 122 – Indigo Blue (IRE) 56 (Bluebird (USA) 125) [1998 NR 1999 5s 8.1m Jun 29] IR 15,000F, IR 9,000Y: fourth foal: half-brother to 4-y-o Ho Leng (by Statoblest) and 9f winner Major Dundee (by Distinctly North): dam sprint maiden half-sister to Mistertopogigo: always behind in claimer (slowly away) and seller: tongue tied on debut. *M. R. Channon*   **–**

KINGSFOLD BLAZE   4 b.f. Mazilier (USA) 107 – Kingsfold Flame 103 (No Loiterer 90) [1998 63: 7s 8.3m⁶ 8.1m³ 8.5d³ 9.9m 1999 8.5s 10s⁶ 11.5g 11.6g⁶ Jul 5] angular filly: has a round action: modest form in maidens in 1998: only poor in 1999: probably stays 1½m: acts on good to firm going, probably on soft: visored (very stiff task) final start. *M. J. Haynes*   **–**

KINGSFOLD PET   10 b.g. Tina's Pet 121 – Bella Lisa (River Chanter 121) [1998 47: 15.4v² 1999 15.4v Apr 20] tall, rangy gelding: poor handicapper, lightly raced on Flat: suited by a test of stamina: acts on heavy ground. *M. J. Haynes*   **–**

KING'S GINGER   2 ch.g. (Mar 13) King's Signet (USA) 110 – Cosset 56 (Comedy Star (USA) 121) [1999 5.1m⁵ 7m³ 7g 8g³ 8.3g 7g⁵ Oct 19] 1,500Y: ninth living foal: half-brother to useful 1¼m/1½m winner Billet (by Nicholas Bill), all-weather 1m/1¼m winner Brackenthwaite (by Faustus): dam very lightly raced: modest maiden: left H. Candy after second outing: stays 1m: joined D. Wintle. *P. R. Chamings*   **62**

KINGS HARMONY (IRE)   6 b.g. Nordico (USA) – Kingston Rose (Tudor Music 131) [1998 63, a79d: a7g* a7g² a6g a7g 7d 7f 6f⁵ 7m 7g 6g a7g 1999 a7g² a8g a8g Mar 18] lengthy gelding: modest performer: below form after reappearance: effective at 6f/7f: acts on firm going and all-weather: blinkered once: usually races prominently: inconsistent. *R. Ingram*   **63**

KING'S HUSSAR   4 b.g. Be My Chief (USA) 122 – Croire (IRE) 74 (Lomond (USA) 128) [1998 54: 9.7d⁶ 12s² 14.1m⁴ a16g 17.2d 1999 12.3m Apr 7] leggy gelding: modest maiden handicapper at best: stays 1¾m: acts on good to firm going and fibresand: blinkered/visored last 4 starts: modest hurdler (successful in November). *G. M. Moore*   **–**

KING SLAYER   4 b.c. Batshoof 122 – Top Sovereign (High Top 131) [1998 98: 7d* 8s³ 7.6m² 8d 7.6m² 7.3m² 8d² 7.3m 10g 1999 8.1s⁵ 8.5f⁵ 8f³ 9f* 11f³ 6.5f³ 6.5f² 8f² Dec 19] well-made colt: useful performer: creditable 8 lengths fifth of 9 to Handsome Ridge in Group 2 event at Sandown (final start for B. Smart) on reappearance in April: awarded allowance race at Del Mar in August: stays 9f: acts on firm and soft going: blinkered last 4 starts: usually held up. *D. Vienna, USA*   **98**

KING'S MILL (IRE)   2 b.c. (Jan 30) Doyoun 124 – Adarika (Kings Lake (USA) 133) [1999 7m 7.5g² 8s² 8d³ Oct 15] IR 15,000Y: angular colt: poor walker, but good mover: sixth foal: brother to smart French 9f (at 2 yrs)/1¼m winner Adaiyka and half-brother to 3 winners abroad: dam unraced: fairly useful maiden: good third of 20 in nursery at Newmarket final start: will stay beyond 1m: acts on soft ground. *N. A. Graham*   **81**

KING SPINNER (IRE)   2 b.c. (May 17) Mujadil (USA) 119 – Money Spinner (USA) 61 (Teenoso (USA) 135) [1999 7g³ 7d⁴ 8d⁵ 8d* Oct 27] IR 16,000Y: third living foal: half-brother to Italian winner up to 9f Windy Day (by Waajib) and Italian 3-y-o 1¼m winner Money Secret (by Paris House): dam 1m winner: fairly useful form: won maiden at Yarmouth in October: not sure to stay much beyond 1m: raced only on good/good to soft going: front runner. *A. P. Jarvis*   **81**

KINGSTON BILL   2 b.g. (Mar 3) Then Again 126 – Tricata (Electric 126) [1999 5d* 5v³ 7.5s⁶ 7g Oct 16] sixth foal: half-brother to 3-y-o Kingston Venture: dam   **73**

unraced: fair form: won maiden at Newcastle in March: well beaten last 2 starts, off course over 3 months before final one: should stay at least 7f. *W. G. M. Turner*

KINGSTON VENTURE   3 b.g. Interrex (CAN) – Tricata (Electric 126) [1998   **99**
74: 6m[4] 7m* 7.1g[6] 8m[6] 1999 10.3d* 9.9g[6] 12m[2] 11.5g* 13.9g 12v[5] Sep 20] good-bodied gelding: useful performer: won handicap at Doncaster in March and minor event at Lingfield in May: well beaten after 3-month break final 2 starts: should stay beyond 1½m: acts on good to firm and good to soft going. *W. G. M. Turner*

KINGS TO OPEN   2 b.c. (Apr 24) First Trump 118 – Shadiyama 58 (Nishapour   **50 p**
(FR) 125) [1999 6.8d Sep 21] 7,200Y: angular, workmanlike colt: fifth foal: half-brother to a winner in Germany by Never So Bold: dam second over 6f at 2 yrs: seventh of 16 to Jamestown in maiden at Warwick: joined J. Osborne: should do better. *D. Marks*

KINGSTREE   3 b.c. Distant Relative 128 – Sinking (Midyan (USA) 124) [1998   **78**
64p: 6g 6s[3] 1999 7d[4] 6m[2] 7m May 3] small, sturdy colt: fair maiden: ran well second outing: carried head awkwardly when well below par next time: should be suited by 7f/1m: sent to UAE. *J. H. M. Gosden*

KING'S VIEW   2 b.g. (May 14) Distant View (USA) 126 – Migiyas 87 (Kings   **70**
Lake (USA) 133) [1999 8.2d[5] 7d Nov 11] 14,000Y: half-brother to several winners, including 1992 2-y-o 6f winner Break My Heart (by Broken Hearted) and fairly useful 1¾m to 17f winner Nanton Point (by Darshaan): dam 5f (at 2 yrs) and 7f winner: better effort in maidens when fifth of 11 to Alva Glen at Nottingham on debut: should stay at least 1¼m: may still do better. *E. A. L. Dunlop*

KING TIARA (USA)   2 b. or br.c. (May 11) Fairy King (USA) – Cap of Dignity   **– p**
(Shirley Heights 130) [1999 8s Oct 25] tall, close-coupled colt: looked rather weak at 2 yrs: first foal: dam unraced daughter of Washington International runner-up Persian Tiara: 4/1 but burly and green, tenderly handled and shaped much more promisingly than bare result suggests when never dangerous in maiden at Leicester: should stay 1¼m+: type to do better with experience. *H. R. A. Cecil*

KING TUT   3 ch.g. Anshan 119 – Fahrenheit 69 (Mount Hagen (FR) 127) [1998   **–**
NR 1999 7m[6] 7.6f 7d 10.4f Sep 2] 1,500Y: half-brother to several winners, including smart sprinter Farhana (by Fayruz) and fairly useful sprinter Alasib (by Siberian Express): dam ran twice at 3 yrs, placed at 7f/1m: sign of ability only in maiden at Newmarket on debut. *W. Jarvis*

KING UNO   5 b.g. Be My Chief (USA) 122 – The Kings Daughter 79 (Indian King   **69**
(USA) 128) [1998 73: 6.1s 5.9d[6] 5.9s 6g 6s[5] 6.1g* 7m 6m* 7g* 7s[2] 7g[4] 8.2v[4] 7s 1999   **a62**
a6g a7g[4] 7g 8v 6d[5] 8.5d 7g Jun 5] strong, good-topped gelding: good mover: modest handicapper: reportedly lame after final start: effective at 6f to 1m: acts on good to firm ground, heavy and fibresand: tried blinkered, effective visored or not: tends to hang, and can get behind. *E. J. Alston*

KINLANO   3 b.g. Cyrano de Bergerac 120 – Kinlacey 74 (Aragon 118) [1998 67:   **–**
6f[5] 6m[6] 6m 6s 6g[5] 1999 7m 7s a6g 6g Oct 14] rather leggy, good-topped gelding: good mover: fair form at 2 yrs: well held in 1999, including in blinkers: should stay 7f: seems unsuited by soft ground: sold 3,000 gns, sent to Kuwait. *W. Jarvis*

KINNESCASH (IRE)   6 ch.g. Persian Heights 129 – Gayla Orchestra (Lord   **90**
Gayle (USA) 124) [1998 79, a–: 12.3m[2] 20d 11.8f[2] 12m[5] 12m a12g 1999 12s* 12s   **a–**
12g 17.2m 12m* Sep 4] small gelding: fairly useful handicapper: better than ever when winning quite valuable events at Epsom in April (had won valuable handicap hurdle at Aintree earlier in month) and September (by 7 lengths): should stay beyond 1½m (though seemed not to get 2½m): acts on fibresand, hard and soft going: usually races prominently/leads: genuine. *P. Bowen*

KINNINO   5 b.g. Polish Precedent (USA) 131 – On Tiptoes 107 (Shareef Dancer   **44**
(USA) 135) [1998 58p: 8g 9m[6] 8.1m 7m 7m 8g[5] a7g[6] a7g 1999 a7g[5] a7g[3] a7g 7f 9d a10g 7f[5] 7.1m 8m[5] 10d a10g[2] a10g Dec 22] poor maiden: will prove best up to 1¼m: acts on equitrack and good to firm going: blinkered twice. *G. L. Moore*

KINSAILE   2 ro.f. (Mar 10) Robellino (USA) 127 – Snowing 88 (Tate Gallery   **56**
(USA) 117) [1999 5m Apr 19] first foal: dam, 5f winner, from family of Middle Park winner Bassenthwaite: green when eighth of 15 to Launfal in maiden at Windsor: looked likely to do better. *R. Charlton*

KINSMAN (IRE)   2 b.g. (Mar 21) Distant Relative 128 – Besito 79 (Wassl 125)   **67**
[1999 5g 6d 5.1g 7g 6g⁶ 6.1m² 6s* a6g⁵ Oct 8] 10,500F, 8,000Y: fourth foal:
half-brother to 1m winner Simlet (by Forzando) and Italian 5f winner Catnil (by
Statoblest): dam 2m winner: fair performer: won nursery at Brighton in September:
should stay at least 7f: acts on soft and good to firm ground: visored/blinkered 5 of
last 6 starts. *I. A. Balding*

KINTAVI   9 b.g. Efisio 120 – Princess Tavi (Sea Hawk II 131) [1998 60: 12d   **60**
13.8d⁴ 11.8s* 14.1v 13g⁵ 12s² 12g 13d³ 15.9g 1999 11.8s 14.1s⁶ 13.8m* 12g³ 14.6m⁴
Jun 26] close-coupled, good-topped gelding: modest handicapper: won at Catterick
in May: effective at 1½m to 1¾m: acts on firm and soft ground: held up: sometimes
bandaged. *T. W. Donnelly*

KINTBURY   4 b.g. Kylian (USA) – Easter Baby (Derrylin 115) [1998 NR 1999   **60**
a10g⁴ a8g a12g⁴ 11.8s³ 14.1s² a16.2g* May 8] second foal: dam, winning hurdler,
little form on Flat: modest performer: won handicap at Wolverhampton in May: will
stay beyond 2m: acts on fibresand and probably on soft going. *P. D. Cundell*

KIRBY PRINCESS   4 ch.f. Weldnaas (USA) 112 – Lovely Greek Lady (Ela-   **45**
Mana-Mou 132) [1998 52: 6m 7s 10g 12g⁵ 12m 1999 12m 12m⁵ 9.9g Aug 28] big,
angular filly: modest maiden at 3 yrs: below form in handicaps in 1999: probably
stays 1½m: acts on good to firm going. *R. A. Fahey*

KIRILOV (IRE)   4 b.g. Roi Danzig (USA) – Ever So 78 (Mummy's Pet 125)   **–**
[1998 74: 9m⁶ 10m⁶ 10f⁴ 10.1g 1999 10.3f⁵ 10g 7m 12g 10d 10.1g⁵ Aug 19] fair
maiden at best, lightly raced: little form in 1999: stays 1¼m: acts on good to firm going:
blinkered final 2 starts: sent to Poland. *R. W. Armstrong*

KIRISNIPPA   4 b.g. Beveled (USA) – Kiri Te (Liboi (USA) 76) [1998 NR 1999   **58 §**
10d 10.1g⁴ 11.6m 6g³ 8s 7d a8g⁶ a8.5g Dec 27] second foal: brother to 5-y-o
Kanawa: dam unraced: modest maiden: probably stays 1¼m: tried blinkered/visored:
swerved and unseated rider after start fifth outing. *Derrick Morris*

KIRK   3 b.f. Selkirk (USA) 129 – Sancta 106 (So Blessed 130) [1998 NR 1999 8g   **79 p**
8g⁶ 8.2s* 8s³ 8d² Oct 29] closely related to smart 7f (at 2 yrs) and 1¼m winner Carmelite House (by Diesis), 1¼m winner Khrisma (by Kris) and a winner in Sweden by
Sharpo, and half-sister to 3 winners, including useful stayer Saint Keyne (by Sadler's
Wells): dam 1m and 1¼m winner: fair form: won maiden at Nottingham (after
4-month break) in October: good efforts in handicaps last 2 starts: will be suited by
1¼m: acts on soft going: should do better still. *W. Jarvis*

KIROV PROTEGE (IRE)   7 b.g. Dancing Dissident (USA) 119 – Still River   **–**
(Kings Lake (USA) 133) [1998 NR 1999 a16g⁶ May 25] smallish gelding: poor
handicapper in 1997: no show on belated return: stays 1½m: acts on firm and good to
soft going: tried in blinkers and visor. *Mrs L. C. Jewell*

KIROVSKI (IRE)   2 b.c. (Mar 30) Common Grounds 118 – Nordic Doll (IRE)   **59**
71 (Royal Academy (USA) 130) [1999 8.1m 8d⁶ 7s Oct 8] IR 21,000Y: tall, quite
attractive colt: first foal: dam 7f winner who stayed 1m: modest form first 2 starts in
maidens: ran no sort of race on soft going final one: not bred to stay much beyond
1m. *P. W. Harris*

KIRSCH   2 ch.f. (Apr 9) Wolfhound (USA) 126 – Pondicherry (USA) 64 (Sir Wim-   **65**
borne (USA) 118) [1999 a5g³ a5g² 5.1m³ 5.1m³ a6g³ 5m⁵ 5m 5.1m⁵ 5g⁶ 6g* 6.1m⁴
5d a6g² a6g³ Nov 17] 1,000F, 2,000Y: small filly: third foal: dam 7f winner: fair
performer: won claimer at Lingfield in August: stays 6f: acts on good to firm going,
good to soft and all-weather: often apprentice ridden: usually waited with: consistent.
C. A. Dwyer

KIRSTENBOSCH   12 b.g. Caerleon (USA) 132 – Flower Petals (Busted 134)   **–**
[1998 NR 1999 17.2m Jun 23] leggy gelding: well held only run on Flat since 1990.
L. Lungo

KISSED BY MOONLITE   3 gr.f. Petong 126 – Rose Bouquet 78 (General   **52**
Assembly (USA) [1998 –: 7g 7m 6s 1999 8m 7g⁶ 8g⁶ 8.5m 8g² 8g 8s Sep 16] modest
maiden: stays 1m: form only on good going: sold 2,400 gns. *P. W. Harris*

KISSIMMEE BAY (IRE)   3 b.f. Brief Truce (USA) 126 – Deer Emily (Alzao   **41**
(USA) 117) [1998 54: 5m⁶ 6g⁶ 5g 6.1g² 6m 6.1d 5m 5s 1999 7m 6g 6.1d 6m⁶ 5g 6m
5m⁵ 5f⁶ 6f⁴ 6f Aug 7] workmanlike filly: poor maiden on balance: barely stays 6f:
tried blinkered/visored: has had tongue tied: sold 800 gns. *N. Tinkler*

KISSING TIME   2 b.f. (May 11) Lugana Beach 116 – Princess Athena 119 (Aho-   **79**
noora 122) [1999 5d 5.1m* 5g⁵ 6g 5d⁶ Sep 30] 6,000Y: sturdy filly: seventh foal:
sister to a winner in Germany and half-sister to useful 6f/7f winner Waypoint (by
Cadeaux Genereux): dam best at 5f, won Queen Mary Stakes but better at 3 and 4
yrs: fair performer: won maiden at Bath in August: good sixth of 16 in nursery at
Newmarket final start: speedy, and will prove best over sharp 5f: yet to race on
extremes of going. *P. F. I. Cole*

KISS ME GOODKNIGHT   3 b.f. First Trump 118 – Flitteriss Park 62§ (Beldale   **–**
Flutter (USA) 130) [1998 86: 6.1g* 7m 6s 7g 1999 6m⁶ 6m 8m Jun 19] leggy,
sparely-made filly: fairly useful form at best at 2 yrs: well beaten in 1999, including
in handicaps. *I. A. Balding*

KISS ME KATE   3 b.f. Aragon 118 – Ingerence (FR) (Akarad (FR) 130) [1998   **73**
59: 5.1g 5.7s⁶ 7m⁵ 7m⁴ 7m 7d⁴ 8m⁶ 8v⁵ 1999 8.3m 10m³ 9.9d² 10m* 10g⁵ 10m³ 9f⁶
10.2g 9.9v 10d 10d* Oct 26] tall, leggy filly: fair performer: won maiden at Ripon in
June and minor event at Redcar in October: stays 1¼m: acts on good to firm and good
to soft going: usually held up: sold 12,000 gns, joined S. Sherwood. *J. W. Hills*

KISSOGRAM   4 b.f. Caerleon (USA) 132 – Alligram (USA) 61 (Alysheba (USA))   **114**
[1998 120: 8g* 9.9g⁴ 8.1m* 10g* 1999 10m⁴ 9.9f⁴ 10.4m Aug 17] rangy, angular
filly: very smart performer at 3 yrs, winner of Sun Chariot Stakes: respectable length
fourth to Zahrat Dubai in Nassau Stakes at Goodwood in July, best effort in 1999:
sweating, edgy and unimpressive in coat on reappearance and well beaten in
Juddmonte International Stakes at York on final start: effective at 1m and 1¼m: raced
only on good ground or firmer. *L. M. Cumani*

KISTY (IRE)   2 b.f. (Mar 17) Kris 135 – Pine Ridge 80 (High Top 131) [1999 7m   **68 p**
8.1d⁵ 8.2s⁴ Oct 5] closely related to a winner in USA by Sharpo and half-sister to
3-y-o Lonesome and several winners, notably In The Groove (by Night Shift): dam
1½m winner: settled better with experience (pulled very hard on debut), best effort in
maidens when fourth of 14 to Embraced at Nottingham final start: should do better
still over 1¼m+. *H. Candy*

KITTIWAKE   3 b.f. Barathea (IRE) 127 – Gull Nook 120 (Mill Reef (USA) 141)   **98**
[1998 NR 1999 7m³ 10m⁴ 11d 10d⁵ 10m* 10.1g² Sep 14] 300,000Y: lengthy, quite
attractive filly: closely related to 2 winners by Sadler's Wells, including smart
middle-distance stayer Spring, and half-sister to 2 winners, notably Pentire (by Be
My Guest): dam, lightly-raced 10.5f and 1½m winner, out of half-sister to Shirley
Heights: useful performer: won maiden at Kempton in June: good short-head second
to Gino's Spirits in listed race at Yarmouth final start, racing freely and leading from
1f out: will stay 1½m: acts on good to firm going, probably on good to soft: sent to
Germany. *G. Wragg*

KI YASE (USA)   2 b.c. (Apr 4) Chief's Crown (USA) – Questionablevirtue (USA)   **53**
(Key To The Mint (USA)) [1999 7d 8s Oct 25] $37,000F, IR 130,000Y: strong, rangy,
attractive colt: has plenty of scope: fifth living foal: half-brother to Sussex Stakes
winner Among Men (by Zilzal): dam unraced half-sister to US 1990 Grade 1 2-y-o
6.5f winner Deposit Ticket: well held in maidens at Newmarket and Leicester: sold
only 9,000 gns in November. *Sir Michael Stoute*

KIZZAZZY   3 b.f. Chilibang 120 – River Fire (IRE) (Petong 126) [1998 NR 1999   **–**
7d Oct 11] second foal: dam little form: broke leg on debut: dead. *J. L. Harris*

KNAVE'S ASH (USA)   8 ch.g. Miswaki (USA) 124 – Quiet Rendezvous (USA)   **69**
(Nureyev (USA) 131) [1998 72: 7g 6s 8d 7.6m² 8g⁶ 8m* 9d 8m 7m 9m² 8.5m³ 7.5m
8g* 9d⁶ 8.9g 1999 7g 7d 7s 8m 8s 8m³ 7.6m² 8f* 7.5m³ 8f 8.5g² 10d³ Aug 17] compact gelding: fair handicapper: won apprentice event at Redcar in July: effective at
7.5f to 1¼m: acts on firm and good to soft going: blinkered once: well beaten when
sweating once: usually held up: joined Martin Todhunter. *D. Nicholls*

KNIGHTHOOD   3 b.c. Highest Honor (FR) 124 – Picardy 61 (Polish Precedent   **63**
(USA) 131) [1998 NR 1999 8f 7.1s 9s⁶ 10f Oct 20] 52,000Y: first foal: dam, third at
1m at 2 yrs on only start, daughter of Irish St Leger winner Opale: form in maidens
only on debut: sold 3,200 gns: sent to Germany. *J. W. Hills*

KNIGHT OF SILVER   2 gr.g. (May 15) Presidium 124 – Misty Rocket 75 (Roan   **55**
Rocket 128) [1999 5.1m 6.1m 6m⁵ 6.1m³ 7m 6g 8s Oct 26] 4,200Y: half-brother to a

winning chaser: dam 1¼m and 1½m seller winner, also successful over hurdles: modest maiden: well held last 3 starts: has raced freely, and best form at 6f (bred to stay further): acts on good to firm going. *S. Mellor*

KNIGHT'S EMPEROR (IRE) 2 b.c. (Apr 4) Grand Lodge (USA) 125 – So **66 p**
Kind 90 (Kind of Hush 118) [1999 6d Oct 14] IR 155,000Y: rangy, good sort: fifth
foal: half-brother to 1994 Mill Reef Stakes winner Princely Hush (by Prince Sabo),
also successful over 5f at 2 yrs, and 1995 2-y-o 6f winner Sweet Nature (by Classic
Secret): dam 6f winner who stayed 7f: better for race, seventh of 14 to Alfini in
Newmarket maiden, not knocked about having chased pace 4f: likely to prove best
up to 1m: sort to do much better. *J. Noseda*

KNIGHT'S RETURN 2 ch.c. (Mar 21) Never So Bold 135 – Return To Romance **–**
71 (Trojan Fen 118) [1999 5.7m 7m 7g Aug 13] fourth foal: dam 7f (at 2 yrs) to 12.5f
seller winner and winning hurdler: no promise in maidens/seller. *P. D. Evans*

KNOBBLEENEEZE 9 ch.g. Aragon 118 – Proud Miss (USA) (Semi-Pro) [1998 **61**
74: 7d 7v³ 8.3d⁵ 8m 7.3g* 7m⁴ 7.1d³ 8m 7g 7d 7m⁵ 8g 7.1g⁵ 8m 1999 8d² 7.6m 8.3s³
8g 8f 8.5m 8d⁴ 8d 7s⁵ 7d⁵ 8g Nov 3] sturdy gelding: modest handicapper: effective at
7f/1m: acts on good to firm and heavy ground (won on equitrack earlier in career):
usually visored: inconsistent. *M. R. Channon*

KNOCKEMBACK NELLIE 3 b.f. Forzando 122 – Sea Clover (IRE) 77 (Ela- **68**
Mana-Mou 132) [1998 72: 5g 5d⁶ 7m 6g 6m 6f² 6d 6m² 5.7g⁴ 1999 7g⁵ 6m⁵ 5g 6d
6m⁵ Jun 24] smallish filly: fair maiden handicapper: stays 6f: acts on firm ground:
often makes running. *D. R. C. Elsworth*

KNOCKHOLT 3 b.g. Be My Chief (USA) 122 – Saffron Crocus 83 (Shareef **102**
Dancer (USA) 135) [1998 NR 1999 10g⁶ 12m* 13.9g⁶ 14.1g² 14.8m³ 14f* 13.9g
14.6m* Sep 10] 22,000F, IR 27,000Y: rather unfurnished, useful-looking gelding:
fluent mover: second foal: half-brother to Norwegian 9f and 11.5f winner Art
Prospector (by Damister): dam Irish 1½m and 13f winner: useful performer: won
maiden at Salisbury in May, rated stakes at Goodwood (given most enterprising ride
by G. Duffield) in July and quite valuable handicap at Doncaster (kept on gamely to
beat Mardani by 1¼ lengths) in September: will stay 2m+: acts on firm ground, well
beaten only start on softer than good. *S. P. C. Woods*

KNOCKTOPHER ABBEY 2 ch.c. (Mar 3) Pursuit of Love 124 – Kukri (Kris **80**
135) [1999 5.1s⁴ 5d² 6.1m 6.1g³ 6m³ 6.1m* 7.3g⁶ 6g 6s Oct 2] 13,000F, 13,000Y:
sixth foal: half-brother to several winners, including useful 1m (including in USA)
winner Blessed Spirit (by Statoblest) and 8-y-o Sharp Rebuff: dam unraced: fairly
useful performer: won maiden at Chepstow in July: best form at 6f on good/good to
firm going. *B. R. Millman*

KNOTTY HILL 7 b.g. Green Ruby (USA) 104 – Esilam 62 (Frimley Park 109) **–**
[1998 64, a73: a7g⁵ a6g⁴ 7d 5v² 5g 6v* 6g² 6m 6.1s a6g 1999 a8g 7g Apr 16] tall,
workmanlike gelding: fair on all-weather, modest on turf: little form in 1999: best at
5f (given good test) to 7f: acts on fibresand and any turf going: usually races prominently. *R. Craggs*

KNYSNA LILY (USA) 3 b.f. Kris S (USA) – Kerygma (USA) (Drone) [1998
78p: 8g³ 1999 10s Apr 23] big, strong filly: promising third in maiden at Doncaster
at 2 yrs: favourite, pulled hard only run of 1999: sold 31,000 gns in December.
J. H. M. Gosden

KOCAL 3 b.g. Warrshan (USA) 117 – Jeethgaya (USA) 61 (Critique (USA) 126) **–**
[1998 NR 1999 8d 7d 7m 7g Jul 26] third reported foal: dam, maiden, best at around
1¼m: well beaten in maidens/handicap (reportedly lame). *D. W. Barker*

KOLBY 4 b.g. Superpower 113 – Abrasive 53 (Absalom 128) [1998 49: 5m* 5g **–**
6.1g 7.1g 7g⁶ 7s⁶ a7g a6g³ a7g 1999 a6g Mar 1] robust gelding: poor performer: well
beaten only run of 1999: probably stayed 7f: acted on fibresand and good to firm
going: seemed effective blinkered or not: dead. *A. Bailey*

KOMASEPH 7 b.g. Komaite (USA) – Starkist 81 (So Blessed 130) [1998 –§, **31 §**
a63§: a6g* a6g⁶ a6g² a7g a6g* a6g a6g a7g a6g a8f 1999 a7g a6f 6m 6g a6g⁵ a5g Jul
24] workmanlike gelding: poor form in 1999, including in visor/blinkers: probably
stays 7f: acts on fibresand and good to firm ground: inconsistent. *R. F. Marvin*

KOMISTAR 4 ch.g. Komaite (USA) – Rosie's Gold 57 (Glint of Gold 128) [1998 **95**
91: 8.2s² 10.4d 8.1g 1999 7.6m³ 8m⁵ 9.9g³ 10.3g* 12.3m 10m⁶ 10m* 9v Oct 23]

workmanlike gelding: useful performer: won handicaps at Doncaster (by head from Pasternak) in June and Newbury (valuable 16-runner event) in September, latter by short head from Senure, having been allowed to dictate pace: stays 1¼m: acts on soft and good to firm going: game front runner. *P. W. Harris*

KOMLUCKY 7 b.m. Komaite (USA) – Sweet And Lucky (Lucky Wednesday 124) [1998 53, a–: a6g⁶ a7g a7g a6g⁵ 7d a7g 7.5d 8m 6.9m² 7g* 7g² 7m 8d² 7m⁵ 1999 a8f⁵ a8g 8g⁵ 8d⁴ 7.1m⁵ 7.5d* 7.1m 8s 8g³ 6.9m 8d* 8m⁶ 6.9m 9.9m 8g 7g Sep 18] leggy mare: modest handicapper: won at Beverley (ladies race) in May and Ripon in July: below form final 5 starts: stays 1m: acts on firm ground, good to soft and fibresand: effective blinkered/visored or not: often claimer ridden. *K. A. Ryan* — **57 a–**

KOMREYEV DANCER 7 b.g. Komaite (USA) – L'Ancressaan 67 (Dalsaan 125) [1998 74, a58: a11g⁵ a11g⁵ a12g⁴ a12g² 12d⁵ 10.1s 12g 10g 10.8d⁶ 1999 8m Jun 16] leggy gelding: has a round action: modest handicapper on all-weather, fair at best nowadays on turf: no show only run of 1999: stays 1½m: acts on firm ground, good to soft and all-weather: blinkered once as 4-y-o. *Mrs L. Williamson* — **–**

KONDOTY (USA) 3 b.g. Mtoto 134 – Princess Haifa (USA) 69 (Mr Prospector (USA)) [1998 95+: 7m² 7.1d³ 1999 11.1g² a6.5f³ Dec 12] angular gelding: fairly useful form: placed in maiden at Kempton (final start for M. Channon) and handicap at Nad Al Sheba: stays 11f. *D. J. Selvaratnam, UAE* — **86**

KONKER 4 ch.g. Selkirk (USA) 129 – Helens Dreamgirl 95 (Caerleon (USA) 132) [1998 73: 9v³ 11.1d³ 12.3m⁵ 10g* 10.2s⁵ 8g 11d 1999 12.3m 9.9m⁶ Apr 14] unfurnished gelding: fair performer: below par in 1999: stays 11f: acts on heavy going. *G. M. Moore* — **–**

KOOKABURRA (FR) 2 b.c. (Apr 21) Zafonic (USA) 130 – Annoconnor (USA) (Nureyev (USA) 131) [1999 7d⁴ 7m² 8m³ 8v³ 8d² 8.3d⁴ Nov 4] 62,000Y: seventh foal: half-brother to winners in Germany by Rainbow Quest and USA by Woodman: dam, Grade 1 9f winner in USA, half-sister to Grand Prix de Paris and Melbourne Cup winner At Talaq: fairly useful maiden: best effort when ½-length second of 11 in nursery at Brighton penultimate start: will stay beyond 1m: acts on good to firm and good to soft going, well below form on heavy. *B. J. Meehan* — **93**

KOOL CAPTAIN 2 b.c. (Apr 27) Distant Relative 128 – Jhansi Ki Rani (USA) 94 (Far North (CAN) 120) [1999 7m 6m⁵ 5.7m* 7f Jul 31] half-brother to 3-y-o Discerning Air and several winners, including useful 1991 2-y-o 6f winner Colway Bold (by Never So Bold) and 12.5f and 1¾m winner Memorable (by Don't Forget Me): dam 7f/1m winner: fair form: awarded maiden at Bath in July: well beaten only subsequent outing: raced only on ground firmer than good: sold 3,000 gns, sent to Slovakia. *S. C. Williams* — **70**

KOSEVO (IRE) 5 b.g. Shareef Dancer (USA) 135 – Kallista (Zeddaan 130) [1998 47, a60: 8m 6.9m⁴ a7g² 6m a7g² a7g* a7g* 7g 5m⁵ 5m a6g² 6g a6g⁵ a7g a7g a6g⁵ a6g² a7g² a7g⁶ a6g 1999 a7g³ a7g² a8g a6g⁵ a6f⁵ a6g a7g³ a7g a7g² a7g 6f⁴ a7g⁵ a6g² a7g⁵ 6g⁶ 5g³ a6g⁵ 5s⁵ 5f* 5m 6f² 5m⁶ 5g 5g 5m Sep 10] angular gelding: fair performer: won handicap at Haydock in July: effective at 5f (given a test) to 7f: acts on firm ground, soft and all-weather: wears visor/blinkers: often bandaged: usually front runner. *D. Shaw* — **68 a62**

KPOLO 4 b.g. Polish Precedent (USA) 131 – Ktolo 80 (Tolomeo 127) [1998 45: 7s 8.3m 8m 11.5g a14g a12g² 1999 a16f a13g a13g a8.5g⁴ 12m 10.5d⁶ 12g a8.5g⁶ a12g Nov 22] unfurnished gelding: poor maiden: left B. Johnson after third start: stays 1½m: acts on fibresand: blinkered second start. *C. N. Kellett* — **–**

KRAKING MAGIC 2 br.f. (Mar 28) Magic Ring (IRE) 115 – Little Kraker 69 (Godswalk (USA) 130) [1999 5g⁶ 5m 7m 8v a8.5g Oct 30] leggy, close-coupled filly: fourth foal: dam best up to 1¼m: modest maiden at best: form only (at 5f) on first 2 starts: acts on good to firm going: tried visored. *J. W. Mullins* — **58 d**

KRAM 5 ch.g. Kris 135 – Balenare (Pharly (FR) 130) [1998 65: 6v 6.1m⁶ 5m³ 6f⁶ 5g² 5m* 5g⁴ 5g³ 5m 6m⁵ 5m 5g³ 6.1s 1999 5d⁵ 5.7g 5.1m⁵ 6g 5g⁴ 6m 5.7m⁴ 5d 5.1m⁶ 5d* Sep 15] leggy gelding: fair performer: most inconsistent in 1999, 25/1 when winning claimer at Sandown in September: best at 5f/6f: acts on good to firm and good to soft ground, probably on firm: blinkered final 2 starts. *Mrs P. N. Dutfield* — **65 ?**

KRIKLES 3 ch.g. Selkirk (USA) 129 – Bumpkin 108 (Free State 125) [1998 60: 8g 8m 7v⁵ 1999 8.3m 7m Jul 7] tall, angular gelding: modest maiden at 2 yrs: well beaten in 1999: stays 7f: pulls hard: sold 4,800 gns. *A. J. McNae*   –

KRISALIGHT (USA) 3 b. or br.f. Kris S (USA) – Dancing Grass (USA) (Northern Dancer) [1998 –p: 8m 1999 10v⁴ 12v⁶ 10.5v⁴ Oct 13] big, good-topped filly: modest form in maidens/handicap, though shaped encouragingly most starts: should stay 1½m: still likely to do better. *J. L. Dunlop*   **61 p**

KRISPY KNIGHT 4 ch.c. Kris 135 – Top Table 65 (Shirley Heights 130) [1998 101: 8v* 8m⁶ 1999 8d⁶ 8g⁴ 8.3m 8d 9v Oct 23] sturdy colt: useful performer at 3 yrs: ran as if something amiss on reappearance in 1999: off course 4½ months and form only on third start: should stay beyond 1m: acts on good to firm and heavy going: sold 14,000 gns, joined L. Comer in Ireland. *J. W. Hills*   **91**

KRISSY (USA) 3 br.f. Kris S (USA) – Rascal Rascal (USA) (Ack Ack (USA)) [1998 64p: 8d 1999 10.5d⁴ 10g Aug 16] big, strong, good-topped filly: fair maiden: sweating when tailed off final start: stays 10.5f: sent to USA. *J. H. M. Gosden*   **74**

KRISTINA 3 ch.f. Kris 135 – Derniere Danse (Gay Mecene (USA) 128) [1998 81p: 8.1g² 8.2s* 1999 10m⁶ 10s 12.4m³ 10m⁵ 12g² 14.8m³ 16m⁴ Sep 11] close-coupled, quite good-topped filly: fairly useful performer: mostly creditable efforts, including in listed/handicap company: stays 14.8f, apparently not 2m: acts on good to firm ground, possibly not at best on soft: visored/blinkered last 4 starts: has worn tongue strap. *Sir Michael Stoute*   **92**

KRYSTAL MAX (IRE) 6 b.g. Classic Music (USA) – Lake Isle (IRE) (Caerleon (USA) 132) [1998 –, a82: a6g² a6g* a5g* a5g* a5g a6g³ a6g⁶ 1999 a6g* a5g* a5f* a6g* a6g³ a6g² a6g² a5g² a6g⁴ a5g² a5g Dec 21] smallish, good-topped gelding: fairly useful performer: won claimers at Lingfield (3) in January and Wolverhampton in February, leaving T. D. Barron after third start: effective at 5f to easy 7f: acts on all-weather, lightly raced on turf of late: blinkered once at 2 yrs: usually claimer ridden. *T. G. Mills*   **– a86**

KUMAIT (USA) 5 b. or br.g. Danzig (USA) – Colour Chart (USA) 122 (Mr Prospector (USA)) [1998 109: 6g² 6m⁴ 6d 7f² 7m 7f³ 6g* 7m⁴ 7d⁴ 1999 6g⁴ 7g 6m 7d 7d² 7f 7d² 7m² 7g* Oct 2] strong-quartered gelding: fluent mover: useful performer: good second to Granny's Pet in rated stakes at Chester and Goodwood prior to winning 5-runner minor event at Redcar final start by length from Black Amber, dictating pace: best at 6f/7f: acts on firm and good to soft going: sometimes wore tongue strap at 3 yrs: has been taken steadily to post: usually leads/races prominently. *E. A. L. Dunlop*   **106**

KUMON EILEEN 3 ch.f. Anshan 119 – Katie Eileen (USA) 49 (Bering 136) [1998 NR 1999 9m 10m Jun 23] first reported foal: dam lightly-raced maiden: well held in maidens. *J. R. Jenkins*   –

KURSIANG 3 gr.f. Petong 126 – Bellyphax (Bellypha 130) [1998 56: 5g 6.1g 7.1m 6.1g⁴ 6f 7g³ 7d⁵ 7s⁶ 1999 7d 7g 6.8m⁶ 6f⁶ 6m Aug 6] smallish, sturdy, close-coupled filly: modest maiden: form in 1999 only on third start: stays 7f: acts on good to firm and good to soft going: has run creditably in blinkers: sold 800 gns in December. *B. R. Millman*   **51**

KUSTER 3 b.c. Indian Ridge 123 – Ustka 60 (Lomond (USA) 128) [1998 62p: 7d 1999 8.5s* 10.2d² 9v Oct 23] fairly useful performer: won maiden at Epsom in April: good second in minor event at Chepstow following month: stays 1¼m. *L. M. Cumani*   **87**

KUSTOM KIT KATE 4 b.f. Tragic Role (USA) – Wing of Freedom (Troy 137) [1998 61: a7g² a7g³ 6.1s* 6.1v a7g⁵ 6d 1999 a7g a8g a8f 7s 8d a5g 7s⁴ a7g⁶ 6s Jun 12] leggy, unfurnished filly: modest handicapper at best: creditable effort in 1999 only on seventh start: effective at 6f and should stay 1m: acts on good to firm going, soft and fibresand: no form blinkered/visored. *S. R. Bowring*   **56**

KUSTOM KIT KEVIN 3 b.g. Local Suitor (USA) 128 – Sweet Revival 41 (Claude Monet (USA) 121) [1998 NR 1999 10.1f⁶ 7m Sep 24] second foal: half-brother to 4-y-o Sweet Reward: dam 1¼m winner at 5 yrs: last in maidens at Newcastle and Redcar (didn't look entirely keen). *S. R. Bowring*   –

KUUIPO 2 b.f. (Jan 10) Puissance 110 – Yankee Special 60 (Bold Lad (IRE) 133) [1999 5d⁴ 5d⁶ 5.1f⁶ 5m³ 6f 6s⁶ 6g 6d Oct 26] 6,200F, 10,500Y: tall, quite good-topped   **55**

filly: half-sister to 6f (at 2 yrs) and 1m winner Langtonian (by Primo Dominie) and French winner up to 11f Soldiers Bay (by Robellino): dam sprint maiden: modest maiden: stays 6f: acts on soft and good to firm going: usually tongue tied. *B. S. Rothwell*

KUWAIT BIRD 3 b.c. Cosmonaut – Loadplan Lass 63 (Nicholas Bill 125) [1998 NR 1999 8g 8m 8m⁴ 6g 6g Oct 15] 1,800Y, resold 7,000Y: tall, leggy, shallow-girthed colt: sixth foal: half-brother to 3 winners, including 8-y-o Hill Farm Dancer and 6-y-o Hill Farm Blues: dam, maiden, bred to stay middle distances: well held all starts: has worn tongue strap: sold 2,000 gns. *K. Mahdi* —

KUWAIT DAWN (IRE) 3 b.f. Pips Pride 117 – Red Note (Rusticaro (FR) 124) [1998 82: 7m² 7f⁴ 6f 6d 8.1g 1999 8d* 7m 8m 8d⁴ 8.1m 7d⁶ 7m 7g 8d 10d 8g 7s Oct 23] big, sturdy, lengthy filly: poor mover: useful performer: won minor event at Doncaster in March: creditable ninth in 1000 Guineas at Newmarket 2 outings later: best effort after when seventh in rated stakes at Goodwood eighth start: best at 7f/1m: acts on good to firm and good to soft going: often sweating/edgy: sold 26,000 gns. *K. Mahdi* 98

KUWAIT FLAVOUR (IRE) 3 b.c. Bluebird (USA) 125 – Plume Magique (Kenmare (FR) 125) [1998 61p: 6s⁴ 1999 6d³ Mar 27] lengthy colt: modest form when in frame in maidens: bandaged off-hind only start in 1999: sold 9,000 gns in October. *K. Mahdi* 67

KUWAIT ROSE 3 b.c. Inchinor 119 – Black Ivor (USA) (Sir Ivor 135) [1998 NR 1999 7.7d 6s³ a6g⁶ a7g² a6g⁶ Dec 21] 5,000Y: smallish, sturdy colt: half-brother to several winners, including 1m winners Tequila and Drive Assured (both by Mystiko): dam unraced: fair maiden: seems better at 7f than 6f: acts on fibresand. *K. Mahdi* 73

KUWAIT SAND 3 b.c. Lugana Beach 116 – Soon To Be 84 (Hot Spark 126) [1998 NR 1999 6.1g⁴ 6s a6g a6g³ a5g Dec 1] 6,400Y: sixth foal: half-brother to 1996 2-y-o 6f winner Mumkin (by Reprimand): dam 6f/7f winner: best effort when fourth in maiden on debut: reportedly lost front plate next time (changed hands 6,500 gns after). *K. Mahdi* 65 a59

KUWAIT THUNDER (IRE) 3 ch.c. Mac's Imp (USA) 116 – Romangoddess (IRE) (Rhoman Rule (USA)) [1998 76: 6m³ 6f⁵ 6g⁴ 6d³ 1999 7d³ 6g 6m 7m⁴ 6.1g 6s⁵ 6d 7g 8.2d 8s Nov 6] rather leggy, quite good-topped colt: unimpressive mover: fair maiden: below form after third in handicap on reappearance: well held final 4 outings, leaving K. Mahdi after penultimate one: effective at 6f/7f: acts on firm and good to soft going: visored eighth start. *J. L. Eyre* 73 d

KUWAIT TROOPER (USA) 2 b. or br.c. (May 8) Cozzene (USA) – Super Fan (USA) (Lear Fan (USA) 130) [1999 a8g⁶ a10g Dec 18] IR 28,000F, $35,000Y, 27,000 2-y-o: fourth foal: half-brother to winners in USA by Dixieland Band and Miswaki: dam US Grade 3 9.5f winner: well beaten in maidens at Lingfield in December: has worn tongue strap. *G. A. Butler* —

KWIKPOINT 5 ch.g. Never So Bold 135 – Try The Duchess 99 (Try My Best (USA) 130) [1998 57: 8d 6.9d 6g⁴ 5m 6m 1999 10m 5g 5.9m⁶ Jun 23] good-bodied gelding: modest maiden at 4 yrs: poor form in 1999: should prove best at 5f/6f: blinkered once at 4 yrs. *Martin Todhunter* 39

KYLKENNY 4 b.g. Kylian (USA) – Fashion Flow (Balidar 133) [1998 NR 1999 10.2s 9s⁵ 8s⁵ Oct 25] fourth reported foal: half-brother to 1992 2-y-o 6f winner Fabriana (by Northern State): dam unraced: signs of ability in maidens/claimer. *H. Morrison* —

L

LAA JADEED (IRE) 4 b.c. Petorius 117 – Sea Mistress (Habitat 134) [1998 56: a8g 6m 8.5m 7d 8.2s⁶ 10v⁵ a12g a8g 1999 a11g* a11g a12g a8g a8g 10m 10.1m 10f 12d 12.3m 10.3m⁵ a8.5g³ 10m Sep 7] modest performer: won apprentice maiden at Southwell in January: changed hands 1,550 gns before final start: stays 11f: acts on good to firm going, soft and fibresand. *M. J. Polglase* 46 a51

LAAL YAN   3 b.f. Anshan 119 – Cromarty 75 (Shareef Dancer (USA) 135) [1998   –
NR 1999 12.4g 11.1g⁴ 10d⁵ May 21] first foal: dam, 1½m winner who stayed well,
also successful over hurdles: little form in maidens. *J. J. O'Neill*

LA BELLE MYSTERE   2 b.f. (Mar 29) Lycius (USA) 124 – Mysterious Plans   48
(IRE) (Last Tycoon 131) [1999 6m 6d Aug 11] 4,000F, 7,500Y: second foal:
half-sister to French 1m winner Ti For Too (by Exit To Nowhere): dam, 10.5f winner
in France, sister to smart sprinter Monde Bleu: showed some ability in maidens at
Kempton and Salisbury. *B. R. Millman*

LA BIRBA (IRE)   2 b.f. (Apr 17) Prince of Birds (USA) 121 – Ariadne 79   44
(Bustino 136) [1999 6m 5d 5.7d a6g⁴ Oct 16] IR 28,000F, 8,500Y: half-sister to
several winners, including useful 1997 2-y-o 5f/6f winner Another Fantasy (by
Danehill) and 3-y-o Baron de Pichon: dam, 2m winner, sister to Italian Group 1
winner Stufida (the grandam of Pivotal): blinkered, form only when fourth of 13 in
claimer at Wolverhampton: should stay at least 1m. *B. J. Meehan*

LABRETT   2 b.c. (Mar 27) Tragic Role (USA) – Play The Game 70 (Mummy's   89
Game 120) [1999 5m⁵ 5d⁴ 5d* 6f⁴ 5m³ 5.1m* 5g⁴ 6m⁵ 5d 6g 6s Oct 23] 8,500Y: sixth
foal: half-brother to several winners, including 6-y-o Power Game and fairly useful
1997 2-y-o 5f winner Lets Be Fair (by Efisio): dam 2-y-o 5f winner: fairly useful
performer: won minor events at Redcar in May and Chester in June: stiff tasks last 3
outings: effective at 5f and 6f and good to soft ground: blinkered last 7
starts: has swished tail in preliminaries: sold 13,000 gns. *B. J. Meehan*

LA CAPRICE (USA)   2 ch.f. (Apr 28) Housebuster (USA) – Shicklah (USA)   75
106 (The Minstrel (CAN) 135) [1999 5d² 5m 5g⁴ 5f⁵ 5.1g² 5g* Aug 24] leggy filly:
half-sister to several winners, including 3-y-o Muqtarib and useful sprinter Ra'a (by
Diesis): dam 2-y-o 5f/6f winner from family of Suave Dancer: fair performer: won
maiden at Lingfield in August: will prove best over sharp 5f: acts on firm going.
J. Berry

LACE WING   2 ch.f. (May 11) Caerleon (USA) 132 – Capo di Monte 118 (Final   57 p
Straw 127) [1999 7d Oct 30] eighth foal: half-sister to 3-y-o Complimentary Pass
and to 3 winners by Danzig, including 8-y-o Daawe and 1m winner Dafrah: dam, 6f
(at 2 yrs) to 11f (Grade 3 event in USA) winner, half-sister to smart 1½m filly Wind
In Her Hair: weak in market, always behind in Newmarket maiden: will be suited by
1m+: should do better. *B. W. Hills*

LA CHARPENTIERE   5 b.g. Robellino (USA) 127 – Antoinette Jane 86 (Ile   –
de Bourbon (USA) 133) [1998 NR 1999 7.5v 9m 7.7m 8m Aug 22] 22,000Y: big,
heavy-topped gelding: third foal: half-brother to 1995 2-y-o 1m winner Ancestral
Jane (by Distant Relative): dam 2-y-o 7f winner: fifth in Leopardstown maiden at 2
yrs (trained by G. Cusack): little form in Britain. *P. Bowen*

LA CHATELAINE   5 b.m. Then Again 126 – La Domaine 89 (Dominion 123)   32
[1998 54, a–: a8g a10g 8d⁶ 8g 11.9g⁶ 11.5s⁴ 12g* 11.5g⁴ 14m 11.5g 11.9m⁶ 11.5f⁶
12g a13g a16g 1999 11.9f 10d⁵ 10m⁶ 10f³ Jun 25] poor handicapper: stays 1½m: acts
on good to firm and good to soft ground: visored once: has worn tongue strap: sold 725
gns, joined Miss Z. Davison. *Miss B. Sanders*

LA CINECITTA (FR)   3 ch.f. Dancing Spree (USA) – Cox's Feather (USA)   –
(Cox's Ridge (USA)) [1998 –: 6g⁶ 6m⁵ 7v 1999 6m 9.9m 7m 8m Aug 4] smallish
filly: poor maiden handicapper: should stay at least 1m: blinkered final start.
C. B. B. Booth

LA DOYENNE (IRE)   5 ch.m. Masterclass (USA) 116 – Sainthill (St Alphage   61
119) [1998 57: a6g⁶ a5g* a5g² a5g⁶ 5s a5g 5m 5.1g⁴ 5m* 5d* 5m 5g 5g 5v a5g   a65
1999 a5g* 5m a5g³ 5v² a5g⁶ 5s a5g⁴ 5g² 5.3d⁵ 5d 5d⁵ a5g⁶ Nov 23] small,
good-topped mare: modest handicapper: made all at Southwell in May: mainly
creditable efforts after: best at 5f: acts on all-weather, good to firm and heavy going:
has carried head awkwardly: often front runner. *C. B. B. Booth*

LADY ALEXANDER (IRE)   4 ch.f. Night Shift (USA) – Sandhurst Goddess   100
103 (Sandhurst Prince 128) [1998 112: 6m² 5m⁶ 5g² 5d 1999 6g⁵ 5m 6d 5d Sep 11]
compact filly: not a good walker: only raced in 1999, best effort when eighth of 17
in King's Stand Stakes at Royal Ascot second start: stays 6f: has won on good to soft

ground, best on good/good to firm: blinkered/tongue tied final outing. *C. Collins, Ireland*

LADY ANGHARAD (IRE)   3 b.f. Tenby 125 – Lavezzola (IRE) (Salmon Leap   **89**
(USA) 131) [1998 95: 5g⁴ 6g* 7m* 6f 7m⁵ 8d 8s 1999 8g⁵ 10m 10s 8.1m 10.1m⁶ 12f
10d² 10m 10d Sep 17] smallish, angular filly: useful performer at 2 yrs: fairly useful
form on occasions in 1999: ran poorly final start: stays 1¼m (raced freely over 1½m):
acts on good to firm and good to soft going, possibly not on soft: visored last 3
outings: sold 16,000 gns. *A. P. Jarvis*

LADY ANNABEL   3 b.f. Alhijaz 122 – Anna Rella (IRE) (Danehill (USA) 126)   –
[1998 54: 5d 6g 1999 8d 8f 6g 7f May 31] leggy filly: poor maiden. *C. W. Fairhurst*

LADY ARDROSS   4 b.f. Flying Tyke 90 – Hatshepsut (Ardross 134) [1998 –:   –
8.2v 1999 8.2s 5g 6g a6g 10s Nov 1] lengthy filly: no form: blinkered fourth start.
A. Smith

LADY BALLA CALM (IRE)   3 b.f. Balla Cove 119 – Across The Ring (IRE)   –
(Auction Ring (USA) 123) [1998 –: 6d 7s 5s 1999 6d a6g a8g Nov 26] first foal: dam
poor Irish maiden: well beaten in maidens, trained by M. Byrne in Ireland at 2 yrs.
J. J. Bridger

LADY BENSON (IRE)   6 b.m. Pennine Walk 120 – Sit Elnaas (USA) 82 (Sir   **49 d**
Ivor 135) [1998 38: 5m 5g⁵ 5g 5d 6d 6s 1999 a5g a8g 9.2d² 10m² 10s 12g 12.3m⁵
10g 10.2m 11.9d 12.1f Aug 24] small, leggy mare: poor maiden handicapper: below
form after fourth start: should stay 1½m: acts on good to firm and good to soft going.
W. M. Brisbourne

LADY BEWARE   3 b.f. Warning 136 – Thewaari (USA) 68 (Eskimo (USA))   **43**
[1998 70d: 5.7s 5g⁴ 5.2m⁵ 7g 6m⁵ 5.1m³ 6.1d⁵ 6m 1999 6m 6.1m 7m 5.9m 5g 5d 5v
7g Oct 19] smallish, well-made filly: poor maiden: stays 6f: acts on good to firm and
good to soft going: visored 3 of last 4 starts. *M. R. Channon*

LADY BOXER   3 b.f. Komaite (USA) – Lady Broker 54 (Petorius 117) [1998 80:   **83**
6d* 6m³ 6g⁵ 6d⁶ 6g 1999 6.1m 6d⁴ 6.1s* 6d 7d Oct 26] close-coupled, unfurnished
filly: fairly useful performer: creditable fourth of 29 in Ayr Silver Cup, then won
minor event at Chester later in September: well below form both starts after: stays 6f:
acts on soft and good to firm going. *M. Mullineaux*

LADY BREANNE (IRE)   3 b.f. Woods of Windsor (USA) – Tootsie Roll   **55**
(Comedy Star (USA) 121) [1998 72: 7s 6d³ 6d 1999 7f⁴ 8f⁶ 6f 7m² a7g⁶ a8g³ a8g⁶
Dec 6] IR 2,200 2-y-o: half-sister to 3 winners, including Irish sprinter Sand Or Stone
(by Sandhurst Prince) and 1m and 1¼m winner Royal Thimble (by Prince Rupert):
dam lightly raced: modest maiden: trained by B. Lawlor in Ireland at 2 yrs: stays 1m:
acts on firm going, good to soft and equitrack. *G. L. Moore*

LADYCAKE (IRE)   3 gr.f. Perugino (USA) 84 – Olivia's Pride (IRE) (Digamist   **51 d**
(USA) 110) [1998 71d: 5g⁴ 5g 5s⁶ 5g² 5.1g 5g* 5d² 5d 5s⁶ a5s a5g³ 1999 a5g³ a5s⁵
a5g⁴ 5g⁶ 6.1s a6g 5g 5d⁶ Jun 28] tall, angular filly: fair form at best at 2 yrs:
deteriorated again in 1999: takes good hold, and best at 5f: acts on good to soft going
and fibresand: blinkered third to sixth starts: has wandered. *J. Berry*

LADY CARBRON (IRE)   3 br.f. Elbio 125 – Smart Turn 67 (His Turn 82) [1998   **60 d**
52: 5v a5g* a5g² a5g⁴ a5g² 5d² 5.1g⁴ 5g 5s³ a5g³ 1999 a5g² a6g⁵ a5g⁶ 6v Apr
20] rather leggy filly: modest performer: little form after reappearance in 1999: best
at 5f: acts on fibresand (well held only try on equitrack), raced only on good going or
softer on turf: often makes running. *J. Berry*

LADY CAROLINE (IRE)   3 b.f. Hamas (IRE) 125§ – Pericolo (IRE) 92 (Kris   **58 d**
135) [1998 71: 6g⁵ 6d² 5.1v 5d a5g² a5g a6g² a6g* a5g⁵ 1999 a5g³ a6g⁶ a8g³ a8.5g⁶
a6g⁵ a7g⁶ 6g³ 6v 5g 8f a7g 10d a7g Dec 6] leggy filly: modest performer: left
M. Johnston after eighth start: changed hands 1,000 gns before final start (blinkered):
stays 6f: acts on good to soft going and all-weather: none too resolute. *A. T. Murphy*

LADY COLDUNELL   3 b.f. Deploy 131 – Beau's Delight (USA) (Lypheor 118)   **72**
[1998 –p: 8m 7d 1999 a7g a11g 12s² 14.1m² 14f² 16m⁴ 12g³ a12g* 11.9f⁴ 12m 12m*   **a81**
16.4g⁵ 16.2g² 17.5d⁵ a12g 12d⁵ Oct 29] workmanlike filly: fairly useful handicapper
on all-weather, fair on turf: won at Lingfield in July and Epsom in August: effective

at 1½m, barely stays 17f: acts on equitrack, good to soft and good to firm going, probably not at best on firm. *N. A. Callaghan*

LADY CONFESS 9 ch.m. Backchat (USA) 98 – Special Branch 83 (Acer 123) **52**
[1998 NR 1999 11.1f³ 17.1g* 16m³ 16f² 17.1s⁵ Oct 4] leggy, sparely-made mare: modest handicapper, lightly raced on Flat: won at Pontefract in August: stays 17f: acts on fibresand and firm ground, possibly not on soft: effective blinkered: held up in 1999. *M. W. Easterby*

LADY CYRANO 2 b.f. (Jan 13) Cyrano de Bergerac 120 – Hazy Kay (IRE) 77 **46**
(Treasure Kay 114) [1999 a5g 5m a5g³ a5g³ a5g⁶ a6g⁴ 6g³ 6.1m 8m a5g Oct 13] 3,500Y: third foal: half-sister to 3-y-o Clara Blue: dam disappointing maiden: poor maiden: stays 6f: yet to race on extremes of going: tried visored. *Mrs N. Macauley*

LADY D'ABO 4 b.f. Ron's Victory (USA) 129 – Lady Sabo 69 (Prince Sabo 123) **– §**
[1998 NR 1999 a6g a7f a5g Feb 18] no sign of ability, including in visor. *Mrs S. Lamyman*

LADY DONATELLA 2 b.f. (Mar 25) Last Tycoon 131 – Nekhbet 74 (Artaius **57**
(USA) 129) [1999 7s⁶ 6.1m 6.1g Sep 25] 30,000Y: half-sister to several winners, including 5-y-o Right Wing and useful 6f/7f performer Cim Bom Bom (by Dowsing): dam, maiden, half-sister to Irish St Leger winner M-Lolshan: best effort when sixth of 13 in maiden at Kempton: hampered both starts after: will stay at least 1m. *M. L. W. Bell*

LADY DORCHESTER 2 b.f. (Feb 21) Then Again 126 – Miramede (Norwick **35**
(USA) 125) [1999 5f⁵ 7g⁵ 6f⁶ 6f⁶ Aug 6] third foal: half-sister to 4-y-o Porlock Lady: dam no form: poor form in sellers: sold 925 gns. *Miss Gay Kelleway*

LADY EXCALIBER 2 b.f. (Apr 22) Sure Blade (USA) 130 – Bewails (IRE) 53 **–**
(Caerleon (USA) 132) [1999 5s 5m a6g⁶ 6.1g⁶ 8m⁵ 10s Oct 5] third foal: dam twice-raced granddaughter of Yorkshire Oaks and Park Hill winner Attica Meli: no form in varied company, including in blinkers. *J. Cullinan*

LADY FEARLESS 2 b.f. (Apr 11) Cosmonaut – Lady Broker 54 (Petorius 117) **–**
[1999 7.1s 6d⁶ Oct 20] unfurnished filly: second foal: half-sister to 3-y-o Lady Boxer: dam 7f winner: signs of ability in maidens at Haydock (sweating and very green, unseated rider to post) and Newcastle in the autumn. *M. Mullineaux*

LADY FLORA 3 b.f. Alflora (IRE) 120 – Lady Marguerrite (Blakeney 126) **–**
[1998 NR 1999 5.9m⁶ Jun 24] first foal: dam, ran twice, from family of St Leger and Gold Cup winner Classic Cliche: behind in maiden at Carlisle. *D. McCain*

LADY FROM LUCCA 2 b.f. (Feb 6) Inchinor 119 – Play With Me (IRE) 73 **49**
(Alzao (USA) 117) [1999 6g⁶ 7g 6d 6m a6g⁶ a7g⁵ Oct 18] third foal: sister to useful **a44**
performer up to 1m in Scandinavia Shawdon, also 5f/6f winner in Britain at 2 yrs, and half-sister to 3-y-o Lincoln Dean: dam, 1¼m winner, out of half-sister to a smart stayer: poor maiden: tried blinkered: sold 4,000 gns, sent to Germany. *Sir Mark Prescott*

LADY GEORGIA 3 gr.f. Arazi (USA) 135 – Petillante 101 (Petong 126) [1998 **78**
94: 5g⁴ 5g² 6g⁶ 7m² 7g³ 7m⁴ 8d⁶ 8d 7g⁵ 8v⁵ 1999 8f³ 7.7m* 8d a8.5g Nov 20] rather leggy, quite good-topped filly: useful form in pattern company at 2 yrs: only fair in 1999, winning maiden at Warwick in August: last in listed race at Ascot next time: stays 1m: acts on good to firm and heavy going. *C. E. Brittain*

LADY HELEN (IRE) 2 b.f. (May 26) Salse (USA) 128 – Old Domesday Book **64**
93 (High Top 131) [1999 6s⁵ 5.9m 7.5m* 7.1m 8d Sep 17] 52,000F: leggy, close-coupled filly: half-sister to several winners, notably very smart sprinter Owington (by Green Desert): dam 10.4f winner: modest form: well held in nurseries final 2 starts: stays 7.5f: acts on good to firm ground: sold 54,000 gns in December. *T. D. Easterby*

LADY IN COLOUR (IRE) 3 b.f. Cadeaux Genereux 131 – Piffle 87 (Shirley **71**
Heights 130) [1998 NR 1999 9.9g² May 25] IR 85,000Y: fifth foal: half-sister to 3 winners, notably smart middle-distance performer in Europe/USA Frenchpark (by Fools Holme): dam, 1½m winner who stayed well, sister to useful stayer El Conquistador: 33/1, 3 lengths second in maiden at Beverley in May: will stay beyond 1¼m: sold 16,000 gns in December. *J. Noseda*

LADY IN WAITING 4 b.f. Kylian (USA) – High Savannah 77 (Rousillon (USA) **113**
133) [1998 110: 8d⁴ 8f 10.2g⁴ 11.9f⁴ 10.2d* 12s² 10m* 1999 10.4s* 10m² 9.9f² 11.9g
10s* 10g⁵ Oct 17] workmanlike filly: did well physically: good mover: smart
performer: won listed race at York in May and Sun Chariot Stakes at Newmarket
(by 8 lengths from Gino's Spirits) in October: ran well when runner-up otherwise,
including when beaten ½ length by Zahrat Dubai in Nassau Stakes at Goodwood on
third start: 4½ lengths fifth of 7 to Insight in E. P. Taylor Stakes at Woodbine final
outing: stays 1½m: acts on firm and soft going: races prominently: game. *P. F. I. Cole*

LADY IONA 3 ch.f. Weldnaas (USA) 112 – Shadha 57 (Shirley Heights 130) **50**
[1998 –: 6g 7.5m 7s⁵ 6s 8g⁶ 1999 10m 8.2f 8g² 8.2f 9.1g⁶ 8.3m 10g 10.9v⁵ Oct 11]
leggy, sparely-made filly: modest maiden: should stay beyond 1m. *Martyn Wane*

LADY IRENE (IRE) 3 br.f. Tirol 127 – Felsen (IRE) 54 (Ballad Rock 122) **52**
[1998 NR 1999 a7g⁶ a8g² a8g⁵ 9.7s⁶ 11.6g 10g a9.4g⁴ 10.1m 11.9s⁴ 10d² a16.2g **a39**
Dec 15] IR 13,500Y: third foal: half-sister to a winner in France/Belgium by Salt
Dome: dam, ran twice in Britain and later 6f winner in Ireland, daughter of German
Oaks winner Alaria: modest maiden on turf, poor on all-weather: runner-up in
Windsor seller penultimate start: stays 1½m: acts on soft going: often claimer ridden.
T. J. Naughton

LADY JO 3 ch.f. Phountzi (USA) 104 – Lady Kalliste (Another Realm 118) [1998 **74**
–: 7m 6f 6.9f 1999 8.3m a10g³ 10g³ 10.1g* 11.5m 10f* 10m⁶ 10.1m 10g⁶ 11.9m Sep
1] fair handicapper: won at Yarmouth and Lingfield in June: stays 1¼m, probably not
1½m: acts on firm going: usually held up. *S. Dow*

LADY JONES 2 b.f. (Mar 17) Emperor Jones (USA) 119 – So Beguiling (USA) **50**
49 (Woodman (USA) 126) [1999 6m⁵ 7m 7.7g 7m* 8s 7d Oct 21] fourth foal: dam 7f
seller winner at 2 yrs: modest performer: won seller at Brighton in September: well
held in nurseries after: stays 7f: acts on good to firm ground. *J. Pearce*

LADY LAUREN 3 b.f. Cyrano de Bergerac 120 – Wandering Stranger 69 (Petong **–**
126) [1998 67: 5g³ 5g³ 6g³ 5m⁵ 6m⁴ 7d 1999 6m 7m 5m 5g 5f 6g a8.5g Dec 1] small,
leggy filly: fair maiden at 2 yrs: little show (mainly in handicaps) in 1999: stays 6f:
acts on good to firm going: blinkered fourth start. *G. Woodward*

LADY LAZARUS 3 ch.f. Beveled (USA) – Swilly Express (Ballacashtal (CAN)) **–**
[1998 75d: 6m⁴ 6m⁶ 7d³ 6.1d 7s 1999 8m 6m 7g 10.2m Jul 15] angular filly:
disappointing maiden: races freely: has been bandaged behind. *M. Blanshard*

LADY-LOVE 2 b.f. (Apr 25) Pursuit of Love 124 – Lady Day (FR) (Lightning (FR) **70**
129) [1999 5g* 6m 6d⁶ 5g Aug 18] quite attractive filly: seventh living foal:
half-sister to several winners, including 3-y-o Day-Boy and 1995 2-y-o 1m winner
Ladykirk (by Slip Anchor), latter later suited by middle distances: dam French 9f
to 12.5f winner: fair form when winning maiden at Musselburgh in June: well held
last 2 starts: races freely, and may prove best at 5f/6f: upset in stalls second start.
Denys Smith

LADY MARGARET 3 b.f. Sir Harry Lewis (USA) 127 – Candarela 41 (Damis- **–**
ter (USA) 123) [1998 NR 1999 10.1g⁶ 12f⁶ 14.8m⁶ a16g⁶ 8s Oct 26] first foal: dam,
poor maiden, half-sister to useful 1¼m performer Game Ploy: poor maiden: left
P. Hedger after penultimate start. *Mrs L. Richards*

LADY MELBOURNE (IRE) 3 b.f. Indian Ridge 123 – Gayshuka 112 (Lord **76 d**
Gayle (USA) 124) [1998 65: 6m 6s² 5s⁴ 5.2s⁴ a5g 1999 6g² 6f* 5.3s 5m a6g 6d Nov
1] angular filly: fair handicapper: won at Thirsk in July: well below form after: will
stay 7f: acts on firm and soft going, probably not on fibresand: sold 23,000 gns.
M. Johnston

LADY MONTDORE 2 b.f. (Jan 28) Pursuit of Love 124 – Kentfield (Busted **43**
134) [1999 5m 8d⁶ a7g 8d Nov 1] 11,000Y: sixth foal: half-sister to 4 winners: dam
once raced: poor maiden: trained by M. Johnston on debut: dead. *T. J. Etherington*

LADY MOORINGS (IRE) 3 b.f. Dolphin Street (FR) 125 – Crimson Ring **39**
(Persian Bold 123) [1998 –: 6g 6g 7d 1999 9.7s 8m⁶ 10m 10.5m 11.7g⁶ 8m⁶ 9.9m Jul
30] close-coupled filly: poor maiden: stayed 1¼m: dead. *M. Blanshard*

LADY MUCK (IRE) 3 b.f. Shalford (IRE) 124§ – Kept In Style 49 (Castle Keep **–**
121) [1998 74: 6m² 6g⁴ 6.3s 7g² 7m* 8m⁵ 8m⁶ 8m 1999 7.1g 8.3m 10g⁶ 10d 8s Oct

26] sturdy filly: fair winner at 2 yrs: little show in 1999: stays 1m: acts on soft and good to firm going: blinkered once. *D. J. S. ffrench Davis*

LADY NAIRN 3 b.f. Mujadil (USA) 119 – Animate (IRE) 62 (Tate Gallery (USA) 117) [1998 41+: 5v³ 5g⁶ 6f 1999 a6g Nov 17] poor maiden. *J. Berry*   –

LADY NOOR 2 b.f. (Apr 9) Lugana Beach 116 – Noor El Houdah (IRE) 61 (Fayruz 116) [1999 5g 5.1f 5s³ 6d 6v³ 5s Nov 5] 5,000Y: leggy, angular filly: first foal: dam 5f (at 2 yrs) to 7f winner: fair maiden: best effort when third of 17 in nursery at Newbury penultimate start: stays 6f: acts on heavy going. *Mrs P. N. Dutfield*   **71**

LADY ODDJOB (IRE) 3 gr.f. Up And At 'em 109 – Thalssa (Rusticaro (FR) 124) [1998 50: 7d a6g⁵ a7g³ 1999 a7g 6.1g a8g³ a9.4g⁵ a8.5g 10d 10d a8g Dec 13] smallish, close-coupled filly: modest maiden: reportedly finished lame on reappearance (off 5 months after): stays 1m, probably 9.4f: acts on fibresand: often blinkered/visored. *K. McAuliffe*   – a53

LADY OF ARAGON 3 b.f. Aragon 118 – Gentle Stream 55 (Sandy Creek 123) [1998 63: 5.7s 6g⁶ 7m⁴ 7m⁴ 8g 1999 10m 11.7g 9.9m⁶ 8.5m⁵ 8.1d Aug 5] leggy, unfurnished filly: modest maiden: should stay 1m: acts on good to firm going: visored final start. *M. J. Heaton-Ellis*   **52**

LADY OF CHAD 2 b.f. (Feb 18) Last Tycoon 131 – Sahara Breeze 85 (Ela-Mana-Mou 132) [1999 8m* 8v* Oct 3]   **109 p**
    Despite the prevailing heavy ground for the weekend at Longchamp featuring the Prix de l'Arc de Triomphe, there were some close finishes, with seven of the ten pattern winners over the two days having a length or less to spare. There were no real shocks among the ten either—Diamond White, successful in the Prix de l'Opera at a shade over 11/1, was the longest priced. One of the most decisive scorers, second only to eight-length Prix Hubert de Chaudenay winner Amilynx, was Lady of Chad, whose emphatic three-length defeat of New Story after making all the running in the Prix Marcel Boussac turned the spotlight on her for the classics. She looks the sort to train on, and should be kept on the right side, but it has to be said that the form of the Marcel Boussac does not look good even by the standards of a race which, from the last five runnings, has produced just one winner to have gone on to Group 1 success the following year. That filly was Ryafan, who won three such races in the States in 1997, including the Yellow Ribbon and the Matriarch. Lady of Chad had won a newcomers' race at Longchamp in September, making all to beat Highest Cool comfortably by a length and a half. All the eleven runners in the Marcel Boussac were winners, including pattern performers Dignify, successful in the Prix d'Aumale, and Lady Vettori, unbeaten in five races, including the Prix du Calvados at Deauville. They were the first and second favourites, with Lady of Chad fourth in the betting at just over 5/1. British hopes rested on Chez Cherie, Miletrian, Issey Rose and Perugia. As soon as the stalls opened Lady of Chad's jockey Olivier Peslier sent her on and nothing else got a look in. Ridden along entering the straight, she had the race in her pocket a long way out as New Story, whose previous form was not outstanding, stayed dourly in second with Lady Vettori half a length away third. Allowing for the fact that not all the runners were suited by the conditions, this was still quite an impres-

Prix Marcel Boussac Royal Barriere, Longchamp—a first Group 1 victory
for the French-based trainer Richard Gibson as Lady of Chad makes all in only her second race;
New Story (rail), Lady Vettori (noseband) and Miletrian are her closest pursuers

sive display and it provided Lady of Chad's trainer, English-born Richard Gibson, with easily his most important win in three years with a licence.

Lady of Chad (b.f. Feb 18, 1997)	Last Tycoon (b 1983)	Try My Best (b 1975)	Northern Dancer
			Sex Appeal
		Mill Princes (b 1977)	Mill Reef
			Irish Lass II
	Sahara Breeze (b 1986)	Ela-Mana-Mou (b 1976)	Pitcairn
			Rose Bertin
		Diamond Land (br 1978)	Sparkler
			Canaan

Last Tycoon, who finished his sprint championship season in 1986 with victory in the Breeders' Cup Mile, has sired several first-class performers to go along with a host of nondescript ones. The stars, all successful in Group 1 company, have been Bigstone, Ezzoud, Lost World, Marju, Taipan and, in Australia, Mahogany. Last Tycoon started off in Ireland but now shuttles between Australia and Japan. A significant proportion of his better progeny have stayed further than he did, and Lady of Chad will probably stay a mile and a half. A 28,000-guinea Newmarket October Yearling Sales purchase, she is out of a mare by stamina influence Ela-Mana-Mou. The mare, Sahara Breeze, placed over seven furlongs and a mile in three of her four starts, showing fair form, and, sold for 4,200 guineas as a filly out of training in 1989, has produced five offspring of racing age. Before Lady of Chad her winners were Rapier (by Sharpo), a fairly useful performer at up to a mile and a quarter, and Alcazar (by Alzao), who showed smart form around a mile and a half as a three-year-old in 1998, putting up his best effort when landing a listed race at Doncaster by five lengths. Sahara Breeze has a yearling filly by Lycius and a filly foal by Lake Coniston. The grandam Diamond Land, a winner over thirteen furlongs in

Mr John Martin's "Lady of Chad"

Ireland out of a half-sister to St Leger victress Cantelo, produced three stakes performers, notably Ivanka, who won the Fillies' Mile and finished second to Armiger in the Racing Post Trophy in 1992 before fracturing her pelvis early the following year. Diamond Land is also grandam of the smart Japanese performer Tsukuba Symphony. *R. Gibson, France*

LADY OF GUADALOPE (IRE)   4 b.f. Tirol 127 – Gorgeous Annie (Hello   **29**
Gorgeous (USA) 128) [1998 –: 12s 7g 1999 a11g⁶ a8g⁶ a8g 10s 10g 10.5m Jul 10]
IR 5,000F, IR 13,000Y: ex-Irish filly: third foal: half-sister to winners abroad by
Mazaad and Mac's Imp: dam, second over 7f at 2 yrs in Ireland, half-sister to smart
performers up to 1m Darcy's Thatcher and Rasa Penang: bad maiden: tried visored.
D. J. S. Cosgrove

LADY OF HONOUR (IRE)   2 b.f. (Jan 18) Bigstone (IRE) 126 – Zabeta (Diesis   **70**
133) [1999 7d³ 7m 7d 7g* 8d Sep 23] 28,000F, 650,000 francs Y: third foal:
half-sister to 3-y-o Turtle's Rising: dam French 1m winner out of half-sister to Prix
de Diane winner Harbour: fair performer: won nursery at Yarmouth in September:
beaten long way out final start: should stay 1m+: sold 8,000 gns, sent to Norway.
E. A. L. Dunlop

LADY OF THE DANCE   4 b.f. Tragic Role (USA) – Waltz 75 (Jimmy Reppin   **–**
131) [1998 –: 11.9m⁴ a13g⁵ 1999 14.1g 10v Sep 24] lengthy, good-topped filly: little
form. *P. Eccles*

LADY OF THE LUNE   4 b.f. Skyliner 117 – Hot Feet (Marching On 101) [1998   **–**
–: 6d 8.3m a9.4g⁶ 7.6m a8.5g 1999 a6g 7.1m Aug 5] of no account. *J. M. Bradley*

LADY OF THE NIGHT (IRE)   4 b.f. Night Shift (USA) – Joma Kaanem   **54**
(Double Form 130) [1998 NR 1999 7m 8.2s⁴ a10g² Dec 29] IR 22,000Y: closely
related to 1m winner Killinghall (by Glow) and half-sister to several winners, including 5-y-o Dellua (by Suave Dancer): dam, ran once, from good family: in frame in
maidens at Nottingham (final start for P. Harris) then Lingfield (best effort): stays
1¼m. *Mrs L. Stubbs*

LADY OF WINDSOR (IRE)   2 ch.f. (Apr 18) Woods of Windsor (USA) –   **70 §**
North Lady (Northfields (USA)) [1999 5f⁴ 6m⁴ 6g⁴ 7g³ 6m² 7d² 7.1g⁴ 8d 8d⁴ 7d 7s⁴
Nov 2] IR 3,000Y: sturdy, lengthy filly: sister to 3-y-o Arbor Ealis and half-sister to
several winners, including 1¼m/1½m winner Eskimo Nel (by Shy Groom): dam
poor half-sister to Lowther winner Miss Demure: fair maiden: stays 1m: acts on soft
and good to firm going: visored/blinkered last 8 starts: has found little, swished tail
and wandered: not one to trust. *I. Semple*

LADY PEPPIATT (IRE)   3 b.f. Tirol 127 – Kirsova (Absalom 128) [1998 54,   **–**
a58: 6m 6.1m³ a6g* a5g³ 5d⁴ 6s⁴ 7f³ a6g* a6g⁴ 6f⁵ 6m 1999 a8g* a7g⁶ a8g² 8.1m   **a52**
a7g a6g⁶ 6m 7g Aug 11] good-topped filly: modest at best: all 3 wins at Southwell,
including claimer in January: below form final 5 starts: stays easy 1m: acts on firm
going, good to soft and fibresand: often forces pace. *J. S. Moore*

LADY PETRA   3 b.f. Petong 126 – Miss Clarinet (Pharly (FR) 130) [1998 –: 6d   **–**
7m 7d 1999 8g 8g 9f a8g 10g Aug 18] sparely-made filly: little sign of ability:
blinkered final 3 starts: sold 1,300 gns in September. *V. Soane*

LADY RACHEL (IRE)   4 b.f. Priolo (USA) 127 – Alpine Spring 95 (Head For   **67 d**
Heights 125) [1998 75: a8.5g² a8g³ 11.1v³ 9.9s⁶ 10d³ 10m* 12s⁴ 12g 12g³ 12d*
11.8m³ 14.1m² 15d² 12g 1999 a12g 12g 14s⁴ 12m 13g⁶ 14d³ 15.9m 14.1g 13.9d
14.1g 12g Nov 3] sparely-made filly: fair handicapper at best: below form after third
start: stays 15f well: has form on good to firm going and fibresand, very best efforts
on softer than good: has been heavily bandaged: joined M. W. Easterby. *J. L. Eyre*

LADY ROCKSTAR   4 b.f. Rock Hopper 124 – Silk St James (Pas de Seul 133)   **88**
[1998 90: 9.7d 10d 9.1m* 9.7m* 8.1m* 10.1d* 8.2d* 10m* 9.7m* 10g* 10f 10.1m³
9d 10g 10.1d⁵ 10s 1999 10s 10m 10.3f⁴ 10s* 10f⁵ 10m² 10m⁵ 10.3g⁴ 10m 10.5s²
10d 10.1m⁴ 10s 10.1d⁵ Oct 27] smallish, sturdy filly: fairly useful handicapper: won
20-runner event at Newbury in May: creditable efforts only when in frame after:
stays 10.5f: acts on soft and good to firm going, possibly not on firm nowadays: often
gives trouble at stalls (has refused to enter): usually held up: below form both starts
blinkered. *M. J. Ryan*

LADY SANDROVITCH (IRE) 2 b.f. (Apr 20) Desert Style (IRE) 121 – Mauras **44**
Pride (IRE) (Cadeaux Genereux 131) [1999 5d⁵ a5g⁴ a5g⁴ a6g³ Dec 13] 2,300Y:
first foal: dam (unraced) from family of William Hill Futurity winner Al Hareb: poor
maiden: stays 6f: acts on fibresand. *R. A. Fahey*

LADY SANTANA (IRE) 2 b.f. (Feb 19) Doyoun 124 – Santana Lady (IRE) 72 **57**
(Blakeney 126) [1999 5m 5d 6m Sep 7] 12,000Y: first foal: dam 8.3f to 1½m winner:
modest maiden: trained by M. Heaton-Ellis on debut, C. Cox next outing: will stay at
least 1m. *Mrs Merrita Jones*

LADY SARKA (IRE) 2 b.f. (Jan 11) Lake Coniston (IRE) 131 – Petite Epaulette **90**
80 (Night Shift (USA)) [1999 5g⁴ 5m* 5g⁴ 6m² 5.2m 6d² 5g* Oct 16] IR 32,000F,
20,000Y: angular, quite attractive filly: second foal: half-sister to fairly useful 1997
2-y-o 5f winner Shalford's Honour (by Shalford): dam, 5f winner, ran only at 2 yrs:
fairly useful performer: won maiden at Warwick in May and minor event at Catterick
in October: effective at 5f/6f: acts on good to firm and good to soft going. *R. Hannon*

LADY'S HEART (IRE) 4 b.f. Broken Hearted 124 – Lady Fawley 86 (He **51**
Loves Me 120) [1998 59: 12g 6.5g³ 5d 8g² 9s⁴ 7d³ 7d 9m 1999 8s a7g 6m⁶ 7g 9g 5g³
5m⁵ 6.5g⁴ 9m a7g Nov 19] half-sister to winners abroad by Runnett and Carmelite
House: dam Irish 2-y-o 1m winner: modest maiden handicapper at best: left L. Reilly,
Ireland before final start: stays 9f: acts on good to firm and good to soft ground:
blinkered once: inconsistent. *D. Carroll*

LADY SO BOLD 4 ch.f. Bold Arrangement 127 – Lady Blues Singer (Chief **–**
Singer 131) [1998 –: a8g 7f 8g⁵ 7m⁶ 1999 10f May 4] unfurnished filly: little sign of
ability. *Mrs L. Stubbs*

LADY STALKER 2 b.f. (Apr 23) Primo Dominie 121 – Tarvie 101 (Swing Easy **57**
(USA) [1999 5.1m 5m⁴ 5.1m⁶ 5g⁶ 5.7s Oct 26] half-sister to several winners,
including fairly useful sprinter Macfarlane and 1985 Middle Park winner Stalker
(both by Kala Shikari): dam sprinter: modest maiden: well beaten in seller final start:
should stay 6f: acts on good to firm going. *M. J. Fetherston-Godley*

LADY TILLY 2 b.f. (Feb 17) Puissance 110 – Lady of Itatiba (BEL) (King of **49**
Macedon 126) [1999 5g⁶ 5m 5m 7d³ 7.1m 7s⁵ 8v⁶ 5g Nov 3] 700Y: sparely-made
filly: fifth foal in Britain: half-sister to 3-y-o Peppers Girl and 5f winner Had A Girl
(by Hadeer): dam won in Belgium: poor maiden: stays 7f: acts on good to soft going,
probably on good to firm: blinkered final start. *Martyn Wane*

LADY UPSTAGE (IRE) 2 b.f. (Apr 25) Alzao (USA) 117 – She's The Tops 83 **90**
(Shernazar 131) [1999 7m³ 7m 7s* 7.3s⁴ Oct 23] IR 36,000Y: well-made filly: fifth
foal: half-sister to 1996 2-y-o 6f winner Lycility (by Lycius) and 4-y-o The Blues
Academy: dam 1½m winner out of half-sister to Most Welcome: fairly useful form:
won maiden at Brighton in September: good fourth in listed event at Newbury final
start: will stay 1¼m+: acts on good going. *B. W. Hills*

LADY VIENNA 2 ch.f. (Mar 28) Weldnaas (USA) 112 – Fresh Lady (IRE) (Fresh **56**
Breeze (USA) 80) [1999 7m a6g 7d 10.2s⁵ Sep 27] first foal: dam placed in Irish
points: form only when 15 lengths fifth of 12 in maiden at Bath: will stay 1½m.
W. G. M. Turner

LADYWELL BLAISE (IRE) 2 b.f. (Feb 13) Turtle Island (IRE) 123 – Duly **– p**
Elected (Persian Bold 123) [1999 a6g⁵ Dec 22] 27,000Y: sister to fairly useful 1998
2-y-o 6f winner Kangaroo Island and half-sister to winners in Italy by Taufan and
Mujtahid: dam, fourth at 1m/9f in Ireland, sister to Phoenix Stakes winner King
Persian: never dangerous fifth of 9 in maiden at Lingfield: should improve.
M. L. W. Bell

LADY WYN 4 ch.f. Mac's Fighter 116 – Wanracine (Dom Racine (FR) 121) **–**
[1998 NR 1999 10g 7m 8.1m Sep 9] fourth foal: dam possibly stayed 13f: never a
threat in sellers. *J. M. Bradley*

LA FAY 2 b.f. (Mar 7) Caerleon (USA) 132 – Fayrooz (USA) 74 (Gulch (USA)) **74**
[1999 7m² 7d⁴ Oct 11] second foal: half-sister to 3-y-o Beryl: dam 2-y-o 7f winner
out of half-sister to El Gran Senor and Try My Best: in frame in maidens at Kempton
and Leicester: will be very well suited by 1¼m+. *J. L. Dunlop*

LAFITE 3 b.f. Robellino (USA) 127 – Gorgeous Dancer (IRE) (Nordico (USA)) **92**
[1998 68: 7g 7m⁴ 7s³ 1999 8.3m³ 8.1m* 8m³ 10.5d⁴ 10m 10d* 10d* 10s Oct 23]
good-bodied filly: fairly useful performer: won handicaps at Chepstow in July,
Newbury (tongue tied) in September and Brighton in October: not discredited in
listed race at Gelsenkirchen final start: stays 1¼m well: acts on good to firm and good
to soft going: sometimes wanders, but is genuine. *J. W. Hills*

LAFLEUR (IRE) 2 ch.f. (Apr 18) Grand Lodge (USA) 125 – Russian Countess **75 p**
(USA) 104 (Nureyev (USA) 131) [1999 8d Oct 22] 75,000Y: medium-sized, lengthy
filly: seventh foal: half-sister to smart 7f (at 2 yrs) to 11f winner and Oaks third
Crown of Light (by Mtoto), and to useful 7f/1m winners Romanzof (by Kris) and
4-y-o Alboostan: dam 2-y-o 1m winner in France: green, seventh of 18 to Interlude
in maiden at Doncaster, staying on having missed break: will be suited by 1¼m+:
sure to improve. *M. R. Channon*

LA GALLERIA 4 ch.f. Royal Academy (USA) 130 – Two And Sixpence (USA) **–**
74 (Chief's Crown (USA)) [1998 NR 1999 11.7g Jun 30] tall, workmanlike filly:
well beaten in maidens at 2 yrs, and in seller on belated reappearance. *J. S. Moore*

LAGAN 6 b.g. Shareef Dancer (USA) 135 – Lagta 75 (Kris 135) [1998 NR 1999 **–**
21.6d 17.2m Jun 23] good-bodied gelding: fair hurdler: poor maiden handicapper on
Flat, well held in 1999: probably stays 1¾m: tried blinkered: tail swisher. *S. Gollings*

L'AGNEAU NOIR 3 br.f. Rock City 120 – Shernborne (Kalaglow 132) [1998 **–**
54: 5.1m² 5g 6s 1999 6.1m 7f 7d 8f Sep 6] modest form at best in 2-y-o maidens: well
held in handicaps in 1999: stays 6f: very slowly away final start. *W. R. Muir*

LAGO DI COMO 2 b.c. (Mar 15) Piccolo 121 – Farmer's Pet 90 (Sharrood **53**
(USA) 124) [1999 7.1m 7m 7.7d 8d Nov 1] 21,000Y: sturdy colt: has a round action:
second foal: half-brother to 3-y-o Never Can Tell: dam stayer: modest maiden: well
held in nursery at Redcar final start: should stay 1m. *T. J. Naughton*

LAGO DI LEVICO 2 ch.c. (Mar 24) Pelder (IRE) 125 – Langton Herring **43**
(Nearly A Hand 115) [1999 6m Aug 13] half-brother to several winners, including
useful but untrustworthy sprinter Sylvan Breeze and 1994 2-y-o 7f winner Chaldon
Herring (both by Sulaafah): dam unraced: eighth of 10 in maiden at Lingfield, left
behind from halfway. *A. P. Jarvis*

LAGO DI VARANO 7 b.g. Clantime 101 – On The Record 72 (Record Token **90**
128) [1998 97: 5g³ 5s⁶ 5.1m 6s⁴ 5s² 5s* 5s 5g⁴ 6s⁶ 5g² 6g² 6m 6f² 6g 5.6g 6s³ 6g 5m
5s⁶ 10m 6m 5s 7m 6m³ 5d* 5m 5m 5m* 5g³ 6f⁶ 6m 5m* 5.6g 5m 5s 5d 5d⁶ 5d⁴
Oct 18] strong gelding: fairly useful handicapper: won at York in June and Sandown
in August: good fourth of 18 at Pontefract final start: best at 5f (given bit of a test)/6f:
unraced on heavy going, acts on any other: usually visored/blinkered: races up with
pace: tough. *R. M. Whitaker*

LAGOON (IRE) 2 ch.c. (Jan 23) Common Grounds 118 – Secret Hideaway **90 +**
(USA) (Key To The Mint (USA)) [1999 5f³ 5.1g⁶ 6d* 6s³ 6s⁵ Oct 23] 30,000Y:
compact colt: half-brother to 3 winners, including fairly useful 5f (at 2 yrs) and 7f
winner Muchtarak (by Try My Best) and a 1¼m winner by Contract Law: dam
unraced: fairly useful form: sweating and on toes, won maiden at Pontefract (after
4-month break) in September: ran creditably in nursery at Newmarket and listed race
at Doncaster subsequently: will be suited by 7f+: acts on soft going. *B. W. Hills*

LAGUNA BAY (IRE) 5 b.m. Arcane (USA) – Meg Daughter (IRE) (Doulab **51**
(USA) 115) [1998 –: a12g 14.1s 17.2d 1999 13.1g 11.9f² 17.2g⁵ 17.2f* 15.8m⁵
14.1m⁵ 16f⁴ 14.4m Sep 8] close-coupled mare: modest handicapper: won seller at
Bath in June: below best after next start: stays 17f: acts on firm and soft going:
usually races prominently/leads. *G. M. McCourt*

LAHAAY 2 ch.g. (Mar 23) Lahib (USA) 129 – Jasarah (IRE) 70 (Green Desert **77 p**
(USA) 127) [1999 7v 8s⁵ Nov 6] quite good-topped gelding: third foal: half-brother
to 3-y-o Muqtarb and 4-y-o Safi: dam, twice runner-up at 7f, from family of Celestial
Storm: much better effort in maidens when fifth of 18 to Summoner at Doncaster,
staying on well: should stay 1¼m: can improve further. *M. P. Tregoning*

LAHAN 2 b.f. (Jan 22) Unfuwain (USA) 131 – Amanah (USA) 100 (Mr Pros- **104 p**
pector (USA)) [1999 7g* 7g* Oct 16] big, lengthy, rather unfurnished filly with
scope: powerful galloper: first foal: dam 1m winner out of US Grade 1 1m and 8.5f

Owen Brown Rockfel Stakes, Newmarket—only two weeks after making her debut, Lahan (striped cap) becomes a pattern winner with a game victory over Clog Dance (white cap) and Total Love (rail)

winner Cheval Volant: won maiden at Redcar and 12-runner Owen Brown Rockfel Stakes at Newmarket, both in October: heavily backed, travelled strongly, led 2f out and held on gamely by neck from Clog Dance in latter: will stay 1m, probably 1¼m: almost certainly a smart filly in the making, sure to win more races. *J. H. M. Gosden*

LAILA MANJA (IRE) 3 b.f. Diesis 133 – London Pride (USA) 106 (Lear Fan (USA) 130) [1998 –: 7d 1999 8.3m 6m 8m a9.4g⁶ Jun 19] little form: sold 4,500 gns in October. *P. F. I. Cole* —

LA ISLA BONITA 4 ch.f. Lion Cavern (USA) 117 – La Dama Bonita (USA) 87 (El Gran Senor (USA) 136) [1998 72: 8.3m² 8.3m⁴ 8m³ 8.1m² 8m² 8.1g 8m 1999 8g 8.2f⁵ a8g³ 9m 8g² 7g² 8d Oct 11] tall, angular filly: fair maiden: acts on good to firm going: sold 3,000 gns in December. *J. W. Hills* **67**

LAIYL (IRE) 3 gr.f. Nureyev (USA) 131 – Alydaress (USA) 124 (Alydar (USA)) [1998 NR 1999 10v* 12s Nov 6] third living foal: closely related to useful French 1¼m and 10.5f winner Allurement (by Sadler's Wells): dam, won Irish Oaks, half-sister to Cheveley Park winners Park Appeal (dam of Cape Cross, grandam of Diktat) and Desirable (dam of Shadayid): created very favourable impression when landing odds by 7 lengths from Deputise in maiden at Ayr in October, winning as rider pleased: favourite, raced freely when last of 7 in listed event at Doncaster next time: should still do better, possibly back around 1¼m. *J. H. M. Gosden* **85 p**

LAJADHAL (FR) 10 gr.g. Bellypha 130 – Rose d'Amour (USA) (Lines of Power (USA)) [1998 –: 17.2g a14g 17.2s 1999 10g 14.1g Jul 2] of little account on Flat. *P. D. Purdy* —

LAKABI (USA) 2 b. or br.f. (May 22) Nureyev (USA) 131 – Lakab (USA) 74 (Manila (USA)) [1999 6d⁶ Oct 29] $260,000Y: third foal: dam, 7.6f winner, half-sister to smart 1m winner Wixim: easy to back, shaped encouragingly when considerately-handled sixth of 19 to Pax in maiden at Newmarket, travelling well long way: will probably stay 1m: sure to improve a fair bit at 3 yrs. *J. H. M. Gosden* **63 p**

LAKE ARIA 6 b.m. Rambo Dancer (CAN) 107 – Hinge (Import 127) [1998 25: a7s a12g² a12g a11g 7g⁶ 8m 16.2m 12m 8v 1999 a8g a7f a12g⁴ a14g 6g a7g a6g Nov 22] lengthy, angular mare: bad maiden: left J. L. Eyre after fourth start: blinkered twice. *J. Balding* —

LAKE DOMINION 10 b.g. Primo Dominie 121 – Piney Lake 54 (Sassafras (FR) 135) [1998 25, a43: 14.1d⁵ 17.2s² a14g³ a16m a14.8g 1999 a16.2g 12g 18m a14g a14g⁶ Nov 30] poor handicapper: no form in 1999: tried blinkered. *K. C. Comerford* —

LAKELAND PADDY (IRE) 2 b.c. (Apr 4) Lake Coniston (IRE) 131 – Inshad 81 (Indian King (USA) 128) [1999 5m 6s⁵ 6m⁴ 5d⁴ 6.1g² 6d⁵ 7.3v⁶ Oct 23] 7,200Y: **73**

workmanlike, rather unfurnished colt: seventh foal: half-brother to useful 7f/1m winner Mareha (by Cadeaux Genereux): dam 7f winner: fair maiden: probably stays 7f: acts on soft and good to firm going. *M. Blanshard*

LAKE MEHRA   3 b.c. Superlative 118 – Westering 54 (Auction Ring (USA) 123)   **38** [1998 45: 5g a7g a7g⁶ 1999 a8g⁴ a9.4g⁴ a8g⁴ a8f a8.5g⁶ Feb 20] poor maiden: stays 1m: acts on all-weather: visored last 3 starts. *M. H. Tompkins*

LAKE MILLSTATT (IRE)   4 b.f. Magical Strike (USA) 114 – Repeat Addition   **77** (IRE) (Hard Fought 125) [1998 NR 1999 9v⁴ 9.5g 12m² 10f* 11m 8.5m² 9g* 9m² 10m 6.2v a8.5g Dec 1] second foal: dam ran twice in Ireland: fair performer: won maiden at Clonmel in June and handicap at Cork in August: stays 1¼m: acts on firm ground, well held on fibresand at Wolverhampton final start. *A. Leahy, Ireland*

LAKE SUNBEAM   3 b.g. Nashwan (USA) 135 – Moon Drop 103 (Dominion   **91** 123) [1998 91p: 8m³ 1999 8s⁶ 7m* 7.3m 8m⁵ 7g³ 8.3m⁶ 8m a8g⁴ a12g⁵ Dec 6] rangy, angular gelding: very good mover: has reportedly had wind operation: fairly useful performer: won 4-runner minor event at Salisbury in June: ran well in handicaps fourth to sixth starts: left R. Hannon after seventh one, G. L. Moore after eighth: will probably prove best at 7f/1m: acts on good to firm going (possibly not on soft), some promise on equitrack. *W. R. Muir*

LAKE TAAL   4 ch.f. Prince Sabo 123 – Calachuchi 74 (Martinmas 128) [1998 59:   **49** 6d 8m³ a8.5g 8.5m 1999 7m² a11g 10m 7.5m Jul 2] poor performer: no form after reappearance: stays 1m: acts on good to firm going: sold 750 gns in July and won in Holland after. *Miss J. A. Camacho*

LA LANDIERE (FR)   4 b. or br.f. Synefos (USA) 114 – As You Are (FR) (Saint   **–** Estephe (FR) 123) [1998 12v² 1999 10m⁵ 12.3d⁶ Aug 20] first reported foal: dam twice-raced daughter of smart French filly at 9f/1¼m Asania: second in minor event at Lyon Parilly on debut in 1998: well held both starts in 1999, leaving J. Bertran de Balanda in France after reappearance: successful twice over hurdles in December for A. King. *D. Nicholson*

LALANDO   2 ch.c. (Mar 29) Forzando 122 – Laleston 73 (Junius (USA) 124)   **76** [1999 5d⁴ 5g³ 6d⁴ 5m² 5g² 5v Sep 24] 19,000Y: rather unfurnished colt: eighth foal: half-brother to four 5f winners, including 3-y-o Ewenny: dam 5f winner: fair maiden: effective at 5f/6f: acts on good to firm ground, well beaten on heavy: has worn tongue strap: possibly no battler. *J. L. Spearing*

LALA SALAMA (IRE)   3 br.f. College Chapel 122 – Sally St Clair (Sallust 134)   **62** [1998 NR 1999 9.9m 10.2s 8.3g Oct 11] IR 3,000Y: half-sister to numerous winners here and abroad, including fairly useful 5f (at 2 yrs) to 9f (in France) winner Ride Sally Ride (by Shalford) and smart winner up to 11f in Ireland/UAE Doreg (by Fools Holme): dam, winner in Canada, half-sister to Superlative: modest form in maidens: eased right off after being hampered final start: may yet do better. *Lady Herries*

LA LYONESSE   4 b.f. Lion Cavern (USA) 117 – Princess Sioux 69 (Commanche   **–** Run 133) [1998 62, a59: 9.9m 11.5g⁵ 11.5m⁶ 10m³ 9.9m a14.8g a10g⁴ a10g³ a10g⁶ 1999 a10g Jan 9] angular filly: modest maiden: well beaten only run of 1999: probably stays 11.5f: acts on good to firm going and equitrack. *J. W. Hills*

LAMBORGHINI LOZ   2 b.c. (Apr 21) King's Signet (USA) 110 – Scented   **60** Goddess (IRE) 54 (Godswalk (USA) 130) [1999 5v 5m⁵ 5f³ 5f 5f* 5.3s³ 5m⁶ a5f⁴ a5g² Oct 13] 5,000Y: good-topped colt: fifth foal: half-brother to Italian 7f to 9f winner Sampei (by Reprimand): dam 7f (at 2 yrs)/1m winner, also successful over hurdles: modest performer: won seller at Lingfield in July: raced at 5f: acts on firm going, soft and fibresand: blinkered/visored 4 of last 5 outings: usually races prominently/leads: sold 5,200 gns in October. *J. Berry*

LAMBSON KATOOSHA   4 b.f. Weldnaas (USA) 112 – Lamsonetti 68 (Never   **–** So Bold 135) [1998 –: 7.9g 12m 1999 12.3m 8s 7d a8g Nov 15] workmanlike filly: no sign of ability. *J. Pearce*

LAMEH   2 ch.f. (Jan 31) Mujtahid (USA) 118 – Tablah (USA) 86 (Silver Hawk   **80 ?** (USA) 123) [1999 6m⁴ 7v 8d⁵ Oct 22] strong, lengthy filly: second foal: half-sister to 3-y-o Ghuroob: dam, 2-y-o 6f winner (stayed 1¼m), from family of Alydar: 25/1, possibly flattered when appearing to show much improved form to finish fifth of 18 to Interlude in maiden at Doncaster, dictating pace much of way: stays 1m: acts on good to soft ground. *P. T. Walwyn*

LAMENT   3 b.f. Phountzi (USA) 104 – Devils Dirge 68 (Song 132) [1998 61+, a–: 5.3g 6m⁵ 7d³ 6m² 6.1d² 6g* 6f⁵ 7g⁶ 7s a6g a8g 1999 6.1s² 6s* 6g⁶ 7d a6g a7g Nov 17] modest performer: left Mrs L. Stubbs after reappearance: won 17-runner claimer at Pontefract in October: stays 6f: acts on soft and good to firm going, little form on all-weather: visored final start: sometimes bandaged behind. *Miss Gay Kelleway*   **64 a–**

LAMERIE (IRE)   3 b.c. Roi Danzig (USA) – Eurosanta (Scorpio (FR) 127) [1998 NR 1999 10.3d⁶ 8s³ 11m⁴ 10f* 12d 12m 11.6d² 10.2m* 10d* 10d² a10g⁴ Nov 16] IR 7,000Y: sturdy, close-coupled colt: half-brother to an Irish bumper winner by Eurobus: dam third in Irish bumper: useful performer: won maiden at Brighton in April and handicaps at Chepstow and Newmarket (apprentice event) in September: stays 1½m: acts on firm going, soft and equitrack: sent to USA. *R. Hannon*   **95**

LAMMOSKI (IRE)   2 ch.g. (Mar 21) Hamas (IRE) 125§ – Penny In My Shoe (USA) (Sir Ivor 135) [1999 6s 6.1f 5m 7m 5m 5.2m⁵ 7m 5.1g 6g 6d a6g a6g a5g a5g⁵ Dec 21] workmanlike gelding: has a round action: half-brother to 1992 2-y-o 5f winner Other One (by Hadeer) and a winner in USA by Believe It: dam, unraced half-sister to Gorytus, out of 1000 Guineas winner Glad Rags: no worthwhile form: visored final start: has been slowly away, got upset in stalls. *M. C. Chapman*   **–**

LAMORNA   5 ch.m. Shavian 125 – Malibasta 83 (Auction Ring (USA) 123) [1998 53: 8g⁶ 8.1g 7m 7f* 7m⁶ a7g 7m 8s 1999 a10g⁶ 8g 7m³ 6.1g 6m⁴ 6.9m Jun 24] lengthy mare: has quick action: modest handicapper: stays 7f: acts on firm and good to soft going: visored last 5 starts. *D. W. P. Arbuthnot*   **53**

LAMORRAN   2 b.g. (May 11) Son Pardo 107 – Sans Diablo (IRE) (Mac's Imp (USA) 116) [1999 5.7f 6.8m 5.1m 6m 6.1m a6f⁴ a6g⁶ 5.7s Oct 26] 5,500Y: leggy gelding: first foal: dam unraced: form only at Wolverhampton sixth start: stays 6f: acts on fibresand: visored/blinkered last 3 outings. *D. Haydn Jones*   **– a60**

LAMZENA (IRE)   3 b.f. Fairy King (USA) – Ezana (Ela-Mana-Mou 132) [1998 71p: 6g³ 1999 7g⁶ 8m 8.5f⁴ Dec 24] has a quick action: quite useful form when sixth to Valentine Waltz in Nell Gwyn Stakes at Newmarket in April: sweating, tailed off last in 1000 Guineas at Newmarket: left G. Wragg and off course 7½ months then 2 lengths fourth in maiden on US debut: bred to need much further than 7f. *A. McKeever, USA*   **92**

LANCASHIRE LEGEND   6 gr.g. Belfort (FR) 89 – Peters Pet Girl (Norwich (USA) 125) [1998 –§, a63d: a7g⁴ a7g³ a6g⁴ a7g⁵ a8g² a8g³ a7g⁶ a7g⁵ a6g a7g a6g a7g⁶ a10g a7g⁵ a6g 1999 a6g⁶ a6g⁵ a7g⁵ a7g 7g Mar 31] poor performer: barely stays 1m: acts on firm ground and all-weather: blinkered/visored earlier in career: carries head high, and finds little: not one to trust: sold 600 gns in October. *W. M. Brisbourne*   **– § a38 §**

LANCER (USA)   7 ch.g. Diesis 133 – Last Bird (USA) (Sea Bird II 145) [1998 78, a39: a14.8g² a16.2g⁴ a14g 12d 12.3v² 11.9d² 11.9g⁵ 13g³ 14.1d⁶ 12m* 9.9d² 12g⁵ 11.6f⁶ 12f⁴ 12g 12d² 12g² 11.9g* 1999 12g 12g⁵ 12s³ 12m* 11.9d² 12m 12m⁶ 12.3m⁵ 10.1m⁴ 12g² 12m a12g a14g⁴ 14.1s² a14g Nov 12] workmanlike gelding: fair performer on turf, poor on all-weather: won amateur minor event at Folkestone in May: effective at 1½m to 15f: acts on all-weather and probably any turf going: blinkered once at 3 yrs, visored nowadays: tends to start slowly and held up: has looked none too keen: not one to trust implicitly. *J. Pearce*   **78 a47**

L'ANCRESS PRINCESS   2 b.f. (Mar 19) Rock City 120 – Premier Princess 45 (Hard Fought 125) [1999 a8g Dec 29] 1,500Y: second foal: half-sister to 9.4f winner Rosie Jaques (by Doyoun): dam won at 2m+ on Flat and up to 3½m over hurdles: tailed off in Lingfield seller. *G. A. Ham*   **–**

LAND AHEAD (USA)   2 ch.f. (Apr 28) Distant View (USA) 126 – Nimble Folly (USA) (Cyane) [1999 7d⁵ Oct 11] strong, close-coupled filly: has quick action: half-sister to several winners, including smart performer up to 1¼m Skimble (by Lyphard), US 1984 Grade 1 2-y-o 1m winner Contredance (by Danzig) and dam of 1000 Guineas winner Wince: dam unraced: burly and green, encouraging fifth of 19 to The Woodstock Lady in maiden at Leicester, keeping on steadily: will probably stay 1¼m: sure to do fair bit better. *H. R. A. Cecil*   **59 p**

LANDFALL LIL (IRE)   2 b.f. (Mar 30) Mujadil (USA) 119 – Local Belle   **55 d**
(Ballymore 123) [1999 5m 5m² 5g⁶ 6s a6g a7g Nov 22] IR 1,500Y: sister to 4-y-o
Comeoutofthefog and half-sister to 7f winner McKellar (by Lomond): dam Irish
1½m winner: modest form first 2 starts only. *I. Semple*

LANDFORD LAD (IRE)   3 ch.g. Mujtahid (USA) 118 – Bold And Bright (FR)   **–**
(Bold Lad (USA)) [1998 70: 8.1m⁴ 8s⁶ 7d 1999 11.6g 14.6s⁶ May 29] fair form on
2-y-o debut, but hasn't repeated it. *B. Palling*

LANDICAN LANE   3 b.g. Handsome Sailor 125 – Harifa (Local Suitor (USA)   **53**
128) [1998 61: 5d⁴ 5.1m⁶ 6m 6m 5g 5.3g* a6g 1999 a6g⁶ 5s² 5s² 6f 5.1g 5.3g 6d 6g   **a–**
7g 10d³ a12g Nov 16] lengthy gelding: modest performer at best: left G. L. Moore
before final start: effective at 5f and seems to stay 1¼m: acts on soft and good to firm
going: usually blinkered: has looked ungenuine. *T. M. Jones*

LANDRFUN   4 b.g. Lugana Beach 116 – Basic Fun (Teenoso (USA) 135) [1998   **39**
57: a8.5g a9.4g⁶ a9.4g⁴ 8.2s a8.5g* 7f³ 6.9m⁶ 8.2g 8m 8m⁶ 7.6m 7g a9.4g a8.5g⁶   **a57**
a8.5g² a8.5g⁵ 1999 a8.5g² a8g² a8g a8g a8.5g 8m 10.5m 11.9f² 11.9g a12g* a12g²
a12g⁴ Oct 13] small gelding: poor walker: modest handicapper on all-weather, poor
on turf: won selling event at Wolverhampton in September: reportedly lame final
start: stays 1½m: acts on firm going and all-weather: effective visored or not.
H. J. Collingridge

LANELLE (USA)   2 b.f. (Jan 31) Trempolino (USA) 135 – Laluche (USA) 100   **70 p**
(Alleged (USA) 138) [1999 7d Oct 30] closely related to smart stayer Landowner
and 1¾m winner Lala Musa (both by Kris) and half-sister to 2 winners, including
useful 1½m winner Lallans (by Old Vic): dam 2-y-o 6f to 1m (including May Hill
Stakes) winner from excellent family: shaped well when ninth of 16 to Garota do
Leblon in Newmarket maiden, racing freely in rear and not knocked about: bred
to be suited by at least 1½m: looks certain to improve given stiffer test of stamina.
J. H. M. Gosden

LANGANS FIGURINE (IRE)   3 b.f. Petardia 113 – Cree's Figurine 63 (Cree-   **55 ?**
town 123) [1998 62: 5g³ 6.1g 5.7d⁴ 5m⁵ 1999 6g 6m 6d 6g⁴ 6m 5g 6g 8s Sep 27]
modest maiden handicapper: stays 6f: acts on good to soft going: no form blinkered/
visored: inconsistent: sold 800 gns, sent to Spain. *M. J. Fetherston-Godley*

LANGUAGE OF LOVE   3 br.f. Rock City 120 – Indian Love Song 68 (Be My   **63**
Guest (USA) 126) [1998 NR 1999 7g 7.1d 7.1s² 6v 8g a7g⁵ Nov 27] lengthy filly:
sixth foal: sister to modest 7f/1m winner Indian Rhapsody and half-sister to 4-y-o
Adjutant and 5-y-o Tomba: dam maiden who stayed 1½m: modest maiden: left
B. Meehan after second start: may stay beyond 7f: acts on soft going. *M. Johnston*

LANIN   4 b.g. Shirley Heights 130 – Minute Waltz (Sadler's Wells (USA) 132)   **–**
[1998 –: 8.2m 7m⁶ 7.1s 10g 11.5g 1999 10v 12d 12.3m Jun 23] lengthy gelding: little
sign of ability: has worn tongue strap: sold 500 gns in August. *D. J. S. Cosgrove*

LANZLO (FR)   2 b. or br.c. (Apr 17) Le Balafre (FR) 116 – L'Eternite (FR) (Cari-   **57**
ellor (FR) 125) [1999 6d 7.1d 7.6g⁵ 7m 10s Oct 5] 105,000 francs Y: sparely-made
colt: second foal: half-brother to winning hurdler Navarre Samson (by Ganges): dam
unraced half-sister to dam of very smart French stayer/hurdler Nononito: modest
form in maidens: should stay 1¼m+. *P. J. Hobbs*

LA PAOLA (IRE)   3 ch.f. Common Grounds 118 – Lotte Lenta (Gorytus (USA)   **66**
132) [1998 68: 6g 6m 5g* 5.3g² 5s 1999 6g 6m a6g 6m 6s⁴ 6d* 5m6 5g Sep 20] leggy
filly: fair performer: won minor event at Folkestone in August: ran poorly after: stays
6f: acts on good to soft going: blinkered (below form) fourth start: sold 3,500 gns.
B. J. Meehan

LA PETITE FLAMECHE   4 b.f. Cigar 68 – Little Missile (Ile de Bourbon   **–**
(USA) 133) [1998 65: 6d 6m⁶ 6d³ 7m a6g⁶ a7g 1999 a7g a8g a6g 9.7v 8.3m Jun 28]
modest maiden at best: no form in 1999: should stay 7f: acts on good to soft going
and fibresand: tried blinkered. *R. J. O'Sullivan*

LA PIAZZA (IRE)   3 ch.f. Polish Patriot (USA) 128 – Blazing Glory (IRE) (Glow   **92**
(USA)) [1998 60: a6g² 1999 a5g² a6g 6g* 5.3f² 6f² 6f* 6f* 5g³ 6g a6g Sep 4]
fairly useful performer: won maiden at Wolverhampton in June: much improved
to win handicaps at Lingfield in July and August: stays 6f: acts on all-weather and

firm going: has been early to post: reluctant to go down when sweating and edgy penultimate start: usually waited with. *W. J. Haggas*

LAPU-LAPU   6 b.m. Prince Sabo 123 – Seleter (Hotfoot 126) [1998 –: 10.4g 12d a11g 1999 a11g Jan 2] lengthy mare: modest performer in 1997: virtually refused to race only outing of 1999: blinkered last 2 starts: one to avoid. *Miss J. A. Camacho* — §

LARAZA   2 ch.f. (Feb 13) Arazi (USA) 135 – Queen Midas 119 (Glint of Gold 128) [1999 7m 7.9m³ Sep 1] 6,500Y: close-coupled filly: eighth foal: half-sister to 3-y-o Spinning Star, 4-y-o Regent and useful 1¼m winner Royal Circle (by Sadler's Wells): dam won Ribblesdale Stakes: much better effort in maidens when third of 20 to Bold State at York, staying on strongly: will be suited by 1¼m/1½m: should improve further. *Miss I. Foustok* **64 p**

LARGESSE   5 b.h. Cadeaux Genereux 131 – Vilanika (FR) 81 (Top Ville 129) [1998 110: 10s* 12s² 11.9d* 11.9m⁶ 14d⁴ 10.9s* 12g⁴ 11s³ 12s⁴ 1999 12d* 12m 13.9s² 15s³ 10.9d⁴ 20v 12s⁵ Nov 6] tall horse: has a long, round action: smart performer: won minor event at Doncaster in March: ran well when neck second to Churlish Charm in Yorkshire Cup at York and when in frame in Prix Kergorlay at Deauville (6 lengths third to Kayf Tara) and listed race at Ayr (behind Leggera): ran poorly final start: effective at 1¼m (given testing conditions) to 15f: has won on good to firm ground, best form on good or softer: game. *John Berry* **110**

LARIMAR BAY   3 b.c. Puissance 110 – Aryaf (CAN) (Vice Regent (CAN)) [1998 70: 6m 6v⁴ 1999 7.1s 12s⁴ 5s 7.1d Jun 3] tall colt: fair form on second 2-y-o start: soundly beaten in 1999: has had tongue tied. *W. M. Brisbourne* —

L'ARITA (FR)   2 ch.f. (Feb 16) Arazi (USA) 135 – Lypharita (FR) 125 (Lightning (FR) 129) [1999 6.1d³ 6g* 7.3s Oct 23] quite attractive filly: sister to useful French 1¼m (at 2 yrs) and 10.5f winner Balizac and half-sister to 2 winners, including useful 1m winner Polinesso (by Polish Precedent): dam, out of half-sister to dam of Belmez, won Prix de Diane: odds on, confirmed promise when winning maiden at Redcar in October by 5 lengths: well beaten in listed race at Newbury final start: should stay at least 1m: possibly unsuited by soft ground: remains likely to do better. *J. H. M. Gosden* **82 p**

LA ROCQUE (IRE)   2 b.g. (Mar 11) Rock Hopper 124 – Unique Treasure (Young Generation 129) [1999 8s³ Oct 26] half-brother to 6f/7f winner Don Pepe (by Dowsing): dam once-raced half-sister to smart middle-distance performer Alriffa: modest form when third of 13 to Riddlesdown in maiden at Bath, taking good hold early and no extra final 1f: bred to stay at least 1¼m: should improve. *P. W. Harris* **68 p**

LA SOEUR D'ALBERT   3 b.f. Puissance 110 – Florentynna Bay 61 (Aragon 118) [1998 47: 5d 5.1m 6d 1999 6m a8g 8d Jul 6] poor form in maidens/handicaps: sold 800 gns in December. *J. Berry* —

LA SPEZIANA (IRE)   2 b.f. (Feb 28) Perugino (USA) 84 – Election Special 78 (Chief Singer 131) [1999 6m⁴ 6.8m⁶ 8s⁶ Oct 25] 9,500Y: second foal: sister to 3-y-o First Ballot: dam, 2-y-o 6f winner, half-sister to dam of smart pair Night Shot (sprinter) and Grey Shot (stayer): modest form in maidens: shapes as though will stay at least 1¼m. *D. R. C. Elsworth* **61**

LAS RAMBLAS (IRE)   2 b.c. (Feb 19) Thatching 131 – Raise A Warning 57 (Warning 136) [1999 5m³ 6g² 5.2m 6s³ 6m* 6m 6s Oct 2] 13,000Y: first foal: dam maiden (ran only at 2 yrs): fairly useful performer: won maiden at Newmarket in August: well beaten in nursery there final start: unlikely to stay much beyond 6f: acts on good to firm going, ran respectably first outing on soft. *R. F. Johnson Houghton* **81**

LAST CHANCE   5 b.g. River Falls 113 – Little Red Hut (Habitat 134) [1998 47: 8m⁵ 6m⁴ 7f 6m 1999 a5g a8g Jan 21] leggy gelding: poor handicapper nowadays: stays 7f: acts on good to firm ground, well beaten on soft and equitrack: has had tongue tied: tried visored/blinkered at 3 yrs. *J. S. Wainwright* —

LAST CHRISTMAS   4 b.g. Salse (USA) 128 – State Ball 61 (Dance In Time (CAN)) [1998 91: 10v² 10.4d 14.1d² 12m⁴ 1999 a12g Jan 2] fairly useful performer in 1998: tailed off only run of 1999: better at 1¼m than shorter: acted on good to firm and heavy ground: dead. *J. R. Jenkins* —

LAST HAVEN (FR) 3 b.c. Slip Anchor 136 – Lady Norcliffe (USA) (Norcliffe (CAN)) [1998 79p: 8.5m⁶ 8g 10d* 8d⁴ 1999 11.9s Sep 24] quite attractive colt: fair performer: last in handicap only run of 1999: should stay 1½m: sent to France. *J. G. FitzGerald* –

LASTMAN (USA) 4 b. or br.g. Fabulous Dancer (USA) 124 – Rivala (USA) (Riverman (USA) 131) [1998 95?: 8g² 10d³ 11.7v⁴ 1999 11.8g⁵ Apr 8] tall, leggy gelding: fairly useful form in France for Mme C. Head: only modest form in maidens in Britain: stays 1¼m: joined J. J. O'Neill. *D. Nicholson* **64**

LAST REPUTATION (IRE) 4 b.f. Zafonic (USA) 130 – Reputation (Tower Walk 130) [1998 82+, a90: 7s⁴ 7d⁵ 8m⁵ 7m* 7g⁶ 7g a7g* a7g⁴ 1999 7m 6g 7f⁶ 7m⁶ 7m⁵ 7f 7g* 6.9g³ 7m Sep 7] lengthy filly: has quick action: fair performer nowadays: won minor event at Leicester in August: stays 7f: acts on equitrack and firm going: usually bandaged: sold 14,000 gns, sent to USA. *B. W. Hills* **73**

LAST WARNING 3 b.g. Warning 136 – Dancing Crystal 76 (Kris 135) [1998 –p: 8g 1999 10g⁶ 10m 8g a10f Dec 23] tall, useful-looking gelding: modest form only on reappearance: left E. Dunlop and off course 7 months before final start. *E. Charpy, UAE* **60**

LATALOMNE (USA) 5 ch.g. Zilzal (USA) 137 – Sanctuary (Welsh Pageant 132) [1998 92: 7m⁴ 8d 1999 8d⁵ 7.5m² 8m* 7.9d 8m Jun 16] strong, good-topped gelding: has a powerful, round action: useful performer, lightly raced: won Thirsk Hunt Cup (Handicap) in May, unseating rider and running loose before start, then making virtually all to beat Jay-Owe-Two a neck: well below form at York and Royal Ascot (Hunt Cup) after: stays 1m: acts on firm and good to soft going: very free-going sort: needs treating with some caution. *B. Ellison* **100**

LA TAVERNETTA (IRE) 3 ch.f. Magical Wonder (USA) 125 – Carolina Rua (USA) 36 (L'Emigrant (USA) 129) [1998 59: 5.3g⁵ 6f* 6f⁴ 7d² a7g* 7g⁵ a7g 7m 7g⁴ 7d³ a8g 1999 a8g⁵ 8g a6g 10.1g 8.2g Sep 25] modest performer at 2 yrs: well beaten in 1999, including in sellers: sold 800 gns, sent to Holland. *J. A. Gilbert* –

LATCH LIFTER 3 b.g. Prince Sabo 123 – Thevetia 65 (Mummy's Pet 125) [1998 –: 5f 5g 6f 5m a5g 1999 5.3g 6m 5.7h a7g Dec 22] no form: left G. Lewis before final start: tried blinkered. *Miss Gay Kelleway* –

LATE ARRIVAL 2 b.g. (Mar 4) Emperor Jones (USA) 119 – Try Vickers (USA) 72 (Fuzzbuster (USA)) [1999 6d 7s⁴ 7.1d Aug 6] 31,000Y: leggy, smallish gelding: seventh foal: half-brother to several winners, including sprinter Nordico Princess (by Nordico) and 1½m winner Hurgill Dancer (by Rambo Dancer): dam, maiden, stayed 1¼m: showed some ability in maidens. *J. J. O'Neill* **51**

LATEEN 4 b.f. Midyan (USA) 124 – Sail Loft 74 (Shirley Heights 130) [1998 –: 9.9f 10m 10.2d⁶ 11.8d 14.1s 1999 11.7s 11.9f 10.5s⁶ 11.7g⁴ 15.8d Sep 21] angular filly: poor form: probably stays 1½m. *Major D. N. Chappell* **30**

LATE NIGHT LADY (IRE) 2 b.f. (Apr 22) Mujadil (USA) 119 – Riverwave (USA) (Riverman (USA) 131) [1999 5d⁵ 5v⁶ 5g* 7m a7g⁶ 6m² 7g 7d a6g Nov 11] 3,800F, IR 13,000Y: compact filly: half-sister to several winners, including temperamental 1998 2-y-o 5f winner Ruanbeg (by Up And At'em) and 1¼m winner Rive-Jumelle (by M Double M): dam placed up to 13f in Ireland: won claimer at Hamilton in June: failed to repeat the form: stays 6f. *P. C. Haslam* **65 d**

LATE NIGHT OUT 4 b.g. Lahib (USA) 129 – Chain Dance 88 (Shareef Dancer (USA) 135) [1998 106: 6s³ 7d⁶ 7d* 7v⁶ 1999 7d³ 7.1g* 7.1d⁴ 6m⁴ 7.3m 7m 7g⁴ 7.3d⁵ 7d² 7s⁴ Oct 31] compact gelding: useful performer: has had knee problems: won listed rated stakes at Haydock in May by a length from Ramooz: good 1½ lengths second to Tarry Flynn in Concorde Stakes at Cork in October: not sure to stay beyond 7f: acts on good to firm and good to soft ground, possibly not on soft. *W. Jarvis* **107**

LATE PARADE (IRE) 8 b.h. Astronef 116 – Skisette (Malinowski (USA) 123) [1998 114: 5g* 5g* 5m* 5g² 1999 5g* 5f* 5m* 5g² Oct 3] strong, good-quartered horse: smart performer: prolific winner, mainly in minor company: quite lightly raced nowadays, though at least as good as ever in 1999, winning minor event at Rome in March, listed race at Milan in May and Gran Premio Citta di Napoli (for second year running, by 2½ lengths from disqualified Su Tirolesu) in July: below **115**

best when 3¾ lengths second to Nuclear Debate in Premio Omenoni at Milan final start: best at 5f: acts on any going: front runner. *A. Renzoni, Italy*

LATIN BAY   4 b.g. Superlative 118 – Hugging 78 (Beveled (USA)) [1998 50: 8m⁵ **50** 11g³ 11.4d 8g 11.9d 9m* 7.6m⁴ 8d 10g 1999 a12g⁶ a13g* a12f* a11g 12.3m 9.3m **a57** 11.5m³ 14.1g a8g Oct 8] small, leggy gelding: modest performer: won selling handicaps at Lingfield in January, first for S. Williams and second for G. Lewis: trained next 3 starts by D. Nicholls before returning to G. Lewis for 2 outings: stays 13f: acts on good to firm going and equitrack: races prominently: inconsistent. *D. J. Wintle*

LATINO BAY (IRE)   2 ch.c. (Apr 26) Perugino (USA) 84 – Slightly Latin (Aho- **49** noora 122) [1999 7.6g 6.1g 7d Oct 12] IR 6,000F, 8,000Y, 12,000 2-y-o: half-brother to 3-y-o Poles Apart and Irish 13f winner Pipes of Peace (both by Distinctly North): dam lightly raced in Ireland: best effort in maidens when seventh of 12 at Nottingham second start: will probably stay 1m. *N. P. Littmoden*

LA TIZIANA   4 b.f. Rudimentary (USA) 118 – Tizona (Pharly (FR) 130) [1998 **76** 83: 10.5d³ 10.1m² 8.1s⁵ 10m 10g* 10.5m² 10.5s⁶ 1999 10.8d 10s 10f⁶ 10.1m 10.2m² Jul 3] lengthy, angular filly: fair handicapper: best effort in 1999 on final start: likely to prove best around 1¼m: acts on good to firm and good to soft ground: has been bandaged: flashes tail under pressure, but seems game: front runner. *W. Jarvis*

LA TORTUGA   2 b.g. (Feb 21) Turtle Island (IRE) 123 – Ville Sainte (FR) (Saint **79** Estephe (FR) 123) [1999 5g 5m* 5d⁴ 6.1d⁴ 7s a7g⁴ a8.5g⁵ a7g Dec 15] 8,600Y: **a66** angular gelding: fifth foal: half-brother to 2 winners by Unfuwain, including 1m (at 2 yrs) and 16.4f winner Chairman's Daughter: dam French 1¼m winner: fair performer, better on turf than all-weather: returned from 4-month break to win maiden at Carlisle in August: some creditable efforts after: probably stays 8.5f: acts on good to firm and good to soft going: visored first outing, blinkered last 2. *P. D. Evans*

L A TOUCH   6 b.m. Tina's Pet 121 – Silvers Era 72 (Balidar 133) [1998 45: 5s⁶ 6g **56** 5m 6g³ 6m 6f* 5m⁶ 6m 1999 6g⁵ 5m³ 6g* 5.9g 7.6m* 7m³ 6m 6f Aug 7] strong, lengthy mare: modest handicapper: won at Yarmouth in June and Chester (apprentices) in July: well below form final 2 starts: stays 7.6f: best on good going or firmer. *M. A. Peill*

LATOUR   2 b. or br.f. (Mar 13) Sri Pekan (USA) 117 – Fenny Rough 114 (Home **79** Guard (USA) 129) [1999 7f⁶ 7m⁴ 7g⁵ Oct 2] 60,000Y: tall filly: half-sister to useful sprinter Watch Me (by Green Desert), 5-y-o Natural Eight and winners abroad by Sharpen Up and Icecapade: dam, 5f to 7f winner, later Grade 2 9f winner in USA: fair form in maidens: best effort when fourth of 9 to My Hansel at Newmarket second start: should stay 1m. *J. W. Hills*

LATVIAN   12 gr.g. Rousillon (USA) 133 – Lorelene (FR) 97 (Lorenzaccio 130) **40 §** [1998 41§: 12s⁵ 14s⁵ 16g² 14.1m 12d⁵ 16g⁴ 12d⁵ 12m 12s 1999 12.1m⁴ 16g⁶ 12g Aug 25] lengthy gelding: poor performer in 1999: stays 15f: acts on hard and good to soft going: sometimes blinkered/visored: none too resolute. *R. Allan*

LAUGHARNE PARK (IRE)   2 b.c. (Mar 28) Fourstars Allstar (USA) 122 – **51** Frantesa (Red Sunset 120) [1999 6.8m 7m 6.1m Aug 23] IR 18,000F, 16,000Y: third foal: half-brother to 1997 2-y-o 7f winner Docklands Dispatch (by Distinctly North): dam Irish 1¼m to 1¾m winner: modest form at best in maidens: should stay 1m. *B. R. Millman*

LAUND VIEW LADY   2 ch.f. (Apr 11) Presidium 124 – Vickenda 52 (Giaco- **73** metti 130) [1999 5m⁵ 6d* 5g 6g 6d Oct 22] 3,000Y: fifth foal: sister to 4-y-o After Eight: dam 7f winner at 4 yrs: fair performer: easily best effort when winning maiden at Ripon in August: stays 6f. *Mrs S. J. Smith*

LAUNFAL   2 gr.c. (Feb 8) Rudimentary (USA) 118 – Laune (AUS) 68 (Kenmare **93** (FR) 125) [1999 5m⁵ 6f³ 6m⁴ 7f³ 7f³ 7g³ 6v² 8s⁵ Oct 22] tall, rather leggy colt: has scope: first living foal: dam, 2-y-o 5f winner, became unenthusiastic: fairly useful performer: won maiden at Windsor in April: in frame in varied races after, including Coventry Stakes at Royal Ascot and Champagne Stakes at Goodwood third and fifth starts: effective at 6f/7f (beaten some way out over 1m): acts on any ground: sometimes gives trouble stalls. *R. Hannon*

LAUREL PRINCE   3 b.g. Reprimand 122 – Laurel Queen (IRE) 76 (Viking **52 d**
(USA)) [1998 59d: 6g⁶ 6m 7s⁶ 7g⁴ 7.5m⁶ 7.1g⁵ 7.5m 1999 8d 6f 8m² 10d 7.5m
8.1m 9m⁵ 12.1m a11g³ Sep 28] smallish, good-bodied gelding: modest maiden,
disappointing: stays 1m: acts on good to firm ground and fibresand: free-going sort
(bolted before start and withdrawn once). *J. Berry*

LAUREN'S LAD   4 ch.g. Tachyon Park 87 – Glory Isle 60 (Hittite Glory 125)   –
[1998 52, a56: a8g⁵ a8.5g⁵ 9.7d 8m² 8.1g 8.1m 1999 11.6m May 24] plain gelding:
modest performer at 3 yrs: last on only run of 1999: best up to 8.5f: acts on firm going
and all-weather: best in blinkers and with forcing tactics. *B. J. Llewellyn*

LAURENTIAN   4 b.f. Shareef Dancer (USA) 135 – Kiomi 65 (Niniski (USA)   **42**
125) [1998 –: a10g 8m 7s 8m 7f 10.1g 7g⁵ 7s 1999 8g a8.5g 7f³ 8f⁴ 8g³ 8g⁵ 7f 7f 7f⁵
Jul 30] small filly: poor form: stays 1m: acts on firm ground: visored penultimate
start. *K. R. Burke*

LAURENTIDE (USA)   4 b.c. Pleasant Colony (USA) – Northern Sunset (North-   **102**
fields (USA)) [1998 109: 12d² 14f* 16.2d² 1999 13.9s 16.4g 20m Jun 17]
deep-bodied colt: useful performer: form in 1999 only when seventh of 11 to Arctic
Owl in Henry II Stakes at Sandown second start: should stay beyond 2m: best efforts
on good/good to soft ground: withdrawn after breaking blood vessel once at 3 yrs:
has been bandaged: sent to USA. *H. R. A. Cecil*

LAUTREC   3 b.g. Shareef Dancer (USA) 135 – Pride of Paris (Troy 137) [1998   **65**
65: 7g⁶ 7f 7m³ 1999 10m⁴ 11.8m³ 9.9m³ 10.5m⁶ a10g Nov 16] fair maiden handi-   **a–**
capper: probably better at 1½m than shorter: raced only on good ground or firmer on
turf. *G. M. McCourt*

LAVACA RIVER   4 b.g. Primo Dominie 121 – Rose Music 86 (Luthier 126)   –
[1998 –: 7m 7g 1999 a8g⁵ Feb 20] smallish gelding: no show in maidens: sold 500
gns in May. *P. Howling*

LAVERY (IRE)   3 b.c. Royal Academy (USA) 130 – Lady Donna 92 (Dominion   **113**
123) [1998 109: 6d⁶ 6m* 7g⁵ 1999 6g* 8m 6f Jul 8] medium-sized, attractive colt:
smart performer: won valuable Tote Shergar Cup Sprint at Goodwood in May by 2½
lengths from Sheer Viking, showing good turn of foot: behind afterwards in Poule
d'Essai des Poulains at Longchamp and July Cup at Newmarket: will prove best up
to 7f: raced mainly on good going or firmer: broke out of stalls once at 2 yrs, refused
to enter them at Royal Ascot third intended outing in 1999. *A. P. O'Brien, Ireland*

LAW COMMISSION   9 ch.g. Ela-Mana-Mou 132 – Adjala 89 (Northfields   **92 d**
(USA)) [1998 98§: 7s 6g 8m⁵ 6d 7f 6g 7g⁵ 7m 1999 6f 7f* 7d⁵ 7g 7g 7g 7m⁶ 7.3m 7s
7d Oct 30] small, sturdy gelding: fairly useful handicapper: won at Newbury in May:
well beaten after next start: stays 1m: acts on any going: sometimes hangs under
pressure: held up: unreliable. *D. R. C. Elsworth*

LAW DANCER (IRE)   6 b.g. Alzao (USA) 117 – Judicial (USA) (Law Society   –
(USA) 130) [1998 –, a66: a9.4g⁶ a8.5g⁶ a9.4g* a8g a9.4g² a12g² a10g⁴ a9.4g 10.1m   **a66**
1999 a12g* a12g* a10g a9.4g⁶ a12g⁴ May 25] small gelding: fair performer: won
minor event at Lingfield in February and handicap at Wolverhampton in March:
below form final 3 starts: stays 1½m: acts on all-weather, lightly raced on turf of late:
visored once at 4 yrs: has been bandaged. *T. G. Mills*

LAW LADY (IRE)   2 ch.f. (Feb 13) Port Lucaya 118 – Law Student (Precocious   –
126) [1999 6m 6g 7m a7g Sep 28] small filly: fourth foal: half-sister to Irish 1996
2-y-o 6f winner Silvestrini (by Maledetto), later successful abroad: dam, poor
maiden, half-sister to Ribblesdale winner Queen Midas: well held, including in
sellers: sold 800 gns in October. *M. H. Tompkins*

LAYAN   2 b.f. (Jan 28) Puissance 110 – Most Uppitty 69 (Absalom 128) [1999 5d⁶   **60**
5d² 5.1m⁴ 5g a5g 5f⁶ Sep 13] first foal: dam 5f (at 2 yrs) and 6f winner: modest
maiden: will prove best at 5f/6f: best effort on good to soft going, ran poorly on
fibresand: sold 3,800 gns in October, joined J. Balding. *J. Berry*

LAY THE BLAME   6 b.g. Reprimand 122 – Rose And The Ring (Welsh Pageant   **56**
132) [1998 –: 8d 10m a8g 10d 10g⁵ 10d⁶ 12m² 12.3f⁶ Aug 2] good-bodied gelding:
modest performer: stays 1½m: acts on good to firm ground: visored fourth start,
blinkered final 2: inconsistent: joined Kate Milligan. *M. D. Hammond*

LAZER MAGIC (USA) 2 b.f. (Mar 2) Personal Hope (USA) 118 – La Caleche   –
(USA) (Gregorian (USA) 124) [1999 6g 6d 7g 7d Oct 21] $17,000F, 21,000Y, resold
20,000Y: fifth foal: half-sister to 3 winners in USA: dam minor stakes winner at 1m
in USA: well held in maidens/nursery: tried visored: sold 900 gns. *J. H. M. Gosden*

LEADING PROSPECTOR (USA) 3 b.c. Mr Prospector (USA) – Araadh   **79 ?**
(USA) 70 (Blushing Groom (FR) 131) [1998 74p: 6g⁶ 1999 10.3m May 4] small,
close-coupled colt: appeared to show fair form in maidens only 2 starts: sent to USA.
C. E. Brittain

LEADING ROLE 2 ch.f. (Mar 22) Cadeaux Genereux 131 – Footlight Fantasy   **90**
(USA) 68 (Nureyev (USA) 131) [1999 7m* 7d Sep 28] 300,000Y: sturdy, lengthy
filly: second foal: half-sister to 3-y-o Dominant Dancer: dam 7f winner out of top-
class miler Milligram: won maiden at Lingfield by 3½ lengths: only tenth of 17 in
sales event at Newmarket later in September, virtually bolting to post: will stay 1m:
sent to USA. *Sir Michael Stoute*

LEADING SPIRIT (IRE) 7 b.g. Fairy King (USA) – Shopping (FR) (Sheshoon   **§§**
132) [1998 90: 12g 12m³ 12d 13.3m² 14m⁵ 12s 10s 1999 14.4m 10m 12f Jun 18]
well-made gelding: fairly useful handicapper at best: has become most temperamental (refused to race last 2 starts): one to leave alone. *D. Sasse*

LEAPING CHARLIE 3 b.g. Puissance 110 – Impala Lass 81 (Kampala 120)   **66**
[1998 61: 6m 6d 5s³ 6d 1999 6.1f 6s 5g 5m 5m* 6m⁶ 5g 5d⁵ 5g 5v² 5s Nov 5] leggy,
angular gelding: fair handicapper: won at Hamilton in June: effective at 5f/6f: acts on
heavy and good to firm going. *Mrs A. Duffield*

LEAR SPEAR (USA) 4 b.c. Lear Fan (USA) 130 – Golden Gorse (USA)   **124**
(His Majesty (USA)) [1998 109: 10.2s 8f² 8d 10d 8.1m³ 8.1g* 8.1m³ 8g³ 9g*
9m⁴ 1999 8.5g⁵ 8.1s⁴ 9.9d⁶ 8.5g* 10m* 10m 9.9m* 10m³ Dec 12]
      Five Cambridgeshire winners in the 'nineties went on to win listed or
pattern contests. Lear Spear is the most recent one to do so, and while his
achievements in the latest season didn't match Halling's they surpassed those
of Mellottie, Penny Drops and Cap Juluca. In finishing fourth in a listed race on
his only start after the Cambridgeshire as a three-year-old, Lear Spear had run
well enough to suggest that he might make an impact outside handicap
company at four years. Yet even the most optimistic of Lear Spear's admirers,
outside his connections, could hardly have envisaged that he'd do quite so well
as he did.
      There were certainly no indications early on in his four-year-old career
that Lear Spear was capable of much better. Though victory in the Vodafone
Diomed Stakes at Epsom on Derby Day ended a run of three early defeats, there
were question marks over the true merit of the performance with hot favourite
Altibr unable to reproduce his Dubai form. Leaving Altibr out of calculations,
Lear Spear almost certainly didn't need to show improved form to win a
substandard renewal of this Group 3 event by a length from Yakareem.
Therefore, when he lined up against much stronger opposition in the Group 2
Prince of Wales's Stakes (a race which has been promoted to Group 1 in 2000)
at Royal Ascot ten days later, Lear Spear was a 20/1 outsider of eight along
with Xaar's pacemaker Limpid. The first and second favourites were the Henry
Cecil-trained pair Chester House, a close second in the previous year's running
and an impressive winner of the Brigadier Gerard Stakes on his most recent
start, and Shiva, the Tattersalls Gold Cup winner. Apart from Lear Spear's form
appearing short of that required to win such a contest, there was also a doubt as
to whether he had the necessary stamina. However, when he'd appeared not to
stay a mile and a quarter fully the going had been on the soft side of good, and
it was a very different story on good to firm ground at Royal Ascot. Lear Spear,
held up as usual, improved under pressure early in the straight, where Chester
House had taken over from the pacemaker, and took the lead inside the final
furlong, the danger now Fantastic Light, the only three-year-old in the field,
who had also made good headway. The latter put in a sustained challenge but
Lear Spear, battling on splendidly, held on by a head as the pair pulled two and

Prince of Wales's Stakes, Royal Ascot—a stirring battle to the line as Lear Spear (rail) belies his odds and holds off the three-year-old Fantastic Light by a head

a half lengths clear of third-placed Xaar. Lear Spear's remaining races were all over a mile and a quarter on good or good to firm ground and he won one of them, the Caffrey's Premium Ale Select Stakes at Goodwood in September. This time Lear Spear had a pacemaker, Wolf Tooth, who set a good gallop. None of those who raced close to it were involved in the finish, which saw Lear Spear get the better of a sustained duel with Kabool, who was in receipt of 5 lb, by half a length. Like several others in the race, Lear Spear would have benefited from a stronger pace when ninth in the Champion Stakes at Newmarket next time, and then he finished third behind Jim And Tonic and Running Stag in the Hong Kong Cup at Sha Tin. Lear Spear was beaten five and a quarter lengths by Jim And Tonic there, but he'd have been a lot closer, almost certainly a clear second, had he not been squeezed when improving from the rear under two furlongs out, running on strongly once clear. Lear Spear's only poor performance during the season came when he trailed home last of eight in the Coral-Eclipse at Sandown. It was Lear Spear's fourth race inside four weeks and it's possible his exertions, especially his hard race at Royal Ascot, had temporarily caught up with him.

		Roberto	Hail To Reason
Lear Spear (USA) (b.c. 1995)	Lear Fan (USA) (b 1981)	(b 1969)	Bramalea
		Wac	Lt Stevens
		(b 1969)	Belthazar
	Golden Gorse (USA) (b 1986)	His Majesty	Ribot
		(b 1968)	Flower Bowl
		Golden Petal	Mr Prospector
		(ch 1981)	Hatton's Rose

Bought as a yearling in Keeneland for 25,000 dollars, Lear Spear is the fifth foal of Golden Gorse, a winning sprinter in the USA and a half-sister to Lotus Pool and Golden Larch, both at least smart performers at up to a mile and a quarter. Golden Gorse has also produced a winner in Hong Kong by Spec-

Mr Raymond Tooth's "Lear Spear"

tacular Bid and the modest Gleaming Heather (by Irish River) who won a two-mile handicap in Ireland as a three-year-old. Lear Spear, a tall, workman-like colt with a long, round action, usually impressess in appearance. He is best on good or firmer ground and is thoroughly genuine. *D. R. C. Elsworth*

LEA VALLEY EXPRESS (IRE) 2 b.f. (Mar 20) Fayruz 116 – Fenland Express (IRE) (Reasonable (FR) 119) [1999 5m 5m 5m⁵ 5.1m⁴ 6g 5.3s³ a5g a6g⁵ Nov 11] IR 1,300F, 4,000Y: second foal: half-sister to 4-y-o Danzig Flyer: dam unraced: poor sprint maiden: visored after fourth start. *J. R. Jenkins* **47**

LEAVE IT TO ME 3 b.f. College Chapel 122 – Enaam 65§ (Shirley Heights 130) [1998 71: 6m² 6g 6.1g 6f⁵ 1999 8.2d⁴ 8.2s* a10g 10d³ Jul 6] quite attractive filly: fair performer: won 15-runner handicap at Nottingham in April: stays 1m, probably not 1¼m: acts on soft going, well beaten on equitrack: sometimes flashes tail: sold 1,000 gns in October. *S. P. C. Woods* **72 a–**

LEAVE IT TO RODNEY 4 b.g. Tina's Pet 121 – Fivesevenfiveo 77 (Enchantment 115) [1998 –: 7f 5.1m⁶ 5d 5.1d 6m 5m 1999 5.7h 5d 8.1m Sep 9] unfurnished gelding: little sign of ability: tried blinkered. *R. J. Hodges* **–**

LE CAVALIER (USA) 2 b.c. (Mar 22) Mister Baileys 123 – Secret Deed (USA) (Shadeed (USA) 135) [1999 7s⁵ 7m 8.3m³ 8m 8.3d a8g⁴ a8g Nov 30] third foal: dam, US winner up to 9f, out of half-sister to Champion Stakes winner Northern Baby: modest maiden: stays 1m: acts on fibresand and good to firm ground, no form on softer than good: blinkered (well beaten) fifth start. *C. N. Allen* **58**

LEDGENDRY LINE 6 b.g. Mtoto 134 – Eider 80 (Niniski (USA) 125) [1998 78: 13v² 1999 14.1s⁵ 14.1s 14g³ 14m⁵ 12.3s³ 16.1m² 17.1g² 17.5d⁴ 17.1s Oct 4] good-topped gelding: useful jumper: fair handicapper on Flat: mostly ran creditably in 1999: barely stays 17f: acts on good to firm and heavy going: usually held up. *Mrs M. Reveley* **68**

LEDHAM (USA) 3 ch.g. Diesis 133 – First Tracks (USA) (Alleged (USA) 138) [1998 75: 7m⁴ 7g⁶ 7s³ 1999 9.9m 10g² 10m² 11.6m² 11m³ 9g* 12g⁴ Aug 28] **87**

useful-looking gelding: fairly useful performer: won maiden at Musselburgh in August: stays 11.6f: acts on good to firm going: has worn tongue strap: sold 7,000 gns, joined C. Mann. *Sir Michael Stoute*

LEEN 2 b.f. (May 15) Distant Relative 128 – St James's Antigua (IRE) 79 (Law Society (USA) 130) [1999 5m⁶ 5.7h² 5.1f* 6s⁴ 6d Oct 14] 1,000Y: neat filly: has a quick action: fourth foal: half-sister to 1¼m winner Ibin St James (by Salse), who stayed 1½m, and 4-y-o Bint St James: dam 8.3f winner: fair form: trained first 2 starts by M. Heaton-Ellis: won maiden at Bath in September: creditable efforts in nurseries at Newmarket both starts after: should stay 7f: acts on hard and soft going: sold 5,000 gns in October. *C. G. Cox* **68**

LEEROY (IRE) 2 b.c. (Mar 13) Dancing Dissident (USA) 119 – Birdhill (IRE) (Petorius 117) [1999 6d⁵ 6g³ 6m² 6s² 6g⁴ Oct 11] IR 6,800Y: first foal: dam once-raced daughter of sister to 1000 Guineas winner Humble Duty: fair maiden: in frame last 4 starts: will stay 7f: acts on soft and good to firm going. *R. Hannon* **76**

LEES FIRST STEP 2 b.f. (Mar 14) Reprimand 122 – Classic Coral (USA) (Seattle Dancer (USA) 119) [1999 5.7g 7m 6.8m² 8f Sep 6] 1,800F, 6,500Y: first foal: dam unraced daughter of half-sister to very smart middle-distance stayers Shining Finish and Bright Finish: modest maiden: best effort when second of 9 at Warwick penultimate start, making most: stays 7f: raced only on good going or firmer: sold 1,300 gns in November. *P. G. Murphy* **61**

LEGACY OF LOVE 3 b.f. Distant Relative 128 – May Hills Legacy (IRE) 68 (Be My Guest (USA) 126) [1998 NR 1999 7.1m⁵ 10m² 7.6f* 8g 8d⁴ 8.2f⁴ Oct 20] 30,000Y: first foal: dam, 6f (at 2 yrs) and 1¼m winner, out of Yorkshire Oaks and Park Hill winner May Hill: fair performer: won maiden at Lingfield in July: creditable efforts in handicaps last 2 starts: stays 1¼m: acts on firm and good to soft going. *B. W. Hills* **68**

LEGAL ISSUE (IRE) 7 b.h. Contract Law (USA) 108 – Natuschka (Authi 123) [1998 76, a58: 8s³ 8s* 9.9m² 8.5d* 9.9d⁴ 9.3g⁵ a8g a8.5g⁵ 10.3m 12d 10.3v⁶ 12s 1999 8d* 10d⁴ 8.5d⁶ 8m² 8.5d* 8g⁵ 8.9d 8.5m⁴ 8m 9g 8.3m 10d³ a9.4f 8.9d 8g⁵ a8.5g⁴ a7g³ a11g* a12g a12g⁴ Dec 17] sturdy horse: poor mover: fair handicapper: won at Thirsk in April, Beverley in June and Southwell in November: effective at 7f to 11f, probably not 1½m: acts on firm going, soft and all-weather: visored at 4 yrs: has been bandaged near-fore: none too consistent. *B. S. Rothwell* **76**

LEGAL LUNCH (USA) 4 b.g. Alleged (USA) 138 – Dinner Surprise (USA) (Lyphard (USA) 132) [1998 95: 10m⁴ 10.5d* 12s 10.5g⁵ 11.9f 13.9g⁵ 16d³ 16.2d 1999 12s 12m 12g² 16.1m 16.4m⁵ 16m² 16.2m⁶ 16.1m³ 12s⁵ 12m 12m 14s⁶ 11.9d⁵ 12s² a16g³ a14g³ Nov 22] well-made gelding: fairly useful handicapper on turf, fair on all-weather: generally ran respectably in 1999: effective at 1½m (given bit of a test) to 2m: acts on good to firm going, soft and equitrack: visored last 5 starts: sometimes finds little, and seems difficult to win with. *P. W. Harris* **90** **a79**

LEGAL SET (IRE) 3 gr.c. Second Set (IRE) 127 – Tiffany's Case (IRE) 65 (Thatching 131) [1998 73p: 8m 6g 1999 7g 8.3m³ 7.1g 9.9g Jun 11] rather leggy, close-coupled colt: fair maiden handicapper: stays 1m (never landed a blow over 1¼m): raced only on good/good to firm ground: free-going sort: has worn tongue strap. *C. A. Horgan* **73**

LEGAL VENTURE (IRE) 3 ch.g. Case Law 113 – We Two (Glenstal (USA) 118) [1998 61: 5s 5.3d 5.1d 5g⁴ 5m* 5g³ 5.3m³ 5m² 5.1m⁴ 5m⁵ a5g² 5.2s a5g² a5s⁶ a5g a5g⁵ 1999 a5g a5s⁴ a6g³ a5g² a5g³ a5g⁴ 5d a5g a5g* a5g 5g⁶ 5g a5g² 5m a5g a5g a5g Dec 10] smallish, sturdy gelding: unimpressive mover: modest performer: won seller at Wolverhampton in May: lost form last 4 starts: best at 5f: acts on good to firm going and fibresand, probably not on soft: usually blinkered/visored, effective without: usually races prominently: none too consistent. *N. P. Littmoden* **53** **a60 d**

LEGEND 3 b.f. Belmez (USA) 131 – Once Upon A Time 77 (Teenoso (USA) 135) [1998 74p: 8d⁵ 8d³ 1999 11.9d³ 12f⁴ Jul 23] leggy, lengthy filly: fair form in maidens at 2 yrs: below form in 1999: will be suited by further than 1½m. *I. A. Balding* **56**

LEGENDAIRE (USA) 2 gr.c. (Apr 4) Fly Till Dawn (USA) – Iolani 59 (Alzao (USA) 117) [1999 6g 6f² 7g 6g⁴ 7m 6s 7d Oct 21] $3,500Y, 12,000 2-y-o: second foal: dam, maiden, daughter of Galtres Stakes winner Sans Blague: modest maiden: well beaten last 3 starts: should be suited by 7f+. *C. A. Dwyer* **59 d**

LEGENDARY LOVER (IRE)   5 b.g. Fairy King (USA) – Broken Romance   **73 d**
(IRE) (Ela-Mana-Mou 132) [1998 NR 1999 12m 11.4m² 12.3m⁶ 12m 14m⁶ a14.8g⁶
Sep 18] strong, rangy gelding: poor mover: fair maiden: runner-up in handicap at
Sandown: ran as if something amiss next 3 starts, though won maiden hurdle in
November: probably best at 1¼m/1½m: acts on good to firm and good to soft going.
J. R. Jenkins

LEGEND FALLS (IRE)   3 ch.f. River Falls 113 – Sister Dympna 63 (Grundy   **73**
137) [1998 73, a55: 6g⁴ 5.8d³ 6.5d² 6.5v² 7g³ 7d⁶ 1999 a7g² a9.4g⁵ a8g² a7g 8g⁵   **a53**
6.5d* 7m⁶ 6.5s* 7d 6s Sep 25] IR 4,000F, IR 1,400Y: small, sparely-made filly:
half-sister to smart Irish winner up to 9f Ger's Royale (by Dominion Royale): dam
stoutly bred: fair on turf, modest on all-weather: trained by J. Noseda first 4 starts:
won maiden at Sligo in June and handicap there in August: best at 6f/7f: acts on
heavy going and equitrack: tried visored: has carried head awkwardly/edged left:
usually held up: sold 2,000 gns in December. *M. J. Grassick, Ireland*

LEGEND OF LOVE   4 b.g. Pursuit of Love 124 – Legendary Dancer 90 (Shareef   **67**
Dancer (USA) 135) [1998 73, a45+: 10v 10v⁵ 14.1m³ 14.1m⁴ 14m a12g⁶ 12m³   **a–**
16.1m⁶ 12m² a14g⁵ 16s³ 15.8d* 1999 a16f 16s 18d⁵ 16.1s 17.2g² 17.2g² 15.9m⁶
16.2m⁴ 16.5f⁴ Jul 29] workmanlike gelding: has a round action: fair handicapper:
ran as though something amiss final start: stays 17f: acts on good to firm going,
good to soft and fibresand: below form blinkered/visored: has worn tongue strap.
B. J. Llewellyn

LEGGERA (IRE)   4 b.f. Sadler's Wells (USA) 132 – Lady Ambassador (General   **116**
Assembly (USA)) [1998 125: 10g² 11d² 11.9m⁴ 13.5s* 12s* 12d² 12f 1999 12d⁵
10.9d* 12v⁴ 15.5v³dis Oct 24] rangy, quite attractive filly: took the eye: had a
powerful, round action: high-class performer in 1998, winner of Prix Vermeille and
second in Prix de l'Arc de Triomphe, both at Longchamp: bit below that form at 4
yrs, though again made the frame in Arc when 11½ lengths fourth to Montjeu: was
having first race for 4 months (had reportedly suffered muscular problem) when
winning listed event at Ayr in September in workmanlike style by 1½ lengths from
Carry The Flag: 2 lengths third of 6 to Amilynx in Prix Royal-Oak at Longchamp on
final start but was disqualified after rider weighed in light: suited by good test at
1½m and stayed 15.5f: went well on ground softer than good: sweating and edgy
penultimate start: stud. *J. L. Dunlop*

LEGGY LADY   3 b.f. Sir Harry Lewis (USA) 127 – Lady Minstrel (Tudor Music   **58**
131) [1998 NR 1999 10m 10g⁶ 10f a16g⁴ Nov 8] tall, angular filly: half-sister to
several winners, including useful 7f (at 2 yrs) and 1¼m winner Mary Davies (by
Tyrnavos): dam, placed over hurdles in Ireland, half-sister to 2000 Guineas winner
Tap On Wood: modest form: stays 2m: acts on equitrack. *J. A. R. Toller*

LEGS BE FRIENDLY (IRE)   4 b.g. Fayruz 116 – Thalssa (Rusticaro (FR) 124)   **78 d**
[1998 –: 6v 7d 6m 6s 1999 5s 5d² 6f 5m a5g 5m Sep 10] angular gelding: fair
handicapper at best: below form after third start: effective at 5f to 7f: acts on firm
and soft going, probably on fibresand: usually blinkered (including when gaining only
win at 2 yrs), tried visored: sold 5,000 gns. *K. McAuliffe*

LEIGH CROFTER   10 ch.g. Son of Shaka 119 – Ganadora (Good Times (ITY))   **–**
[1998 52, a60: a6g³ a7g a7g a6g⁴ a8g⁴ a7g³ a7g² a6g⁵ a8.5g⁴ 6d³ a7g⁴ a8g⁴ 6g⁵ 6v⁵
7g a7g⁴ a7g² 1999 7.7s a7g 6m Jun 23] workmanlike gelding: modest performer: no
form in 1999: barely stays 1m: acts on fibresand, good to firm and heavy going: has
been visored, blinkered nowadays. *J. L. Harris*

LE KHOUMF (FR)   8 ch.g. Son of Silver 123 – Bentry (FR) (Ben Trovato (FR)   **55**
128) [1998 NR 1999 16d⁵ Oct 21] workmanlike gelding: fair maiden in 1996: fifth
in handicap at Nottingham, only Flat run since: probably stays 2m: fair hurdler.
J. Neville

LE LOUP   2 b.c. (Mar 10) Wolfhound (USA) 126 – Chandni (IRE) (Ahonoora 122)   **65 ?**
[1999 5m 5s³ 6m 5g⁶ 6m 5.7d Sep 27] 22,000F, 14,000Y: fourth foal: half-brother to
4-y-o Cold Front and Irish 3-y-o 9f and 1½m winner Chanoud (by Ezzoud): dam (of
no account), sister to smart 1m/1¼m performer Visto Si Stampi, out of a sister to
Kings Lake: appeared to show fair form second start: largely well below that level
afterwards: should stay at least 6f: acts on soft and good to firm going. *Miss
E. C. Lavelle*

LEMON BRIDGE (IRE)   4 b.g. Shalford (IRE) 124§ – Sharply (Sharpman) [1998 81: 7v³ 9.2v² 10.4s³ 9.9g* 11.6g³ 10.2d⁵ 10m⁴ 10.3m⁶ 12.1s 1999 12m² 12m² 12s Aug 18] well-made gelding: fairly useful handicapper: runner-up at Newmarket and Doncaster in 1999: effective at 1¼m/1½m: acts on good to firm and heavy ground: often made running at 3 yrs. *R. T. Phillips*   **81**

LEMON STRIP   3 ch.f. Emarati (USA) 74 – Lon Isa 80 (Grey Desire 115) [1998 –: 6m 6g 5.7g 1999 8.3g 8m a5g 6.1m a5g⁴ 5f² a5g³ 6d 5f a6g⁴ a6g² a7g⁴ a5g⁴ a7g Dec 15] modest maiden on all-weather, poor on turf: will prove best at 5f/6f: acts on firm going and fibresand: has gone early to post. *B. Palling*   **43 a55 ?**

LEND A HAND   4 b.c. Great Commotion (USA) 123 – Janaat 74 (Kris 135) [1998 121: 8d² 8g² 8d³ 8d⁶ 1999 a8f* 7f 7.3g* 7g² 8g⁴ Nov 6]   **124**

The Hungerford Stakes at Newbury will go down in the record books as the race in which Frankie Dettori rode his two hundredth pattern-race winner, and it is doubtful whether many of his one hundred and ninety-nine previous victories were won in such imperious manner, as Lend A Hand, running on British soil for the first time in over a year, laid his claim to be one of the best seven furlong/mile horses in training.

Lend A Hand had joined Godolphin at the end of his 1998 season from Mark Johnston, having finished second to King of Kings in the Two Thousand Guineas at Newmarket. He'd failed to repeat that form in three subsequent races for Johnston, despite a respectable third in the Sussex Stakes at Goodwood. Lend A Hand started the new season impressively, beating Muhtathir and Cape Cross by six lengths and one and a quarter lengths in the Nad Al Sheba Mile on dirt on Dubai World Cup day in March. A disappointing tenth in the Keio Hai Spring Cup in Tokyo in May and a subsequent three-month absence from the course clearly didn't put punters off in the seven-furlong Hungerford Stakes. Lend A Hand started odds on and neither his supporters nor his jockey had any worries as the colt cruised into the lead two furlongs out and put five lengths between himself and Teapot Row when given his head approaching the final furlong, a margin which would undoubtedly have been a few lengths more had he been sent about his business sooner.

After this impressive victory, it may seem surprising that Lend A Hand failed to add to his tally of seven career wins, but in both his subsequent runs he lost nothing in defeat and showed a bare level of form superior to Newbury, while hinting that he possibly could have done better still under different circumstances. With Diktat representing Godolphin in the Prix de la Foret, Lend A Hand's obvious target was the Champions' Gallery Challenge Stakes at Newmarket twenty-four hours earlier. The positioning of the two best seven-furlong races in Europe on the same weekend cannot be in the interests of competitive racing, especially as options for high-class horses at this distance

Hungerford Stakes, Newbury—impressive Lend A Hand provides Frankie Dettori with his two-hundredth pattern-race success; the race for the places is more competitive with Teapot Row (light colours) and Exeat (striped cap) coming out on top over Auction House and Tumbleweed Ridge (left)

are limited anyway. However, with their odds-on favourites beaten in both races, Godolphin arguably found life slightly more competitive than usual. Lend A Hand looked in fine condition before the Newmarket race and, as usual, travelled strongly, still cruising as he went to the front two furlongs out. Arguably, if Olivier Peslier had committed Lend A Hand for home in earnest a bit sooner he might have won, but as it was Susu was able to get her head in front, and Sir Michael Stoute's improving mare was a neck to the good at the line, Lend A Hand rallying and the pair four lengths clear of Josr Algarhoud. The first two met again at Gulfstream in the Breeders' Cup Mile and, while Susu ran no sort of race, Lend A Hand put up another good performance. Despite his being allocated only first reserve in the pre-entries by the handicapping panel, the Godolphin camp always maintained that Lend A Hand represented one of their best hopes to break their Breeders' Cup duck. For a long time during the race, he looked like justifying the confidence, racing close to the pace and taking up the running early in the straight. However, in the last fifty yards his stamina ran out, and in a blanket finish Lend A Hand even missed out on a place, beaten around half a length by the winner Silic.

Lend A Hand (b.c. 1995)	Great Commotion (USA) (b 1986)	Nureyev (b 1977)	Northern Dancer / Special
		Alathea (b 1975)	Lorenzaccio / Vive La Reine
	Janaat (b 1989)	Kris (ch 1976)	Sharpen Up / Doubly Sure
		Triple First (b 1974)	High Top / Field Mouse

Lend A Hand's pedigree has been discussed in detail in previous editions of this Annual and he remains the best runner sired by Great Commotion. On the distaff side, Janaat's three-year-old Opulence (by Arazi) did not

Godolphin's "Lend A Hand"

see the racecourse and her two-year-old Classic Lord (by Wolfhound) failed to win for Mark Johnston in five attempts, showing modest form at best. However, Lend A Hand wasn't left to uphold the family name alone in 1999 as Janaat's half-sister, the Lancashire Oaks winner Three Tails, was responsible for the Goodwood Cup runner-up Three Cheers as well as the very smart Sea Wave. Some more 'black type' was provided by Trefula, a daughter of Janaat's sister Trefoil, who won a listed race in France over eleven and a half furlongs.

The good-bodied Lend A Hand acts on firm going, good to soft and dirt and usually either races prominently or makes the running. Although he stays a mile on dirt and has good form at the trip on turf, he may prove better at seven furlongs on the latter surface, and as he travels so strongly through his races it would be no surprise to see him eventually tried again at even shorter, perhaps in races such as the July Cup and the Prix Maurice de Gheest. All in all Lend A Hand is a genuine colt who should continue to give a good account of himself. *Saeed bin Suroor*

LENNOX 3 b.g. Bustino 136 – Ivory Gull (USA) 80 (Storm Bird (CAN) 134) **72** [1998 74: 7.1m⁴ 8.1m 8d⁵ 1999 12s³ 10s⁴ 12m 8d Oct 29] tall, close-coupled gelding: fair maiden: ran creditably in 1999 in minor event at Nottingham (pulled early on) second start: should be suited by 1½m: acts on good to firm and soft going: sold 6,500 gns, joined C. Weedon. *P. F. I. Cole*

LENNY THE LION 2 b.g. (Feb 22) Bin Ajwaad (IRE) 119 – Patriotic 43 (Hot- **56 +** foot 126) [1999 7g 7.6g 8m⁶ 7d⁵ Oct 21] 8,000Y, 26,000 2-y-o: half-brother to 5-y-o Sweet Patoopie and a winner in Italy by Formidable: dam, 13.8f and 2¼m winner, half-sister to dam of User Friendly: modest maiden: creditable fifth in nursery at Brighton final start: should stay at least 1¼m: sold 16,000 gns. *R. Hannon*

LEOFRIC 4 b.g. Alhijaz 122 – Wandering Stranger 69 (Petong 126) [1998 57, a–: **50** 7d 6.1m⁵ 6d⁴ 7g 8g 6m⁴ 5g³ 6g 5m 5m 5m 5m 5g 6g 6s a6g⁵ a5g a5g 1999 a7g* a6g **a57** a5g⁵ a6f⁶ a6g⁴ a7g a6g 8s a7g⁴ 6.1f 7m⁴ 8d⁵ 8m⁴ 10m⁶ 8f 8h 8.1d* 10m 8m a7g 7s a8g⁴ a7g Nov 30] leggy gelding: modest performer: won claimer at Southwell in January and apprentice handicap at Sandown (taken to race alone stand side in straight and possibly flattered) in August: stays 1m: acts on fibresand and firm going, probably on good to soft: sometimes blinkered/visored, but as effective when not: has looked none too keen. *M. J. Polglase*

LEONATO (FR) 7 b.g. Law Society (USA) 130 – Gala Parade 78 (Alydar (USA)) **?** [1998 105: 12d⁴ 18.7m³ 12.3g² 16.1v 1999 12.3d² 13.9d⁵ Jun 11] tall gelding: has knee action: useful performer at best: lightly raced: second of 3 to The Glow Worm in minor event at Chester: poor last of 5 only other start in 1999: stays 2¼m well: acts on good to firm and good to soft going, tailed off only start on fibresand: has been bandaged/tongue tied. *P. D. Evans*

LEONIE SAMUAL 4 b.f. Safawan 118 – Hy Wilma 52 (Jalmood (USA) 126) **–** [1998 NR 1999 5m 8m Jun 23] 500 3-y-o: first foal: dam 2-y-o 6f seller winner out of Galtres winner Hymettus: well held in claimers. *R. J. Hodges*

LE PIN 2 ch.f. (Feb 14) Persian Bold 123 – Red Rose Garden 87 (Electric 126) **59 ?** [1999 7m⁵ a7g 5.1m 6d Aug 11] 25,000Y: seventh foal: half-sister to 5-y-o Handsome Ridge and fairly useful stayer Red Bustaan (by Aragon): dam Irish 1½m winner: showed only signs of ability in maidens. *M. R. Channon*

LERMONTOV (USA) 2 b. or br.c. (Feb 4) Alleged (USA) 138 – Prospect **112 p** Dalia (USA) (Mr Prospector (USA)) [1999 7d* 8s* 8s² Oct 23]

At least any duel in which Lermontov becomes involved shouldn't have the same tragic consequences as the 'pistols for two, coffee for one' which, in 1841, ended the life of the Russian writer of the same name at an early age. Mikhail Lermontov evidently didn't lack courage—shortly before his death he'd distinguished himself in the infantry—and Lermontov the racehorse doesn't look one to shirk the issue either judged on what has been seen of him so far. After readily landing the odds in a maiden at Gowran in June on his debut, Lermontov became involved in a couple of no-holds-barred contests himself, and he displayed admirable gameness each time. Reappearing in mid-October in the Juddmonte Beresford Stakes at the Curragh, one of three Aidan O'Brien entries in the six-runner field, Lermontov won by a short head from stable-companion Barrier Reef. The latter had looked likely to prevail when heading the front-running Lermontov a furlong out, but Lermontov, despite being hampered as Barrier Reef edged right, fought back with great tenacity to get up. Lermontov was ridden by Paul Scallan, who earlier in the afternoon had been presented with his prize for winning the Derrinstown apprentice series. Scallan was also given the mount on Lermontov, again one of three O'Brien-trained runners, in the Racing Post Trophy at Doncaster a week later. This time Lermontov had a set-to with Ekraar, getting the better of that battle only for his own stable-companion Aristotle to pounce late and beat the pair. Lermontov led until Ekraar took over three furlongs out and kept on splendidly under pressure, beaten a length and a quarter into second.

Lermontov (USA) (b. or br.c. Feb 4, 1997)	Alleged (USA) (b 1974)	Hoist The Flag (b 1968)	Tom Rolfe Wavy Navy
		Princess Pout (b 1966)	Prince John Determined Lady
	Prospect Dalia (USA) (b or br 1990)	Mr Prospector (b 1970)	Raise A Native Gold Digger
		Vidalia (b 1981)	Nijinsky Waya

Judged on his style of racing, Lermontov takes after his sire rather than his dam in that he's a staying type rather than a sprinter. At the time of writing he is prominent in the Derby betting, and, while a mile and a half may prove within his compass, he does have a lot more improvement to make to reach classic-winning standard. Lermontov came into the bargain-basement category when he appeared at the Keeneland September Sale in 1998. The 20,000 dollars it cost to secure him is a paltry sum compared to the prices paid for most of his contemporaries at Ballydoyle, and surprisingly low given his pedigree. Lermontov is the second foal of Prospect Dalia, a minor winner in the States and a granddaughter of Waya. After showing smart form in France, Waya was top class in the States, winning eleven races and receiving the Eclipse Award as best older filly or mare in 1979. Waya's daughter Vidalia, the grandam of Lermontov, won a Group 3 in Italy at two years and finished fourth in the Cheshire Oaks at three, when trained by Ian Balding, and was later successful in the States. Lermontov, who has raced only on good to soft and soft ground, should continue to progress. *A. P. O'Brien, Ireland*

LE SAUVAGE (IRE) 4 b.g. Tirol 127 – Cistus 123 (Sun Prince 128) [1998 –, a37+: 10g 12m a13g⁶ a11g³ 1999 a12g² a11g 16.2d⁵ 16m 17.2m 16d 17.1g⁵ 17.1s⁶ a14g Nov 12] workmanlike gelding: poor maiden handicapper: probably stays 17f. *D. W. Barker* **47**

LESLEY'S ADVENTURE (IRE) 4 b. or br.f. Petardia 113 – Island Adventure (Touching Wood (USA) 127) [1998 39: a7g⁶ 10v 6g 8g⁵ 8m⁵ 8.3d 1999 a7g a8g⁵ Feb 26] poor maiden handicapper: no form in 1999: should stay beyond 1m: sent to Denmark. *E. J. Alston* **–**

L'ESTABLE FLEURIE (IRE) 4 b.f. Common Grounds 118 – Dorado Llave (USA) (Well Decorated (USA)) [1998 71, a76?: a6g³ a6g⁵ a7g³ 7g* 6.1m⁵ a7g* 7.6m⁴ a9.4g⁴ 8d 1999 a7g a7g⁵ a8g⁵ a8g⁴ a8g Feb 25] fair performer: easily best effort in 1999 on fourth start: stays 9.4f: acts on good to firm ground, good to soft and all-weather. *B. Smart* **70**

LET IT RAIN (NZ) 5 b.g. Rainbow Myth (NZ) – Wayside Inn (NZ) (Long Row 124) [1998 7v² 7v* 8v* 1999 6g⁴ 5d³ 7m⁵ 12g⁵ 10m 7.9g⁵ 10d⁴ 10s Oct 2] strong, lengthy ex-New Zealand gelding: half-brother to a 1m winner: dam ran once: won maiden and minor event from 3 starts for R. Manning in native country in 1998: useful form in Britain, including in handicaps: effective at 1m to 1½m: acts on heavy ground, probably on good to firm. *M. Johnston* **95**

LEVEL HEADED 4 b.f. Beveled (USA) – Snowline (Bay Express 132) [1998 – 44: 6.1g 8d 7d⁶ 8v⁴ 1999 6g 8s 8.3g 6d a6g⁵ a8.5g Dec 1] poor maiden: stays 1m: acts on heavy going: often claimer ridden. *E. A. Wheeler*

LEVELLED 5 b.g. Beveled (USA) – Baino Charm (USA) (Diesis 133) [1998 95: 103
6d⁴ 6v 5m⁶ 5g 6g⁶ 6g 5m 5g² 5d 5.1g² 6m* 5.1m 6m 6m* 5g² 5.2g* 5s³ 6s⁴ 5s² 5m
6v⁵ 1999 a6g⁵ 5d 6m* 5.2m 6m 5.1m* 6s¹ 6m⁵ 6d 5m 6m 6f 6m 5m² 6g 5g
5.6g 6m 6d a5f³ 6m² Dec 17] angular gelding: useful handicapper: won at Ripon in
April and Chester in May: left M. Channon before penultimate outing: effective at
5f/6f: acts on any going: has won for apprentice: held up. *P. L. Rudkin, UAE*

LEVEL PEGGING (IRE) 2 ch.f. (Feb 16) Common Grounds 118 – Family At 48
War (USA) 71 (Explodent (USA)) [1999 5m⁶ 5m⁶ Jun 2] IR 40,000Y: quite good-
topped filly: fourth foal: sister to 3 winning sprinters, including 3-y-o Flanders and
fairly useful 6f winner Disputed: dam 2-y-o 5f winner: poor form in maidens: played
up at start second outing. *T. D. Easterby*

LIBERTE BELL (IRE) 4 b.f. Petorius 117 – Ransomed (IRE) (Ballad Rock –
122) [1998 –: a8.5g 1999 a10f a7g 8m May 3] modest maiden as 2-y-o: lightly raced
and no form since. *D. Haydn Jones*

LIBERTY LINES (USA) 3 b.g. Zilzal (USA) 137 – Bold 'n Determined (USA) 79
(Bold And Brave) [1998 77p: 7g 6d² 1999 7m³ 7.5d² 7g² 8.2d Oct 21] quite attractive
gelding: fair maiden: stays 7f, probably not 1m: yet to race on extremes of going:
sold 5,700 gns, sent to Macau. *B. W. Hills*

LICENCE TO THRILL 2 ch.f. (Apr 21) Wolfhound (USA) 126 – Crime of 66
Passion 115 (Dragonara Palace (USA) 115) [1999 6g a6g² a5g⁵ Nov 20] half-sister to
3-y-o Quicksilver Girl and several winners, including 5f/6f winner Master of Passion
(by Primo Dominie), useful at 2 yrs: dam sprinting 2-y-o (won Cherry Hinton) who
didn't train on: fair form in maidens at Lingfield and Wolverhampton last 2 starts.
D. W. P. Arbuthnot

LIEUTENANT FANCY 3 ch.g. Kris 135 – Noirmant (Dominion 123) [1998 47
NR 1999 12g a11g 10.2m 16.2m Jul 19] 12,000Y: tall, useful-looking gelding: fifth
foal: half-brother to fairly useful winning sprinters Ouaisne (by Warning), Portelet
(by Night Shift) and Soviet Leader (by Soviet Star): dam unraced: poor form: sold
3,200 gns, joined R. Ford. *C. A. Cyzer*

LIFE IS LIFE (FR) 3 b.f. Mansonnien (FR) 122 – La Vie Immobile (USA) 108
(Alleged (USA) 138) [1998 NR 1999 10g⁴ 12d³ 12v* 12d 14.6s² Nov 5] fourth foal:
sister to a winner in USA: dam unraced: trained first 2 starts by A. Hosselet in France:
useful performer in Britain, winning maiden at Kempton in September impressively:
best effort when neck second of 5 to Persian Punch in minor event at Doncaster:
should stay 2m: raced only on good ground or softer. *M. A. Jarvis*

LIFE OF RILEY 5 ch.g. Caerleon (USA) 132 – Catina 102 (Nureyev (USA) 107 ?
131) [1998 96: 12d 14.4m* 16g² 14g² 16.4g* 16g 16.2d 18g 1999 14m* 16.1m³
14f 14.8m* 17.3g Oct 16] big, good-topped gelding: useful handicapper: won at
Goodwood in June and Newmarket (beat Loop The Loup by 3½ lengths) in August,
dictating pace in small fields both times: midfield in Cesarewitch at Newmarket final
start: should stay beyond 2m: acts on good to firm and good to soft ground: blinkered
once as 4-y-o: has worn dropped noseband/tongue tie: has run well sweating: sold
25,000 gns and gelded. *B. J. Meehan*

LIFT BOY (USA) 10 b.g. Fighting Fit (USA) – Pressure Seat (USA) (Ginistrelli 35
(USA) 117) [1998 35, a48d: a7g⁵ a8g⁶ a7g⁶ a8g³ a7g³ 6g⁴ 6f 7g a7g 5.3d 7m a8g⁶ 8m
a10g 7s a8g⁶ a7g⁶ a8.5g 1999 a10g a10g a8g⁶ a8g a8g 7m a7g Jun 12] small, sturdy
gelding: poor performer nowadays: probably stays 1m: acts on good to firm going,
soft and all-weather: tried visored. *P. Burgoyne*

LIFT THE OFFER (IRE) 4 ch.g. Ballad Rock 122 – Timissara (USA) (Shah- 53
rastani (USA) 135) [1998 69, a–: 8g 8.2m³ 10.1g 11.4d 8s³ 8.2g⁶ 7.1m 9m⁶ 8g 10v⁵ a58
1999 7g 8d 8m 8.2m⁴ 5.9g⁵ 6m² 7g 6g 6s a6g Dec 21] close-coupled, workmanlike
gelding: modest handicapper: effective at 6f to 1m: acts on equitrack, soft and good
to firm going: visored once at 3 yrs: none too consistent. *J. J. Quinn*

LIGHT BREEZE 3 b.f. Hamas (IRE) 125§ – Fiorini 54 (Formidable (USA) 125) 61 d
[1998 70: 5g⁵ 5f³ 7.8d 5s a6g⁵ 1999 a5g³ a6g* a5g⁴ a6g⁵ a6g a5g⁶ 5.1g⁵ 5f a5g 5m
a5g a6g Dec 6] modest performer: won seller at Lingfield in February: below form

after next start and left G. L. Moore after sixth outing: stays 6f: acts on all-weather, best turf effort on firm going. *N. E. Berry*

LIGHTHOUSE   3 br.f. Warning 136 – Valika 75 (Valiyar 129) [1998 NR 1999   **92** 8.3s* 8m⁴ 8d Oct 1] 220,000Y: good-topped filly: good walker: half-sister to several winners, notably 1993 Middle Park winner First Trump (by Primo Dominie) who stayed 1m: dam, maiden placed up to 1½m, half-sister to high-class sprinter Mr Brooks: won maiden at Windsor in August: not discredited next start (raced freely): tailed off final outing: stays 8.3f: acts on soft going. *H. R. A. Cecil*

LIGHTNING ARROW (USA)   3 br.g. Silver Hawk (USA) 123 – Strait Lane   **110** (USA) (Chieftain II) [1998 101p: 7m⁶ 8m² 7.9g² 8g* 1999 10.1s² 12.3m² 12m 12m⁴ 12d³ 12v Oct 23] close-coupled, quite attractive gelding: smart performer: ran well when 2¼ lengths third (promoted to second) to disqualified Housemaster in Chester Vase second start and when 1¾ lengths third to Kahtan in listed event at Newmarket penultimate outing: stays 1½m: acts on good and good to firm going, possibly not on heavy: blinkered third (reportedly struck into in Derby Italiano) and final starts: mulish exiting paddock at Chester, and seems a tricky ride: gelded at end of season. *J. L. Dunlop*

LIGHTNING BLAZE   3 ch.f. Cosmonaut – Royal Deed (USA) 76 (Shadeed   **58** (USA) 135) [1998 57: 5g 5g³ a5g* 5d 5m* 5m² 5m* 5m* 5m³ 6f 5d 5m 1999 6g⁵ 5m 5.3f⁶ 5f⁴ 5m² 5g 5m 6g Sep 20] small, sturdy filly: modest performer: left B. Meehan following sixth start, and below par after: barely stays 6f: acts on firm ground, seems unsuited by good to soft: often races prominently/leads. *D. Nicholls*

LIGHTNING REBEL   5 b.g. Rambo Dancer (CAN) 107 – Ozra 63 (Red Alert   **30** 127) [1998 –: a9.4g 11.9g a8.5g 1999 a12g³ a12f a12g a12f a11f a12g Feb 16] fair at 2 yrs: retains only a little ability. *P. W. Hiatt*

LIGHT ON THE WAVES   3 b.f. Greensmith 121 – Roof Dancer (Martinmas   **71** 128) [1998 54+: 6.1g⁶ 6m² a8.5g* a8g⁵ 1999 11.7g* 16.2m² 17.2h* Aug 3] fair performer: won seller at Bath in June and 3-runner handicap at same course in August: will stay 2¼m: acts on fibresand and hard going: has carried head awkwardly/flashed tail. *M. C. Pipe*

LIGHT PROGRAMME   5 b.g. El Gran Senor (USA) 136 – Nashmeel (USA)   **–** 121 (Blushing Groom (FR) 131) [1998 NR 1999 10.4g 10s Oct 22] fairly useful winner from 2 starts for H. Cecil in 1997: had knee operation afterwards and sold only 5,000 gns: well held in handicaps both starts since (tongue tied on first occasion): raced only at 1¼m. *J. G. Smyth-Osbourne*

LIGHT THE ROCKET (IRE)   3 ch.c. Pips Pride 117 – Coolrain Lady (IRE)   **112 ?** 74 (Common Grounds 118) [1998 94: 5f 6.1g² 5.2m 5g* 5m* 5d⁴ 5m 1999 5s² 6m² 5m⁶ 6m 6m 5m 6m² 6m 5d 5d² Oct 14] leggy, rather lightly-made colt: smart performer: improved in 1999, finishing second in rated stakes at Sandown, Salisbury and Newmarket and in minor event at Doncaster: appeared to put up best effort at Newmarket on final outing, going down by a head to Ellens Lad: likely to prove best at 5f/easy 6f: acts on good to firm and soft ground: often bandaged behind: upset in stalls and withdrawn on sixth intended start: often makes running: changed hands 44,000 gns after final outing. *R. Hannon*

LIGNE GAGNANTE (IRE)   3 b.g. Turtle Island (IRE) 123 – Lightino (Bustino   **97** 136) [1998 71p: 6m 6f⁶ 6m⁴ 7s 1999 9.1m* 12s* 12.4m* 14f³ 11.9m⁵ 13.3m³ 12s² Sep 26] useful-looking gelding: useful performer: much improved in 1999, winning maiden at Ayr in May and handicaps at Goodwood and Newcastle in June: creditable efforts in valuable handicaps at York (wandered and hampered), Newbury and Ascot (£46,000 event, 3½ lengths second to Vicious Circle) final 3 starts: stays 1¾m, at least when conditions aren't testing: acts on firm and soft going: consistent. *W. J. Haggas*

LILA   3 b.f. Zafonic (USA) 130 – Bint Pasha (USA) 126 (Affirmed (USA)) [1998   **88** NR 1999 8g* 10m² 10.2m³ 10g Sep 25] sixth foal: half-sister to 3 winners, including smart 1m (at 2 yrs) to 11.5f winner Revere (by Dancing Brave) and fairly useful 1½m winner Monarch (by Sadler's Wells): dam won Yorkshire Oaks and Prix Vermeille: fairly useful performer: won maiden at Salisbury in June: good efforts when placed in minor events after: stays 1¼m: raced only on good/good to firm going: sold 105,000 gns in December. *P. F. I. Cole*

LIL

LILANITA 4 b.f. Anita's Prince 126 – Jimlil 99 (Nicholas Bill 125) [1998 62: 7v⁴ **42** 7d 6.1g 8.1d* 10d² 10g 8m³ 8m⁶ 8m 8d 8v⁵ a7g² a7s² 1999 a10g³ a10g a7g a8g 8.1m **a55** 8f 7.1m⁵ 8f 8s⁴ a8g³ a8.5g² a7g a8.5g³ Dec 27] modest handicapper on all-weather, poor on turf nowadays: left B. Palling after eleventh start: effective at 7f to 1¼m: acts on good to firm going, heavy and all-weather: often races freely. *P. D. Evans*

LILARDO 2 b. or br.f. (Apr 12) Son Pardo 107 – Jimlil 99 (Nicholas Bill 125) **48** [1999 6g⁵ 7s 7.6g 7g a8.5g⁴ a8.5g⁶ Oct 30] second foal: half-sister to 4-y-o Lilanita: **a43** dam 6f (at 2 yrs) and 1m winner: poor maiden: stays 8.5f: acts on fibresand. *B. Palling*

LIMA TANGO 3 b.f. Aird Point – Routine (Teenoso (USA) 135) [1998 NR 1999 **–** a9.4g⁶ 16m⁶ 14d a12g Jun 16] lengthy, sparely-made filly: second reported foal: dam unraced daughter of 11.5f winner: no form: blinkered penultimate outing, unruly start final one. *M. Waring*

LIMELIGHTING (USA) 3 b.f. Alleged (USA) 138 – Steal The Thunder (CAN) **102** (Lyphard (USA) 132) [1998 NR 1999 10d 10m² 10g² 10.4m* 11.8d² 10.3s* 10.5v² Nov 26] 130,000Y: rather unfurnished, workmanlike filly: third foal: half-sister to a winner in USA by Afleet: dam, Canadian sprint winner, from family of Grade 1 winners, including Dance Smartly (Breeders' Cup Distaff) and Sky Classic (Roth-man's International): useful performer: won maiden at York in September and minor event at Doncaster (beat Esteraad by 5 lengths) in November: short-headed in listed race at Maisons-Laffitte final start: stays 1½m: acts on good to firm and heavy going: has hung. *J. H. M. Gosden*

LIMPID 4 b.c. Soviet Star (USA) 128 – Isle of Glass (USA) 94 (Affirmed (USA)) **116** [1998 119: 7d* 8m² 9.3g⁴ 10m* 10.4f⁵ 12d 1999 10m⁶ 10m⁶ Jun 15] medium-sized, good-topped colt: smart performer: trained by A. Fabre in France at 3 yrs, winner of Grand Prix de Paris: creditable sixth to Jim And Tonic in Queen Elizabeth II Cup at Sha Tin on reappearance: below best in Prince of Wales's Stakes at Royal Ascot (crossed noseband, tongue tied and bandaged behind, made running) 2 months later: stays 1¼m: acts on firm and good to soft going. *Saeed bin Suroor*

LINCOLN DANCER (IRE) 2 b.c. (Mar 21) Turtle Island (IRE) 123 – Double **96** Grange (IRE) (Double Schwartz 128) [1999 5d* 5d³ 6s* 6m Jun 15] 7,000F, 25,000Y: compact, sturdy, attractive colt: third foal: dam of little account in Ireland: useful form: won maiden at Warwick in April and minor event at York in May, beating Pipadash by 3 lengths in latter: should stay at least 7f: acts on soft going, below form in Coventry Stakes on good to firm: joined M. Jarvis. *G. Lewis*

LINCOLN DEAN 3 b.g. Mtoto 134 – Play With Me (IRE) 73 (Alzao (USA) 117) **64** [1998 62p: 7d 7s a6s⁵ 1999 a8f* a10g a8g² 8m 9.1g⁵ 8d 10f⁴ 10m Aug 10] small, **a76** sturdy gelding: fair handicapper at best: won at Lingfield in January: left Sir Mark Prescott after third start, and well held back on turf after: stays 1m: acts on equitrack, best turf effort on good to soft going: often races prominently. *J. S. Goldie*

LINDAS GEM 3 ch.f. Kasakov – Kabella (Kabour 80) [1998 66d: 5d² 5g 5.3d⁴ **–** 5.3g 1999 a6g 8g 5g Aug 13] leggy filly: little form since 2-y-o debut. *B. Preece*

LINDEN GRACE (USA) 2 b.f. (Mar 16) Mister Bailey 123 – Gracefully Bold **82** (USA) (Nasty And Bold (USA)) [1999 7m* 6m² 7m⁵ 7.3v Oct 23] $19,000Y: big, useful-looking filly: has scope: fifth foal: half-sister to winners in USA by Blue Ensign and Dixie Brass: dam sprint winner in USA on only start: fairly useful form when winning maiden at Epsom and second of 4 to Far Mount in minor event at Doncaster (shade mulish in stalls), both in July: tailed off in listed race at York and nursery at Newbury after: should prove better at 7f than 6f. *M. Johnston*

LINEA-G 5 ch.m. Keen 116 – Horton Line 89 (High Line 125) [1998 –, a42: a12g⁴ **71** 10m 11m 9.9m 1999 a12g* a12g² 16g³ 12.4m* 13.1d² 12g⁵ 12g* 12m² 14.1g Oct 2] fair performer: won maiden at Southwell in March, handicap at Newcastle in May and minor event at Beverley in August: may prove best around 1½m (failed to stay 1¾m final start): acts on fibresand, good to firm and good to soft going: twice successful over hurdles in October. *Mrs M. Reveley*

LINE CALL 3 b.c. Second Set (IRE) 127 – Misguided 106 (Homing 130) [1998 **68** 73p: 7d⁴ 1999 8m 8.3m⁵ 11.6m 8g⁴ 8g 8.5s⁶ 12s Oct 5] fair maiden: well below form

610

after fourth start: stays 1m: acts on good to firm and good to soft going: tongue tied sixth outing: sold 5,600 gns. *D. W. P. Arbuthnot*

LINENS GIRL   3 br.f. Thowra (FR) – Stocktina 42 (Tina's Pet 121) [1998 NR 1999 6.8m 6m⁵ 7m⁴ 7.7m Aug 30] second foal: dam 5f winner: little sign of ability in maidens (pulled up on debut). *R. J. Hodges*

LINGUISTIC DANCER   4 ch.f. Aragon 118 – Linguistic 95 (Porto Bello 118)   **33**
[1998 –: 7s 8m a6g⁶ 8m 7f 8d 8s 1999 a8g³ a8g Mar 22] leggy filly: third in handicap in February, only form. *A. G. Newcombe*

LINK HILL   3 ch.f. Generous (IRE) 139 – Phaleria (USA) (Lyphard (USA) 132)   **68**
[1998 –: 7d 1999 7m 8m⁵ 9.9m 10m³ 11.9s 10d⁴ Oct 21] fair maiden: unlucky when third in minor event at Nottingham: below form in handicaps both starts after: should be suited by 1½m: acts on good to firm going: sold 7,000 gns. *Mrs A. J. Perrett*

LINKSMAN (USA)   4 b.g. Diesis 133 – Wrap Around (AUS) (Bletchingly   **–**
(AUS)) [1998 NR 1999 6g 8s a6g a5g Nov 19] $75,000Y, 1,400 3-y-o: second foal: half-brother to a winner in USA by Wild Again: dam Australian Group 1 6f winner: no form. *D. Shaw*

LIONARDO   3 b.c. Lion Cavern (USA) 117 – Pravolo (Fools Holme (USA))   **75**
[1998 75+: a4.5g* 5f* 7m⁵ 5f* 7f* 5v 1999 8d 8.5f² 8f* 9g* 7m⁵ 6.5s Oct 1] fair performer at best: successful at Ostend in minor event in July and handicap in August: well held in minor event at Goodwood next time: stays 9f: acts on firm ground. *Paul Smith, Belgium*

LION CUB (IRE)   3 b.g. Catrail (USA) 123 – Lightly Dancing (FR) (Groom   **52 ?**
Dancer (USA) 128) [1998 52: 7g 8g 6d 1999 8.2d 8d 14.1g 12s a12g⁴ a12g a12g⁵ Dec 4] tall, leggy gelding: modest maiden: stays 1½m: acts on fibresand: blinkered final start: has worn tongue strap. *R. McGhin*

LIONESS   3 b.f. Lion Cavern (USA) 117 – Pidona (Baillamont (USA) 124) [1998   **74**
NR 1999 8.2m⁴ 8g⁴ 9f³ 10.3m Jul 28] first foal: dam, German 1m winner, daughter of Galtres Stakes winner and from good middle-distance family: fair form in frame in maidens: should stay beyond 9f: sold 2,300 gns in December. *J. R. Fanshawe*

LION GUEST (IRE)   2 ch.c. (Apr 15) Lion Cavern (USA) 117 – Decrescendo   **64**
(IRE) (Polish Precedent (USA) 131) [1999 7d 7d⁶ Oct 27] 24,000F, 50,000Y: sturdy, lengthy colt: first foal: dam unraced half-sister to 3-y-o Calando, out of Oaks winner and St Leger second Diminuendo: better effort when sixth of 12 to Fast Track in maiden at Yarmouth: will stay 1¼m: may improve further. *G. G. Margarson*

LIONHEARTED (IRE)   3 b.c. Catrail (USA) 123 – Quiche 83 (Formidable   **110**
(USA) 125) [1998 –p: 6g 1999 6g* 6g² 6d² 6m⁵ 6s Sep 17] strong, good-topped colt: smart performer: won maiden at Newmarket in April: runner-up in listed race at Ascot (beaten 3 lengths by Sampower Star) then minor event at Newbury (short headed by Vision of Night): off course 3½ months and visored, behind in Group 3 at Chantilly final start: likely to prove best at 5f/6f: acts on good to soft going: has been bandaged in front: sent to UAE. *J. H. M. Gosden*

LION'S DOMANE   2 b.g. (Mar 31) Lion Cavern (USA) 117 – Vilany 87 (Never   **–**
So Bold 135) [1999 7d 6s a5g Nov 30] 10,500F, 18,000Y: strong, workmanlike gelding: third foal: half-brother to winners up to 1m in Italy by Primo Dominie and Forzando: dam 7f winner: little show in maidens, equipped with net muzzle and going markedly left leaving stalls on second start. *P. C. Haslam*

LISA-B (IRE)   2 b.f. (Mar 16) Case Law 113 – Nishiki (USA) (Brogan (USA)   **50**
110) [1999 5.1s⁶ 5d 5m 6m⁵ a6g* a6g* 6d⁶ a5g³ a6g⁵ 6g³ 6m 7g 7s 6d a7g a5g Nov   **a58**
19] IR 5,000Y: leggy, sparely-made filly: second foal: sister to 3-y-o Cashiki: dam, lightly raced on Flat, won over hurdles in Ireland: modest performer: won sellers at Southwell and Wolverhampton in June: best form at 6f: acts on fibresand and good to firm ground: usually blinkered/visored. *J. A. Glover*

LISALA   3 ch.f. Beveled (USA) – Super Style (Artaius (USA) 129) [1998 44: 7d³   **48 §**
7.5d 7m 7f 1999 8.2s⁵ a9.4g³ 9.9d a11g a9.4g Jul 9] sparely-made filly: poor and ungenuine maiden: stays 9.4f. *W. G. M. Turner*

LISIEUX ROSE (IRE)   4 ch.f. Generous (IRE) 139 – Epicure's Garden (USA)   **107**
102 (Affirmed (USA)) [1998 108: 12m* 11g* 12d⁴ 11s* 1999 9g³ 12m³ 12.3g⁴

14.6g[6] 11s[3] Sep 19] sixth foal: half-sister to 3 winners, including Cryptic Pattern (up to 1½m, by Green Dancer): dam Irish 7f (at 2 yrs) to 9f winner, sister to Irish 1,000 Guineas winner Trusted Partner: useful performer: won 3 times at 3 yrs, notably Blandford Stakes at the Curragh: creditable third in listed race at Leopardstown, Premio Legnano (promoted from fourth) at Milan and Blandford Stakes (beaten 10½ lengths by Insatiable) at the Curragh: respectable sixth in Park Hill Stakes at Doncaster: probably stays 1¾m: acts on soft and good to firm going: blinkered final 2 starts: sent to USA. *D. K. Weld, Ireland*

LISTE ROUGE (USA)   6 b.g. Red Ransom (USA) – Bestseller's List (USA) (Going Straight (USA)) [1998 NR 1999 a8.5g Apr 24] $65,000Y: fifth foal: half-brother to a winner in USA by Exclusive Era: dam maiden in USA: signs of ability in bumpers (has pulled too hard) for R. Alner: well held in apprentice claimer at Wolverhampton on Flat debut. *G. L. Moore*   **–**

LITERARY SOCIETY (USA)   6 ch.h. Runaway Groom (CAN) – Dancing Gull (USA) (Northern Dancer) [1998 101: 5f* 6g* 5g[5] 6g 6f* 5m 1999 6m 6s 6f[3] 6m 6m[3] 6f[3] 6m 5.6g Sep 8] small, sturdy horse: has a quick action: useful handicapper: fared clearly best of those on far side when 2 lengths third of 30 to Harmonic Way in Stewards' Cup at Goodwood sixth start: disappointing after, shaping as though something amiss final outing: effective at 5f/6f: best efforts on good ground or firmer: usually comes from off pace: unseated rider leaving stalls fourth start. *J. A. R. Toller*   **102 +**

LITTLE AMIN   3 b.g. Unfuwain (USA) 131 – Ghassanah 73 (Pas de Seul 133) [1998 67: 6g[3] 6d 1999 7d* 7.5m[2] 7.6m 8g[3] 8m[4] 9m[4] 11.9d* 11.6d[6] 12s Oct 23] smallish, well-made gelding: has marked knee action: fairly useful performer: won maiden at Newcastle in March and handicap at Haydock in August (first start since leaving J. Bethell): something possibly amiss final start: stays 1½m: acts on good to firm and good to soft going. *W. R. Muir*   **82**

LITTLE AN (FR)   3 b.f. Sheyrann 81 – Little Miss John (Last Fandango 125) [1998 NR 1999 8v 12s 8.5d 12m Jul 14] first reported foal: dam won several races in Belgium, including at 11f: well beaten in France for A. Hermans and in maiden at Kempton on British debut. *G. L. Moore*   **–**

LITTLE BOY BLUE (IRE)   3 br.g. Petardia 113 – Bluebutton 65 (Blue Cashmere 129) [1998 –: 5v a7g a8.5g a7g 1999 a8g Jan 4] no promise in maidens/sellers: blinkered last 2 starts. *M. Waring*   **–**

LITTLE BRAVE   4 b.g. Kahyasi 130 – Littlemisstrouble (USA) (My Gallant (USA)) [1998 64, a71: a8g* 10s 8m 10m[6] 11.6f[6] 14.1m[3] 16d[2] 16.1g[2] 16s[4] 1999 16d 16.2m[6] 16.4m a16g[4] 16.4d[6] 15.8m* 18.2s* 17.2s 17.3g a16g[2] a16.2g[4] Dec 1] lengthy gelding: fairly useful on all-weather, fair on turf: won minor event at Lingfield in July and handicaps at Warwick in August and Yarmouth in September: stays 2¼m: acts on all-weather, soft and good to firm going: possibly not a straightforward ride. *J. M. P. Eustace*   **67 a85**

LITTLE CAESAR   5 ch.g. Keen 116 – Loredana 64 (Grange Melody) [1998 31: a12g[4] a12g[4] 7m 1999 8d 10.1m May 26] lightly raced and poor form at best, including in handicaps. *S. C. Williams*   **–**

LITTLE CHAPEL (IRE)   3 b.f. College Chapel 122 – Istaraka (IRE) (Darshaan 133) [1998 73: 5m 5.2m[2] 5g[3] 6.1g 6d 7s 1999 6f[4] 6d 7m 6d[5] 7.1m Sep 9] quite good-topped filly: fair maiden at best: disappointing after reappearance: should stay 7f: acts on firm going: sold 1,300 gns in November, joined G. Yardley. *D. J. S. ffrench Davis*   **70 d**

LITTLE CHRISTIAN (IRE)   2 b.g. (Apr 30) Common Grounds 118 – Alexanders Way (FR) 83 (Persian Heights 129) [1999 5d[3] 5m[6] 5d a5g[6] 5m 6m[3] 7m 6g[2] 6m 7.5g[4] 7d a7g Oct 18] 11,000F, 15,000Y: workmanlike gelding: has a round action: first foal: dam, Irish 9f winner, out of half-sister to Irish Oaks winner Give Thanks: modest maiden: stays 7.5f: acts on good to firm and good to soft going. *N. Tinkler*   **53 a–**

LITTLE CINNAMON   3 ch.c. Timeless Times (USA) 99 – Belltina 41 (Belfort (FR) 89) [1998 65: 5m[5] 5d 5m[6] 5g[4] 7d 1999 5.9m 7g 6m 5.9m 5f[6] Sep 4] small, sturdy colt: modest maiden: should prove best up to 7f: probably acts on firm ground: blinkered (ran respectably) final outing: reportedly bled from nose penultimate start. *J. L. Eyre*   **55**

LITTLE DOCKER (IRE)   2 b.g. (Mar 9) Vettori (IRE) 119 – Fair Maid of Kent   **72 p**
(USA) 68 (Diesis 133) [1999 7.1d⁴ Aug 6] 16,000F, 6,500Y: big, workmanlike
gelding: third foal: closely related to a winner in Greece by Machiavellian: dam, 1m
winner from 2 starts at 2 yrs, half-sister to US Grade 1 1¼m winner Clear Choice:
some promise when fourth of 14 to Nicobar in Haydock maiden, chasing pace and
not unduly knocked about: will stay at least 1m: should do better. *T. D. Easterby*

LITTLEFEATHER (IRE)   2 b.f. (Apr 5) Indian Ridge 123 – Marwell 133   **103**
(Habitat 134) [1999 5g² 5m⁴ 5m* 6m* 6.1d* 7m³ 5d⁵ Oct 9] unfurnished filly:
half-sister to several winners, notably very smart miler Marling (by Lomond) and
very smart sprinter/miler Caerwent (by Caerleon): dam top-class sprinter and fourth
in 1000 Guineas: useful performer: won maiden at Ripon, nursery at Newmarket and
minor event at Chester (by 5 lengths, showing fine turn of foot) in July/August: best
effort, though didn't have run of race, when third of 12 to Preseli in Moyglare Stud
Stakes at the Curragh in September, short of room twice: below form final start:
should stay 1m: yet to race on extremes of going. *Sir Mark Prescott*

LITTLE FOX (IRE)   4 br.f. Persian Bold 123 – Dance Land (IRE) (Nordance   **73**
(USA)) [1998 NR 1999 11.9f⁴ 11.7f a13g² a12g⁴ a16g Nov 15] 6,800F, 26,000Y,
3,500 2-y-o: first foal: dam unraced from family of Lord of Men and Sonic Lady: fair
maiden: should stay beyond 13f: acts on equitrack. *Mrs L. Richards*

LITTLE GEM   3 b.f. Night Shift (USA) – Um Lardaff (Mill Reef (USA) 141)   **67**
[1998 72: 5.7m² 6g⁴ 7.1d³ 8m⁴ 8.5s* 8m⁵ 1999 8.3m⁵ 8g Aug 12] sturdy filly: fair
performer: respectable efforts in handicaps in 1999: should stay 1¼m: acts on soft
and good to firm going: sold 40,000 gns in December. *R. Hannon*

LITTLE GREENBIRD   3 b.f. Ardkinglass 114 – Hot Money 50 (Mummy's Pet   **–**
125) [1998 39: a5g 6m 5.1m 1999 a6g 7f 8s 10d Oct 28] poor maiden: well held in
seller final start. *J. G. Portman*

LITTLE HENRY   3 ch.g. My Generation 111 – White African (Carwhite 127)   **47**
[1998 47: 5s 7d⁶ a7g³ 7.5d⁴ 7g³ 7g⁶ 7.5m 7.9g 8g³ 7.5m⁵ 10s³ 8.2v 1999 a9.4g a10g³
a11g a10g⁴ 12.5d⁵ 12d⁶ 8m May 7] smallish gelding: poor maiden: probably stays
1½m: acts on soft and good to firm going and equitrack: wears blinkers/visor:
sometimes tongue tied: joined M. Barnes. *P. D. Evans*

LITTLE IBNR   8 b.g. Formidable (USA) 125 – Zalatia 97 (Music Boy 124) [1998   **–**
–, a37: a6g³ a5g a7g⁶ a6g⁴ a6g⁴ a6g⁶ a6g 1999 a6g⁶ a5g³ a6f² a5g⁴ a6g   **a52**
a6s³ a6g a6g² a6g a5g a6g² a5g⁴ a5g⁶ a6g³ a5g⁶ May 8] workmanlike gelding:
modest performer: stays 7f: best on all-weather, hasn't raced on turf since 1996:
effective blinkered, visored nowadays. *P. D. Evans*

LITTLE IMP (IRE)   4 b.f. Imp Society (USA) – Poka Poka (FR) (King of   **–**
Macedon 126) [1998 –: a7g a7g 6.1s 7g 8f⁶ 8m 1999 a11g Jan 4] no form, mostly
raced in sellers: blinkered last 3 starts. *K. R. Burke*

LITTLE ITALY (IRE)   3 b.f. Common Grounds 118 – Broken Romance (IRE)   **103**
(Ela-Mana-Mou 132) [1998 52: 7f⁵ 6d 1999 a6g* a7g³ 11.8m* 11.8m* 11.5g*
11.5m⁵ 11.9m² 12.4m² 10.5v* 12s* 8.5f⁵ Dec 18] lengthy, angular filly: useful
performer: improved greatly at 3 yrs, winning maiden at Lingfield in April and
handicaps at Leicester (2), Lingfield in May/June and Haydock in October: awarded
listed race at Milan later in October after being beaten ¾ length by Wellanca:
tailed-off last of 5 in Grade 2 at Hollywood final start: stays 1½m: acts on good to
firm and heavy ground and equitrack: free-going sort who usually races prominently.
P. F. I. Cole

LITTLE JOHN   3 b.g. Warrshan (USA) 117 – Silver Venture (USA) (Silver Hawk   **72**
(USA) 123) [1998 69: 7s⁴ 7d⁴ 7s⁴ 1999 9f⁴ 9g² 7.1m⁵ 12f⁵ 10.1m 9.2s³ 10v⁴ 11d⁴
11d⁶ Nov 1] big, lengthy gelding: fair maiden: stays 1½m: acts on any going: has run
creditably when sweating profusely. *Miss L. A. Perratt*

LITTLE LAUREN   2 b.f. (Feb 24) Northern Elegance – Denby Wood (Lord Bud   **–**
121) [1999 7.5s 8g Aug 30] second foal: dam never ran: well held in seller/claimer:
dead. *J. S. Wainwright*

LITTLE LENA   3 b.f. Alhijaz 122 – Killarney Belle (USA) (Irish Castle (USA))   **–**
[1998 NR 1999 6.1s 6s a6g 8m 10g 7.5g Aug 29] sister to fair miler Killarney Belle

and half-sister to 2 winners, including fairly useful Eire-Leath-Sceal (stayed 2m, by Legend of France): dam unraced: no sign of ability. *J. Wharton*

LITTLE LOTTIE   3 gr.f. Nalchik (USA) – Grey Runner 36 (Crofthall 110) [1998 NR 1999 a8.5g Dec 27] second foal: dam, sprint maiden, ran only at 2 yrs: showed little in Wolverhampton maiden. *M. Mullineaux*   –

LITTLE MERMAID (IRE)   3 b.f. Mac's Imp (USA) 116 – Aegean Lady 59 (Lochnager 132) [1998 –: 6d 1999 6d 6v 5d Jun 28] small, close-coupled filly: first foal: dam 9f to 11f winner: no form in maidens/selling handicap. *G. Woodward*   –

LITTLE MIRACLE   2 b.f. (Apr 18) Skyliner 117 – Kalvee Dancer (Kalaglow 132) [1999 5g6 6m 6f 8g Aug 30] 500Y: fifth foal: dam no form: well beaten, including in seller. *Martyn Wane*   –

LITTLE MISS LUCY   5 b.m. Petoski 135 – Puki Puki (Roselier (FR)) [1998 NR 1999 10.1g Jul 14] lightly-raced maiden: blinkered in seller, only outing in 1999: dead. *M. J. Heaton-Ellis*   34

LITTLEPACEPADDOCKS (IRE)   2 b.f. (Mar 20) Accordion – Lady In Pace (Burslem 123) [1999 8g* Nov 3] third reported foal: sister to 7-y-o Yavana's Pace: dam useful Irish sprinter: encouraging debut when winning maiden at Musselburgh by short head from Makasseb, still having lot to do over 2f out but finishing strongly to lead post: likely to be suited by 1¼m/1½m: sure to improve for the experience, and looks a useful prospect. *M. Johnston*   84 p

LITTLE PILGRIM   6 b.g. Precocious 126 – Bonny Bright Eyes 58 (Rarity 129) [1998 –: a8g4 a7g5 a7g a12g6 1999 a8g Nov 23] tall, lengthy gelding: poor maiden. *T. M. Jones*   –

LITTLE PIPPIN   3 ch.f. Rudimentary (USA) 118 – Accuracy 83 (Gunner B 126) [1998 73: 6m 6d6 7g 8s3 1999 10.5s3 10m 10.2d4 12g3 12d4 12s* 13.1d4 11.9d Oct 7] rather unfurnished filly: has a round action: fairly useful handicapper: won at Salisbury and Kempton in August: should stay 1¾m: best efforts on going softer than good: has been bandaged behind/worn tongue strap: sweating (ran poorly) final start. *G. B. Balding*   93

LITTLE ROCK   3 b.c. Warning 136 – Much Too Risky 87 (Bustino 136) [1998 89p: 7d* 1999 8.1s* 10.3m2 8d4 10g 10d* Oct 29] smallish, lengthy, angular colt: smart performer: won minor event at Sandown in April and 7-runner listed race at Newmarket in October, latter ridden out by length from Mujahid: not discredited when 4 lengths eighth to Alborada in Champion Stakes at Newmarket fourth start: finds 1m a bare minimum, and should stay beyond 1¼m: acts on soft and good to firm going: suffered chip on fetlock and off course 5 months after second outing: has edged right, including for last 2 wins. *Sir Michael Stoute*   117

LITTLE TARA   2 b.f. (Mar 11) Pyramus (USA) 78 – Eastwood Heiress (Known Fact (USA) 135) [1999 6s 6g Oct 19] third foal: dam unraced daughter of half-sister to 2000 Guineas winner Mon Fils: well beaten in claimer/maiden. *J. C. Fox*   –

LITTLE TUMBLER (IRE)   4 b.f. Cyrano de Bergerac 120 – Glass Minnow (IRE) 59 (Alzao (USA) 117) [1998 66d: 6m* 6g4 6g4 6m 7m 6f 7s 1999 8g4 7m 9m5 10f* 10g 11.9m a10g Nov 24] neat filly: modest handicapper: won at Brighton in August: stays 1¼m: acts on firm going: has been slowly away: carried head awkwardly and flashed tail once at 3 yrs: none too consistent. *S. Woodman*   54 §

LITTLE WHITE HEART   4 ch.f. Russian Red 72 – Dip N Dot (Golden Dipper 119) [1998 NR 1999 6d 7m 7g 7d a8g Nov 23] third reported foal: dam unraced: of little account. *L. A. Dace*   –

LIVELY JACQ (IRE)   3 ch.f. Case Law 113 – Nordic Living (IRE) 53 (Nordico (USA)) [1998 72: 6m2 6m* 6m* 6f2 6m2 6.5g5 6g 6m6 1999 6.1m 5.3f3 6g4 6m3 6.8m 6m4 6f5 a6g5 7g4 a7g a7g a6g4 a7g6 a6g6 Dec 27] small filly: poor mover: fair on turf, modest on all-weather: may prove best at 5f/6f: acts on equitrack, raced only on good going or firmer on turf: blinkered/visored 4 of last 5 starts. *C. N. Allen*   72 a52

LIVELY LADY   3 b.f. Beveled (USA) – In The Papers 87 (Aragon 118) [1998 67: 5v* 5.1m4 5g2 6g a5g3 5.3g6 6g 5.2s2 5d4 1999 6.1v* a6g 6d 6d2 6g* 5s 6.1s2 5d5 6d 5s* Nov 5] fairly useful handicapper on turf, modest on all-weather: won at Nottingham in March, Kempton in June and 20-runner race at Doncaster in November: 92 effective at 5f/6f: acts on heavy ground and fibresand: tends to wander: visored. *J. R. Jenkins*

LIVELY MILLIE 2 b.f. (Apr 15) Ridgewood Ben 113 – Sweet Pleasure 88 **54** (Sweet Revenge 129) [1999 6m 6m⁵ 6m 7s 8m Oct 19] half-sister to several winners, including useful French 1986 2-y-o sprinter Ma Columbine (by Jaazeiro) and 1½m and 1¾m winner Haddaaj (by Ela-Mana-Mou): dam 2-y-o 6f winner: modest maiden: should stay 1m: acts on good to firm going. *P. T. Walwyn*

LIVELY PROJECT (IRE) 3 b.f. Project Manager 111 – Lovely Ali (IRE) 69 **43** (Dunbeath (USA) 127) [1998 –: 7g 8d⁴ 7g 10s 1999 a7g 7m 10f⁵ 12.1m⁵ 12g 11f² 12.4f⁴ Aug 4] poor maiden: stays 1½m: acts on firm and good to soft going. *M. Dods*

LIVE PROJECT (IRE) 7 b.g. Project Manager 111 – Saturday Live (Junius **–** (USA) 124) [1998 49, a71: a8g⁴ a8g² a7g* a7g* a8g 6m⁴ 8m³ 7g 7d⁴ 8.3s a8g³ a7g **a71** 1999 a8g² a7g³ a7g⁶ a8f a7g* a7g³ a7g² a7g⁴ 10s Apr 19] fair handicapper on all-weather, poor on turf: won amateur event at Southwell in March: fatally injured at Nottingham in April: was effective at 7f to 8.5f: acted on good to firm going, heavy and fibresand: went well for inexperienced rider. *R. Craggs*

LIVE TO TELL 3 ch.f. Primo Dominie 121 – Dreams Are Free (IRE) 71 (Caer- **68** leon (USA) 132) [1998 NR 1999 a6g⁴ a6g* a6g⁶ 5.1s 6m 5g* 5m⁶ 5m² 5d² 5v* 5.2s a6g Dec 27] 10,000F, 7,000Y: second foal: half-sister to 1997 2-y-o 6f winner Truth Teller (by Statoblest): dam, 1¼m winner, from family of Seattle Slew and Lomond: fair performer: won maiden at Wolverhampton in February and handicaps at Warwick in August and Ayr in October: will prove best at 5f/6f: acts on good to firm and heavy going and fibresand: usually forces pace. *M. S. Saunders*

LIVIUS (IRE) 5 b.g. Alzao (USA) 117 – Marie de Beaujeu (FR) 108 (Kenmare **87** (FR) 125) [1998 85: 10d³ 10d⁴ 10m⁴ 10.2g² 13.9g 12d² 13.3g 1999 12m 12m² 12m* Aug 7] big gelding: fairly useful handicapper: won at Ascot in August under strong ride from K. Fallon: should stay beyond 1½m: yet to race on extremes of going: blinkered once. *Major D. N. Chappell*

LIZZIE SIMMONDS (IRE) 2 b.f. (Apr 25) Common Grounds 118 – Able **56** Susan 98 (Formidable (USA) 125) [1999 5d 5m 5g³ 6s 6d Oct 26] 15,000Y: sturdy filly: fourth foal: dam 7f (at 2 yrs)/1m winner and granddaughter of 1000 Guineas winner Full Dress II: form only when third of 17 to Royal Romeo in maiden at Beverley in September: tongue tied last 3 starts. *N. Tinkler*

LOBLITE LEADER (IRE) 2 b.g. (Mar 16) Tirol 127 – Cyrano Beauty (IRE) **63** (Cyrano de Bergerac 120) [1999 6d 7m⁶ 7f⁴ 7m 7s⁴ 8g⁵ 8d Nov 1] IR 5,000Y, 9,600 2-y-o: good-topped gelding: has scope: second foal: dam unraced: modest maiden: stiff task when well held in nursery at Redcar final start: stays 1m. *G. M. Moore*

LOBUCHE (IRE) 4 b.g. Petardia 113 – Lhotse (IRE) 67 (Shernazar 131) [1998 **– §** 66d, a56d: a8g⁵ a8g² a8.5g a10g² 9.9s⁵ 6d* a6g³ 6.1g 6m⁴ 8.2g 7m 6m a6g 6d 7d 1999 a7g a7g a11g⁶ a14.8g 16f 7m 8.2s a12g Nov 19] neat gelding: fair handicapper at best on turf, modest on all-weather: little form in 1999, though successful over hurdles in March: tried blinkered/tongue tied: temperamental. *M. C. Chapman*

LOCHANGEL 5 ch.m. Night Shift (USA) – Peckitts Well 96 (Lochnager 132) **113** [1998 119: 5.1s² 5.7g* 5g² 5d² 5g³ 5f* 6m⁶ 5d⁶ 1999 5g² 5m⁴ 6f 5g 5d⁴ 5.2d Sep 19] big, rangy mare: good walker: has a quick action: smart performer: won Nunthorpe Stakes at York in 1998: not quite so good in 1999, best efforts in Temple Stakes at Sandown (beaten 1¾ lengths by Tipsy Creek) and King's Stand Stakes at Royal Ascot (fourth to Mitcham) on first 2 starts: best at 5f: acted on firm and good to soft going, probably on soft: usually a front runner: reportedly retired. *I. A. Balding*

LOCH DANCER 6 br.m. Lochnager 132 – Cute Dancer (Remainder Man 126§) **–** [1998 –: 10d 10m 7g 1999 6d Aug 6] no form. *W. M. Brisbourne*

LOCHDENE (IRE) 4 b.g. Robellino (USA) 127 – Cat's Claw (USA) (Sharpen **–** Up 127) [1998 –: 8s⁴ 1999 8.3v⁶ 9.2v Apr 10] no form since second of 2 starts at 2 yrs: sold 1,600 gns in May, sent to Sweden. *M. Johnston*

LOCH FYNE 3 b.f. Ardkinglass 114 – Song's Best (Never So Bold 135) [1998 **66** 70: 5g⁵ 5m³ 5g 5.7g 1999 6g 5m³ 5g³ 6d Aug 26] sturdy filly: fair maiden: best effort of 1999 in handicap penultimate start: will prove best at 5f: acts on good to firm going: front runner. *W. R. Muir*

LOCH INCH   2 ch.c. (Mar 31) Inchinor 119 – Carrie Kool 69 (Prince Sabo 123)   **92**
[1999 5.1s³ 6g⁵ 6.1m* 6g 7m⁴ a8g⁶ 8d 6v 6d* 7s Nov 6] 12,000Y: smallish colt: **a?**
second foal: dam 2-y-o 5f winner who stayed 7f: fairly useful performer: won maiden
at Nottingham in August and nursery at Windsor (hung left under very strong ride
from J. Fortune) in October: well held final start: stays 7f: acts on good to firm and
good to soft going: blinkered last 3 starts: none too consistent. *K. McAuliffe*

LOCH LAIRD · 4 b.g. Beveled (USA) – Daisy Loch (Lochnager 132) [1998 80:   **85**
6m³ 6f² 5.7m² 7m 1999 6m* 5.1g 6s* 6g 6f⁶ 6f 6g 6v Sep 29] lengthy gelding: fairly
useful performer: won maiden at Salisbury in May and handicap at Goodwood in
June: mostly at least respectable efforts (met trouble in running final one): stays
6f: acts on firm and soft ground. *M. Madgwick*

LOCHLASS (IRE)   5 b.m. Distinctly North (USA) 115 – Littleton Song 73 (Song   –
132) [1998 –: a8.5g a11g a16g 10s⁶ 1999 12.1m 13.1f Sep 6] angular mare: no form
since 1997: pulled up on reappearance and ran as though something amiss 6 weeks
later: tried blinkered. . *R. J. Price*

LOCH MAGIC   3 b.g. Arazi (USA) 135 – Peckitts Well 96 (Lochnager 132)   –
[1998 NR 1999 6m 7g Jun 8] half-brother to several winners, including high-class
sprinter Lochsong (by Song), 5-y-o Lochangel and 1¼m winner Lochbelle (by
Robellino): dam sprinter: showed little in maidens at Salisbury: sold 1,800 gns in
July: sent to Kuwait. *I. A. Balding*

LOCHON   8 br.g. Lochnager 132 – Sky Mariner 59 (Julio Mariner 127) [1998 NR   –
1999 a7g a6s a6g a6g⁶ 5g 5g Jul 3] compact, workmanlike gelding: modest 6f
handicapper at best: disappointing since 1996: often blinkered/visored. *F. Watson*

LOCH SOUND   3 b.g. Primitive Rising (USA) 113 – Lochcross 65 (Lochnager   –
132) [1998 NR 1999 10g 12.3m 11.9d 14.1m 9.9s Sep 21] leggy, workmanlike
gelding: first reported foal: dam, maiden, should have stayed 7f: well beaten in
maidens/handicaps. *C. W. Thornton*

LOCKERLEY WATER   3 ch.f. Mac's Fighter 116 – Swift Stream 72 (Chief   –
Singer 131) [1998 NR 1999 11.7s Oct 26] first foal: dam poor maiden: 66/1, tailed
off in maiden. *W. G. M. Turner*

LOCOMBE HILL (IRE)   3 b.c. Barathea (IRE) 127 – Roberts Pride 62   **104**
(Roberto (USA) 131) [1998 101: 6s³ 6m* 7g⁶ 6s² 7.3v⁶ 1999 7m⁴ 10g 7g 9m³ 12v*
12d Sep 28] very big, rather dipped-backed colt: useful performer: won 6-runner
minor event at Kempton in September by length from Balladonia: found little in
handicap at Newmarket 8 days later: stays 1½m: acts on good to firm and heavy
going. *M. Blanshard*

LOCOMOTION (IRE)   3 ch.g. Seattle Dancer (USA) 119 – Pipe Opener 58   **80**
(Prince Sabo 123) [1998 NR 1999 a6g a6f² 6.1f³ 6g³ a8g* a8.5g² 7g a7g² 7.1s a8g
a7g Dec 4] IR 9,000Y: sturdy gelding: second foal: dam, disappointing maiden,
half-sister to useful sprinter Viceroy: fairly useful performer: won maiden at
Southwell (flashed tail) in June: good efforts after when runner-up in handicaps: left
W. Haggas 8,500 gns before penultimate start: stays 8.5f: acts on fibresand and firm
going: has worn tongue strap. *S. Dow*

LODEN BLUE   2 b.f. (Mar 18) Anshan 119 – Dolly Bevan 53 (Another Realm   –
118) [1999 6d⁶ 6.8d 8.2d 6.1s Nov 1] 650F, 3,400Y: half-sister to several winners,
including 7-y-o Pengamon and fairly useful sprinter Oggi, both by Efisio, and 3-y-o
Avanti, dam, 2-y-o 6f winner, half-sister to smart sprinter Pips Pride: little sign of
ability: left M. Bell after third start. *C. A. Dwyer*

LOGANLEA (IRE)   5 gr.m. Petong 126 – White's Pet (Mummy's Pet 125) [1998   –
60: 6.1m³ 6g 5f 7m 6d* 6m 1999 a7g a7g 6s Apr 13] tall, close-coupled mare: modest
handicapper at 4 yrs: well beaten in 1999: stays 6f: acts on good to firm and good to
soft ground: none too easy a ride: refused to enter stalls final 2 intended starts: sold
1,400 gns in October. *W. J. Musson*

LOHAN (IRE)   3 b.g. Perugino (USA) 84 – Deep In September (IRE) 50 (Common   –
Grounds 118) [1998 52, a61: 7s 6s a6g⁴ a5g⁴ 1999 6v 7m 8s Sep 16] modest maiden
at 2 yrs: well held in 1999: stays 6f: acts on fibresand. *Miss Z. C. Davison*

LOKOMOTIV   3 b.g. Salse (USA) 128 – Rainbow's End 83 (My Swallow 134)   **62 §**
[1998 68: 7g 7.1g⁶ 7m* 1999 8m 6d 9m 8.2g⁵ 6.9m⁴ 7.1d² 8d⁵ 7.6g³ 7m 8.2f Oct 20]
quite attractive gelding: modest handicapper: stays 1m: acts on good to firm and good
to soft going: looked unenthusiastic in blinkers/visor: not one to trust. *P. D. Evans*

LOLETTE   3 b.f. Arazi (USA) 135 – Wild Pavane (Dancing Brave (USA) 140)   **–**
[1998 NR 1999 9.9m 10d 8.2f Jun 21] fourth foal: sister to useful 7f to 9f winner
Apache Star and half-sister to 1¼m winner Stately Dancer (by Be My Guest) and
French 15f winner Pavenica (by Suave Dancer): dam unraced half-sister to dam of
very smart miler Rebecca Sharp: only a little sign of ability in maidens. *G. Wragg*

LOLITA (FR)   5 b.m. Hellios (USA) – Silver Dime (FR) (Son of Silver 123) [1998   **–**
–: 10m⁵ 6g⁵ 12f⁶ a12g 12s 1999 11.6m 11.8m May 24] leggy mare: winner in France
but no form in Britain. *J. R. Jenkins*

LOMAS (IRE)   8 b.g. Ela-Mana-Mou 132 – Bold Miss (Bold Lad (IRE) 133)   **43**
[1998 NR 1999 a7g a9.4g 13d May 24] sturdy gelding: formerly useful performer:
poor form in handicaps in 1999: seems to stay 13f: acts on good to firm and good to
soft going. *A. G. Newcombe*

LOMOND DANCER (IRE)   2 b.g. (Apr 23) Common Grounds 118 –   **64**
Lomond's Breeze (Lomond (USA) 128) [1999 6d⁴ 7m⁴ 7f 7m⁶ Aug 13] IR 12,500F,
IR 12,000Y: fourth foal: half-brother to fairly useful Irish 9f and 1¼m winner Flying
Blind (by Silver Kite) and fairly useful Irish 7f winner Model Show (by Dominion):
dam lightly raced: modest maiden: best effort when fourth of 15 at Salisbury on
second start: well beaten in nursery at Lingfield final one: should stay 1m.
P. W. Harris

LONELY PLACE (IRE)   2 b.c. (Mar 17) Lake Coniston (IRE) 131 – Aimores   **94**
(IRE) (Persian Heights 129) [1999 6g 6f 6g 7.9f 8d* 7.9d³ 8d* Oct 22] 30,000F, IR
32,000Y: small, lengthy, quite attractive colt: good walker: first foal: dam, 7.5f
winner in Italy, half-sister to Oaks winner Shahtoush: fairly useful performer: won
nurseries at Ayr in September and Doncaster in October: will stay 1¼m: acts on good
to soft going: often taken last to post: sold 60,000 gns, sent to USA. *B. W. Hills*

LONE PIPER   4 b.c. Warning 136 – Shamisen 86 (Diesis 133) [1998 106: 7s⁵ 7g*   **98 +**
7d 7g 7f 6g* 6s 1999 6s 6g² 6m Jun 18] small, close-coupled colt: poor mover: useful
performer: respectable second in minor event at Goodwood, then well beaten in
Wokingham Handicap at Royal Ascot: stays 7f: acts on soft ground, probably on
firm: ran poorly when sweating once: inconsistent. *C. E. Brittain*

LONESOME   3 b.f. Night Shift (USA) – Pine Ridge 80 (High Top 131) [1998 –p: **60**
8.2s 1999 9g⁵ 10m 12m 8.3m Aug 28] stocky filly: modest maiden: well held in
handicaps last 2 starts: should stay 1¼m: visored final outing. *Sir Michael Stoute*

LONESOME DUDE (CAN)   4 b.c. With Approval (CAN) – Local Lass 106   **117**
(Local Suitor (USA) 128) [1998 107: 7m* 9g* 8.9s⁵ 10.4f⁴ 9d² 10g⁶ 1999 8.1g* 8m
8.1m² 8f* 8f Sep 19] angular colt: smart performer: won handicaps at Sandown in

William Hill Mile (Handicap), Goodwood—
Lonesome Dude (spotted cap) puts up a smart weight-carrying performance
to hold the strong-finishing Swallow Flight (noseband) and the gambled-on Indian Lodge (rail)

May and Goodwood (20-runner William Hill Mile, best effort when beating fast-finishing Swallow Flight by a neck) in July: always behind in Atto Mile at Woodbine final start: effective at 1m, and stays 10.4f when conditions aren't testing: acts on firm and soft going: not at best when twice tried in visor: best waited with: stayed in North America. *Sir Michael Stoute*

LONGCHAMP LADY   2 br.f. (May 10) Puissance 110 – Gem of Gold 52   **47** (Jellaby 124) [1999 5g a5g⁵ 5g⁵ 6f 5m⁶ 5m³ 5m Sep 24] 2,000Y: leggy, sparely-made filly: half-sister to several winning sprinters, including 8-y-o Captain Carat and 1996 2-y-o 5f winner Bayford Thrust (later won in Denmark, by Timeless Times): dam sprinter: poor maiden: may prove best at 5f: raced only on good going or firmer on turf, below form on fibresand: sold 2,000 gns, sent to Israel. *J. Berry*

LOOP THE LOUP   3 b.g. Petit Loup (USA) 123 – Mithi Al Gamar (USA) 68   **105** (Blushing Groom (FR) 131) [1998 79p: 7d 8s³ 1999 8s⁵ 9.9g 11.5d* 12g* 14f² 13.9g* 14.8m² 15d² Sep 16] smallish, workmanlike gelding: progressed into useful performer: won maiden at Lingfield in June and handicaps at Salisbury in July and York (quite valuable rated stakes, came from off strong pace to beat Who Cares Wins by 3 lengths) in August: creditable second in handicaps at Newmarket and Ayr after: will stay 2m+: acts on firm and soft ground: sold 70,000 gns, joined M. Hammond. *J. L. Dunlop*

LORD ADVOCATE   11 br.g. Law Society (USA) 130 – Kereolle (Riverman   **41** (USA) 131) [1998 47: 12.1v 13v⁶ 12g⁶ 13d⁶ 12m⁶ 13g* 13s⁴ 13d⁴ 11.1m⁴ 13d² 12.1d 10.9s⁵ 12.1s 1999 13g 13s⁴ 13d⁵ 13g⁵ 13g⁵ 12m 13f⁵ 13f³ 11.1m⁶ 13m⁴ 12.1f² 14m⁵ 12.1m 10.9d⁶ 13s Sep 27] workmanlike gelding: bad mover: poor handicapper: mostly creditable efforts in 1999: effective at 11f to 2m: acts on firm ground, soft and all-weather: usually blinkered/visored: usually front runner. *D. A. Nolan*

LORD BANKES   2 b.c. (Feb 26) Presidium 124 – Marfen (Lochnager 132) [1999   **76 d** 5g² 5g² 5.1s⁵ 6.1m 5.1m 5.1g⁴ 6d 5.3s⁶ a6g Oct 8] 2,600Y: neat colt: fourth foal: half-brother to 2 winners by Timeless Times, including 6-y-o Ramsey Hope: dam unraced: maiden, disappointing after showing fair form first 2 starts: may prove best at 5f: best efforts on good ground: blinkered final start. *W. G. M. Turner*

LORD BERGERAC   3 b.c. Cyrano de Bergerac 120 – Vax Lady 98 (Millfontaine   **53** 114) [1998 76: 6s* 6d⁶ 6s⁵ 1999 6d 5.7g 5.7f⁶ a7g³ 8.2m⁴ 7.1d⁶ 6g 6m Sep 3] modest performer: barely stays 1m: acts on firm and soft going, and fibresand: blinkered/visored last 7 starts: reportedly bled from nose on fifth start, wandered markedly penultimate one: often races prominently. *J. L. Spearing*

LORD DISCORD   5 b.g. Primo Dominie 121 – Busted Harmony (Busted 134)   **45** [1998 NR 1999 a14.8g⁶ 10.9g* 10.9d Sep 16] lengthy, angular gelding: modest handicapper in 1997: won seller at Ayr in July, then left J. Mackie: well beaten final start: stays 11f: acts on soft and good to firm going: visored once. *J. S. Goldie*

LORD EUROLINK (IRE)   5 b.g. Danehill (USA) 126 – Lady Eurolink 55   **84** (Kala Shikari 125) [1998 98: 10g³ 1999 10.1g⁶ 10.9d 10d⁴ 10.4d⁵ Oct 7] sturdy, good sort: useful handicapper at best: form in 1999 only in apprentice race penultimate start: stays 1¼m: acts on soft and good to firm going: held up. *C. A. Dwyer*

LORD FLASHEART (USA)   2 b.c. (Apr 25) Blush Rambler (USA) 119 – Miss   **110** Henderson Co (USA) (Silver Hawk (USA) 123) [1999 4.5g³ 4.5d* 4.3m³ 6s* 6d* 7g² 8m*ᵈⁱˢ 9v* Oct 2] $30,000Y: fifth foal: half-brother to useful performer up to 1m Bouche Bee (by Naevus) and winners abroad by Black Tie Affair and Technology: dam, won at around 1m in USA, half-sister to US Grade 1 8.5f winner By Land By Sea: progressive form: first past post in maiden at Salon-de-Provence in April, 2 minor events at Lyon Parilly in June (second of them final start for J. Rossi), listed race at Craon (disqualified) in September and Prix de Conde Royal Thalasso Barriere (easily best effort, by 2 lengths from Crystal d'Ass) at Longchamp in October: should stay at least 1¼m: acts on good to firm and heavy going. *A. de Royer Dupre, France*

LORD HARLEY   2 b.c. (Apr 27) Formidable (USA) 125 – Nanny Doon   **50** (Dominion 123) [1999 6d 7d 5.7s a8g⁴ Dec 29] 3,800Y: second foal: half-brother to a 7f winner in Czech Republic by Alflora: dam, well beaten in sellers both starts, out of half-sister to high-class middle-distance stayer Mistigri: off 2 months, first form when fourth in seller at Lingfield in December. *B. R. Millman*

LORD HIGH ADMIRAL (CAN)   11 b.g. Bering 136 – Baltic Sea (CAN) (Danzig (USA)) [1998 86: 5d² 5v 5d 5g 6g² 5g² 5g⁵ 5g 5d⁵ 1999 5g³ 5d⁵ 6f* 6g 5m⁵ 5m 5d 5.1m² 6d² 5g 5d³ 5s 5.2s a5g⁴ Nov 19] tall gelding: fair performer at best in 1999: won claimer at Doncaster in May: best at 5f/6f: acts on firm and soft ground: effective blinkered/visored or not: taken down early/alone: usually a front runner: tends to hang right: none too consistent. *C. G. Cox*   **74 d**

LORD KINTYRE   4 b.c. Makbul 104 – Highland Rowena 59 (Royben 125) [1998 109: 5s² 5g⁵ 6g² 5d³ 6f 5.1m³ 5.2g 1999 6g⁵ 5f Jul 27] good-topped colt: useful performer: has reportedly suffered from lung infections: third in King's Stand Stakes at Royal Ascot at 3 yrs: well below form in 1999: stayed 6f: acted on any going: was game: retained 9,000 gns in December: reportedly retired. *B. R. Millman*   **–**

LORD LAMB   7 gr.g. Dunbeath (USA) 127 – Caroline Lamb 74 (Hotfoot 126) [1998 86p: 8f 10.1g⁵ 10.5g⁴ 14.8g³ 14m* 18g 1999 12d³ 16d² 12s³ Nov 6] tall, good-topped gelding: useful hurdler: similar level on Flat (first season to race at 6 yrs), and shaped well all 3 starts in 1999 (after reappearance): very close third of 16 to Flossy in November Handicap at Doncaster final one: stays 2m (reportedly returned with leg injury when well held over 2¼m): acts on good to firm and soft going: tends to be on toes/carry head awkwardly, and isn't an easy ride. *Mrs M. Reveley*   **98**

LORDOFENCHANTMENT (IRE)   2 ch.g. (Apr 2) Soviet Lad (USA) – Sauvignon (IRE) 63 (Alzao (USA) 117) [1999 5g 6m⁶ a6g⁵ 6g 6m* 6d⁵ 6g⁶ 7s⁶ Oct 23] IR 2,000F, 3,500Y, 6,000 2-y-o: strong gelding: fourth foal: half-brother to Swedish 1998 2-y-o 6f/1m winner Polish Panter (by Polish Patriot): dam 7f winner who stayed 1m: modest performer: won seller at Ripon (bought in 9,000 gns) in August: probably stays 7f: acts on good to firm ground, probably on soft: effective visored or not. *N. Tinkler*   **63**

LORD OF MEN   6 ch.h. Groom Dancer (USA) 128 – Upper Strata 109 (Shirley Heights 130) [1998 115: 10.5g² 10.3m* 10s⁵ 10d³ 12s⁵ 10m* 1999 a10f* 10f* a10f³ 10d⁶ Sep 11] robust horse: not the best of walkers (suffered fractured pelvis at 3 yrs): smart performer: won Prix de la Salamandre in 1995: successful in 1999 in 2 conditions events at Nad Al Sheba in February: below-form third to Altibr in very valuable Dubai Duty Free there following month: appeared to run as pacemaker in Irish Champion Stakes at Leopardstown final outing and first for 5½ months: stayed 12.5f: acted on firm and soft going and on dirt: visored final start at 5 yrs: had flashed tail under pressure, but was game: to stand at Haras du Logis, France, fee 15,000 francs, Oct 1st. *Saeed bin Suroor*   **115**

LORD OMNI (USA)   2 ch.c. (Mar 1) El Prado (IRE) 119 – Muskoka Ice (USA) (It's Freezing (USA) 122) [1999 6g⁶ 6.1g 7d⁴ Oct 26] $13,000Y: first foal: dam winning sprinter at 4 yrs in USA, half-sister to 1½m Grade 1-placed performer there: easily best effort when sixth of 21 in maiden at Ripon on debut. *T. D. Barron*   **70**

LORD PACAL (IRE)   2 b.g. (Mar 14) Indian Ridge 123 – Please Believe Me 93 (Try My Best (USA) 130) [1999 5.2f* 5m⁴ 6m⁵ 5.5g⁴ 5m² 6g 6m³ 5v⁴ Oct 25] leggy gelding: third foal: half-brother to 5-y-o Storyteller: dam 2-y-o 5f winner out of Princess Royal Stakes winner Believer: fairly useful performer: won maiden at Newbury in May: at least creditable efforts next 4 starts, fourth in Norfolk Stakes at Royal Ascot on first occasion: below form last 3 outings: should prove better at 6f than shorter: acts on firm ground, well held on heavy. *N. A. Callaghan*   **94**

LORD ROCHESTER   3 b.g. Distant Relative 128 – Kentfield (Busted 134) [1998 66: 7d 8.1m⁵ 7d 1999 10s⁶ 11.6g 10m 8m* 8.2g⁶ 8m 10.5m Sep 3] good-topped gelding: fair performer: won amateur handicap at Salisbury in June: below form after: stays 1m: acts on good to firm going: sold 10,000 gns in October, joined C. Mann. *B. R. Millman*   **66**

LORD STROLLER   3 b.g. Petong 126 – Breakfast Boogie 59 (Sizzling Melody 117) [1998 65: 5.1s 6.1m⁶ 6.1d⁶ 5g⁶ 7d 1999 6m 8m 7m 8m 7.1g Jun 11] quite good-topped gelding: has a quick action: modest maiden at 2 yrs: little form in 1999: likely to prove best at 5f/6f: blinkered twice: has worn tongue strap. *B. R. Millman*   **–**

619

LORD YASMIN (IRE) 2 b.c. (Apr 23) Lahib (USA) 129 – Adieu Cherie (IRE) **53**
(Bustino 136) [1999 6d 6d² Jul 1] 3,000Y: second foal: brother to German 1¼m
winner Albertino: dam (unraced) from family of Prix de la Salamandre winner
Common Grounds: 1½ lengths second to Baytown Melody in Yarmouth seller,
pulling hard: joined C. Wall. *J. Noseda*

LORINER'S LASS 3 b.f. Saddlers' Hall (IRE) 126 – Sixslip (USA) 94 (Diesis **80 +**
133) [1998 –: 7m 8s 1999 10g⁴ 11.6m⁵ 12f³ 14g² 14.6g Sep 8] good-bodied filly:
fairly useful maiden: good second at Lingfield penultimate start: sweating, probably
flattered when seventh of 10 in Park Hill Stakes at Doncaster final one: stays 1¾m
well: joined Lady Herries. *W. Jarvis*

LORINS GOLD 9 ch.g. Rich Charlie 117 – Woolcana 71 (Some Hand 119) **–**
[1998 NR 1999 8.2g Aug 13] well-made gelding: modest handicapper in 1997:
stayed 1m: acted on firm and good to soft going: was effective blinkered: dead.
Andrew Turnell

L'ORPHELINE (FR) 3 b.f. Seattle Song (USA) 130 – Buck's Dame (USA) **64**
(Damascus (USA)) [1998 NR 1999 10m 7.1m 10m Sep 16] 35,000 francs F,
11,000Y: sister to useful performer in Europe up to 1m Dictator's Song, closely
related to a winner in Hong Kong by Septieme Ciel and half-sister to several winners
and to dam of Prix Saint-Alary winner Brilliance: dam French maiden: modest form
at best in maidens. *C. E. Brittain*

LOSADA (IRE) 3 b.g. Unblest 117 – Fickle Femme (Hard Fought 125) [1998 NR **76**
1999 7d⁴ 7m* 6m 7m Jul 15] IR 7,000F, IR 11,000Y: sixth foal: half-brother to 2
winners in Italy: dam French 9f winner: won maiden at Catterick in May: last in
handicaps after: stays 7f: sold 1,600 gns, sent to Spain. *P. Calver*

LOST IN HOOK (IRE) 2 b.f. (Feb 27) Dancing Dissident (USA) 119 – **82**
Rathbawn Realm (Doulab (USA) 115) [1999 5g* 5f⁶ 6d⁴ 5m⁵ 5.2m² Sep 17] IR
7,200Y: good-quartered filly: fourth foal: half-sister to 4-y-o Blundell Lane and a
winner in Holland by Simply Great: dam Irish 5f (at 2 yrs) and 7f winner: fairly
useful performer: won maiden at Ripon in July by 7 lengths: best efforts after in
Molecomb Stakes at Goodwood next outing and in Newbury nursery final start:
likely to prove best at 5f/6f: below par on good to soft ground. *A. P. Jarvis*

LOST IN LUCCA 3 b.f. Inchinor 119 – Poyle Fizz (Damister (USA) 123) [1998 **72 §**
56: 7f⁴ a7g⁶ 6m⁴ 7s 1999 10g 11.4m 11.9d² 13.8g³ 11.9f⁵ 12m* 11.8g⁶ 11.9d **a59 §**
a12g³ a12g⁴ Nov 19] angular filly: fair performer: easily best effort to win
handicap by 9 lengths at Newmarket in July: probably stays 1¾m: acts on firm and
good to soft going, probably on fibresand: below form visored/blinkered once each:
sometimes sweating/edgy: has hung/found little: sold 15,000 gns: one to be wary of.
J. W. Hills

LOST SPIRIT 3 b.g. Strolling Along (USA) – Shoag (USA) (Affirmed (USA)) **53**
[1998 49§: 7m 7m² 6m⁶ 1999 a7g a9.4g⁵ a7f⁶ a11g³ a12g* a12g⁵ 12g³ 11.6m **a67**
a12g 12.1m a12g a12g⁶ a12g⁶ a12g Dec 21] strong, sturdy gelding: fair on
all-weather, modest on turf: won claimer at Southwell in February and handicap at
Wolverhampton in March: stays 1½m: acts on all-weather and good to firm going:
tried blinkered at 2 yrs: carries head high: front runner. *P. W. Hiatt*

LOTS OF MAGIC 3 b.c. Magic Ring (IRE) 115 – Pounelta 91 (Tachypous **122**
128) [1998 93: 7g² 7.1g² 7d⁴ 7d* 7.1g⁴ 1999 7m* 8.1g⁴ 7m* 7m⁴ 7g Oct 16]
    The 33/1-shot Lots of Magic pulled something special out of the hat
when he won the Jersey Stakes at Royal Ascot, though it was a trick he was
unable to repeat. A performance, which at the time was difficult enough to
explain, now looks even more perplexing in the light of Lots of Magic's two
subsequent efforts. At least Lucayan Prince, the 50/1-winner of the 1996
running of the Jersey, went on to show further improvement, developing into a
very smart racehorse. Lots of Magic, on the other hand, didn't even come close
to reproducing his Jersey Stakes form, which represented an advance of over a
stone on his previous best. A lung infection kept Lots of Magic off the course
for almost three months after Ascot, and, in the circumstances, he wasn't

disgraced in finishing fourth of seven behind Tumbleweed Ridge in a listed event at Epsom on his return. That race should have put him spot-on, but six weeks later Lots of Magic ran poorly in the Challenge Stakes at Newmarket, finding little for pressure and finishing last of ten. He'll start the next season with still plenty to prove.

Lots of Magic arrived at Royal Ascot with a record of two wins from seven starts and form which made it hard to envisage his being able to cope with the step up in class. At two years Lots of Magic had landed the odds in a maiden at Epsom, and on his reappearance in May he upset the odds laid on Al Naba in a four-runner minor event at Lingfield. The latter performance showed that Lots of Magic, who'd undergone a wind operation during the winter, had progressed from two to three, but a defeat in a rated stakes handicap at Sandown next time, off a mark of 99, looked to have exposed his limitations. The Sandown race was over a mile, and it was Lots of Magic's only one at a distance other than seven furlongs. He didn't run as though lack of stamina was a problem, but following the Jersey Stakes one obvious conclusion that can be drawn is that Lots of Magic is much more effective at the shorter trip. The field of twelve for the Jersey was the smallest since 1992 but it wasn't lacking in quality. The favourite at 13/8 was Enrique, who had finished second in the Two Thousand Guineas at both Newmarket and the Curragh; second favourite at 9/2 was one of the leading two-year-olds of 1998, Stravinsky. Lots of Magic beat that pair, and the rest, in very good style. Soon in front, racing under the stand rail and tracked by Enrique, Lots of Magic quickened around two and a half furlongs out and ran on very strongly inside the last furlong to extend his advantage over Enrique to three lengths, with Bertolini finishing third and Stravinsky fourth. Enrique ran a long way below form on his only subsequent start, while top sprinter Stravinsky and Bertolini were to prove better at shorter distances, but even so there were enough useful individuals further back in the field to leave no room for doubt that Lots of Magic had put up a very smart performance.

Lots of Magic, a leggy, quite good-topped colt, is the fifth winner from ten foals of racing age produced by Pounelta. It may be six winners before too long in the next season, Lots of Magic's two-year-old full brother and stable-companion Magelta having already finished in the frame in a couple of maidens, showing fair form. None of Pounelta's other produce were better than fairly useful, the pick of them Top Pet (by Petong) who was most effective at two years. Pounelta herself was fairly useful as a two-year-old for Hannon, winning over seven furlongs, but was just a fair performer at three, when she probably stayed a mile and a half; she was suited by forcing tactics. Her dam

Mr Peter Valentine's "Lots of Magic"

Lots of Magic (b.c. 1996)	Magic Ring (IRE) (b 1989)	Green Desert (b 1983)	Danzig
			Foreign Courier
		Emaline (ch 1981)	Empery
			Chere Alise
	Pounelta (br 1983)	Tachypous (b 1974)	Hotfoot
			Stilvi
		Sirnelta (b or br 1971)	Sir Tor
			Finelta

Sirnelta, who won at a mile to a mile and a quarter in France, also produced the very smart if ultimately unreliable filly Dead Certain, winner of the Cheveley Park at two and Prix Maurice de Gheest at three. Sirnelta is out of Finelta, a good French two-year-old and a full sister to the French Derby winner Sanctus II. Lots of Magic, a fluent mover, won on good to soft going at two years, but he goes particularly well on good to firm ground. *R. Hannon*

LOUGHANLEA (USA) 3 b. or br.g. Salt Lake (USA) – Moment of Flight (USA) (My Favorite Moment (USA)) [1998 59p: 5d 7g 6.1g 8d 1999 a7f⁴ a7g a7g⁵ a6g* a7g⁴ a5g a5g³ Mar 22] leggy, unfurnished gelding: modest performer: won seller at Wolverhampton in February: stays 7f: acts on fibresand, well held only try on equitrack: blinkered last 5 starts: has been bandaged behind: not one to trust: sold 3,200 gns, sent to Sweden. *D. Nicholls* **64 d**

LOUGH SWILLY (IRE) 3 b.g. Mukaddamah (USA) 125 – Flooding (USA) (Irish River (FR) 131) [1998 93+: 6m⁴ 6.1g* 6.1d³ 7m* 8s⁵ 1999 8g 9g 10.1d 9m 8m⁴ 8g 9m 8m 8s Sep 29] quite good-topped gelding: fairly useful performer at 2 yrs: disappointing in 1999, mostly in handicaps: may prove best up to 1m: seems unsuited by ground softer than good: sold 5,200 gns, joined V. Soane. *B. W. Hills* **89 d**

LOU'S WISH   2 b.g. (Apr 21) Thatching 131 – Shamaka 53 (Kris 135) [1999 6s   **59**
a7g 5.2g⁵ 7m 6.1m 7.7d⁶ 7.9d a6g Oct 18] leggy, rather unfurnished gelding: second
foal: half-brother to 3-y-o Broke Road: dam lightly-raced maiden: modest maiden:
stays 7.7f: acts on good to firm and good to soft going. *M. J. Polglase*

LOVEABLE ROGUE   3 b.g. Simply Great (FR) 122 – Quick J 61 (Jim J (USA))   **50**
[1998 –: 8v 1999 10m³ 10f⁵ Aug 2] modest maiden: not sure to stay beyond 1¼m.
M. A. Peill

LOVE ACADEMY   4 b.g. Royal Academy (USA) 130 – Quiet Week-End 99   **61**
(Town And Country 124) [1998 62+, a87: 7d 6s 9.2s⁴ 7v a7g 8.5s 7g 5g a8g* 8s³   **a83**
a7g* a7g² a8g⁶ a7g* 1999 a7g a7g a7g² a7g⁶ 7m 7g⁵ 8.3g 7.8m 7m 8.5m 6.5f² 9d
9.6m 6m 6m 7d Sep 7] leggy, good-topped gelding: fairly useful handicapper on
all-weather, modest on turf: second at Lingfield in January (left M. Johnston 4 starts
later) and Galway in August: barely stays 1m: acts on firm and soft going and
all-weather: often blinkered: carries head high and has idled. *Luke Comer, Ireland*

LOVE ALONE   2 b.f. (May 6) Barathea (IRE) 127 – Chepstow Vale (USA) 97   **53 p**
(Key To The Mint (USA)) [1999 7.5g⁵ Sep 15] tall, workmanlike filly: half-sister to
several winners, including French 1995 2-y-o 7.5f winner Amiarma (by Unfuwain),
later useful at 10.5f, and 1¼m winner Studio Thirty (by Rock City): dam 2-y-o sprint
winner who stayed 1m: not knocked about when never-dangerous fifth of 9 to Kind
Regards in maiden at Beverley: will be suited by 1¼m+: sent to France: will improve.
J. G. FitzGerald

LOVE AND KISSES   6 ch.m. Salse (USA) 128 – Soba 127 (Most Secret 119)   **–**
[1998 NR 1999 14.8m⁶ 16.4g Aug 20] fair handicapper in 1996: little form in 2 runs
since: should stay beyond 1¾m. *C. A. Cyzer*

LOVE BLUES (USA)   3 b.g. Hansel (USA) – Jolie Bold (USA) (Bold Forbes   **75 d**
(USA)) [1998 58: 7m⁶ 8.5s⁶ 7d⁶ a6g⁵ a8g³ 1999 a8g² a9.4g* a10f* a12g⁴ 12.3d²
12.4m 12m* 11.6d 12g 10m 8.5s 8.2f Oct 20] well-made gelding: fair performer:
won maiden at Wolverhampton and minor event at Lingfield in January then
4-runner handicap at Carlisle in August: well below form after: stays 1½m: acts on
all-weather, good to firm and good to soft going: visored last 3 starts: none too
consistent: sold 5,500 gns. *M. Johnston*

LOVE CROWN (CAN)   3 br.g. Chief's Crown (USA) – With Style (CAN)   **–**
(Smarten (USA)) [1998 NR 1999 12m May 1] $40,000F, IR 76,000Y: fourth foal:
half-brother to 3 minor winners in North America: dam, 2-y-o sprint winner in North
America, half-sister to Canadian Oaks winner First Summer Day: tongue tied, pulled
up in maiden (reportedly had breathing problem). *M. Johnston*

LOVE DIAMONDS (IRE)   3 b.g. Royal Academy (USA) 130 – Baby   **55 §**
Diamonds (Habitat 134) [1998 ?, a72: 6s⁵ 7s 8.3d⁵ 6d a7g² a8g² a8g* a8g³ 1999   **a76 §**
a8.5g² a8g* a8f² a8.5g⁴ a8g⁵ 8.2d 8d 8m 10m 8m² 8m⁵ 8d³ 8d a8g Nov 23] fair
handicapper on all-weather, modest on turf: won at Lingfield in January: left M.
Johnston before penultimate start: stays 8.5f: acts on good to firm going, good to soft
and all-weather: blinkered (ran creditably) fourth outing: has wandered/flashed tail/
carried head awkwardly: unreliable. *N. P. Littmoden*

LOVE DIVINE   2 b.f. (Feb 12) Diesis 133 – La Sky (IRE) 107 (Law Society   **80 p**
(USA) 130) [1999 7s² Nov 5] rangy filly: fourth foal: sister to 3-y-o Easy To Love
and half-sister to French 1½m winner Laurentine and a winner in USA (both by
Private Account): dam 1¼m winner (probably stayed 1¾m), closely related to
Champion Stakes winner Legal Case: favourite but green and better for race, shaped
well when 2½ lengths second of 20 to Hopeful Light in maiden at Doncaster, never
far away and keeping on willingly: will prove suited by 1¼m/1½m: sure to improve,
and probably at least a useful performer in the making. *H. R. A. Cecil*

LOVE KISS (IRE)   4 b.g. Brief Truce (USA) 126 – Pendulina 102 (Prince Tender-   **–**
foot (USA) 126) [1998 –: 10.5g 1999 12.4m⁶ 14.1g 10d Oct 26] tall, useful-looking
gelding: fairly useful form at 2 yrs, no show since: should stay beyond 1m. *W. Storey*

LOVE LANE (IRE)   2 b.g. (Apr 15) Mujtahid (USA) 118 – Ibda 67 (Mtoto 134)   **77**
[1999 5m⁵ 5g 6m³ 6.3m 7.5g* 8m Aug 27] IR 68,000Y: strong, good-bodied gelding:
has a quick action: third foal: half-brother to 1997 2-y-o 7f winner Burnt Yates (later
won in Malaysia, by Distinctly North) and 3-y-o Oregon Dream: dam, Irish 2-y-o 7f

winner, half-sister to useful sprinter Mubhij (by Mujtahid): fair performer: made all in nursery at Beverley in August, wandering under pressure: well held in similar event at Newmarket final start: should stay 1m: raced only on good/good to firm going: tried visored and blinkered. *M. Johnston*

LOVE LETTERS 2 ch.f. (Apr 13) Pursuit of Love 124 – Pinkie Rose (FR) **81** (Kenmare (FR) 125) [1999 6g² 5m³ 6.8m* 7f 7d Aug 14] 9,000Y: leggy filly: fourth foal: half-sister to 3-y-o Capitalist: dam, 1½m winner, out of half-sister to Vert Amande and Indian Rose: fairly useful performer: best effort when winning maiden at Warwick in July: well held in nursery at Goodwood and listed race at Newmarket (sweating and edgy) after: stays 6.8f: acts on good to firm ground: races prominently. *J. E. Banks*

LOVELY ISLAND (IRE) 3 b.f. Inchinor 119 – Lovely Me (IRE) 70 (Vision **44** (USA)) [1998 60: 6g⁵ 5m⁶ 6d⁵ 5g⁵ a7g a7g⁴ a6g 1999 a8g⁴ 6g 6f 5m⁶ May 26] small filly: poor maiden: stays 7f: acts on good to firm going and equitrack: blinkered second and third starts. *R. F. Johnson Houghton*

LOVEMAN (USA) 5 b.g. Alleged (USA) 138 – Love Someone (USA) **–** (Graustark) [1998 11.8d* 12g* 12v 1999 16.2s⁴ Apr 3] $20,000Y, resold $30,000Y: tall, leggy gelding: half-brother to several minor winners in USA: dam unraced: fairly useful performer: won 2 amateur races in France in 1998 for N. Clement: winner over hurdles in December that year: last of 4 in minor event at Haydock on only run of 1999: stays at least 1½m: acts on soft going. *K. A. Morgan*

LOVE OPERA 4 ch.f. Pursuit of Love 124 – Lets Fall In Love (USA) (Northern **–** Baby (CAN) 127) [1998 54d: 5m³ 5m⁴ 6d 8v a6g³ a6g 1999 a6g² a7g² a6g² a7g⁴ a6g **a53** 9.9g 10m Sep 24] lengthy filly: modest maiden: creditable efforts in frame: left Jack Berry 600 gns and off track 6 months after fifth start: may prove best at 6f/7f: acts on all-weather and good to firm ground: visored twice: has looked none too keen: resold 650 gns, sent to Israel. *Ronald Thompson*

LOVER'S LEAP 3 b.g. Pursuit of Love 124 – Anna Karietta 82 (Precocious 126) **87** [1998 86p: 6m 7g² 1999 8m⁴ 9g 8g³ 7d* 7.1g² 7m Jul 25] unfurnished gelding: has a round action: fairly useful performer: won maiden at Newbury in June, making all: good second of 16 in handicap at Sandown next start: stays 1m: best efforts on good/ good to soft going (yet to race on softer). *H. Candy*

LOVE'S DESIGN (IRE) 2 b. or br.g. (Feb 21) Pursuit of Love 124 – Cephista **71 +** 61 (Shirley Heights 130) [1999 6m 7.1s⁶ 6g³ 7.1g* Nov 3] 28,000F, 65,000Y: lengthy gelding: poor mover: first foal: dam maiden who stayed 1½m: fair form: visored, won maiden at Musselburgh in November by 3 lengths from Hi Buddy, pulling hard early, wandering and flashing tail: should stay 1m. *J. Noseda*

LOVE YOU TOO 2 ch.f. (May 1) Be My Chief (USA) 122 – Nagida 94 (Skyliner **88** 117) [1999 6g* 5m 6m 6m⁶ 5.2g⁴ 6.1d⁵ 5.5g⁴ 6d Oct 15] 4,000Y: quite attractive filly: third foal: sister to modest 1997 2-y-o 7f winner Chief Blade: dam won Wokingham: fairly useful performer: won maiden at Doncaster in June: best efforts when fourth in listed race at Newbury in August and Prix d'Arenberg at Chantilly in September: stays 6f: hung left third start, sweating fourth one. *A. Kelleway*

LOWNDES COURT 3 b.f. Salse (USA) 128 – Basha (USA) (Chief's Crown **69** (USA)) [1998 NR 1999 7s⁴ 10.2m⁴ 10m⁶ 10f³ 11.7m⁴ Aug 22] third foal: half-sister to 5-y-o Robbo: dam twice-raced daughter of high-class (up to 9f) My Darling One: fair form in maidens/handicap: probably needs 1½m+: sold 4,500 gns in December. *M. P. Tregoning*

LOW ON FUNDS (USA) 2 b.g. (Feb 3) Eagle Eyed (USA) 111 – Miss Sanmar **60** (USA) (Recitation (USA) 124) [1999 6g⁶ 6g 7m⁶ Aug 4] $52,000F, IR 52,000Y: quite attractive gelding: fourth foal: half-brother to a winner in USA by Classic Account: dam winning sprinter in USA at 4/5 yrs: modest form in maidens: stays 7f: has been heavily bandaged in front. *T. G. Mills*

LOYAL TOAST (USA) 4 b.g. Lyphard (USA) 132 – Lisieux (USA) (Steady **–** Growth (CAN)) [1998 80: 8s 8g 7.5m⁵ 9.9m* 9.9m⁵ 8f 9d 1999 9.7m⁶ 9.9v⁴ 8m 10.5d 9g 12g 10.4f 10m a11g Sep 28] formerly fairly useful: very much on downgrade: tongue tied final 2 starts. *N. Tinkler*

L S LOWRY (USA)   3 b.g. Thorn Dance (USA) 107 – Queluz (USA) 59   **87**
(Saratoga Six (USA)) [1998 64: 5s 7m* 8d⁵ 1999 9.7s 8f² 10f* 11.5m* 12m² 10m*
10.1m* Aug 4] smallish, robust gelding: has a quick action: fairly useful performer:
won claimer at Newbury in May, handicap at Lingfield and claimer at Newmarket
in July then another claimer at Yarmouth in August: stays 11.5f: acts on firm going:
blinkered second start: has carried head awkwardly: joined Miss K. George.
P. F. I. Cole

LUANSHYA   3 b.f. First Trump 118 – Blues Indigo 103 (Music Boy 124) [1998   **78**
74: 5g³ 5.1d² 5.1g⁴ 5g² 6f⁵ 5g³ 6m⁵ 1999 5.1s⁴ 6.1m² 6m* 6m 6f 6f⁵ 7m Aug 8]
sparely-made filly: fair performer: won maiden at Catterick in May: best effort in
handicap on second start: stays 6f: acts on firm and good to soft going: has been
bandaged behind. *R. M. Whitaker*

LUBOHENRIK (IRE)   2 b.f. (Apr 26) Perugino (USA) 84 – Febian John (FR)   **–**
(Shafaraz (FR) 124) [1999 6g 6d 5g 5g Oct 14] IR 4,600Y: small, unfurnished filly:
seventh foal: half-sister to Irish 1994 2-y-o 6f winner Johns Conquerer (by
Conquering Hero): dam French 11f winner: well beaten in maidens: tried visored.
I. Semple

LUCAYAN BEACH   5 gr.g. Cyrano de Bergerac 120 – Mrs Gray 61 (Red Sunset   **58**
120) [1998 77: 6m* 6m³ 6g⁶ 1999 6g 6m 6g 6d a7g a8g³ Nov 23] angular gelding:
modest form in 1999: stays 1m: acts on equitrack and good to firm going: very slowly
away in blinkers fourth start. *B. Gubby*

LUCIDO (IRE)   3 b.c. Royal Academy (USA) 130 – Lady Ambassador (General   **116**
Assembly (USA)) [1998 98p: 7m⁴ 8s* 8v³ 1999 10m* 11.5g* 12g 12d 12d³ Oct 17]
strong, rangy colt: smart performer: won minor event at Newbury in April by neck
from Oath and 5-runner Pertemps Derby Trial Stakes at Lingfield in May by 1¼
lengths from Daliapour, leading on bridle under 2f out then idling: ran poorly in

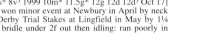

Mrs H. Focke's "Lucido"

Derby at Epsom in June (later reported to have sustained stress fracture to ilium), much the better effort after 4 months off when excellent third of 10 to First Magnitude in Prix du Conseil de Paris at Longchamp, staying on well from rear: stays 1½m: acts on good to firm and heavy ground: waited with. *J. L. Dunlop*

LUCKY ARCHER   6 b.g. North Briton 67 – Preobrajenska 93 (Double Form   **79** 130) [1998 79: 8.2m* 7f* 8d* 8.5d² 7.9m⁵ 7m 8g 7.5m² 8g⁵ 1999 8g 7.7m⁶ 8g* 7.9f 7m 8f⁵ 8h* 8m⁵ 7g⁵ 8g Oct 2] smallish, well-made gelding: fair handicapper: won at Yarmouth in June and Bath in August: rare poor effort final start: stays 8.5f: acts on hard and good to soft going: blinkered once at 3 yrs: often races up with pace. *J. M. Bradley*

LUCKY BEGONIA (IRE)   6 br.m. Simply Great (FR) 122 – Hostess 81 (Be My   **52** Guest (USA) 126) [1998 60, a74+: a8g² a8g* a8.5g⁵ a11g* 12.1m⁵ 12s* a11g⁶ a12g* 12d 11.9g 12g⁴ 1999 a12g 12v⁵ 10.5s³ 10m 12.3g 10d Sep 28] sturdy, workmanlike mare: modest handicapper in 1999: stayed 1½m: acted on fibresand and good to firm going, winner on soft ground: usually claimer ridden: dead. *A. W. Carroll*

LUCKY COVE   3 gr.c. Lugana Beach 116 – Port Na Blath (On Your Mark 125)   **69 d** [1998 67, a61: a5g³ a5g³ a6g 5d² 5m⁴ 1999 5.1s 5.1s 5d³ 5g 5m a5g³ Jun 25] close-coupled, workmanlike colt: fair maiden at best: best at 5f: acts on good to firm going, good to soft and fibresand: sold 3,500 gns in September, joined Don Enrico Incisa. *B. A. McMahon*

LUCKY GITANO (IRE)   3 br. or b.g. Lucky Guest 109 – April Wind 91 (Wind-   **82** jammer (USA)) [1998 81: 8.1m³ 8.3s² 8v⁵ 1999 9g³ 10f² Apr 29] leggy, quite attractive gelding: fairly useful maiden: good third in handicap at Kempton: below form in maiden next time: should stay 1¼m. *J. L. Dunlop*

LUCKY HEATHER (IRE)   2 b.f. (Feb 16) Soviet Lad (USA) – Idrak 68 (Young   **50** Generation 129) [1999 5.1f 5.7g⁶ 6d 5.7m Jul 5] 16,000Y: sixth foal: half-sister to 3 winners, including 1993 2-y-o 6f winner Recaptured Days (by Salse) and 7f winner Marguerite Bay (by Darshaan): dam 5f winner from very good middle-distance family: modest form at best: well held final start: joined R. Baker. *R. J. Hodges*

LUCKY JUDGE   2 b.c. (Apr 20) Saddlers' Hall (IRE) 126 – Lady Lydia 66   **–** (Ela-Mana-Mou 132) [1999 7.1d Aug 6] 6,200F, 6,500Y: close-coupled colt: second foal: dam 11f winner: needed race and showed signs of ability when ninth of 14 in Haydock maiden. *W. W. Haigh*

LUCKY LINDA (IRE)   3 b.f. Bluebird (USA) 125 – Spectacular Dawn 81   **55** (Spectacular Bid (USA)) [1998 66p: 6.1s 7v 7d 1999 10.2s 10g⁶ May 29] leggy, sparely-made filly: modest maiden: stays 1¼m: sold 5,000 gns, sent to Bahrain. *J. L. Dunlop*

LUCKY LOVER (IRE)   4 b. or br.g. Ballad Rock 122 – Petticoat Lane (Ela-   **63** Mana-Mou 132) [1998 68: 8.1m 8.3m⁴ 8.3f⁶ 1999 7m 7f 8g 9.9m Jun 24] modest maiden handicapper, lightly raced: below form final 4-y-o start: stays 1m: raced only on good going or firmer. *G. B. Balding*

LUCKY ME (IRE)   4 g.rg. Maledetto (IRE) 103 – Silver Heart (Yankee Gold   **–** 115) [1998 48: a8g⁴ 7s 8.2m 10d 8.3d 7m 6.9d a7g⁴ 7s³ 7d⁵ 1999 9.7v 7m a7g Jun 12] big, leggy, workmanlike gelding: poor maiden: no form in 1999: best up to 1m: acts on soft ground and all-weather. *P. Butler*

LUCKY MELODY   2 b.c. (Apr 14) Suluk (USA) 72 – Impromptu Melody (IRE)   **35** (Mac's Imp (USA) 116) [1999 6m a5g³ a6g³ 7m Jul 21] leggy colt: first foal: dam no form: poor form when third in sellers at Southwell. *B. S. Rothwell*

LUCKY MYST   4 b.g. Mystiko (USA) 124 – Lucky Omen 99 (Queen's Hussar   **40** 124) [1998 65d: 7.6g⁶ 6f⁵ 9.9m 9.7s 1999 a8g a12g a12g 12v⁴ 11.9f⁴ 16d³ 14.1m   **a–** a13g⁵ 16.2s Jul 3] poor maiden handicapper: reportedly lame final start: stays 2m: acts on any turf going (has hung on firm) and on equitrack. *C. E. Brittain*

LUCKY NEMO   3 b.c. Sabrehill (USA) 120 – Lucky Omen 99 (Queen's Hussar   **70 d** 124) [1998 –: 6s 8s 1999 a8f⁶ a8g³ a10g² 12s* 9.7v 12g⁶ 14.1g⁵ 11.5f* 14.6m 10.1m 12d 11.5g² 11.8d a11g⁶ Dec 13] fair performer at best: won handicaps at Folkestone in March and Lingfield (apprentices) in June: well below form after, leaving C. Brittain before penultimate start: stays 1½m: acts on firm going, soft and equitrack. *Mrs L. Richards*

LUCKY RASCAL (IRE)   3 b.g. Indian Ridge 123 – Chesnut Tree (USA) 97   **60** (Shadeed (USA) 135) [1998 73: 6g⁴ 6g 1999 8.3d 8g⁴ 8s a7g 8d Jul 1] modest maiden: should stay beyond 1m: raced only on good going or softer on turf: blinkered final start: sold 8,000 gns. *B. Hanbury*

LUCKY RED   3 b.g. Presidium 124 – Judys Girl (IRE) (Simply Great (FR) 122)   **53** [1998 56+, a53: 6g² 5g⁶ a6g³ 7m³ 7f⁵ 6s³ 7v a5g a7g a7g 1999 9.7v⁴ 10f 8.1m 8f 6m⁴ 7f 7d Aug 14] tall, unfurnished gelding: modest maiden at best: should stay beyond 7f: acts on good to firm going and fibresand, probably on heavy: blinkered twice in 1998. *Pat Mitchell*

LUCKY STAR   2 b.f. (Mar 5) Emarati (USA) 74 – Child Star (FR) 58 (Bellypha   **59** 130) [1999 5m 6m⁶ 7d⁶ a7g⁶ Dec 18] first foal: dam winning stayer, also successful over hurdles: modest maiden: should stay at least 1m: acts on equitrack and good to firm ground. *D. Marks*

LUCKY SWEEP   2 ch.c. (Mar 27) Cadeaux Genereux 131 – Phantom Gold 119   **65 p** (Machiavellian (USA) 123) [1999 8v⁶ 7d⁴ Oct 12] first foal: dam, 1m winner at 2 yrs, successful in Ribblesdale and in Geoffrey Freer Stakes: fair form in maidens at Salisbury and Leicester: will stay at least 1¼m: should make a better 3-y-o. *R. Hannon*

LUCKY TOUCH   6 ch.g. Broadsword (USA) 104 – Solatia 75 (Kalydon 122)   **70 ?** [1998 NR 1999 a13g³ a12g² a12s³ Feb 10] half-brother to a winner in Hong Kong: dam 1½m winner: modest form in bumpers: probably flattered on belated Flat debut: well below that form after. *W. R. Muir*

LUCKY UNO   3 b.c. Rock City 120 – Free Skip 68 (Free State 125) [1998 –: 7.9g   **55 d** 8s 6d 1999 7d⁶ 5.1s 7.5g³ 10.3m 5m 5.9m⁶ Aug 2] modest maiden at best: stays 7f: acts on good to firm and good to soft going. *C. Smith*

LUCONIC   3 b.c. Zafonic (USA) 130 – Felucca 94 (Green Desert (USA) 127)   **70** [1998 NR 1999 8g⁶ 8m Jul 10] first foal: dam 2-y-o 6f winner: fair form in maiden at Newmarket on debut: last of 7 in similar event at Ascot: sold only 1,400 gns, sent to Sweden. *H. R. A. Cecil*

LUCYLIAM (IRE)   2 b.f. (May 25) College Chapel 122 – Style (Homing 130)   **–** [1999 6f a6g 6v Sep 24] IR 1,400F, 500Y: eighth foal: half-sister to 6-y-o Sharp Shuffle: dam unraced: no sign of ability. *J. S. Moore*

LUCY MARIELLA   3 b.f. Mystiko (USA) 124 – Deanta In Eirinn (Red Sunset   **75** 120) [1998 74: 5.1m³ 5g 5g² 6g 5s⁵ 1999 7.5m 6f* 5.3f² 5g 6g² 6m⁴ 5m Jul 28] sturdy filly: fair handicapper: won maiden event at Brighton in May: effective at 5f/6f: acts on firm going: blinkered (below form) final start: has worn tongue strap/crossed noseband: has been taken last to post. *G. A. Butler*

LUDERE (IRE)   4 ch.g. Desse Zenny (USA) – White Jasmin 53 (Jalmood (USA)   **59** 126) [1998 50, a40: a8g⁵ a11g³ a12g⁴ 12d a8.5g⁶ 12g* 12m² 12m⁵ 14s⁴ 12.1m³ 15.8d⁵ 12g⁵ 1999 9m 12g² 16m² 14d⁴ 13f 13f Jul 16] good-bodied gelding: modest handicapper: seems best around 1½m: acts on soft and good to firm going: blinkered once at 3 yrs: successful over hurdles in July: sold 11,000 gns following month, joined P. Wegmann. *P. Monteith*

LUGANA LADY   3 b.f. Lugana Beach 116 – Mrs Bacon 82 (Balliol 125) [1998   **–** –: 6g 5.1m 1999 8g 7m 7.1g a10g a16.2g Dec 15] no form: left D. Haydn Jones before final outing (visored). *D. Burchell*

LUJAIN (USA)   3 b.c. Seeking The Gold (USA) – Satin Flower (USA) 115   **109 +** (Shadeed (USA) 135) [1998 119: 6f* 6g* 6g* 7g⁶ 1999 6s⁵ 5m Jun 18] rather leggy, close-coupled, quite attractive colt: has a quick action: smart performer at 2 yrs for D. Loder, winner of Middle Park Stakes: below that form in 1999, 4½ lengths fifth to Sampower Star in Duke of York Stakes on reappearance, weakening markedly late on: tongue tied, only twelfth of 17 in King's Stand Stakes at Royal Ascot following month: bred to stay 1m, but almost certainly best at 5f/6f: acts on firm ground: attended by 2 handlers all starts at 2 yrs. *Saeed bin Suroor*

LULLABY 2 b.f. (Jan 26) Unfuwain (USA) 131 – Heart's Harmony (Blushing – Groom (FR) 131) [1999 7m Aug 6] fourth foal: half-sister to 3-y-o National Anthem: dam, second at 1m from 2 starts in France, closely related to useful 1¼m and 1¾m winner Proposing: behind from halfway in maiden at Salisbury. *J. R. Fanshawe*

LUMINANT 2 b.c. (Apr 5) Lammtarra (USA) 134 – Shimmering Sea 89 (Slip **87** Anchor 136) [1999 a7g⁵ 6m² 7m* 7f 7g 7.3v² Oct 23] IR 100,000Y: strong, lengthy colt: fifth foal: half-brother to several winners, including 3-y-o Summer Night, useful 6f/7f winner Sheltering Sky (by Selkirk) and useful sprinter Sea Dane (later won in Scandinavia, by Danehill): dam, 2-y-o 5f/7f winner who stayed 1m, half-sister to Petoski: fairly useful performer: won maiden at Chester in July: good second in nursery at Newbury final start: will be suited by 1m+: acts on good to firm and heavy ground: has shown some reluctance stalls: sold 30,000 gns, sent to Saudi Arabia. *Sir Mark Prescott*

LUNAJAZ 2 ch.g. (Feb 8) Alhijaz 122 – Lunagraphe (USA) (Time For A Change – (USA)) [1999 7g 6m 7d Aug 26] 3,000Y: fourth foal: closely related to 3-y-o Gilou: dam (little form here and in France) out of half-sister to high-class US 7f to 9f winner Polish Navy: well held in maidens/seller. *T. M. Jones*

LUNALUX 2 b.f. (Feb 12) Emarati (USA) 74 – Ragged Moon 72 (Raga Navarro **61** (ITY) 119) [1999 5d a5g⁶ 5g 6g⁵ 6m⁶ 5m³ 5d⁴ 5f⁵ 5m⁵ 6d Oct 15] 8,000Y: unfurnished filly: half-sister to several winners, including useful 1991 2-y-o 6f winner Misterioso (by Forzando), later successful in USA: dam won 1m sellers: modest maiden: stays 6f: acts on good to soft going, probably on firm: visored last 2 starts: usually races up with pace: consistent: sold 3,800 gns. *C. Smith*

LUNAR LORD 3 b.g. Elmaamul (USA) 125 – Cache (Bustino 136) [1998 –: 7s **48** 6g 8d 1999 8.2s 10g 8.1d⁵ 8m Aug 4] sparely-made gelding: poor form: will stay 1½m. *J. S. Moore*

LUNAR MUSIC 5 b.m. Komaite (USA) – Lucky Candy 61 (Lucky Wednesday – 124) [1998 46, a49: 5g 7g⁶ a6g⁶ 5g a5g 7g 5.1g* 5m 6m a7g a6g 1999 a6g Jan 4] angular mare: poor handicapper: no form since winning at Nottingham in 1998: effective at 5f, probably 7f: acts on firm going and all-weather: sometimes blinkered: none too consistent. *S. R. Bowring*

LUNAR PROSPECTOR (IRE) 3 ch.f. Second Set (IRE) 127 – Eastern Aura **?** (IRE) 49 (Ahonoora 122) [1998 73: 5g² 5g³ 5d⁶ 5m³ 5m² 5m² 5g 1999 5m⁶ May 29] big filly: fair maiden at 2 yrs: broke blood vessel only start in Britain in 1999: sold 3,900 gns in July and subsequently won over 5f in Belgium. *M. G. Quinlan*

LUNCH PARTY 7 b.g. Beveled (USA) – Crystal Sprite 74 (Crystal Glitters **72** (USA) 127) [1998 70: 7.1g³ 7.1m* 7d* 8s² 7.6m⁶ 7m* 7.6d⁴ 7s 7.1g⁵ 7s 1999 7g⁴ 7g⁵ 7m¹* 7m¹* 7g 7m¹² 7m 7g 7.1d⁶ 7g Oct 16] good bodied gelding: not a good walker: fair performer: has won 3 times at Catterick, including minor event in May: also successful in handicap at Thirsk following month: below form final 4 starts: effective at 7f/1m: acts on firm and soft going: usually races prominently: has been early to post: usually ridden by claimer Iona Wands. *J. Berry*

LUVADUCK 3 b.f. Pursuit of Love 124 – Pillowing 69 (Good Times (ITY)) [1998 **65** NR 1999 7v⁵ 8m⁴ 8.3g 7.6g Aug 24] 5,500Y: fifth foal: half-sister to 3 winners, including winner up to 1m Greatest (by Superlative) and 8.5f winner Hugging (by Beveled): dam, sprinter, out of half-sister to Blushing Groom: fair form at best in maidens first 3 starts for M. Heaton-Ellis: gave trouble at stalls on debut. *C. G. Cox*

LUZ BAY (IRE) 3 b.g. Tenby 125 – Cabcharge Princess (IRE) 64 (Rambo Dancer **79** (CAN) 107) [1998 70: 7.9g⁵ 8s a8g⁵ 1999 12.5d* 11.8v⁶ 11f⁴ 10m³ 11.6m² 12m² 11.8g* 10g² 15.8m Aug 30] small, quite attractive gelding: fair performer: won claimer at Warwick in April and minor event at Leicester in August: stays 12.5f (failed to stay 2m final start): acts on firm and good to soft going, possibly not on soft/heavy: blinkered last 6 starts: consistent: sold 10,500 gns in October. *R. Charlton*

LUZERN 3 ch.c. Selkirk (USA) 129 – Luana 101 (Shaadi (USA) 126) [1998 79: **63** 7g 6f³ 6m⁵ 1999 7g Apr 5] leggy colt: poor mover: fair maiden at best: should stay 1m: sent to UAE. *C. E. Brittain*

LV GIRL (IRE) 3 ch.f. Mukaddamah (USA) 125 – Penny Fan 58 (Nomination **67 d** 125) [1998 55: 5g 5.2m⁶ 7.1m 7s⁴ 1999 6v⁴ 7d 8.1d⁴ 8m² 8m⁵ 8g 7.1m⁴ 8g 7s 7d⁴

8.2s Nov 1] lengthy, sparely-made filly: fair maiden handicapper: below form after fourth start: stays 1m: acts on good to firm and heavy going: visored final start. *G. B. Balding*

LYCIAN (IRE) 4 b.g. Lycius (USA) 124 – Perfect Time (IRE) (Dance of Life (USA)) [1998 62+, a71+: 8m* a9.4g² 8g* 8m⁵ 8g³ a9.4g² a8g* 1999 a7g⁵ a8g* a8.5s⁵ a8g² 8g 8g⁶ 8f² 9m* 9m² 8m 8m Sep 2] tall, lengthy gelding: fairly useful handicapper on all-weather, fair on turf: won at Lingfield in January and Goodwood in June: well below form last 2 starts: seems best at 1m/9f: acts on all-weather, raced only on good going or firmer on turf. *J. A. R. Toller* — **71 a81**

LYNDAH CHARLOTTE (IRE) 2 ch.f. (Apr 10) Case Law 113 – Elanmatina (IRE) 77 (Burslem 123) [1999 5m⁵ 5m⁵ 5g 5g Nov 3] IR 2,800Y: third foal: dam 2-y-o 6f winner out of half-sister to Superlative: little worthwhile form, including in sellers: will prove best short of 1m. *J. J. O'Neill* — **–**

LYNTON LAD 7 b.g. Superpower 113 – House Maid 95 (Habitat 134) [1998 NR 1999 a8g 8d³ a6g 8d* 8s² 8m⁵ Jun 23] good-topped gelding: fair handicapper: won at Ayr in May: suited by around 1m: acts on soft and good to firm going, well beaten on fibresand: occasionally blinkered. *E. J. Alston* — **72**

LYRIC 2 ch.f. (Apr 6) Lycius (USA) 124 – River Jig (USA) 98 (Irish River (FR) 131) [1999 7m⁴ 7m⁶ 6m 8d 6s Sep 29] seventh foal: closely related to useful 5f (Queen Mary Stakes) and 7f winner Dance Parade and fairly useful 1m winner (stayed 1¼m) Western Reel (both by Gone West) and half-sister to 2 winners, including 3-y-o Jig: dam 9f (at 2 yrs) and 1½m (in Italy) winner: well beaten after debut: tried blinkered: sold 85,000 gns in December. *P. F. I. Cole* — **58 d**

LYRICAL LEGACY (IRE) 2 ch.f. (May 5) Common Grounds 118 – Lyric Junction (IRE) (Classic Secret (USA) 91) [1999 5d 5g 6g Oct 15] IR 14,000Y: first foal: dam unraced: well beaten in maidens, reportedly lame final start. *A. P. Jarvis* — **–**

LYRIST 3 gr.f. Cozzene (USA) – La Llave (USA) (Risen Star (USA)) [1998 –: 7m 1999 7s 8.5s⁴ 8m 10m 11.5g² 10m 8d 10f* 11.9m* 12d Oct 29] fair handicapper: much improved to win at Brighton in July and September, dictating pace both times: stays 11.9f: acts on firm going, below form on softer than good: blinkered last 6 starts. *C. E. Brittain* — **77**

LYSANDROS (IRE) 5 b.g. Lycius (USA) 124 – Trojan Relation (Trojan Fen 118) [1998 11d* 10d 10.5v 9g³ 10g⁶ 12.5m* 15g³ 15.5g² 16d 17s⁶ 1999 a12g² a16.2g³ a12g² a12s* Feb 10] fair performer: ran in Britain for J. Gosden in 1997: sold 21,000 gns and joined R. Gibson in France, winning twice there in 1998: creditable efforts on return, winning handicap at Wolverhampton in February: stays 2m: acts on good to firm going, soft and fibresand: tried blinkered. *Noel T. Chance* — **76**

M

MA-ARIF (IRE) 3 b.f. Alzao (USA) 117 – Taqreem (IRE) 73 (Nashwan (USA) 135) [1998 76: 7g⁴ 8.1g⁴ 7d⁵ 1999 7d* 8m² 8m⁵ 10s Aug 21] strong, deep-girthed filly: type to carry condition: useful performer: won handicap at Newmarket (carried head awkwardly) in June: good efforts after listed rated stakes at Ascot (head second to Holly Blue), Falmouth Stakes at Newmarket (3½ lengths fifth to Ronda) and Prix de la Nonette at Deauville (5 lengths seventh to Star of Akkar): stays 1¼m: acts on soft and good to firm going: sent to USA. *J. H. M. Gosden* — **104**

MAAS (IRE) 4 br.c. Elbio 125 – Payne's Grey (Godswalk (USA) 130) [1998 60: 5f⁴ 6m 5.1d a6g² a6g² 1999 6m 5d 6d a6g² a7g⁶ Nov 24] good-bodied colt: modest maiden: stays 7f: acts on firm going, good to soft and equitrack. *P. J. Makin* — **58**

MABROOKAH 3 b.f. Deploy 131 – Adorable Cherub (USA) 58 (Halo (USA)) [1998 NR 1999 10.3d 10m 8f⁶ 8s² 9s⁴ a8g⁵ Nov 26] 3,200Y: angular, plain filly: fourth foal: half-sister to a 6f/7f winner in Italy by Warrshan: dam, maiden bred to stay at least 1m, from family of Singspiel: fair maiden: best effort (after 4-month break) on fourth start: should stay 1¼m. *K. Mahdi* — **73**

MACARI 5 gr.g. Arzanni 115 – View Halloa (Al Sirat (USA)) [1998 35, a–: 10m – 10.8g 8g 12m³ a9.4g⁶ 10.8m 9.9m 10.3v a10g 1999 10m 8.5g Aug 12] tall gelding: poor maiden at best: has reportedly bled from nose. *B. P. J. Baugh*

MAC BE LUCKY 2 b.c. (Feb 3) Magic Ring (IRE) 115 – Take Heart 84 (Electric **70** 126) [1999 7.1s³ 7v² 6s Nov 5] 42,000Y: strong, workmanlike colt: third living foal: half-brother to useful 1¼m winner Lonely Heart (by Midyan): dam 7f to 1¼m winner: fair form in maidens at Haydock and Ayr (unfortunate not to have landed odds, caught on line by more vigorously ridden winner) in September/October: well held final start: should stay 1m. *J. Noseda*

MACCA LUNA (IRE) 4 b.f. Kahyasi 130 – Medicosma (USA) 80 (The Minstrel **78** (CAN) 135) [1998 –: 11.4d 1999 10d 12f 12m² 13.8m⁶ 12g² 12g* 12m* 10d³ 11.9d⁶ **a–** a12g 12s Nov 6] smallish, sturdy filly: fair performer: won handicap at Beverley in August and minor event at Musselburgh in September: well held last 2 starts, on fibresand penultimate one: should stay beyond 1½m: acts on good to firm and good to soft going: has been bandaged behind. *Miss S. E. Hall*

MACGILLYCUDDY (IRE) 10 b. or br.g. Petorius 117 – My Bonnie 61 (High- – land Melody 112) [1998 –: 6.1m 6m 5g 1999 7g Jun 8] sturdy, close-coupled gelding: modest performer at best: no form since 1997. *Mrs P. N. Dutfield*

MACHAMILLION (USA) 3 ch.c. Machiavellian (USA) 123 – Gracieuse – (USA) (Nureyev (USA) 131) [1998 NR 1999 8m Sep 17] good-bodied colt: first foal: dam unraced half-sister to Prix de la Salamandre winner Oczy Czarnie and Criterium de Saint-Cloud winner Glaieul: fourteenth of 19 in maiden at Newbury: sent to USA. *P. W. Chapple-Hyam*

MACHE 2 b.g. (May 9) Noble Patriarch 115 – Shalta (FR) (Targowice (USA) 130) – [1999 8d 7.9g 7g Oct 15] half-brother to 2 winners in France, including 1990 2-y-o 1m winner Shotkar (by The Wonder): dam French 9f winner: well held in maidens and claimer. *R. D. E. Woodhouse*

MACHIAVELLI 5 b.g. Machiavellian (USA) 123 – Forest Blossom (USA) 56 – (Green Forest (USA) 134) [1998 –: 12m 12m 10s 1999 a12g⁶ Jun 25] strong, good-bodied gelding: fairly useful at 3 yrs for H. Cecil: no form in 1998 and probably flattered only 5-y-o start: blinkered once: successful over fences (has raced moodily) in September. *G. L. Moore*

MACH ONE (FR) 4 b.g. Sanglamore (USA) 126 – Douceur (USA) (Shadeed **50 d** (USA) 135) [1998 –: 7g a7g⁶ 1999 a12g² a12f a16g a12g a12g Mar 27] strong, lengthy gelding: modest maiden: well beaten after reappearance, twice shaping as though something amiss: should stay beyond 1½m: acts on fibresand: blinkered (raced freely) penultimate start: sold 2,800 gns. *Sir Mark Prescott*

MACHRIE BAY 2 b.c. (Apr 12) Emarati (USA) 74 – Fleeting Rainbow 65 **87** (Rainbow Quest (USA) 134) [1999 7d 7d 8s³ Oct 25] 14,000Y: useful-looking colt: fourth foal: half-brother to smart Irish 5f (at 2 yrs) to 11f winner Quws (by Robel- lino): dam, should have stayed 1½m, from good family: easily best effort in maidens (fairly useful form) when third of 19 to Delius at Leicester: likely to stay 1¼m: raced only on ground softer than good. *J. L. Dunlop*

MACHUDI 2 b.f. (Apr 14) Bluebird (USA) 125 – Machaera (Machiavellian **– p** (USA) 123) [1999 5.1g Oct 21] first foal: dam unraced half-sister to smart sprinters Russian Bond and Snaadee: never-dangerous seventh of 15 in maiden at Nottingham, soon nudged along: likely to do better. *B. A. McMahon*

MACLOUD (IRE) 6 b.g. Mac's Imp (USA) 116 – Cloud Nine 97 (Skymaster – 126) [1998 NR 1999 6m 8m Jul 30] 6,300Y: good-topped gelding: half-brother to several winners, including useful 7f/1m performer Sky Cloud (by Formidable): dam 5f to 1¼m winner: well beaten in maiden and seller at Newmarket. *N. A. Graham*

MAC'S DREAM (USA) 4 b.g. Mister Frisky (USA) – Annie's Dream (USA) **51** (Droll Role (USA)) [1998 41+: 7m 8g⁴ 7.1g 8.2g a7g a6g⁶ a7g 1999 8.3m 8.5s 6f 6.1f 6g 8.1m³ 7m 8m² 8m 8f⁵ Sep 6] quite attractive gelding: unimpressive mover: modest maiden handicapper: left A. Carroll before penultimate start: seems best at 1m: acts on equitrack and firm going: usually tongue tied. *W. Jarvis*

MAC'S EXPRESS (IRE)   3 br.g. Mac's Imp (USA) 116 – Almasa 83 (Faustus **86**
(USA) 118) [1998 NR 1999 7m 5.1s³ 5.1s³ 5d 5m³ 5m* 5.1m 6m 5d Jul 30] 18,000Y:
sturdy, good-quartered gelding: first foal: dam 2-y-o 6f winner from family of Ridgewood Pearl: fairly useful handicapper: won at Newmarket in June: was best at 5f:
acted on good to firm going: dead. *A. P. Jarvis*

MADAGASCAR   3 b.f. Puissance 110 – Tabyan (USA) 68 (Topsider (USA))   –
[1998 NR 1999 7m 8g 6g a8g⁴ 6m 7g Aug 11] fourth foal: half-sister to smart 1m   **a43**
to 1¼m winner Cap Juluca (by Mtoto): dam 6f winner: form only when fourth in
maiden at Southwell (visored): sold 6,400 gns in December.
J. W. Hills

MADAM ALISON   3 b.f. Puissance 110 – Copper Burn 68 (Electric 126) [1998 **87**
75p: 5g⁶ 7m 6.1s 5s⁴ 6s* 1999 7m 8m* 8m² 8m³ 8.1m⁶ 7m⁵ 8.1d² 8.1s⁶ Oct 2] sturdy
filly: fairly useful handicapper: won at Newmarket in June: ran creditably most starts
after: may prove best around 1m: acts on soft and good to firm going. *R. Hannon*

MADAME CHINNERY   5 b.m. Weldnaas (USA) 112 – Bel Esprit (Sagaro 133)   –
[1998 70d: 10m⁴ 12m 11.9g* a14g² a12g⁴ 16.4g 14m 11.8d 11.9s a10g⁶ a14.8g⁶ 1999
a13g⁶ Jan 12] lengthy, sparely-made mare: fair at best: well held in 6 starts for current
stable, though has won in Jersey: tried blinkered. *C. Weedon*

MADAME GENEREUX   2 ch.f. (Mar 21) Cadeaux Genereux 131 – Bright   –
Spells 93 (Salse (USA) 128) [1999 6m Sep 18] 11,000Y: close-coupled, sparely-
made filly: second foal: half-sister to fairly useful Irish 1997 2-y-o 7f winner Cultural
Role (by Night Shift): dam 2-y-o 6f winner who stayed 1¾m: well held in maiden at
Newbury. *N. A. Graham*

MADAME JONES (IRE)   4 ch.f. Lycius (USA) 124 – Gold Braisim (IRE) 77   –
(Jareer (USA) 115) [1998 73, a–: 6m² 6.1m* 6g⁴ 6m 5.1m 5.1d 7.6g⁵ 8.1m⁴ a7g⁵
8.1g⁶ 6.1g* 7s 6s 1999 a6g a7g a6g Dec 6] tall filly: fair handicapper at 3 yrs: well
beaten in 1999, off course over a year before reappearance: stays 1m: acts on good to
firm ground. *A. T. Murphy*

MADAME MAXI   5 ch.m. Ron's Victory (USA) 129 – New Pastures (Formid- **64**
able (USA) 125) [1998 61: 8m² 8d* 10d 10v 1999 a8g a8.5g⁵ a8f⁶ 8.3m³ 8m 8g Sep **a–**
20] modest handicapper on turf, poor on all-weather: easily best effort in 1999 when
close third at Windsor in August: best at 1m: acts on good to firm going, good to soft
and fibresand: tried blinkered. *H. S. Howe*

MADAME SISU   2 b.f. (Mar 25) Emarati (USA) 74 – About Face (Midyan (USA) **47**
124) [1999 5m 5m Jul 19] 8,000Y: first foal: dam unraced half-sister to high-class 1m
to 1¼m performer Bijou d'Inde: better effort in maidens (poor form) when seventh of
14 at Windsor: should stay at least 7f. *A. P. Jarvis*

MADAM LUCY   5 ch.m. Efisio 120 – Our Aisling 82 (Blakeney 126) [1998 –:   –
a11g 10.8g 11.5m 1999 a12g a14g Mar 16] poor at best: tried blinkered/visored: sold
500 gns. *Mrs N. Macauley*

MADEMOISELLE PARIS   2 gr.f. (Feb 24) Paris House 123 – Heather Honey **45 §**
(Insan (USA) 119) [1999 5.1f 7d³ 6.8d 5.7s 6.1s⁶ a5g a5g⁴ a8g a7g Dec 15] 2,600
2-y-o: lengthy, unfurnished filly: second foal: sister to 3-y-o Honey House: dam unraced: poor maiden: stays 7f: acts on soft ground and fibresand: tried blinkered: has
looked ungenuine. *A. W. Carroll*

MADGE'S PET   5 b.m. Precious Metal 106 – Lucky Lena (Leander 119) [1998   –
NR 1999 12s 10s Nov 1] no sign of ability. *B. D. Leavy*

MADMAN'S MIRAGE (FR)   4 b.g. Green Desert (USA) 127 – Layaali (USA)   –
(Diesis 133) [1998 56, a73: a6g* a7g² a6g⁵ a6g⁵ 8g 8g⁶ 6g 9.2s² 8d 9g⁴ 1999 a8g
Jan 2] good-topped gelding: fair on all-weather, modest on turf: tailed off only 4-y-o
start: unlikely to stay beyond 9f: acts on soft going and all-weather. *V. Thompson*

MADMUN (IRE)   5 ch.g. Cadeaux Genereux 131 – Kates Cabin 96 (Habitat 134) **83**
[1998 76: 8d 7m³ 6m² 6g³ 6g⁵ 1999 6g⁴ 6v⁵ 6g⁵ 6.1f² 6d* Oct 28] tall gelding:
fairly useful performer, lightly raced: creditable efforts in handicaps in 1999 prior to
winning 21-runner maiden at Windsor in October: seems best at 6f: acts on any
ground: visored (ran poorly) final 4-y-o start. *M. P. Tregoning*

MAESTEG 3 b.f. Reprimand 122 – Eluned May 62 (Clantime 101) [1998 –: 5m –
5.7g 1999 6v 6.1g 8.1m Jul 9] small, unfurnished filly: no form. *M. J. Fetherston-
Godley*

MAESTERSINGER 2 b.c. (Feb 5) Piccolo 121 – Madurai 71 (Chilibang 120) **85**
[1999 6.1m² 6g² 6.1m² 6f 6d* 6m² 6v³ 6d Oct 14] sturdy, well-made colt: good
walker: first foal: dam 6f winner: fairly useful performer: won nursery at Windsor in
August: creditable efforts after: stays 6f: acts on good to firm and heavy going: sold
31,000 gns, sent to Macau. *J. L. Dunlop*

MAFTUN (USA) 7 ch.g. Elmaamul (USA) 125 – Allesheny 85 (Be My Guest **52**
(USA) 126) [1998 56, a52: a11g⁵ a12g a14g⁶ 14.1d⁶ 16.1d⁶ 15.8g² 16.2g 17.1m⁶
a12g a12g 1999 a16g³ a16f⁴ a16g Feb 12] workmanlike gelding: unimpressive
mover: modest handicapper: pulled up final start: stayed 2m: acted on fibresand,
good to firm and good to soft going: sometimes had tongue tied: dead. *G. M. Moore*

MAGDA (IRE) 3 b.f. Turtle Island (IRE) 123 – Pennine Drive (IRE) (Pennine –
Walk 120) [1998 82+: 7m 8.2s* 7g 1999 9.9g⁶ May 19] good-topped filly: won
maiden at Nottingham at 2 yrs: well held in listed race only outing in 1999: should
have stayed at least 1¼m: dead. *C. E. Brittain*

MAGELLA 2 b.f. (May 11) Magic Ring (IRE) 115 – Thatcherella 80 (Thatching **45**
131) [1999 5m 6g 5m Aug 31] 2,000Y: first foal: dam 5f (including at 2 yrs) and 6f
winner: poor maiden: dead. *B. J. Meehan*

MAGELTA 2 b.c. (Apr 14) Magic Ring (IRE) 115 – Pounelta 91 (Tachypous 128) **74**
[1999 6f 6d⁴ 6d³ Oct 29] big, useful-looking colt: brother to 3-y-o Lots of Magic
and half-brother to 4-y-o Rubanna and several winners: dam, 2-y-o 7f winner who
probably stayed 1½m, half-sister to very smart but temperamental sprinter Dead
Certain: fair maiden, in frame at Newmarket final 2 starts: should stay 1m. *R. Hannon*

MAGENKO (IRE) 2 ch.g. (Feb 3) Forest Wind (USA) 111 – Bebe Auction –
(IRE) (Auction Ring (USA) 123) [1999 6g 6d 7d Oct 27] IR 6,000F, IR 5,400Y:
strong, workmanlike gelding: second foal: dam unraced: showed little in maidens.
M. H. Tompkins

MAGHAARB 3 ch.f. Machiavellian (USA) 123 – Fida (IRE) (Persian Heights **104**
129) [1998 103: 6g² 6g* 1999 7m⁴ 7m⁴ 6m* 6m⁴ Aug 27] small, compact filly: useful
performer: won 4-runner minor event at Doncaster in July by length from Light The
Rocket: creditable fourth to Arkadian Hero in listed race at Newmarket next time:
stays 6f: raced only on good/good to firm going: sent to USA. *M. P. Tregoning*

MAGICAL BAILIWICK (IRE) 3 ch.g. Magical Wonder (USA) 125 – Alpine **73**
Dance (USA) 62§ (Apalachee (USA) 137) [1998 NR 1999 7m⁴ 8m⁵ 8.1d³ 9m
Aug 29] sixth reported foal: half-brother to 7f (at 2 yrs) and 1¼m winner Northern
Bailiwick (by Nordance): dam, middle-distance maiden, probably ungenuine: fair
maiden: well beaten in handicap final start: stays 1m: yet to race on extremes of
going. *R. J. Baker*

MAGICAL COLOURS (IRE) 4 b.f. Rainbows For Life (CAN) – Immediate –
Impact (Caerleon (USA) 132) [1998 –: 7s⁵ 9.7v 1999 12m 10d Jun 2] little sign of
ability. *R. Rowe*

MAGICAL DANCER (IRE) 4 b.f. Magical Wonder (USA) 125 – Diva Encore –
74 (Star Appeal 133) [1998 53: 5.3d 6m 8m⁴ 10g 10d³ 8.5m² 8m 8m* 8d 10g³ 1999
11.7s 8m 7f May 12] leggy, unfurnished filly: modest handicapper: well held in 1999:
stays 1¼m: acts on good to firm and good to soft going: held up. *M. R. Channon*

MAGICAL JACK 2 b.c. (Feb 16) Belfort (FR) 89 – Gavea (African Sky 124) –
[1999 6d a5g a8g Dec 17] brother to several maidens: dam twice-raced half-sister to
very smart 1m to 1¼m winner Cataldi: no sign of ability. *G. Woodward*

MAGICAL MILLIE 2 b.f. (Feb 25) Muhtarram (USA) 125 – Milne's Way 83 **71**
(The Noble Player (USA) 126) [1999 5m* 6.1m⁴ 5f 6g⁴ 7d 7g⁵ Oct 15] 9,000Y: fifth
foal: half-sister to 3-y-o Milne's Dream and 3 winners, including 7-y-o That Man
Again and 1¼m winner Who's That Man (by Mystiko): dam 5.8f (at 2 yrs) to 1m
winner: fair performer: won claimer at Folkestone in July: best effort when fourth of
17 in nursery at Leicester fourth start: should stay at least 7f: acts on firm ground.
S. C. Williams

MAGICAL RIVER 2 ch.f. (Jan 21) Lahib (USA) 129 – Awtaar (USA) 67 **60 d**
(Lyphard (USA) 132) [1999 5g 6.1f³ 6g 7d⁶ a6g 7d Oct 21] 7,500Y: second foal:
half-sister to 3-y-o Sharp Stepper: dam disappointing maiden out of half-sister to
Fairy Footsteps and Light Cavalry: modest form on debut: well beaten last 2 starts:
should stay 1m. *C. E. Brittain*

MAGICAL SHOT 4 b.g. Magic Ring (IRE) 115 – Final Shot 91 (Dalsaan 125) **74 d**
[1998 75: 6g³ 7g⁴ 7g³ 7m 7d³ 7.8m³ 7.8d⁴ 8g a12g⁶ a11g⁴ 1999 a8.5g* a11f³ a11g³
a8g² a8g² a8.5g 10v 7.1m a9.4g 9.2m⁶ 10m a7g a8g⁴ a11g Nov 30] fair performer:
won maiden at Wolverhampton in January: mostly well below form after fifth start:
effective at 1m to 11f: acts on good to soft ground and fibresand: effective blinkered
or not: usually apprentice ridden. *D. Carroll*

MAGIC ARROW (USA) 3 b.c. Defensive Play (USA) 118 – Magic Blue (USA) **66**
(Cure The Blues (USA)) [1998 NR 1999 a10g a12g* 14.1m⁶ a14.8g* 16.1s⁵ 14.1g **a78**
Aug 12] $30,000F: brother to a winner in USA and half-brother to a minor stakes
winner there by Star de Naskra: dam unraced half-sister to dam of Breeders' Cup
Classic and Kentucky Derby winner Unbridled: fair performer: won maiden at
Lingfield in February and handicap at Wolverhampton in May: best at 1½m/
1¾m: acts on all-weather and good to firm going, probably on soft: sold 5,000 gns.
J. Noseda

MAGIC BABE 2 b.f. (Mar 28) Magic Ring (IRE) 115 – Head Turner 61 (My Dad **56**
Tom (USA) 109) [1999 5m 5s 5g 6g⁴ 6g 6m 7m 7.1m Aug 21] 6,800Y: first foal: dam
1½m to 2m winner, also successful over hurdles: modest maiden: below form last 4
starts: should stay at least 1m: joined Jamie Poulton. *D. R. C. Elsworth*

MAGIC FLUTE 3 ch.f. Magic Ring (IRE) 115 – Megan's Flight 74 (Welsh **77**
Pageant 132) [1998 NR 1999 7g 7s⁵ 7m⁵ 8.1f 8m² 8d Oct 4] good-bodied filly:
second foal: dam, 1¾m and 2m winner on Flat, also 2¾m winner over hurdles: fair
maiden: best effort when second of 19 in handicap at Kempton in September: may
prove best at 1m: acts on good to firm going, pulled up lame on firm. *Lady Herries*

MAGIC GLOW 3 b.f. Presidium 124 – Mrs Magic (Magic Mirror 105) [1998 NR **–**
1999 6f⁵ 7f a6g Nov 12] tall, unfurnished filly: third foal: dam unraced: no sign of
ability. *N. Bycroft*

MAGIC GRAND 2 b.f. (May 12) Magic Ring (IRE) 115 – Between The Sticks **67**
83 (Pharly (FR) 130) [1999 5.1s 5m² 5s* 5.1m 5f² 5g* 5.1g⁶ 6m³ 5f⁵ Jul 9] 1,000Y:
small, leggy, unfurnished filly: third foal: half-sister to 3-y-o Penalty Miss and
winning Italian sprinter Pichon Lalande (by Forzando): dam sprinter: fair performer:
won maiden in May and minor event in June, both at Hamilton: effective at 5f/6f:
acts on firm and soft ground: sold 4,500 gns in October. *M. R. Channon*

MAGIC LEGS 2 b.f. (Feb 9) Reprimand 122 – Inherent Magic (IRE) 95 (Magical **54 p**
Wonder (USA) 125) [1999 5v Sep 24] 9,500Y: first foal: dam sprinter: weak in
market and green, never-nearer seventh of 17 to Inventive in maiden at Lingfield:
should do better. *W. R. Muir*

MAGIC MEMORIES 3 b.f. Magic Ring (IRE) 115 – Bay Runner (Bay Express **–**
132) [1998 69d, a–: 6f 5m² 6g² 7m* 6d⁴ 8m 7m⁴ 8d⁴ a7g a7g a8g 1999 8.2s Mar 29]
rather sparely-made filly: fair at best: well held only 3-y-o start: stays 7f: acts on
good to firm and good to soft going, no form on equitrack: often bandaged behind:
has edged right and finished weakly. *Mrs L. Stubbs*

MAGIC MILL (IRE) 6 b.g. Simply Great (FR) 122 – Rosy O'Leary (Majetta **74**
115) [1998 82: 7v⁴ 8d⁴ 8d⁴ 7m⁵ 8.1g 7s⁵ 10.1g 8s² 1999 7m 7m⁴ 8.1g May 28]
sparely-made gelding: fair handicapper: form in 1999 only on second start: effective
at 7f/1m, not 1¼m: acts on equitrack and any turf going: tried visored: has been
bandaged in front. *J. S. Goldie*

MAGIC MOMENT 3 b.f. Magic Ring (IRE) 115 – Epithet 105 (Mill Reef **63**
(USA) 141) [1998 –: 6m 6g⁶ 5s⁶ 6s 1999 7m³ 5.9g* 6g⁴ 6m⁴ 6m 6g Oct 14] leggy
filly: modest performer: won maiden at Carlisle in June: ran well next 2 starts, but
poorly last 2: should stay 7f: acts on good to firm going. *E. Weymes*

MAGIC MONDAY (IRE) 3 b.f. Petardia 113 – Ultra (Stanford 121§) [1998 **–**
62d: 5.2s² 5.1d⁵ 7m 5m 7g 1999 6v 6f 6g a5g 7m a8.5g Sep 8] sturdy filly: no form
since debut: left R. Hannon after second 3-y-o start: blinkered last 3. *L. A. Dace*

MAGIC OF LOVE   2 b.f. (Feb 17) Magic Ring (IRE) 115 – Mistitled (USA) 54 **95** (Miswaki (USA) 124) [1999 5m* 6d* 5m³ 6d* Oct 15] 12,000Y: leggy, workmanlike filly: second foal: sister to 4-y-o Jacobina: dam 2-y-o 5f winner: useful form: won maiden at Beverley in July, minor event at Lingfield in August and sales race at Newmarket (favourite, all out by head from Blue Velvet) in October: best effort when very close third of 14 to Mrs P in Flying Childers Stakes at Doncaster: unlikely to stay beyond 6f: yet to race on extremes of going. *M. L. W. Bell*

MAGIC POWERS   4 ch.g. Magical Wonder (USA) 125 – Kissin' Cousin 74 (Be **–** Friendly 130) [1998 59: 7.1g 8m 7d³ 1999 6v Apr 20] sparely-made gelding: modest maiden: well backed, reportedly finished lame in seller only 4-y-o start: stays 7f: acts on good to firm and good to soft going. *G. B. Balding*

MAGIC RAINBOW   4 b.g. Magic Ring (IRE) 115 – Blues Indigo 103 (Music **98** Boy 124) [1998 87: a6g* 6v 6.1m⁴ 6f* 6s 6f⁴ 5f 6f 6.1g⁶ 6g 1999 a6g* a6g⁴ 6m⁵ 5.1m⁶ 6f* 6g⁴ 5m² 6f 5m³ 5.6g Sep 8] leggy gelding: poor mover: useful handi-capper: won at Lingfield in March and Kempton in May: ran at least respectably most other starts, notably when 1¾ lengths second to Rudi's Pet in rated stakes at Ascot: effective at 5f/6f: seems unsuited by soft/heavy going, acts on any other turf/all-weather: sometimes starts slowly. *M. L. W. Bell*

MAGIC SISTER   2 ch.f. (Jan 14) Cadeaux Genereux 131 – Gunner's Belle 69 **63 p** (Gunner B 126) [1999 6s⁶ 6d⁶ Nov 4] 31,000Y: ninth foal: sister to 3-y-o Dalaauna and 2 winners, notably smart 1994 2-y-o sprinter (won Prix Morny) Hoh Magic who later stayed 1m, and half-sister to 2 winners, including 1m winner Gunner's Daughter (by Pharly): dam 7f to 1¼m winner: better effort in maidens when sixth of 18 to Free Rider at Windsor on second start, again slowly away before some late headway: will probably stay 7f: capable of better still. *M. L. W. Bell*

MAGIC SUNSET   2 b.f. (Mar 23) Magic Ring (IRE) 115 – Run To The Sun (Run **57** The Gantlet (USA)) [1999 8.1d 8.2s Oct 5] 10,000Y: half-sister to several winners here and abroad, including ungenuine stayer Go South (by Thatching) and middle-distance stayer Ikdam (by Glint of Gold), latter also successful in Triumph Hurdle: dam unraced half-sister to high-class hurdler Gay George: much better effort in maidens when seventh of 14 to Embraced at Nottingham on second start: will prove suited by 1½m+. *I. A. Balding*

MAGIQUE ETOILE (IRE)   3 b.f. Magical Wonder (USA) 125 – Shes A **64** Dancer (IRE) (Alzao (USA) 117) [1998 59, a62: 5f 6g 5d 7m⁶ 7g 6d⁴ 7s 8s⁶ a6g⁶ a7g³ **a60** a7g³ a6f³ 1999 6m 8.3m⁵ a8g⁵ 6g² 5.3f⁵ 6g 7d³ a6g³ a8g² Nov 26] good-bodied filly: modest maiden: stays 1m: acts on good to soft going and equitrack: tried blinkered/visored: often races prominently. *M. P. Muggeridge*

MAGNO (USA)   3 b.c. El Gran Senor (USA) 136 – Nice Noble (USA) (Vaguely **–** Noble 140) [1998 102: 7g³ 7s³ 7.9g* 8v² 1999 11.5g³ May 22] good-bodied colt: useful at 2 yrs: disappointing last of 3 in minor event at Lingfield (reportedly lame after race) only start in 1999: should stay 1¼m: raced only on good ground or softer: sold 5,500 gns in December. *P. F. I. Cole*

MAIDAAN   3 b.c. Midyan (USA) 124 – Panache Arabelle (Nashwan (USA) **107** 135) [1998 108p: 6m³ 7g* 1999 8.5d² 8d Oct 30] smallish, sturdy colt: good mover: useful form: won 26-runner Houghton Sales race at Newmarket at 2 yrs, then left M. Channon: much better effort in listed races in 1999 when head second to Indian Lodge in falsely-run event at Newmarket, cruising to front 2f out but faltering and caught near line: found little 15 days later: may prove best around 1m: yet to race on extremes of going. *Saeed bin Suroor*

MAIDEN'S BLUSH (USA)   3 ch.f. Silver Hawk (USA) 123 – Barmistress **91** (USA) (Alydar (USA)) [1998 70p: 7d 1999 10m* 11.4m 10d² 10d⁴ Sep 17] tall filly: fairly useful performer: won maiden at Windsor in April: tailed off in listed race at Chester next time, then (after 3-month break) in frame in handicaps at Ripon and Ayr: should prove at least as effective at 1½m as 1¼m: yet to race on extremes of going: has been equipped with rope halter and blanketed for stalls entry. *J. H. M. Gosden*

MAID PLANS (IRE)   3 br.f. Petardia 113 – Ballerina Anna (IRE) (Dance of Life **–** (USA)) [1998 –: 5d 5g 5m⁶ 6s a5s a7g⁶ 1999 a6g a6g⁵ Feb 3] sparely-made filly: little form. *N. P. Littmoden*

MAID TO LOVE (IRE)   2 ch.f. (Apr 19) Petardia 113 – Lomond Heights (IRE)   **65**
(Lomond (USA) 128) [1999 6g³ 6.1g³ 6.8m 7s a8.5g² a8g² a8g³ Dec 8] IR 10,000Y: **a62**
third living foal: sister to 3-y-o Satin Slipper: dam, third at 1m at 2 yrs in Ireland,
daughter of May Hill winner Satinette: fair maiden: creditable efforts in blinkers (on
all-weather) last 3 starts: stays 1m. *G. A. Butler*

MAID TO MEASURE   3 b.f. Inchinor 119 – Walking Saint 73 (Godswalk
(USA) 130) [1998 48: 6s³ 7.5d 7f 6g⁵ 1999 8.2s Apr 19] leggy filly: poor form at best
in sellers: should stay beyond 6f. *M. Brittain*

MAIELLA   4 ch.f. Salse (USA) 128 – Forelino (USA) 62§ (Trempolino (USA)   **50**
135) [1998 63: 10.2s 11.6g 11.9f* 10m³ 11.9g³ 12g 12m⁵ 12m* 11.9m⁴ 11.1m a10g
1999 12.3m 17.1v 16.2d 13.8g 14.1m 10d 8m³ 9.9m⁴ 10g² 10m* Aug 28] unfurnished filly: modest performer: won selling handicap at Nottingham in August: best at
1¼m/1½m: acts on firm ground, well beaten only start on all-weather: blinkered after
second start: has looked none too genuine, and likely to prove best held up: sold
2,700 gns, joined C. Weedon. *T. D. Easterby*

MAI TAI (IRE)   4 b.f. Scenic 128 – Oystons Propweekly 74 (Swing Easy (USA)   **61**
126) [1998 61: 5s⁶ 7.3m 6m³ 7d⁴ 6m⁴ 8m 6g³ 7m⁶ 8d 6g 7g 7d a7s 1999 a7g²   **a65**
a8g a7f* a7g³ 7.1m 7.5d³ 7s* 7m⁶ 7g 6.9m 7.5m 7f 7g 8g a7g³ a7g a7g⁴ a7g³ a8g*
a7g⁴ Dec 8] leggy filly: fair performer: won maiden at Southwell in February and
handicaps at Redcar in May and Lingfield in December: stays 1m: acts on good to
firm going, soft and all-weather: blinkered once at 3 yrs, visored last 6 starts.
D. W. Barker

MAITEAMIA   6 ch.g. Komaite (USA) – Mia Scintilla 54 (Blazing Saddles (AUS))   **77**
[1998 68, a78: 5g² 5d 6s a7g² 7f² a7g⁵ 7g³ 5m 6m² 7g 5g⁶ 5m⁵ 6m³ 5g 5v a7g² a6g⁴   **a86**
a7g 1999 a6g a5g³ a5g³ a5g⁵ a6g² a6g* a6g* a5g² 5d³ 6m⁵ 6d 5m⁶ 7f 7m 5g³ 6m*
8g² 7g Oct 14] robust gelding: fairly useful handicapper on all-weather, fair on turf:
won at Southwell in February and March and Redcar (17-runner apprentice race) by 5
lengths: effective at 5f to 1m: acts on fibresand, firm and soft going:
blinkered/visored: sometimes tongue tied: usually races prominently: tough and
genuine. *S. R. Bowring*

MAITREYA   4 ch.f. Anshan 119 – Princess Fair (Crowned Prince (USA) 128)   **52**
[1998 52: 7g⁴ 8.2m⁶ 8m² 9m 8d 8d 1999 11.6m 11.9f³ 11.6m a10g⁶ 10m Sep 13]
modest maiden: left C. Allen before final start: barely stayed 1½m: acted on firm
ground: dead. *Mrs D. Haine*

MAIYSHA   2 b.f. (Apr 28) Contract Law (USA) 108 – Bint Al Arab (Ahonoora   **–**
122) [1999 7s 7v Oct 25] fourth reported foal: dam tailed off in bumpers: never
dangerous in maidens at Lingfield. *R. M. Flower*

MAJALIS   4 b. or br.f. Mujadil (USA) 119 – Rose Barton (Pas de Seul 133) [1998   **65 d**
79: 6g 5.3g² 6g² 5d* 6m² 6m⁵ 7m³ 6m⁵ 6g 1999 7f³ 6d 8m 7g 8m² 7m 8d 8f³ 10m
10m Sep 24] sparely-made filly: fair performer at best in 1999: stays 1m: acts on firm
and good to soft going: sold 900 gns in November. *J. L. Eyre*

MAJESTIC BAY (IRE)   3 b.g. Unfuwain (USA) 131 – That'll Be The Day (IRE)   **93**
68 (Thatching 131) [1998 NR 1999 10f⁵ 10g² 12m⁴ 12.3m² 12v³ Sep 20] 35,000Y:
sturdy gelding: second foal: half-brother to Italian winner (including in listed race)
up to 7.5f That's The Way (by Hamas): dam, 7f winner and pattern placed up to 1m,
half-sister to Gran Criterium and Premio Parioli winner Candy Glen: fairly useful
maiden: best efforts when placed, though wandered and looked none too keen final
start: stays 1½m: acts on good to firm and heavy ground. *P. W. Harris*

MAJESTIC (IRE)   4 b.g. Belmez (USA) 131 – Noble Lily (USA) (Vaguely Noble   **75**
140) [1998 75: 10m⁴ 12f³ 9m⁴ 11.9m³ 14.4d⁴ 16s⁴ a14g⁴ 11.8s² 1999 10.8d⁵ a12g*
a12f⁶ Oct 2] fair performer: won maiden at Wolverhampton in April by 12 lengths:
ran poorly final start: stays 1¾m well: acts on firm ground, soft and fibresand:
blinkered last 5 starts: has had tongue tied: winner 3 times over hurdles in October/
November, useful form final occasion. *Ian Williams*

MAJOR ATTRACTION   4 gr.g. Major Jacko 78 – My Friend Melody (Sizzling   **41**
Melody 117) [1998 –: 8g 8m 1999 a11g⁶ a11g⁴ a12g³ a12g⁴ a8.5g Dec 27] poor
maiden: stays 1½m: acts on fibresand. *P. Eccles*

MAJOR BART (IRE) 2 gr.g. (Apr 12) Paris House 123 – Kilnoe (IRE) (Rhoman –
Rule (USA)) [1999 5m 5g Aug 24] IR 5,300F, IR 7,500Y, 30,000 2-y-o: second foal:
dam poor Irish maiden: well held in maidens. *N. P. Littmoden*

MAJOR FORCE (USA) 3 b.c. Woodman (USA) 126 – Ready For Action 117
(USA) (Riverman (USA) 131) [1998 80p: 8v⁴ 1999 8d* 7v* 7s* 7d⁶ 7s³ Nov 7]
half-brother to 3 winners in Ireland, including fairly useful 1m/9f winner Dancing
Action (by Danzatore): dam 1¼m winner out of half-sister to Lyphard: smart
performer: won maiden and Desert King EBF Tetrarch Stakes (by 6 lengths from
Namid) in April and Aon MacDonagh Boland Stakes (by 5½ lengths from Artistic
Blue) in September, all at the Curragh: creditable efforts when sixth in Prix de la
Foret at Longchamp (to Field of Hope) and third in listed race at Leopardstown
(giving weight away all round when 1½ lengths behind One Won One): stays 1m:
raced only on ground softer than good (acts on heavy): made all for first 2 wins.
D. K. Weld, Ireland

MAJOR MORRIS (IRE) 4 br.g. New Express 95 – Saul Flower (Saulingo 122) –
[1998 NR 1999 7m a8g Dec 17] brother to winning sprinter Rambo Express: dam
unraced: well beaten in seller/claimer. *J. Mackie*

MAJOR REBUKE 2 b.g. (Apr 8) Reprimand 122 – Ackcontent (USA) (Key To 80
Content (USA)) [1999 6m* 7v⁴ 6d Oct 29] 12,000Y: seventh foal: half-brother to 3
winners, including winners up to 7f Eager To Please (by Keen) and No Sympathy (by
Ron's Victory), both successful at 2 yrs: dam ran once in USA: fairly useful form:
won maiden at Goodwood in September: best effort when fourth of 6 in minor event
at Salisbury later in month: will prove best up to 1m: acts on good to firm and heavy
ground. *S. P. C. Woods*

MAJOR'S LAW (IRE) 10 b.g. Law Society (USA) 130 – Maryinsky (USA) 48
(Northern Dancer) [1998 –: 17.2d⁴ 16.2g 18s⁴ a14g 1999 a16g⁴ a16f⁵ Feb 8] poor
handicapper, lightly raced nowadays: stays 17f: acts on good to firm going, heavy
and equitrack (below form on firesand). *R. Simpson*

MAKAAREM (USA) 2 gr.c. (Mar 18) Danzig (USA) – Sierra Madre (FR) 119 96 p
(Baillamont (USA) 124) [1999 6g* Jun 18] second foal: half-brother to 3-y-o Aljabr:
dam won Prix Marcel Boussac and Prix Vermeille: won minor event at Maisons-
Laffitte in June by 2 lengths from Slew The Red, going well close up and just pushed
out after quickening to lead under 2f out: carried head rather high: sure to improve.
D. R. Loder, France

MAKAHU DON 4 ch.g. Derrylin 115 – Rockalong 35 (Native Bazaar 122) [1998 –
–: a7g a6g 1999 a5g 5d Apr 5] smallish gelding: modest winner at 2 yrs: no form
since. *S. R. Bowring*

MAKAIRA (IRE) 2 b.g. (Apr 1) Thatching 131 Sharnazad (IRE) (Track Barron 45
(USA)) [1999 5m 6s⁶ 7d 6m 6d 6g 8g 7m 8d Sep 16] 40,000F, 10,000Y: strong,
lengthy gelding: fourth foal: half-brother to useful Italian middle-distance filly
Splendida Idea (by Kenmare): dam Italian 7.5f winner from family of Law Society:
poor maiden: should stay at least 1m: tried visored: sold 500 gns. *N. Tinkler*

MAKARIM (IRE) 3 ch.c. Generous (IRE) 139 – Emmaline (USA) (Affirmed 83 d
(USA)) [1998 NR 1999 10.5m⁴ 10m⁶ 11.7m* 12.4m 14.8d a16.2g⁶ a12g⁵ Dec 29]
$170,000F: tall colt: seventh foal: half-brother to smart 6f winner (including at 2
yrs) Zaranni Sidi Anna (stayed 1m, by Danzig) and fairly useful 1¼m/1½m winner
My Ballerina (by Sir Ivor): dam, won up to 9f in USA: fairly useful performer:
won maiden at Bath in August: ran poorly all starts after, reportedly choking
(subsequently sold from N. Graham 11,000 gns) on second occasion (blinkered):
stays 11.7f: acts on good to firm going. *P. Eccles*

MAKASSEB 2 ch.c. (Feb 23) Kris 135 – Shefoog 90 (Kefaah (USA) 124) 86
[1999 8s⁶ 7.9d³ 8d² 8g² 9v* 8v⁵ Nov 30] first foal: dam, 7f winner (including at 2
yrs), half-sister to smart winner in Britain/UAE up to 1¼m Murheb: fairly useful
form: won minor event at Maisons-Laffitte in November: creditable fifth in listed
event at Saint-Cloud later in month: stays 9f: raced only on good going or softer.
M. R. Channon

MAKATI 5 b.g. Efisio 120 – Seleter (Hotfoot 126) [1998 –, a58: 11v⁵ a11g² 13.8d 37
a14g⁴ a14g* a16.2g* a14.8g² a12g² 1999 17.1v a16.2g a16g⁵ 16.1m a14g² a16.2g³ a58

a14.8g² a16.2g⁶ a14g* Oct 18] big, strong gelding: modest handicapper on all-weather, poor on turf: won at Southwell in October: effective at 1½m to 2m: acts on fibresand: sold 16,000 gns. *Miss J. A. Camacho*

MAKEIT MUSIC 3 b.g. Komaite (USA) – Gandoorah 90 (Record Token 128) –
[1998 –: 5g 6d 5d 7m 1999 7.5g Aug 29] sturdy, lengthy gelding: no form. *Mrs A. M. Naughton*

MAKE NO MISTAKE (IRE) 4 b.c. Darshaan 133 – Respectfully (USA) (The **116**
Minstrel (CAN) 135) [1998 112: 10s³ 10m³ 12s² 12v 10g² 10m* 10d⁶ 1999 10.5g³ 12m 10m* 10m 10.2g Oct 23] IR 67,000Y: tall colt: seventh foal: half-brother to 3 winners, including Irish 7f to 8.5f winner Robertolomy (by Roberto) and Irish 1¼m and 2m winner Limbo Lady (by Theatrical): dam, ran once in France, from family of Be My Guest: smart performer: third to Shiva in Tattersalls Gold Cup at the Curragh prior to winning Meld Stakes on same course in July by 4 lengths from Saffron Walden: well held otherwise, including in BMW Cox Plate (had bruised foot in week before) at Moonee Valley on final start: best around 1¼m: acts on soft and good to firm going, well held on heavy: usually blinkered: races prominently: joined C. Clement in USA. *D. K. Weld, Ireland*

MAKE READY 5 b.m. Beveled (USA) – Prepare (IRE) 58 (Millfontaine 114) **76**
[1998 46: a6g a5g 5.1g⁶ 5m⁶ 7.1g 7m a6g 6f² 7g 6g 1999 a6g* a5g⁴ a5g⁵ a5g⁵ 6m² **a62**
6.1g* 6g 5.7g⁵ 6m⁶ 6.1m⁴ 6m* 6m⁵ 6.1m a6g Nov 22] tall mare: fair handicapper on turf, modest on all-weather: won at Wolverhampton in April, Chepstow in May and Newmarket (carried head bit awkwardly) in July: best at 6f: acts on fibresand, firm and good to soft going: visored once at 3 yrs: often races up with pace: often apprentice ridden. *J. Neville*

MAKE RINGS 3 b.f. Rainbow Quest (USA) 134 – Guillem (USA) 76 (Nijinsky –
(CAN) 138) [1998 NR 1999 14g⁶ Aug 14] third foal: dam ran over 11.5f only start, closely related to smart winner at up to 1½m Lydian and half-sister to Ribblesdale winner Ballinderry, herself dam of Sanglamore: soundly beaten in maiden at Lingfield: sold 15,000 gns in December. *H. R. A. Cecil*

MAKE WAY (USA) 3 b.g. Red Ransom (USA) – Way of The World (USA) **92**
(Dance of Life (USA)) [1998 59p: 5.7g 1999 7d² 8.3m* 10m³ 10d⁴ 8.3m³ 8m⁶ Sep 18] quite attractive gelding: fairly useful performer: won maiden at Windsor in June, despite hanging left: creditable efforts in handicaps next 2 starts: stays 1¼m: yet to race on extremes of going: blinkered last 2 starts: has had 2 handlers in paddock: raced up with pace after third outing. *B. J. Meehan*

MAKNAAS 3 ch.c. Wolfhound (USA) 126 – White-Wash 94 (Final Straw 127) **63**
[1998 –: 7g 6g 1999 7m 8g a7g 8s³ 10s⁴ a10g⁵ a13g³ a16.2g* Dec 15] smallish, sturdy, lengthy colt: modest handicapper: left R. Armstrong 11,000 gns after sixth start: won at Wolverhampton in December: effective at 13f to 2m: acts on all-weather and soft going, probably on good to firm: blinkered third to sixth starts: sometimes looked difficult ride for previous stable. *T. G. Mills*

MALAAH (IRE) 3 gr.g. Pips Pride 117 – Lingdale Lass 60 (Petong 126) [1998 **60**
70: 6f 1999 7f 8g 6g 7m⁶ 5f⁶ Jun 26] good-topped gelding: disappointing maiden: will prove best up to 7f: blinkered last 2 starts: sold 4,500 gns, joined Julian Poulton. *R. W. Armstrong*

MALADERIE (IRE) 5 b.g. Thatching 131 – Native Melody (Tudor Music 131) **79**
[1998 78: 6.1v⁵ 6g⁴ 7g³ 7f 6f² 6g² 6g⁶ 5m² 6m² 5f 6m³ 6g⁶ 5m* 5m² 5m⁶ 5.3m⁵ 5m* 5.1d⁴ 6m 5g* 5d⁵ 5d 1999 7g 5d 7m⁶ 5d 5s⁶ 5f⁶ 5.7g* 6m³ 6m 6d 5f² 5m³ 5f³ 5.7m 5g⁵ 5g 5m⁵ 5m 5m 5g 5d 5s a6g Nov 15] close-coupled gelding: fair handicapper: won at Bath in June: lost form towards end of year: probably best at 5f/6f on good going or firmer: usually visored, blinkered final start: has had tongue tied. *M. Dods*

MALAKAL (IRE) 3 b.c. Shernazar 131 – Malmada (USA) (Fappiano (USA)) **76**
[1998 NR 1999 9s⁴ 10m⁴ 10g² a10g a7g Dec 11] first foal: dam unraced daughter of **a–**
very smart French 9f to 10.5f winner Masmouda: fair form in maidens at the Curragh (2) and Roscommon when trained by J.Oxx in Ireland (sold 17,000 gns in October): well beaten on all-weather in Britain: stays 1¼m: acts on soft and good to firm going. *B. J. Curley*

MALCHIK   3 ch.c. Absalom 128 – Very Good (Noalto 120) [1998 48: 5.3g 5m 6f   **–**
a6g 7m 6g 7m³ 7f 8g* 8m 8d 8d 8d a8f⁶ a7g³ 1999 a10g³ a8g² a8f⁴ a10g³ a8g³ a8g⁶   **a48**
a10g⁵ 8.3m 8v 11.6g 8m a9.4g² a12g⁶ a8.5g⁵ a16g³ 10g 8d a10g a10g a7g⁵ a10g a7g⁵
Dec 29] leggy colt: poor handicapper: stays 1¼m: acts on all-weather, no recent form
on turf: blinkered (ran poorly) once at 2 yrs. *P. Howling*

MALE-ANA-MOU (IRE)   6 ch.g. Ela-Mana-Mou 132 – Glasson Lady (GER)   **90**
108 (Priamos (GER) 123) [1998 85d: 12f² 13.3g⁴ 14g 14m⁴ 12m 14m⁶ 1999 14.1m
14.4m 14m* 20m 14m 14.1g* 14m* 16m³ 13.9d⁵ 16s² Oct 22] fairly useful handicapper: won at Sandown in June and Salisbury then Sandown in August: good 6
lengths second of 17 to Nicely at Newbury final start: stays 2m: yet to race on heavy
going, acts on any other: races up with pace: more reliable in 1999 than in the past.
Jamie Poulton

MALIAN (IRE)   3 b. or br.g. Arcane (USA) – Rhein Valley (IRE) (Kings Lake   **68**
(USA) 133) [1998 NR 1999 11.1g 12g 12g⁵ 18m⁵ 14.1m Jul 30] sturdy gelding:
fourth reported foal: brother to 1½m winner Kierans Bridge: dam once-raced sister
to Irish St Leger and Gold Cup runner-up Tyrone Bridge: fair maiden: likely to prove
best at 2m+: raced only on good to firm going. *A. P. Jarvis*

MALIBU MAN   7 ch.g. Ballacashtal (CAN) – National Time (USA) (Lord Avie   **74 §**
(USA)) [1998 80§, a72§: 6v 5s⁴ a5g⁶ 5.1g 5g³ 5m⁶ 5g 5.7d 5.1m 1999 5s* 5.3f   **a87 §**
6f a5g³ 5.7f⁵ Jun 26] quite good-topped gelding: has a round action: fairly useful
handicapper on all-weather, fair on turf: won at Folkestone in March: best at 5f/
sharp 6f: acts on firm ground, soft and on fibresand (yet to race on equitrack): tried
blinkered/visored: sometimes sweating: often starts slowly (has reared stalls): not
one to trust implicitly. *E. A. Wheeler*

MALLEUS   2 ch.g. (Mar 21) Hamas (IRE) 125§ – Queen Warrior 74 (Daring   **75**
March 116) [1999 6s⁵ 7m⁵ 7.6g³ 8s² Sep 22] second live foal: dam won around 1m:
fair maiden: unlikely to stay much beyond 1m: acts on soft and good to firm going.
P. T. Walwyn

MALLIA   6 b.g. Statoblest 120 – Pronetta (USA) (Mr Prospector (USA)) [1998 76:   **82 §**
7d 6v* 6s 6d³ 6g 6s 5s 6.1v a6g⁵ a6g* a5g⁵ 1999 a6g² a6g³ a6g a6f² a6g a6g⁵ a6g*
a6g³ 6v² 6g a6g* 6s³ 6m 6d* 6m⁴ 6s⁶ 6m⁴ 5g 6d 6m² 6g 6d 6d 6d 6d⁴ a6g⁶ a6g
Nov 30] lengthy, dipped-backed gelding: fairly useful performer: won claimer at
Wolverhampton in March and handicaps at same track in May and Haydock in July:
best at 6f: acts on good to firm ground, heavy and all-weather: blinkered/visored:
held up, and sometimes finds little. *T. D. Barron*

MALL QUEEN (USA)   2 b.f. (Feb 14) Sheikh Albadou 128 – Hiaam (USA) 110   **94 +**
(Alydar (USA)) [1999 6g* 5.5g³ 6d Sep 28] good-topped filly: seventh foal: half-
sister to several winners, including useful French 1996 2-y-o 6f winner Sheer Reason
(by Danzig) and useful 11.5f winner Munnaya (by Nijinsky): dam 6f (including
Princess Margaret Stakes at 2 yrs) and 1m winner from family of Swain: won
4-runner listed newcomers race at Deauville in August: 3 lengths third of 8 to Moon
Driver in Prix d'Arenberg at Chantilly (didn't get best of runs), then well held in
Cheveley Park Stakes at Newmarket (pulled hard early) final start: likely to prove
best at 5f/6f. *Mme C. Head, France*

MAMA-SAN (IRE)   4 b.f. Doyoun 124 – Avila 76 (Ajdal (USA) 130) [1998 NR   **58**
1999 a8.5g⁴ a8.5g⁴ 10v 10m 8.3m 10.5m a10g a12g² 10.5d* 9.9v³ Sep 29] lengthy   **a53**
filly: second foal: closely related to a winner in Austria by Shirley Heights: dam,
third once from 2 starts at 7f, half-sister to smart middle-distance colts Nomrood,
Alleging and Monastery: modest handicapper: won 20-runner claiming event at
Warwick in September: seemed best around 1¼m: acted on heavy going and fibresand: dead. *N. A. Callaghan*

MAMBLE'S PENSION (IRE)   4 ch.f. Elmaamul (USA) 125 – Chance All (FR)   **–**
88 (Glenstal (USA) 118) [1998 34?, a–: a9.4g 6s⁴ 6.1v 6.1d a7g 1999 6m May 24]
poor maiden: should stay at least 7f: acts on soft going and fibresand. *A. Bailey*

MAMMA'S BOY   4 b.g. Rock City 120 – Henpot (IRE) 68 (Alzao (USA) 117)   **64**
[1998 74: 6v³ 7.5s 6g⁴ 7.1s² 6d³ 6g* 6g⁵ 6s 5m² a7g⁶ 5g* 6d⁴ 5d 1999 6v 6d 6f 7s*
7.1m* 7m 7.1g³ 6m⁵ 7.1d 5f⁶ 5m³ 6f⁴ 6f 6d⁶ 6g⁶ 6m⁴ 6g 7g Oct 16] sturdy gelding:
modest performer: won seller at Thirsk and claimer at Musselburgh, both in May:

mostly respectable efforts after: effective at 5f (given strong gallop) to 7f: acts on any turf going (below best only run on fibresand): blinkered third start. *J. Berry*

MAMMAS F·C (IRE) 3 ch.f. Case Law 113 – Wasaif (IRE) 79 (Lomond (USA) **65** 128) [1998 66: 5s² a5g² a5g a5g² 5g⁶ a5g* 5m* a5g⁶ 5d² 6m 6m* 6m a6g 1999 a5g⁴ 6g⁴ a5g⁴ a5g⁵ 5.1g² 6m⁴ 7g² 6.8m⁴ 7f* 5.7h³ 6g³ 6m* 6m⁴ 6g 5.1s² 6d Nov 4] good-bodied filly: fair performer: won claimers at Folkestone and Bath and handicap at Ripon in July/August: effective at 5f to easy 7f: acts on hard going, soft and fibresand: usually held up: tough. *J. M. Bradley*

MAMZUG (IRE) 2 b.c. (Apr 23) Hamas (IRE) 125§ – Bellissi (IRE) 77 (Blue- **–** bird (USA) 125) [1999 7d Oct 27] IR 58,000F, 42,000Y: first foal: dam, Irish 7f/1m winner, sister to smart Irish 7f winner Wild Bluebell and half-sister to Moyglare Stud Stakes winner Priory Belle: well beaten in maiden at Yarmouth: sold 3,800 gns in November. *B. Hanbury*

MANA D'ARGENT (IRE) 2 b.c. (Apr 25) Ela-Mana-Mou 132 – Petite-D- **75** Argent 91 (Noalto 120) [1999 7g⁶ 6s³ 6h³ Oct 23] small, quite attractive colt: good walker: first foal: dam 6f (at 2 yrs) to 7f winner: fair maiden: made running when third at Newcastle and Newbury last 2 starts: will stay 7f, probably 1m. *M. Johnston*

MANA-MOU BAY (IRE) 2 b.c. (Feb 12) Ela-Mana-Mou 132 – Summerhill **98 p** (Habitat 134) [1999 6m² 7g* Aug 13] IR 21,000F, 42,000Y: good-bodied colt: sixth foal: half-brother to 3-y-o Top of The Pops, fairly useful Irish 7f/1m winner Two Bandits (by Thatching) and a winner in Italy by Glow: dam Irish 6f winner: confirmed promise when justifying favouritism in 6-runner listed race at Newbury by 1¼ lengths from Tioga, drifting left once leading final 1f: will stay at least 1m: capable of better still. *R. Hannon*

MANCALA 3 ch.f. Deploy 131 – Alghabrah 70 (Lomond (USA) 128) [1998 67: **–** 6.9f 8.5s³ 8.1m⁶ 1999 12.5d 8f⁵ May 27] smallish, good-topped filly: fair maiden at 2 yrs: well below form both 3-y-o starts: should be suited by 1¼m/1½m: sold 1,200 gns. *P. F. I. Cole*

MANCHURIA (IRE) 3 ch.c. Indian Ridge 123 – Shih Ching (USA) (Secreto **75** (USA) 128) [1998 NR 1999 6s 7.1d³ 6m³ 7g² Jul 14] IR 200,000Y: sturdy colt: fifth foal: brother to fairly useful Irish 9.6f winner Hayward and half-brother to fairly useful 1m winner Province (by Dominion) and a winner in Germany (up to 9f, by Taufan): dam unraced half-sister to dual Grade 1 winner Dontstop Themusic: fair maiden: best efforts last 2 starts: headstrong, likely to prove best up to 7f: tongue tied after debut: sent to UAE. *J. H. M. Gosden*

MANCINI 6 b. or br.g. Nomination 125 – Roman Blue (Charlottown 127) [1998 **–** –: 10v 1999 18d May 19] workmanlike gelding: fair at 2 yrs: generally well beaten since, including in visor. *J. A. B. Old*

MANDOOB 2 b.c. (Apr 29) Zafonic (USA) 130 – Thaidah (CAN) 105 (Vice **64 p** Regent (CAN)) [1999 7d⁵ Oct 12] seventh foal: half-brother to several winners, including smart 1m winner Kismah (by Machiavellian) and French middle-distance winner Mawayed (by Blushing Groom): dam, 5f (at 2 yrs) to 7f winner, half-sister to Devil's Bag and top-class filly Glorious Song, latter dam of Singspiel: weak in market and green, 11¾ lengths fifth of 15 to Ferzao in maiden at Leicester, one-paced when shaken up: will stay at least 1m: should do a fair bit better. *A. C. Stewart*

MANE FRAME 4 b.g. Unfuwain (USA) 131 – Moviegoer 104 (Pharly (FR) 130) **73** [1998 69: 10d 10.1g⁵ 12g⁴ 14m³ 17.1m 16s 11.7v² 12s³ 1999 14.1d² 11.6d* 13.3f⁴ 12.3s* 14m* 16.1m⁴ 13s² 13.9d⁶ 16.5s⁴ Nov 6] rangy gelding: fair performer: won minor event at Windsor in April and handicaps at Warwick in June and Sandown in July, making all in first 2-named: effective at 1½m (given good test) to 2m: acts on any going except possibly firm: has been bandaged: game and reliable. *H. Morrison*

MANFUL 7 b.g. Efisio 120 – Mandrian 103 (Mandamus 120) [1998 70, a55: 11.1v **66** 11.1m³ 9.9m⁴ 11.1d² 10s* 10.4g³ 10.9d³ 12.1s⁵ 11.9g 11s² a12g³ a11g 1999 a11g **a33 +** a11g⁶ 11.1v⁶ 13v 11d² 10d³ 10.1m* 10.9s* 10.5s² 11.1f 11.1m 12.1f 10.9d⁶ 13s 10v⁴ 10.1d 11d³ a12g a16.2g Dec 15] fair handicapper on turf, poor on all-weather nowadays: won at Ayr in June: generally below form after, leaving Miss L. Perratt after eighteenth start: effective at 1¼m/1½m: acts on any turf/all-weather: usually blinkered, has been visored: usually held up. *R. Brotherton*

MANGUS (IRE) 5 b.g. Mac's Imp (USA) 116 – Holly Bird (Runnett 125) [1998 **69 §** 82§: a5g 5d⁵ 5.1s 5m 5m* 5m a5g* 5.1d 5g 5.7d⁶ 5.1g 5m⁴ 1999 a5g⁴ a5g⁴ a5g² **a88 §** 5.2m 5s 5.3f³ 5g⁴ 5g 5d³ 5f³ 5m 5.1m² 5m 5d² a5g a5g* a5g⁴ Dec 15] workmanlike gelding: fairly useful on all-weather, fair on turf: won at Wolverhampton in December: has form at 6f, but raced mainly at 5f: acts on firm going, good to soft and all-weather: sometimes starts slowly/fails to go through with effort: not one to trust. *K. O. Cunningham-Brown*

MANICURE (IRE) 3 b.f. Lucky Guest 109 – Mana (GER) (Windwurf (GER)) **78 §** [1998 –: 6.1s 1999 6.1f 8g² 8m² 10m* 10.5s 9.1v Oct 12] leggy, sparely-made filly: fair performer: not at best when landing odds in maiden at Leicester in July: looked ungenuine last 2 starts: may prove best at 1m/1¼m: acts on good to firm going: has been bandaged in front: sold 7,000 gns. *E. A. L. Dunlop*

MANIKATO (USA) 5 b.g. Clever Trick (USA) – Pasampsi (USA) (Crow (FR) **40** 134) [1998 –, a55: a10g⁴ a10g³ a8.5g³ a7g⁴ a2g⁴ a8g⁴ 8.2m 7.1d a10f 1999 a7g⁵ a7g 11.5m⁶ 10d 12.3m Jul 17] close-coupled gelding: poor maiden: left D. Cosgrove after second start: possibly needs further than 7f nowadays, and stays 1½m: acts on firm going, good to soft and all-weather: sometimes visored. *T. T. Clement*

MANILENO 5 ch.g. K-Battery 108 – Andalucia 57 (Rheingold 137) [1998 71: **61** a16g* a14g* 1999 a16.2g⁵ a16.2g* a14.8g* a16.2g⁶ a14.8g⁴ 15.8m Jun 23] small, light-framed gelding: has a round action: modest performer, lightly raced: won seller and claimer at Wolverhampton in February: seems to stay 17f: acts on fibresand and any turf going: tried blinkered: races prominently. *Miss S. J. Wilton*

MANNDAR (IRE) 3 b.c. Doyoun 124 – Madiriya 119 (Diesis 133) [1998 NR **115** 1999 8g² 8m² 10.2g* 10d* 12m⁴ 10g³ 10d³ 9f⁴ 9f² Nov 28] strong, good sort: fluent mover: fourth foal: half-brother to smart 1m/1¼m winner Mandilak (by El Gran Senor): dam won up to 1½m: smart performer: won minor event at Bath in May and listed race at Newmarket in June: creditable efforts after in King Edward VII Stakes at Royal Ascot, Prix Eugene Adam at Maisons-Laffitte, Prix du Prince d'Orange (final start for L. Cumani, length third of 4 to State Shinto) at Longchamp, Grade 2 race at Santa Anita and Hollywood Derby (2 lengths second to Super Quercus): best at 9f/1¼m: acts on firm and good to soft going: has wandered and found little. *C. B. Greely, USA*

MAN OF COURAGE 4 b.g. Nashwan (USA) 135 – Dafrah (USA) 78 (Danzig **76** (USA)) [1998 84: 10f⁶ 10s³ 1999 11.8g² 12m³ 12g Jun 5] deep-bodied, angular gelding: has a long, round action: fair maiden in 1999: stays 1½m: sold 4,500 gns. *E. A. L. Dunlop*

MAN OF THE NIGHT 3 b.g. Clantime 101 – Forbidden Monkey 47 (Gabitat **–** 119) [1998 63: 5d⁴ 6f 7s⁶ 1999 7g 8d 12.3m 12g⁶ Jul 3] leggy gelding: modest at 2 yrs: well held in 1999: blinkered final start: subsequently won over hurdles. *J. J. O'Neill*

MANOLO (FR) 6 b.g. Cricket Ball (USA) 124 – Malouna (FR) (General Holme **60** (USA) 128) [1998 –, a75: a6g a6g* a5g* a6g 5v 1999 7g 6.8d 6.5g 8d³ 7s⁵ 7d Sep 17] small, lengthy gelding: fair handicapper in Britain prior to 1999 season: showed he retains some ability in France for A. de Moussac before only outing for new trainer: probably best at 5f/6f: acts on firm ground and equitrack: usually blinkered/visored (not at 6 yrs). *D. Nicholls*

MAN O'MYSTERY (USA) 2 b.c. (Jan 23) Diesis 133 – Eurostorm (USA) 104 **59** (Storm Bird (CAN) 134) [1999 7m Aug 27] 95,000Y: first foal: dam, Irish 7f (at 2 yrs) to 1¼m winner and later successful in USA, daughter of Irish St Leger winner Eurobird, herself half-sister to Assert and Bikala: raced freely and made only short-lived effort when eleventh of 16 in maiden at Newmarket: may do better. *J. Noseda*

MANSA MUSA (IRE) 4 br.g. Hamas (IRE) 125§ – Marton Maid 74 (Silly **76** Season 127) [1998 73: 8v³ 8s³ 9m² 8f⁵ 10.1g² 9.9g 10.2s³ 12g 1999 a10g⁶ 10.8d 8f* 10s 8m⁶ 8.5d⁴ 9.2g Jun 16] leggy gelding: fair performer: won minor event at Brighton in April: stays 1¼m: below form on heavy going, acts on any other on turf. *M. R. Channon*

MANSTAR (IRE) 2 b.g. (Feb 3) In The Wings 128 – Model Village 101 (Habitat **61** 134) [1999 6m 7d³ 7.5m⁴ 8.3f⁵ 8d Sep 18] 27,000Y: medium-sized, workmanlike gelding: fifth foal: half-brother to fairly useful 1m winner Polska Modelle (by Polish Precedent): dam 7f/1m winner: modest maiden: easily best effort on second start: should stay 1m. *C. W. Fairhurst*

MANTILLA   2 b.f. (Mar 17) Son Pardo 107 – Well Tried (IRE) 43 (Thatching   **73** 131) [1999 5d⁵ 6s³ a5g⁴ Nov 20] second foal: dam poor maiden: fair form in maidens at Redcar, Doncaster and Wolverhampton: stays 6f: acts on fibresand. *R. Hollinshead*

MANTLES PRIDE   4 b.g. Petong 126 – State Romance 67 (Free State 125)   **93** [1998 82: 5s³ 6.1m³ 6f 6s 6d 6g 6m 6g 7.1g³ 6v² 7s 1999 7m³ 7m⁵ 7d³ 7d 8m⁶ 6.9m* 7.6m 7m* 7.1m* 7.1d³ 7g Oct 14] sparely-made gelding: fluent mover: fairly useful handicapper: won at Carlisle in July, Redcar in August and Haydock in September: didn't get run of race final start: best efforts around 7f: acts on good to firm and heavy going: visored/blinkered: has been bandaged: usually held up: tends to carry head awkwardly: joined J. Glover. *P. Calver*

MANTLES PRINCESS   4 b.f. Rock City 120 – Teslemi (USA) 73 (Ogygian   **37** (USA)) [1998 59: 8d 1999 a10g³ 8.2s 12v Apr 20] sturdy filly: poor maiden: sent to Australia. *G. Lewis*

MANTUSIS (IRE)   4 ch.g. Pursuit of Love 124 – Mana (GER) (Windwurf   **92** (GER)) [1998 97: 10v³ 10g 7s² 7g 7m 8s 1999 8m 8g 10f² 10m³ 11.8m³ 10m⁴ 10m 10s 10.1m* Oct 19] sturdy, useful-looking gelding: has a markedly round action: fairly useful handicapper: in frame 4 times before winning at Yarmouth in October: stays 1½m, at least in steadily-run race: acts on firm and soft going. *P. W. Harris*

MANUFAN   4 b.c. Sabrehill (USA) 120 – The Last Empress (IRE) 73 (Last   **55** Tycoon 131) [1998 69: 10m 11.7s⁴ 12.3g³ 14.1m 12m 12g 8m² 7d² 1999 7.1d 7g³ 8s 7.7m⁴ 7f³ 8.2m 10m 8f 7d³ 8d Oct 20] lengthy colt: modest maiden handicapper: best at 7f/1m: acts on firm and good to soft going: blinkered sixth start: inconsistent: sold 3,000 gns, joined G. Woodward. *W. R. Muir*

MANX SHADOW   2 b. or br.f. (May 22) Contract Law (USA) 108 – Inbisat 68   **–** (Beldale Flutter (USA) 130) [1999 5.1s 5m 5m 6m 7f⁵ 8.5g Aug 29] 500Y: sparely-made filly: seventh foal: dam disqualified 1¾m winner: no form. *K. W. Hogg, Isle of Man*

MANXWOOD (IRE)   2 b.c. (Apr 25) Petorius 117 – Eliza Wooding 70 (Faustus   **57** (USA) 118) [1999 6m 7m a6g⁴ 7.9m⁶ 8s Sep 16] IR 5,600F, IR 4,000Y: rather leggy colt: unimpressive mover: half-brother to a winner at up to 9f in Italy by Forest Wind: dam, 7f seller winner at 2 yrs, probably stayed 1m: modest maiden: left R. Ingram after second start: best efforts next 2 outings: will probably stay beyond 1m: acts on good to firm ground and fibresand. *D. J. S. Cosgrove*

MANY HAPPY RETURNS   2 br.f. (Jan 28) Bin Ajwaad (IRE) 119 – Daarat   **–** Alayaam (IRE) (Reference Point 139) [1999 6g 6.1m Jul 3] 5,400Y: first foal: dam unraced daughter of smart 1¼m winner Tralthee: always behind in maidens: will probably be suited by 1m+. *G. B. Balding*

MANZONI   3 b.g. Warrshan (USA) 117 – Arc Empress Jane (IRE) (Rainbow   **58** Quest (USA) 134) [1998 56: 6f 7g⁵ 6g 8d 1999 5g 6s 9.3g⁴ a12g³ a12g* 12m² 12.4g² Aug 20] small gelding: modest handicapper: made all at Southwell in July: seems best around 1½m: acts on good to firm going, good to soft and fibresand: blinkered fifth/sixth starts: usually races prominently. *M. W. Easterby*

MANZOR (FR)   2 b.c. (Apr 26) Cricket Ball (USA) 124 – Amarige (Lesotho   **110 +** (USA) 118) [1999 5d⁵ 5s* 5.5g⁴ 5s* 5v* Oct 24] second foal: brother to French 3-y-o 4.5f (at 2 yrs) to 1m winner Domineguine: dam third at 2 yrs in France: progressive form: won newcomers race at Bordeaux in March, minor event at Longchamp in April (final start for D. Soubagne) and listed race at Maisons-Laffitte then Prix du Petit Couvert at Longchamp (beat Nuclear Debate ¾ length) in October: should stay 6f: acts on heavy ground, yet to race on firmer than good: may do better still. *X. Nakkachdji, France*

MAPLE (IRE)   3 ch.g. Soviet Lad (USA) – Little Red Rose (Precocious 126)   **90 d** [1998 91: 5d 5m² 6m⁶ 6m² 5m⁴ 7d² 6g* 5g³ 7s 1999 7g 6s 6m³ 6d⁵ 6m 6m 7f 6.8g⁶ 5d 7.1s a7g a8g⁶ a10g³ Dec 22] sturdy, lengthy gelding: fairly useful handicapper: finished lame fifth start, and mostly disappointing after, leaving D. Elsworth before eleventh outing: stays easy 1¼m: acts on equitrack, good to firm and good to soft going: has been bandaged behind: inconsistent. *S. Dow*

MARADI (IRE)   5 b.g. Marju (IRE) 127 – Tigora (Ahonoora 122) [1998 47:   **53** 10.3d 10v 10m 12d⁴ 10m² 1999 a13g² a12f² a10g⁶ Jan 21] leggy gelding: modest handicapper: ran creditably first 2 starts in 1999: stays 13f: acts on all-weather, best turf form on good going or firmer: visored final outing: races freely and has looked a difficult ride. *B. J. Curley*

MARAH   2 ch.f. (Jan 18) Machiavellian (USA) 123 – Samheh (USA) 62 (Private   **93** Account (USA)) [1999 7m* 7.1m³ 7m 7.3s⁶ Oct 23] leggy, angular filly: has a quick action: first foal: dam, maiden who stayed 1¼m, daughter of 9f Kentucky Oaks winner Lucky Lucky Lucky: fairly useful form: won maiden at Doncaster in June: best effort when third of 5 to Hypnotize (beaten 2 necks) in listed event at Sandown in July: off course 2 months before well held in another listed race at Newbury (had gone in coat) final start: likely to stay 1¼m: acts on good to firm going. *J. L. Dunlop*

MARAHA   2 ch.f. (Mar 5) Lammtarra (USA) 134 – Taroob (IRE) 72 (Roberto   **79** (USA) 131) [1999 7m⁶ 8.1s* 8d Oct 30] angular filly: fourth foal: half-sister to 3-y-o Hararah (by Barathea) and a winner in Macau: dam, 2-y-o 9f winner who stayed 1¾m, sister to Celestial Storm: fair form: won maiden at Haydock in September: much stiffer task, far from discredited when eighth of 10 in listed event at Newmarket final start: will stay 1½m: may still do better. *J. L. Dunlop*

MARAMBA   3 b.f. Rainbow Quest (USA) 134 – Gayane 125 (Nureyev (USA)   **97** 131) [1998 NR 1999 10s⁴ 8.1m* 8g 9d⁴ 10.5v Nov 26] 33,000 2-y-o: seventh foal: closely related to fairly useful 6f winner Duel At Dawn (by Nashwan) and 5-y-o Giko: dam, 6f/7f winner, half-sister to Sun Chariot winner Ristna from family of Oh So Sharp: useful form: won maiden at Sandown (4 months after debut) in August, making most and flashing tail under pressure: easily best effort in listed races after when ½-length fourth to Shemaya at Longchamp (first run after leaving P. Chapple-Hyam), finishing well from rear: should stay 1¼m. *G. A. Butler*

MARASEM   3 b.f. Cadeaux Genereux 131 – Balaabel (USA) 83 (Sadler's Wells   **86 +** (USA) 132) [1998 NR 1999 7.1m* 8d Aug 8] quite attractive filly: first foal: dam, 1m winner, out of Princess Margaret winner Muhbubh: won maiden at Chepstow in July by 1½ lengths from Umbrian Gold, leading on bridle over 1f out: seemed to flounder on softer ground in listed race at Ascot next time: should stay 1m: sent to USA. *M. P. Tregoning*

MARATHON MAID   5 gr.m. Kalaglow 132 – El Rabab (USA) 70 (Roberto   **–** (USA) 131) [1998 67: 12d 10m 11.8m 8m* 10.1g⁶ 9.9m⁵ 8d 10s 8g⁶ 8d 1999 a8g Feb 15] leggy mare: fluent mover: fair handicapper in 1998: well held (all-weather debut) only 5-y-o start: seems effective at 1m to 1¾m: best on good going or firmer: tried blinkered/visored: inconsistent: sold 8,400 gns. *R. A. Fahey*

MARAUD   5 ch.g. Midyan (USA) 124 – Peak Squaw (USA) 75 (Icecapade (USA))   **27** [1998 NR 1999 13.8m 18g 16.2s³ 17.1g Aug 22] sparely-made gelding: winning hurdler, but only poor form on Flat since 2 yrs: tried blinkered. *M. E. Sowerby*

MARCH PARTY (FR)   3 ch.f. Archway (IRE) 115 – Social Gathering (IRE)   **49** (Dance of Life (USA)) [1998 49: 5.2s⁵ 5.1s 6.1m 7m 7g a7g* a7g 7.1m³ 8g 1999 a7g 10.8d⁶ 9.7v 10m 10f⁴ 8m 8.2f 8.1m 9g⁴ Aug 20] plain filly: poor performer: barely stays 11f: acts on fibresand, firm and good to soft going: blinkered penultimate start: inconsistent. *J. G. Portman*

MARCIANO   3 b.g. Rock Hopper 124 – Raintree Venture (Good Times (ITY))   **–** [1998 –: 6v 1999 a8g 12.1s 17.2m 16.2m Jul 19] little sign of ability: sold 5,200 gns. *C. W. Thornton*

MARCOMIR (USA)   6 b.h. Dayjur (USA) 137 – Mariella (USA) 106 (Roberto   **45 d** (USA) 131) [1998 –: a6g a7g 1999 7m 8d⁵ 12d 10.9s 10d 12.4m Jul 12] big horse: fair winner only 2-y-o start: poor form in 1999. *W. Storey*

MARCO'S PAL   3 ch.g. Timeless Times (USA) 99 – Parijoun (Manado 130)   **–** [1998 –: 5g 6.1m 7m 7m 1999 a8g a8f Jan 19] good-bodied gelding: only a little sign of ability. *A. P. Jarvis*

MARCUS MAXIMUS (USA) 4 ch.c. Woodman (USA) 126 – Star Pastures **120**
124 (Northfields (USA)) [1998 111: 11.5m* 10.3g* 11.9s⁴ 1999 12m 12.4f* May 27]
rather leggy colt: has a round action: very smart performer, lightly raced: needed
run (in Jockey Club Stakes at Newmarket) on reappearance, then improved to win
falsely-run 5-runner minor event at Newcastle by length from Travelmate: stays
1½m: acts on firm ground, ran poorly on soft: bandaged: carries head high, but game:
stays in training. *H. R. A. Cecil*

MARDANI (IRE) 4 b.g. Fairy King (USA) – Marmana (USA) (Blushing Groom **102**
(FR) 131) [1998 95: 10m⁴ 12g² 10s² 12m* 12g* 12.3g⁵ 1999 16.2s³ 13.9d⁴ 12g*
11.9f* 12f² 13.9g 14.6m² 12.3v Sep 26] tall, good sort: half-brother to several
winners, including smart French 1m/9f winner Masslama (by No Pass No Sale): dam
French middle-distance performer: useful performer: trained in Ireland in 1998 by
J. Oxx: won in small fields in handicaps at Beverley in June and York (rated stakes
by ½ length from Tough Leader) in July: ran creditably after when runner-up in
handicaps at Goodwood (behind Danish Rhapsody in listed rated stakes) and
Doncaster (to Knockholt): best at 1½m/1¾m: well held on heavy going final start,
acts on any other: usually races up with pace: carries head high but is genuine.
M. Johnston

MARENGO 5 b.g. Never So Bold 135 – Born To Dance 76 (Dancing Brave **71**
(USA) 140) [1998 71: a6g* a6g* 6s* 6m⁴ 6g³ 6g⁵ 6m a6g 1999 a6g 6d² 6g 5g 5g
5.9g 6f a6g⁶ 6d⁵ a6g 6g³ 6d⁴ 6d a7g⁵ a6g³ a6g a6g* a6g a6g³ Dec 27] small gelding:
fair performer: won handicap at Southwell in December: best at 6f: acts on fibresand,
firm and soft going: tried visored: usually races prominently: none too consistent.
M. J. Polglase

MARGARET'S DANCER 4 b.g. Rambo Dancer (CAN) 107 – Cateryne (Bally- **65 d**
moss 136) [1998 68: a6g 8m 7g³ 8s* 6.9d³ 8m 8g* 8.5m* 8d 8.2v² 8d 1999 a8g 8d⁴
8d 8.3d² 8s 8m 9g 8m⁶ 8.3s⁵ 8.2s⁵ a8.5g Nov 13] sturdy gelding: fair performer:
below form after fourth outing: stays 8.5f: acts on good to firm and heavy ground, no
form on all-weather: often blinkered at 2 yrs: usually tongue tied: often races
prominently: none too consistent. *J. L. Eyre*

MARGARETS FIRST 3 b.f. Puissance 110 – Margaret's Gift 101 (Beveled **–**
(USA)) [1998 NR 1999 6m 6m Jun 24] first foal: dam 5f (at 2 yrs) and 6f winner who
stayed 7f: always behind in maidens at Catterick and Newcastle. *J. Berry*

MARGARITA MOU 2 ch.f. (Apr 29) Clantime 101 – Needle Sharp 64 (Kris **–**
135) [1999 a5g 5m Jul 27] 1,000 2-y-o: second foal: dam maiden, stayed 1m: behind
in seller and maiden. *C. Smith*

MARIA FROM CAPLAW 2 ch.f. (Feb 9) Clantime 101 – Mary From Dunlow **–**
49 (Nicholas Bill 125) [1999 6f⁵ 5m 5f Sep 13] 5,000Y: fourth foal: sister to a winner
in Scandinavia and half-sister to 5-y-o Smokey From Caplaw: dam 2-y-o 5f winner:
well held in varied company. *J. J. O'Neill*

MARIA ISABELLA (USA) 4 ch.f. Kris 135 – Korveya (USA) 116 (Riverman **96**
(USA) 131) [1998 74p: 8.2v* 1999 8.5m² 10.1m² Jun 26] strong, good-bodied filly:
not the best of movers: half-sister to several winners, notably Bosra Sham, Hector
Protector and Shanghai: useful form: second in listed races at Newmarket (to Putuna)
and Newcastle (behind Fictitious): stays 1¼m: acts on good to firm going, successful
on heavy only 2-y-o start. *L. M. Cumani*

MARIANA 4 ch.f. Anshan 119 – Maria Cappuccini 70 (Siberian Express (USA) **38**
125) [1998 50, a48: a6g⁴ a7g² a7g⁴ a8g 8m 8.1g⁴ 6m 8m 7d 8v² a8g a7g a10g 1999
a7f³ a8g³ a7g⁴ 7s a8g⁴ 6s 7f 8d a7g Dec 11] rather leggy filly: disappointing maiden:
best at 7f/1m: acts on good to firm and all-weather: usually visored. *T. T. Clement*

MARIDPOUR (IRE) 4 b.c. Shernazar 131 – Maridana (USA) 86 (Nijinsky **117**
(CAN) 138) [1998 117: 10d 12d² 12.1d* 16.2d* 16.1v 15.9f³ 15d 1999 16.2d 16.4g³
14m* 15.9m 12d 16m Nov 2] strong, lengthy colt: smart performer: good 1½ lengths
third to Arctic Owl in Henry II Stakes at Sandown prior to winning IAWS Curragh
Cup in June by length from Yeoman's Point (made all): behind in Lonsdale Stakes
at York (final start for Sir Michael Stoute) and Caulfield Cup/Melbourne Cup in
Australia: stays 2m well: acts on firm and good to soft going, possibly unsuited by
heavy: has run well when sweating/edgy. *M. Moroney, New Zealand*

MARIGLIANO (USA) 6 b.g. Riverman (USA) 131 – Mount Holyoke 93 (Golden   **67**
Fleece (USA) 133) [1998 73, a79+: 8m⁴ 7.1s* 8m³ a7g* a7g 7f³ 6m 7g 7g² 7d⁴ 7s
1999 10s 7d⁶ Oct 27] tall gelding: has a round action: fair performer: better effort in
1999 on second start: will probably prove best up to 1m: acts on soft going, good
to firm and fibresand: has been bandaged: fairly useful hurdler, successful twice in
November. *K. A. Morgan*

MARILIA (IRE) 4 ch.f. River Falls 113 – Bronze Celtic (Stanford 121§) [1998   **–**
–: 8d⁵ 5m 7v⁵ 1999 a7g a7g 7g 5g 12.3g⁶ Jul 13] IR 1,200F, IR 2,000Y: first foal: dam
unraced: fair winner for J. Bolger in Ireland at 2 yrs: little form since (trained by
E. Lynam in 1998, Gay Kelleway on first 2 starts in 1999): best form at 6f: tried
blinkered. *H. Rogers, Ireland*

MARINO STREET 6 b.m. Totem (USA) 118 – Demerger 61 (Dominion 123)   **55**
[1998 45, a38: a5g⁴ a6g a6g³ a5g³ a5g a7g⁵ a6g³ 5.1g³ 7.6m⁴ 6m³ 7g 5.2g² 6m 7m   **a–**
6f⁴ 5g 1999 5.1m⁶ 5v⁵ 5m* 5d* 5m² 5m⁵ 5g⁶ 5.1m Sep 9] small, leggy mare: modest
handicapper on turf, poor on all-weather: more consistent in 1999 than in the past,
winning at Warwick in June and Haydock in July: best at 5f: acts on any turf/all-
weather: often blinkered/visored before 1999: usually held up. *B. A. McMahon*

MARISOL (IRE) 6 b.m. Mujtahid (USA) 118 – Stanerra's Star (Shadeed (USA)   **38**
135) [1998 33: 10d 9.2s⁵ 7.1s⁵ 13m² 9g³ 1999 16g⁶ 12m 14g 12m 11.1m⁶ 9.2f⁶ Jul
16] poor maiden handicapper: stays 13f: acts on good to firm going, probably on soft:
has worn tongue strap: sold 1,400 gns. *P. Monteith*

MARITUN LAD 2 b.g. (Apr 14) Presidium 124 – Girl Next Door 58 (Local   **50**
Suitor (USA) 128) [1999 6s a7g⁶ a5g⁵ Nov 30] good-topped gelding: second foal:
half-brother to 3-y-o Starvine: dam 6f winner, including at 2 yrs: fifth of 15 in maiden
at Southwell: likely to prove best at 5f/6f: upset in stalls on debut. *D. Shaw*

MARJAANA (IRE) 6 b.m. Shaadi (USA) 126 – Funun (USA) 84 (Fappiano   **–**
(USA)) [1998 NR 1999 a7g 7g a7g Nov 12] lengthy mare: fairly useful at 4 yrs for
P. Walwyn: well beaten in 1999: best at 7f/1m: acts on firm and good to soft ground:
tried visored. *C. Smith*

MARJEUNE 2 b.f. (Feb 11) Marju (IRE) 127 – Ann Veronica (IRE) (Sadler's   **62**
Wells (USA) 132) [1999 7g⁵ 7.5g 7m 8s⁴ 10s* Oct 5] 12,000Y: first foal: dam, un-
raced, from family of Spectrum: modest form: best effort when winning nursery at
Nottingham in October: will stay at least 1½m: acts on soft going. *P. W. Harris*

MARJORIE ROSE (IRE) 6 b.m. Magical Strike (USA) 114 – Arrapata   **–**
(Thatching 131) [1998 –: a5g⁶ 6v 1999 a6g a6g a6g a5g³ a5g⁵ a5g Apr 24] work-
manlike mare: one-time fair handicapper, little show since 1997: tried blinkered.
R. Brotherton

MARJORY POLLEY 2 ch.f. (Mar 13) Timeless Times (USA) 99 – Rubylee 59   **–**
(Persian Bold 123) [1999 a5g⁴ 6g 7m Sep 2] first foal: dam, maiden, best at 2 yrs
when stayed 7.5f: well beaten in maidens. *P. T. Walwyn*

MARJU GUEST (IRE) 2 b.f. (Feb 26) Marju (IRE) 127 – Dance Ahead 81   **67**
(Shareef Dancer (USA) 135) [1999 6m 7m⁴ 7.5g⁴ Sep 15] IR 52,000Y: fourth foal:
sister to useful Irish 6f (at 2 yrs) and 7f winner Dance Clear, later successful up to 9f
in USA, and half-sister to a winner in Italy by Lycius: dam, 2-y-o 7f winner, from
family of Untold and Sally Brown: fair form when fourth in maidens at Salisbury and
Beverley: will stay 1¼m. *M. R. Channon*

MARKAN (USA) 3 ch.c. Affirmed (USA) – Norma (USA) (Procida (USA) 129)   **109**
[1998 105p: 7s 7m* 1999 8.5g⁴ 12m 10m³ 8f Jul 29] big, lengthy colt: fluent mover:
useful performer: in frame at Newmarket in listed race (5 lengths fourth to Golden
Snake) in April and quite valuable handicap (equal-third to Zindabad) in July: stiff
task second start: stays 1¼m: acts on good to firm going: sent to USA. *P. F. I. Cole*

MARKELLIS (USA) 3 b.g. Housebuster (USA) – Crimsons Contender (USA)   **46**
(Monsieur Champlain (USA)) [1998 –: 7s 1999 8d 12m⁵ 12g⁶ 8.2s a12g⁶ a10g a12g⁶
a8g a14g a11g⁴ a12g* Dec 21] $30,000F, IR 80,000Y: first foal: dam unraced: poor
performer: left P. Prendergast, Ireland, for 5,500 gns after third start: won handicap at
Southwell in December: stays 1½m: acts on all-weather: tried blinkered. *D. Carroll*

MARK TIME   4 b.g. Pursuit of Love 124 – Quiet Harbour (Mill Reef (USA) 141)   **43**
[1998 63: 8.2s⁴ 7s 8m 8g 7s⁴ 8d³ 8.2v⁵ 8.2v 1999 a10g⁶ a10g⁴ a11g 7s 8.3m Apr 12]
modest maiden at best: stayed 1¼m: acted on equitrack, turf form only on going
softer than good: dead. *P. R. Hedger*

MARLENE   4 b.f. Komaite (USA) – Kaiserlinde (GER) (Frontal 122) [1998 68:   **–**
10d³ 1999 a12g Mar 8] plain filly: better effort in maidens on debut. *M. R. Channon*

MARMADUKE (IRE)   3 ch.g. Perugino (USA) 84 – Sympathy 77 (Precocious   **84**
126) [1998 75+: 7.5s* 8g 1999 10.2s⁵ 10.3f⁵ 6g⁵ 7.1m³ 7m⁴ 8.1g a7g a7g Nov 24]   **a–**
tall, close-coupled gelding: fairly useful performer: left L. Cumani 18,000 gns after
third start: well below form last 3 outings: may prove best around 7f: acts on soft and
good to firm going, well held on all-weather. *Miss Gay Kelleway*

MARNIE   2 ch.f. (Apr 13) First Trump 118 – Miss Aboyne 64 (Lochnager 132)   **58**
[1999 6d³ 6.8d 6d⁵ 6.1s Nov 1] 4,000F, 2,000Y: sturdy, lengthy filly: third foal: half-
sister to 4-y-o Aberkeen: dam 5f and 1m winner at 4/5 yrs: easily best effort when
third in maiden at Yarmouth on debut: saddle slipped next start: will prove best up to
1m. *M. J. Ryan*

MARNOR (USA)   3 ch.c. Diesis 133 – Love's Reward (Nonoalco (USA) 131)   **114**
[1998 NR 1999 10m² 10f* 10f³ Jul 11] $105,000F, 140,000Y: big, strong, lengthy
colt: type to carry condition: powerful mover, with a round action: sixth foal: brother
to 3 winners, including 4-y-o Altibr and very smart sprinter Keen Hunter, and half-
brother to 2 winners: dam lightly-raced half-sister to Bassenthwaite: long odds-on
winner of maiden at Newmarket in June: much better form when 1½ lengths third
of 4 to Danish Rhapsody in minor event at Newbury: raced only at 1¼m: retired.
H. R. A. Cecil

MAROMITO (IRE)   2 b.c. (Feb 8) Up And At 'em 109 – Amtico (Bairn (USA)   **79**
126) [1999 5m* 5f Jul 9] IR 10,000F, 7,200Y: sixth reported foal: half-brother to
1993 2-y-o 6f winner Kingswell Prince (by Nashamaa): dam unraced: fair form when
winning maiden at Lingfield on debut, making most: reportedly finished lame
following month. *R. Bastiman*

MARON   2 b.g. (Apr 17) Puissance 110 – Will Be Bold 79 (Bold Lad (IRE) 133)   **67**
[1999 5d 5s³ 5g² 5g³ 5.2m 5m* 5g⁴ 5g⁴ 6m³ 6m 6s a6g Oct 18] 7,000Y: rather leggy
gelding: second reported thoroughbred foal: dam, sprint maiden, half-sister to very
smart German middle-distance performer Kornado: fair performer: won minor event
at Hamilton in July: below form last 4 starts: may prove best at 5f: acts on good to
firm going. *J. Berry*

MARQUANTE (IRE)   4 b.f. Brief Truce (USA) 126 – Festive Season (USA)   **–**
(Lypheor 118) [1998 12.5s² 12s⁵ 10s 11d³ 9.5g³ 10m³ 12.5d⁶ 8d 10v* 1999 10m³ Jun
21] IR 8,000F: fourth foal: half-sister to 1995 2-y-o 1m winner D'Naan (by Royal
Academy) and a winner in Japan by Danehill: dam twice-raced half-sister to Prix
Marcel Boussac winner Mary Linoa: trained by Mme M. Bollack-Badel in France in
1998, winning apprentice handicap at Fontainebleau: outclassed in 3-runner minor
event at Windsor only 4-y-o start, but won over hurdles in July: stays 12.5f: acts on
heavy ground: blinkered last 4 starts in France. *D. J. Wintle*

MARRY ME   3 ch.f. Pursuit of Love 124 – Perfect Desire (USA) (Green Forest   **69 d**
(USA) 134) [1998 NR 1999 a10g⁴ 10m³ 8g 9m 8g 7.6f⁶ 10g 8s 10s Sep 29] third
foal: half-sister to useful German winner up to 11f Irish Stainy (by Robellino): dam,
French 4-y-o 1m winner, daughter of very smart French filly up to 1m Mysterieuse
Etoile: fair form second start: well beaten after, virtually refusing to race penultimate
outing: has had tongue tied: sold 1,000 gns, sent to Belgium. *C. E. Brittain*

MARSAD (IRE)   5 ch.g. Fayruz 116 – Broad Haven (IRE) (Be My Guest (USA)   **98**
126) [1998 88: 6v* 6d³ 6g³ 1999 6d* 6m 6d⁵ 6g⁶ 6d⁴ 6v³ 6d³ 7g Oct 16] good-topped
gelding: useful handicapper: won at Doncaster in March: generally good efforts after,
including when fifth to Pipalong in Great St Wilfrid at Ripon (best of those on stand
side), fourth to Grangeville in Ayr Gold Cup and third to Get Stuck In in quite
valuable event at York penultimate start: probably stays 7f: probably best on going
softer than good. *J. Akehurst*

MARSAYAS (IRE)   6 ch.g. Classic Music (USA) – Babiana (CAN) 90 (Sharpen   **–**
Up 127) [1998 NR 1999 a14.8g Jan 27] workmanlike gelding: modest in 1997:

well held only 6-y-o start: stays 2m: acts on firm and good to soft going: races prominently. *F. Jordan*

MARSHALL ST CYR   2 ch.g. (May 15) Emarati (USA) 74 – St Helena (Monsanto (FR) 121) [1999 5.1g 5d² a6g⁵ Nov 15] 11,000Y: half-brother to several winners, including 5-y-o Swino and 4-y-o Oriel Girl: dam, Italian sprinter, half-sister to useful sprinter Up And At'em: clearly best effort in maidens (fair form) when ½-length second of 16 to Footprints at Redcar: should stay 6f. *P. D. Evans*   **71**

MARSH MARIGOLD   5 br.m. Tina's Pet 121 – Pulga (Blakeney 126) [1998 –: 10v 10.5m 10d 1999 14.1s Mar 29] sparely-made mare: one-time fair handicapper: no form since 1997. *G. Fierro*   **–**

MARSKE MACHINE   4 ch.f. Prince Daniel (USA) – Ciboure 74 (Norwick (USA) 125) [1998 70: 8s 11g 7g 8m⁴ 8g³ 9.3m² 8m² 9.9m* 10g⁶ 9m* 8.5m 9d⁴ 9.7s⁴ 9g* 8d 1999 9.9m 8g 9.3m 10g* 10s⁴ 10.3m⁶ 10.5s 8d* 8m 8.5m 8f 9g Aug 20] strong, workmanlike filly: has a round action: fair handicapper: won at Pontefract in May and July: well beaten last 4 starts: effective at 1m/1¼m: acts on good to firm and soft going: gave trouble on way to start third outing, reared badly and unseated rider leaving stalls seventh and final ones: usually comes from off pace. *N. Tinkler*   **74**

MARTELLO   3 b.g. Polish Precedent (USA) 131 – Round Tower 93 (High Top 131) [1998 NR 1999 12m⁴ 10m 10m 11.9d⁶ 10m 8m 8s⁵ Oct 4] strong, rangy gelding: half-brother to several winners, including useful 1986 2-y-o 7f winner Roundlet (by Roberto) and fairly useful 1½m winner Moat Garden (by Sportin' Life): dam, 1¼m winner, out of half-sister to Highclere: fair form first 2 starts: generally disappointing after, visored final start: may prove best at 1¼m/1½m: joined P. Webber. *R. Charlton*   **75 d**

MARTHA REILLY (IRE)   3 ch.f. Rainbows For Life (CAN) – Debach Delight 97 (Great Nephew 126) [1998 45: 6g 7m 6.1g 7f 7m 8.2s a8g a7g⁵ a8g⁵ 1999 a10g⁶ a8g* a8g³ 7s a11g 11.6m a10g⁴ 11.6g a10g a12g³ a14g⁴ a12g⁶ Dec 21] smallish, sparely-made filly: modest performer: won seller at Southwell in February: respectable efforts last 3 starts: stays 1½m: acts on all-weather and firm going: tried blinkered: has looked difficult ride. *Mrs Barbara Waring*   **a51**

MARTINDALE (IRE)   6 b.g. Fairy King (USA) – Whist Awhile (Caerleon (USA) 132) [1998 44: a5g² 6g a5g a7g 6g* 6g 6m a6g 6g a6g 1999 a6g a7g Jan 11] tall, sparely-made gelding: poor handicapper at best: best at 5f/6f: acts on fibresand, best turf run on good going: usually blinkered/visored in 1998: hung left only 5-y-o success: inconsistent. *R. Bastiman*   **–**

MARTINE   5 ch.m. Clantime 101 – Marcroft 91 (Crofthall 110) [1998 45: 6g 7.1g 7.1m 7.1d⁴ 7m 8s 1999 a6g a7g May 10] small, sparely-made mare: poor maiden: well beaten in 1999: stays 7f: acts on good to firm and good to soft going. *W. G. M. Turner*   **–**

MARTINEZ (IRE)   3 b.g. Tirol 127 – Elka (USA) (Val de L'Orne (FR) 133) [1998 NR 1999 5g Aug 28] 15,000F: angular, good-bodied gelding: fifth foal: half-brother to 2 winners abroad, one over 1¼m by Exit To Nowhere: dam, French 1¼m winner, half-sister to smart French sprinter West Man: slowly away in Beverley maiden: likely to need much further than 5f. *C. W. Thornton*   **–**

MARTIN (IRE)   2 b.c. (Apr 21) Dancing Dissident (USA) 119 – Martin's Princess (Martin John) [1999 5g 6f 5m 5m⁴ Aug 26] IR 1,000Y: small, sparely-made colt: first foal: dam lightly raced in Ireland: poor form in sellers. *Martyn Wane*   **42**

MARTON MERE   3 ch.g. Cadeaux Genereux 131 – Hyatti 74 (Habitat 134) [1998 NR 1999 a8f a7g a8.5g 7.5g² 6f 7m⁵ 8g⁶ Jul 3] 30,000Y: half-brother to sprint winners by Absalom and Prince Sabo and to Irish 1,000 Guineas runner-up Goodnight Kiss (by Night Shift): dam, maiden, form only at 9f: poor maiden: joined A. Lockwood. *T. D. Easterby*   **44**

MARTON MOSS (SWE)   4 b.g. Polish Patriot (USA) 128 – Arrastra 79 (Bustino 136) [1998 99: 6v⁴ 5s⁵ 6.1m² 7g⁵ 6s² 6s* 6v⁵ 6m² 7g 7g⁴ 5.6g 6s 6g⁶ 7s³ 6d 1999 6m 7m⁵ 6s 7m* 7.1d* 6d 7.1d² 7.9f Jul 9] tall, angular gelding: useful performer: won handicap at Doncaster (by ¾ length from Deep Space) and minor event at Haydock within 6 days in May/June: best effort after when second to Pulau Tioman in handicap on latter course: better at 7f than shorter, and should stay 1m: **102**

possibly unsuited by firm going, acts on any other: has been bandaged in front: usually held up: game. *T. D. Easterby*

MARVEL 2 b.f. (Apr 2) Rudimentary (USA) 118 – Maravilla 73 (Mandrake Major 122) [1999 6s⁶ 7v* 7s Oct 23] smallish, workmanlike filly: half-sister to several winners, including 6f winner Mu-Arrik (by Aragon) and 6-y-o Calandrella: dam maiden who stayed 1m: 33/1, easily best effort when winning maiden at Ayr in October by short head from less-vigorously-ridden Mac Be Lucky, still green: well held in nursery after: will stay 1m. *Don Enrico Incisa* — **65**

MARWELL MAGNUS 2 b.c. (Mar 15) Beveled (USA) – Lily of France 81 (Monsanto (FR) 121) [1999 6m Aug 13] half-brother to winning sprinters Great Hall (by Hallgate) and Marwell Mitzi (by Interrex): dam sprinter: well beaten in maiden at Lingfield. *M. Madgwick* — **–**

MARX MISTRESS 5 b.m. Batshoof 122 – No Jazz 55 (Jaazeiro (USA) 127) [1998 38: a12g 10m⁵ 1999 10.9s⁴ 14.6m⁵ 14.1m Jul 17] bad maiden, lightly raced: stayed 1¼m: visored once at 4 yrs: winning hurdler: dead. *P. D. Evans* — **28**

MARY 3 b.f. Batshoof 122 – Outward's Gal 78 (Ashmore (FR) 125) [1998 NR 1999 11.7g Jun 30] 1,000 2-y-o: half-sister to useful 5f (at 2 yrs) to 7.5f winner Abbey's Gal (by Efisio) and unreliable 1m winner Princess of Orange (by Master Willie): dam, maiden, should have stayed 1m: little show in seller at Bath. *A. G. Newcombe* — **–**

MARY CULI 5 gr.m. Liboi (USA) 76 – Copper Trader 53 (Faustus (USA) 118) [1998 52: 9.7s 11.7s 11.6g⁶ 11.5s³ 10.8g 12m³ 12f⁶ 10g* 10s 10d 1999 11.7s 10.8m a11g a12g³ a12g 10g⁵ 10m³ a12g⁶ 8.3s Sep 27] smallish, lengthy mare: poor performer: left H. Candy after second start: stays 1½m: acts on fibresand, soft and good to firm going: effective blinkered/visored. *G. M. McCourt* — **34**

MARY HANNAH 6 b.m. Lugana Beach 116 – Bloomsbury Girl 63 (Weepers 52 Boy 124) [1998 50: 6d a6g a8.5g a6g⁴ a6g² 1999 a5g* a6g a5g a5g Jun 16] modest handicapper, lightly raced: well held after winning at Wolverhampton in January: will prove best at 5f/6f: acts on fibresand: joined Miss L. Siddall. *A. Senior* — **52**

MARY JANE 4 b.f. Tina's Pet 121 – Fair Attempt (IRE) (Try My Best (USA) 68 130) [1998 53, a63: a5g a5g⁴ a5g* a5g⁴ a5g³ a5g 5s 5g 5m a5g⁶ 5m 5m⁵ 5m a77 a6g* a6g⁴ a5g⁴ a5g* 1999 a6g⁵ a5g* a5g³ 5m 5m³ a5g⁴ 5m² a5g* 5.1m* 5m 5g² 5m⁵ 5.1m² 5g* 5d⁵ Oct 20] fair handicapper: had a good year, winning at Wolverhampton (twice), Chepstow and Leicester between January and September: has won at 6f, but raced mainly at 5f: acts on good to firm ground, good to soft and all-weather: blinkered once at 3 yrs: usually forces pace: consistent: sold 16,000 gns. *R. M. H. Cowell*

MARY STUART (IRE) 3 b.f. Nashwan (USA) 135 – Scots Lass 79 (Shirley 114 Heights 130) [1998 –p: 8.2s 1999 9.9m* 9.9m* 9.9g* 12f⁶ 11.9g⁵ Aug 18] good-bodied filly: has scope: good mover: smart and progressive performer: favourite when winning steadily-run maiden at Salisbury in May and handicaps at Goodwood (made all) in June and July, last-named Tote Gold Trophy by head from Tabareeh: ran well

Tote Gold Trophy Stakes (Handicap), Goodwood—
a good front-running performance by Mary Stuart (white cap) who holds off Tabareeh (blinkers)
with Timahs (right) back in third

when 4¼ lengths fifth to Ramruma in Yorkshire Oaks final start: will stay beyond 1½m: raced only on good going or firmer since debut: game: may do better yet. *Sir Michael Stoute*

MARZOCCO 11 ch.g. Formidable (USA) 125 – Top Heights (High Top 131) [1998 NR 1999 6f 14.1m 7f 24] of little account nowadays. *T. A. K. Cuthbert* —

MASILIA (IRE) 2 b.f. (Jun 4) Kahyasi 130 – Masmouda 123 (Dalsaan 125) **68 p** [1999 8s⁴ Nov 6] unfurnished filly: sixth living foal: dam, French 9f to 10.5f winner, third in Prix de Diane: weak in market and green, 11½ lengths fourth of 18 to Blusienka in maiden at Doncaster, staying on late: likely to need 1½m+ at 3 yrs: sure to improve. *L. M. Cumani*

MASONIC (IRE) 3 ch.c. Grand Lodge (USA) 125 – Winning Heart 98 (Horage **60 §** 124) [1998 –p: 8m⁵ 8d 8s 1999 12g 14.1g² 14.1m³ 15.8m⁴ 14.1g 12g⁴ 11.5g 13.8g² 12d⁶ Sep 30] good-topped colt: modest maiden: effective at 1½m to 2m: acts on good to firm going: usually visored/blinkered: has run in snatches: found little last 2 starts, and one to treat with caution: sold 5,000 gns, sent to Italy. *M. H. Tompkins*

MASTER BEVELED 9 b.g. Beveled (USA) – Miss Anniversary §§ (Tachypous — 128) [1998 81, a–: a11g 10.3g⁴ 8g 8.1g⁶ 8.9s 12m³ 12.3g² 10.3m 10.9d* 8s a12g 10.4g⁶ 1999 10.4g Oct 6] lengthy gelding: fairly useful handicapper on turf, fair on all-weather: well held only start in 1999: stays 1½m: acts on any turf going and all-weather: sometimes blinkered/visored, but at least as effective without: sometimes bandaged: smart hurdler. *P. D. Evans*

MASTER CASTER (IRE) 4 b.g. Night Shift (USA) – Honourable Sheba **80** (USA) (Roberto (USA) 131) [1998 80: a7g⁵ a8g⁴ a8g³ a10g* a10g³ 9.3d⁶ 10d 8.1m⁴ **a66** 7g² 8g⁶ 6.9d² 7.5m 7.5m² 8.5m* 8.5m² 1999 a9.4g⁵ a10g⁴ 10.8d³ 8f* 9m⁶ May 22] close-coupled, heavy-bodied gelding: fairly useful handicapper on turf, fair on all-weather: won at Brighton in May: stays up to 1¼m: acts on firm going, good to soft and all-weather: seems effective visored or not: usually requires strong handling: successful over hurdles twice in June. *G. M. McCourt*

MASTER FAY (IRE) 2 b.c. (Feb 28) Fayruz 116 – Non Dimenticar Me (IRE) **102** 63 (Don't Forget Me 127) [1999 5s⁵ 5g* 5f* 6f² 6d² 5m² 6m⁴ 6m* 6g⁴ Sep 8] 8,000Y: leggy, angular colt: first foal: dam 5f winner who stayed 7f: useful performer: won minor events at Newcastle in April and Doncaster (awarded race) in May and listed race at Newbury (made all, by 3 lengths) in July: creditable fourth to City On A Hill in July Stakes at Newmarket (pulled hard under restraint) and to Sheer Hamas in sales race at Doncaster: effective at 6f/stiff 5f: acts on firm and good to soft ground: usually races prominently/leads: tough and consistent: sent to Hong Kong. *M. R. Channon*

MASTER GEORGE 2 b.g. (Apr 17) Mtoto 134 – Topwinder (USA) (Topsider **73 p** (USA)) [1999 8v² Sep 29] 25,000Y: third living foal: half-brother to 3-y-o Piper's Clan and 7f seller winner (including at 2 yrs) Fast Spin (by Formidable): dam ran twice in France: 12 lengths second of 11 to Island Sound in maiden at Salisbury, soon bustled along to race prominently and keeping on: will prove suited by 1¼m/1½m: should do better. *I. A. Balding*

MASTER HYDE (USA) 10 gr.g. Trempolino (USA) 135 – Sandspur (USA) (Al **44** Hattab (USA)) [1998 –: 16m⁶ 16g 14.6d 1999 14.1m⁴ 14d 14.1m³ 12m⁴ Aug 3] leggy, workmanlike gelding: fair hurdler: poor on Flat nowadays: stays 1¾m: acts on firm ground, soft and equitrack: tried blinkered/visored: carries head awkwardly and not an easy ride. *J. S. Goldie*

MASTER JONES 2 b.g. (Mar 28) Emperor Jones (USA) 119 – Tight Spin (High **64 ?** Top 131) [1999 5g 5g 6.8m 5s⁶ a7g⁴ a10g Dec 18] 7,000Y: unfurnished gelding: half-brother to several winners, notably 5-y-o Vicious Circle: dam once-raced daughter of smart 5f to 7f winner Petty Purse: modest maiden: seemed to show best form fourth start: should stay 7f: acts on soft ground, probably on equitrack. *Mrs L. Stubbs*

MASTER LODGE 4 ch.c. Night Shift (USA) – Katie Koo 82 (Persian Bold 123) **63** [1998 NR 1999 6g⁵ 7m⁵ 8.2s a10g⁵ a12g Nov 26] closely related to Irish 1987 2-y-o 5f winner Hakari (by Glenstal) and half-brother to 3 winners, including 1m and 1¼m winner Lady Philippa (by Taufan): dam 11.7f and 13f winner: modest maiden: best effort on debut: may prove best short of 1¼m: tongue tied last 2 starts. *S. C. Williams*

MASTER MAC (USA)   4 br.g. Exbourne (USA) 125 – Kentucky Blonde (USA) **78 d**
(General Assembly (USA)) [1998 76: 7d⁶ 6d⁵ 6g⁵ 6g 6f 1999 8f 8f 7d 8.5g 7m 6g Oct
19] small gelding: fluent mover: fair handicapper: generally well beaten in 1999:
probably needs further than 6f, and stays 1m: acts on firm and good to soft going: has
been bandaged near-hind: joined R. O'Sullivan. *N. Hamilton*

MASTER MILLFIELD (IRE)   7 b.g. Prince Rupert (FR) 121 – Calash (Indian   **–**
King (USA) 128) [1998 65, a–: 8g* 8d* 8m⁵ 8.9g 1999 8g 8.1d 8d Aug 17] tall
gelding: fair handicapper at best: well beaten in 1999: effective at 7f to sharp 1½m:
acts on any going: visored once at 4 yrs: held up. *R. J. Hodges*

MASTERMIND (IRE)   2 ch.c. (Feb 24) Dolphin Street (FR) 125 – Glenarff   **103 p**
(USA) (Irish River (FR) 131) [1999 6m² 6m* Jul 31] 52,000F, IR 80,000Y: strong,
lengthy colt: fluent mover: third living foal: half-brother to 3-y-o Housemaster: dam
French 1m winner out of stakes-placed half-sister to very smart French miler
Shaanxi: useful form: length second of 8 to Boast in minor event at Newmarket
before winning maiden there later in July by 1¾ lengths from The Deputy: will stay
7f, probably 1m: remains capable of better if all is well. *P. F. I. Cole*

MASTERPIECE   5 br.g. Primo Dominie 121 – Swift Return 79 (Double Form   **–**
130) [1998 –: 6m 6m 1999 8m 8m Sep 2] big, rangy gelding: fair maiden at 3 yrs: well
beaten since: probably stays 1m: raced only on good going or firmer. *N. J. Henderson*

MASTERPIECE (USA)   2 b. or br.c. (Apr 15) Nureyev (USA) 131 – Lovely   **80 p**
Gemstone (USA) (Alydar (USA)) [1999 7d 7v* Oct 25] $250,000Y: rather leggy,
unfurnished colt: fourth foal: half-brother to a minor winner in USA by Half A Year:
dam unraced half-sister to Lear Fan and smart winner up to 1½m Pirate Army:
improved on debut form at Newmarket to win maiden at Lingfield by ¾ length from
Hypersonic, getting on top final 100 yds: will stay 1m, probably 1¼m: should do
better still. *Sir Michael Stoute*

MASTER REX   4 ch.g. Interrex (CAN) – Whose Lady (USA) (Master Willie 129)   **–**
[1998 –: 11.7m 14.1s⁶ 11.7v a10g⁵ 1999 10m Jul 17] little sign of ability. *W. R. Muir*

MASTER SODEN (USA)   2 b.c. (Feb 14) Pembroke (USA) 113 – Lady Member   **65 p**
(FR) (Saint Estephe (FR) 123) [1999 6m 6m 7s 8d* Nov 1] $15,500F, 46,000Y:
sturdy colt: second foal: dam, French 2-y-o 1m winner, later stayed 1¼m and successful in USA: well held in maidens before 50/1-winner of 27-runner nursery at Redcar,
wandering under pressure (probably still green) but coming clear final 1f: will stay
1¼m: should do better still. *T. G. Mills*

MASTER TIROL (IRE)   3 ro.g. Tirol 127 – Inisfail (Persian Bold 123) [1998   **53**
59: 5d⁶ 6g 5.9d⁵ 7g 1999 9.9g 10s 9.9g 10.9s 8.5m⁵ Jul 13] modest maiden handicapper: well held after reappearance: should stay 1¼m: acts on good to soft going:
blinkered last 2 starts: sold 5,000 gns. *R. A. Fahey*

MATERIAL WITNESS (IRE)   2 b.c. (Feb 6) Barathea (IRE) 127 – Dial Dream   **83 p**
(Gay Mecene (USA) 128) [1999 7.1m³ 6g² Oct 6] 650,000 francs Y: closely related
to useful French 1½m and 15f winner Periple (by In The Wings) and half-brother to
French 9f to 11.5f winner Lyphard's Dream (by Lyphard): dam, French 9f and 10.5f
winner, half-sister to high-class French 1¼m performer Al Nasr: better effort in
maidens when head second of 9 to Strahan at York: takes good hold, but bred to stay
at least 1m: open to further improvement. *W. R. Muir*

MATIN DE PRINTEMPS (FR)   5 ch.h. Kendor (FR) 122 – Zarzaya (USA)   **100**
(Caro 133) [1998 105: 6s* 5.5g³ 6v⁴ 6s 6g 7g³ 8s 8s⁶ 8d 7s² 8d³ 8v* 8v³ 1999 8v* 8d⁵
7m⁵ 8g 8d⁶ 7g² 6g 7m 7m* 8s⁵ 6v² 8s⁵ Nov 22] leggy, quite good-topped horse:
brother to French 1997 2-y-o 5f winner Kavalcadour and half-brother to several
winners, including useful French 1½m winner Zaydiya (by Shernazar): dam unraced
from very good family: useful performer: won minor event at Saint-Cloud in March
and handicap at Longchamp in September: well held in Tote International Handicap
at Ascot eighth outing: effective at 6f to 1m: acts on good to firm ground, goes well
on heavy. *H. Van de Poele, France*

MATTAN   3 b.g. Chaddleworth (IRE) 103 – Gilded Omen (Faustus (USA) 118)   **54**
[1998 NR 1999 12.1g³ 13.4m³ Jun 23] first reported foal: dam no worthwhile form,
including in points: modest form in minor event and maiden. *B. J. Llewellyn*

MA VIE 2 b.f. (May 6) Salse (USA) 128 – One Life (USA) (L'Emigrant (USA) **61**
129) [1999 6m⁶ 7d 7d Oct 11] 40,000Y: sturdy filly: has a quick action: seventh foal:
half-sister to useful 7.5f (at 2 yrs) and 1½m winner Tenorio (by Law Society) and
several winners abroad: dam unraced half-sister to Miesque: easily best effort
(modest form) when eleventh of 17 in sales event at Newmarket on second start: will
probably stay 1¼m. *J. R. Fanshawe*

MAWARED (IRE) 6 ch.h. Nashwan (USA) 135 – Harmless Albatross 115 (Pas **–**
de Seul 133) [1998 107: 14m² 16g* 18.7g* 1999 16.2d Apr 28] tall, good-topped
horse: useful handicapper in 1997 and 1998: reportedly injured in Sagaro Stakes at
Ascot, only 6-y-o outing: stayed 2¼m: easily best efforts on good going or firmer:
had been bandaged: was held up: retired. *J. L. Dunlop*

MAWDSLEY 2 b.f. (Feb 2) Piccolo 121 – Legendary Dancer 90 (Shareef Dancer **–**
(USA) 135) [1999 6g Aug 4] 6,500Y: sixth foal: half-sister to 3 winners, including
6-y-o Riccarton and 4-y-o Legend of Love: dam 1½m winner from family of Wassl:
slowly away and always behind in maiden at Leicester. *G. Woodward*

MAWINGO (IRE) 6 b.g. Taufan (USA) 119 – Tappen Zee (Sandhurst Prince **69**
128) [1998 –: 7.6m⁵ 8.1g 10.1g 8m 1999 7g 8v³ 8m 7.9m 8s³ 9g⁵ a8g⁴ Dec 10]
leggy gelding: fair handicapper nowadays: probably stays 1¼m: acts on any going:
blinkered twice (ran creditably first time): has won for apprentice. *G. Wragg*

MAWKAB (USA) 4 b. or br.g. Gulch (USA) – Up Sail (USA) (Herculean (USA)) **59**
[1998 46: a8g⁶ a8g⁵ a7g⁶ 1999 a6g⁴ a8g* a8g² a8g a8g⁵ a8g⁶ a8g² 7s⁶ a7g² **a71**
8.3m7.6f 8d 8m⁴ 6s a7g* a7g² Oct 25] fair on all-weather, modest on turf: won
maiden at Lingfield in January and claimer at Wolverhampton in October: several
creditable efforts otherwise: effective at 7f/1m: acts on all-weather, good and to
firm going: usually blinkered/visored, but has run well without: races prominently/
leads: has carried head awkwardly/swished tail: sold 8,000 gns, sent to Kuwait.
Miss Gay Kelleway

MAX (FR) 4 gr.g. L'Emigrant (USA) 129 – Miss Mendez (FR) (Bellypha 130) **?**
[1998 10f 12v⁴ 11v⁵ 1999 11g⁴ a13g 10g⁶ 9g⁵ 8g⁴ 11g 9g 8g* 8g³ a7g⁵ 7g³ 8g³ 8g²
8g² 9.5s² 8g* 8.5d* a8g Dec 18] ex-Belgian gelding: half-brother to French 1¼m
winner Marguns (by Cricket Ball): dam, French 1m/9f winner, sister to high-class
French 1m/9f performer Mendez: in good form in Belgium in the autumn for
A. Hermans, winning handicap at Ostend in September and minor event and handicap at same course in November: well beaten on British debut: possibly best at 1m:
has been blinkered. *J. J. Bridger*

MAXIMUM MAKEUP (IRE) 2 b.g. (Apr 9) Mujadil (USA) 119 – Oileann **57 p**
Carrig 80 (Pitcairn 126) [1999 6.1f⁵ Oct 20] IR 8,200F, 6,500Y, 16,500 2-y-o:
half-brother to several winners, including Irish 1½m winner Toordillon (by Contract
Law) and Irish 6f winner Shragraddy Lass (by Jareer): dam, Irish 6f winner at 2 yrs,
fourth in Group 3 at 7f at 3 yrs: modest form when fifth of 6 to Heathyardsblessing in
minor event at Nottingham, slowly away and not unduly knocked about: likely to
prove best up to 1m: should do better. *J. R. Fanshawe*

MAYA COVE 3 b.f. Caerleon (USA) 132 – Shining Water 111 (Kalaglow 132) **72**
[1998 56: 7.1d⁶ 1999 11.5g⁶ 14d⁴ 11m² 11.5f* 12g⁶ 11.9d⁶ Oct 21] lengthy, unfurnished filly: fluent mover: fair performer: won handicap at Lingfield in August: stays
1½m: acts on firm going: sold 76,000 gns in December. *B. W. Hills*

MAYARO BAY 3 b.f. Robellino (USA) 127 – Down The Valley 73 (Kampala **105**
120) [1998 85p: 6g 6d⁴ 6.1g³ 6d* 6m² 1999 8m 7d² 7g* 7d⁶ 8.1g⁵ 7m⁴ 7d⁶ 8d³
8g² Oct 16] sturdy filly: useful performer: won valuable handicap at Goodwood in
May: generally good efforts otherwise (off course 3 months before eighth start),
notably when ¾-length second of 20 to Free Option in handicap at Newmarket final
start: best at 7f/1m: yet to race on extremes of going: held up. *R. Hannon*

MAYARO (FR) 3 br.c. Saumarez 132 – Milesime (USA) (Riverman (USA) 131) **115**
[1998 8v* 8v³ 1999 12d³ 12d* 10g³ 12d* 12d* 12v² 10d* Nov 20] third foal: dam,
French 9f/1¼m winner, half-sister to very smart 1m/9f performer In Extremis and
3-y-o Juvenia: smart performer: off course 3 months after third outing, progressed
well in autumn, winning listed races at Saint-Cloud (2, making all both times) and
Marseilles Borely, beating Milord Fontenaille 3 lengths final start: races freely but

gives impression he'll stay further than 1½m: acts on heavy ground, yet to race on firmer than good. *Mme C. Head, France*

MAYBE'N 2 ch.c. (Apr 22) Deploy 131 – Travel Mystery 99 (Godswalk (USA) 130) [1999 6m 7m⁶ 7f Jul 14] 5,000Y: sturdy colt: sixth foal: dam, suited by test of stamina on Flat (won Sagaro Stakes), also fairly useful hurdler: signs of ability. *C. Smith*   –

MAY CONTESSA (USA) 2 b.f. (Jan 23) Bahri (USA) 125 – Copper Creek 78 (Habitat 134) [1999 6m³ 5.7d⁵ Sep 27] IR 135,000Y: half-sister to several winners, including 5-y-o Tipsy Creek and smart UAE 1m/9f winner Wathik (by Ogygian), latter also 6f/7f winner in Britain at 2 yrs: dam 6f winner: third of 11 in maiden at Goodwood: well held when odds-on for similar event at Bath: gives impression will prove best over bare 5f. *D. R. C. Elsworth*   **67**

MAYDORO 6 b.m. Dominion Royale 112 – Bamdoro 54 (Cavo Doro 124) [1998 57: a6g* a6g a6g a6g⁵ 6d 5s* 5m 6m² a6g⁵ a6g 1999 a7g a7g 6v a5g 5s 6.9g 6f⁶ Jul 9] sparely-made mare: modest in 1998: poor in 1999, leaving M. Dods after previous start: stays 6f: acts on soft ground and fibresand. *W. M. Brisbourne*   **32**

MAY I SAY (IRE) 3 b.f. Night Shift (USA) – Monoglow (Kalaglow 132) [1998 72: 7.1m 7m³ 8g 8m² 8d⁵ 1999 10d 10m 11.4m⁵ 10m 9.7f² 10s 10f Oct 20] close-coupled filly: fair maiden: stays 11.4f: acts on firm and good to soft going: has run well sweating/edgy: tongue tied last 3 starts: sold 2,700 gns, sent to Germany. *P. W. Harris*   **68**

MAY KING MAYHEM 6 ch.g. Great Commotion (USA) 123 – Queen Rana-valona (Sure Blade (USA) 130) [1998 46: 12.5s⁶ 11.8s³ 12v 14.1s 14.9m⁶ 12m⁵ 14.1d³ 16.1d 12m⁶ a14g³ 12m⁴ 11.9d* 14.1m 14g 12g³ 12d* 1999 a12g⁵ a12g⁶ 14.1d⁶ 14.1s 12g 11.8g* 12d* 12.3m⁶ Jun 17] close-coupled gelding: has a round action: modest handicapper: won at Leicester (apprentices) in May and Newmarket (31-runner ladies event) in June: effective at 1½m to 15f: acts on good to firm going, soft and fibresand: blinkered/visored: sometimes goes in snatches. *Mrs A. L. M. King*   **58**

MAYLANE 5 b.g. Mtoto 134 – Possessive Dancer 118 (Shareef Dancer (USA) 135) [1998 110§: 12f 20s 1999 12f 12m³ 11d⁵ 11.9v* 12s* Nov 6] smallish, leggy gelding: smart performer: rejoined former trainer in 1999, winning minor event at Haydock (by ½ length from Muhib) in October and listed event at Doncaster (by 2 lengths from Badaayer) in November, both times better away than usual and just coaxed along to assert: effective at 1½m, seemingly at 2½m: acts on any going: blinkered second/third starts: can spoil chance with very slow start: unreliable. *A. C. Stewart*   **112 §**

MAYLAN (IRE) 4 br.f. Lashkari 128 – Miysam 60 (Supreme Sovereign 119) [1998 NR 1999 10m 11.7f 10.5d 10d a10g a13g Dec 10] poor maiden at best: blinkered once. *W. de Best-Turner*   –

MAYO 3 b.c. Nashwan (USA) 135 – Nuryana 107 (Nureyev (USA) 131) [1998 70: 8g⁶ 8d 1999 10g* 10.5g* 12m 10g Jul 2] sturdy, attractive colt: has a quick action: useful performer: won maiden at Lingfield and rated stakes at Haydock (beat Senure by 5 lengths), both in May: disappointed after in large-field valuable handicaps at Royal Ascot and Sandown, seeming to run moody race in latter: should be well suited by 1½m: yet to race on extremes of going: has awkward head carriage. *H. R. A. Cecil*   **104**

MA YORAM (USA) 2 gr.c. (Jan 26) Dayjur (USA) 137 – Quelle Affaire (USA) (Riverman (USA) 131) [1999 5g* 6g² 6m³ Sep 18] 110,000Y: rather leggy, quite attractive colt: second reported foal: dam, French maiden, sister to smart 7f/1m performer Rami and half-sister to smart French sprinters Crack Regiment and La Grande Epoque: rather coltish, landed odds impressively in maiden at Kempton in April: off course 4 months with various minor problems before showing useful form to be placed in Gimcrack Stakes at York (3 lengths second to Mull of Kintyre) and Mill Reef Stakes at Newbury (2¾ lengths third of 4 to Primo Valentino): stays 6f: led by 2 handlers and constantly on the jog in preliminaries at Newbury: may benefit from being gelded. *M. R. Channon*   **101**

MAY QUEEN MEGAN 6 gr.m. Petorius 117 – Siva (FR) (Bellypha 130) [1998 59: a8.5g 8f 8.2d* 8d⁵ 8m 9m* 10.2d 8m 10m³ 10.2m 8m⁵ 10.4g 1999 8g⁵ 9.9g 10m 10g⁴ 10s² 9m 10g³ 9m² 10.2m⁶ 8.2m 10g⁵ 10m⁵ 10m 8d⁴ Oct 20] leggy mare: modest   **55**

handicapper: generally ran at least respectably in 1999: stays 1¼m: acts on firm and soft going: blinkered once at 3 yrs: often comes from off pace. *Mrs A. L. M. King*

MAY SONG   7 b.g. Gold Song 112 – Kaymay 76 (Maystreak 118) [1998 NR 1999 8d 6.9m Jul 16] sixth reported living foal: half-brother to 5f winner (including at 2 yrs) Brave Melody (by Heroic Air): dam won up to 1m: no show in maidens: broke down second start: dead. *Mrs G. S. Rees*

MAYVILLE'S DANCER (IRE)   3 ch.f. Up And At 'em 109 – Cutlers Corner 111 (Sharpen Up 127) [1998 71: 6g 6g 6s² 1999 6.1v 7m May 3] fair form in maidens at 2 yrs: well beaten in 1999: likely to prove best at 5f/6f: carries head high. *G. A. Butler*

MAZAYA (IRE)   3 b.f. Sadler's Wells (USA) 132 – Sharaniya (USA) 117 (Alleged (USA) 138) [1998 NR 1999 9.9m² 12.1g* 12s² 12d Oct 9] 150,000Y: eighth foal: closely related to French 1m winner Shamsiya (by The Minstrel) and half-sister to 3 winners, including useful Irish 1½m and 2m winner Sharazan (by Akarad): dam, French 1¼m to 12.5f winner, half-sister to Prix Vermeille winner Sharaya: won maiden at Chepstow in June: useful form when length second to Signorina Cattiva in listed race at Ascot 3½ months later: last of 12 in Princess Royal Stakes there final start: stayed 1¾m: acted on soft going: stud. *J. L. Dunlop*   **105**

MAZEED (IRE)   6 ch.g. Lycius (USA) 124 – Maraatib (IRE) 93 (Green Desert (USA) 127) [1998 82, a77: a10g* a9.4g a9.4g³ 10.1f* 10.1m* 10.3g² 9.9d* 10.4f 10m² 9.9m³ 9.9m⁴ a9.4g³ a10g⁶ 1999 a12g⁵ a10g 11.8m 10s 10.5m a12g Oct 1] neat gelding: fairly useful on turf, fair on all-weather: below best in 1999, leaving P. D. Evans 6,000 gns after second start: best up to 1¼m: acts on firm going, good to soft (probably on soft) and all-weather: blinkered twice, usually visored. *Miss K. M. George*   **65 d**

MAZILLA   7 b.m. Mazilier (USA) 107 – Mo Ceri 63 (Kampala 120) [1998 49, a43: 10m 10m³ 9.7m² 10s⁶ 8g 9m 10g⁵ 1999 9.9g⁶ a11g 10.9s Jun 19] leggy mare: poor handicapper: best around 1¼m: acts on good to firm ground, soft and all-weather: effective visored or not: usually waited with: fair hurdler. *A. Streeter*   **34**

MAZZELMO   6 gr.m. Thethingaboutitis (USA) 106 – Nattfari (Tyrnavos 129) [1998 67: a12g³ 14m⁵ a16.2g* 15.8g 15.9m⁴ 16m⁴ 16.5g³ 17.1m⁴ 15.9g* 16v³ 17.5s 15.9g⁴ 16s 1999 a16.2g a16.2g⁵ 18d 17.1v³ 18.7m 16s⁵ 16m⁴ 17.2g³ 18m* 15.8g⁶ 15.9m a16.2g 16.2g⁵ 15.9d³ 16m 15.9s* Sep 22] leggy, quite good-topped mare: fair handicapper: won at Chepstow in June and Chester in September: stays 2¼m: yet to race on firm going, acts on any other turf/fibresand: blinkered second start: none too consistent. *A. Bailey*   **67 a–**

MBELE   2 b.c. (Feb 16) Mtoto 134 – Majestic Image 86 (Niniski (USA) 125) [1999 8s² Oct 26] 8,000Y: third foal: half-brother to smart German 3-y-o 11f and 1½m winner Montalban and German 1997 2-y-o 1m winner Majestic Moon (both by Mondrian): dam 1¾m and 2m winner at 5/6 yrs: 25/1, promising head second of 13 to Riddlesdown in maiden at Bath, not finding stride until approaching final 1f: will prove suited by 1½m+: sure to improve. *W. R. Muir*   **88 p**

MCFARLINE (IRE)   3 b.g. Ela-Mana-Mou 132 – Highland Ball 73 (Bold Lad (IRE) 133) [1998 67: 7.1m 7.5m⁶ 8.1m 1999 11.6m 12f⁴ 12m 12d Aug 26] sturdy gelding: disappointing maiden: should prove suited by at least 1½m: probably acts on firm going: blinkered penultimate start: joined N. Hawke. *J. L. Dunlop*   **63**

MCGILLYCUDDY REEKS (IRE)   8 b.m. Kefaah (USA) 124 – Kilvarnet 78 (Furry Glen 121) [1998 80: 9.9m 12m⁵ 10.1s* 8.9s 8s⁶ 8.5d⁴ 10.4f 9.9m⁴ 12g* 9.9m 11.9f⁶ 10s⁶ 12g 10.5m⁶ 10.4g 10v⁶ 10.1v³ 1999 10.3m 10d³ 12m 10.1m⁵ 8.9d 9.9g* 9.2m⁴ 9.9m² 10.3m* 9.9g⁴ 11.9m 9.9g³ 10.3m 10.5s 10.4g⁶ 12s 10d Nov 1] small mare: fairly useful handicapper: raced more handily than usual when winning at Beverley in June and Doncaster in July: best at 1¼m/1½m: acts on fibresand and any turf going: often slowly away and usually held up: used to have tongue tied, not after fifth start. *Don Enrico Incisa*   **80**

MCQUILLAN   2 b.g. (May 6) Maledetto (IRE) 103 – Macs Maharanee 85 (Indian King (USA) 128) [1999 6s 7g Oct 16] second foal: half-brother to 3-y-o Now Is The Hour: dam sprinter: always behind in maidens. *P. S. Felgate*   **–**

MEADAAAR (USA)   2 ch.c. (Mar 1) Diesis 133 – Katiba (USA) 99 (Gulch   **99 p**
(USA)) [1999 7m² 7m* 7d³ Oct 1] rangy, rather unfurnished colt: has scope: third
foal: half-brother to 3-y-o Badaayer and 1m winner Kariyh (by Shadeed), who stayed
1¼m, both useful: dam 6f (at 2 yrs) and 7f winner who stayed 1¼m, out of half-sister
to a Breeders' Cup Sprint winner: comfortably landed odds in 3-runner minor event
at Yarmouth in August: useful form when 3¾ lengths third of 5 to Scarteen Fox in
listed event at Newmarket final start, setting sound pace until over 1f out: will stay
1m: should make a better 3-y-o. *J. L. Dunlop*

MEADOW LEADER (USA)   9 ro.h. Meadowlake (USA) – Tobriand (USA)   **69**
(Mr Leader (USA)) [1998 53, a68: 6.8s⁴ 7v 8f 7m² 7f* 7d 8f⁵ a7g* 1999 a7g* a5.5s²
a5.5s⁵ a6g² 8g* 8g a6g³ 8s⁵ a6g⁵ Nov 26] Belgian-trained horse: fair performer: won
seller at Lingfield in January and handicap at Ostend in August: ran creditably in
handicap at Lingfield final start: effective at 6f to 1m: acts on firm going, soft and
all-weather: has been blinkered: usually front runner. *C. Dondi, Belgium*

MEDELAI   3 b.f. Marju (IRE) 127 – No Islands (Lomond (USA) 128) [1998 52:   **52**
6m 7.5m⁶ 7g³ 7.1g⁴ 7.5m 10d² 8.2v* 8d 1999 12m 14.1m 12d⁵ 12.1m 12.1m 13.8g⁵
14.1f a16.2g² Dec 15] close-coupled filly: modest handicapper: left J. Bethell before
final start: stays 2m: acts on fibresand, best turf efforts on going softer than good.
Mrs A. E. Johnson

MEDICINE BALL   4 b.f. Rudimentary (USA) 118 – Morica 88 (Mooorestyle   **–**
137) [1998 63?: 7m 9m⁴ 11.5g⁶ 1999 a8g 10m Jul 19] modest maiden at best: well
held both 4-y-o starts: won over hurdles in August. *T. R. Watson*

MEDINA DE RIOSECO   2 b.f. (Mar 2) Puissance 110 – Antonia's Folly 64   **70 d**
(Music Boy 124) [1999 5m⁴ 5.1m³ 5g⁶ 5.1m⁶ 5.3f⁴ 5.2m 5d² 5d 6m 5v⁶ 5.1g⁶ 6s⁵
Nov 2] 14,000Y: tall, rather leggy filly: fluent mover: second foal: half-sister to 3-y-o
Zaragossa: dam 2-y-o 5f winner: maiden: failed to repeat form of first 2 starts: best
efforts at 5f: acts on good to firm and heavy ground: inconsistent. *J. Berry*

MEG   3 b.f. Be My Chief (USA) 122 – Megdale (IRE) 74 (Waajib 121) [1998 49:   **53**
7m 7m 7g³ 7s 1999 7m 8f 10.1g³ a8g⁵ a12g 10.1g⁶ 11.5g Sep 14] leggy, rather
unfurnished filly: modest maiden: stays 1¼m: acts on good to firm going and fibresand: sometimes flashes tail: sold 800 gns, sent to Germany. *C. F. Wall*

MEGA (IRE)   3 b.f. Petardia 113 – Gobolino (Don 128) [1998 66p: 6d 1999   **–**
10m 7m 8m 10d 11g Oct 14] big filly: disappointing maiden: visored once.
M. H. Tompkins

MEGS PEARL   3 gr.f. Petong 126 – Heaven-Liegh-Grey 90 (Grey Desire 115)   **–**
[1998 56: 6g⁵ 6s 5.7g⁶ 1999 8d 10m 7m May 5] sparely-made filly: modest maiden:
no show in 1999: stays 6f: visored final start. *P. D. Evans*

MEHMAAS   3 b.g. Distant Relative 128 – Guest List 85 (Be My Guest (USA)   **79**
126) [1998 79, a69: 6m 7.1d⁵ 7m 8d² a8g² 1999 8.3s 8s⁵ 7m* 8.5m⁵ 8d 8m⁴ Sep 18]
smallish, sturdy gelding: fair performer: won 4-runner maiden at Brighton in August:
creditable effort otherwise only when fourth in handicap at Newbury: stays 1m: acts
on good to firm going, good to soft and fibresand: effective blinkered/visored or not:
has looked difficult ride: sold 5,500 gns, joined R. Barr. *M. R. Channon*

MEILLEUR (IRE)   5 b.g. Nordico (USA) – Lucy Limelight 98 (Hot Spark 126)   **65**
[1998 59: 10d⁴ 11.5g³ 11.5g⁴ 11.1d* 10g 11.9g⁶ 12s 11.9s⁵ 1999 11.6m 12.3g² 12d²
12m* 12d⁵ 11.5g a12g² a12g⁴ Dec 11] workmanlike gelding: fair handicapper: won
21-runner ladies event at Newbury in September: creditable efforts last 2 starts:
effective at 11f to easy 2m: acts on all-weather, soft and good to firm ground: visored
once: usually held up: carries head high. *Lady Herries*

MELANZANA   2 b.f. (Mar 10) Alzao (USA) 117 – Melody Park 104 (Music Boy   **81 p**
124) [1999 6m³ 6m* Sep 24] 18,000Y: sixth live foal: half-sister to 4-y-o Morgan Le
Fay and 1992 2-y-o 5f winner Five Islands and 5f to 7f winner Creche (both by
Bairn): dam sprinter: favourite, confirmed debut promise when winning maiden at
Redcar by 2 lengths from Adamas, travelling strongly and leading final 1f: should
stay 7f: almost certainly open to further improvement. *E. A. L. Dunlop*

MELASUS (IRE)   7 ch.g. Nashamaa 113 – Sweet Camden 62 (Camden Town   **–**
125) [1998 NR 1999 a8f a7g⁵ a7g⁵ 10.8d 8.3m 10v Apr 24] good-topped gelding: fair
6f/7f winner at 2 yrs: lightly raced and little form since. *D. W. P. Arbuthnot*

MELBA (IRE) 2 b.f. (Feb 20) Namaqualand (USA) – Priyanka (Last Tycoon 131) **62** [1999 7d 8d Oct 22] stocky filly: first foal: dam unraced daughter of half-sister to Oaks winner Fair Salinia: modest form when midfield in maiden at Leicester: well held in similar event at Doncaster following week. *A. P. Jarvis*

MELBEN 3 b.c. Dolphin Street (FR) 125 – Shapely Test (USA) (Elocutionist **–** (USA)) [1998 NR 1999 a6g a8f Jan 23] 54,000F, 70,000Y: closely related to 9-y-o Birchwood Sun and a winner in USA (both by Bluebird) and half-brother to several winners, including smart Irish sprinter Lidanna (by Nicholas): dam Irish 1m winner: well beaten in maidens at Lingfield: visored on debut: sold 2,200 gns. *J. Noseda*

MELLORS (IRE) 6 b.g. Common Grounds 118 – Simply Beautiful (IRE) (Simply **65** Great (FR) 122) [1998 62, a72: a9.4g5 a8g* a8g* a7g3 8g* 8f2 8f* 9m5 8g4 a10g 1999 a8g 8f* 8f5 10f* 10g4 10g Jul 5] well-made gelding: fair handicapper: goes well at Brighton, and won there in April and May: stays 1¼m only when emphasis is on speed: acts on firm ground and equitrack: tried blinkered/visored: front runner: sold 7,000 gns, joined John Berry. *M. J. Heaton-Ellis*

MELLOW JAZZ 2 b.f. (Mar 14) Lycius (USA) 124 – Slow Jazz (USA) 106 **77 p** (Chief's Crown (USA)) [1999 6.1g* Sep 25] second foal: dam, French 6f (at 2 yrs) to 1m winner, closely related to smart 6f/7f performers Zieten and Blue Duster: well-backed favourite, won 12-runner maiden at Nottingham by ½ length from Lakeland Paddy, green early but asserting final 1f: will probably stay 1m: sure to improve. *E. A. L. Dunlop*

MELLOW MISS 3 b.f. Danehill (USA) 126 – Like The Sun (USA) 74 (Wood-**60** man (USA) 126) [1998 61: 6g 6g 1999 7m 6m5 5.2s a7g a8g4 a8g4 a10g Dec 18] angular filly: modest maiden: stays 1m: acts on good to firm going and equitrack: blinkered on reappearance. *R. M. Flower*

MELODIAN 4 b.c. Grey Desire 115 – Mere Melody 88 (Dunphy 124) [1998 47: **62** 6d 8m 8g 7g* 5.9d3 7.1g 7d 1999 8f4 6.9m 6.9m2 7.5m* 8.2m3 7f* 7g* 7.5g 8d3 7.5s5 7g Oct 14] leggy colt: modest handicapper: won at Beverley, Doncaster and Catterick in summer, last 2 in large fields: effective at 7f/1m: yet to race on heavy going, acts on any other: blinkered nowadays: usually races up with pace. *M. Brittain*

MELODIC HEIGHTS 2 b.f. (Apr 30) Puissance 110 – Pick A Tune (Music Boy **–** 124) [1999 5d a5g 5m a5g5 Jun 5] 600Y: leggy, unfurnished filly: fourth reported living foal: dam well beaten: no form, including in sellers. *J. Berry*

MELODY BLUES 3 b.f. Merdon Melody 98 – Hsian (Shantung 132) [1998 43: **–** 6g3 a6g3 a7g5 7m 1999 a6g a7g Feb 26] poor maiden at best: should stay 1m: blinkered final start. *M. Dods*

MELODY LADY 3 ch.f. Dilum (USA) 115 – Ansellady 67 (Absalom 128) [1998 **57** 53, a–: 6g 7m 6m5 6m3 6s a6g 1999 7m 8.2m 12g2 10d 12f2 Jul 14] workmanlike **a–** filly: modest maiden: best efforts at 1½m: acts on firm going: blinkered last 3 starts at 2 yrs. *F. Murphy*

MELODY QUEEN 3 b.f. Merdon Melody 98 – Thabeh 57 (Shareef Dancer **81** (USA) 135) [1998 76: 6g 6g5 6g2 7m6 7m* 7.1g2 6g2 8m2 7g* 8m 1999 a8f3 a10g4 a7g2 a8g* a8g* a10g 8s6 10.1m 8.5f6 a8f3 8.5f* a8s Dec 18] small, leggy filly: fairly useful performer: won at Lingfield in February (claimer) and March (handicap): below form next 3 starts, including in listed races, and left K. Burke: successful in claimer at Aqueduct in November: stays 1m: acts on good to firm going, dirt and equitrack. *M. W. Dickinson, USA*

MELOMANIA (USA) 7 b.g. Shadeed (USA) 135 – Medley of Song (USA) **– §** (Secretariat (USA)) [1998 NR 1999 a8g* a8g a7g a8g3 7.5d a8.5g6 11.5m 12d **a49 §** a7g 5g 10m a7g6 Oct 13] poor handicapper: won amateur event at Lingfield in February: stays 1m: acts on equitrack, no form on turf: has looked ungenuine: joined T. Clement. *P. Howling*

MELON PLACE (IRE) 2 b.c. (Mar 31) Dancing Dissident (USA) 119 – Shikari **92 p** Rose (Kala Shikari 125) [1999 5m2 5g3 5g* Aug 28] IR 3,200F, IR 12,000Y: tall, lengthy, rather unfurnished colt: has scope: half-brother to 3 winners, including Italian 3-y-o Scisma (by Ballad Rock), 5f/6f winner at 2 yrs, and Irish 2m winner Coopers Spot-On (by Glenstal): dam, Irish maiden, half-sister to a US Grade 1-winning middle-distance stayer: fairly useful form: best effort when third of 7 to Buy

Or Sell in listed race at York: landed odds in maiden at Goodwood later in month: speedy, and likely to prove best at 5f: probably still capable of better. *K. R. Burke*

MELT THE CLOUDS (CAN) 6 ch.g. Diesis 133 – Population (General **40** Assembly (USA)) [1998 NR 1999 a9.4g⁵ a13g 7m 8.3g 7s 8s Sep 27] quite attractive gelding: fair maiden at 3 yrs: just poor form at best in 1999, leaving M. Pipe after second outing: stays 1¼m: acts on firm and soft ground: blinkered/visored first 4 starts. *J. Neville*

MELVELLA 3 b.f. Mtoto 134 – Trojan Desert 97 (Troy 137) [1998 NR 1999 10d⁶ **70 d** 10m 12d⁶ 10g⁵ 12m⁶ a14.8g³ 11.9d 12d Oct 29] rather sparely-made filly: fifth foal: half-sister to winners abroad by Kalaglow and Local Suitor: dam 7f winner, later successful in USA: fair form first 2 starts, just modest at best after: may prove best around 1½m: acts on good to soft going, good to firm and fibresand. *M. L. W. Bell*

MEMORISE (USA) 5 b.h. Lyphard (USA) 132 – Shirley Valentine 104 (Shirley **104** Heights 130) [1998 112: 13.4m³ 12d⁵ 14v* 13.3m³ 1999 12m³ 12m² 12m* Aug 7] rather leggy, angular horse: has a quick action: smart at 4 yrs, just useful in 1999: won 6-runner minor event at Ascot in August by ½ length from Wales: effective at 1½m, and will stay 2m: acts on any going. *H. R. A. Cecil*

MEMORY'S MUSIC 7 b.g. Dance of Life (USA) – Sheer Luck 72 (Shergar **–** 140) [1998 34, a49?: a12g³ a12g* a12g⁴ 10s² a12g a10g 1999 a12f Jan 14] sturdy gelding: poor handicapper: stays 1½m: acts on equitrack and soft ground: visored once at 3 yrs. *M. Madgwick*

MEMPHIS DANCER 4 b.f. Shareef Dancer (USA) 135 – Wollow Maid 73 **–** (Wollow 132) [1998 67: 8.1m² 8m 10.2s⁶ 10m 12m 12d² 1999 11.1g⁶ May 2] big, strong, lengthy filly: fair maiden at best: well held only 4-y-o start: should stay 1½m: acts on soft and good to firm going: sometimes slowly away. *Miss Lucinda V. Russell*

MENDELUCI (IRE) 7 b.g. Nordico (USA) – Favourite Niece (Busted 134) **36** [1998 –: 10.8m 1999 a12g⁵ Jan 20] fairly useful winner in Ireland in 1995: lightly raced and poor at best since: stays 1½m: acts on firm going and fibresand: usually blinkered/visored. *L. R. Lloyd-James*

MENDOZA 5 b.g. Rambo Dancer (CAN) 107 – Red Poppy (IRE) 58 (Coquelin **52** (USA) 121) [1998 52, a55: a8g⁴ a8g a8.5g 8f³ 9m³ 10g 11.9d⁵ 8m³ 8.1m a8g⁶ a10f⁴ 1999 a10g² a12g⁴ a12g⁵ a10g⁴ 11.9f May 4] modest handicapper: probably stays 1½m: acts on firm ground and equitrack: tried blinkered: usually gets behind. *P. Mitchell*

MEN OF WICKENBY 5 b.g. Shirley Heights 130 – Radiant Bride (USA) **59 d** (Blushing Groom (FR) 131) [1998 NR 1999 12.1m 11.1s⁴ 10d 9.2g* 9.2g⁵ 12m 12g 9.2f 11.1m⁵ 10m Sep 24] won seller at Hamilton in June by 5 lengths: poor at best (mostly in handicaps) otherwise: likely to prove best around 1¼m: best effort on good going. *Martyn Wane*

MENSA 3 ch.g. Rudimentary (USA) 118 – Musianica 92 (Music Boy 124) [1998 **111** 88: 6m⁵ 6d³ 5.9d² 7.1d* 7d⁵ 1999 9m* 8g⁴ 10.4s⁵ 8f² 7m⁵ 7m⁴ 8m⁴ 7m² 7m² Dec 12] lengthy, good-topped gelding: has a quick action: smart performer: won minor event at Ripon in April: ran well after when 3½ lengths fourth to Compton Admiral in Craven Stakes at Newmarket, head second of 6 to Kalanisi in listed race at Kempton and fifth to Lots of Magic in Jersey Stakes at Royal Ascot (final start for M. Tompkins): renamed Industrialist and in frame all 4 starts in Hong Kong: likely to prove best at 1m/9f: acts on firm and good to soft going: blinkered second 2-y-o start. *P. C. Kan, Hong Kong*

MENTEITH (USA) 3 b.g. Dehere (USA) 121 – Bunka Bunka (USA) (Raja Baba **–** (USA)) [1998 NR 1999 11.8g 11.9v Oct 13] $60,000Y: strong, lengthy gelding: third foal: dam, minor stakes winner up to 1½m in USA, from family of Lyphard: well beaten in maidens at Leicester and Haydock 6 months apart, sold from P. Cole's 750 gns in between. *B. P. J. Baugh*

MENTIGA (IRE) 2 b.g. (Jan 5) Dancing Dissident (USA) 119 – Lowtown (Cam- **88** den Town 125) [1999 5s² 5.1s² 6.1d³ 7g 6m 6.8d² 7.3v* 8.3d³ Nov 4] IR 7,600F, 12,000Y: seventh foal: dam Irish 1m/9f and hurdles winner: fairly useful performer: won nursery at Newbury in October: respectable effort in similar event at Windsor final start: probably stays 1m: acts on heavy going: edgy sort. *B. R. Millman*

MERANIE GIRL (IRE)   3 b.f. Mujadil (USA) 119 – Christoph's Girl 50 (Efisio   –
120) [1998 52: 6m 5g 5.1g⁶ 7g 5.1m⁵ 5m 5.2s 1999 6.1s 6g 8.2f 10.2g 7f 8m 5m Aug
30] modest maiden in 1998: little show at 3 yrs: blinkered once. *J. R. Arnold*

MERANTI   6 b.g. Puissance 110 – Sorrowful (Moorestyle 137) [1998 68: 5.7f 6m   **58 d**
6d³ 6m 6g 6m* 7m⁶ 6g* 7m⁵ 6m⁵ 6m 7g 6m 6s 1999 6m 6.1f 6g⁴ 6m 6f 6.1m 6g Aug
14] leggy gelding: modest handicapper: well below form after third outing: has won
at 7f but seems best around 6f: acts on good to firm going, probably on good to soft.
J. M. Bradley

MERCEDE (IRE)   2 b.f. (Apr 20) Perugino (USA) 84 – Miss Busybody (IRE)   –
(Phardante (FR) 123) [1999 8s 8s a6g Nov 27] IR 2,600F, 7,000Y, 9,500 2-y-o: leggy
filly: third foal: half-sister to winners abroad by Don't Forget Me and Case Law: dam
ran twice: well held in maidens. *N. P. Littmoden*

MERCHANT PRINCE   3 b.g. Flying Tyke 90 – Bellinote (FR) 71 (Noir Et Or   –
125) [1998 –: 5g 1999 5g 5d 7f 6f 8.2s Nov 1] leggy gelding: no sign of ability.
A. Smith

MERCURY (IRE)   6 b.g. Contract Law (USA) 108 – Monrovia (FR) (Dancer's   **31**
Image (USA)) [1998 –, a51d: a8.5g a11g² a12g⁶ a12g⁴ a11g 10g 8m a12g a10g
a8g 1999 a9.4g a8g a12g a11g a12g a11g May 17] strong, lengthy gelding: bad
performer: stays 1½m: acts on fibresand: tried blinkered/visored: inconsistent.
B. P. J. Baugh

MERE SLAD   3 b.f. Beveled (USA) – Pallomere 85 (Blue Cashmere 129) [1998   –
–: 7g a6g⁵ 1999 a6g 8.2m a6g 11.6s⁵ 10m a14g Sep 28] no form. *Derrick Morris*

MERLY NOTTY   3 ch.f. Inchinor 119 – Rambadale 68 (Vaigly Great 127) [1998   **34 ?**
–: 5s 5d 7d 1999 7m 8m 9.2f 12.4f⁵ Aug 4] unfurnished filly: poor maiden.
J. S. Haldane

MERRY (IRE)   2 ch.f. (Mar 23) Ridgewood Ben 113 – Speedy Action (Horage   –
124) [1999 7.9m 7s 7.9g Oct 6] 500Y: seventh foal: half-sister to 3-y-o Vale of Leven
and 1m winner Bustle'em (by Burslem): dam Irish 1¼m winner: little sign of ability.
N. Tinkler

MERRY MELODY   4 b.f. Almoojid 69 – Merry Marigold 77 (Sonnen Gold 121)   **45**
[1998 –: 8.1m⁵ 8m 7d 1999 7m⁴ 10m Aug 28] poor maiden: should stay 1m: acts on
good to firm going. *R. J. Hodges*

MERRY MERLIN   2 b.c. (Apr 22) Polar Falcon (USA) 126 – Bronzewing 103   **98 p**
(Beldale Flutter (USA) 130) [1999 7m* 7d⁵ Oct 1] useful-looking colt: half-brother
to several winners, including 4-y-o Minivet, 1996 2-y-o 7f winner Redwing (by
Reprimand) and stayer Sun Grebe (by Arctic Tern), all fairly useful: dam 6f and 1m
winner: made most encouraging winning debut in well-contested 16-runner maiden
at Newmarket in August, pulling clear with short-head runner-up Cabriac: useful
form when last of 5 to Scarteen Fox in listed event there only subsequent start: likely
to stay 1¼m: probably capable of better still. *M. L. W. Bell*

MERRY PRINCE (IRE)   4 b.g. Roi Danzig (USA) – Queen of The Brush (Averof   **62 §**
123) [1998 66: 10d 8g 7.1d⁵ 11.4d⁵ 10g⁶ 8g⁵ 10s a13g⁴ 1999 a10f⁵ a12g a10f³ a12g   **a53 §**
a11g 10g⁵ 9.9m⁵ 11.7g⁵ 11.6m Jul 19] tall, lengthy gelding: modest maiden: stays
1½m: acts on good to firm going, good to soft and equitrack (well beaten on
fibresand): usually blinkered/visored nowadays: ungenuine. *P. R. Hedger*

MERRYVALE MAN   2 b.c. (Apr 7) Rudimentary (USA) 118 – Salu 65 (Ardross   **63**
134) [1999 5m 6g 6.8m 7.5g³ 7s⁵ 7g 6d a8g² Nov 30] 1,200Y, 3,600 2-y-o: leggy,   **a60**
unfurnished colt: second foal: half-brother to 3-y-o Clarinch Claymore: dam, 11f to
2m winner, out of half-sister to Middle Park winner Creag-An-Sgor: modest maiden:
stays 1m: acts on fibresand, well beaten on softer than good on turf. *J. G. Given*

MERSEY MIRAGE   2 b.c. (May 9) King's Signet (USA) 110 – Kirriemuir 51   **84**
(Lochnager 132) [1999 6d⁴ 5m⁴ 6d 6f* 6f³ 5g 6d² Aug 17] 3,000F, 2,200Y, 5,200
2-y-o: neat colt: first foal: dam 5f (at 2 yrs) to 7f winner: fairly useful performer: won
maiden at Brighton in July: good second of 6 in minor event there final start: stays 6f:
acts on firm and good to soft going. *R. Hannon*

METEORITE (IRE)   3 b.g. Bigstone (IRE) 126 – Winning Appeal (FR) 62 (Law   **73**
Society (USA) 130) [1998 61p: 8d 1999 10g⁵ 12m⁵ 11.6m⁴ 12f 14.1g⁴ 15.8m²

14.4m[5] 15d[6] 17.2s 14.8d[4] 16s Oct 22] leggy gelding: fair maiden handicapper: generally creditable efforts in 1999: should stay beyond 2m: acts on good to firm and good to soft going, seemingly not on soft: sold 20,000 gns, joined J. Eustace. *R. Hannon*

METEOR STRIKE (USA)   5 ch.g. Lomond (USA) 128 – Meteoric 102 (High   **73 §**
Line 125) [1998 87+: 10m a12g[5] a12g* 1999 12m[2] 14.4g[6] 10g[4] 9.9m 8.9m[3] 12f 10.4d Oct 7] big, lengthy gelding: fair performer: left Mrs A. Perrett after third start: reportedly finished lame behind on penultimate outing and had breathing problem final one: stays easy 1½m: acts on equitrack and good to firm going (yet to race on soft/heavy): blinkered on reappearance: has been tongue tied: inconsistent. *D. Nicholls*

METHODIST (IRE)   2 b.g. (Feb 9) Rainbows For Life (CAN) – Pass The Rose   **81**
(IRE) (Thatching 131) [1999 6m 6.1m* 6g[2] 8.5g 9f[5] Dec 12] 6,800F: first foal: dam, unraced half-sister to Cheveley Park winner Pass The Peace (probably stayed 1¼m), the dam of Cheveley Park winner Embassy: won seller at Nottingham in August: short-headed in valuable 23-runner similar event at York later in month (claimed from N. Tinkler 10,000 gns): off 3 months, ran well at Calder in valuable non-group event and an allowance race, blinkered both times: stays 9f. *L. Olivares, USA*

MEXICAN ROCK   3 b.c. Rock City 120 – Pink Mex (Tickled Pink 114) [1998   **92**
NR 1999 6v* 6g 7g[5] May 15] well-made colt: sixth foal: half-brother to 3 winners, including fairly useful 1995 2-y-o 6f to 1m winner Believe Me (by Beveled) and 1m and 1¼m winner Tragic Hero (by Tragic Role): dam little form: won maiden at Folkestone in April by 8 lengths: stiffer tasks in listed races after, far from discredited when last of 5 (beaten 5 lengths) behind Fragrant Oasis at Newmarket, though left behind when pace increased: may stay beyond 7f. *J. A. R. Toller*

MEZZORAMIO   7 ch.g. Cadeaux Genereux 131 – Hopeful Search (USA) 71   **55**
(Vaguely Noble 140) [1998 59, a?: 8.2m 7f[3] 6d[4] 6.1g[3] 6m 6.9d 8f a8g a10g 1999 a7g   **a34**
a8g[3] a9.4g[5] 8.2m[5] 7m[6] 8m[3] 7.7m* 8f[4] 7f* 7g[5] 7d Sep 15] workmanlike gelding: modest handicapper on turf, poor on all-weather: won at Warwick (selling event) and Yarmouth in July: best at 6f to 1m: acts on fibresand, best on good going or firmer on turf: effective blinkered/visored or not: good mount for inexperienced rider: best up with pace. *K. A. Morgan*

MHEANMETOO   8 ch.g. Roi Danzig (USA) – Spinster 75 (Grundy 137) [1998   **–**
NR 1999 a12f a8g Mar 8] fair 7f winner at 2 yrs: lightly raced and little form since. *A. P. Jones*

MI AMIGO   2 b.c. (Apr 15) Primo Dominie 121 – Third Movement 75 (Music   **57 p**
Boy 124) [1999 6s Nov 5] 20,000F, IR 36,000Y: sturdy, angular colt: brother to 3-y-o First Hussar and 2 winners, including useful Italian sprinter Bruttina and half-brother to several winners, including useful 1995 2-y-o 6f winner Apple Musashi (by Never So Bold): dam maiden, stayed 7f: very green when seventh of 20 to Royal Highlander in maiden at Doncaster, not punished once fading: will prove capable of better. *L. M. Cumani*

MICE IDEAS (IRE)   3 ch.g. Fayruz 116 – Tender Encounter (Prince Tenderfoot   **63**
(USA) 126) [1998 67: 6d 7d[4] 7f 8.1m[4] 7.5m[2] 8m[5] 1999 10d 12.5m[5] 12g[4] 14.1g a12g[5] a14.8g[4] Sep 18] tall, angular gelding: modest maiden: stays 1½m: acts on good to firm and good to soft going, probably on fibresand: sometimes carries head awkwardly and is usually held up: joined N. Littmoden. *S. Mellor*

MICE WORLD (IRE)   2 b.g. (Mar 30) River Falls 113 – Naglaa (USA) (State   **–**
Dinner (USA)) [1999 7g 8d 8s Oct 25] IR 4,800F, 10,000Y: lengthy, workmanlike gelding: sixth foal: half-brother to Italian 1m winner Real Lady (by Waajib): dam unraced: well behind in maidens. *S. Mellor*

MICHELE MARIESCHI   2 b.g. (Apr 23) Alzao (USA) 117 – Escape Path   **98**
(Wolver Hollow 126) [1999 7m* 8s[6] 8.1m[2] 8.1s[2] Oct 2] 44,000Y: tall, quite good-topped gelding: has scope: easy mover: fourth foal: half-brother to smart 5f (at 2 yrs) to 7f (Jersey Stakes) winner Sergeyev and Irish 1m and 1½m winner Sea Fisher (both by Mulhollande): dam half-sister to William Hill Futurity winner Sandy Creek: useful performer: won maiden at Newmarket in June: placed in minor events at Haydock (jinked and almost unseated rider) and Sandown (pulled hard in blinkers

and carried head high): bred to stay beyond 1m: acts on soft and good to firm going: looks difficult ride. *P. F. I. Cole*

MICKLEY (IRE) 2 b.g. (Apr 17) Ezzoud (IRE) 126 – Dawsha (IRE) 75 (Slip Anchor 136) [1999 6d 6g⁵ 7.1d* 7m* 7m⁵ 8g⁴ 8d 7s Oct 23] IR 15,000F, 11,000Y: tall gelding: first foal: dam 1¼m winner: fairly useful performer: won maiden at Musselburgh in June and nursery at Chester in July: below form last 2 starts, something possibly amiss final one: will stay at least 1¼m: acts on good to firm and good to soft going. *J. D. Bethell* — **83**

MICKY DEE 3 ch.g. Lion Cavern (USA) 117 – Bellagio 68 (Busted 134) [1998 –: 8m 1999 a10g a10g Nov 26] tall gelding: no sign of ability. *P. W. Hiatt* — **–**

MIDDAY COWBOY (USA) 6 b.g. Houston (USA) – Perfect Isn't Easy (USA) (Saratoga Six (USA)) [1998 –: a12s a8g a11g 1999 7.1g 14m 16m 9.2m 16f 12d Sep 26] no longer of any account. *Miss Lucinda V. Russell* — **–**

MIDDELKERKE 3 b.g. College Chapel 122 – Andbell (Trojan Fen 118) [1998 NR 1999 8.3d² 8s⁵ 8g a9.4g Aug 14] 24,000F, 40,000Y: rather unfurnished gelding: sixth foal: half-brother to a 1m winner in Norway by Mango Express: dam, of little account, from family of excellent broodmare Flying Melody: fairly useful form in Windsor maiden on debut: disappointed after, leaving P. Chapple-Hyam cheaply before final start. *D. J. Wintle* — **81 d**

MIDDLETHORPE 2 b.g. (Apr 6) Noble Patriarch 115 – Prime Property (IRE) 60 (Tirol 127) [1999 5d⁶ 6f⁴ 7m 7g⁵ 7.5g³ 7d³ 7.9f 8d Sep 26] unfurnished gelding: first foal: dam 6f winner: modest maiden: well held last 2 starts: should stay at least 1m: acts on good to soft going. *M. W. Easterby* — **55**

MIDHISH TWO (IRE) 3 b.g. Midhish 109 – Tudor Loom (Sallust 134) [1998 84: 5g⁴ 6v* 5.2m⁴ 7.3g 1999 a6g⁶ 6g⁵ 5s³ 6m* 7d 6m⁶ 7f 7m⁶ Sep 7] leggy gelding: has a quick action: fairly useful handicapper: won 20-runner valuable event at Lingfield in May by 1½ lengths from Cubism: ran creditably after only on sixth start: best at 6f: acts on heavy and good to firm going (ran as though something amiss on firm): often taken last/steadily to post. *P. Mitchell* — **91**

MIDNIGHT ALLURE 2 b.f. (Mar 12) Aragon 118 – Executive Lady 59 (Night Shift (USA)) [1999 5m⁵ 6.1m 6.1d Oct 1] third living foal: sister to 6-y-o Midnight Escape: dam stayed 7f: modest form only on debut: raced too freely final start. *C. F. Wall* — **52**

MIDNIGHT DREAM 4 ch.f. Infantry 122 – Enterprise Lady (FR) 69 (Gorytus (USA) 132) [1998 NR 1999 8.2s Mar 29] second foal: dam 8.3f seller winner, half-sister to useful Italian miler Karla Wyller: tongue tied, no show in maiden at Nottingham. *A. Smith* — **–**

MIDNIGHT ESCAPE 6 b.g. Aragon 118 – Executive Lady 59 (Night Shift (USA)) [1998 113: 5m⁶ 5m* 5d 5d³ 5g 5d 1999 5m 5m 5m³ 5.1m 5m 5.2g 6g 5.6g⁴ 6.1g Sep 25] close-coupled gelding: smart at best: only useful nowadays: some creditable efforts in 1999, including third in minor event at Kempton and fourth in Portland Handicap at Doncaster: stays 5.6f: acts on firm and good to soft going: often races prominently/leads. *C. F. Wall* — **99**

MIDNIGHT MAX 2 b.g. (Jun 5) Sure Blade (USA) 130 – Carpadia (Icecapade (USA)) [1999 6.1m 7g⁵ 7g Aug 6] seventh foal: half-brother to 6f (at 2 yrs) and 1m winner Tancred Grange (by Prince Sabo) and 7.6f to 9.4f winner Dia Georgy (by Reesh): dam French maiden: no promise, including in seller. *C. A. Dwyer* — **–**

MIDNIGHT ORCHID (IRE) 3 b.f. Petardia 113 – Rosa Van Fleet (Sallust 134) [1998 74: 6g² 5s² 6d* 6m⁶ a6g⁵ 6g² 6d⁵ 6m 1999 a6g 6.1m 6g 7m³ 7m² 7g 6.8m 7g Jul 26] leggy filly: fair handicapper: stays 7f: acts on good to soft going, good to firm and fibresand: sometimes hangs badly: tail flasher: unreliable. *J. Berry* — **69 §**

MIDNIGHT WATCH (USA) 5 b.g. Capote (USA) – Midnight Air (USA) 111 (Green Dancer (USA) 132) [1998 –: 10s 1999 11.8m 14.4m Sep 8] leggy gelding: fairly useful maiden for H. Cecil at 3 yrs: lightly raced and no show since. *P. Winkworth* — **–**

MIDSUMMER NIGHT (IRE) 4 b.f. Fairy King (USA) – Villota (Top Ville 129) [1998 50: 6d⁶ 6m 6.1g⁵ 5.1d 5m⁵ 1999 a5g a6s Feb 10] lengthy, unfurnished filly: modest maiden at 3 yrs: tailed off on all-weather both 4-y-o starts: should stay 6f: acts on good to firm ground. *J. S. Wainwright*

MIDSUMMER ROMANCE (IRE)   4 b.f. Fairy King (USA) – Jealous One (USA) (Raise A Native) [1998 56: 10.2s 8m 10m 8m 8d⁴ 8s 1999 10.5d³ 12.1m 11.6s 14.1m 12m Sep 17] tall, angular filly: modest maiden handicapper: well held after reappearance: effective at 1m/1¼m: acts on good to soft ground: blinkered final start. *B. J. Meehan*   **54 d**

MIDYAN QUEEN   5 b.m. Midyan (USA) 124 – Queen of Aragon 76 (Aragon 118) [1998 62d: 7s⁶ 7.6m 8g 7.5m a7g⁶ 1999 7.7s⁶ 6.1f 7.6m Jul 9] leggy mare: modest handicapper: no form in 1999: has worn tongue strap: sold 500 gns. *P. D. Evans*   **–**

MIGHTY ARTHUR   3 b.g. Puissance 110 – Fire Gold 48 (Never So Bold 135) [1998 NR 1999 9d⁵ 7.1m a7g a6g 7d Aug 20] tall, leggy, sparely-made gelding: third foal: dam poor maiden on Flat/over hurdles: no form. *D. Shaw*   **–**

MIGHTY MAGIC   4 b.f. Magic Ring (IRE) 115 – Mighty Flash 81 (Rolfe (USA) 77) [1998 63: 8d 8f 10d 7d 10.2d² 9m⁴ 12m² 10m⁴ 14g³ 16m 12s⁵ 1999 7f⁶ 8g⁵ 6m² 6m² 7m³ 6m 8d Oct 4] angular filly: modest maiden handicapper: has form from 6f to 1¾m: acts on soft and good to firm going, probably on firm: blinkered/visored once each: consistent: joined R. Alner. *Mrs P. N. Dutfield*   **61**

MIGRATION   3 b.c. Rainbow Quest (USA) 134 – Armeria (USA) 79 (Northern Dancer) [1998 NR 1999 10.2s* 10.4s⁶ 12d² Oct 1] tall, leggy colt: fifth living foal: brother to 3 at least useful winners, notably Armiger: dam, useful winner by 1¼m, half-sister to Park Hill winner I Want To Be: won maiden at Bath in April: hung right in straight when disappointing in listed race at York following month, but smart form when ¾-length second to Kahtan in similar event at Newmarket (started very slowly) in October: stays 1½m: raced only on good to soft/soft ground: wore crossed noseband final start: seems a difficult ride. *R. Charlton*   **112**

MIGWAR   6 b.g. Unfuwain (USA) 131 – Pick of The Pops 109 (High Top 131) [1998 –: 11.9s⁶ 8s a8.5g a12g 1999 a11g* a12g* a12g⁶ a11g⁴ a11g 10.3d 12.3m 10d a12g a10g a11g⁴ a8g a10g* Dec 22] deep-girthed gelding: one-time useful performer, just fair nowadays: easy winner of 2 sellers at Southwell in January, and also won handicap at Lingfield in December: mostly well beaten in between: stays 1½m: acts on all-weather, no form on turf since 1996: visored twice, including at Lingfield: edgy type. *N. P. Littmoden*   **– a67**

MIKE'S DOUBLE (IRE)   5 br.g. Cyrano de Bergerac 120 – Glass Minnow (IRE) 59 (Alzao (USA) 117) [1998 69: a6g² a6g⁴ a6g⁶ a6g⁶ a7g³ a7g⁵ 6.1s³ a7g* a7g² 6g 6g* 6g 7d⁴ 6s 6m 7m⁶ 8.2m 7g 7.6g a8g a6g 7g⁴ 8.2v a7g⁴ a8g a6g⁶ a6g⁴ a7g⁴ a6g* 1999 a6f³ a6f a6s² a6g a7g⁵ a6g³ 6.1v³ a6g 6s⁶ 6.1f 6s a7g 6g a6g 6g⁵ a6g a8g⁶ 8.2s a7g⁵ a7g⁷ a6g Dec 27] sturdy gelding: modest performer: well below form after seventh start: effective at 6f, probably 1m: acts on good to firm going, heavy and all-weather: tried blinkered, usually visored: sometimes carries head high and hangs: not to be trusted. *Mrs N. Macauley*   **62 d**

MIKE SIMMONS   3 b.g. Ballacashtal (CAN) – Lady Crusty (Golden Dipper 119) [1998 –: 7d 7d a7g 1999 12f 12.1m Jul 23] lengthy, workmanlike gelding: no promise. *L. P. Grassick*   **–**

MIKES WIFE   2 b.f. (Apr 7) Tragic Role (USA) – Grecian Belle 53 (Ilium 121) [1999 7d a8g Nov 15] 700Y, 3,400 2-y-o: second foal: dam maiden who stayed 1m: well beaten in maidens. *N. Bycroft*   **–**

MIKE THE SPUD   2 b.g. (May 9) Emarati (USA) 74 – Zilzilah (USA) 59§ (Zilzal (USA) 137) [1999 5d 6f 5v⁴ 5g 5m³ 6s 5s⁵ 6d a5g⁶ a6g⁶ Nov 19] 3,500Y: unfurnished, angular gelding: first foal: dam, temperamental maiden, probably stayed 1¼m: modest maiden on turf, poor on all-weather: should stay 6f: acts on fibresand, soft and good to firm ground: sent to Holland. *M. W. Easterby*   **52 a38 +**

MILAD (IRE)   4 b.g. Green Desert (USA) 127 – Arctic Winter (CAN) (Briartic (CAN)) [1998 69: 10v 9m 8g 6s 8.3m³ 9.7f 1999 a8g Apr 26] fair maiden in 1998: well beaten only 4-y-o start: stays 1m. *K. Bell*   **–**

MILADY LILLIE (IRE)   3 b.f. Distinctly North (USA) 115 – Millingdale Lillie   **65**
119 (Tumble Wind (USA)) [1998 57: 6m 6m 6g⁶ 1999 a6g⁴ 6m⁴ 6g⁵ 7f* 7g 7m⁴ 7d⁶
6.8m³ 7m⁶ 8.5m 7m³ Sep 1] fair performer: won minor event at Brighton in May:
generally creditable efforts otherwise: effective at 6f/7f: acts on firm going and
fibresand: has worn tongue strap: has been bandaged. *K. T. Ivory*

MILDON (IRE)   3 ch.g. Dolphin Street (FR) 125 – Lycia (Targowice (USA) 130)   **–**
[1998 –: 7m 1999 8m 8d 10g Jul 3] good-topped gelding: little form. *E. Weymes*

MILETRIAN (IRE)   2 b.f. (Feb 8) Marju (IRE) 127 – Warg (Dancing Brave   **101**
(USA) 140) [1999 7m 8.1m² 8.1g⁵ 9m* 8v⁴ Oct 3] IR 70,000Y: leggy, workmanlike
filly: third foal: sister to 1997 2-y-o 6f winner Marksman and half-sister to 3-y-o
Parkside: dam unraced daughter of sister to Shirley Heights: useful performer: easy
winner of maiden at Redcar in September: showed much improved form when fourth
of 11 to Lady of Chad in Prix Marcel Boussac at Longchamp on final start: should be
well suited by 1¼m/1½m: acts on good to firm and heavy ground. *M. R. Channon*

MILL AFRIQUE   3 b.f. Mtoto 134 – Milinetta (Milford 119) [1998 62: 5d 8.5m   **62 d**
8.2g⁵ 1999 11.6m 10.2s 10f² 10g⁴ 8g⁴ 12.4g 9.9s 10g Oct 14] rather leggy filly:
modest maiden: best efforts when dictating pace in small fields on third/fourth starts:
left C. Brittain after fifth: stays 1¼m: acts on firm going: blinkered (well held)
second outing. *Mrs M. Reveley*

MILL EMERALD   2 b.f. (Apr 5) Old Vic 136 – Milinetta (Milford 119) [1999 7s   **–**
Oct 8] fifth live foal: half-sister to 3-y-o Mill Afrique and 1993 2-y-o 1m winner Mill
Force (by Forzando): dam won over hurdles: always behind in maiden at Lingfield.
R. A. Fahey

MILLENARY   2 b.c. (Apr 21) Rainbow Quest (USA) 134 – Ballerina (IRE) 88   **87 p**
(Dancing Brave (USA) 140) [1999 7g³ 8m⁵ Sep 17] leggy, unfurnished colt: good
walker: fluent mover: second foal: dam, 2-y-o 7f winner, half-sister to Princess Royal
winner Dancing Bloom and smart French performer up to 1m River Dancer, herself
dam of Spectrum (by Rainbow Quest): plenty of promise when third of 6 to
Mana-Mou Bay in listed race at Newbury: good 5½ lengths fifth of 8 to Ethmaar in
minor event there (raced freely) following month: should stay at least 1¼m: should
improve again. *J. L. Dunlop*

MILL END QUEST   4 b.f. King's Signet (USA) 110 – Milva 56 (Jellaby 124)   **63**
[1998 60: 6g³ 6m 5.1m⁴ 5g 5g⁶ 5v 1999 5g 5d⁴ 6s³ 6.1f⁴ 6m* 6d⁶ 6f⁶ 6f 6.1m 5g Sep
20] sturdy filly: modest handicapper: made all at Pontefract in June: stays 6f: acts on
firm and soft ground: blinkered (well held) final start. *M. W. Easterby*

MILL END VENTURE (IRE)   3 b.g. Namaqualand (USA) – Risk All 90 (Run   **–**
The Gantlet (USA)) [1998 –: 6f 5m 6g 1999 12d 14.1m Jun 19] no promise: tends to
be slowly away and look tricky ride: sold 700 gns. *M. W. Easterby*

MILLENIUM MOONBEAM (USA)   2 ch.c. (Mar 11) Phone Trick (USA) –   **107 p**
Shywing (USA) (Wing Out (USA)) [1999 6f⁶ 6d* 6g⁴ Oct 2] $35,000Y, IR 34,000Y,
99,000 2-y-o: half-brother to several winners in USA, mostly at sprint distances: dam
won 5 stakes races at 6.5f and 1m: progressive form: won maiden at Salisbury in
August despite still looking green and carrying head awkwardly: did really well
considering lack of experience when never-nearer fourth of 26 to Khasayl in Two-
Year-Old Trophy at Redcar final start: will stay at least 7f: already useful, and will do
better still. *M. Pitman*

MILLENNIUM BUG   3 b.f. Rock Hopper 124 – So Precise (FR) (Balidar 133)   **–**
[1998 NR 1999 8g 10m⁶ 10m⁶ Jul 15] 550Y: half-sister to 11f winner Crystal Park
(by Head For Heights) and a winner in Sweden by Elegant Air: dam once-raced
half-sister to grandam of Shaamit: well beaten in maidens: reportedly finished lame
final start. *A. Streeter*

MILLESIME (IRE)   7 ch.g. Glow (USA) – Persian Myth (Persian Bold 123)   **41**
[1998 47: 5f⁵ 6m 5d⁶ 5g⁶ 6m⁵ 5g 5s 1999 5m 5m 5g⁵ 6f⁴ 6m 5m 6g Oct 14]
unfurnished gelding: poor performer: effective at 5f/6f: acts on firm going, below
form on softer than good: visored once in 1998: has had tongue tied: usually races
prominently. *Martyn Wane*

MILLIGAN (FR)   4 b.g. Exit To Nowhere (USA) 122 – Madigan Mill 86 (Mill   **–**
Reef (USA) 141) [1998 10s⁴ 10.5m² 10d² 1999 6g 6d 5s Sep 21] 300,000 francs Y:

quite attractive gelding: half-brother to several winners, including useful French middle-distance performer Rainbow Reef (by Rainbow Quest): dam, rated on only start at 2 yrs, later successful at 11.5f at 4 yrs: useful performer: in frame in minor events and listed race at Longchamp/Chantilly at 3 yrs for J. Pease in France: well held over inadequate trips in minor events in 1999: stays 10.5f: acts on soft and good to firm going: joined Venetia Williams. *D. Nicholls*

MILLING (IRE)   4 b.f. In The Wings 128 – Princess Pati 124 (Top Ville 129)   **77**
[1998 89: 8.2s⁵ 10d² 12d² 10m³ 9.2d* 9d⁶ 10d 12s 1999 8.5m 8g 10.5g⁴ 10d 10d 10s 11.6g Oct 11] long-backed filly: only fair form in 1999: stays 1½m: acts on good to soft going: sold 40,000 gns in December. *R. Guest*

MILLIONFORMERTHYR   3 b.f. Mon Tresor 113 – Regal Salute 68 (Dara   **–**
Monarch 128) [1998 54, a50: 5d⁶ 5m³ a6g² 7m 7f³ a6g 8g a6g 5.7v a8g⁵ 1999 10f 7.1g⁴ a7g 7f 11.6s Aug 9] modest performer at 2 yrs: little form in 1999: tried blinkered. *B. Palling*

MILLIONS   2 b.g. (Feb 12) Bering 136 – Miznah (IRE) 102 (Sadler's Wells (USA)   **– p**
132) [1999 7m 8s 8d Sep 23] strong individual: fourth foal: half-brother to 3-y-o Zindabad and useful Irish middle-distance stayer Geisha Girl (by Nashwan), 7f winner at 2 yrs: dam, Irish 2-y-o 6f winner, closely related to dam of US champion turf mare Flawlessly: clear signs of ability in maidens: will prove well suited by 1¼m+: has been coltish, and was gelded after final start: should do better. *Sir Michael Stoute*

MILLISCENT   3 b.f. Primo Dominie 121 – Millaine 69 (Formidable (USA) 125)   **49**
[1998 –: 6m 6m 7v 1999 8f⁴ 8f 8.1d a8g Jun 19] workmanlike filly: poor maiden: below form after reappearance: likely to prove best up to 1m: acts on firm going. *M. Johnston*

MILLSEC   2 b.f. (Feb 1) Petong 126 – Harmony Park 55 (Music Boy 124) [1999   **58**
6m 6d 5s⁶ 5g² Nov 3] 3,000Y: leggy filly: sixth foal: sister to fair 1994 2-y-o 6f seller winner Vocalize: dam, 7f winner at 4 yrs, sister to useful sprinter Melody Park: modest maiden: second of 16 in selling nursery at Musselburgh final start: may prove best at 5f. *R. Bastiman*

MILNE'S DREAM   3 b.f. Reprimand 122 – Milne's Way 83 (The Noble Player   **–**
(USA) 126) [1998 47: 6s 5m 5s 5.7v³ 1999 10.1g 8.2f 7f a14g Nov 30] close-coupled filly: poor maiden: no form in 1999: left M. Quinlan before final start. *P. R. Hedger*

MILTON   6 ch.g. Groom Dancer (USA) 128 – Gold Flair 93 (Tap On Wood 130)   **–**
[1998 58: a8g⁵ a11g⁶ 1999 11g 16s Oct 22] formerly fair maiden, very lightly raced: no show in 1999. *P. T. Dalton*

MIMANDI (IRE)   2 b.f. (Mar 9) Pips Pride 117 – Glass Minnow (IRE) 59 (Alzao   **–**
(USA) 117) [1999 6d 6s Sep 29] IR 6,000Y: third foal: half-sister to 4-y-o Little Tumbler and 5-y-o Mike's Double, both by Cyrano de Bergerac: dam placed up to 9f in Ireland: always behind in maidens. *I. Semple*

MINALCO   3 ch.f. Minster Son 130 – La Millie (Nonoalco (USA) 131) [1998 NR   **–**
1999 9m⁵ 8g 8m 12s Nov 2] third reported living foal: dam French maiden: well held in maidens. *R. E. Barr*

MINDANAO   3 b.f. Most Welcome 131 – Salala 83 (Connaught 130) [1998 –: 6g   **98 p**
7d 1999 6g 9m* 9.9m² 10f² 10d* 10d² 10v* Oct 11] leggy filly: useful handicapper: progressed well in 1999, winning at Newcastle in June, Ripon in August and Ayr in October, last-named by 6 lengths from Caerosa, just pushed clear once asserting: likely to stay 1½m: acts on any going: held up: should continue to improve, and type to have another good season. *Miss J. A. Camacho*

MINDRACE   6 b.g. Tina's Pet 121 – High Velocity 53 (Frimley Park 109) [1998   **43**
53: 5m 5.7f 5g 5m⁵ 5m 1999 5m 5g⁶ 6g 5m 5m⁶ Jul 10] leggy gelding: poor handicapper: best at 5f: acts on firm ground: probably effective blinkered/visored or not: has had tongue tied: none too consistent. *K. T. Ivory*

MIND THE SILVER   2 gr.g. (Jan 16) Petong 126 – Marjorie's Memory (IRE) 76   **65**
(Fairy King (USA)) [1999 6m⁶ 6g⁵ 5g⁶ Oct 19] sturdy gelding: first foal: dam 5f winner, including at 2 yrs: fair maiden: well-backed favourite, well below par final start. *V. Soane*

MINERS QUEST   3 b.g. Miner's Lamp 114 – Interrogate 54 (In Fijar (USA) 121)   **66**
[1998 NR 1999 14g⁶ Jul 2] first foal: dam, maiden, best short of 11f: sixth of 7 in
maiden at Sandown, very green after slow start. *G. A. Butler*

MINETTA   4 ch.f. Mujtahid (USA) 118 – Minwah (USA) (Diesis 133) [1998 77:   **85**
10s⁶ 7.9g 10g 8g⁴ 8g² 8f* 8d* 8m² 8m³ 7m⁵ 7g⁵ 1999 8g 8d⁴ 8m 8m 8.3m* 9f 8.3s
8m² 8.3m* 8f* 8d Oct 14] lengthy filly: fairly useful handicapper: won at Windsor in
July/August and Thirsk in September: ran creditably only when in frame otherwise:
best at 7f/1m: acts on firm and good to soft going, probably on soft: blinkered once at
3 yrs: carries head high, and has hung left. *M. L. W. Bell*

MINGLING   2 b.c. (Feb 20) Wolfhound (USA) 126 – On The Tide 72 (Slip Anchor   **75**
136) [1999 7g⁴ 7m⁵ 7d Sep 16] 38,000F, IR 22,000Y: second foal: half-brother to
3-y-o Tier Worker: dam, 1m winner, half-sister to Rock City and Kerrera: fair form
in maidens at Newmarket (2) and Ayr: will stay 1m: sweating second start.
M. H. Tompkins

MINI LODGE (IRE)   3 ch.g. Grand Lodge (USA) 125 – Mirea (USA) 104 (The   **–**
Minstrel (CAN) 135) [1998 96?: 7g* 8g 7s² 7g² 1999 10.4d⁶ 8m 9f⁶ 8m 10.3d Oct
22] tall, close-coupled gelding: useful at 2 yrs: ran poorly in 1999: should be suited
by 1¼m: best form on good or softer going. *J. G. FitzGerald*

MINIMUS TIME   2 ch.f. (Apr 25) Timeless Times (USA) 99 – Glenfield Greta   **36**
72 (Gabitat 119) [1999 6g 5f³ 5.1m 5f⁶ Jul 24] 1,650Y, resold 800Y: dam form (at 2 yrs)
to 7.5f winner: poor form at best in sellers: reportedly gurgled final start. *T. M. Jones*

MINI RED   2 ch.f. (Apr 5) Timeless Times (USA) 99 – Loving Doll 72 (Godswalk   **–**
(USA) 130) [1999 5.3f 6g 8.3d Nov 4] 500F, 2,000Y: half-sister to 4-y-o Just Nobby,
10-y-o Nobby Barnes and 1¼m winner Ash Amour (by Hotfoot): dam maiden who
stayed 7f: soundly beaten in maidens/seller. *G. L. Moore*

MINIVET   4 b.g. Midyan (USA) 124 – Bronzewing 103 (Beldale Flutter (USA)   **94**
130) [1998 82: 9m 8g² 10d³ 8g² 9m* 9m³ 10.2d³ 11.9m⁶ 10.4g² 12.4v² 1999
12g* 12s³ 14g 11.9d³ 16.1m 16.1m⁶ 11.8m⁴ 12g² 11.9s* 10.4d² 12s⁵ Nov 6] leggy,
plain gelding: fairly useful performer: won handicaps at Newmarket in April and
Haydock in September: left M. Bell before creditable fifth in November Handicap at
Doncaster final start: stays 1½m, not 1¾m: acts on soft and good to firm going: often
held up: genuine and consistent: promising hurdler. *T. D. Easterby*

MINJARA   4 b.g. Beveled (USA) – Honey Mill 67 (Milford 119) [1998 –: 7d 8m   **39**
7g 10.2d 14.1s 1999 10.3d 11.8s 10.2g 8m⁴ 8.2m Jul 23] tall, leggy gelding: poor
maiden: stays 1m: acts on good to firm going: blinkered (raced freely) third start:
inconsistent. *Derrick Morris*

MINKASH (IRE)   2 b.c. (Mar 21) Caerleon (USA) 132 – Ingabelle 108 (Taufan   **92**
(USA) 119) [1999 6f⁴ 7f²* 7m² 8m² 8d Oct 9] IR 85,000Y: quite good-topped colt:
half-brother to several winners, including useful Irish 1995 2-y-o 6f and 7f (Moyglare Stud) winner Priory Belle (by Priolo) and smart Irish 6f and 7f winner Wild
Bluebell (by Bluebird): dam won Group 3 Phoenix Sprint: fairly useful performer:
won maiden at York in July: best effort when second of 10 in nursery at Doncaster
penultimate start: should stay 1¼m: acts on firm going, probably on good to soft:
noisy and led by 2 handlers at start on third outing. *B. Hanbury*

MINNESOTA   3 b.g. Danehill (USA) 126 – Santi Sana 80 (Formidable (USA)   **55**
125) [1998 76: 6f³ 6s² a7g* 7m* 6m⁶ 8m 8d 6g 8m 1999 9.9g 10m a8g⁵ 8g 7f 10m
7m⁴ a6g Oct 8] sturdy gelding: poor mover: fair winner at 2 yrs: modest at best in
1999: stays 1m: acts on firm going and fibresand: sometimes blinkered: has swished
tail and seemed difficult ride: sold 4,500 gns, joined M. Pipe. *N. A. Callaghan*

MINNISAM   6 ch.g. Niniski (USA) 125 – Wise Speculation (USA) (Mr Prospector   **–**
(USA)) [1998 50: 14.1g⁶ 11.7d³ 17.2d⁵ 1999 14.6s 17.2m Jul 20] angular gelding:
one-time fair winner: no form in 1999: barely stays 17f: acts on firm and soft ground:
often blinkered, including when winning. *G. A. Ham*

MINTY   3 b.g. Be My Chief (USA) 122 – Mindomica 63 (Dominion 123) [1998 –:   **64 d**
8d a8g 1999 a11g⁶ a11g² 12g⁴ a12g⁵ 9.9g⁵ 8.3m 9.3m⁵ 10.1d Oct 20] useful-looking
gelding: modest maiden: below form after third start, leaving C. Thornton before
final one: stays 11f: acts on fibresand, best turf form on good going: blinkered sixth
outing: tends to race freely. *N. Bycroft*

MINUIT NOIR (IRE)   3 b.g. Machiavellian (USA) 123 – Misbegotten (IRE) 112   **85**
(Baillamont (USA) 124) [1998 NR 1999 7.9d³ 10d* 12.3g 12.4m Sep 19] 580,000
francs Y: rather leggy, useful-looking gelding: first foal: dam, second in Prix de
l'Opera, stayed 10.5f: fairly useful performer: won maiden at Pontefract in July by ½
length from Bellefonte: lost all chance when rearing leaving stalls (after giving
trouble) final start: probably stays 1½m: acts on good to soft going. *J. G. FitzGerald*

MIRACLE ISLAND   4 b.g. Jupiter Island 126 – Running Game 81 (Run The   **74**
Gantlet (USA)) [1998 72: a9.4g² a11g² a9.4g* a11g4 9.9s⁴ 1999 10m 10m Apr 30]
tall gelding: fair handicapper: much better effort in 1999 when eighth of 22 at
Newbury on reappearance: stays 11f: acts on fibresand, soft and good to firm going:
visored once: fair hurdler: sold 10,000 gns, joined K. Burke. *D. R. C. Elsworth*

MIRACULOUS GUEST   3 b.f. Be My Guest (USA) 126 – Mystery Ship 105   **50**
(Decoy Boy 129) [1998 56: 7g⁶ 7m 1999 8s 8g 8.1f 10f⁶ 12m 8g⁶ 7d Oct 11] tall,
leggy filly: poor maiden: stays 1¼m: acts on firm going: visored once. *M. Kettle*

MIRAGGIO   3 b.g. Alhijaz 122 – Doppio 62 (Dublin Taxi) [1998 44: 7d a7g⁵   **52**
1999 a7g⁵ a8g⁶ 10m⁵ 11.6g 10f 17.2f⁴ 11.6m³ 11.6m 10.5m⁴ 10g⁴ 10d⁴ 11.6d Oct
28] angular gelding: modest maiden: ran creditably most starts in 1999, leaving
H. Morrison 1,500 gns before final one: finds 1¼m a bare minimum, and stays 17f:
acts on firm going, good to soft and fibresand: looked none too keen in blinkers
fourth and fifth outings. *B. J. Llewellyn*

MIRAKI (USA)   2 b.c. (May 3) Miswaki (USA) 124 – Lady's Truth (USA) (River-   **84**
man (USA) 131) [1999 6g³ 6f* a7f³ 8.5g 8f Oct 13] $80,000Y: second foal: dam, 9f
winner in France, sister to multiple stakes winner in USA Minneapple: won maiden
at Newmarket in June: left C. Wall and soundly beaten in 3 allowance races in USA:
should stay 1m. *M. Hennig, USA*

MIRBECK (USA)   3 ch.f. Gone West (USA) – Oakmead (IRE) 116 (Lomond   **86**
(USA) 128) [1998 74p: 6d 1999 7g² 7m* 8.1f² 8m² 8.3m Aug 28] strong, lengthy
filly: fairly useful performer: won maiden at Thirsk in June: good second in handicaps at Haydock and Doncaster after: stays 1m: acts on firm going: sent to USA.
P. W. Chapple-Hyam

MIRJAN (IRE)   3 b.g. Tenby 125 – Mirana (IRE) (Ela-Mana-Mou 132) [1998   **102 +**
NR 1999 10g* 12m³ 9.9s² 12m⁴ 10d 10s⁴ Oct 22] small, sturdy gelding: third foal:
half-brother to fairly useful winner Mirarima (by Shernazar): dam useful Irish
1½m winner from good family: useful performer: won maiden at Newmarket in
April: good efforts when fourth in handicaps at Royal Ascot (King George V, behind
Elmutabaki) and Newbury (behind Shadoof, set plenty to do): likely to prove best at
1¼m/1½m: acts on soft and good to firm going: sold 82,000 gns, joined L. Lungo
and gelded. *L. M. Cumani*

MISALLIANCE   4 ch.f. Elmaamul (USA) 125 – Cabaret Artiste (Shareef Dancer   **60**
(USA) 135) [1998 73d: 8g 8m 8.2d⁵ 9s⁶ 10.8m 9.7m³ 8.5m⁵ 8d 1999 8m 8.2g⁴ 8g
9.9s Sep 21] unfurnished filly: modest handicapper nowadays: stays 1m: acts on
good to firm and good to soft going, possibly not on soft: sold 1,000 gns, joined
M. Sowersby. *C. F. Wall*

MISBEHAVE   2 b.f. (Feb 21) Reprimand 122 – Princess Moodyshoe 72 (Jalmood   **95**
(USA) 126) [1999 5.1f² a5g² 5s* 6m* 6m 6g 8d* 8d Oct 30] leggy, unfurnished
filly: second foal: dam winner around 1½m and also successful over hurdles: useful
performer: won minor events at Warwick in May and Windsor in July and 20-runner
nursery at Newmarket in October: ran poorly in listed event at Newmarket final start:
should stay 1¼m: acts on soft and good to firm going: has given trouble at stalls.
M. L. W. Bell

MISCHIEF   3 ch.g. Generous (IRE) 139 – Knight's Baroness 116 (Rainbow Quest   **64**
(USA) 134) [1998 NR 1999 a10g⁵ a12g³ 10g 11.8v³ Apr 24] compact gelding: fifth
foal: closely related to 4-y-o Wales and half-brother to very smart 9f to 1½m winner
Riyadian (by Polish Precedent): dam won Irish Oaks: modest maiden: will stay 1¾m:
blinkered second start: sold 8,000 gns, joined M. Quinn. *P. F. I. Cole*

MISCONDUCT   5 gr.m. Risk Me (FR) 127 – Grey Cree 64 (Creetown 123) [1998   **56**
56: a7g⁵ a7g 8g a8g² 9.9m* 10.2g⁵ 10.2d⁴ a10g* 11.1m 9.9s⁴ 1999 11.7s² a10g May
7] lengthy mare: modest handicapper: better effort in 1999 (after successful spell

hurdling) on reappearance: ran as though something amiss next time: best at 1¼m/ 1½m: acts on good to firm going, soft and all-weather. *Mrs Merrita Jones*

MISHOR 3 b.f. Slip Anchor 136 – Miss Up N Go (Gorytus (USA) 132) [1998 **83** NR 1999 8g 8.2s³ 12.1s³ 14.8m* 14f⁶ 16.2g⁵ 14.8d Oct 15] leggy filly: second foal: half-sister to a winner in Turkey by Damister: dam unraced half-sister to Ribblesdale winner Miss Petard: fairly useful performer: won 6-runner maiden at Newmarket in July: below form in handicaps after: stays 1¾m: best efforts on going firmer than good: sweating and edgy final start, found little penultimate one: usually takes good hold. *W. Jarvis*

MISINTERPRETATION (IRE) 2 b.f. (Apr 26) Perugino (USA) 84 – Steel **44** Tap (IRE) (Flash of Steel 120) [1999 5d³ 6f³ 5v 5m* 5g⁴ 5g 5m 5s Sep 21] 4,200 2-y-o: leggy, close-coupled filly: fourth foal: closely related to a winner in Italy by Classic Music: dam, Irish maiden, out of sister to 2000 Guineas winner Tap On Wood: poor performer: won claimer in June: may prove best at 5f: acts on soft and good to firm ground. *N. Tinkler*

MISMEWMEW 4 b.f. Weldnaas (USA) 112 – Joan's Gift (Doulab (USA) 115) **– §** [1998 47§: a8g⁴ a8g⁴ 9.7v 8g 8f 8d⁴ a7g a10g 1999 a8f a8g 7f 7m 10d 11.5m 12.3m 8g 12m Jul 10] poor maiden: stays 1m: acts on equitrack and good to soft going: tried blinkered: ungenuine. *L. A. Dace*

MISPRINT 3 b.f. Minshaanshu Amad (USA) 91§ – Miss Copyforce (Aragon 118) **48** [1998 48: 5g 5m⁶ 6f⁵ 6m⁵ 5m a6f a8g² 1999 a7g a7f³ a8f⁶ a7g³ a8g a6g⁶ a5g⁴ Mar 4] poor maiden: effective at 6f, barely stays 1m: acts on equitrack: blinkered after reappearance: sent to Holland. *E. A. Wheeler*

MISRAAH (IRE) 2 ch.c. (Feb 27) Lure (USA) 131 – Dwell (USA) 96 (Habitat **94 P** 134) [1999 7d⁴ 7d* Oct 12] 160,000Y: close-coupled, useful-looking colt: sixth foal: half-brother to 3-y-o Doowaley and several winners abroad, including King Leon (by Caerleon), also useful 1m and 8.5f winner in Ireland at 2 yrs, and useful Hong Kong sprinter Quick Action (by Alzao): dam, 1m winner, at least as effective at 6f: shaped well when fourth of 22 to Scarteen Fox in maiden at Newbury, and landed odds in similar event at Leicester following month by 10 lengths from Tap, travelling well and leading well over 1f out: likely to prove best up to 1m: looks sure to go on to much better things. *Sir Michael Stoute*

MISS ALL ALONE 4 ch.f. Crofthall 110 – Uninvited 73 (Be My Guest (USA) **45** 126) [1998 51: 8.2s⁶ 7s³ a7g² 8s⁵ a8g² 8.2d² 8.2g³ a8g² a8.5g 1999 a8g² a8g³ **a52** a8g³ a7f² 10.3d 9.9g⁵ 9.3m⁴ 7m a7g Sep 28] unfurnished filly: modest maiden on all-weather, poor on turf: stays 1¼m: acts on fibresand and good to firm going, probably on soft: often blinkered/visored, effective without. *J. A. Glover*

MISS AMANPURI 3 b.f. Alzao (USA) 117 – Miss Rinjani 83 (Shirley Heights **90** 130) [1998 92: 6f⁵ 7d⁴ /m* 8d 1999 8.5g 9.9g⁴ 12d 10d Oct 14] leggy, unfurnished filly: fairly useful performer: highly tried in 1999, form only when 6½ lengths fourth to Claxon in listed event at Goodwood in May: stays 1¼m: acts on good to firm and good to soft ground: tail flasher, and found little final 2-y-o start. *G. Wragg*

MISS ARCH (IRE) 3 gr.f. Archway (IRE) 115 – Zanskar (Godswalk (USA) 130) **43** [1998 –: 6m 7.5m 9m⁵ 8.2v 1999 9.9d⁵ 8m 8m⁵ 10g³ 10g² 9.9g 10g Sep 20] close-coupled filly: poor maiden: placed in sellers in 1999: will stay 1½m: acts on good to firm ground: often slowly away. *M. A. Buckley*

MISS ASIA QUEST 2 ch.f. (Feb 14) Rainbow Quest (USA) 134 – Miss Kuta **70** Beach 91 (Bold Lad (IRE) 133) [1999 6.1d 7d³ 7d⁵ Nov 1] sister to a fairly useful maiden and half-sister to several winners, including fairly useful middle-distance performer Miss Rinjani (by Shirley Heights), 7f winner at 2 yrs, and to dam of smart 6f/7f performer Andreyev: dam, 6f and 1¼m winner, half-sister to smart 9f winner Bali Dancer: fair form in maidens: will need further than 7f at 3 yrs, and should stay 1¼m. *G. Wragg*

MISS BANANAS 4 b.f. Risk Me (FR) 127 – Astrid Gilberto 75 (Runnett 125) **49** [1998 –, a61: a5g² a5g⁴ a5g* a5g a5g 5m 5g 5v a5g a5g³ a5g a5s³ a5f 1999 a5g **a63** a6g a5g⁵ a6s⁴ a6g² 6f a5g 6g 6s a6g² a7g 6.8m⁵ 6m 5m 5g* a5g a6g a6g a6g Dec 27] workmanlike filly: modest on all-weather, poor on turf: won 20-runner ladies handicap at Leicester in August: effective at 5f/easy 6f: acts on all-weather: has been taken early to post: inconsistent. *C. N. Kellett*

MISS CHIQUITA (IRE) 4 b.f. Waajib 121 – Golden Leap (Salmon Leap (USA) –
131) [1998 63: 8v 9s⁶ 10s⁶ 12m* 12.5g⁴ 14m⁶ 12d⁵ 13m⁵ 10m⁵ 12g* 12s⁵ 1999 10.3d
Mar 25] fair performer: won claimers at Clonmel and Down Royal in 1998, sold from
J. Hayden in Ireland 4,200 gns after final start: no show only 4-y-o outing: stays
1¾m: acts on soft and good to firm going: blinkered. *J. S. Moore*

MISS DANGEROUS 4 b.f. Komaite (USA) – Khadine 79 (Astec 128) [1998 70: **64**
a5g⁵ a5g* a6g² a5g 5s* a6g* 6d⁶ 7.1g⁴ 6g 5d* 5d⁴ 5g 5s a5g a6g a6g 1999 a7g*
a8g a7g a6g a7g 7s⁵ 6s 5.1s a5g 5.7g 7m⁵ 7f 5d² 5.1s a7g a7g a5g⁶ Dec 10] rather
dipped-backed filly: modest handicapper: won at Lingfield in January: below best
after: effective at 5f to 7f: acts on soft ground and all-weather: tried blinkered: often
races prominently: inconsistent. *M. Quinn*

MISS DOODYBUSINESS 3 b.f. Formidable (USA) 125 – Miss Doody 63 (Gory- **30**
tus (USA) 132) [1998 –: 5g a5g a5g 1999 a7g³ a7g⁴ a8g⁵ a8g 10f a8g 12.1m⁶ 12g⁴ **a38**
11.1f⁵ 12m 10g a11g Sep 28] poor maiden: stays 1½m: acts on fibresand and firm
going: sold 500 gns, sent to Belgium. *C. W. Thornton*

MISSED MAY 5 br.m. Petong 126 – Altara (GER) (Tarim) [1998 NR 1999 a12g –
Dec 21] no form: tried blinkered. *M. Mullineaux*

MISS ELIMINATOR 4 b.f. Komaite (USA) – Northern Line 92 (Camden Town **57 d**
125) [1998 –: 6g 6d a5g 6d 1999 6d 7.5d² 7m 7.7s 6.9m 6m 10m⁶ 6f Jul 31] modest
handicapper: form since 2 yrs only when second in ladies race at Beverley in May:
may prove best at 5f/6f: acts on good to firm and good to soft going: tried blinkered,
including when successful: has been bandaged/tongue tied. *J. L. Harris*

MISS FARA (FR) 4 ch.f. Galetto (FR) 118 – Faracha (FR) (Kenmare (FR) 125) **73**
[1998 78: 10.5v⁵ 9g 8v⁶ 8s⁶ 8f 8m³ 8.2m² 8m 10g² 9.9m³ 1999 9.9m² 10m Aug 2]
leggy, angular filly: fair maiden: stays 1¼m: acts on good to firm going: fairly useful
over hurdles, winning 4 times from September to December. *M. C. Pipe*

MISS FIT (IRE) 3 b.f. Hamas (IRE) 125§ – Soucaro (Rusticaro (FR) 124) [1998 **87**
82+: a5g* 5.9m* 5m* 5d² 5d 1999 6m⁵ 5.1m⁶ 5d⁴ 5m 6d³ 5s⁵ 5.1g⁵ 5.1m* 5f 6f² 6m
6m⁵ 5m 5s 5g² Oct 16] unfurnished filly: fairly useful handicapper: won at Chester in
July: best at 5f/6f: acts on fibresand, firm and good to soft going: has hung and
swished tail: none too consistent. *Mrs G. S. Rees*

MISS FLIRTATIOUS 2 b.f. (Mar 8) Piccolo 121 – By Candlelight (IRE) 84 **63**
(Roi Danzig (USA)) [1999 5.1g 6m⁶ 5.7m⁶ 5m⁵ 5.1m⁴ 5.1g 6m 6g² Sep 20] 20,000Y:
tall, useful-looking filly: second foal: half-sister to 3-y-o Candellino: dam 6f winner
from family of Wassl: modest maiden: visored, made best effort when short-head second of
17 to Peruvian Jade in nursery at Leicester final start: effective at 5f/6f: raced only on
good/good to firm going: tends to race freely. *D. Haydn Jones*

MISS GRAPETTE (IRE) 3 b.f. Brief Truce (USA) 126 – Grapette (Nebbiolo **61**
125) [1998 77d: 5d³ 5f³ 5.1m² 6g² 5m 5g⁵ 1999 6g* 6d 6m 6m 6f⁴ 5m³ 5g⁶ 5d 6s 5v
Oct 11] close-coupled filly: modest performer: rather disappointing after winning
maiden at Catterick in March: effective at 5f/6f: acts on firm and good to soft going.
J. Berry

MISS HAMOUSE (IRE) 3 b.f. Hamas (IRE) 125§ – Highland Warning 43 –
(Warning 136) [1998 NR 1999 5.9m 5s⁶ 6f 5f Sep 4] IR 3,600G: first foal: dam,
sprint maiden, half-sister to 1985 Middle Park winner Stalker: little sign of ability.
J. Parkes

MISS HIT 4 b.f. Efisio 120 – Jennies' Gem (Sayf El Arab (USA) 127) [1998 75p: **75**
6g⁴ 6m⁵ 5g² 5m³ 5m 5g* 5d a6g a5g* 1999 a5g* a6g a5g 5m⁴ 5.1d⁵ 5d⁴ 5m⁴ 5.7m² **a78**
5m² 6m* 6g⁴ 5g 5.7f 6g Oct 11] sturdy filly: fair handicapper: trained first 6 starts by
Gay Kelleway, next 7 by D. Elsworth: won at Lingfield in January (awarded race)
and Salisbury in August: ran poorly last 2 starts: effective at 5f/6f: acts on all-weather
and good to firm ground. *G. A. Butler*

MISSILE TOE (IRE) 6 b.g. Exactly Sharp (USA) 121 – Debach Dust 64 (Indian **52**
King (USA) 128) [1998 56: 10s 10m⁵ 10m⁵ 10.1g⁵ 9m³ 10g 8g 1999 8.3m⁶ 8d⁵ **a–**
10.1g⁴ 8f² 8g 10m* 10.1m 10.4d 8s a10g Nov 24] good-topped gelding: poor walker:
modest handicapper: ended long losing run at Newmarket in July: well held after:
effective at 1m/1¼m: acts on firm and good to soft going, no recent form on all-
weather: tried blinkered/visored (not since 1996): pulls hard. *D. Morris*

MISS KIRSTY (USA)   2 ch.f. (Mar 13) Miswaki (USA) 124 – Spit Curl (USA)   **82 p**
(Northern Dancer) [1999 7d³ Oct 30] IR 33,000Y: seventh foal: closely related to a
winner in USA by Mr Prospector and half-sister to winners in USA by Cox's Ridge
and Ogygian: dam US Grade 1 1¼m winner: shaped encouragingly when third of 16
to Garota Do Leblon in maiden at Newmarket, eye-catching headway 2f out but no
extra near finish: raced freely, but will stay at least 1m: sure to improve and win at
least a maiden. *G. A. Butler*

MISS LACROIX   4 b.f. Picea 99 – Smartie Lee 66 (Dominion 123) [1998 –:   **32**
10.5d 12m a8.5g a8.5g 1999 a12g⁴ a16.2g⁴ a12g a16g 11.5m 10g 13.8m 16m Sep 13]
small, sturdy filly: poor maiden: should stay at least 2m: acts on fibresand and good
to firm going: has given trouble at start. *R. Hollinshead*

MISS LADY LYDIA   4 ch.f. Tina's Pet 121 – Kinfauns Dancer (Celtic Cone 116)   **–**
[1998 NR 1999 a10g Feb 16] no sign of ability in sellers/claimers. *Jamie Poulton*

MISS LORILAW (FR)   2 b.f. (Mar 29) Homme de Loi (IRE) 120 – Miss Lorika   **82 p**
(FR) (Bikala 134) [1999 7.9g* Oct 6] 160,000 francs Y: fourth foal: half-sister to 2
winners in France by Kadrou, including 7f (at 2 yrs) to 10.5f winner Miss Karila:
dam French 1¼m winner from family of Prix Jacques le Marois winner Miss Sata-
mixa: weak in market, won 26-runner maiden at York by ½ length from Muntej,
under pressure over 2f out before running on very strongly to lead last 50 yds: will be
very well suited by 1¼m+: sure to do better. *J. W. Hills*

MISS MAGNUM (IRE)   4 b.f. Whitehall Bridge 103 – Illiney Girl 66 (Loch-   **–**
nager 132) [1998 –: 9.9f 10.8m 1999 9.9m Jul 30] no sign of ability. *J. Neville*

MISS MILLENNIUM   2 b.f. (Mar 12) Sabrehill (USA) 120 – Lucky Thing   **42**
(Green Desert (USA) 127) [1999 5m 5.1s Apr 27] 4,000Y: third foal: sister to 2 poor
maidens: dam, unraced, from family of Terimon: poor form at best in early-season
maidens: sold 800 gns in October. *B. W. Hills*

MISS MONEY SPIDER (IRE)   4 b.f. Statoblest 120 – Dream of Jenny 73 (Caer-   **60**
leon (USA) 132) [1998 58: 7m 6g 5g³ 5f 6g⁴ 6f 7g* 8m³ 7s⁵ 1999 7s 6s 6g 7m* 5.9g
7.7m 7f* 7f³ 7f* 8g 7g 7m a7g⁶ Oct 13] leggy filly: modest performer: made all in
claimers at Folkestone in May and July and handicap at Lingfield in August: possibly
best at 7f nowadays: acts on equitrack and any turf going: blinkered once at 3 yrs:
races up with pace. *J. M. Bradley*

MISS MONTROSE   5 b.m. Tina's Pet 121 – Miss Ark Royal (Broadsword   **54**
(USA) 104) [1998 NR 1999 8.1m⁶ 10m 10d⁵ 14.1m 10m Sep 7] unfurnished mare:
second foal: dam winning selling hurdler: modest maiden: stays 1¼m: blinkered
(raced too freely) final start: has been bandaged in front: sent to Belgium. *M. Kettle*

MISS ORAH   2 b.f. (Apr 24) Unfuwain (USA) 131 – Massorah (FR) 108 (Habitat   **91**
134) [1999 7m⁴ 7m² 6d⁴ Oct 9] 30,000Y: quite good-topped filly: good mover with a
long stride: closely related to several winners, including fairly useful 6f winner
Massiba (by Shareef Dancer) and 7f winner Wisham (by Be My Guest), and half-
sister to a winner in Germany by Shadeed: dam French sprinter: fairly useful form:
won maiden at Salisbury in September: best effort when second of 7 to Veil of Avalon
in minor event at Newbury: not discredited in listed race at York final start: may
prove best up to 7f. *J. Noseda*

MISS PETERSHAM (IRE)   2 gr.f. (Apr 24) Petong 126 – Miss Siham (IRE) 59   **–**
(Green Forest (USA) 134) [1999 5.2m⁵ 5m⁶ 5v Sep 24] IR 10,000Y: first foal: dam
winning sprinter: well beaten in maidens. *Miss E. C. Lavelle*

MISS PIN UP   10 gr.m. Kalaglow 132 – Allander Girl (Miralgo 130) [1998 67:   **69**
a12g⁵ 11.8m⁴ 12m⁶ 11.5g² 16m⁴ 11.8m⁵ 14.1m* 14.1g⁴ 12g⁶ 1999 14.1m² 14.1g⁴   **a–**
14.1m² 14.4m² 14.1g 14.6d a16g Nov 8] tall mare: dam of 2-y-o Two's Better: fair
handicapper: creditable efforts in 1999 until last 2 starts: best around 1¾m: acts on
good to firm and good to soft ground, no show on equitrack: blinkered once at 3 yrs:
has been early to post. *R. McGhin*

MISS PIPPIN   3 ch.f. Rudimentary (USA) 118 – Appledorn 99 (Doulab (USA)   **52**
115) [1998 NR 1999 6.1m⁴ 5g⁴ 6.1g a6g⁵ a6g Nov 22] 5,000Y: workmanlike filly:
third foal: sister to poor 1m winner Patina and half-sister to a winner in Italy by
Primo Dominie: dam 6f/7f winner: modest form in maidens: may prove best at 5f.
B. A. McMahon

MISS PORTHCAWL (IRE) 2 b.f. (Apr 12) Tenby 125 – Stella Ann (Ahonoora – 122) [1999 7m a7g Sep 18] 13,000Y: seventh foal: half-sister to 4-y-o Cadmax and 7f/1m winner Indrapura (by Gallic League): dam best around 7f in Ireland: little promise in maiden/seller: sold 800 gns, sent to Kuwait. *M. L. W. Bell*

MISS RIMEX (IRE) 3 b.f. Ezzoud (IRE) 126 – Blue Guitar 88 (Cure The Blues **84** (USA)) [1998 82: 6m 5m 6m² 5m³ 6m* 7.3m 8m² 7s³ 8m 1999 9g⁴ 10m⁶ 10.1d 9m 8m⁵ 8m* 7.1d³ 8d⁵ 10g 8s* Oct 25] close-coupled, rather angular filly: fairly useful performer: won handicap at Newmarket in July and 20-runner claimer at Leicester (hung left) in October: probably finds 7f bare minimum now, and should stay beyond 1¼m: acts on soft and good to firm going: often held up: game. *D. R. C. Elsworth*

MISS ROXANNE 2 b.f. (Feb 6) Cyrano de Bergerac 120 – Conquista 87 (Aragon – 118) [1999 5d 5m 5.1f 5g⁶ a5g a8g Dec 6] 7,800Y: unfurnished filly: third foal: half-sister to 4-y-o Cumbrian Caruso: dam 1m winner: little sign of ability. *K. W. Hogg, Isle of Man*

MISS SCOOTER 4 ch.f. Beveled (USA) – Donosa (Posse (USA) 130) [1998 44, – a–: 5s² 5.1v⁵ 5.1m 7s⁴ 6s a8g⁵ 1999 a10f Jan 23] poor maiden: well beaten only start in 1999. *M. P. Muggeridge*

MISS SHANNON (IRE) 4 ch.f. Mukaddamah (USA) 125 – Lypharden (IRE) – (Lyphard's Special (USA) 122) [1998 –: 12g 8g 7v 7g 1999 a7g a6g Mar 10] ex-Irish filly: no sign of ability, including in blinkers: sold 520 gns. *R. A. Fahey*

MISS SHEMA (USA) 3 b.f. Gulch (USA) – Fire And Shade (USA) 91 (Shadeed **81** (USA) 135) [1998 72p: 6g⁴ 1999 7m³ 7m* 7.1g 7d Jun 5] tall, good-topped filly: good mover: fairly useful performer: won 16-runner maiden at Kempton in May: below form in handicaps after, blinkered final start: likely to stay 1m: acts on good to firm going: has been bit unruly in preliminaries: sold 45,000 gns in December. *B. Hanbury*

MISS SINCERE (IRE) 2 b.f. (Apr 5) Imperial Frontier (USA) 112 – Brite Mist **53** (IRE) (Shy Groom (USA)) [1999 5.1m 5m⁴ 5m⁵ 5g Aug 18] IR 1,000Y: close-coupled filly: unimpressive mover: third foal: dam unraced half-sister to Cyrano de Bergerac: modest sprint maiden: tailed off in seller final start. *B. S. Rothwell*

MISS SKICAP 2 b.f. (Mar 5) Welsh Captain 113 – Miss Nelski 84 (Most Secret **69** 119) [1999 a5g⁴ a5g² a6g* Dec 27] 7,800Y: sister to 3 winners, including fairly useful sprinter Ski Captain, and half-sister to fairly useful 1996 2-y-o 5f/6f winner Burkes Manor (by Presidium): dam 5f winner who stayed 7f: fair performer: won claimer at Wolverhampton in December: stays 6f. *T. D. Barron*

MISS SKYE (IRE) 4 b.f. Common Grounds 118 – Swift Chorus (Music Boy – 124) [1998 46: a8g³ a6g² a7g⁴ a8.5g⁵ a7g* a8g³ a7g⁴ a7g⁴ a6g 6m a8f 1999 a8g a7g 6f 7f 7m May 26] poor performer: stays 1m: acts on good to soft ground and all-weather: visored final start. *Miss B. Sanders*

MISS SPRINGFIELD 2 b.f. (Mar 26) Environment Friend 128 – Esilam 62 (Frim- – ley Park 109) [1999 5v 7d 7d Oct 14] 500Y: lengthy filly: eighth foal: half-sister to several winners, including 3-y-o Pure Elegancia, 4-y-o Pure Coincidence and 7-y-o Knotty Hill: dam, 2-y-o 5f winner here, won up to 1m in Italy: no show in maiden/sellers. *D. Morris*

MISS TAKE (IRE) 3 ch.f. Red Sunset 120 – Grave Error (Northern Treat (USA)) **52** [1998 52, a68: a5g a5g a6g* a7g² 6g⁵ 7m 7g³ 7m 7g 6m 7d a6g a7g a7g² a7g⁴ a8g² **a68** a8.5g* a7g* a7g⁴ 1999 a7g³ a8.5g⁶ a7g⁶ a10g³ a10g³ a8.5g² a12g⁶ a7g a7g a8.5g² 8.1d³ a9.4g* 10.3m a9.4g 9.7m³ 8.1d a9.4g⁵ Aug 14] leggy, sparely-made filly: fair handicapper on all-weather: modest on turf: below form after winning at Wolverhampton in June: stays easy 1¼m: acts on good to firm and good to soft going, better form on fibresand than equitrack: tried blinkered, visored nowadays: sometimes looks less than genuine: joined A. Newcombe. *P. D. Evans*

MISS TANGO 2 b.f. (Apr 14) Batshoof 122 – Spring Flyer (IRE) 66 (Waajib 121) **60** [1999 6f⁵ 6f³ 7m³ 6m³ 6g³ a6f⁵ Oct 2] 6,000Y: second living foal: dam, 7f (at 2 yrs) to 9.4f winner, half-sister to smart sprinter A Prayer For Wings: modest maiden: should stay 7f: acts on firm ground, well held on fibresand. *J. Berry*

MISS TRAXDATA 3 gr.f. Absalom 128 – Princess Sharpenup 63 (Lochnager – 132) [1998 –: 6m 5f 5s 1999 a8f a11g Feb 19] leggy filly: no form. *M. L. W. Bell*

MISS UNIVERSE (IRE)   3 gr.f. Warning 136 – Reine d'Beaute 97 (Caerleon   **97**
(USA) 132) [1998 99: 5d² 6g³ 6m* 7.1m³ 6.5g³ 6g⁴ 6s³ 1999 8g 6g³ 7m⁶ 6d 6s Oct
22] angular filly: useful performer: third in minor event at Yarmouth in August: stays
7f: acts on soft and good to firm going: sold 55,000 gns. *B. W. Hills*

MISS UNIVERSITY (USA)   3 gr.f. Beau Genius (CAN) – Gorgeously Divine   **–**
(USA) (Al Hattab (USA)) [1998 NR 1999 7g 10.5m Jun 23] $20,000Y, 19,000 2-y-o:
half-sister to several winners in USA, including minor 6f stakes winner Reissaurus
(by Country Pine): dam lightly raced in USA: well beaten in Newmarket maiden (for
C. Wall) and Warwick seller (pulled hard): may prove best up to 1m. *C. N. Allen*

MISS VITA (USA)   5 b.m. Alleged (USA) 138 – Torrid Tango (USA) (Green   **43**
Dancer (USA) 132) [1998 56, a51: a10g⁶ 11.8m 12.5d⁴ 12f² a12g² a12g* 16.1m³
a12g⁵ a12g a12g 1999 11.6m⁵ a12g⁶ 16.1s 14.6m 11.8m⁵ 16g² Aug 9] sparely-
made mare: poor handicapper: stays 2m: acts on firm ground, soft and fibresand:
often held up: sent to New Zealand. *R. J. R. Williams*

MISS VIVIEN   4 b.f. Puissance 110 – Madam Bold (Never So Bold 135) [1998   **41**
66d: 7.5s 6.1m 6s⁶ 7g⁴ 7d 6.9d⁶ 7g 7m² 7.1g 6v 7d 8s 1999 6d 7.1m 5m 5m³ 5f 5g⁵
Jun 10] tall filly: poor handicapper nowadays: best up to 7f: acts on firm going,
possibly not on softer than good: has carried head high. *Miss L. A. Perratt*

MISS WORLD (IRE)   2 b.f. (Apr 1) Mujadil (USA) 119 – Great Land (USA)   **54**
(Friend's Choice (USA)) [1999 5m 7.5g⁴ 7f⁶ 7g 7.1m⁴ 8g 7m⁴ a7g* a6g⁴ a6g⁴ 7d⁶   **a74**
a7g² a8g³ a8g² a8g* Dec 21] leggy, angular filly: sister to Italian 7f/1m
winner Jadim and half-sister to several winners, including 3-y-o Ecudamah and 7f
to 1½m winner Able Choice (by Taufan): dam won 9 races up to 9f in USA: fair
performer on all-weather, modest on turf: won seller at Wolverhampton in September
and nursery at Southwell in December: stays 1m: acts on all-weather, best turf form
on good going: tried blinkered once: usually tongue tied. *C. N. Allen*

MISTER BENJAMIN (IRE)   4 b.g. Polish Patriot (USA) 128 – Frau Ahuyen-   **83**
tante (ARG) (Frari (ARG)) [1998 93: 9v* 10.5g* 10g² 10m⁵ 10m* 10g² 12d 1999
10v 10d⁵ 9.9g⁶ 10m 12m² 10.3m² 12m³ 11.5g² 12f Sep 4] tall, quite good-topped
gelding: has a round action: fairly useful handicapper: ran creditably in 1999 when
placed: saddle slipped final outing: effective at 1¼m/1½m: acts on fibresand, good to
firm and heavy ground: visored (ran poorly) third start: usually races prominently: won novice
hurdle in December. *S. P. C. Woods*

MISTER BLOMBERG (IRE)   3 b.g. Distinctly North (USA) 115 – Ruby   **51**
Realm 47 (Valiyar 129) [1998 NR 1999 6g 5m⁶ 6f 8.2g Sep 25] 42,000Y: first foal:
dam poor here but 2m winner at 4 yrs in Ireland: modest maiden: left J. Fanshawe
after second start: may prove best at 5f/6f: acts on good to firm going: slowly away
first 2 outings. *D. Nicholls*

MISTER CLINTON (IRE)   2 ch.g. (Mar 17) Lion Cavern (USA) 117 – The-   **–**
waari (USA) 68 (Eskimo (USA)) [1999 8s 6s 6g Oct 11] 21,000F, 12,500Y, 14,500
2-y-o: fourth foal: half-brother to 3-y-o Lady Beware and 5-y-o Moonshift: dam 7f
winner: well beaten in maidens. *K. T. Ivory*

MISTER DAMASK   4 b.g. Damister (USA) 123 – Smelter 111 (Prominer 125)   **–**
[1998 NR 1999 10d Jul 5] no show in maiden and seller (visored). *E. J. Alston*

MISTER GILL   2 ch.g. (Mar 29) Suave Dancer (USA) 136 – Bundled Up (USA)   **59**
(Sharpen Up 127) [1999 6d 5.7f⁴ 7f 5.1m⁴ 5g³ 5.1g a6g Oct 8] 9,000Y: workmanlike
gelding: half-brother to 4-y-o Above Board and several winners, including 6-y-o
Rififi and 9f winner in Italy by Unfuwain: dam won over 9.7f at 2 yrs in France:
modest maiden: may prove best around 6f: acts on firm going: tongue tied all starts.
A. T. Murphy

MISTER HARVEY (IRE)   3 b.g. Elbio 125 – White Wine (IRE) (Carmelite   **–**
House (USA) 118) [1998 NR 1999 12m 9.9d 8m May 26] IR 2,600F, 8,000Y:
good-bodied gelding: first foal: dam third at 7f/1m at 2 yrs in Ireland: no form: sold
700 gns. *M. Dods*

MISTER JOLSON   10 br.g. Latest Model 115 – Impromptu 88 (My Swanee 122)   **72**
[1998 84: 6v⁵ 5v² 5.1f* 6g 5g⁴ 5m⁴ 5.1d³ 6g 5.2g⁴ 5m² 5d⁵ 6s 5s 5d 1999 5s 5m 5.1d²
5d² 5.7g 5.1h² 5.2g 5.7f 5s 6.1d Oct 5] workmanlike gelding: fair handicapper

nowadays: effective at 5f/6f: acts on any turf going and equitrack: blinkered twice (not since 1997): usually held up: formerly tough and consistent: refused to enter stalls final intended start. *R. J. Hodges*

MISTER MAL (IRE)   3 b.g. Scenic 128 – Fashion Parade (Mount Hagen (FR) 127) [1998 –: 6.1m 7g 1999 7s³ 8m³ 8f² 7g* 7s* a7g² 7m 8g 7g³ 7d* 7s³ Nov 2] fairly useful performer: won apprentice maiden at Catterick in June and handicaps at Leicester later in month and Redcar (18-runner event) in October: good third in handicap at Catterick final start, weakening final 1f having been sent clear before halfway: free-going sort, likely to prove best at 6f/7f: yet to race on heavy going, acts on any other on turf and on fibresand: unruly at stalls and withdrawn ninth intended outing: likely to do better still. *J. A. Glover*   **86 p**

MISTER MUNNELLY (IRE)   6 b.g. Imperial Frontier (USA) 112 – Maid of The Ring (Stetchworth (USA) 120) [1998 62, a43: 10m² 9.7m⁶ 8.3g 7m 8f a7g a8g⁵ a10f 1999 a8g a8g a8g a8g 8.2m May 21] modest handicapper at best: well held in 1999. *J. R. Jenkins*   **–**

MISTER PQ   3 ch.g. Ardkinglass 114 – Well Off (Welsh Pageant 132) [1998 53: 7m 6.1g⁵ 6m 8g 1999 7g 8.5m 10f 11.9d* 12m 12g⁵ 12s⁴ a14g Oct 18] leggy, unfurnished gelding: modest handicapper: won at Brighton in August: should stay 1¾m: best efforts on good to soft/soft ground. *J. G. Smyth-Osbourne*   **62 a–**

MISTER RAIDER   7 ch.g. Ballacashtal (CAN) – Martian Melody 62 (Enchantment 115) [1998 –, a56: a5g⁶ a5g a6g² 5m 6g 6m⁶ 6f a7g⁵ a5g a6g 1999 a6g a8g⁴ a8.5g⁵ 5.3g 5.1m⁶ 5.7h 6d⁴ 5.1m a5g⁵ a5g a5g Dec 10] slightly dipped-backed gelding: poor performer: probably best at 5f/6f: acts on firm ground, good to soft and equitrack: blinkered: inconsistent. *E. A. Wheeler*   **36 a44**

MISTER RAMBO   4 b.g. Rambo Dancer (CAN) 107 – Ozra 63 (Red Alert 127) [1998 92: 7d² 7m⁵ 8g⁵ 7m 7.8m* 7g⁴ 7.3m⁴ 7d⁵ 7.3g 7g⁵ 1999 6d² 6m 6m³ 7g 7g 7d⁴ 7.1m 7m* 7.1d 7m⁵ 7s⁴ 7d Oct 30] strong, lengthy gelding: fairly useful handicapper: won 18-runner ladies event at Ascot in July by short head from Zucchero: ran respectably most other starts: effective at 6f (given test) to 1m: acts on good to firm and good to soft going, probably on soft: blinkered third start: often races up with pace: sometimes finds little. *B. J. Meehan*   **94**

MISTER SUPERB   2 ch.c. (Apr 6) Superlative 118 – Kiveton Komet 71 (Precocious 126) [1999 5g⁵ 5m⁶ 6m⁴ 6d Oct 14] 2,500Y, resold 9,200Y: robust colt: fifth foal: half-brother to 1m seller winner Waltz Time (by Rambo Dancer): dam sprinter: fair maiden: off course 4 months prior to fourth of 15 to Jarn at Newbury: didn't get run of race in Newmarket nursery following month: type to do better in 5f/6f handicaps as 3-y-o. *V. Soane*   **79 p**

MISTER TRICKY   4 ch.g. Magic Ring (IRE) 115 – Splintering 80 (Sharpo 132) [1998 –, a68: a8g³ a8g* a7g* 6m 8.3g a8g⁴ a8f⁶ 1999 a7g a8g² a7g* a7g⁶ 5d* 6f⁵ 5g³ 6m* 6s 6g* 5m⁶ 6f⁵ 6f 5f³ 7d* a7g* a6g* Dec 22] fairly useful performer, seemingly better on all-weather than turf: had an excellent year, winning minor event at Lingfield in March, handicaps at Windsor in April, Lingfield in May and Goodwood in June, minor event at Brighton in October and 2 more handicaps at Lingfield in November and December: effective at 5f to 7f: acts on equitrack (yet to race on fibresand), firm and good to soft going: free-going sort, best with waiting tactics in strongly-run race. *P. Mitchell*   **71 a81**

MISTER WEBB   2 b.g. (Mar 31) Whittingham (IRE) 104 – Ruda (FR) (Free Round (USA)) [1999 7.6g⁶ 8.3s⁴ Sep 27] 11,000Y: half-brother to 1¾m and 2m winner Kikam (by Ardross), 4-y-o Wings Awarded and 2 winners in Spain: dam won 4 times in Spain: modest form in maidens at Lingfield and Hamilton: will probably stay 1¼m. *B. Smart*   **63**

MISTER WESTSOUND   7 b.g. Cyrano de Bergerac 120 – Captivate 79 (Mansingh (USA) 120) [1998 59: 6v 5.9d 5.9s³ 6g⁵ 6d² 6d⁶ 6m² 6m 6s⁵ 6g 6d 6m⁵ 6m⁴ 6v* 7s⁵ 6v³ a7g⁶ 1999 6v 5.9m³ 6d* a7g 6g Jun 16] workmanlike gelding: modest handicapper: won at Ayr (fourth course success) in May: acts on any turf going, showed promise first of 2 starts on fibresand: tried visored, usually blinkered: tends to start slowly/get behind/hang: not one to trust implicitly. *Miss L. A. Perratt*   **61**

Rothmans Royals Park Hill Stakes, Doncaster—an exciting finish to the 'fillies' St Leger'
with Mistle Song proving just too strong for Credit-A-Plenty (rail) and the weakening Valentine Girl

MISTLE SONG   3 b.f. Nashwan (USA) 135 – Mistle Thrush (USA) 90 (Storm   **112**
Bird (CAN) 134) [1998 6 1p: 8.2g 1999 10m³ 12g² 10g³ 12m⁴ 11.9s² 11.9g⁶ 12.3m*
14.6g* 12d⁶ Oct 9] tall, angular, unfurnished filly: has quick action: smart performer:
won maiden at Ripon in August and Rothmans Royals Park Hill Stakes at Doncaster
(by ½ length from Credit-A-Plenty) in September: looked difficult ride when below
form in Princess Royal Stakes at Ascot final start: best at 1½m/1¾m: acts on soft and
good to firm going: sometimes carries head high. *C. E. Brittain*

MIST OVER MEUGHER   2 gr.f. (May 16) Thowra (FR) – Misty View 73 (Ab-   **–**
salom 128) [1999 5d 5m 7.5g 8d a8g Nov 15] 1,500Y: leggy, close-coupled filly: first
foal: dam 7f (at 2 yrs) and 1¼m winner: no sign of ability. *C. W. Fairhurst*

MISTY BOY   2 br.g. (Apr 1) Polar Falcon (USA) 126 – Misty Silks 81 (Scottish   **56**
Reel 123) [1999 5.2g 6g⁶ 8v Sep 20] first foal: dam 1m winner who stayed 1¼m:
form in maidens only on second start: should stay at least 1m. *M. J. Ryan*

Jockey Club of Kenya Molecomb Stakes, Goodwood—Misty Miss shows herself to be a real bargain buy
as she graduates from selling company to pattern winner; Fez (No.7) stays on strongly for second

King's Stand Stakes, Royal Ascot—Mitcham (rail) puts up his best effort, leading on the line to beat Flanders with Sainte Marine (hooped cap) and Lochangel (noseband) not far behind

MISTY MAGIC   2 b.f. (Mar 6) Distinctly North (USA) 115 – Meadmore Magic **52**
68 (Mansingh (USA) 120) [1999 6f 6m³ 6m Sep 24] 10,500Y: neat filly: second
foal: half-sister to useful 1996 2-y-o 5f/6f winner Magical Times (later won in USA,
by Timeless Times): dam 2-y-o 5f winner: modest maiden: unlikely to stay much
beyond 6f. *P. W. Harris*

MISTY MISS   2 b.f. (May 15) Distant Relative 128 – Baino Clinic (USA) (Sove- **95**
reign Dancer (USA)) [1999 5.1m* 5.1m² 5f* a6g* 5m 6d³ Sep 18] 1,800Y: sixth foal:
half-sister to 3-y-o Redeploy and 3 winners, including 1¼m seller winner Boldly So
(by Never So Bold): dam French maiden from good family: useful performer: won
seller at Bath, Jockey Club of Kenya Molecomb Stakes at Goodwood (33/1, came
late to beat Fez by a length) and £19,000 event at Wolverhampton, all in July/August:
good third to Femme Fatale in listed race at Ayr final start: stays 6f: acts on fibresand,
firm and good to soft going. *P. D. Evans*

MISTY ROSE   2 b.f. (Feb 21) Lugana Beach 116 – Rain Splash 74 (Petong 126) **46 +**
[1999 5m 5g 5.1f⁶ a6s³ Dec 21] 9,500Y: small filly: second foal: sister to 3-y-o The
Rain Lady: dam, 6f winner, half-sister to smart performer up to 1m Muchea: poor
form in maidens: sold out of A. Jarvis's stable 2,000 gns before final start: stays 6f.
Madeleine Smith, Sweden

MITCHAM (IRE)   3 br.c. Hamas (IRE) 125§ – Arab Scimetar (IRE) (Sure Blade **113**
(USA) 130) [1998 95p: 6.1m⁴ 6m* 6s² 6g² 6g³ 6g* 5g⁵ 5m* 6f 5.2d⁴ 5v Oct 3]
quite good-topped colt: has scope: takes eye in appearance: smart performer: won
quite valuable handicap at Newmarket in May and 17-runner King's Stand Stakes at
Royal Ascot in June, in latter squeezing through to beat Flanders by short head: easily
best effort after when creditable fourth to Imperial Beauty in listed race at Newbury:
effective at 5f/6f: acts on good to firm and good to soft going, probably on soft: held
up: genuine. *T. G. Mills*

MITCHELLS MAYHEM   2 b.f. (Apr 7) Mistertopogigo (IRE) 118 – Mayday **–**
Kitty 38 (Interrex (CAN)) [1999 a5g⁶ Apr 9] 6,000Y: first foal: dam middle-distance
maiden: well held in maiden at Lingfield. *W. G. M. Turner*

MITHAK (USA)   5 b.g. Silver Hawk (USA) 123 – Kapalua Butterfly (USA) **87**
(Stage Door Johnny) [1998 90§: 18.7m⁵ 16.1v⁶ 13.9f 16.1m⁵ 13.1s⁴ 1999 18d*
20m 15.9d⁶ Aug 21] rather unfurnished gelding: fairly useful handicapper: won at
Chepstow in May: not discredited both starts after: needs 2m+ nowadays: acts on
good to firm and heavy ground: effective blinkered/visored or not: held up: has found
little. *D. Nicholson*

MITHRAIC (IRE)   7 b.g. Kefaah (USA) 124 – Persian's Glory (Prince Tender- **50**
foot (USA) 126) [1998 NR 1999 13.8g³ 11.1m³ 12.4f* 12g³ Aug 13] big, lengthy
gelding: has been tubed: modest performer: won 7-runner seller at Newcastle in
August: stays 1½m: acts on any going: blinkered first 2 starts, looking none too keen
and wandering on second. *W. S. Cunningham*

MITHRAS (USA)   3 ch.c. Theatrical 128 – Star Glimmer (USA) (General **89**
Assembly (USA)) [1998 NR 1999 10m* 12g⁴ 10.3g⁵ Sep 8] close-coupled, rather
leggy colt: third foal: dam lightly-raced half-sister to Breeders' Cup Juvenile Fillies

winner Pleasant Stage: won maiden at Sandown in July: similar form in minor events at Newbury and Doncaster after: stays 1½m: raced only on good/good to firm going: sent to UAE: may still do better. *J. H. M. Gosden*

MITIE ACCESS (IRE) 3 ch.f. Mujtahid (USA) 118 – Simply Marilyn (IRE) 75 – (Simply Great (FR) 122) [1998 ?: 7f 7g³ 7g 1999 7m a8g 10.1g 8f Jun 18] angular filly: little form. *C. A. Dwyer*

MIXED CURRENCY (USA) 3 b. or br.c. Silver Hawk (USA) 123 – Copper- 77 head (USA) (Hawaii) [1998 77p: 8s³ 1999 10.3d 10g 12.3m⁶ May 5] sparely-made colt: brother to 2 winners, notably US Grade 1 9f winner Silver Ending, and half-brother to a winner in USA by Sing Sing: dam sprint winner in USA from very good family: fair maiden: best effort when midfield at Newmarket second start: probably stays 1½m: acts on soft and good to firm going: sent to UAE. *J. H. M. Gosden*

MIXED OPINION (IRE) 6 b.g. Be My Guest (USA) 126 – Outside Pressure 44 (Shernazar 131) [1998 NR 1999 11.6m 14.6m⁴ 16g⁴ Aug 9] second foal: dam, won both her starts (at 1¼m including listed race) in Ireland, out of half-sister to River-man: modest handicapper in 1997 for D. Weld in Ireland: poor form in Britain: stays 1¾m: acts on good to firm going: effective blinkered or not. *C. F. C. Jackson*

MIXSTERTHETRIXSTER (USA) 3 b.g. Alleged (USA) 138 – Parliament 98 House (USA) (General Assembly (USA)) [1998 104p: 7d* 7f³ 8.1m* 8s⁴ 8d³ 1999 10g⁵ 13.9s⁴ 10.4g Aug 18] tall, angular gelding: useful performer: best effort in 1999 when fourth of 7 to Turtle Valley in minor event at York: edgy and pulled too hard both other starts, gelded before final one: appears to stay 1¾m: yet to race on heavy going, seems to act on any other: fairly useful form over hurdles, successful in October/November. *T. D. Easterby*

MIZHAR (USA) 3 b. or br.g. Dayjur (USA) 137 – Futuh (USA) 95 (Diesis 133) – [1998 101p: 7m 7m⁴ 6.1d* 6g* 1999 6g 6m 6g⁶ May 18] sturdy, workmanlike gelding: good walker: useful in 1998: very disappointing (including in listed race) in 1999, shaping as if something amiss and finding little: likely to prove best at 5f/6f: yet to race on extremes of going: visored final start: sold 9,500 gns, joined D. Nicholls. *E. A. L. Dunlop*

MIZ TAW 3 b.f. Mizoram (USA) 105 – Brown Taw 66 (Whistlefield 118) [1998 44: 5m³ 5m 6f⁴ 1999 5s 7m 8.2m May 21] poor maiden at best: no form at 3 yrs. *J. R. Jenkins*

MO-ADDAB (IRE) 9 b.g. Waajib 121 – Tissue Paper 95 (Touch Paper 113) [1998 NR 1999 10m 8.2g 8.3f Aug 24] useful-looking gelding: fair handicapper at 7 yrs: poor at best in 1999, reportedly lame final start: best efforts at 1m: acts on firm and soft going: sometimes flashes tail: has run well when sweating. *A. C. Stewart*

MODEM (IRE) 2 b.g. (Apr 19) Midhish 109 – Holy Water (Monseigneur (USA) 48 127) [1999 7d 7.9g 7g Oct 15] IR 10,500Y: half-brother to 9-y-o Broadstairs Beauty and 1m (at 2 yrs) to 1½m winner Drinks Party (by Camden Town): dam unraced: well beaten in maidens/claimer. *M. H. Tompkins*

MODERN ERA (USA) 3 ch.f. Diesis 133 – Timely 104 (Kings Lake (USA) 133) 87 [1998 NR 1999 7g* 8s 8d⁶ Oct 30] fourth foal: half-sister to 2-y-o Shining Hour: dam 1m winner: won 6-runner maiden at Newcastle in August: far from discredited in listed races at Saint-Cloud (best effort, ninth of 11 on final start for P. Chapple-Hyam) and Newmarket after: may prove best at 7f/1m. *A. G. Foster*

MODEST HOPE (USA) 12 b.g. Blushing Groom (FR) 131 – Key Dancer (USA) 34 (Nijinsky (CAN) 138) [1998 34, a37: a11g³ a12g a11g⁶ a12g⁵ 12.3v⁶ 12m 12m³ 14.1g 11.9m* 12m 11.5d a12g 1999 a11g³ a12f⁵ a13g² a11g 12.3m a14g 12s a11g 14.1d Oct 27] strong gelding: poor performer: stays 1¾m: acts on good to firm going and all-weather: sometimes bandaged: visored once: inconsistent. *Mrs S. Lamyman*

MODESTY FORBIDS 3 b.f. Formidable (USA) 125 – Ming Blue 52 (Primo – Dominie 121) [1998 62: 6.1g⁵ 7m 7m³ 7d 1999 7.1m 7.1m 8g Aug 18] modest maiden at 2 yrs: well held in 1999: should stay 1m. *J. M. Bradley*

MODESTY HALL 4 b.f. Saddlers' Hall (IRE) 126 – Shy Dolly 74 (Cajun 120) – [1998 NR 1999 a12g⁶ a10g 8.2s⁵ 10d Apr 27] fourth foal: half-sister to winning sprinter Bashful Brave and 2 winners in Italy (all by Indian Ridge): dam 1m winner: little sign of ability. *M. Kettle*

672

MODISH (IRE)   2 b.c. (May 8) Tenby 125 – Moorfield Daisy (IRE) (Waajib 121)   **91**
[1999 7m 7.5g* 8d* 8d⁴ Oct 18] 16,500Y: smallish, workmanlike colt: second
foal: half-brother to Swedish 3-y-o 1m to 1½m winner Simply More (by Simply
Great): dam poor Irish maiden: fairly useful form: won minor events at Beverley in
August and Ayr in September: creditable fourth of 6 to Hataab in listed race at
Pontefract final start: will prove well suited by 1¼m+: acts on good to soft going.
M. H. Tompkins

MODUS OPERANDI (USA)   3 b.g. Known Fact (USA) 135 – Proud Lou (USA)   **91**
(Proud Clarion) [1998 NR 1999 8m 10d⁴ 10f* 12m⁵ Jun 23] strong, close-coupled
gelding: seventh foal: brother to useful French 7f/1m winner Proud Fact and half-
brother to 2 winners by Riverman, notably Poule d'Essai des Pouliches winner
Houseproud: dam best at 2 yrs in North America when Grade 1 1m winner: fairly
useful form: workmanlike winner of maiden at Redcar in June: far from discredited
in handicap final start: barely stays 1½m: sold 3,200 gns, joined K. Burke.
H. R. A. Cecil

MOET (IRE)   4 b.f. Mac's Imp (USA) 116 – Comfrey Glen 63 (Glenstal (USA)   **54**
118) [1998 58, a70: 7s³ 5.9d⁴ 8m⁵ 6g⁴ 6.1s⁵ 6.1s a6g⁴ a6g⁶ 1999 a6g⁴ 5g 6d 6d a7g   **a72**
7f Jul 24] lengthy, rather leggy filly: fair handicapper on all-weather, modest on turf:
should stay 7f: acts on soft going and fibresand: has worn tongue strap. *J. L. Eyre*

MOGIN   6 ch.m. Komaite (USA) – Misdevious (USA) (Alleged (USA) 138) [1998   **– §**
39, a50: a8g* a10g² a10g* a10g⁶ a8g a10g² 9.7s⁶ a8g 8f 8g⁴ 10g 10.1m 11.5f 1999   **a50 §**
a10g² a8g a10g a10g a8g⁴ a10g a10g Dec 18] big mare: modest on all-weather, poor
on turf: left A. McNae after sixth start: stays 1¼m: acts on equitrack, soft and good
to firm going: has given trouble stalls/been slowly away (markedly so sometimes):
blinkered fifth and sixth starts: not to be trusted. *L. Montague Hall*

MOHICAN PRINCESS   3 b.f. Shirley Heights 130 – Mohican Girl 112 (Dancing   **–**
Brave (USA) 140) [1998 NR 1999 10.1m⁴ Jul 7] second reported foal: half-sister to
5-y-o The Prince: dam, winner at up to 11f, half-sister to Yorkshire Oaks winners
Sally Brown and Untold: slowly away in maiden at Epsom. *R. M. H. Cowell*

MOIAVA (FR)   3 b.f. Bering 136 – Mona Stella (USA) 117 (Nureyev (USA) 131)   **–**
[1998 112p: 6g² 7m* 7v* 1999 8m 8m May 16] tall, rather angular filly: won
Criterium de Maisons-Laffitte at 2 yrs: not seen out after disappointing (raced too
freely) in 1000 Guineas at Newmarket (second favourite) and French equivalent
at Longchamp (favourite): bred to stay at least 1m: best effort on heavy going.
Mme C. Head, France

MOI CANARD   6 ch.g. Bold Owl 101 – Royal Scots Greys 38 (Blazing Saddles   **–**
(AUS)) [1998 –: a6g a7g⁵ a7g 6g 1999 a7g Jan 7] compact gelding: fair at best: no
show since 1997. *B. A. Pearce*

MOJACK   2 ch.f. (Feb 20) Interrex (CAN) – Jubilata (USA) 65 (The Minstrel   **33**
(CAN) 135) [1999 5d⁴ Apr 21] first foal: dam 11f winner: fourth of 9 in seller at
Catterick: very unruly and withdrawn in June: dead. *W. G. M. Turner*

MOLA (IRE)   4 b.f. Robellino (USA) 127 – Epure (Bellypha 130) [1998 66: 10d⁴   **–**
12g⁵ 12g 1999 a10g 14.1d 15.4v 10.8m May 3] fair form on debut in 1998: no show
since. *M. J. Ryan*

MOLE CREEK   4 gr.f. Unfuwain (USA) 131 – Nicholas Grey 100 (Track Spare   **91**
125) [1998 83: 9.9f² 10g² 12g⁵ 12.4g² 10g² 9.9m² 10.8d* 10.1s² 1999 12m 14g⁵ May
20] rather leggy, useful-looking filly: fairly useful performer: better effort in 1999
when fifth to Salmon Ladder in rated stakes at Goodwood: barely stays 1¾m: acts
on soft and good to firm going: has been bandaged in front/tongue tied: consistent.
J. R. Fanshawe

MOLLY BROWN   2 b.f. (Apr 17) Rudimentary (USA) 118 – Sinking (Midyan   **77 +**
(USA) 124) [1999 5d* 5m 6d⁵ Aug 6] 20,000Y: good-topped, attractive filly: has
scope: third foal: half-sister to 3-y-o Kingstree and useful Italian 7f/1m performer
Stato King (by Statoblest): dam (unraced) from good family: fair form when winning
maiden at Haydock in June: on toes, well held in Norfolk Stakes at Royal Ascot and
minor event at Haydock (tailed off) after: bred to stay at least 1m. *R. Hannon*

MOLLY MACK   3 b.f. Thowra (FR) – Gangawayhame 91 (Lochnager 132) [1998   **–**
–: 6g 7.5g⁵ 6m 6m 1999 6.1f 7g 8.1m Sep 9] of little account. *A. W. Carroll*

MOLLY MUSIC 5 b.m. Music Boy 124 – Carlton Glory (Blakeney 126) [1998 **39** 39, a53d: a8g⁵ a8g a8g² a7g⁴ a8g⁵ 7s 9.9s a8g⁵ a7g⁴ a8g a8g⁶ 8g 8g⁴ 7g a8g⁶ a8.5g 1999 a7g⁵ a8g Jan 18] sturdy mare: modest handicapper on all-weather at best, poor on turf: stays 8.5f: acts on fibresand, good to firm and good to soft going: tried blinkered/visored. *G. G. Margarson*

MOLLYTIME 3 ch.f. Timeless Times (USA) 99 – Merry Molly (Deploy 131) **–** [1998 –: 7d 7v 7d 1999 9.9g 5.9g 8d 8f⁵ 10g a11g Dec 17] little form. *N. Bycroft*

MOLY 3 b.f. Inchinor 119 – Circe's Isle (Be My Guest (USA) 126) [1998 NR 1999 **64** 10v⁴ 8.3d⁵ a12g Nov 22] fourth foal: half-sister to 3 winners, including 5-y-o Flint **a–** Knapper and smart 7f (at 2 yrs) and 1¼m winner Don Micheletto (by Machiavellian): dam unraced half-sister to Sasuru and Sally Rous: modest form in maidens on first 2 starts: should stay 1½m: blanketed for stalls entry: sold 13,000 gns. *R. Charlton*

MOLYNEUX 3 b.g. Marju (IRE) 127 – Mahasin (USA) 90 (Danzig (USA)) [1998 **81** NR 1999 6g⁶ 6g 6f* a6g* a7g 7g 10.3d Oct 22] IR 25,000F, IR 65,000Y: big, good-topped gelding: third foal: half-brother to fairly useful 7f (1m and 9.5f in Italy) winner Musharak (by Mujtahid) and 4-y-o Elhayq: dam 7f/1m winner: fairly useful performer: won maiden at Lingfield in June and handicap at Southwell in July: will prove best up to 1m: acts on firm ground and fibresand: sold 8,500 gns, sent to Macau. *Sir Mark Prescott*

MOMENTOUS JONES 2 b.g. (Mar 17) Emperor Jones (USA) 119 – Ivory **65** Moment (USA) (Sir Ivor 135) [1999 7m a7g⁵ 8.2d⁵ 8.3d² Nov 4] 23,000Y: leggy gelding: third living foal: dam unraced: progressive form in sellers, second of 17 at Windsor final start: should stay beyond 1m. *M. R. Channon*

MONACLE 5 b.g. Saddlers' Hall (IRE) 126 – Endless Joy 90 (Law Society (USA) **47 §** 130) [1998 NR 1999 a12g a16g³ a16.2g⁶ 11.5m* 11.5mᵂᵈⁱˢ 12.3m⁵ 11.5g⁴ 12.1m 16f a14g³ 12s Oct 4] big gelding: poor handicapper nowadays: first past post in amateur events at Yarmouth in May and Lingfield (disqualified for interference) in June: fell soon after halfway final start: effective at 11.5f, probably at 2m: acts on fibresand and good to firm ground: tried blinkered: has been slowly away: looks unenthusiastic. *John Berry*

MONACO GOLD (IRE) 7 b.g. Durgam (USA) – Monaco Ville (Rheingold 137) **37** [1998 43, a55: a14g* 12.3v³ 11.9d³ a16g² a16g* a16g⁵ a16.2g² a13g⁵ 1999 a12g² **a60** a14.8g⁴ a14.8g⁴ a12g⁴ 16m⁴ a16g* a16g⁴ a13g* 14.1g Jul 3] sparely-made gelding: modest on all-weather, poor on turf: won selling handicaps at Lingfield in May and June: effective at 1½m (given a test) to 2m: acts on good to firm ground, heavy and all-weather: visored twice at 6 yrs. *D. J. S. Cosgrove*

MONACO (IRE) 5 b.g. Classic Music (USA) – Larosterna (Busted 134) [1998 –: **37 §** 8s 6.9s 1999 9g 9.2m 5m 9.2m³ 8.3s Sep 27] tall gelding: poor maiden nowadays: best up to 9f: acts on good to firm going: unreliable. *R. Allan*

MONASABA MUBARAKA 5 b.g. Rainbow Quest (USA) 134 – Blessed Event **–** 117 (Kings Lake (USA) 133) [1998 NR 1999 a12g Jan 9] 160,000Y, 1,000 3-y-o: fifth foal: half-brother to 3 winners, notably smart Sacrament (up to 1½m, by Shirley Heights): dam 1¼m winner who stayed 1½m: modest form in bumpers: soundly beaten only run on Flat. *A. Barrow*

MONASHEE MOUNTAIN (USA) 2 b.c. (Feb 10) Danzig (USA) – Pros- **111 p** pectors Delite (USA) (Mr Prospector (USA)) [1999 6g* 7s* Oct 25]
After Monashee Mountain had made it two wins from two starts by landing the odds easily in the Group 3 Killavullan Stakes at the end of October, Aidan O'Brien was asked if he considered the colt to be a Two Thousand Guineas prospect. The reply from a trainer with such a strong hand in the two-year-old division, and one not noted for over-enthusiasm where his horses are concerned, could hardly have been more upbeat. 'He is, big time,' replied O'Brien, adding that 'He is a lovely horse, with a good turn of foot.' Monashee Mountain clearly must have been held in high regard at Ballydoyle from a very early stage. Not for him the usual maiden race introduction. Monashee Mountain made his debut in June in a listed event run over six furlongs at Leopardstown, and despite his inexperience was sent off at odds on to account

for four rivals. The confidence wasn't misplaced, Monashee Mountain soon travelling well in front and not hard pressed to win by a length and a half from Yara. Monashee Mountain was to start at even shorter odds at Leopardstown again over four months later. With an extra furlong to cover and the ground testing, he was ridden with a bit more restraint, racing in second until taking the lead two furlongs out. Shaken up shortly afterwards, Monashee Mountain quickly put distance between himself and his four rivals, carrying his head slightly high and giving the impression he was still green. Even so, he won without coming under anything like strong pressure by three and a half lengths from stable-companion Bashkir, eased a touch close home. It was a smart performance, and, with further improvement virtually assured, it's not hard to see Monashee Mountain, who will stay at least a mile, becoming a leading contender for the Guineas for which he is a best-priced 25/1 at the time of writing.

Monashee Mountain (USA) (b.c. Feb 10, 1997)	Danzig (USA) (b 1977)	Northern Dancer (b 1961)	Nearctic
			Natalma
		Pas de Nom (b or br 1968)	Admiral's Voyage
			Petitioner
	Prospectors Delite (USA) (ch 1989)	Mr Prospector (b 1970)	Raise A Native
			Gold Digger
		Up The Flagpole (b or br 1978)	Hoist The Flag
			The Garden Club

The saying 'he looks a million dollars' could be applied to Monashee Mountain without its being considered a wild exaggeration. That was the sum paid for him at Keeneland, and he wasn't even the top-priced yearling at the sale, not by a long chalk, a Mr Prospector colt having changed hands for four million. As could be deduced from his purchase price, Monashee Mountain is an extremely well-bred colt, by Danzig out of a mare who won Grade 1 races at eight and eight and a half furlongs in the States. Prospectors Delite's two

Mr M. Tabor and Mrs John Magnier's "Monashee Mountain"

previous foals, by A P Indy and Dixieland Band, are both winners. The former, a mare named Tomisue's Delight, is a very smart but quirky Grade 1 winner who stays at least a mile and a quarter. Prospectors Delite herself is a half-sister to numerous winners, including a couple of Grade/Group 1 performers who stayed a mile and a quarter in Runup The Colors (Alabama Stakes) and Flagbird (Premio Presidente della Repubblica). Their dam Up The Flagpole won seven races in the USA, including the nine-furlong Delaware Oaks. *A. P. O'Brien, Ireland*

MONAWARA (IRE)   2 b.f. (Jan 29) Namaqualand (USA) – Monus (IRE) (Thatch-   **73** ing 131) [1999 5m³ Jun 23] second foal: dam unraced: eye-catching third of 11 to Kelso Magic in maiden at Salisbury, tailed off early on but finishing strongly: looked sure to improve. *M. R. Channon*

MON BRUCE   5 ch.g. Beveled (USA) – Pendona 72 (Blue Cashmere 129) [1998   **56 d** 59: 5g 5m 5g 5m 5m³ 5m 5m 5m⁵ 1999 5d 5m 5.7g 5m 5m 5.9m Jun 23] modest handicapper at best nowadays: no form after reappearance: best at 5f/sharp 6f: acts on all-weather and on good to firm going, blinkered final start: has worn plastic strap: sold 650 gns. *M. Dods*

MONCHANIA   4 ch.f. Mon Tresor 113 – Sugar Owl (Bold Owl 101) [1998 70:   **52** a8.5g* a9.4g⁶ 8s a9.4g 1999 a9.4g² a8.5g* a8g a9.4g Feb 6] workmanlike filly: modest performer: won seller at Wolverhampton in January: probably stayed 9.4f: raced mainly on fibresand: blinkered final start: dead. *J. L. Spearing*

MONDRAGON   9 b.g. Niniski (USA) 125 – La Lutine 95 (My Swallow 134)   **56** [1998 70, a62: a16g² a16.2g⁶ a16g⁵ 16.1d³ 16.2m⁴ 18s⁵ 16s² 16.2g² 16m* 16m³ 16.2m* 16v² 17.5s⁵ 16g³ 16s² 1999 14.1m 16.2s⁴ Jul 3] smallish, leggy gelding: good mover: veteran handicapper: modest form second start: best at 2m+: acts on fibresand and any turf going: normally held up. *Mrs M. Reveley*

MONDURU   2 b.c. (Mar 17) Lion Cavern (USA) 117 – Bint Albadou (IRE) 91   **–** (Green Desert (USA) 127) [1999 6g Aug 14] 20,000Y: second foal: half-brother to French 3-y-o 1½m winner Pibale (by Mujtahid): dam Irish 2-y-o 6f winner out of very smart filly up to 1¼m Cistus: never a threat in maiden at Lingfield. *W. R. Muir*

MONICA'S CHOICE (IRE)   8 b.g. Shaadi (USA) 126 – Tendermark (Prince   **–** Tenderfoot (USA) 126) [1998 68: 6.9d³ 7d⁶ 6.9s³ 8m⁴ 8s⁵ 1999 a8g⁵ Dec 17] sturdy gelding: fair in 1998 for Mrs. M. Reveley: well held only outing in 1999: stays 1¼m: acts on soft and good to firm going: blinkered once. *Mrs N. Macauley*

MONIS (IRE)   8 ch.g. Waajib 121 – Gratify 65 (Grundy 137) [1998 43: 8v* 1999   **43** 9.2v 8d 8g 10d² 8g Jun 18] neat gelding: has suffered from fracture of knee: poor performer: stays 1¼m, probably 1½m: acts on any turf going and fibresand: effective blinkered/visored or not. *B. Ellison*

MONKEY BUSINESS   2 b.f. (Mar 11) Warning 136 – Rosie Sweetheart (IRE)   **69** 71 (Sadler's Wells (USA) 132) [1999 6f³ 7d⁴ Aug 26] first foal: dam, maiden who stayed 1½m, sister to smart French middle-distance filly Papago, from family of Dancing Brave: fair form in maidens at Folkestone: will stay 1¼m. *N. A. Callaghan*

MONKSTON POINT (IRE)   3 b.g. Fayruz 116 – Doon Belle (Ardoon 124)   **101** [1998 103: 5.1s* 5d³ 5.1d* 5s³ 5.2m³ 6d⁴ 5d* 5s³ 1999 6g⁵ 6g6 6g 6m 5.6g 6d 5s² 5d 6s Oct 22] sturdy, good sort: useful handicapper: not so consistent in 1999 as at 2 yrs, creditable second to First Maite in rated stakes at Ascot in September: badly hampered final outing: probably best at 5f: acts on soft and good to firm going: has been bandaged: visored seventh/eighth starts. *D. W. P. Arbuthnot*

MONO LADY (IRE)   6 b.m. Polish Patriot (USA) 128 – Phylella (Persian Bold   **77** 123) [1998 77: 10s 10m² 10.5g⁶ 12.3g² 10.2g 11.8m* 10s⁵ 10g 10v 10s 1999 a8.5g³ a10g 11.6m² 12.3m* 12.1g⁵ 11.6m⁴ 12.3m² 11.9m Aug 17] leggy mare: fair handicapper: won at Chester in May: ran respectably most other starts: effective at 1¼m to easy 1½m: acts on good to firm going, good to soft and all-weather: tried visored, effective blinkered or not. *D. Haydn Jones*

MONSAJEM (USA)   4 ch.c. Woodman (USA) 126 – Fairy Dancer (USA) 94   **114** (Nijinsky (CAN) 138) [1998 98p: 10m³ 11.9g³ 10g⁴ 12s⁶ 10.1d* 10.1s* 1999 10g³ 10m 10.4s 10.1g* 10g 11g* 10.1m³ 9.9s³ 10d* 10d³ Oct 29] rangy colt: smart performer: won handicaps at Epsom (£32,000 race) in June, Newbury in August and

*Vodafone Handicap, Epsom—the first-time visor has the desired effect
as Monsajem holds off Brave Reward (spotted cap) with Supply And Demand in third*

Ascot in October, last-named by 1¼ lengths from Backcloth: creditable third of 7 to Little Rock, beaten just over a length, in listed race at Newmarket final start: seems best around 1¼m, possibly on good going or softer: visored fourth to eighth starts: best held up: often looks a difficult ride (tends to wander for pressure), but goes very well for T. Quinn. *E. A. L. Dunlop*

MONTAGUE TIGG (IRE)   3 b.g. Common Grounds 118 – Astra (IRE) (Glenstal (USA) 118) [1998 65: 6g⁴ 6g 7m 6m² 6m³ 6m 6m 6d* 1999 7.5m 6g 8.2m 8.1d 8.3g⁴ 8m 7g Oct 15] good-bodied gelding: has a round action: only modest performer in 1999: probably stays 1m: yet to race on extremes of ground: visored penultimate outing: sold 2,400 gns, sent to Kuwait. *N. Tinkler*   **55**

MONTALCINO (IRE)   3 b.g. Robellino (USA) 127 – Only Gossip (USA) (Trempolino (USA) 135) [1998 65p: 7.1m⁴ 1999 10m² 12g* 11.9d⁴ 11.5g⁵ 12g³ 13.1d² 12s Oct 23] good-bodied gelding: useful performer: won maiden at Goodwood in May: good efforts next 4 starts, second to Top Cees in steadily-run rated stakes at Ayr (final outing for P. Chapple-Hyam) in September: stays 13f: acts on good to firm and good to soft ground, well held on soft final start: subsequently gelded. *P. J. Makin*   **101**

MONTE CALVO   3 b.f. Shirley Heights 130 – Slava (USA) (Diesis 133) [1998 –p: 8.2s⁵ 1999 9.9m⁶ 12d² 14.1m⁴ 13.8m* 17.2m* 17.5d⁶ 16.5s Nov 6] rather sparely-made filly: fairly useful performer: won maiden at Catterick in July and handicap at Bath in August: below form last 2 starts: stays 17f: acts on good to firm and good to soft going. *J. L. Dunlop*   **85**

MONTE CARLO (IRE)   2 b.c. (Apr 22) Rainbows For Life (CAN) – Roberts Pride 62 (Roberto (USA) 131) [1999 7m⁴ 7.1m³ 8.1g³ 8.5m* 10d* Oct 30] IR 42,000Y: big, close-coupled colt: has a quick action: sixth foal: closely related to smart Italian/US performer around 1¼m Alpride (by Alzao) and half-brother to 2 winners, including 3-y-o Locombe Hill: dam, maiden, daughter of Park Hill runner-up Glowing With Pride: fair form first 4 starts, winning maiden at Epsom in September: much improved when beating Galleon Beach by 3 lengths in listed event at Newmarket following month, improving to lead 1½f out and staying on strongly: will be suited by 1½m+: acts on good to firm and good to soft going: good sort physically, and looks a smart prospect. *R. Hannon*   **104 p**

MONTECRISTO   6 br.g. Warning 136 – Sutosky 78 (Great Nephew 126) [1998 97: a12g* a12g³ 12.5s* 14.1v³ 14m⁴ 12g⁴ 11.9m* 12m³ 12s* 12s³ 1999 12s² 11.9d 12g 11.9d 12g* 13s* 12d 12s Nov 6] leggy, sparely-made gelding: useful performer: won minor event at Newbury in August and handicap at Hamilton (by short head from Mane Frame) in September: well held in handicaps last 2 starts: effective from 11f to 1¾m: acts on good to firm going, heavy and on all-weather: held up: has won twice for a lady rider: genuine. *R. Guest*   **97**

677

MONTE MAYOR   3 b.f. Magic Ring (IRE) 115 – Giblet Pie (Henbit (USA) 130)   –
[1998 –: 5.7g 1999 6m 5d⁴ 5.7f Sep 6] signs of only a little abilty. *D. Haydn Jones*

MONTENDRE   12 b.g. Longleat (USA) 109 – La Lutine 95 (My Swallow 134)   **68 d**
[1998 80: 5.1v* 5.1g 6m³ 6g 5.7d⁴ 6m² 5.1d³ 6g* 6m 6s⁴ 6s 1999 6.1s 6f³ 6g⁶ 5m³
6.1f⁵ 6m* 6d⁴ 6s 6g³ 6d Nov 4] leggy gelding: shows traces of stringhalt: fluent
mover: one-time smart performer, only fair in 1999: won claimer at Kempton in July:
has form at 7f, races at 5f/6f nowadays: acts on any going: formerly tongue tied:
comes from behind. *R. J. Hodges*

MONTFORT (USA)   5 b.g. Manila (USA) – Sable Coated (Caerleon (USA) 132)   **80 §**
[1998 –: 16d 1999 18g⁵ 16.2d 12g⁴ 15.9m 11.9s² 12.1g⁴ a16.2g Sep 8] angular
gelding: one-time useful performer, fairly useful at best in 1999: stays 1¾m: acts on
firm and soft ground: tends to go in snatches, and has hung/flashed tail/given trouble
stalls: effective blinkered or not: unreliable: sold 3,600 gns. *P. F. I. Cole*

MONTJEU (IRE)   3 b.c. Sadler's Wells (USA) 132 – Floripedes (FR) 121   **137**
(Top Ville 129) [1998 113p: 8g* 9v* 1999 10.5s* 10.5m² 12s* 12g* 12m*
12v* 12f⁴ Nov 28]
  Over a mile and a half in 1999, a top-form Montjeu was a staggering
seven lengths in front of any other three-year-old in Europe. He is the sort of
competitor who could give his rivals a healthy start and still beat them, and in
this case that claim would be more than mere rhetoric because that is what he
usually did. The rest were a lightweight bunch, it's true, but Montjeu was good
enough to have dominated in most other seasons as well. For three-year-olds
over any distance in the 'nineties, he was almost unsurpassed: Generous had
the edge over him but Montjeu is right up there with Dayjur, Mark of Esteem
and Peintre Celebre. None of those other paragons saw a racecourse at four,
Peintre Celebre being prevented from doing so by injury. Thankfully, Montjeu
is due to buck the trend.
  Three of his races in the latest season, however, demonstrated that
Montjeu was not invulnerable. In two of them he was beaten. The first of those
defeats came in the Prix Lupin at Longchamp in May, before which Montjeu's
racecourse career had been plain sailing. A minor event at Chantilly and listed
race at Longchamp had fallen without any fuss to Montjeu as a two-year-old, to
which he added the Prix Greffulhe at Longchamp in April on his reappearance
as a three-year-old. The fuss on this occasion was considerable, in that by
beating his 6/4 joint-favourite Sendawar by a length, Montjeu was widely
hailed as the next Prix du Jockey Club winner and was also made one of the
market leaders, as low as 10/1, for Epsom. Three weeks before those classics,
however, and an hour and a half after Sendawar had bolted up in the Poule
d'Essai des Poulains, Montjeu lost his unbeaten record in the Lupin. Gracioso,
who had been five lengths behind him in the Greffulhe, turned the tables to win
by a length as Montjeu, whose starting price on the pari-mutuel was 10/1-on,
carried his head high and looked to hang fire when first sent in pursuit. The only
other occasion on which Montjeu appeared to be in even a semblance of trouble
during the European season came five months and three races later in the Prix
Niel Majestic Barriere. With not one of the main events run at a true pace, the
'day of Arc trials' at Longchamp turned into something more resembling a day
of trials for the Prix de l'Abbaye, and Montjeu only just came through his with

*Emirates Airline Prix du Jockey Club, Chantilly—the smallest field since 1991, but the best
winning performance in a decade as Montjeu beats Nowhere To Exit and Rhagaas most impressively*

Budweiser Irish Derby, the Curragh—Montjeu needs correcting as he hangs but puts up
another very good performance; Daliapour and Tchaikovsky make it a clean sweep for stallion Sadler's Wells

a win. Held up last of the four runners, he took third soon enough in the straight, took second from First Magnitude just inside the final furlong and first from Bienamado in the final strides, subjected to firm hand riding over the last two furlongs. In the context of a slowly-run race, Montjeu had done well to come from last, but, as in the Lupin, his supposed superiority beforehand had resulted in a pari-mutuel starting price of 10/1-on.

Montjeu's two rather scrambling performances have more in common than their starting prices. Both were run on good to firm ground—the firmest conditions that Montjeu encountered in Europe—and, despite their Group 1 and Group 2 status, both were basically trials. For our money, Montjeu definitely looked ill at ease on the ground in the Lupin and, although excuses in horseracing are seldom hard to come by and should often be taken with a pinch of salt, it is worth noting that after both of these races, and on other occasions, Montjeu's connections reported that the colt was better with some give. 'It was the ground,' trainer John Hammond stated after the Lupin. 'He's not the same horse on firm ground.' Montjeu looked in fine condition before both events, while giving the impression that he would come on a good deal for the Prix Niel, his first race for two and a half months, after which Hammond observed that 'he needed the run, mentally as well as physically.' Of Montjeu's defeat in the Lupin, his jockey Cash Asmussen reflected that 'This is the first time he has had to fight, and it will make a man of him. I had the same experience with Suave Dancer, who was also beaten in the Lupin [at 10/1-on] but went on to win the Prix du Jockey Club and Arc.'

On his three other starts in Europe, Montjeu was imperious. With the last-time-out winners of the Prix Noailles (the Andre Fabre-trained Slickly) and Prix Hocquart (Pascal Bary's Falcon Flight), as well as Lupin winner Gracioso, all in opposition, the Emirates Airline Prix du Jockey Club promised to establish the pecking order among the home team and did so unequivocally as, with foreign challengers Rhagaas, Tchaikovsky, Nowhere To Exit and Royal Rebel thrown in for good measure, Montjeu beat them all with ease. No sooner had a gap appeared between Nowhere To Exit and Rhagaas up front two furlongs out than Montjeu was through it; with all the rest virtually flat out, as the field came up the centre of the course in the soft ground, the race was effectively over, and when Asmussen gave Montjeu his head another half furlong later they went on to score by four lengths. In the Budweiser Irish Derby at the Curragh three weeks later, it was a strikingly similar story except that Montjeu was if anything even more impressive. Held up even further behind this time, a detached last of the ten runners at halfway, he weaved his way through into striking distance in sixth place entering the straight, was kept firmly under restraint while joining Daliapour for the lead approaching the furlong pole and needed only hand riding and two slaps down the shoulder (as he again hung right onto the rail) thereafter to surge five lengths clear. Tchaikovsky, a further five and a half lengths away, completed a 1-2-3 for sire Sadler's Wells, who was responsible for fifty percent of the field. Languishing in fourth and fifth were Beat All and Mutafaweq; on good ground and in a supposedly stronger field here, Montjeu had his rivals even more strung out than at Chantilly. These two performances looked good and they were good, equal best of the 'nineties as far as the Prix du Jockey Club is concerned and the the best since 1994 in the Irish Derby. On form, Salsabil, Generous (in particular), St Jovite and Balanchine all achieved more in their victories at the Curragh early in the decade. However, the best was still to come with Montjeu.

The Prix de l'Arc de Triomphe Lucien Barriere (Arc day again having a sponsor, the same as that for the day of Arc trials) attracted fourteen runners, with the King George and Irish Champion Stakes winner Daylami allowed to take his place in a gruelling contest on heavy ground only after a sporting decision on the day of the race. Without the previous week's downpour Daylami might have disputed favouritism with Montjeu, but, as it was, Montjeu was a best-priced 6/4 with British bookmakers in the morning (that was also his starting price, coupled with apparent pacemaker Genghis Khan) and Daylami was 5/2. Sagamix, whose season had been planned round another tilt at the Prix de l'Arc, had left the scene following his sale to Godolphin, but the 1998 Arc form was still represented by the second, third and fourth that day in Leggera, Tiger Hill and Croco Rouge. Croco Rouge had been last of three in another tight finish at Longchamp on the day of trials, behind two more Arc contenders in the 1998 Japan Cup and 1999 Grand Prix de Saint-Cloud winner El Condor Pasa and the 1997 Arc third Borgia. Impressive Prix Vermeille winner Daryaba was, after Montjeu, easily the most fancied of six three-year-olds, the others being Voltigeur winner Fantastic Light, Vermeille third Cerulean Sky, top German filly Flamingo Road and Genghis Khan. Completing the field were International Stakes runner-up Greek Dance and the Norwegian-trained six-year-old Albaran, who had just won the Stockholm Cup.

John Hammond reckoned that El Condor Pasa posed the greatest threat and was thoroughly vindicated. While Montjeu was ridden further up the field than normal, on the rail in seventh, the Japanese challenger made the running and did so at a strong pace. That, it transpired, was a considerable surprise to his trainer and owner. If they believed afterwards that things could have gone better in different circumstances, perhaps they would have swopped positions with Montjeu who was four lengths off the pace and boxed in as the field entered the straight. Extricated from that pocket, Montjeu set off in pursuit and the race came down to a decision between him and El Condor Pasa; Croco Rouge had also been travelling well as the field turned in but was rapidly competing only for third. El Condor Pasa was not stopping, but with a furlong to go it became clear that Montjeu was going to reel him in, the inevitable happening with about a hundred yards of the race remaining, Montjeu pushed out to hold on by half a length; there were six lengths back to Croco Rouge and another five to Leggera in fourth. Plenty of Arc de Triomphes end with most of the runners in a bunch. This was not one of them.

With no reason to believe that Croco Rouge did not run near to his best, the inescapable conclusion is that Montjeu and El Condor Pasa both produced performances of the highest order. Peintre Celebre's 1997 win had been the best since Dancing Brave, and Montjeu is right up there with him. Montjeu was eighteen and a half lengths in front of the next three-year-old (eighth-placed Cerulean Sky) in the Arc, and over the season as a whole Montjeu's superiority over his contemporaries at a mile and a half is still extraordinary. Mutafaweq's annual rating is 8 lb lower, but the Godolphin colt's best effort was put up over the St Leger distance and his three performances at a mile and a half do not come close. Oath was the next best, but the Derby winner is rated 12 lb inferior to his French counterpart. It can be argued that Peintre Celebre enjoyed a similar superiority two years earlier—as the next best over middle distances in his year, Desert King and Benny The Dip, both recorded their very best form, by our reckoning at least, at a mile and a quarter—but certainly no other horse over the past decade can claim such dominance in the division.

Montjeu was the sixth consecutive winning favourite in the Arc, a sequence which will still quicken the pulse of followers of such trends even though the 1994 winner Carnegie was one of four contenders who sported variations of the Sheikh Mohammed colours and were coupled in betting on the pari-mutuel. Another striking trend came to an end, of course, when Olivier Peslier and Andre Fabre managed no better than seventh (with Borgia). Both Montjeu's trainer and jockey were enjoying success for the second time, though this was not the Hammond/Asmussen partnership associated with Montjeu's first six races; Asmussen suffered an injury after the Irish Derby which led to Michael Kinane taking over in the Prix Niel. Commenting on Montjeu's performance in that race, and having previously been on the receiving end of such sizeable beatings when riding Tchaikovsky in the French and Irish Derby, Kinane reported with marvellous understatement after the Prix Niel that 'I'd be happy to ride that horse in three weeks.' Kinane's consequent second Arc win came ten years after his first successful ride in the race on Carroll House.

Montjeu carries the colours of Michael Tabor. The idea of Tabor and his Coolmore associates buying top-priced yearlings and foals is familiar, and they must have had a contender (along with Godolphin's many recruits) for the top-priced two-year-old of 1998 because Montjeu was owned by Tsega Ltd during his first season. Despite not having contested a pattern race, Montjeu's form in his first season was only 3 lb below the top-rated French two-year-old. Tsega Ltd (who still own a sizeable share in him) is owned by Laure Boulay de la Meurthe, friend of the late Sir James Goldsmith, the multi-millionaire financier who bred the colt. Goldsmith died in 1997 and Montjeu is named after his chateau in Burgundy. Montjeu's dam Floripedes carried the Goldsmith colours in a career which began in July as a three-year-old and ended that October. She improved dramatically in what little time she had, coming third in two maiden events before getting off the mark in a quite valuable conditions race at Clairefontaine, registering her own win at the Arc meeting in the Prix de Lutece and having her swansong in a still more important staying prize, the Prix Royal-Oak, in which she finished two lengths second of sixteen to Star Lift. Before Montjeu, Floripedes had had four foals, two of whom failed to see the racecourse. One of the latter pair was Cumbres (by Kahyasi) who made 200,000 guineas at the latest December Sales, the other is Cuixmala, dam of smart French four-year-old Mont Rocher. Of the two who did so race, one did so only once and another, Le Paillard (by Sanglamore) made some amends with a French listed win in 1998 and second place in the Grade 1 San Juan Capistrano Handicap in 1999. Floripedes' 1999 two-year-old was the filly La Leuze (by Caerleon); there is also a yearling brother to Montjeu and the dam visited Sadler's Wells again in 1999. Floripedes is half-sister to Dadarissime, who himself won the Lutece, among other good staying prizes, and grandam Toute Cy is a half-sister to the John Hammond-trained Dear Doctor, whose many high-class efforts in far-flung locations included a win in the Arlington Million and a third place in the Japan Cup in 1992.

Prix de l'Arc de Triomphe Lucien Barriere, Longchamp—Montjeu does well to catch El Condor Pasa (rail) in a memorable finish; Croco Rouge is clear of the others in third

Seven years after Dear Doctor's effort at Tokyo, Hammond was back there with his latest stable star. It was a bold move, particularly given all that had previously been observed and said about Montjeu's ground preferences—the going for the Japan Cup is almost invariably firm, so perhaps this was a sporting challenge almost on a par with Daylami's participation in the Arc, only with an awful lot further to travel. After Montjeu had performed below his best in fourth, beaten two and a quarter lengths by the winner Special Week and three quarters of a length by third-placed High-Rise, connections blamed Montjeu's long and delayed journey rather than the ground. 'I wasn't able to do as much as I think he needed before the race,' said Hammond. 'He was very tired after the journey and I don't think he was in top form.' Kinane reported that 'the ground was beautiful—that wasn't his undoing. It's a tough trip for a three-year-old, especially when things go wrong.'

		Northern Dancer (b 1961)	Nearctic
Montjeu (IRE) (b.c. 1996)	Sadler's Wells (USA) (b 1981)		Natalma
		Fairy Bridge (b 1975)	Bold Reason
			Special
	Floripedes (FR) (b 1985)	Top Ville (b 1976)	High Top
			Sega Ville
		Toute Cy (b 1979)	Tennyson
			Adele Toumignon

Montjeu's performance in Japan detracts little from his spectacular achievements in Europe or from the anticipation of what he might achieve as a four-year-old. In fact, this newly-found attitude to his ground preferences must increase the chances of British racegoers seeing him in action in the country's

Mr M. Tabor's "Montjeu"

premier middle-distance event, the King George and Queen Elizabeth Stakes. It is possible he might also appear at a mile and a quarter given that in the latest season he was declared to run—and his trainer fined IR£15,000 (later reduced to IR£6,750) when he failed to do so—in the Irish Champion Stakes as an alternative engagement to the Prix Niel. It is far more likely that Montjeu will stay beyond a mile and a half than prove capable of reproducing his best at a mile and a quarter, but the former option is, of course, most unlikely to be taken up. Either way, it will take a very special horse indeed to beat Montjeu as long as he makes normal improvement from three to four. He gave the firm impression in 1999 that he still had scope for physical development. A tall, rangy colt, he has a rather short, unimpressive action, but also has a fine turn of foot. Much was made of his growing maturity as a three-year-old after improvement on his tendency to become edgy during the preliminaries. He can still take a strong hold in the early stages of a race. After his four-year-old season, he is reportedly due to stand at Coolmore Stud. That, of course, would be alongside his sire Sadler's Wells, and of all the accolades heaped on Montjeu, one of the most telling must be that he is rated more highly than any other son or daughter of that outstanding stallion. *J. E. Hammond, France*

MONUMENT   7 ch.g. Cadeaux Genereux 131 – In Perpetuity 90 (Great Nephew 126) [1998 65, a–: 10.8m⁵ 10g⁵ 11.8m³ 12m* 14.1m 12.1m² a12g 1999 10m⁶ 8f* 11.8m⁴ 12m⁵ 10m Aug 28] quite good-topped gelding: fair handicapper: won claimer at Bath in June: effective at 1m to easy 1½m: acts on firm and good to soft ground: has won for an apprentice: usually races prominently: game: won selling hurdle in October. *J. S. King* **67**
a–

MOOCHA CHA MAN   3 b.c. Sizzling Melody 117 – Nilu (IRE) 58 (Ballad Rock 122) [1998 68: 5.1d³ 5.1g⁵ a5g* a6g 5s⁶ 5d 1999 6.1v² 6.1s 6.1s⁵ a6g 5d 6g³ a6g a5g⁶ 5m* 6.1g² 5.1s⁴ 5d Sep 30] lengthy colt: fair performer: won claimer at Pontefract in August: good efforts in handicaps next 2 starts, poorly drawn final one: effective at 5f/6f: acts on fibresand, good to firm and heavy going: blinkered last 4 starts: usually comes from off pace nowadays. *B. A. McMahon* **78**

MOON AT NIGHT   4 gr.g. Pursuit of Love 124 – La Nureyeva (USA) 83 (Nureyev (USA) 131) [1998 60p: 7m 6m 7d 7.1g 8m 8m* 1999 8f³ 7.1d⁶ 6m 8.5m 7.1m* 8d* 7.1m Sep 9] leggy gelding: fair handicapper: won at Chepstow (17 ran) in July and Brighton in August: raced on unfavoured side and not given hard time final start: effective at 6f to 1m: acts on firm and good to soft going: front runner. *L. G. Cottrell* **71**

MOON BLAST   5 gr.g. Reprimand 122 – Castle Moon 79 (Kalamoun 129) [1998 65: 13.3m⁶ 12d³ 1999 10m 12m 10g⁶ 12g 12.3m 11.6m Jul 26] useful-looking gelding: fluent mover: fair performer: became disappointing: possibly best at 1½m nowadays: raced mostly on good going or firmer: tried visored: sometimes pulls hard and wanders. *M. Salaman* **74 d**

MOON COLONY   6 b.g. Top Ville 129 – Honeymooning (USA) (Blushing Groom (FR) 131) [1998 86: 14.1d² 14d³ 14.6g 16.4g 12m* 12g* 12m⁶ 12m 11.9g⁴ 14.6d 1999 14.1s 12m 14.1g³ 12m 12s⁶ 16m⁵ a14g Nov 30] quite attractive gelding: fair handicapper: disappointing after third outing: effective at 1½m to 2m: acts on soft and good to firm going: often tongue tied (reportedly had wind infirmity final 5-y-o start): blinkered penultimate start: joined A. Forbes. *Lady Herries* **75 d**

MOON DRAGON (IRE)   3 b.c. Sadler's Wells (USA) 132 – Moonsilk (Solinus 130) [1998 88+: 8.5g² 8g 9g⁵ 8v³ 1999 12g* 16.2m⁶ 14.8m* 14d Sep 11] IR 98,000Y: big, strong, lengthy colt: has a fluent, round action: closely related to 2 winners, including Irish 1995 2-y-o 1m winner Night Spell (by Fairy King) and half-brother to several winners, notably very smart but untrustworthy stayer Moonax (by Caerleon): dam, placed over 9f in France, half-sister to 1000 Guineas winner Nocturnal Spree: useful performer: won maiden at Leopardstown in May: better form when sixth of 11 to Endorsement in Queen's Vase at Royal Ascot and 1½ lengths second (promoted to first) of 4 to Royal Line in listed race at Newmarket in June/July: visored, reportedly finished distressed when last of 10 final start: stayed 2m: acted on good to firm going: dead. *A. P. O'Brien, Ireland* **104**

MOON DREAM   3 ch.f. Interrex (CAN) – Zamoon (Zambrano) [1998 NR 1999   –
6s 7m 6d Oct 28] third reported foal: sister to modest 6f winner Moon Fairy: dam
unraced: no show in maidens: gave trouble stalls final start. *J. G. Smyth-Osbourne*

MOON DRIVER (USA)   2 b.f. (Jan 5) Mr Prospector (USA) – East of The Moon   **98 p**
(USA) 123 (Private Account (USA)) [1999 6.5v² 5.5g* 6d Sep 28] tall, leggy filly:
second foal: dam, triple Group 1 winner in France at 1m and 10.5f, half-sister to
Kingmambo and daughter of Miesque: useful form when winning Prix d'Arenberg at
Chantilly in September by 2½ lengths from Harbour Island, forging clear final 1f:
favourite, only ninth of 14 in Cheveley Park Stakes at Newmarket (had 2 handlers)
later in month, still last over 1f out then running on all too late: likely to do better at 3
yrs, stepped up to 7f/1m. *J. E. Pease, France*

MOON EMPEROR   2 b.c. (Apr 11) Emperor Jones (USA) 119 – Sir Hollow   **97**
(USA) (Sir Ivor 135) [1999 8.1m³ 8v⁵ 7d⁴ 8f⁵ Oct 17] 25,000Y: close-coupled colt:
fifth foal: half-brother to 2 winners abroad by Highest Honor, including French 1¼m
to 11.5f winner Knight of Honor: dam French 1m winner: best effort in maidens
when fourth of 14 to Qamous at Newmarket: improved again when fifth of 9 to
Night Style in Gran Criterium at Milan final start: not sure to stay much beyond 1m:
possibly unsuited by heavy ground. *H. Akbary*

MOON GLOW (IRE)   3 b.g. Fayruz 116 – Jarmar Moon (Unfuwain (USA) 131)   **74**
[1998 69p: 7m⁵ 7m² 6m⁴ 1999 9.1m³ 8m 7m³ 8m⁴ 8g 8m Sep 19] big, heavy-topped
gelding: fair maiden: ran at least respectably most starts: likely to prove best at 1m/
9f: raced only on good/good to firm going: won over hurdles in October. *Miss
S. E. Hall*

MOONLIGHT FLIT   4 b.f. Presidium 124 – Moonwalker (Night Shift (USA))   **44**
[1998 46: 9.3d 10g⁶ 9.9m⁵ 10m* 12m 9.9m⁶ 8v 1999 a8g³ a8g a8f³ a8g³ a8g⁴ a8g*   **a51**
a8g³ 9.2d³ 10g 9.2f a8g a8g⁵ a8g Dec 13] small, sturdy filly: modest handicapper on
all-weather, poor on turf: won apprentice event at Southwell in March: effective at
1m/1¼m: acts on firm ground, good to soft and all-weather: effective blinkered/
visored or not. *J. L. Eyre*

MOONLIGHT (IRE)   3 b.f. Night Shift (USA) – Local Custom (IRE) (Be My   **69**
Native (USA) 122) [1998 –: 6f 1999 7m 10.2m³ 10m 12m Aug 6] fair maiden: ran as
though something amiss final start: stays 1¼m: raced only on good to firm/firm
going. *B. J. Meehan*

MOONLIGHT MONTY   3 ch.c. Elmaamul (USA) 125 – Lovers Light (Grundy   **59**
137) [1998 67: 7.3g 7m³ 8.1m 10s 1999 11.5m⁵ 14.1g Sep 25] lengthy, rather
unfurnished colt: modest maiden: likely to stay at least 2m: acts on good to firm
going, possibly not on soft: sold 3,500 gns. *J. L. Dunlop*

MOONLIGHT SEAS   3 b.f. Sabrehill (USA) 120   Fair Seas 72 (General   **36**
Assembly (USA)) [1998 NR 1999 8.3g 8m 10m⁵ a12g Aug 14] 500Y: third foal:
half-sister to 4-y-o Blue Anchor: dam, lightly-raced maiden, best at 1¼m: poor
maiden: stays 1½m: acts on fibresand: visored final start: has given trouble stalls:
successful over hurdles in September. *A. W. Carroll*

MOONLIT WATER   3 b.f. Rainbow Quest (USA) 134 – Shimmer (FR) (Green   **?**
Dancer (USA) 132) [1998 –p: 7m 8.1g 1999 10m a12g 10.3s 10g³ 9.5g* 10.5v⁵ 8.5g*
a9g 8s Nov 13] close-coupled, useful-looking filly: well beaten in maiden/handicap
before sold from J. Fanshawe 4,800 gns after second start: successful for new stable
in maiden at Dresden in September and handicap at Gotha in October: stays 9.5f:
blinkered last 5 starts. *H. W. Hiller, Germany*

MOON MISSION   4 br.f. Interrex (CAN) – Zamoon (Zambrano) [1998 –: 8m   –
1999 7f 5m Jun 11] lengthy filly: no form. *J. G. Smyth-Osbourne*

MOON OF ALABAMA   2 b.f. (Mar 24) Sadler's Wells (USA) 132 – Military   **59**
Tune (IRE) (Nashwan (USA) 135) [1999 7.9d⁵ 7d Oct 30] 50,000Y: second foal: dam
unraced half-sister to Prix Saint-Alary winner Muncie (by Sadler's Wells) and Prix
Royal-Oak winner Mersey: better effort in maidens at York and Newmarket on latter
course: raced freely both starts: should stay 1½m+. *J. W. Hills*

MOONRAKING   6 gr.g. Rusticaro (FR) 124 – Lunaire (Try My Best (USA) 130)   –
[1998 –, a74: a12g² a12g² a11g² a11g* a8g* a8g⁵ 10s 10.1v 1999 a11g a8g* a12g*   **a67**
a12g² a12g⁵ a12g³ 11.8s 10v a12g⁵ 10m Aug 28] leggy, close-coupled gelding: fair

on all-weather, lightly raced and modest at best on turf: has gained all 6 wins at Southwell, including 2 claimers in February, first one for T. Etherington: effective at 1m to 1½m: acts on fibresand: blinkered nowadays: sometimes carries head high and wanders: won twice over hurdles in November. *Miss S. J. Wilton*

MOONRIDGE (IRE)   2 b.f. (Apr 21) Common Grounds 118 – Concave (Connaught 130) [1999 5s⁵ 6g 6d³ 5g 5m Jun 30] IR 4,000Y: half-sister to 3 winners, including useful Irish 1987 2-y-o 7f winner Impressive Lady (by Mr Fluorocarbon) and 8.5f winner Pillow Talk (by Taufan): dam lightly raced: appeared to show modest form when third in maiden at Ballinrobe in May: tailed off at Hamilton next start: stays 6f. *Gerard O'Leary, Ireland*   **56 ?**

MOON RIVER WONDER (IRE)   3 b.g. Doyoun 124 – Bayazida (Bustino 136) [1998 –: 7m 7s a8g 1999 12g Nov 3] rather sparely-made gelding: little form. *C. W. Thornton*   **–**

MOONSHIFT   5 b.g. Cadeaux Genereux 131 – Thewaari (USA) 68 (Eskimo (USA)) [1998 40: 12s 10.1g⁴ 11.5g⁵ 11.8d 14.1s 1999 a11g 10.1m* a12g a11g⁵ a12g Dec 21] lengthy, quite good-topped gelding: poor performer: won apprentice handicap at Yarmouth in May: stays 11.5f: acts on good to firm ground and fibresand: sometimes visored, including for win: tongue tied. *H. J. Collingridge*   **38**

MOON SHOT   3 gr.g. Pistolet Bleu (IRE) 133 – La Luna (USA) (Lyphard (USA) 132) [1998 77p: 6g 6m 6d a6g* 1999 10s 11.5g² 11.7g⁵ a10g* 11f* 10.9s 10m 10g 10d⁶ 10g⁴ Oct 19] good-bodied gelding: fair handicapper: made all at Lingfield and Redcar in July: stays 11.5f: acts on firm going, good to soft and all-weather: has been tongue tied: has dropped out tamely: sold 32,000 gns. *Sir Mark Prescott*   **79**

MOON SOLITAIRE (IRE)   2 b.c. (May 1) Night Shift (USA) – Gay Fantastic (Ela-Mana-Mou 132) [1999 7s⁶ Oct 8] 120,000Y: brother to 3-y-o Fantastic Belle, closely related to French 1m to 1¼m winner Fantastic Don (by Sovereign Dancer) and half-brother to several winners, notably smart middle-distance performer Germano (by Generous): dam unraced sister to smart middle-distance filly Gay Hellene: weak in market and unfavourably drawn, shaped fairly well when nevernearer sixth of 18 to Frontier in maiden at Lingfield: will stay 1m: sure to do better. *E. A. L. Dunlop*   **62 p**

MOONSTONE (IRE)   4 b.f. Statoblest 120 – Opening Day (Day Is Done 115) [1998 69d: 9.4g⁴ 7.1g 7g 8.2d 7g* 7m 7m⁵ 7m 8m 7.1m⁴ 8m 8m a8.5g 1999 a11g 10m 8f Sep 6] lengthy filly: modest handicapper: no form in 1999: stays 1m: acts on good to firm ground: tried visored. *B. P. J. Baugh*   **–**

MOON STRIKE (FR)   9 b. or br.g. Strike Gold (USA) – Lady Lamia (USA) (Secreto (USA) 128) [1998 102: 5m 5g 5g³ 5f 5m⁵ 5m 1999 5.2m⁶ 5m 5d³ 5m Jun 25] lengthy gelding: usually looks very well: fairly useful handicapper: best effort in 1999 when third at York in June: best at 5f: acts on equitrack, firm and good to soft ground (tailed off on heavy): effective blinkered: often bandaged in front: comes from off pace. *Miss I. Foustok*   **92**

MOOSE MALLOY   2 ch.g. (Jan 31) Formidable (USA) 125 – Jolimo 92 (Fortissimo 111) [1999 7m⁶ 8s 6v Oct 23] big, workmanlike gelding: half-brother to several winners, including 5-y-o Doc Ryan's and fairly useful performer up to 1½m/highclass hurdler Osric (by Radetzky): dam won from 1½m to 2¼m: burly, well held in minor event and maidens. *M. J. Ryan*   **–**

MORE BILLS (IRE)   7 b.g. Gallic League 119 – Lady Portobello (Porto Bello 118) [1998 –: 14.1g 1999 18m Jul 3] poor winning hurdler: lightly raced and of little account on Flat nowadays. *B. J. Llewellyn*   **–**

MORE MAGIC   2 b.g. (Feb 12) Cyrano de Bergerac 120 – Maziere 45 (Mazilier (USA) 107) [1999 5.2m 5m 5f⁴ 6g⁶ 7m⁴ 6.1m⁶ 5v* 5.3d* 5s Oct 13] 16,500Y: usefullooking gelding: first foal: dam, poor maiden, half-sister to very smart performer up to 1½m in France/USA Millkom (by Cyrano de Bergerac): fair performer: won nurseries at Lingfield in September and Brighton in October: well-beaten favourite on final start: headstrong, and likely to prove best at 5f: acts on heavy going, probably on firm: has worn net muzzle to post and flashed tail under pressure: front runner. *W. J. Haggas*   **73 +**

MORGAN LE FAY   4 b.f. Magic Ring (IRE) 115 – Melody Park 104 (Music Boy   **69**
124) [1998 70: 7d 6d 6d³ 7g 7m² 7f² 8m 7.1g² 8.1g 7m³ 7s 1999 7g⁵ 6f² 8m³ 7g Aug
18] leggy filly: fair maiden: left B. Meehan after reappearance: effective at 6f to 1m:
acts on firm and good to soft ground: has sweated. *Don Enrico Incisa*

MORGANS ORCHARD (IRE)   3 ch.g. Forest Wind (USA) 111 – Regina St   **75**
Cyr (IRE) (Doulab (USA) 115) [1998 NR 1999 10g 10.5s⁵ a12g³ Nov 22] 13,000F:
third foal: half-brother to useful winner up to 2m Cyrian (by Persian Bold): dam,
Irish 9f winner, half-sister to Cyrano de Bergerac: first form in maidens when third at
Southwell: likely to stay beyond 1½m: acts on fibresand. *A. G. Newcombe*

MORNING DAWN (USA)   2 b. or br.c. (Apr 19) Dayjur (USA) 137 – Istiska   **72 d**
(FR) (Irish River (FR) 131) [1999 5d⁵ 6d 5m² 6g³ 5.2m² 5.3g² 5.3m⁶ 7g Sep 18]
$85,000F, 100,000Y: half-brother to several winners, including fairly useful Irish 1m
winner Fairy Water (by Warning) and 7f (fairly useful at 2 yrs) and 13f winner Noyan
(by Northern Baby): dam French maiden: fair maiden: below form last 3 starts: stays
6f: yet to race on extremes of going: has taken strong hold and finished weakly: sold
12,000 gns, sent to Macau. *E. A. L. Dunlop*

MORNING GLORY   3 b.f. Polar Falcon (USA) 126 – Round Midnight 64 (Star   **62**
Appeal 133) [1998 53: 6m 7g 1999 6v⁵ 7m May 3] sturdy filly: modest maiden:
should stay at least 7f: acts on heavy going: sold 1,200 gns in September. *R. A. Fahey*

MORNING LOVER (IRE)   2 b.c. (Feb 6) Ela-Mana-Mou 132 – The Dawn   **47**
Trader (USA) 70 (Naskra (USA)) [1999 7d Nov 1] IR 26,000F, IR 40,000Y, 20,000
2-y-o: second foal: half-brother to a winner in Germany by Seattle Dancer: dam, 7f
winner, half-sister to smart filly up to 1¼m here and in USA Party Cited: green,
slowly away and never on terms in Redcar maiden. *K. R. Burke*

MORNING MUSIC   3 b.f. Green Desert (USA) 127 – Blushing Storm (USA)   **78**
102 (Blushing Groom (FR) 131) [1998 82: 5m² 6g 6f⁵ 6g 7m² 7m³ 7m* 1999 10g
9.9m 8.3d³ 9m⁴ 8.1m 8m* 8.5m⁶ 9m 10g³ Oct 19] leggy, workmanlike filly: fair
performer: won 5-runner minor event at Bath in July: ran creditably when in frame
otherwise: stays 1¼m: acts on firm and good to soft going: has looked headstrong:
sold 55,000 gns in December. *R. Hannon*

MORNING PRIDE (IRE)   2 b.f. (Jan 27) Machiavellian (USA) 123 – Wilayif   **113 p**
(USA) 75 (Danzig (USA)) [1999 5s³ 5.5g* 5.5g* 5g* Jul 2]
      At the time of her impressive win in France's first pattern race for
two-year-olds, the Prix du Bois run at Chantilly in early-July, Morning Pride
looked at least as good as any filly of her age in Europe. She wasn't seen out
again, but, in a muddling year for the latest crop of two-year-old fillies,
Morning Pride's claims to being the top filly of her generation remarkably seem
every bit as strong at the end of the year as they seemed then. After finishing
third to Manzor at Longchamp on her debut in April (the winner showed smart
form in beating older horses in the Prix du Petit Couvert in the autumn),
Morning Pride made no mistake in winning minor events at Chantilly and
Maisons-Laffitte the following month by three and four lengths respectively.
The Prix du Bois yielded another wide-margin victory over five other winners,
Morning Pride forging clear inside the final furlong to put four lengths between

*Prix du Bois, Chantilly—Morning Pride puts up the best performance by a two-year-old filly in Europe,
beating Legend of Spring by four lengths*

herself and Legend of Spring, who'd set the early pace. The form of the race stood up well as the first four home behind Morning Pride were all successful in races of some consequence afterwards; runner-up Legend of Spring won the valuable Prix des Reves d'Or at Vichy next time, third- and fourth-placed Perugina and Harbour Island went on to win pattern races themselves, taking the Prix Eclipse and Prix de Cabourg respectively, and fifth-placed Radhwa later won a listed event at Maisons-Laffitte. As for Morning Pride, she looked as though she would have taken all the beating in the Prix Robert Papin but missed that race with what was described as a 'slight flake on one of her joints', and, although reported to have recovered fully, wasn't seen out again. Her transfer to Godolphin (who also acquired another of Fabre's two-year-olds in River's Curtain) means that she probably won't have another race, in public at any rate, until the Guineas at the earliest. Although raced only at around five furlongs so far, she's bred to stay a mile, and a good showing in one of Godolphin's private trials in Dubai would make her winter odds of 16/1 for the One Thousand Guineas look long.

		Mr Prospector (b 1987)	Raise A Native
	Machiavellian (USA) (b 1987)		Gold Digger
		Coup de Folie (b 1982)	Halo
Morning Pride (IRE) (b.f. Jan 27, 1997)			Raise The Standard
		Danzig (b 1977)	Northern Dancer
	Wilayif (USA) (b 1988)		Pas de Nom
		Kamar (b 1976)	Key To The Mint
			Square Angel

Judged on her pedigree, speed and precocity are not the most obvious qualities that could have been expected from Morning Pride, though she's not the first filly in her family to show plenty of ability at two. She's the fourth foal, and third winner from as many to race, out of her dam Wilayif, following on from useful stayer Wilawander (by Nashwan), runner-up in the Sagaro Stakes, and French mile winner Royal Allegiance (by Kris), who has since run over hurdles in Britain. Wilayif didn't race at two and was one of the Stoute stable's lesser lights at three, beaten twice at Musselburgh before getting off the mark at the expense of just one rival in a seven-furlong maiden at York. Wilayif, who stayed a mile and a quarter, could also be described as one of the lesser lights of her dam, the Canadian Oaks winner Kamar. Among Kamar's offspring are champion Canadian three-year-old colt Key To The Moon, Princess Margaret Stakes winner Hiaam, Hollywood Oaks winner Gorgeous, Kentucky Oaks winner Seaside Attraction (herself dam of several good horses, including Grade 1 winners Cape Town and Golden Attraction and Cherry Hinton winner Red Carnival) and the dam of the latest Great Voltigeur winner Fantastic Light. Kamar's own dam Square Angel was also a champion three-year-old filly in Canada, while Kamar's full sister Love Smitten, a Grade 1 winner in her own right, is now better known as the dam of Swain. *A. Fabre, France*

MORNINGSIDE (IRE) 2 b.f. (Mar 25) Night Shift (USA) – Recipe 66 (Bustino 136) [1999 8v⁶ Sep 29] IR 12,000Y: half-sister to 6-y-o Heart and winners in Scandinavia by Warning and Last Tycoon: dam, maiden, half-sister to smart stayer Teamster: well held in maiden at Salisbury: should do better. *D. R. C. Elsworth* – p

MOROCCO (IRE) 10 b.g. Cyrano de Bergerac 120 – Lightning Laser 68 (Monseigneur (USA) 127) [1998 65: 7.6m 7m* 7m 7m⁴ 8f⁴ 8g 8g 7m³ 7v 1999 8f 7f 7m 7g⁶ Jun 8] small, workmanlike gelding: unimpressive mover: modest handicapper: effective at 7f/1m: acts on any going: tried blinkered/visored earlier in career: sometimes finds little (usually held up): usually apprentice ridden: none too consistent. *M. R. Channon* 57

MORSELL 3 br.f. Dilum (USA) 115 – Count On Me 77 (No Mercy 126) [1998 56: 6m² 1999 5.1s⁶ 6m 8g 7.1d 8.2f³ Jun 21] leggy filly: modest maiden: stayed 1m: acted on firm going: dead. *R. J. Hodges* 58

MORTEENO 3 b.g. Perpendicular 119 – Petticoat Rule (Stanford 121§) [1998 –: 8d 8.3s 7s 1999 a9.4g³ 8g 7g 12.1m Sep 6] no form. *J. Mackie* –

MOSAIC TIMES   2 ch.c. (Apr 22) Timeless Times (USA) 99 – Pastelle 52 (Tate   **45** Gallery (USA) 117) [1999 a5g² a6g a5g⁶ Dec 21] 3,000Y: first foal: dam maiden: form in Southwell sellers only on debut. *Mrs G. S. Rees*

MOSCOW MIST (IRE)   8 b.g. Soviet Star (USA) 128 – Ivory Dawn (USA) (Sir   **–** Ivor 135) [1998 78: 8.3f 7m² 7g 1999 a9.4g 8d 8m May 1] lengthy, good-topped gelding: fair handicapper: no show in 1999, swerving and unseating rider leaving stalls penultimate start: stays 1m: best on good going or firmer. *B. Palling*

MOSELLE   2 b.f. (Apr 22) Mtoto 134 – Miquette (FR) (Fabulous Dancer (USA)   **89 p** 124) [1999 8d³ Oct 30] eighth foal: sister to Irish 3-y-o 9f winner Macabeo and half-sister to several winners, including fairly useful winner around 1¼m Oops Pettie (by Machiavellian): dam French 1½m and 13.5f winner: 25/1, encouraging third of 10 to Silver Colours in steadily-run listed event at Newmarket, held up and keeping on willingly despite being rather short of room: will stay at least 1½m: sure to improve and win a race. *W. J. Haggas*

MOSEY ALONG   3 b.f. Petong 126 – Mo's Star 63 (Most Welcome 131) [1998   **–** –: 6m 1999 6v Apr 20] tailed off in seller and maiden. *L. A. Dace*

MOSI-OA-TUNYA (IRE)   3 ch.c. River Falls 113 – Heart To Heart (IRE)   **–** (Double Schwartz 128) [1998 –: 7d 1999 a8g 7.1m Jun 12] sparely-made colt: well beaten in maidens: sold 800 gns. *K. McAuliffe*

MOSQUERO (USA)   3 b.c. Sky Classic (CAN) – Mosella (USA) (Lord At War   **63** (ARG)) [1998 76p: 7g⁵ 8g⁴ 1999 a9.4g⁵ 10d 12.5m May 3] modest maiden: probably stays 1¼m: yet to race on extremes of going on turf (ran poorly on fibresand): sent to UAE. *J. H. M. Gosden*

MOSS ROSE   3 ch.f. Wolfhound (USA) 126 – Champagne 'n Roses 63 (Chief   **–** Singer 131) [1998 NR 1999 7g 8s 7g a10g a10g Nov 24] 30,000Y: sparely-made filly: second foal: half-sister to a 9f and 11f winner in Hong Kong by Last Tycoon: dam, Irish 4-y-o 7f winner, half-sister to Nell Gwyn winner Thrilling Day: no sign of ability: has been bandaged: sold 1,000 gns. *B. W. Hills*

MOSS SIDE MONKEY   4 b.g. Presidium 124 – Lady of Leisure 75 (Record   **– §** Run 127) [1998 NR 1999 11.8g 12g 8g 12.4m 13f⁶ 16.2g 15.8g Sep 18] tempera-mental maiden: stays 7f: tried blinkered/visored at 2 yrs. *K. W. Hogg, Isle of Man*

MOSSY MOOR   2 ch.f. (Feb 17) Sanglamore (USA) 126 – Moss (Alzao (USA)   **66 p** 117) [1999 7v⁴ Oct 25] second foal: dam, French 1¼m winner, half-sister to Toulon: weak in market and green, fourth of 11 to Decision Maid in maiden at Lingfield, keeping on well: will stay at least 1½m: sure to do better. *Mrs A. J. Perrett*

MOST RESPECTFUL   6 ch.g. Respect 95 – Active Movement 36§ (Music Boy   **52 +** 124) [1998 57, a61: 5.9d⁵ 8g 6m 6g 6g³ 5m* 6m⁴ a6g* 5v a6g⁴ a7g⁴ a7g² a6g⁶ 1999   **a61** a7g⁴ a7g⁴ a6g³ a6f a6g⁵ 6d 6m 5.9g² a7g* 7.5m a7g⁵ 6m⁶ 6s a6g⁶ 6g Oct 14] plain gelding: modest handicapper: won apprentice selling event at Southwell in June: effective at 5f to 7f: acts on good to firm going and fibresand (untried on equitrack): tongue tied. *N. Tinkler*

MOST-SAUCY   3 br.f. Most Welcome 131 – So Saucy 59 (Teenoso (USA) 135)   **84** [1998 NR 1999 10s 10g³ 9g⁴ 8.1d 7m² 7m* 7m⁴ 6g* 8.1d⁴ Sep 15] lengthy filly: first foal: dam 1¼m and 17f winner: fairly useful handicapper: won at Leicester in July and Lingfield in August: likely to prove best at 7f/1m: acts on good to firm and good to soft going. *B. J. Meehan*

MOTET   5 b.g. Mtoto 134 – Guest Artiste 110 (Be My Guest (USA) 126) [1998   **89** 99: 16d 16g 15m² 14g 12m³ 11.9m 1999 16f May 29] good-bodied gelding: useful handicapper at best: respectable effort only outing in 1999: stays 2¼m: acts on firm and good to soft going: blinkered twice, visored once: has worn tongue strap: winning hurdler. *M. Pitman*

MOTHER CORRIGAN (IRE)   3 gr.f. Paris House 123 – Missed Opportunity   **61** (IRE) (Exhibitioner 111) [1998 ?: 7.5s 1999 10d 10f 7.7m⁴ 6m⁶ Aug 6] modest maiden: stays 1m: acts on good to firm going: joined M. Brittain. *L. M. Cumani*

MOTHER MOLLY (USA)   2 b. or br.f. (Mar 23) Irish River (FR) 131 – Charm-   **78** ing Molly (USA) 86 (Diesis 133) [1999 6m² Jun 25] $10,000F, 17,000Y: smallish filly: fifth foal: half-sister to a winner in USA by Black Tie Affair: dam, 2-y-o 6f winner, later successful up to 9f in USA: stayed on well to pull clear of remainder when second of 6 to Jeed in maiden at Newmarket: looked sure to improve. *R. Guest*

MOTHER OF PEARL (IRE)   3 b.f. Sadler's Wells (USA) 132 – Sisania (High   **113**
Top 131) [1998 104p: 7g* 8v* 1999 10.4d² 10d⁵ 12m⁴ 10s³ 12m 12.5v⁶ 10g⁶ Oct 17]
deep-girthed, rather unfurnished filly: smart performer: best effort when very close
third to Star of Akkar in Prix de la Nonette at Deauville in August: also in frame in
Musidora Stakes at York (second to Zahrat Dubai) and Irish Oaks at the Curragh
(fourth to Ramruma): below form last 2 starts, including in Canada, trained until
penultimate one by P. Chapple-Hyam: may prove best around 1¼m: acts on heavy
going, probably on good to firm: stayed in North America. *A. G. Foster*

MOTHERS HELP   4 b.f. Relief Pitcher 120 – Laundry Maid 89 (Forzando 122)   **–**
[1998 64: 8g 8m⁴ 8g 8d³ 8d⁵ 1999 11.6m May 24] modest maiden handicapper:
winning hurdler. *D. L. Williams*

MOUJEEDA   2 ch.f. (Apr 8) Zafonic (USA) 130 – Dafinah (USA) 89 (Graustark)   **64 p**
[1999 7d Oct 30] eighth foal: half-sister to 3 winners, including 1m winner El Gahar
(by Green Desert) and useful 1¼m winner (better at 1½m) Alhamad (by Slip
Anchor): dam 1¼m/1½m winner: green, tenth of 16 to Premier Prize in steadily-run
Newmarket maiden, getting the hang of things late on and finishing strongly: will
stay 1m, probably 1¼m: likely to do fair bit better: joined W. Jarvis. *Sir Michael
Stoute*

MOUNT ABU (IRE)   2 b.c. (Apr 8) Foxhound (USA) 103 – Twany Angel (Double   **99**
Form 130) [1999 5m⁴ 6d* 6m⁵ 6g² 6s⁶ Aug 22] IR 16,500F, 60,000Y: rather leggy,
quite attractive colt: eighth foal: closely related to fairly useful Irish 1996 2-y-o 5f
winner Melleray (by Danehill), later 1m winner in USA, and half-brother to several
winners: dam French maiden: useful performer: won maiden at Newbury in May:
short-neck second of 6 to Harbour Island in Prix de Cabourg at Deauville in July:
creditable sixth of 7 to Fasliyev in Prix Morny at Deauville final outing: should stay
at least 7f: acts on soft and good to firm going. *P. W. Chapple-Hyam*

MOUNTAIN BIRD   3 ch.f. Superlative 118 – Northern Bird 86 (Interrex (CAN))   **–**
[1998 50: 5d 5g⁵ 6g 1999 6.1s 6d 6g a8g Jul 8] smallish, sturdy filly: modest maiden
at best: little form in 1999. *M. Brittain*

MOUNTAIN DREAM   6 b.g. Batshoof 122 – Echoing 93 (Formidable (USA)   **–**
125) [1998 –: 6.9d 9.3s 8d 9.2d⁵ 8g 11.1d 1999 16g⁵ Jul 5] disappointing maiden:
tried visored: poor hurdler, won in November. *R. Allan*

MOUNTAIN MAGIC   4 b.f. Magic Ring (IRE) 115 – Nevis 61 (Connaught 130)   **55**
[1998 58: 7.3m* 7m 6m 7g⁵ 7.1m 8m 8m 8g 1999 7.7s 8.3g 8.1m⁴ 10m a10g 8m³
8s Oct 25] close-coupled filly: modest handicapper: in frame in sellers in 1999: best
at 7f/1m: acts on good to firm going: blinkered final 2 starts: joined A. Juckes.
D. J. S. ffrench Davis

MOUNTAIN SONG   4 b.c. Tirol 127 – Persian Song 45 (Persian Bold 123) [1998   **107**
112: 10.3g² 10d⁶ 10f* 10m² 8s* 1999 a10f² 9.9d May 8] smart performer in 1998: 4
lengths second of 4 to Lord of Men in minor event at Nad Al Sheba: off 3 months and
always behind in valuable contest at Goodwood: stays 1¼m: acts on firm going, soft
and dirt: usually races prominently. *Saeed bin Suroor*

MOUNT HOLLY (USA)   5 b.h. Woodman (USA) 126 – Mount Helena 82 (Danzig   **89**
(USA)) [1998 82: a8g³ 10g 8.5m 7.1d 7g⁶ 8f* 8.1m³ 8m 7f 8.3f 1999 8d⁴ 8.1s³ 8m
7m² 8.5d 8m 8.1s³ 7s Oct 2] good-bodied horse: has a short, round action: fairly useful handicapper: ran well in 1999 when in frame: best at 7f/1m: acts on firm ground,
soft and equitrack: tongue tied: usually races up with pace: sold 8,500 gns. *K. Mahdi*

MOUNT PARK (IRE)   2 b.f. (Mar 10) Colonel Collins (USA) 122 – Make Hay   **73**
(Nomination 125) [1999 6.1m 6.8d 5.7d² 5g⁵ 6d³ Oct 28] 5,000 2-y-o: smallish, quite
attractive filly: fourth foal: half-sister to a 7f winner in Japan by Kefaah: dam unraced
half-sister to dam of smart middle-distance stayer/very smart hurdler Midnight
Legend: fair maiden: close third of 10 in nursery at Windsor final start: should stay
7f. *H. S. Howe*

MOUNTRATH ROCK   2 b.f. (Mar 3) Rock Hopper 124 – Point of Law (Law   **53**
Society (USA) 130) [1999 7m 6f² 6f² 7.1m Aug 21] 2,000F, 4,200 2-y-o: tall, leggy
filly: has a round action: third foal: half-sister to 4-y-o First Frame: dam unraced

daughter of half-sister to Tirol: modest form: runner-up in sellers at Newcastle and Redcar in July/August: should stay at least 1m. *N. Tinkler*

MOURAMARA (IRE) 2 b.f. (Mar 2) Kahyasi 130 – Mamoura (IRE) 97 (Lomond (USA) 128) [1999 8s³ Nov 6] quite good-topped filly: third foal: half-sister to French 3-y-o Mouriyana (by Akarad), 1m winner at 2 yrs: dam Irish 1¼m and 1½m winner from good family: green (swished tail in paddock), plenty of promise when 5 lengths third of 18 to Summoner in maiden at Doncaster, getting hang of things late on and never nearer: will stay at least 1½m: sure to progress. *L. M. Cumani* **74 p**

MOUSEHOLE 7 b.g. Statoblest 120 – Alo Ez 100 (Alzao (USA) 117) [1998 74: 6v 5d 5m 5g⁶ 5g³ 5g³ 5f² 5m* 5g² 5m 5.1m* 5f 5g⁵ 5.2g 5m 5s 5.1v 1999 5d 5d 5.1m* 5g 5m⁴ 5f² 5m³ 5m* 5.1m* 5m* 5g² 5m³ 5.2g⁶ 5d 5g⁶ 5d Oct 28] strong gelding: fairly useful performer: better than ever in 1999, winning handicaps at Nottingham and Windsor (2) and minor event at Nottingham between May and August: ran well when placed after: effective at 5f/easy 6f: best on good ground or firmer: successful in blinkers, not tried since 1996: comes from behind, and often soon off bridle. *R. Guest* **84**

MOUTAHDDEE (IRE) 3 b.c. Alzao (USA) 117 – Ah Ya Zein (Artaius (USA) 129) [1998 83+: 7f 7m 8g* 1999 10.5s² 10g* 12d³ 9.9g* 10g* 9.9f⁵ 10.5d³ 9.9m⁶ Sep 11] strong, angular colt: has a powerful, round action: smart performer: progressed well in 1999, winning handicaps at Newmarket in April, Goodwood in June and Sandown (Hong Kong Jockey Club Trophy by 1½ lengths from King Darius) in July: sweating, good fifth of 17 to Azouz Pasha in Globetrotter Handicap at Goodwood: well below form in Group 3 events last 2 starts: best around 1¼m: yet to race on heavy going, acts on any other: races up with pace: genuine: sent to UAE. *M. P. Tregoning* **110**

MOUTON (IRE) 3 b.f. Dolphin Street (FR) 125 – The Queen of Soul 75 (Chief Singer 131) [1998 65p: 7m 7.6f² 1999 8g⁵ 8d³ 9m² 9m² Aug 8] unfurnished filly: fair maiden: best effort on reappearance: probably stays 9f: acts on firm going: sold 4,000 gns in December, joined J. Bridger. *J. W. Hills* **70**

Hong Kong Jockey Club Trophy (Handicap), Sandown—
a smart front-running performance by Moutahddee, who is not especially troubled
to beat King Darius (right) and Algunnaas

MOVE THE MOUSE (IRE) 2 b.f. (Apr 26) Foxhound (USA) 103 – Kip's Sister **?**
(Cawston's Clown 113) [1999 5m⁶ 7m 7g Aug 6] seventh foal: half-sister to a 2-y-o
6f seller winner and 1½m winner by Homing and an Italian 7f (at 2 yrs) to 1¼m
winner by Statoblest: dam unraced: well held in sellers, for M. Tompkins on debut:
sold 600 gns in August and subsequently won over 9f in Holland. *N. A. Callaghan*

MOVIE STAR (IRE) 3 b.f. Barathea (IRE) 127 – Mary Astor (FR) (Groom **–**
Dancer (USA) 128) [1998 NR 1999 7d⁶ Oct 11] 680,000 francs Y: first foal: dam,
French 1¼m to 11.5f winner, half-sister to dam of 3-y-o Commander Collins: slowly
away in apprentice maiden at Leicester: sold 8,000 gns in December. *L. M. Cumani*

MOVING ARROW 8 ch.g. Indian Ridge 123 – Another Move 69 (Farm Walk **56**
111) [1998 81d: 8.5m 8.1g 10.5g 8g 8m 8m 8m² 9m 8g 8v 1999 a8g 10m⁴ Jun 16]
lengthy gelding: formerly useful handicapper: on the downgrade nowadays: stays
1¼m: probably acts on any turf going (well held on fibresand): visored twice at 4 yrs:
inconsistent. *Mrs M. Reveley*

MOVING EXPERIENCE (IRE) 2 b.f. (May 14) Nicolotte 118 – Sound **60**
Performance (IRE) 63 (Ahonoora 122) [1999 6g 8s⁴ Oct 26] 6,400Y: third foal:
half-sister to 3-y-o Dolphin Friendly: dam Irish 1½m winner out of half-sister to
Stanerra: much better effort in maidens in October when fourth at Bath: will be suited
by 1¼m+: may do better again. *M. J. Fetherston-Godley*

MOVING PRINCESS 4 b.f. Prince Sabo 123 – Another Move 69 (Farm Walk **61**
111) [1998 71: 8g³ 10s⁴ 8.1g² 8m⁶ 8m⁴ 10m² 10g⁵ 8.3d 9d 1999 a8g a8g Mar 19]
smallish, strong filly: fair maiden handicapper at best: stays 1¼m: acts on fibresand,
seems best on good ground or firmer on turf: has been bandaged off-hind. *Miss
S. E. Hall*

MOWBRAY (USA) 4 b. or br.g. Opening Verse (USA) 126 – Peppy Raja (USA) **108**
(Raja Baba (USA)) [1998 106: 9.9m⁴ 12m⁴ 12g² 12g⁶ 11.8s* 14.6d⁴ 1999 12g⁴
12g 12m 14.1m² 12m 14f* 13.9g³ 20v 14.6s⁵ Nov 5] tall gelding: good mover: useful
performer: won Grosvenor Casinos Cup (Handicap) at Goodwood in July by 2
lengths from Pairumani Star: very good third of 21 to Vicious Circle in Ebor at York
next start, but tailed off last 2 outings, including in Prix du Cadran at Longchamp:
stays 1¾m: acts on firm and soft ground: has gone in snatches/carried head high/
wandered under pressure: blinkered fourth start: none too consistent. *P. F. I. Cole*

MOY (IRE) 4 ch.f. Beveled (USA) – Exceptional Beauty 94 (Sallust 134) [1998 **–**
49: 8s 6d³ a6g 6g a8g 5.9g 7g² 8m 6s⁶ 5s 6v 8s 1999 5s a6g³ 7.1m a7g a7g⁴ a7g 6d **a54**
a12g 8.3f Aug 24] leggy filly: modest maiden handicapper: stays 7f: acts on
fibresand, probably on soft going: blinkered once at 2 yrs. *W. M. Brisbourne*

MR BERGERAC (IRE) 8 b.g. Cyrano de Bergerac 120 – Makalu 79 (Godswalk **72**
(USA) 130) [1998 89, a–: 7d³ 6.1g³ 6m 6m 6m³ 6d⁶ 6s 6.1g 6g 1999 7g 6s⁵ 6m 6g⁵ **a70**
6.1m⁵ 6m 8.2m⁵ 8.3s⁵ 8m* 8m² 8m 8s⁶ a7g⁵ a9.4g⁵ a9.4g⁶ Dec 11] sparely-made
gelding: fair handicapper nowadays: won at Bath in August: effective at 6f to 1m:
acts on all-weather, firm and soft going: visored once, usually blinkered nowadays:
has looked less than keen. *B. Palling*

Grosvenor Casinos Cup (Handicap), Goodwood—
Mowbray ends Pairumani Star's winning sequence; Red Ramona (striped cap) runs on for third

MR BOMBASTIQUE (IRE)   5 b.g. Classic Music (USA) – Duende 75 (High   –
Top 131) [1998 80: 10.5g 10s² 10.5m⁶ 9.9m⁵ 1999 10.3d 9.9m 13.3m Jul 17] sturdy
gelding: fairly useful handicapper at best: well beaten in 1999, leaving Mrs J. Brown
2,800 gns after reappearance: stays 10.5f: acts on soft and good to firm going:
successful over hurdles twice in July. *P. Bowen*

MR COSPECTOR   2 b.c. (Mar 6) Cosmonaut – L'Ancressaan 67 (Dalsaan 125)   62
[1999 6m⁵ 6m⁴ 6g 6.8m Aug 30] 7,200Y: tall colt: fourth foal: half-brother to fairly
useful 1m/1¼m winner Komreyev Dancer (by Komaite): dam 2-y-o 6f winner:
modest maiden: well below form final start. *T. H. Caldwell*

MR CUBE (IRE)   9 ch.g. Tate Gallery (USA) 117 – Truly Thankful (CAN) (Grau-   49
stark) [1998 49d, a–: 8g⁵ 7.5m 8g 8.2d 7g⁶ 7m 8m 8.1d 7g⁴ a7g 1999 7m⁴ 7f³ 7m 7m   a–
8f 7.7m³ 8.1m⁶ 7f 6f³ 8d⁴ 8.1m⁵ 7g⁴ 7d² Sep 15] sturdy gelding: poor performer:
effective at 6f to 1m: acts on firm going, soft and all-weather: blinkered/visored: gets
behind and tends to wander: has won for apprentice. *J. M. Bradley*

MR FORTYWINKS (IRE)   5 ch.g. Fools Holme (USA) – Dream On 54 (Absa-   71
lom 128) [1998 66, a77: a12g² a11g* a12g³ 11.1v² 10v* 12g² 10m 12g 10.9d 12.1s⁴   a77
11.9g 10d 1999 a12g² 11.1v² 13v⁵ 13g² 13s* 12g 12.3m* 12g* 13f⁴ 16.5f³ 13m
15.9s³ 14.1g 13.8g Oct 16] sparely-made gelding: fair handicapper: won at Hamilton
in May, Ripon (ladies race) in June and Carlisle in July: effective at 1¼m (given good
test) to 2m: acts on any turf going and all-weather: often races prominently/leads:
tends to sweat: game and genuine. *J. L. Eyre*

MR GEORGE SMITH   2 b.c. (Mar 3) Prince Sabo 123 – Nellie's Gamble 66   58
(Mummy's Game 120) [1999 6m 6m 7m 7d a7g³ a7g* Dec 6] 7,500Y, 7,000 2-y-o:
second foal: dam 7f (including at 2 yrs) and 1m winner: modest performer: won
nursery at Lingfield in December: stays 7f: acts on equitrack: hung left fourth start.
G. L. Moore

MR JONES   2 b. or br.c. (Feb 23) Emperor Jones (USA) 119 – Roxy Hart (High   66
Top 131) [1999 6g³ 5m 7m 8m a8.5g⁴ 8d Oct 18] 19,500F, 22,000Y: close-coupled,
attractive colt: half-brother to several winners, including 6f (at 2 yrs) and 1m winner
Don't Presume (by Pharly) and 1½m to 2m winner Chahaya Timor (by Slip Anchor):
dam unraced: fair maiden: stays 8.5f: acts on fibresand: sold 2,400 gns. *R. Hannon*

MR MAJICA   5 b.h. Rudimentary (USA) 118 – Pellinora (USA) (King Pellinore   62
(USA) 127) [1998 84d: a7s⁴ 8d⁵ 8s 8.1s² 8d 8.3d⁴ 8s⁶ 8m* 8m⁴ 8f 8.1m⁴ 8m²
1999 8g 7m 8.3m⁴ 8.3m 7s 8g Sep 20] robust horse: modest handicapper nowadays:
stays 1m: acts on soft and good to firm going: usually blinkered, though has won
without: none too consistent. *A. J. McNae*

MR MERTON   2 b.c. (May 11) Distant Relative 128 – Merton Mill 68 (Dominion   –
123) [1999 7.1m Sep 9] brother to 5-y-o Bicton Park and half-brother to 1¼m winner
General Monck (by Formidable): dam stayed 2¼m: always behind in Chepstow
maiden: sold 2,800 gns, sent to Spain. *B. Hanbury*

MR MIYAGI   4 b.g. Full Extent (USA) 113 – All The Girls (IRE) 49 (Alzao   –
(USA) 117) [1998 46: 8g 7.5g⁴ a6g 7s 1999 a7g Jan 23] small gelding: poor maiden:
seems to stay 1m: acts on fibresand: usually blinkered. *A. Bailey*

MR MONTAGUE (IRE)   7 b.g. Pennine Walk 120 – Ballyewry (Prince Tender-   30
foot (USA) 126) [1998 –: 10.3d 10m 1999 10.8m 13.8m⁶ 14.1f 11.9d Aug 6] lengthy
gelding: poor maiden: stays 1¾m: acts on good to firm going: blinkered final start:
modest winning jumper. *T. W. Donnelly*

MR MORIARTY (IRE)   8 ch.g. Tate Gallery (USA) 117 – Bernica (FR) 114   –
(Caro 133) [1998 39, a–: 16d⁶ 12m⁴* 12.3s⁵ 1999 14.1m Aug 28] neat gelding: poor
handicapper: stays 1½m: acts on fibresand, best efforts on good to firm going on
turf: tried blinkered: often bandaged: has had tongue tied: usually races prominently.
S. R. Bowring

MR PARADISE (IRE)   5 b.g. Salt Dome (USA) – Glowlamp (IRE) 93 (Glow   –
(USA)) [1998 67, a77: a7g² a7g⁵ a7g³ 7d 7f⁴ a7g* 7g⁵ a7g² a7g⁴ 7s³ 6.1v⁴ 7s⁴ a7g⁵   a70
1999 a7g⁵ Feb 24] leggy gelding: fair performer: effective at 6f (given a test) to 8.5f:
acts on good to firm going, heavy and fibresand: visored (raced freely) twice at 4 yrs:
usually races prominently. *W. R. Muir*

692

MR PEABODY   2 b.g. (Feb 1) Tigani 120 – Benten 61 (Sharrood (USA) 124)   –
[1999 5m 6m a6g 5m Sep 24] leggy gelding: first foal: dam disappointing maiden
who stayed 7f: no sign of ability. *D. W. Chapman*

MR PERRY (IRE)   3 br.g. Perugino (USA) 84 – Elegant Tune (USA) 51 (Aly-   **76**
sheba (USA)) [1998 NR 1999 7v² 8.3d 7g⁶ 8f a8g² 10g a8.5g⁴ a8.5g* 8.1s⁵ 7d 8.2f
Oct 20] 5,000F, 12,000Y, 18,000 2-y-o: second foal: dam fourth at 9f in Ireland on
only start: fair performer: won maiden handicap at Wolverhampton in September:
below form last 2 starts: stays 8.5f well: acts on fibresand, best turf form on soft/
heavy going: sold 18,500 gns, joined M. Hammond. *J. S. Moore*

MR ROUGH   8 b.g. Fayruz 116 – Rheinbloom 66 (Rheingold 137) [1998 46, a35:   **46**
8s 8.3m 8g 8m² 8d* 8m 8m 8f³ 8m³ 8m a8g⁴ 1999 a8f⁵ a8g³ a10g⁴ a8g³ 8.5m 8f⁵ 8g⁴   **a52**
8d³ 8f⁴ a8.5g 8m a8g a8g⁵ a8.5g² Dec 1] sturdy gelding: modest performer: effective
at 1m/1¼m: acts on firm going, good to soft and all-weather: usually blinkered/
visored. *D. Morris*

MRS BOSSY BOOTS   3 gr.f. Mystiko (USA) 124 – Rich Pickings 44 (Dominion   **44**
123) [1998 NR 1999 8m 10f⁶ 10.5m⁶ Jun 23] 5,600Y: second foal: dam, 2¼m winner
at 4 yrs, also successful over hurdles: poor form: stays 1¼m: acts on firm going:
tongue tied final start: joined C. Egerton, and successful over hurdles in October.
G. A. Butler

MRS JODI   3 b.f. Yaheeb (USA) 95§ – Knayton Lass 94 (Presidium 124) [1998   **59 ?**
NR 1999 8d 7f 12d³ 10g 8m Jun 21] unfurnished filly: first foal: dam sprinter, best at
2 yrs: modest maiden: form only at 1½m: won juvenile hurdles in November and
December. *J. M. Jefferson*

MRS MIDDLE   4 b.f. Puissance 110 – Ibadiyya 120 (Tap On Wood 130) [1998   –
47: 6s 7g 8g² 8.2d 8g 6.9d 9.2s 8d 10g² 8.5m 10m 1999 a8g a8g Feb 25] leggy filly:
has a round action: poor handicapper: stays 1¼m: acts on good to firm and good to
soft going (well beaten on equitrack): inconsistent. *D. W. Chapman*

MRS P   2 b.f. (Mar 27) First Trump 118 – Zinzi (Song 132) [1999 6f 5.9m² 6m² 6f²   **96**
6d³ 5g* 5g² 5m* Sep 11] tall, good-quartered filly: eighth foal: closely related to 2

*Polypipe plc Flying Childers Stakes, Doncaster—in a blanket finish
the late burst of Mrs P (far side) proves decisive over Emerald Peace (diamonds),
Magic of Love and Fez (nearest camera)*

winning sprinters by Primo Dominie, including smart Sarcita, and half-sister to 2 winners, including Pussy Galore (7f, by Pursuit of Love): dam Irish 4-y-o 5f winner: useful performer: won nursery at Sandown in August: 33/1, easily best effort when winning 14-runner Polypipe plc Flying Childers Stakes at Doncaster by head from Emerald Peace, held up after tardy start and bursting through final 1f: acts on good to firm and good to soft going: shade edgy at stalls at Doncaster. *Mrs L. Stubbs*

MR SPEAKER (IRE)   6 ch.g. Statoblest 120 – Casting Vote (USA) 54 (Monteverdi 129) [1998 65, a51+: a10g 7g⁶ 7.5m* 7g a7g³ 1999 7m 7.5s 8d* 9g³ 8s Oct 25] close-coupled, workmanlike gelding: fair handicapper: won ladies race at Brighton in October: very good third at Redcar next time: stays 9f: yet to race on heavy going, acts on any other (some promise on equitrack): inconsistent. *C. F. Wall*   **68 a–**

MR SPECULATOR 6 ch.g. Kefaah (USA) 124 – Humanity (Ahonoora 122) [1998 –, a48: a16.2g 1999 a14.8g³ Dec 11] strong, lengthy gelding: modest performer: should stay 2m: acts on good to firm ground and fibresand: usually visored/blinkered. *J. L. Spearing*   **– a51**

MRS PICKLES   4 gr.f. Northern Park (USA) 107 – Able Mabel 77 (Absalom 128) [1998 39: a9.4g⁵ a12g⁶ 8f 10g 6g 10m 16m⁴ 16.4m² 1999 a16g⁴ a14g* 14.1d a14g a16g⁶ May 17] poor handicapper: won apprentice event at Southwell in March: below form after: stays easy 2m: acts on fibresand and good to firm going: blinkered final start. *M. D. I. Usher*   **43**

MRS SIDDONS (IRE)   3 ch.f. Royal Academy (USA) 130 – White Water (FR) (Pharly (FR) 130) [1998 82p: 7d² 1999 7m⁴ 8d⁵ 10d Nov 4] plenty of promise only start at 2 yrs: disappointing in 1999 (not seen out until September): should stay at least 1¼m. *G. Wragg*   **60**

MR STICKYWICKET   2 b.c. (May 16) Mistertopogigo (IRE) 118 – Low Road (Lomond (USA) 128) [1999 a5g Nov 30] third foal: dam unraced daughter of sister to smart 1¼m performer Perpendicular: well beaten in maiden at Southwell. *M. J. Polglase*   **–**

MR STYLISH   3 b.g. Mazilier (USA) 107 – Moore Stylish 65 (Moorestyle 137) [1998 NR 1999 7s 6v⁵ 6.1f 6.1g³ 6m² 6.1m² 6m² 6f³ 7.1s⁴ a6g 6g⁴ Oct 14] 6,200F, 5,500Y: third foal: dam, middle-distance maiden, winning hurdler: fair maiden handicapper: most recent starts in 1999: effective at 6f/7f: acts on soft and good to firm going. *I. A. Balding*   **78 +**

MT SPECULATION (IRE)   3 b.c. Common Grounds 118 – Blue Alicia (Wolver Hollow 126) [1998 75: 7.1d² 7m 7s² 1999 8m 7d⁵ 7m³ 7.1g 9m² 8s* Aug 6] fair performer: made all in claimer at Clairefontaine in August: claimed 200,555 francs to join E. Lellouche in France and won over hurdles following month: stays 9f: acts on soft and good to firm going. *P. W. Chapple-Hyam*   **75**

MUARA BAY   5 gr.g. Absalom 128 – Inca Girl (Tribal Chief 125) [1998 57§, a59§: a8s* a8.5g² a7g⁴ 8s 8m³ 8m 8g a8g 8.3g 8d² 8g⁵ 8.2s 7v³ 1999 a8g 7m 8s Jun 12] good-bodied gelding: modest handicapper: no form in 1999: barely stays 1¼m: acts on firm going and fibresand, probably on heavy: effective blinkered: sometimes very slowly away: sold 1,600 gns. *J. A. Glover*   **– §**

MUBRIK (IRE)   4 b.c. Lahib (USA) 129 – Bequeath (USA) (Lyphard (USA) 132) [1998 107p: 7s² 7s* 7.1d* 8f² 7g⁴ 1999 7d⁵ 7m² 7d Aug 14] well-made colt: fluent mover: useful performer: 2 lengths second of 27 to stable-mate Russian Revival in Tote International Handicap at Ascot in August: heavily-backed favourite, gave impression something amiss 7 days later: likely to prove best at 7f/1m: acts on firm and soft going: sent to UAE. *J. H. M. Gosden*   **106**

MUCHANA YETU   2 b.f. (Mar 21) Mtoto 134 – Bobbie Dee 93 (Blakeney 126) [1999 6f³ 6d 7m⁵ 7m⁴ Jul 10] close-coupled filly: first foal: dam, maiden who should have stayed 1½m, also placed over hurdles: fair maiden: bred to be well suited by 1½m+. *Mrs P. N. Dutfield*   **65**

MUCHMOORE   3 b.g. (Apr 17) Casteddu 111 – Tassagh Bridge (IRE) (Double Schwartz 128) [1999 6f 7g 7.9m a8.5g Sep 8] 2,300Y: workmanlike gelding: has a round action: second foal: dam bad maiden: well held in maidens. *J. S. Moore*   **–**

MUCHO COLOR (IRE) 3 ch.c. Pips Pride 117 – Aubretia (USA) 84 (Hatchet –
Man (USA)) [1998 66?: 5g⁶ 6s 5m⁵ 5.7d 5.1d 1999 a6g a6g Jan 27] fair maiden at
best: showed little in 1999: blinkered last 2 starts at 2 yrs. *S. R. Bowring*

MUDALAL (USA) 4 b.g. Dixieland Band (USA) – Barakat 93 (Bustino 136) –
[1998 91: 10m* 12s 1999 10g 12m 11.9d May 11] angular gelding: fairly useful
performer at 3 yrs: well below par in 1999: should stay 1½m: acts on good to firm
going: sold 16,500 gns, sent to Bahrain. *B. W. Hills*

MUDDY WATER 3 b.f. Salse (USA) 128 – Rainbow Fleet 66 (Nomination 125) 57
[1998 –: a5g a12g⁶ 1999 a6g² a6g³ a6g⁶ a9.4g 6g⁶ 6m⁴ 6f⁶ 7m² Jul 26] modest maiden:
effective at 6f/7f: acts on fibresand and good to firm going: none too consistent.
D. Marks

MUDLARK 7 b.g. Salse (USA) 128 – Mortal Sin (USA) 65 (Green Forest (USA) 44
134) [1998 NR 1999 a16g³ a16f² a16g⁵ a16g³ a16g² 17.1v⁴ 21.6d a16g 17.2m⁵ Jun
23] good-bodied gelding: poor maiden handicapper: stays 17f: acts on heavy going
and fibresand: wears blinkers/visor: usually soon off bridle. *J. Norton*

MUFFIN MAN 2 b.c. (Feb 7) Timeless Times (USA) 99 – Allessca 69 (Alleging 71
(USA) 120) [1999 5g 5.2m⁵ 5.1s⁴ 5.1g⁴ 6m 6d⁴ 6m⁵ 6m⁵ 7g² 7g⁴ 7m 7m 7.3v Oct
23] 4,000F: workmanlike colt: first foal: dam 1¼m to 1½m winner: fair maiden:
creditable fourth of 17 in nursery at York tenth start: below form after: should stay
1m: acts on good to firm and good to soft going. *M. D. I. Usher*

MUFFLED (USA) 2 ch.f. (Apr 6) Mizaaya 104 – Sound It (USA) (Believe It 67
(USA)) [1999 7m⁴ 8s Sep 22] $21,000F: second foal: dam, fourth at 7f at 2 yrs in
France, half-sister to Cheveley Park winner Pas de Reponse and Poule d'Essai des
Poulains winner Green Tune: much better effort in maidens when fourth of 7 to Zyz
at Leicester: should stay 1m. *J. L. Dunlop*

MUHAAJIM (IRE) 2 ch.c. (May 9) Lake Coniston (IRE) 131 – Maellen (River 69
Beauty 105) [1999 6g 7m³ 7m⁶ 7m 7s 7d Oct 21] 48,000Y: closely related to a winner
up to 11f in Hong Kong by Bluebird and half-brother to several winners, including 7f
winner Hujoom (by Fairy King) and 6f (at 2 yrs) to 1½m winner Lifewatch Vision
(by Vision), both useful: dam Irish 1½m winner: fair maiden: well held in nurseries
last 3 starts, blinkered final one: should stay 1m: acts on good to firm going: sold
8,000 gns. *J. L. Dunlop*

MUHANDIS 6 b.h. Persian Bold 123 – Night At Sea 107 (Night Shift (USA)) 79
[1998 58: 11.9s³ a10g a13g² 1999 a12g a12f⁴ a12g⁴ a13g* a13g* Feb 6] fair handicapper: won selling events at Lingfield in January and February: stayed 13f: acted on
soft ground and equitrack: tried visored, usually blinkered: dead. *G. L. Moore*

MUHASSIL (IRE) 6 ch.g. Persian Bold 123 – Nouvelle Star (AUS) (Luskin Star 54
(AUS) [1998 NR 1999 10m⁵ 10g⁵ a11g² 10.3m Jun 23] rangy gelding: modest
maiden, lightly raced: probably stays 11f: acts on good to firm going and fibresand:
blinkered/visored in 1999. *K. A. Morgan*

MUHIB (USA) 4 b.c. Red Ransom (USA) – Sensorious (CAN) (Vice Regent 111
(CAN)) [1998 111: 8m² 9m* 10.4f 12d⁴ 12s 1999 12d² 11.8s³ 10s³ 12f³ 10.1g²
11.9v² 11.8s* Oct 25] well-made colt: smart performer: won minor event at Leicester
in October: ran creditably most other starts, notably when third in listed race at
Leicester (behind Yavana's Pace) on second and listed rated stakes at Goodwood
(behind Danish Rhapsody) on fourth: stays 1½m: acts on any going: visored last 2
starts: sent to Australia. *Sir Michael Stoute*

MUHTAFEL 5 b.g. Nashwan (USA) 135 – The Perfect Life (IRE) 106 (Try My 100
Best (USA) 130) [1998 100: a12g⁶ 12d 10v 8m 8s 8m 8m⁵ 8d³ 10.2d² 10m* 10m²
10.2m* 10m³ 10.3m*ᵈⁱˢ 1999 10g⁶ 10m* May 1] big, lengthy, good-topped gelding:
useful handicapper: better effort in 1999 when second of 17 to Elhayq in rated stakes
at Newmarket: stays 1¼m: acts on firm and good to soft ground: has won in visor, but
is at least as effective without: held up, and has good turn of foot. *J. R. Jenkins*

MUHTATHIR 4 ch.c. Elmaamul (USA) 125 – Majmu (USA) 105 (Al Nasr (FR) 120
126) [1998 123: 10s³ 8f² 8g* 7.3m* 8m* 8g 7v 1999 a8f² 8f⁵ 8m⁴ 8m⁴ Dec
12] rangy, good-topped colt: has a round action: very smart performer: won Premio
Vittorio di Capua at Milan in October by 2½ lengths from Stanott: in frame in listed

Premio Vittorio di Capua, Milan—another Group 1 win for Godolphin
as Muhtathir sets a new course record; fellow British raider Stanott (far side) runs on for second,
ahead of Midyan Call and Crisos Il Monaco

race at Nad Al Sheba (6 lengths second to Lend A Hand) in March, Park Stakes at
Doncaster (fourth to Sugarfoot) in September and when 2½ lengths fourth to Docksider in Hong Kong Mile at Sha Tin: best around 1m on good to firm/firm going
and dirt (though has won on good to soft): usually races prominently/leads: stays in
training. *Saeed bin Suroor*

MUJAHID (USA) 3 b.c. Danzig (USA) – Elrafa Ah (USA) 105 (Storm Cat **118**
(USA)) [1998 125p: 6f* 6m* 6f⁵ 7g* 1999 8g⁵ 8m³ 8m⁵ 8m 7g⁴ 10d² Oct 29] sturdy,
good-bodied colt: has a round action: the leading 2-y-o of 1998, winner of Dewhurst
Stakes: bit below that form in 1999, best efforts when 1½ lengths third to Island
Sands in 2000 Guineas in May, 5 lengths fourth to Susu in Challenge Stakes in October and length second to Little Rock in listed race later in month, all at Newmarket:
effective at 7f, barely stays 1¼m: acts on firm and good to soft going: mulish at stalls
third and fourth (blinkered) starts: has shown tendency to drift left. *J. L. Dunlop*

MUJA'S MAGIC (IRE) 4 b.f. Mujadil (USA) 119 – Grave Error (Northern **57**
Treat (USA)) [1998 62, a65: a7g² a7g³ a5g⁵ a6g 6m⁶ 5.3f⁵ 6g* 6m⁴ 6g⁶ 7m 6m² 7m **a70**
6f⁵ 6m³ 6.1d 5.1v 1999 6.1v 6s 5.3f 6f 6g⁵ 5m⁶ 6g² 6m² 5m⁵ 7f 5.7h⁵ 6f 5g* 5.7f⁶ 5d⁵
5d³ a6g⁴ a7g a7g* Dec 15] leggy, workmanlike filly: fair handicapper on all-weather,
modest on turf: won at Beverley in August and at Wolverhampton in December:
left K. Ivory after sixteenth start: stays 7f: acts on good to firm going, good to soft
and all-weather: occasionally blinkered, usually visored: none too consistent.
Mrs N. Macauley

MUJKARI (IRE) 3 ch.g. Mujtahid (USA) 118 – Hot Curry (USA) (Sharpen Up **49**
127) [1998 –: 5d 5.3d 7d⁶ 7d 7d 8.2v 1999 8.2s 7m⁶ 8g 6.1g 8.1m⁵ 7f² 7f* 8d⁶ a7g
Sep 4] lengthy gelding: poor performer: won maiden handicap at Brighton in August:
stays 7f: acts on firm and good to soft going, some promise on fibresand: visored last
4 starts, blinkered (well beaten) once at 2 yrs. *J. M. Bradley*

Mr Hamdan Al Maktoum's "Mujahid"

MUJODA 2 b.f. (Apr 22) Mizoram (USA) 105 – Titian Beauty (Auction Ring – (USA) 123) [1999 7m 7m 5.7d Sep 27] fifth reported foal: half-sister to 1m winner Pastiche (by Kylian) and 1992 2-y-o 5f seller winner Petite Lass (by Lidhame): dam Irish maiden: well held in maidens. *R. Brotherton*

MUKAABED (USA) 2 ch.c. (Apr 3) Phone Trick (USA) – Slick Delivery (USA) **76** (Topsider (USA)) [1999 6d³ 6d Oct 29] $200,000Y: well-made, quite attractive colt: fluent mover: second foal: dam winner up to 1m in USA: promising third of 14 to Alfini in Newmarket maiden on debut: 7/4, only tenth of 19 to Pax in similar event there 2 weeks later: should stay 1m. *M. P. Tregoning*

MUKARRAB (USA) 5 b. or br.g. Dayjur (USA) 137 – Mahassin (NZ) (Biscay **59** (AUS)) [1998 56, a60+: a7g a7g⁶ a6g 5s³ 5.9d 5g² 5m 5g⁴ 5g a5g² a5g³ 5g 5s³ **a91** 5m² 5m³ 5g* 5d 5m 5d 5v 6v⁵ a6g* a5f⁵ a5g* 1999 a6g* a5g³ a6f* a6g³ a6g² a6g² a5g* a6g* a6g³ a6g 5d 5g⁵ a5g³ 5s² 5m 5d³ 5m² 6.1f 5g⁶ 5m 6g⁵ 5g³ 5g 5m³ 5g⁵ a5g a6g a5g⁶ Dec 15] good-bodied gelding: fairly useful handicapper on all-weather, modest on turf: won 4 times at Lingfield in January/February: best at 5f/6f: acts on all-weather, good to firm and heavy going: tried blinkered: usually races up with pace. *D. W. Chapman*

MUKASOL 3 b.c. Mukaddamah (USA) 125 – So Long Boys (FR) (Beldale Flutter **94** (USA) 130) [1998 74: 8m⁴ 7.9g³ 8v³ 1999 7v* 8f* 8.1m 8m 7m⁶ 7g² 6s⁴ Nov 7] tall, attractive colt: shows knee action: fairly useful performer: won maiden at Folkestone in April and 5-runner minor event at Milan (made all) in May: best effort when second in minor event at Milan in September: stays 1m: probably acts on any going. *L. M. Cumani*

MUKAYED (IRE) 3 ro.c. Cadeaux Genereux 131 – Al Sylah 118 (Nureyev **88 §** (USA) 131) [1998 NR 1999 7g⁶ 8s 6g⁵ 7m⁴ 7m³ 7m³ 6g² Oct 15] leggy, lengthy colt:

good mover: seventh foal: half-brother to fairly useful 7f winner Yaqthan (by Kris), later successful around 1m/9f in UAE and USA, and useful 6f/7f winner in Britain and in UAE/1m in USA Laafee (by Machiavellian): dam sprinter: fairly useful maiden: best effort when fourth to Nice One Clare in handicap at Newmarket (after 3-month break) in August, hanging left: stays 7f: blinkered/visored last 3 starts: probably not one to trust implicitly: sold 9,000 gns. *J. L. Dunlop*

MUKHALIF (IRE)   3 ch.c. Caerleon (USA) 132 – Potri Pe (ARG) (Potrillazo (ARG)) [1998 108p: 7g* 7s* 1999 10m² 10.4s² 12m* 12m Jul 4] close-coupled colt: has a quick action: smart performer: good second in listed races at Newmarket (behind Beat All) and York (behind Zaajer) before winning Derby Italiano at Rome in May by 1½ lengths from Iscan: down the field in 17-finisher Deutsches Derby at Hamburg final start: better at 1½m than shorter: acts on soft and good to firm going. *Saeed bin Suroor*   **114**

MUKHLLES (USA)   6 b.g. Diesis 133 – Serenely (USA) (Alydar (USA)) [1998 47, a53+: a8g 8.2m 8g 7g 7f 8m 8d 1999 10g* 10.1d⁴ 11.5g⁵ 10m 12d Aug 26] small gelding: modest handicapper: won at Lingfield in June: effective at 7f to 1¼m: acts on firm going, good to soft and fibresand: has had tongue tied: has run well sweating: none too consistent. *Bob Jones*   **60**

MULLAGH HILL LAD (IRE)   6 b.g. Cyrano de Bergerac 120 – Fantasise (FR) (General Assembly (USA)) [1998 –, a66d: a7s⁶ a6g² a5g⁶ a6g a6g a6g a6g a7g⁶ 1999 a8.5g a7g⁵ a8g a6g Apr 29] dipped-backed gelding: formerly fair winner, just poor nowadays: probably stays 7f: acts on good to firm ground, soft and fibresand: visored once, effective blinkered or not: slowly away second/third starts: tends to hang: one to treat with caution. *N. P. Littmoden*   **– §**
a39 §

Godolphin's "Mukhalif"

MULLAGHMORE (IRE)   3 b.g. Petardia 113 – Comfrey Glen 63 (Glenstal   **65**
(USA) 118) [1998 –: 8s 7.9g 1999 8m 8g³ 8.1m 8m⁶ 8g⁵ 8g³ 8s⁶ 9g 8g⁴ Nov 3] strong
gelding: fair maiden handicapper: probably stays 9f: best efforts on good going:
blinkered last 4 starts: has worn tongue strap. *M. Kettle*

MULLITOVER   9 ch.g. Interrex (CAN) – Atlantic Air (Air Trooper 115) [1998   **75**
76, a70: 7m 7g³ 7d² 7m 8.3f⁴ 8m⁶ 7g 7g² 7s a7g⁴ a8g 1999 7m⁵ 7m 8g² 7m 8m Sep 2]
close-coupled, workmanlike gelding: fair handicapper: trained by M. Heaton-Ellis
first 4 starts: best at 7f/1m: acts on firm going, soft and all-weather: usually races
prominently: none too consistent. *C. G. Cox*

MULL OF KINTYRE (USA)   2 b.c. (Jan 24) Danzig (USA) – Retrospective   **112**
(USA) (Easy Goer (USA)) [1999 6g* 6m² 6g* a8.5f⁴ Nov 6]
          The Kentucky Derby is a possible target for Mull of Kintyre after he
acquitted himself so well on his first run on dirt when fourth of fourteen to
Anees in the Breeders' Cup Juvenile in November. Mull of Kintyre, who didn't
get the best of breaks at Gulfstream and was in the rear in the back straight,
improved into fourth turning for home and stayed on to be beaten five and a
quarter lengths by the winner. The colt's three previous races had all been over
six furlongs, and he'd won two of them, a maiden at Leopardstown in June
and the Scottish Equitable Gimcrack Stakes at York in August. In between he
finished a creditable second to City On A Hill in the July Stakes at Newmarket.
Mull of Kintyre had comfortably the best form in a ten-runner field for the
Gimcrack, and he landed the odds with the minimum of fuss, asserting when
pushed along approaching the final two furlongs and gradually pulling clear
without needing to be hard ridden, winning by three lengths from Ma Yoram.
Mull of Kintyre still has plenty of improvement to make if he's to win the
Kentucky Derby, or for that matter the Two Thousand Guineas, which is an
alternative should it be decided not to send him to Churchill Downs. He won't
be short of opportunities to pick up good prizes elsewhere, though.

		Northern Dancer	Nearctic
	Danzig (USA)	(b 1961)	Natalma
	(b 1977)	Pas de Nom	Admiral's Voyage
Mull of Kintyre (USA)		(b or br 1968)	Petitioner
(b.c. Jan 24, 1997)		Easy Goer	Alydar
	Retrospective (USA)	(ch 1986)	Relaxing
	(b 1992)	Hay Patcher	Hoist The Flag
		(b 1973)	Turn To Talent

          Mull of Kintyre, like his stable-companions Monashee Mountain and
Brahms, was bought for a million dollars at Keeneland as a yearling. He's the
first foal of Retrospective, who was bought by John Magnier at the 1999
Keeneland November Sale for 2,900,000 dollars. She was a winner at up to
nine furlongs in the USA and is a half-sister to the high-class US Grade 1
nine-furlong and ten-furlong winner Broad Brush. The next two dams were
both stakes winners, with Hay Patcher one of nine winners out of the good
racemare Turn To Talent. The latter is a half-sister to the high-class stakes
winner Too Bald, herself the dam of the top-class colt Exceller. Mull of Kintyre
may stay the Kentucky Derby distance of a mile and a quarter, but he's unlikely
to get any further. A sturdy, good-topped colt with plenty of scope, he has raced
only on good and good to firm ground on turf. *A. P. O'Brien, Ireland*

Scottish Equitable Gimcrack Stakes, York—
Mull of Kintyre gradually pulls clear of Ma Yoram, Bally Pride (rail) and Day Journey

MULTI FRANCHISE   6 ch.g. Gabitat 119 – Gabibti (IRE) 82 (Dara Monarch   –
128) [1998 48: a10g⁴ a10g⁴ a8g⁶ a10g³ a10g⁶ 10g 8f⁴ a7g⁴ 10g⁴ 8.3m a10g⁶ 8.3m
a10g⁶ 1999 a10g a11g May 17] leggy gelding: poor performer: stays 1¼m: acts on
firm ground (has won on heavy over hurdles) and all-weather: tried in visor/blinkers.
Mrs L. C. Jewell

MUMBAI   3 b.g. Theatrical Charmer 114 – Lehzen (Posse (USA) 130) [1998 NR   –
1999 10.5s⁴ 8.3m 8.1m Jun 29] fourth living foal: dam (unraced) from family of
Celtic Swing: no sign of ability in maidens/seller. *D. J. Wintle*

MUMMY NOSE BEST   3 b.f. Cyrano de Bergerac 120 – Wendy's Way 53   **37**
(Merdon Melody 98) [1998 54: 5g 1999 a7g⁶ 6m 5m 6.1m 6g 7m 7d Oct 11] poor
maiden: stays 6f. *V. Soane*

MUNASIB (IRE)   4 br.g. Treasure Kay 114 – Pipe Opener 58 (Prince Sabo 123)   –
[1998 57: 8m 6.5v³ 5m 7m 7d⁶ a8.5g 1999 7.1m 8m a7g Nov 19] modest maiden: no
form in 1999, leaving S. Kettlewell after second start: tried blinkered. *G. Brown*

MUNDAKA (IRE)   2 ch.c. (Apr 29) Mukaddamah (USA) 125 – Frau Ahuyen-   **64**
tante (ARG) (Frari (ARG)) [1999 7m 7m⁵ 8f³ 8d 8m 8d Oct 30] 2,800F, IR 11,000Y:
close-coupled colt: has a quick action: half-brother to several winners, including
4-y-o Mister Benjamin: dam unraced: modest maiden: below form in nurseries/
seller last 3 starts, in tongue strap final outing: should stay 1¼m: acts on firm going.
S. P. C. Woods

MUNDO RARO   4 b.c. Zafonic (USA) 130 – Star Spectacle (Spectacular Bid   **92**
(USA)) [1998 94: 8d² 9g³ 8m* 10.3m 8d² 8s 1999 7.5m⁶ 8.5g² 8.9d 7.6m 7d 8g Oct
2] fairly useful performer: easily best effort in 1999 when second in handicap in May:
stays 8.5f: acts on good to firm and good to soft going: pulled too hard third start.
J. G. FitzGerald

MUNGO DUFF (IRE)   4 b.g. Priolo (USA) 127 – Noble Dust (USA) (Dust   **68**
Commander (USA)) [1998 –: 10d 10d 1999 8.3s⁵ 9.9m Aug 29] tall gelding: has
scope: fair maiden: should stay beyond 1m: acts on soft going. *J. R. Fanshawe*

MUNGO PARK   5 b.g. Selkirk (USA) 129 – River Dove (USA) 86 (Riverman   **88**
(USA) 131) [1998 88: 5g² 5s⁴ 5v* 5d² 6s 5m* 5g⁵ 5.1g* 5s 5d 5g⁵ 5g* 5g⁴ 5m⁴ 5d
5g⁵ 5s⁶ 5d³ 1999 5d 5g⁴ 5d* 5m 5.1g⁴ 5d⁶ 5m 5.1g² 5s 5f⁶ 5d⁵ 5.7m⁴ 5g² 5m⁴ 5m⁵
6m² 6d 5d Oct 18] big, strong gelding: impresses in appearance: has a round action:
fairly useful performer: won minor event at Thirsk in April: ran at least respectably
most other starts: best at 5f: acts on any going: blinkered tenth to twelfth starts,
visored once at 3 yrs: sometimes unruly in stalls: tends to flash tail/find little, and
best with exaggerated waiting tactics. *M. Dods*

MUNIF (USA)   4 ch.g. Woodman (USA) 126 – Garvin's Gal (USA) (Seattle Slew   **69**
(USA)) [1998 –: 7g 1999 12.4g³ 7f⁶ a9.4g 10.3d³ 8d Jun 9] quite attractive gelding:
fair maiden: seems to stay 1½m: acts on firm and good to soft going: tends to carry
head high: sold 12,000 gns. *B. Hanbury*

MUNJIZ (IRE)   3 b. or br.c. Marju (IRE) 127 – Absaar (USA) 76 (Alleged (USA)   **118**
138) [1998 99: 6g⁴ 6f² 6d* 7g³ 1999 6g* 6g⁶ 6m² 6d⁶ 6m² 6.1m⁶ 6s² Sep 26]
good-topped, attractive colt: smart performer: won handicap at Newmarket in April:
good efforts after when runner-up in rated stakes at Haydock (listed event) and
Newmarket (behind Haafiz) and Diadem Stakes at Ascot (best effort, short-headed
by Bold Edge): best at 6f: yet to race on heavy going, acts on any other: sent to UAE.
B. W. Hills

MUNTEJ   2 ch.c. (Apr 11) Muhtarram (USA) 125 – El Rabab (USA) 70 (Roberto   **86**
(USA) 131) [1999 7m⁶ 7.1d² 7m² 7d² 7.9g² 7d³ Oct 21] tall, quite good-topped colt:
fourth foal: half-brother to 3-y-o Awwaliya, useful 6f (including at 2 yrs) and 7f
winner Filfilah (by Cadeaux Genereux) and 5f (at 2 yrs) to 1m winner Marathon
Maid (by Kalaglow): dam 2-y-o 1m winner out of Breeders' Cup Juvenile Fillies
winner Brave Raj: fairly useful maiden: beaten favourite last 4 starts: may prove
best around 7f: yet to race on extremes of going: sold 65,000 gns, reportedly to join
R. Attfield in Canada. *B. W. Hills*

MUQTARB (IRE)   3 ch.g. Cadeaux Genereux 131 – Jasarah (IRE) 70 (Green   **93**
Desert (USA) 127) [1998 98p: 6m* 7f⁵ 1999 7g⁴ 6s Oct 22] strong, good sort: fairly

useful form: found to have cracked cannon bone after final 2-y-o start: respectable fourth of 5 to Kumait in Redcar minor event on reappearance, travelling best long way: last in rated stakes at Newbury later in October: could well prove best at 5f/6f: joined W. Musson. *M. P. Tregoning*

MUQTARIB (USA) 3 b.c. Gone West (USA) – Shicklah (USA) 106 (The Minstrel **109** (CAN) 135) [1998 108p: 6m* 6g² 6d* 1999 6d 6s Nov 6] strong colt: has a short, rather scratchy action: useful performer: won Richmond Stakes at Goodwood at 2 yrs: creditable 3¾ lengths ninth of 20 to Gaelic Storm in listed race at Newmarket in October, first and better effort in 1999: will probably prove best up to 7f: best efforts on good to soft going. *J. L. Dunlop*

MURCHAN TYNE (IRE) 6 ch.m. Good Thyne (USA) 98 – Ardnamurchan **66** (Ardross 134) [1998 66: 11v² 11.8m⁴ 12.3g³ 11.9g⁴ 16.2g⁴ 15.9g² 14g 15.9g² 1999 12.3m³ 15.9m 12.3d 15.9d⁵ 16m* 16f⁵ 17.3g Oct 16] smallish, workmanlike mare: fair handicapper: won 5-runner race at Ripon in August: effective at 1½m to 17f: acts on any going: usually held up. *E. J. Alston*

MURGHEM (IRE) 4 b.c. Common Grounds 118 – Fabulous Pet (Something- **103 +** fabulous (USA)) [1998 103: 8m² 8.1g⁵ 10g 10.3g² 12m* 12d³ 13.9f² 11.9g² 16g² 15d³ 1999 14.1s⁴ 14d 12g⁶ 12f⁴ 14d* 11.9m³ 16.1g² 12m 12d³ 11.8s² 12s Nov 12] rangy colt: useful performer: won handicap at Sandown in August by short head from Danegold: ran well when placed after, particularly when ½-length second to Muhib in minor event at Leicester on penultimate start: left B. Hanbury after eighth outing: effective at 1½m to 2m: yet to race on heavy going, acts on any other: blinkered fourth start. *M. Johnston*

MURJAN (FR) 2 ch.g. (Mar 4) Lycius (USA) 124 – Raknah (IRE) 91 (Night Shift **76** (USA)) [1999 8g⁴ 8.5g³ 9m⁴ Sep 24] good-topped gelding: second foal: half-brother to 3-y-o My Pleasure: dam 5f to 7f winner: fair form in minor event/maidens: likely to prove best at 1m/9f: joined E. Dunlop. *M. Johnston*

MURMOON 4 b.g. Danehill (USA) 126 – Reflection 111 (Mill Reef (USA) 141) **72** [1998 68: 8.2m⁴ 9s 10g³ 10.9s 12m⁶ 9.7f 6g⁴ 8g 9.2s² 8.2s⁴ 1999 a8g² a7g³ a9.4g⁶ a8.5f a5f a7.5f⁵ Dec 16] strong gelding: fair maiden: left B. Hanbury after third start: off 8 months and well below form subsequently: has form at 1½m, but headstrong and may prove best at 7f/1m: acts on soft going, good to firm and equitrack. *E. Charpy, UAE*

MURPHY'S GOLD (IRE) 8 ch.g. Salt Dome (USA) – Winter Harvest (Grundy **56** 137) [1998 58: 8.5m⁴ 7.1m⁶ 8.5d³ 8d³ 6.9d 8.5d⁶ 7.5m⁶ 8.5g* 6.9d 8.5m³ 7.5m⁵ 8g 1999 8m 8.5d 6.9m 7.5m³ 8m 8f⁴ 8d 8.5g⁴ 8.3f² 8.9m 9.2m* 8m Sep 16] tall gelding: modest performer: won seller at Hamilton in September: probably best at 1m/9f nowadays: acts on firm and good to soft going: blinkered twice as 3-y-o: successful for apprentice/amateur: broke blood vessel once: none too consistent. *R. A. Fahey*

MURPHY'S LAW 3 b.g. High Kicker (USA) – Mio Mementa 61 (Streak 119) **–** [1998 –: 6.1m 5.1v 7s 1999 7s 11.6m 16m⁴ 11.9d Aug 6] little sign of ability. *M. J. Ryan*

MUSALSE 4 b.g. Salse (USA) 128 – Musical Sally (USA) (The Minstrel (CAN) **a60** 135) [1998 66, a60+: a8t a11g³ a8g⁵ a11g³ 10d5 14.1g* a14.8g² 16m² a14.8g⁴ a16g* 15.8m* 16.1m* 15.8d³ a14.8g 1999 a16f⁴ a16f³ a16g³ a16g⁴ 17.1v 16m 16d⁶ 16d 15.8g a16.2g Dec 15] sturdy, workmanlike gelding: modest handicapper: below form after third start: stays 2m: acts on all-weather, good to firm and good to soft ground (possibly not on heavy): visored once at 3 yrs: usually held up. *P. C. Haslam*

MUSCHANA 2 ch.f. (Mar 5) Deploy 131 – Youthful (FR) (Green Dancer (USA) **76 p** 132) [1999 7v⁵ 7d³ 8s² Oct 26] sturdy, workmanlike filly: has quick action: half-sister to several winners, including smart 7f (at 2 yrs) to 1½m (King Edward VII Stakes) winner Beneficial (by Top Ville) and very smart 6f (at 2 yrs) to 2m (Melbourne Cup) winner Jeune (by Kalaglow): dam, French 1½m winner, out of high-class French staying 2-y-o First Bloom: fair form in maidens: neck second of 12 to Top Hand at Bath final start: will be suited by 1¼m+: raced only on good to soft going or softer: well bred, and remains capable of better. *J. L. Dunlop*

MUSH (IRE) 2 b.c. (May 15) Thatching 131 – Petite Jameel (IRE) (Ahonoora **70 p** 122) [1999 6d 7m³ Sep 3] 10,000F, 6,000Y: rather unfurnished colt: fourth foal:

half-brother to winner up to 11f in USA Ready To Roll (by Priolo): dam unraced sister to Don't Forget Me: much better effort in maidens when third of 12 to The Deputy at Epsom, keeping on: will stay 1m: should improve further. *P. W. Harris*

MUSICAL FRUITS   2 b.f. (Mar 1) Tuam – Golden Apple 68 (Athens Wood 126)   –
[1999 5m a6g a7g Sep 18] half-sister to poor animals: dam thorough stayer: no form: trained on debut by R. Phillips. *Mrs P. N. Dutfield*

MUSICAL MAYHEM (IRE)   6 b.g. Shernazar 131 – Minstrels Folly (USA)   –
(The Minstrel (CAN) 135) [1998 89: 16d² 16d* 16m⁵ 16v⁴ 1999 20m 16m Jul 11] first foal: dam Irish 1m winner: fairly useful handicapper in 1998: well held at Royal Ascot and the Curragh at 6 yrs: should stay 2½m: acts on soft ground: blinkered (respectable effort) once in 1998: won over hurdles in September. *D. K. Weld, Ireland*

MUSICAL TONES (USA)   3 b.f. Diesis 133 – Arsaan (USA) 106 (Nureyev   **94 §**
(USA) 131) [1998 7p: 8d² 1999 10m⁵ 8.3g² 10d⁴ 8m² 8d⁴ 8g* Jul 17] leggy, unfurnished filly: has a round action: fairly useful performer: ran very well when fifth to Alabaq in listed race at Newmarket in May: failed to repeat that form, including when making all in 5-runner maiden at Ayr in July by 7 lengths: may prove best at 1m/1¼m: has found little and wandered: not one to trust: sent to Australia. *B. W. Hills*

MUSICAL TREAT (IRE)   3 ch.f. Royal Academy (USA) 130 – Mountain Ash   **98**
107 (Dominion 123) [1998 98: 7d² 1999 7g² 7m* 9.9g² 10.1m⁴ 10.2m³ 10.1g Aug 30] angular, rather unfurnished filly: useful performer: won maiden at Chester in May: ran well after when placed in listed races at Goodwood (second to Claxon) and Chepstow (third to Ela Athena): better at 1¼m than shorter: yet to race on extremes of going: sent to USA. *P. W. Chapple-Hyam*

MUSIC EXPRESS (IRE)   5 b.m. Classic Music (USA) – Hetty Green (Bay   –
Express 132) [1998 –: a12g⁵ 7d 1999 8g 8d 7m May 29] modest maiden at best: tried visored. *J. L. Eyre*

MUSICIAN   3 b.f. Shirley Heights 130 – Rose Alto 98 (Adonijah 126) [1998 78p: **104**
8.2g⁴ 7v³ 1999 8.3m³ 10.5s* 12m* 12m* 12m* 12s⁵ Sep 26] angular filly: developed into a useful handicapper: won at Warwick in May, Thirsk and Newmarket in June and Doncaster (by length from Prince Alex) in September: set plenty to do when creditable fifth of 16 to Vicious Circle in Ritz Club Stakes at Ascot final start: will stay 1¾m: acts on soft and good to firm going: usually held up: genuine. *J. R. Fanshawe*

MUS-IF   3 b.c. Lahib (USA) 129 – Navajo Love Song (IRE) 43 (Dancing Brave   **116**
(USA) 140) [1998 108: 6s² 7v* 7m² 7g² 8d* 1999 8m² 8g⁴ 9g⁵ 8d⁴ Sep 25] leggy, angular colt: smart performer: best efforts on first 2 outings when in frame behind Saffron Walden in listed race at Leopardstown (went down by a head) and Irish 2,000 Guineas at the Curragh (beaten 3½ lengths): last of 5 in International Stakes at the Curragh and fourth of 7 (well below best) in Grosse Europcar-Meile at Cologne after: stays 1m: acts on good to firm going, probably on heavy: blinkered: carries head high: sent to USA. *D. K. Weld, Ireland*

MUSKETRY   3 b.c. Terimon 124 – Mousquetade (Moulton 128) [1998 NR 1999   –
8m 10m 10s 16d a16.2g Dec 15] half-brother to fairly useful stayer Shtaifeh (by Welsh Pageant): dam unraced: well beaten in maidens/handicaps: tried blinkered. *N. A. Graham*

MUSTAFHEL   3 b. or br.c. Wolfhound (USA) 126 – Kadwah (USA) 80 (Mr   **81**
Prospector (USA)) [1998 81p: 7g 8g 8s⁴ 1999 8m⁶ 7.9s⁵ 8d² 8.1d² 7.9f³ 8s³ Oct 4] strong, sturdy colt: has a round action: fairly useful maiden: likely to prove best around 1m: yet to race on heavy going, acts on any other: consistent: sent to UAE. *J. H. M. Gosden*

MUSTANG   6 ch.g. Thatching 131 – Lassoo 87 (Caerleon (USA) 132) [1998 55,   **51**
a60: a7g² a7g² a7g² a7g² a8g 5.9d² 5.9s⁴ a6g² 6g⁶ 6.9m⁶ 6.9d 9m a7g⁴ a7g⁶ 1999 a7f⁴ a8g a8g⁴ a7g⁴ a7g⁵ a10g⁴ Dec 18] strong, lengthy gelding: modest handicapper: seems to stay easy 1¼m: acts on soft going, races mainly on all-weather: often blinkered/visored: races prominently. *J. Pearce*

MUST BE MAGIC 2 b.c. (May 16) Magic Ring (IRE) 115 – Sequin Lady (Star **70**
Appeal 133) [1999 6.8m 8.2m⁴ 8s³ 8v 8.3d Nov 4] 5,500Y, 6,200 2-y-o: half-brother
to several winners, including fairly useful Italian 3-y-o 6f (at 2 yrs) and 1m winner
She's So Lovely (by Distant Relative): dam unraced daughter of Oaks winner
Scintillate: fair maiden: well held in nurseries last 2 starts: should stay 1¼m: acts on
soft and good to firm going. *H. J. Collingridge*

MUSTN'T GRUMBLE (IRE) 9 b.g. Orchestra 118 – Gentle Heiress (Prince **–**
Tenderfoot (USA) 126) [1998 48, a53: a7g⁴ a8.5g⁶ a8g* a8g 7s⁶ a7g⁶ a8g 6g² 8g a7g⁵
5.7g⁶ 1999 a7g 7s a7g Jun 17] sturdy gelding: poor performer: stays 1m: acts on
all-weather, best turf efforts on good going or firmer: effective blinkered/visored: has
had tongue tied: tends to carry head high: usually starts slowly. *Miss S. J. Wilton*

MUTAAHAB (CAN) 3 b.c. Dixieland Band (USA) – Serene Nobility (USA) **103**
(His Majesty (USA)) [1998 111: 6f* 6d⁴ 6f⁵ 7m* 8d* 8s* 1999 7m⁴ 10.4s⁴ 10.1m⁵
Jul 7] medium-sized, good-topped, quite attractive colt: has a quick action: useful
performer: successful in Royal Lodge Stakes at 2 yrs: best effort in 1999 when 6¾
lengths fourth to Salford Express in Dante Stakes at York second start: stays 1¼m:
has form on firm ground, but best efforts on good to soft/soft (yet to race on heavy):
sold 115,000 gns. *E. A. L. Dunlop*

MUTAAKKID (USA) 3 b. or br.c. Dayjur (USA) 137 – Arjuzah (IRE) 110 (Aho- **109**
noora 122) [1998 77p: 7s⁵ 6d* 1999 6g* 6g⁵ 7g 6m 6f⁴ 6.1g³ 6d Sep 18] smallish
colt: useful form: won minor event at Leicester in April: best effort when 3¾ lengths
third to Deep Space in similar contest at Nottingham in August: ran poorly (tongue
tied) in Ayr Gold Cup final start: likely to prove best at 6f/7f: acts on good to firm and
good to soft ground: sent to UAE. *J. H. M. Gosden*

MUTABARI (USA) 5 ch.g. Seeking The Gold (USA) – Cagey Exuberance (USA) **58**
(Exuberant (USA)) [1998 –, a54: 7v⁶ 6.9v⁶ 8d a7g 11.9s a9.4g⁵ a12g 1999 a8g² a7g* **a66**
a8f a7f⁵ a7g* a7g* 6.1v a7g² 6d⁵ 7.5d 7m⁶ 7m⁴ 6m⁴ 6d⁴ 6d 6.9m⁵ 10m⁵ 7m a6g⁵ a7g⁶
a7g a7g Nov 16] rangy gelding: fluent mover: fair handicapper on all-weather,
modest on turf: won at Southwell in January, Lingfield in February and Wolverhampton in March: best at 6f/7f: acts on all-weather and probably any turf going:
usually visored nowadays. *Mrs S. Lamyman*

Constant Security Handicap, Doncaster—a fourth win in succession for Musician,
who responds well to beat Prince Alex and Alberich (far side)

MUTABASSIR (IRE)   5 ch.g. Soviet Star (USA) 128 – Anghaam (USA) 80   **77**
(Diesis 133) [1998 68: a10g² a10g a12g⁴ 10.3d 9m⁵ 8g³ 7g⁵ 7m* 7d* 7m* 7s² a7g*
a7g* a6g² 1999 a7g² 8f* 7f² 7g⁴ 7g⁴ 7g³ 8d Aug 17] fair performer: won handicap
at Brighton in April by 8 lengths: reportedly finished distressed final start: effective
at 6f to 1m: acts on firm going, soft and all-weather: usually races prominently:
consistent. *G. L. Moore*

MUTADARRA (IRE)   6 ch.g. Mujtahid (USA) 118 – Silver Echo (Caerleon   **77**
(USA) 132) [1998 70: 10d 10g⁵ 8g 10m² 10g² 10f⁴ᵈⁱˢ 1999 10m 10g² 10m* 10m
10m⁴ 10m⁶ 12m 10m 10s 8.9d Oct 9] tall, angular gelding: fair handicapper: won at
Sandown in June: ran respectably most other starts: effective at 1¼m to 1½m: acts
on firm going, below form on softer than good: tried blinkered: held up: probably
best with sound pace and strong handling: sold 10,500 gns, joined G. McCourt.
W. J. Musson

MU-TADIL   7 gr.g. Be My Chief (USA) 122 – Inveraven 53 (Alias Smith (USA))   **48 §**
[1998 38: 17.2g⁶ 17.2m 17.2s³ 18g² 14.1m⁶ 17.2m³ 14.1s 1999 18d 17.2g⁴ 17.2f⁵
18m³ 17.2m⁴ 16.4d 17.2m² 16m 17.2s Sep 27] sturdy gelding: poor maiden
handicapper: stays 2¼m: acts on firm and soft going: blinkered fifth/sixth starts:
often slowly away: ungenuine. *R. J. Baker*

MUTAFAWEQ (USA)   3 b.c. Silver Hawk (USA) 123 – The Caretaker 113   **129**
(Caerleon (USA) 132) [1998 99p: 8g² 8m* 1999 10.3f* 12m* 12g⁵ 11.9m⁴
14.6m* Sep 11]
   It is easy to fall into the trap of being too anthropomorphic when talking
or writing about racehorses, but it was there for all to see that winning the St
Leger required Mutafaweq to 'go through the pain barrier'. Talk of guts and
gameness sometimes comes very cheaply, but after this race the physical cost
of competition was demonstrated graphically to a racecourse and television
audience which must have watched aghast as Mutafaweq entered the unsaddling enclosure in front of the grandstand in a state of uncomprehending panic,
lashing out frenziedly. When he was led away, seemingly close to collapse,
many onlookers must have feared the worst, but expert veterinary treatment
was on hand. Buckets of water, a sedative, an anti-inflammatory drug and
painkillers were administered in the hour after the St Leger, in addition to ten
litres of a glucose saline solution fed through an intravenous drip attached to
the horse's jugular vein.
   On a day of unusual heat and humidity for the time of year, the St Leger
had shown again what high demands it can make on its participants. Mutafaweq's reaction, however, is, thankfully, an aberration. But the St Leger still
provides a special test, increasingly special given that so few of the St Leger
runners nowadays have previously run over a mile and three quarters. Those
who had not been seen out over as much as thirteen furlongs formed the
majority of St Leger runners in all but one renewal in the 'nineties, the exception being 1991 when five of ten had done so. The group who had previously
been tried over the longer distances boast a single St Leger runner-up, the
French-trained Vertical Speed in 1997, and not one St Leger winner. The latest
edition featured nine runners and only two who had been tried beyond a mile
and a half, the unlucky March Stakes runner-up Iscan (13/2) and ordinary
staying maiden Praslin Island (200/1). Both could count themselves fortunate
to appear in the classic field, as the Jockey Club had bent the rules regarding
stalls tests to enable the participation of Iscan. The remainder of the field
included two Royal Ascot winners in Mutafaweq (11/2) and Elmutabaki (16/1),
victorious in the King Edward VII Stakes and King George V Handicap
respectively, the largely unknown quantity of Godolphin's American import
Adair (9/1) and four representatives of the classic form, in the Oaks first and
second Ramruma (11/10-on) and Noushkey (11/1), Derby fifth All The Way
(8/1) and the Irish Derby third and French Derby fifth Tchaikovsky (20/1).
Ramruma, of course, had additional triumphs in the Irish Oaks and Yorkshire
Oaks to back up her claims.

Mutafaweq too had classic form, but his fifteen and a half lengths fifth to Montjeu at the Curragh was just about the least of his accomplishments as a three-year-old. Following his win in a Newmarket maiden the previous October, he had justified favouritism in a minor event at Doncaster and the King Edward VII, in clear-cut style on both occasions and by two lengths from Iscan at Royal Ascot. Mutafaweq's one remaining race before going to Town Moor was the Great Voltigeur Stakes at York, as reliable a guide to St Leger prospects as any race in recent years, and one which promised to be so again in 1999 as all but one of the runners held St Leger entries. When the only one who hadn't, Fantastic Light, won the race after the early pace had been pedestrian, the Voltigeur no longer looked like proving quite so informative. Those who ignored the bare result, however, and the fact that Mutafaweq had finished only fourth of seven, might instead have taken notice that Mutafaweq had dropped back to last three furlongs out before staying on as well as anything towards the finish.

Ramruma and Adair ensured that every ounce of battling quality was required from Mutafaweq in the St Leger. All The Way accompanied them into the straight but gave way at the four-furlong marker as Ramruma set sail for home flanked by Adair on her inside and Mutafaweq on her outside. The three of them matched strides for almost another quarter mile before Adair cracked, while Mutafaweq went a neck up at the furlong marker and extended his advantage to a length over the next hundred yards, at which point Ramruma's jockey finally accepted defeat. The margins at the line were two lengths between Mutafaweq and Ramruma, another two between Ramruma and Adair, and seven lengths back to the rest. It was the best performance in the race since Snurge beat Hellenic in 1990. For Richard Hills, gaining his second British classic win, there was virtually no time before celebration turned to anxiety.

Mutafaweq's battle to assert superiority inch by inch over the length of the straight at Doncaster demonstrated what a hard race the St Leger can be to win, hard that is for everyone except his owners. Following Moonax, Classic Cliche, Shantou and Nedawi, this was the fifth time in six years that the classic winner has carried the colours of either Godolphin or Sheikh Mohammed. Mutafaweq was acquired for 310,000 dollars as a yearling and his yearling

Rothmans Royals St Leger Stakes, Doncaster—
Mutafaweq puts up the best display seen in the race since 1990 to defeat Ramruma in a gruelling battle

brother must now be short odds to carry the royal blue as well after he fell to John Ferguson's bid of 500,000 dollars at Keeneland two days after the St Leger. They are the first and third foals—there is also a two-year-old by King-mambo—out of the 1989 Cartier Million winner The Caretaker. Winner of a listed race at both seven furlongs and a mile as a three-year-old, when she was also fourth in the Irish One Thousand Guineas, The Caretaker was sold for 230,000 guineas at the December Sales before racing without success in the United States at four, five and six years. Her dam Go Feather Go and grandam Feather Bed were both minor winners and dependable broodmares, with nine and thirteen (from twenty foals) winners respectively. Go Feather Go is a sister to the 1977 Grande Course de Haies de Quatre Ans winner Tepatitlan, while, besides The Caretaker, the most illustrious of her own progeny are US Grade 3 handicap winner Go Honey Go and useful Irish sprinter Feathers Lad. It was not always so, but Mutafaweq's sire Silver Hawk is now well established as a producer of pattern-class horses, though his two other British classic runners of 1999, Glamis and Zaajer, had much less successful campaigns.

		Silver Hawk (USA) (b 1979)	Roberto (b 1969)	Hail To Reason
Mutafaweq (USA) (b.c. 1996)				Bramalea
			Gris Vitesse (gr 1966)	Amerigo
				Matchiche II
		The Caretaker (b 1987)	Caerleon (b 1980)	Nijinsky
				Foreseer
			Go Feather Go (b 1972)	Go Marching
				Feather Bed

Mutafaweq, unsurprisingly retired for the season, was said to be in good health again a few days after the St Leger but his future prospects depend

Godolphin's "Mutafaweq"

largely on his recovery, mental as well as physical. He also has to show that he can repeat the St Leger form, which is easily his best, in all probability over other distances. For most St Leger winners in the last twenty years, that has meant a mile and a half but Sheikh Mohammed has bucked that trend, sending Nedawi over both shorter and longer trips in 1999, having let Moonax and Classic Cliche tackle the top staying races before that. Mutafaweq should stay two miles. All of his races have been on good ground or firmer. A sturdy, attractive colt, Mutafaweq has drifted left under pressure on his last two starts and tends to swish his tail in the preliminaries; he was also sweating (a tendency of many by his sire) and edgy before the St Leger. *Saeed bin Suroor*

MUTAHADETH 5 ch.g. Rudimentary (USA) 118 – Music In My Life (IRE) 59 (Law Society (USA) 130) [1998 52, a70: a8s⁴ a7s* a7g a7g² a8g a8g³ a9.4g⁶ a8g 7d 8f² a8.5g 7d⁵ 8d 8m 1999 a8g³ a8g a7g³ a8f⁴ a8.5g* a8g* a8g² a7g a8g a6g⁴ a8.5g a6g⁴ a6g Dec 21] angular gelding: fair on all-weather, modest on turf: won creditably at Wolverhampton in February and handicap at Southwell in March: ran creditably after only when in frame: seems best at 7f to 8.5f: acts on firm going, good to soft and all-weather: visored once, usually blinkered. *D. Shaw* — a70

MUTAMAM 4 b.c. Darshaan 133 – Petal Girl 96 (Caerleon (USA) 132) [1998 119: 9.9m² 12m 10m* 10.5g* 9.9d* 10g⁴ 1999 12m Mar 28] smallish, quite attractive colt: good mover: smart performer: did well at 3 yrs (trained by A. Stewart), when wins included Rose of Lancaster Stakes at Haydock and Select Stakes at Goodwood and creditable fourth to Alborada in Champion Stakes at Newmarket: behind in Dubai Turf Classic at Nad Al Sheba only outing in 1999: probably best forcing pace at 1¼m: yet to race on extremes of going: rejoined A. Stewart. *Saeed bin Suroor* —

MUTAMAYYAZ (USA) 3 b. or br.c. Nureyev (USA) 131 – Ajfan (USA) 112 (Woodman (USA) 126) [1998 99p: 6m² 6m* 1999 7d 7m² 6.1g² 6d Oct 15] quite attractive colt: useful performer: best effort when ½-length second of 19 to Easy Dollar in handicap at Nottingham in September: ran creditably when twelfth of 20 in Newmarket listed race next time: likely to prove best at 6f/7f: yet to race on extremes of going: tongue tied (reportedly had breathing problem) on reappearance: usually races prominently: sent to UAE. *J. H. M. Gosden* — 107

MUTANASSIB (IRE) 6 b.g. Mtoto 134 – Lightning Legacy (USA) 78 (Super Concorde (USA) 128) [1998 NR 1999 18m* 20f² 17.2s³ 17.3g Oct 16] tall, rather leggy gelding: fairly useful handicapper: won maiden event at Chepstow in July by 12 lengths: ran creditably next 2 starts, paid price for setting strong pace in Cesarewitch at Newmarket final one: stays 2½m: yet to race on heavy going, acts on any other: wears crossed noseband/tongue strap: races prominently. *M. C. Pipe* — 82

MUTASADER (IRE) 2 b.f. (Mar 14) Unfuwain (USA) 131 – Bawaeth (USA) 72 (Blushing Groom (FR) 131) [1999 7d Oct 30] third foal: sister to 3-y-o Elmutabaki and half-sister to 4-y-o Bawsian: dam, middle-distance maiden, half-sister to useful 7f/1m winner Ruznama out of Oaks third Last Feather: weak in market and considerately handled when eighth of 16 in Newmarket maiden: will be suited by 1¼m+: sure to improve. *B. W. Hills* — 72 p

MUTASAWWAR 5 ch.g. Clantime 101 – Keen Melody (USA) 60 (Sharpen Up 127) [1998 61, a71: a6s* a6g⁴ a6g² a6g⁶ a6g⁶ 5.7f 5.7d 5.7d 6.1m⁶ 5.3m⁴ 5.1d* 5m 6.1s 5.1v a7g a6g² 1999 a6g⁴ a6f a6g³ 5.1m⁵ a5g 5.1m Sep 9] fair handicapper on all-weather, modest on turf: possibly best at 6f/7f nowadays: acts on good to firm going, good to soft and all-weather: has won in blinkers, but is as effective without: tail flasher: sometimes bandaged in front. *M. S. Saunders* — 55 a66

MUWAKALL (IRE) 2 b.c. (Feb 10) Doyoun 124 – Sabayik (IRE) 93 (Unfuwain (USA) 131) [1999 7m 8m³ 9m 8m⁶ Oct 19] second foal: half-brother to 3-y-o Khibrah: dam 1m winner who should have stayed 1½m: fair maiden: best effort on debut: ran in snatches in Yarmouth nursery final start: will stay 1¼m: sold 12,000 gns in November. *R. W. Armstrong* — 60

H & K Commissions Bookmakers Stakes (Handicap), Newmarket—
the stand side has it with Muyassir winning from Iron Mountain (rail), Redswan (right) and Topton (noseband);
this result led to the controversial re-positioning of the stalls halfway through the day's racing

MUYASSIR (IRE)   4 b.c. Brief Truce (USA) 126 – Twine (Thatching 131) [1998   **84**
74: 8f² 8s 8m³ 8.5m 8m a10g* a10g⁴ 1999 8g³ 10g⁶ 9.9m² 8m* 9f⁴ 7.9m Sep 1]
compact, deep-bodied colt: fairly useful handicapper: won 20-runner event at Newmarket in July: met trouble final start: effective at 1m/1¼m: acts on firm going and
equitrack: usually held up: consistent. *P. J. Makin*

MUZAHEM (IRE)   2 b.c. (Feb 11) Grand Lodge (USA) 125 – Annsfield Lady   **–**
(Red Sunset 120) [1999 7s⁴ Aug 18] 275,000Y: seventh foal: half-brother to several
winners, including smart 6f (at 2 yrs) to 1m winner Pipe Major (by Tirol) and useful
1m to 10.4f winner Give Me A Ring (by Be My Guest): dam Irish 1¼m performer:
very green when well-held fourth of 5 in minor event at Kempton: sold 17,000 gns in
October, sent to Kuwait. *Sir Michael Stoute*

MY ALIBI (USA)   3 b.f. Sheikh Albadou 128 – Fellwaati (USA) (Alydar (USA))   **61**
[1998 –p: 7v 1999 10g 10.5m 8g⁵ 8s⁶ Sep 16] good-topped filly: modest maiden: ran
creditably in handicaps last 2 starts, not finding much in front final one: stays 1m:
acts on soft going: sold 2,800 gns in December. *E. A. L. Dunlop*

MY ANNETTE (USA)   3 b.f. Red Ransom (USA) – Andover Way (USA) (His   **78**
Majesty (USA)) [1998 NR 1999 10m⁵ 10.5g⁶ 10d³ 10d Oct 1] big filly: closely
related to 1997 2-y-o 1m winner Publisher (by Kris S) and smart US winner up to
1½m Dynaformer (by Roberto) and half-brother to several winners in USA: dam,
Grade 1 9f winner in USA, half-sister to Belmont Stakes third Darby Creek Road:
fair maiden: well held in handicap final start: may prove best up to 1¼m: acts on
good to soft going: sent to USA. *J. R. Fanshawe*

MY BOLD BOYO   4 b.g. Never So Bold 135 – My Rosie (Forzando 122) [1998   **71**
78: 7s⁴ 7v³ 8d⁴ 7f³ 7.6g* 8.5s⁵ 7m 8s 1999 7m⁶ 8g⁶ 8m⁵ 7m 6g 7v a8g Dec 10] sturdy,
close-coupled gelding: fair performer: ran creditably in 1999 first 3 starts only: left

708

D. Elsworth before penultimate one: stays 1m when conditions aren't testing: acts on firm going, probably on soft: tried blinkered. *Jamie Poulton*

MY BOLD GIRL   2 ch.f. (May 26) Bold Arrangement 127 – Oh My Oh My   **40**
(Ballacashtal (CAN)) [1999 5.1s⁵ a5g³ 6m a6g⁵ 5m⁵ Jun 21] 500Y: half-sister to 3 winning sprinters, including 3-y-o Cartmel Park: form only in sellers: dead. *J. Berry*

MYBOTYE   6 br.g. Rambo Dancer (CAN) 107 – Sigh 75 (Highland Melody 112)   **–**
[1998 64: 7s⁴ 7.1g⁵ 7.5m 7g⁵ 7g⁶ 7s³ 7d⁴ 1999 8d 7.1m 8.2s a7g a7g Dec 15] sturdy gelding: modest handicapper: no form in 1999: tried blinkered: has had tongue tied. *A. B. Mulholland*

MY BOY HARRY (IRE)   2 b.c. (Feb 15) Efisio 120 – Caroline Connors (Fairy   **–**
King (USA)) [1999 6m⁴ Jul 14] 16,000F: smallish, well-made colt: second foal: brother to 3-y-o Zola Power: dam, won 10 times in Sweden from 6f to 1m, half-sister to useful sprinter El Yasaf: last of 4 in minor event at Doncaster. *J. Berry*

MY BROADSTAIRS JOY   3 b.g. Terimon 124 – Al Raja 79 (Kings Lake (USA)   **–**
133) [1998 –: 7m 7g 8.3s⁶ 1999 12s Oct 5] rather leggy, unfurnished gelding: only a little sign of ability. *J. J. O'Neill*

MY BROTHER   5 b.g. Lugana Beach 116 – Lucky Love 65 (Mummy's Pet ‡25)   **45**
[1998 –: 8.1m 8g 1999 8m⁵ 7.7m 7m a7g 7m Sep 7] poor maiden: may prove best up to 1m: acts on good to firm going: visored final start. *P. Eccles*

MY DARLING DODO (IRE)   3 b.f. Anita's Prince 126 – Seldovia (Charlot-   **–**
town 127) [1998 NR 1999 10.2s 7d⁵ 10d⁶ 9.4g a8.5g Dec 27] half-sister to several winners abroad, including Saurez (up to 1½m in Germany by Waajib): dam won over 1m in France at 2 yrs: little form. *B. Palling*

MY DESPERADO (IRE)   6 b.m. Un Desperado (FR) 125 – Lady Kasbah (Lord   **70**
Gayle (USA) 124) [1998 77: 8g⁶ 6.9m³ 10.1g³ 8g* 10m 7.5m⁴ 8m⁶ 8g 8g 10m 12.1s 10d 10s* 10s* 10.1v⁵ 10.3d⁵ 1999 10d 8s Nov 6] angular mare: fair performer: ran creditably on belated reappearance, poorly 7 days later: probably stays 1½m: acts on soft and good to firm going: none too consistent. *M. A. Peill*

MY DILEMMA   3 b.f. Pursuit of Love 124 – Butosky 71 (Busted 134) [1998 42:   **–**
a7g⁴ 7m 8s³ 1999 a8g a12g 7m 10f 10d⁶ 8d Oct 29] lengthy filly: poor maiden at best: blinkered once: gave trouble at stalls penultimate start. *M. J. Ryan*

MY EMILY   3 b.f. King's Signet (USA) 110 – Flying Wind 51 (Forzando 122)   **81**
[1998 63: 5d³ 5.7s² 7g 7g 7m 1999 8g 7g* 6m² 7m 6.1g Aug 13] smallish filly: fairly useful handicapper: won 16-runner event at Brighton in June: very good effort (sweating) at Newmarket next time: saddle slipped penultimate start, ran as though something amiss final one: effective at 6f/7f: acts on good to firm going, showed promise on soft: has raced freely. *G. L. Moore*

MY FLOOSIE   4 b.f. Unfuwain (USA) 131 – My Chiara 95 (Ardross 134) [1998   **–**
–: 10.5d 12.1s³ 12g 15.8d 1999 14.1d 9.9g 11.8m⁵ 14.1m Jun 16] small filly: only a little sign of ability. *B. D. Leavy*

MY HANSEL (USA)   2 b.c. (May 15) Hansel (USA) – My Shafy 92 (Rou-   **98 p**
sillon (USA) 133) [1999 7m* 8s³ Sep 26] tall, leggy, angular filly: has plenty of scope: fourth foal: half-sister to 6-y-o Ramooz and 3-y-o Zulal: dam 1m winner out of smart French middle-distance performer Lys River: won maiden at Newmarket in August: useful form when 1½ lengths third of 6 to Teggiano in Fillies' Mile at Ascot, keeping on gamely: should stay at least 1¼m: acts on soft and good to firm ground: seems sure to improve further. *B. Hanbury*

MY HEARTS DESIRE   4 b.f. Deploy 131 – Blue Room 70 (Gorytus (USA)   **–**
132) [1998 –: 10g 10d 8.2g 1999 10m 10m 10m Sep 13] angular filly: little form. *D. Haydn Jones*

MY KIND   6 ch.m. Mon Tresor 113 – Kind of Shy 61 (Kind of Hush 118) [1998   **–**
NR 1999 7s Apr 1] poor up to 1m for N. Tinkler in 1996: soundly beaten in seller only start since: tried visored/blinkered: sold 540 gns. *N. M. Babbage*

MY LADY   2 b.f. (Apr 8) Derrylin 115 – Brianstan Rose (The Brianstan 128) [1999   **52**
7.7g Aug 13] first reported foal: dam little form: never a threat in maiden at Warwick. *W. M. Brisbourne*

MYLANIA   3 b.f. Midyan (USA) 124 – Appelania 63 (Star Appeal 133) [1998 –:   **70**
6m 1999 8.2m 8g 8s⁴ 8s² 8.2f Oct 20] good-bodied filly: fair maiden: best efforts

when in frame in handicaps at Yarmouth (after 4-month break) and Newcastle in September: may prove best up to 1m: goes well on soft going. *M. H. Tompkins*

MY LASS 3 b.f. Elmaamul (USA) 125 – Be My Lass (IRE) (Be My Guest (USA) 126) [1998 69: 7d⁴ 7s² a7g⁵ 1999 12.1s* a10g³ 14d³ a12g⁴ a12g⁶ 12d⁶ 10d³ 10s⁶ 8d Oct 10] sturdy filly: unimpressive mover: fairly useful on turf, fair on all-weather: won maiden at Hamilton in May: left Sir Mark Prescott after fifth start: seemed to run very well when third in listed race at Leopardstown seventh one: probably stays 1¾m: acts on all-weather, raced only on going softer than good on turf. *L. Browne, Ireland* **91 ?** **a66**

MY LEGAL EAGLE (IRE) 5 b.g. Law Society (USA) 130 – Majestic Nurse 80 (On Your Mark 125) [1998 53: a8g a9.4g³ 8.1d 8s 7f⁴ 7g* 8m³ 7d a8.5g⁴ 1999 a7g 10.8d⁶ 10s⁵ 10v³ 10.8m³ 10m³ 10.2g 10.5s⁴ 10.3d² 10.2g⁵ 9m 12.1m 10.3s² 9.9v* 11.9d³ 11.5g 10s⁴ a12g a12g⁵ a11g³ a16.2g² a12g a16.2g⁴ Dec 15] smallish gelding: fair handicapper on turf, modest on all-weather: won apprentice event at Salisbury in September: ran respectably most other starts: stays easy 2m: acts on good to firm going, heavy and fibresand: sometimes blinkered, better form when not: usually held up: sometimes looks none too keen. *R. J. Price* **65** **a51**

MY LITTLE MAN 4 b.g. Lugana Beach 116 – Gay Ming 50 (Gay Meadow 52) [1998 61, a45: 10.2g 8m⁶ 9.2s⁴ 11.7v a10g³ a11g 1999 a9.4g² a10g⁵ a8.5g⁵ Mar 13] short-backed gelding: modest maiden: stays 1¼m: acts on good to firm going, soft and all-weather: visored last 2 starts. *B. Smart* **50**

MY MAN FRIDAY 3 b.g. Lugana Beach 116 – My Ruby Ring 72 (Blushing Scribe (USA) 107) [1998 54: 5.1g 7m 6d⁵ 1999 6g 6m 6g 6.1g⁵ 7m³ 7m⁴ 8s a7g Oct 16] unfurnished gelding: modest maiden: effective at 6f/7f: acts on good to firm and good to soft going, well held on fibresand: has carried head high/flashed tail. *W. R. Muir* **54**

MY MOTHER'S DREAM (IRE) 3 b.f. Fayruz 116 – With Diamonds (Shirley Heights 130) [1998 47, a33: a5g a5g 5g³ a6g 6m⁴ 5.1g³ a6g³ 6g 6m⁶ 5.1m⁵ a7g a6g⁶ 1999 a5g 6g Apr 8] neat filly: poor maiden: no form in sellers in 1999: barely stays 6f: acts on good to firm going and fibresand: tried visored. *A. T. Murphy* **–**

MYNAH BIRD (IRE) 3 b.f. Bluebird (USA) 125 – Maribiya (FR) (Natroun (FR) 128) [1998 67: 7.5m⁵ 7.5m⁵ 8m³ 8v 1999 10g 9.9g a14g Jul 8] leggy, lengthy filly: fair maiden for Mrs J. Ramsden at 2 yrs: no show in handicaps in 1999: should stay at least 1m: acts on good to firm going. *J. G. FitzGerald* **–**

MY PETAL 3 gr.f. Petong 126 – Najariya (Northfields (USA)) [1998 90: 5.7g² 5.2m* 6g* 6d 1999 6m 7d 7f 6m Sep 11] fairly useful at 2 yrs: little show in handicaps in 1999: best at 5f/6f: acts on good to firm going. *R. Hannon* **–**

MY PLEASURE 3 b.g. Cadeaux Genereux 131 – Raknah (IRE) 91 (Night Shift (USA)) [1998 NR 1999 8s 8d⁴ 7m² 7f² 7.1d* 7.1d⁴ 8m* 8f 8.1g² 7m 7s Oct 2] sturdy gelding: first foal: dam 5f to 7f winner: fairly useful performer: won maiden at Haydock in June and handicap at Salisbury (dictated pace) in July: below form last 2 starts, in visor on penultimate one: will prove best at 7f/1m: acts on firm and good to soft going: sent to UAE. *E. A. L. Dunlop* **87**

MY PLEDGE (IRE) 4 b.g. Waajib 121 – Pollys Glow (IRE) 91 (Glow (USA)) [1998 72: 8m⁴ 8m 10d* 10g 11.9m⁶ 1999 13.3f 12g 12m⁴ 14.1g⁵ 12d Oct 9] unfurnished gelding: fair handicapper at 3 yrs: just modest at best in 1999: stays 1½m: acts on good to soft going: has worn tongue strap/crossed noseband. *C. A. Horgan* **61**

MY POPPET 4 b.f. Midyan (USA) 124 – Pretty Poppy 67 (Song 132) [1998 –: 9.9f 1999 6m 9.9m May 13] well beaten in maidens. *S. G. Knight* **–**

MY RAMONA 2 b.f. (Apr 8) Alhijaz 122 – Petriece 64 (Mummy's Pet 125) [1999 5d 5.1f May 7] 10,000Y: sixth foal: half-sister to 3-y-o Natural Pearl, 1993 2-y-o 5f winner Smart Pet (by Petong) and useful sprinter Amazing Bay (by Mazilier): dam, 7f winner, half-sister to dam of Lochsong and Lochangel: signs of ability on debut: blinkered, reared and unseated rider stalls only subsequent start. *C. A. Dwyer* **–**

MY RETREAT (USA) 2 b.c. (Feb 12) Hermitage (USA) – My Jessica Ann (USA) (Native Rythm) [1999 6m⁵ 7d² Oct 21] 16,500Y: half-brother to several winners in USA, including minor 1m stakes winner by Lac Ouimet: dam won twice in USA: **86**

much better effort in maidens when ¾-length second of 11 to Wurzel at Brighton: should stay 1m+: sold 44,000 gns. *L. M. Cumani*

MYRMIDON 5 b.g. Midyan (USA) 124 – Moorish Idol 90 (Aragon 118) [1998 –: 6v⁴ 7.6m 1999 7d Apr 29] rather sparely-made gelding: good walker: one-time fairly useful performer: ran badly only 5-y-o start: best at 5f on good ground or softer: blinkered once at 3 yrs. *Mrs L. Stubbs* –

MYSTAGOGUE 4 ch.g. Mystiko (USA) 124 – Malibasta 83 (Auction Ring (USA) 123) [1998 70: a8g² a10g² a10g* a10g⁶ 12m² 14.1m³ 16.4f⁵ 11.5g⁴ 12g⁶ 12s³ a12g 1999 a12g* a13g³ a13g² a12f³ a12g 12.4m³ 10.9s 11.1m* 11.1f³ 13f² 12.1m³ 14.1f² 15m³ 16m 16f 16g Nov 3] angular gelding: fair performer: won claimers at Lingfield in January and Hamilton in June: left R. Hannon after fifth start, well held last 3: stays 15f: acts on equitrack and firm going: blinkered twice at 3 yrs. *J. S. Goldie* **64 a70**

MYSTERIOUS ECOLOGY 4 gr.f. Mystiko (USA) 124 – Ecologically Kind (Alleged (USA) 138) [1998 57: 10f 12.1m⁴ 11.5g² 12g 1999 10d Oct 26] tall, sparely-made filly: modest maiden for B. Hills at 3 yrs: claimed out of M. Pipe's stable after making winning debut over hurdles in January: well beaten only Flat start in 1999: stays 11.5f. *J. L. Spearing* –

MYSTERIOUS MISS (IRE) 4 b.f. Imp Society (USA) – Hotel du Lac (Lomond (USA) 128) [1998 67: 7v 10s 12s³ 12g⁴ 12m² 12g⁵ 12.5g⁵ 10d⁶ 14g 1999 a12g May 8] third foal: dam unraced: fair maiden for A. Leahy in Ireland at 3 yrs: well held only 4-y-o start: stays 1½m: acts on good to firm and good to soft ground. *A. W. Carroll* –

MYSTERIUM 5 gr.g. Mystiko (USA) 124 – Way To Go 69 (Troy 137) [1998 –: a12g⁴ a9.4g 1999 a12g⁵ a12g⁶ a12g³ a12g⁴ a9.4g³ a9.4g⁵ 10.1m⁴ 10.1g³ a12g⁵ 10.5m³ 11.5g* 10m⁵ 10f a12g⁴ a9.4g* a12g² a11g⁴ a10g Dec 18] tall, leggy gelding: modest handicapper: trained by J. Given eleventh to thirteenth starts: won at Yarmouth in July and Wolverhampton in November: effective at 9.4f to 1½m: acts on good to firm going and all-weather: visored once at 4 yrs. *N. P. Littmoden* **59**

MYSTICAL 5 gr.m. Mystiko (USA) 124 – Midnight Imperial (Night Shift (USA)) [1998 –, a77: a6g² a6g* a6g³ a6g² a6g a5g* a5g⁴ a6g² a6g² a5g 5.1g 6d a5g⁵ 6v 1999 a5g⁴ 5m³ 6m² a6g⁴ 5g⁴ 5m* Aug 30] lengthy mare: modest performer: generally creditable efforts before winning claimer at Warwick in August: effective at 5f/6f: acted on firm going, good to soft and equitrack: usually visored: raced prominently: reportedly in foal. *N. Tinkler* **52**

MYSTICAL WISDOM 2 b.f. (Mar 25) Mystiko (USA) 124 – Surprise Surprise 91 (Robellino (USA) 127) [1999 7m 6m 7m⁵ 7f⁶ 7g 8m⁶ Sep 7] 1,050Y: third foal: half-sister to 3-y-o Secret Treasure and Italian 7f winner Dark Impulse (by Damister): dam 2-y-o 7f winner who stayed 1¼m: modest maiden: should stay beyond 1m: raced only on good ground or firmer. *P. R. Chamings* **51**

MYSTICISM 4 ch.f. Mystiko (USA) 124 – Abuzz 101 (Absalom 128) [1998 55: a5g³ 6v⁶ 6m 1999 a6g a6g⁵ 6.1v 6s 7f* 8f³ 10g 6g³ 7f 8d⁵ Aug 17] small filly: fair handicapper: won 18-runner apprentice event at Brighton in May: effective at 6f to 1m: acts on firm ground and equitrack: unseated rider on way to post on fourth start, blinkered after: none too reliable: sold 4,500 gns. *C. E. Brittain* **65**

MYSTIC QUEST (IRE) 5 b.g. Arcane (USA) – Tales of Wisdom 70 (Rousillon (USA) 133) [1998 60, a77: a12g³ 14.1s 11.5g 14.9g 12m* 12f⁵ 12m 12s 1999 11.9f a12g³ 12d Sep 30] fair handicapper on all-weather, modest on turf: stayed 1½m, seemingly not 1¾m: acted on firm ground, good to soft (probably not on soft) and all-weather: usually blinkered/visored: sold 1,500 gns: dead. *K. McAuliffe* –

MYSTIC RIDGE 5 ch.g. Mystiko (USA) 124 – Vallauris 94 (Faustus (USA) 118) [1998 58: 12d 12s 14.1s 12m 12g³ 12s 14.9d⁶ 10g³ 9g² 9.9m 11.9g 12s 10d 1999 a8g 11.9f 8f* 7m* 7m³ 7m* a8g a6g Dec 11] good-bodied gelding: fairly useful handicapper: formerly none too reliable but in good heart in 1999, winning at Brighton in May, Leopardstown and Galway in July and Lingfield in September: well held on all-weather last 2 starts: has form at 1¼m, but best with forcing tactics at 7f/1m: acts on firm going, probably not on soft: usually blinkered, though is as effective without. *B. J. Curley* **81 a–**

MYSTIC SPRING (IRE)   3 gr.f. Royal Academy (USA) 130 – Secret Sunday **72**
(USA) (Secreto (USA) 128) [1998 66p: 7d 7d⁵ 1999 7f⁴ 8f a8g³ a9.4g⁴ a9.4g* Aug
6] fair performer: won maiden at Wolverhampton in August: stays 9.4f: acts on
fibresand and good to soft going: sent to South Africa. *J. Noseda*

MYSTIFY   2 b.f. (Feb 21) Batshoof 122 – Santa Linda (USA) (Sir Ivor 135) [1999 **78 p**
7m⁵ 7m⁵ Aug 27] half-sister to several winners, including 4-y-o Key Academy and
7f (at 2 yrs) and 1½m (Lancashire Oaks) winner Squeak (by Selkirk), latter later very
smart Grade 1 9f/1¼m winner in USA: dam unraced from very good American
family: fair form in maidens at Salisbury (unseated rider before start) and Newmarket
(blanketed for stalls entry) in August: raced freely, but will stay at least 1m: remains
capable of better. *J. H. M. Gosden*

MY TESS   3 br.f. Lugana Beach 116 – Barachois Princess (USA) 62 (Barachois **77**
(CAN)) [1998 71: 8.2s⁶ 8d³ 8d⁵ 1999 10.3d⁶ 10d³ 8m 8.2s* 8g 8m 10.5s⁵ a8.5g³
8s 8s⁶ a8.5g* a7g⁴ Dec 4] big, strong, lengthy filly: fair performer: won maiden at
Nottingham in April and handicap at Wolverhampton in December: mostly below
form in between: barely stays 1¼m: acts on fibresand, goes well on ground softer
than good on turf: has hung left: races up with pace. *B. A. McMahon*

MYTHICAL GIRL (USA)   3 b.f. Gone West (USA) – Yousefia (USA) 84 (Dan- **107**
zig (USA)) [1998 104: 6f* 6m* 6f⁶ 1999 8d* 8g May 23] leggy, good-topped filly:
good mover: useful performer: won European Breeders Fund Shergar Cup Distaff at
Goodwood in May by 1½ lengths from Choirgirl: got upset and unseated rider exiting
paddock when tailed-off last of 17 in Irish 1,000 Guineas at the Curragh only start
after: likely to prove best up to 1m: tended to carry head awkwardly at 2 yrs. *Saeed
bin Suroor*

MYTHICAL KING (IRE)   2 b.c. (Apr 5) Fairy King (USA) – Whatcombe (USA) **68**
88 (Alleged (USA) 138) [1999 7m³ 7.1d⁵ 7d Oct 12] 58,000Y: second foal: brother
to an Italian 2-y-o 5f winner: dam winner in Italy at 7.5f: fair maiden: well beaten
final start: likely to prove best up to 1m. *B. Palling*

MYTTON'S AGAIN   2 b.g. (Apr 30) Rambo Dancer (CAN) 107 – Sigh 75 **77**
(Highland Melody 112) [1999 5.1d⁵ 7.1m² 7m 7.5g⁵ 7d 8g⁵ 6d 7s* 6s 6g 8d⁴ 8d² **a61**
a8g⁶ a8g Dec 21] 5,200Y, 6,000 2-y-o: close-coupled gelding: brother to fair 5f (at 2
yrs) to 7f winner Mybotye and a winner in Scandinavia and half-brother to a winner
in Hong Kong by Nicholas Bill: dam 1m winner: fair performer: won nursery at
Chester in September: best effort when second of 27 in Redcar nursery (made most):
stays 1m: acts on soft going, below form on all-weather: blinkered from sixth to
penultimate starts. *A. Bailey*

MYTTONS MISTAKE   6 b.g. Rambo Dancer (CAN) 107 – Hi-Hunsley 82 **69**
(Swing Easy (USA) 126) [1998 79, a–: 6.1s 8.5s³ 7g 8f 7f² 7g² 7.1d 6g⁶ 6g³ 5.7d* **a–**
6m³ 7m* 7g 7s 7g 6s 1999 6.1v 8.3m 6f³ 7f¹ 7g 7f⁴ 6ᴵᴵᴵ 6m⁵ 7f⁶ 7f 7.1m 6d⁴ 5m⁵ a6g
6d a8g Nov 23] leggy, workmanlike gelding: fair performer: won 17-runner seller at
Brighton in August: left R. Hodges after thirteenth start: effective at 5.7f (given a
test) to 1m: acts on firm and good to soft going, little recent form on all-weather: tried
blinkered: good mount for apprentice. *R. J. Baker*

MYTTON'S MOMENT (IRE)   3 b.g. Waajib 121 – Late Swallow (My Swallow **62 §**
134) [1998 68: 5.1m 6g 7.4s⁴ 7g⁴ 7.9g 8s⁴ 8v 1999 10.3d 8g 10.3m 8f 8d* 8m 8.5s⁵
10.3m⁴ 10.9g⁶ 8.1d³ a8g³ Nov 22] leggy, useful-looking gelding: modest performer:
won seller at Newmarket in June: stays 1¼m: acts on good to firm going, soft and
fibresand: often blinkered: unreliable: successful over hurdles in September and
November. *A. Bailey*

MY TYSON (IRE)   4 b.g. Don't Forget Me 127 – Shuckran Habibi (Thatching **–**
131) [1998 –: 6g a6g 8.1s 5d 8.2g 6g 1999 a6g⁶ a6g Dec 21] lengthy, good-bodied
gelding: little form since 2 yrs: has started very slowly, and possibly temperamental.
K. A. Ryan

N

NABADHAAT (USA)   2 b.f. (Jan 29) Mr Prospector (USA) – Roseate Tern 123 **72**
(Blakeney 126) [1999 8.2g⁴ 8d Oct 22] sturdy, good-bodied filly: poor walker: fifth

foal: sister to useful 1¼m winner Siyadah and half-sister to fairly useful 1997 2-y-o 7f winner Fakhr (by Riverman) who stayed 1½m: dam, won Yorkshire Oaks and third in Oaks and St Leger, half-sister to Ibn Bey out of half-sister to Teleprompter: fair form in maidens at Nottingham and Doncaster: will stay at least 1¼m. *E. A. L. Dunlop*

NABONASSAR   3 ch.g. Lion Cavern (USA) 117 – Negligent 118 (Ahonoora 122) **106**
[1998 78p: 7d² 1999 7d² 7f* 8.5s² 7m⁴ 8f* Jul 31] useful performer: made all at Brighton (maiden) in May and Thirsk (handicap) in July, latter clearly best effort, by 2 lengths from Amalia: likely to prove best at 7f/1m: yet to race on heavy going, acts on any other: sent to UAE. *Sir Michael Stoute*

NADDER   4 ch.g. Lion Cavern (USA) 117 – Nadia Nerina (CAN) (Northern **44**
Dancer) [1998 NR 1999 6g 5g 6s 6f a6g⁵ a6g a7g⁵ 6.8m 6v a7g a8.5g Dec 27] 45,000F, 60,000Y, 5,000 2-y-o: close-coupled gelding: sixth foal: half-brother to several winners, including smart French 10.5f winner Nadina (by Shirley Heights): dam 6f winner: poor maiden: probably stays 7f: acts on fibresand: has had tongue tied. *W. M. Brisbourne*

NADISHA (IRE)   3 b.f. Rainbows For Life (CAN) – Gracieuse Amie (FR) (Gay **68**
Mecene (USA) 128) [1998 NR 1999 a10g³ a12g³ 10m⁶ a14.8g² 13.1g* 14d² a14g³ 13.1g³ a16.2g³ 15.8d³ 16s³ Oct 5] 6,800F, IR 22,000Y: workmanlike filly: sixth foal: half-sister to 3 winners, including really useful Irish 1m/1¼m winner Euphoric (by Common Grounds): dam French maiden: fair handicapper: won apprentice maiden event at Ayr in June: will prove best at 1¾m/2m: acts on all-weather, good to firm and good to soft going (probably on soft): blinkered (raced freely and wandered) final start: has found little: consistent: sold 16,000 gns, joined A. King. *W. J. Haggas*

NAFITH   3 ch.g. Elmaamul (USA) 125 – Wanisa (USA) (Topsider (USA)) [1998 **60**
68: 8m⁶ 7s⁶ 1999 8d⁶ 8v⁵ 8m 8g 10g Jun 12] modest maiden: stays 1m: acts on heavy going: free-going sort: sold 10,000 gns. *M. P. Tregoning*

NAGOYA (GER)   3 b.f. Goofalik (USA) 118 – Nuas (GER) (Aspros (GER)) **106**
[1998 6g 7.8d² 8.5v² 7.8s* 1999 11g⁴ 11m* May 23] half-sister to fairly useful 10.8f winner Nuez (by Shareef Dancer) and several winners in Germany: dam won at up to 1¼m in Germany, including Group 2 event: useful performer: won maiden at Frankfurt at 2 yrs and Oaks d'Italia at Milan (by 1¼ lengths from Janestra) in May: stays 11f: acts on soft ground, best effort on good to firm. *H. Blume, Germany*

NAILER (IRE)   3 b.g. Darshaan 133 – Raysiya (Cure The Blues (USA)) [1998 **–**
NR 1999 a9.4g 11.7m Aug 22] 3,800Y: fourth foal: half-brother to useful Irish 7f and 11f winner Profit Alert (by Alzao) and 1¼m winner Razana (by Kahyasi): dam Irish 1¼m and 1½m winner: well beaten in maidens. *E. J. O'Neill*

NAISSANT   6 b.m. Shaadi (USA) 126 – Nophe (USA) 95 (Super Concorde (USA) **71**
128) [1998 63§: 6.1s 6d⁴ 7.1m 6g 5.9g² 6d* 6d⁵ 6g 6m 6d* 6m 6.1m 6s⁵ 6v 1999 6v² **a–**
6g⁴ 7s³ 5s* 6d⁴ 6d⁶ 5g³ 6g 7d³ 6m⁶ 6m⁴ 6m 6g⁵ 6.9g* 7.1m⁵ 7d a7g 6v Oct 12] sparely-made mare: has a round action: fair performer: won handicap at Hamilton in May and minor event at Carlisle in August: effective at 5f to 7f: probably acts on any turf going, seemingly not on all-weather. *J. S. Goldie*

NAJJM (USA)   2 br.c. (Mar 27) Dynaformer (USA) – Azusa (USA) (Flying Paster **76**
(USA)) [1999 7f² 8f² 8d³ 8d³ Oct 22] $57,000Y: leggy, workmanlike colt: fourth foal: half-brother to winners in USA by Broad Brush and Majestic Light: dam stakes winner up to 9f: fair maiden: good third in nursery at Doncaster final start: will be suited by 1¼m+: acts on firm and good to soft going. *J. L. Dunlop*

NAKED OAT   4 b.g. Imp Society (USA) – Bajina (Dancing Brave (USA) 140) **64**
[1998 61: a8g³ a9.4g² a8.5g⁴ a9.4g³ 8.2s a8.5g² a7g³ a8.5g² 1999 a10f⁴ a9.4g* a9.4g 9.7v⁵ 10v⁶ 8m* 8g 10g⁶ 8.3m 8.3g Jul 5] strong gelding: modest performer: won maiden at Wolverhampton in February and apprentice handicap at Warwick in May: generally below form otherwise: best at 1m/9f: acts on good to firm and good to soft going, better form on fibresand than equitrack: blinkered once at 3 yrs. *B. Smart*

NAMAQUALASS (IRE)   2 b.f. (Mar 27) Namaqualand (USA) – Joyful Lass **53 d**
(USA) (Danzig (USA)) [1999 5.1s⁴ a5g 5.7g 5g⁵ 6g 5m³ 5f² 5.1m 5m⁶ 6g⁵ 6g 7m⁵ 8m 5.3s Sep 29] IR 6,200Y: half-sister to 1991 2-y-o 7f seller winner Rustic Wedding (by Red Sunset), later successful in Germany, and a winner in Italy by Lear Fan: dam

modest maiden: generally on downgrade after debut: stays 7f: acts on soft and good to firm going: sold 1,000 gns in November. *M. Quinn*

NAME OF OUR FATHER (USA) 6 b.g. Northern Baby (CAN) 127 – Ten Hail Marys (USA) (Halo (USA)) [1998 –: 20d 1999 17.2s Sep 27] winning hurdler/chaser: formerly fair maiden on Flat, no form since 1996. *P. Bowen* –

NAMPARA BAY 5 b.m. Emarati (USA) 74 – Dewberry 68 (Bay Express 132) [1998 –: a5g 1999 a6g Feb 22] modest maiden at 3 yrs: no show since, found to be lame in front only outing in 1999: blinkered once. *J. Hetherton* –

NANOUSHKA (IRE) 4 b.f. Taufan (USA) 119 – West Chazy (USA) (Gone West (USA)) [1998 106: 7d⁶ 7m* 8d 6m* 6m³ 6g⁴ 7m 1999 6g⁶ 6g* 7m⁶ 6m 7f⁴ 7m⁵ Sep 3] tall, close-coupled filly: useful performer: won listed race at Newmarket in May by 1½ lengths from Aunt Flo: creditable fourth of 6 to Selfish in similar event at Goodwood in July: best at 6f/7f: acts on firm going, probably on good to soft: edgy type: often races prominently/leads: sold 155,000 gns in December. *R. Hannon* **106**

NANSEN (GER) 6 ch.g. Orfano (GER) – Nanja (Surumu (GER)) [1998 9.3v⁶ 10g 9g⁴ 10.8v² 10.5g² 9g² 10.5s² 9.3d³ 11v 1999 8.1m³ 11.9s⁵ Aug 18] big, workmanlike ex-German gelding: fair performer: won 5 times at 3 and 4 yrs for P. Rau: fair form in claimer on reappearance, much better effort in Britain: stayed 11f: acted on good to firm and heavy ground: dead. *Miss E. C. Lavelle* **75**

NANTUCKET (IRE) 2 b.c. (Mar 19) Turtle Island (IRE) 123 – Pericolo (IRE) 92 (Kris 135) [1999 5.2m 5g 6d 6m⁴ 5g* 5.2m Sep 17] IR 19,000Y: quite good-topped colt: fourth foal: half-brother to 3-y-o Lady Caroline and a winner in Norway by Royal Academy: dam third at 7f at 2 yrs on only start: fair performer: won maiden at Lingfield in August: effective at 5f and 6f: yet to race on extremes of going. *D. R. C. Elsworth* **79**

Thurloe Thoroughbreds II's "Nanoushka"

NANY'S AFFAIR (USA)   3 b.f. Colonial Affair (USA) 126 – Nuryette (USA)   **57**
(Nureyev (USA) 131) [1998 NR 1999 a7f² a7g* a7g* 8.3v² 10g⁵ 12f³ Jul 14]
$110,000F, $190,000Y: sixth foal: closely related to smart US performer up to 1¼m
Tap To Music (by Pleasant Tap) and half-sister to several winners, including smart
US miler Northern Afleet (by Afleet): dam unraced half-sister to smart filly Cuddles:
modest performer: won maiden at Lingfield in February and minor event at South-
well in March: stays 1½m: acts on all-weather and firm going: blinkered final start.
Sir Mark Prescott

NAPIER STAR   6 b.m. Inca Chief (USA) – America Star (Norwick (USA) 125)   **–**
[1998 –: a6s 1999 a6g a6g Sep 28] lightly raced and no form since 1997: visored.
A. B. Mulholland

NAPOLEON'S RETURN   6 gr.g. Daring March 116 – Miss Colenca (Petong   **53**
126) [1998 45, a–: 8d⁶ 8.3s⁴ 12d 8v³ 8s² a7g a11g 1999 8.3g² 8.3s² 9m 8m* 10.1m 9g   **a–**
8.9m 8m 8.3s Sep 27] close-coupled gelding: modest handicapper: won 20-runner
apprentice selling event at Ripon in June: stays 1m well, not 1½m: acts on fibresand
and probably on any turf going: effective in blinkers/visor (not tried since 1997).
J. L. Eyre

NAPOLEON STAR (IRE)   8 ch.g. Mulhollande (USA) 107 – Lady Portobello   **–**
(Porto Bello 118) [1998 52, a–: a6g³ a6g a7g⁶ 8s 5d 6g⁶ 6.1m 6m⁶ 5.1g² 6.1g⁵ 6.1g
7g⁶ 6m 7.6g 7d 5m 6g 6.1g⁵ a7g 8v 1999 5d 7d 7s 10.3d 8m 6.9g 7.6m 7.6m 8.5g
8f Sep 4] sparely-made gelding: formerly fair performer: no show in 1999: often
blinkered/visored. *Miss J. F. Craze*

NASAIEB (IRE)   2 b.f. (Mar 30) Fairy King (USA) – Atyaaf (USA) 48 (Irish   **89**
River (FR) 131) [1999 5g 5.1m* 5m³ 5g⁴ 7g Oct 16] 100,000Y: quite attractive filly:
fifth foal: half-sister to 3-y-o Raise A Grand, 4-y-o Dushanbe and fairly useful 1m
winner Royal Aty (by Royal Academy): dam lightly-raced half-sister to smart 6f/7f
winner Weldnaas: fairly useful form: won maiden at Nottingham in May: in frame
in 2 listed races at Sandown before running as though something amiss in Rockfel
Stakes at Newmarket (bandaged behind) final start: bred to stay 7f. *C. E. Brittain*

NASHEED (USA)   3 b. or br.f. Riverman (USA) 131 – Thawakib (IRE) 108   **113**
(Sadler's Wells (USA) 132) [1998 90p: 7.3g³ 7g* 7s* 1999 10s* 10.5d Jun 13] small
filly: smart performer: improved to win listed race at Newbury in May by ¾ length
from Samoa, leading 2f out and battling on well: only tenth in Prix de Diane at
Chantilly: stayed 1¼m: raced only on good going or softer: stud. *J. L. Dunlop*

NASH HOUSE (IRE)   6 b.h. Nashwan (USA) 135 – River Dancer 118 (Irish   **97 d**
River (FR) 131) [1998 NR 1999 8g⁶ 10g⁵ 12g² 12.3g 10m 10d 7s Oct 25] leggy
horse: useful form second and third starts in 1999 (after 3-year absence): well beaten
after, leaving W. Roper, Ireland, before penultimate outing: stayed 1½m: acted on
good to firm and good to soft going: dead. *N. P. Littmoden*

NATALIE JAY   3 b.f. Ballacashtal (CAN) – Falls of Lora 107 (Scottish Rifle 127)   **73**
[1998 73: 7g³ 7g⁶ 8s³ 8v³ 1999 9m a10g² 9f 8g* 7g⁵ 8.3m 8m 10d⁵ 8s² 8.2f⁵
Oct 20] angular filly: fair handicapper: won at Salisbury in August: ran creditably
otherwise only when runner-up: best at 1m/easy 1¼m: acts on equitrack and soft
going, probably on firm: often races prominently. *M. R. Channon*

NATASHA   2 b.f. (Apr 7) Mujtahid (USA) 118 – Wakayi 87 (Persian Bold 123)   **–**
[1999 7.5g Aug 11] sturdy, lengthy filly: shows knee action: sixth foal: sister to fairly
useful 5f (at 2 yrs) and 7f winner Arruhan and half-sister to 6f winner Fata (by
Machiavellian): dam, 2-y-o 5f winner, half-sister to smart sprinter Reesh: backward,
well beaten in maiden at Beverley. *T. D. Easterby*

NATHAN'S BOY   3 gr.g. Tragic Role (USA) – Gold Belt (IRE) 61 (Bellypha   **84**
130) [1998 78+: 6m 6g 6d³ 7f 7.5m³ a8g⁶ 8d² 7d² 1999 10.3d⁴ 9.9g* 12.3m 10g 9.9g²
12v² 12g³ 11.9f⁴ 11.9m 10.2m Sep 9] leggy gelding: fairly useful handicapper: won
at Beverley in April: ran at least respectably when in frame otherwise: reportedly
bled from nose final start: effective at 1¼m/1½m: acts on heavy going, probably on
firm: often gets behind. *R. Hollinshead*

NATHAN'S HERO (IRE)   3 ch.g. Forest Wind (USA) 111 – Lapland Lights   **–**
(USA) 85 (Northern Prospect (USA)) [1998 46, a57: 5.1m 5g 5.1d a5g 7d 6m 7m   **a54**
7.5m³ a7g⁵ a7g³ a8g² a8.5g 1999 a8g² a8g⁶ a12g⁴ a9.4g² a12g⁴ a14.8g⁴ 10.5s⁴ a11g

a9.4g[5] a8.5g Oct 30] close-coupled gelding: modest maiden: left R. Hollinshead after second start: stays 9.4f: acts on good to firm going and fibresand: visored eighth outing: has looked ungenuine. *Miss A. Stokell*

NATIONAL ANTHEM 3 b.c. Royal Academy (USA) 130 – Heart's Harmony **102** (Blushing Groom (FR) 131) [1998 81p: 7g 7d[2] 1999 7g[4] 10.4d[2] 10.1d[3] 10g[6] 10d* 10m[4] Sep 18] angular, unfurnished, quite attractive colt: easy mover: made into useful performer: easily landed odds in maiden at Sandown in August: good fourth to Komistar in Courage Handicap at Newbury final start: will probably stay 1½m: yet to race on extremes of going. *Sir Michael Stoute*

NATIONAL WISH (USA) 4 ch.g. Forty Niner (USA) – Regent's Walk (CAN) **60** (Vice Regent (CAN)) [1998 67: 8d 9m[3] 1999 7m 7f 8m[5] 7m 8h Aug 3] heavy-topped gelding: modest maiden handicapper: stayed 9f: acted on good to firm and good to soft going: blinkered final start: dead. *Mrs Merrita Jones*

NATSMAGIRL (IRE) 2 b.f. (Apr 26) Blues Traveller (IRE) 119 – Top The Rest **53** (Top Ville 129) [1999 5g[6] 5m[5] 6m[3] 6m* 6m 5m[5] 5f[2] 7f[4] 5g[4] 6g[2] 6m[6] 6m[3] 6.1m 7g 7g **a42** a6g[5] a7g Dec 15] IR 1,200F, IR 1,200Y: small, sparely-made filly: third living foal: dam French 11f winner: modest performer: won seller at Thirsk in June: effective at 5f to 7f: raced only on good going or firmer on turf, well held in visor on fibresand last 2 starts: has flashed tail. *Martyn Wane*

NATURAL EIGHT (IRE) 5 b.g. In The Wings 128 – Fenny Rough 114 (Home **67** Guard (USA) 129) [1998 –: 10d 10g 10.1g 1999 12m 12m[5] 12m 11.6m[6] 11.5f[4] 11.6s[6] 12d[4] 13.1f* 14d[3] 16d[2] a16g[6] a13g* Dec 10] unfurnished gelding: fair handicapper: won at Bath (maiden event) in September and Lingfield in December: stays 2m: acts on firm going, good to soft and equitrack: blinkered/visored first 6 starts in 1999: usually held up. *Jamie Poulton*

NATURAL (IRE) 2 b.g. (Apr 28) Bigstone (IRE) 126 – You Make Me Real (USA) **–** (Give Me Strength (USA)) [1999 7d Sep 30] 180,000Y: strong, rangy gelding: fifth foal: half-brother to 3 winners in Ireland, including useful 1998 2-y-o 5f/6f winner Camargo (by Brief Truce) and 9f and 1¾m winner Real Guest (by Be My Guest): dam sprint winner in USA: well beaten in maiden at Newmarket: sold 3,200 gns in October, joined John Berry. *J. Noseda*

NATURAL PEARL 3 gr.f. Petong 126 – Petriece 64 (Mummy's Pet 125) [1998 **–** –p: 6g 1999 6.1f 6g 6d 6.1m 6.1g 7.1s Sep 24] good-bodied filly: little sign of ability: sold from C. Wall 5,500 gns after fourth start: visored/blinkered last 2. *J. J. Quinn*

Brook Street Stakes (Handicap), Goodwood—Naviasky follows up his win on the course a month earlier;
Asef Alhind (No.3) and Stoppes Brow (No.5) win the battle for the places
whilst Polish Spirit (No.16) manages fourth despite a slipping saddle

NAUGHTY BUT NICE   3 b.f. Sizzling Melody 117 – Aldington Peach (Cree-   –
town 123) [1998 NR 1999 a7g a9.4g 9.9d 10.5s⁵ May 29] angular filly: second foal:
dam, no worthwhile form on Flat, winning selling hurdler: no form. *T. Wall*

NAUGHTY CROWN (USA)   3 b.f. Chief's Crown (USA) – Native Twine 114   **84**
(Be My Native (USA) 122) [1998 77p: 8.2s³ 7v⁴ 1999 10m⁶ 10.4d⁶ 10.1d 8m⁶ 8g⁵
7m² 7f* 6.8g 10.2m⁶ a7.5f* a8s⁵ Dec 18] strong, sturdy filly: fairly useful performer:
won maiden at Thirsk in July: left P. Cole then successful in allowance race at
Churchill Downs in November: effective at 7f to 1¼m: acts on firm ground and dirt:
blinkered seventh/eighth starts. *N. M. O'Callaghan, USA*

NAUTICAL STAR   4 b.c. Slip Anchor 136 – Comic Talent 105 (Pharly (FR) 130)   **100**
[1998 97: 10s* 10.4d⁴ 12s 10m³ 10.3g³ 12m* 1999 10g 12s⁵ 12g² 12g² 12m 12g*
Jun 27] workmanlike, good-topped colt: useful performer: awarded minor event at
Goodwood in June: good efforts earlier when runner-up, beaten by Tough Leader in
handicap at Epsom on second occasion: stays 1½m: acts on firm and soft going:
visored fifth 3-y-o start: races up with pace: sold 29,000 gns. *J. W. Hills*

NAUTICAL WARNING   4 b.g. Warning 136 – Night At Sea 107 (Night Shift   **61**
(USA)) [1998 57, a60: a7g* a7g⁵ 7.1g 8g⁴ 7m 7d 1999 a7g a8g* a8g³ 7s⁵ a8g* a8g²   **a84**
8m 7.6f* 8g⁴ a8g* a7g² Dec 4] sturdy gelding: fairly useful on all-weather, modest on
turf: won 3 handicaps and a minor event at Lingfield between February and November: effective at 7f/1m: acts on all-weather, firm and soft ground: tongue tied after
fourth start. *B. R. Johnson*

NAVAL AFFAIR (IRE)   2 b.f. (Feb 16) Last Tycoon 131 – Sailor's Mate 114   **86 p**
(Shirley Heights 130) [1999 7m³ 7s* Aug 18] seventh foal: half-sister to several
winners, notably 3-y-o King Adam: dam, 1½m winner, half-sister to high-class
Hellenic, dam of Greek Dance: still seemed green when justifying favouritism in
13-runner maiden at Kempton by length from Island Princess, disputing lead and
staying on well despite carrying head awkwardly: should stay at least 1¼m: remains
open to improvement, and likely to prove useful. *Sir Michael Stoute*

NAVAN PROJECT (IRE)   5 gr.g. Project Manager 111 – Just Possible (Kala-   –
glow 132) [1998 NR 1999 9.2m 12.4m 13.1g⁵ 10.1d Oct 20] first foal: dam unraced:
fair handicapper for J. Bolger in Ireland at 3 yrs: well held in 1999, sold from C.
Mann before reappearance: best form at up to 9.6f: acts on good to firm and good to
soft ground: effective blinkered or not. *A. R. Dicken*

NAVIASKY (IRE)   4 b. or br.g. Scenic 128 – Black Molly (IRE) (High Top 131)   **91**
[1998 72: 7d 7s 8d 8g⁴ 8g⁴ 8d* 8.5d³ 10.3f³ 8g² 8m 8m⁵ 8g 1999 7g³ 8.5d³ 8g* 8f*
8f 8m* 8s⁶ Sep 26] big, strong gelding: fairly useful handicapper: better than ever
in 1999, winning at Goodwood in June and July and Leicester in August, on last
2-named occasions in large fields: best at 7f/1m: acts on firm and good to soft going:
held up, and suited by truly-run race. *W. R. Muir*

NEBL   4 ch.f. Persian Bold 123 – Maraatib (IRE) 93 (Green Desert (USA) 127)   **66**
[1998 –: 8.1g 8d 1999 10.3m 10d 8f 10.1f a10g⁵ 10g* 10g² a9.4g⁶ Sep 8] sturdy filly:
has had a soft palate operation: fair performer: left P. D. Evans after third outing:
didn't need to be at best to win seller at Lingfield in August: ran well in handicap
there next time: stays 1¼m: acts on firm going and equitrack: has been slowly away/
given trouble at start. *N. P. Littmoden*

NEDAWI   4 ch.c. Rainbow Quest (USA) 134 – Wajd (USA) 121 (Northern   **126**
Dancer) [1998 124p: 12m* 11.9m³ 12g* 14.6m* 1999 12m² 20m⁵ 12m² Jul 24]
    The distance of two and a half miles did look a shade too far for Nedawi
as he failed in his attempt to complete the St Leger/Gold Cup double achieved
by another Godolphin representative, Classic Cliche, three years earlier.
Nedawi, preferred by Frankie Dettori to the previous year's Gold Cup winner
Kayf Tara, was pushed along to improve his position approaching the home
turn but couldn't sustain his effort in the last couple of furlongs and finished
fifth to Enzeli, beaten six and a half lengths by the winner and two and a half by
third-placed Kayf Tara. Other factors possibly counted against Nedawi besides
the trip, as he sweated in the preliminaries and took a stronger hold than ideal
held up in mid-field. Even so, he certainly didn't look a thorough stayer and as

far as the Cup races go, leaving aside the possibility of a small field and a steady gallop at Ascot, he'll be seen to better advantage over the shorter distances at York, Goodwood and Doncaster. Not that there won't be plenty of other opportunities—all being well—for Nedawi to pick up good prizes, even at a mile and a half. That was the distance of both his other starts during the season and, though he failed to win either, Nedawi did enhance his reputation with a couple of high-class performances. Reappearing in the Dubai Turf Classic at Nad Al Sheba at the end of March, Nedawi looked the likely winner when ridden clear soon after being sent to the front early in the straight. However, though he ran on gamely to pull six lengths and more clear of the remainder, he was just unable to hold the late challenge of Fruits of Love, going down by a neck. The first two met again in the King George VI and Queen Elizabeth Stakes, run at Ascot just over five weeks after the Gold Cup, and this time Nedawi came out ahead of Fruits of Love as Daylami surged away for a five-length success. With Dettori having chosen to ride Daylami, Gary Stevens took the mount on Nedawi and was seen to very good advantage, making the most of his mount's stamina. After racing close up in second as Daliapour cut out the running, Nedawi nosed ahead around half a mile out and briefly had all his rivals stretching when sent for home on the turn, but, in the end, he had no answer when Daylami quickened past him well over a furlong out. Nedawi stuck to his task, though, holding on to second place by half a length from Fruits of Love, who didn't enjoy the clearest of runs. Unfortunately Nedawi suffered an injury during the race, reportedly twisting an ankle, and in mid-September it was announced that he had been retired for the season.

			Blushing Groom		Red God
	Rainbow Quest (USA)		(ch 1974)		Runaway Bride
	(b 1981)		I Will Follow		Herbager
Nedawi			(b 1975)		Where You Lead
(ch.c. 1995)			Northern Dancer		Nearctic
	Wajd (USA)		(b 1961)		Natalma
	(ch 1987)		Dahlia		Vaguely Noble
			(ch 1970)		Charming Alibi

    Nedawi, whose pedigree was dealt with fully in *Racehorses of 1998*, is the third foal of the Prix Minerve and Grand Prix d'Evry winner Wajd, a daughter of the brilliant racemare Dahlia. Wajd's first foal Wall Street (by Mr Prospector) won the 1996 Cumberland Lodge Stakes; her fourth Wajina, a sister to Nedawi, was successful in a newcomers event for fillies run over ten and a half furlongs at Saint-Cloud in May. Nedawi, a big, leggy colt, has raced only on good and good to firm ground in just seven races to date. *Saeed bin Suroor*

NEEDWOOD MAESTRO 3 b.g. Sizzling Melody 117 – Needwood Poppy 29 (Rolfe (USA) 77) [1998 NR 1999 8.2s³ 8.2s³ 9.2m⁴ 11.8m 12.1m a12g 12s 10d 14.1f⁴ 14.1d Oct 27] first foal: dam, bad maiden on Flat, winning stayer over hurdles: modest maiden: below form after third start: shapes as though will stay 2m: acts on firm and soft going. *B. C. Morgan*   **53 d**

NEEDWOOD MERLIN 3 b.c. Sizzling Melody 117 – Enchanting Kate (Enchantment 115) [1998 54: a6g 6m 7m⁵ 7.3g 1999 8.2d 7s 7.1d⁵ 7g³ 7.1d 8.3m 7d a8g a12g Nov 22] close-coupled colt: modest maiden handicapper: ran creditably in 1999 only on fourth start: should stay 1m. *B. C. Morgan*   **53 a–**

NEEDWOOD MINSTREL 3 b.g. Clantime 101 – Azubah 67 (Castle Keep 121) [1998 56: 6m 6m⁵ 5g⁶ 6d 1999 6.1s 6s⁴ 5m⁶ 5.1m 5g⁵ 6g 6f⁶ a6g a6g Dec 1] small, angular gelding: modest maiden: stays 6f: acts on soft and good to firm going: none too consistent. *B. C. Morgan*   **51 a–**

NEEDWOOD MYSTIC 4 b.f. Rolfe (USA) 77 – Enchanting Kate (Enchantment 115) [1998 54: 10.5g⁵ 10m 8m⁴ 12m 10.5s 10v 1999 10.3d 10s⁶ 10s 8.3m 10g 12.3m* 12.3m³ 12m³ 11.9d² 12.3g* 12d⁵ 11.9d 12d a12g Nov 19] smallish, workmanlike filly: modest handicapper: won at Warwick in June and August: stays 1½m: acts on soft and good to firm going: has been very slowly away. *B. C. Morgan*   **55**

NEEDWOOD SPIRIT 4 b.g. Rolfe (USA) 77 – Needwood Nymph 45 (Bold Owl **73**
101) [1998 68, a56+: 8s⁴ 11.1d⁴ 10m 10m 12s³ 12.3s⁶ 12.3g⁵ 11.9g⁴ a14.8g⁴ 13.8s*
1999 13.8g⁴ 13v⁴ 15.4v* 14g⁵ 13.9s² 16.1s 13.9d 16s³ 13.8s⁴ 16.5s⁵ Nov 6] smallish
gelding: fair handicapper: won at Folkestone in April: ran creditably when in frame
otherwise: should stay beyond 2m: acts good to firm and heavy going, showed
promise only run on fibresand: ran poorly in visor once as 3-y-o. *B. C. Morgan*

NEEDWOOD SPITFIRE 4 b.f. Rolfe (USA) 77 – Lime Brook 56 (Rapid River **49**
127) [1998 49: 7g a8g 10.8m⁵ 13.8m³ 12g³ 1999 14.1s 12v 12.1m⁶ 13.8g⁶ 11.9d
17.2m 13m³ 12.1f⁵ 11.9s* 11.7s Oct 26] small, leggy filly: poor handicapper: won
maiden event at Brighton in September: needs good test at 1½m and should stay 2m:
acts on firm and soft going: none too consistent. *B. C. Morgan*

NEEDWOOD TRIDENT 2 b.f. (Feb 14) Minshaanshu Amad (USA) 91§ – **–**
Needwood Nymph 45 (Bold Owl 101) [1999 7d 6s Nov 5] small filly: seventh foal:
half-sister to 4-y-o Needwood Spirit: dam 1½m winner: well beaten in maidens at
Doncaster. *B. C. Morgan*

NEEDWOOD TROOPER 2 br.c. (Apr 30) Puissance 110 – Blueit (FR) 101 **–**
(Bold Lad (IRE) 133) [1999 5.1g Oct 21] 7,500Y: half-brother to several winners,
mostly sprinters, including useful Blues Indigo (by Music Boy) and fairly useful
Indigo (by Primo Dominie), the dam of smart sprinters Astonished and Bishops
Court: dam 2-y-o 5f winner: always behind in maiden at Nottingham. *B. C. Morgan*

NEEDWOOD TRUFFLE (IRE) 2 ch.f. (Apr 4) Brief Truce (USA) 126 – Green **76**
Wings (General Assembly (USA)) [1999 6g⁶ 6.1f³ 5.1m⁵ 6.1m³ 5f* 5g 5s Oct 13]
9,000F, 22,000Y: lengthy, angular filly: seventh foal: half-sister to 3-y-o Entertainer,
1995 2-y-o 1m seller winner Addie Pray (by Great Commotion) and 5-y-o Key To
The City: dam Irish 1½m winner: fair performer: won nursery at Goodwood in July:
well below form last 2 starts: stays 6f: raced only on good ground or firmer prior to
final start: has flashed tail. *B. C. Morgan*

NEEDWOOD TRUMP (IRE) 2 br.g. (Apr 8) Marju (IRE) 127 – Play The **35**
Queen (IRE) (King of Clubs 124) [1999 5m a5g⁴ 7m Jul 21] IR 8,000Y: smallish,
close-coupled gelding: fifth foal: half-brother to several winners, including 3-y-o
Franco Mina and 5-y-o Salty Jack: dam Irish 7f winner: poor form. *B. C. Morgan*

NEELA (IRE) 3 ch.f. Bluebird (USA) 125 – Scammony (IRE) (Persian Bold 123) **66 ?**
[1998 NR 1999 6.1g 6d⁴ a6g Nov 11] 130,000Y: first foal: dam once-raced sister to
dam of Lake Coniston (by Bluebird): easily best effort when fourth of 21 in maiden
at Windsor in October: likely to prove best up to 7f. *R. Hannon*

NEGRONI 2 br.f. (Feb 4) Mtoto 134 – Carousel Music 56 (On Your Mark 125) **65 p**
[1999 8.2g⁶ Sep 25] second foal: half-sister to 3-y-o Credenza: dam 1¼m to 1½m
winner: green, around 6 lengths sixth of 11 to Dollar Bird in maiden at Nottingham,
not knocked about: will be suited by 1¼m/1½m: sure to do better. *J. W. Hills*

NEIGES ETERNELLES (FR) 4 b.f. Exit To Nowhere (USA) 122 – Nabita **–**
(FR) (Akarad (FR) 130) [1998 95: 10.5d² 10.5s* 10g 11.5d² 12.8d² 12.5m³ 12.5d
12s⁴ 14s⁵ 1999 10.2m 14s⁵ 10.3s⁵ Nov 5] leggy filly: half-sister to several winners,
including high-class chaser Nakir (by Nikos): dam 13f winner in France: useful
performer at best: won twice in French Provinces at 2 yrs and minor event at
Maisons-Laffitte early at 3 yrs (in frame subsequently in listed races) for H. Pantall:
no show in listed race/minor events in 1999: stays 12.8f: acts on soft and good to firm
going. *P. R. Webber*

NELIA 3 b.f. Local Suitor (USA) 128 – La Ciotat (IRE) 40 (Gallic League 119) **–**
[1998 NR 1999 7f 8.5g 10g Aug 18] no form: dead. *J. G. FitzGerald*

NELLIE NORTH 6 b.m. Northern State (USA) 91 – Kimble Princess (Kala **–**
Shikari 125) [1998 40: 6.1v 6.1m 6f 6m³ 5.1g 6m⁶ 5g⁴ 5g 5m³ 6m⁴ 5m 5f 5m 1999
5m 5g 8g 5.1m Jul 5] poor at 5 yrs: no form in 1999. *A. J. Chamberlain*

NEPTUNE 3 b.g. Dolphin Street (FR) 125 – Seal Indigo (IRE) 93 (Glenstal (USA) **44**
118) [1998 NR 1999 7g 8.5s 7g 10g⁶ 11.9d 10d⁵ a11g⁴ a8g Nov 22] 31,000F,
35,000Y: leggy, unfurnished gelding: third foal: dam best at 1½m: poor maiden: left
G. Lewis before penultimate start: should stay 1½m: acts on good to soft going,
probably on fibresand: has given trouble stalls. *K. C. Comerford*

NERONIAN (IRE) 5 ch.g. Mujtahid (USA) 118 – Nimieza (USA) 70 (Nijinsky **43**
(CAN) 138) [1998 NR 1999 10.1m 10g² 11.1f⁴ 10m 8.2g 8f⁴ 10m⁵ 10d a8g⁶ a8g **a38**
a10g⁵ a13g⁶ Dec 10] tall, lengthy gelding: poor nowadays: stays 1¼m: acts on firm
going: tried blinkered/visored: has been bandaged. *K. R. Burke*

NERO TIROL (IRE) 3 b. or br.g. Tirol 127 – Saltoki 86 (Ballad Rock 122) **–**
[1998 72: 6g⁴ 5.1d⁵ 6.3s 1999 a8f a6f* a6g* a6g³ 6.1s 6m 7m a8g⁵ 7s a7g a7g a8g **a72**
Dec 27] fair performer: won maiden (made all) and handicap at Southwell in
February: patchy form after, off 5 months before final start: likely to prove best up to
1m: acts on all-weather, little form on turf in 1999: often blinkered (including for
both wins). *A. Kelleway*

NERVOUS REX 5 b.g. Reprimand 122 – Spinner 59 (Blue Cashmere 129) [1998 **–**
60: 6s 6m* 5.9d 7.1g* 5m 7d 7.1m³ 6m 1999 a7g Jan 4] useful-looking gelding:
modest handicapper: best at 6f/7f: acts on firm and good to soft going, well held on
fibresand: below form in blinkers/visor. *D. Nicholls*

NESTING 4 ch.f. Thatching 131 – Tatouma (USA) 79 (The Minstrel (CAN) 135) **47**
[1998 NR 1999 5g⁵ 6f 5g⁶ Sep 15] workmanlike filly: fifth foal: sister to 1994 2-y-o
7f winner Trimming and half-sister to a German 7.5f and 1m winner by Dowsing:
dam 2-y-o 5f/6f winner: poor maiden. *J. S. Wainwright*

NESYRED (IRE) 3 b.f. Paris House 123 – Abrika (Dominion 123) [1998 NR **75**
1999 7.6f⁶ 6d* 6d Oct 29] IR 1,200Y: sixth foal: dam lightly raced: won maiden at
Folkestone in August: stiff task, last in minor event at Newmarket 2 months later:
may prove best at 5f/6f: joined M. Ryan. *Mrs D. Haine*

NETHERHALL 3 ch.g. Rudimentary 118 – Legal Precedent (Star Appeal **–**
133) [1998 –: 5g 6m 6g 7.5m 10d 1999 a7g⁴ a11g³ a12g² a12g² a14.8g* a12g* **a55**
a12g⁴ᵈⁱˢ a14.8g⁵ a14g⁶ Sep 28] modest handicapper: won at Wolverhampton and
Southwell in June: stays 15f: no form on turf at 2 yrs, raced only on fibresand in
1999: genuine and reliable. *M. G. Meagher*

NETTA RUFINA (IRE) 4 ch.g. Night Shift (USA) – Age of Elegance (Troy **79**
137) [1998 79: a8.5g a8g⁴ a10g* a9.4g² 13s⁶ 12d 10g⁵ 13.1d⁵ 12.3g* 14.1g² 16g²
14g⁴ 16.1m 1999 14g 16s a14.8g 13g⁴ 16m³ 14d* 12m³ 12.3m 14.8m² 12m⁶ 15m⁵
14m 12f 12g² a12g⁵ 16g³ a16g³ a16.2g² Dec 1] sturdy, close-coupled gelding: fair
handicapper: won at Musselburgh in June: stayed 2m: acted on good to firm ground,
good to soft and all-weather: usually visored: often raced up with pace: sometimes
hung: dead. *M. Johnston*

NEUWEST (USA) 7 b.h. Gone West (USA) – White Mischief 103 (Dance In **–**
Time (CAN)) [1998 –: 7d 7g 1999 8m 7m 7m⁶ 7g 7d Sep 15] robust horse: useful
handicapper for R. Akehurst in 1997: little form since, leaving M. Pipe after second
7-y-o start. *K. R. Burke*

NEVER CAN TELL 3 ch.g. Emarati (USA) 74 – Farmer's Pet 90 (Sharrood **–**
(USA) 124) [1998 77: 6.1g 6m 7m⁴ 6s² 6g 1999 6.1m⁵ a8.5g 7g a9.4f 7d 10s Nov 1]
fair maiden at 2 yrs: no show in 1999, leaving J. FitzGerald after reappearance: has
given trouble stalls: visored once. *B. P. J. Baugh*

NEVER DISS MISS 2 b.f. (Mar 19) Owington 123 – Pennine Pink (IRE) 72 **75**
(Pennine Walk 120) [1999 5g 5s* 5m⁴ 6m 6m³ 7d 6d Oct 15] 9,000Y: small, sturdy
filly: second foal: dam 1m/1¼m winner: fair performer: 20/1-winner of maiden at
Sandown in April: in frame in minor events at Salisbury and Windsor after: should
stay 7f: acts on soft and good to firm ground. *R. J. R. Williams*

NEVER LEAVE 2 b.f. (Apr 25) Never So Bold 135 – Leave It To Lib 66 (Tender **–**
King 123) [1999 5m⁵ Jun 16] 1,500Y: first foal: dam 7f/1m winner: always behind in
minor event at Ripon: dead. *P. Calver*

NEW ABBEY 4 b.f. Sadler's Wells (USA) 132 – Bahamian 115 (Mill Reef (USA) **104**
141) [1998 82: 12d* 1999 11.6m* 12s³ 12d² 12s Nov 29] useful performer: won
minor event at Windsor (after near 16-month absence, beat Azouz Pasha a neck) in
August: ran creditably at Ascot behind Signorina Cattiva in listed race and Princess
Royal Stakes (beaten 7 lengths) next 2 starts: stayed 1½m: acted on soft and good to
firm going: stud. *H. R. A. Cecil*

NEW ASSEMBLY (IRE) 2 b.f. (Apr 15) Machiavellian (USA) 123 – Abbey **73 p**
Strand (USA) 78 (Shadeed (USA) 135) [1999 7d 7d Oct 30] useful-looking filly:

good walker: fourth foal: half-sister to 4-y-o Celtic Cross and 3-y-o Temple Way: dam, 1m winner, half-sister to 6f to 10.5f winner Church Parade and middle-distance stayer Castle Rising, both smart: much better effort in maidens (very slowly away on debut) when seventh of 16 at Newmarket, still green and keeping on from mid-field: will stay 1¼m: should improve and win races. *Sir Michael Stoute*

NEW CAPRICORN (USA)   9 ch.g. Green Forest (USA) 134 – Size Six (USA)   **48** (Caerleon (USA) 132) [1998 54: 7m 7s⁶ 7.1g 6v⁵ 7s 1999 8d 7g 8m² 9.2m⁴ 8.3s⁶ 8d Oct 20] sturdy gelding: poor handicapper: stays 1m: acts on good to firm and heavy going: blinkered once in 1995: tongue tied. *C. Parker*

NEW EARTH MAIDEN   2 b.f. (Apr 19) Ezzoud (IRE) 126 – Susie's Baby   **–** (Balidar 133) [1999 7.1m 6m 7g 5.7m Jul 20] half-sister to several sprint winners, notably 6-y-o Repertory: dam lightly raced: well held in maidens/seller. *J. Cullinan*

NEW FORTUNE (FR)   2 ch.f. (Feb 11) Exit To Nowhere (USA) 122 – Fortuna   **–** Redux (Primo Dominie 121) [1999 7m Jul 25] 350,000 francs Y: second foal: dam, French 7f winner, half-sister to 2 smart French milers: last of 9 in maiden at Newmarket. *W. R. Muir*

NEWGATE CASTLE   3 b.f. Rambo Dancer (CAN) 107 – Gemgem 54 (Loch-   **–** nager 132) [1998 NR 1999 8g Jun 14] unfurnished filly: seventh foal: dam 7f seller winner: no show in seller at Pontefract. *B. W. Murray*

NEWLANDS CORNER   6 b.m. Forzando 122 – Nice Lady 65 (Connaught 130)   **53** [1998 61, a–: 6.1s 4g 6.1m⁴ 6d⁶ 6m 6d a7g 6.1v⁵ 6s⁴ 6s a6g 1999 6s⁶ 6v 6f Apr 29]   **a–** stocky mare: modest handicapper: best at 6f: acts on any turf going and fibresand: usually slowly away: often blinkered: sold 5,000 gns. *J. Akehurst*

NEW MOON   3 ch.g. Good Times (ITY) – Two Moons (Bold Lad (IRE) 133)   **–** [1998 –: 5g 6m 6g 1999 a11g⁵ a12g 12.1m May 6] workmanlike gelding: little sign of ability: blinkered final start: sold 3,000 gns. *C. W. Thornton*

NEWSCASTER   3 b.g. Bluebird (USA) 125 – Sharp Girl (FR) 114 (Sharpman)   **76** [1998 NR 1999 6m⁶ 8s⁵ 8.3m⁴ a9.4g* 9g* Aug 20] 30,000Y: close-coupled gelding: half-brother to several winners, including middle-distance performer Tart (by Warning), 10-y-o Gold Blade and fairly useful 7f and 1¼m winner Robsart (by Robellino): dam French 1¼m winner who stayed 1½m: fair performer: won 5-runner claimer at Sandown (joined M. Pipe £20,000) in August: will stay 1¼m: acts on fibresand, soft and good to firm ground. *P. F. I. Cole*

NEWSHAN   3 b.f. Anshan 119 – New Pastures (Formidable (USA) 125) [1998 NR   **–** 1999 8.3m 11.7m 7.7d Sep 21] workmanlike filly: fifth living foal: half-sister to 5-y-o Madame Maxi: dam unraced: well held in maidens. *H. S. Howe*

NEW VICTORIA (USA)   3 b.f. Colonel Collins (USA) 122 – Distinctiveness   **63** (USA) (Distinctive (USA)) [1998 NR 1999 a7g⁵ 6m³ 6g⁵ Jun 2] half-sister to several winners, notably smart 1990 2-y-o 5f winner and Middle Park runner-up Distinctly North (by Minshaanshu Amad): dam half-sister to Grade 2 1¼m winner Determined King: best effort in maidens on second start: should stay at least 7f: jinked right under whip final start: sold 17,000 gns, sent to New Zealand. *P. W. Chapple-Hyam*

NEW YORKER (USA)   4 ch.g. Gilded Time (USA) – Doris's Secret (USA)   **42** (Nikoli 125) [1998 61: a10g a12g² a12g² a12g⁶ 14.6d a14g a8.5g⁴ a14.8g a8g³ 1999 a8g⁴ Jan 2] modest maiden at best: very slowly away only 4-y-o start: stays 1½m: acts on fibresand: visored last 5 starts: carries head high, and possibly none too genuine. *Miss A. Stokell*

NIAGARA (IRE)   2 b.c. (Jan 4) Rainbows For Life (CAN) – Highbrook (USA)   **83** 88 (Alphabatim (USA) 126) [1999 5g⁴ 5m² 6d* 7.3g⁴ 8g⁶ 6d Sep 17] stocky colt: first foal: dam 1¼m to 13f winner, also useful over hurdles: fairly useful performer: won maiden at Ayr in May: good fourth in nursery at Newbury nearly 3 months later, but well held in similar events last 2 starts: stays 7f: usually races prominently. *M. H. Tompkins*

NICE BALANCE (USA)   4 b.g. Shadeed (USA) 135 – Fellwaati (USA) (Alydar   **37** (USA)) [1998 NR 1999 a11g 10.3m⁶ 10d 6f 7f⁵ 8m 6g2 a7g Nov 19] 2,700 3-y-o: big, good-topped gelding: first foal: dam unraced: poor maiden: stays 7f: acts on firm going: blinkered fourth start. *M. C. Chapman*

NICE GUY (IRE)   4 ch.g. Persian Bold 123 – Flying Bid 71 (Auction Ring (USA)   **51**
123) [1998 67: 12s⁵ 8.5s⁴ 10s⁴ 12s 1999 11.9f 14m 18m Jun 29] half-brother to
several winners, including useful 1987 Irish 2-y-o 5f/6f winner Flutter Away (by
Lomond) and 1½m winner Rahwah (by Northern Baby): dam 1¼m winner: fair
maiden (also winning hurdler) for F. Berry in Ireland at 3 yrs: just modest at best in
1999: stays 1¾m. *S. Dow*

NICELY (IRE)   3 gr.f. Bustino 136 – Nichodoula 65 (Doulab (USA) 115) [1998   **94 p**
74p: 7.9g 8v* 1999 11.4m⁵ 11m 14.1g⁵ 12g⁶ 10.1m⁵ 10.5s 13.9d⁴ 16s* 16.1d Oct 29]
lengthy, sparely-made filly: fairly useful handicapper: much improved when winning
17-runner race at Newbury in October by 6 lengths from Male-Ana-Mou: 18 lb out
of weights and shuffled back to rear 5f out when not discredited in listed rated stakes
at Newmarket final start: will stay beyond 2m: goes well on ground softer than good:
may well do better still. *J. W. Hills*

NICE 'N EASY (IRE)   2 b.f. (May 2) Perugino (USA) 84 – Oystons Propweekly   **50 d**
74 (Swing Easy (USA) 126) [1999 5m a5g 6s⁴ 7g 6m 6g 6g 7m 8m Sep 7] IR 3,000Y,
resold IR 18,000Y: half-sister to 3 winners, including 4-y-o Mai Tai: dam 2-y-o 5f
winner: modest maiden: generally well beaten after third start: tried blinkered: has
been bandaged. *K. T. Ivory*

NICE ONE CLARE (IRE)   3 b.f. Mukaddamah (USA) 125 – Sarah-Clare 67   **104 p**
(Reach 122) [1998 NR 1999 7m* 7m³ 6.8m² 7m* 7m* Aug 28] second foal: dam
1m/1¼m winner: progressive form: won maiden at Folkestone in May and handicaps
at Kempton and Newmarket in August, last-named by head from Holly Blue, idling
in front: likely to prove best at 6f/7f: raced only on good to firm going: held up: open
to further improvement and should have another good season at 4 yrs. *J. W. Payne*

NICHOLAS DUDLEY (USA)   2 b.c. (Apr 28) Caerleon (USA) 132 – Flood   **81**
(USA) (Riverman (USA) 131) [1999 7s² 6g⁸* 7m³ 7d 8v⁶ Oct 12] rather leggy,
unfurnished colt: seventh foal: brother to smart 1m (at 2 yrs) and 11.6f winner King
Sound, closely related to a winner in Japan by Shadeed and half-brother to fairly
useful 1½m winner Mr Flood (by Al Nasr): dam, 6f winner in USA, from family of
Generous (by Caerleon) and Triptych: fairly useful performer: won maiden at Ayr in
July: good third in nursery at Lingfield next time, but below form in similar events
after: should stay 1¼m: sold 10,000 gns. *Sir Mark Prescott*

NICHOLAS MISTRESS   3 b.f. Beveled (USA) – Foreign Mistress (Darshaan   **46**
133) [1998 56, a45: 5m² 5m⁵ 5.1g³ 5.3m² 5m 6g⁶ 5s⁴ 5.7v⁵ 5s² a5g⁵ a6g³ a5s⁴ a5g⁶
1999 a5g⁴ a7g⁴ a8f³ a6g² a6g* a6g⁶ a8g⁵ a5g 6g 7.1d 7.1g 8.2f Jun 21] small, leggy
filly: poor performer: won handicap at Lingfield in February: below form most starts
after: best at 5f/6f: acts on good to firm ground, soft and all-weather: tried visored.
P. D. Evans

NICHOL FIFTY   5 b.g. Old Vic 136 – Jawaher (IRE) 60 (Dancing Brave (USA)   **83**
140) [1998 –: 12.5d 1999 14.1s* 18.7m 14m⁶ 14.4g* 16.1m 14d² 14m² 13.1d⁵
17.3g 16.5s Nov 6] workmanlike gelding: fairly useful performer: won handicap at
Nottingham in April and minor event at Kempton in June: some creditable efforts
after, including when seventh in Cesarewitch at Newmarket penultimate start:
effective at 1¾m to 17f: acts on soft and good to firm going. *M. H. Tompkins*

NICIARA (IRE)   2 b.g. (Mar 9) Soviet Lad (USA) – Verusa (IRE) (Petorius 117)   **51**
[1999 6.1m 8d 8d a8g a6g³ a8g³ a5g a8g Dec 21] IR 5,800F, 3,000 2-y-o: lengthy
gelding: third foal: half-brother to Irish 7f and 9f winner Sterling High (by Mujadil):
dam lightly raced at 2 yrs in Ireland: modest maiden: pulled up penultimate start:
stays 1m: acts on fibresand. *M. C. Chapman*

NICKLES   4 b.g. Lugana Beach 116 – Instinction (Never So Bold 135) [1998 75:   **71 d**
5s³ 5g³ 5.7m 1999 5s⁴ 5s 5g³ 5f 5d 5d* 5m³ 5s 5.3d 5.2s 5s Nov 2] fair performer:
won claimer at Lingfield in August: well held last 4 starts: best at 5f: yet to race on
heavy going, acts up when raced up with pace. *L. G. Cottrell*

NICK'S CHOICE   3 b.g. Sula Bula 109 – Clare's Choice (Pragmatic 115) [1998   **–**
NR 1999 a8.5g 5.1g 7m 6.1m 7f 7d 9.9s Sep 21] 500Y: first foal: dam third in bumper
only start: signs of only a little ability: blinkered penultimate start: looked wayward
third outing. *J. M. Bradley*

NICK'S JULE (IRE)   2 ch.f. (Apr 7) Perugino (USA) 84 – Miss Lee Ann   **57**
(Tumble Wind (USA)) [1999 6f⁵ 7s Aug 18] IR 3,500F, IR 16,000Y: big, strong,

workmanlike filly: sixth foal: closely related to 2 winners in Ireland, including fairly useful Irish 1995 2-y-o 1m winner Errazuriz (by Classic Music), and half-sister to 6f winner John Emms (by Shalford): dam unraced: modest form in maiden at Goodwood: well held in similar event at Kempton following month. *A. P. Jarvis*

NICOBAR 2 b.c. (Mar 1) Indian Ridge 123 – Duchess of Alba 75 (Belmez (USA) 131) [1999 7.3f³ 7.1d* 7d⁵ 7.1d² 7d⁵ Sep 28] 45,000Y: quite attractive colt: first foal: dam, 13.8f winner (stayed 17f), out of Oaks winner Juliette Marny: useful performer: impressive winner of maiden at Haydock in August: best efforts when second of 5 to Adilabad in minor event at Sandown and fifth of 17 to Inchlonaig in sales event at Newmarket, setting good pace and finishing clear on his side of course in latter: will prove suited by 1m+: gave impression something amiss at Deauville third start. *I. A. Balding* **99**

NICOLA BELLA (IRE) 4 b.f. Sadler's Wells (USA) 132 – Valley of Hope (USA) (Riverman (USA) 131) [1998 98: 8s² 10g² 10s⁵ 9.6g* 9g⁶ 12g 10m⁶ 1999 10m May 1] workmanlike filly: first foal: dam unraced half-sister to Mill Reef Stakes winner Vacarme and Prix Jacques le Marois winner Vin de France: useful for J. Oxx in Ireland at 3 yrs, winning maiden at Gowran: wrong in coat and showed little in minor event at Newmarket only 4-y-o start: stays 1¼m. *J. L. Dunlop* **–**

NIFTY MAJOR 2 b.g. (Mar 27) Be My Chief (USA) 122 – Nifty Fifty (IRE) 97 (Runnett 125) [1999 5s⁶ 5m* 5d² 5f⁵ 5d⁴ 5m⁵ 5g* 5m⁵ 5d Sep 16] 10,000Y: tall, rather unfurnished gelding: third foal: half-brother to 5-y-o Nifty Norman: dam 2-y-o 5f winner who probably stayed 7f: fair performer: won maiden in April and nursery in August, both at Musselburgh: will prove best at 5f: acts on good to firm and good to soft going: often forces pace: consistent. *J. Berry* **78**

NIFTY NORMAN 5 b.g. Rock City 120 – Nifty Fifty (IRE) 97 (Runnett 125) [1998 77d: 6v² 5v 6d 5g 5d 5d 5m 5d 5d 1999 a7g a5g⁵ a5g a6g* a5g⁵ a6g² a6g² a5g* a6g³ 5d 5m⁵ 5d³ 5.7g³ 5m⁴ 5.1d* 5d² 5g⁶ 5m 5d⁴ 6d 5g 5d⁴ 5s a5g⁶ a5g⁶ a5g⁵ Dec 21] leggy, angular gelding: fairly useful handicapper on all-weather, fair on turf: won at Southwell in February and March and Chester in June: effective at 5f/easy 6f: acts on all-weather and heavy going, probably on good to firm: tried blinkered: has been early to post: sometimes slowly away (has reared in stalls): usually races prominently. *D. Nicholls* **74 a81**

NIGEL'S LAD (IRE) 7 b.g. Dominion Royale 112 – Back To Earth (FR) (Vayrann 133) [1998 90, a–: 16g* 13s* 13.9g 14.6d 1999 13.9s 16.2d⁵ 11.9d 17.1g* 14d⁵ 18.7m³ 20f Jul 28] sturdy gelding: fairly useful handicapper: won 5-runner race at Pontefract in June by 11 lengths: creditable third of 6 to Kahtan in rated stakes at Chester: well held 4 days later: effective at 13f (given good test) to 2¼m: acts on good to firm ground, soft and all-weather: game front runner: won over fences in November. *P. C. Haslam* **87 a–**

NIGHT ADVENTURE (IRE) 3 ch.g. Night Shift (USA) – Mary Hinge 100 (Dowsing (USA) 124) [1998 NR 1999 8m 7m³ 6.1g Sep 25] IR 34,000Y: first foal: dam sprinter: easily best effort in maidens on second start: sold 3,000 gns. *J. L. Dunlop* **59**

NIGHT AND DAY 2 ch.f. (May 3) Anshan 119 – Midnight Break 78 (Night Shift (USA)) [1999 a6g³ Nov 27] first foal: dam 5f/6f winner: 10 lengths third to The Prosecutor in maiden at Wolverhampton: should improve. *W. Jarvis* **53 p**

NIGHT AUCTION (IRE) 4 b.f. Night Shift (USA) – Maria Stuarda (Royal And Regal (USA)) [1998 64, a54: 7f 6d* 6g² 6m⁴ 6m⁵ 6m 6.1d 6.1s a7g a6g a7g⁵ a8.5g² 1999 a8g a12f³ a12g⁴ 8g⁶ 12.3g Aug 13] sturdy filly: modest performer: stays easy 1½m: acts on good to firm going, good to soft and all-weather: inconsistent. *B. Palling* **– a54**

NIGHT CHIME (IRE) 4 b.f. Night Shift (USA) – Baydon Belle (USA) 64 (Al Nasr (FR) 126) [1998 –: a7g 1999 a6g⁴ a6g 6g 6.8s a5g a5g a5g 14.1m Jul 17] little form: tried visored: tongue tied. *Miss A. Stokell* **–**

NIGHT CHORUS 5 b.g. Most Welcome 131 – Choral Sundown 81 (Night Shift (USA)) [1998 72, a–: a9.4g 8.3d⁵ 8m⁶ 8.2d⁴ 8s* 7.9m³ 8g³ 7.1g⁴ 8.9g 8m 8.1m 8.2s 8.2v 1999 8d* 8m² 8.3g⁴ 7.7m* Jun 23] strong, lengthy gelding: fairly useful performer: won minor event at Pontefract (19 ran) in April and handicap at Warwick **80 a–**

in June: stays 9f: acts on soft and good to firm ground, possibly not on fibresand: tried visored: sometimes edges left: sold 7,000 gns, sent to Sweden. *B. S. Rothwell*

NIGHT CITY   8 b.g. Kris 135 – Night Secret 86 (Nijinsky (CAN) 138) [1998 94: a12s³ a13g³ a12g* a10g³ a12g* a12g³ a12g⁶ 11.1v* 12.3m 11.9d 12g* 12.1d² 11.9g² 12.1m* 12d* 11.5f* 12m 12.1s 11.9g* 10.4g* 10s a12g* a13g² a12g³ 1999 a12g⁵ a8f³ a10g² a11g⁵ 11.1v 11.9d² 11.6d² 11.1m* 11.9g⁴ 11.5g 10.4f 10.4d* 10s⁵ 10d* a8g* a10g a13g³ a12g² Dec 29] sturdy gelding: fairly useful performer: won claimers at Hamilton, York and Lingfield and handicap at Brighton (by 5 lengths) between June and November: ran well final start: finds 1m a bare minimum and stays 13f: acts on any turf going and on equitrack: blinkered once: sometimes early to post: has given trouble at stalls: quirky sort, and less than ideal mount for inexperienced rider: front runner (often goes clear): tough. *K. R. Burke*   **83**
a90

NIGHT DANCE   7 ch.g. Weldnaas (USA) 112 – Shift Over (USA) 62 (Night Shift (USA)) [1998 –: a8g 8.2m 8f 1999 8.3g⁶ 8.2m² 7m May 26] good-topped gelding: formerly useful, modest nowadays: best up to 1m: acts on soft and good to firm going (possibly not on firm): has worn tongue strap. *K. A. Morgan*   **57**

NIGHT DIAMOND   2 b.g. (Feb 4) Night Shift (USA) – Dashing Water 87 (Dashing Blade 117) [1999 6f 6d⁵ 6m³ 7m Sep 11] good-topped gelding: first foal: dam, 2-y-o 7f winner, half-sister to Nunthorpe winners Lochangel (by Night Shift) and Lochsong: fair maiden: best efforts on second and third starts: has been bandaged in front. *I. A. Balding*   **72**

NIGHT EMPRESS   2 br.f. (Mar 29) Emperor Jones (USA) 119 – Night Trader (USA) (Melyno 130) [1999 6f⁴ 6s² 7v³ 7s Oct 23] 8,500F: leggy, close-coupled filly: second foal: dam lightly-raced daughter of sister to Prix de la Salamandre winner Maximova: fair maiden: best efforts on second and third starts: should stay 1m: acts on heavy ground. *J. R. Fanshawe*   **76**

NIGHT FLIGHT   5 gr.g. Night Shift (USA) – Ancestry (Persepolis (FR) 127) [1998 85: 6g⁴ 6g² 6s⁵ 6d* 6g⁶ 6f 6g³ 5m⁵ 5g 6s 5g³ 6s 1999 a6g³ 5d² 6m 5.2m 5s* 5m* 5g³ 5m⁴ 5m* 6f 5g 5.6g 5s 6d 5s⁶ Oct 23] good-bodied gelding: useful handicapper: won at York and Haydock in May and Ascot (easily best effort, by 1¼ lengths from Rudi's Pet) in July: not in same heart afterwards: successful at 6f, but best at 5f: acts on soft and good to firm going, ran well only try on fibresand: often claimer ridden. *R. A. Fahey*   **108**

Grosvenor Casino Newcastle Sprint (Handicap), York—
Night Flight and Robert Winston record the first of their three victories in 1999,
always holding Iris May (nearer camera)

NIGHT FLYER   4 b.g. Midyan (USA) 124 – Scandalette (Niniski (USA) 125)   **92**
[1998 80: 7.5d⁴ 7.6m⁶ 8m² 8d 8m 8m⁴ 8g² 10.4g a10g 1999 a9s a10g³ a10g
9.9m² 10.3f³ a10g 10.1m³ 12m* 11.7m² 12m* 12m 12g⁴ 12m⁵ Sep 4] angular, good-
quartered gelding: fairly useful performer: won 2 handicaps at Epsom in July: stiff
task there final start: stays 1½m: acts on firm going, good to soft and snow (well held
on equitrack): usually races prominently/leads. *J. W. Hills*

NIGHTGLADE (IRE)   3 b.c. Night Shift (USA) – Woodland Garden (Godswalk   **49**
(USA) 130) [1998 –: 7f 7.9g 7.5m 1999 12g 10m³ a12g 12d⁴ 12.1m 12.3d 16.2m
10g⁶ 15.8g⁵ 12.4g Aug 20] small, sturdy colt: poor maiden handicapper: reportedly
found to have injured his back seventh start: stays 1½m: acts on good to firm and
good to soft ground: inconsistent. *M. Brittain*

NIGHTINGALE   3 ro.f. Night Shift (USA) – Grey Angel (Kenmare (FR) 125)   **–**
[1998 –: 5m 6d 8s 1999 a7f Jan 19] little form. *P. D. Evans*

NIGHTINGALE SONG   5 b.m. Tina's Pet 121 – Songlines 78 (Night Shift   **58**
(USA)) [1998 49: 6m 5g⁵ 5.1g 1999 7f 5g 6g* 6s* 6m³ 5g³ 5g* 5.1m 7v⁶ 5.2s a6g
Nov 20] sparely-made mare: modest handicapper: won at Lingfield and Leicester (18
ran) in June and Sandown in August: best at 5f/6f: acts on firm going, soft (probably
on heavy) and all-weather: usually races prominently: game. *L. Montague Hall*

NIGHT LIFE (IRE)   3 gr.f. Night Shift (USA) – Petula 103 (Petong 126) [1998   **75**
60p: 5m 6g 5s 5.2s* 5d 1999 6.1s³ a6g³ a6g* 6g² 6g* 6.1f⁶ 7.1d 6g² 6m⁴ 6s⁶ 7g Oct
15] sturdy filly: fair handicapper: won at Wolverhampton in April and Catterick in
May: ran well in frame otherwise, unlucky at Yarmouth (jumped litter twice inside
final 1f) on eighth start: likely to prove best at 5f/6f: acts on fibresand, soft and good
to firm going: sold 40,000 gns in December. *M. L. W. Bell*

NIGHT MUSIC   2 br.f. (Jan 26) Piccolo 121 – Oribi 59 (Top Ville 129) [1999 7g⁴   **58**
7.7d 7g Oct 19] 13,000F, 8,000Y: sparely-made filly: second living foal: dam, ran
twice, from family of middle-distance performers Ascot Knight (top class) and Petit
Loup (very smart): well beaten after showing modest form when fourth of 18 to
Noble Pursuit in maiden at Salisbury on debut: should stay 1m. *Major D. N. Chappell*

NIGHT OF GLASS   6 b.g. Mazilier (USA) 107 – Donna Elvira 80 (Chief Singer   **97**
131) [1998 95: 7d⁴ 7s* 8d* 7d* 8.5m* 7m³ 7g² 8.1g 8s³ 7.1g³ 8.1g 7.9f 7m 8m 8s³
7.1g* 7g⁵ 8g 7s 1999 8d³ 7g⁵ 8m 7.9d³ 8.5g* 8.9d⁵ 7m³ 10.4f 7.6m⁵ 8.1d 7.9g³ 8m⁵
7d⁴ Oct 7] small gelding: useful handicapper: won rated stakes at Beverley in May:
mostly at least respectable efforts otherwise, including when third in Lincoln at
Doncaster on reappearance and in Bradford & Bingley Stakes at York on eleventh
outing: effective at 7f to 9f: acts on any going: usually blinkered/visored/bandaged:
tends to do just enough once in front (held up): tough and consistent. *J. L. Eyre*

NIGHT OF GLORY   4 b.f. Perpendicular 119 – Donna Elvira 80 (Chief Singer   **–**
131) [1998 NR 1999 13.8m⁵ 10g Aug 21] second foal: half-sister to 6-y-o Night of
Glass: dam best at 7f: last in maidens at Catterick and Ripon. *J. L. Eyre*

NIGHT OMEN (IRE)   2 ch.g. (Feb 1) Night Shift (USA) – Propitious (IRE) 101   **54**
(Doyoun 124) [1999 6m 5m⁵ Aug 13] 25,000F, 30,000Y: sturdy, heavy-topped gelding: first foal: dam Irish 1m winner: modest form in maidens at Pontefract (bandaged
off fore) and Lingfield (galloped loose before start). *S. C. Williams*

NIGHT SHIFTER (IRE)   2 b.f. (Feb 7) Night Shift (USA) – Atsuko (IRE) (Mtoto   **74**
134) [1999 5g 5.2m⁴ 5m 5g 5g* 6m² 7g⁶ 6m³ Sep 3] IR 40,000Y: sturdy, close-
coupled filly: second foal: dam, second over 1m at 2 yrs in Ireland, closely related to
very smart French middle-distance performer Muroto: fair performer: won nursery
at Lingfield in August: best effort when second in similar event at Thirsk later in
month: should stay 7f: raced only on good/good to firm going. *M. R. Channon*

NIGHT SHOT   4 br.g. Night Shift (USA) – Optaria 83 (Song 132) [1998 112p: **112**
5s* 6m⁵ 5g² 6f³ 6s 5g* 6g⁶ 6g⁶ 5f* 5.6g⁴ 5.2g² 6m 1999 5d* 5m 6s⁴ 6m³ 6m² 6m² 6f
5g⁴ 5.1m³ 5m 5m Dec 12] good-quartered gelding: smart performer: won handicap
at Doncaster (under 10-0) in March by head from Night Flight: several creditable
efforts after, including when second to Arkadian Hero in listed race at Newbury
on sixth start and 4 lengths fourth to Stravinsky in Nunthorpe Stakes at York on
eighth: left I. Balding and renamed Night Star, below form in Hong Kong last 2 starts:
has form at 6f, but probably best at strongly-run 5f: yet to race on heavy going, acts

on any other: has run well when sweating/on toes: usually held up. *D. Oughton, Hong Kong*

NIGHT STYLE (FR) 2 b.c. (Apr 22) Night Shift (USA) – Style For Life (IRE) **104** (Law Society (USA) 130) [1999 6g² 6m* 7f³ 6m⁵ 7m² 6m 7g* 8f* Oct 17] 850,000 francs Y: attractive, good-topped colt with scope: progressed well physically: second foal: dam, French 1¼m and 1½m winner, half-sister to useful French 1m winner Central Lobby: useful performer: won maiden at Ripon in June, minor event at Leicester in September and Gran Criterium at Milan in October, last-named gamely by ½ length from demoted Winning Venture: should stay beyond 1m: raced only on good going or firmer: visored once: has worn crossed noseband: often a front runner. *E. A. L. Dunlop*

NIGHT VENTURE (USA) 3 b.c. Dynaformer (USA) – Charming Ballerina 89 **94** (Caerleon (USA) 132) [1998 NR 1999 8d⁴ 10.3m³ 10m* 10.1m* 12f 10.4g⁵ 10m 12d⁶ Oct 14] $300,000Y: good-topped, quite attractive colt: has a round action: third foal: dam 2-y-o 7f winner, later successful in minor stakes up to 9f in USA, half-sister to Hawaiian Sound: fairly useful performer: made all in maiden at Ripon in May and handicap at Newcastle in June: well held afterwards: should stay 1½m: acts on good and to firm going, possibly not on firm. *B. W. Hills*

NIGHT WINK (USA) 7 ch.g. Rahy (USA) 115 – Lady In White 94 (Shareef **–** Dancer (USA) 135) [1998 –: a7g 1999 7g 8s 9g 10d Oct 21] fair at 5 yrs: little form since: tried visored: tongue tied. *Mrs V. C. Ward*

NIGRASINE 5 b.h. Mon Tresor 113 – Early Gales (Precocious 126) [1998 112: **114** 8d⁵ 6s³ 7.9g 7.1g* 6s⁴ 7g 6g⁴ 6m⁵ 6g² 6s 6.1g² 7g 7v³ 1999 a8.5g 8d 6d* 6s 6g* 6m² 6m⁴ 6.1m² 6d⁴ 7g³ 6d 6s⁴ 6d 6s Nov 6] close-coupled horse: fluent mover: smart performer: best efforts when winning minor events at Thirsk (beat Eastern Purple short head) in April and Yarmouth (by 2 lengths from Cretan Gift) in June: ran creditably after runner-up in listed races at Newcastle (behind Halmahera) and Chester (behind Tedburrow): best at 5.6f to 7f: acts on good to firm and heavy going: usually visored/blinkered nowadays: normally races up with pace: game. *J. L. Eyre*

NIKA NESGODA 3 b.f. Suave Dancer (USA) 136 – Highland Ceilidh (IRE) 100 **75** (Scottish Reel 123) [1998 64p: 8d 7d⁶ 1999 10m² 12g* 12d 12m⁴ 16.2m⁵ 16g⁵ 12g Aug 29] tall, lengthy, unfurnished filly: has a round action: fair performer: won maiden at Beverley in April: ran creditably after only on fourth and penultimate starts: stays 1½m, not 2m: acts on good to firm going: looked bit wayward fifth start: sold 9,000 gns in December. *J. L. Dunlop*

NIKITA'S STAR (IRE) 6 ch.g. Soviet Lad (USA) – Sally Chase 101 (Sallust **48** 134) [1998 –, a63: a16.2g⁵ a12g⁴ a14.8g³ a14g⁴ a14.8g⁶ a14g³ 13d a16g³ a16.2g⁴ **a67** a12g³ 14g⁵ a14.8g⁶ a14.8g⁴ a12g* 1999 a16g⁴ a16.2g⁴ a12f⁶ a12g* a12g* a12g² a12g 14.1s² 14.1d 17.1v a14.8g³ a16g² 13g⁶ a12g³ Jun 19] sturdy gelding: unimpressive mover: fair on all-weather, poor on turf: won handicap at Wolverhampton then minor event at Southwell in February: ran well when placed after: effective at 1½m to 2m: acts on firm going, soft and fibresand: tried visored/blinkered (not since 1997): usually races prominently: game. *M. Brittain*

NILOUPHAR 2 b.f. (Apr 8) Pharly (FR) 130 – White African (Carwhite 127) **–** [1999 a5g 5.3f 7m Jun 24] fifth foal: half-sister to 1996 2-y-o 5f winner Bold African and 6-y-o White Emir (both by Emarati) and to 3-y-o Little Henry: dam unraced: well held in maidens/minor event. *W. G. M. Turner*

NIMELLO (USA) 3 b.c. Kingmambo (USA) 125 – Zakota (IRE) (Polish Pre- **96** cedent (USA) 131) [1998 90: 7f* 1999 9m⁵ 8v² 8d Oct 30] smallish, well-made colt: useful performer: best effort (off 14 months before reappearance) when second of 4 to Island House in minor event at Ayr in October, carrying head awkwardly: not well drawn final start: should stay 1¼m: seems to act on any going. *P. F. I. Cole*

NIMINY-PIMINY (IRE) 3 ch.f. Polish Patriot (USA) 128 – Recherchee (Rain- **23** bow Quest (USA) 134) [1998 –: 6m 6s 5d 1999 a7g a12g 6f a8g⁴ Jun 4] bad maiden: blinkered last 3 starts. *M. Johnston*

NINEACRES 8 b.g. Sayf El Arab (USA) 127 – Mayor 86 (Laxton 105) [1998 NR **52** 1999 5m 5s 5.3d 6.1f 5.2s⁴ a6g* a6g a5g² Dec 21] angular, workmanlike gelding: **a65** modest performer: won claimer at Wolverhampton in December: effective at testing

5f to easy 7f: acts on all-weather, possibly needs good ground or softer on turf nowadays: usually blinkered/visored. *J. M. Bradley*

NINETEENNINETYNINE 2 b.c. (Mar 7) Warning 136 – Flower Girl 108 **56** (Pharly (FR) 130) [1999 7d⁵ 7d 8d⁶ Oct 29] 41,000Y: leggy, lightly-made colt: fourth foal: half-brother to 4-y-o Eco Friendly and 5-y-o Water Flower: dam 6f winner: well held in maidens/minor event. *R. W. Armstrong*

NINETY DEGREES 2 ch.g. (Apr 25) Piccolo 121 – Champagne Grandy 84 **75** (Vaigly Great 127) [1999 5d⁵ 5.1m² 5.2m* 5g⁵ Aug 5] 10,500Y, resold 22,000Y: leggy, good-topped gelding: first foal: dam 5f to 7.3f winner: fair form: won maiden at Yarmouth in July: below best in nursery at Haydock final start: likely to prove best at 5f: acts on good to firm going: sent to Hong Kong. *J. Berry*

NISIBIS 3 b.f. In The Wings 128 – Nibabu (FR) 101§ (Nishapour (FR) 125) [1998 – NR 1999 10g a12g a14.8g Dec 11] 7,500 2-y-o: lengthy filly: half-sister to several winners, including smart 7f/1m performer Nijo (by Top Ville) and 1¼m winner Nisaba (by Belmez): dam, mainly disappointing, best at 7f/1m: no show in maidens/ seller: slowly away. *N. A. Callaghan*

NISR 2 b.g. (Apr 28) Grand Lodge (USA) 125 – Tharwa (IRE) 63 (Last Tycoon **82** 131) [1999 6m 5g 6g² Oct 11] 30,000Y: well-made gelding: first foal: dam 5f (at 2 yrs) and 6f winner: easily best effort (fairly useful form) when ¾-length second of 22 to Spencers Wood in maiden at Windsor, leading 2f out: unlikely to stay much beyond 6f. *J. W. Payne*

NITE OWLER 5 b.g. Saddlers' Hall (IRE) 126 – Lorne Lady (Local Suitor (USA) **–** 128) [1998 –, a54: 6g 5s a6g⁶ a6g* 5m a5g a6g⁶ 6g a6g² a6g⁵ 1999 a6g* a6g⁶ **a64** a6g³ a6g a7g* a6g² a7g* a7g a7g Nov 19] sturdy gelding: modest handicapper: won at Southwell in March (selling event) then June and Wolverhampton in July: effective at 6f/7f: acts on fibresand, lightly raced and little form on turf. *J. Balding*

NITWITTY 5 b.g. Nomination 125 – Dawn Ditty 100 (Song 132) [1998 71d: 8.2s **63** 7s³ 7f 6m 5g⁴ 5.7s² 5m 7.1g 5.1m 6s 1999 6.1s 7.1d 7m 6.1g⁴ 6g* 7m 5.7h⁴ 5.7m 6d a6f 7d⁴ Oct 29] modest performer: won 20-runner claiming handicap at Salisbury in July: barely stays 7f: yet to race on heavy going, acts on any other turf (below form only try on fibresand): none too consistent. *R. J. Hodges*

NO ANIMOSITY (IRE) 6 ch.g. Ajraas (USA) 88 – Arctic Ford (FR) 85 (Arctic **–** Tern (USA) [1998 69, a?: 7d⁶ 6.3v 6s³ 7d 7g 9d⁶ 8s² 8v 1999 a6g a7g Feb 15] smallish, strong gelding: useful winner at 2 yrs in Ireland: still capable of fair form in handicaps in 1998 (left D. Hassett after final start): well held both 6-y-o starts: stays 1m: acts on soft and good to firm going: tried blinkered: sold 800 gns. *W. T. Kemp*

NOBALINO 5 ch.h. Sharpo 132 – Zipperti Do 70 (Precocious 126) [1998 81, a72: **73** a5g a6g⁵ a5g a6g² 5.1s⁵ 5g⁵ 5m² 5g⁵ a5g⁴ 5.1g 5.1d 1999 a5g⁶ a5g 7g² 7f 7v 7g **a78** a7g³ a7g³ a7g* a7g³ a7g⁵ Dec 8] small horse: fair handicapper: left A. Newcombe after second start: won at Lingfield in November: stays 7f: acts on all-weather and firm going, probably on soft: effective visored or not. *Mrs V. C. Ward*

NOBBY BARNES 10 b.g. Nordance (USA) – Loving Doll 72 (Godswalk (USA) **43** 130) [1998 49, a38: a8s⁶ a8g⁵ a8g⁶ a7g³ a8g a8g 9.2v² 8s³ 8.3d³ 9.3s 8.3d 8.5d⁶ 7.5g **a–** 9.2d* 9.2g⁶ 9.2m⁶ 9m⁴ 8.9g⁶ 9.2d³ 8.3s⁶ 10.4g 9.1v³ 8v⁶ 8v³ 1999 8.5m 7d⁴ 8.3m 8.5d⁶ 8g⁴ 9.2g⁴ 8d 8m⁵ 8.5g³ 8.3f 8.9m 9.1v Oct 12] neat gelding: has a round action: poor performer: stays 1¼m: acts on any turf/all-weather: tends to get behind and find trouble, and suited by strong pace. *Don Enrico Incisa*

NOBLE CALLING (FR) 2 b.c. (Feb 20) Caller I D (USA) – Specificity (USA) **62** 103 (Alleged (USA) 138) [1999 7m 8.1m⁶ 8d 8s Nov 6] 550,000 francs Y: angular colt: fourth foal: half-brother to a winner in USA by Sky Classic: dam, suited by test of stamina, half-sister to St Leger winner Touching Wood: modest maiden: best efforts on first 2 starts: will stay at least 1¼m. *N. A. Graham*

NOBLE CHARGER (IRE) 4 ch.g. Cadeaux Genereux 131 – Shawgatny (USA) **–** 83 (Danzig Connection (USA)) [1998 –: 8d 1999 8.2s 5g⁵ 7m a6g 6.1f 6f 6m a5g Jul 24] big gelding: little form: blinkered/visored last 2 starts: has flashed tail. *R. F. Marvin*

NOBLE CYRANO 4 ch.g. Generous (IRE) 139 – Miss Bergerac (Bold Lad (IRE) **68** 133) [1998 68: 8m³ 10g 1999 7.5v⁵ 8.3m 8.1d* 7.9m 10m a8g² Dec 13] leggy, angular gelding: fair handicapper: won at Haydock in August: reportedly finished lame penultimate start: stays 1m: acts on good to firm going, good to soft and fibresand. *G. Woodward*

NOBLE FALCON   3 gr.g. Polar Falcon (USA) 126 – Noble Haven 74 (Indian   –
King (USA) 128) [1998 NR 1999 10f Oct 20] fifth foal: half-brother to 3 winners, including useful French 1993 2-y-o 5f winner Shoalhaven and 5f winner Sky Red (both by Night Shift): dam, 2-y-o 6f winner, half-sister to useful sprinter Night At Sea: behind in maiden at Nottingham: sold 800 gns. *J. W. Hills*

NOBLELY (USA)   12 b.g. Lyphard (USA) 132 – Nonoalca (FR) 120 (Nonoalco   **64**
(USA) 131) [1998 NR 1999 7.7s² 10.5s* a8.5g 10m Jul 17] modest handicapper, lightly raced on Flat: won apprentice race at Warwick in June: probably best around 1¼m: acts on good to firm ground, soft and equitrack (well beaten on fibresand): tried visored: fairly useful hurdler. *M. Tate*

NOBLE ONE   3 ch.f. Primo Dominie 121 – Noble Destiny 89 (Dancing Brave   **107**
(USA) 140) [1998 92p: 5g* 1999 5m* 6g⁶ 6d 6s Nov 6] lengthy filly: useful performer: won minor event at Newmarket in July by neck from Flanders, rallying when headed briefly: best effort in listed races after when 4 lengths eleventh of 20 to Gaelic Storm on same course third start, finding little room: should stay 6f: acts on good to firm going: has been blanketed for stalls entry. *Sir Mark Prescott*

NOBLE PASAO (IRE)   2 b.g. (Mar 26) Alzao (USA) 117 – Belle Passe (Be My   **68**
Guest (USA) 126) [1999 5d 5m 5m 6g 8d* 7.9d Oct 7] IR 30,000Y: tall, rangy gelding: has a round action: sixth foal: half-brother to 3-y-o Belleme and smart Irish 6f to 1m performer Burden of Proof (both by Fairy King) and Italian winner up to 1¼m Revenger (by Persian Heights): dam ran once: fair performer: best effort when winning nursery at Musselburgh in September: acts on good to soft ground: blinkered third start. *Andrew Turnell*

NOBLE PATRIOT   4 b.g. Polish Patriot (USA) 128 – Noble Form (Double Form   **44**
130) [1998 44: 6.1s 8m 5g³ 7g 5s a5s a6g a6g³ 1999 a5g a5g⁴ a7g⁵ a6g a7g² a7g a6g a6g a9.4g 6f³ 6m 6f⁴ 5m 6g 8s a7g² a8.5g a7g³ Dec 11] tall gelding: poor maiden handicapper: stays 7f: acts on firm going and fibresand: blinkered once. *R. Hollinshead*

NOBLE PURSUIT   2 b.c. (Feb 22) Pursuit of Love 124 – Noble Peregrine   **85 p**
(Lomond (USA) 128) [1999 7m⁴ 7g* 7g² Aug 30] 18,000F, 10,000Y, 52,000 2-y-o: third foal: half-brother to useful French 1m/9f performer Nobelist (by Bering), 7.5f winner at 2 yrs, and 3-y-o Cockatrice: dam Italian 1¼m winner, from family of Armiger: fairly useful form: won maiden at Salisbury in August: good neck second of 8 to Queens Bench in nursery at Epsom final start: will stay at least 1m: open to further improvement. *T. G. Mills*

NOBLE REEF   2 b.c. (Mar 19) Deploy 131 – Penny Mint 79 (Mummy's Game   **65**
120) [1999 a5g 5g⁴ 5m 7m³ 7g⁶ 7g 7g⁶ 8d Nov 1] 10,000F, 15,000Y: smallish, good-bodied colt: fourth foal: half-brother to 4-y-o Ron's Pet and 6-y-o Present Generation: dam 2-y-o 6f winner: fair maiden: had excuses last 3 starts: will stay 1m: acts on good to firm going. *Mrs G. S. Rees*

NOBLE SPLENDOUR   2 ch.c. (Feb 17) Grand Lodge (USA) 125 – Haskeir   **72**
(Final Straw 127) [1999 6m 6d 7m³ 6s⁵ 7s Oct 23] 12,000F: tall, good-topped colt: has scope: sixth foal: half-brother to 1¼m winner Salanka (by Persian Heights): dam unraced daughter of half-sister to St Leger winner Athens Wood: fair maiden: favourite, only eighth of 13 to Avezzano in nursery at Doncaster final start: will be suited by 1m+: best effort on good to firm ground. *L. M. Cumani*

NOBLE WATER (FR)   4 b.f. Noblequest (FR) 124 – Bulle d'Eau (FR) (Faraway   –
Son (USA) 130) [1998 31: 7g 8m 9d 7m* 6m² 7g 9f³ 9f⁶ 7m⁵ 5g 8.2s 7s a7g a8g   **a46**
1999 a6f³ a7g a6g* a7g⁵ 5m 6g 6m 5g⁶ 6m Jul 9] poor handicapper: well held after winning at Lingfield in February: seems best at 6f/7f: acts on equitrack: sold 2,000 gns. *J. J. Bridger*

NOBODY'S FOOL   4 ch.g. St Ninian 104 – Majestic Form (IRE) (Double   –
Schwartz 128) [1998 NR 1999 a12g Jul 9] first foal: dam of little account: well held in seller at Wolverhampton. *M. G. Meagher*

NOCCIOLA   3 ch.f. Cadeaux Genereux 131 – Norpella 95 (Northfields (USA))   –
[1998 NR 1999 5d May 8] 70,000Y: lengthy, rather unfurnished filly: sixth foal:

sister to useful 5f (at 2 yrs) to 1m winner Ultimo Imperatore and half-sister to several winners, including 5-y-o Sugarfoot: dam, 1¼m and 1½m winner who stayed 14.8f, from good family: carrying plenty of condition and uneasy in stalls, outpaced in maiden at Beverley. *Sir Mark Prescott*

NOCKSKY (IRE) 6 b.g. Niniski (USA) 125 – Olivana (GER) (Sparkler 130) **63**
[1998 NR 1999 18.7m 20m Jun 15] half-brother to several winners abroad: fair handicapper: won at Listowel final start in 1997 for L. Browne in Ireland: much better effort in 1999 when eighth to High And Mighty in Ascot Stakes second start, running on well despite meeting trouble: probably needs 2m+: acts on firm and soft ground: useful jumper. *M. C. Pipe*

NO CLICHES 6 ch.g. Risk Me (FR) 127 – Always On A Sunday 101 (Star **–**
Appeal 133) [1998 68: 10.3d* 10s⁵ 11.9d⁶ 13.8d 11.9s⁶ 10g³ 9.9d³ 10.3g² 10g³ 9.9m³ 9d⁴ 9.9m⁶ 1999 8g 12m May 24] lengthy, workmanlike gelding: fair handicapper: well held both starts in 1999: probably best at 1m to 1¼m: acts on good to firm and good to soft ground: effective blinkered/visored or not: sometimes reluctant. *N. Tinkler*

NO COMMITMENT (IRE) 2 b.g. (Feb 21) Brief Truce (USA) 126 – Pleasant **–**
Memories 63 (Danehill (USA) 126) [1999 7g 7d 6s a8g a8g a10g Dec 11] 6,500Y: first foal: dam, 1m winner, half-sister to Belmont Stakes runner-up My Memoirs: little sign of ability, including in seller. *H. J. Collingridge*

NOCTURNE (IRE) 4 b.f. Tenby 125 – Phylella (Persian Bold 123) [1998 61: 8g **30**
8f⁴ 10m⁵ 9.9d⁴ 9g⁴ 12g⁴ 16.4m⁴ a16g⁵ a13g² a12g² a12g³ 1999 a11g⁴ Jan 4] modest maiden in 1998: well below best only 4-y-o outing: stays 13f: acts on all-weather. *S. E. Kettlewell*

NOD'S NEPHEW 2 b.g. (Apr 8) Efisio 120 – Nordan Raider 81 (Domynsky 110) **–**
[1999 6g 6d Oct 20] first foal: dam, 6f winner, half-sister to useful 7f/1m performer Hi Nod: signs of ability in maidens at Ripon and Newcastle: may do better in long term. *Miss J. A. Camacho*

NO EXTRAS (IRE) 9 b.g. Efisio 120 – Parkland Rose (Sweet Candy (VEN)) **83**
[1998 101: 7s 8d⁴ 8m 7m³ 7g* 7.6m⁴ 8d 6g 7m 7d 8m² 7g 1999 7g 7g 7m 8g⁴ 8.1m² 8.3d* 8m 7m 8d 9g⁵ 9g⁶ 8s 10d⁴ 10d Oct 29] quite good-topped gelding: fairly useful nowadays: won 6-runner minor event at Windsor in June: stays 9f: acts on soft and good to firm going: tried blinkered/visored: held up. *G. L. Moore*

NO FOOL (IRE) 3 b.f. Distinctly North (USA) 115 – Chez Nous (Habitat 134) **–**
[1998 NR 1999 8.1m 8f 8m Jul 21] IR 4,100Y, resold IR 1,000Y: sister to fairly useful 1997 2-y-o 5f winner Mislead: dam, lightly raced in France, from good family: soundly beaten in sellers. *J. S. Moore*

NOIRIE 5 br.g. Warning 136 – Callipoli (USA) 81 (Green Dancer (USA) 132) **40**
[1998 37: 8d 10s* 8d⁴ 8g 10g⁶ 12m 1999 12.3m 10v 10v⁴ 12.4m 10m 10g 9.9s³ 10v 10.1d Oct 20] sparely-made gelding: poor handicapper: stays 1¼m, not 2m: form only on good going or softer: blinkered/visored once each: has won for apprentice: inconsistent. *M. Brittain*

NO MERCY 3 ch.c. Faustus (USA) 118 – Nashville Blues (IRE) 94 (Try My Best **76**
(USA) 130) [1998 70: 7.1m 7.9g⁴ 8v⁴ 1999 a10g* 9.9m⁴ 8.1m³ 8f³ 8.5g³ 8.5g⁴ Aug 30] quite attractive colt: fair performer: won 4-runner handicap at Lingfield in April: ran at least respectably after: will prove best up to 1¼m: acts on any turf going and equitrack: tongue tied final start: edgy penultimate outing. *J. W. Hills*

NOM FRANCAIS 3 b.f. First Trump 118 – Eastern Ember 85 (Indian King **39 §**
(USA) 128) [1998 –: 5s⁶ 7s 7d 1999 9.7v 9.9d 16m² 17.2f 16.2m 12m² 15.8m³ 14.1g Aug 29] small filly: poor maiden: seems to stay 2m: acts on good to firm going: blinkered last 3 starts: difficult ride, and probably ungenuine. *R. Guest*

NOMINATOR LAD 5 b.g. Nomination 125 – Ankara's Princess (USA) 81 **89**
(Ankara (USA) 106) [1998 85: 8g 7g⁶ a8.5g* 6.9d a8.5g⁴ 8g⁴ 8.1g⁵ 7.6d² 8s* 7g 7s 8s⁶ 1999 8d 8m 8v* 10m 8.1g² 7.9f 7.9g 8d 10s Oct 2] sturdy gelding: poor mover: fairly useful handicapper: won at Pontefract in April: best effort after when good second at Haydock in May: stays 8.5f: has won on good to firm going, but best form on good or softer: usually held up. *B. A. McMahon*

NOM

NO MORE HASSLE (IRE) 6 ch.g. Magical Wonder (USA) 125 – Friendly –
Ann (Artaius (USA) 129) [1998 NR 1999 15.8s Oct 5] big gelding: fairly useful
hurdler/chaser: only poor handicapper on Flat: stays 17.2f: acts on any going.
Mrs M. Reveley

NOMORE MR NICEGUY 5 b.h. Rambo Dancer (CAN) 107 – Lariston Gale 97
81 (Pas de Seul 133) [1998 97, a104: a8.5g² 8d 6v⁶ 6d⁵ 7.6m⁴ 6g 7m³ 7g* 6.1g² 7v⁴ a104
7f 7m 6.1g³ 7m 7g 6s 7g⁴ 7g 7g³ a7g* a8f* 1999 a6g⁵ a8.5g³ 8d⁴ 8d 7.6m 8m² 7d⁴
7.1m 6.1m* 7.1d³ 7m² 7m⁶ 7m 7d⁶ 7.6d⁵ 7d² 7d 8g Oct 16] big, good-bodied horse:
useful performer: won handicap at Chester in June: ran respectably most starts after,
including when neck second to Trans Island in valuable handicap at Leopardstown
on sixteenth one: effective from 6f to easy 8.5f: acts on any turf/all-weather: ran
poorly in blinkers: possibly needs strong handling: tough. *E. J. Alston*

NON VINTAGE (IRE) 8 ch.g. Shy Groom (USA) – Great Alexandra (Runnett –
125) [1998 –: 16.2m 12m⁶ 1999 18g May 18] lengthy gelding: poor at best on Flat
nowadays. *M. C. Chapman*

NOOSHMAN (USA) 2 ch.g. (Apr 10) Woodman (USA) 126 – Knoosh (USA) 81
113 (Storm Bird (CAN) 134) [1999 7g² 7d⁵ 7.1v² Oct 25] seventh foal: closely
related to useful 1¼m/1½m winner in Britain/UAE Rocky Oasis and 3-y-o All Our
Hope (both by Gulch): dam 7f (at 2 yrs) to 1½m (Galtres Stakes) winner: fairly useful
form in maidens: short-head second of 9 to Cavalier at Haydock final start: tends to
race freely, but should stay at least 1m. *Sir Michael Stoute*

NOPALEA 5 b.m. Warrshan (USA) 117 – Nophe (USA) 95 (Super Concorde 56 d
(USA) 128) [1998 –: 6d 5m 5.1m 1999 5s⁴ 5s⁵ 5m 5.3g 5.3f 6g Aug 24] lengthy,
good-quartered mare: modest handicapper: on the downgrade: effective at 5f/6f: acts
on firm and soft going: blinkered penultimate start. *T. J. Naughton*

NO PASS NO HONOR (FR) 2 b.c. (Mar 5) Highest Honor (FR) 124 – Marzi- –
pan (IRE) 74 (Green Desert (USA) 127) [1999 7m 7v Oct 25] 600,000 francs Y: tall
colt: first foal: dam, maiden who should have stayed beyond 1¼m, half-sister to
smart 7f to 9f performer Anshan: well held in maidens at Ascot and Lingfield. *S. Dow*

NORCROFT JOY 4 b.f. Rock Hopper 124 – Greenhills Joy 90 (Radetzky 123) 82 §
[1998 77: 8.2s 12d² 14.1d* 14.1g² 12d⁵ 12.1s* 12m* 11.9m* 12.1s 11.8d⁵ 1999
12.5s* 13v 14.1s 12.1g 12g* 12g⁵ 11.9d⁴ 12g³ 12m⁶ 13.3m 11.6g⁵ 12s⁶ Nov 6] workmanlike filly: fairly useful handicapper: won at Warwick in March and Doncaster in
June: left M. Ryan after tenth start: stays 1¾m: acts on soft and good to firm going:
often held up: sometimes looks a difficult ride and finds little. *N. A. Callaghan*

NORDANSK 10 ch.g. Nordance (USA) – Free On Board 73 (Free State 125) [1998 –
NR 1999 11.6m May 24] workmanlike gelding: modest handicapper up to 1¾m in
1997: well held only start since. *M. Madgwick*

NORDIC STAR 3 b.g. Cosmonaut – Could Have Been (Nomination 125) [1998 –
NR 1999 7s 7.1d 8m Jul 15] 5,600Y, 20,000 2-y-o: heavy-topped gelding: first foal:
dam unraced half-sister to Prix du Jockey Club winner Polytain: tailed-off last in
maidens: has refused to enter stalls: has worn net muzzle. *J. J. Quinn*

NORDINEX (IRE) 7 b.g. Nordico (USA) – Debbie's Next (USA) 82 (Arctic 37
Tern (USA) 126) [1998 42: 8m 8.1d 10.8d⁴ 8.3d 8d a7g a7g a10g 1999 7.7m⁶ 10.5m
10d Oct 21] well-made gelding: poor handicapper: stays 1m: acts on good to firm
going, good to soft and equitrack: blinkered/visored once each. *P. Hayward*

NO REGRETS 2 b.c. (Apr 25) Bin Ajwaad (IRE) 119 – Marton Maid 74 (Silly 57
Season 127) [1999 6.1d 8.2m³ 8.5m⁴ 10.2s⁶ 8.2d a8g Nov 11] 7,000F, IR 13,500Y:
half-brother to several winners, including 4-y-o Mansa Musa and 6f (at 2 yrs) to 1½m
winner Mr Devious (by Superpower): dam inconsistent maiden: modest maiden:
should stay beyond 1m: acts on good to firm going. *M. Quinn*

NO RESERVE (USA) 3 b.f. Gone West (USA) – Milly Ha Ha 106 (Dancing 68
Brave (USA) 140) [1998 63p: 8d 1999 10m⁵ 10.2d 11.6m Jun 28] smallish, quite
attractive filly: fair maiden: ran poorly final start: stays 1¼m: acts on good to firm
going: sent to New Zealand. *H. R. A. Cecil*

NORFOLK REED (IRE) 2 b.g. (Mar 13) Thatching 131 – Sawaki 71 (Song 132) 86 +
[1999 5m* 6d 6m² 6m Aug 28] 9,000F, 13,000Y, resold 5,600Y: leggy, close-coupled

730

gelding: fifth foal: half-brother to 4-y-o Discretion: dam best at 7f: fairly useful performer: won minor event at Lingfield in May: best effort when ¾-length second of 11 in nursery at Kempton: should stay 7f. *R. Hannon*

NORLING (IRE) 9 ch.g. Nashamaa 113 – Now Then (Sandford Lad 133) [1998 –: 6d 6m 1999 5.9g 5.9m 6m Jun 29] sturdy gelding: no longer of much account. *J. S. Wainwright* —

NORTH ARDAR 9 b.g. Ardar 87 – Langwaite (Seaepic (USA) 100) [1998 –, a55: a9.4g⁵ a10g* a10g⁴ a12g* a12g⁶ a12g⁶ 1999 a7g a8f a12g⁵ a12g⁵ a8.5g⁶ a11g³ 11.6m³ a11g* a11g² a13g³ 10.5m 8.2s a8g a10g a11g² a12g⁴ a12g⁶ Dec 27] close-coupled, angular gelding: modest performer: won seller at Southwell in June: effective at 11f to 13f: acts on all-weather, best turf form on good going or firmer: visored once: held up. *R. Brotherton* **52**

NORTHERN ACCORD 5 b.g. Akarad (FR) 130 – Sioux City (Simply Great (FR) 122) [1998 52: 12.3g 8.3d* 12.1d⁴ 10.9d 9.9m* 10s⁴ 1999 14.1s Mar 29] modest handicapper: well beaten only run of 1999: probably stays 1½m: acts on good to firm and good to soft going. *M. Dods* —

NORTHERN CHARMER 7 br.g. Charmer 123 – Trading 74 (Forlorn River 124) [1998 NR 1999 a16g Jan 4] poor maiden: sold 1,200 gns. *E. J. Alston* —

NORTHERN ECHO 2 b.g. (Jan 26) Pursuit of Love 124 – Stop Press (USA) 93 (Sharpen Up 127) [1999 5.9m Jun 23] 7,000F, IR 7,000Y: second foal: half-brother to 9.4f winner Hever Golf Machine (by Rudimentary): dam, 1¼m winner, also successful at 1m and 11.5f in France at 4 yrs: behind in maiden at Carlisle. *M. Dods* —

NORTHERN FLEET 6 b.g. Slip Anchor 136 – Kamkova (USA) 62 (Northern Dancer) [1998 NR 1999 16.2m⁵ 14.1m* 14d 14.4m Sep 8] quite good-topped gelding: fair handicapper: won at Salisbury in July: below form after: best at 1¾m+: acts on good to firm going: blinkered once: made running in 1999. *Mrs A. J. Perrett* **76**

NORTHERN LAW 7 gr.g. Law Society (USA) 130 – Pharland (FR) (Bellypha 130) [1998 NR 1999 14g 15.8m Jul 10] tall gelding: one-time fair winner: no form in 1999. *J. G. Smyth-Osbourne* —

NORTHERN LIFE (IRE) 2 b.f. (Mar 10) Distinctly North (USA) 115 – Another Way 68 (Wolverlife 115) [1999 7.6g 7s 7d Oct 21] IR 10,000Y, 9,500Y: half-sister to several winners, including listed winners in Scandinavia and Germany by Red Sunset: dam sprint maiden: well beaten in maidens. *P. Shakespeare* —

NORTHERN LORD 3 ch.g. Northern Park (USA) 107 – Miss Trilli 89 (Ardoon 124) [1998 NR 1999 8m 8m 7g 11.5g 10g Sep 20] big, workmanlike gelding: half-brother to several winners: dam won over 5f: little sign of ability. *R. J. R. Williams* —

NORTHERN MOTTO 6 b.g. Mtoto 134 – Soulful (FR) (Zino 127) [1998 64, a48: a12g³ a12g a14g 16s* 16d³ 16g⁵ 16d* 16m* 15.9m* 16.2g 15s² 16m 17.5s 1999 16g⁴ 13v 16m⁵ 18g³ 16m* 15.9m* 16.2m 15m⁴ 16m² 16f⁴ 16d⁴ 16g Nov 3] leggy gelding: modest handicapper: won at Musselburgh in June and Chester in July: ran respectably most other starts: needs further than 13f and stays 2½m: acts on fibresand, soft and good to firm ground: usually held up. *J. S. Goldie* **64 a–**

NORTHERN SPRING (IRE) 3 ch.c. Common Grounds 118 – North Telstar 104 (Sallust 134) [1998 82: 6g⁵ 5.7g² 1999 6d² 7g² 7d* 8.1d² 8m 8f 7m⁴ 8f² Nov 14] quite good-topped colt: useful performer: won maiden at Redcar in May: ran creditably in handicaps after, seventh in Britannia at Royal Ascot fifth outing: trained by M. Heaton-Ellis until after penultimate start: beaten a head in allowance race at Aqueduct on US debut: stays 1m: acts on firm and good to soft going: tends to sweat/get on edge: free-going sort: game and consistent. *M. Hennig, USA* **96**

NORTHERN SUN 5 b.g. Charmer 123 – Princess Dancer (Alzao (USA) 117) [1998 83?, a–: a10g⁶ 10v 10m² 12m 9.9d⁶ a12g a10g 1999 a13g⁵ 8.5s³ 10g² 8f 10f³ a12g Nov 13] small, close-coupled gelding: fair performer: left T. Mills 1,200 gns and off over 5 months before final start: probably stays 1½m: acts on firm and soft going, possibly not on all-weather: has drifted under pressure: none too consistent. *W. G. M. Turner* **76 a–**

NORTHERN SVENGALI (IRE) 3 b.g. Distinctly North (USA) 115 – Trilby's **84**
Dream (IRE) (Mansooj 118) [1998 81+: 5d 5g² 5s 5m² 5d² 5f² 5f² 6m² 6g 6m* 5g
5d* a5g⁵ a6g³ a5g⁵ a6g³ 1999 5d 6v⁴ 6g⁴ 6m⁴ May 29] small, sturdy gelding: fairly
useful performer: best effort when fourth to Mitcham in valuable handicap at Newmarket third start: will prove best at 5f/6f: acts on any turf/all-weather: usually races
up with pace. *T. D. Barron*

NORTHERN TIMES (USA) 2 ch.g. (Feb 6) Cahill Road (USA) – Northern **–**
Nation (USA) (Northrop (USA)) [1999 6d May 16] second foal: dam winning
sprinter in USA: well held in maiden at Ripon. *T. D. Easterby*

NORTHERN TRIO (FR) 2 b.g. (Feb 4) Aragon 118 – Northern Notion (USA) **–**
(Northern Baby (CAN) 127) [1999 6.1g 6d 6s Nov 5] 105,000 francs F, 5,000Y,
7,500 2-y-o: workmanlike gelding: half-brother to 2 winners abroad, including
Italian winner up to 1½m Fingertip (by Alhijaz): dam French maiden: well held in
maidens. *D. Carroll*

NORTHERN VILLAGE 12 ch.g. Norwick (USA) 125 – Merokette 83 (Blast **–**
125) [1998 NR 1999 a16g a16f 22.2m Jun 18] winning jumper: very lightly raced on
Flat and no form. *L. A. Dace*

NORTH FACE 2 ch.g. (Mar 15) Factual (USA) 108 – Northgate Dancer 57 (Ile **64**
de Bourbon (USA) 133) [1999 5.9g³ 6f Aug 4] 2,000Y, 2,200 2-y-o: leggy gelding:
fourth foal: dam 1½m winner: modest form in minor event at Carlisle and maiden at
Newcastle: should stay 1m. *J. J. O'Neill*

NORTHGATE (IRE) 3 b.c. Thatching 131 – Tender Time (Tender King 123) **55 §**
[1998 –: 6m 6g⁶ 7f 7g 1999 8v 8f⁴ 7m⁴ 8m 9m 8m⁴ 7.1m⁵ 7.1f² 7g 7d Oct 22] leggy
colt: modest maiden handicapper: should stay beyond 1m: acts on firm going: usually
blinkered: often races prominently: unreliable. *M. Brittain*

NORTH OF KALA (IRE) 6 b.g. Distinctly North (USA) 115 – Hi Kala (Kam- **36**
pala 120) [1998 42: 12v 16v 13s 13d 15.4m⁶ 1999 a16g a16g⁵ a11g 11.9s Sep 29]
poor performer: seems to stay 2m: acts on good to firm going and equitrack:
blinkered penultimate start: won over hurdles in November. *G. L. Moore*

NORTHWING 3 b.g. Minshaanshu Amad (USA) 91§ – Kicking Bird (Bold Owl **–**
101) [1998 –: 6m 8s 1999 10m 10.2s 14.1s Nov 1] no sign of ability: left E. Wheeler
before final start. *G. B. Balding*

NORTON (IRE) 2 ch.c. (Feb 19) Barathea (IRE) 127 – Primrose Valley 99 (Mill **87 p**
Reef (USA) 141) [1999 7d⁵ 8d 7d* Nov 1] IR 350,000Y: smallish, useful-looking
colt: half-brother to several winners, including 3-y-o Turtle Valley, useful French 1m/
1¼m performer Veiled Threat (by Be My Guest) and leading 1991 Italian 2-y-o
Prime Glade (by Green Forest): dam, 1½m winner, later successful in USA: confirmed debut promise when winning 15-runner maiden at Redcar by 2 lengths from
Wathbat Mujtahid, off bridle at halfway before running on strongly to lead entering
final 1f: will stay at least 1¼m: appears a slow learner, and should do better still at 3
yrs. *T. G. Mills*

NOSEY NATIVE 6 b.g. Cyrano de Bergerac 120 – Native Flair 87 (Be My **44**
Native (USA) 122) [1998 55, a47: a11g⁴ a10g⁵ a12g⁶ a13g³ a13g⁶ 10.3d 10v 10.5m⁵
12.3s* 11.1m⁵ 16.5g² 12m* 14.1f⁵ a14g⁶ a14g⁵ 1999 a16g⁵ a13g³ 7.5v 12.3m 12m
Jul 10] leggy gelding: poor handicapper: usually runs in amateur/lady races: effective
at 1½m to 2m: acts on all-weather and probably any turf going: tried visored: tends to
get behind. *J. Pearce*

NO SHOES NO NEWS (IRE) 4 br.g. Be My Native (USA) 122 – Buffs **–**
Express 68 (Bay Express 132) [1998 –: 8g 12g 14.1g 1999 a12g* a12g³ 14.1f May **a48**
31] workmanlike gelding: poor performer: won maiden at Southwell in January:
should stay beyond 1½m: acts on fibresand, no show on turf. *M. A. Buckley*

NOTAGAINTHEN 3 b.f. Then Again 126 – Fairy Ballerina (Fairy King (USA)) **–**
[1998 58?: 5.7d⁵ 6m⁴ 8v 1999 6m 8g a9.4g⁶ 12.1m Jul 9] seemingly modest maiden
at best: well held in 1999. *S. G. Knight*

NOTATION (IRE) 5 b.g. Arazi (USA) 135 – Grace Note (FR) 99 (Top Ville 129) **31**
[1998 37, a57d: a16s⁴ a16g⁴ a16g³ a16g² a16g² a14.8g 16s 16d a14g⁴ a14g⁶ 16d³ 18s
a14g a14g 1999 a16g a12f 11d a14g⁴ a16g 16d 16m a16.2g Sep 8] quite good-topped
gelding: poor performer nowadays: stays 2m well: acts on fibresand and good to soft
ground: tried blinkered: usually gets well behind. *D. W. Chapman*

NOTEWORTHY   3 br.f. Saddlers' Hall (IRE) 126 – Rushing River (USA) (Irish **68**
River (FR) 131) [1998 –: 8.2s 1999 10g⁶ 12.1g⁴ 14.1m³ 17.2m⁴ 14g⁵ Aug 14] leggy
filly: fair maiden: below form last 2 starts: stays 1¾m: acts on good to firm going:
sold 1,200 gns. *J. Noseda*

NOT FORGOTTEN (USA)   5 b.g. St Jovite (USA) 135 – Past Remembered   **–**
(USA) (Solford (USA) 127) [1998 –: a16g 21.6s 11.9g 1999 11.9d Oct 4] smallish
gelding: disappointing staying maiden on Flat: often blinkered/visored: winning
hurdler. *R. P. C. Hoad*

NOTHING DAUNTED   2 ch.c. (Apr 13) Selkirk (USA) 129 – Khubza 86   **98 p**
(Green Desert (USA) 127) [1999 5g⁶ 7.1d² 7g* 8m³ 6s² Oct 2] 60,000F, 120,000Y:
quite attractive colt: fluent mover: third foal: brother to 4-y-o Trans Island and half-
brother to 3-y-o Bread Winner: dam, lightly-raced 7f winner out of smart 6f/7f
winner Breadcrumb, herself half-sister to College Chapel: progressive form: won
maiden at Goodwood in August: improved efforts in nurseries at Doncaster and
Newmarket (second of 16 to CD Flyer) after, in latter caught near finish: stays 1m:
acts on soft and good to firm going: type to do better still and win more races at 3 yrs.
E. A. L. Dunlop

NOTHING DOING (IRE)   10 b.g. Sarab 123 – Spoons (Orchestra 118) [1998   **44 §**
NR 1999 a13g a13g a16g 12.1m³ 11.1s May 14] poor handicapper: stays 2m: acts on   **a– §**
any turf/all-weather: tried blinkered: temperamental. *W. J. Musson*

NOTIONAL (IRE)   3 b.f. Lucky Guest 109 – Sportin' Notion (USA) (Sportin'   **65 d**
Life (USA)) [1998 69p: 7.5d⁵ 1999 9d⁴ 7d⁶ 10m² 9g⁴ 11f² 9g³ 9m³ 10m a8.5g a10g
Dec 29] IR 1,000Y: second foal: half-sister to 1¼m and 11.5f winner Coalminers-
daughter (by Dynaformer): dam, placed in USA, out of half-sister to Cacoethes: fair
maiden: runner-up at Naas and Kilbeggan: left L. Browne in Ireland, before well held
last 2 starts: stays 11f: acts on firm and good to soft going: tried blinkered and tongue
tied. *P. D. Evans*

NOUF   3 b.f. Efisio 120 – Miss Witch 59 (High Line 125) [1998 NR 1999 7d* 7g   **96**
8d⁴ Oct 12] 5,000Y, 12,000 2-y-o: leggy filly: unimpressive mover: third foal: half-
sister to 1m seller winner Circle of Magic (by Midyan): dam, middle-distance
maiden, sister to very smart French 7.5f to 10.5f winner Metal Precieux: won maiden
at Doncaster in March by 10 lengths: failed to confirm that form in Nell Gwyn Stakes
at Newmarket following month and minor event at Leicester. *K. Mahdi*

NOUFARI (FR)   8 b.g. Kahyasi 130 – Noufiyla 68 (Top Ville 129) [1998 75, a87:   **82**
a16s* a16.2g² a16g* a14.8g* 18d a14.8g* a14.8g* 16.2m³ 16g² 18s 14.6g⁵ 16m³   **a87**
16.1g* 15.9g 16.1m² 18g 16.5d a14.8s² a14.8g* 1999 a16.2g² a16.2g⁴ a16.2g⁴
a14.8g³ 16.2d⁶ a14.8g² 16.2d a16.2g³ 16g* 15.9d² 16m* 16d⁵ 14.1g 14.6d a14.8g*
a14.8g* Dec 11] quite good-topped gelding: bad walker: fairly useful performer:
won handicaps at Nottingham and Thirsk then claimer and seller (by 12 lengths) at
Wolverhampton between August and December: finds 1¾m a bare minimum, and
stays 2½m: acts on fibresand, firm and good to soft going: not an easy ride and sometimes gets behind/hangs (usually ridden by P. Quinn): tough. *R. Hollinshead*

NOUKARI (IRE)   6 b.g. Darshaan 133 – Noufiyla 68 (Top Ville 129) [1998   **87**
70: 12m² 12s a12g² a12g² a12g* a14g³ a14.8s a12g⁶ a13g* a16g⁵ 1999 a13g*
a12g² a12f² a12g⁵ a12g⁵ a12s³ a12g⁴ a12g⁴ a12g³ a12g³ a12g⁵ 12g² a14.8g⁴
12.3m³ 12s⁵ 12m² 11.6m² 11.5m³ 12g 10.3m* 10.3m 12g⁴ 10.3m² 11.9f² 10m*
12.3m⁶ 9.9m³ 12g* 12g* 11.8m⁴ 10.5m⁵ 10.9d a12g* a14g³ a12g* a12g*
a12g* a12g⁴ Dec 29]
    In racing, as in life in general, the back-room boys and girls seldom get
the recognition they deserve, so, with that in mind, we take time here to pay
tribute to one of the relatively unsung heroes of the latest Flat season, Noukari.
    He might not have run in a pattern race, much less have the ability to
win one, but it could reasonably be argued that no horse did more to keep the
racing show on the road in 1999 than Noukari. Thirty-eight runs between
January 7th and December 29th inclusive yielded nine victories, four handicaps
and a minor event on the all-weather at Lingfield, a claimer at Chester, handicaps at Newmarket and Catterick and a minor contest at Pontefract. Not one of

Pontefract Apprentice Series (Round 4) Classified Stakes—
twenty-ninth race of the year for the indomitable Noukari,
who snatches the verdict on the line from Macca Luna (far side)

these wins could fairly have been described as representing a simple task for
Noukari, yet for good measure the horse also ran five times over hurdles,
winning twice. At times, it seemed as if he was running each and every day, and
on one occasion in January he did indeed turn out at Lingfield then twenty-four
hours later at Wolverhampton. He was, however, spared the fate that faced one
of his stable-companions, Amington Girl, who ran (unsuccessfully) in both the
7 o'clock and the 9 o'clock races at Wolverhampton on May 22nd! If Noukari
has a serious rival for the title of the toughest horse around then it is surely in
the shape of another of his stable-mates, Italian Symphony, who also ran in the
colours of Noukari's owner. Italian Symphony chalked up a remarkable forty-
one runs on the Flat during the year, though in his case they resulted in 'just'
seven victories. Then again, Italian Symphony wasn't tried over jumps and ran
at shorter trips than did Noukari, resulting in a good deal less mileage on the
clock. On the Flat alone, Noukari covered the equivalent of more than two
human marathons during the year! His last three wins, all in handicaps at
Lingfield, saw him at his best and demonstrated his battling qualities to the
full, notably when accounting for another all-weather success story in Virgin
Soldier by a head for the penultimate one. It's possible that even Noukari can
be taken to the well too often, as he ran a lacklustre race on his final start, at
Lingfield again. On the other hand, after a break of more than three weeks,
perhaps it was just a case of him being a bit rusty!

A horse of Noukari's toughness is essentially a product of his trainer's
unique approach. However, Noukari's dam, Noufiyla, who is part of the Aga
Khan's breeding operation, had already bred another horse in a similar mould
before Noukari, her fourth living foal. The two-years-older Noufari (by
Kahyasi) was having the eighty-sixth race of his career when winning at
Wolverhampton in December. Noukari will, in all probability, continue to be

seen frequently on the track well into the next millennium. Effective at a mile and a quarter to a mile and three quarters (he pulled too hard at two miles) and on any all-weather or turf going (with the exception of heavy, on which he's yet to race on the level), he should add to his excellent record. *P. D. Evans*

NOUSHKEY 3 b.f. Polish Precedent (USA) 131 – Top of The League 85 **118** (High Top 131) [1998 80p: 7d* 1999 11.5g³ 12d² 11.9s* 11.9g 14.6m⁶ Sep 11]

Noushkey was dogged by the shadow of Ramruma in the latest season but on the one occasion in five outings that she managed to avoid her, Noushkey took full advantage to win the Payne And Gunter Lancashire Oaks at Haydock. The poor showings of Katiykha and Ramruma's stable-companion Samoa did devalue to some extent what had looked a good renewal of the race. Yet, even if they'd given their running, it's doubtful they would have coped with Noushkey, who couldn't have been more impressive in dealing with some other useful fillies. Sent on turning for home, Noushkey began to draw clear over three furlongs out and ran on very strongly to increase her advantage. She was ridden out to the line, passing it eight lengths ahead of her nearest pursuer, the subsequent Park Hill Stakes winner Mistle Song. The St Leger rather than the Park Hill was the race for Noushkey at Doncaster in September, and at that stage of her career her credentials were such that she was prominent in the ante-post betting on the event. The step up to a mile and three quarters was unlikely to be a problem, and she was a lightly-raced filly who was progressing very well. A winner of a maiden at Newmarket on her only outing at two years, Noushkey shaped well when third to Ramruma in the Oaks Trial at Lingfield on her reappearance and then went on to finish second to that filly in the Oaks itself. Noushkey was beaten three lengths at Epsom, trying hard to close on the winner from halfway up the straight but always playing second fiddle, nevertheless pulling five lengths clear of third-placed Zahrat Dubai. Following Noushkey's Haydock victory there seemed a chance that she could make a closer race of it with Ramruma when they met again in the Yorkshire Oaks, but the encounter proved an anti-climax, Noushkey trailing in eighth behind Ramruma, apparently having broken a small blood vessel. Allowed to take her chance in the St Leger, Noushkey again ran poorly, never threatening to take a hand as Ramruma fought a losing battle up front with Mutafaweq.

Noushkey was well bought as a yearling for 55,000 guineas, at a time when her half-brother San Sebastian (by Niniski) had still to show his worth. By the time Noushkey made her debut, smart stayer San Sebastian had stormed home in the Ascot Stakes, and he returned to Royal Ascot in the latest season to win the Queen Alexandra Stakes. Their dam Top of The League had made an impact at stud before this pair saw the racecourse, her winners including San

Payne And Gunter Lancashire Oaks, Haydock—Noushkey confirms the form of her second in the Oaks, turning the Lancashire version into a one-horse race; Mistle Song (striped cap) and String Quartet are left toiling

Sheikh Ahmed Al Maktoum's "Noushkey"

Noushkey (b.f. 1996)	Polish Precedent (USA) (b 1986)	Danzig (b 1977)	Northern Dancer Pas de Nom
		Past Example (ch 1976)	Buckpasser Bold Example
	Top of The League (br 1982)	High Top (br 1969)	Derring-Do Camenae
		Home And Away (ch 1977)	Home Guard Garden of Eden

Sebastian's sister Chesa Plana, one of the leading three-year-old fillies in Germany in 1992. In the same year Top of The League produced the useful staying hurdler Metastasio (by Petoski), while her second foal, the filly Fariba (by Chief Singer), was named champion older horse in Holland. Top of The League herself won over seven furlongs as a two-year-old and showed her best form over a mile and a quarter at three. Her dam Home And Away was an unraced half-sister to Galaxy Libra, just useful in Britain but high-class in North America, and the Prix du Conseil de Paris winner Garden of Heaven. Noushkey, a rangy, unfurnished filly, raced on ground firmer than good only in the St Leger, and she acts well on soft. *M. A. Jarvis*

NOUVEAU CHEVAL   4 b.f. Picea 99 – Freeracer (Free State 125) [1998 61: a7g 8.2s 8g* a9.4g³ 9.9m⁵ 1999 12.3m² 12.3m* 12.1m³ Jul 23] leggy filly: fair performer: made all in 4-runner minor event at Chester in July: ran well both other starts in 1999: stays 1½m: acts on good to firm going. *M. C. Pipe*   **72**

NOVADREAM   2 b.f. (May 6) Aragon 118 – Please Please Me (IRE) 45 (Tender King 123) [1999 7m 6m 7.6g Aug 25] second live foal: dam poor winning hurdler: no sign of ability. *J. J. Bridger*   **–**

NOVELLINI GOLD   2 ch.g. (Mar 15) Mystiko (USA) 124 – Glittering World (USA) (Diesis 133) [1999 7f Jul 22] second foal: dam French 1¼m winner: no promise in maiden at Brighton. *N. M. Babbage*   **–**

NOVELTY   4 b.f. Primo Dominie 121 – Nophe (USA) 95 (Super Concorde (USA)   –
128) [1998 –: 7.5g 8d 1999 8d 8.5g Aug 11] little sign of ability. *M. Brittain*

NOWELL HOUSE   3 ch.g. Polar Falcon (USA) 126 – Langtry Lady 91 (Pas de   **81**
Seul 133) [1998 64: 5g 5d³ 5g³ 7f 6g 8d 8d 1999 6m 5g⁴ 5m 7g³ 12g* 9.9s² 12s*
10g* Oct 14] smallish, lengthy gelding: fairly useful handicapper: much improved
upped in trip, winning at Beverley in September then Pontefract (apprentice race)
and Redcar (despite tending to hang) in October: stays 1½m well: acts on soft going,
some promise on good to firm: held up: may do better still. *M. W. Easterby*

NOWHERE TO EXIT   3 b.c. Exit To Nowhere (USA) 122 – Tromond 94   **120**
(Lomond (USA) 128) [1998 87p: 7m 8.5m² 8s* 1999 10.5s* 12d* 12v* 12s² 14g⁵
Aug 28] leggy, quite attractive colt: very smart performer: successful in April/May in
rated stakes at Haydock, listed race at Chantilly and Prix La Force (made most to
beat First Magnitude 2 lengths) at Longchamp: best effort when 4 lengths second to
Montjeu in Prix du Jockey Club at Chantilly in June, headed around 2f out and
keeping on well: last in listed race at Goodwood (reportedly returned with cuts on
hind legs) when next seen out: stays 1½m well: best form on ground softer than good:
joined Godolphin. *J. L. Dunlop*

NOW IS THE HOUR   3 ch.g. Timeless Times (USA) 99 – Macs Maharanee 85   –
(Indian King (USA) 128) [1998 40: a5g 5g 5.1m⁴ 6s 5m⁶ 7d 1999 a6g⁴ 6g 5g 6g 6m
8f⁶ 8m Aug 4] small gelding: poor maiden at best. *P. S. Felgate*

NOW LOOK HERE   3 b.c. Reprimand 122 – Where's Carol 67 (Anfield 117)   **96**
[1998 76: 6s⁶ 5.1v³ 6d⁴ 1999 7.1s* 7m 6m⁴ 7d³ 6m 6f 6d³ 6d 7d³ 6d³ Oct 29] tall,
leggy colt: useful performer: won maiden at Haydock in April: ran creditably most
starts after, third to Pipalong in Great St Wilfrid Handicap at Ripon on seventh: may
prove best at 6f/7f: acts on soft and good to firm going. *B. A. McMahon*

Mr & Mrs Gary Pinchen's "Nowhere To Exit"

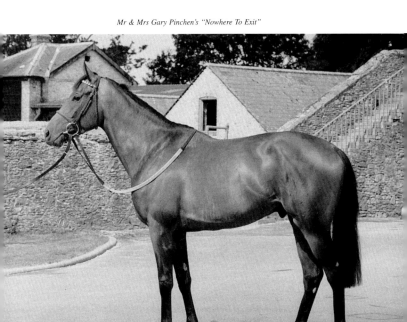

NOWT FLASH (IRE) 2 ch.c. (Apr 4) Petardia 113 – Mantlepiece (IRE) (Common **53**
Grounds 118) [1999 5m⁶ 5m a6g a5f⁶ 7g a5g² Dec 21] IR 4,700Y: compact colt:
third foal: half-brother to 3-y-o Weetrain: dam no worthwhile form: modest maiden:
blinkered third start. *B. S. Rothwell*

NOYAN 9 ch.g. Northern Baby (CAN) 127 – Istiska (FR) (Irish River (FR) 131) **–**
[1998 NR 1999 16m May 22] big, rangy gelding: better known as a staying chaser
nowadays. *K. A. Ryan*

NOZOMI (IRE) 3 b.f. Mujadil (USA) 119 – Crimbourne 83 (Mummy's Pet 125) **–**
[1998 69+: 6m 5g⁶ a6g* 6v a7g⁵ 1999 7d 6d 10.2g Jun 30] fair performer: well held
in handicaps in 1999: blinkered penultimate start. *P. J. Makin*

NUBILE 5 b.m. Pursuit of Love 124 – Trojan Lady (USA) (Irish River (FR) 131) **36**
[1998 –, a24: a16s⁵ a16g⁵ a16g⁴ 11.6g 1999 a14g 14.1s 14.1s a14g 13d a12g*
a14.8g⁶ a12g Nov 19] poor handicapper: won at Southwell in July: appears to stay
2m: acts on firm going and all-weather: blinkered fifth to seventh starts: inconsistent.
W. J. Musson

NUCLEAR DEBATE (USA) 4 b.g. Geiger Counter (USA) – I'm An Issue **116**
(USA) (Cox's Ridge (USA)) [1998 105: 6s³ 6m² 6g* 6f⁵ 5s⁴ 6g 6m 5.6g² 5s⁴ 1999
5.5d² 5m 5g* 6g⁴ 5s* 6g³ 5.2d³ 5g* 5v² 5m Dec 12] big, strong gelding: smart
performer: better than ever in 1999, winning listed races at Maisons-Laffitte in June
and Deauville in August and Premio Omenoni at Milan (by 3¾ lengths from Late
Parade) in October: ran well most other times, ½-length third to Vision of Night in
Prix de Meautry at Deauville on sixth outing and ¾-length second to Manzor in Prix
du Petit Couvert at Longchamp (not clearest of runs) penultimate one: effective at 5f/
6f: best on good ground or softer (acts on heavy): held up. *J. E. Hammond, France*

NUCLEAR FREEZE (USA) 3 b.c. Danzig (USA) – Razyana (USA) 87 (His **95 p**
Majesty (USA)) [1998 NR 1999 8m³ 8f* 8m⁴ Sep 10] well-made, attractive colt:
brother to 4 winners, notably Danehill and US Grade 2 9f winner Eagle Eyed, and
half-brother to smart French/US performer up to 1m Euphonic (by The Minstrel):
dam, placed over 7f and 1¼m from 3 starts, out of half-sister to Northern Dancer:
improved to win maiden at Thirsk in July by 2½ lengths from Palm Tree: not
discredited when 8 lengths fourth of 5 to Swallow Flight in minor event at Doncaster,
seeming to lose action in latter stages: will prove as effective at 6f/7f as 1m: may well
do better yet. *H. R. A. Cecil*

NUIT D'OR (IRE) 4 ch.g. Night Shift (USA) – Sister Golden Hair (IRE) (Glint **–**
of Gold 128) [1998 60: a6s⁶ a8.5g⁴ a8g² a8.5g* a8.5g a7g⁵ 1999 a8.5g a12g
a9.4g a9.4g a8.5g Feb 24] small gelding: modest at best: no form in 1999 (trained by
W. G. M. Turner on reappearance): tried blinkered: sold 900 gns. *M. Waring*

NUIT SAINT 3 b.f. College Chapel 122 – Nuit Blanche (Night Shift (USA)) **68**
[1998 72: 8d 7s² 7s⁵ 5s 6v 6v 1999 6d 6.5d⁵ 9d⁴ 8.5g³ 6.5g² 6.5s⁴ 8m 10m⁵ 8.5s 7g⁶
8s Oct 16] first foal: dam, ran once in Ireland at 2 yrs, from family of Doyoun: fair
maiden: below form in Ayr handicap seventh start: effective at 6.5f to 8.5f: acts on
soft ground: blinkered (below form) third start. *T. Hogan, Ireland*

NULLI SECUNDUS 3 b.c. Polar Falcon (USA) 126 – Exclusive Virtue (USA) **69**
94 (Shadeed (USA) 135) [1998 60p: 7s⁶ 1999 8.1m⁴ a8.5g⁵ 8s Sep 29] rather
unfurnished colt: fair maiden: should stay beyond 1m: acts on good to firm going,
showed promise first try on soft: tongue tied penultimate start: sold 2,000 gns, sent to
Germany. *J. A. R. Toller*

NUMERATOR 3 ch.f. Rudimentary (USA) 118 – Half A Dozen (USA) 57 (Sara- **72**
toga Six (USA)) [1998 76p: 8v³ 1999 a9.4g* 10g 7s⁶ 8m* 8d⁶ Jul 1] rangy filly: fairly **a82**
useful on all-weather, fair on turf: made all in maiden at Wolverhampton in May and
claimer at Newmarket in June: stays easy 9.4f: acts on good to firm going, heavy and
fibresand: sold 21,000 gns, sent to Saudi Arabia. *W. J. Haggas*

NUNTHORPE 4 ch.f. Mystiko (USA) 124 – Enchanting Melody 71 (Chief **–**
Singer 131) [1998 79d: 7d 8.5m* 8g 8.5d⁵ 8m 8.5m⁶ 8d 1999 7.5d 6.1f Jun 21] big,
workmanlike filly: fair handicapper at best: better around 1m than shorter: acts on
good to firm going. *G. Woodward*

NUTCHAT 3 ch.g. Beveled (USA) – Shapina 105 (Sharp Edge 123) [1998 60?: **52**
5m⁶ 7s 6.1g 7.1d⁴ 8m 1999 8g 8g 8m⁴ 8.1m Jul 9] modest maiden: stayed 1m: acted
on good to firm going: inconsistent: dead. *R. G. Frost*

NUTMEG (IRE)   2 ch.f. (Mar 9) Lake Coniston (IRE) 131 – Overdue Reaction   **70 +**
(Be My Guest (USA) 126) [1999 5m 7m 6g 7d 7g⁴ 6d⁵ Oct 28] 41,000F, IR 26,000Y:
half-sister to several winners, including Atlantic Mist (around 11.5f, by Elmaamul)
and 3-y-o Divorce Action: dam lightly-raced half-sister to smart Irish 1½m performer Token Gesture: fair maiden: best effort over 7f. *M. H. Tompkins*

NUTS IN MAY (USA)   2 b.f. (Feb 24) A P Indy (USA) 131 – Regal State (USA)   **63**
122 (Affirmed (USA)) [1999 6g 6.1m² 6.1d Oct 5] useful-looking filly: sixth
reported foal: half-sister to useful 6f and 6.5f winner Hurricane State (by
Miswaki): dam won Prix Morny and later stayed 1m: form in maidens only when
second of 12 to Aljawf at Nottingham: possibly unsuited by ground when last of 15
there final start: should stay 1m. *J. L. Dunlop*

NUTTY STAN (IRE)   5 ch.g. Shahrastani (USA) 135 – Coconut Grove (What A   **–**
Guest 119) [1998 NR 1999 a11g Jun 17] half-brother to a winner in Sweden: dam
French 1m winner: fair maiden for P. Flynn in Ireland at 2 and 3 yrs: no show only
outing since: stays 9f: acts on good to firm ground. *Miss M. E. Rowland*

O

OAKBURY (IRE)   7 ch.g. Common Grounds 118 – Doon Belle (Ardoon 124)   **–**
[1998 45: 12d³ 12.1d 16d 1999 17.2m Jun 23] sparely-made gelding: winning
hurdler: poor maiden on Flat: tried blinkered. *Miss L. C. Siddall*

OAKWELL ACE   3 b.f. Clantime 101 – Fardella (ITY) (Molvedo 137) [1998 NR   **57 d**
1999 8m 6s* 8m 8g 8.5s 6s 7d 10d 8.2s³ a7g Nov 19] eighth foal: half-sister to 1¼m
winner Melancolia (by Legend of France): dam French 11f winner: modest performer: won claimer at Warwick in June: effective at 6f (given a test) to 1m: acts on soft
going: visored surly start: inconsistent. *J. A. Glover*

OARE KITE   4 b.f. Batshoof 122 – Portvasco 90 (Sharpo 132) [1998 68: 8.2s 6g   **56**
6.1m 7m 6s⁵ 6.9d 5m³ 5m² 6g 8d² 7d* a8g 1999 6f 7f⁶ 7g 8g⁵ 6g 7f² 7f⁶ 7.1m⁴ 7m*   **a44**
8f⁴ 7g a7f 7d³ 8s⁶ a7g⁶ Dec 8] close-coupled filly: modest on turf, poor on all-
weather: won 11-runner seller at Leicester in August: ran creditably after when in
frame: effective at 7f/1m: acts on firm and good to soft ground: wears visor/blinkers:
has carried head awkwardly under pressure. *G. L. Moore*

OARE LINNET   3 ch.f. Polish Precedent (USA) 131 – Portvasco 90 (Sharpo 132)   **58**
[1998 –: 7d 1999 6m 6g 8.2m 6.1m Jul 3] modest maiden: easily best effort on
reappearance: bred to prove best up to 1m: sold 1,000 gns. *P. T. Walwyn*

OARE PINTAIL   2 b.f. (Feb 8) Distant Relative 128 – Oare Sparrow 75 (Night   **60**
Shift (USA)) [1999 7.7d⁶ 7g 7g⁶ 7.3v Oct 23] smallish, sturdy filly: first foal: dam 6f/
7f winner: modest maiden: seemed not to stay final start. *P. T. Walwyn*

OATH (IRE)   3 b.c. Fairy King (USA) – Sheer Audacity (Troy 137) [1998   **125**
89p: 6m⁵ 7g³ 8.2s* 1999 10m² 10.3m* 12g* 12m Jul 24]
Nothing recedes like success. By the end of the season, Oath's Derby
victory was already a fading memory for some, injury having deprived him of
the opportunity to cement his newly-found reputation after a clear-cut victory
at Epsom. Oath damaged a knee when a well-beaten favourite on his only
subsequent start, in the King George VI and Queen Elizabeth Stakes, and his
name is not one that will resonate in the same way as those of Daylami and
Montjeu, or those of some other Derby winners of the 'nineties such as
Generous and Lammtarra. More's the pity. Oath progressed really well as a
three-year-old up to Epsom and there seemed every likelihood at the time that
he would go on improving. His sale to Japan for a reported eight million dollars
(around £5m) continued a sad trend—from a British point of view—among
Derby winners, and, indeed, among potential sires of middle-distance horses
generally. Both Generous and Lammtarra, by some way the two best horses to
win the Derby in the 'nineties, have joined the exodus to Japan in recent years,
Generous leaving behind four crops, Lammtarra only one. The three Derby

Vodafone Derby Stakes, Epsom—All The Way leads round Tattenham Corner,
followed by Salford Express with Daliapour on the outside of Val Royal coming next;
eventual winner Oath (striped sleeves) is in fifth

winners between Generous and Lammtarra—Dr Devious, Commander In Chief and Erhaab—were all exported directly to Japan (though Dr Devious has since been returned to stand in Ireland and Erhaab will be covering in the US in 2000). The chief executive of the National Stud struck a note of realism when asked about the export of Oath. 'You only have to look at our experience with Shaamit [1996 Derby winner] to see why Oath has gone abroad,' he said. 'Shaamit has been available at between £7,500 and £5,000 for a nomination during his time with us and we haven't exactly been knocked over in the rush. People do not favour middle-distance sires.' Shaamit, now based at Scarvagh House Stud in County Down, Northern Ireland, at a fee of £5,000 (1st October), has his first runners in 2000.

If it was ever true that the history of the breed was inextricably linked to the history of the Derby, it is certainly not so now. Tesio's famous quote that 'The thoroughbred is what it is because of the piece of wood that marks the finish of the Derby' belongs firmly to an age when the Derby was universally regarded as the greatest race in the world. The international all-aged events are the benchmark now, rather than the domestic classic races. When Andre Fabre created controversy in the latest season with some comments about the Derby—including 'It is too hard a race for three-year-olds . . . it lives on its reputation'—he was at least right about one thing. His claim that 'the Derby hasn't produced a decent stallion in years' could perhaps have been put more delicately, but discounting Generous—whose export is a blow—so far only Nashwan among the Derby winners of the past twenty years has gone on to figure as a sire in Europe. One of the Derby runners to have had most 'influence on the breed' in recent times was Linamix, an above-average winner of the Poule d'Essai des Poulains who seemed not to stay the trip at Epsom, managing only ninth in Quest For Fame's year. It was while greeting the smart Slickly, a son of Linamix, after his win in the Prix Noailles, at Longchamp in April, that Fabre made his much publicised remarks. Slickly went on to become one of two Fabre-trained runners in the Prix du Jockey Club, a race the trainer said he would always rather win than the Epsom version. Fabre won the Prix du Jockey Club with Peintre Celebre in 1997 but has yet to come close to winning the

740

Derby. The unbeaten Val Royal, supplemented for Epsom at the £8,000 second entry stage in the spring but reportedly inferior at home to Fabre's Prix du Jockey Club pair, became his seventh Derby runner. He was one of two overseas-trained challengers for the latest edition, the other being the Irish Two Thousand Guineas winner Saffron Walden, saddled by Aidan O'Brien.

Eighteen were declared for the Derby at the forty-eight hour stage— runners and riders for all Group 1 races in Britain will be known two days beforehand in the next season—but two of them, Tchaikovsky (on standby for Saffron Walden) and Rhagaas, ran instead next day in the Prix du Jockey Club, their trainers incurring fines of £5,000. The Derby, with total prize money of a million pounds for the third year running, brought together a representative collection of Britain's leading middle-distance three-year-olds at that stage. It is often said that the Two Thousand Guineas is the best trial for the Derby but none of the first three in the latest edition was entered at Epsom, which contributed to a wide-open betting market on the Derby. The only two Guineas runners to go on to Epsom, incidentally, fourth-placed Brancaster and Compton Admiral, started at 20/1 and 25/1 respectively. The Guineas also saw the winter favourite for the Derby, Racing Post Trophy winner Commander Collins, finish well down the field. He was displaced at the head of the Derby betting by an expensively-bought Godolphin recruit from North America, Adair, whose claims on the form-book rested on an easy win in a maiden at Belmont Park on his only start. Adair did make the Derby line-up, but, in the end, he wasn't Godolphin's number-one. That mantle fell on the Predominate Stakes winner Dubai Millennium, who was sent off 5/1 favourite. Among the other leading contenders were: the first and second in the Lingfield Derby Trial, Lucido (supplemented afterwards for the Derby at a cost of £75,000) and Daliapour; the winner of the Dante Stakes, Salford Express; and the disqualified winner of the Chester Vase, Housemaster. Also near the head of the betting were Beat All (7/1) and Oath (13/2), both of whom had won less important races, the Newmarket Stakes and the Dee Stakes respectively, in good style. The very promising Beat All's Derby preparation didn't go so smoothly as it might because of a bruised foot.

Oath's emergence as a Derby candidate seemed to take even those closest to him by surprise. His name was not mentioned among twenty-one three-year-olds in a two-page feature (covering fifty horses in all) in the *Racing Post* in mid-April when Henry Cecil discussed his stable's prospects for 1999. Warren Place's winter hopes for the colts' classics had been centred on such as Ballet Master, Enrique and, in the same ownership as Oath, Killer Instinct. Cecil also mentioned Yaralino as one 'to keep an eye on' with the Derby in mind and said he hoped unraced Adelphi 'might be our Commander In Chief' (Adelphi subsequently cracked a cannon bone). Oath had had three outings as a two-year-old—the first of them for Roger Charlton—and a victory in a Nottingham maiden on his final start marked him down as the type to make a useful three-year-old at least. Oath held the Derby engagement but, frankly, looked unlikely to live up to such aspirations after his second in a Newbury conditions stakes on his reappearance in mid-April. He had the run of a falsely-run affair, quickening three furlongs out and keeping on strongly, but was caught close home by Lucido who had to be extricated from a pocket with a furlong or so left to go. Lucido had been taken out of the Derby at the forfeit stage in early-March because connections felt he wasn't good enough. Oath's connections must have felt glad they hadn't taken a similar course of action when Oath ran out an impressive winner of the Dee Stakes at Chester next time. The Dee Stakes winner rarely enters seriously into classic calculations nowadays—the 1990 winner Blue Stag was the last to go on to reach a place in the Derby—but Oath, available generally at 16/1 for Epsom the next day, certainly did enough to justify a crack at the big race. Coming on a lot from his reappearance (as did several of his stable-companions in the latest season), Oath put up as good a performance as has been seen in the Dee Stakes for a long time, soon drawing clear after taking it up inside the two-furlong marker and romping home by five lengths and three from hitherto-unbeaten Little Rock and the Sandown Classic Trial fourth Bombard. Oath continued to thrive, his trainer reporting in Derby week that 'he looks terrific at the moment and is getting stronger all the time . . . he has improved since Chester.' Oath's jockey Kieren Fallon was asked whether he thought the protracted Derby preliminaries, involving a parade and a long canter down, would affect his mount. 'It's a big occasion, some horses can spoil their chances in the Derby before they start . . . but Oath will thrive on it.' The effects of the Derby parade on the runners are usually much exaggerated, but Cecil took the precaution—wisely as things turned out—of telling Fallon to leave the parade prematurely if Oath showed signs of getting above himself. When Oath, who had two handlers, began to sweat and become edgy, Fallon broke from the parade, for which he was later fined £1,000. Oath calmed down at the start, though he was a little mulish entering the stalls, where Saffron Walden gave most trouble.

The lack of an obviously outstanding contender suggested that the field for the last Derby of the nineteen hundreds was probably little better than average. In fairness, the same had been said in the years of Generous and Lammtarra, whose true merit few had suspected beforehand, but this time the preconceptions turned out to be accurate. As usual, a few of the runners had to contend with interference (most of it in the early stages), among them Compton Admiral, Brancaster and Adair, but there were no real hard-luck stories. Oath had raced as if he would be suited by the Derby trip and was ridden like a proven stayer, handy from the start and perfectly placed when the pace quickened on the run down to Tattenham Corner. Daliapour, who also got a copybook Derby ride, was the first to tackle the front-running outsider All The Way in the home straight, taking over two furlongs out and keeping on gamely. Fallon was forced to check Oath for a stride or two at Tattenham Corner, when nudged by the under-pressure Val Royal, but once the field straightened for home Oath was soon in pursuit of Daliapour and stayed on strongly after catching him a furlong out. Oath won by a length and three quarters from

Vodafone Derby Stakes, Epsom—
Oath provides Henry Cecil and Kieren Fallon with their third British classic of the season;
Daliapour battles on gamely in second whilst Beat All (spotted cap) runs on to pip Housemaster for third

Daliapour, both horses drifting left with the camber of the track in the closing stages. Beat All, nothing like so well placed as the first two early on, stayed on for third, a further length and a half behind, with Housemaster a short head back in fourth and All The Way a creditable fifth. Dubai Millennium was a major disappointment, pulling hard before meeting some trouble.

Andre Fabre's Derby remarks, perhaps fuelled partly by the fate of his Two Thousand Guineas winner Pennekamp, who sustained a hairline fracture when a disappointing favourite in 1995, included views about the high physical demands placed on Derby runners, partly because of the unusual conformation of the track. These were echoed by nine-times Derby winning jockey Lester Piggott before the race. 'What Fabre said was absolutely right . . . every year horses run in the Derby that are never heard of again. An immature horse can be finished off for good.' Thankfully, the aftermath of the latest Derby provided little to fuel the controversy further. Lucido returned with a stress fracture and was off the course for four months but all the Derby runners were seen out at least once more. The best horse in the Derby field turned out to be Dubai Millennium who, reverting to ten furlongs and then a mile, won all three of his subsequent races, including the Prix Jacques le Marois and the Queen Elizabeth II Stakes. Daliapour went on to finish second to Prix du Jockey Club winner Montjeu in the Irish Derby, Adair and All The Way were in the frame in the St Leger, Compton Admiral won the Coral-Eclipse and Val Royal won two Group/Grade 2 races. Injury contributed to curtailed campaigns for at least five of the Derby runners, but Epsom couldn't be blamed directly for any of them. Oath and Daliapour (gashed heel) were both side-lined after the King George VI and Queen Elizabeth Stakes at Ascot; Saffron Walden finished lame in the Meld Stakes at the Curragh and wasn't seen out after running poorly next time in the International at York; Compton Admiral reportedly fractured a bone in his off-fore knee in the International; and Glamis, third in the Great Voltigeur, fractured a cannon bone afterwards while being prepared for the St Leger. Epsom may have its detractors but it is as well to remember that injury is an occupational hazard for the thoroughbred, with risks attached to running on the fairest of tracks, as well as to taking exercise at home.

Oath's trainer Henry Cecil has achieved nearly all there is to achieve in the sport and Oath's victory made him the most successful trainer of the century in the domestic classic races. Cecil has saddled the winners of all five classics at least twice, his total of twenty-two including the Derby with Slip Anchor and Reference Point in the 'eighties, and Commander in Chief and now Oath in the 'nineties. He also won the One Thousand Guineas with Wince and the Oaks with Ramruma in the latest season, when all three Warren Place classic winners were ridden by Kieren Fallon. Cecil and Fallon were the first trainer/jockey team to complete the Epsom classic double since Cecil shared the feat with Steve Cauthen in 1985, when Reference Point and Oh So Sharp completed the double. The partnership between Cecil and Fallon was ended abruptly in Goodwood week, however, amid the whiff of scandal, after stories about the private life of Cecil's wife were splashed across the national Press. Richard Quinn will be the number-one jockey at Warren Place in the next season, while Fallon is set to team up with Sir Michael Stoute.

The smallish, strong, close-coupled Oath, a well-balanced, nimble individual who handled the Epsom course very well, again showed a tendency to become excited when lining up for the King George VI and Queen Elizabeth Stakes. Fallon once more allowed Oath to leave the parade early, the stewards fining him £1,250 for acting 'without sufficient reason.' Oath, incidentally, never looked better than before the King George, really impressing with his well-being despite being on his toes; unfortunately, he wasn't able to show what he was capable of, dropping out quickly in the home straight after moving well for a long way, eventually bringing up the rear with Daliapour. The initial prognosis was that Oath would need eight weeks on the easy list to recover from his knee injury, but, as the season wore on, it became increasingly apparent that he was unlikely to be seen out again as a three-year-old. The Japanese stepped in and Oath's sale was confirmed in late-October. He is to stand at Yushun Farm, alongside Commander In Chief, who is making an impact at stud.

Oath (IRE) (b.c. 1996)	Fairy King (USA) (b 1982)	Northern Dancer (b 1961)	Nearctic
			Natalma
		Fairy Bridge (b 1975)	Bold Reason
			Special
	Sheer Audacity (b 1984)	Troy (b 1976)	Petingo
			La Milo
		Miss Upward (b 1964)	Alcide
			Aiming High

Before Oath's Derby victory, his now-deceased sire Fairy King had had only one major winner over a mile and a half, the Arc victor Helissio. He was also represented by Ribblesdale winner Fairy Queen in the latest season. Though a full brother to Sadler's Wells, once-raced Fairy King took more after his three-parts brother Nureyev as a sire. Like Nureyev, for whom top-class mile and a half winners such as Peintre Celebre and Theatrical were the exception, Fairy King became known for endowing his progeny with speed rather than stamina. The average distance of races won by the offspring of Fairy King is less than a mile and the distaff side of Oath's pedigree is the most likely source of his stamina. His dam Sheer Audacity, placed twice in Italy, was bred to stay, being by Derby winner Troy out of the fair racemare Miss Upward, who stayed at least a mile and a half. Sheer Audacity is closely related to Miss Petard (by Troy's sire Petingo out of Miss Upward) who won a Ribblesdale; Miss

The Thoroughbred Corporation's "Oath"

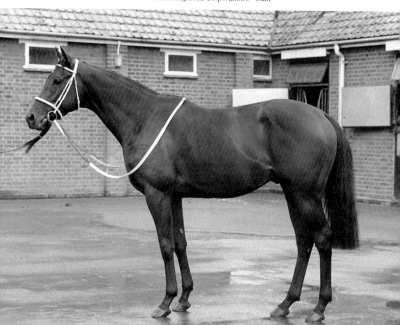

Petard has produced a Park Hill winner in Rejuvenate and the dam of a Park Hill winner (Casey) in the fair sprinter Kiss. Oath is the second classic winner out of Sheer Audacity, who is also the dam of Premio Parioli winner Pelder (by Be My Guest). Pelder went on to win the Prix Ganay as a five-year-old; he never ran beyond the Ganay distance of ten and a half furlongs but was in training that season for the Arc when an old leg injury flared up. Another of Sheer Audacity's winning offspring is Sheer Danzig (by Roi Danzig), a smart performer who won at up to a mile and three quarters, and she is also responsible for the Lupe Stakes winner Napoleon's Sister (by Alzao), who was also placed in listed company at a mile and three quarters. *H. R. A. Cecil*

OBSERVATORY (USA) 2 ch.c. (Feb 17) Distant View (USA) 126 – Stellaria **97 p** (USA) 98 (Roberto (USA) 131) [1999 6g* 6m⁴ 6m* Oct 19] well-made, attractive colt: fifth foal: half-brother to several winners, including fairly useful 1998 2-y-o 5.7f winner En Garde (by Irish River) and useful 9f/1¼m winner Ninette (by Alleged): dam 5f (at 2 yrs) to 8.5f (in USA) winner: useful form: won maiden in June and minor event in October, both at Yarmouth, latter by ¾ length from Final Row: far from discredited when last of 4 to Primo Valentino in Mill Reef Stakes at Newbury in between: will stay 7f/1m: should improve further and win more races at 3 yrs. *J. H. M. Gosden*

OCCAM (IRE) 5 ch.g. Sharp Victor (USA) 114 – Monterana 99 (Sallust 134) **–** [1998 NR 1999 10.5m 10v⁵ a9.4g Dec 15] leggy gelding: fluent mover: fair maiden for G. Wragg at 3 yrs: no show in 1999: should stay at least 1¼m: well beaten on ground softer than good. *L. J. Barratt*

OCEAN DRIVE (IRE) 3 b. or br.g. Dolphin Street (FR) 125 – Blonde Goddess **69 d** (IRE) (Godswalk (USA) 130) [1998 69?: 7d³ 7s⁶ 8v⁴ 1999 8g 7d⁶ 9d 10.9m⁵ 10f 13.1g³ 12.1m⁴ 12.1m* 12.3d⁴ 14.1m⁵ 12m⁴ 13m⁶ 12.1f 10.9d 10g³ 10.1d Oct 20] fair handicapper: won 6-runner apprentice race at Hamilton in June: largely well below form afterwards: may prove best at 1¼m/1½m: acts on good to firm going, probably on good to soft: often held up. *Miss L. A. Perratt*

OCEAN LINE (IRE) 4 b.g. Kefaah (USA) 124 – Tropic Sea (IRE) (Sure Blade **51** (USA) 130) [1998 51: a8g 9.3d 10g 10g⁴ 8.5m⁵ 8.9g 1999 10s 11.9f 14.6s a7g⁴ 10m⁵ 10.5m² 10.5m⁵ 11.6m* 10f⁴ 10m* 8f³ 8m Sep 16] leggy, angular gelding: modest performer: left K. Bell after second start: won selling handicap at Windsor in July and claimer at Brighton in August: finds 1m on sharp side and stays 11.6f: acts on firm going. *G. M. McCourt*

OCEAN OF STORMS (IRE) 4 b. or br.c. Arazi (USA) 135 – Moon Cactus 118 **112** (Kris 135) [1998 110: 13m* 12g* 15g² 15s* 15d² 1999 8g 7d⁶ 9d 10.9m⁵ Oct 20] half-brother to Oaks winner Moonshell (by Sadler's Wells): dam, 7f (at 2 yrs) and 1¼m winner, second in Prix de Diane: smart performer: trained by A. Fabre in France at 3 yrs, winning listed race at Chantilly: better effort in 1999 when good 2 lengths third to stable-companion Opera King in valuable handicap at Goodwood: stays 15f: winner on good to firm and soft ground. *Saeed bin Suroor*

OCEAN PARK 8 b.g. Dominion 123 – Chiming Melody 71 (Cure The Blues **72** (USA)) [1998 65, a–: 10g 8m 9.7f² 10m 10.8m* 11.9s⁵ 1999 11.9f⁴ 11.5f* 11.5f² Jul **a–** 31] good-bodied gelding: good mover: fair handicapper: won at Lingfield in June: ran well only subsequent start: stays 1½m: acts on all-weather and probably any turf going: blinkered once as 3-y-o: best held up. *Lady Herries*

OCEAN PRINCE (FR) 3 b.g. Dolphin Street (FR) 125 – Dumayla 78 (Sher- **59 ?** nazar 131) [1998 59: 8s⁶ 8m 1999 7s 11.6g 10.5s³ May 29] modest maiden: probably stays 1¼m and acts on soft going: blinkered final start: joined D. Bridgwater. *W. R. Muir*

OCEAN RAIN (IRE) 2 ch.c. (Mar 8) Lake Coniston (IRE) 131 – Alicedale (USA) **77** (Trempolino (USA) 135) [1999 5.7m 6m² 6d⁴ 7g 7s⁵ Oct 23] 22,000F, 16,000Y: sturdy colt: first foal: dam, placed at 1m/9f in France, from family of 1000 Guineas winner Las Meninas: fair performer: won maiden at Haydock in August on final start for M. Heaton-Ellis: creditable efforts in nurseries at York and Doncaster after: should stay 1m: acts on soft and good to firm ground. *C. G. Cox*

OCEANS FRIENDLY (USA) 3 br.f. Green Dancer (USA) 132 – Sedra 116   **89**
(Nebbiolo 125) [1998 77p: 8g⁴ 8s 1999 10m 10s⁶ 12m 10m* 9.9f 10.1g⁶ 10.1g⁵ Sep
14] tall, unfurnished filly: good mover: fairly useful performer: best efforts in listed
races at Newmarket, Newbury and Newcastle (rated stakes) on first, second and sixth
starts: vastly superior to sole rival in maiden at Nottingham in July: should stay 1½m:
acts on soft and good to firm going: takes good hold. *B. W. Hills*

OCEAN SPRAY 6 ch.g. Cadeaux Genereux 131 – Shore Line 107 (High Line   **–**
125) [1998 NR 1999 10.9g Jul 26] half-brother to very smart Soviet Line: dam 2-y-o
7f winner and fourth in Oaks: twice-raced in bumpers before tailed off in seller at
Ayr. *D. Eddy*

OCEAN VIEW 3 ch.f. Rope Trick – Nashya (Rousillon (USA) 133) [1998 NR   **–**
1999 8g⁶ Apr 5] second reported foal: half-sister to 5f winner General Sir Peter (by
Last Tycoon): dam unraced: last in maiden at Newcastle. *W. T. Kemp*

OCHOS RIOS (IRE) 8 br.g. Horage 124 – Morgiana (Godswalk (USA) 130)   **44 §**
[1998 57, a–: 7d 7g 7.5g* 7s* 7.5d⁶ 7f 7d 1999 7m³ 7s 8g 9.9m 8.5g Aug 12] small,   **a– §**
lengthy gelding: good mover: poor performer: stays 1m: acts on good to firm going,
heavy and fibresand: tried blinkered: unreliable. *B. S. Rothwell*

OCKERBRIDGE 2 b.f. (Mar 23) Casteddu 111 – Grey Twig 68 (Godswalk (USA)   **44**
130) [1999 a6g 6v⁶ 7d Oct 14] leggy, lengthy filly: half-sister to several winners,
including fairly useful 1986 2-y-o 6f winner Grey Wolf Tiger (by Rolfe): dam ran
only at 2 yrs: poor maiden: best effort when ninth of 19 in seller at Newmarket final
start: should stay 1m: has been bandaged behind. *J. S. Moore*

OCKER (IRE) 5 br.g. Astronef 116 – Violet Somers (Will Somers 114§) [1998   **107**
85: 6.1s* 5s² 6d 6.9d 6.1m² 6g² 5g² 5.1g² 6s 6g 5g* 5g³ 6m³ 5.2g* 6g 5g 6s 5g³ 5g 6s   **a85**
6s 5d* a6g² a6g³ 1999 a6g a6g² a6g³ a6g³ a6g² 6d⁶ 5d* 6v³ 6m 6d 6m⁴ 6d³ 7f 6m⁵
6m 6f³ 6d 5.7m⁶ 5.1m* 6g 6m* 5.6g³ 5m 6.1g 5s⁵ 6s⁵ a6g⁴ a5g⁶ a6g a6g Dec 13]
leggy gelding: useful performer on turf, fairly useful on all-weather: won handicap
at Thirsk in April and minor events at Nottingham in August and Haydock in
September: best effort when third to Astonished in Portland Handicap at Doncaster
later in September: best at 5f/6f: acts on any turf going and fibresand: tried visored:
often wears net muzzle to post, and has worn blanket for stalls entry: has been
bandaged in front: has spoilt chance by rearing stalls/starting slowly/hanging left:
tends to carry head high: tough. *Mrs N. Macauley*

OCTANE (USA) 3 b.g. Cryptoclearance (USA) – Something True (USA) 119   **73 d**
(Sir Ivor 135) [1998 NR 1999 8g⁶ 8m 8m⁵ 10m 10m Jul 12] $35,000Y: good-bodied,
quite attractive gelding: fluent mover: fifth foal: half-brother to a winner in USA by
Devil's Bag: dam French 1¼m and (Grand Prix d'Evry) 1½m winner: fair maiden:
form only on first and third starts: should be suited by further than 1m: blinkered third
and final outings: possibly temperamental: sold 10,000 gns, joined W. Brisbourne.
H. R. A. Cecil

OCTAVIUS CAESAR (USA) 2 ch.c. (Apr 24) Affirmed (USA) – Secret Impera-   **74**
trice (USA) (Secretariat (USA)) [1999 8.5m² 8d Sep 23] angular colt: fourth foal:
half-brother to winners in USA by Rubiano and Storm Bird: dam minor stakes
winner up to 9f in USA: promising second of 8 to Monte Carlo in maiden at Epsom
on debut, but well held in similar event at Pontefract next time: should stay 1¼m.
P. F. I. Cole

ODDSANENDS 3 b.c. Alhijaz 122 – Jans Contessa 68 (Rabdan 129) [1998 78:   **78**
6s⁵ a6g⁴ 7f⁴ 7m* a6g³ 1999 a7g⁴ a7g⁶ a8g a7g² a8g² Dec 17] small colt: fair
performer: stays 7f, probably not 1m: acts on good to firm going and fibresand: wears
bandages. *C. N. Allen*

ODYN DANCER 2 b.f. (May 11) Minshaanshu Amad (USA) 91§ – Themeda 69   **47**
(Sure Blade (USA) 130) [1999 6g 6.8m a7g² a7g⁵ a8.5g⁴ 8d a8g a8g a8g³ Dec 6]
500Y, 8,000 2-y-o: third foal: half-sister to 3-y-o Chief Abba: dam, unreliable 11f
winner, half-sister to smart sprinter Cathedral: poor maiden: stays 1m: acts on fibresand. *M. D. I. Usher*

ODYSSEY 3 b.g. Slip Anchor 136 – Circe 73 (Main Reef 126) [1998 70+: 7m⁵   **71**
8.1m⁶ 8d 1999 10.2s⁵ 11.6g⁴ 11.4m⁵ 15.8m³ 14.1m³ 14.1g⁵ 13.1f³ 12s 10f Oct 20]
good-bodied gelding: fair maiden: likely to prove best at 1½m/1¾m: acts on firm and

good to soft going, probably on soft: visored/blinkered last 3 starts: front runner: consistent: sold 19,000 gns. *P. T. Walwyn*

OFFENBURG   2 b.g. (Feb 5) Petong 126 – Bold County 70 (Never So Bold 135) [1999 8m⁵ 8v 7d 8.2d Oct 21] 2,800Y: workmanlike gelding: third foal: half-brother to 3-y-o Paradise County: dam, 2-y-o 5f winner, half-sister to smart middle-distance filly Tants: well beaten in maidens/sellers: tried blinkered. *J. S. Moore*

OFF HIRE   3 b.g. Clantime 101 – Lady Pennington 51 (Blue Cashmere 129) [1998 65: 5m 7g 8g 5s* a5g⁴ a5s³ a5g³ 1999 a6g⁴ 5g² 6s a6g 5.3f⁶ 5d 5v a6g a5g³ Dec 21] leggy, angular gelding: fair handicapper: effective at 5f/6f: acts on soft going and fibresand: effective visored or not: reportedly finished lame fifth start: inconsistent. *C. Smith*   **61 a65**

OFFICE HOURS   7 b.g. Danehill (USA) 126 – Charmina (FR) (Nonoalco (USA) 131) [1998 –: 12.4g⁵ 1999 5.1m 6.8m a12g Aug 14] no longer of any account. *R. Lee*   **–**

O'GARNEY PARK (IRE)   5 b.g. Shalford (IRE) 124§ – Rince Si (Malinowski (USA) 123) [1998 25: 11g 13d 12.5g 13m 12m 13m⁴ a13g a16g⁶ 1999 a13g Jan 28] bad maiden handicapper: usually blinkered, visored once. *P. Mitchell*   **–**

OGILIA   2 b.f. (Mar 27) Bin Ajwaad (IRE) 119 – Littlemisstrouble (USA) (My Gallant (USA)) [1999 5.7m*ᵈⁱˢ 5.7h* 6d² 6m³ 6.5g³ 7d 6d³ Oct 22] 11,000Y: unfurnished filly: half-sister to 7.5f and 9f winner/smart hurdler Polar Prospect (by Polar Falcon) and 4-y-o Little Brave: dam won up to 9f in USA: fairly useful performer: first past post in maidens at Bath in July (disqualified) and August: unfortunate (badly hampered) not to have won valuable nursery at Doncaster in September: below form both starts after: likely to prove suited by 1m+: acts on hard and good to soft ground. *I. A. Balding*   **88**

OH I SAY   3 b.f. Primo Dominie 121 – Isotonic 74 (Absalom 128) [1998 74d: a5g² 5.1d* 5.1g⁶ 5m* 5d⁶ 5f⁵ 5f⁴ 6m⁴ 6f 5.3g a6g 1999 a5g² a5g⁴ a6g a6g 6d Jun 7] good-topped filly: modest at best in 1999: acts on firm going, good to soft and equitrack. *Miss Gay Kelleway*   **60 d**

OH NO NOT HIM   3 b.g. Reprimand 122 – Lucky Mill 50 (Midyan (USA) 124) [1998 –: 7g 7g 7.1s⁵ 1999 8d a9.4g a12g Sep 4] rather sparely-made gelding: no form: tried blinkered. *M. Mullineaux*   **–**

OH SO GRAND   3 ch.f. Grand Lodge (USA) 125 – Cutleaf 81 (Kris 135) [1998 56: 7.5m⁶ 8.2s a8g a8.5g² a7g³ a7g⁵ 1999 a8g 8g Jun 14] angular, quite good-topped filly: modest maiden: stays 8.5f: acts on all-weather: has wandered: visored last 5 starts: has worn tongue strap: sold 11,000 gns, in foal to Be My Guest, sent to Bahrain. *R. M. H. Cowell*   **–**

OK BABE   4 b.f. Bold Arrangement 127 – Celtic Bird 77 (Celtic Cone 116) [1998 –, a68: a7g⁴ a6g² a6g* a6g 6.1d 7g 6.1v 6s 1999 7s 7m 7d 6d a10g a8g Dec 17] fair at 3 yrs: little show in 1999: best form at 6f: acts on all-weather and good to soft going: visored fourth start. *G. P. Enright*   **–**

OK JOHN (IRE)   4 b.g. Mac's Imp (USA) 116 – Ching A Ling (Pampapaul 121) [1998 60: 5d 5.3d⁶ 5m 5m 6d 5.3m 6g a6g a6g² a6f⁴ a6f⁴ 5g 7.8d 5s 5.8d a5g³ a6g a6g³ Dec 17] modest maiden: left J. Akehurst third start and L. Reilly, Ireland, seventh: stays 6f: acts on good to firm going and all-weather: tried blinkered. *G. P. Enright*   **a63**

OLD FEATHERS (IRE)   2 b.g. (May 16) Hernando (FR) 127 – Undiscovered (Tap On Wood 130) [1999 6m⁶ 8.1m⁶ 8.2m⁶ Sep 13] 19,000F, 30,000Y: leggy, quite attractive gelding: seventh foal: half-brother to several winners, including useful Italian 7f to 1¼m winner Broken Detraeh (by Broken Hearted) and 1992 2-y-o 7f winner (stayed 1½m) Taahhub (by Nordico): dam Irish maiden: modest form in maidens at Pontefract, Haydock and Nottingham: may prove best around 1m. *J. G. FitzGerald*   **61**

OLD GOLD N TAN   6 ch.g. Ballacashtal (CAN) – Raleigh Gazelle (Absalom 128) [1998 –: a8g⁵ a12g⁵ 15.8d⁶ 12.4g⁴ 1999 a8.5g May 22] little form: dead. *A. G. Juckes*   **–**

OLD HOOK (IRE)   8 b. or br.h. Digamist (USA) 110 – Day Dress (Ashmore (FR) 125) [1998 51, a?: a7g⁶ 8d 8.3v a7g³ 6f³ 7f* 7m 8f³ 6m* 6f² 7f* 8f* a7g a8g a7g   **37 +**

1999 7g⁴ 8d 7m 7m⁵ May 26] neat horse: poor performer: stays 8.5f: acts on firm going and equitrack. *Paul Smith, Belgium*

OLD HUSH WING (IRE)   6 b.g. Tirol 127 – Saneena 80 (Kris 135) [1998   **60** 49: a16s a16.2g⁵ 13d² a16.2g⁵ 1999 a16f³ a16g² 16.1d* 17.1v* 17.1s Oct 4] good-   **a43** topped gelding: modest handicapper on turf, poor on all-weather: won at Newcastle in March and Pontefract in April: well held final start: needs 2m+: acts on good to firm going, heavy and all-weather: visored once: held up: fairly useful hurdler. *Mrs M. Reveley*

OLD JOHN (IRE)   2 b.c. (Apr 7) Port Lucaya 118 – Bradwell (IRE) 76 (Taufan   **– §** (USA) 119) [1999 6d 7f⁶ Jul 14] IR 4,600F, 2,800 2-y-o: close-coupled colt: second foal: half-brother to a 5f to 1m winner in Spain by Bob's Return: dam 5f winner who probably stayed 7f: reportedly lame when soon pulled up on debut, but looked decidedly reluctant in blinkers next time: one to avoid. *J. J. O'Neill*

OLD RED (IRE)   9 ch.g. Ela-Mana-Mou 132 – Sea Port (Averof 123) [1998 53:   **52** 16g 14.1d 16.1d⁵ 15.8g³ 16.1g² 16g* 14.1m⁵ 16d* 1999 16.2s² 16g⁶ Aug 9] modest handicapper nowadays: best at 2m+: acts on any turf going and fibresand: usually held up. *Mrs M. Reveley*

OLD SCHOOL HOUSE   6 ch.h. Polar Falcon (USA) 126 – Farewell Letter   **–** (USA) (Arts And Letters (USA)) [1998 NR 1999 8.1m 8.3m 12m Jun 23] quite attractive horse: fairly useful on all-weather, fair on turf at 3 yrs: no show in 1999. *T. J. Naughton*

OLIBERI   3 b.g. First Trump 118 – Rhiannon 65 (Welsh Pageant 132) [1998 53:   **58** 5v⁴ 5s⁵ 7.5m⁵ 1999 8.3g⁶ 11.1m² 11.1f 11f* Jul 24] modest performer: won seller at Redcar in July: better at 11f than shorter: acts on firm going: joined Mrs J. Oliver. *J. Berry*

OLIVE THE TWIST (USA)   4 ch.f. Theatrical 128 – Lady of The Light (USA)   **94** (The Minstrel (CAN) 135) [1998 90: 10g* 10.2g 1999 10f⁴ 10m² 10.1g Aug 30] fairly useful performer: best efforts when in frame in minor events at Newbury (carried head awkwardly) and Ascot: stays 1¼m: acts on firm going: sent to USA. *J. H. M. Gosden*

OLIVIAS CHOICE   2 b.f. (Apr 22) Pyramus (USA) 78 – Navarino Bay 102   **64** (Averof 123) [1999 5d⁵ 6s* 6.8m⁵ 7g 6g 6d Sep 17] 1,500Y: leggy, unfurnished filly: eighth foal: half-sister to 3 winners, including 5-y-o Pension Fund: dam 2-y-o 5f winner who stayed 1½m: modest performer: won seller at Goodwood in June: good efforts next 2 starts, but ran poorly in visor after: may prove best at 7f/1m: acts on soft and good to firm ground: sent to Norway. *K. R. Burke*

OLIVO (IRE)   5 ch.g. Priolo (USA) 127 – Honourable Sheba (USA) (Roberto   **69** (USA) 131) [1998 75: 8g⁴ 12g⁴ 14.1m* 14.8f⁶ 16.2g² 13.3m 16.1m⁴ 16d 17.2d 1999 13.3m² 16.2m 12m 14.4m⁶ Sep 8] strong, close-coupled gelding: fair handicapper: stays 2m well: possibly needs good going or firmer: has gone in snatches: has been bandaged behind. *C. A. Horgan*

OLLIE'S CHUCKLE (IRE)   4 b.g. Mac's Imp (USA) 116 – Chenya (Beldale   **64** Flutter (USA) 130) [1998 67: a6g³ a6g⁶ 6d 7d² 7s⁶ 7g 10g² 9.2d³ 10m 8.5m 10s 1999   **a46** a8g⁵ a8g 9d* 9.3m 8.3d³ 8m 8d³ 7.5s 8g 9g Oct 15] angular gelding: modest on turf, poor on all-weather: won apprentice maiden handicap at Redcar in April: stays 1¼m: acts on soft and good ground (possibly not on good to firm) and fibresand: none too consistent. *J. J. Quinn*

OMAHA CITY (IRE)   5 b.g. Night Shift (USA) – Be Discreet (Junius (USA)   **101** 124) [1998 101§: 6g 7s 8d 7f⁴ 7g³ 7.3m 7m 7d 6.1g 1999 7g 7g⁵ 6f⁵ 8m* 8g 7.6m⁴ 7m 8f⁴ 7.3g⁶ 7g³ 7m³ 8s³ 7d* 7g 7s⁶ Oct 23] strong, useful-looking gelding: useful performer: won handicaps at Goodwood in June and York (rated stakes by 1½ lengths from Granny's Pet) in October: below form last 2 starts: effective at 7f/1m: acts on firm and soft ground: sometimes edgy/on toes: usually held up. *B. Gubby*

OMAR DANCER   3 b.g. Shareef Dancer (USA) 135 – Happydrome (Ahonoora   **–** 122) [1998 NR 1999 8s 7m Oct 19] 5,400Y: second foal: dam unraced: well beaten in maidens at Pontefract (slowly away) and Yarmouth. *C. Smith*

OMAR'S ODYSSEY (IRE)   4 ch.g. Sharifabad (IRE) 96 – Tales of Homer   –
(Home Guard (USA) 129) [1998 –: a10g⁴ a10g 11.6m 11.5m 9m a16g 1999 a13g⁴
10.1m 8m⁵ 11.5m Sep 7] little form: tried visored/blinkered: sold 975 gns. *P. Mitchell*

OMNIHEAT   2 b.f. (May 24) Ezzoud (IRE) 126 – Lady Bequick 81 (Sharpen Up   **70**
127) [1999 7f⁵ 7f⁵ 7m⁴ 6g 7d⁴ 8d⁶ 7s* Nov 6] 5,000Y: half-sister to numerous
winners, including smart 6f (at 2 yrs) to 1m winner Cloud of Dust (by Aragon), 7-y-o
Crowded Avenue and 6-y-o Scathebury: dam 2-y-o 5f winner: fair performer: best
effort when winning 22-runner nursery at Doncaster by head from Slick Willie,
checked 3f out but leading final 100 yds: should stay 1m: acts on soft going, probably
on firm. *M. J. Ryan*

ONCE MORE FOR LUCK (IRE)   8 b.g. Petorius 117 – Mrs Lucky (Royal   **81**
Match 117) [1998 81: a12g 12m² 10.4g* 12d* 12g⁴ 10.4g³ 12s* 10.3v⁴ 1999 13.8g³
14.1s³ 11.9d 14.6d⁴ Oct 22] sturdy gelding: fairly useful handicapper: effective at
1¼m (given good gallop) to 1¾m: acts on fibresand and probably any turf going:
held up: consistent. *Mrs M. Reveley*

ON CREDIT (IRE)   2 ch.g. (Apr 8) Magical Wonder (USA) 125 – Forest Trea-   **52**
sure (USA) (Green Forest (USA) 134) [1999 8d 8g a8g⁶ Nov 11] brother to 3-y-o
Priestess and useful sprinter Open Credit, and half-brother to a winner in USA by
Siberian Express: dam unraced: modest form second start in maidens: blinkered last
2 outings: sold 1,000 gns, sent to Denmark. *Miss I. Foustok*

ONE DINAR (FR)   4 b.c. Generous (IRE) 139 – Lypharitissima (FR) (Lightning   **70**
(FR) 129) [1998 68, a53: 10d 7d 8d⁵ 10g⁵ 9d 10d a10g⁴ 1999 7f² 8d³ 8g⁵ 10g⁵ 8m⁴ 8g   **a–**
7g² 8m⁴ 8.5g⁶ 7m* 8m Sep 10] big, good-topped colt: has a markedly round action:
fair on turf, modest on all-weather: won maiden at Lingfield in September: has form
at 1¼m, at least as effective at 7f/1m: acts on firm going, good to soft and equitrack:
visored sixth start: sold 13,000 gns. *K. Mahdi*

ONE DOMINO   2 ch.g. (Feb 23) Efisio 120 – Dom One 92 (Dominion 123) [1999   **65**
7m⁵ 7s³ 8.3f⁴ 8d 8s⁶ Sep 29] quite good-topped gelding: first foal: dam 2-y-o 5f and
7f winner: fair maiden: well beaten last 2 starts: stays 8.3f: acts on firm and soft
going. *J. Berry*

ONE FOR ALL   4 gr.g. Petong 126 – Go Tally-Ho 66 (Gorytus (USA) 132) [1998   **–**
NR 1999 8f 6g Sep 20] second foal: dam 2-y-o 5f winner, also successful over
hurdles: tongue tied, well beaten in seller and claimer. *Mrs S. J. Smith*

ONE IN THE EYE   6 br.g. Arrasas (USA) 100 – Mingalles 65 (Prince de Galles   **– §**
125) [1998 NR 1999 8.1m a11g 8.1m Jul 21] small gelding: poor maiden handicapper: little show in 1999: probably stays 1½m: acts on soft and good to firm going:
tried blinkered: has been bandaged in front: ungenuine. *Jamie Poulton*

ONE OF THE FAMILY   4 b.f. Alzao (USA) 117 – Someone Special 105 (Habitat   **73**
134) [1998 NR 1999 8m 8g⁵ 9m⁵ 11.4m 10m⁵ 12d⁵ 8g² 8d⁶ 10f⁶ Oct 20] 72,000Y:
lengthy, rather angular filly: seventh foal: sister to 1993 2-y-o 6f/7f winner Relatively
Special (later smart up to 1¼m) and half-sister to several winners, notably very smart
1¼m performers One So Wonderful (by Nashwan) and Alnasr Alwasheek (by
Sadler's Wells): dam, 7f winner, half-sister to top-class miler Milligram: fair maiden:
second of 19 in minor event at Leicester in September: below form both starts after:
should stay at least 1¼m: acts on good to firm going. *J. R. Fanshawe*

ONE QUICK LION   3 b.c. Lion Cavern (USA) 117 – One Quick Bid (USA)   **74**
(Commemorate (USA)) [1998 NR 1999 7m 8.3g⁶ 8.3d⁵ Nov 4] 38,000Y: second
foal: half-brother to 4-y-o Swift Alliance, fairly useful 6f winner at 2 yrs: dam,
winning sprinter at 4 yrs in USA, half-sister to very smart 1¼m performer Tamayaz:
best effort in maidens (5 months after debut) second start. *R. W. Armstrong*

ONES ENOUGH   3 b.c. Reprimand 122 – Sea Fairy 64 (Wollow 132) [1998 88:   **79 d**
5d³ 6m⁶ 5m³ 7.6f⁶ 6m⁵ 5m* 5v* 1999 6g 5s⁵ 6m 5g 6g 6m 7v 7s Oct 1] close-coupled
colt: has only one eye: fairly useful at 2 yrs: lost his form in 1999: will prove best at
5f/6f: acts on good to firm and heavy going: wore eyecover first 5 starts, blinkered
third one at 3 yrs: sometimes wanders: edgy sort. *G. L. Moore*

ONE STEP AT A TIME   2 b.f. (Feb 12) Sabrehill (USA) 120 – Ghost Tree (IRE)   **98**
88 (Caerleon (USA) 132) [1999 7m² a7g* 7m 8d³ 8d² Oct 9] 6,000F: third foal:
half-sister to 3-y-o Trawling: dam 7f winner out of Cheveley Park winner Embla:

useful performer: won maiden at Southwell in July: best effort when neck second of 11 to French Fellow in listed race at Ascot final start: stays 1m: flashed tail third start, found little fourth: sold 90,000 gns, sent to Saudi Arabia. *B. W. Hills*

ONE TO GO (IRE) 4 b.g. Peterius 117 – Caroline's Mark (On Your Mark 125) –
[1998 62, a56: 8.3v^4 7s a6g^4 6g 7g^2 5m^2 7.1s^3 a6g^2 6g a6g 8.1g 5g 7.1d^2 6g* 7d 1999 a8g a6g^6 8f 6g 7d Oct 4] close-coupled gelding: modest at best: little show in 1999: best at up to 7f: acts on fibresand and soft going, probably on good to firm: blinkered penultimate start: sold 520 gns. *G. F. H. Charles-Jones*

ONE WON ONE (USA) 5 b.g. Naevus (USA) – Harvard's Bay (ARG) (Halpern 110
Bay (USA)) [1998 108: 6v^4 6v* 5s* 6d 6.3v^2 6d* 5s^3 6s 1999 8s 6d* 6g^3 5g^4 6m 6.3g^4 6m^6 8m 7d 6s^3 5s^6 6s^2 7s* Nov 7] good-topped, attractive gelding: smart performer: won handicap at the Curragh in April and (having reportedly suffered hairline fracture of pastern after sixth outing) listed race at Leopardstown in November, in latter beating Wray by length: well held in Cork And Orrery Stakes at Royal Ascot fifth start: effective at 5f (given test) to 7f: best form on good ground or softer (acts on heavy): blinkered eleventh start: genuine. *Mrs J. Morgan, Ireland*

ONLY FOR GOLD 4 b.c. Presidium 124 – Calvanne Miss 48 (Martinmas 128) 70
[1998 79: 6.1m 6d 7g 6v 6g^6 6f 6s^4 7g 6v 6d 1999 6m^2 7.6m^5 6d 7d^6 6g^6 6d 7.6m 6f 7.6m 6.9m^2 7.6d^2 7.9m 8.1s^2 7g^3 7d^3 a7g^6 Nov 12] rangy colt: fair handicapper: ran creditably several times in 1999: effective at 6f to 1m: acts on soft and good to firm going, well below form on fibresand: visored eighth start. *J. Berry*

ONLY JOSH (IRE) 5 gr.g. Waajib 121 – Carlyle Suite (USA) (Icecapade (USA)) –
[1998 –: 7g 8m 1999 8g 8f Jul 17] tall gelding: disappointing maiden: tried blinkered. *R. A. Fahey*

ONLYONEUNITED 2 b.f. (Apr 10) Pelder (IRE) 125 – Supreme Rose 95 72
(Frimley Park 109) [1999 6.1f 6s^5 5s^2 Oct 1] half-sister to several winning sprinters, including 4-y-o Faute de Mieux, 5-y-o Bramble Bear and 6-y-o Rambling Bear: dam sprinter: fair maiden: best effort when second of 13 to easy winner Kier Park at Lingfield: likely to prove best at 5f/6f: acts on soft ground. *M. Blanshard*

ON PORPOISE 3 b.g. Dolphin Street (FR) 125 – Floppie (FR) (Law Society –
(USA) 130) [1998 NR 1999 8s 10s 8.3d Nov 4] 36,000F, 18,000Y: first foal: dam, French 1m winner, half-sister to 6-y-o Raise A Prince: little sign of ability. *P. W. D'Arcy*

ON SHADE 2 ch.f. (Mar 5) Polar Falcon (USA) 126 – Vagrant Maid (USA) 85 –
(Honest Pleasure (USA)) [1999 8.1s^6 8d Oct 22] 38,000Y: quite good-topped filly: eighth foal: half-sister to several winners, including a useful Irish 2-y-o 1m/9f winner by Robellino and useful French 10.5f winner Wayfaring (by Be My Guest), latter later winner in Australia: dam 1½m winner out of sister to Oaks winner Valoris: burly, well beaten in maidens at Haydock and Doncaster (sweating). *N. Tinkler*

ON THE RIDGE (IRE) 4 ch.c. Risk Me (FR) 127 – Star Ridge (USA) (Storm 115
Bird (CAN) 134) [1998 104: 8m^3 8f^3 7.9s* 10.3m^2 1999 8.1s^2 8m Jun 15] rangy, angular colt: has a round action: smart performer: improved when neck second to Handsome Ridge in Sandown Mile in April, dictating pace: well held in Queen Anne Stakes at Royal Ascot (reportedly lost near-fore plate) only start after: may prove best around 1m: acts on soft ground, seems unsuited by good to firm: has been bandaged in front. *H. R. A. Cecil*

ON THE TRAIL 2 ch.c. (Mar 15) Catrail (USA) 123 – From The Rooftops (IRE) 56
(Thatching 131) [1999 7s 6g^6 Oct 19] 15,000F, 21,000Y: fourth foal: dam unraced daughter of half-sister to Molecomb winner Hatta: modest form in maidens. *S. Dow*

ON TILL MORNING (IRE) 3 ch.f. Never So Bold 135 – Shamasiya (FR) 73
(Vayrann 133) [1998 67: 5.1g^3 6m^2 5m 6m^3 5d* 1999 5d^4 6m^5 6m 6g^3 6m* 7g* 7.1m 8m Sep 19] angular filly: fair performer: won minor event at Pontefract and handicap at Ayr in July: below form last 2 starts: effective at 6f/7f: yet to race on extremes of going: has been bandaged behind: game. *P. Calver*

ON TIME (IRE) 2 b.c. (Mar 8) Blues Traveller (IRE) 119 – Go Flightline (IRE) 101
63 (Common Grounds 118) [1999 6.8m* 7s* 7d^3 Oct 7] IR 5,000Y, 7,800 2-y-o: smallish, quite attractive colt: good walker: first foal: dam 2-y-o 5f winner: useful form: won maiden at Warwick in August and minor event at Goodwood (beat Sir

Ninja by 5 lengths) in September: good third of 6 to Zoning in minor event at York final start, travelling strongly long way but tending to hang under pressure: will stay 1m: may do better still. *J. R. Fanshawe*

ONYOUROWN (IRE) 6 b.g. Treasure Kay 114 – Mursuma (Rarity 129) [1998 NR 1999 a14g⁶ Nov 22] half-brother to several winners over jumps, notably top-class chaser Direct Route (by Executive Perk): dam half-sister to Galmoy: fair hurdler/poor chaser (possibly temperamental) nowadays: fairly useful 11f/1½m winner in Ireland in 1996: tailed off in visor on only Flat start since. *Mrs N. Macauley* —

OO EE BE 3 b.g. Whittingham (IRE) 104 – Miss Derby (USA) (Master Derby (USA)) [1998 78+: 6g 5g 7m⁵ 7m³ 5.7d 6m⁶ 6m a6g⁵ 8v⁵ a8g* a8g² a8f³ 1999 a10g² 10.3d 9v 10g Oct 11] good-topped gelding: fluent mover: fair handicapper on all-weather, little form on turf in 1999: off 6 months after second start: stays 1¼m: acts on good to firm going, heavy and equitrack: blinkered once at 2 yrs: best ridden up with pace. *A. T. Murphy* **a78**

OPEN ARMS 3 ch.g. Most Welcome 131 – Amber Fizz (USA) (Effervescing (USA)) [1998 75: 6d⁵ 7.6f⁴ 8.5s⁴ 8g² 7.9g 8d³ 1999 7.5m³ Apr 14] strong gelding: fair maiden: creditable third in handicap at Beverley only 3-y-o start: will be suited by 1¼m: acts on good to firm and good to soft going. *Mrs A. L. M. King* **78**

OPEN GROUND (IRE) 2 ch.c. (Apr 27) Common Grounds 118 – Poplina (USA) (Roberto (USA) 131) [1998 8g a7g⁶ a10g³ Dec 18] IR 17,000Y: sixth foal: brother to useful 1998 2-y-o 7f winner Come What May and half-brother to winners abroad by Damister and Belmez: dam, French 11f winner, half-sister to champion US older horse Vanlandingham and to dam of Distant Music: poor maiden: best effort at Lingfield final start. *P. Howling* **47**

OPENING NIGHT 4 b.g. Theatrical Charmer 114 – First Time Over (Derrylin 115) [1998 –: 8m a9.4g 1999 10.5m Jul 10] little sign of ability. *Miss K. M. George* —

OPENING RANGE 8 b.m. Nordico (USA) – Waveguide 76 (Double Form 130) [1998 –: 5g a5g⁶ a5g 1999 a6g a5f⁶ a5g² a6s a5g⁶ a5g 5m 5g 5m 5.1m⁵ 5.1m 5m⁴ 5d⁶ 5.1m Sep 9] workmanlike mare: poor handicapper: best at 5f/6f: acts on firm going, good to soft and all-weather: has been blinkered, including on last 3 starts: often leads: has hung right. *N. E. Berry* **36**

OPERA BUFF (IRE) 8 br.g. Rousillon (USA) 133 – Obertura (USA) 100 (Roberto (USA) 131) [1998 65§, a86§: a10g⁴ 12d a12g² 12d 12f 11.9f³ 12m 12m 12.1g⁴ 12m⁶ 11.5g⁴ 11.5f² 16.4m⁵ 12m² 12g⁶ 12m⁶ a12g⁶ a12g³ a16.2g² a12g³ a13g⁵ a12g 1999 a12g³ a12g* a12g³ 14.1m 11.9f* 12m a12g⁵ 11.5f 11.9f³ Jul 13] big, good-topped gelding: fair performer: won claimer at Lingfield in February and handicap at Brighton in May: effective at 1½m to 2m: unraced on heavy going, acts on any other turf/all-weather: effective blinkered/visored or not: tends to hang left and find little: usually held up: unreliable. *Miss Gay Kelleway* **65 §**
a76 §

OPERA KING (USA) 4 ch.c. Storm Bird (CAN) 134 – Jewel In My Crown (CAN) (Secretariat (USA)) [1998 103: 11.5g* 12s 1999 a12f² 14d* 12m³ Aug 7] sturdy, angular colt: useful performer, lightly raced: better than ever to win Theo Fennell Shergar Cup Stayers (Handicap) at Goodwood in May by 1¼ lengths from Perfect Paradigm, coming from well back to lead near finish: sweating between legs, disappointing favourite in minor event at Ascot next time, finding little and changing legs several times under pressure: stays 1¾m: raced only on good going or softer on turf prior to Ascot: usually held up. *Saeed bin Suroor* **109**

OPERATIC 4 b.f. Goofalik (USA) 118 – Choir Mistress (Chief Singer 131) [1998 72: a10g⁴ a8.5g² a12g² a12g³ a12g³ 12d³ 12.3s⁶ a12g³ a11g 16f* 14m³ a14.8g³ 14.1d³ 14.1d 16m⁶ 14g² 14.1g³ a14.8g² 16m³ 15.4m² 14.1g² a14.8g 17.1m a16m³ 11.9m a14.8g* 15.8d² 13.8s² a12g² a14.8g a14g⁵ a16.2g⁴ a16g³ 1999 a16f a16f⁶ Feb 1] sparely-made filly: fair performer: well beaten both starts in 1999: should stay beyond 2m: acts on firm ground, good to soft (probably on soft) and all-weather: usually blinkered/visored. *P. R. Hedger* —

OPERATIONDESERTFOX 2 ch.f. (Apr 21) Foxhound (USA) 103 – Scravels Saran (IRE) 57 (Indian King (USA) 128) [1999 7d Oct 30] 500Y: fourth foal: dam, became ungenuine: tailed off in Newmarket maiden. *Dr J. D. Scargill* —

OPERETTA (FR) 4 b.f. Lashkari 128 – Lyric Opera (Sadler's Wells (USA) 132) –
[1998 59d: 10g³ 9g 10g 12d 1999 a12g Sep 4] smallish filly: little form since debut:
blinkered only 4-y-o start. *Ian Williams*

OPTIMAITE 2 b.c. (Mar 16) Komaite (USA) – Leprechaun Lady 57 (Royal 98
Blend 117) [1999 5m* 5g* 5m 5.2m 6m² 6g 8d⁴ 8s Oct 23] 7,200Y: tall, workmanlike
colt: easy mover: seventh foal: half-brother to 3 winners, including 4-y-o Chimes of
Peace and 6f (at 2 yrs) to 1¾m winner Goodbye Millie (by Sayf El Arab): dam stayer:
useful performer: won maiden at Windsor and minor event at Ascot (made all) in
April: best effort after when fourth of 11 to French Fellow in listed race at Ascot: out
of depth in Racing Post Trophy at Doncaster final start: stays 1m: acts on good to
firm and good to soft ground: reportedly lame behind third start. *B. R. Millman*

OPTIMISTIC 4 b.f. Reprimand 122 – Arminda (Blakeney 126) [1998 90: 10.4d⁵ –
10g 1999 10m 10d Sep 17] unfurnished filly: fairly useful handicapper: well beaten
both 4-y-o starts: stays 1¼m well: acts on good to soft going, probably on firm.
M. H. Tompkins

OPULENT 8 b.g. Robellino (USA) 127 – One Half Silver (CAN) (Plugged Nickle 62
(USA)) [1998 71: 8d 8d 10.1s⁵ 9.9d⁵ 8.5d 1999 10s 9.9m³ 8s 9g Oct 15] sturdy
gelding: modest handicapper: stays 1¼m: acts on good to firm and heavy ground:
often tongue tied: tends to carry head high, and not an easy ride. *Mrs M. Reveley*

ORANGE ORDER (IRE) 6 ch.g. Generous (IRE) 139 – Fleur d'Oranger 110 43
(Northfields (USA)) [1998 –: 12d⁴ 14g 1999 12g 14.1m 12m⁵ 11m Aug 28] poor
handicapper nowadays: stays 1½m: acts on good to firm ground: successful over
hurdles in July (twice) and September. *G. M. Moore*

ORANGEVILLE (USA) 2 b. or br.c. (Feb 12) Dynaformer (USA) – Orange 88 P
Sickle (USA) (Rich Cream (USA)) [1999 7s² Nov 5] $150,000Y: heavy-topped colt:
fourth foal: brother to smart 1m (at 2 yrs) to 1¼m winner Voyagers Quest and half-
brother to 2 winners in USA: dam won up to 9f in USA, including minor stakes at 2
yrs: sire (by Roberto) Grade 2 1¼m winner: very green when promising 2 lengths
second of 20 to Golovin in maiden at Doncaster, starting slowly, improving well from
halfway and running on strongly despite hanging left final 1f: should stay 1¼m/1½m:
type to improve considerably and win races at 3 yrs. *J. H. M. Gosden*

ORBITAL STAR (IRE) 3 b.c. Contract Law (USA) 108 – Sun Gift (Guillaume 79
Tell (USA) 121) [1998 60: 7d 8v 8d⁴ a8g⁵ 1999 a10g 10g* 9.3g* 9m⁶ 9g 9.7d² Aug
26] leggy, plain colt: fair handicapper: won at Lingfield in May and Carlisle
in June: stayed 1¼m: acted on equitrack and good to soft ground: dead. *P. W. Harris*

ORDAINED 6 b.m. Mtoto 134 – In The Habit (USA) 88 (Lyphard (USA) 132) 49
[1998 66, a–: a12g⁶ 12g² 10m 12g² 1999 12m 11.1m 10m 12f a12g 12d Oct a–
29] dipped-backed mare: poor handicapper nowadays: best at 1¼m/1½m on good
going or firmer (little form on all-weather): sold 600 gns in November, joined Gay
Kelleway. *E. J. Alston*

ORDER IN COURT (IRE) 5 ch.m. Imp Society (USA) – Fair Flutter (Beldale 44
Flutter (USA) 130) [1998 –: a8.5g 1999 a9.4g⁶ a12s² Feb 10] form only when second
of 7 in maiden at Wolverhampton: should stay beyond 1½m. *A. Bailey*

OREGON DREAM (IRE) 3 b.f. Seattle Dancer (USA) 119 – Ibda 67 (Mtoto 68
134) [1998 50: 5g a6g³ 5s 1999 10d⁵ 8m² 8f* 8m⁵ 8g³ 8.2g* 8m⁶ 8g 8.5s 8d* Oct
11] fair performer: won handicaps at Musselburgh in May and Nottingham in July
and minor event at Leicester (20 ran) in October: should stay 1¼m: acts on firm
and good to soft going (ran respectably on fibresand): often held up: sold 7,000 gns.
M. L. W. Bell

ORIEL GIRL 4 b.f. Beveled (USA) – St Helena (Monsanto (FR) 121) [1998 61, 62
a47: a5s⁵ a5g a5g³ a5g a5g⁵ a7g 5d 8g 7d 8d 7d 7s* 6s⁴ a7g a7g a6g a7s 1999 7s⁶ 6v a–
6.1s* 6s 6g 6g³ 6s 6m 7d² 8g 6g⁴ 6m 6s 6d Oct 29] small, leggy filly: modest
handicapper on turf, poor on all-weather: won at Nottingham in April: effective at 6f/
7f (not 1m): acts on good to firm ground, soft and all-weather: effective blinkered/
visored (rarely tried nowadays) or not: inconsistent. *N. A. Callaghan*

ORIEL STAR 3 b.f. Safawan 118 – Silvers Era 72 (Balidar 133) [1998 65: 5.1d³ 68 d
5s 5d⁴ 5d* 5d 5.2g³ 5m³ 5g 6g 5.2s³ 5d 1999 a5g 6.1v 5d⁴ 5m 5s 5g* 5.3f 5g 5s 5m
5g 5.1d 5m 5m 5m 5m 5d Sep 16] leggy, plain filly: modest handicapper: won at

752

Windsor in May: disappointing after: best at 5f: acts on soft and good to firm going, well held only all-weather start: usually blinkered/visored: has been bandaged/tongue tied: none too consistent. *P. D. Evans*

ORIENTAL 4 b.c. Inchinor 119 – Orient 106 (Bay Express 132) [1998 NR 1999 **101** 7g³ 6d* 7g* 8m 7f 7g Aug 14] 100,000Y: well-made colt: has a quick action: half-brother to 7-y-o Yeast: dam sprinter: useful performer: won maiden at Thirsk (easily) in April and 18-runner handicap at Goodwood in May, latter impressively by 1¾ lengths from Tayseer: disappointing in competitive handicaps after: likely to prove best up to 7f: possibly unsuited by ground firmer than good: visored final start: wears rope halter: blanketed for stalls entry on debut: sent to UAE. *J. H. M. Gosden*

ORIENTAL FASHION (IRE) 3 b.f. Marju (IRE) 127 – Wijdan (USA) 101 (Mr **110** Prospector (USA)) [1998 93p: 7m² 8.2g* 1999 9.9g³ 8g³ 8s² 8g* 8s* Nov 7] small-ish, sturdy filly: smart performer: progressed well, placed in listed races prior to winning similar event at Chantilly in September then Premio Ribot at Rome (by 2¼ lengths from Alabama Jacks) in November: best at 1m: acts on soft ground: usually bandaged. *Saeed bin Suroor*

ORIENTAL PRIDE (IRE) 3 ch.g. Indian Ridge 123 – Mercy Bien (IRE) 63 **63** (Be My Guest (USA) 126) [1998 –p: 7s 7d 1999 11.1g 12.5m 12g May 25] lengthy, rather unfurnished gelding: modest maiden: stays 11f: blinkered final start: slowly away all outings: sold 3,200 gns, joined J. Cullinan. *E. A. L. Dunlop*

ORIGINAL SPIN 2 b.f. (Feb 15) Machiavellian (USA) 123 – Not Before Time **75 p** (IRE) (Polish Precedent (USA) 131) [1999 7d⁴ 8.3d² Oct 28] lengthy, unfurnished filly: good walker: third foal: half-sister to 3-y-o Time Mill and 4-y-o Time Loss: dam, unraced half-sister to smart 1½m winner Time Allowed and smart stayer Zinaad, out of Time Charter: fair form in maidens at Leicester and Windsor (second of 13 to Coeur de la Mer) in October: should stay at least 1¼m: remains capable of better. *J. L. Dunlop*

ORIOLE 6 b.g. Mazilier (USA) 107 – Odielese 82 (Mummy's Pet 125) [1998 55, **59** a–: 7s 5.9s⁵ 8g 7g 7s² 6.9d* 8g 8g 6.9m 7.5m 7g 7m* 8m⁴ 8v⁵ 7s 1999 8d 7g 6.9m⁴ **a48** 7m² 7f⁵ 7m 8m⁵ 7m 8g 7g 7d⁴ a7g⁵ Nov 19] leggy gelding: modest handicapper on turf, poor on all-weather: effective at 7f/1m: acts on firm and soft going, and on fibre-sand: tried blinkered/visored: ridden by Kim Tinkler and usually comes from behind. *Don Enrico Incisa*

ORLANDO SUNSHINE 2 ch.g. (May 11) Beveled (USA) – Harvest Rose 55 **63** (Bairn (USA) 126) [1999 5.7f² a6g 6.8m 6.1m 6.8d Sep 21] 500Y, 4,200 2-y-o: smallish gelding: first foal: dam won 1m seller: runner-up in maiden at Bath on debut: well beaten after. *J. L. Spearing*

ORMELIE (IRE) 4 gr.c. Jade Hunter (USA) – Trolley Song (USA) (Caro 133) **101** [1998 95: 8s⁵ 10d² 12m³ 12m³ 13.3m³ 15d⁵ 12v 1999 13.4m⁶ 13.3d⁵ 12m⁵ 9.9f* Jul 27] leggy, lightly-made colt: unimpressive mover: useful performer: well backed and

Marchpole Cup (Handicap), Goodwood—
a morning gamble is landed as Jimmy Fortune galvanises Ormelie (right);
Achilles (left) and Brave Reward lose no caste in defeat

returned to best when winning Marchpole Cup (Handicap) at Goodwood in July by neck from Achilles, despite carrying head rather awkwardly: effective at 1¼m to 13.4f: acts on firm and good to soft going, possibly not on heavy. *P. W. Chapple-Hyam*

ORO STREET (IRE) 3 b.g. Dolphin Street (FR) 125 – Love Unlimited (Dominion 123) [1998 NR 1999 8g 8m⁶ 8s⁴ 10m 10f⁴ Aug 2] IR 15,500F, 20,000Y: big, lengthy gelding: sixth foal: half-brother to several winners in Germany, including 1m and 9.5f winner Lenya (by Zampano): dam won in Germany: fair maiden: left A. Kelleway before final start: probably stays 1¼m: acts on soft and good to firm going: joined D. Bridgwater. *G. C. H. Chung* **76**

ORPEN (USA) 3 b.c. Lure (USA) 131 – Bonita Francita (CAN) (Devil's Bag (USA)) [1998 114p: 6g* 6d* 1999 8m 8g³ 8m 6.5s Aug 8] strong, lengthy colt: smart performer: won Prix Morny at Deauville in 1998: ran well when 3½ lengths third to Saffron Walden in Irish 2,000 Guineas at the Curragh in May: disappointing otherwise at 3 yrs in 2000 Guineas at Newmarket (favourite, refused to settle), St James's Palace Stakes at Royal Ascot and Prix Maurice de Gheest at Deauville (visored): stayed 1m: acted on good to soft going: has worn crossed noseband: to stand at Coolmore, Co. Tipperary, Ireland, fee IR 7,000 gns. *A. P. O'Brien, Ireland* **116**

ORSAY 7 gr.g. Royal Academy (USA) 130 – Bellifontaine (FR) (Bellypha 130) [1998 86: 9.9m⁴ 10.2g 10m* 10.3m 8.1m 10.1d⁶ 1999 a10f⁴ a10g* a10g⁶ a10g⁶ 9.7m⁵ 8.9m* Sep 1] big, lengthy gelding: fairly useful on all-weather, fair on turf: won claimers at Lingfield in February and York (after 3-month break) in September: best at 9f/1¼m: acts on good to firm going, good to soft and equitrack: usually held up: has run well sweating: sold 10,500 gns, sent to USA. *W. R. Muir* **75 a86**

OSCAR PEPPER (USA) 2 b.g. (May 13) Brunswick (USA) 119 – Princess Baja (USA) (Conquistador Cielo (USA)) [1999 7m 5m⁵ 5m 6v 8d Oct 18] $28,000Y: fifth foal: half-brother to 3 winners in USA, including stakes-placed sprint winner Princess Pietrina (by Spectacular Bid): dam winning sprinter in USA: modest maiden: best effort second start: not sure to stay 1m. *T. D. Barron* **54 +**

OSCIETRA 3 b.f. Robellino (USA) 127 – Top Treat (USA) 101 (Topsider (USA)) [1998 NR 1999 7.1m 7m⁵ 8m⁶ 8g⁵ 9s* 9.7d⁴ 10.2m 10d⁶ 12d Oct 9] 11,000Y: seventh foal: half-sister to 1¼m/1½m winner Rehaab and 13f/1¾m winner Ela Man Howa (by Mtoto): dam 6f winner who probably stayed 1m: fair handicapper: won apprentice event at Kempton in August: ran poorly last 2 starts: should stay 1¼m: goes well on soft ground: has been bandaged in front. *G. B. Balding* **72**

OSOOD (IRE) 2 b.c. (Mar 30) Caerleon (USA) 132 – Ozette 99 (Dancing Brave (USA) 140) [1999 8v* 10d⁶ 7d* Oct 26] small, angular colt: first foal: dam, Irish 11f to 1¾m winner, half-sister to smart French middle-distance performer Takfa Yahmed: won maiden at Salisbury in September and minor event at Redcar in October, showing fairly useful form when beating Secret Agent gamely by a length on second occasion: should stay at least 1¼m: raced only on good to soft/heavy going. *M. P. Tregoning* **92**

OSOOL (USA) 3 b.c. Danzig (USA) – Histoire (FR) (Riverman (USA) 131) [1998 NR 1999 8m Sep 19] closely related to 3 winners, notably Erhaab: dam French 10.5f winner: well held in maiden at Newcastle: sold 3,500 gns, sent to Greece. *J. L. Dunlop* **–**

OSTARA (IRE) 2 b.g. (May 1) Petorius 117 – Onde de Choc (USA) (L'Enjoleur (CAN)) [1999 5m 6d 6d 6m² 7m⁴ 6d Jul 2] 9,800Y: tall gelding: half-brother to a French 1m winner by Mister Majestic and 2 Irish 9f winners by Stanford and Woods of Windsor: dam never ran: poor performer: in frame in sellers at Thirsk (blinkered) and Redcar: stays 7f: edgy sort, and has gone freely/hung. *K. A. Ryan* **49**

OSWALD 3 b.g. Distant Relative 128 – River Dove (USA) 86 (Riverman (USA) 131) [1998 NR 1999 5d 5g 5g 5g Sep 15] 28,000Y: well-made gelding: sixth foal: half-brother to 5-y-o Mungo Park and 7f/1m winner Square Deal (by Sharpo): dam, 2-y-o 6f winner, half-sister to 5-y-o Running Stag: outpaced in maidens, slowly away first 2 starts. *C. W. Thornton* **–**

OTAHUNA 3 b.c. Selkirk (USA) 129 – Stara (Star Appeal 133) [1998 76: 7.1m 7.1s⁴ 7d² 1999 10.3d 10.3m⁴ 10.5g⁵ 8.5g³ 8f⁵ 9g⁴ 12g⁵ 8m 10m* 8s⁶ 10g 10d Oct **76 d**

21] leggy, unfurnished colt: fair performer: won minor event at Nottingham in September: stays 1¼m, probably not 1½m: acts on firm and good to soft going: held up: sold 12,500 gns. *R. Hollinshead*

OTIME (IRE) 2 b.g. (Apr 20) Mujadil (USA) 119 – Kick The Habit 94 (Habitat 134) [1999 6s 5.1h* 5g⁴ 5g 6s 5.7s⁵ a6g* a7g³ a7g a6g* a5g⁴ Dec 17] lengthy, quite good-topped gelding: seventh foal: half-brother to 3-y-o Three Green Leaves and untrustworthy 9f and 1¼m winner Shining Example (by Hadeer): dam, 1¼m winner, became one to leave well alone: fair on all-weather, modest on turf: won seller at Bath in August, claimer at Lingfield in November (then left M. Channon) and nursery at latter course (made most, hung right) in December: probably best at 5f/6f: acts on hard ground and all-weather: visored final 2 starts. *Mrs N. Macauley* **56 a76**

OTTERINGTON GIRL 3 b.f. Noble Patriarch 115 – Bidweaya (USA) 45 (Lear Fan (USA) 130) [1998 44: 5s 5g 7g 6g⁵ 8d 1999 8f 9.3g 8m 8f 6f Jul 31] small filly: poor mover: poor maiden at best: visored once. *Miss S. E. Hall* **–**

OTTO 4 b.g. Sure Blade (USA) 130 – Nikatino 63 (Bustino 136) [1998 –: 14d 11.9m⁵ 12.1m 13.8m 1999 a13g⁵ Jan 9] of little account. *K. McAuliffe* **–**

OUDALMUTEENA (IRE) 4 b.g. Lahib (USA) 129 – Roxy Music (IRE) 63 (Song 132) [1998 74: 6.1g 7d³ 1999 a8g a8g⁶ a7f⁴ 7g⁴ 7v⁵ 8f⁶ 10m 10d³ 9m² 8m⁵ 9.9m⁶ 8d 8d Oct 11] quite attractive gelding: fair maiden handicapper: effective at 7f, barely stays 1¼m: acts on good to soft going, probably on firm (no form on all-weather): has carried head awkwardly and found little: attempted to bite rival tenth start: one to treat with caution: sold 5,000 gns in November. *V. Soane* **72 § a– §**

OULTON BROAD 3 b.g. Midyan (USA) 124 – Lady Quachita (USA) (Sovereign Dancer (USA)) [1998 –: 7.6f 7.1d 8s 1999 a8g³ a11g 8.2s² a9.4g⁵ 8.2m 10m 9g⁵ Aug 20] modest maiden: stays 9f: acts on soft ground: visored final start: joined Mrs J. Ewer. *J. G. Portman* **55**

OUR AMBITION (IRE) 2 b.c. (May 1) Great Commotion (USA) 123 – Sea Power 88 (Welsh Pageant 132) [1999 5g* 6d³ 6m 6f⁶ 6m* 6g 6m⁶ 6s Oct 2] IR 7,000F, IR 7,200Y: leggy, angular colt: ninth foal: dam staying maiden: fairly useful performer: won maiden in May and nursery in August, both at Kempton: well below form last 3 starts: stays 6f: acts on good to soft and good to firm going: sold 10,500 gns, sent to USA. *B. J. Meehan* **89**

OUR BANDBOX 3 ch.g. Risk Me (FR) 127 – Treble Top (USA) (Miswaki (USA) 124) [1998 55: 5m 6g 6.1g 5m 6g 1999 6g 6.1g 5.9m 6g 10m 10g Aug 4] poor maiden handicapper: not sure to stay much beyond 6f: sold 800 gns. *S. Mellor* **–**

OUR FIRST LADY 2 b.f. (Apr 13) Alzao (USA) 117 – Eclipsing (IRE) 93 (Baillamont (USA) 124) [1999 7d Oct 30] 54,000Y: fourth foal: half-sister to 3-y-o Esteraad, 4-y-o Franklin Lakes and 5-y-o Vagabond Chanteuse: dam 1m winner: eleventh of 16 in steadily-run Newmarket maiden, challenging 2f out before weakening and eased: will do better. *D. W. P. Arbuthnot* **61 p**

OUR FRED 2 ch.c. (Jan 23) Prince Sabo 123 – Sheila's Secret (IRE) 97 (Bluebird (USA) 125) [1999 5.1m³ 5g⁴ 5d³ 6s³ Sep 29] 2,500Y: first foal: dam 5f winner (including at 2 yrs) who stayed 6f: fair maiden: best effort in nursery at Brighton final start: stays 6f: acts on soft and good to firm going. *T. G. Mills* **76**

OUR JACK 4 ch.g. Rock City 120 – Queen Canute (IRE) (Ahonoora 122) [1998 NR 1999 a8.5g⁶ May 22] second foal: half-brother to a German 7f/1m winner by Rudimentary: dam well beaten: mid-division in seller at Wolverhampton. *C. N. Kellett* **–**

OUR MAIN MAN 9 ch.g. Superlative 118 – Ophrys 90 (Nonoalco (USA) 131) [1998 –, a63: a13g⁶ a14g² 16.1d a12g² a14g⁵ 1999 a16g⁶ a12g⁴ a14g Jul 8] good-topped gelding: poor nowadays: stays 1¾m: sometimes visored/blinkered: has hung and tends to find little: sold 1,000 gns, joined Mrs S. Smith. *R. M. Whitaker* **– a46**

OUR MEMOIRS 2 ch.c. (Apr 22) Lake Coniston (IRE) 131 – Julip 99 (Track Spare 125) [1999 7d Sep 19] 18,000F, 240,000 francs Y: good-topped colt: half-brother to several winners, including 4-y-o Tumbleweed Hero, Dee Stakes winner and Belmont Stakes runner-up My Memoirs (by Don't Forget Me) and smart miler

Patriach (by London Bells): dam 2-y-o 7f winner who stayed 1¼m: burly, tailed off in maiden at Newbury. *P. R. Chamings*

OUR MONOGRAM   3 b.g. Deploy 131 – Darling Splodge (Elegant Air 119) **66**
[1998 NR 1999 12g 11.9d 14.1m⁵ 16m⁴ 16.1s Sep 29] second foal: dam unraced half-sister to a fairly useful middle-distance stayer: fair maiden: best effort when fourth in handicap: stays 2m: acts on good to firm going. *A. C. Stewart*

OUR PEOPLE   5 ch.g. Indian Ridge 123 – Fair And Wise 75 (High Line 125) **57 §**
[1998 68§, a–§: a10g 11.1v 8s⁴ 7s³ 7.1m a6g 8m* 10s² 11m* 12g⁵ 10g 11.9g³ 10v⁴   **a43 §**
10.1v 12s a12g 1999 10v 10d⁶ a10g a10g⁵ a12g⁵ a12g a12g Dec 21] leggy, useful-looking gelding: modest handicapper on turf, poor on all-weather: probably stays 1½m: acts on any turf going and fibresand: blinkered (ran well)/visored once each: has worn tongue strap: has won for apprentice: carries head high: unreliable. *M. Johnston*

OUR POPPET (IRE)   2 b.f. (Apr 2) Warning 136 – Upend 120 (Main Reef 126) **58 p**
[1999 7g⁶ Oct 19] 16,000Y: seventh foal: half-sister to 3-y-o Up And About, 5-y-o Al Azhar and useful winner around 1¼m winner Shortfall (by Last Tycoon): dam, won St Simon Stakes, half-sister to dam of Royal Gait: green, under 7 lengths sixth of 16 to Azur in maiden at Lingfield: will be suited by 1¼m+: seems sure to do better. *R. Guest*

OUR ROBERT   7 b.g. Faustus (USA) 118 – Duck Soup 55 (Decoy Boy 129)   **–**
[1998 NR 1999 14.1m Jun 16] no show only 2 starts since 1996. *A. Streeter*

OURS FOR LIFE   2 b.f. (May 5) Rainbows For Life (CAN) – Kaliala (FR)   **–**
(Pharly (FR) 130) [1999 5m 5m 5v 7m Jun 19] 2,700Y: good-bodied filly: half-sister to 1m seller winner Chauvelin (by Durgam) and 2 winners abroad: dam French 1m winner: little sign of ability: dead. *Ronald Thompson*

OUR TIMMY   2 gr.c. (Mar 23) Petong 126 – Doppio 62 (Dublin Taxi) [1999 6d⁶ **75**
6m² 6.8d³ 6g Oct 2] 10,000Y: tall colt: brother to 1990 2-y-o 5f winner Garth and 6f winner Wandering Stranger and half-brother to 6f (including at 2 yrs) and 7f winner Thordis (by Mazilier): dam 2-y-o 5f winner: fair maiden: placed at Lingfield and Warwick: very stiff task final start: sold 15,000 gns: sent to USA. *P. J. Makin*

OUTCRY   3 b.f. Caerleon (USA) 132 – In Full Cry (USA) (Seattle Slew (USA))   **–**
[1998 73+: 6m 7d 1999 10m 10g 8d 8s Oct 26] leggy filly: fair form on debut: little show since: should stay at least 1m. *G. Wragg*

OUTER LIMIT (IRE)   3 b.g. Caerleon (USA) 132 – Lady Liberty (NZ) (Noble **103**
Bijou (USA)) [1998 NR 1999 11m³ 12m³ 12g² 16.2m⁴ 14g⁴ Jul 2] strong, good-bodied gelding: unimpressive mover: closely related to smart 1996 2-y-o 7f/1m winner Equal Rights (by Royal Academy) and half-brother to 2 winners in Australasia: dam Australian Group 1 1½m winner: useful maiden: well backed, best effort when 6¾ lengths fourth to Endorsement in Queen's Vase at Royal Ascot penultimate start: gave impression something amiss next time: will stay beyond 2m: raced only on good/good to firm ground: sold 26,000 gns, joined J. Old and gelded. *P. W. Chapple-Hyam*

OUT FOR A CRUISE   6 ch.m. Cruise Missile – Real Beauty (Kinglet 98) [1998   **–**
NR 1999 a12g⁵ Feb 12] National Hunt bred mare: no sign of ability over jumps or on Flat debut. *D. E. Cantillon*

OUT LIKE MAGIC   4 ch.f. Magic Ring (IRE) 115 – Thevetia 65 (Mummy's Pet **48**
125) [1998 –, a52: 7m⁵ 5.1g 6m 8m 8d a7g⁵ a8g⁴ 1999 a6g a7g⁵ a8g⁶ a10g 8f 8m 7g⁵ a7g Nov 11] small filly: poor nowadays: left P. D. Evans after fourth start: barely stays 1m: acts on firm going and equitrack: visored (ran poorly) once at 2 yrs: none too consistent. *J. L. Eyre*

OUT LINE   7 gr.m. Beveled (USA) – Free Range 78 (Birdbrook 110) [1998 86: **98**
7g⁴ 8f² 6g* 7m³ 6g 7m* 6m 7g 7.3g⁵ 1999 7m 6m⁴ 7.1g⁵ 7m* 7f² 8f 7f* 8d⁴ 8.1m³ 7m 6d Oct 1] good-topped mare: useful performer, better than ever in 1999: won handicap in June and minor event in July, both at Goodwood: creditable fourth (promoted to third) behind Etizaaz in listed race at Sandown in August: best at 7f/easy 1m: acted on firm and good to soft ground, probably on soft: usually came with late run: retired. *M. Madgwick*

Coldstream Guards Rockingham Stakes, York—some deserved 'black type' for the consistent Out of Africa (No.6) as she comes out best in a finish of short heads against Bally Pride (blinkers) and Rudik

OUT OF AFRICA (IRE) 2 b.f. (Jan 29) Common Grounds 118 – Limpopo 49 (Green Desert (USA) 127) [1999 5g⁵ 5.2f² 5s² 5.1g³ 5m² 6m³ 6m² 6.5g* 7d* 6d* Oct 9] IR 50,000Y: leggy, angular filly: fifth foal: sister to a winner in USA and half-sister to 3-y-o Pipalong: dam, poor maiden, out of smart Irish 7f to 8.5f winner Grey Goddess: useful performer: improved with virtually every run, winning well-contested nurseries at Doncaster and Newmarket in September and listed event at York (by short head from Bally Pride) in October: effective at 6f/7f: acts on firm and good to soft going, probably on soft: best held up: game and consistent: sold 200,000 gns in December. *B. W. Hills*   **98**

OUT OF REACH 2 b.f. (May 22) Warning 136 – Well Beyond (IRE) 101 (Don't Forget Me 127) [1999 6v* Oct 23] smallish, angular filly: fourth foal: sister to useful 1996 2-y-o 6f winner Well Warned (stayed 7f) and half-sister to 4-y-o Fuegian: dam 5f (at 2 yrs) to 1m winner out of sister to dam of Zafonic: well-backed second favourite, won 14-runner maiden at Newbury by head from Free Rider, pair pulling well clear final 2f: should stay 1m: probably a better than useful performer in the making, sure to win more races. *B. W. Hills*   **93 p**

OUT OF SIGHT (IRE) 5 ch.g. Salse (USA) 128 – Starr Danias (USA) (Sensitive Prince (USA)) [1998 79: 8.1s⁴ 8d⁶ 8.5m 1999 7.9f⁴ 8.1d⁶ 8g⁵ 7.1m 8.1s 8d a7g* Nov 19] deep-girthed gelding: fairly useful handicapper: won at Southwell on all-weather debut in November: stays 1m: acts on firm and soft going and fibresand: has run creditably sweating. *B. A. McMahon*   **79**

OUT OF THE WOOD 2 ch.g. (Mar 13) Prince Daniel (USA) – Spring Garden 54 (Silly Prices 110) [1999 5g⁶ 7m Jun 19] 1,400Y: ninth foal: dam poor maiden: well beaten in sellers. *M. W. Easterby*   **–**

OUT ON THE LIFFEY (IRE) 7 b.g. West China 107 – Eurotin (Shack (USA) 118) [1998 NR 1999 14g Aug 14] half-brother to useful jumper Boardroom Shuffle (by Executive Perk): modest form in Irish bumpers for S. Donohoe: no form in 2 outings over hurdles and only one on Flat (slowly away). *John A. Harris*   **–**

OUTSTANDING TALENT   2 gr.f. (Apr 20) Environment Friend 128 –   **51**
Chaleureuse (Final Straw 127) [1999 5m 6.1m⁴ 5.7d³ 6.1d 5.1g Oct 21] 500Y: half-
sister to a winner in Holland by Liboi: dam ran once: modest maiden: trained first 2
starts by R. Simpson: should stay 1m. *V. Soane*

OVERCOME   4 b.f. Belmez (USA) 131 – Olivana (GER) (Sparkler 130) [1998   –
11d² 12g³ 10m* 8.5s⁴ 9s⁵ 1999 7s 11.6m Jul 12] half-sister to several winners,
including 6-y-o Nocksky: dam unraced half-sister to German Derby winners Orofino
and Ordos: won maiden at Frankfurt in 1998 (left U. Ostmann, Germany, 5,000 gns
after final start): no show in sellers in 1999: probably better at 1¼m+ than shorter:
acts on good to firm ground: blinkered final start at 3 yrs. *R. G. Frost*

OVERENTHUSE (USA)   3 b.g. Alleged (USA) 138 – Zealous Lady (USA)   –
(Highland Blade (USA)) [1998 NR 1999 12g 12g⁶ Jun 11] fifth foal: half-brother to
7f winner Utmost Zeal (by Cozzene) and winners in USA by Northern Prospect and
Majestic Light: dam 6f winner in USA from family of very smart middle-distance
stayers Raintrap and Sunshack: only signs of ability in maidens at Newmarket
(blinkered) and Goodwood (visored): sent to UAE. *J. H. M. Gosden*

OVER KEEN   5 b.m. Keen 116 – Shift Over (USA) 62 (Night Shift (USA)) [1998   –
58, a55: 8m⁵ 10m⁶ 9.7m 7v⁴ a8g² a8.5g 1999 a8g 7m Jun 26] sturdy mare: modest
maiden at best: left Gay Kelleway and off nearly 6 months before final start: likely to
prove best at 7f/1m: acts on good to firm going, heavy and equitrack: blinkered on
reappearance. *Miss L. C. Siddall*

OVERSMAN   6 b.g. Keen 116 – Jamaican Punch (IRE) (Shareef Dancer (USA)   **53 §**
135) [1998 NR 1999 a12g³ 12s 13.8g² 13.8g³ 10m³ a11g Jun 28] robust gelding: **a64 §**
modest performer: probably stays 1¾m: acts on fibresand, best turf run on good
going: blinkered/tongue tied: irresolute. *J. G. FitzGerald*

OVER THE MARCH   3 b.f. Deploy 131 – Carn Maire 83 (Northern Prospect   **49**
(USA)) [1998 53: 6.1g 8.2s⁶ 8d 1999 9.7v⁶ 11.6g 11.8m³ 14.1g³ 14.1m³ 16m 12s Oct
4] sturdy, workmanlike filly: has a round action: poor maiden handicapper: stays
1¾m: acts on good to firm going, probably on soft: visored third to fifth starts,
blinkered final one: sold 5,500 gns. *J. E. Banks*

OVER THE MOON   5 ch.m. Beveled (USA) – Beyond The Moon (IRE) 58   –
(Ballad Rock 122) [1998 –, a59: a7g³ a8g⁶ a8g⁵ a9.4g⁵ a9.4g a7g³ a8.5g 6.9s a7g*   **a57**
a8.5g⁶ a8.5g* a8.5g a7g* a7g 1999 a8g⁶ a8.5g* a7g a7g6 a8.5g³ a8.4g a7g a7g a7g⁵
a8.5g⁶ a11g Dec 13] modest performer: won apprentice claimer at Wolverhampton
(fourth course success) in April: effective at 7f to 8.5f: acts on fibresand, lightly raced
and no form on turf: tried visored: none too consistent. *Miss S. J. Wilton*

OVER TO YOU (USA)   5 ch.g. Rubiano (USA) – Overnight (USA) (Mr Leader   **85**
(USA)) [1998 77: 7d 7v² 8d 10m³ 10d 10s⁵ 1999 a12g* a10g 18.7m⁶ 16s 12g⁴ 12m²
12m⁶ 15.9m 12.3m* 12.3m⁵ 12f⁵ a9.4g* 8m 10m² 10.3m a13f⁵ Dec 26] leggy, close-
coupled gelding: fairly useful handicapper: successful at Southwell in February,
Ripon in July and Wolverhampton in August: left T. D. Barron before final start:
effective at 9f to 1½m: acts on fibresand and good to firm ground, probably on heavy:
tough and consistent. *M. W. Dickinson, USA*

OWENBRISTY (IRE)   2 b.f. (Jan 18) Ridgewood Ben 113 – Dance In The   –
Wings (In The Wings 128) [1999 6s Oct 25] smallish, leggy filly: first foal: dam
unraced out of smart 1982 2-y-o Dancing Meg, a winner over 6f and 1m: showed
nothing in Leicester maiden: wore crossed noseband. *G. A. Butler*

OXBANE   5 b.m. Soviet Star (USA) 128 – Oxslip 106 (Owen Dudley 121) [1998   **44**
54, a–: a6g 6m⁶ 7f 7g 7m 9.9m⁴ 11.9g⁵ 10s² 8s 10d² a12g 1999 a12g a8g⁵ a8g² a8f
a10g³ 10.3d 9.9v⁵ 9.9g⁵ 7.5m 9.9s 8d⁴ 14.1d⁴ Oct 27] deep-girthed mare: poor
maiden: effective at 1m to 1¾m: acts on all-weather, firm and soft going: has been
bandaged in front: sometimes pulls hard/hangs/finishes weakly: tried visored:
inconsistent. *Mrs S. Lamyman*

OZAWA (IRE)   2 gr.g. (Apr 21) Brief Truce (USA) 126 – Classy 59 (Kalaglow   –
132) [1999 6m Aug 28] IR 13,500F, 20,000Y: second foal: half-brother to Italian
1998 2-y-o 5f winner Blake Relative (by Distant Relative): dam third at 1m and
1½m: looked wayward when well beaten in minor event at Windsor. *J. W. Payne*

OZZIE 3 br.f. Ezzoud (IRE) 126 – Australia Fair (AUS) (Without Fear (FR) 128) – [1998 –: a6s a7g 1999 a7g a8.5g 10.5m 8.2m⁶ 5.9m 10g Aug 18] leggy, sparely-made filly: no form: left M. Waring after second start. *Mrs N. Macauley*

P

PAARL ROCK 4 ch.c. Common Grounds 118 – Markievicz (IRE) 73 (Doyoun **59** 124) [1998 NR 1999 10m 7.7m 7.1d 7m 8.1d³ 8g 10m 7g Oct 16] quite good-topped colt: modest maiden handicapper: stays 1m: yet to race on extremes of going: blinkered last 4 starts. *G. Barnett*

PACAERA (GER) 3 b.f. Caerleon (USA) 132 – Pamplona (GER) (Surumu **67** (GER)) [1998 –p: 8m 1999 12v² 14.1m 11m 10.3d* 10g² 10.3g⁴ 9s Oct 23] leggy, angular filly: best effort in maidens in Britain when second at Folkestone on reappearance: left J. Dunlop after next start and won similar event at Krefeld in August: stays 1½m: acts on heavy ground: has worn tongue strap. *P. Lautner, Germany*

PACIFIC ALLIANCE (IRE) 3 b.c. Fayruz 116 – La Gravotte (FR) (Habitat **70** 134) [1998 70: 6m⁵ 6m 1999 a8g⁴ a8g* a10g³ 8.2d 8.3m 8.1m* 8m⁴ Jul 25] quite attractive colt: fair performer: won maiden at Lingfield in February and handicap at Sandown in June: ran creditably final start: may prove best around 1m: acts on equitrack and good to firm going: blinkered last 2 starts: sold 8,000 gns in November. *R. W. Armstrong*

PACIFIC PLACE (IRE) 2 gr.c. (Apr 20) College Chapel 122 – Kaitlin (IRE) – (Salmon Leap (USA) 131) [1999 6v 6d Nov 4] IR 11,500F, 30,000Y: good-bodied colt: second foal: dam Irish 1½m and hurdles winner: well held in maidens at Newbury and Windsor. *M. Quinn*

PACINO 2 b.c. (Mar 5) Zafonic (USA) 130 – June Moon (IRE) (Sadler's Wells **81 +** (USA) 132) [1999 7m* 7m² Jul 30] 50,000Y: good-bodied colt: third foal: brother to smart Japanese 3-y-o 7f/1m winner (Group 1-placed) Zachariah and half-brother to 4-y-o Winsome George: dam unraced daughter of 1000 Guineas runner-up and smart sprinter Kerrera: fairly useful form when second in maidens at Salisbury (awarded race after winner failed dope test) and Newmarket (odds on), on latter course flashing tail and beaten length by Reflex Blue: likely to prove best at 7f/1m: didn't walk freely beforehand and got upset in stalls at Newmarket: joined Godolphin. *J. L. Dunlop*

PACK-A-PUNCH (IRE) 2 b.f. (Mar 22) Up And At 'em 109 – Soul Fire (IRE) **54** (Exactly Sharp (USA) 121) [1999 a5g⁴ a5g⁶ Dec 13] IR 4,400Y: second foal: dam unraced: modest form in all-weather maidens. *Miss L. A. Perratt*

PADAUK 5 b.h. Warrshan (USA) 117 – Free On Board 73 (Free State 125) [1998 **42 §** 62, a55: 14.4m⁴ 16.4m³ 14.4s² 12m 14m² 14g⁵ 13.1m 14g⁵ 15.4m⁵ 12s a16g² **a61 §** 1999 a16f² a16f* a16g² a16g³ 16.4s⁶ 16d⁵ 16.2m 14m⁶ a16g Nov 8] lengthy horse: has a round action: modest handicapper: won for first time at Lingfield in January: effective at 1½m to 2m: acts on good to firm ground, soft and equitrack: usually blinkered: best held up: thoroughly irresolute. *M. J. Haynes*

PADDOCK INSPECTION (IRE) 3 ch.g. Archway (IRE) 115 – Lauretta Blue – (IRE) (Bluebird (USA) 125) [1998 43+, a64: a5g 7m³ 5g 7d a6g* a7g⁴ 1999 a8g² **a60** a8g³ 9.9d a8g Jun 22] sturdy gelding: modest on all-weather, poor on turf: tailed off last 2 starts: stays 1m: acts on equitrack: usually blinkered. *Mrs L. Stubbs*

PADDY MCGOON (USA) 4 ch.g. Irish River (FR) 131 – Flame McGoon (USA) – (Staff Writer (USA) 72) [1998 72: 12d⁵ 11.6m⁵ 9.9g³ 11.6m⁵ 1999 9.7v 10d Oct 12] fair maiden handicapper: no show in 1999: stays 1½m: acts on good to firm and good to soft going. *D. R. C. Elsworth*

PADDY MUL 2 ch.c. (Apr 24) Democratic (USA) 101 – My Pretty Niece (Great – Nephew 126) [1999 7m 7m 8s 6d Oct 26] sparely-made colt: second live foal: dam, of little account, half-sister to 5-y-o Royal Amaretto: tongue tied, little sign of ability. *W. Storey*

PADDYWACK (IRE) 2 b.g. (Feb 20) Bigstone (IRE) 126 – Millie's Return (IRE) **58 +** 71 (Ballad Rock 122) [1999 5m 5.3f 6m 6m⁶ 5m³ a5f a7g 6d* 7s a5g⁶ a8g Nov 30] **a41**

IR 11,500F, IR 13,000Y: small gelding: first foal: dam, Irish middle-distance maiden, out of sister to very smart stayer Assessor: modest on turf, poor on all-weather: left G. Lewis after fifth start: won 22-runner nursery at Redcar in October: should stay 7f: acts on good to soft going, good to firm and fibresand: blinkered 5 times, including for win: rather inconsistent. *D. W. Chapman*

PADHAMS GREEN   3 b.g. Aragon 118 – Double Dutch 100 (Nicholas Bill 125)   **73**
[1998 67p: 5.2m⁴ 5m 6g⁴ 1999 9g 8m⁴ 7m³ 7g⁵ 7m³ 7m* 7m 7g⁶ a7g 7s Oct 23]
sturdy, short-backed gelding: fair handicapper: won apprentice event at Salisbury in August: below form after, including on all-weather: effective at 7f/1m: acts on good to firm ground: sold 10,000 gns. *M. H. Tompkins*

PADOUKI (USA)   3 b.g. Dayjur (USA) 137 – Gesedeh 117 (Ela-Mana-Mou 132)   –
[1998 NR 1999 7v 7f⁶ 7m 6g Aug 14] 8,500 2-y-o: half-brother to useful 11.5f winner Elbaaha and 9.4f and (in Spain) 1¼m winner El Ghaazee (both by Arazi): dam, best at 1¼m, half-sister to Ardross: little form: dead. *B. A. Pearce*

PAGAN   4 b.g. Last Tycoon 131 – Temple Row (Ardross 134) [1998 –: 11.5m⁴
12m⁴ 1999 10.1m⁴ 12f 15.8g⁶ 17.2g Aug 25] little sign of ability: blinkered final start. *M. W. Easterby*

PAGAN KING (IRE)   3 b.c. Unblest 117 – Starinka (Risen Star (USA)) [1998   **79**
89p: 6m 6m⁴ 7s* 1999 8m 9.9m 8m⁴ 9.9g 8m⁴ 8g³ 7s* a8g⁵ a10g⁶ Dec 8] fairly useful at 2 yrs, just fair in 1999: won handicap at Brighton in August: effective at 7f (given a test)/1m: acts on equitrack, soft and good to firm going. *J. A. R. Toller*

PAGEANT   2 br.f. (Feb 16) Inchinor 119 – Positive Attitude 82 (Red Sunset 120)   **68**
[1999 7m⁴ 7v⁴ 7g³ Oct 19] 9,000Y: sixth living foal: half-sister to 5-y-o Epworth and 1m seller winner Guto Nyth Bran (by Bairn): dam best at 1m: fair form in frame, third of 16 to Azur in maiden at Lingfield final start: should stay 1m: joined W. Jarvis. *R. J. R. Williams*

PAGEBOY   10 b.g. Tina's Pet 121 – Edwins' Princess 75 (Owen Dudley 121) [1998   **41**
–, a79: a6g* a6g⁵ a6g a6g⁵ 6d 6m 6g 6m 7m 1999 a6g a6f a6f⁵ a6s⁴ a6g² a7g² a6g 6m   **a60 d**
5.9m⁵ 7g a7g a7g⁶ a8.5g⁶ Dec 1] small, sturdy gelding: modest on all-weather, poor on turf: stays 7f: acts on all-weather and firm going: sometimes blinkered/visored: none too consistent. *P. C. Haslam*

PAINT IT BLACK   6 ch.g. Double Schwartz 128 – Tableaux (FR) (Welsh Pageant   –
132) [1998 54: a8s a8g³ a7g* a7g⁶ a8g³ 1999 a8g a9.4g⁶ Feb 20] sturdy gelding: modest at best: well held both 6-y-o starts: best form at 7f/1m: acts on all-weather, best turf form on good going or firmer: tried blinkered. *Mrs A. Duffield*

PAIRUMANI STAR (IRE)   4 ch.c. Caerleon (USA) 132 – Dawn Star 94 (High   **101**
Line 125) [1998 96: 12.3s² 14.6g² 14m* 14g³ 12g* 14g⁶ 12m* 13.3g² 14m³ 1999 16m⁴ 14g⁶ 13.9d* 14 1m* 16f* 14f⁷ 13.9g 16.1d Oct 29] leggy, lengthy colt: useful performer: better than ever in 1999, winning in small fields at York (rated stakes), Salisbury (minor event) and Newbury (handicap, by ½ length from Benatom) in June/July: creditable second to Mowbray in Grosvenor Casinos Cup (Handicap) at Goodwood, but well held last 2 starts: best at 1¾m/2m: yet to race on heavy going, acts on any other: has won in blinkers: tends to run in snatches and may be best with strong handling. *J. L. Dunlop*

PALACEGATE GOLD (IRE)   10 b.g. Sarab 123 – Habilite 94 (Habitat 134)   –
[1998 53, a–: 7f 7m 6f 5g⁴ a6g 1999 a6g 5.3f 6g 5m Jun 11] sturdy gelding: one-time modest performer: only a little form since 1994. *J. E. Long*

PALACEGATE JACK (IRE)   8 gr.g. Mazilier (USA) 108 – Pasadena Lady   **57**
(Captain James 123) [1998 60, a67: a5g² a6g⁵ a5g⁵ a5g² a5g⁴ 5d 5m⁵ 5d* 5s⁶ 5d⁵ 5g   **a67**
a5g² a5g 5g 5m³ 5.1d² 5g⁵ 5.1m 1999 a5g a5f² a5g⁴ a5g a5g 5g² 5m 5m 5s⁶ 5m 5m* 5g 5g⁴ 5g a5g 5g 5g⁶ 5m³ 5m⁴ 5s a5g⁵ a5g² Dec 15] lengthy, workmanlike gelding: fair on all-weather, modest on turf: made all in seller at Newcastle in June: best at 5f: acts on any all-weather/turf: visored twice, usually blinkered: often races prominently/leads: tends to hang left. *J. Berry*

PALACEGATE JO (IRE)   8 b.m. Drumalis 125 – Welsh Rhyme (Welsh Term   –
126) [1998 34: a8g² a8g⁶ a8g³ a12g* a12g³ a12g a12g a12g a12g 1999 a8g 12.1v⁶ a11g 11.1s May 14] poor handicapper: stays 1½m: won in visor at 2 yrs, blinkered once. *D. W. Chapman*

PALACEGATE TOUCH   9 gr.g. Petong 126 – Dancing Chimes (London Bells   **57**
(CAN) 109) [1998 66, a80: a7s³ a7g a6g* a7g⁴ a6g² a6g³ a6g⁵ 6v 5.1v⁶ 6g* 5.9g⁵ 5s⁵   **a72**
6d⁴ 5m⁴ 6m* 6m* 6g* 6g 5m³ 5.1m 6s 1999 a6g⁴ a6g* a6f³ a6g³ a6g* a6g⁵ 6s a6g²
6f⁵ 5.9m 6d 6g³ 5g 5m 6f² 6m³ 5.7h³ 5d³ 5m⁵ 5m⁶ 5.1s 6g 5s⁶ a7g³ a8g² a7g⁵ Nov
30] tall, good-topped gelding: fair on all-weather, modest on turf: won claimers at
Lingfield in January and March: effective at 5f to easy 1m: acts on hard going, soft
and all-weather: usually blinkered/visored: tends to hang left and race with head
high: effective from front or held up: tough. *J. Berry*

PALACE GREEN (IRE)   3 ch.f. Rudimentary (USA) 118 – Show Home 90   **71 d**
(Music Boy 124) [1998 68: 5v² 5g 5m⁶ a5g* a6g* 5f⁴ 5g³ 6s 5g³ a5g² a6g⁴ a6g² 6m³
5d⁶ 6s⁵ a6g² a5g⁶ 1999 a6g* a7g² a6g a6g a5g a7g 6g Dec 17] workmanlike filly:
fair performer: won handicap at Southwell in January: ran creditably next start, well
below form after: acts on fibresand and any turf going: not an easy ride
(has hung badly right). *D. W. Chapman*

PALACE HOUSE   2 b.g. (May 14) Never So Bold 135 – Cardinal Palace 85   **–**
(Royal Palace 131) [1999 7m Jul 21] 2,000 2-y-o: leggy gelding: brother to 4-y-o
Appyabo, Irish 1¼m and 11f winner Bold Habibti and half-brother to several
winners: dam 9.4f to 1½m winner: last of 18 in seller at Catterick. *J. J. O'Neill*

PALAIS (IRE)   4 b.g. Darshaan 133 – Dance Festival 101 (Nureyev (USA) 131)   **63**
[1998 75: 8d⁴ 8.2m⁵ 9.9m⁶ 11.5m⁶ 12d⁴ 1999 a8g³ a11g* a11g² a12g⁵ a11g   **a69**
10d⁵ 10m⁴ 10d 16m⁵ 16m 14.1g a14g Nov 12] sparely-made gelding: fair performer:
won maiden at Southwell in January: mostly below form after: stays 1¾m: acts on
firm going, good to soft and fibresand: visored once: has been bandaged behind.
J. L. Harris

PALAWAN   3 br.g. Polar Falcon (USA) 126 – Krameria 72 (Kris 135) [1998 63p: **75**
6v 6d 1999 7.1m² 7.1g⁵ 6f² 5d² 5g Sep 15] lengthy gelding: fair maiden: best efforts
at Sandown (including in handicap) first 2 starts: likely to prove best up to 7f: acts on
good to firm going (looked none too keen on firm), probably on good to soft: has
been bandaged. *I. A. Balding*

PALERIA (USA)   3 ch.f. Zilzal (USA) 137 – Placer Queen (Habitat 134) [1998   **77**
71: 6g 6m* 6g⁵ 1999 7m 8g⁵ 7d a7g Nov 11] tall, unfurnished filly: fair performer:
best effort when fifth of 22 in handicap in October: free-going sort, but should stay
beyond 1m: acts on good to firm ground, possibly not on good to soft: has been early
to post. *P. W. Harris*

PALHA   2 b.g. (Mar 9) Jalmood (USA) 126 – Alioli (Nishapour (FR) 125) [1999 7g   **56**
7.1d³ 7f⁵ 7g 10s Oct 5] IR 5,000Y: first foal: dam (no worthwhile form) from
family of Last Second and Alborada: modest maiden: well held in nurseries at Ayr
(well-backed favourite, looked difficult ride) and Nottingham last 2 starts: should
stay 1m (seemed not to get 1¼m): sold 3,000 gns, sent to Kuwait. *Sir Mark Prescott*

PALIO SKY   5 b.h. Niniski (USA) 125 – Live Ammo 94 (Home Guard (USA)   **112**
129) [1998 113: 12s 13.4m² 16g 16.4g⁵ 15g* 12g⁶ 15d 16g 1999 15g⁴ 13.9f⁵ 12.5g²
13.4d⁵ 14.1m³ Sep 2] leggy, attractive, good-topped horse: smart performer: best
efforts in 1999 when in frame behind Lucky Dream in listed race at Chantilly on
reappearance and Prix Maurice de Nieuil (beaten ¾ length) at Maisons-Laffitte on
third start: effective at 1½m to 15f: acts on good to firm and good to soft ground:
races rather lazily: none too consistent: sold only 13,000 gns in October. *J. L. Dunlop*

PALLIUM (IRE)   11 b.g. Try My Best (USA) 130 – Jungle Gardenia (Nonoalco   **33**
(USA) 131) [1998 46: 6v 5s 5g 5d⁵ 5m² 5f 5g³ 5s⁴ 5d 5g⁶ 6m 5d⁴ 5s 5g 5d⁶ 1999
5g 5m 5m 5m 5m⁵ 6d 5g 5m 6m 5f 5m⁵ 5m 5m Sep 6] good-bodied gelding: poor
handicapper: effective at 5f/6f: acts on any going: usually blinkered/tongue tied: has
hung. *D. A. Nolan*

PALMSTEAD BELLE (IRE)   2 b.f. (Mar 18) Wolfhound (USA) 126 – Fiction   **79**
59 (Dominion 123) [1999 5m³ 5.1m* 5d 5g 5m⁴ 5g⁵ Aug 20] 3,000Y: close-coupled,
quite attractive filly: fourth foal: half-sister to Italian 3-y-o Uragano Meri (by Kris),
1m winner at 2 yrs: dam 2-y-o 5f winner out of Galtres winner Sans Blague: fair
performer: won minor event at Nottingham in May: appeared to run best race when
seventh of 10 to Vita Spericolata in listed race at Sandown (though reportedly
swallowed tongue) fourth start: should prove best at 5f. *C. B. B. Booth*

PALM TREE   3 b.f. Alzao (USA) 117 – Swan Heights 70 (Shirley Heights 130)   **84**
[1998 NR 1999 8g² 8.3g 8f² 10g³ Aug 21] third foal: half-sister to Italian 1m/9f
winner Kafenion (by Fairy King): dam, won around 1½m, half-sister to very smart
sprinter Primo Dominie: fairly useful maiden: runner-up at Newmarket and Thirsk:
may prove best at 1m: raced only on good going or firmer: sent to Saudi Arabia. *Sir
Michael Stoute*

PALO BLANCO   8 b.m. Precocious 126 – Linpac Mapleleaf 69 (Dominion 123)   **–**
[1998 69: a6g⁶ a7g⁶ a5g² a5g a6g⁴ 5m⁴ 6m⁶ 5.2g³ 6m⁵ 5m⁵ 7m⁵ 6.9d² 7g 6.1d⁶
1999 a6g Nov 15] leggy, workmanlike mare: fair performer for G. L. Moore and
M. Ryan in 1998: no show only outing in 1999. *Andrew Reid*

PAL OF MINE   3 b.c. Zafonic (USA) 130 – Dana Springs (IRE) 111 (Aragon   **75 d**
118) [1998 81p: 6m 5m² 6s* 1999 8m 7m⁶ 7.9s⁴ 9.9d⁴ 9m 7.1m 8s Oct 25] smallish,
workmanlike colt: fair handicapper: ran creditably second to fourth starts, but poorly
otherwise: stays 1¼m: acts on soft and good to firm going: has been free to post: sold
3,000 gns, sent to Sweden. *R. Hannon*

PALUA   2 b.c. (Feb 6) Sri Pekan (USA) 117 – Reticent Bride (IRE) 71 (Shy Groom   **76**
(USA)) [1999 7m 6d 7.1m³ 7m Sep 18] 14,000Y, 42,000 2-y-o: tall, useful-looking
colt: third foal: half-brother to 3-y-o Barnacla and a 6f winner in Italy by Night Shift:
dam, Irish 6f winner, sister to Lowther winner Miss Demure: fair maiden: best effort
when third at Chepstow: not bred to stay much beyond 7f. *Mrs A. J. Bowlby*

PALVIC LADY   3 b.f. Cotation – Palvic Grey (Kampala 120) [1998 –: 7m 7g   **60 +**
6.1g 1999 6.1v 6.1s⁶ 5g³ 5d⁶ 5g 8.1f 6g⁵ 5g³ 5g* 5d Sep 23] tall, leggy filly: modest
performer: won maiden at Beverley in September: well held in handicap final start:
may prove best at 5f: acts on soft going: looks difficult ride. *C. Smith*

PAMELA ANSHAN   2 b.f. (Feb 18) Anshan 119 – Have Form (Haveroid 122)   **–**
[1999 6.1d 6g 6v Oct 23] big, lengthy filly: half-sister to useful sprinter (also won up
to 1m) Shikari's Son (by Kala Shikari): dam poor maiden who stayed 7f: well held in
maidens. *J. Cullinan*

PAMS PRINCESS   3 b. or br.f. King's Signet (USA) 110 – Good Skills 57   **–**
(Bustino 136) [1998 NR 1999 a6g a7g 7.1m 5.1m Jul 15] 500Y: third foal: dam,
headstrong maiden, bred to stay 1½m: no sign of ability. *K. Bishop*

PANAMA HOUSE   4 ch.g. Rudimentary (USA) 118 – Lustrous 73 (Golden Act   **78**
(USA)) [1998 78: 7d⁶ 8s 9m 8m 8.5m³ 8d 8g 10.3d* 1999 10m³ 10.3g⁶ 12m⁴ 10.1f⁴
9.9g* 9g³ 10m⁵ 10.3m Sep 11] lengthy, useful-looking gelding: fair handicapper:
won at Beverley in August: below form last 2 starts: stays 1¼m, not 1½m: acts on
good to firm and good to soft going: blinkered last 4 starts: has worn tongue strap: has
been blanketed/worn rope halter for stalls: usually races up with pace. *T. D. Easterby*

PANCAKE WOOD   3 b.g. Saddlers' Hall (IRE) 126 – Dame Ashfield 90 (Grundy   **–**
137) [1998 NR 1999 12.4g⁶ 12g⁶ 14.1m 16.1m Jun 24] half-brother to several
winners, including stayers Rosina Mae (by Rousillon) and Shirley Sue (by Shirley
Heights): dam 1½m winner out of Park Hill winner African Dancer: well held in
maidens/handicap: sold 4,400 gns, joined D. Bridgwater. *M. Johnston*

PANDJOJOE (IRE)   3 b.g. Archway (IRE) 115 – Vital Princess (Prince Sabo   **81 d**
123) [1998 52: 5v 5g⁵ 5d⁶ 6m 6m⁵ 1999 6m* 6g* 6g* 6m⁴ 6m⁵ 6f 6.1g 6m 6g 5s
Nov 5] sturdy gelding: fairly useful handicapper: won impressively in large fields at
Newcastle, Windsor and Haydock (apprentices) in May: generally below form after:
should prove as effective at 5f as 6f: acts on good to firm ground: slowly away final
start: usually races up with pace. *R. A. Fahey*

PANSY   3 br.f. Lugana Beach 116 – Smah (Mtoto 134) [1998 65: 6m⁵ 5g⁴ 6m 1999   **59**
8m 7d 6m⁶ 7g⁴ 6m 7m⁶ Jul 7] small, close-coupled filly: modest maiden: should stay
1m: acts on good to firm going: visored penultimate start. *H. Morrison*

PANTANAL   2 b.c. (Apr 22) Wolfhound (USA) 126 – Forest Blossom (USA) 56   **61**
(Green Forest (USA) 134) [1999 6m 7f⁴ 6.8m⁶ 8s⁵ 7g Oct 15] 7,500Y: sixth foal:
half-brother to 3 winners at around 1½m, including fairly useful Forest Heights (by
Slip Anchor) and 5-y-o Machiavelli: dam, winner in Holland, half-sister to Yorkshire
Oaks winner Magnificent Star: modest maiden: below form last 2 starts: should be
suited by 1¼m+: sold 2,500 gns, sent to Spain. *J. L. Dunlop*

PANTAR (IRE)   4 b.g. Shirley Heights 130 – Spring Daffodil 97 (Pharly (FR)   **104**
130) [1998 109: 10d 8g³ 8m⁴ 8d² 8g* 7.6m³ 8d 7.5g⁵ 8s 9g³ 1999 10g⁵ 8m⁴ 8.1g⁵ 8m
8m⁵ 8d⁶ 7.9g 8m³ 8m³ 10s Oct 2] rangy gelding: useful handicapper: best efforts in
1999 on first 2 starts, including when fourth to Bomb Alaska in Spring Cup at
Newbury: effective at 1m/easy 1¼m: acts on good to firm and good to soft going
(possibly not on soft): waited with, and best with end-to-end gallop. *I. A. Balding*

PANTO QUEEN   8 b.m. Lepanto (GER) – Tyqueen (Tycoon II) [1998 NR 1999   **37**
9.9m 18m² 16g Aug 9] poor maiden handicapper: stays 2¼m: acts on good to firm
going, well held on fibresand. *J. Neville*

PAPABILE (USA)   2 b.f. (Apr 13) Chief's Crown (USA) – La Papagena (Habitat   **82 p**
134) [1999 7m⁵ 7d² Oct 30] sister to high-class 1m/1¼m performer Grand Lodge,
Dewhurst winner at 2 yrs, and half-sister to 11.5f winner Rose Noble (by Vaguely
Noble) and 7-y-o Zygo: dam unraced daughter of very smart 5f to 1m winner Magic
Flute: promising efforts in Newmarket maidens 3 months apart, favourite when
always-prominent second of 16 to Garota Do Leblon on second occasion: will stay
1¼m: capable of better still and well up to winning races. *W. Jarvis*

PAPAGENA (USA)   2 b. or br.f. (Apr 25) Robellino (USA) 127 – Morning Crown   **58**
(USA) (Chief's Crown (USA)) [1999 6d 6d 5m⁶ 5f² 6m 6s³ 6s a5g⁵ a7g⁶ a8g⁴ Dec   **a54**
21] $1,200F, $7,000Y: has a round action: second foal: half-sister to 4-y-o
Ayem: dam winning sprinter in USA: modest maiden: creditable third of 16 in
nursery at Hamilton in September: probably stays 1m: acts on fibresand, soft and
firm going: blinkered final start. *C. W. Thornton*

PAPE DIOUF   2 b.g. (Mar 10) Prince Sabo 123 – Born To Dance 76 (Dancing   **59**
Brave (USA) 140) [1999 5v 5g a5g² a5g⁴ 5m² 5m⁵ 6f⁵ 5.7s Oct 26] 9,200F, IR
17,000Y: close-coupled gelding: fourth foal: brother to 3-y-o Song 'N Dance Man
and a winner in France, and half-brother to 5-y-o Marengo: left K. McAuliffe before
well beaten in seller at Bath (after 3-month break) final start: stays 6f: acts on
fibresand and firm going: blinkered both outings on all-weather. *B. Smart*

PAPERWEIGHT   3 b.f. In The Wings 128 – Crystal Reay 59 (Sovereign Dancer   **77**
(USA)) [1998 NR 1999 10f² 10d⁵ 10v² 10.4g³ 10g Oct 19] second foal: dam, maiden,
closely related to 1000 Guineas third Crystal Gazing: fair maiden: well held on
handicap debut final start: should stay 1½m: seems to act on any going: sold 20,000
gns in December. *L. M. Cumani*

PAPILLON SAUVAGE   4 b.f. Theatrical Charmer 114 – Gotcher 74 (Jalmood   **–**
(USA) 126) [1998 –: 8.2v a8.5g a8g 1999 12m Jul 26] no sign of ability. *W. R. Muir*

PAPI SPECIAL (IRE)   2 b.g. (Feb 8) Tragic Role (USA) – Practical 95 (Bally-   **72 +**
more 123) [1999 8.3f 8f⁴ 8.3s² 8v² Oct 12] IR 11,000F, 13,000Y, 7,500 2-y-o: brother
to fairly useful 6f winner Be Practical and half-brother to several winners, including
fairly useful 1m (at 2 yrs) and 1¼m winner Shrewd Partner (by Ahonoora): dam Irish
9f and 1¼m winner: progressive form: second of 11 to Clever Girl in nursery at Ayr
final start: will stay at least 1¼m: acts on heavy ground: visored after debut. *I. Semple*

PAPUA   5 ch.g. Green Dancer (USA) 132 – Fairy Tern 109 (Mill Reef (USA) 141)   **86**
[1998 96: 12m² 12m 1999 a12g⁴ a12g Jan 20] tall gelding: useful handicapper at best
on turf, fairly useful on all-weather: better effort in 1999 on reappearance: stays
1½m: acts on firm ground, good to soft and equitrack: tried visored, blinkered second
start: sometimes gets on edge: takes strong hold: may not be one to trust implicitly:
useful hurdler. *I. A. Balding*

PARABLE   3 b.c. Midyan (USA) 124 – Top Table 65 (Shirley Heights 130) [1998   **76**
NR 1999 10.5s⁶ 8.3g⁵ 8.2d⁶ Oct 21] 53,000Y: third foal: half-brother to 4-y-o Krispy
Knight: dam, maiden who stayed 1½m, half-sister to smart miler Centre Stalls: best
effort in maidens when close fifth at Windsor: should be suited by 1¼m+: raced only
on good going or softer: sold 16,000 gns, joined D. Barker. *L. M. Cumani*

PARADISE COUNTY   3 b.f. Prince Sabo 123 – Bold County 70 (Never So Bold   **–**
135) [1998 NR 1999 10.1m⁵ 10d 9s Oct 8] second foal: dam, 2-y-o 5f winner, half-
sister to smart middle-distance filly Tants: well beaten in maidens. *Miss B. Sanders*

PARADISE GARDEN (USA)   2 b.c. (Mar 3) Septieme Ciel (USA) 123 – Water   **98**
Course (USA) (Irish River (FR) 131) [1999 7m³ 8g* 8m² 8d² 10d⁴ Oct 30] IR
21,000Y: tall, leggy colt: fluent mover: fifth living foal: half-brother to top juvenile

hurdler of 1997/8 Deep Water (by Diesis), Irish 3-y-o 1m (at 2 yrs)/1¼m winner King of The Wire (by Danzig Connection) and 4-y-o Star of The Course: dam (unraced) from good family: useful performer: won minor event at Newcastle in August: in frame after in minor event at Newbury and listed races at Pontefract (neck second to Hataab) and Newmarket (didn't quite last home when fourth to Monte Carlo): stays 1m: acts on good to firm and good to soft going. *M. Johnston*

PARADISE (IRE) 2 b.g. (Apr 4) Distinctly North (USA) 115 – Why Not Glow (IRE) (Glow (USA)) [1999 6d Sep 16] 20,000 2-y-o: fifth foal: half-brother to 3-y-o Bartholomew and 5-y-o Vasari: dam unraced: well beaten in maiden at Ayr. *J. J. O'Neill* —

PARADISE LANE 3 ch.g. Alnasr Alwasheek 117 – La Belle Vie 73 (Indian King (USA) 128) [1998 62: 5m⁴ 1999 5.1s² 5.1s* 5.1m* 6m⁵ 5g 5m 5.1m 6m Jul 25] close-coupled gelding: fairly useful performer: won maiden at Nottingham in April and handicap at Chester in May: well beaten last 3 starts: best at 5f: acts on soft and good to firm going: trail-blazing front-runner. *B. R. Millman* 94

PARADISE NAVY 10 b.g. Slip Anchor 136 – Ivory Waltz (USA) (Sir Ivor 135) [1998 75, a68+: a12g⁶ 15.4s⁴ 15.4v³ 17.2g³ 16m* 14.1g³ 16m² 16.5g 16.1m⁴ 14.1m* 14.1m 14.4d 12g 15.4m 17.2d² 16.2s 14.1v⁴ a14.8g⁴ a14g* a16.2g* a14.8g⁵ 1999 a16g* a16f⁵ a16f⁴ a16.2g⁶ 14.1m³ 14.1g² 12m 17.2m⁶ 14.1m⁴ 16g⁶ 14.4m Sep 8] close-coupled gelding: fair handicapper: won amateur event at Lingfield in January: effective at 1¾m to 2½m: acts on any turf/all-weather: wears blinkers: held up: sometimes finds little: none too consistent. *C. R. Egerton* 70

PARADISE YANGSHUO 2 b.f. (Mar 14) Whittingham (IRE) 104 – Poly Static (IRE) 43 (Statoblest 120) [1999 5d 5.1s² 5d² 5g 5m⁵ 5.1m² 5g 5g⁶ 5m 5f Sep 13] angular filly: first foal: dam ran twice at 2 yrs: modest maiden: runner-up in seller, claimer and nursery: left M. Channon after third start: raced only at 5f: acts on soft and good to firm going: sold 800 gns in October. *E. J. Alston* 54

PARDAN 5 b.g. Pharly (FR) 130 – Silent Pool 68 (Relkino 131) [1998 48, a32: a6g⁵ a7g 16g³ a13g⁴ 14.1g³ 17.2d⁴ 14.1m⁵ 15.8d² 15.8m 14.1s 1999 12.3m 14.1g* 15.8m 14.1m Jul 17] sturdy gelding: poor handicapper: won 18-runner selling event at Nottingham in July: stays 2m: acts on good to firm and good to soft ground: blinkered once: often front runner: none too consistent. *B. Palling* 48 a–

PARDY PET (IRE) 2 ch.f. (Mar 16) Petardia 113 – Elite Exhibition (Exhibitioner 111) [1999 5g 6m 6g 5m* 5.1h⁴ 6m 6.1m a6g⁶ Nov 17] IR 6,500Y: sixth foal: half-sister to fairly useful Irish 7f winner Diesel Dan (by Mac's Imp): dam Irish maiden: poor performer: trained by M. Heaton-Ellis first 5 starts, winning seller at Leicester in July: probably stays 6f: raced only on good going or firmer on turf: races freely. *C. G. Cox* 48

PARIJAZZ (IRE) 5 b.m. Astronef 116 – Brandywell (Skyliner 117) [1998 NR 1999 6g May 21] fair at 2 yrs: little form since. *M. A. Buckley* –

PARISIAN LADY (IRE) 4 b.f. Paris House 123 – Mia Gigi (Hard Fought 125) [1998 91: 6d⁴ 7m³ 7g 7.3m 7f⁴ 6m 6s 8g 1999 6v 7m 7g 7f a6g⁴ a7g a7g a8g* a7g a9.4g⁶ Dec 27] tall, rather shallow-girthed filly: modest handicapper nowadays: won at Lingfield in December: stays 1m: acts on firm going and all-weather: effective blinkered or not: very reluctant to post penultimate start, ran moody race final outing. *A. G. Newcombe* 62

PARISIENNE HILL 3 b.f. Lapierre 119 – Snarry Hill 34 (Vitiges (FR) 132) [1998 –: 6m 7d 8.2v 1999 12m 8m 10m 9.9m⁶ 12m⁶ 16.2g 7.5g a11g 11.8d 14.1f Oct 20] workmanlike filly: poor maiden. *B. W. Murray* 36

PARISIEN STAR (IRE) 3 ch.g. Paris House 123 – Auction Maid (IRE) (Auction Ring (USA) 123) [1998 96p: 6g 6m 5m 5.3f³ 6d* 7.3g* 7s² 8g⁴ 1999 8d⁵ 8.1s⁴ 7.6m 8m² 7d 7.6m² 8f⁶ 7g 8.5g 8.1s Sep 24] leggy, useful-looking gelding: fairly useful performer: only a few creditable efforts in 1999, including in William Hill Mile at Goodwood seventh start: left G. Lewis before final one: stays 1m: yet to race on heavy going, acts on any other: none too consistent. *N. Hamilton* 94

PARIS LIGHTS (IRE) 2 gr.c. (May 11) Paris House 123 – Visible Form 99 (Formidable (USA) 125) [1999 5.1g³ 5m⁴ a5g* 5m⁴ 5.2m 5.1m³ 5d⁶ 5g⁵ 6m Sep 3] IR 5,800F, IR 10,000Y: good-topped colt: half-brother to several winners, including 3-y-o Royal Preview and useful 1m/1¼m winner Living Image (by Taufan): dam 6f 79 d and 1¼m winner: fair performer: won maiden at Southwell in June: below form last 4 starts: well below form on final one: should stay 6f: acts on fibresand, best efforts on good to firm going: blinkered 6 of last 7 starts. *B. J. Meehan*

PARIS PUDDLES (IRE) 2 gr.f. (Apr 14) Paris House 123 – Bright Puddles (IRE) **35** (Bold Arrangement 127) [1999 a5g⁶ 6m 5m 5m⁵ 5m⁴ 7s Oct 5] second foal: dam (unraced) from family of Pebbles: poor maiden: best efforts at 5f: tried blinkered. *C. W. Fairhurst*

PARIS STAR (IRE) 2 gr.c. (Feb 9) Paris House 123 – Glenista (IRE) 79 (Glen- **74** stal (USA) 118) [1999 5g a5g* 5.1m 5g⁵ 5d* 5m⁶ 5s³ 7g⁵ 7g⁴ 8g* 8d⁵ 9s 8g⁶ 8v 6s⁴ 6v⁵ Nov 24] IR 10,500F, IR 16,000Y: rather leggy, quite good-topped colt: first foal: dam Irish 7f winner: fair performer: won maiden at Lingfield in April and 3-runner claimer at Hamilton in May (made it, final start for J. Berry): trained by M. Pimbonnet next 3 starts: won claimer at Compiegne in September: stays 1m: acts on equitrack and probably on soft ground. *A. Bonin, France*

PARKER 2 b.c. (Apr 27) Magic Ring (IRE) 115 – Miss Loving 89 (Northfields **69 +** (USA)) [1999 6.8d³ 7s 6g⁴ Oct 19] 15,000F, 10,500Y: neat colt: fluent mover: brother to 3-y-o Adornment and half-brother to several winners, including fairly useful sprinter Love Returned (by Taufan): dam 2-y-o 5f/7f winner: fair maiden: in frame at Warwick and Lingfield: hung right under pressure on debut. *B. Palling*

PARKER'S PEACE (IRE) 2 b.g. (Feb 1) Common Grounds 118 – Harmer (IRE) **49** 72 (Alzao (USA) 117) [1999 7m 7d 7v Oct 25] IR 40,000Y: fourth living foal: brother to fairly useful 2-y-o 5f winner Amaretto Bay, later successful abroad, and half-brother to a 1m winner in Germany by Silver Kite: dam stayed 7f: poor form in maidens last 2 starts. *M. L. W. Bell*

PARK ROYAL 4 b.g. Secret Appeal – Mohibbah (USA) 86 (Conquistador Cielo **–** (USA)) [1998 58d: 7s⁵ 7v 10g a8g 8.1d 10v 1999 8s a8g Nov 22] modest winning hurdler, but disappointing maiden on Flat. *P. Butler*

PARKSIDE (IRE) 3 b.g. Common Grounds 118 – Warg (Dancing Brave (USA) **85** 140) [1998 NR 1999 8g⁵ 8m⁶ 7.7g* 8.1s³ 8d Oct 14] 28,000Y: angular, useful-looking gelding: has short, round action: second foal: half-brother to 1997 2-y-o 6f winner Marksman (by Marju): dam unraced daughter of sister to Shirley Heights: fairly useful performer: won 3-runner maiden at Warwick (after 3-month break) in August: good third in handicap at Sandown next start, possibly something amiss final one: raced only around 1m: acts on soft ground: went left stalls and under pressure second start. *W. R. Muir*

PARKSIDE PREMIER 2 ch.f. (Apr 11) First Trump 118 – Golden Scissors 76 **–** (Kalaglow 132) [1999 7m Aug 27] big, workmanlike filly: sixth foal: half-sister to 3 winners, including 7-y-o Scissor Ridge and 4-y-o Cutting Anshake: dam stayer: bolted to post, well held in Thirsk seller. *C. Grant*

PARKSIDE PROSPECT 2 b.f. (Feb 16) Piccolo 121 – Banner (USA) 75 **65** (Known Fact (USA) 135) [1999 6d 6.1m³ 6f³ 5g³ 6g⁴ 6m* 7.5s 6m 7.5g 6v⁵ 6s a6g² 5g* a5g² a6g³ a6g* Dec 18] leggy filly: first foal: dam 7f winner out of Queen Mary and Flying Childers winner Abeer: fair performer: won sellers at Newcastle in June and Musselburgh (nursery) in November and claimer at Lingfield in December: effective at 5f/6f: acts on all-weather and firm going, probably on heavy: joined T. McCarthy. *M. R. Channon*

PARLEZ MOI D'AMOUR (IRE) 4 gr.f. Precocious 126 – Normanby Lass **38** 100 (Bustino 136) [1998 39, a45?: a7g³ 11.1d 12g³ 1999 a7g⁴ 6v 7.1m 5.9g 8g a8g Dec 17] compact filly: poor maiden: no form after reappearance: stays 1½m: acts on fibresand: tried blinkered. *Denys Smith*

PARONOMASIA 7 b.g. Precocious 126 – The Crying Game 55 (Manor Farm **–** Boy 114) [1998 25: a10g⁵ a10g a12g⁵ a16g a11g 12m 17.2d 12m 11.1d⁴ 9.9m 15.8m 1999 a12f a13g Jan 28] poor maiden handicapper: stays 11f: acts on equitrack and good to soft going. *J. L. Harris*

PARTE PRIMA 3 b.g. Perpendicular 119 – Pendle's Secret 73 (Le Johnstan 123) **47** [1998 NR 1999 a8f a7f³ a8g³ a8g³ a8.5g 12g⁶ 8f 7m³ 7.1m Sep 2] 2,800Y: half- **a51** brother to fair 6f (at 2 yrs) to 1m winner Pride of Pendle (by Grey Desire) and 1986 2-y-o 8.2f winner River's Secret (by Young Man): dam 1¼m winner: modest maiden: effective at 7f/1m: acts on all-weather and good to firm going. *S. E. Kettlewell*

PARTING ECHO   4 ch.g. Aragon 118 – Annabrianna 88 (Night Shift (USA))   **61**
[1998 66, a49: 7d⁵ 8g⁴ 7g⁴ 7.6g⁴ 7m a7g³ a8.5g 1999 8f 8d 8g⁶ 8.3m 9.9m³ 11.8d Oct   **a–**
12] modest maiden: stays 1¼m: acts on good to firm ground, poor form on fibresand:
looked none too keen under pressure last 2 starts: sold 4,000 gns. *J. A. R. Toller*

PARTY GIRL   2 b.f. (Feb 14) Unfuwain (USA) 131 – Prima Domina (FR) 89   **–**
(Dominion 123) [1999 7d Oct 30] 24,000F, 8,800Y: seventh foal: half-sister to 6f (at
2 yrs) to 1¾m winner Primo Figlio (by Assert): dam sprinting sister to very smart
sprinter Primo Dominie: well held in Newmarket maiden. *E. A. L. Dunlop*

PARTY ROMANCE (USA)   5 gr.h. Black Tie Affair 128 – Tia Juanita (USA)   **77**
(My Gallant (USA)) [1998 91: 10.3g⁴ 10m* 8.1g⁶ 10g⁵ 10m⁵ 10m 9.9m⁴ 10m⁶ 10.1g
1999 10m 12.3m⁶ 10.5g⁵ 16s Oct 22] close-coupled, good-bodied horse: just fair
form in 1999: free-going sort, probably best forcing pace around 1¼m: best on good
or firmer ground: ran creditably only try in blinkers: sometimes tongue tied: winner
3 times over hurdles between June and September. *R. G. Frost*

PAS DE MEMOIRES (IRE)   4 b.g. Don't Forget Me 127 – Bally Pourri (IRE)   **97**
(Law Society (USA) 130) [1998 79, a91: 10.3g⁶ 6m⁶ 8g³ 8s⁴ 7g³ 7g a8.5g⁵ a7g⁶ a7g   **a99**
a10g² a9.4g 1999 a9.4g* a8.5s³ a10g* a10g⁵ 10g⁶ 8m⁵ 8.9d⁴ 8m* 10g 7.9f² 8d²
7.9g⁶ a8g⁴ 7.9g⁵ 9v⁶ a10g³ Nov 16] tall gelding: useful performer: won handicap at
Wolverhampton in January, minor event at Lingfield in February and handicap at
Carlisle in June: largely in good form otherwise, second in handicap at Ascot on
eleventh start and in listed race at Taby (demoted to fourth) on thirteenth: effective at
1m/1¼m: acts on all-weather, firm and soft going: has shown some reluctance at
stalls: usually races up with pace: tough and genuine: sent to M. Dickinson in USA.
K. R. Burke

PAS DE PROBLEME (IRE)   3 ch.g. Ela-Mana-Mou 132 – Torriglia (USA)   **69**
(Nijinsky (CAN) 138) [1998 72: 6g² 6m⁶ 6f⁵ 7d 1999 9g⁶ 8.3m⁶ 10m 10.5m⁵ 12s
Aug 18] lengthy gelding: fair maiden handicapper: stays 9f: acts on good to firm
ground: tends to swish tail in preliminaries/get on toes. *M. Blanshard*

PASHA   3 b.f. Ardkinglass 114 – Infanta Maria 82 (King of Spain 121) [1998 –,   **–**
a54: 5.1d⁶ a5g² a5g⁴ 5d a5g 5f 1999 a5g⁶ a5g a7g⁵ Mar 19] quite good-topped filly:
modest maiden at best: should stay 6f: acts on fibresand: tried blinkered/visored.
Miss J. F. Craze

PASSE PASSE (USA)   3 b.f. Lear Fan (USA) 130 – Madame L'Enjoleur (USA)   **78**
(L'Enjoleur (CAN)) [1998 NR 1999 7m⁴ 10.5g³ 11.9g³ 12.1g² 11.7s a8g⁵ a10g Dec   **a–**
8] lengthy, angular filly: first reported foal: dam, 2-y-o stakes winner in USA and
third in two Grade 1 8.5f events, half-sister to 3-y-o Alrassaam and to very good
performers up to 1¼m Fanmore and Labeeb: fair maiden: well below form last 3
starts: should be suited by further than 1½m: best efforts on good ground: blinkered
on all-weather. *G. Wragg*

PASSIONATE PURSUIT   4 b.f. Pursuit of Love 124 – Flambera (FR) (Akarad   **85**
(FR) 130) [1998 82: 10m 10m⁴ 12g⁵ 10g* 10f 1999 9.9g⁶ 12g 12m 11.6g⁴ 13.3m⁴
14f 12m 12m² 12m⁴ Sep 11] tall, leggy, useful-looking filly: fairly useful performer:
generally respectable efforts at least in 1999: stays 13f: acts on good to firm going,
yet to race on softer than good. *S. Dow*

PASSION FLOWER   2 b.f. (Mar 3) Forzando 122 – Carn Maire 83 (Northern   **85**
Prospect (USA)) [1999 5g* 5.1m* 5.2g 6m⁶ 5d 8f Dec 26] strong, angular filly: fifth
foal: sister to 4-y-o High Carry and half-sister to 2 winners, including 6f winner
Maple Burl (by Dominion): dam 2-y-o 5f winner: fairly useful performer: won
maiden at Windsor and minor event at Bath in July for J. Banks: stiff tasks in listed
races/Group 3 next 3 starts: sold 26,000 gns in October and last of 8 in blinkers in
conditions event only outing in USA: should stay 6f: acts on good to firm going.
D. Vienna, USA

PASSION FOR LIFE   6 br.g. Charmer 123 – Party Game 70 (Red Alert 127)   **90**
[1998 83: 5d 6d 6m⁶ 6g 1999 6g* 5s³ 6m 5m 6m 5d² 5g 6m⁶ 6v* Sep 29] good-topped
gelding: unimpressive mover: fairly useful handicapper nowadays: made most when
winning in large fields at Kempton in April and Salisbury in September: best at 5f
(given a test)/6f: acts on good to firm and heavy going: tried blinkered earlier in
career: usually early to post. *J. Akehurst*

PASSIONS PLAYTHING 3 ch.g. Pursuit of Love 124 – Maiyaasah 75 (Kris 135) **69**
[1998 NR 1999 8s 8.2m⁴ 8d⁴ Jun 4] 21,000F, 220,000 francs Y: good-bodied gelding:
sixth foal: half-brother to 3 winners, including useful 6f (at 2 yrs) and 1m winner
Lead The Dance (by Lead On Time) and fairly useful 9.4f winner Serious Sensation
(by Be My Chief): dam lightly-raced maiden who ran only at 1m: fair form in
maidens when fourth at Nottingham and Goodwood: not sure to stay beyond 1m.
W. R. Muir

PASS THE REST (IRE) 4 b.c. Shalford (IRE) 124§ – Brown Foam (Horage **68**
124) [1998 81, a89: 7s² 7g 8s* 8g a8.5g* a8g² 9d a8.5g a9.4g 1999 8.1g 10.5d a8.5g
a7g 12g 7.5s 8.1s Sep 24] close-coupled colt: fairly useful handicapper at 3 yrs, fair
at best in 1999: likely to prove best around 1m: acts on soft going and fibresand: tried
blinkered/visored. *D. Shaw*

PASTERNAK 6 b.h. Soviet Star (USA) 128 – Princess Pati 124 (Top Ville 129) **109**
[1998 111: 10.4f² 9m² 8d 9g 9m⁶ a9.4g⁴ 1999 10.3g² 10.4f 10g⁴ Aug 6] good-topped
horse: smart performer: won Magnet Cup and Cambridgeshire in 1997: good head
second to Komistar in handicap at Doncaster on reappearance: disappointing in valuable handicap at York (looked less well than usual) and minor event at Newmarket
(found little) after: effective at 9f/1¼m: acted on firm and good to soft ground, below
form only on very soft ground: free going sort and usually tracked pace: to stand at
Scarvagh House Stud, Co. Down, N. Ireland. *Sir Mark Prescott*

PATACAKE PATACAKE (USA) 2 b.f. (Mar 17) Bahri (USA) 125 – Chaleur **67**
(CAN) (Rouge Sang (USA)) [1999 8.3s⁶ 8v⁴ 6d⁴ Oct 20] 43,000 2-y-o: closely
related to smart 7f winners Bog Trotter and Poteen (both by Irish River), latter also
effective at 1m, and half-sister to several winners abroad: dam won at up to 1m in
Canada: fair maiden: in frame at Ayr and Newcastle: raced only on ground softer than
good. *M. Johnston*

PATRINIA 3 ch.f. Superlative 118 – Dame du Moulin 81 (Shiny Tenth 120) [1998 **–**
–: 6m 8.1m 7s 1999 7.1d 6g 7f 7.1s Sep 24] big, workmanlike filly: no form.
M. J. Ryan

PATRIOT 3 b.c. Whittingham (IRE) 104 – Gibaltarik (IRE) 68 (Jareer (USA) 115) **97**
[1998 99+: 5.1s² 5m* 5s⁵ 6m² 6d³ 6s³ 6s⁶ 1999 5d⁴ 6d⁴ 6m⁴ 6d 6m 7.1g⁵ Aug 30] tall,
angular colt: poor mover: useful performer: best efforts in 1999 in minor events at
Newbury, Leicester and Chepstow on second, third and final starts: probably stays
7f: acts on soft and good to firm going: sent to UAE. *B. Smart*

PATRITA PARK 5 br.m. Flying Tyke 90 – Bellinote (FR) 71 (Noir Et Or 155) **52**
[1998 37: 7g³ 8d⁶ 10g⁵ 12m 9.9g⁶ 8.1m 10f⁵ 10m* 1999 9d³ 12.3m² 12m² 10m²
14.1m³ 10m² 12m⁴ 14.1v Sep 29] small mare: modest handicapper: generally good
efforts in 1999: effective at 1¼m to 1¾m: acts on good to firm ground, good to soft
and fibresand: usually held up. *Mrs P. N. Dutfield*

PATSY CULSYTH 4 b.f. Tragic Role (USA) – Regal Salute 68 (Dara Monarch **56 d**
128) [1998 52: a7g 6d 6m⁶ 5m⁴ 5m 7s* 6m 1999 6d² 7s 5f 6g 6g 7g 7s Oct 23]
useful-looking filly: modest performer: below form after reappearance: stays 7f: acts
on firm and soft going: effective visored or not. *Don Enrico Incisa*

PATSY STONE 3 b.f. Jester 119 – Third Dam (Slip Anchor 136) [1998 60: 5m **69**
5.7d² 6m 6f³ 6m 7g⁴ 6m³ 7s² 7d 1999 a8g⁴ 8.2d⁵ a7g⁶ 7d³ 7.1g⁶ 7g⁴ 7m 7m 7g³ 7g⁴ **a–**
7m⁶ a8.5g 8s* 10d 8d Oct 11] leggy, sparely-made filly: poor mover: fair performer:
left M. Kettle after eleventh start: best effort when winning handicap at Yarmouth
in September: stays 8.3f: acts on soft and good to firm going, below form on
all-weather: inconsistent: sold 5,000 gns. *W. J. Musson*

PAULINES STAR 3 b. or br.f. Superlative 118 – Champion Girl 81 (Blazing **–**
Saddles (AUS)) [1998 –: 6.1s 8.2s 5.7v 1999 a7g Nov 8] no form. *E. A. Wheeler*

PAWN BROKER 2 ch.c. (Mar 7) Selkirk (USA) 129 – Dime Bag 87 (High Line **89 p**
125) [1999 7d⁶ 8d* Oct 15] 25,000F, 38,000Y: tall, leggy, angular colt: second
foal: half-brother to fairly useful Irish 7f winner Blushing Melody (by Never So
Bold): dam 1½m to 2m winner: confirmed debut promise when winning slowly-run
13-runner maiden at Newmarket from River Bann, strong run from unpromising
position to lead post: will be suited by 1¼m/1½m: has scope, and very much the type
to make a useful 3-y-o at the least. *D. R. C. Elsworth*

PAWSIBLE (IRE)   3 b.f. Mujadil (USA) 119 – Kentucky Wildcat 64 (Be My   **52**
Guest (USA) 126) [1998 –: 5f 7d a8g 1999 11.6g 11.8m 10m a12g³ a14.8g* 16.4d⁶
a16.2g³ Nov 17] modest handicapper: won apprentice race at Wolverhampton in
August: ran very wide on first turn at Folkestone next time: stays 2m: acts on fibresand and good to firm ground. *D. W. P. Arbuthnot*

PAX   2 ch.c. (Feb 13) Brief Truce (USA) 126 – Child's Play (USA) (Sharpen Up   **86 p**
127) [1999 6d* Oct 29] 75,000Y: third foal: half-brother to smart 7f (at 2 yrs) to 9f
winner Sharp Play (by Robellino): dam, ran twice here then 10.5f winner in France,
from very good family: 40/1, won 19-runner maiden at Newmarket by 1¾ lengths
from Kathology, showing good turn of foot to stride clear on stand side inside final 1f
(nearest pursuer on that part of course finished only eleventh): will probably stay 1m:
looks a useful colt in the making, sure to win more races. *J. W. Payne*

PAY HOMAGE   11 ch.g. Primo Dominie 121 – Embraceable Slew (USA) (Seattle   **62**
Slew (USA)) [1998 70: 9.7s 10.8g* 10m 10.8d⁶ 11.6m 12.1g⁶ 11.7d³ 11.6m 11.7m³
12f 14.1g 1999 12v³ 11.9f² 9m⁵ 10.5s³ 10g 11.5f 12.1m² 11.1f⁵ 12m³ 12d 10.5d⁴ 12s⁶
Oct 4] workmanlike gelding: modest handicapper: stays 1½m, probably not 1¾m:
acts on any going: blinkered/visored earlier in career: usually held up: often ridden
by inexperienced apprentice. *I. A. Balding*

PAYS D'AMOUR (IRE)   2 b.c. (Feb 27) Pursuit of Love 124 – Lady of The Land   **72 +**
75 (Wollow 132) [1999 5m 7m⁵ 6d⁶ 6m⁶ 6s Oct 2] 17,000Y: half-brother to several
winners, including 5-y-o Jawhari and 1¼m winner Sharquin (by Indian King): dam
1m winner: fair performer: best effort when winning 4-runner nursery at Epsom in
September: saddle slipped final start: stays 7f: acts on good to firm and good to soft
going. *R. Hannon*

PAY THE PIED PIPER (USA)   3 b.g. Red Ransom (USA) – Fife (IRE) 95   **87**
(Lomond (USA) 128) [1998 –: 7d 7d 1999 8d 11.6g² 14.1m² 15.8g* 14.1g* 16d⁶
14.8d Oct 15] good-topped gelding: fairly useful handicapper: won at Catterick
(maiden event) and Yarmouth in August: was effective at 1¾m/2m: didn't race on
extremes of ground: usually raced prominently: dead. *E. A. L. Dunlop*

PC'S EUROCRUISER (IRE)   3 b.g. Fayruz 116 – Kuwait Night 67 (Morston   **43 §**
(FR) 125) [1998 –: a5g 5.1g 5g a6g a6g a7g a8.5g⁶ 1999 6.1f 6d⁵ 8m a8g 8.2f⁴ 8g
Jul 5] poor maiden: stays 1m: acts on firm going: has given trouble stalls and been
withdrawn: temperamental. *G. Woodward*

PEACEFUL   3 br.f. Primo Dominie 121 – Ideal Home 104 (Home Guard (USA)   **–**
129) [1998 67+: 5g² 5m* 6g² 6m 1999 8m 6m 6f Jul 29] sparely-made filly: fair at 2
yrs, no show in 1999: should stay 7f: blinkered penultimate start: has flicked tail: sent
to Australia. *T. D. Easterby*

PEACEFUL PROMISE   2 b.c. (Mar 22) Cadeaux Genereux 131 – Island   **67 p**
Wedding (USA) 89 (Blushing Groom (FR) 131) [1999 7d Sep 30] well-made colt:
fifth foal: brother to smart 1m and 1¼m performer Winter Romance and half-brother
to useful middle-distance performer Due South (by Darshaan), 7.5f winner at 2 yrs:
dam 7f and 8.5f winner out of sister to Storm Bird: green, not knocked about when
tenth of 14 in maiden at Newmarket: should stay at least 1m: type to do better.
E. A. L. Dunlop

PEACEFUL SARAH   4 b.f. Sharpo 132 – Red Gloves 83 (Red God 128§) [1998   **75 d**
80: 10s⁵ 9.7m⁶ 10d 7g² 7f³ 7m* 7m⁴ 8d 7s* 7s³ 8d⁶ 1999 8d⁵ 8g 8.5s² 7g 7g 7s Sep
19] leggy, angular filly: fair performer: ran creditably only on first and third outings
in 1999, leaving R. Ingram before penultimate one: barely stays 8.5f: has won on
good to firm going, goes well on softer than good. *S. Donohoe, Ireland*

PEACE OF MIND   3 ch.c. Nashwan (USA) 135 – De Stael (USA) 93 (Nijinsky   **104**
(CAN) 138) [1998 94p: 7m³ 8m* 1999 10g² 12.3m 8f⁵ May 29] close-coupled colt:
good walker: fine mover: useful performer: best efforts when second of 5 to Glamis
in minor event in April and fifth of 6 to Kalanisi in listed race (beaten under 3 lengths)
in May, both at Kempton: may prove best at 1¼m: raced only on good ground or
firmer: free-going sort. *R. Charlton*

PEACE PACT   3 b.f. Brief Truce (USA) 126 – Royal Mazi 58 (Kings Lake (USA)   **–**
133) [1998 –: 6v a5g 1999 9d⁶ 6m 5.9m 5m 7m 12.3f Aug 2] of little account.
G. P. Kelly

PEACOCK ALLEY (IRE) 2 gr.f. (Mar 21) Salse (USA) 128 – Tagiki (IRE) **75** (Doyoun 124) [1999 6g⁵ 6g 7d² 8g³ Nov 3] smallish filly: good walker: second foal: dam Italian 2-y-o 7f winner: fair maiden: placed at Newcastle and Musselburgh in autumn: should stay 1¼m. *W. J. Haggas*

PEACOCK JEWEL 2 ch.c. (May 15) Rainbow Quest (USA) 134 – Dafrah (USA) **94 p** 78 (Danzig (USA)) [1999 8s² 8d* Sep 28] quite attractive colt: has fluent, rather round action: fifth foal: brother to useful 1¼m winner Bold Demand and half-brother to 3-y-o Gold Angel: dam 1m winner from family of Nashwan and Unfuwain: confirmed promise when winning maiden at Newmarket by 1¾ lengths from Capa, racing freely early on then quickening impressively to lead over 2f out: will stay at least 1¼m: likeable type who should go on to better things. *E. A. L. Dunlop*

PEAJAY (USA) 3 b.c. Dehere (USA) 121 – Petroleuse 104 (Habitat 134) [1998 **83** –p: 8m 1999 10f³ 12.3m⁴ 12d⁵ 11.5m² 11.9d 11.7f⁴ a13g* Oct 1] quite attractive colt: fairly useful performer: won maiden at Lingfield in October: stays 13f: acts on firm going and equitrack, below form on good to soft: blinkered after second start: tends to wander: has found little: possibly not one to trust implicitly: sold 8,500 gns, joined D. Cosgrove. *M. A. Jarvis*

PEAK PATH (IRE) 4 b.c. Polish Precedent (USA) 131 – Road To The Top 84 **105** (Shirley Heights 130) [1998 115p: 10.2s* 10m⁴ 11.9f⁴ 1999 12m⁶ 12m Apr 30] big, rangy colt: shows a quick, rather round action: smart performer in 1998: below best in John Porter Stakes at Newbury (sixth to Sadian) and Jockey Club Stakes at Newmarket: should be well suited by 1¾m+: yet to race on heavy going, seems to act on any other: sold only 32,000 gns. *Sir Michael Stoute*

PEARL ANNIVERSARY (IRE) 6 ch.g. Priolo (USA) 127 – Tony Award (USA) **–** (Kirtling 129) [1998 –, a37: a12g⁵ a14.8g³ 12m a12g⁶ a14g 1999 a14.8g Jan 27] leggy, lengthy gelding: poor nowadays: stays 2m: best efforts on fibresand. *Miss S. J. Wilton*

PEARL BARLEY (IRE) 3 ch.f. Polish Precedent (USA) 131 – Pearl Kite **79 d** (USA) 106§ (Silver Hawk (USA) 123) [1998 –: 6g 1999 7g⁶ 8d 10g⁶ 10.2m 8.3g 10.2m 7v Sep 24] good-topped filly: fair maiden: disappointing after second start, leaving C. Brittain's stable 8,000 gns before penultimate one: stays 1m: tried visored. *J. S. Moore*

PEARL BUTTON (IRE) 3 b.f. Seattle Dancer (USA) 119 – Riflelina (Mill Reef **–** (USA) 141) [1998 NR 1999 8m 9.9m 10g 10m a8g a10g Dec 18] 14,000Y: leggy, workmanlike filly: fifth foal: half-sister to 3 winners in Italy, including by Tibullo (up to 11f): dam Italian 8.5f to 11f winner: no form. *C. A. Cyzer*

PEARL CROWN (USA) 3 gr.f. Diesis 133 – Peach of It (USA) (Navajo (USA)) **80** [1998 NR 1999 9.9m 10g⁶ 10v* 10d Nov 4] $150,000Y: good-topped filly: third foal: half-sister to a 2-y-o minor stakes winner in USA by Black Tie Affair: dam won 15 races in USA, including Grade 3 9f event: easily best effort when winning maiden at Newbury in October by neck from Raji, wandering and looking none too keen when first put under pressure: should stay 1½m: visored last 3 starts: sold 15,000 gns in December. *J. H. M. Gosden*

PEARLY QUEEN 4 ch.f. Superlative 118 – Miss Kimmy (Tower Walk 130) **–** [1998 –, a54: a5s³ a6g³ a6g³ a7g² a7g³ a7g⁴ a8g⁶ a7g a6g³ 7g 6.9m 7s a7g⁵ a7g² 1999 **a45 d** a6g⁶ a6f a7g a8g a6g⁵ a7g a5g Mar 27] workmanlike filly: poor maiden at best: stays 7f: sold 650 gns. *G. C. Bravery*

PEARTREE HOUSE (IRE) 5 b.g. Simply Majestic (USA) – Fashion Front **94** (Habitat 134) [1998 94, a–: 8d 8s 7.6m* 8m⁴ 8s a8.5g a9.4g 1999 8.1g 8m 7m² 7f⁴ **a–** 8m 8f 8g Oct 16] rangy, workmanlike gelding: fairly useful handicapper: in frame at Newcastle in June and Newmarket (fourth to Grangeville in Bunbury Cup, despite being hampered) in July: reportedly coughing penultimate start, off 2½ months after: effective at 7f/1m: acts on firm and good to soft ground, no form on all-weather (including in visor): sometimes carries head high: usually races prominently: sold 22,000 gns. *W. R. Muir*

PEBBLE MOON 3 gr.g. Efisio 120 – Jazz 76 (Sharrood (USA) 124) [1998 68: **68** 6g 7.3g⁴ 7m 7.3g 7d 1999 8v² 8m 10m a9.4g³ a12g 10.2g 10s³ 8d² Oct 11] big, good-topped gelding: fair maiden: stays 1¼m, not 1½m: acts on heavy going, probably on good to firm: blinkered (well held) once at 2 yrs: sold 24,000 gns, joined P. Hobbs. *M. A. Jarvis*

PECULIARITY   3 b.c. Perpendicular 119 – Pretty Pollyanna (General Assembly   **106**
(USA)) [1998 87p: 8g 8m³ 7.9g* 1999 8g⁴ 8d² 10.3m⁵ 8.2m* 8f³ 8g² 8m⁵ 7m³ 7g
Aug 19] leggy, workmanlike colt: useful performer: won minor event at Nottingham
in May: ran creditably after in listed races at Kempton and Goodwood (½ length
second to Ramooz) and Tote International Handicap at Ascot (third to Russian
Revival but first home on stand side): best at 7f/1m: acts on firm and good to soft
going: races prominently/leads: has run well when sweating: sent to UAE. *B. Smart*

PEDRO JACK (IRE)   2 b.g. (May 6) Mujadil (USA) 119 – Festival of Light   **79 p**
(High Top 131) [1999 6s 6.1m* 6.1m* 6d Oct 14] IR 7,000F, IR 10,000Y: tall, leggy
gelding: sixth foal: half-brother to a winner up to 9f in Germany by Soughaan: dam
unraced: fair form: won maiden in August and nursery in September, both at
Nottingham: not certain to stay beyond 6f: acts on good to firm ground, well held on
good to soft: probably remains capable of better. *B. J. Meehan*

PEDRO PETE   2 ch.g. (Feb 27) Fraam 114 – Stride Home 78 (Absalom 128)   **55**
[1999 7.1d 8.1m Sep 9] third foal: half-brother to 4-y-o Striding King: dam 5f (at 2
yrs) to 1¼m winner who stayed 1½m: modest form in maidens at Sandown and
Chepstow: should stay 1¼m. *M. R. Channon*

PEGASUS BAY   8 b.g. Tina's Pet 121 – Mossberry Fair 28 (Mossberry 97) [1998   **69**
53§, a58§: a8g⁶ a8g⁴ 12m² 10m³ 10.1g a7g³ a10g 1999 10.5m² 11.6m² 8m* 9.2m*
8.3f* 8m⁶ 8m² Sep 16] big gelding: fair performer: won seller at Newmarket in July
and claimer then selling handicap at Hamilton in August: in good form otherwise:
possibly best at 1m/1¼m: acts on firm going and all-weather: tried visored: sometimes slowly away: used to find little (usually held up): successful over fences in
October. *D. E. Cantillon*

PEGASUS STAR (IRE)   2 ch.g. (Feb 26) Lycius (USA) 124 – Boranwood (IRE)   **82**
(Exhibitioner 111) [1999 5m³ 5d* 5m³ Jul 2] IR 18,000Y: second foal: dam Irish
2-y-o 6f winner, sister to useful Irish sprinter Wicked Folly: fairly useful form: won
minor event at Ayr in June: sent to Hong Kong. *J. S. Wainwright*

PEGNITZ (USA)   4 b.c. Lear Fan (USA) 130 – Likely Split (USA) (Little Current   **112**
(USA)) [1998 106: 9s⁴ 8d 9.9m³ 12d 9g² 10f* 1999 a10g⁴ 12m⁵ 10f² 10m⁴ 10.1m*
10m² 10.4m 10m⁵ 11d³ Sep 19] tall colt: has a long stride: smart performer: won
minor event at Epsom in July by short head from Timahs: best efforts when neck
second at Newbury in minor event (to Elhayq) and listed race (to Rhapsodist) and
when fifth in Winter Hill Stakes at Windsor on penultimate start: probably stays
1½m: best on good or firmer ground: usually races up with pace. *C. E. Brittain*

PEKAN HEIGHTS (USA)   3 b.g. Green Dancer (USA) 132 – Battle Drum   **82**
(USA) (Alydar (USA)) [1998 74: 7.5g³ 8.5m⁵ 8g 1999 10d* 9.9g 12.3d⁴ 10m 10g
Oct 2] quite attractive gelding: fairly useful performer: won handicap at Nottingham
in April: below form after, in visor penultimate start: stays 1¼m, possibly not 1½m:
best effort on good to soft going: joined C. Egerton. *E. A. L. Dunlop*

PEKANSKI (IRE)   2 b.f. (Mar 8) Sri Pekan (USA) 117 – Karinski (USA) (Palace   **89 p**
Music (USA) 129) [1999 6m⁶ 7s⁶ Oct 2] rangy, rather unfurnished filly: has scope:
first foal: dam unraced half-sister to Italian Group 3 1¼m winner Riverullah: won
maiden at Goodwood in August: improved fair bit when sixth of 12 to Agrippina in
listed race at Newmarket only subsequent outing, keeping on from rear whilst
carrying head high (possibly still green): will probably stay 1¼m: capable of better
still. *P. W. Chapple-Hyam*

PEKAN'S PRIDE   2 b.f. (Mar 30) Sri Pekan (USA) 117 – London Pride (USA)   **84**
106 (Lear Fan (USA) 130) [1999 7m* Jun 23] fourth foal: half-sister to 3-y-o Laila
Manja, 4-y-o Ameena and German 1m winner Bremen Rose (by Shadeed): dam, 1m
winner and third in Fred Darling on only starts in Britain, ran 3 times in USA:
favourite, won maiden at Kempton in June by 1¾ lengths from Terra Nova, despite
hanging left late on: looked sure to improve. *P. F. I. Cole*

PELARGONIUM   3 b.f. Danehill (USA) 126 – Sweet Jaffa 73§ (Never So Bold   **–**
135) [1998 NR 1999 7.1d⁶ 7m 8d 9.9g Aug 28] unfurnished filly: second foal: dam

untrustworthy 7f winner: no sign of ability: slowly away first 2 starts: withdrawn after bolting before start on intended debut: sold 1,000 gns. *C. W. Thornton*

PENALTY MISS   3 gr.f. Midyan (USA) 124 – Between The Sticks 83 (Pharly   –
(FR) 130) [1998 –: 6.1d 7m 5.7v a7g 1999 6g 8m Sep 1] leggy filly: no form.
A. G. Newcombe

PENANG PEARL (FR)   3 b.f. Bering 136 – Guapa (Shareef Dancer (USA) 135)   **106**
[1998 64: 7d⁵ 6.1g⁵ 7f⁵ 8.3d² 10s 1999 8.3m* 8.1m² 9m* 10m² 10g³ 10.2m² 10.5s⁴
8d* Oct 9] neat filly: useful performer: progressed well in 1999, winning handicaps
at Windsor in May and Kempton in June and listed race at Ascot (by 3½ lengths from
Ras Shaikh) in October: better form at 1m than over further: acts on soft and good to
firm going: held up: reliable. *G. A. Butler*

PENDANT   4 b.g. Warning 136 – Emerald (USA) (El Gran Senor (USA) 136)   **61**
[1998 80: 12g³ 11.5m* 12d 1999 12m⁴ 12m⁴ Jun 25] sturdy gelding: poor walker:
fairly useful winner for H. Cecil at 3 yrs (reportedly made a noise final appearance):
just modest in 1999: raced only around 1½m: visored final start. *K. A. Morgan*

PENDOGGETT (USA)   4 b.g. Alleged (USA) 138 – Waaria (Shareef Dancer   –
(USA) 135) [1998 NR 1999 10m Aug 23] 35,000Y: fourth foal: half-brother to
winners in USA by Arctic Tern and Irish River: dam unraced: behind when pulled up
in claimer: dead. *D. R. C. Elsworth*

PENDOLINO (IRE)   8 b.g. Thatching 131 – Pendulina 102 (Prince Tenderfoot   –
(USA) 126) [1998 NR 1999 10v 12.4m 12m 10d 10.9s 10d Jul 5] lengthy gelding:
has a markedly round action: little form since 1997: tried blinkered/visored.
A. B. Mulholland

PEN FRIEND   5 b.g. Robellino (USA) 127 – Nibbs Point (IRE) 107 (Sure Blade   –
(USA) 130) [1998 66: 16.2d² 1999 12.4m May 3] workmanlike gelding: fair
handicapper: below form only 5-y-o start: will stay beyond 2m: acts on good to firm
and good to soft going. *W. J. Haggas*

Mr B. H. Voak's "Pegnitz"

PENGAMON 7 b.g. Efisio 120 – Dolly Bevan 53 (Another Realm 118) [1998 NR **a69** 1999 a8.5g 7d a7g² a7g² a7g* a8g² Dec 18] smallish, well-made gelding: carries condition: fair handicapper: left H. Collingridge after second start: good efforts after, winning at Lingfield in November: effective at 7f/1m: acts on firm going and all-weather: usually held up. *D. T. Thom*

PENMAR 7 b.g. Reprimand 122 – Latakia 80 (Morston (FR) 125) [1998 63: 8g³ — 8g 8s* 1999 8d Apr 16] good-topped gelding: modest handicapper: well held only 7-y-o start: has form at 1½m, better at 1m: acts on firm ground, soft and fibresand: sometimes blinkered earlier in career: has worn tongue strap. *A. B. Mulholland*

PENMAYNE 3 ch.f. Inchinor 119 – Salanka (IRE) 68 (Persian Heights 129) [1998 **95** 86+: 5.1g 5.2m 6g² 6m⁴ 7.1m* 7.1m³ 7.1g⁴ 7g² 7g 1999 8.5d⁵ 8m⁵ 8.1g⁴ 7.3m⁴ 9m⁶ Sep 18] smallish filly: useful performer: good fifth in listed rated stakes at Ascot second start: not discredited in minor events at Sandown and Newbury next 2: stays 1m: raced mainly on good/good to firm going: sometimes bandaged: tends to wander: sold 20,000 gns in December. *D. R. C. Elsworth*

PENN 3 ch.f. Be My Guest (USA) 126 – Scribbling (USA) 88 (Secretariat (USA)) — [1998 NR 1999 7m May 16] third living foal: dam 1¼m winner: slowly away and behind in Kempton maiden (flashed tail to post and in race): sold 4,500 gns in December. *J. H. M. Gosden*

PENNILESS (IRE) 4 b.f. Common Grounds 118 – Tizzy 79 (Formidable (USA) **49** 125) [1998 53: a6s³ a6g⁵ a6g a6g⁵ 6s 7.5m⁵ 6g 5g* 5s⁵ 6g² 5m 5.9d 5m 5m 1999 a5g 5m 6m 6d May 24] close-coupled, angular filly: poor handicapper: stays 6f: acts on fibresand, best turf form on good ground. *N. Tinkler*

PENNY BLACK 3 br.f. Cyrano de Bergerac 120 – Cow Pastures (Homing 130) — [1998 NR 1999 7.1m 7g Aug 12] half-sister to a 2-y-o 7f seller winner by Petong and a winner in Italy: dam unraced daughter of useful sprinter Pennycuick: behind in maidens at Chepstow and Salisbury: sold 600 gns. *V. Soane*

PENNYGOWN 3 b.f. Rainbow Quest (USA) 134 – Applecross 117 (Glint of Gold **91 p** 128) [1998 NR 1999 12s* Jun 27] small, sparely-made filly: fifth foal: half-sister to several winners, including 4-y-o Craigsteel, 5-y-o Invermark and useful Inchrory (best up to 1½m in Scandinavia, by Midyan): dam, 1¼m to 13.3f winner, second in Park Hill Stakes: 8/1 and green, won 5-runner maiden at Doncaster by 2 lengths from Inigo Jones: sent to USA: looked sure to progress. *H. R. A. Cecil*

PENSHIEL (USA) 2 b.g. (Mar 2) Mtoto 134 – Highland Ceilidh (IRE) 100 **– p** (Scottish Reel 123) [1999 7.1d 7.6g 8.1m Sep 9] fourth living foal: half-brother to 3-y-o Nika Nesgoda: dam 1m (at 2 yrs) and 1¼m winner who stayed 1½m: behind in maidens: likely to be suited by 1¼m+: should do better at 3 yrs. *J. L. Dunlop*

PENSION FUND 5 b.g. Emperor Fountain 112 – Navarino Bay 102 (Averof 123) **87** [1998 87: 12.3m 10m 10.1g² 11.9f³ 10s* 10m 10.4g 12d⁴ 1999 7.9m* 10s 8.2d⁶ Oct 21] tall, leggy gelding: fairly useful handicapper: won 21-runner race at York in September by ½ length from Arterxerxes: not discredited both starts after: effective at 1m to 1½m (when conditions aren't testing): yet to race on heavy going, acts on any other: blinkered once: not an easy ride: held up. *M. W. Easterby*

PENTAGONAL (USA) 2 b.c. (Mar 1) Dynaformer (USA) – Pent (USA) (Mr **72 P** Prospector (USA)) [1999 7d Sep 30] \$300,000Y: angular colt: first foal: dam, unraced, from family of Nureyev and Sadler's Wells: green and in need of race, shaped very well when seventh of 14 to Qamous in maiden at Newmarket, never on terms and not at all knocked, keeping on most encouragingly: will stay at least 1m: sort to improve considerably, and sure to win races at 3 yrs. *Sir Michael Stoute*

PENTAGON LAD 3 ch.g. Secret Appeal – Gilboa 48 (Shirley Heights 130) **81** [1998 –: 6m 7.9g 7d 1999 8m* 8d* 8g 8m* 8m⁴ 10.3m* 10m 9f⁶ 8d⁴ 10.3d 8.9d 10.3d Oct 22] sparely-made gelding: fairly useful handicapper: much improved in 1999, winning at Carlisle and Thirsk in May, Ripon in June and Chester in July: generally below form after: effective at 1m/1¼m: acts on firm and good to soft ground: effective ridden from front or held up. *J. L. Eyre*

PENYBONT 3 b.f. Unfuwain (USA) 131 – Morgannwg (IRE) 86 (Simply Great **77** (FR) 122) [1998 77: 6g 7d 7v³ 1999 7s² 8m 12g⁵ 8.3d⁴ 8f⁴ 8m³ 8.1d 7s* 7s 7s Nov 2] smallish filly: fair handicapper: won at Lingfield in October: well held both starts after: effective at 7f/1m: best efforts on ground softer than good. *M. L. W. Bell*

PEPETA   2 b.f. (Feb 25) Presidium 124 – Mighty Flash 81 (Rolfe (USA) 77) [1999   **63 p**
6m⁶ 6m 7v⁶ Sep 20] 14,000F, 20,000Y: tall, unfurnished filly: seventh foal: sister to
1993 2-y-o 7f winner Mighty Forum, later smart up to 8.5f in USA, and half-sister to
4-y-o Mighty Magic: dam staying sister to Derby third Mighty Flutter: fair form in
maidens at York, Ascot and Kempton, taking good hold in lead for much of way on
last-named course: should stay 1m: type to do better. *I. A. Balding*

PEPPERCORN   2 b.f. (Feb 6) Totem (USA) 118 – Sparkling Roberta 55 (Kind of   **33**
Hush 118) [1999 a6g⁵ a7g 7d⁵ 8m a7g a8g Nov 30] first foal: dam 1m winner who   **a–**
stayed 1¾m: poor maiden: should stay 1¼m: no form on all-weather. *M. D. I. Usher*

PEPPERDINE (IRE)   3 b.g. Indian Ridge 123 – Rahwah 73 (Northern Baby   **102 p**
(CAN) 127) [1998 81: 6g² 6d² 7g⁵ 7f 6m⁶ 7d* 1999 6m² 6m 6m² 6d* 6f 6d 6d² Oct
9] lengthy gelding: useful handicapper: won William Hill Trophy at York in June by
½ length from First Musical, showing fine turn of foot, despite drifting left as saddle
started to slip: in mid-field in Stewards' Cup at Goodwood and Gold Cup at Ayr
(poorly drawn) next 2 starts, then ran well when length second of 22 to Get Stuck In
in Coral Sprint Trophy back at York, carried towards stand rail by winner having
quickened well to challenge: will prove best at 5f/6f: acts on good to firm and good
to soft ground: blinkered once at 2 yrs: should make a smart sprinter in 2000.
D. Nicholls

PEPPERS GIRL   3 b.f. Mon Tresor 113 – Lady of Itatiba (BEL) (King of Mace-   **–**
don 126) [1998 NR 1999 10.1m⁵ 8.1d 8g 13.8g 11d Oct 26] 920Y, resold 1,200Y:
fourth foal in Britain: sister to a poor maiden, and half-sister to 5f winner Had A Girl
(by Hadeer): dam won in Belgium: no form: blinkered once. *Martyn Wane*

PEPPIATT   5 ch.g. Efisio 120 – Fleur du Val (Valiyar 129) [1998 81: 8d 6g 6s 6m⁴   **77 d**
7s 6m⁴ 7.1g³ 6m³ 6m³ 7m³ 7g² 6d* 8s 7g 6d⁵ 1999 7g⁶ 6g 6d 6d⁵ 6d 6m 7f
6s* 5g⁵ 6f 6d 6g 7g⁶ 6d 5s⁶ 6v 6d⁵ 7d Oct 26] robust gelding: fair handicapper:
disappointed after winning at Ayr in July: needs good test at 5f, and stays 7f: well
held on heavy going, acts on any other: tried blinkered: usually comes from off pace:
none too consistent. *N. Bycroft*

William Hill Trophy, York—the principal race on the 29th Timeform Charity Day,
which raised a record £163,396, taking total proceeds to over £2½m;
Pepperdine shows a fine turn of foot to collar 50/1-shot First Musical (No.3)

PERADVENTURE (IRE) 4 b.g. Persian Bold 123 – Missed Opportunity (IRE) –
(Exhibitioner 111) [1998 93: 8s 8d³ 9m² 10.5g⁴ 12s⁵ 11.9m⁵ 11.9g⁵ 10.4g* 12.5d³
10v 1999 12g⁵ Sep 18] angular, good-topped gelding: fairly useful in 1998 for
R. Hannon: well below form only 4-y-o start: stays 1½m: acts on soft and good to
firm going, ran poorly on heavy: goes well ridden up with pace. *M. D. Hammond*

PERCHANCER (IRE) 3 ch.g. Perugino (USA) 84 – Irish Hope (Nishapour 59
(FR) 125) [1998 57: 6g 6g 6s³ 6g 6m⁶ 6d 1999 a7g⁴ a9.4g³ a7f² a8f³ a8g 9.3g 8.3m⁴
10d³ 7f* 8.1d² 9g 10m a9.4g a11g⁶ Nov 30] strong, close-coupled gelding: modest
handicapper: won apprentice maiden event at Thirsk in July: ran creditably most
other starts: stays 1¼m: acts on all-weather, firm and soft ground: tried blinkered/
visored: has carried head high and found little. *P. C. Haslam*

PERCHCOURT STEEL (IRE) 3 b.g. Grand Lodge (USA) 125 – Scaravie –
(IRE) (Drumalis 125) [1998 NR 1999 a9.4g 10g Aug 21] 14,000F, 17,500Y: third
foal: dam from family of Ardross: no promise in maidens. *R. M. Whitaker*

PERECAPA (IRE) 4 b.f. Archway (IRE) 115 – Cupid Miss (Anita's Prince 126) – §
[1998 44: 10.2s 8f⁵ a9.4g⁴ 10.8g 11.6g³ 11m³ 11.6f³ 10m³ a11g* 1999 10m a12g 10g
Aug 14] poor performer: no form in 1999: should stay beyond 11.6f: acts on good to
firm going and fibresand: slowly away last 2 starts. *B. Palling*

PERFECT MOMENT (IRE) 2 b.f. (Feb 19) Mujadil (USA) 119 – Flashing 66
Raven (IRE) (Maelstrom Lake 118) [1999 6g⁵ 5m⁵ 7m* 7f 7g 7g Oct 15] IR 1,500F,
4,000Y: second foal: dam unraced: fair performer: won maiden at Leicester in
July: well below form last 3 starts: stays 7f: raced only on good ground or firmer.
A. P. Jarvis

PERFECT PARADIGM (IRE) 5 b.h. Alzao (USA) 117 – Brilleaux 73 (Manado 107
130) [1998 107: 12s 14m⁶ 13.9s 11.9m* 14g 12m² 13.4d³ 11.9m³ 12s 1999
a10f² a10f² 12f² 14d² May 8] finely-made, attractive horse: fluent mover: useful
performer: runner-up in 1999 at Nad Al Sheba (3 times) and Goodwood (1¼ lengths
behind Opera King in valuable handicap): stays 1¾m: acts on firm and soft ground:
effective visored or not. *Saeed bin Suroor*

PERFECT PEACH 4 b.f. Lycius (USA) 124 – Perfect Timing 107 (Comedy 78
Star (USA) 121) [1998 82: 5g⁴ 5m⁶ 5m³ 5f⁴ 5f 5m 5m 5f 7m² 7.6d
7f 6m 7.1d* 7g 7d Oct 26] quite good-topped filly: fair handicapper: won at
Musselburgh in September: well held both starts after: effective at 5f to 7f: acts on
firm and good to soft going: blinkered (ran poorly) sixth start: none too consistent.
C. W. Fairhurst

PERFECT PITCH 2 b.f. (Jan 6) Dashing Blade 117 – Singer On The Roof 62 63
(Chief Singer 131) [1999 7m⁵ 6.1g⁶ Sep 25] third foal: half-sister to 3-y-o Sole
Singer and a winner in Holland by Bluebird: dam, 1m winner, half-sister to Prix
Saint-Alary winner Air de Rien: modest form in minor event at Kempton and maiden
at Nottingham: sold 4,200 gns, sent to Sweden. *I. A. Balding*

PERFECT VINTAGE 9 b.g. Shirley Heights 130 – Fair Salinia 125 (Petingo 111
135) [1998 111: 10d² 10d 8g* 1999 7g⁵ 8m⁵ 8g⁴ 10d Sep 22] good-topped gelding:
reportedly has 2 screws in right cannon bone: smart performer: formerly trained in
Britain and Germany: won Prix Quincey at Deauville in 1998 and at least as good as
ever first 3 starts on return in Prix du Palais-Royal at Longchamp, Queen Anne
Stakes at Royal Ascot (3¾ lengths fifth to Cape Cross) and Prix Messidor at
Deauville: effective at 7f, won up to 11f earlier in career: acts on good to firm and
good to soft going. *Mme C. Barbe, France*

PERFORMING MAGIC (USA) 2 ch.c. (Apr 4) Gone West (USA) – Perform- 98
ing Arts 104 (The Minstrel (CAN) 135) [1999 6g³ 6g² 7m³ 6m³ 5g* 5g⁶ 8.1m* 8d
Oct 9] 300,000Y: close-coupled colt: has a quick, fluent action: fifth foal: closely
related to smart Woodborough (by Woodman), 2-y-o 6f winner in 1995, and half-
brother to useful 1997 2-y-o 6f winner Dance Trick (by Diesis): dam, 2-y-o 5f/6f
winner, third in Irish 1,000 Guineas: useful performer: won maiden at Leicester in
August and minor event at Haydock (best effort) in September: stays 1m: acts on
good to firm going, well held on good to soft: visored (found little) fourth start: joined
S. Shulman in USA. *H. R. A. Cecil*

774

PERICLES 5 b.g. Primo Dominie 121 – Egalite (FR) (Luthier 126) [1998 76: **58**
a8.5g a7g⁶ 7d 8g³ 7m 7m* 7g³ 8m⁶ 7f 7m 7.5m⁶ 7.1g² 7.1g⁵ a8g a8f a7g 1999 a7g
a7f a7g a7g² a7g³ a7g⁴ a7g a7g 8m³ 6.9g 7f³ 8m⁴ 8d⁵ a8g⁵ 10m⁶ Sep 7] sturdy, close-
coupled gelding: modest performer: effective at 7f to easy 1¼m: acts on firm going,
soft and all-weather: visored penultimate start, effective blinkered or not: sometimes
makes running: tail swisher: inconsistent, joined M. Pipe. *Miss Gay Kelleway*

PERIGEUX (IRE) 3 b.c. Perugino (USA) 84 – Rock On (IRE) (Ballad Rock **71**
122) [1998 82+: 6g² 6g⁵ a6g* 6d* a6g* 6s 1999 6g⁴ 6.1d 6m⁶ 6.9g³ a7g² 6s 7f² 6d **a76**
7g² 7g 6m Aug 30] small, good-bodied colt: fair performer: likely to prove best at 6f/
7f: acts on fibresand and good to soft going, possibly unsuited by soft: sometimes
blinkered: has been unruly stalls (including final start). *J. Berry*

PERIQUITUM 2 br.f. (Feb 3) Dilum (USA) 115 – Periquito (USA) (Olden **56**
Times) [1999 6d⁵ 7m Jun 23] half-sister to several winners, including 1½m to 2m
winner Grey Power (by Wolf Power) and smart stayer Primitive Rising (by Raise A
Man): dam ran 4 times: modest form when well-held fifth of 7 to Kingsclere in minor
event at Newbury: well beaten only subsequent outing: should stay at least 1m: sent
to France. *R. Hannon*

PERLE DE SAGESSE 2 b.f. (Mar 19) Namaqualand (USA) – Pearl of Dubai **66**
(USA) (Red Ransom (USA)) [1999 5.3f³ 6g³ 7.5g 6g 5m* a5g 6s⁵ a6g² a7g* a6g
a7g* Dec 8] 2,500Y: leggy filly: first foal: dam unraced: fair performer: won seller at
Windsor in August: sold out of P. Cole's stable 1,000 gns after seventh start:
subsequently won seller at Lingfield in November and claimer there in December:
stays 7f: acts on firm ground and equitrack: sometimes awkward leaving stalls, very
slowly away once: occasionally wanders. *Julian Poulton*

PERPETUAL PRIDE (IRE) 2 b.c. (Mar 2) Pips Pride 117 – Miss Springtime **–**
65 (Bluebird (USA) 125) [1999 5m a6g Jun 5] 10,000Y: first foal: dam, 7f/1m
winner, became one to treat with caution: well beaten in maiden/minor event: sold
2,500 gns in October. *E. J. Alston*

PERRYSTON VIEW 7 b.h. Primo Dominie 121 – Eastern Ember 85 (Indian **104**
King (USA) 128) [1998 97: 6d⁶ 6d 5d⁵ 6g* 6f 6s 1999 6m* 6m 6f 6d⁴ 5.6g 6d 6d⁴
5d 5s* Oct 23] lengthy, angular horse: has been hobdayed: useful handicapper, better
than ever at 7 yrs: won at Newmarket in May and Doncaster (by 1¼ lengths from
Ellens Lad) in October: effective at 5f/6f: acts on firm and soft going: blinkered/
visored: usually races up with pace: tends to wander: tough: joined J. Glover.
P. Calver

*Ladbrokes Handicap, Newmarket—Perryston View (blinkers) blazes the trail
to repeat his 1997 win in the race, beating Rushcutter Bay*

PERSEPHONE 6 ch.m. Lycius (USA) 124 – Elarrih (USA) (Sharpen Up 127) –
[1998 –: 15.8m a13g 1999 a10g a13g⁶ Jan 9] of little account nowadays. *C. N. Allen*

PERSIAN FAYRE 7 b.g. Persian Heights 129 – Dominion Fayre 49 (Dominion **84**
123) [1998 92, a–: 7v 7d 7m⁴ 7.1m* 7v⁵ 7.1g⁵ 7s² 7f 7g 7s 7g³ a7g 1999 7g 7d* **a–**
6.9m* 7m* 7d² 7m 7s 7.1g 6d 7.1d 6v 7s Nov 2] sturdy gelding: fairly useful
performer: won seller at Redcar, claimer at Carlisle and handicap at Ayr in April/
May: below form after fifth start: best at 7f/1m: appears to act on any turf going, well
beaten on fibresand: races up with pace. *J. Berry*

PERSIANO 4 ch.g. Efisio 120 – Persiandale (Persian Bold 123) [1998 102: 6v⁴ **102**
7g* 7f* 7g* 1999 8m 8.1g³ 8m 7f⁵ 8g³ 7.9g 8s⁵ 8g Oct 16] big, lengthy gelding:
unimpressive mover: useful handicapper: best efforts in 1999 when third to Lonesome Dude in rated stakes at Sandown in May and fifth to Grangeville in Bunbury
Cup at Newmarket in July: best at 7f/1m on good going or firmer: visored final start.
J. R. Fanshawe

PERSIAN POINT 3 ch.g. Persian Bold 123 – Kind Thoughts 71 (Kashmir II –
125) [1998 NR 1999 8g 8g 10m 10.1d Oct 20] 6,000F, IR 13,000Y, 9,000 2-y-o:
half-brother to several winners, including useful 6f (at 2 yrs) and 7f winner Kayus
(by Junius), later successful in USA, and stayer Penny Forum (by Pas de Seul): dam
stayer: little form in maidens/handicap. *Mrs A. Duffield*

PERSIAN PUNCH (IRE) 6 ch.g. Persian Heights 129 – Rum Cay (USA) 75 **111**
(Our Native (USA)) [1998 122: 16d* 13.9g³ 16.4g* 20s⁶ 15.9f* 16m³ 1999 12m⁴
12m 13.9s⁵ 16.4g⁴ 20m 14.6s* Nov 5] big, strong gelding: impresses in appearance:
has a powerful, round action: very smart at 5 yrs, when successful in 3 pattern races
and third in Melbourne Cup: not so good in 1999, best effort when fourth to Sadian in
John Porter Stakes at Newbury on reappearance: off 4½ months after suffering minor
pelvic injury, won 5-runner minor event at Doncaster in November by neck from Life
Is Life: effective at 13f (given a test) to 2½m: acts on firm and soft ground: game.
D. R. C. Elsworth

Mr J. C. Smith's "Persian Punch"

PERSIAN SABRE   4 b.f. Sabrehill (USA) 120 – Wassl's Sister (Troy 137) [1998   **45**
63: 8.5s⁵ 8g 10g 8m² 8m⁴ 10m* 12d 1999 10d⁶ 10g 10.2m⁶ 10.2m 7d Oct 12] rather
sparely-made filly: modest winner at 3 yrs: poor at best in 1999: stays 1¼m: acts on
good to firm going: has given trouble stalls/flashed tail: sold 800 gns. *V. Soane*

PERSIAN WATERS (IRE)   3 b.g. Persian Bold 123 – Emerald Waters (Kings   **69**
Lake (USA) 133) [1998 67p: 7m⁴ 7m 7.5m 10s⁴ 8d* 1999 12m 12.3m³ 13.9d 14.1g
Oct 15] lengthy, quite good-topped gelding: fair performer: best effort when seventh
of 19 in King George V Handicap at Royal Ascot on reappearance: left M. Pipe and
off 3 months after next start: should stay 1¾m+: acts on soft and good to firm going:
half reared leaving stalls and looked none too keen under pressure final start: fairly
useful winner over hurdles in November. *J. R. Fanshawe*

PERTEMPS CRAIC   3 b.g. Gildoran 123 – Pertemps Partner 47 (Bairn (USA)   **–**
126) [1998 48: 8s a8.5g⁴ 1999 a10g a11g 10.8d a8g a9.4g⁵ Jun 16] poor maiden at
best: left A. Newcombe after third start: pulled too hard in visor final one. *A. Streeter*

PERTEMPS FC   2 b.g. (Feb 14) Prince Sabo 123 – Top Mouse (High Top 131)   **64**
[1999 5d⁴ 5m 6m 6f* 5g² 5g* 6d⁶ 5d Sep 30] 9,000Y, 8,500 2-y-o: lengthy gelding:
closely related to 5f winner Idrak (by Young Generation) and half-brother to several
winners, including 6-y-o Chief Mouse: dam, ran twice, from very good middle-
distance family: modest performer: won seller at Newcastle in July and nursery at
Beverley in August: acts on firm going: well held in blinkers: often
slowly away: swerved violently left and unseated rider leaving stalls second start.
T. D. Easterby

PERTEMPS MISSION   5 b.g. Safawan 118 – Heresheis 69 (Free State 125)   **50**
[1998 52: 14.1s 15.4v 16d⁴ 17.2d 14.9g³ 14.1m 15.8m* 16v 15.8m 16m² a14.8g⁶
a14.8g* a16g² 1999 a16g² a16f³ a16f⁵ a16g⁶ a16g² Feb 25] workmanlike gelding:
has a roundish action: modest handicapper: stays 2m well: acts on firm going, good
to soft and all-weather: usually visored/blinkered. *J. Pearce*

PERTEMPS STAR   2 b.g. (Apr 25) Imperial Frontier (USA) 112 – Stella Royale   **–**
(Astronef 116) [1999 5m 6m 6g 5.7s a5g a5g Nov 19] 500Y: third foal: dam unraced:
little form. *A. D. Smith*

PERU GENIE (IRE)   2 b.g. (Feb 22) Perugino (USA) 84 – High Concept (IRE)   **69 d**
(Thatching 131) [1999 6.1g⁴ 6.1m⁶ 6.8m⁶ 7g 7d Oct 14] 14,500F, 5,000Y: good-
topped gelding: first foal: dam unraced: fair form when fourth of 6 in minor event at
Chepstow on debut: long way below that level all starts after, sweating and edgy final
one. *R. Hannon*

PERUGIA (IRE)   2 gr.f. (Mar 3) Perugino (USA) 84 – Lightning Bug (Prince Bee   **94**
128) [1999 6g* 7.1m² 8v 7g Oct 16] IR 38,000Y: lengthy, quite attractive filly:
second foal: dam Irish 1½m and 2m winner from family of Barathea: fairly useful
performer: won maiden at Goodwood in May, and ran well when neck second of 5 to
Hypnotize in listed race at Sandown in July: well below form in Prix Marcel Boussac
at Longchamp and Rockfel Stakes at Newmarket last 2 starts: should stay 1m.
B. W. Hills

PERUGIA LADY (IRE)   3 ch.f. Perugino (USA) 84 – Love Hurts (IRE) 64   **–**
(Broken Hearted 124) [1998 NR 1999 7d 10f Jun 11] IR 3,500Y: second foal: half-
sister to Irish 1m to 1¼m winner Simply Monarch (by Simply Great): dam ran twice
in Ireland: always behind in maidens at Redcar. *J. S. Wainwright*

PERUGINO BAY (IRE)   3 b.c. Perugino (USA) 84 – Dublah (USA) (Private   **109**
Account (USA)) [1998 104p: 5d² 5v* 5.1g⁵ 5f* 5g⁴ 5m³ 5f 5d³ 6v³ 6s² 1999 5s 7m³
8.5f* 8f⁴ 8.5f Aug 15] good-topped colt: useful performer: ran well when 1¼ lengths
third to Enrique in Tripleprint (Greenham) Stakes at Newbury in April, final outing
for B. McMahon: won conditions event at Hollywood in June: stays 8.5f: acts on any
going. *D. Vienna, USA*

PERUGINO PEARL (IRE)   2 b.f. (Feb 23) Perugino (USA) 84 – Farnacliffe   **–**
(Taufan (USA) 119) [1999 6g 6m Jul 10] IR 3,000F, 2,000Y: leggy, sparely-made
filly: sixth foal: half-sister to Irish 7f/1m winner Gerrydardis (by The Noble Player)
and 2 winners in Italy: dam Irish 7f winner: well beaten in maidens. *M. Brittain*

PERUGINO'S MALT (IRE)   3 ch.f. Perugino (USA) 84 – Malt Leaf (IRE) 48   **76**
(Nearly A Nose (USA) 84) [1998 –: 6v 1999 8m* 10g⁴ 9g³ 10m 7g a10g⁶ Nov 26]

first foal: dam poor Irish maiden: fair performer: won apprentice minor event at Naas in July: left A. O'Brien in Ireland before well held in sellers in Britain last 2 starts: may prove best at 1m/1¼m: acts on good to firm going. *A. T. Murphy*

PERUVIAN CHIEF (IRE) 2 b.c. (Apr 13) Foxhound (USA) 103 – John's Ballad (IRE) (Ballad Rock 122) [1999 6s 6g a6f² a6g* a7g* a7g³ Dec 18] IR 12,000F, IR 21,000Y, 50,000 2-y-o: good-topped colt: second foal: half-brother to fairly useful Irish 3-y-o 5f winner Black Paddy (by Mujadil): dam unraced daughter of half-sister to Dewhurst winner Monteverdi: fairly useful performer: improved to win maiden at Wolverhampton in October and nursery at Lingfield (edged left) in November: stays 7f: acts well on all-weather: gave trouble stalls final outing. *N. P. Littmoden* **88**

PERUVIAN JADE 2 gr.f. (Jan 23) Petong 126 – Rion River (IRE) (Taufan (USA) 119) [1999 5g⁶ a6g³ a5g⁴ a6g² 6m* 6g* 5d 6d⁴ 6d⁴ Oct 28] 5,500Y, 8,000 2-y-o: leggy filly: fourth foal: half-sister to 1995 2-y-o 5f winner Gagajulu (by Al Hareb): dam Irish 1¼m winner: fair performer: won nurseries at Goodwood and Leicester in September: will prove best at 5f/6f: acts on good to firm going, good to soft and fibresand: consistent. *N. P. Littmoden* **76**

PERUVIAN STAR 3 b.g. Emarati (USA) 74 – Julie's Star (IRE) 45 (Thatching 131) [1998 84: a6g² a6s* a7g³ 1999 6m a7g a7g Jun 25] fairly useful at 2 yrs: below form in 1999: stays 7f: raced mainly on fibresand: tends to sweat. *N. P. Littmoden* **–**

PESCARA (IRE) 3 b.f. Common Grounds 118 – Mackla 109 (Caerleon (USA) 132) [1998 100: 5.5d² 5.5g* 6f³ 6d⁵ 1999 8m⁵ 8m⁵ 7m² Sep 9] tall, angular filly: has a fluent, round action: useful performer: ran well when fifth in 1000 Guineas at Newmarket (beaten 3¾ lengths by Wince) and Coronation Stakes at Ascot (over 2 lengths behind Balisada) and second in listed race at Doncaster (beaten 1¼ lengths by Susu): should stay 1¼m: acts on firm and good to soft ground. *Saeed bin Suroor* **108**

Maktoum Al Maktoum's "Peshtigo"

PESHTIGO (USA) 3 b.c. Kris S (USA) – Fume (USA) (Secretariat (USA)) **112**
[1998 82p: 7g⁵ 8g⁵ 1999 11m² 12.3m* 12m⁵ 12g⁵ 12m⁴ Sep 4] strong, well-made
colt: not a good walker, but fluent mover: smart performer: awarded race after
finishing length second to Housemaster in Chester Vase in May: ran respectably in
King Edward VII Stakes at Royal Ascot (to Mutafaweq) next time and in September
Stakes at Epsom (pulled hard when fourth of 5) final outing: stays 1½m: raced only
on good/good to firm going: has been bandaged off-hind: usually races up with pace:
sent to UAE. *B. W. Hills*

PETAL (IRE) 3 b.f. Common Grounds 118 – Bayadere (USA) 61 (Green Dancer **82**
(USA) 132) [1998 NR 1999 10d² 10m³ 10.5d² 12.3m⁴ 13.3m 10.1m³ 12d⁶ Oct 29]
unfurnished filly: third foal: closely related to 4-y-o Bryony Brind: dam staying
maiden: fairly useful maiden: should stay 1½m when conditions aren't testing: yet to
race on extremes of going: edgy and led part of way to post fourth outing: sold 11,000
gns in December. *Lady Herries*

PETANE (IRE) 4 b.g. Petardia 113 – Senane 86 (Vitiges (FR) 132) [1998 57: –
10.3d 11.6g 10g⁴ 10d 10g⁵ 14.1m 12m* 12f 11.9g³ a12g 1999 11.5m 14m 12m
16m Sep 13] good-bodied gelding: has a quick action: modest at best: well beaten in
1999: stays 1½m: acts on good to firm going: sometimes blinkered: inconsistent.
John A. Harris

PETARA (IRE) 4 ch.g. Petardia 113 – Romangoddess (IRE) (Rhoman Rule **49**
(USA)) [1998 54: 8d⁴ 8g 8m 7g⁵ 7d⁵ 12m⁴ 8g² 8m⁶ 10.4g 9m⁵ 8.5m 8v 1999 7.5m
9g 8.9m 10m* 8m 10m Sep 24] close-coupled gelding: unimpressive mover: poor
handicapper: won 16-runner selling event at Lingfield in September: probably best at
1m/1¼m nowadays: probably best on good/good to firm going: usually blinkered/
visored: seems a difficult ride (usually held up). *J. S. Wainwright*

PETARGA 4 b.f. Petong 126 – One Half Silver (CAN) (Plugged Nickle (USA)) **83**
[1998 83: 6m³ 6f 6m⁶ 5.1g⁴ 5g³ 1999 6f 6f³ 5g 5.7g 5.7f² 6f* 6g 5.7m³ 6g 6m Sep 11]
close-coupled filly: fairly useful handicapper: won at Folkestone in July: possibly
best at 6f nowadays: raced only on good ground or firmer: has been bandaged in
front: sometimes flashes tail: none too consistent. *J. A. R. Toller*

PETARY 2 gr.g. (Feb 1) Petong 126 – Daffodil Fields (Try My Best (USA) 130) **97**
[1999 6m* 6d³ 6g 6g⁵ 7d Oct 12] 42,000Y: quite good-topped gelding: sixth foal:
brother to useful sprinter Petula and 2 winners in Italy and half-brother to useful
Italian performer up to 1m Pappa Reale (by Indian Ridge): dam Irish maiden from
family of Environment Friend: useful performer: won maiden at Newmarket in July:
ran well next start and when fifth of 26 to Khasayl in Two-Year-Old Trophy at Redcar
penultimate one: may prove best up to 6f: withdrawn after unseating and injuring
rider on intended debut: visored (coltish, found little) third outing: sent to UAE.
J. H. M. Gosden

PETER PERFECT 5 gr.g. Chilibang 120 – Misdevious (USA) (Alleged (USA) –
138) [1998 40: a6g 7d a7g a8g a11g 1999 a16g a11g Feb 5] lengthy gelding: poor
maiden: stays 1m: acts on good to firm ground, good to soft and all-weather: often
blinkered/visored. *Mrs S. Lamyman*

PETER'S IMP (IRE) 4 b.g. Imp Society (USA) – Catherine Clare 58 (Sallust **86**
134) [1998 77, a–: 7.6g 6s 7g 6d³ 7.1g* 7m² 7m 7.1m⁶ a7g 1999 6v 6m* 5.7g² 7f* **a–**
6s² 7g 7f⁶ 7.6m 6f⁵ 6m 7g 7m 7d Oct 26] good-bodied gelding: fairly useful
performer: won minor events at Hamilton (amateurs) in May and Redcar (broke
loose before start) in June: generally below form after: best up to 7f: yet to race on
heavy going, acts on any other: effective blinkered or not: usually held up. *J. Berry*

PETER'S PRINCESS (IRE) 2 ch.f. (Apr 21) Lycius (USA) 124 – Regal Scin- –
tilla 103 (King of Spain 121) [1999 6g 6m⁶ 6f⁵ 6s Nov 5] 21,000Y: tall, unfurnished
filly: second foal: dam, 5f performer, won Prix d'Arenberg at 2 yrs: well beaten in
maidens/minor event. *J. Berry*

PETEURESQUE (USA) 2 ch.c. (Feb 19) Peteski (CAN) 125 – Miss Ultimo **74 p**
(USA) (Screen King (USA)) [1999 7m² 7.9g⁵ Oct 6] $14,000Y: half-brother to
several winners abroad, including French 1m to 1½m winner Ultimate Glory (by Our
Native): dam minor 8.5f stakes winner at 2 yrs in USA: fair form in maidens at York,
runner-up to easy winner Akeed on first occasion: will be well suited by 1¼m+:
should do better. *T. D. Barron*

PET EXPRESS FLYER (IRE) 3 b.g. Mukaddamah (USA) 125 – Take The Option (USA) (Bold Bidder) [1998 89: 5d³ 6g* 6s² 7.1m* 7m³ 7d* 7f 6s 8m³ 8d 1999 10.5d 8g Aug 16] close-coupled gelding: fairly useful at 2 yrs: well held in handicaps in 1999: stays 1m well: acts on soft and good to firm going. *P. C. Haslam* –

PETITE DANSEUSE 5 b.m. Aragon 118 – Let Her Dance (USA) (Sovereign Dancer (USA)) [1998 62, a52: a7s⁵ a6g a6g a6g⁶ a6g⁴ 5s 6.1s³ 6g 5s 6d³ a6g⁴ 6m 7g 6m³ 7g² 7g 6d⁴ 6m⁵ 7d⁶ 1999 a5g 5f 6g⁶ 6s⁵ 6m 5.9g 6m³ 7m⁵ 5f⁴ 5f² 6v⁶ a6g Nov 22] small mare: poor handicapper: possibly best at 6f/7f nowadays: acts on firm ground, soft and all-weather: visored/blinkered once each: has carried head awkwardly. *D. W. Chapman* **45 a34**

PETIT MARQUIS (FR) 2 b.c. (Apr 9) Lost World (IRE) 119 – Ephemeride (USA) (Al Nasr (FR) 126) [1999 6g² Aug 4] 140,000 francs F, IR 30,000Y: fourth foal: half-brother to French 11f and 1½m winner Cricket Bat (by Cricket Ball): dam placed up to 1m in France: shaped well when neck second of 13 to Trinculo in maiden at Leicester, green under pressure 2f out but running on well towards finish: should stay 1m: seems sure to improve. *J. R. Fanshawe* **72 p**

PETIT PALAIS (IRE) 3 gr.g. Paris House 123 – Renzola (Dragonara Palace (USA) 115) [1998 –: 7g 1999 8.2s 6.1s* 8f 6g 6.1d a6g a6g a7g a8.5g Dec 1] tall gelding: only form when winning seller at Nottingham (bought out of B. Meehan's stable 6,200 gns) in April: will prove best at 5f/6f: acts on soft going: visored/blinkered. *P. D. Evans* **65 d**

PETRACO (IRE) 11 b.g. Petorius 117 – Merrie Moira (Bold Lad (IRE) 133) [1998 54, a47: 6.1m 6g³ 5g⁵ a6g⁴ a6g² 5.1g 5g⁵ 6g* 6g 7m 6m 1999 a6g a6g 6m 6g Jul 2] workmanlike gelding: had a quick action: fairly useful at best, winner of 9 races during career: no form in 1999 though was second in Jersey in June: effective at 5f/6f: acted on all-weather and any turf going: tried blinkered: sometimes hung: often apprentice ridden: retired. *N. A. Smith* –

PETRA NOVA 3 ch.f. First Trump 118 – Spinner 59 (Blue Cashmere 129) [1998 51?: 5g² 5m 6m 5.1v 1999 5d 7m⁶ 5m 6m 7m 5m 5g⁵ 5g 6s Oct 5] lengthy, good-quartered filly: poor maiden: seems to stay 7f: acts on good to firm going. *R. M. Whitaker* **47**

PETRIE 2 ch.g. (Apr 12) Fraam 114 – Canadian Capers 70 (Ballacashtal (CAN)) [1999 5.7m 5f⁵ 7f⁵ 5.3s⁴ 5.7s² a5g³ a6g² a7g² a6g⁵ a6g⁶ Dec 22] second foal: dam, 5.7f (at 2 yrs) and 7.6f winner, probably stayed 1¼m: modest maiden: in frame in 5 sellers: stays 7f: acts on soft ground and fibresand: tends to hang left. *M. R. Channon* **60 a52**

PETRISK 2 b.f. (Mar 31) Risk Me (FR) 127 – Bernstein Bette 76 (Petong 126) [1999 6g 6g 8d Oct 22] 2,200F, 4,200Y: third foal: sister to 4-y-o Cape Hope and to a 9f winner in Spain: dam best up to 7f: tailed off in maidens. *T. E. Powell* –

PETROSELLI (IRE) 2 b.c. (Apr 12) Grand Lodge (USA) 125 – Will Be Blue (IRE) (Darshaan 133) [1999 7.5s² 8s* 8m³ 9v³ 10v² Oct 31] 500,000 francs Y: big, close-coupled colt: fifth foal: half-brother to French 1½m winner Blue Bering (by Bering) and French 11.5f winner High And Blue (by Highest Honor): dam French 10.5f winner, half-sister to Prix Vermeille winner Walensee: smart performer: won minor event at Deauville in August: third at Longchamp in Prix des Chenes and Prix de Conde before improved effort in first-time blinkers when running-on length second of 7 to Goldamix in Criterium de Saint-Cloud: will stay 1½m: carries head awkwardly and has been mulish at stalls. *Mme C. Head, France* **110**

PETROVNA (IRE) 3 ch.f. Petardia 113 – Efficient Funding (IRE) 65 (Entitled 126) [1998 74: 6m⁵ 5f* 6m⁵ 5g² 7g 1999 5s⁶ 6g 5.1g 7.1g a7g Jul 10] fair performer: form in 1999 only on reappearance: should prove best at 5f/6f: yet to race on heavy going, acts on any other: sometimes blinkered. *P. L. Gilligan* **78 d**

PETRUSHKA (IRE) 2 ch.f. (May 3) Unfuwain (USA) 131 – Ballet Shoes (IRE) 75 (Ela-Mana-Mou 132) [1999 7d* Oct 11] IR 110,000Y: strong, rangy filly: good walker: third foal: closely related to Irish 3-y-o 7f winner Danse Classique (by Night Shift): dam, 5f winner, half-sister to Spectrum, family of Sun Princess: won 19-runner maiden at Leicester, taking while to get hang of things but finishing strongly to beat Shamah by ¾ length: will stay at least 1m: probably a smart performer in the making, sure to win more races. *Sir Michael Stoute* **95 p**

PETRUS (IRE) 3 b.c. Perugino (USA) 84 – Love With Honey (USA) (Full **92**
Pocket (USA)) [1998 ?: 7f⁶ 7g 6g 6d⁶ 1999 7d 7v 7m* 7d 8m³ 7g 7g⁴ 7f* 7m⁶ 7m⁶
8g Oct 16] smallish, compact colt: fairly useful handicapper: won at Kempton in
May and Yarmouth and Goodwood (quite valuable race) in July: good sixth to
Russian Revival in Tote International Stakes at Ascot in August: failed to handle
track at Epsom penultimate start, not well drawn final one: probably best at 7f/1m
on good going or firmer: has worn net muzzle to post: usually races prominently.
C. E. Brittain

PETTY FRANCE (IRE) 3 b. or br.f. Petardia 113 – Business Centre (IRE) 58 **54**
(Digamist (USA) 110) [1998 78p: 6f² 1999 7.6f⁴ 5.7f⁶ Sep 6] looked promising only
2-y-o start: just modest form at best in 1999: raced only on firm going: sold 2,000
gns. J. A. R. Toller

PETUNTSE 5 b.g. Phountzi (USA) 104 – Alipampa (IRE) (Glenstal (USA) 118) **46**
[1998 48, a39: a8.5g⁴ 10m⁶ 6.9m² 8m* 1999 10m⁶ 10.2g 10.2g⁵ 7d Sep 15] tall
gelding: poor handicapper: headstrong, and will prove best at 7f/1m: acts on good to
firm ground: usually bandaged behind. R. G. Frost

PETURA (IRE) 3 br.g. Petardia 113 – Roman Heights (IRE) (Head For Heights **–**
125) [1998 63?: 6g⁴ 6g 7m⁴ 8m⁴ 1999 8.9d 10g 10d Oct 21] lengthy, good-topped
gelding: little form: gave impression something amiss final start. J. S. Wainwright

PHANTOM STAR (IRE) 2 b.g. (Mar 18) Foxhound (USA) 103 – Une Paris- **41**
ienne (FR) (Bolkonski 134) [1999 6m 7.5s⁵ 7m 7g⁴ 7.1m 7m⁵ 6m 7d⁵ Oct 15] IR
8,600F, 9,500Y, 6,200 2-y-o: good-topped colt: good mover: half-brother to 6f to 1m
winner Commander Glen (by Glenstal) and a winner in Italy by Distinctly North:
dam ran once: poor form at best, mostly in sellers: sometimes visored. Mrs
A. E. Johnson

PHANTOM THREEONINE 3 ch.f. Hatim (USA) 121 – Glenrock Dancer (IRE) **–**
(Glenstal (USA) 118) [1998 –: 5g 6g 5g⁴ 5d⁶ 6s 6g 6s⁶ 7m 1999 11.1g⁵ 9.2m⁵ 10m
Jun 16] lengthy filly: little form: tried blinkered/tongue tied. W. T. Kemp

PHANTOM WATERS 4 b.f. Pharly (FR) 130 – Idle Waters 116 (Mill Reef **73**
(USA) 141) [1998 79: 9.9d⁴ 11.6g⁴ 12.1m* 11.8m² 12g² 11.9d* 12d⁶ 14m 12d 1999
11.6m⁴ 11.7s 12s 12m³ 12m⁴ 13.3m³ 14.1m 12m⁵ 14.4m³ 12m 14.1g Oct 2] fair
handicapper: best at 1½m/1¾m: acts on good to firm and good to soft going (well
below form on soft): sold 68,000 gns in December. R. F. Johnson Houghton

PHARAOH'S HOUSE (IRE) 2 b.g. (Apr 19) Desert Style (IRE) 121 – Cella- **64 d**
tica (USA) 67 (Sir Ivor 135) [1999 5d 6d³ 6s³ 7m 6s 7s Sep 29] IR 20,500F, IR
10,000Y: second foal: dam Irish 13f/hurdles winner: modest form second and third
starts only: should stay 1m: blinkered penultimate outing. T. D. Easterby

PHARLY REEF 7 b.g. Pharly (FR) 130 – Hay Reef 72 (Mill Reef (USA) 141) **50**
[1998 NR 1999 10.3d⁵ 12m⁴ 12g Jun 30] modest maiden handicapper: stays 1½m:
acts on good to firm going: tried visored: fair hurdler. D. Burchell

PHASE EIGHT GIRL 3 b.f. Warrshan (USA) 117 – Bugsy's Sister (Aragon **52**
118) [1998 –: 6g 5d 5d⁶ 7d 1999 9.9g 9.9d 12g 16.2m³ 12m* 16d³ Aug 9] small filly:
modest handicapper: won selling event at Beverley in July: effective at 1½m to 2m:
yet to race on extremes of going. J. Hetherton

PHAYUHA KIRI LOVE 4 b.g. Pursuit of Love 124 – My Moody Girl (IRE) **–**
(Alzao (USA) 117) [1998 –: 10.2m⁴ 10d 1999 a12g Feb 6] no sign of ability: dead.
B. R. Johnson

PHEISTY 2 b.f. (Feb 19) Faustus (USA) 118 – Phlirty (Pharly (FR) 130) [1999 **72**
5g* 5.1s³ 5s⁶ 5.1m 6m Aug 30] 1,000Y: smallish, good-quartered filly: first foal: dam
tailed off both starts: fair performer: won maiden at Leicester in April: off course
over 3 months before respectable effort final start. R. F. Johnson Houghton

PHILAGAIN 2 b.f. (Apr 29) Ardkinglass 114 – Andalucia 57 (Rheingold 137) **–**
[1999 8d 8.3s 8g Oct 15] half-sister to several winners, including 5-y-o Manileno and
7-y-o Philmist: dam won 1¼m seller: well beaten, including in seller. J. Hetherton

PHILANTHA (USA) 2 b.f. (Feb 17) Woodman (USA) 126 – Tiger Flower 103 **89 p**
(Sadler's Wells (USA) 132) [1999 6s* Oct 2] lengthy, quite attractive filly: fifth foal:
half-sister to 1½m winners Zibeth (by Rainbow Quest) and Tiger Lake (by Nash-

wan): dam, 1¼m winner, better at 1½m: fairly useful form when winning 11-runner maiden at Newmarket by ½ length from Double Platinum, sweeping through from off pace: should be suited by 1m+: seems sure to improve. *J. H. M. Gosden*

PHILATELIC LADY (IRE) 3 ch.f. Pips Pride 117 – Gold Stamp (Golden Act (USA)) [1998 70: 6d 7m⁶ a8g² a8g* a8f⁵ 1999 10d* 10m² 11.6m 9g 10g⁴ 11.6d² 10d* Nov 4] unfurnished filly: fairly useful handicapper: won at Lingfield in June and Windsor (20 ran) in November: barely stays 11.6f: acts on equitrack, yet to race on extremes of going on turf: usually held up. *M. J. Haynes* **89**

PHILISTAR 6 ch.h. Bairn (USA) 126 – Philgwyn 66 (Milford 119) [1998 84: a7g³ a9.4g a7g* a8g³ a7g* a8g⁴ 8g⁴ 9g²ᵈⁱˢ 8.5g* 8.9s 8g⁶ 10.4f 9.9g 9.3g 8.5m⁴ 7.6f³ 8.5m² 8.9g 8m a7g⁵ 1999 a10g* a8g³ a10f⁵ a10g² a10g 10.3d 7g 10.1s 9m 8.5d⁶ 8m 8g 10.2m⁶ 9m³ 10.1m³ 10.1m⁵ 8.5g⁵ 10.1m³ 8.9d⁵ 8s⁵ a8g² a8.5g⁶ a10g⁵ Dec 8] good-topped horse: fair handicapper: won apprentice event at Lingfield in January: mostly respectable efforts after: probably best at 1m/1¼m: acts on all-weather, firm and good to soft going (possibly not on soft): tried blinkered/visored: has run well sweating: takes strong hold, and usually held up: tough. *K. R. Burke* **73 a79**

PHILMIST 7 b.m. Hard Fought 125 – Andalucia 57 (Rheingold 137) [1998 49: 11.1g³ 13.1d⁶ 12.1d* 13d⁵ 12.1d 10.9d 10s 1999 12.1v 12.1m* 11.1s³ 13d² 13g³ 13g* 12m⁶ 11.1m⁴ Jun 29] leggy mare: modest handicapper: won at Hamilton in May (selling event) and June (apprentice race): effective at 11f to 1¾m: acts on good to firm ground, soft and fibresand, probably on equitrack: wears blinkers: best patiently ridden: not one to trust implicitly. *Miss L. A. Perratt* **53**

PHILOSOPHIC 5 b.g. Be My Chief (USA) 122 – Metaphysique (FR) (Law Society (USA) 130) [1998 55, a78: a16g³ a13g* a16g* 12m 16.4m⁶ 14.9g⁴ 14m³ a14.8g* a16g² 17.1m a16m* 16d 15.4m* a12g² 12s 1999 a12g³ a16f⁶ a16g a13g⁶ a14.8g² 14.1m a16g May 17] big, workmanlike gelding: fair handicapper on all-weather, modest on turf: probably best at 1¾m/2m: acts on all-weather, possibly needs good going or firmer on turf: reportedly bled from nose final start. *Mrs L. C. Jewell* **– a68**

PHOEBE BUFFAY (IRE) 2 b.f. (Apr 21) Petardia 113 – Art Duo 86 (Artaius (USA) 129) [1999 a6g² 7.1d² a6g* 6m² 6.5g 6d Oct 15] 6,500Y: close-coupled filly: sixth foal: sister to 3-y-o Annie Apple and half-sister to 3 winners, including useful 6f (at 2 yrs) to 10.4f winner Amyas (by Waajib): dam, fourth in 7f listed event at 2 yrs, failed to train on: fair performer: won maiden at Southwell in July: creditable efforts next 2 starts: best form around 6f: acts on good to firm going and fibresand: well held only try in blinkers: races prominently. *C. N. Allen* **78**

PHOEBUS 2 b.c. (Apr 14) Piccolo 121 – Slava (USA) (Diesis 133) [1999 7d 7d 7g a6g⁴ a7g* a7g⁵ Nov 26] 14,000Y: sturdy colt: fifth foal: half-brother to several winners, including 3-y-o Monte Calvo, fairly useful 7f to 1m winner Transylvania (by Wolfhound) and 1995 2-y-o 6f winner Sava River (by Lycius): dam French 11f winner out of close relative to Soviet Star: fair performer: won nursery at Southwell in November: stays 7f: acts on fibresand, well below form only start on equitrack. *W. R. Muir* **66**

PHOTOFIRST 6 ch.g. Derrylin 115 – Fedelm (Celtic Cone 116) [1998 NR 1999 14.1m Jul 10] 850 4-y-o, resold 7,000 4-y-o: fourth foal: half-brother to winning jumpers by Oats and Rakaposhi King: dam unraced: little form in novice hurdles: well beaten in maiden at Salisbury only run on Flat. *R. M. Flower* **–**

PHYLOZZO 3 ch.f. Michelozzo (USA) 127 – Phyllida Fox (Healaugh Fox) [1998 –: 5d⁵ 6s a7g⁶ a5g 1999 a7g⁵ a8f⁴ a8f Feb 1] sparely-made filly: poor maiden. *P. D. Evans* **31**

PIAF 3 b.f. Pursuit of Love 124 – Pippas Song 75 (Reference Point 139) [1998 62: 6m 6m 6d 1999 9.7s 8g⁶ 10m⁴ 9.9m 12m 12m a10g³ a16g a11g⁵ Nov 30] strong, lengthy filly: modest maiden at best: stays 1¼m: acts on good to firm going and all-weather: blinkered (hung left) sixth start. *B. W. Hills* **62 d**

PICCADILLY 4 ch.f. Belmez (USA) 131 – Polly's Pear (USA) (Sassafras (FR) 135) [1998 62d: 12.4d³ 14.1m³ 14.1d 12m⁶ 10m⁵ 10g 12m 16.1g⁶ 18s 14.1s 1999 12.3m* 9.9g 13.8m 12g Jun 4] lengthy filly: poor handicapper: had run of race when **43**

winning 19-runner selling event at Ripon in April: below form after: stays 1¾m: acts on soft and good to firm going: tried blinkered. *Miss Kate Milligan*

PICCATA 2 b.g. (May 25) Piccolo 121 – Katya (IRE) 93 (Dancing Dissident (USA) 119) [1999 6s 5m Aug 28] first foal: dam 5f (at 2 yrs) and 6f winner: well beaten in maiden and seller. *M. R. Channon*

PICCOLA BELLA 3 b.f. Picea 99 – Blushing Belle 74 (Local Suitor (USA) 128) – [1998 NR 1999 10m 11.8m 14g Aug 14] first foal: dam 10.6f seller winner at 2 yrs, also successful over hurdles: tailed off in claimers/maiden. *J. G. Portman*

PICCOLO CATIVO 4 b.f. Komaite (USA) – Malcesine (IRE) 46 (Auction Ring **65 d** (USA) 123) [1998 67, a–: a7s a7g 5d* 6g⁴ a5g 5g⁶ 5d* 6g² 5m 6d⁴ 6m² 5.1d 5d **a–** 6s 5v⁶ 6v⁴ 5d a6g 1999 6s* 5.1s⁵ 5.9m 7m⁵ 6g 6g 7m 6m² 6m⁵ 6g 5f⁴ 5m⁵ 5d 6v Oct 12] modest performer: won apprentice minor event at Catterick in April: mostly disappointing in handicaps after: effective at 5f (given test)/6f: acts on good to firm going, heavy and fibresand: has flashed tail under pressure: usually ridden by 7-lb claimer Angela Hartley. *Mrs G. S. Rees*

PICEA'S PAST 5 b.g. Picea 99 – Atoka 97 (March Past 124) [1998 NR 1999 – a8.5g Jan 20] 1,700Y: half-brother to 1¼m and 2m winner Edge of Darkness (by Vaigly Great) and useful 1985 2-y-o 5f winner Oh Boyar (by Young Generation): dam won from 6f to 15f: little sign of ability in bumpers/hurdles and on Flat debut. *J. Neville*

PICHON BARON (USA) 4 ch.g. Zilzal (USA) 137 – Flora Lady (USA) (Track – Barron (USA)) [1998 –: 8.2s 8s 11d a8g 1999 8.2m Jun 16] leggy, sparely-made gelding: well beaten since 2 yrs: sold 500 gns. *Andrew Reid*

PICKENS (USA) 7 b.g. Theatrical 128 – Alchi (USA) 112 (Alleged (USA) 138) **68** [1998 75: a11s² a12g² a12g* a11g* a11g* a11g² a12g* a12g* a12g⁶ a12g² 1999 a11g⁶ a11g a11g* a12g⁴ Feb 12] stocky gelding: fair performer: won seller at South-well (fifth course success) in February: effective at 11f to 1¾m: acts on fibresand and firm ground, possibly not on good to soft: tried blinkered earlier in career: has had tongue tied: usually races up with pace. *Don Enrico Incisa*

PICK OF AFFECTION 3 gr.c. Salse (USA) 128 – High Matinee (Shirley **75** Heights 130) [1998 –p: 8s 7d 1999 12m³ 11.9d Aug 7] well-made colt: easily best effort in maidens when third of 4 at Newmarket (only start on ground firmer than good) on reappearance: stays 1½m: sold 14,000 gns. *E. A. L. Dunlop*

PICOLETTE 2 ch.f. (Apr 23) Piccolo 121 – Poyle Jezebelle 58 (Sharpo 132) **56** [1999 6g 5.1f⁴ 6.8d⁵ a6g 6d a7g⁵ a8g⁵ a8g⁶ Dec 6] 3,500F, 5,500Y: close-coupled **a47** filly: first foal: dam, 6f winner, sister to smart sprinter Poyle George: modest maiden: stays 6.8f: acts on firm and good to soft ground. *W. R. Muir*

PICOT 2 b. or br.f. (Feb 24) Piccolo 121 – Special Guest 67 (Be My Guest (USA) **76** 126) [1999 6g 6.1m³ 6s* Oct 25] 50,000Y: close-coupled, useful-looking filly: half-sister to several winners, including 3-y-o Guest of Honour and 1997 2-y-o 5f/6f winner Hoh Chi Min (by Efisio), who stays 1m, and 7f winner Cragganmore (by Faustus), last pair both useful: dam 2-y-o 7f winner who stayed 9f: fair performer: made most when winning maiden at Leicester in October by neck from Branston Fizz, drifting right under pressure: will stay at least 7f: acts on soft going. *H. Candy*

PICTURE PUZZLE 3 b.f. Royal Academy (USA) 130 – Cloudslea (USA) **78** (Chief's Crown (USA)) [1998 –: 7d 1999 7s⁴ 7m* 8m* 7d⁶ 8.1f 7g⁶ 8m* 8d⁶ Sep 26] tall, angular, dipped-backed filly: fair performer: won maiden at Thirsk and handicaps at Yarmouth in May and Newcastle in September: may prove best at 7f/ 1m: best form on good/good to firm going. *W. J. Haggas*

PICULA BIERE (IRE) 4 ch.g. Balla Cove 119 – Loreo (IRE) (Lord Chancellor – (USA)) [1998 –: 8g⁶ 7.1d⁵ 10.8d 8f 1999 11.6d Apr 27] no form: tried blinkered. *N. M. Babbage*

PIERPOINT (IRE) 4 ch.g. Archway (IRE) 115 – Lavinia (Habitat 134) [1998 **78** 73: 6v 6d² 7.1g 6.1g² 6s 7g² 6m 8f⁵ 7g 7d 5d 1999 7g 7g 6f 7.6m 7m⁵ 6d 6g a6g* a6g³ 6f* 6g* 5g 5g 5g Oct 16] smallish gelding: poor mover: fair handicapper: won at Southwell in June and Redcar and Pontefract in August, last 2 in large fields: has form at 1m, but best form ridden prominently at 6f: acts on firm going, good to soft and fibresand: visored (ran respectably) once at 2 yrs, often blinkered. *D. Nicholls*

PIGEON 4 b.f. Casteddu 111 – Wigeon 80 (Divine Gift 127) [1998 84: a6g 6v 6d   **78**
6g² 6d* 6g* 6s² 6g⁵ 6g² 5d³ 5m 6m 6m 5m 5g³ 5d 5.1m* 6g⁴ 5d⁵ 1999 a6g 6d 5g 5d
6f 5d 6s 7m 6d² 6m 6d Jul 1] fair handicapper: not so consistent in 1999 as at 3 yrs,
best effort when short-head second of 22 at York: effective at 5f/6f: acts on soft and
good to firm going: gave impression something amiss eighth start, hung badly right
penultimate one: front runner. *D. W. Barker*

PIGGY BANK 3 b.f. Emarati (USA) 74 – Granny's Bank 88 (Music Boy 124)   **68**
[1998 71: 5v⁵ 5s⁶ 5g 5m⁴ 6m 7.9g 5m⁵ 6d⁶ 6g⁴ 5s* 5d² 5d² 1999 5g 5d 5m 5d⁴ 5g⁵
5v⁴ 6g* 5g 6g 5m 5s 5d⁴ a5g⁶ Nov 13] tall, lengthy filly: has a round action: fair
handicapper: made all at Ripon in July: best at 5f/6f: acts on heavy going, probably
on good to firm and fibresand. *M. W. Easterby*

PILGRIM'S WAY (USA) 3 br.f. Gone West (USA) – Marling (IRE) 124   **84**
(Lomond (USA) 128) [1998 NR 1999 6v² 6.9m* 8m* 8.1g³ 8m Aug 28] good-topped
filly: third foal: half-sister to 1997 2-y-o 6f winner Half-Hitch (by Diesis) and 7f
winner Moonshiner (by Irish River), both fairly useful: dam won Cheveley Park and
Sussex Stakes, daughter of Marwell: fairly useful performer: won maiden at Carlisle
and handicap at Doncaster in July: ran respectably (reared leaving stalls) penultimate
start, but as though something amiss (tongue tied) final one: will prove best up to 1m:
acts on good to firm going, showed promise on heavy. *Sir Mark Prescott*

PILLAGER 2 b.c. (May 3) Reprimand 122 – Emerald Ring 74 (Auction Ring   **–**
(USA) [1999 6d Oct 18] 1,900Y, good-topped colt: has scope:
half-brother to 2 winners, including 5-y-o Warring: dam 6f winner: burly and green,
always behind in maiden at Pontefract. *Mrs A. J. Bowlby*

PILOT'S HARBOUR 3 b.g. Distant Relative 128 – Lillemor (Connaught 130)   **– §**
[1998 86: 6m³ 6.1g⁵ 7.1m² 7.5g* 8m* 8d 1999 10g 9.9m⁵ 12m 14m 11.5g 10d
12g Nov 3] smallish, workmanlike gelding: fairly useful at 2 yrs: generally looked
unenthusiastic in 1999, leaving J. Dunlop for 5,200 gns after fifth start: blinkered
once. *D. W. Chapman*

PIMPINELLA (IRE) 3 b.f. Reprimand 122 – Lady Leman 74 (Pitskelly 122)   **–**
[1998 NR 1999 a8.5g⁶ 10.3d 8m 10m a12g Dec 21] IR 4,800Y: leggy filly: half-sister
to 1m winner Winston (by Safawan) and Irish 9f winner Points Pass (by Primo
Dominie): dam 2-y-o 5.3f winner later suited by 1m: little promise: blinkered final
start. *B. S. Rothwell*

PINCHANINCH 2 ch.g. (May 11) Inchinor 119 – Wollow Maid 73 (Wollow 132)   **59**
[1999 8v⁵ 8d 8s Oct 25] 10,000Y: small, lengthy gelding: half-brother to several
winners, including 1m and 1¼m winner Janglynyve (by Sharpo) and 7f/1m winner
Reverand Thickness (by Prince Sabo): dam, 1¼m winner, refused to race once:
modest form in maidens at Leicester last 2 starts. *J. G. Portman*

PINCHINCHA (FR) 5 b.g. Priolo (USA) 127 – Western Heights (Shirley Heights   **85**
130) [1998 86: 10m⁶ 10.3m⁴ 10.2m⁴ 11.5f 10.1g 1999 10s⁶ 10m⁵ 10m 10s 10m²
10.2m⁴ 10.4f 10.3m⁴ 10.1d² 10.4g² 8.9d 10.1m² 10.1d³ Oct 27] workmanlike
gelding: fairly useful handicapper: several creditable efforts in 1999: stays 1¼m: acts
on all-weather, good to firm and good to soft going: tried visored: sweated freely (ran
poorly) seventh start. *D. Morris*

PINE RIDGE LAD (IRE) 9 gr.g. Taufan (USA) 119 – Rosserk (Roan Rocket   **54 §**
128) [1998 64: a8s³ a7g* a8g a8g³ a7g⁶ a8g² a8g⁴ 8s² 6d a8g² 8d* 9g 8g 1999 a7g
a8g a8g⁶ a8g 8.5m⁴ a8g* a9.4g 8g a7g a7g 10.1g² a12g⁶ 10d³ 10g 10m⁵ a12g Dec
21] good-topped gelding: modest performer: won amateur handicap at Southwell in
April: stays 1¼m: acts on any turf/all-weather: sometimes blinkered/visored: inconsistent. *J. L. Harris*

PINHEIROS DREAM (IRE) 2 ch.f. (Apr 14) Grand Lodge (USA) 125 – Nikki's   **69**
Groom (Shy Groom (USA)) [1999 6m 7f³ 6g 7d Sep 28] IR 8,000F, IR 10,000Y,
resold IR 7,000Y: tall, close-coupled, quite attractive filly: has a quick action: fifth
foal: half-sister to 3-y-o Heathyards Tipple, fairly useful 6f winner Compatibility (by
Common Grounds) and a German 1½m winner by Ballad Rock: dam fourth at 1¼m

in Ireland: fair form in maidens: stiffish task and well held in nursery final start: should stay 1m. *B. J. Meehan*

PINK CRISTAL   3 b.f. Dilum (USA) 115 – Crystal Fountain (Great Nephew 126) **113** [1998 NR 1999 7m 7m² 7g* 8d* 9.3v 10d Oct 14] big, rangy filly: half-sister to several winners, including smart 7f (at 2 yrs) to 10.3f winner in Britain/Germany/ USA Crystal Hearted (by Broken Hearted) and useful stayer High Fountain (by High Line): dam once-raced half-sister to Royal Palace: smart performer: won maiden at Salisbury in June and listed race at Ascot in August, in latter improving markedly to beat Diamond White by 1½ lengths: below form last 2 starts: best up to 1m: showed promise on good to firm going, easily best effort on good to soft. *H. Candy*

PINK MOSAIC   3 b.f. Safawan 118 – Stoneydale 83 (Tickled Pink 114) [1998 **60 +** NR 1999 6v 5m⁵ 5g 5d Sep 30] 6,000Y: half-sister to several winners, including sprinters Halbert (by Song) and Runs In The Family (by Distant Relative): dam sprinter: modest maiden: not punished in handicap (after 4-month break) final start: should be suited by 6f. *J. G. Smyth-Osbourne*

PINNACLE   3 b.f. Shirley Heights 130 – Manhattan Sunset (USA) 76 (El Gran **87** Senor (USA) 136) [1998 75p: 7m² 7m³ 1999 11.4m³ May 5] angular filly: placed both starts: 2 lengths third to Valentine Girl in Cheshire Oaks at Chester only 3-y-o outing, plenty to do 2f out: will stay at least 1½m. *W. J. Haggas*

PIPA   3 b.f. Suave Dancer (USA) 136 – Pipitina 91 (Bustino 136) [1998 68: 7m **72** 8.2s² 8s⁵ 1999 11.6m 12.5m 14.1m⁵ 16.4d² 16v² 18d Oct 18] workmanlike filly: fair maiden handicapper: may prove best at 1¾m/2m: goes well on ground softer than good: effective visored or not: sold 10,000 gns. *J. L. Dunlop*

PIPADASH (IRE)   2 b.f. (Feb 14) Pips Pride 117 – Petite Maxine 70 (Sharpo 132) **91** [1999 5s* 5d* 6s² 5d³ 5m 6m³ 5m* 6g⁵ 6g Oct 2] 5,200Y: big, leggy filly: good walker: second foal: dam, maiden who stayed 7f, out of smart 2-y-o 5f winner Penny Blessing: fairly useful performer: won maiden at Haydock and minor events at Pontefract in April and Ascot in August: creditable fifth of 21 in sales race at Doncaster penultimate start: likely to prove best at 5f: acts on soft and good to firm ground: blinkered fifth and last 3 starts: often races prominently. *T. D. Easterby*

PIPADOR (IRE)   3 ch.g. Pips Pride 117 – Dorado Llave (USA) (Well Decorated **52** (USA)) [1998 59: 5m 5g 6d⁵ 1999 a7g a5g 5m 8s 6d a10g⁵ Dec 29] good-topped gelding: modest maiden: stays 1¼m: tried blinkered. *R. Guest*

PIPALONG (IRE)   3 b.f. Pips Pride 117 – Limpopo 49 (Green Desert (USA) 127) **112** [1998 103: 5s* 5g* 5d² 6f² 7g⁴ 6v* 8d⁴ 6g⁴ 6g⁵ 6d² 5m⁴ 6m² 6.1m⁴ 6d* 6g² 6m

William Hill Great St Wilfrid Handicap, Ripon—
Pipalong (No.4) gets to the front in the final stride to deny Bon Ami,
with Now Look Here and Perryston View, both on the far side, taking third and fourth places

Mr T. H. Bennett's "Pipalong"

6d⁵ 6d² 6s* Nov 6] neat filly: smart performer: won 23-runner William Hill Great St Wilfrid Handicap at Ripon (by short head from Bon Ami) in August and 20-runner listed event at Doncaster (by short head from Two Clubs) in November: creditable 1¼ lengths second to Gaelic Storm in listed race at Newmarket on penultimate start: should stay 7f: acts on any going: has been bandaged in front: game and genuine. *T. D. Easterby*

PIPED ABOARD (IRE) 4 b.g. Pips Pride 117 – Last Gunboat 50 (Dominion **79** 123) [1998 90: 7s* 8d² 8.1s² 8s² 8.1m² 10.3g⁴ 10.3d⁶ 1999 10.3m 11.9d Jun 12] good-bodied gelding: poor walker: just fair form in 1999: probably stays 1½m: acts on soft and good to firm going: blinkered/visored 4 of last 5 starts: one to treat with caution over hurdles but has shown fairly useful form. *M. C. Pipe*

PIPE DREAM 3 b.g. King's Signet (USA) 110 – Rather Warm 103 (Tribal Chief **66** 125) [1998 NR 1999 8v 7d⁶ 7.8m⁶ 9.5g³ 11m 8g⁴ 8m 7s 6d a10g a8g a7g Dec 22] 26,000Y: half-brother to several winners, including fairly useful winner up to 7.6f Sparky Lad (by Hot Spark) and 1¼m winner Woodurather (by Touching Wood): dam won up to 7.6f at 2 yrs: fair maiden handicapper: left K. Prendergast in Ireland after seventh start: no form in Britain: stays 1m. *P. Burgoyne*

PIPE MUSIC (IRE) 4 b.g. Mujadil (USA) 119 – Sunset Cafe (IRE) 68 (Red **56** Sunset 120) [1998 69: a7g⁵ a8g* 10.3d⁴ 9.9s 10m 11.5m 8.3d⁵ 11.1d³ 12.3g² 12m⁴ **a75** a8.5g⁵ 1999 a16g² a16.2g³ a16f² a16f* a16g⁵ a16g⁶ 13.8m 18g 14d⁵ 16d 17.1g a16.2g² a14g³ a14g⁶ Dec 13] compact gelding: fair handicapper on all-weather, modest on turf: won at Southwell in February: probably best at 2m+ in truly-run race: acts on good to firm ground, good to soft and all-weather: effective blinkered/visored or not: reportedly injured pelvis eleventh start. *P. C. Haslam*

PIPER'S CLAN   3 b.c. Aragon 118 – Topwinder (USA) (Topsider (USA)) [1998   **65**
NR 1999 a5g* a6f Aug 14] 18,000Y, 4,400 2-y-o: second living foal: half-brother to
7f seller winner Fast Spin (by Formidable): dam ran twice in France: won maiden at
Lingfield in February, despite carrying head awkwardly: left N. Callaghan and last of
10 in allowance race only outing in USA. *B. D. A. Cecil, USA*

PIPIJI (IRE)   4 gr.f. Pips Pride 117 – Blue Alicia (Wolver Hollow 126) [1998 –:   **41**
a12g 10.5d 8.1g⁴ a14.8g 11.9d 10v 1999 8.3s⁴ 8d² 7m⁵ 6.9m 7f² Jul 30] tall, lengthy
filly: poor maiden handicapper: effective at 7f/1m: acts on firm ground, probably on
soft. *Mrs G. S. Rees*

PIPPAS PRIDE (IRE)   4 ch.g. Pips Pride 117 – Al Shany 92 (Burslem 123) [1998   **–**
–: 8d 7v 8v⁶ a8g⁶ a10g 1999 a8g* a6f⁴ a8g a7g⁴ 8d a8g* Dec 17] strong gelding: **a57**
modest performer: won handicap at Lingfield in January and (first run after leaving
M. Fetherston-Godley 800 gns) claimer at Southwell in December: stays 1m: acts on
all-weather, little form on turf. *S. R. Bowring*

PIP'S BRAVE   3 b.g. Be My Chief (USA) 122 – Pipistrelle 62 (Shareef Dancer   **58**
(USA) 135) [1998 58, a52: 7g⁶ a9.4g³ a7g a8g⁶ 1999 a8f* a8g⁴ a8g⁴ a8.5g⁶ 10g 14.6f
14.1m 10m a8g⁵ a8g⁶ 8m⁴ 10.5m* 10m⁵ 12m 14.1m 10m 11.5g 12s 10d Oct 21]
tall, lengthy gelding: unimpressive mover: modest performer: won maiden at
Southwell in January and handicap at Warwick in July: stays 10.5f, probably not
further: acts on fibresand and good to firm going: usually blinkered: none too
consistent. *M. J. Polglase*

PIPSISEWA (IRE)   3 ch.f. Pips Pride 117 – Algonquin Park (High Line 125)   **53**
[1998 61: 5d 7m 1999 6v⁴ 6m 8.3g 6m 7g Jun 8] rangy, useful-looking filly: modest
maiden: may prove best up to 7f: yet to race on heavy going, seems to act on any
other: sold 2,400 gns, sent to Kuwait. *D. R. C. Elsworth*

PIPS MAGIC (IRE)   3 b.g. Pips Pride 117 – Kentucky Starlet (USA) 69 (Cox's   **100**
Ridge (USA)) [1998 90: 5d 5v³ 5d 6m* 5f* 5s 5.2m 6m⁵ 6d 5d² 6g⁴ 6s⁴ 6d 1999 5d
6m 6m 6g² 6m³ 6d 5m* 5m 5m 5m 5g 6m 6d Sep 18] good-bodied gelding: useful
handicapper: in good heart in first half of season, winning at Ascot in June by ½
length from Henry Hall: below form after and gelded at end of season: stays 6f when
conditions aren't testing: acts on firm and soft ground: usually waited with.
J. S. Goldie

PIPSSALIO (SPA)   2 b.c. (Apr 8) Pips Pride 117 – Tesalia (SPA) (Finissimo   **54**
(SPA)) [1999 6m 6g 6d Nov 4] 6,000Y, 11,000 2-y-o: first foal: dam won in Spain:
modest form at best in minor event/maidens. *Jamie Poulton*

PIPS SONG (IRE)   4 ch.g. Pips Pride 117 – Friendly Song 48 (Song 132) [1998   **88**
75: a6g* 6.1m 6f⁴ 5g⁶ 6d⁴ 6m³ 7f 1999 a6g a7g a6g* 6v 6v* a6g³ 6d 6v⁶ 6d 6d² 5d²
a6g Nov 30] lengthy gelding: fairly useful handicapper: won at Wolverhampton in
March and Leicester (20 ran) in April: effective at 6f (given good test)/7f: acts on any
turf going and fibresand. *Dr J. D. Scargill*

PIPS STAR   2 b.f. (Mar 19) Pips Pride 117 – Kentucky Starlet (USA) 69 (Cox's   **65**
Ridge (USA)) [1999 5d 5g² 5g⁵ 5g⁵ 5g³ 5.1g 5v a5f* Oct 2] 1,800F, 18,000Y: fourth
foal: sister to 3-y-o Pips Magic and half-sister to 1997 2-y-o 7f winner Wildcat (by
Lion Cavern): dam 7f winner: fair performer: won seller at Wolverhampton in
October: likely to prove best at 5f/6f: acts on fibresand, raced only on good going or
softer on turf. *D. W. P. Arbuthnot*

PIPS TANGO (IRE)   2 ch.f. (Feb 26) Pips Pride 117 – Suppression (Kind of   **–**
Hush 118) [1999 6s 6f 6f Jul 26] sparely-made filly: third foal: sister to a couple of
poor/modest maidens: dam ran once: well held in maidens/seller. *M. Mullineaux*

PIPS WAY (IRE)   2 ch.f. (Mar 24) Pips Pride 117 – Algonquin Park (High Line   **77**
125) [1999 6d* 6d⁶ 6m 7m³ 7g 8g 8d⁴ 7d Sep 28] IR 13,000Y: rangy filly: fluent
mover: sister to 3-y-o Pipsisewa and half-sister to several winners, including 1997
2-y-o 5f seller winner Wilfred Sherman and French 7.5f (at 2 yrs) to 1¼m winner
Silver Wings (both by Silver Kite): dam Irish 1½m winner: fair performer: won
maiden at Ripon in May: creditable fourth of 20 in nursery at Ayr penultimate start:
stays 1m: yet to race on extremes of going: visored (well held) fifth start. *K. R. Burke*

PISCES LAD   3 b.g. Cyrano de Bergerac 120 – Tarnside Rosal 68 (Mummy's   **60**
Game 120) [1998 71: 5s⁴ 5.1g² 5m⁵ 5.1d² 5m³ 6m⁶ a6g 1999 a5g³ a6g² 5.1s 6m 7m

6g 7m 5.3f⁵ 6g⁴ 6d 5m 5d Sep 30] smallish, sturdy gelding: modest maiden handicapper: best at 5f/easy 6f: acts on firm going, good to soft and equitrack: sometimes starts slowly/wanders: inconsistent. *S. Dow*

PISSARO   2 b.c. (Apr 10) Green Desert (USA) 127 – Panache Arabelle (Nashwan (USA) 135) [1999 6m* 7d Sep 28] 500,000Y: good-topped colt: half-brother to 3-y-o Maidaan: dam once-raced half-sister to high-class 1¼m performer Stagecraft, an excellent family: 4/1-on, won maiden at Cork in June by 6 lengths: only eighth of 17 to Inchlonaig when favourite for sales event at Newmarket 3 months later: should stay 1m. *A. P. O'Brien, Ireland*   **92**

PIX ME UP (IRE)   2 b.f. (May 8) Up And At 'em 109 – Water Pixie (IRE) (Dance of Life (USA)) [1999 6d⁶ 7m 6m³ 7f² 6d Oct 26] small filly: second foal: dam unraced: fair maiden: off course 3 months before well beaten in nursery at Redcar final start: stays 7f: acts on firm and good to soft ground. *K. A. Ryan*   **66**

PLAN-B   4 b.c. Polish Precedent (USA) 131 – Draft Board 78 (Rainbow Quest (USA) 134) [1998 103: 7s⁶ 7.6g³ 8d* 8f² 1999 7g 7.9d⁶ 8m² Jun 16] leggy, useful-looking colt: useful performer, lightly raced: fractured knee in 1998: probably needed first 2 outings in 1999, then ran well when 6 lengths second to Showboat in Hunt Cup at Royal Ascot: likely to stay 1¼m: acts on firm and good to soft going: has worn crossed noseband/been early to post: held up: sent to UAE. *J. H. M. Gosden*   **107**

PLAS UCHA   2 b.c. (Apr 22) Forest Wind (USA) 111 – Adivara 58 (Tyrnavos 129) [1999 a5g² 5d Jun 7] 4,200Y: leggy, useful-looking colt: seventh foal: half-brother to a 7f winner in Italy by Gallic League: dam 1¼m winner: fair form in maidens at Wolverhampton and Pontefract: should stay at least 6f. *J. Berry*   **68**

PLAYINAROUND   2 ch.f. (Feb 27) Anshan 119 – Karonga (Main Reef 126) [1999 5v⁶ 5.7g 6f* 7g⁴ 6.1m⁵ 5.1m⁵ 6f³ a7g Sep 28] eighth foal: half-sister to 3-y-o Spendtheproc-Ede's and 2-y-o winners abroad by Nicholas and Salse: dam 9f winner: modest performer: won seller at Brighton in May: stays 7f: acts on firm ground: has hung and pulled hard. *W. G. M. Turner*   **51**

PLAZZOTTA (IRE)   2 b.g. (May 1) Sri Pekan (USA) 117 – Porte Des Iles (IRE) 76 (Kris 135) [1999 6v Oct 23] IR 18,000Y: good-topped gelding: second foal: dam, middle-distance maiden, half-sister to Gold Cup winner Gildoran, from family of Detroit and Carnegie: no promise in maiden at Newbury. *B. J. Meehan*   **–**

PLEADING   6 b.g. Never So Bold 135 – Ask Mama 83 (Mummy's Pet 125) [1998 77: 6.1s 6v 6s* 6m 6g 6v⁶ 1999 a6g a6g a6g⁵ 6.1v² 6.1s 6d³ 7.1d a7g⁴ 6g³ 6m² 6d 6g 7s³ 6m 7.1m* 7d 7s 7d Oct 9] smallish, good-topped gelding: fairly useful handicapper on turf, fair on all-weather: won 20-runner race at Chepstow in September by 4 lengths: effective at 6f (given good test)/7f: acts on good to firm ground, heavy and fibresand: blinkered last 4 starts: usually held up: tough: sold 8,000 gns, joined M. Buckley. *W. J. Musson*   **81 a63**

PLEASANT DREAMS   4 ch.f. Sabrehill (USA) 120 – Tafila 101 (Adonijah 126) [1998 58: 9.9s⁵ 10d 9.1m⁴ 9.3d⁵ 8m² 9.3m* 10m 9.9m 8s* 9.1s 8d a12g 1999 a8g a8f 8d⁵ 8d⁴ 9m⁴ 10g⁶ 8g 10g* 8m 10d⁴ 8g² 12f 10d Nov 1] leggy filly: modest handicapper: won apprentice event at Pontefract in June: best at 1m/1¼m: acts on soft and good to firm going, no form on all-weather: usually races prominently. *Denys Smith*   **64 a–**

PLEASANT MOUNT   3 b.g. First Trump 118 – Alo Ez 100 (Alzao (USA) 117) [1998 –: 6m 7.5m 1999 6d 10s³ 12g³ 14.1f² 14d³ 16.2m* 16d* 14.1m* 15.9s² Sep 22] good-bodied gelding: fair handicapper: progressed well in 1999, winning at Beverley, Thirsk and Redcar in summer: will stay beyond 2m: yet to race on heavy going, acts on any other: type to do better still. *Miss J. A. Camacho*   **72 p**

PLEASING PROSPECT (USA)   3 b.f. Mr Prospector (USA) – Promising Girl (USA) (Youth (USA) 135) [1998 68p: 7m⁶ 1999 7g⁶ 7.6m³ 8m² Jul 25] good-topped, attractive filly: has reportedly had a wind infirmity: fair maiden: best effort at Ascot final start, despite tending to carry head awkwardly: will stay beyond 1m: has worn tongue strap and crossed noseband: hung left on reappearance. *J. H. M. Gosden*   **76**

PLEASURE   4 ch.f. Most Welcome 131 – Peak Squaw (USA) 75 (Icecapade (USA)) [1998 60, a53: 6.1s³ 5m 6g 5g 7d* a7g⁵ a7g 1999 6s 7m 6g 5v* 5d⁵ 5s 7.5s Sep 21] unfurnished filly: fair handicapper: won at Beverley in June, making all on   **65 a–**

favoured stand rail: effective at 5f to 7f: acts on heavy ground and fibresand: blinkered last 4 starts: inconsistent. *A. Smith*

PLEASURE CENTER (USA) 2 ch.f. (Apr 20) Diesis 133 – Creaking Board (Night Shift (USA)) [1999 7d⁴ Oct 30] third foal: half-sister to smart US 9f to 11f performer Crowd Pleaser (by A P Indy): dam, US Grade 1 2-y-o 8.5f winner (earlier successful at 5.5f in France), sister to smart French sprinter Dyhim Diamond: encouraging fourth of 16 to Premier Prize in steadily-run maiden at Newmarket, always close up: will stay at least 1m: sure to improve. *J. H. M. Gosden* **81 p**

PLEASURE PRINCESS 2 b.f. (Feb 8) Presidium 124 – Harem Queen 66 (Prince Regent (FR) 129) [1999 5d 6d 7s Nov 2] 3,200Y: small, leggy filly: half-sister to 1989 2-y-o 6f/7f seller winner Little Ripper and 3 winners abroad (all by Belfort): dam lightly raced: last in maidens, twice mulish stalls. *A. Bailey* **–**

PLEASURE TIME 6 ch.g. Clantime 101 – First Experience 58 (Le Johnstan 123) [1998 76: 5.1m* 5d² 5s² 5f 5m 5m* 5g 5g 5s 1999 5.1m² 5.7f* 5f 5.1d 5m³ 5g 5g Oct 16] leggy, good-topped gelding: fairly useful performer: won minor event at Bath in June: ran well when placed in handicaps otherwise: best up to 5.7f on good going or firmer: has worn blinkers, visored nowadays: races up with pace. *C. Smith* **85**

PLEASURE TRICK (USA) 8 br.g. Clever Trick (USA) – Pleasure Garden (USA) (Foolish Pleasure (USA)) [1998 45, a63: a7g* a8g³ a7g² a8g³ a8g a7g* a8g⁶ a8g³ 8.5g 8m 7.9g 8s⁶ 8s⁵ a7g⁶ a8g 1999 a7g⁶ a7g⁴ a8f⁶ a7g⁶ a8g 6.9m 7s 8m⁵ 8g 8m Jun 24] good-quartered gelding: modest on all-weather, poor on turf: left Don Enrico Incisa before final start: stays 1m: acts on fibresand, firm and soft going: occasionally blinkered/visored: usually gets well behind: none too consistent. *N. Tinkler* **38 a57**

PLEIN GAZ (FR) 6 b.g. Lesotho (USA) 118 – Gazzara (USA) (Irish River (FR) 131) [1998 –, a61d: a6g a5g³ a5g a5g a6g* a7g⁴ a5g⁴ a6g a6g³ 6s 6g⁶ 5m 6.9m a7g⁵ 6m a7g a6g 1999 a6g a8f² a8g a8g⁶ a5g⁴ a7g⁵ 10f 10f 6g May 17] angular, good-quartered gelding: poor performer: seems effective at 5f to 1m: acts on soft ground and all-weather: tried blinkered earlier in career: often a front runner: sold 500 gns. *R. J. O'Sullivan* **45**

PLENTY OF SUNSHINE 6 ch.m. Pharly (FR) 130 – Zipperti Do 70 (Precocious 126) [1998 –: 8g a8g 8m 12d 1999 8g Jun 3] of no account. *A. G. Newcombe* **–**

PLUM FIRST 9 b.g. Nomination 125 – Plum Bold 83 (Be My Guest (USA) 126) [1998 56, a–: 5g⁴ 5m³ 5g 5g³ 5m 5m 6m 5m 6m 7d 6g 1999 6m 7.5d 6g 5.9m 5s⁶ 6d⁴ 5m 6m⁵ 7f⁶ Jul 24] lengthy, workmanlike gelding: modest performer: effective at stiff 5f to 7f: acts on fibresand and any turf going: effective in visor/blinkers, rarely tried of late: often bandaged behind: sometimes starts slowly: tends to hang left. *J. S. Wainwright* **57 a–**

PLURALIST (IRE) 3 b.c. Mujadil (USA) 119 – Encore Une Fois (IRE) 84 (Shirley Heights 130) [1998 71: 6m⁵ 6f² 7m² 7.3m 1999 9g 10g⁴ 9.2m² 11.5g⁶ 10.5s⁵ 10.4d⁶ 10g² a11g* Dec 17] strong, lengthy colt: fairly useful performer: best effort in handicap at Newmarket second start: landed odds easily in maiden at Southwell in December: may prove best around 1¼m: acts on fibresand and firm going, below form on other than good. *W. Jarvis* **81**

PLUTOCRAT 3 b.g. Polar Falcon (USA) 126 – Choire Mhor 100 (Dominion 123) [1998 NR 1999 7d² 6g 7f² 8s³ 9m* Aug 26] 27,000Y: leggy, shallow-girthed gelding: half-brother to several winners, including smart 5f winner Cathedral (by Prince Sabo) and 11f winner Themeda (by Sure Blade): dam, 6f winner, ran only at 2 yrs: fair performer: won claimer (joined L. Lungo for £9,000) at Musselburgh by 6 lengths final start: stays 9f: acts on firm going: has been bandaged in front. *J. Noseda* **75 +**

PODIUM 3 b.g. Presidium 124 – Sally Tadpole 44 (Jester 119) [1998 52: 8m 7.9g 10s⁴ 1999 7m 7f 6s Sep 16] leggy, unfurnished gelding: poor maiden. *P. W. Harris* **–**

POETRY IN MOTION (IRE) 4 gr.f. Ballad Rock 122 – Nasseem (FR) 118 (Zeddaan 130) [1998 76: 5d² 5m 6g 5m 5g 1999 8d a7g 5f² 5m* 5m 5m 6m 5.3s² 5d 5s² 5d Oct 20] big filly: fair performer: won maiden at Musselburgh in June: creditable second in handicaps at Newcastle (twice) and Brighton: poorly drawn final one: best at 5f: yet to race on heavy going, acts on any other: blinkered once. *E. J. Alston* **72**

POETTO   4 ch.g. Casteddu 111 – Steamy Windows § (Dominion 123) [1998 53,   –
a62: a6s a6g⁵ a7g² a8g³ a7g⁴ a7g⁴ 6d 7.1g 6g⁵ 7d⁵ 8d 10m 1999 a8f a8g⁶ Feb 26]
sturdy gelding: modest maiden handicapper at best: stays 1m: acts on good to soft
going and fibresand: tried blinkered/visored: often soon off bridle and not an easy
ride. *Mrs J. Brown*

POINT OF DISPUTE   4 b.g. Cyrano de Bergerac 120 – Opuntia (Rousillon   89
(USA) 133) [1998 82: 7s 6g* 6g 6s 1999 6m 5m 7m* 6g 6d 6d 6.1f* Oct 20] fairly
useful handicapper: won at Lingfield in August and Nottingham in October, in latter
despite carrying head high: may prove best at 6f/7f: acts on firm and good to soft
going: visored after second start: has tended to sweat and get on edge: has been early
to post: inconsistent. *P. J. Makin*

POKEIT   3 b.g. Cyrano de Bergerac 120 – Entourage 75 (Posse (USA) 130) [1998   –
58d: 5.3g⁴ 6f⁴ 6m a5g³ a6g 6g 5.3g⁴ 7s a6g a7g⁵ 1999 a6g Jan 11] poor maiden:
probably stays 7f: acts on fibresand, best turf runs on good going: blinkered once at 2
yrs: sent to Denmark. *N. P. Littmoden*

POKER POLKA   2 b.f. (Apr 11) Salse (USA) 128 – Poker Chip 106 (Bluebird   67
(USA) 125) [1999 6m 6m⁶ 5.1g* 6m⁵ a5g⁵ 5.2m Sep 17] sturdy filly: second foal:
dam, sprinter, won Flying Childers Stakes: fair performer: won maiden at Nottingham in August: should stay 6f: acts on fibresand, raced only on good/good to firm
going on turf. *J. M. P. Eustace*

POKER SCHOOL (IRE)   5 b.g. Night Shift (USA) – Mosaique Bleue (Shirley   –
Heights 130) [1998 –, a68: a10g a10g³ a12g³ 12d 11.9g 8m 10g 11.6d 1999 a11g*   a62
a11g a16f³ a12g⁴ 10s⁵ 10.8d 10s a14g³ a16g³ May 17] smallish, sturdy gelding:
modest handicapper: won amateur event at Southwell in January: ran creditably after
when in frame: effective at 11f to 2m: acts on all-weather, little form on turf since
1997: tried blinkered: has worn tongue strap. *M. R. Bosley*

POLAR CHALLENGE   2 b.c. (May 20) Polar Falcon (USA) 126 – Warning   74 p
Light (High Top 131) [1999 7m⁵ 7d⁴ Aug 21] fifth foal: half-brother to 1996 2-y-o 7f
winner Qui Vivra Verra (by Saddlers' Hall) and 6f (at 2yrs) to 1m winner Twilight
Patrol (by Robellino), both fairly useful: dam, unraced, from family of Nashwan and
Unfuwain: better effort in maidens when fourth of 6 to Rainbow Melody at Chester,
keeping on after slow start: will stay 1m: should do better still. *Sir Michael Stoute*

POLAR ECLIPSE   6 ch.g. Polar Falcon (USA) 126 – Princess Zepoli 61 (Perse-   58
polis (FR) 127) [1998 60: 6.1s⁴ 7s⁵ 7g 6f 7m³ 8m 1999 10s 8f⁴ 10m² 10m² 10m 9g⁴
10.1d a9.4g⁶ a11g Nov 30] rangy gelding: modest handicapper: trained by K. Burke
first 3 starts: stays 1¼m when conditions aren't testing: acts on firm ground, soft and
fibresand: often front runner. *J. G. Given*

POLAR FAIR   3 ch.f. Polar Falcon (USA) 126 – Fair Country 89 (Town And   62
Country 124) [1998 62: 6g 6m 1999 8m 8m a8g 9s³ 11.7s a8.5g* a8.5g a10g Dec 18]
good-topped filly: fluent mover: modest performer: won maiden at Wolverhampton
in November: stays 9f: acts on fibresand, soft and good to firm going: inconsistent.
J. Noseda

POLAR HAZE   2 ch.g. (Mar 25) Polar Falcon (USA) 126 – Sky Music 85 (Absa-   69
lom 128) [1999 5m² 6d 5g² 6d⁶ Oct 22] 5,600Y: lengthy, good-quartered gelding:
second foal: half-brother to 3-y-o Darras Sky: dam 6f/7f winner: fair maiden:
runner-up at Ripon and Musselburgh: effective at 5f/6f: yet to race on extremes of
going. *Miss S. E. Hall*

POLAR ICE   3 b.c. Polar Falcon (USA) 126 – Sweet Slew (USA) 96 (Seattle Slew   79
(USA)) [1998 70p: 6g² 6v⁵ 1999 5.1s⁴ 7m² a7g² a7g* a7g* a8.5g³ 7d a7g a7g Dec 4]   a89
rangy, rather unfurnished colt: fairly useful on all-weather, fair on turf: won maiden
and handicap at Wolverhampton in June: below form after, leaving Sir Mark Prescott
after seventh start: stays 7f, probably not 1m: acts on fibresand and good to firm
going. *D. J. S. Cosgrove*

POLAR LADY   2 ch.f. (May 23) Polar Falcon (USA) 126 – Soluce 98 (Junius   69 p
(USA) 124) [1999 6.1d⁶ Oct 5] half-sister to several winners, including 3-y-o Tarawan, smart sprinter Splice (by Sharpo) and fairly useful miler Alfujairah (by Diesis):
dam Irish 7f winner: very weak in market, some promise when sixth of 15 to
Resounding in Nottingham maiden, losing several lengths when carried left stalls

but travelling well long way and not knocked about: should improve a fair bit. *J. R. Fanshawe*

POLAR MIST 4 b.g. Polar Falcon (USA) 126 – Post Mistress (IRE) 79 (Cyrano **71**
de Bergerac 120) [1998 70: a6g³ a6g* a5g⁵ 6m a6g⁶ a7g a5g² a5g a5g a5g² a5g 1999
a6g³ a6g* a6g² a6f⁵ a6g⁴ a7g a5g² a5g* 5d³ 5s* 5d 5m 5s a5g⁵ a5g² a5g² a5g* a6g⁶
a5g² 5g a6g 5.1s Sep 22] quite good-topped gelding: fair performer: won claimer,
seller and handicap at Wolverhampton and minor event at Folkestone between January and June: effective at 5f/6f: acts on fibresand and soft going: visored/blinkered:
often tongue tied: usually races prominently: tough. *Mrs N. Macauley*

POLAR RED 2 ch.g. (Mar 31) Polar Falcon (USA) 126 – Sharp Top 62 (Sharpo **73**
132) [1999 5.2g⁶ 7m⁴ 6g 7m 7.7d⁵ 8.3g* 8m² 8d³ Nov 1] good-topped, workmanlike
gelding: fourth foal: closely related to 3-y-o Hi Nicky and half-brother to 5-y-o Top
Jem: dam stayed 2m: fair performer: good efforts in nurseries last 3 starts, winning at
Windsor in October: should stay 1¼m: yet to race on extremes of going: blinkered
first 3 starts: has had to be mounted in saddling boxes and worn rope halter: may
prove best with waiting tactics: withdrawn after refusing to go to post intended final
outing. *M. J. Ryan*

POLAR REFRAIN 6 ch.m. Polar Falcon (USA) 126 – Cut No Ice 97 (Great **35**
Nephew 126) [1998 35: 8d* 6.9d² 1999 a8g a8g a12g 10d 9g 8g 7m⁶ 8f 8m⁴ 8f⁵ 8.3s
a8g Dec 17] workmanlike mare: poor handicapper: probably stays 1¼m: acts on firm
ground, soft and fibresand: tried blinkered: inconsistent. *J. L. Eyre*

POLAR STAR 2 b.c. (Feb 1) Polar Falcon (USA) 126 – Glowing With Pride 114 **78 p**
(Ile de Bourbon (USA) 133) [1999 6d 6s² Nov 5] 30,000Y: quite good-topped colt:
closely related to 1994 2-y-o 6f winner Alusha (by Soviet Star) and half-brother to
several winners, including smart 7f (at 2 yrs) and 1¼m winner Prize Giving (by Most
Welcome) and useful 6f/7f performer Everglades (by Green Desert): dam 7f and
10.5f winner, second in Park Hill Stakes: still in need of race, much better effort in
maidens when 1½ lengths second of 20 to very easy winner Royal Highlander at
Doncaster, staying on from well off pace: will stay at least 1m: should make a fairly
useful performer at least. *C. F. Wall*

POLES APART (IRE) 3 b.g. Distinctly North (USA) 115 – Slightly Latin **91**
(Ahonoora 122) [1998 94: 6f³ 6m* 6g⁴ 6m⁵ 1999 6g⁶ 7m 7d 6g⁵ 7.1g 8m 6f* 6m
Aug 22] rangy gelding: fairly useful handicapper: won at Doncaster in July: ran
poorly only start after: best efforts at 6f on good going or firmer: has had tongue tied.
M. H. Tompkins

POLISHED UP 2 b.f. (Apr 23) Polish Precedent (USA) 131 – Smarten Up 119 **–**
(Sharpen Up 127) [1999 7v Sep 20] half-sister to several winners, notably Cadeaux
Genereux (by Young Generation) and useful stayer Brightner (by Sparkler): dam
sprinter: very green when remote seventh of 9 in maiden at Kempton. *P. T. Walwyn*

POLISH FALCON (IRE) 3 b.g. Polish Patriot (USA) 128 – Marie de Fresnaye **59**
(USA) (Dom Racine (FR) 121) [1998 NR 1999 10v a8g a9.4g⁴ Dec 15] 32,000Y:
third reported foal: dam unraced half-sister to very smart French middle-distance
stayer Marie de Litz and to the dam of Polar Falcon: first form in maidens when
fourth at Wolverhampton: should stay 1¼m: acts on fibresand. *R. Hannon*

POLISH GIRL 3 b.f. Polish Precedent (USA) 131 – Stack Rock 111 (Ballad **–**
Rock 122) [1998 NR 1999 8m Sep 17] 54,000Y: lengthy filly: first foal: dam sprinter:
9/1 and in need of race, last of 19 in maiden at Newbury. *B. J. Meehan*

POLISH LEGION 6 b.g. Polish Precedent (USA) 131 – Crystal Bright 75 (Bold **–**
Lad (IRE) 133) [1998 –: 8.3d 6m 6d 6m 6.1s 1999 a6f a5f a7g a8g 8.3m 8f Apr
29] big gelding: fairly useful winner only 2-y-o start: no form since: sold 500 gns.
J. Akehurst

POLISH PILOT (IRE) 4 b.g. Polish Patriot (USA) 128 – Va Toujours 109 (Alzao **–**
(USA) 117) [1998 64: 8m⁶ 10g 9m⁵ 10.2m 13.1m 10m 10g 1999 9m 10.5m 8.1m Jul
9] leggy, workmanlike gelding: modest maiden handicapper at best: stays 9f: acts on
soft and good to firm going, ran poorly only outing on equitrack: tried blinkered:
inconsistent: won over hurdles in November. *W. R. Muir*

POLISH SPIRIT 4 b.g. Emarati (USA) 74 – Gentle Star 77 (Comedy Star (USA) **70**
121) [1998 61: 8.1m 8.3m 7g* 7.1m 7.1g 7.1m⁵ 6s 1999 6s⁴ 7.1d³ 8g³ 8m² 8g³ 8m⁵

8f[4] 8.3s* 8m 8s 10d 10.2s[3] Oct 26] lengthy, workmanlike gelding: fair handicapper: generally in good form in 1999, winning at Windsor in August: effective at 7f to 1¼m: yet to race on heavy going, acts on any other: usually races prominently. *B. R. Millman*

POLIZIANO (USA)   3 ch.c. Storm Bird (CAN) 134 – Polemic (USA) 114 **81** (Roberto (USA) 131) [1998 81p: 6s[2] 1999 8.1m[3] 8g[3] Aug 22] deep-girthed, attractive colt: has a quick action: fairly useful maiden: may stay beyond 1m: sold 10,500 gns, joined W. Haigh. *H. R. A. Cecil*

POLKA   4 b.g. Slip Anchor 136 – Peace Dance (Bikala 134) [1998 –: 9g[6] 1999 **–** a9.4g 11.1v[5] 13s[5] May 14] well beaten in maidens/handicap: sold 1,100 gns. *C. W. Thornton*

POLLY GOLIGHTLY   6 ch.m. Weldnaas (USA) 112 – Polly's Teahouse 68 **77** (Shack (USA) 118) [1998 83: 5s 5s[4] 5.1m[4] 5m 5.1g* 5s* 5s 5m[2] 5f[3] 5d 5.1d[4] 5d[5] 5.2g 5m 5g 5m 5d 1999 5d[5] 5d[6] 5.1d[4] 5d 5f 5f 5.2g[5] 5.1d* 5.1s[6] 5s 5g 5d[4] 5s[4] Nov 5] smallish mare: fair handicapper: won at Chester in August: best at 5f: untried on heavy going, acts on any other: has been visored, blinkered nowadays: has swished tail and tends to edge left: best racing up with pace. *M. Blanshard*

POLLY MILLS   3 b.f. Lugana Beach 116 – Danseuse Davis (FR) (Glow (USA)) **74** [1998 84: 5g 5d* 5m[2] a5g[4] 5f[3] 6g[5] 6m 6.1g[4] 5f[4] 5m 5d 5g 5d[4] 5g[6] a5g* a6g[2] a6g[2] **a89** a5g[4] a6g[2] a5g[4] 1999 a6g[5] a7g[3] a7f[5] a6g[3] a7g[4] a6g[2] a6g* 6g 5d a6g[3] 6.1m[6] 5d[3] 5f 6d[6] 6m 5m[5] 6f[4] 5d 6d a6g a6g[2] a5g Dec 21] small filly: fairly useful handicapper on all-weather, fair on turf: won at Southwell in March: mostly well below form after: probably stays 7f: acts on firm going, good to soft and all-weather: wears visor/ blinkers: has been bandaged: often soon off bridle. *P. D. Evans*

POLLYOLLY (IRE)   2 b.f. (Mar 15) Emarati (USA) 74 – Eurolink Virago **–** (Charmer 123) [1999 5m[5] 6m 6g 5g a5g Dec 29] 500Y: second foal: half-sister to German 3-y-o 5f winner Eternal Moon (by Be My Chief): dam unraced half-sister to smart 7f/1m performer Eurolink Thunder: no form. *M. J. Haynes*

POLO   3 b.f. Warning 136 – Peace Dance (Bikala 134) [1998 NR 1999 8d[5] 10g* **83** 10d Sep 17] rather leggy filly: second foal: dam unraced sister to Prix du Jockey Club winner Polytain: won maiden at Pontefract in August by neck from Horatia, finding plenty under pressure: stiff task in handicap final start: will stay 1½m: may still do better. *C. W. Thornton*

POLO VENTURE   4 ch.g. Polar Falcon (USA) 126 – Ceramic (USA) (Raja Baba **–** (USA)) [1998 64, a71: a9.4g[3] 10v[3] a12g[2] a10g* a12g[5] 12g[5] 12m 1999 11.9d Oct 7] fair form at 3 yrs for S. Woods: well held only start in 1999 (having been successful over hurdles in April): stays 1½m: acts on good to firm ground and all-weather: usually races prominently. *M. D. Hammond*

POLRUAN   3 ch.g. Elmaamul (USA) 125 – Trelissick (Electric 126) [1998 78: 6s[2] **70** 5.7s[4] 5.2m 7d[2] 7.3g[5] 6d* 7d 1999 7m 7d[6] 7g 6.8g[5] 5m 8m 8s[4] Oct 4] tall, leggy gelding: fair handicapper: inconsistent in 1999: should prove best up to easy 1m: acts on soft ground, probably good to firm: has worn tongue strap. *Lady Herries*

POLY BLUE (IRE)   4 ch.f. Thatching 131 – Mazarine Blue (USA) (Chief's **–** Crown (USA)) [1998 82: 6d[2] 7.3m[6] 7g 7s[4] 7f[3] 7.1m 7m[4] 7.1g[5] 7s 7s 1999 a8f 8g Jun 14] quite good-topped filly: fairly useful at best: well held both starts (5 months apart) in 1999: stays 7f: acts on firm and good to soft going: blinkered once. *Miss Gay Kelleway*

POLY RULER (IRE)   3 b.g. Dancing Dissident (USA) 119 – Love Me Tight **–** (Tyrant (USA)) [1998 43: 8.1m 7.1d 8d 10d[5] 1999 10d Oct 11] poor maiden: sold 1,500 gns. *Miss K. M. George*

POMME DUCHESSE (USA)   3 b.f. Alleged (USA) 138 – Quilesse (USA) **75** (Fulmar (USA)) [1998 NR 1999 12m 11.9d 9s* Oct 8] fourth foal: half-sister to a winner in USA by Woodman: dam French 1m/9f winner: easily best effort in maidens when winning at Lingfield in October by 1½ lengths: bred to stay beyond 9f: sold 26,000 gns. *C. E. Brittain*

POMPEII (IRE)   2 b.c. (Feb 11) Salse (USA) 128 – Before Dawn (USA) (Raise A **75 p** Cup (USA)) [1999 8m[6] 8v[2] 8d Oct 21] 52,000Y: rangy colt: half-brother to numerous winners in France/USA, including useful 1½m winner Blue Saddle and 13f/15f winner Daybreak Express (both by Sadler's Wells): dam, champion 1981 2-y-o filly in USA, winner of Grade 1 events at 6f and 7f: trained by P. Chapple-Hyam on debut: favourite, best effort when short-headed by Osood in 8-runner maiden at Salisbury: well beaten at Brighton final start: will stay 1¼m: has scope, and should still do better. *P. F. I. Cole*

PONTIKONISI 2 b.c. (May 22) Mistertopogigo (IRE) 118 – Anse Chastanet **45** (Cavo Doro 124) [1999 6.8m 6.8d 6v a7g a5g⁵ a8g⁴ a7g⁵ Dec 8] 6,500Y: seventh foal: half-brother to 1996 2-y-o 6f/7f seller winner Our Kevin (by Chilibang) and 7f winner Euphyllia (by Superpower): dam ran 3 times: poor maiden: likely to prove best up to 1m: blinkered/visored last 3 starts. *K. McAuliffe*

POPLAR JAY 3 gr. or ro.f. Totem (USA) 118 – Proclaimer 43 (Town Crier 119) **–** [1998 NR 1999 6m 7f 6.9g Jul 3] sixth foal: dam sprint plater: behind in varied company. *J. R. Turner*

POPPADAM 2 ch.f. (Apr 21) Salse (USA) 128 – Wanton 106 (Kris 135) [1999 7d **65 p** Oct 30] half-sister to several winners, including 3-y-o Indian Warrior, useful 5f (at 2 yrs) and 9f (in UAE) winner Magongo (by Be My Chief) and Irish 1,000 Guineas winner Classic Park (by Robellino): dam, sprinter (best at 2 yrs), half-sister to smart sprinter Easy Option: green, tenth of 16 in Newmarket maiden, held up and never a threat: will stay 1m: should do better. *L. M. Cumani*

POPPY'S SONG 2 b.f. (Feb 14) Owington 123 – Pretty Poppy 67 (Song 132) **70** [1999 5.2m³ 5g³ 5g⁴ 5.2m⁴ 5s* Oct 5] 8,000Y: fifth foal: half-sister to 3-y-o Borders, 6-y-o Speed On and Loving And Giving, another 5f winner, (at 2 yrs, by Sharpo): dam 2-y-o 5f winner who stayed 7f: fair performer: didn't have to be at best to win maiden at Catterick in October: may prove best at 5f: acts on soft ground, best efforts on good or firmer. *H. Candy*

POP SHOP 2 b.c. (Jan 14) Owington 123 – Diamond Park (IRE) 91 (Alzao (USA) **77** 117) [1999 5m⁴ 5d⁴ 5.1m⁵ 5m⁶ 5m⁶ 5m² Aug 28] 7,000Y: strong, good-topped colt: has scope: second foal: half-brother to 3-y-o Key: dam disappointing maiden from good middle-distance family: fair performer: won maiden at Nottingham in June: good second to Harryana in minor event at Redcar final start: should stay 6f: acts on good to firm and good to soft going: consistent. *J. W. Payne*

POP THE CORK 2 ch.g. (May 7) Clantime 101 – Hyde Princess 75 (Touch Paper **–** 113) [1999 a5g Nov 20] 5,600Y: brother to 5f winner The Fed and half-brother to 3-y-o Angie Baby and 4-y-o Durham Flyer: dam sprinter: needed experience when behind in maiden at Wolverhampton. *R. M. Whitaker*

PORCINI (IRE) 2 b.c. (Apr 17) Alzao (USA) 117 – Zurarah (Siberian Express **85** (USA) 125) [1999 5.2m* 6s⁶ 6v⁶ 7d⁴ 7m⁴ Oct 19] IR 50,000Y: lengthy, attractive colt: fluent mover: seventh foal: half-brother to fairly useful 1995 Irish 2-y-o 6f winner Magarah (by Magical Strike) and winners in Italy by Digamist and Mujadil: dam unraced half-sister to smart 7f/1m performer Gabr: fairly useful performer: won minor event at Newbury in April: generally below that form after: stays 7f: takes good hold: wandered and looked less than keen penultimate start: sold 25,000 gns. *P. F. I. Cole*

PORLOCK LADY 4 b.f. King's Signet (USA) 110 – Miramede (Norwick (USA) **–** 125) [1998 –: 5.1d⁶ 6m 5m 1999 5.3f 6.1g Jun 11] little sign of ability. *R. J. Hodges*

PORTIA LADY 2 b.f. (Apr 21) Noble Patriarch 115 – Gymcrak Lovebird 84 **47** (Taufan (USA) 119) [1999 6m 7m 7m⁶ 7m⁴ 7.5g 7.5g² 10s Oct 5] close-coupled filly: sixth foal: half-sister to 2 winning sprinters, including 7-y-o Dominelle: dam 5f (at 2 yrs) to 1¼m winner: poor maiden: in frame in sellers: failed to stay 1¼m on soft ground: raced mainly on good going or firmer: blinkered fourth to sixth starts. *T. D. Easterby*

PORTITE SOPHIE 8 b.m. Doulab (USA) 115 – Impropriety (Law Society **41** (USA) 130) [1998 46: a12g⁵ a12g a8g 11.1d² a9.4g 10g⁴ 12.1s⁵ 9.2d* 10.9d 9.9m³ **a35** a11g⁶ a12g³ 1999 a9.4g⁵ a12g⁶ a11g a11g 12.3m⁴ 9.9g³ 11d 12g² 10d³ a9.4g⁶ 10g⁵ 10.5m³ 12s⁴ a11g⁵ Sep 28] small, wiry mare: poor performer: effective at 9f (given test) to 1½m: acts on fibresand, firm and soft going (unraced on heavy): blinkered twice at 3 yrs. *M. Brittain*

PORTLAND 2 ch.c. (Feb 4) Mujtahid (USA) 118 – Princess Dixieland (USA) **79** (Dixieland Band (USA)) [1999 8m 8s² 9d⁶ a7g³ a10g Dec 18] IR 25,000Y: fourth foal: half-brother to 3 winners, including 4-y-o Rafters Music and fairly useful Irish 1½m winner Piranesi (by Grand Lodge): dam fairly useful Irish 7f (at 2 yrs) and 1¼m winner: trained by D. Gillespie in Ireland first 4 starts: broke leg at Lingfield in December: stayed 9f: acted on soft going: dead. *Sir Mark Prescott*

PORT MEADOW (IRE) 3 b.g. Common Grounds 118 – Kharimata (IRE) **64** (Kahyasi 130) [1998 67p: 8g 8d⁶ 1999 a9.4g³ 10.3d 10.8d⁵ 15.8d 11.8d² Oct 12] rather sparely-made gelding: shows plenty of knee action: modest maiden: best effort in 1999 when second of 19 in claimer at Leicester: stays 1½m: below form on fibresand, raced only on good/good to soft going otherwise: joined M. Pipe, won over hurdles in November. *R. Charlton*

PORTRACK JUNCTION (IRE) 2 b.c. (Feb 6) Common Grounds 118 – Bold- **?** absa 96 (Persian Bold 123) [1999 5g 6m 6d 8s⁵ Sep 29] 15,000Y: seventh foal: brother to 4 winners, including 3-y-o Downland, useful 1994 2-y-o sprinter Painted Madam and fair winner around 1½m Double Eight: dam Irish 9f and 1¼m winner: showed only signs of ability: has had tongue tied. *N. Tinkler*

PORT ST CHARLES (IRE) 2 b. or br.c. (Apr 30) Night Shift (USA) – Safe **76** Haven (Blakeney 126) [1999 6m³ 5g³ Aug 24] IR 26,000F, IR 130,000Y: half-brother to several winners, including smart sprinter Lugana Beach (by Tumble Wind) and useful 1¼m winner Delve (by Shernazar): dam, French maiden, half-sister to Mtoto: fair form in maidens at Epsom and Lingfield. *N. A. Callaghan*

PORT VILA (FR) 2 b.c. (Apr 5) Barathea (IRE) 127 – Girouette (USA) (Nodouble **104** (USA)) [1999 7g* 7m* 7g⁴ Oct 16] 65,000F, IR 400,000Y: well-made colt: half-brother to several winners in France, including useful 6f/7f winner Roi Gironde (by Fairy King) and useful 10.5f Prix Cleopatre winner Garendare (by Vacarme), latter later successful in USA: dam unraced half-sister to top-class French miler Gravelines: useful form: well-supported favourite when winning maiden at Newbury in August and minor event at Kempton following month: creditable fourth of 5 to Distant Music in Dewhurst Stakes at Newmarket final start, beaten 5½ lengths: will probably stay at least 1¼m. *J. H. M. Gosden*

POSATIVE 5 ch.m. Charmer 123 – Suprette 64 (Superlative 118) [1998 –: a7g **–** a6g⁵ 8d 1999 8g 8f⁶ 12g Jun 8] little form: dead. *M. P. Muggeridge*

POSIDONAS 7 b.h. Slip Anchor 136 – Tamassos 67 (Dance In Time (CAN)) **–** [1998 120: 12s* 12g⁶ 12d* 11g³ 12d 12s² 1999 12m 12m⁶ Jun 18] good-topped horse: usually impressed in appearance: showed knee action: very smart at best: winner of 4 pattern races, including Gran Premio d'Italia at Milan in 1995, Princess of Wales's Stakes at Newmarket in 1996 and Hardwicke Stakes at Royal Ascot as 6-y-o: well below form both starts in 1999: best around 1½m: acted on any going: blinkered (ran creditably) twice: tended to carry head shade high, but was genuine and consistent: sold 40,000 gns in October, to stand at Sweet Wall Stud, Co. Antrim, Northern Ireland, fee £1,000. *P. F. I. Cole*

POSITIVE AIR 4 b.f. Puissance 110 – Breezy Day 85 (Day Is Done 115) [1998 **–** 81: 6s 6.1m 6g³ 6s 6g* 7g⁶ 7f⁶ 6g 6.1m 7d 6g 1999 6m 7m 8g⁵ 10g⁶ 6.1m a8g Dec 13] tall filly: fairly useful handicapper in 1998: well beaten in 1999, leaving B. McMahon after fifth start: stays 6f: acts on good to firm and good to soft going: tried blinkered/visored. *Mrs A. M. Naughton*

POWDER RIVER 5 b.h. Alzao (USA) 117 – Nest 65 (Sharpo 132) [1998 6g 7g⁴ **71** 1999 a12g a7g a8g³ a10g* a9.4g 10.3m 10g 10m 12.3f⁵ 12s 11m* 12g³ 10.3m⁴ 11.9s² Sep 24] smallish, sturdy horse: fair handicapper: ran in Czech Republic (won up to 11f) in 1997/8: won at Lingfield in March and Redcar in August: probably best at 1¼m/1½m: acts on equitrack (possibly not fibresand), firm and soft going: blinkered (ran well) 4 times as 2-y-o: usually held up. *A. G. Newcombe*

POWER AND DEMAND 2 b.c. (Apr 9) Formidable (USA) 125 – Mazurka- **43** nova 63 (Song 132) [1999 5d 5s 5.1s⁶ a5g a5g⁴ Dec 29] 5,800Y: half-brother to 3-y-o Charmanova, 1997 2-y-o 6f winner Touchanova (by Touch of Grey) and winning sprinter Matthew David (by Indian Forest): dam 2-y-o 6f winner: poor maiden: off 4 months before final start. *D. Shaw*

POWER FLAME (GER)   6 ch.g. Dashing Blade 117 – Pikante (GER) (Surumu (GER)) [1998 116: 8s⁴ 8g 8v* 8d* 8g* 8d* 1999 8.8m² 8m⁴ Jul 11] smart performer: in excellent form at 5 yrs, winning last 4 starts, including pattern races at Cologne (2) and Baden-Baden: much the better effort in 1999 when creditable 1½ lengths second to Gonlargo in Group 3 event at Dortmund in June: stays 9.5f: acts on good to firm and heavy going. *A. Wohler, Germany*   **116**

POWER GAME   6 b.g. Puissance 110 – Play The Game 70 (Mummy's Game 120) [1998 –: 8.3g⁵ 8g 9.1d 8.3s 8.3s 1999 8g 6m⁶ 6f 6m 9.2m 8d 8.3s Sep 27] leggy gelding: modest at 4 yrs: little form since: usually blinkered/visored. *D. A. Nolan*   **–**

POWER GLOW   3 gr.g. Puissance 110 – Kala Rosa 79 (Kalaglow 132) [1998 –: 5.7d 5.1g 6.1g 1999 5.1g 8.1m 8f 7m Aug 22] little sign of ability, including in blinkers. *J. M. Bradley*   **–**

POWER HIT (USA)   3 b.g. Leo Castelli (USA) – Rajana (USA) (Rajab (USA)) [1998 9d 10v 1999 10.2s 10.2g⁵ 10m 12.3m⁵ 12m³ 16.2m⁶ 11.6m 11.9d² Aug 17] rather leggy gelding: half-brother to several winners, including smart 1m/1¼m performer Honor Rajana (by Hero's Honor): dam graded winner in Puerto Rico: well held in France at 2 yrs when trained by P. Bary: fair maiden handicapper in Britain: stays 1½m: acts on good to firm and good to soft going: visored/blinkered last 4 outings: joined M. Pipe. *B. R. Millman*   **66**

POWERLINE   2 b.f. (Jan 25) Warning 136 – Kantikoy (Alzao (USA) 117) [1999 6m 8.1g⁶ Aug 30] 30,000Y: heavy-topped filly: second foal: dam unraced half-sister to smart middle-distance performer Kithanga from family of Kahyasi: modest form in maidens at Ascot and Chepstow (unseated rider to post, still green, sixth of 9 to Idolize) in the summer: will stay 1¼m: open to improvement. *R. Hannon*   **61 p**

POWER PACKED   2 b.c. (Jan 16) Puissance 110 – My First Romance 61 (Danehill (USA) 126) [1999 6d⁵ 5.1m² 5g* 5d² Sep 30] 27,000Y: quite good-topped colt: has scope: first foal: dam ran twice: progressive form: won maiden at Pontefract in August: short-headed by Blue Velvet in 16-runner nursery at Newmarket final start, showing fine speed to help force pace: will prove best at 5f/6f: yet to race on extremes of going: open to further improvement, and should prove smart. *M. A. Jarvis*   **98 p**

POZARICA   4 b.c. Rainbow Quest (USA) 134 – Anna Matrushka (Mill Reef (USA) 141) [1998 111p: 11d⁴ 11.5s⁴ 12g* 15g* 15g* 1999 14d⁴ 15.5m² 11d⁶ Sep 19] rather lightly-raced colt: smart performer, lightly raced: ran creditably in valuable handicap at Goodwood (3 lengths fourth to Opera King) in May and Prix Gladiateur at Longchamp (length second to Tajoun) in September: last in valuable listed race at Newbury final start: stays 15.5f: acts on good to firm and good to soft going: sent to USA. *Saeed bin Suroor*   **112**

PRAETORIAN GOLD   4 ch.g. Presidium 124 – Chinese Princess (Sunny Way 120) [1998 89: 10d 10m³ 9.9g* 10.2s* 10g² 10m 9m⁴ 11.8d 1999 10g 10m 11.9d 9.7m² 10.3d⁶ 10m 10.3g³ 10m⁵ 10m³ 10.1m² 10.3m⁶ 10.4d⁴ Oct 7] rather leggy gelding: fairly useful handicapper: best around 1¼m: acts on soft and good to firm going: blinkered (ran creditably) ninth start: none too consistent. *R. Hannon*   **81**

PRAIRIE DOWNS (USA)   2 ch.f. (May 11) Thunder Gulch (USA) 129 – Tough As Nails (USA) (Majestic Light (USA)) [1999 5g³ 5d⁵ Jun 2] lengthy, angular filly: shows a quick action: half-sister to very smart 6f/7f performer Catrail (by Storm Cat) and winners in USA by Mogambo and Storm Cat: dam unraced half-sister to US Grade 2 9f winner John's Gold: fair form in maiden at Windsor and minor event at Beverley (edgy, showed speed from poor draw) in May/June. *J. Berry*   **71 +**

PRAIRIE FALCON (IRE)   5 b.g. Alzao (USA) 117 – Sea Harrier (Grundy 137) [1998 90: 10m 12m 12m² 12.3g³ 10.5m* 12m* 12s 12v 1999 16g² 18.7m⁴ May 5] attractive gelding: good mover: useful handicapper: ran well both starts in 1999, beaten a head by Far Cry in Queen's Prize at Kempton and 4½ lengths when fourth to Rainbow High in Chester Cup, in latter pulling hard yet seeing longer trip out well: stays 19f: acts on good to firm and good to soft going, well beaten on soft/heavy. *B. W. Hills*   **95**

PRAIRIE WOLF 3 ch.g. Wolfhound (USA) 126 – Bay Queen 85 (Damister (USA) 123) [1998 58: 8m 7v⁶ 1999 a8.5g* 8s³ 8d* 8m³ 8.2m* 8m 8f⁶ 9.9f³ 9.2f² 10.1g* 10s Oct 2] strong, workmanlike gelding: useful performer: had a good year, winning maiden at Wolverhampton in March, handicaps at Ripon in April and Nottingham in May and minor event at Yarmouth in August: below form in Cambridgeshire at Newmarket final start: effective at 1m/1¼m: acts on firm ground, good to soft and fibresand: consistent. *M. L. W. Bell* **96**

PRASLIN ISLAND 3 ch.c. Be My Chief (USA) 122 – Hence (USA) (Mr Prospector (USA)) [1998 NR 1999 12g 14.1m² 13.8g² 14.1m⁶ 14.8m⁴ 17.1g⁴ 14.6m 16s a14.8g² 17.3g 16g⁶ a12g² a12g* a13g² a14g* Dec 13] 6,500Y: brother to 4-y-o Be Gone and half-brother to 3 winners, including 1¼m winner Ruby Heights (by Shirley Heights): dam 7f winner in USA from good family: fairly useful on all-weather, fair on turf: won maiden at Wolverhampton and handicap at Southwell in December: effective at 1½m to 17f: acts on fibresand and good to firm going: blinkered (well out of depth in St Leger) seventh start: tongue tied on debut: has run in snatches: usually races prominently. *A. Kelleway* **74 a89**

PRECIOUS PERSIAN (IRE) 3 b.f. Persian Bold 123 – Cliveden Gail (IRE) 102 (Law Society (USA) 130) [1998 NR 1999 11.8m³ 12g⁴ 14g³ 14.8m² 14g 16.4d² 15.8d* 16.1s⁶ 14.6d⁶ Oct 22] IR 16,500 and 17,000Y: unfurnished filly: first foal: dam, 1¾m/2m winner, half-sister to Rock Hopper: fairly useful performer: best effort when winning apprentice handicap at Warwick in September: likely to prove best at 1¾m/2m: acts on good to firm and good to soft going. *S. P. C. Woods* **82**

PRECIOUS YEARS 4 ch.g. Dilum (USA) 115 – Tantot 65 (Charlottown 127) [1998 –: 7m 8.2s 1999 10g 5f Sep 4] compact gelding: no form. *L. R. Lloyd-James* **–**

PRECOCIOUS MISS (USA) 3 b.f. Diesis 133 – Kissogram Girl (USA) 100 (Danzig (USA)) [1998 88: 6m² 6f* 1999 6g May 3] won maiden at Lingfield in 1998: ran as though something amiss in minor event at Kempton only 3-y-o start: should stay 1m: sold 36,000 gns in December. *Sir Michael Stoute* **–**

PREDATOR 2 b.g. (Feb 4) Polar Falcon (USA) 126 – Red Azalea 95 (Shirley Heights 130) [1999 6g⁵ 5.1g Oct 21] 90,000Y: first foal: dam, 7f (at 2 yrs) and 1¼m winner, half-sister to smart 7f/1m performer Red Camelia (by Polar Falcon) from family of Ibn Bey and Teleprompter: much better effort in maidens (fair form) when fifth of 21 at Windsor: sold 9,000 gns, sent to Spain. *Sir Mark Prescott* **67**

PREDOMINANT (USA) 3 ch.g. Sky Classic (CAN) – Hard Knocker (USA) (Raja Baba (USA)) [1998 NR 1999 a9.4g a10g⁴ Dec 29] $50,000F, $45,000Y: seventh foal: closely related to a winner in USA by Green Dancer and half-brother to 3 winners, including French 1½m winner Anglona (by Polish Navy): dam unraced half-sister to very smart middle-distance stayer Mashaallah: better effort in maidens on second start: will stay 1½m. *W. J. Haggas* **52**

PREMIER BARON 4 b.g. Primo Dominie 121 – Anna Karietta 82 (Precocious 126) [1998 81: a6g⁶ a8g³ 6d⁴ 6d² a6g⁶ 7s⁴ 6m 7g³ 7g 1999 7g² 8g⁵ a7g³ 7.1d* 7g⁴ 7.1s⁶ 7d² 7s² 8d Oct 30] smallish gelding: fairly useful handicapper on turf, fair on all-weather: won at Sandown in August: good efforts after when runner-up: stays 7f: acts on fibresand and soft going. *Pat Mitchell* **93 a71**

PREMIER DANCE 12 ch.g. Bairn (USA) 126 – Gigiolina (King Emperor (USA)) [1998 45, a70d: a12s a14.8g² a16.2g⁴ a14.8g⁴ a14g a12g³ a14g⁶ 11.1d⁴ a14.8g⁶ a14.8g⁶ 1999 a14.8g² a12g* a12g⁵ a12g² a16.2g May 8] compact gelding: has a quick action: modest handicapper on all-weather, poor on turf: won at Wolverhampton (ninth course win) in February: reportedly struck into final start: effective at 1½m to 2m: better form on fibresand than equitrack, acts on any turf going except possibly heavy: has run well in blinkers/visor, not tried since 6 yrs: sometimes carries head high/edges left: usually held up. *D. Haydn Jones* **– a60**

PREMIERE DIVISION 3 b.f. Be My Chief (USA) 122 – One Half Silver (CAN) (Plugged Nickle (USA)) [1998 –: 6d 6g 6s 6d 1999 8f a8g 8m³ 8m 9.3m* 10.9s 12f⁶ 10m 10m Sep 24] modest handicapper: won at Carlisle in July: below form after: stays 9f: acts on good to firm going: has been slowly away: sold 2,200 gns, sent to Israel. *Miss L. A. Perratt* **51**

PREMIERE FOULEE (FR)   4 ch.f. Sillery (USA) 122 – Dee (Caerleon (USA) **45**
132) [1998 8s 10.5m 8.3d 10.5g⁴ 12s² 13d 12.5s² 12d⁵ 14.5d* 12d² 1999 8m⁴ 11.9d⁴
a14g⁴ 11.6m⁶ 14.1v a12g² 11.7s a12g Nov 19] first foal: dam unraced: trained in
1998 by F. Chappet in France, winning handicap at Clairefontaine: poor form in
Britain: stays 14.5f: acts on soft going and fibresand: tried blinkered. *F. Jordan*

PREMIERE VALENTINO   2 b.g. (Apr 2) Tragic Role (USA) – Mirkan Honey   **–**
83 (Ballymore 123) [1999 6d Nov 4] 12,000F, 19,000Y: half-brother to several
winners, including 4-y-o Gypsy Hill, useful 5f/6f winner Lee Artiste (by Tate
Gallery) and useful 6f/7f winner (later stayed 1¼m) Fleet Hill (by Warrshan): dam
Irish 2m winner: always behind (not knocked about) in maiden at Windsor.
D. W. P. Arbuthnot

PREMIER FOIS   2 b.f. (Mar 12) Pelder (IRE) 125 – Doris Doors 61 (Beveled   **67**
(USA)) [1999 6m* 7d⁵ Sep 17] 5,000Y: second foal: half-sister to 3-y-o Helen's
Wedding: dam 5f/6f winner: 25/1, won maiden at Lingfield in August by short head
from Victor's Crown: much stiffer task when well-beaten last of 5 in minor event at
Ayr following month: should stay at least 7f. *G. C. H. Chung*

PREMIER LEAGUE (IRE)   9 gr.g. Don't Forget Me 127 – Kilmara (USA) 78   **43⁻**
(Caro 133) [1998 60, a53?: a12g 10s 12s⁶ 11.6m³ 12m 11.6g* 11.6m* 12d 14g 12s
a12g² a16g⁵ 1999 a13g⁴ a16g⁵ 10d 12m 11.6d a13g⁴ 11.6m⁵ a12g Nov 16] big, strong
gelding: poor handicapper: stays 13f: acts on firm going, soft and equitrack: none too
consistent. *K. O. Cunningham-Brown*

PREMIER PRIZE   2 ch.f. (Feb 4) Selkirk (USA) 129 – Spot Prize (USA) 108   **87 p**
(Seattle Dancer (USA) 119) [1999 6s⁶ 7d* Oct 30] big, lengthy filly: has scope: first
foal: dam, 5f winner at 2 yrs, fourth in Oaks: confirmed promise when winning
steadily-run 16-runner maiden at Newmarket by ½ length from Arabesque, switched
2f out and getting on top final 1f: will stay 1¼m: should make a useful 3-y-o.
D. R. C. Elsworth

European Breeders Fund Balaton Lodge Maiden Fillies' Stakes, Newmarket—
Premier Prize (near side) begins to get the better of Arabesque

PREMIER PROJECT (IRE) 7 b.g. Project Manager 111 – Lady Beck (FR) 104 **73**
(Sir Gaylord) [1998 NR 1999 9.9m⁶ 12.3f² 10m⁵ 12.3g Aug 21] big, workmanlike
gelding: half-brother to several winners, including useful Irish sprinter Tornabuoni
(by Dance In Time): dam French 2-y-o 1m winner: fairly useful in Ireland (winner 5
times), leaving J. Bolger at end of 5-y-o season: just fair in 1999: best effort when
second in handicap at Ripon: likely to stay 1¾m: probably acts on any ground: has
been early to post. *M. Johnston*

PREMIUM PRINCESS 4 b.f. Distant Relative 128 – Solemn Occasion (USA) **66**
(Secreto (USA) 128) [1998 68, a43: 7d 6d⁴ 7g 7m⁴ 7m³ 6.9d⁴ 8g 7m² 7d a8.5g⁵ **a–**
a10g 1999 6s 5f* 6g⁴ 6m Jun 19] good-bodied filly: fair handicapper on turf, poor on
all-weather: won at Newcastle in May: effective at 5f to 7f: acts on firm going, good
to soft and fibresand: none too consistent. *J. J. Quinn*

PREMIUM PURSUIT 4 b.g. Pursuit of Love 124 – Music In My Life (IRE) 59 **–**
(Law Society (USA) 130) [1998 77d: 7d 7.6g⁵ 8.1d 7d⁶ 7.5g⁶ 6m 6g 6m 1999 8d 7m
8m Jul 16] sturdy, good-bodied gelding: fair at best: well held since second 3-y-o
start. *R. A. Fahey*

PREMIUM QUEST 4 b.g. Forzando 122 – Sabonis (USA) 68 (The Minstrel **–**
(CAN) 135) [1998 52, a58: 9.9s 10.5g 8.1m 8.3d⁶ 9s³ 12d a12g² a11g 1999 12.1v
Mar 29] lengthy gelding: modest handicapper: tailed off only 4-y-o start: stays 1½m:
acts on soft going and fibresand: tried visored/blinkered. *R. A. Fahey*

PRESELI (IRE) 2 b.f. (Feb 10) Caerleon (USA) 132 – Hill of Snow 80 **110 p**
(Reference Point 139) [1999 7g* 7g* 7m* Sep 5]
    Preseli retained her unbeaten record and provided trainer Michael
Grassick and former champion apprentice Eddie Ahern with their first Group 1
success when she won the Moyglare Stud Stakes at the Curragh in September.
It represented further significant improvement from a filly who has the Irish
One Thousand Guineas and Irish Oaks as her main objectives, and there's
almost certainly a fair bit better still to come. Preseli, whose three races to date
have all been at seven furlongs, should prove very well suited by further judged
on her pedigree.

Moyglare Stud Stakes, the Curragh—Preseli (centre) retains her unbeaten record;
Torgau (second left), Littlefeather (behind winner, dark cap) and Amethyst (right) fill the frame

A 7/1-shot when successful in an ordinary maiden at Roscommon in July on her debut, Preseli was sent off at the same odds when second favourite for a six-runner listed event at Leopardstown the following month. The favourite, at 4/1-on, was the full sister to King of Kings, Amethyst, who'd impressed when winning on her only start. Preseli was one of those already off the bridle to stay in touch with the front-running Amethyst before the turn, but she responded gamely and gradually reduced the deficit, leading well inside the final furlong to win by three quarters of a length. The pair met again in the Moyglare Stud Stakes, ten others also lining up in a race for which there were five British challengers, including the favourite Littlefeather and the Cherry Hinton winner Torgau, both stepping up in trip. In a race run at a steady pace, Preseli travelled smoothly in mid-division then ran on strongly after being switched left to challenge, leading close home to win by three quarters of a length and one and a half lengths from Torgau and Littlefeather. The last-named, who met trouble, gave the impression that she would have gone very close with a clear run, but nothing should be taken away from Preseli.

	Caerleon (USA) (b 1980)	Nijinsky (b 1967) — Northern Dancer / Flaming Page
Preseli (IRE) (b.f. Feb 10, 1997)		Foreseer (b or br 1969) — Round Table / Regal Gleam
	Hill of Snow (b 1992)	Reference Point (b 1984) — Mill Reef / Home On The Range
		White Star Line (b 1975) — Northern Dancer / Fast Line

The step up to a mile will suit Preseli, but not so much as the step up to a mile and a quarter or more, and she is likely to be seen to better advantage in the Oaks rather than the Guineas. Her dam Hill of Snow, bred by Sheikh

Mr L. Neil Jones's "Preseli"

799

Mohammed, showed fairly useful form at a mile and a quarter and a mile and a half in Ireland, winning a maiden over the former trip, and was then sold for 160,000 guineas at the 1995 December Sales. Hill of Snow is out the high-class performer White Star Line, who won three Grade 1 races in the States from eight and a half furlongs to a mile and a quarter. White Star Line, a half-sister to the Prix Morny winner Filiberto and to the dam of Northern Trick, has produced numerous other winners, the best of them Whitehaven, who won the Prix de Pomone and finished third in the Park Hill. White Star Line is also the grandam of the Italian Oaks winner Valley of Gold. Preseli, who should make up into a very smart filly at the least, has so far raced only on good and good to firm ground. *M. J. Grassick, Ireland*

PRESELI MAGIC   3 gr.f. Puissance 110 – Swallow Bay 54 (Penmarric (USA) **43** 111) [1998 53: 5.1d⁶ 6m³ 5d⁶ 5f⁶ 6m 1999 6f 5m 6.1m 7.1m⁶ 7f⁵ 5.7f⁵ a6g⁵ a6g⁵ a7g a6g Dec 17] poor maiden: stays 7f: acts on firm going, probably on all-weather: tried visored and blinkered: has been slowly away/hung badly. *D. Haydn Jones*

PRESENTATION (IRE)   2 b.f. (Mar 17) Mujadil (USA) 119 – Beechwood **94** (USA) (Blushing Groom (FR) 131) [1999 5g* 5m⁵ 6m⁴ 5f 5.2g⁶ 6.1d³ 6g³ Oct 2] smallish, lengthy filly: fluent mover: sister to useful 1996 2-y-o 5f winner Conne-mara, and half-sister to 7f winners Ned's Contessa (by Persian Heights) and Imposing Groom (by Posen): dam French 10.8f winner: fairly useful performer: won maiden at Windsor in May: good third of 26 to Khasayl in Two-Year-Old Trophy at Redcar final start: will stay 7f: acts on good to firm and good to soft ground: consistent. *R. Hannon*

PRESENT CHANCE   5 ch.g. Cadeaux Genereux 131 – Chance All (FR) 88 **77** (Glenstal (USA) 118) [1998 85, a64: 5s² a5g⁴ 5m³ 6g⁴ 6s³ 6f³ 6g* 6m⁵ 5m 6.1g 7g **a71** 1999 6d 7g³ a7g⁶ 6f a5g* 6s⁵ 6d³ a6g⁴ Jun 19] strong, good-bodied gelding: fair handicapper: won at Southwell in June: good efforts next 2 starts: effective at 5f to 7f: acts on firm ground, soft and fibresand: blinkered last 4 starts: has worn tongue strap: sometimes wanders under pressure. *D. Shaw*

PRESENT GENERATION   6 ch.g. Cadeaux Genereux 131 – Penny Mint 79 **–** (Mummy's Game 120) [1998 89: 8g* 8g 7.6d 8.5m⁵ 7.1g 7g 6.1v 1999 6f Jul 14] big, good-topped gelding: fairly useful handicapper: reportedly bled when tailed off both starts in 1999: effective at 6f to 1m: acts on good to firm and heavy going: sometimes sweating. *R. Guest*

PRESENT LAUGHTER   3 b.c. Cadeaux Genereux 131 – Ever Genial 117 (Brig- **90** adier Gerard 144) [1998 83p: 7s² 1999 5s* 6g 7.1d² 6d⁵ 5m a7g Sep 4] leggy colt: fairly useful performer: won maiden at Warwick in March: creditable staying-on fifth in William Hill Trophy Handicap at York in June: off 2½ months before final start: effective at 6f/7f: acts on soft going: has been bandaged near-hind. *P. F. I. Cole*

PRESENT 'N CORRECT   6 ch.g. Cadeaux Genereux 131 – Emerald Eagle 78 **52** (Sandy Creek 123) [1998 50: 6g⁵ 5g 5m⁶ 5m⁵ 5m⁴ 6d² 5v³ a7g* a6g a6g⁴ 1999 a6g⁵ **a45** a6g³ a7f 5.1s² 5m 7m² 6f⁵ 6m⁴ 6m⁵ 5.9g³ 6m⁶ 6.8m³ 6f⁵ 5.1h⁵ 6g Aug 13] workman-like gelding: modest handicapper on turf, poor on all-weather: generally respectable efforts in 1999: effective at testing 5f to easy 7f: acts on any turf going and all-weather: often races prominently. *J. M. Bradley*

PRESIDENTS LADY   2 b.f. (Apr 18) Superpower 113 – Flirty Lady (Never So **–** Bold 135) [1999 7.9g Oct 6] 500Y: third foal: dam unraced: well held in maiden at York. *J. G. Smyth-Osbourne*

PRESS AGAIN   7 ch.m. Then Again 126 – Silver Empress 63 (Octavo (USA) **47** 115) [1998 42, a–: 8g 11.6d 8.3m³ 7m a7g 1999 8f 9.9m 7.1g 8.3m Aug 28] rather **a–** sparely-made mare: poor maiden handicapper: stays 1m: acts on good to firm ground: inconsistent. *P. Hayward*

PRESS AHEAD   4 b.g. Precocious 126 – By Line 64 (High Line 125) [1998 48, **55** a63: 8s⁵ 5.1m a5g² a6g 5g a6g* 1999 a6g a6g 5d² a6g Nov 20] leggy gelding: modest performer: effective at 5f/6f: acts on fibresand and good to soft going: well held both starts in blinkers. *B. A. McMahon*

PRESS TIMES (USA)   3 b.g. Press Card (USA) – Doubling Time (USA) 117   –
(Timeless Moment (USA)) [1998 56: 6s⁶ 1999 a8g⁶ 6g 9.3m 8.5m Jul 13] modest
form only 2-y-o start: only a little sign of retaining ability in 1999: should stay
beyond 6f: sold 2,800 gns. *T. D. Easterby*

PRESSURISE   4 ch.g. Sanglamore (USA) 126 – Employ Force (USA) (Alleged   **75**
(USA) 138) [1998 67p: 14.1m* 16m* 1999 16.2m³ 18m a14g* Jul 8] big, good-
bodied gelding: fair handicapper: won at Southwell in July: should stay beyond 2m:
acts on good to firm ground and fibresand: has run in snatches: sold 31,000 gns,
joined M. Pitman. *Sir Mark Prescott*

PRESTO   2 b.g. (Mar 25) Namaqualand (USA) – Polish Dancer (USA) (Malinowski   **53**
(USA) 123) [1999 6g 7s a6g Nov 15] 14,000F, 12,500Y: fourth live foal: dam poor
Irish maiden: modest form at best in maidens: should stay 1m. *W. J. Haggas*

PRESUMED (USA)   3 br.f. Dynaformer (USA) – Prebend (USA) (L'Emigrant   **108**
(USA) 129) [1998 NR 1999 7m* 7m* 8m 8m⁴ 8g³ 7m⁴ 7g Oct 16] strong, good sort:
second foal: closely related to a winner in USA by Silver Hawk: dam French 1m
winner, later successful in USA: useful performer: won newcomers race at Newbury
in April and listed race at Lingfield in May: ran well after in Coronation Stakes at
Royal Ascot (over 3 lengths seventh to Balisada), Falmouth Stakes at Newmarket
(fourth behind Ronda), Prix d'Astarte at Deauville (2½ lengths third to Field of
Hope) and listed race at Doncaster (fourth behind Susu, not getting best of runs):
may prove best up to 1m: raced only on good/good to firm ground: free-going sort: sent to
USA. *P. J. Makin*

PRETENDING   2 b.g. (Apr 17) Primo Dominie 121 – Red Salute (Soviet Star   **61**
(USA) 128) [1999 6.1m⁶ 5g² 6m 6d 6.8d⁶ 7s Oct 25] 5,800F, 14,000Y: leggy gelding:
first foal: dam, unraced, from family of Shiva and Prix de Diane winner/Arc
runner-up Northern Trick: modest maiden: well below form 3 of last 4 starts: should
stay 7f. *J. D. Bethell*

PRETRAIL (IRE)   2 b.c. (May 12) Catrail (USA) 123 – Pretty Lady 98 (High   **75 p**
Top 131) [1999 6v 6d² Nov 4] 14,000Y: well-made, quite attractive colt: half-brother
to useful Irish 6f (at 2 yrs) and 11f winner Lacinia (by Groom Dancer): dam 2-y-o 5f/
6f winner (her only starts) from good middle-distance family: better effort in maidens
when 9 lengths second of 17 to impressive Scarlett Ribbon at Windsor: will stay 7f:
capable of better still. *A. C. Stewart*

PRETTY FLY GUY (IRE)   3 ch.g. Forest Wind (USA) 111 – Achtung Lady   –
(IRE) 53 (Warning 136) [1998 NR 1999 8.5s 9g a8g Dec 17] first foal: dam, ran 3
times in Ireland at 2 yrs, daughter of half-sister to disqualified Oaks winner Aliysa:
no form in maidens/claimer: trained first 2 starts by J. Harley in Ireland. *J. Parkes*

PRETTY INDULGENT   2 b.g. (May 19) Mistertopogigo (IRE) 118 – American   –
Beauty 74 (Mill Reef (USA) 141) [1999 7s 6d Nov 4] 3,000Y: half-brother to several
winners, including smart Stephany's Dream (up to 9f in France, by Reform) and
5-y-o Chief Monarch: dam second twice over 1¼m: signs of ability in maidens at
Lingfield and Windsor. *B. Smart*

PRETTY OBVIOUS   3 ch.f. Pursuit of Love 124 – Settlement (USA) 75 (Irish   **69**
River (FR) 131) [1998 60: 6m⁴ 6g⁶ 6s 8v² 1999 9d 12g 10m⁴ 12.1m 11f⁵ 15.8m*
14.1g⁶ 16.1s* 16s* Oct 5] fair performer: left R. Fahey after fourth start: won seller
at Catterick in August and handicaps at Newcastle in September and Nottingham in
October: will stay beyond 2m: acts on good to firm and heavy going: blinkered fourth
start: often soon off bridle, and not an easy ride: won over hurdles in December.
Mrs M. Reveley

PRETTY WOMAN (IRE)   3 b.f. Alzao (USA) 117 – Simply Gorgeous (Hello   **63**
Gorgeous (USA) 128) [1998 71p: 8.2s⁴ 8s⁴ 1999 8.3m⁴ 9.1m⁴ 11.4m⁶ 11.5f⁵ 11.9d⁴
11.9m 13.1f Sep 6] angular filly: fair maiden: stayed 11f: acted on soft and good to
firm going: blinkered once: had been reluctant at stalls: dead. *P. F. I. Cole*

PRICELESS SECOND   2 b.g. (Mar 21) Lugana Beach 116 – Early Gales   **51**
(Precocious 126) [1999 6d 6m⁶ 6d a8.5g⁵ a6g² a5g⁴ Dec 21] 15,000Y: close-coupled,
sparely-made gelding: third foal: half-brother to 5-y-o Nigrasine: dam lightly raced:
modest maiden: trained first 3 starts by P. Calver, blinkered last 3: effective at 5f/6f:
acts on fibresand: slowly away/edged left final start. *J. A. Glover*

PRICE OF PASSION   3 b.f. Dolphin Street (FR) 125 – Food of Love 109 (Music   **78**
Boy 124) [1998 83: 5m 5d 5m 6.1g^6 5.1m^2 5m^3 6m 5m* 6v 1999 7m 6m 6f 5d
5.3m^4 5.7f 5m* 5g Sep 20] strong filly: fair handicapper: won at Goodwood in
September: best at 5f: probably acts on firm going: blinkered/visored last 4 starts.
D. W. P. Arbuthnot

PRIDE OF BRIXTON   6 b.g. Dominion 123 – Caviar Blini 80 (What A Guest   **75 d**
119) [1998 69, a78: 5s* 5m 5f^4 6g^5 5m a5g* 5.1d a6g^5 a6g 5.1m 5s a5g* a5g^3 a6g*
a5g* a5f 1999 a5g^5 a5g^2 a5g^2 a6g^4 a5g a5g^5 a6g a5g 5m a6g 5.3d a6g a7g Nov 17]
lengthy gelding: fair performer: left P. D. Evans after second start: long way below
form after next one, including in visor: effective at 5f/easy 6f: acts on firm ground,
soft and fibresand (last both outings on equitrack): has won for apprentice. *Andrew
Reid*

PRIDE OF DINGLE (IRE)   3 b.g. Dolphin Street (FR) 125 – Aneeda (Rainbow   **78**
Quest (USA) 134) [1998 90: 8.5v* 9v^3 1999 8d 10m 10.2s^4 7d 8m 8g 7s 7.1g* 7.1s
Oct 2] big gelding: fair performer: won minor event at Musselburgh in August: well
beaten in handicap final start: stays 9f: acts on heavy ground, probably on good to
firm: blinkered/visored once each. *M. L. W. Bell*

PRIDE OF INDIA (IRE)   2 b.g. (Mar 30) Ezzoud (IRE) 126 – Indian Queen   **–**
115 (Electric 126) [1999 8s Nov 6] 30,000Y: big, good-topped gelding: fifth foal:
half-brother to 3-y-o Royal Patron and useful performer up to 9f Prince of India (by
Night Shift): dam won Ascot Gold Cup: backward, very slowly away in maiden at
Doncaster. *J. L. Dunlop*

PRIDE OF PERU (IRE)   2 b.f. (Jan 26) Perugino (USA) 84 – Nation's Game 51   **53**
(Mummy's Game 120) [1999 5m^4 6m 6d 6.1d 5g 6d Oct 22] 3,500Y: tall, unfurnished
filly: sixth foal: half-sister to 3 fairly useful winners, including 1993 2-y-o 6f winner
Mazentre Forward and Irish 1¼m/11f winner Jalber (both by Mazaad): dam 2-y-o
5f winner: modest maiden: stays 6f: acts on good to firm and good to soft ground.
M. Brittain

PRIDEWAY (IRE)   3 b.f. Pips Pride 117 – Up The Gates (Captain James 123)   **78 §**
[1998 67: 5.1m 6m^5 7m^3 7g^6 7d^2 6s^4 6.5g 7g^6 1999 a7s* 7d^6 7.5m 7.6m 7.1d^2 7m 8m^2
8g a7g Sep 4] leggy, sparely-made filly: fair handicapper: won at Wolverhampton in
February: should stay 1m: acts on soft going, good to firm and fibresand: tried
blinkered, including last 4 starts: joined W. Brisbourne: has looked none too keen,
and one to treat with caution. *A. Bailey*

PRIESTESS (IRE)   3 b.f. Magical Wonder (USA) 125 – Forest Treasure (USA)   **–**
(Green Forest (USA) 134) [1998 NR 1999 6.8m^5 5m 6.1m 7.7m Aug 30] 6,300Y:
sister to useful sprinter Open Credit and half-sister to a winner in USA by Siberian
Express: dam unraced daughter of very smart French filly at up to 1m Mysterious
Etoile, herself half-sister to Yorkshire Oaks winner Magnificent Star: no sign of
ability in maidens: visored final start: has swished tail. *V. Soane*

PRIESTLAW (USA)   2 ch.c. (Apr 5) El Gran Senor (USA) 136 – Schwanensee   **85 +**
(USA) (Mr Leader (USA)) [1999 8d^4 9v^3 Oct 24] 30,000Y: eighth foal: half-brother
to several winners in Italy, including useful 1m (at 2 yrs) and 11f winner Yavlensky
(by Caerleon): dam unraced: won maiden at Milan in September: 11 lengths third to
Dedi Boy in listed race there month later: should stay 1¼m. *J. L. Dunlop*

PRIMA   2 b.f. (Apr 6) Primo Dominie 121 – Phyliel (USA) 82 (Lyphard (USA)   **76**
132) [1999 6g 6m^2 5m^3 Sep 16] fourth foal: dam 2-y-o 6f winner out of half-sister
to Royal Academy: easily best effort in maidens when ½-length second of 19 to
Iftiraas at Lingfield: beaten 4 lengths when odds on at Pontefract final start: stays 6f.
W. J. Haggas

PRIMARY COLOURS   4 b.f. Saddlers' Hall (IRE) 126 – Go For Red (IRE)   **100 ?**
(Thatching 131) [1998 71, a100: a8.5g^4 10f a9.4g* 8.5s a12g* 10.5s* 10v^4 a12g*
a9.4g^6 1999 a12g^3 a12g^4 10.8d 8.5m 10.4s^2 12m^6 9.9d 9.9s^6 10s Oct 2] tall, lengthy
filly: useful performer: ran well when in frame in handicaps at Wolverhampton and
Southwell and listed race at York (easily best effort on turf, possibly flattered when
2½ lengths second of 6 to Lady In Waiting): ran poorly last 4 starts: stays 1½m: acts
on all-weather and soft going: usually held up. *J. Pearce*

PRIME MUSIC   2 ch.g. (May 11) Primo Dominie 121 – Rose Music 86 (Luthier **52**
126) [1999 5g 5.1m 6s 6.8d Sep 21] half-brother to several winners, including
middle-distance performer Rose Alto (by Adonijah) and 7f to 1¼m performer
Jalmusique (by Jalmood), both useful: dam 7f/1m winner: modest form in maidens,
racing freely final start. *S. Mellor*

PRIME OFFER   3 b.c. Primo Dominie 121 – Single Bid 68 (Auction Ring (USA) **75**
123) [1998 –: 5.1v 1999 6m³ 5g 6m³ 5s⁴ 6f* 6f Jul 29] useful-looking colt: fair
performer: won 3-runner maiden at Hamilton in July: well beaten only start after:
likely to stay beyond 6f: acts on firm going. *K. A. Morgan*

PRIME RECREATION   2 b.g. (Jan 31) Primo Dominie 121 – Night Trans- **70**
action 59 (Tina's Pet 121) [1999 6.1g 6g 5.1g³ Oct 21] 3,200Y: fourth foal:
half-brother to 4-y-o Spanish Eyes and fairly useful 6f winner (including at 2 yrs)
Silca Key Silca (by Polar Falcon): dam stayed 1¼m: form in maidens only when
third of 15 to The Bull Macabe at Nottingham: should stay 6f. *P. S. Felgate*

PRIME SURPRISE   3 b.f. Primo Dominie 121 – My Surprise (Welsh Pageant **–**
132) [1998 –: 7g 6g 8.2v⁶ 1999 a7g a7f⁴ 8m 6m 10.9g 8.1d a7g a8g Dec 17] sparely- **a35**
made filly: poor maiden at best: left C. Dwyer after reappearance. *D. W. Barker*

PRIMEVAL   5 b.g. Primo Dominie 121 – Class Adorns (Sadler's Wells (USA) **57**
132) [1998 69: a10g² 1999 a9.4g⁵ a8g 13.3f 10m a8g a12g* a16.2g Jul 23] modest
performer: won seller at Wolverhampton in July: stays 1½m (probably not 2m): acts
on all-weather, best turf effort on good to soft ground: visored/tongue tied last 2
starts: inconsistent. *K. C. Comerford*

PRIMO LARA   7 ch.h. Primo Dominie 121 – Clara Barton (Youth (USA) 135) **108**
[1998 101, a106: 6m² 7.3g 7g 6g* 6d a7g² a6g* 1999 a5g* 5.2m⁵ 6m* 6s 6d⁴ 6m **a110**
6f³ 6f Jul 31] big, strong, lengthy horse: poor mover: useful handicapper: won at
Wolverhampton (beat Mangus 1¾ lengths) in February and Newmarket (rated stakes
by short head from Halmahera) in May: creditable third of 10 to Tajasur in rated
stakes at Newbury penultimate start: well beaten in Wokingham at Royal Ascot
and Stewards' Cup at Goodwood starts either side: effective at 5f to 7f: acts on
all-weather, best turf form on good ground or firmer: usually races up with pace:
genuine. *P. W. Harris*

PRIMORDIAL (FR)   4 b.g. Lesotho (USA) 118 – Prilly (FR) (Saint Cyrien (FR) **63**
128) [1998 62: a6g⁵ a7g³ 1999 a10g⁴ a7f⁵ 5.5s Jun 28] close-coupled gelding: modest
maiden, lightly raced: left S. Dow after second start: well beaten in claimer 5 months
later: best efforts at 7f: acts on equitrack. *W. J. S. Cargeeg, France*

PRIMO VALENTINO (IRE)   2 b.c. (Feb 14) Primo Dominie 121 – Dorothea **116**
Brooke (IRE) 80 (Dancing Brave (USA) 140) [1999 5g² 5m⁴ 6s* 6m* 6m*
6m* 6d* Sep 30]
          Primo Valentino's career so far has been the stuff of adverts, full-page
ones. This is what anyone who has ever contemplated owning a racehorse, or
owning a leg of a racehorse, has dreamt of, the best-case scenario. Primo
Valentino's owners actually own less than a leg each. There are twelve of them
in the Primo Donnas syndicate, each reportedly paying £325 a month—the
proverbial small outlay in the hope of a big return. That sum might not seem
that small on a wider social scale, but it is minute compared to the investments
of, say, Sheikhs Hamdan, Mohammed, Ahmed and Maktoum Al Maktoum, the
Saudi princes A. A. Faisal and Khalid Abdulla, or Messrs Magnier and Tabor.
Taking these owners with the double glazier, farmer, retired personnel manager,
and others in the Primo Donnas may hardly appear a case of comparing like
with like, but those were the turf celebrities who had to go home disappointed
when Primo Valentino triumphed in the Mill Reef Stakes at Newbury and the
Saudi Arabian Airlines Middle Park Stakes at Newmarket. It is not just every
racehorse owner who dreams of results like these. So too does the BHB marketing department.
          Away from the stud farm and sale-ring and on to the comparatively
level playing field of the Newmarket July course on September 30th, Primo
Valentino was anything but a long-shot for success. Whereas most owners and

most racehorses never win a race, Primo Valentino was going for his fifth win on the trot. A gamble down to favouritism at 5/4 in a £7,000 event at Windsor in May had gone astray, as had Primo Valentino, hitting the front approaching the final furlong only to veer away badly to his left, and the listed National Stakes at Sandown proved even more disappointing, when second-favourite Primo Valentino managed only fourth of seven. But after that he was unbeatable. At odds on in a maiden at Leicester and a minor event at Goodwood in June, he won by six lengths and two lengths respectively, with ease on both occasions and doing so at Goodwood despite the presence of the useful Halland Park Girl in second. A pulled muscle kept Primo Valentino off the track until September, when he made up for lost time with three wins in little more than three weeks. In a listed race at Kempton he was value for rather more than his half-length winning margin over gambled-on Seazun, who went on to win the Cheveley Park later in the month. By that time, Primo Valentino had also made a successful graduation to pattern events in the Mill Reef. Starting favourite for the fifth time, on this occasion at 6/5, Primo Valentino made all and was well on top through the final furlong as he went on to win by a length and a quarter; in a field of only four runners, those who gave pursuit in vain were Sheikh Maktoum's Trouble Mountain, Sheikh Ahmed's Ma Yoram and Khalid Abdulla's Observatory.

One vital ingredient in the Primo Valentino transformation had been a change in tactics. Held up for a turn of foot on his first two outings, he resented being restrained and took a strong hold. Allowed to proceed at his own rhythm, either making the running or racing close to the leaders, he kept plenty in reserve for when it was really needed. The Middle Park, in which Primo Valentino started at 100/30, revealed just how much that was when Fath challenged on the bridle two furlongs out. About a length and a half behind them came the four other runners, Prince Faisal's impressive Ripon listed winner Invincible Spirit (the 2/1 favourite), Sheikh Mohammed's Morny runner-up Warm Heart, Ballydoyle's selected Brahms and 33/1-shot Trinculo. None of that quartet ever threatened the pacesetter, but Fath, in the colours of Sheikh Hamdan, got upsides near the furlong marker. If Fath led it was only for a stride or two as Primo Valentino answered Pat Eddery's every call, stuck his head out and went on again to win by a neck, with Brahms third and Warm Heart fourth.

Whether Primo Valentino can also keep pulling out enough in the top grade as a three-year-old must be in doubt. There is a chance he will do so at six furlongs, but we think his prospects will recede at a mile—speed looks to be his forte. Those willing to take the 33/1 on offer for his next giant killing assignment, the Two Thousand Guineas, will, however, find something to cheer them in his pedigree. His sire Primo Dominie probably isn't it, though. As a racehorse he was a sprinter pure and simple, beaten favourite for the Middle Park in his otherwise highly productive first season and winner of the King George Stakes at Goodwood at three. Primo Dominie the stallion has been basically an influence for speed, with a few significant winners over a mile or more thrown

Saudi Arabian Airlines Middle Park Stakes, Newmarket—fifth win in a row for the tough Primo Valentino, who gets the better of Fath (nearer camera) as Brahms stays on strongly for third

in, such as Sunstreak and Shaylan, who were running in the latest season. More to the point is Primo Valentino's dam Dorothea Brooke, whose sire and dam are Dancing Brave and the Nassau Stakes and Yorkshire Oaks winner Connaught Bridge. Even with that pedigree, Dorothea Brooke failed to win beyond an extended mile—showing fairly useful form at a mile and a quarter but then dropped back in trip for the Epsom maiden in which she made all for her sole success. Dorothea Brooke used to take a good hold and, according to her trainer, was 'quite temperamental.' She is a half-sister to several winners, including the smart French 1986 two-year-old Conmaiche and the useful middle-distance stayer Wassl Reef.

Primo Valentino (IRE) (b.c. Feb 14, 1997)	Primo Dominie (b 1982)	Dominion (b 1972)	Derring-Do / Picture Palace
		Swan Ann (ch 1971)	My Swanee / Anna Barry
	Dorothea Brooke (IRE) (b 1992)	Dancing Brave (b 1983)	Lyphard / Navajo Princess
		Connaught Bridge (ch 1976)	Connaught / Fishermans Bridge

Primo Valentino is a quite good-topped colt, who shows a quick, fluent action; he was taken early to post in his later starts. He has not yet raced beyond six furlongs but has already shown some versatility so far as ground requirements are concerned, seemingly effective on soft and good to firm ground. His trainer Peter Harris also bred him, and bred, owned and trained Dorothea Brooke (Primo Valentino is Dorothea Brooke's first foal), having purchased Primo Valentino's grandam Connaught Bridge in 1979 privately before her final start. Also from the late-'seventies, Harris's best-known horse is probably the high-class chaser Bachelor's Hall. Since taking out his own licence to train, Harris has become a fine advocate for ownership syndicates, which usually take up the majority of the horses he has in training. Half an hour before Primo Valentino took the Mill Reef, the Courage Handicap on the same card provided £43,000 and plenty more advertising material when it was won by another of his partnerships, via Komistar. As Harris has cropped up on the *Sunday Times* list of Britain's richest people, it would be stretching the truth to claim that Primo Valentino's story is entirely that of victory for the small man. Flat racing will have to wait a little longer for its Norton's Coin and Sirrell Griffiths, but Primo Valentino has probably been inspiration enough. *P. W. Harris*

PRINCE ALEX (IRE) 5 b.g. Night Shift (USA) – Finalist 78 (Star Appeal 133) **98** [1998 NR 1999 10m 12m* 12g* 12m* 13.9g 12m² Sep 11] sturdy gelding: has a quick action: improved into a useful handicapper: won at Kempton in May and June and at Ascot in July: raced too freely in Ebor at York, but ran very well when length second to Musician in quite valuable event at Doncaster final start: stays 1½m: acts on good to firm going, yet to race on soft/heavy: tongue tied. *Mrs A. J. Perrett*

PRINCE AMONG MEN 2 b.c. (Mar 22) Robellino (USA) 127 – Forelino **78** (USA) 62§ (Trempolino (USA) 135) [1999 7g 7m⁶ 6d³ 7g³ 7d³ 6d³ 7d⁶ Oct 27] 20,000F, 50,000Y: third foal: half-brother to 5-y-o Tough Act and 4-y-o Maiella: dam 10.6f winner: fair maiden: left E. Lynam in Ireland before final outing: should stay 1m: raced mainly on good/good to soft going: blinkered sixth start. *P. D. Evans*

PRINCE BABAR 8 b.g. Fairy King (USA) – Bell Toll 87 (High Line 125) [1998 **82** 104: 8.1g 10d⁵ 7f 9.9g 9g 7g* 8s² 1999 8.1d⁶ 8m 8f 7m 8g 8s Sep 26] sparely-made gelding: has a round action: fractured off-hind at 6 yrs: useful performer at best, just fairly useful in 1999: effective at 7f/1m, seemingly not quite 1¼m: acts on firm and soft ground: sometimes bandaged: visored once: tends to drift left, but is game. *J. E. Banks*

PRINCE BATSHOOF 4 b.g. Batshoof 122 – Sipsi Fach 100 (Prince Sabo 123) **–** [1998 71: 8s² 9d² 10d 9.9m² 9.9g⁴ 9g³ 10.5d³ 1999 9.9m⁶ Jul 30] smallish, good-topped gelding: fair maiden at 3 yrs: ran as if something amiss only 4-y-o start: stays 10.5f: acts on soft and good to firm going: often makes running. *M. C. Pipe*

PRINCE CONSORT 3 b.g. Clantime 101 – Miss Petella (Dunphy 124) [1998 **62** 68: 5g² 6g⁴ 6m⁵ 7.9g 5d 6m² a5g⁵ 1999 a8g⁵ a10g⁴ a12s 8.2s⁵ 6g 7f⁴ 8.2m² 7m* 8f⁵ 7.7m 7f⁴ 6.9m⁵ 7g* 7m 6s 6g⁶ 7s 7d Oct 12] smallish gelding: modest performer: won claimers at Folkestone in May and Leicester in August: effective at 7f, probably at 1¼m: acts on good to firm going and equitrack: has been bandaged: usually blinkered: has worn tongue strap: sold 4,000 gns. *S. C. Williams*

PRINCE DANZIG (IRE) 8 ch.g. Roi Danzig (USA) – Veldt (High Top 131) **–** [1998 –, a76: a12s 11.9g⁶ 11.9g a12g⁶ a13g* 1999 a12g a13g* a12f⁴ a16f⁵ **a74** a14.8g³ 11.9f a12g² a12g⁵ a13g⁶ Dec 10] close-coupled gelding: good mover: fair performer nowadays: races mainly on all-weather, and won claimer at Lingfield in January: stays 13f: often blinkered/visored earlier in career: inconsistent. *D. J. G. Murray Smith*

PRINCE DARKHAN (IRE) 3 b.g. Doyoun 124 – Sovereign Dona 117 (Sove-**61** reign Path 125) [1998 NR 1999 10d 10m⁴ 10d⁵ 10s Oct 5] IR 30,000Y: rather unfurnished gelding: half-brother to several winners, notably 7f to 9f performer Royal Touch (by Tap On Wood) and Irish Derby/Irish St Leger third Foresee (by Vision), both very smart: dam won 1¼m Prix de Psyche: modest maiden: needs to settle better to stay beyond 1¼m: bandaged in front first 2 starts: hung right final outing. *P. W. Harris*

PRINCE ELMAR 2 b.c. (Apr 8) Elmaamul (USA) 125 – Dramatic Mood **74** (Jalmood (USA) 126) [1999 8d³ 8s Nov 6] 31,000Y: rather leggy colt: fifth foal: half-brother to 3-y-o Dramatic Scenes and 3 winners, including useful 1997 2-y-o 6f/ 7f winner Merlin's Ring (later won in USA, by Magic Ring) and Irish 1½m winner Lifesforliving (by Aragon): dam unraced: fair form in maidens at Leicester (better effort) and Doncaster in autumn: should stay at least 1¼m. *W. R. Muir*

PRINCE KINSKY 6 ch.g. Master Willie 129 – Princess Lieven (Royal Palace **62** 131) [1998 NR 1999 12s 14.4m 12m³ 11.9f³ Jul 12] angular gelding: fairly useful handicapper at 4 yrs: modest in 1999: stays 1½m: acts on equitrack and firm going, below form on softer than good: carries head high. *J. A. B. Old*

PRINCELY DREAM (IRE) 3 br.c. Night Shift (USA) – Princess of Zurich **92** (IRE) (Law Society (USA) 130) [1998 84p: 5g² 6s² 6.3s 5m* 6s⁴ 1999 5m 6g³ 6d 6s² 6m 7f 6m* 6m³ 6d² 6d Oct 9] good-topped colt: fairly useful performer: won 4-runner minor event at Ayr in August: good efforts when placed otherwise, second of 29 to Grey Kingdom in Ayr Silver Cup (Handicap) penultimate start: best at 5f/6f, below form in visor only outing over 7f: acts on soft and good to firm going: usually waited with. *R. A. Fahey*

PRINCELY HEIR (IRE) 4 b.c. Fairy King (USA) – Meis El-Reem 124 **98** (Auction Ring (USA) 123) [1998 108: 8s⁴ 8g⁴ 6s 8m³ 7.3m³ 8g⁵ 8d² 1999 9.9d 6g⁴ 8.8m 7d⁴ Jul 1] smallish, good-quartered colt: smart performer at best: won Heinz 57 Phoenix Stakes at Leopardstown at 2 yrs: placed twice in Group 3 races in 1998: only useful form in 1999: probably best at 1m: acted on good to firm and heavy going: blinkered once at 3 yrs: has been bandaged behind: to stand at Abbeyleix Stud, Co. Laois, Ireland, fee IR£5,000. *M. Johnston*

PRINCELY SPARK (IRE) 4 ch.g. Balla Cove 119 – Tigeen (Habitat 134) [1998 **38** 58: 10v² 11.9m* 13d³ 12.5g 11g 9m⁶ 12s 1999 a10g 11.6d a16.2g⁴ a16g⁶ a12g⁴ a14g Jul 8] IR 6,400Y: closely related/half-brother to several winners: dam won twice at 5f in Ireland: modest handicapper in Ireland for D. Weld in 1998, winner at Downpatrick: only poor form in 1999: stays 13f: acts on good to firm ground, heavy and fibresand: usually blinkered/visored: has worn tongue strap. *Noel T. Chance*

PRINCE NICHOLAS 4 ch.g. Midyan (USA) 124 – Its My Turn 80 (Palm Track **64** 122) [1998 55: 8.3v² 10v² 9v 10d⁵ 11.1d 1999 12g* 12.1v* Mar 29] sparely-made gelding: modest handicapper: won at Doncaster (apprentice event) and Hamilton (easily), both in March: stays 1½m well: acts on heavy going. *K. W. Hogg, Isle of Man*

PRINCE OF ABACO (USA) 4 b.g. Geiger Counter (USA) – Abala (FR) (Bal-**–** dric II 131) [1998 NR 1999 a6g a7f Feb 1] 30,000Y: half-brother to several winners in France, including very smart 6f (at 2 yrs) and 1m winner Art Francais (by

Lyphard's Wish), later successful in USA: dam, smart French miler, closely related to All Along: green, well beaten in maidens. *D. Nicholls*

PRINCE OF ARAGON   3 b.g. Aragon 118 – Queens Welcome 60 (Northfields (USA)) [1998 59: 6m 5m 6g 5g 5s 1999 a6g² 6.1v 7d* 7m 6g⁶ 8.3m 7g a6g⁴ 6m 6s 6s⁴ 7g 5.1s Oct 26] tall, leggy gelding: modest performer: won maiden at Thirsk in April: stays 7f: acts on soft ground, good to firm and fibresand: visored/blinkered 6 of last 7 starts: has wandered, and tends to carry head high: none too consistent. *K. T. Ivory*   **55 a59**

PRINCE OF DENIAL   5 b.g. Soviet Star (USA) 128 – Gleaming Water 81 (Kalaglow 132) [1998 109: 10v⁴ 10.1s³ 10.4g* 12m⁵ 10g 10d 10.4f 10.5g³ 10m⁶ 9.9d² 10.9s⁴ 12s⁵ 12d² 1999 12m 10s⁴ 12d⁵ 12.4f⁴ 12g³ 11m² 10g 10m Jul 24] rather leggy gelding: useful performer: ran creditably several times in 1999, including in Gordon Richards Stakes at Sandown (2 lengths fourth to Generous Rosi) on second start, valuable rated stakes at Epsom (third to Tough Leader) and Idee Hansa-Preis at Hamburg (8 lengths second to Caitano): injured fatally when slipping up at Ascot: was effective at 1¼m/1½m: acted on good to firm and heavy going: was held up. *D. W. P. Arbuthnot*   **106**

PRINCE OF MY HEART   6 ch.h. Prince Daniel (USA) – Blue Room 70 (Gorytus (USA) 130) [1998 100: 8d⁴ 10v 8d 8m 8d³ 8d⁴ 10g 9g 1999 10.5d⁶ Jun 3] tall horse: impresses in appearance: good mover: useful handicapper: well held only 6-y-o start: needs good test at 1m, and probably stays 1½m: acts on firm and soft ground: visored once at 5 yrs: joined H. Cecil. *D. Haydn Jones*   **–**

PRINCE OF MYSTERY (IRE)   2 b. or br.g. (Apr 24) Shalford (IRE) 124§ – Mary Kate Danagher (Petoski 135) [1999 7g⁶ 7f³ 7.5g Aug 12] IR 2,400F, IR 6,000Y: sturdy gelding: second foal: dam ran once in Ireland: only placed effort when last of 3 at Goodwood. *A. P. Jarvis*   **62 ?**

PRINCE OMID (USA)   2 b.c. (Jan 28) Shuailaan (USA) 122 – Matilda The Hun (USA) (Young Bob (USA)) [1999 7.9g 7g⁵ Oct 19] $52,000F, 14,000Y: half-brother to several winners abroad, including a minor US stakes winner by Steady Beat: dam ran 4 times in USA: fair form when fifth in maiden at Lingfield: likely to prove suited by 1m+. *J. R. Fanshawe*   **66 +**

PRINCE PROSPECT   3 b.g. Lycius (USA) 124 – Princess Dechtra (IRE) 65 (Bellypha 130) [1998 84+: 6f⁴ 6d² 6g² 6m³ 6g³ 5s a6g³ a6g* 1999 a6g³ a5g³ 6g⁴ 5s 6g 6m⁴ 5.1g³ 5.1m⁵ 5m* 5f³ 6f⁶ 5d⁴ a6g Dec 22] sturdy gelding: unimpressive mover: fairly useful handicapper: made all at Sandown in July: off course 3 months before final start: may prove best at 5f: acts on firm going, good to soft and equitrack: visored once at 2 yrs: often races up with pace. *Mrs L. Stubbs*   **88**

PRINCE ROCK   2 ch.c. (Mar 16) Rock City 120 – Masuri Kabisa (USA) 48 (Ascot Knight (CAN) 130) [1999 5d 5.1s Apr 5] 2,800Y: workmanlike colt: first foal: dam 1½m winner: well beaten in sellers at Doncaster and Nottingham. *M. Dods*   **–**

PRINCE SLAYER   3 b.c. Batshoof 122 – Top Sovereign (High Top 131) [1998 73p: 7d⁵ 1999 8.2s² 10m³ 10.2s⁵ 9.2s² Sep 27] well-made colt: fairly useful maiden: best efforts at Windsor and Hamilton on second and final starts: stays 1¼m: acts on soft and good to firm going: has carried head high. *B. Smart*   **80**

PRINCESS AURORA   2 ch.f. (Mar 29) Prince Sabo 123 – Made In Heaven 76 (Primo Dominie 121) [1999 6f 6g 5.1m 5.3m² 5m Sep 24] 9,000Y: first foal: dam 2-y-o 5f/6f winner (didn't train on) from very good family: modest maiden: may prove best at 5f. *P. W. Harris*   **58 +**

PRINCESS BELFORT   6 b.m. Belfort (FR) 89 – Domino Rose 67 (Dominion 123) [1998 –: a12g a12g 1999 a9.4g 7g 6s 5g a5g 6.8m 6.1s 8d a8g Nov 15] poor maiden at best: tried visored. *B. D. Leavy*   **–**

PRINCESS ELLEN   2 br.f. (Feb 11) Tirol 127 – Celt Song (IRE) (Unfuwain (USA) 131) [1999 6m* 7d* 8m 7g⁵ Oct 16] sturdy, good-bodied filly: first foal: dam unraced: useful form: won maiden at Ascot in July and listed race at Newmarket (calmer in preliminaries, by ¾ length from Eurolink Raindance) in August: well held in May Hill Stakes at Doncaster (favourite, final outing for P. Chapple-Hyam) and only respectable fifth in Rockfel Stakes at Newmarket following month: should stay 1m: acts on good to firm and good to soft going. *G. A. Butler*   **100**

PRINCESSE ZELDA (FR) 5 b.m. Defensive Play (USA) 118 – Brisk Waters **45** (USA) (Saratoga Six (USA)) [1998 37: a9.4g a8.5g⁶ a8.5g 1999 a12g a16g 8.2f⁶ 10g 10s³ 12m 10f⁴ Aug 6] poor maiden: seems to stay 1½m: acts on firm going, soft and fibresand. *Miss L. C. Siddall*

PRINCESS FOLEY (IRE) 3 ch.f. Forest Wind (USA) 111 – Taniokey (Grundy **49** 137) [1998 64, a–: 5.7m⁵ 6.1g⁶ 5.3d³ 5.3m⁴ 5m³ 7d a6g 1999 a6g 5.1m³ 5.7h a5g 6d² **a42** 7g⁶ a7g a6g a6g Dec 1] poor maiden: effective at 5f/6f: acts on good to soft going (probably on hard) and fibresand. *W. G. M. Turner*

PRINCESS KALI (IRE) 3 ch.f. Fayruz 116 – Carriglegan Girl (Don 128) [1998 **46** –: 8d 7v 6d 1999 5.8v 7g 7m 8g⁶ 8.5m 8.5m⁵ a6g³ a7g a6g* a6g a6g⁶ a7g² a7g⁵ **a61** a8g⁵ a8g² Dec 17] IR 3,400Y: sister to fairly useful 1993 2-y-o 6f/7f winner Friendly Champ: dam Irish maiden: poor form on turf, leaving J. Coogan in Ireland after sixth start: raced only on all-weather in Britain, showing modest form: won claimer at Southwell in November: stays 7f: acts on fibresand: usually blinkered. *D. Carroll*

PRINCESS LATIFA 3 b.f. Wolfhound (USA) 126 – Moorish Idol 90 (Aragon **59** 118) [1998 63: 6m 6g⁴ 1999 7m⁵ 7d May 15] useful-looking, unfurnished filly: modest maiden: stays 7f: acts on good to firm going. *B. J. Meehan*

PRINCESS LONDIS 4 ch.f. Interrex (CAN) – Princess Lucianne (Stanford 121§) **29** [1998 –: 6g 7.1g 6m 7v 1999 7.1m 7f 10m Sep 1] small, sturdy filly: bad maiden: probably stays 1¼m: acts on good to firm going. *B. De Haan*

PRINCESS LOUISE 2 b.f. (Feb 10) Efisio 120 – Louis' Queen (IRE) 102 (Tragic **86** Role (USA)) [1999 6m* Sep 8] first foal: dam 5f (at 2 yrs) to 1m winner: 8/1, won 12-runner maiden at Kempton by short head from Harmonic, prominent throughout: should stay 7f: looked likely to improve. *J. L. Dunlop*

PRINCESS MO 3 b.f. Prince Sabo 123 – Morica 88 (Moorestyle 137) [1998 55: **39** 5s⁵ 5.1v 5v⁶ 1999 5d 7d 8m 5.3d a6g a10g⁵ Dec 22] sturdy filly: poor maiden: left Pat Mitchell after reappearance: barely stays 1¼m: acts on soft going and equi-track: bandaged behind: blinkered/visored once each: refused to enter stalls second intended 3-y-o start. *B. R. Johnson*

PRINCESS OF HEARTS 5 b.m. Prince Sabo 123 – Constant Delight 80 (Never **– §** So Bold 135) [1998 46§: a10g⁵ a12g⁶ a8g a8g 8g 10.1m 8d 1999 10.5m Jul 10] lengthy mare: poor handicapper nowadays: reportedly finished distressed only 5-y-o start: stays 1¼m: acts on good to firm ground: usually blinkered/visored: ungenuine: sold 600 gns. *Andrew Reid*

PRINCESS RIA (IRE) 2 b.f. (Mar 19) Petong 126 – Walking Saint 73 (Gods- **65** walk (USA) 130) [1999 6s* 6m³ 5g⁵ 6.5g 7s Sep 22] IR 4,500F, 16,000Y: leggy, sparely-made filly: third foal: dam 7f (at 2 yrs) to 8.5f winner: fair form when winning minor event at Haydock in July: mostly well below that form after: stays 6f: acts on soft going. *A. Bailey*

PRINCESS TOPAZ 5 b.m. Midyan (USA) 124 – Diamond Princess 69 (Horage **76** 124) [1998 85: a12g⁴ 16.1v 14.8f* 16.2g⁶ 13.9f 14.8g 16.2d 1999 12m⁶ 16.2m 15.9m 14.8m³ 11.8m⁵ Aug 22] leggy, angular mare: fair handicapper: best at 1¾m/2m: acts on firm going, soundly beaten on softer than good: held up: none too consistent. *G. M. McCourt*

PRINCESS VICTORIA 2 b.f. (May 14) Deploy 131 – Scierpan (USA) 86 **61** (Sharpen Up 127) [1999 5g* 7m a6g² a6g⁶ Dec 18] 2,200Y: smallish filly: half-sister to several winners, including useful 6f winner Specified (by Known Fact) and useful French miler Pan Galactic (by Lear Fan): dam second at 5f/6f at 2 yrs: modest performer: won seller at Beverley in May, and ran well when second in Lingfield nursery in December: well beaten both other starts, off 5 months after second one: stays 6f: acts on equitrack. *N. A. Callaghan*

PRINCIPAL BOY (IRE) 6 br.g. Cyrano de Bergerac 120 – Shenley Lass (Prince **55** Tenderfoot (USA) 126) [1998 46: a8g* a8g² a8g⁵ a8g 8.3v⁴ a7g a7g a8g 1999 a11g **a51** a8g⁶ a7g⁶ a6f a6s³ a6g a6g⁴ 7g³ 6v³ 5m⁵ 5m⁵ 6m 7.5d 5.9g⁵ 6.1f 6m 5.9g 7g² 7f 7m⁵ 8.2g 8.3f⁶ 8m 8.3s⁴ 9.1v⁶ 8d⁵ a8g³ a7g a8g⁴ Dec 17] compact gelding: has a round action: modest handicapper: effective at 5f to 9f: acts on fibresand and any turf ground: tried blinkered/visored: takes good hold: tough. *Miss J. F. Craze*

PRINCIPAL DANCER 3 b.f. Shareef Dancer (USA) 135 – Little Beaut 72 –
(Prince Sabo 123) [1998 64: 5s⁴ 5g 6g³ 6s 5m 8d 1999 8.2f a6g 5m 8m Aug 4]
workmanlike filly: modest maiden at 2 yrs: no form in 1999. *R. F. Marvin*

PRINCIPLE ACCOUNT 2 b.c. (Apr 18) Rudimentary (USA) 118 – Fairy Story 73
(IRE) 80 (Persian Bold 123) [1999 7m⁴ 7m² 6g³ 8g 6d⁶ Oct 15] 8,000Y: tall, lengthy
colt: has scope: second foal: half-brother to 3-y-o Uncle Oberon: dam 7f winner,
including at 2 yrs: fair maiden: sweating and edgy, creditable sixth of 20 to Magic of
Love in sales race at Newmarket final start: best efforts at 6f: acts on good to soft
going. *C. A. Dwyer*

PRINCIPLE (IRE) 2 b.c. (May 3) Caerleon (USA) 132 – Point of Honour (Kris 71 p
135) [1999 a8.5g⁶ 8f² 7g⁴ Oct 19] IR 20,000Y: seventh foal: brother to 2 winners,
notably smart 9f and 1¼m winner Del Deya: dam, behind both starts, sister to Oaks
winner Unite: progressive form: fourth of 15 to Atavus in maiden at Lingfield final
start: will prove suited by 1¼m+: remains open to improvement. *Sir Mark Prescott*

PRINTSMITH (IRE) 2 br.f. (Apr 11) Petardia 113 – Black And Blaze (Taufan 53
(USA) 119) [1999 5g⁶ 6m 5g* 5m 5g³ 5g 6g Sep 20] leggy, unfurnished filly: second
reported foal: dam Irish 7f winner: modest performer: won seller at Catterick in July:
ran creditably in nurseries next 2 starts: should stay 6f: raced only on good/good to
firm going. *J. Norton*

PRIOLETTE (IRE) 4 b.f. Priolo (USA) 127 – Celestial Path 101 (Godswalk 40 §
(USA) 130) [1998 48: 8m 8g⁶ 10s³ 9s⁴ 10m⁶ 8d 9.2d² 1999 8d 12g⁴ 10d 10m⁴ 11.1m
Jun 29] compact filly: poor maiden: stays 1½m: acts on firm and soft going: virtually
refused to race on 2 of last 3 starts, and often hangs: joined S. Kettlewell: one to
avoid. *Don Enrico Incisa*

PRIORS MOOR 4 br.g. Petong 126 – Jaziyah (IRE) (Lead On Time (USA) 123) 52 d
[1998 63, a–: 11.4d 8.5m 8d* a7g a10g 1999 a10g³ a8g³ a8g 7m a8g⁵ 7m 7s Aug 18]
sparely-made gelding: modest handicapper: well beaten after second start: stays
1¼m: acts on good to soft going and equitrack: tried blinkered: joined K. Bell.
R. W. Armstrong

PRIORY GARDENS (IRE) 5 b.g. Broken Hearted 124 – Rosy O'Leary (Majetta 49
115) [1998 46: 6s 7.5m 7g⁴ 6m* 6.9d⁴ 6.1m 7d 6d 1999 7.1m 7f⁶ 6f⁴ 6g* 6m 8f⁶ 6g
7f² 7m⁴ 6.1m 5g⁵ 7m Sep 3] poor handicapper: won at Leicester in May: effective at
6f to 1m: acts on firm and good to soft going. *J. M. Bradley*

PRIVATE FIXTURE (IRE) 8 ch.g. The Noble Player (USA) 126 – Pennyala 38
(Skyliner 117) [1998 –, a71: a16g² 1999 12m 17.2g a12g 12.1m 11.9f⁴ 14.1g Aug
12] quite good-topped gelding: fair on all-weather at best, poor on turf nowadays:
stays 2m: acts on all-weather, firm and soft going: twice blinkered (ran creditably
first time). *D. Marks*

PRIVATE SEAL 4 b.g. King's Signet (USA) 110 – Slender 79 (Aragon 118) –
[1998 –, a45+: 7g 7g 8m⁵ 10m⁵ 8g a7g⁴ 1999 a7g⁴ a6g³ a7g a7g a8g⁶ a10g⁵ a12g a7g a47
10f 7m a7g 7f Jul 14] workmanlike gelding: poor nowadays: usually runs in sellers/
claimers: probably stays 1¼m: acts on equitrack, no form on turf since 1997: often
blinkered: has worn tongue strap: has carried head awkwardly. *Julian Poulton*

PRIX DE CLERMONT (IRE) 5 b.g. Petorius 117 – Sandra's Choice 57 (Sandy –
Creek 123) [1998 –, a52d: a12g a12g³ a12g a12g³ a12g 11.6m 12m a16m a12g a12g³
1999 a13g a12f⁶ Jan 14] sturdy gelding: modest handicapper on all-weather at best,
little form on turf: stays 1½m: better form on fibresand than equitrack: sometimes
blinkered: sometimes pulls hard and looks wayward. *G. L. Moore*

PRIX STAR 4 ch.g. Superpower 113 – Celestine 62 (Skyliner 117) [1998 84: 6s³ 67
6s³ 6m 6g 6v 6d 1999 a6g a6g 6.1s 5.9m 6d 6g* 6m 7g² 6m 7f 7g 7g⁶ 7d 6d² a57
a7g⁴ a6g⁵ a6g⁵ Nov 20] angular gelding: fair handicapper: won at Catterick in June:
ran well after when runner-up: effective at 6f/7f: has form on good to firm ground,
but best on good or softer: seems effective visored or not: has been bandaged.
C. W. Fairhurst

PROCEDURE (USA) 3 b. or br.g. Strolling Along (USA) – Bold Courtesan 105
(USA) (Bold Bidder) [1998 78p: 7d⁶ 7v³ 1999 8.2m⁶ 10m* 12m* 13.9g⁶ Aug 19]
big, useful-looking gelding: has plenty of scope: useful handicapper: made all at
Leicester in May and Salisbury in June, latter by ¾ length from Tabareeh, pair clear:

free to post and in race itself when below form in rated stakes at York final start: will prove best up to 1½m: acts on good to firm and heavy ground: tends to carry head high but is genuine: joined J. Old. *Sir Michael Stoute*

PRODIGAL SON (IRE) 4 b.g. Waajib 121 – Nouveau Lady (IRE) (Taufan 81 (USA) 119) [1998 57, a54: 10.3d 14.6g⁴.14.1g 8g⁴ 10g⁵ 8.5m³ 8f² 8m a7g² 1999 a7g* a8g* a8.5g* a8g² 8.2m* 8d² 10g⁵ 10m² 10m² 10d⁶ a9.4g² a10g Dec 8] leggy gelding: fairly useful handicapper: won at Wolverhampton (twice), Lingfield and Nottingham between February and June: stays 1¼m: acts on firm going, good to soft and all-weather: blinkered once at 3 yrs: has wandered/flashed tail: game and consistent. *Mrs V. C. Ward*

PROKOFIEV (USA) 3 br.g. Nureyev (USA) 131 – Aviara (USA) (Cox's Ridge 78 (USA)) [1998 74p: 7s³ 1999 10m⁵ 10m³ 11.4m Jul 3] fair maiden: didn't progress as expected in 1999, finding little in visor final start: stays 1¼m: acts on soft and good to firm ground: tends to run in snatches: won over hurdles in December for J. J. O'Neill. *Sir Michael Stoute*

PROLIX 4 ch.c. Kris 135 – Ajuga (USA) 102 (The Minstrel (CAN) 135) [1998 116 115: 8d² 8s* 10.3m* 12g⁵ 10m⁵ 11.9f³ 10.3g³ 1999 9.9d 10.3g* 10m² 10s* 10.5d² 10m³ 9.9s² Sep 22] big, strong, good-topped colt: has a quick action: smart performer: won minor event at Doncaster in June and Tennent Caledonian Breweries Scottish Classic at Ayr (soon clear, beat Housemaster by 3 lengths) in July: ran creditably after in Rose of Lancaster Stakes (second to easy winner Greek Dance) at Haydock, Winter Hill Stakes (third to Zindabad) at Windsor and listed race at Goodwood: effective at 1¼m/1½m: acts on firm and soft going: tends to sweat and race freely to the post: genuine: sent to Saudi Arabia. *B. W. Hills*

PROMESSA 3 b.f. Reprimand 122 – Congress (IRE) 86 (Dancing Brave (USA) 62 140) [1998 NR 1999 6.1f⁵ 7s⁴ 5.9m² 7f³ a6g* 8m 6g Aug 19] third foal: dam, 1m a76 winner, sister to very smart 6f/7f performer Cherokee Rose: fair on all-weather, modest on turf: won maiden at Wolverhampton in July by 8 lengths: well held in handicaps last 2 starts: stays 7f: acts on firm going, soft and fibresand: blinkered fourth start: often tongue tied: sold 7,000 gns in December. *W. J. Haggas*

PROMISE OF GLORY 2 ch.c. (Apr 4) Lammtarra (USA) 134 – Vana Turns – (USA) (Wavering Monarch (USA)) [1999 7g 8g Sep 8] strong, good sort: sixth foal: half-brother to smart French 3-y-o 7f/1m winner Midnight Foxtrot and fairly useful 10.5f winner King Tango (both by Kingmambo), multiple graded-stakes winner Petionville (by Seeking The Gold) and Kentucky Oaks winner Pike Place Dancer (by Seattle Dancer): dam minor stakes winner at around 1m: saddle slipped on debut: took fierce hold and pulled up 3f out in maiden at Doncaster next time: looks very difficult ride. *B. W. Hills*

PROPER GENT 2 b.g. (Mar 19) Alhijaz 122 – Proper Madam 93 (Mummy's Pet – 125) [1999 6m 7.5g 7.9g 8d Nov 1] 9,500Y: close-coupled, unfurnished gelding: poor mover: half-brother to several winners, including Swedish 3-y-o 6.5f winner Enthaisingh, 5f/6f winner here at 2 yrs, and fairly useful 1996 2-y-o 5f winner Osomental (both by Petong): dam sprinter: well held in maidens/nursery. *M. Brittain*

PROPER SQUIRE (USA) 2 b.c. (Feb 9) Bien Bien (USA) 125 – La Cumbre 79 (Sadler's Wells (USA) 132) [1999 8.1m³ 9v⁶ 8d² Oct 27] first foal: dam, lightly raced in USA, out of sister to Cherry Hinton winner Turkish Treasure: fair maiden: trained by P. Chapple-Hyam first 2 starts (very stiff task second one): 4 lengths second of 10 to Scotty Guest at Yarmouth final outing: will stay 1½m. *A. G. Foster*

PROPHITS PRIDE (IRE) 7 ch.g. Carmelite House (USA) 118 – Asinara (Julio 33 Mariner 127) [1998 47: 10m* 12.1d⁴ 12s² 1999 9g 9.2v⁶ 9.2g⁵ 12.1m 9m 11.1m 11.1f 12.1m⁵ 16g⁴ Aug 18] poor performer: stays 1½m: acts on soft and good to firm ground. *P. Monteith*

PROSPECTOR'S COVE 6 b.g. Dowsing (USA) 124 – Pearl Cove 63 (Town 82 And Country 124) [1998 70: a13g⁵ 16.2g³ 11.8s 11.9m 11.9g⁵ 8.2m⁴ 8.1d 8f* 8d⁴ a68 8m 8g 8.2s³ 8.2v⁵ a9.4g² a11g² a10g⁵ a10f* a10g² 1999 a10g⁵ a8g⁶ a9.4g³ a9.4g² a8g⁵ a8.5g⁵ 8.3m³ 8f² a9.4g⁵ a10g³ 8.9d 8m 8g² 8f³ 9f 8m² 8g* 8m⁶ 7.9m 8d* 8v 8g 8s Oct 25] angular, workmanlike gelding: fairly useful handicapper on turf, fair on all-weather: won in large fields at Newmarket in August and Yarmouth in September: generally ran respectably otherwise: has form at 2m, best at 1m to 1¼m: acts on any all-weather/turf: visored (ran poorly) twice: usually held up: tends to wander. *J. Pearce*

PROSPERITY (IRE) 3 b.g. Catrail (USA) 123 – Bequeath (USA) (Lyphard **61** (USA) 132) [1998 72: 6s⁴ 6g³ 6g⁴ 1999 8g 9m 9.9s⁴ 12m 11m Aug 28] tall gelding: modest maiden handicapper: stayed 1¼m: acted on soft and good to firm going: blinkered once: dead. *T. D. Easterby*

PROSPERO 6 b.g. Petong 126 – Pennies To Pounds 80 (Ile de Bourbon (USA) **–** 133) [1998 NR 1999 16.2m Jun 19] big, strong, lengthy gelding: fair handicapper in 1997: well beaten only 6-y-o start: stays 17f: acts on firm and good to soft ground. *Mrs A. J. Perrett*

PROSPEROUS (IRE) 3 ch.f. Generous (IRE) 139 – Amwag (USA) 106 (El **71** Gran Senor (USA) 136) [1998 88p: 7v² 1999 12g⁶ 10g³ 12.3d² 12v⁵ 10d 7s 10s⁵ Nov 1] smallish, close-coupled filly: fair maiden: left B. Hills after fourth start: stays 1½m: acts on heavy going. *P. F. Cashman, Ireland*

PROTARAS BAY 5 b.g. Superpower 113 – Vivid Impression (Cure The Blues **39** (USA)) [1998 54, a41: a11g³ a9.4g⁵ 9.3s² 12m⁵ 10.5m⁶ 10g² 10g⁵ 10g 8v* 8s 1999 9m 10m⁶ 8d 10m⁶ Sep 24] angular gelding: poor handicapper: effective at 1m to 11f: has form on good to firm going, but best on good or softer: usually visored/blinkered. *P. L. Gilligan*

PROTECTOR 2 b.c. (Feb 26) Be My Chief (USA) 122 – Clicquot 101 (Bold Lad **69** (IRE) 133) [1999 6m⁵ 6s Aug 18] 28,000F, 60,000Y: strong, well-made colt: half-brother to smart 5f (at 2yrs) to 1m winner Fizzed (by Efisio) and useful 5f/6f winner Premiere Cuvee (by Formidable): dam best at 5f: fair form when fifth of 6 in newcomers race at Ascot: tailed-off last of 17 in maiden at Kempton following month. *J. W. Hills*

PROTOCOL (IRE) 5 b.g. Taufan (USA) 119 – Ukraine's Affair (USA) (The **63** Minstrel (CAN) 135) [1998 91d, a84: a12g⁵ a11g³ a16g⁶ a16g⁵ a7g a9.4g³ 12d* 10s* **a–** 10d⁴ 9.9m⁶ 10.5g 12g 16.1f 10.3m⁶ 12v 8d 1999 a12g a11g 10d 13.8m 11.5m 10.1m³ 10.3m⁴ 10m⁶ 10m⁶ 10g⁴ 12.3d³ 10.5m² 12m⁵ 12d² 10d⁵ 14.1s* a12g Nov 16] rather leggy gelding: modest performer: won amateur minor event at Nottingham in November: best at 1¼m to 1¾m: acts on soft and good to firm going, no form on all-weather in 1999: tried visored: has had soft palate operation, and wears tongue strap: none too consistent. *Mrs S. Lamyman*

PROUD CAVALIER 3 b.g. Pharly (FR) 130 – Midnight Flit 89 (Bold Lad (IRE) **–** 133) [1998 –: a8g 1999 8.3g 8g May 17] no sign of ability. *K. Bell*

PROUD CHIEF 2 ch.c. (Mar 14) Be My Chief (USA) 122 – Fleur de Foret **74** (USA) 61§ (Green Forest (USA) 134) [1999 6g 6g* 5.2m 6m 6d 6d Oct 14] 17,000Y: smallish, strong colt: sixth foal: half-brother to 3 winners, including useful 1997 2-y-o 5f winner Mugello (by Emarati) and 7f/1m winner Proud Image (by Zalazl): dam, sprint maiden, became ungenuine at 3 yrs: fair performer: reportedly lame on debut: won maiden at Goodwood in June: ran creditably after only on final start: should stay 1m: acts on good to soft going *A. P. Jarvis*

PROUD MONK 6 gr.g. Aragon 118 – Silent Sister 78 (Kind of Hush 118) [1998 **40** 40: a8s⁵ a8g a10g 7s 8.2s 8m 8d 9m⁴ 8g 10g⁶ 10g 8.3m 10m³ 12.3g⁵ 10m 10.5m⁴ 12s 10s 1999 10g 8.2m⁴ 10m⁴ 9d⁴ 10.5s⁴ 10d 10.5m⁶ 11.6m⁴ 12.1m 11.6m⁴ 10m⁴ Aug 4] strong, lengthy gelding: poor handicapper: probably stays 1½m: acts on soft and good to firm going: tried blinkered/visored: often tongue tied: has worn crossed noseband/been bandaged in front. *K. Bell*

PROUD NATIVE (IRE) 5 b.g. Imp Society (USA) – Karamana (Habitat 134) **115** [1998 113: 5d⁵ 6d 6g 5g 5s 6g 6g 5g* 6m 5.1m⁵ 5d⁵ 5.2g⁶ 1999 5d⁵ 5s 5m* 5g* 5m⁵ 5m³ 5g³ 5.8g* 5m Dec 12] sturdy gelding: smart walker/mover: smart performer: won listed race at Kempton in May, Ballyogan Stakes at Leopardstown in June and Taby Open Sprint Championship (by head) in September: best efforts when third to Timote (under 10-1) in listed handicap at the Curragh and to Stravinsky, beaten 3 lengths, in Nunthorpe Stakes at York: off 3 months, behind in Hong Kong Sprint at Sha Tin final start: effective at 5f/easy 6f: acts on good to firm and good to soft going, possibly not on soft: edgy sort: often early to post: has been bandaged in front: waited with: tough and reliable. *D. Nicholls*

PROUD PICTURE (IRE) 3 b.g. Pips Pride 117 – Mint Addition 50 (Tate Gallery –
(USA) 117) [1998 59: 5.1g 6m 6m 7g 1999 6g 6s 6g Oct 11] modest maiden at 2 yrs:
no form in 1999: likely to prove best up to 1m: visored final start: sold 800 gns, sent
to Italy. *J. G. Smyth-Osbourne*

PRU'S VENTURE 3 b.f. Tragic Role (USA) – Indivisible 56 (Remainder Man –
126§) [1998 NR 1999 a8g⁶ 12m⁵ 7.5m Jul 13] 600Y: small filly: fourth foal: half-
sister to 5-y-o Divide And Rule (5f winner at 2 yrs): dam stayed 1¼m: no sign of
ability. *R. Hollinshead*

PTAH (IRE) 2 b.c. (Jan 16) Petardia 113 – Davenport Goddess (IRE) (Classic 58
Secret (USA) 91) [1999 5d⁴ 5d 5m⁵ 6s 7.9d 7g Oct 16] 10,000Y: leggy colt: first
living foal: dam unraced: modest maiden: form only on first and third starts: stays 6f:
has given trouble in preliminaries/reared stalls. *J. L. Eyre*

PTARMIGAN RIDGE 3 b.c. Sea Raven (IRE) 75 – Panayr (Faraway Times 88 d
(USA) 123) [1998 81p: 5s* 1999 8m 5s² 5g 6m⁴ 5g 5d 6d 5s Sep 25] fairly useful
handicapper: easily best effort in 1999 when second at Ayr in June: should stay 6f:
goes well on soft going. *Miss L. A. Perratt*

PUBLIC PURSE (USA) 5 b.h. Private Account (USA) – Prodigious (FR) (Pharly 119
(FR) 130) [1998 122: 10g* 12.5d* 12s³ 1999 12d³ 12d* 12g⁶ 12.5g³ 12f* 12f² Dec
4] tall horse: has a powerful, round action: smart performer: won Prix Jean de
Chaudenay at Saint-Cloud in May by ½ length from Sestino and (having left
A. Fabre) Grade 3 event at Santa Anita in October: good 1¼ lengths second to Lazy
Lode in Hollywood Turf Cup final start: stays 12.5f: acts on firm and soft going:
genuine and consistent. *R. Frankel, USA*

PUDDING LANE (IRE) 2 b.f. (Feb 15) College Chapel 122 – Fire of London 64
78 (Shirley Heights 130) [1999 5d 6d 6g³ 6s a7g² a7g⁵ Dec 18] 8,000Y: small,
workmanlike filly: first foal: dam second at 1¼m: modest maiden: stays 7f: acts on
equitrack: visored final start. *R. F. Johnson Houghton*

PUISSANTKOOLA 3 b.g. Puissance 110 – Nikoola Eve 69 (Roscoe Blake 120) –
[1998 NR 1999 a8g 8s 8g 15.8g 7s Oct 23] tall gelding: fourth reported foal: half-
brother to 1¼m winner Vin St Koola (by Vin St Benet): dam 1½m and 15.8f winner,
also successful over hurdles: no sign of ability: blinkered final start. *D. Shaw*

PUIWEE 4 b.f. Puissance 110 – Glow Again 78 (The Brianstan 128) [1998 49: 7d 35
6.1v a8g 8g³ 7s⁶ 7g³ 8.1g 8m² 7g 8.2g 8v a11g⁴ 1999 a9.4g⁴ a12g a11g 8m 7m 7.7m⁵
a8g 11.5m 11d Oct 26] leggy filly: has a round action: poor maiden: stays 9.4f: acts
on fibresand and good to firm going: blinkered final start: has been edgy and
mounted on track: has started slowly: inconsistent. *P. T. Dalton*

PULAU PINANG (IRE) 3 ch.f. Dolphin Street (FR) 125 – Inner Pearl (Gulf 75
Pearl 117) [1998 NR 1999 11.7m³ 11.5m* 10g Oct 11] 15,000Y: half-sister to several
winners, including useful 1992 2-y-o 6f and 1m winner Iommelli (by Don't Forget
Me) who stayed 1¼m: dam French 4f (at 2 yrs) to 9f winner: confirmed promise
when landing odds in falsely-run maiden at Lingfield in September: found little in
handicap next time: stays 11.5f. *G. A. Butler*

PULAU TIOMAN 3 b.c. Robellino (USA) 127 – Ella Mon Amour 65 105
(Ela-Mana-Mou 132) [1998 89: 7.1g³ 7g⁴ 8.2m* 7.9g⁵ 1999 9m² 9g² 8m 7.1d* 7f
7.1d* 7g⁵ 7d 8d Oct 30] compact, quite attractive colt: useful performer: won rated
stakes at Haydock (by 1½ lengths from Marton Moss) in July and minor event at
Sandown (beat Granny's Pet 1¾ lengths in 4-runner race) in August: below form last
3 starts: effective at 7f, probably at 9f: has won on good to firm going, best efforts on
good to soft: none too consistent. *M. A. Jarvis*

PUNCTUATE 2 b.c. (Apr 3) Distant Relative 128 – Niggle 65 (Night Shift (USA)) 98 p
[1999 5d* 5m* Aug 31] 10,000F, 50,000Y: first foal: dam twice-raced daughter of
smart 1975 2-y-o sprinter Enchanted: won minor events at Sandown and Ripon in
August, showing useful form when beating Jailhouse Rocket by ½ length on second
occasion: likely to prove best at 5f/6f: should improve further. *W. J. Haggas*

PUNISHMENT 8 b.h. Midyan (USA) 124 – In The Shade 89 (Bustino 136) [1998 105 d
105, a102: 8d² 8d 10.6g⁴ 12v 10d⁶ 10d² 9.9g⁵ 13.9f 12s² 12s 10s* 12d a12g⁵
a9.4g⁴ 1999 a12g⁶ a10g³ a10g⁶ 10m³ 12d 10m⁶ 10m² 10g 14f 11g⁴ 11.6m³ 12s 10d
10d³ 12s a10g⁶ Dec 8] workmanlike horse: useful handicapper: ¾-length second to

Brilliant Red in valuable contest at Ascot in June: mostly disappointing otherwise: effective at 1¼m/1½m: acts on all-weather, soft and good to firm going: tried visored: usually tongue tied: usually held up: inconsistent. *K. O. Cunningham-Brown*

PUNKAH (USA) 6 b.g. Lear Fan (USA) 130 – Gentle Persuasion 95 (Bustino 136) [1998 –: a10g 10m 10.1m⁵ a10g 1999 10d Apr 27] well-made gelding: one-time fairly useful performer: no show since 1997 (though won over hurdles in July): tried visored. *G. M. McCourt* —

PUPPET PLAY (IRE) 4 ch.f. Broken Hearted 124 – Fantoccini (Taufan (USA) 119) [1998 66: 9m⁴ 11.9m² 1999 9g 11s⁶ 8g² 8m 8m 7d a7g⁶ a8.5g⁴ a7g² a8.5g² Dec 27] fourth foal: half-sister to 2-y-o 5f winners by Dancing Dissident (in Ireland) and Dominion: dam Irish maiden: modest maiden: left J. O'Haire in Ireland after fifth start: effective at 7f to 1½m: acts on good to firm ground and all-weather: tried blinkered, including final start: has awkward head carriage. *E. J. Alston* **65** **a58**

PUP'S PRIDE 2 b.g. (Apr 23) Efisio 120 – Moogie 103 (Young Generation 129) [1999 6d 5.1m 5g⁶ 5m 6d Oct 26] 13,000Y: seventh foal: half-brother to fairly useful 1996 2-y-o 7f winner Catwalk and 1994 2-y-o 6f winner Mood Swings (both by Shirley Heights): dam 2-y-o 6f winner later suited by 9f: modest maiden at best: well held last 2 starts: should be suited by 6f+. *R. A. Fahey* **54**

PURE BRIEF (IRE) 2 b.g. (Mar 22) Brief Truce (USA) 126 – Epure (Bellypha 130) [1999 6.8m⁵ 7m 6.8m 10s a8g a8g Dec 21] 11,000F, 5,000Y, 7,200 2-y-o: half-brother to 4-y-o Mola and several winners, including fairly useful 6f (at 2 yrs) and 1m winner Cinema Paradiso (by Polar Falcon) and useful stayer Pashto (by Persian Bold): dam French 11.5f winner: modest maiden: form only on first and third starts: should stay 1m+. *D. J. G. Murray Smith* **56** **a–**

PURE COINCIDENCE 4 b.g. Lugana Beach 116 – Esilam 62 (Frimley Park 109) [1998 88: a5g 5d 5m 7.3g 6.1g 5s³ 5s⁴ 1999 6v a6g 6g⁴ 5m 5g* 5d³ 5d⁶ 5d a5g Nov 17] rather leggy gelding: has a short action: fairly useful handicapper: left W. Musson before winning at Carlisle in August: probably best at 5f: acts on firm ground, soft and fibresand: blinkered once: wore crossed noseband/very slowly away fourth start: front runner. *K. R. Burke* **88**

PURE ELEGANCIA 3 b.f. Lugana Beach 116 – Esilam 62 (Frimley Park 109) [1998 NR 1999 6g⁶ 6d⁴ 5g 5g* 5g⁵ 5f* 5g⁶ Aug 18] 16,000Y: rather leggy, workmanlike filly: seventh foal: sister to 4-y-o Pure Coincidence and half-sister to 2 winners, including 7-y-o Knotty Hill: dam, 2-y-o 5f winner here, won up to 1m in Italy: fairly useful handicapper: won at Catterick in June and Goodwood in July: best of those towards stand rail when sixth of 20 to Emma Peel at York final start: will prove best at bare 5f: acts on firm going: type to do well in 2000. *D. Nicholls* **82 p**

PURNADAS ROAD (IRE) 4 ch.f. Petardia 113 – Choral Park (Music Boy 124) [1998 53: 6d 7m⁵ 7d 1999 5.1s 5.7g a8g a6g Dec 27] modest form second 3-y-o start, well beaten otherwise (said to have bled from nose on reappearance): left J. Toller before final 2 starts, when blinkered. *H. E. Haynes* —

PURPLE DAWN (IRE) 3 b.f. Tirol 127 – Tuesday Morning (Sadler's Wells (USA) 132) [1998 60: 6g 7g 7f 7.1g² 7m 7.3g 10s 8.2v⁵ 8d⁵ 1999 8v 10f⁵ 8g 10m* 12.1m 9m⁵ 10g a11g⁶ 10d 14.1f 10d Oct 28] tall, leggy filly: modest performer: won selling handicap at Nottingham in June: stays 1¼m: acts on good to firm going, probably on heavy: inconsistent: sold 900 gns. *J. S. Moore* **50**

PURPLE FLAME (IRE) 3 b.f. Thatching 131 – Polistatic 53 (Free State 125) [1998 NR 1999 7m 7m 7g⁶ 8.1m⁵ 9.9d 8m Sep 8] workmanlike filly: third foal: dam, 11f/1½m, sister to Ebor winner Western Dancer: modest maiden handicapper: should stay beyond 1m: acts on good to firm going. *C. A. Horgan* **63**

PURPLE FLING 8 ch.g. Music Boy 124 – Divine Fling (Imperial Fling (USA) 116) [1998 69: a6g 6m 7.3g⁵ 6g⁵ 5m 5m⁵ 5m 6m 6.1s 1999 6g⁵ 5d⁴ 6.1f⁶ 6f 7.1g 6g³ a6g* a6g² a6g* a6g⁶ Dec 11] strong gelding: fair performer on all-weather, modest on turf: won handicap at Southwell in September and minor event at Wolverhampton in November: stays 7f: acts on any turf/all-weather. *A. J. McNae* **63** **a69**

PURPLE HEATHER (USA) 2 b.f. (Mar 10) Rahy (USA) 115 – Clear Attraction (USA) (Lear Fan (USA) 130) [1999 6g⁶ 8m⁴ 8.2g² Sep 25] smallish, sturdy filly: first foal: dam, well held only outing, out of 1000 Guineas winner Highclere: fairly **93**

useful form: did particularly well considering still very green when fourth of 12 to Teggiano in May Hill Stakes at Doncaster in September: odds on, ridden to lead final 1f but caught post in maiden at Nottingham later in month: should stay 1¼m: sure to win a race. *R. Hannon*

PURPLE LACE 7 b.m. Salse (USA) 128 – Purple Prose (Rainbow Quest (USA) – 134) [1998 –: 16.4g 1999 10m 8.3s 17.2m 15.8d Sep 21] little form, unraced on Flat before 1998. *H. S. Howe*

PURSE 3 b.f. Pursuit of Love 124 – Rose Noble (USA) 62 (Vaguely Noble 140) **78** [1998 NR 1999 8.3g³ 8m⁴ 8m⁵ 8.2s Oct 5] well-made filly: second foal: closely related to 4-y-o Dower House: dam, 11.5f winner, half-sister to Grand Lodge: fair form in maidens on first and third starts: reportedly finished lame in between and looked none too keen final one: likely to stay beyond 1m. *H. R. A. Cecil*

PURSUANT 3 b.g. Puissance 110 – Payvashooz 78 (Ballacashtal (CAN)) [1998 – –: 5g 7m 7m 1999 7d 6g 7m Jul 12] leggy gelding: little sign of ability. *M. Brittain*

PURSUIVANT 5 b.g. Pursuit of Love 124 – Collapse 107 (Busted 134) [1998 63: **67** 7s⁶ 7d⁶ 9m³ 10d 1999 a8g³ a9.4g² 8d⁵ 8.3g² a8.5g³ 8.1s 10s Oct 2] sturdy gelding: **a71** fair maiden: stays 9f: acts on fibresand and good to firm going: tried blinkered. *M. D. Hammond*

PURSUMI 3 b.f. Pursuit of Love 124 – Alacrity 62 (Alzao (USA) 117) [1998 –: 6s – 6m⁶ 1999 8.2m 12.1m 11f 8m Aug 4] lengthy filly: of little account. *R. M. Whitaker*

PUSSIE WILLOW (IRE) 2 b. or br.f. (Mar 5) Catrail (USA) 123 – Quiche 83 **77** (Formidable (USA) 125) [1999 5g² 6s Oct 2] good-topped filly: has scope: sixth living foal: sister to 3-y-o Lionhearted and half-sister to 3 winners, including useful sprinter Symboli Kildare (by Kaldoun) and UAE 7f winner Doraid (by Danehill): dam 6f winner: fair form in maidens at Newmarket 6 months apart: unlikely to stay much beyond 6f. *P. F. I. Cole*

PUSSY GALORE 4 b.f. Pursuit of Love 124 – Zinzi (Song 132) [1998 72: 7d⁵ **72 d** 8m 8.2v 1999 7s* 8.3d 8g 7g 8m Sep 5] strong, attractive filly: fair performer at best: won maiden at Folkestone in April: well held in handicaps after, sold from D. Elsworth 9,000 gns prior to penultimate start: stays 7f: acts on soft going: blinkered final outing. *A. Slattery, Ireland*

PUTERI WENTWORTH 5 b.m. Sadler's Wells (USA) 132 – Sweeping 104 – (Indian King (USA) 128) [1998 88: 16.2g 14.6g* 14.8f⁴ 20d* 13.9g 16.2d⁴ 18g⁴ 1999 14m 17.5d Sep 17] lengthy mare: fairly useful handicapper at 4 yrs: well held both starts in 1999: best at 2m+: acts on soft going, probably on firm: often bandaged nowadays: held up. *Miss Gay Kelleway*

PUTUNA 4 b.f. Generous (IRE) 139 – Ivoronica 89 (Targowice (USA) 130) [1998 **98** 98: 8.5s* 11.5m⁶ 9.9m² 10s* 12s 10.2g⁵ 9.9m 10.1m 10s⁶ 1999 10.1s⁴ 8.5m* 10.1m⁶ 10m³ 10.4g⁴ 10.1g³ 8m³ 10s Oct 2] rangy filly: useful performer: sweating, won listed race at Newmarket in April: ran well when in frame after, notably when third to Fickle in listed rated stakes at Newcastle and third to Dazzling Park in Matron Stakes at the Curragh on sixth/seventh starts: best at 1m/1¼m: acts on soft and good to firm going: has ungainly head carriage: rather headstrong (usually held up). *I. A. Balding*

PUZZLEMENT 5 gr.g. Mystiko (USA) 124 – Abuzz 101 (Absalom 128) [1998 **78** 78: a10g a8g 9.7m 8s 10.1g⁶ 10m⁶ 11.5g⁵ 9.9m* 9.9m* 10s³ 10.1g 10.4g² 10d 1999 a11g⁵ a9.4g a10g⁴ a8g⁵ 10s² 10m⁶ 12m⁴ 10.5s⁵ May 29] big, good-bodied gelding: fair handicapper: best at 1¼m/1½m (at least when conditions aren't testing): acts on all-weather, soft and good to firm going: usually held up: tough and consistent. *C. E. Brittain*

PYJAMA GIRL (USA) 2 gr.f. (Mar 3) Night Shift (USA) – Permissible Tender **63** (USA) (Al Hattab (USA)) [1999 6g⁵ 6f⁶ 6m 6m⁴ 6m⁵ a6g a6g⁶ Nov 8] $12,500F, **a49** $40,000Y: half-sister to 1989 Richmond Stakes winner Contract Law (by Lypheor) and several winners abroad: dam, won at up to 9f in USA, out of half-sister to Law Society: modest maiden: raced only at 6f: acts on good to firm going, below form on all-weather: has flicked tail/shown signs of temperament. *P. R. Chamings*

Britannia Stakes (Handicap), Ascot—Pythios is clear of Siege (No.1), Harlequin Dancer (far side) and Tobruk (spotted cap), all four making their handicap debuts

PYRAMID PRINCESS   2 b.f. (Feb 15) Pyramus (USA) 78 – Sancilia (Dalsaan   **53**
125) [1999 5m³ Jul 19] 500Y: sixth foal: half-sister to 6f (at 2 yrs)/7f winner Stardust
Express (by Sylvan Express) and a 6f winner in Sweden by Floose: dam sprint
maiden: broke leg after finishing third in Beverley claimer: dead. *J. S. Wainwright*

PYTHAGORAS   2 ch.c. (Feb 10) Kris 135 – Tricorne 92 (Green Desert (USA)   **82**
127) [1999 8.1g⁴ 8d Oct 9] 38,000Y: second foal: half-brother to 3-y-o Tricolore:
dam 2-y-o 6f winner out of half-sister to Old Vic: shaped quite well when fourth of 9
in maiden at Chepstow on debut: much stiffer task, well held in listed race at Ascot 6
weeks later: should stay 1¼m. *W. R. Muir*

PYTHIOS (IRE)   3 b.c. Danehill (USA) 126 – Pithara (GR) (Never So Bold 135)   **107 p**
[1998 –: 6g 1999 7f* 7m³ 8m*] strong, well-made colt: has scope: progressive
form: won maiden at Doncaster in May and 32-runner Britannia Handicap at Royal
Ascot in June, latter by 2 lengths from Siege, soon nudged along but staying on
strongly to lead inside final 1f: will stay beyond 1m: raced only on good ground or
firmer: tongue tied: looks capable of better still. *H. R. A. Cecil*

Q

QAMOUS (USA)   2 gr.c. (Jan 24) Bahri (USA) 125 – Bel Ray (USA) (Restivo   **89 p**
(USA)) [1999 8m⁴ 7d* Sep 30] $180,000Y: strong, lengthy colt: unimpressive
mover: second foal: dam won 10 races in USA, including 6f minor stakes at 2 yrs:
fairly useful form in maidens, winning at Newmarket by a head from Holding Court,
looking likely to score decisively 1½f out but all out to hold on: will probably prove
best short of 1m: almost certainly capable of better, and should win more races at 3
yrs. *E. A. L. Dunlop*

QANDIL (USA)   3 ch.g. Riverman (USA) 131 – Confirmed Affair (USA)   **–**
(Affirmed (USA)) [1998 –: 7g 1999 10.1g a8.5g Sep 8] little sign of ability.
H. J. Collingridge

QHAZEENAH   3 b.f. Marju (IRE) 127 – Nafhaat (USA) 91 (Roberto (USA) 131)   **95**
[1998 101+: 6f³ 7d⁵ 6.9f* 6.5g* 6s 1999 6m⁴ 7g* 8d⁵ 7d Oct 7] lengthy filly: useful
performer: best effort in 1999 when winning 4-runner minor event at Yarmouth in
July by head from Hot Tin Roof: should stay at least 1m: acts on firm ground,
possibly not on softer than good: has been bandaged behind: tail flasher, but genuine
in a finish: sent to USA. *J. L. Dunlop*

QILIN (IRE)   4 b.f. Second Set (IRE) 127 – Usance (GER) (Kronenkranich (GER)   **94**
118) [1998 90: 8g 6g² 7d 6g* 6m³ 6g 6f 6g⁵ 6s 5m 1999 6m² 6g 5m 7m* 7f 7s³ 7s⁴
6s³ 6v⁵ Nov 17] big, strong filly: fairly useful performer: won handicap at Newcastle
in June: flattered when 3 lengths third of 20 to Pipalong in listed event at Doncaster
penultimate start but ran creditably (despite slow start) when fifth behind Two
Clubs in similar event at Maisons-Laffitte final outing: headstrong, and will prove
best up to 7f: acts on good to firm and heavy going: reportedly bled from nose on
reappearance. *M. H. Tompkins*

QOSHEEYYA   3 b.f. Robellino (USA) 127 – Sharanella (Shareef Dancer (USA)   **–**
135) [1998 NR 1999 7.5v Jun 9] 20,000Y: fifth foal: closely related to useful 5f (at 2
yrs) to 1m winner Sonic Boy (by Celestial Storm), later successful in USA, and
half-sister to a winner in Germany by Miller's Mate: dam unraced: 8/1, slowly away
and never dangerous in maiden at Beverley. *N. A. Graham*

QUAESTIO (USA)   2 b.f. (Jan 23) Seeking The Gold (USA) – Oscillate (USA)   **90 +**
(Seattle Slew (USA)) [1999 6d* 6m⁵ Jun 26] close-coupled filly: sixth foal: sister to
smart 6f to 1m performer Mutakddim, closely related to a winner in Japan by Mr
Prospector and half-sister to a Grade 1-placed winner in USA by Easy Goer: dam,
winning sprinter in USA, half-sister to Breeders' Cup Juvenile winner Rhythm: fairly
useful form: won maiden at Newmarket in June: better effort when fifth of 8 to Hoh
Dear in listed race there: sent to race in USA. *J. L. Dunlop*

QUAINT DESIRE   6 br.g. Grey Desire 115 – Aquainted 63 (Known Fact (USA)   **–**
135) [1998 NR 1999 9.9s a11g Sep 28] of little account. *M. Brittain*

QUAKERESS (IRE)   4 b.f. Brief Truce (USA) 126 – Deer Emily (Alzao (USA)   **–**
117) [1998 NR 1999 5g 6f⁴ 6f 8m 8.9m 8g 6.1d a6g a8g a11g Dec 13] sturdy filly:
modest maiden: easily best effort in 1999 when fourth in handicap at Brighton in
July: may prove best up to 1m: acts on firm ground: blinkered twice. *John Berry*

QUAKERS FIELD   6 br.h. Anshan 119 – Nosey 96 (Nebbiolo 125) [1998 NR   **–**
1999 10s 12s Nov 6] smart in 1996: first runs of any sort since 1997 when never
dangerous in handicaps in 1999: stays 1½m: acts on good to firm and good to soft
going: useful hurdler, won in November. *G. L. Moore*

QUALITAIR SILVER   5 gr.m. Absalom 128 – Irish Limerick 89 (Try My Best   **–**
(USA) 130) [1998 –: a6g a8.5g⁶ 1999 a6g a7g Feb 12] poor maiden at best: stays 7f:
raced almost exclusively on fibresand: tried blinkered/visored. *Miss L. C. Siddall*

QUALITAIR SURVIVOR   4 gr.g. Terimon 124 – Comtec Princess 73 (Gulf   **40**
Pearl 117) [1998 NR 1999 10m⁴ 10g 8.9m 14.1g 11d a8g⁴ a11g⁵ Nov 30] half-brother
to several winners, including fairly useful performer up to 2m Qualitair Aviator (by
Valiyar): dam 1m to 1¼m winner: modest form in bumpers: poor maiden at best on
Flat: trained by T. Etherington on debut: bred to stay at least 1½m. *J. Hetherton*

QUEDEX   3 b.c. Deploy 131 – Alwal (Pharly (FR) 130) [1998 58+: 5.1d⁴ 6.1g 7g⁴   **75**
8m 7d 8s⁴ 1999 8m² 9.9d* 11.7g* 12g⁴ Jul 2] neat colt: has a round action: fair
performer: won at Goodwood (handicap) and Bath (minor event) in June: good
fourth of 6 in handicap at Salisbury final start: stays 1½m: acts on good to firm and
good to soft going (probably on soft): held up: carried head awkwardly and wandered
final 2-y-o start. *E. L. James*

QUEEN FOR A DAY   2 b.f. (Mar 14) Emperor Jones (USA) 119 – Could Have   **63**
Been (Nomination 125) [1999 6g 6g³ 7f⁴ 8s² 7s 7g a8g Dec 29] 9,600F, 7,500Y:
second foal: half-sister to 3-y-o Nordic Star: dam unraced half-sister to Prix du
Jockey Club winner Polytain: modest maiden: well beaten last 3 starts, leaving
C. Wall before final one: stays 1m: acts on soft ground. *H. J. Collingridge*

QUEEN OF THE KEYS   3 b.f. Royal Academy (USA) 130 – Piano Belle   **–**
(USA) (Fappiano (USA)) [1998 –: 6g 7g 1999 7g 8g a10g a7g a8g³ a8.5g⁶ Dec 27]   **a47**

small, strong filly: poor maiden: probably stays 8.5f: acts on equitrack, probably on fibresand. *S. Dow*

QUEEN OF THE MAY (IRE) 2 b.f. (Feb 15) Nicolotte 118 – Varnish 85 (Final Straw 127) [1999 5.3f* 5m 7g⁴ 6m⁴ 6s 5.3m⁴ 6s⁴ a6g* a6g³ Nov 24] 7,500Y: small filly: fourth foal: half-sister to fairly useful 1996 2-y-o 5f winner Cherry Blossom (by Primo Dominie): dam 2-y-o 7f winner: fair performer: won maiden at Brighton in May and nursery at Lingfield in November: likely to prove best at 5f/6f: acts on equitrack, firm and soft going: races freely: consistent. *M. R. Channon* **72**

QUEEN OF TIDES (IRE) 4 b.f. Soviet Star (USA) 128 – Tidesong (Top Ville 129) [1998 62d, a–: 11.8m² 11.8d 10.8d 9m² 10g⁶ 11.9g 14.1v a10g a13g 1999 a13g⁶ a16f 9m a10g Jul 31] leggy, sparely-made filly: modest maiden at best: little form in 1999. *S. Dow* **–**

QUEEN OMAH (IRE) 3 b.f. Dolphin Street (FR) 125 – Quilting 80 (Mummy's Pet 125) [1998 65: 7g⁴ 6s⁴ 7v 1999 9m 9.7m⁴ 9m⁴ 10g⁶ 10g 10d Oct 11] leggy, unfurnished filly: modest maiden: well beaten in sellers last 2 starts: stays 1¼m: acts on soft and good to firm going: sold 2,700 gns, sent to Germany. *R. Hannon* **58 d**

QUEENS BENCH (IRE) 2 ch.f. (Feb 2) Wolfhound (USA) 126 – Zafaaf 105 (Kris 135) [1999 5s⁴ 6d² 6m³ 6m³ 5g* 7g* Aug 30] lengthy, rather unfurnished filly: second foal: half-sister to 3-y-o Ashover Amber: dam 7f/1m winner: fairly useful performer: won maiden at Beverley and nursery at Epsom in August, making virtually all on latter occasion: stays 7f: acts on good to firm and good to soft ground: has run well when sweating: consistent. *B. Hanbury* **86 +**

QUEEN'S HAT 4 b.f. Cadeaux Genereux 131 – Greenlet (IRE) 79 (Green Desert (USA) 127) [1998 72d: 9g 6d³ 7m⁴ a8g⁶ a7g⁴ a10g⁵ 1999 a8g 7.7s 9m 8g 9m a10g Nov 26] robust filly: fair maiden at best: no form in 1999. *J. J. Bridger* **–**

QUEENSMEAD 2 b.f. (Apr 18) Rudimentary (USA) 118 – Shernborne (Kalaglow 132) [1999 5m⁵ 5m 6d⁴ 5d⁶ 5g² 5d⁶ 5g² 5.2d⁵ Oct 27] 4,000Y: sturdy filly: fifth foal: half-sister to 3-y-o L'Agneau Noir: dam, lightly raced in France, from family of Blakeney and Morston: modest maiden: may prove best at 5f: yet to race on extremes of going: below form in blinkers final start. *R. Hannon* **61**

QUEEN'S PAGEANT 5 ch.m. Risk Me (FR) 127 – Mistral's Dancer (Shareef Dancer (USA) 135) [1998 80, a88: a8.5g² a9.4g 8.1s 6d 7.3g 7g⁵ 7g* 8s 8d 1999 8d* 8.1d 8g³ 8.1s 7d 7d 7d 7s⁵ a9.4g Nov 27] big mare: fair handicapper: won at Thirsk in April: off nearly 4 months before next outing: below form after third start: effective at 7f (given good test) to 8.5f: acts on heavy ground and fibresand: blinkered once at 4 yrs: often held up: inconsistent. *J. L. Spearing* **80**

QUEEN'S SIGNET 3 ch.f. King's Signet (USA) 110 – Axe Valley 89 (Royben 125) [1998 NR 1999 7m 7.7d a6g a6g Dec 6] 7,000Y: long-backed filly: half-sister to several winners, including fairly useful sprinter For The Present (by Then Again) and 5-y-o Ginger Rogers: dam sprinter: no form. *D. W. P. Arbuthnot* **–**

QUEEN TITANIA (IRE) 3 b.f. Elbio 125 – Astania (GER) (Arratos (FR)) [1998 –p: 6f⁶ 8g 7g 1999 a7g 8m 11.6s 10s Sep 29] angular, workmanlike filly: little form: blinkered final start: sold 5,000 gns. *A. J. McNae* **–**

QUEEN ZENOBIA 3 b.f. Danehill (USA) 126 – Persia (IRE) (Persian Bold 123) [1998 70p: 6m⁶ 7m⁶ 1999 8.3m* 8.2m 7d⁵ 6.8m Jul 10] quite attractive, unfurnished filly: fair performer: won maiden at Windsor in April: bit below that form in handicaps after: stays 1m: yet to race on extremes of going: sold 39,000 gns in December. *J. H. M. Gosden* **78**

QUESTABELLE 3 ch.f. Rainbow Quest (USA) 134 – Bella Colora 119 (Bellypha 130) [1998 NR 1999 10v⁵ 10.3s⁴ Nov 5] 470,000Y: half-sister to several winners, including high-class 1¼m performer Stagecraft (by Sadler's Wells) and smart 1m winner Hyabella (by Shirley Heights): dam 6f (at 2 yrs) to 1¼m winner, half-sister to Irish Oaks winner Colorspin, the dam of Opera House and Kayf Tara: signs of only a little ability in maiden (favourite) then minor event. *L. M. Cumani* **–**

QUESTAN 7 b.g. Rainbow Quest (USA) 134 – Vallee Dansante (USA) (Lyphard (USA) 132) [1998 64, a–: a10g⁶ a14g⁵ a12g⁴ 8f* 7.5g² a8g 8d⁵ 8.2m⁵ 8.3m 7m 8g **–**

1999 a8g Mar 8] modest handicapper: stays 1m: acts on firm and good to soft going, little form on all-weather: inconsistent. *B. Smart*

QUESTUARY (IRE)   3 b.f. Rainbow Quest (USA) 134 – Pelf (USA) 79 (Al Nasr (FR) 126) [1998 63: 7g 8g a8g* 1999 a8g⁴ a10g Jan 26] angular filly: has a round action: modest performer: stays 1m, probably not 1¼m: raced only on good going and equitrack. *M. R. Channon*   **58**

QUEZON CITY   5 ch.g. Keen 116 – Calachuchi 74 (Martinmas 128) [1998 –: 12m a12g a11g⁵ 1999 a16f* a16g⁴ a16g* 16.1d² a16.2g² a14.8g⁶ Apr 24] tall gelding: fair handicapper: won at Southwell in February and March: better at 2m than shorter: acts on fibresand, good to firm and good to soft going: best held up. *Miss J. A. Camacho*   **69**

QUIBBLING   5 b.m. Salse (USA) 128 – Great Exception 84 (Grundy 137) [1998 42: a11g⁵ 11.6g a12g⁴ 11.6g⁴ 12.5m⁴ 15.8d³ 1999 a12g⁵ a11g a12g⁶ a16g⁵ 14.1m⁶ Aug 23] rather leggy mare: bad maiden nowadays: stays 2m: acts on soft ground and fibresand: blinkered once at 3 yrs, visored nowadays. *K. C. Comerford*   **26**

QUICK SILVER   3 b.f. Anshan 119 – Tabeeba (Diesis 133) [1998 –: a7g 1999 a10g 10m Jun 18] no sign of ability: sold 500 gns from R. Hannon after reappearance. *R. E. Barr*   **–**

QUICKSILVER GIRL   3 b.f. Danehill (USA) 126 – Crime of Passion 115 (Dragonara Palace (USA) 115) [1998 NR 1999 7.1d⁴ 7g⁵ Aug 12] big filly: half-sister to several winners, including sprinter Master of Passion (by Primo Dominie), useful at 2 yrs: dam sprinting 2-y-o who didn't train on: modest form in maidens at Haydock and Salisbury 10 weeks apart: may prove best up to 7f. *J. W. Hills*   **52**

QUICKSTEP   3 ch.f. Salse (USA) 128 – Short And Sharp 88 (Sharpen Up 127) [1998 85: 7m⁶ 7g³ 7g 1999 9g 10m 14.6f 8g⁶ 8.1g⁵ 11.5m⁴ 10.2m³ 10m 8m 8d Oct 11] leggy, close-coupled filly: good mover: fair maiden: effective at 1m to 11.5f: acts on good to firm going: sold 5,000 gns. *R. Hannon*   **70**

QUICKTIME   2 ch.f. (Apr 15) Timeless Times (USA) 99 – Sally Weld 65 (Weldnaas (USA) 112) [1999 6m 6m 6v⁴ a7g Dec 8] 4,500Y: first foal: dam 6f (at 2 yrs) and 7f winner: best effort when fourth of 19 in claimer at Lingfield. *B. Smart*   **48**

QUIDS INN   2 b.rg. (Mar 27) Timeless Times (USA) 99 – Waltz On Air 86 (Doc Marten 84) [1999 5d⁶ 5m⁵ 5g 6g 8d 8d Nov 1] leggy gelding: fifth reported foal: dam 6f winner: modest form second start: poor form otherwise, in blinkers final start. *T. D. Easterby*   **64 d**

QUIET AFFAIR   2 b.f. (Feb 28) Distant Relative 128 – Princess Eboli 108 (Brigadier Gerard 144) [1999 6g* 6m⁴ 7m* 8.1m³ Aug 21] half-sister to several winners, including fairly useful 8.5f winner Affair To Remember (by Persian Bold) and ungenuine 11.5f winner Ebolito (by Welsh Pageant): dam won Cheshire Oaks and Lancashire Oaks: fairly useful performer: won maiden at Lingfield in June and nursery at Newmarket in July: should have stayed at least 1m: dead. *J. L. Dunlop*   **87**

QUIET ARCH (IRE)   6 b.g. Archway (IRE) 115 – My Natalie 64 (Rheingold 137) [1998 67, a79: a12s² a10g² a12g* a12g² a12g* a13g³ a12g* 11.9g a12g³ 11.8g⁴ 10g* 11.9g⁶ a12g⁴ a12g 1999 a13g⁴ a16f Jan 19] good-topped gelding: has a round action: fair performer: below form both 6-y-o starts: stays 1½m: acts on good to firm and good to soft going, better form on equitrack than fibresand: visored once at 4 yrs: held up. *J. G. M. O'Shea*   **–**

QUIET DIGNITY   3 b.f. Unfuwain (USA) 131 – Docklands 91 (On Your Mark 125) [1998 NR 1999 8g⁶ 8m 10m⁵ 10f⁵ 8m⁵ 8s⁵ Sep 29] workmanlike filly: has a quick action: half-sister to 3 winners, notably useful 1½m winner Port Helene (by Troy): dam, best up to 1m, half-sister to 1000 Guineas winner Night Off: fair maiden: stays 1¼m: acts on firm going: free-going sort: sold 19,000 gns. *B. W. Hills*   **71**

QUIET MILLFIT (USA)   3 b.g. Quiet American (USA) – Millfit (USA) 62 (Blushing Groom (FR) 131) [1998 –: 6g 7d 1999 6g 7m³ 10f⁴ 7.9d⁵ 9f* 10m 9g⁶ 8.9m⁴ 9.1d⁵ 10d³ Oct 11] lengthy gelding: has a round action: fairly useful performer: won maiden at Lingfield in June: below form last 3 starts: stays 1¼m: best form on good going or firmer: has worn tongue strap: usually races up with pace: sold 7,500 gns. *B. Hanbury*   **83**

QUIET MISSION   8 ch.g. Hubbly Bubbly (USA) – Woodlands Arabella VII – (Damsire Unregistered) [1998 NR 1999 a6g Dec 1] leggy gelding: of little account. *B. P. J. Baugh*

QUIET VENTURE   5 b.g. Rainbow Quest (USA) 134 – Jameelaty (USA) 96   **87** (Nureyev (USA) 131) [1998 87, a94: a12g 8.3d 9.1d 8m* 7.1g* 7m* 7g a6g* a7g 1999 7m 7f² 6m³ 8m⁶ 7.1m⁶ 7g⁵ Oct 2] big, lengthy gelding: fairly useful performer: best effort in 1999 when second of 4 in handicap at Newcastle (after 3-month break) in August: effective at 6f to 1m: acts on fibresand and firm going: visored penultimate start: tongue tied: races prominently. *I. Semple*

QUILT   3 b.f. Terimon 124 – Quaranta 83 (Hotfoot 126) [1998 53: a8g 10s² 8v – 1999 10g 11.9f a12g Jul 24] leggy filly: modest form second 2-y-o start: behind in handicaps and minor event in 1999: stays 1¼m. *Sir Mark Prescott*

QUINTRELL DOWNS   4 b.g. Efisio 120 – Nineteenth of May 86 (Homing 130)   **48 +** [1998 52: 9v 8.5m 8g⁶ 8.5s 7d 9d 1999 9d⁵ a11g* 12m⁴ 11.8g a12g* a12g* a12g³   **a85** a12g² Dec 17] 8,700F: fifth foal: half-brother to a 1m winner in Italy by Sharpo: dam 1m winner: fairly useful handicapper on all-weather, poor form on turf: trained by M. Brassil in Ireland at 3 yrs: won at Southwell (twice) and Wolverhampton in May/June: successful over hurdles in July for T. George before returning to Flat with best efforts last 2 starts: should prove best at 1¼m/1½m: acts on fibresand, good to soft and good to firm going: blinkered (well held) once at 3 yrs. *R. M. H. Cowell*

QUITE HAPPY (IRE)   4 b.f. Statoblest 120 – Four-Legged Friend 101 (Aragon   **78 d** 118) [1998 73: 6d 5m³ 5m* 5f 5g³ 5g 1999 5d 5m² 5f 6m 6g 5m 5.1m 5m³ 5g* 5m⁴ 5m 5d Sep 15] sturdy filly: fair performer: below best after second start, including when winning claimer at Catterick in August: best at 5f: acts on firm ground: tried visored/blinkered: has been bandaged behind. *M. H. Tompkins*

QUITE INCREDIBLE (USA)   3 ch.f. Anjiz (USA) 104 – Jacqueline Alice   **72** (USA) (Riverman (USA) 131) [1998 NR 1999 7g* 7m 7.1d Aug 12] $18,000F: smallish filly: fractured tibia at 2 yrs: first foal: dam raced in USA: won maiden at Kempton in April: behind subsequently in listed race and (after 3-month break) handicap: stays 7f: sold 4,500 gns, sent to Greece. *E. A. L. Dunlop*

QUITO (IRE)   2 b.c. (Apr 10) Machiavellian (USA) 123 – Qirmazi (USA) 113   **84 p** (Riverman (USA) 131) [1999 8.2d³ Oct 21] fifth foal: closely related to fairly useful 1m winner Quinwood (by Woodman) and half-brother to 3 winners, including useful 5f to (in Dubai) 7f winner Saheeel (by Dayjur): dam, French 6f (at 2 yrs) and 9f winner, third in Prix Saint-Alary: weak in market, third of 11 to Western Summer in maiden at Nottingham, one-paced after making smooth headway to dispute lead 2f out: not sure to be suited by much further than 1m: will improve. *M. P. Tregoning*

QUIZ MASTER   4 ch.g. Superpower 113 – Ask Away (Midyan (USA) 124)   **40 §** [1998 61d: 6.1g 6d² 5.9d⁶ 6d⁵ 5m 6g 7s 7.1g 6m a8.5g⁶ 1999 7g 9d 11.1s⁶ 5g⁶ 6f⁵ 8f Jul 17] workmanlike gelding: poor maiden: seems to stay 11f: acts on soft ground, good to firm and fibresand: effective blinkered/visored (tried only once at 4 yrs): difficult ride and not to be trusted: joined R. Ford. *E. Weymes*

R

RAAQI   3 b.c. Nashwan (USA) 135 – Mehtaaf (USA) 121 (Nureyev (USA) 131)   **92** [1998 84p: 7g⁵ 8g⁵ 1999 8g² 8.2m³ 10f² 12.3m* 11.9f⁶ Jul 11] strong, lengthy colt: good mover with a long stride: first foal: dam 6f (at 2 yrs) to 1m (Irish 1,000 Guineas) winner, closely related to Elnadim and granddaughter of outstanding broodmare Fall Aspen: fairly useful performer: best effort when winning maiden at Ripon in June by 7 lengths: saddle reportedly slipped in handicap final start: stays 1½m well: raced only on good ground or firmer: has worn crossed noseband. *J. L. Dunlop*

RAASED   7 b.g. Unfuwain (USA) 131 – Sajjaya (USA) 97 (Blushing Groom (FR)   **52** 131) [1998 46: a8g⁴ a8g* a8g 8m 8g² 8.2m 8d³ 8.9g 8.3s² 10d a7g 1999 9g 9.2g² 9m⁵ 8g 8g⁴ 6.9m* 8.2g* 8m 8m 8d Oct 20] tall gelding: modest handicapper: won at Carlisle (ladies race) in June and Nottingham in August: below form last 3 starts: effective at 7f to 1¼m: acts on fibresand, firm and soft going: has worn visor (including for both 7-y-o wins)/blinkers: usually tongue tied. *F. Watson*

RABAH 4 b.c. Nashwan (USA) 135 – The Perfect Life (IRE) 106 (Try My Best – (USA) 130) [1998 118: 10d⁶ 9.9m* 11.9m* 12g* 11.9f² 12m² 1999 12m 12m 11.6m⁵ Aug 28] smallish, strong, well-made colt: usually looks in fine shape: good mover: smart at 3 yrs, winner of Gordon Stakes at Goodwood: well below form in 1999: stays 1½m: acts on firm ground, seemingly not on softer than good: usually front runner: sent to USA. *J. L. Dunlop*

RACE LEADER (USA) 2 b.c. (Apr 24) Gone West (USA) – Dubian 120 **111** (High Line 125) [1999 7m* 7m³ 7d² Sep 18] rather lightly-made colt: ninth foal: half-brother to several winners, including 3-y-o Golden Snake and Sayyedati (by Shadeed): dam, 7f (at 2 yrs) to 1½m winner, third in Oaks and Irish Oaks: won maiden at Newmarket in July: third of 5 to King's Best in listed race at York following month: clearly best effort when 2 lengths second of 5 to Giant's Causeway in Prix de la Salamandre at Longchamp, keeping on: should stay 1m: free to post on debut, and in early stages at York. *B. W. Hills*

RACINGAGAINSTTIME (IRE) 2 b.f. (Feb 15) Night Shift (USA) – Mysistra – (FR) (Machiavellian (USA) 123) [1999 5g 7v⁶ Oct 11] IR 3,800Y: first foal: dam, French 11f winner, out of half-sister to Irish St Leger winner Dark Lomond: well held in maidens in Scotland: sold 1,600 gns in November. *M. Johnston*

RACING TELEGRAPH 9 b.g. Claude Monet (USA) 121 – Near Enough – (English Prince 129) [1998 –: a8s⁶ 1999 a8g a11f Feb 8] tall gelding: has had wind operation: no form since 1997: tried blinkered/visored. *M. Brittain*

RADAR (IRE) 4 b.g. Petardia 113 – Soignee (Night Shift (USA)) [1998 89: 9v⁴ **89** 8g 9s* 9.9g⁶ 8m⁵ 8.5m⁵ 8g⁵ 8d² 8s 1999 8m³ 8m⁶ 10m a8.5g 10m⁵ 10g² 8d Oct 14] close-coupled gelding: fairly useful handicapper: best effort when head second of 16 at Redcar in October: probably best at 1¼m nowadays: acts on soft and good to firm going: visored (well held on all-weather debut) once: sweating final start: sometimes carries head high, and is held up: sold 20,000 gns, joined C. Mann. *M. A. Jarvis*

RADA'S DAUGHTER 3 br.f. Robellino (USA) 127 – Drama School 72 (Young **101** Generation 129) [1998 68p: 7m⁴ 8.2s⁵ 1999 10m 10.2s* 11.6g* 12s³ 12g⁵ 12m* 11.9g⁵ 11.9f⁶ 12d* 12s Oct 10] leggy, lengthy filly: useful performer: had an excellent season, winning handicaps at Bath in April, Windsor in May, Ascot in July and Newmarket (beat Canta Ke Brave by 1¼ lengths in rated stakes) in September: tailed off in listed race at Longchamp (reportedly in season) final start: will stay 1¾m: acts on soft and good to firm ground: has run lazily and probably needs strong handling. *I. A. Balding*

Strutt & Parker Maiden Stakes, Newmarket—
a very pleasing debut by Race Leader, who is ridden clear to beat Ekraar

RADICAL JACK 2 b.g. (Apr 1) Presidium 124 – Luckifosome 45 (Smackover –
107) [1999 5m 5g 5f 5d 7.1g Aug 18] 3,000Y: tall, close-coupled gelding: third foal:
half-brother to 3-y-o Allrighthen: dam, 5f winner, ran only at 2 yrs: well held in
maidens: blinkered (very slowly away) third start: refused to leave stalls on debut.
Denys Smith

RAED 6 b.g. Nashwan (USA) 135 – Awayed (USA) 108 (Sir Ivor 135) [1998 66 §
74, a81: a11g* a11g* a12g² a9.4g 9.9m² 9.2g² 9.2m² 9.9g² 1999 a11g 11d⁶ a11g²
10d² 10s* 10.1g 10m² 10d 10s 10.1d a16g a14.8g⁶ a12g Dec 21] sturdy gelding:
fair performer: won apprentice handicap at Windsor (first run since leaving Mrs
A. Swinbank) in August: below form after: effective at 9f to 1½m: acts on fibresand,
firm and soft going: tends to find little. *J. Pearce*

RAELEEN 3 b.f. Jupiter Island 126 – Ballintava (Better By Far 91) [1998 –: 7s – §
1999 7.7m 8.1m 9s Oct 8] no form: best left alone. *G. M. McCourt*

RAFTERS MUSIC (IRE) 4 b.g. Thatching 131 – Princess Dixieland (USA) 64
(Dixieland Band (USA)) [1998 –: 7g 8g 8d 1999 8f 7m 8.3m 7f⁵ 6m* 6.1m⁴ 6g⁶ 6m
5s⁴ 6g⁶ 6g Oct 19] good-bodied gelding: modest performer: won claimer at Epsom in
July: effective at 5f/6f: acts on firm and soft going: tried blinkered, including last 3
starts (tended to hang final one): often tongue tied: sold 4,500 gns. *Mrs A. J. Perrett*

RAFTING (IRE) 4 b.f. Darshaan 133 – White Water (FR) (Pharly (FR) 130) [1998 87
82: 11.1d² 12g* 14m⁴ 14g⁴ 12d³ 11.9f 1999 14.1s 12m* 12s⁶ 12m⁴ 12g⁴ 12m² 12m⁴
12m⁶ 13.3m⁶ 12.3m* 12f* 12m 13.1v⁴ 12s⁵ Oct 25] sturdy, useful-looking filly:
fairly useful performer: won handicaps at Musselburgh in April and at Chester and
Thirsk in July: several creditable efforts otherwise, including when fifth to Peach Out
of Reach in listed race at Leopardstown: effective at 1½m/1¾m: acts on firm and soft
ground: visored (ran poorly) final 3-y-o start: tends to carry head awkwardly: often
races up with pace. *M. Johnston*

RAGLAN ACCOLADE 2 b.f. (May 7) New Reputation 93 – Ophiuchus (Nader –
62) [1999 6g 6m 7.1m Sep 9] first reported foal: dam (non-thoroughbred) unraced:
little show in maidens. *Derrick Morris*

RAGTIME COWGIRL 6 ch.m. Aragon 118 – Echo Chamber 89 (Music Boy –
124) [1998 –: 6v 5d 9.2s⁶ 7.1s 11.1d 9.2d 9.2s 1999 9.2v 12.1m 5s May 14] of no
account nowadays. *D. A. Nolan*

RAHAYEB 3 b.f. Arazi (USA) 135 – Bashayer (USA) 103 (Mr Prospector (USA)) 76
[1998 79: 7m³ 7m⁵ 8g² 1999 8d⁵ 10g⁶ 12v⁴ 12f² 12.3d* 12s⁴ Sep 22] unfurnished,
shallow-girthed filly: tended not to impress in appearance: fair performer: won
maiden at Chester in August: ran creditably most other starts: stayed 1½m: acted on
any going: blinkered last 3 outings: hung right first and third starts: stud. *J. L. Dunlop*

RAHCAK (IRE) 3 b.f. Generous (IRE) 139 – Homage (Ajdal (USA) 130) [1998 80
76p: 8s³ 1999 11.7f⁵ 10.4g² Oct 6] fairly useful form in maidens: should stay 1½m:
seems to act on firm and soft going. *J. H. M. Gosden*

RAHEEN (USA) 6 b.h. Danzig (USA) – Belle de Jour (USA) (Speak John) 103
[1998 96: 8.1g³ 8d 9.3g⁴ 7.9f⁵ 8m 10m⁶ 9g 8g 7s 8s* 1999 a8.5g 8d⁴ 8m⁶ 10.4s* a–
9.8m³ 8m⁴ 10g 10.4f 8m⁶ 8d 10s⁵ 10d³ 12v⁵ 8d⁴ a10g Nov 16] rather leggy horse:
useful handicapper: won rated stakes at York in May by length from Achilles: ran
well several other starts, including when fourth to Showboat in Hunt Cup at Royal
Ascot on sixth and fifth to She's Our Mare in Cambridgeshire at Newmarket on
eleventh: effective at 1m to 1¼m: stiff task when well held at 1½m: acts on firm and
soft ground, no form on all-weather since 1996: often blinkered/visored earlier in
career: held up. *R. A. Fahey*

RAILROADER 2 ch.g. (Apr 15) Piccolo 121 – Poyle Amber 55 (Sharrood (USA) 75
124) [1999 6d 6d³ 6m 5s³ 6d⁴ 6v Oct 23] 14,000F, 15,500Y: sturdy gelding: has a
quick action: third foal: half-brother to 3-y-o Sue's Reprimand and 4-y-o Wilton:
dam, sprint maiden, half-sister to smart sprinter Poyle George: fair maiden: best
efforts when in frame in nurseries at Sandown and Newmarket in October: didn't
stay final start: acts on soft ground. *G. B. Balding*

RAINBOW FRONTIER (IRE) 5 b.g. Law Society (USA) 130 – Tatchers Mate –
(Thatching 131) [1998 93: 20d² 16.1v² 1999 20m Jun 15] leggy, angular gelding:
fairly useful handicapper: mid-field in Ascot Stakes only 5-y-o start: stays 2½m:
raced mainly on good ground and softer: smart hurdler. *M. C. Pipe*

RAINBOW HIGH   4 b.c. Rainbow Quest (USA) 134 – Imaginary (IRE) 94   **117**
(Dancing Brave (USA) 140) [1998 101: 12.3s* 12d² 13.9f⁵ 11.9g⁵ 12g² 12m⁴
1999 16m* 18.7m* 16.4g² 20m 15.9m³ 18m² 16.1s* Oct 2]

An above-average renewal of the Tote Chester Cup witnessed performances from the first and third that would have been good enough to win
many a pattern race for stayers. Third-placed Invermark was that most unusual
sight, a Group 1 winner in a handicap, carrying top weight on the strength of his
win in the Prix du Cadran the previous October. His next target was the Gold
Cup at Royal Ascot, and Rainbow High came firmly on course for that race too
when he gave favourite backers minimum cause for concern in the Chester
Cup. When stepping up from a mile and a half to two miles at Newbury on his
reappearance the previous month, Rainbow High had hacked up by nine
lengths. His triumph off a mark 10 lb higher against fifteen rivals at Chester
was not so easy, but, despite receiving a bump a mile from home, Rainbow
High again treated jockey Michael Hills to an armchair ride. Rainbow High's
only problem, albeit minor, was keeping a straight line once hitting the front
just inside the final furlong as he ran on strongly to beat Generosity by two
lengths, with Invermark a length and three quarters back in third.

When Rainbow High and Invermark met again in the Gold Cup, they
put up contrasting performances. The Chester Cup winner finished around
twenty lengths behind the Chester Cup third, but that was the only cause for
complaint with Rainbow High's five appearances in pattern events. In the
Lonsdale Stakes at York in August he was a respectable third to Celeric, beaten
four lengths and never threatening to get much closer, but in the Henry II Stakes
at Sandown in May, the Doncaster Cup in September and the Deloitte & Touche
Jockey Club Cup at Newmarket in October, Rainbow High was involved in
very tight finishes. With Arctic Owl pipping him on the line at Sandown and
Far Cry pulling out just enough at Doncaster, however, Rainbow High had to
wait until his final start of the year for his first pattern victory. The Jockey Club
Cup has been a happy hunting ground for the Hills team in the 'nineties, with
Further Flight winning five consecutive runnings, from 1991 to 1995. The field
for this race has only twice (in 1985 and 1987) made it into double figures in
the last thirty years, but it was nonetheless far more typical of the century's
opening decades when only three turned up for the 1999 renewal. Hopefully,
the 2000 running will attract more runners as it will be run two weeks later,
thus avoiding a clash with Longchamp's Prix du Cadran, though that will bring
it closer to the Prix Royal-Oak. Rainbow High was the 11/4 second favourite
in the Jockey Club Cup, bidding to reverse previous form with Arctic Owl

*Tote Chester Cup (Handicap)—Rainbow High confirms his improvement,
beating the course record; Generosity is second*

Mr K. Abdulla's "Rainbow High"

(11/8-on) and Celeric (100/30). The confidence behind Arctic Owl was partly due to his proven effectiveness on soft ground. Celeric's comparative ineffectiveness under such conditions was well known, while the last time Rainbow High had encountered soft going was when he won a maiden at Ripon in June 1998, his only success, incidentally, before the latest season. With none of the three runners accustomed to setting out in front, tactics also proved of major importance. Celeric was the first to crack when things finally hotted up, and finished tailed off, but Rainbow High and Arctic Owl gave spectators their money's worth with a battle up the hill in which Rainbow High, who had made the running, held on by a neck.

		Blushing Groom (ch 1974)	Red God
	Rainbow Quest (USA) (b 1981)		Runaway Bride
		I Will Follow (b 1975)	Herbager
Rainbow High (b.c. 1995)			Where You Lead
		Dancing Brave (b 1983)	Lyphard
	Imaginary (IRE) (b 1990)		Navajo Princess
		Bold Fantasy (b 1974)	Bold Lad
			Ribot's Fantasy

Rainbow High's Jockey Club Cup provided a belated high for his sire Rainbow Quest—his first British pattern success of the season. For the dam Imaginary, Rainbow High is a first pattern winner at the first attempt, and her second living foal the 1999 two-year-old Imaginative (by Last Tycoon) won over nine furlongs for Maurice Zilber in France. Imaginary herself won just a maiden, over a mile and a quarter at Newmarket, and had only four races, but tales of more substantial achievement abound in her family. Rainbow High's fourth dam Fantan II was the dam of Ragusa and also figures on the bottom line in the pedigrees of such as Sarah Siddons, Princess Pati, Seymour Hicks, Crofter and Leggera. Third dam Ribot's Fantasy produced only two winners, but they were the smart 1981 US two-year-old Chilling Thought and Bold Fantasy, winner of two seven-furlong races and runner-up in the Irish One Thousand Guineas and the Cork And Orrery. Bold Fantasy had eight winners in addition to Imaginary, including smart 1985 two-year-old Kingscote. Fifth in the Fred Darling on her only start at three, Kingscote went on to foal Rainbow Corner, who showed very smart form as a two-year-old in 1991, playing second fiddle only to Arazi, but failed by a short neck to take advantage of Arazi's absence in the the Poule d'Essai des Poulains. His close relation Rainbow High is a very different type who should stay two and a half miles. A rather lightly-made, quite attractive colt, he has not yet raced on heavy going but acts on any other. Usually held up, Rainbow High kept his form really well as a four-year-old and should figure prominently in pattern races in 2000. *B. W. Hills*

RAINBOW MELODY (IRE) 2 ch.f. (Mar 17) Rainbows For Life (CAN) – Lingering Melody (IRE) 59 (Nordico (USA)) [1999 7g² 6m⁵ 8.5f⁵ 7f² 7d* 6m 8d⁴ 7d⁵ Sep 28] rather lightly-made, close-coupled filly: first foal: dam, Irish maiden who stayed 1m, half-sister to very smart miler Alflora: fairly useful performer: trained first 4 starts by K. Prendergast in Ireland: won maiden at Chester in August: best effort after when fifth of 19 in nursery at Newmarket final start: stays 1m: acts on firm and good to soft ground. *E. J. Alston*   **81**

RAINBOW RAIN (USA) 5 b.g. Capote (USA) – Grana (USA) (Miswaki (USA) 124) [1998 64, a78: 8s 8d 13g 8d 7f 8g⁶ 10d 10.1g 7m 8g 7m³ 6g² 6f⁵ 6m⁶ a7g* 7d 7m 7g a7g⁵ a7g⁴ a10g a10g² 1999 a10g³ a8g⁶ a8g 5m 6f² 7f 6g 6g⁴ 6m⁵ 7f* 6m 6f* 6g⁴ 6m a7g² a7g³ a7g a8.5g⁵ Dec 27] well-made gelding: has a long stride: fair performer: won handicap and minor event at Brighton in July: has form at up to 1¼m, but races mainly at 6f/7f: acts on firm ground, good to soft and all-weather: edgy sort, and has been early to post: none too consistent. *S. Dow*   **75 a71**

RAINBOW RAVER (IRE) 3 ch.f. Rainbows For Life (CAN) – Foolish Passion (USA) (Secretariat (USA)) [1998 57: 5s⁵ 6.1m 5m 7.5m⁵ 7.9g⁶ 8d 8d 1999 12g 7m 8.2m⁶ 9.9m³ a12g 12f² 10f² 12g⁶ 12.1f⁴ 16.1s⁵ Sep 29] sturdy filly: modest maiden handicapper: left C. Smith after third start: runner-up at Thirsk and Redcar in summer: should prove best at 1¼m/1½m: acts on firm going, below form only start on fibresand: visored (below form) eighth start. *J. L. Eyre*   **57 a–**

RAINBOW REALM (IRE) 2 ch.f. (Apr 15) Rainbows For Life (CAN) – Sakanda (IRE) (Vayrann 133) [1999 7g⁵ 7.6g a6f 7s Oct 25] smallish, close-coupled filly: third foal: half-sister to Irish 3-y-o 13f winner McCracken (by Scenic): dam 1¼m winner and winning hurdler: appeared to show fair form when fifth of 11 in maiden at Leicester on debut: well held after: hard to assess. *S. C. Williams*   **?**

RAINBOW ROMEO (IRE) 3 br.c. Rainbows For Life (CAN) – Splendid Chance (Random Shot 116) [1998 59, a48: 6g⁵ 7m 5.7d 6m⁵ 7s a6g a7g⁵ 1999 a5g a8g⁶ 7v* 8m⁵ 8.3m² 8.1m 8f 8m 7m 7d 7g Oct 19] rather sparely-made colt: fair performer: won maiden at Folkestone in April: mostly well held after: stays 1m: acts on good to firm and heavy ground: has had tongue tied: tends to wander and look less than keen: sold 5,000 gns, sent to Norway. *Jamie Poulton*   **65 a–**

RAINBOW SPIRIT (IRE) 2 b.g. (Mar 24) Rainbows For Life (CAN) – Merrie Moment (IRE) (Taufan (USA) 119) [1999 7.9m Sep 1] IR 4,800F, 8,500Y: big, lengthy gelding: has scope: fifth foal: half-brother to 4-y-o Sassy: dam unraced half-sister to Stewards' Cup winner Autumn Sunset: green and in need of race when always in rear in maiden at York. *A. P. Jarvis*   **–**

RAINBOW VIEW (IRE) 3 b.g. Rainbows For Life (CAN) – L'Anno d'Oro (Habitat 134) [1998 NR 1999 7m 6f* 6g 8m 10.9s 7m 8.5g⁵ 8.5s³ Sep 21] 5,500Y: good-bodied gelding: poor mover: fourth foal: half-brother to useful 1995 2-y-o

6f winner Lacryma Christi (by Green Desert): dam lightly-raced sister to Habibti: modest performer: won 6-runner maiden at Redcar in May: best effort in handicap at Beverley penultimate start: should stay beyond 1m: acts on firm going, probably on soft. *Mrs G. S. Rees*

RAINBOW WAYS 4 b.c. Rainbow Quest (USA) 134 – Siwaayib 97 (Green **106** Desert (USA) 127) [1998 100: 10.3d³ 12m⁴ 12f² 12f* 11.9m* 12m* 1999 12g² 14g 16.1m⁴ 13.9f* 13.9g⁶ 14.6m⁵ Sep 10] quite good-topped colt: has a quick, fluent action: useful handicapper: good fourth to Far Cry in Northumberland Plate at Newcastle before winning listed rated stakes at York (by neck from Banbury) in July: also ran creditably last 2 starts, sixth to Vicious Circle in Ebor at York on penultimate: best at 1¾m/2m nowadays: acts on firm going, probably on good to soft: effective blinkered or not. *B. W. Hills*

RAINDROP 3 b.f. Primo Dominie 121 – Thundercloud 70 (Electric 126) [1998 **59** NR 1999 a8.5g 8m 7.1s⁴ 8d Oct 11] 42,000Y: leggy filly: unimpressive mover: fifth foal: sister to fair 1994 2-y-o 5f and 6f winner Made In Heaven and half-sister to useful Irish 9f/1¼m winner Moving On Up (by Salse) and useful 6f (at 2 yrs) to 9f winner Al Shafa (by Midyan): dam, third at 1½m from 2 starts, closely related to Julio Mariner and Juliette Marny: modest maiden: may prove best up to 7f: acts on soft going. *H. Morrison*

RAIN IN SPAIN 3 b.c. Unfuwain (USA) 131 – Maria Isabella (FR) (Young **101 +** Generation 129) [1998 NR 1999 12g* 11.6g* 12m³ Jul 16] 17,000Y, 40,000Y: rangy, unfurnished colt: brother to useful Italian middle-distance performer Streisand and half-brother to 3 winners, including fairly useful 1¼m and 1½m winner Top Royal (by High Top): dam French maiden: won maiden at Kempton in June and minor event at Windsor (impressively by 5 lengths from Veronica Franco) in July: far from discredited when 7½ lengths third of 6 to Adnaan in steadily-run minor event at Newmarket: will be suited by further than 1½m: already useful, and may still do better. *J. Noseda*

RAIN RAIN GO AWAY (USA) 3 ch.g. Miswaki (USA) 124 – Stormagain **50** (USA) 102 (Storm Cat (USA)) [1998 69p: 7s³ 1999 6g 8.5m 8s a8g a7g⁴ a7g³ a8.5g³ Dec 27] strong gelding: fair form only 2-y-o start: modest at best in 1999, leaving E. Dunlop after reappearance: stays 8.5f: acts on all-weather: headstrong, and has bolted to post. *D. J. S. Cosgrove*

RAINSHACK 4 ch.c. Rainbow Quest (USA) 134 – Suntrap (USA) 112 (Roberto **84** (USA) 131) [1998 NR 1999 10g³ 10.1m² 10d May 21] stocky colt: fifth foal: brother to very smart middle-distance stayers Raintrap and Sunshack and useful 1998 French 2-y-o 1m winner Summer Breeze: dam 2-y-o 6f/7f winner who stayed 1m: unraced for A. Fabre, reportedly due to leg problems: fairly useful form in maidens when placed at Leicester and Newcastle: reportedly lost action final start: will stay 1½m: has been bandaged in front. *B. W. Hills*

RAINSTORM 4 b.c. Rainbow Quest (USA) 134 – Katsina (USA) 98 (Cox's **–** Ridge (USA)) [1998 –, a83: 10.4g⁶ 10g 8.2s⁵ a8g² a7g* a7g⁴ 1999 a8g⁴ a7f⁵ 7g 8m **a79** 7.1m 8g Sep 20] stocky colt: fair performer: stays 1m: acts on equitrack, little form on turf: tried visored. *E. J. O'Neill*

RAINWORTH LADY 2 b.f. (Apr 2) Governor General 116 – Monongelia 98 **–** (Welsh Pageant 132) [1999 a7g 6.1m⁴ 7m a7g Nov 12] half-sister to 3 winners, including fairly useful Italian winner up to 1½m Dancer Shareef (by Shareef Dancer) and 13f and 2m winner Hattaafeh (by Mtoto): dam 1m to 1¼m winner: well beaten all starts: has hung left. *M. J. Polglase*

RAISE A GRAND (IRE) 3 ch.c. Grand Lodge (USA) 125 – Atyaaf (USA) 48 **111** (Irish River (FR) 131) [1998 114p: 6m³ 6.1d* 7m* 7d² 7.1m* 7g⁵ 1999 8g 8m⁵ 7m² 8f 8f³ 7.1d³ Aug 11] close-coupled colt: has a fluent, rounded action: smart performer: best efforts in 1999 in St James's Palace Stakes at Royal Ascot (fifth to Sendawar) on second start, Criterion Stakes at Newmarket (1½ lengths second to Diktat) on third and listed race at Goodwood (third of 4 to Slip Stream) on penultimate: barely stays 1m: acts on firm and good to soft ground: usually held up: sent to USA. *J. W. Payne*

RAISE A PRINCE (FR) 6 b.g. Machiavellian (USA) 123 – Enfant d'Amour **108** (USA) (Lyphard (USA) 132) [1998 108: 12s* 12g² 14m⁴ 13.9s⁵ 11.9m⁴ 12g 13.1s* 12s* 11.9s³ 12d⁴ 1999 16.2s² 14.1s* 13.3d³ 15.5d 16.1m 14.6m 12s³ 17.3g 16.1d³ 14.6s³ Nov 5] rather leggy gelding: unimpressive mover: useful performer: won minor event at Nottingham in April: ran creditably otherwise when placed, including when third in Ritz Club Handicap at Ascot (behind Vicious Circle) on seventh start and listed rated stakes at Newmarket (behind Eilean Shona) on penultimate: effective at 1½m (given a test) to 2m: has form on good to firm ground and equitrack, goes very well on good or softer: visored (won) once at 4 yrs: usually tongue tied: usually held up. *S. P. C. Woods*

RAJI 3 b.c. Green Desert (USA) 127 – Cancan Madame (USA) (Mr Prospector **84** (USA)) [1998 NR 1999 8m⁴ 8.3g 10v² Oct 23] smallish, good-bodied colt: eighth foal: closely related to 7f winner Tarhhib (by Danzig) and half-brother to 2 winners in France, notably high-class middle-distance performer Dancehall (by Assert): dam 9f winner in USA: fairly useful form in maidens when in frame, neck second to Pearl Crown at Newbury final start, shaping as though conditions stretched stamina: sent to UAE. *A. C. Stewart*

RAJMATA (IRE) 3 b.f. Prince Sabo 123 – Heart of India (IRE) (Try My Best **66** (USA) 130) [1998 66p: 5d⁵ 5g⁶ 5m⁵ 5s 5.2s a5g² a5g² 1999 a6g a5g² 5g⁵ a5g 6m² 5d⁵ 6g 6.1m Aug 28] leggy, lengthy filly: fair handicapper on all-weather, modest on turf: left Sir Mark Prescott after reappearance: lost form last 3 starts: effective at 5f/6f: acts on fibresand and good to firm going: visored after reappearance: has been early to post: has looked difficult ride. *Mrs N. Macauley*

RAJWHAN (USA) 3 br.g. Lear Fan (USA) 130 – Samra (USA) 62 (Solford (USA) **83** 127) [1998 83: 6m 7g⁴ 1999 7g³ 8d⁵ 8m 8.5d 10m 8.5s⁴ 9.7m* 8m⁵ 9.7d³ 10.1m Sep 4] strong, heavy-topped gelding: fairly useful handicapper: won at Folkestone in July: better at 1¼m than shorter: acts on good to firm and good to soft going: blinkered once: inconsistent: sent to UAE. *C. E. Brittain*

RAKEEB (USA) 4 ch.g. Irish River (FR) 131 – Ice House 89 (Northfields (USA)) **78 d** [1998 92: 8g 10.5d³ 10d³ 10s* 11.9g* 12g 1999 12m 12g 12m 12.3d 12.3g⁶

11.9s 13.9d 14.1s⁴ Nov 1] big, strong gelding: fairly useful at 3 yrs: deteriorated in 1999: stays 1½m: acts on soft going: blinkered penultimate start: tends to hang. *M. W. Easterby*

RAKIS (IRE)   9 b. or br.g. Alzao (USA) 117 – Bristle 96 (Thatch (USA) 136)   **61** [1998 84: a7g 8m 7.1d² 6.9d⁴ 8.1m⁵ 7.1g⁴ 7.6f 7.1g 7.5m³ 8.2v a8g⁴ 1999 a7g **a73** a8g⁵ a8g 8m 7.1d 7.5m 6.9m 8d Oct 20] good-topped gelding: fair handicapper on all-weather, modest on turf nowadays: effective at 7f/1m: acts on firm ground, soft and all-weather: effective blinkered, not tried for long time: has worn tongue strap: usually held up. *Mrs L. Stubbs*

RAMBLING BEAR   6 ch.h. Sharrood (USA) 124 – Supreme Rose 95 (Frimley   **115** Park 109) [1998 112: 6m* 6g⁶ 6s⁶ 5d 6m 5g 6m² 5f⁵ 6g 5d⁶ 5.2g 1999 5m* 5m⁴ 5m⁵ 5f 5g 6m 5d³ 6d⁵ 6s Nov 6] leggy, workmanlike horse: smart performer: won Palace House Stakes at Newmarket in May by 1½ lengths from Red Prairie: best efforts after in listed races at Kempton (fourth to Proud Native) and Newmarket (1¾ lengths third to Sakha then 2 lengths fifth of 20 to Gaelic Storm): brought down in Nunthorpe at York fifth outing: barely stays 6f: unraced on heavy going, acts on any other: below form in blinkers fourth start: often taken alone to post: free-going sort, patiently ridden. *M. Blanshard*

RAMBOLD   8 b.m. Rambo Dancer (CAN) 107 – Boldie 81 (Bold Lad (IRE) 133)   **53 d** [1998 65§: 6.1m 6.1m* 6m 6f 6g* 6m⁴ 6g 6g 6.1s 6s 1999 6.1f 6.1g² 6m 6m 6f 6.1m⁶ 6g 5m 6d a7g Nov 24] angular mare: modest handicapper: well below par in 1999: stays 6f: acts on firm and good to soft going: sometimes sweats: possibly needs to dominate: unreliable. *N. E. Berry*

Mrs Michael Hill's "Rambling Bear"

Minstrel Stakes, the Curragh—third career win in Ireland for Ramooz, who is clear of Risque Lady

RAMBO NINE 2 b.g. (Apr 9) Rambo Dancer (CAN) 107 – Asmarina 50 (Ascendant 96) [1999 5g a6g⁵ 8.5g⁶ a8.5g Sep 8] 6,000 2-y-o: first foal: dam, 9.4f winner, half-sister to 6-y-o First Maite: well held in maidens. *S. R. Bowring* –

RAMBO WALTZER 7 b.g. Rambo Dancer (CAN) 107 – Vindictive Lady (USA) (Foolish Pleasure (USA)) [1998 77, a96: a8s² a9.4g³ a8g² a9.4g* a9.4g² a7g⁶ a8.5g³ 7d² a8g* 7v 10.3g 8.9g 9.1s⁵ a7g³ 8.2s⁵ a8g* 1999 a8g³ a8g² 7g* 8g 7g* 8m a7g* 8g³ 8.9d 7m 9.1d 10.4d 8d a8g* a7g⁴ a8g* Dec 17] smallish, sturdy gelding: carries plenty of condition: prone to lameness: fair performer: successful in handicaps at Catterick and Thirsk and 2 claimers and a seller at Southwell, all between March and December: effective at 7f to 9.4f: acts on good to firm ground, good to soft and fibresand: visored once as 3-y-o: usually bandaged in front: good mount for inexperienced rider: none too consistent. *D. Nicholls* **77**
a73

RAMIN (IRE) 2 b.c. (Mar 28) Night Shift (USA) – Shady Leaf (IRE) 56 (Glint of Gold 128) [1999 8s Sep 22] IR 16,000Y, 32,000 2-y-o: closely related to fairly useful Irish 2m winner Academy House (by Sadler's Wells): dam maiden who stayed 1½m: broke leg in maiden at Goodwood: dead. *S. Dow* –

RAMOOZ (USA) 6 b.h. Rambo Dancer (CAN) 107 – My Shafy 92 (Rousillon (USA) 133) [1998 115: 7.1d² 7.9g* 8.5m⁴ 7g² 8d⁴ 7m³ 7.3m 8.5d³ 7d* 8d 8s³ 6d⁴ 1999 8d³ 7d⁵ 7.1g² 7d⁵ 8.5g⁶ 8g* 8m* 7f⁴ 8m⁴ 8.9f⁴ 7s⁶ Sep 18] rangy horse: takes the eye: smart performer: won listed race at Goodwood (by ½ length from Peculiarity) in June and Minstrel Stakes at the Curragh (by 3½ lengths from Risque Lady) in July, both in small fields: ran creditably otherwise only in rated stakes at Haydock (second to Late Night Out) on third start and listed race at York (didn't travel with usual fluency) on penultimate one: best at 7f/1m: acts on firm and soft going: blinkered twice (including final start): usually bandaged: has a turn of foot and best held up: sold only 11,500 gns in December. *B. Hanbury* **115**

RAMPART 2 b.c. (Mar 13) Kris 135 – Balliasta (USA) (Lyphard (USA) 132) [1999 7d 7s³ Nov 5] rangy colt: has scope: third living foal: half-brother to 3-y-o Kilting: dam twice-raced half-sister to Sanglamore out of Ribblesdale winner Ballinderry: better effort in maidens at Doncaster when third of 20 to Hopeful Light, settling better and keeping on: should stay 1¼m: should do better. *B. W. Hills* **78 p**

RAMRUMA (USA)   3 ch.f. Diesis 133 – Princess of Man 104 (Green God   **123**
128) [1998 78: 8.1g³ 8.2s² 1999 12g* 11.5g* 12d* 12m* 11.9g* 14.6m²
Sep 11]

    Anyone glancing at the race-finish photographs of the Vodafone Oaks
and the Kildangan Stud Irish Oaks reproduced with this essay might run away
with the idea that the winner Ramruma is a really top-notch middle-distance
filly. Ramruma had the opposition at Epsom strung out like a field of three-mile
steeplechasers—there was nearly sixty lengths between first and last—and she
landed the odds by seven lengths at the Curragh. But looks can be deceptive.
The Irish Oaks, in particular, lacked strength in depth for a classic and when
Ramruma finally came up against high-class colts—in the St Leger—she was
just found wanting.

    Ramruma and the Oaks runner-up Noushkey became the first bene-
ficiaries in the St Leger of the decision to extend the fillies' allowance from 3 lb
to 5 lb in all three-year-old pattern races open to both sexes. It was already 5 lb
in the Two Thousand Guineas and Derby but the St Leger was, surprisingly,
only brought into line in the latest season. High And Low, winner of the
Cheshire Oaks and runner-up in the Yorkshire Oaks, went down by half a length
to Nedawi in the 1998 St Leger and with the additional allowance would
arguably have won. Ramruma won five races off the reel as a three-year-old
and started odds on for the latest St Leger. She had gone on to add the Yorkshire
Oaks to her tally after her Oaks/Irish Oaks double, becoming only the fourth
filly, after Fair Salinia, Diminuendo and User Friendly, to land that three-timer.
Diminuendo and User Friendly both contested the St Leger and both started
favourite, Diminuendo at odds on. The outstandingly tough and genuine User
Friendly, who like Ramruma lined up at Doncaster with five successive
victories under her belt, put the six colts who took her on firmly in their place;
Diminuendo, the only filly in a field of six, went down by a length to Minster
Son after a hard-fought struggle. Ramruma's performance at Doncaster was
similar to that of Diminuendo in that the nine-runner race developed into a
three-way contest from early in the straight, Ramruma battling it out with the
Godolphin pair Mutafaweq and Adair before the finish came down to a match.
Mutafaweq and Ramruma couldn't have responded more gamely to strong
pressure, Ramruma keeping on dourly after Mutafaweq edged ahead entering
the final furlong and giving best only in the last hundred yards, Pat Eddery
easing her towards the finish where she was two lengths behind the all-out
Mutafaweq, with two lengths back to Adair and a further seven to fourth-placed
All The Way; Noushkey came sixth, beaten seventeen lengths. Ramruma's
rider reportedly felt that the filly didn't get the trip at Doncaster but, considering the way the field finished strung out behind the first three, it is not a view to

*Vodafone Oaks, Epsom—a real test and Ramruma gallops her rivals into the ground;
Noushkey, in second, is clear of Zahrat Dubai (right) and Sunday Picnic*

Kildangan Stud Irish Oaks, the Curragh—more of the same from Ramruma as, from left to right, Sister Bella, Sunspangled and Mother of Pearl battle it out for the minor places

which we subscribe. In all probability, Ramruma, whose appearance beforehand betrayed no signs of her season catching up with her, ran very close to her best in the St Leger. Ramruma will remain in training as a four-year-old, when she will presumably be seen mostly at a mile and a half. The precedents are not encouraging—User Friendly's four-year-old campaign, for example, was a disappointment—especially as Ramruma will have to shoulder a Group 1 penalty in lesser pattern races. Grand performer that she is, Ramruma will have plenty on to beat top-class colts in races such as the Coronation Cup and the King George VI and Queen Elizabeth Stakes, which have both been mentioned as targets.

Whatever the future holds, Ramruma's connections can take enormous credit from her splendid three-year-old campaign. Placed in maidens at Sandown and Nottingham at two, she soon left that form well behind, winning the opening maiden at the Newmarket Craven meeting by three and a half lengths from All The Way, sent on some way from home. Ramruma was well on top at the end of her next pattern race too, the Victor Chandler Oaks Trial at Lingfield, though she needed some firm backhanders after pricking her ears and idling once in front. Credit-A-Plenty (whose stable had a leading Oaks candidate in Claxon) and Noushkey filled the places behind Ramruma at Lingfield, where the early pace wasn't strong. Judged on that running, Ramruma looked sure to show herself a good-class filly given a truer test of stamina, and so it proved at Epsom. The Lingfield Oaks Trial had been used as a stepping-stone to Epsom most recently by User Friendly and by Lady Carla, one of two earlier Cecil-trained Oaks winners in the 'nineties, and Ramruma was made ante-post favourite for the Oaks after Lingfield. She was supplanted three days later, though, by the most impressive Musidora Stakes winner Zahrat Dubai, seeking to become the third Oaks winner for Godolphin in the 'nineties. Zahrat Dubai kept her place at the head of the market, at 9/4 with Ramruma at 3/1, despite adverse rumours about her well-being in the days leading up to the Oaks. The Lupe Stakes winner Claxon (third favourite at 11/2), French challenger Sunday Picnic, Irish challengers Sunspangled and Crystal Downs and Godolphin's second string Kilting all hailed from stables that had also won the Oaks in the 'nineties. Sunday Picnic (Prix Cleopatre), Sunspangled (winner of the Fillies' Mile at Ascot as a two-year-old) and Zahrat Dubai were the only pattern winners among the ten runners. The going on Oaks day was good to soft and, with Claxon setting the tempo, the race turned into a thorough test. Ramruma was handy from the start, though she tended to race lazily early on and had to be niggled at. Kieren Fallon, who rode Ramruma in her first four races as a three-year-old, began to roust her along in earnest soon after Tattenham Corner and Ramruma took the lead early in the home straight, galloping on relentlessly and gradually drawing away to win by three lengths and five from Noushkey and Zahrat Dubai, with Sunday Picnic, Claxon and Sunspangled next.

Ramruma was the sixth Oaks winner saddled by Henry Cecil, whose success the following day with Oath in the Derby gave him a twentieth-century record of twenty-two domestic classics. Cecil's first two Oaks winners, Oh So Sharp (who went on to land the fillies' triple crown) and Diminuendo, won in devastating fashion at Epsom, Oh So Sharp by six lengths and Diminuendo by four (though the photo-finish strip showed it to be five). They are the only two of Cecil's Oaks winners that we have rated superior to Ramruma. Cecil's third winner Snow Bride was eventually awarded the race on the disqualification of Aliysa, who failed a dope test, though, because of protracted legal argument, the winner of the race remained technically undecided until after the end of the following season. Next came Lady Carla, whose nine-length winning margin in the Oaks was exceeded in the twentieth century only by Sun Princess (twelve lengths in 1983) and Noblesse and Jet Ski Lady (ten lengths in 1963 and 1991 respectively). Reams of Verse became Cecil's fifth Oaks winner in 1997. Ramruma followed in the footsteps of Diminuendo and Lady Carla by being sent next for the Irish Oaks at the Curragh. Diminuendo got up in the final strides to force a dead-heat with the Oaks d'Italia winner Melodist (in the same ownership) at the Curragh whereas Lady Carla managed only fourth. Ramruma started odds on, as had Diminuendo and Lady Carla, and, unlike her predecessors, she made as straightforward a job of following up her Epsom victory as the form-book indicated she would. Ramruma won by seven lengths from Sunspangled, stretching clear from three furlongs out and eased a little in the closing stages once the race was in safe-keeping. Ramruma became the ninth to complete the Oaks/Irish Oaks double, following Masaka, Altesse Royale, Juliette Marny, Fair Salinia, Blue Wind, Unite, Diminuendo and User Friendly.

Ramruma's victory in the Aston Upthorpe Yorkshire Oaks at the York August meeting was gained against the biggest field for the race since it was

Aston Upthorpe Yorkshire Oaks, York—
Ramruma becomes the first since User Friendly in 1992 to complete the Oaks Group 1 treble;
she has a bit more in hand over Ela Athena (left) than the bare result implies;
Silver Rhapsody and Zahrat Dubai (right) come next

opened to four-year-olds and upwards in 1991 (Fair Salinia and Diminuendo won it in the days when it was for three-year-olds only). Re-opposed by Noushkey and Zahrat Dubai, winners respectively of the Lancashire Oaks and the Nassau Stakes on their only outings since Epsom, Ramruma was again odds on. There were two older fillies in the eleven-strong line-up, Ramruma's smart stable-companion Silver Rhapsody and the previous year's fourth Lady In Waiting, runner-up to Zahrat Dubai in the Nassau on her latest outing. Ramruma kept her unbeaten record for the season, going on after a couple of furlongs and responding every time a challenger threatened in the straight. The 33/1-shot Ela Athena came out best of the opposition on the day, Ramruma seeming to have more in hand than her winning margin of a length and a quarter (Pat Eddery, riding her for the first time, reported that 'she was doing nothing in front but waiting'); Silver Rhapsody was a further two lengths behind, with Zahrat Dubai half a length away in fourth and Noushkey a disappointing eighth.

Plans for Ramruma after York were at first unclear. Although she had been ante-post favourite for the St Leger from the time the entries were published in July—and had shortened from around 7/1 to around 4/1 after winning the Irish Oaks—her owner had always maintained that she might run in the Arc. Corals removed Ramruma from their advertised St Leger betting at first after York saying they would lay her at 6/4 for Doncaster to 'those who insist'; she was in the Arc betting at around 8/1. Ramruma's connections took a week to decide that she would go for the St Leger rather than the Arc. Diminuendo and User Friendly had gone on to contest both races after completing their Oaks treble, Diminuendo managing only tenth at Longchamp to Tony Bin, running as if she had not recovered from her exertions at Doncaster, and User Friendly covering herself in glory with a close second to Subotica after her St Leger win. It was never likely that Ramruma would run at both Doncaster and Longchamp, her owner making it clear after the Yorkshire Oaks that, because he was keeping her in training, he felt she should have only one more outing as a three-year-old. Staying seemed to be Ramruma's game and the decision to go for the St Leger looked the correct one at the time. With hindsight, though, the strong pace set by El Condor Pasa in the Arc would have suited Ramruma down to the ground. Also with hindsight, however, the best connections could really have hoped for was third or fourth at Longchamp; the first two Montjeu and El Condor Pasa finished six lengths clear of the rest. The first filly home in the Arc was the previous year's runner-up, the four-year-old Leggera, who came fourth; Ramruma's form—which entitled her to be regarded as the best three-year-old filly in Europe—was some way in advance of the best form shown by Leggera in the latest season.

Ramruma (USA) (ch.f. 1996)	Diesis (ch 1980)	Sharpen Up (ch 1969)	Atan Rocchetta
		Doubly Sure (b 1971)	Reliance II Soft Angels
	Princess of Man (ch 1975)	Green God (ch 1968)	Red God Thetis II
		White Legs (ch 1957)	Preciptic Caspian Sea

The angular, sparely-made Ramruma is by Diminuendo's sire Diesis, who stands in Kentucky. Diesis was a top-class two-year-old, successful in the Middle Park and the Dewhurst, but, like his brother the champion miler Kris, was never raced beyond a mile. Kris, incidentally, has also sired two Oaks winners, Oh So Sharp and Unite. Ramruma and Diminuendo are not the only notable offspring of Diesis to shine at middle distances; Halling and Elmaamul made their mark at a mile and a quarter, while, somewhat surprisingly, Keen Hunter is the only specialist sprinter among the dozen or so Group 1 winners by Diesis. Ramruma's dam the Musidora Stakes winner Princess of Man has bred ten winners from eleven runners in all on both sides of the Atlantic. Her three visits to Diesis have yielded the pick of her produce, with Lingfield Oaks

H.R.H. Prince Fahd Salman's "Ramruma"

Trial winner Ausherra and the useful middle-distance stayer Royal Scimitar preceding Ramruma. Ausherra, Royal Scimitar and Ramruma are the only offspring of Princess of Man to have won beyond a mile and a quarter, and the only ones successful at listed level or above. Ausherra is the dam of the smart stayer Yorkshire. Princess of Man, who cost 5,800 guineas as a yearling, was much improved at three and made all to win the Musidora; she stayed a mile and a quarter well and connections were clearly confident that she would get a good deal further, giving her a crack at the Park Hill Stakes on her final start. Princess of Man was a product of a mating between a sprinter, Green God, and a middle-distance maiden, White Legs. She was a half-sister to six other winners who met with success over differing distances, ranging from the smart sprinter Long Johns, by the very fast Whistling Wind, to the smart stayer Danton, by the stoutly-bred Gulf Pearl. Ramruma's year-younger half-sister Zarara (by Manila), her dam's thirteenth foal, was in training at Warren Place in the latest season but did not reach the racecourse. Ramruma, who, as we've stated, sometimes races lazily, both in behind and once in front, is a relentless galloper in full cry and needs a strongly-run race to bring the best out of her over a mile and a half. She acts on good to firm and good to soft going. *H. R. A. Cecil*

RAMSEY HOPE   6 b.h. Timeless Times (USA) 99 – Marfen (Lochnager 132) [1998 –§, a70d: a5g⁴ a5g⁵ a6g⁴ a6g² a5g⁶ a5g a5g⁵ a6g⁴ a6g 5g 6m⁵ 6g⁶ a6g 6m a6g⁵ a7g a8.5g a6g⁴ a7g⁵ a6g⁶ 1999 a6g a7g a6g³ a6g⁴ a6g Mar 1] compact horse: just a poor handicapper in 1999: best at 5f/6f: acts on firm going and all-weather: has been blinkered, effective visored or not: sometimes hangs left: unreliable. *D. W. Chapman*   — §   a48 §

RANAAN (IRE)   3 ch.c. Brief Truce (USA) 126 – Ma Minti 62 (Mummy's Pet 125) [1998 77: 5v² 6d⁶ a5g* a6g 1999 6g² 6g⁵ 6.1m³ 6d⁶ 5g 6m⁴ 8m 7m Dec 22] sturdy, lengthy colt: fair handicapper: generally ran creditably in 1999 before leaving   **79**

M. Channon before penultimate start: will prove best at 5f/6f: acts on heavy going and fibresand, probably on good to firm: carries head high. *D. J. Selvaratnam, UAE*

RANDOM KINDNESS 6 b.g. Alzao (USA) 117 – Lady Tippins (USA) 83 (Star de Naskra (USA)) [1998 79, a91: a16.2g⁶ 12.5s a12g* 11.9g² 12m³ 11.9f* 14m² 12m² 12m 12m⁴ 12m 16.2d 18g a12g* a12g³ a12g⁴ 1999 a12g 12m⁶ 14.4m² 14m⁴ 14m⁴ 11.9g² 12m 12m 11.8m Aug 22] sturdy, angular gelding: fair handicapper on turf, fairly useful on all-weather: well held last 3 starts: effective at 1½m to 2m: acts on firm going and all-weather, below form on softer than good: joined R. Rowe. *R. Ingram* **79 a85**

RANDOM TASK (IRE) 2 b.c. (Feb 18) Tirol 127 – Minami (IRE) (Caerleon (USA) 132) [1999 a6g* 6d⁴ Aug 14] IR 34,000Y: good-topped, workmanlike colt: has scope: third foal: brother to fairly useful Irish 1998 2-y-o 5f winner African Skimmer: dam unraced: won maiden at Wolverhampton in May: well-held last of 4 in minor event at Ripon only subsequent start. *D. Shaw* **79**

RANEEN NASHWAN 3 b.g. Nashwan (USA) 135 – Raneen Alwatar 80 (Sadler's Wells (USA) 132) [1998 80p: 7.1d⁶ 8s⁵ 8s⁴ 8s* 1999 10.5s⁴ 9.9m May 2] lengthy, angular gelding: fairly useful performer: much better effort in 1999 when 12 lengths fourth to Nowhere To Exit in rated stakes at Haydock: will stay 1½m: raced only on good to soft/soft going before final start. *M. R. Channon* **80**

RANELLE (USA) 3 ch.f. Rahy (USA) 115 – Aspenelle (CAN) (Vice Regent (CAN)) [1998 NR 1999 7.1m 7.7m² 10m* 12.4m⁵ Sep 19] $300,000Y: first foal: dam won up to 9f in Canada and second in Canadian Oaks: fair performer: won maiden at Leicester in September: ran poorly in minor event at Newbury final start: stays 1¼m: raced only on good to firm going: visored after debut: sent to USA. *J. Noseda* **77**

RANGATIRA (IRE) 4 ch.g. Royal Academy (USA) 130 – Chief's Quest (USA) (Chief's Crown (USA)) [1998 66: 8d⁴ 8v³ 9.2s⁵ 1999 8.3m 8.3m 9.3d³ 11g⁶ 8g⁶ 8s⁶ a9.8g a9g⁵ a9.8g⁴ Nov 21] fair form in maidens: sold from M. Johnston 4,500 gns after second start in 1999: in frame in maidens for new stable: stays 9.8f: acts on heavy going: blinkered last 2 starts. *B. Hellier, Germany* **?**

RANGER SLOANE 7 ch.g. Gunner B 126 – Lucky Amy (Lucky Wednesday 124) [1998 43, a–: 16.2m 16m⁴ 1999 16.1d⁵ 14.1d 15.8s Oct 5] leggy gelding: poor handicapper: stays 2m: acts on good to firm ground, good to soft and fibresand: tried blinkered at 3 yrs. *G. Fierro* **36 a–**

RAPIDASH 2 gr.g. (Mar 20) Petong 126 – Join The Clan 95 (Clantime 101) [1999 5.1g 6.1g Sep 25] 8,500Y: first foal: dam multiple 5f/6f winner: well held in maidens: tried visored. *Mrs N. Macauley* **–**

RAPID DEPLOYMENT 2 b.c. (Apr 27) Deploy 131 – City Times (IRE) 65 (Last Tycoon 131) [1999 7m⁵ 7g 6.8m³ 6d Oct 15] 10,000Y: rangy colt: second foal: dam, maiden best up to 7.6f, half-sister to smart middle-distance performer Water Boatman: modest form in maidens/sales race: should stay at least 1m: has scope to do better at 3 yrs. *J. G. Smyth-Osbourne* **63 p**

RAPID LINER 6 b.g. Skyliner 117 – Stellaris (Star Appeal 133) [1998 NR 1999 14.1m 17.2m 10m Sep 13] bad maiden. *R. J. Baker* **–**

RAPID RELIANCE 4 b.f. Emarati (USA) 74 – Chiquitita 44 (Reliance II 137) [1998 50: 5s⁴ 6m 6.9m 10m⁴ 12m 10.2d 7g 1999 12.3m 7.1m Aug 5] little form since 2 yrs. *H. J. Manners* **–**

RAPIER 5 b.g. Sharpo 132 – Sahara Breeze 85 (Ela-Mana-Mou 132) [1998 93: 8d 8.1g³ 8.9s* 10.4f 10.1g 8.3d⁵ 1999 10.4s 10d* 10.5d Jun 3] leggy gelding: has a fluent, quick action: fairly useful handicapper: won at Ayr in May: broke blood vessel final start: stays 1¼m: has some form on firm ground, best efforts on good to soft/soft. *M. D. Hammond* **87**

RA RA RASPUTIN 4 b.g. Petong 126 – Ra Ra Girl 77 (Shack (USA) 118) [1998 59, a–: 7d 6g 5.1g⁵ 7g³ 8.2g 7m⁴ 7.6g 7.1g 8m 8d⁴ 8d 8v² 1999 8d 8d 10d 10m 8m⁶ a8.5g a8.5g² 8.2s a6g a7g³ a7g a8g Dec 13] workmanlike gelding: has a quick action: fair handicapper on all-weather, poor on turf: stays 1m: acts on good to firm ground, heavy and fibresand: sometimes blinkered: sometimes slowly away: none too reliable. *B. A. McMahon* **46 § a67 §**

RARE GENIUS (USA) 3 ch.g. Beau Genius (CAN) – Aunt Nola (USA) (Olden **72** Times) [1998 NR 1999 10g 10m⁵ 10.1g⁶ 10m³ 12m 11.9s⁵ 14.1g² Oct 15] $50,000Y: half-brother to several winners in USA, including a 2-y-o 8.5f minor stakes winner by Farma Way: dam winning sprinter: fair maiden: good efforts in handicaps last 2 starts: stays 1¾m, at least when conditions aren't testing: acts on soft and good to firm ground. *P. W. Harris*

RARE TALENT 5 b.g. Mtoto 134 – Bold As Love (Lomond (USA) 128) [1998 **67** 67: 8g³ 8.2d 10.3g* 10.1m⁴ 10.3g* 9.9m³ 10m 10.4g 10m 10g 1999 8d⁵ 10m 10f⁶ 10.3m 8m⁶ 10m 9.9m* 10m² 11.6m* 10m² 9.9g⁶ 10.1g² 12g 10.4f 10f Oct 20] leggy, angular gelding: unimpressive mover: fair handicapper: won at Beverley (ladies race) in July and Windsor (amateurs) in August: ran creditably otherwise only when runner-up: effective at 1¼m/1½m: acts on soft and good to firm going: visored (ran poorly) fourth start. *S. Gollings*

RASM 2 b.c. (Feb 1) Darshaan 133 – Northshiel 85 (Northfields (USA)) [1999 7s³ **86 p** Oct 8] 100,000Y: half-brother to several winners, including useful middle-distance stayer Asterita (by Rainbow Quest): dam, 2-y-o 7f winner, closely related to very smart miler Waajib: weak in market, plenty of promise when third of 18 to Frontier in maiden at Lingfield, keeping on well under hands and heels after slow start: will probably stay 1¼m: sure to improve. *A. C. Stewart*

RASPBERRY SAUCE 5 b.m. Niniski (USA) 125 – Sobranie 86 (High Top 131) **62** [1998 65: a13g² a10g³ a8g⁶ a12g² a10g* 11.7s* a10g⁴ a10g 12m³ 10.2d⁶ a10g⁴ a12g a10g a8g* a8f⁵ 1999 a7g a8g 11.7s⁴ a10g* a10g⁵ 10g a8g⁶ Jun 22] modest handicapper: best effort in 1999 when winning at Lingfield in May: effective at 1m to 1½m: acts on equitrack and soft ground, probably on good to firm: none too consistent: reportedly in foal to Fleetwood. *C. A. Cyzer*

RAS SHAIKH (USA) 3 b.f. Sheikh Albadou 128 – Aneesati 85 (Kris 135) [1998 **105** 89p: 6g³ 6m* 6g³ 1999 7m⁶ 10d² 10.1m 8d² 8d² 8d⁵ Oct 30] tall, rather unfurnished filly: useful performer: best efforts in 1999 when second in listed races at Newbury (1¼ lengths behind Fairy Godmother) and Newmarket (beaten ½ length by Indian Lodge) on second and fourth starts: may prove best around 1m: yet to race on extremes of going: tends to race freely, and is held up: hung first 2 starts, found little penultimate one: sent to USA. *B. W. Hills*

RATATUIA 3 b.f. Zafonic (USA) 130 – Refilee (IRE) (Sadler's Wells (USA) 132) **91** [1998 76: 7.5m 8.2s² 8s³ 1999 8.3m* 9g³ 8m* 9f⁵ Oct 9] angular filly: fairly useful performer: won maiden at Windsor in April and handicap at Thirsk in June, latter final outing for L. Cumani: off 4 months before fifth in allowance race at Belmont, only start in USA: will stay 1¼m: acts on soft and good to firm going. *M. Hennig, USA*

RATHCLOGHEENDANCER (IRE) 2 ch.g. (Mar 19) Colonel Collins (USA) **40** 122 – Fleeting Quart (Rainbow Quest (USA) 134) [1999 5d⁴ 5g a5g 6m 5g⁴ 8.3f⁶ 8d Sep 16] IR 4,200F, 6,000Y: rather leggy, quite attractive gelding: first foal: dam unraced half-sister to Oaks second Bourbon Girl: poor maiden: form only when fourth in 5f sellers: ran too freely when blinkered fourth outing. *K. A. Ryan*

RATHER DIZZY 4 b.g. Sizzling Melody 117 – Rather Dark (Nomination 125) **–** [1998 NR 1999 7m 8s Sep 29] first reported foal: dam unraced: tailed-off last in maidens at Lingfield and Brighton. *P. Butler*

RATHLEA 5 b.h. Risk Me (FR) 127 – Star of Jupiter (Jupiter Island 126) [1998 **–** NR 1999 a7f 8.3g 8.2s Nov 1] third foal: dam unraced half-sister to useful sprinter Boozy: no show in maidens/minor event. *R. Hollinshead*

RATIFIED 2 b.g. (Apr 4) Not In Doubt (USA) 101 – Festival of Magic (USA) 73 **–** (Clever Trick (USA)) [1999 7m 7.1m 8.1g a8g Nov 24] half-brother to fairly useful Irish 5f winner Afrostar (by Soviet Lad), also 5f winner in USA at 2 yrs, and a winner in Italy by Alzao: dam 1m winner: well beaten in maidens. *H. Candy*

RATTLE 6 b.g. Mazilier (USA) 107 – Snake Song 94 (Mansingh (USA) 120) **–** [1998 NR 1999 16g Nov 3] small gelding: no longer of any account. *D. A. Nolan*

RAVENSWOOD (IRE) 2 b.c. (May 15) Warning 136 – Green Lucia 116 (Green **79** Dancer (USA) 132) [1999 7m⁶ 7f* 7.7d 8d Oct 15] IR 15,000Y: half-brother to several winners, including Irish 3-y-o 1¼m winner Serena (by Rainbow Quest) and smart 1½m performer Luchiroverte (by Slip Anchor): dam, placed in Irish and Yorkshire Oaks, half-sister to Old Vic: fair form when winning maiden at Brighton in August: ran badly in nurseries after, tongue tied and unimpressive to post final start: should stay at least 1m: acts on firm ground. *M. C. Pipe*

RAVENWOOD LADY   3 ch.f. Unfuwain (USA) 131 – Sylvatica 99 (Thatching 131) [1998 56p: 7d 1999 12v³ 12.5f³ 10m 10.5m Jul 2] modest maiden: third at Folkestone and Duindigt (handicap), Holland: stays 12.5f: probably acts on any going. *S. C. Williams*   **61**

RAVINE   2 ch.f. (Feb 12) Indian Ridge 123 – Cubby Hole (Town And Country 124) [1999 6g⁶ Oct 6] half-sister to several winners, including useful 6f to 1m (in USA) winner Wolf Mountain (by Selkirk), 1000 Guineas runner-up Niche (by Risk Me) and winner up to 1½m Alcove (by Faustus): dam, poor maiden, half-sister to Gold Cup winner Little Wolf and to dam of Sheikh Albadou: green, sixth of 9 to Strahan in maiden at York: should stay 1m: will do better. *R. Hannon*   **59 p**

RAVISHING (IRE)   2 b.f. (Mar 26) Bigstone (IRE) 126 – Dazzling Maid (IRE) 64 (Tate Gallery (USA) 117) [1999 6d* Oct 18] 7,500Y: angular, quite attractive filly: fourth foal: half-sister to 3 winners, including 3-y-o Crystal Creek and fairly useful 1995 2-y-o 7f winner Al Abraq (by Reprimand): dam placed at 5f/6f at 2 yrs: won maiden at Pontefract, travelling smoothly and quickening in good style to beat Risky Reef by 3 lengths: will stay 7f: sure to improve. *W. J. Haggas*   **88 p**

RAWAFED   3 b.f. Arazi (USA) 135 – Princess Sucree (USA) (Roberto (USA) 131) [1998 NR 1999 10f⁴ Jun 18] half-sister to several winners, including smart 7f (at 2 yrs) to 1½m winner Burooj (by Danzig): dam, placed at 6f and 8.5f at 4 yrs in USA, half-sister to Kentucky Derby winner Cannonade: 20/1, under 5 lengths fourth to Marnor in maiden at Newmarket: sent to stud. *A. C. Stewart*   **72**

RAWI   6 ch.g. Forzando 122 – Finally (Final Straw 127) [1998 NR 1999 a7g 9d 11.5m 12m⁵ 10m 8.1m⁵ 10m a10g³ a10g Dec 18] workmanlike gelding: modest handicapper on all-weather, poor on turf: trained by J. Charlton on reappearance: stays 1½m: acts on firm ground and all-weather: sometimes blinkered/visored. *Mrs A. J. Perrett*   **37 a52**

RAYIK   4 br.g. Marju (IRE) 127 – Matila (IRE) 98 (Persian Bold 123) [1998 77: 8m⁴ 10g⁵ a10g³ a10g⁶ a10g* 1999 a12g² a8.5g⁶ 12s 10m⁶ 10f 9.9m 10.2m 11.5g 9f 8.1d 10.2s a8g a12g⁶ a12g Dec 6] sparely-made gelding: fairly useful on all-weather, fair on turf: mostly below form after reappearance, leaving N. Berry after tenth start: best at 1¼m/easy 1½m: acts on good to firm going and all-weather: tried visored. *G. L. Moore*   **69 a81**

RAYWARE BOY (IRE)   3 b.c. Scenic 128 – Amata (USA) (Nodouble (USA)) [1998 –: a7g 6.1m a6g 6s 1999 a8g* a8g* a10g⁴ a12g² 10.3d 10m 8g a9.4f 7g a8g Dec 18] leggy, short-backed colt: fair handicapper: won at Southwell in January/February: mostly below form after: effective at 1m to easy 1½m: better form on fibresand than equitrack, little show on turf: visored/blinkered. *D. Shaw*   **– a71**

RAYYAAN (IRE)   2 ch.c. (Feb 21) Cadeaux Genereux 131 – Anam 79 (Persian Bold 123) [1999 6d⁵ 6g⁴ 7.7d² 6d² Oct 4] medium-sized, quite attractive colt: first foal: dam, 7f winner, half-sister to useful middle-distance performer Estimraar: fairly useful maiden: narrowly beaten at Warwick and Brighton: should stay 1m: raced only on good/good to soft going. *P. T. Walwyn*   **83**

REACHFORYOURPOCKET (IRE)   4 b.g. Royal Academy (USA) 130 – Gemaasheh (Habitat 134) [1998 NR 1999 7g 7.1m 6g 7m 8.3g 7m 7g 6g⁶ 6g⁶ 8s⁶ 9s Oct 8] 30,000F: fifth foal: brother to fairly useful Irish 7.8f and 9f winner Dance Academy: dam unraced half-sister to smart 1¼m performer Dartrey: modest maiden: stays 7f: acts on good to firm going: tried blinkered: has had tongue tied: sold 5,000 gns, joined M. Usher. *K. Mahdi*   **62**

REACTION BALL   3 b.f. Simply Great (FR) 122 – Empty Purse (Pennine Walk 120) [1998 –: 7m 1999 8g⁵ 8g 8g² 8f⁵ 8f⁵ Jul 22] fair maiden: best efforts at Brighton third and fourth starts: will be suited by 1¼m: raced only on good going or firmer. *T. R. Watson*   **71**

READY FONTAINE   4 b.g. Dilum (USA) 115 – Prepare (IRE) 58 (Millfontaine 114) [1998 44: 6g² 5.7f⁵ 6g³ 6s³ 6.1g² 7f 7.1g 8v 1999 5m Jun 11] robust gelding: poor maiden handicapper: seems best at 6f: acts on firm and soft going. *J. Neville*   **–**

READY TO ROCK (IRE)   3 b.g. Up And At 'em 109 – Rocklands Rosie **50**
(Muscatite 122) [1998 73d: 5d⁵ 5g⁵ 5g 6f⁶ 5g 5d 7m 1999 6.5d 5m 5s 5.8d 5s a6g³
a6g Dec 27] fifth foal: dam ran 3 times in Ireland: modest maiden: trained by
B. Lawlor in Ireland until after fifth start: stays 6f: acts on fibresand and soft going:
sometimes blinkered, not in Britain. *J. S. Moore*

REAGANESQUE (USA)   7 b.g. Nijinsky (CAN) 138 – Basoof (USA) 83 (Believe **46**
It (USA)) [1998 NR 1999 14.6m² Jul 2] tall, lengthy gelding: has a round action:
modest handicapper at 5 yrs: just poor form only outing in 1999: effective at 1½m/
1¾m: acts on firm going, below form on softer than good: often a front runner: game:
fairly useful chaser, reportedly finished lame when fourth in Galway Plate in July.
P. G. Murphy

REALMS OF GOLD (USA)   3 ch.f. Gulch (USA) – Royal Pageant (USA) **–**
(Majestic Light (USA)) [1998 –: 6g 6.1s 1999 7.1m⁶ 8.5m 9.9d a7g Aug 25] strong,
angular filly: little form. *I. A. Balding*

REAL TING   3 br.g. Forzando 122 – St Helena (Monsanto (FR) 121) [1998 –: 6m **34**
a5g 6s 1999 a5g a5g a6g⁵ Dec 6] neat gelding: poor mover: poor maiden handicapper: stays 6f: visored at 3 yrs: has worn tongue strap. *P. D. Evans*

REAMZAFONIC   3 b.f. Grand Lodge (USA) 125 – Eye Witness (IRE) 72 (Don't **46 p**
Forget Me 127) [1998 –: 7.1s 1999 10g 10m⁶ 10.5v 7g Oct 15] tall filly: poor maiden:
best effort when staying-on seventh of 30 in handicap at Redcar (best of those drawn
high) final start: should be suited by 1m: may well do better. *E. J. Alston*

REAR GUARD ACTION   3 b.c. Almoojid 69 – Belle Deirdrie (Mandamus 120) **–**
[1998 –: a8g 1999 12g 11.9f³ May 28] rangy colt: no sign of ability. *P. Butler*

REAR WINDOW   5 b.g. Night Shift (USA) – Last Clear Chance (USA) (Alleged **57**
(USA) 138) [1998 67: a12g* 9.7s² 12v² 10m* 10m² 16.2g⁶ 11.6m 10g 1999 11.8s⁴
14.1s⁴ 14.1m⁴ a11g⁵ a14g⁵ a14.8g Aug 6] compact gelding: modest performer:
effective at 1¼m to easy 2m: acts on good to firm ground, heavy and fibresand:
visored twice in 1997, blinkered third start: has worn tongue strap. *G. M. McCourt*

REASON WHY (IRE)   3 b.g. College Chapel 122 – Stifen (Burslem 123) [1998 **76**
NR 1999 7g 7f 7m 8.1d⁶ 8g² 7m² 7.1d 8g 8m* Sep 8] IR 9,000Y, 10,000 2-y-o:
lengthy gelding: half-brother to 4-y-o Ruzen and a winner in Italy by Common
Grounds: dam unraced: fair handicapper: made all in 19-runner event at Kempton in
September: effective at 7f/1m: acts on good to firm going: visored 4 of last 5 starts.
Bob Jones

REBECCA JAY   3 b.f. Rambo Dancer (CAN) 107 – Having Fun (Hard Fought **a56**
125) [1998 –: 5s 7g 7g⁵ 6d a6g⁵ 1999 a7g² 6g a8g 7.1d 6g a8.5g a7g a7g Nov 17]
angular filly: modest maiden: left M. Meagher before final outing: stays 7f: acts on
fibresand, no form on turf: has had tongue tied. *R. Simpson*

REBEL COUNTY (IRE)   6 b.m. Maelstrom Lake 118 – Haven Bridge 88 (Con- **63**
naught 130) [1998 75: 8d 12s 10.3g 12.3m 8.1g 9m 9.1d² 8d* 9.3g² 8f⁵ 8.5m* 8.1m⁴
8m 7.9g 8m 8s 8g 8s⁴ 1999 8d⁴ 10f 10.3d⁴ 10g 8m³ 10.1d⁵ 8.3m 8.1m 8m² 8g Aug
16] good-topped mare: modest handicapper nowadays: seems best at 1m/1¼m: acts
on any turf going: tried blinkered/visored: has worn tongue strap: usually held up:
tends to carry head awkwardly. *A. Bailey*

REBEL ROSE   2 ch.f. (May 31) Factual (USA) 108 – Ragtime Rose (Ragstone **–**
128) [1999 5.3f⁶ a5g⁵ Jun 11] half-sister to several winners, including sprinter
Supreme Rose (by Frimley Park), dam of 6-y-o Rambling Bear, and 7f winner
Mel's Rose (by Anfield), both fairly useful: dam ran 3 times: little sign of ability in
maidens. *E. A. Wheeler*

RECOLETA   2 b.f. (Mar 13) Ezzoud (IRE) 126 – Hug Me 96 (Shareef Dancer **–**
(USA) 135) [1999 6g 7d a7g Nov 23] 8,800Y: half-sister to 3-y-o Hug Me Rob and
several winners, including 1995 2-y-o 7f winner Villeggiatura (by Machiavellian),
who stayed 1¾m, and 1½m/1¾m winner Embracing (by Reference Point), latter
fairly useful: dam 7f (at 2 yrs) and 1½m winner: well held in maidens: bred to stay
1¼m+. *D. R. C. Elsworth*

RECORD TIME   3 ch.f. Clantime 101 – On The Record 72 (Record Token 128) **69**
[1998 61: 5g 5.1m⁶ 1999 5.1s 5m⁶ 6g⁵ 5g² 5m⁵ 5m 5d² 5g⁴ 5g² 5f⁴ 5d* 5v Oct 11]

lengthy filly: fair handicapper: best effort when winning 20-runner race at New-market in September: ran creditably most other starts: best at 5f: acts on good to soft going, probably on firm. *E. J. Alston*

RED APOLLO 3 gr.g. Petong 126 – Scarlet Veil 75 (Tyrnavos 129) [1998 73: 6s 6d a6g² 1999 7g 8m 6g a7g² 7m⁴ 7m 7m a9.4f a8.5g Oct 16] small gelding: modest maiden: left A. Stewart after fourth start: stays 7f: acts on fibresand and good to firm going: blinkered (ran creditably) twice. *P. Howling* **51 a56**

RED BARRON (IRE) 2 b.g. (May 11) Brief Truce (USA) 126 – Miss Sandman 86 (Manacle 123) [1999 6m⁶ 5.1g 5m⁶ Jun 21] IR 3,500Y: half-brother to several winners, including useful 7f (at 2 yrs) to 1¼m winner Arman's Sax (by Waajib): dam 2-y-o 5f winner: poor form only in seller on debut: blinkered final start: sold 500 gns. *J. Berry* **46**

RED BORDEAUX 4 b.g. Alzao (USA) 117 – Marie de Flandre (FR) 109 (Crystal Palace (FR) 132) [1998 70: 7d⁵ 7d 9.9m 10.2s³ 11.9m 15d⁵ 16.1g⁴ 12d⁴ 1999 14.1s Mar 29] leggy, quite attractive gelding: fair in 1998 for B. Hills: well held only 4-y-o start: stays 1½m well: acts on soft ground: has been bandaged: has looked reluctant (including over hurdles): not one to trust implicitly. *J. Akehurst* **–**

REDBRIDGE (USA) 5 b.h. Alleged (USA) 138 – Red Slippers (USA) 111 (Nureyev (USA) 131) [1998 110: a12g* 13.4m⁴ 10.3g* 11.8d* 12g⁴ 10m⁵ 10.9s³ 1999 a10f³ a10f 10f² 12f Jul 30] lengthy, good-topped horse: smart performer: creditable efforts in 1999 when placed in listed race at Nad Al Sheba (penultimate start for S. bin Suroor) in March and minor event at Newbury (½-length second of 4 to Danish Rhapsody) in July: stumbled and unseated rider early final start: stays 1½m: acts on fibresand/dirt, good to firm and good to soft ground: visored (ran poorly) second start: has flashed tail: returned to UAE. *J. H. M. Gosden* **115**

RED BROOK LAD 4 ch.g. Nomadic Way (USA) 104 – Silently Yours (USA) 53 (Silent Screen (USA)) [1998 39: 10g 11.8g a13g⁵ 1999 a16g* a16g⁶ a16g a16g May 29] poor performer: won handicap at Lingfield in February: stays 2m: acts on equitrack: blinkered first 3 starts of 1999. *S. Dow* **46**

RED CANYON (IRE) 2 b.g. (Feb 10) Zieten (USA) 118 – Bayazida (Bustino 136) [1999 6m 6s⁶ 5m 6s 8m Oct 19] 38,000F, IR 100,000Y: half-brother to several winners, including 1996 2-y-o 5f winner Natalia Bay (by Dancing Dissident), useful Irish 1¼m winner Balawhar (by Doyoun) and top-class staying hurdler Paddy's Return (by Kahyasi): dam French maiden: modest maiden: probably stays 1m: acts on soft and good to firm going. *M. L. W. Bell* **59**

RED CASTILE 2 ch.f. (Apr 16) Casteddu 111 – La Fontainova (IRE) (Lafontaine (USA) 117) [1999 a6g⁵ 6m⁶ Jun 23] 2,800Y: third foal: sister to 4-y-o Cosmic Case and Italian winner up to 1¼m Juan Dolio: dam unraced: no show in seller/maiden: sent to Greece. *J. Berry* **–**

RED CHARGER (IRE) 3 ch.g. Up And At 'em 109 – Smashing Pet (Mummy's Pet 125) [1998 75: 5.1s³ 5d* 5g⁵ a6g⁴ 7m* 7m³ 7.5m⁵ 6f* 6m 7.1g⁶ 1999 a6g 7d 7.5m 6g² 6m⁵ 5d⁵ 6m 7m 6f 5d* Aug 9] tall, leggy gelding: fair performer: blinkered, won handicap at Thirsk final start: likely to prove best at 5f/6f: yet to race on heavy going, acts on any other: none too consistent. *D. Nicholls* **75 +**

RED CITY (IRE) 2 b.c. (Mar 12) Mujadil (USA) 119 – Prim (USA) (Diesis 133) [1999 6s⁴ 7d⁴ Oct 15] IR 34,000F, IR 36,000Y: quite attractive colt: poor walker/mover: first foal: dam unraced: modest form in maiden at Lingfield and minor event at Newmarket (last of 4): unlikely to stay much beyond 7f. *R. Hannon* **63**

RED DECEMBER (IRE) 3 b.g. Soviet Lad (USA) – Late Date (Goldhill 125) [1998 –: 8m 8g⁵ 1999 11.1g 8.2s Apr 19] neat gelding: no form. *A. P. Jarvis* **–**

RED DELIRIUM 3 b.g. Robellino (USA) 127 – Made of Pearl (USA) 107 (Nureyev (USA) 131) [1998 95: 5d⁶ 6m* 6g 6d 6f⁶ 5.1d² 6m 7f⁵ 8m 7m² 7s⁴ 1999 7g 7m 7d 8m 8f 7.6g⁵ 7.3m 7g 7s Oct 22] small, sturdy, close-coupled gelding: useful at 2 yrs: fair at best in 1999: barely stays 7.6f: acts on firm and good to soft going: visored second start: none too consistent: sold 12,000 gns. *R. Hannon* **77**

REDEPLOY 3 b.g. Deploy 131 – Baino Clinic (USA) (Sovereign Dancer (USA)) [1998 –p: 8.1m⁶ 10.2d⁶ 8d 1999 14m 12m 16.4g Aug 20] good-topped gelding: **54**

modest maiden handicapper: should prove best at 1¾m+: yet to race on extremes of going: has worn crossed noseband. *B. R. Millman*

RED GUARD   5 ch.g. Soviet Star (USA) 128 – Zinzara (USA) 119 (Stage Door   **79** Johnny) [1998 NR 1999 10g⁴ 10g² May 22] big, useful-looking gelding: fluent mover: fairly useful maiden: stays 1¼m: raced only on good/good to firm ground on Flat: successful twice over hurdles in October. *J. T. Gifford*

RED HEATHER   2 b.f. (Apr 17) Mistertopogigo (IRE) 118 – That's Rich (Hot   **–** Spark 126) [1999 7m 7g 7m Aug 27] 1,000Y: strong filly: sixth living foal: half-sister to 3-y-o Crystal Lass and a winner in Belgium by Star Appeal: dam unraced: well beaten in sellers: sold 600 gns in October. *J. Berry*

RED KING   2 b.g. (Apr 27) King Among Kings 60 – Market Blues (Porto Bello   **–** 118) [1999 6d 7f 8d 8.3s 8d a8g Nov 12] 4,000Y: neat gelding: seventh foal: brother to 3-y-o Ferny Factors, 6f/7f winner Palacegate King and 6f (at 2 yrs) to 9.2f winner Gospel Song: dam poor maiden: little sign of ability, including in sellers: sold 700 gns. *J. Berry*

RED LETTER   2 b.f. (Feb 9) Sri Pekan (USA) 117 – Never Explain (IRE) 80   **84** (Fairy King (USA)) [1999 6m* 6m 6g 6m⁴ 7d Sep 28] 41,000F, IR 67,000Y: rangy, unfurnished filly: first foal: dam, 1¼m winner, half-sister to Irish 1,000 Guineas winner Matiya: fairly useful performer: overcame greenness to win minor event at Ascot in June: failed to progress, highly tried third start: should prove better at 7f than 6f: acts on good to firm going, probably on good to soft. *R. Hannon*

RED LION   3 ch.g. Lion Cavern (USA) 117 – Fleur Rouge 71 (Pharly (FR) 130)   **105** [1998 91: 5g* 6g⁴ 5m* 6m 6g³ 7v⁶ 1999 6m* 6g⁵ 6m 6m 6m* 6f 6m⁵ 6d⁵ 6.1g 6d 5s Oct 23] useful-looking gelding: useful performer: won minor event at Leicester in June and handicap at Yarmouth (by ½ length from Bon Ami) in July: also ran creditably on several other occasions: stays 6f: poorly drawn on firm going, acts on any other: usually held up. *J. W. Payne*

RED MAY (IRE)   3 b. or br.f. Persian Bold 123 – Stay That Way (Be My Guest   **70** (USA) 126) [1998 62: 6m⁵ 7.1m 9mm 10m⁴ 12.3m⁵ 11.6g⁵ 11.8m 10m 11.6m² 11.8g² 12d⁴ 12.3d⁴ 11.9m a12g⁴ 9.5v* Dec 10] smallish, well-made filly: fair performer: ran creditably most starts before sold from R. Hannon 20,000 gns prior to final outing: won minor event at Bordeaux in December: stays 1½m: acts on good to firm and heavy ground, showed promise on fibresand. *J-C. Rouget, France*

RED MITTENS   2 ch.f. (Apr 3) Wolfhound (USA) 126 – Red Gloves 83 (Red   **–** God 128§) [1999 6m⁵ 5m⁶ 6d 6s Oct 4] 4,500Y: half-sister to several winners, including 4-y-o Peaceful Sarah, 1995 2-y-o 6f winner Red Nymph and 6f and 1m winner Takdeer, all 3 by Sharpo: dam, second in Britain at 2 yrs, later won in Norway: poor maiden. *Martyn Wane*

RED N' SOCKS (USA)   2 ch.c. (May 10) Devil's Bag (USA) – Racing Blue   **84** (Reference Point 139) [1999 7m⁴ 7m⁴ 7.1m⁵ 8m* 10d Oct 30] third foal: half-brother to Irish 3-y-o 1¼m winner Rominten (by Danzig): dam German 1½m winner and third in German St Leger: fairly useful performer: best effort when winning nursery at Yarmouth in October: well held in listed event at Newmarket final start: bred to stay 1¼m. *J. L. Dunlop*

REDOUBLE   3 b.c. First Trump 118 – Sunflower Seed 70 (Mummy's Pet 125)   **75 d** [1998 70: 5d⁶ 6m³ 7g⁶ 7m⁶ 7.6f² 6d 7s³ 7d a8g 1999 a7g⁵ 8.2s² 10g⁴ 10m 9f 9g   **a–** 11.8m³ 11.9m⁵ 14d⁴ 12d⁵ 10g⁵ a10g Dec 18] smallish, good-topped colt: fair maiden handicapper: below form after second start: barely stays 1¾m: yet to race on heavy going, acts on any other turf (well beaten on equitrack). *R. J. O'Sullivan*

REDOUBTABLE (USA)   8 b.h. Grey Dawn II 132 – Seattle Rockette (USA)   **88** (Seattle Slew (USA)) [1998 83, a86: a7g* a6g⁴ a7g³ a5g 5s 6g 6g³ 7m* 8.1g 7m⁵ 7v*   **a81** 7f 7m 6m 7.6d⁶ 7d 6s⁶ 6m² 6s 6v 7s 1999 a6g a6g a8g³ a6g a6g⁶ a7g² a7g⁶ a8g² a6g 6d 7g² 7g² 8m 6d* 7m³ 7m² 6m⁵ 7g⁴ 7m 6d⁵ 7f 6s⁴ 7m 6d a6g⁶ a7g³ Dec 8] small, sturdy horse: usually looks well: fairly useful handicapper: won at Thirsk in May: mostly creditable efforts after: effective at 6f to easy 1m: acts on any turf going/all-weather: blinkered (well held) once: sometimes finds little: tough. *D. W. Chapman*

RED PRAIRIE (USA)   3 b.c. El Prado (IRE) 119 – Kates Delimma (USA)   **102** (Tank's Prospect (USA)) [1998 99: 5d 5d* 6m* 6d 6m³ 5f* 5m³ 5s⁶ 1999 5m² 6g

5m⁵ 5g³ 5m³ 5f 5.1m² 5m⁴ 5s⁵ 5.5g Dec 19] strong, lengthy colt: useful performer: mostly creditable efforts in 1999, including when placed in Palace House Stakes at Newmarket (behind Rambling Bear), Prix du Gros-Chene at Chantilly, Gran Premio Citta di Napoli at Naples (promoted from fourth) and minor event at Nottingham (beaten head by Ocker): sold from M. Bell 55,000 gns before final start: best at 5f: acts on firm and good to soft ground, probably on soft: blinkered/visored fifth, sixth and final starts: has been tongue tied. *T. Amoss, USA*

RED RAJA 6 b.g. Persian Heights 129 – Jenny Splendid 101 (John Splendid 116) **63**
[1998 –: 12f 1999 a16f* a16f a16g³ 16d* 18m 14m⁴ 20f⁵ a16g⁶ a16g Nov 8] workmanlike gelding: modest handicapper: won at Lingfield in January and June: effective at 2m, probably at 2½m: acts on firm going, good to soft and equitrack: visored final start. *P. Mitchell*

RED RAMONA 4 b.c. Rudimentary (USA) 118 – Apply 87 (Kings Lake (USA) **97 §**
133) [1998 97: 10.2s² 12m* 12g⁵ 11.9m⁶ 13.3g 12s⁴ 12d⁵ 1999 12s 14f³ 13.9g 14.6m 12s Nov 6] lengthy, quite attractive colt: useful handicapper: ran creditably in 1999 only when third to Mowbray in Grosvenor Casinos Cup at Goodwood (3 months after reappearance) in July: slowly away and took little interest final start: effective at 1½m/1¾m: yet to race on heavy going, acts on any other: not one to rely on. *J. Akehurst*

RED REVOLUTION (USA) 2 ch.c. (Feb 17) Explosive Red (CAN) 119 – **69 p**
Braided Way (USA) (Mining (USA)) [1999 5m³ a5g² Nov 30] $20,000Y: second foal: dam winning sprinter in USA, including at 2 yrs: placed in maidens at Musselburgh and Southwell 7 months apart: likely to improve. *T. D. Barron*

RED RISK 4 ch.g. Risk Me (FR) 127 – Red Sails (Town And Country 124) [1998 **–**
–, a40: a7g³ a8g⁶ a7g 9.7d 10s⁶ 10.1g 10m 8m 8s 1999 a7g a7g Feb 3] poor maiden: form only at 7f on fibresand. *S. G. Knight*

RED ROSES (IRE) 3 b.f. Mukaddamah (USA) 125 – Roses Red (IRE) 64 (Exhib- **70 d**
itioner 111) [1998 95: 7.5s 1999 8.2s² 8g 7m 10.2m 12f⁵ 12.4g 10.4d 11g³ 12s⁶ Nov 2] leggy, close-coupled filly: fair maiden at best: disappointing after reappearance, leaving L. Cumani 6,200 gns after fourth start: stays 11f: acts on soft ground: has been sweating and edgy. *Don Enrico Incisa*

RED SEA 3 b.c. Barathea (IRE) 127 – Up Anchor (IRE) 114 (Slip Anchor 136) **113**
[1998 113: 5d 6g* 6d* 6d 8v² a8.5f 1999 8m 9.9g² 12m³ 11.9s⁴ 12f⁴ Jul 27] strong, good-quartered colt: smart performer: ran creditably when 3½ lengths second to Dubai Millennium in listed race at Goodwood and 3¼ lengths third to Mutafaweq in King Edward VII Stakes at Royal Ascot: stays 1½m: acts on good to firm and heavy going: effective blinkered or not: twice gave good deal of trouble stalls at 2 yrs, more settled in 1999: sent to USA. *P. F. I. Cole*

RED SEPTEMBER 2 b.g. (May 18) Presidium 124 – Tangalooma 56 (Hotfoot **52**
126) [1999 6d⁴ 6g 5.9g⁶ 6m⁶ 6d⁵ Oct 18] 3,000Y: tall, leggy gelding: seventh reported foal: half-brother to 3-y-o Time Temptress and 5f/6f winner Time To Tango (by Timeless Times) and an 11f winner by Belfort (in Italy): dam won over hurdles: modest maiden: should stay at least 7f. *G. M. Moore*

RED SHIFT (IRE) 4 b.g. Night Shift (USA) – Histoire Douce (USA) (Chief's **–**
Crown (USA)) [1998 69: 6m⁵ 5.7m⁵ 1999 6.1g 5g 5.1m 8.3m a8.5g 10m Aug 28] disappointing maiden handicapper: blinkered last 2 starts. *C. R. Egerton*

RED SONNY (IRE) 2 ch.g. (Mar 31) Foxhound (USA) 103 – Olivia's Pride **53**
(IRE) (Digamist (USA) 110) [1999 6g⁵ 5.9g 5g 5d Oct 26] IR 11,000Y: good-topped gelding with scope: second foal: half-brother to 3-y-o Ladycake: dam, unraced, from family of Only Royale and Oscar Schindler: modest maiden: stays 6f: raced only on good/good to soft going: sold 2,000 gns in November. *J. Berry*

RED SUN 2 b.g. (Apr 28) Foxhound (USA) 103 – Superetta 65 (Superlative 118) **59 d**
[1999 5d³ 6d 5m 6m⁶ 7d⁶ 7g Sep 18] 16,000F, 24,000Y: third foal: half-brother to 6f (at 2 yrs) to 1¼m winner Domettes (by Archway): dam 1¼m and hurdles winner: long way below debut form subsequently. *J. Berry*

REDSWAN 4 ch.g. Risk Me (FR) 127 – Bocas Rose 106 (Jalmood (USA) 126) **80**
[1998 79: 8m⁵ a8g² 8g* 7f² 1999 8v 7m 7.5d⁶ 7f⁵ 8m³ 7m* 7m⁵ 8d⁵ 7g⁴ 7f 7m* Sep 9] big, workmanlike gelding: fairly useful handicapper: won at Leicester in July

and Doncaster (21 ran) in September: effective at 7f/1m: acts on firm ground, good to soft and fibresand: blinkered last 2 starts: often tongue tied: has been bandaged: held up: has carried head awkwardly, drifted left and unseated rider in preliminaries: consistent, but has his quirks. *S. C. Williams*

RED SYMPHONY 3 b.f. Merdon Melody 98 – Woodland Steps 86 (Bold Owl **61 §** 101) [1998 64: a5g⁴ a5g* 5d² 5g* 5d³ 5m⁴ 5g⁶ 5d* 5d 1999 6g 5m 5g 5g³ 5g 5m 5d 5d 5v³ a6g Nov 22] modest performer: should stay 6f: acts on heavy going and fibresand: has looked difficult ride: inconsistent. *I. Semple*

RED THATCH 2 ch.c. (May 2) Pelder (IRE) 125 – Straw Castle (Final Straw 127) **–** [1999 6m 7g⁶ Jul 2] fourth reported foal: dam, poor maiden, best treated with caution: well beaten in maiden at Windsor and minor event at Salisbury, looking none too keen on second occasion. *G. F. H. Charles-Jones*

RED TIARA (USA) 3 b. or br.f. Mr Prospector (USA) – Heart of Joy (USA) 120 **52** (Lypheor 118) [1998 60p: 7d 1999 8.3m 7.6m⁴ 8g Aug 18] quite attractive filly: showed promise only 2-y-o start: disappointing in 1999: bred to prove best up to 1m. *Sir Michael Stoute*

RED TOWER 4 b.g. Damister (USA) 123 – Tower of Ivory (IRE) (Cyrano de **58** Bergerac 120) [1998 NR 1999 10m 11.9f² Aug 4] 500 3-y-o: good-topped gelding: second reported foal: dam tailed off only start at 2 yrs: better effort in maidens on Flat when second at Brighton, tending to hang left once headed. *L. Wells*

RED TYPHOON 2 ro.f. (Feb 16) Belfort (FR) 89 – Dash Cascade (Absalom 128) **73** [1999 5m⁴ a5g⁵ 5g⁴ 5.2m 7f⁶ 7.1g³ 7.1m³ 6m* 6.1m⁶ 6s* 6d Oct 22] 2,600Y: leggy filly: fourth foal: half-sister to 2 winners abroad by Petong, including Swedish 3-y-o Swiss Toni, 1m winner in Britain at 2 yrs: dam unraced: fair performer: won claimers at Haydock in September and Lingfield in October: easily best form at 6f: acts on soft and good to firm going: sold 9,400 gns, joined M. Kettle. *J. Berry*

RED VENUS (IRE) 3 ch.f. Perugino (USA) 84 – Reflection Time (IRE) (Fayruz **56** 116) [1998 62, a59: 5d 5d a5g³ 5d a5g⁶ a5g⁶ 5s³ a5g⁵ a5g 1999 a6g⁴ a6g³ a7f* a7g² **a62** a10g⁶ a7g⁴ a7g* 7d 7g 7m a8g 8d⁶ 7m⁵ a7g⁴ Sep 28] modest performer: won seller (penultimate start for J. Berry) in January and handicap in April, both at Southwell: stays 7f: acts on soft going (probably on good to firm) and all-weather: often blinkered/visored. *Miss Gay Kelleway*

RED WOLF 3 ch.g. Timeless Times (USA) 99 – Stealthy 73 (Kind of Hush 118) **–** [1998 NR 1999 7.1s⁶ 8s 10f a8.5g Dec 27] 7,000Y: fourth foal: half-brother to an Italian winner up to 7.5f by Presidium: dam 1m winner: signs of a little ability. *J. G. Given*

REDWOOD GROVE (USA) 3 b.c. Woodman (USA) 126 – Ikebana (IRE) 93 **79** (Sadler's Wells (USA) 132) [1998 NR 1999 10d 12g 12.3m⁵ 14.1m* 14m⁶ 14d⁶ 17.5d Sep 17] tall, rather leggy, quite attractive colt: brother to Derby runner-up City Honours (by Darshaan), useful 1m winner at 2 yrs, and a winner up to 9f in Spain by High Estate: dam, 1¼m winner who stayed 1½m, out of very smart Miss Toshiba: fair performer: won maiden at Salisbury in July: below form in handicaps after: stays 1¾m: yet to race on extremes of going: sold 16,000 gns. *P. W. Chapple-Hyam*

REEMATNA 2 b.f. (Mar 8) Sabrehill (USA) 120 – Reem Albaraari 81 (Sadler's **75 p** Wells (USA) 132) [1999 7d Oct 30] fourth foal: half-sister to 3-y-o Reken: dam (stayed 9f) maiden daughter of Habibti: shaped well when eighth of 16 to Premier Prize in steadily-run Newmarket maiden, travelling strongly and not knocked about after becoming short of room: will be suited by 1m+: likely to do a fair bit better. *M. A. Jarvis*

REFERENDUM (IRE) 5 b.g. Common Grounds 118 – Final Decision (Tap On **100** Wood 130) [1998 99: 6f 5g² 6s 7d⁵ 1999 6d⁴ 6m⁴ 7g⁶ 6m 6m 6d Sep 18] good-topped gelding: has a fluent, round action: useful performer: best effort in rated stakes at Newmarket on second start: stiff tasks next 2, but well held back in handicaps last 2: has form at 1m, but probably best at 5f/6f: acts on good to firm and good to soft ground. *D. Nicholls*

REFLEX BLUE 2 b.c. (Mar 28) Ezzoud (IRE) 126 – Briggsmaid 70 (Elegant Air **89** 119) [1999 7.3f² 7m* 8g² 10d⁵ Oct 11] 12,500Y: lengthy, angular colt: good walker:

has a quick action: third foal: closely related to French 1m/9f winner Goldfill (by Marju) and half-brother to 3-y-o Kez: dam 1½m to 2m winner: fairly useful performer: won maiden at Newmarket in July: seemed reluctant early on when good second of 5 to Whyome in minor event at Pontefract: below form final start: should stay at least 1¼m. *J. W. Hills*

REFUSE TO LOSE   5 ch.h. Emarati (USA) 74 – Petrol 73 (Troy 137) [1998 98, **103** a111: a8g* a8.5g⁴ a10g² 8d² a8g* 8.1g⁴ 7.1m² 8d* 10.4f 8d a9.4g* 1999 a10g² a10g 8m³ 8m* 7m 7.9g 8m Sep 9] big, lengthy horse: useful performer: won handicap at Ascot in July by ½ length from Rock Falcon: also ran well when placed in minor event at Lingfield (short-head second to Pas de Memoires) and in Royal Hunt Cup at Royal Ascot (third to Showboat, a race he'd won in 1998): behind in Park Stakes at Doncaster final start: stays 1¼m: acts on all-weather, firm and good to soft ground: races up with pace: game and consistent: sent to Saudi Arabia. *J. M. P. Eustace*

REGAL ACADEMY (IRE)   5 b.m. Royal Academy (USA) 130 – Polistatic 53 **53** (Free State 125) [1998 57: 9.9f⁵ 10d 9m 11.5g 11.9m⁵ 8g⁶ 1999 8.3m 11.9f³ 11.6m 11.5g 10f 11.9m⁴ Sep 1] modest maiden: stays 1½m: acts on firm going: blinkered in 1999: has worn tongue strap: has hung badly. *C. A. Horgan*

REGAL BRIDGET   4 ch.f. Gildoran 123 – Bridge Street Lady 93 (Decoy Boy **56 d** 129) [1998 71: 12m⁵ 10m² 10m³ 10m 12m 10.2d⁴ 1999 10s⁴ 10s⁴ 12s 10g 10g 8.2m a12g Sep 18] lengthy filly: disappointing maiden handicapper: probably stays 1½m: acts on soft and good to firm going: has found little: sold 800 gns. *B. A. McMahon*

REGAL CHARM (IRE)   2 b.f. (Feb 8) Sadler's Wells (USA) 132 – Abury (IRE) **56 p** 104 (Law Society (USA) 130) [1999 8d Oct 22] close-coupled, quite good-topped filly: turns fore-legs in markedly: third foal: closely related to 3-y-o Westbrook and half-brother to 4-y-o Glory of Grosvenor: dam, 7f (at 2 yrs) and 11.4f (Cheshire Oaks) winner, should have stayed further: 12 lengths tenth of 18 to Interlude in maiden at Doncaster: should stay 1½m+: likely to do better. *A. G. Foster*

REGAL EXIT (FR)   3 ch.g. Exit To Nowhere (USA) 122 – Regalante (Gairloch **73** 122) [1998 79p: 7.1m⁵ 7.9g³ 1999 7v⁴ 10.4d 9.9d⁵ 9m⁶ 8.5s³ 8.1m⁵ 8.1g⁶ Aug 20] good-topped gelding: fair maiden: generally respectable efforts in 1999 without managing to fulfil 2-y-o promise: may prove best at 1¼m/1½m: yet to race on firm going, acts on any other: joined N. Henderson. *M. L. W. Bell*

REGAL GLOW   3 b.g. Regal Embers (IRE) – Kimmy's Princess 34 (Prince Sabo **–** 123) [1998 NR 1999 6.8s⁶ 7.7m 7.1m 5g Aug 18] first foal: dam sprint maiden: no sign of ability: tongue tied final start. *T. Keddy*

REGALITY (IRE)   3 ch.f. Lion Cavern (USA) 117 – Broadway Gal (USA) **–** (Foolish Pleasure (USA)) [1998 73: 8s⁶ 8s 1999 10d 10m 12f 12m a9.4g a11g Nov 30] 7,000Y: fourth foal: dam third once from 4 starts in North America: maiden, seemingly fair form on debut: no show in 1999, leaving Miss S. Collins in Ireland before penultimate start. *M. Johnston*

REGALO   4 b.c. Nalchik (USA) – Stardrop (Starch Reduced 112) [1998 –: 8d 5m **–** 1999 5m Jul 8] lengthy, angular colt: modest maiden at 2 yrs: well beaten since. *W. de Best-Turner*

REGAL PHILOSOPHER   3 b.c. Faustus (USA) 118 – Princess Lucy 42 (Local **96** Suitor (USA) 128) [1998 79p: 7g³ 7g 7.9g² 8v² 1999 8g* 8m* 8m 8.1m² 7.9g 10m⁴ 10.1m² 10s Oct 2] big, strong, lengthy colt: useful performer: won maiden at Bath in May and handicap at Newcastle in June: ran at least respectably in handicaps after, runner-up at Chepstow and Newcastle: effective at 1m/1¼m: yet to race on firm going, acts on any other: held up: hung left penultimate start, didn't look entirely keen final one. *J. W. Hills*

REGAL RAMBLER (CAN)   8 ch.g. Regal Classic (CAN) – Rushing Rachel **–** (USA) (Breezing On (USA)) [1998 NR 1999 a14g Jul 8] bad maiden: tried blinkered: dead. *L. J. Barratt*

REGAL SONG (IRE)   3 b.g. Anita's Prince 126 – Song Beam 84 (Song 132) **64** [1998 61: 5d 6g⁵ 6g 8v⁶ 6s³ 5d³ 1999 a6g a6g 6m⁴ 5.9g² 5g* Jun 16] useful-looking **a54** gelding: modest performer: won maiden at Hamilton in June, despite tending to hang right: stays 6f, probably not 1m: acts on good to firm going, soft and fibresand: best efforts in blinkers. *T. J. Etherington*

REGAL SPLENDOUR (CAN)   6 ch.g. Vice Regent (CAN) – Seattle Princess   **41 §**
(USA) (Seattle Slew (USA)) [1998 –§: 9m 10s 9g a10g 10g 7.6g 8m 10m 12g   **a52 §**
16m 1999 a7g⁵ a7g⁶ 8m² 8.5g⁶ a8g⁶ a11g Nov 30] good-topped gelding: modest
handicapper on all-weather, poor on turf: should stay 1¼m: acts on firm going and
all-weather: temperamental. *B. A. McMahon*

REGARDEZ-MOI   2 b.f. (Mar 12) Distinctly North (USA) 115 – Tomard   **64**
(Thatching 131) [1999 5d 5g 6g a5g 5.7h 5d³ 5.1g⁶ 5v⁶ 7s⁴ 7d³ 8d³ Oct 30] 7,000Y:
sparely-made filly: half-sister to 3-y-o Bodfari Vista and several winners, including
useful Irish 5f performer Tourandot (by Emarati), later successful in North America,
and 15f winner Tophard (by Lyphard's Special): dam Irish 2-y-o 5f winner: modest
maiden: in frame in nursery at Catterick and sellers at Newmarket last 3 starts: likely
to prove best up to 1m: acts on soft going. *A. W. Carroll*

REGENT   4 ch.g. Zafonic (USA) 130 – Queen Midas 119 (Glint of Gold 128)   **53**
[1998 –: 8d 10v a6g 1999 10.8m 8.3g⁴ 8.1m⁶ 10d⁵ 9m⁶ 8.3m⁴ 8.3g 7m Jul 16] big,
workmanlike gelding: modest maiden handicapper: best at 1m/1¼m: acts on good to
firm and good to soft ground: often slowly away. *C. P. Morlock*

REGGIE BUCK (USA)   5 b. or br.g. Alleged (USA) 138 – Hello Memphis   **40**
(USA) (Super Concorde (USA) 128) [1998 –, a53: a8g³ a16g a11g⁶ 14.1s 10m a11g
1999 12g 10.2g 10m Sep 24] leggy, sparely-made gelding: poor maiden handicapper:
should stay 1½m: tried blinkered: sold 2,000 gns in November, joined J. Mackie:
modest winning hurdler. *J. L. Harris*

REGGIE BYRNE   3 b.g. Mon Tresor 113 – Failand 36 (Kala Shikari 125) [1998   **–**
–: 6d 1999 8.2s Oct 5] tailed off in maidens. *R. Dickin*

REINE DE LA CHASSE (FR)   7 ch.m. Ti King (FR) 121 – Hunting Cottage   **–**
(Pyjama Hunt 126) [1998 NR 1999 11.8d 11.8s⁶ a12g a14.8g⁵ Nov 27] smallish,
workmanlike mare: second reported foal: dam unraced: fair performer in France at 3
yrs for D. Sepulchre, winning claimers at Saint-Cloud (10.5f) and Longchamp (15f):
had a foal in 1998: well beaten in claimers/minor events in 1999. *N. M. Babbage*

REKEN   3 b.c. Mujtahid (USA) 118 – Reem Albaraari 81 (Sadler's Wells (USA)   **64 d**
132) [1998 NR 1999 8.3d⁵ 8s 7m 8.3m 10g a8.5g 8.2g a7g Oct 25] small colt: has a
quick action: third foal: dam maiden (stayed 9f) daughter of Habibti: little form after
debut. *P. Burgoyne*

REMEMBER STAR   6 ch.m. Don't Forget Me 127 – Star Girl Gay (Lord Gayle   **–**
(USA) 124) [1998 NR 1999 a16g 18m Jun 29] of little account. *R. J. Baker*

RENAISSANCE LADY (IRE)   3 ch.f. Imp Society (USA) – Easter Morning   **59**
(FR) (Nice Havrais (USA) 124) [1998 –: 7m 7g 1999 7s 10f⁴ 11.6g⁴ 11.4m⁶
11.9g* 14.6m⁶ 10f 12m² 14.1m 11.9m Sep 1] unfurnished filly: modest performer:
won 4-runner maiden at Brighton in June, despite looking wayward: ran creditably
after only when second in handicap at Newmarket (saddle slipped previous start):
stays 1½m, probably not 1¾m: acts on good to firm going: successful over hurdles in
October. *T. R. Watson*

RENDITA (IRE)   3 b.f. Waajib 121 – Rend Rover (FR) (Monseigneur (USA)   **57**
127) [1998 52: a6s³ a6g⁴ 1999 a7g a8.5g⁶ a7g* 7m 8.3m 8g² 7m 10d 8s Oct 25]
modest handicapper: won at Lingfield in April: ran well after only when second of 20
at Leicester (after 3-month break) in August: best at 7f/1m: acts on equitrack: visored
final start. *D. Haydn Jones*

RENDITION   2 b.f. (May 25) Polish Precedent (USA) 131 – Rensaler (USA)   **72**
(Stop The Music (USA)) [1999 7s⁵ 7m³ 7d Oct 11] good-topped filly: half-sister to
several winners, including 6-y-o Sadler's Realm, useful 1¼m winner Silence Reigns
(by Saddlers' Hall) and 1989 2-y-o 6f winner Jovial (by Northern Jove), latter later
very smart graded-stakes winner in USA up to 1¼m: dam won around 1m in USA:
fair form in maidens last 2 starts: should stay 1m. *J. H. M. Gosden*

RENNYHOLME   8 ch.g. Rich Charlie 117 – Jacqui Joy 63 (Music Boy 124)   **–**
[1998 a35: a6g⁵ a5g a5g 5d 6g⁴ 6m⁵ 1999 a5g a6g a6g³ a7g⁶ a5g 5m Apr 30]
close-coupled gelding: little form in 1999: best at 5f/6f: acts on firm ground and all-
weather: effective blinkered/visored or not: inconsistent. *K. A. Ryan*

RENOWN 7 b.g. Soviet Star (USA) 128 – Starlet 119 (Teenoso (USA) 135) [1998 **72** 72, a–: a10g 11.7d 9.9m* 9m³ 1999 8g* 8.5d 9.9m⁵ 8.5m⁴ 9m⁵ 9f 9g Aug 28] **a–** small, angular gelding: fair handicapper: won 21-runner race at Goodwood in May: generally ran creditably after: effective at 1m to 1½m: acts on all-weather and firm ground: often held up: sold 2,000 gns. *I. A. Balding*

RENZO (IRE) 6 b.g. Alzao (USA) 117 – Watership (USA) (Foolish Pleasure **80 §** (USA)) [1998 89: 14.1d⁵ 16.4g 14g 14m² 14.8g⁵ 18g 16.5d* 1999 16g 16.4s⁴ 14.4m 14m 16.2m 13.9d 14.6d 16.5s Nov 6] strong gelding: fairly useful handicapper: deteriorated after second start in 1999: stays 2m: acts on firm and soft going: tried blinkered: sometimes slowly away: held up: has very high head carriage: ungenuine. *J. L. Harris*

REPEAT WARNING 3 b.f. Warning 136 – Reprocolor 114 (Jimmy Reppin 131) **72** [1998 NR 1999 7m 8.3d³ Nov 4] half-sister to several winners, including very smart middle-distance horse Cezanne (by Ajdal), Irish Oaks winner Colorspin (by High Top), now dam of Opera House and Kayf Tara, and very smart filly at up to 1¼m Bella Colora (by Bellypha), the dam of Stagecraft: dam won Lancashire Oaks: much better effort in maidens when third of 17 to Beleaguer at Windsor: will probably stay beyond 1m: slowly away on debut: impeccably bred, and may improve further. *G. Wragg*

REPERTORY 6 b.g. Anshan 119 – Susie's Baby (Balidar 133) [1998 110: 5.1g² **107** 6m 5m² 5g² 5d* 5g 5f* 5.2g⁴ 5s² 5v³ 1999 5.5s⁴ 5m 5d⁵ 5g⁶ 5m 5f 5g⁶ 5m² 5.2d² 5s⁵ 5d⁴ Oct 24] tall, angular gelding: useful performer: seemingly best effort in 1999 when ½-length second to Imperial Beauty in listed race at Newbury ninth start: several respectable efforts otherwise, including when fourth in similar events at Maisons-Laffitte in April and Newmarket (behind Sakha) in September: trail-blazing front runner, best at 5f: acts on any going. *M. S. Saunders*

REPOSE (IRE) 4 gr.f. Posen (USA) – Dream Trader (Auction Ring (USA) 123) **–** [1998 –: 6s 8.2g 13.8g⁵ 11m 7m 8v 1999 7m 8d May 16] no sign of ability. *A. B. Mulholland*

REPTON 4 ch.g. Rock City 120 – Hasty Key (USA) (Key To The Mint (USA)) **59** [1998 59: 7.5g 10s* 9.3m 8m a12g⁶ 10s³ a11g³ a12g³ 1999 a11g a12g* 12.1v³ 11d 10.5s 11.5g 11.7s⁶ a12g a12g Dec 21] modest handicapper: won apprentice event at Southwell in March: below form after next start: left Mrs A. Swinbank and off 4 months after fifth start: will stay beyond 1½m: acts on fibresand, form only on soft/heavy going on turf: blinkered once: very slowly away sixth start. *B. Smart*

REPUBLIC (IRE) 3 b.g. Anita's Prince 126 – Sweet Finale (Sallust 134) [1998 **55 d** 67: 5m⁴ 6.1m⁵ 5m⁵ 5.1m³ 5g 5.3g⁴ 1999 a6g a7g 8g⁶ 8.3v³ 7.1m 8m 5.9m 7.5g⁴ 8.3s 5v⁵ a6g Oct 18] disappointing maiden: stays 1m: acts on good to firm going, probably on heavy: has worn severe noseband. *J. Hetherton*

REQUESTOR 4 br.g. Distinctly North (USA) 115 – Bebe Altesse (GER) (Alpen- **70** konig (GER)) [1998 –: 7.6g 7g 1999 7g 8v 8.5d 8m⁶ 8d⁶ 7.9f³ Jul 9] smallish, good-bodied gelding: has a fluent action: fair maiden handicapper: stays 1m: acts on firm ground, probably on heavy: blinkered once. *J. G. FitzGerald*

RESALAH 3 ch.f. Zafonic (USA) 130 – Ghzaalh (USA) 87 (Northern Dancer) **75 +** [1998 75p: 6m³ 6d* 1999 7.7m² 7g Oct 14] fair performer: second of 6 in minor event at Warwick on reappearance: very stiff task, not discredited in 29-runner handicap at Redcar 3 months later: stays 1m: yet to race on extremes of going: sent to USA. *M. P. Tregoning*

RESEARCH MASTER 2 br.g. (Mar 4) Primo Dominie 121 – Nutmeg Point **50** (Nashwan (USA) 135) [1999 6m 6.1m 7f⁴ Jul 22] first reported foal: dam unraced half-sister to very smart middle-distance performer John French: modest form in maidens: should stay 1m. *P. R. Chamings*

RESERVATION (IRE) 3 ch.f. Common Grounds 118 – Chief's Quest (USA) **78** (Chief's Crown (USA)) [1998 NR 1999 8m⁵ 7.1m* 7.1g⁴ 8f 7d Oct 9] deep-girthed, workmanlike filly: fifth foal: half-sister to 5-y-o Rich In Love and a winner up to 1½m in Hong Kong by Groom Dancer: dam, French 8.5f winner, half-sister to Prix de la Salamandre winner Noblequest and the dam of Pursuit of Love: fair performer: won maiden at Sandown in June: easily best effort in handicaps after when good fourth to Daytime at Sandown: off track 2½ months before (considerably handled) final start: should stay 1m: acts on good to firm going. *A. C. Stewart*

RESIDUAL VALUE (USA)   3 b.c. Lear Fan (USA) 130 – Riverlyph (USA)   **108** (Lyphard (USA) 132) [1998 79p: 7g 1999 10m* 9.9g* 10m⁵ Jul 17] good-bodied colt: won maiden at Windsor in June and minor event at Salisbury in July, latter by 6 lengths from Annapurna: well-backed favourite, ran respectably in listed race at Newbury final start, not for first time wandering and swishing tail: will stay beyond 1¼m: raced only on good/good to firm going: sent to USA. *Sir Michael Stoute*

RESIST THE FORCE (USA)   9 br.g. Shadeed (USA) 135 – Countess Tully   **81** 112 (Hotfoot 126) [1998 87: 6m* 6g² 5m 6g³ 7m* 7.6f⁴ 6m 1999 a8g² a7g Dec 29] big, lengthy gelding: fairly useful handicapper: off 16 months before landing gamble in handicap at Lingfield: ran poorly just 11 days later: effective at 6f to 1m: acts on firm going and equitrack: best held up. *R. Rowe*

RESOUNDING (IRE)   2 b.f. (Mar 1) Elmaamul (USA) 125 – Echoing 93 (Form-   **83 p** idable (USA) 125) [1999 6m⁵ 6.1d* Oct 5] 20,000Y: rather unfurnished filly: half-sister to several winners, including 3-y-o Calcutta and 1½m winner Sommersby (by Vision): dam 2-y-o 5f winner, from family of Time Charter: favourite, confirmed debut promise when winning 15-runner maiden at Nottingham by ½ length from Dancemma, always well placed and leading close home: bred to stay 1m, but clearly not short of speed: should improve further. *A. C. Stewart*

RESPLENDENT STAR (IRE)   2 b.g. (Feb 24) Northern Baby (CAN) 127 –   **85** Whitethroat (Artaius (USA) 129) [1999 6g 7m³ 7m² 7f* 7g 8d a8g* 8d Oct 22] IR 16,000Y: useful-looking gelding: good mover: half-brother to fairly useful Irish 2m winner Woodren (by Woodman) and 4m winner aboard by Storm Cat: dam lightly-raced half-sister to Assert, Bikala and Eurobird: fairly useful performer: won nursery at Newcastle in August and minor event at Southwell in September: should stay 1¼m: acts on firm ground and fibresand, below form on softer than good: visored last 2 starts: tends to hang, and looks difficult ride. *P. W. Harris*

RESPOND   4 b.f. Reprimand 122 – Kina (USA) (Bering 136) [1998 75: 9d⁴ 10g   **63** 8.2d 8m* 8m⁶ 9d 9m⁵ 8.1g⁵ 9.9m⁶ 8g⁴ 9.7s 1999 a12g⁶ 10s 8.3d 10d³ a8g⁶ 10m* Jun 22] leggy, close-coupled filly: modest handicapper: won apprentice race at Lingfield in June: will prove best at 1m/1¼m: acts on equitrack, good to firm and good to soft going, probably not on soft: seems effective blinkered or not: rather headstrong, and likely to prove best held up (downed tools ridden prominently penultimate start): sent to Saudi Arabia. *G. L. Moore*

RESURRECTION (IRE)   4 b.f. Midyan (USA) 124 – Tolstoya (Northfields   **–** (USA)) [1998 –: 10.3d 8f 6g a6g 1999 a8g a12g Jan 18] leggy filly: no sign of ability. *M. C. Chapman*

RETALIATOR   3 b.f. Rudimentary (USA) 118 – Redgrave Design 77 (Nebbiolo   **80** 125) [1998 69: a5g⁶ 5m³ 5g³ 6m* 7m⁵ 6.5g⁴ 6g³ 6m 1999 7s² 7g 7f³ 6.1d* 6d 6m   **a–** 7m* 6d 5.1m 7m⁴ 6.1m 6f⁵ a7g 6.1s a7f a6g Oct 30] rather sparely-made filly: fairly useful performer: won claimer (final start for M. Bell) and handicap at Chester in June, forcing pace both times: below form after: best at 6f/7f: acts on soft and good to firm going, no show on fibresand: visored once: has been bandaged: edgy sort, has given trouble in preliminaries. *P. D. Evans*

RETURN OF AMIN   5 ch.h. Salse (USA) 128 – Ghassanah 73 (Pas de Seul 133)   **99** [1998 102, a83: a7g⁶ 6v 6g⁶ 6s* 6d⁶ 6v² 6g² 7m 6s 7g² 7g⁶ 6s⁵ 1999 7g 7.1g⁵   **a–** 6s⁵ 7.1d⁵ 6m 7m Jun 26] angular, good-bodied horse: has a quick action: useful performer on turf: ran creditably in 1999 only when fifth in rated stakes at Haydock (listed event) and York and listed race at Haydock (behind Warningford): effective at 6f/7f: acts on fibresand, very best turf efforts on good ground or softer: blinkered penultimate start: often held up: game: joined W. Muir. *J. D. Bethell*

RETURN TO BASE   2 b.g. (May 12) Whittingham (IRE) 104 – Isla Bonita (Kings   **–** Lake (USA) 133) [1999 5g Sep 15] 1,200Y, resold 2,000Y: close-coupled gelding: half-brother to 2 winners abroad, including Italian winner at around 11f Ercole Il Grande (by Persian Heights): dam unraced half-sister to dam of Almushtarak: well held in maiden at Beverley. *C. W. Fairhurst*

RETURN TO BRIGHTON   7 b.m. Then Again 126 – Regency Brighton (Royal   **29**
Palace 131) [1998 39, a–: 8m 10g² 10m 1999 10g 10.1g⁶ 10g 12.3m 12.1m Jul 23]
rather leggy mare: poor handicapper: stays 1¼m: acts on good to firm ground, well
beaten on all-weather: successful over hurdles in August. *J. M. Bradley*

REVENGE   3 b.g. Saddlers' Hall (IRE) 126 – Classic Heights (Shirley Heights   **77**
130) [1998 NR 1999 10m 11.9d⁴ Aug 7] 50,000Y: lengthy, quite good-topped
gelding: poor mover: fifth foal: brother to a winner in Greece: dam unraced sister
to high-class middle-distance performer Head For Heights: much better effort in
maidens when staying-on fourth at Haydock, soon off bridle: may improve further,
particularly at 1¾m+. *R. T. Phillips*

REVERSE CHARGE   7 b.g. Teenoso (USA) 135 – Ebb And Flo 82 (Forlorn   **–**
River 124) [1998 NR 1999 17.2g Aug 25] very lightly raced and no form on Flat:
joined C. Grant, and successful 3 times over hurdles in November and December.
D. Nicholls

REVIEWING (USA)   3 ch.c. Irish River (FR) 131 – Be Exclusive 110 (Be My   **87 p**
Guest (USA) 126) [1998 NR 1999 8s³ 8.3m* 8g 10g 8.2d* Oct 21] useful-looking
colt: fourth foal: half-brother to 3 winners, including fairly useful 1997 2-y-o 6f
winner Vignette (by Diesis), later successful in USA, and US minor 1m stakes winner
Be Elusive (by With Approval): dam French winner up to 9f (Prix Chloe), also
successful at 5 yrs in USA: fairly useful form: won maiden at Windsor in August
and handicap at Nottingham in October, latter by short head from Katy Nowaitee,
dictating pace and rallying: likely to prove best at 7f/1m: acts on good to firm and
good to soft going, showed promise on soft: should improve further. *J. H. M. Gosden*

REVIVAL   2 b.f. (Feb 7) Sadler's Wells (USA) 132 – Fearless Revival 102 (Cozzene   **– P**
(USA)) [1999 6d Oct 14] lengthy filly: fifth foal: half-sister to 3 winners, including
very smart sprinter Pivotal (by Polar Falcon) and fairly useful 1m winner (stayed
1¼m) Brave Revival (by Dancing Brave): dam 2-y-o 6f/7f winner who stayed 1¼m:
weak in market and very green when promising ninth of 14 to Alfini in Newmarket
maiden, never placed to challenge nor knocked about: should stay at least 7f: sure to
do a lot better and win races at 3 yrs. *Sir Michael Stoute*

REVOLUTION   5 b.h. Suave Dancer (USA) 136 – Sunny Flower (FR) (Dom   **–**
Racine (FR) 121) [1998 –: 8.2s⁵ 8v⁴ a12g⁴ 12d⁴ 8m 1999 a8g Jan 18] big, good-
topped horse: signs of a little ability. *D. Nicholls*

REWARD   5 gr.g. Highest Honor (FR) 124 – Intimate Guest 110§ (Be My Guest   **–**
(USA) 126) [1998 NR 1999 7v⁶ 6.1s 5.3f 10.2g May 21] tall, angular gelding:
disappointing maiden: should be suited by further than 1m: blinkered (looked none
too keen) penultimate start. *D. L. Williams*

REX IS OKAY   3 ch.g. Mazilier (USA) 107 – Cocked Hat Girl 47 (Ballacashtal   **82**
(CAN)) [1998 80: 6s 5d³ 7d⁵ 6s⁵ 6d³ 8d³ 7s* 7d* 1999 8s 7s 5s 8g 8m³ 8.5s² 7s³ 7d³
6g³ 7s Oct 22] quite good-topped gelding: fairly useful handicapper: placed 5 times
in 1999, running particularly well at York on eighth start: probably best at 7f: has
form on good to firm going, goes well on good to soft/soft: blinkered last 3 outings:
races up with pace. *S. R. Bowring*

REYNOLDS (IRE)   3 b.g. Royal Academy (USA) 130 – In Perpetuity 90 (Great   **59**
Nephew 126) [1998 –p: 7d 1999 7g 7v⁶ 7m⁶ Jul 17] rangy, unfurnished gelding:
shaped well in maidens first 2 starts: very disappointing after, dropping away tamely
in handicap at Newmarket (after 3-month break) final start: has looked headstrong
and possibly quirky: sold 3,000 gns. *R. Charlton*

RHAGAAS   3 b.c. Sadler's Wells (USA) 132 – Darara 129 (Top Ville 129) [1998   **115**
107p] 1999 12m² 12s³ 16.2m⁵ 15m² 14s³ Oct 3] rangy, rather unfurnished colt:
fluent mover: smart performer: best effort when 7 lengths third to Montjeu in Prix du
Jockey Club at Chantilly in June: ran respectably at best after, finding little when fifth
in Queen's Vase at Royal Ascot, then keeping-on length second to Northerntown in
Prix de Lutece at Longchamp and 4½ lengths third to Win For Us in Deutsches St
Leger at Dortmund: probably stays 15f: has form on good to firm going, goes well on
good to soft/soft: blinkered/visored last 4 starts: has worn crossed noseband: has high
head carriage. *Saeed bin Suroor*

RHAPSODIST (USA) 3 b.c. Affirmed (USA) – Secret Rhapsody (USA) (Secreto **112**
(USA) 128) [1998 107: 6m² 7s* 7f² 7d 8g³ 1999 10.3s² 10m* 10m⁴ 9f Oct 23]
useful-looking, unfurnished colt: smart performer: won listed race at Newbury in
July by neck from Pegnitz: creditable 3 lengths fourth to Zindabad in Winter Hill
Stakes at Windsor in August: only eighth of 9 in Grade 2 event at Santa Anita final
start: stays 1¼m: yet to race on heavy going, acts on any other: hung markedly left in
visor on reappearance: sent to UAE. *J. H. M. Gosden*

RHAPSODY IN BLUE (IRE) 4 b.g. Magical Strike (USA) 114 – Palace Blue –
(IRE) (Dara Monarch 128) [1998 –: 8f 11.6m 11.5g 1999 11.1m Jun 23] close-
coupled gelding: no form: blinkered only 4-y-o start: sold 500 gns. *Andrew Turnell*

RHAPSODY IN WHITE (IRE) 5 b.g. Contract Law (USA) 108 – Lux Aeterna –
(Sandhurst Prince 128) [1998 NR 1999 12.3m 10m Aug 10] smallish gelding: fair
form for M. Jarvis in 1997: well held over hurdles and on Flat since: tried blinkered.
S. E. Kettlewell

RHEINBOLD 5 br.g. Never So Bold 135 – Rheinbloom 66 (Rheingold 137) [1998 **67**
76d: 8d 10.3g⁵ 12m⁶ 12g 12s⁶ 10.3g³ 12g³ 9m 7.5m⁶ a9.4g⁵ 1999 10d² 11.6m 12g³
9.7f⁵ Jul 14] strong gelding: shows knee action: fair handicapper: stays 1½m: acts on
firm going, good to soft and fibresand. *Mrs A. E. Johnson*

RHODAMINE (IRE) 2 b.c. (Apr 22) Mukaddamah (USA) 125 – Persian Empress **72**
(IRE) 51 (Persian Bold 123) [1999 5.9m 7m 6m* 7f⁴ 6g 8g³ 8m⁵ 7.9d⁴ Oct 7]
IR 9,000F, 12,000 2-y-o: smallish, close-coupled colt: fourth foal: half-brother to
winners in Italy by Imp Society and Namaqualand: dam, maiden who ran only at 2

yrs, stayed 7f: fair performer: won maiden at Newcastle in July: best efforts in nurseries last 3 starts: stays 1m: acts on firm and good to soft going. *J. L. Eyre*

RHODE ISLAND (IRE) 2 b.c. (May 6) Dolphin Street (FR) 125 – Far From **83 p**
Home 73 (Habitat 134) [1999 6f 6m⁴ 6m⁴ 6s* Sep 24] IR 35,000Y: smallish, sturdy, quite attractive colt: very good walker: fifth foal: half-brother to fairly useful Irish 1998 2-y-o 5f winner My Chief (by Perugino) and useful Irish 6f and 7.8f winner Poker-B (by Shalford): dam, 6f winner, half-sister to smart 6f to 1m winner Missed Blessing (dam of Unblest): fairly useful form: left G. Lewis after third start, then showed much improved form when winning 18-runner nursery at Haydock (under top weight) in September by 1¾ lengths from Glendamah, leading inside final 1f: will stay 7f: acts on soft going: sold 28,000 gns in October. *N. Hamilton*

RHYTHM BAND (USA) 3 gr. or ro.c. Cozzene (USA) – Golden Wave Band **109 p**
(USA) (Dixieland Band (USA)) [1998 8f* 1999 8m* Jul 14] tall, rather leggy colt: second foal: half-brother to a winner in US by Silver Deputy: dam won up to 9f in USA, mainly in sprints: won maiden at Belmont (for H. J. Bond) in 1998 and 5-runner minor event at Doncaster only 3-y-o start, latter by length from Sunstreak, finding plenty for pressure: stays 1m: looks a smart prospect. *Saeed bin Suroor*

RIBBLE ASSEMBLY 4 ch.g. Presidium 124 – Spring Sparkle 95 (Lord Gayle **59 d**
(USA) 124) [1998 59: 8s⁵ 8.2m² 8m 8d 9.3m⁵ 7g 8m 8m 12m 10g 9m³ 9.9m 1999 8.3v* 9.2v 11d 10.5d 8.2m 7.5m 8f 9g 8.3f Aug 24] smallish gelding: modest performer: won on reappearance for a second successive year in minor event at Hamilton in March: well beaten after: probably stays 1¼m: acts on good to firm and heavy ground: tried blinkered/visored: has been very slowly away. *K. A. Ryan*

RIBBLE PRINCESS 4 b.f. Selkirk (USA) 129 – Ricochet Romance (USA) –
(Shadeed (USA) 135) [1998 65: 8.5m⁴ 8g³ 7m 1999 11.1v Mar 29] unfurnished filly: fair maiden at 3 yrs: soundly beaten only 4-y-o start: stays 8.5f. *K. A. Ryan*

RIBBON LAKE (IRE) 2 b.f. (Jan 24) Namaqualand (USA) – Topmost (IRE) **73**
(Top Ville 129) [1999 6g³ 7m² 6m* 6m⁶ 6.5g 8d Oct 15] IR 4,500F, IR 4,800Y: third foal: half-sister to Irish 1998 2-y-o 7f winner Ray of Light (by Rainbows For Life) and a winner in Scandinavia by Roi Danzig: dam poor Irish maiden: fair performer: won maiden at Lingfield in July: well beaten in Newmarket nursery final start: should stay 7f: acts on good to firm going. *Mrs P. N. Dutfield*

RIBERAC 3 b.f. Efisio 120 – Ciboure 74 (Norwick (USA) 125) [1998 49: 6g 5m* **87 ?**
5.2m³ 5d⁵ 6s⁶ 1999 6m 6m³ 6m⁶ 6d Nov 1] angular filly: has a round action: fairly useful performer: seemed to run well when third of 5 in minor event at Newmarket in July: below that form otherwise, leaving W. Haggas and off over 2 months before final start: should stay 7f: best efforts on good to firm going: frequently gives trouble stalls, twice withdrawn as a result in 1999. *M. Johnston*

RICCARTON 6 b.g. Nomination 125 – Legendary Dancer 90 (Shareef Dancer **67 d**
(USA) 135) [1998 68: 11v* 10m 9.2g* 10.9m⁴ 9.2m³ 10.3m* 10s⁴ 10.9d 10s 1999 10m⁴ 10.2g⁶ 9m⁴ 10m⁵ 9g 10.2g 10m Sep 7] big gelding: modest handicapper: disappointing after reappearance: stays 1½m: acts on good to firm and heavy going: blinkered twice: usually held up: sometimes hangs left: successful over hurdles in September. *J. M. Bradley*

RICHARD ANSDELL 2 gr.g. (Mar 24) Absalom 128 – Reina 24 (Homeboy **78**
114) [1999 a5g* 5m⁴ a6g⁴ 5m 5g 6g a6g⁵ Oct 16] 6,500Y, 20,000 2-y-o: third foal: **a70**
brother to a winner in Macau: dam maiden who stayed 7f: fair performer: won maiden at Wolverhampton in April: mostly well below form after next start: probably stays 6f: acts on good to firm going and fibresand: tried visored: sold 7,200 gns. *N. P. Littmoden*

RICH BALLERINA (USA) 3 b.f. Strike The Gold (USA) – Corps de Ballet 89 **58**
(Green Dancer (USA) 132) [1998 72p: 7s a7g* 1999 a8g² a8.5g⁴ a7g³ a7g³ a7g Mar 19] fair winner at 2 yrs: just modest in 1999, seeming to go amiss before falling at early stage final start: should stay 1m: raced mainly on fibresand: blinkered second and third starts. *D. Carroll*

RICH DOMINION 3 ch.g. First Trump 118 – Tiszta Sharok 81 (Song 132) [1998 –
55: 5d 5g 5d⁵ 6g 6s 5d 5m 6s 1999 a6g 8.2s⁴ a9.4g⁵ 7m a8g May 6] modest maiden

at 2 yrs: just poor at best in 1999: seems to stay 1m: acts on soft going: effective blinkered or not. *J. D. Bethell*

RICH GLOW 8 b.g. Rich Charlie 117 – Mayglow (Sparkling Boy 110) [1998 44d, a–: a6g 5f⁶ 5g⁶ 5g⁶ 5g⁶ 5d⁶ 5d⁶ 6m 6g 5m 7m 5m 5m 6m 1999 5d Apr 15] leggy, angular gelding: poor performer nowadays: well beaten only 8-y-o start: stays 6f: acts on firm and soft going, no show on fibresand: occasionally blinkered: held up. *N. Bycroft* —

RICH IN LOVE (IRE) 5 b.m. Alzao (USA) 117 – Chief's Quest (USA) (Chief's Crown (USA)) [1998 89: 8g² 10.4g 6.1m² 6g 7m 7m 8g 7m* 7m* 7f² 7g² 7d⁶ 7g 10m 1999 8.5m⁴ 7m² 6m⁴ 8m 7d³ 7g⁵ 7m⁶ 8.1m⁴ 7m 7m 7m Sep 11] angular mare: useful performer: ran creditably on several occasions in 1999, including in listed races at Lingfield (to Presumed then Bold Fact) on second and third starts and Sandown (fourth to Etizaaz) on eighth: possibly finds 6f on sharp side nowadays, and stays 1m: acts on firm and good to soft going: below form blinkered. *C. A. Cyzer* 95

RICH VEIN (IRE) 2 b.g. (May 2) Up And At 'em 109 – Timissara (USA) (Shahrastani (USA) 135) [1999 7s⁵ 7g 8s Oct 25] 12,000Y: fifth foal: half-brother to 3 winners, including 4-y-o Lift The Offer and fairly useful Irish 11f and 1½m winner Timidjar (by Doyoun): dam Irish 1m and 1½m winner: form in maidens only at Lingfield on debut. *S. P. C. Woods* 63

RIDDLE 3 ch.f. Superlative 118 – Griddle Cake (IRE) 62 (Be My Guest (USA) 126) [1998 55d, a–: 6g⁵ 5g 5d a7g a6f a5g⁶ 1999 a5g⁴ a7g⁴ a7g² a7f a6g³ a7g a6g Feb 17] sparely-made filly: poor maiden: effective at 5f to 7f: acts on equitrack: visored last 2 starts at 2 yrs, blinkered in 1999. *P. D. Evans* 44

RIDDLESDOWN (IRE) 2 ch.c. (Apr 24) Common Grounds 118 – Neat Dish (CAN) 90 (Stalwart (USA)) [1999 8s³ 8g² 8s* Oct 26] 25,000Y: fourth foal: brother to Irish 9f winner Flags Up and half-brother to useful Irish 7f (at 2 yrs) to 1¼m winner Fill The Bill (by Bob Back): dam 6f winner at 2 yrs: fairly useful form in maidens, making all in 13-runner event at Bath eased by head from Mbele: will stay 1¼m: acts on soft going. *S. P. C. Woods* 91

RIDE THE TIGER (IRE) 2 ch.c. (Feb 13) Imp Society (USA) – Krisdaline (USA) 98 (Kris S (USA)) [1999 6g 7g 7d Aug 11] 4,000Y: second foal: half-brother to a 1998 2-y-o 7f winner in Germany by Rainbows For Life: dam, Irish 1¼m winner, half-sister to smart sprinter Freddie Lloyd: well beaten in maidens/claimer. *M. D. I. Usher* —

RIDGECREST 2 ch.c. (May 2) Anshan 119 – Lady Sabo 69 (Prince Sabo 123) [1999 5m 5.1m 5.7s³ a6g a7g⁴ a8g² a7g⁴ a8g² Dec 29] 650F: third foal: dam 5f (at 2 yrs)/6f winner who stayed 1m: modest maiden: runs mainly in sellers: stays 1m: acts on all-weather and soft going. *R. Ingram* 56

RIDGEWAY (IRE) 4 b.c. Indian Ridge 123 – Regal Promise (Pitskelly 122) [1998 107: 8.2s* 8s² 12.3g⁴ 1999 8.1g⁴ May 28] tall colt: useful performer,lightly raced: signs of retaining ability when fourth of 7 to Alrassaam in minor event at Haydock only 4-y-o start: seems to stay 1½m: acts on soft going: sold 17,000 gns. *G. Wragg* 92 +

RIDGEWOOD BAY (IRE) 2 b.f. (Mar 20) Ridgewood Ben 113 – Another Baileys 60 (Deploy 131) [1999 6.1d 6g 6g 8.1m⁶ 5v 7d 8s 8.3d Nov 4] IR 9,500Y: big, heavy-topped filly: second foal: half-sister to 3-y-o Irish Cream: dam, 7f winner, ran only at 2 yrs: no sign of ability: has been bandaged. *J. C. Fox* —

RIDGEWOOD RUBY (IRE) 4 b.f. Indian Ridge 123 – Glen Kella Manx 97 (Tickled Pink 114) [1998 77: 8v 8m⁵ 7d³ 8g⁵ 7g³ 8d 1999 6g 5m Jun 11] fifth reported foal: half-sister to 1992 2-y-o 6f seller winner Pat Poindestres (by Interrex): dam, 5f/6f winner who stayed 7f, half-sister to dam of Ridgewood Pearl (by Indian Ridge): fair maiden at 3 yrs for J. Oxx in Ireland: below form both 4-y-o starts: stays 7f: acts on good to soft ground. *D. R. C. Elsworth* —

RIFIFI 6 ch.g. Aragon 115 – Bundled Up (USA) (Sharpen Up 127) [1998 84: 6d 6g 6g 6g 6g 6m 6m⁶ 6m⁶ 6m* 5m* 6m⁴ 6d³ 6s 7g a6g a7g* 1999 a7g⁴ a7g 6g² 6m 6f 6m 6m Jun 19] small, sturdy gelding: poor mover: fairly useful handicapper: good second of 23 at Kempton in April: well held after: stays easy 7f: acts on equitrack, raced mainly between good to firm and good to soft ground on turf: has worn bandages: usually comes from off pace. *R. Ingram* 86

Worthington Lincoln (Handicap), Doncaster—
Right Wing (visor) gets to the front under a splendid ride from Richard Quinn,
beating Captain Scott; the other horse pictured, Raheen, finishes fourth

RIGADOON (IRE) 3 b.g. Be My Chief (USA) 122 – Loucoum (FR) 93 (Iron **63**
Duke (FR) 122) [1998 –: 5g 6g 7.5m 1999 7s 8m 8d 14.1f⁶ 17.2m* 12.1m³ 16m*
16d⁶ 15.8g* Sep 18] tall, unfurnished gelding: modest handicapper: won at Carlisle
(maiden event) in June, Nottingham in July and Catterick in September: will prove
best at 2m+: acts on good to firm ground, possibly not on softer than good: blinkered
after fourth start: won juvenile hurdle in November. *M. W. Easterby*

RIGGING 3 b.f. Warning 136 – Pilot 117 (Kris 135) [1998 60: 5m 1999 7m 8s a8g **64**
8d Oct 11] small, good-quartered filly: modest maiden: saddle slipped on return from
4-month break final start: seems rather headstrong, and likely to prove best up to 1m:
best efforts on good to firm going: has been early to post. *B. W. Hills*

RIGHT WING (IRE) 5 b.h. In The Wings 128 – Nekhbet 74 (Artaius (USA) **111**
129) [1998 108: 8d³ 8s⁴ 7.1d 8d 8d³ 8m* 7.9g⁶ 1999 8d* 8d² 7.9d⁵ 10g 10.4g³ 10s
8.2s* Nov 1] smallish horse: smart performer: won Worthington Lincoln (Handicap)
at Doncaster (beat Captain Scott by ½ length, landing gamble) in March and minor
event at Nottingham (beat Weet-A-Minute by 1½ lengths) in November: ran creditably 3 times in between, including when third to Algunnaas in rated stakes at York:
stays 10.4f: acts on firm and soft going: visored nowadays: has rather high head
carriage and has wandered under pressure: suited by exaggerated waiting tactics, and
well handled by T. Quinn: stays in training. *J. L. Dunlop*

RIGHTY HO 5 b.g. Reprimand 122 – Challanging 95 (Mill Reef (USA) 141) **61**
[1998 NR 1999 12s⁶ 10f³ 12.4m² 12m⁴ 12m⁶ 9.9m⁶ 10.5d 10.4d³ Oct 7] tall, leggy
gelding: modest performer: creditable efforts when placed in 1999: effective at 1¼m/
easy 1½m: probably acts on any going: often visored earlier in career. *C. B. B. Booth*

RIGOLETTO 4 ch.g. Machiavellian (USA) 123 – Sally Brown 120 (Posse (USA) **53 d**
130) [1998 59: 7.1g⁶ 8m 8.2v 1999 a8g⁴ a11g⁴ a12g 15.8m⁶ 15.8d Sep 21] big
gelding: modest maiden at best: sold out of C. Thornton's stable 500 gns after third
start: probably stays 11f: acts on fibresand, form on turf only on debut. *R. Ford*

RIMATARA   3 ch.g. Selkirk (USA) 129 – Humble Pie 92 (Known Fact (USA)   **74**
135) [1998 NR 1999 9m⁶ Jun 18] 115,000Y: seventh foal: closely related to smart
sprinter Leap For Joy (by Sharpo) and half-brother to 2 winners, including fairly
useful 7f winner West Humble (by Pharly): dam, 2-y-o 6f winner, half-sister to
College Chapel: slowly away in maiden at Goodwood: sold 3,400 gns. *I. A. Balding*

RIMBA (USA)   3 b.f. Dayjur (USA) 137 – Ristna 120 (Kris 135) [1998 82: 6g⁶   **73**
6m⁴ 1999 7g 7d 7g³ Jun 3] rangy filly: has no off-eye: has a round action: fair maiden:
form in 1999 only at Yarmouth final start: free-going sort, may prove best up to 7f:
acts on good to firm going. *J. H. M. Gosden*

RING CHEQUER'S   4 ch.g. Magic Ring (IRE) 115 – Sharp Silk (Sharpo 132)   **–**
[1998 –: 7g 1999 a10g Jan 1] well beaten in seller and maiden. *T. T. Clement*

RING DANCER   4 b.c. Polar Falcon (USA) 126 – Ring Cycle 64 (Auction Ring   **87**
(USA) 123) [1998 95: 7m² 6f 5g 6f⁴ 6.1g³ 6d 1999 6g 6v Sep 29] useful-looking colt:
good walker: fairly useful performer: better effort in handicaps 3 months apart in
1999 when ninth of 26 at Goodwood on reappearance: slowly away next start: stays
easy 7f: acts on firm and good to soft ground: has worn crossed noseband, been
attended by 2 handlers and early to post. *P. J. Makin*

RING FENCE   3 b.f. Polar Falcon (USA) 126 – Ring Cycle 64 (Auction Ring   **74**
(USA) 123) [1998 NR 1999 6g⁴ 6m³ 5d* Aug 11] deep-girthed, lengthy filly: third
foal: sister to 4-y-o Ring Dancer and half-sister to 7f winner Farley Green (by
Pharly): dam 6f winner from 2 starts at 2 yrs: fair form: won maiden at Sandown in
August by a head, overcoming trouble: may prove best at stiff 5f/6f: blanketed for
stalls entry last 2 starts: may still do better. *H. Candy*

RING MY MATE   2 ch.c. (Apr 22) Komaite (USA) – My Ruby Ring 72 (Blushing   **61**
Scribe (USA) 107) [1999 7s⁶ a8g³ a7g⁴ Dec 10] 3,000Y: second foal: half-brother to
3-y-o My Man Friday: dam 6f winner: modest form in maidens, in frame at Southwell and Lingfield: likely to prove best up to 1m. *W. R. Muir*

RING OF LOVE   3 b.f. Magic Ring (IRE) 115 – Fine Honey (USA) 90 (Drone)   **77**
[1998 73: 5.1s⁵ 5v² 5.1m* 5.2m 5.1g³ 5m 1999 6.1h* 6g 5s 5m² 5m⁶ 5d⁶ 5m* 5m*
5.2g 5g⁵ a5g a6g⁴ a6g⁵ Dec 11] good-topped filly: fair performer: won handicaps at
Musselburgh in August (apprentices) and September: left M. Bell for 7,000 gns after
eleventh start: likely to prove best at 5f: has form on heavy going/fibresand, best
efforts on good to firm/firm: visored seventh start: has pulled hard: usually comes
from off pace. *J. L. Eyre*

RING OF VISION (IRE)   7 br.g. Scenic 128 – Circus Lady (High Top 131)   **34**
[1998 NR 1999 a12f 10d 13d May 24] fair handicapper for Mrs M. Reveley in 1996:
poor form in 1999: probably stays 1½m: acts on good to firm going, good to soft and
fibresand: winning hurdler. *J. J. Quinn*

RINGSIDE JACK   3 b.g. Batshoof 122 – Celestine 62 (Skyliner 117) [1998 73:   **82 d**
5d 6g 5d* 6d³ 7.5m² 7.9g 7m⁴ 1999 8d 8m² 8.2m 8m 10.5d 10m 10.2m 10g³ 10g
10.3d⁵ 10d Nov 1] quite good-topped gelding: fairly useful handicapper: well below
form after fifth start: stays 1¼m: yet to race on extremes of going: visored last 4
starts. *C. W. Fairhurst*

RING THE CHIEF   7 b.g. Chief Singer 131 – Lomond Ring (Lomond (USA)   **44**
128) [1998 37: a8s³ a6g a8.5g⁴ 1999 a8g* a8g² a7f³ a7g a7g⁶ Mar 13] poor handicapper: won apprentice event at Southwell in January: ran creditably next 2 starts:
stays 1¼m: acts on fibresand, firm and good to soft ground (possibly not on soft).
M. D. I. Usher

RING THE RAFTERS   4 b.f. Batshoof 122 – Soprano 112 (Kris 135) [1998 –:   **–**
7.1m 8d a8g 1999 a12g a9.4g Feb 6] sturdy filly: no form: tried visored/blinkered.
B. P. J. Baugh

RING THE RELATIVES   3 b.f. Bering 136 – Relatively Special 112 (Alzao   **75**
(USA) 117) [1998 NR 1999 7g⁴ 10g² Aug 2] 50,000Y: first foal: dam, 2-y-o 6f and
7f (Rockfel) winner who was later ideally suited by 1¼m, half-sister to very smart
1¼m performer One So Wonderful, from family of Milligram: in frame in maidens,
8 lengths second to Didifon at Ripon. *L. M. Cumani*

RIO'S DIAMOND   2 b.f. (May 5) Formidable (USA) 125 – Rio Piedras 86 (Kala   **33**
Shikari 125) [1999 5g 5v 5.1f 6s a6g³ 8d 8d a6g a6g Nov 17] 1,600Y: small filly: **a42**

third living foal: dam best at 1¼m: poor maiden: stays 6f, seemingly not 1m: acts on fibresand: visored penultimate start. *M. J. Ryan*

RIPARIAN 2 b.g. (Apr 7) Last Tycoon 131 – La Riveraine (USA) 90 (Riverman (USA) 131) [1999 7.1m⁵ Sep 4] second foal: half-brother to 3-y-o Riverblue: dam won twice around 1½m: fifth of 14 to Hunting Tiger in maiden at Haydock, not given unduly hard time: will stay at least 1¼m: should do better. *Sir Michael Stoute* **75 p**

RIPLEY 2 b.f. (Apr 16) Presidium 124 – Hannie Caulder (Workboy 123) [1999 6m Jun 15] 4,500Y: half-sister to several winners, including 5-y-o Jedi Knight: dam unraced half-sister to Mrs McArdy: tailed off in seller at Thirsk. *M. W. Easterby* **–**

RIPSNORTER (IRE) 10 ch.h. Rousillon (USA) 133 – Formulate 119 (Reform 132) [1998 –, a38: a8g a8g⁶ a8g* a8g³ a8g⁶ a10g a8.5g 9m a8g a9.4g 8.2s 8s a9.4g a8g 1999 a8g a10g Jan 9] poor performer: stays 8.5f: acts on good to firm going, good to soft and all-weather: visored both 10-y-o starts: inconsistent. *P. D. Purdy* **–**

RISCATTO (USA) 5 b.g. Red Ransom (USA) – Ultima Cena (USA) (Leonardo Da Vinci (FR)) [1998 44, a–: 10s³ a12g a10g 1999 a13g⁴ a10g Feb 16] tall gelding: poor handicapper: stays 1¼m: acts on good to firm ground, soft and fibresand: tried blinkered: carries head high. *W. R. Muir* **–**

RISE 'N SHINE 5 ch.m. Night Shift (USA) – Clunk Click 72 (Star Appeal 133) [1998 –, a59: a6g³ a8g² a5g* a5g³ a6g² a5g³ a6g⁶ a5g 5.1g a5g a5f⁶ 1999 a5g a5f a5g² a5g⁴ a5g⁵ 5m⁶ 5g May 29] workmanlike mare: poor handicapper: effective at 5f/6f: acts on equitrack and firm ground: effective blinkered or not. *C. A. Cyzer* **41 a47**

RISING SPRAY 8 ch.g. Waajib 121 – Rose Bouquet 78 (General Assembly (USA)) [1998 72: 12m⁴ 11.4g⁵ 14m⁶ 12g³ 14g 12m² 1999 12m 10m² 10g 14g⁶ Jun 11] quite good-topped gelding: has a quick action: fair handicapper: effective at 1¼m to 1¾m: acts on good to firm and good to soft going: sometimes slowly away (markedly so in blinkers penultimate start), and usually held up. *C. A. Horgan* **75**

RISK FREE 2 ch.g. (Feb 12) Risk Me (FR) 127 – Princess Lily 65 (Blakeney 126) [1999 5g a5g* 5g a5g² 6s 6d a7g² Nov 26] 5,000Y: tall, leggy gelding: brother to 3 winners, including 1991 2-y-o 7f winner Personal Hazard and 1m to 2m winner Royal Roulette: dam maiden who stayed 1½m: fairly useful performer: won maiden at Southwell in May: good second in nursery on same course in July: well below form last 2 starts: bred to be suited by further than 5f: acts on fibresand. *N. P. Littmoden* **79 ? a88**

RISK MATERIAL (IRE) 4 b.c. Danehill (USA) 126 – Spear Dance (Gay Fandango (USA) 132) [1998 113: 10s² 10g* 10m* 10g³ 12v 12m 10m⁴ 9d* 11s⁶ 1999 10s⁶ 14m² 14m⁵ 8.5m 10m Aug 14] sturdy, close-coupled colt: useful performer: best effort in 1999 when second to Enzeli in listed race at Leopardstown: sixth in Gordon Richards Stakes at Sandown previous start: stays 1¾m: acts to race on firm ground, acts on any other: blinkered final outing. *A. P. O'Brien, Ireland* **108**

RISKNOWT GETNOWT 4 b.g. Ron's Victory (USA) 129 – Scottish Tina (Scottish Reel 123) [1998 NR 1999 a12g Feb 6] of no account. *R. J. Price* **–**

RISKY EXPERIENCE 3 ch.f. Risk Me (FR) 127 – First Experience 58 (Le Johnstan 123) [1998 55d: 5d⁶ 6m 5.1g³ 5.1g 5f⁶ a6g 5.1g⁵ a5g² 6d 6s a5g a6g⁵ 1999 a6g a6g 6g Apr 8] modest maiden at best: should stay 6f: acts on fibresand and good to soft going: tried visored. *B. P. J. Baugh* **–**

RISKY GEM 2 ch.c. (Jan 5) Risk Me (FR) 127 – Dark Kristal (IRE) 66 (Gorytus (USA) 132) [1999 5m 6d 5m² 6d a6g* 7m 7m⁶ 6s a6g Oct 18] 4,000F: fourth foal (all by Risk Me): dam winner at 6f: modest performer: won nursery at Wolverhampton in July: stays 7f: acts on good to firm going and fibresand: has found little and looked less than keen: sold 5,500 gns. *R. Hannon* **57 a62**

RISKY MONEY 4 b.c. Risk Me (FR) 127 – Where's The Money 87 (Lochnager 132) [1998 –: a6g 7v 8g 7d 1999 8.3g May 10] no form. *V. Soane* **–**

RISKY REEF 2 ch.g. (May 5) Risk Me (FR) 127 – Pas de Reef 49 (Pas de Seul 133) [1999 6g⁵ 6d² Oct 18] 2,000F, 6,200Y: workmanlike gelding: second foal: dam 1¼m and 11f winner: fair form in maidens at Windsor and Pontefract, better effort when second of 12 to Ravishing on second occasion: should stay 7f: capable of further improvement. *I. A. Balding* **82 p**

RISKY VALENTINE 3 ch.f. Risk Me (FR) 127 – Mandrake Madam 88 **68**
(Mandrake Major 122) [1998 63: 5.1d³ a5g* 5.1s³ 5.1m 5d² a6g a6g⁵ a7g² a7g³ 6s⁵
a6g 6.1v³ 5.7v² 5d 1999 6.1v⁴ 6.1s* 6.1s 6d 5s Oct 2] sparely-made filly: fair
handicapper: well below form after winning 20-runner event at Nottingham in April:
barely stays 7f: acts on fibresand, raced mainly on ground softer than good on turf:
hung left penultimate 2-y-o start. *J. L. Spearing*

RISKY WAY 3 b.g. Risk Me (FR) 127 – Hot Sunday Sport 42 (Star Appeal 133) **47**
[1998 55: a5g6 5g⁵ 6s⁶ 7.5d² 7g* a7g³ 6d 7m³ 7m 1999 a6g a8g⁵ a7s⁵ 7s⁶ 7.5d
8f 8m⁵ 8g Jun 14] sparely-made, close-coupled gelding: poor performer: best at
7f/1m: acts on fibresand, soft and good to firm going: won over hurdles in September.
B. S. Rothwell

RISQUE LADY 4 ch.f. Kenmare (FR) 125 – Christine Daae 74 (Sadler's Wells **104**
(USA) 132) [1998 109: 7d³ 7g 7g⁵ 8d 7f³ 7m³ 7d² 8m³ 8g* 1999 8d⁴ 8d³ 8g³
8.5d² 8m* 8m² 8m⁴ 7.9g 10.1g³ 8d Sep 30] smallish, good-quartered filly: useful
performer: won minor event at Newcastle in June by length from Celtic Cross: ran
creditably several times otherwise, including in listed races at Goodwood (third to
Hawriyah) and Epsom (3½ lengths second to Fairy Queen) and Minstrel Stakes at the
Curragh (second to Ramooz) on third, fourth and sixth starts: stays 1m: acts on firm
and good to soft going (yet to race on soft/heavy): has been bandaged near-hind:
often early to post: tends to carry head high: has won from the front, but best held up:
sold 85,000 gns in December. *P. W. Harris*

RITA MACKINTOSH (IRE) 2 b.f. (Apr 12) Port Lucaya 118 – Silver Stream **48**
(USA) (Silver Hawk (USA) 123) [1999 7g⁶ 7g³ 7d 8m⁴ 10s a8.5g³ a8g Nov 15] IR **a45**
5,000Y: third foal: dam, maiden in USA, half-sister to 2-y-o 1m pattern winners
Mesange Bleue (in Italy) and Un Reitre (in France): poor maiden: left M. Tompkins
for 4,000 gns after penultimate start: stays 8.5f: acts on good to firm going and fibresand: ran creditably tried visored. *R. Brotherton*

RITA'S ROCK APE 4 b.f. Mon Tresor 113 – Failand 36 (Kala Shikari 125) **84**
[1998 67, a64: 5m³ 5g 5d 5f⁶ 5m 5.1d³ 5m² 5.3g³ a5g³ a5g⁵ a5g⁴ 1999 a5g⁶ 5.1s
5.1m 5m⁴ 5.3g* 5.1m* 5m* 5.3f* 5m³ 5.3m² 5m* 5.2g³ 5d Oct 18] workmanlike
filly: fairly useful performer: better than ever in 1999, winning handicaps (including
2 apprentice races) at Brighton, Bath, Lingfield and Salisbury and minor event at
Brighton between June and September: best at 5f: acts on firm going, good to soft
and all-weather: reportedly broke blood vessel once at 3 yrs: makes running: tough
and reliable. *R. Brotherton*

RITUAL 4 ch.g. Selkirk (USA) 129 – Pure Formality 84 (Forzando 122) [1998 77: **59**
7g⁴ 7.1s³ 8g 8.1m⁶ a8g* 1999 10s 10g a10g 9.7v 8g 12m 10g 9.9m 10g Jul 5] leggy,
sparely-made gelding: modest performer: stays 1¼m: acts on equitrack and soft
ground, probably on good to firm: awarded novice hurdle in October. *S. Dow*

RITUAL RUN 4 b.g. Rudimentary (USA) 118 – Roussalka 123 (Habitat 134) **–**
[1998 55: 7g 7.1g⁶ 7s 8m 9.9m 1999 a12g⁵ Jan 11] good-topped gelding: modest
maiden at best: may prove best up to 1m: sold 700 gns. *Ronald Thompson*

RIVAL BID (USA) 11 b.g. Cannonade (USA) – Love Triangle (USA) (Nodouble **–**
(USA)) [1998 44, a–: a8.5g a12g a11g⁶ 10g* 10d⁶ 10d a12g a9.4g⁶ 12m 10m 1999
a10g a10g Feb 16] workmanlike gelding: poor handicapper: effective at 9f to 1½m:
acts on firm going, good to soft and all-weather: tried visored. *Mrs N. Macauley*

RIVENDELL 3 b.f. Saddlers' Hall (IRE) 126 – Fairy Kingdom (Prince Sabo 123) **–**
[1998 –: 8g 1999 8.3d 8m 8m⁵ 10g Sep 20] angular, unfurnished filly: little form.
A. G. Newcombe

RIVER BANN (USA) 2 ch.c. (Apr 11) Irish River (FR) 131 – Spiritual Star (USA) **89 p**
(Soviet Star (USA) 128) [1999 8d² Oct 15] $140,000F, 120,000Y: big, rather leggy,
useful-looking colt: second foal: dam minor stakes winner in USA, including 1m
event at 2 yrs: weak in market, better for race and green to post, short-head second of
13 to Pawn Broker in slowly-run maiden at Newmarket, improving to lead final 1f
but just pipped: should stay beyond 1m: has scope, and should do better and win
races. *P. F. I. Cole*

RIVER BEAT (IRE) 4 b.g. River Falls 113 – Aughamore Beauty (IRE) (Dara **85**
Monarch 128) [1998 92: 9.3d³ 11.6g 8.3g* 9.3d* 9.1g* 9.9g* 10f 10g 10s 10s 1999

10g 10m 10m 10f⁴ 10.1g⁵ 10f³ 10m 7.9f 9.1d* 10.4g 10.1m⁵ 8s Oct 25] leggy gelding: fairly useful performer: won claimer at Ayr (final start for K. Burke) in September: probably best at 9f/1¼m nowadays: acts on firm and good to soft going: held up: sold 8,000 gns, sent to Switzerland. *D. Sasse*

RIVERBIRD (IRE) 3 b.f. Mujadil (USA) 119 – Ruby River (Red God 128§) **73**
[1998 65p: 5m 6g⁵ 1999 7g 7m 7m* 8m Sep 18] fair performer: best effort when winning maiden at Goodwood in August: pulled hard and broke blood vessel final start: raced only on good/good to firm ground: sold 4,600 gns in December. *Major D. N. Chappell*

RIVER BLEST (IRE) 3 b.g. Unblest 117 – Vaal Salmon (IRE) (Salmon Leap **57**
(USA) 131) [1998 NR 1999 7d 6s 6f³ 6m³ 6g⁶ Aug 20] 4,800F: tall, angular gelding: second foal: dam unraced: modest maiden: likely to prove best at 5f/6f: acts on firm going, probably on soft: free-going sort. *Mrs A. Duffield*

RIVERBLUE (IRE) 3 b.c. Bluebird (USA) 125 – La Riveraine (USA) 90 (River- **93**
man (USA) 131) [1998 87p: 5.1g³ 7m⁴ 7.5g² 7d* 6m⁵ 6m* 1999 10.4d 8.1m² 8m 8m⁵ 8.1m 7.6d 8.1s 8.2d⁴ a7g Nov 12] rather leggy, quite attractive colt: fairly useful handicapper: ran very well when second to Date in valuable event at Haydock in May: inconsistent after, leaving M. Channon after seventh start: should stay 1¼m: acts on good to firm and good to soft going: visored fourth/fifth starts: may prove best held up: has flashed tail. *D. J. Wintle*

RIVER BOY (IRE) 3 b.g. River Falls 113 – Natty Gann (IRE) (Mister Majestic **49**
122) [1998 42: 7f 7m⁴ a7g⁶ 8g a8g 1999 a11g⁶ a12g⁵ 9.9d² 10f 8g⁶ 10m⁶ 11.6m⁶ Jul 12] small, angular gelding: poor maiden: probably best at 1¼m: acts on good to firm and good to soft ground, probably on fibresand: blinkered once, visored last 2 starts: has worn dropped noseband: possibly none too genuine. *P. Shakespeare*

RIVER CAPTAIN (USA) 6 ch.g. Riverman (USA) 131 – Katsura (USA) (North- **–**
ern Dancer) [1998 –, a64: a12g a12g* a12g⁵ a14g³ 12g a11g² a12g a12g* 1999 a11g **a64**
a12g⁵ a12g* a12g² 11.8s⁶ a14g⁵ a12g a11g Nov 30] close-coupled gelding: modest handicapper: won at Southwell in March: ran creditably after only when second in apprentice event there: stays 1½m: acts on fibresand, well held all 3 starts on turf. *D. J. G. Murray Smith*

RIVER COLN (USA) 2 b.f. (Mar 29) Irish River (FR) 131 – Erwinna (USA) **54 p**
(Lyphard (USA) 132) [1999 7m 7d Nov 1] $36,000F, IR 75,000Y: seventh foal: half-sister to 5-y-o Wild Sky and several winners in Italy: dam, French maiden, daughter of half-sister to Blushing Groom: modest form in maidens at Salisbury (very green) and Redcar 2 months apart: will stay at least 1m: should do better. *L. M. Cumani*

RIVERDANCE (IRE) 3 ch.g. College Chapel 122 – Valmarana (USA) 51 **64**
(Danzig Connection (USA)) [1998 67: 5.2m⁵ 5s 6d⁶ 5g⁴ 5.1v 1999 6m 8d⁵ 5m 7.1m⁶ **a–**
8s² 8g 8s⁶ 8s a7g a5g a7g⁶ Dec 15] fair maiden handicapper: left Mrs L. Jewell after third start: stays 1m: acts on soft going, probably on good to firm, below best on fibresand: sometimes visored/blinkered. *P. D. Evans*

RIVER ENSIGN 6 br.m. River God (USA) 121 – Ensigns Kit (Saucy Kit 76) **58**
[1998 48: a6s* a6g⁵ a6g³ a8g³ a6g⁴ a6g² a7g a5g⁵ a5g⁵ 6.1s* 6.1m a6g a7g² 6g⁴ 6d⁴ 6d⁶ a6g⁵ 7.6m 6g 6v³ 6.1v 6s⁵ a6g⁶ a6g 1999 a6g³ a7g² a7g a8g² 7s 6d⁵ a6g* a7g² a6g a7g 6d a9.4g² a8.5g⁵ a8.5g² 11.9d³ a9.4g⁴ 10.3s* 10v a12g a8.5g⁴ a8g a8.5g⁶ Dec 27] smallish, plain mare: modest performer: won amateur claimer at Wolverhampton in April and handicap at Chester in September: effective at 6f, barely stays 1½m: acts on fibresand and heavy going (below form on good to firm): often races up with pace: none too consistent. *W. M. Brisbourne*

RIVER JUNCTION (IRE) 8 b.g. Cyrano de Bergerac 120 – Lovestream (Sandy **–**
Creek 123) [1998 35, a–: 10v 10s⁵ 12m⁴ 14.1m⁵ 11.7d 1999 a12g Feb 17] tall gelding: poor handicapper nowadays: effective at 1m to 1½m: acts on good to firm ground, soft and fibresand. *B. Smart*

RIVER SAINT (USA) 3 ch.f. Irish River (FR) 131 – Imagining (USA) (North- **73 §**
fields (USA)) [1998 72p: 6g⁵ 1999 7m⁴ 8m⁵ 7.7m² 7f³ 7.1g⁶ Aug 18] unfurnished filly: fair maiden: should stay 1m: acts on good to firm going: tongue tied/slowly away penultimate start: has flashed tail/tended to hang/find little: not to be relied on. *Sir Michael Stoute*

854

RIVER'S CURTAIN (USA)   2 b.c. (Jan 29) Theatrical 128 – Marshua's River **103 p**
(USA) (Riverman (USA) 131) [1999 7.5v* Oct 31] $210,000Y: second foal: dam US
Grade 3 8.5f winner: easily won 6-runner minor event at Saint-Cloud in October by 4
lengths from Roscius: will be suited by at least 1m: joined Godolphin: looks a good
prospect. *A. Fabre, France*

RIVERSDALE (IRE)   3 b.g. Elbio 125 – Embustera 73 (Sparkler 130) [1998 **61**
57p: 7g 6d⁶ 1999 8m³ 8g⁴ 8.5s 10g 8g² a8.5g Nov 13] good-topped gelding: modest **a–**
maiden: stays 1m, not 1¼m: acts on good to firm ground, well held on soft/fibresand.
J. G. FitzGerald

RIVER'S SOURCE (USA)   5 b.g. Irish River (FR) 131 – Singing (USA) 91 **79 §**
(The Minstrel (CAN) 135) [1998 80: 10.1s⁵ 12g 10s² 9.9d⁶ 8m⁴ 10m⁶ 10m* 9m²
10.9d² 10.4g 10v⁴ 1999 10.2g 12g 10.1m 10m* 10.5m 10.9d 9v Sep 20] sturdy
gelding: fair handicapper: usually runs in amateur races, and won at Pontefract in
August for second year in a row: effective at 9f to 11f: acts on good to firm and
heavy going: visored once, effective blinkered or not: has been bandaged: pulls hard:
probably best held up: none too genuine: sold 5,000 gns. *B. W. Hills*

RIVER'S SPARKLE (IRE)   3 b.f. River Falls 113 – El Zaana (Priamos (GER) **41**
123) [1998 –: 7m 6.1g 7m⁶ 7m 1999 10.8d 11.6m 11.6g⁶ 10f 12.3m⁴ 12m 12.1g⁵ Aug
30] small, plain filly: poor maiden: stayed 1½m: dead. *G. B. Balding*

RIVER TERN   6 b.g. Puissance 110 – Millaine 69 (Formidable (USA) 125) [1998 **79**
72§: 5m 5g³ 5.1d 5d 5.1g⁵ 5m⁴ 5.2g² 5m³ 5m 5m⁶ 1999 5m³ 5m* 5f³ 5m³ 5m⁴ 5m*
5m 5m 5f² 5.1h⁴ 5.7m⁵ 5g⁶ 6g 5.2g⁴ 5.2g⁵ Sep 14] tall gelding: has a high knee action:
fair handicapper: won at Thirsk in May and York in July: ran creditably most other
starts: has won at 6f, races mainly at 5f nowadays: acts on firm going: often visored/
blinkered at 3 yrs: sometimes starts slowly: carries head high, has flashed tail and
often finds little: best held up behind strong pace. *J. M. Bradley*

RIVER TIMES (USA)   3 b.c. Runaway Groom (CAN) – Miss Riverton (USA) **100**
(Fred Astaire (USA)) [1998 84: 5g⁵ 7g³ 6f⁴ 8.1m* 1999 10.5s 7.5m* 7.5g² 7.6m
8.1m 10.1m⁵ 8m* 8m⁵ 8m Sep 11] smallish, quite attractive colt: useful performer:
won minor event at Beverley in April and rated stakes at Newmarket (gamely by
neck from Calcutta) in July: best around 1m: acts on firm going (trip too far on soft):
blinkered last 3 starts: usually races up with pace. *T. D. Easterby*

RM AGAIN   3 b.g. Primo Dominie 121 – La Cabrilla 89 (Carwhite 127) [1998 –: **48 d**
5m 5m 1999 5.1s 6f 5.3f 5g³ 5g⁶ 5g 5.3g 5.3m 5f Sep 4] poor maiden: will prove
best at 5f: has worn blinkers (including for best effort): sold 800 gns, sent to Spain.
R. Guest

ROAR ON TOUR   10 b.g. Dunbeath (USA) 127 – Tickled Trout 70 (Red Alert **– §**
127) [1998 NR 1999 a8g a8g⁴ a8g Jan 18] good-bodied gelding: one-time fair **a42 §**
handicapper: poor performer nowadays: unreliable. *Mrs P. Sly*

ROBANDELA (USA)   2 b.c. (May 15) Kingmambo (USA) 125 – Yemanja (USA) **52 p**
(Alleged (USA) 138) [1999 7m Sep 1] 55,000Y: big, good-topped colt: has plenty
of scope: fourth foal: dam, showed signs of ability in 3 starts, half-sister to Hector
Protector, Shanghai and Bosra Sham: weak in market and green, ninth of 10 in
maiden at York: should do better. *M. Johnston*

ROBANNA   4 b.f. Robellino (USA) 127 – Pounelta 91 (Tachypous 128) [1998 59: **52**
8.2s 6g 8.3g 7g 10.2d⁴ 9.7f 10m 10.8m 14.1s⁴ 14.1v² 1999 13.1g³ 12.1g⁴ 12g a16g
Nov 8] tall, leggy filly: modest maiden handicapper: stays 1¾m: possibly best on
good ground or softer. *J. Akehurst*

ROBBER RED   3 b.g. Mon Tresor 113 – Starisk 47 (Risk Me (FR) 127) [1998 74: **65**
5d⁵ 5.1f⁴ 5d² 5d 5.1g² 6g² 7m⁵ 6f* 6m² 6d 5g² 6g⁵ 1999 8.1s⁵ 8m 6d 6m 6f⁶ 8f²
7.6f 8g⁵ 8d 8m 7m⁶ 8m Sep 10] tall, close-coupled gelding: has a round action: fair
handicapper: stays 1m: acts on firm and good to soft ground: blinkered (ran poorly)
once at 2 yrs: has worn tongue strap: often held up: carried head awkwardly tenth
start: none too reliable. *R. M. Flower*

ROBBIES DREAM (IRE)   3 ch.g. Balla Cove 119 – Royal Golden (IRE) **–**
(Digamist (USA) 110) [1998 69+: 7g 6f 6s⁶ 8m 1999 8.2m 8m 8g Aug 11] small,
sparely-made gelding: poor mover: fair maiden at 2 yrs: well held in 1999: should
stay beyond 6f: acts well on soft going. *D. Morris*

ROBBO   5 b.g. Robellino (USA) 127 – Basha (USA) (Chief's Crown (USA)) [1998 –
67, a–: 15.9g³ 17.1d³ 18g 1999 17.1v⁶ Apr 20] small gelding: fair handicapper:
below form only 5-y-o start: will prove best at 15f+: acts on fibresand and soft
ground: best form when blinkered: won twice over fences in November. *Mrs
M. Reveley*

ROBEENA   4 b.f. Robellino (USA) 127 – Raheena (USA) 69 (Lyphard (USA)   54
132) [1998 –: a7g a10g⁶ 6v a7g 1999 8.3v 7d² 7.1m 7m 6f 7.6m 6f 7f 8.3f 6f⁵ Sep 4]
small filly: modest maiden: stays 7f: acts on good to firm and good to soft going:
tried visored. *J. L. Eyre*

ROBELLION   8 b.g. Robellino (USA) 127 – Tickled Trout 70 (Red Alert 127)   66
[1998 66, a70: a7s² a8g² a8g* a8g³ a8g* a7g⁵ a7g* a8g⁵ 6v² 6g 7m⁶ 7m³ 8.1m 1999
7m* 7.1g 8f 7m 7s 6g Oct 11] sturdy gelding: fair handicapper: below form after
winning ladies event at Lingfield in May: has won at easy 1¼m, best recent form at
6f (given a test) to 1m: acts on any all-weather/turf: often visored earlier in career,
blinkered last 2 starts: bandaged behind: usually held up. *Miss E. C. Lavelle*

ROBELLITA   5 b.g. Robellino (USA) 127 – Miellita 98 (King Emperor (USA))   74
[1998 –: 10d 10d 11.7s 1999 a12g² a12g³ a12g² a12g* 14.1s* a12g² a12g⁶
Dec 6] angular gelding: fair performer: won maiden at Southwell and handicap at
Nottingham (18 ran) in March: will stay 2m: acts on all-weather and soft going: game
and consistent. *B. Smart*

ROBERT ELLIS   3 ch.c. Anshan 119 – Susie's Baby (Balidar 133) [1998 –: 6m   51
5v 1999 5m⁵ Jul 21] lengthy colt: modest form on only 3-y-o start: bred to prove best
at 5f/6f: joined B. Smart. *J. Cullinan*

ROBERT'S TOY (IRE)   8 b.g. Salt Dome (USA) – Zazu 58 (Cure The Blues
(USA)) [1998 –: a14.8g⁴ 1999 a12g⁴ 11.7m⁴ Jul 15] fair winner on Flat at 3 yrs when
trained in Ireland: of similar merit over jumps at best for M. Pipe, but little form in 3
runs on Flat for present stable: blinkered on reappearance. *G. A. Ham*

ROBIN HOOD   2 b.c. (Mar 21) Komaite (USA) – Plough Hill (North Briton 67)   –
[1999 5g Oct 14] 3,200F, 2,000Y: second foal: dam unraced: some late headway after
missing break in 22-runner maiden at Redcar. *Miss L. A. Perratt*

ROBIN LANE   4 b.f. Tenby 125 – Hiawatha's Song (USA) (Chief's Crown (USA))   95
[1998 98: 10v⁴ 10v² 10d 10g* 12d² 9.2g* 9.2m* 10g⁴ 10.1g 10.1m⁴ 10s 8g 12s*
12v* 1999 11.9s 14.1s⁵ 11.9d 12m⁵ 11.9s 11.8m² 14f 10.5g* 10.1g² 10.3m² 12s
10d⁶ 12s 12s Nov 29] small filly: useful performer: won minor event at Warwick in
August: also ran well when second to Fickle in listed rated stakes at Newcastle (ninth
start) and fourth to Vicious Circle in Ritz Club Stakes at Ascot: effective at 1¼m/
1½m (well beaten over 1¾m on firm ground): acts on good to firm and heavy ground:
usually races up with pace: blinkered final start: game: visits Dr Fong. *M. Johnston*

ROBOASTAR (USA)   2 b. or br.c. (Jan 30) Green Dancer (USA) 132 – Sweet   72
Alabastar (USA) (Gulch (USA)) [1999 7.1m 7.5g³ 8.5m² Sep 4] $72,000F: useful-
looking colt: second foal: dam unraced half-sister to dam (by Green Dancer) of smart
French/US middle-distance performer Majorien: fair form in maidens: third of 8 to
Monte Carlo at Epsom final start: should stay 1¼m. *W. Jarvis*

ROBO MAGIC (USA)   7 b.g. Tejano (USA) – Bubble Magic (USA) (Clever   48
Trick (USA)) [1998 40, a85: a8g a6g* a6g⁵ a6g² a6g a5g² a6g* a5g⁵ 5m⁴ 7g 6m a7g²   **a82 d**
a6g a8g⁵ 1999 a7g a7g³ a6g a6g 6g³ 6m⁴ 6g a5g³ 7m a7g⁶ a6g a7g Dec 8] neat
gelding: fairly useful at best on all-weather, poor on turf: stays 7f: acts on good to
firm ground, good to soft and all-weather: effective blinkered, not tried since 1996.
L. Montague Hall

ROBORANT   4 b.g. Robellino (USA) 127 – Sunny Davis (USA) 71 (Alydar   –
(USA)) [1998 84: 8g 9.9m³ 9.9m* 10.2g 9d 9.7f 10g* 10.3d³ 1999 10.1s Apr 21]
useful-looking gelding: fairly useful handicapper in 1998 for J. Dunlop: well held
only 4-y-o start (though won over hurdles later in April): stays 1¼m: acts on good to
firm and good to soft ground: blinkered (below form) twice: lazy sort, and probably
requires strong handling: not one to trust implicitly: sold 800 gns. *J. Akehurst*

ROCCIOSO   2 br.c. (May 7) Pelder (IRE) 125 – Priory Bay 54 (Petong 126) [1999   –
6s 6d Nov 4] third reported live foal: dam poor maiden: well held in maidens.
J. C. Fox

ROCCO TOWER (IRE) 3 b.c. Thatching 131 – Tatra (Niniski (USA) 125) [1998 **101**
NR 1999 5d⁴ 6g* 5m² 5m⁶ Jun 19] IR 8,000Y: good-topped colt: half-brother to
fairly useful Irish 5f winner Zilina (by Pips Pride) and a winner in USA by Tirol:
dam Irish 1½m winner: useful performer: won maiden at Pontefract in May: very
good 1¾-length second of 5 to Dashing Blue in minor event at Sandown, then not
disgraced in handicap at Ascot: stayed 6f: dead. *John Berry*

ROCK FALCON (IRE) 6 ch.g. Polar Falcon (USA) 126 – Rockfest (USA) 104 **104**
(Stage Door Johnny) [1998 107: 8s 8m* 8d 7.1g² 7f 7m* 7d⁴ 8d* 7m* 7m⁴
6f 8m² 7d³ 8m 8m 8d 6.1g 7g³ Oct 16] useful handicapper: best efforts in 1999 when
second to Refuse To Lose at Ascot in July and third to Granny's Pet in rated stakes at
Chester in August, leaving Lady Herries for 32,000 gns before latter: best at 7f/1m:
acts on good to firm and heavy ground: visored once, often blinkered (seems as
effective without): taken early to post: refused to race twice in 1997: slowly away last
2 outings: usually held up nowadays: not one to trust implicitly. *D. Nicholls*

ROCK ISLAND LINE (IRE) 5 b.g. New Express 95 – Gail's Crystal (Crofter **–**
(USA) 124) [1998 62, a59: a7s a7g* a8g⁵ a8g* a7g³ a7g³ a8g⁵ a7g⁴ 8.3v 6.9d³ 6.9m⁴ **a70**
a7g⁴ a7g² a7g³ 1999 a6f* a7g⁶ a6g³ a7g* 7m a7g* 6g Aug 20] fair performer: won
seller in February and claimer and handicap in July, all at Southwell: well held both
starts on turf in 1999: effective at 6f to 1m: acts on good to firm going, good to soft
and fibresand (untried on equitrack). *G. Woodward*

ROCKLANDS LANE 3 b.g. Puissance 110 – Dancing Daughter 79 (Dance In **67 d**
Time (CAN)) [1998 61: 5s⁴ 5v 1999 6d² 6.1m 5d 6g 5.1m 7f 5.7h 5.1m Sep 9] fair
maiden: well beaten after reappearance: likely to prove best at 5f/6f: has worn tongue
strap: sold 500 gns. *R. F. Johnson Houghton*

ROCK ON ROBIN 2 br.g. (Feb 1) Rock City 120 – Volcalmeh 67 (Lidhame 109) **43**
[1999 5d 7.5s⁶ 7m⁵ 10s⁶ a8.5g 8d a8g Nov 12] 900F, 500Y: workmanlike gelding: **a–**
fourth foal: half-brother to winning stayer Lady Felix (by Batshoof) and a winner in
Czech Republic by Petong: dam 7f winner: poor maiden: will stay 1½m: well beaten
twice on fibresand: usually visored. *C. W. Fairhurst*

ROCK TO THE TOP (IRE) 5 b.g. Rudimentary (USA) 118 – Well Bought **–**
(IRE) 35 (Auction Ring (USA) 123) [1998 –: 12d 8d 7g 6m 5.1g 7m a7g 1999 a6g 7f
a6g a7g May 22] one-time fair handicapper: no form since 1997: visored final start.
J. J. Sheehan

ROCKY ISLAND 2 b.g. (Mar 28) Rock Hopper 124 – Queen's Eyot 79 (Grundy **–**
137) [1999 5m 5d 6d May 21] half-brother to winning middle-distance stayers Island
Blade (by Sure Blade) and Persuasive (by Sharpo): dam best at 1¼m: little sign of
ability. *Mrs M. Reveley*

ROCKY STALLONE 4 b.g. Rock City 120 – City Link Pet 79 (Tina's Pet 121) **–**
[1998 –: 6g 1999 6d Apr 16] big, workmanlike gelding: well beaten in maidens at
Thirsk 11 months apart. *W. McKeown*

RODERICK HUDSON 7 b.g. Elmaamul (USA) 125 – Moviegoer 104 (Pharly **–**
(FR) 130) [1998 83d: a9.4g² a8g 8.5m a10g² a9.4s 1999 a8g a8g 11.9f 10f 12d Jun 5]
fairly useful at best: generally well beaten since 6-y-o reappearance, including in
blinkers. *Jamie Poulton*

ROFFEY SPINNEY (IRE) 5 ch.g. Masterclass (USA) 116 – Crossed Line **60 §**
(Thatching 131) [1998 68§, a63§: a6g a6g³ a8g³ a7g a7g 6.1s 6g 7g 7g 7f* 6g² 6g
8m³ 6f⁵ 7g⁶ 8m 7d* a7g a7g² a8.5g 1999 a9.4g* a8.5g⁶ a9.4g a11g⁴ 7s 7g a8.5g a8g
a7g⁶ Oct 25] angular gelding: modest performer: won seller at Wolverhampton in
January: stays 9.4f: acts on firm ground, good to soft and all-weather: blinkered/
visored once each: carries head high: unreliable: sold 1,500 gns. *J. Cullinan*

ROGER ROSS 4 b.g. Touch of Grey 90 – Foggy Dew 45 (Smoggy 115) [1998 **60 §**
84: a8g³ a7g a8g a8g⁶ a8g² 8d* 8.1s* 9m 8m* 8m² 9m a8d³ 8.1g³ 8g 8s* 8g 1999
8g 8g 8d 8m 8d 9.9d 8g 8v 7v 8s a10g⁶ a8g a10g* a10g a10g Dec 18] small,
good-bodied gelding: fairly useful handicapper at 3 yrs: modest at best in 1999,
winning at Lingfield in November: stays easy 1¼m: acts on good to firm going, soft
and equitrack: occasionally blinkered: usually held up: thoroughly inconsistent.
R. M. Flower

ROGUE SPIRIT 3 b.g. Petong 126 – Quick Profit 78 (Formidable (USA) 125) **82**
[1998 NR 1999 6s 6m* 6m 6d³ 7f 6f 5g³ 6s 6d⁵ Oct 9] 18,500Y: rangy gelding: good
walker: fourth foal: brother to fairly useful 1996 2-y-o 5f winner Smokey Pete and
half-brother to 1m/1¼m winner Battleship Bruce (by Mazilier): dam 7f winner: fairly
useful performer: won maiden at Folkestone in May: ran well after when third in
handicaps: may prove best at 5f/6f: won on good to firm going, best efforts on good
and good to soft: has reared badly stalls. *P. W. Harris*

ROI DE DANSE 4 ch.g. Komaite 89 – Princess Lucy 42 (Local Suitor (USA) **–**
128) [1998 79, a60: 7.5s 7g 8.1m 8.9g⁵ 8g 8g* 7g² 7v a8g a9.4s⁶ a7g⁶ a8.5g⁴ 1999 **a60**
a7g⁴ a10f² a10f² 10s 10m 8f a7g 7.1d 8d a8g⁶ 8d 7s a7g a10g⁶ a10g³ a10g* a8.5g²
Dec 27] lengthy, workmanlike gelding: has a round action: modest performer: won
handicap at Lingfield in December: stays easy 1¼m: acts on all-weather, no recent
form on turf: visored seventh start. *M. Quinn*

ROISIN SPLENDOUR (IRE) 4 ch.f. Inchinor 119 – Oriental Splendour 85 **72**
(Runnett 125) [1998 77: 7m⁴ 6m³ 7m² 7.1g⁴ 7g* 7g 7g 6d 7m 7g a7g² a8f² 1999 a7g² **a77**
a8g⁵ a7g* a8.5g⁵ 7m 8g⁶ 7m³ 7m* 7g⁶ 7m 7m⁵ 8m 7m a7g a8g Nov 23] good-topped
filly: fair handicapper: won at Lingfield in February and Goodwood (apprentice
event) in June: effective at 7f/easy 1m: acts on equitrack, raced mainly on good
ground or firmer on turf: has been early to post: free-going sort: none too consistent.
S. Dow

ROKEBY BOWL 7 b.g. Salse (USA) 128 – Rose Bowl (USA) 131 (Habitat 134) **110**
[1998 110: 10d⁵ 9.9g² 12m² 12m* 11.9f* 11.9m² 12s 12m² 1999 10g² 13.4m³ 12g
12m Jun 16] small gelding: has had leg trouble: smart performer: ran well when neck
second of 20 to Carry The Flag in valuable handicap at Kempton and over length
third to Sadian in Ormonde Stakes at Chester in April/May: bit below best both
outings in handicaps after: effective at 1¼m (given good pace) to 13.4f: acts well on
good going or firmer, below form on softer than good: has run well sweating: usually
waited with: genuine. *I. A. Balding*

ROLE MODEL 3 b.f. Tragic Role (USA) – Emerald Gulf (IRE) (Wassl 125) **47**
[1998 –: 6g 1999 8m⁶ 7.5d 10.5m 10d⁴ 13.8g 9.9s 11.8d⁶ 14.1f² Oct 20] tall, leggy
filly: poor maiden: stays 1¾m: acts on firm and good to soft going: best form racing
up with pace. *R. M. Whitaker*

ROLLER 3 b.c. Bluebird (USA) 125 – Tight Spin (High Top 131) [1998 76p: 6m⁴ **77**
6f³ 1999 8m 6.8s* 7.1g⁵ 8.1m³ 8g 8m 10.2m 9.9v 11.8d⁵ Oct 11] small, angular colt:
has a quick action: fair performer: won maiden at Warwick in May: ran well in
handicaps after only on next 2 starts: best up to 1m: acts on firm and soft ground:
blinkered second to sixth starts: sold 11,000 gns, joined G. Woodward. *H. Candy*

ROLLESTON ROCKET 2 ch.f. (Mar 30) King's Signet (USA) 110 – Jubilee
Line 33 (High Line 125) [1999 a6g Nov 19] first foal: dam maiden who stayed 10.8f:
33/1, well beaten in seller at Southwell. *M. J. Polglase*

ROLLING RIO 3 b.g. Chaddleworth (IRE) 103 – Broughton's Gold (IRE) (Trojan **60**
Fen 118) [1998 59+: 5s 6g 5m⁴ a7g⁶ 6s 1999 a10g² a10g 8g a12g Sep 8] modest
maiden: sold out of P. Haslam's stable for 950 gns before final start: stayed 1¼m:
acted on equitrack and good to firm ground: dead. *Ronald Thompson*

ROLLING STONE 5 b.h. Northern Amethyst 99 – First Sapphire (Simply Great **99**
(FR) 122) [1998 NR 1999 10m⁴ 11.7f³ 10.2s* Sep 27] leggy horse: reportedly
suffered 2 fractured knees after debut at 3 yrs: best effort in maidens when winning
at Bath by 6 lengths from Total Delight, making all and eased: should stay 1½m: may
do better still. *Mrs A. J. Perrett*

ROMA 4 b.f. Second Set (IRE) 127 – Villasanta (Corvaro (USA) 124) [1998 61: **54**
a7g 8m 9.2s³ 10.5s⁵ a12g² a12g⁶ 1999 a12g⁵ a9.4g 9g 10m 12m* 12g² 12g a12g
Nov 19] modest handicapper: left C. Thornton's stable 10,000 gns before winning at
Musselburgh in June: stays 1½m: acts on good to firm ground, soft and fibresand.
A. R. Dicken

ROMAN CANDLE (IRE) 3 b.c. Sabrehill (USA) 120 – Penny Banger (IRE) 74 **81**
(Pennine Walk 120) [1998 NR 1999 8g 10v⁶ 10g⁵ 11.8m² 11.6m* 12.3d* 12s⁵ 11.6g
Oct 11] 18,000F, 17,000Y: strong, rangy colt: has scope: second foal: dam 7f winner:
fair performer: won handicaps at Windsor in June and Ripon in July: below form in

minor events last 2 starts, off course 11 weeks before penultimate: better around 1½m than shorter: acts on good to firm and good to soft going. *C. F. Wall*

ROMANECH (IRE) 2 b.c. (Apr 30) Nicolotte 118 – O La Bamba (IRE) **58** (Commanche Run 133) [1999 5m 6d⁵ 6.8m 8m Oct 19] 5,000Y, 6,400 2-y-o: neat colt: third foal: half-brother to Italian 3-y-o 8.5f to 1¼m winner Namabamba (by Namaqualand): dam unraced: modest maiden: best effort on second start: should stay at least 7f. *J. G. Smyth-Osbourne*

ROMAN EMPEROR 2 ch.g. (Feb 24) Lycius (USA) 124 – Subya 107 (Night **46** Shift (USA)) [1999 5d⁶ 6d 5m 6m 7f 6d Oct 26] 17,000Y: first foal: dam 5f (at 2 yrs) to 1¼m winner: poor form at best. *M. W. Easterby*

ROMAN HOLIDAY (IRE) 3 ch.g. Lahib (USA) 129 – Beneficiary 69 (Jalmood **50** (USA) 126) [1998 NR 1999 6g⁶ 5d⁶ 6.1g Sep 25] 8,000Y: stocky gelding: first foal: dam, 6f and (including at 2 yrs) 7f winner, half-sister to very smart 7f/1m performer Decorated Hero: modest form in maidens. *M. A. Buckley*

ROMAN KING (IRE) 4 b.g. Sadler's Wells (USA) 132 – Romantic Feeling 88 **92** (Shirley Heights 130) [1998 NR 1999 12.3m⁵ 12d⁴ 11.9v* Oct 13] 44,000Y: sturdy gelding: sixth foal: half-brother to several winners, including useful 7f (at 2 yrs) and 1¼m winner Bridal Toast (by Rousillon): dam 1½m winner from family of El Gran Senor and Xaar: progressive form in maidens, winning at Haydock by 1¾ lengths from Historic, though edging right: will stay beyond 1½m: has been bandaged: blanketed for stalls entry: sold 95,000 gns, joined M. Hammond. *J. H. M. Gosden*

ROMAN LEGIONNAIRE 2 b.c. (Mar 25) Ezzoud (IRE) 126 – Zalfa (Luthier **67** 126) [1999 6g 7m 6.8m⁶ 7g³ 7m 7s Oct 11] 10,000Y: half-brother to several winners, including 7f winner Henry Heald (by Anshan) and 1995 2-y-o 6f winner Truancy (by Polar Falcon): dam French 1m to 12.5f winner: fair maiden: third of 17 at Salisbury in August: should be suited by 1m+. *G. B. Balding*

ROMAN REEL (USA) 8 ch.g. Sword Dance – Our Mimi (USA) (Believe It **48** (USA)) [1998 70: a10g* a8g a10g⁶ a8g* 8m2 a7g 10g² 10m³ 9d 8f⁶ 10f* 10m a12g² **a58** a10g 1999 a10g a12g⁵ 10m 10f 10d 10m 12m a12g⁴ a12g Nov 16] lengthy, good-quartered gelding: good mover: modest nowadays: effective at 1m to 1½m: acts on equitrack (possibly not fibresand), seems best on good going or firmer on turf: usually apprentice/lady ridden and held up. *G. L. Moore*

ROMANTIC AFFAIR (IRE) 2 ch.g. (Apr 15) Persian Bold 123 – Broken **75 p** Romance (IRE) (Ela-Mana-Mou 132) [1999 7.1m 7s* 7s³ Oct 25] 11,000Y: leggy, useful-looking gelding: fourth foal: half-brother to 5-y-o Legendary Form and 3-y-o Little Italy: dam unraced half-sister to US Grade 1 9f winner Foscarini and smart performer up to 1¼m Guns of Navarone: won maiden at Newcastle in September: good third of 20 to French Horn in nursery at Leicester final start: will stay at least 1¼m: likely to improve further. *J. L. Dunlop*

ROMERO 3 b.g. Robellino (USA) 127 – Casamurrae 87 (Be My Guest (USA) **68** 126) [1998 58: 6m 8.3d³ 7s 1999 10.3d² 12g² 12.3d³ 14.6f⁶ 14.1g Oct 15] leggy, good-quartered gelding: fair maiden handicapper: ran well when placed in the spring: left C. Thornton and off 5 months before final start: should be suited by 1¾m: acts on good to soft going: fairly useful form over hurdles, winning 2 juveniles in October/November. *J. Akehurst*

ROMNEY 2 ch.g. (May 18) Timeless Times (USA) 99 – Ewe Lamb 86 (Free State **–** 125) [1999 7f 8d Oct 12] 3,000Y: fifth foal: half-brother to 3-y-o Ryeland and a winner in Denmark by Music Boy: dam, 2-y-o 5f winner, also successful over hurdles: showed little in maidens at Thirsk and Leicester. *Mrs P. Sly*

ROMOLA 3 b.f. Wolfhound (USA) 126 – Myth 89 (Troy 137) [1998 NR 1999 **82** 8.3g 8g⁴ 9.9m³ 8.3m⁶ 12d² 12d Oct 29] 22,000Y: half-sister to several winners, including smart middle-distance stayer/hurdler Midnight Legend (by Night Shift) and useful middle-distance performer Spillo (by Midyan): dam 1½m to 13.4f winner: fairly useful maiden: best effort when short-head second at Musselburgh in September: will stay beyond 1½m: sold 7,500 gns. *L. M. Cumani*

RONDA 3 b.f. Bluebird (USA) 125 – Memory's Gold (USA) 68 (Java Gold **112** (USA)) [1998 95: 5s² 5.5d* 5.5d* 5g³ 7g⁶ 1999 8s² 7d² 8m² 8s* 8m* 9d³ 9d⁶ Oct 9] 30,000Y: tall, lengthy filly: first foal: dam, 7.6f winner, out of a sister to Mill

RON

859

Greene King Falmouth Stakes, Newmarket—
the improved Ronda shows a fine turn of foot to go past Balisada (right) and Cape Verdi

Reef: smart performer: progressed well in 1999, winning Prix de Sandringham at Chantilly in June by 2½ lengths from Venize and Greene King Falmouth Stakes at Newmarket in July by 1¼ lengths from Balisada, showing fine turn of foot: creditable third to Perfect Sting in Garden City Breeders' Cup Handicap at Belmont, better effort in Grade 1s in USA last 2 starts: stays 9f: acts on soft and good to firm going. *C. Laffon-Parias, France*

RONNI PANCAKE 2 b.f. (Apr 26) Mujadil (USA) 119 – Funny Choice (IRE) 68 (Commanche Run 133) [1999 6m 6g 6m² 6.8d a7g⁶ 7g a7g⁶ Nov 16] 1,600Y: first foal: dam won from 6.5f (at 2 yrs) to 15f: modest maiden on turf: stays 7f: acts on good to firm ground, poor form in sellers on fibresand. *J. S. Moore* — **56 a39**

RONQUISTA D'OR 5 b.g. Ron's Victory (USA) 129 – Gild The Lily 83 (Ile de Bourbon (USA) 133) [1998 55, a58: a12s* a13g⁴ a12g a16.2g 11.6g a11g⁵ 12.5m* 14.1m⁴ 12.1m² 14.4d 14.1s a14g a12g* 1999 a11g³ a12g² a12g³ a16.2g³ 11.6m⁴ a12g² 12.1m⁵ 12.3g³ Aug 13] sturdy gelding: modest handicapper: probably best at 1½m/13/4m: acts on good to firm going and fibresand, below form on softer than good and equitrack: usually blinkered: consistent. *G. A. Ham* — **55**

RON'S PET 4 ch.g. Ron's Victory (USA) 129 – Penny Mint 79 (Mummy's Game 120) [1998 75: 7d 10s 10m 8m 8m⁵ 8m⁵ 8m 7v⁵ 1999 a7g* a8g⁴ a7g* a8.5g⁴ 6s⁶ 7.6m a8g 7f a7g² a8g⁶ a7g Dec 21] tall gelding: fairly useful form on all-weather in 1999: won claimer (final start for R. Hannon) and handicap at Wolverhampton in March: reportedly lame eighth start, then off 5½ months before second in handicap at Southwell next time: stays 1m: acts on fibresand, good to firm and good to soft ground, probably on heavy: effective blinkered/visored or not: has had tongue tied: sometimes carries head high. *K. R. Burke* — **– a80**

ROO 2 b.f. (Apr 16) Rudimentary (USA) 118 – Shall We Run 59 (Hotfoot 126) [1999 5.1s* 5.1g 5g³ 5m² 5.2m⁶ 6f² 6d* 6.1d⁴ 6d² 7.3s Oct 23] 7,000Y: workmanlike filly: fourth foal: half-sister to 4-y-o Absolute Majority and 3-y-o Startoo: dam, third at 5f at 2 yrs, sister to useful 1¼m performer Fire Top and half-sister to very smart but unreliable sprinter Dead Certain: fairly useful performer: won maiden at Bath in April and minor event at Haydock in August: good second of 6 in listed race at Ayr penultimate start: should stay 7f: acts on firm and soft ground: has worn tongue strap: edgy final outing. *R. F. Johnson Houghton* — **88**

ROOFTOP PROTEST (IRE) 2 b.g. (Apr 10) Thatching 131 – Seattle Siren (USA) 101 (Seattle Slew (USA)) [1999 6m 7m⁶ 7.5g⁵ Aug 11] IR 19,000F, 13,500Y: tall gelding: half-brother to several winners, including 1991 2-y-o 7f winner Sea — **61 ?**

Clover and 5-y-o Il Principe (both by Ela-Mana-Mou): dam 6f winner at 2 yrs: maiden: apparently best effort when fifth of 8 at Beverley (possibly flattered in steadily-run race) final start: should stay 1m. *N. Tinkler*

ROOKIE 3 b.g. Magic Ring (IRE) 115 – Shot At Love (IRE) 79 (Last Tycoon 131) **59** [1998 –: 6g 1999 a10g² 8.2m² 7f 10.1g a16g⁵ 10d a10g² a10g Dec 22] modest maiden: stays 1¼m: acts on equitrack and good to firm going: left C. Cyzer 4,000 gns before final start. *Mrs A. E. Johnson*

ROONAH QUAY (IRE) 3 br.f. Soviet Lad (USA) – Piney Lake 54 (Sassafras (FR) 135) [1998 NR 1999 a8g 12.4g 9.9d⁶ 7.6m⁶ a6g 7f a9.4g Aug 14] 8,000Y: half-sister to numerous winners, including 2m winner Lake Dominion (by Primo Dominie): dam third at 1m and 1¼m: little form: trained first 3 starts by J. L. Eyre. *D. McCain*

ROOSTER 4 b.g. Roi Danzig (USA) – Jussoli (Don 128) [1998 76: 10.5g⁴ **–** 12.3g⁶ 8m 1999 11.1g 11.9d⁴ Jun 11] good-topped gelding: disappointing maiden. *Miss S. E. Hall*

ROSA CANINA 3 b.f. Bustino 136 – Moon Spin 83 (Night Shift (USA)) [1998 **91** –p: 8d 8v 1999 10m 14.1m³ 14.1f* 16.2m* 16f* 16.1f³ 16m* 18d* 16.1d Oct 29] unfurnished filly: fairly useful handicapper: progressed really well in 1999, winning at Redcar, Beverley, Lingfield, Nottingham and Pontefract between June and October: ran well from 22 lb out of weights in listed rated stakes at Newmarket final start: stayed 2¼m: acted on firm and good to soft going: stud. *J. L. Dunlop*

ROSA ROYALE 5 b.m. Arazi (USA) 135 – Gussy Marlowe 118 (Final Straw **49** 127) [1998 53, a–: 16d 8.3d³ 8d² 8s 9.2g³ 9.2m 12.4g⁴ a12g 9m 12d 1999 10g⁴ a8g² a10g⁵ 8m Aug 2] poor maiden handicapper: stays 1½m when conditions aren't testing: acts on fibresand, best turf efforts on good/good to soft going: tongue tied (reportedly choked on 4-y-o reappearance): none too consistent. *Mrs L. Stubbs*

ROSEAU 3 b.f. Nashwan (USA) 135 – Fair Rosamunda (Try My Best (USA) 130) **75** [1998 NR 1999 10g⁴ 12s a12g² Dec 4] fifth foal: sister to French 7.6f and 11f winner Spanish Serenade and half-sister to French 1m winner Mille Roses (by Cadeaux Genereux): dam French 1¼m/1½m winner: best efforts on first and final starts: stays 1½m: acts on fibresand: sold 12,000 gns. *J. H. M. Gosden*

ROSE BAY 3 b.f. Shareef Dancer (USA) 135 – Cormorant Bay 55 (Don't Forget **64** Me 127) [1998 62p: 7d 1999 12v⁵ 9.9g⁵ 9m⁴ 10.2m⁵ 11f⁵ 12f⁴ Jul 30] fair maiden: should prove best at 1½m+: acts on good to firm and good to soft going, below form on firm last 2 starts. *C. E. Brittain*

ROSE HILL 3 b.f. Sabrehill (USA) 120 – Petite Rosanna 89 (Ile de Bourbon **–** (USA) 133) [1998 73p: 7m* 8.1g⁶ 8m 1999 10.2s Apr 27] angular filly: fair at 2 yrs: well held in handicap only 3-y-o start: should stay at least 1¼m: sold 1,100 gns. *T. G. Mills*

ROSE OF HYMUS 2 ch.f. (Feb 7) Rudimentary (USA) 118 – Green's Cassatt **–** (USA) 74 (Apalachee (USA) 137) [1999 6.8d Sep 21] 1,200Y: leggy, lengthy filly: third foal: half-sister to 1m winner Swan Island (by Hubbly Bubbly): dam 6f (at 2 yrs) to 1½m winner: green, towards rear in maiden at Warwick. *J. E. Banks*

ROSE OF MOONCOIN (IRE) 3 b.f. Brief Truce (USA) 126 – Sharp Deposit **–** (Sharpo 132) [1998 99: 6m* 6f⁴ 6m⁵ 1999 8.1m 10.1g Sep 14] good-topped filly: good walker: useful form in 1998: well beaten in listed races at 3 yrs: should stay beyond 6f: retained 8,000 gns in November. *J. E. Banks*

ROSE'S TREASURE (IRE) 3 b.f. Treasure Kay 114 – Euro Miss (IRE) 51 **70 d** (Double Schwartz 128) [1998 77: 5d* 5s² 5g² 5g² 5m⁵ 5f⁴ 6f⁵ 5m⁵ 6m 1999 5d **a–** 5d² 5d 6g 6m 5g⁵ 5m 6g 5g 5d a5g a5g Dec 21] workmanlike filly: fair handicapper: best effort in 1999 on second start: mostly well beaten after: probably best at 5f on good ground or softer, no form on all-weather: sometimes blinkered/visored. *B. S. Rothwell*

ROSETTA 2 b.f. (Apr 20) Fraam 114 – Starawak 68 (Star Appeal 133) [1999 5.1g **52** 6s⁶ 6g⁴ 5.1m³ 7m⁵ 7m⁴ 8.1m⁵ 7m⁵ 6s Oct 1] 3,200Y: leggy, sparely-made filly: half-sister to several winners, including 4-y-o Baby Spice, fairly useful 6f to 1m (at 2 yrs) winner Fame Again (by Then Again) and useful 1¼m to 15f winner Army of

Stars (by Posse): dam 1½m winner: modest maiden: probably stays 1m: acts on good to firm ground, well held on soft. *R. J. Hodges*

ROSEUM   3 b.f. Lahib (USA) 129 – Rose Barton (Pas de Seul 133) [1998 –: 6s 1999 6v* 6d* 7d 6s* Jul 3] good-quartered filly: useful performer: won maiden at Pontefract in April and handicaps at Newbury in May and Haydock in July, last-named by 2½ lengths from Princely Dream: likely to prove best at 5f/6f: raced only on ground softer than good: held up: capable of better still. *R. Guest*   **102 p**

ROSHANI (IRE)   2 b.f. (Mar 28) Kris 135 – Maratona (Be My Guest (USA) 126) [1999 6d⁵ 7d³ 7d Sep 28] 130,000Y: closely related to 3-y-o Buckle, and half-sister to several winners in USA: dam twice-raced half-sister to Oh So Sharp (by Kris): best effort (fair form) when close third of 10 in maiden at Folkestone: well held in sales race at Newmarket final start: should stay 1m. *M. R. Channon*   **79**

ROSIE DREAM   3 ch.f. Cadeaux Genereux 131 – Impudent Miss 105 (Persian Bold 123) [1998 NR 1999 8g² 8m³ 9m⁶ 8m³ 8g 8.5g 7d⁵ Oct 4] 40,000Y: small, close-coupled filly: has quick action: half-sister to several winners, including 6f to 7.6f winner King Al (by Indian King) and May Hill Stakes runner-up Self Assured (by Ahonoora), both useful: dam, Irish 2-y-o 5f winner, half-sister to very smart sprinter Sayyaf: fair maiden: best efforts first 2 starts: should stay beyond 1m: acts on good to firm going: has given trouble at stalls: sold 9,500 gns. *E. A. L. Dunlop*   **70 d**

ROSIE JAQUES   4 b.f. Doyoun 124 – Premier Princess 45 (Hard Fought 125) [1998 47: 9.9f 11.8m 12.1s⁵ a9.4g⁴ a9.4g* a9.4g a12g⁶ 1999 a12g a10g⁶ a8g Mar 22] poor at best: bred to stay beyond 9.4f: acts on fibresand: blinkered final start. *N. P. Littmoden*   **–**

ROSIES ALL THE WAY   3 b.f. Robellino (USA) 127 – No More Rosies 74 (Warpath 113) [1998 NR 1999 7.1d 10s⁴ 10g 12g Sep 15] lengthy, unfurnished filly: half-sister to several winners, including 1¼m and 1½m winner Eau de Cologne (by Persian Bold) and 1990 2-y-o 7f winner (stayed 15f), later useful jumper, Beachy Head (by Damister): dam 1¼m winner from 2 starts: poor maiden: should stay beyond 1¼m: raced only on good going or softer. *C. W. Thornton*   **43**

ROSSE   2 ch.f. (Apr 19) Kris 135 – Nuryana 107 (Nureyev (USA) 131) [1999 6d Oct 29] seventh foal: half-sister to several winners, including 3-y-o Mayo, very smart miler Rebecca Sharp (by Machiavellian) and smart 1m (at 2 yrs) and 11.5f winner Mystic Knight (by Caerleon): dam 1m winner out of half-sister to 1000 Guineas winner On The House: weak in market and green, shaped quite well when seventh of 19 to Pax in maiden at Newmarket, staying on from rear once switched: should stay 1m: sure to do better. *G. Wragg*   **63 p**

ROSSELLI (USA)   3 b.c. Puissance 110 – Miss Rossi (Artaius (USA) 129) [1998 107: 5m* 5d* 5s* 6d³ 6f 1999 5g 6m 5d⁵ 5.2d Sep 19] tall, good-topped colt: won Norfolk Stakes at Royal Ascot at 2 yrs: reported in May to have injured a tendon on gallops: made belated return 3 months later: easily best effort when fifth to Tedburrow in Flying Five at Leopardstown: may prove best at 5f/6f: acts on soft and good to firm ground. *J. Berry*   **106**

ROSSEL (USA)   6 b.g. Blushing John (USA) 120 – Northern Aspen (USA) 120 (Northern Dancer) [1998 70: 13v* 16s³ 12d³ 10.9d 12.1s² 13.1v² 1999 11.1v⁴ 13v 13s⁶ 12g* Nov 3] rangy gelding: fair handicapper: second start after 5½-month break when winning easily at Musselburgh in November: effective at 1½m to 15f: acts on any going: visored once at 3 yrs: fair form over jumps. *P. Monteith*   **79**

ROSSINI (USA)   2 b.c. (Feb 17) Miswaki (USA) 124 – Touch of Greatness (USA) (Hero's Honor (USA)) [1999 5v* 6.3m* 5.5g* 7m² Sep 10]   **118**
          When Rossini started at 5/2-on for his debut at the Curragh in April, it was partly as a consequence of his being trained by Aidan O'Brien, for whom he duly completed a clean sweep of the first five two-year-old races in Ireland. A similar starting price in the Prix Robert Papin at Maisons-Laffitte three months later, however, owed almost everything to the horse himself and to his eye-catching victories in that Curragh maiden and in the Anglesey Stakes over the same course. Rossini made it three wins in a row in the Robert Papin before

losing his unbeaten record to the impressive Distant Music in the Champagne Stakes at Doncaster, after which he was put away for the season.

The absence through injury of the Prix du Bois winner Morning Pride from the field for the five and a half furlong Prix Robert Papin robbed the race of its potential major attraction. Only four took on Rossini, including his stable-mate Finnan, with whom he was coupled in the betting. Rossini was always prominent and stretched clear in the closing stages, edging left, to beat the German colt Auenklang by five lengths. Auenklang improved to win one of Germany's only two pattern races for two-year-olds, the Group 2 Baustoffe-Cup at Baden-Baden, next time. Rossini had blotted his copybook when refusing to enter the stalls at Royal Ascot for the Windsor Castle Stakes, but his clear-cut victory over Still Going On when odds on for the Anglesey Stakes at the Curragh in July dispelled doubts about his temperament. Rossini progressed well during the season and put up his best performance in the Champagne Stakes in September, when, for the first time, he wasn't favourite. Rossini travelled strongly in third, moving through to dispute the lead two furlongs out, but he had no answer to Distant Music's turn of foot, eventually going down by two and a half lengths. Rossini was conceding 4 lb to Distant Music and, in pulling five lengths clear of the third Winning Venture, in our opinion he put up one of the best performances of the season by a two-year-old.

At 500,000 dollars, Rossini was the most expensive yearling by Miswaki sold at public auction in 1999. Other notable representatives for the stallion in 1999 were the smart German sprinter Tertullian and the promising juvenile Tough Speed. Although most often noted as an influence for speed, Miswaki has sired such as the Arc winner Urban Sea, the Japan Cup winner Marvelous Crown, the Eclipse second Misil and the Breeders' Cup Classic winner Black Tie Affair, all of whom won over at least ten furlongs. Rossini's

Prix Robert Papin, Maisons-Laffitte—
Rossini stretches clear of Auenklang (blinkers), Finnan, Lord Pacal (rail) and Vinceslass

dam Touch of Greatness was unraced but she has produced three winners, including Mystic Eagle (by Woodman), who was fairly useful at best and won twice at a mile on fibresand before going on to win another five races in America, and another miler Elusive Quality (by Gone West), winner of two Grade 3 Handicaps, over seven furlongs and a mile, as a five-year-old. Mystic Eagle and Elusive Quality are closely related to Rossini, all three being by sons of Mr Prospector. Ivory Idol, a half-sister to Touch of Greatness, produced the 1999 Breeders' Cup Juvenile winner Anees to a grandson of Mr Prospector, Unbridled. Two more half-sisters to Touch of Greatness have also produced good juveniles—Land of Ivory and Radiant being responsible for the National Stakes winner Heart of Darkness and the Moyglare Stud Stakes runner-up Poolesta respectively. Touch of Greatness is also a half-sister to the high-class middle-distance performer Gold And Ivory. Rossini's great grandam is Natashka who has the likes of Dark Lomond, Mukaddamah and Eclipse- and King George-placed Gregorian among her descendants. Sheikh Hamdan Al Maktoum's Shadwell Stud paid 575,000 dollars for a half-sister to Rossini (by Gone West) at the 1999 Keeneland September Sale.

Rossini (USA) (b.c. Feb 17, 1997)	Miswaki (USA) (ch 1978)	Mr Prospector (b 1970)	Raise A Native / Gold Digger
		Hopespringseternal (ch 1971)	Buckpasser / Rose Bower
	Touch of Greatness (USA) (b 1986)	Hero's Honor (b 1980)	Northern Dancer / Glowing Tribute
		Ivory Wand (b 1973)	Sir Ivor / Natashka

Mr M. Tabor & Mrs John Magnier's "Rossini"

Rossini acts on good to firm and heavy ground. He should stay a mile and give a good account of himself when given the opportunity to represent his powerful stable in good races. *A. P. O'Brien, Ireland*

ROSSLYN CHAPEL 2 b.g. (Mar 12) Petong 126 – Stoneydale 83 (Tickled Pink 114) [1999 5f 6.1m 5g 5.3d Oct 4] 9,000Y: small gelding: half-brother to several winners, including sprinters Halbert (by Song) and Runs In The Family (by Distant Relative): dam sprinter: no form: has sweated up. *Bob Jones* —

ROTHERHITHE 3 ch.g. Lycius (USA) 124 – Cariellor's Miss (FR) (Cariello (FR) 125) [1998 NR 1999 6.1g 8.2d a8g³ a9.4g a7g⁶ Dec 22] IR 36,000Y: second foal: dam French 7.5f (at 2 yrs) and 1¼m winner: modest maiden: easily best effort when third at Lingfield: stays 1m: acts on equitrack: carries head high. *T. J. Naughton* **59**

ROTOR MAN (IRE) 5 b.g. River Falls 113 – Need For Cash (USA) (Raise A Native) [1998 NR 1999 a9.4g 6f 17] leggy, useful-looking gelding: modest maiden handicapper at 3 yrs: well beaten only 5-y-o start: best form at 7f: tried blinkered/visored. *J. D. Bethell* —

ROTOSTAR 3 ch.f. Aragon 118 – Davinia 92 (Gold Form 108) [1998 50: a5g 5.1m⁶ 6m⁶ 6m⁴ 6m⁴ 7.1g 1999 6f 8m 8g⁶ Jul 5] small, leggy filly: poor maiden handicapper: probably stays 1m. *P. D. Evans* **43**

ROUBLES GALORE (IRE) 3 b.g. Unblest 117 – Cut The Red Tape (IRE) 75 (Sure Blade (USA) 130) [1998 NR 1999 a8g⁴ 6s Jun 7] IR 5,000Y, 10,500 2-y-o: first foal: dam, 2-y-o 7f winner who later stayed 1m, half-sister to smart miler Bold Russian: better effort in claimers when fourth of 7 at Southwell. *Dr J. D. Scargill* **51**

ROUGE 4 gr.f. Rudimentary (USA) 118 – Couleur de Rose (Kalaglow 132) [1998 52: a7g⁴ 8.2s a8.5g³ 1999 a8f² a8g² a8.5g² a8.5g² 8g⁵ a8.5g⁶ 7.5s a7g² a8g³ a7g* a7g² a6g a8g⁴ Dec 17] big, lengthy filly: fairly useful on all-weather, modest on turf: won for first time in handicap at Wolverhampton in October: ran creditably most other starts: best form forcing pace at 7f: acts on fibresand, best turf effort on good going: often makes running. *J. P. Leigh* **51 a82**

ROUGE ETOILE 3 b.f. Most Welcome 131 – Choral Sundown 81 (Night Shift (USA)) [1998 81p: 6s³ 6s* 1999 7g 7d 7.1g 9.7d Aug 26] lengthy filly: fairly useful winner at 2 yrs: well held in 1999: should stay at least 1m. *A. J. McNae* —

ROUSING THUNDER 2 b.c. (Mar 27) Theatrical 128 – Moss (USA) (Woodman (USA) 126) [1999 7.1m³ 7m³ 8g⁶ Sep 8] 82,000F, 85,000Y: leggy, rather unfurnished colt: first foal: dam once-raced half-sister to high-class sprinter Committed: third of 14 to Blue Gold in maiden at Sandown on debut: well below that form final start: should stay at least 1m. *E. A. L. Dunlop* **80**

ROUTE SIXTY SIX (IRE) 3 b.f. Brief Truce (USA) 126 – Lyphards Goddess (IRE) (Lyphard's Special (USA) 122) [1998 74: 6f 7m² 7d 7f⁶ 7g⁶ 7s* 1999 7g 8m* 8m 7d⁴ 7.1g 8m 7f 8.1d⁵ 8s 7.1s² 8d 7d Oct 30] close-coupled filly: fairly useful handicapper: won 22-runner race at Newmarket in May: several creditable efforts after: effective at 7f/1m: yet to race on heavy going, acts on any other: none too consistent. *G. L. Moore* **82**

ROWAASI 2 gr.f. (Feb 27) Green Desert (USA) 127 – Pamela Peach 81 (Habitat 134) [1999 5.2d² 5m* 5m² 6g⁴ Aug 19] 150,000Y: rangy, angular filly: good walker: has a quick action: fifth living foal: half-sister to 3 winners, including 1995 2-y-o 5f winner Marl (by Lycius) and 1¼m winner Davoski (by Niniski), both fairly useful: dam, maiden in Britain, later sprint winner in USA: useful performer: impressive 6-length winner of listed race at Sandown in June: in frame in Queen Mary Stakes at Royal Ascot (favourite, beaten ½ length by Shining Hour) and Lowther Stakes at York (made running, below-par fourth of 9 to Jemima) last 2 starts: yet to race on extremes of going. *M. R. Channon* **103**

ROWA (USA) 2 ch.f. (Mar 28) Cozzene (USA) – Met Her Dream (USA) (Mehmet (USA)) [1999 7m⁶ 7f* 8.2m² 8m⁶ Sep 9] $65,000F: strong, lengthy filly: has a quick action: first foal: dam, won at up to 9f in USA, second in Grade 3 8.5f event at 2 yrs: fairly useful performer: won maiden at Redcar in August: creditable efforts after, sixth of 12 to Teggiano in May Hill Stakes at Doncaster on final start: should stay beyond 1m: raced only on good to firm/firm going. *H. R. A. Cecil* **89**

ROWLANDSONS CHARM (IRE) 6 b.m. Fayruz 116 – Magic Gold (Sallust –
134) [1998 49: a13g* a16g² a16g 8.3d a13g² 11.6g 1999 a13g⁵ a16f⁵ a16g Feb 25]
sturdy, workmanlike mare: poor handicapper: stays 2m: acts on all-weather, rarely
tried on turf nowadays: usually visored: often forces pace: carries head awkwardly:
not one to trust implicitly. *Miss B. Sanders*

ROWLANDSONS STUD (IRE) 6 b. or br.g. Distinctly North (USA) 115 – Be –
My Million (Taufan (USA) 119) [1998 –, a53: a5g⁴ a6g³ a6g a7g* a6g 7m a8g
a7g a7g 1999 a7g a6g a6g Dec 17] modest handicapper: no form since winning at
Lingfield in June 1998: stays 7f: goes well on equitrack, and acts on firm ground and
fibresand: tried blinkered: has been tongue tied: inconsistent. *K. C. Comerford*

ROYAL ALIBI 5 b.g. Royal Academy (USA) 130 – Excellent Alibi (USA) –
(Exceller (USA) 129) [1998 –: 11.5g⁴ 1999 a13g 12.3m Jun 16] signs of ability in
maidens only on debut for H. Cecil: has worn tongue strap. *D. J. G. Murray Smith*

ROYAL AMARETTO (IRE) 5 b.g. Fairy King (USA) – Melbourne Miss **107**
(Chaparral (FR) 128) [1998 107: 12s 10d 10d³ 10m⁵ 1999 10g 10.1s² 12d 10.1g
12m 11g² 12d 10d Oct 9] big, strong gelding: useful handicapper: best efforts in
1999 when runner-up at Epsom (beaten 2 lengths by Chief Cashier) in April and
Newbury (beaten neck by Monsajem) in August: stays 11f: has won on firm ground,
best efforts on good or softer: tongue tied: takes good hold: none too consistent.
B. J. Meehan

ROYAL ANTHEM (USA) 4 b.c. Theatrical 128 – In Neon (USA) (Ack Ack **135**
(USA)) [1998 129: 10m* 10m* 12d* 12m³ 12f* 12f 1999 12d² 12m² 10.4m*
10d⁵ 12g² Nov 6]

Stravinsky in the July Cup and Daylami in the King George both put up
the best performances seen in their respective divisions in Britain for many a
year. This was a remarkable season, however, and after the Juddmonte International at York there were strong grounds for thinking that Daylami's Ascot
showing had merely become the best performance in his division for a few
weeks. Royal Anthem's International win was another exhibition which took
the breath away.

They went a strong pace at York. Frankie Dettori said later that they had
gone too fast, but if that had been the case Royal Anthem would have been
inconvenienced a good deal more than most; racing on the outside, he was
scarcely any more than two lengths behind the leader from the off and was
disputing the lead himself fully five furlongs out. The truth is that from that
point onwards Royal Anthem just went too fast for everything else. Greek
Dance was the only other runner still on the bridle approaching the three-
furlong marker and, when Gary Stevens asked Royal Anthem to show what he
could really do soon afterwards, Greek Dance was transformed into an also-ran
as well. Royal Anthem was eight lengths clear at the line, if anything still
drawing further clear, Greek Dance holding off Chester House for second. It
was not a vintage field but, behind the second and third, Royal Anthem had also
shown a clean pair of heels to Group 1 winners Almutawakel, Central Park,

*Juddmonte International Stakes, York—a breathtaking performance from Royal Anthem;
Greek Dance and Chester House (rail) have no chance with the eight-length winner*

Compton Admiral (fifth), Golden Snake and Saffron Walden, and to Group 2 winners Almushtarak (fourth), Kissogram and Salford Express. Whatever the accomplishments of those behind him, Royal Anthem had won in such a manner that no-one needed telling this was an outstanding performance. That impression was fully confirmed by a timefigure of 1.53 fast (equivalent to a timerating of 138), which was bettered only once in any race in Britain during the decade, by Dayjur (1.69 fast) in the 1990 Nunthorpe. Royal Anthem's was the widest winning distance in the International, eclipsing Assert's six lengths in 1982, and also, arguably, the best form shown in the race's twenty eight year history.

Amazing as it may seem, Royal Anthem's four-year-old campaign might still be considered a disappointment. It would certainly have been hard to match the expectations that were held for him when the season started. One indication of those was that Royal Anthem was selected more often than any other horse in the Tote/Racing Post Horses To Follow competition. When the competition ended, however, the least popular ten selections had outperformed the top ten and Royal Anthem had scored just the once. His first two starts of 1999 were at a mile and a half, the distance of his wins in the 1998 King Edward VII Stakes and Canadian International and of his two and a half lengths third to Swain in the King George. With that form behind him and the confident predictions from all and sundry that he would make marked improvement from three to four, Royal Anthem was sent off favourite in the Coronation Cup and Hardwicke Stakes, at 2/1 and 6/5 respectively. Second place to Daylami in a muddling race at Epsom seemed to be forgiven readily enough, but connections could not hide their dismay when he finished second again, to Fruits of Love, at Royal Ascot a fortnight later. In both races, the prospect of something better had been there when, after taking a strong hold, Royal Anthem had taken up the running early in the straight.

Three days after Royal Ascot, Henry Cecil revealed his interpretation of these performances—Royal Anthem would revert to a mile and a quarter and the 1999 King George was off the agenda. After vindication had come in such spectacular fashion at York, Cecil stated 'He's not going to tackle a mile and a half again in his life.' Instead, however, Royal Anthem was to have only one more race for Henry Cecil. An imminent transfer to the United States was announced two days after his tame effort had helped Daylami to make victory so laughably easy in the Irish Champion Stakes, the supposed showdown between these two top-class colts who could barely be split in the betting (Royal Anthem at 11/8; Daylami at 6/4) but had thirteen and a half lengths and three other horses between them at the line. Leopardstown would never have suited Royal Anthem so well as the wide open spaces of York, while rain-softened ground and the so-called spoiling tactics of Godolphin pacemaker Lord of Men were also mentioned as reasons for Royal Anthem's dismal response to pressure in the straight. None, taken on its own, provides an adequate explanation.

The following month another trainer was able to have his say on the horse. It was reported that his new handler, Bill Mott, had now familiarised himself with Royal Anthem and that the horse struck him as a bit one-paced, especially for American racing with its tighter courses. A bid for the Breeders' Cup Classic had been mooted originally, but instead of that Royal Anthem was stepped back up to a mile and a half, for the Breeders' Cup Turf, in which Mott wanted him to be ridden much more prominently than in 1998, when he had been a disappointing favourite after a set-back. On the colt's aptitude for dirt as opposed to turf, Mott observed: 'I guess there are some horses who can handle both, but he hasn't indicated to me that he is one of them . . . a horse like him will either adapt or he won't. There's really not much I can do to help him.' What would have helped Royal Anthem the most would have been a below-form effort by Daylami, whom he had to take on for the third time in the season; at 87/10, Royal Anthem put up a bold display but no sooner had he mastered Buck's Boy early in the straight than the grey horse went past him a stride or two later. Royal Anthem's form in the Breeders' Cup Turf would, nonetheless, have been good enough to have won eight of the nine other renewals of the race during the decade. There was nothing of the non-stayer about this display. Royal Anthem's best performance, however, remains the one he put up over the one mile, two furlongs and eighty-five yards on good to firm ground at York.

The International Stakes also represented the highlight of a colourful sojourn in Britain for the champion US jockey Gary Stevens, whose career in 1999 took an even greater number of about-turns than that of Royal Anthem. Arriving to take the job of stable jockey to Sir Michael Stoute, Stevens made his first British ride of 1999 a winning one, just four days before partnering Beat All into third place in the Derby. The respect and enthusiasm he expressed for British racing immediately on his arrival, stating that he hoped to see out the remainder of his career here, helped to endear Stevens to the racing public before he did so in more tangible fashion by registering a total of forty-five winners from two hundred and ten rides. Ready to admit some of the inevitable teething difficulties, Stevens went on to impress particularly with the knack of putting his mount in front in unflappable fashion where it mattered, something exhibited most clearly when winning the William Hill Mile at Goodwood by a neck on Lonesome Dude. One day earlier he had dictated the pace to win another major prize at the track on Mary Stuart, whilst Zahrat Dubai (Nassau Stakes), Cape Cross (Queen Anne Stakes), Greek Dance (Rose of Lancaster Stakes) and Torgau (Cherry Hinton Stakes), as well as Royal Anthem, were all guided by Stevens to pattern-race victories. Glorious Goodwood also, however,

The Thoroughbred Corporation's "Royal Anthem"

brought the news that he would be leaving Stoute and heading back to the States again at the end of August to take up a five-year contract with the Thoroughbred Corporation, less of a shock than it might have been seeing that Kieren Fallon had so recently become available as a suitable replacement. Stevens ended his stay in Britain, as he began it, with a winner. In the United States, Anees (in the Juvenile) gave him a seventh success at the Breeders' Cup meeting, to go with three Kentucky Derby triumphs and 4,512 victories in all before he announced his retirement from the saddle in December because of irreparable damage inflicted by arthritis on his right knee. The following month, however, Stevens seemed to be having a rethink, the news coming that, armed with 'new supplements and herbal remedies,' he was hoping to make a comeback. Stevens, however, played down the reports over the next few days.

Royal Anthem (USA) (b.c. 1995)	Theatrical (b 1982)	Nureyev (b 1977)	Northern Dancer
			Special
		Tree of Knowledge (b 1977)	Sassafras
			Sensibility
	In Neon (USA) (b 1982)	Ack Ack (b 1966)	Battle Joined
			Fast Turn
		Shamara (ch 1973)	Dewan
			Palsy Walsy

The very tall, close-coupled Royal Anthem will hopefully attempt to make it third time lucky in the Breeders' Cup Turf and emulate his sire Theatrical, who won the race as a five-year-old in 1987. He will be most unlucky to come up against a rival of Daylami's quality again, while his dam In Neon is also perhaps due for a change of luck at the breeding because her 1998 four-year-old Sharp Cat (by Storm Cat) would have started favourite for the Distaff but for illness one week before the race which necessitated her withdrawal. By that stage, Sharp Cat had already notched five Group 1 victories. Royal Anthem's score stands at one Group 1 and one Grade 1. He is worth a lot more. *W. I. Mott, USA*

ROYAL ARROW (USA) 3 b.g. Dayjur (USA) 137 – Buy The Firm (USA) (Affirmed (USA)) [1998 6s* 6d 6.5d 1999 5.5s 8d 6.1m 6.1g 7g Aug 19] $65,000Y: fourth foal: half-brother to a winner in USA by Storm Cat: dam US Grade 1 9f winner: won newcomers listed race at Deauville on debut: disappointing since (left A. Fabre in France after second 3-y-o start). *F. Murphy* –

ROYAL ARTIST 3 b.g. Royal Academy (USA) 130 – Council Rock 74 (General Assembly (USA)) [1998 NR 1999 6g 5g⁴ 7m² 6d³ a7g* Nov 8] 44,000Y: workmanlike gelding: seventh foal: brother to a winner in Macau and half-brother to winners abroad by Anshan and Keen: dam, maiden suited by 1¼m, daughter of Nassau winner Dancing Rocks: fair performer: off 6 months after second start: won maiden at Lingfield in November: will stay 1m: acts on equitrack, yet to race on extremes of going on turf: has been bandaged behind. *W. J. Haggas* **75**

ROYAL AXMINSTER 4 b.g. Alzao (USA) 117 – Number One Spot 71 (Reference Point 139) [1998 NR 1999 10m 10m 17.2g⁵ 14.1g 13.1f⁶ Sep 6] useful-looking gelding: modest maiden handicapper: may prove best up to 1½m: acts on firm going. *Mrs P. N. Dutfield* **50**

ROYAL BLUE 4 ch.g. Ron's Victory (USA) 129 – Angels Are Blue 73 (Stanford 121§) [1998 –: 6s 6m 6s⁴ 5d 6g a8.5g a8g 1999 a7f⁶ 8m May 3] unfurnished gelding: fluent mover: modest maiden at 2 yrs: little form since. *M. D. I. Usher* –

ROYAL CANARY (IRE) 2 ch.c. (Jan 23) Prince of Birds (USA) 121 – Inesse (Simply Great (FR) 122) [1999 5s 5m² 6f 5g⁵ Jun 16] IR 6,500F, 6,000Y: first foal: dam unraced: poor maiden: best effort when second in seller at Musselburgh in May: should be suited by 6f+. *Miss L. A. Perratt* **49**

ROYAL CARLTON (IRE) 7 b.c.c. Mulhollande (USA) 107 – Saintly Angel 87 (So Blessed 130) [1998 39, a–: a10g a8g 8d 8g 10g 9m⁶ 8.5g 8g 8d⁴ 10v 1999 7.7m Jul 2] poor handicapper nowadays: stays 1m: acts on good to firm going, good to soft and all-weather: usually held up. *K. C. Comerford* –

ROYAL CASCADE (IRE) 5 b.g. River Falls 113 – Relative Stranger (Cragador 110) [1998 49, a69: a7g⁵ a6g* a6g⁴ a6g* a6g* 5s⁶ 5.9d 6.1m a6g² 5.7g⁵ a6g a6g a6g² a6g* 1999 a7g² a6g a7g* a6g* a7g* 7.5v a8.5g 7.5g a7g³ a7g⁵ a6g Nov 30] **–a88** lengthy gelding: fairly useful on all-weather, poor on turf: won claimer at Southwell in January and handicaps at Wolverhampton and Southwell in February: needs good pace at 6f, and should stay 1m: raced mainly on fibresand, acts on soft going on turf: usually blinkered. *B. A. McMahon*

ROYAL CASTLE (IRE) 5 b.g. Caerleon (USA) 132 – Sun Princess 130 (English Prince 129) [1998 84: 12.5s³ 12s 12g³ 15.5g⁴ 16g⁵ 15.5g 12g⁴ 14.1m² 14.6d 1999 18.7m⁵ 16f³ 20m Jun 15] sturdy, lengthy gelding: good mover: fairly useful handicapper: ran creditably first 2 starts in 1999, fifth to Rainbow High from out of handicap in Chester Cup on reappearance: well held in Ascot Stakes final one: likely to prove best at 2m+: acts on firm and good to soft going. *M. H. Tompkins* **84**

ROYAL CAVALIER 2 b.g. (May 16) Prince of Birds (USA) 121 – Gold Belt (IRE) 61 (Bellypha 130) [1999 5m⁴ 7.9g³ 8g⁴ 8s² a8g² Nov 22] sturdy gelding: third foal: half-brother to 1996 2-y-o 5f seller winner Fearless Cavalier (by Bold Arrangement) and 3-y-o Nathan's Boy (by Tragic Role): dam 1m winner: fair maiden: creditable second of 18 to Summoner at Doncaster final turf start: should stay 1¼m: acts on soft going, looked none too keen only outing on fibresand: refused to enter stalls on intended debut. *R. Hollinshead* **79**

ROYAL CIRCUS 10 b.g. Kris 135 – Circus Ring 122 (High Top 131) [1998 30, a35: a13g³ a16g³ a12g a16g⁵ a13g a13g³ 12.5m 12m⁴ a12g a14.8g 1999 a16f 15.8m 12g⁴ a12g Oct 1] workmanlike gelding: poor handicapper: effective at 1½m to 2m: acts on firm ground, good to soft and equitrack, possibly not on fibresand: front runner. *P. W. Hiatt* **–**

ROYAL CZARINA 2 ch.f. (Mar 27) Czaravich (USA) – Sabrata (IRE) (Zino 127) [1999 a8g Dec 17] 1,400Y: good-bodied filly: first foal: dam French 2-y-o 5f winner: gave trouble at start and withdrawn in October: seventh of 14 in Southwell maiden 2 months later. *M. Salaman* **–**

ROYAL DANCE (USA) 3 b.c. Trempolino (USA) 135 – Rosey Ramble (USA) (Chieftain II) [1998 NR 1999 12m⁶ 10.5m 8g⁴ 8m³ 7.6m⁴ 8.5m a8.5f⁵ a7f⁵ a8f⁴ Dec 9] \$35,000F, 60,000Y: small, quite attractive colt: half-brother to several winners, including smart 6f (at 2 yrs) and 7f winner Cliveden (by Valdez) and US Grade 3 9.5f winner Assert Oneself (by Affirmed): dam unraced: fair maiden: left C. Brittain after sixth start: stays 1¼m: raced only on good/good to firm going on turf, below form on dirt: blinkered fourth start. *P. L. Rudkin, UAE* **75**

ROYAL DOLPHIN (IRE) 3 b.c. Dolphin Street (FR) 125 – Diamond Lake (Kings Lake (USA) 133) [1998 –: 7d 1999 6s 6g 10g⁶ a9.4g 9.9s a12g Nov 19] sturdy, heavy-topped colt: little sign of ability. *B. A. McMahon* **–**

ROYAL DOME (IRE) 7 b.g. Salt Dome (USA) – Brook's Dilemma 80 (Known Fact (USA) 135) [1998 77: 5g 5d⁶ 5g 5d⁴ 5g⁴ 5m³ 5m² 5g⁵ 5g 5m⁵ 5m* 5g* 5g 5d 1999 5s 5m 6d 5g⁴ 5m 5g 5m⁶ 5f Jul 24] good-quartered gelding: fair handicapper at best: won 9 of his 67 starts: best effort in 1999 when fourth of 17 at Pontefract: died on gallops early in August: stayed easy 6f: acted on firm and good to soft ground: probably best visored. *Martyn Wane* **64**

ROYAL EAGLE (USA) 2 b.c. (Jan 28) Eagle Eyed (USA) 111 – Accountin-question (USA) (Classic Account (USA)) [1999 6d² 6m⁴ 7m* 7d² Aug 11] 40,000Y: medium-sized, angular colt: has a fluent, round action: first foal: dam won up to 9f in USA and placed in Grade 3 event: useful form: won maiden at Epsom in July: best effort when second of 5 to Barathea Guest in minor event at Salisbury following month, rallying after making running: will be suited by 1m+: yet to race on extremes of going: probably capable of better still. *P. F. I. Cole* **97 p**

ROYAL EXPRESSION 7 b.g. Sylvan Express 117 – Edwins' Princess 75 (Owen Dudley 121) [1998 NR 1999 18d 14.4g³ 15.8m 15.9m 16.2m 16.1f² 16g* 15.9d⁴ 15.8m⁶ 17.2s² 16s a16g⁵ a14.8g² a16.2g a16.2g* Dec 15] tall gelding: fair handicapper: won at Nottingham in August and Wolverhampton (by 10 lengths) in December: stays 17f: acts on firm ground, soft and equitrack: blinkered (ran well) once at 2 yrs, visored (no form) penultimate start: sometimes races freely. *F. Jordan* **77**

ROYAL FLAME (IRE) 3 b.f. Royal Academy (USA) 130 – Samnaun (USA) **72**
(Stop The Music (USA)) [1998 NR 1999 10m⁶ 12f⁵ 10g⁵ 8m⁴ 8d⁴ 9s² a10g⁶ a10g⁴
a9.4g³ Dec 15] IR 46,000F, 25,000Y: deep-girthed, angular filly: third foal: dam
unraced half-sister to useful miler Lonely Leader (by Royal Academy) and German
1000 Guineas winner Quebrada: fair maiden: stays 1¼m: acts on soft going and all-
weather, probably on firm. *J. W. Hills*

ROYAL FONTAINE (IRE) 4 b.f. Royal Academy (USA) 130 – Bellifontaine **69**
(FR) (Bellypha 130) [1998 84: 8.1g² 10m² 10.4g² 10g* 1999 10m 10g 10m³ Jun 17]
tall, quite attractive filly: fair performer, lightly raced: stays 10.4f: raced only on
good/good to firm ground: has given trouble stalls. *J. W. Hills*

ROYAL FUSILIER (IRE) 3 b.g. Case Law 113 – Tropical Rain (Rainbow **70**
Quest (USA) 134) [1998 65?: 7g 7m² 7m 8s 6d 1999 8.3g* 8m 8.5m² 10m⁵ a8g Nov
15] close-coupled gelding: fair performer: won minor event at Hamilton in June: ran
well after only on third outing: left M. Bell for 3,500 gns in October: broke blood
vessel following month: stayed 8.5f: acted on good to firm going: was inconsistent:
dead. *J. L. Harris*

ROYAL HIGHLANDER (IRE) 2 b.c. (Feb 15) Foxhound (USA) 103 – Sky **101 p**
Lover (Ela-Mana-Mou 132) [1999 6s* Nov 5] IR 13,000F, 39,000Y: small, angular
colt: has quick action: fourth foal: half-brother to 4-y-o Al Mabrook and fairly useful
Irish 11f and 1½m winner Rainbow Warrior (by Imperial Frontier): dam Irish 2-y-o
5f winner: favourite, created very favourable impression when easily winning
20-runner maiden at Doncaster by 1½ lengths (value more like 12, rated accordingly)
from Polar Star, striding well clear from over 2f out before being heavily eased:
should stay 1m: sold for a reported £400,000, joined J. Hills: looks a smart performer
in the making, sure to win more races. *A. G. Foster*

ROYAL HUSSAR 3 gr.c. Efisio 120 – Altaia (FR) 90 (Sicyos (USA) 126) [1998 **51**
NR 1999 7.1s 6s⁵ 6g a6g Nov 11] 32,000Y: third foal: half-brother to 1994 2-y-o 7f
winner Silver Tzar (by Dominion): dam 6f/7f winner: modest form at best: sold 1,800
gns after third start: disputed lead long way and eased final outing. *P. Howling*

ROYAL INSULT 2 ch.c. (Apr 21) Lion Cavern (USA) 117 – Home Truth 98 **81 p**
(Known Fact (USA) 135) [1999 6s² 6g* Oct 14] 18,000Y: fifth foal: closely related
to 6-y-o Susu and 1½m winner Return of The Mac (both by Machiavellian) and
half-brother to 5-y-o Cadeaux Cher: dam 7f/1m winner: improved on form of
encouraging debut when beating Kareeb by ¾ length in 13-runner maiden at Redcar,
leading over 1f out: will probably stay 1m: type to progress. *K. R. Burke*

ROYAL IVY 2 ch.f. (Mar 19) Mujtahid (USA) 118 – Royal Climber (Kings Lake **71**
(USA) 133) [1999 5s⁴ 5.1m⁴ 6g⁴ 6m⁵ 7m⁴ 7d 8v³ a7g² Dec 6] 20,000Y: sturdy filly:
has a quick action: fifth foal: half-sister to 1¼m winner Heboob Alshemaal (by
Nordico) and fairly useful 1¼m/1½m winner General Macarthur (by Alzao): dam
Irish 7f (at 2 yrs) and 13f winner: fair maiden: stays 1m: acts on good to firm and
heavy going and equitrack: sold 15,000 gns, joined J. Akehurst. *B. W. Hills*

ROYAL KINGDOM (IRE) 2 b.c. (Apr 17) Fairy King (USA) – Alliance **109**
(USA) 113 (Alleged (USA) 138) [1999 7m* 7m* 8s* 10v⁵ Oct 31] $170,000F: rather
leggy, unfurnished colt: closely related to several winners, including useful middle-

*Serpentine Gallery Royal Lodge Stakes, Ascot—Royal Kingdom (left) rallies admirably to hold off the challenge
of Best of The Bests, with Kingsclere (No.5) battling on well for third ahead of Chinatown*

Mr M. Tabor & Mrs John Magnier's "Royal Kingdom"

distance stayer Matador (by Nureyev) and half-brother to 3 winners abroad: dam, French 10.5f winner who stayed 1½m, half-sister to Blushing Groom: useful form: won maiden in July and listed race (by 2½ lengths from Anzari) in August, both at the Curragh, and 6-runner Serpentine Gallery Royal Lodge Stakes at Ascot (ran on strongly to beat Best of The Bests by ½ length) in September: favourite, beaten 10 lengths when fifth of 7 to Goldamix in Criterium de Saint-Cloud final start: should stay at least 1¼m: acts on soft and good to firm ground. *A. P. O'Brien, Ireland*

ROYAL LEGEND   7 b.g. Fairy King (USA) – Legend of Arabia (Great Nephew   –
126) [1998 71: 11.9g⁴ 8m 10g³ 10s* 9.9m* 10m⁵ 10g 10g³ 10g⁶ 10g⁵ 1999 10s 10g
9.9m Jun 18] leggy gelding: fair handicapper: below form in 1999: effective at 1¼m/
easy 1½m: acts on fibresand, soft and good to firm going: blinkered/visored earlier in
career. *R. M. Flower*

ROYAL LINE   3 b.c. Saint Estephe (FR) 123 – Double Line (FR) (What A Guest   **106**
119) [1998 9s* 1999 14.8m*ᵈⁱˢ 15g⁴ Jul 30] 620,000 francs Y: rather leggy, angular
ex-French-trained colt: fourth foal: dam, third over 1½m in France at 4 yrs, half-sister
to dam of Poule d'Essai des Pouliches winner Pearl Bracelet: first past post in
newcomers event at Longchamp (by 1½ lengths from Sendawar) in 1998 for A. Fabre
and 4-runner listed race at Newmarket (by 1½ lengths from Moon Dragon) in July:
disqualified on latter occasion after failing dope test: creditable length fourth of 7 to
Artistique in Prix Berteux at Chantilly later in month: stays 15f: acts on soft and good
to firm going. *Saeed bin Suroor*

ROYAL MARK (IRE)   6 b.g. Fairy King (USA) – Take Your Mark (USA)   **74 +**
(Round Table) [1998 91: 6d 6v 7d 7g⁴ 7m⁴ 8m² 7g* 7f 7g 6g 7g 1999 7g 6d 7m⁶ 7m
5g⁴ Aug 25] good-topped gelding: fairly useful handicapper at 5 yrs: below best in
1999, though very much caught the eye final start, going strongly long way and not
given hard time: stays 1m, seems likely to prove at least as effective at 5f/6f: acts on
firm and good to soft ground: blinkered once as 3-y-o: best held up. *D. Nicholls*

ROYAL MEASURE   3 b.c. Inchinor 119 – Sveltissima 48 (Dunphy 124) [1998   **63**
NR 1999 a9.4g⁵ a9.4g⁶ 11.8g⁴ 11.8v⁵ 11.6g 10.2g 12m 10m Aug 23] 8,500Y: leggy,
angular colt: fourth reported foal: dam 7f/1m winner: modest maiden: best efforts at
Leicester (including in handicap) on third/fourth starts: stays 1½m: acts on heavy
going. *B. R. Millman*

ROYAL MINSTREL (IRE)   2 ch.c. (May 15) Be My Guest (USA) 126 – Shann-   **74**
tabariya (IRE) (Shernazar 131) [1999 7g⁶ 8g⁶ 8d⁴ Sep 28] IR 17,000Y: lengthy,
workmanlike colt: fifth foal: half-brother to winners abroad by Kahyasi and Dancing
Dissident: dam French 11.5f winner: fair maiden: best effort when fourth of 8 to
Peacock Jewel in steadily-run race at Newmarket final start: will stay at least 1¼m.
M. H. Tompkins

ROYAL MOUNT   3 ch.g. Cadeaux Genereux 131 – Hawait Al Barr 100 (Green   **–**
Desert (USA) 127) [1998 75: 6s⁵ 1999 a9.4g Dec 15] third foal: half-brother to useful
1m (at 2 yrs) and 9f winner Equity Princess (by Warning): dam best at 2m: fair form
when promising fifth of 9 in maiden at York in 1998: said to have suffered minor
injury (sold from M. Johnston only 2,100 gns in October 1999) and no show on
return. *K. T. Ivory*

ROYAL OCCASION (USA)   2 b.f. (Apr 5) El Gran Senor (USA) 136 – Hot   **56 p**
Princess 101 (Hot Spark 126) [1999 7m⁶ 7s Nov 5] angular, useful-looking filly:
sister to Rodrigo de Triano, closely related to 2 winners, including 7f winner Musick
House (by Sadler's Wells), and half-sister to a 7f winner by Assert: dam, Irish 5f to 7f
winner, later successful in USA: well held on debut for P. Chapple-Hyam: modest
form when seventh of 20 to Hopeful Light in maiden at Doncaster 4½ months later:
should stay 1¼m: probably remains capable of better. *A. G. Foster*

ROYAL ORIGINE (IRE)   3 b.g. Royal Academy (USA) 130 – Belle Origine   **–**
(USA) (Exclusive Native (USA)) [1998 78: 5.1m³ 6m³ 6m⁴ 1999 8s 7.1g 6m⁶ 8s a6g
a5g Dec 18] well-made gelding: has a quick action: disappointing maiden: trained by
M. Channon until third start and by M. Quinn next 2: bred to stay beyond 6f: form
only on good to firm going: wore blinkers and tongue strap final outing. *J. R. Jenkins*

ROYAL PARADE (IRE)   4 b.g. Pips Pride 117 – Route Royale (Roi Soleil 125)   **25**
[1998 –: 8g 8.2m 8.1m 6.1d 7g 7g 6g 1999 6f 6g 11.8g 10.2g 17.2f Jun 26] bad
maiden: tried blinkered. *J. M. Bradley*

ROYAL PASTIMES   2 b.f. (Apr 15) Ezzoud (IRE) 126 – Royal Recreation (USA)   **45**
(His Majesty (USA)) [1999 5m 6m⁵ 6m 7.1m⁶ 7.1d⁵ 7m 7m Aug 27] 3,000Y: small, sparely-
made filly: fifth foal: closely related to 1½m winner Royal Diversion (by Marju) and
half-sister to a 1m winner in USA by Lycius: dam Irish maiden who stayed 2m: poor
maiden: well beaten in sellers last 2 outings. *Martyn Wane*

ROYAL PATRON   3 ch.f. Royal Academy (USA) 130 – Indian Queen 115 (Elec-   **78**
tric 126) [1998 –p: 7d 1999 10m⁶ 14g* 15.8m⁵ 14d⁵ 14.1g⁶ 11.9d² Oct 29] leggy,
lightly-made filly: fair performer: won maiden at Lingfield in August: ran creditably
most starts after: likely to prove best at 1½m/1¾m: yet to race on extremes of going.
J. L. Dunlop

ROYAL PREVIEW (IRE)   3 b.f. Prince Sabo 123 – Visible Form 99 (Formid-   **76**
able (USA) 125) [1998 –: 5m 6m⁵ 6m 1999 a7g* a6g* a6g* a6g² a8g* 6m⁶ 6g 6d   **a81**
5.7f⁴ 5m⁶ 5f⁵ 5d 5m⁴ a7f³ Oct 2] quite good-topped filly: fairly useful handicapper
on all-weather, fair on turf: won at Lingfield (twice), Southwell and Wolverhampton
in January/February: ran respectably most other starts: effective at 5f to easy 1m:
acts on firm going and all-weather (possibly not on softer than good): often races
prominently: sold 14,500 gns, sent to Saudi Arabia. *M. L. W. Bell*

ROYAL REBEL   3 b.g. Robellino (USA) 127 – Greenvera (USA) (Riverman   **109**
(USA) 131) [1998 98p: 7f³ 7f 8d⁴ 1999 8d³ 8g* 10m² 11.5g³ 12s 9.9f 14g* 12g Sep
12] good-topped gelding: smart performer: won maiden at Newcastle in April and
listed race at Leopardstown in August, latter by 2 lengths from Try For Ever, staying
on having been pushed along some way out: ran well when placed in between in
listed race at Leopardstown (beaten neck by Cupid) and Derby Trial at Lingfield (1¾
lengths third of 5 to Lucido): stiff task when seventh of 8 in Prix du Jockey Club at
Chantilly on fifth outing: disappointing in Stockholm Cup at Taby final start: gelded

afterwards: should stay further than 1¾m: acts on firm and good to soft going: blinkered second to sixth starts. *M. Johnston*

ROYAL REPRIMAND (IRE)   4 b.g. Reprimand 122 – Lake Ormond (Kings   **44** Lake (USA) 133) [1998 58?: 9g⁶ 8g 9m² 1999 8g 9d⁶ 8m⁶ 9f 8m 8f⁵ 9m⁴ 7g⁵ 9.9s⁴ 10.1d⁵ Oct 20] close-coupled, good-topped gelding: poor maiden: stays 1¼m: acts on good to firm going, probably soft: visored twice: usually races up with pace. *R. E. Barr*

ROYAL RESULT (USA)   6 b. or br.g. Gone West (USA) – Norette (Northfields   **98** (USA)) [1998 87: 8d 8d 8.5m 7.5d³ 7.9m 7f⁴ 8m³ 7m⁶ 7m² 8m 7g* 7d⁴ 6s* 7.1g 1999 6m 6f 6d 7g 6d² 6m* 6m³ 6s²⁷ 7m 6g* 6d³ 6.1g Sep 25] good-bodied gelding: useful handicapper: again took a few runs to come to himself, and won at York in July and Goodwood in August, latter by neck from Flak Jacket in 27-runner race: good narrowly-beaten third to Grangeville in Ayr Gold Cup penultimate start, got very upset in stalls when below form final one: likely to prove best at 5f/6f nowadays: yet to race on heavy going, acts on any other: blinkered once at 5 yrs: usually held up, raced more prominently at Ayr: sold 34,000 gns. *D. Nicholls*

ROYAL ROMEO   2 ch.g. (May 18) Timeless Times (USA) 99 – Farinara (Dragon-   **66** ara Palace (USA) 115) [1999 5f⁶ 6d 5g⁵ 5g³ 5g* Sep 15] 16,000Y: good-bodied gelding: unimpressive mover: seventh foal: brother to fair 6f/7f winner (including at 2 yrs) Miss Offset and half-brother to useful performer Croft Imperial (by Crofthall): dam unraced: fair performer: won 17-runner maiden at Beverley in September by 1¼ lengths from Ducie: should stay 6f: has been bandaged behind. *T. D. Easterby*

ROYAL ROULETTE   5 ch.m. Risk Me (FR) 127 – Princess Lily 65 (Blakeney   **57** 126) [1998 –, a68: a12g⁶ 12s a12g⁵ a16.2g³ a14.8g² a16g* 1999 a16g³ a16f* a16f   **a77** 14.1s 16.4m 16m⁵ 16.4d³ 16.4g Aug 20] small mare: fair handicapper on all-weather, modest on turf: easy winner at Lingfield in January: best effort after when third at Sandown in August: stays 2m: acts on good to firm ground, good to soft and all-weather: effective visored/blinkered (not tried since 1997): has raced freely. *Miss B. Sanders*

ROYAL SIGNET   4 ch.f. King's Signet (USA) 110 – Ladiz (Persian Bold 123)   **53** [1998 –: 7.1g⁶ 8m 10m⁶ 10.2d 9.7m⁶ 1999 11.7s 13.1g⁴ 16d⁶ 17.2m⁵ 12d 17.2m Aug 22] modest maiden handicapper: stays 2m: acts on good to soft going: has had tongue tied. *M. J. Weeden*

ROYAL TARRAGON   3 b.f. Aragon 118 – Lady Philippa (IRE) 77 (Taufan   **–** (USA) 119) [1998 48?, a–: 5g 6m 7f 6.1g 5.1g⁴ 6m 5.7v a6g a7g 1999 8m a7g 6.1m 5.1m 7g Aug 11] poor maiden: tried blinkered/visored. *J. R. Arnold*

ROYAL TIPPLE   3 b.g. Noble Patriarch 115 – Mashin Time 73 (Palm Track 122)   **69** [1998 NR 1999 10g 12.3m 10m⁵ 11g Oct 14] 1,400Y: leggy gelding: half-brother to 1m seller winner Tiffin Time (by Lochnager): dam 6f and 1m winner: fair maiden: should stay bit beyond 1¼m: raced only on good/good to firm going: won over hurdles in November. *T. D. Easterby*

ROYAL WAVE (IRE)   3 b. or br.g. Polish Precedent (USA) 131 – Mashmoon   **72 d** (USA) 80 (Habitat 134) [1998 71p: 7g⁵ 1999 6g* 7m 8.1s 7d 7d a8g Dec 13] plain, lengthy gelding: fair performer: won maiden at Pontefract in May: well held after, leaving Mrs A. Swinbank after third start: should be suited by 7f+. *J. L. Eyre*

ROYRACE   7 b.g. Wace (USA) 82 – Royal Tycoon (Tycoon II) [1998 –: 15.9g   **–** 1999 13.1v⁶ Oct 12] tall gelding: no form on Flat: poor novice hurdler/chaser. *W. M. Brisbourne*

ROYS SUPER CLAN   2 ch.c. (Apr 24) Clantime 101 – Hello Hobson's (IRE) 67   **–** (Fayruz 116) [1999 5m May 26] sturdy colt: first foal: dam 5f/6f winner, including at 2 yrs: tailed off in maiden at Ripon: dead. *R. Bastiman*

RUACANA FALLS (USA)   3 b.f. Storm Bird (CAN) 134 – Obeah 112 (Cure   **86** The Blues (USA)) [1998 85p: 7d⁴ 8.1m* 7g 1999 11.4m⁴ 11m 8m⁴ 9.9g³ 8m a7f⁴ 8.5f a6f⁵ Nov 20] angular, useful-looking filly: fairly useful performer: ran at least respectably first 5 outings in 1999, including when fourth in listed race at Chester in May and minor event at Ascot in June: left P. Chapple-Hyam: blinkered, well held all 3 starts at Woodbine: effective at 1m to 11.4f: acts on good to firm and good to soft going: has worn bandages. *S. Hall, Canada*

RUBAMMA   4 b.g. Kris 135 – Idle Gossip (USA) (Lyphard (USA) 132) [1998 61,   –
a–: 9v⁶ 7.5s⁶ 11.6m 9.9m⁵ 10d⁴ 10g 8d 10.9d 1999 a8.5g a11g⁶ Mar 10] smallish,
robust gelding: modest maiden for P. Walwyn at 3 yrs: well beaten in 1999: pulls
hard, and may prove best up to 1m: acts on all-weather, very best turf effort on soft
going: blinkered final start: sold 2,100 gns. *D. J. G. Murray Smith*

RUBY BEAR   4 gr.f. Thethingaboutitis (USA) 106 – Hitravelscene (Mansingh   –
(USA) 120) [1998 42, a33: 8.3v² 10s 12g² 14m² 14.1g a14.8g 13.4g³ 12.1g² 13.8g³
a9.4g³ 10.9s⁶ 1999 a12g 9.2v³ 12.3m 11.1v⁶ 11.1s May 14] workmanlike filly: poor
maiden: little form in 1999: stays 1¾m: acts on good to firm and heavy going: tried
blinkered: has been bandaged: sold 4,200 gns. *W. M. Brisbourne*

RUBY LASER   3 b.f. Bustino 136 – Ower (IRE) 71 (Lomond (USA) 128) [1998   56
NR 1999 12m 14g 14.1m⁴ 13.1f 14.1v³ Sep 29] fourth foal: dam, 7f winner, half-
sister to several winners, including smart middle-distance colts Weigh Anchor and
Dr Massini: modest maiden: will stay 2m: acts on heavy ground, probably on good to
firm: gave plenty of trouble stalls on debut, got loose before start next time: sold
10,000 gns, joined E. James. *R. F. Johnson Houghton*

RUBYS REPLY   2 ch.f. (Mar 17) Deploy 131 – Ruby Venture 56 (Ballad Rock   56
122) [1999 6g 7m 7m* Jul 20] first foal: dam maiden who stayed 1¼m: well beaten
in maidens prior to narrowly winning Yarmouth seller, getting up close home having
been in rear long way: will stay 1m. *S. C. Williams*

RUDE AWAKENING   5 b.g. Rudimentary (USA) 118 – Final Call 79 (Town Crier   52
119) [1998 58: a6g a6g* a6g³ a6g a5g³ a6g² a7g⁶ a5g⁵ 5s⁴ 5d⁵ a5g³ a6g⁶ a6g 5g⁵ 5g²   a54
6m 5m 6m 5m 1999 a6g⁴ a6g² a6g a5g a6g 5s³ 5m⁴ 5m⁵ 5g 5m⁶ Aug 27]
sturdy gelding: modest handicapper: has form up to 7.5f, races mainly at 5f/6f
nowadays: acts on fibresand, firm and soft going: effective blinkered/visored or not:
carries head high: races up with pace. *C. W. Fairhurst*

RUDIK (USA)   2 b. or br.c. (Apr 13) Nureyev (USA) 131 – Nervous Baba (USA)   95 p
(Raja Baba (USA)) [1999 7.1m² 6m³ 6s* 6d³ Oct 9] $200,000Y: compact colt:
closely related to 3 winners in USA by Danzig and half-brother to winners abroad by
Saratoga Six and Gone West (2): dam US Grade 2 6f winner: progressive form: won
maiden at Newcastle in September: narrowly-beaten third of 6 to Out of Africa in
listed event at York final start, keeping on gamely: should stay 1m: acts on soft and
good to firm ground: should still do better. *Sir Michael Stoute*

RUDI'S PET (IRE)   5 ch.g. Don't Forget Me 127 – Pink Fondant (North-   118
fields (USA)) [1998 90d: 5d 6v 5.1m⁵ 5d⁶ 6d 7f 6g 8.1g 6f 5.6g 6s 7g 6g 5d
1999 5d⁴ 5d⁴ 5m* 5s 5m⁶ 5m* 5m² 5m* 5f* 5m⁶ Dec 12]
   Cases of mistaken identity within the racehorse population still crop up
on a regular basis, and one could be forgiven for thinking that this was one of
them. The Rudi's Pet of 1999 was simply unrecognisable. Gone was the habit-

Northern Rock Gosforth Park Cup (Handicap), Newcastle—
the rejuvenated Rudi's Pet has no trouble accounting for the opposition
and is able to be eased close home as Storyteller stays on well for second place

King George Grosvenor Casinos Stakes, Goodwood—
Rudi's Pet continues his fine season and never looks like being caught after taking over at halfway;
Imperial Beauty does her best to close the gap

ual under-achiever usually spotted skulking among the also-rans in handicaps. In his stead, there was a spirited trail-blazer who could match strides with the fastest in his division and ended the season with competing in handicaps behind him. Incredibly, that horse who began the year running (and being beaten) off a BHB mark of 73 in handicaps was the same one who ended the year as the horse with the best five-furlong form trained in Britain.

The preamble to Rudi's Pet's emergence as a sprinter to be reckoned with lasted three seasons, two of them with Richard Hannon and one with Lynda Ramsden. For the former he was hard to pin down, successful twice at both two and three but also prone to disappointments. Reserving easily his best until last for Hannon, when he showed useful form to win a handicap at Doncaster, helped push his price up to 42,000 guineas at the sales. Trained by Mrs Ramsden, appearing at eye-catchingly short odds in the morning betting on several occasions and mentioned as a market mover in the early exchanges on several others, Rudi's Pet never came close to rewarding even each-way support—in twelve of his fourteen outings that season he managed no better than tenth. His BHB mark slid from 97 and 20,000 guineas was enough to secure him when he was sent back to the sale-ring.

It did not take long in 1999 before Rudi's Pet revealed himself a bargain and a very different character to go with the same old chestnut shown on his equine passport. Fourth places in large fields on his first two starts gave little sign of what was to come, but he was sent off favourite or joint-favourite on all of his remaining starts in Britain. These resulted in clear-cut wins in handicaps, making all or most of the running, at Thirsk in May, Newcastle (the Gosforth Park Cup) in June and Ascot (a rated stakes) in July. When he romped home off 97 at Ascot, his connections could no longer be described as capitalising on a lenient handicap mark.

Rudi's Pet was in the form of his life and his next assignment was to take on pattern-class rivals over one of the fastest tracks in the country in the King George Grosvenor Casinos Stakes at Goodwood. The supposed gap between handicaps and pattern races can seldom have seemed so small as when Rudi's Pet showed a clean pair of heels to the fourteen others who took him on at Goodwood, twelve of whom had made their previous start in either a pattern or a listed race. The 6/1 favourite, Rudi's Pet raced close to the pace in the early stages rather than setting it himself, but he was in front on the stand side at halfway and had stretched a length and three quarters clear at the line. Imperial Beauty, who was hampered early on and unlucky not to have finished closer, and Dashing Blue did best of those who chased him. Dashing Blue finished fifth in the Nunthorpe on his next start whilst Imperial Beauty later came within a short neck of being the Abbaye winner. Rudi's Pet had not been entered for the Nunthorpe and was ineligible for the Abbaye because he is a gelding, but his one race after Goodwood offered a more valuable prize than either of them. Nearly £250,000 was at stake in the Hong Kong Sprint at Sha Tin in December. Although below his Goodwood form, Rudi's Pet was beaten only about two and a half lengths, fading after hitting the front despite missing the break, in sixth of thirteen to Fairy King Prawn. In every respect Rudi's Pet had come a very long way in 1999.

			Ahonoora	Lorenzaccio
Rudi's Pet (IRE) (ch.g. 1994)	Don't Forget Me (b 1984)		(ch 1975)	Helen Nichols
		African Doll	African Sky
		(b 1978)	Mithril
	Pink Fondant (ch 1984)	Northfields	Northern Dancer
		(ch 1968)	Little Hut
		Sheelin Rose	Bold Lad
		(ch 1979)	Motacilla

So how could this be the same horse who had languished so badly in 1998? For a start, it was not exactly the same horse, as one of the first results of Rudi's Pet's latest change of stables had been a gelding operation. Additionally, although his improvement in the latest season is remarkable by almost any standards, it is rather less remarkable in the context of the many other success stories emanating from the stables near Thirsk run by David Nicholls. Since he took out a training licence in 1993, Soba's jockey has had to found his second reputation in the sport on raw material already used by other trainers. In the latest season, that material included multiple winners Nifty Norman, Further Outlook, American Cousin, Atlantic Viking, Cryhavoc, Daawe, Brecongill Lad, Tayseer and Zuhair, and Pepperdine who won the William Hill Trophy at York. Having had forty-six and fifty-eight horses listed in his care in *Horses In Training* in the last two seasons, Nicholls sent out a total of ninety different

Mr G. H. Leatham's "Rudi's Pet"

runners in 1999. He is known as a trainer of sprinters and an earlier flag-bearer for the yard was the rejuvenated 1997 Nunthorpe Stakes dead-heater Ya Malak who nearly died of colic early in 1999. The Nunthorpe will presumably be on the agenda for Rudi's Pet in 2000 and he should be in the shake-up given an ideal surface; he has form on soft going, but is probably best on good or firmer. However, his first target in the forthcoming season is the Dubai Golden Shaheen (formerly the Nad Al Sheba Sprint) over six furlongs on dirt on Dubai World Cup day. A strong gelding, Rudi's Pet is nearly always blinkered nowadays (but was not on his first two starts in 1999) and was visored twice as a four-year-old. In the latest season, having come from the back to register his Doncaster win in 1997, he was able to overcome the odd slow start to demonstrate on a regular basis that he is well suited by forcing tactics.

With Rudi's Pet and the very smart middle-distance horse Insatiable to represent him in the latest season, the dual Guineas winner Don't Forget Me has made a late bid for prominence as a stallion, five years too late though to prevent his taking up residence in India. Rudi's Pet's dam Pink Fondant was well beaten in two maiden events as a two-year-old. Her dam Sheelin Rose also raced only as a juvenile; she won over five furlongs on her debut and, although failing to score again, she ran mostly in pattern events and showed fairly useful form at up to a mile. Her only winners as a mare followed her export to South Africa. Pink Fondant has done well as a broodmare but Rudi's Pet is the last of her six foals to reach racing age. Five were winners and, in addition to Rudi's Pet, they include Sue Me (by Contract Law) and Fionn de Cool (by Mazaad) who were still running in the latest season, both fair performers in their time. More noteworthy, however, is the 1994 Victoria Cup and Royal Hunt Cup winner Face North (by Fayruz). He did not reach his peak until he was a six-year-old, so, who knows, maybe there is better still to come from Rudi's Pet. *D. Nicholls*

RUFF   3 b.f. First Trump 118 – Hotel California (IRE) 58 (Last Tycoon 131) [1998 **58** NR 1999 7m² 6.1g⁶ 7m 8v Nov 24] 10,000Y: second foal: dam 2-y-o 7.5f winner from good family: best effort when second of 18 in claimer at Newmarket on debut: sold from W. Jarvis 3,600 gns after third start: stays 7f. *J. E. Hammond, France*

RULE OF THUMB   2 ch.g. (Apr 19) Inchinor 119 – Rockin' Rosie 59 (Song **85 p** 132) [1999 6d* 6d⁶ Oct 29] 5,000Y, 6,500 2-y-o: tall, rather leggy gelding: fifth foal: dam 5f winner: fairly useful form: won maiden at Pontefract in October: didn't have run of race when sixth of 11 to Don't Surrender in minor event at Newmarket later in month: should stay 7f: equipped with severe noseband and taken steadily to post on debut: remains capable of better. *G. L. Moore*

RUM BABA (IRE)   5 b.g. Tirol 127 – Rum Cay (USA) 75 (Our Native (USA)) **51** [1998 70: 12s⁶ 12g² 12m 16s 13g⁵ 11g³ 12g 12s 12v 1999 12.3m 13g⁴ 16m⁴ 16.1s 17.1g² Jun 28] 34,000F, IR 38,000Y: fourth foal: half-brother to 3 winners, notably very smart stayer Persian Punch (by Persian Heights): dam 14.6f winner out of Premio Lydia Tesio winner Oraston: fair handicapper for C. Collins in Ireland in 1998: modest form at 5 yrs: should stay further than 2m: acts on good to firm and heavy going: blinkered (ran respectably) once. *Mrs M. Reveley*

RUM LAD   5 gr.g. Efisio 120 – She's Smart 88 (Absalom 128) [1998 71: 6.1s 5s **70** 6s³ 5m 6g 6g³ 5m³ 6m⁶ 5d² 7g⁴ 5m⁵ a6g* 6s 6s 1999 6.1v⁵ 6.1s² 6f⁴ 6s 6g³ 6s* 5g* 7m⁴ 6m 6g⁵ 6g⁴ 5g⁵ a6g 6m Sep 24] sturdy gelding: fair performer: won handicap and minor event at Pontefract in June: ran creditably most other starts: probably best at 6f/stiff 5f: acts on any turf going and fibresand: usually held up. *J. J. Quinn*

RUM LASS   2 gr.f. (May 15) Distant Relative 128 – She's Smart 88 (Absalom 128) **54** [1999 5m⁶ 5g⁵ 5s Oct 5] unfurnished filly: fourth foal: half-sister to 5-y-o Rum Lad and 3-y-o Smart Predator: dam sprinter: best effort (modest form) when fifth of 17 to Royal Romeo in maiden at Beverley: something seemingly amiss final start: may prove best at 5f/6f. *J. J. Quinn*

RUM POINTER (IRE)   3 b.g. Turtle Island (IRE) 123 – Osmunda (Mill Reef **101** (USA) 141) [1998 64: 7m⁴ 7.5d⁵ 7m⁶ 10s 8d 1999 12g* 10m 14.6f² 12.3d* 14.1f²

11.9d* 12.4m⁴ 11.9f³ 13.9g⁴ 11.9f⁵ 15d* 17.3g 16.1d Oct 29] small, sturdy gelding: useful handicapper: progressed well in 1999, winning at Catterick in March, Ripon in May, Haydock in June and Ayr (by 3½ lengths from Loop The Loup) in September, last 3-named in small fields: better at 15f than shorter: acts on firm and good to soft ground, probably on soft: races up with pace: game and consistent. *T. D. Easterby*

RUM PUNCH 2 b.c. (Apr 13) Shirley Heights 130 – Gentle Persuasion 95 **69 p** (Bustino 136) [1999 8d Oct 15] big, lengthy colt: half-brother to several winners, including 3-y-o Gracious Gift, smart performer up to 7f Sharp Prod (by Sharpo) and fairly useful 1¼m winner Punkah (by Lear Fan): dam 2-y-o 6f winner, later best at 1m: wearing special noseband and very weak in market when ninth of 13 to Pawn Broker in maiden at Newmarket, racing freely: bred to stay beyond 1m: should do better. *Sir Michael Stoute*

RUNAWAY BAY 3 gr.g. Lugana Beach 116 – Absaloui 64 (Absalom 128) [1998 **42** 49: 5g 5.1m 5m⁴ 6s 1999 5d Jun 28] leggy gelding: poor maiden: likely to prove best at 5f/6f: hung badly left penultimate 2-y-o start. *Mrs L. Stubbs*

RUN FOR GLORY (IRE) 2 ch.c. (May 5) Lahib (USA) 129 – Blazing Glory **–** (IRE) (Glow (USA)) [1999 5s Oct 1] 15,000Y, 30,000 2-y-o: fourth foal: half-brother to 3 winners, including 3-y-o La Piazza (by Polish Patriot) and 5f/6f winner Prince Dome (by Salt Dome): dam, Irish 5f winner, including at 2 yrs: soundly beaten in maiden at Lingfield. *D. R. C. Elsworth*

RUNIN CIRCLES 2 b.g. (May 3) Presidium 124 – True Ring (High Top 131) **52** [1999 6d 7.9g 6d Oct 20] 15,000Y: leggy, unfurnished gelding: sixth reported foal: half-brother to useful 7f (at 2 yrs) to 1¼m winner Future Perfect (by Efisio) and 4-y-o Semi Circle: dam, well beaten both starts at 2 yrs, out of half-sister to Circus Ring: easily best effort in maidens when ninth of 26 to Miss Lorilaw at York second start: may still improve. *M. W. Easterby*

RUN MACHINE (IRE) 2 ch.c. (Apr 5) Fayruz 116 – Anita's Love (IRE) 53 **–** (Anita's Prince 126) [1999 5.1g 5.1m 5d Sep 15] IR 12,500Y: second foal: brother to 3-y-o Thornaby Girl: dam sprint maiden: last in minor event/maidens. *Mrs P. N. Dutfield*

RUNNING BEAR 5 ch.g. Sylvan Express 117 – Royal Girl 67 (Kafu 120) [1998 **–** –: 6g 1999 6d 7f a6g a6g a8.5g⁵ a7g⁵ a8g Dec 17] tall gelding: poor maiden: left **a46** Mrs A. Naughton after fourth start: stays 8.5f: acts on all-weather: has been slowly away. *Miss J. F. Craze*

RUNNING STAG (USA) 5 b.h. Cozzene (USA) – Fruhlingstag (FR) 112 **117** (Orsini 124) [1998 120: a10g* 10v⁵ 12s⁶ 12m 10g³ 10d* a9f³ a10s⁴ a10f a9f⁴ **a124** 1999 a10f 9.9d² a9f² a9f* 10m⁵ a10f* a9f⁴ a10g² 10m² Dec 12]
The description 'tough and consistent' barely does justice to the much travelled Running Stag, who added another memorable chapter in the latest season to what is shaping up into a pretty remarkable story. Only three of Running Stag's nine outings came in Britain, his principal targets being big races abroad, first in Dubai, then in the United States and finally in Hong Kong. Running Stag travelled in excess of 35,000 miles during the course of the year and stood up very well to a demanding schedule, repaying the enterprise of his connections by earning a fistful of dollars with victories in two Grade 2 events in the States, the Brooklyn Handicap at Belmont Park in June and the Saratoga Breeders' Cup Handicap in August. Running Stag had put up some good efforts on dirt when raiding the States as a four-year-old, including finishing third in the Grade 1 Woodward Stakes and seventh in the Breeders' Cup Classic, but he did even better on his four outings there in the latest season. After dividing two of the top older horses in North America, Behrens and the previous year's Kentucky Derby and Preakness winner Real Quiet, in the Massachusetts Handicap at Suffolk Downs in May, Running Stag was an impressive winner of the Brooklyn, taking it up on the home turn and drawing seven and a quarter lengths clear of runner-up Deputy Diamond. After being flown back to Britain for the Coral-Eclipse (in which he managed only fifth of eight), Running Stag followed up with his second big victory, defying top weight at Saratoga to win

Saratoga Breeders' Cup Handicap, Saratoga—a second win in the States for Running Stag

with something in hand from Catienus and Golden Missile, the latter going on to finish third in the Breeders' Cup Classic later in the season. Running Stag's growing status was highlighted by the fact that he started a short-priced favourite for the Woodward Stakes at Belmont Park in September for which there was a second British-based challenger in Dubai World Cup winner Almutawakel (who had Running Stag, below form tried in blinkers, well behind at Nad Al Sheba). Running Stag looked the likely winner of the Woodward when looming up in the home straight but failed to find as much as expected and weakened near the finish, coming around two lengths fourth (Almutawakel second) to River Keen, a former British-trained all-weather performer who was better than ever in the latest season. Running Stag's final overseas venture was in the Hong Kong Cup at Sha Tin in December when—after being beaten at 3/1-on in a preparatory race at Lingfield—he ran close to his best turf form, finishing second of twelve to Jim And Tonic. Running Stag seems best on dirt nowadays though he put up another smart effort on turf in the latest season when running Handsome Ridge to half a length in the Shergar Cup Classic, a pattern race in all but name run at Goodwood in May.

Running Stag (USA) (b.h. 1994)	Cozzene (USA) (gr 1980)	Caro (gr 1967)	Fortino II
			Chambord
		Ride The Trails (b 1971)	Prince John
			Wildwook
	Fruhlingstag (FR) (br 1975)	Orsini (b 1954)	Ticino
			Oranien
		Revada (b 1966)	Iron Liege
			Dalama

The well-made Running Stag, taking after his sire Cozzene who improved with age, is a half-brother to several winners, including the smart

French miler Blackwater (by Irish River); the dam Fruhlingstag was runner-up in the Poule d'Essai des Pouliches. The versatile Running Stag is effective at nine furlongs to eleven furlongs and acts on firm going, soft, all-weather and dirt. He seems effective held up (which he usually is) or making the running (as he did in the Massachusetts Handicap). North American racegoers are again likely to see more of him than their British counterparts in the next season when his major target is said to be the Breeders' Cup Classic at Churchills Downs in November. Doubtless we'll be hearing plenty more of his exploits in the interim. *P. Mitchell*

RUNNING TIMES (USA)   2 b.c. (Jan 29) Brocco (USA) – Concert Peace (USA)   **66**
(Hold Your Peace (USA)) [1999 7.5s³ 7m⁴ 7m⁴ 7g 8d Sep 17] $15,000F, $30,000Y:
workmanlike colt: second foal: half-brother to a winner in USA by Cryptoclearance:
dam unraced half-sister to US Grade 2 8.5f winner Spectacular Sue: fair maiden: best
effort on debut: should be suited by 1m+: acts on soft ground, probably on good to
firm. *T. D. Easterby*

RUN SILENT (IRE)   3 b.c. Sadler's Wells (USA) 132 – Fair of The Furze 112   **68**
(Ela-Mana-Mou 132) [1998 NR 1999 12m 12g 14d³ 14d a14.8g⁴ Oct 13] IR
90,000Y: big, good-topped colt: unimpressive mover: brother to 1½m winner Bel
Canto and half-brother to 3 winners, including high-class White Muzzle (up to 1½m,
by Dancing Brave) and Elfaslah, dam of Almutawakel: dam Irish 1m/1¼m winner
who stayed 1½m: fair maiden: better than result suggests in handicaps at Haydock
(eased when beaten) and Wolverhampton (probably needed race after 3-month
break) last 2 starts: will stay 2m+: acts on good to soft going: sold 13,000 gns.
J. W. Hills

RUSH (BEL)   6 b.h. Abbey's Grey – La Bretonne (Naamiri) [1998 a9.3g² a8.5g*   **?**
a8g* 8m 8f² 9m 9.3v⁵ 1999 a9.8g* 8g³ 8g³ 10g² 8.5g³ a9.8g* 11s a10g⁶ Nov 26]
Belgian-bred horse: winner of 6 races in Belgium prior to 1999, including 2 handicaps at Sterrebeek at 5 yrs: won similar events at Boitsfort in May and October: only
poor form in seller at Lingfield on final start: stays 1¼m: acts on firm ground and
dirt. *C. Dondi, Belgium*

RUSHCUTTER BAY   6 br.g. Mon Tresor 113 – Llwy Bren (Lidhame 109) [1998   **90**
86: 6m 6m* 6m 6f 5.2g 5m⁴ 6.1g⁴ 1999 6m² 6f 6m* 6m 5m⁵ 6m⁵ 5.2g 6.1g⁵ 5d Oct
18] close-coupled gelding: impresses in appearance: fairly useful performer: won
minor event at Windsor in May: mostly ran respectably in handicaps otherwise:
effective at 5f/6f: acts on firm going, probably on good to soft: effective visored or
not: tends to drift left and idle in front. *P. L. Gilligan*

RUSHED (IRE)   4 b.g. Fairy King (USA) – Exotic Bride (USA) (Blushing Groom   **– §**
(FR) 131) [1998 34: 7s a8g³ a10g⁶ 1999 a10f a12g² 11.9f 12.1m 11.6m Jul 19] rangy   **a43 §**
gelding: poor maiden: should stay beyond 1½m: acts on equitrack: virtually refused
to race on reappearance and very slowly away last 2 starts: swished tail and looked
none too keen second start: not to be trusted. *G. P. Enright*

RUSHEN RAIDER   7 br.g. Reprimand 122 – Travel Storm 77 (Lord Gayle (USA)   **50**
124) [1998 60: 14.1g⁴ 14s⁶ 16.1g⁵ 16m⁴ 17.1m 15.8m⁴ 16.1m² 1999 21.6d
16.2d 16m 18g 16.2g* 14.1m³ 15.8g Sep 18] leggy, shallow-girthed gelding: poor
performer: won selling handicap at Beverley in August by 6 lengths, making all:
stays 2m: best form on good going or firmer: sold 3,800 gns, joined P. Needham.
K. W. Hogg, Isle of Man

RUSHMORE (USA)   2 b.c. (May 7) Mt Livermore (USA) – Crafty Nan (USA)   **73 p**
(Crafty Prospector (USA)) [1999 6g³ Oct 6] $100,000Y: sixth foal: brother to smart
performer up to 7f Lucky Lionel, Norfolk Stakes and Prix Robert Papin winner at 2
yrs, and half-brother to a winner in USA by The Prime Minister: dam unraced: weak
in market and green, third of 9 to Strahan in maiden at York, unable to quicken inside
final 2f and eased: will stay 7f: should improve. *P. F. I. Cole*

RUSSIAN ABOUT (IRE)   4 b.f. Polish Patriot (USA) 128 – Molly Carter (IRE)   **56**
(Dr Carter (USA)) [1998 –: a7g a9.4g 1999 8s³ 7d Oct 27] leggy filly: modest
maiden: stays 1m: acts on good to firm and soft going. *H. J. Collingridge*

RUSSIAN FOX (IRE) 2 ch.c. (Jan 20) Foxhound (USA) 103 – La Petruschka **91**
(Ballad Rock 122) [1999 5.2m³ 5d⁴ 5.3f² 5g³ 5s⁴ 5f* 5m* 5f 5g³ 5g² 5d 6d* Oct 14]
IR 12,500F, IR 20,000Y: angular, quite good-topped colt: seventh foal: half-brother
to a winner in Czech Republic by Fairy King: dam ran twice: fairly useful performer:
won maiden and nursery at Lingfield in June/July and nursery at Newmarket (best
effort, dictated pace) in October: effective at 5f/6f: acts on firm and good to soft
going: tends to race prominently/edge left. *R. Hannon*

RUSSIAN MUSIC 6 b.g. Forzando 122 – Sunfleet 59 (Red Sunset 120) [1998 **80**
94: 8d² 10v⁴ 10.2g³ 7.9g 8g 8m 7m 1999 8d 7g 7.1d⁴ 7.1s 7s 7d Oct 27] smallish,
good-quartered gelding: fairly useful performer nowadays: possibly finds 7f on sharp
side nowadays, and barely stays 1¼m: acts on firm and soft ground, below best on
fibresand: effective blinkered or not: has tended to hang left: sold only 500 gns in
November, joined M. Sowersby. *Miss Gay Kelleway*

RUSSIAN RELATION (IRE) 5 ch.g. Soviet Star (USA) 128 – Anjaab (USA) **41**
(Alydar (USA)) [1998 59: 10s⁶ 10m 7.3g 6g⁴ 8m 7.1g 8d 1999 8m 8g 8.3m⁶ 8g 6g
7m Aug 6] poor maiden handicapper nowadays: stays 9f: acts on good to firm and
good to soft ground: effective blinkered (not tried in 1999): has been tongue tied:
carries head awkwardly. *Mrs P. N. Dutfield*

RUSSIAN REVIVAL (USA) 6 ch.h. Nureyev (USA) 131 – Memories **125**
(USA) (Hail The Pirates (USA) 126) [1998 116: 7g³ 7g⁴ 6f 7.3g* 6m² 7g⁵ 1999
7d² 7g* 6m² 7m* Aug 7]
    An admirable racing career spanning five seasons fittingly ended on a
high note when Russian Revival won the Tote International Stakes at Ascot in
August. In terms of merit it was the finest handicap performance on the Flat in
Britain for many a year, Russian Revival defying a BHB mark of 114 under top
weight of 9-7 in the most valuable race of its type in Europe. A close finish
might have been expected from such a competitive-looking contest, but, as with
Jo Mell in the inaugural running in 1998, there was plenty of daylight between
the winner and his nearest pursuer at the line. Whereas Jo Mell had come up the
stand rail, Russian Revival and runner-up Mubrik, a stable companion, raced
under the far rail and were thought by some to have gained an advantage by
racing on a fresh strip of ground. Both were drawn near the rail and stuck close
to it, Dettori on Russian Revival electing to make the running. Two furlongs out
Russian Revival was still travelling well within himself, and he soon settled
the issue when pushed along, justifying strong support—he was co-favourite at
9/1—by two lengths.
    It was Russian Revival's seventh success, the first of which had come
as a two-year-old when he was owned by Robert Sangster and trained by Peter
Chapple-Hyam. Russian Revival was then bought by Godolphin and won twice
for them as a three-year-old, since when he's been with John Gosden. Gosden
won the listed Dubai Duty Free Cup at Newbury in 1997 and 1998 with Russian
Revival; and in the latest season the Group 3 Prix du Palais-Royal at Longchamp in May as well as the Tote International. Russian Revival, who started
favourite for the Palais-Royal following his excellent second to Diktat in the
Shergar Cup Seven at Goodwood, broke the course record in winning by three
lengths at Longchamp.

		Nearctic
Russian Revival (USA) (ch.h. 1993)	Nureyev (USA) (b 1977)	Northern Dancer (b 1961)	Nearctic Natalma
		Special (b 1969)	Forli Thong
	Memories (USA) (b or br 1986)	Hail The Pirates (b 1970)	Hail To Reason Bravura
		All My Memories (b 1979)	Little Current Java Moon

    Russian Revival did the majority of his racing over seven furlongs in
the latter part of his career. He was almost effective over a stiff six furlongs,
though, as he demonstrated when finishing one and a quarter lengths second to
Bold Edge in the Cork And Orrery Stakes at Royal Ascot in June. Russian

Prix du Palais-Royal, Longchamp—a new course record for Russian Revival as Tycoon's Dolce (near side), Massimo (No.4) and King Country (rail) fight it out for the minor honours

Revival is the third foal of Memories, who won a Grade 2 nine-furlong event in the USA as a four-year-old. Memories has produced a couple of other winners, including the smart three-year-old Tobruk (by Red Ransom). The next dam, All My Memories, is a winning daughter of Java Moon, whose nine successes in the States included one in a Grade 3. Both All My Memories and Java Moon proved successful as broodmares, particularly the former. Her other produce include the very smart Memories of Silver, the winner of two Grade 1 races. Russian Revival, an angular horse, was a fine mover who acted on soft and

Tote International Stakes (Handicap), Ascot—
Russian Revival produces the finest handicap performance for years;
Mubrik, in second place, finishes ahead of those on the other side of the course

good to firm ground. He usually made the running or raced prominently. Thoroughly game and consistent, he deserves to prove popular at a fee of IR £3,000, standing at the Killarkin Stud, Co. Meath, Ireland. *J. H. M. Gosden*

RUSSIAN ROMEO (IRE) 4 b.g. Soviet Lad (USA) – Aotearoa (IRE) (Flash **68** of Steel 120) [1998 70§: a6g⁴ a5g a6g² a6g 6.1s 6.1g* a5g 5.1m a6g 5g 5m a5g **a79** a5g 1999 a6g* a6g* 6g² a6g³ 5g a5g³ a5g Dec 4] leggy gelding: fair performer: won handicap at Wolverhampton in June and minor event at Southwell in July: good efforts after when placed in handicaps: stays 6f: acts on fibresand, best turf effort on good ground: has been visored, blinkered nowadays: races prominently. *B. A. McMahon*

RUSSIAN ROUGE (IRE) 4 b.f. Soviet Lad (USA) – Red Lory 87 (Bay Express **36** 132) [1998 –: a11g 1999 8.5m 6v 7m⁵ a11g 10g Aug 16] sparely-made filly: poor maiden: should stay beyond 6f: acts on heavy going. *M. Brittain*

RUSSIAN SILVER (USA) 2 ch.f. (Apr 16) Red Bishop (USA) 121 – Russian **70** Maid 85 (Cadeaux Genereux 131) [1999 5.7g 7m³ 7d⁴ 7g Sep 14] first reported foal: dam, 7f winner, out of half-sister to high-class sprinter/miler Golden Opinion: fair maiden: stiff task (well beaten) in Yarmouth nursery final start: stays 7f: yet to race on extremes of going. *C. E. Brittain*

RUSSIAN VELVET (IRE) 3 br.f. Soviet Lad (USA) – Ballylesson Girl (IRE) **–** (Nashamaa 113) [1998 –: 6s 5s a5g a7g⁶ a7g 1999 a5g a6g a8f Feb 1] sparely-made filly: little form. *M. Quinn*

RUSTIC (IRE) 3 b.f. Grand Lodge (USA) 125 – Style of Life (USA) (The **94** Minstrel (CAN) 135) [1998 99: 6m⁶ 6m* 6m³ 1999 7m⁶ 7m² 8m⁴ 6m 7f³ 7g Aug 14] sturdy, good sort: good walker: has a quick action: fairly useful performer: best efforts in 1999 when placed in minor events at Leicester in May and Goodwood (found little in front) in July: best at 7f: raced only on good going or firmer: visored after second start: stud. *R. Charlton*

RUTLAND CHANTRY (USA) 5 b.g. Dixieland Band (USA) – Christchurch **82** (FR) 88 (So Blessed 130) [1998 82: 10s* 12m⁶ 10.3m 10.4g 1999 10d⁴ 9.9v* 11.9d 10.1m² 9.9s² 9.9g⁵ 12.3d² 12g 10.1m 10.4g 10d Nov 1] robust gelding: fairly useful handicapper: won at Beverley in June: ran creditably after when runner-up: effective at 1¼m/1½m: acts on good to firm and heavy going: often a front runner. *S. Gollings*

RUZEN (IRE) 4 b.g. Fayruz 116 – Stifen (Burslem 123) [1998 91: 5.1s⁶ 6g* 6g* **78 d** 6s 6m⁶ 5.1d 5g 5g a6g* a6g 1999 a5g 5.1d 5m 5.7m 5m 5d Sep 15] sturdy, good-quartered gelding: reportedly had wind operation after 2-y-o season: fairly useful performer at 3 yrs: form in 1999 only on reappearance: stays 6f: acts on equitrack, good to firm and good to soft ground: below form when blinkered: often front runner. *B. Palling*

RYEFIELD 4 b.g. Petong 126 – Octavia (Sallust 134) [1998 80: 6d⁴ 6.1m³ 6g² 6s **72** 6.9m* 8s 8s 7.1g 8m⁴ 7s 8d 1999 8m² 7m 8g 7s⁵ 8f* 8m⁵ 8m* 7.9m 8d 7.1d 7g 8g⁶ 8s Nov 6] small gelding: fair handicapper: won at Newcastle in July and Ayr (after being switched markedly) in August: stays 1m, at least when conditions aren't testing: acts on firm and good to soft going: sometimes slowly away: races freely and best held up in truly-run race. *Miss L. A. Perratt*

RYEFIELD STAR 4 b.g. Marju (IRE) 127 – Awayed (USA) 108 (Sir Ivor 135) **–** [1998 43: a6g a8g 7.5m³ 8m 10m⁶ 9.2s⁴ 10.8m 1999 a12g 7g a6g⁶ a8.5g a8.5g May 22] compact gelding: poor maiden: no form in 1999: tried blinkered/visored. *D. McCain*

RYELAND 3 b.f. Presidium 124 – Ewe Lamb 86 (Free State 125) [1998 NR 1999 **–** 7g 10g Aug 16] angular filly: half-sister to a winner in Denmark by Music Boy: dam 2-y-o 5f winner, also successful over hurdles: well held in maidens. *Mrs P. Sly*

RYMER'S RASCAL 7 b.g. Rymer 121 – City Sound 63 (On Your Mark 125) **73** [1998 67: 7s 7.1m⁵ 7d⁵ 7.5g⁴ 6.9d 7d² 7f⁵ 8m³ 7m³ 7g 8m 7.1g³ 7.5m⁵ 8m 8g 7s* 1999 6.1s 5.9m 7m² 7.5v 7m⁴ 7m³ 7.9f⁵ 7.6m* 8m³ 7.9m⁶ 7m 7d⁵ 8s 7d⁵ 7g 8d Oct 26] sturdy gelding: carries condition: fair handicapper: won at Chester in July: effective at 7f/easy 1m: acts on firm and soft going: sometimes pulls hard, and usually held up. *E. J. Alston*

RYTHM N TIME   2 b.f. (Feb 19) Timeless Times (USA) 99 – Primum Tempus **75**
49 (Primo Dominie 121) [1999 5.9m 5m⁵ 5.1m³ 5g* 6.1d² 6m³ 6.5g 7s⁴ 6g³ 7s Nov
6] smallish filly: second foal: half-sister to 3-y-o Springs Noblequest: dam sprint
maiden: fair performer: won nursery at Beverley in August: creditable third of 15 in
similar event at York penultimate start: stays 7f: acts on soft and good to firm going:
has been bandaged near-hind. *T. D. Easterby*

S

SAAFEND BOY   2 b.c. (Apr 6) Marju (IRE) 127 – Perfect Alibi (Law Society **73**
(USA) 130) [1999 5g³ 5g⁶ 6d 7m 7g³ 7d⁵ 8m* 8m⁴ 8d Oct 15] 15,000Y: rather leggy,
good-topped colt: good walker/mover: fifth foal: closely related to 5-y-o Final Trial
and half-brother to 3-y-o Beggars Belief, 7-y-o Acquittal and fairly useful 6f winner
(including at 2 yrs) Likely Story (by Night Shift): dam unraced half-sister to Phoenix
Stakes winner Aviance and Prix du Cadran winner Chief Contender, an excellent
family: fair performer: won nursery at Newmarket in August: should stay 1¼m: acts
on good to firm going, possibly not on good to soft: tends to race freely: sold 14,000
gns. *R. Hannon*

SAANEN (IRE)   2 b.c. (Mar 30) Port Lucaya 118 – Ziffany 68 (Taufan (USA) **61**
119) [1999 6g 6f⁴ 6m 8d Nov 1] IR 12,500F, 9,000Y, 15,000 2-y-o: lengthy, angular
colt: first foal: dam, 7f seller winner, ran only at 2 yrs: modest maiden: best effort
on second start: off course 2 months before final one: should stay at least 7f. *Mrs
A. Duffield*

SABADILLA (USA)   5 b.h. Sadler's Wells (USA) 132 – Jasmina (USA) (Forli **115**
(ARG)) [1998 116: 12m² 12d² 12f⁵ 12g* 1999 12f² 12m⁴ Mar 28] strong, lengthy
horse: has a short, round action: smart performer: won Glorious Rated Stakes at
Goodwood for J. Gosden at 4 yrs: better effort in 1999 when creditable fourth to
Fruits of Love in Dubai Turf Classic at Nad Al Sheba: stays 1½m: acts on firm and
soft ground. *Saeed bin Suroor, UAE*

SABANG   3 ch.f. Sabrehill (USA) 120 – Seleter (Hotfoot 126) [1998 NR 1999 8d
a8g 8s May 14] workmanlike filly: half-sister to several winners, including 1¼m
performer Alabang (by Valiyar) and 5-y-o Makati: dam no form: well beaten in
maidens (unruly final start). *Miss J. A. Camacho*

SABICA   2 b.f. (Jan 29) Prince Sabo 123 – Mindomica 63 (Dominion 123)   **–**
[1999 6m 6g Oct 15] second living foal: half-sister to 3-y-o Minty: dam, 7f winner
(including at 2 yrs), half-sister to Fred Darling winner/Oaks fourth Sueboog (dam of
2-y-o Best of The Bests): well held in maidens at Redcar. *C. W. Thornton*

SABOT   6 b.g. Polar Falcon 126 – Power Take Off 109 (Aragon 118) [1998 **62**
–: 6v 6d 6g 7m a7g 1999 8g² 7.5v⁶ 9.2g 7.1d a7g⁴ a8.5g 9g 9v⁵ 8.2s⁵ a9.4g⁴ Nov
17] tall, good-topped gelding: modest performer nowadays: left C. Thornton's stable
6,000 gns after sixth start: stays 9.4f: acts on good to firm going, heavy and fibresand:
usually held up. *John A. Harris*

SABRE BUTT   4 gr.g. Sabrehill (USA) 120 – Butsova 93 (Formidable (USA) **45**
125) [1998 45: 11.1d⁴ 11s⁵ 8.5g⁶ 10m 8.3d 6.9d a7g 1999 a10g⁴ 9g 10g³ 11.9s⁶ Aug
18] strong, sturdy gelding: poor maiden: seems to stay 11f: acts on soft going: usually
blinkered: often a weak finisher: winning hurdler: sold 3,000 gns. *M. H. Tompkins*

SABRE LADY   2 ch.f. (Mar 31) Sabrehill (USA) 120 – Cal Norma's Lady (IRE) **82**
87 (Lyphard's Special (USA) 122) [1999 5f* 6f² 6d³ 6s Sep 27] 35,000Y: third
foal: half-sister to 1996 2-y-o 5f winner Under Pressure (by Keen) and 1997 2-y-o 6f
winner Magical (by Magic Ring), latter subsequently Grade 3 1m winner in USA:
dam 2-y-o 6f/7f winner who stayed 1¼m: fairly useful form: won maiden at Hamilton in July: best effort when third of 13 in nursery at Ayr: will prove best at 5f/6f: acts
on firm and good to soft ground (badly drawn on soft). *Miss L. A. Perratt*

SABREON   2 b.f. (May 11) Caerleon (USA) 132 – Sabria (USA) (Miswaki (USA) **78**
124) [1999 7m⁴ 8.1g² 7.7d² 8v² 8.3d Nov 4] 78,000F: small filly: second foal:
half-sister to French 3-y-o 1m winner Ghita (by Zilzal): dam, unraced half-sister to

smart middle-distance colt King Sound, from family of Generous and Triptych: fair maiden: runner-up at Chepstow, Warwick and Ayr: will stay at least 1¼m: acts on good to firm and heavy going. *J. L. Dunlop*

SACRED HEART (IRE)   2 b.f. (Apr 29) Catrail (USA) 123 – Merry Devil   **45** (IRE) (Sadler's Wells (USA) 132) [1999 8.3d Nov 4] 8,000Y: fourth foal: half-sister to 2 winners abroad, including UAE 1m to 9f winner Meshty (by Lahib): dam once-raced close relative to smart French 9f to 11f winner Lichine: poor form when eighth of 17 in seller at Windsor. *K. McAuliffe*

SACRED SONG (USA)   2 b.f. (Mar 13) Diesis 133 – Ruby Ransom (CAN)   **95** (Red Ransom (USA)) [1999 6.1m* Jul 17] $300,000F: first foal: dam, Canadian 1m stakes winner, half-sister to Breeders' Cup Turf winner Chief Bearhart and Holly-wood Derby winner Explosive Red: very green when winning 4-runner maiden at Nottingham, swishing tail and wandering but comfortably on top at line: should stay 1m: looked sure to improve. *H. R. A. Cecil*

SADAKA (USA)   2 ch.f. (Apr 11) Kingmambo (USA) 125 – Basma (USA) 104   **69** (Grey Dawn II 132) [1999 7m³ 6.1g Sep 25] third living foal: dam, 2-y-o 6f winner, third in Cheveley Park Stakes: much better effort in maidens when third of 11 to Leading Role at Lingfield on debut: should stay 1m. *E. A. L. Dunlop*

SADDLE MOUNTAIN   3 b.f. Saddlers' Hall (IRE) 126 – Rainbow Mountain 71   **53 ?** (Rainbow Quest (USA) 134) [1998 NR 1999 8.5g⁴ a12g⁶ Dec 4] first foal: closely related to 2-y-o Cornelius: dam 11.5f winner out of useful sister to Italian Derby winner My Top: modest form at best in maidens: sold 6,500 gns. *Lady Herries*

SADDLERS' GLORY   3 b.f. Saddlers' Hall (IRE) 126 – Hope And Glory (USA)   **–** 87 (Well Decorated (USA)) [1998 –: 7g 8g 8.1m 1999 12g 12m Apr 14] lengthy filly: little sign of ability. *C. W. Fairhurst*

SADDLER'S QUEST   2 b.c. (Mar 15) Saddlers' Hall (IRE) 126 – Seren Quest   **93 p** 90 (Rainbow Quest (USA) 134) [1999 10.2s* Sep 27] second foal: half-brother to 3-y-o Seren Hill: dam 1¼m winner: won maiden at Bath in good style by 1¾ lengths from Duchamp: will be suited by 1½m+: sure to improve, and looks at least a useful stayer in the making. *G. A. Butler*

SADEEBAH   4 b.g. Prince Sabo 123 – Adeebah (USA) 94 (Damascus (USA))   **– §** [1998 48§: 8s 7g 8.2g² 8.3d⁶ 7.5d 7d 8m⁴ 9g⁴ 1999 10.9s Jun 19] very tall gelding: poor maiden handicapper: probably stays 9f: acts on good to firm ground: blinkered once: none too consistent and not to be trusted. *Martin Todhunter*

SADIAN   4 b.c. Shirley Heights 130 – Rafha 123 (Kris 135) [1998 118: 10.2s*   **116** 11.5m² 12m 12v 12m* 14.1g* 14.6m⁴ 1999 12m* 13.4m* 12m 13.3g³ 12.5g⁴ Aug 29] small, quite attractive colt: fluent mover: smart performer: won Lanes End (John Porter) Stakes at Newbury (by ¾ length from The Glow-Worm) in April and Ormonde Stakes at Chester (by neck from Secret Saver) in May: ran well when 2¼ lengths third of 4 to Silver Patriarch in steadily-run Geoffrey Freer Stakes at New-bury in August: below best in Grand Prix de Deauville final start: will stay beyond 14.6f: acts on soft and good to firm going (reportedly finished lame on heavy): usually held up: game: sold privately. *J. L. Dunlop*

SADLER'S REALM   6 b.g. Sadler's Wells (USA) 132 – Rensaler (USA) (Stop   **81** The Music (USA)) [1998 NR 1999 14g* 20m Jun 15] leggy gelding: fairly useful handicapper: trained by M. Stoute in 1996: first outing on Flat since when winning at Haydock in May in good style by 4 lengths: didn't stay in Ascot Stakes next time: should stay 2m: raced only on good going or firmer on Flat, acts on heavy over jumps (useful hurdler). *P. J. Hobbs*

SADLER'S SONG   2 b.f. (Apr 4) Saddlers' Hall (IRE) 126 – Life Watch (USA)   **44** (Highland Park (USA)) [1999 5g⁶ 7m 6g 8g⁵ Aug 30] lengthy filly: second foal: dam twice-raced sister to Poule d'Essai des Pouliches runner-up Duckling Park: poor maiden: should stay 1¼m: raced only on good/good to firm going. *P. C. Haslam*

SADLERS SWING (USA)   3 b.c. Red Ransom (USA) – Noblissima (IRE) 77   **–** (Sadler's Wells (USA) 132) [1998 NR 1999 8.1m Jul 22] 25,000 2-y-o: first foal: dam 13.4f winner, sister to a useful 1¼m performer out of half-sister to Grand Prix de Paris and Melbourne Cup winner At Talaq: little promise in maiden at Sandown: withdrawn after refusing to enter stalls there next intended start. *J. J. Sheehan*

SAD MAD BAD (USA)   5 b.g. Sunny's Halo (CAN) – Quite Attractive (USA)   **64 +**
(Well Decorated (USA)) [1998 62: 13d 15.8d⁴ 18s² 1999 13.8s* Nov 2] strong,
workmanlike gelding: modest handicapper: won at Catterick only 5-y-o start:
stays 2¼m well: best efforts on good ground or softer: winning hurdler/chaser.
Mrs M. Reveley

SAFARANDO (IRE)   2 b.c. (Apr 9) Turtle Island (IRE) 123 – Hertford Castle   **75**
(Reference Point 139) [1999 6f⁴ 6s⁵ 7g* 7.5s⁵ 7f² 7m³ 7m³ 7f⁶ 8m³ 7.9f⁵ 8m 7s* 7g²
7s² 7s Nov 6] IR 9,000Y: well-made colt: second foal: half-brother to a 1m winner in
Norway by Priolo: dam lightly-raced daughter of Irish 1,000 Guineas winner Forest
Flower: fair performer: won seller at Yarmouth (bought out of R. Hannon's stable
8,500 gns) in June and nursery at Lingfield in October: stays 1m: acts on firm and
soft going: often leads: tough and consistent. *N. P. Littmoden*

SAFARASIKNOW   2 ch.c. (Feb 23) Safawan 118 – Lutine Royal 46 (Formidable   **49**
(USA) 125) [1999 5.7m 6m 6s 5g a6g Nov 8] 5,400F, 4,200Y: fourth foal: half-
brother to 1½m winner Sam Peeb (by Keen): dam, lightly raced, from very good
family: poor form: should stay beyond 6f. *Major D. N. Chappell*

SAFARI BLUES (IRE)   2 b.f. (Jan 20) Blues Traveller (IRE) 119 – North Hut   **77 +**
(Northfields (USA)) [1999 5.1s 5.1f⁴ 5.3f² 6g⁴ 6.1g⁴ 7m³ 7g⁵ 7s² a8g* a8g* Nov 16]   **a92**
11,500Y: half-sister to several winners, including smart 5f performer Dublin Lad (by
Dublin Taxi): dam ran twice: fairly useful performer: improved efforts on all-weather
at Lingfield last 2 starts, winning maiden and nursery, both in November: stays 1m:
acts on firm and soft ground, goes well on equitrack. *R. Hannon*

SAFECRACKER   6 ch.g. Sayf El Arab (USA) 127 – My Polished Corner (IRE)   **–**
53 (Tate Gallery (USA) 117) [1998 NR 1999 a8g a12f a12g Mar 19] one-time fair   **a48**
performer, poor at best nowadays: stays 1¼m: acts on firm going and all-weather:
tried blinkered/visored: sold 1,850 gns. *T. J. Etherington*

Prince A. A. Faisal's "Sadian"

SAFERJEL   3 b.f. Elmaamul (USA) 125 – Band of Fire (USA) (Chief's Crown   –
(USA)) [1998 NR 1999 8g 10m⁶ 10m⁶ Jun 25] unfurnished filly: first foal: dam 1½m
winner in Dubai: well beaten in maiden and claimers. *J. W. Hills*

SAFE SHARP JO (IRE)   4 ch.g. Case Law 113 – Kentucky Wildcat 64 (Be My   –
Guest (USA) 126) [1998 57: 6g 7.6m 8.2m⁴ 8.5s 8.5m 9d a10g 1999 a7g Jan 27]
modest maiden at best: form only at 1m on good to firm going. *M. A. Jarvis*

SAFEY ANA (USA)   8 b.g. Dixieland Band (USA) – Whatsoraire (USA) (Mr   **63**
Prospector (USA)) [1998 77: 7f² 7.3g 7g³ 8g³ 8f⁴ 7f 7m⁶ 8m* 7.9g 8m 1999 7g 8g
8.5m⁶ 10m 8f 8.2g⁶ Aug 13] good-bodied gelding: poor mover: fair handicapper:
generally below form in 1999: races mainly at 7f/1m nowadays: acts on firm and
good to soft going: effective blinkered or not: wears bandages. *B. Hanbury*

SAFFIZZ   2 ch.g. (Mar 4) Safawan 118 – Polar Fizz (Polar Falcon (USA) 126)   **83**
[1999 5v* 5d² 6s 6g³ 5m⁶ 6m³ 6f³ 6g 6d Sep 17] 9,500Y: leggy, close-coupled
gelding: first foal: dam, unraced half-sister to smart 1m to 1¼m performer Port
Lucaya, out of half-sister to Diminuendo: fairly useful performer: won maiden at
Hamilton in March: well below form last 2 starts: should be well suited by further
than 6f: acts on any going: sold 13,000 gns. *K. A. Ryan*

SAFFRON   3 ch.f. Alhijaz 122 – Silver Lodge (Homing 130) [1998 70: 5d³ 6g² 6s²   **70**
6.1g 5g² 7m⁵ a6g⁵ 7m* 1999 8g 7g 8m⁴ 8d 7g 8g Aug 25] workmanlike filly: fair
performer: generally below form in 1999: stays 1m: acts on good to firm going and
fibresand, probably on soft. *J. A. Glover*

SAFFRON ROSE   5 b.m. Polar Falcon (USA) 126 – Tweedling (USA) (Sir Ivor   **65**
135) [1998 77: 8s³ 8g⁴ 8.1m⁵ 8s² 8.2d 8m 8.3g⁴ 10m 8m 8d 1999 a9.4g⁵ 8d 12m
12m⁶ a9.4g Sep 8] tall, unfurnished mare: has a round action: fair handicapper: best
around 1m: has form on firm ground and fibresand, but goes well on softer than good:
usually races up with pace: sometimes flashes tail: withdrawn after refusing to enter
stalls fifth intended start: none too consistent: won maiden hurdle in November: sold
2,400 gns in December. *M. Blanshard*

SAFFRON WALDEN (FR)   3 b.c. Sadler's Wells (USA) 132 – Or Vision   **123**
(USA) 108 (Irish River (FR) 131) [1998 98p: 7s² 1999 8s* 8m* 8g* 12g 10m²
10.4m Aug 17]
          There are times when it appears that the team from Ballydoyle really
does suffer an embarrassment of riches. In the vast majority of stables, if there
is a really good horse in the yard its programme of races will virtually plan
itself. Aidan O'Brien, however, has so many high-class horses that on some
occasions there are not enough high-class races to go round, while on others it
seems as if the stable is unclear about which is its strongest candidate. The
situation reached comic proportions in November when it was reported that the
bookmakers Sean Graham had taken money for Saffron Walden in the Triumph
Hurdle from 'the right sources' and had cut his odds from 20/1 to 14/1 second
favourite. Saffron Walden is the 1999 Irish Two Thousand Guineas winner.
          As a Ballydoyle classic candidate at the start of the latest Flat season,
Saffron Walden was one of many. To be precise, he was one of eight O'Brien
entries in the Two Thousand Guineas at Newmarket and one of eighteen in
the Derby (there were also five in the One Thousand and nine in the Oaks).
What marked Saffron Walden out from the rest was that he had been the
most expensive yearling sold at auction in Britain and Ireland in 1997.
There was also something out of the ordinary, for one from his stable anyway,
in his having run but lost as a two-year-old, but the high regard in which he was
held was nevertheless clear enough on that one outing, as his assignment was
the Group 3 Killavullan Stakes at Leopardstown and Saffron Walden started
favourite. The Dewhurst had apparently been a target initially, but his
appearance on a racecourse had been delayed until late-October after he had
pulled some muscles. He was beaten one and a half lengths into second by
Athlumney Lady at Leopardstown, a highly promising effort. In the close
season, Stravinsky, Orpen, Black Rock Desert and Saffron Walden were all at
some stage rumoured to be the best in the stable.

Only Orpen made it to Newmarket on May 1st, but Saffron Walden was alongside him in the Entenmann's Irish Two Thousand Guineas at the Curragh three weeks later. For Orpen it was a retrieving mission, whereas Saffron Walden was making his first venture into a pattern event since the Killavullan. In the meantime he had justified odds of 6/4-on in a maiden at the Curragh in March, pushed out by a length, and of 11/8-on in the listed Guineas trial at Leopardstown in April. Victory at Leopardstown by a head in receipt of 7 lb, from Mus-If, was a long way removed from classic-winning form, even if Saffron Walden had been ridden largely just to win the race, and it was no surprise that Michael Kinane chose to ride Orpen again in the Guineas. The issue looked somewhat academic though, given that the Newmarket one-two, Island Sands and Enrique, were also in the field and they headed the market at 2/1 and 5/2; Orpen was at 9/2 with two other Irish-trained runners, Access All Areas (10/1) and Mus-If (11/1), also preferred to 12/1-chance Saffron Walden. Marius Petipa and Lucky Legend took Aidan O'Brien's entry to four, all but one carrying the colours of Mrs Magnier. Those outsiders helped set the pace while Saffron Walden, ridden with patience by Olivier Peslier initially, and with great persistence up the straight, emerged to win by three lengths going away. Island Sands never got in a blow in the closing stages, but at the furlong marker Mus-If, Enrique and Orpen were virtually in line abreast up front. Enrique narrowly got the better of that battle, but not before Saffron Walden, who had been ninth of ten at the three-furlong pole, arrived on the outside to surge past all three.

In the last two seasons, Aidan O'Brien has shown an adventurous policy towards the Derby, prompting scratching of heads over both the Bally-doyle pecking order and over whether any of his runners had much chance of staying a mile and a half. Following the Irish Derby success of doubtful stayer Desert King in 1997, one can hardly blame him for having a go again. The Derby has been a much richer event as a result. However, while Saratoga Springs had at least won the Dante, Second Empire, King of Kings and now Saffron Walden, for all their ability, were unlikely stayers. For punters, support-ing these colts in the Derby has represented a considerable act of faith, one they were willing to make with Second Empire and King of Kings, who started at 9/2 and 11/2 respectively, in 1998. Twelve months later, Saffron Walden was sent off at 8/1 fifth favourite of sixteen. Settling well under restraint, he entered the straight on the outside with only four behind him and kept on past some beaten rivals to finish seventh, six lengths behind the winner. He did not shape like an obvious non-stayer, but on the other hand was clearly below the form he showed in the Irish Guineas.

Saffron Walden's season after Epsom was likewise not a success. In the Meld Stakes at the Curragh he was below even his Derby form when beaten

Entenmann's Irish 2,000 Guineas, the Curragh—
Saffron Walden is a convincing winner, one of trainer Aidan O'Brien's four runners in the race;
Newmarket runner-up Enrique (No.2) fills the same spot, ahead of Orpen and Mus-If (rail)

four lengths into second at 5/4-on, reportedly wrenching a joint and finishing very sore. He was back in action less than four weeks later though, in the International at York, but his contribution to the spectacle at York amounted only to pulling hard up with the leaders for six furlongs before dropping away rapidly to finish last of twelve. Both of those races were at around a mile and a quarter. There was strong visual evidence that the application of a visor at York had been hugely counter-productive, but his trainer admitted culpability for running Saffron Walden too soon after the Meld Stakes. Three months later, one day after the Triumph 'gamble', O'Brien described the notion of Saffron Walden going hurdling as 'nonsense' and reported that he would be campaigned as a four-year-old 'over one mile and possibly a bit further.'

For most of his career, Saffron Walden the racehorse has been known as Saffron Waldon, the mis-spelling. Aggrieved residents of the Essex market town must have been disappointed that he flew the flag for them with such little success after a corrective name change was sanctioned by the turf authorities shortly before the Derby. Back in October 1997, when he was known merely as a bay colt by Sadler's Wells out of Or Vision, Saffron Walden went through the ring for IR 1,200,000 guineas at the Goff's Orby Sale. This was almost twice as much as was paid for the second highest-priced Sadler's Wells, the Irish Derby third Tchaikovsky; the third-highest, incidentally, was another colt who went on to run in a classic, Rhagaas.

A tall, good-topped colt, Saffron Walden had an imposing pedigree to go with his physical presence, as he is a half-brother to the high-class Dolphin Street (by Bluebird). Winner of the Prix de la Foret and second in the July Cup as a three-year-old, Dolphin Street won the Prix Maurice de Gheest at four. Dolphin Street's first crop were three-year-olds in 1999 and lacked a star

Mrs J. Magnier/M. Tabor/Niarchos Family's "Saffron Walden"

performer, the best of them being the useful but very lightly-raced Berlioz. Or Vision had six other foals before Saffron Walden and four were winners, easily the best of them being Saffron Walden's year-older brother, the Prix de l'Opera and E. P. Taylor Stakes winner Insight. The next two representatives are the 1999 two-year-old Vision's Flight (by Bluebird) and a yearling filly by Lure. Vision's Flight started favourite for the Criterium de Maisons-Laffitte, finishing fifth, after making a winning debut in October. Or Vision herself won twice as a two-year-old, got the following year off to a good start with victory in the Prix Imprudence, but failed to win again; behind in the Poule d'Essai des Pouliches, she was second in one listed race at a mile. Her dam Luv Luvin'and grandam Ringing Bells were both minor winners in the United States, the former also runner-up at three in two small stakes races over six furlongs. Ringing Bells was a half-sister to Silent Screen, the top American two-year-old of 1969.

Saffron Walden (FR) (b.c. 1996)	Sadler's Wells (USA) (b 1981)	Northern Dancer (b 1961)	Nearctic Natalma
		Fairy Bridge (b 1975)	Bold Reason Special
	Or Vision (USA) (ch 1983)	Irish River (ch 1976)	Riverman Irish Star
		Luv Luvin' (ch 1977)	Raise A Native Ringing Bells

At the moment, despite his being a classic winner, it is hard to be that definitive about Saffron Walden's racing character. He has yet to repeat his Irish Guineas form or prove that he stays beyond a mile, though he shapes as if he should prove effective at a mile and a quarter. A winner on soft ground and good to firm, easily his best effort was registered on good. He has been mulish at the stalls, including before his biggest win, and the application of a visor at York presumably indicated some dissatisfaction on behalf of connections with his style of running. The name issue aside, will the real Saffron Walden please step forward? *A. P. O'Brien, Ireland*

SAFI 4 b.g. Generous (IRE) 139 – Jasarah (IRE) 70 (Green Desert (USA) 127) **58**
[1998 66: 6m⁴ 7.1g³ 7.1g⁵ 9.4g 1999 a8g a11g⁶ a9.4g 8.2m⁵ 10.5d 6.9m 10.5m 11.1f² 9.9m⁶ 11.9d 12g Aug 13] robust, close-coupled gelding: modest maiden: stays 11f: acts on firm going: blinkered after fifth start: has had tongue tied: inconsistent. *D. McCain*

SAFRANINE (IRE) 2 b.f. (Mar 7) Dolphin Street (FR) 125 – Webbiana (African **85**
Sky 124) [1999 a5g 6f* 6.1m² 6.1d Aug 20] IR 1,400Y, 8,700 2-y-o: half-sister to several winners, including 1994 2-y-o 7f winner Rupiana (by Prince Rupert) and Irish 9f winner Two Firsts (by Burslem): dam, Irish middle-distance maiden, half-sister to Moyglare Stud Stakes winner Gala Event: fairly useful form: won maiden at Redcar in July: short-head second of 5 to Asturian Lady in minor event at Nottingham, hanging badly left when shaken up but battling on: should stay 7f: acts on firm going, ran poorly on good to soft. *J. L. Eyre*

SAGAMIX (FR) 4 gr.c. Linamix (FR) 127 – Saganeca (USA) 120 (Sagace **122**
(FR) 135) [1998 129: 12s* 12s* 12s* 12d* 1999 10.5g⁴ 12g⁴ Jul 4]
Sagamix's absence from the latest Prix de l'Arc de Triomphe was ironic, given that the thoroughly testing conditions would have suited him better than most; he had remained unbeaten through his three-year-old career on ground softer than good, culminating in a splendid performance to win the Prix de l'Arc de Triomphe. There was further irony in that he missed the 1999 Arc because he'd had to forego a prep race in the Prix Foy three weeks earlier owing to the ground being considered too firm! However, there was more to his late defection from the Prix Foy than that. At the same time, it emerged that both Sagamix, and his stable-companion Slickly, the Grand Prix de Paris winner also owned by Jean-Luc Lagardere, were in the process of being sold to race in Dubai. While original reports suggested Godolphin were not the buyers,

it was announced after the Arc that Sagamix and Slickly would, in fact, be joining Saeed bin Suroor's stable.

Sagamix's aborted autumn campaign followed on from his missing the King George at Ascot in July; named as a five-day acceptor, he was pulled out the following day after failing to scope cleanly. He'd reportedly coughed a little after his previous start. For the two races he did contest, Sagamix was sent off a short-priced favourite but both ventures ended in disappointment. His return in the steadily-run Prix Ganay over an inadequate ten and a half furlongs was best overlooked but there was some encouragement from his fourth place in a strong field for the Grand Prix de Saint-Cloud. First off the bridle in typical fashion, Sagamix was doing his best work at the finish to be beaten around five lengths by the winner El Condor Pasa, though he was also beaten by two of his own Arc victims from the previous autumn, Tiger Hill and Dream Well.

Sagamix (FR) (gr.c. 1995)	Linamix (FR) (gr 1987)	Mendez (gr 1981)	Bellypha
			Miss Carina
		Lunadix (gr 1972)	Breton
			Lutine
	Saganeca (USA) (b 1988)	Sagace (b 1980)	Luthier
			Seneca
		Haglette (b 1978)	Hagley
			Sucrette

It will be interesting to see how, and where, the still lightly-raced Sagamix is campaigned by his new stable. He'd no doubt stay further than a mile and a half given the chance but if the top races around the world at that trip are on the agenda, his best chance of winning one is likely to be on ground softer

Mr J-L. Lagardere's "Sagamix"

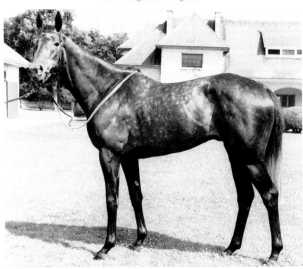

than good. Andre Fabre's assertion after Sagamix had won the Arc that 'his action is really good; he'll be a good horse on any ground' remains unproven and the fact that he was taken out of the Prix Foy suggests that his former connections have since decided otherwise. The leggy Sagamix was bandaged in front for both his starts in the latest season, as he has been in the past.

Sagamix's year-younger full sister Sage Et Jolie also progressed well through her three-year-old campaign without reaching the same heights; she won the Prix de Malleret at Longchamp in June and ran her best race (on soft ground) when short-headed in the Prix de la Nonette at Deauville, showing smart form. Two-year-old Sagazon (by Zafonic) and yearling Sagacity (by Highest Honor) have the task of keeping up their dam's pattern-winner producing record. Sagamix's pedigree was covered fully in *Racehorses of 1998*, but it remains to be added that his sire Linamix, still under-appreciated on the English side of the Channel, doubled his Group 1 winners thanks to Slickly (Grand Prix de Paris), Amilynx (Prix Royal-Oak) and Goldamix (Criterium de Saint-Cloud) in the latest season. *A. Fabre, France*

SAGUARO　5 b.g. Green Desert (USA) 127 – Badawi (USA) 103 (Diesis 133) [1998 –: 8.2s 8.5s 7g 6g 1999 a8g* a9.4g* a8g⁴ a8.5g 8g 8d 8g 8m Sep 2] quite attractive gelding: has a quick action: fairly useful handicapper: won at Southwell (apprentice maiden event by 13 lengths) in February and Wolverhampton in March: stays 9.4f: acts on fibresand, little turf form: visored twice at 4 yrs. *K. A. Morgan* — **a81**

SAHARA SPIRIT (IRE)　2 b.g. (Feb 24) College Chapel 122 – Desert Palace (Green Desert (USA) 127) [1999 6s³ 7.1s⁴ 7d Oct 22] IR 11,500F, IR 34,000Y: smallish, quite attractive gelding: unimpressive mover: fourth foal: brother to fairly useful 1998 2-y-o 5f winner Principality (later successful in Norway): dam Irish 5f winner out of half-sister to Kalaglow: fair form in frame in maidens at Leicester and Haydock over 3 months apart: well held in similar event at Doncaster final start: not sure to stay much beyond 7f. *E. A. L. Dunlop* — **75**

SAIFAN　10 ch.g. Beveled (USA) – Superfrost 49 (Tickled Pink 114) [1998 78§, a–§: 8d 8s 8m³ 8g 8m² 8g 8m 8g a7g 1999 8g 8g 8m³ 8s 8d* 8m 8m 7m* 7f⁶ 7.9m 7f 8d⁶ 8s Oct 25] tall, angular gelding: has a round action: fair performer: won claimer and handicap at Yarmouth in July: best at 7f/1m: probably acts on any going: usually blinkered/visored: usually held up: has reportedly bled from nose: unreliable. *D. Morris* — **70 §** **a– §**

SAILING　2 ch.f. (Feb 6) Arazi (USA) 135 – Up Anchor (IRE) 114 (Slip Anchor 136) [1999 6g² 7m* 8.1m* 8m 7.3s⁵ Oct 23] lengthy, workmanlike filly: third foal: closely related to useful 1997 2-y-o 7f winner Fleetwood (by Groom Dancer) and half-sister to 3-y-o Red Sea: dam 1m (at 2 yrs) to 12.5f (St Simon Stakes) winner: fairly useful performer: won maiden at Goodwood (made all) in June and minor event at Sandown (waited with) in August: creditable fifth in listed event at Newbury final start: stays 1m: acts on soft and good to firm going. *P. F. I. Cole* — **94 +**

SAILING SHOES (IRE)　3 b.g. Lahib (USA) 129 – Born To Glamour (Ajdal (USA) 130) [1998 103: 6g⁴ 5.1g* 5s⁴ 6f² 6g⁵ 6v 1999 6g³ 6m² 6g⁴ 5.2d 5s 6s⁵ 6d Oct 29] smallish gelding: useful performer: best efforts in 1999 when second of 6 to Red Lion in minor event at Leicester in April and fifth in rated stakes at Newbury in October: may prove best around 6f: ran no sort of race on heavy going, acts on any other: often races up with pace. *R. Hannon* — **99 d**

SAIL-ON BUN　3 gr.f. Beveled (USA) – Sea Farer Lake 74 (Gairloch 122) [1998 –: 7.5m 7m 8s 1999 a11g 12.1g 14.1g Sep 25] unfurnished filly: signs of only a little ability. *K. McAuliffe* — **–**

SAIL ON SALLY　3 ch.f. Clantime 101 – Croft Sally (Crofthall 110) [1998 52: 7v 6s⁵ 1999 6g Oct 15] form in maidens only on final 2-y-o start: should stay 7f. *C. F. Wall* — **–**

SAILOR A'HOY　3 b.g. Handsome Sailor 125 – Eye Sight 67 (Roscoe Blake 120) [1998 NR 1999 8m⁴ 10.3m⁶ 9.9m² 10m⁵ 12m⁵ 11.7m⁵ Aug 22] rangy, angular gelding: fourth foal: brother to modest 1½m winner The Roundsills and half-brother to 1994 2-y-o 7.5f seller winner Kings Vision (by Absalom): dam middle-distance — **81**

maiden: fairly useful maiden: stays 1½m: raced only on good to firm ground: has been reluctant to enter stalls, gone in snatches and flashed tail. *R. F. Johnson Houghton*

SAILOR JACK (USA) 3 b.g. Green Dancer (USA) 132 – Chateaubrook (USA) **54** (Alleged (USA) 138) [1998 65p: 6d 7s⁴ 1999 10m 11.6g 11.8m⁵ 14.1m⁶ 12m³ 14.1g 10d⁴ 9.9s 11.5m⁶ Oct 19] modest maiden handicapper: stays 1½m: acts on soft and good to firm going: usually blinkered/visored: sold 3,000 gns, joined D. McCain. *C. E. Brittain*

SAIL WITH THE WIND 2 b.f. (Mar 17) Saddlers' Hall (IRE) 126 – Shesa- **–** delight 67 (Shirley Heights 130) [1999 8.3d 8s Nov 6] fourth foal: sister to 11.6f winner Tikopia and half-sister to 3-y-o Total Delight and a winner in Italy by Reprimand: dam maiden, from family of High-Rise and In The Wings: backward, well held in maidens. *T. D. McCarthy*

SAINT ALBERT 4 ch.g. Keen 116 – Thimbalina 63 (Salmon Leap (USA) 131) **?** [1998 76: 7.5m 10.5m² 12.3s³ 11.1m² 12m* 12.1g² 16.5g* 14.1f² 1999 9d⁶ Jun 4] plain gelding: fair handicapper: shaped as though retaining ability only 4-y-o start: effective at 1½m to 2m: acts on firm and soft ground: visored second 2-y-o start: usually held up. *P. T. Walwyn*

SAINTE MARINE (IRE) 4 b.f. Kenmare (FR) 125 – Pont-Aven 113 (Try My **116** Best (USA) 130) [1998 116: 5f* 5g* 5d⁵ 5f² 5d³ 1999 5m⁶ 5g* 5m³ 5g² 5v⁶ 5m Dec 12] big filly: smart performer: won Prix du Gros-Chene at Chantilly for second year running in June by 3 lengths from Dream Chief: placed afterwards in King's Stand Stakes at Royal Ascot and Nunthorpe Stakes at York (1½ lengths second of 16 to Stravinsky): below form in Prix de l'Abbaye de Longchamp and Hong Kong Sprint at Sha Tin last 2 outings: ideally suited by 5f and good going or firmer: very speedy front runner: had flashed tail under pressure but was genuine: stud. *R. Collet, France*

Mr R. C. Strauss's "Sainte Marine"

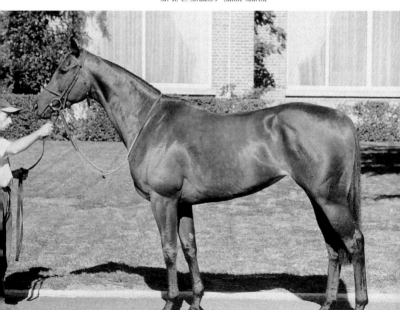

Princess Margaret Stakes, Ascot—a ready success for Saintly Speech over Journalist (rail); Bandanna is third

SAINT EXPRESS   9 ch.g. Clantime 101 – Redgrave Design 77 (Nebbiolo 125)   –
[1998 86: 6d 7d 7f² 7g 6g 8m* 7g⁵ 8m³ 7d 6.1g 7g 7s² 6d⁴ 1999 6m 6d 7f Jul 10]
lengthy, workmanlike gelding: has quick action: fairly useful handicapper in 1998:
never able to challenge at 9 yrs: possibly needs good test at 6f, and stays easy 1m:
acts on firm and soft going: blinkered twice in 1996. *Mrs M. Reveley*

SAINT GEORGE (IRE)   3 b.g. Unblest 117 – Jumana (Windjammer (USA))   –
[1998 55: 5.7d 6m 6m⁶ 5g 1999 6m 7g Jun 8] modest maiden at 2 yrs: well beaten
both 3-y-o starts: should stay 7f. *G. B. Balding*

SAINTLY SPEECH (USA)   2 br.f. (Jan 18) Southern Halo (USA) – Eloquent   **103 p**
Minister (USA) 109 (Deputy Minister (CAN)) [1999 6g* 6m* Jul 24] rangy filly: has
plenty of scope: has a fluent, round action: half-sister to several winners, including
useful 1997 2-y-o 6f/7f winner Woodland Melody (by Woodman) and a good winner
in Japan by Diesis: dam, sprinter, won in Europe and USA: won maiden at Pontefract
in May and Princess Margaret Stakes at Ascot in July: useful performance when
accounting for Journalist readily by ½ length in latter, leading final 1f having pulled
hard in rear: should stay at least 7f: swished tail in preliminaries at Ascot: already
useful, and should win more races at 3 yrs. *P. W. Chapple-Hyam*

SAKHA   3 ch.f. Wolfhound (USA) 126 – Harmless Albatross 115 (Pas de Seul 133)   **109**
[1998 105p: 6g³ 6m* 6g* 1999 7m⁵ 6m⁴ 6d⁵ 5d* 5v⁵ Oct 24] quite attractive filly:
found to have chipped a bone in a knee after final 2-y-o start: useful performer: won
minor event at Yarmouth and listed race at Newmarket, both in September, latter by
1¼ lengths from Andreyev: below form in Prix du Petit Couvert at Longchamp final
start: best at 5f/6f: acted on good to firm and good to soft ground: stud. *J. L. Dunlop*

*JRA Nakayama Rous Stakes, Newmarket—Sakha is a decisive winner from Andreyev (black sleeves);
Afaan (rail) finishes fifth*

SAKHEE (USA)   2 b.c. (Feb 14) Bahri (USA) 125 – Thawakib (IRE) 108 (Sad- **106 p**
ler's Wells (USA) 132) [1999 7m⁴ 8.2m* 8.1s* Oct 2] third foal: closely related to
3-y-o Nasheed and half-brother to useful 1997 2-y-o 7f winner Alharir (by Zafonic):
dam, won Ribblesdale Stakes, half-sister to Celestial Storm: progressive form: won
maiden at Nottingham in September and minor event at Sandown in October, leading
2f out when beating Michele Marieschi by 3½ lengths on second occasion: will stay
1¼m: sure to improve further and win more races. *J. L. Dunlop*

SALABUE (USA)   2 b.c. (Mar 5) Affirmed (USA) – Parliament House (USA) **58**
(General Assembly (USA)) [1999 7.1v⁵ 8s Oct 25] $55,000F, 55,000Y: has a round
action: fourth foal: half-brother to 3 winners, including 3-y-o Mixsterthetrixster:
dam, American sprint winner at 4 yrs, half-sister to Prix du Cadran winner Molesnes:
well held in maidens at Haydock and Leicester. *J. L. Dunlop*

SALALAH   3 gr.f. Lion Cavern (USA) 117 – Sea Fret 96 (Habat 127) [1998 NR **62**
1999 8m 7g⁶ 8.1m⁶ 7.1f* 8.3s 7g 8s³ 8.2s Nov 1] half-sister to several winners,
including 4-y-o Shanillo and 5-y-o Cauda Equina: dam 2-y-o 6f winner out of
smart half-sister to Buoy and Bireme: modest handicapper: won maiden event at
Musselburgh in September: ran well after when third at Bath, albeit hanging right
under pressure: effective at 7f/1m: yet to race on heavy going, acts on any other.
H. Morrison

SALAMAN (FR)   7 b.g. Saumarez 132 – Merry Sharp (Sharpen Up 127) [1998 –: **57**
14.4s³ 20d 1999 16g 16d 16.2m Jun 19] lengthy gelding: modest handicapper: needs
2m+: best form on good going or firmer: tried blinkered. *D. C. O'Brien*

SALEE (IRE)   2 b.f. (Apr 1) Caerleon (USA) 132 – Almaaseh (IRE) 63 (Dancing **73 p**
Brave (USA) 140) [1999 7d⁶ Oct 30] 125,000F, IR 110,000Y: fourth foal: half-sister
to 2 winning sprinters, notably 6-y-o Almaty: dam twice-raced daughter of Irish
1,000 Guineas winner Al Bahathri: promising sixth of 16 to Garota Do Leblon in
Newmarket maiden: should stay 1m: should do better. *A. G. Foster*

SALESTRIA   3 b.f. Salse (USA) 128 – Lydia Maria 70 (Dancing Brave (USA) **82**
140) [1998 76p: 7d⁶ 7m³ 7.5m² 7.5m³ 1999 8.2m 9.9g⁵ 12m⁴ 12d² 14.8m⁴ 16m²
16m⁶ 12s² 11.9d⁵ Oct 21] good-bodied filly: fairly useful maiden handicapper: will
prove best at 1¾m/2m: acts on soft and good to firm going: visored (ran as if
something amiss) seventh start: sold 14,000 gns. *P. W. Harris*

*Grosvenor Casinos Dante Stakes, York—Salford Express beats Golden Snake,
who doesn't enjoy the clearest of runs; Slip Stream (left) is third*

SALFORD EXPRESS (IRE) 3 ch.c. Be My Guest (USA) 126 – Summer **116**
Fashion 84 (Moorestyle 137) [1998 93p: 7d² 7g 1999 11m* 10.4s* 12g 10g⁵ 10.4m
11d⁴ 10g 12v² Oct 23] leggy colt: fluent mover: smart performer: made all in maiden
at Newbury in April and Grosvenor Casinos Dante Stakes (by 1½ lengths from
Golden Snake) at York in May: returned to near best when 7 lengths second to
Signorina Cattiva in St Simon Stakes at Newbury final start: below form in between,
including in Derby at Epsom, International Stakes at York (ran lifeless race in
blinkers fifth start) and Champion Stakes at Newmarket: will prove best at 1¼m/
1½m: successful on good to firm ground, best efforts on soft/heavy: often takes
strong hold. *D. R. C. Elsworth*

SALFORD FLYER 3 b.g. Pharly (FR) 130 – Edge of Darkness 62 (Vaigly Great **82**
127) [1998 65, a–: 6g 7m⁴ a7g 8g⁴ 7.9g 8d² 1999 10s 12.3d⁶ 11.9d* 11.7g³ 14.1m*
14.1g* 15.9m⁴ 16.2m⁴ 14.1g² 14.1m² 16s⁵ Oct 5] rather sparely-made gelding: fairly
useful performer: won claimer at Haydock and handicap at Yarmouth in June and
minor event at Salisbury in July: generally in good form otherwise: likely to prove
best at 1¾m/2m: acts on good to firm and good to soft going, ran poorly on fibresand
and soft: carries head awkwardly and has flashed tail: usually held up: sold 26,000
gns, joined D. Elsworth. *G. Wragg*

SALFORD LAD 5 b.h. Don't Forget Me 127 – Adjusting (IRE) (Busted 134) **–**
[1998 –: a8g a7g 10.8g 8g 8g 7g 1999 a8.5g Jan 13] of little account. *J. Pearce*

SALIGO (IRE) 4 b.f. Elbio 125 – Doppio Filo (Vision (USA)) [1998 87: 6.1s⁴ 7s² **87**
7g² 8f* 10m* 10g 12d⁶ 8.9g* 1999 8m 10.4s⁵ 10f 8m² 8.1m⁵ 8m⁴ 8g² 10m 10.3g³
10s 8d 7d Oct 30] plain filly: fairly useful performer: ran creditably most starts in
1999: sold out of H. Morrison's stable 22,000 gns prior to final one: best at 1m/1¼m:
acts on firm and soft going: blinkered twice at 2 yrs: game and reliable. *N. Tinkler*

Chester Rated Stakes (Handicap)—Salmon Ladder dominates in a field of five; Kadaka is second

SALIM   2 b.c. (May 9) Salse (USA) 128 – Moviegoer 104 (Pharly (FR) 130) [1999 7d Oct 27] 65,000Y: fifth foal: half-brother to fairly useful 1993 2-y-o 5.7f winner Kissininthebackrow (by Trempolino), 4-y-o Mane Frame and 7-y-o Roderick Hudson: dam, 7f winner, half-sister to dam of Oaks winner Lady Carla: weak in market and probably in need of race when eighth of 11 to Shaibani in maiden at Yarmouth: likely to do better. *Sir Michael Stoute*   **63 p**

SALLYANDAR   3 b.f. Milieu 111 – Megan's Move 66 (Move Off 112) [1998 –: 6m 7d 1999 9.1d Sep 17] no form: pulled up only 3-y-o start. *W. Storey*   **–**

SALLY-ANN (IRE)   2 b.f. (Apr 11) Petardia 113 – Curie Express (IRE) 65 (Fayruz 116) [1999 5m 5.1f⁵ 5m 5.7f⁵ 5.1m⁴ 7f² 7.1m 6g 7.5g 5.3d⁵ 5.7s a8g Nov 12] IR 3,200Y: rather leggy filly: second foal: half-sister to 1998 2-y-o 5f winner Acuria (by Contract Law): dam 2-y-o 5f winner: poor maiden: well below form last 6 starts: stays 7f: acts on firm ground: sold 1,250 gns, sent to Holland. *Mrs P. N. Dutfield*   **48**

SALLY GARDENS   2 b.f. (Mar 22) Alzao (USA) 117 – Polina 69 (Polish Precedent (USA) 131) [1999 6d⁵ 7m 6f⁵ a7g* 7g⁵ 7s a8g Nov 16] leggy filly: first foal: dam, second over 1m on only start, daughter of Yorkshire Oaks winner Sally Brown: modest performer: won seller at Wolverhampton in July (final start for M. Channon): well below form in nurseries after: should stay at least 1m: acts on good to firm going, good to soft and fibresand. *T. J. Naughton*   **60 d**

SALLY HOPPER   3 b.f. Rock Hopper 124 – Super Sally 108 (Superlative 118) [1998 NR 1999 8g⁵ 10.5g 10m⁵ Jun 17] 5,000Y: half-sister to useful 1996 2-y-o 7f winner Shii-Take (by Deploy) who should have stayed beyond 1¼m: dam effective at 1m to 1¼m: little form in maidens. *J. J. O'Neill*   **–**

SALMON LADDER (USA)   7 b.h. Bering 136 – Ballerina Princess (USA) (Mr Prospector (USA)) [1998 105: 9.2d* 10.2g* 12.4m³ 11.8d⁵ 11.9m 10.9s² 12s 12m 12d 1999 12d² 10m 14g* 16.1m 13.9g 13.4d* 12v³ 12s³ Nov 6] good-topped horse: impresses in appearance: formerly smart, useful nowadays: won rated stakes at Goodwood in May and listed rated stakes at Chester in August, latter by 3½ lengths from Kadaka: respectable third in St Simon Stakes at Newbury (behind Signorina Cattiva) and listed event at Doncaster (to Maylane) last 2 starts: stays 1¾m: acts on any going: tried blinkered: often sweating: usually races up with pace. *P. F. I. Cole*   **107**

SALORY 3 b.c. Salse (USA) 128 – Mory Kante (USA) (Icecapade (USA)) [1998 –
–: 7d 6g 1999 11.9v 10v 8.3d a10g Nov 24] quite attractive colt: signs of ability but
no form: has worn tongue strap. *Miss Jacqueline S. Doyle*

SALSA DANCER (IRE) 3 b.f. Seattle Dancer (USA) 119 – Rince Deas (IRE) **78**
53 (Alzao (USA) 117) [1998 NR 1999 8.3g⁴ 8g³ 8.3g⁵ 10d 10g Oct 11] well-made
filly: fifth foal: half-sister to 3 winners, including fairly useful 7f to 9f winner Panata
(by Tirol) and UAE 1¼m winner Royal Shock (by Brief Truce): dam, placed at 5f at
2 yrs, sister to smart miler Mirror Black: fairly useful maiden: well held in handicaps
last 2 starts, visored final one: should stay 1¼m. *P. J. Makin*

SALSIFY 3 b.c. Salse (USA) 128 – Amaranthus (Shirley Heights 130) [1998 66p: –
8g 1999 8s Apr 1] sturdy colt: fair form only outing at 2 yrs: well beaten only 3-y-o
start: sold 1,500 gns. *R. Charlton*

SALSKA 8 b.m. Salse (USA) 128 – Anzeige (GER) (Soderini 123) [1998 75: **75**
14.1d* 16.1d* 16m² 16m⁵ 13.9g⁶ 1999 16.1m 14d⁶ 15.9m² 16f* 15.9d 14.8m⁶
14.1m 16d 17.3g Oct 16] strong, lengthy mare: fair handicapper: won 7-runner race
at Redcar in July: stays 2m: acts on firm and good to soft going: tried visored earlier
in career. *A. Streeter*

SALTENBY (IRE) 3 b.g. Tenby 125 – Salt 90 (Sallust 134) [1998 NR 1999 8f –
a12g 8g⁵ 10g 10.5m 13.8g Sep 18] IR 7,000F: half-brother to several winners, including 1993 2-y-o 5f winner Iva's Flyer (by Imperial Frontier) and fairly useful Irish
5f/6f winner Two Seats (by Hays): dam 2-y-o 5f/6f winner: little sign of ability in
sellers/claimers: blinkered last 3 starts. *P. T. Dalton*

SALTY BEHAVIOUR (IRE) 5 ch.h. Salt Dome (USA) – Good Behaviour –
(Artaius (USA) 129) [1998 80, a65: a8g 5d⁴ 6d² 6m⁵ 6m* 5.7g 7.1m* 6m⁴ a7g a7g²
a7g* a8.5g⁶ a7g⁴dis a7g² a8g⁴ 1999 a8g Jan 2] rangy horse: fair performer: reportedly
lame after only 5-y-o start: ideally needs further than 5f, and stays 1m: acts on good
to firm going, heavy and all-weather: held up: sometimes hangs left: visored final
4-y-o start. *P. D. Evans*

SALTY JACK (IRE) 5 b.h. Salt Dome (USA) – Play The Queen (IRE) (King of **94**
Clubs 124) [1998 94, a80+: a7g a7g³ 6.9v* a8g³ 7m⁶ 7.1d⁴ 7d 7m² 7m* 7m² 7g³ 7d*
7g* 7s 1999 7g 7g 7.6m⁴ 7f 7f² 7m 7d 7.3m 7s² Dec 8] small horse: has a
round action: fairly useful handicapper: runner-up in large fields at Newmarket in
July (beaten 1¼ lengths by Grangeville in Bunbury Cup) and October before winning
at Lingfield in December: best form at 7f: acts on equitrack and any turf going: has
turn of foot, and best patiently ridden in truly-run race. *V. Soane*

SALVA 3 b.f. Grand Lodge (USA) 125 – Salvezza (IRE) 97 (Superpower 113) **73**
[1998 NR 1999 7.7m³ 8m Sep 17] first foal: dam 2-y-o 6f winner who stayed 7f:
better effort in maidens when third of 17 at Warwick. *P. J. Makin*

SALVAGE 4 b.g. Kahyasi 130 – Storm Weaver (USA) (Storm Bird (CAN) 134) **58**
[1998 NR 1999 12g 10m 14.1m⁶ 15.8g² 17.2g⁴ 15.8g⁶ 15.8s* 16d Oct 21] big,
workmanlike gelding: sixth foal: half-brother to fairly useful 2-y-o winners Storm
Master (9f in Ireland, by Generous) and Cape Weaver (6f, by Pampabird): dam
second at 9f: modest handicapper: won at Catterick in October: stays 17f: acts on soft
going. *W. W. Haigh*

SALVIATI (USA) 2 b.c. (Mar 23) Lahib (USA) 129 – Mother Courage 67 **76 +**
(Busted 134) [1999 6d³ 6f* Jul 14] fourth foal: half-brother to a winner in Spain by
Scottish Reel: dam, staying maiden, half-sister to dam of Halling: confirmed promise
when winning maiden at Folkestone in July: should stay 1m: seemed likely to do
better. *Mrs A. J. Perrett*

SALZGITTER 2 b.f. (Apr 24) Salse (USA) 128 – Anna of Brunswick 78 (Rain- **71 p**
bow Quest (USA) 134) [1999 7d⁵ Oct 11] smallish, close-coupled filly: has a quick
action: first foal: dam, 9.7f winner (stayed 1¾m), half-sister to dams of Annus Mirabilis, Anna of Saxony and Annaba: shaped quite well when fifth of 19 to Petrushka in
maiden at Leicester, travelling well until unable to quicken final 2f: should stay at
least 1¼m: seems sure to improve. *H. Candy*

SAMANGIE 3 b.f. Sure Blade (USA) 130 – Beauchamp Queen (Known Fact **45**
(USA) 135) [1998 NR 1999 7d 6f⁴ Jun 25] fourth reported live foal: dam unraced
half-sister to useful stayer Beauchamp Express: better effort in maidens when fourth
of 6 at Lingfield: joined V. Soane. *R. Simpson*

SAMARARDO 2 b.g. (Mar 11) Son Pardo 107 – Kinlet Vision (IRE) 56 (Vision **42**
(USA)) [1999 5m 5m 6d 6d⁵ 6.1m a7g⁶ a8.5g* a8.5g² a8g a7g³ Dec 15] 5,000F, **a60 +**
6,800Y: leggy gelding: third foal: half-brother to 1997 2-y-o 1m winner Ringleader
(by Magic Ring), who became ungenuine, and 3-y-o Brave Vision: dam, 2-y-o sprint
winner, also won over hurdles: modest performer: won selling nursery at Wolverhampton in October: creditable efforts 2 of 3 starts after: stays 8.5f: acts on good to
firm going, good to soft and fibresand: tried visored. *N. P. Littmoden*

SAMARA SONG 6 ch.g. Savahra Sound 111 – Hosting (Thatching 131) [1998 **81**
72: 7g⁶ 7.1d 7g⁴ 7m⁵ 7m² 7.1g² 7.1g* 7.6f⁶ 7g³ 7.1g 8m⁴ 7g 1999 a7g a7g 7m* a8g **a53**
a7g⁶ 7g² 8m 7.9f* 7m⁵ 8f 7.9m 7f 8d 8g Oct 2] lengthy gelding: fairly useful
handicapper on turf, modest on all-weather: won at Salisbury in May and
York in July: better than bare result suggests on occasions after, but disappointing
last 2 starts: best at 7f/1m: acts on firm going, good to soft and all-weather: tried
blinkered/visored early in career: best held up. *Ian Williams*

SAMASAKHAN (IRE) 3 b.c. Slip Anchor 136 – Samarzana (USA) 95 **95**
(Blushing Groom (FR) 131) [1998 NR 1999 10d⁶ 10.5m* 16.2m 13.9g⁵ 13.9m³
14.1m⁶ Sep 24] rangy, angular colt: fifth foal: closely related to useful Irish 1½m/
1¾m winner Samakaan (by Darshaan) and half-brother to fairly useful Irish 1¼m
winner Samanid (by Shardari): dam 1½m winner: useful performer: won maiden at
Haydock in May: best effort when third to Borgia in handicap at York in September,
making most: may prove best at 1½m/1¾m: yet to race on extremes of going: visored
final start: edgy third and fourth ones: may prove best with strong handling: sold
55,000 gns. *Sir Michael Stoute*

SAMATA ONE (IRE) 4 b.c. River Falls 113 – Abadila (IRE) (Shernazar 131) **–**
[1998 63: 7m⁵ 7g² 8g⁵ 8.2g² 9.3m 7m 1999 a8.5g* a8g a8g Jun 28] unfurnished colt:
modest maiden: well held on fibresand in 1999, leaving W. Haggas before final
outing: should stay beyond 1m: best form on good/good to firm going: blinkered: has
been bandaged behind. *D. G. Bridgwater*

SAMEEAH (IRE) 3 br.f. Perugino (USA) 84 – Kayrava (Irish River (FR) 131) **–**
[1998 NR 1999 8.2m⁵ Jul 23] 3,700Y, 9,000 2-y-o: half-sister to French 1m winner
(including at 2 yrs) Kenavo (by Un Desperado): dam unraced half-sister to very smart
1¼m filly Kartajana: last of 5 in maiden at Nottingham. *K. Mahdi*

SAMIYAH (IRE) 3 b.f. Anshan 119 – Fujairah 98 (In Fijar (USA) 121) [1998 **51**
NR 1999 7s⁵ 7s⁴ a8g 10g 10.1g 10m Aug 28] 4,500Y: leggy, angular filly: fourth
foal: half-sister to 3 winners, including 7f seller winner Fahema and Italian 9f to 13f
winner Lycksale (both by Most Welcome): dam 2-y-o 6f winner who later stayed
1¼m: modest maiden: stays 1¼m: wears tongue strap: sold 1,700 gns, joined
Mrs P. Sly. *Miss I. Foustok*

SAMMAL (IRE) 3 b.g. Petardia 113 – Prime Site (IRE) (Burslem 123) [1998 **58**
75d: 5d³ 5d* 5m² 5f 6m 6d 5g 1999 5d 5g 5g⁶ 5m 5m⁴ 5f³ Jul 17] close-coupled
gelding: modest performer: possibly best at 5f: acts on firm and good to soft going:
visored third and fourth starts. *J. A. Glover*

SAMMIE DUROSE (IRE) 2 b.g. (Apr 26) Forest Wind (USA) 111 – La Calera **–**
(Corvaro (USA) 124) [1999 5m 6f 7f Jul 30] IR 7,000Y: half-brother to several
winners, including fairly useful 1990 2-y-o 6f/7f winner Spice Trader (by Burslem):
dam Irish 1¼m winner: well held in maiden and claimers. *R. A. Fahey*

SAMMY'S SHUFFLE 4 b.c. Touch of Grey 90 – Cabinet Shuffle (Thatching **45**
131) [1998 57: a8g a7g⁶ a10g a10g⁶ 11.9g a8g⁴ 10d⁵ 10g* 10m² 10f⁴ 9.9m 10g* 9g⁶ **a63**
a10g* 1999 a12g³ a12g² a10g⁵ a12g⁴ 10m 12m⁶ 10d 10m⁴ a10g³ a10g³ a10g² a10g⁵
a10g* Dec 22] modest handicapper on all-weather, poor on turf: dam, 7f (at 2 yrs) and 1¼m
winner off nearly 6 months after fourth start: creditable efforts final 5 outings, winning at
Lingfield in December: effective at 1¼m/1½m: acts on equitrack and firm going:
blinkered: has been bandaged in front: reliable. *Jamie Poulton*

SAMOA 3 b.f. Rainbow Quest (USA) 134 – Sardegna 111 (Pharly (FR) 130) [1998 **112**
NR 1999 10s* 10s² 12m² 11.9s Jul 3] tall, useful-looking, unfurnished filly: third
foal: half-sister to useful 1¼m winner Sardonic (by Kris): dam, 7f (at 2 yrs) and 1¼m
winner who stayed 13f, daughter of Lancashire Oaks winner Sandy Island, herself
closely related to Slip Anchor: smart performer: won maiden at Sandown in April:

improved when runner-up in listed race at Newbury (beaten ¾ length by Nasheed) and Ribblesdale Stakes at Royal Ascot (beaten length by Fairy Queen): ran badly in Lancashire Oaks at Haydock: stays 1½m. *H. R. A. Cecil*

SAMOL 2 ch.f. (Apr 3) Timeless Times (USA) 99 – Le Bal 41 (Rambo Dancer –
(CAN) 107) [1999 6s 5g Oct 16] first foal: dam maiden: no sign of ability.
A. B. Mulholland

SAMPOWER STAR 3 b.c. Cyrano de Bergerac 120 – Green Supreme (Primo **118**
Dominie 121) [1998 83, a?: 6f² 5d 6m* 7g* 7.1g³ 5m⁵ a6g 8.1g⁴ 7s⁴ 1999 8s² 8.3m³
6m* 6g* 6s* 5g⁴ 6f 6.5s 6g² 6m⁵ 6s⁶ 6s⁴ 5v⁴ Oct 3] sturdy, lengthy, strong-quartered
colt: smart performer: vastly improved in 1999, winning minor event at Windsor and
listed race at Ascot in April and Duke of York Victor Chandler Stakes at York (by 1¾
lengths from Warningford) in May: ran well several times after, including in Prix de
Meautry at Deauville (short-headed by Vision of Night), Sprint Cup at Haydock (2½
lengths fifth to Diktat) and Prix de l'Abbaye de Longchamp (1¾ lengths fourth to
Agnes World) on ninth, tenth and final starts: very best form at 6f: acts on good to
firm and heavy ground: effective racing prominently or held up: tough: sold, and sent
to UAE. *R. Hannon*

SAMRAAN (USA) 6 br.h. Green Dancer (USA) 132 – Sedra 116 (Nebbiolo 125) **105**
[1998 116: 16d³ 16.4g² 16d 15.9f⁵ 16g³ 1999 16.2s* 16.2d⁶ Apr 28] useful-looking
horse: smart at best: just useful in 1999, including when landing odds in minor event
at Haydock: respectable sixth in Sagaro Stakes at Ascot later in April: stays 2m: acts
on firm and good to soft going, seemingly on soft: usually held up: sometimes
bandaged: sold only 7,000 gns in December. *J. L. Dunlop*

SAMSAAM (IRE) 2 b.c. (Mar 28) Sadler's Wells (USA) 132 – Azyaa 101 (Kris **65 p**
135) [1999 7g 8v 8d Oct 12] eighth foal: closely related to 6-y-o Yarob and half-
brother to several winners, including useful 7f/1m performer Ihtiraz (by Soviet Star),
later successful in UAE/USA up to 11f: dam 7.5f winner from good middle-distance
family: steady improvement in maidens, seventh of 19 to Imperial Rocket at
Leicester final start: will stay 1¼m: likely to do better still. *J. L. Dunlop*

Sampower Racing Club's "Sampower Star"

SAMUEL WHISKERS 2 b.c. (Apr 10) Son Pardo 107 – Yah Dancer 52 (Shareef Dancer (USA) 135) [1999 a5g a5g⁶ a6g⁶ a8.5g⁵ 6s 10d Oct 11] 3,500Y, 7,500 2-y-o: small colt: second foal: dam, ran only at 5f/6f at 2 yrs, bred to stay further: only a little sign of ability in varied company: sold 800 gns, sent to Norway. *R. T. Phillips* —

SAMUT (IRE) 3 b.f. Danehill (USA) 126 – Simaat (USA) 72 (Mr Prospector (USA)) [1998 89+: 7m⁵ 7.5m* 7g 1999 8m⁴ 7m⁶ 8d Aug 8] strong, good-topped filly: fairly useful performer: best effort when fourth of 15 to Holly Blue in listed rated stakes at Ascot on reappearance: will prove best at 7f/1m: acts on good to firm ground: visored final start: sent to USA. *J. H. M. Gosden* **92**

SAMWAR 7 b.g. Warning 136 – Samaza (USA) 90 (Arctic Tern (USA) 126) [1998 77§, a85§: 6g 5.1g⁴ 6g a6g⁴ 5g 6m 6m³ 6m a7g⁶ 5d⁵ 5.7m a6g 6.1v³ 7s a6g² 1999 a6g² a7g⁴ a6g⁴ a5g³ a6g⁶ a5g³ a5g² 5.1s a5g³ a5g² a5g⁵ a5g³ 5g a5g* a6g⁵ a6g³ a6g⁵ a5g* a5g* 5g a7g 5g⁶ 6.1d a5g a5g* a5g* a5g⁵ a5g a5g* Dec 21] small gelding: unimpressive mover: fair on all-weather, moderate on turf: won seller at Wolverhampton and handicaps at Southwell and Wolverhampton in the summer, and 2 claimers at Southwell and handicap at Wolverhampton in November/December: best at 5f/6f: acts on any all-weather/turf going: blinkered/visored: sometimes slowly away, and usually waited with: tough. *Mrs N. Macauley* **58 a82**

SANARIYA (IRE) 3 b. or br.f. Darshaan 133 – Sanamia (Top Ville 129) [1998 NR 1999 11.9g 10.1g² 12.3m⁶ a9.4f⁵ 10.5v Oct 13] big, lengthy filly: third foal: half-sister to fairly useful Irish winners around 13f Sanaka (by Kahyasi) and Saninka (by Doyoun): dam fairly useful Irish 1½m winner: fair maiden: should stay beyond 1½m: acts on good to firm going, insufficient test of stamina on fibresand: has swished tail. *Sir Michael Stoute* **67**

SANDABAR 6 b.g. Green Desert (USA) 127 – Children's Corner (FR) 106 (Top Ville 129) [1998 NR 1999 8g 8m³ 10d 10m⁴ 9g⁴ 10m* 10g 9g 10d⁴ Nov 1] strong gelding: fair handicapper: won at Ripon in July: ran creditably when in frame otherwise: stays 1¼m: acts on good to firm and good to soft going: often tongue tied. *Mrs M. Reveley* **67**

SANDBAGGEDAGAIN 5 b.g. Prince Daniel (USA) – Paircullis (Tower Walk 130) [1998 83p: 7m 7g 7d 10s³ 12s³ 12m² 15.8g* 16.2g* 16m³ 15.9g* 1999 12g Aug 22] leggy, shallow-girthed gelding: fairly useful handicapper: tailed off only 5-y-o start: will stay 2¼m: acts on good to firm and good to soft ground: hung and pulled hard when blinkered on 1998 reappearance. *M. W. Easterby* —

SAND CAY (USA) 5 ch.g. Geiger Counter (USA) – Lily Lily Rose (USA) (Lypheor 118) [1998 59: 8d 12f⁶ 11.6g 10d 16m 11.9g⁶ a12g a10g* a10g a10f⁵ 1999 a10g a13g a10f a13g Feb 6] rangy gelding: modest performer: well held in 1999: barely stays 1½m: acts on firm going and equitrack: has carried head high. *Miss Gay Kelleway* —

SANDERLING (IRE) 3 b.f. Exit To Nowhere (USA) 122 – Tartique Twist (USA) 78 (Arctic Tern (USA) 126) [1998 71: 7m⁶ 8m 7s⁵ 1999 11.4m Jun 1] lengthy, quite good-topped filly: best effort (fair form) on debut: should stay at least 1¼m: sold 1,500 gns. *J. L. Dunlop* —

SAND FALCON 4 ch.g. Polar Falcon (USA) 126 – Sand Grouse (USA) (Arctic Tern (USA) 126) [1998 108: 8g* 8g* 8g² 1999 8s² 7g³ 8g* 8d⁶ 8v³ 8v⁵ Nov 6] big, strong, lengthy gelding: fifth foal: half-brother to several winners, 3 by Danehill, including 1996 2-y-o 1m winner Desert Horizon, later useful at 1¼m, and useful 7f winner Sandhill: dam French 1¼m winner: improved into smart performer in 1999: won listed race at Vichy in July: best efforts when 1½ lengths second to Gold Away in Prix Edmond Blanc at Saint-Cloud and close third to Trans Island in 1m Prix du Rond-Point at Longchamp: stays 1m: raced only on good ground or softer. *P. Bary, France* **117**

SAND HAWK 4 ch.g. Polar Falcon (USA) 126 – Ghassanah 73 (Pas de Seul 133) [1998 59: a6g 6d 5s³ 6.1m 6g 8d³ 7d² 8v a8g² a8.5g 1999 a8g⁴ 9d 8d² 8s 8s⁶ 8m a8g 7.5m⁵ 6m 7.1m 6g a8.5g⁴ a6g⁵ a7g* a7g² Dec 15] workmanlike gelding: fair performer: won maiden at Wolverhampton in December: ran well in handicap there final start: probably finds 6f on sharp side, and stays 8.5f: acts on fibresand, good to firm and good to soft going: usually blinkered: has been slowly away. *D. Shaw* **67**

SANDICLIFFE (USA) 6 b.m. Imp Society (USA) – Sad Song (USA) (Roberto (USA) 131) [1998 61: 8g⁶ 8g⁶ 8f³ 8m⁵ 1999 8m* 8h² Aug 3] tall, lengthy mare: **62**

modest handicapper: has reportedly had problems with her hocks and quarters: won at Bath in July: ran well there only start after: effective at 7f/1m: acts on hard going, well held only try on equitrack. *J. A. R. Toller*

SAN DIMAS (USA) 2 gr.c. (Mar 15) Distant View (USA) 126 – Chrystophard (USA) (Lypheor 118) [1999 6g 8s Oct 25] $50,000F, IR 65,000Y: strong colt: fourth foal: half-brother to winners in USA: dam won at up to 9f in USA: burly, well held in maidens at York (very green) and Leicester. *Andrew Turnell* —

SANDMASON 2 ch.c. (Feb 26) Grand Lodge (USA) 125 – Sandy Island 110 (Mill Reef (USA) 141) [1999 8v* Sep 20] half-brother to several winners, including 7f (at 2 yrs) and 1¼m winner Sardegna (by Pharly) and 1½m winner Sebastian (by Sadler's Wells), both smart: dam, won Pretty Polly Stakes and Lancashire Oaks, closely related to Slip Anchor: second favourite, won maiden at Kempton by 2 lengths from Spirit of Light, soon prominent after slow start and running on strongly to assert final 1f: will stay at least 1½m: should make a much better 3-y-o. *H. R. A. Cecil* **74 P**

SANDMOOR CHAMBRAY 8 ch.g. Most Welcome 131 – Valadon 72 (High Line 125) [1998 NR 1999 10.4s 8.5g 8.1d⁵ 8.9d 10g 10.4f 10m 12f³ 11.9m 12g* 12f 13.9d 12s Oct 23] lengthy gelding: poor mover: smart at 6 yrs, fairly useful at best in 1999: won handicap at Pontefract in August: stays 1½m: acts on soft and good to firm ground: sometimes blinkered, including when successful: inconsistent. *T. D. Easterby* **80**

SANDMOOR DENIM 12 b.g. Red Sunset 120 – Holernzaye 93 (Sallust 134) [1998 –: a8g a11g 1999 a8g a11g a8g Jan 18] close-coupled gelding: veteran handicapper, tough and game in his prime: well beaten since 1997: tried blinkered. *S. R. Bowring* —

SANDOVA (IRE) 3 b.f. Green Desert (USA) 127 – Alinova (USA) 89 (Alleged (USA) 138) [1998 70p: 7v 1999 7m* 7m* 7d⁴ 7f⁶ Jul 29] lengthy, workmanlike filly: good walker: useful performer: impressive winner of maiden at Lingfield and minor event at Leicester in May: disappointing in listed races at Epsom and Goodwood after: free-going sort, likely to prove best up to 1m: acts on good to firm ground, showed promise on heavy: has worn crossed noseband: tail swisher, and temperament under suspicion. *Sir Michael Stoute* **101**

SANDPOINT 3 b.f. Lugana Beach 116 – Instinction (Never So Bold 135) [1998 –: 6m 1999 6m 5d 5.1m 5s⁶ 5.2s Oct 22] poor form: shaped well in handicaps at Goodwood (travelled strongly long way) and Newbury (raced on unfavoured side) last 2 starts: will prove best at 5f/6f: form only on good to soft/soft going: likely to do better. *L. G. Cottrell* **44 p**

SAND STORM (IRE) 3 ch.f. Forest Wind (USA) 111 – Clifton Beach (Auction Ring (USA) 123) [1998 NR 1999 a6g³ a6g⁴ a5s* a6g a6g a5g a5g a5g May 8] 4,000Y: fifth foal: half-sister to a winner in Singapore by Digamist: dam unraced: poor performer: easily best effort when winning seller at Wolverhampton (final start for B. Meehan) in February: may prove best at 5f: usually blinkered. *M. Waring* **46 d**

SANDY FLOSS (IRE) 6 b.g. Green Desert (USA) 127 – Mill On The Floss 117 (Mill Reef (USA) 141) [1998 NR 1999 14.1m 16.4g Aug 20] good-topped gelding: good walker and easy mover: fair maiden handicapper at 4 yrs: well beaten both 6-y-o starts: stays 2m: acts on soft when conditions aren't testing): probably acts on any going: has been mulish at stalls and gone in snatches. *P. R. Hedger* —

SANDY SHORE 4 b.f. Lugana Beach 116 – City Link Lass 92 (Double Jump 131) [1998 –: 8g 6d a7g⁶ 1999 7s 6.1s Apr 27] fair maiden at 2 yrs: no form since, including in blinkers. *J. Wharton* —

SANGRA (USA) 2 b.f. (Feb 15) El Gran Senor (USA) 136 – Water Song (CAN) (Clever Trick (USA)) [1999 7m³ 7d⁵ 8.2s⁶ Oct 5] $125,000Y: rather unfurnished filly: third foal: dam, won at up to 9f in Canada, out of half-sister to Champion Stakes winner Northern Baby: fair maiden: best effort on debut: should be suited by 1m+. *N. A. Callaghan* **69**

SANGUINE 2 gr.c. (Mar 4) Sanglamore (USA) 126 – Sacristy 54 (Godswalk (USA) 130) [1999 7m³ 7.1m² 7m* 7g⁵ 8m⁶ 8d Oct 15] angular colt: fluent mover: sixth living foal: half-brother to 3 winners, including 7f (at 2 yrs) and 9f winner Holtye (both by Danehill): dam lightly-raced half-sister to Desirable, Park Appeal and Alydaress: fairly useful performer: won maiden at **82**

Catterick in August: respectable efforts at best in nurseries after: should be suited by 1m+: acts on good to firm going: sold 37,000 gns, sent to USA. *B. W. Hills*

SANKATY LIGHT (USA)   3 b.f. Summer Squall (USA) – Brave And True (USA) (Fappiano (USA)) [1998 –p: 6g 7d 1999 7.5d⁴ 7m 6.8m a9.4g 8s Oct 26] modest maiden: should stay beyond 1m: acts on good to soft going, well below form both starts on good to firm: has worn tongue strap. *I. A. Balding*   **55**

SAN MICHEL (IRE)   7 b.g. Scenic 128 – The Top Diesis (USA) (Diesis 133) [1998 63, a–: 5g 5d³ 5s² 6m⁶ 5g⁴ 5d 5d⁴ 6v 5v³ 1999 a7g a7g 7g⁵ 6v³ 6s 6d 7.1m 7.5v 6v⁵ a7g a6g⁶ a6g³ a6g a6g⁵ Dec 21] sturdy gelding: half-brother to 2-y-o Charlottevalentina: dam Italian 6.5f and 7.5f winner: modest handicapper: trained by E. Hughes in Ireland in 1998: best effort at 7 yrs when third of 17 at Hamilton: stays 7f: acts on good to firm and heavy going, poor at best on all-weather: usually blinkered/visored. *J. L. Eyre*   **62 a48**

SAN SEBASTIAN   5 ch.g. Niniski (USA) 125 – Top of The League 85 (High Top 131) [1998 109: 14s² 16g² 14g* 20d* 20d³ 18g 1999 16.2d 14m³ 22.2m* 14m⁵ 14g⁴ 18m⁴ 20v² Oct 2] sturdy gelding: smart performer: beat Jaseur by a head in Queen Alexandra Stakes at Royal Ascot in June: ran well when 1¾ lengths fourth of 6 to Far Cry in Doncaster Cup and neck second to Tajoun in Prix du Cadran at Longchamp last 2 starts: finds 1¾m on sharp side nowadays, and stays 2¾m: acts on any going: wears blinkers: tends to wander under pressure, but is genuine: sold 170,000 gns, joined J. Dunlop. *M. J. Grassick, Ireland*   **113**

SANS RIVALE   4 ch.f. Elmaamul (USA) 125 – Strawberry Song 87 (Final Straw 127) [1998 57, a–: a6s a5g a7g⁶ 5d* 5m² 5m 6m 6m 6d a6g 1999 5g 5d 5m 5m 5g 7m 6f Jul 31] poor performer: left J. L. Eyre after third start: should stay beyond 5f: acts on good to firm and good to soft ground, little form on fibresand. *D. W. Chapman*   **–**

SANTA COURT   4 b.g. Be My Native (USA) 122 – Christmas Show (Petorius 117) [1998 57: 8d 8.2s⁵ 10g 8d⁶ 1999 10d 10.8m⁵ 10.2g² 10d Jun 10] leggy gelding: modest maiden handicapper: best effort when short-head second of 20 in amateur event at Bath: shapes as though will stay 1½m: acts on soft and good to firm going. *R. Dickin*   **63**

Queen Alexandra Stakes, Royal Ascot—San Sebastian follows up his win in the Ascot Stakes the previous year, but has to dig deep to hold off Jaseur (right), with Canon Can third

SANTA LUCIA   3 b.f. Namaqualand (USA) – Villasanta (Corvaro (USA) 124)   **71**
[1998 NR 1999 8g⁶ 8g⁶ 8m⁶ 10d 11d² a14g Nov 12] 8,500Y: half-sister to 1½m   **a–**
winners Hamilton Lady (by Zino) and 4-y-o Roma and several winners (mainly
middle distances) abroad: dam French maiden from poor family: fair maiden: easily
best effort when second in handicap at Redcar final start: will stay 1½m: yet to race
on extremes of going, well beaten on fibresand: sold 8,600 gns, joined M. Dods.
C. W. Thornton

SANTANDRE   3 ch.g. Democratic (USA) 101 – Smartie Lee 66 (Dominion 123)   **66**
[1998 75: a6g⁴ 6.1d⁴ 5g⁴ 5g* 5.7m⁴ 6m⁶ 6m 6m² 7s³ 6g⁶ 7s 1999 7g a7g³ 8.2m 7m⁵   **a79**
a7g⁴ 6g 5m⁴ 5d⁵ a6g* 6s 6.1d 7d³ 6d a5g⁴ a7g⁵ a6g³ Dec 21] leggy gelding: fair
handicapper: won at Wolverhampton in September: creditable efforts final 3 starts:
effective at 5f to 7f: acts on fibresand, soft and good to firm going: often ridden by
claimer. *R. Hollinshead*

SANTARENE (IRE)   4 b.f. Scenic 128 – Rising Spirits 77 (Cure The Blues   **46**
(USA)) [1998 46, a36: a11g⁵ 8f 8m 10m 10m² 10g⁴ 11.5d a10g⁵ 1999 a10g⁶ a11g³   **a33**
a12f³ a13g a13g⁵ a13g⁵ 9m 10g 10m 10.1g*¹ 11.6m 8m⁵ 10m³ 10.1d⁴ Sep 15] leggy
filly: poor performer: won seller at Yarmouth in July: best at 1¼m/1½m: acts on all-
weather and good to firm going, probably on good to soft. *P. Howling*

SANTIBURI GIRL   2 b.f. (Mar 12) Casteddu 111 – Lake Mastissiu 86 (Tina's   **75**
Pet 121) [1999 5d³ 5s 5m 6g² 6.8m² 7g* 7m³ 7m⁴ 7m⁵ 8m⁶ 6.5g⁵ 7g⁴ 7d 6d Oct 14]
5,600Y, resold 5,000Y: small, workmanlike filly: keen walker/unimpressive mover:
second living foal: sister to a poor maiden: dam 5f winner, including at 2 yrs: fair
performer: trained by J. J. O'Neill on debut: won minor event at Salisbury in July:
mainly creditable efforts after: finds 6f on sharp side, but barely stays 1m: acts on
good to firm going, below form on softer than good: has had 2 handlers and been
rather edgy. *J. R. Best*

SANTONE (IRE)   4 b.c. Fairy King (USA) – Olivia Jane (IRE) (Ela-Mana-Mou   **52**
132) [1998 65, a–: 10.3d 8g⁵ 8m⁵ a10g a7g 1999 a7g⁶ a10g⁶ a8.5g Feb 24] small,
compact colt: has a quick action: disappointing maiden: should be well suited by
further than 7f. *R. Hannon*

SAPHIRE   3 ch.f. College Chapel 122 – Emerald Eagle 78 (Sandy Creek 123)   **87**
[1998 92: 5v² 5d 5g 5s* 6s* 5d³ 5d² 5d⁵ 5m⁵ 6s 1999 5s⁵ 5s 6d³ 6d 5g 5s 6s Nov 6]
sturdy filly: fairly useful performer: probably flattered when third of 5 in slowly-run
listed race at Haydock in June: well held last 3 starts: stays 6f: ran respectably on
good to firm going, raced mainly on good or softer: tends to drift right: sometimes
gets on edge: sometimes reluctant stalls. *C. B. B. Booth*

SAPPHIRE SON (IRE)   7 ch.g. Maelstrom Lake 118 – Gluhwein (Ballymoss   **–**
136) [1998 –, a36?: 11.9d 12m 10m 11.6f 12f a12g a12g² a13g 1999 a12g a13g
11.6m a12g Oct 1] sparely-made gelding: poor handicapper at best nowadays: left
P. Clarke after third start. *P. Butler*

SAPPHIRE TRIO   3 b.c. Bluebird (USA) 125 – Triode (USA) 105 (Sharpen Up   **92**
127) [1998 NR 1999 8.2f² 10d⁴ 7.8m* 8.5f² 12d⁴ 8m³ 6m 9g 8g⁵ 12d 9s 9g 8s⁵ Oct
23] 150,000Y: fifth foal: closely related to a 6f to 9f winner in Germany by Storm
Bird and half-brother to Italian 1997 2-y-o 1m winner Taleban (by Alleged) and
fairly useful 1996 2-y-o 6f winner Blane Water (by Lomond): dam 1m winner: fairly
useful performer: sold out of Sir Michael Stoute's stable 20,000 gns after second
start: won maiden at Dundalk in July: faced several stiff tasks after, best effort when
fifth in listed race at Tralee on ninth outing: stays 9f: acts on firm going, probably
good to soft: blinkered (ran creditably) sixth start. *Luke Comer, Ireland*

SARAFAN (USA)   2 b.c. (May 9) Lear Fan (USA) 130 – Saraa Ree (USA) 102   **106**
(Caro 133) [1999 6g* 6m* 7.5s* 7f² 7.1g² 8m* Sep 10] $90,000Y: big, good-topped
colt with plenty of scope: sixth foal: half-brother to 3-y-o Shanghai Crab and useful
1m to 1½m winner Hagwah (by Dancing Brave): dam, 7f winner who stayed 1m, out
of sister to Irish River: useful performer: won maiden at Hamilton and minor events
at Pontefract and Beverley in June/July: good placed efforts in Group 3 events at
Goodwood (beaten 2 lengths by Ekraar) and Sandown (beaten 2 lengths by Best of
The Bests) prior to winning listed event at Goodwood (by 1¾ lengths from Kingsclere) in September: stays 1m: acts on firm and soft ground: has shown reluctance to
enter stalls, and blanketed for entry last 3 starts. *Sir Mark Prescott*

SARAH'S SONG (IRE) 3 b.f. Warning 136 – Two And Sixpence (USA) 74 **75**
(Chief's Crown (USA)) [1998 NR 1999 7m⁵ 7m⁶ 8s 7.1g⁵ 7g² 7m* 7g³ Jul 1]
20,000Y: angular, workmanlike filly: has a quick action: third foal: dam 17f winner:
fair performer: comfortable winner of minor event at Lingfield in June: ran creditably
in handicap at Catterick final start: should stay 1m: acts on good to firm going (below
form only try on soft): sent to USA. *B. J. Meehan*

SARA MOON CLASSIC (IRE) 4 b.g. Fayruz 116 – Irish Affaire (IRE) (Fairy **49**
King (USA)) [1998 66, a62: a6g² a7g³ 6v³ 6.1m⁶ 6m⁶ 8d 8g a7g⁵ a6g 8.3s 6.1s a7g
1999 a9.4g a7g 7.1m 8.5g⁶ 8s³ Oct 25] leggy gelding: poor maiden handicapper:
barely stays 1m when conditions are testing: acts on good to firm going, heavy and
all-weather: often blinkered/visored: has worn dropped noseband: sold 800 gns.
K. McAuliffe

SARANGANI 3 b.c. Polish Precedent (USA) 131 – Height of Folly 81 (Shirley **98**
Heights 130) [1998 NR 1999 10.2s² 10.4s⁴ 11.5g² 12g* 12.4m² Jun 24] 94,000Y: big,
rather leggy, good-topped colt: has plenty of scope: seventh foal: half-brother to 3
winners, including 8-y-o Charity Crusader and 9.7f and 1¼m winner Opalette (by
Sharrood): dam stayer: useful performer: didn't have to be at best to win maiden at
Goodwood in June: creditable second in rated stakes at Newcastle final start: will
stay beyond 1½m: acts on soft and good to firm going. *I. A. Balding*

SARATOGA RED (USA) 5 ch.g. Saratoga Six (USA) – Wajibird (USA) (Storm **–**
Bird (CAN) 134) [1998 51, a–: 7m 7f⁵ 7g 6d⁶ 8m 8m 9.2s* 1999 a11g⁴ a8f³ a9.4g⁶ **a60**
a8g⁶ 10v 8.3g 11.9d Jun 3] strong gelding: has a poor, round action: modest handicapper: effective at 1m, probably at 11f: acts on all-weather, soft and good to firm
going: effective blinkered/visored, not tried in 1999. *E. J. Alston*

SARENA PRIDE (IRE) 2 b.f. (Apr 29) Persian Bold 123 – Avidal Park 68 **76**
(Horage 124) [1999 5g 6d* 6m⁶ 6m⁵ 6m* 6s² 7.3v Oct 23] 4,000F, 5,500Y: leggy
filly: half-sister to 3-y-o Diletto and 3 winners, including 1m winner Projectvision
and 1½m winner Real Popcorn (by Jareer): dam 2-y-o 5f winner: fair performer:
won maiden at Windsor in June and nursery at Warwick in August: stays 6f well, but
not testing 7f: acts on soft and good to firm going. *R. J. O'Sullivan*

SARENA SPECIAL 2 b.c. (Feb 16) Lucky Guest 109 – Lariston Gale 81 (Pas de **72**
Seul 133) [1999 6d 6g² 7.1m⁴ 6.8m² 6.1m⁶ Jul 23] 5,000Y: strong colt: seventh foal:
half-brother to several winners, including 3-y-o Dolly Day Dream and 5-y-o Nomore
Mr Niceguy: dam 2-y-o 6f winner: fair form in frame in maidens at Lingfield,
Sandown and Warwick: races freely, but stays 7f. *R. J. O'Sullivan*

SARI 3 b.f. Faustus (USA) 118 – Fire Lily (Unfuwain (USA) 131) [1998 79: 6g³ **83**
6m 6g⁴ 6m² 7d² 7d* 1999 8.3d 7d² 7m 7m 8.3m⁴ 8.1d 7.1s* 7d a8g a7g Nov 20] **a–**
fairly useful handicapper: won at Sandown in October: seems best at 7f: acts on soft
and good to firm going, no form on all-weather: well beaten in blinkers: usually races
prominently: none too consistent. *P. F. I. Cole*

SARPEDON (IRE) 3 ch.g. Be My Chief (USA) 122 – Sariza 79 (Posse (USA) **–**
130) [1998 NR 1999 9.8.3d 10g 8.9m a6g Oct 18] heavy-topped gelding: half-brother
to 8.5f winner Aratos (by Night Shift) and 5-y-o Selfish: dam, best at 7f, out of 1000
Guineas second Tolmi, an excellent family: well held in maidens/claimer, leaving
L. Cumani's stable 4,200 gns after second start. *M. C. Chapman*

SARSON 3 b.g. Efisio 120 – Sarcita 111 (Primo Dominie 121) [1998 103: 5g² 5g² **98 d**
5d² 5d* 6d² 1999 6d⁵ 6m⁶ 8g⁵ 7g 7m 6v Sep 29] neat gelding: has a quick action:
useful performer: form in 1999 only when sixth to Arkadian Hero in listed race at
Newbury in July: ran as if something amiss fourth and fifth starts: should stay 7f: acts
on good to firm and good to soft going. *R. Hannon*

SARTEANO 5 ch.m. Anshan 119 – Daisy Girl 69 (Main Reef 126) [1998 –: 10g **–**
10m 8.2m 1999 9.9m Aug 28] leggy mare: no form. *D. Shaw*

SARTORIAL (IRE) 3 b.g. Elbio 125 – Madam Slaney 92 (Prince Tenderfoot **84 +**
(USA) 126) [1998 75p: 6g⁴ 1999 6g² 6m³ a6g² Jul 9] strong, good-topped gelding:
has scope: fair maiden: best efforts when runner-up at Newmarket and Wolverhampton: reportedly returned lame after second start: free-going sort, likely to prove best
at 5f/6f: has been bandaged in front. *P. J. Makin*

SARUM 13 b.g. Tina's Pet 121 – Contessa (HUN) (Peleid 125) [1998 –, a30: a10g⁶ – a13g a8g² a7g 7m a7g a8.5g 12m 8m a8g 9m 10m a12g 1999 a8g a10g a8g a8g a7g 11.5m Jun 19] tall gelding: poor mover: no longer of any account. *J. E. Long*

SASEEDO (USA) 9 ch.g. Afleet (CAN) – Barbara's Moment (USA) (Super **61 §** Moment (USA)) [1998 –§: a8s a8g⁶ a11g⁵ a12g⁶ 8m⁶ 10s⁴ 11.5g 11.9m 1999 a8g⁵ a8g² a7g⁶ a8g a8g a10g* 10d 10g a10g⁶ 10g³ 12g 9.9m 10g 11.6m 9g 10m 9.9v 10s⁶ 12d 10d 7d⁶ a10g a10g Nov 11] modest at best nowadays: trained first 2 starts by K. Morgan: gained first win since 1996 in seller at Lingfield in April: stays 1¼m: acts on all-weather and any turf going: temperamental (often slowly away and off bridle in rear) and not one to trust. *J. J. Bridger*

SASHA 2 ch.c. (Mar 20) Factual (USA) 108 – Twice In Bundoran (IRE) 70 (Bold – Arrangement 127) [1999 5m Sep 16] first foal: dam 5f winner, including at 2 yrs: slowly away and always behind in maiden at Pontefract. *J. L. Eyre*

SASSY (IRE) 4 b.f. Imp Society (USA) – Merrie Moment (IRE) (Taufan (USA) **28** 119) [1998 52: a8.5g⁴ a8.5g⁴ a9.4g 8.3g 10.1d⁵ 8g 10.1g³ a12g⁵ a10g² a12g⁵ 10.1g³ a11g* 11.5d a10g a14g 1999 11.9f 12d a11g a11g a10g⁶ 12m⁴ Jul 26] poor nowadays: stays 1½m: acts on good to firm going (possibly not softer than good) and all-weather: visored last 3 starts: sold 4,000 gns in November. *Mrs L. C. Jewell*

SATIN SLIPPER (IRE) 3 ch.f. Petardia 113 – Lomond Heights (IRE) (Lomond **?** (USA) 128) [1998 65: 5g 5m 5.3d* 5.1d⁴ 6m³ 5.3f 1999 a7g⁵ a8f⁶ 8.2s 6.1s Apr 27] modest at 2 yrs: well held in sellers in 1999: subsequently won over 9f in Spain. *K. T. Ivory*

SATIRE 2 br.f. (May 24) Terimon 124 – Salchow 116 (Niniski (USA) 125) [1999 – 8g Oct 15] 4,000Y: half-sister to several winners, including 7.5f winner Kalko (by Kalaglow) and 11.5f winner Meltemison (by Charmer): dam, 2-y-o 7f winner who stayed 1¾m (second in Park Hill), half-sister to 4-y-o Gulland: soundly beaten in Redcar maiden. *T. J. Etherington*

SATRIA (IRE) 3 b.c. Shareef Dancer (USA) 135 – Inderaputeri 67 (Bold Fort **42** 100) [1998 –: 7d 1999 a10g⁶ a9.4g⁴ a10g³ a11g 9.7s a10g³ Apr 9] small colt: poor maiden: should stay beyond 1¼m: acts on all-weather, well held both starts on turf: sold 2,000 gns, sent to Spain. *Miss Gay Kelleway*

SATZUMA (IRE) 2 ch.g. (Feb 5) Lycius (USA) 124 – Satz (USA) 50 (The Min- – strel (CAN) 135) [1999 6s Nov 5] 27,000Y: good-topped gelding: third foal: half-brother to a winner in USA by Quiet American: dam, lightly raced in Britain and in USA, half-sister to useful 7f/1m performer Satin Flower (dam of 3-y-o Lujain) and US Grade 1 1¼m winner Martial Law: well beaten in maiden at Doncaster. *C. F. Wall*

SAUCY DANCER 6 ch.m. Chilibang 120 – Silent Dancer 76 (Quiet Fling (USA) – 124) [1998 –: a12g⁶ a12g³ a14.8g 1999 13.8f³ May 26] no form. *G. A. Ham*

SAUCY NIGHT 3 ch.g. Anshan 119 – Kiss In The Dark 55 (Starry Night (USA)) – [1998 NR 1999 10d 7.5m Jul 13] 5,400Y: first foal: dam 1m winner at 2 yrs, and successful 2m hurdler: no promise in maiden and claimer. *M. Dods*

SAUSALITO BAY 5 b.g. Salse (USA) 128 – Cantico 58 (Green Dancer (USA) **100** 132) [1998 108: 15.5s⁵ 13.3m⁴ 12d 16.1v 13.9f 13.9f 14.6d⁵ 13.3g 1999 16m 14.1m³ 13.9d³ 11.4m* 12d 11.5s* Oct 8] rangy gelding: useful handicapper: made all at Sandown in July and Lingfield (rallied to beat Angels Venture by ¾ length) in Oct-ober: best at 1½m/1¾m: acts on soft and good to firm going: tends to race freely: sometimes blinkered (for wins only in 1999): sold 66,000 gns, won over hurdles in December for N. Meade, Ireland. *I. A. Balding*

SAVANNAH BELLE 2 b.f. (Mar 17) Green Desert (USA) 127 – Third Watch **84** 114 (Slip Anchor 136) [1999 5d³ 5m³ 5.1m⁴ 5g* 5g² 6m⁵ 5d⁶ 5d Sep 30] 60,000Y: small filly: fourth foal: half-sister to useful 1½m winner Rainwatch (by Rainbow Quest) and fairly useful 1995 2-y-o 7f winner Tria Kemata (by Kris): dam, won Rib-blesdale Stakes, from very good middle-distance family: fairly useful performer: won nursery at Haydock in August: creditable efforts next 3 starts: effective at 5f/6f: yet to race on extremes of going: wears net muzzle: races freely. *J. A. Glover*

SAVMO ONE 3 b.f. Distinctly North (USA) 115 – Dear Heart (Blakeney 126) – [1998 –: 5m 7g 10d 1999 9.9g 7.5g Aug 29] tall filly: no form: has been bandaged in front. *D. Shaw*

SAVOIR FAIRE (IRE) 3 b.f. College Chapel 122 – Arctic Splendour (USA) 66 – (Arctic Tern (USA) 126) [1998 –: 5.7g 7m 6d 1999 12s Nov 2] tall, leggy, unfurnished filly: no form. *M. A. Buckley*

SAWLAJAN (USA) 8 ch.g. Woodman (USA) 126 – Crafty Satin (USA) – (Crimson Satan) [1998 NR 1999 a10g 11.9f⁶ Jul 13] useful 1m winner in Britain in 1994: no form since, including in Dubai in 1996: successful over hurdles in August. *T. R. Watson*

SAWWAAH (IRE) 2 ch.c. (May 18) Marju (IRE) 127 – Just A Mirage 76 (Green 94 Desert (USA) 127) [1999 7.1m³ 7d² Sep 30] big, useful-looking colt: has plenty of scope: fourth foal: half-brother to 7f performers Kahal (5-y-o, very smart) and Doomna (useful), both by Machiavellian: dam, maiden (stayed 1m), sister to smart 1m winner Distant Oasis and half-sister to very smart Reprimand and Wiorno: better effort in maidens (fairly useful form) when head second of 14 to Zentsov Street at Newmarket, wandering under pressure but rallying: will stay 1m. *E. A. L. Dunlop*

SAYARSHAN (FR) 4 b.c. Darshaan 133 – Sayyara 81 (Kris 135) [1998 117: 117 10.5s⁵ 10.5v* 11s* 12g 1999 10s⁶ 10d⁴ 11f* 12f 11f* 10f⁴ Oct 3] leggy colt: smart performer: off course over 10 months, ran creditably when sixth to Barbola in Prix Exbury at Saint-Cloud and 2½ lengths last of 4 to Dark Moondancer in Prix d'Harcourt at Longchamp (final start for P. Bary) in spring: won Grade 3 handicap at Golden Gate in June and Grade 2 handicap at Del Mar in August: creditable 4½ lengths fourth to Mash One in Oak Tree Turf Championship at Santa Anita final start: stays 11f: acts on any ground. *N. Canani, USA*

SAYEDATI ELJAMILAH (USA) 2 b. or br.f. (Apr 16) Mr Prospector (USA) 64 – Histoire (FR) (Riverman (USA) 131) [1999 6s 7d Oct 30] smallish, quite good-topped filly: has a quick action: half-sister to 3-y-o Osood and several winners, notably Erhaab (by Chief's Crown) and smart 7f (at 2 yrs) to 1¼m winner Oumaldaaya (by Nureyev): dam French 10.5f winner: better effort in maidens at Newmarket on debut: should stay 1m. *J. L. Dunlop*

SAYEH (IRE) 7 b.g. Fools Holme (USA) – Piffle 87 (Shirley Heights 130) [1998 79 NR 1999 8m 10.3m³ Sep 11] big, deep-girthed gelding: has a round action: useful at best: missed 1997 and 1998 seasons, but won 4 of 5 starts over hurdles for current stable: well backed, much better effort on return to Flat when third of 17 in handicap at Doncaster, briefly short of room: will stay 1½m: yet to race on firm going, acts on any other turf and dirt: pulls hard, and has won special bridle. *P. Bowen*

SAYSO 3 b.f. Anshan 119 – Total Sa (IRE) (Gallic League 119) [1998 NR 1999 – 10m Jul 12] first foal: dam little form in 3 starts: always behind in maiden at Windsor: sold 1,000 gns. *P. J. Hobbs*

SCAFELL 2 b.c. (Feb 13) Puissance 110 – One Half Silver (CAN) (Plugged 69 Nickle (USA)) [1999 5f⁶ 5m² 5m 6g³ 6m³ 5f² 5.1m⁵ 5m Aug 31] 6,200Y: workmanlike colt: half-brother to several winners, including 3-y-o Premiere Division, 4-y-o Petarga and French 1½m winner Garboesque (by Priolo): dam unraced half-sister to smart French middle-distance filly Gamberta: fair maiden: below form last 2 starts: effective at 5f/6f: raced only on good going or firmer. *C. Smith*

Somerville Tattersall Stakes, Newmarket—
Scarteen Fox gradually extends his advantage, beating Winning Venture

SCARLET CRESCENT   5 b.m. Midyan (USA) 124 – Scarlet Veil 75 (Tyrnavos   –
129) [1998 60, a49: 10g⁶ 8d a12g a13g⁵ a16g 1999 a12f a13g Jan 28] close-coupled,
angular mare: modest handicapper: probably stayed 13f: acted on firm going, good
to soft and equitrack: tried visored/blinkered: dead. *M. D. I. Usher*

SCARLET LIVERY   3 b.f. Saddlers' Hall (IRE) 126 – Go For Red (IRE)   **63**
(Thatching 131) [1998 NR 1999 10v⁶ 8m 7m³ 7d⁴ 7m 8g 8s⁶ 10d Oct 21] smallish,
useful-looking filly: second foal: sister to 4-y-o Primary Colours: dam unraced
granddaughter of smart French/US 5.5f to 11f winner Warfever: modest maiden: left
R. Cowell after fourth start: should stay beyond 7f: acts on good to firm and good to
soft going. *C. B. B. Booth*

SCARLET RAIDER (USA)   3 b.f. Red Ransom (USA) – Dariela (USA)   **81**
(Manila (USA)) [1998 81p: 7g* 7g⁴ 1999 10.4d⁶ 7m⁶ 10d Oct 1] lengthy, good-
quartered filly: has a quick action: fairly useful performer: beaten over 16 lengths
when last of 6 in Musidora Stakes at York on reappearance: disappointing both starts
after, shaping as though something amiss after 4-month break final one: seems to stay
1¼m: sold 36,000 gns in December. *P. F. I. Cole*

SCARLET SCEPTRE (USA)   3 b.f. Red Ransom (USA) – Wand (IRE) 69   **63**
(Reference Point 139) [1998 67p: 8d⁶ a8g⁴ 1999 a9.4g² a9.4g³ 11.6m 12m³ a16g²
Aug 25] rather leggy, sparely-made filly: modest maiden: stays 2m: acts on good to
firm going, good to soft and all-weather: races prominently. *R. Charlton*

SCARLET TANAGER   2 ch.f. (Apr 18) Formidable (USA) 125 – Twosixty-   –
threewest (FR) 69 (Kris 135) [1999 a8g Nov 12] 5,000Y: third foal: half-sister to
German 7f winner Twosixty Four (by Beldale Flutter): dam, 1m winner, from family
of Fruits of Love: well held in seller at Southwell. *G. C. Bravery*

SCARLETTA (USA)   2 b.f. (Jan 25) Red Ransom (USA) – Snowtown (IRE) 103   **79**
(Alzao (USA) 117) [1999 7d² 8.3d² Oct 28] smallish, compact filly: first foal: dam 7f
winner (at 2 yrs) who stayed 1½m: fair form in maidens at Leicester and Windsor in
October: should stay 1¼m. *A. G. Foster*

SCARLETT RIBBON   2 b.f. (Mar 13) Most Welcome 131 – Scarlett Holly 81   **92 +**
(Red Sunset 120) [1999 6d* 6s Nov 22] fifth foal: half-sister to 3 winners, including
6f winner Siouxrouge (by Indian Ridge), later 1m/9f winner in USA: dam 6f/7f
winner: weak in market, made impressive winning debut in 17-runner maiden at
Windsor by 9 lengths from Pretrail, quickening clear 2f out: only eighth of 11 in listed
race at Maisons-Laffitte later in November: will stay 7f: looked potentially useful at
Windsor. *P. J. Makin*

SCARLETT'S BOY   3 b.g. Emarati (USA) 74 – Katie Scarlett 70 (Lochnager   **67**
132) [1998 81: a7g² a6g a6g* 1999 a7g⁵ a6g 6.1s⁶ a6g⁶ 5d a7g Oct 30] fair
performer: form in 1999 only on fourth start (off track over 7 months after second):
should prove best short of 1m: acts on fibresand, probably equitrack (well beaten
both starts on turf). *N. P. Littmoden*

SCARTEEN FOX (IRE)   2 ch.c. (Apr 15) Foxhound (USA) 103 – Best Swinger   **108 p**
(IRE) (Ela-Mana-Mou 132) [1999 7m³ 7d* 7d* 8s Oct 23] IR 50,000Y: smallish,
sturdy colt: fourth foal: half-brother to 1997 2-y-o 7f seller winner Mari-Ela and an
8.5f winner in Norway (both by River Falls): dam Irish 7f winner: useful form: won
22-runner maiden at Newbury in September and 5-runner Somerville Tattersall
Stakes at Newmarket following month, latter by 2 lengths from Winning Venture:
favourite, only seventh of 9 to Aristotle in Racing Post Trophy at Doncaster final
start, finding little: should stay 1m: acts on good to soft going, showed promise on
good to firm. *D. R. C. Elsworth*

SCATHEBURY   6 b.g. Aragon 118 – Lady Bequick 81 (Sharpen Up 127) [1998   **50**
62, a58: a7g³ a8.5g³ a7g⁴ 7d⁴ 7s⁵ 7s² 8.3m 8s⁴ 8.3m⁴ 7m 7g⁶ 8.3m² 8.3f a7g⁶ 8.3s
8.2s 8v* 7s⁶ 1999 a7g⁴ a8g 7g⁶ 6.9m 8d 8f 8.3f³ 8.3s 6g 8d Oct 20] compact gelding:
modest performer: effective at 6f to 8.5f: acts on fibresand and probably any turf
going: effective blinkered/visored or not: has run poorly when sweating: carries head
awkwardly: best held up: none too consistent: sold 2,000 gns. *R. Craggs*

SCENE (IRE)   4 b.f. Scenic 128 – Avebury Ring (Auction Ring (USA) 123) [1998   **84**
82: 10.3d 7d 8s* 8d 8.1g* 7f³ 8m 10m 8m 10.5m³ 8.9g 8g⁴ 8.2v² 1999 8d 8g³ 8d 8g*
8m⁴ 10d² 8m³ 8.5d* 8m 8m 8m 10d 8s 8s⁴ 10s* Nov 1] plain filly: fairly useful

handicapper: won at Ascot in April, Epsom in June and Nottingham (edged left) in October, first- and last-named in large fields: effective at 1m to 1¼m: acts on good to firm and heavy ground, probably on firm: visored thirteenth start. *J. A. Glover*

SCENIC LADY (IRE) 3 b.f. Scenic 128 – Tu Tu Maori (IRE) (Kings Lake **40** (USA) 133) [1998 –: 7g 8s 1999 7v⁵ 10f² 11.6d 10.5m⁵ 10g 14.1m a16g⁶ 11.9g 11.5g⁶ Sep 14] poor maiden: stays 1¾m: acts on firm going. *L. A. Dace*

SCHATZI 2 gr.f. (Mar 4) Chilibang 120 – Fluorescent Flo (Ballad Rock 122) **53** [1999 5d³ 5d 6m² 5g² 6m² 6f 5m³ 5s⁵ a6g 6d 5g⁵ Nov 3] second reported foal: dam little worthwhile form: modest maiden: effective at 5f/6f: acts on firm and soft going, well held only try on fibresand. *D. Moffatt*

SCHIEHALLION 2 b.f. (Apr 20) Polar Falcon (USA) 126 – Frisson (Slip **58** Anchor 136) [1999 6d 5m⁴ 6m 5m⁶ 6.1s Nov 1] 5,000F, 13,500Y: leggy, rather unfurnished filly: first foal: dam unraced daughter of useful 7f to 9f winner Comic Talent: modest maiden: should stay 7f. *W. J. Musson*

SCHNITZEL (IRE) 3 b.f. Tirol 127 – Good Reference (IRE) 84 (Reference **84 §** Point 139) [1998 78: 7g⁵ a7g* 7m 7m² 7d* 7g⁴ 1999 8m⁴ 7.6m² 7d 7m⁴ 7g⁴ 7m 7.1d* 7.1s 7d 8d⁴ a7g Nov 20] deep-girthed, lengthy filly: fairly useful performer: won minor event at Sandown in September: below form after: effective at 7f/1m: acts on good to firm going, good to soft and fibresand: races prominently: sometimes hangs right/carries head awkwardly: sold 12,000 gns in December. *M. L. W. Bell*

SCINTILATING SOUND 4 ch.f. Savahra Sound 111 – Mia Scintilla 54 **38** (Blazing Saddles (AUS)) [1998 43: 5d 5g³ 5m 5g 8v 8s a6g⁶ a6g³ 1999 a6g a8.5g⁵ **a51** a7g² a7f a7g³ a6g a5g³ 5f 5g 5g a5g Jul 9] leggy, angular filly: modest maiden handicapper on all-weather, poor on turf: effective at 5f to 7f: acts on firm going and fibresand: blinkered (well held) once at 3 yrs. *S. R. Bowring*

SCISSOR RIDGE 7 ch.g. Indian Ridge 123 – Golden Scissors 76 (Kalaglow **54** 132) [1998 63, a76: a7g³ a7g⁶ a7g⁴ a6g³ a7g⁴ a6g⁶ a6g⁴ 6m⁵ 7g 6m² 6f* 5d² 6f 6m **a66** 5m 6m 6d 6m 6.1s 7v a6g 1999 a5g⁶ a6f a7g a7f⁴ a6g⁵ a7g³ a6g⁵ a7g³ 7m 5f 7m⁵ 6g a7g 7m 8m a6f⁵ a8.5g⁴ 7s⁴ a7g² a7g³ a7g a7g² Dec 29] sparely-made gelding: fair handicapper on all-weather, modest on turf: won at Lingfield in November: finds 5f on sharp side nowadays, and stays easy 8.5f: acts on firm ground, soft and all-weather: tried blinkered (not since 1996): has run well sweating: tough and reliable. *J. J. Bridger*

SCOLD 4 gr.f. Reprimand 122 – Hopea (USA) 60 (Drone) [1998 –: 8m 7.5d 12g **–** 1999 a7g Mar 22] leggy filly: no sign of ability, including in blinkers. *G. P. Kelly*

SCOLDING 4 b.f. Reprimand 122 – Tinkerbird 76 (Music Boy 124) [1998 49: 6g **39** 8.2d 8.2g 8.2g⁴ 8m* 8m 10m 8.2s⁶ 8v 1999 8d 8f 10g⁶ 8.9m 8f Sep 4] rather sparely-made filly: poor mover: poor performer: stays 1m: acts on good to firm and heavy going. *G. Woodward*

SCONCED (USA) 4 ch.g. Affirmed (USA) – Quaff (USA) 115 (Raise A Cup **41** (USA)) [1998 76p: 10g³ 9.2s* 11.8d⁴ 1999 10.1m⁶ 13g 12g 11.1m⁴ 13f 17.1g a14g⁵ a14g³ a16.2g³ Dec 15] leggy gelding: fair at 3 yrs: poor in 1999: probably stays 2m: acts on fibresand, firm and soft going: visored (ran creditably) final start. *Martyn Wane*

SCOOP (IRE) 3 b.f. Scenic 128 – Big Story 50 (Cadeaux Genereux 131) [1998 **58 d** 66: 6d³ 6g* 7.5m³ 7f 8m⁴ 8d³ 7.9g 8d⁶ 1999 12m 8d⁴ 10s⁴ 9.2d⁶ 8.2m³ 8m⁴ 8g⁴ 8m 8f⁶ 13.8g³ 8d Oct 20] tall, quite good-topped filly: modest performer: stays 1¾m: acts on good to firm and good to soft going: visored (dropped out tamely) once at 2 yrs: joined G. M. Moore. *S. E. Kettlewell*

SCORCHED AIR 9 b.m. Elegant Air 119 – Misfire 56 (Gunner B 126) [1998 –: **–** a11g⁴ a16g a14g a14g 13.8g⁴ 16.2g 1999 a12f a16f 12g 10.5m Sep 3] has been to stud: formerly fair winner, little form since 1994 (tried visored): modest hurdler. *Mrs S. Lamyman*

SCOTLAND BAY 4 b.f. Then Again 126 – Down The Valley 73 (Kampala 120) **–** [1998 59, a66: a7g* a6g⁴ a7g² 6s³ 7g³ 7f⁴ 6.9m⁶ 7d 7s⁎ 7s a8f⁴ 1999 a7g a7g² a10f⁵ **a55** a7g⁴ a7g 7s 8f a7g a7g a7g Dec 8] good-topped filly: modest performer: barely stays 1m: acts on soft going and all-weather, probably on firm: tried visored: inconsistent. *P. Butler*

SCOTTIE YORK 3 b.g. Noble Patriarch 115 – Devon Dancer 73 (Shareef **49**
Dancer (USA) 135) [1998 NR 1999 9m⁴ 10f 9m³ 17.2g 9.9s⁵ Sep 21] leggy, workmanlike gelding: third foal: dam 2-y-o 7f winner who stayed 1m: poor maiden: stays
1¼m (pulled too hard at 17f): acts on soft and good to firm going. *T. D. Easterby*

SCOTTISH SPICE 2 b.f. (Feb 6) Selkirk (USA) 129 – Dilwara (IRE) (Lashkari **89 +**
128) [1999 7m⁶ 7f⁴ 7d* 7m* Sep 18] 19,000F: tall, leggy filly: first foal: dam French
10.5f winner: fairly useful performer: won maiden at Folkestone (tended to hang) in
August and nursery at Newbury (got up near finish to beat Travelling Lite a head) in
September: will stay 1m. *I. A. Balding*

SCOTTY GUEST (IRE) 2 b.c. (Apr 29) Distinctly North (USA) 115 – Tartan **85**
Lady (IRE) 88 (Taufan (USA) 119) [1999 8d 8d* Oct 27] IR 20,000F: tall, unfurnished colt: third foal: half-brother to Irish 1¼m winner Lady For Life (by Rainbows
For Life): dam 7f winner (at 2 yrs) and 9f winner in Ireland: much better effort in
maidens when making all at Yarmouth by 4 lengths from Proper Squire, kicking clear
3f out: not sure to stay beyond 1m: may do better. *G. G. Margarson*

SCRAGGYS DREAM (IRE) 3 ch.c. Shalford (IRE) 124§ – Massive Powder **92**
(Caerleon (USA) 132) [1998 –: 8s 1999 a10g* a10g² a10g* a10g* 12f 10.1g³ 10m
Sep 18] quite attractive colt: fairly useful performer: won maiden and handicaps at
Lingfield between January and March: best effort on turf when third of 6 in minor
event at Yarmouth: stays 1¼m: acts on equitrack: usually held up. *P. Mitchell*

SCROOGE (IRE) 3 b.g. Tirol 127 – Gay Appeal 76 (Star Appeal 133) [1998 –: **52**
7g 7d 7s 1999 6.1s 6g 5.9m⁶ 5.9g⁶ 6g 6g 7g 10d⁵ 10s Nov 1] robust gelding: poor
mover: modest maiden handicapper: seems to stay 1¼m: acts on good to firm and
good to soft going: visored final start: has looked none too keen. *M. H. Tompkins*

SCURRILOUS 4 ch.f. Sharpo 132 – Tea And Scandals (USA) (Key To The **46**
Kingdom (USA)) [1998 56: a6g² a6g⁵ a6g 1999 a6g a6g³ a6g⁵ a6g⁶ a5g³ a5g Mar 16]
poor maiden: likely to prove best at 5f/6f: no form on turf, raced mainly on all-
weather: usually races prominently. *J. L. Harris*

SEA-BELLE (IRE) 3 ch.f. Mukaddamah (USA) 125 – Blue Bell Lady 75 **52 d**
(Dunphy 124) [1998 75: 6g⁴ 6m³ 7m⁴ 7g 1999 a7g² a6g a9.4g 8.2s a7g 8.2m³ 12m
9.9m⁴ 8d 10.5m 10g Sep 20] modest maiden on all-weather, no form on turf: may prove
best at 7f/1m: acts on good to firm going and fibresand: tried visored/blinkered: has
carried head awkwardly and hung right: inconsistent. *J. G. Portman*

SEABOUND 3 b.f. Prince Sabo 123 – Shore Line 107 (High Line 125) [1998 NR **65**
1999 6.1f 7m 8.3s⁴ Aug 9] half-sister to several winners, including very smart
performer (best at 7f/1m) Soviet Line (by Soviet Star) and useful middle-distance
performers Mamdooh (by Green Desert) and South Shore (by Caerleon): dam, 7f
winner at 2 yrs and fourth in Oaks, sister to Park Hill winner Quay Line: best effort in
maidens when fourth at Windsor (reluctant stalls), held when losing footing close
home: stays 1m well: slowly away first 2 starts. *J. R. Fanshawe*

SEA DANZIG 6 ch.g. Roi Danzig (USA) – Tosara 84 (Main Reef 126) [1998 70, **64**
a80: a12s⁴ a10g* a10g* a10g² a10g⁴ a10g⁵ 10m 9m* 9g⁶ 12m⁴ 9.7f* 9d 10f⁵ 8.1m³ **a72**
8g² 8m 9.9s 10d 1999 a10g⁵ a10g⁵ 10.8d 11.6d⁶ 10m³ 10s² 9.9m 10.2m³ 10m 10m²
10s 12m⁴ 10m³ 10.1m* 9.9v a8.5g 10f Oct 20] big, plain gelding: fair handicapper:
won at Epsom in September: probably best around 1¼m: possibly unsuited by heavy
going, acts on any other turf/all-weather: usually races prominently. *J. J. Bridger*

SEA-DEER 10 ch.g. Hadeer 118 – Hi-Tech Girl 98 (Homeboy 114) [1998 77, a–: **90**
6d 6d⁶ 6g⁴ 7g⁶ 6d⁴ 6m³ 6f³ 7m 6m* 6m 6m⁴ 6m³ 5.7m 5.2g 6g 6s 7s⁵ 1999 6g⁴ 6g 6m
6g² 6m⁴ 6m 7f⁴ 7m³ 6d 6m³ 7f⁴ 7g* 7d* 7v 7d Oct 9] strong, deep-girthed gelding:
fairly useful performer: won seller and apprentice handicap at Yarmouth on consecutive days in September: effective at 6f/7f: acts on fibresand, firm and good to soft
going, probably on soft: has been bandaged. *C. A. Dwyer*

SEA DRIFT (FR) 2 gr.f. (Mar 14) Warning 136 – Night At Sea 107 (Night Shift **53 p**
(USA)) [1999 6.1m Aug 28] sixth foal: sister to 4-y-o Nautical Warning and half-
sister to 2 winners, including 7-y-o Muhandis: dam sprinter: joint favourite but green,
seventh of 13 to Shuruk in maiden at Nottingham, some late headway after slow start:
will stay 7f, probably 1m: sure to do better. *L. M. Cumani*

SEA EMPEROR   2 br.g. (Jan 13) Emperor Jones (USA) 119 – Blumarin (IRE)   **53**
(Scenic 128) [1999 6d 6m 6d Aug 5] 23,000F, 16,000Y: leggy gelding: first foal:
dam, German 11f winner, half-sister to dam of very smart 7f/1m winner Wizard
King: modest maiden: should stay at least 1m. *Mrs G. S. Rees*

SEA FIG   4 gr.f. Robellino (USA) 127 – Aimee Jane (USA) 76 (Our Native (USA))
[1998 56, a62: a8.5g⁶ a6g² 7s a6g 6d a8g 7g² 8g 7s 5.9d² 7g 6g 6g 5.9d 5g⁶ a7s a10f
1999 10.2g 9.9m Jun 24] workmanlike filly: modest maiden handicapper: best efforts
at 6f, doesn't stay 1¼m: acts on fibresand, raced mainly on good ground or softer on
turf: tried blinkered: often a front runner. *S. G. Knight*

SEA FREEDOM   8 b.h. Slip Anchor 136 – Rostova 91 (Blakeney 126) [1998 75:   **64**
16v⁴ 16.4s³ 14.1d³ 16g⁶ 20d³ 18s* 16g 16.2d 18g 16.5d⁴ 1999 18d⁴ 16g 16m 16.4s³
12g⁵ 20m 16.4m Jul 3] strong, workmanlike horse: modest handicapper: best efforts
in 1999 when in frame at Doncaster and Sandown in the spring: stays 2½m well:
probably acts on any ground: usually visored. *G. B. Balding*

SEA GOD   8 ch.g. Rainbow Quest (USA) 134 – Sea Pageant (Welsh Pageant 132)   **–**
[1998 –: a11g⁶ a12g a14g 12d 12.3v 12m 14.1f 1999 10.1g a11g Dec 13] one-time
modest performer: no form since 1997. *M. C. Chapman*

SEAGREEN (IRE)   2 b.f. (Apr 30) Green Desert (USA) 127 – Ocean Ballad 104
(Grundy 137) [1999 6d 8.2m⁶ Aug 23] 31,000Y: seventh foal: half-sister to 8-y-o
Frozen Sea: dam 1½m winner from family of 6-y-o Indigenous: tailed off in minor
events at Haydock and Nottingham. *Mrs A. L. M. King*

SEA HAZE   2 ch.g. (Mar 27) Emarati (USA) 74 – Unveiled 76 (Sayf El Arab   **70**
(USA) 127) [1999 5m 5m⁶ 6d 5.7f* 6m⁵ 6d³ 6m⁴ 6m Sep 10] 5,000F, 9,000Y: third
foal: half-brother to 4-y-o Kathies Pet and 3-y-o Unmasked: dam 5f (at 2 yrs) to 7f
winner: fair performer: won maiden at Bath in June: creditable efforts next 3 starts:
will stay 7f: acts on firm and good to soft going: sweating (stiff task, well beaten)
final outing: joined R. Baker. *R. J. Hodges*

SEA ISLE   3 ch.f. Selkirk (USA) 129 – Miss Blitz 83 (Formidable (USA) 125)   **73**
[1998 NR 1999 7m⁵ 8m⁶ 8s³ 7g⁵ 8d Oct 26] 49,000Y: workmanlike filly: seventh
foal: half-sister to fairly useful 5f to 7f winner Berge (by Most Welcome) and a
winner in Hong Kong by Alzao: dam 6f winner from family of Mummy's Pet and
College Chapel: fair maiden: may prove best up to 1m: acts on good to firm going
(below form both starts on softer than good). *I. A. Balding*

SEALED BY FATE (IRE)   4 b.g. Mac's Imp (USA) 116 – Fairy Don (Don 128)   **67**
[1998 57, a50: a7s⁴ a6g³ a6g⁶ a7g³ 6.1s 5m 6d 5.9g 5m² 5s⁴ 5g³ 5m⁶ 5m 1999 5d   **a–**
5g³ 6f 5m² 5m³ 5m² 5g* 5g² 5g⁶ 5m 5g⁴ 6f⁶ 5m⁴ 5m² 5d⁶ 5g 6g 6d Oct 9] big,
workmanlike gelding: fair on turf, modest on all-weather: won apprentice handicap
at Carlisle in June: has form at 7f but races mainly at 5f nowadays: acts on fibresand
and good to firm ground, probably not on soft: usually visored/blinkered: best in
strongly-run race. *J. S. Wainwright*

SEA MARK   3 gr.c. Warning 136 – Mettlesome (Lomond (USA) 128) [1998 89p: **79 +**
6g 6m² 1999 7d* Oct 11] big, rangy colt: has a round action: fairly useful form: didn't
need to reproduce best to win apprentice maiden at Leicester only 3-y-o start: will
stay 1m: yet to race on extremes of going. *B. W. Hills*

SEA MINSTREL   3 b.f. Sea Raven (IRE) 75 – Give Us A Treat (Cree Song 99)
[1998 56: 5g⁵ 5d 6f 6m³ 5m⁴ 7.9g 6m 1999 6f 8f 6f 6f 10m 12g 5s Nov 2] workmanlike filly: modest maiden: well beaten in 1999: stays 6f: acts on firm going.
M. E. Sowersby

SEAMUS   5 ch.g. Almoojid 69 – Royal Celerity (USA) (Riverman (USA) 131)   **–**
[1998 NR 1999 17.2f Jun 26] sturdy gelding: no form. *A. G. Newcombe*

SEA PICTURE (IRE)   3 b.f. Royal Academy (USA) 130 – Grecian Sea (FR) 107   **82**
(Homeric 133) [1998 77p: 7d² 1999 10s⁶ 10.4d⁵ 7.9d 8m⁵ Jun 26] tall, leggy, quite
good-topped filly: good mover: fairly useful maiden: best efforts at York (over 16
lengths fifth of 6 in Musidora Stakes) on second start and Sandown (handicap) on
final: bred to stay 1½m, but races freely. *Sir Michael Stoute*

SEASAME PARK   2 b.f. (Mar 23) Elmaamul (USA) 125 – Holyrood Park   **41**
(Sharrood (USA) 124) [1999 6.1g³ a6g² a7g* 7d⁴ 8m a7g² a8g Nov 12] 1,500Y: neat   **a50**

filly: second foal: half-sister to 3-y-o Forest Grey: dam unraced: modest performer on all-weather, poor on turf: raced only in selling events, winning at Wolverhampton in June: stays 7f, seemingly not 1m: acts on fibresand: races prominently. *B. Palling*

SEASON OF HOPE   3 ch.f. Komaite (USA) – Honour And Glory 46 (Hotfoot 126) [1998 –: 6m⁵ 7f 7m 1999 a9.4g³ a9.4g 8m 10m 12g⁵ 10f⁵ a10g⁴ Jul 24] lengthy filly: poor maiden: stays 1¼m: acts on fibresand and good to firm going: blinkered/visored first 3 starts. *D. E. Cantillon*   **41**

SEA SPOUSE   8 ch.g. Jalmood (USA) 126 – Bambolona 108 (Bustino 136) [1998 40, a75: a8g a8g² a8g* a8g⁴ 6.9d³ a8g 8g a8g⁵ 11.6d⁶ a8g* a8g* a8.5g² a8g a9.4g³ 10g 8d 1999 a9.4g a10g 8f a9.4g a8.5g⁴ a7g a11g³ a8g a10g² a9.4g³ a12g⁶ 8.1m a11g⁶ 9.9v a8g Oct 8] workmanlike gelding: modest on all-weather, poor on turf: effective at 1m/easy 1¼m: acts on all-weather, best turf efforts on good going or softer: often races prominently. *M. Blanshard*   **– a59**

SEA SQUIRT (IRE)   2 b.g. (Apr 29) Fourstars Allstar (USA) 122 – Polynesian Goddess (IRE) (Salmon Leap (USA) 131) [1999 8g⁶ 7s² a8g² Dec 17] 8,000F, 12,000Y: fourth foal: half-brother to 4-y-o Jay Gee and German 11f winner Casito (by Law Society): dam third at 7f in Ireland: fair form when runner-up in maidens at Catterick and Southwell: will stay 1¼m. *M. Johnston*   **76**

SEATTLE ALLEY (USA)   6 b.g. Seattle Dancer (USA) 119 – Alyanaabi (USA) 74 (Roberto (USA) 131) [1998 NR 1999 10.2g May 21] good-topped gelding: easy mover: fair handicapper in 1997: well beaten only 6-y-o start: probably stays 1½m: acts on good to firm ground and equitrack. *P. R. Webber*   **–**

SEATTLE ART (USA)   5 b.g. Seattle Slew (USA) – Artiste 95 (Artaius (USA) 129) [1998 NR 1999 13.1g⁶ 12d⁶ Sep 26] big gelding: fairly useful maiden for H. Cecil in 1997 (best run at 1½m on good to soft ground): soundly beaten both starts at 5 yrs. *P. Monteith*   **–**

SEA WAVE (IRE)   4 b.c. Sadler's Wells (USA) 132 – Three Tails 121 (Blakeney 126) [1998 124: 12d² 10g* 11.8d* 11.9f* 12s 12d 1999 12m³ 12m⁴ 12m³ Dec 12] strong, angular colt: type to carry condition: fluent mover: very smart performer in

Godolphin's "Sea Wave"

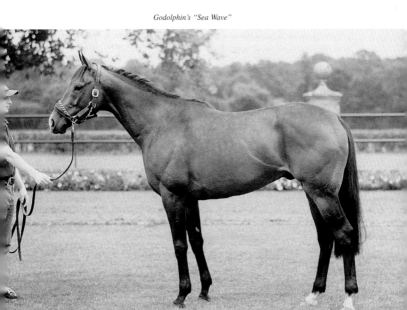

1998, winner of Great Voltigeur Stakes: bit below that form at 4 yrs when in frame behind Fruits of Love in Hardwicke Stakes at Royal Ascot, Craigsteel in Princess of Wales's Stakes at Newmarket and Borgia (beaten ¾ length after setting steady pace) in Hong Kong Vase at Sha Tin: will stay 1¾m: acts on firm and good to soft ground: tongue tied in 1999: ducked left and unseated rider leaving stalls penultimate 3-y-o start: temperament under suspicion. *Saeed bin Suroor*

SEA YA MAITE 5 b.g. Komaite (USA) – Marina Plata (Julio Mariner 127) [1998 53, a72: a8g a7g³ 6g a8g* 7d a8g³ 9m³ 10.4g 12g 9.9m a8g⁴ a8.5g a9.4g 1999 a7g² a8g⁶ a6g a9.4g⁶ a6g a7g 8d 8g a8.5g⁵ 8.5g a9.4g a8g² a7g* a7g a11g a8g Dec 13] tall, rangy gelding: fair handicapper: won at Southwell in November: best at 7f/1m: acts on fibresand, lightly raced and little form on turf recently: tried blinkered: has worn tongue strap. *S. R. Bowring*   **a69**

SEAZUN (IRE) 2 b.f. (Apr 29) Zieten (USA) 118 – Sunset Cafe (IRE) 68 (Red Sunset 120) [1999 5g⁶ 5.3f* 6m² 6d* Sep 28]   **110**

West Ilsley stables, from where Dick Hern sent out fifteen of his sixteen British classic winners, will be the base in the next season of Mick Channon. While Channon himself has yet to train a classic winner, it's surely only a matter of time before he does. Hopes that Bint Allayl, the best juvenile filly of 1998, would become Channon's first were cruelly dashed when she fractured a shoulder on the gallops in February. Now he has another contender for the One Thousand Guineas—the last classic won by a West Ilsley representative, Harayir in 1995—in Seazun.

Seazun has won two of her four starts to date, notably the Shadwell Stud Cheveley Park Stakes at Newmarket, a race in which Harayir finished third. Like the majority of her trainer's juveniles, Seazun improved a great deal for her first run, and a couple of weeks later she easily won a maiden at Brighton in April. Sore shins then kept her off the course until September, and she was stepped up markedly in class on return. Backed at long odds, Seazun left her previous form well behind in finishing a half-length second to the subsequent Middle Park winner Primo Valentino in a listed race at Kempton, a performance which made her well worth her place in the Cheveley Park field. Her thirteen opponents at Newmarket included the French-trained pair Mall Queen and Moon Driver, and it was the latter, winner of the Prix d'Arenberg on her previous start, who was sent off favourite at 5/2 after Warrior Queen was withdrawn at the start. Next in the betting at 9/2 came the unbeaten three-time

Shadwell Stud Cheveley Park Stakes, Newmarket—
Seazun is a game winner from Torgau, Crimplene and Seraphina

winner Elaflaak, followed by Torgau, winner of the Cherry Hinton Stakes over the course and distance, at 11/2. Seazun, a 10/1-shot, settled well in a race run at a steady pace early on, whereas several others, including Elaflaak, went too freely. The field split into two groups of seven, Torgau leading those racing towards the stand side, who included Seazun and looked to have a decided advantage over the far side. Asked for her effort when the pace was stepped up at halfway, Seazun quickened well to edge ahead entering the final furlong and, pushed along vigorously, ran on gamely to hold the rallying Torgau by a head. The pair had the finish to themselves, pulling two and a half lengths clear of third-placed Crimplene, who in turn was a length and a half ahead of the fourth, Seraphina. Moon Driver, who raced in the far group, was soon outpaced and never threatened. At best it was an average running of the Cheveley Park. However, it still required a smart performance to win it, and, as there's a fair chance that she'll prove effective at a mile, Seazun has to be on the short-list for the One Thousand Guineas. All being well, she's likely to be seen in the Fred Darling Stakes at Newbury before then.

Seazun (IRE) (b.f. Apr 29, 1997)	Zieten (USA) (b 1990)	Danzig (b 1977)	Northern Dancer / Pas de Nom
		Blue Note (b 1985)	Habitat / Balsamique
	Sunset Cafe (IRE) (b 1990)	Red Sunset (b 1979)	Red God / Centre Piece
		Cafe Au Lait (ch 1968)	Espresso / Blue Sash

Seazun's sire Zieten (also responsible for the Cheveley Park runner-up Torgau) showed his best form at up to seven furlongs, though he did land the odds in a slowly-run race over a mile; her dam Sunset Cafe was just a fair performer in Ireland who gained her sole win in a mile and a half maiden, and she was usually blinkered. Sunset Cafe is a sister to the Prix Foy winner Beeshi, who was suited by a mile and a half, and she is a half-sister to the useful ten- and twelve-furlong performer Chaumiere, successful in two Magnet Cups at York, and to the dam of the very smart six-year-old Insatiable. Their dam Cafe Au Lait was a fairly useful winner who stayed middle distances. She is out of the useful two-year-old six-furlong winner Blue Sash, a daughter of the leading 1955 two-year-old Star of India and grandam of the 1977 One Thousand Guineas winner Mrs McArdy. Seazun, a 60,000-guinea yearling, is the third foal and second winner of Sunset Cafe. Her first, the fair handicapper Pipe Music, won over two miles in the latest season; her second, a colt by Thatching called Hamadeen, is unraced. A rather leggy, quite attractive individual and a good walker, Seazun acts on firm and good to soft ground. With such an able filly in his team, Seazun's trainer has good reason to be optimistic about his first season in his new surroundings. *M. R. Channon*

SECOND EMPIRE (IRE)   4 b.c. Fairy King (USA) – Welsh Love (Ela-Mana-Mou 132) [1998 124: 8m³ 12m 8m* 8s³ 8g³ 8f⁶ 1999 10.5g⁶ 7g Jun 9] rangy, good-topped colt: very smart at best: unbeaten in 3 races at 2 yrs, including Grand Criterium at Longchamp: won Desmond Stakes at the Curragh and third in 3 Group 1 events in 1998, including Irish 2,000 Guineas at the Curragh and Queen Elizabeth II Stakes at Ascot: reportedly finished lame when well below form in Tattersalls Gold Cup (sweating and edgy) at the Curragh and Ballycorus Stakes at Leopardstown in 1999: best at 1m: acted on soft and good to firm going: looked a difficult ride (pulled hard and also tended to carry head awkwardly): reported in June to have had recurrence of muscle problem in hind-quarters: to stand at Coolmore, Co. Tipperary, Ireland, fee IR 8,000 gns. *A. P. O'Brien, Ireland*   –

SECOND PAIGE (IRE)   2 b.g. (Apr 25) Nicolotte 118 – My First Paige (IRE) 53 (Runnett 125) [1999 7.1m a8.5g 7g Oct 19] IR 14,000Y: tall, lightly-made gelding: second foal: half-brother to 3-y-o Sweet As A Nut: dam, 6f seller winner, ran only at 2 yrs: modest maiden: will probably stay 1m. *N. A. Graham*   55 ?

SECONDS AWAY 8 b.g. Hard Fought 125 – Keep Mum 63 (Mummy's Pet 125) **41**
[1998 41, a–: 8d 8s⁵ 8g* 8g³ 9.1d³ 10g 8m 8.3s 1999 5d 9g 8g² 10.3m² 9.2f³ 8f 8f
11.1m³ 9.2m² 8.3f 9.2m Sep 6] small gelding: poor performer: stays 1¼m: acts on
good to firm and good to soft going: tried blinkered/visored. *J. S. Goldie*

SECOND TERM (IRE) 4 b.f. Second Set (IRE) 127 – Trinida (Jaazeiro (USA) **–**
127) [1998 50: 8s 8s⁴ 9.9d² 13m 12g 9.9m 8.3s 1999 a11f a12g⁶ Feb 22] modest
maiden handicapper at best: stays 1¼m: acts on good to soft going, well held on
all-weather: visored final start. *W. Storey*

SECOND TIME AROUND (IRE) 2 b.f. (Apr 12) Mukaddamah (USA) 125 – **35**
Up The Gates (Captain James 123) [1999 a5g 5g 7g 6g 7m 6f 6.1m³ 7g Oct 15]
IR 1,400Y: half-sister to several winners, including 3-y-o Prideway and a winner in
Denmark up to 1½m by Flash of Steel: dam unraced: poor form, often in sellers.
M. C. Chapman

SECOND WIND 4 ch.g. Kris 135 – Rimosa's Pet 109 (Petingo 135) [1998 88d: **78**
8.2g⁵ 7m⁵ 6f² 5.1d 7m 6f⁶ 7g 6s 1999 8m 7m 6m⁶ 6g⁶ 5f 7f* 7m⁸ 8h 8m 5m 7f⁶ 7s³
7d 7s⁴ Oct 23] lengthy, workmanlike gelding: unimpressive mover: fair performer:
won claimer at Brighton (final start for Gay Kelleway) and handicap at Epsom in
July: stays 7f, not 1m: yet to race on heavy going: acts on any other: has had tongue
tied: often races up with pace: has hung badly right. *C. A. Dwyer*

SECRET AGENT 2 b.c. (Mar 15) Machiavellian (USA) 123 – Secret Obsession **89 p**
(USA) 89 (Secretariat (USA)) [1999 7.7d* 7d² Oct 26] tall, quite attractive colt:
closely related to 1995 2-y-o 6f winner Obsessive (by Seeking The Gold), later useful
at 1¼m, and to a winner in USA by Woodman, and half-brother to 3 winners, including 3-y-o Secret's Out: dam, 1¼m winner, half-sister to smart 1½m performer
Beyton: fairly useful form: won maiden at Warwick in September: length second of 7
to Osood in minor event at Redcar following month, still looking green under
pressure: should stay 1¼m: remains capable of better. *Sir Michael Stoute*

SECRET ARCHIVE 4 b.g. Salse (USA) 128 – Lycia (USA) (Lyphard (USA) **93**
132) [1998 109: 12f* 12g⁴ 11.9m⁵ 12d 11m* 14.1g² 14m² 1999 12m 13.3d⁶ 12.3d³
12m 12m⁵ 14f 12g⁵ Aug 14] quite good-topped gelding: useful in 1998, fairly useful
at 4 yrs: best efforts when mid-division in valuable handicaps at Royal Ascot
(visored) and Goodwood on fourth and penultimate starts: likely to stay 2m: acts on
firm going, well held on softer than good: has been bandaged in front: usually races
up with pace: gelded at end of season. *R. Hannon*

SECRETARIO 2 b.f. (Feb 12) Efisio 120 – Lucidity 67 (Vision (USA)) [1999 6m **55**
7d Oct 20] first foal: dam 1m winner who stayed 1½m: modest form when seventh of
13 to Melanzana in maiden at Redcar on debut, but well held in similar event at
Newcastle following month: likely to stay 1m. *C. W. Thornton*

SECRET CONQUEST 2 b.f. (Mar 23) Secret Appeal – Mohibbah (USA) 86 **80**
(Conquistador Cielo (USA)) [1999 6m³ 6g 5.9m 6d* 7m² 7m* 6f² 6g* 6m 6d Sep 17]
600Y: strong, close-coupled filly: seventh foal: sister to 4-y-o Park Royal: dam 2-y-o
5f winner: fair performer: won seller at Haydock and 2 nurseries at Catterick in the
summer: well held final start: stays 7f: acts on firm and good to soft going: front
runner. *D. W. Barker*

SECRET DELL (IRE) 3 b.g. Doyoun 124 – Summer Silence (USA) (Stop The **75**
Music (USA)) [1998 –: 8d 7s⁶ 7d 1999 9.7s² 12.3d⁶ 12g³ 11.4m⁴ 12m⁴ 14.1g⁶ 16.4d*
17.5d Sep 17] rather sparely-made gelding: fair handicapper: won apprentice race at
Folkestone in August: ran creditably when in frame otherwise: stays 2m well: acts on
soft and good to firm ground: sold 18,000 gns, joined J. Spearing. *E. A. L. Dunlop*

SECRET DESTINY (USA) 2 b.f. (Jan 29) Cozzene (USA) – Dramatrix (USA) **83 p**
(Forty Niner (USA)) [1999 7f 7d³ 7d³ Oct 30] $100,000Y: close-coupled, quite
attractive filly: has a quick action: first foal: dam, won at up to 1¼m in USA, closely
related to US Grade 1 1m winner Aptostar: fairly useful maiden: trained by
P. Chapple-Hyam on debut: would have gone close to winning with clear run when
third of 16 to Premier Prize in steadily-run event at Newmarket final start: should
stay 1¼m: capable of better still. *A. G. Foster*

SECRET DROP 3 b.f. Bustino 136 – Safe House 81§ (Lyphard (USA) 132) **74**
[1998 NR 1999 11.5m⁶ 8m 10v³ a12g⁶ 12d Oct 29] angular filly: half-sister to several

winners, including 1988 2-y-o 1m winner Ivory Tower (by Shirley Heights) and 9f seller winner Northern Rainbow (by Rainbow Quest): dam, temperamental, won at 10.8f: fair maiden: should stay at least 1½m: acts on heavy going, ran respectably on fibresand. *K. McAuliffe*

SECRET RENDEZVOUS (IRE) 2 br.f. (Jan 30) Petong 126 – Heaven-Liegh-Grey 90 (Grey Desire 115) [1999 5.7g 5.1d⁶ 6.8m 6g Sep 20] 9,500Y: fourth foal: sister to 3-y-o Megs Pearl and half-sister to 4-y-o French Connection and a winner in Denmark by Timeless Times: dam, out of half-sister to Lochnager, best at 5f: modest maiden: best effort penultimate start: should stay 7f: tongue tied second start. *A. T. Murphy* **54**

SECRET SAVER (USA) 4 ch.c. Green Dancer (USA) 132 – Vachti (FR) 114 (Crystal Palace (FR) 132) [1998 108p: 8s 11.1d* 10.2f² 12.4d* 1999 10s⁵ 13.4m² 12m⁵ 12m 12m³ 12d⁴ 12v⁴ Oct 23] angular, attractive colt: usually looks well: useful performer: ran well in 1999 in Ormonde Stakes at Chester (neck second to Sadian), Hardwicke Stakes at Royal Ascot (tongue tied, fifth to Fruits of Love) and listed race at Newmarket (fourth to Kahtan) on second, third and penultimate starts: better at 1½m/13f than shorter: acts on good to firm and soft ground: has worn net muzzle in parade/been taken early to post: looks difficult ride, and one to treat with some caution: sold 105,000 gns, sent to USA. *Sir Michael Stoute* **109 §**

SECRET'S OUT 3 b.g. Polish Precedent (USA) 131 – Secret Obsession (USA) 89 (Secretariat (USA)) [1998 86: 7m² 7m² 8.1m² 8g² 1999 10m* 12.3m 9g May 18] leggy, quite good-topped gelding: fairly useful performer: won 17-runner maiden at Windsor in April by short head from Montalcino, making most: disappointing in handicaps after, finding little in visor final start: stays 1¼m: raced only on good/good to firm going: sold 26,000 gns, joined J. Quinn. *Sir Michael Stoute* **90**

SECRET SPICE 2 br.g. (Feb 27) Dilum (USA) 115 – Ancient Secret (Warrshan (USA) 117) [1999 a6g*¹ 8v a6f* a6f* Dec 21] first foal: dam unraced half-sister to smart stayer Primitive Rising: had different trainer for each start, but won 3 times, seller at Wolverhampton in September (for J. Eustace) and, after leaving S. Williams, 2 claimers at Calder in December (for J. Calascibetta on first occasion): should stay 7f+: acts on dirt/all-weather. *J. Canet, USA* **72 +**

SECRET SPRING (FR) 7 b.g. Dowsing (USA) 124 – Nordica 99 (Northfields (USA)) [1998 95: 8g⁶ 9.7m² 8.5g² 8g⁵ 10m* 9.9g⁶ 10.2m² 9g 1999 a8g 10m 12g² 10m² 9.9f⁴ 9g⁴ 8d a8g* a8g a10g² a8g* a8g* Dec 18] leggy gelding: useful performer on all-weather, fairly useful on turf: won 2 handicaps and a minor event, all at Lingfield, in November/December: best at 1m to 1¼m: acts on firm ground and equitrack: usually held up: consistent. *Mrs L. Richards* **87 a98**

SECRET STYLE 4 b.g. Shirley Heights 130 – Rosie Potts 83 (Shareef Dancer (USA) 135) [1998 77: 11s* 11g³ 12m⁴ 11.6m⁴ 1999 14.1s 14.1m⁶ 13.9s 14m 14.4g⁴ 16f⁶ Jun 21] lengthy, quite good-topped gelding: fairly useful performer: won claimer at Nottingham in June and handicap (for Mrs A. Malzard) in Jersey following month: stays 2m: acts on firm going. *E. A. L. Dunlop* **86**

SECRET TANGO 4 ch.f. Interrex (CAN) – Seymour Ann (Krayyan 117) [1998 –: a6g 1999 a6g a6g⁶ a8g 8.1m 7f⁶ 7m⁶ 7.1m Aug 5] poor maiden: stays 7f: acts on firm ground. *J. R. Best* **28**

SECRET TREASURE 3 b.f. Dilum (USA) 115 – Surprise Surprise 91 (Robellino (USA) 127) [1998 –p: 6m 6.1d 7d 1999 7s 7m⁶ 10g 8s⁵ 7d Oct 11] leggy filly: modest maiden: probably stays 1m, not 1¼m: acts on soft and good to firm going: sold 2,500 gns, sent to Czech Republic. *H. Candy* **59**

SEDONA (IRE) 2 b.g. (May 24) Namaqualand (USA) – Talahari (IRE) (Roi Danzig (USA)) [1999 5g 6g Aug 21] IR 9,000Y: second foal: dam lightly raced in Ireland: well beaten in maidens. *Andrew Turnell* **–**

SEDRAH (USA) 3 ch.f. Dixieland Band (USA) – Madame Secretary (USA) (Secretariat (USA)) [1998 76: 7m⁵ 7m⁶ 1999 9g² 9m⁴ 12m* 12m⁵ Jul 30] sturdy, angular filly: fairly useful performer: won 5-runner maiden at Catterick in June: raced freely and reportedly finished distressed final start: stays 1½m: raced only on good/good to firm ground: sent to USA. *E. A. L. Dunlop* **82**

SEEK   3 br.c. Rainbow Quest (USA) 134 – Souk (IRE) 98 (Ahonoora 122) [1998 **88 p**
NR 1999 12.3m² 12d* Jul 6] 50,000Y: fourth foal: half-brother to several winners,
including 10.5f winner Shouk (by Shirley Heights) and smart middle-distance stayer
Puce (by Darshaan): dam, 7f winner better at 1m, out of half-sister to dam of Doyoun:
shaped most promisingly in maiden at Ripon on debut: easily landed odds in similar
event at Pontefract following month by 1¾ lengths from Salestria, smooth headway
to lead 3f out and eased considerably: will stay beyond 1½m: looked capable of a
good deal better. *L. M. Cumani*

SEEKING SANCTUARY   2 ch.f. (Mar 29) Most Welcome 131 – Tjakka (USA) **–**
(Little Missouri (USA)) [1999 7d Oct 11] first reported foal: dam unraced: always
behind in maiden at Leicester. *Dr J. D. Scargill*

SEEKING UTOPIA   2 b.f. (Mar 6) Wolfhound (USA) 126 – Sakura Queen (IRE) **76**
52 (Woodman (USA) 126) [1999 7m³ 7f² 7f² 7.1g* 8f² 8d 8d⁵ Oct 15] 12,000F,
6,500Y: fluent mover: third foal: half-sister to 2 winners by Shareef Dancer, including 1½m winner Reine Cerise: dam, maiden who stayed 1¼m, out of half-sister
to Riverman: fair performer: won maiden at Musselburgh in August: good efforts
in nurseries 2 of last 3 starts: stays 1m: acts on firm and good to soft going.
S. P. C. Woods

SEE YOU LATER   2 b.f. (Mar 17) Emarati (USA) 74 – Rivers Rhapsody 104 **87**
(Dominion 123) [1999 5m* 5.2g³ 6m³ Sep 2] third foal: half-sister to 5-y-o For Your
Eyes Only: dam sprinter: fairly useful form: won maiden at Sandown in June by 5
lengths: third in listed race at Newbury then minor event at Salisbury after, taking
strong hold in latter: likely to prove best at 5f/6f. *Major D. N. Chappell*

SEFTON BLAKE   5 b.g. Roscoe Blake 120 – Rainbow Lady 65 (Jaazeiro (USA) **–**
127) [1998 –: 12m 1999 a14g Nov 12] lengthy, workmanlike gelding: lightly raced
and no form on Flat since 1997, though successful 3 times over hurdles in 1999: tried
visored. *R. Simpson*

SEGAVIEW (IRE)   3 b.g. Scenic 128 – Little Sega (FR) (Bellypha 130) [1998 **77**
58?: 7s 7f 7.5m⁴ 8g⁶ 1999 10g⁴ 9.9g 12.3d² 11.9d* 12.3m 11.9m 11.8d⁶ Oct 11]
smallish, workmanlike gelding: has a round action: fair performer: runner-up in
handicap at Ripon before justifying favouritism in 5-runner maiden at York in June
easily by 5 lengths: below form after: will stay beyond 1½m: acts on good to soft
going. *Mrs P. Sly*

SEIGNORIAL (USA)   4 b.c. Kingmambo (USA) 125 – Suavite (USA) (Alleged **92**
(USA) 138) [1998 102: 12s* 12.3g⁵ 11.9m 14g* 13.4d 15d⁶ 15v* 1999 12m 15.5g
14m⁶ 13.9f 16f Jul 29] leggy, lightly-made colt: useful at 3 yrs, fairly useful in 1999
(mostly stiff tasks): should be suited by 2m+: acts on heavy ground: blinkered twice:
lazy sort: sent to USA. *P. W. Chapple-Hyam*

SELECT EQUINAME   4 b.g. Soviet Star (USA) 128 – Dame Ashfield 90 **49**
(Grundy 137) [1998 NR 1999 12.4g⁵ 16m⁵ 12.1s⁵ 16m 12g 16d² 14.1m Jul 16]
13,000Y: half-brother to several winners, including stayers Rosina Mae (by Rousillon) and Shirley Sue (by Shirley Heights): dam 1½m winner out of Park Hill winner
African Dancer: poor handicapper: stayed 2m: acted on good to soft going: visored
(well beaten) once: dead. *D. Eddy*

SELFISH   5 ch.m. Bluebird (USA) 125 – Sariza 79 (Posse (USA) 130) [1998 89: **111**
7m* 1999 8m² 7.6m* 7f* 8.1m² 7m² 7m² 7s³ Oct 23] strong, good-bodied mare: easy
mover: smart performer: better than ever in 1999, winning minor event at Lingfield
and listed race at Goodwood, both in July, latter by head from Wannabe Grand: ran at
least respectably after, including when runner-up in listed races at Sandown (behind
Etizaaz) and Epsom (beaten head by Tumbleweed Ridge): stayed 1m: acted on firm
going: visits Daylami. *H. R. A. Cecil*

SELHURSTPARK FLYER (IRE)   8 b.g. Northiam (USA) – Wisdom To **90 d**
Know (Bay Express 132) [1998 110: 6d 6s⁴ 6d⁶ 6m* 6d* 6g 6m⁶ 6s 1999 6d⁶ 6d⁶ 6g⁶
6d 6m 6m 6m Sep 1] leggy, workmanlike gelding: smart handicapper at best: won
Wokingham at Royal Ascot at 6 and 7 yrs: well below form in 1999: races solely at 6f
nowadays: acts on any ground: below form in blinkers/visor in 1994: usually bandaged: races up with pace. *J. Berry*

SELIANA   3 b.f. Unfuwain (USA) 131 – Anafi 95 (Slip Anchor 136) [1998 –p: 7d **79 p**
1999 12s³ Nov 2] strong, lengthy filly: has scope: better effort in maidens 12 months

apart when third at Catterick only 3-y-o start: always handy: will stay 1¾m: withdrawn after giving trouble stalls intended reappearance: should do better still. *G. Wragg*

SELKING (IRE)   2 ch.c. (Apr 20) Selkirk (USA) 129 – Stay That Way (Be My   **93**
Guest (USA) 126) [1999 5m³ 6g⁴ 5m* 5g³ 5d⁴ 6g a6g² Oct 13] 15,000Y: brother to
fairly useful German 1m winner Susi Wong, closely related to fairly useful 1m
winner Delirious Moment (by Kris), and half-brother to 3 winners, including 3-y-o
Red May: dam unraced half-sister to high-class miler Chalon: fairly useful performer: won maiden at Carlisle in June: in frame in listed races at Sandown and Ayr next
2 outings: headstrong, and may prove best at 5f: acts on fibresand, yet to race on
extremes of going on turf. *K. R. Burke*

SELKIRK ROSE (IRE)   4 b.f. Pips Pride 117 – Red Note (Rusticaro (FR) 124)   **63**
[1998 72§: 8m⁴ 7m 8.1g⁴ 7s⁶ 7g 7.1g⁴ 7g 7s 5s⁵ 1999 a5g a6g a5g⁴ a6g a6s a5g a5g   **a66**
6.1s⁴ 5.9m 7m⁴ 7.5d 6s⁴ 6.1f* 5.9g² 6m 7m⁴ 7m 6g⁶ 6.1m³ 7g⁶ 7d Oct 12] modest
handicapper: won 20-runner race at Nottingham in June: has form at 1m, seems best
at 6f nowadays: acts on firm going, soft and fibresand: blinkered/visored once each:
sometimes starts very slowly: has flashed tail: not one to trust implicitly. *J. G. Given*

SELTON HILL (IRE)   2 b.g. (May 2) Bin Ajwaad (IRE) 119 – Ivory Gull (USA)   **62**
80 (Storm Bird (CAN) 134) [1999 8.5m⁻ 8.2m⁵ 7.7d⁶ 8m⁴ 8d⁴ Oct 29] 33,000F,
56,000Y: useful-looking gelding: seventh foal: half-brother to 3-y-o Lennox, 11f
winner Mister Kite (by Damister) and a winner in USA by Local Suitor: dam, 2-y-o
6f winner who became disappointing, also winner to Bluebird: modest maiden: should stay
1¼m: yet to race on extremes of going. *N. A. Callaghan*

SEMI CIRCLE   4 b.f. Noble Patriarch 115 – True Ring (High Top 131) [1998 61:   **52**
12d⁴ 14.1m 12d* 12.3s² 14.1s* 12.3g* 11m³ 12g 12m⁴ 16m⁶ 12g⁴ 15.8d⁵ 1999
12.3m 12.4m 13.8m 15.8g⁴ 16.2m⁴ 12.3f⁴ 16g³ 14m* 16m⁴ 12f 15.8s⁴ 13.8s² Nov 2]
modest handicapper: won at Musselburgh in August: ran at least respectably most
other starts: probably needs good test at 1½m now, and stays 2m: acts on firm and
soft going: often blinkered, but is as effective without: has been early to post: won 2
novice hurdles late in year. *T. D. Easterby*

SEMIRAMIS   2 b.f. (Mar 10) Darshaan 133 – Sulitelma (USA) 63 (The Minstrel   **56**
(CAN) 135) [1999 6g⁴ 6m⁶ 7g 8m a6g⁴ a7g Nov 26] second foal: half-sister to 3-y-o
Border Glen: dam, 5f winner who ran only at 2 yrs, out of half-sister to Petoski:
modest maiden: bred to be suited by 1m+ (stiff task when tried). *Sir Mark Prescott*

SENA DESERT   3 b.f. Green Desert (USA) 127 – Sueboog (IRE) 109 (Darshaan   **89**
133) [1998 86?: 7m 8g³ 8s⁶ 1999 8g⁶ 10m 12g² 11.9g² 9m² 10.2m* 9f³ 11.9g 10.1g
10g² 10.1m⁶ Oct 19] close-coupled, quite attractive filly: has a round action: fairly
useful performer: won 6-runner maiden at Chepstow in July: ran well after when
placed in handicaps at Goodwood and Windsor: seems best ridden prominently at 9f/
1¼m: acts on firm going: visored last 2 starts. *C. E. Brittain*

SENDAWAR (IRE)   3 b.c. Priolo (USA) 127 – Sendana (FR) (Darshaan 133)   **129**
[1998 9s² 7.5s² 1999 10d* 10.5s² 8m* 8m* 8m* Sep 5]

The Aga Khan has enjoyed success in Group 1 races in a big way but, even by his high standards, the achievements of the horses he bred in the latest season were phenomenal. In Britain he landed the title 'leading breeder' for the first time since the 'eighties thanks chiefly to Daylami (Coronation Cup and King George VI and Queen Elizabeth Stakes), Enzeli (Gold Cup), Sendawar (St James's Palace Stakes) and Derby runner-up Daliapour, who between them earned almost a million pounds. In France the Aga Khan's winners included Daryaba (Prix de Diane and Prix Vermeille), Tajoun (Prix du Cadran) and Sendawar again (Poule d'Essai des Poulains and Prix du Moulin), while in Ireland Daylami (ESAT Digifone Champion Stakes) and Sinndar (National Stakes) were on the mark and Daliapour finished second in the Irish Derby. All these apart from Daylami carried their breeder's colours and Sendawar was the best of them. Although his campaign was compromised by the elements, he showed form over a mile almost on a par with Dubai Millennium's, and, as he stays in training, has every chance of boosting his reputation as well as his earnings.

Dubai Poule d'Essai des Poulains, Longchamp—third victory in the race in four years for the Aga Khan, Alain Royer Dupre and Gerald Mosse; Sendawar is a convincing winner from Dansili

Sendawar did not give much early indication of top quality, losing both his starts at two, minor events at Longchamp and Saint-Cloud, the former over nine furlongs. He started off his classic campaign by winning a seven-runner minor event at Longchamp early in April, then took on Montjeu and five others in the Prix Greffulhe on the same course later in the month. Considering the trip was an extended mile and a quarter on soft going, Sendawar put up a cracking performance, leading over a furlong out and being hard ridden but failing to quicken, going down by a length to Montjeu, the pair four lengths clear of Gracioso. Next time out Gracioso beat Montjeu in the Prix Lupin, so Sendawar's capabilities should not be underestimated if he happens to be campaigned over a mile and a quarter again. However, he spent the rest of the

St James's Palace Stakes, Royal Ascot—Sendawar succeeds where Ashkalani and Daylami failed by adding this race to the Poulains; Aljabr (rail) runs a good race on his belated reappearance

920

latest season over a mile, beginning with the Poule d'Essai des Poulains at Longchamp again in mid-May, in which fifteen colts faced the starter. The others included two of the best juveniles of 1998, Mujahid and Way of Light, who had not won at three (though Mujahid had run creditably to be third in the Two Thousand Guineas); Free Handicap winner Bertolini; Lavery, successful in a valuable six-furlong event at Goodwood; Prix de Fontainebleau winner Indian Danehill; and Dansili, making his debut in pattern company after collecting two minor events. Sendawar soon tracked the pace, took up the running entering the straight and ran on strongly to defeat Dansili by a length and a half, with Kingsalsa three lengths further back. Way of Light finished fourth and Mujahid fifth.

The win was the third in four years for Sendawar's connections, following those of Ashkalani and Daylami, and the colt was soon nominated as a contender for the St James's Palace Stakes at Royal Ascot, in which both his predecessors had been defeated. As noted in the essay on Zalaiyka last year, trainer Alain de Royer-Dupre had not won a race of any kind in England despite sending some good horses, but Sendawar looked a very likely candidate to end this run of ill-luck. He started favourite to beat ten others, notably unbeaten Aljabr, back from an abortive visit to the States for the Kentucky Derby, much-touted Killer Instinct from the Henry Cecil stable, Mujahid again and Two Thousand Guineas fifth Gold Academy. In the closing stages the race concerned just the market leaders as Sendawar, who had been moving comfortably throughout, edged ahead of Aljabr over a furlong from home and strode on to win by a length and a quarter. The pair had drawn five lengths clear of Gold Academy, with Killer Instinct fourth. Interestingly, Ladbrokes quoted odds a few days after the race about which three-year-old colt would head the International Classification. Sendawar was favourite at 7/2, ahead of Montjeu at 4/1, Beat All and Oath at 5/1 and Aljabr at 7/1 (Montjeu gained the day eventually).

The ground at Ascot, as at Longchamp for the Poulains, was on the firm side and, although Sendawar failed to impress going to post, these conditions evidently suit him. Not that he is incapable of showing form on soft—the Prix Greffulhe proved that—but his connections perceived good going or firmer as a necessity, and this assessment played a significant part in the remainder of his campaign. The Prix du Haras de Fresnay-le-Buffard Jacques le Marois at Deauville was his preferred target to the Sussex Stakes at Goodwood, which Aljabr won on firm going, but relentless rain turned the ground heavy and Sendawar was taken out. Aljabr tried his luck against Sendawar again in the Emirates Prix du Moulin de Longchamp in September, when there was never

Emirates Prix du Moulin de Longchamp—
a third Group 1 win for Sendawar as he lands the odds from Gold Away and Dansili

any doubt about the French colt's participation—the going was good to firm. The other runners included the second and third from the Jacques le Marois, Dansili and Slickly, Prix d'Astarte winner Field of Hope, Gold Away, recently runner-up to Diktat in the Prix Maurice de Gheest, and Fly To The Stars. Unfortunately, Aljabr ended up lame in fourth place, but he would have had to have been in the form of his life to have defeated Sendawar that day, as the odds-on favourite produced a terrific turn of foot to lead a furlong out and win, pushed out, by one and a half lengths from the staying-on Gold Away. Dansili was third and Slickly fifth but Fly To The Stars ran no sort of race in eighth. On this form a showdown between Sendawar and Dubai Millennium was something to look forward to, and it should have taken place in the Queen Elizabeth II Stakes at Ascot later in the month. Sadly the elements intervened again, turning the ground soft, and de Royer-Dupre withdrew his colt after inspecting the track a couple of days before the race was scheduled. The trainer also opposed the idea of running the colt in the Breeders' Cup Mile on the grounds of the climate and the tightness of the track at Gulfstream, so Sendawar was retired for the season.

			Sovereign Dancer (b 1975)	Northern Dancer
		Priolo (USA) (b 1987)		Bold Princess
			Primevere (br 1982)	Irish River
Sendawar (IRE) (b.c. 1996)				Spring Is Sprung
			Darshaan (br 1981)	Shirley Heights
		Sendana (FR) (b 1987)		Delsy
			Sherniya (b or br 1980)	Empery
				Sherkala

H.H. Aga Khan's "Sendawar"

The Aga Khan is no slavish follower of fashion with his breeding policy and he uses a wide range of sires, some of whom are not that commercial, to devastating effect. His loyalty to his own stallions has resulted in Daylami (by Doyoun) and Enzeli (by Kahyasi) among others, while Sendawar's sire Priolo, a high-class miler who won the Prix Jean Prat, Prix Jacques le Marois and Prix du Moulin, stood at only IR 3,000 guineas when mated with Sendana. He is responsible for two other Group 1 winners, Priory Belle (Moyglare Stud Stakes) and Brilliance (Prix Saint-Alary), but his ratio of stakes performers to foals is low. Sendawar, whose turn of foot is a chip of the old block, is Priolo's best runner by far. Sendana did not race and is out of a twice-raced maiden. At stud she started out with visits to Glenstal, Shardari, Shahrastani and Kahyasi, producing winners to the last two sires. Sendoro (by Shahrastani) was a useful performer over middle distances, winning twice and gaining places in the Criterium de Saint-Cloud and Prix Noailles, and Senanjar (by Kahyasi) won at up to eleven furlongs in France and has made a very promising start over hurdles in Ireland. Sendana had a colt by Tirol in 1997 called Sembar, then a filly by Linamix and visited Valanour after being barren in 1999. Sendana is a half-sister to two winners from nine foals out of her dam, notably the smart filly Sherarda, who won a listed race, finished second in the Prix de l'Opera and has produced a listed winner. The third dam, who was Group 3-placed, had only two foals. Going much further back, the family produced plenty of stars in the pre-war period, and the fact that the Aga Khan has persevered with the line despite few real successes in the time he has been an owner is another comment on his breeding policies. Sendawar, a small, sturdy colt, has repaid this patience superbly, and should continue to do so. *A. de Royer Dupre, France*

SEND IT TO PENNY (IRE)   2 b.f. (Mar 9) Marju (IRE) 127 – Sparkish (IRE)   **43** (Persian Bold 123) [1999 5m 5m[5] 5m 6m[4] Aug 30] 11,000Y: big, lengthy filly: third foal: half-sister to 3-y-o Clarendon: dam unraced: poor maiden: bred to stay at least 1m: raced only on good to firm going: swished tail and went poorly to post final start. *M. W. Easterby*

SEND ME AN ANGEL (IRE)   2 ch.f. (Apr 17) Lycius (USA) 124 – Niamh   **– p** Cinn Oir (IRE) (King of Clubs) 124) [1999 7d Oct 11] 15,000Y: tall, workmanlike filly: fifth foal: half-sister to 3-y-o Cindesti: dam, Irish 1½m and 1¾m winner, half-sister to Sun Chariot winner Home On The Range, dam of Reference Point: in need of race when seventh of 19 to The Woodstock Lady in maiden at Leicester: should stay 1¼m: should do better. *S. P. C. Woods*

SENOR HURST   4 b.g. Young Senor (USA) 113 – Broadhurst 68 (Workboy 123)   **50** [1998 50: 10.8m[2] 10d 8m* 7.5m 7d 1999 8d[3] 10d 8d Jul 1] smallish gelding: modest performer: best form at 1m: yet to race on extremes of going. *Mrs P. Sly*

SENURE (USA)   3 b.c. Nureyev (USA) 131 – Diese (USA) 111 (Diesis 133)   **105** [1998 87p: 6m 7g 7d* 1999 8m[3] 9.9m* 10.5g[2] 10.4d[5] 10m[2] 10s Oct 2] close-coupled, well-made colt: has a quick action: useful handicapper: won at Salisbury in May: good efforts when runner-up after, beaten short head by Komistar in Courage Stakes at Newbury (looked fit and well after 3-month break) penultimate start, racing bit too freely but staying on strongly: stays 1¼m: best form on good/good to firm ground: stirred up at start fourth run: wandered first 2 outings: sent to R. Frankel in USA. *R. Charlton*

SEPTEMBER HARVEST (USA)   3 ch.g. Mujtahid (USA) 118 – Shawgatny   **65** (USA) 83 (Danzig Connection (USA)) [1998 74: 5.2m 7.3g 7.1m[5] 7m 7m[3] 8m[5] 8m 7.3g 7s[3] 1999 12m 10s 5.1g[6] 6s[2] 8f[2] 10m[4] 6m[6] 8.5m[5] 8m* 9.9g 8g[5] 10m[6] 8.5s[4] 16.1s 10.1d 10d Nov 4] tall, angular gelding: fair handicapper: won at Pontefract in August: generally below form after: stays 1¼m: acts on firm and soft going: tried blinkered: not an easy ride. *Mrs S. Lamyman*

SERAPE   6 b.m. Primo Dominie 121 – Absaloute Service 96 (Absalom 128) [1998   **34** 44, a–: 9v 7.5m 6g[2] 6g[3] a7g 7g[2] 8g 7g 6g[5] 6m 8v 1999 6f 8g 7m[6] Sep 24] plain mare: **a–** poor maiden handicapper: effective at 6f, seemingly 1m: acts on good to firm going, possibly not heavy: has been tongue tied. *M. A. Peill*

SERAPHINA (IRE) 2 ch.f. (Feb 12) Pips Pride 117 – Angelic Sounds (IRE) **99**
(The Noble Player (USA) 126) [1999 5g* 5s³ 5m 5.2m 5.2g 6g² 6g 6d⁴ Sep 28]
IR 7,500F, 19,000Y: strong, lengthy filly: carries condition: unimpressive mover:
second foal: sister to 3-y-o Harp Player: dam Irish 2-y-o 5f winner from 3 starts: useful performer: won minor event at Doncaster in March: best efforts when second in
Lowther Stakes at York (beaten neck by Jemima) in August and Cheveley Park
Stakes at Newmarket (4 lengths fourth to Seazun) in September: takes strong hold
(best held up), and likely to prove as effective at 5f as 6f: acts on soft ground, gave
impression wasn't entirely at ease on good to firm. *B. A. McMahon*

SERDAL (USA) 3 b.g. Gulch (USA) – Ginny Dare (USA) (Pilgrim (USA) 108) **68**
[1998 NR 1999 7m³ 10s³ May 10] $400,000Y: quite attractive gelding: first foal:
dam, won up to 9f and third in Grade 2 1¼m event in USA, from family of US Horse
of The Year Fort Marcy and champion 3-y-o Key To The Mint: visored, fair form in
maidens at Thirsk and Redcar: withdrawn after getting very upset in stalls intended
debut: sold 10,500 gns, joined J. Mackie and won over hurdles in November.
Sir Michael Stoute

SEREN HILL 3 ch.f. Sabrehill (USA) 120 – Seren Quest 90 (Rainbow Quest **94**
(USA) 134) [1998 74: 7m⁶ 7m⁶ 7m⁴ 8d* 1999 12.5m³ 12.1g² 12m³ 12g³ 14s* 16.5s³
15v Nov 30] small filly: fairly useful handicapper: won at Haydock (after near
3-month break) in September, slowly away: creditable third at Doncaster penultimate
start: needs good test at 1¾m, and will stay beyond 2m: has form on good to firm
going, goes well on good to soft/soft (stiff task on heavy). *G. A. Butler*

SEREN TEG 3 ch.f. Timeless Times (USA) 99 – Hill of Fare (Brigadier Gerard **80 d**
144) [1998 64, a78: 5.1m⁵ 5f³ 6.1m⁵ 6.1d⁶ 6m⁵ 6.1s a6g* a6g⁴ a6f* 1999 a6g² a6g⁴
5g² 6.1g 6g² 5m³ 6s⁵ 6m³ 6m⁴ 6f⁵ 5d 7d 6g 6d Nov 14] quite good-topped filly:
unimpressive mover: fairly useful handicapper: left B. Palling and well below form
after ninth start: will prove best at 5f/6f: acts on firm going, good to soft (below
form both starts on soft) and all-weather: sometimes sweating/edgy: usually races
prominently. *R. M. Flower*

SERENUS (USA) 6 b.g. Sunshine Forever (USA) – Curl And Set (USA) **86**
(Nijinsky (CAN) 138) [1998 NR 1999 12m* 14.4m May 16] leggy gelding: fairly
useful handicapper: first run on Flat since 1996 when winning at Kempton in May by
½ length from Borgia: unable to challenge in steadily-run race at Kempton next time:
should stay beyond 1½m: raced only on good/good to firm ground on Flat, acts on
soft over hurdles (capable of useful form in that sphere/also successful in novice
chase in November). *N. J. Henderson*

SERGEANT IMP (IRE) 4 b.g. Mac's Imp (USA) 116 – Genzyme Gene 38 **53**
(Riboboy (USA) 124) [1998 57, a–: a7g 6d⁶ 6d* 6g 6.9m 6g 8g 6m⁵ 7m⁵ 8.5s 9.9m **a–**
10g⁶ a10g 1999 7f⁶ 8f⁴ 8f 8s ⁷/m² 8.5m 8f 10m 8m 8m⁶ 7d a8g Dec 18] workmanlike
gelding: modest performer: stays 1m: acts on firm and good to soft going, no worthwhile form on equitrack: tried blinkered/visored: has been early to post: inconsistent.
P. Mitchell

SERGEANT SLIPPER 2 ch.c. (Apr 25) Never So Bold 135 – Pretty Scarce **59**
(Handsome Sailor 125) [1999 5g a5g 5g⁶ 5g² a5g² a5g⁵ 5m 6s 5g⁴ a5g a5g* a5g*
Dec 21] 800Y: workmanlike colt: first foal: dam little sign of ability: modest performer: won sellers at Wolverhampton and Southwell in December: raced only at 5f/
6f: acts on fibresand: usually visored: usually claimer ridden, and often slowly away:
formerly untrustworthy. *C. Smith*

SERGEANT YORK 3 b.c. Be My Chief (USA) 122 – Metaphysique (FR) (Law **92**
Society (USA) 130) [1998 90: 5v* 6d 7m³ 5.2m 6m² 6g⁴ 6s³ 1999 8d⁶ 9m² 10m⁶
10m⁵ 10.4d 8.1m⁶ 8m² 8f⁶ 8m 8m³ 10g 10.4d Oct 7] big, good-topped colt: fairly
useful performer: ran creditably several times in 1999: stays 1¼m: acts on good to
firm and heavy going: has been bandaged behind. *C. Smith*

SERPENTINE 3 ch.c. Grand Lodge (USA) 125 – Lake Pleasant (IRE) 90 **106**
(Elegant Air 119) [1998 87p: 6g³ 6m³ 7m* 1999 7.5m⁴ 8m 10m* 10.3m* 9.9f⁶ 10d³
11.9f* Sep 2] deep-girthed colt: has a short action: useful performer: won minor
event at Lingfield and handicap at Doncaster in July and rated stakes at York (beat
dead-heaters Agitando and Toto Caelo by neck) in September, all in small fields: ran

Sun Life of Canada Garrowby Rated Stakes (Handicap), York—Serpentine (centre) is given a forceful ride by Ray Cochrane to beat dead-heaters Toto Caelo and Agitando (right)

at least respectably otherwise: shapes as though will stay beyond 1½m: acts on firm and good to soft going: game: sent to Bahrain. *J. R. Fanshawe*

SERRA NEGRA 2 b.f. (Apr 8) Kris 135 – Congress (IRE) 86 (Dancing Brave (USA) 140) [1999 7d Oct 30] fourth foal: half-sister to 3-y-o Promessa: dam, 1m winner, sister to very smart 6f/7f performer Cherokee Rose: twelfth of 16 in Newmarket maiden. *W. J. Haggas* **57**

SERRATE 5 ch.m. Sharpo 132 – Baino Clinic (USA) (Sovereign Dancer (USA)) [1998 41: a8.5g a8.5g 8.2s⁶ 6.1v a5g⁵ 5.1m 1999 a8g a8f a6g⁵ a7g a5g⁶ a5g 6f Jun 1] sparely-made maiden: bad maiden: tried blinkered/visored. *R. F. Marvin* **27**

SERVICE CHARGE 3 ch.f. Pharly (FR) 130 – Absaloute Service 96 (Absalom 128) [1998 NR 1999 5g 6m³ a6g⁴ 7d⁵ 6s Oct 4] seventh foal: half-sister to 3 winners, including 1991 2-y-o 6f winner Ring Cycle (by Auction Ring): dam 2-y-o 5f winner: modest maiden: probably stays 7f: sold 3,200 gns, sent to Sweden. *J. M. P. Eustace* **63**

SERVICE STAR (IRE) 2 b. or br.c. (Mar 29) Namaqualand (USA) – Shenley Lass (Prince Tenderfoot (USA) 126) [1999 6f 6.8m⁴ a7g⁴ 8m² 7.9m² 8s a8g* a8.5g³ Dec 11] IR 7,200F, 8,000Y: useful-looking colt: unimpressive mover: sixth foal: half-brother to 1992 2-y-o 1¼m seller winner Trepidation (by Cyrano de Bergerac) and 6-y-o Principal Boy: dam Irish maiden: fair performer: won maiden at Southwell in November: will prove best up to 1m: acts on good to firm going and fibresand: blinkered final 2 starts: tends to carry head high, and has hung and flashed tail under pressure. *M. A. Jarvis* **75**

SESTINO (IRE) 4 b.c. Shirley Heights 130 – Stellina (IRE) (Caerleon (USA) 132) [1998 118: 10.5v* 11s² 12g³ 10s³ 12v⁵ 1999 12d² 12d³ 11f⁵ Aug 28] rangy, good sort: smart performer: ½-length second of 5 to Public Purse in Prix Jean de Chaudenay at Saint-Cloud on reappearance: bit below best after in 4-runner Grand Prix de Chantilly (final start for Mme C. Head) and Grade 2 handicap at Del Mar: stays 1½m: acts on good to firm and heavy going. *N. Drysdale, USA* **115**

SET AND MATCH (IRE) 3 ch.g. Second Set (IRE) 127 – Kate Labelle 58 (Teenoso (USA) 135) [1998 57p: 7v⁵ 1999 10m 12m 11.5g a12g Nov 19] some promise only 2-y-o start: disappointing in 1999. *Miss Gay Kelleway* **–**

SET SAIL 2 b.f. (May 5) Distant Relative 128 – Sail Loft 74 (Shirley Heights 130) [1999 5g⁴ 6d⁶ Nov 4] sister to an 8.5f winner in Italy and half-sister to several **60 p**

winners here and abroad, including fairly useful 1¼m winner Chandlery (by Woodman): dam, maiden, best at 1½m, half-sister to Juliette Marny, Julio Mariner and Scintillate: modest form in maidens at Lingfield and Windsor: will be suited by 7f+. *D. R. C. Elsworth*

SEVEN 4 ch.g. Weldnaas (USA) 112 – Polly's Teahouse 68 (Shack (USA) 118) **69**
[1998 69: 6d 6.1m 7.5d⁶ 9g⁵ 7.6g² 7g⁵ 7s⁶ 1999 a7g* a8g a7g² a7g⁴ 7.1m³ a7g² 7s⁶ a6g² a7g² Nov 17] lengthy gelding: fair performer: won claimer at Southwell in March on final start for B. Smart: ran creditably when in frame after: will prove best up to 1m: acts on good to firm going, good to soft and fibresand: usually blinkered: has hung and flashed tail under pressure: usually races up with pace: consistent. *Miss S. J. Wilton*

SEVEN NO TRUMPS 2 ch.c. (Mar 22) Pips Pride 117 – Classic Ring (IRE) 50 **106**
(Auction Ring (USA) 123) [1999 6d 6.1m* 5f* 6d⁵ 5m⁵ 6d² 6g 5d³ 6g² 6s² Oct 23] 29,000Y: rangy, good-topped colt: fourth foal: brother to 3-y-o Bonds Gully and half-brother to a winner in Denmark: dam 2-y-o 7f seller winner who stayed 1m: useful performer: won maiden at Nottingham and minor event at Newcastle in May: excellent second in nursery at York (to Avezzano) and listed race at Doncaster (beaten ¾ length by Halland Park Girl) last 2 starts, making running each time: best efforts at 6f: acts on firm and soft ground: tends to carry head high: edgy sort: races prominently. *B. W. Hills*

SEVEN OF SPADES 2 b.c. (Apr 15) Mistertopogigo (IRE) 118 – Misty Arch **63**
(Starch Reduced 112) [1999 5.1m⁵ 5g² a6f a5g 5d³ 5s⁵ Nov 5] 5,200F, 2,400Y, 6,200 **a–**
2-y-o: compact colt: half-brother to 3 winners, including 6f/7f winner here and in Belgium Vax New Way (by Siberian Express): dam ran twice: modest maiden: should stay 6f: acts on soft going, probably on good to firm, well held on all-weather. *R. A. Fahey*

SEVEN O SEVEN 6 b.g. Skyliner 117 – Fille de Phaeton (Sun Prince 128) [1998 **–**
NR 1999 a8.5g⁴ a10f³ a8.5g⁴ a12g⁴ 10.2s a14.8g Oct 13] half-brother to 11f winner **a63**
Happy Brave (by Daring March) and 2 winners in Belgium: dam unraced: modest maiden: stays 1¼m: acts on all-weather, well held (after 7-month break) only start on turf: reportedly lame final start. *P. D. Cundell*

SEVEN SPRINGS (IRE) 3 b.c. Unblest 117 – Zaydeen (Sassafras (FR) 135) **67 d**
[1998 79p: 7m 6.1v² a6g* 1999 a6g 6g 5.1m 6.1f 5m a6g⁴ a7g⁵ 7.1d 6.1g a6g a6f 7g a6g a6g a6g Nov 20] tall, workmanlike colt: fair handicapper: disappointing in 1999: should stay 7f: acts on fibresand and heavy going. *R. Hollinshead*

SEVEN STARS 3 b.g. Rudimentary (USA) 118 – Carlton Glory (Blakeney 126) **–**
[1998 –: 5g 6m 7m 1999 8g 8d 5.9m a7g 11d Oct 26] no form: left M. Tompkins before final start. *W. Storey*

SEVENTII HEAVEN 4 ch.g. Clantime 101 – Portvally (Import 127) [1998 NR **–**
1999 5m Sep 19] close-coupled gelding: modest maiden at 2 yrs for J. Berry and D. Nicholls: soon tailed off only 4-y-o start: stays 6f: blinkered once. *J. S. Wainwright*

SEWARDS FOLLY 3 b.f. Rudimentary (USA) 118 – Anchorage (IRE) 86 (Slip **63**
Anchor 136) [1998 70: 6m⁴ 1999 7m 7m⁴ 6g 7.6m⁶ 6m 6s⁵ Aug 18] modest maiden: should stay beyond 7f: acts on good to firm going: sold 1,300 gns, joined P. Bowen. *J. A. R. Toller*

SHAAN MADARY (FR) 2 b. or br.f. (Feb 16) Darshaan 133 – Madary (CAN) **– p**
93 (Green Desert (USA) 127) [1999 7d Sep 30] medium-sized, good-bodied filly: second foal: dam 7f/1m winner: well held in maiden at Newmarket, probably needing race: will stay at least 1m: should do better. *B. W. Hills*

SHAANXI ROMANCE (IRE) 4 b.g. Darshaan 133 – Easy Romance (USA) **55**
(Northern Jove (CAN)) [1998 81, a71: a8.5g* 8s² 10.1d a9.4g 1999 8d 7f 8g 8d⁶ 6.9m* 8m⁴ 6.9g 8.3m Sep 6] tall gelding: one-time fairly useful at best, modest nowadays: given enterprising ride to win minor event at Carlisle in August: ran creditably otherwise only on next start: effective at 7f to 8.5f: acts on fibresand, good to firm and soft ground: visored after second start. *I. Semple*

SHABAASH (IRE) 3 b.c. Mujadil (USA) 119 – Folly Vision (IRE) 58 (Vision **59**
(USA)) [1998 57: 5s⁴ 5.1s 5m 5m* 6g 5m⁴ 5.3m⁵ 5g⁵ 6g³ a6g⁵ 1999 a7g² a8f⁵ a7g⁶ a7g* a8g⁴ a8g⁶ 7f 8f 8f a7g³ a7g⁴ 8m³ a8g a8g a10g a8g⁵ a10g³ a8g Dec 13] close-

coupled colt: easy mover: modest performer: won claimer at Lingfield in February: stays 1m: acts on equitrack and good to firm going (soundly beaten on soft): none too consistent. *P. Howling*

SHABLAM (USA) 2 b.c. (Feb 4) Lear Fan (USA) 130 – Awestamind (USA) (Flying Paster (USA)) [1999 6m³ 7d* Sep 17] $100,000Y: second foal: half-brother to a winner in USA by Runaway Groom: dam sprint winner in USA, including minor stakes at 2 yrs: confirmed promise when winning slowly-run 5-runner minor event at Ayr by head from Muntej, challenging 1f out and keeping on well despite carrying head awkwardly: will stay 1m: should improve further, and probably a useful colt in the making. *Sir Michael Stoute*   **87 p**

SHADE D'AMETHYSTE (FR) 4 b.f. Shadeed (USA) 135 – Coastal Jewel (IRE) (Kris 135) [1998 53: 10.5v 9.5m³ a8.5g² a8g 1999 8m⁶ 8.1m Jul 9] modest maiden: below form both 4-y-o starts: should stay 1¼m: acts on fibresand: visored final start: returned to France. *M. C. Pipe*   **–**

SHADES OF JADE 11 gr.m. General Wade 93 – Gellifawr 80 (Saulingo 122) [1998 NR 1999 a7g Nov 11] poor 5f handicapper in 1995: well beaten only start since. *J. J. Bridger*   **–**

SHADES OF LOVE 5 b.h. Pursuit of Love 124 – Shadiliya 90 (Red Alert 127) [1998 53, a74: a8g⁵ a7g* a8g a7g 7g 8.2d 7.1d⁴ 8m a7g* a7g⁴ 1999 a7g⁶ a7f* a7f² a7g³ 8f 7.1d 7m⁵ Sep 3] good-topped horse: fair handicapper on all-weather, poor on turf: won at Lingfield in January: below form last 3 starts: likely to prove best at 6f/7f: acts on all-weather, good to firm and good to soft going: usually held up. *V. Soane*   **35 + a78**

SHADIANN (IRE) 5 b.g. Darshaan 133 – Shakanda (IRE) (Shernazar 131) [1998 NR 1999 12m⁵ 11.9d⁴ 13.3f² 11.9d 11.9m Aug 17] smallish, sturdy gelding: unimpressive mover: fair maiden handicapper: ran creditably first 3 starts: will stay 1¾m: acts on firm and soft going: fairly useful hurdler. *P. G. Murphy*   **80**

SHADOOF 5 b.h. Green Desert (USA) 127 – Bermuda Classic 98 (Double Form 130) [1998 92: 10d⁵ 10g* 10.1m* 10d 10.1m² 10.4f 10.1d² 10g 9g 1999 10.2d³ 10.1g 10.5g² 10.1m* 10s³ 10s* Oct 22] lengthy horse: useful handicapper: won at Epsom in September and Newbury (comfortably by 1¾ lengths from Flossy) in October: excellent third to She's Our Mare in Cambridgeshire at Newmarket in between: probably best around 1¼m: acts on soft and good to firm ground: usually held up, but raced more handily last 3 starts: game and reliable: sold 105,000 gns, sent to Saudi Arabia. *W. R. Muir*   **106**

SHADOW PRINCE 2 ch.c. (Apr 6) Machiavellian (USA) 123 – Shadywood 96 (Habitat 134) [1999 7.1m⁶ Sep 9] 30,000Y: half-brother to several winners, including very smart 9f to 14.6f winner Madame Dubois (by Legend of France) and to dam of smart 1997 2-y-o Daggers Drawn: dam 1¼m winner from very good family: sixth of 12 in Chepstow maiden, off bridle halfway: should improve. *R. Charlton*   **– p**

SHADY DEAL 3 b.g. No Big Deal – Taskalady 47 (Touching Wood (USA) 127) [1998 ?: 6m 6m 6s a9.4g⁵ 1999 a6g⁴ a8f⁴ a7g² a8g² a7g 6d³ 7.1g 6g⁶ 6m 7m 6g 6m 7s a7g Dec 8] angular gelding: fair maiden on turf, modest on all-weather: well below form 6 of last 7 starts: effective at 6f (given bit of a test) to 1m: acts on equitrack, probably on soft ground. *M. D. I. Usher*   **70 d a54**

SHADY POINT (IRE) 2 b.f. (Apr 13) Unfuwain (USA) 131 – Warning Shadows (IRE) 113 (Cadeaux Genereux 131) [1999 7f 7m³ Sep 2] medium-sized, lengthy filly: first foal: dam 7f and 1¼m (Sun Chariot Stakes) winner: green, fair form in maidens at Goodwood and Salisbury: will stay at least 1m. *C. E. Brittain*   **72**

SHAFAQ (USA) 2 b.f. (Jan 28) Dayjur (USA) 137 – Shemaq (USA) 98 (Blushing John (USA) 120) [1999 6m* 6m³ Jul 23] first foal: dam 7f (at 2 yrs) and 1m winner, out of US Grade 2 9f winning half-sister to Al Bahathri: favourite, won maiden at Lingfield in July, making most: bit below that form when third of 4 to Day Journey in minor event at Newmarket only subsequent start: should stay 7f. *R. W. Armstrong*   **90**

SHAFFISHAYES 7 ch.g. Clantime 101 – Mischievous Miss 73 (Niniski (USA) 125) [1998 73: 11.1v⁵ 12s* 10s 12m⁴ 11.9s 12.3m⁵ 12.3m⁵ 12.4g³ 10.5m² 10d* 10g 10s² 1999 12d² 10d³ 12m³ 12g 12m⁵ 12.3f 12.3g* 10d⁴ 14.1g⁴ 14.6d⁵ 13.8s⁵ Nov 2] lengthy gelding: fair handicapper: won at Ripon in August: ran creditably most other   **73**

starts: effective at 1¼m to 1¾m: acts on fibresand and probably any turf going: usually early to post: takes good hold, and is waited with. *Mrs M. Reveley*

SHAFTESBURY (IRE)　3 b.c. Sadler's Wells (USA) 132 – Surmise (USA) 75　–
(Alleged (USA) 138) [1998 NR 1999 10s Oct 2] IR 275,000Y: sixth foal: closely related to a winner in Italy by Be My Guest and half-brother to a winner in Macau by Royal Academy: dam 7f winner, half-sister to smart 7f/1m performer Aim For The Top: tailed off in maiden at Sandown: dead. *Sir Michael Stoute*

SHAHED　2 ch.c. (Feb 9) Arazi (USA) 135 – Nafhaat (USA) 91 (Roberto (USA)　73
131) [1999 7.1m⁴ 7s⁴ 7v³ Oct 25] sixth foal: half-brother to several winners, including 5-y-o Ghalib and 3-y-o Qhazeenah: dam 1½m winner who stayed 15f: fair form in maidens, third of 12 to Masterpiece at Lingfield on final start: will stay at least 1m: acts on good to firm and heavy going. *M. P. Tregoning*

SHAHIK (USA)　9 b.g. Spectacular Bid (USA) – Sham Street (USA) (Sham　–
(USA)) [1998 62: a8g a8g 8m 9m⁴ 1999 12.3m 11.6m Aug 2] good-bodied gelding: carries condition: modest handicapper: stays 1¼m: acts on fibresand, good to firm and good to soft going: no form in visor/blinkers. *K. C. Comerford*

SHAHRANI　7 b.g. Lear Fan (USA) 130 – Windmill Princess 55 (Gorytus (USA)　28
132) [1998 38: 14.1m⁶ 16m² 16.1m 18s 1999 a12g a16g⁴ a16g³ a16g 17.1v Apr 20]
lengthy gelding: poor maiden: probably stayed 2m: acted on good to firm ground and fibresand: inconsistent: dead. *M. C. Chapman*

SHAHRUR (USA)　6 b. or br.g. Riverman (USA) 131 – Give Thanks 123 (Relko　69
136) [1998 76: 16g³ 16d 18g 16.5d⁶ 1999 14f 14d⁵ 14.4m* 16.5s Nov 6] strong, good sort: fair handicapper: won at Kempton in September: effective at 1¾m/2m: acts on good to firm and good to soft going: bolted to post and withdrawn once at 5 yrs. *G. L. Moore*

SHAIBANI　2 b.c. (Apr 16) Muhtarram (USA) 125 – Haboobti (Habitat 134) [1999　88 p
7d* Oct 27] 40,000Y: sixth foal: half-brother to 7f/1m winner Abeyr (by Unfuwain) and 1996 2-y-o 6f/7f winner Boojum (by Mujtahid), both useful: dam lightly-raced daughter of sister to high-class miler Noalcoholic: odds-on winner of 11-runner maiden at Yarmouth by 1½ lengths from Fair Impression, quickening to lead over 1f out and running on well despite seeming green: will stay 1m: almost certainly a useful colt in the making, sure to win more races. *B. W. Hills*

SHAKESPEARE　2 b.c. (Feb 1) Rainbow Quest (USA) 134 – Silver Lane　93 P
(USA) 115 (Silver Hawk (USA) 123) [1999 7m* Jul 11]
'For now sits Expectation in the air . . .' seldom can one stable have gone into a season holding a stronger hand in the classics. Ballydoyle's dominance in the top European two-year-old races was well-nigh unprecedented and left Aidan O'Brien with some difficult choices when he was inevitably asked to mark everyone's card. In an interview at the turn of the year, O'Brien produced a list of more than half a dozen colts whom he predicted would form the backbone of his classic challenge. One he didn't mention, however, was once-raced Shakespeare, whom Ladbrokes have as joint favourite for the Derby (at 20/1, compared to 33/1 with Hills and the Tote at the time of writing). Shakespeare's narrow victory in a seven-runner maiden over seven furlongs at the Curragh in July is light years removed from Derby-winning form, but he was asked to do no more than necessary and will clearly prove capable of a good deal better over middle distances as a three-year-old.

		Rainbow Quest (USA)		Blushing Groom		Red God
		(b 1981)		(ch 1974)		Runaway Bride
				I Will Follow		Herbager
Shakespeare				(b 1975)		Where You Lead
(b.c. Feb 1, 1997)		Silver Lane (USA)		Silver Hawk		Roberto
		(b or br 1985)		(b 1979)		Gris Vitesse
				Strait Lane		Chieftain II
				(b or br 1974)		Level Sands

Shakespeare, a 2,200,000-guinea yearling, is by Rainbow Quest, who is not an influence for precocity, even though he, himself, showed top-class form at two, as well as at three and four. Rainbow Quest retired to stud with two other prerequisites for a very successful career as a stallion—good looks and an excellent pedigree—and he made the good start imperative for a stallion in an age renowned for breeders' fickleness. The Derby winner Quest For Fame, the Arc winner Saumarez and the Irish Oaks winner Knight's Baroness were among Rainbow Quest's first crop, but his subsequent achievements have been something of an anti-climax. Most of his pattern-race winners have, however, made their mark at a mile and a half or more and there is little doubt that Shakespeare will be well suited by the Derby trip. His dam, the smart Silver Lane, did not win beyond a mile but stayed well enough to gain third place in the Irish Oaks, beaten a length by dead-heaters Diminuendo and Melodist, and is a sister to the high-class North American middle-distance performer Hawkster. Shakespeare is Silver Lane's fifth foal, and her third winner, following the useful French miler Starmaniac (by Septieme Ciel) and the very smart Japanese horse Black Hawk (by Nureyev), who beat Agnes World in the Group 1 Sprinters Stakes in the latest season. *A. P. O'Brien, Ireland*

SHAKIEYL (IRE) 3 b.c. Grand Lodge (USA) 125 – Frill (Henbit (USA) 130) **82** [1998 NR 1999 10.3d⁵ 11.1v* 12m⁵ 12d 10.1d Jun 4] 38,000Y: smallish, workmanlike colt: sixth foal: half-brother to 5-y-o Sudest and French 6f/7f winner Lady Frill (by Standaan): dam, Irish 1½m winner, half-sister to high-class miler Pitcairn: fairly useful performer: won maiden at Hamilton in April: not disgraced in minor event at Newmarket next start, but well held in handicaps last 2 (raced too freely in visor and reportedly returned home lame final one): stays 1½m: acts on good to firm and heavy going: sold 4,500 gns. *M. R. Channon*

SHAKIYR (FR) 8 gr.g. Lashkari 128 – Shakamiyn (Nishapour (FR) 125) [1998 – 48, a67+: a16.2g* 16s² 21.6s 16d 14.1d 16m³ 18s⁶ 14.9g⁵ 14.1m 1999 a16.2g 15.8g 17.1s Oct 4] workmanlike gelding: poor handicapper on turf, fair on all-weather: no show in 1999: stays 2m: acts on fibresand, soft and good to firm going: tried visored, effective blinkered or not. *R. Hollinshead*

SHALAD'OR 4 b.f. Golden Heights 82 – Shalati (FR) (High Line 125) [1998 97: **76** 8s⁴ 7g³ 8s* 8.3g* 10m² 10m⁶ 8.3m² 8g 1999 8.1s 8d 10.2d⁴ 9.9g⁵ 11.4m 10m⁵ 8g⁶ 10m Aug 23] leggy, quite attractive filly: useful and reliable handicapper in 1998, fair at best in 1999: effective at 1m to 1¼m: acts on soft and good to firm ground: rather headstrong and best forcing pace. *B. R. Millman*

SHALARI (IRE) 3 b.f. Shalford (IRE) 124§ – Hinari Disk Deck 75 (Indian King – (USA) 128) [1998 50, a–: 5s⁵ 6m 5s 5d⁶ 5g⁵ 7m a7g 8d 1999 a7g 5d 8g Jun 14] smallish, workmanlike filly: poor maiden: best efforts at 5f: well beaten on fibresand. *Miss Kate Milligan*

SHALARISE (IRE) 2 ch.f. (Feb 28) Shalford (IRE) 124§ – Orthorising (Aragon **71** 118) [1999 5g⁴ 5d⁵ 5f² 5m² 5m⁴ a6g³ 5g* a5g Sep 8] second foal: dam unraced: fair performer: blinkered, best effort when winning minor event at Newcastle in August: effective at 5f/6f: acts on firm going, some promise on fibresand. *Miss L. A. Perratt*

SHALATEENO 6 b.m. Teenoso (USA) 135 – Shalati (FR) (High Line 125) [1998 **73** 80: 10s 10g³ 13.1f² 12.1m⁶ 12d* 14g 13.3g 12.5d⁶ 16s³ 16v 1999 11.6m 14.1m² 12m 12g⁶ 18m⁵ 14m⁵ 12d² 12d³ Aug 26] sturdy mare: fair handicapper: often runs well at Salisbury, and put up best 6-y-o efforts when twice runner-up there: effective at 1½m to 2m: acts on firm and soft going: has worn severe bridle and gone early to post: has twice broken blood vessel, including third start: front runner: game. *B. R. Millman*

SHALIMAR (IRE) 2 b.f. (Feb 23) Indian Ridge 123 – Athens Belle (IRE) 101 **86** (Groom Dancer (USA) 128) [1999 7g² 7d⁶ Oct 30] IR 85,000Y: third foal: sister to 4-y-o India and half-sister to 3-y-o Grecian Tale: dam, 7f (at 2 yrs) and 1¼m winner (probably stayed 1½m), out of half-sister to Prix du Cadran winner Sought Out: fairly useful form in maidens at Redcar (½-length second of 15 to Lahan, final start for P. Chapple-Hyam) and Newmarket (raced too freely, no extra final 1f) in October: will need to settle better to stay 1m: may still improve. *A. G. Foster*

SHALL WE DANCE 3 b.f. Rambo Dancer (CAN) 107 – Angel Fire (Nashwan **83** (USA) 135) [1998 NR 1999 6g⁵ 7m⁴ 8d* 8.1d² 10g⁶ 8m⁴ 8s Oct 4] angular filly: first foal: dam unraced granddaughter of Arc winner All Along: fairly useful performer: won maiden at Ripon in July: ran creditably in handicaps after when in frame: races freely, and likely to prove best up to 1m: acts on good to firm and good to soft going. *C. W. Thornton*

SHALYAH (IRE)   4 ch.f. Shalford (IRE) 124§ – Baheejah (Northfields (USA)) [1998 52: 8m 8g⁴ 8.2d 8g² 10g 7g 8m³ a8.5g² a6g a8.5g a7g⁶ a7g 1999 8g Apr 8] strong, lengthy filly: modest maiden: seems best at 7f/1m: acts on fibresand, yet to race on extremes of going on turf: blinkered once. *N. P. Littmoden*   –

SHAMAH   2 ch.f. (Apr 28) Unfuwain (USA) 131 – Shurooq (USA) 94 (Affirmed (USA)) [1999 8m² 7d² Oct 11] quite attractive filly: sister to UAE 9f/1¼m winner Ajlaan and 1¼m winner Ijlal (both fairly useful) and half-sister to several winners, including 3-y-o Ghaazi: dam 2-y-o 6f/7f winner who stayed 1¼m: fairly useful form when second in maidens at Leicester, beaten length by High Walden on debut, ¾ length by Petrushka on second start (took good hold to post): should stay 1¼m. *B. W. Hills*   87

SHAMAN   2 b.c. (Apr 21) Fraam 114 – Magic Maggie 38 (Beveled (USA)) [1999 7m 7m² 6f² 7g⁴ 7d* 7m 6v³ 7d a8g a7g⁴ a8g* Dec 29] fluent mover: first reported foal: dam, poor sprint maiden, ran only at 2 yrs: fair performer: won sellers at Folkestone in August (final start for M. Channon) and Lingfield in December: better at 1m than shorter: acts on good to firm and heavy ground, and equitrack. *G. L. Moore*   65

SHAMAYNE   3 ch.f. Most Welcome 131 – La Primavera (Northfields (USA)) [1998 NR 1999 7.7m 7.7d 8.3d Nov 4] big filly: half-sister to several winners here and abroad, notably very smart middle-distance performer Highland Chieftain (by Kampala): dam Irish 1½m winner: easily best effort in maidens on debut: bred to be suited by at least 1¼m. *P. J. Makin*   65

SHAMBLES   4 ch.f. Elmaamul (USA) 125 – Rambadale 68 (Vaigly Great 127) [1998 45, a–: 7d a7g 8f 10m 11.5m 11.6g³ 12g³ 11.6f² a16g 11.5g³ 12m⁴ 12d⁵ 11.5d⁴ 14.1s⁴ 1999 11.8s Apr 1] leggy filly: poor maiden handicapper: stays 1¾m: acts on soft and good to firm ground, well beaten on all-weather. *G. G. Margarson*   –

SHAMEL   3 b.c. Unfuwain (USA) 131 – Narjis (USA) 87 (Blushing Groom (FR) 131) [1998 74+: 7m² 8.2d 8.2s⁶ 1999 10s⁵ 11.6g² 14.1g* 12.3m³ 16.2m⁴ Jul 23] lengthy, good-bodied colt: has scope: fair handicapper: comfortable winner at Yarmouth in June: ran well next start, then sold out of J. Dunlop's stable 21,000 gns before final one: should stay beyond 1¾m: best form on good ground or firmer. *D. Shaw*   77

SHAMOKIN   7 b.g. Green Desert (USA) 127 – Shajan (Kris 135) [1998 35: a8g a8g³ a8g a8g 8m 8m 1999 a7g² a7g⁴ a8g³ 7d 6.9m⁵ 8g⁶ 6.9g 8m⁶ 11m Aug 28] workmanlike gelding: poor maiden: stays 1¼m: acts on fibresand and good to firm going, possibly not on soft: visored once. *F. Watson*   41 a47

SHAMROCK CITY (IRE)   2 b.c. (Mar 17) Rock City 120 – Actualite (Polish Precedent (USA)) 131) [1999 7m⁴ 7m² 8g* Sep 8] 25,000 2-y-o: leggy, useful-looking colt: first foal: dam French 10.5f winner from family of Old Vic and High Top: useful form: odds on, won maiden at Doncaster by 3½ lengths from Capa, storming clear from 2f out and eased near finish: 2-length second to King's Best in listed race at York time before: will stay at least 1¼m: should continue to progress. *P. Howling*   96 p

SHAMSAN (IRE)   2 ch.c. (Feb 25) Night Shift (USA) – Awayi] (USA) 82 (Woodman (USA) 126) [1999 6g 5.2m⁶ a6g⁴ Dec 22] 36,000Y: first foal: dam, 6f winner, half-sister to smart 6f/7f performer here and in USA Musafi and from family of Suave Dancer: trained first 2 starts by B. Hanbury: best effort when fourth of 9 to D'Accord in maiden at Lingfield, leading 4f. *M. Johnston*   62

SHAMSAT MTOTO   3 b.f. Mtoto 134 – Jasoorah (IRE) 98 (Sadler's Wells (USA) 132) [1998 NR 1999 12g⁴ 10m⁵ 12m⁵ Jul 28] third foal: half-sister to German middle-distance stayer Aljaarif (by Rainbow Quest): dam, 1m (at 2 yrs) and 1½m winner, granddaughter of Irish 1,000 Guineas and St Leger winner Pidget: best effort in maidens at Kempton second start: should stay 1½m: raced only on good/good to firm going: sold 3,000 gns in December. *M. A. Jarvis*   69

SHAM SHARIF 2 b.f. (Mar 28) Be My Chief (USA) 122 – Syrian Queen 82 (Slip   **– p**
Anchor 136) [1999 7g 7d Sep 19] first foal: dam, 1¼m winner, half-sister to Rock
City and Kerrera: backward, behind in maidens at Newbury: should do fair bit better.
B. W. Hills

SHAMWARI SONG 4 b.g. Sizzling Melody 117 – Spark Out (Sparkler 130)   **–**
[1998 77d, a55: 8.2s⁶ 7.5m* 8m* 8s² 8g³ a7g⁴ 7m 7g 8.2v 7s 8d a7g a8f 1999 a10g⁵
a7f 10m 8f 8g 8f 8.5g⁶ a10g⁵ Dec 10] tall gelding: one-time fair performer: little form
in 1999: trained reappearance by N. Callaghan: tried visored. *Mrs L. C. Jewell*

SHANAZ 4 b.f. Then Again 126 – Trecauldah 69 (Treboro (USA) 114) [1998 –:   **–**
10.2s 8m⁵ 7.1g 10m 10m 8.1d 1999 10.2m 8.1m Sep 9] no form. *D. Burchell*

SHANGHAI CRAB (USA) 3 b.c. Manila (USA) – Saraa Ree (USA) 102 (Caro   **73**
133) [1998 NR 1999 a8g* 8f⁴ 8m³ 8g 10m⁴ 9.2m² 10d 10m⁵ 9.9v a8.5g⁵ Oct 13] big,
strong colt: has scope: fifth foal: closely related to useful 1m to 1½m winner Hagwah
(by Dancing Brave): dam, 7f winner who stayed 1m, out of sister to Irish River: fair
performer: landed odds comfortably in maiden at Southwell in March: some creditable efforts in handicaps after: probably stays 1¼m: acts on fibresand and good to
firm going, probably on good to soft: sold 20,000 gns. *M. L. W. Bell*

SHANGHAI LADY 3 b.f. Sabrehill (USA) 120 – Session 80 (Reform 132)   **77**
[1998 –p: 7d 1999 8g 8.1m⁴ 8s* 8.2f 8s Nov 6] sturdy filly: fair performer: won
maiden at Brighton in September comfortably: well held in handicaps next 2 starts:
stays 1m: acts on soft going, probably on good to firm: tongue tied last 3 starts.
J. H. M. Gosden

SHANGHAI LIL 7 b.m. Petong 126 – Toccata (USA) 64 (Mr Leader (USA))   **a57**
[1998 37?, a54: a12g⁴ a12g² a12g³ a10g* a12g* a11g a11g⁴ a12g⁵ a10g 12g⁵
1999 a13g a12g a12g* a10g* a13g³ a12g a11.7s a12g⁴ 11.6m a12g⁶ a12g* a12g a11g
a12g Dec 11] smallish mare: modest handicapper on all-weather, poor on turf: won at
Lingfield (twice) in February and Wolverhampton in October: left M. Fetherston-
Godley after twelfth start: effective at 1¼m, probably at 13f: acts on good to firm
going, good to soft and all-weather: tried blinkered earlier in career: has reportedly
bled from nose twice: inconsistent. *P. D. Evans*

SHANILLO 4 gr.g. Anshan 119 – Sea Fret 96 (Habat 127) [1998 73: 6d⁴ 6v* 7g   **58**
1999 6v 6f 7.1d 7f 7.1g 6g 8f² 7d⁵ 8.3s³ Sep 27] very tall gelding: modest handicapper nowadays: stays 1m: acts on any going: sold 17,000 gns. *M. R. Channon*

SHANNON DORE (IRE) 2 b.f. (Mar 26) Turtle Island (IRE) 123 – Solas Abu   **81**
(IRE) 82 (Red Sunset (120)) [1999 5m² 6m² 5f² 6.5g 6.1g* 7s Oct 2] 12,500Y:
useful-looking filly: second foal: half-sister to 3-y-o Ballymorris Boy: dam Irish 9f/
1¼m winner: fairly useful performer: won maiden at Nottingham in September:
bandaged behind, never on terms (but creditable effort nonetheless) in listed race at
Newmarket final start: bred to stay 1m: acts on good to firm ground, probably on soft.
B. Hanbury

SHANTUNG (IRE) 4 ch.f. Anshan 119 – Bamian (USA) (Topsider (USA))   **–**
[1998 59d: 10g 7g 7m⁶ 7m 7m 6g⁵ a12g a8g⁵ 1999 a10g Feb 4] leggy filly: disappointing maiden: probably stays 1¼m: tried blinkered/visored. *K. McAuliffe*

SHANUKE (IRE) 7 b.m. Contract Law (USA) 108 – Auntie Ponny (Last   **–**
Fandango 125) [1998 38: 10g 8m 7f 11.9g* 14.1m 11.1m 14.1s 11.9g 1999 a13g⁵
a16g⁶ 11.9f 11.9f 11.6d 11.9f Jul 22] smallish mare: dam of 2-y-o Grove Lodge: poor
form at 6 yrs: showed little in 1999. *S. Woodman*

SHAPOUR (IRE) 2 b.c. (Feb 20) Sadler's Wells (USA) 132 – Sharamana (IRE)   **76 p**
110 (Darshaan 133) [1999 7m 8d² Oct 12] first foal: dam, French 1¼m and 1½m
(Prix Minerve) winner, half-sister to Shergar and Shernazar: better effort in maidens
when 1½ lengths second of 19 to Imperial Rocket at Leicester, staying on well having
been caught flat-footed when race began in earnest: will be well suited by 1¼m/1½m:
sure to improve further. *Sir Michael Stoute*

SHARAF (IRE) 6 b.g. Sadler's Wells (USA) 132 – Marie de Flandre (FR) 109   **58 §**
(Crystal Palace (FR) 132) [1998 58: 14d⁵ 16.4m⁴ 17.2d³ 16.2g⁵ 14.1g² 17.2d*
17.1m³ 16.4m² 16d⁴ 17.5s² 17.2d 18s⁶ 1999 18d² 16.1s 16m a14.8g³ 16.4d 15.8m⁴
a14.8g⁵ Sep 18] lengthy gelding: modest on all-weather, poor on turf: stays 2¼m:

acts on soft ground, good to firm and fibresand: tried blinkered/visored, not since 1997: carries head high: inconsistent and irresolute. *W. R. Muir*

SHARAVAWN (IRE)   2 b.f. (May 7) College Chapel 122 – My My Marie – (Artaius (USA) 129) [1999 5.1m 6.8m 7g 6d a7g a7g a8g a10g Dec 18] IR 7,000Y: half-sister to several winners, including 1993 2-y-o 6f winner Connect (by Waajib) and 1¼m winner Don't Forget Marie (by Don't Forget Me): dam ran twice: no form: tried blinkered. *N. P. Littmoden*

SHARAZAN (IRE)   6 b.g. Akarad (FR) 130 – Sharaniya (USA) 117 (Alleged **62** (USA) 138) [1998 –: 18.7m 16.4g 1999 a12g a12s⁶ 17.2g 12.1m⁶ 14.1s Nov 1] smallish gelding: useful in Ireland at 3 and 4 yrs: modest at best in Britain: stays 17f: acts on good to firm going, probably on soft: sometimes blinkered. *O. O'Neill*

SHAREEF KHAN (FR)   2 b.c. (Feb 9) Alzao (USA) 117 – Sharenara (USA) – (Vaguely Noble 140) [1999 7s Nov 5] 900,000 francs Y: stocky colt: half-brother to several winners, including fairly useful 1¼m winner Sharera (by Kahyasi) and 1½m winner Sharbadarid (by Night Shift): dam twice-raced half-sister to Shahrastani: burly, well held in maiden at Doncaster. *N. A. Graham*

SHARH   3 ch.c. Elmaamul (USA) 125 – Depeche (FR) (Kings Lake (USA) 133) **88** [1998 60: 7m 1999 10f³ 8s² 10.1f* 10.4d⁴ 10m⁶ 10g* 8.1d 9.2f⁶ 10.3g⁶ 11.9s⁶ Sep 24] good-topped colt: fairly useful performer: won maiden at Newcastle (carried head high) in May and minor event at Ayr in July, both in small fields: ran creditably most other starts: stays 1¼m, not 1½m: acts on firm and soft ground: tongue tied: has been attended by 2 handlers in preliminaries: sent to UAE. *B. Hanbury*

SHARMY (IRE)   3 b.c. Caerleon (USA) 132 – Petticoat Lane (Ela-Mana-Mou **95 p** 132) [1998 NR 1999 8.1d* 10.1g² Aug 29] 180,000F, 160,000Y: fifth foal: half-brother to 3 winners, including Irish 1m winner Mindless Miss (by Dominion): dam Irish maiden half-sister to Irish 2000 Guineas winner Northern Treasure: won maiden at Sandown by 2 lengths from Mustafhel: again favourite, 1½ lengths second of 6 to Prairie Wolf in minor event at Yarmouth later in August, outbattled by more experienced rival inside final 1f: may prove best at 1m/1¼m: capable of further progress. *Sir Michael Stoute*

SHAROURA   3 ch.f. Inchinor 119 – Kinkajoo 53 (Precocious 126) [1998 66p: **90** 7m² 1999 6d* 7g⁶ 6g⁶ 6m 6m 7.7m⁵ 6g 5.2g* 5s 5s Oct 23] angular filly: poor mover: fairly useful performer: won maiden at Doncaster in March and handicap (easily best effort) at Yarmouth in September: likely to prove best at 5f/6f: acts on good to firm and good to soft going, well held on soft last 2 starts. *K. Mahdi*

SHARP EDGE BOY   3 gr.g. Mystiko (USA) 124 – Leap Castle (Never So Bold **73** 135) [1998 67?: 5s 6g 7g 5d⁵ 5g⁶ 5m³ 5g 1999 a5g a6f⁵ 6v* 7s 6m² 6m³ 7.1d* 7m⁶ 6g **a–** 6f³ 7.1d⁵ 6.8g⁴ 6m 7.1s 6s Oct 4] good-bodied, close-coupled gelding: fair handicapper: won at Hamilton in March and Haydock in June: best at 7f/testing 6f: acts on any turf ground: visored (no show on fibresand) twice. *E. J. Alston*

SHARP ENDING (IRE)   3 b.g. Keen 116 – Last Finale (USA) (Stop The Music **50 ?** (USA)) [1998 –: 7m 7m 7.1m 8m 1999 12g³ 11.6d 14.1m May 7] rather leggy gelding: poor maiden: stays 1½m: visored final outing: joined J. Cromwell in Ireland. *A. P. Jarvis*

SHARPEN THE ARROW (IRE)   3 br.g. Elbio 125 – Clodianus (Bay Express – 132) [1998 NR 1999 a6g 6.1g 7d Oct 11] IR 2,800F, IR 6,200Y: half-brother to 3 winning sprinters, including useful Terrhars (by Anita's Prince): dam unraced: well held in maidens: dead. *N. P. Littmoden*

SHARP HAT   5 ch.g. Shavian 125 – Madam Trilby (Grundy 137) [1998 86: 5d **79** 6d 6g 6m⁶ 6g³ 8d 6g 6g 6m 5g 1999 5d⁶ 5.1m 6m 6d 5m 6d 6m 6s a6g a5g* a5g³ **a67** a6g a6g Dec 27] leggy, angular gelding: fair handicapper nowadays: sold out of T. Etherington's stable 3,200 gns prior to winning at Lingfield in November: stays 6f: acts on all-weather, soft and good to firm ground: well held in blinkers: has run well sweating: has gone freely to post, and often taken down early. *D. W. Chapman*

SHARP HINT   4 ch.f. Sharpo 132 – May Hinton 82 (Main Reef 126) [1998 60: 7d **54** 6v⁴ 5g 5d 5g 5g⁵ 5v a6g³ 1999 a5g a5g³ a6g a5g² Mar 4] modest maiden: will prove best at 5f: acts on all-weather, best turf run on heavy going: races freely. *D. Nicholls*

SHARP HOLLY (IRE)   7 b.m. Exactly Sharp (USA) 121 – Children's Hour   –
(Mummy's Pet 125) [1998 NR 1999 a5g a5g⁵ a6g a7g Mar 22] shallow-girthed mare:
poor maiden: tried blinkered/visored. *M. Bradstock*

SHARP IMP   9 b.g. Sharpo 132 – Implore 71 (Ile de Bourbon (USA) 133) [1998   46
63, a57: a6s⁴ a7g a6g* a6g⁴ a7g⁶ a6g⁵ 7g 7m 7f³ 6m 6g 7g 6g³ 6m² 6f⁶ 6.9m⁴ 7m a7g
a7g⁵ a7g⁵ 1999 a6g a6g⁴ 5.3m 5m 5.7f a7g a7g a7g Dec 8] workmanlike gelding:
poor handicapper: trained first 2 starts by R. M. Flower: effective at 6f/7f: acts on
all-weather, best turf efforts on good going or firmer: wears blinkers: tends to get
behind/hang left (has worn near-side pricker). *Jamie Poulton*

SHARP LOVE   3 b.f. Pursuit of Love 124 – Sweet Decision (IRE) 70 (Common   –
Grounds 118) [1998 –: 6m 5m⁶ 7m 6m 1999 8.2d 7.5m 9.7v 7d Oct 12] useful-
looking filly: no form: left M. Ryan before final start. *N. A. Callaghan*

SHARP MONKEY   4 b.g. Man Among Men (IRE) – Sharp Thistle 87 (Sharpo   a44
132) [1998 –, a61: a8s³ a9.4g⁴ a8g* a8g* a7g⁶ a7g² a8g² a8g⁵ a7g 8.2s a8g³ 8.2g
a11g³ a9.4g 7m 8m a7g² a8g a7g a8g 1999 a11g⁴ a8.5g a8f³ a8g a8g⁵ a8g Mar 19]
tall, leggy gelding: poor performer: probably stays 11f: raced almost exclusively on
fibresand: usually visored: has run in snatches: sold 2,000 gns, joined G. M. Moore.
Mrs N. Macauley

SHARP MOVE   7 ch.m. Night Shift (USA) – Judeah 69 (Great Nephew 126)   –
[1998 –: a6g 1999 a12g Feb 16] of no account. *Miss H. C. Knight*

SHARP PEARL   6 ch.g. Sharpo 132 – Silent Pearl (USA) (Silent Screen (USA))   –
[1998 88d: 5f 5d³ 5.2g 7g 6s 7s 1999 a7g a6g⁶ a6g 7g Apr 8] good-topped gelding:
fairly useful handicapper at best: well beaten since second 5-y-o start: effective at 5f/
easy 6f: acts on firm ground, good to soft and equitrack: usually blinkered: has had
tongue tied: held up. *D. J. S. Cosgrove*

SHARP REBUFF   8 b.h. Reprimand 122 – Kukri (Kris 135) [1998 96, a–: 8d⁴ 8d   93
7.1d* 7.1g⁴ 8.2s² a8.5g 1999 8.1s 7d⁵ 7s⁴ 7.1d² 7.6d³ 7g⁵ 7d Oct 30] lengthy horse: a–
poor mover: fairly useful handicapper: ran creditably in 1999 fourth to sixth starts:
effective at 7f/1m: acts on soft and good to firm going, below form on fibresand: held
up. *P. J. Makin*

SHARP RHYTHM (IRE)   3 b.f. Mujadil (USA) 119 – Welsh Note (USA) 111   45
(Sharpen Up 127) [1998 45: 5s 5d 5v⁵ 6s⁴ 1999 a5g⁵ a6g⁴ a8f³ a7s a8g² a6g a7g Mar
10] leggy filly: poor maiden handicapper: stays 1m: acts on all-weather, raced only
on ground worse than good on turf: sold 3,000 gns, sent to Israel. *M. Johnston*

SHARP SCOTCH   6 b.g. Sharpo 132 – Scotch Thistle 73 (Sassafras (FR) 135)   57
[1998 69, a72: 6m⁶ a7g² 8s* 8v a7g³ a9.4g* a9.4s³ a12g³ 1999 a8g a8g* a8f* a8f*   a89
a8g* a7g⁵ 10s 10m 6v 5d 6.1d 10d 8.2s³ Nov 1] smallish, sturdy gelding: fairly useful
handicapper on all-weather, modest on turf: won 4 times at Southwell between
January and March: generally well held after: seems best at 1m/9f: acts on soft
ground and fibresand (below form only start on equitrack): blinkered once at 4 yrs:
usually held up: genuine. *D. Carroll*

SHARP SHOOTER (IRE)   4 b.g. Sabrehill (USA) 120 – Kermesse (IRE)   –
(Reference Point 139) [1998 49: 8s 10m³ 12g² 13m⁵ 12g 1999 12g 12.1f Aug 24]
workmanlike gelding: poor maiden handicapper: tailed off both 4-y-o starts: stays
1½m: won maiden hurdle in October. *B. Ellison*

SHARP SHUFFLE (IRE)   6 ch.g. Exactly Sharp (USA) 121 – Style (Homing   65
130) [1998 74, a68: 8.1d⁵ 8g⁵ 8s 8m² 10m³ 8g 7g² 8m* 7f* 8s³ 8.1m 8.2s 7d² a7g²
1999 a9.4g 7m⁴ 7d a7f² a8g a7g* a8.5g* a8g Dec 13] smallish gelding: unimpressive
mover: fair performer: left J. O'Shea after reappearance: won sellers at Wolverhampton in November and December (left I. Williams): best at 7f/1m: acts on firm going,
good to soft and all-weather: sometimes bandaged: held up. *Miss S. J. Wilton*

SHARP SMOKE   2 br.f. (May 18) Cigar 68 – Abrasive 53 (Absalom 128) [1999   –
5m⁴ Jun 16] half-sister to 3 winning sprinters, including 4-y-o Kolby: dam, maiden
who stayed 6f, ran only at 2 yrs: well held in minor event at Ripon. *D. W. Barker*

SHARP SPICE   3 b.f. Lugana Beach 116 – Ewar Empress (IRE) 57 (Persian Bold   70
123) [1998 60: 6.1d 6s⁵ a7g 1999 8.2d⁶ 8.2s 7d 7g 7m⁵ 7m 9.9m* 10.1m⁴ 10d³ 10.5v³

10.3d⁴ Oct 22] angular filly: fair handicapper: won maiden event at Goodwood in August: stays 1¼m well: acts on good to firm and heavy ground. *D. J. Coakley*

SHARP STEEL 4 ch.g. Beveled (USA) – Shift Over (USA) 62 (Night Shift **56** (USA)) [1998 56: a7g² a7g⁵ a7g* a8.5g⁵ 1999 a7g³ a7g⁵ 8g a8g a8g² Nov 15] leggy, workmanlike gelding: modest performer: stays 8.5f: easily best form on fibresand. *Miss S. J. Wilton*

SHARP STEPPER 3 b.f. Selkirk (USA) 129 – Awtaar (USA) 67 (Lyphard **91 p** (USA) 132) [1998 NR 1999 9.9m⁴ 10d 10m⁵ 9.9g⁶ 10d³ 10g³ 12d² a12g* Nov 22] 88,000Y: rather unfurnished filly: first foal: dam disappointing maiden out of half-sister to Fairy Footsteps and Light Cavalry: fairly useful form: good second in handi-cap at Newmarket before winning maiden at Southwell easily: stays 1½m: acts on fibresand, yet to race on extremes of going on turf: probably open to improvement. *J. H. M. Gosden*

SHARP STOCK 6 b.g. Tina's Pet 121 – Mrewa (Runnymede 123) [1998 65: 5d **64** 5.1s 5m⁷ 6g⁶ 5g* 5d 5d 1999 5d 5g 5d⁵ 5g 5g 5.2g 5s Sep 22] sturdy gelding: modest handicapper: won at Haydock in June: probably best at 5f: acts on good to firm and good to soft going: visored once at 4 yrs: has hung and shown signs of temperament, but well handled by N. Pollard for last 3 wins. *R. J. Hodges*

SHARVIE 2 b.g. (Feb 1) Rock Hopper 124 – Heresheis 69 (Free State 125) [1999 **–** 8d Oct 21] fifth foal: half-brother to 3 winning stayers, including 6-y-o Athenry and 4-y-o Cry For Freedom: dam stayed 2m: well beaten in maiden at Brighton. *J. Pearce*

SHATIN BEAUTY 2 b.f. (Apr 15) Mistertopogigo (IRE) 118 – Starisk 47 (Risk **66** Me (FR) 127) [1999 5f* 5m² 5g⁴ 5f⁴ 5m⁴ 6s Sep 27] 2,700F, 6,500Y: second foal: half-sister to 3-y-o Robber Red: dam, maiden, should have stayed beyond 1m: fair performer: won minor event at Hamilton in July: creditable efforts most starts after: may prove best at 5f: acts on firm ground. *Miss L. A. Perratt*

SHATIN LAD 2 b.c. (May 10) Timeless Times (USA) 99 – Fauve 71 (Dominion **–** 123) [1999 6g Jul 26] 10,500Y: seventh foal: brother to 5f (at 2 yrs) to 7f winner Masterstroke and half-brother to a winner in Yugoslavia by Weldnaas: dam, stayed 6f, best at 2 yrs: last of 10 in maiden at Ayr. *Miss L. A. Perratt*

SHATIN VENTURE (IRE) 2 b.c. (Mar 3) Lake Coniston (IRE) 131 – Justitia **90 +** (Dunbeath (USA) 127) [1999 5m* 5d⁴ 5m² 5m⁴ Aug 7] 20,000F, 21,000Y: good-topped, imposing colt: fifth foal: half-brother to 7-y-o Justinianus, a 1m winner in Italy by Lycius and very smart hurdler Bacchanal (by Bob Back): dam won 6 races at 3 yrs in Belgium: fairly useful performer: won minor event at Ayr in May: best effort when neck second of 7 to Dorchester in similar contest at Doncaster in July: will be suited by 6f. *Miss L. A. Perratt*

SHAUBAN (IRE) 2 b.f. (Mar 12) Dolphin Street (FR) 125 – Boristova (IRE) 79 **44** (Royal Academy (USA) 130) [1999 5m a5g 6f³ 6g 6g Aug 11] 3,300Y: first foal: dam, Irish 2-y-o 9f winner, half-sister to useful Irish middle-distance stayer Judicial Field: poor maiden: sold 2,200 gns in October. *N. A. Callaghan*

SHAW VENTURE 2 ch.c. (Apr 30) Whittingham (IRE) 104 – Al Shany 92 **71** (Burslem 123) [1999 5s 5m⁵ 5s⁴ 5.1g⁵ 5m* 6m⁶ 5.1g 5g⁶ 6d Oct 22] 1,100Y, resold 2,000Y: short-backed colt: fourth foal: half-brother to 4-y-o Pippas Pride: dam 5f (at 2 yrs) to 1½m winner: fair performer: won maiden at Windsor in July: well held last 3 starts, including in blinkers: should prove better at 6f than 5f: acts on good to firm going. *B. Palling*

SHAYA 5 ch.h. Nashwan (USA) 135 – Gharam (USA) 108 (Green Dancer (USA) **111** 132) [1998 –: 11m⁵ 19m⁵ 10g² 12m³ 16.2d² 14d⁵ 20m 15d³ 12m⁴ Jul 16] big, lengthy horse: smart performer: best efforts in 1999 when placed in Lanes End (John Porter) Stakes at Newbury (2¼ lengths third to Sadian) then Sagaro Stakes at Ascot (1½ lengths second to Celeric) in April: far from discredited when seventh of 17 in Gold Cup at Royal Ascot on fifth start: well below form final one: effective at 1½m, probably at 2½m: acts on firm and good to soft ground: tends to carry head high: sold 26,000 gns. *G. C. Bravery*

SHAYLAN (IRE) 3 br.c. Primo Dominie 121 – Shayraz 110 (Darshaan 133) **98** [1998 69p: 7.1s² 1999 8.3d⁴ 8s* 8m³ 10m⁶ 8m³ 9.9f 10.1m* 10s Oct 2] tall colt: has a quick, fluent action: useful performer: won maiden at Thirsk (veered away from whip) in May and handicap at Newcastle in September: well held in Cambridgeshire at Newmarket final start: stays 1¼m: acts on soft and good to firm ground: sold 45,000 gns, sent to USA. *Sir Michael Stoute*

SHAYZAN (USA)   2 b.c. (Mar 4) Shadeed (USA) 135 – Espuela (USA) (Gone West (USA)) [1999 7d 7s a7g⁴ a7g⁶ Nov 26] 17,000Y: heavy-topped colt: not a good walker: second foal: dam unraced half-sister to useful stayer Jaseur, family of Solford: modest form in maidens: well held in nursery at Lingfield final start: should stay 1m. *W. R. Muir*   **56 a50**

SHEATH KEFAAH   6 ch.g. Kefaah (USA) 124 – Wasslaweyeh (USA) 66 (Damascus (USA)) [1998 NR 1999 12d 10g³ Aug 14] poor maiden: should be suited by 1½m: winning hurdler: joined P. Rich. *J. R. Jenkins*   **45**

SHEBA SPRING (IRE)   3 b.f. Brief Truce (USA) 126 – Shebasis (USA) (General Holme (USA) 128) [1998 NR 1999 8g 8.3g* 10m* 9.9d⁴ 8s⁶ 8d⁴ Oct 9] 40,000Y: sixth foal: half-sister to 4-y-o Bank House and listed placed winners abroad by Bluebird (up to 2m in Sweden) and Be My Guest (USA): dam unraced daughter of half-sister to Alysheba: useful performer: won maiden at Windsor and 5-runner minor event at Ascot in July: best effort in listed races after when fourth to Ajhiba at Salisbury on fourth start: effective at 1m/1¼m: acts on good to firm and good to soft ground: sent to USA. *R. Charlton*   **100**

SHEBEG   2 ch.f. (Apr 4) Rudimentary (USA) 118 – Oakbrook Tern (USA) (Arctic Tern (USA) 126) [1999 5g Oct 19] sixth foal: half-sister to 1997 2-y-o 1m winner Lady Eil (by Elmaamul) and French 1m winner Highest Oak (by Highest Honor): dam French 2-y-o 1m winner: well beaten in maiden at Lingfield. *Mrs L. C. Jewell*   **–**

SHEEP STEALER   11 gr.g. Absalom 128 – Kilroe's Calin (Be Friendly 130) [1998 NR 1999 a13g a14g Mar 16] workmanlike gelding: winning jumper but little sign of ability on Flat. *R. E. Peacock*   **–**

SHEER FACE   5 b.g. Midyan (USA) 124 – Rock Face 77 (Ballad Rock 122) [1998 82§: 8g 8m 8m* 9g 8g⁵ 8.3f a9.4g 7d² 9g 8s 8m 1999 8f³ 8m⁴ 10d⁶ 8m 8f⁶ 8m³ 8h⁴ 7g⁴ 8d Aug 17] close-coupled gelding: fair handicapper: blinkered final start at 3 yrs: yet to race on heavy going, acts on any other: blinkered final start at 3 yrs. *W. R. Muir*   **79**

SHEER HAMAS (IRE)   2 b.c. (Mar 4) Hamas (IRE) 125§ – Kilcoy (USA) (Secreto (USA) 128) [1999 6m³ 7f* 6g* Sep 8] 16,000F, 20,000Y: big, workmanlike colt: has scope: fourth foal: half-brother to 3-y-o Free-Valley-Mou, 1996 2-y-o 1m winner Double Espresso (by Taufan) and a winner abroad by Anshan: dam unraced: progressive form: won maiden at Yarmouth in July and 21-runner £200000 St Leger Yearling Stakes at Doncaster (held on gamely by short head from Blue Bolivar) in September: effective at 6f/7f: sent to UAE: already useful, and should improve further. *B. W. Hills*   **99 p**

£200000 St Leger Yearling Stakes, Doncaster—
Sheer Hamas (right) holds on gamely for this valuable prize;
Blue Bolivar (stripes), The Deputy (left) and Master Fay (centre) are very close behind

SHEER HARMONY (USA)　3 b. or br.f. Woodman (USA) 126 – Memories of **78**
Pam (USA) (Graustark) [1998 –p: 7g 1999 8m² 8s² 8.3g* 10d Nov 4] fair performer:
won maiden at Windsor in October, in blanket finish: well backed when down field
in handicap there next time: should stay 1¼m: acts on soft going, probably on good
to firm: carried head high on reappearance. *Sir Michael Stoute*

SHEER NATIVE　3 b.f. In The Wings 128 – Native Magic 97 (Be My Native　**–**
(USA) 122) [1998 66p: 7g 7.1g 7m 7m⁵ 1999 a10g* a12g³ 8.9m 9.1d a8g* a10g³　**a77**
Nov 23] sparely-made filly: fair performer: won maiden at Lingfield in March and
seller there (sold from B. Hills 9,000 gns) in November: should stay beyond 1¼m:
acts on equitrack, no form on turf in 1999: inconsistent. *Miss Gay Kelleway*

SHEERNESS ESSITY　2 b.f. (Mar 30) Fraam 114 – Reclusive (Sunley Builds　**57 d**
102) [1999 6m 6m 8d² a7g⁴ a8.5g* a8.5g a7g Nov 22] second reported foal: half-
sister to 7f winner Solianna (by Beveled): dam unraced: modest performer: won
seller at Wolverhampton in October on final start for M. Channon: no form after:
stays 8.5f: acts on good to soft going and fibresand. *M. Dods*

SHEER SABO　2 b.c. (Feb 2) Prince Sabo 123 – Sunfleet 59 (Red Sunset 120)　**74**
[1999 5g² 5.1m³ 6d³ May 21] 52,000Y: tall, attractive colt: good mover: seventh foal:
half-brother to several winners, including useful 1997 2-y-o sprinter Pool Music,
later 8.5f winner in USA, and 6-y-o Russian Music (both by Forzando): dam 1¼m
maiden from family of Insatiable: fair form in maidens at Newmarket, Chester and
Ayr: likely to prove best at 5f/6f: sent to Hong Kong. *B. W. Hills*

SHEER VIKING (IRE)　3 b.g. Danehill (USA) 126 – Schlefalora (Mas Media)　**105 d**
[1998 101: 5d* 6g³ 5s² 6f⁴ 6f⁶ 5m* 6g 1999 6g² 5m 6f 5g 5.2d 6s 6s Oct 22] lengthy,
good-quartered gelding: useful performer: disappointing (though faced some stiff
tasks) after second to Lavery in valuable conditions race at Goodwood on reappearance: seems best at 5f/easy 6f: acts on soft and good to firm going: blinkered fifth
outing, tongue tied next 2: usually held up. *B. W. Hills*

SHEER WARNING (IRE)　5 b.g. Warning 136 – Native Magic 97 (Be My　**–**
Native (USA) 122) [1998 –: 7m 8f 8m a12g a7g 1999 7.1m 8.3m 11.1s May 14] little
sign of ability: tried blinkered/visored. *I. Semple*

SHEHAB (IRE)　6 b.g. Persian Bold 123 – Fenjaan 77 (Trojan Fen 118) [1998 NR　**–**
1999 12m 10m Jul 19] workmanlike gelding: fairly useful 1¼m winner at 3 yrs: well
held in handicaps both 6-y-o starts. *P. R. Hedger*

SHEILA-B　4 ch.f. Formidable (USA) 125 – Good Woman 60 (Good Times (ITY))　**–**
[1998 –: 5s 1999 6m 6f 7g 8f Jun 26] lightly raced and little form: sold 900 gns.
P. J. Makin

SHEILAS DREAM　6 b.m. Inca Chief (USA) – Windlass (Persian Bold 123)　**–**
[1998 NR 1999 11.8g 10d Jun 10] poor maiden handicapper for G. L. Moore at 4 yrs:
well beaten both 6-y-o starts: stays 1¼m: acts on firm going and fibresand: below
form in visor/blinkers: successful over hurdles in August. *H. S. Howe*

SHELTERED COVE (IRE)　8 ch.g. Bold Arrangement 127 – Racing Home　**–**
(FR) 89 (Dom Racine (FR) 121) [1998 39, a45: a16g⁵ a16.2g 17.2s⁶ 14m⁶ 11.6f
a16m² 14.1s* a12g⁴ a14.8s 1999 a13g Dec 10] angular gelding: poor handicapper:
well beaten only start in 1999. *J. E. Long*

SHEPHERDS REST (IRE)　7 b.g. Accordion – Mandy's Last (Krayyan 117)　**47**
[1998 NR 1999 a14g² a12g² 14.1d³ 15.4v² 21.6d Apr 28] poor maiden handicapper,
lightly raced: stays 15f: acts on fibresand and heavy going: often ridden by claimer:
has found little: fair jumper. *S. Mellor*

SHERATON HEIGHTS　2 b.f. (May 12) Deploy 131 – Norbella (Nordico　**52**
(USA) [1999 6m⁵ a8.5g⁶ 7g Oct 2] second foal: sister to 3-y-o Achilles Star: dam
unraced: modest form at best in maidens: gave temperamental display to post on
debut. *K. R. Burke*

SHERGANZAR　4 b.g. Shernazar 131 – Victory Kingdom (CAN) (Viceregal　**– §**
(CAN)) [1998 78: 8g⁵ 9m 11.4d⁶ 12m² 12s² 12m⁵ 11.4g⁴ 1999 11.9g³ 12s Sep
22] lengthy, good-topped gelding: fair maiden handicapper for R. Hannon in 1998:
had looked faint-hearted when juvenile hurdler for O. Sherwood and again left
that impression both starts on return to Flat, finding nothing: stays 1½m: acts on

soft and good to firm ground: has been bandaged behind: one to treat with caution. *G. L. Moore*

SHERIFF 8 b.g. Midyan (USA) 124 – Daisy Warwick (USA) 91 (Ribot 142) [1998 –, a81: a16g* a16g* a16g* 14.9g⁴ 1999 a16f² a16g⁴ Feb 20] small, close-coupled gelding: bad mover: fairly useful handicapper: stays 2m: acts on equitrack, little recent Flat form on turf: blinkered once at 4 yrs. *J. W. Hills*   **–** **a81**

SHERIFF OFFICER (IRE) 2 b.g. (Mar 20) Distinctly North (USA) 115 – Skip The Nonsense (IRE) (Astronef 116) [1999 6.1m 6d Sep 23] IR 13,000Y: second foal: half-brother to Italian 3-y-o Treewaddy (by Taufan), 6.5f and 7.5f winner at 2 yrs: dam unraced: well beaten in maidens: sold 1,000 gns in October. *P. Calver*   **–**

SHERZABAD (IRE) 2 b. or br.c. (Feb 6) Doyoun 124 – Sheriya (USA) (Green Dancer (USA) 132) [1999 7d 7d Oct 12] sturdy, lengthy colt: first foal: dam unraced daughter of smart French 1m to 12.5f winner Sherarda: green, well held in maidens at Newmarket and Leicester: should do better at 1¼m/1½m. *Sir Michael Stoute*   **– p**

SHE'S A GEM 4 b.f. Robellino (USA) 127 – Rose Gem (IRE) 62 (Taufan (USA) 119) [1998 51, a70: a7g* a7g* a7g⁶ a7g* a7g³ a7g⁶ a6g 7s a7g³ 7m 5.9d⁴ 5.1g 6m⁶ a6g 1999 5d 6g⁴ a6g 6g⁵ 6.1m⁵ 6g⁴ a7g a7g³ a6g Dec 21] smallish filly: modest performer: left A. Newcombe after third start: best at 6f/7f: acts on good to soft ground and fibresand: visored last 4 starts, running creditably twice: usually races prominently. *Mrs V. C. Ward*   **47** **a59**

SHE'S MAGIC 2 b.f. (Apr 18) Magic Ring (IRE) 115 – Norfolk Serenade 83 (Blakeney 126) [1999 6g 7m Jun 15] 1,200F, 6,100Y: half-sister to fairly useful winner up to 7f Samsolom (by Absolom), useful 1m/9f winner North Song (by Anshan) and 6f (at 2 yrs) and 2m winner Secret Serenade (by Classic Secret): dam 11.7f winner: well held in maidens. *M. Brittain*   **–**

SHE'S OUR MARE (IRE) 6 b.m. Commanche Run 133 – Miss Polymer (Doulab (USA) 115) [1998 70: a10g* 16g 14m⁵ 10m⁴ 8.5d 12s² 10d* 14v⁴ 1999 8.3f* 11.9s³ 9m⁵ 11.9m 8s* 10s* Oct 2]   **100**

In 1999 the Cesarewitch and, much more unusually, the Cambridge-shire were both won by horses who had also made their names as hurdlers. In addition to their triumphs in the autumn double, Top Cees had already won the 1998 Coral Cup at the Cheltenham Festival, She's Our Mare the Powers Handicap Hurdle at Fairyhouse and the Swinton Hurdle at Haydock, both in 1999. In its own rather different way, She's Our Mare's story is as remarkable as that of the hugely better known Top Cees, because a little over twelve months earlier, at the age of five, there was little reason for her to be known at all.

At the end of the 1997/8 jumping season, She's Our Mare had run nine times for two wins, operating at a modest level. Her Flat career had not even begun at that stage, but when it did, over a mile and a quarter on the beach at Laytown in June 1998, she made a winning start. Since then, with her Flat and hurdling careers operating in harness, She's Our Mare has risen through the ranks at a seemingly exponential rate. Three more hurdles wins and one on the Flat (in a mile and a quarter handicap at Leopardstown) were added before 1998 was over. The spring of 1999 brought those two major handicap hurdles, worth IR £48,750 and £23,800 respectively, before She's Our Mare had her attention turned again to action on the level. Trainer Tony Martin had plundered eight wins and £137,473 in Britain during the 1998/9 jumps season and two months after her Swinton triumph, having warmed up with a win over a mile at Navan, She's Our Mare was back at Haydock for the Old Newton Cup, in which she finished a creditable third. Hampered when bidding for £20,000+ prizes at Leopardstown and York, victory over a mile at the Curragh in September preceded her challenge for the Cambridgeshire.

The riding tactics adopted with She's Our Mare, brought smoothly from behind to deliver a late challenge, risked trouble in running and kept the verdict in doubt in the races she won until the last moment. Her Curragh win came in last-gasp fashion, with She's Our Mare not travelling so smoothly as usual back over a mile. Because of building works on the Rowley Mile, all racing at

Tote Cambridgeshire (Handicap) Newmarket—
the versatile She's Our Mare (noseband) becomes the first Irish-trained winner since Tarqogan in 1965;
she catches Bomb Alaska (right) close home; Shadoof (striped sleeves) is third

Newmarket in the latest season was on the July course, which necessitated a change in distance for the Cambridgeshire. When the race was also transferred in 1986, this had meant a reduction to eight and a half furlongs. In 1999 there was an increase to a mile and a quarter and the disturbing prospect of thirty-three runners negotiating a turn after a couple of furlongs. That hazard passed with only a small amount of scrimmaging, and a far greater inconvenience to many was the soft ground which saw the closing stages dominated by just two horses, She's Our Mare and Bomb Alaska, whose effectiveness in the mud was thoroughly proven. Bomb Alaska got first run, hampering She's Our Mare in the process, but, having still been biding his time towards the rear three furlongs out, Francis Norton produced She's Our Mare with a perfectly-timed run to win by a neck. Bomb Alaska franked the form by winning a listed race at the end of the month. She's Our Mare did the same in her own way by going close in a £31,728 handicap hurdle at Cheltenham in November and finishing third in the Ladbroke shortly after the turn of the year.

She's Our Mare's sire, the 1984 St Leger winner Commanche Run, is better known as a National Hunt sire these days but not that well known in that sphere either, his previous standard-bearer being Triumph Hurdle winner Commanche Court. There are echoes of Commanche Run, who won two Group 1 events at a mile and a quarter as a four-year-old, in the way that She's Our Mare has successfully been dropped back in distance. Thankfully, there is no resemblance to the careers of her dam or grandam, Miss Polymer and Deer Park, who were both maidens. Miss Polymer's other progeny have so far failed to register a win, and for a winner of much consequence in this family one has to go back to Deer Park's half-brother Gelas who was a smart jumper in France.

She's Our Mare (IRE) (b.m. 1993)	Commanche Run (b 1981)	Run The Gantlet (b 1981)	Tom Rolfe
			First Feather
		Sorceress (b 1987)	Ratification
			Mitrailleuse
	Miss Polymer (b 1987)	Doulab (ch 1982)	Topsider
			Passerine
		Deer Park (b or br 1977)	Faraway Son
			Bury

The rather sparely-made She's Our Mare has her tongue tied. She finds a mile a minimum for her these days, though her form at around a mile and a quarter is much better than at a mile and a half. She acts on firm and soft going and, to stress her versatility a little further, it is as well to remember that success at Laytown. *A. J. Martin, Ireland*

SHE-WOLFF (IRE)   3 b.f. Pips Pride 117 – Royal Wolff (Prince Tenderfoot (USA) 126) [1998 89+: 5.7m* 5d⁵ 6m² 1999 5m³ 5s² 5m Aug 21] good-topped filly: useful performer: good third to Pips Magic in handicap at Ascot in June: below that form both starts after, including when 1½ lengths second to Nuclear Debate in listed race at Deauville: likely to prove best at 5f/6f: goes well on good to firm going. *P. J. Makin*   **104**

SHIFTING   4 ch.f. Night Shift (USA) – Preening 62 (Persian Bold 123) [1998 –, a44: a11g³ 11.9g⁶ 8d a8.5g 8d a8g 1999 a7g³ a9.4g⁵ a9.4g⁴ a12g Feb 20] lengthy, workmanlike filly: poor maiden: probably stayed 11f: acted on good to firm going, good to soft and fibresand: blinkered once at 3 yrs: dead. *B. A. McMahon*   **– a50**

SHIFTING MOON   7 b.g. Night Shift (USA) – Moonscape 87 (Ribero 126) [1998 NR 1999 14.1v Sep 29] stocky gelding: fairly useful handicapper at 3 yrs: lightly raced and well beaten on Flat since, though won over hurdles in November: tried visored/blinkered. *F. Jordan*   **–**

SHIKASTA (IRE)   3 ch.f. Kris 135 – India Atlanta (Ahonoora 122) [1998 NR 1999 10m² 12.1g⁶ 10.1m³ Jul 7] 75,000Y: tall, leggy, sparely-made filly: half-sister to several winners, including smart 1m/9f performer Ventiquattrofogli (by Persian Bold) and useful German 6f (at 2 yrs) and 11f winner Irish Fighter (by Persian Heights): dam unraced: promising debut in maiden at Ripon: disappointing both starts after: sent to Greece. *H. R. A. Cecil*   **74**

SHINBONE ALLEY   2 b.c. (Mar 30) Lake Coniston (IRE) 131 – Villota (Top Ville 129) [1999 5m² 5m 6f² 5f 5g⁵ Aug 18] 28,000F, IR 24,000Y, 43,000 2-y-o: lengthy, quite attractive colt: has a quick action: fourth foal: half-brother to a winning sprinter abroad by Lycius: dam once-raced daughter of high-class sprinter/miler Vilikaia: fairly useful form: second in maidens: respectable fifth of 7 to Buy Or Sell in listed race at York final start: effective at 5f/6f: raced only on good ground or firmer: takes good hold: has hung left and carried head high. *J. Berry*   **91**

SHINEROLLA   7 b.g. Thatching 131 – Primrolla 64 (Relko 136) [1998 78, a–: 8m 7m 10.3m² 1999 11.9d 8.3m Sep 6] tall gelding: fairly useful handicapper on all-weather, fair on turf: well held both starts in 1999, though won over hurdles earlier in year: stays 10.3f: acts on fibresand and probably any turf going: tried blinkered earlier in career: held up. *C. Parker*   **–**

SHINING DANCER   7 b.m. Rainbow Quest (USA) 134 – Strike Home 82 (Be My Guest (USA) 126) [1998 61: 14.1d⁶ 12g 14.1d 16.2g 14.9g⁵ 14m⁵ 16.2g 16.4m³ 14g* 15.4m² 16.2s 1999 12g⁵ 16f 14m⁴ 14m³ 16.2m⁴ 16.4m³ 14m² 14m³ 14.1m Jul 30] angular mare: has a markedly round action: modest handicapper: effective at 1¾m to 2½m: acts on good to firm and good to soft ground, probably not soft: usually taken early to post: takes good hold, and waited with. *S. Dow*   **61**

SHINING DESERT (IRE)   3 b.f. Green Desert (USA) 127 – Riyoom (USA) 83 (Vaguely Noble 140) [1998 82: 5g* 5d 6g³ 6.1g⁵ 6g⁶ 1999 6m⁶ 6.8g Aug 13] leggy, good-topped filly: fairly useful at 2 yrs: no form in 1999: should stay 7f: may not be altogether genuine. *J. Berry*   **–**

SHINING HOUR (USA)   2 b.f. (Apr 14) Red Ransom (USA) – Timely 104 (Kings Lake (USA) 133) [1999 5.1m² 5.7g* 5m* Jun 16] deep-girthed filly: fifth foal: half-sister to 3-y-o Modern Era: dam 1m winner: progressive form: won maiden   **104**

Queen Mary Stakes, Royal Ascot—
Shining Hour (No.8) produces a plucky performance for a narrow success;
Rowaasi (black epaulets) is second with Warrior Queen (in between them) in third

at Bath in May and 13-runner Queen Mary Stakes at Royal Ascot in June: 20/1, off bridle halfway before weaving through to lead close home when beating Rowaasi by ½ length in latter: reportedly ripped muscles in pelvic area during work in July: should stay at least 7f/1m: looked a smart performer in the making. *P. W. Chapple-Hyam*

SHINING STAR   2 ch.f. (Jan 26) Selkirk (USA) 129 – Mystery Ship 105 (Decoy **56** Boy 129) [1999 6g 6.1g⁵ 5.1m⁶ 5g⁵ Sep 26] 17,500F, 10,000Y: compact filly: sister to 1996 2-y-o 6f winner Serenity, later useful at 7f, and half-sister to several winners, including 7f/1m winner Final Enigma (by Final Straw): dam 2 y o 5f and 7f winner: modest maiden: best effort final start: races freely, and likely to prove best at 5f. *J. Berry*

SHIPLEY GLEN   4 b.c. Green Desert (USA) 127 – Lady Shipley 111 (Shirley **71** Heights 130) [1998 72: 9.3d² a9.4g* 10g⁴ 1999 9.3m* 8f² 10f⁴ a8.5g* 9.1g³ 8.5g⁵ **a87** Aug 11] sturdy colt: fairly useful handicapper on all-weather, fair on turf: won at Carlisle in May and Wolverhampton in July: effective at 1m to 9.4f: acts on fibresand, firm and good to soft going: has been bandaged in front. *Sir Mark Prescott*

SHIRLEY NOT   3 gr.g. Paris House 123 – Hollia 72 (Touch Boy 109) [1998 74+: **77** a5g* 5g² 5g² 5f⁵ 5.1g* 5f 5m² 1999 5d 5m⁶ 5s⁴ 5.1m² 5m² 5d³ 5g 5m 6g Oct 14] tall, lengthy gelding: fair handicapper: should stay 6f: acts on firm going, soft and fibresand: has looked wayward. *S. Gollings*

SHIVA (JPN)   4 ch.f. Hector Protector (USA) 124 – Lingerie (Shirley Heights **119** 130) [1998 95p: 9g* 1999 8.5g* 10.5g* 10m 10g² Oct 16]

      Shiva looked set to be a force to be reckoned with at the highest level throughout 1999 following her victory in the Tattersalls Gold Cup at the Curragh in May on only her third start. As it was, Shiva could manage only two more runs, both unsuccessful ones. But this lightly-raced filly should prove capable of winning more top races as a five-year-old, provided of course she can be kept sound.

Tattersalls Gold Cup, the Curragh—in a race upgraded to Group 1, Shiva puts up a smart performance to beat Daylami on only her third start; Make No Mistake and Insatiable come next

A history of knee problems had restricted Shiva to only one outing up to the end of her three-year-old campaign, which comprised winning a maiden impressively at Kempton in May. Despite this, trainer Henry Cecil had no qualms about pitching her into pattern company on her return nearly eleven months later. His faith was rewarded when Shiva won the Weatherbys Earl of Sefton Stakes at Newmarket's Craven meeting by one and a quarter lengths from Haami, sensibly moved into a prominent position before the steady pace quickened and running on willingly to edge ahead inside the final furlong. An understandably pleased Cecil pronounced Shiva 'exciting' following the victory; exciting enough to be given her chance in Group 1 company on her next start, in fact. She faced five rivals at the Curragh, chief amongst them the previous year's winner Daylami. On that day, though, Daylami was nowhere near his best and Shiva proved too strong, scoring decisively by two and a half lengths, held up and off the bit early in the straight before responding gamely to forge ahead inside the final furlong. Euphoria was to turn to disappointment next time in the Prince of Wales's Stakes at Royal Ascot. Shiva's knees were, apparently, once again the source of her troubles as, discarded by Fallon, she finished over twelve lengths seventh of eight to Lear Spear, jarred on the good to firm ground. The injury was serious enough to prevent Shiva from cantering for two months and meant she wasn't seen on the racecourse until the Champion Stakes at Newmarket in October, her final start of the year. In finishing one and a quarter lengths second to another lightly-raced filly, Alborada, Shiva performed most creditably in view of her absence. Cecil went on record before the race as saying he would have liked an extra week with Shiva, and in the event she was found out towards the finish, after seeming likely to come through and take the steadily-run affair. There would have been every chance that Shiva could have turned the tables if she and Alborada had met their next intended engagement, the Premio Roma in Italy, but the rematch never took place.

Strictly speaking, Shiva is a Japanese-bred. In reality, though, there is little Japanese about her pedigree. Her sire, Hector Protector, is an American-bred and her dam, Lingerie, was bred in Britain. Both did their racing in Europe, more notably Hector Protector, who, having won three Group 1s in 1990, was crowned champion two-year-old. A classic, the Poule d'Essai des Poulains, and the Prix Jacques le Marois were added at three years. Hector Protector was subsequently twice disappointing, after failing to stay in the Derby in between, before being exported to stand in Japan. His best season was 1998, when he finished eighth in the sires' table, and he has sired only four pattern winners in Japan. Hector Protector is now at the National Stud and he can build on his good start in Europe: two pattern winners from two runners,

Niarchos Family's "Shiva"

		Woodman	Mr Prospector
	Hector Protector (USA)	(ch 1983)	Playmate
	(ch 1988)	Korveya	Riverman
Shiva (JPN)		(ch 1982)	Konafa
(ch.f. 1995)		Shirley Heights	Mill Reef
	Lingerie	(b 1975)	Hardiemma
	(b 1988)	Northern Trick	Northern Dancer
		(ch 1981)	Trick Chick

namely the full siblings Limnos and Shiva. The very smart year-older Limnos, like Shiva, also prospered at four, winning two Group 2 races in France. Their dam, Lingerie, had none of their ability on the racecourse, ending her career as a five-times placed maiden from twelve starts in France. She is, however, out of the top-class Northern Trick, 1984 Prix de Diane and Vermeille winner and runner-up to Sagace in the Prix de l'Arc de Triomphe. Lingerie's three-year-old Ipso Facto (by Sunday Silence) ran a couple of times in France for Dominique Sepulchre, while two-year-old Burning Sunset showed some promise for Henry Cecil in the latest season. Shiva, a quite good-topped, attractive filly with a round action, has raced only once on good to firm going, with the rest on good ground. She stays a mile and a quarter well. *H. R. A. Cecil*

SHOESTRING   3 br.g. Petong 126 – Wantage Park 104 (Pas de Seul 133) [1998   – NR 1999 6d 5.7f 10.2s Sep 27] fifth foal: half-brother to 3 winners, including stayers Izza and Thornby Park (both by Unfuwain), latter fairly useful: dam stayed 7f: well beaten in maidens: sold 1,600 gns, sent to Italy. *D. W. P. Arbuthnot*

SHOGUN (IRE)   4 b.g. Zafonic (USA) 130 – Sheriyna (FR) (Darshaan 133)   **70**
[1998 84: 8f⁴ 8f² 8m² 10m⁴ 1999 20m* a10f* a11g a12g⁴ 14.1s 10s 10s Nov 1] good-
topped gelding: has a quick action: fair performer: won maiden at Lingfield in
January, hanging fire briefly before asserting: left K. Burke and off nearly 6 months
before penultimate start: stays 1¼m (pulled too hard over 1¾m): acts on equitrack
and firm ground: has given trouble stalls/carried head awkwardly. *B. A. McMahon*

SHONTAINE   6 b.g. Pharly (FR) 130 – Hinari Televideo 97 (Caerleon (USA)   **56**
132) [1998 –, a74d: a8s⁵ a8g² a8g² a8g² a8g* a8.5g⁵ 8.2v a7g a8g a10g a10g 1999   **a50**
a7g a7f a8g⁴ a8g³ a7g⁶ 8g 7.1m⁴ 8.3s⁵ 7.1m 7.7s a7g 8m² 8g* 7.5m⁴ 8g³ 8.1m² 7g
8m⁶ 7g³ 8.3f 8m 8m 8.3s² 8d 8.2s a7g Nov 16] small gelding: modest handicapper:
won selling event at Ayr in June: ran creditably otherwise when in frame: best at 7f/
1m nowadays: possibly unsuited by heavy going, acts on any other turf/all-weather:
tried blinkered: tough. *M. Johnston*

SHOOFHA (IRE)   2 b.f. (Mar 11) Bluebird (USA) 125 – Courtesane (USA)   **70 p**
(Majestic Light (USA)) [1999 8.3d Oct 28] 110,000Y: fifth foal: sister to smart
middle-distance stayer Delilah and half-sister to winners abroad by Vigors and
Assert: dam placed twice in USA: weak in market and green, fair form when eighth
of 13 in Windsor maiden: will be suited by 1¼m+: should do better. *M. P. Tregoning*

SHOOGLE (USA)   3 ch.f. A P Indy (USA) 131 – Dokki (USA) (Northern   **86**
Dancer) [1998 73: 7m* 7.1m⁶ 7d⁵ 1999 8m³ 10.3m³ 10.1m Oct 19] fairly useful
performer: good third in minor event at Yarmouth and handicap at Chepstow: well
held (after 3-month break) final start: stayed 1¼m: unraced on extremes of going:
stud. *J. H. M. Gosden*

SHOO-IN   3 b.f. Minshaanshu Amad (USA) 91§ – Heavenly State (Enchantment   **–**
115) [1998 NR 1999 8f 11.6d Jun 7] fourth reported foal: dam unraced: always
behind in maiden and claimer. *M. Madgwick*

SHOP WINDOW   3 b.f. Noble Patriarch 115 – Warning Bell 88 (Bustino 136)   **54**
[1998 54d: 6m³ 7m⁶ 7.5m 8d 1999 12m⁴ a12g 12g 12g 9.3g 8g³ 7.5m Jul 2] close-
coupled filly: modest maiden: seems to stay 1½m: acts on good to firm going: tried
visored: has worn tongue strap. *T. D. Easterby*

SHORT ROMANCE (IRE)   4 b.f. Brief Truce (USA) 126 – Lady's Turn   **66**
(Rymer 121) [1998 66: 8.3g 9.9g⁵ 10.2d 9.7f⁴ 12f* 12d 11.1m 1999 14.1s⁶ 13.1g²
12.1g 15.8m² 16m 14.1m⁵ 12d 11.8d⁵ Oct 12] leggy filly: fair handicapper: stays 2m:
yet to race on heavy ground, acts on any other: takes good hold: sold 5,500 gns.
J. W. Hills

SHOTACROSS THE BOW (IRE)   2 b.c. (Feb 24) Warning 136 – Nordica 99   **80 p**
(Northfields (USA)) [1999 6f 6d⁴ 6m* Sep 4] 70,000Y: tall, angular colt: has scope:
half-brother to several winners, including useful 7f winner (including at 2 yrs) and
Oaks fourth Sueboog (by Darshaan), the dam of 2-y-o Best of The Bests, and 7-y-o
Secret Spring: dam 6f (in Ireland) and 1m winner: progressive form: won maiden at
Epsom in September by ¾ length from Golden Harvest: will be suited by 7f+: should
make useful 3-y-o. *B. W. Hills*

SHOTLEY MARIE (IRE)   4 b.f. Scenic 128 – Hana Marie 101§ (Formidable   **– §**
(USA) 125) [1998 –: 8m 9.1m⁶ 10.9m 8m 1999 12.3m a12g 12.4m a16g 9.1v 7s a8g⁵
a11g⁶ Dec 17] plain filly: little sign of ability: tried blinkered: ungenuine. *N. Bycroft*

SHOUF AL BADOU (USA)   2 b.c. (Mar 18) Sheikh Albadou 128 – Millfit   **97 p**
(USA) 62 (Blushing Groom (FR) 131) [1999 7m³ 6g⁴ a6f* a6g* 8s* Nov 5] good-
bodied, attractive colt: fourth foal: brother to 5-y-o Tayseer and half-brother to
3-y-o Quiet Millfit: dam 7f winner: won maiden and minor event at
Wolverhampton in October and minor event at Doncaster (beat French Lieutenant by
2 lengths) in November: may prove best up to 1m: acts on soft going, good to firm
and fibresand: capable of better still. *B. W. Hills*

SHOULDHAVEGONEHOME (IRE)   2 ch.f. (Apr 29) Up And At 'em 109 –   **65 d**
Gentle Papoose (Commanche Run 133) [1999 5d 5s⁴ 5g² 5.1m⁵ 5m⁴ 5g 5m* 5m²
6m⁴ a5f³ 5s a6g 5.7s 5g a5g² a6g Dec 27] IR 4,000Y: leggy, workmanlike filly: third
foal: half-sister to 1998 2-y-o 5f/6f winner Cheyenne Gold (by Anita's Prince): dam
poor Irish maiden: fair performer: deteriorated after fourth start, though won seller at
Musselburgh in August: should prove best at 5f/easy 6f: acts on soft and good to firm
going, and on fibresand: tried blinkered/visored. *P. D. Evans*

Royal Hunt Cup (Handicap), Royal Ascot—Showboat draws six lengths clear of his thirty-one rivals; Plan-B and Refuse To Lose (rail) make it a 1–2–3 for the far-side group

SHOWBOAT 5 b.h. Warning 136 – Boathouse 116 (Habitat 134) [1998 99: 7s³ **113** 7.9g³ 8d 7f⁶ 7m⁴ 7m 7g 7g⁶ 7g 1999 7g* 7g 8g² 7m³ 8m* 8m⁴ 8f² 7m⁴ 8.9f⁶ 9m* 10g Oct 16] strong, close-coupled horse: has a short, unimpressive action: smart performer: won handicaps in large fields at Newmarket in April and Royal Ascot (Hunt Cup by 6 lengths from Plan-B) and 7-runner minor event at Newbury (by short head from Diamond White) in September: respectable fourth to Russian Revival in Tote International at Ascot eighth start, and not discredited in Champion Stakes at Newmarket final one: effective at 7f, probably at 1¼m: yet to race on heavy going, acts on any other: best held up in strongly-run race. *B. W. Hills*

SHOWING 2 b.c. (May 14) Owington 123 – Sharanella (Shareef Dancer (USA) **–** 135) [1999 6d 6d Oct 29] 14,000Y: good-topped colt: sixth foal: half-brother to useful 5f (at 2 yrs) to 1m winner Sonic Boy (by Celestial Storm), later successful in USA, and a winner in Germany by Miller's Mate: dam unraced: well beaten in Newmarket maidens. *N. A. Graham*

SHOW ME HEAVEN 2 b.f. (Apr 11) Rock City 120 – Tufty Lady 91 (Riboboy **–** (USA) 124) [1999 5m a6g⁶ Jul 24] 700Y: fourth foal: half-sister to 7f winner Second Cello (by Music Boy): dam 6f and 1m winner: showed nothing in claimers. *J. P. Leigh*

SHOW ME THE MONEY (IRE) 3 b.f. Mujadil (USA) 119 – Snappy Dresser **111** (Nishapour (FR) 125) [1998 108p: 5v* 5m⁴ 6m³ 6.3s³ 5g* 6d* 5s* 1999 7m* 8g 5d 7s³ 6s³ 7d⁶ Oct 9] close-coupled, workmanlike filly: smart performer: won listed race at Leopardstown in April by head from Apparatchik: ran at least respectably after when third in Boland Stakes at the Curragh (beaten over 5 lengths by Major Force) and Diadem Stakes at Ascot (beaten over a length by Bold Edge): best at 6f/7f: acts on good to firm and heavy ground. *N. Meade, Ireland*

SHRIVAR (IRE) 2 b.g. (Mar 15) Sri Pekan (USA) 117 – Kriva 69 (Reference **73** Point 139) [1999 7d⁶ 7s 7d⁵ Oct 27] 42,000Y: first foal: dam 17f winner, from family of Shaanxi: fair form in maidens, racing freely: bred to stay at least 1m, but needs to settle better. *M. R. Channon*

SHUDDER 4 b.g. Distant Relative 128 – Oublier L'Ennui (FR) 79 (Bellman (FR) **85 d** 123) [1998 –: 7g⁶ 1999 6m⁵ 6d* 7m⁵ 5m 6g 6d 5.1s Oct 26] fairly useful performer: won claimer at Haydock in July: generally below form after: should stay 7f: acts on good to soft going: visored second to fifth starts. *R. J. Hodges*

SHURUK 2 ch.f. (Mar 9) Cadeaux Genereux 131 – Harmless Albatross 115 (Pas **73 +** de Seul 133) [1999 6g 6.1m* 7m Sep 17] quite good-topped filly: half-sister to several winners (most at least useful), including smart 11f and 1½m winner Ghataas (by Sadler's Wells), 3-y-o Sakha, 4-y-o Kahtan, 6-y-o Mawared and very smart performer up to 1½m Volochine (by Soviet Star): dam French miler: fair form: won maiden at Nottingham in August: stiff task and seemed to run well when last of 7 in minor event at Newbury on final start: has raced freely, and may prove best up to 1m. *J. L. Dunlop*

SHUTTLECOCK 8 ch.g. Pharly (FR) 130 – Upper Sister (Upper Case (USA)) **30** [1998 30, a37: a13g⁴ a12g a12g 12.1v³ a11g⁴ 11.1d⁶ 10.9m a12g² a14g³ a14g⁴ a11g a11g⁶ 1999 a16g⁴ a12f a13g a16g a16g⁵ Feb 19] angular gelding: poor handicapper nowadays: stays 2m: acts on good to firm ground, heavy and all-weather: effective blinkered or not: usually races up with pace. *D. W. Chapman*

SIANA SPRINGS (IRE) 2 b.f. (Mar 15) Emarati (USA) 74 – Psylla 96 (Beldale **59** Flutter (USA) 130) [1999 5g⁵ 5d 5g* 5m⁶ 5m² 5g 6.5g 6s Sep 24] 1,400F: tall, rather unfurnished filly: half-sister to several winners, including 1997 2-y-o 5f winner Balance The Books (by Elmaamul) and 1¼m winners Akayid (by Old Vic) and Kabayil (by Dancing Brave): dam, 9f/1¼m winner, from family of Kris and Diesis: modest performer: won seller at Haydock in May: below form after fifth start: should be suited by 6f+: acts on good to firm going. *J. J. Quinn*

SIAN'S MILLENNIUM 2 b.f. (Apr 1) Whittingham (IRE) 104 – Special One **62** 66 (Aragon 118) [1999 5g⁵ 5m⁶ 5m⁴ 5g⁶ 6g 5m Jun 23] 24,000Y: quite attractive filly: has a quick action: second foal: sister to 3-y-o Inya Lake: dam, 2-y-o 5f winner, best at 6f: modest maiden: tried blinkered: dead. *B. Palling*

SIBERIAN MYSTIC 6 gr.m. Siberian Express (USA) 125 – Mystic Crystal **–** (IRE) 85 (Caerleon (USA) 132) [1998 48: 11.8g³ 12m² 14.1d² 12g⁵ 12.1g 1999 13.1g May 17] lengthy mare: modest handicapper: gave impression something amiss only 6-y-o start: stays 1¾m: acts on good to firm and good to soft going: good mount for inexperienced rider. *P. G. Murphy*

SIBERTIGO 3 b.g. Touch of Grey 90 – Young Lady (Young Generation 129) **–** [1998 NR 1999 7f 7.6m Jul 8] fifth reported foal: brother to 6-y-o Billaddie: dam never ran: well beaten in maidens at Lingfield. *R. M. Flower*

SIBLING RIVAL (USA) 5 b.h. Quest For Fame 127 – Perfect Sister (USA) **117** (Perrault 130) [1998 117: 12d* 12d² 12.5g² 10m 1999 12f* 12m 20m Jun 17] leggy, useful-looking horse: smart performer: won 5-runner prestige race at Nad Al Sheba in February by 5½ lengths from Perfect Paradigm: well beaten in Dubai Turf Classic there and Ascot Gold Cup (refused to settle) after: should stay beyond 12.5f: acts on firm and good ground. *Saeed bin Suroor*

SICK AS A PARROT 4 ch.g. Casteddu 111 – Sianiski (Niniski (USA) 125) **87** [1998 87: 8g 8.5m* 9.9g² 10g⁶ 9.9g⁶ 11m* 9m⁶ 10.1g 9g 1999 a10g³ a10g² 10.1s **a108** 10m 8.5g⁵ 8m 9.9g³ 9f⁵ 10m 8.5g 10.1d⁵ a10g⁶ a8.5g² a10g Dec 8] angular gelding: useful on all-weather, fairly useful on turf: good second to Supreme Sound in listed race at Lingfield in March: ran creditably only a few times after: effective at 1m to 11f: acts on firm going and equitrack: effective visored or not: has ungainly head carriage, but is game: sent to M. Dickinson in USA. *K. R. Burke*

SICNEE (USA) 3 gr.c. Rubiano (USA) – Lets Be Personal (CAN) (Grey Dawn II **120** 132) [1998 107: 7m⁵ 7.1g² 7g* 7.3v² 1999 a6.5f² 7m 7.1g* Aug 30] well-made colt: very smart performer: beaten a head in allowance race at Churchill Downs on reappearance, then respectable seventh in Jersey Stakes at Royal Ascot: best effort when winning minor event at Chepstow in August impressively by 2½ lengths from Trans Island: free-going sort, but likely to stay 1m: acts on good to firm and heavy ground. *Saeed bin Suroor*

SIDDONS COMMON (IRE) 3 b.c. Common Grounds 118 – Miss Siddons **–** (Cure The Blues (USA)) [1998 NR 1999 8m 10g 10m 10g 11g Oct 14] 12,000F, 17,000Y: well-made colt: poor mover: half-brother to several winners, including fairly useful 1¼m winner The Feltmaker (by Shernazar) and Irish 1¾m winner Any Minute Now (by Alzao): dam twice-raced half-sister to Seymour Hicks and Princess Pati: no sign of ability: has had breathing problems/been tongue tied: sold 800 gns: sent to Italy. *J. W. Hills*

SIDNEY THE KIDNEY 5 b.m. Mystiko (USA) 124 – Martin-Lavell Mail **–** (Dominion 123) [1998 32: a12s⁵ a11g³ a12g⁵ a11g⁵ a12g⁴ a11g a12g³ a12g⁴ 11.5d³ 10s a12g 1999 a11g⁶ a12f a12g a12f Jan 29] poor maiden handicapper: appears to stay 1½m: acts on good to firm ground, good to soft and fibresand: sent to Holland. *M. J. Ryan*

SIEGE (IRE) 3 br.c. Indian Ridge 123 – Above Water (IRE) (Reference Point **109** 139) [1998 97: 6m² 6f³ 6g³ 7g⁵ 1999 7f² 7m* 8m² 10.4f² Jul 10] strong, well-made colt: fluent mover: useful performer: won maiden at Kempton in May: very good second in Britannia Handicap at Royal Ascot (went down by 2 lengths to Pythios) and John Smith's Cup at York (sweating, beaten ½ length by Achilles) in June/July: stays 10.4f: raced only on good going or firmer: has worn net muzzle: sold to race in Dubai. *Sir Michael Stoute*

SIEGE PERILOUS (IRE) 6 b.g. Taufan (USA) 119 – Carado 82 (Manado 130) **74** [1998 NR 1999 16.4s⁵ 16s⁶ 16f May 29] rangy gelding: fairly useful handicapper in 1997, fair in 1999: stays 2¼m well: has form on good to firm ground, goes well on good or softer: sold 4,200 gns. *S. C. Williams*

SIEGFRIED 3 ch.g. Magic Ring (IRE) 115 – Spirit of The Wind (USA) (Little **–** Current (USA)) [1998 NR 1999 8m 7m a7g⁵ Jun 5] half-brother to fairly useful 1m winner Moon Mistress (by Storm Cat) and useful 11f winner North Wind (by Lomond): dam unraced: little sign of ability in maidens: will stay beyond 1m. *B. W. Hills*

SIFAT 4 b.f. Marju (IRE) 127 – Reine Maid (USA) (Mr Prospector (USA)) [1998 **66** 77: 8.1m⁴ 8m⁶ 10m³ 9.9m⁵ 8.1g⁵ 8d* 8.2v³ 1999 10s 8g 8g 10m⁵ 10m 10s⁴ 12d Oct 29] fair performer: effective at 1m to 1¼m: acts on good to firm and heavy ground: sometimes blinkered/visored: has looked less than keen: joined J. Jenkins. *N. A. Graham*

SIFT 2 b.f. (Mar 25) Salse (USA) 128 – Lake Pleasant (IRE) 90 (Elegant Air 119) **59** [1999 7g³ 6m 6.1m³ 7.5g⁶ 7g 8d³ Sep 16] 21,000Y: leggy, unfurnished filly: third foal: half-sister to 3-y-o Serpentine: dam, 6f winner from 3 starts at 2 yrs, from family of Bireme and Buoy: modest maiden: left Sir Mark Prescott after first 2 outings in sellers: will stay 1¼m: yet to race on extremes of going. *D. Haydn Jones*

SIGGIEWI 5 ro.m. Mystiko (USA) 124 – Shadiyama 58 (Nishapour (FR) 125) **23** [1998 –: a12g 11.9m 1999 11.8m⁴ 12g 14.1m Jun 16] bad maiden: stays 1½m. *N. M. Babbage*

SIGNET RING 3 ch.f. King's Signet (USA) 110 – Geoffreys Bird (Master Willie **–** 129) [1998 NR 1999 8m 7m 7.1m 8f 10g Sep 20] third foal: dam unraced half-sister to useful sprinter Mac's Fighter: little form: blinkered once: sold 1,000 gns, sent to Spain. *H. Candy*

SIGNIFY 3 b.c. Marju (IRE) 127 – Windmill Princess 55 (Gorytus (USA) 132) **80** [1998 NR 1999 8m 10m⁵ 12s³ 10.5m² 10g⁶ Aug 11] 30,000F, IR 21,000Y: tall, strong colt: fourth foal: half-brother to 1997 2-y-o 6f winner Cosmic Countess (by Lahib) and fairly useful 7f winner (including at 2 yrs) Cosmic Prince (by Teenoso): dam, placed at 1m and 11f, out of half-sister to Blakeney and Morston: fairly useful maiden: will prove best up to 10.5f: acts on good to firm going: swished tail in preliminaries, pulled hard and tended to hang third start: sold 7,000 gns, sent to Italy. *L. M. Cumani*

SIGN OF HOPE 2 ch.g. (Mar 3) Selkirk (USA) 129 – Rainbow's End 83 (My **78** Swallow 134) [1999 7.1d 7g⁴ 8m 7s 8d³ Oct 18] 42,000Y: tall, leggy gelding: half-brother to numerous winners, including 3-y-o Lokomotiv, useful 1993 2-y-o 6f/7f winner Carmot (by Cadeaux Genereux) and fairly useful stayer Cap del Mond (by Troy): dam 2-y-o 6f winner: fair maiden: visored, best effort when close third of 19 in nursery at Pontefract final outing: will stay 1¼m: pulled hard third start. *I. A. Balding*

SIGN OF THE TIGER 2 b.g. (Mar 12) Beveled (USA) – Me Spede (Valiyar **57 p** 129) [1999 6d 6g 5g a6g⁴ a8g³ Nov 30] 10,000F: fifth foal: brother to 5-y-o Gablesea: dam ran twice at 2 yrs: modest maiden: best effort in nursery at Southwell on final start despite racing wide: stays 1m: acts on fibresand: should improve further. *P. C. Haslam*

SIGNORINA CATTIVA (USA) 3 b.f. El Gran Senor (USA) 136 – Assez Cuite **117** (USA) 114 (Graustark) [1998 93p: 7g 8s* 1999 11.4m² 11m³ 12m⁴ 10.1g 12s* 12d* 12v* 10s³ Nov 7] angular filly: not a fluent mover: smart performer: improved in the autumn, winning listed race and Princess Royal Willmott Dixon Stakes (by 7 lengths from New Abbey) at Ascot and Perpetual (St Simon) Stakes at Newbury (by 7

lengths from Salford Express, sweating and on toes, flashed tail under whip): bit below best in Premio Roma final start: stayed 1½m: had form on good to firm ground, went very well on softer than good: stud. *J. L. Dunlop*

SIGNS AND WONDERS   5 b.m. Danehill (USA) 126 – Front Line Romance 89 (Caerleon (USA) 132) [1998 75§, a72§: a10g* a8g 6g⁵ a10g⁵ 8.3g² 9d 9.9m⁶ 6f 8.1m⁴ 1999 8.3m 7.6f³ 8g 8.3m⁶ 7m⁴ 8d² 7d Oct 27] lengthy, angular mare: fair handicapper: barely stays 1¼m: acts on firm going, good to soft and equitrack: edgy sort: not an easy ride. *C. A. Cyzer*   **68**

SIHAFI (USA)   6 ch.g. Elmaamul (USA) 125 – Kit's Double (USA) (Spring Double) [1998 79, a88: a6g⁵ a6g* a6g a6g 5s 5.9d 7g³ 6m* 5.3m² 5.1g* 5m* 5m* 5g* 5.7d⁴ 5m* 5m² 6m⁶ 6f³ 5.1d⁵ 5m² 5g 5g 5d 5m* a6g* 5d a6g a5g² a6g a5g² a6g a7g⁵ 1999 5g 5m 5m⁵ 6g 5f³ 5f³ 5f⁵ 6f⁶ 5g 6g 5m 5d 5s 6v Oct 12] tall gelding: fair handicapper: had a terrific year in 1998, successful 9 times: several creditable efforts in 1999, though lost form late on: has won at easy 6f, but probably best at strongly-run 5f: acts on firm going, good to soft and all-weather: often apprentice ridden: takes good hold and best covered up. *D. Nicholls*   **79**
 a–

SILCA BLANKA (IRE)   7 b.h. Law Society (USA) 130 – Reality 88 (Known Fact (USA) 135) [1998 92: 8d 7.6m³ 8m³ 8.5m 8d 8g 7f⁴ 7m* 7m 8d² 7m 7g a8g² 1999 a7g a7g* a8.5g 8d a8g² 7m² a8g 7d² 7g* 6f 7m 7d⁴ 7.1m⁴ 6v 7d 8d 7s a7g Nov 24] smallish, quite attractive horse: went to stud in 1997: useful handicapper: won at Lingfield in January and Epsom in June: well below form last 4 starts: effective at 7f to 8.5f: acts on firm ground, good to soft (probably on heavy) and equitrack: band-aged nowadays. *A. G. Newcombe*   **92**
 a89

SILCA FANTASY   2 b.f. (May 13) Piccolo 121 – Fantasy Racing (IRE) 86 (Tirol 127) [1999 6d May 15] first foal: dam 5f (including at 2 yrs) to 7f winner: ninth of 16 in maiden at Newbury: sold 3,400 gns in October. *M. R. Channon*   **–**

SILENTLY   7 b.g. Slip Anchor 136 – Land of Ivory (USA) 109 (The Minstrel (CAN) 135) [1998 89: 14.4m 13.3g³ 14.9d² 16.4g 14.8f³ 16.2g 14.1m* 12.3m³ 14g* 13.9g³ 13.1s⁵ 16g* 13.9g 14.6d⁶ 16.5d 1999 12m⁶ 18.7m 16s 12m 15.9m 16f 14.1f³ 14m⁶ 16m⁶ 14.1g Sep 25] good-topped gelding: one-time fairly useful performer, deteriorated in 1999: stays 2m: acts on firm and good to soft going, possibly not on soft: blinkered once at 4 yrs: tends to find little/look less than keen. *K. A. Ryan*   **71 d**

SILENT NIGHT   2 gr.f. (Mar 9) Night Shift (USA) – Catch The Sun (Kalaglow 132) [1999 7m⁷ 8.1s⁵ 7.3s Oct 23] 27,000Y: tall, close-coupled filly: seventh foal: half-sister to several winners, including smart stayer Tioman Island (by Midyan) and fairly useful middle-distance stayer Remaadi Sun (by Cadeaux Genereux): dam unraced: fairly useful form when winning minor event at Kempton in September, quickening 2f out and pushed out to beat La Fay by 2½ lengths: well held in stronger company after: should stay at least 1m. *D. R. C. Elsworth*   **80 +**

SILENT PRIDE (IRE)   4 ch.f. Pips Pride 117 – Suppression (Kind of Hush 118) [1998 39: a7g⁴ 9.9m⁴ 10.8m⁵ 10.1m 10g 8.1d 7.5d 11.9g⁶ 10m a8g² a8g⁵ a7g⁵ 1999 a6g a8g⁶ a7g Feb 4] leggy filly: poor mover: poor maiden: stays 1¼m: acts on good to firm ground and all-weather: virtually refused to race ninth 3-y-o start. *G. L. Moore*   **37**

SILENT SOUND (IRE) 3 b.g. Be My Guest (USA) 126 – Whist Awhile (Caer- **64**
leon (USA) 132) [1998 62: 7m⁵ 7m⁵ 8m⁶ 8d 1999 10m 10.9m⁴ 14.1f 12.1m 12f²
16m³ 10f* 12.4g⁶ 12.1m⁶ 12f 9.9s² 10g Oct 14] rather leggy, quite attractive gelding:
modest handicapper: won at Redcar in August: not clear run when creditable second
at Beverley after: likely to prove best at 1¼m: acts on any heavy going, acts on any
other: blinkered after fourth start: sold 13,000 gns, joined Mrs A. Perrett. *P. Calver*

SILENT VALLEY 5 b.m. Forzando 122 – Tremmin 67 (Horage 124) [1998 –§: **– §**
a9.4g 12.4d⁵ 1999 12g 10m Jul 17] sparely-made mare: modest in 1997: very lightly
raced and no form since: usually blinkered/visored: unreliable. *Miss L. C. Siddall*

SILENT WARNING 4 b.g. Ela-Mana-Mou 132 – Buzzbomb 98 (Bustino 136) **90**
[1998 93p: 7.1g⁴ 10m 9.2d⁴ a14g* 11.8s* 16s* a14g* 1999 13.1d 16d³ 17.3g Oct 16]
fairly useful handicapper: creditable third of 7 at Musselburgh in September: may
prove best at 1¾m/2m (possibly failed to stay 17f in Cesarewitch): acts on soft
ground and fibresand, poor efforts on good to firm: has won for amateur. *Sir Mark
Prescott*

SILK COTTAGE 7 b.g. Superpower 113 – Flute Royale 74 (Horage 124) [1998 **58**
56, a62: a6g³ a5g a6g⁴ a6g² a7g 5s 5g³ 5v⁵ 5d² 5s 5g 5m³ 5m⁶ 5g⁴ 5m 5g 5m 5m⁶ 5v² **a62**
6v a5g² a5s* a5g 1999 a6g a5g² a5g⁶ 5d⁴ 5g* 5m³ 5m² 5.1d May 19] sturdy, good-
quartered gelding: modest handicapper: won at Newcastle in April: was effective
at 5f/6f: acted on heavy ground, good to firm and all-weather: usually visored/
blinkered: dead. *R. Bastiman*

SILK DAISY 3 b.f. Barathea (IRE) 127 – Scene Galante (FR) (Sicyos (USA) 126) **74**
[1998 NR 1999 6m⁵ 7.1m³ 7g³ 7.7m 8.2s² 8.3d³ Nov 4] 35,000Y: third foal: half-
sister to German 1996 2-y-o 6f winner Sospel (by Kendor) and French 1¼m winner
Cold Encounter (by Polar Falcon): dam French 1¼m winner: fair maiden: should
stay beyond 1m: acts on soft and good to firm ground. *H. Candy*

SILKEN 3 b.f. Danehill (USA) 126 – Our Reverie (USA) (J O Tobin (USA) 130) **85**
[1998 73p: 7g⁶ 6m⁶ 1999 7m³ 8g² 9m³ 10.1m* 9f⁴ 11.6d³ 12m⁶ Aug 29] quite attractive filly: fairly useful performer: won 5-runner maiden at Epsom in July: ran at least
respectably in handicaps after: barely stays 1½m: acts on firm going, probably on
good to soft: sent to USA. *Mrs A. J. Perrett*

SILKEN DALLIANCE 4 b.f. Rambo Dancer (CAN) 107 – A Sharp (Sharpo **91**
132) [1998 88: a6g² a6g* 8s⁵ 8.2g² 8.5m 8d* 8g 8s* 8g* 8v 1999 8m 7.9f² 8f⁵ 8m⁵ 8s
7.9g 8g Oct 16] neat filly: fairly useful handicapper: creditable fifth to Lonesome
Dude in William Hill Mile at Goodwood on third start: stays 1m: acts on fibresand,
firm and soft going: races prominently. *I. A. Balding*

SILKEN FOX (IRE) 2 b.g. (May 19) Foxhound (USA) 103 – Crown Witness 95 **–**
(Crowned Prince (USA) 128) [1999 7s 6g 7d Oct 27] IR 7,200F, 3,000Y, 10,500
2 y o: half-brother to several winners, including won 1990 2-y-o 7f winner Trojan
Crown (by Trojan Fen) who stayed 1m: dam, 1m winner, half-sister to dam of Vintage Crop: well held in maidens. *J. S. Moore*

SILKEN LADY 3 br.f. Rock Hopper 124 – Silk St James (Pas de Seul 133) [1998 **–**
NR 1999 8.3m 9.9m 10.5s Sep 24] sister to 4-y-o Lady Rockstar and half-sister to
several winners, including 5-y-o Silk St John: dam unraced: well beaten in maidens.
M. J. Ryan

SILK PRINCESS 4 gr.f. Touch of Grey 90 – Young Lady (Young Generation **50**
129) [1998 62p: 7g 10g 10v⁶ 1999 10m 10s 12g a10g⁵ Jul 9] lengthy filly: modest
maiden: should stay 1½m. *R. M. Flower*

SILK ST BRIDGET 2 b.f. (May 12) Rock Hopper 124 – Silk St James (Pas de **– p**
Seul 133) [1999 6d 6s 6g Oct 15] sister to 3-y-o Silken Lady and 4-y-o Lady Rockstar, and half-sister to several winners, including 5-y-o Silk St John and 10-y-o Kingchip Boy: dam unraced: 50/1, first sign of ability in maidens when seventh of 12 to
L'Arita at Redcar final start, staying on encouragingly from rear: will stay at least
1m: type to do much better in handicaps at 3 yrs. *M. J. Ryan*

SILK ST JOHN 5 b.g. Damister (USA) 123 – Silk St James (Pas de Seul 133) **103**
[1998 103, a71: a11g⁶ a11g⁴ 8d 8.1g*dis 8.1m* 7g² 8.3d* 8m³ 8g* 8m⁶ 8.1g 7.6f **a–**
8.3m* 8m² 8s² 9g 8s⁵ 1999 8d 8m 8.1s* 8m 7.9d⁴ 8m⁴ 8.1g 8s² 8m 8.1m⁴ 8f* 8m⁶
8d⁴ 8m³ 8s⁴ 7.9g 8.5d³ 9v 8d Oct 30] close-coupled gelding: useful performer: won

handicaps at Sandown (rated stakes) in April and Newbury in July: ran well several times otherwise, including when third to Indian Lodge in falsely-run listed contest at Newmarket seventeenth start: ran poorly last 2: probably best around 1m: acts on fibresand and any turf going: usually held up, and has turn of foot: tough. *M. J. Ryan*

SILK WING 3 b.f. Wing Park 104 – Little Park 39 (Cragador 110) [1998 –: 5g 6m6 5g 1999 a6g a7g a8g 6.1v a7g 9.9g Apr 22] of little account. *T. T. Clement* —

SILVANO'S EXPRESS 3 b.g. Sizzling Melody 117 – Penny Hasset 73 (Lochnager 132) [1998 NR 1999 7d 6d 5d 6f 7g 5g 5d2 5f 5m 5f 5g 5f 6s6 8d Oct 20] 2,100Y: big, workmanlike gelding: second foal: dam winning sprinter: poor maiden: likely to prove best at 5f/6f: best efforts on good to soft/soft going: blinkered/visored seventh to twelfth starts. *Miss J. F. Craze* **39**

SILVER APPLE (IRE) 3 gr.c. Danehill (USA) 126 – Moon Festival 74 (Be My Guest (USA) 126) [1998 95: 7m2 1999 12m4 10d 11.8m4 7.9d6 10m3 8.1m* 8.1m* Aug 5] angular, workmanlike colt: useful performer: won maiden at Sandown in July and handicap at Chepstow in August (dictated pace): may prove best at 1m: acts on good to firm going, below form both starts on good to soft: blinkered fourth start: sold 35,000 gns, sent to Macau. *P. F. I. Cole* **95**

SILVER ARROW (USA) 2 b. or br.f. (Jan 19) Shadeed (USA) 135 – Aneesati 85 (Kris 135) [1999 5m4 Jun 12] third foal: half-sister to 3-y-o Ras Shaikh and 4-y-o Epsom Cyclone: dam, 1m winner, out of 1000 Guineas runner-up Dabaweyaa: odds on but green, slowly away and never on terms when well-held fourth of 5 to See You Later in maiden at Sandown. *B. W. Hills* **67 +**

SILVER BLADE 3 gr.f. Mystiko (USA) 124 – Blade of Grass 78 (Kris 135) [1998 –: 6g 6.1g 7m 8.1m6 7s 1999 10m 14.1g Jul 3] little sign of ability. *A. T. Murphy* —

SILVER BULLET 3 gr.g. Grey Desire 115 – Spanish Realm 69 (King of Spain 121) [1998 NR 1999 7f6 6d 8f Sep 4] 550Y: tall, angular gelding: has a round action: third reported foal: dam, winning sprinter, half-sister to 8-y-o Grey Kingdom: no form, including in seller. *W. W. Haigh* —

SILVER CASTOR (IRE) 4 b.f. Indian Ridge 123 – Bayazida (Bustino 136) [1998 –, a50: 12.3g4 11.7m 12m 14.1v a14.8g a13g6 1999 16d 12.3m6 14m5 Jul 8] angular filly: poor handicapper: stays 1¾m: acts on good to firm going (probably heavy) and equitrack: joined A. Martin in Ireland. *P. W. Harris* **48**

SILVER COLOURS (USA) 2 b. or br.f. (Feb 9) Silver Hawk (USA) 123 – Team Colors (USA) (Mr Prospector (USA)) [1999 7d6 8d* Oct 30] quite goodtopped filly: has scope: fourth foal: half-sister to 3-y-o Desaru and a winner in USA by Seattle Dancer: dam unraced daughter of sister to US Grade 1 winners Personal Ensign and Personal Flag: confirmed debut (burly and green) promise when winning steadily-run 10-runner listed event at Newmarket by 1¼ lengths from Bedara, leading 2f out and responding gamely: will be suited by 1¼m+: should improve further. *L. M. Cumani* **94 p**

SILVERDALE LAD 8 b.g. Presidium 124 – Its My Turn 80 (Palm Track 122) [1998 NR 1999 12g 14.1m5 Aug 28] fourth foal: half-brother to 1989 2-y-o 6f winner Silverdale Fox (by Sweet Monday): dam miler: fair hurdler at best: poor form in claimer/seller on Flat: joined Kate Milligan. *K. W. Hogg, Isle of Man* **40**

SILVER GROOM (IRE) 9 gr.g. Shy Groom (USA) – Rustic Lawn (Rusticaro (FR) 124) [1998 59: 10g 10.1m 12g 10g 11.5g 9.9m2 10.1s 10g a10g5 1999 9.9m Apr 14] smallish, angular gelding: modest handicapper nowadays: well held only start in 1999: stays 1¼m: has won on soft ground, best efforts on firm/good to firm: used to be held up: visored once. *M. R. Channon* **65**

SILVER GYRE (IRE) 3 b.f. Silver Hawk (USA) 123 – Kraemer (USA) (Lyphard (USA) 132) [1998 63p: 7.5m4 7g 8d 1999 7s 12v 8m 11.6g6 12.3m2 17.2m* 15.8d4 17.1s 16d a16.2g6 Nov 17] lengthy, useful-looking filly: fair handicapper: won at Bath in July: mostly below form after: stays 17f: acts on good to firm and good to soft going. *D. J. Wintle* **65**

SILVER MIST 3 b.f. Lugana Beach 116 – Highland Bonnie (Dreams To Reality (USA) 113) [1998 54: 5g 6m 5m4 6.1s 1999 8m 10.1g 7m* 8m 7f 7.1m 7g Sep 14] **54**

good-quartered filly: modest performer: form in 1999 only when winning handicap at Newcastle in July: stays 7f: acts on good to firm going: usually blinkered: has been bandaged: has raced freely. *G. G. Margarson*

SILVER PATRIARCH (IRE)   5 gr.h. Saddlers' Hall (IRE) 126 – Early **125** Rising (USA) (Grey Dawn II 132) [1998 125: 12d² 12g* 12m⁴ 12m⁶ 13.3m² 14d² 12s* 1999 12m* 12d⁴ 12m⁴ 13.3g* 14s³ 12f² 12m Dec 12]

As a result of Peter Winfield's bequeathing a half-share in Silver Patriarch to the National Stud, the horse will be taking up stallion duties there in the next year at a fee of £2,500. Winfield, a sporting owner, must have derived special pleasure from being so closely involved with a horse who achieved so much in four seasons' racing. Silver Patriarch won eight races, including the St Leger, Coronation Cup and Gran Premio del Jockey Club and around £920,000 in win and place prize money, but he will be remembered as much for the part he played in the 1997 Derby. In last place and under pressure as the field came down Tattenham Hill, Silver Patriarch put in such a strong run up the straight that he went down by only a short head to Benny The Dip in one of the finest finishes to the classic. Silver Patriarch was in front just before the line and just after it.

Silver Patriarch was as good as ever in the latest season and won a couple of Group 2 contests, the Sagitta Jockey Club Stakes at Newmarket in April and the Geoffrey Freer Stakes at Newbury in August. Beaten a neck in the race the previous year, Silver Patriarch had that margin to spare over Silver Rhapsody in the latest running of the Jockey Club Stakes. He was soon off the bridle as usual, but responded in generous fashion to edge ahead in the final furlong. Silver Patriarch gave a similar performance at Newbury, where, as at Newmarket, his penalty for his Group 1 successes meant that he had to concede weight all round. His three rivals included his stable-companion Sadian, who had won both the John Porter Stakes and Ormonde Stakes, along with the Princess of Wales's Stakes winner Craigsteel and the progressive Blueprint, who was going for a fourth straight win. A steady pace wasn't ideal for Silver Patriarch, and he also wasn't helped when Blueprint hung left around two furlongs out, causing him to be checked in his run. He quickly regained his momentum, though, and ran on strongly to collar the leader Craigsteel inside the final furlong, going on to beat him by half a length. Silver Patriarch wasn't disgraced in his two races in between those wins, finishing fourth to Daylami in both the Coronation Cup at Epsom and King George VI and Queen Elizabeth Diamond Stakes at Ascot.

Silver Patriarch ran some way below his best in his final three races, even though he was beaten only a nose when going for a second successive win

Geoffrey Freer Stakes, Newbury—Silver Patriarch shows himself to be as good as ever, overcoming Craigsteel, Sadian and Blueprint (outside)

in the Gran Premio del Jockey Club in Milan, where he was struck into on the outside of his off-fore. The ground had been soft when Silver Patriarch had won it, but it was very firm this time around. It certainly wasn't ideal for a horse who seemed to be less at ease on ground firmer than good as he got older. However, it shouldn't be forgotten that the ground was good to firm when he won the St Leger and the Jockey Club Stakes.

Silver Patriarch (IRE) (gr.h. 1994)	Saddlers' Hall (IRE) (b 1988)	Sadler's Wells (b 1981)	Northern Dancer Fairy Bridge
		Sunny Valley (b 1972)	Val de Loir Sunland
	Early Rising (USA) (gr 1980)	Grey Dawn II (gr 1962)	Herbager Polamia
		Gliding By (b 1975)	Tom Rolfe Key Bridge

Silver Patriarch's pedigree details have been well documented in previous Annuals. Suffice to say here that he's the ninth foal of Early Rising, a mare from one of Paul Mellon's most successful families who won a small race at around a mile in the United States for him. She then produced four foals, three of them winners, before being bought by Mr Winfield for 160,000 dollars in 1988. Early Rising has also been responsible for plenty of winners since, apart from Silver Patriarch. The best of the rest are the useful sprinter Silver Singing (by Topsider) and the smart stayer My Patriarch (by Be My Guest). Silver Patriarch, a rather leggy, good-topped individual, was effective at a mile and a half and a mile and three quarters and would probably have stayed further. Apparently a Cup campaign would have been on the agenda had he been kept in training for another season. *J. L. Dunlop*

SILVER PREY (USA) 6 b.g. Silver Hawk (USA) 123 – Truly My Style (USA) **58**
(Mount Hagen (FR) 127) [1998 76: 8.1g⁵ 8.1g 8d 8m 7.1g 8m 8.9g 7s 1999 7m 7f 10g⁶ 11.7m* Jul 15] modest in 1999: won seller at Bath in July: stayed 1½m: acted on good to firm ground: dead. *M. J. Bolton*

SILVER PRINCE 4 gr.g. Mystiko (USA) 124 – Hawaiian Song 63 (Henbit **–**
(USA) 130) [1998 NR 1999 7d 8m 6d Apr 16] 5,000F, 7,500Y: leggy, lengthy, sparely-made gelding: fourth reported foal: dam 7f winner: well beaten in maidens. *D. Nicholls*

SILVER QUEEN 2 ch.f. (Apr 10) Arazi (USA) 135 – Love of Silver (USA) 110 **71**
(Arctic Tern (USA) 126) [1999 5m⁵ 6f⁵ 6m⁴ 8.1m⁴ 7.5g Sep 15] leggy filly: third foal: half-sister to 3-y-o Silver Tongued: dam, 2-y-o 6f and 7f winner and third in Prix Marcel Boussac, should have been well suited by 1½m: fair maiden: best efforts second to fourth starts: will stay 1¼m. *C. E. Brittain*

SILVER RHAPSODY (USA) 4 b.f. Silver Hawk (USA) 123 – Sister Chrys **115**
(USA) (Fit To Fight (USA)) [1998 115: 10m* 11.9m³ 12s* 12s⁵ 1999 12m² 12d⁴ 12m³ 11.9g³ 12d⁶ 12d⁵ Oct 9] big, strong, rangy filly: has a powerful, round action: smart performer: best efforts in 1999 when placed in Jockey Club Stakes (neck second to Silver Patriarch) and Princess of Wales's Stakes (2¼ lengths third to Craigsteel) both at Newmarket and Yorkshire Oaks (3¼ lengths third to Ramruma) at York: well held in Europa-Preis at Cologne and Princess Royal Stakes at Ascot last 2 starts: should be suited by further than 1½m: acts on soft and good to firm going: refused to enter stalls third intended start, and equipped with rope halter after: sent to USA. *H. R. A. Cecil*

SILVER ROBIN (USA) 3 b. or br.c. Silver Hawk (USA) 123 – Wedge Musical **99**
(What A Guest 119) [1998 90P: 7d² 1999 10m³ Apr 30] big, strong colt: has scope: has a powerful, round action: highly promising only start at 2 yrs: better for race, again shaped well when 5½ lengths third to Beat All in listed race at Newmarket in April: will be suited by 1½m: sold only 14,000 gns. *L. M. Cumani*

SILVER SECRET 5 gr.g. Absalom 128 – Secret Dance (Sadler's Wells (USA) **50**
132) [1998 60: 7f⁶ 7.5m⁴ 10g 9.9m 8v⁴ 7s 1999 7.5d 8g³ 8m 12d⁴ 10.3m⁴ 8m* 10m⁶ 7f⁴ 8m 8.5g⁴ 10.5m⁶ 12m³ Sep 10] well-made gelding: modest handicapper: won

amateur event at Newmarket in July: effective at 1m, probably at 1½m: acts on any ground: tried visored. *S. Gollings*

SILVER SKY 3 gr.f. Chilibang 120 – Sizzling Sista (Sizzling Melody 117) [1998 NR 1999 6.1g 6d 8.3d a7g a8g Dec 6] 3,000Y, 8,500 2-y-o: second reported foal: dam unraced: little sign of ability. *M. D. I. Usher* —

SILVERSMITH (FR) 4 b.g. Always Fair (USA) 121 – Phargette (USA) (Lyphard (USA) 132) [1998 69d: 7.1d⁶ 7m 7f⁵ 8g 7.6g 5.7m a7g a12g⁶ 1999 a12g a8g⁵ a7f⁴ 7.5m² 8d² 7.6g⁴ 9g³ 8g 7.6g 9.3m⁶ 7.6m 9s Nov 20] close-coupled gelding: modest maiden on turf, poor on all-weather: left S. Dow after third start (blinkered, raced freely): stays 1m: acts on good to firm ground, good to soft and equitrack. *W. J. S. Cargeeg, France* **64 a49**

SILVER SNAKE (IRE) 3 b.c. Salse (USA) 128 – Ibtisamm (USA) 71 (Caucasus (USA) 127) [1998 –p: 7m⁵ 1999 8s⁶ Sep 29] small colt: little impact in minor event and maiden 11 months apart: sold 800 gns: dead. *C. E. Brittain* —

SILVER SOCKS 2 gr.g. (Mar 31) Petong 126 – Tasmim 63 (Be My Guest (USA) 126) [1999 7f⁵ 5f 6g 6s Oct 4] quite good-topped gelding: fourth foal: half-brother to 3-y-o Itsanothergirl: dam 11f winner: modest maiden: best effort when eleventh of 23 in valuable seller at York third start: probably stays 7f: may still do better. *M. W. Easterby* **52 +**

SILVER SPIDER 4 gr.g. Terimon 124 – Quetta's Girl (Orchestra 118) [1998 –: 9.9m 8.5m 1999 a12g⁶ a11g Feb 5] lengthy gelding: soundly beaten in maidens. *Mrs S. Lamyman* —

SILVER SUN 4 gr.f. Green Desert (USA) 127 – Catch The Sun (Kalaglow 132) [1998 74: 8d 10m³ 8g 10g⁴ 8m² 7m 9.9d² 9.9m⁵ 8d⁶ a10g⁶ 1999 8f² 9m* 9m³ 9.9g⁴ Jul 2] rather leggy, sparely-made filly: fairly useful performer: won maiden at Goodwood in June: ran creditably all other starts: effective at 1m/1¼m: acts on firm and good to soft going. *D. R. C. Elsworth* **83**

SILVER SYMPHONY 4 gr.f. Kylian (USA) – Brave Maiden 63 (Three Legs 128) [1998 –: 8f⁶ 1999 10v 10.2d 12.1g⁶ 14.1m⁶ 17.2m³ 16.4d⁵ Aug 12] big, close-coupled filly: modest maiden handicapper: stays 17f: acts on good to firm and good to soft going. *B. R. Millman* **53**

SILVER TONGUED 3 b.c. Green Desert (USA) 127 – Love of Silver (USA) 110 (Arctic Tern (USA) 126) [1998 NR 1999 10f 7g 8.3m⁵ 8g 7.1m Sep 9] second foal: dam, 2-y-o 6f/7f winner and third in Prix Marcel Boussac, should have been well suited by 1½m: seemed to show fair form when fifth in steadily-run maiden at Windsor in August: well beaten otherwise. *C. E. Brittain* —

SILVERTOWN 4 b.g. Danehill (USA) 126 – Docklands (USA) (Theatrical 128) [1998 69d: 7.1d³ 8.1s 9s⁵ 10g⁴ 11.6f² 12d⁶ 11.9m 12g 10v 11d 1999 a12g⁵ 10d⁶ 11.9d³ 10.1m* 11.5g³ 10.4f* 12m 11.5g 10s a9.4g² a12g Dec 11] lengthy gelding: fair handicapper: won at Epsom in August and York (22-runner apprentice race) in September: well held after other than penultimate run: has form at 1½m, likely to prove best at 1m/1¼m: acts on fibresand, firm and good to soft going: sometimes pulls hard, and often races up with pace. *B. J. Curley* **66**

SILVER VEIL (IRE) 3 gr.f. Shirley Heights 130 – Papago (IRE) 110 (Sadler's Wells (USA) 132) [1998 NR 1999 10d Aug 16] first foal: dam, French 2-y-o 1m winner who stayed 1½m, out of sister to dam of Dancing Brave and Jolypha: 5/2, well beaten in maiden at Windsor (swished tail to post and throughout race): sold 18,500 gns in December. *M. P. Tregoning* —

SIMBATU 2 b.f. (Feb 7) Muhtarram (USA) 125 – Kantado 93 (Saulingo 122) [1999 5m⁵ 5g³ 7.1g a6g Nov 24] half-sister to several winners, notably In Excess (by Siberian Express), 6f/7f winner here and later top-class in USA at 1m/1¼m: dam raced mainly at 5f: modest maiden: may prove best at 5f/6f. *Miss I. Foustok* **60**

SIMPLE IDEALS (USA) 5 b. or br.g. Woodman (USA) 126 – Comfort And Style 95 (Be My Guest (USA) 126) [1998 60d: 11s⁵ 10s 12.3m 10.5v 12g 12m 14m 11.9g 11.5d⁵ 1999 9g⁵ 12.3m 11d 12.1m⁴ 12s⁴ 13.8g⁴ 14.1f⁴ 10.9s² 12m³ 12.4m⁶ 12m³ 11.9d* 15m* 11m² 12g⁴ 14s⁵ 14.1g⁶ 13.9d³ 14.1g* 14.6d³ 13.8s³ Nov 2] sparely-made gelding: has a round action: modest handicapper: left N. Tinkler after **54**

fourth start: won at Haydock and Ayr in August and Redcar in October: effective at 1½m to 15f: acts on firm and soft ground: blinkered twice in 1997: sometimes races freely/hangs, and usually held up: tough and consistent. *Don Enrico Incisa*

SIMPLY MAGICAL   3 b.f. Magic Ring (IRE) 115 – Naulakha (Bustino 136) [1998 73: 7d 8s⁵ 7v⁵ a8g⁴ a8f² 1999 a10g⁴ 7d 8.5m⁶ 8s Sep 27] fair on all-weather in 1998: little form at 3 yrs: stays 1m: acts on equitrack: sold 3,000 gns, sent to Kuwait. *P. Mitchell* —

SIMPLY NOBLE   3 b.c. Noble Patriarch 115 – Simply Candy (IRE) 42 (Simply Great (FR) 122) [1998 81: 6.1g 8g 8.3s* 1999 12s⁵ 12m 10.1m² 10.3d⁶ 11.9m³ 12m Sep 11] useful-looking colt: fairly useful handicapper: ran creditably in 1999 when placed: stays 1½m: acts on soft and good to firm going: free-going sort. *K. McAuliffe* **81**

SIMPSON'S DOMAIN (IRE)   3 b.f. Woods of Windsor (USA) – Admiralella 71 (Dominion 123) [1998 51, a42: 5d⁶ 5d³ 5.3d⁵ 6g⁴ 7d⁵ 7m⁵ a7g⁶ 6m 6m a7g⁶ 8d³ a8g a7g⁵ a8g⁶ 1999 a8g⁴ a10g⁶ a10g⁴ a12g⁵ 6m 8m 8m⁶ 10d⁴ 12m 12.1m 8.1m 10m⁴ 10m Sep 1] lengthy, sparely-made filly: poor maiden handicapper: left J. S. Moore after fourth start: probably best around 1m nowadays: acts on good to firm going, good to soft and fibresand: tried visored: none too consistent: joined P. Jones. *Simon Earle* **46 a36**

SING AND DANCE   6 b.m. Rambo Dancer (CAN) 107 – Musical Princess 66 (Cavo Doro 124) [1998 54: 9.9s⁴ 9.3s 12m³ 12g⁴ 10.9m³ 12m* 12g² 12.4g* 10s⁶ 11m⁴ 12d⁴ 12m 12d* 12s⁵ 1999 12m⁴ 12m* 12.4m⁴ 10.9s⁵ 12m³ 12g⁶ 12.4m³ 13.8m 11.1m³ 12.1f* 12g² 11.9d 13.8g² Oct 16] big, workmanlike mare: modest handicapper: won in large fields at Musselburgh in May and Hamilton (apprentices) in August: probably best at 1½m/1¾m: acts on firm and good to soft ground: tried in visor/blinkers: held up: consistent. *E. Weymes* **59**

SING CHEONG (IRE)   3 b.c. Forest Wind (USA) 111 – Lady Counsel (IRE) 43 (Law Society (USA) 130) [1998 NR 1999 7g 7.1m⁵ 9g³ 8d 7d a6g a7g² a8g⁴ a10g³ Dec 29] IR 8,000F, 10,000Y: medium-sized, good-bodied colt: first foal: dam poor Irish maiden: fair maiden: best efforts first 2 starts: probably stays 1¼m: acts on good to firm going and equitrack. *G. C. H. Chung* **70 d**

SING FOR ME (IRE)   4 b. or br.f. Songlines (FR) 121 – Running For You (FR) (Pampabird 124) [1998 43: a8g a6g³ a5g* a5g⁴ a6g⁶ a6g 6.1s² 6g⁵ 6d 8.5g 6g³ 5m⁶ 5m 6g a6g⁵ a5g a6g⁵ a6g 1999 a7g a8.5g⁵ a8f a6s⁶ a7g⁵ a7g a8g⁵ a8g a8g 5v a5g⁵ a6g⁶ 5m⁶ 5m⁶ 6g 6g 5s⁵ a6g a5g a6g a6g Dec 17] sparely-made filly: poor mover: poor performer: stays 7f: acts on soft ground, good to firm and fibresand: visored (ran creditably) once. *R. Hollinshead* —

SINGING WINDS (IRE)   3 b.f. Turtle Island (IRE) 123 – Shamiyda (USA) (Sir Ivor 135) [1998 NR 1999 7f² 7g⁴ 8g² 8d Sep 26] 70,000Y: seventh foal: half-sister to 3 winners, including smart Irish stayer Shaiybara (by Kahyasi): dam middle-distance maiden: fair maiden: will stay beyond 1m: acts on firm going: wandered/seemed none too keen penultimate start, found nothing final one: temperament under suspicion: sold 6,000 gns in December. *M. Johnston* **73**

SINGLE CURRENCY   3 b.c. Barathea (IRE) 127 – Kithanga (IRE) 117 (Darshaan 133) [1998 NR 1999 10.5s³ Sep 24] 160,000Y: first foal: dam won St Simon Stakes and third in Irish St Leger: weak 10/1-shot, looked in need of experience when 2¾ lengths third to Tariyfa in maiden at Haydock, keeping on from mid-field: will improve. *P. F. I. Cole* **78 p**

SINGLE SHOT (USA)   3 b.c. Hermitage (USA) – Bourbon Miss (USA) (Smile (USA)) [1998 85: 7m 6m³ 6g² 7.1g² 8v² 7.1s* 1999 7.9s⁶ 7m⁶ 7f³ 8.1m³ 9m 7m 8d* Oct 21] good-topped colt: fairly useful performer: won minor event at Brighton in October: should prove best up to 1m: acts on any going: sold 36,000 gns, joined N. Canani in USA. *L. M. Cumani* **86**

SINGSONG   2 b.g. (Mar 20) Paris House 123 – Miss Whittingham (IRE) 68 (Fayruz 116) [1999 5d* 5g³ 5f⁴ 5d 5m* 5m⁵ 5m² 6m Jul 31] 6,000Y: small, leggy gelding: first foal: dam 5f/6f winner who stayed 7f: fairly useful performer: won maiden at Doncaster in March and minor event at Ripon in June: good head second of 10 in nursery at York penultimate start: may prove best at 5f: acts on good to firm and good to soft going: has edged right. *J. Berry* **81**

H.H. Aga Khan's "Sinndar"

SINNDAR (IRE) 2 b.c. (Feb 27) Grand Lodge (USA) 125 – Sinntara (IRE) (Lash- **105 p**
kari 128) [1999 8m* 8s* Sep 19] useful-looking, slightly unfurnished colt: third foal:
half-brother to useful Irish 1½m winner Sirinndi (by Shahrastani) who stayed 2m and
Irish 3-y-o 12.5f winner Sinndiya (by Pharly): dam Irish 1½m and (including listed
race) 2m winner: won both his starts at the Curragh in September, namely maiden by
1½ lengths and Aga Khan Studs National Stakes (by head from Murawwi) fortnight
later, soon off bridle in latter, but forging ahead near finish: will stay 1½m: tongue
tied final start: type to progress further and win more races. *J. Oxx, Ireland*

SINON (IRE) 4 ch.g. Ela-Mana-Mou 132 – Come In (Be My Guest (USA) 126) **111**
[1998 105: 13.9d* 16.2d⁴ 14.8f⁴ 1999 17.3g 15v* Nov 30] tall, leggy gelding: smart
performer, lightly raced: off 17 months before reappearance: won listed race at
Saint-Cloud 6 weeks later by 5 lengths: stays 2m: acts on good to firm and good to
soft going, moved poorly on firm. *M. Johnston*

SIOUX 5 ch.m. Kris 135 – Lassoo 87 (Caerleon (USA) 132) [1998 68: 12m⁵ 12.1s **64**
a12g³ a12g* a13g 1999 a12g² Jan 6] leggy mare: fair performer: ran creditably only
5-y-o start: stays 1½m: acts on soft going, good to firm and fibresand: usually tongue
tied: none too reliable. *C. W. Thornton*

SIOUX CHEF 2 b.f. (May 2) Be My Chief (USA) 122 – Sea Fret 96 (Habat 127) **78**
[1999 6m⁴ 5.7m* Jul 20] 36,000Y: sister to useful 1995 2-y-o 5f/6f winner Flying
Squaw and half-sister to several winners, including 3-y-o Salalah, 4-y-o Shanillo
and 5-y-o Cauda Equina: dam 2-y-o 6f winner: fair form: won maiden at Bath by
head from Enaaq, getting up under strong pressure close home: will stay 7f: looked
capable of better. *M. R. Channon*

SIOUX WARRIOR 7 br.g. Mandrake Major 122 – Seminole 79 (Amber Rama **–**
(USA) 133) [1998 NR 1999 10.1m 12g 14d Jun 4] good-topped gelding: half-brother
to 2 winning hurdlers by Great Nephew: dam 11f and 1½m winner: modest bumper
winner in 1996: little show over jumps/on Flat since: blinkered final start. *N. Tinkler*

SIRDHANA   2 ch.f. (Feb 5) Selkirk (USA) 129 – Vicky Dolman (USA) (Slew **79 p**
O'Gold (USA)) [1999 8s² Oct 31] 15,000Y: sixth foal: half-sister to several winners
in Italy, including at up to 1½m Kocin (by Be My Guest): dam Italian 1m winner:
beaten nose by Green Reew in 7-runner minor event at Milan: likely to improve.
L. M. Cumani

SIR ECHO (FR)   3 b.g. Saumarez 132 – Echoes (FR) 112 (Niniski (USA) 125) **92 p**
[1998 73: 7.1m 8d⁶ 8s⁴ 7d⁶ 1999 11.8v⁴ 11.6g² 12d⁷ 12.4m⁵ Jun 24] big, good-
topped gelding: has scope: fairly useful performer: best effort when winning
6-runner handicap at Newbury in June by 1¼ lengths from Thames Dancer: ran
respectably in rated stakes at Newcastle final start: will be suited by at least 1¾m:
acts on good to soft going, probably good to firm: game front runner: type to improve
again at 4 yrs. *H. Candy*

SIR EFFENDI (IRE)   3 ch.c. Nashwan (USA) 135 – Jeema 102 (Thatch (USA) **99 p**
136) [1998 NR 1999 8s 7.6m* 8m² Aug 22] tall, good-topped colt: has scope: closely
related to 1995 2-y-o 5f winner Unfuwaanah and Italian 1¼m winner Stravos (both
by Unfuwain) and half-brother to 2 winners, including useful Irish 1997 2-y-o 6f
winner Wish Me Luck (by Lycius): dam, best at 2 yrs, won 3 times at 5f: progressive
form: won maiden at Lingfield (well backed) in July: head second of 5 to Bathwick
in minor event at Bath only start after, rather awkward on bend: will stay 1¼m: likely
to improve further. *M. P. Tregoning*

SIRENE   2 ch.f. (May 16) Mystiko (USA) 124 – Breakaway 98 (Song 132) [1999 **61**
6.8d 6g 7s a7g* a8g a5g² Dec 17] 3,400Y: leggy, lengthy filly: half-sister to fairly
useful 1m winner Hippy (by Damister), who stayed 1¼m, and winners abroad by
Damister and Superlative: dam 5f winner: modest performer: won seller at Southwell
in November: blinkered, good second in nursery there final start: stays 7f: acts on
fibresand. *M. J. Polglase*

SIR FERBET (IRE)   2 b.c. (Mar 16) Mujadil (USA) 119 – Mirabiliary (USA) 74 **77 p**
(Crow (FR) 134) [1999 6d⁴ 7g³ Oct 11] IR 28,000Y: brother to 1997 2-y-o 5f winner
Hirst Bridge and half-brother to several winners, including 6-y-o Fairly Sure and
7-y-o Tribal Peace: dam 1¼m winner: much better effort in maidens when narrowly-
beaten third of 21 to Toleration at Windsor: will stay 7f: can do better still. *B. W. Hills*

SIR FOLEY   2 ch.g. (Feb 12) Elmaamul (USA) 125 – Light Fantastic 66 (Deploy **44**
131) [1999 a5g a6g⁴ a6g³ a7g⁵ a6g Jul 10] 2,600Y: first foal: dam, second from 2
starts at 1m, out of half-sister to smart middle-distance performer Icona: poor
maiden: stays 6f: raced only on fibresand. *W. G. M. Turner*

SIRIUS PROSPECT   3 b.g. Sanglamore (USA) 126 – Star of The Future (USA) **57**
100 (El Gran Senor (USA) 136) [1998 NR 1999 10v⁶ 10d 12d 9.9m⁴ Jun 24] 8,000
2-y-o: sturdy gelding: fourth foal: half-brother to fairly useful 7f winner Starry Eyed
(by Warning): dam 7f (at 2 yrs)/1m winner who stayed 1¼m, half-sister to smart
performer up to 1¼m Man From Eldorado: modest maiden: stays 1¼m: acts on good
to firm going: hung right final start. *H. J. Collingridge*

SIR JACK   3 b.g. Distant Relative 128 – Frasquita (Song 132) [1998 83p: 6.1d² **84**
6g* 6v 1999 6g 6g 7m Jun 23] quite good-topped gelding: fairly useful performer:
well beaten in 1999 after reappearance (hung badly right): stays 6f: blinkered once as
2-y-o: sold 1,000 gns. *J. Noseda*

SIR LEGEND (USA)   3 br.c. El Gran Senor (USA) 136 – Tadkiyra (IRE) (Dar- **74**
shaan 133) [1998 NR 1999 10g 11.8m⁵ 12d³ 14d⁵ 11.5g⁵ Sep 14] $100,000Y: big,
good-topped colt: second foal: dam, French 1¼m winner, half-sister to several
useful/smart performers, including Princess Royal winner Tashtiya: fair maiden:
should stay 1¾m: yet to race on extremes of going: visored final start: has been
tongue tied: sold 3,800 gns, sent to Italy. *E. A. L. Dunlop*

SIR NICHOLAS   2 b.c. (Mar 21) Cadeaux Genereux 131 – Final Shot 91 (Dalsaan **106**
125) [1999 6m* 6m² 6m³ Jul 7] 42,000Y: smallish, well-made, quite attractive colt:
fifth foal: half-brother to 3-y-o Durham Dancer and 3 winners, including 5-y-o
Double Action and 4-y-o Magical Shot: dam won Ayr Gold Cup: won maiden at
Doncaster in May: useful form after when 2½ lengths second of 18 to Fasliyev in
Coventry Stakes at Royal Ascot in June and 2 lengths third of 7 to City On A Hill in
July Stakes at Newmarket (unimpressive to post) in July: may prove best at 5f/6f.
J. Noseda

SIR NINJA (IRE) 2 b.c. (Feb 27) Turtle Island (IRE) 123 – The Poachers Lady **98**
(IRE) (Salmon Leap (USA) 131) [1999 6.1d⁴ 6d⁶ 7m² 7d* 7g² 8g 7s² 7d* 7.3s Oct
22] 4,500Y: sturdy colt: fourth foal: half-brother to winners in Scandinavia and
Hong Kong: dam, Irish 1¼m/1½m winner, half-sister to very smart 1¼m performer
Insatiable: useful performer: won maiden at Thirsk in August and minor event at
Ascot (by 1½ lengths from Compton Bolter) in October: well held in Horris Hill
Stakes at Newbury final start: will stay 1m: has form on good to firm going, easily
best runs on softer than good. *D. J. S. ffrench Davis*

SIR PERSE 3 b.g. Precocious 126 – Anne's Bank (IRE) 77 (Burslem 123) [1998 **53**
66: 6m 6g 6s⁶ a8g a7g² 1999 6f a8g⁴ 8m 8d 9.9m 10g Oct 19] modest maiden: left **a66**
G. L. Moore before final start: should stay beyond 1m: acts on equitrack, probably on
good to firm going: blinkered (below form) penultimate start. *Jamie Poulton*

SIR SANDROVITCH (IRE) 3 b.g. Polish Patriot (USA) 128 – Old Downie **81**
(Be My Guest (USA) 126) [1998 58: 5m⁶ 1999 5g 5m* 5.1d 5s 5g² 5.1m⁴ 6m⁶ 5g
5m Sep 19] tall gelding: has scope: fairly useful performer: readily won maiden at
Musselburgh in May: settled better than usual when in frame in handicaps in July:
reportedly pulled a muscle in near-hind final start: pulls hard, and may prove best at
strongly-run 5f: acts on good to firm going: has worn dropped noseband and gone
early to post. *R. A. Fahey*

SIR WALTER (IRE) 6 b.g. The Bart (USA) 108 – Glenbalda (Kambalda 108) **46**
[1998 50, a42+: 12s⁵ 11m 10d⁴ 9m 9m* 8g a9.4g⁵ a8.5g⁵ 1999 a10g a10g⁴ a13g³
a13g² a12g a14g⁶ a8.5g³ a12g⁴ a9.4g⁴ 10g 11.5f a12g⁶ a10g a12g Dec 27] poor
performer: barely stays 13f: acts on good to firm going and all-weather: tried in
blinkers/tongue strap: takes strong hold: tends to finish weakly. *A. T. Murphy*

SISAO (IRE) 3 ch.c. College Chapel 122 – Copt Hall Princess 70 (Crowned **65**
Prince (USA) 128) [1998 NR 1999 6.1g 6g 6d a6g⁶ a6g³ a6g² Nov 23] 8,000Y,
2,300 2-y-o: half-brother to several winners, including 1m/1¼m winner Prince
Merandi (by Blakeney) and 1¼m/1½m winner Dovedon Lady (by Castle Keep): dam
7f winner: fair maiden: stays 6f: best efforts on all-weather: blinkered last 4 starts:
races prominently. *Miss Gay Kelleway*

SISTER KATE 2 b.f. (Jan 27) Barathea (IRE) 127 – Norpella 95 (Northfields
(USA)) [1999 7.9d⁶ Oct 9] 60,000Y: half-sister to several winners, notably useful 5f
(at 2 yrs) to 1m winner Ultimo Imperatore (by Cadeaux Genereux) and 5-y-o
Sugarfoot: dam, 1¼m/1½m winner who stayed 15f, from good family: tailed-off last
of 6 in maiden at York. *N. Tinkler*

SISTER PATRICE (IRE) 3 b.f. Petorius 117 – Top Nurse (High Top 131) [1998 **–**
–: 5f 6g 5m 6m⁶ 5g⁶ 5.1m 5.1m 5.3g 1999 10.8d 7m May 13] little form. *Mrs
P. N. Dutfield*

SITTING PRETTY 3 b.f. Presidium 124 – Malvern Madam (Reesh 117) [1998 **–**
NR 1999 10d 7f 8f Jul 30] first foal: dam poor maiden hurdler: tailed off in maidens.
D. Nicholls

SIX FOR LUCK 7 b.g. Handsome Sailor 125 – Fire Sprite 83 (Mummy's Game **– §**
120) [1998 –§: 5g 5s⁶ 5g 5d 5g 1999 5m 6d 5m 6s Sep 27] disappointing handicapper.
D. A. Nolan

SIZZLING 7 b.g. Sizzling Melody 117 – Oriental Splendour 85 (Runnett 125) **53**
[1998 56: a6g³ 6f* 6m 7g⁵ 6m 7m a6g³ 1999 a6g⁵ a7f⁶ a8g Jan 28] smallish, sturdy
gelding: modest handicapper: barely stays 7f: acts on firm going, good to soft and
equitrack: blinkered once at 4 yrs. *R. Hannon*

SKELTON MONARCH (IRE) 2 ch.c. (Apr 20) Prince of Birds (USA) 121 – **–**
Toda 53 (Absalom 128) [1999 5m a6g 6.1m 7.5g 7s Nov 5] 8,000Y: smallish, strong
colt: fourth foal: half-brother to 3-y-o Adelphi Boy: dam, 1¼m seller winner, also
successful over hurdles: well held in maidens: tongue tied final start. *R. Hollinshead*

SKEPTICAL (USA) 2 br.c. (Mar 19) Kris S (USA) – Skep (USA) (Fappiano **76**
(USA)) [1999 6m⁶ 7.1d⁵ 7g⁶ Aug 28] $170,000Y: rather leggy, close-coupled,
useful-looking colt: fourth foal: half-brother to winners in USA by Pine Bluff and
Japan by Storm Cat: dam, US maiden, half-sister to minor 1m stakes winner in USA
Minority Dater: fair form in maidens, better than result suggests (hampered) when
sixth of 7 to Nothing Daunted at Goodwood final start: will stay 1m: sold 42,000 gns
in October, sent to USA. *Sir Michael Stoute*

SKERRAY   4 b.f. Soviet Star (USA) 128 – Reuval 102 (Sharpen Up 127) [1998 71: 8.1g³ 8m 7m³ 8v⁶ 1999 8.2m⁶ May 22] fair maiden: below form only 4-y-o start: stays 1m: well held on heavy ground. *J. R. Fanshawe* — —

SKIBO (JPN)   2 b.c. (May 9) Carnegie (IRE) 129 – Dyna Avenue (JPN) (Northern Taste (CAN) 129) [1999 8d⁴ 7d⁴ Oct 22] angular, unfurnished colt: half-brother to Japanese 1996 2-y-o 7f winner Sunday Story (by Sunday Silence): dam unraced: fair form in maidens at Leicester and Doncaster, travelling comfortably and staying on when fourth of 22 to Fame At Last on second occasion: may well do better at 1¼m+. *M. P. Tregoning* — **78 p**

SKIFFLE MAN   3 b.g. Alhijaz 122 – Laundry Maid 89 (Forzando 122) [1998 NR 1999 a9.4g³ 10g a12g Nov 22] third foal: dam 7f winner: best effort in maidens when third at Wolverhampton (trained by M. Heaton-Ellis) on debut: something seemingly amiss both starts after, trained on first one by C. Cox: should stay at least 1¼m. *B. I. Case* — **61**

SKI FREE   2 b.f. (Mar 10) Factual (USA) 108 – Ski Blade (Niniski (USA) 125) [1999 5.3f⁵ 5.2m³ a5g⁶ a5g a5g⁵ Dec 29] first foal: dam, tailed off both starts, granddaughter of useful Clare Island (herself half-sister to very smart 1½m horse Caliban): poor form in maiden/sellers on turf: will stay 6f: no show on fibresand: tongue tied penultimate start (final one for R. Guest). *J. L. Harris* — **43 a–**

SKI LODGE (IRE)   3 br.f. Persian Bold 123 – Place of Honour (Be My Guest (USA) 126) [1998 78p: 6s⁵ 7m 7d* 1999 7g 11.4m⁶ 9.9g May 19] leggy, unfurnished filly: unimpressive mover: fair performer: edgy, best effort in 1999 when 6½ lengths sixth to Valentine Girl in listed race at Chester: tailed off next time: will stay 1½m: acts on good to firm and good to soft going. *C. E. Brittain* — **78**

SKIMRA   2 b.f. (Apr 28) Hernando (FR) 127 – Skuld (Kris 135) [1999 8.2s² 8.3d⁶ Oct 28] second living foal: dam unraced half-sister to Petoski (by Niniski, also sire of Hernando): fair form in maidens at Nottingham and Windsor, favourite on second occasion: should stay at least 1½m: remains capable of better. *R. Guest* — **74 p**

SKI RUN   3 b.f. Petoski 135 – Cut And Run (Slip Anchor 136) [1998 NR 1999 12v 11.9v 11.7s* Oct 26] first foal: dam (no worthwhile form) out of half-sister to champion US filly Go For Wand: 66/1, easily best effort in maidens when winning at Bath by 2 lengths: will stay 1¾m: raced only on soft/heavy ground. *R. F. Johnson Houghton* — **83**

SKY BELLE (IRE)   2 b.f. (Apr 20) Mujadil (USA) 119 – Astronomer Lady (IRE) (Montekin 125) [1999 5.1g 6.1g 6.8m 5.7h⁶ 6g 6v Sep 24] IR 3,000F, 3,000Y: second foal: dam unraced: poor maiden: acted on hard ground. *J. L. Spearing* — —

SKY CITY   3 b.f. Be My Chief (USA) 122 – Pellinora (USA) (King Pellinore (USA) 127) [1998 –: a8g 1999 a10g² a8g⁶ a12g 10.1g 8d a10g a10g a13g a10g Dec 29] modest maiden: well held after reappearance: should stay 1½m: acts on equitrack. *P. Howling* — **63 d**

SKY DOME (IRE)   6 ch.g. Bluebird (USA) 125 – God Speed Her (Pas de Seul 133) [1998 81: 10m² 10d⁶ 8d 8s 10.4f 8g 8s⁴ 7g⁴ 8s 7s 1999 8d³ 8f² 7m² 8g* 7m 8.3d⁶ 8d Oct 14] lengthy, leggy gelding: poor mover: fairly useful handicapper: below form after winning amateur event at Newmarket in May: effective at 7f to easy 1¼m: acts on soft and good to firm going: has carried head awkwardly. *M. H. Tompkins* — **86**

SKYE   2 ch.f. (Feb 25) Timeless Times (USA) 99 – Excavator Lady 65 (Most Secret 119) [1999 5m 5g 5d a5g Nov 12] 5,500Y: half-sister to several winners, including fairly useful 5f performer Tuscan Dawn (by Clantime) and 1¼m winner Glenugie (by Insan): dam 9.4f and 13f winner, also successful over hurdles: signs of just a little ability in maidens. *J. Balding* — —

SKYE BLUE (IRE)   2 b.g. (Apr 25) Blues Traveller (IRE) 119 – Hitopah (Bustino 136) [1999 6v⁵ a6g Nov 15] 7,500Y: tall gelding: half-brother to several winners, including 3-y-o Thomas Henry and 7f winner Queen of Scotland (by Mujadil): dam unraced: better run in maidens (modest form) at Newbury on debut: suffered kick-back at Southwell next time: should stay 1m. *M. R. Channon* — **61**

SKYERS A KITE   4 b.f. Deploy 131 – Milady Jade (IRE) (Drumalis 125) [1998 56: 8g 12m³ 11m² 12g* 10m 12m² 12m⁵ 12g* 15.8d³ 1999 a12g a14g 14g⁶ 12g³ — **56 a–**

16.2g^6 17.1g 9.9s* 12s^3 10.1d Oct 20] modest handicapper: won 18-runner event at Beverley in September: effective at 1¼m (given test) to 2m: acts on soft and good to firm ground (no form on all-weather). *Ronald Thompson*

SKYERS FLYER (IRE)   5 b. or br.m. Magical Wonder (USA) 125 – Siwana (IRE) (Dom Racine (FR) 121) [1998 68d: 5.9d^3 7.1g^2 7d^5 6.1m 7d^3 7.5g 6.9d 6s^4 7g^6 6d 7m 5m 6m 7m 6g^6 6v 1999 6.1f a6g 5m^5 5.9g* 5g^2 5m 7m 6g^4 6m^5 5d 6d^3 Oct 29] rangy, angular mare: has a round action: modest handicapper: won 19-runner race at Carlisle in July: generally ran creditably after: effective at 5f, probably at 1m: acts on firm and soft going, well beaten on fibresand: tends to carry head high. *Ronald Thompson*   **56**

SKY HOOK   2 ch.c. (Feb 23) Superlative 118 – Lady Eccentric (IRE) (Magical Wonder (USA) 125) [1999 a6g 6.1m 7f^5 a6g 6d^3 6.1s a6g^5 Dec 6] 4,000Y, 4,500 2-y-o: fifth foal: half-brother to 5-y-o Dubai Nurse: dam unraced: modest maiden: best effort when close third of 22 in nursery at Redcar: stays 7f: acts on equitrack, firm and good to soft going: has looked none too keen. *N. P. Littmoden*   **59 a52**

SKYLARK   2 ch.f. (Apr 25) Polar Falcon (USA) 126 – Boozy 111 (Absalom 128) [1999 5.2m^2 5m^3 6m 6d a5g Nov 30] fifth foal: half-sister to 3-y-o Brew and 5f winner (including at 2 yrs) Gwespyr (by Sharpo): dam best at 5f: fair maiden: below best last 3 outings: may prove best at 5f: acts on good to firm going: races up with pace. *R. Hannon*   **74**

SKY OF HOPE (FR)   3 b.g. Zieten (USA) 118 – Rain Or Shine (FR) (Nonoalco (USA) 131) [1998 65: 7g 6g 7d 1999 7g 7m^3 7m^5 7.1g^4 8f 7s^2 Oct 23] lengthy gelding: fairly useful maiden: best efforts when in frame in handicaps at Newmarket and Sandown on second and fourth starts: stays 7f: acts on good to firm going, probably on soft: sold 4,200 gns, joined John Berry. *R. Hannon*   **82**

SKY STORM   3 ch.g. Lycius (USA) 124 – Beijing (USA) 89 (Northjet 136) [1998 –: 7d 8.2v 1999 a7g^4 a8g 10.5m Sep 3] tall, close-coupled gelding: poor maiden at best: left B. Meehan 500 gns before final start: bred to stay beyond 1m: tried blinkered. *J. Norton*   **45**

SLAM BID   2 b.g. (Mar 1) First Trump 118 – Nadema (Artaius (USA) 129) [1999 6s 6m Aug 28] 29,000F, 38,000Y: half-brother to several winners, including 5-y-o Dizzy Tilly: dam unraced half-sister to smart and prolific 1984 2-y-o Provideo: considerably handled and signs of ability in maiden at Kempton and minor event at Windsor: will probably stay 1m: should do better. *R. Charlton*   **– p**

SLANDER (USA)   3 b.f. Miswaki (USA) 124 – Slam Bid (USA) (Forli (ARG)) [1998 –: 5d 1999 a6g^6 Jan 13] half-sister to several winners, including useful Cydalia (by Cresta Rider) and fairly useful Storm Bid (by Storm Cat), both successful at 7f: dam lightly-raced French 1m winner out of half-sister to L'Emigrant and Salpinx: signs of just a little ability in maidens at Tipperary (for D. Weld) and Wolverhampton: in foal to Unfuwain: sent to France. *Sir Mark Prescott*   **–**

SLAPY DAM   7 b.g. Deploy 131 – Key To The River (USA) (Irish River (FR) 131) [1998 –§: 11.5d 1999 12.1m^4 11.6m^2 11.9s* 12.1g* 12m 10.5d 11.9d^5 a16.2g Nov 17] close-coupled gelding: fair performer: won claimers in small fields at Brighton and Chepstow (final start for D. Burchell) in August: long way below form after: stays 1½m: acts on soft and good to firm going: sometimes visored (not in 1999): unreliable. *J. M. Bradley*   **67 § a– §**

Grand Prix de Paris, Longchamp—Slickly provides trainer Andre Fabre with his seventh success in the last nine runnings; stable-companion Indian Danehill is second with Sardaukar third

SLASHER JACK (IRE)   8 b.g. Alzao (USA) 117 – Sherkraine 98 (Shergar 140)   **41**
[1998 66: a16g 12.3v² 14.1v 12.4d⁴ 12m⁴ 12g⁵ 11.9s 11.9g* 1999 16m² Apr 30]
good-bodied gelding: fair in 1998 for R. Fahey: below form only 8-y-o start:
stays 1¾m: acts on any ground: has run well in blinkers: joined Mrs D. Thomson.
K. A. Ryan

SLAVE TO THE RYTHM (IRE)   2 br.f. (Mar 26) Hamas (IRE) 125§ – Silver   **63**
Singing (USA) 96 (Topsider (USA)) [1999 6g⁶ 6m Sep 7] IR 32,000Y: sixth foal:
half-sister to 3 winners, including fairly useful Irish 1996 2-y-o 5f winner Nevada
(by Marju) and 1½m winner Troubadour Song (by King of Clubs): dam, sprinter,
closely related to smart stayer My Patriarch and half-sister to Silver Patriarch: early
speed in maidens at Goodwood (much better effort) then Lingfield 3 months apart.
J. L. Dunlop

SLEAVE SILK (IRE)   4 b.f. Unfuwain (USA) 131 – Shanira (Shirley Heights   **46**
130) [1998 35p: 9.2s 8.2s 10.3v a11g³ 1999 a12g* a12f² a12g² a16g³ a16g* 14.1d   **a55**
16.1m⁶ a16.2g⁴ Jul 23] workmanlike filly: modest handicapper on all-weather, poor
on turf: won 3 times at Lingfield between January and March: stays easy 2m: acts on
all-weather and good to firm going. *W. J. Musson*

SLEEPLESS   5 b.m. Night Shift (USA) – Late Evening (USA) (Riverman (USA)   **92**
131) [1998 92: 7s* 7.1d 7.1g⁶ 7s⁵ 8m⁵ 7g* 7s 1999 8m 7s 8.5d³ Jun 4] sturdy,
good-topped mare: fairly useful performer: seemingly best effort when 5¼ lengths
third of 6 to Fairy Queen in steadily-run listed race at Epsom final start: effective at
7f/1m: seems best on going softer than good: usually held up. *N. A. Graham*

SLEEPTITE (FR)   9 gr.g. Double Bed (FR) 121 – Rajan Grey (Absalom 128)   **–**
[1998 NR 1999 a13g Feb 6] well beaten on only 2 starts after showing fair form in
1995: dead. *Mrs S. D. Williams*

SLICKLY (FR)   3 gr.c. Linamix (FR) 127 – Slipstream Queen (USA) (Conquis-   **119**
tador Cielo (USA)) [1998 112p: 7.5g* 8g* 1999 11d* 12s⁴ 10g* 8v² 8m⁵ Sep 5]

Mr J-L. Lagardere's "Slickly"

smart performer: won Prix Noailles (by 2½ lengths from State Shinto) in April and Grand Prix de Paris (by 2 lengths from Indian Danehill) in June, both at Longchamp: creditable efforts when 2½ lengths second of 5 to Dubai Millennium in Prix Jacques le Marois at Deauville and when keeping-on 5 lengths fifth to Sendawar in Prix du Moulin de Longchamp: may prove best around 1¼m (not discredited in Prix du Jockey Club at Chantilly at 1½m): acts on good to firm and heavy going: joined Godolphin. *A. Fabre, France*

SLICK WILLIE (IRE)   2 b.g. (Apr 4) Up And At 'em 109 – Perfectly Entitled **78** (IRE) (Entitled 126) [1999 5m³ 5m³ 6m⁵ 6g 6d⁴ 5m* 6f 5g³ 5g⁶ 7m 7g 6s² 6v² 7s³ 7s² Nov 6] IR 5,500F, 14,000Y: workmanlike gelding: third foal: dam soundly beaten both starts: fair performer: won maiden at Beverley in July: good efforts in nurseries last 4 starts, very unlucky not to win when head second of 22 to Omniheat at Doncaster on final one: should stay 1m: acts on good to firm and heavy going: effective blinkered or not: usually hangs and seems suited by strong handling: consistent. *T. D. Easterby*

SLIGHTLY DUSTY   3 b.f. Deploy 131 – Dusty's Darling (Doyoun 124) [1998 **44** 40: 5g a6g⁴ 8d 10.8d 8.2s⁴ a7g a9.4g Apr 29] small, lightly-made filly: poor maiden: should stay beyond 1m: acts on soft going and fibresand: has been bandaged behind: visored last 3 starts. *P. D. Evans*

SLIMS LADY   3 b.f. Theatrical Charmer 114 – Lady Antoinette (Pharly (FR) 130) **59** [1998 59: 5.7m 6m⁶ 7g³ 7m³ 8s³ a8g 1999 10.1g⁵ 12.3m⁵ 11.5f³ 10m 11.6s² 10.9d³ 10s³ 11.7s⁴ Oct 26] modest maiden handicapper: effective at 1¼m/1½m: yet to race on heavy ground, acts on any other: consistent. *K. R. Burke*

SLIP JIG (IRE)   6 b.g. Marju (IRE) 127 – Taking Steps 100 (Gay Fandango **63** (USA) 132) [1998 –, a61+: a12g⁵ a12g 1999 a10g³ a11g a10g³ a12g⁴ a11g⁴ a12s⁵ a8.5g² a8g⁴ a8g³ 13v Apr 10] sturdy gelding: modest performer: effective at 1m to 1½m: acts on good to firm ground, heavy and all-weather: visored (looked less than keen) final start, usually blinkered: often races prominently. *K. R. Burke*

SLIP KILLICK   2 b.f. (May 13) Cosmonaut – Killick 69 (Slip Anchor 136) [1999 **61** 7s⁵ 6g⁴ 7.1g Nov 3] first foal: dam 1m to 1¼m winner: easily best effort in maidens when fourth of 12 to L'Arita at Redcar: carried head awkwardly and found little final start: should stay 7f. *M. Mullineaux*

SLIP OF THE TONGUE   3 b.f. Slip Anchor 136 – Plaything 69 (High Top 131) **47** [1998 –: a7g 1999 a7g 7m 14.1f⁵ a12g⁶ 16.2m² 16d 10g a16g³ 13.8g⁴ 14.1f* Oct 20] poor handicapper: visored, won selling event at Nottingham, making virtually all: effective at 1¾m/2m: acts on firm going and equitrack: blinkered (looked less than genuine) once: sold 2,800 gns in November, joined N. Waggott. *S. C. Williams*

SLIPSTREAM   5 b.g. Slip Anchor 136 – Butosky 71 (Busted 134) [1998 64, a–:   – a9.4g 12v⁶ 14.1s² 16d 14d⁴ 13.1d* 20d 14s³ 14.9g 1999 a13g a16g⁴ Jan 15] big, lengthy gelding: fair performer: should stay 2m: no form on all-weather: raced mostly on good going or softer on turf. *G. M. McCourt*

SLIP STREAM (USA)   3 ch.c. Irish River (FR) 131 – Sous Entendu (USA) **118** (Shadeed (USA) 135) [1998 90P: 7s* 7m 10.4s³ 9s² 8f* 8m⁵ 8v⁵ Oct 3] angular colt: smart performer: neck second to Golden Snake in Prix Jean Prat at Chantilly in June, then landed odds with minimum of fuss in 4-runner listed race at Goodwood (by 3 lengths from Bahamian Bandit) in July: respectable fifth to Trans Island in Prix du Rond-Point at Longchamp final start: may prove best up to 9f: acts on any ground: usually races prominently. *Saeed bin Suroor*

SLOANE   3 ch.c. Machiavellian (USA) 123 – Gussy Marlowe 118 (Final Straw **83** 127) [1998 NR 1999 8.3m⁴ 8m⁶ 8m² 8.2d Oct 21] third foal: dam won Falmouth and Musidora Stakes: fairly useful maiden: best effort when short-head second to Ermine at Newcastle in September: will be suited by 1¼m. *G. Wragg*

SLUMBERING (IRE)   3 b.g. Thatching 131 – Bedspread (USA) (Seattle Dancer **86** (USA) 119) [1998 95: 7g 6g⁴ 6g* 6d⁵ 7d⁵ 1999 8m 7m 7g⁶ May 19] tall, unfurnished gelding: has scope: useful at 2 yrs: just fairly useful in 1999, best effort when sixth in handicap at Goodwood (not well drawn): likely to prove best up to 1m: acts on good to soft going, probably on good to firm. *B. J. Meehan*

SMALL RISK   5 b.m. Risk Me (FR) 127 – Small Double (IRE) 55 (Double – Schwartz 128) [1998 –: 8m 1999 a7g Jan 7] no form since 1996. *J. W. Hills*

SMART BOY (IRE)   5 ch.g. Polish Patriot (USA) 128 – Bouffant (High Top 131) – § [1998 72, a74: a10g⁶ a12g* a12g⁵ 14.1s² 12s⁴ 14d⁴ 12d a12g 13.9g 11.9s² 1999 a11g a9.4g Jan 27] small gelding: fair handicapper in 1998 for P. Cole: no show both 5-y-o starts, pulled up lame final one: stays 1¾m: acts on all-weather, best turf efforts on soft going (though has won on good to firm): blinkered twice, looking ungenuine on reappearance: sold 8,000 gns, joined J. Given. *M. P. Bielby*

SMARTER CHARTER   6 br.g. Master Willie 129 – Irene's Charter 72 (Persian   57 Bold 123) [1998 69: 8f² 8m* 7.5m* 8m 8m 8g 7v⁶ 1999 8d 8.2m³ 8f 8.5d⁴ 9g* 8d 8.5m⁵ 8m 9.9m⁵ 8.5m 8.1d³ 8m⁴ 8.5g 8.3s⁴ 10s² 10.1d⁴ 8.2s⁶ 8g³ Nov 3] leggy gelding: modest handicapper: won at Musselburgh in June: generally ran creditably after: effective at 1m/1¼m: acts on firm and soft going: held up. *Mrs L. Stubbs*

SMART (IRE)   4 b.f. Last Tycoon 131 – Belle Origine (USA) (Exclusive Native – (USA)) [1998 –: a7g a7g⁵ a8.5g 1999 a7g 8.3m 11.8g Aug 18] no sign of ability. *Andrew Reid*

SMART KID (IRE)   5 b.g. Lahib (USA) 129 – Diamond Lake (Kings Lake (USA) – 133) [1998 70, a81: 8g 8m 9.7m 8m a8g* a8f* a8g⁶ 1999 a8g Jan 16] workmanlike gelding: fair on turf, fairly useful on all-weather: no show only 5-y-o start: stays 1m: acts on good to firm going and equitrack: used to look unenthusiastic: broke leg on gallops in February. *Miss Gay Kelleway*

SMART PREDATOR   3 gr.g. Polar Falcon (USA) 126 – She's Smart 88 (Absalom   86 p 128) [1998 NR 1999 6g⁴ 6g⁴ 7.5v² 7.1d 7.5m² 8m² 7.9f* 8m 7d 7d⁶ Oct 26] big, lengthy, good-quartered gelding: third foal: half-brother to 5-y-o Rum Lad: dam sprinter: fairly useful performer: best effort when winning 7-runner maiden at York in September: stays 1m, may well prove effective at 6f/7f: acts on any ground: has scope and should do better at 4 yrs. *J. J. Quinn*

Godolphin's "Slip Stream"

SMART RIDGE 2 ch.c. (Apr 1) Indian Ridge 123 – Guanhumara (Caerleon (USA) **97**
132) [1999 5m 5m² 5.3f* 6s⁵ 5m⁵ 5m 6m⁶ 6m* 5.3g* 6g Oct 2] 50,000Y: close-
coupled colt: has a quick action: third foal: dam, poor maiden, half-sister to Cadeaux
Genereux: useful performer: won maiden at Brighton in May and nurseries at
Hamilton in July and Brighton (last start for M. Channon) in August: stiff task, well
held final outing: effective at 5f/6f: acts on firm ground, possibly not on soft: tends to
carry head awkwardly. *K. R. Burke*

SMART SAVANNAH 3 b.g. Primo Dominie 121 – High Savannah 77 (Rousillon **108**
(USA) 133) [1998 102p: 7m³ 7.1g* 7g 1999 8.1g⁶ 8m 10m 8f 8d* 7.9g 8m⁵ 8s 10s
Oct 22] big, lengthy gelding: useful handicapper: clearly best effort when winning at
Ascot in August by 1¼ lengths from Pas de Memoires: better than bare result
suggests on couple of occasions after: should prove best at 1m/easy 1¼m: acts on
good to firm and good to soft going, seemed ill-at-ease on firm: often mounted in
saddling boxes: tongue tied after fourth start: gelded after final one. *R. Charlton*

SMARTS MEGAN 3 b.f. Marju (IRE) 127 – Taschkent (IRE) (Sure Blade (USA) **–**
130) [1998 NR 1999 10m 12v Sep 20] 1,000F, 4,800Y: first foal: dam German 10.5f
winner from very good family: always behind in maidens. *Ian Williams*

SMART SPIRIT (IRE) 5 b.m. Persian Bold 123 – Sharp Ego (USA) (Sharpen **56**
Up 127) [1998 49: 8s⁶ 9v 8d 11s² 11.9d 9.9m 1999 9.9g⁴ 10m* 10f⁴ 10g⁴ 10m Sep
16] tall, good-topped mare: modest handicapper: won at Nottingham in May: seems
best around 1¼m: acts on firm and soft going: often on toes/takes strong hold: fair
winner over hurdles in November. *Mrs M. Reveley*

SMART SQUALL (USA) 4 b.c. Summer Squall (USA) – Greek Wedding (USA) **–**
(Blushing Groom (FR) 131) [1998 108: 10.4d 10g⁴ 12g² 12s³ 14s² 1999 12d
Oct 1] smallish, good-bodied colt: useful at 3 yrs for Lord Huntingdon: no show in
listed event at Newmarket only 4-y-o start: stays 1¾m: acts on heavy going: joined
E. Stanners. *D. J. Coakley*

SMOGAR (IRE) 2 ch.c. (Mar 25) Catrail (USA) 123 – Piney River 63 (Pharly **55 p**
(FR) 130) [1999 a6g³ Dec 6] 27,000F, 25,000Y: sixth foal: half-brother to fairly
useful 1996 2-y-o 5f winner Eye Shadow (by Mujtahid) and 1m winner Gushing
(by Formidable): dam maiden from family of Bassenthwaite: 5 lengths third of 7 to
Cruise in maiden at Lingfield: should improve. *P. J. Makin*

SMOKE SIGNAL (IRE) 3 ch.f. College Chapel 122 – Indian Express 61 (Indian **72 d**
Ridge 123) [1998 NR 1999 6v 7m⁵ 5d² 6m² 6m 5m⁴ 6m⁶ 5m⁶ 6m 6m⁵ 5g a8.5g²
a8.5g 10d Oct 21] IR 10,000Y: sturdy filly: first foal: dam, 8.5f and 1¼m winner,
sister to useful 6f/7f performer Cheyenne Spirit: disappointing maiden handicapper:
stays 8.5f: acts on good to firm going, good to soft and fibresand: has wandered
markedly: sold 4,000 gns. *M. Johnston*

SMOKEY FROM CAPLAW 5 b.g. Sizzling Melody 117 – Mary From Dunlow **68 d**
49 (Nicholas Bill 125) [1998 74: 8d 7v⁶ 6s 5.9s 6.1m³ 7g² 7m² 8g 6.9m* 7g 1999 7g
8.3g⁵ 5.9m 7m 8d 7g 6.9m Jul 16] strong, compact gelding: has a round action: fair
handicapper: generally well beaten in 1999: finds 6f a minimum, barely stays 1m:
seems to need good going or firmer: has carried head awkwardly: blinkered once.
J. J. O'Neill

SMOKIN BEAU 2 b.g. (Mar 6) Cigar 68 – Beau Dada (IRE) 66 (Pine Circle **74 +**
(USA)) [1999 6s 5.1g⁴ 6d³ a5g³ a5g* a6g⁵ Dec 22] third reported foal: half-brother
to Swedish 3-y-o 1m and 1¼m winner Big Oz (by Kylian): dam 6f (at 2 yrs) and
1m winner who stayed 1¼m: fair performer: favourite, won maiden at Southwell in
November: likely to prove best at 5f: acts on all-weather, yet to race on ground firmer
than good. *J. Cullinan*

SMOOTH SAILING 4 gr.g. Beveled (USA) – Sea Farer Lake 74 (Gairloch 122) **93**
[1998 93, a–: 7s 7d 6g 7g⁶ 6g 6m⁵ 7g² 7d* 8m³ 7d 7m⁴ 7m 7d 7.1g² 7s² a7g 1999 7m
7.6m³ 7g 7d² 6m 7.1d 7.1d 7d 7g 10.3m 8d² 8d Oct 30] leggy gelding: fairly useful
handicapper: ran creditably several times in 1999, including when short-head second
of 20 at Newmarket penultimate start: likely to prove best at 7f/1m: acts on soft and
good to firm ground, well beaten both all-weather outings: tried visored/blinkered at
2 yrs: has been slowly away/taken good hold. *K. McAuliffe*

SMOOTH SAND (USA) 2 b.c. (Mar 12) Desert Secret (IRE) 106 – Baby **68**
Smooth (USA) (Apalachee (USA) 137) [1999 8.1m 6.1g⁴ 6g Oct 11] 21,000Y: sixth

foal: half-brother to 3 winners in USA: dam winner up to 7f in USA: form in maidens only when fourth of 12 to Mellow Jazz at Nottingham: never going well final start. *M. A. Jarvis*

SMUDGER SMITH   2 ch.g. (May 3) Deploy 131 – Parfait Amour 73 (Clantime   **64** 101) [1999 7.5m³ 7.5g 8g² 8d 7s Sep 29] 11,000Y: third foal: half-brother to 3-y-o Just Gifted: dam 6f (at 2 yrs) to 1m winner: modest maiden: clearly best effort when second of 5 to Paradise Garden in minor event at Newcastle: stiff tasks last 2 starts: will stay 1¼m. *B. S. Rothwell*

SNAP CRACKER   3 b.f. Inchinor 119 – Valkyrie 87 (Bold Lad (IRE) 133) [1998   **74** 82: 5v* 5.1m⁶ 5g³ 5d* 5.1g* 5d⁵ 5.2g² 5d⁴ 5f⁶ 5d³ 5.2g 6s 1999 6m 5.1d⁴ 5g 5m 5.7m   **a–** 5.1s 5d⁴ 6g 6d⁴ 6d a6g a5g Dec 29] small, sturdy filly: fair performer: left H. Howe before penultimate start: probably best at 5f on good going or softer (well beaten on all-weather). *D. W. Chapman*

SNOW PARTRIDGE (USA)   5 ch.g. Arctic Tern (USA) 126 – Lady Sharp (FR)   **–** (Sharpman) [1998 64: 12d 10g⁴ 14.1d 9.9m³ 10.1m 11.7d⁶ 10.8m² 12f² 13.1m 11.9g* 11.9g 1999 12g 11.5f⁶ Jun 25] leggy gelding: modest handicapper at 4 yrs for P. Cole: below form both 5-y-o starts: stays 1¾m: acts on firm going, below form on good to soft: blinkered (well held) twice: has worn tongue strap: wears dropped noseband: none too consistent. *R. T. Phillips*

SNOWY MANTLE   6 gr.m. Siberian Express (USA) 125 – Mollified 67 (Lom-   **42 §** bard (GER) 126) [1998 44, a47: 8.5m 8g² a8g⁴ a8g 1999 a8g a8f⁴ a8g 9.9g 8d 7m May 29] tall, lengthy mare: poor handicapper: best around 1m: acts on good to firm going, soft and fibresand: blinkered final start: reportedly broke blood vessel once at 4 yrs: not one to trust. *J. D. Bethell*

SNOWY RANGE (USA)   3 b.f. Seattle Slew (USA) – November Snow (USA)   **76** (Storm Cat (USA)) [1998 NR 1999 8g³ 8m⁴ 7m* Sep 7] $400,000Y: unfurnished filly: fluent mover: first foal: dam US Grade 1 7f and 1¼m winner: fair form in maidens (off 4 months after debut), making all Lingfield in September: may stay beyond 1m: has been bandaged in front: sent to USA. *J. Noseda*

SNUGFIT ROSIE (GER)   3 ch.f. Kris 135 – Sorceress (FR) 108 (Fabulous   **74** Dancer (USA) 124) [1998 NR 1999 9.9m⁵ 10g⁶ 12.1g³ 14.1m 14g⁴ 16.2g³ 13.1f 16v³ 16s Oct 5] 45,000Y: tall, unfurnished filly: third foal: half-sister to useful 1½m and 2m winner in Austria/Ireland Commanche Court (by Commanche Run), also very smart hurdler: dam French 1m/1¼m winner: fair maiden: stays 2m: best efforts on good ground: unseated rider leaving stalls fourth start. *M. R. Channon*

SO   3 b.f. Mystiko (USA) 124 – High And Bright 95 (Shirley Heights 130) [1998 NR   **–** 1999 8m 10d 11.9d⁵ Jun 11] big, lengthy, plain filly: has a round action: sixth foal: half-sister to 1997 2-y-o 1m winner Bullion (by Sabrehill): dam, twice-raced 1¼m winner, closely related to Main Reef: no form in maidens: sold 4,600 gns, joined M. Hourigan in Ireland. *B. W. Hills*

SOAKED   6 b.g. Dowsing (USA) 124 – Water Well 96 (Sadler's Wells (USA) 132)   **61** [1998 74, a88: a5g² a7g⁴ a6g⁵ a6g* a6g a5g³ 5s 5d⁴ 5g* 5.1m² 5g* 6g* a5g* a5g* 5g   **a92** 6m 5m* 5g a6g⁴ 5s a6g a5g² a5g* a6g* a5g⁴ a5g⁶ a6g 1999 a5g* a5g³ a6g⁴ a5g³ 5s 5m 6m⁵ 5d⁶ 5g 5m⁴ Aug 26] fairly useful handicapper on all-weather, modest on turf nowadays: won at Lingfield in January: has won at 6f, best form at 5f: acts on all-weather, best turf form on good going or firmer: visored once in 1996, effective blinkered or not: front runner. *D. W. Chapman*

SOAKING   9 b.g. Dowsing (USA) 124 – Moaning Low 85 (Burglar 128) [1998 49:   **–** a8g a8g⁵ a8g⁴ a7g a8g 7f⁵ 8m⁴ a8g* a10g a8g³ a10f 1999 a8f* a8g a8g² a8g a8g⁴   **a55** 8.3m a8g⁶ a8g 8m⁶ a8g Oct 8] strong, useful-looking gelding: modest performer: won claimer at Lingfield in January: stayed 1m, not 1¼m: acted on equitrack, firm and soft ground: tried blinkered: sometimes swished tail/finished weakly: none too consistent: dead. *P. Burgoyne*

SOAP STONE   4 b.f. Gunner B 126 – Tzarina (USA) (Gallant Romeo (USA))   **–** [1998 –: 11.9d 1999 17.2g Aug 25] no sign of ability. *A. Bailey*

SOBA JONES   2 b.c. (Apr 20) Emperor Jones (USA) 119 – Soba 127 (Most Secret   **55 p** 119) [1999 5m³ Jul 17] 20,000Y: rather unfurnished, workmanlike colt: half-brother to several winners, including 3-y-o Spitzbergen (by Polar Falcon), 7f/1m winner at 2 yrs, and to dam of very smart middle-distance performer Dark Moondancer: dam high-class sprinter: modest form when third of 5 to Littlefeather in maiden at Ripon: should do better at 6f+. *T. D. Easterby*

SOBER AS A JUDGE 2 b.g. (Apr 16) Mon Tresor 113 – Flicker Toa Flame –
(USA) 85 (Empery (USA) 128) [1999 6m⁵ 6s 7f Jul 13] 6,200Y: half-brother to several winners, including useful 1m/1¼m winner Quavering (by The Minstrel) and fairly useful 6f (at 2 yrs) and 9f winner Trailblazer (by Efisio): dam, stayed 1m, half-sister to smart colt up to 1m Motavato: little form. *C. A. Dwyer*

SOBRIETY (IRE) 2 b.c. (Feb 26) Namaqualand (USA) – Scanno's Choice (IRE) 90
54 (Pennine Walk 120) [1999 7g* 7m² 7d⁴ Oct 9] IR 18,000F, IR 20,000Y: third foal: half-brother to 3-y-o Violet and a 9f winner in Japan (both by Mukaddamah): dam Irish middle-distance maiden: fairly useful form: won maiden at Salisbury in August: creditable efforts in minor events at Kempton and Ascot (fourth of 7 to Sir Ninja) after: will stay 1m. *R. F. Johnson Houghton*

SOCIAL CONTRACT 2 b.g. (Mar 9) Emarati (USA) 74 – Just Buy Baileys 69 76
(Formidable (USA) 125) [1999 5m³ 6m³ 6.5v a6g* 5m⁴ 7m* 7d Aug 20] 7,500F, 10,000Y: first foal: dam 6f winner at 2 yrs: fair performer: won seller at Southwell (subsequently left T. Stack, Ireland) in July and nursery at Lingfield in August: should stay 1m: acts on good to firm going and fibresand, well below form on going softer than good. *W. J. Haggas*

SOCIALIZER (USA) 3 b.c. Glitterman (USA) – Speckofsun (USA) (Sunny –
North (USA)) [1998 60: 5.1v⁵ a5g⁵ a6s⁶ a5g⁴ 1999 a5g⁵ Jan 20] modest maiden: should stay 6f: acts on fibresand, showed promise on heavy ground. *W. Jarvis*

SOCIAL SCENE (IRE) 3 ch.f. Grand Lodge (USA) 125 – Ardmelody (Law 86
Society (USA) 130) [1998 91+: 6.9f² 8.1g* 8d 1999 11.5g⁵ 12m⁴ 10.3m⁶ Jul 15] leggy, angular, useful-looking filly: fairly useful performer: not discredited in listed races first 2 starts in 1999: usually bandaged behind: free-going sort: sent to Australia. *P. W. Chapple-Hyam*

SOCIETY KING (IRE) 4 b.g. Fairy King (USA) – Volga (USA) (Riverman 44
(USA) 131) [1998 62d: 7s³ 7v 8g 10g 1999 a7g a7g a11g a8g Apr 26] lengthy gelding: poor maiden: should stay 1m: bled from nose once. *J. E. Banks*

SO DAINTY (IRE) 2 b. or br.f. (Apr 2) Common Grounds 118 – Naxos (USA) 53
(Big Spruce (USA)) [1999 5.1g 5m⁶ 7m 6.8m a7g³ Oct 18] 10,000Y: angular filly: sixth foal: half-sister to several winners, including 11f to 1¾m winner Nornax Lad (by Northern Baby): dam, won in USA, half-sister to Irish 1,000 Guineas winner Nicer: modest maiden: stays 7f: acts on fibresand, raced only on good/good to firm going on turf: sold 6,500 gns. *B. W. Hills*

SODELK 5 ch.m. Interrex (CAN) – Summoned By Bells 55 (Stanford 121§) [1998 –
NR 1999 a16.2g 10f 11.9f May 27] no form. *J. Pearce*

SOFISIO 2 ch.c. (Mar 17) Efisio 120 – Legal Embrace (CAN) 73 (Legal Bid 73
(USA) 120) [1999 7m 7g⁴ 7.6g a8g² a7g* a8g⁴ a7g⁴ Dec 15] 12,000 2-y-o: second foal: dam 1¼m winner who stayed 1½m: fair performer: won maiden at Lingfield in November: creditable fourth in nurseries after: stays 1m: acts on all-weather, some promise on turf: tongue tied first 3 starts (reportedly had breathing problem last of them). *W. R. Muir*

SOHO TOMMY 5 b.g. Tina's Pet 121 – Absalantra (Absalom 128) [1998 NR 72
1999 10g⁵ 8.5s⁵ 10g³ May 8] strong gelding: first foal: dam unraced: fair form in maidens: stayed 1¼m: dead. *N. Hamilton*

SOLAIA (USA) 2 ch.f. (Apr 11) Miswaki (USA) 124 – Indian Fashion (USA) 71 96
(General Holme (USA) 128) [1999 7m* 7g⁵ 7s⁵ 8g⁵ Oct 19] $120,000Y: lengthy, quite attractive filly: second foal: closely related to a winner in USA by Crafty Prospector: dam, second at 1m in Britain at 2 yrs, later won 8 times in USA and second in Grade 2 1½m event: useful form: won maiden at Newmarket in July: fifth afterwards in Prix du Calvados at Deauville, listed race at Newmarket and Prix des Reservoirs at Deauville: not sure to stay much beyond 1m: acts on soft and good to firm ground. *P. F. I. Cole*

SOLDIER COVE (USA) 9 ch.g. Manila (USA) – Secret Form 120 (Formidable –
(USA) 125) [1998 50: a9.4g³ a12g 1999 a9.4g⁶ Jan 6] sparely-made gelding: modest
performer: seems to stay 1½m: acts on all-weather and soft ground. *D. Burchell*

SOLDIER (USA) 4 b.g. Sheikh Albadou 128 – His Ginger (USA) (Fred Astaire –
(USA)) [1998 –: 8.2s 7d a7g 1999 a8.5g a11g a7g 6.1f a5g 5m 8m Aug 4] of no
account. *R. F. Marvin*

SOLE SINGER (GER) 3 b.g. Slip Anchor 136 – Singer On The Roof 62 (Chief **63 §**
Singer 131) [1998 73p: 7d 7v⁴ 1999 8.5s 11.4m 9.9m 10m³ 10s² a12g³ Dec 11]
deep-girthed gelding: modest maiden: left I. Balding after third start: stays 1½m:
acts on soft ground and fibresand: has worn tongue strap: tends to hang: probably
ungenuine. *D. Haydn Jones*

SOLFEGGI (USA) 3 b.c. Irish River (FR) 131 – Never A Care (USA) 88 **75**
(Roberto (USA) 131) [1998 NR 1999 8m² 10m⁵ 8m⁶ 10d Sep 23] compact colt:
second foal: dam 2-y-o 7f winner who stayed 1¼m: fair form in maiden on debut, but
failed to progress: free-going sort: sold 3,000 gns, sent to Germnay. *B. W. Hills*

SOLITARY 2 b.c. (Feb 23) Sanglamore (USA) 126 – Set Fair (USA) (Alleged **70 p**
(USA) 138) [1999 6v⁴ Oct 23] leggy, lengthy colt: second foal: half-brother to 3-y-o
Valentine Girl: dam, French 1¼m winner, sister to smart French stayer Non Partisan
and half-sister to dam of Sunshack and Raintrap: green and edgy, shaped well when
fourth of 14 to Another Pearl in maiden at Newbury, staying on well from halfway:
will be suited by 1¼m+: sure to do better. *B. W. Hills*

SOLLER BAY 2 b.g. (Apr 3) Contract Law (USA) 108 – Bichette 66 (Lidhame **69 p**
109) [1999 7g² Oct 19] 3,200Y: second foal: dam 7f winner, including at 2 yrs: weak
25/1-shot, encouraging second of 15 to Atavus in maiden at Lingfield, rallying: will
stay 1m: sure to do better. *K. R. Burke*

SOLLY'S PAL 4 gr.g. Petong 126 – Petriece 64 (Mummy's Pet 125) [1998 –: 6d **56**
6m 1999 6d a7g a8g⁴ Dec 13] tall, leggy gelding: modest maiden: should prove best
up to 7f: acts on fibresand. *P. J. Makin*

SOLO FLIGHT 2 gr.c. (Mar 18) Mtoto 134 – Silver Singer 65 (Pharly (FR) 130) **83 p**
[1999 8g⁴ 7d⁵ Sep 30] 24,000Y: angular, unfurnished colt: first foal: dam maiden
sister to Busy Flight, out of half-sister to Further Flight: fairly useful form in
maidens: shaped particularly well when fourth of 12 to Shamrock City at Doncaster:
fifth of 14 to Zentsov Street at Newmarket later in September: will be suited by
1¼m+: seems an edgy sort: should improve and win races. *B. W. Hills*

SOLOIST (IRE) 2 ch.f. (May 2) Elmaamul (USA) 125 – Alyara (USA) (Alydar –
(USA)) [1999 7s 7g Oct 15] IR 2,100Y: fourth living foal: half-sister to 3-y-o Tonic:
dam, French 10.7f winner, half-sister to smart middle-distance performer Tralos:
well held in maiden and claimer. *J. L. Eyre*

SOLO MIO (IRE) 5 b.h. Sadler's Wells (USA) 132 – Marie de Flandre (FR) 109 **114**
(Crystal Palace (FR) 132) [1998 114: 15.5s³ 15.5s³ 16g* 15s³ 15.5s² 1999 15.5g⁶
16g* 20m 12g⁶ Sep 12] rangy, good-bodied horse: impresses in appearance: fine
mover: smart performer: trained by B. Hills in 1996/7: won Betty Barclay-Rennen at
Baden-Baden (made all, by 2 lengths from Graf Philipp) in May for second year
running: well held in Ascot Gold Cup and (blinkered) Stockholm Cup at Taby: stays
2m: acts on soft and good to firm ground: joined A. King. *J. E. Hammond, France*

SOLO SONG 4 ch.f. Executive Man 119 – Aosta (Shack (USA) 118) [1998 –: 5g –
7d 7.1g 5g 5s 8s 1999 a7g Jun 17] of little account. *P. D. Evans*

SOLO SPIRIT 4 b.f. Northern Park (USA) 107 – Brown Taw 66 (Whistlefield –
118) [1998 64, a48: 6v 6m 5m 6g 5d 7.1m 6f 6.1d a6g a6g⁶ 1999 a6g a6g a6f a8g⁵ Feb
13] close-coupled filly: formerly fair 6f winner: little show in 1999: tried visored.
J. R. Jenkins

SOMAYDA (IRE) 4 b.c. Last Tycoon 131 – Flame of Tara 124 (Artaius (USA) **98 ?**
129) [1998 98p: 8d* 8g⁵ 9d* 10s³ 1999 10g 10v² 11.9d⁶ 11.9d² 12g 13.1d 10d⁶ 10s
Oct 22] unfurnished colt: poor mover: fairly useful performer: best efforts in 1999
when runner-up in minor events at Pontefract (behind Cugina) and York (behind
Achilles in 3-runner race): tongue tied, ran as if something amiss final start: barely

stays 1½m: acts on heavy going: blinkered/visored last 3 starts, also tongue tied final one: sold only 5,500 gns in December. *J. L. Dunlop*

SOME MIGHT SAY   4 b.g. Be My Chief (USA) 122 – Willowbed 66 (Wollow   –
132) [1998 72, a77: a10g² a8g² a9.4g³ a10g* 14.1m² 1999 a12g Dec 27] fair winner at 3 yrs: well beaten only start in 1999. *N. J. Hawke*

SOMER SOLO   6 b.m. Prince Daniel (USA) – Shift Over (USA) 62 (Night Shift   –
(USA)) [1998 –: a8.5g 1999 8.2m 10m Jul 30] modest maiden at 2 yrs for P. Mitchell: lightly raced and well beaten since. *Miss L. C. Siddall*

SOMERTON BOY (IRE)   9 b.h. Thatching 131 – Bonnie Bess 95 (Ardoon 124)   **68**
[1998 71: 7s 8.1g 8g 9.1d* 8s³ 8.9g³ 9.1s³ 10.4g 10.3v 1999 10s⁴ 8d May 21] good-topped horse: fair handicapper: reportedly lame on off-fore final start: stays 1¼m: acts on any going: blinkered twice early in career: held up. *P. Calver*

SONBELLE   2 b.f. (Apr 26) Son Pardo 107 – Ty-With-Belle 67 (Pamroy 99) [1999   **68**
5.7g* 6d⁵ 6m⁶ 5v 6d⁶ a7g⁴ Dec 6] half-sister to 4-y-o Chikal, 1989 2-y-o 5f seller winner Starchy Belle (by Starch Reduced) and 8.5f (at 2 yrs) and 12.5f winner Belle's Boy (by Nalchik): dam, maiden, best at 2 yrs: fair performer: won minor event at Bath in June: ran creditably in nursery penultimate start: stays 6f: acts on good to soft going, some promise on equitrack. *B. Palling*

SONEVA (IRE)   4 b.f. Alzao (USA) 117 – Rathvindon 93 (Realm 129) [1998 –:   **39**
8.1g 10.3g 10.2g 10m 8d⁶ 1999 9.9g a8g 8m Jul 17] tall filly: poor maiden. *M. A. Buckley*

SONG 'N DANCE MAN   3 b.c. Prince Sabo 123 – Born To Dance 76 (Dancing   **81**
Brave (USA) 140) [1998 74: 6g 6m⁵ 7d⁵ 8m 1999 9g 7m² 7d² 8m 7f* 7s Oct 2] angular, unfurnished colt: fairly useful performer: best efforts when second in handicaps at Kempton and Epsom in May/June: made hard work of landing odds in 4-runner maiden at Brighton in July, flashing tail under whip: will prove best up to 1m: acts on firm and good to soft going: has been bandaged behind: reportedly injured going to races on intended final start: sold 2,300 gns, sent to Kuwait. *J. Noseda*

SONG OF FREEDOM   5 ch.h. Arazi (USA) 135 – Glorious Song (CAN) (Halo   **107**
(USA)) [1998 107: 10g² 10.1m 10.4f⁴ 10m* 10.1m⁵ 10.4f 1999 a8f³ a10f* a10f⁴ 12d May 8] rangy horse: carries condition: useful handicapper: won at Nad Al Sheba in February by 5½ lengths from Perfect Paradigm: respectable seventh in valuable handicap at Goodwood final start: best around 1¼m: acts on firm ground and dirt, well beaten on soft: tends to sweat: usually held up. *Saeed bin Suroor*

SONG OF SKYE   5 b.m. Warning 136 – Song of Hope 103 (Chief Singer 131)   **83**
[1998 79§: 8s 8.1s⁶ 7.1g³ 8.5g 8g 8.1m 8.3g 7f 7.6f 1999 6f² 7.1g* 7.1m⁴ 8m 7f* 7m⁶ 7m³ 7.1d⁵ 8m⁴ 7m³ 8s a8 5g² a8g² Dec 10] leggy, close-coupled mare: fairly useful handicapper: won at Sandown in May and Lingfield in June: good second final 2 starts: effective at 7f to 8.5f: acts on firm and soft ground, and all-weather: tried blinkered: has hung left and usually held up. *T. J. Naughton*

SONICOS   3 ch.g. Cosmonaut – Bella Bambola (IRE) 42 (Tate Gallery (USA) 117)   –
[1998 NR 1999 7d Apr 29] second foal: dam sprint maiden: soon tailed off in maiden at Redcar. *J. S. Wainwright*

SON OF SKELTON   4 ch.g. Minster Son 130 – Skelton 70 (Derrylin 115) [1998   –
–: 8d 8s 11g⁵ 13.8s 1999 9.3m 14.1g Oct 2] plain, good-topped gelding: maiden, no longer of much account. *J. S. Haldane*

SON OF SNURGE (FR)   3 b.g. Snurge 130 – Swift Spring (FR) 56 (Bluebird   **87**
(USA) 125) [1998 72: 10.2d² 10d⁶ 8s⁵ 1999 10.3d a10g² 12.5m 10m⁵ 8g 9.9m 11.9f* 14m* 16.2m² 13.9g 14.8d³ Oct 15] good-topped gelding: fairly useful performer: won minor event at Brighton then handicap at Sandown in July: good efforts when placed in handicaps after: effective at 1½m to 2m: acts on firm and good to soft going, probably on equitrack: effective blinkered (was for both wins) or not: best forcing pace. *P. F. I. Cole*

SONTIME   2 b.f. (May 4) Son Pardo 107 – Fact of Time (Known Fact (USA) 135)   **65**
[1999 5d³ 5.3f 5.1g⁴ 5f* 5.1m³ 5.1m⁵ 6f* 6s 5.1g 6.1m Sep 13] 6,000Y: fifth foal: half-sister to winning sprinter Camionneur (by Cyrano de Bergerac): dam unraced:

fair performer: won seller and claimer at Lingfield in June and July: likely to prove best at 5f/6f: acts on firm and good to soft going, well beaten on soft. *B. Palling*

SOPHALA 2 b.f. (Apr 27) Magical Wonder (USA) 125 – Fujaiyrah 98 (In Fijar (USA) 121) [1999 8s Sep 16] 3,700Y: fifth foal: half-sister to 3-y-o Samiyah, 7f seller winner Fahema (by Most Welcome) and winners abroad by Most Welcome and Priolo: dam 2-y-o 6f winner who later stayed 1¼m: signs of ability when seventh of 12 in maiden at Yarmouth: should do better. *D. Morris* **– p**

SOPHIE JONES 2 ch.f. (Mar 26) Sabrehill (USA) 120 – Noble Singer 66 (Vaguely Noble 140) [1999 5.7f a7g³ 7g 5.7d 6s 8s a8.5g Oct 30] 7,200Y: fourth foal: dam, 1¼m winner, out of half-sister to Prince Sabo: poor maiden: stays 7f: form only on fibresand: tried blinkered: sold 750 gns in November. *A. T. Murphy* **– a45**

SOPHIE LOCKETT 6 b.m. Mon Tresor 113 – Silverdale Rose (Nomination 125) [1998 NR 1999 14.1s Apr 27] of no account. *K. W. Hogg, Isle of Man* **–**

SOPRAN ZANCHI (IRE) 2 ch.c. (Mar 13) College Chapel 122 – Star Gazing (IRE) (Caerleon (USA) 132) [1999 6f² 6g³ Aug 21] fourth foal: half-brother to 6-y-o Western Venture: dam unraced: second in minor event in Milan in July: fair form when third of 21 to Abderian in maiden at Ripon following month, finishing strongly: likely to prove suited by 7f/1m: remains capable of better. *L. M. Cumani* **76 p**

SO PRECIOUS (IRE) 2 b.f. (Mar 3) Batshoof 122 – Golden Form (Formidable (USA) 125) [1999 6m⁶ 7v* Sep 20] 6,500Y: seventh foal: half-sister to fairly useful 7f (at 2 yrs) and 1¼m (in USA) winner Rug (by Persian Bold): dam Irish 8.5f (at 2 yrs) and 9f (listed race) winner: much better effort in maidens at Kempton when winning 9-runner race by neck from Able Native, jinking at path over 1f out but staying on strongly to lead close home: will probably stay 1¼m: should improve again. *N. P. Littmoden* **69 p**

SORBETT 2 b.c. (Feb 23) Dolphin Street (FR) 125 – Midnight Imperial (Night Shift (USA)) [1999 7.5s* Oct 31] 16,500F, 35,000Y: half-brother to several winners, including 5-y-o Mystical and useful Irish/US 6f to 1m winner Harveys Point (by Keen): dam poor maiden: won 6-runner minor event at Milan by ½ length: will probably improve. *L. M. Cumani* **70 p**

SORBIE TOWER (IRE) 6 b.h. Soviet Lad (USA) – Nozet (Nishapour (FR) 125) [1998 NR 1999 8.1g³ 8m⁶ 8g⁶ 7.3m⁶ 8m Jul 24] tall horse: very smart in 1996: found to be suffering from minor tendon problem on off-fore in 1997, went to stud in 1998: length third of 7 to Alrassaam in minor event at Haydock on reappearance: disappointing after: effective at 7f/1m: used to act on firm and soft going: sometimes bandaged behind: tends to hang under pressure: sold 15,000 gns in December. *Miss Gay Kelleway* **109 d**

SORRENTO KING 2 ch.c. (May 17) First Trump 118 – Star Face (African Sky 124) [1999 7d 6g 7.9m 7g⁴ 7.9d 7s Oct 25] 4,000Y, 12,000 2-y-o: strong colt: half-brother to several winners, notably smart performer up to 1½f Lord of The Field (by Jalmood): dam French 10.5f winner: modest maiden: easily best effort when fourth of 15 in nursery at Catterick: edgy, well held after: should stay 1m: blinkered last 3 starts. *M. W. Easterby* **56**

SOSSUS VLEI 3 b.c. Inchinor 119 – Sassalya (Sassafras (FR) 135) [1998 97: 7m 7m* 7g 8g² 1999 8s* 8.5d⁶ 8v² Nov 6] lengthy, attractive colt: had slight fracture of cannon bone before reappearance: smart performer, lightly raced: won minor event at Bath in September by 6 lengths from Emily's Luck Charm: better effort after when creditable 3 lengths second to Danzigaway in Prix Perth at Saint-Cloud: likely to stay 1¼m: has won on good to firm going, goes well on soft/heavy: has given trouble stalls. *G. Wragg* **112**

SOTONIAN (HOL) 6 br.g. Statoblest 120 – Visage 75 (Vision (USA)) [1998 56: a5g⁵ a5g 5.1m a5g a6g³ 5g³ a5g⁶ a5g* 5m² 5m³ 5.1d² 6g a5s⁴ a5g a6g³ 1999 a5g² a5g² a5g* a5g* a5g* a5g³ 5d* a6g a5g 5g* a5g 5m⁶ 5f⁶ 5m³ 5.1d 5.2g⁶ 5.1s² 5g Oct 16] rather sparely-made gelding: fair handicapper: better than ever at 6 yrs, winning at Wolverhampton, Lingfield (twice), Warwick and Catterick between January and May: best at 5f: acts on firm ground, soft and all-weather: blinkered twice earlier in career: effective held up/from the front: reportedly bled final start. *P. S. Felgate* **74**

SOUHAITE (FR) 3 b.g. Salse (USA) 128 – Parannda 117 (Bold Lad (IRE) 133) **57**
[1998 NR 1999 10d 8.1g 7.1m⁶ a12g* a11g³ a16.2g a12g³ Dec 21] 450,000 francs Y,
65,000 2-y-o: robust gelding: seventh foal: half-brother to 3 winners, including
Italian Oaks winner Shahmiad (by Alleged): dam French 6f to 1m winner (and fourth
in French 1000 Guineas) who stayed 1¼m: modest handicapper, lightly raced: won
at Southwell in November: races freely, and will prove best at 1¼m/1½m: acts on
fibresand: virtually refused to race when tongue tied third start. *W. R. Muir*

SOUND APPEAL 5 b.m. Robellino (USA) 127 – Son Et Lumiere (Rainbow **62**
Quest (USA) 134) [1998 54: 16m⁶ 1999 13.1g* May 17] leggy mare: fairly useful
hurdler: modest on Flat: won handicap at Bath only 5-y-o start: effective at 13f,
barely stays 2m: acts on firm and soft going: often blinkered/visored, wasn't at Bath.
G. M. McCourt

SOUND'S ACE 3 ch.f. Savahra Sound 111 – Ace Girl 58 (Stanford 121§) [1998 **60**
67: 5s 6m⁵ 5m* 5d³ 5g* 5d⁶ 1999 6g 5d 5g 5g 5m⁶ Jun 25] leggy filly: fair at 2 yrs,
modest at best in 1999: raced mainly at 5f: acts on good to firm and good to soft
ground: effective blinkered or not: has been bandaged: has twice refused to enter
stalls. *D. Shaw*

SOUNDS COOL 3 b.g. Savahra Sound 111 – Lucky Candy 61 (Lucky Wednes- **48 d**
day 124) [1998 45, a53?: 5g 6s 6.1g 5m a8g³ a7g⁶ 1999 8.2s² 8.2s a9.4g⁶ 6.1f 8.2m⁴
10f³ 8g 10g 7.5g a7g a11g Dec 13] tall, sparely-made gelding: poor maiden: effective
at 1m/1¼m: yet to race on heavy going, acts on any other turf and fibresand: tried
blinkered. *S. R. Bowring*

SOUNDS CRAZY 2 b.f. (Mar 14) Savahra Sound 111 – Sugar Token 66 (Record **42 §**
Token 128) [1999 5d⁴ 6d 5f a5g⁵ 5m 5g a5g a5g Dec 21] sister to 3-y-o Taz Mania,
and half-sister to winning sprinters Hershebar (by Stanford) and Lunar Mist (by
Komaite), latter fairly useful at 2 yrs: dam 6f/7f winner, including at 2 yrs: poor
maiden: tried blinkered: looked temperamental sixth start. *S. R. Bowring*

SOUNDS FAB 2 ch.f. (Apr 8) Savahra Sound 111 – Ace Girl 58 (Stanford 121§) **41**
[1999 5d⁵ 6d 5.1h⁵ 5g⁵ 5m⁶ 5m a5g Oct 13] tall, angular filly: third reported foal:
sister to 3-y-o Sound's Ace: dam 1m winner: poor maiden: may prove best at 5f: acts
on good to firm and good to soft ground: visored last 4 starts. *D. Shaw*

SOUNDS LUCKY 3 b.g. Savahra Sound 111 – Sweet And Lucky (Lucky Wed- **67**
nesday 124) [1998 45: a6g⁵ 5.1g⁶ a5g 1999 a6g a5g⁶ a6g a8g² a5g* a6g* a6g⁵ a5g **a59**
a6g 6m⁵ 6g 6g 5m⁴ 5g 6f⁴ 5d⁵ 5g 6d Aug 26] leggy gelding: has round action: fair
handicapper on turf, modest on all-weather: successful at Wolverhampton (twice
within 3 days, including selling event) in March and Lingfield in May: some
creditable runs after: effective at 5f/6f: acts on fibresand and good to firm going:
visored (stiff task) once: has swished tail. *N. P. Littmoden*

SOUNDS SOLO 3 b.g. Savahra Sound 111 – Sola Mia 78 (Tolomeo 127) [1998 **–**
64: a7g² a7g* 1999 a7g⁵ 8.2s Mar 29] modest at 2 yrs: well beaten in 1999 (upset
stalls on reappearance): likely to prove best up to 7f: acts on fibresand: wears visor/
eyecover (has only one eye). *S. R. Bowring*

SOUNDS SPECIAL 2 b.f. (May 6) Savahra Sound 111 – Sola Mia 78 (Tolomeo **58**
127) [1999 6.1m⁵ 5g Sep 15] tall filly: fourth foal: sister to 3-y-o Sounds Solo: dam,
2-y-o 6f winner, best up to 1m: signs of ability in maidens at Nottingham and
Beverley, good early speed in latter. *S. R. Bowring*

SOUNDS SWEET 3 ch.f. Savahra Sound 111 – Be My Sweet 78 (Galivanter **39**
131) [1998 39: 5d 5d⁵ 6m⁵ 7m⁶ 7m⁴ 7.5m a6g 1999 a7g a7g a6g 7.5g³ a8g a6g a7g **a–**
Dec 4] leggy filly: poor maiden: stays 7.5f: acts on good to firm going: tried
blinkered: sometimes looks headstrong. *D. Shaw*

SOUND THE TRUMPET (IRE) 7 b.g. Fayruz 116 – Red Note (Rusticaro (FR) **46**
124) [1998 56d: a5g* a5g⁵ a5g 5d a6g 1999 a5g⁴ a6f⁴ a7g 5d³ 5g 7m⁶ 6g 6g 6f⁵ 7g **a52**
a7g⁴ a7g⁴ a8g* a10g³ a10g Dec 18] rangy gelding: modest handicapper on all-
weather, poor on turf: won at Lingfield in November: best form at 7f/1m: acts on
all-weather, firm and good to soft going: often blinkered/visored earlier in career:
usually tongue tied. *R. C. Spicer*

SOUPERFICIAL 8 gr.g. Petong 126 – Duck Soup 55 (Decoy Boy 129) [1998 **58**
58: 5s² 5.9g* 5d* 6g 7f 6m⁶ 6g⁵ 6m³ 5m 6v² 6v 1999 5d 6v⁴ 5.9m⁴ 5.9g 6g³ 5.9m⁴

6m⁴ 6f⁴ 6f 6g* 5g 6v Oct 12] sturdy gelding: modest performer: won 20-runner handicap at Newcastle in August: best at 6f/stiff 5f: acts on fibresand and any turf going: effective visored or not: often slowly away. *Don Enrico Incisa*

SOURCE 4 b.g. Rudimentary (USA) 118 – Sakala (NZ) (Gold And Ivory (USA) 128) [1998 NR 1999 a9.4g a6g⁴ a7g 6f 10d Oct 21] 2,000 3-y-o: second foal: half-brother to French 7f winner Sakti (by Kenmare): dam, Australian sprinter, half-sister to smart middle-distance horses Spritsail and Emperor Fountain: poor maiden. *T. T. Clement* **40**

SOUTHAMPTON 9 b.g. Ballacashtal (CAN) – Petingo Gold 69 (Pitskelly 122) [1998 NR 1999 14.1m⁶ 17.2g⁵ Aug 25] plain gelding: poor maiden handicapper: stays 2m: acts on good to firm and good to soft going: blinkered once, visored last 3 starts: winning jumper. *G. B. Balding* **36**

SOUTHBOUND TRAIN 3 ch.g. Superlative 118 – Louisianalightning (Music Boy 124) [1998 54: 7m 6s 7m 5.7v⁶ 1999 8.3d a8g Nov 22] poor maiden. *G. B. Balding* **–**

SOUTHERN DOMINION 7 ch.g. Dominion 123 – Southern Sky 89 (Comedy Star (USA) 121) [1998 63: a5g 5s 5g 5g⁴ 5g 5s⁶ 5g* 5m⁵ 5d⁶ 5m⁵ 5g* 5d 5g 5v 5v a5g² a5s² 1999 5m 5m a5g 5m⁴ 5d 5g 6m⁵ 5g 6g³ 6m 6s² 5d 6v a6g a5g² a5g² a5g a5g⁴ Dec 21] small gelding: modest handicapper: effective at 5f/6f: acts on any all-weather/turf: often visored/blinkered: successful for apprentice: usually races up with pace. *Miss J. F. Craze* **63**

SOUTHERN DUNES 3 b.g. Ardkinglass 114 – Leprechaun Lady 57 (Royal Blend 117) [1998 –: 6g 1999 8d 9.9g⁵ 12g 12f⁵ Jul 14] little sign of ability: blinkered on debut. *Don Enrico Incisa* **–**

SOUTHERN MIST 2 b.f. (Feb 13) Forzando 122 – Southern Sky 89 (Comedy Star (USA) 121) [1999 5s 5m⁵ a6g⁶ 5.3f 5.1m Aug 5] sixth live foal: half-sister to fairly useful 1993 2-y-o 6f winner Southern Ridge (by Indian Ridge) and 7-y-o Southern Dominion: dam 7f/1m winner: fair maiden: best effort when fifth of 10 in minor event at Salisbury: should stay 6f: has worn tongue strap. *W. G. M. Turner* **66**

SOUTH LANE 2 br.g. (May 27) Rock City 120 – Steppey Lane 95 (Tachypous 128) [1999 6g 6d Oct 20] 600F: third living foal: dam 1¾m winner: tailed off in maidens. *G. P. Kelly* **–**

SOVEREIGN ABBEY (IRE) 3 b.f. Royal Academy (USA) 130 – Elabella (Ela-Mana-Mou 132) [1998 68: 7v 7v³ a7g³ 1999 a8.5g⁵ a6g⁴ a7g⁶ Nov 27] modest maiden: stays 7f: acts on heavy going and fibresand. *Sir Mark Prescott* **57 +**

SOVEREIGN CREST (IRE) 6 gr.g. Priolo (USA) 127 – Abergwrle (Absalom 128) [1998 52§: 11.9f⁴ 11.9g³ 11.9m 14m* 14.1m 11.9m 11.5f⁵ 16m 1999 10g 11.9g⁵ Aug 5] workmanlike gelding: modest handicapper: stays 1¾m: acts on firm going: effective visored/blinkered or not: often slowly away, and comes from off pace: has tended to hang, and looks temperamental. *C. A. Horgan* **45 §**

SOVEREIGN STATE (IRE) 2 b.g. (Mar 16) Soviet Lad (USA) – Portree 82 (Slip Anchor 136) [1999 7m⁶ 7.6g⁵ 8f* 7.7d⁴ Sep 21] IR 24,000Y: small, well-made gelding: third foal: half-brother to 3-y-o Best Port: dam maiden half-sister to Park Hill winner Coigach and dam of 4-y-o Craigsteel and 5-y-o Invermark: best effort in maidens (seemed in need of race first 2 starts) when dictating pace to win at Thirsk in September: respectable fourth of 12 in nursery at Warwick: should stay 1¼m: acts on firm ground. *M. A. Jarvis* **73 +**

SOVIET FLASH (IRE) 2 b.c. (Feb 26) Warning 136 – Mrs Moonlight (Ajdal (USA) 130) [1999 7f⁴ 7m* Aug 22] 100,000Y: fourth foal: half-brother to a 1m winner in Japan by Machiavellian: dam unraced half-sister to Pushy, Jupiter Island and Precocious: confirmed debut promise when winning maiden at Leicester by 2 lengths from Thari, leading final 1f: will stay 1m: already useful, and should improve further. *E. A. L. Dunlop* **95 p**

SOVIET KING (IRE) 6 b.g. Soviet Lad (USA) – Finessing (Indian King (USA) 128) [1998 NR 1999 10d a13g a14g⁶ Jul 8] angular gelding: has a round action: poor performer: stays 1¾m: acts on firm ground and all-weather. *P. Mitchell* **33**

SOVIET LADY (IRE)   5 b.m. Soviet Lad (USA) – La Vosgienne (Ashmore (FR)   –
125) [1998 37, a–: a6g a8g 6g⁵ 8.3m⁴ 8f 7g 8g³ 7f 16v 1999 a10g a13g a16g Feb 25]
sparely-made mare: no longer of much account. *R. Ingram*

SO WILLING   3 gr.g. Keen 116 – Sweet Whisper 63 (Petong 126) [1998 63: 5d³   **67**
5f⁵ 5g⁴ 6g a6g⁶ 5d⁴ 5d 1999 a6g a6g* 6v² a6g 6m 7.1d a6g² a6g a7g a7g a6g a6g   **a74 d**
Dec 21] leggy gelding: fair performer: won maiden at Southwell in March: ran
creditably in handicaps after only when runner-up: stays 6f, probably not 7f: acts on
heavy going and fibresand: visored final start. *M. Dods*

SPACE BABE   3 br.f. Cosmonaut – Concorde Lady 66 (Hotfoot 126) [1998 50:   **50**
7f⁶ 7m 5.1m 7d 1999 6.1g 6m 6g⁵ 7f³ Aug 4] poor maiden: stays 7f: acts on firm
going: sold 2,000 gns, sent to Sweden. *R. Hannon*

SPACE RACE   5 b.g. Rock Hopper 124 – Melanoura (Imperial Fling (USA) 116)   **73**
[1998 83: a8.5g² a9.4g a8g a10g 1999 a12g* a10g⁵ a12g² a12g⁴ 12s 10d² 10g⁵ 11.7s   **a83**
a10g² a10g a12g² Dec 6] workmanlike gelding: fairly useful on all-weather, fair on
turf: won 6-runner handicap at Lingfield in January: creditable second in handicaps
and minor events after: effective at 1¼m/easy 1½m: acts on all-weather, firm and
good to soft ground: free-going sort, used to make running: sometimes finds little:
none too consistent. *C. A. Cyzer*

SPA LANE   6 ch.g. Presidium 124 – Sleekit 78 (Blakeney 126) [1998 60, a39:   **60**
16.2m* 16g³ 14.1d² 18s⁴ 16.2d⁶ 16.2m² 17.1m² 16m² 16v 18.2g³ 17.1d⁵ 14.6d a14g   **a43**
a11g⁴ a12g⁴ 1999 a16g* a16f² a16g a16g⁴ 14.1s 17.1v 16.2d 12g* 16.1m⁴ 12m²
16.2m² 12m 17.1g 16m a14g Sep 28] leggy gelding: modest handicapper on turf,
poor on all-weather: won at Southwell in January and Pontefract in May: well below
form final 4 starts (reportedly lame first of them): effective at 1½m to 17f: acts on
firm ground, soft and fibresand. *Mrs S. Lamyman*

SPANISH EYES   4 b.f. Belmez (USA) 131 – Night Transaction 59 (Tina's Pet   –
121) [1998 60, a52: 8m⁴ 10d a8g³ 10.1g² 9.7f³ 8g³ 1999 10.8m May 3] modest
maiden: stays 1¼m: acts on firm going. *J. L. Spearing*

SPANISH LADY (IRE)   3 b.f. Bering 136 – Belle Arrivee 87 (Bustino 136)   **61**
[1998 –p: 7d 1999 10m 12d⁴ 14.1g⁵ 16v Sep 24] strong, good sort: modest maiden:
stayed 1½m: acted on good to soft going: stud. *J. L. Dunlop*

SPANISH STAR   2 b.g. (Mar 27) Hernando (FR) 127 – Desert Girl (Green Desert   **72 p**
(USA) 127) [1999 7.5g⁴ 8s³ Sep 29] 20,000Y: third foal: half-brother to 1997 2-y-o
6f winner Moontabeh (by Mujtahid): dam lightly-raced daughter of smart middle-
distance filly Upend from family of Royal Gait: better effort in maidens when third
of 7 to High Cheviot at Newcastle: should prove well suited by 1¼m/1½m: open to
further improvement. *W. Jarvis*

SPANKER   3 ch.f. Suave Dancer (USA) 136 – Yawl 112 (Rainbow Quest (USA)   **71 §**
134) [1998 NR 1999 8g⁵ 12g⁴ 12.3m⁶ 12m³ 10.5f⁴ a10g² a12g³ a9.4g Dec 15] leggy   **a66 §**
filly: second foal: half-sister to 11.5f winner Genoa (by Zafonic): dam, 7f (Rockfel)
winner at 2 yrs but mostly disappointing afterwards, daughter of Oaks winner
Bireme: fair maiden: stays 1½m: acts on good to firm going and all-weather: has
flashed tail/found little: blinkered final outing: one to treat with caution. *B. W. Hills*

SPARKLING HARRY   5 ch.g. Tina's Pet 121 – Sparkling Hock (Hot Spark 126)   –
[1998 45, a64: 7s⁶ 7d 6m a7g² a8g a8g a7g⁴ 8.1d 8.3d³ a8.5g* 8.3s a9.4g*   **a56**
10.1v a8.5g⁴ a9.4g⁴ 1999 a9.4g a11g a9.4g 10d 9.3m⁶ a9.4g⁴ 10m 8m Jul 16] smallish
gelding: modest handicapper on all-weather, poor on turf: generally well beaten in
1999: stays 9.4f: acts on soft going, good to firm and fibresand: tried blinkered/
visored. *Miss L. C. Siddall*

SPARKLING ISLE   2 ch.f. (Apr 18) Inchinor 119 – Brillante (FR) 118 (Green   **66**
Dancer (USA) 132) [1999 6m⁴ 7d⁶ 7v⁴ 6v Oct 23] 30,000Y: half-sister to winning
stayer Arc Bright (by Trempolino), 3-y-o Intensity and several winners abroad: dam,
French 1m (at 2 yrs) and 11f winner, half-sister to Bellypha: fair form in maidens:
lost all chance when rearing leaving stalls in nursery at Newbury final start: will stay
at least 1m. *M. Blanshard*

SPARK OF LIFE   2 b.f. (Apr 11) Rainbows For Life (CAN) – Sparkly Girl (IRE)   **59**
79 (Danehill (USA) 126) [1999 7g 8s⁶ 8s Nov 6] 4,000Y: first foal: dam Irish 1m to

1½m winner: form in maidens only when sixth of 13 at Bath in October: should stay 1½m: blinkered last 2 starts: has flashed tail under pressure. *P. R. Chamings*

SPARKY   5 b.g. Warrshan (USA) 117 – Pebble Creek (IRE) (Reference Point 139)   – [1998 67, a80: a9.4g⁵ 10m⁴ 8g⁵ 8.5d 1999 8d 8m Aug 2] workmanlike gelding: has a round action: fair handicapper: well beaten both 5-y-o starts: has form at 1¼m, possibly best at strongly-run 1m: acts on firm ground and fibresand: best in blinkers, visored once. *M. W. Easterby*

SPARTAN HEARTBEAT   6 b.g. Shareef Dancer (USA) 135 – Helen's Dream   – §
(Troy 137) [1998 65§: 18d a12g² 1999 a12g a16.2g Dec 15] good-bodied gelding: disappointing maiden on Flat: tried blinkered. *J. G. M. O'Shea*

SPARTAN ROYALE   5 b.g. Shareef Dancer (USA) 135 – Cormorant Creek 73   72
(Gorytus (USA) 132) [1998 64: 12.1d³ 11.1d 12.1s² 17.2d* 12.1d 17.5s⁶ 1999 13g 13s² 13d⁶ 13g² 13g² 10.9d 13s³ 17.1s⁴ 13.1v² Oct 12] sturdy, close-coupled gelding: fair handicapper: effective at 13f to 17f: acts on heavy going. *P. Monteith*

SPECIALIZE   7 b.g. Faustus (USA) 118 – Scholastika (GER) (Alpenkonig (GER))   39
[1998 34: a12g² a12g⁴ a12g 1999 a11g³ Mar 10] poor maiden handicapper: stays 1½m: acts on firm going and fibresand: visored/blinkered last 4 starts: fairly useful handicap chaser. *K. R. Burke*

SPECIAL-K   7 br.m. Treasure Kay 114 – Lissi Gori (FR) (Bolkonski 134) [1998   51
47: 7d⁴ 8m 8m³ 7.5d 5g 8s⁵ 7.5d a7g 8d 8d 1999 8g* 8m⁶ 8m⁶ 8f³ 8m⁵ 10g³ 9g 8.3f⁴ 8m 9.2m Sep 6] leggy mare: modest performer: won claimer at Pontefract in May: ran creditably after when in frame (hampered and unseated rider early penultimate start): barely stays 1¼m: acts on any ground: tried blinkered/visored: usually races prominently. *E. Weymes*

SPECIAL PERSON (IRE)   4 ch.f. Ballad Rock 122 – Hada Rani (Jaazeiro (USA)   46
127) [1998 49, a64: 7v⁴ 7m a8g* 9m a8g² a10g 1999 a10g⁵ a12f 8g a10g 10d 6m⁶ 6m 7m a7g Nov 16] poor handicapper: stays 1m, probably not 1¼m: acts on equitrack, good to firm and heavy going. *P. Mitchell*

SPECIAL PROMISE (IRE)   2 ch.g. (Mar 27) Anjiz (USA) 104 – Wooden-   51
itbenice (USA) (Nasty And Bold (USA)) [1999 6d⁶ 5m⁶ 5d 7s a7g⁵ Dec 15] 13,000Y: strong, workmanlike gelding: fourth foal: half-brother to 2 winners in USA by World Appeal: dam unraced: modest maiden: should stay 1m. *P. C. Haslam*

SPECKLED GEM   3 b.f. Precocious 126 – My Diamond Ring 65 (Sparkling Boy   – 110) [1998 –: a5g⁵ 5d a5g⁵ 6s⁵ a8.5g 5.7v a7g⁶ a6f 1999 a6g Dec 6] little form. *J. R. Best*

SPECTROMETER   2 ch.c. (Mar 1) Rainbow Quest (USA) 134 – Selection Board   65 p
75 (Welsh Pageant 132) [1999 7m⁵ 8s 7s⁶ Sep 29] seventh foal: brother to useful 1m winner (stayed 1½m) Star Selection and half-brother to 3 winners, including 4-y-o Cruinn A Bhord: dam twice-raced sister to Teleprompter and half-sister to Chato-yant: best effort in maidens when sixth of 11 at Brighton on final start, slowly away and never dangerous: will need at least 1¼m at 3 yrs: capable of better. *Sir Mark Prescott*

SPEEDFIT FREE (IRE)   2 b.g. (Jan 24) Night Shift (USA) – Dedicated Lady   78
(IRE) 101 (Pennine Walk 120) [1999 5g 5g 6m* 5m 7m⁶ 6m 6s⁴ Sep 16] 82,000Y: good-bodied gelding: third living foal: closely related to 3-y-o Fairy Queen: dam, Irish 2-y-o 5f/6f winner, out of half-sister to Irish St Leger winner M-Lolshan: fair performer: made all in steadily-run minor event at Yarmouth in May: well held after, including in blinkers: stays 6f: acts on good to firm going: sold 6,200 gns in October, joined M. Buckley. *G. G. Margarson*

SPEED ON   6 b.g. Sharpo 132 – Pretty Poppy 67 (Song 132) [1998 100d: 5.1s* 5m   94
5s 5.2g 5m⁶ 6d 6s⁵ 6s 1999 5.2m* 5s⁶ 5d⁵ 5.1m* 5.2g 5m⁶ 5d Oct 18] small, strong gelding: reportedly chipped knee as 2-y-o: fairly useful handicapper: won at Newbury (rated stakes by ½ length from Cortachy Castle) in April and Chepstow in June: below form after: best at 5f: acts on firm and soft ground: tried visored: usually tracks leaders/held up. *H. Candy*

SPEEDY CLASSIC (USA)   10 br.g. Storm Cat (USA) – Shadows Lengthen 73   –
(Star Appeal 133) [1998 67, a92d: a7s* a7g a8g⁵ a6g³ 7f 7m 7m 6.1m* 7m a8g* a6g   a67 d

1999 a6g² a8f⁴ a7g² a7g² a7g² 7m 7.1g 7.1m a7g 7.1m a8g⁴ a8g Nov 23] workman-like gelding: has a round action: modest performer: trained by M. Heaton-Ellis until after eighth start: ran poorly after: best at 6f/7f: acts on all-weather, no recent form on turf: has won in blinkers (not tried since 1997): has given trouble at stalls and often taken down early: races prominently. *C. G. Cox*

SPEEDY JAMES (IRE)   3 ch.g. Fayruz 116 – Haraabah (USA) 99 (Topsider   **102** (USA)) [1998 97+: 5g* 5s* 5d² 5s 5g³ 5f 5m 1999 5m³ 5.1m⁶ 5d Sep 30] strong, good-topped gelding: good mover: useful performer: first run since being gelded when good third to Noble One in minor event at Newmarket: well held in similar race (final start for Jack Berry) and listed event after: will prove best at 5f: acts on soft and good to firm going: visored once at 2 yrs. *D. Nicholls*

SPELLBINDER (IRE)   3 b.f. Magical Wonder (USA) 125 – Shamanka (IRE)   **– p** (Shernazar 131) [1998 NR 1999 8.3d Nov 4] 25,000Y: first foal: dam French 1¼m winner: 14/1, some promise when eighth of 17 in Windsor maiden: should do better. *G. B. Balding*

SPENCER'S REVENGE   10 ch.g. Bay Express 132 – Armour of Light (Hot   **–** Spark 126) [1998 –: 8.3m 9m a8g 1999 a8g a13g Feb 6] sturdy gelding: formerly fairly useful winner: little form since 1997. *P. Butler*

SPENCERS WOOD (IRE)   2 b.c. (Mar 10) Pips Pride 117 – Ascoli (Skyliner   **84 p** 117) [1999 6g* Oct 11] IR 17,500F, 35,000Y: third foal: half-brother to a winner in Turkey by Prince Rupert: dam won in Ireland up to 1¼m and over hurdles: 10/1 and green, won 22-runner maiden at Windsor, staying on well to beat Nisr by ¾ length: will stay at least 7f+: seems sure to improve and win more races. *P. J. Makin*

SPENDER   10 b. or br.g. Last Tycoon 131 – Lady Hester (Native Prince) [1998 71,   **78 d** a–: 5d 5s⁶ 5m 5.7m 5.2g 5.3g 5v³ 5.1v 1999 a5g a5g⁴ a6g⁵ 6f 5.7g 5g 5g 5.7g 6m 6g 5m 5.1m 5d a5g a7g³ Dec 8] small, well-made gelding: fair performer, on the downgrade in 1999 (ran in seller final start): effective at 5f/6f: acts on any all-weather/turf: reportedly retired. *V. Soane*

SPENDTHEPROC-EDE'S   3 b.f. Dilum (USA) 115 – Karonga (Main Reef   **–** 126) [1998 56: 5g⁵ 5d⁵ 6.1m² 7s⁵ 7m 7m⁵ 1999 a10g Apr 1] robust filly: modest maiden: stays 6f: acts on good to firm and good to soft going. *W. G. M. Turner*

SPICK AND SPAN   5 b.g. Anshan 119 – Pretty Thing 83 (Star Appeal 133) [1998   **61** 55: a12g³ 16m⁴ 1999 a12g⁴ a16f* a16f² a16g⁶ Feb 9] modest handicapper: got off mark at Lingfield in January: stays 2m: acts on all-weather and good to firm going. *P. R. Hedger*

SPIN A YARN   2 b.c. (Jan 24) Wolfhound (USA) 126 – Green Flower (USA) 56   **85** (Fappiano (USA)) [1999 6d 6.1f⁴ 5.7m⁴ 7m⁴ 7 3g* Aug 14] fourth foal: half-brother to French 10.5f winner Green Laafe (by Green Desert): dam lightly-raced sister to champion 1985 US 2-y-o Tasso: fairly useful performer: best effort when winning nursery at Newbury in August: will stay 1m. *B. W. Hills*

SPINDRIFT (IRE)   4 b.c. Mukaddamah (USA) 125 – Win For Me (Bonne Noel   **116** 115) [1998 110p: 8g² 8f* 7m* 1999 a8f* a9f³ a10f* a10f² 8.9f³ Sep 2] rangy colt: smart performer: won listed races (from Altibr both times) at Nad Al Sheba early in 1999: ran creditably in Dubai Duty Free there (3½ lengths second to Altibr) and listed contest at York (3½ lengths third to Gold Academy) after: stays 1¼m: acts on firm going and dirt. *Saeed bin Suroor*

SPINNER TOY   4 ch.g. Seven Hearts 98 – Priory Bay 54 (Petong 126) [1998 –:   **–** 7.6m 1999 a10g Mar 2] no form in maidens at Lingfield. *J. C. Fox*

SPINNING STAR   3 ch.f. Arazi (USA) 135 – Queen Midas 119 (Glint of Gold   **70** 128) [1998 NR 1999 11.9d⁶ 12.3d³ 10v⁵ 11g⁴ 16g Nov 3] 25,000Y: seventh foal: half-sister to useful 1¼m winner Royal Circle (by Sadler's Wells): dam won Ribbles-dale Stakes: fair maiden: may prove best around 1½m: acts on good to soft going. *C. F. Wall*

SPINNING THE YARN   3 b.f. Barathea (IRE) 127 – Colorspin (FR) 118 (High   **70** Top 131) [1998 NR 1999 10d Jun 5] closely related to 5-y-o Kayf Tara and Opera House (both by Sadler's Wells), and half-sister to smart middle-distance winner

Highland Dress (by Lomond): dam, Irish Oaks winner, half-sister to Bella Colora and Cezanne: seventh in maiden at Newmarket, seeming green. *Sir Michael Stoute*

SPIRIT OF KHAMBANI (IRE) 2 ch.f. (Apr 28) Indian Ridge 123 – Khambani (IRE) 80 (Royal Academy (USA) 130) [1999 6m 7v³ Oct 11] IR 80,000Y: first foal: dam, Irish 6.5f winner, half-sister to Celestial Storm: modest form in maidens at Redcar and Ayr: should prove best at 7f/1m. *M. Johnston* — **53**

SPIRIT OF LIGHT (IRE) 2 b.g. (Apr 8) Unblest 117 – Light Thatch (Thatch (USA) 136) [1999 7m 8v² 7.9g 7d⁵ Oct 21] 7,000F, 12,500Y: half-brother to several winners, including 1988 2-y-o 5f winner Before The Crash (by Stanford): dam temperamental half-sister to dam of very smart sprinter Paris House: fair maiden: second of 11 at Kempton in September: races freely, and likely to prove best up to 1m. *M. R. Channon* — **70**

SPIRIT OF LOVE (USA) 4 ch.g. Trempolino (USA) 135 – Dream Mary (USA) (Marfa (USA)) [1998 121: a11g* a10g³ a11g² a12g³ 14.6g* 16.2m* 14m⁴ 14.6d* 14m³ 18g* 1999 16.2d⁴ 16.4g 20m 17.3g 17s* Nov 7] tall, lengthy gelding: has a long stride: very smart at 3 yrs, when 9-length winner of Cesarewitch: reportedly had some problems in 1999 and showed just useful form, not needing to be anywhere near best to win listed race at Mulheim by 12 lengths: best earlier efforts when fourth to Celeric in Sagaro Stakes and eighth of 17 to Enzeli in Gold Cup, both at Ascot: best at 2m+: acts on fibresand, soft going and good to firm: has wandered/run wide on bends and worn brush pricker on near-side: heavily bandaged in front second start: gelded after final outing. *M. Johnston* — **109**

SPIRIT OF TENBY (IRE) 2 b.g. (Apr 14) Tenby 125 – Asturiana (Julio Mariner 127) [1999 7m³ 7m⁵ 7m⁵ 8d 8d a8g⁵ Nov 11] IR 6,700Y, 15,000 2-y-o: half-brother to 5f winner (including at 2 yrs) Twice In Bundoran (by Bold Arrangement) and 3 winners abroad: dam lightly raced: fair maiden: ran poorly final 2 starts: should stay beyond 1m. *S. Dow* — **65**

SPIRIT OF THE NILE (FR) 4 b.f. Generous (IRE) 139 – Egyptale (Crystal Glitters (USA) 127) [1998 NR 1999 a13g* 16m⁴ 13.1g² a16g² 11.8m Aug 22] tall, leggy filly: fair performer, lightly raced: won maiden at Lingfield in January: ran poorly last 2 starts, finding nothing in blinkers final one: stays 2m: acts on equitrack, yet to race on extremes of going on turf. *P. F. I. Cole* — **72**

SPITZBERGEN 3 ch.g. Polar Falcon (USA) 126 – Soba 127 (Most Secret 119) [1998 84p: 6g 7s* 8s* 1999 8d 12.3d⁵ 11f² 8.3d² 10g⁶ 10m 10.3m⁶ 10d Sep 28] big, angular gelding: fairly useful performer: ran poorly final 4 starts: stays easy 11f: yet to race on heavy ground, acts on any other: has hung under pressure: sold 6,700 gns, sent to Spain. *M. Johnston* — **84 d**

SPLASH OUT (USA) 2 b.c. (May 5) Prized (USA) – Splash Em Baby (CAN) (Bucksplasher (USA)) [1999 6g⁵ 7.5s² 7f³ 7m* 7g Aug 17] $7,000F, $18,000Y: big, good-topped colt: has plenty of scope: fifth foal: half-brother to 3 winners in USA, including smart gelding Unruled (by Notebook), runner-up in Grade 1 races at 9f/ 1¼m: dam won up to 9f in USA: fair performer: won maiden at Ayr in August: ran no sort of race final outing: will stay 1m: acts on firm and soft going. *M. Johnston* — **78**

SPLIT THE ACES (IRE) 3 gr.g. Balla Cove 119 – Hazy Lady (Habitat 134) [1998 56: 5v⁴ 5.1s 6.1d a7g 1999 6g² 7v 6.1s³ 5.1g* 6.1d 5.1m 5.1m 8m 6g Aug 24] rather leggy, useful-looking gelding: fluent mover: modest performer: won claimer at Bath in May: well below form after: effective at 5f/6f: acts on heavy going: blinkered final start: inconsistent. *R. J. Hodges* — **64 d**

SPONDULICKS (IRE) 5 b.g. Silver Kite (USA) 111 – Greek Music (Tachypous 128) [1998 –§: a12g a16g 1999 12.3m Apr 7] workmanlike gelding: poor maiden: unreliable. *B. P. J. Baugh* — **– §**

SPONTANEITY (IRE) 3 ch.f. Shalford (IRE) 124§ – Mariyda (IRE) (Vayrann 133) [1998 70: 6.1g⁵ 6m³ 7m* 6g a8g⁵ 8d⁶ 1999 10.3d 8d 12f Jul 30] smallish filly: fair at 2 yrs: showed little in 1999: should stay beyond 1m: acts on good to firm and good to soft going: blinkered final start. *P. D. Evans* — **–**

SPOONFUL OF SUGAR 3 b.f. Sabrehill (USA) 120 – Pacific Gull (USA) 67 (Storm Bird (CAN) 134) [1998 76p: 7d⁶ 8d² 1999 7g Apr 14] leggy filly: fair maiden: stayed 1m: sold 3,000 gns: dead. *C. A. Cyzer* — **70**

SPORTING GESTURE 2 ch.g. (May 15) Safawan 118 – Polly Packer 81 **79 p**
(Reform 132) [1999 5g 6m⁵ 6m⁶ 6f⁶ 7.9m 7g* 7.9d Oct 7] 4,000Y: leggy, unfurnished
gelding: has a round action: half-brother to several winners, notably useful stayer
Regal Reform (by Prince Tenderfoot): dam second at 7f/1m: fair form: improved to
win nursery at Catterick in September in good style: much better than ninth of 20 to
Duchamp in similar event at York (met good deal of trouble and eased) final outing:
will stay 1m: acts on good to firm going, probably on good to soft: probably capable
of better still. *M. W. Easterby*

SPORTING LAD (USA) 3 b.c. Danzig (USA) – Lydara (USA) (Alydar (USA)) **108**
[1998 98+: 6f⁵ 7.3g² 7g² 7g* 7.3v⁴ 1999 7g⁵ 7.6m* 7g 7.3d⁴ 8d 7s⁵ Oct 25] quite
good-topped colt: useful performer: won handicap at Chester in May: ran creditably
after only when ½-length fourth to Trans Island in listed race at Newbury on return
from 4-month break: likely to be best at 7f/1m: acts on good to firm and good to soft
going: has worn crossed noseband. *P. F. I. Cole*

SPORTY MO (IRE) 2 b.g. (Apr 25) Namaqualand (USA) – Miss Fortunate **65**
(IRE) (Taufan (USA) 119) [1999 a6g* a6g⁶ 7g 8d⁵ 7s a7g* Oct 18] IR 3,400Y:
third foal: dam unraced: fair performer: won sellers at Southwell in May and October: stays 1m: acts on good to soft going and fibresand: well beaten in blinkers.
K. R. Burke

SPORTY SPICE (IRE) 4 b.f. Indian Ridge 123 – Intrinsic (Troy 137) [1998 –: **32**
8.2d 11.1d 10g 14.1g⁵ a12g⁴ 11.5g 11.5d 9g 1999 a11g² a12f⁵ a8g⁶ 11.5g 10g Aug
16] sturdy filly: poor mover: poor maiden handicapper: stays 11f: acts on fibresand:
blinkered (too free) once at 3 yrs: looked unenthusiastic final start: sold 1,000 gns in
November. *J. L. Harris*

SPOTTED EAGLE 6 ch.g. Risk Me (FR) 127 – Egnoussa 76 (Swing Easy (USA) **–**
126) [1998 59, a–: a5g a5g 6g 6g² 6m² 5m⁶ 5d 5m⁴ 1999 5m 6f 5f Aug 2]
close-coupled gelding: has a quick action: modest handicapper: no show in 1999,
pulled up lame final start: stays 6f: acts on firm going, no form on ground softer than
good. *D. Nicholls*

SPREE VISION 3 b.g. Suave Dancer (USA) 136 – Regent's Folly (IRE) 101 **86 d**
(Touching Wood (USA) 127) [1998 75p: 8.2d 7d⁴ 8v* 1999 10g⁶ 7.9s 12f² 10.4d
12m⁵ 10d⁶ 12m 10d 11.8d Oct 11] smallish, good-topped gelding: fairly useful
handicapper: mostly disappointing after third start: stays 1½m: acts on any going:
visored final start: has worn severe noseband: joined P. Monteith. *S. C. Williams*

SPRING BLADE 7 b.g. Jester 119 – Runfawit Pet 41 (Welsh Saint 126) [1998 –:
a12g 1999 a13g Jan 12] tailed off in claimers. *L. A. Dace*

SPRINGER 3 b.g. Cyrano de Bergerac 120 – Spring Collection (Tina's Pet 121) **– §**
[1998 –: 7g 6v a6g 1999 6v 6f Aug 7] no form: reluctant to race on final outing.
J. L. Eyre

SPRING PURSUIT 3 b.g. Rudimentary (USA) 118 – Pursuit of Truth (USA) 69 **88**
(Irish River (FR) 131) [1998 84+: 6m 6g* 7s 7d 1999 6m 8m 7.1g³ 8.1m⁴ 8.2m⁵ 7.1m
6.9m 7.1d³ 6.8g 10.2g² 12g 10s* 8.9d* 10g* 10g* 10d⁶ 10d² Nov 4] close-coupled
gelding: fairly useful handicapper: completed 4-timer at Brighton, York, Windsor
and Lingfield in September/October: effective at 9f/1¼m (well held at 1½m): best
form on good going or softer: blinkered once at 2 yrs: has been early to post: often
held up. *R. J. Price*

SPRINGS 3 b.f. Anshan 119 – College Supreme (Mansingh (USA) 120) [1998 39: **39**
7m 6g⁶ 7g 7d 10s⁶ 1999 10g 10.5d Sep 21] rather leggy filly: poor maiden at best.
J. L. Spearing

SPRINGS ETERNAL 2 b.f. (Mar 5) Salse (USA) 128 – Corn Futures 78 (Nom- **69**
ination 125) [1999 6.1m 7m 6d⁴ 8d² 8.3g a7g³ a8g Nov 30] fourth foal: half-sister to
3-y-o Inviramental, useful 1997 2-y-o 6f winner Crazee Mental (by Magic Ring) and
6f (at 2 yrs) and 7f winner Trading Aces (by Be My Chief): dam 2-y-o 6f winner out
of half-sister to Wassl: fair maiden: placed in nurseries at Musselburgh and
Southwell: stays 1m: acts on fibresand: difficult ride. *Sir Mark Prescott*

SPRINGS NOBLEQUEST 3 b.f. Noble Patriarch 115 – Primum Tempus 49 **59**
(Primo Dominie 121) [1998 68: 5d³ 5s* 5m³ 6s 6m 6s 1999 7.5m 8m⁶ 7m 8.1d 6m⁵
5.9m² 5.9g 6g 7m³ 8g Aug 16] workmanlike filly: modest handicapper: placed at

Carlisle and Newcastle in summer: effective at 6f/7f: acts on soft and good to firm ground. *T. D. Easterby*

SPRING SONG 2 b.f. (Apr 9) Petong 126 – Naturally Fresh 91 (Thatching 131) **46**
[1999 5d 5s⁵ 5d 7m⁵ 7.5g 8.5g⁵ 7.5g 9m Sep 24] 700Y: big, workmanlike filly: half-sister to 3 winners abroad, including German winner up to 10.5f Never To Louse (by Petoski): dam 2-y-o 5f winner: poor maiden: seems to stay 8.5f: acts on soft going, probably good to firm: visored last 2 starts. *M. E. Sowersby*

SPRINGTIME LADY 3 ch.f. Desert Dirham (USA) 108 – Affaire de Coeur 55 **69**
(Imperial Fling (USA) 116) [1998 NR 1999 8.3m 8m 6m² 8g⁵ 6m 7m 6g⁴ 8.1d a7g⁵ a8g² a8g² a8g Dec 18] second reported living foal: sister to 4-y-o Desert Song: dam 1m winner, also won over hurdles: fair maiden: trainer fined and horse and jockey subject of bans under non-triers' rule on fifth start: runner-up 3 times, including in 2 handicaps at Lingfield: stays 1m: acts on equitrack and good to firm going. *S. Dow*

SPRING TO GLORY 12 b.g. Teenoso (USA) 135 – English Spring (USA) 116 **–**
(Grey Dawn II 132) [1998 NR 1999 17.2f⁶ 14.1m Jul 17] winner over jumps: no longer of much account on Flat. *P. Hayward*

SPRINGWOOD 4 b.g. Green Desert (USA) 127 – Prosperous Lady (Prince **60**
Tenderfoot (USA) 126) [1998 NR 1999 8.5g⁵ 7d⁶ 8g⁴ 8d 8d⁴ 8m Jul 16] tall, good-topped gelding: fifth foal: half-brother to 3 winners, including smart 7f/1m performer Eurolink Thunder (by Fairy King): dam unraced: modest maiden: best efforts when fourth at Ripon, including in handicap: pulled up lame final start: may prove best at 7f/1m: acts on good to soft going, showed promise on fibresand. *R. A. Fahey*

SPRY 3 b.f. Suave Dancer (USA) 136 – Sandy Island 110 (Mill Reef (USA) 141) **84**
[1998 NR 1999 12m* 11.9g Aug 19] close-coupled filly: ninth foal: half-sister to 3 winners, including 7f (at 2 yrs) and 1¼m winner Sardegna (by Pharly) and 1½m winner Sebastian (by Sadler's Wells), both smart: dam, winner of Pretty Polly Stakes and Lancashire Oaks, closely related to Slip Anchor: fairly useful form when winning 4-runner maiden at Newmarket in July by 1¼ lengths from WilliamShakespeare: last in listed race at York: likely to stay beyond 1½m. *H. R. A. Cecil*

SPUNKIE 6 ch.g. Jupiter Island 126 – Super Sol (Rolfe (USA) 77) [1998 97p: **94**
14.1g* 12m⁵ 12m⁶ 16.2d* 18g³ 1999 16g⁵ 18.7m 20m 16g² 16d* 17.3g Oct 16] tall, leggy gelding: fairly useful performer: second in listed race at Baden-Baden prior to making all in 4-runner handicap at Newbury in September: well beaten in Cesarewitch at Newmarket final start: will prove best at 2m+: acts on good to soft going, seemingly not on good to firm. *R. F. Johnson Houghton*

SPY (IRE) 3 b.c. Mac's Imp (USA) 116 – Mystery Bid (Auction Ring (USA) 123) **82**
[1998 80: 5d 6g⁴ 6g² 6s⁵ 7.1g* 1999 7.5g⁵ 10m 8.2m² 8m² 8m⁵ Jun 17] fairly useful handicapper: runner-up at Nottingham and Newcastle in May/June: reportedly finished lame final start: stays 8.3f: acts on good to firm going, possibly not on softer than good: sold 11,500 gns. *C. W. Thornton*

SPY KNOLL 5 b.g. Shirley Heights 130 – Garden Pink (FR) (Bellypha 130) **81**
[1998 NR 1999 14m² 16.2m 14m Aug 21] very tall, rangy gelding: fairly useful handicapper: stays 2m: acts on soft going, probably on firm: visored once at 3 yrs. *Mrs L. Richards*

SQUANDAMANIA 6 b.g. Ela-Mana-Mou 132 – Garden Pink (FR) (Bellypha **35**
130) [1998 NR 1999 a12g⁴ 11.8d 12g Oct 16] poor maiden, lightly raced. *J. Norton*

SQUARE DANCER 3 b.g. Then Again 126 – Cubist (IRE) 71 (Tate Gallery **79 +**
(USA) 117) [1998 69: 6m⁵ 6m⁴ 6m 8d 7.9g 1999 8g 6m⁴ 7.1d³ 6.1g⁵ 6m² 5.9m* 6g² 6f² 6f 6m 6s* 6d 6g Oct 14] tall, good-bodied gelding: fair performer: won maiden at Carlisle in June and minor event at Brighton in August: has form at 1m, raced mainly at 6f in 1999: acts on firm and soft going: tends to get on toes, and has given trouble at stalls: has worn crossed noseband and been early to post. *M. Dods*

SQUARE MILE MISS (IRE) 6 b.m. Last Tycoon 131 – Call Me Miss (Hello **–**
Gorgeous (USA) 128) [1998 –, a51: a3g* a7g a8g⁶ a8g⁵ a8g³ 7m 1999 a8g a8g² a7g **a41**
a8g 8f 9m a7g a8g Dec 6] leggy mare: poor performer: stays 9f: acts on equitrack (possibly not fibresand) and good to firm going. *N. E. Berry*

SQUIRE CORRIE 7 b.g. Distant Relative 128 – Fast Car (FR) (Carwhite 127) **67 d**
[1998 79, a71: a5g 5s a5g 5g 5g⁵ 5g 5s a5g 6v 5m 5m 7m 5m² 5m² 6d⁵ 5d³ 5.1m 5m
5g a5g a5g³ 1999 a5g⁵ a6f a5g* a5g³ a5g⁴ a5g⁶ a5g a5g⁵ 5d 6s 5m⁴ 5g⁴ 5m a5g 5f 5m
a5g Aug 6] tall, workmanlike gelding: unimpressive mover: fair handicapper: won at
Lingfield in February: not so good later on: barely stays 6f: acts on all-weather, firm
and soft going: effective blinkered/visored or not: tends to sweat: has broken blood
vessel: has won for apprentice: usually leads. *D. W. Chapman*

STACCATO 4 b.g. Forzando 122 – Fast Car (FR) (Carwhite 127) [1998 –: 6g **–**
1999 a11g Feb 5] well beaten in maiden and seller. *Denys Smith*

STAFFORD KING (IRE) 2 b.c. (Feb 20) Nicolotte 118 – Opening Day (Day Is **–**
Done 115) [1999 6g 7d Oct 22] IR 27,000F, 10,000Y: lengthy, workmanlike colt: has
scope: half-brother to 3-y-o Just A Snack and several winners, including fairly useful
sprinter Norwegian Blue (by Mac's Imp) and 4-y-o Moonstone: dam Irish 1m
winner: well beaten in maidens. *J. G. M. O'Shea*

STAFFORD PRINCE 2 br.c. (Feb 21) Bin Ajwaad (IRE) 119 – Petonellajill **47**
73 (Petong 126) [1999 5m 5.1m 6.1m⁶ 7.9m 8d Oct 22] 7,000Y: first foal: dam
7f winner: poor maiden: stays 6f: visored (very stiff task in nursery) final start.
J. G. M. O'Shea

STAGE WHISPER 4 b.g. Alzao (USA) 117 – Starlet 119 (Teenoso (USA) 135) **70**
[1998 –: 10.5g⁶ 1999 12m 18g 14.6m³ Jun 26] sparely-made gelding: fair performer,
lightly raced: stays 1¾m: won only start on fibresand, raced only on good/good to
firm going on turf. *M. D. Hammond*

STAKIS CASINOS BOY (IRE) 5 ch.g. Magical Wonder (USA) 125 – Har-
diona (FR) (Hard To Beat 132) [1998 NR 1999 10d 9.9v Jun 9] sturdy gelding: fairly
useful for M. Johnston at 3 yrs: well held in 1999: stays 1½m: acts on good to firm
going: tried visored: winning hurdler. *B. Ellison*

STAND ASIDE 3 b.g. In The Wings 128 – Honourable Sheba (USA) (Roberto **–**
(USA) 131) [1998 –p: 7d⁶ 1999 8g 10m 14.1g 15.8m Jul 10] leggy, quite good-
topped gelding: only a little sign of ability. *Lady Herries*

STAND BY 2 b.f. (Mar 3) Missed Flight 123 – Ma Rivale (Last Tycoon 131) [1999 **53 p**
5d 7s a5g⁵ Dec 13] 6,200Y, resold 6,000Y: second foal: dam placed in Belgium:
best effort in maidens (modest form) when fifth at Southwell: likely to progress.
T. D. Easterby

STAND TALL 7 b.g. Unfuwain (USA) 131 – Antilla 87 (Averof 123) [1998 88: **82 d**
6m⁴ 5.8s² 6g 6m³ 6s² 6m 7g 6g 6.1v 6s* 6d 1999 6v⁶ 6g 5.7g 6m⁴ 6m³ 6m 6g 6s 6g⁵
6g⁶ 7d Oct 30] big, strong gelding: fairly useful handicapper: below best after fifth
start: stays easy 7f: acts on any turf/all-weather: none too consistent. *Lady Herries*

STANLEY WIGFIELD (USA) 3 b.c. Woodman (USA) 126 – Las Meninas **–**
(IRE) 115 (Glenstal (USA) 118) [1998 –: 8.2d 7.1m 1999 a8f⁵ a6g a8g⁴ a7g 12g⁴ **a59**
a12g³ 10.9m 12g Sep 15] small, sturdy, lengthy colt: modest maiden: left D. Nicholls
and off 4 months before final start: stays 1½m: acts on fibresand, yet to race on
extremes of going on turf: has been bandaged in front: carries head high. *L. McAteer,
Ireland*

STANOTT (IRE) 4 b.c. Mukaddamah (USA) 125 – Seme de Lys (USA) 61 (Slew **111**
O'Gold (USA)) [1998 103: 7s* 7m⁴ 8m* 10.3g⁴ 8m² 1999 7g³ 7.9d² 8m* 10s⁵ 10g³
8m² Oct 10] good-quartered colt: smart performer: better than ever in 1999, ½-length
second to Sugarfoot in listed rated stakes at York before winning Premio Emilio
Turati at Milan in June by short neck from demoted Sole Che Sorgi, leading final
strides: creditable 2½ lengths second to Muhtathir in Premio Vittorio di Capua at
Milan final start: best at 1m: acts on good to firm and good to soft going, has won on
soft: sent to USA. *L. M. Cumani*

STARBOARD TACK (FR) 3 b.f. Saddlers' Hall (IRE) 126 – North Wind (IRE) **76**
101 (Lomond (USA) 128) [1998 66p: 7d⁵ 1999 11.4m 10.2g³ 11.7f³ 12d³ 10d⁵
10.2s⁴ Sep 27] sturdy filly: fair maiden: effective at 1¼m/1½m: acts on good to soft
ground, carried head awkwardly and found little on firm: has been bandaged in front.
B. W. Hills

STAR CAST (IRE) 2 ch.f. (Feb 3) In The Wings 128 – Thank One's Stars (Alzao **68 ?**
(USA) 117) [1999 7m 7.3f⁵ 7m 7m Sep 18] small filly: half-sister to several winners,

including 3-y-o Be Thankfull, fairly useful 1997 2-y-o 5f winner Thanksgiving (by Indian Ridge) and fairly useful 6f (at 2 yrs) to 11f (in Italy) winner Suris (by Taufan): dam unraced: seemed to show fair form second outing: well held in Newbury nursery final one: should be suited by 1m+. *Major D. N. Chappell*

STAR DYNASTY (IRE)   2 b.c. (Mar 12) Bering 136 – Siwaayib 97 (Green **70 p** Desert (USA) 127) [1999 7d⁴ Nov 1] third foal: half-brother to 3-y-o Happy Lady and 4-y-o Rainbow Ways: dam 6f winner, including at 2 yrs: weak in market, encouraging fourth of 15 to Norton in maiden at Redcar, no extra final 1f: should stay at least 1m: sure to improve. *E. A. L. Dunlop*

STAR FANTASY (USA)   4 ch.g. Sky Classic (CAN) – Wanda's Dream (USA) **61** 74 (Miswaki (USA) 124) [1998 68: 10f⁵ 1999 a9.4g² a12g³ a10g Jul 7] modest maiden: should stay beyond 1¼m: joined N. Twiston-Davies: winner over hurdles. *D. G. Bridgwater*

STARLIGHT   2 b.f. (Apr 8) King's Signet (USA) 110 – Petinata (Petong 126) **65** [1999 6m 7.5g 8.2s⁵ 7s⁴ 8d⁵ Nov 1] 1,100F: sparely-made filly: second foal: half-sister to a sprint winner in Sweden by Beveled: dam, ran twice at 2 yrs, half-sister to useful sprinter Peatswood Shooter: fair maiden: trained by N. Graham on debut: best effort when fourth of 20 to French Horn in nursery at Leicester: stays 1m: acts on soft ground. *E. A. L. Dunlop*

STARLINER (IRE)   4 ch.f. Statoblest 120 – Dancing Line (High Line 125) [1998 **43** 53, a?: 6g⁶ 8.1m 5.9g 5.9d 8m² 8m 7.5m⁵ 10g 8d⁶ 8.2g a8.5g 1999 a8g a11g 9d³ 8.3m **a–** 9m 8m Jun 16] unfurnished filly: modest maiden handicapper: stays 9f: well beaten on all-weather, yet to race on extremes of going on turf: effective visored or not: sold 3,200 gns, joined L. Wells. *M. Brittain*

Scuderia Rencati Srl's "Stanott"

STARLYTE GIRL (IRE) 2 b.f. (Feb 12) Fairy King (USA) – Blushing Storm **83**
(USA) 102 (Blushing Groom (FR) 131) [1999 6m² 6f³ 7.7g* 7m Aug 29] close-
coupled filly: has a quick action: fourth foal: half-sister to 3-y-o Morning Music and
4-y-o Churlish Charm: dam (maiden) third in Ribblesdale and Lancashire Oaks:
fairly useful form: made all in maiden at Warwick in August: stiff task in Group 3
event at Goodwood final outing: will stay 1¼m. *R. Hannon*

STAR MANAGER (USA) 9 b.g. Lyphard (USA) 132 – Angel Clare (FR) (Mill **62 d**
Reef (USA) 141) [1998 79: 8.1s⁵ 8d 10.8m⁶ 8.5g* 9m 10.1m⁶ a8.5g 1999 a10g⁶ a12g
15.4v 10d 12s 10m 9.9g⁴ 10g 10f 10g 10s Nov 1] close-coupled gelding: fluent
mover: one-time fairly useful winner: modest at best in 1999: stays 1¼m: acts on any
turf going, little form on all-weather: tried blinkered: sometimes sweating/edgy: has
worn crossed noseband. *R. C. Spicer*

STAR OF AKKAR 3 b.f. Distant Relative 128 – Donna Star (Stately Don (USA) **115**
122) [1998 8v* 8v² 1999 8d* 9.3g* 10.5d² 9g* 10s* 9.3v Oct 3] 5,000Y, 120,000
francs 2-y-o: first foal: dam third at 1m at 2 yrs in France: smart performer: won
minor event in April and Prix Vanteaux (by ¾ length from Hello Soso) in May, both
at Longchamp, 4-runner Prix Chloe at Chantilly (by ¾ length from Visionnaire, made
all but shied away from winning post) in July and Prix de la Nonette-Japan Racing
Association at Deauville (led near line to beat Sage Et Jolie by short head) in August:
also ran well when length second to Daryaba in Prix de Diane at Chantilly in June:
stays 10.5f: raced only on good ground or softer: seems a nervy sort (reportedly
reared over at stalls before running poorly final start). *J-C. Rouget, France*

STAR OF THE COURSE (USA) 4 b.f. Theatrical 128 – Water Course (USA) **95**
(Irish River (FR) 131) [1998 81: 7m 12d⁵ 12f* 11.9f* 11.9m* 10.5s² 1999 11.6m³
12.1g* 11.9d* 11.7m* 11.9g³ 12d³ 12v⁴ Nov 19] leggy filly: useful performer: better
than ever in 1999, winning handicaps at Chepstow and Haydock and minor event at
Bath between May and July: respectable fourth in listed race at Lyon Parilly: seems
best around 1½m: probably acts on any going: tends to start slowly: consistent.
P. F. I. Cole

Marquesa de Moratalla's "Star of Akkar"

STAR PRECISION   5 ch.m. Shavian 125 – Accuracy 83 (Gunner B 126) [1998   **100**
100d: 10v³ 9d³ 10.4g² 12d 10m⁵ 12g 8s⁴ 10.3d⁴ 1999 10m⁶ 11.9d* 10.2d* 12g 9.9d⁶
10.4g 10.1g 12s 10d 12s⁴ 12s Nov 6] sparely-made, angular mare: has a long, round
action: useful performer: emphatic winner of 20-runner handicap at York (by 3
lengths from Banbury) and 6-runner minor event at Chepstow (by 7 lengths from
Kuster) in May: signs of retaining ability late in year: stays 13f: acts on soft ground,
probably not on good to firm. *G. B. Balding*

STAR PRINCESS   2 b.f. (Apr 28) Up And At 'em 109 – Princess Sharpenup 63   **71**
(Lochnager 132) [1999 5s 5g³ 6v² 6s⁴ Nov 5] 2,000Y: workmanlike filly: half-sister
to 3-y-o Miss Traxdata and several winners by Belfort, including sprinter Sharp Anne
and 5f to 7f winner Prince Belfort: dam, third at 5f at 2 yrs, only start: fair maiden: in
frame at Redcar, Newbury (bandaged in front) and Doncaster (hung markedly right):
stays 6f: raced only on good going or softer (acts on heavy). *K. T. Ivory*

STAR RAGE (IRE)   9 b.g. Horage 124 – Star Bound (Crowned Prince (USA)   **93**
128) [1998 80, a83: a14.8g⁵ a14.8g* 13.9g 16g⁶ 17.2d² 16m² 16.4g⁵ 1999 a16g*
a16.2g⁵ 16g 16.2d* 16f⁶ 15s⁵ 17.1g³ 16f² 16f* 16.2g* 16.1g³ 16m* Sep 11] sturdy,
angular gelding: fairly useful handicapper: better than ever at 9 yrs, winning at
Lingfield, Beverley (first run since leaving D. Elsworth and returning to former
trainer), Redcar, Beverley and Goodwood between March and September: needs
thorough test at 1½m, and probably stays 2¼m: acts on all-weather, firm and good to
soft ground (well below form on soft): sometimes idles, but seems effective held up
or front running: game. *M. Johnston*

STARRY NIGHT   3 b.f. Sheikh Albadou 128 – My Ballerina (USA) 94 (Sir Ivor   **89**
135) [1998 74p: 7.1s* 1999 10m 10g 10.5s* 10.5v² 11.6d⁵ Oct 28] strong, lengthy
filly: fairly useful performer: won handicap at Haydock in September by 5 lengths:
looked a difficult ride last 2 starts, though ran creditably on penultimate: should stay
1½m: goes well on soft/heavy going: blinkered last 3 starts: sold 20,000 gns in
December. *J. L. Dunlop*

STARTOO   3 ch.f. King's Signet (USA) 110 – Shall We Run 59 (Hotfoot 126)   **–**
[1998 64: 5m 6g³ 1999 8.3m 6g 7g 7g Jun 14] smallish, leggy filly: signs of ability at
2 yrs but well held in 1999: headstrong: sent to Italy. *R. F. Johnson Houghton*

STAR TURN (IRE)   5 ch.g. Night Shift (USA) – Ringtail 102 (Auction Ring   **64**
(USA) 123) [1998 –, a56: a7g⁴ a8.5g⁵ a8g² 7g⁵ 8g a12g a10f⁴ 1999 a10g* a10g 10d*   **a56**
8.9d Oct 9] strong gelding: has reportedly suffered knee problems: modest handicapper: won at Lingfield in January and (having been off 7 months after finishing
lame second start) Newmarket in August, latter ladies race: stays 1¼m: acts on firm
ground, soft and equitrack. *R. M. Flower*

STARVINE   3 b.f. Superlative 118 – Girl Next Door 58 (Local Suitor (USA) 128)   **–**
[1998 40: 5s 5.1m a5g⁶ a5g⁶ a5g³ a5g 5m a5g 5m 1999 a7g a6g 6g 5v a5g a5g⁶
Jun 19] poor maiden at best: left R. Spicer after second start: visored/blinkered after
reappearance. *D. Shaw*

STATAJACK (IRE)   11 b.g. King of Clubs 124 – Statira 103 (Skymaster 126)   **78**
[1998 68, a64+: 9.7s* 10.8g 12f 10g 12g* 12s 12.5g⁴ 12m⁶ 12g 11.9g² 11.8d* 12s   **a–**
a12g⁴ a12g 1999 a12g⁶ 10d* 12m⁶ 12g² 11.5m⁶ 12g* 12m³ 11.6m* 12m² 11.6s⁴ 12m
12m⁶ Sep 17] leggy, sparely-made gelding: fair handicapper: won at Windsor (19
ran) in May, Epsom in June and Windsor in July: effective at 1¼m/1½m: acts on any
turf ground and equitrack: wears blinkers/bandages: not an easy ride, best produced
very late and handled by T. Quinn. *D. R. C. Elsworth*

STATE APPROVAL   6 b.g. Pharly (FR) 130 – Tabeeba (Diesis 133) [1998 –,   **44**
a67: a12g* a12g* a11g⁴ a12g² a11g* a12g⁵ a12g* a12g* a12g* a11g² 1999 a12g*   **a76**
a11g² a12g⁶ 11.8s 10s a12g⁶ 10m⁶ a9.4g* a9.4g² a8.5g⁵ Jul 23] small gelding: fair
on all-weather, poor and lightly raced on turf nowadays: won claimers at Southwell
(penultimate run for Miss S. Wilton) in March and Wolverhampton in May: effective
at 9.4f to 13f: acts on fibresand and good to firm going: usually races up with pace.
D. Shaw

STATELY FAVOUR   4 ch.f. Statoblest 120 – Dixie Favor (USA) 82 (Dixieland   **–**
Band (USA)) [1998 –, a48: a6g³ a7g² a5g* a6g⁵ a6g 6.1g a6g a6g 1999 a7g⁶ a7g a6g

Mar 1] smallish, useful-looking filly: poor performer: stays 7f: acts on fibresand: has been bandaged behind: inconsistent: sold 1,350 gns. *Miss J. A. Camacho*

STATE OF CAUTION 6 b.g. Reprimand 122 – Hithermoor Lass 75 (Red Alert 127) [1998 86, a111: a5g² 5d⁶ 5g⁶ 6v³ 6d a6g⁵ 7g 7s 5g 6s 7g 6g⁴ 5v² 6s² 6s³ a7g a8f⁵ 1999 a5g⁶ a6g⁶ a10g⁶ a7g* 5.8g a6g² a6g* a6g² a6g* a6s² Dec 5] quite attractive gelding: useful on all-weather, fair on turf: won claimer at Wolverhampton (claimed out of K. Burke's stable £16,000) in February, listed race at Jagersro (back to near best, with Gaelic Storm third) in August and handicap at Taby in October: effective at 5f to easy 7f: acts on good to firm going, heavy and fibresand/dirt: blinkered/visored: sometimes bandaged: has broken blood vessel. *C. Bjorling, Sweden* — **a108**

STATE SHINTO (USA) 3 br.c. Pleasant Colony (USA) – Sha Tha (USA) 118 (Mr Prospector (USA)) [1998 9v² 8v* 1999 11d² 11g² 10.5g* 10g² 10d* 9.8v* Oct 2] **121**

Sheikh Mohammed's silks may not be quite so omnipresent as they once were in pre-Godolphin days but they were certainly to the fore, if rather mud-spattered, at the finish of the Prix Dollar at Longchamp in October. Two progressive three-year-old colts in the maroon and white colours, State Shinto and the Irish-trained Strategic, fought out the finish of the Group 2 contest run in heavy rain and ever-worsening ground. State Shinto emerged three quarters of a length to the good over Strategic after taking up the running over a furlong out and holding on well despite tending to edge right. The pair finished two lengths clear of Kabool, representing Godolphin, in third. Before the month was out it was announced that both State Shinto and Strategic would themselves be part of the Godolphin team in the next season.

State Shinto ended his three-year-old season with the admirable record of four wins and four seconds from his eight career starts. Having won the listed Prix Saraca at Saint-Cloud on his final two-year-old start, State Shinto contested two trials in the spring for the Prix du Jockey Club but defeat in both—he was second to Slickly in the Prix Noailles at Longchamp and Falcon Flight in the Prix Hocquart at Chantilly—meant he was not one of his stable's representatives in the French Derby. Instead, State Shinto was returned to listed company for the Prix Pelleas at Maisons-Laffitte at the end of June and gained a length win from Chelsea Manor in a falsely-run four-runner race after setting a steady pace. He then failed to trouble Dubai Millennium when finishing three lengths second in the Prix Eugene Adam at the same course the following month, though that represented improvement on his earlier form, and State Shinto confirmed that progress when again having to account for only three rivals to win the Prix du Prince d'Orange at Longchamp in September by a length from Way of Light. Taking on older horses for the first time in the Prix Dollar, State Shinto ran his best race yet, giving Thierry Jarnet the chance to atone for mistaking the winning post in the Prix de Royallieu earlier on the card, for which he received a twenty-day suspension.

		Pleasant Colony (USA) (b 1978)	His Majesty (b 1968)	Ribot
				Flower Bowl
State Shinto (USA) (br.c. 1996)			Sun Colony (b 1968)	Sunrise Flight
				Colonia
		Sha Tha (USA) (b or br 1988)	Mr Prospector (b 1970)	Raise A Native
				Gold Digger
			Savannah Dancer (b or br 1982)	Northern Dancer
				Valoris II

State Shinto comes from an excellent middle-distance family. Great grandam Valoris won the One Thousand Guineas and Oaks and was a half-sister to the top-class Prix du Jockey Club winner Val de Loir and the grandam of King George winner Petoski. Both State Shinto's dam and grandam were Grade 2 winners over nine furlongs in the States, Sha Tha winning the All Along Stakes and Savannah Dancer the Del Mar Oaks. Sha Tha also showed smart form in France, being placed in the Prix Marcel Boussac and the Poule

d'Essai des Pouliches. Savannah Dancer's half-sisters Val's Girl and Vincennes were runners-up in the Oaks and Irish Oaks respectively, and Savannah Dancer herself was closely related to the Geoffrey Freer winner Valinsky. Savannah Dancer is also the dam of the smart middle-distance stayer Brier Creek. State Shinto is his dam's second foal and winner after the fair Irish stayer Shastri (by Alleged). State Shinto himself should have no trouble staying a mile and a half. He's raced only on good ground or softer so far and acts on heavy. He may not have stopped improving yet and should win another good race or two. *A. Fabre, France*

STATE WIND (IRE)   3 ch.g. Forest Wind (USA) 111 – Kowalski (IRE) (Cyrano **55** de Bergerac 120) [1998 –: a7g 6m a6g a6g a6g 1999 a8g³ a9.4g² a8g⁶ a7f⁶ a7s² a7g³ a8.5g⁶ 8m⁶ 8m a9.4g Aug 14] close-coupled gelding: poor mover: modest maiden: stays 9.4f: acts on fibresand, some promise on turf: usually blinkered/visored: has carried head awkwardly. *N. P. Littmoden*

STATISTICIAN   7 b.g. Statoblest 120 – Sharp Lady 70 (Sharpen Up 127) [1998 **64** 51: a6g⁵ a6g* a7g⁴ a7g³ a7g³ a8g³ 1999 a6f⁴ a7g⁶ a7g³ a8g a7g* a8g* Mar 18] tall gelding: modest handicapper: won at Wolverhampton and Lingfield (amateurs) within 6 days in March: later won in Jersey: effective at 6f to 1¼m: acts on firm ground and all-weather: tried blinkered. *John Berry*

STATOYORK   6 b.g. Statoblest 120 – Ultimate Dream 74 (Kafu 120) [1998 63, **77** a47: a6g a6g⁶ a5g⁶ 5d³ a5g³ a5g⁴ 6s 5.1m⁶ 6m³ a5g 5g² 6.1g² 6d⁵ 5m⁶ 5g⁶ 6g² 5m **a51** 5m* 5m⁶ 5.1d⁵ 6d⁶ 5m³ 5m 1999 5g² 5m 5m* 5d* 5g 6.1f³ 5.1d³ 5d² 5m* 5m 5m 5f 5f⁶ 6f 5g⁴ 5g 5s 5g⁴ 6.1f 5d 7s Nov 2] strong, attractive gelding: fair on turf, modest on all-weather: won minor event at Carlisle and handicaps at Ripon (2) in May/June: has form at 6f/7f, but probably best at truly-run 5f: acts on fibresand, firm and good to soft going (probably on soft): visored (well beaten) twice: has been early to post: has bled from nose (including on reappearance): sometimes finds little, and best produced late. *D. Shaw*

STAVANGER (IRE)   3 b.g. Distinctly North (USA) 115 – Card Queen (Lord **54** Gayle (USA) 124) [1998 57d: a5g³ 5d 5.1g⁶ 5.7g 6m 1999 6.1s 6f 5.9g⁶ 6.9m⁴ 6.9m² 8.1d⁴ 7m⁴ 7.5g⁴ 7g³ 8.2g⁶ Sep 25] strong gelding: modest maiden: may prove best around 7f: acts on good to firm ground and equitrack: sent to UAE. *J. Berry*

STAYIN ALIVE (USA)   2 b. or br.c. (Jan 27) Sword Dance – Marilyn's Mystique **93 p** (USA) (Dearest Doctor (USA)) [1999 7g⁴ 8d⁴ a7g* Dec 18] angular, workmanlike colt: fifth foal: brother to 2 winners in USA and half-brother to a winner in USA by Sejm: dam winner at up to 7f in USA: fairly useful form when winning minor event at Lingfield in December easily by 6 lengths from Insightful, quickening well clear on turn: better effort on turf in maiden at Yarmouth (for A. G. Foster) second start (trained by P. Chapple-Hyam on debut): stays 7f: acts on equitrack: tongue tied final outing: should improve again. *G. A. Butler*

STEALTHY TIMES   2 ch.f. (May 3) Timeless Times (USA) 99 – Stealthy 73 **80** (Kind of Hush 118) [1999 6.1g* Jul 3] 5,000 2-y-o: sister to 3-y-o Red Wolf and half-sister to a 5f to 7.5f winner in Italy by Presidium: dam 1m winner: 33/1, made all in 17-runner maiden at Nottingham, hanging badly left but holding Ecstasy by 3 lengths: looked sure to improve. *J. G. Given*

STEAMROLLER STANLY   6 b.g. Shirley Heights 130 – Miss Demure 106   – §
(Shy Groom (USA)) [1998 79, a105: a10g* a10g* a10g⁵ 13.8d 14.6g 10.1m³ 14m   **a95 §**
1999 a8g³ a10g a12g³ 11.9s⁵ a14.8g* a9.4g³ a16g³ a16g* a14g² 20m a12g³ a8.5g⁶
a9.4g⁶ a12g⁴ a12g³ a12g³ Dec 29] sturdy gelding: useful performer: won handicap
at Wolverhampton in April and claimer at Southwell in June: stays 2m: acts on
all-weather, little form on turf of late: tried blinkered/visored: often races up with
pace: usually flashes tail: none too reliable. *K. R. Burke*

STELLIO (USA)   3 b.f. Dynaformer (USA) – Stella Mystika (USA) 92 (Diesis   **81**
133) [1998 NR 1999 8m² 8m Aug 28] second foal: dam 7f/1m winner out of Grade 1
2-y-o 6f winner Share The Fantasy: better effort in maidens when ½-length second to
Badaayer at Salisbury: hampered next time: not sure to stay beyond 1m: carries head
high: sold 6,500 gns in December. *J. H. M. Gosden*

STEP AHEAD (IRE)   2 b.f. (Apr 17) Shalford (IRE) 124§ – Tidal Reach (USA)   **54**
68 (Kris S (USA)) [1999 5d 5.1s 5g² 5v* 6.1m³ a6g⁶ 6s 6s a8.5g Oct 16] IR 3,000Y: **a–**
first foal: dam 2-y-o 1m winner who stayed 10.5f: modest performer: won claimer at
Beverley in June: well below form last 4 starts: stays 6f: acts on good to firm and
heavy going: has edged left: sold 600 gns in November. *P. G. Murphy*

STEPASTRAY   2 gr.g. (Apr 28) Alhijaz 122 – Wandering Stranger 69 (Petong   –
126) [1999 7m 7m 7g Aug 12] 6,000Y: third foal: brother to 4-y-o Leofric and half-
brother to 3-y-o Lady Lauren: dam 6f winner: well held in maidens: sold 900 gns in
November. *P. G. Murphy*

STEP FREE   2 ch.g. (Apr 25) Factual (USA) 108 – Angel's Sing (Mansingh   **40**
(USA) 120) [1999 6d 6m 7d⁵ a7g Sep 28] 2,200Y: leggy gelding: sixth foal: dam
unraced: poor maiden: best effort third start. *P. G. Murphy*

STEP ON DEGAS   6 b.m. Superpower 113 – Vivid Impression (Cure The Blues   **60**
(USA)) [1998 64: a8g 6f* 7g⁶ 6.9d² 7.6m⁵ 7m 7m 6f⁵ 7g 8m 7g 1999 a7g a7g³ a7g
6s⁵ 7m⁴ 7.7s³ 8g⁶ 7.7m² 8f 7m³ 7s 6d² 7m² 8v 8d Oct 4] rather leggy mare: modest
handicapper: probably needs good test at 6f nowadays, and stays 1m: acts on firm
going, soft and all-weather: visored twice at 3 yrs. *Mrs A. L. M. King*

STEPS IN TIME (IRE)   2 b.c. (Mar 18) Dancing Dissident (USA) 119 – After-   **55**
glow (IRE) 61 (Glow (USA)) [1999 5s a5g⁴ Oct 13] IR 7,600F, 10,500Y: second foal:
half-brother to a 5f to 8.5f winner in Scandinavia by Petorius: dam Irish 5f winner:
better effort when fourth of 13 in seller at Wolverhampton: should stay 6f: sold 1,400
gns. *R. Hannon*

STEPSTONE   3 b.f. Slip Anchor 136 – Stedham 84 (Jaazeiro (USA) 127) [1998   **56**
65p: 7g⁵ 1999 10.2g⁶ 12m⁶ 14.1m 9.9d⁵ 11.9m² 12g 11.9s Sep 29] unfurnished filly:
modest maiden handicapper: should stay beyond 1½m: acts on good to firm going:
blinkered third and fourth starts: sold 2,500 gns. *H. Candy*

STEP UP   2 ch.g. (Feb 7) Mizoram (USA) 105 – Arabian Nymph 49 (Sayf El Arab   **52 d**
(USA) 127) [1999 5s⁶ 5m⁴ 5.1s 6.1g² a6g⁴ 8m a6g 5.7s Oct 26] 500Y, resold 1,700Y:
half-brother to 3 winners, including 3-y-o Arabian Desert and 6f seller winner
Copper Bright (by Mon Tresor), latter subsequently successful up to 10.5f in Scandinavia: dam, sprint maiden, ran only at 2 yrs: modest maiden: off course nearly 3
months before well beaten last 3 outings: stays 6f: acts on soft and good to firm
going: sold 550 gns. *P. G. Murphy*

STERO HEIGHTS (IRE)   4 b.c. Shirley Heights 130 – Trystero (Shareef   **66**
Dancer (USA) 135) [1998 80: 10g 10.5m³ 11.9s⁵ a10g⁴ 1999 a13g⁴ a16.2g²
a16f⁵ Feb 1] leggy, angular colt: fair maiden: stays 2m: acts on good to firm going
and all-weather: joined A. Broad in Ireland. *D. J. S. Cosgrove*

STERT   4 ch.f. Petrizzo 109 – Ziggy's Pearl (USA) (Ziggy's Boy (USA)) [1998 –:   –
a10g 1999 a6g 9.9m 11.7g Jun 30] of little account. *A. J. Chamberlain*

STEVAL   2 ch.f. (May 14) Efisio 120 – Vannozza 58 (Kris 135) [1999 5s 5.1g 6d   –
Nov 4] 12,000Y: fourth living foal: dam, ran twice at 2 yrs, out of high-class French
7f to 1m winner Vilikaia: well held in maidens. *R. Guest*

STEVIE CRUISE (IRE)   2 b.g. (Apr 20) Foxhound (USA) 103 – Petticoat Louis   –
(Absalom 128) [1999 5f 6m Jun 17] IR 6,200F, 12,000Y: strong, quite good-topped
gelding: fourth reported foal: dam unraced half-sister to a useful 2-y-o 5f winner:
well held in minor event at Redcar and maiden at Ripon. *P. C. Haslam*

ST EXPEDIT   2 b.c. (Mar 23) Sadler's Wells (USA) 132 – Miss Rinjani 83 (Shirley   **84 p**
Heights 130) [1999 7d³ Oct 27] second foal: half-brother to 3-y-o Miss Amanpuri:
dam 2-y-o 7f winner who stayed 1½m: weak in market, shaped well when third of 11
to Shaibani in maiden at Yarmouth, pulling hard early on but keeping on well: should
stay at least 1¼m: sure to improve and win races. *G. Wragg*

ST GEORGE'S BOY   2 b.c. (Apr 23) Inchinor 119 – Deanta In Eirinn (Red Sunset   –
120) [1999 7d 7s a8g Nov 22] 8,000Y: strong colt: half-brother to several winners,
including 4-y-o Welcome Sunset and 3-y-o Lucy Mariella: dam ran once at 2 yrs:
well beaten in maidens: has given trouble at start. *J. Wharton*

ST HELENSFIELD   4 ch.g. Kris 135 – On Credit (FR) (No Pass No Sale 120)   **95**
[1998 –: 12s⁴ 1999 11.9s 13.9f⁶ 10.1f* 9.9g 9.2f³ 10m 10s 10.1d⁴ Oct 27] strong,
angular gelding: useful handicapper: won 5-runner event at Newcastle in July: ran
creditably after only when third at Hamilton: likely to prove best around 1¼m: goes
well on ground firmer than good. *M. Johnston*

ST HILARY   4 b.f. Formidable (USA) 125 – Positive Attitude 82 (Red Sunset   –
120) [1998 –: 8.3m 8.2m 1999 12v Apr 13] no sign of ability in maidens. *Mrs
A. J. Perrett*

STILL IN LOVE   2 b.f. (Feb 15) Emarati (USA) 74 – In Love Again (IRE) 86   **75 p**
(Prince Rupert (FR) 121) [1999 6s³ Oct 25] 28,000Y: strong, sturdy filly: first foal:
dam, 2-y-o 5f winner, half-sister to high-class sprinter Hallgate: better for race,
prominent throughout when very close third of 13 to Picot in maiden at Leicester
(gave trouble at stalls): unlikely to stay much beyond 6f: sure to improve.
H. R. A. Cecil

STILL WATERS   4 b.g. Rainbow Quest (USA) 134 – Krill (Kris 135) [1998 63:   **69**
8.2s 8g² 10m a8.5g 1999 a8f* a11g 8.3m a9.4g Dec 11] sturdy gelding: fair
performer: won handicap at Southwell in January: well held after (leaving K. Bell
before fourth start): should stay 1¼m: acts on fibresand. *I. A. Wood*

STITCH IN TIME   3 ch.g. Inchinor 119 – Late Matinee 84 (Red Sunset 120)   **53**
[1998 NR 1999 7g 8m 10g 10m 10m 8.3s Sep 27] 27,000F, 20,000Y: big, leggy
gelding: good mover: sixth foal: dam 2-y-o 6f winner: modest maiden: likely to
prove best up to easy 1m: acts on soft ground: has carried head high/hung right.
G. C. Bravery

ST IVES   2 b.c. (Jan 26) Puissance 110 – Clan Scotia 47 (Clantime 101) [1999 6.8d   –
7s 6v⁶ Oct 23] 6,500Y: leggy, rather unfurnished colt: first foal: dam 2-y-o 5f winner:
burly, well held in maidens. *V. Soane*

ST LAWRENCE (CAN)   5 gr.g. With Approval (CAN) – Mingan Isle (USA)   **62**
(Lord Avie (USA)) [1998 79: 12f 10s 10.3m³ 11.9m⁴ 1999 12g 10m 9.7m 10.1g
10.1m⁶ 10.5m 10m³ 10m⁵ 12g 12.3d⁴ 10.9d a14g² 14.1s a14g⁶ a14g Nov 30]
smallish gelding: modest maiden handicapper: trained first 6 starts by C. Brittain:
stays 1¾m: acts on firm ground and fibresand: tried blinkered: has gone in snatches:
often amateur ridden. *N. Tinkler*

STOCKBROOK   6 b.g. Marju (IRE) 127 – Burning Ambition (Troy 137) [1998   **25 §**
NR 1999 14.1g 14.1m 16.2g⁵ 17.2g Aug 25] poor maiden: stays 2m: ungenuine.
K. R. Burke

STOLEN MUSIC (IRE)   6 b.m. Taufan (USA) 119 – Causa Sua (Try My Best   **51**
(USA) 130) [1998 44: 7d 9.9s 7.1s³ 8.3d 11s⁴ 10g 12m⁴ 9.9g 10m⁴ 11.1d⁶ 9.9m*
9.9m* 12d⁵ 14.1v* 16s 1999 10v⁶ 11d 13.8m³ 14.1f⁶ 12g 14.1m* 14d 16f³ 13.8m*
17.1g 12g 15.8g 14.1g² 13.9d 14.1g Oct 15] short-backed mare: modest handicapper:
won at Redcar in June and Catterick in August: effective at 1¾m, probably at 2m:
acts on good to firm and heavy going: visored once at 4 yrs: sometimes slowly away,
and often gets behind. *R. E. Barr*

STOLEN TEAR (FR)   3 ch.f. Cadeaux Genereux 131 – Durrah (USA) 93   **76**
(Nijinsky (CAN) 138) [1998 76p: 7m³ 8.3d* 8m 1999 10.5s 12.3d Apr 15] angular,

unfurnished filly: fair at 2 yrs: well held last in handicaps both 3-y-o starts: should stay 1¼m: sold 200,000 gns (well bred) in July. *M. Johnston*

STONE BECK   4 b.f. Lapierre 119 – Dovey (Welsh Pageant 132) [1998 71: 8.5m⁴ 9.9m⁴ 11.8m 12.3s³ 12d 11.9m⁴ 15d³ 1999 13v Apr 10] lengthy, sparely-made filly: fair maiden handicapper: stays 15f: acts on soft and good to firm going: blinkered once as 3-y-o: won novice hurdle in November. *J. M. Jefferson*

STONE COLD   2 ch.g. (May 16) Inchinor 119 – Vaula 49 (Henbit (USA) 130) –
[1999 8.1m 7.5g 7s Nov 2] 10,000Y: leggy gelding: eighth foal: half-brother to 7f winner Time Again (by Then Again), 1991 French 2-y-o 5f winner Amizour (by Midyan) and 4-y-o Flak Jacket: dam won at 13f at 4 yrs: signs of a little ability in maidens. *T. D. Easterby*

STONE OF DESTINY   4 ch.g. Ballad Rock 122 – Shamasiya (FR) (Vayrann –
133) [1998 85: 7g⁴ 7g 7.1d 8f 7m 7.3g 6d* 1999 7s 8s a8.5g a6g Nov 20] big, imposing gelding: fairly useful at 3 yrs for B. Meehan: no form in 1999: stays 7f: acts on good to firm and good to soft going: tried blinkered. *Mrs L. Williamson*

STONE RIDGE (IRE)   7 b.g. Indian Ridge 123 – Cut In Stone (USA) 72 (Assert   56
134) [1998 80: 10v 10.3g 10g* 12m 10g² 10d⁵ 9.9m⁵ 10d 10g 8.1m⁶ 8.3m 10g 9.9s⁶ 10.3v* 1999 a12g 8d 9.2g* May 2] useful-looking gelding: fairly useful for R. Hannon at 6 yrs: modest in 1999, winning claimer at Hamilton final start: stays 1¼m: yet to race on firm going, acts on any other turf: no improvement in blinkers/visor: inconsistent: sold 2,200 gns, joined M. Evans. *J. Pearce*

STONEY GARNETT   2 b.f. (Mar 28) Emarati (USA) 74 – Etourdie (USA)   66
(Arctic Tern (USA) 126) [1999 5.1g 5.1g 5.7m² 5.7h³ 5g³ 5.1f 6.1m⁵ 6d Oct 15] 1,800Y: tall filly: half-sister to 2 winners abroad by Glint of Gold, including French winner up to 1½m Easy Gold: dam unraced: fair maiden: best effort when third of 19 in nursery at Nottingham: stays 6f: acts on hard going: twice blinkered: sweating and much too free to post final start. *M. S. Saunders*

STOPPES BROW   7 b.g. Primo Dominie 121 – So Bold (Never So Bold 135)   86
[1998 78, a81: a7g⁴ a7g a7g⁴ a7g² a7g⁶ a7g² 6.9d 8.5s² 7g⁵ 8m* 9.7m⁶ 7.1d 7g⁵ 8m² 8g³ 7g⁶ 7g 8g² 8m⁶ 7s 8d 1999 a8g⁶ a8g⁴ a7g* 8.5s⁵ a8g⁶ 8d* 8m⁴ 8.5m² 8f³ 7m³ 8.5g* 10d 8d Oct 30] strong, lengthy gelding: poor mover: fairly useful handicapper: won at Lingfield (twice) in April, Kempton in June and Epsom (no headgear) in August: best at 7f to 8.5f: acts on all-weather, firm and soft going: used to be visored, usually blinkered nowadays: usually held up: consistent. *G. L. Moore*

STOP THE TRAFFIC (IRE)   2 b.f. (Mar 26) College Chapel 122 – Miss Baga-   66
telle 70 (Mummy's Pet 125) [1999 6f 5.7f³ 5d³ 6m Sep 10] IR 6,800F, 5,000Y, 9,000 2-y-o: lengthy filly: half-sister to French 1997 2-y-o 7f winner Baghamas (by Hamas) and a 7f/1m winner in Hong Kong by Nabeel Dancer: dam, Irish 6f winner, out of sister to Gold Cup winner Arcadian Heights: fair maiden: best effort when third of 6 in minor event at Sandown on third start: should stay 7f: acts on good to soft going. *C. N. Allen*

STOPWATCH (IRE)   4 b.g. Lead On Time (USA) 123 – Rose Bonbon (FR)   –
(High Top 131) [1998 87, a?: 10v 8s* 10g 8s⁵ 8s⁵ 8.5d² 9f⁴ 9d⁶ 1999 a7f⁶ 8g 8g 9d Jun 4] seventh foal: half-brother to 3 winners in France, including 1¼m winner Marie La Rose (by Night Shift): dam, French 13f winner, half-sister to French Group 1 winners Le Nain Jaune, Indian Rose and Verte Amande: fairly useful performer: won maiden at Cork early in 1998 (sold from T. Stack for 13,000 gns after final start): well held in 1999 (though successful over hurdles in April): stays 1m: acts on soft ground: blinkered once. *Mrs L. C. Jewell*

STORM CAT   4 ch.g. Interrex (CAN) – Albion Polka (Dance In Time (CAN))   69
[1998 72: 10d 11.8d⁴ 9g² 9d a9.4g⁵ 8m 8d 1999 a7f* a7g⁴ 7s⁴ a7g* 7g⁶ 6m a7g a7g   a78
Jul 24] tall, angular gelding: fair performer: won maiden at Southwell in February and handicap at Wolverhampton in April: leading when breaking leg at Southwell final start: stayed 9f: acted on soft going and fibresand (well held only try on equitrack): usually blinkered/visored: dead. *K. McAuliffe*

STORM COMMAND   5 b.g. Gildoran 123 – Summer Sky 75 (Skyliner 117)   42
[1998 –: 8g 10d 1999 a12g⁶ a12g⁴ a14g 15.4v Apr 20] big gelding: poor maiden, lightly raced: should stay beyond 1½m: acts on fibresand. *D. W. P. Arbuthnot*

STORM CRY (USA) 4 b.c. Hermitage (USA) – Doonesbury Lady (USA) **81 §**
(Doonesbury (USA)) [1998 81: 8f* 9s⁵ 8f³ 7g 1999 8.1s⁴ 8g 8g 7.1g 8h⁵ 7s⁴ 8m 7d⁶
7v* 7.1s 7s Oct 22] tall, leggy colt: poor mover: fairly useful handicapper: back to
best to win apprentice race at Lingfield in September: likely to prove best at 7f/1m
(didn't stay testing 9f): acts on any going: tongue tied after fifth start: often races up
with pace: inconsistent. *M. S. Saunders*

STORMDANCER (IRE) 2 ch.c. (Feb 8) Bluebird (USA) 125 – Unspoiled **62**
(Tina's Pet 121) [1999 7m 7.1m 10.2s Sep 27] 50,000Y: good-topped colt: seventh
foal: half-brother to 3 winners, including 1998 2-y-o 7f winner Caledonian Colours
(by Indian Ridge) and 1991 2-y-o 6f winner Sylvan (by Taufan): dam unraced:
modest maiden: should stay at least 1m: well beaten on soft going. *R. Hannon*

STORM HILL (IRE) 3 b.c. Caerleon (USA) 132 – Jackie Berry 97 (Connaught **87**
130) [1998 NR 1999 10g³ 10.3m⁵ 8.3m⁴ 10f⁵ Oct 20] rather leggy, close-coupled
colt: eighth foal: brother to smart 1½m performer (7f winner at 2 yrs) Pencader and
half-brother to 3 winners, including useful 7f (at 2 yrs) to 1½m winner Coneybury
(by Last Tycoon): dam Irish 7f and 8.5f winner: fairly useful form when close third
in Newmarket maiden on debut: below that level in similar races after, failing to
settle on first 2 occasions (trained by P. Chapple-Hyam): bred to stay 1½m: tongue
tied second start. *A. G. Foster*

STORMIN (IRE) 3 b.g. Perugino (USA) 84 – Unalaska (IRE) 65 (High Estate **–**
127) [1998 51: 6f 7f 1999 8s 9.7v a12g 14.6s a14.8g⁶ Jun 5] no form: visored at 2 yrs.
D. J. Wintle

STORMLESS 8 b.g. Silly Prices 110 – Phyl's Pet (Aberdeen 109) [1998 74: 8.3v² **–**
8d⁶ 8.3v* 10d⁴ 1999 9.1g 11.1m 9g 10.9d 8.3s 10.1d Oct 20] tall gelding: fair
handicapper for J. Goldie in 1998: poor in 1999: effective at 1m (given good test) to
1¼m: acts on good to firm and heavy ground. *J. S. Haldane*

STORM PRINCE (IRE) 2 ch.c. (Apr 19) Prince of Birds (USA) 121 – Peters- **68**
ford Girl (IRE) 84 (Taufan (USA) 119) [1999 6m 7m⁶ 6m⁴ 7.1m⁴ 8m* a8g² Sep 28]
17,500Y: first foal: dam 6f winner who stayed 7f: fair performer: won selling nursery
at Leicester (left S. Williams 8,500 gns) in September: ran well final start: should
stay beyond 1m: acts on fibresand, raced only on good to firm going on turf: has had
tongue tied. *J. L. Spearing*

STORM SONG (IRE) 2 ch.c. (Mar 21) Prince of Birds (USA) 121 – Wolviston **47**
(Wolverlife 115) [1999 6f⁶ 6m a7g⁶ 6.8m 5.3s⁵ a7g Dec 8] IR 6,700F, 10,000Y: **a44**
half-brother to several winners, including 3-y-o Three Leaders, 7f/1m winner Sie
Amato (by Soughaan) and a 2-y-o 5f winner in Germany by Homo Sapien: dam Irish
2-y-o 5f winner: poor maiden: left N. Hamilton after third start: stays 6f: acts on firm
going, soft and fibresand. *R. J. O'Sullivan*

STORMSWELL 2 ch.f. (May 10) Persian Bold 123 – Stormswept (USA) 74 **56**
(Storm Bird (CAN) 134) [1999 6f 6g 6m⁶ 6d Oct 26] small filly: poor walker: fourth
foal: half-sister to 3-y-o Vanille and 1m winner Amico (by Efisio): dam, 2-y-o 5f
winner, closely related to Colonel Collins, Commander Collins and Breeders' Cup
Sprint winner Lit de Justice: best effort when sixth of 19 to Sudra in maiden at Thirsk:
should stay 1m: acts on good to firm ground (stiff task in nursery on good to soft).
R. A. Fahey

STORMVILLE (IRE) 2 b.g. (May 23) Catrail (USA) 123 – Haut Volee (Top **75**
Ville 129) [1999 7f⁶ 7.5g³ 6.8m⁵ 6d⁵ Oct 15] 7,000Y: unfurnished gelding: third foal:
half-brother to German 11f winner La Peregrina (by Shirley Heights): dam German
2-y-o 6f and 1m winner: fair maiden: best effort when close fifth of 20 to Magic of
Love in sales race at Newmarket on final start: should stay 1m. *M. Brittain*

STORM WEAVE (IRE) 3 ch.f. Polar Falcon (USA) 126 – Kaliala (FR) (Pharly **–**
(FR) 130) [1998 –p: 6.1g⁶ 8.2g 1999 a8.5g 10s 9m 8f Jul 23] lengthy, sparely-made
filly: little form. *Mrs A. Duffield*

STORM WIZARD (IRE) 2 b.c. (Mar 25) Catrail (USA) 123 – Society Ball 72 **–**
(Law Society (USA) 130) [1999 7d Sep 19] 15,000F, 28,000Y: workmanlike colt:
fourth foal: half-brother to 4-y-o Keld and Italian 3-y-o 7f (at 2 yrs) and 10.5f winner
Zanic (by Ezzoud): dam 1½m winner out of sister to dam of Zafonic: backward,
always in rear in maiden won by Scarteen Fox at Newbury. *M. R. Channon*

STORMY RAINBOW 2 b.c. (May 3) Red Rainbow 105 – Stormy Heights 62 –
(Golden Heights 82) [1999 6d Jun 10] second foal: dam sprinter: well beaten in
minor event at Newbury. *R. Simpson*

STORMY SKYE (IRE) 3 b.g. Bluebird (USA) 125 – Canna (Caerleon (USA) **85**
132) [1998 92: 7.1g⁵ 7.1m 8s³ 8v⁵ 1999 11.1g⁴ 14.1m⁴ 12.1g² May 31] angular
gelding: fairly useful performer: may prove best at 1¼m/1½m: best efforts on good
going or softer: blinkered final start: reluctant stalls first 2: sold 21,000 gns, joined
G. Bravery. *A. J. McNae*

STORYTELLER (IRE) 5 b.g. Thatching 131 – Please Believe Me 93 (Try My **94**
Best (USA) 130) [1998 92: 5d⁶ 5m² 5g² 5f² 5g* 6s⁴ 5g* 5g* 5d* 5d² 5g* 5m² 5g⁵
5.6g 5d² 1999 5d 5m 6d⁴ 6m* 5g* 5m² 5m⁴ 5m⁴ Jul 23] quite good-topped gelding:
impresses in appearance: fairly useful performer: won minor event at Doncaster in
May and handicap at Salisbury in June: in frame in handicaps at Newcastle (good
second in quite valuable event), Sandown and Ascot after: effective at 5f/6f: acts on
firm and good to soft going, probably on soft: best in visor: held up: genuine and
consistent. *M. Dods*

ST PACKOISE (IRE) 2 b.f. (Apr 5) Brief Truce (USA) 126 – Classic Opera **52**
(Lomond (USA) 128) [1999 5m⁵ 7g 6d⁴ Oct 18] IR 4,800Y: workmanlike filly: fifth
foal: half-sister to 5f (in Ireland at 2 yrs) and 9f (in USA) winner Without Doubt (by
Kenmare): dam ran once: modest maiden: should stay 7f. *A. B. Mulholland*

STRAHAN (IRE) 2 b.c. (Apr 2) Catrail (USA) 123 – Soreze (IRE) 102 (Gallic **83 p**
League 119) [1999 6m³ 6.1g² 6g* Oct 6] IR 31,000Y: first foal: dam Irish 5f
performer: fairly useful form: placed at Goodwood and Nottingham before winning
maiden at York by head (rider suspended for use of whip) from Material Witness:
should stay 7f: can improve further. *J. H. M. Gosden*

STRAND OF GOLD 2 b.c. (Apr 13) Lugana Beach 116 – Miss Display 47 **74**
(Touch Paper 113) [1999 6d 5d² 6.8d 6d⁴ Oct 18] 3,800Y, 16,000 2-y-o: leggy, quite
good-topped colt: half-brother to 3 winning sprinters, including 3-y-o Dazzling
Quintet and 5-y-o Dyce: dam 5f maiden: well drawn, clearly best effort in maidens
when close second to Brandon Rock at Sandown: should stay at least 6f. *R. Hannon*

STRASBOURG (USA) 2 ch.c. (Apr 1) Dehere (USA) 121 – Pixie Erin 110 **94 p**
(Golden Fleece (USA) 133) [1999 7.1m* 7d² 7.3s Oct 22] half-brother to 1¼m
winner Ericolin (by Ahonoora) and useful 6f winner (including at 2 yrs) Bint
Albaadiya (by Woodman): dam, 7f to 1¼m winner, half-sister to smart colt (up to
1¾m) Skaramanga and very smart filly (up to 1¼m) Star Pastures: won maiden at
Chepstow in September on only outing for P. Chapple-Hyam: still green, 1¾ lengths
second of 8 to Sun Charm in minor event at Leicester, finishing strongly: well held in
Horris Hill Stakes at Newbury final start: should be suited by 1m+: still likely to
make a useful 3-y-o at least. *A. G. Foster*

STRATEGIC 3 b.c. Caerleon (USA) 132 – Game Plan 118 (Darshaan 133) [1998 **120**
106p: 7v⁴ 8g* 1999 10m* 10m² 10d* 9.8v² Oct 2] close-coupled colt: fourth foal:
half-brother to 1m (at 2 yrs) and 1¼m winner Night Vigil (by Night Shift) and useful
Irish 1¼m and 1½m winner Power Play (by Nashwan): dam, 1¼m winner and second
in Oaks, half-sister to Oaks winner Shahtoush: very smart performer: won maiden at
Leopardstown at 2 yrs, minor event at the Curragh on reappearance in July and listed
race at Leopardstown (by 6 lengths from Scottish Memories) in September:
runner-up to Zomaradah in Royal Whip Stakes (beaten ½ length) at the Curragh and
to State Shinto in Prix Dollar (best effort, beaten ¾ length) at Longchamp on other 2
starts: acts on good to firm and heavy ground: has been bandaged
near-hind: joined Godolphin: well up to winning a pattern race. *J. Oxx, Ireland*

STRATEGIC CHOICE (USA) 8 b.h. Alleged (USA) 138 – Danlu (USA) –
(Danzig (USA)) [1998 116: 13.9g² 13.3m⁴ 12.5g³ 12m⁶ 12d⁵ 12m 1999 12m⁴ 12m⁶
Jul 16] big, strong horse: has suffered from foot trouble: has an easy action: very
smart performer in his prime: well-held last in listed race and minor event at
Newmarket in 1999: effective at 1½m/1¾m: best on good ground or firmer:
sometimes blinkered (including when successful). *P. F. I. Cole*

STRATHBLAIR 3 b.g. Bustino 136 – Orlaith 68 (Final Straw 127) [1998 NR –
1999 8m Jun 19] sixth living foal: half-brother to 1¼m winner Telopea (by Teenoso):

dam, third over 6f only start, out of half-sister to Irish Oaks winner Swiftfoot: 66/1, tailed off in maiden at Redcar. *G. M. Moore*

STRAT'S QUEST 5 b.m. Nicholas (USA) 111 – Eagle's Quest 62 (Legal Eagle **54** 126) [1998 65d, a–: 7s 6v 5v³ 6g⁶ 6.1m 6g 5d⁵ 6d 5.1v 6s a6g a5s⁵ 1999 a6g a6g⁴ a6s² **a51** a6g* 7s² a6g⁶ 6v a7g 5.3d⁴ a6g⁵ Nov 22] leggy, sparely-made mare: has a quick action: modest handicapper: won selling event at Southwell in March: stays 7f: acts on fibresand, best turf efforts on ground softer than good: visored. *D. W. P. Arbuthnot*

STRATTON (IRE) 2 b.c. (Mar 5) Fairy King (USA) – Golden Bloom (Main **70 p** Reef 126) [1999 6d⁶ Oct 14] 110,000F, 85,000Y: half-brother to 2 winners, including smart US Grade 2 1½m winner Golden Pond (by Don't Forget Me), earlier 6f (at 2 yrs) to 1m winner here: dam unraced: very backward and free to post, shaped quite well when sixth of 14 to Alfini in Newmarket maiden, keeping on after pulling hard early: should stay at least 7f: seems sure to improve. *C. F. Wall*

STRAVINSKY (USA) 3 b.c. Nureyev (USA) 131 – Fire The Groom (USA) **133** 115 (Blushing Groom (FR) 131) [1998 120: 6f* 7s⁶ 7g³ 1999 7s² 7m⁴ 6f* 5g* a6f⁶ Nov 6]

    Every season has its share of unforgettable performances and 1999 offered more than usual. Montjeu in the Budweiser Irish Derby, Daylami in the King George VI and Queen Elizabeth Diamond Stakes and in the Irish Champion Stakes, Royal Anthem in the Juddmonte International and Dubai Millennium in the Queen Elizabeth II Stakes all displayed devastating superiority over far-from-ordinary opponents. Stravinsky's success in the July Cup loses nothing by comparison with any of that quartet and arguably was even more stunning, as it came straight after two indifferent performances. The colt didn't just beat his rivals in the July Cup—he destroyed them, and from the moment he passed the post there was little doubt where the title 'champion sprinter' was going.

    Our remarks on Stravinsky in *Racehorses of 1998* indicated that there was no guarantee he would be suited by a mile, judged on his performances in the seven-furlong Prix de la Salamandre (second, demoted to last) and Dewhurst Stakes (third). The incentives to race three-year-olds over sprint distances from the outset of their second season are, however, minimal, and Aidan O'Brien was being hard on himself after the July Cup when he said: 'I've just made an awful mess of it up to now. Blame me. I was asking him to do something he just wasn't able to do.' Co-owner John Magnier put the issue in better perspective: 'There is great commercial pressure to get the mile [and] you have to keep trying to get it if you possibly can'. Magnier might have added that there are no European Group 1 races over five or six furlongs until the July Cup, which, like all sprints at that level, is also open to four-year-olds and up.

Darley July Cup, Newmarket—
the return to sprinting and the application of a visor has a dramatic effect on Stravinsky;
he is hugely impressive in beating Bold Edge and Bertolini (visor)

In contrast, over a mile or nine furlongs there are nine such races restricted to the classic crop. The financial rewards for speed merchants, and the prestige obtained for showing supreme ability, do not compare with those for milers either. The first-prize money for the three British Group 1 sprints in the latest season (the July Cup, Nunthorpe Stakes and Sprint Cup at Haydock) amounted to just under £260,000, an average of £86,500. The figure for the four mile races open to three-year-old colts—the Two Thousand Guineas, St James's Palace Stakes, Sussex Stakes and Queen Elizabeth II Stakes—was £664,000, at an average of £166,000. The difference (even after taking into account the fact that top milers have generally achieved a slightly higher level of form than top sprinters in recent times) is alarming and unsatisfactory. Suffice to say that, like a number of other post-war sprint champions, including Abernant, Amber Rama, Huntercombe, Marwell, Habibti and Ajdal, Stravinsky spent the first part of the season doing what did not come naturally for him. He did not make much of a job of it either, making his debut in a minor event at the Curragh at the end of March, by which time he was 5/1 favourite in ante-post lists for the Two Thousand Guineas. Starting at 5/2-on, he was shaken up to take a narrow lead with a furlong to go but lost out to Tarfaa by a head. The going was soft, but Stravinsky had run well enough in such conditions in the Prix de la Salamandre, and he was promptly pushed out to 12/1 for the Guineas, from which race he was withdrawn at the five-day stage because of fears about the ground. The Poule d'Essai des Poulains was mooted, but bypassed as well, and Stravinsky's next start came in the Jersey Stakes at Royal Ascot, his absence from the much more prestigious St James's Palace Stakes suggesting a mile was now deemed too far. Held up, Stravinsky carried his head awkwardly under pressure when asked to make ground after halfway and could finish only five lengths fourth to Lots of Magic.

So, Stravinsky arrived at Newmarket for the July Cup with the record of one win from five starts, in the Convivial Maiden at York the previous August, and the suspicion that he would never take high rank. His star was not so low, however, as to make him an outsider in a most open July Cup, for which he started 8/1 third favourite. The sixteen other runners included thirteen pattern winners, among them proven speed merchants Bold Edge, successful in the Cork And Orrery Stakes and second favourite at 7/1, King's Stand Stakes winner Mitcham, Duke of York Stakes winner Sampower Star and 1998

Persimmon Homes Nunthorpe Stakes, York—
Stravinsky becomes the first since Cadeaux Genereux in 1989 to complete the Newmarket/York double;
Sainte Marine is runner-up for the second successive year

Nunthorpe winner Lochangel. There were also several other three-year-olds coming back in distance, headed by the 11/2 favourite Wannabe Grand, placed in the One Thousand Guineas and Coronation Stakes, and 9/1-shot Bertolini, who had finished one place ahead of Stravinsky at Royal Ascot. The best sprinter of 1979, Thatching, had been trained at Ballydoyle (by Vincent O'Brien) and had improved dramatically when tried in blinkers, storming home in the Cork And Orrery Stakes and the July Cup, which he won by five lengths. Another Ballydoyle inmate, Marinsky, had been blinkered (and muzzled) when winning the 1977 July Cup, only to be disqualified. Stravinsky was fitted with a visor for the first time—he wore this headgear in his remaining starts as well—and, combined with the shorter trip, the result was devastating. Cool as a cucumber in the preliminaries, Stravinsky was held up, travelling smoothly, as Bold Edge and Bertolini set a good pace. Cruising through on the bridle from halfway, he unleashed a spectacular turn of foot to lead inside the final furlong and strode away to score by four lengths. The time was a track record (if not an outstanding time performance), beating that set by Elnadim the year before, and the winning margin equalled Lake Coniston's in 1995, with only Thatching having scored by further in recent times. For the record, Bold Edge was second and Bertolini third, a neck away, but nothing really mattered besides the winner, who was in a class of his own and clearly very much at home on firm going.

The July Cup had been won by the season's designated Timeform champion sprinter in nineteen of the previous thirty years and Stravinsky's display put him up there with the best of them. On this win he was the best sprinter since Dayjur in 1990, and inferior to only five others in the period, namely Deep Diver, Flirting Around, Moorestyle, Habibti and Never So Bold. In style, Stravinsky and Dayjur were as different as chalk and cheese. Dayjur, who won the King's Stand Stakes, Nunthorpe Stakes, Haydock Sprint Cup and Prix de l'Abbaye and finished a famously unlucky second in the Breeders' Cup Sprint, always showed blistering early pace, putting paid to his rivals by halfway. Stravinsky fitted in with the majority of sprint champions by being able to produce a thrilling burst of speed to zip past his opponents in the closing stages. If horses of Dayjur's type aren't always able to last out six furlongs, horses of Stravinsky's type are not always so effective when stepped back to the minimum trip. Stravinsky faced that test on his next start, in the Persimmon Homes Nunthorpe Stakes at York in August. Evens favourite, he had to deal with the French five-furlong specialist Sainte Marine, who had won the Prix du Gros-Chene in June, Lochangel over her best trip, Dashing Blue, third in the race the previous year, and twelve others, all of whom were 14/1 or longer in the betting. As the field edged towards the stand side, and Rambling Bear was brought down as Tipsy Creek got badly hampered two furlongs out, Stravinsky travelled on the bridle in mid-field while Sainte Marine blazing away up front, made ground impressively to lead a furlong out and pulled away without being asked for everything to beat the filly by one and a half lengths, with the good handicapper Proud Native the same distance back in third. This was the first time the July Cup-Nunthorpe double had been achieved since Cadeaux Genereux in 1989, whereas five had managed the feat from 1978 to 1987.

The two remaining Group 1 events for sprinters, the Stanley Leisure Sprint Cup and Prix de l'Abbaye, were soon discounted as Stravinsky's connections decided to let him try to go one better than Dayjur in the Breeders' Cup Sprint at Gulfstream. There were suggestions early in October, and again in the week leading up to the event, that he might challenge for the Mile instead, as the Nunthorpe winner Last Tycoon and the July Cup victor Royal Academy had done successfully in 1986 and 1990 respectively, but the Sprint won. The difficulties facing European runners in this race are hard to understate. American sprints are run round two turns, they are run on dirt, and they are usually run at a breakneck pace from start to finish. This presents a serious obstacle to challengers from abroad, and in the fifteen years from the start of the Breeders' Cup in 1984, up to and including 1998, twenty-seven different horses had contested the race, with Sheikh Albadou's win in 1991 and Dayjur's second year before the only placings. Some grand horses had run abysmally, including July Cup victors Lake Coniston and Green Desert, Nunthorpe winner Lochsong and Haydock Sprint Cup winner Royal Applause, the last three-named all finishing last. Stravinsky, who started third favourite of the fourteen runners, ran a lot better than that group without managing to maintain his winning run. Close up from the outset, he chased the eventual winner Artax into the straight but could not sustain his effort in the closing stages and came in sixth, beaten over four lengths. The self-effacing O'Brien tended to blame himself for the defeat, saying he should have run the colt again after his Nunthorpe win, or should maybe have given him another gallop, but that's being wise after the event and the argument isn't entirely convincing anyway.

Stravinsky (USA) (b.c. 1996)	Nureyev (USA) (b 1977)	Northern Dancer (b 1961)	Nearctic
			Natalma
		Special (b 1969)	Forli
			Thong
	Fire The Groom (USA) (b 1987)	Blushing Groom (ch 1974)	Red God
			Runaway Bride
		Prospector's Fire (b or br 1976)	Mr Prospector
			Native Street

The Breeders' Cup took nothing away from what Stravinsky had achieved in Europe but he will not have the chance to thrill racegoers anywhere again. He was retired after the race and, with due deference to the composer after whom he was named, will begin his own rite of spring at Coolmore Stud's American arm, Ashford Stud in Kentucky, at a fee of 35,000 dollars. Sending him there made sense because another son of Nureyev, Fasliyev, will be at

Mr M. Tabor & Mrs John Magnier's "Stravinsky"

Coolmore in 2000, but the previous records of top European sprinters sent to stand in the States is not exactly encouraging. Neither Dayjur nor Sheikh Albadou, who died in 1999, has excelled, but that may just be one facet of a wider inconsistency, as even in Europe very few of the best sprinters have surpassed themselves at stud in the last thirty years. Stravinsky's looks should stand him in good stead—he is a strong, well-made, attractive colt. The pedigree lends encouragement too, as he can be backed to get horses who stay at least a mile. He is by a superb sire, responsible for winners over a wide range of distances (though he doesn't have an outstanding record as a sire of sires), out of a very smart mare who gained her biggest success over nine and a half furlongs in the Beverly D Stakes. There are speedier elements in the background though, notably Fire The Groom's half-brother Dowsing, a high-class sprinter who landed the Vernons Sprint Cup at Haydock. This is also the family of Florida Derby winner Regal And Royal. Since foaling Stravinsky, Fire The Groom has produced the two-year-old Madame Modjeska (by Danzig) and a colt foal by Deputy Minister. *A. P. O'Brien, Ireland*

STRAVSEA   4 b.f. Handsome Sailor 125 – La Stravaganza 74 (Slip Anchor 136)   – [1998 –, a56: a7g² a6g² a7g⁵ a6g² a7g² a7g³ 6.1m a6g³ a5g 6m 8.2g 1999 a6g a7g⁴   **a57** a7g³ a8.5g³ a7g a7g a8g² a8g² a8g² 7m a8g* 8g a8.5g a7g⁶ a8g a7g a8g* Dec 13] tall, leggy filly: modest handicapper: won at Southwell in July and December: stays 1m: acts on fibresand, no recent form on turf. *R. Hollinshead*

STRAZO (IRE)   6 b.g. Alzao (USA) 117 – Ministra (USA) (Deputy Minister   **84 d** (CAN)) [1998 103d: 8d⁵ 7m⁵ 8.1g 8d 8g⁴ 8m 10m a9.4g 1999 8m 10f 8g 10m 9v 10d⁵ 7s 8s Nov 6] good-bodied gelding: fairly useful handicapper nowadays: best at 1m/9f: acts on firm and good to soft ground: visored once at 5 yrs. *Lady Herries*

STREAK OF DAWN   2 b.f. (Apr 19) Old Vic 136 – Nafla (FR) (Arctic Tern (USA)   – 126) [1999 6f 6m Jul 16] 3,000Y: leggy, unfurnished filly: ninth foal: half-sister to 1993 2-y-o 5f and 7f winner Lambent (by Rambo Dancer), later successful in USA: dam French 7f (at 2 yrs) and 1¼m winner: behind in maidens, weakening quickly each time. *K. A. Ryan*

STREET WALKER (IRE)   3 b.f. Dolphin Street (FR) 125 – Foolish Dame   **62** (USA) (Foolish Pleasure (USA)) [1998 –: 7d 1999 8.3m⁶ 8m 8.2m 10g² 10g⁴ 9m² 8s⁵ 8.2g³ Sep 25] rather leggy filly: modest maiden: effective at 1m/1¼m: acts on soft and good to firm going: sold 7,000 gns. *C. F. Wall*

STRENSALL   2 b.c. (May 21) Beveled (USA) – Payvashooz 78 (Ballacashtal   – (CAN)) [1999 6m 6m Jun 25] 900Y: fifth reported foal: half-brother to 3-y-o Pursuant: dam stayed 1m: no promise in maiden/seller. *M. Brittain*

STRETCHING (IRE)   6 br.g. Contract Law (USA) 108 – Mrs Mutton 89   – (Dancer's Image (USA)) [1998 NR 1999 a12g Jan 25] winning hurdler: poor maiden and lightly raced on Flat: tried blinkered. *A. G. Juckes*

STRICTLY SPEAKING (IRE)   2 b.c. (Feb 16) Sri Pekan (USA) 117 – Gaijin   **68** 97 (Caerleon (USA) 132) [1999 6m⁶ 8v³ 10.2s⁴ 8.3g⁵ Oct 11] 52,000Y: tall, quite attractive colt: half-brother to several winners, notably high-class 1m/9f performer in USA Hawksley Hill (by Rahy), earlier 7f to 11f winner in Britain: dam, 2-y-o 6f winner, best at 7f: fair maiden: best efforts first 2 starts: did not stay testing 1¼m. *P. F. I. Cole*

STRIDHANA   3 ch.f. Indian Ridge 123 – French Gift 99 (Cadeaux Genereux 131)   **70** [1998 NR 1999 6g⁴ 7.1m 6m³ 6g* 8.1d 6g 7s Oct 22] first foal: dam, daughter of Soba, won at 6f at 2 yrs: fair performer: won maiden at Lingfield in August: stiff tasks and well beaten in handicaps after: may prove best at 6f: acts on good to firm going. *D. R. C. Elsworth*

STRIDING KING   4 ch.g. King's Signet (USA) 110 – Stride Home 78 (Absalom   – 128) [1998 66: a6g² a7g² a7g³ 6.1d⁵ 1999 6g 5g 6m 7.1m Jul 23] good mover: fair maiden at 3 yrs: below form in handicaps in 1999: may prove best up to 7f: acts on good to soft going and all-weather. *M. R. Channon*

STRIMMER 11 ch.h. Sharpo 132 – Toppeshamme (USA) 94 (Topsider (USA)) **?**
[1998 5v² a6g* 5g² 5m 7f* 7m* 7g* 7g⁵ 7.6g 1999 a7g⁶ Jan 7] winner of claimer for
W. Jarvis at 3 yrs: successful 4 times in Belgium/France in 1998 and won another 4
races in Belgium in 1999 after mid-division in seller at Lingfield on reappearance:
stays 7f: seems to act on any turf going and on dirt: has been blinkered. *C. Dondi,
Belgium*

STRINDBERG 3 b.c. Bering 136 – Dagny Juel (USA) 75 (Danzig (USA)) [1998 **–**
NR 1999 10v Apr 24] good-bodied colt: second foal: half-brother to a winner in
Japan by Selkirk: dam lightly-raced 7f winner from family of Nureyev: 7/2, well held
in maiden at Leicester: sold 800 gns: sent to Spain. *J. L. Dunlop*

STRINGERS (IRE) 4 ch.g. Shalford (IRE) 124§ – Rebecca's Girl (IRE) **–**
(Nashamaa 113) [1998 –: 10.3d 10d 7.1g 1999 a8g Feb 26] lengthy, sturdy gelding:
no sign of ability. *S. E. Kettlewell*

STRING QUARTET (IRE) 3 b.f. Sadler's Wells (USA) 132 – Fleur Royale **109**
111 (Mill Reef (USA) 141) [1998 NR 1999 10m 10.2d* 10d³ 11.9s³ 12.5s* 12d⁴ Oct
9] IR 85,000Y: unfurnished filly: sister to 3 winners, notably smart Irish 7f (at 2 yrs)
to 1¼m winner Casey Tibbs (also won in USA), and closely related to 1992 Irish
2-y-o 7f winner Oiseau de Feu (by Nijinsky): dam, won Pretty Polly Stakes and
second in Irish Oaks, from family of Levmoss and Le Moss: useful performer: won
maiden at Chepstow in May and listed race at Deauville (awarded race having been
1½ lengths second to Hijaz) in August, latter final start for P. Chapple-Hyam: ran
well when third otherwise, beaten 8½ lengths by Noushkey in Lancashire Oaks at
Haydock fourth start: better at 1½m than shorter: acts on soft ground. *A. G. Foster*

STRIP SEARCH 3 b.f. Bluebird (USA) 125 – Swift Pursuit 57 (Posse (USA) **–**
130) [1998 –: 6g⁶ 6.1g 6m 8m 1999 a7g⁶ a10g 10m 12m 7d Oct 11] unfurnished filly:
little form: blinkered penultimate start. *J. G. Smyth-Osbourne*

STROMSHOLM (IRE) 3 ch.g. Indian Ridge 123 – Upward Trend 112 (Salmon **78**
Leap (USA) 131) [1998 NR 1999 7.7m 8.3g² Oct 11] fourth foal: dam Irish 1m/1¼m
performer: better effort in maidens when head second at Windsor, running on well.
J. R. Fanshawe

STRONGDAKA (IRE) 6 b.m. Strong Gale 116 – Randaka (Main Reef 126) **–**
[1998 –: 10s 14g⁶ 12s 1999 a16g Feb 9] first foal: dam Irish bumper winner/useful
hurdler: no form: trained by T. Taaffe in Ireland at 5 yrs: dead. *P. J. Hobbs*

STRONG PRESENCE 2 b.c. (Apr 2) Anshan 119 – Lazybird Blue (IRE) (Blue- **70 p**
bird (USA) 125) [1999 6s⁵ Nov 5] 3,500Y: big, strong, rangy colt: first foal: dam
unraced: shaped encouragingly when fifth of 20 to easy winner Royal Highlander in
maiden at Doncaster: should stay at least 7f: should improve. *T. P. Tate*

STUDLEY PARK 3 b.f. Northern Park (USA) 107 – B A Poundstretcher 82 **60**
(Laser Light 118) [1998 68: 6.1g³ 7f 7.9g* 1999 8.2m 8m 9.9m 8m⁶ 9g⁴ 10.4f⁵ 12s
10.1d Oct 20] tall, unfurnished filly: modest performer: stays 10.4f: acts on firm
going: sold 800 gns. *P. Calver*

STURGEON (IRE) 5 ch.g. Caerleon (USA) 132 – Ridge The Times (USA) 78 **74**
(Riva Ridge (USA)) [1998 74: 8.2g³ 9.9d 10g⁴ 10.5d⁴ 9m⁶ 8.3d⁶ 1999 8g 10m* 10g⁴
10m 9.9g 12m Sep 2] smallish gelding: fair handicapper: won at Ripon in June:
stays 1¼m: acts on good to firm and good to soft going: visored penultimate start.
K. A. Morgan

STUTTON GAL (IRE) 3 b.f. Up And At 'em 109 – Sashi Woo (Rusticaro (FR) **44**
124) [1998 44, a49?: a5g⁴ 7g⁴ 6.1g 8g 7m a5g a5g³ a5s⁵ 1999 a7g² a8f⁵ a7g⁵ a5g⁴
6.1s⁵ 7.5g a6g⁴ 5s a6g Nov 12] rather leggy filly: poor maiden: stays 7f: acts on
fibresand: usually blinkered: possibly none too genuine. *J. Wharton*

STYLE DANCER (IRE) 5 b.g. Dancing Dissident (USA) 119 – Showing Style **77**
(Pas de Seul 133) [1998 78: 6d 6g 7f* 7g⁶ 8.3f 7.6d⁵ 7g⁵ 7d 7.1g⁶ 1999 7g 6f 7g **a64**
8m⁵ 7g 8m⁶ 8m⁴ 7.1d* 7f⁵ 7m⁴ 7f 8.1d 8g³ 7f³ 7d⁴ 8d⁴ 7.1s 8.9d 7s a7g a7g³ a8g³ a8g
Dec 10] tall gelding: good mover: fair handicapper: won at Haydock in July:
creditable efforts when in frame after: effective at 7f/1m: acts on firm going, good to
soft and all-weather: blinkered once, usually visored (though effective when not).
R. M. Whitaker

STYLISH BEAUTY   2 b.f. (Jan 29) Night Shift (USA) – Reine de Neige 96 (Kris   **76 d**
135) [1999 5m* 5g⁵ 6s³ 7d Sep 28] smallish, sturdy, close-coupled filly: has a short
action: second foal: dam 1m winner from excellent North American family: fair form
when winning maiden at Leicester in May: seemed amiss next 2 starts, sweating and
attended by 2 handlers on final one: should stay 7f: sold 7,500 gns in December.
E. A. L. Dunlop

STYLISH WAYS (IRE)   7 b.g. Thatching 131 – Style of Life (USA) (The Minstrel   **89 d**
(CAN) 135) [1998 85: 6v³ 6g³ 6s² 6d² 6f 6m² 6g* 6m 6s* 6v⁵ 6d⁶ 1999 6g⁴ 6s⁵
6g³ 6s 6d⁶ 6s 6m 6d 6g² 6m 7f 6d 7s 6.1f⁵ 6d Nov 1] compact gelding: fluent mover:
fairly useful performer at best: excelled himself when fourth in listed race at
Newmarket on reappearance: deteriorated after third start: effective at 6f/7f: acts on
any ground: best covered up, and suited by good gallop: none too consistent.
J. Pearce

SUALTACH (IRE)   6 b.h. Marju (IRE) 127 – Astra Adastra (Mount Hagen (FR)   **67**
127) [1998 81, a87: a7g² a9.4g* a8.5g a9.4g³ a9.4g⁶ a8.5g* a9.4g⁵ a8g⁶ a8.5g* a9.4g   **a89**
10.3g⁶ 8.5m² 8g 10.3g⁵ 8d² a8.5g² 8d 7.1g² 8m⁴ a8.5g* 8.1g⁴ 7.6d 8m 8.1m* 10.3v
a8.5g² a8g² 1999 a8g² a8.5g⁴ a9.4g* a8.5g 9g a9.4g⁵ a9.4g³ a8.5g 8d 10s a8.5g 8.1m
10.5d a9.4g⁴ 10m⁶ 10m⁵ 10s 10d 10f Oct 20] strong, lengthy horse: has a round
action: fairly useful handicapper on all-weather, fair on turf: won at Wolverhampton
in January: effective at 7f to bare 1¼m: acts on soft going, good to firm and fibresand:
visored once at 3 yrs: sometimes looks less than genuine: usually held up: reportedly
lame final start. *R. Hollinshead*

SUAVE FRANKIE   3 ch.g. Suave Dancer (USA) 136 – Francia 59 (Legend of   **54 ?**
France (USA) 124) [1998 –p: 7g 7d 6g 1999 12g² 11.6m 11.5m⁴ 16f² 13.8m a14.8g
Oct 13] smallish, lengthy gelding: modest maiden: reportedly lame behind
penultimate start: stays 2m: acts on firm going: blinkered last 3 starts: has looked
difficult ride: inconsistent: sold 500 gns in November. *S. C. Williams*

SUBADAR MAJOR   2 b.g. (May 20) Komaite (USA) – Rather Gorgeous 37§   **–**
(Billion (USA) 120) [1999 a8g Dec 17] 1,250Y: third foal: dam temperamental 1¾m
winner, also won over hurdles: well beaten in maiden at Southwell. *Mrs G. S. Rees*

SUBEEN   3 b.f. Caerleon (USA) 132 – Khamsin (USA) (Mr Prospector (USA))   **93**
[1998 100p: 6m³ 6g* 6g³ 1999 7m³ May 2] small, leggy filly: has a quick, fluent
action: useful at 2 yrs for D. Loder, third in Cheveley Park Stakes at Newmarket final
start: respectable third of 4 to Kalinisi in minor event there only 3-y-o outing: may
prove best up to 7f: raced only on good/good to firm going: sent to USA. *Saeed bin
Suroor*

SUCH BOLDNESS   5 b.h. Persian Bold 123 – Bone China (IRE) (Sadler's Wells   **59**
(USA) 132) [1998 66: 12d³ 14m³ 17.2d 14.1m³ 14.1m⁴ 12f⁴ 10d³ a10g² 1999 a10g³   **a71**
a13g² a12g* a12g* a11g⁵ 12g a12g² 11.6m 10g³ 11.5f⁵ Jun 25] tall horse: fair on
all-weather, modest on turf: won apprentice maiden handicap at Southwell and minor
event at Lingfield in January: effective at 1¼m to 1¾m: acts on good to firm going
(probably on firm), good to soft and all-weather: usually races up with pace. *Miss
Gay Kelleway*

SUCH FLAIR (USA)   2 b.f. (Mar 27) Kingmambo (USA) 125 – Lady Fairfax   **65 p**
106 (Sharrood (USA) 124) [1999 7d Oct 30] $100,000Y: first foal: dam, 1m winner,
from family of Balla Cove: fair form when ninth of 16 in steadily-run Newmarket
maiden, fading final 2f: should stay at least 1m: should improve. *J. Noseda*

SUDDEN FLIGHT (IRE)   2 b.c. (Apr 29) In The Wings 128 – Ma Petite Cherie   **71**
(USA) 93 (Caro 133) [1999 7m⁵ 7m 7m 8s* 10s³ 8d Oct 18] tall colt: half-brother to
several winners, including fairly useful 6f winner Siwaayib (by Green Desert) and
2m winner Fatack and useful 7f/1m winner Zafaaf (both by Kris): dam French 1m (at
2 yrs) to 1¼m winner: fair performer: won nursery at Yarmouth in September: met
trouble in similar events both subsequent starts: will stay 1½m: acts on soft and good
to firm going: may do better. *E. A. L. Dunlop*

SUDDEN SPIN   9 b.g. Doulab (USA) 115 – Lightning Legacy (USA) 78 (Super   **–**
Concorde (USA) 128) [1998 –: 16.1d 1999 a14g a14g⁵ Dec 13] leggy, good-topped
gelding: well beaten both 9-y-o starts. *J. L. Eyre*

SUDDEN SQUALL (USA)   3 ch.c. Gulch (USA) – Sudden Storm Bird (USA) –
(Storm Bird (CAN) 134) [1998 78+: 7.3g⁶ 7m⁶ 8.5s⁵ 7s* 8d³ 1999 10.3d 12.3d a10f
Dec 23] lengthy colt: fair at 2 yrs: little form in handicaps in 1999, leaving J. Gosden
after second start: should stay beyond 1m: acts on soft ground: reportedly had
breathing problem third 2-y-o start. *W. D. Mather, UAE*

SUDEST (IRE)   5 b.g. Taufan (USA) 119 – Frill (Henbit (USA) 130) [1998 72:   **90 d**
16v 16.4s 12m 16.2g⁴ 14.6g² 14.1v 14.6d 1999 a16.2g* a14.8g* a16.2g* a16f²
a16.2g² 16.2m 14d a12g Dec 17] quite attractive gelding: fairly useful handicapper:
won 3 times in small fields at Wolverhampton in January: tailed off last 3 starts, sold
out of I. Balding's stable 3,400 gns before final one: stays 17f: acts on firm going,
soft and fibresand. *J. L. Harris*

SUDRA   2 b.g. (Feb 7) Indian Ridge 123 – Bunting 102 (Shaadi (USA) 126) [1999   **92**
6d³ 6m* 6g Oct 2] first foal: dam, 1m (at 2 yrs)/1¼m winner, third in Italian Oaks and
from good family: favourite first 2 starts, fairly useful form when winning maiden at
Thirsk in August by 5 lengths from Jaybird: stiff task final start: will stay 7f, probably
1m. *E. A. L. Dunlop*

SUE ME (IRE)   7 b. or br.g. Contract Law (USA) 108 – Pink Fondant (Northfields   **71**
(USA)) [1998 78: a5g⁴ a7g³ a6g* a6g* a6g 6.1s 5v⁴ 5s 5d* 6s⁵ 6g⁶ 6m⁶ 5f⁴ 5m* 6s
a5g² a6g⁵ 5d 5d 5m a6g* 5g² 6v a5g⁴ 1999 a6g* a6g³ a6g⁴ a6g a6g 6d³ 5m 5m³ 6g
5d* a6g 5s a5g a6g⁶ Dec 17] smallish, sturdy gelding: fair performer: won claimer at
Southwell in January and handicap at Ayr in September: effective at 5f/6f: acts on
fibresand (probably on equitrack) and any turf: effective with blinkers and without:
unreliable. *D. Nicholls*

SUE'S REPREMAND   3 b.f. Reprimand 122 – Poyle Amber 55 (Sharrood   –
(USA) 124) [1998 NR 1999 10d 8m Jul 21] 14,000Y: second foal: half-sister to 4-y-o
Wilton: dam sprint maiden half-sister to smart sprinter Poyle George: well held in
sellers at Ripon and Leicester. *A. P. Jarvis*

SUEZ TORNADO (IRE)   6 ch.g. Mujtahid (USA) 118 – So Stylish 77 (Great   **66**
Nephew 126) [1998 66, a70: a9.4g⁵ a8.5g⁴ a8g⁵ a9.4g⁴ 8g³ 7.6g⁴ 8m 7.9g² 8m 8s
8g 8s⁴ 8s⁴ a9.4g a8f 1999 8.3v⁴ 7m 9m⁶ 10d³ 10.3m² 10d⁵ 9.1g* 10m³ 10.5d⁵ 10m³
12f 10.3s⁴ 12d* 10v⁶ 10.1d⁵ 11d Oct 26] lengthy, good-topped gelding: modest
performer: won handicap at Ayr in July and claimer at Newmarket in September:
effective at 9f to 1½m: acts on firm going, soft and fibresand (below form on heavy
and equitrack): effective blinkered/visored or not: usually held up: sold 6,400 gns.
E. J. Alston

SUGAR CUBE TREAT   3 b.f. Lugana Beach 116 – Fair Eleanor (Saritamer   **65**
(USA) 130) [1998 61: 5g 5s⁴ 5g⁵ 5g⁵ 7d³ 7.9g 7g 1999 8m 6g⁵ 6.1d³ 6g³ 7m⁵ 7.1f⁶
6m 6g 6v* 6d Nov 4] small, close-coupled filly: fair performer: improved to win
27-runner handicap at Ayr in October by 3 lengths, short of room halfway but
quickening in fine style despite edging left: likely to prove best at 6f/7f: has form on
good to firm going, but goes well on heavy: has pulled hard and been early to post:
none too consistent. *M. Mullineaux*

SUGARFOOT   5 ch.h. Thatching 131 – Norpella 95 (Northfields (USA))   **118**
[1998 107: 10d 10.4g 7g² 8d⁴ 8g² 8m* 7m⁵ 7.9f* 7g² 7.9g* 1999 8d³ 7.9d* 8m⁶
8m³ 7m 7.9g* 8m* 8v² 7g⁵ Oct 16]
    In his four seasons on the racecourse, Sugarfoot has undergone several
transformations. Best known will be Sugarfoot the good-class handicapper,

Bradford & Bingley Rated Stakes (Handicap), York—
Sugarfoot repeats his 1998 win off a 13-lb higher mark and lands a gamble in the process

GNER Park Stakes, Doncaster—Pat Eddery is at his strongest, forcing the game Sugarfoot (left) in front of Wallace; Touch 'N' Fly is third

and a highly successful one at that; and now there is the Sugarfoot who has graduated successfully to pattern races. At different stages, he has been described as a course specialist on both the straight course at Ascot and the round course at York, before he added performances which were as at least good as anything he has achieved at either of those tracks when making his first appearances, in the latest season, at both Doncaster and Longchamp. There are several constants in the story as well though, as throughout the last three seasons Sugarfoot has raced almost exclusively at seven furlongs or a mile and, just as strikingly, performed with the utmost consistency and gameness.

Sugarfoot became a first pattern winner for his trainer Nigel Tinkler in the latest season, after adding a £16,367 listed rated stakes at York in May and a second Bradford & Bingley Handicap on the same course (worth £29,482) in August. Landing a gamble by three and a half lengths from Calcutta off a mark of 105, in what had looked an extremely competitive latest renewal of the Bradford & Bingley, effectively saw Sugarfoot wave handicaps goodbye for the time being.

He rubbed shoulders with some very different types in the GNER Park Stakes at Doncaster, the Prix du Rond-Point at Longchamp and the Challenge Stakes at Newmarket. In the Park Stakes, there could hardly have been a greater contrast than that between the seasoned handicapper Sugarfoot, sent off 15/2

Mrs D. Wright's "Sugarfoot"

fourth favourite, and the 6/4 favourite Touch 'N' Fly, veteran of just a maiden and a conditions stakes, both of which he had won by seven lengths at odds of 2/1-on. All of the eight other runners were either listed or pattern winners, including the Godolphin pair Muhtathir and Slip Stream, who had come close to winning a Group 1. Sugarfoot was not out of place. When Touch 'N' Fly and Muhtathir went on three furlongs out, he was able to stay in touch, and when the three-year-old Wallace went past them on the inside at the furlong marker, Sugarfoot threw down his challenge on the outer; the same willing response to pressure that he had always produced in handicap company was good enough to see him get up in the final stride. That was on good to firm ground. On heavy going in the Rond-Point, Sugarfoot again dug deep but on this occasion the post came just in time for the front-running, short-neck winner Trans Island. Fifth place in the Challenge Stakes did not represent form of the same order, but in dropping back to seven furlongs, which is shorter than ideal for him these days, Sugarfoot was certainly not disgraced.

After the Park Stakes, owner Derek Wright commented on one transformation which Sugarfoot would never be asked to make. 'We've turned down an offer of £200,000,' he revealed, 'and we won't sell him to go to America to continue his career for another two or three years and get drugged up to the eyeballs.' The preferred plan is for Sugarfoot to race on in 2000 and then be sold as a stallion. His own sire, Thatching, died in February. Not seen on the racecourse until October of his three-year-old season, and then over the wrong trip, Thatching showed startling improvement when put back to sprint distances as a four-year-old and was a clear-cut winner of the Duke of York Stakes, the Cork And Orrery, the July Cup and the Nunthorpe (then known as the William Hill Sprint Championship), though he lost the last of those prizes in the stewards' room after veering across the track when he hit the front. As a sire, Thatching has produced sprinters such as Shalford, Archway, Mistertopogigo and Wiganthorpe, as well as classic winners in Tirol and Danseuse du Soir, though none of those has had a huge impact at stud themselves.

Sugarfoot's dam Norpella, a fairly useful winner at a mile and a quarter and a mile and a half, comes from a famous family, as her dam Palmella, another middle-distance performer, is a half-sister to the Derby and King George winner Teenoso. Another offspring of the Oaks second Furioso is Topsy, winner of the Sun Chariot and the dam of Most Welcome. Norpella established a very solid record at stud herself, all four of her foals prior to Sugarfoot winning and showing fairly useful form at least, the best of them Easter Stakes winner Ultimo Imperatore (by Cadeaux Genereux). Things took a turn for the worse, however, when the three-year-old Nocciola (by Cadeaux Genereux) and two-year-old Sister Kate (by Barathea) both appeared for one uninspiring outing in the latest season. The latter represents Sugarfoot's connections, having been purchased for 60,000 guineas at the Houghton Sales.

Sugarfoot (ch.h. 1994)	Thatching (b 1975)	Thatch (b 1970)	Forli
			Thong
		Abella (ch 1968)	Abernant
			Darrica
	Norpella (ch 1983)	Northfields (ch 1968)	Northern Dancer
			Little Hut
		Palmella (ch 1977)	Grundy
			Furioso

Sugarfoot himself cost 31,000 guineas at the October Sales. He is a big, good-topped horse who habitually impresses in appearance. Below-form efforts on both starts at seven furlongs in the latest season (in the Tote International Handicap at Ascot and the Challenge Stakes), indicated that Sugarfoot is almost certainly better at a mile nowadays. Three runs at a mile and a quarter much earlier in his career saw him finish among the backmarkers. Apart from that, Sugarfoot has had virtually no need for excuses. He acts on any going and is as game and consistent a racehorse as one could wish to find, a great credit to himself and to his connections. *N. Tinkler*

SUGAR MILL 9 b.g. Slip Anchor 136 – Great Tom 99 (Great Nephew 126) [1998 NR 1999 14g May 1] tall, angular gelding: has a round action: fairly useful handicapper: missed 1998: never dangerous only 9-y-o start: finds 1½m a bare minimum and stays 14.6f: acts on good to firm and heavy ground: often soon off bridle. *Mrs M. Reveley* –

SUGAR REEF 5 br.g. High Kicker (USA) – Miss Poll Flinders (Swing Easy (USA) 126) [1998 NR 1999 10g 11.8d 14.1d Oct 27] no form. *M. J. Ryan* –

SUGGEST 4 b.g. Midyan (USA) 124 – Awham (USA) (Lear Fan (USA) 130) [1998 54: 12d 8m 6.9d 8g 9.3m 10m³ 8g⁶ 12m⁵ 11m 16d 12m⁶ 12g² 12d³ 12.4v⁵ 1999 12m 12g 8m 8g 10d⁵ 12.4m⁵ 17.1g Aug 22] smallish gelding: poor handicapper: stays 1½m: well beaten on extremes of ground: sometimes blinkered/visored. *W. Storey* 35

SUHAAD 3 ch.f. Unfuwain (USA) 131 – Forest Lair (Habitat 134) [1998 NR 1999 10m* 11.9s⁵ 12m* Jul 17] rather unfurnished filly: has a round action: seventh foal: sister to useful Irish 1½m winner Rajjaaf, closely related to useful Irish 1¼m to 1¾m winner Layik and Irish 1½m winner Kuwah (both by Be My Guest) and half-sister to 3 winners: dam, 1m winner at 2 yrs in Ireland, half-sister to very smart French miler Pampabird: progressive form: won maiden at Sandown in June and listed race at 111

Mr Hamdan Al Maktoum's "Suhaad"

Newmarket (beat Innuendo by a head) in July: over 12 lengths fifth of 7 to Noushkey in Lancashire Oaks at Haydock: will stay 1¾m: smart and may do better still. *A. C. Stewart*

SUHAIL (IRE)   3 b.g. Wolfhound (USA) 126 – Sharayif (IRE) (Green Desert   **53** (USA) 127) [1998 54: 7m 8.5m 1999 a8f² a8g 6.1s 6.1s 8.2f Jun 21] unfurnished gelding: modest maiden: stays 1m: acts on fibresand, best turf form on good to firm going: sold 550 gns. *P. L. Gilligan*

SUITE FACTORS   5 b.g. Timeless Times (USA) 99 – Uptown Girl 65 (Caruso   **62 d** 112) [1998 74, a–: 6d² 5.1g 7m⁴ 7m* 7m³ 6f* 6m³ 7f⁶ 7g* a6g 7s 1999 a7f³ a7g⁵ a7g   **a51** a8g 7s 6v 5d⁶ 6f 6g⁵ 6g 5.9g 7f⁴ 7m 6f⁵ 5g 6m 6g Oct 14] rather leggy gelding: modest handicapper: seems best at 6f/7f: acts on equitrack, firm and good to soft going: no improvement in visor/blinkers: usually races up with pace: none too consistent nowadays: sold 2,800 gns, sent to Kuwait. *K. R. Burke*

SUITYOUSIR (IRE)   3 br.g. Midhish 109 – Bel Ria (Gay Fandango (USA) 132)   **–** [1998 NR 1999 6g Jun 2] 15,000F, 5,000Y: half-brother to 1994 2-y-o 7f seller winner Magical Belle (by Magical Strike) and Irish 1m winner Municipal (by Common Grounds): dam maiden half-sister to Topanoora: slowly away and no show in Lingfield maiden (bandaged). *Jamie Poulton*

SULALAT   3 br.f. Hamas (IRE) 125§ – Enaya 99 (Caerleon (USA) 132) [1998   **82 §** 76: 6m⁵ 1999 7g⁴ 7g⁵ 7g² 7m⁵ 6d* 6d Oct 9] strong, lengthy filly: has a fluent, round action: fairly useful performer: made all in maiden at Newmarket in August: below form in valuable handicap at York final start: effective at 6f/7f: yet to

998

race on extremes of going: has given trouble at stalls: flashes tail: none too genuine. *R. W. Armstrong*

SULEYMAN 4 b.g. Alhijaz 122 – Aonia 97 (Mummy's Pet 125) [1998 73: 8m 8m³ 8.3m a9.4g³ 9.7f 8m a6g* a7g³ 1999 7g 7m 7f⁶ 8f Jun 26] smallish, quite attractive gelding: fair at 3 yrs for R. Charlton: little form in 1999, losing chance by rearing stalls on second start: stays 7f: acts on all-weather, raced only on good to firm/firm going on turf: sometimes blinkered, including for only success: sold 4,800 gns. *D. Nicholls* –

SULU (IRE) 3 b.g. Elbio 125 – Foxy Fairy (IRE) (Fairy King (USA)) [1998 70: 7m⁴ 1999 6d³ 7m⁵ 7d⁶ 7f² 6.1m³ 5.7f³ Sep 6] good-topped gelding: second foal: dam showed little at 2 yrs in Ireland: fair maiden: likely to stay beyond 7f: best efforts on going firmer than good: sold 9,000 gns. *I. A. Balding* **74**

SUMATI 3 b.c. Warning 136 – Swell Time (IRE) 30 (Sadler's Wells (USA) 132) [1998 6m⁴ 7.5d 6m* 8m 7s* 9v 1999 7.5d⁴ 8d² 7.5m* 7.5d³ 8m* 8d³ 11d² 8f* 10f³ 10g² 12g⁵ 9v* 12f* 9f Nov 28] approx 60,000Y in Italy: fourth foal: half-brother to winners in Italy by Formidable and Slip Anchor: dam maiden half-sister to smart 7f to 9f performer Bluegrass Prince: improved into smart performer: won handicap at Pisa, minor event at Milan and listed race at Rome in first half of year (also beaten 2 noses behind Alabama Jacks in Premio Parioli at Rome sixth start), then won minor event at Milan in October before best effort there later in month (final start for B. Grizetti) when beating below-form Silver Patriarch a nose in Gran Premio del Jockey Club: always behind in Hollywood Derby final start: stays 1½m: probably acts on any ground. *W. Dollase, USA* **114**

SUMBAWA (IRE) 4 ch.f. Magic Ring (IRE) 115 – Tittlemouse 86 (Castle Keep 121) [1998 58d: 8.2s 8.3g⁵ 11.7d⁴ 9.7m 8.3m⁴ 10.8m⁴ 10m 8m a8.5g⁵ 10g 1999 a8g a8.5g⁴ 7m⁵ 10f* 10.2g 8f³ 9f 8f 10g 10.5m 12.3m 11.9f⁵ Jul 22] angular filly: poor performer: won claimer at Brighton in May by 6 lengths: best at 1m/easy 1¼m: acts on firm going: tried blinkered/visored: none too consistent. *J. M. Bradley* **46**

SUMITAS (GER) 3 br.c. Lomitas 129 – Subia (GER) (Konigsstuhl (GER)) [1998 111p: 8d* 8v* 8v* 1999 8.5s* 8g* 11g⁵ 12m⁵ 12m² 12g⁴ 12d⁴ Sep 26] smart performer: the top 2-y-o in Germany in 1998: extended winning run when successful in listed race at Krefeld in April and Mehl-Mulhens-Rennen at Cologne (by 1¼ lengths from Gonlargo) in May: mostly disappointing subsequently (only fifth to Belenus in Deutsches Derby at Hamburg fourth start) but ran best race when short-head second of 5 to Ungaro in WGZ Bank-Deutschlandpreis at Dusseldorf in July: stays 1½m: acts on good to firm and heavy ground. *P. Schiergen, Germany* **117**

SUMITRA 3 b.f. Tragic Role (USA) – Nipotina 51 (Simply Great (FR) 122) [1998 NR 1999 9g⁶ 10.5s² 10.1g⁵ 16.4d³ 13.1f Sep 6] 4,200Y: third foal: dam, 11f/1½m winner, half-sister to smart sprinter Roman Prose: modest maiden: stays 2m: acts on soft going, probably not on firm. *Major D. N. Chappell* **56**

SUMMER BOUNTY 3 b.g. Lugana Beach 116 – Tender Moment (IRE) 78 (Caerleon (USA) 132) [1998 69: 7m 7d³ 7g⁵ 1999 a10g* 10g⁴ 10.1d⁴ 9.9g³ 10.3m⁶ 12f 12.1g² Aug 30] close-coupled gelding: fairly useful performer: easily landed odds in 5-runner maiden at Lingfield in February: ran well after when in frame in handicaps: claimed (to join F. Jordan) £10,000 final start: stays 1¼m, seemingly not 1½m: acts on equitrack and good to soft going: blinkered penultimate start. *B. W. Hills* **85**

SUMMER CHERRY (USA) 2 b.c. (Mar 7) Summer Squall (USA) – Cherryrob (USA) (Roberto (USA) 131) [1999 7g 8s Sep 22] $220,000Y: seventh foal: half-brother to winners in USA by Danzig Connection and Dixieland Band: dam, ran twice in France, half-sister to US Grade 1 1¼m winner Willow Hour: modest form, pulling hard, in maidens at Newmarket and Goodwood, still seeming in need of race on second occasion: should stay 1¼m. *P. F. I. Cole* **59**

SUMMERHILL SPECIAL (IRE) 8 b.m. Roi Danzig (USA) – Special Thanks (Kampala 120) [1998 73, a–: 12d⁶ 12.3v⁴ 12g* 12d² 12m 12g² 11.9s 12.3s² 12d⁴ 10g⁶ 12.3g⁵ 12d 12m² 12.1s 11.9g⁵ 12d 12s a12g⁴ 1999 a1f² a12g⁴ 12.3m 12m⁶ 12s Jun 30] sturdy, good-bodied mare: modest handicapper nowadays: effective at 1½m/ 1¾m: acts on good to firm going, probably on heavy (no form on all-weather): tried **56** **a–**

blinkered (not since 1996): not an easy ride but has won for lady/amateur: none too consistent. *D. W. Barker*

SUMMER NIGHT 3 b.f. Nashwan (USA) 135 – Shimmering Sea 89 (Slip Anchor 136) [1998 NR 1999 6g* 8d⁵ Oct 9] fourth foal: half-sister to several winners, including useful 6f/7f winner Sheltering Sky (by Selkirk) and useful 5f/6f winner Sea Dane (later won in Scandinavia, by Danehill): dam, 2-y-o 5f and 7f winner who stayed 1m, half-sister to top-class middle-distance performer Petoski: won 7-runner maiden at Yarmouth easily: again favourite, plenty of improvement when over 5 lengths fifth to Penang Pearl in listed race at Ascot following month, having pulled hard and been bumped 2f out: may prove best up to 1m: open to further progress. *Sir Mark Prescott*   **94 p**

SUMMER SONG 2 b.f. (Jan 25) Green Desert (USA) 127 – High Standard 83 (Kris 135) [1999 7d* Oct 15] quite good-topped filly: first foal: dam, 2-y-o 1m winner who stayed 1½m, from family of Nureyev and Sadler's Wells: green, won 5-runner private race at Newmarket readily by 3 lengths from John Company: moved poorly to post: will probably stay 1m: should improve. *E. A. L. Dunlop*   **69 p**

SUMMER SPLENDOUR (USA) 3 ch.f. Summer Squall (USA) – Sin Lucha (USA) (Northfields (USA)) [1998 71: 8.1m² 8.2g³ 1999 11.9g* 11.9f² 13.9g Aug 19] rather unfurnished filly: fairly useful performer: won maiden at Haydock in May: good second of 7 in handicap there in July: gave impression something amiss final start: stays 1½m: raced only on good going or firmer: sold 17,000 gns in December. *B. W. Hills*   **86**

SUMMER THYME 5 b.m. Henbit (USA) 130 – Hasty Sarah 56 (Gone Native) [1998 –: 9.9s 1999 a12g 9.9g Aug 28] close-coupled mare: very lightly raced and no form. *R. A. Fahey*   **–**

SUMMERTIME JOY 2 b.f. (Feb 18) Muhtarram (USA) 125 – Phylian 77 (Glint of Gold 128) [1999 7m 7g* 8s⁶ 7s Oct 25] rather leggy filly: first foal: dam 1¼m and 11f winner: poor performer: won seller at Catterick in August: should stay 1¼m: sold 2,500 gns. *S. C. Williams*   **46**

SUMMONER 2 b.c. (Mar 2) Inchinor 119 – Sumoto 101 (Mtoto 134) [1999 7.6g⁶ 8s* Nov 6] 50,000Y: angular, useful-looking colt: third foal: half-brother to 3-y-o Compton Admiral: dam 6f (at 2 yrs) and 7f winner: green when running in snatches on debut: created most favourable impression when making all in 18-runner maiden at Doncaster 10 weeks later by 3 lengths from Royal Cavalier, clear entering final 1f and eased: unlikely to stay much beyond 1m: useful performer in the making at least, and sure to win more races. *R. Charlton*   **90 p**

SUMTHINELSE 2 ch.g. (Apr 14) Magic Ring (IRE) 115 – Minne Love 67 (Homeric 133) [1999 5.1m⁵ 5.1g³ 5m³ 6m⁴ 6m Aug 13] 5,800Y, 12,000 2-y-o: stocky, good-quartered gelding: unimpressive mover: half-brother to several winners, including 3-y-o Gunner Sam and fairly useful sprinter Micro Love (by Vaigly Great): dam 6f (at 2 yrs) and 1m winner: fairly useful maiden: good fourth of 13 in nursery at Newmarket: reportedly choked when disappointing final outing: effective at 5f/6f: raced only on good going or firmer. *N. P. Littmoden*   **81**

SUN CHARM (USA) 2 b. or br.c. (Mar 28) Gone West (USA) – Argon Laser 107 (Kris 135) [1999 7d* 7.3s⁵ Oct 22] $220,000Y: half-brother to several winners, including smart middle-distance performers Weigh Anchor (by Slip Anchor) and Dr Massini (by Sadler's Wells), latter became one to avoid: dam 7f winner: useful form: won minor event at Leicester by 1¾ lengths from Strasbourg: only fifth of 9 to Umistim in Horris Hill Stakes at Newbury 10 days later, weakening when slightly hampered over 1f out: raced freely at Newbury, but should stay at least 1m: slowly away both starts: joined Godolphin: almost certainly remains capable of better, and should win more races. *Sir Michael Stoute*   **96 p**

SUN DANCING (IRE) 4 ch.f. Magical Wonder (USA) 125 – Lockwood Girl 81 (Prince Tenderfoot (USA) 126) [1998 –: 7g 6d 1999 5g 9.2v 8m⁵ 6g⁶ 6d² 5g 7g Jul 17] good-topped filly: modest performer: likely to prove best at 5f/6f: acts on good to firm going, good to soft and all-weather. *P. Monteith*   **64**

SUNDAY MAIL TOO (IRE) 7 b.m. Fayruz 116 – Slick Chick 89 (Shiny Tenth 120) [1998 32: 5v⁴ 5d⁵ 5g⁵ 5g 5g 5d³ 5d 5g³ 1999 5m⁴ 5g 5m⁶ 5g 5f Aug 2]   **30**

sparely-made mare: poor handicapper: has form at 6f, raced mainly at 5f nowadays: acts on any going: tried visored/blinkered, not for long time: usually held up: sometimes hangs. *Miss L. A. Perratt*

SUNDAY PICNIC (JPN)   3 b.f. Sunday Silence (USA) – Atoll 115 (Caerleon   **109** (USA) 132) [1998 8v* 1999 10.5s³ 10.2d* 12d⁴ Jun 4] rangy, good sort: third foal: dam won Italian 1000 Guineas and Oaks and second in Irish Oaks: useful form: won minor event at Longchamp at 2 yrs and Prix Cleopatre (by 2 lengths from Side Saddle) at Saint-Cloud in May: creditable fourth to Ramruma, beaten over 8 lengths, in Oaks at Epsom following month: stays 1½m well: raced only on going softer than good: somewhat quirky (proved difficult to saddle and swished tail throughout preliminaries at Epsom). *A. Fabre, France*

SUNDAY RAIN (USA)   2 b.c. (Feb 4) Summer Squall (USA) – Oxava (FR) 112   **68** (Antheus (USA) 122) [1999 7.1m⁴ 8g 8v⁴ 10s⁴ 8.3d Nov 4] $100,000Y: lengthy, attractive, unfurnished colt: fluent mover: first foal: dam, French 1m (including at 2 yrs) and 10.5f (Prix de Flore) winner, half-sister to smart French 7f to 1¼m performer Goofalik: fair maiden: blinkered, creditable fourth of 16 in nursery at Nottingham penultimate start: stays 1¼m: acts on good to firm and heavy going. *P. F. I. Cole*

SUN FAIRY   5 ch.m. Hatim (USA) 121 – Petite Melusine (IRE) 50 (Fairy King   **–** (USA)) [1998 42: a7g a11g² a12g 1999 a12g Jan 18] leggy, unfurnished mare: poor maiden: stays 11f: acts on fibresand and soft going: tried blinkered/visored. *D. Burchell*

SUNGLO   2 b.f. (Mar 30) Lugana Beach 116 – Mo Ceri 63 (Kampala 120) [1999   **50** 5.7d 5g⁵ Oct 19] 2,000Y: fifth foal: half-sister to 3 winners, including 4-y-o Desert Valentine and 7-y-o Mazilla: dam stayed 1¾m: modest form in maidens: should prove suited by 6f+: sold 5,000 gns, sent to Sweden. *P. J. Makin*

Mr Teruya Yoshida's "Sunday Picnic"

SUN HAT   3 b.c. Warning 136 – Instant Desire (USA) 86 (Northern Dancer) [1998   **92**
NR 1999 10g 10.1m³ 12g* 12m 16.2m² 16.1m⁵ 13.9m⁶ Sep 1] leggy, useful-looking
colt: fourth foal: half-brother to 1¼m winner Monitor (by Machiavellian) and
out-and-out stayer Speed To Lead (by Darshaan), both fairly useful: dam, stayed
1¼m, half-sister to Poule d'Essai des Poulains and Prix Lupin winner Fast Topaze:
fairly useful performer: won maiden at Catterick in May: best effort in handicaps
after when second of 5 at Chepstow: should prove best at 1¾m+: raced only on good/
good to firm going: sold 22,000 gns. *H. R. A. Cecil*

SUNLEY SENSE   3 b.g. Komaite (USA) – Brown Velvet 68 (Mansingh (USA)   **94**
120) [1998 97: 5d⁵ 5g² 5m⁵ 5.1g⁵ 5g² 5.1m³ 5m² 5g* 5.2g* 5g² 5s⁵ 1999 6m 6g 6m⁶
5g 5m Jun 19] sturdy, workmanlike gelding: fairly useful handicapper: best effort in
1999 when seventh (promoted a place) in listed rated stakes at Haydock: effective at
5f/6f: acts on soft and good to firm going: sometimes slowly away and rears stalls.
M. R. Channon

SUNLEY SOLAIRE   3 b.f. Aragon 118 – Pharsical 80 (Pharly (FR) 130) [1998   **–**
NR 1999 a7g 8.2s Apr 27] first foal: dam 6f/7f winner from family of Sonic Lady:
slowly away and tailed off in seller and maiden. *M. R. Channon*

SUNLEY'S PICC   2 b.f. (Mar 12) Piccolo 121 – Pharsical 80 (Pharly (FR) 130)   **60**
[1999 6g⁶ Jun 2] second foal: half-sister to 3-y-o Sunley Solaire: dam 6f/7f winner
from family of Sonic Lady: green, sixth of 11 in weak maiden at Lingfield, never on
terms. *M. R. Channon*

SUN LION (IRE)   4 b.g. Shalford (IRE) 124§ – Susie Sunshine (IRE) 81 (Waajib   **–**
121) [1998 55: 9v 9.9s 8f 8d 7.6m 8d 9.9s² 9g 1999 10.8d 10m 10.2g 8m 9.9v Sep
29] disappointing maiden handicapper: tried blinkered. *Mrs P. N. Dutfield*

SUN MARK (IRE)   8 ch.g. Red Sunset 120 – Vivungi (USA) (Exbury 138) [1998   **–**
–: 12.3v 1999 a8g 12.1v Mar 29] modest in 1997 for Mrs A. Swinbank: well beaten
all 3 starts since. *Miss J. F. Craze*

SUNNY CHIEF   3 ch.g. Be My Chief (USA) 122 – Sunny Davis (USA) 71 (Alydar   **a81**
(USA)) [1998 –: 6g⁶ 6m 6.1g 1999 a12g* a12g* 14.1m May 7] fair handicapper:
won at Wolverhampton in April and Southwell in May: broke leg and destroyed at
Nottingham: stayed 1½m well. *Sir Mark Prescott*

SUNNY FACT   3 ch.g. Known Fact (USA) 135 – Sunerta (USA) 75   **57**
(Roberto (USA) 131) [1998 72?: 6m² 6m⁵ 1999 6m⁴ Jul 30] maiden, just modest
form only 3-y-o outing: bred to stay beyond 6f: dead. *P. R. Webber*

SUNNY SLOPE   3 ch.f. Mujtahid (USA) 118 – Scottish Eyes (USA) (Green   **59 ?**
Dancer (USA) 132) [1998 57: 7g⁵ 7s 1999 7s 7f 6s⁵ 6m 5v 9.5d 10d Oct 19] IR
3,000Y: lengthy filly: first foal: dam unraced daughter of Coronation Stakes winner
Kesar Queen: modest maiden: trained both starts at 2 yrs by K. Prendergast in Ireland
and first 5 in 1999 by R. Fahey: stays 7f: acts on soft going: has worn tongue strap:
has tended to hang left. *Gerard Keane, Ireland*

SUNRISE (IRE)   2 b. or br.f. (Feb 3) Sri Pekan (USA) 117 – Grade A Star (IRE)   **58**
(Alzao (USA) 117) [1999 5m 5g 5g³ Aug 12] IR 27,000Y: smallish, sturdy, lengthy
filly: third foal: half-sister to useful sprinter March Star (by Mac's Imp) and fairly
useful Irish 1¼m winner Jimmy Swift (by Petardia): dam, Irish 2-y-o 1m winner who
stayed 11f, out of half-sister to smart stayer Saronicos: withdrawn after being injured
at start on intended debut: best effort in maidens when keeping-on third of 8 at
Beverley: will be suited by 6f+. *W. R. Muir*

SUNSET GLOW   2 gr.c. (Jan 21) Rainbow Quest (USA) 134 – Oscura (USA) 82   **77 p**
(Caro 133) [1999 8d⁴ Oct 29] brother to very smart middle-distance horse in Britain/
North America Urgent Request and half-brother to 3 winners, notably dual stayer/
very smart hurdler Sanmartino (by Salse): dam 1m winner: raced far too freely when
fourth of 6 to Autonomy in minor event at Newmarket, left behind final 2f: bred to be
well suited by 1¼m+: should do fair bit better provided he settles down. *B. W. Hills*

SUNSET HARBOUR (IRE)   6 br.m. Prince Sabo 123 – City Link Pet 79 (Tina's   **48**
Pet 121) [1998 56, a48: a5g⁵ a6g⁶ 5s a5g* a5g 5m* 5g³ 5d 5d* 5.1g⁶ 6f³ 5m² a6g² a5s
1999 a5f⁴ a5g⁶ a6g⁴ 5f 5m 5m a5g 5f 5m Aug 26] tall mare: poor handicapper:
effective at 5f/6f: acts on all-weather, firm and good to soft going: tried blinkered at
3 yrs, visored penultimate start: has won for apprentice. *S. E. Kettlewell*

SUP

SUNSET LADY (IRE) 3 b. or br.f. Red Sunset 120 – Lady of Man 85 (So Blessed **75**
130) [1998 75: 5d 6g* 6g⁴ 7g⁵ 7g⁵ 8m* 10s² 8v* a8g 1999 a8g⁶ a8.5g 9.9g³ 8d² 9.2d⁵
9.2f 9m⁴ Aug 26] leggy filly: fair handicapper: probably best at 1m: acts on good to
firm and heavy going, below form on fibresand: tongue tied final start: sold 3,000
gns, joined M. Sowersby. *P. C. Haslam*

SUNSHINE BOY 3 b.g. Cadeaux Genereux 131 – Sahara Baladee (USA) 79 **80**
(Shadeed (USA) 135) [1998 NR 1999 8g³ 8.3d⁶ 9d² 10m* 12d⁵ 10.5d 10m⁴
10.2m² 10m³ 10d Sep 28] fourth foal: big, rangy, good-topped gelding: has scope:
has round action: half-brother to 3 winners, including 1m and 1¼m winner Bint
Baladee (by Nashwan) and 1¼m winner Shanaladee (by Darshaan), both useful: dam
(maiden) would have stayed beyond 1m: fairly useful handicapper: won at Leicester
in June: ran well after when in frame: may prove best around 1¼m: acts on good to
firm going: visored last 3 starts: has flashed tail under pressure: sold 11,000 gns.
E. A. L. Dunlop

SUNSHINE STREET (USA) 4 b.c. Sunshine Forever (USA) – Meadow Spirit **118**
(USA) (Chief's Crown (USA)) [1998 120: 10v² 10s² 10g² 12m⁴ 12v 12g* 10m²
14.6m³ 12f⁵ 1999 10s² 12m⁴ 12m⁵ 10m⁴ 10d⁴ 12g⁵ Oct 9] tall, leggy colt: smart
performer: in frame in Derby and St Leger at 3 yrs: best effort in 1999 when staying-
on 9½ lengths fifth to Daylami in King George VI And Queen Elizabeth Stakes at
Ascot (ridden with restraint) third start: not entirely discredited when fourth to same
rival (would probably have finished third with clear run) in Champion Stakes at
Leopardstown and when 5½ lengths fifth of 7 to Val's Prince in Turf Classic at
Belmont last 2 starts: needs further than 1¼m and stays 1¾m: best on good ground
or firmer: often races prominently/leads: has been sweating and edgy this term:
sometimes tongue tied: joined N. Drysdale in USA. *N. Meade, Ireland*

SUNSPANGLED (IRE) 3 ch.f. Caerleon (USA) 132 – Filia Ardross 121 **108**
(Ardross 134) [1998 111p: 7d* 7d² 7d⁵ 8s* 1999 8m 8g 12d⁶ 12m² 11.9g 10d Sep 11]
tall, angular filly: smart at 2 yrs, winning Fillies' Mile at Ascot: didn't improve as
expected in 1999, best effort when 7 lengths second to Ramruma in Irish Oaks at the
Curragh: little impact in Group 1 races otherwise, including in 1000 Guineas, Oaks
and Yorkshire Oaks: should prove better at 1½m than shorter: acts on soft and good
to firm going. *A. P. O'Brien, Ireland*

SUNSTREAK 4 ch.c. Primo Dominie 121 – Florentynna Bay 61 (Aragon 118) **109**
[1998 112p: 7m⁴ 7.1g 8.2g* 8m* 8.1m* 8g² 1999 8m² 8m² 7f³ 7m 8d³ Sep 30]
unfurnished colt: useful performer: ran creditably in 1999 when placed, including
in Jubilee Handicap at Kempton (short-head second to Tertium) on reappearance,
Beeswing Stakes at Newcastle (3 lengths third to Josr Algarhoud) on third start and
listed race at Newmarket (length third to Indian Lodge) on final one: likely to prove
best at 7f/1m: acts on firm and good to soft going: sometimes tongue tied: usually
waited with. *C. F. Wall*

SUPERAPPAROS 5 b.g. Superpower 113 – Ayodessa 78 (Lochnager 132) [1998 **–**
–, a43: a8s⁴ a7g 1999 a6g⁶ Nov 12] poor maiden: probably stays 1m: form only on
fibresand: tried blinkered. *S. R. Bowring*

SUPERBIT 7 b.g. Superpower 113 – On A Bit 66 (Mummy's Pet 125) [1998 63, **68**
a–: 6.1m 5d³ 5g 6.1g 5g⁴ 6m⁶ 5g* 5m 5d 5m 6m⁵ 5m 6.1s² 5.1v⁴ 1999 5.1m³ 5m
5.1m⁴ 5m a5g² 5g 6m a6g³ 6.1d* Oct 5] small, good-bodied gelding: poor mover: fair
handicapper on turf, modest on all-weather: best effort for some time when winning
20-runner minor event at Nottingham final start: best at 5f/6f: acts on fibresand and
any turf going: tried blinkered/visored. *B. A. McMahon*

SUPERBOB 3 b.g. Superlative 118 – Beebob 85 (Norwick (USA) 125) [1998 –: **35**
6m 7m 7m⁶ a8g a8g 1999 a8f⁵ a10g⁵ a12s⁶ a11g 12s 8.2s Apr 27] leggy, unfurnished
gelding: poor maiden: stays 1¼m: blinkered fourth start. *R. J. R. Williams*

SUPERCHIEF 4 b.g. Precocious 126 – Rome Express (Siberian Express (USA) **50**
125) [1998 54: 9m⁶ 10g 7g 5.3d 5m 6m⁶ 6m 1999 7.6f 5d a7g a8.5g a10g³ a12g a10g³
a10g⁴ Dec 22] smallish, sturdy gelding: modest maiden handicapper: barely stays
1¼m: acts on good to firm going and equitrack: often tongue tied: tried visored/
blinkered. *Miss B. Sanders*

SUPER DOLLAR (IRE) 3 ch.g. Great Commotion (USA) 123 – L'Americaine **67**
(USA) (Verbatim (USA)) [1998 65: 6d³ 7d⁵ 7v 1999 a10g 9.7s 10s 9m 12.1m²

1003

12f* 12m* 12m 12.1m 12g 12m⁵ Sep 17] modest handicapper: left P. Cole after reappearance: won twice at Folkestone in July under good rides: stays 1½m: acts on firm and good to soft going: blinkered (raced quite freely) twice: has worn tongue strap/crossed noseband: sold 3,000 gns, joined K. Bailey. *S. C. Williams*

SUPERFRILLS 6 b.m. Superpower 113 – Pod's Daughter (IRE) 43 (Tender King **54** 123) [1998 52: a5g 5m a5g 5g 5d² 5g* 5g³ 5g 5m 5s* 5d⁴ 5d 5v* a5g a6g² 1999 5v 5m⁶ 5m² 5d⁶ 5m 5g a6g 5.2s 5d⁶ Nov 1] small mare: modest handicapper: effective at 5f/easy 6f: acts on fibresand and any turf going. *Miss L. C. Siddall*

SUPER-GEM 4 ch.g. Superpower 113 – Ela-Yianni-Mou 73 (Anfield 117) [1998 **37** –: 10.5g 10g 10.1g 9g 1999 a10g a12g a16g⁴ a11g² 12.3m³ a12g Apr 26] quite good-topped gelding: poor mover: poor maiden handicapper: stays 1½m, possibly not quite 2m: acts on all-weather, best turf effort on good to firm going: visored once at 3 yrs. *J. S. Wainwright*

SUPER HELEN 5 b.m. Superlative 118 – Sweet Helen (No Mercy 126) [1998 **–** NR 1999 a8g Jan 2] eighth foal: half-sister to winning sprinters Grange Farm Lad and Grange Farm Lady (both by Faraway Times) and a winner in Germany by Pharly: dam ran once: soundly beaten in claimer at Southwell. *C. Drew*

SUPERIOR PREMIUM 5 br.h. Forzando 122 – Devils Dirge 68 (Song 132) **116** [1998 110: 6d 6d² 6g 6m 6d³ 6.1g* 6g* 6g* 6m⁵ 6s 1999 6g² 6s 5.8m* 6m⁴ 6f 6f 6d⁶ 6d 5d* 6s* 6s Nov 6] good-topped horse: impresses in appearance: smart performer, better than ever in 1999, winning listed race at Taby in June and handicaps at Ascot then Newbury (rated stakes, by neck from Gaelic Storm) in October: also ran well when 2¼ lengths fourth to Bold Edge in Cork And Orrery Stakes at Royal Ascot: effective at 5f (given test)/6f: probably acts on any ground: sometimes edgy: has been tongue tied: best form coming with late run. *R. A. Fahey*

Mr J. C. Parsons' "Superior Premium"

SUPER KIM 2 b.f. (Apr 28) Superpower 113 – Kimble Blue 56 (Blue Refrain **46**
121) [1999 5m a7g 7d Oct 14] 1,000 2-y-o: smallish filly: sixth foal: half-sister to
5-y-o Blue Hopper: dam 2-y-o 5f winner: poor form in maiden/sellers. *P. L. Gilligan*

SUPERLAO (BEL) 7 b.m. Bacalao (USA) – Princess of Import (Import 127) **38**
[1998 –, a36: a6s⁶ a6g⁶ a5g⁵ a6g⁵ a6g⁴ a6g⁴ a5g⁶ a7g 1999 a6g⁵ 5s⁶ 5d 7m 7m³ 6g⁴
6m⁴ 5m⁶ 6m 5m 6m 5d⁴ 5s a6g⁶ Dec 6] smallish, sturdy mare: poor handicapper:
effective at 5f to 7f: acts on firm ground, soft and equitrack: tried blinkered/visored.
J. J. Bridger

SUPERLOU 3 br.f. Superpower 113 – Louise Moulton 90 (Moulton 128) [1998 **50**
NR 1999 7.5v⁴ 8.5g⁴ 7f⁴ 6f 8.3f 8.2g 11.5m Oct 19] smallish, leggy filly: half-sister
to several winners, including 1½m winner Kalou (by K-Battery) and useful 1985
2-y-o 7f winner Kolgong Heights (by Shirley Heights): dam 9f winner: poor maiden:
sold 700 gns. *J. G. FitzGerald*

SUPER MONARCH 5 ch.g. Cadeaux Genereux 131 – Miss Fancy That (USA) **76**
99 (The Minstrel (CAN) 135) [1998 85, a67+: a10g 6.5d 8d⁵ 11g a7g* a8g 8d 6v 7d² **a70**
7.6m 8.1m 8g 7.1g⁶ 8m² 10g 8.9g² 8m* 8s a9.4g 1999 a7g⁵ a8g 8d 10m 8g⁶ a8g⁴ 8g
8g 8f⁵ 8m³ 8g Oct 2] sturdy gelding: fair handicapper: best around 1m: acts on
equitrack, firm and good to soft going (probably not on soft): used to start slowly:
usually held up: has got upset in stalls. *K. R. Burke*

SUPER SAINT 5 b.g. Superpower 113 – Martyrdom (USA) (Exceller (USA) **?**
129) [1998 –, a45: a7g⁴ 8g 7f 8f 8s a8g² 1999 a8g⁵ a7.5g³ a7.5g³ a7.5g a9.8g² a9.8g*
a9.8g* 8g⁶ a9.8g⁴ a8g Nov 23] tall gelding: poor performer: won handicaps at
Boitsfort in May (amateurs) and June (apprentices): well held in claimers at Lingfield
on reappearance and final start: stays 9.8f: best turf form on good ground, acts on
equitrack and dirt. *Alex Vanderhaeghen, Belgium*

SUPER SECRET 2 ch.f. (Apr 3) Elmaamul (USA) 125 – Supreme (USA) **50**
(Lomond (USA) 128) [1999 7v⁵ 8g Nov 3] 4,500Y: first foal: dam no worthwhile
form: better effort in maidens when fifth of 6 at Ayr on debut: should stay at least 1m.
Miss L. A. Perratt

SUPERSONIC 3 b.f. Shirley Heights 130 – Bright Landing 78 (Sun Prince 128) **80**
[1998 –p: 7d 1999 8g 12.1g⁵ 10m³ 10.5d² 10m² 10.2m⁵ 10.2s² 8.9d Oct 9]
workmanlike filly: fair maiden: should be suited by 1½m+: acts on soft and good to
firm going. *R. F. Johnson Houghton*

SUPER STORY 2 b.f. (Mar 27) Superlative 118 – Princess Story 64 (Prince de **–**
Galles 125) [1999 6m Sep 7] 500Y: half-sister to several winners, including 6f
winner Aquarian Prince (by Mansingh) and 1¼m to 1½m winner Kiki Star (by Some
Hand): dam won sellers around 1m: tailed-off last of 19 in maiden at Lingfield.
M. Madgwick

SUPER STRIDES 3 b.f. Superpower 113 – Go Tally-Ho 66 (Gorytus (USA) 132) **–**
[1998 44: a5g⁴ a5g a5g 5d a6g² a6g² a5g² a6g 6g⁴ 6m a5g⁵ 6g 5s⁵ a5g⁴ a5s a5g 1999 a6g
Jan 2] angular, unfurnished filly: poor maiden: barely stays 6f: acts on fibresand and
good to soft going: inconsistent. *C. W. Fairhurst*

SUPLIZI (IRE) 8 b.h. Alzao (USA) 117 – Sphinx (GER) (Alpenkonig (GER)) **–**
[1998 100: 10v³ 12d⁶ 8m² 1999 10.1g 10g 10.4f 12m Jul 24] smallish, deep-bodied
horse: smart performer at 3 yrs: lightly raced since and little show in handicaps in
1999, pulled up lame final start: best at 1¼m/1½m: acts on good to firm and heavy
ground. *P. Bowen*

SUPPLY AND DEMAND 5 b.g. Belmez (USA) 131 – Sipsi Fach 100 (Prince **99**
Sabo 123) [1998 106: 12d 10g³ 9.9g* 10.4f 10.1m² 9g 10s⁵ a9.4g 1999 10m 8m 8.5g⁶
10.1g³ 10g 9.9f⁶ 10m 12g⁶ Aug 30] well-made gelding: impresses in appearance:
useful handicapper: best effort in 1999 when third to Monsajem in valuable event at
Epsom in June: finds 9f on short side, and should stay 1½m: acts on soft and good to
firm ground, below form on firm and fibresand: best blinkered nowadays: has gained
all 3 wins for K. Fallon. *G. L. Moore*

SUPREME ANGEL 4 b.f. Beveled (USA) – Blue Angel (Lord Gayle (USA) **–**
124) [1998 85d: 6d³ 6m 6g* 6m 5g 6.1g 6s 6v 1999 5s 6f 6f 6g 5.2g 6s 5s Sep 25]
angular filly: fairly useful at best: little show in 1999: stays 6f: acts on soft and good
to firm ground: blinkered last 3 starts. *M. P. Muggeridge*

Mitsubishi Shogun Winter Derby, Lingfield—
Supreme Sound and Sick As A Parrot finish clear in the second running of this race

SUPREMELY DEVIOUS 2 ch.f. (May 11) Wolfhound (USA) 126 – Clearly **58**
Devious 71 (Machiavellian (USA) 123) [1999 5m 6m⁵ 5.7h⁴ 6.1m² 7m⁶ 7s a6g **a48**
a6g⁶ a7g² a6g⁶ Dec 27] 4,000Y: first foal: dam, second from 2 starts at 1m, out of
smart 1983 2-y-o filly Shoot Clear, herself half-sister to Yorkshire Oaks winners
Sally Brown and Untold: modest maiden: stays 7f: acts on good to firm going and
equitrack: visored final 4 starts. *R. M. H. Cowell*

SUPREME MAIMOON 5 b.h. Jareer (USA) 115 – Princess Zena 96 (Habitat **–**
134) [1998 NR 1999 a6g⁶ a6g a7g⁶ a8g⁶ 10m a8.5g³ a12g³ a11g* a8g a12g³ a11g **a55**
Nov 30] workmanlike horse: modest performer: won claimer at Southwell in September: stays easy 1½m: acts on all-weather, well beaten only run on turf in 1999.
M. J. Polglase

SUPREME SALUTATION 3 ch.g. Most Welcome 131 – Cardinal Press (Sharrood (USA) 124) [1998 NR 1999 a6g a8f⁶ 6g⁵ 8m 8f³ 7g² 7m² 7g* 8f² 8d* Aug 9] leggy, sparely-made gelding: fairly useful handicapper: progressed well in first season, winning impressively at Catterick in July and Thirsk (by 3 lengths) in August: effective at 7f/1m: acts on firm and good to soft going: sweated profusely and got on toes (though ran well) penultimate start: has looked difficult ride: likely to improve further. *T. D. Barron* **89 p**

SUPREME SOUND 5 b.h. Superlative 118 – Sing Softly 112 (Luthier 126) [1998 104: 10s⁴ 12s 9.9m* 10g 9.7m* 10.5g² 9m* 10m 10.1g⁴ 10.1m* 10.4f* 10.1m³ 10g 9g 1999 a10g* 10g 10.3m² 9.9g 10.3g² 11f² 12g⁶ a10f* a10f* Nov 6] strong horse: has a round action: smart performer: won listed Mitsubishi Shogun Winter Derby at Lingfield (by 2½ lengths from Sick As A Parrot) in March and Grade 3 event at Hawthorne in October: also ran well when runner-up in between in listed race at Chester, minor event at Doncaster (final start for P. Harris) and United Nations Handicap (beaten 1½ lengths by Yagli, who gave 11 lb) at Monmouth Park: last of 14 in Breeders' Cup Classic at Gulfstream final outing: stays 11f: best on good or firmer turf going and acts on equitrack/dirt: game front runner. *M. W. Dickinson, USA* **111**

SURE DANCER (USA) 4 b.c. Affirmed (USA) – Danlu (USA) (Danzig (USA)) [1998 NR 1999 10g* 8f* 9.8v Oct 2] tall, good sort: fifth reported foal: half-brother to 4 winners, notably very smart middle-distance stayer Strategic Choice (by Alleged): dam, probably stayed 1¼m in Ireland, sister to smart 6f/7f performer Nicholas: won maiden at Leicester in April and 7-runner minor event at Doncaster in July, latter by head from Showboat: well held in Prix Dollar at Longchamp final start: stays 1¼m: already smart. *P. F. I. Cole* **114**

SURE FIRE 2 b.c. (May 14) Deploy 131 – Certain Story (Known Fact (USA) 135) [1999 6s Oct 1] half-brother to several winners, including 7f winner Fairy Story (by Persian Bold) and useful middle-distance performer Pharly Story (by Pharly): dam unraced half-sister to dam of Shaamit: always outpaced in maiden at Lingfield: sold 3,000 gns. *C. A. Dwyer* **–**

SURE FUTURE 3 b.g. Kylian (USA) – Lady Ever-So-Sure 80 (Malicious) [1998 NR 1999 10v⁵ 12g 10f 11.6m⁵ 14.1g a12g 11.9s² Sep 29] 17,000Y: short-backed gelding: eighth foal: half-brother to winning Irish stayer Ruano (by Belfort) and a winner in Italy by Superpower: dam won from 6f to 1½m, mostly in sellers: fair maiden: stays 1½m: acts on soft and good to firm ground: sold 21,000 gns, joined N. Gaselee. *A. C. Stewart* **66 a–**

SURE QUEST 4 b.f. Sure Blade (USA) 130 – Eagle's Quest 62 (Legal Eagle 126) [1998 65: 8.1m⁵ 10d 10g³ 10g³ 9.7f* 10.2m⁶ 11.1m⁴ 1999 8g 9m 10m 10m Jul 26] close-coupled filly: fair at 3 yrs: modest at best in 1999: finds 1m a bare minimum, and stays 1½m: acts on firm ground, probably on good to soft: visored final start. *D. W. P. Arbuthnot* **61**

SURE TO DREAM (IRE) 6 b.m. Common Grounds 118 – Hard To Stop 77 (Hard Fought 125) [1998 49, a53: a6g² a6g³ a6g* 5.1d² 6g⁴ 6s a5g⁵ 1999 a6g³ a7g* a7g 7f a6g a7g a7g a6g Dec 6] sturdy mare: modest handicapper: below form after winning at Southwell in May: stays 7f: acts on good to soft ground and all-weather: blinkered final start: usually races prominently. *R. T. Phillips* **– a61**

SURPRESA CARA 4 ch.f. Risk Me (FR) 127 – Yukosan 69 (Absalom 128) [1998 –: 6g 7d a6g a7g⁵ a10f 1999 a8g a8g Feb 13] good-bodied filly: no form: tried blinkered. *B. R. Johnson* **–**

SURPRISED 4 b.g. Superpower 113 – Indigo 86 (Primo Dominie 121) [1998 64: 6s 6s 6d⁶ 7f 1999 6.1f² 6g* 6m³ 6d⁵ 7.5m² 7m⁵ 5m² 5d Sep 16] big, useful-looking gelding: fair handicapper: won 18-runner race at Pontefract in June: ran creditably most other starts: effective at 5f to 7.5f: acts on firm going, probably on good to soft: blinkered (below best) sixth start. *R. A. Fahey* **78**

SURPRISE ENCOUNTER 3 ch.g. Cadeaux Genereux 131 – Scandalette (Niniski (USA) 125) [1998 87p: 7g 7g 1999 7g* 7m⁵ 7d⁶ May 11] quite good-topped gelding: fairly useful performer: won maiden at Kempton in April: ran well in handicaps at Newmarket (early to post) and York after: may prove best at 6f/7f: yet to race on extremes of going. *E. A. L. Dunlop* **88**

SURREY LASS 3 b.f. Chaddleworth (IRE) 103 – Aquarula 88 (Dominion 123) – [1998 NR 1999 7m 11.5m 11.5g Sep 14] half-sister to 3 winners, including 6f winner Aquatic Queen (by Rudimentary) and 1½m winner To Be Fair (by Adonijah): dam 2-y-o 5f/6f winner: no form in claimers/maiden. *C. A. Dwyer*

SURTSEY 5 ch.g. Nashwan (USA) 135 – Fire And Shade (USA) 91 (Shadeed – (USA) 135) [1998 NR 1999 12.4m 11.1s May 14] lengthy, angular gelding: disappointing maiden: stays 1½m. *Mrs A. Duffield*

SURVEILLANCE (USA) 3 ch.c. Woodman (USA) 126 – Eye Drop (USA) 96 **91** (Irish River (FR) 131) [1998 NR 1999 8m* 8g⁵ 8.1d³ 10f³ 12.3m³ 12v Sep 20] $300,000F: leggy, workmanlike colt: has a quick action: eighth foal: half-brother to 3 winners, including fairly useful stayer Latahaab (by Lyphard): dam, 2-y-o 6f winner, daughter of Queen Mary winner Pushy: easily beat sole rival in Newmarket Challenge Whip in April: fairly useful form in maidens after: stays 1½m: acts on firm and good to soft going, well beaten on heavy: sent to UAE. *J. H. M. Gosden*

SURVEYOR 4 ch.c. Lycius (USA) 124 – Atacama (Green Desert (USA) 127) **86 +** [1998 101p: 6m 6g³ 6g 6f 6.1g⁵ 1999 5m 6.1g Sep 25] smallish, quite attractive colt: useful handicapper: shaped as though in need of race when well held both 4-y-o starts: should prove best at 6f/7f: acts on good to firm ground, not discredited only outing on soft: held up, and has turn of foot: sometimes sweating/edgy: sold 16,000 gns. *J. L. Dunlop*

SURVIVAL VENTURE 3 b.g. Unfuwain (USA) 131 – Sherkraine 98 (Shergar **71** 140) [1998 –: 7m 8g 8g 8d 1999 a10g³ 7f² 7f 6g a7g* a8g² 7s⁴ a7g³ Aug 25] close-coupled, useful-looking gelding: fair performer: won claimer at Lingfield in June: effective at 7f/1m: acts on firm ground and equitrack: races up with pace: sold 4,000 gns. *S. P. C. Woods*

SUSAN'S DOWRY 3 b.f. Efisio 120 – Adjusting (IRE) (Busted 134) [1998 72: – 5s⁶ 5g⁴ 6s* 7d⁶ 5.9m⁴ 1999 8.5s Sep 21] leggy, angular filly: has a round action: fair at 2 yrs for T. Easterby: no show only start in 1999: should stay beyond 6f: acts on soft going, probably good to firm: has swished tail. *Andrew Turnell*

SUSAN'S PRIDE (IRE) 3 b.g. Pips Pride 117 – Piney Pass (Persian Bold 123) **85** [1998 NR 1999 5s² 5s⁶ 6g 6.1f* 6d 7d³ 8m 7.1g⁶ 7.7m⁶ 7.1m⁴ 8.5m⁶ 6.1s⁵ 7s* 7d* Oct 29] 60,000Y: good-topped gelding: has a quick action: brother to 4-y-o Easter Ogil and half-brother to several winners, including 11-y-o Allinson's Mate: dam Irish 2-y-o 8.5f winner: fairly useful performer: won maiden at Nottingham in May and claimers at Doncaster (21 ran) and Brighton in October: effective at 6f/7f: yet to race on heavy going, acts on any other: blinkered once. *B. J. Meehan*

SUSEJEBHA (IRE) 3 ch.f. Magical Wonder (USA) 125 – Tribute To Viqueen – (Furry Glen 121) [1998 NR 1999 10m 14g 11.7s Oct 26] second reported foal: half-sister to 10.8f winner Imperial Glen (by Imperial Frontier): dam pulled up lame only start over hurdles: soundly beaten in maidens. *M. J. Weeden*

SUSHI BAR (IRE) 8 gr.g. Petorius 117 – Sashi Woo (Rusticaro (FR) 124) [1998 **52** NR 1999 17.1v 14.1g² 14.1m³ 16.2g⁴ 14.1m⁵ 12s* 11.8d⁴ Oct 12] big gelding: modest performer: won seller at Beverley in September: effective at 1½m (given good test) to 2m: acts on all-weather, firm and soft going: fair form over hurdles, won in November and December. *Mrs M. Reveley*

SUSIE'S FLYER (IRE) 2 br.f. (Mar 30) Frimaire – Wisdom To Know (Bay **90** Express 132) [1999 5.1d² 5m⁵ 5m* 5.2m* 5v⁵ Sep 24] tall, leggy filly: half-sister to 8-y-o Selhurstpark Flyer and Irish 9f and 1¼m winner Chuck's Treasure (by Treasure Kay): dam placed at 6f: fairly useful performer: won maiden at Lingfield in August and nursery (by 4 lengths) at Newbury in September: hot favourite, only fifth of 11 in another nursery at Lingfield final start: should stay 6f: acts on good to firm ground, possibly not on heavy: withdrawn at start having gone to post freely on intended third outing: races prominently. *J. Berry*

SUSSEX LAD 2 b.c. (May 4) Prince Sabo 123 – Pea Green 98 (Try My Best **76** (USA) 130) [1999 5g⁶ 5m Jun 18] workmanlike colt: sixth foal: half-brother to 3 winners, including fairly useful 5f winner Jade Pet (by Petong) and 5-y-o The Grey Grey: dam probably stayed 1m: showed ability in maiden at Goodwood (green) and Windsor Castle Stakes at Royal Ascot (better effort when tenth of 16). *R. Hannon*

SUSU 6 ch.m. Machiavellian (USA) 123 – Home Truth 98 (Known Fact **122** (USA) 135) [1998 97: a7f* a7f^2 7m^2 a7f^2 a7f^2 a7f^2 1999 7m* a9f^5 a7f^4 8d^3 7m* 7g* 8g Nov 6]

Racing boasts numerous examples of horses who started off in the foothills before scaling the heights, most notably Rockfel, winner of the 1938 One Thousand Guineas, Oaks and Champion Stakes after finishing eighth of eleven at 100/8 in a selling race at Sandown Park on her juvenile debut. Now another can be added to the list in the shape of the late-developing Susu, whose first run, in January 1997 when just turned four, was little short of deplorable. Up against eight opponents in a maiden race over seven furlongs at Nad Al Sheba, she dwelt and was always behind, finishing tailed-off last, beaten around thirty lengths. The winner, La Maffarr, had been beaten at odds on in a maiden at Redcar on his previous start. Susu's improvement in the following three seasons was phenomenal, and it was a shame that British racegoers had the opportunity of seeing her only three times, culminating in a game defeat of Lend A Hand in the Champions' Gallery Challenge Stakes at Newmarket in October. Her record in between that abysmal debut and the Challenge bears close scrutiny, since she won five times and was second five times over six and seven furlongs in the UAE, including landing The President Cup, a listed event, at Abu Dhabi in January.

Sent to Sir Michael Stoute in the summer, Susu made her British debut in a one mile listed race at Ascot in August and shaped fairly well in third, running on without being knocked about to be around seven lengths behind Pink Cristal. She reverted to seven furlongs in the eleven-runner Kyoto Sceptre Stakes at Doncaster in September, a listed race which is consistently better contested than some pattern events and perhaps ought to be upgraded to Group 3. Susu started at 11/1 in a market headed by Cruinn A Bhord, successful in two fairly valuable handicaps at Newmarket, Pescara and Selfish, and proved a revelation. Held up, Susu had trouble finding a passage but produced a tremendous burst of speed to hit the front in the final furlong and defeat Pescara by one and a quarter lengths. Susu impressed in appearance as well as in the race—a sturdy, close-coupled mare, she really caught the eye beforehand and evidently was thriving in her new surroundings. She looked superb before her next start, too, in the ten-runner Challenge Stakes, which presented an altogether tougher task than the Sceptre. The first two in the 1998 Dewhurst Stakes, Mujahid and Auction House, were trying to get off the mark for the year but more serious opposition was promised by easy Hungerford Stakes winner

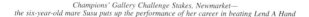

Champions' Gallery Challenge Stakes, Newmarket—
the six-year-old mare Susu puts up the performance of her career in beating Lend A Hand

Lend A Hand, who started at odds on, his smart stable-companion Josr Algarhoud and admirable handicapper turned pattern performer Sugarfoot. Susu was a little troublesome at the stalls but raced sweetly enough, making ground from the rear under pressure to get into contention two furlongs out, leading entering the final furlong and maintaining her run to hold off Lend A Hand by a neck, the pair four lengths clear of Josr Algarhoud. Not all of Susu's rivals had the run of the race—Josr Algarhoud was stopped in his tracks at the distance—but this was still a cracking display, the best of the mare's career by some way. Regrettably she failed to reproduce the form in the Breeders' Cup Mile at Gulfstream, starting at over 50/1 and finishing twelfth of fourteen, eight places behind Lend A Hand, unable to get into contention from her wide draw after a slowish start. A planned run in the Hong Kong Mile was ruled out when she failed to please in her work.

Susu (ch.m. 1993)	Machiavellian (USA) (b 1987)	Mr Prospector (b 1970)	Raise A Native
			Gold Digger
		Coup de Folie (b 1982)	Halo
			Raise The Standard
	Home Truth (ch 1987)	Known Fact (b 1977)	In Reality
			Tamerett
		Dance Card (ch 1980)	Be My Guest
			Ivor's Honey

Susu's sire Machiavellian has had his stud fee for 2000 increased from 40,000 guineas to 50,000, presumably thanks to the achievements of Almutawakel, Best of The Bests, Morning Pride and Susu herself. His ratio of 'black-type' winners to foals is just over ten per cent, a good score, and he gets winners over all sorts of distances—he is the sire of Ascot Gold Cup runner-up Invermark. Susu's best form is all at seven furlongs. She cost 55,000 guineas at the 1994 Houghton Sales and is one of four winners out of her dam Home Truth. The pick of the others is Cadeaux Cher (by Cadeaux Genereux), one of the best sprint handicappers of 1998 when successful in the Great St Wilfrid Handicap and Portland Handicap. The two-year-old, Royal Insult (by Lion Cavern), won a maiden race at Redcar on the second of his two starts. Home Truth was a useful performer at up to a mile, winning three times and running some good races in defeat, notably when a close second in a listed event at Leopardstown. Her dam Dance Card, a disappointing maiden, produced another useful performer in Chief's Image, who ran third in the Phoenix Stakes as a juvenile. *Sir Michael Stoute*

SUSY WELLS (IRE)   4 b.f. Masad (IRE) 119 – My Best Susy (IRE) (Try My   **50 d**
Best (USA) 130) [1998 50: 10s⁵ 7.5g³ 8.2m 8.1g² 10m⁶ 7.1d 8.2g⁶ 8v⁵ 1999 7d⁴ 8m 8d 9g 8m 7m⁵ 8d⁶ 7s Oct 23] lengthy filly: modest maiden at best: stays 1m: acts on heavy ground: tried blinkered: has worn tongue strap: none too consistent. *J. Parkes*

SUTTON COMMON (IRE)   2 b.c. (May 10) Common Grounds 118 – Fadaki   **62**
Hawaki (USA) 60 (Vice Regent (CAN)) [1999 6s 7.9d⁴ Oct 9] 25,000F, 15,000Y: third foal: dam maiden half-sister to 4-y-o Fruits of Love and smart 1990 2-y-o sprinter Mujadil: modest form in maidens at Newcastle and York: should stay 1¼m. *K. A. Ryan*

SWAGGER   3 ch.g. Generous (IRE) 139 – Widows Walk (Habitat 134) [1998 –p: **53**
6v 1999 a6g 7f 8f 9.9g 17.2g³ 16v⁴ a14g⁸ 16d⁶ Oct 21] sturdy gelding: modest handicapper: given good front-running ride to win amateur event at Southwell in September: barely stays 17f: acts on fibresand, best turf run on good going: has looked difficult ride (early reminders final start). *Sir Mark Prescott*

SWALDO   2 ch.c. (Apr 19) Muhtarram (USA) 125 – Ethel Knight (Thatch (USA)   **65**
136) [1999 6.1m a6f 8.2d² 8.3d³ Nov 4] 6,000F, 9,000Y: small, lightly-made colt: half-brother to several winners, including 1993 2-y-o 5f winner Battling Blue and moody 6f (at 2 yrs) and 1m winner Roly Wallace (both by Primo Dominie): dam, daughter of useful 1¼m winner, lightly raced: fair maiden: blinkered and trained by A. Kelleway on debut: placed in sellers at Nottingham and Windsor: should stay 1¼m: joined N. Berry. *G. C. H. Chung*

William Hill Stakes (Handicap), York—Swallow Flight (left) makes a successful handicap debut from Mayaro Bay (blaze) and Now Look Here (stars)

SWALLOW FLIGHT (IRE)   3 b.c. Bluebird (USA) 125 – Mirage 60 (Red Sunset 120) [1998 95: 6m 6m² 7g³ 8d² 1999 7g⁵ 8m³ 7d* 8.1m³ 10.4d³ 8f² 7m⁵ 8m* 8s² 8d⁴ Oct 30] tall, attractive colt: has a quick action: smart performer: won quite valuable handicap at York in May and minor event at Doncaster (beat Desert Knight by 3½ lengths) in September: ran creditably most other starts, including when runner-up to Lonesome Dude in William Hill Mile (Handicap) at Goodwood and Spadoun in listed race at Longchamp: effective at 7f, probably at 10.4f: yet to race on heavy going, acts on any other. *G. Wragg*   **111**

SWALLOW JAZ   2 b.g. (Apr 20) Alhijaz 122 – Marguerite Bay (IRE) 73 (Darshaan 133) [1999 7.1d 7m 8f⁵ 8d Sep 26] leggy gelding: first foal: dam 7f winner: poor form in maidens: stiff task final outing: stays 1m. *T. J. Etherington*   **47**

SWAMPY (IRE)   3 b.c. Second Set (IRE) 127 – Mystery Lady (USA) (Vaguely Noble 140) [1998 71: 7.3g 5.1d 7.1d⁶ 1999 a8g⁴ a8g⁴ a10g⁵ 9.7s³ 9.7v² 9d² 8.3m a7g 8f⁶ 9v 8s² a9.4g Dec 15] fair maiden on turf, modest on all-weather: stays 9.7f: acts on equitrack and heavy ground, possibly not on firm/good to firm. *J. Wharton*   **71 a51**

SWAN AT WHALLEY   7 b.g. Statoblest 120 – My Precious Daisy (Sharpo 132) [1998 70d, a–: a5g a5g 5s 5d 5m 5m² 5s 5m² 5g 5g 5m⁶ 5.1d 1999 5g 5d 5m* 5m² 5d 5m⁶ 5f 5g Aug 22] compact gelding: modest handicapper: won at Musselburgh in April: below form after next start: raced only at 5f: acts on firm and soft going: tailed off in visor/blinkers: often early to post/troublesome stalls: has reportedly broken blood vessels. *K. A. Ryan*   **56**

SWANDALE FLYER   7 ch.g. Weldnaas (USA) 112 – Misfire 56 (Gunner B 126) [1998 32: a12g a11g 12.3v 13g 13.1g³ 16.1d 13m 1999 a12g 12g⁵ 12.4m Jul 12] big, workmanlike gelding: poor handicapper: probably stays 13f: acts on good to firm going, good to soft and fibresand. *N. Bycroft*   **32**

SWAN HUNTER   6 b.h. Sharrood (USA) 124 – Cache (Bustino 136) [1998 76, a93: a12g* a12g⁶ a9.4g⁵ 12d⁴ 17.2d 13.9g a12g² 1999 a12g² a12g 11.8d 14.1d a14.8g² a12g⁵ Dec 27] leggy, angular horse: bad mover: fairly useful on all-weather, poor on turf: below form after reappearance (ran in sellers final 2 starts): effective at 1½m to 2m: acts on all-weather and soft going. *D. J. S. Cosgrove*   **– a93 d**

SWAN KNIGHT (USA)   3 b. or br.c. Sadler's Wells (USA) 132 – Shannkara (IRE) (Akarad (FR) 130) [1998 NR 1999 8g* 10m Apr 30] $600,000Y: good-topped colt: good walker and mover: second foal: closely related to minor US stakes winner (second in Grade 2 event at 8.5f) Tekken (by Nureyev): dam 1m (at 2 yrs in France) and 8.5f (Grade 3 event in USA) winner, half-sister to smart/very smart French   **81 +**

middle-distance fillies Sharaniya and Sharaya: well-backed favourite, won new-comers event at Newmarket by short head from Manndar: raced much too freely when last in listed race there 16 days later: should stay 1¼m: sent to UAE. *J. H. M. Gosden.*

SWAN LAKE (FR) 3 b.f. Lyphard (USA) 132 – Dame Au Faucon (USA) (Silver **56 d** Hawk (USA) 123) [1998 7m⁶ 7g⁵ 8s 7.8m³ 8v⁵ 8v 8v 1999 a10g⁵ 10m 10s 8m⁶ 11.8m⁶ 10g 11.5f⁵ 8s⁶ a10g a10g Nov 8] first reported foal: dam, French 7f and 9f winner, half-sister to US Grade 2 1½m winner Copper Mel: modest maiden: trained by J. Hammond in France in 1998: appears to stay 1¼m: tried blinkered at 2 yrs. *K. O. Cunningham-Brown*

SWAN PRINCE 2 b.c. (Apr 9) King's Signet (USA) 110 – Princess Tallulah 43 **42** (Chief Singer 131) [1999 a6g 6.1g⁴ 6m a7g 7f⁶ 6g Aug 25] first foal: dam poor maiden who stayed 1m: poor maiden. *W. G. M. Turner*

SWCI 2 ch.f. (Apr 17) Shalford (IRE) 124§ – Plucky Pet 50 (Petong 126) [1999 **–** 5m Jul 15] 1,200Y: first foal: dam poor maiden: well beaten in seller at Leicester. *B. Palling*

SWEET ANGELINE 2 b.f. (May 1) Deploy 131 – Fiveofive (IRE) 61 (Fairy **70** King (USA)) [1999 6.1m 7m⁴ 7.7g⁴ 8m⁴ 8m 10.2s³ 8.3g Oct 11] third foal: half-sister to 3-y-o Canyouhearme: dam 5f (at 2 yrs) and 1m winner: fair maiden: seems barely to stay 1¼m: acts on soft and good to firm ground: tongue tied on debut. *A. T. Murphy*

SWEET AS A NUT (IRE) 3 ch.f. Pips Pride 117 – My First Paige (IRE) 53 **64** (Runnett 125) [1998 75: 5d⁴ a5g 5m² 6g 5g* 5d⁴ 6g³ 5f* 6g 5m⁵ 5d⁵ 6s 1999 6g 6m a6g⁵ 5.1g⁴ 6.1d² 5g 6g² 6m⁵ 5m Aug 4] leggy, lengthy filly: fair at 2 yrs: modest in 1999: effective at 5f/6f: acts on firm going, good to soft and fibresand: joined D. Carroll. *C. A. Dwyer*

SWEET BETTSIE 5 b.m. Presidium 124 – Sweet And Sure (Known Fact (USA) **34** 135) [1998 49: 8s⁵ 7g 6m 6g⁵ 6m 6v 6s 1999 7f 10m Sep 7] leggy mare: poor maiden handicapper: should prove best up to 1m: acts on soft going: visored final 4-y-o start. *D. J. Coakley*

SWEET CHARITY (IRE) 3 ch.f. Bigstone (IRE) 126 – Tolstoya (Northfields **78** (USA)) [1998 70: 5d⁴ 6m³ 6f² 5m³ 6m³ 6m⁴ 1999 7d 7d³ 7m⁴ 6f* 6f⁴ 5.3s 6g* Sep 20] fair performer: won maiden handicap at Brighton in July and 22-runner claimer at Leicester in September: stays 7f: acts on firm and good to soft going: often races up with pace: sent to Saudi Arabia. *M. A. Jarvis*

SWEET CICELY (IRE) 2 b.f. (May 21) Darshaan 133 – Glendora (Glenstal **63 p** (USA) 118) [1999 7s 8.3d Oct 28] 3,400Y, 15,000 2-y-o: sixth foal: half-sister to Irish 7f winner Caduga (by Dancing Dissident) and 3 winners abroad. dam ran 3 times in Ireland: better effort in maidens (modest form) when seventh of 13 at Windsor: should stay 1¼m: should improve further. *D. R. C. Elsworth*

SWEET COMPLIANCE 3 ch.f. Safawan 118 – Sianiski (Niniski (USA) 125) **–** [1998 71, a60: 5g a5g² 6m³ 6g⁶ a5g 7m 7g* 7g a7g 1999 a8f⁶ a8g 7m 6.1g 6g Jul 2] workmanlike filly: fair at 2 yrs: little show in 1999: usually blinkered/visored. *P. Shakespeare*

SWEET EMOTION (IRE) 3 b.f. Bering 136 – Hiwaayati (Shadeed (USA) **97** 135) [1998 NR 1999 8g* 8d² 9.9g 8d Oct 12] strong, lengthy filly: has a quick, fluent action: second foal: dam unraced half-sister to very smart colts at 6f/7f Lead On Time and Great Commotion, the family of Vaguely Noble: won newcomers race at Newmarket in April: unlucky when head second of 7 to Insinuate in listed race at Ascot later in month, hampered over 1f out then staying on strongly: well held both starts after, reportedly finishing distressed penultimate: should stay beyond 1m: restless in preliminaries first 2 starts: sold 56,000 gns in December. *E. A. L. Dunlop*

SWEET GLOW (FR) 12 b.g. Crystal Glitters (USA) 127 – Very Sweet (Belly-pha 130) [1998 65: 17.2s* 16.2d⁶ 16v 1999 21.6d Apr 28] small gelding: fairly useful hurdler nowadays: fair and lightly raced on Flat: pulled up only start in 1999: stays 2½m well: acts on firm and soft ground. *M. C. Pipe*

SWEET HAVEN 2 b.f. (Apr 6) Lugana Beach 116 – Sweet Enough 79 (Caerleon **60** (USA) 132) [1999 5s 5m* 5f 6m 6g⁶ 6s 6d Oct 22] 2,000Y: small filly: sixth foal:

sister to a fair maiden up to 11.5f and half-sister to 1995 2-y-o 7f winner Bold Enough (by Bold Arrangement): dam, stayer, from very good family: modest performer: trained by M. Heaton-Ellis first 3 starts, winning maiden at Beverley in April: out of depth final start: may prove better at 6f than 5f: acts on good to firm going, possibly unsuited by softer than good. *C. G. Cox*

SWEET MAGIC   8 ch.g. Sweet Monday 122 – Charm Bird 60 (Daring March   **68** 116) [1998 61: 5d 5.1m⁵ 5g 5d a5g⁵ a5g² a5g³ 1999 a5g 5g² a5g* 5m a5g² 5m⁴ a5g a5g⁵ 5m* 5d 5f⁵ a5g²] lengthy, plain gelding: tends to look dull in coat: fair performer: won seller at Wolverhampton in April and handicap at Catterick in June: off 5 months before well beaten final start: best at 5f: acts on firm going, soft and all-weather: blinkered (tailed off) once at 6 yrs: wears tongue strap. *L. R. Lloyd-James*

SWEET PATOOPIE   5 b.m. Indian Ridge 123 – Patriotic 43 (Hotfoot 126) [1998   **57** 49, a69: a6g² 8s 8.5m⁶ 10.1g³ a10g² 10.1m⁴ 1999 a12g* 11.5g³ a12g² a12g⁵ 13.8s   **a72** a16g Nov 15] leggy, quite good-topped mare: fair on all-weather, modest on turf: won handicap at Lingfield in May: left B. Hanbury after third start: ran poorly final 2: stays 1½m: acts on all-weather and good to firm going, possibly not on soft: tried blinkered. *Mrs P. Ford*

SWEET PEA   4 b.f. Persian Bold 123 – Silk Petal 105 (Petorius 117) [1998 81: 7d   **94** 8g² 8m* 8g* 8.3g² 9d 1999 8m 8.3d* 8.1d⁴ 8.1d* 8.1m⁶ 8d Oct 9] rangy filly: fairly useful handicapper: won at Windsor in April and Haydock in August: stiffish tasks in listed races last 2 starts: stayed 1m well: won on good to firm, but better form on good/good to soft ground: usually held up: stud. *J. L. Dunlop*

SWEET REWARD   4 ch.g. Beveled (USA) – Sweet Revival 41 (Claude Monet   **79** (USA) 121) [1998 81: 7.5s³ 8g 10.4d⁶ 8.1s³ 8s³ 8.2g⁵ 8.1g 10d 8d 1999 9.7v² 8g² 7.5v 10m³ 8v³ 8.9d Oct 9] leggy, short-backed gelding: shows knee action: fair handicapper: stays 1¼m: acts on good to firm and heavy going: not an easy ride. *J. G. Smyth-Osbourne*

SWEET ROSIE (IRE)   4 b.f. Petardia 113 – White's Pet (Mummy's Pet 125)   **–** [1998 NR 1999 a7g⁶ 6d 6d a8g Dec 6] disappointing maiden. *P. Mitchell*

SWEET SENORITA   4 b.f. Young Senor (USA) 113 – Sweet N' Twenty 74   **51** (High Top 131) [1998 –: 7m 10f⁶ 16.4f⁶ 11.5g 1999 10g⁶ 11.6m² 11.9f* Jul 22] poor performer: landed odds in selling handicap at Brighton (sold 7,200 gns) final start: stays 1½m: raced only on good going or firmer: won 4 times over hurdles for M. Pipe between August and December. *M. Madgwick*

SWEET SERENATA   4 gr.f. Keen 116 – Serenata (Larringa 97) [1998 51, a43:   **44** a9.4g⁴ 7v 10g 12d 14.1g⁴ 16.2g 16m 10m⁵ 13.8m* a13g⁴ 1999 a16g² a16f⁶ a13g⁶ 13d³ 11.5f⁴ 14.1g⁶ Jul 3] poor performer: effective at 1½m to easy 2m: acts on good to firm going, good to soft and equitrack: often races prominently: sold 4,400 gns, joined M. Sowersby. *S. C. Williams*

SWEET SORROW (IRE)   4 b.f. Lahib (USA) 129 – So Long Boys (FR) (Bel-   **100** dale Flutter (USA) 130) [1998 84: 8d³ 8.3g³ 10m³ 10g³ 10.5s³ 1999 10m² 10d* 12m* 12m⁵ 11.9g³ 12g⁴ 12s⁴ 10d⁵ Oct 14] big, useful-looking filly: useful performer: won maiden at Ayr in May and minor event at Goodwood in June, both in small fields: best efforts in listed races after when in frame, third at York (behind Innuendo), and fourth at Chantilly and Ascot (behind Signorina Cattiva): will stay beyond 1½m: acts on soft and good to firm ground. *C. F. Wall*

SWEET TEDDY   2 b.f. (Feb 14) Namaqualand (USA) – Nashville Blues (IRE)   **66** 94 (Try My Best (USA) 130) [1999 5g⁵ 6g⁵ 6m⁴ Jul 10] big, leggy filly: third foal: half-sister to 4-y-o Francesca's Folly and 3-y-o No Mercy: dam, 7f/1m winner, not one to trust implicitly: fair form in maidens at Sandown, Goodwood (carried head awkwardly) and York, sweating freely on last-named course: bred to stay 1m. *J. W. Hills*

SWEET TRENTINO (IRE)   8 b.g. High Estate 127 – Sweet Adelaide (USA)   **46** 98 (The Minstrel (CAN) 135) [1998 –: 10v 8m 12m 10.8d 8.1m 1999 a12g⁴ a16.2g⁶ Jul 23] compact gelding: poor nowadays: seems to stay 2m: tried blinkered: won over hurdles in August. *M. Tate*

SWEET WILHELMINA   6 b.m. Indian Ridge 123 – Henpot (IRE) 68 (Alzao (USA) 117) [1998 87: 7s² 8s a8g² 7m* 8g² 8.5d 8.5m 8g⁶ 7g 8g a8g 1999 a8g* 8.3m⁶ 7m* Aug 13] sturdy mare: fairly useful performer: won handicap at Lingfield in January and minor event at Epsom (second start after 6-month break) in August: stays 1m only when conditions aren't testing: acts on soft going, good to firm and all-weather: sometimes tongue tied: usually held up: reportedly in foal to First Trump. *W. R. Muir*   **87**

SWELL BETTY (IRE)   3 b.f. Distinctly North (USA) 115 – Cambridge Lodge 65 (Tower Walk 130) [1998 63: 5g⁶ 5m⁵ 7m⁶ 6d³ 7g 1999 7s³ 8m³ 7s 8m* 7g² 7m Aug 28] rather leggy, quite good-topped filly: fair performer: improved to win handicap at Salisbury in July: ran well next start, but poorly final one: stays 1m: acts on soft and good to firm going: consistent: sold 7,000 gns. *R. Hannon*   **77**

SWIFT   5 ch.g. Sharpo 132 – Three Terns (USA) (Arctic Tern (USA) 126) [1998 71§: a8g⁴ a7g³ a8g a8g² a8g 8d⁶ 10s⁶ 7.1g⁶ 8.3g³ 7g 7.3g² 7m 8g⁵ 8f 8.1m⁴ 8d² 8g 8.3s⁵ 7.5m 7g 8g⁴ 8s⁴ 8s 8d 1999 a8g⁴ a8f⁵ a9.4g³ a11g² a12g⁵ a11g² a12g* a12g* 12g 10s* 10.8d* 12.3m⁴ 10d⁶ 12m 13.9s* 14m 12g 11.9s 11.9s⁵ 13.8s a14g Nov 12] strong, lengthy gelding: poor mover: fairly useful on all-weather, fair on turf: won at Southwell (twice), Nottingham and Warwick in March/April and at York in May: mostly below best after: effective at 1¼m to 1¾m: acts on all-weather, soft going and probably good to firm: usually held up. *M. J. Polglase*   **73 a84**

SWIFT ALLIANCE   4 b.g. Belong To Me (USA) – One Quick Bid (USA) (Commemorate (USA)) [1998 NR 1999 6g Jun 27] robust gelding: fairly useful at 2 yrs for R. Akehurst: well beaten only 4-y-o start. *Lady Herries*   **–**

SWIFT MAIDEN   6 gr.m. Sharrood (USA) 124 – Gunner Girl 85 (Gunner B 126) [1998 NR 1999 10.2s Oct 26] sturdy mare: fair at 3 yrs: tailed off only start since: should stay further than 1¼m: goes well on soft ground. *J. Neville*   **–**

SWIFTUR   2 b.f. (Mar 6) Snurge 130 – Swift Spring (FR) 56 (Bluebird (USA) 125) [1999 7g Jun 12] 5,000Y: third foal: sister to 3-y-o Son of Snurge and half-sister to fairly useful 11.5f winner Spring Anchor (by Slip Anchor): dam, 7f winner who seemed as effective at 2m, out of close relative to Arc winner April Run: considerably handicapped when well held in maiden at Lingfield: seemed likely to improve. *P. F. I. Cole*   **–**

SWIFTWAY   5 ch.g. Anshan 119 – Solemn Occasion (USA) (Secreto (USA) 128) [1998 56: 14d⁶ 16.2m 16.2d⁵ 16.2g* 16.2m⁴ 16g 1999 16.1d³ 16.2g⁴ Aug 11] tall, plain gelding: modest handicapper: will stay beyond 2m: acts on firm and good to soft going: none too consistent: winning hurdler. *K. W. Hogg, Isle of Man*   **56**

SWING ALONG   4 ch.f. Alhijaz 122 – So It Goes 73 (Free State 125) [1998 84: 7d² 7m 1999 7v³ 6m⁵ 7m 7g 6m⁵ 7g³ 8s 8d⁵ 7d³ a7g* a7g⁶ Dec 29] strong filly: fair handicapper: won at Wolverhampton in November before leaving C. Wall only 1,000 gns: respectable effort final start: best efforts around 7f: acts on good to firm going, heavy and all-weather: has got worked up before start. *R. Guest*   **68 a78**

SWING BALL   4 b.f. Always Fair (USA) 121 – Lady Anchor (Slip Anchor 136) [1998 –: 8.2s 8f 1999 11.8g 8f 11.6m 9.9m Jun 24] sturdy filly: little sign of ability on Flat. *T. R. Watson*   **–**

SWING BAR   6 b.m. Sadeem (USA) 122 – Murex (Royalty 130) [1998 NR 1999 7.7m 6.8m⁴ 8f⁶ 8.3m² 10m⁴ 9.9g* 10m 10m Sep 16] angular, workmanlike mare: fourth foal: half-sister to 2 winning jumpers: dam bumper winner: modest handicapper: won apprentice maiden event at Beverley in August: ran poorly both starts after: will be suited by 1½m: raced only on good going or firmer. *J. M. Bradley*   **59**

SWING CITY (IRE)   2 ch.f. (Jan 9) Indian Ridge 123 – Menominee (Soviet Star (USA) 128) [1999 6d⁴ 6m 5g Sep 26] IR 10,000Y: lengthy filly: third foal: half-sister to 3-y-o Touch 'n' Fly and 4-y-o Count de Money: dam unraced half-sister to very smart French middle-distance stayer Mersey and smart French middle-distance filly Muncie: modest form in maidens: should stay 1m: tends to race freely. *R. Guest*   **58**

SWINGING THE BLUES (IRE)   5 b.g. Bluebird (USA) 125 – Winsong Melody (Music Maestro 119) [1998 73: 8f³ 8.3d 8g² 8.2m* 8m³ 8g³ 8g² 9d* 8.2v 1999 10s 8.3m 8g 8.2m⁶ 10.1m 8.2m 10m⁴ 8d 9g* 10d² Nov 1] useful-looking gelding: modest handicapper: dropped in weights before winning at Redcar in   **62**

October for second successive year: ran well there final start: stays 1¼m: acts on good to firm and good to soft going: tried visored, including last 4 starts: has had tongue tied: often held up. *C. A. Dwyer*

SWINGING TRIO (USA) 2 b.c. (Mar 29) Woodman (USA) 126 – Las Meninas   –
(IRE) 115 (Glenstal (USA) 118) [1999 6m Jul 31] IR 130,000Y: smallish colt: second foal: brother to 3-y-o Stanley Wigfield: dam won 1000 Guineas: last of 9 in maiden at Newmarket. *T. G. Mills*

SWING JOB 3 b.f. Ezzoud (IRE) 126 – Leave Her Be (USA) (Known Fact (USA)   –
135) [1998 57, a47: 6.9f⁵ 7g⁶ 6g⁶ a8g⁶ a8g 1999 a10g a11g 11.5f⁶ 8d Aug 17] maiden: little show in 1999: tried blinkered. *T. G. Mills*

SWING OF THE TIDE 2 b.f. (Feb 9) Sri Pekan (USA) 117 – Rawya (USA) 80   **70**
(Woodman (USA) 126) [1999 5.1g² 6f⁴ 6d Aug 7] 25,000Y: sturdy, quite attractive filly: first foal: dam, 2-y-o 7f winner (later stayed 1¼m), half-sister to useful performer up to 1m Elegant Warning: fair form in maidens at Bath and Goodwood first 2 starts: well held (softer ground) final one: will stay 1m. *J. Berry*

SWINO 5 b.g. Forzando 122 – St Helena (Monsanto (FR) 121) [1998 91: 5g⁵ 5s²   **77 d**
5s* 6.1v⁶ 5.1m 6g* 6g⁴ 5d⁵ 5.1g⁴ 6s 6.1g 5d 6s 6.1g² 6g 7g 6s 1999 6d 6d 6s²   **a61 §**
6d 5.1d⁶ 6d 5f 5m³ 6.1m⁵ 5g 5.1d 7d 5s⁵ 6.1d⁴ 6.1f 6d³ a6g⁴ a6g a8g a6g²
Dec 21] leggy gelding: unimpressive mover: fair handicapper on turf, modest on all-weather: effective at 6f/stiff 5f: below form on heavy going, acts on any other turf and fibresand: sometimes blinkered, usually visored: has carried head awkwardly: inconsistent and not one to trust. *P. D. Evans*

SWISS ALPS (IRE) 2 b.c. (Feb 2) Common Grounds 118 – Lady of Zurich (IRE)   –
(Danehill (USA) 126) [1999 6g Aug 25] IR 11,500Y, resold 15,000Y: first foal: dam French 1¼m winner out of champion US sprinter What A Summer: well held in claimer at Lingfield. *R. W. Armstrong*

SWISS ENSIGN 2 b.c. (Apr 15) Tirol 127 – Rosa Van Fleet (Sallust 134) [1999   **64**
7g³ 7f⁴ 6.1m⁵ 6s⁵ Oct 1] 4,200Y: fifth foal: half-brother to several winners, including 9f (at 2 yrs) and 1½m winner Buddy Marvel (by Law Society) and 9.6f to 11f winner Rossmore Girl (by Scenic), both useful in Ireland: dam, Irish maiden, half-sister to To-Agori-Mou: modest maiden: probably needs 1m+: sold 2,200 gns, sent to Kuwait. *R. Hannon*

SWYNFORD DREAM 6 b.g. Statoblest 120 – Qualitair Dream 80 (Dreams To   **72**
Reality (USA) 113) [1998 62: a5g a5g 5d 5s 5m 5g 5m⁶ 5g⁴ 5f² 5s 5f 5g* 5m⁶ 5d 5g   **a–**
1999 5g* 5d a5g 5g² 5f 5d 5m² 5m⁶ 5f 5m 5m⁶ 5g a5g Nov 19] workmanlike gelding: fair handicapper: won at Musselburgh in April: left T. Etherington after tenth start: raced only at 5f: acts on firm and good to soft ground, only a little sign of ability on all-weather: has given trouble at start: inconsistent. *J. Hetherton*

SWYNFORD ELEGANCE 2 ch.f. (Apr 15) Charmer 123 – Qualitairess 49   –
(Kampala 120) [1999 5m 7s⁶ 5g a6g⁵ a5g Dec 13] 2,200Y: half-sister to 1½m winner Qualitair Pride (by Siberian Express) and 1m to 11.6f winner Swynford Flyer (by Valiyar): dam 1m winner: little form. *J. Hetherton*

SWYNFORD LORD 3 b.g. Formidable (USA) 125 – Princess Lieven (Royal   **33**
Palace 131) [1998 –: 7m 6m 8m⁵ 8d 1999 8m 7.5g⁴ 8m 12m 12.3m⁵ 12m⁵ 10g 8.9m Sep 1] close-coupled gelding: poor maiden: left T. Etherington after sixth start: stays 1½m: acts on good to firm going: tried blinkered/visored. *J. Hetherton*

SWYNFORD PLEASURE 3 b.f. Reprimand 122 – Pleasuring 68 (Good Times   **55 d**
(ITY)) [1998 60: 6d⁴ 8m² 7g² 8v 7d 1999 8f⁵ 7d 8.3g² 9m⁵ 12g 11f³ 12m 11d 8.2s a9.4g Nov 17] angular filly: modest maiden: left T. Etherington after sixth start, then disappointing: stays 9f, possibly not 11f: acts on good to firm and good to soft going: tried blinkered: none too consistent. *J. Hetherton*

SWYNFORD WELCOME 3 b.f. Most Welcome 131 – Qualitair Dream 80   **67 ?**
(Dreams To Reality (USA) 113) [1998 71: 5g² 5g⁴ 5m* 6m³ 6m 5g 6m 1999 6g   **a–**
5f 5.9m 6g 5m 6.1m 5m 6d* a7g a7g a8g a6g Dec 27] good-topped filly: not a good walker: fair handicapper: left T. Etherington after fifth start: form only when winning 18-runner event at Brighton in October by 5 lengths, racing alone far side and making all (possibly flattered): likely to prove best at 5f/6f: acts on good to firm and good to soft going. *J. Pearce*

SYCAMORE LODGE (IRE) 8 ch.g. Thatching 131 – Bell Tower 98 (Lyphard's **73**
Wish (FR) 124) [1998 61, a–: a7g 7d⁵ 5g 6g⁵ 6.9d² 6d³ 6g⁵ 6m² 6d³ 7d⁵ 1999 7g⁴ 6f **a–**
5m⁵ 6g* 7m 6f* 7m* 7f⁶ 7g⁵ 7f 6m 6g Oct 14] strong gelding: fair performer: won
claimer in May (ended 3-year losing sequence) and seller and apprentice handicap in
July, all at Catterick: effective at 6f and had form over 1¼m earlier in career: acts on
firm and soft going (below form on fibresand): bandaged: usually held up, and suited
by strong pace. *D. Nicholls*

SYLPHIDE 4 b.f. Ballet Royal (USA) – Shafayif 43 (Ela-Mana-Mou 132) [1998 **–**
–: a7g a10g a7g 1999 a13g Feb 6] of no account. *H. J. Manners*

SYLVA LEGEND (USA) 3 b.g. Lear Fan (USA) 130 – Likeashot (CAN) (Gun **90 d**
Shot) [1998 ?: 6m 6g⁶ 1999 8m² 9g³ 8.1m 8m 10m⁶ 11.9m 12m³ 12s³ 11.6g⁶ 10d⁴
Oct 29] tall, good-topped gelding: has scope: shows plenty of knee action: fairly
useful maiden: clearly best efforts in 1999 at Kempton and Goodwood (handicap) on
first 2 starts: stays 1½m: acts on soft and good to firm going: seemed ill-at-ease on
track at Epsom seventh start: visored final one. *C. E. Brittain*

SYLVA PARADISE (IRE) 6 b.g. Dancing Dissident (USA) 119 – Brentsville **88**
(USA) (Arctic Tern (USA) 126) [1998 90: 6d 5g 5f³ 6g⁵ 5g⁴ 6g 5.2g 5m³ 5.2g⁴ 5m⁴
5s 1999 5d³ 5.2m⁴ 5s⁶ 5m³ 6d 6m² 5m⁴ 6f⁵ 5m³ 6m⁵ 6.1g 6d Oct 20] smallish, lengthy
gelding: fairly useful handicapper: best at 5f/6f (when conditions aren't testing): acts
on firm and good to soft going: often blinkered/visored. *C. E. Brittain*

SYRAH 3 b.f. Minshaanshu Amad (USA) 91§ – La Domaine 89 (Dominion 123) **–**
[1998 41: 8d a8.5g⁴ a8g⁵ 1999 8.2m 10f a12g 8.3d Nov 4] workmanlike filly: poor
maiden at best. *R. T. Phillips*

T

TAAKID (USA) 4 b.g. Diesis 133 – Tanwi 101 (Vision (USA)) [1998 80: 8v 12d² **57**
10g² 13g⁶ 9g⁶ 12d 9g 9m² 12s³ 10d 8s⁵ 12s 1999 12.3g 12f⁵ 9.9s 11g Oct 14] fourth
foal: half-brother to fairly useful 9f winner Sofyaan (by Silver Hawk) and 7-y-o Fahs:
dam, Irish 5f to 1m winner, from family of Marju and Salsabil: fairly useful maiden
for K. Prendergast in Ireland at 3 yrs: modest at best in Britain: stays 1½m: acts on
firm going, probably on soft. *M. D. Hammond*

TAARISH (IRE) 6 b.g. Priolo (USA) 127 – Strike It Rich (FR) (Rheingold 137) **75 ?**
[1998 NR 1999 11.8g² 14g 14.4m 12d Oct 9] IR 65,000Y: half-brother to several
winners, including Italian Oaks winner Lady Bentley (by Bellypha): dam, Irish
1¼m winner, half-sister to smart stayer Yawa: fairly useful winner in Ireland at 3 yrs
(sold out of D. Weld's stable 26,000 gns): fair at best in handicaps in Britain, leaving
S. Mellor and off 3 months after second start: probably stays 1¾m: yet to race on
extremes of going: blinkered in Ireland. *P. Mitchell*

TABARAK (IRE) 3 b.c. Nashwan (USA) 135 – Select Sale (Auction Ring (USA) **61**
123) [1998 NR 1999 10g 8.2d Oct 21] 20,000Y: strong, angular colt: brother to fair
1½m winner Top Shop and half-brother to several winners, notably King Edward
VII Stakes winner Private Tender (by Shirley Heights): dam unraced half-sister to
Ribblesdale winner Queen Midas: blinkered, better effort in maidens (6 months
apart) when seventh of 18 at Nottingham final start, looking less than keen: bred to
need at least 1¼m. *K. Mahdi*

TABAREEH (IRE) 3 b.c. Marju (IRE) 127 – Rosia Bay 102 (High Top 131) **115**
[1998 92p: 8s² 1999 8d* 8.5g 12m⁴ 12m² 11.9s⁵ 12f² 14.1m* 12d⁶ Oct 1] angular,
quite attractive colt: smart performer: won maiden at Doncaster in March and minor
event at Salisbury in September, latter by 3½ lengths from Bryony Brind: ran well
otherwise when runner-up in handicaps at Salisbury and Goodwood (beaten head by
Mary Stuart in Tote Gold Trophy): will stay 2m: acts on firm and good to soft going:
blinkered after second start: sometimes sweating/on toes: has shown signs of temperament. *M. P. Tregoning*

TABASCO (IRE) 4 b.f. Salse (USA) 128 – El Taranda 61 (Ela-Mana-Mou 132) **60**
[1998 64: 8.2s 11.5m⁵ 1999 11.6m 10v 8m² a8g 8.2m May 21] leggy filly: modest
maiden: effective at 1m, probably at 11.5f: acts on good to firm ground: visored final
start. *M. R. Channon*

TABBETINNA BLUE   2 b.f. (Mar 14) Interrex (CAN) – True Is Blue (Gabitat   – p
119) [1999 6d Oct 18] 500Y: leggy, lengthy filly: has a round action: first foal: dam
unraced: seventh of 12 in maiden at Pontefract, leading briefly halfway: should do
better. *J. W. Payne*

TABHEEJ (IRE)   2 ch.f. (Jan 24) Mujtahid (USA) 118 – Abhaaj 91 (Kris 135)   100
[1999 5m* 6g³ 6m* 7s³ Oct 2] big, lengthy, rather unfurnished filly: has plenty of
scope: has a quick, fluent action: fifth foal: sister to useful 1995 2-y-o 5f winner
Mubhij and half-sister to 2 winners, including 1m winner Dalu (by Dancing Brave):
dam, 2-y-o 5f winner who ran once at 3 yrs, out of 5f-winning half-sister to Danzig:
useful form: won maiden at Haydock in May and minor event at Doncaster (by head
from Kier Park) in September: sweating, respectable third of 12 to Agrippina in listed
race at Newmarket final start, headed only inside final 1f: will prove best up to 7f:
acts on good to firm going. *B. W. Hills*

TACHELLE (IRE)   3 b.f. Elbio 125 – Tacheo 64 (Tachypous 128) [1998 NR   –
1999 8m⁵ Jun 26] sister to 4-y-o Happy Days Again and half-sister to 2 winners by
Carmelite House, including 7f winner Vilamar: dam 2-y-o 5f winner, later successful
over hurdles: tailed off in maiden at Newcastle. *E. J. Alston*

TACHYCARDIA   7 ch.m. Weldnaas (USA) 112 – Gold Ducat 74 (Young Gener-   –
ation 129) [1998 –, a45: 5m 8d 6s a6g⁶ a7g⁴ 1999 a6g a6f² a7g a6g a7g Mar 13]   a45
rather sparely-made mare: poor performer: has form at 8.5f, raced mainly up to 7f
nowadays: acts on firm going, soft and all-weather: has run well for 7-lb claimer:
usually a front runner. *N. E. Berry*

TACTFUL REMARK (USA)   3 ch.c. Lord At War (ARG) – Right Word (USA)   103
(Verbatim (USA)) [1998 77p: 8.2m 8m 8s 1999 9g* 9m³ 10.5g⁴ 9m* 9.9f 9m³
Sep 18] strong, attractive colt: useful handicapper: won at Kempton in April and
Newbury (by 6 lengths from Lycian) in July: creditable length third of 7 to Showboat
in minor event at Newbury final start: should stay 1¼m: acts on good to firm ground:
possibly needs to dominate: joined J. Osborne. *J. H. M. Gosden*

TADBEER (USA)   2 ch.c. (Jan 28) Kris S (USA) – Ra'a (USA) 106 (Diesis 133)   79 p
[1999 7g³ 7d⁶ Sep 19] good-topped colt: fifth foal: half-brother to 6f/7f performer
Musafi (by Dayjur), now smart in USA, and fairly useful 6f winner Awayil (by
Woodman): dam sprinter: burly, fair form in maidens at Goodwood (third of 7 to
Nothing Daunted) and Newbury (sixth of 22 to Scarteen Fox, first of those drawn
low): likely to prove best up to 1m: slowly away both starts: should do better.
M. P. Tregoning

TADEO   6 ch.g. Primo Dominie 121 – Royal Passion 78 (Ahonoora 122) [1998   113 d
108: 5g⁴ 5d* 5m³ 6d 5d 5g 6m 6m* 5f³ 5.8s⁶ 1999 5m² 5g 5m⁶ 5m 5.1m⁶ 6m⁴ Jul 28]
small, strong gelding: smart performer: better than ever when head second of 18 to
Night Flight in handicap at Haydock on reappearance: well below best final 3 starts,
including in listed races: barely stays 6f: acts on firm and soft going: races up with
pace: game. *B. J. Meehan*

TADREEJ (IRE)   2 b.g. (Feb 5) Fairy King (USA) – Rose Bonbon (FR) (High   78
Top 131) [1999 6d 7m³ a8.5g² Sep 18] 120,000Y: compact gelding: closely related to
French 1¼m winner Marie La Rose (by Night Shift) and half-brother to several
winners, including Irish 1m winner Stopwatch (by Lead On Time): dam, French 13f
winner, half-sister to 3 French Group 1 winners and to the dam of Groom Dancer:
placed in maidens at Leicester (best effort) and Wolverhampton, wandering under
pressure on latter course: should prove suited by 1¼m+. *M. R. Channon*

TAFFS WELL   6 b.g. Dowsing (USA) 124 – Zahiah 90 (So Blessed 130) [1998   86
80: 6d 6v⁵ 8d² 8d⁵ 8.1g⁶ 8.9s 7m⁶ 8g 7.9m 8g 7.6g 9d 6v² 1999 6.1v 6v 7.1m* 7.6m*
7m² 8.1g* 7.1m 8m* 8m³ 8f 8m 7.1m 8d 8.9d⁶ 8.2d 7s⁶ Nov 2] small gelding: fairly
useful handicapper: won at Musselburgh in April, Chester and Haydock in May and
Newcastle in June: generally below form in second half of season: has form at 6f
(given test), raced mostly at 7f/1m: acts on good to firm and heavy going: often held
up. *B. Ellison*

TAGADOO (IRE)   2 b.c. (Apr 22) Desse Zenny (USA) – Conquering Kate (IRE)   –
(Conquering Hero (USA) 116) [1999 6d 7.5g 7s Sep 29] IR 1,600Y: small,
sparely-made colt: first foal: dam unraced: little sign of ability. *B. S. Rothwell*

Prix du Cadran Casino Croisette Barriere, Longchamp—Tajoun wins his fourth pattern race, staying on too strongly for San Sebastian, Divination and Invermark

TAHSEEN (USA) 2 b.f. (Jan 30) Hansel (USA) – Aljawza (USA) 86 (Riverman **54** (USA) 131) [1999 6m⁶ Aug 29] second foal: closely related to fairly useful 1998 2-y-o 6f winner Ishtihar (by Woodman): dam, Irish 2-y-o 6f winner, half-sister to 1994 Cheveley Park winner Gay Gallanta and very smart Irish 1¼m performer Sportsworld: sixth of 11 in maiden at Goodwood: dead. *M. P. Tregoning*

TAI TAI 3 b.f. Mujtahid (USA) 118 – Duwon (IRE) 55 (Polish Precedent (USA) **–** 131) [1998 –: 7m 1999 10m 10m 11.5m⁶ 10d Oct 11] rather leggy filly: no form. *M. Blanshard*

TAJAR (USA) 7 b.g. Slew O'Gold (USA) – Mashaarif (USA) (Mr Prospector **58 §** (USA) 55: 11.8g 10.5m³ 11.6m 10g* 10m 11.9d 10.8m* 10m³ 12g 9.9m 1999 10.3d 10s² 10m 11.6m* 10.2g 10m³ 11.6m⁵ 12.3g 10.4f⁶ 10m 12m³ 11.5g Oct 19] angular gelding: modest handicapper: won 20-runner race at Windsor in May: effective at 1¼m to 1½m: acts on soft and good to firm going: blinkered twice at 5 yrs: sometimes looks less than keen, and best held up: unreliable. *T. Keddy*

TAJASUR (IRE) 4 ch.g. Imperial Frontier (USA) 112 – Safiya (USA) (Riverman **112** (USA) 131) [1998 98: 6s² 7g³ 1999 6d⁵ 6f* 7m 6d 6s* 6.5s³ Oct 10] strong, lengthy gelding: smart performer, lightly raced: won rated stakes at Newbury (by ¾ length from Harmonic Way) in July and minor event at Hamilton in September: also ran well when ¾-length third to Tomba in Group 3 event at Munich (best form around 6f: yet to race on heavy going, acts on any other: joined I. Allan in Hong Kong. *J. L. Dunlop*

TAJMIL (IRE) 4 ch.f. Wolfhound (USA) 126 – Nouvelle Star (AUS) (Luskin **–** Star (AUS)) [1998 62: 6d 7m 8f⁴ 7m 7m⁵ 7m 7m² 7m 7s⁶ a7g 1999 6.1s⁵ 7s May 10] sturdy, angular filly: good walker: has a round action: modest maiden handicapper: stays 7f: acts on good to firm going: tried visored: none too consistent: sent to New Zealand. *D. Morris*

TAJOUN (FR) 5 b.g. General Holme (USA) 128 – Taeesha (Mill Reef (USA) **117** 141) [1998 117: 15.5s* 15.5s* 15.5m* 15d³ 1999 15.5d* 15.5g² 15.5d² 20m 15.5m* 20v* 15.5v² Oct 24] tall, angular gelding: has a round action: smart performer: won listed race at Maisons-Laffitte in April, Prix Gladiateur at Longchamp (by length from Pozarica) in September and Prix du Cadran Casino Croisette Barriere at Longchamp (by neck from San Sebastian) in October: ran poorly in Gold Cup at Royal Ascot fourth start but runner-up in pattern events at Longchamp on other outings, beaten 1½ lengths by Amilynx in Prix Royal-Oak final one: stays 2½m: acts on good to firm and heavy ground: not the most straightforward of rides (tends to hang and idle) and best held up: stays in training. *A. de Royer Dupre, France*

TAKE ACTION (IRE) 2 b.c. (Apr 30) Shalford (IRE) 124§ – Action Belle **41** (Auction Ring (USA) 123) [1999 5.7m 8.2m⁵ 8.1m 7.7d 10s Oct 5] 3,400F: smallish, good-bodied colt: unimpressive mover: half-brother to 3 winners, including 1988 2-y-o 5f/6f winner Holster (by Gorytus) and 6-y-o Batoutoftheblue: dam, maiden, sister to 1000 Guineas runner-up Meis El-Reem, herself dam of 4-y-o Princely Heir:

form only when seventh of 16 in nursery at Nottingham final start: will stay 1½m+. *F. Jordan*

TAKE A TURN   4 br.g. Forzando 122 – Honeychurch (USA) 93 (Bering 136)   –
[1998 79: a7g³ 7d 9v² 8s⁵ 9d⁶ a8g 8d⁶ 8m* a8.5g⁴ 9.7f⁵ 8.5s³ 9.9m⁵ a12g 1999 10g
8.3m 8.3g 8.3m 10.1m Aug 13] smallish gelding: has a quick action: fair handicapper
in 1998: well below form in 1999: stays 1¼m: acts on good to firm ground, heavy
and all-weather: tried blinkered, effective visored or not: possibly none too genuine.
Miss Gay Kelleway

TAKE CARE (IRE)   4 b.f. Treasure Kay 114 – Miss Tuko (Good Times (ITY))   –
[1998 –: 8g 9m⁶ 10m 6d 5g a6g a5g 1999 a7g Jan 4] little form: tried blinkered.
M. H. Tompkins

TAKE FLITE   2 b.c. (Feb 15) Cadeaux Genereux 131 – Green Seed (IRE) 78   **77**
(Lead On Time (USA) 123) [1999 5m⁵ 6m³ 6m 6d³ 7m⁴ Aug 29] 45,000Y: tall,
angular colt: first foal: dam 2-y-o 6f winner, later stayed 10.3f: fair maiden: creditable fourth in nursery at Goodwood final start: should stay 1m: yet to race on
extremes of going. *W. R. Muir*

TAKE MANHATTAN (IRE)   2 b. or br.g. (Mar 18) Hamas (IRE) 125§ – Arab   **50 p**
Scimetar (IRE) (Sure Blade (USA) 130) [1999 5g Sep 26] IR 9,200F, IR 15,000Y:
fifth foal: brother to 3-y-o Mitcham and half-brother to a winner in Germany/Austria
by Jareer: dam unraced: second favourite, eighth of 13 to Jaybird in maiden at Musselburgh, never on terms and tending to edge right: bred to prove best at 5f/6f: should
do better. *M. R. Channon*

TAKER CHANCE   3 b.g. Puissance 110 – Flower Princess (Slip Anchor 136)   **58**
[1998 69d, a–: 6g³ 6g 7.5m⁶ a6g a7g 1999 a7g 8g⁵ 7d⁵ 6v 7.5g* 8m 7.5s⁴ 8s Oct 4]
angular gelding: shows knee action: modest performer: won claimer at Beverley in
August: should prove best up to 1m: acts on soft going: visored last 2 starts: none too
consistent. *J. Hetherton*

TAKHLID (USA)   8 b.h. Nureyev (USA) 131 – Savonnerie (USA) 108 (Irish   **72**
River (FR) 131) [1998 81, a66: a8s a6g⁴ a6g a7g²ᵈⁱˢ a6g³ a8g⁶ 8g² 8g* 8.5d⁴ 8.3s*   **a91**
a8g⁴ 8.5d³ 6m 8m³ a7g⁶ 7m³ 8m 8m 8.3d 7g 8s 1999 a6g² a6g⁶ a8g* a7g* a8g* a6g⁴
a8.5s⁴ a6g* 7.5d a7g* 7m a7g* a7g* a8.5g* 7f⁴ a7f* 7g 9g a7g² a8g³ a6g* a7g* a8g⁶
Dec 17] strong, compact horse: fairly useful on all-weather, fair on turf: had very
successful year, winning 11 of his 23 races, namely at Southwell (handicap and 2
claimers), Lingfield (minor event and amateur handicap) and Wolverhampton (6
claimers, including amateurs): effective at 6f to 8.5f: acts on firm going, soft and all-
weather: tough. *D. W. Chapman*

TALARIA (IRE)   3 ch.f. Petardia 113 – Million At Dawn (IRE) 63 (Fayruz 116)   **82**
[1998 75+: 5m⁴ 5d⁶ 1999 6g⁵ 6m 6m* 6m⁴ 6.1m 5.2g 6.1f Oct 20] rather leggy,
useful-looking filly: fluent mover: fairly useful performer: won maiden at Newmarket in July: seemed to run well in minor event there next start, but well held in
handicaps after: may prove best at 5f/6f: acts on good to firm and good to soft going:
reportedly had a wind infirmity second start, tongue tied after: free-going sort: sold
4,500 gns in December, joined S. Williams. *G. Wragg*

TALAUD (IRE)   3 ch.g. Salse (USA) 128 – Furry Friend (USA) (Bold Bidder)   **72**
[1998 NR 1999 7v 8g⁵ 8.3m 8m⁶ 10f⁶ 8s Sep 29] 36,000Y: half-brother to 1¼m
winner (including at 2 yrs) Thorntoun Estate (by Durgam) and 1990 2-y-o 6f winner
Russian Mink (by L'Emigrant): dam lightly raced: fair maiden: should stay 1¼m:
acts on good to firm going: blinkered final start: reared leaving stalls fourth outing:
sold 2,800 gns, sent to Germany. *I. A. Balding*

TALECA SON (IRE)   4 b.g. Conquering Hero (USA) 116 – Lady Taleca (IRE)   **44**
49 (Exhibitioner 111) [1998 53: 8v 9s⁴ 10s 12m 8g⁵ 8m⁵ 9.6g 9m 8g⁵ 9m 8g² 8.5s 7d
9g³ 9d 8v 1999 9m 8m 7g³ 7f 7m 8g⁴ 8m⁴ 8.5f 7.8m 9m⁶ 7s³ 9g 9.5g⁵ a12g a12g⁴
a11g³ a12g⁴ Dec 21] smallish gelding: first foal: dam maiden who should have stayed
further than 6f: poor maiden handicapper: left P. Matthews in Ireland after thirteenth
start: will prove best up to 1½m: acts on good to firm going, soft and fibresand:
sometimes blinkered in Ireland. *D. Carroll*

TALENTS LITTLE GEM   2 b.f. (Jun 6) Democratic (USA) 101 – Le Saule   **48 ?**
d'Or 70 (Sonnen Gold 121) [1999 5.3f⁶ 5m a6g 6d³ a6g a7g Dec 8] third live foal: **a–**

dam, 2-y-o 1m winner, stayed 1¼m: poor maiden: trained on debut by R. Simpson. *V. Soane*

TALES OF BOUNTY (IRE)   4 b.g. Ela-Mana-Mou 132 – Tales of Wisdom 70   **68**
(Rousillon (USA) 133) [1998 68: 10.2s⁶ 10m 12s 12g³ 11.6m 12m⁴ 11.7v³ 1999 12m
14m⁶ 17.2g⁶ Jun 12] lengthy gelding: fair maiden handicapper: should stay beyond
1¾m: acts on good to firm ground, possibly not soft: inconsistent: won over hurdles
in November. *D. R. C. Elsworth*

TALIB (USA)   5 b.g. Silver Hawk (USA) 123 – Dance For Lucy (USA) (Dance   **– §**
Bid (USA) 114) [1998 65: 12.4d² 10.8m 11.6d* 11.5m 12g 1999 a12s a10g 11.6d⁵
11.9f 13g 12g⁵ 14m 18.7m⁶ a14.8g 14d⁶ 15.8d a16.2g Dec 15] tall gelding: fair
winner at 4 yrs: very disappointing in 1999, leaving P. Mitchell after fourth start: has
worn tongue strap: difficult ride, and not to be trusted. *P. W. Hiatt*

TA-LIM   4 b.c. Ela-Mana-Mou 132 – Alkaffeyeh (IRE) (Sadler's Wells (USA)   **110**
132) [1998 116: 11.8m³ 12g* 10m⁶ 13.9f⁴ 14m* 14.6m⁵ 1999 12m³ 13.9s 16f⁴ 18m⁵
16.1d Oct 29] strong, lengthy colt: smart performer: best efforts in 1999 in Jockey
Club Stakes at Newmarket (1½ lengths third to Silver Patriarch), Goodwood Cup
(6½ lengths fourth to Kayf Tara) and Doncaster Cup (5¼ lengths fifth to Far Cry):
effective at 1½m to 2¼m: acts on firm going, well beaten on softer than good: visored
final start: has worn rope halter for stalls entry. *Sir Michael Stoute*

TALLULAH   2 b.f. (May 25) Puissance 110 – Dame de L'Oise (USA) (Riverman   **–**
(USA) 131) [1999 a6g⁶ Jun 16] 2,200F, 500Y: third foal: dam ran once at 2 yrs in
France: very slowly away when tailed off in seller. *N. P. Littmoden*

TALLULAH BELLE   6 b.m. Crowning Honors (CAN) – Fine A Leau (USA) 51   **77**
(Youth (USA) 135) [1998 75, a83: a9.4g² 10d a10g* 10m³ 12g⁶ a9.4g³ 10.2g 10m⁴   **a92**
9.9m² 9d* 10.1m⁴ 10.1f* 9m 1999 a9.4g² a9.4g² a10g³ a10g⁵ a8.5g⁴ a10g³ a12g*
11.6m⁶ 11.9f² 9.2d* 10g a9.4g* 9.9m⁶ 9.2f³ 9f² 9f 10d 10s 10d 10d a12g³ a8.5g⁶
a9.4g* a10g⁵ a9.4g Dec 11] smallish mare: fairly useful on all-weather, fair on turf:
won minor event at Lingfield in April and handicaps at Hamilton in May and Wolverhampton in June and November: effective at 8.5f to easy 1½m: acts on all-weather,
firm and good to soft going: visored once at 3 yrs: tough. *N. P. Littmoden*

TALLYWHACKER   2 b.f. (Mar 14) Bon Secret (IRE) 71 – Nomadic Rose 45   **–**
(Nomination 125) [1999 6.1g a7g Dec 15] first reported foal: dam winning hurdler:
well beaten in maiden and seller. *T. J. Naughton*

TAMARA   3 b.f. Marju (IRE) 127 – Ivory Palm (USA) 93 (Sir Ivor 135) [1998 83:   **–**
5d 5d* 5d 6m² 7m 7g 1999 8m Aug 6] fairly useful at 2 yrs: no show in minor event
at Salisbury only 3-y-o start: should stay 1m+: acts on good to firm and good to soft
going: sold 5,400 gns. *J. D. Bethell*

TAMARAN (IRE)   2 br.c. (May 26) Doyoun 124 – Tamarzana (IRE) (Lear Fan   **64**
(USA) 130) [1999 7.6g a8.5g⁵ Sep 18] sturdy colt: second foal: half-brother to a
winner in Austria by Ezzoud: dam French 7f winner: modest form in maidens at
Lingfield and Wolverhampton, still not fully wound up on second occasion: should
stay at least 1m: sold 10,000 gns, sent to Sweden. *Sir Michael Stoute*

TAMASHAN   3 b.c. Puissance 110 – Wild Truffes (IRE) (Danehill (USA) 126)   **–**
[1998 NR 1999 a8g 8.3m⁶ 10.1g a8.5g Sep 4] 17,000Y: lengthy colt: first foal: dam
behind all 4 starts: little form. *G. C. H. Chung*

TAMBOURINAIRE (IRE)   2 gr.g. (Feb 6) Kendor (FR) 122 – Rotina (FR)   **83**
(Crystal Glitters (USA) 127) [1999 6d³ 6m³ 6m Jul 7] 230,000 francs Y: big, angular
gelding: third living foal: brother to French 1997 2-y-o 9f winner Rendorina: dam
placed at 10.5f in France: encouraging third of 16 to Mount Abu in maiden at
Newbury, but disappointing after in minor events at Yarmouth (changed legs and
hung behind winner) and Newmarket (very edgy and finished last after forcing pace):
should stay 1m. *B. J. Meehan*

TAMGEED (USA)   3 ch.f. Woodman (USA) 126 – Toujours Elle (USA) (Lyphard   **66**
(USA) 132) [1998 –: 6m 7v⁶ 1999 7s⁶ 7d² 10.1g⁶ 10f³ 11.9d 13.1f⁵ Sep 6] strong
filly: fair maiden handicapper: may prove best at 1¼m/1½m: acts on firm going,
probably on good to soft: blinkered after reappearance: sent to USA. *J. L. Dunlop*

TAMING (IRE)   3 ch.g. Lycius (USA) 124 – Black Fighter (USA) 79 (Secretariat   **86**
(USA)) [1998 81p: 7m⁵ 8.2d³ 1999 12m* Jul 14] tall, leggy, close-coupled gelding:

fairly useful form: won maiden at Kempton by 3½ lengths from First Cut, settling better than at 2 yrs: stays 1½m: sold 36,000 gns, joined D. Bridgwater. *H. R. A. Cecil*

TAMMAM (IRE)   3 b.c. Priolo (USA) 127 – Bristle 96 (Thatch (USA) 136) [1998 75: 6m² 6.1g³ 7.1m³ 7m³ 1999 10.3m* 9g⁵ 9.9s³ 10.3d⁴ Aug 20] good-bodied colt: useful performer: won maiden at Chester in May: ran creditably next 2 starts: stays 1¼m: acts on soft and good to firm going: blinkered final start: sold 22,000 gns, joined Mrs L. Stubbs. *B. Hanbury*   **97**

TANCRED ARMS   3 b.f. Clantime 101 – Mischievous Miss 73 (Niniski (USA) 125) [1998 59: 5d⁶ 5g 6g 5s² 5m⁶ 6g⁶ 5d 6d² 6s² 6s⁶ 1999 a8g a6g³ 7g 6d² 6m 6g⁵ 6m 6f 5.9m 6m⁵ 6g* 6g 6f 6g 6m a6g Sep 28] sturdy filly: fair handicapper: won at Catterick in July: stays 6f: easily best efforts on good going or softer: tends to hang: usually races prominently: visored final start: inconsistent. *D. W. Barker*   **73 ?** **a45**

TANCRED MISCHIEF   8 b.m. Northern State (USA) 91 – Mischievous Miss 73 (Niniski (USA) 125) [1998 44: 13.8d⁶ 21.6s 16d 13.8d⁵ 13.8g 16m⁵ 15.8m⁶ 15.8d 17.1d⁴ 18s* 16s 1999 15.8g Jul 1] small mare: poor handicapper: stays 2¼m: acts on soft and good to firm ground: blinkered last 4 starts at 7 yrs. *D. W. Barker*   **–**

TANCRED TIMES   4 ch.f. Clantime 101 – Mischievous Miss 73 (Niniski (USA) 125) [1998 69, a52: 10v 7.5m 6s⁴ 5.9d³ 6g⁴ 5m 5m⁵ 5.9d* 5m² 6f³ 6g 6m 6d³ 5s a6g³ a5g⁴ a6g a5g⁵ 1999 a7g⁴ a5g a7g 7s 6s 7f 8f 5.9g 7.6m 5m² 5f² 6f⁶ 6g⁵ 5s a6g² a6g⁶ Dec 6] small, sparely-made filly: modest on turf, poor on all-weather: left J. Cullinan after eighth start: has won at 7f, raced mainly at 5f/6f: acts on good to firm going, soft and all-weather: tried blinkered: often a front runner. *D. W. Barker*   **52** **a49**

TANGERINE   2 ch.f. (Jan 9) Primo Dominie 121 – Sweet Jaffa 73§ (Never So Bold 135) [1999 6g 6m 5.7d* 7g Oct 16] lengthy filly: good walker: third foal: half-sister to 3-y-o Pelargonium: dam untrustworthy 7f winner: form only when winning 17-runner maiden at Bath in September: should stay 7f: acts on good to soft going. *B. W. Hills*   **70 +**

TANGO (IRE)   4 b.c. Dancing Dissident (USA) 119 – Tunguska 76 (Busted 134) [1998 87: a8g⁵ 6d 6m* 6g² 6g 6f 7g 1999 8.1m 6d Aug 6] leggy, close-coupled colt: has a quick action: fairly useful at 3 yrs for R. Hannon: no show both 4-y-o starts: should stay 7f: acts on good to firm going. *K. C. Bailey*   **–**

TANGO MAN (IRE)   7 ch.g. King Luthier 113 – Amour Libre (He Loves Me 120) [1998 NR 1999 11.7m Jul 15] no form on Flat: poor winning hurdler. *J. G. M. O'Shea*   **–**

TANIMBAR (IRE)   4 b.g. Persian Bold 123 – Try My Rosie 93 (Try My Best (USA) 130) [1998 49: 7d 6m 8.2g 7s⁵ 8f⁴ 1999 8d 8f 10m 11.9s Sep 29] close-coupled gelding: poor maiden: left D. Haydn Jones and off 3 months after second start: probably stays 1¼m: acts on firm ground, probably on soft: blinkered (ran well)/visored once each: has carried head awkwardly. *G. L. Moore*   **40**

TANKERSLEY   4 ch.g. Timeless Times (USA) 99 – Busted Love (Busted 134) [1998 89: 7d² 7d* 8d 10.3f⁶ 10.3m² 11.9f 12g 1999 7m 10f* 11.9f⁵ 9.9m⁴ 10.3m 12.3d 8v 10.4g 10d⁵ Oct 26] lengthy, workmanlike gelding: fairly useful performer: won handicap at Nottingham in June: generally below form after: stays 1¼m: acts on firm and good to soft ground: visored penultimate start: has been bandaged: tends to carry head high under pressure. *P. W. D'Arcy*   **83 d**

TANNENKONIG (IRE)   4 b.c. Fairy King (USA) – Tannenalm (GER) (Luciano) [1998 111: 8s* 8g³ 10g³ 8g⁴ 8d² 8g⁴ 8d² 8s⁶ 7s² 1999 8v 7d 8g May 30] half-brother to winners in Germany by Windwurf and Local Suitor: dam German 6f and 1m winner: smart performer at 3 yrs, in frame in 7 pattern races after winning maiden at Munich, including third to Tiger Hill in Mehl-Mulhens-Rennen at Cologne: below form in 1999, including in valuable event at Goodwood second start: effective at 7f to 1¼m: acted on soft ground: stud. *W. Kujath, Germany*   **98**

TANSHAN   4 ch.g. Anshan 119 – Nafla (FR) (Arctic Tern (USA) 126) [1998 71: 8g⁴ 10.8s³ 9g⁴ 7.6m 1999 10s 10f⁶ 12m⁵ 11.4m 10m⁴ Jul 17] good-bodied gelding: modest maiden: stays easy 1½m: acts on soft and good to firm going. *R. Rowe*   **62**

TANTALUS   2 ch.c. (Feb 20) Unfuwain (USA) 131 – Water Quest (IRE) (Rainbow Quest (USA) 134) [1999 7d² Oct 27] first foal: dam unraced half-sister to Grand   **91 p**

Criterium and Dante winner Tenby: 13/2, promising second of 12 to Fast Track in maiden at Yarmouth, short of room then staying on strongly: will stay at least 1¼m: sure to improve and win races. *B. W. Hills*

TANTISPER 3 ch.g. Anshan 119 – Fine Asset (Hot Spark 126) [1998 –: 8v⁵ a7g a8g 1999 a11g⁵ Dec 17] leggy gelding: poor maiden: stays 11f. *Mrs A. Duffield* **34**

TANUSIUS 3 b.c. Warning 136 – Tanz (IRE) 79 (Sadler's Wells 132) [1998 75: 7g² 7g³ 8d⁵ 1999 12d³ 11.9d² 12m 14g² 12f³ Jul 11] quite attractive colt: fairly useful maiden: stays 1¾m: acts on firm and good to soft going: sent to UAE. *C. E. Brittain* **86**

TAOISTE 6 b.h. Kris 135 – Tenue de Soiree (USA) 120 (Lyphard (USA) 132) [1998 85: 5m 6g⁴ 5s² 6g² 5f 7m 1999 6g Apr 5] good-bodied horse: fairly useful at 5 yrs: well held only 6-y-o start: effective at 5f/6f, not 7f: acts on soft and good to firm going: blinkered (too free) once at 5 yrs: usually bandaged. *M. S. Saunders* **–**

TAP 2 b.c. (May 29) Emarati (USA) 74 – Pubby 73 (Doctor Wall 107) [1999 7d² Oct 12] half-brother to 7f winner Nellie Dean (by Song) and 7f (at 2 yrs) to 2m winner Landlord (by Be My Chief): dam 1¼m to 1¾m winner: shaped quite well when 10 lengths second of 15 to easy winner Misraah in maiden at Leicester, disputing lead much of way: should stay 1m: should improve. *J. A. R. Toller* **70 p**

TAPAGE (IRE) 3 b.g. Great Commotion (USA) 123 – Irena (Bold Lad (IRE) 133) [1998 85: 7s a7g* a7g² 1999 8f⁵ 8.2m² a8.5g⁵ 8g² 7d 8m 8m a7g a10g a10g³ a9.4g Nov 17] fair performer: left W. Muir after fifth start: stays 1m: acts on equitrack and good to firm going, probably on soft: blinkered once: has pulled hard. *Andrew Reid* **71 d**

TAPAUA (IRE) 3 b.g. Common Grounds 118 – Tap The Line (Tap On Wood 130) [1998 NR 1999 6d⁵ 10.1m 8s 5.9g² 6.1m 7m 6.1g 7m³ 7g 8.2g a7g⁴ a6g Dec 17] 7,000Y, 8,200 2-y-o: leggy, short-backed gelding: brother to fairly useful 1995 2-y-o 5f winner Hear The Music, later successful in USA, and to a winner in Japan, and half-brother to 2 winners, including 7f (at 2 yrs) and 2½m winner Southern Power (by Midyan): dam French middle-distance winner: modest maiden: stays 7f: acts on good to firm going and fibresand: blinkered last 3 starts. *M. Dods* **59 d**

TARA HALL 3 b.f. (Mar 28) Saddlers' Hall (IRE) 126 – Katie Scarlett 70 (Loch-nager 132) [1999 7d 6f a7g a8.5g 7.7d⁵ 8d Oct 18] smallish, close-coupled filly: fourth foal: half-sister to 3-y-o Scarlett's Boy and 6-y-o Antarctic Storm: dam 1¼m and hurdles winner: poor maiden on balance of form: should stay beyond 1m: blinkered (stiff task and probably flattered) penultimate start. *N. P. Littmoden* **?**

TARA (IRE) 3 br.f. Petardia 113 – Genzyme Gene 38 (Riboboy (USA) 124) [1998 41: a5g⁶ a5g 6g a7g 6m⁴ 8g 5g 1999 a7g a7g Jan 12] close-coupled filly: little sign of ability: tried blinkered. *K. T. Ivory* **–**

TARAJAN (USA) 7 ch.g. Shahrastani (USA) 135 – Tarafa 93 (Akarad (FR) 130) [1998 NR 1999 16d⁵ Jun 28] third foal: brother to useful Irish 9f winner Tarakana who stayed 1½m: dam 1½m winner: lightly raced on Flat: useful (stayed 1½m) for J. Oxx at 3 yrs: no form at 4/5 yrs for P. Prendergast (blinkered once) and well beaten only start in 1999: winning jumper. *Miss Lucinda V. Russell* **–**

TARA'S GIRL (IRE) 2 b.f. (Mar 31) Fayruz 116 – Florissa (FR) (Persepolis (FR) 127) [1999 5s² 5m* 5d 5d* 5m⁴ 6m 6g 5d² 5d Oct 9] IR 6,600Y: leggy, useful-looking filly: progressed well physically: sixth foal: sister to fair 5f (at 2 yrs) to 7f winner Santa Faye and half-sister to 3-y-o Haystacks and a winner in Belgium by Common Grounds: dam French 2-y-o 7f winner: useful performer: won maiden at Beverley in April and minor event there in June: creditable efforts after in frame in Queen Mary Stakes at Royal Ascot and listed race (4 lengths second of 10 to Khasayl) at Ayr: should stay 6f: acts on soft and good to firm ground. *J. J. Quinn* **95**

TARAWAN 3 ch.g. Nashwan (USA) 135 – Soluce 98 (Junius (USA) 124) [1998 76p: 7m 7g 7d² 1999 8s² 8m⁵ 9.9m⁶ 9m² 9.9g⁴ 10m² 8m³ 8.3s² 8g² 8g* 8m² 8.1s*⁵ 8g Oct 16] strong, long-backed gelding: fairly useful performer: won maiden at Newcastle (made all) in August and handicap at Sandown in October: effective at 1m/1¼m: acts on soft and good to firm going: blinkered sixth start, visored after next: effective from front or held up: consistent. *I. A. Balding* **94**

TAR BABY   4 b.f. Handsome Sailor 125 – Queen of Aragon 76 (Aragon 118)   –
[1998 –: 7.1m 7d a7g 1999 a11g⁶ a11g Feb 5] lengthy, unfurnished filly: no form in
maidens: sold 700 gns. *R. Hollinshead*

TARCOOLA   2 ch.c. (Feb 3) Pursuit of Love 124 – Miswaki Belle (USA) 73   **61 p**
(Miswaki (USA) 124) [1999 6m 6v⁴ Oct 23] 4,200Y: tall, quite attractive colt: first
foal: dam, second over 7f on only start, closely related to smart performer up to 1m
Dazzle: backward, showed ability in maidens at Newbury: should prove suited by 7f/
1m: type to do better in long term. *V. Soane*

TARIYFA (IRE)   3 b.f. Bigstone (IRE) 126 – Tarafa 93 (Akarad (FR) 130)   **86**
[1998 NR 1999 10.2d² 10.5s* Sep 24] half-sister to several winners in Ireland,
including 9f winner Tarakana and 7-y-o Tarajan, both useful performers by Shahrastani: dam 1½m winner: runner-up in maiden at Chepstow before landing odds in
similar race at Haydock 4 months later (flashed tail): would have stayed 1½m: dead.
Sir Michael Stoute

TARPON TALE (IRE)   2 b.g. (Apr 27) Mujadil (USA) 119 – Lady of The Mist   –
(IRE) 46 (Digamist (USA) 110) [1999 5.1s 5m 6.1m⁵ Aug 9] 8,800Y: first foal: dam
poor maiden: well beaten, including in seller. *Mrs A. L. M. King*

TARRADALE   5 br.g. Interrex (CAN) – Encore L'Amour (USA) § (Monteverdi   **56**
129) [1998 50: 9.3s 8m⁴ 8.3d* 8m² 9.1d⁶ 12.1d⁵ 10.1v 8s² a10g³ a10f a10g⁵ 1999   **a35**
a8g a8g⁶ 9.2v² 9.2v 8d 9f² 8f³ 8.1d 8.2g³ 10.4f 8d² 8d³ 8g Nov 3] heavy-topped, plain
gelding: modest handicapper: effective at 1m to easy 1¼m: acts on any turf going and
equitrack (no show only run on fibresand): has hung. *C. B. B. Booth*

TARRIFA (IRE)   2 ch.f. (Apr 29) Mujtahid (USA) 118 – Gibraltar Heights (High
Top 131) [1999 8.3d Oct 28] 6,200F, 12,000Y: fourth foal: dam unraced half-sister to
Prix de la Foret winner Brocade, herself dam of Barathea: always behind in Windsor
maiden. *J. G. Smyth-Osbourne*

TARRY FLYNN (IRE)   5 br.g. Kenmare (FR) 125 – Danzig Lass (USA) (Danzig   **117**
(USA)) [1998 97: 8v* 7s² 9v² 1999 8s 7m* 6g* 7g* 6m 7d⁴ 7d* Oct 9] third foal:
half-brother to 3 winners, including Irish 13f winner Any Dream (by Shernazar):
dam Irish 2-y-o 6f winner: improved into smart performer in 1999, winning handicaps at Leopardstown (2) and the Curragh in April/May and 6-runner Coolmore Stud
Home of Champions Concorde Stakes at Cork (made all, comfortably by 1½ lengths
from Late Night Out) in October: also ran very well when fourth to Trans Island in
valuable handicap at Leopardstown: has won at 9.6f, best around 7f: acts on good to
firm and heavy ground: usually blinkered nowadays. *D. K. Weld, Ireland*

TARSKI   5 ch.g. Polish Precedent (USA) 131 – Illusory 81 (Kings Lake (USA)   **63**
133) [1998 –: 8.1g 8m⁶ 8g 9.9g 9d 12m 8s 1999 8g 12g⁶ 9d² 9.9m* 10.2m² 9g 9g³
10.1m⁶ 9.9v⁵ 10.2s Oct 26] sturdy gelding: modest handicapper: won at Goodwood
in June: effective at 9f/1¼m: acts on good to firm and good to soft going: blinkered
once: held up. *L. G. Cottrell*

TARTAN ISLAND (IRE)   2 b.g. (Apr 19) Turtle Island (IRE) 123 – Welsh Harp
(Mtoto 134) [1999 6d 5s 6g Oct 14] IR 5,500Y: first foal: dam unraced daughter of
half-sister to Poule d'Essai des Poulains winner Recitation: towards rear in maidens.
I. Semple

TARTAN LASS   4 b.f. Selkirk (USA) 129 – Gwiffina 87 (Welsh Saint 126) [1998   **86**
71: 7d⁵ 6.1d 1999 6.1g* 6.1g* 6m 7f 6s* 6v 6d 6d a6g Nov 30] big, angular filly:
fairly useful handicapper: easily best efforts when winning at Chepstow (maiden
event) in June and Kempton (22 ran) in September: likely to prove best at 6f: acts on
soft going: has worn tongue strap: none too consistent. *R. Guest*

TARXIEN   5 b.g. Kendor (FR) 122 – Tanz (IRE) 79 (Sadler's Wells (USA) 132)   **86**
[1998 94: 12s³ 12g³ 14d* 13.3g* 13.9s⁴ 14g* 14g 12m⁵ 13.9f 11.9m 13.1v⁴ 1999
16g⁴ 16m Apr 16] deep-girthed gelding: poor mover: fairly useful handicapper:
better effort in 1999 on reappearance: may prove best at 1½m/1¾m: acts on good to
firm and good to soft going, probably on soft. *Mrs Merrita Jones*

TASHANNAH   6 b.m. Sizzling Melody 117 – Liu Liu San (IRE) 44 (Bairn (USA)   –
126) [1998 NR 1999 7m Sep 7] last in maidens/claimer. *P. Butler*

TASKONE 3 ch.f. Be My Chief (USA) 122 – Good As Gold (IRE) 50 (Glint of –
Gold 128) [1998 –: 6s 1999 12d⁵ 12g 14.1f 17.2m 16.2m Jul 19] lengthy, unfurnished
filly: little form: blinkered final start. *R. A. Fahey*

TASTE OF SUCCESS 4 b.c. Thatching 131 – Tastiera (USA) (Diesis 133) –
[1998 –: 7.1m⁴ 1999 a8.5g Sep 18] small colt: fair maiden at best. *P. W. Harris*

TATTENHAM STAR 2 b.c. (Feb 10) Mistertopogigo (IRE) 118 – Candane 73 **63**
(Danehill (USA) 126) [1999 5m 6g 6s⁵ 7g⁶ a6g³ a8g⁵ a7g Dec 18] 500Y: second foal:
dam 1½m winner: modest maiden: stays 1m: acts on equitrack. *M. J. Haynes*

TATTOO 4 b.f. Casteddu 111 – Ebony Park (Local Suitor (USA) 128) [1998 NR –
1999 a8.5g Dec 27] 2,200Y: fourth foal: dam (unraced) from family of Shaamit: last
in Wolverhampton maiden. *K. Mahdi*

TAUFAN BOY 6 b.g. Taufan (USA) 119 – Lydia Maria 70 (Dancing Brave (USA) **68**
140) [1998 72: 14.1v⁵ 14.1s⁴ 14d* 12m⁴ 13.9g² 1999 14.1m⁵ 13.9s⁶ 13.3f 14.1v⁴
16s⁵ Oct 22] quite attractive gelding: has a round action: fair handicapper: should
stay 2m: has form on firm going, possibly best on good or softer nowadays: tried
visored/blinkered earlier in career: has gone in snatches. *G. B. Balding*

TAUREAN 4 b.g. Dilum (USA) 115 – Herora (IRE) 98 (Heraldiste (USA) 121) –
[1998 –: a6g⁶ a8g a8g⁵ 1999 a7g Jun 12] little form. *N. A. Graham*

TAURUS BAY (IRE) 3 b.g. River Falls 113 – Farriers Slipper (Prince Tenderfoot – §
(USA) 126) [1998 –§: 5g 5g 5g⁶ 7g 1999 a8g Feb 22] temperamental and of no
account. *Ronald Thompson*

TAVERNER SOCIETY (IRE) 4 b.c. Imp Society (USA) – Straw Boater 89 –
(Thatch (USA) 136) [1998 101: 10d⁴ 10.3m³ 12g⁶ 10m² 10m⁵ 12s⁵ 12g 12s 1999
10g 10m 7g 11.7m³ Jul 20] strong, close-coupled colt: has a quick action: useful in
1998: little show in 1999 for new trainer: stays 1½m: acts on soft and good to firm
ground: blinkered penultimate start: has worn tongue strap: sometimes pulls hard.
M. S. Saunders

TAWN AGAIN 3 b.g. Then Again 126 – Tawny 81 (Grey Ghost 98) [1998 NR –
1999 a5g⁶ Jan 5] 3,800Y: fourth living foal: half-brother to 4-y-o Angel Hill and
Italian 7.5f and 1¼m winner Patsy Jo (by Absalom): dam 2-y-o 5f/6f winner: not
knocked about in 8-runner maiden at Lingfield. *T. D. Barron*

TAWWAG (IRE) 3 b.g. Shirley Heights 130 – Albertville (USA) 108 (Polish **67**
Precedent (USA) 131) [1998 78: 7f⁵ 1999 10v⁵ 12g⁵ 10.5m 8m⁶ a6.5f Dec 16] sturdy
gelding: good mover: fair maiden: left M. Jarvis before final start: may prove best at
1¼m/1½m: acts on firm going, possibly not heavy: blinkered third and fourth starts.
D. J. Selvaratnam, UAE

TAXI-FOR-ROBBO (IRE) 2 b.f. (Feb 26) Shalford (IRE) 124§ – Miromaid **43**
(Simply Great (FR) 122) [1999 6m 5g³ 6f⁶ 7g Oct 15] third living foal: half-sister to
4-y-o Durgams Delight and Durgams First (both by Durgam): dam placed at 1½m in
Ireland: poor maiden: likely to prove best at 5f/6f. *J. L. Eyre*

TAXMERE 2 ch.f. (Apr 21) Lake Coniston (IRE) 131 – Maculatus (USA) –
(Sharpen Up 127) [1999 7m⁶ 8d Oct 21] 7,200F: fifth foal: half-sister to 3 winners,
including useful 1998 2-y-o sprinter Chomper (by Mujtahid) and 7f winner Nordic
Doll (by Royal Academy): dam, ran twice, from family of high-class sprinter/miler
Golden Opinion: well beaten in maidens. *A. T. Murphy*

TAYIF 3 gr.c. Taufan (USA) 119 – Rich Lass (Broxted 120) [1998 78p: 6s² 1999 **105 +**
5.1s* 7.1g³ 7.1m* 7d⁵ 7g* 7g Oct 16] quite good-topped colt: useful performer: won
maiden at Nottingham in April and handicaps at Sandown in July and Newcastle (by
1¾ lengths from Donna's Double) in August: below form (not punished after being
slightly hampered) final start: likely to prove best at 6f/7f: acts on soft and good to
firm going: tongue tied last 2 starts: held up: may do better still. *J. W. Payne*

TAYIL (IRE) 3 b.c. Caerleon (USA) 132 – Desert Bluebell 83 (Kalaglow 132) **97**
[1998 97: 7g* 7f* 7d⁶ 7.1m⁶ 7g⁴ 1999 8g⁵ 10.3m⁶ 12f² Jun 18] small, quite attractive
colt: useful performer: ran well in 1999 when fifth in listed race at Kempton and
second of 4 to Wales in handicap at Newmarket: may prove best at 1¼m/1½m: acts
on firm going, below form only start on softer than good: sold 11,000 gns, sent to
Macau. *J. L. Dunlop*

TAYOVULLIN (IRE) 5 ch.m. Shalford (IRE) 124§ – Fifth Quarter (Cure The **56**
Blues (USA)) [1998 61, a58: a8g a8g 7s 8g 11.8g 8d 7g* 7m⁵ 7.1g a7g² 7d 7g⁵ 7d² **a65**
7v 7s² a7g³ a7s⁵ 1999 7m a7g* a7g² 7m³ a6g Dec 21] leggy mare: fair handicapper
on all-weather, modest on turf: won at Wolverhampton in May: left H. Morrison and
off 14 weeks before well beaten final start: stays 1m: acts on firm ground and
fibresand, probably on soft: visored once. *K. A. Ryan*

TAYSEER (USA) 5 ch.g. Sheikh Albadou 128 – Millfit (USA) 62 (Blushing **96 +**
Groom (FR) 131) [1998 78: 7m⁵ 8s a6g* a7g a6g⁵ 1999 6m 7g² 8.1g² 7f 7g 7m
8f 7.1g⁵ 8m* 8d* 8d* Oct 30] lightly-made gelding: has a quick action: useful
performer: won claimer at Brighton (left W. Muir £10,000) and valuable handicaps
at Ayr (by length from Bomb Alaska) and Newmarket (landed gamble in 19-runner
Ladbroke Autumn Stakes by neck from Brilliant Red, idling in front) in September/
October: effective at 7f/1m: acts on firm going, good to soft and fibresand: usually
waited with: rejuvenated, and likely to have another good season in 2000. *D. Nicholls*

TAZKIYA 4 ch.f. King's Signet (USA) 110 – Irene's Charter 72 (Persian Bold **32**
123) [1998 52d: 7m⁶ 7m³ 7d 9.9m 7m 7m 9.9m 1999 a13g a16f⁵ a13g a16g⁵ a16g⁶
a13g³ 12v Apr 13] quite attractive filly: poor maiden: probably stays 2m: blinkered/
visored last 4 starts. *R. Ingram*

TAZ MANIA 3 b.g. Savahra Sound 111 – Sugar Token 66 (Record Token 128) **–**
[1998 –: 5d 5.1f⁵ 6g⁶ 5m a6g a5g 1999 a7g a6g a5g 6.1v 5g 8g 8.2g 8.2m 7.5g
a6g a5g Dec 21] lengthy, rather unfurnished gelding: no form: blinkered/visored
nowadays: has worn tongue strap. *S. R. Bowring*

TCHAIKOVSKY (IRE) 3 b.c. Sadler's Wells (USA) 132 – Crystal Spray 75 **114**
(Beldale Flutter (USA) 130) [1998 92p: 7d* 1999 10s* 10g² 12s⁵ 12g³ 14.6m⁵ Sep
11] smart performer: won 3-runner minor event at Gowran in April: best efforts when
behind Montjeu in Prix du Jockey Club at Chantilly (11½ lengths fifth in visor) and
Irish Derby at the Curragh (10½ lengths third in blinkers), both in June: left
A. O'Brien before respectable 15 lengths fifth to Mutafaweq in St Leger at Doncaster
final start: may prove best at 1½m/1¾m: acts on soft ground, probably on good to
firm: sent to Saudi Arabia. *G. A. Butler*

TEA FOR TEXAS 2 ch.f. (May 6) Weldnaas (USA) 112 – Polly's Teahouse 68 **48 p**
(Shack (USA) 118) [1999 a6g⁴ Dec 6] eighth foal: sister to 3-y-o Fas and 3 winners,
including 4-y-o Seven and 6-y-o Polly Golightly: dam sprint maiden: 14/1, 5¾
lengths fourth of 7 in maiden at Lingfield, green but keeping on well: should
improve. *H. Morrison*

TE AKAU DAN (NZ) 5 b.g. Dance Floor (USA) – Bellandaan (NZ) (Standaan **–**
(FR) 118) [1998 NR 1999 7s May 14] New Zealand-bred gelding: poor maiden
hurdler: blinkered, behind in seller only Flat run. *J. M. Bradley*

TE ANAU 2 b.f. (Feb 25) Reprimand 122 – Neenah 107 (Bold Lad (IRE) 133) **–**
[1999 6.1m a7g³ 7g 7.1m Aug 21] half-sister to several winners, notably smart N C **a52**
Owen (up to 1½m, by Bustino): dam, half-sister to Irish Oaks winner Swiftfoot, won
at 6f at 2 yrs and stayed 1½m: form only when third of 11 in seller at Wolverhampton:
should stay 1m: joined W. Musson. *B. J. McMath*

TEAPOT ROW (IRE) 4 b.c. Generous (IRE) 139 – Secrage (USA) 105 (Secreto **110**
(USA) 128) [1998 110: 10.4g⁶ 8m² 10.5g² 8m 9m⁵ 1999 8.1s⁶ 8.1g² 8g⁴ 7.3m* 7.3g²
Aug 13] smallish, leggy colt: easy mover: smart performer: comfortably won minor
event at Newbury in July by 2 lengths from Caballero: ran creditably otherwise when
runner-up in similar race at Haydock (beaten ½ length by Alrassaam) and Hungerford Stakes (beaten 5 lengths by impressive Lend A Hand having been set lot to do):
effective at 7f to 10.5f: acts on good to firm going: reportedly finished distressed
third start: usually held up. *J. A. R. Toller*

TEAR WHITE (IRE) 5 b.g. Mac's Imp (USA) 116 – Exemplary 106 (Sovereign **73**
Lord 120) [1998 70, a75: 5m⁶ 5m⁵ a5g⁴ 5m⁴ 5m 5.3g* a5f* a5g³ 1999 a5g² a5g* **a87**
a5g*ᵈⁱˢ a5g⁴ a5g* a5g 5g³ 5m 5m 5f Jul 28] sturdy gelding: fairly useful handicapper on all-weather, fair on turf: first past post twice at Lingfield in January
(disqualified for interference on second occasion) and once in March: effective at 5f/
easy 6f: acts on·firm ground (tailed off on good to soft) and equitrack: effective
blinkered/visored, not tried since 1997: reportedly bled from nose final start: used to
wander: often races prominently. *T. G. Mills*

*Stillorgan Park Hotel Flying Five, Leopardstown—at seven years of age,
Tedburrow shows himself to be as good as ever with a second successive win in the race;
the fillies Timote (noseband) and Antinnaz (striped cap) battle it out for the places*

TEBYAAN (USA)   3 b.f. Silver Hawk (USA) 123 – Umniyatee 104 (Green Desert (USA) 127) [1998 85p: 6m² 1999 7g² 7.1m⁴ 8.1m² 8m⁵ Sep 19] fair maiden: effective at 7f/1m: raced only on good/good to firm going: blinkered final start: sent to USA. *B. Hanbury*   **79**

TECHNICIAN (IRE)   4 ch.g. Archway (IRE) 115 – How It Works (Commanche Run 133) [1998 69: a8s² a7g a8g³ a8.5g² 8s⁴ 8s² 8g 7.1g 7g⁴ 8d² 7d² 9.2d⁵ 7.1g³ 7.1g³ 8m⁵ 7.1d² 7d 8g 1999 a7g³ 7g⁶ 7.1m² 7.1m² 7m³ 8g 7m⁶ 7g³ 7.6m 7s² 7.6m 8.1d 6g³ 7f 6f² 8s a6f³ 6.1d Oct 5] leggy gelding: poor mover: fair maiden on turf, modest on all-weather: effective at 6f to 8.5f: acts on soft ground, firm and fibresand: best in blinkers/visor: usually races prominently: tough. *E. J. Alston*   **73**
a60

TEDBURROW   7 b.g. Dowsing (USA) 124 – Gwiffina 87 (Welsh Saint 126) [1998 115: 6d³ 6d* 5d⁵ 6g 5d 5.1m* 5g⁶ 5d* 5s² 6m² 1999 6d* 6g 5m 5m 5.1m* 6.1m* 5d* 5m Dec 12] leggy, workmanlike gelding: smart performer: had a good season, winning listed races at Doncaster (by 3 lengths from Yorkies Boy) in March and Chester (twice, first occasion same race for third year running and second one by head from Nigrasine) in July and Flying Five at Leopardstown (for second year running, comfortably beat Timote by length) in September: effective at 5f/6f: acts on firm and soft ground: has won when sweating: usually held up: genuine. *E. J. Alston*   **115**

TEDDY BOY   3 b.g. Midyan (USA) 124 – Likeable Lady 67 (Piaffer (USA) 113) [1998 NR 1999 9f 7f⁴ 10g⁴ 11.6s⁶ Aug 9] fifth foal: dam 9f and 11f winner: no sign of ability in maidens/seller: blinkered final start: sold 640 gns. *M. Madgwick*   **–**

TE-DEUM (IRE)   2 ch.c. (Feb 23) Ridgewood Ben 113 – Tabessa (USA) (Shahrastani (USA) 135) [1999 6.8m 8v³ 8s Oct 26] IR 9,400Y: third foal: half-brother to fairly useful 1¼m winner Taberann (by Doyoun) and a winner in Italy by Statoblest: dam Irish 7f/1m winner: best effort in maidens (fair form) when third of 8 to Osood at Salisbury: should stay 1¼m: acts on heavy going. *J. C. Fox*   **67**

TEEN IDOL (IRE)   3 ch.f. Red Sunset 120 – Truly Flattering (Hard Fought 125) [1998 –: 7d 5m 7g 7m 1999 7f 11.6g 10m a13g 11.6m⁵ 14.1m 11.6s Aug 9] poor maiden: probably stays 11.6f: acts on good to firm going: sold 500 gns. *J. J. Bridger*   **36**

TEEPLOY GIRL   4 b.f. Deploy 131 – Intoxication 73 (Great Nephew 126) [1998 –: a8g a6g a12g 1999 8.2s Oct 5] little form. *J. P. Smith*   **–**

TEE TEE TOO (IRE)   7 ch.g. Hatim (USA) 121 – Scottish Welcome (Be My Guest (USA) 126) [1998 NR 1999 a9.4g Jul 9] stocky gelding: no form on Flat since 1995. *C. F. C. Jackson*   **–**

TEGGIANO (IRE)   2 b.f. (Mar 3) Mujtahid (USA) 118 – Tegwen (USA) 79 (Nijinsky (CAN) 138) [1999 7m⁴ 6g* 8m* 8s* Sep 26]   **107 p**

Racing bonuses seem to spring up with all the regularity of a crop of exotic fruit in the tropics, and sometimes they have an equally odd shape. The latest season saw at least three new bonus schemes for performances announced, led by one for a million dollars to be awarded to a colt winning the Irish

Derby in 2000 after landing the Derby, the Prix du Jockey Club or the Kentucky Derby. The Kentucky Derby looks a bit of a red herring here, but as four colts—Shahrastani, Kahyasi, Generous and Commander In Chief—have won the Derby and Irish Derby since 1986, and three—Old Vic, Dream Well and Montjeu—have won the Prix du Jockey Club and the Curragh classic, the bonus looks much more achievable than most. The next bonus announced was one of a million pounds to be given to a colt winning the Racing Post Trophy, the Derby and the St Leger. Aristotle is the great white hope for this, and, if he goes for it, he will be trying to emulate Reference Point, the only colt to have completed the treble. A tough task. The third bonus, the grandly-titled 'Millennium Million Miler Challenge', isn't so much tough as well-nigh impossible. This involves a horse adding victory in the Queen Elizabeth II Stakes at Ascot to earlier ones on the same course in the Royal Lodge Stakes and St James's Palace Stakes, or the Fillies' Mile and Coronation Stakes. Sure Blade and Milligram were the most recent to win two of the three, but no horse has ever landed the treble, and it is long odds against one managing it in the foreseeable future. The Royal Lodge Stakes, as a Group 2, is not a championship event and has been won by some distinctly ordinary colts in the last decade, as well as by two good ones in Mister Baileys and Benny The Dip. Essentially, though, it is a race for aspiring middle-distance performers rather than milers. The latter types are much more likely to go for the seven-furlong Champagne Stakes—Sure Blade won this before completing the St James's Palace/Queen Elizabeth II Stakes double in 1986—or Dewhurst Stakes. The Fillies' Mile, as a Group 1, attracts better fields, but again, many have middle-distance potential and three-year-old fillies capable of beating colts of all ages over a mile in the Queen Elizabeth II Stakes are few and far between. Apart from Milligram, who won that race in 1987, only four others have done so, most of them in the early days—Cigalon in 1956, Rosalba in 1959, when she also won the Coronation Stakes, The Creditor in 1963 (at Newbury) and Rose Bowl in 1975. All of which is doubtless comforting news for Ladbrokes, who are underwriting the Challenge.

What of the two contenders for the bonus? Royal Kingdom, successful in the Royal Lodge Stakes, doesn't look like a miler and, on what we've seen so far, is nowhere near good enough anyway. Teggiano, a narrow and determined winner of the Meon Valley Stud Fillies' Mile, is indeed winter favourite for the One Thousand Guineas but she doesn't look an out-and-out miler to us. Nor, for that matter, to Frankie Dettori, who had ridden her to victory in the May Hill Stakes at Doncaster after which he declared 'she's a mile and a half filly'. Teggiano, who has joined the Godolphin team and was sent to winter in Dubai, arrived at Doncaster with one win to her name, in a sixteen-runner maiden race

Meon Valley Stud Fillies' Mile, Ascot—Teggiano earns a winter in Dubai
after her gutsy victory over Britannia (noseband), My Hansel (partly hidden by the winner) and Issey Rose

at Newbury in August, in which she showed improvement on her debut run in a similar event at Newmarket and beat Femme Fatale decisively under a confident ride. The May Hill Stakes attracts a mixture of exposed and unexposed fillies, and, in the latest running, sponsored by Rothmans, all but one of the twelve runners had won. Teggiano started third favourite behind Princess Ellen, successful on both her starts including a listed race, and once-raced Aunty Rose, winner of the Newmarket maiden in which Teggiano had made her debut. However, Teggiano scored in good style, travelling easily among the back-markers after missing the break, quickening well to lead entering the final furlong and running on strongly to beat Everlasting Love by three lengths, with Aunty Rose over a length away third. Princess Ellen ran poorly.

The Fillies' Mile at Ascot is the British mile championship for juvenile fillies and it was fortunate that the elements relented and allowed the race, together with the Queen Elizabeth II Stakes, to be transferred from the cancelled Saturday card to Sunday. Not that the six-runner field was outstanding. Teggiano was the only one to have contested an important race of any kind and she started a warm favourite to account for maiden and/or minor winners Barakula, Issey Rose, My Hansel and Veil of Avalon plus the maiden Britannia. It was the last-named who gave the favourite most to do as she made the running and kept on well once challenged by Teggiano, who responded gamely to pressure after joining the leader two furlongs out and landed the odds by three quarters of a length. My Hansel was a similar distance away third with Issey Rose close up in fourth. By no stretch of the imagination can this be regarded as top-class form, and in all probability the testing conditions did not suit Teggiano anything like so well as the good to firm ground she had encountered at Doncaster. She also got a bit stirred up in the preliminaries.

			Woodman	Mr Prospector
		Mujtahid (USA)	(ch 1983)	Playmate
		(ch 1988)	Mesmerize	Mill Reef
Teggiano (IRE)			(b 1982)	Jeanie Duff
(b.f. Mar 3, 1997)			Nijinsky	Northern Dancer
		Tegwen (USA)	(b 1967)	Flaming Page
		(b or br 1991)	Beautiful Aly	Alydar
			(b 1986)	Beautiful Glass

There can have been few, if any, previous winter favourites for the One Thousand Guineas or Oaks sired by a stallion residing in Turkey, but that's the case with Teggiano (Turkey is also where Daylami's sire, Doyoun, has ended up). Mujtahid was a smart juvenile, landing the July Stakes by seven lengths and the Gimcrack Stakes by four before running indifferently at odds on in the Dewhurst Stakes on his only outing over further than six furlongs. He did not race again, so his stamina remained unproven. Retired to Derrinstown Stud in Ireland he got winners, finishing second in the first-crop sires' table in 1995 thanks mainly to Cornwallis Stakes victor Mubhij, but he did not get sufficient stakes performers to make him commercial and he was exported to Turkey in 1997. Mujtahid should have stayed at least seven furlongs but not necessarily much beyond a mile—the average winning distance of races won by his progeny is around seven and a half furlongs, and hardly any have shone over a mile and a quarter plus. The stamina Teggiano seems to possess can be assumed to come principally from her dam Tegwen, a Nijinsky filly who won a maiden race at Yarmouth over a mile and a half and stayed a mile and three quarters well. Teggiano's three-year-old half-sister Tegyra (by Trempolino) was also successful in a maiden event, winning at a mile and three quarters at the same track in the latest season. Tegwen, who cost 625,000 dollars as a yearling, is a half-sister to a stakes-placed winner by Mujtahid's sire Woodman out of a half-sister to Jeanne Jones (by Nijinsky), a Grade 1 winner over eight and a half furlongs in the Fantasy Stakes and second in the Breeders' Cup Juvenile Fillies. The third dam Beautiful Glass was a Grade 3 winner and a half-sister to Beautiful Melody, successful in the Grade 1 Beverly Hills Handicap and,

like Teggiano's grandam Beautiful Aly, a daughter of Alydar. This is not a truly stamina-packed pedigree but the way a horse races often says nearly as much about its staying potential as the names in its tabulated pedigree, and Teggiano's style suggests she will stay a mile and a quarter, probably a mile and a half. Not that she is devoid of pace, so a One Thousand Guineas challenge looks a certainty. Teggiano will need to improve, but expect her to run her heart out whatever the company and whatever demands are made of her. *C. E. Brittain*

TEGYRA (IRE) 3 ch.f. Trempolino (USA) 135 – Tegwen (USA) 79 (Nijinsky **69** (CAN) 138) [1998 73p: 7m 8.1m³ 1999 11.9g⁵ 14.1m* 16.2m⁵ 14.1m⁵ 14.6d 12d Oct 29] tall, leggy, lengthy filly: fair performer: won 5-runner maiden at Yarmouth in June: ran creditably next 2 starts: stays 1¾m: acts on good to firm going, yet to race on soft/heavy. *M. A. Jarvis*

TELECASTER (IRE) 3 ch.g. Indian Ridge 123 – Monashee (USA) (Sovereign **–** Dancer (USA)) [1998 NR 1999 a8.5g 8.3d 6d Oct 28] 37,000F, 38,000Y: fourth foal: dam unraced granddaughter of top American 2-y-o filly Queen Empress: well held in maidens. *C. R. Egerton*

TELLION 5 b.g. Mystiko (USA) 124 – Salchow 116 (Niniski (USA) 125) [1998 **–** 69: 12s⁶ 11.9g³ 12g⁶ 12m 1999 14.1s 11.9s Sep 29] workmanlike, good-bodied gelding: fair maiden handicapper at best: barely stays 1½m: acts on good to firm going, soft and fibresand: visored on reappearance: has refused to race over hurdles, though won novice event in November. *J. R. Jenkins*

TEMERAIRE (USA) 4 b.c. Dayjur (USA) 137 – Key Dancer (USA) (Nijinsky **96** (CAN) 138) [1998 96: 7g² 8.3m* 7.6m* 8d 7g a9.4g 1999 a9.4g⁶ 8d 7g² 6m 7m 7m **a98** 7f 7f 7d 6m⁵ 7.1d² 7.3m* 7s a8g⁵ a7g* a7g Dec 4] strong, good-topped colt: useful performer: left R. Ingram after eighth start: won handicap at Newbury (by ¾ length from Adjutant) in September and minor event at Lingfield in November:

likely to prove best with good test at 6f, and stays 1m: acts on equitrack (yet to show same form on fibresand), good to firm and good to soft going: visored twice, running respectably first time: often front runner: none too consistent. *D. J. S. Cosgrove*

TEMESIDE TINA 3 ch.f. Tina's Pet 121 – Expletive 77 (Shiny Tenth 120) [1998 NR 1999 9g 7.9f⁶ 7.1s 8s⁶ a9.4g a8g⁶ Nov 26] workmanlike filly: fourth foal: dam 5f (at 2 yrs) to 1¼m winner: poor maiden. *P. D. Evans*   **43**

TEMPERATE 3 ch.g. Librate 91 – Miss Moody 67 (Jalmood (USA) 126) [1998 –: 6.1g 7.1d 1999 6.8m⁶ 8f 7f Aug 4] workmanlike gelding: no sign of ability: tried blinkered. *J. M. Bradley*   **–**

TEMPLE WAY 3 b.g. Shirley Heights 130 – Abbey Strand (USA) 78 (Shadeed (USA) 135) [1998 NR 1999 10m 12m³ 12g⁴ 14.1m⁴ 16.2m* 16.2m⁵ 17.2m⁴ 16m² 14.8d Oct 15] workmanlike gelding: third foal: dam, 1m winner, half-sister to smart 6f to 10.5f winner Church Parade and smart middle-distance stayer Castle Rising: fairly useful handicapper: won at Chepstow in July: ran creditably next 3 starts: likely to prove best at 1¾m/2m: acts on good to firm going, possibly not on good to soft: blinkered after fourth start: found little penultimate start. *R. Charlton*   **84**

TEMPRAMENTAL (IRE) 3 ch.f. Midhish 109 – Musical Horn (Music Boy 124) [1998 55: 5v 5d⁴ 6m⁵ 6g 5m³ 7d⁵ 6d⁶ 6m⁶ 5.1m* 5.2g 5.3g⁵ 1999 6g 5m⁵ 5m 6g 7d³ a6g⁴ 7g 8.2s a7g a8g⁵ a8.5g⁵ a8g³ a8.5g Dec 27] good-topped filly: modest handicapper: stays 1m: acts on good to firm going, soft and all-weather: sometimes blinkered/visored (including when successful): has given trouble to start. *D. Haydn Jones*   **51**

TEMPUS FUGIT 4 ch.f. Timeless Times (USA) 99 – Kabella (Kabour 80) [1998 –: 5g 5m 6s a6g 1999 a7g Jan 23] sturdy filly: fairly useful 5f performer at 2 yrs: well beaten since. *B. R. Millman*   **–**

TENBY HEIGHTS (IRE) 3 b.g. Tenby 125 – Alpine Spring 95 (Head For Heights 125) [1998 –: 6m⁴ 7m 6m⁵ 6g 7.9g 10d 1999 10v 12d 8.2m 14.1f Jun 1] small, sturdy gelding: little sign of ability. *R. Hollinshead*   **–**

TEN KINGDOMS (USA) 3 b.c. Mr Prospector (USA) – Chinese Empress (USA) (Nijinsky (CAN) 138) [1998 74p: 7m 7m 1999 8m³ 9g 8g³ 10.3m* 11.9f* 10v 10.3m Sep 11] big, lengthy colt: useful performer: made all in maiden at Doncaster in June and handicap at Haydock in July: tailed off last 2 starts, in listed race at Deauville on penultimate: stays 1½m: acts on firm ground: tends to sweat, get on edge and carry head high: sent to UAE. *J. H. M. Gosden*   **96**

TENNESSEE (IRE) 2 b.c. (Feb 8) Blues Traveller (IRE) 119 – Valiant Friend (USA) (Shahrastani (USA) 135) [1999 7m⁵ 7.1d³ 8.1m⁴ Sep 3] IR 12,000F, IR 36,000Y: quite attractive, unfurnished colt: third foal: half-brother to 4-y-o King Darius: dam, ran twice in France, granddaughter of Oaks winner Valoris: fair maiden: best effort when third of 13 at Sandown: should stay 1¼m: made the running final 2 starts. *S. P. C. Woods*   **75**

TENOR BELL (IRE) 3 b.g. Tenby 125 – Top Bloom (Thatch (USA) 136) [1998 64p: 8g 8d⁵ 1999 10m 14.1s Nov 1] smallish, good-topped gelding: good mover: modest maiden: disappointing both 3-y-o starts, leaving L. Cumani 5,500 gns after reappearance. *M. R. Bosley*   **–**

TEN PAST SIX 7 ch.g. Kris 135 – Tashinsky (USA) (Nijinsky (CAN) 138) [1998 62: 8s⁵ 12.4d a11g* a16g 12.3s 11.1g* 9.2m² 12m² 9.2d² 12d* 12.1d 12d⁵ 9.9m 1999 12.4m⁵ 12m May 17] lengthy, good-quartered gelding: modest performer: effective at 9f to 1½m: acts on good to firm ground, soft and fibresand: usually blinkered/visored nowadays: often makes running. *Martyn Wane*   **59**

TENSILE (IRE) 4 b.g. Tenby 125 – Bonnie Isle 115 (Pitcairn 126) [1998 87: 9.9s* 10.5g⁵ 12s 11.9g² 14g⁵ 14m 1999 12m 13.9d² 14m⁵ 11.9d³ 16s Oct 22] small, sturdy gelding: has a quick action: fairly useful handicapper: hung left when short-head second of 5 in rated stakes at York in June: below form after, though set strong pace final start: should stay 2m: possibly needs good going or softer (unraced on heavy): usually held up, and not an easy ride. *J. R. Fanshawe*   **92**

TEODORA (IRE) 2 b.f. (May 10) Fairy King (USA) – Pinta (IRE) (Ahonoora 122) [1999 6m* 6m⁴ 6m⁵ 7d³ Sep 28] 35,000Y: angular, quite attractive filly: second foal: dam, 2-y-o 5f (in Ireland) and 7.5f (Italian listed race) winner, also 7f winner in Italy at 3 yrs, out of half-sister to Timarida: fairly useful performer: won maiden at   **93**

Windsor in July: best effort when third of 17 to Inchlonaig in valuable sales event at Newmarket final start: likely to prove best at 6f/7f. *S. Dow*

TEOFILIO (IRE) 5 ch.h. Night Shift (USA) – Rivoltade (USA) (Sir Ivor 135) **81** [1998 –: 8.5m 7.6f 5m⁶ 6.1v 7s a8f⁵ 1999 a6g a7g a10g⁴ a8g² a8g* 8.3m⁵ 7f² **a69** 7.1m* 7f* 7f³ 7g² 7d⁶ 6g Aug 28] good-topped horse: fairly useful on turf, fair on all-weather: won minor event at Lingfield in February and handicaps at Sandown and Newmarket in June: effective at 7f to 8.5f: acts on equitrack, firm and good to soft going: blinkered after third start: has choked/worn tongue strap: has hung left/carried head awkwardly: held up. *A. J. McNae*

TERM OF ENDEARMENT 2 b.f. (Mar 26) First Trump 118 – Twilight Secret **73 d** 70 (Vaigly Great 127) [1999 5.7g⁵ 5.1g* 5.7g⁴ 7f⁴ 6g⁶ 7.9f 6.1m 6g 7s⁶ 7s Oct 25] 11,500Y: small filly: fourth foal: half-sister to Irish 9f winner Consider It Done (by Robellino): dam 1¼m winner: fair performer: won maiden at Bath in June: below that form last 7 starts, claimed from M. Channon 10,000 gns after second of them: should stay beyond 6f: best efforts on good ground. *J. Pearce*

TERRA NOVA 2 ch.f. (Feb 18) Polar Falcon (USA) 126 – Tarsa 81 (Ballad Rock **71** 122) [1999 6.1f⁴ 7m² 7m⁵ 6f² 7s⁴ 6g⁶ Oct 11] 28,000Y: angular filly: half-sister to useful 1996 2-y-o 6f/7f winner Churchland (by Kylian) and a 2-y-o 6f winner in Italy by Primo Dominie: dam 6f winner also successful in Italy: fair maiden: races freely, but stays 7f: acts on firm and soft going. *R. W. Armstrong*

TERRAZZO (USA) 4 b.g. Nureyev (USA) 131 – Diese (USA) 111 (Diesis 133) **68** [1998 NR 1999 a12g² a9.4g³ a8.5g⁵ 12m⁵ 9m⁴ 10.1m⁴ Jun 2] 21,000 3-y-o: first foal: brother to 3-y-o Senure: dam, French 1¼m winner, half-sister to Xaar, from family of Try My Best and El Gran Senor: modest form in 2 bumpers in January: fair on Flat: best effort when winning handicap at Musselburgh in May, despite showing ungainly head carriage under pressure: stays 1½m: raced only on fibresand and good to firm ground. *J. G. FitzGerald*

TERTIUM (IRE) 7 b.g. Nordico (USA) – Nouniya (Vayrann 133) [1998 93§, **96 §** a73§: a8g 8d⁴ a8.5g³ 8d⁵ 8d* 8m 8g 8.5g 8.9s 8s 7v³ 7f 8m² 8d 7f* 7.9f 8m 7g 8s 7g **a– §** 1999 a7g 8d 7g⁴ 8m* May 3] strong, good-bodied gelding: useful handicapper: better than ever when winning Jubilee Stakes at Kempton (for second year in succession) in May by short head from Sunstreak: effective at 7f (given test) to 1¼m: acts on any turf going, lightly-raced on all-weather of late: has reportedly choked, and sometimes tongue tied: usually held up: sometimes slowly away, and has refused to race: not one to trust implicitly: sold 10,000 gns. *N. P. Littmoden*

TERTULLIAN (USA) 4 ch.c. Miswaki (USA) 124 – Turbaine (USA) (Trempo- **115** lino (USA) 135) [1998 112: 8v* 7.5s⁴ 10g⁵ 8.8g² 8g* 8d⁴ 8g⁶ 8d 7s* 1999 6.5s* 6.5s* 6.5s* 6d⁴ 6m³ 6.5g* 6g³ 6.5s² 7s* Oct 31] dam, French 9.5f and 1¼m winner and listed placed, half-sister to Urban Sea (by Miswaki): smart performer: in fine form in 1999, winning listed races at Hanover, Krefeld and Munich between March and May, Grosser Preis von Berlin at Hoppegarten (by 3½ lengths from below-form Tomba) in July and Premio Chiusura at Milan (for second year running, by 1½ lengths from Onice Nero) in October: good neck second to Tomba in Group 3 event at Munich penultimate start: has form up to 9f but best at 6f/7f: has form on good to firm ground, goes very well on soft/heavy: reliable. *P. Schiergen, Germany*

TESS 3 b.f. Emarati (USA) 74 – Everdene (Bustino 136) [1998 ?: 5.2m⁵ 7g 7g 1999 **58 d** a7g² a8g⁵ 8m³ 7g⁵ 7f 7f Aug 4] smallish, lengthy filly: disappointing maiden: left B. Hills before final start: stays 7f. *G. F. H. Charles-Jones*

TESSARA 4 ch.f. Kasakov – Sum Music 56 (Music Boy 124) [1998 –: 6d 1999 **–** a7g 7.5d⁶ a8g 8d 12f⁶ Jul 14] workmanlike filly: no form in varied company: has been mulish in preliminaries/slowly away. *C. W. Thornton*

TESS TOO 3 b.f. Lugana Beach 116 – Ankara's Princess (USA) 81 (Ankara **67** (USA) 106) [1998 NR 1999 6.1m² 5.1m Aug 28] fourth live foal: half-sister to 5-y-o Nominator Lad: dam 2-y-o 5f winner who stayed 6f: second in maiden at Notting-ham: pulled up lame there later in August: dead. *B. A. McMahon*

TEST THE WATER (IRE) 5 ch.h. Maelstrom Lake 118 – Baliana (CAN) **68** (Riverman (USA) 131) [1998 80: 8d 8d⁶ 8d 7.3g 8.5g³ 9m 8.1m* 8.9g² 9.1s 8d⁴ 1999 8d 7g⁵ 8v 8.1m a8.5g⁶ 8m² Jul 30] dipped-backed horse: poor walker and mover: fair performer: stays 9f: acts on soft and good to firm ground: blinkered (below form) once at 4 yrs: has been bandaged: has looked none too keen. *R. Hannon*

TETHKAR 3 b.f. Machiavellian (USA) 123 – Munnaya (USA) 101 (Nijinsky **62** (CAN) 138) [1998 75: 7m 8.1m⁴ 1999 8s 7.1m⁴ 11.5m⁴ 8m Sep 8] quite attractive filly: good mover: modest maiden: should stay beyond 1m: acts on good to firm going: visored final start: sent to USA. *E. A. L. Dunlop*

TEYAAR 3 b.g. Polar Falcon (USA) 126 – Music In My Life (IRE) 59 (Law **78** Society (USA) 130) [1998 NR 1999 8m⁵ 7m 7s² 8m 6m 7s³ Aug 8] 30,000F, 32,000Y: strong gelding: third foal: closely related to 5-y-o Mutahadeth and half-brother to 4-y-o Premium Pursuit (6f winner at 2 yrs): dam (maiden) stayed 1m: fair maiden: left J. Dunlop 7,500 gns after penultimate outing: likely to prove best at 7f/1m: acts on soft and good to firm going: has been bandaged: has hung. *D. Shaw*

T G'S GIRL 2 gr.f. (Feb 7) Selkirk (USA) 129 – River's Rising (FR) 88 (Mendez **57** (FR) 128) [1999 5m 6m⁴ 5g Jul 5] 9,500F, 18,000Y: leggy filly: sixth foal: closely related to a winner abroad by Sharpo and half-sister to 2 winners, including fairly useful 1996 2-y-o 7f winner Mudflap (by Slip Anchor): dam 1m winner: modest form in maidens, showing good early speed last 2 starts: bred to stay at least 7f. *R. Hannon*

THAAYER 4 b.g. Wolfhound (USA) 126 – Hamaya (USA) 60 (Mr Prospector **–** (USA)) [1998 68: 6d 7m⁶ 7g 6v a5g⁶ a6g³ a6g⁵ 1999 a6f* a6g² 6.1f 6f a5g a6g³ a6g **a72 +** a6g* a6g⁴ Dec 27] fair performer: won minor event at Southwell in January, and handicap there in good style in December: raced too freely from wide draw final outing: left K. Bell after sixth start (found little): should stay 7f: acts on fibresand, no form on turf. *I. A. Wood*

THADY QUILL (USA) 2 ch.c. (Mar 14) Nureyev (USA) 131 – Alleged Devot- **96** ion (USA) (Alleged (USA) 138) [1999 7m* 7f* 9g³ Nov 5] 425,000Y: leggy, attract-ive colt, somewhat unfurnished: sixth foal: closely related to fairly useful Irish 1998 2-y-o 6f winner April Starlight (by Storm Bird) and half-brother to 2 winners in USA, including Grade 3 8.5f winner Humble Eight (by Seattle Battle): dam unraced half-sister to smart middle-distance colt Romanov and Sun Chariot winner Red Slippers (both by Nureyev) and top-class 1½m filly Balanchine: won maiden at Gowran (landed odds by 5½ lengths) in June and 5-runner listed race at Newmarket (beat Full Flow by short head) in July: creditable third in non-graded stakes at Gulfstream final start: likely to stay beyond 9f: useful. *A. P. O'Brien, Ireland*

THAMES DANCER (USA) 3 ch.c. Green Dancer (USA) 132 – Hata (FR) **79** (Kaldoun (FR) 122) [1998 79: 7g⁶ 8g 1999 11.1g⁶ 12.5m⁶ 12d² a12g³ Jun 28] close-coupled colt: has a short action: fair maiden handicapper: should stay beyond 1½m: acts on good to soft going, showed promise on fibresand. *K. McAuliffe*

THARI (USA) 2 b. or br.c. (Apr 4) Silver Hawk (USA) 123 – Magic Slipper 97 **90** (Habitat 134) [1999 7m² 7.1m* 7s³ 7d⁶ Oct 12] strong, sturdy colt: half-brother to 3-y-o Al Nakhlah and several winners, including useful 1994 2-y-o 7f winner Muhab (by Lyphard) and 1¼m winner Atnab (by Riverman): dam, 1¼m and 11.5f winner, half-sister to Fairy Footsteps and Light Cavalry: fairly useful form: won maiden at Chepstow in September in good style: well held when favourite for minor event at Leicester on final start: will stay 1¼m+. *P. T. Walwyn*

THATCHAM (IRE) 3 ch.g. Thatching 131 – Calaloo Sioux (USA) 100 (Our **64 d** Native (USA)) [1998 NR 1999 8f 7.1m⁵ 8.2f⁴ a8g 7m 7d Oct 27] IR 17,000Y: half-brother to several winners, including useful 1994 2-y-o 7f winner Muhab and useful Irish 1m winner/hurdler Master Tribe (by Master Willie): dam 7.6f winner: disappointing maiden. *R. W. Armstrong*

THATCHED (IRE) 9 b.g. Thatching 131 – Shadia (USA) 53 (Naskra (USA)) **52** [1998 53: 9.3s 9g* 7.5g⁶ 8d 8.5d⁵ 8g 9.9m² 8.5g² 8m 9.9m 7.9g 1999 9.3m⁵ 7.1m 8m 9g³ 9d³ 8.5m 8f² 8.5m⁴ 8f⁶ Aug 7] leggy gelding: has a quick action: modest handicapper: effective at 7.5f to 1¼m: acts on hard going, not at best on soft/heavy: effective blinkered/visored or not: suitable mount for apprentice: usually held up. *R. E. Barr*

THATCHING LAD 6 gr.g. Belfort (FR) 89 – Sing Out Loud (Thatching 131) **–** [1998 NR 1999 a6g Dec 17] third foal: dam well beaten: no show in bumpers (virtually refused to race once) or in seller at Southwell. *D. Eddy*

THATCHMASTER (IRE) 8 b.g. Thatching 131 – Key Maneuver (USA) (Key 74
To Content (USA)) [1998 77: 10m⁵ 10g 9.9m 11.6m* 13.3m⁵ 11.6m* 12m⁵ 9.9m²
12m³ 12s 1999 12m 12g 11.6m³ 12m 9g* 12m⁴ 9v⁴ Sep 20] tall gelding: fair handicapper: won amateur event at Goodwood in August: effective at 9f, barely stays
1½m: acts on any ground: has worn crossed noseband/tongue strap: usually races
prominently. *C. A. Horgan*

THATCHROYAL (IRE) 3 ch.c. Thatching 131 – Wish You Were Here (USA) 74
81 (Secretariat (USA)) [1998 NR 1999 11m⁶ 12.1s² 12d⁵ 10.2m³ 12m⁴ 11.5m⁴ 8s a–
a14.8g⁵ Oct 13] approx 50,000Y in Italy: workmanlike colt: half-brother to several
winners, including useful 1997 Italian 2-y-o 6f and 7.5f winner Tenbyssimo (by
Tenby) and 1¼m winner Duveen (by Tate Gallery): dam 7f and 1¼m winner: fair
maiden: effective at 1¼m/1½m: acts on good to firm going, probably on soft (showed
little on fibresand): blinkered (below best) twice: sold 3,200 gns. *S. P. C. Woods*

THAT MAN AGAIN 7 ch.g. Prince Sabo 123 – Milne's Way 83 (The Noble 86
Player (USA) 126) [1998 78: a5g³ a5g³ 6g 6g 6s 5m* 5m⁴ 5.7d 5m 5m* 5m⁴ 5g 1999
5d 5g⁶ 5g² 5m⁶ 5m* 5m⁴ 5m⁶ 5.2g⁶ 5m⁶ 5f Sep 4] robust gelding: fairly useful
handicapper: won at Sandown then Newmarket within 4 days in July: best at 5f/easy
6f: acts on any turf/all-weather, except possibly heavy going: visored once, usually
blinkered nowadays: often leads. *S. C. Williams*

THATOLDBLACKMAGIC (IRE) 4 b.f. Contract Law (USA) 108 – Spinelle –
88§ (Great Nephew 126) [1998 –: 7m³ 7m 5m 10m 1999 a7f Feb 8] small filly: has a
round action: little form. *W. Storey*

THAT OLD FEELING (IRE) 7 b.g. Waajib 121 – Swift Reply (He Loves Me –
120) [1998 NR 1999 5d 7d 5s May 14] quite good-topped gelding: no longer of any
account. *G. P. Kelly*

THATS ALL FOLKS 2 b.c. (May 17) Alhijaz 122 – So It Goes 73 (Free State 71
125) [1999 6.8m 7s⁶ a8g³ a7g³ Dec 15] 8,000Y: sixth foal: brother to 4-y-o 7f winner
Swing Along and half-brother to 3 winners, including fairly useful 1993 2-y-o 5f
winner Eleuthera (by Mazilier) and 1½m winner Ttyfran (by Petong): dam 2-y-o 6f
winner: progressive maiden: fair form when 4¾ lengths third of 11 to Church Farm
Flyer in nursery at Wolverhampton final start: will stay beyond 1m: acts on all-
weather: slowly away first 2 starts: may do better yet. *P. J. Makin*

THATS LIFE 4 b.g. Mukaddamah (USA) 125 – Run Faster (IRE) (Commanche 66
Run 133) [1998 79: 8g⁴ 7g⁵ 7.1g 6m* 6m 6g a6g³ a6g a7g⁶ 1999 a6g* a6g³ 7d⁶ 5m⁵ a71
a5g* 5d 5s a6g³ Dec 1] leggy, quite good-topped gelding: fair performer: won seller
in February and claimer (final outing for T. Mills) in July, both at Lingfield: effective
at 5f and barely stays 1m: acts on all-weather and good to firm going. *R. Bastiman*

THE ANGEL GABRIEL 4 ch.c. My Generation 111 – Minsk 36 (Kabour 80) –
[1998 –: 9.2s 1999 11.1g 5m 5g Jun 16] no show in maidens. *D. A. Nolan*

THE ARTFUL DODGER 4 b.g. Alhijaz 122 – Madam Millie 99 (Milford 119) 58
[1998 58, a–: 7m⁴ 8.1s⁶ 8g⁵ 7m 10.1g⁴ 9m³ a8.5g 1999 10f 7g³ 7m 7g² Sep 14] leggy a–
gelding: modest maiden: effective at 7f to 1¼m: acts on good to firm ground, well
beaten on fibresand: wandered under pressure final start: joined Mrs V. Ward.
R. J. R. Williams

THEATRELAND (USA) 2 b.g. (May 28) Dynaformer (USA) – Mime (Cure 68
The Blues (USA)) [1999 7d 7d 7v⁵ Oct 25] $90,000Y: close-coupled, attractive
gelding: fifth foal: half-brother to a winner in Japan by Capote: dam, won up to 9f in
USA, half-sister to top-class US colt General Assembly: fair form in maidens: will
be suited by 1m/1¼m. *Sir Michael Stoute*

THEATRE MAGIC 6 b.g. Sayf El Arab (USA) 127 – Miss Orient (Damister –
(USA) 123) [1998 –, a71+: a7s* a7g a7g² a6g² a7g a7g⁴ a7g⁶ a6g³ a6g a5g 6g a76
a7g⁵ a6g² a7g⁵ a7g² a6g* a6g³ a6g⁴ 1999 a6g³ a7g* a6g* a6g⁶ a6g Feb 5] close-
coupled gelding: unimpressive mover: fair handicapper: won twice at Southwell in
January: effective at 6f to 9.4f: acted on fibresand, lightly raced on equitrack and turf:
tried visored, effective blinkered or not: often took strong hold: dead. *D. Shaw*

THEATREWORLD (IRE) 7 b.g. Sadler's Wells (USA) 132 – Chamonis 111
(USA) 101 (Affirmed (USA)) [1998 104: 12d⁴ 14s³ 12s³ 22.2d⁶ 14v³ 16d³ 12g* 13.9f
1999 14g* 12g⁴ 12m* 13.9g 12d⁶ 11s² Sep 19] close-coupled gelding: runner-up in

last 3 Champion Hurdles: smart on Flat: better than ever in 1999, winning minor event at Navan in May and handicap and listed race, both at Galway, in July/September: creditable 8 lengths second of 5 to Insatiable in Blandford Stakes at the Curragh final start: effective at 11f to 2m: acts on soft and good to firm going: visored (reluctant stalls and in race) fourth start (Ebor at York): has worn tongue strap: tends to race lazily. *A. P. O'Brien, Ireland*

THE BARGATE FOX   3 b.g. Magic Ring (IRE) 115 – Hithermoor Lass 75 (Red **62** Alert 127) [1998 NR 1999 7.7m a8.5g 7.7d a8g⁵ a9.4g* a8g a8g⁴ a8.5g* Dec 27] 11,500F, 21,000Y: sturdy, well-made gelding: half-brother to several winners, notably smart sprinter Poyle George (by Sharpo) and 6-y-o State of Caution: dam placed from 5f to 7f: modest handicapper: won at Wolverhampton in November and December: stays 9.4f: acts on fibresand. *D. J. G. Murray Smith*

THE BARNSLEY BELLE (IRE)   6 b.m. Distinctly North (USA) 115 – La **–** Tanque (USA) (Last Raise (USA)) [1998 –, a56d: a7s a7g⁵ a7g⁴ a8g³ 8.3v a7g a8g 8d **a44** a8g a7g⁶ a8g 1999 a7g a8f⁸ a7f a8g 9.9g a8g⁶ a8g⁵ a11g⁶ Jun 17] leggy, angular mare: poor handicapper: won at Southwell in February: effective at 7f/1m: acts on good to firm ground, good to soft and fibresand: inconsistent. *G. Woodward*

THE BAT   6 b.h. Chauve Souris 108 – Jamra 69 (Upper Case (USA)) [1998 64: **–** 12g⁵ 11.5m³ 10m 10.4g 1999 12.3m 10g 12m Jul 26] maiden: well beaten in 1999. *Mark Campion*

THE BIZZ   6 b.m. Devon Missile – Kingmon's Girl (Saucy Kit 76) [1998 NR 1999 **–** 7f May 12] second reported foal: dam winning 2m chaser: behind in maiden at Brighton only Flat run. *B. A. Pearce*

THE BLUE BRAZIL (IRE)   3 b.g. Thatching 131 – Approche (FR) (Sharp- **–** man) [1998 NR 1999 7g³ 10g⁶ 10m⁵ 7.1f 9.2s 6s 9.1v a6g Dec 17] 15,000 francs F, 9,200Y, 14,000 2-y-o: lengthy gelding: half-brother to 3 winners, including French 10.5f/11f winner Stage Exit (by In The Wings): dam once-raced half-sister to Prix Greffulhe winner Arokar: little form: blinkered penultimate start. *Denys Smith*

THE BLUES ACADEMY (IRE)   4 b.g. Royal Academy (USA) 130 – She's **75 d** The Tops 83 (Shernazar 131) [1998 75: 10.2s 10.5g 14.9m² 14.9d⁴ 17.2g* 16.2g³ 20d 15.9g 17.1d 1999 16m² 17.1g⁴ 16.2m 16m³ 16m⁴ 15.8g⁴ Sep 18] tall, sturdy gelding: fair handicapper: will prove best at 2m+: acts on good to firm going: visored at 2 yrs: inconsistent, and possibly moody. *M. A. Buckley*

THE BULL MACABE   2 ch.c. (Jan 22) Efisio 120 – Tranquillity 70 (Night Shift **77** (USA)) [1999 5.7d⁶ 6g 5.1g* a6g³ Nov 11] 25,000Y: first foal: dam, 1m winner, out of half-sister to smart performer up to 1m Lemon Souffle: easily best effort in maidens (fair form) when winning 15-runner contest at Nottingham in October by head from Kind Emperor: will prove best at 5f/6f: joined A. Reid. *R. Hannon*

THE BUTTERWICK KID   6 ch.g. Interrex (CAN) – Ville Air 85 (Town Crier **80** 119) [1998 73: a11g* 11.1v³ 13v³ 13d³ 14.1g* 12g³ 20d 1999 11.1v* 13v² 18.7m May 5] workmanlike gelding: fairly useful handicapper: won at Hamilton in March: good second of 17 there next month: took little interest final start: effective at 11f (given good test), probably at 2½m: acts on fibresand and probably any turf going: tried blinkered/visored at 3 yrs: held up: has shown temperament over hurdles. *R. A. Fahey*

THE CANNIE ROVER   4 ch.g. Beveled (USA) – Sister Rosarii (USA) (Proper- **–** antes (USA)) [1998 45, a38: a8g⁶ 9.1m³ a8g 1999 a8g a11g 8g Apr 5] tall gelding: poor maiden handicapper: barely stays 9f: acts on firm ground, soft and fibresand: blinkered final start: sent to Holland. *M. W. Easterby*

THE CASTIGATOR   2 b.g. (Feb 15) Reprimand 122 – Summer Eve 63 (Hotfoot **48** 126) [1999 7m 5.9g 7m⁴ Aug 10] 4,500F, 3,000Y, 7,200 2-y-o: half-brother to a 2-y-o winner in Holland by Chilibang: dam (maiden) best at 6f: poor maiden: should stay 1m. *J. J. O'Neill*

THE COME BACK KID   2 b.c. (Feb 9) Shareef Dancer (USA) 135 – Clock- **69** watch (USA) (Alleged (USA) 138) [1999 8d 8d 8s⁶ Nov 6] good-topped colt: third foal: half-brother to a winner in Denmark by Mystiko: dam, ran twice in France, out of US Grade 3 6f winner Clocks Secret: first form in maidens when sixth of 18 to Blusienka at Doncaster: should prove suited by 1¼m+. *B. W. Hills*

THECOMEBACKKING 4 ch.c. Mystiko (USA) 124 – Nitouche 68 (Scottish –
Reel 123) [1998 47: a9.4g³ a8g a10g 1999 a8.5g Jul 23] poor maiden: tailed off only
4-y-o start. *R. Ford*

THE COTTONWOOL KID 7 b.g. Blakeney 126 – Relatively Smart 76 (Great –
Nephew 126) [1998 –: 14.1g 1999 a8g a11g⁶ a12g 12.3m 12.1m 14g a11g 16.2g Aug
12] of no account nowadays. *Mrs A. M. Naughton*

THE DEALER 4 b.c. No Big Deal – Not Alone 84 (Pas de Seul 133) [1998 62: 7g **48 d**
6m⁶ 6.1g 5.3g⁴ 5s⁶ 1999 7m 5g 10g 8f 8g⁴ a8.5g 6.8m a10g Jul 24] poor maiden:
seems to stay 1m: tried blinkered: looked virtually unrideable penultimate start:
reared leaving stalls final one. *M. D. I. Usher*

THE DEPUTY (IRE) 2 b.c. (Mar 29) Petardia 113 – Manfath (IRE) 65 (Last **102 p**
Tycoon 131) [1999 6m³ 6m² 7d³ 7m* 6g³ Sep 8] 14,000Y: good-bodied colt: first
living foal: dam staying maiden: progressive form: won maiden at Epsom in
September: again well backed, beaten only 2 short heads in 21-runner sales race won
by Sheer Hamas at Doncaster 5 days later, giving impression would have won had
run started sooner: stays 7f: best form on good ground or firmer: sold privately,
joined Jenine Sahadi in USA. *J. W. Hills*

THE DONK (IRE) 3 b.g. Case Law 113 – Peep of Day (USA) (Lypheor 118) –
[1998 68d: a5g³ 5s³ a5g a6g³ a6g³ 7d² 6s 8.2v a8g 1999 11g Oct 14] small, sturdy
gelding: modest maiden: demoted to second in seller at Redcar sixth 2-y-o start: well
held since: stays 7f: acts on good to soft going and fibresand. *B. S. Rothwell*

THE DOWNTOWN FOX 4 br.g. Primo Dominie 121 – Sara Sprint (Formid- **83**
able (USA) 125) [1998 85: 6d² 7v* 7.5s 7.6g⁶ 7g 6s⁵ 6m⁵ 7g 7m 7g 6s 1999 6d
7g⁶ 7m 6d 6d 6g 6d* 6d Nov 1] leggy gelding: unimpressive mover: fairly useful
performer: best effort in 1999 when winning 23-runner minor event at York in
October: effective at 6f to 7.6f: acts on good to firm and heavy going: tried blinkered/
visored: tends to hang left. *B. A. McMahon*

THE DRUMMER (IRE) 3 b.g. River Falls 113 – Tribal Rhythm (IRE) (Double **45**
Schwartz 128) [1998 60: 5v⁵ 5d⁵ 5m 1999 6v 7s 8m 8d⁶ 8f 8g 8g 7g³ 7g 9m Aug 26]
poor maiden handicapper: pulled up having reportedly lost action final start: stays
1m: acts on heavy going. *Miss L. A. Perratt*

THE DUKE OF BELAIR 2 b.c. (Feb 12) Cosmonaut – Gay Hostess (FR) –
(Direct Flight) [1999 5m 5g 7.1g Nov 3] half-brother to 3 winners, including 6f (at 2
yrs) and 7f winner Clare Kerry Lass (by Alleging) and 7-y-o Dally Boy: dam French
7f (at 2 yrs) and 1¼m winner: soundly beaten, including in seller. *D. A. Nolan*

THE EXHIBITION FOX 3 b.c. Be My Chief (USA) 122 – Swift Return 79 **87**
(Double Form 130) [1998 –p: 7.9g 1999 10g² 10.4s 10.3f⁴ 7.9d* 8m 10.5d Aug 5]
tall, close-coupled colt: fairly useful performer: won maiden at York in June: well
beaten in handicaps after: stays 1m: acts on good to soft going. *B. A. McMahon*

THE FINAL WORD 2 ch.f. (Mar 13) Cosmonaut – Jolizal 52 (Good Times **66**
(ITY)) [1999 8s⁵ Nov 5] sturdy filly: second foal: sister to 3-y-o The Last Word: dam
1m seller winner: awkward stalls, never-nearer fifth of 18 to Blusienka in maiden at
Doncaster: should stay beyond 1m. *R. Hollinshead*

THE FLY 5 gr.h. Pharly (FR) 130 – Nelly Do Da 78 (Derring-Do 131) [1998 116d: **111**
12d³ 12s³ 12d³ 12d 13.3m⁵ 11.6m² 12g⁴ 12g⁵ 1999 14.1s² 13.4m⁴ 12.4f³ 10s 11.8s³
12f⁴ 9f² Dec 29] leggy, useful-looking horse: good mover: smart performer: won
over hurdles early in year but below form on return to Flat and sold from B. Hills
70,000 gns after fifth start: back to near best when 5¾ lengths fourth to Lazy Lode in
Hollywood Turf Cup then second in allowance race at Santa Anita: stays 14.6f: acts
on firm and soft going: tends to find little, and seems best held up. *D. Vienna, USA*

THE FLYER (IRE) 2 b.c. (Apr 18) Blues Traveller (IRE) 119 – National Ballet **67**
(Shareef Dancer (USA) 135) [1999 7m⁶ Jun 24] 32,000Y: fourth foal: half-brother to
useful 2-y-o 7f winner Name of Love (by Petardia) and 3-y-o Annapurna: dam,
unraced close relative of useful middle-distance stayer Saxon Maid, out of Oaks third
Britannia's Rule: weak in market and green when sixth of 16 to Breathless Dreams in
maiden at Salisbury, getting hang of things late on: likely to stay 1¼m: should
improve. *P. F. I. Cole*

THE FOSSICK (IRE)   3 ch.g. Forest Wind (USA) 111 – Rose of Summer (IRE)   –
(Taufan (USA) 119) [1998 NR 1999 a8g⁵ Jun 11] 12,000Y, 11,000Y: second foal:
half-brother to a winner in Belgium by River Falls: dam once-raced half-sister to
useful Irish performer up to 1¼m Lord Bud: well beaten in Southwell maiden.
M. A. Peill

THE FRENCH FURZE (IRE)   5 ch.g. Be My Guest (USA) 126 – Exciting   **71 d**
(Mill Reef (USA) 141) [1998 NR 1999 a13g 10s³ 12g⁶ 11.5m 12g⁴ 14m⁶ 12.1m⁵ Aug
5] IR 14,000Y: leggy gelding: related to several winners, notably 6-y-o Almushtarak:
dam (ran once) sister to a smart stayer and from family of smart juveniles: fair
maiden handicapper on Flat: trained by C. Roche in Ireland at 3 yrs: became disappointing in 1999: should stay beyond 1½m: acts on soft going: blinkered final start:
has shown useful form over hurdles for M. Pipe, including in December, but not one
to trust. *R. E. Peacock*

THE FROG QUEEN   2 b.f. (Mar 3) Bin Ajwaad (IRE) 119 – The Frog Lady   **64**
(IRE) 52 (Al Hareb (USA) 123) [1999 6g³ 6m³ 6m 7m a7g* Sep 28] lengthy, unfurnished filly: first foal: dam, maiden, best form at 1¼m/1½m: fair performer: won
seller at Southwell in September: should stay 1m. *D. W. P. Arbuthnot*

THE FUGATIVE   6 b.m. Nicholas (USA) 111 – Miss Runaway 73 (Runnett 125)   **94 +**
[1998 78, a57: 5d 5s* 6s³ 6g³ 5m² 5m⁴ 6g* 6m 6g* 7m⁶ 5d⁵ 5g 7m² 7m⁶ 5d⁶ a7g⁶   **a58 +**
1999 a6g⁴ 6s* 7m⁵ 6g⁶ 6d² 6g* 6f 5s³ 6s⁵ᵈⁱˢ 6v Nov 17] small mare: fairly useful on
turf, modest on all-weather: won handicaps at Epsom (has good record there) in April
and June: good efforts when third to Nuclear Debate in listed race at Deauville in
August and fifth (disqualified, having got poor run and forced way out) to Superior
Premium in rated stakes at Newbury in October: effective at 5f (given test) to easy 7f:
acts on good to firm going, soft and equitrack. *P. Mitchell*

THE GAMBOLLER (USA)   4 b.g. Irish Tower (USA) – Lady Limbo (USA)   –
(Dance Spell (USA)) [1998 84d: 8g⁴ 8f² 10g 10m* 10.2d 12g 9.9m 9.7s 1999 9.9g
15.8g Jul 1] big, close-coupled gelding: fairly useful performer at best: well held
both 4-y-o starts, blinkered final one: stays 1¼m: looks a tricky ride: successful over
hurdles in September/October. *M. E. Sowersby*

THE GAY FOX   5 gr.g. Never So Bold 135 – School Concert 80 (Music Boy 124)   **83 d**
[1998 95: 5d³ 6v 5v* 6d 5.1m³ 5d 5s⁶ 6.1g⁶ 5m⁵ 6g 5g 6f 5m 6s 5s 5d² 5s⁵ 1999 5.2m
5.1m⁴ 5s 5m 5d⁶ 6d 5m³ 5f⁵ 5d⁴ 5.2g⁴ 5.1d⁴ 5m⁵ 5s 5g⁵ 5.1s Oct 26] good-topped
gelding: unimpressive mover: fairly useful handicapper: has won at easy 7f, very best
form at 5f: acts on any ground: blinkered 4 of last 5 starts: usually bandaged/wears
tongue strap: tends to race lazily. *B. A. McMahon*

THE GIRLS' FILLY   2 b.f. (Feb 3) Emperor Jones (USA) 119 – Sioux City   **64**
(Simply Great (FR) 122) [1999 6m³ 7m⁴ 6m 7g Sep 14] 15,500F, 19,000Y: strong,
good-bodied filly: third foal: half-sister to 5-y-o Northern Accord and French 9.5f to
11.5f winner Dorsoduro (by Highest Honor): dam useful French 1¼m/1½m winner:
best effort in maidens when fourth of 8 to Solaia at Newmarket: will stay
at least 1m: sold 3,000 gns in October. *J. H. M. Gosden*

THE GLOW-WORM (IRE)   4 b.c. Doyoun 124 – Shakanda (IRE) (Shernazar   **113 §**
131) [1998 113: 12s* 12.3g² 12m⁶ 11.9f⁵ 14.6m 12s³ 1999 12m² 16.2d⁵ 13.9s 12.3d*
22.2m⁶ 13.4d³ 10.9d⁵ 11.9v⁴ 12v Oct 23] lengthy colt: smart performer: creditable
¾-length second to Sadian in John Porter Stakes at Newbury on reappearance: below
form after, including when landing odds in 3-runner minor event at Chester in May:
effective at 1½m to 2m: probably acts on any going: blinkered (ran poorly having
made running) third start: usually held up: inconsistent and probably ungenuine: sold
20,000 gns, joined P. O'Brady in Ireland. *B. W. Hills*

THE GREAT FLOOD   6 ch.g. Risk Me (FR) 127 – Yukosan 69 (Absalom 128)   **53**
[1998 NR 1999 13.8g⁵ 15.4v⁶ a16.2g⁵ a14.8g Aug 6] modest handicapper: left
C. Dwyer after second start: stays 2m: acts on fibresand. *G. F. H. Charles-Jones*

THE GREEN GREY   5 gr.g. Environment Friend 128 – Pea Green 98 (Try My   **73**
Best (USA) 130) [1998 75: 8g 9.7m 8g* 8m* 8f² 8m* 8m* 8g⁵ a7g³ a8g* 1999 a10g²
a8g² 8m 8.5g Aug 30] big, workmanlike gelding: good mover: fair performer: left
D. Morris and off 7 months after second start: stays easy 1¼m: acts on equitrack,
goes well on going firmer than good on turf: visored once at 3 yrs. *L. Montague Hall*

THE GROOVER 3 ch.g. Beveled (USA) – Taffidale 67 (Welsh Pageant 132) – [1998 NR 1999 8m 8.2s Oct 5] tall, unfurnished gelding: sixth foal: dam maiden who stayed 1½m: no show in maidens at Newbury and Nottingham, looking less than keen. *G. M. McCourt*

THE GROVELLER 4 b.g. Prince Sabo 123 – Estonia (Kings Lake (USA) 133) **58** [1998 NR 1999 7d 8m 8.3g 10m 7.6m 8h⁶ 8.1d⁵ 7m³ 8d³ 8m³ 7m³ 7.1m Sep 9] strong, useful-looking gelding: has a round action: modest handicapper: pulled up lame final start: effective at 7f/1m: acts on good to firm going, soft and fibresand: often blinkered/visored. *P. D. Evans*

THE GYPSY TIPPLER 4 ch.f. Romany Rye 102 – Eidolon (Rousillon (USA) **56** 133) [1998 60: 7.6m⁵ 7m 6m⁶ 7m 6.1d 6.1g³ 6.1s 6s⁵ 6s 6.1f 6g⁵ 6.1g 6.1f a6g Jul 10] plain filly: modest maiden: best efforts at 6f: acts on soft and good to firm ground, well beaten only run on fibresand. *B. Palling*

THE HAKA 3 ch.g. Sabrehill (USA) 120 – Exotic Forest 66 (Dominion 123) **62** [1998 62: 5g 6s⁶ a7g⁵ 6.1g³ 6m⁵ 6.9m 7m 10s⁶ 8d 1999 7s² 7f 7.1g⁵ 8g⁵ 8.2f 7m Aug 10] good-bodied gelding: has a short, round action: modest maiden: stays 1¼m: acts on good to firm going, soft and fibresand: tried visored, blinkered after second outing: edgy sort, has been early to post. *M. Dods*

THE HAULIER 3 ch.g. Ardkinglass 114 – Ask Away (Midyan (USA) 124) **77** [1998 77: 5s⁵ 7s³ 5d⁶ 6g⁵ 7m⁵ 7g* 7f 8s⁵ 7.9g 6s² 1999 7.5g⁴ 8.5d 7m⁶ 7g 7.5m* 7m⁶ 7.1g³ 8m 7f 7.1d⁵ 7g² Oct 15] sparely-made gelding: fair handicapper: made all in 4-runner race at Beverley in July: may prove best at 7f/1m: acts on soft and good to firm going: game: sold 10,000 gns. *T. D. Easterby*

THE HIGHGATE POT 2 b.f. (Feb 9) Never So Bold 135 – Sea Farer Lake 74 **50** (Gairloch 122) [1999 5g 7g 6m a7g 8s 6d Nov 4] eighth foal: half-sister to 3-y-o Sail-On Bun, 4-y-o Smooth Sailing and 1989 2-y-o 6f seller winner Sirse (by Enchantment): dam 1m/1¼m winner: modest maiden at best: stays 7f: sent to Belgium. *M. D. I. Usher*

THE IMPOSTER (IRE) 4 ch.g. Imp Society (USA) – Phoenix Dancer (IRE) – (Gorytus (USA) 132) [1998 55: a8s⁵ a8g 7g⁶ a9.4g³ a8g a7g⁵ a8.5g⁶ a8.5g² a8g 1999 **a68** a8.5g* a11g⁴ a8.5g² Jun 19] fair performer: won seller at Wolverhampton (final start for D. Murray Smith) in May: best efforts around 1m: acts on good to firm going, good to soft and fibresand. *Miss S. J. Wilton*

THE JAM SAHEB 2 b.c. (Apr 6) Petong 126 – Reem El Fala (FR) (Fabulous – Dancer (USA) 124) [1999 7g 7v Oct 25] 10,000F, 9,600Y: fourth foal: dam French 7.6f/11f winner: always behind in maidens at Lingfield: tongue tied. *Lady Herries*

THEKRYAATI (IRE) 4 ch.c. Indian Ridge 123 – Lamu Lady (IRE) 70 (Lomond **90** (USA) 128) [1998 –p: 8g 1999 a10g* a11g a8.5g² a9.4g² a10g² a9.4g² a10g² 12g a8.5g² 10.3f² 10d 10m⁴ 9f* Jul 29] strong, angular colt: fairly useful performer: won maiden at Lingfield and handicaps at Wolverhampton in January/February and at Goodwood (22 ran) in July: effective at 8.5f to 1¼m: acts on all-weather and firm ground (well held on good to soft): usually races prominently: game and reliable: sent to UAE. *M. Johnston*

THE LAMBTON WORM 5 b.g. Superpower 113 – Springwell 73 (Miami **46** Springs 121) [1998 50: 8.3v⁶ 7.1m 7m 6d 8g 6.9m⁵ 7g 1999 a8g 5.9m⁶ 8d 7f⁵ 6.9m⁵ 6.9m⁶ Jul 16] strong, well-made gelding: poor handicapper nowadays: seems to stay 7f: acts on good to firm and soft ground: blinkered (signs of temperament)/visored once each. *N. Bycroft*

THELANDY 4 b.g. Noble Patriarch 115 – Choir (High Top 131) [1998 –: 8g⁶ a8g – 7m 12d⁶ 1999 a7f 12.4g 14.1f⁶ Aug 7] of no account. *W. S. Cunningham*

THE LAST RAMBO 2 b.c. (Mar 16) Rambo Dancer (CAN) 107 – Under The – Wing 69 (Aragon 118) [1999 7m Jun 15] fifth known foal: dam, maiden, from good middle-distance staying family: always behind in Thirsk maiden. *J. L. Eyre*

THE LAST WORD 3 b.g. Cosmonaut – Jolizal 52 (Good Times (ITY)) [1998 – 48: 6s 5.7v a7g a6g⁵ a7g² 1999 a9.4g² a8g* a8.5g³ 12g⁵ a11g² a12g⁴ a11g⁴ a8g **a67** a8g³ a8.5g² Jul 9] compact gelding: fair handicapper: won at Southwell in February: effective at 1m to 11f: acts on fibresand, little form in 3 runs on turf. *R. Hollinshead*

THE MANX TOUCH (IRE)   3 gr.f. Petardia 113 – Chapter And Verse   **70**
(Dancer's Image (USA)) [1998 –: 7m 6m 6.1g 1999 6.1s 6.1g⁶ 8d⁵ 7g⁴ 9s⁴ 10.5d 8s*
7d* Oct 12] leggy filly: fair handicapper: won apprentice maiden event at Bath in
September and selling event at Leicester (sold to join Miss K. Marks 7,700 gns) in
October, latter despite hanging/swishing tail: should stay 1¼m: acts on soft going.
M. A. Peill

THEME TIME (USA)   3 b.c. Stop The Music (USA) – Ranales (USA) (Majestic   **–**
Light (USA)) [1998 NR 1999 10m 11.9f⁵ Aug 4] first foal: dam 2-y-o 1m winner
from 2 starts in USA: tongue tied, well beaten in maidens at Sandown (slowly away)
and Brighton: sold 800 gns. *Mrs A. J. Perrett*

THEME TUNE   4 b.f. Dilum (USA) 115 – Souadah (USA) (General Holme   **46**
(USA) 128) [1998 –: 7s 1999 a8g 7m 8f a8g 7d 11.5m* Oct 19] poor performer:
easily best effort in 1999 when winning selling handicap at Yarmouth: stays 11.5f:
acts on good to firm going: visored twice: sold 1,400 gns, joined M. Pipe.
Dr J. D. Scargill

THE NURSE (IRE)   3 b.f. Mujadil (USA) 119 – Nurse Jo (USA) (J O Tobin   **64 d**
(USA) 130) [1998 64: 5d⁴ a5g⁶ 6m* 6f⁴ 6m² 6s³ 5d 6g 1999 6v⁵ 6m 6m 8m³ 7g 8m
6m 6m 8.2g Sep 25] angular, unfurnished filly: modest handicapper: stays 1m: acts
on firm and soft ground: inconsistent: sold 2,000 gns. *K. A. Ryan*

THEO'S LAD (IRE)   2 b.g. (Apr 6) Shareef Dancer (USA) 135 – Inshirah (USA)   **54**
90 (Caro 133) [1999 6m* 6.1m⁵ 6g 5m⁶ 7.5g Sep 15] 10,000F, 6,500Y: good-bodied
gelding: half-brother to several winners, including a French middle-distance winner
by Mtoto and 4-y-o Days of Grace: dam 2-y-o 5f and 7f winner: modest form: best
effort when winning seller at Catterick in May: should stay 7f: tried blinkered: sold
800 gns. *R. Guest*

THE OUTBACK   2 ch.g. (May 19) Timeless Times (USA) 99 – Ninety-Five 70   **–**
(Superpower 113) [1999 5g Jul 1] 3,000Y: first foal: dam 5f winner: well beaten in
seller at Catterick. *J. G. FitzGerald*

THE PRESIDENT   4 b.g. Yaheeb (USA) 95§ – When The Saints (Bay Express   **58**
132) [1998 72: 10d⁶ 12.3s⁴ 12g⁶ 11m⁵ 12d 1999 12.3m 12s 13f⁴ 14.1g Oct 2] tall,
lengthy gelding: modest maiden: stays 13f: acts on firm and soft going: awkward
stalls second/third starts, unseating rider having reared on first occasion: successful
over hurdles in October. *Mrs M. Reveley*

THE PRINCE   5 b.g. Machiavellian (USA) 123 – Mohican Girl 112 (Dancing   **98**
Brave (USA) 140) [1998 NR 1999 8.3m² 7.6m* 8.1g 8m⁶ 7f 10m⁴ᵈⁱˢ 9g 8.3m² 8.3m*
7.9g³ 8g 8.2d³ Oct 21] well-made gelding: has a quick action: useful performer: won
minor event at Lingfield in May and handicap at Hamilton in September: ran well
when placed otherwise: best around 1m: acts on good to firm and good to soft
ground: versatile last 5 starts: wears tongue strap: often slowly away: needs exaggerated waiting tactics: not one to trust implicitly: sold 22,000 gns. *R. M. H. Cowell*

THE PROOF   2 b.g. (Apr 16) Rudimentary (USA) 118 – Indubitable 87 (Sharpo   **– p**
132) [1999 8v 6v 6d Nov 4] big, lengthy gelding: fifth foal: half-brother to 3-y-o City
Guild, 4-y-o Bronzino and 5-y-o Cugina: dam 1¼m winner who stayed 1¾m: green,
signs of ability in maidens at Salisbury, Newbury and Windsor: comes from family
of late developers, and should do better at 3 yrs. *G. B. Balding*

THE PROSECUTOR   2 b.c. (Mar 15) Contract Law (USA) 108 – Elsocko 76   **63**
(Swing Easy (USA) 126) [1999 a5g² 6d² 5g⁶ 6s a6g³ 7s a6g* Nov 27] 4,500Y: **a79**
seventh foal: half-brother to several winners, including fairly useful 1997 2-y-o 5f/6f
winner Socket Set (by Tragic Role): dam maiden who stayed 7f: easily best effort
when winning maiden at Wolverhampton in November: stays 6f: acts on fibresand,
raced only on good going or softer on turf. *B. A. McMahon*

THE PUZZLER (IRE)   8 br.g. Sharpo 132 – Enigma 87 (Ahonoora 122) [1998   **94 §**
102d: 6d⁶ 6g⁴ 6g³ 6d 5.1d⁶ 6g 5g 5g 6f 6.1g 6g 1999 6m⁶ 5s* 6m 5s 5d⁵ 5s Oct 23]
leggy gelding: bad mover: fairly useful handicapper: best effort in 1999 when
winning at Sandown in April: has form at 7f, raced mainly at 5f/6f: needs good going
or softer: blinkered once in 1998: usually bandaged, and has gone lame while racing:
cannot be relied on. *B. W. Hills*

THE QUARE FELLOW 3 ch.c. Elmaamul (USA) 125 – Bizarre Lady (Dalsaan **80** 125) [1998 69p: 8m⁵ 1999 8g* 8m 9.9g⁵ 8d Oct 21] rangy, rather unfurnished colt: fairly useful performer: won maiden at Ripon in April: ran creditably after only when fifth in handicap at Goodwood: stays 1¼m: yet to race on extremes of going: sold 7,500 gns. *J. H. M. Gosden*

THE RAIN LADY 3 b.f. Lugana Beach 116 – Rain Splash 74 (Petong 126) [1998 **–** 55: 5.1g 5g 5m⁵ 1999 5.1s 6g a5g 6.1m 6f 7.1d 6.1g Aug 13] poor mover: poor maiden: left R. Hollinshead after fourth start: should stay 6f. *P. D. Evans*

THE REAL MCCOY 5 b.g. Deploy 131 – Mukhayyalah (Dancing Brave (USA) **–** 140) [1998 42, a47: a12g* 10.3d⁵ 9.9m 1999 a11g Sep 28] rangy, good-topped gelding: poor performer: stays 1½m: acts on fibresand, probably on good to soft going. *M. A. Peill*

THE REPUBLICAN 2 b.g. (Jun 17) Democratic (USA) 101 – Loving You **–** (Thatch (USA) 136) [1999 5d 7.1g Nov 3] half-brother to several winners in Italy, including 1¼m and 1½m winner Last Long (by Commanche Run): dam unraced: well held in maidens. *W. Storey*

THERHEA (IRE) 6 b.g. Pennine Walk 120 – Arab Art (Artaius (USA) 129) **98** [1998 94: 7s⁴ 8s³ 8.1s* 8d 8m² 8.1g³ 8g⁵ 8m 8d⁵ 9d⁵ 8s³ 8s² 1999 8d⁶ 8m⁵ 7g³ 8m 8.1d³ 7d* 8.1m³ 7m 7g⁵ 8.3m Aug 28] close-coupled, good-bodied gelding: takes the eye: useful handicapper: won rated stakes at Newbury in June: good efforts otherwise when third in Victoria Cup at Ascot on third start and rated stakes at Sandown (to Brilliant Red) on seventh: effective at 7f, barely stays 9f: acts on soft and good to firm ground: twice blinkered earlier in career: has been bandaged off-fore: sometimes early to post: effective ridden from front or held up: genuine. *B. R. Millman*

THERMAL SPRING 2 ch.f. (Apr 24) Zafonic (USA) 130 – Seven Springs **66 p** (USA) 114 (Irish River (FR) 131) [1999 7m⁵ Sep 7] half-sister to several winners, notably high-class miler Distant View (by Mr Prospector): dam won Prix Robert Papin and Prix Morny and later stayed 1m: weak in market and green, sixth of 11 to Leading Role in maiden at Lingfield, slowly away and never dangerous: should stay 1m: will do better. *H. R. A. Cecil*

THERMOPYLAE 3 b.f. Tenby 125 – Tamassos 67 (Dance In Time (CAN)) **81** [1998 74p: 8.2s⁴ 7v² 1999 10m² 10.5g⁴ 10d² a8.5g 10d a13g⁶ Oct 1] leggy, angular filly: fairly useful maiden: best efforts when runner-up at Newbury in April and Windsor in August: should stay 1½m: acts on good to firm and heavy going (below form on all-weather): has worn crossed noseband: sold 16,000 gns. *P. F. I. Cole*

THE ROBE 4 b.f. Robellino (USA) 127 – Outward's Gal 78 (Ashmore (FR) 125) **43** [1998 50, a–: 10.8g 11.6g 12g⁶ 16.2m³ a16g⁶ 16d³ 14.1s² 1999 14.1d⁵ 15.4v⁵ Apr 20] sturdy filly: poor maiden handicapper: stays beyond 2m: acts on equitrack, good to firm and heavy ground: not an easy ride: joined M. Pipe, and won over hurdles in November. *A. W. Carroll*

THE ROBSTER (USA) 2 ch.c. (Mar 13) Woodman (USA) 126 – Country **66** Cruise (USA) (Riverman (USA) 131) [1999 7v 7s Nov 5] $100,000F, IR 45,000Y: strong colt: has scope: second foal: brother to a winner in USA: dam won up to 9f in USA: better effort in maidens (fair form) when seventh of 20 to Golovin at Doncaster on second start, making much of running: should stay 1m. *B. J. Meehan*

THESEUS (IRE) 3 b.c. Danehill (USA) 126 – Graecia Magna (USA) 109 **86** (Private Account (USA)) [1998 72p: 7m 8.2d⁶ 7d⁶ 1999 11.4m² 11.9d Jun 12] big, strong, good-topped colt: has a quick action: fairly useful performer: 1¼ lengths second to Compton Amica in handicap at Sandown: found to be suffering from respiratory distress next time: stays 11.4f: sold 21,000 gns. *Sir Michael Stoute*

THE SHADOW 3 br.g. Polar Falcon (USA) 126 – Shadiliya 90 (Red Alert 127) **69** [1998 67p: 8s 7s³ 1999 8m 10g a7g⁶ a9.4g* 9s⁵ Aug 18] fair handicapper: best effort when winning at Wolverhampton in July: stays 9.4f: acts on soft going and fibresand. *D. W. P. Arbuthnot*

THE SHEIKH (IRE) 2 b.g. (Mar 8) Sri Pekan (USA) 117 – Arabian Dream **–** (IRE) (Royal Academy (USA) 130) [1999 6g 6.8m 7m Jul 7] 11,000Y: leggy, lengthy gelding: has a quick action: first foal: dam unraced granddaughter of Allez France: some promise on debut, but well held (including in seller) after. *M. L. W. Bell*

THE SILK THIEF 4 b.g. Thowra (FR) – Fine N Fancy (Netherkelly 112) [1998 –
–: 7d 8s 1999 a12g⁶ a11g a16g Feb 11] no sign of ability: tried visored. *J. R. Jenkins*

THE STAGER (IRE) 7 b.g. Danehill (USA) 126 – Wedgewood Blue (USA) 87 –
(Sir Ivor 135) [1998 61: a7g⁵ a8g⁶ a8g 7m a8g a8g* 1999 a8g a8g* 8.3m 8f a8.5g⁶ **a69**
a8.5g a10g² Dec 18] tall, lengthy gelding: good mover: fair handicapper on all-
weather: won at Southwell in April: easily best effort after when good second at
Lingfield: stays easy 1¼m: acts on firm ground and all-weather: tried blinkered/
visored: has worn tongue strap: takes good hold. *J. R. Jenkins*

THE TATLING (IRE) 2 b.c. (Apr 23) Perugino (USA) 84 – Aunty Eileen **104**
(Ahonoora 122) [1999 6g³ 5m⁶ 6g⁴ 5.2g⁶ 6m² 5.3s* 6g² 6m⁶ 5d² Oct 9] IR 54,000Y:
half-brother to several winners, including 3-y-o Amazing Dream and 5-y-o Daintree:
dam unraced half-sister to smart sprinter Lugana Beach: useful performer: won
maiden at Yarmouth in July and minor event at Brighton in August: best effort when
1¼ lengths second of 13 to Kier Park in Cornwallis Stakes at Ascot final start, leading
from over 1f out until last 100 yds: has form at 6f, but may well prove best at 5f: acts
on soft and good to firm going: races freely. *M. L. W. Bell*

THE THIRD CURATE (IRE) 4 b.g. Fairy King (USA) – Lassalia (Sallust **84 d**
134) [1998 67: 8v⁶ 10v⁴ 1999 16s 12s 7m* 7.1d 8m 7.3m 7d 6g 6d a7g a7g Dec 15]
105,000Y: rangy gelding: brother to 1994 2-y-o 1m winner King Balant and a winner
in Italy and half-brother to several winners, notably smart 1¼m performer Free Flyer
(by Bluebird), 7f winner at 2 yrs: dam placed from 6f to 9.5f in Ireland: easily best
effort when winning 24-runner handicap at the Curragh (final start for D. Weld) in
June: well below that form in Britain: bred to stay beyond 7f: has worn blinkers,
including for success. *B. J. Curley*

THE THRUSTER 4 b.g. Elmaamul (USA) 125 – Moon Spin 83 (Night Shift **61**
(USA)) [1998 73: 8m 7m² 7.6m* 7m 1999 10.3d 8d 9.3m 12s³ 13.8m⁴ a12g 12m **a–**
14.6m⁵ 8m* 7m² 7m 7.5g³ 8f 7d³ 6g² 7d Oct 12] lengthy gelding: modest handicapper: won at Pontefract in July: ran creditably after when placed: likely to prove
best up to 1¼m: acts on good to firm and good to soft going (probably on soft), below
form only start on equitrack: usually blinkered/visored: usually races prominently:
sold 5,000 gns, sent to Italy. *D. Nicholls*

THE WHISTLING TEAL 3 b.c. Rudimentary (USA) 118 – Lonely Shore **93**
(Blakeney 126) [1998 66: 7s⁶ 7d⁶ 1999 7s³ 8.3m* 8m 8g² 9m⁵ a8.5g* a9.4g² 10.3d³
8s² 10s Oct 2] strong, compact colt: fairly useful handicapper: won at Windsor in
April and Wolverhampton in August: good short-head second of 22 to Indium in
valuable contest at Ascot penultimate start: respectable eighth in Cambridgeshire at
Newmarket (hampered early) final one: effective at 1m, probably at 1¼m: acts on
good to firm going, soft and fibresand: genuine. *J. G. Smyth-Osbourne*

THE WIFE 2 b.f. (Feb 15) Efisio 120 – Great Steps 88 (Vaigly Great 127) [1999 **85**
5d 6g³ 7.5g* 7.5m² 7.5g² 7.9f* 7.9d 8d Oct 22] 6,500Y: rather leggy, useful-looking
filly: second foal: sister to 3-y-o Birth of The Blues: dam 2-y-o 7f winner: fairly
useful performer: won maiden at Beverley in June and nursery at York in September:
will stay beyond 1m: acts on firm going, not at best on softer than good: tends to
sweat, and edgy last 2 starts. *T. D. Easterby*

THE WILD WIDOW 5 gr.m. Saddlers' Hall (IRE) 126 – No Cards 109 (No **53**
Mercy 126) [1998 71: 8.2s³ 8g⁴ 10d² 12.3g⁵ 10m⁶ 10s 10s 1999 a11g a8g a9.4g* **a63**
a9.4g² a9.4g a8.5g 8.5m a8.5g a11g³ a9.4g² a8.5g³ a9.4g* 10.5m* 8.1m 10.5d 10f
a10g Nov 26] deep-girthed mare: has had leg problems: modest performer: won
sellers at Wolverhampton in February and Warwick in August: probably best at 9f to
10.5f: acts on good to firm ground, soft and fibresand: blinkered last 5 starts: often
leads: none too consistent. *Miss S. J. Wilton*

THE WOODCOCK 4 b.g. Handsome Sailor 125 – Game Germaine (Mummy's **67 §**
Game 120) [1998 74: 6d⁶ 6s 6.1m⁴ 5g 6.1g* 6m⁶ 6g 7d 7d 1999 a7g⁴ 7g* 8d a7g³ 7m
6d⁵ a7g⁴ a6g² a7g⁵ a6g 7m a7g⁵ Aug 25] lengthy gelding: fair performer: left B. Hills
after second start: won seller at Catterick in March: best at 6f/7f: acts on good to firm
ground and all-weather: effective visored or not: sometimes wanders/finds little: not
one to trust implicitly: sold 1,000 gns. *K. R. Burke*

THE WOODSTOCK LADY 2 ch.f. (Apr 10) Barathea (IRE) 127 – Howlin' **80 p**
(USA) (Alleged (USA) 138) [1999 7d* Oct 11] 17,000F: tall, quite good-topped

filly: second foal: sister to French 3-y-o 1½m winner Les Hurlants: dam French 11f winner from good US family: green to post, won 19-runner maiden at Leicester by neck from Scarletta, good headway to lead entering final 1f: should stay 1¼m: open to plenty of improvement, and could well make a useful performer. *B. W. Hills*

THIEVES WELCOME 2 b.f. (Jan 27) Most Welcome 131 – Miss Tealeaf (USA) (Lear Fan (USA) 130) [1999 a6g⁶ 6f³ Aug 4] workmanlike filly: fourth reported foal: sister to a modest maiden: dam, once-raced, from good middle-distance family: much better effort in maidens when staying-on third of 13 to Glendamah at Newcastle: should be suited by 1m+. *E. Weymes* **61 +**

THIHN (IRE) 4 ch.g. Machiavellian (USA) 123 – Hasana (USA) (Private Account (USA)) [1998 62: 8d 8.2v 1999 10g⁶ 8g³ 8g 8m⁵ 9.9v² 10s² Nov 1] leggy gelding: modest maiden handicapper: stays 1¼m: acts on heavy going: wandered final start. *N. E. Berry* **62**

THINK AGAIN (IRE) 5 b.g. Long Pond 113 – Either Or (Boreen (FR) 123) [1998 –: 16s 1999 9.9m 16d 12.1f Aug 24] bad maiden. *R. Craggs* **25**

THIRTY SIX CEE 2 b.f. (Feb 27) Rudimentary (USA) 118 – Dear Person (Rainbow Quest (USA) 134) [1999 5m⁵ 6d⁵ 5d⁴ 6m⁶ 7d 6s a8.5g Dec 11] 2,400Y: fourth foal: sister to 4-y-o Figawin: dam twice-raced half-sister to Galtres Stakes winner Startino: modest maiden: headstrong (has worn crossed noseband and been early to post), and may prove best at 5f/6f: sometimes tongue tied. *A. W. Carroll* **59**

THOMAS CROWN (IRE) 7 ch.g. Last Tycoon 131 – Upward Trend 112 (Salmon Leap (USA) 131) [1998 NR 1999 17.2f Jun 26] quite good-topped gelding: little form on Flat since 1994. *D. L. Williams* **–**

THOMAS HENRY (IRE) 3 br.g. Petardia 113 – Hitopah (Bustino 136) [1998 69: 7.3g 6m 7m⁴ 8.2d 7m⁴ 7s 1999 a6g⁶ a7f* a8g³ a8g⁴ 8.3m⁴ 9.9m 8.1m⁴ a10g* a10g⁶ Dec 10] leggy, close-coupled gelding: fair performer: won maiden at Lingfield in January and seller on same course in November: stays easy 1¼m: acts on equitrack and good to firm going: tried visored: none too consistent. *J. S. Moore* **73**

THORNABY GIRL (IRE) 3 b.f. Fayruz 116 – Anita's Love (IRE) 53 (Anita's Prince 126) [1998 67: 5d* 5g³ a5g² 1999 a5g⁶ a5g a5g² 5m 5g Jun 4] modest performer: will prove best at 5f: acts on all-weather and good to soft going: sold 1,100 gns. *T. D. Barron* **59**

THORNCLIFF FOX (IRE) 2 ch.g. (Mar 29) Foxhound (USA) 103 – Godly Light (FR) 47 (Vayrann 133) [1999 5m a5g³ 5d³ 5g Aug 29] IR 12,500F, IR 13,500Y: workmanlike gelding: fourth foal: half-brother to 3-y-o Beverley Monkey: dam third in 1m seller at 4 yrs: dam poorly in maidens: ran poorly in nursery at Beverley final start: raced only at 5f: blinkered last 3 starts: looks quirky. *J. A. Glover* **72**

THORNTOUN BELLE (IRE) 4 b.f. Rainbows For Life (CAN) – Manzala (USA) 71 (Irish River (FR) 131) [1998 51: 6s 8d 8m³ 9.1m 9.3d 11.1d 1999 9.2g⁵ 13.1g 8.3m 6.9m Jul 16] maiden, little form in 1999. *D. A. Nolan* **–**

THORNTOUN GOLD (IRE) 3 ch.f. Lycius (USA) 124 – Gold Braisim (IRE) 77 (Jareer (USA) 115) [1998 52: 6d⁵ 6g⁴ 7g 8d⁴ 7d 8v 1999 8d 8.1d 8g 8g⁴ 9.1g⁴ 8f* 7g² 8m 8m³ 10m 8.3s 8s Oct 4] workmanlike filly: modest handicapper: won selling event at Thirsk in July: effective at 7f to 9f: acts on firm and good to soft ground. *J. S. Goldie* **56**

THRASHING 4 b.c. Kahyasi 130 – White-Wash 94 (Final Straw 127) [1998 85d: 12d³ 13.9d⁴ 14g 11.6f 8m⁵ 1999 8m Aug 22] small, quite attractive colt: has a quick action: disappointing maiden. *J. G. M. O'Shea* **–**

THREADNEEDLE (USA) 6 b.g. Danzig Connection (USA) – Sleeping Beauty 87 (Mill Reef (USA) 141) [1998 –, a95+: a10g⁵ a10g* a10g* a12g a8.5g a10g² 8d 8m 9d 8.1d a8g a9.4g⁶ 11.9g a10g⁶ a8g* a7g 1999 a7g* a7g³ a9.4g a7g a8g a10g 7g a8f a8f* a10f a7s⁶ a8f Dec 13] workmanlike gelding: useful performer on all-weather: better than ever when winning handicap at Lingfield in January: ran creditably next time: left K. Burke after seventh outing: nowhere near best in USA after, including when winning claimer at Philadelphia Park in October: effective at 7f to 1¼m: acts on equitrack/dirt, little form on fibresand or recently on turf: blinkered once at 5 yrs and on final start: often front runner. *G. Rennison, USA* **– a99 d**

THREAT   3 br.g. Zafonic (USA) 130 – Prophecy (IRE) 109 (Warning 136) [1998 **103**
93+: 6d* 6m³ 1999 6g 6m⁴ 6d 6d² Jul 2] rather unfurnished, quite attractive gelding:
has been freeze-fired: useful performer: best efforts in 1999 when in frame at
Haydock in listed rated stakes (2 lengths fifth to Cubism, promoted a place) and
minor event (1½ lengths second of 5 to Tomba): likely to prove best at 5f/6f: yet to
race on extremes of going: has worn crossed noseband/tongue strap: ran in snatches
penultimate start: not a straightforward ride: sold 28,000 gns. *J. H. M. Gosden*

THREE ANGELS (IRE)   4 b.g. Houmayoun (FR) 114 – Mullaghroe (Tarboosh **82**
(USA)) [1998 79: 12d 9d 7m* 7.1g* 7.1d⁵ 7g³ 7m² 7.1m³ 7m⁴ 7.1g⁶ 6g³ 1999 7m
7m⁴ 7f² 7.1m 6.9m² 8m 8m² 7f³ 8g 7.1g² 7.9m 7m⁶ 7d Sep 15] robust gelding: fairly
useful performer: ran creditably several times in 1999: effective at 6f to 1m: acts on
firm ground: effective visored or not. *M. H. Tompkins*

THREE BAY TREES (IRE)   3 b.f. Polish Patriot (USA) 128 – Suggia (Alzao **63**
(USA) 117) [1998 –p: a7g 1999 a6g⁵ a8f* a10g⁶ Feb 13] modest performer: clearly
best effort when winning maiden at Lingfield in January: should stay 1¼m: sold
3,000 gns, sent to Israel. *M. Johnston*

THREE CHEERS (IRE)   5 b. or br.g. Slip Anchor 136 – Three Tails 121 **115 §**
(Blakeney 126) [1998 118§: 16d 16.4g⁴ 20s³ 16d⁴ 18d⁴ 20d⁵ 15.5v⁵ 1999 18g² 20m⁶
16f² Jul 29] smallish, sturdy gelding: smart performer: looked to have simple task
but proved most reluctant in minor event at Pontefract on reappearance: ran at least
respectably both starts after, 7½ lengths sixth of 17 to Enzeli in Ascot Gold Cup and
4 lengths second of 7 to Kayf Tara in Goodwood Cup: best at 2m+: acts on firm
and soft going: wears blinkers/visor: tends to run in snatches, and not one to trust.
J. H. M. Gosden

THREE CHERRIES   3 ch.f. Formidable (USA) 125 – Mistral's Dancer (Shareef **–**
Dancer (USA) 135) [1998 NR 1999 6v 6m 6m⁵ 6.1g Sep 25] half-sister to 5-y-o
Queen's Pageant and 1¼m to 1½m winner Kristal Breeze (both by Risk Me): dam,
maiden, best at 7f: signs of a little ability in maidens. *R. Hannon*

THREE FOR A POUND   5 b.g. Risk Me (FR) 127 – Lompoa (Lomond (USA) **61**
128) [1998 76: 7d⁴ 8s* 8.5m 7d 10s⁶ 8.5g 8.5m² 7.9f 8.9g 8.9g⁵ 8.2v 10s² 10d
1999 8d 8v 8.5d 8m 7.5v² 7d⁴ 8m⁵ 7.9f 8m 8m 8g Sep 20] sturdy, lengthy gelding: modest handicapper: stays 8.5f: acts on any going: held up: looked none too
keen when blinkered only all-weather outing in 1997: sold 1,600 gns, joined
A. Juckes. *Don Enrico Incisa*

THREEFORTYCASH (IRE)   2 b.g. (Apr 16) Balla Cove 119 – Tigeen **–**
(Habitat 134) [1999 5g 5m Jun 24] IR 7,200Y: brother to 4-y-o Princely Spark,
closely related to a winner in Hong Kong by Ballad Rock, and half-brother to several
winners, including useful sprinter Alkaaseh (by Ela-Mana-Mou): dam Irish 5f
winner: in rear in maidens at Carlisle. *Andrew Turnell*

THREE GREEN LEAVES (IRE)   3 ch.f. Environment Friend 128 – Kick The **97**
Habit 94 (Habitat 134) [1998 95: 5s 5m 6m³ 6g² 7.5m* 7d³ 7.5m* 8m* 7d* 8d* 10s⁴
1999 8v 10s⁴ May 14] leggy, quite good-topped filly: useful performer: behind in
Italian 1000 Guineas on reappearance, then ran well when 7 lengths fourth to
Nasheed in listed event at Newbury: will stay 1½m: acts on soft and good to firm
ground: used to give trouble stalls. *M. Johnston*

THREE LEADERS (IRE)   3 ch.g. Up And At 'em 109 – Wolviston (Wolverlife **60**
115) [1998 –: 5.9d 5m 5g 1999 a6g 7s³ 6g² 7.1d 5g* 5.9m⁵ 5m⁶ 5m 6m 5m⁵ 5v 6g⁵
Oct 14] workmanlike gelding: modest handicapper: won 19-runner apprentice race
at Beverley in June: effective at 5f/6f: best efforts on good/good to firm ground:
blinkered twice: sold 7,000 gns, joined E. Alston. *D. Nicholls*

THREE LIONS   2 ch.g. (Feb 20) Jupiter Island 126 – Super Sol (Rolfe (USA) 77 **64 p**
[1999 6g 6d⁴ 6d Nov 4] third reported foal: brother to 6-y-o Spunkie: dam winning
selling hurdler: shaped promisingly without landing a blow in maidens at Brighton
and Windsor (2), not at all knocked about by inexperienced rider last 2 starts: will be
well suited by 1m+: sure to do better in handicaps. *R. F. Johnson Houghton*

THREE POINTS   2 b.c. (Mar 11) Bering 136 – Trazl (IRE) 88 (Zalazl (USA) **98 p**
120) [1999 7m* 8.2m* 8m³ Sep 10] first foal: dam, from good middle-distance
staying family, won 4 times around 1¾m: useful form: won maiden at Kempton and

minor event at Nottingham in August: creditable third of 5 to Sarafan in listed event at Goodwood (gave trouble stalls) final start: will be well suited by 1¼m+: raced only on good to firm going: remains capable of better. *J. L. Dunlop*

THREE WHITE SOX 2 ch.f. (Mar 13) Most Welcome 131 – Empty Purse – (Pennine Walk 120) [1999 7s Sep 29] 1,000Y: fourth foal: half-sister to 1994 2-y-o 1m seller winner Gigfy (by Warrshan), 3-y-o Reaction Ball and 1m to 1¼m winner Going For Broke (both by Simply Great): dam unraced: very green, well held in maiden at Newcastle. *P. W. Harris*

THRIFTY 3 b.f. Night Shift (USA) – Gena Ivor (USA) (Sir Ivor 135) [1998 –p: 8g **64** 6g 7m 1999 6.1s⁵ 6m 6.1g May 31] sturdy, close-coupled filly: modest maiden: should have stayed 7f: acted on soft going: dead. *M. J. Ryan*

THROUGH THE RYE 3 ch.c. Sabrehill (USA) 120 – Baharlilys 67 (Green **99** Dancer (USA) 132) [1998 87p: 7s⁴ 8g⁵ 1999 11.1g³ 10.3m⁴ 12g 8m* 8d 9v⁴ Oct 23] rangy colt: good mover: useful performer: 10 lengths fourth to easy winner Oath in listed race at Chester in May: below that form after, including when landing odds in maiden at Newcastle in June: may prove best around 1¼m: acts on good to firm going, probably on heavy: sometimes sweats: sold 60,000 gns, joined M. Pipe. *B. W. Hills*

THROWER 8 b.g. Thowra (FR) – Atlantic Line (Capricorn Line 111) [1998 NR **60** 1999 11.8s* 10s* Apr 19] sparely-made gelding: useful hurdler: modest handicapper on Flat: won at Leicester (first race of any sort for 15 months) and Nottingham (18-runner ladies race) in April: effective at 1¼m/1½m: acts on good to firm ground, soft and fibresand. *S. A. Brookshaw*

THUNDERBIRD LADY (IRE) 3 b.f. Mukaddamah (USA) 125 – Shenley **31** Lass (Prince Tenderfoot (USA) 126) [1998 NR 1999 8.3g 10m² 9.9m 12.1g a12g Sep 4] IR 2,500Y: compact filly: half-sister to 1992 2-y-o 1¼m seller winner Trepidation and 6-y-o Principal Boy (both by Cyrano de Bergerac): dam Irish maiden: poor maiden at best. *L. A. Dace*

THUNDERHEART 8 b.g. Celestial Storm (USA) 132 – Lorelene (FR) 97 **43** (Lorenzaccio 130) [1998 NR 1999 14g² 16m⁵ 16d³ Jun 28] poor handicapper: best at 1¾m/2m: acts on any going: below form in blinkers once as 6-y-o: successful over hurdles in July. *R. Allan*

THUNDERING SURF 2 b.c. (Apr 17) Lugana Beach 116 – Thunder Bug **72 ?** (USA) 66 (Secreto (USA) 128) [1999 8d⁵ Oct 29] third foal: dam 1¼m winner from good American family: 50/1, 10¾ lengths fifth of 6 to Autonomy in minor event at Newmarket: joined J. Jenkins. *N. A. Graham*

THWAAB 7 b.g. Dominion 123 – Velvet Habit 89 (Habitat 134) [1998 70: 6g 6g – 6d 7f* 7g² 7m 8m 7g 7g⁴ 6g a7g 1999 7m 7g 8m Aug 28] strong, good-bodied gelding: fair handicapper: well beaten in 1999: effective at 6f to 1m: acts on firm and good to soft going: effective blinkered/visored or not: usually held up: none too consistent. *F. Watson*

TIAPHENA 8 b.m. Derrylin 115 – Velda 74 (Thatch (USA) 136) [1998 NR 1999 – a16g Feb 19] big mare: poor handicapper: stays 2m, possibly not 2¼m: acts on fibresand, best turf effort on good ground. *T. W. Donnelly*

TICKA TICKA TIMING 6 b.g. Timeless Times (USA) 99 – Belltina 41 (Bel- – fort (FR) 89) [1998 42?: a6g⁴ a6g⁵ a6g⁵ a5g 1999 5d 9m May 22] small, sparely-made gelding: poor handicapper: stays 6f: best efforts on fibresand: tried blinkered/visored: has worn tongue strap. *L. R. Lloyd-James*

TICKLISH 3 b.f. Cadeaux Genereux 131 – Exit Laughing (Shaab 85) [1998 67: **77** 6g³ 7g⁶ 5g³ 6f³ 6s* 6s⁵ 6g* 7s 1999 7d⁴ 7d⁶ a7g⁵ 7g⁵ 6.8g* 7m 7v² 7s⁵ Oct 1] quite attractive filly: fair handicapper: won at Warwick in August: ran creditably after when runner-up at Lingfield: may prove best at 6f/7f: raced mainly on good going or softer (acts on heavy), below form only start on fibresand: held up. *W. J. Haggas*

TICK N PICK 3 br.f. Reprimand 122 – My Preference (Reference Point 139) – [1998 62, a–: 7m 7.9g 7s⁵ a7g a6g 1999 a7g³ 8.5s 7f a10g a7g a8g² a8g⁵ a10g⁶ 10d **a48** Oct 21] leggy, sparely-made filly: poor maiden: stays 1m: acts on equitrack, best turf effort on soft going. *B. R. Johnson*

TICK TOCK 2 ch.f. (Mar 6) Timeless Times (USA) 99 – Aquiletta 67 (Bairn **55** (USA) 126) [1999 5d⁵ 5g 5m 5m² 5d Oct 26] small, sturdy filly: first foal: dam, maiden, effective at 6f/7f: modest maiden: best effort when second of 21 to Branston Lucy in nursery at Redcar: will stay 6f: acts on good to firm going. *M. Mullineaux*

TIC TAC MAC 2 b.c. (Apr 7) Mac's Fighter 116 – Tickle Me Too (Tickled Pink **–** 114) [1999 7g 7d 6v a7g a10g Dec 18] first reported foal: dam unraced: no sign of ability, including in seller. *L. A. Dace*

TIEBREAKER (IRE) 4 b.g. Second Set (IRE) 127 – Millionetta (IRE) 75 **–** (Danehill (USA) 126) [1998 70, a–: 8.2s 8d 8g a8g 10g* 10m³ 12m⁴ 1999 10s May 14] heavy-topped gelding: fair performer: pulled up only 4-y-o start: stays 1½m: acts on good to firm going, ran poorly on equitrack: has hung left. *N. A. Graham*

TIERGARTEN (IRE) 3 b.f. Brief Truce (USA) 126 – Lady In The Park (IRE) **66** (Last Tycoon 131) [1998 –p: 8s 1999 8.3m² 8m⁴ 8d Oct 11] fair maiden: may stay beyond 1m: best efforts on good to firm going: sold 3,000 gns. *A. C. Stewart*

TIERRA DEL FUEGO 5 b.m. Chilibang 120 – Dolly Bevan 53 (Another **32** Realm 118) [1998 –: 7g 10v 1999 a10g a8g⁵ a11g a11g 7g Sep 14] poor maiden. *H. J. Collingridge*

TIER WORKER 3 b.c. Tenby 125 – On The Tide 72 (Slip Anchor 136) [1998 **102** 79: 7.9g 6v³ 8s² 1999 7d³ 8m* 10.4d* 10.1d* 12m² Jun 17] smallish, angular colt: useful performer: much improved at 3 yrs, completing hat-trick in maiden at Ripon in April, rated stakes at York in May and handicap at Epsom in June: good 3½ lengths second of 19 to Elmutabaki in King George V Handicap at Royal Ascot final start: stays 1½m: acts on good to firm and good to soft going: idles in front, but is perfectly genuine. *T. D. Easterby*

TIGER GRASS (IRE) 3 gr.g. Ezzoud (IRE) 126 – Rustic Lawn (Rusticaro (FR) **65** 124) [1998 76: 8g 7g² 7m⁴ 1999 8m 9g 8m 10m 13.1f 10d² 11.6d⁴ 10d Nov 4] tall, leggy gelding: fair maiden: probably best at 1¼m/1½m: acts on good to firm and good to soft going: blinkered third start: won over hurdles in December. *W. R. Muir*

TIGER HILL (IRE) 4 b.c. Danehill (USA) 126 – The Filly (GER) (Appiani **127** II 128) [1998 127: 8v* 8g* 10g* 12v 12g² 12s* 12d³ 1999 12m* 11s² 12g² 10g* 12g* 12v⁵ 12f Nov 28]

Plans to keep top German colt Tiger Hill in training for a fourth season were abandoned when he was found to have sustained a tendon injury when failing to do himself justice in the Japan Cup in November. He has been retired to the Haras du Val Henry in Normandy, where he will stand at a fee of 60,000 francs (£5,700). Tiger Hill won ten races worth over half a million pounds in total, all of them in Germany, including the Mehl-Mulhens-Rennen (the equivalent of the Two Thousand Guineas) and two runnings of the prestigious Mercedes Benz Grosser Preis von Baden. His second success in the latter was one of three gained by Tiger Hill in his final season, having earlier picked up the Gerling-Preis at Cologne and the Grosser Dallmayr-Preis Bayerisches Zuchtrennen at Munich. Tiger Hill, who had shown improvement when winning the previous year's Grosser Preis von Baden by four lengths from Caitano, gave a performance of similar merit in accounting for Germany's leading three-year-old colt Belenus and leading three-year-old filly Flamingo Road in the latest edition. Strongly pressed by that pair around two furlongs out, Tiger Hill found plenty under pressure and drew clear in the final furlong to win by three lengths from Flamingo Road, who was just a head in front of Belenus. Tiger Hill didn't just reserve his best for Germany. On his first appearance abroad he ran a cracking race when a close third behind Sagamix and Leggera in the 1998 Prix de l'Arc de Triomphe; and on his return to France in July he performed right up to his best in finishing two and a half lengths second to El Condor Pasa in the Grand Prix de Saint-Cloud. The heavy ground possibly wasn't ideal for Tiger Hill when he made his second Arc de Triomphe bid, though he won on such a surface at three years, and in the circumstances he wasn't disgraced, finishing fifth of fourteen to Montjeu.

Mercedes Benz Grosser Preis von Baden, Baden-Baden—
in a smart field, Tiger Hill repeats his win of the previous year;
the German Oaks winner Flamingo Road (right) beats the German Derby winner, Belenus, for second

Tiger Hill (IRE) (b.c. 1995)	Danehill (USA) (b 1986)	Danzig (b 1977)	Northern Dancer Pas de Nom
		Razyana (b 1981)	His Majesty Spring Adieu
	The Filly (GER) (b 1981)	Appiani II (b 1963)	Herbager Angela Rucellai
		Tigress Silver (gr 1973)	St Chad Templeogue

Tiger Hill's pedigree was dealt with fully in *Racehorses of 1998*. Suffice to say here that his dam, The Filly, won four times in Germany at around ten and eleven furlongs; his grandam, Tigress Silver, won seven times in Holland, including that country's version of the Cesarewitch, and his great grandam, Templeogue, was successful at a mile in Ireland. Tiger Hill is The Filly's sixth foal and fifth winner, the others all being successful at up to at least a mile and a quarter in Germany, the best of them probably Toyah (by Lidhame) who was third in a Group 3. Tiger Hill, a good-topped colt, stayed a mile and a half and acted on soft and good to firm ground. He usually raced prominently, and was genuine and consistent. *P. Schiergen, Germany*

TIGER IMP (IRE)   3 b.g. Imp Society (USA) – Mrs Merry Man (Bellypha 130)   **83**
[1998 NR 1999 7.1m² 7m² 6g³ Aug 24] IR 2,000F: fourth foal: half-brother to Italian 1½m winner Golden Taufan (by Taufan): dam French 9f winner: fairly useful form in maidens, just caught at Lingfield final start: likely to prove best at 5f/6f. *I. A. Balding*

TIGER SHARK (USA)   3 b.c. Chief's Crown (USA) – Life At The Top 107   **115**
(Habitat 134) [1998 94p: 7s⁶ 7s⁴ a7g² a7g* 8v* 1999 12g 9m* 8.5m* 8g 7s⁶ Nov 7] good-bodied, attractive colt: smart performer: trained by Lord Huntingdon at 2 yrs: won handicaps at Leopardstown and Galway (made all, by length from Golden Fact in listed event) in July: well below form in listed races after: stays 9f: has won on heavy ground and equitrack, best efforts on good to firm. *J. S. Bolger, Ireland*

TIGER TALK 3 ch.c. Sabrehill (USA) 120 – Tebre (USA) 70 (Sir Ivor 135) [1998 **87** 82: 7g 7g 8m 8v² 8d² 1999 7s* 8.1s* 7.9s 8m 7g 7d Oct 30] workmanlike colt: fairly useful performer: won maiden at Folkestone in March and handicap at Sandown (made all in 5-runner race) in April: well held after, sold out of B. Hills's stable 33,000 gns before penultimate start (orginally intended for export to Macau but failed veterinary examination): will stay 1¼m: acts on heavy going. *N. P. Littmoden*

TIGGY SILVANO 4 b.f. Tigani 120 – Infanta Maria 82 (King of Spain 121) **–** [1998 –, a35: a8g⁵ a8g⁴ a10g⁴ 10s 9.9s 9.2d 10m a14g 12s 14.1v⁵ a13g a14.8g 1999 a13g a16f Jan 14] leggy filly: poor maiden at best: tried blinkered/visored. *M. Quinn*

TIGHTROPE 4 b.g. Alzao (USA) 117 – Circus Act (Shirley Heights 130) [1998 **71** –: 9.1g⁵ 8m 10d 1999 10.1d* 9.9v 9.1v² a10g² a11g a9.4g² a9.4g⁴ Dec 27] quite good-topped gelding: fair nowadays: comfortably landed odds in seller at Yarmouth in September: left Sir Mark Prescott 5,000 gns after third start: stays 1¼m: acts on good to firm and heavy going, and all-weather. *N. P. Littmoden*

TIGI 4 ch.f. Tigani 120 – Molly Brazen 51 (Risk Me (FR) 127) [1998 36: 5m⁴ 5.9d **43** 5g 1999 7.5d 6f 5v 5g³ 5g 5m 6f 5f Aug 2] sparely-made filly: poor maiden handicapper: stays 6f: often blinkered/visored: inconsistent. *J. J. Quinn*

TIGRE 2 b.c. (Feb 16) Mujtahid (USA) 118 – Vice Vixen (CAN) (Vice Regent **82** (CAN)) [1999 6s⁴ 7m² 8.1m² 7d² 7.9d² Oct 9] 16,000F, 52,000Y: sturdy colt: has quick action: seventh foal: half-brother to 3 winners, including smart 1¼m/1½m winner Cunning (by Bustino) and useful 6f (at 2 yrs) to 1m winner Mushraaf (by Zafonic): dam unraced: fairly useful maiden: runner-up last 4 starts, beaten 2½ lengths by easy winner Zafonium at York on final one: finds 7f a bare minimum, and should stay 1¼m: acts on good to firm and good to soft going. *B. W. Hills*

TIGRE BOIS 2 b.c. (Apr 27) Mon Tresor 113 – Gentle Star 77 (Comedy Star **–** (USA) 121) [1999 7d 7d Oct 12] 1,200Y: sturdy, well-made colt: half-brother to 1988 2-y-o 5f seller winner Tell Me This (by Goldhills Pride) and 4-y-o Polish Spirit: dam 6f winner: well beaten in maidens. *B. R. Millman*

TIGRELLO 5 ch.g. Efisio 120 – Prejudice 83 (Young Generation 129) [1998 –: **71** 8d 1999 7g 7m 10.3d 8f* Jul 12] leggy, quite good-topped gelding: modest nowadays: made all in seller at Brighton: best at 1m: acts on firm and good to soft ground: has been tongue tied: joined T. Mills. *J. Berry*

TIJUANA 3 ch.f. Gabitat 119 – Gabibti (IRE) 82 (Dara Monarch 128) [1998 –: **–** 5.1g 6g 1999 6g 8.3m Jun 21] workmanlike filly: no form. *B. Gubby*

TIKOTINO 3 ch.f. Mystiko (USA) 124 – Tino-Ella 73 (Bustino 136) [1998 46: 6g **58 d** 6.1m 6m 7s⁶ 1999 8.2s⁶ 9.9g² 12g 14.1f 8d 10m 10g 10d⁵ Oct 21] modest maiden: stays 1½m: best efforts on good going: tried blinkered/visored: carries head awkwardly and has looked difficult ride. *J. A. Glover*

TILAAL (USA) 7 ch.g. Gulch (USA) – Eye Drop (USA) 96 (Irish River (FR) **42** 131) [1998 47: 7.5m⁵ 8.2m⁴ 10.5m⁴ 8d⁴ 8d⁵ 8m 9.9g⁴ 7g³ 8.3d⁵ 1999 a8g⁴ a8g 7.5d⁵ **a48** 10.5d 8m⁴ 6.9m 12g⁵ Aug 13] strong, angular gelding: has run tubed: poor maiden handicapper: effective at 7f to 10.5f: acts on fibresand, good to firm and good to soft going: tried blinkered/visored. *M. D. Hammond*

TILBURG 4 b.f. High Kicker (USA) – Touch My Heart 61 (Steel Heart 128) [1998 **– §** –, a42: a8s⁵ a6g⁴ a5g² a6g⁵ a5g⁶ a6g⁵ a5g a7g a5g⁵ a6g 1999 a5g⁵ a5g a8g Jul 8] leggy filly: poor maiden: threw jockey and withdrawn when visored once: ungenuine. *Mrs N. Macauley*

TILE IT 2 b.g. (May 2) Distinctly North (USA) 115 – Simmie's Special 75 **58** (Precocious 126) [1999 5.1m 5m³ May 17] 7,500F, 4,800Y, resold 1,600Y: good-topped gelding: second foal: dam sprinter: still green, much better effort when third of 9 in maiden at Musselburgh: dead. *A. Bailey*

TILER (IRE) 7 br.g. Ballad Rock 122 – Fair Siobahn (Petingo 135) [1998 86: 6d **89** 6g³ 6g² 6g⁶ 6g⁶ 6.1g 6f 6m 7.6g³ 7g⁴ 7.6d* 7m² 7.1m 6s⁵ 7g 7s 6d³ 1999 7g* 7g 7d⁵ 7m⁴ Jun 26] tall, lengthy gelding: fairly useful handicapper: made all at Newcastle in April: stays 7.6f: acts on fibresand, firm and soft going: blinkered once in 1996: sometimes gives trouble at stalls: none too consistent. *M. Johnston*

TILIA 3 b.f. Primo Dominie 121 – Bermuda Lily 78 (Dunbeath (USA) 127) [1998 **56** 51: 6f 6m 5.1m 6g 1999 6m 5.1s 5.3f⁶ 6d⁴ 6m 5.3g⁶ 5.1m Jul 5] small filly: has a round action: modest maiden handicapper: stays 6f: acts on good to firm and good to soft ground: blinkered last 4 starts. *R. Hannon*

TILLERMAN   3 b.c. In The Wings 128 – Autumn Tint (USA) (Roberto (USA) **111 p**
131) [1998 NR 1999 9g* 8d* Oct 1] big, strong, good sort: has plenty of scope: sixth foal: half-brother to 3 winners, including useful French 1m winner (including at 2 yrs) Welsh Autumn (by Tenby) and 1¼m winner Minatina (by Ela-Mana-Mou): dam French 1½m winner, half-sister to dam of very smart 1m to 1¼m filly Ryafan: created good impression when winning maiden at Lingfield in August and minor event at Newmarket (last and steadily to post) in October, latter by 4 lengths from Chief Rebel, again slowly away but running on strongly after leading under 2f out: bred to stay at least 1¼m, but doesn't seem short of speed: sure to improve further, and looks well worth his place in stronger company. *Mrs A. J. Perrett*

TILLYBOY   9 b.g. Little Wolf 127 – Redgrave Creative 67 (Swing Easy (USA) **30**
126) [1998 –: a12g a14.8g 1999 a16g⁶ a16g² Feb 19] poor maiden: will stay beyond 2m: acts on fibresand, showed promise (on good to soft going) only run on turf. *Mrs M. Reveley*

TIMAHS   3 b.c. Mtoto 134 – Shomoose (Habitat 134) [1998 96p: 8g* 8v⁴ 1999 **112**
10.1m² 12f³ 10.3m* 9.9s Sep 22] close-coupled, attractive colt: very good walker: smart performer: best efforts when third to Mary Stuart in Tote Gold Trophy Handicap at Goodwood (wandered briefly and found little) in July and winning 6-runner minor event at Doncaster (by neck from Goombayland, just getting better of sustained duel) in September: may prove best at 1¼m/1½m on good going or firmer. *Saeed bin Suroor*

TIMARU (IRE)   2 ch.c. (Feb 13) Shalford (IRE) 124§ – Wide Outside (IRE) 50 **68**
(Don't Forget Me 127) [1999 6.1d 6d 7g² 7m³ 6m⁶ 7.5g² 8g 8d* 7d Oct 14] IR 2,500F, IR 7,000Y: sturdy, close-coupled colt: first foal: dam, maiden, sister to smart US Grade 3 9f winner Eastern Memories: fair performer: won seller at Ayr in September: unimpressive to post and something probably amiss final start: stays 1m: yet to race on extremes of going: visored last 2 outings: sent to Macau. *A. P. Jarvis*

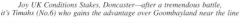

Joy UK Conditions Stakes, Doncaster—after a tremendous battle,
it's Timahs (No.6) who gains the advantage over Goombayland near the line

TIME   2 b.g. (Apr 11) Timeless Times (USA) 99 – Petrina Bay 67 (Clantime 101) – [1999 a6g Dec 22] 15,000Y: second foal: dam, 5f winner, sister to 9-y-o sprinter Saint Express: last of 9 in maiden at Lingfield. *T. G. Mills*   –

TIME AND AGAIN   3 ch.f. Timeless Times (USA) 99 – Busted Love (Busted 134) [1998 52: 6g 5d³ 6d 8d 1999 8f 12m 10.5d⁶ 12.4g 12s 11d a6g Dec 17] workmanlike filly: poor maiden: sold from Mrs G. Rees 7,000 gns before final outing: seems to stay 10.5f: acts on good to soft going. *D. W. Chapman*   –

TIME BOMB   2 b.f. (Mar 2) Great Commotion (USA) 123 – Play For Time (Comedy Star (USA) 121) [1999 5.7d Sep 27] half-sister to 1995 2-y-o 5f/6f winner Red River Valley (by Belfort) and a winner abroad by Sulaafah: dam unraced: eighth of 17 to Tangerine in maiden at Bath: will stay at least 6f: should improve. *B. R. Millman*   – p

TIME CAN TELL   5 ch.g. Sylvan Express 117 – Stellaris (Star Appeal 133) [1998 –, a68: a10g⁴ a12g² a13g* a12g³ a16g² a16g⁴ a16.2g³ a16.2g⁶ a16.2g³ 12m⁴ 1999 a16g a12g⁴ a13g² a12g⁴ a16g⁴ a16.2g* a16g² 18m a14g⁶ a13g² a14g⁵ a16.2g Dec 4] big, heavy-topped gelding: fair handicapper: won at Wolverhampton in April: disappointing after next start: needs at least 1½m and stays 2m: acts on firm ground and all-weather, not softer than good: tried visored/blinkered: usually bandaged. *A. G. Juckes*   – a68 d

TIME FOR LAGER   4 gr.f. Timeless Times (USA) 99 – Laura Lager (Warpath 113) [1998 41: a6g a7g 8.2s⁴ 9.9s³ a12g⁴ 1999 a12g⁴ a12g⁵ a11g 12g⁴ a12g⁴ a12g⁶ 15.8g 14.1d⁵ Oct 27] sparely-made filly: poor maiden handicapper: stays 1¾m: acts on fibresand and soft going or firmer: joined I. Park. *J. Wharton*   37 a41

TIME FOR MUSIC (IRE)   2 b.c. (Jan 23) Mukaddamah (USA) 125 – Shrewd Girl (USA) 79 (Sagace (FR) 135) [1999 6f⁵ 7m² 7m² 7g⁶ 6.1m* Aug 23] IR 66,000Y: lengthy, quite attractive colt: third foal: half-brother to 1¼m/1½m winner in France and 1m/9f winner in Ireland, both by Taufan: dam, disappointing maiden, daughter of half-sister to Palace Music: fair performer: won nursery at Nottingham in August: races freely, and may prove best at 6f/7f: raced only on good going or firmer: hung third start. *T. G. Mills*   77

TIME FOR THE CLAN   2 ch.g. (Mar 20) Clantime 101 – Fyas 52 (Sayf El Arab (USA) 127) [1999 5m 6m 5.9m 5g 6f⁴ 5g 5m Aug 11] 9,000Y: angular gelding: second foal: brother to 3-y-o Chorus of Approval: dam, placed at 6f/7f (ran only at 2 yrs), from good family: modest maiden at best: form only on first and fifth starts: stays 6f: raced only on good going or firmer: tried blinkered. *J. J. O'Neill*   54 ?

TIME GOES BY (IRE)   2 ch.g. (Apr 23) Shalford (IRE) 124§ – Alva Clare (IRE) (Pennine Walk 120) [1999 5d⁵ a5g 5d 5g⁴ a5g³ 6m⁵ 6m* 6m⁴ 5.1m² 5.1h Aug 3] IR 750F, 3,200Y: quite good-topped gelding: first foal: dam showed little in Ireland: modest performer: won seller at Lingfield in June: effective at 5f/6f: acts on good to firm going: blinkered (ran respectably) once: tends to hang: sold 6,500 gns, sent to Macau. *J. Berry*   57

TIME IS MONEY (IRE)   7 br.g. Sizzling Melody 117 – Tiempo 50 (King of Spain 121) [1998 NR 1999 8d 6.9m² 6d 7.1g⁵ Jun 14] poor maiden: off 3½ years before reappearance: stays 7f: best form on good going or firmer: visored once at 3 yrs. *M. H. Tompkins*   52

TIMELESS CHICK   2 ch.f. (Apr 8) Timeless Times (USA) 99 – Be My Bird 65 (Be My Chief (USA) 122) [1999 a5g 6m⁶ a7g⁶ 6m⁶ 7.6g Aug 25] quite good-topped filly: has a round action: first foal: dam, third at 7f/8.5f at 2 yrs, should have stayed further: poor maiden: unlikely to stay beyond 7f: tried blinkered. *Andrew Reid*   47

TIMELESS QUEST   2 ch.f. (Mar 30) Timeless Times (USA) 99 – Animate (IRE) 62 (Tate Gallery (USA) 117) [1999 6.1g a7g⁴ 7.5g a7g² 7s Oct 5] 8,000Y: leggy filly: third foal: half-sister to 4-y-o Frankie Fair and 3-y-o Lady Nairn: dam Irish maiden from family of Saratoga Springs: fair maiden: best effort when second in seller at Southwell: stays 7f: acts on fibresand, little form on turf: blinkered last 2 starts. *T. J. Etherington*   40 a58

TIME LOSS   4 ch.g. Kenmare (FR) 125 – Not Before Time (IRE) (Polish Precedent (USA) 131) [1998 85: 8d⁶ 8f 10.2s* 10.1g 12.5d 1999 11.1m² 11.1m 10.4f 10m Sep 16] good-topped gelding: fair performer: ran as if something amiss after   70 ?

creditable reappearance: should stay 1½m: acts on soft and good to firm ground: blinkered final start. *Mrs A. Duffield*

TIME MILL   3 b.c. Shirley Heights 130 – Not Before Time (IRE) (Polish   **80**
Precedent (USA) 131) [1998 –p: 7g 1999 10.2g² 10m⁴ 11.5g² 10f³ Aug 2] fairly
useful maiden: should stay at least 1¾m: acts on good to firm going, yet to race on
softer than good: ruined chance by hanging left final start. *J. W. Hills*

TIME N TIDE (IRE)   3 b.g. Namaqualand (USA) – Now Then (Sandford Lad   **93**
133) [1998 NR 1999 8s* 8.1s⁵ 10.2g² 11.9d³ 10m 12d 10.1d⁶ Oct 27] 12,000F,
27,000Y: tall, quite attractive gelding: has a fluent, rather round action: half-brother to
9-y-o Norling (modest 5f/6f winner) and 1½m winner Salubrious (by Sallust): dam
placed in Ireland from 7f to 1¼m: fairly useful handicapper: 40/1-winner of maiden at
Leicester in April: good third of 6 to Rum Pointer in rated stakes at Haydock
(penultimate run for B. Meehan) in June: well held after: stays 1½m: acts on soft
ground. *G. M. McCourt*

TIME OF NIGHT (USA)   6 gr. or ro.m. Night Shift (USA) – Tihama (USA)   **52**
(Sassafras (FR) 135) [1998 49, a63: a8s² a8g a8.5g² a7g* a7g² a7g* a7g* 8s⁶ 8.3v⁴   **a60**
7d³ 7m⁴ a7g³ a7g⁴ 1999 a7g⁴ a8f a7f⁶ a11g⁶ 8d² 7.1m 7.5d 7.5d⁵ 8g 8d⁵ 8d 8f*
8m* 8g 10.4f⁴ 10m a7g Nov 12] leggy mare: modest handicapper: won apprentice
races at Thirsk in July and Carlisle in August: effective at 7f to 10.4f: acts on
fibresand and probably any turf going: tried blinkered/visored: has had tongue tied.
J. L. Eyre

TIME ON MY HANDS   3 b.g. Most Welcome 131 – Zareeta (Free State 125)   **–**
[1998 –: 6g 6d 7.1s⁵ 1999 a8f⁶ a8g³ a7g 9.9g a8g* 8f a9.4g 10g 8s a8g a11g a8g   **a53**
Dec 13] modest performer: best effort when winning 7-runner claimer at Southwell
(claimed from C. Thornton £2,000) in May: should stay beyond 1m: acts on
fibresand, little show on turf: blinkered last 2 starts, tongue tied last 3. *S. R. Bowring*

TIME OUT   4 ch.f. Timeless Times (USA) 99 – Tangalooma 56 (Hotfoot 126)   **42 d**
[1998 42: a7g⁵ 8d 6m 7d a7g⁵ a11g* 1999 a12f² a12g³ a16g a12g a8g a14g a12g a11g
a11g Jun 28] small filly: poor performer: left G. M. Moore after second start (no
subsequent form), M. Polglase after sixth: should stay beyond 1½m: acts on
fibresand: blinkered once: sometimes slowly away. *D. Carroll*

TIME SAVED   3 b.f. Green Desert (USA) 127 – Time Charter 131 (Saritamer   **89**
(USA) 130) [1998 NR 1999 8g 10m* 9.9d 10.1g Aug 30] sister to useful 1m winner
Illusion and half-sister to several winners, including 4-y-o Generous Terms and 1½m
winner Time Allowed (by Sadler's Wells) and stayer Zinaad (by Shirley Heights),
both smart: dam top-class middle-distance performer: won maiden at Windsor in
July: better effort in listed races after when creditable seventh to Ajhiba at Salisbury
next time: stays 1¼m. *Sir Michael Stoute*

TIME TEMPTRESS   3 b.f. Timeless Times (USA) 99 – Tangalooma 56   **69**
(Hotfoot 126) [1998 58: a5g 5m⁵ 5g 5d⁴ 6g⁴ 7.5m 7d² 8d⁴ 1999 8m* 8.2m⁴ 8m³ 9m
9f³ 8g 8m⁵ 8s 10d⁶ Oct 26] leggy, lengthy filly: has a rather round action: fair performer:
won handicap at Newcastle in May: ran creditably most starts after: effective at 1m,
probably at 1¼m: acts on firm and good to soft going, well held on soft: carries head
awkwardly. *G. M. Moore*

TIME TO FLY   6 b.g. Timeless Times (USA) 99 – Dauntless Flight (Golden   **55**
Mallard 103) [1998 –, a86: a6g* a5g* a6g* a6g² a5g² a5g⁴ 5d a6g a5g 1999 a6g⁵   **a74**
a5g⁴ a6g a6g* a5g 6g 6f 5g 5m² 5m 6m³ a6g Oct 16] smallish, good-bodied gelding:
poor mover: fair handicapper on all-weather, modest on turf: won at Lingfield in
April: effective at 5f/6f: acts on all-weather and hard ground, yet to race on soft/
heavy: usually blinkered: races prominently: carries head high: reportedly
bled from nose sixth start: inconsistent. *B. W. Murray*

TIME TO SKIP   2 b.f. (Apr 24) Timeless Times (USA) 99 – North Pine (Import   **–**
127) [1999 6m 6m 7.7g 5m 7m Sep 1] 4,400Y: half-sister to several winners,
including useful Echo-Logical (up to 7f, by Belfort) and fairly useful 5f performer
Heaven-Liegh-Grey (by Grey Desire): dam poor half-sister to top-class sprinter
Lochnager: well held in maidens/sellers: not certain to stay beyond 6f. *R. Hannon*

TIME TO WYN   3 b.g. Timeless Times (USA) 99 – Wyn-Bank 82 (Green God   **62**
128) [1998 58: 7s a7g⁶ 7g 6s⁶ 7.5m* 7d³ 8d 1999 9.9g 9.9g³ 8m* 8g² 8m 8.2g 8.5g

9.9s 8.2f 8d Oct 29] smallish gelding: modest performer: won minor event at Carlisle in June: below form after next start: effective at 1m/1¼m: acts on good to firm and good to soft going, tailed off on fibresand: sold 4,000 gns. *J. G. FitzGerald*

TIME VALLY 2 ch.f. (Feb 2) Timeless Times (USA) 99 – Fort Vally 58 (Belfort (FR) 89) [1999 7v 7d 7v⁶ Oct 25] 550Y: leggy filly: first foal: dam 1m/9f winner at 4/5 yrs: modest maiden: races freely, but should stay 1m. *S. Dow* **60**

TIME ZONE 3 b.c. Shirley Heights 130 – Forthwith 104 (Midyan (USA) 124) [1998 96p: 10d² 10s³ 1999 12g³ 12m²* 16.2m² 12f² 11.9m⁶ Aug 17] lengthy, sparely-made colt: has a quick, fluent action: smart performer: won minor event at Salisbury in May: fine efforts when second in Queen's Vase at Royal Ascot (went down by ½ length to Endorsement) and Gordon Stakes at Goodwood (beaten 1½ lengths by Compton Ace), making running both times: possibly something amiss when only sixth of 7 in Great Voltigeur Stakes at York final start: should stay beyond 2m: acts on firm ground, probably on soft: genuine. *C. E. Brittain* **111**

TIMOTE (IRE) 3 ch.f. Indian Ridge 123 – Across The Ice (USA) (General Holme (USA) 128) [1998 88: 8g² 6d² 7s 5s² 1999 6s² 5.8v* 6m* 5m* 5f⁴ 5d² 5v Oct 3] 68,000Y: leggy, lengthy filly: has plenty of scope: third reported foal: half-sister to French 1¼m winner Glissando (by In The Wings): dam, French 6.5f winner, half-sister to smart French 6.5f (at 2 yrs) to 1m winner Northern Premier: smart performer: won maiden in April and handicaps at Cork in June and the Curragh in July: ran creditably after in King George Stakes at Goodwood (2½ lengths fourth to Rudi's Pet), Flying Five at Leopardstown (length second to Tedburrow) and Prix de l'Abbaye de Longchamp (3¾ lengths seventh to Agnes World, snatched up when beginning strong challenge): effective at 5f/6f: acts on any ground: blinkered twice at 2 yrs. *D. K. Weld, Ireland* **110**

TINA'S ROYALE 3 b.f. Prince Sabo 123 – Aventina 83 (Averof 123) [1998 67: 5m 5g⁵ 6.1d⁶ 5s³ 5s³ 1999 6g⁴ 5m 5g⁶ 5d² 5g⁴ 5s 5.2s Oct 22] small, leggy filly: fair maiden at best: barely stays 6f: acts on soft ground: sold 6,000 gns. *H. Candy* **68 d**

TIN DRUM (IRE) 3 b.c. Roi Danzig (USA) – Triumphant 90 (Track Spare 125) – [1998 –: 7m 7g 1999 10m 11.6g 9.9d a12g Oct 13] sturdy colt: no form, shaping as if something amiss last 2 outings: sent to Italy. *R. Hannon* **–**

TINGED WITH GOLD (IRE) 4 ch.g. Kris 135 – Touch And Love (IRE) (Green Desert (USA) 127) [1998 7s 7s* 8d⁶ 7g² 8d⁵ 7g 1999 10.1m³ Aug 4] third foal: dam, useful French sprinter, out of half-sister to Sure Blade (by Kris): trained by C. Laffon-Parias in France at 3 yrs, winning minor event at Strasbourg in the spring: poor form over hurdles and probably flattered only start on Flat in 1999: stays 7f: acts on soft ground: returned to France. *M. D. Hammond* **?**

TING (IRE) 2 b.g. (May 27) Magical Wonder (USA) 125 – Rozmiyn (Caerleon (USA) 132) [1999 5d 6m 6m⁵ a5g⁵ Dec 17] IR 7,500Y: leggy, quite good-topped gelding: fifth foal: dam French 1½m winner: modest maiden: good fifth in Southwell nursery final start: should stay 7f: acts on fibresand. *P. C. Haslam* **56**

TINKER OSMASTON 8 br.m. Dunbeath (USA) 127 – Miss Primula 81 (Dominion 123) [1998 69: 6.1v 5.1s 5.7f 6.1m³ 5.7d² 6d³ 6m³ 6m 5.1g 6m⁵ 5.1g⁶ 5.7m 1999 6s* 5.1s³ 6.1f 5.7g 6.1g³ 5g 5d 5m 7v³ 6.1d 8d Oct 11] workmanlike mare: fair handicapper: won 16-runner apprentice event at Folkestone in April: ran creditably after only when placed: effective at 5f to 7f: acts on any going: tried in visor/blinkers: usually held up. *R. J. Hodges* **70 d**

TINKER'S SURPRISE (IRE) 5 b.g. Cyrano de Bergerac 120 – Lils Fairy (Fairy King (USA)) [1998 50§: 5g⁶ 5d 5g⁴ 5s 5g a6g⁵ a5g 5g a5g² 5m² a6g a5s⁶ a5g⁴ 1999 a5g⁴ a5g* a5g³ a5g a5g⁴ a5g⁶ a5g⁴ a5g 5m² 5d² 5f 6m⁴ 5f⁵ 5d a5g Nov 27] strong, good-topped gelding: modest handicapper on all-weather, poor on turf: won at Wolverhampton in January: has form at 6f, races mainly at 5f: acts on good to firm going, good to soft and all-weather: blinkered nowadays: pulls hard: none too resolute. *J. Balding* **49 §**
a58 §

TINSEL WHISTLE 2 b.c. (Mar 27) Piccolo 121 – Pewter Lass 56 (Dowsing (USA) 124) [1999 5m⁶ 5m 5g³ 5m 5.2m* 5m 6f* 6g⁴ 6m² 6d⁶ Oct 14] 6,200F, 7,000Y: leggy, close-coupled colt: first foal: dam, maiden, half-sister to useful 1991 2-y-o 6f winner Misterioso: fair performer: won sellers at Yarmouth in June and July: **71**

good efforts in nurseries at Goodwood and Newmarket last 2 starts: probably better at 6f than 5f: acts on firm and good to soft going: tried blinkered, better form when not: has carried head awkwardly. *M. A. Jarvis*

TINTORANO   2 b.g. (Mar 1) Presidium 124 – Junuh 80 (Jalmood (USA) 126)   – [1999 7m Jun 19] third reported living foal: dam 2-y-o 7f winner: last in seller at Redcar. *Miss J. F. Craze*

TIOGA   2 br.g. (Apr 23) Unfuwain (USA) 131 – Susquehanna Days (USA) 68   **89** (Chief's Crown (USA)) [1999 6g* 7m⁵ 7m⁴ 7g² 7m⁶ 7.7d 8d Oct 15] 32,000Y: useful-looking gelding: third foal: half-brother to 4-y-o Clef of Silver and 3-y-o Balladonia: dam, 1m winner, half-sister to dam of Silver Patriarch, from very good family: fairly useful performer: won maiden at Lingfield in May: good second of 6 to Mana-Mou Bay in listed race at Newbury: well held in nurseries last 2 outings: should stay at least 1m: acts on good to firm going: often leads. *B. J. Meehan*

TIPPERARY SUNSET (IRE)   5 gr.g. Red Sunset 120 – Chapter And Verse   **71** (Dancer's Image (USA)) [1998 66, a–: 7s 8d 7.5m⁵ 9.3g 8f⁴ 8.3s* 9.9m 8.5m² 8.3s⁵   **a–** 8.9g 10v³ 8s³ 8d³ a9.4s 1999 8.5d³ 7m 7.5d* 7.5v⁴ 8m⁴ 8m 8.5g 7.5g 8.5g² 7.5s³ 8s 7g 8s² 8s⁵ Nov 6] strong, close-coupled gelding: fair handicapper: won at Beverley in June: effective at 7.5f (given good test) to 1¼m: acts on any turf going, no form on all-weather: has hung left: usually held up: goes well on stiff tracks. *J. J. Quinn*

TIPSY   3 ch.f. Kris 135 – Heady (Rousillon (USA) 133) [1998 –: 7g 1999 a8.5g*   **95** 8m⁴ 10.9m* 11.4m⁴ 12.3g⁴ 12s* 12d³ 12s⁶ Nov 6] unfurnished filly: useful performer: won maiden at Wolverhampton in April, handicap at Ayr in May and minor event at Goodwood in September: best effort when 13 lengths third to Signorina Cattiva in Princess Royal Stakes at Ascot penultimate start: will stay beyond 1½m: acts on good to firm ground, soft and fibresand. *W. J. Haggas*

TIPSY CREEK (USA)   5 b.h. Dayjur (USA) 137 – Copper Creek 78 (Habitat   **115** 134) [1998 114: 5g 6g* 5d 6v 5f⁴ 6m* 6m* 6m⁶ 1999 6m³ 6m² 5g* 6m 6f⁶ 5f⁶ 5g Aug

Mr Hamdan Al Maktoum's "Tipsy Creek"

19] robust, good-quartered horse: reportedly broke a bone in a hock before reappearance in 1997: smart performer: won Temple Stakes at Sandown in May by 1¾ lengths from Lochangel: ran creditably most other starts, including when sixth in July Cup at Newmarket and King George Stakes at Goodwood: badly hampered and pulled up 2f out in Nunthorpe Stakes at York (blinkered) final outing: effective at 5f/6f: acts on firm ground: sometimes bandaged: front runner. *B. Hanbury*

TIP THE BALANCE (IRE)   3 b.f. Ballad Rock 122 – Daidis 66 (Welsh Pageant   –
132) [1998 41: 5m⁵ 6g 1999 8.5m 9.9g Apr 22] poor maiden at best. *J. Parkes*

TIRMIZI (USA)   8 b.g. Shahrastani (USA) 135 – Tikarna (FR) (Targowice (USA)   –
130) [1998 NR 1999 a16.2g 17.1v 18g Jun 14] poor maiden: sold 500 gns.
Mrs A. Duffield

TISSIFER   3 b.c. Polish Precedent (USA) 131 – Ingozi 91 (Warning 136) [1998   **114**
97p: 6m* 7d* 8s⁵ 1999 8d³ 8g 10.3f² 10d² 10.4f Jul 10] smart performer: won minor
event at Thirsk in April by 2½ lengths from Peculiarity: ran creditably after when
runner-up in similar race at Doncaster and listed event at Newmarket (beaten length
by Manndar, carrying head bit high and wandering): stiffish task in John Smith's Cup
(Handicap) at York final start: stays 1¼m: acts on firm and good to soft going:
blinkered last 2 starts. *M. Johnston*

TITAN   4 b.g. Lion Cavern (USA) 117 – Sutosky 78 (Great Nephew 126) [1998 71:   **57 §**
7s 6v 7m³ 7.1g 8m 7g 1999 7m 7g 8.1m 8d 8.5g⁵ 8m 8d² 8m 8d⁵ 7d 7d a8g⁶ a8.5g   **a– §**
Dec 27] good-topped gelding: modest performer: left S. Dow before penultimate
outing: stays 1m: acts on good to firm and good to soft going: has been early to post:
races freely: inconsistent. *N. E. Berry*

TITAN LAD   2 b.g. (Apr 9) Puissance 110 – Sister Sal 74 (Bairn (USA) 126) [1999   –
6.1d a6g 7m 6.8m 8.2d 8s Oct 26] 1,050Y, 4,000 2-y-o: fifth foal: half-brother to
3-y-o Fulham and 2-y-o 5f winners Exosal (seller in 1994, by Exodal) and Northern
Sal (in 1996, by Aragon): dam 2-y-o 6f winner who later stayed 1¼m: signs of ability
only on third start. *G. A. Ham*

TITIAN ANGEL (IRE)   2 ch.f. (Apr 21) Brief Truce (USA) 126 – Kuwah (IRE)   **60 p**
77 (Be My Guest (USA) 126) [1999 8g² Aug 29] IR 10,000F, 2,200 2-y-o: second
foal: half-sister to 3-y-o Honey Guest: dam, Irish 1½m winner, closely related to
smart 1¼m and 1½m winner Suhaad: 33/1, second of 12 to Bow Strada in maiden at
Yarmouth, finishing well: will stay at least 1¼m: should do better. *C. N. Allen*

TITTA RUFFO   5 b.g. Reprimand 122 – Hithermoor Lass 75 (Red Alert 127)   **65**
[1998 83d: 10g 9.9d 9.9m³ 11.4g 10g 10m 11.6f* 10m 12m 10.8m 1999 a8g⁶
a7f² a8.5g⁴ a7g⁴ 6.1d Oct 5] quite attractive gelding: unimpressive mover: fair
handicapper: probably stays 11.6f: yet to race on soft/heavy going on turf, probably
acts on any other and fibresand: usually blinkered nowadays: sometimes carries head
high. *D. Shaw*

TITUS BRAMBLE   2 b.c. (Apr 23) Puissance 110 – Norska 67 (Northfields   **62**
(USA)) [1999 5g 6g 7m⁶ 7m 7d Aug 11] 12,500Y: tall, rather unfurnished colt: half-
brother to several winners, including 1990 2-y-o 7f winner Neroli (by Nishapour)
and 1¾m winner Eponine (by Sharpo): dam, staying maiden at 2 yrs, not so good as
3-y-o: best effort in maidens when sixth of 11 at Salisbury in July: stays 7f: acts on
good to firm ground: pulled hard in blinkers final start. *B. R. Millman*

TIVOLI (IRE)   3 b.g. Ela-Mana-Mou 132 – Solac (FR) (Gay Lussac (ITY) 116)   **75**
[1998 NR 1999 14d⁵ 14.1m² 14.8m³ Jul 25] tall gelding: brother to very smart stayers
Double Eclipse and Double Trigger and half-brother to several winners: dam lightly-
raced half-sister to Derby Italiano winner Sirlad: fair form in maidens when placed
at Redcar and Newmarket: will stay beyond 1¾m: carried head high first 2 starts.
M. Johnston

TOBLERSONG   4 b.g. Tirol 127 – Winsong Melody (Music Maestro 119) [1998   **69**
86d: 6d⁶ 7g 7g 7m 6d⁵ 8s⁵ 1999 a8g⁶ 7g 7m a7g 7.7s⁴ 7g² 6.9m² 7g³ 7.9f⁶ 7.6m² 7g
7g 5m 7m⁵ 7m 8s 6.1d⁵ 6.1f Oct 20] good-bodied gelding: fair performer: stays 7.5f:
acts on soft and good to firm ground: tried visored: has worn tongue strap: usually
held up: sold 5,000 gns, joined Mrs L. Stubbs. *C. A. Dwyer*

TOBRUK (IRE)   3 b.c. Red Ransom (USA) – Memories (USA) (Hail The Pirates   **110**
(USA) 126) [1998 97p: 7g² 1999 8m³ 8m* 8.2m² 8m⁴ 8s² 10m⁶ 9.9s⁴ Sep 22] rather

leggy, quite good-topped colt: smart performer: won maiden at Kempton in May: ran at least respectably after, including when fourth to Pythios in Britannia Handicap at Royal Ascot then ¾-length second of 5 to Raucous Lad in listed race at Deauville: possibly needs good test at 1m and stays 1¼m: acts on soft and good to firm ground: blinkered fifth start, visored sixth: sold 70,000 gns. *P. W. Chapple-Hyam*

TOBY GRIMES (IRE)   2 ch.g. (Apr 28) Forest Wind (USA) 111 – Emma   –
Grimes (IRE) 54 (Nordico (USA)) [1999 7m 7g 7s Sep 22] IR 3,400Y: first foal: dam second at 1¼m: well beaten in maidens/minor event. *J. S. Moore*

TOEJAM   6 ch.g. Move Off 112 – Cheeky Pigeon (Brave Invader (USA)) [1998   **43**
NR 1999 13.8g 13.8g⁶ 14.1m⁵ 8f 10f⁴ 11m Aug 28] fourth foal: half-brother to a winner over hurdles by Wonderful Surprise: dam poor half-sister to winning hurdlers: poor maiden handicapper: should prove best at 1¼m+: raced only on good going or firmer. *R. E. Barr*

TOLDYA   2 b.f. (Apr 18) Beveled (USA) – Run Amber Run (Run The Gantlet   **50**
(USA)) [1999 5m 5m 6d a6g² Dec 6] sister to several winners, including 4-y-o Dare and useful 5f (at 2 yrs) and 7f winner Moon Over Miami, and half-sister to smart middle-distance stayer Quick Ransom (by Hostage): dam won up to 9f at 5 yrs in USA: modest maiden: best effort final start: stays 6f: acts on equitrack: has reared stalls/wandered under pressure, and possibly not the easiest of rides. *E. A. Wheeler*

TOLERATION   2 b.f. (Feb 1) Petong 126 – Dancing Chimes (London Bells   **82 p**
(CAN) 109) [1999 6s⁴ 6g* Oct 11] 6,500Y: lengthy, unfurnished filly: seventh foal: sister to 9-y-o Palacegate Touch and half-sister to three 2-y-o sprint winners: dam unraced: promising fourth of 11 to Philantha in maiden at Newmarket: didn't need to repeat that form to justify favouritism in 21-runner similar event at Windsor 9 days later: should stay 7f: remains capable of better. *D. R. C. Elsworth*

TOLSTOY   2 b.c. (Feb 6) Nashwan (USA) 135 – Millazure (USA) 71 (Dayjur   **85**
(USA) 137) [1999 7.1m² 8.2d² Oct 21] 425,000Y: first foal: dam, ran 4 times (should have stayed beyond 7f), daughter of top-class miler Milligram, from very good family: runner-up in maidens at Chepstow and Nottingham, fairly useful form when beaten 1¾ lengths by Western Summer on second occasion: will prove suited by 1¼m+. *Sir Michael Stoute*

TOM   4 gr.g. Petong 126 – Wanton 106 (Kris 135) [1998 34, a52: 8.3v⁵ 9.3d 6m   **34**
7.1s² 7g⁵ 5.9d a6g⁵ 8g⁶ a7g³ 7.5m 5.9d 7s 6d 6m a7g⁵ a8g³ a7g⁶ 1999 a8g* a8g²   **a57**
a8g⁴ a8g⁶ a8g⁶ a8g³ a8g⁴ a8g² 7.5d⁶ 8d a7g 8f a8.5g Aug 14] smallish, good-bodied gelding: modest handicapper on all-weather, poor on turf: won amateur event at Southwell in January: stays 1m: acts on firm ground, soft and fibresand (below form only try on equitrack): blinkered once in 1997, visored nowadays. *C. W. Fairhurst*

TOMASEAN   3 b.c. Forzando 122 – Bunny Gee (Last Tycoon 131) [1998 81p: **76**
6m² 6s⁴ 1999 6d⁴ 6m² 7.7g² 9g⁴ 8.5m⁴ 7g⁴ Sep 18] lengthy, quite attractive colt: fair maiden: stays 9f: acts on soft and good to firm going: visored/blinkered after reappearance: sold 7,000 gns, sent to Sweden. *J. Noseda*

TOMBA   5 ch.h. Efisio 120 – Indian Love Song 68 (Be My Guest (USA) 126)   **117**
[1998 119: 6s⁴ 6g⁴ 6s* 6.5m 6m³ 6m⁴ 6.5s* 7v* 1999 7d⁴ 8d⁵ 6d* 6.5g² 6.5s⁵ 6m⁶ 7.3d³ 6s 6.5s* 7d Oct 17] well-made horse: smart performer: winner of 13 of his 37 starts, including Cork And Orrery Stakes and Prix de la Foret in 1998: successful in minor event at Haydock in July and Grosser Buchmacher Springer Sprint-Preis at Munich (for second year in succession, by neck from Tertullian) in October: ran creditably otherwise when 3 lengths sixth to Diktat in Sprint Cup at Haydock on sixth start and 3 lengths eighth to Bold Edge in Diadem Stakes at Ascot on eighth: best at 6f/7f: had form on good to firm going, though went particularly well on soft/heavy: usually soon off bridle, and came from behind when in front: to stand at Rossenarra Stud, Co. Kilkenny, Ireland, fee IR£3,000. *B. J. Meehan*

TOM DOUGAL   4 b.c. Ron's Victory (USA) 129 – Fabulous Rina (FR) (Fabulous   **95**
Dancer (USA) 124) [1998 94: 8.2s³ 7s 8g* 7.9g* 8.1d³ 8d 8m 8s 7g 1999 8d 7.5m⁵ 8m* 8.9d² 10.3g 7.9f⁴ 8m⁵ 8m 8.3m 7.9g Oct 6] leggy, quite good-topped colt: useful performer: won minor event at Ayr in May: ran creditably after when in frame in

handicaps at York: finds 7.5f on sharp side and likely to stay 1¼m: acts on firm and soft ground, probably on fibresand: held up. *C. Smith*

TOMETOYOUTOYOUTOME   2 br.f. (May 24) Timeless Times (USA) 99 –
Ping Pong 65 (Petong 126) [1999 5m 5.1m 6.1g 5.1h 7g Aug 13] 3,700Y: leggy filly: third living foal: half-sister to 1996 2-y-o 6f winner Calchou (by Barrys Gamble) and 3-y-o Ascari: dam 2-y-o 6f winner: behind in maidens/sellers: tried visored/ blinkered. *P. D. Evans*

TOMMY CARSON   4 b.g. Last Tycoon 131 – Ivory Palm (USA) 93 (Sir Ivor **65**
135) [1998 73: 10g 10v³ 1999 14g 14.1m⁴ 9.9m² 11.6s³ 11.9s³ 14.1v² Sep 29] sturdy gelding: fair maiden: left D. Elsworth before final start: will stay 2m: acts on good to firm and heavy going. *Jamie Poulton*

TOMMY TITTLEMOUSE   3 ch.g. Chilibang 120 – Fire Sprite 83 (Mummy's **55 +**
Game 120) [1998 NR 1999 7d⁵ Mar 26] 10,000Y, 15,000 2-y-o: sixth foal: half- brother to 3 winners, including 5-y-o Always Alight and 4-y-o Demolition Jo: dam 2-y-o 5f winner: 20/1 and green, not at all knocked about when never-dangerous fifth in maiden at Doncaster, subsequently banned for 30 days under non-triers' rule: has reportedly broken blood vessels: looked likely to do better. *P. D. Evans*

TOMMY TROJAN (IRE)   2 b.c. (May 2) Namaqualand (USA) – Bilander 78 **69 d**
(High Line 125) [1999 6d* 6g³ 6m⁶ 7f 8d 7d⁶ 8d Oct 18] IR 5,200F, IR 13,000Y: sturdy colt: fifth foal: half-brother to 3 winners, including useful sprinter Humbert's Landing (by Cyrano de Bergerac) and 1m (at 2 yrs) and 1½m winner White Sea (by Soviet Lad): dam maiden who stayed 1½m: fair performer: won maiden at Good- wood in June: became disappointing: stays 6f: best effort on good to soft going: visored final 2 starts: sold 7,000 gns, sent to Sweden. *A. P. Jarvis*

TOMOE GOZEN (IRE)   3 b.f. Brief Truce (USA) 126 – Deelish (IRE) 76 –
(Caerleon (USA) 132) [1998 78: 6g² 6g⁶ 7m 1999 7g⁵ Jun 3] angular filly: fair maiden: ran as if something amiss only start in 1999: should stay at least 7f: twice withdrawn after refusing to enter stalls: sold 10,000 gns. *S. P. C. Woods*

TOMOOJID   4 b.g. Almoojid 69 – Misty Arch (Starch Reduced 112) [1998 NR –
1999 11.8d 8s Oct 25] half-brother to 3 winners, including 6-y-o Vax New Way (by Siberian Express): dam ran twice: tailed off in claimers. *Pat Mitchell*

TOM TAILOR (GER)   5 b.g. Beldale Flutter (USA) 130 – Thoughtful 86 **65**
(Northfields (USA)) [1998 –: 17.2d 13.9g 1999 11.6d⁴ 12m 11.6m⁶ 14m² 16.4m* 16.2m 16.4d 16.4g Aug 20] tall gelding: reportedly operated on for his wind: fair handicapper: won at Sandown in July, despite carrying head awkwardly: disap- pointing after: better around 2m than shorter: acts on soft and good to firm ground. *D. R. C. Elsworth*

TOM TUN   4 b.g. Bold Arrangement 127 – B Grade 59 (Lucky Wednesday 124) **87**
[1998 61p, a67p: 7g 7s 5.9d a6g* a5g⁵ 5m⁵ 6m* a6g 6.1s⁶ a5g* a5f 1999 a6g* a6g* **a83**
a6g³ 5d* 5d³ 6f* 6s⁴ 6d⁶ 6m⁴ 6m⁵ 6f* 6m² 6m⁴ 5m² 6d³ 5s 6d a6g² a6g⁶ Nov 30] workmanlike gelding: has a round action: fairly useful performer: had another good year, winning handicaps at Southwell in January and February, Newcastle in March and Doncaster in May and minor event at Doncaster in July: effective at 5f/6f: acts on firm going, soft and all-weather: usually races prominently: tough, game and consistent: a credit to connections. *Miss J. F. Craze*

TONDYNE   2 b.g. (Feb 27) Owington 123 – Anodyne 100 (Dominion 123) [1999 –
6m 7.1m Sep 4] 29,000Y: leggy, useful-looking gelding: sixth foal: closely related to 8.5f winner Desert Mirage (by Green Desert) and half-brother to 3 winners, including fairly useful 1993 2-y-o 5f winner Stimulant (by Sharpo), later successful in USA: dam 6f winner, including at 2 yrs: well beaten in maidens. *T. D. Easterby*

TONGA   2 gr.f. (Jan 31) Petong 126 – Pegs 60 (Mandrake Major 122) [1999 5g a7g –
a7g Nov 22] leggy filly: first foal: dam well beaten after third over 1m on debut at 2 yrs: well held in maiden/sellers. *C. W. Thornton*

TONG ROAD   3 gr.g. Petong 126 – Wayzgoose (USA) (Diesis 133) [1998 –: 5d **48**
6.1d 5.1v 1999 5g 5m 5m 5g 6s⁶ 6d a6g Nov 17] workmanlike gelding: poor maiden: stays 6f: acts on soft and good to firm going: has been slowly away. *B. R. Cambidge*

TONIC 3 b.g. Robellino (USA) 127 – Alyara (USA) (Alydar (USA)) [1998 83: **89**
8g³ 8v² 1999 8d* 8m 7.9s May 13] leggy, angular gelding: fairly useful performer:
won maiden at Ripon in April: below form in handicaps after: will stay at least 1¼m:
acts on good to soft going, probably on good to firm: carries head awkwardly.
M. Johnston

TONIGHT'S PRIZE (IRE) 5 b.g. Night Shift (USA) – Bestow 76 (Shirley **83**
Heights 130) [1998 93: 10d 8.5g 9g³ 9m⁵ 8m* 8.3m⁵ 8g³ 9g 8g 1999 7.6m⁶ 8.1g 8.5m
8m² 8f 8g 8.3m 10d³ 10.4g⁵ Oct 6] leggy gelding: fairly useful handicapper: effective
at 1m to 1¼m: acts on good to firm and good to soft going: usually held up. *C. F. Wall*

TONNERRE 7 b.g. Unfuwain (USA) 131 – Supper Time 71 (Shantung 132) **61**
[1998 61: 12.3m⁶ 11.8g 10.5m 10s* 9.9m³ 10.5m⁴ 10g⁶ 1999 a12g³ a8g 10m 10g **a–**
16f³ 16.2s* 13f a16.2g 14.1d* 16.5s⁶ Nov 6] close-coupled gelding: modest performer: won handicap at Beverley in July and claimer at Yarmouth in October: stays 2m:
acts on firm ground, though all 5 wins on good to soft/soft: has been bandaged: tends
to pull hard: none too consistent: fair hurdler, won twice in November/December.
K. A. Morgan

TONY TIE 3 b.g. Ardkinglass 114 – Queen of The Quorn 53 (Governor General **87**
116) [1998 84: 5d* 6d 7g⁴ 6.9m³ 7d* 7.9g 8d⁶ 1999 8m 9.2f 8.3m 8d 8.9d 8d² 8s*
a8.5g Dec 1] leggy, angular gelding: fairly useful handicapper: back to best to win
22-runner ladies event at Doncaster in November: acts on soft and
good to firm going (well held only run on all-weather). *J. S. Goldie*

TOORAK (USA) 2 b.c. (Apr 7) Irish River (FR) 131 – Just Juliet (USA) (What A **76 p**
Pleasure (USA)) [1999 8d⁶ Oct 15] rangy, angular colt: fluent mover: half-brother to
3-y-o Fair Verona, 1996 2-y-o 7f winner Julietta Mia (by Woodman) and several
winners abroad: dam, 2-y-o sprint winner in USA, half-sister to US Grade 1 winners
Tis Juliet and Stella Madrid: in need of race, never-nearer sixth of 13 to Pawn Broker
in slowly-run maiden at Newmarket: should stay beyond 1m: sure to do better.
J. W. Hills

TOPACIO 3 b.g. Saddlers' Hall (IRE) 126 – Teresa (SPA) 117 (Rheffissimo (FR) **81 p**
120) [1998 –: 8s 1999 10m⁶ 10.2m 14.1g³ 17.2g² 16.1s² 16d* Oct 21] fairly useful
handicapper: progressed well in 1999, winning at Nottingham final start by 4 lengths:
better at 2m than shorter: acts on soft going: sold 45,000 gns, joined P. Hughes in
Ireland: probably open to further improvement. *S. C. Williams*

TOP ACT 3 b.g. Inchinor 119 – Actress 73 (Known Fact (USA) 135) [1998 –: 6g⁶ **–**
6f 8m 7.9g 1999 8d 9.9g 7.9f 7m 12s Oct 4] tall, lengthy gelding: shows knee action:
little sign of ability, including in visor. *J. S. Wainwright*

TOPATORI (IRE) 5 ch.m. Topanoora 118 – Partygoer (General Assembly **89**
(USA)) [1998 89: 8s* 10v⁵ 9d⁵ 8d 8g³ 10d 9d⁶ 10s 9g 8.9g 8s³ 10s³ 1999 8g* 8m² 8m
8m⁴ 8m 8.1d³ 9g² 8m 8d 8s 10s Oct 2] angular mare: fairly useful handicapper: won
at Leicester in April: ran creditably most other starts after: effective at 1m/1¼m: acts
on soft and good to firm ground: usually held up. *M. H. Tompkins*

TOPAZ 4 b.g. Alhijaz 122 – Daisy Topper (Top Ville 129) [1998 –: 10.2s⁶ 11.9f **–**
11.7d⁶ 9m 10g 9.9m 11.9s 1999 10.8m 10g 8m 9.9v 10.1d Oct 20] rather leggy
gelding: signs of only a little ability. *H. J. Collingridge*

TOP BANANA 8 ch.g. Pharly (FR) 130 – Oxslip 106 (Owen Dudley 121) [1998 **68**
82: 6g³ 6g 6g 7d⁴ 6m⁶ 6g 7.1g 1999 6v 6.1f 7m 6s² 6m 7.1d 6g⁶ 6s² 6g Oct 11] close-
coupled, workmanlike gelding: fair handicapper: stays 7f: acts on firm and soft
ground: blinkered once in 1996: ridden by inexperienced riders nowadays: none too
consistent. *H. Candy*

TOP CEES 9 b.g. Shirley Heights 130 – Sing Softly 112 (Luthier 126) [1998 **106**
106: 12s³ 18.7m 13.9s² 15m* 18.7g² 12m* 1999 13.4d⁴ 13.1d* 17.3g* Oct 16]
Even at the age of nine, the last had not been heard of Top Cees.
Through no fault of his own, he has not always been everybody's favourite
racehorse, but he is leaving plenty of memories—other than the Swaffham
Handicap and events in Court 13 during the successful libel case prosecuted by
the Ramsdens and Kieren Fallon against the owners of *The Sporting Life*. The

latest step in Top Cees' evolution from cause celebre into celebrated elder statesman came in October with victory in the Cesarewitch.

The sight of Top Cees returning to the winner's enclosure at Newmarket while Channel 4 man Derek Thompson conducted an interview with his jockey Kieren Fallon was somewhat bizarre, and would have been long odds against for anyone who had seen the two men take the witness stand to contradict each other in February 1998. Top Cees' part in this reunion was also an unlikely one seeing he had spent most of the intervening period on the side-lines with an injury. He had won the Coral Cup at the Cheltenham Festival, to a mixed reception, only weeks after his starring role on video at the High Court and then added two more wins when switched back to the Flat before the 1998 Cesarewitch and 1999 Coral Cup passed by without him. When Lynda Ramsden retired, Top Cees moved to Ian Balding's along with the latter's son Andrew, who had been associated with Top Cees for two years when he was assistant trainer at Mrs Ramsden's. Under his guidance, and trained largely in the swimming pool, Top Cees was prepared for the latest Cesarewitch. Two previous attempts in the race, in 1995 and 1997, had resulted in a third and a second. Fourth of five in a rated stakes at Chester in August gave no indication that Top Cees would improve on that record. However, another rated stakes over a mile and five furlongs at the Ayr Western meeting, a race whose relevance to the Cesarewitch in pre-publicity had largely been confined to the reappearance run of ante-post gamble Silent Warning, instead proved hugely more encouraging for Top Cees when he got up close home. This was as good a performance as Top Cees had ever given and he was sent off 7/1 second favourite at Newmarket, behind the Northumberland Plate and Doncaster Cup winner Far Cry. In a thirty-two runner field, the favourite's bid for a four-timer was thwarted by three outsiders and by Top Cees. The last-named could be called the winner from some way out as he crept through the field into a challenging position and then quickened well approaching the final furlong to win by a length and a quarter from the fast-finishing Dominant Duchess. A bad bump as he took over up front did nothing to stop Top Cees in the race but was described as probably career-ending in the immediate aftermath, when it was blamed for an apparent recurrence of an old suspensory injury on the near-fore. The potential seriousness of the injury was downgraded a few days later, however, and Top Cees is reportedly on course for another appearance in the Coral Cup and, all being well, another season on the Flat.

The close-coupled Top Cees, who has a round action, has not raced on firm going but acts on any other. His stamina and temperament were both the subject of no little discussion at the High Court. The latest evidence is that he stays two and a quarter miles well (while in 1998 he also demonstrated his

Tote Cesarewitch (Handicap), Newmarket—Top Cees adds to his good record in big handicaps with a comfortable defeat of Dominant Duchess (right), Heros Fatal (third right) and Eastwell Hall (fourth right)

effectiveness at a mile and a half on a stiff track) and is notable for his gameness. Top Cees was bred by Peter Harris, who also owned and trained him until his sale for 15,000 guineas at the Autumn Sales in 1994. Five years, two Chester Cups, one Coral Cup and one Cesarewitch later, Top Cees is still going strongly. *I. A. Balding*

TOP FIT 3 b.c. Thatching 131 – Diplomatist 69 (Dominion 123) [1998 65: 5m 5m 5m 7s⁴ 8d² a8g⁴ a8g³ a8.5g³ Jan 6] unfurnished colt: has a quick action: fair performer: stays 8.5f: acts on all-weather and good to soft going: blinkered last 4 starts: sent to Macau. *W. J. Haggas* **69**

TOP FLOOR (IRE) 4 ch.g. Waajib 121 – Keen Note 69 (Sharpo 132) [1998 59, a51: a6g a6g a7g⁵ a7g³ 8.3v* 8.2s 8s 7.5g⁵ 8f⁵ 6.9d 8.2s⁴ 8v² 1999 a9.4g² a9.4g 10d 12s 10g⁶ May 31] sparely-made gelding: poor performer: barely stays 1¼m: acts on fibresand and good to firm going, goes well on heavy. *J. L. Spearing* **49**

TOP HAND 2 ch.f. (Mar 2) First Trump 118 – Gold Luck (USA) (Slew O'Gold (USA)) [1999 8d⁶ 8s* Oct 26] first reported foal: dam unraced daughter of smart winner up to 1¼m Rambushka: confirmed debut promise when winning maiden at Bath by neck from Muschana, gamely making all: should stay 1¼m: remains capable of better. *B. W. Hills* **77 p**

TOP JEM 5 b.m. Damister (USA) 123 – Sharp Top 62 (Sharpo 132) [1998 80, a64: a12g a10g a11g⁶ 10s⁴ 10s 10.3g 10d³ 10.1s⁶ 9.9s 10d 1999 10s 10s* 9.2v* 9.9m* 10s³ 10.5d⁴ 10d⁴ 9.9v³ a12g² 10f a12g Jun 28] sparely-made mare: has a round action: fairly useful handicapper on turf, fair on all-weather: won at Leicester, Hamilton and Beverley in April: stays 1½m: acts on good to firm going, heavy and fibresand: has hung left and looked less than keen. *M. J. Ryan* **82 a75**

TOP MAITE 4 ch.g. Komaite (USA) – Top Yard (Teekay) [1998 40: 7d 11.1v⁵ 8f 7g 8m 10d 8f⁴ 8m 8m⁶ 8.3s 1999 a8g Jan 2] good-bodied gelding: poor maiden handicapper: tried blinkered. *G. F. H. Charles-Jones* **–**

TOPMAN 2 ch.c. (Mar 25) Komaite (USA) – Top Yard (Teekay) [1999 5.2m Apr 16] leggy, plain colt: fifth foal: brother to 4-y-o Top Maite: dam unraced: tailed-off last of 8 in minor event at Newbury. *G. F. H. Charles-Jones* **–**

TOP OF THE CHARTS 3 b.g. Salse (USA) 128 – Celebrity 101 (Troy 137) [1998 –: 7g 7d 7s 1999 8.2f⁴ 11.4m a12g⁴ 16.2m⁴ Jul 19] quite attractive maiden: poor maiden handicapper: stays 1½m: acts on fibresand and firm ground: visored/ blinkered last 2 starts, hanging and carrying head awkwardly final one: joined Mrs M. Reveley. *J. Noseda* **41 §**

TOP OF THE CLASS (IRE) 2 b.f. (Jan 29) Rudimentary (USA) 118 – School Mum (Reprimand 122) [1999 5g³ 5s⁵ 5v⁵ 6f 6g³ 7.5g⁵ 5.9g⁴ 6g³ 6d* 6s⁶ 6g Oct 6] 600F, IR 2,400Y: unfurnished filly: has a round action: first foal: dam ran once: fair performer: won nursery at Ayr in September: better than bare form of final 2 starts: should stay 7f: acts on soft going. *Martyn Wane* **69**

TOP OF THE FORM (IRE) 5 ch.m. Masterclass (USA) 116 – Haraabah (USA) 99 (Topsider (USA)) [1998 65: 5d 5m⁶ 6m 5g⁴ 5.1g⁵ 5m 6.1m 5.1m⁵ 5g⁶ 5s⁵ a5g³ 1999 a6f Feb 1] sparely-made mare: modest handicapper: has won at easy 6f, but best at 5f: raced mainly on good going or firmer on turf: no improvement in blinkers/visor: often leads: carries head high. *K. A. Ryan* **–**

TOP OF THE MORNING 3 b.f. Keen 116 – Kelimutu 58 (Top Ville 129) [1998 48: 6m 6.9f 8g 6m⁴ a7g⁵ 1999 10m⁵ 8g Jun 30] modest maiden: free-going sort, likely to prove best up to 1¼m: raced only on good going or firmer on turf: reared stalls final start. *G. A. Butler* **56**

TOP OF THE PARKES 2 b.f. (Mar 14) Mistertopogigo (IRE) 118 – Bella Parkes 83 (Tina's Pet 121) [1999 5.7m³ 5g⁵ 5v Sep 24] first foal: dam, 6f winner (including at 2 yrs), half-sister to useful sprinter Lucky Parkes: modest form in maidens first 2 starts: likely to prove best at 5f/6f: acts on good to firm ground, well held on heavy. *N. P. Littmoden* **60**

TOP OF THE POPS (IRE) 3 b.g. Ballad Rock 122 – Summerhill (Habitat 134) [1998 NR 1999 6d⁵ 6s⁶ a7g⁴ a6g⁴ 6.1g⁶ 6m⁵ Aug 30] 12,000Y: big, workmanlike **66**

gelding: has plenty of scope: fourth living foal: half-brother to fairly useful Irish 7f/
1m winner Two Bandits (by Thatching) and a winner in Italy by Glow: dam Irish 6f
winner: fair maiden: effective at 6f/7f: acts on good to firm going, soft and fibresand.
C. W. Thornton

TOP OF THE SNOBS (IRE)   5 b.g. Top of The World 103 – Little Snob   –
(Aristocracy 111) [1998 NR 1999 10d Jun 7] IR 11,500Y, 8,200 4-y-o: seventh foal:
half-brother to useful chaser Pennybridge (by Orchestra): dam unraced: modest form
in bumpers: well beaten in seller only Flat run. *Mrs G. S. Rees*

TOP ORDER (USA)   3 b. or br.f. Dayjur (USA) 137 – Victoria Cross (USA)   **94**
(Spectacular Bid (USA)) [1998 82: 5g⁵ 5d⁴ 5d* 5s 5.1d⁶ 1999 6g⁴ 7m 5.5f² 8f² 8f²
6.5f* 5.5f² 5.5f² Nov 25] leggy, close-coupled filly: fairly useful performer: trained
by P. Cole first 2 starts in 1999, better effort when fourth at Newmarket on reappearance: ran well all starts in USA, winning allowance race at Santa Anita in October:
probably stays 1m, at least as effective around 6f: acts on good to soft and firm
ground. *N. Drysdale, USA*

TOPPO'S GEM   2 b.c. (Apr 26) Mistertopogigo (IRE) 118 – Rosy Diamond 57   **62**
(Jalmood (USA) 126) [1999 5m 5d* 5d⁴ 5d⁶ 5.9g Jul 3] 3,600Y: rather leggy colt:
sixth foal: dam 6f winner: modest form: won maiden at Redcar in April: well beaten
last 2 starts: may prove best at 5f. *K. A. Ryan*

TOP STAR (IRE)   3 b.g. Thatching 131 – Decadence Star (IRE) (High Estate   **69**
127) [1998 69: 6d⁴ 6g 6v⁶ 1999 7d² 6m 8m 7m 6m 7d⁵ Oct 22] close-coupled
gelding: fair maiden handicapper: left M. Channon and off 5 months before final
start: should stay 1m: acts on good to soft ground, possibly not on firmer than good:
visored/blinkered first 5 starts: inconsistent: sold 3,700 gns. *D. W. P. Arbuthnot*

TOP TARN (IRE)   3 b.f. Royal Academy (USA) 130 – Laugharne (Known Fact   –
(USA) 135) [1998 50: 6g 5g 5.1m 1999 6g 6d Jun 7] quite attractive filly: modest
maiden at 2 yrs: no form in 1999: sold 6,200 gns. *C. F. Wall*

*Charles Heidsieck Champagne Cherry Hinton Stakes, Newmarket—Torgau strikes a blow for smaller stables,
making all and holding the late run of Hoh Dear (dark cap); Presentation (dark colours) does best of
those on the far side, finishing fourth, while the other horse in the picture, Areydha, is only ninth*

TOPTON (IRE) 5 b.g. Royal Academy (USA) 130 – Circo 77 (High Top 131) **85**
[1998 77, a89: 6d 6d 7m² 8f⁶ 7g* 7g⁵ 7v⁶ 7.1g³ 8g 6m 7f 7m 7g 7g 7s 7s² a7g* a7g³ **a91**
a7g* a8g⁴ a7g⁴ a8g⁴ 1999 a7g² a7g a7g* a7f³ a8g² a8g⁶ a8.5g 8d⁶ 8g 7m 8g 7m³ 7g*
7f 7m³ 8m⁴ 7m* 7m⁴ 7m* 7d 7g³ 7m 8d 7s a8g a7g² a8g³ a7g² Dec 21] tall, angular
gelding: fairly useful handicapper: had another good year, winning at Lingfield in
January, Doncaster in June (awarded race) and July and Yarmouth in August: good
placed efforts final 3 starts: best at 7f/1m: acts on good to firm going, soft and all-
weather: has won in visor, blinkered nowadays: usually held up (forced pace final
start): tough, but not an easy ride. *P. Howling*

TORCH SONG 3 ch.c. Zafonic (USA) 130 – River Lullaby (USA) (Riverman **86 p**
(USA) 131) [1998 NR 1999 8m² 8s* Oct 4] smallish, stocky colt: sixth foal: half-
brother to several winners, including useful French middle-distance performer
Berceau (by Alleged) and very smart miler Wixim (by Diesis): dam, Irish 2-y-o 6f
winner, third in 1¼m listed race at 3 yrs: won maiden at Pontefract comfortably by ½
length from Sheer Harmony: will improve further: sold 87,000 gns, sent to USA.
R. Charlton

TOREERO 4 b.g. Cadeaux Genereux 131 – Free City (USA) (Danzig (USA)) **36**
[1998 –: 8v 1999 a8.5g a10f a8f 8f 7.8m⁵ 12d Sep 13] poor maiden: left B. Curley
after fourth start: likely to prove best short of 1m. *T. Carmody, Ireland*

TORGAU (IRE) 2 b.f. (Jan 15) Zieten (USA) 118 – Snoozy Time 65 (Cavo Doro **109**
124) [1999 5g* 5m⁶ 6m* 7m² 6d² Sep 28] 13,000F, 13,000Y: close-coupled, rather
leggy filly: half-sister to several winners, including 1m winner Dream of Fame (by

The TT Partnership's "Torgau"

Petorius) and 7-y-o Fujiyama Crest, both fairly useful: dam, 2-y-o 5f winner, half-sister to Grey Desire: useful performer: won minor event at Catterick in June and Charles Heidsieck Champagne Cherry Hinton Stakes at Newmarket (by 1¼ lengths from Hoh Dear) in July: good second to Preseli (beaten ¾ length) in Moyglare Stud Stakes at the Curragh and to Seazun (beaten head) in Cheveley Park Stakes at Newmarket last 2 starts: will probably stay 1m: acts on good to firm and good to soft ground. *G. C. Bravery*

TORMENTOSO   2 b.g. (Apr 26) Catrail (USA) 123 – Chita Rivera 61 (Chief   **70**
Singer 131) [1999 7.1m 7g⁵ 8.1g Aug 30] 18,000F, 31,000Y: first foal: dam, staying maiden, half-sister to Oaks winner Lady Carla: best effort in maidens (fair form) when fifth of 13 to Port Vila at Newbury: should stay 1m. *M. R. Channon*

TORNADO PRINCE (IRE)   4 ch.g. Caerleon (USA) 132 – Welsh Flame 106   **73**
(Welsh Pageant 132) [1998 70: 10d 8g 9.7m* 10m³ 11.9f⁶ 1999 a8g a9.4g⁶ 9.2v 8d 7m⁴ 7m 7.1m³ a7g⁶ 7g⁴ 8g² 8m 8m* 8.5m 6d 7g 7m⁵ 6m 8f* 8m* 10g 9g 8g Nov 3] quite good-topped gelding: fair performer: won sellers at Ripon (made all) in July and Thirsk and Pontefract (20-runner handicap) in September: has form at 1¼m, but probably best around 1m: acts on firm going (no form on all-weather): sometimes takes strong hold. *E. J. Alston*

TORRENT   4 ch.g. Prince Sabo 123 – Maiden Pool 85 (Sharpen Up 127) [1998   **81**
83: 6d* 6.1m⁶ 5g* 6f 6s⁶ 5g 5g 5d 1999 5d 5m³ 6d 5d 7m 5g 5m⁴ 5m* 5d 6g⁶ 5m⁴ 5m 6g³ 6g² 6d 5s² a5g² a6g³ a5g² a6g* a5g* a5g³ Dec 29] strong, lengthy gelding: fairly useful performer: left T. D. Barron after sixth start: won minor event at Beverley in July and 2 handicaps (for 7-lb claimer) at Lingfield in December: best at 5f/6f: yet to race on heavy going, acts on any other: blinkered last 9 starts: has worn tongue strap: carries head high, and has found little in front. *D. W. Chapman*

TORROS STRAITS (USA)   2 b.f. (Feb 10) Boundary (USA) 117 – Preparation   **82 +**
(USA) (Easy Goer (USA)) [1999 6m⁴ Jul 7] $110,000Y: strong, useful-looking filly: first foal: dam unraced half-sister to high-class American mare Heavenly Prize (best at 1¼m) out of sister to Breeders' Cup Sprint winner Dancing Spree: favourite but in need of race, fourth of 8 to Boast in minor event at Newmarket, taking fierce hold early on and not knocked about once held: green and short to post: seemed sure to do better. *N. A. Callaghan*

TORY BOY   4 b.g. Deploy 131 – Mukhayyalah (Dancing Brave (USA) 140) [1998   **68**
73: 10.5d 10.8s* 11.6g⁵ 14g 14g⁴ 1999 a16g² 14.6s a14g³ 15.8m² 20f⁶ 16.5s a16g⁴   **a54**
a16.2g³ Dec 1] smallish, lengthy gelding: fair on turf, modest on all-weather: stays 2m: acts on soft and good to firm going, and all-weather: probably best blinkered nowadays: has hung left: won 3 times over hurdles in 1999. *Ian Williams*

TOSHIBA TIMES   3 b.g. Persian Bold 123 – Kirkby Belle 44 (Bay Express 132)   **–**
[1998 –: 7d 1999 10f 7.5v 6m 5g 9g Aug 18] little sign of ability. *B. Ellison*

Vodafone 'Dash' Rated Stakes (Handicap), Epsom—
To The Roof repeats his 1996 success under a fine ride from Jimmy Fortune,
winning a shade cosily from Dashing Blue (noseband) and Night Flight (rail)

TOTAL DELIGHT   3 b.g. Mtoto 134 – Shesadelight 67 (Shirley Heights 130)   **81**
[1998 60p: 7d⁵ 1999 9.9m³ 10.2s² 11.8d Oct 11] fairly useful maiden: should stay
1½m: acts on soft and good to firm going: sold 16,000 gns. *Lady Herries*

TOTAL LOVE   2 ch.f. (Mar 11) Cadeaux Genereux 131 – Favorable Exchange   **102**
(USA) (Exceller (USA) 129) [1999 5s² 6g* 5m 6d³ 6m⁶ 5d 7d² 8d³ 7g³ Oct 16]
52,000Y: rather leggy, quite good-topped filly: half-sister to several winners, including 1989 2-y-o 5f/6f winner Nobodys Sweetheart (by Pharly) and 7-y-o Unchanged:
dam French 1¼m to 1½m winner: useful performer: won maiden at Leicester in May:
progressed well after, close third of 12 to Lahan in Rockfel Stakes at Newmarket
final start: much better at 7f/1m than less: acts on soft and good to firm ground.
E. A. L. Dunlop

TOTALLY SCOTTISH   3 b.g. Mtoto 134 – Glenfinlass (Lomond (USA) 128)   **–**
[1998 NR 1999 12d 10f 12s⁴ Nov 2] 24,000Y: smallish, quite attractive gelding: third
reported foal: half-brother to French 9f winner Bolder Still (by Never So Bold): dam
unraced sister to 10-y-o Inchcailloch and half-sister to smart middle-distance
performer Prize Giving: poor form in maidens. *Mrs M. Reveley*

TOTEM DANCER   6 b.m. Mtoto 134 – Ballad Opera (Sadler's Wells (USA)   **78 §**
132) [1998 88: a14g⁴ 12d³ 13v⁵ 14.1v⁴ 13.9g² 11.9s³ 12.3g* 13.9g² 13.1s² 12s⁴ 12d⁶
1999 a16.2g 9.9m⁵ 13.9s 12m 12f 11.9d⁴ 14d³ 11.8m² 14s 12d Oct 9] sparely-made
mare: has a short action: fair performer: effective at 1½m/1¾m: acts on soft and good
to firm going: visored twice: has run in snatches: sold 11,500 gns. *J. L. Eyre*

TO THE LAST MAN   3 b.g. Warrshan (USA) 117 – Shirley's Touch (Touching   **70**
Wood (USA) 127) [1998 69: a5g² a5g⁶ 7d⁴ 7g² 7m 7m 8v⁴ 1999 10.8d⁴ 10s 8m
10f⁵ 8g* 8.2m⁵ 8f⁴ 8.5m⁴ 10m 8m⁴ 8g³ 8d* 7.9m 8s⁵ 8.9d 7d⁶ Oct 22] leggy
gelding: fair performer: won apprentice handicap at Salisbury in June and minor
event at Brighton in August: probably best around 1m: acts on good to firm and
heavy going: visored once: usually bandaged: held up: sold 7,000 gns, joined
G. M. Moore. *M. D. I. Usher*

TO THE ROOF (IRE)   7 b.g. Thatching 131 – Christine Daae 74 (Sadler's Wells   **112**
(USA) 132) [1998 108: 6g³ 6m² 5m⁴ 5f 5.6g⁵ 6g² 5s* 5s 1999 5d⁶ 6g³ 5d* 5m³ 5g*
5m⁶ 5.1m² 5f 5m 5s 5d Sep 30] big, lengthy, good-bodied gelding: usually impresses
in appearance: has a quick action: smart performer: won minor event at Beverley in
May and listed rated stakes at Epsom (by ½ length from Dashing Blue) in June: ran
creditably otherwise when placed in listed races at Kempton (close third to Proud
Native) on fourth start and Chester (2 lengths second to Tedburrow) on seventh:
effective at 5f/6f: acts on firm ground, soft and fibresand: often bandaged behind:
usually races prominently. *P. W. Harris*

TOTIMETO   3 b.g. Mtoto 134 – Stolon Time 80 (Good Times (ITY)) [1998 NR   **64 p**
1999 7.7m⁵ 8m 8g⁵ Aug 22] leggy, sparely-made gelding: fourth reported foal: dam,
2-y-o 6f winner, bred to stay at least 1m: modest form in maidens, not knocked about
final start: likely to do better, particularly beyond 1m. *J. A. Glover*

TOTO CAELO   3 b.c. Mtoto 134 – Octavia Girl 104 (Octavo (USA) 115) [1998   **97**
80p: 7f⁶ 8g⁶ 1999 11.8g* 12s² 12m 11.9s⁶ 11.6d* 11.9f² 13.3m 12s Sep 26] smallish,
good-topped colt: useful performer: won maiden at Leicester in April and handicap
at Windsor in August: ran creditably in handicaps after only when second at York:
should stay beyond 1½m: yet to race on heavy going, acts on any other: has raced
freely and wandered: sold 46,000 gns. *B. W. Hills*

TOTOM   4 b.f. Mtoto 134 – A Lyph (USA) 78 (Lypheor 118) [1998 74, a80+:   **80**
8.3m³ 7.6m² 8.1g⁴ 10g 9g a10g* a9.4g⁵ 1999 a10g* a10g 10g 9.9m⁴ 10g* 10m*
10m⁵ 11.5g* 13.3m⁴ 11.5s⁵ Oct 8] lengthy filly: fairly useful performer: had a good
year in 1999, winning handicap at Lingfield in February, minor event/handicap at
Windsor in June/July and handicap at Lingfield in August: will stay 1¾m: acts on
good to firm going and all-weather: visored all starts on all-weather. *J. R. Fanshawe*

TOUCH 'N' FLY (IRE)   3 b.c. Catrail (USA) 123 – Menominee (Soviet Star   **116**
(USA) 128) [1998 NR 1999 8.2m* 8g* 8m³ 8.5d⁴ Oct 15] IR 210,000Y: leggy,
lengthy colt: second foal: half-brother to 4-y-o Count de Money: dam unraced half-
sister to very smart French middle-distance stayer Mersey and smart French middle-
distance filly Muncie: quickly made into a smart performer: landed odds impres-

The Thoroughbred Corporation's "Touch 'N' Fly"

sively in maiden at Nottingham in May and minor event at Salisbury (by 7 lengths from Al Waffi) in August: under 2 lengths third to Sugarfoot in Park Stakes at Doncaster penultimate start: pulled hard and not best of runs final one: raced only at 1m: joined A. Hassinger in USA. *H. R. A. Cecil*

TOUCH'N'GO   5 b.g. Rainbow Quest (USA) 134 – Mary Martin (Be My Guest (USA) 126) [1998 –, a60: a11g a9.4g³ 1999 a14.8g⁵ May 14] modest performer: stays 11f: best efforts on all-weather: races up with pace. *G. Woodward*   –

TOUCH OF FAIRY (IRE)   3 b.c. Fairy King (USA) – Decadence (Vaigly Great 127) [1998 NR 1999 6d² Oct 28] 11,500Y: brother to useful 5f performer Fairy Wind and fairly useful 5f to 7f winner Angaar and half-brother to 2 winners, notably smart 5f performer Mistertopogigo (by Thatching): dam lightly-raced sister to smart sprinter Hallgate: 10/1, ¾-length second of 21 to Madmun in Windsor maiden, showing plenty of speed: should improve. *K. Mahdi*   **78 p**

TOUCH OF LOVE   3 b.c. Pursuit of Love 124 – Nitouche 68 (Scottish Reel 123) [1998 73p: 7g 8m 1999 8.2s⁶ 10g 10g 8s 11g* 14.6d Oct 22] good-topped colt: fair performer: clearly best effort in 1999 when winning maiden handicap at Redcar in October: should stay beyond 11f: sold 9,000 gns. *J. Noseda*   **73**

TOUGH ACT   5 b.g. Be My Chief (USA) 122 – Forelino (USA) 62§ (Trempolino (USA) 135) [1998 88: 12m* 11.4g⁶ 14m² 14g³ 12d* 13.3g⁵ 18g 1999 16.4s 14g² 12m² 14m 14f 13.3g⁴ 11.5g⁴ 12m⁶ Sep 4] neat gelding: fairly useful performer: effective at 1½m/1¾m: acts on good to firm and good to soft ground: blinkered last 3 starts: sometimes starts slowly (very much so final outing), and tends to carry head awkwardly: not one to trust implicitly: sold 12,000 gns, joined Mrs P. Sly. *Mrs A. J. Perrett*   **83 §**

TOUGH GUY (IRE)   3 b.c. Namaqualand (USA) – Supreme Crown (USA) (Chief's Crown (USA)) [1998 93: 6.1m⁴ 6m 6s* 6f⁶ 7m* 8g 7s⁵ 7v² 1999 7g⁵ 7m 7d⁵ 7f 7.1s* 7g Oct 16] smallish, good-topped colt: fluent mover: useful handicapper: **103**

clearly best effort in 1999 when winning handicap at Haydock (after 3-month break) in September by 1½ lengths from Haymaker: gave impression something amiss next time: should stay 1m: has form on good to firm going, goes well on soft/heavy: reportedly bled from nose second start: sold 8,000 gns, sent to Sweden. *M. A. Jarvis*

TOUGH LEADER   5 b.g. Lead On Time (USA) 123 – Al Guswa 98 (Shernazar   **106**
131) [1998 101: a8g a9.4g* a10g⁴ a12g* 10s³ 10g* 12m³ 10g⁴ 11.9m* 14g⁶ 12m²
12m³ 10.1m⁴ 13.3g 1999 10m 14g³ 12g* 12m 11.9s⁴ 11.9f² 12f⁵ Jul 30] robust
gelding: useful handicapper: won rated stakes at Epsom in June by neck from
Nautical Star: ran well after in Old Newton Cup at Haydock (fourth to Celestial
Welcome) and rated stakes at York (second to Mardani) within 6 days in July:
effective at 1½m/1¾m: acts on all-weather, firm and soft going: usually tongue tied:
genuine and consistent: sent to USA. *B. Hanbury*

TOUGH SPEED (USA)   2 b.c. (Jan 28) Miswaki (USA) 124 – Nature's   **108 p**
Magic (USA) (Nijinsky (CAN) 138) [1999 6g² 7g* 7d⁴ Oct 1]
      Owner Saeed Suhail and trainer Sir Michael Stoute must have been
delighted with the performances of two-year-olds King's Best and Tough
Speed at the York August meeting. The smashing-looking King's Best won the
Acomb Stakes in tremendous style and debutant Tough Speed ran a race full of
promise when runner-up to Fath in the Convivial Maiden. King's Best was
clearly regarded as the pick of the pair at the time—he was aimed next at the
Dewhurst while Tough Speed held no entries in the big autumn races—but
Tough Speed could yet make the bigger name for himself. He was the least
forward of the Convivial runners and it was clear from his performance,
finishing well without being given a hard race, that he was going to take plenty
of beating next time. He bolted up three weeks later in the Queen's Own
Yorkshire Dragoons Conditions Stakes at the Doncaster St Leger meeting,
value for at least double his four-length winning margin over the subsequent
listed race winner Hataab. After such an impressive display, Tough Speed's
third and final outing in his first season, in the Somerville Tattersall Stakes at
Newmarket in October, was something of a let-down. Starting at odds on and
the clear pick of the paddock, he managed only fourth of five to Scarteen Fox,
held up and unable to quicken when given the office two furlongs out. The good
to soft going may not have suited Tough Speed and, for the time being, we
prefer to judge him on the potential of his eye-catching victory on good at

Queen's Own Yorkshire Dragoons Conditions Stakes, Doncaster—
Tough Speed puts distance between himself and Hataab, as he confirms the promise of his debut behind Fath

Doncaster. He might even make up into a Two Thousand Guineas contender and looks temptingly priced at 50/1 with Ladbrokes at the time of writing.

Tough Speed (USA) (b.c. Jan 28, 1997)	Miswaki (USA) (ch 1978)	Mr Prospector (b 1970)	Raise A Native / Gold Digger
		Hopespringseternal (ch 1971)	Buckpasser / Rose Bower
	Nature's Magic (USA) (b 1992)	Nijinsky (b 1967)	Northern Dancer / Flaming Page
		Joy Returned (b 1977)	Big Spruce / Imajoy

Tough Speed, a 230,000-dollar yearling, is a tall, good sort; he was rather unfurnished as a two-year-old and has the scope to develop into an even better-looking individual at three. A mile is likely to prove the limit of his stamina. Tough Speed's sire Miswaki, who is also the sire of Rossini, won the Prix de la Salamandre over seven furlongs and none of his four victories as a three-year-old in the United States was achieved at much beyond a mile; Tough Speed's dam, the maiden Nature's Magic, whose first foal he is, is a half-sister to a Grade 3 nine-furlong winner in the States called Stalwars. Miswaki, it should be said, has sired good-class winners over a variety of distances, his best offspring including the Arc winner Urban Sea, the Japan Cup winner Marvelous Crown, the Breeders' Cup Classic winner Black Tie Affair and the Abbaye winner Kistena. However, Tough Speed's general demeanour—he got rather above himself in the preliminaries at Doncaster and took some holding at first on the canter to the start—is that of a horse for whom speed rather than stamina will be the forte. *Sir Michael Stoute*

TOUS LES JOURS (USA)   3 b.f. Dayjur (USA) 137 – Humility (USA) (Cox's Ridge (USA)) [1998 70: 5g³ 6s⁴ 5d 5f⁴ 7.5m* 8m 8s³ 8v³ 1999 7s⁵ 10s 8m 6g⁴ 6g³ 7.1g² 7d⁶ 6m 7g* 7m⁴ 7s⁶ 7m 7g 8g⁴ 8.3m⁴ 10g Oct 19] big, rangy filly: has scope: fair performer: won minor event at Catterick in July: may prove best at 7f/1m: acts on good to firm and heavy ground: blinkered eighth start: has run well when sweating. *M. Johnston*   **70**

TOWER OF SONG (IRE)   2 ch.g. (Feb 9) Perugino (USA) 84 – New Rochelle (IRE) 65 (Lafontaine (USA) 117) [1999 7m² 7m 7m⁵ 7m³ 10s⁵ a8.5g a8g* a7g⁴ a8g² a8g Dec 21] IR 17,000F, IR 28,000Y: useful-looking gelding: has a quick action: first foal: dam, Irish 1¾m winner at 5 yrs, sister to smart middle-distance stayer Shambo: modest on turf, fair on all-weather: won 16-runner seller (left M. Channon 5,000 gns) at Southwell in November by 8 lengths: needs further than 7f and stays 1¼m: acts on soft and good to firm going, and fibresand. *D. W. Chapman*   **64 a71**

TOWN GIRL (IRE)   2 ch.f. (Feb 19) Lammtarra (USA) 134 – Greektown (Ela-Mana-Mou 132) [1999 8d Oct 22] rangy filly: sixth living foal: half-sister to 3-y-o Greek Myth, useful 7f (at 2 yrs) and 1¼m winner Athens Belle (by Groom Dancer) and smart 1¼m and 13f winner Multicoloured (by Rainbow Quest): dam, French 1¼m/1½m winner, half-sister to Prix du Cadran winner Sought Out: very green, slowly away and never dangerous under considerate handling when well held in maiden at Doncaster: should stay at least 1½m: almost certainly capable of better. *Sir Michael Stoute*   **– p**

TOWN GOSSIP (IRE)   2 ch.f. (Apr 7) Indian Ridge 123 – Only Gossip (USA) (Trempolino (USA) 135) [1999 7d Oct 11] third foal: half-sister to 3-y-o Montalcino and a middle-distance winner in Italy by Marju: dam French 1½m winner: bandaged near-hind, well beaten in maiden at Leicester. *P. J. Makin*   **–**

TOWNVILLE CEE CEE   4 b.f. Anshan 119 – Holy Day 82 (Sallust 134) [1998 42: 7.5m 6g 8.1m⁶ 8s 8.2g 7m⁴ 8m 6v a11g⁵ 1999 a12g a7g a9.4g 8m⁵ 8.5m⁶ Apr 14] poor maiden: stays 1m: acts on good to firm ground, no form on soft or all-weather: none too consistent: sold 1,200 gns, sent to Israel. *G. Woodward*   **42 a–**

TOY STORY (FR)   3 b.g. Fijar Tango (FR) 127 – Grundygold (FR) (Grundy 137) [1998 NR 1999 10g 9s⁶ 11.7s a11g² Dec 17] 120,000 francs Y, 21,000 2-y-o: half-brother to several winners in France, including useful 7.5f (at 2 yrs) to 11.5f   **46 +**

winner Farceur du Mesnil (by Pharly): dam French 1¼m to 11.5f winner: poor maiden on balance: should stay beyond 11f. *Miss Gay Kelleway*

TRAFFORD 3 b.f. Prince Sabo 123 – Number One Spot 71 (Reference Point 139) **58** [1998 NR 1999 7.1s⁵ a7g a8.5g² Oct 30] 52,000Y: second foal: dam, 7f winner, closely related to top-class miler Milligram: best effort in maidens when 4 lengths second at Wolverhampton. *B. A. McMahon*

TRAGIC DANCER 3 b.g. Tragic Role (USA) – Chantallee's Pride (Mansooj **77** 118) [1998 63: 6g a7g 7m 10.2d³ 10s a8g⁵ 1999 a11g² a10g* a10g⁵ 11.6m⁴ 14.1m⁴ a10g⁵ 11.4m* a12g² a12g a12g Dec 6] workmanlike gelding: fair handicapper: won at Lingfield in January and Sandown (led near finish) in June: barely stays 1¾m: acts on all-weather, good to firm and good to soft ground: carries head high. *K. McAuliffe*

TRAGIC LADY 3 b.f. Tragic Role (USA) – Rainbow Lady 65 (Jaazeiro (USA) **–** 127) [1998 NR 1999 8g⁶ 5.9m a6g Jul 9] half-sister to a couple of winning hurdlers: dam, staying maiden on Flat, winner over hurdles: form only when sixth of 16 in seller at Pontefract: will stay beyond 1m. *M. G. Meagher*

TRAIKEY (IRE) 7 b.g. Scenic 128 – Swordlestown Miss (USA) (Apalachee **–** (USA) 137) [1998 NR 1999 8f 8m 5s 5d 7d 6d Nov 4] trained by J. Banks, winner on only 2-y-o start and showed useful form only one at 3 yrs (subsequently discovered to have damaged sesamoid in near-hind): only a little sign of retaining ability in 1999. *Mrs S. Lamyman*

TRAJAN (IRE) 2 b.c. (May 5) Dolphin Street (FR) 125 – Lavezzola (IRE) **79** (Salmon Leap (USA) 131) [1999 6d² 6m⁵ 6f⁴ 6d² 6g⁵ 6d⁶ 6d⁵ 5.1g⁵ Oct 21] 12,000Y: sturdy, useful-looking colt: third foal: half-brother to 3-y-o Lady Angharad: dam Italian 7f to 1¼m winner: fair maiden: below form last 3 starts: should stay 7f: acts on firm and good to soft ground: often races prominently. *A. P. Jarvis*

TRAMLINE 6 b.h. Shirley Heights 130 – Trampship 110 (High Line 125) [1998 **71** 57, a–: a16g a13g 11.9s 14.1s³ 16.5d 1999 11.9f 12m 14m² 14m* 14.6m* 16.4m² 16.1m⁶ 16.4g* 16d² 17.1s 16s 16.5s Nov 6] strong, lengthy horse: carries plenty of condition: fair handicapper: won at Sandown then Doncaster (5 ran) in June and Sandown in August: well below form last 3 starts: best at 1¾m/2m: acts on soft and good to firm going, well beaten both starts on all-weather. *M. Blanshard*

TRANS ISLAND 4 b.c. Selkirk (USA) 129 – Khubza 86 (Green Desert **119** (USA) 127) [1998 109: 7s² 8m² 8g 1999 8d⁵ 7.1g² 7d* 7.3d* 8v* 7d³ Oct 17]
 Ian Balding will no doubt be delighted that he will have the much improved Trans Island in his yard for another season at least, something that had seemed unlikely to happen when the Al Muallim Partnership, which owned

Prix du Rond-Point Grand Hotel Barriere, Longchamp—Trans Island is given a fine front-running ride by Kieren Fallon, just holding off Sugarfoot and Sand Falcon

the horse, was dissolved. One of the four partners has taken on the ownership himself, and should Trans Island prove as successful in the next season as he was in 1999 then he'll have no cause to regret it.

A winner three times as a two-year-old, Trans Island was unsuccessful in a restricted three-year-old campaign, though he did pass the post first in the Premio Parioli, the Italian Two Thousand Guineas, only to be demoted to second for causing interference. Well held on his reappearance in the latest season, his first start for about a year, Trans Island was then subsequently off the course for four months. He quickly made up for lost time on his return, following a promising second behind Sicnee at Chepstow with three straight wins, the first of them under 9-10 in the valuable eighteen-runner Tote Ireland Handicap at Leopardstown. Eight days later, Trans Island lined up for a listed race at Newbury, the Dubai Duty Free Cup, in which he was ridden by Olivier Peslier for the first time since winning a similar event at Deauville two years previously. Peslier failed to carry out orders on Trans Island, normally a front runner, but managed to escape any criticism that would surely have come his way had the horse been beaten. He cut it fine, though, Trans Island getting up only in the final strides in a very close finish which also involved Warningford, Tomba and Sporting Lad, in that order. 'He did exactly the opposite to what he was told,' said Balding. '[The horse] likes to bowl along but Olivier had other ideas. Luckily it worked out!' Kieren Fallon had the mount on Trans Island in the Prix du Rond-Point Grand Hotel Barriere at Longchamp on Arc day. Peslier was on board Grazalema, who started favourite, coupled with Slip Stream, the last-named along with Sugarfoot the other British-trained contestants in the nine-runner field. This time Trans Island made the running, Fallon riding the

Al Muallim Partnership's "Trans Island"

perfect race in setting just a steady pace then kicking clear early in the straight. Trans Island began to come to the end of his tether near the finish, but held on by a short neck from Sugarfoot, with Sand Falcon the same distance away in third. Trans Island had more on his plate when returned to Longchamp a fortnight later for the Prix de la Foret, and in finishing around a length third to Field of Hope he ran right up to his best.

		Sharpen Up	Atan
	Selkirk (USA)	(ch 1969)	Rocchetta
	(ch 1988)	Annie Edge	Nebbiolo
Trans Island		(ch 1980)	Friendly Court
(b.c. 1995)		Green Desert	Danzig
	Khubza	(b 1983)	Foreign Courier
	(b 1990)	Breadcrumb	Final Straw
		(ch 1982)	Scarcely Blessed

Trans Island, a 45,000-guinea foal who fetched 100,000 guineas as a yearling, is the first produce of the lightly-raced Khubza, a fairly useful winner over seven furlongs. Her second foal Bread Winner (by Reprimand), also trained by Balding, is still a maiden; her third, a two-year-old full brother to Trans Island named Nothing Daunted, has already shown useful form at up to a mile, winning once. Khubza is out of the smart six- and seven-furlong winner Breadcrumb, also the dam of useful sprinter Heard A Whisper and a half-sister to the very smart sprinter College Chapel. Trans Island's great grandam Scarcely Blessed won the King George Stakes at Goodwood and comes from a family noted for producing important sprint winners. Trans Island has more stamina in his make-up, though a mile in ground as testing as that which he encountered in the Rond-Point is plenty far enough for him, and he's just as effective at seven furlongs. Trans Island, a big, lengthy colt, acts on any going. *I. A. Balding*

TRANSPARENT (IRE) 7 b.m. Dance of Life (USA) – Clear Picture 121 – (Polyfoto 124) [1998 42: 10g⁵ 10d 9g³ 10m 7d 9g a12g⁵ 1999 a8g a11g a12f a11g a16g Feb 12] poor handicapper: no form in 1999: stays 1½m: acts on soft ground, probably on firm. *D. Carroll*

TRAPPER NORMAN 7 b.g. Mazilier (USA) 107 – Free Skip 68 (Free State 52 125) [1998 45?: 8.5m⁴ 1999 6f⁶ 6m³ 5.9m² 6m³ 7f³ Jul 30] smallish, workmanlike gelding: modest maiden: stays 8.5f: acts on firm ground. *C. Smith*

TRAVELLING CLOCK 4 ch.c. Deploy 131 – Travel Mystery 99 (Godswalk – (USA) 130) [1998 –: 14.1s³ 12d 14m 1999 18m Jul 3] big, workmanlike colt: signs of ability but no form. *B. A. McMahon*

TRAVELLING LITE (IRE) 2 b.c. (Apr 21) Blues Traveller (IRE) 119 – Lute 82 And Lyre (IRE) 96 (The Noble Player (USA) 126) [1999 6m⁵ 7.1m⁵ 7g 7m* 7m² 7.9d⁶ 7s Oct 23] 16,500Y: rather leggy, angular colt: third foal: half-brother to 3-y-o College Music: dam Irish 2-y-o 5f winner: fairly useful performer: won nursery at Lingfield in September: not at best on softer ground last 2 starts: stays 1m: acts on good to firm ground. *B. R. Millman*

TRAVELLING STAR (USA) 3 b.c. Lear Fan (USA) 130 – Ladanum (USA) 86 (Green Dancer (USA) 132) [1998 NR 1999 7m⁶ 10g* 9.9g² 9.9g⁵ 8.5f 8f³ 8.5f Nov 21] $145,000F, 105,000Y: tall, leggy colt: third foal: half-brother to a winner in Japan by Woodman: dam French 1½m winner, later successful in USA where Grade 1 placed: fairly useful form: won maiden at Pontefract in May: best efforts after when placed in minor event at Salisbury (5 lengths second of 6 to Fredora, penultimate start for C. Brittain) and allowance race at Santa Anita: stays 1¼m: blinkered last 2 starts. *A. L. Hassinger, USA*

TRAVELMATE 5 b.g. Persian Bold 123 – Ustka 60 (Lomond (USA) 128) [1998 116 103+: 12d⁵ 12g* 12d⁶ 14.8g* 14.6d⁶ 12g* 1999 12.4f² 16.1m² 13.9g² 16m⁵ Nov 2] lengthy, useful-looking gelding: smart performer, better than ever in 1999: good second in Northumberland Plate at Newcastle (beaten short head by Far Cry) and Ebor at York (beaten 2 lengths by Vicious Circle) on second and third starts: ran creditably when close fifth of 24 to Rogan Josh in Foster's Melbourne Cup at Flemington final one, despite being involved in barging match late on: stays 2m: acts on firm and good to soft ground: has wandered, and may prove best held up: reliable. *J. R. Fanshawe*

TRAVESTY OF LAW (IRE) 2 ch.g. (May 2) Case Law 113 – Bold As Love **95** (Lomond (USA) 128) [1999 5v⁶ 5.3f⁴ 5m* 5m² 5m⁵ 5m 5m* 5.2m 5f⁴ 5s 5m⁵ 5d Oct 9] IR 3,500F, 10,000Y: smallish, strong, angular gelding: progressing well physically: second foal: half-brother to 5-y-o Rare Talent: dam, unraced, from quite speedy family: useful performer: made all in maiden at Salisbury in May and minor event at Windsor in June: best efforts when beaten in Molecomb Stakes at Goodwood and fifth in Flying Childers Stakes at Doncaster: will prove best over bare 5f: acts on firm going, well beaten on softer than good: trail-blazing front-runner: sold 15,000 gns. *B. J. Meehan*

TRAWLING 3 b.f. Mtoto 134 – Ghost Tree (IRE) 88 (Caerleon (USA) 132) [1998 **71** 75: 7m² 7g² 1999 a8g* 12m³ 8m 10.2m a8g Dec 6] sparely-made filly: fair performer: landed odds in 5-runner maiden at Lingfield in February by 16 lengths: sold from B. Hills 11,000 gns after fourth start: free-going sort, best form at 1m: acts on equitrack. *C. A. Dwyer*

TREAD SOFTLY (IRE) 3 b.f. Roi Danzig (USA) – Albenita (IRE) (Alzao **60 d** (USA) 117) [1998 70: 5d² 6d* 5d 1999 a6g⁶ a7f 6m 5s 7g Oct 15] small, close-coupled filly: fair at 2 yrs: form in 1999 only on reappearance: should stay 7f: has carried head high. *R. A. Fahey*

TREASURE CHEST (IRE) 4 b.g. Last Tycoon 131 – Sought Out (IRE) 119 **82 §** (Rainbow Quest (USA) 134) [1998 89: 10.2s⁵ 14.4m³ 14s 16.1m² 18.2g² 14m⁶ 1999 20m 17.2g³ 16.1m⁵ 16.2m² 16.5f⁵ 14d Aug 11] leggy, angular gelding: fluent mover: fairly useful maiden handicapper: stays 2¼m: acts on good to firm going, possibly not on soft: visored/tongue tied: sometimes slowly away/hangs: not one to trust. *M. C. Pipe*

TREASURE COVE (IRE) 3 b.f. Treasure Kay 114 – Shydico (IRE) 64 **41** (Nordico (USA)) [1998 NR 1999 a7g 7s⁶ 7d 8m 12.1m⁶ 11.1f 9m³ 7.1m 9.2m Sep 6] IR 4,500Y: first foal: dam, placed over 7f at 2 yrs in Ireland, half-sister to smart Italian middle-distance colt Toto Le Moko: poor maiden: stays 9f: acts on good to firm going. *Miss L. A. Perratt*

TREASURE ISLAND 4 b.f. Rainbow Quest (USA) 134 – Cockatoo Island 99 **41** (High Top 131) [1998 50: a12g 11.1d* 14.1s⁶ 10d 1999 12s⁴ Apr 21] lengthy, sparely-made filly: poor handicapper: probably stays 1½m: acts on good to soft ground: very headstrong and no easy ride. *F. Murphy*

TREASURE TOUCH (IRE) 5 b.g. Treasure Kay 114 – Bally Pourri (IRE) **67** (Law Society (USA) 130) [1998 77?: 5g 5s 6g 5g 6s 5d⁶ 6g 5m 1999 5m⁴ 6s 6.1d² 6v Oct 12] tall gelding: fair nowadays: best effort in 1999 when second of 20 in minor event at Nottingham in October, drifting right: effective at 5f/6f: acts on good to firm ground, good to soft (probably heavy) and fibresand: often apprentice ridden: usually races prominently. *D. Nicholls*

TREASURY 3 ch.f. Generous (IRE) 139 – Atlantic Flyer (USA) 98 (Storm Bird **–** (CAN) 134) [1998 67p: 7.5m 7m 7d 7d 1999 10.2m Jun 29] good-topped filly: fair form at best at 2 yrs in maidens/nursery: suffered fatal injury when losing footing only 3-y-o start: should have been suited by 1m+. *Sir Mark Prescott*

TREASURY GARDENS (USA) 3 ro.f. Miswaki (USA) 124 – Tira (FR) **88 +** (Bellypha 130) [1998 NR 1999 6g* 8s Aug 22] $37,000F, $50,000Y: rather unfurnished, good-quartered filly: half-sister to several winners, including minor stakes-winning sprinter Silver Spool (by Strike Gold): dam 7f (at 2 yrs)/1m winner in France: green, won maiden at Pontefract in May by head, leading close home: far from discredited when over 6 lengths eighth of 9 to Tycoon's Dolce in listed race at Deauville 3 months later: may do better yet. *P. W. Chapple-Hyam*

TREATY (USA) 5 b.g. Trempolino (USA) 135 – Zonda 100 (Fabulous Dancer **§§** (USA) 124) [1998 NR 1999 12.3m Aug 30] ungenuine maiden. *Mrs S. Lamyman*

TRELLIS BAY 3 b.f. Sadler's Wells (USA) 132 – Bahamian 115 (Mill Reef **100** (USA) 141) [1998 NR 1999 10.2d 12f⁴ 12m* 11.8g 14.8d² 16.1d² Oct 29] sixth foal:

sister to 1½m winners Coraline, Spanish Wells and 4-y-o New Abbey and half-sister to Irish Oaks winner Wemyss Bight (by Dancing Brave): dam 1½m winner who stayed 15f: useful performer: won maiden at Doncaster in July: best efforts when second in handicaps at Newmarket in October, beaten 2 lengths by Eilean Shona in listed rated stakes on final one: stayed 2m: acted on good to firm and good to soft going: stud. *R. Charlton*

TREMBLEY 2 b.c. (Apr 19) Komaite (USA) – Cold Blow 67 (Posse (USA) 130) **72**
[1999 6m⁵ 5g² 7m⁴ Sep 1] 2,000Y: close-coupled colt: third foal: brother to 3-y-o Katy Nowaitee and half-brother to a 9f winner in Holland by Tina's Pet: dam, second at 7f at 2 yrs, from family of Yorkshire Oaks winners Sally Brown and Untold: fair form in maidens last 2 starts, fourth of 10 to easy winner Akeed at York on final one: will stay 1m: raced only on good/good to firm going. *J. L. Eyre*

TREMENDISTO 9 b.g. Petoski 135 – Misty Halo 93 (High Top 131) [1998 –: –
a16.2g 1999 10d Apr 28] strong gelding: poor maiden handicapper on Flat: successful but very temperamental hurdler (often refuses to race). *T. Wall*

TREMONNOW 4 b.f. Reprimand 122 – Tree Mallow 71 (Malicious) [1998 45: –
6g 6g² 6s 6.1g⁶ 6g 7g⁴ 7m 8m 1999 6f 6g May 17] poor maiden handicapper: stays 7f: below form both starts on ground softer than good: tried visored. *J. M. Bradley*

TREMPLIN (USA) 7 gr.g. Trempolino (USA) 135 – Stresa (Mill Reef (USA) –
141) [1998 70, a–: 8d⁶ 10m⁶ 1999 12f Sep 13] short-necked gelding: fair handi-capper, lightly raced nowadays: well held only 7-y-o start: stays 10.5f: acts on good to firm and heavy going: tried blinkered: has looked none too hearty. *N. A. Callaghan*

TREWORNAN 2 b.f. (Mar 22) Midyan (USA) 124 – Miss Silca Key 102 (Welsh **79**
Saint 126) [1999 7m⁵ 6d* 6v⁶ Oct 23] 32,000Y: tall, angular filly: sister to smart Central City (best up to 7f), and half-sister to 3-y-o Gone In The Wind and several winners, including useful 6f (at 2 yrs) and 7f (in France) winner Miss Zafonic and useful 6f winner Silca Supreme (by Chief Singer): dam won Jersey Stakes: fair form when winning maiden at Brighton in October by ½ length from Rayyaan: stays 7f: below best on heavy going. *D. R. C. Elsworth*

TRIBAL MOON (IRE) 6 b.g. Ela-Mana-Mou 132 – Silk Blend (Busted 134) –
[1998 –: a12g⁶ a14g 1999 21.6d Apr 28] close-coupled gelding: lightly-raced maiden, fair at best: should stay 1½m. *J. G. Portman*

TRIBAL NOTE (USA) 2 ch.c. (Apr 15) Eagle Eyed (USA) 111 – Ada Ruckus **69**
(CAN) (Bold Ruckus (USA)) [1999 6f⁴ 7m³ 6m² 8g 6.1g³ 8v Oct 12] $140,000Y: big, strong, lengthy colt: has scope: has a round action: first foal: dam winning sprinter in North America: fair maiden: trained by P. Chapple-Hyam first 5 starts: best efforts at 6f: acts on firm going: sold 30,000 gns, sent to USA. *A. G. Foster*

TRIBAL PEACE (IRE) 7 ch.g. Red Sunset 120 – Mirabiliary (USA) 74 (Crow **54 d**
(FR) 134) [1998 58, a65: a10g³ a10g⁴ 9m 9d 10f⁴ 9m⁴ 8d 8s a10g a10g⁶ 1999 a10g³ a10f⁴ a12g 8m 8.3s 9g 10m⁵ 10.4d a10g a10g Dec 22] small gelding: modest on all-weather, poor on turf: well below form last 3 starts: stays 1¼m: acts on firm going, soft and equitrack (probably on fibresand): usually waited with. *B. Gubby*

TRIBAL PRINCE 2 b.g. (Feb 6) Prince Sabo 123 – Tshusick 81 (Dancing Brave **77**
(USA) 140) [1999 5g² 6d⁵ 6g 6d² 7s⁵ Nov 6] 16,000Y: sturdy gelding: first foal: dam 7f winner: fair maiden: beaten head in Windsor nursery penultimate start: barely stays 7f, at least under testing conditions: raced only on good ground or softer: took little interest in visor third start: slowly away first 3 outings: has been bandaged behind. *P. W. Harris*

TRICCOLO 2 b.c. (Mar 31) Piccolo 121 – Tribal Lady 80 (Absalom 128) [1999 **68 p**
6.1m⁵ 6s⁵ Sep 29] 21,000F, 70,000Y: fourth foal: half-brother to Italian winner up to 7.5f Tito Claudio (by Aragon): dam 2-y-o 5f/6f winner who stayed 7f: shaped well in maidens at Nottingham (not at all knocked about) and Newcastle (fared best of those who raced on unfavoured part of track) in September: remains capable of better, and could well prove useful. *A. C. Stewart*

TRICKS (IRE) 3 b.f. First Trump 118 – Party Line 63 (Never So Bold 135) [1998 **59**
73p: 6g a6g³ a8g² a7g* 1999 7d 7m 8.1m 7f⁶ 8d Aug 17] modest on turf, fair on all-weather: stays 1m: acts on equitrack and good to firm ground: blinkered final start: joined D. Coakley. *I. A. Balding*

TRICOLORE 3 b.f. Sadler's Wells (USA) 132 – Tricorne 92 (Green Desert **82**
(USA) 127) [1998 68p: 7d³ 1999 10s² 10.2d⁶ 10.2m⁵ Jun 29] smallish, rather sparely-
made filly: fairly useful maiden: best effort when second to Samoa at Sandown on
reappearance: will stay beyond 1¼m: stud. *J. L. Dunlop*

TRIGGER HAPPY (IRE) 4 ch.f. Ela-Mana-Mou 132 – Happy Tidings (Hello **–**
Gorgeous (USA) 128) [1998 98: 11.5m² 11.9f 1999 16.4g May 31] leggy, plain filly:
useful performer, lightly raced: well held in Henry II Stakes at Sandown only 4-y-o
start: should stay beyond 1½m: raced only on good ground or firmer. *M. Johnston*

TRIMILKI (IRE) 3 b.f. Lahib (USA) 129 – Timissara (USA) (Shahrastani **–**
(USA) 135) [1998 –: 7g 1999 a8g⁵ 8m a12g 14.1f 17.2f Jun 26] tall, leggy filly: no
form. *T. J. Etherington*

TRIM STAR 3 gr.f. Terimon 124 – Western Star 107 (Alcide 136) [1998 NR 1999 **–**
9.9m 11.5d 11.9g⁴ 12m 12m³ 14g 16d Sep 21] sister to Italian 6.5f to 9.5f winner
Terimore, closely related to smart 1m and 1½m winner Startino (by Bustino) and
half-sister to several winners: dam, 7f and 1¼m winner, half-sister to Queen Anne
winner Mr Fluorocarbon: little form: left C. Brittain 4,400 gns after third start
(looked none too keen in blinkers). *A. Slattery, Ireland*

TRINA'S PET 3 ch.f. Efisio 120 – Lindy Belle 32 (Alleging (USA) 120) [1998 **–**
56, a65: 5m 6g a5g⁴ a5g* 6g³ a5g* 6.1d 5m a6g⁵ a5g 1999 a6g³ a7g³ a7s³ a6g² a6g⁵ **a65**
a6g Mar 6] fair handicapper on all-weather, modest on turf: effective at 6f (given
bit of a test)/7f: acts on all-weather, best turf run on good going: blinkered in 1999.
J. Balding

TRINCULO (IRE) 2 b.c. (Apr 2) Anita's Prince 126 – Fandangerina (USA) **102**
(Grey Dawn II 132) [1999 a6g³ 6g* 6g³ 6d⁵ 6s⁴ Oct 23] IR 13,000Y: tall, rather
unfurnished colt: has a long, rounded action: half-brother to several winners, including smart 1987 2-y-o 6f/7f winner Western Gun (by Lypheor) and useful 7f (at 2 yrs)
to 1½m winner Ocean Air (by Elegant Air): dam won up to 1m in USA: won maiden
at Leicester in August: useful form when third of 24 to Halland Park Girl in sales race
at the Curragh, fifth of 6 to Primo Valentino in Middle Park Stakes at Newmarket and
fourth in listed race at Doncaster: should stay 7f: raced only on good ground or softer
on turf. *N. P. Littmoden*

TRINITY (IRE) 3 b.c. College Chapel 122 – Kaskazi (Dancing Brave (USA) **92 d**
140) [1998 91: 5g⁴ 6s⁶ 6g² 5.2m⁵ 6g³ 5f² 6g² 5m 6g⁴ 1999 5m* 6d 5m 6m 5m⁵ 5f 6m
5m 6d Nov 1] close-coupled colt: fairly useful performer: won maiden at Doncaster
in May: below form last 4 starts: effective at 5f/6f: acts on firm going: has worn
crossed noseband: has had tongue tied: sometimes finds little. *M. Brittain*

TRIO 3 b.g. Cyrano de Bergerac 120 – May Light 62 (Midyan (USA) 124) [1998 **87**
89: 6g³ 7.1d⁵ 6f⁶ 6.9m 7m³ 8d* 8g⁴ 8d³ 1999 10.1s⁵ 9m⁴ 9g⁴ 10.1d⁶ 8m 10m 9ᵢᵢᵢ 10s
10g 8.2d Oct 21] quite good-topped gelding: fairly useful performer: ran creditably
in 1999 only on second to fourth starts: may prove best at 1m/9f: acts on good to firm
and good to soft going: has been early to post and taken good hold, and likely to
prove best waited with: has looked difficult ride. *N. Hamilton*

TRIPLE CONCERTO 2 ch.f. (Feb 5) Grand Lodge (USA) 125 – On The Bank **–**
(IRE) (In The Wings 128) [1999 8d Oct 15] leggy, unfurnished filly: first foal: dam
unraced half-sister to dam of 4-y-o Limpid: moved poorly down and always rear in
maiden at Newmarket. *C. F. Wall*

TRIPLE DASH 3 ch.g. Nashwan (USA) 135 – Triple Joy 104 (Most Welcome **112**
131) [1998 97p: 6v* 6d² 1999 8m 8.1g* 8s³ 8g 8v³ Oct 11] strong, good-topped
gelding: smart performer: won 5-runner minor event at Sandown in July by 1¼
lengths from Exeat, despite flashing tail: ran creditably otherwise when 7 lengths
eighth to Sendawar in Poule d'Essai des Poulains at Longchamp on reappearance and
third of 5 to Raucous Lad in listed race at Deauville on third start: may stay 1¼m:
acts on good to firm and heavy going. *Sir Mark Prescott*

TRIPLE GREEN 3 b.f. Green Desert (USA) 127 – Triple Reef (Mill Reef (USA) **69**
141) [1998 NR 1999 8s 8m³ 8.1d⁵ 10m 12g 8.2f³ 6d⁶ Oct 28] well-made filly:
half-sister to several winners, including smart Talented (1¼m, by Bustino) and useful pair Trifolio (up to 15f, by Touching Wood) and Triple Joy (6f/7f, by Most
Welcome): dam unraced from excellent middle-distance staying family: fair maiden:

may prove best at 7f/1m: acts on firm going, yet to race on soft/heavy: blinkered final 2 starts. *J. L. Dunlop*

TRIPLE TREASURE (USA)   4 b.f. Gone West (USA) – Lemhi Go (USA)   **70** (Lemhi Gold (USA) 123) [1998 81p: 8s³ 1999 10g 10d⁴ 8m a8.5g³ Sep 8] smallish filly: fairly useful form only 3-y-o start: fair in 1999: seems to stay 1¼m: acts on fibresand and soft going. *H. R. A. Cecil*

TRIPLE WOOD (USA)   2 b. or br.f. (Feb 1) Woodman (USA) 126 – Triple Kiss   **77** 106 (Shareef Dancer (USA) 135) [1999 6f⁵ 7d² Jul 1] fifth foal: half-sister to 3 winners, including 3-y-o Gudlage and 8.5f to 1¾m winner Rawy (by Rahy), both useful: dam, Irish 1m winner who stayed 1¾m, out of twice-raced sister to Relko: fair form in maidens at Newmarket and Yarmouth (second of 8) in the summer: should stay at least 1m. *B. Hanbury*

TROILUS (USA)   2 ch.c. (Apr 12) Bien Bien (USA) 125 – Nakterjal (Vitiges   **71 p** (FR) 132) [1999 8d⁵ 8.2d Oct 21] very big, rangy colt: ninth foal: brother to 3-y-o Bienamado and half-brother to 2 winners in France, including 1¼m winner Mousquetaire (by Woodman): dam, little sign of ability, from family of Nureyev and Sadler's Wells: much better effort in maidens when fifth of 8 at Newmarket (trained by P. Chapple-Hyam), burly and green but showing up long way: will prove suited to 1¼m+: type to do better in long term. *A. G. Foster*

TROIS   3 b.g. Efisio 120 – Drei (USA) 67 (Lyphard (USA) 132) [1998 ?: 10s⁵ 1999   **72** 7v⁴ 7f 8g a9.4g* Dec 15] fair form: left L. Cumani for 2,500 gns in September, then first form when winning maiden at Wolverhampton (after near 7-month absence): may prove best up to 1¼m: acts on fibresand. *G. Woodward*

TROIS ELLES   3 b.c. Elmaamul (USA) 125 – Ca Ira (IRE) 48 (Dancing Dissident   **54** (USA) 119) [1998 –: 8d a7g a6f 1999 a7g a7f* a8f 10m² 8.2s 10.1m 8m⁵ 8m² 8.2g²   **a37 +** 9.3m³ 8m² 8g⁶ 8d 7g 8d 8d³ Oct 29] sparely-made colt: modest handicapper on turf, poor on all-weather: won apprentice race at Lingfield in January: ran creditably when placed after: stays easy 1¼m: acts on good to firm going, good to soft (possibly not on soft) and equitrack. *R. C. Spicer*

TROJAN GIRL (IRE)   3 b.f. Up And At 'em 109 – Lady-Mumtaz (Martin John)   **74** [1998 67: a5g² a5g² 5g⁴ a5g 5.3m⁶ a5g³ 5.7v a6g² a5g³ a6g a5s* a6g² 1999 a5g* a5g⁴ a5g* a5g* a5g² a5g³ a5g* a5g a5g⁶ a6g a5g³ a5g Jun 16] fair performer: won 2 handicaps and 2 claimers at Wolverhampton between January and April for N. Littmoden: well below form last 3 starts: stays easy 6f: acts on all-weather, best turf effort on good going: game. *Miss S. J. Wilton*

TROJAN HERO (SAF)   8 ch.g. Raise A Man (USA) – Helleness (SAF)   **40 §** (Northfields (USA)) [1998 68, a75: a7g³ a8g⁴ a8.5g⁵ a6g² a7g² 7g* 7s 7g⁴ 7f 7s 7d   **a70 §** 6d² 5s 5d a7g a6g 1999 a6g² a7g² a7g³ a7g⁴ 7d 6d 7s 6f a5g 5f 6g a7g³ a6g² a7g² a7g⁶ a6g² a6g* a5g a6g Dec 27] workmanlike gelding: unimpressive walker/mover (has reportedly gone lame on off-fore a few times): fair performer on all-weather, poor on turf: trained first 7 starts by Mrs M. Reveley: won seller at Southwell (first start since leaving M. Buckley) in December: effective at 6f to easy 1m: acts on any turf/all-weather: tried blinkered: has worn tongue strap: usually races up with pace: none too consistent, and often finishes weakly. *K. C. Comerford*

TROJAN RISK   6 ch.g. Risk Me (FR) 127 – Troyes 81 (Troy 137) [1998 69: 10.1s   **69 §** 10s² 12m⁴ 1999 a12g a12g⁴ 12g⁶ 12.3m 12g Aug 25] sturdy, good-bodied gelding: fair performer: stayed 1½m: acted on soft and good to firm ground, probably on fibresand: tried blinkered: had been slowly away (virtually refused to race final start): was one to be wary of: dead. *Mrs M. Reveley*

TROJAN WOLF   4 ch.g. Wolfhound (USA) 126 – Trojan Lady (USA) (Irish   **85** River (FR) 131) [1998 74: 8g 9m⁴ 9s⁶ 10g⁴ 10.3f⁴ 8m⁴ 10.9s⁴ 1999 8g 10f⁵ 10g 8m 7m² 6g⁴ a7g² 7m 7g⁵ a8g* a11g* Nov 30] strong, workmanlike gelding: fairly useful handicapper: sold out of D. Sasse's stable 4,000 gns then won twice at Southwell (first an amateur event) in November: effective at 7f to 11f: acts on firm going (not on soft) and all-weather: tried visored/tongue tied. *P. Howling*

TROPICAL BEACH   6 b.g. Lugana Beach 116 – Hitravelscene (Mansingh   **62** (USA) 120) [1998 51, a77: 5g 6g 5s⁵ 6.9d⁵ 6m 7g⁴ 7m 7d² 8.1m⁶ 5m a8.5g* a8.5g*   **a68** a8g³ a9.4s* a10g⁵ 1999 a11g a9.4g a8f⁵ 7.5d² 8f* 6.9m⁴ 8d 7f 7.6f* 8.1d 7m 8.5g a8.5g⁴ Oct 13] leggy gelding: fair handicapper on all-weather, modest on turf: won apprentice races at Newmarket in June and Lingfield in July: effective at 7f to 9f: acts on firm going, soft and fibresand: tried blinkered, usually visored: reportedly bled from nose third start: often slowly away and tends to get behind. *J. Pearce*

TROPICAL BEAT (USA)   2 b.f. (Feb 12) Kingmambo (USA) 125 – Ropa Usada (USA) (Danzig (USA)) [1999 6g 7m Jun 25] $135,000F, 60,000Y: fourth foal: dam, unraced half-sister to US Grade 1 2-y-o 1m winner Mogambo, out of champion US 2-y-o filly Lakeville Miss: broke down badly in 7f maiden at Goodwood: dead. *J. L. Dunlop*

TROUBLE   3 b.g. Kris 135 – Ringlet (USA) 58 (Secreto (USA) 128) [1998 NR   **61** 1999 7g⁶ 7g 8m a8.5g⁶ Sep 4] 21,000Y: rangy, rather unfurnished gelding: poor walker/mover: second foal: closely related to 4-y-o Incepta: dam, 1¼m and 13f winner, half-sister to milers Sure Blade (top class, by Kris) and Sure Sharp (smart, by Sharpen Up): modest maiden: stays 8.5f: acts on fibresand: sold only 500 gns in November. *B. W. Hills*

TROUBLED TIMES   2 ch.f. (Apr 1) Timeless Times (USA) 99 – Lurking 69   **–** (Formidable (USA) 125) [1999 5m³ 5m 6g 6g 5m Sep 24] 1,000Y: sixth foal: half-sister to 3-y-o Bayard Lady and fairly useful 5f (at 2 yrs) to 7f winner Whittle Rock (by Rock City): dam 6f winner: well beaten all starts, leaving D. Moffatt after third. *L. R. Lloyd-James*

TROUBLE MOUNTAIN (USA)   2 br.c. (Jan 27) Mt Livermore (USA) –   **105** Trouble Free (USA) (Nodouble (USA)) [1999 6f* 7f* 6.1d³ 6m² Sep 18] $225,000Y: small, quite attractive colt: good mover: has a quick action: sixth foal: closely related to a winner in USA by Rahy and half-brother to several winners abroad, including smart US Grade 3 6f winner Demaloot Demashoot (by Bold Ruckus): dam ran twice in USA: useful performer: won maiden at Haydock and minor event at Doncaster in July: good second of 4 to Primo Valentino in Mill Reef Stakes at Newbury final start: stays 7f: acts on firm going, well below form at Chester on good to soft. *B. W. Hills*

TRUANT (USA)   3 b.c. Alleged (USA) 138 – Top Roberto (USA) (Topsider   **85** (USA)) [1998 98p: 7m³ 8g³ 8s⁴ 1999 10v² 10m³ 10.1m² 10s² 8f 9g² 9.2s* Sep 27] small, quite good-topped colt: fairly useful performer: mostly ran creditably before winning maiden at Hamilton final start, tending to idle in front: will stay beyond 1¼m: acts on good to firm and heavy ground: sold 37,000 gns. *W. Jarvis*

TRUE FLYER   3 b.f. Midyan (USA) 124 – Surf Bird (Shareef Dancer (USA) 135)   **40** [1998 –: 7v 1999 10.1m⁶ 12g 10m 11f³ 14.1g 14.1m Aug 28] sparely-made filly: poor maiden: seems to stay 1¾m: acts on firm going: visored last 3 starts: sold 1,000 gns. *J. D. Bethell*

TRUE LOVE WAYS   3 ch.f. Anshan 119 – Halimah 56 (Be My Guest (USA)   **–** 126) [1998 54d: 5d 5v³ 5v⁵ 5m 5g a5g 6m³ 5g 5.3g⁶ 5.7v⁴ 5s⁵ 1999 6g 5s 7f a6g Jun 25] lengthy, unfurnished filly: poor maiden: probably stays 6f: acts on good to firm and heavy going: tried blinkered/visored: often finds little. *W. G. M. Turner*

TRUE OBSESSION (USA)   2 br.c. (Mar 13) Lear Fan (USA) 130 – Valid   **81** Fixation (USA) (Valid Appeal (USA)) [1999 5.1s³ a7g* 7m² 7m² 7f³ 7g⁶ 8g 8d Oct 29] close-coupled, quite attractive colt: first reported foal: dam winning sprinter in USA from good North American family: fairly useful performer: won maiden at Southwell in June: good efforts in nurseries next 4 starts, but well below form on last 2: should stay 1m: acts on firm ground (probably on soft) and fibresand. *P. F. I. Cole*

TRUFFLE (IRE)   3 b.f. Ezzoud (IRE) 126 – Queen Cake (Sandhurst Prince 128)   **–** [1998 75p: 7g³ 7g* 1999 8m 10d 7s a7g Nov 24] sparely-made filly: fair form at 2 yrs: well below that level in handicaps in 1999, fly-jumped leaving stalls on reappearance (final start for J. Fanshawe): should stay 1m. *K. McAuliffe*

TRULY BEWITCHED (USA)   3 ch.f. Affirmed (USA) – Fabulous Fairy   **–** (USA) 75 (Alydar (USA)) [1998 81p: 6m* 7g 1999 7m 10s 8m 7m Jul 6] smallish, close-coupled filly: fairly useful form at 2 yrs: disappointing in 1999, highly tried first 2 starts and blinkered/visored last 2: should stay 1¼m: sold 65,000 gns in December. *J. Noseda*

TRUMBLE   7 b.g. Tragic Role (USA) – Sideloader Special 66 (Song 132) [1998   **– §** NR 1999 9.2g⁶ 10.9s 11.1m 11.1m 11.1f 12g Aug 13] small, quite attractive gelding:

poor performer: should stay 1¾m: acts on fibresand and probably on any turf ground: has looked none too keen: one to treat with caution. *D. A. Nolan*

TRUMPET BLUES (USA) 3 br.g. Dayjur (USA) 137 – Iosifa 108 (Top Ville 129) [1998 72: 6d 6s² 1999 7.1s⁶ Apr 3] unfurnished gelding: easily best effort in maidens on final 2-y-o start: raced far too freely only one at 3 yrs: should stay at least 7f: has been bandaged near-fore: sold 4,200 gns, joined D. Nicholls. *J. L. Dunlop* —

TRUMPET SOUND (IRE) 2 b.c. (Feb 14) Theatrical 128 – Free At Last 115 (Shirley Heights 130) [1999 7m⁴ Aug 27] third foal: half-brother to 1¼m winner Coretta (by Caerleon), later smart winner up to 1½m in USA, and 4-y-o Fisherman's Cove: dam, 2-y-o 7f winner and fourth in 1000 Guineas (later stakes winner up to 1½m in USA), half-sister to Barathea: green, shaped with plenty of encouragement when 4½ lengths fourth of 16 to Merry Merlin in well-contested maiden at Newmarket, staying on well under considerate handling having been in rear halfway: will be suited by 1¼m+: sure to improve considerably and win races. *L. M. Cumani* **77 P**

TRUMP STREET 3 b.f. First Trump 118 – Pepeke 78 (Mummy's Pet 125) [1998 77+: 6m⁴ 7g² 6m⁴ 1999 8.3m 7m 7.1m³ 8.2g Sep 25] leggy, workmanlike filly: disappointing maiden: should stay 1m: raced only on good/good to firm going: has carried head awkwardly/tended to hang/found little. *N. A. Graham* **51**

TRUST GEORGE 4 ch.g. Lancastrian 126 – Lingdale Lady 66 (Sandford Lad 133) [1998 NR 1999 a16.2g Feb 6] tenth live foal: dam sprinter: no show in Wolverhampton seller. *C. N. Kellett* —

TRYARDIA-ON-AGAIN (IRE) 3 ch.f. Petardia 113 – Trysinger (IRE) (Try My Best (USA) 130) [1998 55: 5d⁵ 6m 5.1d⁴ 5d⁴ 1999 a9.4g 7f 6.9m⁶ 8.1d 7m⁶ Aug 22] leggy, sparely-made filly: poor maiden: probably stays 7f: acts on firm and good to soft going (looked reluctant on all-weather): visored final start. *P. D. Evans* **48**

TRY IT AGAIN (IRE) 3 br.g. Mujtahid (USA) 118 – Pursue 78 (Auction Ring (USA) 123) [1998 NR 1999 7m May 3] IR 8,000Y: good-topped, workmanlike gelding: half-brother to several winners, including useful winner up to 1½m Bold Pursuit (by Thatching): dam, 2-y-o 5f winner, half-sister to smart miler Alert: 5/1, last in claimer at Newcastle. *M. Johnston* —

TRY PARIS (IRE) 3 b.c. Paris House 123 – Try My Rosie 93 (Try My Best (USA) 130) [1998 71: 6d⁶ 6d 6s⁶ 9d 1999 6m 5m 5s 7d a6g⁶ 6d Oct 28] IR 17,000Y: sixth foal: half-brother to Irish 1995 2-y-o 5f winner Zebra Stripes (by Tirol) and 1992 2-y-o 6f winner Red Leader (by Vision): dam Irish 2-y-o 6f winner best at 1m: fair form at best in maidens at 2 yrs in Ireland for K. Prendergast: little show in 1999: stays 6f: acts on soft going: visored last 3 starts. *Mrs L. C. Jewell* **44**

TSUNAMI 3 b.f. Beveled (USA) – Alvecote Lady 50 (Touching Wood (USA) 127) [1998 66?: 7.5d 7g 7m 7v⁴ 1999 7g⁴ 7d³ 8g⁶ 8m⁶ 8m⁶ 7s 10s⁴ 8d⁶ 10v⁴ Oct 23] leggy, unfurnished filly: fair maiden: may prove best at 7f/1m: acts on good to firm going, probably on heavy: sold 3,000 gns, joined P. D. Evans. *D. R. C. Elsworth* **66**

TSWALU 2 b.f. (Feb 2) Cosmonaut – Madam Taylor 81 (Free State 125) [1999 8.1s³ 7.1v 8g⁶ Nov 3] unfurnished filly: fourth living foal: dam stayed 1½m: modest form in maidens first and third starts: should stay 1¼m. *M. Mullineaux* **52**

TUCSON (IRE) 2 ch.c. (Mar 28) Gabitat 119 – Gabibti (IRE) 82 (Dara Monarch 128) [1999 7s Oct 8] fourth foal: brother to 3-y-o Tijuana and 6-y-o Multi Franchise: dam stayed 7f: no show in maiden at Lingfield. *B. Gubby* —

TUDOR KING (IRE) 5 br.g. Orchestra 118 – Jane Bond 59 (Good Bond 122) [1998 NR 1999 14g Aug 14] brother to a winning jumper and half-brother to several winners, including 1¼m winner Clurican (by Dara Monarch) and an Italian listed winner by Bustomi: dam 2-y-o 5f winner: poor form over hurdles: soundly beaten in Lingfield maiden on Flat debut. *J. S. King* —

TUFAMORE (USA) 3 ch.g. Mt Livermore (USA) – Tufa 78 (Warning 136) [1998 NR 1999 a6g⁴ a8.5g⁴ a7g⁴ 8f⁵ 11.5g³ 12.1m 10m 11.5f⁵ Aug 6] 3,000 2-y-o: first foal: dam 2-y-o 7f winner (her only start) out of close relative to Danehill: modest maiden: stays 11.5f: acts on fibresand: sometimes visored: none too genuine. *K. R. Burke* **55 §**

TUFTY HOPPER 2 b.g. (May 5) Rock Hopper 124 – Melancolia 77 (Legend of France (USA) 124) [1999 8.2d Oct 21] third reported foal: half-brother to 3-y-o Game Tufty: dam 1¼m winner: modest form when seventh of 11 in maiden at Nottingham. *J. Pearce* **59**

TUFTY STAR 4 b.f. Sirgame – Raffles Virginia 73 (Whistling Deer 117) [1998 –: 8.2s 12s⁴ 16f⁵ 12g 12g 9.7f 16.4f 10m 11.5d 1999 a13g 14.1m⁶ Jul 20] angular filly: little form. *J. Pearce* **–**

TUI 4 b.f. Tina's Pet 121 – Curious Feeling (Nishapour (FR) 125) [1998 59, a–: a6g 10m 12d 10.2d³ 10m² 8.1d² 9.9d* 10g⁵ 8.1g⁵ 12m* 10m⁵ 10m⁶ 12m 10.2m 10g 1999 a11g a8f a12s a12g 11.7s⁶ 13.1g 12d 12m Sep 8] poor handicapper: stays 1½m: acts on good to firm and good to soft going, probably on soft: won 3 times over hurdles in 1999. *P. Bowen* **39**

TUKANO (CAN) 8 ch.g. Halo (USA) – Northern Prancer (USA) (Northern Dancer) [1998 NR 1999 a16g 15.4v³ 15.4v 22.2m a16.2g² 16.4g⁶ 15.9s⁵ 16d³ Oct 21] tall gelding: has been hobdayed: modest on all-weather, poor on turf: should stay beyond 2m: probably acts on any turf going and fibresand: visored/blinkered after third start: has worn tongue strap. *J. R. Jenkins* **47 a53**

TULLYNESSLE 3 ch.f. King's Signet (USA) 110 – Miss Klew (Never So Bold 135) [1998 –: 5s⁶ 5d⁶ 5g 1999 a7g Apr 26] small, lengthy filly: no form: dead. *M. W. Easterby* **–**

TULSA (IRE) 5 b.g. Priolo (USA) 127 – Lagrion (USA) 68 (Diesis 133) [1998 58d: 8.1d⁴ 10d⁶ 8m⁶ 11.6f 9.9m 10s 1999 9.9m 10g³ a10g* 11.6s a12g Oct 25] poor nowadays: won apprentice maiden handicap at Lingfield in July: stays 1¼m: acts on equitrack, best turf efforts on good going or softer: tried blinkered/visored. *L. Montague Hall* **46**

TUMBLEWEED GLEN (IRE) 3 ch.g. Mukaddamah (USA) 125 – Mistic Glen (IRE) (Mister Majestic 122) [1998 83+: 6g 7.1g 7g³ 7m⁵ 8d⁵ 8m* 7s 1999 9m⁵ 10.4d⁴ 10g³ 12s⁴ 9m 10.2m 10.5m⁴ 10g* Sep 20] lengthy, useful-looking gelding: has a round action: fairly useful performer: didn't need to be anywhere near best to win seller at Leicester (joined N. Twiston-Davies for 9,000 gns) final start: stays 1¼m, not 1½m: acts on good to firm and good to soft ground: blinkered twice, including at Leicester: races up with pace. *B. J. Meehan* **86**

TUMBLEWEED HERO 4 b.g. Alzao (USA) 117 – Julip 99 (Track Spare 125) [1998 84: 10.3d 7d³ 8m 8.2v² a8g* 1999 10s 7g³ 7m 8.3g* 7.1f⁵ 8f 9f 8s 10d Oct 18] good-topped gelding: fair performer: didn't have to be at best to win 18-runner claimer at Windsor (final start for B. Meehan) in May: well held after: was best at 7f/1m: acted on heavy going and equitrack: blinkered for both wins: dead. *D. Nicholls* **79 d**

TUMBLEWEED INCA (IRE) 2 b.g. (May 5) Ezzoud (IRE) 126 – Atacama (Green Desert (USA) 127) [1999 6f² 7f* 7m³ 7d 7.1m 7d 7m⁶ Sep 1] 12,000Y: third foal: half-brother to 4-y-o Surveyor: dam unraced granddaughter of Oaks third The Dancer: fair form when winning maiden at Brighton in July: failed to repeat it, finding little and looking none too keen last 2 outings: should stay 1m: acts on firm ground: tried blinkered, no improvement: sent to Macau. *B. J. Meehan* **72 d**

TUMBLEWEED QUARTET (USA) 3 b.g. Manila (USA) – Peggy's String (USA) (Highland Park (USA)) [1998 104p: 6s* 7m³ 7g³ 8v⁶ 1999 8g 10m 10s 9.9f 10g 10.3m 10d Oct 1] strong, rangy gelding: useful at 2 yrs: deteriorated in 1999: should stay at least 1m: blinkered once. *B. J. Meehan* **96 d**

TUMBLEWEED RIDGE 6 ch.h. Indian Ridge 123 – Billie Blue 63 (Ballad Rock 122) [1998 112§: 7s* 7.1d⁶ 7s* 7.3m 7m 7.3g 7g 7s⁴ 1999 7g 7v³ 7.1d² 7g* 7g* 7.3g⁵ 7g² 7m* 7g Oct 16] well-made horse: impresses in appearance: smart performer: won Ballycorus Stakes at Leopardstown (for second year running) and Prix de la Porte Maillot at Longchamp (by ½ length from Warningford), both in June and listed race at Epsom (by head from Selfish) in September: ran well otherwise when runner-up in listed events at Haydock and York (beaten ½ length by Fa-Eq): best around 7f: probably acts on any turf going, ran poorly on fibresand: blinkered nowadays: often wears tongue strap and has worn dropped noseband: has found little. *B. J. Meehan* **117**

TUMBLEWEED RIVER (IRE)   3 ch.g. Thatching 131 – Daphne Indica (IRE)   **90**
(Ballad Rock 122) [1998 82p: 7s² 1999 7m⁴ 7.1s* 7g 6d⁵ Oct 29] good-topped
gelding: has scope: fairly useful performer: landed odds in maiden at Haydock in
September: best effort in minor event at Newmarket final start: likely to stay 1m: acts
on soft going. *B. J. Meehan*

TUMBLEWEED TOR   2 b.g. (Mar 2) Rudimentary (USA) 118 – Hilly 96   **86**
(Town Crier 119) [1999 7m⁶ 7s⁴ 8g³ Oct 15] 9,200F, 12,000Y: eighth foal: half-
brother to 4-y-o Arpeggio: dam 2-y-o 6f winner: best effort (fairly useful form) when
fourth of 12 to On Time in Goodwood minor event: stays 1m. *B. J. Meehan*

TUMBLEWEED WIZARD   2 ch.g. (Mar 16) Magic Ring (IRE) 115 –   **57**
Chiquitita 44 (Reliance II 137) [1999 7.6g 8g 6d Oct 14] 6,000F, IR 26,000Y: close-
coupled, unfurnished gelding: half-brother to 4-y-o Rapid Reliance and 3 winners,
including 1992 2-y-o 6f/7f winner Another Kingdom (by Another Realm), later
middle-distance winner in Germany: dam won 1¼m seller: modest maiden: stiff task
and went freely to post when well held final start: should stay bit beyond 1m.
B. J. Meehan

TUNNEL BRIDGE   3 b.g. Merdon Melody 98 – Tripolitaine (FR) (Nonoalco   **51**
(USA) 131) [1998 63: 6f 6g⁵ 6s⁴ 8s 1999 a8g a8.5g⁵ 12g 17.2g Aug 25] modest
maiden: likely to prove best up to 7f: best effort on good going: blinkered second
start: sold 1,500 gns, sent to Denmark. *K. A. Ryan*

TURAATH (IRE)   3 b.c. Sadler's Wells (USA) 132 – Diamond Field (USA) 71   **93 +**
(Mr Prospector (USA)) [1998 90p: 7g⁴ 7d³ 1999 10.3d* Mar 26] smallish, attractive
colt: fluent mover: best effort when winning maiden at Doncaster only 3-y-o start,
making all to beat Ipledgeallegiance readily by 5 lengths: will stay 1½m: looked open
to further progress. *B. W. Hills*

The Tumbleweed Partnership's "Tumbleweed Ridge"

TURGENEV (IRE)   10 b.g. Sadler's Wells (USA) 132 – Tilia (ITY) (Dschingis   –
Khan) [1998 74: 13.8d 17.1d⁵ 14d⁵ 14d² 14s* 14.6g 14g⁴ 14g 14.4d² 13.9g 16.5d
1999 13.8g 14g 10.1d 11d 14.1s a14g Nov 30] fair at 9 yrs: no form in 1999: tried
visored/blinkered, not since 1997. *R. Bastiman*

TURNED OUT WELL   2 b.g. (Apr 23) Robellino (USA) 127 – In The Shade 89   –
(Bustino 136) [1999 5d 5m 7d Oct 22] 10,000Y: useful-looking gelding: has a round
action: half-brother to 3 winners, including fairly useful 1998 2-y-o 6f/7f winner
Relative Shade (by Distant Relative) and 8-y-o Punishment: dam 1½m to 14.8f
winner: well beaten in maidens: should prove suited by 1¼m+. *P. C. Haslam*

TURNOFACARD   3 ch.f. First Trump 118 – Barbary Court (Grundy 137) [1998   –
–p: 7d 1999 8g 8g⁶ 9.9m a12g Jul 24] workmanlike filly: modest maiden: should stay
beyond 1m. *P. J. Makin*

TURNTABLE (IRE)   3 b.f. Dolphin Street (FR) 125 – Sharp Circle (IRE) 83   **59 d**
(Sure Blade (USA) 130) [1998 –: 7d 1999 8.3m⁵ 8m 10g 11.5g 8d Oct 29] modest
maiden: form only on reappearance: sold from G. Wragg 3,000 gns after next start:
blinkered final one. *H. J. Collingridge*

TURQUOISE GEM (IRE)   2 b.f. (Apr 3) Fayruz 116 – Pepilin (Coquelin   **52**
(USA) 121) [1999 6s 6m 5v 6g⁶ Oct 11] 11,500Y: sixth foal: half-sister to UAE 6f
winner Adrien de Vries (by Thatching): dam Irish 2-y-o 6f winner: modest maiden:
not sure to stay beyond 6f: acts on good to firm and heavy ground. *V. Soane*

TURRILL HOUSE   7 b.m. Charmer 123 – Megabucks (Buckskin (FR) 133)   **35**
[1998 –: 16.4m⁵ 1999 a16g* a12g⁶ a14.8g Aug 6] poor handicapper, lightly raced:
easily best effort when winning at Southwell in January: will prove best at 2m+: acts
on fibresand. *W. J. Musson*

TURTLE   3 b.g. Turtle Island (IRE) 123 – Kate Marie (USA) (Bering 136) [1998   **54**
74: 5.1m⁵ 5g 6m³ 6s³ 7m 1999 8g a8.5g³ a12g⁵ 7s 10f 10d* 10g 12.3g 16.1s⁴ 16g
Nov 3] leggy, shallow-girthed gelding: modest performer: won seller at Pontefract
(left M. Johnston 6,800 gns) in June: stays 1¼m: acts on good to firm going, soft and
fibresand: tends to sweat and look difficult ride: none too consistent. *W. Storey*

TURTLE SONG (IRE)   2 br.g. (Mar 12) Turtle Island (IRE) 123 – Miss   **72 +**
Bojangles (Gay Fandango (USA) 132) [1999 6d 6g³ 5g⁴ Aug 22] IR 13,000Y:
seventh foal: half-brother to several winners, including Irish 1993 2-y-o 7f winner
Ziravello (by Roi Danzig) and Irish 1994 2-y-o 1m winner Onenineten (by Petorius):
dam Irish 2m winner: best effort in maidens (fair form) when third of 16 to Veil of
Avalon at Lingfield: reportedly finished lame when favourite on final start: should
prove suited by 7f+. *M. L. W. Bell*

TURTLE SOUP (IRE)   3 b.c. Turtle Island (IRE) 123 – Lisa's Favourite   **83**
(Gorytus (USA) 132) [1998 NR 1999 8s 8f⁶ 8.3m 10.9s* 12m² 10m 11.6g⁴ Oct 11]
13,000F, 22,000Y: sturdy colt: sixth foal: half-brother to 1993 2-y-o 7f winner
Majestic Heights (by High Estate) and a winner in USA by Brief Truce: dam Irish
maiden best around 1m: fairly useful performer: improved to win handicap at Ayr in
July: ran well after when in frame: may prove best around 1½m: acts on soft and
good to firm going: sold 32,000 gns, joined Mrs L. Richards. *L. M. Cumani*

TURTLE'S RISING (IRE)   3 b.f. Turtle Island (IRE) 123 – Zabeta (Diesis 133)   **76**
[1998 76: 5.2m³ 5m* 5f⁵ 5.2m⁴ 5m 5m⁴ 1999 5.1m 5g 5m² 5m⁵ 5g 6.8g³ 7d* 6m
7s 7g Oct 15] sturdy, close-coupled filly: fair handicapper: won at Lingfield in
August: probably best at 7f nowadays: acts on good to firm and good to soft going
(possibly not on firm): blinkered (raced freely) fifth start: usually races prominently.
B. J. Meehan

TURTLE SURPRISE   2 b.f. (Mar 10) Turtle Island (IRE) 123 – Foreno   **71 d**
(Formidable (USA) 125) [1999 5v* a5g* 6m 6.1m³ 6d⁴ a8.5g³ a7g³ 6s a7g Oct 18]
5,000F, 10,000Y: compact filly: half-sister to 1½m seller winner Early To Rise (by
Don't Forget Me) and a winner in Italy by Persian Heights: dam lightly-raced sister
to smart French sprinter Reasonable: fair performer: won maidens at Leicester
(awarded race) in April and Southwell in May: became very disappointing: should
stay 1m, though needs to settle better: acts on good to firm going, heavy and fibresand: refused to enter stalls fourth intended outing: has been early to post: often
sweating and edgy: sold 4,800 gns, sent to Sweden. *R. M. H. Cowell*

TWI

TURTLE VALLEY (IRE) 3 b.c. Turtle Island (IRE) 123 – Primrose Valley 99 **102**
(Mill Reef (USA) 141) [1998 80: 6m 6m⁶ 7d² 7m 8g⁶ 7.1g⁴ 1999 a10g⁵ 8g 12.5d²
11.6m⁶ 11.8v² 13.9s* 12d* 14.1g* 16.2m 13g 15s⁵ 16d⁴ 13s Sep 27] small, strong
colt: unimpressive mover: useful performer: won minor event at York (by 4 lengths
from Compton Ace, despite hanging markedly left) then rated stakes at Newbury and
Salisbury (by short head from Knockholt) in May/June: ran creditably most starts
after: stays 2m: has form on good to firm going, probably best on good or softer
(some promise only run on equitrack): blinkered (looked unenthusiastic) final 2-y-o
start: sold 28,000 gns. *S. Dow*

TUSCAN DREAM 4 b.g. Clantime 101 – Excavator Lady 65 (Most Secret 119) **81**
[1998 64: a5g² 5f³ 6m 5m² 5.7m⁶ 5m 5s 1999 5d a5g³ a5g 5m* a5g* a5g⁴ 5m³ 5f*
5m² 5f² 5f 5f* 5.2g⁴ Sep 14] fairly useful on turf, modest on all-weather: won seller
at Musselburgh and claimer at Wolverhampton in May and handicaps at Lingfield in
June and Epsom in September: best at bare 5f: acts on fibresand, raced mainly on
ground firmer than good on turf: below form (on soft ground) in blinkers: has bolted
to post/been taken down early: often leads. *J. Berry*

TUSSLE 4 b.g. Salse (USA) 128 – Crime Ofthecentury 80 (Pharly (FR) 130) [1998 **102**
102: 6s⁴ 6m 6d 1999 6m⁵ 6m⁵ 5m 6f 6m 6m⁴ 6v Sep 29] good-topped, attractive
gelding: good walker, and has a quick, fluent action: useful handicapper, lightly raced
(suffered chipped knee in 1998): ran creditably on first 2 starts and on penultimate
outing in 1999, fifth in Wokingham at Royal Ascot on second one: will prove best at
6f: acts on good to firm and heavy ground. *M. L. W. Bell*

TWEED 2 ch.c. (Feb 21) Barathea (IRE) 127 – In Perpetuity 90 (Great Nephew **60 p**
126) [1999 7s 8s⁵ 7s Nov 5] good-bodied colt: type to carry condition: half-brother to
3-y-o Reynolds and several winners, notably smart 1¼m winner Baron Ferdinand
(by Ferdinand): dam, winner around 1¼m, half-sister to Shirley Heights: modest
form in maidens at Leicester (still burly and green) and Doncaster second and third
starts: will stay at least 1¼m: likely to do better in handicaps. *R. Charlton*

TWEED MILL 2 b.f. (Mar 3) Selkirk (USA) 129 – Island Mill 79 (Mill Reef **73**
(USA) 141) [1999 6m³ Jul 12] closely related to 4-y-o Gaily Mill and half-sister to
several winners, including fairly useful 6f (at 2 yrs) to 1m winner Mara River (by
Efisio) and 1¾m winner Arrastra (by Bustino): dam stayer: green, third of 7 to
Teodora in maiden at Windsor: looked sure to do better. *I. A. Balding*

TWENTY FIRST 3 ch.f. Inchinor 119 – Picnicing 104 (Good Times (ITY)) **70**
[1998 –: 6m 1999 8.2m³ 8.1m⁵ 8m 10d² 10s⁶ Nov 1] lengthy filly: fair maiden: stays
1¼m: probably acts on soft going. *G. Wragg*

TWICE 3 b.c. Rainbow Quest (USA) 134 – Bolas 118 (Unfuwain (USA) 131) **82**
[1998 NR 1999 10d⁴ 10.4m⁴ 12v Sep 20] quite good-topped colt: first foal: dam Irish
Oaks winner out of half-sister to Gold Cup winner Longboat: fairly useful form in
maidens when fourth at Windsor and York: should stay beyond 1¼m: sweating final
start: sold 11,000 gns, joined G. L. Moore. *B. W. Hills*

TWICE AS SHARP 7 ch.h. Sharpo 132 – Shadiliya 90 (Red Alert 127) [1998 **97**
90: 6d 5g 6d² a6g 1999 6d 6g 6s² 6m 6m³ 6m⁴ 6f⁴ 5m 5.6g⁶ 6d Sep 18] big,
close-coupled horse: useful handicapper: ran creditably several times in 1999,
including when fourth to Harmonic Way in Stewards' Cup at Goodwood seventh
start: effective at 5f/6f: acts on firm and soft ground: usually races prominently.
P. W. Harris

TWICE BLESSED (IRE) 2 ch.c. (Feb 26) Thatching 131 – Fairy Blesse (IRE) **77**
(Fairy King (USA)) [1999 6v 6d a6g² a7g* Dec 10] 20,000F: strong, lengthy colt
with scope: good walker: first foal: dam, unraced sister to useful Irish 1m/9f winner
City Nights, later successful up to 1½m in USA: fair performer: made all in maiden
at Lingfield in December: will probably stay 1m: acts on all-weather, some promise
on turf. *R. Hannon*

TWICKERS 3 b.f. Primo Dominie 121 – Songstead 92 (Song 132) [1998 71p] **63**
5.1m⁴ 1999 5g² 5m³ 5d⁶ 5m⁴ 5m² 5m⁵ 5d Sep 30] modest maiden: likely to prove
best at 5f: acts on good to firm going: bolted before start on third outing: sold 5,200
gns. *R. Guest*

1077

TWILIGHT SLEEP (USA)   7 b.g. Shadeed (USA) 135 – Sleeping Beauty 87   –
(Mill Reef (USA) 141) [1998 NR 1999 a12g⁶ a16g Jan 15] fairly useful in 1997 for
Lord Huntingdon: sold only 525 gns from M. Pipe in 1998 and no show both 7-y-o
starts (pulled up in blinkers final one). *C. N. Kellett*

TWILIGHT WORLD   2 b.g. (May 22) Night Shift (USA) – Masskana (IRE)   –
(Darshaan 133) [1999 6.1m 6.1g 6d⁶ Oct 4] 25,000Y: third foal: half-brother to 3-y-o
Wallace: dam, French 9f and 1¼m winner at 4/5 yrs, out of Poule d'Essai des
Pouliches winner Masarika: well held in maidens. *Sir Mark Prescott*

TWIN CREEKS   8 b.g. Alzao (USA) 117 – Double River (USA) (Irish River   **59**
(FR) 131) [1998 68, a83: a7g⁵ a7g 7d⁴ 7.6m² 7f⁴ 8d⁴ 8.3g² 8.1m 7m 6.9m³ 8m a7g⁶   **a76**
a7g 1999 a7g a7g⁴ a8g⁴ a10g 8g 8d⁶ 7.7m⁵ Jun 23] small, close-coupled gelding: fair
handicapper on all-weather, modest on turf: effective at 6f to 9f: acts on firm and
good to soft going, probably better on equitrack than fibresand: none too consistent.
V. Soane

TWIN TIME   5 b.m. Syrtos 106 – Carramba (CZE) (Tumble Wind (USA)) [1998   **68**
68: 8f³ 9g⁶ 10g² 10.2g⁵ 9m⁶ 10.2g* 11.8m 10g 1999 8g* 10d⁴ 9m³ 10.2m* 8h³ 10.2g⁵
10m 8d Oct 11] quite good-topped mare: fair handicapper: won at Bath in May and
July (dead-heated): stays 1¼m: acts on hard and good to soft going: has won for an
apprentice: races prominently. *J. S. King*

TWIST   2 b.c. (Apr 22) Suave Dancer (USA) 136 – Reason To Dance 96 (Damister   **75**
(USA) 123) [1999 6m 7m⁶ 8s⁴ Oct 26] 17,000Y: first foal: dam, 2-y-o 5f and 5.8f
winner, later stayed 1m and successful in USA at 4 yrs: best effort in maidens (fair
form) when fourth of 12 to Top Hand at Bath, taking good hold: should stay beyond
1m if he settles. *W. R. Muir*

TWO CLUBS   3 br.f. First Trump 118 – Miss Cindy 95 (Mansingh (USA) 120)   **111**
[1998 100p: 6g⁸ 6g* 6v⁴ 6s* 1999 6g 6g⁴ 6d² 6d* 6d 6s² 6v* 7v³ Dec 1] good-bodied
filly: has a quick action: smart performer: won rated stakes at Newmarket (by neck
from Fragrant Oasis) in October and listed race at Maisons-Laffitte (by 2 lengths
from Matin de Printemps) in November: best effort when short-head second of 20 to
Pipalong listed event at Doncaster in between: best at 6f: raced only on good going or
softer: sold 100,000 gns. *W. Jarvis*

TWOFORTEN   4 b.g. Robellino (USA) 127 – Grown At Rowan 75 (Gabitat 119)   **47**
[1998 49: 6g 7g 6g 10g⁵ 12m 9m³ 8d 10g 1999 11.6m⁴ 11.6m³ 12m² 12m⁴ 16.4g   **a41**
11.9s³ 10d³ a10g a12g⁵ Nov 26] small, strong gelding: poor maiden handicapper:
effective at 1¼m (given a test)/1½m: acts on soft and good to firm ground, and
equitrack: sometimes visored/blinkered. *M. Madgwick*

TWO JACKS (IRE)   2 b.g. (Apr 4) Fayruz 116 – Kaya (GER) (Young Generation 129) [1999 5m 5g Sep 15] 10,000F, 8,000Y: workmanlike gelding: half-
brother to 3-y-o Windstorm and several winners in Germany/Austria: dam placed in
Germany: little show in maidens. *W. S. Cunningham*

TWO ON THE BRIDGE   5 gr.g. Chilibang 120 – Constant Companion 84 (Pas
de Seul 133) [1998 53: 8.3d 7.5m 6m 7.1d 1999 a8.5g⁶ a8.5g³ a9.4g⁴ a12g³ a12g   **a50**
a11g⁵ a14g³ 12.1v⁴ Mar 29] leggy, lengthy gelding: modest maiden: probably stays
1¾m: acts on good to firm going, soft and fibresand: tried blinkered, not since 1997:
usually races prominently: has hung left. *J. G. Given*

TWO PACK   3 b.c. Diesis 133 – Zonda 100 (Fabulous Dancer (USA) 124) [1998
–: 7m a8g 1999 11m 8.3g 8g 11.5m a10g a16g⁶ a10g a6g a7g Dec 8] good-bodied
colt: no form: tried blinkered: has worn tongue strap. *B. A. Pearce*

TWO'S BETTER   2 b.g. (Apr 10) Rock City 120 – Miss Pin Up 86 (Kalaglow   **65**
132) [1999 7.6g 8v 8s Oct 26] 5,000F: first foal: dam, 11.5f to 14.6f winner, racing
again in 1999: marginally best run in maidens (fair form) at Bath on final start: should
stay 1¼m. *G. L. Moore*

TWO SOCKS   6 ch.g. Phountzi (USA) 104 – Mrs Feathers 57 (Pyjama Hunt 126)   **73**
[1998 75: 10.8d⁴ 12g³ 11.4g² 1999 12g⁶ 12m* 11.4m⁶ 11.8m⁵ 12.1g³ 12m⁶ 12d
14.6d 11.7s Oct 26] leggy gelding: fair handicapper: won at Kempton in June: ran
poorly final 3 starts: stays 12.5f: acts on firm going, good to soft and fibresand:
blinkered (below form) once at 2 yrs: effective held up/from front. *J. S. King*

TWO STEP 3 b.f. Mujtahid (USA) 118 – Polka Dancer 93 (Dancing Brave (USA) –
140) [1998 NR 1999 a8.5g a8.5g⁶ a9.4g Dec 15] first foal: dam 1m/1¼m winner:
little show in maidens at Wolverhampton. *R. M. H. Cowell*

TWO-TWENTY-TWO (IRE) 4 b.c. Fairy King (USA) – Easy To Copy (USA) 110
108 (Affirmed (USA)) [1998 110: 7v* 8s* 7v* 8m⁶ 10g⁴ 9g⁴ 7d² 7s* 1999 7d*
8.1s 7g³ 8m⁵ Aug 14] closely related to Irish 1m winner Clear Procedure (by The
Minstrel) and half-brother to 2 winners, including Irish 7f/1m winner Easy Defini-
tion (by Alzao): dam, 1m (at 2 yrs) and 1½m winner, sister to Irish 1,000 Guineas
winner Trusted Partner: smart performer: made most when winning Gladness Stakes
at the Curragh in April by 1½ lengths from Gaelic Storm: creditable length third to
Tumbleweed Ridge in Ballycorus Stakes at Leopardstown, easily best subsequent
effort: well held in Sandown Mile second start: effective at 7f to 1¼m: acts on heavy
ground, below form both starts on firmer than good: blinkered nowadays: sold
34,000 gns in December. *D. K. Weld, Ireland*

TWO WILLIAMS 4 b.g. Polar Falcon (USA) 126 – Long View 68 (Persian Bold –
123) [1998 58, a–: 6d 5s³ 5.9d 5d 5v⁵ a7g 1999 5g 5g Jun 9] big gelding: has a round
action: has reportedly had tie-back operation and been hobdayed: modest handicapper: showed nothing in 1999: has given trouble at start. *M. W. Easterby*

TYCANDO 2 ch.g. (Apr 15) Forzando 122 – Running Tycoon (IRE) 62 (Last 73
Tycoon 131) [1999 6f⁵ 6m³ 5f³ 6d⁶ 6g² 5.7d a6g* 6v a7g² a6g² Dec 22] second foal: a79
half-brother to 1998 2-y-o 6f winner Dillionaire (by Dilum), also 6f winner at 3 yrs
in USA: dam, ran only at 2 yrs, from good family: fair performer: won claimer at
Wolverhampton in October, making all: sold from R. Hannon 11,000 gns after next
start: good efforts in Lingfield nurseries last 2 outings: stays 7f: acts on firm going
and all-weather, seems unsuited by softer than good: races up with pace. *K. R. Burke*

TYCOON'S LAST 2 b.f. (May 8) Nalchik (USA) – Royal Tycoon (Tycoon II) 58
[1999 5.2d⁶ 5f⁶ 6m 5.1g⁴ 6g 6v 6.1s Nov 1] big, lengthy filly: fifth reported foal:
half-sister to 5-y-o Tycoon Tina: dam won selling hurdle: modest maiden: should
be suited by 1m+: no form on going softer than good: none too consistent.
W. M. Brisbourne

TYCOON TINA 5 b.m. Tina's Pet 121 – Royal Tycoon (Tycoon II) [1998 61, 38
a40: a12g² 12.1v* 12.3v 9.9s* 11.7s⁶ 13d² 11.8g 13.1d⁵ 13d⁵ 12.3g⁶ 10s⁵ 10s³ a12g
12s 1999 a12g 11.1v⁵ 13v 9.9g 11.9d⁵ 13g 11.1m² 11.1m 11.9d⁶ 11.1f 9.1v Oct 12]
tall mare: poor maiden: effective at 11f to 13f: acts on good to firm ground, heavy
and fibresand: blinkered sixth start: sometimes slowly away: none too consistent.
W. M. Brisbourne

TYLER'S TOAST 3 ch.g. Grand Lodge (USA) 125 – Catawba 98 (Mill Reef 71
(USA) 141) [1998 74p: 7d³ 1999 10f⁶ 10m⁶ 10g⁴ a8.5g Sep 8] lengthy gelding: fair
maiden: stays 1¼m: acts on firm and good to soft going (well beaten on fibresand):
sold 4,500 gns, joined S. Dow. *W. Jarvis*

TYPHOON EIGHT (IRE) 7 b.g. High Estate 127 – Dance Date (IRE) (Sadler's 52
Wells (USA) 132) [1998 –: 8s⁶ 8s⁶ 10.3g 12g 1999 a8g a8g 13.8g 12.3m 10d² 11d a–
a11g⁵ 12m 13.8g⁵ May 21] smallish, sturdy gelding: poor mover: modest handicapper: stays 1½m: acts on soft and good to firm going: has run well in blinkers:
sometimes tongue tied: joined L. Lungo. *D. Nicholls*

TYPHOON GINGER (IRE) 4 ch.f. Archway (IRE) 115 – Pallas Viking 70
(Viking (USA)) [1998 73: 6g² 5m⁶ 6g² 7g 7d³ 1999 7s 6g 7m³ 8.2m⁴ 8g⁵ 10.4f² 8g⁴
10.4g³ Oct 6] close-coupled filly: fair maiden handicapper: stays 10.4f: acts on firm
and good to soft going: has been slowly away. *G. Woodward*

TYPHOON TILLY 2 b.g. (Mar 31) Hernando (FR) 127 – Meavy 86 (Kalaglow –
132) [1999 8d 8d 7s Nov 5] 14,000Y: quite good-topped gelding: third foal: dam
1½m winner, should have stayed further: green, well held in maidens: bred to be
suited by 1½m+. *C. F. Wall*

TYRA 3 b.f. Lion Cavern (USA) 117 – Lara (USA) 90 (Lyphard (USA) 132) [1998 78
NR 1999 8.3m² Aug 2] half-sister to French 1m winner The Empress (by In Fijar)
and 2 winners in USA by Siberian Express: dam 1m winner: 1½ lengths second to
Reviewing in maiden at Windsor: sold only 800 gns in December, joined D. Burchell.
H. R. A. Cecil

TYROLEAN DANCER (IRE)   5 b.m. Tirol 127 – Waffling 68 (Lomond (USA)   –
128) [1998 –: a8g 17.2g 12d 1999 a16g 12g Jun 8] no longer of any account.
A. J. Chamberlain

TYROLEAN DREAM (IRE)   5 b.g. Tirol 127 – Heavenly Hope (Glenstal   –
(USA) 118) [1998 71: 10s 12d 12m⁶ 1999 12m May 22] fair performer: cracked
cannon bone earlier in career: well held only 5-y-o start: stays 1½m: acts on soft and
good to firm going: useful jumper. *M. H. Tompkins*

TYROLEAN LOVE (IRE)   3 b.f. Tirol 127 – Paradise Forum 78 (Prince Sabo   **53**
123) [1998 –: 7s 7d 1999 10m 8f⁴ 7g Jun 8] leggy filly: second foal: dam 2-y-o 5f
winner: form only in maiden at Brighton penultimate start. *C. A. Horgan*

TZARINASSILOUHETTE   2 b.f. (Mar 4) Puissance 110 – Tzarina (USA)   **42**
(Gallant Romeo (USA)) [1999 6d⁴ 7m 6f⁴ 5g³ 5m a5f Oct 2] 500Y: leggy filly:
half-sister to 3-y-o Wilomeno and 3 winners, including useful sprinter Mandub (by
Topsider): dam placed in USA: poor maiden: should prove best at 5f/6f: visored (best
effort) fourth start, blinkered fifth. *B. Palling*

U

UBITOO   2 b.c. (Apr 26) Puissance 110 – Cassiar 84 (Connaught 130) [1999 6d   –
a8g a7g a7g Dec 10] 4,000Y: brother to 7-y-o Ultra Beet and half-brother to several
winners: dam 11.5f winner: soundly beaten in maidens. *R. M. Flower*

U K MAGIC (IRE)   4 b.g. Alzao (USA) 117 – Lightino (Bustino 136) [1998 65:   –
7s⁶ 10.8d² 11.6m 12m 10m⁴ 1999 a11g 9.7v 11.9f Apr 29] workmanlike gelding: fair
maiden handicapper for J. Banks in 1998: no form at 4 yrs: should stay further than
10.8f: acts on good to firm and good to soft going: visored once. *J. R. Jenkins*

ULSHAW   2 ch.g. (Mar 14) Salse (USA) 128 – Kintail 76 (Kris 135) [1999 7m 8f⁵   **60 ?**
Sep 13] 20,000Y: fourth foal: half-brother to 6f winner Invergordon (by Efisio): dam,
runner-up on debut over 1¼m, out of smart Sleat, half-sister to St Leger winner
Athens Wood: apparently better effort in maidens when last of 5 to Cool Investment
at Musselburgh: should stay 1¼m. *J. D. Bethell*

ULTIMATELY LUCKY (IRE)   4 b.c. Kris 135 – Oczy Czarnie (USA) 109   **115**
(Lomond (USA) 128) [1998 112: 8d⁴ 8d 11g* 12d* 12d* 12d³ 10m* 1999 10g* Jun
24] fourth foal: half-brother to useful French 1m winners Berine (also 6f winner at 2
yrs, by Bering) and Teobaldo (by Green Desert): dam won Prix de la Salamandre and
9f Grade 3 event in USA: smart performer: well beaten for A. Fabre first 2 starts in
1998, but much improved in second half of year, winning 4 times, including listed
races at Saint-Cloud and Cagnes: returned better than ever to win La Coupe at Longchamp by ¾ length from Native Justice: reportedly received a knock during race and
not seen out again: stays 1½m: yet to race on extremes of ground. *J-P. Gallorini,
France*

ULTRA BEET   7 b.g. Puissance 110 – Cassiar 84 (Connaught 130) [1998 61, a56:   –
a6g³ a6g a6g² a6g² a6g² a6g a6g⁶ 6g³ 6g 6m 7m⁵ 7g a7g a7g a7g⁶ a8g a10f 1999
a7g 8m 6g 7f 8.1m Jul 21] compact gelding: modest performer: little show in 1999:
probably stays easy 1m: acts on firm ground and all-weather: sometimes blinkered/
visored: has been bandaged in front. *R. M. Flower*

ULTRA CALM (IRE)   3 ch.g. Doubletour (USA) – Shyonn (IRE) (Shy Groom   **71**
(USA)) [1998 –: 5m 6s 5g 1999 a7g⁴ a8.5g⁴ a9.4g* a8g² a10g a8.5g* 10m* 10s²
10.9m⁶ 9m⁵ a8g a10g Nov 11] fair performer: won claimer and minor event at
Wolverhampton and handicap at Ripon (23 ran) between January and April: below
form final 4 starts: effective at 8.5f to 1¼m: acts on good to firm going, soft and
fibresand (below form both starts on equitrack): blinkered fourth start, visored fifth.
P. C. Haslam

UMBRIAN GOLD (IRE)   3 b.f. Perugino (USA) 84 – Golden Sunlight (Ile de   **82**
Bourbon (USA) 133) [1998 66p: 7s² 1999 8g 7g² 7.1m² 7.1m² 7.7m² 7s* 7m Sep 2] fairly
useful performer: made all in maiden at Ascot in August: well held on handicap debut
next time: will prove best up to 1m: acts on soft and good to firm going. *J. A. R. Toller*

*Vodafone Horris Hill Stakes, Newbury—a 1–2 for trainer Richard Hannon
with Umistim (No.8) beating the better-backed Cape Town (blaze);
Zyz (striped sleeves) battles on for third place with Zoning (right) in fourth*

UMISTIM   2 ch.c. (Jan 17) Inchinor 119 – Simply Sooty 78 (Absalom 128) [1999   **107**
5.7g³ 7.3f* 6s* 7d⁵ 7.3s* Oct 22] third foal: half-brother to a 7.5f winner in Denmark
by First Trump: dam 2-y-o 5f winner: useful performer: won maiden at Newbury in
July, minor event at Windsor in August and 9-runner Vodafone Horris Hill Stakes at
Newbury (20/1, best effort when rallying to beat Cape Town by 1¼ lengths) in
October: should stay 1m, but not necessarily further: has won on firm going, best
efforts on soft: races prominently. *R. Hannon*

UNA (IRE)   3 b.f. Lion Cavern (USA) 117 – Prosperous Lady (Prince Tenderfoot   **–**
(USA) 126) [1998 NR 1999 9.2s 7d a8.5g Oct 30] sixth foal: half-sister to 3 winners,
including smart 7f/1m performer Eurolink Thunder and fairly useful Irish 1m winner
Eternal Joy (both by Fairy King): dam unraced: little form in maidens (slowly away
and badly in need of experience first 2 starts): tongue tied last 2 outings. *R. A. Fahey*

UNAWARE   2 b.c. (Mar 20) Unfuwain (USA) 131 – Rainbow Lake 113 (Rainbow   **92**
Quest (USA) 134) [1999 7g⁴ 8.1g* 8m 8.1s⁴ Oct 2] quite good-topped, attractive
colt: third foal: half-brother to smart 13.3f and 1¾m winner Brimming (by Generous): dam 1¼m and 1½m (Lancashire Oaks) winner: fairly useful performer: won
maiden at Chepstow in August: gave impression something amiss next time, but ran
well when fourth of 5 to Sakhee in minor event at Sandown on final start: will be
suited by 1¼m+: acts on soft ground. *R. Charlton*

UNCHAIN MY HEART   3 b.f. Pursuit of Love 124 – Addicted To Love 73   **70**
(Touching Wood (USA) 127) [1998 66: 6g 7d 6d³ 1999 8.2d³ 10s³ 10s 8m³ 8.2m 8m³
7m⁴ 7f² 7f² 7f⁴ 8d² 8s a8g* a8g³ a8g Dec 18] lengthy, good-bodied filly: fair
performer: won maiden at Lingfield in November: has form at 1¼m but seems best
at 7f/1m: acts on firm ground, soft and equitrack (untried on fibresand): often
blinkered, but is as effective without: races prominently. *B. J. Meehan*

UNCHANGED   7 b.m. Unfuwain (USA) 131 – Favorable Exchange (USA)   **68**
(Exceller (USA) 129) [1998 73: 14.1v⁶ 14.1s⁶ 16g* 20d 14.9d³ 1999 16.2d 16s 14.1f
15.8g³ 15.9m 16.2m Jul 23] angular mare: fair handicapper: best at 2m to 2½m:
unsuited by heavy going, probably acts on any other turf: blinkered once earlier in
career: often bandaged. *J. L. Harris*

UNCLE DOUG   8 b.g. Common Grounds 118 – Taqa 85 (Blakeney 126) [1998   **–**
61: a16g⁶ 16d⁵ 13.8d⁴ 12m 1999 17.1g⁵ Jun 28] close-coupled gelding: modest
handicapper: has form at 2½m, but at least as effective at 1¾m/2m: acts on firm and
soft going, well beaten on all-weather: sometimes looks reluctant, and best held up:
has run well sweating. *J. L. Eyre*

UNCLE EXACT   2 b.g. (Feb 28) Distant Relative 128 – True Precision 84   **77**
(Presidium 124) [1999 5d³ 5m* 5m⁴ 5.1m⁴ 5m⁵ 6g 5s⁵ 6s 5g² 5s Nov 5] 7,000Y:
well-made gelding: second foal: half-brother to 3-y-o Foreign Editor: dam 5f to 7f

winner: fair performer: won maiden at Hamilton in May: left Jack Berry after next start: inconsistent after: should stay 6f: acts on soft and good to firm going. *K. A. Ryan*

UNCLE OBERON 3 b.g. Distant Relative 128 – Fairy Story (IRE) 80 (Persian   **57**
Bold 123) [1998 54: 6g 7d 1999 7m^5 6.1g Jun 11] tall gelding: modest maiden: stays 7f: acts on good to firm going: has worn tongue strap. *G. A. Butler*

UNDER THE CLOCK 5 ch.m. Anshan 119 – Worthy Venture 76 (Northfields   **67 §**
(USA)) [1998 NR 1999 8m^5 8g 7.7m Aug 30] 4,800 4-y-o: unfurnished mare: half-sister to several winners, including 10-y-o Canovas Heart and useful Marbella Silks (both sprinters by Balidar): dam placed over 5f at 2 yrs: best effort in maidens when fifth of 7 at Pontefract on debut (possibly flattered): refused to race final start, or to enter stalls next intended one. *J. G. Given*

UNDETERRED 3 ch.c. Zafonic (USA) 130 – Mint Crisp (IRE) 108 (Green   **104**
Desert (USA) 127) [1998 105p: 6f^4 6f* 6g^4 6g* 1999 7g^4 7g^3 6d^4 6d 6d Oct 15] sturdy, deep-girthed colt: has a quick action: useful performer: best effort in 1999 when 2 lengths third of 5 to Fragrant Oasis in listed event at Newmarket in May: may prove best at 6f/7f: acts on firm going, possibly not on good to soft. *C. F. Wall*

UNFORTUNATE 2 ch.f. (Apr 5) Komaite (USA) – Honour And Glory 46   **49**
(Hotfoot 126) [1999 6d 7m a7g^6 6.1s a6g a5g^2 a6g* a6g^4 Dec 18] 1,000Y: sturdy filly: fourth foal: sister to 3-y-o Season of Hope: dam, poor maiden, half-sister to smart sprinter Singing Steven: poor performer: won seller at Southwell in December: probably stays 7f: form only on all-weather: looked very reluctant from stalls when blinkered fifth start. *Miss J. F. Craze*

UNGARO (GER) 5 b.h. Goofalik (USA) 118 – Ustina (GER) (Star Appeal   **119**
133) [1998 119: 12s^3 11g 12m* 12g* 12m^2 12d^4 12s^3 12f 12m 1999 12m^2 12m^2 12m* 12s* Aug 15]

It would probably have taken more than a few guesses—or a long trawl through the alphabet—to come up with the name of the European-trained horse, a four-time Group 1 winner and a classic winner in his own country, who'd been allotted just two kilos less than top weight Kayf Tara in the entries for the 1999 Melbourne Cup. Ungaro might not have done enough to become well known in Britain, but he'll be all too familiar to rivals who have tried to get past him in Germany or Italy in the last couple of seasons.

At Dusseldorf in July, the front-running Ungaro managed to keep four rivals at bay to win the WGZ Bank-Deutschlandpreis for the second year, holding on by a short head from the three-year-old Sumitas with the British-trained Dark Shell a length and a half away third. Three weeks later at Gelsenkirchen he had the relative luxury of a half-length verdict over outsider Wins Fiction, who was probably flattered by staying on the far side of the course as the three other runners came up the centre, in another Group 1 contest, the ELE Pokal Grosser Erdgas-Preis. Ungaro's rider received a suspension for excessive use of the whip both times. Ungaro's first two starts had been closely-run affairs too, but he was on the receiving end in those races. On his reappearance in the Group 2 Gerling-Preis at Cologne he was beaten three quarters of a length by Germany's best older horse Tiger Hill and then went down by just a nose to Dark Moondancer when attempting a repeat win in the Gran Premio di Milano. That was the second time in his career that Ungaro had lost out by a nose in an Italian Group 1 event; Single Empire pipped him by the same margin in the Derby Italiano as a three-year-old. But Ungaro's classic success had only been delayed, as he won the German version of the St Leger, a Group 2 contest at Dortmund, later that year. Group 1 wins the following season at Milan and Dusseldorf booked Ungaro a place in the Japan Cup and in Hong Kong at the end of his four-year-old campaign, and, although he failed to figure in either contest, that didn't stop connections drawing up plans for another ambitious programme in the latest season. In the event, Ungaro didn't make it to Australia for either the Caulfield Cup or the Melbourne Cup and nor did he take up an alternative engagement in the Canadian International, owing to a slight injury.

Unusually for a German-trained horse, Ungaro has been raced mainly on good going or firmer, deliberately it would seem, but he probably ran at least as well as ever when the ground was soft on his final start at Gelsenkirchen. He stays a mile and three quarters but has raced almost exclusively at a mile and a half since his win in the German St Leger, though there were plans for him to contest the Irish St Leger as a four-year-old.

	Goofalik (USA) (b 1987)	Lyphard (b 1969)	Northern Dancer
			Goofed
		Alik (br 1978)	Targowice
Ungaro (GER) (b.h. 1994)			Kaliope
	Ustina (GER) (b 1983)	Star Appeal (b 1970)	Appiani II
			Sterna
		Unwetter (ch 1970)	Waldcanter
			Union

Ungaro is by the smart seven furlong to mile and a quarter performer Goofalik, a tough and consistent horse trained by John Hammond, whose three pattern wins included a Group 2 event at Frankfurt and third place in the Grade 1 Budweiser International. Goofalik was also responsible for Ungaro's stable-companion Nagoya, who won the Oaks d'Italia, and the German Derby runner-up Acambaro in the latest season. All five previous foals out of the German six furlong (at two) and mile winner Ustina have won, the best of them being Upper Class (by Konigsstuhl), a useful stayer. Ungaro's four-year-old half-sister Umbria (by Mondrian) and three-year-old half-brother Universus (by Unfuwain) are also winners, the latter finishing fifth and seventh respectively in the Italian and German Derby and second in a Group 3 at Baden-Baden, showing useful form. Ungaro didn't contest the German Derby as a three-year-old but his grandam Unwetter was fourth in it and his great grandam Union was a full sister to the 1959 winner Uomo. *H. Blume, Germany*

UNICAMP 3 ch.f. Royal Academy (USA) 130 – Honeyspike (IRE) 79 (Chief's Crown (USA)) [1998 84: 6.1m* 6g⁴ 6m⁵ 5.3f² 1999 6m 8m⁶ May 26] sturdy filly: poor walker: fairly useful at 2 yrs: disappointing in 1999: should stay beyond 6f. *E. A. L. Dunlop*   –

UNICORN STAR (IRE) 2 b.g. (Apr 6) Persian Bold 123 – Highland Warning 43 (Warning 136) [1999 7d 7.1g⁴ a8g Nov 22] IR 26,000F, IR 24,000Y: tall gelding: second foal: dam, sprint maiden, half-sister to Middle Park winner Stalker: modest form first 2 starts in maidens, racing freely when fourth at Musselburgh: seemed to need experience on fibresand. *J. S. Wainwright*   53 +

UNIFORM 4 ch.f. Unfuwain (USA) 131 – Trachelium 65 (Formidable (USA) 125) [1998 61: 10v 8d⁴ 10m⁶ 12m³ 12.1d* 17.5s³ 16.1g 14.1v³ 1999 a16g* a16g⁵ 16g⁵ 13g* 13.1d³ 13g* 16.1m³ 15.8g Jul 1] angular filly: fair handicapper: won at Southwell in February and Hamilton in May and June: finds 1½m a bare minimum, and stays 17.5f: acts on good to firm going, soft and fibresand: held up: game. *Miss S. E. Hall*   65

UNIMPEACHABLE (IRE) 2 b.f. (Feb 16) Namaqualand (USA) – Bourbon Topsy 108 (Ile de Bourbon (USA) 133) [1999 6.1m 7v³ 7.9g 8.2d* 8.3d⁵ Nov 4] 17,000Y: sixth foal: half-sister to 11.5f to 2m winner Anjou (by Saumarez): dam, middle-distance stayer, half-sister to Most Welcome from family of Teenoso: fair performer: best effort when third in maiden at Kempton in September: justified favouritism in seller at Nottingham in October: will be well suited by 1¼m+: acts on heavy ground. *P. F. I. Cole*   65

UNITUS (IRE) 6 b.h. Soviet Star (USA) 128 – Unite 126 (Kris 135) [1998 55: 10.3g 10.4g 10g 7g 8m⁵ 10.1f⁴ 8.9g 18.2g⁴ 11.9g a12g 1999 a7g a16g a11g³ a11g a12g⁶ a11g⁴ a12g 18g May 18] good-bodied horse: poor handicapper nowadays: stays 11f: acts on fibresand and good to firm going: has had tongue tied: inconsistent. *M. C. Chapman*   47

UNLIKELY LADY   3 b.f. Clantime 101 – Casbar Lady 79 (Native Bazaar 122)   **49**
[1998 NR 1999 6g⁴ 6m⁶ 6s a6g a6g Dec 1] 1,000Y: smallish filly: sister to modest 6f   **a–**
winner Tailwind (who stays 1m) and half-sister to 3 winning sprinters: dam 5f
winner: poor form in maiden on debut, little show after. *D. W. Barker*

UNMASKED   3 ch.f. Safawan 118 – Unveiled 76 (Sayf El Arab (USA) 127) [1998   **–**
35: 5m⁴ a6g 1999 8s Oct 4] form only on debut. *J. S. Goldie*

U-NO-HARRY (IRE)   6 b.g. Mansooj 118 – Lady Roberta (USA) (Roberto   **48**
(USA) 131) [1998 44, a64: a6g a6g⁶ a7g* a7g² a8g³ a7g a8.5g a7g² a7g⁵ a7g³ 6.9s⁴
6m⁵ a7g⁵ a7g³ a8g a8.5g³ a7g* a7g a8.5g a7g 1999 a8.5g a7g 8.5m 6v⁶ a7g⁵ a6g⁶
a8.5g⁵ a7g⁵ 5.9g a8.5g Jun 19] sturdy gelding: poor mover: poor performer: stays
8.5f: acts on fibresand, firm and good to soft going, possibly not on soft: blinkered
once. *R. Hollinshead*

UNREAL CITY (IRE)   6 b.g. Rock City 120 – Tolmi 122 (Great Nephew 126)   **74**
[1998 91+: a10g² a8f⁶ 1999 a10g³ Feb 9] sturdy gelding: very lightly raced, useful in
1996 for H. Cecil: just fair form only start in 1999: seems better at 1¼m than 1m: acts
on equitrack, best turf effort on good to soft going. *G. Wragg*

UNSEEDED   2 ch.f. (Feb 10) Unfuwain (USA) 131 – Sesame 117 (Derrylin 115)   **81 p**
[1999 7d 8d⁴ Oct 22] big, rangy filly: fourth foal: closely related to 1¼m and 1½m
winner Calendula (by Be My Guest): dam, middle-distance stayer, half-sister to
Celeric: much better effort in maidens (fairly useful form) when fourth of 18 to
Interlude at Doncaster, staying on strongly: will be well suited by 1½m+: should
make a useful performer, and seems sure to win races. *J. L. Dunlop*

UNSHAKEN   5 b.h. Environment Friend 128 – Reel Foyle (USA) 77 (Irish River   **85**
(FR) 131) [1998 73: a6g³ a6g³ 5.9d⁵ 6s² 5.9s* 6g³ 5.1g6 6g* 6g² 6s³ 6m 5m² 6s⁵ 6v
1999 a6f³ a6g³ 5d² 6v* 5d 6g* 6d 5m 6s⁴ 6m* 6m 6s³ 6d 6m 6d 6.1s⁴ 5s³ 6d 6d Oct
20] strong, sturdy horse: fairly useful handicapper: won at Hamilton in April and
May and at Newcastle in June: generally in good form otherwise: effective at 5f
(given test)/6f: acts on good to firm going, heavy and fibresand: tried blinkered/
visored: held up. *E. J. Alston*

UNTOLD RICHES (USA)   3 b.f. Red Ransom (USA) – Asdaf (USA) 63 (Forty   **94**
Niner (USA)) [1998 68p: 7m 7g 7g 1999 7.5m⁵ 6f 8m² 8.2m* 7d³ 8.1f* 9f* 8s⁴ 7m
a8f 7.5f⁴ Dec 16] well-made, useful-looking filly: good mover: fairly useful performer: won handicaps at Nottingham in June and Haydock then Goodwood in July:
creditable efforts after when fourth in listed race at Deauville (to Tycoon's Dolce,
final start for J. Gosden) and handicap at Nad Al Sheba: stays 9f: acts on firm and
soft ground, well beaten only start on dirt: visored first 2 outings: seems suited by
forcing tactics. *P. L. Rudkin, UAE*

UNTOLD STORY (USA)   4 b.g. Theatrical 128 – Committed Miss (USA) (Key   **62 d**
To Content (USA)) [1998 65: 8v 8k⁶ 8m 8v 1999 10v a7g³ 8m 8g 7.1m 10.2g 10f 8.2s
Nov 1] $4,000F, $200,000Y: seventh foal: half-brother to winners in USA by Mistral
Dancer and Strawberry Road: dam twice-raced half-sister to high-class sprinter
Committed: modest maiden: left D. Weld in Ireland, after fourth start for 7,500 gns:
may prove best up to 1m: acts on heavy going and sand: tried blinkered. *T. Keddy*

UP AND ABOUT   3 b.f. Barathea (IRE) 127 – Upend 120 (Main Reef 126) [1998   **a77**
66p: 8.2g⁶ 1999 7m⁶ 7g 10s a14.8g* 13.8g⁶ 13.8s Nov 2] fair performer: easily best
effort in 1999 when winning handicap at Wolverhampton in October, making most:
stays 15f: acts on fibresand: tongue tied (found little) final start. *Sir Mark Prescott*

UP IN FLAMES (IRE)   8 br.g. Nashamaa 113 – Bella Lucia (Camden Town 125)   **–**
[1998 54, a59: a12g⁴ a8g* a9.4g⁵ 8d 9g 8g² 8.2d⁶ 8g a11g 8s⁴ a8.5g³ a9.4g a11g6
1999 a8g a8g Jan 18] leggy gelding: modest handicapper: effective at 1m to 11f: acts
on soft going, firm and fibresand: blinkered final start: has had tongue tied: usually
held up: none too consistent. *S. R. Bowring*

UPLIFTING   4 b.f. Magic Ring (IRE) 115 – Strapless 84 (Bustino 136) [1998 77:   **77**
6d² 6d² 5.1d⁵ 5f* 5f 6d 5s 5.1v 1999 6f² 6g* 6s⁶ 6m 6f 6g³ 5f 5.1s Oct 26] smallish,
good-topped filly: fair handicapper: won at Goodwood in May: ran creditably after
when third of 27 there (made most) in August: effective at 5f/6f: acts on firm and
good to soft going: tried visored. *L. G. Cottrell*

UPON A WISH 3 ch.g. Alzao (USA) 117 – Imprecise 64 (Polish Precedent **79**
(USA) 131) [1998 NR 1999 12m² 10g 12g 13.4m² 14.8m⁵ 14g³ 12v 10.9v⁴ Oct 11]
85,000Y: useful-looking gelding: poor mover: first foal: dam, 1m winner, half-sister
to high-class 1¼m performer Shady Heights: fair maiden: stays 13f: acts on good to
firm going, possibly not on heavy: sold 10,000 gns. *B. Hanbury*

UPPER BULLENS 2 ch.g. (Apr 26) Rock City 120 – Monstrosa 70 (Monsanto **60**
(FR) 121) [1999 7m⁶ 7d⁴ 7.5s⁴ Jul 3] 13,000Y: half-brother to several winners,
including 4-y-o Bens Gift, fairly useful 5f to 7f winner Champagne Grandy (by
Vaigly Great) and 1¼m seller winner Muddy Lane (by Ilium): dam 2-y-o 5f winner
who stayed 1m: modest maiden: best effort when fourth of 8 in minor event at
Beverley: should stay 1m. *A. Bailey*

UPPER CHAMBER 3 b.g. Presidium 124 – Vanishing Trick 83 (Silly Season **64 d**
127) [1998 64: 5g³ 5.1g⁴ 5g⁶ 5g⁶ 5m² 5g 1999 5m² 5d 5m⁵ 6f a5g⁵ 5m⁶ 6g 5g 6m Sep
3] leggy gelding: disappointing maiden: may prove best at 5f: acts on good to firm
going: visored/blinkered last 4 starts: headstrong, and sometimes looks less than
keen: sold 1,100 gns. *J. G. FitzGerald*

UP THE KYBER 2 b.c. (Mar 24) Missed Flight 123 – Najariya (Northfields –
(USA)) [1999 7d 8s Oct 26] 29,000F, 11,000Y: closely related to useful 1992 2-y-o
6f/7f performer Nominator (by Nomination) and half-brother to several winners,
including 3-y-o My Petal: dam unraced half-sister to Cherry Hinton winner
Nasseem: signs of ability though well held in maidens. *R. F. Johnson Houghton*

URGENT REPLY (USA) 6 b.g. Green Dancer (USA) 132 – Bowl of Honey **48**
(USA) (Lyphard (USA) 132) [1998 59: 11.8s⁶ 14.1s⁵ 11.9f 13d* 16s* 12.1g* 12.1g
12.1s⁶ 12.1d 12g 11.8d 1999 a14g 16g 12v⁶ 12.1m 14.6s⁵ 16.1s* 14.1m 16.4g⁴ 17.2s
15.8s Oct 5] sturdy gelding: poor handicapper nowadays: won at Warwick in June:
reportedly finished lame seventh start: effective at 1½m to 2m: acts on soft and good
to firm going (well beaten both runs on all-weather): visored once at 5 yrs: has worn
tongue strap: none too reliable. *C. A. Dwyer*

URGENT SWIFT 6 ch.g. Beveled (USA) – Good Natured § (Troy 137) [1998 –: **81**
16v 14.1v 12m⁵ 14.1d 1999 12g³ 14.1s 12m* 14.4m³ 12f 14g³ 20m 14d* 16m⁶ 16f³
14f 11.9m 13.9m⁵ 17.5d 14.1g⁵ 14.1d² a14g³ Dec 13] rangy gelding: fairly useful
handicapper: won at Salisbury in May and Haydock in July: not discredited on
all-weather debut at Southwell final start: effective at 1½m to 2m: acts on firm and
good to soft going (some promise only run on fibresand), possibly not on heavy/soft:
blinkered final 5-y-o start: often ridden by S. Clancy: best held up. *A. P. Jarvis*

URSA MAJOR 5 b.g. Warning 136 – Double Entendre 81 (Dominion 123) [1998 **71**
–, a92: a8s* a8g⁴ a8g* a8g* a8g* a7g⁴ a8g* a8.5g 7.6m 7g a6g³ a7g³ a7g⁶ 1999 **a74**
a8g 7m 8g 10f² 10g 10.1m⁴ 10.3m⁶ 9f 6d⁴ 7f* 6g 7d a7g a8g⁴ a7g Dec 29] small
gelding: fair handicapper: won 22-runner race at York in September: best at 7f to
easy 1¼m: acts on all-weather and firm going, probably on soft: blinkered 6 of last 7
starts: usually races up with pace: none too reliable. *C. N. Allen*

US AND THEM (IRE) 2 ch.f. (Feb 1) Pips Pride 117 – Tasskeen (FR) (Lyphard –
(USA) 132) [1999 6s⁵ Jul 3] 25,000Y: workmanlike filly: half-sister to several
winners abroad, including fairly useful Irish 1993 2-y-o 7f winner Yahthab (by
Common Grounds): dam ran once in France: bandaged in front and very green when
well beaten in minor event at Haydock. *Mrs N. Macauley*

UTAH (IRE) 5 b.g. High Estate 127 – Easy Romance (USA) (Northern Jove **57**
(CAN)) [1998 –: 10s 1999 a8.5g⁵ a8.5g² 8s a8.5g a10g Dec 22] strong, lengthy
gelding: modest maiden handicapper: stays 8.5f: acts on fibresand:
blinkered penultimate start, subsequently left L. Montague Hall. *G. L. Moore*

UTHER PENDRAGON (IRE) 4 b.g. Petardia 113 – Mountain Stage (IRE) –
(Pennine Walk 120) [1998 –: a5g a8g 8g 1999 8f Jul 12] workmanlike gelding: no
form, including in blinkers. *M. Bradstock*

UZY 3 ch.g. Common Grounds 118 – Loch Clair (IRE) 53 (Lomond (USA) 128) **65 d**
[1998 65p: 6v 6s² 1999 6d⁴ 6g 6g³ 8g 7m 5.7h² 6g 7m⁶ 9v 8s Sep 29] lengthy,
robust gelding: modest maiden: below form after third start, leaving I. Balding after
seventh: effective at 6f/7f: acts on soft and good to firm going: effective visored/
blinkered or not. *M. J. Ryan*

V

VALANTINE ANNA   3 b.f. Perpendicular 119 – Fool's Errand (Milford 119)   **41**
[1998 –: 6g 5.1m 7.6f 7d 1999 a9.4g⁶ a9.4g⁵ 10.5m² a12g 8.1m 10g⁶ a11g Sep 28]   **a–**
poor maiden: stays 1¼m: acts on good to firm going: reportedly swallowed tongue
second start, tongue tied next 2. *D. Haydn Jones*

VALDINI (IRE)   3 b.f. Common Grounds 118 – Windini (Windjammer (USA))   **73**
[1998 68: 7m 7m 7g³ 1999 8s³ 8g 8m⁶ 10.2m⁴ 8m a8.5g 9.9m Aug 29] close-coupled
filly: fair maiden: best effort at 1m: acts on soft and good to firm going, well beaten
only try on fibresand: visored once: sold 2,000 gns, sent to Italy. *P. W. Harris*

VALEDICTORY   6 b.g. Slip Anchor 136 – Khandjar 77 (Kris 135) [1998 NR   **85 ?**
1999 10d⁶ 12.4f⁵ May 27] strong, well-made gelding: had a markedly round action
(reportedly jarred tendons as a 3-y-o): useful for H. Cecil in 1996/7: signs of retaining
ability in 1999: stayed 2m: acted on good to firm and good to soft ground: dead.
P. Monteith

VALENTINE BAND (USA)   2 b.f. (Mar 23) Dixieland Band (USA) – Shirley   **88 P**
Valentine 104 (Shirley Heights 130) [1999 8d⁶ Oct 30] fourth foal: closely related to
5-y-o Memorise: dam, 1½m winner, sister to Deploy and half-sister to Commander
In Chief, Warning and Dushyantor: shaped really well when 3 lengths sixth of 10 to
Silver Colours in listed race at Newmarket, leading going well 3f out but unable to
sustain effort and eased: will be suited by 1¼m+: sure to improve considerably, and
could well be a smart performer in the making. *R. Charlton*

VALENTINE GIRL   3 b.f. Alzao (USA) 117 – Set Fair (USA) (Alleged (USA)   **109**
138) [1998 92+: 7m* 8d 8d 1999 11.4m* 12m 12m⁴ 9.9d³ 14.6g³ 12v⁶ Oct 23]

*Shadwell Stud Cheshire Oaks, Chester—Valentine Girl gives owner Khalid Abdulla
and trainer Barry Hills their fourth win in the race in the last eight years,
making most of the running with Signorina Cattiva proving the biggest threat*

well-made filly: fluent mover: useful performer: made all in listed race at Chester in May by ¾ length from Signorina Cattiva: ran well when in frame in similar events at Newmarket, Salisbury (2 lengths third to Ajhiba) and Park Hill Stakes at Doncaster (4 lengths third to Mistle Song): barely stayed 14.6f: acted on good to firm and good to soft going, ran poorly on heavy final start: tongue tied: stud. *B. W. Hills*

VALENTINES VISION   2 b.c. (Feb 14) Distinctly North (USA) 115 – Sharp   **52**
Anne 74§ (Belfort (FR) 89) [1999 5m⁶ 5s⁵ 7d Oct 21] 17,000Y, 6,000 2-y-o: half-brother to 4-y-o Its All Relative (5f winner at 2 yrs) and 6f (seller) and 7f (in Italy) winner Sharp Monty (by Mon Tresor): dam unreliable sprinter: form in maidens only at Beverley on debut: tended to hang in testing conditions on second start, off course 5 months before final one. *N. P. Littmoden*

VALENTINE WALTZ (IRE)   3 b.f. Be My Guest (USA) 126 – Save Me   **116**
The Waltz 86 (Kings Lake (USA) 133) [1998 99: 5v⁴ 5s³ 5m³ 6s⁴ 7g* 6g³ 7g² 1999 7g* 8m³ 8m* 8m³ Jun 16]
    For only the third time, but also the third time in the 'nineties, the Dubai Poule d'Essai des Pouliches was won by a filly trained in Britain. Paul Cole's Culture Vulture started the trend in 1992, to be followed by Ed Dunlop's Ta Rib in 1996 and now Valentine Waltz for John Gosden. The latest Pouliches winner was an authoritative one—indeed, only Zalaiyka in 1998 among the decade's earlier winners had won by a wider margin than the two lengths by which Valentine Waltz beat Karmifira. Six of the fourteen runners had won last time out, including Italian Guineas winner Shenck and the listed winners Sao and Karmifira, all three having had two starts and two wins earlier in the season; in addition, Venize had won the Prix de la Grotte, Alexis (trained by Jeremy Noseda) a listed race at Chantilly and Rangoon Ruby a Longchamp minor event nine days earlier. At the head of the betting, however, was Moiava, a filly with the last-time-out credentials of having finished nineteenth of twenty-two. Headstrong under restraint when second favourite in the One Thousand Guineas, Moiava was allowed to bowl along in front in the Pouliches and performed just as poorly. Valentine Waltz was held up off the strong pace in mid-division and switched to the outside by Ray Cochrane just inside the final two furlongs; just as Karmifira, Godolphin representative Calando and Italian challenger Shenck emerged at the head of proceedings, Valentine Waltz swept past them all.
    It was a perplexing foible of the Pouliches betting, betraying some spectacularly short memories, to send Moiava off favourite when the One Thousand Guineas result two weeks earlier also included a Pouliches rival who

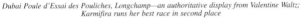

Dubai Poule d'Essai des Pouliches, Longchamp—an authoritative display from Valentine Waltz; Karmifira runs her best race in second place

had finished no fewer than sixteen places in front of her and gone close to winning. That filly was Valentine Waltz. Making impressive headway at Newmarket to take firm control of the far-side group approaching the final furlong, 11/1-chance Valentine Waltz also led overall at that stage, only to be collared by Wince and Wannabe Grand close home, losing out by half a length and a short head. This result had itself been a triumph for traditional thinking in terms of classic calculations, because the first three were graduating from wins in the two most prestigious trials and the top British race for two-year-old fillies, Wince in the Fred Darling, Wannabe Grand in the Cheveley Park and Valentine Waltz in the Nell Gwyn. Valentine Waltz's Nell Gwyn had been the most decisive of those triumphs as she justified favouritism by three lengths from Hawriyah, exhibiting her trademark fine turn of foot. Valentine Waltz ended the season vying for top position among the three-year-old fillies at a mile, but this was not an exclusive collection and she herself failed to enhance her claims on her only remaining start, in a steadily-run race for the Coronation Stakes at Royal Ascot, meeting some trouble in running but for which she would probably have finished second to Balisada instead of equal third.

Valentine Waltz (IRE) (b.f. 1996)	Be My Guest (USA) (ch 1974)	Northern Dancer (b 1961)	Nearctic / Natalma
		What A Treat (b 1962)	Tudor Minstrel / Rare Treat
	Save Me The Waltz (b or br 1986)	Kings Lake (b 1978)	Nijinsky / Fish-Bar
		Mill Princess (b 1977)	Mill Reef / Irish Lass II

The syndicate whose colours Valentine Waltz carried in the latest season reportedly tried to sell her late on as a two-year-old only for her to fail the vet—she subsequently underwent a knee operation—but they succeeded

Kirby Maher Syndicate's "Valentine Waltz"

after the Coronation Stakes, the buyer being George Strawbridge, and she is now under the care of Neil Drysdale in America. Valentine Waltz was originally bought for 75,000 guineas at the Houghton Sales and there were plenty of auspicious connections in her pedigree. For a sire who has produced several top-class animals in his time, Be My Guest has been something of a bargain in recent years—he stood at IR 6,000 guineas in 1999—and Valentine Waltz provided an echo of his spectacular first-crop achievements because her grandam Mill Princess is a half-sister to Irish Bird who produced Be My Guest's superb Prix du Jockey Club, Irish Derby and Benson & Hedges Gold Cup winner Assert, as well as two other classic winners in Bikala and Eurobird to other sires. Mill Princess, a French mile and a quarter winner, went on to visit Be My Guest as well and the result was a smart sprinter, Astronef. Two of her other foals are the Group 3 winner The Perfect Life (dam of Rabah) and the sprint champion and Breeders' Cup Mile winner Last Tycoon. In short, Valentine Waltz is extremely well related. Save Me The Waltz won over six and a half furlongs in France on her only start as a two-year-old but failed to score in one listed race and two pattern events at three, her best effort being a two and a half lengths fifth in the six-furlong Prix de Meautry. Two of her four foals before Valentine Waltz were minor winners in France; her sixth foal, Ignite (by Bluebird), showed fair form in the latest season but remained a maiden after ten starts.

Valentine Waltz, a lengthy, quite attractive filly, had herself failed to score in four runs as a two-year-old when she was trained by Aidan O'Brien. Switched to John Gosden, placed efforts in the Rockingham Stakes and the Rockfel Stakes showed her true potential after she had won at the first attempt in Britain, a success which, following the Oaks d'Italia winner Zomaradah, made her the second classic winner to get off the mark in a 1998 Brighton maiden race. *J. H. M. Gosden*

VALENTINO   2 ch.c. (Apr 9) Nureyev (USA) 131 – Divine Danse (FR) 118 (Kris 135) [1999 6m* 7d⁴ Sep 18] 110,000Y: big, lengthy colt: has a markedly round action: fourth foal: brother to French 1m winner Divin Danseur and half-brother to French/US 7f to 9f winner Djinn (by Mr Prospector): dam French sprinting half-sister to Pursuit of Love: very green when winning newcomers race at Ascot in July: useful form when 5 lengths fourth of 5 to Giant's Causeway in Prix de la Salamandre at Longchamp: should stay 1m: likely to do better still. *P. W. Chapple-Hyam*   **103 p**

VALE OF LEVEN (IRE)   3 b.g. Fayruz 116 – Speedy Action (Horage 124) [1998 58, a68: 6s 6m 8d 7d⁴ a7g² 6s* a7g* a8g⁶ 1999 a8g a7g⁶ a6g 8m 8d 10g a7g 6g a8g 6g 6g 6m 7g Oct 15] sturdy gelding: modest handicapper: should stay 1m: acts on soft ground and fibresand: sometimes last to post: sold 1,000 gns. *K. A. Ryan*   **54**

VALES ALES   6 b.g. Dominion Royale 112 – Keep Mum 63 (Mummy's Pet 125) [1998 –: a8.5g 1999 8f 7f 10g Aug 16] sparely-made gelding: no form. *M. A. Peill*   **–**

VALLEY FLYER (IRE)   2 b.f. (Apr 9) Magical Wonder (USA) 125 – River Low (IRE) (Lafontaine (USA) 117) [1999 7g⁶ Jun 30] fifth foal: half-sister to 3-y-o Highfielder and 1¼m winner River Frontier (by Imperial Frontier): dam unraced half-sister to useful sprinter Imperial Bailiwick: showed little in Brighton seller: refused to enter stalls next intended outing. *R. P. C. Hoad*   **–**

VAL ROYAL (FR)   3 b.c. Royal Academy (USA) 130 – Vadlava (FR) (Bikala 134) [1998 9v* 1999 9g* 9.3v* 12g 9m² 10v* 9f* Sep 6] tall, lengthy colt: half-brother to several winners in France, including smart 1m winner Vadlamixa (by Linamix) and useful 1¼m/1½m winner Vadlawys (by Always Fair): dam French 2-y-o 9f winner: smart performer: won listed race at Chantilly and Prix de Guiche (comfortably beat Fils de Viane ½ length) at Longchamp in May, 5-runner Prix Guillaume d'Ornano (by head from Alrassaam, final start for A. Fabre) at Deauville in August and Grade 2 Del Mar Derby (by ½ length from Fighting Falcon, reportedly returned with cut near-hind) in September: stays 1¼m, well held in Derby at Epsom (decidedly edgy beforehand) when tried at 1½m: acts on any going. *J. C. Canani, USA*   **116**

VALS WHISPA   2 ch.c. (Jan 7) Timeless Times (USA) 99 – Skiddaw Bird (Bold **53 d**
Owl 101) [1999 5g⁴ 5m⁵ 5m 6f⁵ 7m⁶ 7.5s³ 7f⁵ 7m⁶ 7.5g 8g 8g Aug 30] 6,500Y: small
colt: fifth foal: brother to 5f (at 2 yrs)/6f winner Foreman: dam unraced: modest
maiden: well held last 4 starts: stays 7.5f: acts on soft and good to firm going: tried
visored. *S. E. Kettlewell*

VALUABLE IDEA (USA)   2 b.f. (Jan 26) Distant View (USA) 126 – Viviana **65 p**
(USA) (Nureyev (USA) 131) [1999 6m⁵ Jul 23] strong, lengthy filly: first foal: dam,
French 1m to 1¼m (listed race) winner, granddaughter of champion US filly Chris
Evert: favourite but better for race and bandaged behind, fifth of 10 to Princess Ellen
in maiden at Ascot, not knocked about after slow start: should do better. *B. W. Hills*

VANADIUM ORE   6 b.g. Precious Metal 106 – Rockefillee (Tycoon II) [1998 **56**
67: 10.3d⁶ 10m⁶ 10m 10.3g* 10.9m* 10.1s* 12m⁵ 12.4g² 10m 10s⁵ 10.1v 1999
12.4m⁵ 9.9v 10.1m⁵ 12m 12.1f³ 11m 12.1m⁵ 10.9d 10.1d Oct 20] leggy gelding:
modest handicapper: effective at 1¼m/1½m: acts on soft and good to firm going: tried
visored at 3 yrs, blinkered final start: has worn near-side pricker: held up.
W. McKeown

VANBOROUGH LAD   10 b.g. Precocious 126 – Lustrous 73 (Golden Act **56 d**
(USA)) [1998 48: 8f⁴ 8g⁵ 7g 8d⁴ 8.3d² 8s 8.3m 8.3g⁵ 10g⁶ 10m* 1999 10.2g* 10m⁵
10.5d* 12g⁴ 10.2m 12m⁶ 10m⁶ 10m 10.1m 10m 10.5m 9.9v 10s⁴ 10.2s⁶ Oct 26]
strong, lengthy gelding: modest handicapper: won amateur events at Bath (20 ran) in
May and Haydock in June: left M. Bolton after tenth start and not so good late in
year: stays 1½m: acts on any going: usually held up. *Dr J. R. J. Naylor*

VANCOUVER ISLE (IRE)   3 b.g. Erins Isle 121 – Eileenog (IRE) 62 (Kahyasi **68**
130) [1998 68: 7g⁵ 5d⁶ 6s 7.5v⁶ 1999 8.3v³ 10s³ 12g 12f⁵ 12m⁶ 14.1g⁴ 16.4d⁴ Aug
26] first foal: dam maiden daughter of Moyglare Stud Stakes winner Gayle Gal: fair
maiden handicapper: trained by J. Bolger in Ireland first 4 starts: probably stays
1¾m: acts on heavy ground: blinkered/visored in 1999. *G. B. Balding*

VAN DANTZIG (USA)   2 b.c. (Mar 9) Danzig (USA) – Sexy Slew (USA) (Slew **96 p**
O'Gold (USA)) [1999 6g³ 6d⁴ 6d* Oct 10] $675,000Y: strong, lengthy, good sort:
has plenty of scope: fifth foal: brother to a winner in Japan and closely related to a
winner in USA by Nureyev: dam graded stakes-placed winner up to 1m in USA from
family of El Gran Senor: shaped well when 2½ lengths third of 5 to Fath in maiden at
York (green to post) on debut: didn't need to repeat that form when winning
17-runner similar event at Naas in October by 2½ lengths from Crusoe: reportedly
thought to have injured himself in stalls when disappointing in between: may prove
best up to 1m: remains open to improvement. *A. P. O'Brien, Ireland*

VAN GURP   6 ch.g. Generous (IRE) 139 – Atlantic Flyer (USA) 98 (Storm Bird **63 §**
(CAN) 134) [1998 58§: 6.9m⁵ 8g 7s 7d 1999 a8g⁶ a8g⁴ a8g* a10g* a12g⁴ a9.4g
a10g⁵ a11g 8.3g* 9.2g³ 8f³ 9.2f 9.2m Aug 11] small, close-coupled gelding: modest
performer: won seller and claimer (left G. L. Moore) at Lingfield in February and
handicap at Hamilton in June: stays easy 1¼m: acts on equitrack, best turf form on
good going or firmer: blinkered once: refused to race last 2 starts, and one to treat
with considerable caution. *K. R. Burke*

VANILLE (IRE)   3 b.f. Selkirk (USA) 129 – Stormswept (USA) 74 (Storm Bird **72**
(CAN) 134) [1998 NR 1999 10m 8m³ 7m² 7m² 8.2f Oct 20] 38,000Y: angular filly:
third foal: half-sister to 1m winner Amico (by Efisio): dam, 2-y-o 5f winner, closely
related to Colonel Collins, Commander Collins and Breeders' Cup Sprint winner Lit
de Justice: fair maiden: trained by P. Chapple-Hyam first 4 starts: should stay 1m:
raced only on going firmer than good. *A. G. Foster*

VANISHING DANCER (SWI)   2 ch.g. (Feb 17) Llandaff (USA) – Vanishing **–**
Prairie (USA) 93 (Alysheba (USA)) [1999 8.1m 8d Sep 18] 11,000Y: third foal:
half-brother to smart French 3-y-o 1¼m winner La Sylphide (by Barathea) and
French 9.5f winner Verzasca (by Sadler's Wells): dam, Irish 1¼m and 1½m winner,
half-sister to very smart French performers Vetheuil (miler) and Verveine (up to
1½m): last in maiden at Haydock and minor event at Ayr. *K. R. Burke*

VANTAGE POINT   3 b.c. Casteddu 111 – Rosie Dickins 59 (Blue Cashmere 129) **57**
[1998 –: 6.1g 8v 8d a8g 1999 11.9f² 14.1g⁴ 11.9g² 12m⁴ 15.4m⁴ 11.9f³ 12d* 12.1m³ **a63**
12g⁴ 11.5g a12g³ a16.2g³ a13g² a12g² Dec 21] angular colt: shows plenty of knee

action: modest handicapper: won at Folkestone in August: creditable efforts last 4 starts: probably stays easy 2m: acts on all-weather and any turf going: often races prominently: tough and consistent. *K. McAuliffe*

VARIETY SHOP (USA)   3 b.f. Mr Prospector (USA) – Nimble Feet (USA) 82 **83 p** (Danzig (USA)) [1998 NR 1999 10s² Oct 2] seventh foal: closely related to useful 8.3f winner Yamuna (by Forty Niner) and half-sister to several winners, including smart sprinter Forest Gazelle (by Green Forest) and very smart performer up to 1¼m Eltish (by Cox's Ridge): dam 2-y-o 5f winner from family of 3-y-o Wince: 2 lengths second to Anamore in maiden at Sandown, looking likely winner when challenging 2f out but unable to sustain effort: sure to improve. *H. R. A. Cecil*

VASARI (IRE)   5 ch.g. Imperial Frontier (USA) 112 – Why Not Glow (IRE) **75 d** (Glow (USA)) [1998 81: 5d⁵ 5g⁶ 6g⁴ 6m⁶ 6m 7.1m³ 7.3g⁴ 1999 a8g³ 6d⁴ 6g⁶ 7g 6g 5g 5g 6s 5.2s 6d⁶ a7g Nov 24] close-coupled gelding: fair handicapper: sold out of W. Musson's stable 7,000 gns after ninth start: well below form last 4: effective at 6f, barely stays 1m: acts on good to firm going, heavy and equitrack: tried blinkered. *John A. Harris*

VAX NEW WAY   6 gr.g. Siberian Express (USA) 125 – Misty Arch (Starch **?** Reduced 112) [1998 7s a6g² 8g 6f 7f 5m² 5f 6d 5m⁶ 1999 a6g a7g a6g² a7.5g* a7.5g a6g³ a7g Jun 12] sturdy, lengthy gelding: fair performer for J. Spearing at 3 yrs: first win since in handicap at Boitsfort in April: well held in apprentice seller at Lingfield final start: stays 7.5f: acts on dirt, both wins in Britain on fibresand: often blinkered. *Alex Vanderhaeghen, Belgium*

VEGA NEUTRAL   3 ch.f. King's Signet (USA) 110 – Factuelle 43 (Known Fact **–** (USA) 135) [1998 –: 5.7m 5f a5g a6g a7g a5g 1999 a6g Jan 11] little sign of ability. *P. Shakespeare*

VEGAS   3 ch.f. Then Again 126 – Cazanove's Pet 51 (Tina's Pet 121) [1998 NR **44** 1999 a8g⁶ a7g⁶ a8f⁵ a8g Feb 2] 2,300Y: first foal: dam 7f winner: poor maiden: stays 1m: raced only on equitrack. *J. S. Moore*

VEIL OF AVALON (USA)   2 b.f. (Mar 31) Thunder Gulch (USA) 129 – Wind **95** In Her Hair (IRE) 114 (Alzao (USA) 117) [1999 6m³ 6g* 7m* 8s⁶ Sep 26] 200,000Y: well-made filly: fluent mover: second foal: half-sister to 3-y-o Glint In Her Eye: dam, 1¼m and 1½m winner and second in Oaks, from family of Nashwan and Unfuwain: useful form: won maiden at Lingfield in August and minor event at Newbury in September: under 7 lengths last of 6 in Fillies' Mile at Ascot final start: should stay at least 1¼m: acts on good to firm ground. *R. Charlton*

VELVET JONES   6 gr.g. Sharrood (USA) 124 – Cradle of Love (USA) 87 **43** (Roberto (USA) 131) [1998 43: 6g 7g⁵ 8g 7g⁶ 8m⁴ 6m 8d 1999 a6g⁵ a8g⁶ a8g⁵ 8.1m Aug 5] angular gelding: poor maiden: needs further than 6f and stays 1m well: acts on firm ground and all-weather: blinkered once. *G. F. H. Charles-Jones*

VENETIAN PEARL (IRE)   3 ch.f. Generous (IRE) 139 – Veronica (Persian **78** Bold 123) [1998 –p: 6m 1999 10m 12m² 11.8g³ 12s⁶ 14.1g⁴ 16g⁵ Nov 3] fair maiden: stays 2m: acts on good to firm going, below form on soft: sold 15,000 gns. *G. Wragg*

VENIKA VITESSE   3 b.g. Puissance 110 – Vilanika (FR) 81 (Top Ville 129) **77** [1998 –: a6s a7g 1999 a5g* 6s 6m a6m³ 5.9m* 6m³ 6.1g* 6m Aug 30] fair performer: won maiden at Lingfield in January and handicaps in large fields at Carlisle in June and Nottingham in August: likely to prove best at 5f/6f: acts on equitrack and good to firm going, probably on soft: races prominently. *T. D. Barron*

VENTURE CAPITALIST   10 ch.g. Never So Bold 135 – Brave Advance **74** (USA) 98 (Bold Laddie (USA)) [1998 96: 6s 5m⁴ 6g 5s 5d⁴ 6f² 6g⁴ 6m* 6f⁵ 6g 6s 1999 5d³ 6f² 6d 6g 5m⁴ 5m* 5m⁴ 6f⁵ 5g Aug 25] lengthy, deep-girthed gelding: unimpressive mover: fair nowadays: won claimer at Catterick in July: never dangerous in handicap at Carlisle (banned 40 days under non-triers' rule) final start: stays 6f: best on good going or firmer/straight track: effective blinkered, not tried for some time: best coming with late challenge off strong pace. *D. Nicholls*

VENTURE ISLAND (IRE)   3 br.f. Petardia 113 – Island Adventure (Touching **29** Wood (USA) 127) [1998 41: 6m 7f 7m⁴ 7.1m 7.5m 1999 a8.5g 8.2s 8g 8m 10.2g Jun 30] bad maiden: probably stays 1m: acts on good to firm going: blinkered last 2 starts: sold 3,100 gns, sent to Bahrain. *W. J. Musson*

VENUS 2 ch.f. (Feb 25) Bering 136 – Historiette (Chief's Crown (USA)) [1999 7d   –
Oct 11] tall, leggy filly: fourth foal: half-sister to 3-y-o Keebaar: dam unraced close
relative of high-class sprinter Polish Patriot: looked headstrong when well beaten in
maiden at Leicester: sold 5,500 gns. *Sir Mark Prescott*

VERBOSE (USA) 2 b.f. (Mar 17) Storm Bird (CAN) 134 – Alvernia (USA)   **79 p**
(Alydar (USA)) [1999 7d⁵ Oct 30] third foal: dam US 8.5f and 9f winner from family
of Sanglamore and Matiara: encouraging fifth of 16 to Garota Do Leblon in Newmarket maiden, keeping on well from rear under considerate handling: will stay at least
1m: sure to improve. *J. H. M. Gosden*

VERDURA 2 b.f. (Mar 16) Green Desert (USA) 127 – Spirit of The Wind (USA)   **– p**
(Little Current (USA)) [1999 6m Sep 18] quite good-topped filly: half-sister to 3-y-o
Siegfried, fairly useful 1m winner Moon Mistress (by Storm Cat) and useful 11f
winner North Wind (by Lomond): dam unraced half-sister to US Grade 1 1¼m
winner Dawn's Curtsey: bandaged off-hind and green, well held in Newbury maiden:
bred to stay 1m: should do better. *B. W. Hills*

VERONICA FRANCO 6 b.m. Darshaan 133 – Maiden Eileen (Stradavinsky   **86**
121) [1998 90: 12f* 14d* 16g* 14g⁵ 14m³ 12m* 12m³ 14m² 13.3g* 12m⁵ 12d 1999
14.1m 9.9g⁴ 11.6g² 14.8m 12m Aug 29] plain, leggy mare: fairly useful performer:
best effort in 1999 when 5 lengths second of 7 in minor event at Windsor in July:
effective at 1½m to 2m (at least when conditions aren't testing): acts on firm and
good to soft going: blinkered twice as 3-y-o: travels strongly and is held up: sold
50,000 gns in December. *P. R. Hedger*

VERPOSEN (IRE) 3 b.c. Posen (USA) – Jet Set Bunny (USA) (Northjet 136)   **47**
[1998 60: 6m³ 6.1m 7g² 8d⁶ 7s⁵ 7s 7s a8g 1999 9.7v 8.2m 10f⁶ 12d 11.6s² Aug 9]
compact colt: poor maiden: probably stays 1½m: acts on soft going: has worn visor/
tongue strap: unreliable: sold 1,200 gns, joined M. Hill. *J. Pearce*

VERSATILITY 6 b.m. Teenoso (USA) 135 – Gay Criselle (Decoy Boy 129)   **61**
[1998 NR 1999 11.9f 14.6s* 16.1s⁶ 16d Oct 21] leggy mare: modest handicapper:
won at Warwick in May: stays 15f: acts on soft going. *G. M. McCourt*

VIA CAMP 2 b.f. (Mar 4) Kris 135 – Honeyspike (IRE) 79 (Chief's Crown   **88**
(USA)) [1999 7f³ 7.5g* 7s Oct 2] good-topped filly: has a powerful, rounded action:
second foal: half-sister to 3-y-o Unicamp: dam, second over 1m in Ireland, half-sister
to smart 7f to 1¼m winner Casey Tibbs and granddaughter of Prix de Diane winner
Sweet Mimosa: fairly useful form: landed odds in maiden at Beverley in August:
creditable seventh of 12 to Agrippina in listed race at Newmarket final start: will be
suited by 1m+: acts on firm and soft ground. *E. A. L. Dunlop*

VIA DOLOROSA 3 ch.f. Chaddleworth (IRE) 103 – Ophrys 90 (Nonoalco   –
(USA) 131) [1998 NR 1999 7m May 16] closely related to 4-y-o Fredora and half-
sister to 2 winners, including 9-y-o Our Main Man: dam 2-y-o 7f winner from good
family: last of 16 in Kempton maiden (reportedly broke blood vessel). *M. Blanshard*

VIBRANCE (IRE) 3 b.c. College Chapel 122 – Shalara (Dancer's Image (USA))   –
[1998 77: 5d⁴ 1999 5m Jun 2] quite attractive colt: some promise in maiden at
Newmarket only 2-y-o start: no show in Newcastle seller 13 months later: sold 800
gns. *J. Noseda*

VICARS MISTRESS 2 b.f. (Apr 20) Today And Tomorrow 78 – Rectory Maid   –
74 (Tina's Pet 121) [1999 8v 7g Oct 19] 500Y: fifth foal: dam 2-y-o 6f winner: tailed
off in maidens. *J. S. Moore*

VICE PRESIDENTIAL 4 ch.g. Presidium 124 – Steelock 68 (Lochnager 132)   **60**
[1998 78d: 7.5s 6d⁵ 6g 7s* 7.1s* a7g³ a7g⁵ a6g 6.9d⁵ 6g 7.1m 7d 6g 1999 6v 5.1s 5m
6d a7g 7s a6g* a6g Dec 1] big gelding: easy mover: modest performer: won claimer
at Southwell in November: seems best at 6f/7f: acts on fibresand, raced mainly on
good ground or softer on turf: has won when sweating: inconsistent. *J. G. Given*

VICIOUS CIRCLE 5 b.g. Lahib (USA) 129 – Tight Spin (High Top 131)   **117**
[1998 92: 8.3f⁴ 10m² 10v* 10s 1999 10.1m* 10m² 13.9g* 12s* Sep 26]
Vicious Circle's change of ownership just days before winning the Tote
Ebor Handicap at York in August appeared to benefit all concerned. The jump
jockey Graham Bradley, who has now retired to concentrate on his bloodstock

Tote Ebor (Handicap), York—
a comfortable victory for Vicious Circle in Europe's most valuable handicap
over Travelmate (No.3), Mowbray and Eminence Grise, who is hampered near the line

agency, earned some good free publicity for brokering the deal—after being embroiled in controversy for what seemed an age over unrelated incidents. Ex-owner Graham Shiel made a tidy profit on his initial 9,000 guineas investment after selling Vicious Circle for a reputed six-figure sum (as well as securing a canny percentage of the Ebor prize-money). And Vicious Circle's new owners had taken on a gelding that was to provide them with two handsome paydays. Furthermore, Vicious Circle should have little trouble reaping further reward in 2000, when he looks set to make his mark in pattern company.

Vicious Circle made quite an impressive winning return to action in 1999 when taking a four-runner minor event by three lengths from Truant at Newcastle in June. He ran to a similar level of form next time out when second of five to Zindabad in a handicap at Ascot in July, but when stepped up markedly in trip and encountering a strong pace Vicious Circle was to show a great deal of improvement in the Ebor. He beat Travelmate by two lengths in a soundly-run twenty-one-runner race, held up and meeting a little trouble before quickening ahead under two furlongs out and staying on really strongly, despite drifting left. Incidentally, the win provided jockey Kevin Darley with a big staying handicap double—he also finished one place ahead of Travelmate when winning the Northumberland Plate on Far Cry. Even better was to come from Vicious Circle in the sixteen-runner Ritz Club Handicap at Ascot in September. Dropped back to one and a half miles, he showed himself a smart performer by beating Ligne Gagnante by three and a half lengths, pushed along with a fair bit to do over three furlongs out before producing a strong run to lead in the final furlong, soon going clear. Vicious Circle was originally bought with a view to contesting the top races over hurdles during the 1999/2000 season, but those plans were shelved in favour of a campaign on the level in 2000.

However, if he is given his chance over timber Vicious Circle will be a most interesting proposition.

Vicious Circle (b.g. 1994)	Lahib (USA) (b 1988)	Riverman (b 1969)	Never Bend
			River Lady
		Lady Cutlass (b 1978)	Cutlass
			Generals Sister
	Tight Spin (b 1985)	High Top (br 1969)	Derring-Do
			Camanae
		Petty Purse (b 1975)	Petingo
			Parsimony

The lightly-raced Vicious Circle is just about the best performer thus far by the high-class miler and winner of the 1992 Queen Elizabeth II Stakes, Lahib. Unlike his exploits on the track, Lahib's stud record is nothing out of the ordinary—though he has sired the pattern-race winners La-Faah and Mus-If. Vicious Circle's dam, Tight Spin, a daughter of the smart sprinter Petty Purse and a granddaughter of the smart sprinter Parsimony, finished well beaten in a maiden at Yarmouth as a three-year-old. Her stud record is equally uninspiring, her five other offspring having achieved no better than fair form. Vicious Circle

Ritz Club Stakes (Handicap), Ascot—Vicious Circle takes another valuable prize; Ligne Gagnante stays on for second place but has no chance with the winner

Mr D. Metcalf and Mr J. Samuel's "Vicious Circle"

is a tall, lengthy, angular gelding and an easy mover. He is effective at a mile and a half, though his style of racing suggests he will stay beyond a mile and three quarters—a distance much further than the average for Lahib's progeny—and he acts on any going. *L. M. Cumani*

VICKYBERTO 10 b.m. Laxton 105 – Silberto (Dadda Bert 95) [1998 NR 1999 11.1v Apr 10] third reported foal: dam winning staying chaser: of little account over hurdles/in points (has refused to race): tailed off in maiden at Hamilton on Flat debut. *D. A. Nolan*   —

VICKY VETTORI 2 b.f. (Mar 18) Vettori (IRE) 119 – Key West (FR) (Highest Honor (FR) 124) [1999 5m a6g a7g⁶ a8.5g a8g Dec 6] 1,800F, 1,800Y: first foal: dam unraced: no sign of ability. *A. G. Newcombe*   —

VICTOIRE 3 b.f. Makbul 104 – Boxit (General Ironside 121) [1998 NR 1999 7.7m 8g⁴ 8m 10d Oct 12] 2,200Y: close-coupled, angular filly: fourth reported foal: dam won selling hurdle: fair maiden: may prove best up to 1m: acts on good to firm going: reportedly pulled muscle in back second start, ran as if something amiss (tongue tied) final one. *H. Akbary*   **72**

VICTORIET 2 ch.f. (Feb 16) Hamas (IRE) 125§ – Wedgewood (USA) (Woodman (USA) 126) [1999 5s 5g⁴ 5m 5.1m 7m 7g Oct 19] 20,000Y: first foal: dam unraced daughter of Cheveley Park winner/Irish 1,000 Guineas runner-up Woodstream: no form after second start: often slowly away: tried blinkered. *A. T. Murphy*   **54 d**

VICTORIOUS 3 ch.c. Formidable (USA) 125 – Careful Dancer (Gorytus (USA) 132) [1998 66p: 6g 6.1d 6d⁴ 1999 7g 8.2m 7.1d* 7m 7m 8.5s 7.1s⁵ 7d Oct 26] strong   **72**

colt: fair handicapper: best effort to win at Haydock in August (16 ran): should prove best at 7f/1m: acts on good to soft going: has been slowly away. *B. A. McMahon*

VICTOR'S CROWN (IRE)   2 b.c. (Apr 30) Desert Style (IRE) 121 – Royal   **65**
Wolff (Prince Tenderfoot (USA) 126) [1999 6g⁶ 6m² 6.8m 6d Sep 16] IR 11,000F, IR 8,500Y: half-brother to several winners, including 3-y-o She-Wolff and 7f winner Cappuchino (by Roi Danzig): dam winning Irish sprinter: best effort in maidens (fair form) when short-head second of 10 to Premier Fois at Lingfield: below that form after: may prove best around 6f. *M. H. Tompkins*

VICTORY DAY (IRE)   2 b.c. (Apr 16) Fairy King (USA) – Inanna 105 (Persian   **105**
Bold 123) [1999 5m² 5g* 5m² 5.1m* 5f 5d Oct 9] IR 80,000Y: unfurnished colt: seventh foal: half-brother to 3-y-o Green God, fairly useful 6f (at 2 yrs) and 1m (in France) winner Leonine (by Danehill) and 12.5f winner Mrs Snuggs (by Law Society): dam Irish 2-y-o 6f and 1m winner: useful performer: won minor events at Windsor in May and Chester (beat Heathyardsblessing 3½ lengths) in July: ¾-length second of 13 to Warm Heart in Norfolk Stakes at Royal Ascot (attended by 2 handlers, edgy, found less than seemed likely) in between: below form in Group 3 events last 2 starts: may prove best at 5f: acts on good to firm going: joined D. Nicholls. *J. Noseda*

VICTORY SPIN   3 ch.g. Beveled (USA) – Victoria Mill 59 (Free State 125)   **82 +**
[1998 92p: 6m² 1999 7.5g* 8m Jun 19] fairly useful form: 66f (at 2 yrs) and 1m on Beverley in May: raced much too freely in falsely-run minor event at Ascot: stays 7.5f: sold 22,000 gns: sent to France. *L. M. Cumani*

VICTORY STAR   4 ch.g. Soviet Star (USA) 128 – Victoriana (USA) (Storm Bird   **–**
(CAN) 134) [1998 NR 1999 8.5s 10g⁶ 10m 10.5m 8.1m Jul 9] 6,000 3-y-o: smallish, sturdy gelding: fourth foal: half-brother to fairly useful winner around 1m Victorian Style (by Nashwan) and fairly useful stayer Sea Victor (by Slip Anchor): dam, French 5f winner, half-sister to 4-y-o Xaar: poor form at best (twice slowly away) in maidens/handicaps: sold 8,500 gns, and won over hurdles for M. Pipe in September. *Lady Herries*

VIDAME (FR)   4 b.g. Kaldoun (FR) 122 – Vallee Normande (FR) (Bellypha 130)   **49**
[1998 61, a–: 10d³ 11.5g³ 10v 11.7v⁵ a10g 1999 a12g 12v 11.9f⁶ 13.3f 12g Jun 9] compact gelding: poor maiden: should stay beyond 1½m: has been bandaged. *R. M. Flower*

VIE INDIENNE   3 ch.f. Indian Ridge 123 – La Strada (Niniski (USA) 125) [1998   **58**
NR 1999 7m 6m 6f³ a6g Nov 20] leggy, plain filly: first foal: dam, champion 2-y-o filly in Spain, sister to smart German/New Zealand middle-distance horse Vialli: modest maiden at best: should stay 1m: blinkered final start: sold 15,000 gns. *I. A. Balding*

VIGOROUS STROLL (USA)   3 b. or br.c. Strolling Along (USA) – Student of   **–**
Prague (USA) (Vigors (USA)) [1998 NR 1999 a8f a12g⁵ 7d 7m Aug 22] $4,000F, IR 24,000Y: second foal: half-brother to a winner in USA by Farma Way: dam, winner in USA up to 9f, half-sister to US Grade 3 1m winner Play For Love: no sign of ability. *P. S. McEntee*

VIGOUR   2 ch.f. (Jan 25) Lion Cavern (USA) 117 – Brave Revival 93 (Dancing   **78 +**
Brave (USA) 140) [1999 6m² 7g* Aug 11] first foal: dam, 1m winner (including at 2 yrs) who stayed 1¼m, half-sister to very smart sprinter Pivotal: barely needed to improve on promising debut to win maiden at Leicester in August by 1½ lengths from Grace And Power: should stay 1m: looked capable of better: sold 25,000 gns, sent to Kuwait. *Sir Michael Stoute*

VIKING PRINCE   2 b.g. (Apr 9) Chilibang 120 – Fire Sprite 83 (Mummy's   **–**
Game 120) [1999 5m⁵ 5m 6.1m a6g 5.1g Oct 21] 7,000Y: seventh foal: brother to 3-y-o Tommy Tittlemouse and half-brother to 3 winners, including 5-y-o Always Alight and 4-y-o Demolition Jo: dam 2-y-o 5f winner: no form. *M. Quinn*

VILLAGE NATIVE (FR)   6 ch.g. Village Star (FR) 131 – Zedative (FR) 74   **64**
(Zeddaan 130) [1998 67: a5g³ a5g⁵ a7g⁴ a6g⁶ 6.9d a7g 6g⁵ 7f 8.1d* 8s 8.3m 5.1d* 5m⁶ 7d⁵ a7g a6g* a6g a7g² 1999 a6g a5g a5g⁵ a7g⁵ a7g² a7g⁴ 6f 6g 8m² 5m⁶ 8m* Jun 23] lengthy, angular gelding: modest performer: made most to win claimer at

Salisbury in June: effective from 5f to 1m: acts on all-weather, firm and good to soft going: blinkered/visored nowadays. *K. O. Cunningham-Brown*

VILLAGE PUB (FR)   5 ch.g. Village Star (FR) 131 – Sloe Berry 82 (Sharpo 132) [1998 –: a6g a6g⁶ 6.1d⁶ 8.1g 1999 a7g a12g⁶ Feb 6] sparely-made gelding: disappointing maiden handicapper: effective at 5f to 1m: often blinkered. *B. J. Llewellyn*

VILLAMINTA (IRE)   2 b.f. (Apr 6) Grand Lodge (USA) 125 – Mrs Fisher (IRE) –
94 (Salmon Leap (USA) 131) [1999 6g Jun 2] fourth foal: half-sister to 3-y-o Gigetta and fairly useful 1m and (at 2 yrs) 8.5f winner Pedro (by Brief Truce): dam 7f winner, including at 2 yrs: second favourite, well held in Lingfield maiden. *Sir Mark Prescott*

VILLA ROMANA   2 b.f. (Mar 29) Komaite (USA) – Keep Quiet 54 (Reprimand   73
122) [1999 5.1m⁶ 5g³ 5.1m² 7m 6g⁴ 6m 6s⁴ 7s³ 5g⁴ 7d* 8d⁵ 8g Nov 30] 800F,
3,500Y: strong, lengthy filly: first foal: dam, maiden, bred to be suited by further than
1m: fair performer: won nursery at Brighton in October: stays 7f, possibly not 1m:
acts on good to firm and soft going. *A. Bailey*

VILLA WANDA   3 ch.f. Grand Lodge (USA) 125 – Gisarne (USA) 104 (Diesis –
133) [1998 –: 7d 1999 10m Apr 12] rangy, unfurnished filly: only a little promise in
maidens: sent to Australia. *W. Jarvis*

VINCENT   4 b.g. Anshan 119 – Top-Anna (IRE) 71 (Ela-Mana-Mou 132) [1998 –,   54 §
a54: 10s⁵ a12g² 11.6g 12d a14.8g 1999 a12g⁵ a12f* a16f⁶ a12g⁴ a12g 9.9m⁴ 12.4m   a58 §
12m 10g a11g³ 12m a14g⁴ a16.2g* a16.2g³ a16.2g⁴ a14g⁴ Sep 28] moody maiden
handicapper: won at Southwell (amateurs) in January and Wolverhampton (apprentices) in July: effective at 1½m to 2m: acts on all-weather and good to firm going:
visored twice (looked virtually unrideable on second occasion) at 3 yrs: carries head
high and tends to hang: unreliable. *J. L. Harris*

VINTAGE PREMIUM   2 b.c. (Apr 28) Forzando 122 – Julia Domna (Dominion   81
123) [1999 6d² 6g² 7.5g* 7.9d Oct 7] 17,000Y: tall, useful-looking colt: second foal:
dam poor half-sister to very smart 7f/1m winner Norwich: fairly useful performer:
won maiden at Beverley in September: stiff task in nursery at York final start: will
stay 1m. *R. A. Fahey*

VINTAGE TAITTINGER (IRE)   7 b.g. Nordico (USA) – Kalonji (Red Alert   26
127) [1998 –: 16s 16m 1999 16m³ 14g 16d⁴ Jun 28] small, plain gelding: bad handicapper: stays 2m: acts on good to firm going, good to soft and fibresand: successful
over fences in July. *J. S. Goldie*

VIOLET (IRE)   3 b.f. Mukaddamah (USA) 125 – Scanno's Choice (IRE) 54   70 d
(Pennine Walk 120) [1998 77: 7m 7d⁵ 7s⁴ a7g² a8g³ 1999 a8.5g* 7.1g 7.6g 7s a8.5g
a7g a8.5g a10g Dec 8] fair performer: didn't need to be at best to win maiden at
Wolverhampton (final start for Lord Huntingdon) in January: generally well held
after: stays 8.5f: acts on all-weather and soft going: left C. Dwyer after visored on
sixth start. *R. C. Spicer*

VIPEE   2 ch.g. (May 8) Risk Me (FR) 127 – Snow Wonder (Music Boy 124) [1999   63 d
5v² 5m a5g⁴ 6s² 5g 7s 5.3s Sep 29] 5,400Y: workmanlike gelding: has a round action:
fourth foal: brother to 6-y-o Bowlers Boy: dam little form: modest form first 4 starts,
including when second in seller at Goodwood: well held after, looking none too keen
once: stays 6f: acts on good to firm ground, soft and fibresand: blinkered final outing:
sent to Belgium. *A. Kelleway*

VIRBIUS (IRE)   3 ch.g. Wolfhound (USA) 126 – Virelai 72 (Kris 135) [1998 –: –
8g⁶ 8m 1999 a7g⁶ a7g 8g 10m 9.9d 8d 10.1d Oct 20] deep-girthed gelding: little
form: blinkered penultimate start. *J. Hetherton*

VIRGIN SOLDIER (IRE)   3 ch.g. Waajib 121 – Never Been Chaste (Posse   91
(USA) 130) [1998 60: 6m 10d³ 8v⁶ 1999 8f⁶ 12d³ 10.9s 12m 16.2m 12.1m
10.1d² a12g* 16g* a16g* a14g* a16.2g* a14g* a12.2g² a12g² Nov 29] angular, unfurnished
gelding: fairly useful handicapper: left T. Etherington after sixth start: much improved after, winning handicaps at Lingfield (twice), Musselburgh, Southwell (twice)
and Wolverhampton in October/November: better at 1¾m than shorter, and stays 2m:
acts on good to soft ground and all-weather: blinkered (tailed off) once: has won for
amateur: used to start slowly. *M. Johnston*

Hesmonds Stud's "Vision of Night"

VIRGOS BAMBINO (IRE)   2 ch.f. (Apr 30) Perugino (USA) 84 – Deep In   –
September (IRE) 50 (Common Grounds 118) [1999 6m 6m 7d 8m Sep 7] 2,200Y:
third foal: sister to 3-y-o Lohan: dam ran 3 times at 2 yrs in Ireland: little sign of
ability. *M. J. Fetherston-Godley*

VIRTUAL REALITY   8 b.g. Diamond Shoal 130 – Warning Bell 88 (Bustino   93
136) [1998 93: 8g* 7.3g⁶ 8d 8m* 8m² 9g 1999 8m³ 8.5d 8m⁵ 7.7m* 8m² 8d³ 8g Oct
16] angular gelding: fluent mover: fairly useful performer: made all in 6-runner
minor event at Warwick in July: effective at 1m, barely stays 1¼m: acts on firm and
good to soft going: visored once: often runs well fresh. *J. A. R. Toller*

VISION OF NIGHT   3 b.c. Night Shift (USA) – Dreamawhile 85 (Known Fact   115
(USA) 135) [1998 106p: 6m² 6m* 6m* 6g³ 1999 7g⁵ 6d* 6m³ 6f⁵ 6.5s⁴ 6g* 6s Sep
26] smallish, strong colt: smart performer: won minor event at Newbury in May and
Prix de Meautry at Deauville (by short head from Sampower Star, racing handily) in
August: ran creditably in between in Cork And Orrery Stakes at Royal Ascot (1¾
lengths third to Bold Edge), July Cup at Newmarket (5¾ lengths fifth to Stravinsky)
and Prix Maurice de Gheest at Deauville (3½ lengths fourth to Diktat): stays 6f: yet
to race on heavy going, acts on any other: usually waited with: game: sent to USA.
J. L. Dunlop

VISTA ALEGRE   4 b.g. Petong 126 – Duxyana (IRE) (Cyrano de Bergerac 120)   –
[1998 –, a84: a6g* a6g⁶ a5g² 5m 6g 5m 1999 5g 6.1f a5g² 6g Aug 14] sturdy gelding: a70
fair on all-weather: stays 6f: acts on equitrack, little recent form on turf. *P. J. Makin*

VITA SPERICOLATA (IRE)   2 b.f. (Feb 16) Prince Sabo 123 – Ahonita 90   94
(Ahonoora 122) [1999 5m* 5d² 5m⁵ 5g* 6m³ 5f⁵ 5m 6d⁶ 5d Oct 9] 1,800Y: lengthy,
rather plain filly: seventh foal: half-sister to 3 winners, including 1998 2-y-o 5f

1098

winner Head Honcho (by Primo Dominie) and 1½m/1¾m winner Special Risk (by Simply Great): dam 2-y-o 5f winner: fairly useful performer: won seller at Mussel-burgh (bought in 17,000 gns) in May and listed race at Sandown in July: mostly creditable efforts otherwise, dead-heating for sixth behind Seazun in Cheveley Park Stakes at Newmarket penultimate start: barely stays 6f: acts on firm and good to soft ground: sold to race in USA. *J. S. Wainwright*

VOGUE 3 b.f. Clantime 101 – Slipperose 72 (Persepolis (FR) 127) [1998 56: 6g 5.7g 1999 6m 5m 6.1m 8.5m 7f 6s Oct 4] modest maiden at best. *J. S. Moore* —

VOILA PREMIERE (IRE) 7 b.g. Roi Danzig (USA) – Salustrina (Sallust 134) [1998 72: 12.5s 12d⁵ 11.6m⁵ 13d* 14.4d 12.1s* 11.8s⁵ 1999 13v 14.1m* 14.4m 14m 14d² Jul 2] compact gelding: fair handicapper: won at Salisbury in May: stays 1¾m: acts on good to firm and heavy ground: tried visored. *Lady Herries* 76

VOLCANIC STAR 3 ch.f. Primo Dominie 121 – Lava Star (IRE) (Salse (USA) 128) [1998 58d: 5.3d 5.3g² 5d⁶ 6.9m⁵ 7g 7s 1999 8.2f⁶ 7g 9.3d³ 6g⁴ 7.5g⁵ 8s a8.5g* a9g³ a9g Dec 11] sturdy filly: modest form at best in Britain, well out of M. Bell's stable after second start: won maiden at Dortmund in October: stays 8.5f: acts on good to firm going and sand. *B. Hellier, Germany* ?

VOLONTIERS (FR) 4 b.g. Common Grounds 118 – Senlis (USA) 101 (Sensitive Prince (USA)) [1998 101: 7v⁴ 8.2m² 7.1d* 7m* 7d 7m 6g 7d³ 7g 1999 7g³ 7f 7g 7d 7d a8g² a7g⁵ Nov 24] close-coupled, quite attractive gelding: has a round action: useful on turf, fairly useful on all-weather: mostly disappointing after good reappearance effort: stays easy 1m: acts on good to firm going, good to soft and equitrack: free-going sort. *P. W. Harris* 96 a88

VOSBURGH 3 br.g. Petong 126 – Pour Moi 73 (Bay Express 132) [1998 55: 5s 5s³ 6g 6d² 6d⁴ 6m⁶ 1999 6m⁶ 6m 6m 6m² 7.1f³ a6g⁴ a6g Dec 17] quite attractive gelding: modest maiden handicapper on turf, poor on all-weather: left P. Calver before final start: should prove best at 5f/6f: acts on firm going, soft and fibresand: below form both outings in blinkers: drifted badly left fourth start: possibly none too genuine. *D. Carroll* 55 a46

VRENNAN 5 ch.m. Suave Dancer (USA) 136 – Advie Bridge 90§ (High Line 125) [1998 51, a69: a12g⁶ a11g 16v 14.1s a12g a12g³ 13.8s⁴ 1999 12g Jun 9] plain mare: modest handicapper nowadays: stays 14.8f: acts on all-weather and good to soft going: blinkered once at 4 yrs. *J. Akehurst* 51

W

WAABL (IRE) 3 b.c. Caerleon (USA) 132 – Amandine (IRE) (Darshaan 133) [1998 82p: 7s² 1999 8m⁴ 8g* 10m⁵ 9m² Sep 10] useful performer: landed odds in 6-runner maiden at Goodwood in June: ran well while shaping as though stamina being stretched in handicaps at Newmarket and Goodwood (1¼ lengths second to World Alert) after, travelling best but finding little both times: should prove best around 1m: acts on good to firm going, showed promise on soft: sent to UAE: may still do better. *J. H. M. Gosden* 99 +

WAASEF 6 b.g. Warning 136 – Thubut (USA) (Tank's Prospect (USA)) [1998 61: 8.1g 7m a10g² 9.7f⁶ a10g² a12g* a13g* a13g³ 1999 a12g a12g a12g a12g³ 12g a10g a12g May 25] big, rangy gelding: modest handicapper: broke a leg at Lingfield: stayed 13f: acted on equitrack, best turf run on good to firm going: dead. *Miss Gay Kelleway* 61

WADENHOE (IRE) 2 b.f. (Apr 4) Persian Bold 123 – Frill (Henbit (USA) 130) [1999 5.7g 7.1m² 7d* 7m 8m 8f 7.9d Oct 7] IR 20,000Y: workmanlike filly: seventh foal: half-sister to 3 winners, including 3-y-o Shakieyl and 5-y-o Sudest: dam, Irish 1½m winner, half-sister to high-class miler Pitcairn: fair performer: made all in maiden at Ayr in June: reportedly lame fourth start and well held after: should stay at least 1m: acts on good to firm and good to soft going. *M. R. Channon* 69

WADI 4 b.g. Green Desert (USA) 127 – Eternal (Kris 135) [1998 83: 10g 10g* 11.8f⁶ 1999 a10g a10g³ 8.5m² 8.3g⁶ 10m² 8f⁴ a10g⁴ 12.3m* 9.9m* 10m 12d Oct 9] 71 fair performer: won selling handicap at Warwick and claimer at Salisbury (final start for G. McCourt) in July: ran as if something amiss final 2 starts (broke blood vessel first of them): stays 1½m: acts on equitrack and firm ground: twice blinkered: has worn tongue strap: sometimes looks less than keen. *Dr J. R. J. Naylor*

WAFFLES OF AMIN 2 b.c. (Mar 15) Owington 123 – Alzianah 102 (Alzao 78 (USA) 117) [1999 6m⁵ 6m² 6m⁶ 6d² 6d³ a5g* a6g⁶ Nov 24] small colt: first foal: dam 5f/6f winner, including at 2 yrs, and second in Wokingham: fair performer: trained by J. Bethell on debut: won maiden at Wolverhampton in November: stays 6f: acts on all-weather, yet to race on extremes of going on turf. *R. Hannon*

WAFF'S FOLLY 4 b.f. Handsome Sailor 125 – Shirl 52 (Shirley Heights 130) 63 [1998 63: 6d* 6g 6s⁶ 6m 7g 7d⁶ 1999 6.1f³ 6s 6m³ 7m⁵ 6g³ 6d 6.1d³ 6d⁴ Nov 4] sparely-made filly: modest handicapper: may prove best at 5f/6f: acts on firm and good to soft ground: reportedly suffered heart problem once as 3-y-o. *G. F. H. Charles-Jones*

WAFIR (IRE) 7 b.g. Scenic 128 – Taniokey (Grundy 137) [1998 85: 10.3g⁵ 62 11.9d⁵ 10g⁴ 10.1s⁴ 10g⁴ 12m³ 12.4g* 12m 1999 12g 8.5d 8s⁴ 10m* 12g³ 10.3m⁵ 12.3m² 12m⁵ 12f⁶ Jul 31] rangy gelding: modest nowadays: won claimer at Redcar in June: effective at 1¼m/1½m: acts on good to firm and heavy ground: effective blinkered at 3 yrs: sometimes looks a hard ride: joined M. Hammond. *D. Nicholls*

WAGGA MOON (IRE) 5 b.g. Mac's Imp (USA) 116 – Faapette (Runnett 125) 47 § [1998 47: a12g⁵ 8d⁴ 8.3v 8.3d 8d⁶ 8.3d⁵ 8m 9.2m⁵ 8g a8.5g 1999 a8g 7m⁶ 8.2f² 8f a– § 10g 8m 8f 7f 8.5g 8f Sep 4] lengthy, good-bodied gelding: poor maiden handicapper: stays 1m, probably not 1¼m: acts on firm and good to soft going (well beaten on fibresand): tried visored/blinkered: inconsistent: sold 700 gns. *M. Brittain*

WAHJ (IRE) 4 ch.g. Indian Ridge 123 – Sabaah (USA) 65 (Nureyev (USA) 131) 102 [1998 105p: 8.3m* 7.1m* 1999 8.1s 7.1d³ 6m 7.1g⁴ 7d Oct 1] sturdy gelding: useful performer: generally disappointing in 1999 (raced too freely on occasions), best effort when 2¾ lengths third of 6 to Warningford in listed race at Haydock: will prove best up to 1m: acts on good to firm and good to soft going: has worn tongue strap: sold only 12,500 gns, joined C. Dwyer and gelded. *Sir Michael Stoute*

WAIKATO 2 ch.f. (Mar 15) Clantime 101 – Naufrage (Main Reef 126) [1999 5m – a5g⁴ 5m⁵ 6g 5g⁶ 5m Aug 26] 500Y: half-sister to 6-y-o Dovebrace and 1¼m/1½m winner Kismetim (both by Dowsing): dam unraced: little form, including in sellers: tends to carry head awkwardly: sent to Holland. *M. W. Easterby*

WAIKIKI BEACH (USA) 8 ch.g. Fighting Fit (USA) – Running Melody 86 40 § (Rheingold 137) [1998 48§, a69§: a8g³ a8g⁵ a8g* 8.3m a8g a8.5g² 10g a8g³ 8.1m a69 § 9.9m 8d a9.4g a10g* a8f 1999 a10f⁵ a8g⁴ a8g⁴ a8g* 10s 7m a7g³ a8.5g⁵ a10g³ a8g³ 8.1m a8g³ a8g⁴ a8g a8.5g* Dec 1] lengthy gelding: fair on all-weather, poor on turf: won amateur handicap at Lingfield in March and seller at Wolverhampton in December: effective at 1m to easy 1¼m: acts on firm going, good to soft and all-weather: tried visored, usually blinkered nowadays: unreliable. *G. L. Moore*

WAIN MOUNTAIN 3 b.g. Unfuwain (USA) 131 – Mountain Memory 109 (High – Top 131) [1998 74: a8g a7g² 1999 a10g Jan 2] best effort in maidens on final 2-y-o start: bred to stay well beyond 7f. *Sir Mark Prescott*

WAIT FOR THE WILL (USA) 3 ch.c. Seeking The Gold (USA) – You'd Be 87 Surprised (USA) 117 (Blushing Groom (FR) 131) [1998 76: 8.1g⁵ 10.2d⁵ 1999 10m⁶ 12m¹² 12m³ 13.9g 13.3m⁶ 12d Oct 9] tall colt: fairly useful handicapper: comfortably won amateur event at Salisbury in July: should stay beyond 13.3f: yet to race on extremes of going: blinkered last 2 starts. *G. L. Moore*

WAITING KNIGHT (USA) 4 b. or br.c. St Jovite (USA) 135 – Phydilla (FR) 64 126 (Lyphard (USA) 132) [1998 74§: 7d² 7s 8g 10g 8v² 8d³ 8m 9m²⁷ 7m 8.9g⁴ a8.5g⁶ 1999 a7g² a6g⁴ a8g* a8g³ a8g⁶ a7g² a8g⁶ a7g⁶ a7g⁵ a7g a12g² a11g a8.5g Dec 27] tall, workmanlike colt: poor mover: modest performer: won maiden at Lingfield in February: effective at 7f, probably 1½m: acts on all-weather, good to firm and heavy going: visored: sometimes races prominently/leads and looks less than hearty. *Mrs N. Macauley*

WAIT'N'SEE 4 b.g. Komaite (USA) – Kakisa 81 (Forlorn River 124) [1998 67, 53 a57: 6d² 6g 6s⁵ 6f 5m⁶ 7.1g⁴ 7.5m 7.5m a6g³ a6g a8g 1999 7g 5d⁶ a7g⁶ 7.8d 5s Oct 2] tall, workmanlike gelding: shows marked knee action: modest handicapper: left M. W. Easterby after third start: probably stays 7f: acts on firm going, soft and fibresand: tried blinkered: has worn tongue strap/crossed noseband and got upset in paddock: inconsistent. *Michael McElhone, Ireland*

WALES 4 ch.c. Caerleon (USA) 132 – Knight's Baroness 116 (Rainbow Quest (USA) 134) [1998 101: 12f⁴ 12.1m² 16.2d⁶ 14.8f⁵ 12d 11.9s² 1999 13.4m 12g* 10.1g 12f* 13.9f 12f⁶ 12m² 11.6m⁴ 11.9m⁴ 11.9v³ 11.8s⁴ Oct 25] compact colt: useful performer: made all in small fields in minor event at Goodwood in May and handicap at Newmarket (by 3½ lengths from Tayil) in June: ran creditably after only when placed in minor events at Ascot (second to Memorise) and Haydock (third to Maylane): effective at 1½m, probably 2m: acts on any going: tried blinkered: has worn crossed noseband: unreliable: sent to USA. *P. F. I. Cole* **108 §**

WALLACE 3 b.c. Royal Academy (USA) 130 – Masskana (IRE) (Darshaan 133) [1998 91p: 7g³ 7f⁴ 7m³ 7g⁵ 1999 8g² 8g 8g* 8.5g³ 8m* 8g⁴ 8m² 8d 8m Dec 12] rangy, rather finely-made colt: has scope: has a powerful, round action: smart performer: won maiden at Goodwood in May and listed event at Ascot (beat Haami by short head) in July: best effort when short-head second to Sugarfoot in Park Stakes at Doncaster in September, leading 1f out but caught on line: stays 8.5f: raced mainly on good going or firmer: reportedly pulled muscles in back second start: held up. *R. Hannon* **117**

WALNUT LADY 2 ch.f. (Mar 16) Forzando 122 – Princess Tateum (IRE) 69 (Tate Gallery (USA) 117) [1999 5d⁵ 5.1s⁶ a5g* 6s² 6d* 6d² 5g² 7g* 6s² 5s³ 5.5g⁶ 5s⁶ 6.5d 5.5v⁴ 6s² Nov 22] well-grown, lengthy filly: second foal: dam 1m/1¼m winner, also successful over hurdles: fairly useful performer: won seller at Southwell in May (left W. Turner), minor event at Lyon-Parilly in June and claimer at Maisons-Laffitte (claimed from A. Bonin) in July: ran well when third past post in listed race at Maisons-Laffitte (3 lengths behind Zeiting, promoted a place) final outing: stays 7f: acts on soft going and fibresand. *R. Collet, France* **91**

Gary A. Tanaka's "Wallace"

WALNUT WONDER 2 b.f. (Apr 22) Pyramus (USA) 78 – Super Style (Artaius —
(USA) 129) [1999 a7g Jul 23] eighth foal: half-sister to 3-y-o Lisala and 3 winners,
including 2-y-o 6f winners Yours By Right (by Entitled) and Threepenny-Bridge
(by Ballacashtal): dam French 11f winner: last in seller at Wolverhampton.
W. G. M. Turner

WALTER PLINGE 3 b.g. Theatrical Charmer 114 – Carousel Zingira (Reesh **44**
117) [1998 –: 8d a7g 1999 a7g⁶ 10f² 10m⁵ 12g³ 14.1m⁶ 12m 14.1f Oct 20] sturdy
gelding: poor mover: poor maiden handicapper: trained first 5 starts by S. Williams:
stays 1½m: acts on firm going. *A. G. Juckes*

WALTER THE WHISTLE 2 b.c. (Mar 5) Pips Pride 117 – Fleur de Lyphard —
(USA) 73§ (Lyphard (USA) 132) [1999 6s Aug 18] 9,000F, 13,000Y: half-brother to
a winner in Sweden by Sure Blade: dam, none too reliable 5f winner, half-sister to
high-class sprinter Faliraki: badly drawn, always behind in maiden at Kempton.
A. P. Jarvis

WALTHAM SKYLARK 4 b.f. Puissance 110 – Pear Drop 74 (Bustino 136) —
[1998 40: 5d 5m⁵ 5m 6g 1999 6m 8.2g 6g 6g Sep 20] poor maiden. *K. A. Morgan*

WANDERING WOLF 4 ch.g. Wolfhound (USA) 126 – Circle of Chalk (FR) 74 **72 d**
(Kris 135) [1998 –: 7.5s⁵ 7g 1999 7.1m 7.1g 7m⁶ 7d Aug 14] smallish, lengthy
gelding: fair maiden at best, lightly raced: should prove best up to 1m: has been
tongue tied. *S. P. C. Woods*

WANLASS DANCER 2 b.f. (Apr 2) King's Signet (USA) 110 – Consistent Queen —
55 (Queen's Hussar 124) [1999 5g 5m 6f 5m 5m 6d Oct 18] 1,000Y: plain, leggy
filly: closely related to 1½m winner Drama King (by Tragic Role) and half-sister to
several winners, including 1995 2-y-o 6f/7f winner Oriel Lad (by Colmore Row):
dam 1m seller winner: well beaten, including in sellers. *M. E. Sowersby*

WANNABE GRAND (IRE) 3 b.f. Danehill (USA) 126 – Wannabe 84 **116**
(Shirley Heights 130) [1998 107: 6g⁴ 6m² 6g* 6f* 6m⁴ 6f² 7d⁴ 6g* 1999 8m²
8m³ 6f 7f² 6g* 6m 9d³ 9f⁵ Nov 28]

Wannabe Grand, who had provided trainer Jeremy Noseda with his first
Group 1 winner when taking the Cheveley Park Stakes on her final outing at
two years, came close to giving him a second when she reappeared seven
months later in the One Thousand Guineas. With doubts about her stamina on
her first attempt beyond seven furlongs, Wannabe Grand didn't attract much
support and went off at 16/1; but in finishing half a length second of twenty-two
to the favourite Wince, Wannabe Grand left no-one in any doubt that she stayed
a mile well. Held up in the stand-side group, Wannabe Grand followed Wince
through from two furlongs out and stayed on strongly, leaving the impression
she'd have finished even closer had she been kept a little nearer to the leaders.
It represented further improvement from this smart filly, but she wasn't quite
able to reproduce that form in seven subsequent starts, which included
respectable efforts in the July Cup and the Stanley Leisure Sprint Cup.

Wannabe Grand gained her only win of the season in a six-furlong listed
event at Pontefract in August. The Flying Fillies' Stakes, worth just over
£18,000 to the winner, is the richest race run at the course, and the seven-runner
field also included a couple of well above average sprinters in Pipalong and
Noble One, as well as the subsequent Ayr Gold Cup runner-up Evening
Promise. As when she'd won the Cherry Hinton Stakes as a two-year-old,
Wannabe Grand was given most to do by Pipalong. Wannabe Grand, who had
found little off the bridle when second to Selfish in a listed race at Goodwood
on her previous start, was produced late at Pontefract, her rider going so far as
to take a pull halfway up the short straight. This allowed Pipalong to make first
run, but Wannabe Grand responded well to pressure this time and overhauled
her well inside the final furlong to win by half a length. Two of Wannabe
Grand's three subsequent races took place in the States, both of them over nine
furlongs. She ran respectably enough to say she's effective at that trip, finishing
four lengths third of nine to Perfect Sting in the Queen Elizabeth II Challenge
Cup at Keeneland on the first occasion.

*Flying Fillies' Stakes, Pontefract—a deserved win for Guineas runner-up Wannabe Grand,
who wears down Pipalong (nearer camera)*

		Danzig	Northern Dancer
	Danehill (USA)	(b 1977)	Pas de Nom
	(b 1986)	Razyana	His Majesty
Wannabe Grand (IRE)		(b 1981)	Spring Adieu
(b.f. 1996)		Shirley Heights	Mill Reef
	Wannabe	(b 1975)	Hardiemma
	(b 1990)	Propensity	Habitat
		(br 1984)	Kalamac

Wannabe Grand, who has been retired to stud, is the first foal of Wannabe, a fairly useful winner at a mile in Britain at three years and at a mile and a quarter in France at four. Wannabe's second foal Generic (by Fairy King), who cost IR 150,000 gns as a yearling, showed enough on the second of his two starts to suggest that he should win a race or two in the next season. Her 1998 foal by Alzao and her 1999 foal by Night Shift were bought for 330,000 gns and 170,000 gns respectively, making Wannabe herself seem all the more a bargain at just 15,000 gns at the 1994 December Sales. Wannabe Grand's grandam Propensity (the dam of the Cheveley Park runner-up Tanami) showed fairly useful form over five and six furlongs at two years, but disappointed on her only start at three; her great grandam Kalamac was fairly useful up to a mile in France. Wannabe Grand, a sturdy, lengthy filly, is a good walker with a quick, fluent action. She acted on firm and good to soft going. *J. Noseda*

WANSFORD LADY   3 b.f. Michelozzo (USA) 127 – Marnie's Girl (Crooner –
119) [1998 –: 10s 1999 10f Apr 29] workmanlike filly: no promise in maidens.
C. N. Kellett

WAR BABY   3 b.f. Warrshan (USA) 117 – Dutch Czarina 45 (Prince Sabo 123) –
[1998 NR 1999 7g 8.5s 8m 15.4m[5] 11.5m 10g Oct 11] lengthy filly: second foal:
sister to 4-y-o Czar Wars: dam, 1¼m winner at 4 yrs, half-sister to useful stayer
Double Dutch: little sign of ability. *Miss B. Sanders*

Norfolk Stakes, Royal Ascot—Warm Heart forges ahead of Victory Day in the closing stages

WAR CABINET 3 b.c. Rainbow Quest (USA) 134 – Balleta (USA) 87 (Lyphard **100** (USA) 132) [1998 NR 1999 12g⁵ 12m² 14.1m* 16.2m Jun 16] smallish, good-topped colt: fourth foal: half-brother to smart French 6f (at 2 yrs) and 1m winner Barricade (by Riverman): dam, 1m to 1¼m winner, sister to Dancing Brave and Prix de Diane/Vermeille winner Jolypha: useful form: won maiden at Nottingham in May: best effort when about 9 lengths equal eighth to Endorsement in Queen's Vase at Royal Ascot final start, though unimpressive to post and drifted markedly left in straight: may prove best at 1¾m/2m: raced only on good/good to firm going. sold only 10,000 gns in October. *H. R. A. Cecil*

WARDAT ALLAYL (IRE) 2 b.f. (Jan 28) Mtoto 134 – Society Lady (USA) 75 **87** (Mr Prospector (USA)) [1999 7m³ 7m* 7m 8m Sep 9] third foal: half-sister to smart 1998 2-y-o 5f/6f winner Bint Allayl (by Green Desert): dam, ran 4 times at 2 yrs (second at 7f), daughter of champion Canadian filly La Voyageuse and grand-daughter of Fanfreluche: fairly useful form: won minor event at Newbury in July, racing freely and leading late on: disappointing in Group 3 events at Goodwood and Doncaster after: should stay at least 1m: swished tail on debut. *M. R. Channon*

WARM HEART (USA) 2 ch.c. (Mar 25) Diesis 133 – Warm Mood (USA) **109** (Alydar (USA)) [1999 5m* 5m* 6s² 6d⁴ Sep 30] $350,000Y: sturdy, attractive colt: has a quick, fluent action: second foal: dam, unbeaten in 4 starts up to 9f in USA, daughter of champion Canadian sprinter Summer Mood: useful form: won maiden at Newcastle and Norfolk Stakes at Royal Ascot (by ¾ length from Victory Day) in June: beaten 4 lengths when in frame after in Prix Morny at Deauville (best effort, second of 7 to Fasliyev) and Middle Park Stakes at Newmarket (fourth of 6 to Primo Valentino): should stay 7f: acts on soft and good to firm going. *J. H. M. Gosden*

WARNINGFORD 5 b.h. Warning 136 – Barford Lady 93 (Stanford 121§) [1998 **117** 110: 7s 7d² 7.9g⁶ 7g 7g² 7g⁵ 7g* 7m 6g⁶ 7d* 7g 7g³ 7g 1999 7d* 7v* 6s² 7.1d* 7g² 7.3d² 6s 7g⁶ Oct 16] lengthy, good-topped horse: smart performer: better than ever in 1999, winning minor event at Warwick and Peter Sandrovitch Leicestershire Stakes

Barford Bloodstock's "Warningford"

at Leicester (by 2 lengths from Wind Cheetah) in April and listed race at Haydock (by length from Tumbleweed Ridge) in June: ran creditably otherwise when runner-up, beaten 1¾ lengths by Sampower Star in Duke of York Stakes at York, ½ length by Tumbleweed Ridge in Prix de la Porte Maillot at Longchamp and a head by Trans Island in listed race at Newbury: best form at 6f/7f on good going or softer (acts on heavy): effective visored or not: usually held up: consistent. *J. R. Fanshawe*

WARNING NOTE (IRE) 2 b.c. (Mar 25) Zieten (USA) 118 – Cachet (IRE) **83 p** (Warning 136) [1999 7s a8g² Nov 24] 38,000F, 15,000Y: big, lengthy, good-topped colt: second foal: dam unraced half-sister to smart middle-distance performer Papering: much better effort in maidens when neck second of 11 to Forbearing, pair clear, at Lingfield, still looking bit green: joined M. Dickinson in USA: should improve again and win a race. *R. Hannon*

WARNING REEF 6 b.g. Warning 136 – Horseshoe Reef 88 (Mill Reef (USA) **71** 141) [1998 73, a62: 8.3v⁵ a9.4g² 9v a11g⁶ 12m³ 9.9d² 12d* 11.4g* 12m² 12m* 12.3m² 12g⁵ 12.1s³ 10.4g³ 12v 1999 10d 11.9d 12m² 10.5d³ 12m⁵ 11.4m⁵ 12m³ 12.3m³ 12m³ 12m² 11.9m⁴ 12m 10.4g⁴ 10d Oct 18] small, workmanlike gelding: poor mover: fair handicapper: best at 1¼m/1½m: acts on fibresand, good to firm and soft going: sometimes flashes tail and looks none too keen (best held up): consistent, but needs things to go his way: sold 5,000 gns. *E. J. Alston*

WARREN KNIGHT 6 b.g. Weldnaas (USA) 112 – Trigamy 112 (Tribal Chief **–** 125) [1998 51: 8m⁴ 9.9m 1999 8g 9d Jun 4] good-quartered gelding: modest maiden handicapper: stays 9f: acts on good to firm ground: sometimes slowly away. *C. A. Horgan*

WARRING 5 b.g. Warrshan (USA) 117 – Emerald Ring 74 (Auction Ring (USA) **58** 123) [1998 66, a–: 8f 8d⁵ 8s² 8.3g* 8d⁴ 8g² 8.3f* 8m 8.5m⁴ 8d 8.2s a10g a8.5g 1999 **a–** 8.3m 8g² 8g 8.3s² 8d 7.1m⁵ 8d⁴ 8.2s Nov 1] sturdy gelding: modest handicapper: stays 1m well: acts on firm and soft going, no form on all-weather: has had tongue tied: none too consistent. *M. S. Saunders*

WARRING KINGDOM   3 b.g. Warrshan (USA) 117 – Rise And Fall (Mill Reef   **78**
(USA) 141) [1998 –: 5s a6g a8g 1999 8m⁶ 10f³ 10f⁵ 16d² 17.2g* 16m* 16f* 16.1s³
18d² 16g Nov 3] leggy, plain gelding: fair handicapper: won at Carlisle in August
and Musselburgh (twice) in September: broke down fatally returned to latter course:
stayed 2¼m: acted on firm and soft going. *John Berry*

WARRIOR KING (IRE)   5 b.g. Fairy King (USA) – It's All Academic (IRE) 91   **32**
(Mazaad 106) [1998 43, a–: 6.9d 8g 7g⁶ 6g⁴ 6d 8g a9.4g a8g 1999 8.2m 10.1m⁶ 10s
16.2m a8.5g a8g Dec 17] poor performer: probably stays 1¼m: acts on soft and good
to firm ground: tried blinkered/visored: has wandered. *Mrs S. Lamyman*

WARRIOR QUEEN (USA)   2 b.f. (Mar 11) Quiet American (USA) – Call Me   **103 +**
Fleet (USA) (Afleet (CAN)) [1999 6m* 5m³ 6g⁶ 6m* a8.5f Nov 6] $215,000Y: tall,
rangy, good sort: first foal: dam unraced half-sister to dam of high-class French 1m
to 1¼m winner Green Tune and Cheveley Park winner Pas de Reponse out of
half-sister to Storm Bird: useful performer: won maiden at Leopardstown in May and
5-runner listed race at the Curragh (comfortably by length from Poco A Poco) in
September: close third to Shining Hour in Queen Mary Stakes at Royal Ascot second
start: disappointing in Lowther Stakes at York (led by 2 handlers and on toes) and
Breeders' Cup Juvenile Fillies at Gulfstream otherwise: stays 6f: upset in stalls
(reportedly hit head as consequence) at Ascot, and withdrawn lame at start before
Cheveley Park Stakes intended fifth start. *A. P. O'Brien, Ireland*

WARS (IRE)   4 b.f. Green Desert (USA) 127 – Ardassine (Ahonoora 122) [1998   **60**
NR 1999 7s 8.5m⁶ 7m 6g 7d⁵ 7m 7f 7m Sep 7] 34,000 3-y-o: strong, well-made filly:
ninth foal: sister to very smart 7f to 9f performer Gabr and fairly useful 6f winner
Intisab and half-sister to 2 winners, including smart 1¼m and 13.3f winner Kutta (by
Old Vic): dam 1½m winner from family of Slip Anchor: flattered in listed race on
second start, and just modest form at best after: blinkered penultimate start: has been
bandaged in front/tongue tied. *J. E. Banks*

WASEYLA (IRE)   2 b.f. (Feb 8) Sri Pekan (USA) 117 – Lady Windley (Bail-   **71**
lamont (USA) 124) [1999 7m 8v⁵ 8g⁴ Nov 3] 40,000F, 60,000Y: second foal: dam,
French 11f winner, out of Prix de Diane winner and Arc second Northern Trick, the
family of 4-y-o Shiva: fair form in maidens on first and third starts, though carried
head awkwardly and found little in visor on latter occasion: bred to stay 1¼m+: well
held on heavy ground. *J. H. M. Gosden*

WASI   2 b. or br.c. (Feb 13) Emperor Jones (USA) 119 – Miss Ivory Coast (USA)   **–**
(Sir Ivor 135) [1999 7d Oct 22] 7,000F, 50,000Y: fourth foal: half-brother to 5-y-o
Abajany: dam French 9f winner: burly, well beaten in maiden at Doncaster: sold
10,000 gns. *J. H. M. Gosden*

WASP RANGER (USA)   5 b.g. Red Ransom (USA) – Lady Climber (USA)   **79**
(Mount Hagen (FR) 127) [1998 NR 1999 8g 8.1m⁴ 9.9m 8g⁴ 10m* 9f 12s 10m²
10.3m 10m Sep 18] very tall gelding: easy mover: fair handicapper: well backed
when convincing winner at Kempton in July: stays 1¼m, probably not 1½m: acts on
good to firm and good to soft ground, probably on firm: blinkered (ran well) once at
3 yrs: usually held up. *G. L. Moore*

WATCHING   2 ch.c. (May 18) Indian Ridge 123 – Sweeping 104 (Indian King   **103**
(USA) 128) [1999 6m³ 5.1d* 5m³ 6m² 6g² 7g⁵ 6m⁴ 5s² 5d³ Oct 9] 65,000F, 16,000Y:
neat colt: sixth foal: half-brother to 3 winners, including 6f winner Desert Lynx (by
Green Desert) and 5-y-o Puteri Wentworth: dam, 2-y-o 6f winner, out of half-sister to
Middle Park winner Bassenthwaite: useful performer: won maiden at Chester in
June: progressed steadily after, good third to Kier Park in Cornwallis Stakes at Ascot
final start: effective at 5f/6f: acts on soft and good to firm going. *R. Hannon*

WATER BABE   2 b.f. (Feb 10) Lake Coniston (IRE) 131 – Isabella Sharp 83   **59**
(Sharpo 132) [1999 5d 5.1f⁵ 5.1g Oct 21] 16,000Y: second foal: dam, 2-y-o 5f
winner, out of half-sister to Arc winner Saumarez: modest form on first 2 starts in
maidens, well beaten final one: should stay 6f: slowly away last 2 outings.
J. W. Payne

WATER ECHO (USA)   2 b.f. (Mar 5) Mr Prospector (USA) – Magic of Life   **79**
(USA) 118 (Seattle Slew (USA)) [1999 6f⁶ 6m² 6f³ 6d* 7g³ 8s 5.5v³ Nov 2] tall,
lengthy, rather unfurnished filly: has scope: seventh foal: half-sister to 3 winners at

1¼m+, notably useful From Beyond (by Kris): dam, Mill Reef and Coronation Stakes winner, from excellent family: fair performer: won minor event at Brighton in August: creditable third afterwards in nursery at Yarmouth (final start for Sir Michael Stoute) and in 4-runner minor event at Maisons-Laffitte: stays 7f: acts on good to firm and heavy going: sweating, edgy (swished tail) and shade mulish to post third start. *D. Sepulchre, France*

WATER FLOWER   5 b.m. Environment Friend 128 – Flower Girl 108 (Pharly (FR) 130) [1998 NR 1999 12g* 16.2m 12.3m² 12.1m* 12g 17.2s Sep 27] fair handicapper: won at Salisbury in June and Chepstow in July and August, first 2-named 18-runner amateur races: stays 1½m: acts on good to firm going: has been bandaged behind. *B. R. Millman*   **79**

WATERFORD SPIRIT (IRE)   3 ch.g. Shalford (IRE) 124§ – Rebecca's Girl (IRE) (Nashamaa 113) [1998 77: 6.1d⁵ 5m⁵ 5g² 5s² 1999 6d⁶ 6v 5d 5m⁴ 5d* 5g 5s⁴ 5g Jul 2] big, good-topped gelding: has scope: fairly useful handicapper: won at Thirsk in May: reportedly lame final start: headstrong, and may prove best at 5f: has form on good to firm going, goes well on good to soft/soft. *T. D. Barron*   **82**

WATERFRONT (IRE)   3 b.g. Turtle Island (IRE) 123 – Rising Tide 101 (Red Alert 127) [1998 75: 7f 1999 6g⁵ 7m² 8d 6g 7f⁵ 9f 6g 7.1f 8m 8s Oct 4] angular, deep-girthed gelding: fair maiden: left P. Chapple-Hyam after fourth start: may prove best up to 7f: acts on good to firm going: visored once. *R. Bastiman*   **75 d**

WATERGOLD (IRE)   2 ch.g. (Apr 24) Shalford (IRE) 124§ – Trust Sally 65 (Sallust 134) [1999 7d 8g 7.1g Nov 3] IR 3,900F: half-brother to several winners, including 7f (at 2 yrs) to 1½m (in France) winner Pinocchio Boy (by Soviet Lad): dam 5f seller winner: soundly beaten in maidens. *I. Semple*   **–**

WATERGRASSHILL   2 b.f. (Mar 17) Terimon 124 – Party Game 70 (Red Alert 127) [1999 6m 7d 6d a6g² a8g⁵ a6g⁴ Dec 22] sister to modest 6f winner Third Party and half-sister to several winners, including 6-y-o Passion For Life: dam 6f winner: modest form: takes good hold, and likely to prove best at 6f/7f: acts on equitrack, yet to race on extremes of going on turf. *N. A. Callaghan*   **56**

WATER HUNTER   2 ch.g. (Feb 22) Mukaddamah (USA) 125 – Oasis (Valiyar 129) [1999 5m 5m 6m a6g* a7g* 7d² a8.5g² 7.6s² 9g² Sep 22] 13,500F, 10,000Y: rather leggy gelding: fifth foal: half-brother to 3-y-o Jaguar, 7f/1m winner White Settler (by Polish Patriot) and 7f winner Bold Spring (by Never So Bold): dam, won twice over hurdles, half-sister to smart 1991 2-y-o 5f winner Magic Ring: fairly useful performer: won claimer at Southwell in July and nursery at Wolverhampton in August: faded in testing conditions in minor event at Chester final start: will prove best at 7f/1m: acts on fibresand and good to soft going: sold 36,000 gns, sent to USA. *J. W. Payne*   **81 a89**

WATER JUMP (IRE)   2 b.c. (Apr 17) Suave Dancer (USA) 136 – Jolies Eaux 73 (Shirley Heights 130) [1999 7.6g² 8.1m² 8.3s* Sep 27] 14,000Y: fourth foal: half-brother to a winner in USA by Aragon: dam, maiden who probably stayed 1¼m, half-sister to Galtres winners Deadly Serious and Sans Blague: fairly useful form when second in maidens at Lingfield and Chepstow: didn't need to be at best to win similar event at Hamilton, edging left under pressure: will stay at least 1¼m. *J. L. Dunlop*   **84**

WATER LOUP   3 b.f. Wolfhound (USA) 126 – Heavenly Waters 64 (Celestial Storm (USA) 132) [1998 54: 6g⁵ 7s⁶ 1999 8.3m³ 8.1m⁴ 10m 9m⁴ 10g 8s 8s Sep 27] modest maiden handicapper: stays 1¼m: acts on good to firm going. *W. R. Muir*   **63**

WATHBAT MUJTAHID   2 ch.c. (Jan 30) Mujtahid (USA) 118 – Wathbat Mtoto 88 (Mtoto 134) [1999 7d 7g³ 7d² Nov 1] strong, long-backed colt: first foal: dam, 1¼m winner who stayed 1½m, from family of Stravinsky: progressive form in maidens, second of 15 to Norton at Redcar on final outing: should stay 1m: got worked up beforehand on debut. *A. C. Stewart*   **78**

WATKINS   4 ch.g. King's Signet (USA) 110 – Windbound Lass 60 (Crofter (USA) 124) [1998 –, a57: a8g² a8g 10g 8f 12.1m⁶ 11.7d 1999 11.8g 18m 17.2m⁵ Jul 5] modest maiden handicapper: no form since 3-y-o reappearance, but successful over hurdles in July. *A. T. Murphy*   **–**

WAVE OF OPTIMISM 4 ch.g. Elmaamul (USA) 125 – Ballerina Bay 75 **81**
(Myjinski (USA)) [1998 74: 11.5m³ 11.5g² 12g² 14.1s* 1999 12g 16.4s* 16s³ 20m
Jun 15] tall, rather sparely-made gelding: fairly useful handicapper: won at Sandown
in April: ran well next time: stays 2m, probably not 2½m: acts on soft and good to
firm ground: takes good hold: has given trouble stalls. *J. Pearce*

WAVERLEY ROAD 2 ch.c. (Mar 25) Pelder (IRE) 125 – Lillicara (FR) (Cara- **66 p**
colero (USA) 131) [1999 8d⁴ Oct 27] half-brother to several winners, including
useful 6f (at 2 yrs) to 8.5f winner Lilli Claire (by Beveled): dam unraced: 14/1, fair
form when fourth of 10 to Scotty Guest in maiden at Yarmouth: should stay 1¼m:
should improve. *A. P. Jarvis*

WAX LYRICAL 3 b.f. Safawan 118 – Hannah's Music 85 (Music Boy 124) **94**
[1998 NR 1999 6m* 6d Sep 15] first foal: dam, 5f winner, ran only at 2 yrs: won
maiden at Salisbury in May by 3 lengths from Borders, travelling strongly before
sent on 2f out: well held in minor event at Yarmouth final start: joined Dr J. Naylor.
J. A. R. Toller

WAY BACK (IRE) 3 b.g. Toca Madera 111 – My Robin (IRE) (Cyrano de –
Bergerac 120) [1998 53: 7.5m³ 6g 7m 7.9g 1999 9.9g 8m 7m 7.5m 9.9g Aug 28]
smallish gelding: modest maiden at best: should stay at least 1m. *B. S. Rothwell*

WAYNE LUKAS 4 b.g. Don't Forget Me 127 – Modern Dance (USA) (Nureyev –
(USA) 131) [1998 72: 9m⁶ 10g⁵ 9m* 8.1g 8g 1999 9v 10f Oct 20] fair 9f winner in
1998 for H. Cecil: no form since. *P. R. Hedger*

WAY OF LIGHT (USA) 3 b. or br.c. Woodman (USA) 126 – Salchow (USA) **115**
(Nijinsky (CAN) 138) [1998 116p: 6.5d* 8s² 8v* 1999 8s⁵ 8m⁴ 9s⁵ 8v⁴ 8m 10d² 12d⁵
Oct 17] big, good-topped colt: smart performer: successful in Grand Criterium at
Longchamp at 2 yrs: ran creditably most starts in 1999 without winning: in frame in
Poule d'Essai des Poulains at Longchamp (5¼ lengths fourth to Sendawar) in May,
Prix Jacques le Marois at Deauville (3½ lengths fourth of 5 to Dubai Millennium)
in August and Prix du Prince d'Orange at Longchamp (length second of 4 to State
Shinto) in September: stayed 1½m: acted on good to firm going, though went well on
heavy: blinkered (below form) third start: normally held up but made running second
outing: reportedly to stud in Australia. *P. Bary, France*

WEALTHY STAR (IRE) 4 b.c. Soviet Star (USA) 128 – Catalonda (African **101**
Sky 124) [1998 90p: 8f⁶ 8.2g* 1999 6d⁴ 7d 7g 8d Oct 30] rangy, attractive colt: useful
performer: ran creditably first 3 starts in 1999, about 3 lengths fourth to Sakha in
minor event at Yarmouth on first: not certain to stay beyond 1m: acts on good to soft
going: has had tongue tied. *B. Hanbury*

WEAVER OF WORDS 3 b.f. Danehill (USA) 126 – Canadian Mill (USA) 115 **78**
(Mill Reef (USA) 141) [1998 81: 6m⁵ 7g² 7d² 7g² 1999 6v³ 6g² 6g⁴ 7f* 7.1f 7m³
Jul 21] leggy, quite good-topped filly: good mover: fair performer: won maiden at
Lingfield in June: saddle slipped penultimate start: ran well final one: will be suited
by 1m: acts on firm going, probably not on softer than good: has been bandaged: sent
to Australia. *B. W. Hills*

WEAVER SAM 4 ch.g. Ron's Victory (USA) 129 – Grove Star (Upper Case –
(USA)) [1998 NR 1999 10.3m⁵ 10.5f⁵ 12m⁵ 17.1s 18d Oct 18] 700 3-y-o: quite
good-topped gelding: half-brother to several winners, including smart Stella Grande
(by Record Token), best up to 1¼m: dam ran once: bumper winner: well beaten in
maidens/handicaps. *J. Norton*

WEDOUDAH (IRE) 3 b.f. Sadler's Wells (USA) 132 – Salvora (USA) **80**
(Spectacular Bid (USA)) [1998 NR 1999 8m⁶ 10g³ 11.7f⁶ 12d³ 14.8d⁶ 11.7s² Oct
26] 80,000Y: closely related to 2 winners abroad by Tate Gallery, including Special
Gallery, also 6f winner here at 2 yrs in 1991, and half-sister to several winners,
including US Grade 1 1¼m winner Aube Indienne (by Bluebird): dam French 1¼m
winner: fairly useful maiden: should be suited by at least 1¾m: acts on soft ground,
possibly not on firmer than good. *M. R. Channon*

WEE BARNEY 2 b.g. (Mar 19) Balnibarbi 95 – Never So True 52 (Never So **46**
Bold 135) [1999 7m 7m 7g² 8g 8.2d 8d Nov 1] lengthy, plain gelding: first foal: dam
11f winner: poor maiden: best effort when second in seller at Catterick in August:
should stay at least 1m: yet to race on extremes of going: tried visored. *B. Ellison*

WEE CHRISTY (IRE) 4 gr.g. Contract Law (USA) 108 – Eternal Optimist **34** (Relko 136) [1998 38, a–: 7g 12g³ 12.1v 12m 14.1g 8g⁴ 12g a9.4g⁵ 1999 7m 11.1s⁵ **a–** 13d⁴ 10.9s Jun 19] lengthy, sparely-made gelding: poor maiden: stays 13f: acts on soft and good to firm going: tried blinkered. *W. McKeown*

WEEHEBY (USA) 10 ch.g. Woodman (USA) 126 – Fearless Dame (USA) **–** (Fearless Knight) [1998 43: a12g⁴ 1999 a16g a12g Jan 20] modest winning hurdler: very lightly raced and poor at best on Flat nowadays: visored final start: has looked unenthusiastic. *Miss A. Stokell*

WEE JIMMY 3 b.g. Lugana Beach 116 – Cutlass Princess (USA) 41 (Cutlass **–** (USA)) [1998 57: 5.1g⁴ 6.1d⁴ 7g 1999 6.1m 8.2g Sep 25] close-coupled, sparely-made gelding: modest maiden at best: may prove best at 5f/6f: sold 500 gns in November. *B. A. McMahon*

WEET-A-MINUTE (IRE) 6 ro.h. Nabeel Dancer (USA) 120 – Ludovica **104** (Bustino 136) [1998 105: 10.5g³ 7.9g⁴ 8.1g² 8.2g² 10.3g⁵ 7.9m³ 8m⁵ 8g² 7.9f 8.9g³ 8m 9g 10s² a9.4g⁶ a9.4g* 1999 a9g a9.4g² a9.4g² 11.9s⁶ 8m 10m 10.3m⁴ 10.4s⁵ 8.1g⁶ 8.9d³ 7.9f⁶ 10.4g 10d² 7.9g² 8.2s² a8.5g a9.4g* Dec 27] lengthy horse: carries condition: useful performer: won handicaps at Wolverhampton in March and December: good efforts when runner-up in rated stakes at Pontefract and York (beaten short head by John Ferneley) and minor event at Nottingham (beaten 1½ lengths by Right Wing) in autumn: has form at 1½m, raced mainly at 1m/1¼m these days: acts on firm going, soft and fibresand: sometimes carries head awkwardly. *R. Hollinshead*

WEET AND SEE 5 b.g. Lochnager 132 – Simply Style (Bairn (USA) 126) [1998 **–** NR 1999 a7f a12g Feb 20] fair handicapper on all-weather, modest on turf in 1997: no show both 5-y-o starts, but won over hurdles in July (2) and September. *T. Wall*

WEET FOR ME 3 b.c. Warning 136 – Naswara (USA) 88 (Al Nasr (FR) 126) **83** [1998 82: 8g⁴ 8s² 8d² 1999 10.5s⁶ 10.5m 10.5f* 11.9d⁴ 10m 11.9m⁴ 12.4m⁴ 14s 16s² Oct 5] big colt: fairly useful performer: won 5-runner maiden at Haydock in July: ran creditably a few times after: effective at 10.5f to 2m: yet to race on heavy going, acts on any other: often races prominently. *R. Hollinshead*

WEETMAN'S WEIGH (IRE) 6 b.h. Archway (IRE) 115 – Indian Sand (Indian **86** King (USA) 128) [1998 82, a96: a7g* a8.5g a8g⁴ 8d⁶ 8.5m 8.1g 7f 7m³ 7g* 7m⁵ 7d **a104** 7g² 7g⁶ 7s* 8d a8.5g³ a7g² 1999 a7g* a8.5s* a7g² a8.5g⁶ 7g 7.6m² 8.1g⁴ 7m² 8m 7.6m 8m 7.1m 7m⁵ 7.1d⁴ 8g³ 7g⁴ 7d² 8s² a8g² Nov 15] useful-looking horse: fairly useful handicapper on turf, useful on all-weather: won at Southwell and Wolverhampton in January/February: best effort when second to King Priam on former course on final start: effective at 7f to 8.5f: acts on firm going, soft and fibresand: often tongue tied: sometimes hangs left: usually held up, and best with strong gallop: tough and consistent. *R. Hollinshead*

WEETRAIN (IRE) 3 b.f. Fayruz 116 – Mantlepiece (IRE) (Common Grounds **45** 118) [1998 57: 6.5d 7.5d 7d 6v⁵ 1999 a6g⁵ a5g³ a5g⁶ 6.1s 5s³ 5d a6g Dec 27] 1,800Y: second foal: dam no worthwhile form: poor maiden: trained at 2 yrs by M. Cunningham in Ireland: stays 6f: acts on heavy going and fibresand. *J. G. Given*

WEET U THERE (IRE) 3 b.c. Forest Wind (USA) 111 – Lady Aladdin (Persian **53** Bold 123) [1998 67?, a61: a6g⁶ a6g 8d⁵ 7.9g⁵ 7g³ 7.9g 5d a7g a7g* 1999 a7g⁴ a7g³ **a63** a8.5g⁵ a6g* a7s a7g a7g² 8.2s⁶ a9.4g⁴ a9.4g* 10s a9.4g⁶ 9.3g a9.4g³ 14d⁴ a12g a8.5g Aug 6] close-coupled colt: modest performer: won sellers at Wolverhampton in February and April: finds 6f a bare minimum, and stays 9f: acts on fibresand, well beaten on equitrack: blinkered twice: inconsistent: joined T. Wall. *R. Hollinshead*

WEKIWA SPRINGS (FR) 2 gr.c. (Apr 7) Kendor (FR) 122 – Ti Mamaille (FR) **99 P** (Dom Racine (FR) 121) [1999 7d² Sep 19] 620,000 francs Y: big, good-topped colt: has plenty of scope: fifth foal: half-brother to 3 winners in France, including 13.5f listed winner Sea Mamaille (by Sea Full): dam unraced half-sister to smart French/ US middle-distance performer Coeur de Lion: shaped with good deal of promise when head second of 22 to Scarteen Fox in well-contested maiden at Newbury, travelling strongly in front rank throughout and keeping on well: will stay at least 1¼m: joined Godolphin: smart performer in the making, sure to win races. *B. J. Meehan*

WELCH'S DREAM (IRE) 2 b.f. (Feb 13) Brief Truce (USA) 126 – Swift **76**
Chorus (Music Boy 124) [1999 5m² a5g 5m* 5m⁴ 5.1m⁴ 5m³ 5g⁴ a6g⁴ a6g² a6g⁴ Dec **a65**
27] IR 10,000F, IR 9,000Y: leggy, lengthy filly: fourth foal: half-sister to 3 winners,
including 2-y-o winners at 7f by Common Grounds and 5f by Taufan: dam, Irish
2-y-o 6f winner, from good middle-distance family: fair performer: made all in
maiden at Ripon in May: stays 6f: acts on fibresand, raced only on good or firmer on
turf: has got worked up in preliminaries: races prominently. *J. Berry*

WELCOME BACK 2 ch.g. (May 12) Most Welcome 131 – Villavina 59 (Top **–**
Ville 129) [1999 6d 7m 7m 7m⁶ Aug 27] 1,250F, 4,000Y: leggy gelding: second foal:
dam 8.5f winner: poor maiden at best. *K. A. Ryan*

WELCOME GIFT 3 b.g. Prince Sabo 123 – Ausonia (Beldale Flutter (USA) **40 p**
130) [1998 NR 1999 a7g² Dec 11] 30,000F, IR 37,000Y: fifth foal: half-brother to a
winner in Italy by Last Tycoon: dam, little sign of ability, half-sister to Laurent
Perrier Champagne Stakes winner Young Runaway: 10/3, 8 lengths second of 8 to
Sand Hawk in maiden at Wolverhampton: should do better. *W. J. Haggas*

WELCOME HEIGHTS 5 b.g. Most Welcome 131 – Mount Ida (USA) 79 **49**
(Conquistador Cielo (USA)) [1998 71: a10g³ a8g⁶ 8g* 8g 8g 8g 9m³ 8g⁵ 8.3f⁶ 8g
8g 10s 1999 8.3g 10m 8m 8m⁶ a9.4g 10.5d⁵ 8d² 8.2s a11g Nov 30] good-topped,
workmanlike gelding: bad mover: poor handicapper: left M. Fetherston-Godley
5,200 gns after seventh start: effective at 1m to 1¼m: acts on equitrack, good to firm
and good to soft going: held up, and best in strongly-run race. *R. C. Spicer*

WELCOME SHADE 2 gr.g. (Mar 8) Green Desert (USA) 127 – Grey Angel **67**
(Kenmare (FR) 125) [1999 6m 7d 6v a6g* a6g⁴ Dec 10] good-topped gelding:
second foal: half-brother to 3-y-o Nightingale: dam won 8 races in South Africa at
7f/1m, including Grade 3 event: fair performer: won nursery at Lingfield in
November: may prove best at 5f/6f: acts on equitrack, ran badly on heavy ground:
usually races handily. *R. Hannon*

WELCOME SUNSET 4 b.g. Most Welcome 131 – Deanta In Eirinn (Red **78**
Sunset 120) [1998 78: 8.2g⁴ 8m² 8m³ 7m 9m9 7g 7v³ 8d 10m² 8m 10g² 10m³ 10.1m³
10g 8.9d² 10s Oct 22] tall gelding: fair handicapper: effective at 1m to 1¼m (when
conditions aren't testing): acts on soft and good to firm going, probably on heavy:
blinkered once at 3 yrs: has wandered under pressure, and probably needs strong
handling: consistent: sold 25,000 gns. *J. Wharton*

WELCOME TO UNOS 2 ch.g. (Mar 3) Exit To Nowhere (USA) 122 – Royal **69 ?**
Loft 105 (Homing 130) [1999 7m⁵ 6m 6g² Sep 18] 11,500Y: close-coupled gelding:
half-brother to several winners, including 1994 2-y-o 7f winner Wigberto (by Old
Vic) and Irish 7f/9f winner Sir Slaves (by Salse), both fairly useful, and 8-y-o Duello:
dam 6f/7f winner who stayed 1m: progressive form in maidens, disputing lead when
second of 6 to Ile Michel at Catterick on final start (possibly flattered): should stay
7f. *M. Dods*

WELLBEING 2 b.c. (Mar 9) Sadler's Wells (USA) 132 – Charming Life (NZ) **70 p**
(Sir Tristram 115) [1999 8s³ Nov 5] big, good-topped colt: fourth foal: half-brother
to 3-y-o Caerau, very smart 1¼m/1½m winner Kingfisher Mill (by Riverman) and
useful 1½m winner Dear Life (by Lear Fan): dam, Australian 7f winner, sister to
Zabeel and half-sister to Baryshnikov, both Australian Group 1 winners: green and
not right in coat, 9 lengths third of 5 to Shouf Al Badou in minor event at Doncaster,
tending to go in snatches: will be well suited by 1¼m+: sure to do a fair bit better at
least. *H. R. A. Cecil*

WELLCOME INN 5 ch.g. Most Welcome 131 – Mimining 83 (Tower Walk 130) **45**
[1998 NR 1999 9.9v 11.1m 10.9g 12g² 15.8d 12s⁵ 14.1d a12g Dec 21] big, lengthy
gelding: poor handicapper nowadays: may prove best around 1½m: acts on good to
soft going, probably on fibresand: has worn tongue strap. *G. Woodward*

WELL DRAWN 6 b.g. Dowsing (USA) 124 – Classic Design (Busted 134) [1998 **44**
50: 8.2m 8.3m⁶ 10.2m⁵ 10s⁵ 10d a8g 1999 11.6d 9m⁴ May 22] poor handicapper:
stays 1¼m, possibly not 1½m: acts on equitrack, good to firm and soft going:
headstrong: sold 4,000 gns. *H. Candy*

WELLOW (IRE) 3 b.g. Unblest 117 – Alpine Sunset (Auction Ring (USA) 123) **60 d**
[1998 NR 1999 a7g⁶ a6g² a9.4g 7m a8.5g a6g 7d a6g Nov 12] IR 2,200Y, resold IR

4,400Y: workmanlike gelding: sixth foal: half-brother to 2 winners, notably useful 5f/6f winner Afif (by Midyan): dam unraced half-sister to Cyrano de Bergerac: modest maiden: no form after second start: may prove best up to 7f: acts on fibresand: blinkered final outing. *J. A. Glover*

WELODY   3 ch.g. Weldnaas (USA) 112 – The Boozy News (USA) 44 (L'Emigrant   **75** (USA) 129) [1998 –: 7d 1999 7g⁵ 8s⁴ 7m Oct 19] reluctant stalls, best effort in maidens when fifth of 7 at Catterick on reappearance: bred to stay 1m. *K. Mahdi*

WELSH ASSEMBLY   3 ch.g. Presidium 124 – Celtic Chimes (Celtic Cone 116)   **39** [1998 –, a49: a5g³ a5g³ 6.1m⁵ 5d a6g* a6g a7g 10d 1999 9.7s⁵ 9.7v a12g 10.1g⁵ 11.5m Oct 19] poor performer: stays 1¼m: acts on fibresand and soft going: blinkered (ran as though something amiss) final start: sold 800 gns. *G. P. Enright*

WELSH DREAM   2 b.c. (Apr 25) Mtoto 134 – Morgannwg (IRE) 86 (Simply   **51** Great (FR) 122) [1999 7d 8s 8s Nov 6] 7,000Y: useful-looking colt: third foal: half-brother to 3-y-o Penybont and 4-y-o Black Army: dam 7f winner: best effort in maidens when seventh of 15 at Leicester on debut: will be suited by 1¼m+. *A. C. Stewart*

WELSH FAIRING   3 b.f. King's Signet (USA) 110 – Princess Fair (Crowned   **–** Prince (USA) 128) [1998 –: 5s 6s 1999 a8.5g 7m 5.1g May 21] small filly: no form. *M. Blanshard*

WELSH MOUNTAIN   6 b.g. Welsh Captain 113 – Miss Nelski 84 (Most Secret   **42** 119) [1998 47: 10.1f⁴ 10g⁵ 8m 8d* 10g 10.8m 1999 13g⁶ May 2] smallish, good-bodied gelding: poor handicapper: best around 1m: acts on good to firm and good to soft ground: tried visored earlier in career: fair hurdler. *K. A. Morgan*

WELSH PLOY   2 b.f. (Apr 27) Deploy 131 – Safe House 81§ (Lyphard (USA)   **78** 132) [1999 7m 7d³ 7v² 7s⁵ 6d 8.3d⁵ a8g* a8g² Dec 21] 500Y: angular, unfurnished filly: closely related to 1988 2-y-o 1m winner Ivory Tower (by Shirley Heights) and half-sister to several winners, including 9f seller winner Northern Rainbow (by Rainbow Quest): dam temperamental 11f winner: fair performer: won nursery at Lingfield in December: good second in similar event at Southwell: will stay 1½m: acts on heavy going and all-weather. *K. McAuliffe*

WELSH VALLEY (USA)   2 b.f. (Mar 27) Irish River (FR) 131 – Sweet Snow   **64** (USA) (Lyphard (USA) 132) [1999 5s 6g² Oct 15] 120,000Y: half-sister to several winners, including smart 1994 2-y-o 6f winner (Gimcrack Stakes) Chilly Billy, later 1m winner in USA, and fairly useful 6f (at 2 yrs) and 1m winner Weaver Bird (both by Master Willie), and 3-y-o Global Concept: dam, won at 1¼m in France, daughter of Kentucky Oaks winner Sun And Snow: better effort in maidens (modest form) when second of 12 to L'Arita at Redcar, leading until halfway: should stay 7f. *M. L. W. Bell*

WELTON ARSENAL   7 b.g. Statoblest 120 – Miller's Gait 74§ (Mill Reef   **– §** (USA) 141) [1998 86§: 8d 8m 7d⁶ 6.1g² 8g³ 7m⁴ 8s 7s 1999 6v 6d 7.1m Jun 12] sturdy gelding: fairly useful performer: little show in 1999: effective at 6f to 1m: acts on firm and soft ground: tried visored: held up: often finds little, and not one to trust. *K. Bishop*

WELVILLE   6 b.g. Most Welcome 131 – Miss Top Ville (FR) (Top Ville 129) [1998   **–** –, a82+: 6g 7d 7g a7g⁵ 1999 a8g* a8g* a8.5g² a8.5g* 8m May 3] rangy gelding: **a103** useful handicapper, lightly raced: better than ever at 6 yrs, winning at Lingfield (twice) and Wolverhampton (made all by 2 lengths from Thekryaati) between February and April: well held back on turf final start: stays 8.5f: acts on good to firm going and all-weather: has had tongue tied. *P. J. Makin*

WEND'S DAY (IRE)   4 br.g. Brief Truce (USA) 126 – Iswara (USA) (Alleged   **69** (USA) 138) [1998 63: 10g 10.2s⁴ 12g⁵ 1999 11.9d³ Oct 21] fair maiden: stays 1½m: raced only on good going or softer: sold 4,200 gns: won novice hurdle in December. *S. E. H. Sherwood*

WENTOBUYABAY   6 ch.m. Henbit (USA) 130 – Deep Ocean (Deep Run 119)   **–** [1998 NR 1999 a12g Aug 13] half-sister to a winning pointer by Baron Blakeney: dam winning pointer in Ireland: always behind in seller at Lingfield. *E. A. Wheeler*

WE'RE NOT JOKEN 2 b.f. (Apr 7) Foxhound (USA) 103 – We're Joken 62 **54** (Statoblest 120) [1999 a6g 5.1g⁶ 6.1m⁶ a6f 6d Oct 22] 1,800Y: small filly: first foal: **a–** dam 5f/6f winner, including at 2 yrs: modest maiden at best: out of depth in sales race at Doncaster final start: likely to prove best at 5f/6f. *Mrs N. Macauley*

WERE NOT STOPPIN 4 b.g. Mystiko (USA) 124 – Power Take Off 109 **– §** (Aragon 118) [1998 NR 1999 12m 12.3m 10d 11m Aug 28] workmanlike gelding: well beaten in maidens/handicap: twice refused to enter stalls: one to avoid. *R. Bastiman*

WESTBROOK (IRE) 3 b.g. Fairy King (USA) – Abury (IRE) 104 (Law Society **64** (USA) 130) [1998 NR 1999 10.5d⁶ 12.3m 10m⁵ 10.3s 8d Oct 11] good-topped gelding: second foal: half-brother to 4-y-o Glory of Grosvenor: dam 7f (at 2 yrs) and 11.4f (Cheshire Oaks) winner, should have stayed further: left P. Chapple-Hyam 17,000 gns after debut: only sign of ability on third start: has swished tail. *C. N. Kellett*

WESTCOURT MAGIC 6 b.g. Emarati (USA) 74 – Magic Milly 60 (Simply **85** Great (FR) 122) [1998 95§: 6d⁵ 5g⁴ 6v 5.1m* 5d 5m⁶ 5s⁴ 5s 5m 5g⁴ 5g 5.1d* 5m 6s 5m 6g 6v 5d 1999 5d 5.1m² 5s 5.1d² 6.1m 5s 5.1d 5m 5d⁶ 5.1s* 5g 5g Oct 16] smallish, sturdy gelding: fairly useful handicapper: won at Chester (fourth course success) in September: has won at 6f, best at 5f: acts on firm and soft going, well beaten on heavy: rather edgy, and usually early to post: usually leads: none too reliable. *M. W. Easterby*

WEST END DANCER (USA) 2 b.f. (May 28) West By West (USA) 116 – **52** Chateau Dancer (USA) 104 (Giacometti 130) [1999 a8g⁵ a8.5g Dec 11] $6,500Y, 12,000 2-y-o: half-sister to several winners, including Irish 1998 2-y-o 6f winner Man of The Sea and 1¼m winner Rejoneo, both fairly useful performers by El Gran Senor: dam 2-y-o 6f winner and third in May Hill: modest form when fifth of 15 to Heathyards Mate in maiden at Southwell on debut: well beaten next time (slowly away). *G. C. H. Chung*

WESTENDER (FR) 3 b.g. In The Wings 128 – Trude (GER) (Windwurf (GER)) **98 p** [1998 –p: 7d 1999 7g* 8m² 10m² 10m* 10.1d³ Sep 15] leggy, quite good-topped gelding: useful performer: won maiden at Yarmouth (4 ran) in July and handicap at Ripon (came from well off strong pace) in August: good third to First Fantasy in rated stakes at Yarmouth final start, edging left: will stay 1½m: yet to race on extremes of going: likely to improve further. *W. J. Haggas*

WESTERN CHIEF (IRE) 5 b.h. Caerleon (USA) 132 – Go Honey Go (General **74** Assembly (USA)) [1998 NR 1999 a13g 15.4v 20m³ Jun 15] IR 80,000Y: half-brother to 2 winners, including 7f to 1½m winner Sweet Supposin (by Posen): dam French 7.5f winner, later Grade 3 8.5f winner in USA, half-sister to dam of 3-y-o Muta-faweq: useful handicapper for D. Weld in Ireland at 3 yrs: fair in 1999, best effort when third of 29 to High And Mighty in Ascot Stakes: stays 2½m: acts on firm ground, seemingly not on softer than good: effective blinkered, not tried at 5 yrs: has worn tongue strap. *D. L. Williams*

WESTERN COMMAND (GER) 3 b.g. Saddlers' Hall (IRE) 126 – Western **–** Friend (USA) (Gone West (USA)) [1998 65: a7g⁵ a7g² 1999 a10g³ a8g³ a11g* a12g* **a79** 10.3d 12s³ a14.8g a8.5g a12g⁵ 12f⁴ a9.4g⁶ 10g a12g² a12f⁴ a14g² a12g a12g⁶ a12g² a11g² a12g* Dec 11] quite good-topped gelding: fair handicapper: won at Southwell (twice) in March and Wolverhampton in December: probably best around 1½m: acts on fibresand, lightly raced and little form on turf: tried blinkered/visored: takes good hold. *Mrs N. Macauley*

WESTERN COUNTRY 7 ch.g. Beveled (USA) – Country Singer (Town And **–** Country 124) [1998 NR 1999 14d 8s 7d Oct 4] of little account. *M. P. Muggeridge*

WESTERN GENERAL 8 ch.g. Cadeaux Genereux 131 – Patsy Western 81 **58** (Precocious 126) [1998 NR 1999 9.2v⁴ 9.2g² Jun 9] quite attractive gelding: fair handicapper in 1997: just modest form both 8-y-o starts: stays 10.5f: acts on good to firm and heavy going: effective blinkered or not. *Miss Kate Milligan*

WESTERN PYRAMID (USA) 3 b.c. West By West (USA) 116 – Pyramid **–** Power (USA) (Upper Nile (USA)) [1998 NR 1999 a8f 6.1f 7m Aug 27] $52,000F, IR 30,000Y: half-brother to several winners in North America, including 11f Canadian

Derby winner Steady Power (by Steady Growth): dam unraced: well beaten in maidens/claimer. *P. S. McEntee*

WESTERN RAINBOW (IRE)   3 b.g. Rainbows For Life (CAN) – Miss Gal-   **56**
wegian (Sandford Lad 133) [1998 –: 6m 6g 7d 6v 1999 6f 8.3s 8g a8g² a8g² Dec
13] 6,500F, IR 7,500Y: quite good-topped gelding: half-brother to several winners,
including 1991 2-y-o 7f seller winner Jubal Early (by The Noble Player), later
successful abroad: dam placed over 6f at 2 yrs in Ireland: modest maiden: trained by
D. Hughes in Ireland at 2 yrs, by H. Akbary first 3 starts in 1999: best efforts in
handicaps last 2 outings: should stay 1¼m: acts on fibresand. *P. D. Evans*

WESTERN RIDGE (FR)   2 b.c. (Apr 17) Darshaan 133 – Helvellyn (USA) 83   **92 p**
(Gone West (USA)) [1999 7g⁴ 8d⁵ Oct 9] 1,300,000 francs Y: close-coupled,
unfurnished colt: third foal: half-brother to fairly useful Irish 3-y-o 9f winner
Musketeer (by Danehill): dam 8.3f winner who stayed 1¼m: fairly useful form in
listed races at Newbury and Ascot 2 months apart, fifth of 11 to French Fellow on
latter track: will be suited by 1¼m+: capable of better still. *L. M. Cumani*

WESTERN SUMMER (USA)   2 ch.c. (Feb 11) Summer Squall (USA) – Mrs   **94 p**
West (USA) 86 (Gone West (USA)) [1999 8.2d* Oct 21] third foal: half-brother to
fairly useful 1998 2-y-o 7f winner Meneer (by Silver Hawk): dam 2-y-o 6f and 7.5f
winner, later placed in USA: 7/2, looked a good prospect when winning maiden at
Nottingham by 1¾ lengths from Tolstoy, travelling well in mid-field, leading 1f out
and running on strongly: will stay 1¼m: sure to do better, and should prove at least
useful. *H. R. A. Cecil*

WESTERN VENTURE (IRE)   6 ch.g. Two Timing (USA) 124 – Star Gazing   **40**
(IRE) (Caerleon (USA) 132) [1998 41?: 9.2s⁶ 9.9m 9.2d⁵ 9.1v 1999 8g 10.1m 9.2m⁵
a11g⁴ Sep 28] poor performer: trained by L. Lungo first 2 starts: stays 9f: acts on firm
going, possibly on soft: blinkered (below form) once at 4 yrs. *Martyn Wane*

WEST ESCAPE   3 ch.f. Gone West (USA) – Sans Escale (USA) (Diesis 133)   **95**
[1998 78: 6m⁶ 6f⁴ 7.5m³ 7v⁴ 8s² 1999 8m* 10.1d⁵ 9m² 10.3m² 9.9f² 10.1g⁵ 10d² 10d
Oct 9] close-coupled, useful-looking filly: useful performer: won maiden at Warwick
in May: ran well most starts after, including when 1¼ lengths second of 17 to Azouz
Pasha in Globetrotter Handicap at Goodwood on fifth: stays 1¼m well: acts on firm
and soft ground: sometimes slowly away (markedly so penultimate start): usually
held up. *M. A. Jarvis*

WESTGATE RUN   2 b.f. (Feb 14) Emperor Jones (USA) 119 – Glowing Refer-   **68 d**
ence (Reference Point 139) [1999 5g⁶ 6g³ 6d⁶ 7m⁴ 7f² 7.5g⁴ 6m 7m 6s 6v Oct 11]
22,000F, 25,000Y: close-coupled filly: third foal: half-sister to fairly useful 1996
2-y-o 7f winner White Hot (by Weldnaas), later minor stakes winner up to 1¼m in
USA: dam unraced close relative of King Edward VII winner Private Tender: modest
maiden: below form in nurseries last 4 starts: will stay 1m: acts on firm going.
R. A. Fahey

WESTMINSTER CITY (USA)   3 b.c. Alleged (USA) 138 – Promenade Fan   **56**
(USA) (Timeless Moment (USA)) [1998 85: 5m* 7s 6m³ 8g 1999 a10g 11.6g⁵ 10.3m
10.3m⁵ 7.6g 9.9v 11.5g a9.4g⁵ a12g a16.2g Dec 4] tall colt: fairly useful at 2 yrs:
modest at best in 1999, leaving C. Brittain after firm start: probably stays 1m: acts
on soft and good to firm going, well held on equitrack: visored 5 of last 6 starts.
K. O. Cunningham-Brown

WESTMINSTER (IRE)   7 ch.g. Nashamaa 113 – Our Galadrial (Salmon Leap   **78 d**
(USA) 131) [1998 72: 11.6g* 10d² 12s 12d* 10.1s⁶ 12m³ 13.1d² 12.1g⁵ 11.6f³ 1999
11.5m⁵ 12.3m 13.1g* 10.9d 11.9d 11.7s 14.1s⁶ a14g Nov 12] angular gelding: fair
performer: easily best effort in 1999 when winning 5-runner minor event at Ayr in
July: stays 13f: acts on firm and good to soft going (possibly not on soft): has been
blinkered, usually visored: has wandered, and normally held up. *M. H. Tompkins*

WEST ONE   3 ch.f. Gone West (USA) – Bequest (USA) 108 (Sharpen Up 127)   **67**
[1998 NR 1999 7.1m 8d⁶ Jul 5] first reported foal: dam 6f winner in Britain, later
successful in USA, including in Grade 1 1¼m event: showed ability in maidens at
Haydock and Ripon. *L. M. Cumani*

WESTORM (IRE)   8 br.g. Strong Gale 116 – Little Peach (Ragapan 118) [1998   **–**
NR 1999 a12g⁴ a12g Mar 10] seventh foal: half-brother to 2 winning jumpers: dam

winning hurdler: poor form in bumpers/hurdles in Ireland in 1996 for L. Woods: well beaten in maiden and claimer on Flat. *Miss Gay Kelleway*

WESTSIDE FLYER   3 ch.f. Risk Me (FR) 127 – Celtic River (IRE) (Caerleon (USA) 132) [1998 59: 5d 5s⁵ 5m⁶ 6d⁶ a7g³ 7f⁵ 6.9m⁴ a8.5g⁶ 6g 1999 a6g* a6g² a6g a6g⁴ a6g⁶ 6v 6m a6g 6g 8s a6g Oct 30] good-bodied filly: modest performer: won claimer at Southwell in January: left A. Kelleway 3,000 gns after ninth start: effective at 6f/7f: acts on firm going, soft and all-weather: tried blinkered. *J. C. McConnochie*   **–** **a53**

WEST STREET BLUES   3 ch.f. Then Again 126 – Calametta (Oats 126) [1998 –: 5f 6m 5m 6s 1999 6s⁵ 5s 5g 5m 10f Jul 22] no form: left T. McCarthy after fourth start. *R. Ingram*   **–**

WESTWOOD VIEW   3 b.f. Puissance 110 – Long View 68 (Persian Bold 123) [1998 58: 5s³ 5s 5m 6d 7d⁵ 1999 5g⁵ 6d 5m 6g⁴ 6g 5v³ 5.9m³ 7.1d 6g 5f 8s 8d a7g a11g⁴ Dec 17] rather leggy filly: shows knee action: modest maiden handicapper: left J. Quinn 1,300 gns after tenth start: probably stays easy 11f: acts on good to firm and heavy going, probably on fibresand: tried visored/blinkered: usually gets behind: sometimes hangs left. *Ronald Thompson*   **58 d** **a36**

WETHAAB (USA)   2 b.c. (Jan 6) Pleasant Colony (USA) – Binntastic (USA) (Lyphard's Wish (FR) 124) [1999 7.1d Aug 6] $270,000F, $275,000Y: sturdy, well-made colt: second foal: half-brother to a winner in USA by Eastern Echo: dam, won up to 9f in USA at 4 yrs, from family of graded-stakes winners: favourite but very green (scratched to post), well held in maiden at Haydock: will be suited by 1m+: likely to do better. *B. W. Hills*   **– p**

WHAT A CRACKER   2 b.f. (Mar 11) Bustino 136 – Moon Spin 83 (Night Shift (USA)) [1999 6g 8s 8s Nov 6] 4,800Y: third foal: sister to 3-y-o Rosa Canina and half-sister to 4-y-o The Thruster: dam 1m to 1½m winner: well held in maidens: likely to need 1½m+. *M. P. Tregoning*   **–**

WHAT A FUSS   6 b.g. Great Commotion (USA) 123 – Hafwah (Gorytus (USA) 132) [1998 NR 1999 16.2m 12f Jul 31] good-topped gelding: one-time fair handicapper on all-weather: modest on turf: well held both starts in 1999, though won 3 times over hurdles. *M. W. Easterby*   **–**

WHATEVER'S RIGHT (IRE)   10 b.g. Doulab (USA) 115 – Souveniers (Relko 136) [1998 67, a48: a8g⁴ 8f 8.3d⁶ 8.3m a10g⁵ 8.2m 7.6g⁶ 7m* 7m⁴ 10f 7m² 1999 a10g* a10g⁶ Jan 28] strong, workmanlike gelding: modest handicapper: won at Lingfield in January: stays 1¼m: acts on equitrack (yet to race on fibresand), firm and good to soft ground: tried blinkered: has won for apprentice. *M. D. I. Usher*   **53**

WHAT GROUNDS (FR)   2 b.g. (May 11) Exit To Nowhere (USA) 122 – Solving (USA) (Bering 136) [1999 6d⁵ Oct 29] 90,000 francs Y: second foal: half-brother to French 1998 2-y-o 7f winner Linaving (by Linamix): dam, French 8.5f winner, sister to smart French 1¼m winner Vaguely Gay: encouraging fifth of 19 to Pax in maiden at Newmarket, keeping on well from mid-division: will stay at least 1m: sure to improve. *B. J. Meehan*   **71 p**

WHATSITSNAME   3 br.g. Tragic Role (USA) – Princess Yasmin (USA) (Le Fabuleux 133) [1998 –: a6g 1999 a7g a8.5g⁵ a12g Dec 21] lightly-raced maiden: little form. *J. L. Eyre*   **–**

WHATTA MADAM   3 gr.f. Whittingham (IRE) 104 – Sylvan Song (Song 132) [1998 60: 5m 6m² 5.7d³ 6g⁴ 6f² 1999 7s 6s² 6f³ 5.3f⁵ 6d a5g a7g 5.3d³ 6g 5.2s 6d a5g⁶ a6g⁴ Dec 6] close-coupled filly: modest maiden handicapper: should prove best at 5f/6f: acts on firm and soft going: tried blinkered/visored: inconsistent. *G. L. Moore*   **65** **a51**

WHAT THE DEVIL   6 ch.m. Devil To Play 55 – Whats Yours Called 52 (Wind-jammer (USA)) [1998 –: a12g⁶ a12g⁴ 14m⁶ a16.2g 1999 a14g a12g Apr 24] sparely-made mare: of no account. *J. P. Smith*   **–**

WHENWILLIEMETHARRY   2 b.f. (Apr 15) Sabrehill (USA) 120 – William's Bird (USA) 104 (Master Willie 129) [1999 5m 6f 7.1d⁴ 7m⁵ 8.1d 8.3g Oct 11] 9,000Y: sixth foal: sister to fairly useful 1997 2-y-o 1m winner Chim Chiminey and half-sister to 3-y-o Erith's Chill Wind and a winner abroad by Hadeer: dam 2-y-o 5f   **69**

and 7f winner: fair maiden: pulled hard and well beaten last 2 starts: best efforts at 7f. *D. R. C. Elsworth*

WHERE EAGLES DARE (USA)   2 b.c. (Mar 15) Eagle Eyed (USA) 111 –   **60**
Velveteen (USA) (Pirateer (USA)) [1999 7m 7.7d 7g Oct 19] 15,000Y: big, useful-looking colt: sixth foal: half-brother to a winner in USA by Snow Chief: dam, won up to 9f in USA, out of sister to grandam of Swain: modest form in maiden at Epsom on debut: will stay at least 1m: has scope, and may do better at 3 yrs: joined J. Osborne. *D. Marks*

WHERE'S ALBERT   4 ch.g. Out of Hand 84 – Stellajoe 39 (Le Dauphin 73)   **37**
[1998 –: 8.3g 10g 11.6d 1999 a16g² May 29] poor maiden: will stay beyond 2m: acts on equitrack: joined R. Buckler. *A. J. McNae*

WHERE'S CHARLOTTE   2 b.f. (Mar 7) Sure Blade (USA) 130 – One Degree   **53**
80 (Crooner 119) [1999 5.1g⁶ 6m 7m 5.3s² 6g 5.3d 5.7s a6g³ a6g a7g Dec 8]   **a45**
ninth foal: half-sister to 1m winner Waldo (by Northern State) and useful 1987 2-y-o 5f winner Pea Green (by Try My Best): dam 6f winner: modest maiden: below form after fourth start, including in seller: may prove best at 5f: acts on soft going. *R. Hannon*

WHISKY CHASER   2 ch.f. (Jan 30) Never So Bold 135 – Highland Spirit 78   **59**
(Scottish Reel 123) [1999 6g⁴ 6.8m 6m Sep 10] 5,000Y: second foal: dam, 2-y-o 6f/ 7f winner, also fairly useful hurdler: modest form when fourth of 13 in maiden at Salisbury on debut: off course 3 months before well held in similar event at Warwick and sales race at Doncaster (early and led to post): should stay 7f. *B. Smart*

WHISPERING (IRE)   3 b.f. Royal Academy (USA) 130 – Alligatrix (USA) 111   **81**
(Alleged (USA) 138) [1998 NR 1999 9m⁴ 10m² 10.2m² 10m² Jul 21] leggy, lightly-made filly: half-sister to several winners, notably 4-y-o Croco Rouge and useful winner up to 1m Alidiva (by Chief Singer), latter the dam of good performers Ali-Royal, Sleepytime (both by Royal Academy) and Taipan: dam 2-y-o 7f winner (should have stayed much further): fairly useful maiden: likely to prove best up to 1¼m: raced only on good to firm going: drifted left final start. *H. R. A. Cecil*

WHISPERING WIND   3 b.g. Danehill (USA) 126 – Meadow Pipit (CAN) 113   **65**
(Meadowlake (USA)) [1998 NR 1999 8g Apr 14] rather leggy, close-coupled gelding: first foal: dam 4-y-o 7f to 1¼m winner: 6/1 and short to post, very green when eighth in newcomers race at Newmarket: sold 6,000 gns. *E. A. L. Dunlop*

WHISTLER   2 ch.g. (Jan 20) Selkirk (USA) 129 – French Gift 99 (Cadeaux   **74**
Genereux 131) [1999 6d⁴ 5m² 6f 5m³ Aug 13] well-grown, quite attractive gelding: has a quick action: second foal: half-brother to 3-y-o Stridhana: dam 2-y-o 6f winner out of high-class sprinter Soba: fair maiden: best effort when second of 5 in minor event at Windsor on second start: likely to prove best at 5f/6f. *R. Hannon*

WHISTLE TEST   4 gr.g. Kris 135 – Cut Velvet (USA) (Northern Dancer) [1998   **–**
77d: 8s⁶ 10m 8m 11.5m⁶ 10.5d 8g 1999 12g 13f 10f Aug 7] workmanlike gelding: disappointing maiden: tried blinkered. *Mrs M. Reveley*

WHISTLING DIXIE (IRE)   3 ch.g. Forest Wind (USA) 111 – Camden's Gift   **67 d**
(Camden Town 125) [1998 74: 6m 6.1g⁴ 6g 7.3m² 8m 1999 10.1f³ 7m 8m⁶ 6g 10.9s⁶ 12f 14.1g² 12.4g⁴ 14.1m⁴ 16m⁶ 16v⁵ 15.8s⁶ a14.8g 14.1f Oct 20] workmanlike gelding: fair maiden handicapper at best: stays 2m when conditions aren't testing: acts on firm and soft going, ran poorly only start on fibresand: blinkered twice: sold 6,000 gns in November. *T. J. Etherington*

WHISTLING JACK (IRE)   3 b.g. Roi Danzig (USA) – Candy's Sister (Great   **–**
Nephew 126) [1998 66: 7m⁶ 7m a8g³ 10s* 1999 12.5m 11.7s Oct 26] tall gelding: poor mover: fair performer: well held both starts (5 months apart) in 1999: stays 1¼m: acts on soft going and fibresand, probably on good to firm. *B. J. Meehan*

WHITE EMIR   6 b.g. Emarati (USA) 74 – White African (Carwhite 127) [1998   **77 d**
80: 6m² 6m² 6g 5m 5d 5f⁶ 5.7m³ 5s 5.1v³ 5d⁶ 1999 6s³ 6f³ 6d 5m 6f 5m 5d³ 5s 6g⁴ 5.1s 6d a6g Dec 1] good-quartered gelding: fair handicapper: below form after second start: effective at 5f/6f: acts on any turf going (once-raced on all-weather): sometimes wanders under pressure, and best with strong handling and waiting tactics: effective blinkered or not: none too consistent. *B. R. Millman*

WHITEFOOT 2 b.f. (Feb 18) Be My Chief (USA) 122 – Kelimutu 58 (Top Ville **95 p**
129) [1999 7d 8.1d* 10d³ Oct 30] second live foal: half-sister to 3-y-o Top of The
Morning: dam, 1¼m/1½m winner, half-sister to useful 6f to 1m winners Sumonda
and Sumoto, latter the dam of Compton Admiral: useful performer: 40/1-winner of
maiden at Sandown in September, leading near finish: joint favourite, 7 lengths third
of 10 to Monte Carlo in listed event at Newmarket final start, staying on strongly
having been off bridle long way out: will need at least 1½m at 3 yrs, and should stay
2m: will probably do better. *J. Pearce*

WHITEGATE'S SON 5 ch.g. Minster Son 130 – Whitegates Lady (Le Coq d'Or –
101) [1998 –: 9.9m 1999 8f 10g 12.1m Sep 6] of no account on Flat: winning hurdler.
B. Ellison

WHITE HEART 4 b.g. Green Desert (USA) 127 – Barari (USA) (Blushing **114**
Groom (FR) 131) [1998 106p: 7g* 6.1g* 7g² 6s⁴ 7g* 1999 8d* 8.5g 7v⁴ 7d⁶ 7g⁴ 7m³
8m³ 8f 8g* 8m⁶ Sep 9] tall, useful-looking gelding: easy mover: smart performer:
won listed event at Doncaster (by 2½ lengths from Generous Libra) in March and
Darley-Oettingen-Rennen at Baden-Baden (by length from Intruder) in August: ran
creditably otherwise in Criterion Stakes at Newmarket (under 2 lengths third to
Diktat) on sixth start and William Hill Mile Handicap at Goodwood (seventh to
Lonesome Dude) on eighth: effective at 7f/1m: acts on firm and soft going: effective
blinkered/visored or not: has started slowly and wandered: joined N. Drysdale in
USA. *M. Johnston*

WHITE HOUSE 2 b.f. (Apr 29) Pursuit of Love 124 – Much Too Risky 87 **– p**
(Bustino 136) [1999 8s Nov 6] big, lengthy filly: has scope: half-sister to several
winners, including 3-y-o Little Rock and smart 1m to 13.5f winner Whitewater
Affair (by Machiavellian): dam 2-y-o 7f/1m winner: very green when twelfth of 18
to Summoner in maiden at Doncaster: swished tail in paddock: will stay 1¼m: looks
type to do better. *W. Jarvis*

Maktoum Al Maktoum's "White Heart"

WHITE MAGIC (IRE) 2 b.f. (Apr 18) Rainbows For Life (CAN) – Shamanka **–**
(IRE) (Shernazar 131) [1999 8.3d Nov 4] 12,000Y: second foal: half-sister to 3-y-o
Spellbinder: dam French 1¼m winner: well held in seller at Windsor. *G. B. Balding*

WHITE PLAINS (IRE) 6 b.g. Nordico (USA) – Flying Diva 100 (Chief Singer **65**
131) [1998 –, a99: a10g² a12g* a10g² a8.5g⁶ a12g⁵ a12g a10g⁵ a12g² 1999 a12g **a91**
a9.4g⁶ a10g* a10g⁵ a12g³ a10g⁴ 10g 10m a12g 12.3m⁴ a8.5g³ 12g³ 10d⁶ 10.1g⁶ 10m
a7g⁵ a7g⁴ a9.4g³ a9.4g³ a12g* Dec 29] good-bodied gelding: fairly useful on
all-weather, fair on turf: won minor event at Lingfield in February and handicap there
in December: effective around 1¼m to easy 1½m: acts on all-weather, firm and good
to soft going: usually tongue tied: often slowly away. *K. R. Burke*

WHITE SANDS 2 b.f. (Mar 2) Green Desert (USA) 127 – Carte Blanche 67 **55**
(Cadeaux Genereux 131) [1999 6f Jul 8] rather unfurnished, workmanlike filly:
second foal: half-sister to 3-y-o Fudge Brownie: dam 1m winner: eighth of 10 in
maiden at Newmarket. *C. A. Cyzer*

WHITE SETTLER 6 b.g. Polish Patriot (USA) 128 – Oasis (Valiyar 129) [1998
67: 7s* 6.1v 8s² 7g³ a7g 8.2m 7.1m² 8.1d* 1999 7g 7.1d May 19] sturdy gelding: fair
performer: well beaten both starts in 1999: effective at 6f to 1m: acts on soft and good
to firm going: tried blinkered: normally held up. *Miss S. J. Wilton*

WHITE SUMMIT . 2 b.g. (May 4) Mistertopogigo (IRE) 118 – White Heat 67 **53**
(Last Tycoon 131) [1999 6.1m⁵ 5.7m⁶ 5.7d 5g Oct 19] 3,700F, 3,700Y: first foal: dam
maiden who stayed 1m: modest maiden: raced too freely in visor final start: may
prove best over bare 5f. *B. Palling*

WHITE VALLEY (IRE) 4 b. or br.f. Tirol 127 – Royal Wolff (Prince Tender- **54**
foot (USA) 126) [1998 –: 7m 1999 7g 7v 6.1s⁶ a7g⁴ a8g Jun 4] quite good-topped
filly: unimpressive mover: modest maiden: stays 7f: acts on fibresand. *S. Dow*

WHITEWATER BOY 3 b.g. Emarati (USA) 74 – Chacewater 61 (Electric 126) **86**
[1998 83p: 7v² 1999 8m⁵ 8s 8f* 9.9g³ 8f² 8f Jul 8] big, useful-looking gelding: fairly
useful performer: won maiden at Brighton in May: ran well in handicaps after when
placed: stays 1¼m: seems to act on any going. *B. J. Meehan*

WHITE WATERS (IRE) 3 b.g. Great Commotion (USA) 123 – Water Spirit **50**
(USA) (Riverman (USA) 131) [1998 NR 1999 5s⁴ 7f⁵ 10g May 22] IR 13,500F, IR
24,000Y, 30,000 2-y-o: half-brother to several winners, including 6f (at 2 yrs) to 9f
winner Daytona Beach (by Bluebird): dam unraced: modest form in claimers/
maiden: should stay beyond 7f: joined Mrs P. Townsley. *C. A. Dwyer*

WHITLEY GRANGE BOY 6 b.g. Hubbly Bubbly (USA) – Choir (High Top **54**
131) [1998 60, a70: a16g* a16.2g⁵ 18d⁶ 13d⁴ 14m 15.8d a14g a12g⁴ 1999 a16g* **a70**
a14.8g⁴ a16f⁴ a16f 18d 16m 18g⁶ 15.8m⁴ 15.8g* 16m² 17.1g 16m⁴ 17.5d Sep 17]
tall, sparely-made gelding: fair handicapper on all-weather, modest on turf: won at
Southwell in January and Catterick in July: needs good test at 1½m, probably stays
2¼m: acts on fibresand, soft and good to firm going: has worn bitless bridle: looked
moody towards end of year in 1999, but won over hurdles in October. *J. L. Eyre*

WHIZZ KID 5 b.m. Puissance 110 – Panienka (POL) 70 (Dom Racine (FR) 121) **68**
[1998 NR 1999 a6g⁵ 5d* 5d* a5g 5s⁴ 5.1d* 5f⁵ 5g⁵ 6m 6m 5m 5g* 5.2g 5.1d 5.1m⁵ **a–**
5s 5s³ 5g 5d* 6d 5s Nov 5] tall mare: fair handicapper on turf, poor on all-weather:
had excellent 1999, winning at Ripon (apprentices) and Redcar in April, Chepstow
in May, Ayr in July and Newcastle in October: has form at 6f, probably best at 5f: acts
on all-weather, best on good going or softer on turf nowadays (yet to race on heavy):
blinkered twice at 3 yrs: held up: consistent. *J. M. Bradley*

WHO CARES WINS 3 ch.c. Kris 135 – Anne Bonny 105 (Ajdal (USA) 130) **87**
[1998 NR 1999 8g 10g³ 12g³ 13.4m* 13.9g² 13.3m Sep 18] 52,000Y: rather leggy,
quite good-topped colt: first live foal: dam 1m and 1¼m winner (stayed 1½m) out of
Yorkshire Oaks winner Sally Brown: fairly useful performer: won maiden at Chester
in June: better effort after when good 3 lengths second to Loop The Loup in rated
stakes at York: will stay beyond 1¾m: raced only on good/good to firm going: edged
left final start. *C. E. Brittain*

WHO DA LEADER (IRE) 2 b.g. (Feb 3) Brief Truce (USA) 126 – Lingdale **73 d**
Lass 60 (Petong 126) [1999 5.2m⁴ 5g² 6d 5g 7m 5.3g⁶ Aug 5] 24,000F, 39,000Y:
good-topped gelding: fluent mover: third foal: half-brother to 3-y-o Malaah and 6f

(at 2 yrs) and 7f winner Blue Shadow (both by Pips Pride): dam 2-y-o 6f winner: fair form in minor event at Newbury and maiden at Kempton first 2 starts: well beaten after, including in blinkers: best form at 5f: acts on good to firm going. *R. Hannon*

WHO GOES THERE   3 ch.f. Wolfhound (USA) 126 – Challanging 95 (Mill Reef (USA) 141) [1998 –: 6m 7m 6m 1999 a7g a8g 11.6m 10.2s 7m² 7g 8.2f² 8.2g³ 7m⁵ 8.5m⁴ 9s² 9.9m⁵ 8s Sep 16] modest maiden handicapper: stays 9f: acts on firm and soft going. *T. M. Jones*   **53**

WHOOPS   3 b.f. Shernazar 131 – Ten To Six 66 (Night Shift (USA)) [1998 –: 7.5m 7d⁶ 1999 7f⁵ 8.3m Aug 11] workmanlike filly: signs of a little ability. *E. Weymes*   **–**

WHOSAPRETTYGIRL   2 ch.f. (Apr 5) Clantime 101 – She's A Breeze 35 (Crofthall 110) [1999 5g 5g a6g⁶ a7g 6.1m⁴ Aug 9] 2,600Y: third foal: sister to 3-y-o Dispol Clan: dam poor maiden: well held in maiden/sellers. *Ronald Thompson*   **–**

WHYOME (IRE)   2 b.c. (Mar 20) Owington 123 – Al Corniche (IRE) 62 (Bluebird (USA) 125) [1999 5m 6d² 6.1m* 6m⁴ 7f³ 8g* 8m² 8f² Oct 17] 30,000Y: quite good-topped colt: first foal: dam 2-y-o 5f winner who stayed 1¾m: useful performer: won minor events at Nottingham in June and Pontefract (made all) in August: ran well when 1½ lengths second to Jokerman in Prix des Chenes at Longchamp and length third (promoted to second) behind Night Style in Gran Criterium at Milan last 2 starts: should stay beyond 1m: acts on firm and good to soft ground: has been bandaged: tends to sweat. *M. L. W. Bell*   **102**

WHY WORRY NOW (IRE)   3 ch.f. College Chapel 122 – Pretext (Polish Precedent (USA) 131) [1998 75+: 5m 6m 6g 7v⁶ 7s² 1999 7s⁵ 7m 7d⁵ 7g³ 8s³ 7d⁴ 7d 8d⁶ a7g⁵ a8.5g a7g Nov 27] smallish filly: fair maiden: effective at 7f/1m: acts on soft and firm going: sometimes blinkered. *R. Hannon*   **74 d**

WICKED   2 ch.f. (Apr 26) Common Grounds 118 – Azallya (FR) (Habitat 134) [1999 6m 6f⁶ 6f a7g⁶ Dec 8] 6,500Y: big, lengthy filly: half-sister to 1992 2-y-o 6f winner Serious (by Shadeed), useful at best and effective up to 10.5f, and 1¾m winner Height of Heights (by Shirley Heights): dam French 8.3f winner: poor form: trained first 3 starts by G. L. Moore: visored final outing: sold 3,700 gns. *J. H. M. Gosden*   **40**

WIDDECOMBE   2 b.f. (Mar 12) Mon Tresor 113 – Fifth Movement (Puissance 110) [1999 5.3f a5g³ 6f⁴ Jul 25] 850Y: second foal: half-sister to a winner in Poland by Tragic Role: dam unraced: better effort in Britain when third in seller at Southwell, looking awkward ride: left J. S. Moore then fourth of 6 in maiden at Divonne-Les-Bains. *X. Betron, France*   **46 +**

WIGMAN LADY (IRE)   2 b.f. (Apr 11) Tenby 125 – Height of Elegance 82 (Shirley Heights 130) [1999 7s³ Sep 29] IR 3,000F, 2,800Y: half-sister to 3 winners, including 3-y-o Jane Ann: dam French 10.5f winner: 2 lengths third of 11 to Chapel Royale in maiden at Newcastle: should stay at least 1¼m: should improve. *M. Brittain*   **64 p**

WILBY WILLIE   3 bl.g. Bob's Return (IRE) 123 – Kev's Lass (IRE) (Kemal (FR) 120) [1998 NR 1999 11.5m Jul 20] first foal: dam winning hurdler: tailed off in Yarmouth maiden. *G. A. Hubbard*   **–**

Timeform Futurity, Pontefract—
an emphatic success for Whyome over Reflex Blue, Atwaar (rail) and Murjan (partly hidden)

WILCOY WARRIER 3 ch.g. Desert Dirham (USA) 108 – Noirianna 71 – (Morston (FR) 125) [1998 NR 1999 a8.5g Oct 30] third foal: dam, out of smart performer at up to 1m Noirima, ran twice at 2 yrs: last in maiden at Wolverhampton. *P. Eccles*

WILCUMA 8 b.g. Most Welcome 131 – Miss Top Ville (FR) (Top Ville 129) – [1998 92: 10g 8.1g⁵ 10.4f 1999 9m Sep 18] sturdy gelding: useful performer at best: form since 1997 only on second 7-y-o start: stays 10.4f: acts on soft and good to firm going: held up: has run well when sweating/blinkered. *P. J. Makin*

WILD CANARY 4 ch.f. Groom Dancer (USA) 128 – Nest 65 (Sharpo 132) [1998   **51** 64, a71: a11g* 12.5g⁵ 10m 11.5g⁴ 10d a12g⁴ a10g a12g a14g² a12g⁵ 1999 a16g⁶ Jan 4] modest handicapper: stays 1¾m: best efforts on fibresand: often visored/ blinkered: none too consistent. *D. Marks*

WILD CITY (USA) 5 b. or br.g. Wild Again (USA) – Garvin's Gal (USA) – (Seattle Slew (USA)) [1998 –: a7g a8g a11g a5g a6g 8m a7g 6g 10m 6g 1999 a8g⁶ a11g a8g a6g Jan 25] poor maiden: best effort at 1m on fibresand: tried visored/ blinkered: dead. *R. F. Marvin*

WILD COLONIAL BOY (IRE) 4 b.g. Warning 136 – Loch Clair (IRE) 53 – (Lomond (USA) 128) [1998 63: 7s 8d 8m 7f⁵ 8.1m³ 10d⁶ 10g 10g² 12m³ 11.9f² 13.1m³ 14g 16m⁵ 16s⁴ 15.8d⁴ 1999 11.4m 10m 12.3g Aug 13] quite good-topped gelding: modest maiden handicapper in 1998 for R. Hannon: well held in 1999, twice looking somewhat unenthusiastic: stays 2m: acts on firm going, probably on soft. *G. P. Enright*

WILDERNESS (USA) 2 b.f. (Feb 27) Gilded Time (USA) – Dark of The Moon – (Dancing Brave (USA) 140) [1999 7m Aug 6] first foal: dam unraced, from family of high-class middle-distance performers Diamond Shoal and Glint of Gold: badly in need of experience in maiden at Salisbury: refused to enter stalls on same course in September: sold 2,800 gns. *I. A. Balding*

WILD FLIGHT 2 b.g. (Mar 20) Alflora (IRE) 120 – Absolutely Nuts 73 – (Absalom 128) [1999 8.2d a8g Nov 22] 2,600Y: second foal: dam 5f/6f winner: well held in maidens. *T. P. Tate*

WILD MAGIC 2 ch.f. (Mar 28) Magic Ring (IRE) 115 – Wild Humour (IRE) 60 – (Fayruz 116) [1999 5g Oct 19] 1,000Y: first foal: dam lightly raced at 2 yrs: well beaten in maiden at Lingfield. *W. R. Muir*

WILD NETTLE 5 ch.m. Beveled (USA) – Pink Pumpkin 52 (Tickled Pink 114)   **38** [1998 38: a6s² a6g³ a6g a6g³ a6g⁴ 6g 8.3m 8g⁴ 8g 8s⁶ 8g⁴ 8s 7s a7g a7g⁴ a8g³ 1999 a8g⁴ a10g² a10g² a10g⁴ a10g⁶ a7g Dec 22] close-coupled mare: poor maiden: off course 7½ months before final start: stays easy 1¼m: acts on firm going, soft and equitrack: has been tongue tied: often comes from off pace. *J. C. Fox*

WILD RICE 7 b.g. Green Desert (USA) 127 – On Show 92 (Welsh Pageant 132)   **49** [1998 –: a10g 1999 a10g⁴ a7g Dec 8] strong gelding: formerly fairly useful, poor now: left P. Winkworth after reappearance: stays 1¼m: acts on equitrack and firm going: tried blinkered/visored. *L. A. Dace*

WILD SKY (IRE) 5 br.g. Warning 136 – Erwinna (USA) (Lyphard (USA) 132)   **89** [1998 87: 8d² 8m 8f² 8f² 8m 8m⁶ 8g 9g⁵ 8g³ 1999 8d⁵ 7g 8g* 8m 7f 8m 8d Oct 30] close-coupled gelding: fairly useful handicapper: won at Leicester in May: trained by M. Heaton-Ellis until after fifth start: stays 9f well: acts on firm and good to soft ground (poorly drawn on soft): effective visored or not: tongue tied: usually comes from behind: goes well on straight tracks. *C. G. Cox*

WILD THING 3 b.c. Never So Bold 135 – Tame Duchess 71 (Saritamer (USA)   **66** 130) [1998 –: 6g 1999 a6g² a8g² a7g³ 6s 7d² a6g* 7d⁵ a6g² a7g a7g a5g³ Dec 18] fair performer: won maiden at Southwell in October by 5 lengths: left R. Hannon after eighth outing: easily best effort after when strong-finishing third in handicap at Lingfield: has form at 7f, probably best at 5f/6f: acts good to soft going and all-weather: blinkered final 2 starts. *J. J. Bridger*

WILD TIMES 3 b.g. Emarati (USA) 74 – Pink Pumpkin 52 (Tickled Pink 114) – [1998 –: 5.3g 6m 7m 1999 a8.5g Jan 6] no sign of ability. *E. A. Wheeler*

WILD WILLIE-D (IRE) 4 b.g. Balla Cove 119 – Fine Print (IRE) (Taufan –
(USA) 119) [1998 –: a9.4g⁴ 1999 7f 5.7h Aug 3] little form. *John Berry*

WILEMMGEO 2 b.f. (Apr 7) Emarati (USA) 74 – Floral Spark 69 (Forzando **56**
122) [1999 5v a7g⁴ 7m² 7.5g³ a7g a8.5g* a8g Dec 8] 3,800Y: sturdy filly: second **a51**
foal: half-sister to 3-y-o Angus The Bold: dam 5f winner: modest form: won seller at
Wolverhampton in November: stays 8.5f: acts on fibresand, below form on equitrack.
P. C. Haslam

WILFRAM 2 b.g. (May 7) Fraam 114 – Ming Blue 52 (Primo Dominie 121) [1999 **56**
6g 6.1f⁴ 6d Nov 4] 4,000Y: third foal: half-brother to 3-y-o Modesty Forbids: dam
poor maiden on Flat/over hurdles: modest form in maiden/minor event first 2 starts:
will be suited by 7f+: acts on firm ground, well held on good to soft. *J. M. Bradley*

WILLIAM BARRAUD (IRE) 2 b.g. (Apr 6) Tenby 125 – Vibrant Hue (USA) **87**
(Exclusive Native (USA)) [1999 6m 6.8d* 7.9d² 8d Oct 15] IR 15,000F, 4,500Y,
21,000 2-y-o: angular gelding: half-brother to 1993 2-y-o 7f winner Gingerbird (by
Salt Dome), later successful in Belgium, and Irish 6.5f and 9.7f winner Brackloon
Boy (by Lemhi Gold): dam placed in Ireland/USA: fairly useful form: won maiden at
Warwick in September: good neck second of 20 to Duchamp in nursery at York: short
to post and never going well in similar event at Newmarket final start: should stay
1¼m. *P. F. I. Cole*

WILLIAMSHAKESPEARE (IRE) 3 b.c. Slip Anchor 136 – Rostova 91 **87**
(Blakeney 126) [1998 81p: 8g⁶ 1999 10g² 12g³ 12m 12f² 12m² 11.9d³ 14.1m² Aug
23] sparely-made colt: fairly useful maiden: may prove best up to 1½m: raced mainly
on good going or firmer. *B. W. Hills*

WILLIAM'S WELL 5 ch.g. Superpower 113 – Catherines Well 99 (Junius (USA) **77**
124) [1998 63: 5d⁴ 5m⁵ 5d³ 5g³ 5d 5m⁴ a5g⁵ 6m 5m⁴ 5g² 5m³ 1999 5g³ 5m 5g* 5f*
5m² 5m² 5g⁶ 5m² 5m⁵ 5d 5g 5g⁴ Oct 16] useful-looking gelding: fair handicapper:
won at Carlisle and Catterick in July: has form at 6f, races mainly at 5f nowadays:
acts on firm and soft ground, respectable effort only run on fibresand: wears blinkers:
has been slowly away: consistent. *M. W. Easterby*

WILLIAM THE LION 2 b.g. (Feb 9) Puissance 110 – Last Note (Welsh Pageant –
132) [1999 6g 5.9m 7.1d Aug 6] 11,000Y: rather leggy, quite good-topped gelding:
sixth foal: dam, ran once, out of half-sister to smart stayer Fortissimo: no show in
maidens. *J. Berry*

WILLIE CONQUER 7 ch.g. Master Willie 129 – Maryland Cookie (USA) 101 **92**
(Bold Hour) [1998 –: 12m 12d 12g³ 12m 1999 11.9g* 12m⁵ 13.3m 14f⁵ 14.8m⁴ 16s
Oct 22] smallish, lengthy, good-bodied gelding: fairly useful handicapper: won
6-runner race at Brighton in June: ran creditably most starts after: stays 1¾m: acts on
firm ground: ran as if something amiss third start, tongue tied after: often held up.
D. R. C. Elsworth

WILL IVESON (IRE) 2 b.g. (Apr 1) Mukaddamah (USA) 125 – Cherlinoa (FR) **60**
(Crystal Palace (FR) 132) [1999 5d⁴ a6g⁵ 5m⁶ 6g 7m⁵ a7g⁶ a8g⁵ a8g⁵ Dec 21] IR
5,000F, 13,000Y: leggy gelding: eighth foal: half-brother to a multiple winner in
Italy, including at 2 yrs, by Cyrano de Bergerac: dam French maiden: modest maiden:
not at best final 3 starts: stays 7f: acts on fibresand and good to firm going, probably
on good to soft. *P. C. Haslam*

WILLOW MAGIC 2 b.f. (Mar 28) Petong 126 – Love Street 62 (Mummy's Pet **57**
125) [1999 5g⁶ 6g 5g a5g² Dec 29] 13,500Y, 13,000 2-y-o: fifth foal: half-sister to
3-y-o Another Lover, 5.3f winner La Belle Dominique (by Dominion) and 4-y-o
Contrary Mary: dam, sprint maiden, out of smart sprinting 2-y-o Crime of Passion:
modest maiden: left A. McNae, good second in nursery at Lingfield final start: likely
to prove best at 5f/6f: acts on equitrack. *S. Dow*

WILLRACK TIMES 2 b.f. (Feb 5) Timeless Times (USA) 99 – Willrack Farrier **55**
73 (Lugana Beach 116) [1999 5s 5d³ a5g 5.1m 5m⁴ Jul 15] 9,000Y: smallish, sturdy
filly: first foal: dam 5f winner at 2 yrs: modest maiden: good fourth of 8 in nursery at
Doncaster final start, making most: may prove best at 5f: acts on soft and good to
firm going. *B. A. McMahon*

WILL TO WIN 5 b.m. Mazilier (USA) 107 – Adana (FR) (Green Dancer (USA) –
132) [1998 48: a7g 7s 5.1s 5.7f a7g⁶ 6m⁴ 6m 6g 6m⁶ 5m⁶ 5.1d 6m a7g a6g 1999 a8f

Jan 14] unfurnished mare: poor handicapper: stays 6f: acts on firm going, good to soft and fibresand: tried visored. *T. Keddy*

WILLY WILLY   6 ch.g. Master Willie 129 – Monsoon 66 (Royal Palace 131)   –
[1998 84: 9m* 12m⁵ 10.1s 10g⁴ 10.1d 1999 10m May 24] tall, lengthy, unfurnished gelding: unraced before 1998, when fairly useful winner on debut: little show on Flat since, but winning hurdler. *D. L. Williams*

WILMORE   3 gr.g. Elmaamul (USA) 125 – Kibitka (FR) (Baby Turk 120) [1998   **63**
NR 1999 10g 10m 10.5s* 10g³ 11.6m⁶ 11.6s³ 10s⁶ 10f a10g Nov 8] second foal: half-brother to fairly useful 7f (at 2 yrs) to 1½m winner Colleville (by Pharly): dam unraced from family of very smart French stayer Shafaraz: modest performer: won 5-runner maiden at Warwick in June, despite carrying head very high: may prove best around 1¼m: acts on soft going. *M. A. Jarvis*

WILOMENO   3 b.f. Efisio 120 – Tzarina (USA) (Gallant Romeo (USA)) [1998   –
NR 1999 8.3d a8g Nov 26] 450Y: half-sister to 3 winners, including useful sprinter Mandub (by Topsider): dam placed in USA: behind in 2 maidens. *Mrs L. C. Jewell*

WILTON   4 ch.g. Sharpo 132 – Poyle Amber 55 (Sharrood (USA) 124) [1998 88:   –
5v 6m 6g a7g² 7s⁴ 8.3s³ 8d* 8m⁵ 8v* 7s⁶ 8s² a8g* a9.4s² a8g 1999 a7f a8.5g Oct 13] compact gelding: fairly useful handicapper: well beaten both 4-y-o starts: stays 9.4f: acts on all-weather, best turf efforts on good to soft going or softer. *J. Hetherton*

WINCE   3 b.f. Selkirk (USA) 129 – Flit (USA) 72 (Lyphard (USA) 132) [1998   **117**
94+: 5m³ 7d* 7.1m² 6.1g* 7g⁵ 7g 1999 7m* 8m* 8g⁵ May 23]
    With the Rowley Mile course resembling a bomb site due to major building work, Newmarket's two classic races were run on the July course in 1999 for the first time since the Second World War, and, as on the previous occasion it was held there, the One Thousand Guineas was won by the favourite. Whereas Sun Stream, successful in 1945, had looked a major contender for the race from early on in her two-year-old career, the latest winner Wince was generally ignored until around a couple of weeks beforehand, having spent her time in the shadow of her much vaunted stable-companion Bionic. The latter was vying for favouritism for the Guineas

Sagitta 1000 Guineas Stakes, Newmarket—in the largest field for nearly two decades,
Wince (right) gives her trainer his third win in the race in four years;
Wannabe Grand and Capistrano Day (striped cap) are second and fourth respectively; third-placed Valentine
Waltz is off the picture to the right

when having to be scratched after going lame in a gallop in early-April, but even then Wince, who was in the same ownership, wasn't regarded as an automatic replacement. Her two-year-old form, though fairly useful, hardly entitled her to be regarded as a likely classic winner, her only wins in six starts coming in a maiden at Kempton and a minor event at Chester, and on the eve of her reappearance run, in the Dubai Duty Free (Fred Darling) Stakes at Newbury, 33/1 was available about her for the Guineas. Even after a length and a half victory at Newbury, odds of around half that were still on offer. Wince's performance in accounting for Golden Silca and nine others was a workmanlike rather than spectacular one in a no more than useful renewal of this Group 3 event, although it did at least show that she had trained on well.

Five of those who finished behind Wince took her on again in the Sagitta One Thousand Guineas, including Golden Silca and the third and fourth Capistrano Day and Boomerang Blade. There were another sixteen fillies to contend with, too, in what was the biggest field for the race since 1980, when twenty-three had taken part. Apart from Bionic, two others who had figured prominently in the ante-post betting through the winter were missing from the line-up, Etizaaz having failed to please in her preparation and the top juvenile filly of 1998 Bint Allayl tragically having been put down after fracturing a shoulder on the gallops in February. The French challenger Moiava, winner of the Criterium de Maisons-Laffitte, and Sunspangled, winner of the Fillies' Mile at Ascot and one of two Irish-trained runners, headed the betting on the morning of the race. Both were making their seasonal reappearance, as were the two Godolphin runners Fairy Queen and Pescara, the Rockfel Stakes winner Hula Angel, and Wannabe Grand and Imperial Beauty, first and second respectively in the Cheveley Park Stakes. Apart from Wince and the 50/1-shot Kuwait Dawn, the only contender to have been successful in the current season was

Mr K. Abdulla's "Wince"

Valentine Waltz, an impressive winner of the Nell Gwyn Stakes over the course the previous month. Wince, whose odds had contracted steadily, was generally third favourite at this stage. However, confidence behind her was growing following very encouraging reports of her work at home since Newbury with Enrique, and, while Moiava and Sunspangled drifted in the betting, Wince came in for such strong support that she was down to 4/1 at the off.

The field split into two groups with Wince, who looked in magnificent shape, held up on the stand side where Fairy Queen took them along, whilst that filly's stable-companion Pescara led the far-side runners. Wince, who settled well enough, unlike Moiava, began to make progress over two furlongs out and soon took over in the stand-side group as Valentine Waltz, ridden in similar fashion, did the same on the far side. Entering the final furlong Wince held a narrow advantage over Valentine Waltz and continued to run on strongly to maintain it, despite drifting quite badly left and ending up virtually alongside the latter. As they were fighting it out Wannabe Grand, also coming from behind on the stand side, finished strongly to split the pair, Wince having half a length to spare at the line. She provided a sixth One Thousand Guineas win for Henry Cecil, who equalled Sir Noel Murless' tally in the race, and his third in the last four runnings. Although Valentine Waltz went on to win the Poule d'Essai des Pouliches and sixth-placed Hula Angel the Irish One Thousand Guineas, it was still only an average renewal of the One Thousand Guineas and we rate Wince inferior to the other Cecil winners, One In A Million, Fairy Footsteps, Oh So Sharp, Bosra Sham and Sleepytime. Wince herself finished behind Hula Angel and Golden Silca when only fifth in the Irish One Thousand, for which she started a hot favourite. It transpired that she wasn't quite right behind, and she was given a break with a view to preparing her for an autumn campaign. Unfortunately, problems with a hind joint resulted in the decision being made to retire her, the announcement coming in mid-August at the same time as that which stated the previous year's One Thousand Guineas winner Cape Verdi, who had been kept in training, would also not race again.

		Sharpen Up (ch 1969)	Atan
	Selkirk (USA)		Rocchetta
	(ch 1988)	Annie Edge (ch 1980)	Nebbiolo
Wince			Friendly Court
(b.f. 1996)		Lyphard (b 1969)	Northern Dancer
	Flit (USA)		Goofed
	(b 1988)	Nimble Folly (ch 1977)	Cyane
			Instant Sin

Wince, by the Queen Elizabeth II Stakes winner Selkirk, should continue to do her owner/breeder proud at stud, as have so many of her family. Her dam Flit, who won only a ten-furlong maiden at Beverley from six starts as a three-year-old, must have exceeded expectations already with Wince, her fourth foal. Two of her previous produce, both by Rainbow Quest, are also winners, Fleeting Glimpse showing useful form at ten furlongs in France and Ulundi successful in a couple of bumpers in the summer and twice over hurdles in the autumn. Wince's grandam, the unraced Nimble Folly, has produced a host of winners, including the smart performer at up to ten furlongs Skimble and the useful French miler Nimble Mind, both full sisters to Flit, and their close relative Contredance, a Grade 1 winning juvenile in the States. Contredance's full sister Nimble Feet is the dam of Eltish, winner of the Royal Lodge Stakes and runner-up in the Breeders' Cup Juvenile when trained by Cecil. The third dam of Wince, Instant Sin, won over six furlongs in the States as a three-year-old and also bred the smart Misgivings, dam of the 1986 Rockfel winner At Risk. Wince, a tall, attractive filly (her posed portrait was taken in late-summer after her retirement), and a fluent mover, raced only at up to a mile and is unlikely to have stayed much further. Apart from when successful on good to soft ground on her second start, all her races took place on good or good to firm ground. *H. R. A. Cecil*

WIND CHEETAH (USA) 5 b. or br.h. Storm Cat (USA) – Won't She Tell (USA) **111** (Banner Sport (USA)) [1998 101: 6d 1999 7v² 7.9d 6m³ 6m Jul 17] good-topped horse: has a round action: smart performer, lightly raced: better than ever when 2 lengths second of 7 to Warningford in Leicestershire Stakes at Leicester in April: below that form after, including when third to Halmahera in listed race at Newcastle: may prove best at 7f: has won on good to firm going, goes well on heavy: has been tongue tied/bandaged behind: sent to USA. *Sir Michael Stoute*

WIND CHIME (IRE) 2 ch.c. (Jan 31) Arazi (USA) 135 – Shamisen 86 (Diesis **70** 133) [1999 6m² 6d⁴ Nov 4] second foal: half-brother to 4-y-o Lone Piper: dam, 2-y-o 7f winner, half-sister to smart miler Enharmonic: fair form in maidens at Windsor over 3 months apart, fourth of 17 to Scarlett Ribbon on second occasion: will stay 7f, probably 1m: may do better. *C. E. Brittain*

WINDFALL 2 b.g. (Apr 29) Polish Precedent (USA) 131 – Captive Heart (Con- **–** quistador Cielo (USA)) [1999 7s Oct 8] 11,000Y: third living foal: half-brother to French 1m winner Impose Toi (by Pursuit of Love) and a winner in Australia by Serheed: dam, maiden best at 7f, half-sister to Irish Oaks winner Knight's Baroness: little promise in maiden at Lingfield. *C. A. Cyzer*

WIND IN WINNIPEG (IRE) 3 b.f. Midhish 109 – Tara View (IRE) (Wassl **62** 125) [1998 66: 5m 5g⁵ 5g⁴ 5m³ 6m 5m² 5g² 5d* 6s 6s² 6m 1999 6g 5s 5m⁴ 5s 5m⁴ 6m 5d⁵ 5g⁵ 5m 5g 5s 6s Oct 4] lengthy, good-bodied filly: modest handicapper: reportedly lame behind final start: stays 6f: acts on soft and good to firm going: visored penultimate start: swishes tail and often takes time to warm to task: often apprentice ridden: none too consistent. *J. S. Wainwright*

WINDMILL LANE 2 b.f. (Apr 21) Saddlers' Hall (IRE) 126 – Alpi Dora (Valiyar **58** 129) [1999 7g 7.9m⁵ 8d⁵ 8d 8d⁵ Oct 30] 7,600Y, resold 7,500Y: close-coupled filly: fifth foal: half-sister to winners in Italy by Don't Forget Me and High Estate: dam Italian 7.5f (at 2 yrs) and 8.5f winner: modest maiden: will stay at least 1¼m. *A. P. Jarvis*

WINDRUSH BOY 9 br.g. Dowsing (USA) 124 – Bridge Street Lady 93 (Decoy **49 ?** Boy 129) [1998 44+, a–: 5g 5g* 5g⁶ 5.1g 5m 5m⁴ 5m 5m⁶ 5m³ 1999 5g 5g 5m 5.3g² **a–** 5m⁵ 5.1m* 5.1m 5m⁶ 5g 5m⁵ 5.1m⁴ Sep 9] lengthy, leggy gelding: poor performer: 20/1-winner of claimer at Bath in July: best at 5f: raced only on good going or firmer on turf: has won when sweating: sometimes gives trouble at stalls and slowly away: inconsistent. *M. R. Bosley*

WINDRUSH (IRE) 3 gr.g. Conquering Hero (USA) 116 – Linda Dudley 81 **–** (Owen Dudley 121) [1998 –: 7m 1999 8m 10m 13.8g⁵ Jul 1] IR 4,000Y: half-brother to 1½m winner Hostess Quickly (by Hotfoot): dam lightly-raced half-sister to high-class 1981 2-y-o Count Pahlen: little sign of ability, trained by K. O' Sullivan in Ireland only 2-y-o start: visored final one. *B. S. Rothwell*

WINDSHIFT (IRE) 3 b.g. Forest Wind (USA) 111 – Beautyofthepeace (IRE) **81** (Exactly Sharp (USA) 121) [1998 58: 10d⁴ 10s 7s a8g* 1999 a8.5g⁵ a8.5g² a8g* a8g* a8g⁵ a7g³ 8s* 10.5s⁵ 8d 8g⁴ a7g³ 8m a7g Dec 21] leggy, workmanlike gelding: fairly useful handicapper: won at Southwell (twice) and Warwick in February/ March: mostly below form after: stays 1m, not testing 10.5f: acts on firebrand and soft going: visored after reappearance: has been bandaged in front. *D. Shaw*

WINDSOR BOY (IRE) 2 b.c. (Jan 24) Mtoto 134 – Fragrant Belle (USA) 90 **94** (Al Nasr (FR) 126) [1999 8.5g* 8s⁶ 10d⁵ Oct 30] 110,000Y: rangy colt: good walker: has scope: first foal: dam, 1m winner who stayed 1¼m, half-sister to very smart French 1984 2-y-o River Drummer: fairly useful form: won maiden at Beverley in August, despite handling turn none too well: better efforts when sixth of 8 to Sinndar in National Stakes at the Curragh and fifth of 10 to Monte Carlo in listed event at Newmarket: will be suited by 1½m+. *P. F. I. Cole*

WINDSTORM (IRE) 3 b.f. Forest Wind (USA) 111 – Kaya (GER) (Young **–** Generation 129) [1998 –: 5.1m 6m 6m 8g 5.3g 1999 a6g a8f 8m 7g 6g Jul 5] of no account: blinkered once. *H. Morrison*

WINDYEDGE (USA) 6 ch.g. Woodman (USA) 126 – Abeesh (USA) 77 **–** (Nijinsky (CAN) 138) [1998 NR 1999 10m Sep 7] tall, angular gelding: modest maiden at 3 yrs for B. Hills: no form in 3 runs since. *Mrs A. M. Naughton*

WINDY GULCH (USA)   4 b.f. Gulch (USA) – Wyndalia (USA) (Seattle Slew **86** (USA)) [1998 67, a72: 10d⁵ 10g³ 8.1m⁶ 10.2g⁵ 11.9m 8.1g⁶ a9.4g² 8d⁶ 9.7s³ a9.4s 1999 6.1f 6g⁵ 6s² 6g* 7m⁶ 6f* 6m² 7f* 6m⁶ 7.1m³ 6m³ 7.1d 7d² 7d* Oct 30] lengthy, sparely-made filly: fairly useful handicapper: had a good 1999, winning at Hamilton in June and July, Newcastle (4 ran) in August and Newmarket (20 ran, tended to carry head to one side) in October: best at 6f/7f: yet to race on heavy going, acts on any other turf and fibresand: blinkered last 2 starts in 1998: tough, genuine and consistent. *M. Johnston*

WINGED GREYBIRD   5 gr.m. Batshoof 122 – To Oneiro 69 (Absalom 128) **37** [1998 –: 9.7m 8s 1999 a13g³ 15.4v Apr 13] poor maiden. *Miss A. M. Newton-Smith*

WINGED KNIGHT (IRE)   8 ch.g. Kefaah (USA) 124 – Excuse Slip (USA) **–** (Damascus (USA)) [1998 NR 1999 a14g 14.1g Jul 3] poor maiden: well held in Britain both starts in 1999. *Basil King, Ireland*

WINGS AWARDED   4 b.f. Shareef Dancer (USA) 135 – Ruda (FR) (Free Round **62** (USA)) [1998 67, a59: 10.2s 10.5d 8.3g* 9.1m⁵ 12d⁶ 11.5s⁵ a12g² 12m* 11.9g² **a65** 9.9m⁵ 12g² 12m⁵ 11.9m⁵ 10d² 10s² 10v³ 9g 1999 a10g⁴ 10.2m 10.2m 11.6m 10f⁵ 9.9d² 10g³ 11.9m a12g⁵ Sep 18] workmanlike filly: modest handicapper: effective at 1¼m/1½m: acts on any turf/all-weather: visored last 5 starts (looked none too keen final one). *M. R. Channon*

WINLEAH   3 grc. Petong 126 – Tower Glades 90 (Tower Walk 130) [1998 –: 5s **–** 6g a6g 1999 8m 5d 7d a8.5g Dec 1] little sign of ability. *A. G. Newcombe*

WINNING VENTURE   2 b.c. (Feb 21) Owington 123 – Push A Button (Bold **103** Lad (IRE) 133) [1999 6m² 6m³ 7s* 7m³ 7d² 8f³ Oct 17] good-topped colt: half-brother to several winners, including 4-y-o Wuxi Venture and Irish 1¼m winner Outside Pressure (by Shernazar): dam, Irish 2-y-o 6f winner, half-sister to Riverman: useful performer: won minor event at Kempton in August: placed after in Champagne Stakes at Doncaster (7½ lengths third to Distant Music), listed race at Newmarket (second of 5 to Scarteen Fox) and Gran Criterium at Milan (½-length second of 9 to Night Style, demoted to third): not sure to stay beyond 1m: acts on firm and soft ground. *S. P. C. Woods*

WINNIPEG (IRE)   3 ch.f. Mac's Imp (USA) 116 – Cadasi 68 (Persian Bold 123) **–** [1998 NR 1999 a6g a7g Dec 8] 5,800Y: half-sister to several winners, including 1¼m winner Trade Wind (by Rambo Dancer) and 7f and 2m winner Karamoja (by Auction Ring): dam 2-y-o 6f winner later placed up to 1m in Ireland: well beaten in maiden and seller at Lingfield. *B. Gubby*

WINNOWER   3 b.f. Robellino (USA) 127 – Corn Circle (IRE) 65 (Thatching **–** 131) [1998 –: 6m 6m 1999 a10g a11g⁵ 10.2s 10d Oct 28] neat filly: little sign of ability. *Mrs L. Stubbs*

WINSOME GEORGE   4 b.g. Marju (IRE) 127 – June Moon (IRE) (Sadler's **72 d** Wells (USA) 132) [1998 80: 10.3d⁵ 10.5g⁶ 12m* 11g* 12g² 12m³ 12.3g³ 14m² 16.2m⁵ 13.9f 13.9g 15d⁶ 14.1m 1999 12.3m 14.1m 12f⁴ 12g 14.1m⁶ 12m 12g⁴ 12f 12.1m 17.5d 14.1g 16g Nov 3] compact gelding: has a round action: fairly useful handicapper in 1998: deteriorated at 4 yrs: effective at 1½m to 2m: acts on firm and good to soft going: usually visored: has been tongue tied: unreliable. *C. W. Fairhurst*

WINSTON   6 b.g. Safawan 118 – Lady Leman 74 (Pitskelly 122) [1998 45: 8.3d⁴ **32 +** 7g 8s⁵ 8g 7g 8.1d 8m² 8d⁴ 8.3s³ 8s 1999 a8g⁶ Jan 2] sturdy gelding: poor handicapper: worth a try beyond 1m: acts on soft and good to firm ground, not at best on all-weather: sometimes blinkered. *J. D. Bethell*

WINTZIG   2 b.f. (Mar 30) Piccolo 121 – Wrangbrook (Shirley Heights 130) [1999 **70** 7d⁴ 7m⁵ 7.7g⁶ 8d* Sep 23] 5,500F: seventh live foal: half-sister to 5-y-o Kingdom Emperor, useful 1990 2-y-o 6f/7f winner Punch N'Run (by Forzando) and a winner in Italy by Sharrood: dam little form: fair form: best effort when winning 16-runner nursery at Pontefract by neck from Katy Ivory: stays 1m well: slowly away first 2 starts, on toes preliminaries last 2 (mounted on track at Pontefract). *M. L. W. Bell*

WIRA (IRE)   5 ch.h. Lahib (USA) 129 – Mother Courage 67 (Busted 134) [1998 **–** NR 1999 8.2s⁶ 8m⁶ 10m 8m 8s 8.9m Sep 1] big horse: little form. *M. Brittain*

WISHBONE ALLEY (IRE)   4 b.g. Common Grounds 118 – Dul Dul (USA) **60** (Shadeed (USA) 135) [1998 70: 5d² 6d³ 6g 5.9g² 5.9d⁶ 5m² 5.9d⁵ 5m* 5m 5m³ 6m

5v 6v⁶ 5d 1999 6.1v 5m 6s⁵ 5m 6g² 6.1f² 6m* 5.9g 6m² 6f 7f 6g 6g 5m³ a6g 6s³ a6g a7g a6g² a5g² Dec 29] strong, close-coupled gelding: modest handicapper: won at Newcastle in June: effective at 5f/6f: acts on good to firm going (probably heavy) and equitrack: blinkered/visored after firth start: has run well sweating: often early to post: has hung/looked none too keen. *M. Dods*

WISHEDHADGONEHOME (IRE)   2 b.f. (Mar 8) Archway (IRE) 115 – Yavarro 44 (Raga Navarro (ITY) 119) [1999 5.1s⁵ 5.1m⁴ 6d 6g 8d 6d 7.1g⁵ a7g a7g a7g² a8g⁶ Dec 29] IR 17,000Y: leggy filly: seventh foal: sister to useful 1m winner Pelham, also 5f/6f winner at 2 yrs: dam poor daughter of Cheshire Oaks winner Yelda: modest maiden: below form after third start: should stay 1m: acts on fibresand, good to firm and good to soft going: slowly away 3 of last 4 starts: visored (ran creditably)/blinkered final 2 outings: not to be trusted. *P. D. Evans*   **63 d a50 §**

WISHFUL THINKER   2 b.g. (Mar 27) Prince Sabo 123 – Estonia (Kings Lake (USA) 133) [1999 6.1m³ 6m² 5g 7m 7.9g 7g Oct 16] fourth foal: brother to 4-y-o The Groveller and half-brother to 11f winner Cry Baby (by Bairn): dam Irish 11f/hurdles winner: fair form in minor event at Nottingham and maiden at Windsor first 2 starts: well below that form after, leaving B. Meehan after fourth start: should stay 7f. *J. W. Hills*   **70 d**

WISH LIST (IRE)   3 b.f. Mujadil (USA) 119 – Final Moment 100 (Nishapour (FR) 125) [1998 91: 6g 6m⁴ 5g³ 6.3s 5f* 5g* 5d 6d² 1999 7m⁵ 6m 6g⁵ 5g 6d Sep 18] workmanlike filly: third foal: dam best at 1m to 1¼m in Ireland: useful performer: won maiden at Tipperary and nursery at Cork at 2 yrs: best effort when fifth to Tifosi in handicap at Fairyhouse (final outing for C. Collins) in August: stays 6f: acts on firm and good to soft ground: sold 8,500 gns. *D. Nicholls*   **98**

WITCHFINDER (USA)   7 b.g. Diesis 133 – Colonial Witch (USA) (Pleasant Colony (USA)) [1998 61, a82: a7g* a7g* a7g* a6g⁴ a7g⁵ 7g⁶ 7f a7g a8g 1999 a7g Jan 2] big gelding: has a long, round stride: fairly useful handicapper on all-weather, fair on turf: held only 7-y-o start: likely to prove best at 7f/1m: acts on equitrack (unraced on fibresand) and good to soft going: usually visored. *Mrs L. Stubbs*   **–**

WITCH'S BREW   2 b.f. (Feb 25) Simply Great (FR) 122 – New Broom (IRE) (Brush Aside (USA) 125) [1999 a7g⁵ 7m⁶ 7.5g⁶ Aug 11] unfurnished filly: first foal: dam, ran twice on Flat, half-sister to top-class chaser Simply Dashing (by Simply Great): modest form at best in maidens: will stay 1¼m. *T. D. Easterby*   **50**

WITH A WILL   5 b.g. Rambo Dancer (CAN) 107 – Henceforth 58 (Full of Hope 125) [1998 65: 8.2s 8g³ 8f⁶ 9g* 9m* 10g⁴ 9d 1999 8s 8.1m⁴ 10m⁶ 8.2g 7v⁴ 8d Oct 11] good-bodied gelding: modest performer: effective at 7f (given good test) to 1¼m: acts on any going. *H. Candy*   **63**

WITH IRIS (USA)   2 ch.c. (Mar 27) Schossberg (CAN) 117 – Classical Dance (CAN) (Regal Classic (CAN)) [1999 6d* 7m² 7f² 6s³ 7.6s⁴ 5v² Oct 25] $12,000Y: tall, lengthy colt: has scope: first foal: dam unraced half-sister to top 1982 2-y-o Danzatore: fairly useful performer: won maiden at Newbury in June: good efforts after when runner-up in minor events, beaten head by Inventive at Lingfield (rider dropped whip) on final start: effective at 5f (at least in testing conditions) to 7f: acts on any going: has pulled hard/hung left. *P. F. I. Cole*   **94**

WITHOUT FRIENDS (IRE)   5 b.g. Thatching 131 – Soha (USA) 58 (Dancing Brave (USA) 140) [1998 46, a66: a10g⁴ a8g* a8g* a8g³ a8g* 8g a8g 8f 8d³ a8g 10m 9.9m 1999 a7g² a8g⁶ a8g³ a8g* a8g³ a8.5g a8g a10g a9.4g a8g⁵ a8g⁴ 7.7m a10g⁶ 11.6m 8.5g a8g⁴ a8g a12g a8g⁶ Dec 17] leggy, narrow, hollow-backed gelding: modest handicapper: left Miss G. Kelleway after second start: won at Southwell in March: ended year mostly out of form: effective at 1m/1¼m: acts on good to soft going, firm and all-weather: usually visored/blinkered: has worn tongue strap: sometimes slowly away: tends to carry head high. *Mrs N. Macauley*   **– a61 d**

WITH RESPECT (USA)   2 b.f. (Feb 27) Rakeen (USA) 99 – Low Approach (Artaius (USA) 129) [1999 7g 8d Oct 22] leggy filly: half-sister to useful Irish 1m (at 2 yrs) and 2m winner Regal Access (by Lear Fan) and 1992 2-y-o 7f winner Known Approach (by Known Fact): dam, placed 3 times in USA, half-sister to Irish 1,000 Guineas winner More So: modest form though well held in maidens at Redcar and Doncaster: should stay 1¼m. *J. G. Given*   **53**

WITNEY-DE-BERGERAC (IRE)   7 b.g. Cyrano de Bergerac 120 – Spy Girl   **63** (Tanfirion 110) [1998 72, a–: 17.2g* 16g 17.2d* 20d⁵ 16g⁵ 16m 16.1g⁴ a16m 1999   **a–** 14.1m 18d⁴ 17.2g 22.2m 16.4d 15.8d⁶ 17.2s Sep 27] close-coupled gelding: modest handicapper: stays 2½m: acts on firm and good to soft ground, had form on equitrack earlier in career: visored once as 2-y-o: held up. *J. S. Moore*

WITTON WOOD (IRE)   2 b.g. (Feb 25) Bluebird (USA) 125 – Leyete Gulf   **–** (IRE) (Slip Anchor 136) [1999 7m 8d 7s Sep 29] IR 40,000Y: useful-looking gelding: fourth foal: half-brother to 3 winners, including 1995 2-y-o 6f winner Ocean Grove (by Fairy King) and Irish 1m winner Absoluta (by Royal Academy), both fairly useful: dam unraced half-sister to Missionary Ridge out of 1000 Guineas third Shellshock: behind in maidens: tried blinkered. *M. H. Tompkins*

WIZADORA   4 gr.f. Safawan 118 – Shrood Biddy (Sharrood (USA) 124) [1998   **–** NR 1999 a7g Jun 5] 1,500F, 800 3-y-o, resold 1,600 3-y-o: third foal: dam unraced: poor form over hurdles: last in claimer at Wolverhampton on Flat debut. *Ian Williams*

WOLF TOOTH   3 ch.c. Wolfhound (USA) 126 – Collide 102 (High Line 125)   **92** [1998 82: 5f 6f⁶ 7m⁶ 7.1m⁴ 7m⁴ 8.1g³ 1999 9.9m³ 10d 10m⁴ 10m⁴ 8m⁶ 7.7m⁴ 8m⁴ 8.1g* 9.9m 8g⁶ 9v Oct 23] strong, close-coupled colt: fairly useful performer: won maiden at Warwick in July and handicap at Sandown (dictated pace) in August, both in small fields: creditable sixth of 20 in handicap at Newmarket penultimate start: effective at 1m/1¼m: acts on good to firm ground, well beaten on heavy: sold 47,000 gns, sent to Macau. *D. R. C. Elsworth*

WONDERFUL MAN   3 ch.c. Magical Wonder (USA) 125 – Gleeful 72 (Sayf El   **58** Arab (USA) 127) [1998 –: 6m⁵ 6s 6d 1999 8g⁴ 8v⁶ 8.3m May 24] compact colt: modest maiden: may prove best at 7f/easy 1m: joined Merrita Jones. *M. J. Heaton-Ellis*

WONDERLAND (IRE)   2 b.f. (Mar 19) Dolphin Street (FR) 125 – Smart Pet 77   **55** (Petong 126) [1999 6f⁶ 5g⁵ 6g⁶ Jul 17] IR 12,000Y: second foal: dam, 2-y-o 5f winner, from family of Lochsong and Lochangel: modest form at best in maidens: played up in stalls and started slowly penultimate start, well beaten final one: should stay 7f. *J. J. O'Neill*

WONTCOSTALOTBUT   5 b.m. Nicholas Bill 125 – Brave Maiden 63 (Three   **63** Legs 128) [1998 –: 16.1m 1999 15.4v* 15.4v³ 16s⁴ Oct 22] smallish, workmanlike mare: fair handicapper: won at Folkestone in April by 17 lengths: ran creditably later in month: will stay beyond 2m: acts on heavy going: fairly useful hurdler. *M. J. Wilkinson*

WON'T FORGET ME (IRE)   4 br.g. Don't Forget Me 127 – Lucky Realm   **52** (Realm 129) [1998 52: 9.3d 11g⁶ 10.9s⁴ 12m⁵ 12g² 10.9d 10m⁴ 10.9s⁵ a12g 1999 12.1m 12.4f⁶ 9.2m 12g Aug 13] leggy, angular gelding: modest performer: well held in 1999: stays 1½m: acts on good to firm ground: tried visored/blinkered. *I. Semple*

WOODBASTWICK CHARM   2 b.c. (Mar 30) Charmer 123 – Miss Mint   **–** (Music Maestro 119) [1999 7d Oct 12] 3,800Y: fifth foal: half-brother to a winner in Belgium by Tina's Pet: dam disappointing maiden: always behind in maiden at Leicester. *J. Pearce*

WOODCOTE WARRIOR (IRE)   3 b.c. Barathea (IRE) 127 – Overact (IRE)   **74** 92 (Law Society (USA) 130) [1998 NR 1999 8g 10.2s 10g³ 10g³ 10g⁵ 12d⁴ 11.6m⁴ 12.1m* 10f⁴ Jul 12] quite attractive colt: first foal: dam, 2-y-o 7f winner, later stayed 12.5f: fair performer: won apprentice handicap at Chepstow in July: stayed 1½m: acted on good to firm going, finished lame on firm final start: dead. *R. Hannon*

WOODCUT (IRE)   3 ch.g. Woods of Windsor (USA) – Lady of State (IRE)   **–** (Petong 126) [1998 –: 6.1m 6g 6.1d 1999 a6g 6g 5.9m 5f a5g Aug 6] smallish, sturdy gelding: of little account. *P. S. Felgate*

WOODLANDS   2 b.g. (Apr 26) Common Grounds 118 – Forest of Arden (Tap On   **90 ?** Wood 130) [1999 5m 6m³ 6g Oct 2] 12,000Y: half-brother to several winners, including 5-y-o Ardent, useful 6f (at 2 yrs) to 7.3f winner Forest Cat (by Petorius) and 1¼m and 1½m winner Annacurragh (by Shardari): dam Irish 7f winner from good middle-distance family: easily best effort when eighth of 26 in Two-Year-Old Trophy at Redcar final start, no extra late on: should stay at least 7f. *R. McGhin*

WOODLANDS PRIDE (IRE)   4 ch.f. Petardia 113 – Valediction 71 (Town   –
Crier 119) [1998 –: a6s a6g⁶ a6g a7g 10.3d 10s a7g a8g⁶ 8f 10.1d 7g 1999 a8g 10.1g
10.1d Sep 15] workmanlike filly: of no account: sold 500 gns. *M. C. Chapman*

WOOD POUND (USA)   3 b.c. Woodman (USA) 126 – Poundzig (USA) (Danzig   **82**
(USA)) [1998 80p: 8s⁵ 1999 10f² 11.7s Oct 26] fairly useful maiden: best effort when
second at Nottingham on reappearance: gave impression something amiss 6 days
later: should stay 1½m: joined R. Hollinshead. *Sir Michael Stoute*

WOODWIND DOWN   2 b.f. (Jan 23) Piccolo 121 – Bint El Oumara (Al Nasr   –
(FR) 126) [1999 7.1m 6m Sep 18] 7,000Y: sturdy filly: second foal: half-sister to
Italian 3-y-o 5f winner (including at 2 yrs) Sacaletta (by Aragon): dam, ran once in
France, out of half-sister to US Grade 1 9f winner Moment To Buy: backward, well
held in maidens: may prove best around 6f. *M. R. Channon*

WOOLLY WINSOME   3 br.g. Lugana Beach 116 – Gay Ming 50 (Gay Meadow   **59**
52) [1998 62, a55: 7.5m² 8.3s⁵ 7s a8g⁵ a8g⁶ a7g³ 1999 a8g² a8f⁴ a8g³ 8.3d a8.5g a8g⁶
a7g⁵ Dec 22] neat gelding: modest maiden: stays 1m: acts on all-weather and good to
firm going, probably on soft: tried blinkered/visored. *B. Smart*

WOORE LASS (IRE)   3 ch.f. Persian Bold 123 – Miss Ballylea 82 (Junius   **75 d**
(USA) 124) [1998 72: 5g 6m⁴ 6g* 7m⁵ 7m² 7g 7m 7g 1999 10d⁴ 8.5s⁶ 10s⁵ 8m 8f*
8g 10m² 9m⁶ 8.1f⁶ 9f 8.1d 7m⁴ 8d a10g⁴ Oct 25] smallish, sturdy filly: fair performer:
won handicap at Brighton in May: mainly well below form after: effective at 1m/
1¼m: acts on firm and good to soft going, possibly not on soft: has worn tongue
strap: sold 6,000 gns. *R. Hannon*

WORLD ALERT (IRE)   3 b.c. Alzao (USA) 117 – Steady The Buffs 62 (Balidar   **106**
133) [1998 86p: 6m⁵ 8g⁴ 1999 7g² 8d⁴ 9d* 8.1m 10m⁵ 10v 9m* 8d Sep 30] rather
leggy, close-coupled colt: useful performer: won maiden at Ripon in May and
handicap at Goodwood (dictated pace to beat Waabl by 1¼ lengths) in September:
too headstrong to post and in race final start: stays 1¼m: acts on good to firm and
good to soft ground, possibly not on heavy: has high head carriage: races freely (has
worn crossed/dropped noseband), and has been taken last and steadily to post: sold
36,000 gns, sent to Saudi Arabia. *P. W. Chapple-Hyam*

WORSHIP (USA)   3 ch.f. Irish River (FR) 131 – Pedestal (High Line 125) [1998   **69**
NR 1999 8m⁶ 9.9m³ 10g⁵ 10.2m 12f³ Jul 23] 100,000Y: rather leggy filly: fifth foal:
closely related to 1¼m winner Plinth (by Dowsing) and half-sister to useful 7f to 8.5f
winner Lionize (by Storm Cat): dam once-raced half-sister to Precocious and Jupiter
Island: fair maiden: stays 1¼m: raced only on good going or firmer: blinkered (didn't
stay) final start: sold 38,000 gns in December. *P. F. I. Cole*

WORSTED   2 ch.f. (Mar 15) Whittingham (IRE) 104 – Calamanco 71 (Clantime   **53**
101) [1999 5d 6g Oct 11] 11,000Y: first foal: dam, 5f winner, sister to useful
sprinter Cape Merino: green, signs of ability in maidens at Sandown then Windsor
(not knocked about): likely to prove best at 5f/6f: may still do better. *Major
D. N. Chappell*

WORTH A TURN   3 ch.f. Chaddleworth (IRE) 103 – Taciturn (USA) 32 (Tasso   –
(USA)) [1998 –: 7v 1999 8.3g 8.3m 7m 10m 10m Sep 1] no form. *R. Rowe*

WORTH THE EFFORT   4 b.f. Beveled (USA) – Haiti Mill 68 (Free State 125)   **48 §**
[1998 71§: 7d² 8d³ 7m³ 8s⁵ 7g⁵ 9g 8m 8d 8d 7g³ 8d 1999 8.3m 8f 7f 8s Jun 12] rather
leggy filly: disappointing maiden: stays 1m: acts on good to firm and good to soft
ground: has given trouble in preliminaries, and refused to race in visor on sixth 3-y-o
start: untrustworthy. *M. H. Tompkins*

WORTH THE RISK   2 b.f. (Feb 7) Chaddleworth (IRE) 103 – Bay Risk (Risk   –
Me (FR) 127) [1999 5d⁶ 5m 5.7m⁵ 6m 6.1m 6v a8.5g⁵ 8d Nov 1] first foal: dam well
beaten both starts: little form: trained by B. Meehan before final start. *Don Enrico
Incisa*

WROTHAM ARMS (IRE)   2 b.f. (Feb 15) Second Set (IRE) 127 – Usance   –
(GER) (Kronenkranich (GER) 118) [1999 8.2s Oct 5] 15,000F: sister to 4-y-o Qilin
and half-sister to several winners, including Irish 9f/1¼m winner Magical Lady
(by Magical Strike): dam German 1m winner: well held in maiden at Nottingham.
Dr J. D. Scargill

WRY ARDOUR 3 b.g. Pursuit of Love 124 – Wryneck 89 (Niniski (USA) 125) **– §**
[1998 –: 6m 7m 7s 1999 5.1s 6g 8f 7m 10s⁵ a8g a12g Dec 21] sturdy gelding: signs
of only a little ability: looked reluctant penultimate start. *A. G. Newcombe*

WURZEL 2 ch.c. (Mar 27) Weldnaas (USA) 112 – Down The Valley 73 (Kampala **88**
120) [1999 7d 6g³ 7d* Oct 21] sixth foal: half-brother to 3 winners, including 4-y-o
Scotland Bay, useful 3-y-o Mayaro Bay and fairly useful 7f/1m winner (including at
2 yrs) Down D Islands (by Then Again): dam 2-y-o 5f winner who stayed 11f:
progressive form in maidens, beating No Retreat by ¾ length at Brighton on final
start: should stay 1m: raced only on good/good to soft going. *R. Hannon*

WUXI VENTURE 4 b.g. Wolfhound (USA) 126 – Push A Button (Bold Lad **87**
(IRE) 133) [1998 97: 8v* 8.1s² 9m⁵ 8.1g² 9g² 10.4s³ 8.1g 9.9g 8.1g* 8g⁵ 8.3d* 8s
8g² 1999 8.3m⁶ 8.1s⁵ 8g⁶ 10.1g 8m 8.1d⁵ 8.3m 8d⁶ 7.9g⁴ Oct 6] sturdy, good-bodied
gelding: has a fluent, round action: useful handicapper at 3 yrs: fairly useful in 1999:
best at 1m/9f: acts on good to firm and heavy ground: blinkered/visored last 2 starts
at 2 yrs: often held up: sold 20,000 gns. *S. P. C. Woods*

WYCHWOOD CHARMER 2 b.f. (Feb 28) Theatrical Charmer 114 – **–**
Lanzamar (Buzzards Bay 128§) [1999 6d a6g Nov 27] second reported foal: dam bad
maiden: well held in 2 maidens. *E. A. Wheeler*

X

XAAR 4 b.c. Zafonic (USA) 130 – Monroe (USA) 102 (Sir Ivor 135) [1998 124: **122**
8s* 8d⁴ 10d² 10d³ 1999 10m³ 10m² Jul 3] smallish, attractive colt: very smart
performer: 7-length winner of Dewhurst Stakes in 1997: best effort at 3 yrs when
third in Champion Stakes at Leopardstown on final start, then left A. Fabre: placed in
Prince of Wales's Stakes at Royal Ascot (2½ lengths third to Lear Spear) and in
Eclipse Stakes at Sandown (headed close home when neck second to Compton
Admiral) only outings in 1999: had an infection afterwards and not seen out again:

Godolphin's "Xaar"

stays 1¼m: acts on soft and good to firm going: tended to race lazily as 3-y-o: suffered further setback after end of season. *Saeed bin Suroor*

XANADU 3 ch.g. Casteddu 111 – Bellatrix 45 (Persian Bold 123) [1998 –: 7s 5s⁵ 1999 7g⁵ 5g 6f* 5m 5m 5.9m* 6m 5m³ Sep 6] fair performer: won seller at Hamilton in July and handicap at Carlisle in August: good effort final start: effective at 5f/6f: goes well on firm ground: sometimes slowly away: none too consistent. *Miss L. A. Perratt*   **66**

XANIA 2 b.f. (Feb 15) Mujtahid (USA) 118 – Polish Honour (USA) 61 (Danzig Connection (USA)) [1999 7v 6s a6g Nov 27] 17,000Y: half-sister to 2 winners abroad, including French 3-y-o 9f and 11.5f winner Salsicaia (by Pursuit of Love): dam, ran once, from very good family: well held in maidens. *M. Johnston*   **–**

XATIVA (IRE) 2 b.f. (May 8) Thatching 131 – Abergwrle (Absalom 128) [1999 5m⁵ 6s 6d Oct 14] IR 35,000Y: smallish, workmanlike filly: half-sister to several winners, including 6-y-o Sovereign Crest, French 3-y-o Felicita (by Catrail), useful 5.5f to 7f winner at 2 yrs, and useful Irish performer up to 1m Anemone Garden (by Dancing Dissident): dam twice-raced daughter of 1000 Guineas winner Caergwrle: shaped quite well in maiden at Warwick on debut: off course 5 months, well held last 2 starts: should stay 6f. *M. R. Channon*   **61**

XCARET (IRE) 2 b.f. (Mar 10) Ezzoud (IRE) 126 – Nyali Beach (IRE) 59 (Treasure Kay 114) [1999 5d⁴ 6d* 6.3m 5.2m 6d 6s 6m Aug 30] IR 11,000Y: first foal: dam, maiden who stayed 7f, from family of top-class French miler Gravelines: fair performer: won maiden at Hamilton in May: very stiff tasks in nurseries final 2 starts (visored final one): should stay 7f. *M. H. Tompkins*   **67**

XELLANCE (IRE) 2 b.g. (May 28) Be My Guest (USA) 126 – Excellent Alibi (USA) (Exceller (USA) 129) [1999 5m 7s 6d Oct 20] 14,000Y: closely related to smart stayer Witness Box (by Lyphard) and half-brother to several winners, including 3-y-o Arabian Moon: dam, French 1¼m to 1½m winner, closely related to Dahlia: well beaten in maidens. *M. Johnston*   **–**

XENOS 2 b.g. (Feb 14) Owington 123 – Little Change 70 (Grundy 137) [1999 5s 5m 5.7f a5g Dec 21] 9,200Y: smallish, workmanlike gelding: half-brother to several winners, including 7f and 1½m winner Spring Sixpence (by Dowsing) and 1m to 1½m winner Forfun (by Jalmood): dam beat at 2 yrs when third over 5f: modest form in maiden at Haydock on debut: achieved little after, twice after long absences: left M. Channon for 8,000 gns after third start. *P. Howling*   **58 d**

XIBALBA 2 b.c. (Apr 11) Zafonic (USA) 130 – Satanic Dance (FR) 80 (Shareef Dancer (USA) 135) [1999 7m 6m 10d Oct 30] leggy colt: third foal: half-brother to French 1¼m to 1½m winner Demonic Dancer (by Subotica): dam, maiden who stayed 1m, half-sister to smart winner up to 1¼m Satin Wood: well held all starts, though showed modest form in maidens at Newmarket and Newbury on first 2: out of depth final start: should stay at least 1m. *C. E. Brittain*   **59**

XSYNNA 3 b.g. Cyrano de Bergerac 120 – Rose Ciel (IRE) 80 (Red Sunset 120) [1998 66: 5g 6g 5m² 6m 6m³ 6m⁵ 5d 7s a6g a6g* 1999 a6g³ 6m 7m 5.9m⁴ 5d³ a6g⁵ Dec 21] tall gelding: unimpressive mover: modest handicapper: best at 5f/6f: acts on good to firm going, good to soft and all-weather: effective blinkered or not. *T. T. Clement*   **58 a63**

XYLEM (USA) 8 ch.g. Woodman (USA) 126 – Careful (USA) (Tampa Trouble (USA)) [1998 67, a33: 10s 8.5m 8m⁵ 10s³ 8m 10m³ 10m⁴ 10m 8.5m a11g a12g⁴ 1999 a11g a12f⁶ a13g⁴ 10.3d 10d 10g³ 10d⁵ 12.3m 12d 12s² 12d 11.8d 10.1d Oct 20] leggy gelding: poor performer nowadays: stays 1½m: acts on all-weather, soft and good to firm going: tried blinkered/visored. *J. Pearce*   **48**

Y

YA-AIN 3 b.c. Warning 136 – Ahbab (IRE) 81 (Ajdal (USA) 130) [1998 83p: 6s 7d² 1999 8.2m² 8g⁴ 8f⁴ 10d 9.7d 10d⁵ 8s³ 8.2f Oct 20] sturdy colt: has scope: fair maiden: below best final 4 starts: probably stays 1¼m: acts on firm and good to soft going: visored last 3 outings: sold 22,000 gns. *P. T. Walwyn*   **78**

YABINT EL SHAM 3 b.f. Sizzling Melody 117 – Dalby Dancer 71 (Bustiki) **77**
[1998 83p: 6g⁵ 5m* 6f 6.5g⁶ 1999 6d 5.1m 5.2g 5g 6m 7d a6g a5g* Dec 15]
leggy, unfurnished filly: fair handicapper: back to form to win at Wolverhampton in
December: pulls hard and best at 5f/6f: acts on good to firm going and fibresand: has
been tongue tied. *B. A. McMahon*

YAHESKA (IRE) 2 b.f. (Mar 26) Prince of Birds (USA) 121 – How Ya Been –
(IRE) (Last Tycoon 131) [1999 5g 5.1f a7g Sep 18] IR 1,900Y: sparely-made filly:
second foal: dam unraced sister to useful winner up to 1¼m Najm Mubeen: no
promise in maidens/seller. *E. J. O'Neill*

YAJTAHED (IRE) 4 ch.g. Mujtahid (USA) 118 – Rainstone 57 (Rainbow Quest –
(USA) 134) [1998 65: 5.7m 9.9d⁶ 11.9g 10d 8v* 1999 a12g⁶ a10g a8f a8g 9.9v Sep
29] close-coupled gelding: fair handicapper: below form in 1999: should stay 1¼m:
acts on heavy going (below form on all-weather): has worn blinkers, including for
win. *G. L. Moore*

YAKAREEM (IRE) 3 b.c. Rainbows For Life (CAN) – Brandywell (Skyliner **103**
117) [1998 80: 7v² 7d³ 1999 a9.4g* a10g 8.5g⁵ 10m⁴ 10.4s⁶ 8f⁶ 8.5g² 7m 10s 8.5d
a8.5g Dec 1] leggy colt: useful performer: won minor event at Wolverhampton in
March: much stiffer tasks after, running particularly well when length second of 6 to
Lear Spear in Diomed Stakes at Epsom seventh start: poor efforts final 4: probably
stays 1¼m: acts on fibresand (possibly not equitrack), soft and good to firm ground.
K. Mahdi

YALAIL (IRE) 3 b.c. Perugino (USA) 84 – Cristalga 90 (High Top 131) [1998 –
NR 1999 8.2m⁴ 6d 9g⁶ 8.2d a10g a16.2g a12g Nov 26] 8,000F, 2,200 C 2-y-o: half-
brother to two 1¼m winners, including useful General Sikorski (by Petoski): dam
1¼m winner: well held all starts: retained 5,000 gns before fifth outing. *K. Mahdi*

YALLAH YABINT 2 b.f. (Feb 8) Puissance 110 – Great Intent (Aragon 118) –
[1999 5.1f 5g a7g Aug 14] 6,000F: first foal: dam once-raced sister to smart sprinter
Argentum: last in minor event/maidens. *D. Shaw*

YANOMAMI (USA) 4 ch.f. Slew O'Gold (USA) – Sunerta (USA) 75 (Roberto **61**
(USA) 131) [1998 71: 5s² 7m 6s 6d 5d a6g⁶ a6g* 1999 a6g a8g⁴ Jan 25] good-bodied
filly: fluent mover: modest performer nowadays: stays 1m: acts on fibresand, soft
and good to firm going. *J. Berry*

YANSHAN 4 b.g. Anshan 119 – Joy of Freedom 57 (Damister (USA) 123) [1998 –
53: 12d 12.3s 16.2m⁵ a14g² 1999 a14g 14.1s a14g Jul 8] useful-looking gelding:
modest maiden handicapper: no form in 1999, including in visor: stays 1¾m: acts on
fibresand. *Bob Jones*

YARALINO 3 b.c. Caerleon (USA) 132 – Wemyss Bight 121 (Dancing Brave **100**
(USA) 140) [1998 NR 1999 10g* 12m 10.1m³ Jul 7] quite attractive colt: second
foal: dam won Irish Oaks: landed odds in good style by 5 lengths in maiden at
Lingfield in May: reportedly lost shoe when last in King Edward VII Stakes at Royal
Ascot: best effort when 2 lengths third to Pegnitz in minor event at Epsom: should
be well suited by 1½m+: tongue tied: sold 45,000 gns, joined W. Dollase in USA.
H. R. A. Cecil

YAROB (IRE) 6 ch.g. Unfuwain (USA) 131 – Azyaa 101 (Kris 135) [1998 87: **87**
a11g⁴ a9.4g² a8.5g 1999 a7g 10s⁵ 8m 10.3f* 10f⁵ 8m⁵ 8g 8.5m⁵ 8f 8f⁵ Jul 31] quite
good-topped gelding: fairly useful handicapper: won at Doncaster in May: some
respectable efforts after but well below form final 2 starts: effective at 1m to 11f: acts
on firm ground and fibresand: edgy sort: often makes running. *D. Nicholls*

YARUBA 2 b.f. (Mar 1) Warning 136 – Khandjar 77 (Kris 135) [1999 6m⁴ 7m 7d **65**
6g³ 6s⁶ 7s⁴ Oct 23] tall, lengthy filly: has scope: half-sister to several winners,
including 3-y-o Zamat and useful 1½m and 1¾m winner Valedictory (both by Slip
Anchor): dam, 9f winner, sister to Shavian and half-sister to Paean: fair maiden:
creditable efforts in frame in nurseries 2 of last 3 starts: should stay at least 1m: acts
on soft and good to firm ground: sold 12,000 gns. *R. Hannon*

YASALAM (IRE) 3 b.f. Fairy King (USA) – Hana Marie 101§ (Formidable –
(USA) 125) [1998 NR 1999 8g Jun 9] fourth foal: dam, 2-y-o sprint winner, became
untrustworthy: lost all chance in maiden at Salisbury when badly hampered: sold
21,000 gns, joined J. Noseda. *V. Soane*

Victor Chandler September Stakes, Epsom—a well deserved first pattern win for Yavana's Pace,
who comes out the better after a tussle with Blueprint

YAVANA'S PACE (IRE)   7 ch.g. Accordion – Lady In Pace (Burslem 123) [1998   **118**
118: 8.5m³ 10d* 10d* 11.9m⁴ 10m² 9.9g² 12g² 13.9f³ 12v* 12s² 12d* 1999 13.9s⁴
11.8s* 12m² 12f² 13.9g 14g* 12m* 14s² 16m 12g⁶ Nov 13] tall, angular gelding: has
a markedly round action: smart performer: won listed races at Leicester in June and
Goodwood in August and Victor Chandler September Stakes (by ½ length from
Blueprint) at Epsom in September: creditable 8 lengths second of 5 to Kayf Tara
in Irish St Leger at the Curragh later in September: ran in Australia final 2 starts,
mid-division in 24-runner Melbourne Cup at Flemington and 1¾ lengths sixth to
Aerosmith in Group 2 event at Sandown: stays 1¾m: acts on good to firm and heavy
going: has proved troublesome to post and got loose before start (taken down alone
before Melbourne Cup): tough and reliable. *M. Johnston*

YAVERLAND (IRE)   7 b.g. Astronef 116 – Lautreamont (Auction Ring (USA)   **33**
123) [1998 –, a57: a12g³ a12g² a12g⁵ 12m 11.5g a12g³ 14.1d a14g² 1999 16d⁴
Jun 2] big, strong gelding: maiden: poor form in 1999: stays 2m: acts on fibresand,
probably on good to soft. *John Berry*

YAZEYDD   2 b.c. (Mar 5) Primo Dominie 121 – Murooj (USA) (Diesis 133) [1999   **–**
7m 7.1m 6v Sep 24] fifth foal: half-brother to German winner around 7f Dubai
College (by Old Vic): dam unraced half-sister to very smart middle-distance stayer
Mashkour: soundly beaten in maidens and (blinkered) claimer: sold 1,400 gns, sent
to Kuwait. *B. Hanbury*

YAZMIN (IRE)   2 b.f. (Jan 12) Green Desert (USA) 127 – All My Heart (USA)   **94**
(Sharpen Up 127) [1999 6.1m² 6m* 6m³ 6.5d⁴ Oct 15] IR 110,000Y: fourth foal:
half-sister to a winner in Japan by Caerleon: dam unraced daughter of sister to
Rainbow Quest: progressive form: won maiden at Windsor in August: close fourth of
9 to Perugina in Prix Eclipse at Saint-Cloud final start: will stay 7f. *J. L. Dunlop*

YEAHYEAHYEAH   2 b.g. (Mar 24) King's Signet (USA) 110 – Witch (Risk Me   **–**
(FR) 127) [1999 7.1v 7g 5d Oct 26] 1,300F, 5,200Y: first foal: dam unraced: no sign
of ability. *M. W. Easterby*

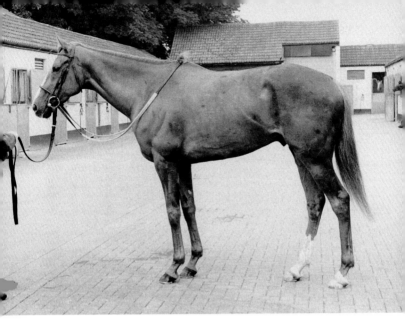

Mrs Joan Keaney's "Yavana's Pace"

YEAST 7 b.g. Salse (USA) 128 – Orient 106 (Bay Express 132) [1998 87: 7.1d **94**
7m[6] 7g[5] 10g[4] 8g 10m[4] 12.3m[6] 10s 8m[3] 1999 8g[5] 8.1g* 8m* 8m 8f[2] 8m 8m* 9.1d 8d
Oct 14] big, good-bodied gelding: one-time smart performer, fairly useful nowadays:
won minor event at Chepstow in May, handicap at Salisbury in June and claimer at
Ripon in August: best form at 1m/1¼m on good going or firmer: has swished tail:
front runner. *W. J. Haggas*

YELLOW RIBBON (IRE) 3 b.f. Hamas (IRE) 125§ – Busker (Bustino 136) **72**
[1998 72: 5s[3] 7m 6m 1999 a10g[4] 7m* 7d 7m 6.8m 7g a9.4f Oct 2] lengthy filly: fair **a–**
handicapper: won 20-runner event at Warwick in May: below form after: may prove
best around 7f: acts on soft and good to firm ground: has given trouble in preliminaries: none too consistent: sold 3,000 gns. *B. W. Hills*

YENALED 2 gr.g. (Apr 19) Rambo Dancer (CAN) 107 – Fancy Flight (FR) 74 **59**
(Arctic Tern (USA) 126) [1999 5m 6d 7.1m[4] 7.1d[6] 6f[3] 7.1m[2] 8d[3] 8v[5] 8d[6] 7.1g[3]
Nov 3] 7,000Y: half-brother to 3 winners, including useful 1994 2-y-o sprinter
Sumoquinn (by Then Again) and 1¼m seller winner Barley Cake (by Midyan): dam
1¼m winner: modest maiden: best efforts when placed, including in 2 nurseries:
stays 1m: acts on good to firm going, probably on heavy: edgy (below form)
penultimate start. *J. S. Goldie*

YEOMAN OLIVER 6 b.h. Precocious 126 – Impala Lass 81 (Kampala 120) **72**
[1998 77: a8s[2] a7s[2] a9.4g[3] a8g[2] a8g[4] a8.5g[4] a9.4g a8.5g[6] 8.2s[3] a8.5g[6] a7g[3] a9.4g[2]
a8.5g[2] a8g[6] 8d* 8.2s* 8d[2] a8.5g a8g[3] 1999 a8g[2] a8g[3] a9.4g Feb 6] fair handicapper:
respectable placed efforts in 1999: ran poorly final start: stayed 9.4f: acted on soft
ground and fibresand: blinkered/visored: sometimes hung: dead. *B. A. McMahon*

YES COLONEL (IRE) 2 gr.c. (Mar 22) Colonel Collins (USA) 122 – Lesley's **–**
Fashion 67 (Dominion 123) [1999 6d a8g Nov 11] first foal: dam 1¼m winner:
soundly beaten in maidens at Windsor (slowly away) and Lingfield. *Derrick Morris*

YES KEEMO SABEE   4 b.g. Arazi (USA) 135 – Nazeera (FR) (Lashkari 128)   **77**
[1998 63: 14m⁴ 12.3s⁵ 10.3g a8.5g a11g² 1999 a11f⁵ a12g² a11g² a12g⁶ 18d² 16g
16.2d² 16s* 16m May 26] tall, angular gelding: fair handicapper: good efforts when
runner-up before winning at Thirsk in May, idling in front: stays 2¼m: acts on fibresand, soft and good to firm going: sometimes edgy: has been bandaged: consistent.
D. Shaw

YET AGAIN   7 ch.g. Weldnaas (USA) 112 – Brightelmstone 105 (Prince Regent   **–**
(FR) 129) [1998 66: a12g² a12g* 12g⁴ 11.9g* 12d⁵ 11.9m² 11.9d³ 1999 12m Aug 4]
compact, good-bodied gelding: fair handicapper: well held only run in 1999: stays
13f: acts on firm going, good to soft and equitrack: blinkered 5 times (winning once)
in 1996: has been bandaged. *Miss Gay Kelleway*

YORKIES BOY   4 gr.c. Clantime 101 – Slipperose 72 (Persepolis (FR) 127)   **107 d**
[1998 111: 5s* 5d* 5.1m 5f 6m 5.2g 6d² 1999 6d² 6g 5m 5m⁵ 6s³ 7g 6m 5v 6d 6s Nov 6]
leggy, useful-looking colt: useful performer: placed in listed race at Doncaster (to
Tedburrow) on reappearance and Duke of York Stakes at York (flattered when third
to Sampower Star): mostly disappointing otherwise: effective at 5f/6f: acts on soft
and good to firm going: usually races prominently: blinkered final start: joined
A. Berry. *B. A. McMahon*

YORKIE TOO   3 b.g. Prince Sabo 123 – Petonica (IRE) 77 (Petoski 135) [1998   **54**
NR 1999 8m 7m 8g 9.9m 10m⁴ 10d 10.1g Aug 19] 20,000Y, 5,000 2-y-o: leggy
gelding: third foal: half-brother to useful 6f (at 2 yrs)/7f winner Yorkie George (by
Efisio): dam lightly raced: modest maiden: will prove best short of 1¼m: blinkered
final 3 starts: has looked difficult ride: inconsistent. *H. J. Collingridge*

YORKSHIRE GRIT   3 ch.f. Ardkinglass 114 – Jarrettelle (All Systems Go 119)   **– §**
[1998 50: 5s 5d⁶ a5g 5g* 5m 5g³ 5d 1999 6m 5g 5m 5g 7m 5m Aug 30] poor
performer: likely to prove best at 5f: blinkered final 3 starts: has reared/played up in
stalls: one to leave alone. *J. Balding*

YORKSHIRE PRIDE (IRE)   2 b.f. (Apr 26) Night Shift (USA) – Shajara (FR)   **–**
(Kendor (FR) 122) [1999 6d Aug 5] 16,000Y: first foal: dam, French middle-distance
maiden, out of half-sister to Shergar: well held in maiden at Haydock. *R. A. Fahey*

YOU DA MAN (IRE)   2 b.c. (Mar 16) Alzao (USA) 117 – Fabled Lifestyle (Kings   **65**
Lake (USA) 133) [1999 7m 8v⁶ 7d 7s Oct 25] 79,000F, 150,000Y: well-made,
attractive colt: fifth living foal: brother to useful 1¼m winner Old Hickory and fairly
useful 1½m winner Fabled Light and half-brother to 2 winners, including useful 1997
2-y-o 5f/6f winner Mijana (by Tenby): dam, Irish 9f winner, half-sister to Dante
winner Lyphard's Wish: fair maiden: well held in nursery at Leicester final start: bred
to be suited by 1¼m+. *R. Hannon*

YOUNG BEN (IRE)   7 ch.g. Fayruz 116 – Jive (Ahonoora 122) [1998 52§, a37§:   **39 §**
a6g³ a5g⁶ a6g 5m³ 5g² 5s⁵ 5d 5m² 5g 5g 1999 5m 5m⁶ 5m 5f 5g 5m Aug 26] smallish   **a– §**
gelding: poor handicapper: best at 5f: acts on good going or firmer and fibresand:
blinkered/visored: reared leaving stalls final start: unreliable. *J. S. Wainwright*

YOUNG BIGWIG (IRE)   5 b.g. Anita's Prince 126 – Humble Mission (Shack   **73**
(USA) 118) [1998 82, a–: a6g 5s 5d* 5m 6g 5s* 6d² 5s⁴ 6g⁵ 6g 6m³ 6g³ 5.1d⁶   **a79**
5d 6d 5m 6v a6g 1999 a6g² a6g a6g⁵ 5d⁵ 6m³ 5d 6d 5d 6d² 6d³ 7m 7.7s a5g⁵
6d⁵ 6m* 6m 5.1m⁵ a6g⁶ 5g 5g 5s a6f* 6v a6g* a7g² 6d⁵ a6g a6g a6g Dec 21]
strong, lengthy gelding: fair handicapper: won at Redcar in June and twice at
Wolverhampton in October: below form final 3 starts: stays easy 7f: acts on
fibresand, firm and soft going: has won for amateur: has run creditably in blinkers,
but looked unenthusiastic and ran poorly in them nineteenth start: usually races up
with pace: tough. *D. W. Chapman*

YOUNG BUTT   6 ch.g. Bold Owl 101 – Cymbal 80 (Ribero 126) [1998 NR 1999   **–**
8.3m 10.8m 7f 7m 8g Jun 3] leggy gelding: one-time fair winner: no form since 1996.
B. A. Pearce

YOUNG IBNR (IRE)   4 b.g. Imperial Frontier (USA) 112 – Zalatia 97 (Music   **52**
Boy 124) [1998 66: a5g⁴ a5g a6g a5g² a5g² 5s 5g⁴ 5s³ a6g 5g⁵ 5.1m 5m³ 5.1m⁴ 5m
5m⁶ 5m 5s⁶ a5g a5g a5g 1999 a5g⁵ a5g³ a5g³ Dec 10] small gelding: modest
handicapper: best form at 5f: acts on all-weather, soft and good to firm going: tried
blinkered/visored earlier in career. *B. A. McMahon*

YOUNG JOSH   4 b.g. Warning 136 – Title Roll (IRE) 107 (Tate Gallery (USA)   **95**
117) [1998 94: 7d 7m² 7g 1999 6m³ 6.1m* 6m 7m 8m³ 7d 7g Oct 16] compact
gelding: has a quick action: useful performer: off course over a year before excellent
third of 30 to Deep Space in Wokingham Handicap at Royal Ascot: landed odds very
easily in minor event at Chepstow in July: mostly well below form otherwise: likely
to prove best at 6f/7f: acts on good to firm going: sent to Singapore. *A. C. Stewart*

YOUNG MARCIUS (USA)   5 ch.g. Green Dancer (USA) 132 – Manhatten   **39**
Miss 94 (Artaius (USA) 129) [1998 NR 1999 10g 10v⁵ 11.8g 12g⁵ 14.1g 15.8m⁴ Aug
3] strong, compact gelding: poor maiden on balance: best efforts at 1¼m: has had
tongue tied. *K. A. Morgan*

YOUNG MAZAAD (IRE)   6 b.g. Mazaad 106 – Lucky Charm (IRE) (Pennine   **52**
Walk 120) [1998 62: 7f³ 8m 7g 6f⁶ a7g 1999 7s 9.7v⁶ 10m 9m Jun 19] workmanlike
gelding: fair performer in 1996: generally disappointing since 5-y-o reappearance:
stays 1m well: acts on equitrack, soft and firm ground: usually races prominently:
tried visored, often blinkered including on final 3 starts. *D. C. O'Brien*

YOUNG PRECEDENT   5 b.g. Polish Precedent (USA) 131 – Guyum (Rousil-   **88**
lon (USA) 133) [1998 95: 8d 8g³ 8.1g* 7.1m⁵ 8g⁴ 7.9m* 8m⁴ 8.5m⁶ 8m³ 8.5m⁶ 7.9g⁴
7s* 8s 1999 8m⁴ 8m 8d⁴ 7g Oct 16] rangy gelding: useful handicapper at 4 yrs:
respectable efforts in 1999 only when fourth in minor events: stays 1m when
conditions aren't testing: acts on soft and good to firm going: front runner/races
prominently. *P. W. Harris*

YOUNG ROOSTER   2 b.c. (Mar 29) Timeless Times (USA) 99 – Jussoli (Don   **–**
128) [1999 6d 6f Aug 4] 1,300Y: rather leggy colt: seventh foal: half-brother to 4-y-o
Rooster and 7f/1m winner So Amazing (by Hallgate): dam Irish 7f (at 2 yrs) and
1¼m winner: well held in maidens. *Miss S. E. Hall*

YOUNG ROSEIN   3 b.f. Distant Relative 128 – Red Rosein 97 (Red Sunset 120)   **66**
[1998 56: 6d⁶ 6d 6s⁵ 1999 8.1d 8.2m 7m 6m⁵ 6.1g⁴ 7.1m* 6.1m 7g² 7g Oct 15] quite
attractive filly: fair handicapper: won at Musselburgh in August: best effort when
second at Catterick following month: stays 7f: acts on good to firm going, probably
on good to soft: unseated rider leaving stalls seventh start. *Mrs G. S. Rees*

YOUNG SUE   3 b.f. Local Suitor (USA) 128 – Young Wilkie (Callernish) [1998   **76**
NR 1999 8d³ 9m* 12m⁴ 10.4g Oct 6] strong, well-made filly: fourth live foal:
half-sister to two 1½m winners by Good Times and 4-y-o Younico: dam fourth both
starts over hurdles: fair performer: won 4-runner maiden at Ripon in July: well held
in handicaps after: should stay beyond 9f. *M. Johnston*

YOUNG TOBY   2 ch.c. (Jan 30) Timeless Times (USA) 99 – Promise Fulfilled   **45**
(USA) 90 (Bet Twice (USA)) [1999 6d 5m 7g 7m⁴ 8m Sep 7] 10,500Y: lengthy colt:
first foal: dam, 2-y-o 6f winner, probably stayed 8.5f: poor form in maidens/selling
events: stays 6f: blinkered last 2 outings: slowly away first 3 starts: sold 500 gns, sent
to Denmark. *T. D. Easterby*

YOUNG-UN   4 b.c. Efisio 120 – Stardyn (Star Appeal 133) [1998 –: 6d 7m 7m 7m   **71**
6.9m⁵ 8d 7s 1999 7s 7g 8f 10m⁴ 8d 10m³ 9.9g 9.9d 9g* 10m* 10.2g⁴ 10.4f³ 10.1d⁴
10d 9g² 10f⁵ 10d* Nov 1] quite good-topped colt: fair handicapper: won at Newcastle
and Nottingham in August and Redcar in November: best at 9f/1¼m: acts on firm
and good to soft going: blinkered (well held) third start: has had tongue tied (not
when successful): held up. *M. J. Ryan*

YOUNICO   4 b.g. Nordico (USA) – Young Wilkie (Callernish) [1998 68§, a59§:   **– §**
a10s² a10g³ a12g⁶ 13.8g* 12m² 14.1m⁴ 13.8d³ 17.1m a14.8g⁵ 1999 16f 16m⁵
12.1f Aug 24] fair performer at best: well held in 1999: tried blinkered/visored:
temperamental. *Mrs M. Reveley*

YOU'RE SPECIAL (USA)   2 b.g. (Apr 12) Northern Flagship (USA) 96 – Pillow   **77 p**
Mint (USA) (Stage Door Johnny) [1999 5d⁵ 6d⁵ 6d² 8d a8.5g² Dec 11] $7,000F,
13,000Y: third foal: brother to a winner in USA: dam won up to 1¾m in USA: fair
maiden: good second in minor event at Wolverhampton final start: should stay
beyond 1m: acts on fibresand, raced only on good to soft going on turf: type to do
better yet. *P. C. Haslam*

YULARA (IRE)   4 b.f. Night Shift (USA) – Fifth Quarter (Cure The Blues   **80 d**
(USA)) [1998 99: 7.3m 7.1g 7m* 7g⁶ 7f 8g⁶ 7s³ 8d 1999 8.3m⁵ 7.5m 7m 7f 7.1g

7f Aug 1] useful at 3 yrs: disappointing in 1999, leaving B. Meehan after fifth start: stays 1m: acts on soft and good to firm going: usually races prominently: blinkered fourth outing. *M. Halford, Ireland*

Z

ZAAJER (USA)   3 ch.c. Silver Hawk (USA) 123 – Crown Quest (USA) (Chief's   **117** Crown (USA)) [1998 104p: 7s² 7s* 1999 10.4s* 12g 12m⁶ 8d 10d⁴ Oct 29] good-topped colt: has a markedly round action: smart performer: won listed race at York in May by 1½ lengths from Mukhalif, boxed in before quickening in good style: well beaten in Derby at Epsom then probably didn't have ideal conditions next 2 starts: best effort when over 2 lengths fourth of 7 to Little Rock in listed race at Newmarket: needs further than 1m, and should stay 1½m: acts on soft ground, possibly not on good to firm. *E. A. L. Dunlop*

ZABAAD (USA)   3 b.f. Kingmambo (USA) 125 – Skeeb (USA) 94 (Topsider   **65** (USA)) [1998 69: 7m⁵ 6m⁵ 7g³ 1999 7d 7.7m³ 9.9g 10m Aug 23] angular filly: fair maiden: likely to prove best up to 1m: yet to race on extremes of going: visored/ blinkered in 1999: sent to USA. *M. P. Tregoning*

ZABIONIC (IRE)   2 ch.c. (Apr 27) Zafonic (USA) 130 – Scene Galante (FR)   **68 p** (Sicyos (USA) 126) [1999 7.1d⁶ 6g 7.1s Sep 25] 66,000F: good-topped colt: has scope: fourth foal: half-brother to 3-y-o Silk Daisy, German 1996 2-y-o 6f winner Sospel (by Kendor) and French 1¼m winner Cold Encounter (by Polar Falcon): dam French 1¼m winner: fair form in maidens at Haydock first and third starts: out-classed in Gimcrack Stakes at York in between: should stay at least 1m: still carrying plenty of condition final outing, and sort to do better at 3 yrs. *B. A. McMahon*

ZABRISKIE   5 b.g. Polish Precedent (USA) 131 – Somfas (USA) (What A Plea-   **– §** sure (USA)) [1998 –: 7g 8m 6s a8g 1999 a8g² a7g⁶ a8g⁵ a10g 9d a10g⁵ a10g⁶ 10f 10g   **a42 §** Aug 14] sturdy gelding: poor maiden handicapper: stays easy 1¼m: acts on all-weather, no recent form on turf: tried blinkered: sometimes flashes tail: inconsistent and not to be trusted. *G. L. Moore*

ZADA   4 b.g. Distant Relative 128 – Handy Dancer 87 (Green God 128) [1998 –,   **–** a60: a10g³ 8d 10g a10g² a10f⁶ a10g³ 1999 a10g⁶ a12g⁶ Feb 6] good-topped gelding: modest maiden: well beaten both starts in 1999: stays 1¼m: acts on equitrack (untried on fibresand), little form on turf: sometimes takes strong hold: blinkered last 5 starts: has shown signs of temperament. *G. L. Moore*

ZAFFIA   2 b.f. (Apr 2) Zilzal (USA) 137 – Zeffirella 88 (Known Fact (USA) 135)   **61** [1999 6.8m⁴ 6.8d² Sep 21] 3,000Y: leggy filly: seventh foal: half-sister to useful Irish 1m winner Charillus (by Be My Chief) and a winner in Denmark by In The Wings: dam 7f winner: modest form in maidens at Warwick, finishing well when head second of 16 to Jamestown second outing: should stay 1m. *P. R. Chamings*

ZAFOIR   2 br.c. (Mar 31) Zafonic (USA) 130 – Reveuse du Soir (Vision (USA))   **74** [1999 5m⁶ 6g 5.7m⁵ 6f² 6.1m⁴ 6m Sep 4] third living foal: half-brother to French 6f and (at 2 yrs) 9f winner Panfilo (by Thatching): dam, French 2-y-o 7f winner, closely related to smart middle-distance performer Don Corleone and half-sister to Poule d'Essai des Pouliches winner Danseuse du Soir: fair maiden: best efforts fourth and fifth starts, ran as if something amiss final one: stays 6f: raced only on good going or firmer: races prominently: sold 6,000 gns, sent to Norway. *Mrs A. J. Perrett*

ZAFONIC'S SONG (FR)   2 br.c. (Feb 20) Zafonic (USA) 130 – Savoureuse   **86 P** Lady 111 (Caerleon (USA) 132) [1999 7s⁴ Nov 5] big, rangy colt: has plenty of scope: fourth reported foal: half-brother to 3 winners abroad, including useful French 1½m winner Quest For Ladies (by Rainbow Quest), later successful in USA: dam, won Prix Fille de l'Air and stayed 12.5f, half-sister to Mtoto: very promising fourth of 20 to Golovin in maiden at Doncaster, doing well to finish so close having lost ground at start and been hampered twice final 2f: will stay at least 1¼m: imposing sort, likely to prove at least useful and sure to win races. *Sir Michael Stoute*

ZAFONIUM (USA)   2 ch.c. (Mar 28) Zafonic (USA) 130 – Bint Pasha (USA)   **89 p** 126 (Affirmed (USA)) [1999 7d³ 7.9d* Oct 9] big, lengthy colt: has plenty of scope:

seventh foal: brother to 3-y-o Lila and half-brother to 3 winners, including smart 1m (at 2 yrs) and 11.5f winner Revere (by Dancing Brave) and fairly useful 1½m winner Monarch (by Sadler's Wells): dam won Yorkshire Oaks and Prix Vermeille: favourite both starts in maidens, confirming debut promise (third of 22 to Scarteen Fox at Newbury) when landing odds in 6-runner event at York by 2½ lengths from Tigre, leading 2f out before wandering through greenness: should stay at least 1¼m: remains open to plenty of improvement, and sure to win more races. *P. F. I. Cole*

ZAGALETA   2 b.f. (Mar 16) Sri Pekan (USA) 117 – Persian Song 45 (Persian   **73** Bold 123) [1999 6d³ 6m² 6f² Jul 23] 120,000Y: tall, good-topped filly: has scope: third foal: half-sister to 4-y-o Mountain Song and fairly useful but untrustworthy 1996 2-y-o 6f winner Raindancing (both by Tyrol): dam lightly-raced sister to high-class performer up to 1¼m Bold Arrangement: fair form: placed in maidens at York, Catterick and (sweating, very much on toes and not striding out on firm ground) Thirsk: bred to stay at least 1m. *Andrew Turnell*

ZAHA (IRE)   4 b.c. Lahib (USA) 129 – Mayaasa (USA) 70 (Lyphard (USA) 132)   **65** [1998 60: 9.9m 10d 10d 12m³ 1999 a10f² a11g* a12g⁶ 10s³ 9.7v³ 10m⁶ 10s⁵ 10.1m⁵ 9.9v² 8g 10.1g* 9.9s 10d⁵ 10f Oct 20] leggy colt: fair performer: won maiden at Southwell in February and minor event at Yarmouth in August: probably best at 1¼m/11f: acts on good to firm going, heavy and all-weather: effective visored/blinkered or not: sometimes slowly away and not an easy ride. *J. Pearce*

ZAHIR (USA)   5 b.g. Riverman (USA) 131 – Manwah (USA) 72 (Lyphard (USA)   **–** 132) [1998 NR 1999 a7g a12g⁵ a12g⁶ 16.2d a16g 8m May 24] of little account. *R. F. Marvin*

ZAHRAN (IRE)   8 b.h. Groom Dancer (USA) 128 – Welsh Berry (USA) (Sir Ivor   **41 §** 135) [1998 41§, a48§: a8.5g 8m² 10g 8m 8d 8s 10g 8.1g² 8m 8.1m² 8m 10.2m 8.1d² 7g² 10.1g 8v a7g⁴ a7g³ a8f 1999 a8g a9.4g³ Jan 6] good-topped horse: unimpressive mover: poor performer: effective at 7f to 1¼m: acts on firm ground, soft and all-weather: tried visored/blinkered earlier in career: tends to get behind: unreliable. *J. M. Bradley*

ZAHRAT DUBAI   3 b.f. Unfuwain (USA) 131 – Walesiana (GER) (Star   **114** Appeal 133) [1998 79P: 7g⁶ 1999 10.4d* 12d³ 9.9f* 11.9g⁴ 9.3v⁵ Oct 3]

Royal Anthem provided American jockey Gary Stevens with his most spectacular pattern victory during his European stint in the International at York, but it was Zahrat Dubai who got him off the mark in Group 1 company in the Nassau Stakes. Opposed by seven rivals, Zahrat Dubai started third favourite behind two top fillies from the previous season in Alborada, making her reappearance, and Cape Verdi, who had finished third in the Falmouth Stakes on her comeback. Kissogram was another four-year-old attempting to prove she had trained on, while Diamond White and Lady In Waiting had both been running creditably without showing anything like Group 1-winning form. There were two other three-year-olds, the French contender Juvenia, seeking her first win since the Marcel Boussac, and listed winner Alabaq. Zahrat Dubai was sent straight into the lead and, though pressed on all sides when the race finally began in earnest only a furlong out, she ran on well, despite initially idling and hanging into Kissogram, to win by half a length from Lady In Waiting with Diamond White third and Kissogram fourth. Alborada, who briefly lost her footing on the top bend, came fifth, with Cape Verdi, who was subsequently retired, last. The way Zahrat Dubai had won the Tattersalls Musidora Stakes at York in May suggested she might well land a Group 1 event, and a better one than the Nassau Stakes turned out to be. A Vodafone Oaks victory looked very much on the cards after the filly trotted up by five lengths from Mother of Pearl at York, leading two furlongs out and sprinting clear before being eased. Her only previous run had seen her finish an eye-catching sixth in a maiden race at Newmarket in the autumn, though she had reportedly run second to Pescara in the private fillies' trial in Dubai in March. A best-priced 2/1 for the Oaks after her York victory, Zahrat Dubai was odds on at one point but drifted after reportedly failing to please in a workout,

Tattersalls Musidora Stakes, York—
Zahrat Dubai shoots to the head of the Oaks market after this most impressive display;
Mother of Pearl is clear of the rest in second

starting 9/4 favourite. Wearing a tongue strap, as she also did in the Nassau and
Yorkshire Oaks, she became edgy in the preliminaries and could not reproduce
the sparkling turn of foot she had shown in the Musidora, being left behind in
the closing stages and finishing eight lengths third to Ramruma. Connections
thought Zahrat Dubai did not stay the trip, but her run in the Aston Upthorpe
Yorkshire Oaks just over a fortnight after the Nassau confirmed that she did,
under slightly less testing conditions at least; it was more the case that she
wasn't up to beating the best. Having tracked the leaders, she battled away in
the straight without accelerating noticeably to finish under four lengths fourth

Vodafone Nassau Stakes, Goodwood—in a close finish to the first running of the race as a Group 1,
Zahrat Dubai (No.8) comes out on top from Lady In Waiting (No.5), Diamond White (noseband)
and Kissogram (spots); the grey Alborada makes her belated reappearance in fifth

to Ramruma. On her only subsequent start she ran below form on heavy ground after setting the pace in the Prix de l'Opera at Longchamp.

Zahrat Dubai (b.f. 1996)	Unfuwain (USA) (b 1985)	Northern Dancer (b 1961)	Nearctic / Natalma
		Height of Fashion (b 1979)	Bustino / Highclere
	Walesiana (GER) (b 1987)	Star Appeal (b 1970)	Appiani II / Sterna
		Wondrous Pearl (br 1980)	Prince Ippi / Weltwunder

Zahrat Dubai has been retired to stud and visits Rahy. A tall, attractive filly with a fluent, quick action who acted on firm and good to soft ground, she impressed in appearance and is a good advert for her sire Unfuwain. He was rather in the shadow of his half-brother Nashwan as a racehorse but has done a good job at stud after starting at a fee of £15,000, compared with Nashwan's £100,000. His fee is now £10,000, while Nashwan's is £45,000, and his other stars have been Alhaarth and Bolas. The dam Walesiana won three races headed by the Arag-Preis (German One Thousand Guineas) and finished a close fifth in the Deutsches Derby. She produced two minor winners before Zahrat Dubai, namely Warluskee (a winner at a mile and a half, by Dancing Brave) and Waiting Game (a two-year-old seven-furlong winner, by Reprimand). Her 1997 foal, by Lammtarra, is called Edhkerini and is in training with Michael Jarvis. The grandam Wondrous Pearl foaled seven winners from the same number of starters including multiple listed scorer Wondras. Wondrous Pearl landed a nine-furlong listed event and was out of a mare who finished second in the Preis der Diana (German Oaks), with a grandam, Wacholdis, who was the best of her sex at two and three and runner-up in the Deutsches Derby. *Saeed bin Suroor*

Godolphin's "Zahrat Dubai"

ZAL

ZALABIA (IRE) 3 ch.f. Perugino (USA) 84 – Lamya 73 (Hittite Glory 125) –
[1998 NR 1999 6g Oct 15] 10,500 2-y-o: half-sister to 6f/7f winner Murray's Mazda
(by M Double M) and a winner in Belgium by Welsh Term: dam won in Sweden:
20/1, always behind in maiden at Redcar. *K. Mahdi*

ZALAL (IRE) 4 b.c. Darshaan 133 – Zallaka (IRE) (Shardari 134) [1998 96: **103**
12m⁶ 10g⁵ 10.2g* 12d 10.1g 11.9g* 1999 12s 12g*ᵈⁱˢ Jun 27] small, good-bodied
colt: useful performer: off over 2 months before winning 6-runner minor event at
Goodwood by ½ length from Nautical Star (subsequently disqualified after failing a
dope test): probably better at 1½m than shorter: seems to act on good to soft going,
showed promise on good to firm: sold 6,500 gns in October. *L. M. Cumani*

ZALOTTO (IRE) 5 b.g. Polish Patriot (USA) 128 – Honest Penny (USA) – §
(Honest Pleasure (USA)) [1998 –§, a67§: a7g³ a7g* a7g² a8g⁶ a7g⁶ a8g a7g⁴ a8g⁵ **a44 §**
a9.4g 1999 a8g⁶ a7g⁶ a8g Jan 15] leggy gelding: poor performer now: effective at 7f/
1m: acts on fibresand, lightly raced on equitrack and turf: blinkered/visored:
sometimes unruly in stalls and hangs left: not one to trust: joined I. Williams, and
successful over hurdles in July. *M. P. Bielby*

ZAMAN 3 b.c. Caerleon (USA) 132 – Zafadola (IRE) 112 (Darshaan 133) [1998 **94 +**
64p: 7s⁵ 1999 8d² 10m* 10.5d⁶ Aug 5] well-made colt: fairly useful performer: won
maiden at Pontefract in July: respectable sixth in handicap at Haydock: will stay
beyond 1¼m: acts on good to firm and good to soft going. *Sir Michael Stoute*

ZAMAT 3 b.g. Slip Anchor 136 – Khandjar 77 (Kris 135) [1998 NR 1999 12v Sep –
20] brother to 6-y-o Valedictory and half-brother to several winners, including fairly
useful 1½m winner Iridal (by Rainbow Quest): dam 9f winner, sister to Shavian and
half-sister to Paean: showed little in maiden at Kempton: sold 3,000 gns. *W. Jarvis*

ZANAY 3 b.c. Forzando 122 – Nineteenth of May 86 (Homing 130) [1998 75: 7g⁴ **85 +**
7.1s² 7s² 1999 7.7g³ 8.2d* 9v a8g⁴ a10g* Dec 8] useful-looking, rather unfurnished **a107 p**
colt: useful form on all-weather, fairly useful on turf: trained by K. Bell on reappearance only: won maiden at Nottingham in October and minor event (much improved,
by 4 lengths from Secret Spring) at Lingfield in December: better at 1¼m than 1m:
acts on equitrack, raced only on good going or softer on turf: should do better still.
Miss Jacqueline S. Doyle

ZANY LADY 4 gr.f. Arzanni 115 – Lady Antonia 66 (Owen Anthony 102) [1998 **47**
55: 9.9f⁵ 8.1m⁴ 7d 10.2g⁶ 10m 8d⁴ 8v 1999 10g⁶ 10m 8f³ 10.2m⁵ 9.9m 8s Sep 27]
poor maiden: stays 1¼m: acts on firm ground, probably on good to soft. *R. J. Hodges*

ZARAGOSSA 3 gr.f. Paris House 123 – Antonia's Folly 64 (Music Boy 124) **80**
[1998 76: 5g⁴ 5.2m 5d⁵ 1999 5.1m³ 5g 5m⁵ 5.1g⁴ 5.1m 5f⁴ 5d 5f 5m Sep 10] leggy,
sparely-made filly: fairly useful handicapper: rather in-and-out form, well below best
final 3 starts: raced only at 5f: acts on firm ground and good to soft: equipped with
blanket for stalls entry: usually races prominently. *J. Berry*

ZARA ZAREEN (IRE) 8 ch.g. Mazaad 106 – Nesreen (The Parson 119) [1998 –
NR 1999 a16g Aug 20] seventh foal: half-brother to Flat and hurdles winner Marius
(by Cyrano de Bergerac): dam won on Flat and over hurdles in Ireland: fair maiden at
best on Flat in Ireland for T. Kinane, last ran 1995: no show over hurdles or in
Lingfield maiden since. *N. M. Babbage*

ZARFOOT 3 br.c. Zafonic (USA) 130 – Harefoot 92 (Rainbow Quest (USA) 134) **116**
[1998 78P: 6g³ 1999 8s* 8m² 12m* 12f⁵ 12d⁵ 12d² Oct 17] strong, lengthy, good
sort: impresses in appearance: has a quick action: smart performer: won maiden at
Newbury in May and 4-runner listed race at Ascot in June: best efforts final 2 starts,
notably when beaten short neck by First Magnitude in steadily-run Prix du Conseil
de Paris at Longchamp: stays 1½m, should prove at least as effective at 1¼m: acts on
soft ground, probably on firm. *L. M. Cumani*

ZARILIYA (IRE) 3 b.f. Darshaan 133 – Zariya (USA) 88 (Blushing Groom (FR) **82**
131) [1998 71p: 8.2s³ 1999 10.5g² 10m² 12d* 11.5s⁶ Oct 8] good-bodied filly: fairly
useful performer: landed odds in maiden at Musselburgh in September in workmanlike style: below form final start: stays 1½m: acts on good to firm and good to soft
going. *Sir Michael Stoute*

ZECHARIAH 3 b.g. Kasakov – Runfawit Pet 41 (Welsh Saint 126) [1998 61: **57**
a5g⁵ a5g³ a5g 7m 7g⁵ 7m² 6d⁵ 7s a8.5g* a8g a7g⁶ 1999 7.5m² 7f³ 8.1d⁶ a8.5g 6.9g

7d[5] Oct 12] modest performer: stays 8.5f: acts on good to firm going, good to soft and fibresand: leads/races prominently: none too consistent. *J. L. Eyre*

ZELBECK 3 b.f. Komaite (USA) – Kakisa 81 (Forlorn River 124) [1998 NR 1999 – 7.1s 6s 8.2d Oct 21] sister to 1997 2-y-o 5f winner Wait'n'See and half-sister to several winning sprinters, including fairly useful 5f performer Lake Mistassiu (by Tina's Pet): dam 5f/6f winner: well held in maidens/claimer. *P. D. Evans*

ZENTSOV STREET (USA) 2 b.c. (Apr 3) Nureyev (USA) 131 – Storm Fear **109** (USA) (Coastal (USA)) [1999 7m[2] 7d* 7g[3] 8s[5] Oct 23] $260,000F: close-coupled, good-topped colt: has a quick action: sixth foal: half-brother to 2 winners in USA by Hawkster: dam maiden half-sister to dam of William Hill Futurity winner Bakharoff and smart miler Emperor Jones: useful form: won maiden at Newmarket in September: 3 lengths third of 5 to Distant Music in Dewhurst Stakes there following month, again dictating pace: weak in market, below form in Racing Post Trophy at Doncaster final start: should stay 1m: wears crossed noseband: sent to USA. *A. P. O'Brien, Ireland*

ZEPPO (IRE) 4 ch.g. Fayruz 116 – Chase Paperchase 79 (Malinowski (USA) **63** 123) [1998 67: 6.1s 6g[2] 6g[6] 6m* 6g[5] 5.1d[6] 5m[6] 5f[2] 5g[4] 6m 1999 6.1s 5m[3] 6m[5] 6f[4] 5.7g 6m 6f 6.1m* 5d 6m[6] 7.1m a6g Sep 18] close-coupled gelding: modest handicapper: won at Chepstow in August: probably stays 7f: acts on firm going, not on softer than good (well beaten on fibresand): too free when blinkered fifth start. *B. R. Millman*

ZESTFUL (USA) 2 ch.f. (Feb 20) Zilzal (USA) 137 – Crown of Sheba (USA) 74 **57** (Alysheba (USA)) [1999 6m[6] 5g[5] Aug 24] 45,000Y: first foal: dam, 8.3f winner (should have been suited by further), half-sister to Kentucky Derby winner Spend A Buck and to dam of 3-y-o Hula Angel: modest form in maidens at Windsor and Lingfield: will be suited by 7f+. *C. F. Wall*

ZESTRIL 2 ch.f. (Apr 26) Zilzal (USA) 137 – Rynavey 67 (Rousillon (USA) 133) **76** [1999 5.9m* 6m 5s[4] Sep 21] tall, unfurnished filly: third foal: closely related to 3-y-o 6f (at 2 yrs) and 1m (in Norway) winner Dipple (by Komaite): dam, middle-distance maiden, half-sister to Applecross, the dam of 5-y-o Invermark and 4-y-o Craigsteel: fair form: showed good turn of foot to win maiden at Carlisle in June after missing break: very stiff task next start (scratched to post): seemed to find trip too short final one: should stay 7f: may still do better. *Denys Smith*

ZEYAARAH (USA) 2 ch.f. (May 1) Rahy (USA) 115 – Princess Haifa (USA) 69 **80** (Mr Prospector (USA)) [1999 8.2g[3] 8d Oct 22] leggy, lengthy filly: second reported foal: half-sister to 3-y-o Kondoty: dam, 1m winner later successful up to 9f in USA, closely related to very smart performer around 1¼m in USA Signal Tap, out of sister to Storm Bird: fairly useful form when close third of 11 to Dollar Bird in maiden at Nottingham: only ninth of 18 when favourite for similar event at Doncaster later in October: should stay 1¼m. *M. P. Tregoning*

ZIBAK (USA) 5 b. or br.g. Capote (USA) – Minifah (USA) 69 (Nureyev (USA) **48** 131) [1998 47: a10g 10.9m 8m 6.9m 7g[2] 8.3d 7.1d[6] 6m 6v 1999 8d 8d 7m 7.1g[6] 6m[4] 6f[3] 7g* 6f* 6f[3] 6m[3] 5g 5f 6m Sep 3] poor handicapper: won sellers at Ayr and Thirsk (ladies race) in July: below form final 3 starts: stays 7f: acts on firm and good to soft ground. *J. S. Goldie*

ZIBELINE (IRE) 2 b.c. (Mar 10) Cadeaux Genereux 131 – Zia (USA) 88 (Shareef **70** Dancer (USA) 135) [1999 7m[5] 7.1m[4] 6.1g[5] 7d Oct 27] quite attractive colt: sixth foal: half-brother to winner around 1½m Zeliba (by Doyoun), 3-y-o Zigere and a winner in Sweden by Mujtahid: dam, 1½m winner, closely related to very smart 1¼m performer Media Starguest: fair form in maidens: should stay at least 1m. *C. E. Brittain*

ZIDAC 7 br.g. Statoblest 120 – Sule Skerry 78 (Scottish Rifle 127) [1998 69, a–: **79** 8.2m 9m 10m[3] 10.8m* 10s[6] a12g 1999 a10g[2] a10g* 10.8m a10g 10.2g* 10.3m[6] 8.9m 10d* 10s[3] Nov 1] tall gelding: fair performer: won minor event at Lingfield in February, claimer at Bath in June and selling handicap at Brighton in October: raced too freely final start: stays 11f: acts on good to firm ground, soft and all-weather: sometimes flashes tail/finds little: none too consistent. *P. J. Makin*

ZIETZIG (IRE)   2 b.c. (Feb 7) Zieten (USA) 118 – Missing You 89 (Ahonoora   **81**
122) [1999 5d⁵ 5g 5m⁵ 6g* 6m⁴ 6m² 6g Oct 6] 10,000F, 9,500Y: shallow-girthed
colt: fifth foal: half-brother to 1994 2-y-o 6f winner Miss Mercy (by Law Society)
and a winner in Italy by Rahy: dam, Irish maiden, daughter of Lincoln winner Saving
Mercy: fairly useful performer: won valuable seller at York in August: sweating,
good head second of 22 to Kilbrannan Sound in sales race at Doncaster penultimate
start: will stay 7f: yet to race on extremes of going: seems best held up. *K. R. Burke*

ZIGERE   3 ch.c. Lycius (USA) 124 – Zia (USA) 88 (Shareef Dancer (USA) 135)   **85**
[1998 67: 6s⁵ 1999 8.2s⁴ 10m² 10m 8.3m⁶ 10g* Aug 5] tall, close-coupled colt: fairly
useful performer: easily best effort when second in maiden at Lingfield in June:
wide-margin winner of weak 4-runner similar event at Brighton in August: better at
1¼m than shorter: acts on good to firm ground: carries head awkwardly and tends to
hang: sent to UAE. *C. E. Brittain*

ZIGGY'S DANCER (USA)   8 b.h. Ziggy's Boy (USA) – My Shy Dancer (USA)   **90**
(Northjet 136) [1998 95, a84: a7g a6g⁵ a6g* a7g⁵ a7g³ a6g² 6d 5s² 5.1m² 6g a6g   **a81**
6.1g⁴ 5g³ 5.1m⁴ 5g⁵ 6.1g⁶ 5d³ 6s 5m⁴ 5m⁶ a6g² a6g² 1999 a6g a6g⁵ a6g 5d 6m 5.1m³
5d² 5.1d⁵ 6.1m² 5m² 5.1m³ 5m 5d⁶ 5.1d⁵ 6m⁴ 5.1s 5d a6g Dec 22] lengthy horse:
usually looks well: poor mover: fairly useful performer: generally creditable efforts
in 1999 until last 3 starts: effective at 5f to 7f: acts on all-weather, firm and soft
ground: tough and consistent. *E. J. Alston*

ZIGGY STARDUST (IRE)   4 b.g. Roi Danzig (USA) – Si Princess (Coquelin   **46**
(USA) 121) [1998 52, a–: a8g⁶ a11g 11.6g⁵ 10s² 11.6m³ 10.8g 11.9g² 11.9s⁴ a12g   **a–**
1999 12v a12g⁶ 9d⁵ 10.1m 11.9g³ 10g² 10m⁴ 11.9d⁴ Oct 4] poor maiden handicapper:
stays 1½m: acts on soft and good to firm going: tends to be soon off bridle. *Mrs
A. J. Bowlby*

ZIG ZIG (IRE)   2 b.c. (Apr 23) Perugino (USA) 84 – Queen of Erin (IRE) (King   **–**
of Clubs 124) [1999 6s Sep 29] IR 10,500Y: fourth foal: dam unraced: always behind
in maiden at Newcastle. *Mrs A. Duffield*

ZILARATOR (USA)   3 b.g. Zilzal (USA) 137 – Allegedly (USA) (Sir Ivor 135)   **96**
[1998 NR 1999 12g 10v* 12d² 12.1g 16.2m 13d³ 13s⁵ 14.8d⁵ Oct 15] 100,000Y:
tall, close-coupled gelding: has scope: half-brother to several winners, notably very
smart middle-distance stayer Per Quod (by Lyllos): dam unraced half-sister to
Alleged: useful performer: won maiden at Leicester in April: creditable placed
efforts in handicaps at Newbury and Ayr after, and when fifth in similar contest at
Newmarket final start: stays 15f: acts on heavy ground (stiffish task on good to firm):
has looked tricky ride. *W. J. Haggas*

ZILVA   4 b.f. Mazilier (USA) 107 – Thulium (Mansingh (USA) 120) [1998 57: 8g   **–**
8g⁵ 8.2s 7d a7g³ a8g 1999 a7g Feb 23] sturdy, good-quartered filly: maiden:
reportedly lost action only run of 1999. *P. J. Makin*

ZIMIRI   5 ch.g. Keen 116 – Annabrianna 88 (Night Shift (USA)) [1998 63, a89d: **–**
a8g* 8g² a8.5g³ 7m 8d a8.5g a8g⁵ a8g 1999 a8g* a8g a8g⁶ Mar 2] compact, deep-   **a56**
bodied gelding: has had wind operation, but reportedly still suffers from breathing
problems: fairly useful at best, modest of late: won weak claimer at Lingfield in
January: stays 1m: acts on all-weather, turf form only on good ground. *J. A. R. Toller*

ZINCALO (USA)   3 gr.g. Zilzal (USA) 137 – Silver Glitz (USA) (Grey Dawn II   **75 d**
132) [1998 NR 1999 10g 14.1m² 14d 14.1m⁴ 16s⁶ 14.8d 14.1d Oct 27] IR 45,000Y:
strong gelding: fourth foal: dam minor 1m stakes winner in USA: fair form when
runner-up in maidens at Nottingham and Haydock: reportedly had breathing problem
next start: well beaten after: likely to stay 2m: acts on good to firm and good to soft
going: visored final start. *C. E. Brittain*

ZINDABAD (FR)   3 b.c. Shirley Heights 130 – Miznah (IRE) 102 (Sadler's Wells   **117**
(USA) 132) [1998 104p: 8d² 8m* 8s² 1999 12.3m⁶ 9.9g⁶ 10m* 10m* 10m* 9.9m⁵
Sep 11] good-topped colt: fluent mover: smart performer: won valuable handicaps at
Newmarket and Ascot (only 3 finished, beat Vicious Circle) in July, and Winter Hill
Stakes at Windsor (beat Alabaq by 1½ lengths) in August: below-form fifth in Select
Stakes at Goodwood: will stay 1½m: acts on soft and good to firm ground: game.
B. Hanbury

ZINNIA 2 b.f. (Feb 24) Zilzal (USA) 137 – Ibtihaj (USA) 97 (Raja Baba (USA)) [1999 6.1g Jul 3] 8,000Y: half-sister to several winners, including fairly useful 2-y-o 5f winner Abhaaj (by Kris): dam, 2-y-o 5f winner, half-sister to Danzig: mid-field in maiden at Nottingham. *J. L. Dunlop* —

ZIPPERGATE 3 b.c. Mystiko (USA) 124 – Branitska (Mummy's Pet 125) [1998 94p: 6m 6g* 6s³ 1999 8g 7m⁴ 6m 6s 7g 6m 6v 8.9d 10g Oct 19] unfurnished colt: fluent mover: fairly useful performer: best efforts in 1999 on second and third starts: stays 7f: acts on soft and good to firm ground: blinkered (looked none too keen) sixth start: has been bandaged: usually held up: sold 10,000 gns. *B. W. Hills* **90 d**

ZIRCONI (FR) 3 b.c. Zieten (USA) 118 – Muirfield (FR) (Crystal Glitters (USA) 127) [1998 109: 5s* 5.5g* 5.5d² 5g² 6d³ 6d⁶ 7s³ 6.5d² 7v³ 1999 7g³ 6d⁶ 7s⁵ 8m 8s 7s⁶ 8.2s⁴ 6s Nov 6] useful in France at 2 yrs, though reportedly had knee operation at end of season: best effort in 1999 on reappearance: left Mme C. Head following sixth start: stays 7f: acts on heavy going: tried blinkered. *D. Nicholls* **99 d**

ZMILE 3 b.c. Ezzoud (IRE) 126 – Mountain Bluebird (USA) 79 (Clever Trick (USA)) [1998 78: 5.1g⁴ 6g² 6f 7v³ 1999 a8g⁶ May 6] small, workmanlike colt: fair maiden at 2 yrs: favourite, well beaten in claimer only run of 1999: should stay at least 1¼m: acts on heavy ground, well beaten on firm. *R. Guest* —

ZOENA 2 ch.f. (Apr 2) Emarati (USA) 74 – Exotic Forest 66 (Dominion 123) [1999 6m⁴ 5g 6m³ 6g 5d⁴ a6g Nov 8] second foal: half-sister to 3-y-o The Haka: dam 1m winner: modest maiden: should stay 7f. *J. G. Portman* **60**

ZOE'S NEWSBOX 5 b.m. Inca Chief (USA) – Let's Go Lochy 42 (Lochnager 132) [1998 NR 1999 a6g a6g Dec 1] first reported foal: dam sprint maiden: well held in maiden at Lingfield and claimer at Wolverhampton. *A. G. Newcombe* —

ZOFFI 3 b.f. Most Welcome 131 – Highsplasher (USA) (Bucksplasher (USA)) [1998 NR 1999 8.3g Jul 5] fourth reported foal: half-sister to fairly useful 1¼m winner Sunny Isle (by Cadeaux Genereux) and 1993 2-y-o 7f winner Dulford Lad (by In Fijar), later useful winner in Scandinavia up to 1¾m: dam, won 6 races in USA, from family of Park Hill winner Quay Line: slowly away and very green when behind in maiden at Windsor. *C. F. Wall* —

ZOLA (IRE) 3 ch.g. Indian Ridge 123 – Fluella 74 (Welsh Pageant 132) [1998 45: 8.1m 7.1d 10.2d 10d⁴ 1999 a10g⁴ a11g³ a10g⁴ a12g a11g⁵ a12g⁴ 12s⁵ 11.8v 12d⁵ 16m* 14d⁴ 16f⁴ 17.2h² a16g² a16g* 16v Sep 24] rangy, angular gelding: modest performer: won claimer at Yarmouth in May and handicap at Lingfield in August: should stay 2¼m: acts on all-weather, good to soft (possibly not on softer) and hard going: visored eighth start: none too consistent. *M. Quinn* **51**

Winter Hill Stakes, Windsor—Zindabad continues his progression up the ranks, making most and finding plenty to hold Alabaq (striped cap) and Prolix

ZOLA POWER 3 ch.f. Efisio 120 – Caroline Connors (Fairy King (USA)) [1998 –
56, a49: 5.7m⁶ 5.1d² 5m⁴ 5m⁶ 5g⁴ 5.1m⁴ 6.1d 5.3g³ a6g a6g² a6g a6f⁴ a8g⁴ 1999 a6g
7m a8g a5g 5d⁵ 6g 5.3d Oct 4] neat filly: poor mover: poor maiden: stays 6f: acts on
good to firm going, good to soft and all-weather: tried blinkered. *B. A. Pearce*

ZOMARADAH 4 b.f. Deploy 131 – Jawaher (IRE) 60 (Dancing Brave **118**
(USA) 140) [1998 114: 10g* 11s* 12s 11g⁵ 10f* 1999 10s 10.3s* 10m* 11s²
10g* 11g³ Nov 6]
    Sheikh Mohammed Obaid Al Maktoum had good reason to question
the wisdom of keeping four-year-olds in training at the beginning of the 1999
Flat season, for within a month he witnessed both High-Rise (who had been
transferred to the ownership of Godolphin) and Zomaradah being virtually
pulled up on their respective reappearances. By the end of the year, however,
his decision to persevere with his Italian Oaks and E. P. Taylor winner had been
more than justified, with Zomaradah following on from other Luca Cumani-
trained older fillies, such as Infamy, Only Royale and One So Wonderful, by
becoming one of the best of her age and sex in Europe.
    Apart from her seasonal debut at Sandown in April and a below-par
second in a Group 3 at Milan in September, Zomaradah's races showed a
consistent level of form, her best performances arguably coming in beating
Rhapsodist by ten lengths in a minor race at Doncaster in June and when
winning the Royal Whip Stakes at the Curragh in August. Zomaradah was the
3/1 second favourite in the nine-runner field at the Curragh, her rivals including
Make No Mistake and Sunshine Street. Although she was favoured by coming
off the strong pace, Zomaradah was a worthy winner on the day, travelling well
behind the leaders and taking up the running over a furlong out. Headed by
Strategic, she rallied well close home to establish a half-length winning margin,

Sheikh Mohammed Obaid Al Maktoum's "Zomaradah"

with Polaire six lengths back in third. An all-the-way two and three quarter length defeat of Calando in the Premio Lydia Tesio in Rome over ten furlongs at the end of September booked Zomaradah a place in the inaugural running of the Breeders' Cup Filly & Mare Turf at Gulfstream. This race, not surprisingly, attracted several European runners, as well as the ex-British-trained fillies Coretta and Spanish Fern, who had both improved since going to North America. As he had done for Barathea five years earlier, Luca Cumani trained Zomaradah around a specially created turn at Newmarket, and in the race this seemed to pay off because, although the filly could not emulate Barathea's victory in the Mile, she ran a fine race in defeat. In a falsely-run contest, Zomaradah was beaten under a length into third by Soaring Softly and the ex-Cumani-trained Coretta, looking threatening but failing to quicken when it really mattered, earning just under 130,000 dollars for her efforts nonetheless.

Zomaradah (b.f. 1995)	Deploy (b 1987)	Shirley Heights (b 1975)	Mill Reef
			Hardiemma
		Slightly Dangerous (b 1979)	Roberto
			Where You Lead
	Jawaher (IRE) (b 1989)	Dancing Brave (b 1983)	Lyphard
			Navajo Princess
		High Tern (gr 1982)	High Line
			Sunbittern

Zomaradah's sire, Deploy, although second in the Irish Derby, is probably known more for being a son of Slightly Dangerous, and therefore a half-brother to Warning, Yashmak, Dushyantor and Commander In Chief. It is the last-named who is of interest in relation to Zomaradah's pedigree, as Zomaradah is out of a Dancing Brave mare and that sire is the sire of Commander In Chief. The link can also be seen in the pedigree of Deploy's best other runner, Mons, as that horse's dam is by Lyphard, the sire of Dancing Brave.

Zomaradah's dam, Jawaher, failed to win in five attempts and was sold at the December Sales for 16,000 guineas to go to Saudi Arabia. The only other foal she left behind was Nichol Fifty (by Old Vic), who is effective at up to seventeen furlongs on the Flat and has also won over hurdles. However, Zomaradah is one in a long list of pattern-race winners in her family, for Jawaher is a half-sister to none other than High-Rise and Zomaradah's great-grandam Sunbittern has the Group/Grade 1 winners High Hawk, In The Wings and Infamy among her descendents.

The strong, deep-girthed Zomaradah has a powerful, round action and acts on firm and soft going. Although she was down the field in the Ribblesdale Stakes on her one attempt at the distance, she should stay a mile and a half. Her success in 1999 was a just reward for her sporting connections. *L. M. Cumani*

ZONING   2 b.c. (Mar 14) Warning 136 – Zonda 100 (Fabulous Dancer (USA) 124)   **101 p**
[1999 6f⁵ 6g* 7d* 7.3s⁴ Oct 22] quite attractive colt: has a fluent, slightly round action: fourth foal: half-brother to 5-y-o Treaty, 3-y-o Two Pack and French 1m winner Zambezi (by Rahy): dam, 5f/6f winner who probably stayed 1m, from family of Oh So Sharp: progressive form: won maiden at Yarmouth in August and minor event at York (idled) in October: good fourth of 9 to Umistim in Horris Hill Stakes at Newbury on final start, looking a threat over 1f out but bumped and no extra: likely to prove best up to 1m: acts on soft going: joined Godolphin: useful already, and should still do better. *J. H. M. Gosden*

ZOOM UP (IRE)   5 ch.g. Bluebird (USA) 125 – Senane 86 (Vitiges (FR) 132)   **76**
[1998 69: 10s 10d 10m 12g⁶ 10g 10g⁴ 10.1d 1999 a7g⁶ 7m³ 8g⁵ 7.5v* 7m³ 7.1d³ Aug 12] leggy, lengthy gelding: easy mover: fair handicapper: won at Beverley in June: effective at 7f to 1¼m: acts on good to firm and heavy going: usually visored/blinkered: has looked a difficult ride: very slowly away penultimate start: withdrawn after refusing to enter stalls in September. *N. A. Graham*

ZORBA   5 b.g. Shareef Dancer (USA) 135 – Zabelina (USA) 57 (Diesis 133) [1998   –
65, a54: a8s a8g³ a8.5g³ a10g⁶ 9.2v* 10v² 8.3d⁶ 8.3v² a11g* 1999 a9.4g a12g a11g

Jun 28] leggy gelding: fair on turf, modest on all-weather: well beaten in 1999: stays 11f: acts on heavy ground and firesand: visored/blinkered last 5 starts: has looked none too hearty. *J. G. M. O'Shea*

ZORRO 5 gr.g. Touch of Grey 90 – Snow Huntress 80 (Shirley Heights 130) [1998 **69** 59: a10g⁶ a12g² a12g² a10g² a12g⁴ 1999 11.5g⁵ a13g* Dec 10] leggy, plain gelding: fair handicapper: better than ever when winning at Lingfield in December: stays easy 13f: acts on firm ground (well beaten on going softer than good) and equitrack: sometimes led to post. *Jamie Poulton*

ZSARABAK 2 br.g. (Mar 11) Soviet Lad (USA) – Moorefield Girl (IRE) 57 **–** (Gorytus (USA) 132) [1999 7m⁶ 6d 7d⁶ 7.9m Sep 1] 8,000Y: leggy, lightly-made gelding: first foal: dam winning stayer on Flat and over hurdles in Ireland: poor maiden: should stay 1¼m. *B. S. Rothwell*

ZUCCHERO 3 br.g. Dilum (USA) 115 – Legal Sound 85 (Legal Eagle 126) [1998 **84** –: 6g 6m 7m 1999 8.3m 6.1m* 7m* 7m* 7m² 7f⁶ Jul 30] fairly useful handicapper: won at Chepstow, Lingfield and Newmarket (by 5 lengths) in July: better effort after when creditable short-head second in ladies event at Ascot: should prove best at 6f/ 7f: raced only on good going or firmer: blinkered final 5 starts: often races prominently. *D. W. P. Arbuthnot*

ZUHAIR 6 ch.g. Mujtahid (USA) 118 – Ghzaalh (USA) 87 (Northern Dancer) **95** [1998 88§, a84§: a5g 5g 6g⁶ 6d⁴ 6d 6f 6g⁵ 6.1m² 6g 7.1m 6g a6g⁴ 1999 5g 5d 6f⁶ 5d⁴ 5m² 6d 5m* 6m 5f⁴ 5f* 6f* 5d 6d 6m* 6g 5.6g 6d Sep 18] strong gelding: useful handicapper: reformed character for much of 1999 for new trainer, and won at Lingfield in June, Goodwood (twice within 2 days) in July and York (quite valuable 23-runner event) in August: below form final 3 starts: effective at 5f/6f: acts on firm ground, good to soft and firesand, probably unsuited by heavy: well beaten in blinkers: wears bandages: tends to sweat: usually held up nowadays, and suited by strongly-run race. *D. Nicholls*

ZULAL (USA) 3 ch.c. Zilzal (USA) 137 – My Shafy 92 (Rousillon (USA) 133) **82** [1998 67p: 7d 7d 7d⁴ 1999 7s⁴ 7.5m* 8m 10g* 10.1m³ 11.9d 12g⁵ 8g 11d³ Dec 11] good-topped, short-backed colt: fairly useful handicapper: won at Beverley in April and Pontefract in June: well below form after next start and sold from E. Dunlop 7,000 gns before final outing: stays 1¼m: acts on good to firm going: visored penultimate appearance. *C. Campi, Italy*

Charter Design Stakes (Handicap), York—another example of David Nicholls' training skills as Zuhair (white cap) wins his fourth race of the season, beating Mallia (spotted cap), Emerging Market (No.7) and Tom Tun (checks)

ZULU DAWN (USA)   3 b.c. El Gran Senor (USA) 136 – Celtic Loot (USA) (Irish **86**
River (FR) 131) [1998 85: 7m⁵ 1999 7m² 8m⁴ 8.3s³ 8g 8m* 7.9g⁶ 8d⁴ Oct 14]
lengthy, rather unfurnished colt: fairly useful performer: won 19-runner maiden at
Newbury in September: creditable efforts in handicaps after, particularly so when
fourth of 20 at Newmarket: stays 1m: acts on soft and good to firm going: blinkered
(ran poorly) fourth start: has taken little interest: sold 24,000 gns. *J. W. Hills*

ZURS (IRE)   6 b.g. Tirol 127 – Needy (High Top 131) [1998 76: 8s 8m² 7m⁵ 8m⁴ **79 §**
7d³ 8g⁵ 9d³ 8.3f³ 8.1m* 8m³ 8.3m 10.1s³ 8m 9.9s* 10v⁵ 11.9s⁴ 1999 8d² 10.1s⁶ 8g
10g⁴ 10s 10g* 10m 9m 9f 9.9v Sep 29] sturdy gelding: fair handicapper: inconsistent
in 1999, winning at Sandown in May: stays 1¼m: acts on any turf going/all-weather:
blinkered once earlier in career: has worn bandages: often slowly away: not an easy
ride: won over hurdles in November. *Jamie Poulton*

ZYGO (USA)   7 b.g. Diesis 133 – La Papagena (Habitat 134) [1998 65, a54: 7f⁵ 7f⁶ **56**
8d 7.1d a8.5g⁵ a10f⁶ 1999 a10g⁶ 10f⁵ 7f⁵ May 12] lengthy gelding: modest maiden
handicapper: barely stays 1¼m: well beaten on heavy going, acts on any other turf/
all-weather. *R. T. Phillips*

ZYZ   2 b.c. (Feb 18) Unfuwain (USA) 131 – Girette (USA) (General Assembly **103 p**
(USA)) [1999 7g² 7m* 7.3s³ Oct 22] seventh foal: closely related to winning French
sprinter Gold Heaven (by Tate Gallery) and half-brother to 2 winners: dam French
1¼m winner: useful form: won maiden at Leicester in September: best effort when
1½ lengths third of 9 to Umistim in Horris Hill Stakes at Newbury: should stay 1¼m:
acts on soft and good to firm ground: made running and wandered last 2 starts: useful
already, and looks capable of better still. *B. W. Hills*

The following unraced horses appeared in ante-post lists for the
2000 classics, and are included for information purposes:

ABSHURR (USA)   2 b.c. (Feb 7) Nureyev (USA) 131 – Go Solo (USA)
(Riverman (USA) 131) $360,000F, 3,000,000Y: seventh foal: half-brother to 2
winners in USA, including Grade 3 winner (placed in Grade 1 at 9f) Gold Fleece (by
Deputed Testamony): dam won up to 9f in USA. *D. R. Loder, France*

AVITRIX (USA)   2 b.f. (Apr 4) Storm Bird (CAN) 134 – Dellagrazia (USA)
(Trempolino (USA) 135) $275,000F, 6,000,000 francs Y: third foal: sister to smart
French 7.5f/1m winner (including at 2 yrs) Grazalema and half-sister to a winner in
Japan by Caerleon: dam, French 1½m winner, half-sister to dam of White Muzzle/
grandam of Almutawakel. *D. R. Loder, France*

DANCE WEST (USA)   2 b.c. (Feb 23) Gone West (USA) – Danzante (USA) 107
(Danzig (USA)) fourth foal: closely related to fairly useful 1998 2-y-o 5f winner
Forante (by Forty Niner), useful 1996 French 2-y-o 7f winner Alpha Plus (by Mr
Prospector) and 4-y-o Gilgamesh: dam, sprint winner in France/USA, half-sister to
Breeders' Cup Classic winner Skywalker. *H. R. A. Cecil*

DEAR GIRL (IRE)   2 b.f. (Apr 23) Fairy King (USA) – Alidiva 105 (Chief
Singer 131) sixth foal: sister to a winner in USA and half-sister to 1000 Guineas
winner Sleepytime and high-class 7f (at 2 yrs) to 9f winner Ali-Royal (both by Royal
Academy), and very smart middle-distance horse Taipan (by Last Tycoon): dam, 6f
to 1m winner, half-sister to 4-y-o Croco Rouge. *H. R. A. Cecil*

EL MASHADD   2 b.c. (Apr 8) Sadler's Wells (USA) 132 – Safa 109 (Shirley
Heights 130) fourth foal: brother to smart 1m to 10.5f winner Saafeya and
half-brother to 3-y-o Bayt Alasad: dam 2-y-o 6f winner who stayed 1½m. *D. R.
Loder, France*

EXECUTIVE ORDER   2 b.c. (May 2) Rainbow Quest (USA) 134 – Exclusive
Order (USA) 120 (Exclusive Native (USA)) half-brother to several winners, notably

2000 Guineas winner Entrepreneur and smart middle-distance performers Dance A Dream and Sadler's Image (all by Sadler's Wells) and smart 7f (at 2 yrs)/1m (Coronation Stakes) winner Exclusive (by Polar Falcon): dam French 6f/7f winner who stayed 1m. *Sir Michael Stoute*

HARDY (USA) 2 b.c. (May 24) Mr Prospector (USA) – Korveya (USA) 116 (Riverman (USA) 131) $2,100,000Y: closely related to top-class 1m/1¼m filly Bosra Sham and Poule d'Essai des Poulains winner (also champion 2-y-o) Hector Protector (both by Woodman) and half-brother to several winners, including Poule d'Essai des Poulains winner Shanghai (by Procida): dam French 9f winner from very good family. *A. P. O'Brien, Ireland*

MOUNT MCKINLEY (USA) 2 ch.c. (Mar 14) Mr Prospector (USA) – Julie's Jazz (USA) (Nureyev (USA) 131) second foal: dam lightly-raced half-sister to Breeders' Cup Distaff winner Princess Rooney. *J. Noseda*

OTTOMAN (IRE) 2 b.c. (Mar 12) Sadler's Wells (USA) 132 – Morning Devotion (USA) 102 (Affirmed (USA)) brother to 3-y-o First Night and closely related to several winners, including Oaks and Irish Derby winner Balanchine (by Storm Bird) and smart winner up to 1½m Romanov (by Nureyev): dam, 2-y-o 6f winner, stayed 1½m. *J. Gosden*

PADUA'S PRIDE (IRE) 2 b.c. (Jan 25) Caerleon (USA) 132 – Doff The Derby (USA) (Master Derby (USA)) 2,500,000F: brother to outstanding winner up to 1½m Generous and half-brother to several winners, notably Irish 1,000 Guineas runner-up Strawberry Roan (by Sadler's Wells): dam unraced half-sister to Trillion, dam of Triptych. *D. K. Weld, Ireland*

PAPER MOON (IRE) 2 b.f. (Mar 10) Lake Coniston (IRE) 131 – Marie Noelle (FR) 114 (Brigadier Gerard 144) 90,000F, 120,000Y: half-sister to numerous winners, including Marcel Boussac winner Mary Linoa (by L'Emigrant) and smart French 1½m to 2m winner Ming Dynasty (by Sadler's Wells): dam French 2-y-o 7.5f winner, later won up to 1¼m in USA. *A. P. O'Brien, Ireland*

REACH THE TOP 2 b.c. (Feb 20) Zafonic (USA) 130 – Andaleeb (USA) 104 (Lyphard (USA) 132) fifth foal: half-brother to 1993 Cheveley Park winner Prophecy (by Warning), stayed 1m: dam won Lancashire Oaks. *J. H. M. Gosden*

RETURN (USA) 2 b.f. (Feb 7) Sadler's Wells (USA) 132 – Slightly Dangerous (USA) 122 (Roberto (USA) 131) sister to very smart middle-distance stayer Dushyantor, closely related to 4-y-o Jibe and smart winner up to 1½m Yashmak (by Danzig) and half-sister to several winners, notably Warning (by Known Fact), Deploy (by Shirley Heights) and Commander In Chief (by Dancing Brave): dam second in Oaks. *H. R. A. Cecil*

SHIBBOLETH (USA) 2 b.c. (Mar 29) Danzig (USA) – Razyana (USA) 87 (His Majesty (USA)) brother to 5 winners, notably high-class sprinter/2000 Guineas third Danehill and US Grade 2 9f winner Eagle Eyed, and closely related to smart French/US performer up to 1m Euphonic (by The Minstrel): dam, placed at 7f and 1¼m from 3 starts, out of half-sister to Northern Dancer. *H. R. A. Cecil*

TOTAL CARE 2 br.c. (Feb 24) Caerleon (USA) 132 – Totality 103 (Dancing Brave (USA) 140) first foal: dam 1¾m winner, sister to Derby winner Commander In Chief and half-sister to Warning, Deploy and Dushyantor. *H. R. A. Cecil*

TOUGH MEN (USA) 2 b.c. (Feb 28) Woodman (USA) 126 – Rhumba Rage (USA) (Nureyev (USA) 131) $185,000Y: second foal: dam, lightly raced in France, sister to smart French 1986 2-y-o Fotitieng from family of Wolfhound and A P Indy. *H. R. A. Cecil*

VELVET LADY 2 b.f. (Mar 22) Nashwan (USA) 135 – Velvet Moon (IRE) 108 (Shaadi (USA) 126) first living foal: dam 6f (at 2 yrs, including Lowther Stakes) and 1¼m winner, half-sister to 4-y-o Central Park. *P. F. I. Cole*

WELSH MAIN 2 br.c. (Mar 2) Zafonic (USA) 130 – Welsh Daylight (Welsh Pageant 132) half-brother to several winners, including useful 1m winner Dawna (by Polish Precedent) and smart French middle-distance performer Ordinance (by Henbit): dam Irish 1¼m winner, from very good family. *H. R. A. Cecil*

1148

PROMISING HORSES

All British-trained horses in *Racehorses of 1999* thought capable of noteworthy improvement are listed below under the trainers for whom they last ran (strings for trainers who have retired or relocated, or where horses are known to have been transferred, have been omitted).

H. AKBARY
Jamadyan (IRE) 2 b.c 82p

C. N. ALLEN
Titian Angel (IRE) 2 ch.f 60p

E. J. ALSTON
Intricate Web (IRE) 3 b.g 79p
Reamzafonic 3 b.f 46p

D. W. P. ARBUTHNOT
Our First Lady 2 b.f 61p

G. B. BALDING
Duke of Modena 2 ch.g 78p
The Proof 2 b.g —p
Spellbinder (IRE) 3 b.f —p

I. A. BALDING
Amazed 2 ch.f 51P
Brisbane Road (IRE) 2 b.g —p
Duchamp (USA) 2 b.c 84p
Exorcet (FR) 2 b.f 60p
First Manassas (USA) 2 b.c 87p
Free Rider 2 b.c 97p
Master George 2 b.g 73p
Pepeta 2 b.f 63p
Risky Reef 2 ch.g 82p
Dorissio (IRE) 3 b.f 75p

T. D. BARRON
Peteuresque (USA) 2 ch.c 74p
Red Revolution (USA) 2 ch.c 69p
Supreme Salutation 3 ch.g 89p

M. L. W. BELL
Autonomy (IRE) 2 b.c 100p
Ladywell Blaise (IRE) 2 b.f —p
Magic Sister 2 ch.f 63p
Merry Merlin 2 b.c 98p

M. BRITTAIN
Grey Cossack 2 gr.g 65p
Wigman Lady (IRE) 2 b.f 64p

K. R. BURKE
Melon Place (IRE) 2 b.c 92p
Royal Insult 2 ch.c 81p
Soller Bay 2 b.g 69p
Achilles Sky 3 b.c 79p

G. A. BUTLER
Blusienka (IRE) 2 b.f 89p
Compton Banker (IRE) 2 br.c 82p
French Lieutenant 2 b.c 83p
Miss Kirsty (USA) 2 ch.f 82p
Saddler's Quest 2 b.c 93p
Stayin Alive (USA) 2 b.c 93p

MISS J. A. CAMACHO
Dancing Bay 2 b.g 64p
Mindanao 3 b.f 98p
Pleasant Mount 3 b.g 72p

H. CANDY
Dixielake (IRE) 2 b.f 59p
Kisty (IRE) 2 b.f 68p
Salzgitter 2 b.f 71p
Borders 3 b.g 109p
Sir Echo (FR) 3 b.g 92p

H. R. A. CECIL
Andromedes (USA) 2 b.c 84p
Arabesque 2 b.f 84p
Beat Hollow 2 b.c 97P
Burning Sunset 2 ch.f 78p
Corinium (IRE) 2 br.f 101p
Decarchy (USA) 2 b.c 91p
Demeter (USA) 2 b.f 79p
High Walden (USA) 2 b.f 98p
Jolly Sharp (USA) 2 ch.c 82p
King Tiara (USA) 2 b.c —p
Land Ahead (USA) 2 ch.f 59p
Love Divine 2 b.f 80p
Sandmason 2 ch.c 74P
Still In Love 2 b.f 75p
Thermal Spring 2 ch.f 66p
Wellbeing 2 b.c 70p
Western Summer (USA) 2 ch.c 94p
Galette 3 b.f 94p
Nuclear Freeze (USA) 3 b.c 95p
Pythios (IRE) 3 b.c 107p
Variety Shop (USA) 3 b.f 83p

M. R. CHANNON
After The Blue (IRE) 2 b.c 63p
Budelli (IRE) 2 b.c 68p
Halhoo Lammtarra 2 ch.c 89p
Lafleur (IRE) 2 ch.f 75p
Take Manhattan (IRE) 2 b.g 50p
Doowaley (IRE) 3 b.c 98p

MAJOR D. N. CHAPPELL
Colette (IRE) 2 b.f 67p
Be Thankfull (IRE) 3 gr.f 95p

R. CHARLTON
Inchlonaig 2 ch.c 105P
Shadow Prince 2 ch.c —p
Slam Bid 2 b.g —p
Summoner 2 b.c 90p
Tweed 2 ch.c 60p
Valentine Band (USA) 2 b.f 88P
Another Question (USA) 3 b.c —p

G. C. H. CHUNG
Grand Oro 2 ch.c 93p

P. F. I. COLE
Akeed (USA) 2 ch.c 102p
Barakula 2 b.f 89p
Cultured Pearl (IRE) 2 ch.f 72p
Dandanna (IRE) 2 gr.f 97p
Everest (IRE) 2 ch.c 87p
Francesco Guardi (IRE) 2 b.c 95p
Mastermind (IRE) 2 ch.c 103p
Pompeii (IRE) 2 b.c 75p
River Bann (USA) 2 ch.c 89p
Royal Eagle (USA) 2 b.c 97p
Rushmore (USA) 2 b.c 73p
Zafonium (USA) 2 ch.c 89p
Freetown (IRE) 3 b.g 74p
Single Currency 3 b.c 78p

L. G. COTTRELL
Another Pearl 2 br.f 73p
Sandpoint 3 b.f 44p

L. M. CUMANI
Happy Omen 2 b.f —p
Mi Amigo 2 b.c 57p
Poppadam 2 ch.f 65p
River Coln (USA) 2 b.f 54p
Sea Drift (FR) 2 gr.f 53p
Silver Colours (USA) 2 b.f 94p
Sirdhana 2 ch.f 79p
Sopran Zanchi (IRE) 2 ch.c 76p
Sorbett 2 b.c 70p
Trumpet Sound (IRE) 2 b.c 77P
Western Ridge (FR) 2 b.c 92p
Seek 3 br.c 88p

P. W. D'ARCY
Circle of Light 2 b.f 87p

MISS JACQUELINE S. DOYLE
Zanay 3 b.c 85+ a107p

E. A. L. DUNLOP
Aljawf (USA) 2 gr.c 80p
Autumn Rain (USA) 2 br.c 72p
Break The Glass (USA) 2 b.g 61p
Count On Thunder (USA) 2 ch.c 58p
Golden Way (IRE) 2 ch.f 60p
Hataab (USA) 2 ch.c 99p
Melanzana 2 b.f 81p
Mellow Jazz 2 b.f 77p
Moon Solitaire (IRE) 2 b.c 62p
Nothing Daunted 2 ch.c 98p
Peaceful Promise 2 b.c 67p
Peacock Jewel 2 ch.c 94p
Qamous (USA) 2 gr.c 89p
Soviet Flash (IRE) 2 b.c 95p
Star Dynasty (IRE) 2 b.c 70p
Summer Song 2 b.f 69p

J. L. DUNLOP
Abuzaid (USA) 2 br.c 88p
Aegean Wind 2 b.c —p
Al Ataya (USA) 2 b.g 59p
All Good Things (IRE) 2 b.c 56p

Al Towd (USA) 2 b.c 94p
Aunty Rose (IRE) 2 b.f 96p
Barrow (SWI) 2 br.c 70p
Bless The Bride (IRE) 2 b.f 65p
Busy Lizzie (IRE) 2 b.f —p
Cabriac 2 b.c 86p
Cephalonia 2 b.f 71p
Dollar Bird (IRE) 2 b.f 93p
Don't Surrender (IRE) 2 b.c 93p
Fantastic Fantasy (IRE) 2 b.f 64p
Firecrest (IRE) 2 b.f —p
Five of Wands 2 b.f 64p
Intrum Morshaan (IRE) 2 b.f 70p
Invincible Spirit (IRE) 2 b.c 111p
Meadaaar (USA) 2 ch.c 99p
Millenary 2 b.c 87p
Muschana 2 ch.f 76p
Original Spin 2 b.f 75p
Penshiel (USA) 2 b.g —p
Romantic Affair (IRE) 2 ch.g 75p
Sakhee (USA) 2 b.c 106p
Samsaam (IRE) 2 b.c 65p
Three Points 2 b.c 98p
Unseeded 2 ch.f 81p
Fantasy Hill (IRE) 3 b.g 101p
Krisalight (USA) 3 b.f 61p

M. W. EASTERBY
Sporting Gesture 2 ch.g 79p
Bodfari Komaite 3 b.g 69p

T. D. EASTERBY
Little Docker (IRE) 2 b.g 72p
Soba Jones 2 b.c 55p
Stand By 2 b.f 53p

D. R. C. ELSWORTH
Alfini 2 ch.c 101p
Bold Saboteur 2 b.g —p
Finished Article (IRE) 2 b.c 66p
Golden Retriever (USA) 2 b.c 60p
Hamlyn (IRE) 2 gr.c 68p
Island Sound 2 b.g 104p
Morningside (IRE) 2 b.f —p
Pawn Broker 2 ch.c 89p
Premier Prize 2 ch.f 87p
Scarteen Fox (IRE) 2 ch.c 108p
Set Sail 2 b.f 60p
Sweet Cicely (IRE) 2 b.f 63p
Toleration 2 b.f 82p
Chief Wallah 3 b.c —p
Deadly Nightshade (IRE) 3 b.f 105p

R. A. FAHEY
Dakota Sioux (IRE) 2 ch.f 62p

J. R. FANSHAWE
Acrobatic 2 br.c 84p
Azur (IRE) 2 b.f 76p
Birdsand 2 ch.f —p
Blue Sugar 2 ch.c 90p
Court of Appeal 2 ch.c 66p
Diver's Pearl (FR) 2 b.f 74p
El Emperador 2 b.c 69p
Embraced 2 b.f 77P

Goldfinch 2 b.f —p
Incredulous (FR) 2 ch.f —p
Maximum Makeup (IRE) 2 b.g 57p
Petit Marquis (FR) 2 b.c 72p
Polar Lady 2 ch.f 69p
Eilean Shona 3 b.f 102p
Fantazia 3 b.f 89p
First Fantasy 3 b.f 91p

J. G. FITZGERALD
Love Alone 2 b.f 53p

MISS I. FOUSTOK
Laraza 2 ch.f 64p

J. A. GLOVER
Catalonia (IRE) 2 ch.f 72p
Mister Mal (IRE) 3 b.g 86p
Totimeto 3 b.g 64p

N. A. GRAHAM
Haikal 2 b.f —p

R. GUEST
Hounds of Love (IRE) 2 b.f —p
Our Poppet (IRE) 2 b.f 58p
Skimra 2 b.f 74p
Roseum 3 b.f 102p

W. J. HAGGAS
Charalambous (USA) 2 b.c 54p
Moselle 2 b.f 89p
Punctuate 2 b.c 98p
Ravishing (IRE) 2 b.f 88p
Welcome Gift 3 b.g 40p
Westender (FR) 3 b.g 98p

N. HAMILTON
Rhode Island (IRE) 2 b.g 83p

B. HANBURY
Desert Fury 2 b.c 104p
Jarn 2 b.c 100p
My Hansel (USA) 2 b.f 98p

R. HANNON
Cape Town (IRE) 2 gr.c 106p
Center Stage (IRE) 2 ch.c 72p
Criss Cross (IRE) 2 b.c 71p
Cruise 2 ch.c 70p
Freddy Flintstone 2 b.c 71p
Frontier 2 b.c 93p
Imperial Rocket (USA) 2 b.c 90p
Lucky Sweep 2 ch.c 65p
Mana-Mou Bay (IRE) 2 b.c 98p
Monte Carlo (IRE) 2 b.c 104p
Powerline 2 b.f 61p
Ravine 2 ch.f 59p
Golden Prince (IRE) 3 b.c 78p

P. W. HARRIS
Bow Strada 2 ch.c 92p
Dynamic Dream (USA) 2 b.f 81p
El Curioso (USA) 2 b.c 96p
La Rocque (IRE) 2 b.g 68p
Mush (IRE) 2 b.c 70p
Katy Nowaitee 3 b.f 92p

P. C. HASLAM
Sign of The Tiger 2 b.g 57p
You're Special (USA) 2 b.g 77p

LADY HERRIES
Cloth of Gold 2 b.c —p
Celtic Fling 3 b.f 77p

B. W. HILLS
Air Defence 2 br.c 82p
Banco Suivi (IRE) 2 b.f 81p
Bedara 2 b.f 91p
Bright Question 2 ch.c 72p
Capa 2 gr.c 85p
Clipper 2 b.f 88p
Clog Dance 2 b.f 103p
Distant Music (USA) 2 b.c 121p
Fame At Last (USA) 2 b.f 87p
Flowering 2 b.f —p
Forest Friendly 2 b.f 81p
In The Arena (USA) 2 ch.c —p
Lace Wing 2 ch.f 57p
Mutasader (IRE) 2 b.f 72p
Out of Reach 2 b.f 93p
Rampart 2 b.c 78p
Shaan Madary (FR) 2 b.f —p
Shaibani 2 b.c 88p
Sham Sharif 2 b.f —p
Sheer Hamas (IRE) 2 b.c 99p
Shotacross The Bow (IRE) 2 b.c 80p
Shouf Al Badou (USA) 2 b.c 97p
Sir Ferbet (IRE) 2 b.c 77p
Solitary 2 b.c 70p
Solo Flight 2 gr.c 83p
Sunset Glow 2 gr.c 77p
Tantalus 2 ch.c 91p
The Woodstock Lady 2 ch.f 80p
Top Hand 2 ch.f 77p
Valuable Idea (USA) 2 b.f 65p
Verdura 2 b.f —p
Wethaab (USA) 2 b.c —p
Zyz 2 b.c 103p
Ex Gratia (USA) 3 b.g 95p

J. W. HILLS
Al Ghabraa 2 ch.f 86p
Broadway Legend (IRE) 2 b.f 69p
Ipanema Beach 2 ch.f 58p
Karajan (IRE) 2 b.c 88p
Miss Lorilaw (FR) 2 b.f 82p
Negroni 2 br.f 65p
Toorak (USA) 2 b.c 76p
Nicely (IRE) 3 gr.f 94p

C. A. HORGAN
Alzola (IRE) 2 b.f 63p

R. F. JOHNSON HOUGHTON
Callas 2 b.f 72p
Three Lions 2 ch.g 64p

P. HOWLING
Shamrock City (IRE) 2 b.c 96p

A. P. JARVIS
Waverley Road 2 ch.c 66p

M. A. JARVIS
Gabidia 2 br.f 73p
Jathaabeh 2 ch.f 55p
Kier Park (IRE) 2 b.c 107p
Power Packed 2 b.c 98p
Reematna 2 b.f 75p
Bachelor 3 b.c 79p

W. JARVIS
Canford (IRE) 2 b.c 80p
Dena 2 b.f 75p
De Tramuntana 2 b.f 71p
Dr Cool 2 b.c 66p
Fraternity 2 b.c 81p
Night And Day 2 ch.f 53p
Papabile (USA) 2 b.f 82p
Spanish Star 2 b.g 72p
White House 2 b.f —p
Kattegat 3 b.g 97p
Kirk 3 b.f 79p

M. JOHNSTON
Awake 2 ch.c 97p
Carousing 2 b.c 94p
Champfis 2 b.c 66p
Cool Investment (IRE) 2 b.c 76p
Double Banger (IRE) 2 b.c 80p
Eastways 2 ch.c 93p
Footprints (IRE) 2 b.f 73p
Hidden Brave 2 b.c 90p
High Topper (FR) 2 b.c 56p
Inca Star (USA) 2 b.c 78p
Kind Regards (IRE) 2 b.f 88p
Littlepacepaddocks (IRE) 2 b.f 84p
Robandela (USA) 2 b.c 52p

BOB JONES
Antonio Canova 3 ch.g 78p

MISS GAY KELLEWAY
Camberley (IRE) 2 b.c 80p
Glory Quest (USA) 2 b.c 86p

N. P. LITTMODEN
So Precious (IRE) 2 b.f 69p

K. MAHDI
Honourable Chief 2 b.c 54p
Touch of Fairy (IRE) 3 b.c 78p

P. J. MAKIN
Caxton Lad 2 b.c 93p
Clotted Cream (USA) 2 gr.f 76p
Guarded Secret 2 ch.c 76p
Smogar (IRE) 2 ch.c 55p
Spencers Wood (IRE) 2 b.c 84p

G. G. MARGARSON
Barathea Guest 2 b.c 110p

D. MARKS
Kings To Open 2 b.c 50p

B. A. MCMAHON
Auchonvillers 2 b.c 65p
Bulawayo 2 b.c 46p
Machudi 2 b.f —p
Zabionic (IRE) 2 ch.c 68p

A. J. MCNAE
Bluebell Wood (IRE) 2 ch.f —p

B. J. MEEHAN
Jeune Premier (FR) 2 ch.g —p
Pedro Jack (IRE) 2 b.g 79p
Wekiwa Springs (FR) 2 gr.c 99P
What Grounds (FR) 2 b.g 71p

B. R. MILLMAN
Time Bomb 2 b.f —p

T. G. MILLS
Master Soden (USA) 2 b.c 65p
Noble Pursuit 2 b.c 85p
Norton (IRE) 2 ch.c 87p

G. L. MOORE
Buxted's First 2 gr.f —p
Rule of Thumb 2 ch.g 85p

D. MORRIS
Sophala 2 b.f —p

H. MORRISON
Tea For Texas 2 ch.f 48p

W. R. MUIR
Atavus 2 b.c 77p
Chem's Truce (IRE) 2 b.c 83p
Grenadier (IRE) 2 b.c 67p
Magic Legs 2 b.f 54p
Material Witness (IRE) 2 b.c 83p
Mbele 2 b.c 88p

D. NICHOLLS
Emley 3 b.f 61p
Pepperdine (IRE) 3 b.g 102p
Pure Elegancia 3 b.f 82p
Bahamian Pirate (USA) 4 ch.g 75p
Beveled Hawthorn 4 b.f 40p

J. NOSEDA
Abderian (IRE) 2 b.c 92p
Blinding Mission (IRE) 2 b.f 67p
Bold Bahamian (IRE) 2 b.g 68p
Dashing Duke (IRE) 2 b.c 89p
Kalypso Katie (IRE) 2 gr.f 97p
Knight's Emperor (IRE) 2 b.c 66p
Such Flair (USA) 2 b.f 65p
Desert Knight 3 b.c 103p

J. W. PAYNE
Pax 2 ch.c 86p
Tabbetinna Blue 2 b.f —p
Nice One Clare (IRE) 3 b.f 104p

J. PEARCE
Whitefoot 2 b.f 95p

MISS L. A. PERRATT
Highland Gold (IRE) 2 ch.c 64p

MRS A. J. PERRETT
Brig O'Turk 2 ch.g 62p
Carens Hero (IRE) 2 ch.g 62p
Ferzao (IRE) 2 b.c 88p
Mossy Moor 2 ch.f 66p
Tillerman 3 b.c 111p

M. PITMAN
Millenium Moonbeam (USA) 2 ch.c   107p

SIR MARK PRESCOTT
Alexandrine (IRE) 2 b.f   —p
Arpello 2 b.f   —p
Bahamas (IRE) 2 b.g   —p
Coruscating 2 gr.g   65p
Dive 2 b.g   —p
Fashion 2 b.f   74p
Forbearing (IRE) 2 b.c   95p
Principle (IRE) 2 b.c   71p
Spectrometer 2 ch.c   65p
French Spice 3 b.f   63p
Summer Night 3 b.f   94p

J. J. QUINN
Smart Predator 3 gr.g   86p

MRS G. S. REES
Elegant Escort (USA) 2 b.c   80p

M. J. RYAN
Silk St Bridget 2 b.f   —p

J. G. SMYTH-OSBOURNE
Rapid Deployment 2 b.g   63p

V. SOANE
Mister Superb 2 ch.c   79p
Tarcoola 2 ch.c   61p
Clarendon (IRE) 3 ch.c   85p

A. C. STEWART
Kathir (USA) 2 ch.c   87p
Mandoob 2 b.c   64p
Pretrail (IRE) 2 b.c   75p
Rasm 2 b.c   86p
Resounding (IRE) 2 b.f   83p
Triccolo 2 b.c   68p

SIR MICHAEL STOUTE
Abscond (USA) 2 b.f   97p
Adilabad (USA) 2 b.c   95p
Air Marshall (IRE) 2 ch.c   99p
Alva Glen (USA) 2 b.c   94p
Ballsbridge (IRE) 2 b.c   —p
Baniyar (IRE) 2 ch.c   62p
Coco (USA) 2 ch.f   —p
Cover Up (IRE) 2 b.g   84p
Daniysha (IRE) 2 b.f   73p
Delius (USA) 2 b.c   89P
Fast Track (IRE) 2 b.c   93p
Foreign Secretary (USA) 2 b.c   78P
Gallant 2 b.c   —p
Gold Quest (IRE) 2 ch.c   —p
Green Casket (IRE) 2 b.c   71P
Interlude 2 b.f   91P
Karaliyfa (IRE) 2 b.f   86P
King's Best (USA) 2 b.c   112p
Masterpiece (USA) 2 b.c   80p
Millions 2 b.g   —p
Misraah (IRE) 2 ch.c   94P
Moujeeda 2 ch.f   64p
Naval Affair (IRE) 2 b.f   86p
New Assembly (IRE) 2 b.f   73p

Pentagonal (USA) 2 b.c   72P
Petrushka (IRE) 2 ch.f   95p
Polar Challenge 2 b.c   74p
Revival 2 b.f   —P
Riparian 2 b.g   75p
Rudik (USA) 2 b.c   95p
Rum Punch 2 b.c   69p
Salim 2 b.c   63p
Secret Agent 2 b.c   89p
Shablam (USA) 2 b.c   87p
Shapour (IRE) 2 b.c   76p
Sherzabad (IRE) 2 b.c   —p
Sun Charm (USA) 2 b.c   96p
Tough Speed (USA) 2 b.c   108p
Town Girl (IRE) 2 ch.f   —p
Zafonic's Song (FR) 2 br.c   86P
Sharmy (IRE) 3 b.c   95p

SAEED BIN SUROOR
Adair (USA) 3 ch.c   123p
Anaam 3 b.f   81p
Rhythm Band (USA) 3 gr.c   109p

T. P. TATE
Strong Presence 2 b.c   70p

C. W. THORNTON
Geronimo 2 b.c   56p

J. A. R. TOLLER
Tap 2 b.c   70p
Blackheath (IRE) 3 ch.c   103p

M. P. TREGONING
Alhufoof (USA) 2 b.f   90p
Eljariha 2 b.f   71p
Ethmaar (USA) 2 b.c   100p
Fath (USA) 2 b.c   115p
Iljasoor (USA) 2 b.c   60p
Lahaay 2 ch.g   77p
Quito (IRE) 2 b.c   84p
Shoofha (IRE) 2 b.f   70p
Skibo (JPN) 2 b.c   78p
Tadbeer (USA) 2 ch.c   79p
Sir Effendi (IRE) 3 ch.c   99p

ANDREW TURNELL
Adamas (IRE) 2 b.f   73p

C. F. WALL
Bonaguil (USA) 2 b.g   65p
Polar Star 2 b.c   78p
Stratton (IRE) 2 b.c   70p

S. P. C. WOODS
Caballe (USA) 2 ch.f   84p
Going Global (IRE) 2 ch.c   84p
Send Me An Angel (IRE) 2 ch.f   —p

G. WRAGG
Bali Batik (IRE) 2 b.g   —p
Decision Maid (USA) 2 b.f   81p
Golden Legend (IRE) 2 b.c   —p
Judicious (IRE) 2 b.c   57p
Rosse 2 ch.f   63p
St Expedit 2 b.c   84p
Seliana 3 b.f   79p

SELECTED BIG RACES 1999

Prize money for racing abroad has been converted to £ sterling at the exchange rate current at the time of the race. The figures are correct to the nearest £. The Timeform ratings (TR) recorded by the principals in each race appear on the last line.

NAD AL SHEBA Sunday, Mar 28   FAST

1   **Dubai World Cup (Gr 1) (4yo+)** £1,855,827   1¼m

ALMUTAWAKEL *SaeedbinSuroor,GB* 4-9-0 RHills (6)............................... 1
MALEK (CHI) *RMandella,USA* 6-9-0 ASolis (7)... ¾ 2
VICTORY GALLOP (CAN) *WEWalden,USA* 4-9-0 JBailey (4) .... ¾ 3
Central Park (IRE) *SaeedbinSuroor,GB* 4-9-0 DO'Donohoe (2) 1½ 4
Daylami (IRE) *SaeedbinSuroor,GB* 5-9-0 JRVelazquez (5)....................... 1¼ 5
Silver Charm (USA) *RBaffert,USA* 5-9-0 GaryStevens (3)........................ 10 6
Running Stag (USA) *PMitchell,GB* 5-9-0 (b) RCochrane (8)...................... nk 7
High-Rise (IRE) *SaeedbinSuroor,GB* 4-9-0 LDettori (1).......................... dist 8
Mr Hamdan Al Maktoum 8ran 2m00.65   TR: 126/124/123/121/118

LONGCHAMP Sunday, Apr 25   SOFT

2   **Prix Greffulhe (Gr 2) (3yo c+f)** £30,334   1¼m110y

MONTJEU (IRE) *JEHammond,France* 3-9-2 CAsmussen 6/4jf 1
SENDAWAR (IRE) *AdeRoyerDupre,France* 3-9-2 GMosse................. 6/4jf 1 2
GRACIOSO (USA) *AFabre,France* 3-9-2 TJarnet............................. 86/10 4 3
First Magnitude (IRE) *AFabre,France* 3-9-2 OPeslier .... 77/10 ½ 4
Fils de Viane (FR) *J-CRouget,France* 3-9-2 J-RDubosc 97/10 3 5
Spadoun (FR) *CLaffon-Parias,France* 3-9-2 DBoeuf....................... 62/10 4 6
Max Tyson (IRE) *PHDemercastel,France* 3-9-2 DBonilla.................. 42/1 2 7
Mr M. Tabor 7ran 2m20.10   TR: 121/119/112/111/105

NEWMARKET Saturday, May 1   GOOD to FIRM (July Course)

3   **Sagitta 2000 Guineas Stks (Gr 1) (3yo c+f)** £171,800   1m

ISLAND SANDS (IRE) *SaeedbinSuroor* 3-9-0 LDettori (3) 10/1 1
ENRIQUE *HRACecil* 3-9-0 KFallon (10) .... 7/1 nk 2
MUJAHID (IRE) *JLDunlop* 3-9-0 RHills (13)... 9/1 1¼ 3
Brancaster (USA) *PWChapple-Hyam* 3-9-0 TQuinn (14) 20/1 1 4
Gold Academy (IRE) *RHannon* 3-9-0 DaneO'Neill (9) 66/1 1 5
Bahamian Bandit *RHannon* 3-9-0 OPeslier (5).................................... 20/1 nk 6
Debbie's Warning *KMahdi* 3-9-0 SSentore(1).. 66/1 hd 7
Exeat (USA) *JHMGosden* 3-9-0 DHolland (12) .... 20/1 sh 8
Desaru (USA) *JNoseda* 3-9-0 GCarter (16) 50/1 1¼ 9
Easaar *SaeedbinSuroor* 3-9-0 MRoberts (4)...................................... 25/1 1½ 10
Commander Collins (IRE) *PWChapple-Hyam* 3-9-0 JFortune (17)......... 8/1 ½ 11
Red Sea *PFICole* 3-9-0 (b) DBoeuf (8) .... 33/1 nk 12
Compton Admiral *GAButler* 3-9-0 PatEddery (7)................................. 10/1 ½ 13
Alrassaam *MAJarvis* 3-9-0 PRobinson (1) .... 14/1 nk 14
Orpen (USA) *APO'Brien,Ireland* 3-9-0 MJKinane (11) .... 7/2f ¾ 15
Auction House (USA) *BWHills* 3-9-0 MHills (6)................................. 15/2 1½ 16
Godolphin 16ran 1m37.14   TR: 122/121/118/115/112/111

NEWMARKET Sunday, May 2   GOOD to FIRM (July Course)

4   **Sagitta 1000 Guineas Stks (Gr 1) (3yo f)** £128,500   1m

WINCE *HRACecil* 3-9-0 KFallon (19)... 4/1f 1
WANNABE GRAND (IRE) *JNoseda* 3-9-0 PatEddery (13)................... 16/1 ½ 2
VALENTINE WALTZ (IRE) *JHMGosden* 3-9-0 RCochrane (1)........... 11/1 sh 3
Capistrano Day (USA) *JHMGosden* 3-9-0 DHolland (14)................... 14/1 2½ 4
Pescara (IRE) *SaeedbinSuroor* 3-9-0 LDettori (7) .... 10/1 ¾ 5
Hula Angel (USA) *BWHills* 3-9-0 MHills (15)...................................... 14/1 sh 6
Golden Silca *MRChannon* 3-9-0 SDrowne (18)..................................... 50/1 hd 7
Fragrant Oasis (USA) *EALDunlop* 3-9-0 GCarter (10)......................... 40/1 1¼ 8
Kuwait Dawn (IRE) *KMahdi* 3-9-0 JQuinn (3)..................................... 50/1 ½ 9
Fairy Queen (IRE) *SaeedbinSuroor* 3-9-0 RHills (20)......................... 12/1 ¾ 10
Atlantic Destiny (IRE) *MJohnston* 3-9-0 PStrydom (4) .... 66/1 sh 11

1154

Boomerang Blade *BSmart* 3-9-0 JStack (6) .... 100/1 ½ 12
Fear And Greed (IRE) *TStack,Ireland* 3-9-0 JPSpencer (22) 20/1 1¼ 13
Circle of Gold (IRE) *PWChapple-Hyam* 3-9-0 (b) JFortune (11) .... 33/1 nk 14
Sunspangled (IRE) *APO'Brien,Ireland* 3-9-0 MJKinane (2) .... 7/1 nk 15
Evening Promise *BAMcMahon* 3-9-0 RFfrench (17) .... 100/1 ½ 16
Bountiful Lady (USA) *SirMichaelStoute* 3-9-0 WRyan (8) .... 33/1 ½ 17
Imperial Beauty (USA) *PJMakin* 3-9-0 SSanders (9) .... 16/1 nk 18
Moiava (FR) *MmeCHead,France* 3-9-0 TQuinn (21) .... 5/1 ¾ 19
Greensand *RHannon* 3-9-0 RHughes (5) .... 66/1 sh 20
Hasty Words (IRE) *BWHills* 3-9-0 KDarley (12) .... 33/1 ¾ 21
Lamzena (IRE) *GWragg* 3-9-0 MRoberts (16) 66/1 10 22

Mr K. Abdulla 22ran 1m37.91   TR: 117/116/116/110/108/108

LONGCHAMP Sunday, May 2   GOOD
5 **Prix Ganay (Gr 1) (4yo+ c+f) £50,201**   1¼m110y

DARK MOONDANCER *AdeRoyerDupre,France* 4-9-2 GMosse 43/10 1
DREAM WELL (FR) *PBary,France* 4-9-2 CAsmussen..................... 54/10 hd 2
CROCO ROUGE (IRE) *PBary,France* 4-9-2 TJarnet 21/10 1 3
Sagamix (FR) *AFabre,France* 4-9-2 OPeslier..................................... 3/5cpf 6 4
Northern Quest (FR) *AFabre,France* 4-9-2 (b) AJunk 3/5cpf 3 5

Mr B. Arbib 5ran 2m11.30   TR: 122/122/120

NEWBURY Saturday, May 15   GOOD to SOFT
6 **Juddmonte Lockinge Stks (Gr 1) (4yo+) £76,750**   1m

FLY TO THE STARS *SaeedbinSuroor* 5-9-0 WSupple (6)..................... 9/1 1
JIM AND TONIC (FR) *FDoumen,France* 5-9-0 GMosse (4)................. 9/2 1½ 2
ALMUSHTARAK (IRE) *KMahdi* 6-9-0 OPeslier (1)............................ 9/1 nk 3
Intikhab (USA) *SaeedbinSuroor* 5-9-0 RHills (2).................................. 4/7f ½ 4
Tomba *BJMeehan* 5-9-0 KFallon (5)... 14/1 13 5
Duck Row (USA) *JARToller* 4-9-0 MRoberts (3)................................ 20/1 ¾ 6

Godolphin 6ran 1m39.64   TR: 124/120/119/118

LONGCHAMP Sunday, May 16   GOOD to FIRM
7 **Dubai Poule d'Essai des Poulains (Gr 1) (3yo c) £100,705**   1m

2 SENDAWAR (IRE) *AdeRoyerDupre,France* 3-9-2 GMosse 37/10 1
DANSILI *AFabre,France* 3-9-2 TJarnet 34/10jf 1½ 2
KINGSALSA (USA) *AFabre,France* 3-9-2 OPeslier 107/10 3 3
Way of Light (USA) *PBary,France* 3-9-2 CAsmussen...................... 34/10jf ¾ 4
3 Mujahid (USA) *JLDunlop,GB* 3-9-2 RHills....................................... 62/10 ½ 5
Indian Danehill (IRE) *AFabre,France* 3-9-2 TGillet .... 18/1 dh 5
Irish Prize (USA) *MmeCHead,France* 3-9-2 ODoleuze .... 37/1 nk 7
Triple Dash *SirMarkPrescott,GB* 3-9-2 GDuffield 27/1 1 8
Bertolini (USA) *JHMGosden,GB* 3-9-2 RCochrane .... 11/1 nk 9
Lavery (IRE) *APO'Brien,Ireland* 3-9-2 MJKinane .... 15/1 sn 10
Grazalema (USA) *AFabre,France* 3-9-2 AJunk.................................... 11/1 2 11
Iridanos *CLaffon-Parias,France* 3-9-2 DBoeuf 20/1 1¾ 12
Le Roi Chic (FR) *NClement,France* 3-9-2 DBonilla .... 28/1 sh 13
Berkoutchi (FR) *H-APantall,France* 3-9-2 GToupel 67/1 1½ 14
Indiana Legend (IRE) *BJMeehan,GB* 3-9-2 PatEddery .... 66/1 ½ 15

H.H. Aga Khan 15ran 1m36.20   TR: 127+/123+/116/114/112/112

8 **Dubai Poule d'Essai des Pouliches (Gr 1) (3yo f) £100,705**   1m

4 VALENTINE WALTZ (IRE) *JHMGosden,GB* 3-9-0 RCochrane......... 43/10 1
KARMIFIRA (FR) *PHDemercastel,France* 3-9-0 DBonilla 416/10 2 2
CALANDO (USA) *SaeedbinSuroor,GB* 3-9-0 MJKinane .... 7/1 ½ 3
Shenck *BGrizzetti,Italy* 3-9-0 MDemuro... 28/10 hd 4
Venize (IRE) *RCollet,France* 3-9-0 TGillet 10/1 2½ 5
Fairlee Mixa (FR) *AFabre,France* 3-9-0 OPeslier 11/1 1 6
Tycoon's Dolce (IRE) *RCollet,France* 3-9-0 CAsmussen 32/1 1½ 7
Rangoon Ruby (USA) *JEPease,France* 3-9-0 CAsmussen 4/1 2½ 8
Alexis (IRE) *JNoseda,GB* 3-9-0 PatEddery .... 26/1 ½ 9
Silver Star *AFabre,France* 3-9-0 TJarnet 24/1 2 10
4 Moiava (FR) *MmeCHead,France* 3-9-0 ODoleuze............................. 39/10f 2 11
Sao (IRE) *DSmaga,France* 3-9-0 DBoeuf.. 9/1 sh 12
Noble Pearl (GER) *WKujath,Germany* 3-9-0 SDavies .... 68/1 nk 13

Comillas (FR) *JdeRoualle,France* 3-9-0 GMosse 8/1   2 14
Kirby Maher Syndicate 14ran 1m36.00   TR: 116/111/110/110/103/101

9   Prix Lupin (Gr 1) (3yo c+f) £50,352   1¼m110y

2 GRACIOSO (USA) *AFabre,France* 3-9-2 OPeslier 6/4   1
2 MONTJEU (IRE) *JEHammond,France* 3-9-2 CAsmussen 1/10cpf 1 2
    OBVIOUSLY FUN (IRE) *JEHammond,France* 3-9-2 FSpanu 1/10cpf 6 3
    Al Waffi *SaeedbinSuroor,GB* 3-9-2 MJKinane.. 6/4 2½ 4
Sheikh Mohammed 4ran 2m10.90   TR: 118/116/104

CURRAGH Saturday, May 22   GOOD

10 Entenmann's Irish 2,000 Guineas (Gr 1) (3yo c+f) £94,706   1m

    SAFFRON WALDEN (FR) *APO'Brien* 3-9-0 OPeslier 12/1   1
3 ENRIQUE *HRACecil,GB* 3-9-0 KFallon 5/2   3 2
3 ORPEN (USA) *APO'Brien* 3-9-0 MJKinane.. 9/2 ½ 3
    Mus-If *DKWeld* (b) PJSmullen .... 11/1 sh 4
3 Island Sands (IRE) *SaeedbinSuroor,GB* 3-9-0 LDettori............................ 2/1f 3½ 5
    Access All Areas (IRE) *JEMulhern* 3-9-0 PatEddery 10/1 1 6
    Lucky Legend (IRE) *APO'Brien* 3-9-0 JAHeffernan............................. 66/1 1½ 7
    Marius Petipa (USA) *APO'Brien* 3-9-0 JPSpencer.............................. 33/1 10 8
    Peace Upholds (IRE) *JohnJMcLoughlin* 3-9-0 NGMcCullagh............ 100/1 2 9
    Tarfaa (IRE) *KPrendergast* 3-9-0 SCraine .... 14/1 ¾ 10
Mrs John Magnier 10ran 1m38.10   TR: 123/117/116/116/109/107

CURRAGH Sunday, May 23   GOOD

11 Tattersalls Gold Cup (Gr 1) (4yo+) £52,101   1¼m110y

    SHIVA (JPN) *HRACecil,GB* 4-8-11 KFallon 10/3   1
1 DAYLAMI (IRE) *SaeedbinSuroor,GB* 5-9-0 LDettori............................ 1/1f 2½ 2
    MAKE NO MISTAKE (IRE) *DKWeld* 4-9-0 (b) PJSmullen............... 16/1 1 3
    Insatiable (IRE) *SirMichaelStoute,GB* 6-9-0 PatEddery .... 9/2 ½ 4
    Lil's Boy (USA) *JSBolger* 5-9-0 KJManning 20/1 8 5
    Second Empire (IRE) *APO'Brien* 4-9-0 MJKinane 13/2 8 6
Niarchos Family 6ran 2m10.20   TR: 119/117/116/114

12 Entenmann's Irish 1,000 Guineas (Gr 1) (3yo f) £94,748   1m

4 HULA ANGEL (USA) *BWHills,GB* 3-9-0 MHills............................... 16/1   1
4 GOLDEN SILCA *MRChannon,GB* 3-9-0 SDrowne .... 25/1 nk 2
    DAZZLING PARK (IRE) *JSBolger* 3-9-0 KJManning .... 40/1 hd 3
    Crystal Downs (USA) *APO'Brien* 3-9-0 JAHeffernan 25/1 2½ 4
4 Wince *HRACecil,GB* 3-9-0 KFallon 5/4f 1½ 5
    Carambola (IRE) *APO'Brien* 3-9-0 PatEddery .... 20/1 ½ 6
4 Sunspangled (IRE) *APO'Brien* 3-9-0 MJKinane.............................. 10/1 hd 7
    Edabiya (IRE) *JOxx* 3-9-0 JPMurtagh... 8/1 1½ 8
4 Capistrano Day (USA) *JHMGosden,GB* 3-9-0 DHolland.................. 12/1 ½ 9
4 Fear And Greed (IRE) *TStack* 3-9-0 JPSpencer............................... 16/1 2½ 10
    Desert Magic (IRE) *CCollins* 3-9-0 PShanahan............................... 66/1 1 11
    Rivana *JOxx* 3-9-0 NGMcCullagh .... 100/1 ¾ 12
    Polaire (IRE) *KPrendergast* 3-9-0 WJSupple.................................. 50/1 ½ 13
    Pink Coral (IRE) *APO'Brien* 3-9-0 PJSmullen 40/1 2 14
    Show Me The Money (IRE) *NMeade* 3-9-0 RHughes....................... 10/1 hd 15
    Cassandra Go (IRE) *GWragg,GB* 3-9-0 MRoberts 40/1 2½ 16
    Mythical Girl (USA) *SaeedbinSuroor,GB* 3-9-0 LDettori....................... 8/1 dist 17
Mr J. R. Fleming 17ran 1m38.80   TR: 111/110/110/105/101/100

LONGCHAMP Sunday, May 23   GOOD to SOFT

13 Prix d'Ispahan (Gr 1) (4yo+ c+f) £50,302   1m1f55y

5 CROCO ROUGE (IRE) *PBary,France* 4-9-2 TJarnet 21/10   1
    EL CONDOR PASA (USA) *YNinomiya,Japan* 4-9-2 MEbina........... 17/10f ¾ 2
    GOLD AWAY (IRE) *MmeCHead,France* 4-9-2 ODoleuze................. 42/10 1 3
    Kabool *SaeedbinSuroor,GB* 4-9-2 SGuillot 107/10 1½ 4
    Handsome Ridge *JHMGosden,GB* 5-9-2 DBoeuf .... 53/10 ¾ 5
    Insight (FR) *JEHammond,France* 4-8-13 (b) CAsmussen.................. 119/10 ns 6
    Loudeac (USA) *AFabre,France* 4-9-2 OPeslier 95/10 2 7
    Renazig *MmeCHead,France* 4-9-2 NGuesdon.................................. 42/10 10 8
Mr Wafic Said 8ran 1m53.70   TR: 126/124/122/119/117/114

SUFFOLK DOWNS Saturday, May 29 FAST

14 Massachusetts Hcap (Gr 2) (3yo+) £250,000 — 1m1f

	BEHRENS (USA) *HJBond,USA* 5-8-6 (b) JChavez	9/10		1
1	RUNNING STAG (USA) *PMitchell,GB* 5-8-1 SSellers	82/10	½	2
	REAL QUIET (USA) *RBaffert,USA* 4-8-9 (b) GaryStevens	8/10f	2¾	3
	Brushing Up (USA) *VSimone,USA* 6-8-2 (b) RBaez	67/1	4½	4
	Galloping Gael (USA) *MLCatalanojnr,USA* 5-7-13 HVega	23/1	1½	5
	Personal Moon (USA) *MJCollins,USA* 4-8-4 (b) JCCaraballo	126/1	20	6

William L. Clifton, jnr 6ran 1m49.14 — TR: 130/124/127/112

EPSOM DOWNS Friday, Jun 4 GOOD to SOFT

15 Vodafone Coronation Cup (Gr 1) (4yo+) £118,000 — 1½m10y

11	DAYLAMI (IRE) *SaeedbinSuroor* 5-9-0 LDettori (3)	9/2		1
	ROYAL ANTHEM (USA) *HRACecil* 4-9-0 KFallon (2)	2/1f	¾	2
5	DREAM WELL (FR) *PBary,France* 4-9-0 CAsmussen (7)	7/2	½	3
	Silver Patriarch (IRE) *JLDunlop* 5-9-0 PatEddery (5)	9/2	1	4
	Borgia (GER) *AFabre,France* 5-8-11 OPeslier (1)	16/1	1¼	5
	Fruits of Love (USA) *MJohnston* 4-9-0 (v) GaryStevens (4)	14/1	2½	6
1	Central Park (IRE) *SaeedbinSuroor* 4-9-0 DO'Donohoe (6)	14/1	5	7

Godolphin 7ran 2m40.26 — TR: 123/123/122/119/114/114

16 Vodafone Oaks (Gr 1) (3yo f) £177,000 — 1½m10y

	RAMRUMA (USA) *HRACecil* 3-9-0 KFallon (5)	3/1		1
	NOUSHKEY *MAJarvis* 3-9-0 PRobinson (9)	33/1	3	2
	ZAHRAT DUBAI *SaeedbinSuroor* 3-9-0 (t) LDettori (3)	9/4f	5	3
	Sunday Picnic (JPN) *AFabre,France* 3-9-0 OPeslier (4)	8/1	nk	4
	Claxon *JLDunlop* 3-9-0 PatEddery (8)	11/2	5	5
12	Sunspangled (IRE) *APO'Brien,Ireland* 3-9-0 MJKinane (10)	8/1	1¼	6
	Miss Amanpuri *GWragg* 3-9-0 MRoberts (6)	50/1	17	7
12	Crystal Downs (USA) *APO'Brien,Ireland* 3-9-0 CAsmussen (7)	14/1	1½	8
	Kilting *SaeedbinSuroor* 3-9-0 GaryStevens (1)	10/1	2½	9
	Frippet (IRE) *SDow* 3-9-0 TQuinn (2)	66/1	21	10

H.R.H. Prince Fahd Salman 10ran 2m38.72 — TR: 123/118/110/109/101/99

EPSOM DOWNS Saturday, Jun 5 GOOD

17 Vodafone Derby Stks (Gr 1) (3yo c+f) £611,450 — 1½m10y

	OATH (IRE) *HRACecil* 3-9-0 KFallon (1)	13/2		1
	DALIAPOUR (IRE) *LMCumani* 3-9-0 GMosse (5)	10/1	1¾	2
	BEAT ALL (USA) *SirMichaelStoute* 3-9-0 GaryStevens (17)	7/1	1½	3
	Housemaster (IRE) *MLWBell* 3-9-0 WRyan (15)	12/1	sh	4
	All The Way (IRE) *TGMills* 3-9-0 JPMurtagh (3)	33/1	1¼	5
	Glamis (USA) *JHMGosden* 3-9-0 RCochrane (10)	40/1	nk	6
10	Saffron Walden (FR) *APO'Brien,Ireland* 3-9-0 MJKinane (14)	8/1	1¼	7
3	Compton Admiral *GAButler* 3-9-0 TJarnet (8)	25/1	1½	8
	Dubai Millennium *SaeedbinSuroor* 3-9-0 LDettori (2)	5/1f	1½	9
3	Brancaster (USA) *PWChapple-Hyam* 3-9-0 JFortune (7)	20/1	3	10
	Val Royal (FR) *AFabre,France* 3-9-0 OPeslier (6)	14/1	hd	11
	Zaajer (USA) *EALDunlop* 3-9-0 RHills (4)	16/1	1¼	12
	Adair (USA) *SaeedbinSuroor* 3-9-0 DO'Donohoe (12)	16/1	sh	13
	Salford Express (IRE) *DRCElsworth* 3-9-0 PatEddery (18)	12/1	1¼	14
	Lucido (IRE) *JLDunlop* 3-9-0 TQuinn (13)	13/2	9	15
	Through The Rye *BWHills* 3-9-0 MHills (16)	100/1	1	16

The Thoroughbred Corporation 16ran 2m37.43 — TR: 125/122/120/119/117/117

BADEN-BADEN Sunday, Jun 6 SOFT

18 Grosser Preis der Baden-Airpark (Gr 2) (4yo+) £53,334 — 1m3f

	CAITANO *ASchutz,Germany* 5-9-0 (b) AStarke	27/10		1
	TIGER HILL (IRE) *PSchiergen,Germany* 4-9-6 ASuborics	2/5f	½	2
	MARCH GROOM (USA) *EPils,Germany* 5-9-0 KWoodburn	82/10	7	3
	Elle Danzig (GER) *ASchutz,Germany* 4-9-2 THellier	63/10	½	4
	Ebisu (GER) *ASchutz,Germany* 4-9-0 NGrant	169/10	6	5

Mr Gary A. Tanaka 5ran 2m23.70 — TR: 121/127/107/110

CHANTILLY Sunday, Jun 6   SOFT

19   Prix Jean Prat Emirates Airline (Gr 1) (3yo c+f) £39,801   1m1f

	GOLDEN SNAKE (USA) *BWHills,GB* 3-9-2 MHills	6/1	1
	SLIP STREAM (USA) *SaeedbinSuroor,GB* 3-9-2 LDettori	83/10	nk 2
7	INDIAN DANEHILL (IRE) *AFabre,France* 3-9-2 OPeslier	81/10	¾ 3
7	Dansili *AFabre,France* 3-9-2 TJarnet	2/5f	2 4
7	Way of Light (USA) *PBary,France* 3-9-2 (b) CAsmussen	43/10	3 5
7	Le Roi Chic (FR) *NClement,France* 3-9-2 GMosse	15/1	6 6

Mr Mohamed Obaida 6ran 1m54.50   TR: 119/118/116/112/105

20   Emirates Airline Prix du Jockey Club (Gr 1) (3yo c+f) £248,757   1½m

	MONTJEU (IRE) *JEHammond,France* 3-9-2 CAsmussen	7/5cpf	1
	NOWHERE TO EXIT *JLDunlop,GB* 3-9-2 TQuinn	5/1	4 2
	RHAGAAS *SaeedbinSuroor,GB* 3-9-2 (b) LDettori	48/10	3 3
	Slickly (FR) *AFabre,France* 3-9-2 OPeslier	18/10	2½ 4
	Tchaikovsky (IRE) *APO'Brien,Ireland* 3-9-2 (v) MJKinane	7/5cpf	2 5
9	Gracioso (USA) *AFabre,France* 3-9-2 TJarnet	48/10	1½ 6
	Royal Rebel *MJohnston,GB* 3-9-2 (b) KFallon	17/1	3 7
	Falcon Flight (FR) *PBary,France* 3-9-2 SGuillot	69/10	8 8

Mr M. Tabor 8ran 2m34.12   TR: 127/120/115/112/109/107

CHANTILLY Sunday, Jun 13   GOOD to SOFT

21   Prix de Diane Hermes (Gr 1) (3yo f) £136,853   1¼m110y

	DARYABA (IRE) *AdeRoyerDupre,France* 3-9-0 GMosse	58/10	1
	STAR OF AKKAR *J-CRouget,France* 3-9-0 TGillet	37/10f	1 2
	VISIONNAIRE (FR) *AFabre,France* 3-9-0 TJarnet	88/10	1½ 3
	Louve (USA) *AFabre,France* 3-9-0 OPeslier	114/10	sh 4
	Juvenia (USA) *MmeCHead,France* 3-9-0 ODoleuze	65/10	1½ 5
	All Glory *JEPease,France* 3-9-0 CAsmussen	22/1	hd 6
	Cerulean Sky (IRE) *RCollet,France* 3-9-0 SGuillot	66/10	dh 6
8	Calando (FR) *SaeedbinSuroor,GB* 3-9-0 LDettori	64/10	1½ 8
	La Sylphide (SWI) *NClement,France* 3-9-0 DBoeuf	83/10	1½ 9
	Nasheed (USA) *JLDunlop,GB* 3-9-0 RHills	13/1	1½ 10
8	Karmifira (FR) *PHDemercastel,France* 3-9-0 DBonilla	20/1	nk 11
	Farfala (FR) *AFabre,France* 3-9-0 AJunk	88/10	3 12
	Zenne (IRE) *RCollet,France* 3-9-0 SCoffigny	53/1	4 13
	Apple of Kent (USA) *JHMGosden,GB* 3-9-0 KFallon	29/1	14

H.H. Aga Khan 14ran 2m16.10   TR: 117/115/112/112/109/109

ASCOT Tuesday, Jun 15   GOOD to FIRM

22   Queen Anne Stks (Gr 2) (3yo+) £71,150   1m (Str.)

	CAPE CROSS (IRE) *SaeedbinSuroor* 5-9-7 GaryStevens (2)	7/1	1
	DOCKSIDER (USA) *JWHills* 4-9-7 MHills (1)	9/1	sh 2
6	ALMUSHTARAK (IRE) *KMahdi* 6-9-5 OPeslier (3)	10/1	1½ 3
	Fa-Eq (IRE) *SaeedbinSuroor* 4-9-2 LDettori (4)	2/1f	¾ 4
	Perfect Vintage *MmeCBarbe,France* 4-9-2 PJSmullen (7)	40/1	1½ 5
	Sorbie Tower (IRE) *MissGayKelleway* 6-9-2 RCochrane (6)	16/1	8 6
6	Fly To The Stars *SaeedbinSuroor* 5-9-7 WSupple (5)	4/1	11 7
	On The Ridge (IRE) *HRACecil* 4-9-2 KFallon (8)	11/2	½ 8

Godolphin 8ran 1m39.72   TR: 125+/120+/119/114/111

23   Prince of Wales's Stks (Gr 2) (3yo+) £88,945   1¼m

	LEAR SPEAR (USA) *DRCElsworth* 4-9-3 MJKinane (5)	20/1	1
	FANTASTIC LIGHT (USA) *SirMichaelStoute* 3-8-5 GaryStevens (2)	14/1	hd 2
	XAAR *SaeedbinSuroor* 4-9-3 LDettori (4)	4/1	2½ 3
	Chester House (USA) *HRACecil* 4-9-3 KFallon (3)	2/1f	1 4
13	Handsome Ridge *JHMGosden* 5-9-6 OPeslier (1)	12/1	½ 5
	Limpid *SaeedbinSuroor* 4-9-8 (t) DO'Donohoe (8)	20/1	6 6
11	Shiva (JPN) *HRACecil* 4-9-5 WRyan (7)	7/2	2 7
	Generous Rosi *JLDunlop* 4-9-3 PatEddery (6)	14/1	4 8

Mr Raymond Tooth 8ran 2m04.37   TR: 124/123/118/116/118

24   St James's Palace Stks (Gr 1) (3yo c) £154,410   1m (Rnd)

7	SENDAWAR (IRE) *AdeRoyerDupre,France* 3-9-0 GMosse (11)	12/1	1
	ALJABR (USA) *SaeedbinSuroor* 3-9-0 LDettori (2)	10/3	1¼ 2
3	GOLD ACADEMY (IRE) *RHannon* 3-9-0 DaneO'Neill (6)	12/1	5 3

1158

Killer Instinct *HRACecil* 3-9-0 KFallon (4) 9/1   1 4
Raise A Grand (IRE) *JWPayne* 3-9-0 MHills (8) 40/1   1 5
3 Alrassaam *MAJarvis* 3-9-0 PRobinson (1) .... 16/1   ¾ 6
7 Mujahid (USA) *JLDunlop* 3-9-0 (b) RHills (3) 9/1   13¾ 7
3 Exeat (USA) *JHMGosden* 3-9-0 OPeslier (10) 10/1   2 8
10 Orpen (USA) *APO'Brien,Ireland* 3-9-0 MJKinane (5) 10/1   4 9
3 Debbie's Warning *KMahdi* 3-9-0 GaryStevens (7) 66/1   1 10
Be The Chief *TGMills* 3-9-0 PatEddery (9) 50/1   22 11
H.H. Aga Khan 11ran 1m39.99   TR: 128/125/113/111+/108/106

ASCOT Wednesday, Jun 16   GOOD to FIRM

25   **Jersey Stks (Gr 3) (3yo) £41,700**   7f

LOTS OF MAGIC *RHannon* 3-8-11 DaneO'Neill (3) 33/1   1
10 ENRIQUE *HRACecil* 3-9-3 KFallon (2) 13/8f   3 2
7 BERTOLINI (USA) *JHMGosden* 3-9-3 OPeslier (7) 10/1   1 3
Stravinsky (USA) *APO'Brien,Ireland* 3-8-11 MJKinane (6) 9/1   1 4
Mensa *MHTompkins* 3-8-11 SDrowne (9) .... 8/1   nk 5
7 Indiana Legend (IRE) *BJMeehan* 3-8-11 GMosse (1) .... 33/1   hd 6
Sicnee (USA) *SaeedbinSuroor* 3-9-0 LDettori (10) .... 10/1   sh 7
Blackheath (IRE) *JARToller* 3-8-11 MRoberts (4) 50/1   2 8
4 Kuwait Dawn (IRE) *KMahdi* 3-8-6 JQuinn (12) 66/1   8 9
Yakareem (IRE) *KMahdi* 3-8-11 GaryStevens (5) 40/1   1½ 10
3 Desaru (USA) *JNoseda* 3-8-11 PatEddery (8).......................... 13/2   2½ 11
Arctic Char *BJMeehan* 3-8-6 JFortune (11) 40/1   20 12
Mr Peter Valentine 12ran 1m26.45   TR: 122/120/118/109/108

26   **Coronation Stks (Gr 1) (3yo f) £134,240**   1m (Rnd)

BALISADA *GWragg* 3-9-0 MRoberts (8) 16/1   1
12 GOLDEN SILCA *MRChannon* 3-9-0 KFallon (4) 15/2   13¾ 2
8 VALENTINE WALTZ (IRE) *JHMGosden* 3-9-0 RCochrane (7) .... 7/2   sh 3
4 WANNABE GRAND (IRE) *JNoseda* 3-9-0 PatEddery (1).................. 11/4f   dh 3
4 Pescara (IRE) *SaeedbinSuroor* 3-9-0 LDettori (3) .... 13/2   nk 5
Choirgirl *JHMGosden* 3-9-0 OPeslier (9) .... 25/1   ¾ 6
Presumed (USA) *PJMakin* 3-9-0 SSanders (2) .... 10/1   ½ 7
12 Hula Angel (USA) *BWHills* 3-9-0 MHills (5)............................. 7/1   2 8
Hawriyah (USA) *JLDunlop* 3-9-0 RHills (6)............................ 10/1   5 9
Mr A. E. Oppenheimer 9ran 1m41.43   TR: 113/109/109/109/108/106

ASCOT Thursday, Jun 17   GOOD to FIRM

27   **Gold Cup (Gr 1) (4yo+) £120,300**   2½m

ENZELI (IRE) *JOxx,Ireland* 4-9-0 JPMurtagh (16) 20/1   1
INVERMARK *JRFanshawe* 5-9-2 RHughes (12) 8/1   1½ 2
KAYF TARA *SaeedbinSuroor* 5-9-2 GaryStevens (9)...................... 7/1   2½ 3
Celeric *JLDunlop* 7-9-2 PatEddery (13).......................... 6/1   13¾ 4
Nedawi *SaeedbinSuroor* 4-9-0 LDettori (3) .... 7/2f   ¾ 5
Three Cheers (IRE) *JHMGosden* 5-9-2 (v) WRyan (14)...................... 20/1   1 6
Shaya *GCBravery* 5-9-2 MFenton (7) 50/1   5 7
Spirit of Love (USA) *MJohnston* 4-9-0 DHolland (11)...................... 20/1   2½ 8
Katun (FR) *XNakkachdji,France* 6-9-2 TThulliez (8)...................... 50/1   5 9
Rainbow High *BWHills* 4-9-0 MHills (6)............................. 13/2   2 10
Churlish Charm *RHannon* 4-9-0 DaneO'Neill (1) .... 12/1   sh 11
Persian Punch (IRE) *DRCElsworth* 6-9-2 MJKinane (17)............. 16/1   2 12
Solo Mio (IRE) *JEHammond,France* 5-9-2 CAsmussen (2).................. 40/1   15 13
Sibling Rival (USA) *SaeedbinSuroor* 5-9-2 DO'Donohoe (5) 40/1   2½ 14
Athenry *JPearce* 6-9-2 NDay (4) 100/1   4 15
Laurentide (USA) *HRACecil* 4-9-0 KFallon (10) .... 20/1   ¾ 16
Tajoun (FR) *AdeRoyerDupre,France* 5-9-2 GMosse (15)...................... 20/1   dist 17
H.H. Aga Khan 17ran 4m18.85   TR: 126/122/119/117/118/115

28   **Cork And Orrery Stks (Gr 2) (3yo+) £65,250**   6f

BOLD EDGE *RHannon* 4-9-0 DaneO'Neill (16) 16/1   1
RUSSIAN REVIVAL (USA) *JHMGosden* 6-9-0 LDettori (6).............. 13/2   1¼ 2
VISION OF NIGHT *JLDunlop* 3-8-7 PatEddery (11)...................... 10/1   ½ 3
Superior Premium *RAFahey* 5-9-0 (t) RWinston (19)...................... 25/1   ½ 4
Eastern Purple (IRE) *KARyan* 4-9-0 JFortune (9) .... 20/1   ¾ 5
Arkadian Hero (USA) *LMCumani* 4-9-0 GMosse (20)........................... 7/1   hd 6
4 Fragrant Oasis (USA) *EALDunlop* 3-8-4 GCarter (3)........................... 20/1   1½ 7

Keos (USA) *JEHammond,France* 5-9-0 CAsmussen (13) .... 16/1 ¾ 8
Monkston Point (IRE) *DWPArbuthnot* 3-8-7 JWeaver (17).................... 66/1 1 9
Daylight In Dubai (USA) *DNicholls* 5-9-0 JCarroll (1)........................ 100/1 sh 10
Bianconi (USA) *APO'Brien,Ireland* 4-9-4 MJKinane (7) .... 6/1 ½ 11
Easy Dollar *BGubby* 7-9-0 (v) RHughes (8)... 100/1 1 12
4 Atlantic Destiny (IRE) *MJohnston* 3-8-4 MRoberts (4) .... 50/1 ½ 13
Referendum (IRE) *DNicholls* 5-9-0 AlexGreaves (2)............................. 66/1 nk 14
Tipsy Creek (USA) *BHanbury* 5-9-4 RHills (14) .... 12/1 ¾ 15
Wahj (IRE) *SirMichaelStoute* 4-9-0 GaryStevens (5) 16/1 3½ 16
Bold Fact (USA) *HRACecil* 4-9-0 KFallon (21).................................... 11/2f 3 17
Andreyev (IRE) *RHannon* 5-9-0 DHolland (12)..................................... 12/1 14 18
One Won One (USA) *MrsJMorgan,Ireland* 5-9-0 KJManning (15)....... 25/1 hd 19
Lady Whent and Friends 19ran 1m13.80 TR: 122/119/115/116/113/113

ASCOT Friday, Jun 18 GOOD to FIRM
29 Hardwicke Stks (Gr 2) (4yo+) £80,050 1½m
15 FRUITS OF LOVE (USA) *MJohnston* 4-8-12 (v) OPeslier (9)............ 12/1 1
15 ROYAL ANTHEM (USA) *HRACecil* 4-9-0 KFallon (3) 6/5f 3 2
SEA WAVE (IRE) *SaeedbinSuroor* 4-8-12 (t) LDettori (8)...................... 5/1 1½ 3
Sunshine Street (USA) *NMeade,Ireland* 4-8-9 JPMurtagh (7) .... 9/1 hd 4
Secret Saver (USA) *SirMichaelStoute* 4-8-9 (t) GaryStevens (10).......... 9/1 2½ 5
Posidonas *PFICole* 7-8-12 JFortune (4).. 33/1 12 6
Sadian *JLDunlop* 4-8-9 PatEddery (1).. 9/1 2½ 7
Rabah *JLDunlop* 4-8-9 RHills (2) 20/1 4 8
Mr M. Doyle 8ran 2m28.70 TR: 125+/122+/117/114/109

MILAN Sunday, Jun 20 GOOD to FIRM
30 Gran Premio di Milano (Gr 1) (4yo+ c+f) £86,198 1½m
5 DARK MOONDANCER *AdeRoyerDupre,France* 4-9-6 GMosse.......... 2/5f 1
UNGARO (GER) *HBlume,Germany* 5-9-6 THellier .... 63/10 ns 2
18 MARCH GROOM (USA) *OGervai,Germany* 5-9-6 (b) JHillis 32/1 3¾ 3
Ivan Luis (FR) *LCamici,Italy* 5-9-6 MDemuro..................................... 91/10 sh 4
Poseidon *LBrogi,Italy* 5-9-6 MPasquale... 34/1 ¾ 5
Robertico *ASchutz,Germany* 4-9-6 AStarke 89/10 1½ 6
11 Make No Mistake (IRE) *DKWeld,Ireland* 4-9-6 PJSmullen 4/1 2½ 7
Mr B. Arbib 7ran 2m30.80 TR: 119+/118+/112/111/110/108

CURRAGH Sunday, Jun 27 GOOD
31 Budweiser Irish Derby (Gr 1) (3yo c+f) £364,095 1½m
20 MONTJEU (IRE) *JEHammond,France* 3-9-0 CAsmussen 13/8f 1
17 DALIAPOUR (IRE) *LMCumani,GB* 3-9-0 GMosse................................ 4/1 5 2
20 TCHAIKOVSKY (IRE) *APO'Brien* 3-9-0 (b) MJKinane 16/1 5½ 3
17 Beat All (USA) *SirMichaelStoute,GB* 3-9-0 GaryStevens........................ 4/1 1½ 4
Mutafaweq (USA) *SaeedbinSuroor,GB* 3-9-0 LDettori............................. 9/2 3½ 5
Urban Ocean (FR) *APO'Brien* 3-9-0 JAHeffernan 25/1 11 6
Mudaa-Eb *KPrendergast* 3-9-0 SCraine .... 66/1 sh 7
Port Bayou (USA) *DKWeld* 3-9-0 (b) PJSmullen 22/1 2½ 8
Genghis Khan (IRE) *APO'Brien* 3-9-0 KFallon 20/1 3½ 9
Festival Hall (IRE) *APO'Brien* 3-9-0 JPSpencer 100/1 15 10
Mr M. Tabor 10ran 2m30.10 TR: 129+/122/114/111/105

LONGCHAMP Sunday, Jun 27 GOOD
32 Grand Prix de Paris (Gr 1) (3yo c+f) £119,284 1¼m
20 SLICKLY (FR) *AFabre,France* 3-9-2 TJarnet 9/5f 1
19 INDIAN DANEHILL (IRE) *AFabre,France* 3-9-2 TGillet.................. 91/10 2 2
SARDAUKAR *ELellouche,France* 3-9-2 DBonilla........................... 143/10 ½ 3
20 Gracioso (USA) *AFabre,France* 3-9-2 SGuillot 42/10 4 4
7 Kingsalsa (USA) *AFabre,France* 3-9-2 OPeslier.................................. 31/10 1 5
2 Fils de Viane (FR) *J-CRouget,France* 3-9-2 J-RDubosc .... 74/10 ½ 6
Golden Marvel (FR) *MmeCHead,France* 3-9-2 ODoleuze...................... 11/1 2½ 7
17 Brancaster (USA) *PWChapple-Hyam,GB* 3-9-2 (v) TQuinn 74/10 10 8
Mr J-L. Lagardere 8ran 2m03.90 TR: 119/115/114/106/103/102

SANDOWN Saturday, Jul 3 GOOD to FIRM
33 Coral-Eclipse Stks (Gr 1) (3yo+) £174,600 1¼m7y
17 COMPTON ADMIRAL *GAButler* 3-8-10 DHolland (7)........................ 20/1 1

23	XAAR *SaeedbinSuroor* 4-9-7 LDettori (5)	6/1	nk	2
23	FANTASTIC LIGHT (USA) *SirMichaelStoute* 3-8-10 GaryStevens (1)	6/1	½	3
23	Chester House (USA) *HRACecil* 4-9-7 KFallon (3)	6/1	1½	4
14	Running Stag (USA) *PMitchell* 5-9-7 RCochrane (4)	9/1	2½	5
11	Insatiable (IRE) *SirMichaelStoute* 6-9-7 RHughes (8)	8/1	1¾	6
13	Croco Rouge (IRE) *PBary,France* 4-9-7 TJarnet (6)	5/2f	¾	7
23	Lear Spear (USA) *DRCElsworth* 4-9-7 TQuinn (2)	7/1	12	8

Mr E. Penser 8ran 2m06.42 TR: 121/122/119/118/113/110

SAINT-CLOUD Sunday, Jul 4 GOOD

34 Grand Prix de Saint-Cloud (Gr 1) (3yo+ c+f) £120,482 1½m

13	EL CONDOR PASA (USA) *YNinomiya,Japan* 4-9-8 MEbina	22/10		1
18	TIGER HILL (IRE) *PSchiergen,Germany* 4-9-8 THellier	54/10	2½	2
15	DREAM WELL (FR) *PBary,France* 4-9-8 (b) CAsmussen	5/2	2½	3
5	Sagamix (FR) *AFabre,France* 4-9-8 OPeslier	19/10f	sn	4
15	Borgia (GER) *AFabre,France* 5-9-5 KFallon	38/1	1	5
	Public Purse (USA) *AFabre,France* 5-9-8 TJarnet	11/1	3	6
	Greek Dance (IRE) *SirMichaelStoute,GB* 4-9-8 GaryStevens	32/1	nk	7
	Blushing Risk (FR) *H-APantall,France* 4-9-8 (b) GMosse	26/1	6	8
	Res Judicata *JEPease,France* 4-9-8 SGuillot	5/2	20	9
	Saugerties (USA) *PSchiergen,Germany* 5-9-8 PvandeKeere	54/10	8	10

Mr Takashi Watanabe 10ran 2m28.80 TR: 131/127/122/122/117+/115

NEWMARKET Tuesday, Jul 6 GOOD to FIRM (July Course)

35 Princess of Wales's Greene King Stks (Gr 2) (3yo+) £31,400 1½m

	CRAIGSTEEL *HRACecil* 4-9-2 KFallon (6)	13/2		1
	ARCTIC OWL *JRFanshawe* 5-9-5 MHills (8)	7/1	1	2
	SILVER RHAPSODY (USA) *HRACecil* 4-8-13 MJKinane (7)	9/1	1¼	3
29	Sea Wave (IRE) *SaeedbinSuroor* 4-9-5 (t) LDettori (4)	13/8f	nk	4
	Bienamado (USA) *PWChapple-Hyam* 3-8-3 TQuinn (3)	14/1	6	5
17	Zaajer (USA) *EALDunlop* 3-8-3 RHills (1)	8/1	11	6
	Capri *HRACecil* 4-9-5 WRyan (5)	12/1	16	7
29	Secret Saver (USA) *SirMichaelStoute* 4-9-2 GaryStevens (2)	10/1	4	8

Sir David Wills 8ran 2m25.38 TR: 121/122/114/119/106+

NEWMARKET Wednesday, Jul 7 GOOD to FIRM (July Course)

36 Tnt International Aviation July Stks (Gr 3) (2yo c+g) £18,260 6f

	CITY ON A HILL (USA) *DRLoder,France* 2-8-13 SGuillot (2)	11/2		1
	MULL OF KINTYRE (USA) *APO'Brien,Ireland* 2-8-10 MJKinane (4)	15/8	1¼	2
	SIR NICHOLAS *JNoseda* 2-8-10 KFallon (5)	11/8f	¾	3
	Master Fay (IRE) *MRChannon* 2-8-10 TQuinn (6)	12/1	3½	4
	Lord Pacal (IRE) *NACallaghan* 2-8-10 GaryStevens (3)	12/1	2½	5
	Digital Image *RHannon* 2-8-10 DaneO'Neill (7)	66/1	¾	6
	Our Ambition (IRE) *BJMeehan* 2-8-10 JFortune (1)	66/1	3	7

Godolphin S.N.C. 7ran 1m10.70 TR: 114/107/105/97

NEWMARKET Thursday, Jul 8 FIRM (July Course)

37 Darley July Cup (Gr 1) (3yo+) £94,300 6f

25	STRAVINSKY (USA) *APO'Brien,Ireland* 3-8-13 (v) MJKinane (6)	8/1		1
28	BOLD EDGE *RHannon* 4-9-5 DaneO'Neill (8)	7/1	4	2
25	BERTOLINI (USA) *JHMGosden* 3-8-13 (v) GaryStevens (13)	9/1	nk	3
28	Arkadian Hero (USA) *LMCumani* 4-9-5 GMosse (1)	12/1	½	4
28	Vision of Night *JLDunlop* 3-8-13 OPeslier (16)	10/1	1	5
28	Tipsy Creek (USA) *BHanbury* 5-9-5 WRyan (18)	20/1	hd	6
26	Wannabe Grand (IRE) *JNoseda* 3-8-10 RCochrane (12)	11/2f	nk	7
	Sampower Star *RHannon* 3-8-13 RHughes (10)	14/1	hd	8
28	Bianconi (USA) *APO'Brien,Ireland* 4-9-5 JPMurtagh (9)	25/1	¾	9
28	Superior Premium *RAFahey* 5-9-5 (t) MRoberts (7)	25/1	nk	10
	Lochangel *IABalding* 5-9-2 KDarley (14)	14/1	½	11
22	Fa-Eq (IRE) *SaeedbinSuroor* 4-9-5 RHills (4)	14/1	2½	12
	Mitcham (IRE) *TGMills* 3-8-13 TQuinn (11)	10/1	½	13
7	Lavery (IRE) *APO'Brien,Ireland* 3-8-13 WSupple (3)	20/1	1¼	14
28	Bold Fact (USA) *HRACecil* 4-9-5 KFallon (15)	12/1	1¼	15
	Dyhim Diamond (IRE) *CLaffon-Parias,France* 5-9-5 DBoeuf (5)	25/1	3	16

	Sheer Viking (IRE) *BWHills* 3-8-13 MHills (17)	33/1	13 17

Mr M. Tabor & Mrs John Magnier 17ran 1m09.51 TR: 133/122/119/120/115/115

CURRAGH Sunday, Jul 11 GOOD to FIRM

38 Kildangan Stud Irish Oaks (Gr 1) (3yo f) £98,099 1½m

16	RAMRUMA (USA) *HRACecil,GB* 3-9-0 KFallon	4/9f	1
16	SUNSPANGLED (IRE) *APO'Brien* 3-9-0 MJKinane	12/1	7 2
	SISTER BELLA (IRE) *JOxx* 3-9-0 JPMurtagh	14/1	nk 3
	Mother of Pearl (IRE) *PWChapple-Hyam,GB* 3-9-0 JFortune	12/1	½ 4
	Blend of Pace (IRE) *DKWeld* 3-9-0 PJSmullen	20/1	7 5
12	Polaire (IRE) *KPrendergast* 3-9-0 DPMcDonogh	8/1	sh 6
	Rose of Tara (IRE) *MJGrassick* 3-9-0 EAhern	200/1	1½ 7

H.R.H. Prince Fahd Salman 7ran 2m33.00 TR: 121+/108/107/106

MAISONS-LAFFITTE Sunday, Jul 18 GOOD

39 Prix Eugene Adam (Gr 2) (3yo) £29,851 1¼m

17	DUBAI MILLENNIUM *SaeedbinSuroor,GB* 3-8-12 LDettori	7/10cpf	1
	STATE SHINTO (USA) *AFabre,France* 3-8-12 TJarnet	7/10cpf	3 2
	MANNDAR (IRE) *LMCumani,GB* 3-8-12 GMosse	3/1	½ 3
32	Sardaukar *ELellouche,France* 3-8-12 DBonilla	32/10	6 4
17	Salford Express (IRE) *DRCElsworth,GB* 3-9-2 TQuinn	56/10	10 5

Godolphin 5ran 2m03.60 TR: 122/116/115/102

ASCOT Saturday, Jul 24 GOOD to FIRM

40 King George VI And Queen Elizabeth Diamond Stks (Gr 1) (3yo+) £342,000 1½m

15	DAYLAMI (IRE) *SaeedbinSuroor* 5-9-7 LDettori (8)	3/1	1
27	NEDAWI *SaeedbinSuroor* 4-9-7 GaryStevens (2)	8/1	5 2
29	FRUITS OF LOVE (USA) *MJohnston* 4-9-7 (v) OPeslier (5)	4/1	½ 3
15	Silver Patriarch (IRE) *JLDunlop* 5-9-7 TQuinn (6)	10/1	2½ 4
29	Sunshine Street (USA) *NMeade,Ireland* 4-9-7 (t) JPMurtagh (1)	25/1	1½ 5
	Indigenous (IRE) *IWAllan,HongKong* 6-9-7 (t) CAsmussen (4)	20/1	½ 6
17	Oath (IRE) *HRACecil* 3-8-9 KFallon (3)	9/4f	1¼ 7
31	Daliapour (IRE) *LMCumani* 3-8-9 GMosse (7)	8/1	5 8

Godolphin 8ran 2m29.35 TR: 135/126/125+/121/118/118

GOODWOOD Wednesday, Jul 28 FIRM

41 Champagne Lanson Sussex Stks (Gr 1) (3yo+) £143,000 1m

24	ALJABR (USA) *SaeedbinSuroor* 3-8-13 LDettori (6)	11/10f	1
22	DOCKSIDER (USA) *JWHills* 4-9-7 MHills (8)	9/1	1 2
22	ALMUSHTARAK (IRE) *KMahdi* 6-9-7 OPeslier (5)	20/1	5 3
26	Balisada *GWragg* 3-8-10 MRoberts (3)	13/2	¾ 4
25	Enrique *HRACecil* 3-8-13 KFallon (1)	6/1	½ 5
6	Jim And Tonic (FR) *FDoumen,France* 5-9-7 GMosse (2)	5/1	½ 6
24	Raise A Grand (IRE) *JWPayne* 3-8-13 TQuinn (4)	33/1	nk 7
24	Gold Academy (IRE) *RHannon* 3-8-13 DaneO'Neill (7)	25/1	5 8

Godolphin 8ran 1m35.66 TR: 125/124/112/105/107/107

GOODWOOD Thursday, Jul 29 FIRM

42 Goodwood Cup (Gr 2) (3yo+) £40,100 2m

27	KAYF TARA *SaeedbinSuroor* 5-9-7 LDettori (5)	9/4jf	1
27	THREE CHEERS (IRE) *JHMGosden* 5-9-2 (v) WRyan (8)	10/1	4 2
	JASEUR (USA) *JHMGosden* 6-9-2 (v) GaryStevens (4)	16/1	¾ 3
	Ta-Lim *SirMichaelStoute* 4-9-2 RHills (6)	9/2	1¾ 4
	Canon Can (USA) *HRACecil* 6-9-2 KFallon (2)	7/1	2 5
27	Celeric *JLDunlop* 7-9-2 TQuinn (3)	9/4jf	1¾ 6
	Seignorial (USA) *PWChapple-Hyam* 4-9-2 (b) JFortune (7)	50/1	17 7

Godolphin 7ran 3m23.67 TR: 119+/109/108/108/103/101

DEAUVILLE Sunday, Aug 8 SOFT

43 Prix Maurice de Gheest (Gr 1) (3yo+) £50,352 6f110y

	DIKTAT *SaeedbinSuroor,GB* 4-9-2 LDettori	4/5jf	1
13	GOLD AWAY (IRE) *MmeCHead,France* 4-9-2 ODoleuze	38/10	1 2
37	BERTOLINI (USA) *JHMGosden,GB* 3-8-12 (v) GaryStevens	4/5jf	½ 3

37	Vision of Night *JLDunlop,GB* 3-8-12 PatEddery	155/10	2 4
6	Tomba *BJMeehan,GB* 5-9-2 MTebbutt	107/10	¾ 5
28	Keos (USA) *JEHammond,France* 5-9-2 (b) TJarnet	59/10	½ 6
37	Sampower Star *RHannon,GB* 3-8-12 RHughes	131/10	2½ 7
37	Bianconi (USA) *APO'Brien,Ireland* 4-9-2 (v) FSanchez	6/1	½ 8
	Special Discount (FR) *MmeCHead,France* 5-9-2 (b) NGuesdon	38/10	5 9
24	Orpen (USA) *APO'Brien,Ireland* 3-8-12 (v) OPeslier	6/1	10

Godolphin 10ran 1m18.20   TR: 126/122/121/115/113/112

NEWBURY Saturday, Aug 14   GOOD

44   Geoffrey Freer Stks (Gr 2) (3yo+) £38,500   1m5f61y

40	SILVER PATRIARCH (IRE) *JLDunlop* 5-9-9 PatEddery (1)	7/2	1
35	CRAIGSTEEL *HRACecil* 4-9-6 TQuinn (3)	10/11f	½ 2
29	SADIAN *JLDunlop* 4-9-3 SSanders (5)	12/1	1¾ 3
	Blueprint (IRE) *SirMichaelStoute* 4-9-3 KFallon (2)	5/2	sh 4

Mr Peter S. Winfield 4ran 2m50.62   TR: 125/121/116/116

DEAUVILLE Sunday, Aug 15   HEAVY

45   Prix du Haras de Fresnay-le-Buffard Jacques le Marois (Gr 1) (3yo+ c+f) £101,626   1m

39	DUBAI MILLENNIUM *SaeedbinSuroor,GB* 3-8-11 LDettori	14/10jf	1
32	SLICKLY (FR) *AFabre,France* 3-8-11 TJarnet	5/2	2½ 2
19	DANSILI *AFabre,France* 3-8-11 OPeslier	14/10jf	1 3
19	Way of Light (USA) *PBary,France* 3-8-11 YTake	69/10	hd 4
8	Venize (IRE) *RCollet,France* 3-8-8 SGuillot	137/10	1 5

Godolphin 5ran 1m44.30   TR: 124+/118+/116/115/110

YORK Tuesday, Aug 17   GOOD to FIRM

46   Juddmonte International Stks (Gr 1) (3yo+) £210,625   1¼m85y

29	ROYAL ANTHEM (USA) *HRACecil* 4-9-5 GaryStevens (9)	3/1jf	1
34	GREEK DANCE (IRE) *SirMichaelStoute* 4-9-5 KFallon (10)	3/1jf	8 2
33	CHESTER HOUSE (USA) *HRACecil* 4-9-5 TQuinn (3)	14/1	1¾ 3
41	Almushtarak (IRE) *KMahdi* 6-9-5 GMosse (11)	25/1	sh 4
33	Compton Admiral *GAButler* 3-8-11 DHolland (1)	10/1	hd 5
19	Golden Snake (USA) *BWHills* 3-8-11 MHills (2)	10/1	5 6
1	Almutawakel *SaeedbinSuroor* 4-9-5 LDettori (4)	6/1	hd 7
	Pegnitz (USA) *CEBrittain* 4-9-5 PRobinson (5)	100/1	4 8
	Kissogram *LMCumani* 4-9-2 JReid (12)	12/1	1½ 9
34	Salford Express (IRE) *DRCElsworth* 3-8-11 (b) PatEddery (8)	33/1	2½ 10
15	Central Park (IRE) *SaeedbinSuroor* 4-9-5 DO'Donohoe (7)	33/1	14 11
17	Saffron Walden (FR) *APO'Brien,Ireland* 3-8-11 (v) MJKinane (6)	11/1	5 12

The Thoroughbred Corporation 12ran 2m06.91   TR: 135/119/115/115/114/104

47   Stakis Casinos Great Voltigeur Stks (Gr 2) (3yo c+g) £57,000   1m3f195y

33	FANTASTIC LIGHT (USA) *SirMichaelStoute* 3-8-9 GaryStevens (6)	4/1	1
35	BIENAMADO (USA) *PWChapple-Hyam* 3-8-9 RHughes (2)	11/2	1¼ 2
17	GLAMIS (USA) *JHMGosden* 3-8-9 RCochrane (4)	9/1	1¼ 3
31	Mutafaweq (USA) *SaeedbinSuroor* 3-8-12 LDettori (1)	3/1f	1 4
	Elmutabaki *BWHills* 3-8-9 RHills (3)	4/1	7 5
	Time Zone *CEBrittain* 3-8-9 GDuffield (5)	9/1	1¼ 6
	Flaming Quest *SirMichaelStoute* 3-8-9 KFallon (7)	10/1	6 7

Maktoum Al Maktoum 7ran 2m29.05   TR: 121/119/117/118/103/100

YORK Wednesday, Aug 18   GOOD

48   Aston Upthorpe Yorkshire Oaks (Gr 1) (3yo+ f+m) £119,550   1m3f195y

38	RAMRUMA (USA) *HRACecil* 3-8-8 PatEddery (9)	5/6f	1
	ELA ATHENA *MAJarvis* 3-8-8 MRoberts (5)	33/1	1¼ 2
35	SILVER RHAPSODY (USA) *HRACecil* 4-9-4 TQuinn (6)	11/1	2 3
16	Zahrat Dubai *SaeedbinSuroor* 3-8-8 (t) LDettori (8)	7/1	½ 4
	Mary Stuart (IRE) *SirMichaelStoute* 3-8-8 GaryStevens (11)	20/1	½ 5
	Mistle Song *CEBrittain* 3-8-8 RHughes (10)	50/1	1 6
21	Cerulean Sky (IRE) *RCollet,France* 3-8-8 MHills (3)	20/1	¾ 7
16	Noushkey *MAJarvis* 3-8-8 PRobinson (7)	4/1	hd 8
21	Calando (USA) *SaeedbinSuroor* 3-8-8 JReid (4)	25/1	1½ 9
38	Sunspangled (IRE) *APO'Brien,Ireland* 3-8-8 MJKinane (1)	16/1	5 10

Lady In Waiting *PFICole* 4-9-4 KFallon (2).. 14/1   4 11
H.R.H. Prince Fahd Salman 11ran 2m29.17   TR: 121+/119/115/114/112

YORK Thursday, Aug 19   GOOD

49   Persimmon Homes Nunthorpe Stks (Gr 1) (2yo+) £88,175   5f
  37   STRAVINSKY (USA) *APO'Brien,Ireland* 3-9-7 (v) MJKinane (13) 1/1f   1
       SAINTE MARINE (IRE) *RCollet,France* 4-9-6 SGuillot (1) 7/1   1½ 2
       PROUD NATIVE (IRE) *DNicholls* 5-9-9 AlexGreaves (3) 16/1   1½ 3
       Night Shot *IABalding* 4-9-9 MartinDwyer (9) 20/1   1 4
       Dashing Blue *IABalding* 6-9-9 KFallon (2) .... 10/1   nk 5
       Almaty (IRE) *WRMuir* 6-9-9 DHolland (4) 50/1   1 6
  37   Lochangel *IABalding* 5-9-6 LDettori (7).. 7/1   ¾ 7
       Cortachy Castle (IRE) *BJMeehan* 4-9-9 PatEddery (8) 25/1   3½ 8
       Rosselli (USA) *JBerry* 3-9-7 JCarroll (14)..................................... 33/1   1½ 9
  37   Sheer Viking (IRE) *BWHills* 3-9-7 MHills (10).............................. 40/1   1 10
       Afaan (IRE) *RFMarvin* 6-9-9 (b) TGMcLaughlin (15) .... 100/1   nk 11
       Night Flight *RAFahey* 5-9-9 RWinston (6) .... 20/1   ¾ 12
       Flanders (IRE) *TDEasterby* 3-9-4 LCharnock (16)........................ 14/1   ¾ 13
       Averti (IRE) *WRMuir* 8-9-9 JReid (5).. 16/1   5 14
       Rambling Bear *MBlanshard* 6-9-9 RCochrane (12)....................... 20/1   bd
  37   Tipsy Creek (USA) *BHanbury* 5-9-9 (b) RHills (11).................... 25/1   pu
       Mr M. Tabor & Mrs John Magnier 16ran 59.33secs TR: 124+/116/115/112/111+/108

DEAUVILLE Sunday, Aug 22   SOFT

50   Prix Morny (Gr 1) (2yo c+f) £80,321   6f
       FASLIYEV (USA) *APO'Brien,Ireland* 2-9-0 MJKinane 6/5cp   1
       WARM HEART (USA) *JHMGosden,GB* 2-9-0 SGuillot 2/5cpf   4 2
       BACHIR (IRE) *JHMGosden,GB* 2-9-0 DBoeuf 2/5cpf   2½ 3
       Grigorovich (USA) *AFabre,France* 2-9-0 OPeslier .... 6/5cp   sn 4
       Harbour Island (FR) *PBary,France* 2-8-11 TJarnet 17/2   2 5
       Mount Abu (IRE) *PWChapple-Hyam,GB* 2-9-0 GMosse .... 16/1   hd 6
  36   City On A Hill (USA) *DRLoder,France* 2-9-0 LDettori.................... 2/5cpf   sn 7
       Mr M. Tabor 7ran 1m11.00   TR: 120/109/104/104/97/99

51   Prix Kergorlay (Gr 2) (3yo+) £30,121   1m7f
  42   KAYF TARA *SaeedbinSuroor,GB* 5-9-6 LDettori 4/5f   1
  27   INVERMARK *JRFanshawe,GB* 5-9-6 RHughes................................. 17/10   5 2
       LARGESSE *JohnBerry,GB* 5-9-9 JFEgan....................................... 79/10   1 3
       Alpha Blues *AWohler,Germany* 4-9-4 OPeslier 38/10   5 4
       Mayshiel (IRE) *JEHammond,France* 6-9-4 FSpanu 15/2   1½ 5
       Godolphin 5ran 3m21.90   TR: 120+/113/110/105/102

GOODWOOD Saturday, Aug 28   GOOD

52   Celebration Mile (Gr 2) (3yo+) £44,125   1m
  22   CAPE CROSS (IRE) *SaeedbinSuroor* 5-9-7 JReid (4)........................... 5/2   1
       JOSR ALGARHOUD (IRE) *SaeedbinSuroor* 3-8-9 LDettori (1) 8/11f   1½ 2
  46   ALMUSHTARAK (IRE) *KMahdi* 6-9-4 GMosse (5)............................. 7/1   2 3
       Wallace *RHannon* 3-8-9 RHughes (3).. 8/1   1¼ 4
  24   Debbie's Warning *KMahdi* 3-8-9 (t) TQuinn (2) .... 33/1   dist 5
       Godolphin 5ran 1m38.64   TR: 129/118/117/110

HAYDOCK Saturday, Sep 4   GOOD to FIRM

53   Stanley Leisure Sprint Cup (Gr 1) (3yo+) £76,800   6f
  43   DIKTAT *SaeedbinSuroor* 4-9-0 LDettori (16).............................. 13/8f   1
  43   BERTOLINI (USA) *JHMGosden* 3-8-12 (v) SGuillot (10)................. 8/1   nk 2
  37   ARKADIAN HERO (USA) *LMCumani* 4-9-0 GMosse (5) 4/1   1¾ 3
  37   Bold Edge *RHannon* 4-9-0 TQuinn (6) .... 8/1   hd 4
  43   Sampower Star *RHannon* 3-8-12 RHughes (14) .... 16/1   ½ 5
  43   Tomba *BJMeehan* 5-9-0 MTebbutt (12) .... 20/1   nk 6
  37   Wannabe Grand (IRE) *JNoseda* 3-8-9 PatEddery (2) .... 11/1   sh 7
   4   Imperial Beauty (USA) *PJMakin* 3-8-9 JFortune (11)...................... 9/1   1¾ 8
       Halmahera (IRE) *IABalding* 4-9-0 KDarley (7)............................. 25/1   nk 9
       Gaelic Storm *MJohnston* 5-9-0 DHolland (3) .... 50/1   ½ 10
       Pipalong (IRE) *TDEasterby* 3-8-9 LCharnock (1) 25/1   1¼ 11
  28   Eastern Purple (IRE) *KARyan* 4-9-0 RHills (4) .... 50/1   nk 12

1164

Yorkies Boy *BAMcMahon* 4-9-0 MRoberts (9).. 66/1 nk 13
49 Rosselli (USA) *JBerry* 3-8-12 JCarroll (15).. 50/1 3½ 14
49 Rambling Bear *MBlanshard* 6-9-0 JWeaver (8).................................... 40/1 2½ 15
Grazia *SirMarkPrescott* 4-8-11 SSanders (13)..................................... 16/1 1½ 16

Godolphin 16ran 1m11.04   TR: 126/125/120/120/118/117

CURRAGH Sunday, Sep 5   GOOD to FIRM
54   **Moyglare Stud Stks (Gr 1) (2yo) £81,875**   7f

PRESELI (IRE) *MJGrassick* 2-8-11 EAhern 9/1   1
TORGAU (IRE) *GCBravery,GB* 2-8-11 MHills .... 5/1   ¾ 2
LITTLEFEATHER (IRE) *SirMarkPrescott,GB* 2-8-11 GDuffield 7/2f   1½ 3
Amethyst (IRE) *APO'Brien* 2-8-11 MJKinane....................................... 9/2   nk 4
Eurolink Raindance (IRE) *JLDunlop,GB* 2-8-11 TQuinn...................... 7/1   1 5
Fairy Gem (IRE) *RHannon,GB* 2-8-11 DaneO'Neill .... 14/1   sh 6
Mandama (IRE) *JOxx* 2-8-11 JPMurtagh... 7/1   nk 7
Aretha (IRE) *JSBolger* 2-8-11 KJManning... 16/1   1 8
Sand Partridge (IRE) *KPrendergast* 2-8-11 PShanahan .... 33/1   ½ 9
Gifts Galore (IRE) *DKWeld* 2-8-11 PJSmullen 16/1   1 10
Lady Upstage (IRE) *BWHills,GB* 2-8-11 RHughes 20/1   2¼ 11
Inforapenny *KPrendergast* 2-8-11 SCraine.. 20/1   ¾ 12

Mr L. Neil Jones 12ran 1m24.20   TR: 107+/105/100+/99+/96/95

BADEN-BADEN Sunday, Sep 5   GOOD
55   **Mercedes Benz Grosser Preis von Baden (Gr 1) (3yo+) £109,428**   1½m

34 TIGER HILL (IRE) *PSchiergen,Germany* 4-9-6 THellier................. 13/10f   1
FLAMINGO ROAD (GER) *ASchutz,Germany* 3-8-7 AStarke........... 64/10   3 2
BELENUS (GER) *AWohler,Germany* 3-8-9 ABoschert..................... 26/10   hd 3
Sumitas (GER) *PSchiergen,Germany* 3-8-9 ASuborics 31/10   12 4
Lucky Dream (FR) *H-APantall,France* 5-9-6 TMundry....................... 82/10   6 5
34 Saugerties (USA) *PSchiergen,Germany* 5-9-6 PvandeKeere .... 189/10   dist 6

Baron G. von Ullmann 6ran 2m29.91   TR: 127/118/120

LONGCHAMP Sunday, Sep 5   GOOD to FIRM
56   **Emirates Prix du Moulin de Longchamp (Gr 1) (3yo+ c+f) £90,361**   1m

24 SENDAWAR (IRE) *AdeRoyerDupre,France* 3-8-11 GMosse 4/5f   1
43 GOLD AWAY (IRE) *MmeCHead,France* 4-9-1 DBoeuf 88/10   1½ 2
45 DANSILI *AFabre,France* 3-8-11 OPeslier....................................... 9/1   hd 3
41 Aljabr (USA) *SaeedbinSuroor,GB* 3-8-11 LDettori.............................. 8/5   2 4
45 Slickly (FR) *AFabre,France* 3-8-11 TJarnet..................................... 10/1   1½ 5
Field of Hope (IRE) *PBary,France* 4-8-12 SGuillot............................ 29/1   hd 6
45 Way of Light (USA) *PBary,France* 3-8-11 KFallon 308/10   4 7
22 Fly To The Stars *SaeedbinSuroor,GB* 5-9-1 RHills.............................. 8/5   1 8
Sabrinsky (FR) *MmeCHead,France* 3-8-11 NGuesdon 88/10   20 9

H.H. Aga Khan 9ran 1m35.20   TR: 129/125/125/121/118/114

DONCASTER Friday, Sep 10   GOOD to FIRM
57   **Frigidaire Champagne Stks (Gr 2) (2yo c+g) £60,840**   7f

DISTANT MUSIC (USA) *BWHills* 2-8-10 MHills (1)........................ 13/8f   1
ROSSINI (USA) *APO'Brien,Ireland* 2-9-0 MJKinane (3) 5/2   2½ 2
WINNING VENTURE *SPCWoods* 2-8-10 JReid (6) 66/1   5 3
Ekraar (USA) *MPTregoning* 2-9-0 RHills (5) .... 9/4   nk 4
Dramatic Quest *MJohnston* 2-8-10 DHolland (2) 8/1   2½ 5
Tioga *BJMeehan* 2-8-10 PatEddery (4) .... 33/1   ¾ 6

Mr K. Abdulla 6ran 1m24.16   TR: 121/118/101/104

DONCASTER Saturday, Sep 11   GOOD to FIRM
58   **Rothmans Royals St Leger Stks (Gr 1) (3yo c+f) £218,500**   1¾m132y

47 MUTAFAWEQ (USA) *SaeedbinSuroor* 3-9-0 RHills (6) 11/2   1
48 RAMRUMA (USA) *HRACecil* 3-8-9 PatEddery (5) 10/11f   2 2
17 ADAIR (IRE) *SaeedbinSuroor* 3-9-0 OPeslier (8) 9/1   2 3
17 All The Way (IRE) *TGMills* 3-9-0 JMurtagh (2) 8/1   7 4
31 Tchaikovsky (IRE) *GAButler* 3-9-0 GMosse (9)................................ 20/1   4 5
48 Noushkey *MAJarvis* 3-8-9 PRobinson (3).. 11/1   2 6
Iscan (IRE) *SirMichaelStoute* 3-9-0 JReid (1) 13/2   11 7

47 Elmutabaki *BWHills* 3-9-0 MHills (4)... 16/1   3 8
    Praslin Island *AKelleway* 3-9-0 (b) MRoberts (7)................................ 200/1 dist 9
    Godolphin 9ran 3m02.75   TR: 129/121+/123/113/107/100

GOODWOOD Saturday, Sep 11   GOOD to FIRM

59   Caffrey's Premium Ale Select Stks (Gr 3) (3yo+) £22,500   1m1f192y

33 LEAR SPEAR (USA) *DRCElsworth* 4-9-5 TQuinn (4) 9/2   1
13 KABOOL *SaeedbinSuroor* 4-9-0 DHolland (3) .... 15/8f   ½ 2
    DIAMOND WHITE *MJRyan* 4-8-11 RCochrane (2)............................. 9/1   ¾ 3
    Alabaq (USA) *JLDunlop* 3-8-4 GCarter (7)....................................... 13/2   1¾ 4
    Zindabad (FR) *BHanbury* 3-8-10 JFortune (5)................................... 3/1   7 5
    Moutahddee (IRE) *MPTregoning* 3-8-7 DaneO'Neill (6)..................... 8/1   2½ 6
    Wolf Tooth *DRCElsworth* 3-8-7 NPollard (1)................................... 50/1   20 7
    Mr Raymond Tooth 7ran 2m05.12   TR: 124/118/113/110

LEOPARDSTOWN Saturday, Sep 11   GOOD to SOFT

60   Esat Digifone Champion Stks (Gr 1) (3yo+) £354,118   1¼m

40 DAYLAMI (IRE) *SaeedbinSuroor,GB* 5-9-4 LDettori (4)...................... 6/4   1
12 DAZZLING PARK (IRE) *JSBolger* 3-8-8 KJManning (8) 33/1   9 2
34 DREAM WELL (FR) *PBary,France* 4-9-4 (b) CAsmussen (6).............. 7/2   2½ 3
40 Sunshine Street (USA) *NMeade* 4-9-4 PShanahan (5).......................... 66/1   ½ 4
46 Royal Anthem (USA) *HRACecil,GB* 4-9-4 GaryStevens (3)................. 11/8f   1½ 5
    Lord of Men *SaeedbinSuroor,GB* 6-9-4 DJO'Donohoe (9) 100/1   9 6
48 Sunspangled (IRE) *APO'Brien* 3-8-8 MJKinane (1)........................... 40/1   3½ 7
    Godolphin 7ran 2m08.40   TR: 135/116/114/113+/110

LONGCHAMP Sunday, Sep 12   GOOD to FIRM

61   Prix Foy Gray d'Albion Barriere (Gr 2) (4yo+ c+f) £40,282   1½m

34 EL CONDOR PASA (USA) *YNinomiya,Japan* 4-9-2 MEbina............. 3/10f   1
34 BORGIA (GER) *AFabre,France* 5-8-13 KFallon .... 49/10   sn 2
33 CROCO ROUGE (IRE) *PBary,France* 4-9-2 TJarnet 17/10   1½ 3
    Mr Takashi Watanabe 3ran 2m31.40   TR: 124/120/120

62   Prix Vermeille Normandy Barriere (Gr 1) (3yo f) £80,564   1½m

21 DARYABA (IRE) *AdeRoyerDupre,France* 3-9-0 GMosse................. 4/5cpf   1
    ETIZAAZ (USA) *SaeedbinSuroor,GB* 3-9-0 LDettori 28/10   2½ 2
48 CERULEAN SKY (IRE) *RCollet,France* 3-9-0 SGuillot.................... 177/10   1½ 3
4 Fairy Queen (IRE) *SaeedbinSuroor,GB* 3-9-0 KFallon 28/10   2½ 4
12 Edabiya (IRE) *JOxx,Ireland* 3-9-0 (b) JPMurtagh .... 4/5cpf   ns 5
21 Juvenia (IRE) *MmeCHead,France* 3-9-0 DBoeuf 11/1   1 6
38 Mother of Pearl (IRE) *PWChapple-Hyam,GB* 3-9-0 RHughes .... 132/10   sh 7
    Side Saddle (IRE) *DSmaga,France* 3-9-0 PatEddery .... 31/1   hd 8
    Sweet Opera (FR) *FHead,France* 3-9-0 DBonilla 12/1   1½ 9
    Ares Vallis (IRE) *AFabre,France* 3-9-0 OPeslier .... 62/10   ns 10
21 La Sylphide (SWI) *NClement,France* 3-9-0 TJarnet......................... 41/1   2½ 11
    H.H. Aga Khan 11ran 2m30.60   TR: 121/117/114/110/110/108

63   Prix Niel Majestic Barriere (Gr 2) (3yo c+f) £40,282   1½m

31 MONTJEU (IRE) *JEHammond,France* 3-9-2 MJKinane...................... 1/10f   1
47 BIENAMADO (USA) *PWChapple-Hyam,GB* 3-9-2 RHughes .... 104/10   hd 2
2 FIRST MAGNITUDE (IRE) *AFabre,France* 3-9-2 OPeslier.............. 51/10   2 3
    Espionage *AFabre,France* 3-9-2 TJarnet.. 76/10   3 4
    Mr M. Tabor 4ran 2m32.80   TR: 119+/119/115/110

CURRAGH Saturday, Sep 18   SOFT

64   Jefferson Smurfit Memorial Irish St Leger (Gr 1) (3yo+) £94,918   1¾m

51 KAYF TARA *SaeedbinSuroor,GB* 5-9-8 LDettori (1) 1/2f   1
    YAVANA'S PACE (IRE) *MJohnston,GB* 7-9-8 JFanning (4)................... 7/1   8 2
44 SILVER PATRIARCH (IRE) *JLDunlop,GB* 5-9-8 PatEddery (6) 5/1   11 3
27 Enzeli (IRE) *JOxx* 4-9-8 JPMurtagh (3)... 5/1   5 4
31 Genghis Khan (IRE) *APO'Brien* 3-8-12 JAHeffernan (2).................... 25/1   2 5
    Godolphin 5ran 3m12.50   TR: 129+/118/103/96

BELMONT PARK Saturday, Sep 18   FAST

65   Woodward Stks (Gr 1) (3yo+) £185,184   1m1f

    RIVER KEEN (IRE) *RBaffert,USA* 7-9-0 CAntley 11/2   1

	46	ALMUTAWAKEL *SaeedbinSuroor,GB* 4-9-0 JBailey	46/10	ns 2
		STEPHEN GOT EVEN (USA) *NicholasPZito,USA* 3-8-9 GaryStevens	1½ 3
			41/10	
	33	Running Stag (USA) *PMitchell,GB* 5-9-0 SSellers	19/20f	nk 4
		Gander (USA) *CAssimakopoulos,USA* 3-8-9 PDay	39/1	4½ 5
		Black Cash (USA) *JOrseno,USA* 4-9-0 (b) EPrado	14/1	6 6
		Barter Town (USA) *RFrankel,USA* 4-9-0 (b) JChavez	18/1	9 7

Hugo Reynolds 7ran 1m46.85 TR: 126/126/123/123/114

LONGCHAMP Saturday, Sep 18 GOOD to SOFT

66 **Prix de la Salamandre (Gr 1) (2yo c+f)** £39,331 7f

		GIANT'S CAUSEWAY (USA) *APO'Brien,Ireland* 2-9-0 MJKinane (4)		1
			3/5cpf	
		RACE LEADER (USA) *BWHills,GB* 2-9-0 TJarnet (1)	69/10	2 2
	50	BACHIR (IRE) *JHMGosden,GB* 2-9-0 DBoeuf (3)	24/10	2 3
		Valentino *PWChapple-Hyam,GB* 2-9-0 MRoberts (5)	36/10	1 4
	50	Grigorovich (USA) *AFabre,France* 2-9-0 OPeslier (2)	3/5cpf	2½ 5

Mrs John Magnier & Mr M. Tabor 5ran 1m22.90 TR: 116/111/106/103/96

CURRAGH Sunday, Sep 19 SOFT

67 **Aga Khan Studs Blandford Stks (Gr 3) (3yo+)** £37,295 1m3f

	33	INSATIABLE (IRE) *SirMichaelStoute,GB* 6-9-3 MJKinane	2/7f	1
		THEATREWORLD (IRE) *APO'Brien* 7-9-3 JAHeffernan	6/1	8 2
		LISIEUX ROSE (IRE) *DKWeld* 4-9-0 (b) PJSmullen	9/1	2½ 3
		Golden Rule *MissFMCrowley* 4-9-3 PShanahan	10/1	5½ 4
	38	Rose of Tara (IRE) *MJGrassick* 3-8-7 EAhern	33/1	15 5

Sir Evelyn De Rothschild 5ran 2m31.50 TR: 124/111/104/98

WOODBINE Sunday, Sep 19 FIRM

68 **Atto Mile (Gr 1) (3yo+)** £263,599 1m

Order as they passed the post; Hawksley Hill was disqualified and placed fourth.

		HAWKSLEY HILL (IRE) *NDrysdale,USA* 6-8-5 (b) PDay	52/10	1
		QUIET RESOLVE (USA) *MFrostad,Canada* 4-8-5 RLandry	45/1	hd 2
		ROB 'N GIN (USA) *RBarbara,USA* 5-8-7 (b) JChavez	20/1	nk 3
	41	Jim And Tonic (FR) *FDoumen,France* 5-8-9 GMosse	62/10	nk 4
		Silic (FR) *JCCanani,USA* 4-8-9 CNakatani	53/10	1½ 5
	52	Cape Cross (IRE) *SaeedbinSuroor,GB* 5-8-9 LDettori	71/10	¾ 6
		Poteen (USA) *BenCecil,USA* 5-8-7 CAntley	84/10	½ 7
		Garbu (USA) *WIMott,USA* 5-8-7 JBailey	38/10f	¾ 8
		Incitatus *RonaldGBurke,USA* 6-8-9 SCallaghan	142/1	2¾ 9
		Bomfim (USA) *PJKelly,USA* 6-8-5 (b) RDavis	48/1	½ 10
		Lonesome Dude (CAN) *SirMichaelStoute,GB* 4-8-7 GaryStevens	72/10	4 11
		Lord Smith *BJackson,USA* 4-8-9 GGomez	22/1	1 12
		Karra Kul (USA) *PEngland,Canada* 4-8-5 RDosRamos	119/1	1 13
		Charge d'Affaires *CClement,USA* 4-8-5 JSantos	34/1	1¼ 14
		Sky Colony (USA) *MFrostad,Canada* 6-8-5 (b) TKabel	45/1	1½ 15

David & Jill Heerensperger 15ran 1m33.10 TR: 121/121/122/123/119/117

ASCOT Sunday, Sep 26 SOFT

69 **Queen Elizabeth II Stks (Gr 1) (3yo+)** £195,275 1m (Rnd)

	45	DUBAI MILLENNIUM *SaeedbinSuroor* 3-8-11 LDettori (3)	4/9f	1
	52	ALMUSHTARAK (IRE) *KMahdi* 6-9-1 OPeslier (1)	5/1	6 2
	41	GOLD ACADEMY (IRE) *RHannon* 3-8-11 PatEddery (2)	14/1	3½ 3
	41	Balisada *GWragg* 3-8-8 MRoberts (4)	13/2	20 4

Godolphin 4ran 1m46.24 TR: 132/119/111

70 **Gardner Merchant Diadem Stks (Gr 2) (3yo+)** £59,250 6f

	53	BOLD EDGE *RHannon* 4-9-4 DaneO'Neill (7)	12/1	1
		MUNJIZ (IRE) *BWHills* 3-8-12 RHills (4)	20/1	sh 2
	12	SHOW ME THE MONEY (IRE) *NMeade,Ireland* 3-8-9 JMurtagh (2)	14/1	1½ 3
	53	Sampower Star *RHannon* 3-8-12 RHughes (9)	13/2	hd 4
		Gorse *HCandy* 4-9-0 JReid (10)	5/1	½ 5
	53	Halmahera (IRE) *IABalding* 4-9-0 KFallon (3)	9/1	sh 6
	43	Vision of Night *JLDunlop* 3-8-12 PatEddery (11)	6/1	½ 7
	53	Tomba *BJMeehan* 5-9-6 MJKinane (8)	7/1	nk 8

Warningford *JRFanshawe* 5-9-0 RCochrane (8) .... 3/1f hd 9
Black Amber (IRE) *NACallaghan* 3-8-12 LDettori (6) 25/1 6 10
49 Sheer Viking (IRE) *BWHills* 3-8-12 (t) MHills (5)................................. 33/1 13 11
    Lady Whent and Friends 11ran 1m20.12   TR: 123/118/111/115/114/114

71 **Serpentine Gallery Royal Lodge Stks (Gr 2) (2yo c+g)** £71,250   1m (Rnd)

ROYAL KINGDOM (IRE) *APO'Brien,Ireland* 2-8-11 MJKinane (5) 10/11f 1
BEST OF THE BESTS (IRE) *CEBrittain* 2-9-0 PRobinson (4) .... 9/2 ½ 2
KINGSCLERE *IABalding* 2-8-11 KFallon (3)....................................... 10/1 2 3
Chinatown (IRE) *PWChapple-Hyam* 2-8-11 JReid (1) .... 9/1 nk 4
Blue Bolivar (IRE) *RHannon* 2-8-11 DaneO'Neill (2) 10/1 2½ 5
Jalad (IRE) *BHanbury* 2-8-11 RHills (6)... 8/1 sh 6
    Mr M. Tabor & Mrs John Magnier 6ran 1m50.06   TR: 109/111/104/104/99/99

NEWMARKET Tuesday, Sep 28   GOOD to SOFT (July Course)

72 **Shadwell Stud Cheveley Park Stks (Gr 1) (2yo f)** £78,460   6f

SEAZUN (IRE) *MRChannon* 2-8-11 TQuinn (8) 10/1 1
54 TORGAU (IRE) *GCBravery* 2-8-11 MHills (12)................................... 11/2 hd 2
CRIMPLENE (IRE) *CEBrittain* 2-8-11 LDettori (11) 14/1 2½ 3
Seraphina (IRE) *BAMcMahon* 2-8-11 KDarley (14)............................ 25/1 1½ 4
Jemima *TDEasterby* 2-8-11 LCharnock (5) 14/1 1 5
Bethesda *JMPEustace* 2-8-11 JTate (6).. 33/1 1¼ 6
Imperialist (IRE) *RHannon* 2-8-11 RHughes (13) .... 33/1 dh 6
Vita Spericolata (IRE) *JSWainwright* 2-8-11 KFallon (7)....................... 20/1 dh 6
Moon Driver (USA) *JEPease,France* 2-8-11 CAsmussen (4)................. 5/2 1 9
Kalindi *MRChannon* 2-8-11 JReid (10)... 25/1 sh 10
Mall Queen (USA) *MmeCHead,France* 2-8-11 ODoleuze (3) 8/1 2 11
Bailey's Whirlwind (USA) *MLWBell* 2-8-11 MFenton (15)................... 14/1 ½ 12
Forever Midnight (IRE) *BWHills* 2-8-11 DHolland (2) 20/1 3½ 13
Elaflaak (USA) *MPTregoning* 2-8-11 RHills (1) 9/2 12 14
    Mr John Breslin 14ran 1m12.92   TR: 110/109/102/98/95/91

NEWMARKET Thursday, Sep 30   GOOD to SOFT

73 **Saudi Arabian Airlines Middle Park Stks (Gr 1) (2yo c)** £68,600   6f

PRIMO VALENTINO (IRE) *PWHarris* 2-8-11 PatEddery (1) 10/3 1
FATH (USA) *MPTregoning* 2-8-11 RHills (4) .... 4/1 nk 2
BRAHMS (USA) *APO'Brien,Ireland* 2-8-11 (v) MJKinane (3) 9/1 1¼ 3
50 Warm Heart (USA) *JHMGosden* 2-8-11 LDettori (7)............................ 10/3 2½ 4
Trinculo (IRE) *NPLittmoden* 2-8-11 KFallon (5).................................. 33/1 ½ 5
Invincible Spirit (IRE) *JLDunlop* 2-8-11 TQuinn (6) .... 2/1f nk 6
    Primo Donnas 6ran 1m12.83   TR: 116/115/112/104/102/101

NEWMARKET Saturday, Oct 2   SOFT (July Course)

74 **Deloitte & Touche Jockey Club Cup (Gr 3) (3yo+)** £23,150   2m24y

27 RAINBOW HIGH *BWHills* 4-9-0 MHills (1).. 11/4 1
35 ARCTIC OWL *JRFanshawe* 5-9-5 RCochrane (2) .... 8/11f nk 2
42 CELERIC *JLDunlop* 7-9-3 PatEddery (3)... 10/3 25 3
    Mr K. Abdulla 3ran 3m38.35   TR: 117/122

LONGCHAMP Saturday, Oct 2   HEAVY

75 **Prix du Cadran Casino Croisette Barriere (Gr 1) (4yo+)** £48,591   2½m

27 TAJOUN (FR) *AdeRoyerDupre,France* 5-9-2 GMosse 6/5f 1
SAN SEBASTIAN *MJGrassick,Ireland* 5-9-2 (b) JPMurtagh .... 94/10 nk 2
DIVINATION (FR) *FHead,France* 4-8-13 DBonilla 127/10 4 3
51 Invermark *JRFanshawe,GB* 5-9-2 RHughes .... 8/5 hd 4
Antarctique (IRE) *RCollet,France* 5-9-2 (b) TJarnet 25/2 8 5
Arctic (FR) *FChappet,France* 4-9-2 (b) MBoutin 37/1 4 6
Mowbray (USA) *PFICole,GB* 4-9-2 DBoeuf 17/1 20 7
51 Largesse *JohnBerry,GB* 5-9-2 OPeslier 73/10 3 8
    H.H. Aga Khan 8ran 4m51.80   TR: 114+/113/106/108

76 **Prix Dollar "Le Saint Denac" Barriere (Gr 2) (3yo+)** £29,155   1m1f165y

39 STATE SHINTO (USA) *AFabre,France* 3-8-10 TJarnet..................... 4/5cf 1
STRATEGIC *JOxx,Ireland* 3-8-10 JPMurtagh .... 4/5cf ¾ 2
59 KABOOL *SaeedbinSuroor,GB* 4-9-0 SGuillot 4/5cf 2 3

	Barbola (USA) *JdeRoualle,France* 4-9-0 GMosse	36/10	1 4
39	Sardaukar *ELellouche,France* 3-8-10 DBonilla	123/10	4 5
23	Handsome Ridge *JHMGosden,GB* 5-9-4 GMosse	37/10	¾ 6
	Sure Dancer (USA) *PFICole,GB* 4-9-0 DBoeuf	61/10	2 7
	Inchrory *AHyldmo,Norway* 6-9-0 JMcLaughlin	134/10	1½ 8
	Happy Woodman (USA) *YNinomiya,Japan* 6-9-0 MEbina	43/1	15 9

Sheikh Mohammed 9ran 2m19.00   TR: 121/120/114/112/107/108

LONGCHAMP Sunday, Oct 3   HEAVY

77 **Prix Marcel Boussac (Criterium des Pouliches) Royal Barriere (Gr 1)** 1m
(2yo f) £77,745

	LADY OF CHAD *RGibson,France* 2-8-11 OPeslier	53/10	1
	NEW STORY (USA) *RCollet,France* 2-8-11 SGuillot	567/10	3 2
	LADY VETTORI *FRohaut,France* 2-8-11 TGillet	29/10	½ 3
	Miletrian (IRE) *MRChannon,GB* 2-8-11 MRoberts	564/10	ns 4
	Chez Cherie *PWChapple-Hyam,GB* 2-8-11 KFallon	132/10	2 5
	Darakiyla (IRE) *AdeRoyerDupre,France* 2-8-11 GMosse	43/10	2½ 6
	Dignify (IRE) *DRLoder,France* 2-8-11 LDettori	21/10f	1½ 7
	Lippe Lippe (IRE) *LCamici,Italy* 2-8-11 VMezzatesta	279/10	10 8
	Abime (USA) *PBary,France* 2-8-11 CAsmussen	146/10	hd 9
	Perugia (IRE) *BWHills,GB* 2-8-11 MHills	142/10	1½ 10
	Issey Rose (IRE) *TGMills,GB* 2-8-11 TQuinn	119/10	11

Mr John Martin 11ran 1m44.81   TR: 109/103/102/101/97/92

78 **Prix de l'Abbaye de Longchamp Majestic Barriere (Gr 1) (2yo+ c+f)** 5f
£48,591

	AGNES WORLD (USA) *HMori,Japan* 4-9-11 YTake	68/10	1
53	IMPERIAL BEAUTY (USA) *PJMakin,GB* 3-9-8 PatEddery	62/10	sn 2
43	KEOS (USA) *JEHammond,France* 5-9-11 (b) CAsmussen	69/10	1½ 3
70	Sampower Star *RHannon,GB* 3-9-8 RHughes	221/10	ns 4
	Antinnaz (IRE) *TStack,Ireland* 3-9-8 JPMurtagh	794/10	½ 5
49	Sainte Marine (IRE) *RCollet,France* 4-9-8 SGuillot	37/10	1 6
	Timote (IRE) *DKWeld,Ireland* 3-9-8 KFallon	108/10	½ 7
53	Arkadian Hero (USA) *LMCumani,GB* 4-9-11 GMosse	74/10	sh 8
37	Mitcham (IRE) *TGMills,GB* 3-9-11 TQuinn	237/10	2½ 9
49	Averti (IRE) *WRMuir,GB* 8-9-11 JReid	437/10	1½ 10
53	Yorkies Boy *BAMcMahon,GB* 4-9-11 KDarley	757/10	2½ 11
53	Bertolini (USA) *JHMGosden,GB* 3-9-11 (b) LDettori	2/1f	¾ 12
	Dojima Muteki (JPN) *HMori,Japan* 9-9-11 MEbina	68/10	2 13
	Black Rock Desert (USA) *APO'Brien,Ireland* 3-9-11 MJKinane	74/10	5 14

Mr Takashi Watanabe 14ran 1m00.92   TR: 120/117/115+/115/111/107

79 **Prix de l'Arc de Triomphe Lucien Barriere (Gr 1) (3yo+ c+f)** £485,909 1½m

63	MONTJEU (IRE) *JEHammond,France* 3-8-11 MJKinane	6/4cpf	1
61	EL CONDOR PASA (USA) *YNinomiya,Japan* 4-9-5 MEbina	36/10	½ 2
61	CROCO ROUGE (IRE) *PBary,France* 4-9-5 TJarnet	14/1	6 3
	Leggera (IRE) *JLDunlop,GB* 4-9-2 TQuinn	209/10	5 4
55	Tiger Hill (IRE) *PSchiergen,Germany* 4-9-5 THellier	154/10	¾ 5
46	Greek Dance (IRE) *SirMichaelStoute,GB* 4-9-5 KFallon	344/10	nk 6
61	Borgia (GER) *AFabre,France* 5-9-2 OPeslier	142/10	2 7
62	Cerulean Sky (IRE) *RCollet,France* 3-8-8 SGuillot	578/10	4 8
60	Daylami (IRE) *SaeedbinSuroor,GB* 5-9-5 LDettori	4/1	5 9
55	Flamingo Road (GER) *ASchutz,Germany* 3-8-8 AStarke	554/10	3 10
47	Fantastic Light (USA) *SirMichaelStoute,GB* 3-8-11 JReid	334/10	2½ 11
	Albaran (GER) *MsCErichsen,Norway* 6-9-9 JTandari	817/10	3 12
62	Daryaba (IRE) *AdeRoyerDupre,France* 3-8-8 GMosse	76/10	15 13
64	Genghis Khan (IRE) *APO'Brien,Ireland* 3-8-11 JPMurtagh	6/4cpf	10 14

Mr M. Tabor 14ran 2m38.35   TR: 137/136/126/116/118/117

80 **Prix du Rond-Point Grand Hotel Barriere (Gr 2) (3yo+)** £38,873 1m

	TRANS ISLAND *IABalding,GB* 4-9-1 KFallon	31/10	1
	SUGARFOOT *NTinkler,GB* 5-9-1 PatEddery	5/2	sn 2
	SAND FALCON *PBary,France* 4-9-1 TJarnet	17/1	sn 3
	Mahboob (IRE) *JEHammond,France* 4-9-1 CAsmussen	58/10	1½ 4
19	Slip Stream (USA) *SaeedbinSuroor,GB* 3-8-11 LDettori	21/10jf	ns 5
45	Venize (IRE) *RCollet,France* 3-8-8 SGuillot	58/10	hd 6
	Orso (FR) *FHead,France* 3-8-11 DBonilla	162/10	1½ 7
7	Grazalema (USA) *AFabre,France* 3-8-11 OPeslier	21/10jf	10 8

Sole Che Sorgi (IRE) *RCollet,France* 5-9-1 DVargiu .... 403/10   ½ 9
Al Muallim Partnership 9ran 1m45.10   TR: 119/118/117/114/114/110

LONGCHAMP Sunday, Oct 10   SOFT

81   **Grand Criterium (Gr 1) (2yo c+f)** £98,523   1m

Order as they passed the post: Barathea Guest was disqualified and placed
second for hampering Ciro.

BARATHEA GUEST *GGMargarson,GB* 2-9-0 PRobinson 26/10   1
CIRO (USA) *APO'Brien,Ireland* 2-9-0 MJKinane .... 4/5f   nk 2
OCEAN OF WISDOM (USA) *PBary,France* 2-9-0 CAsmussen 11/10   15 3
Mr M Tabor,Mrs J Magnier & Mr R Santulli 3ran 1m50.50   TR: 110/109

NEWMARKET Saturday, Oct 16   GOOD

82   **Champions' Gallery Challenge Stks (Gr 2) (3yo+)** £51,450   7f

	SUSU *SirMichaelStoute* 6-8-11 KFallon (10) 8/1		1
	LEND A HAND *SaeedbinSuroor* 4-9-0 OPeslier (4) 8/11f	nk	2
52	JOSR ALGARHOUD (IRE) *SaeedbinSuroor* 3-8-12 JReid (6) 7/1	4	3
24	Mujahid (USA) *JLDunlop* 3-8-12 RHills (7) 14/1	½	4
80	Sugarfoot *NTinkler* 5-9-0 PatEddery (3) 9/1	½	5
70	Warningford *JRFanshawe* 5-9-0 RCochrane (8) 20/1	nk	6
3	Auction House (USA) *BWHills* 3-8-12 MHills (9) 40/1	3	7
26	Presumed (USA) *PJMakin* 3-8-9 MJKinane (2) 25/1	1¾	8
	Tumbleweed Ridge *BJMeehan* 6-9-0 (b+t) MTebbutt (1)...................... 16/1	nk	9
25	Lots of Magic *RHannon* 3-8-12 DaneO'Neill (5) 16/1	¾	10

H.E. Sheikh Rashid Al Maktoum 10ran 1m24.20   TR: 122/124/114+/113/110/110

83   **Dewhurst Stks (Gr 1) (2yo c+f)** £117,600   7f

57	DISTANT MUSIC (USA) *BWHills* 2-9-0 MHills (2).............................. 4/6f		1
73	BRAHMS (USA) *APO'Brien,Ireland* 2-9-0 (v) OPeslier (5) 14/1	1	2
	ZENTSOV STREET (USA) *APO'Brien,Ireland* 2-9-0 MJKinane (3)... 14/1	2	3
	Port Vila (FR) *JHMGosden* 2-9-0 RHills (4) 10/1	2½	4
	King's Best (USA) *SirMichaelStoute* 2-9-0 KFallon (1) 11/4	nk	5

Mr K. Abdulla 5ran 1m26.84   TR: 117+/114/109/102/101

84   **Dubai Champion Stks (Gr 1) (3yo+)** £228,200   1¼m

	ALBORADA *SirMarkPrescott* 4-8-13 GDuffield (10) 5/1		1
23	SHIVA (JPN) *HRACecil* 4-8-13 TQuinn (3) 7/2f	1¼	2
76	KABOOL *SaeedbinSuroor* 4-9-2 JReid (8).. 20/1	nk	3
69	Gold Academy (IRE) *RHannon* 3-8-11 DaneO'Neill (4) 20/1	½	4
79	Greek Dance (IRE) *SirMichaelStoute* 4-9-2 KFallon (2)...................... 13/2	¾	5
1	High-Rise (IRE) *SaeedbinSuroor* 4-9-2 OPeslier (6)............................. 5/1	nk	6
76	Handsome Ridge *JHMGosden* 5-9-2 WRyan (12)................................. 33/1	nk	7
	Little Rock *SirMichaelStoute* 3-8-11 JFortune (7) 33/1	nk	8
59	Lear Spear (USA) *DRCElsworth* 4-9-2 MJKinane (11).......................... 9/2	hd	9
46	Golden Snake (USA) *BWHills* 3-8-11 MHills (5).................................. 12/1	½	10
	Showboat *BWHills* 5-9-2 RHughes (13).. 33/1	1¼	11
69	Almushtarak (IRE) *KMahdi* 6-9-2 PatEddery (1) 20/1	3	12
46	Salford Express (IRE) *DRCElsworth* 3-8-11 RCochrane (9)................. 50/1	nk	13

Miss K. Rausing 13ran 2m05.57   TR: 118+/115+/118/118/115/115

LONGCHAMP Sunday, Oct 17   GOOD to SOFT

85   **Prix de la Foret (Gr 1) (3yo+ c+f)** £48,971   7f

56	FIELD OF HOPE (IRE) *PBary,France* 4-8-13 SGuillot 185/10		1
78	KEOS (USA) *JEHammond,France* 5-9-2 (b) CAsmussen 37/10	¾	2
80	TRANS ISLAND *IABalding,GB* 4-9-2 KDarley 128/10	sn	3
	Danzigaway (USA) *MmeCHead,France* 3-8-10 ODoleuze 21/1	hd	4
53	Diktat *SaeedbinSuroor,GB* 4-9-2 LDettori..................................... 6/10f	sh	5
	Major Force (USA) *DKWeld,Ireland* 3-9-0 PJSmullen 43/10	2	6
80	Mahboob (IRE) *JEHammond,France* 4-9-2 FSpanu......................... 352/10	sn	7
70	Tomba *BJMeehan,GB* 5-9-2 MTebbutt.. 187/10	2	8
	Seltitude (IRE) *JEHammond,France* 3-8-10 TGillet 27/1	½	9
80	Venize (IRE) *RCollet,France* 3-8-10 OPeslier 23/1	½	10
	Atalante (GER) *BHellier,Germany* 3-8-10 GMosse 58/1		11

Grundy Bloodstock Limited 11ran 1m20.80   TR: 119/120/119/115/119/114

86 **Canadian International (Gr 1) (3yo+)** £368,853 1½m

THORNFIELD (CAN) *PEngland,Canada* 5-9-0 RDosRamos.............. 19/1 1
40 FRUITS OF LOVE (USA) *MJohnston,GB* 4-9-0 (v) KFallon 18/10f 1 2
COURTEOUS *PFICole,GB* 4-9-0 JFortune 161/10 1 3
Tanaasa (IRE) *NDrysdale,USA* 5-9-0 PDay 57/10 1 4
63 Bienamado (USA) *AGFoster,GB* 3-8-7 CMcCarron 42/10 1 5
Gritty Sandie (USA) *JJToner,USA* 3-8-7 (b) MESmith 11/1 1½ 6
Dawson's Legacy (USA) *NormanMcKnight,USA* 4-9-0 CMontpellier 73/10 3 7
Beautiful Dancer (BRZ) *RViolettejnr,USA* 5-9-0 (b) MLuzzi 86/10 25 8
Dancing Place (CHI) *NDrysdale,USA* 6-9-0 (b) DFlores 11/1 8 9
Knob Hill Stable 9ran 2m32.39 TR: 123/121/120/119/117/115

87 **Racing Post Trophy (Gr 1) (2yo c+f)** £106,900 1m (Rnd)

ARISTOTLE (IRE) *APO'Brien,Ireland* 2-9-0 GDuffield (8) 10/1 1
LERMONTOV (USA) *APO'Brien,Ireland* 2-9-0 PaulScallan (2).......... 10/1 1¼ 2
57 EKRAAR (USA) *MPTregoning* 2-9-0 (b) RHills (6) .... 10/1 nk 3
Air Marshall (IRE) *SirMichaelStoute* 2-9-0 KFallon (4) 7/1 7 4
83 Zentsov Street (USA) *APO'Brien,Ireland* 2-9-0 MJKinane (9) 11/2 1¾ 5
Cornelius *PFICole* 2-9-0 JFortune (1)...................................... 6/1 1½ 6
Scarteen Fox (IRE) *DRCElsworth* 2-9-0 RCochrane (3) 2/1f 1 7
Holding Court *BJMeehan* 2-9-0 LDettori (5)..................................... 13/2 2½ 8
Optimaite *BRMillman* 2-9-0 MFenton (7).. 50/1 ½ 9
Mrs John Magnier 9ran 1m45.00 TR: 115/112/111+/95+/91/87

88 **Prix Royal-Oak (Gr 1) (3yo+)** £39,762 1m7f110y

Order as they passed the post: Leggera was disqualified after her rider was found
to have weighed in light.

AMILYNX (FR) *AFabre,France* 3-8-9 OPeslier 2/1 1
75 TAJOUN (FR) *AdeRoyerDupre,France* 5-9-4 GMosse 2/1 1½ 2
79 LEGGERA (IRE) *JLDunlop,GB* 4-9-1 TQuinn .... 14/10f ½ 3
Northerntown (USA) *FHead,France* 3-8-9 DBonilla 77/10 6 4
Shebane (USA) *MmeCHead,France* 3-8-6 ODoleuze .... 77/10 sn 5
Win For Us (GER) *PSchiergen,Germany* 3-8-6 DBoeuf 237/10 2 6
74 Arctic Owl *JRFanshawe,GB* 5-9-4 MHills.. 5/1 sh 7
Mr J-L. Lagardere 7ran 3m40.60 TR: 121/117/114/111/108/106

89 **Foster's Melbourne Cup (Hcap) (Gr 1) (3yo+)** £714,008 2m

ROGAN JOSH (AUS) *BCummings,Australia* 7-7-12 (b) JMarshall........ 5/1 1
46 CENTRAL PARK (IRE) *SaeedbinSuroor,GB* 4-9-1 LDettori .... 50/1 ½ 2
LAHAR (AUS) *PCave,Australia* 5-7-13 CBrown .... 140/1 sn 3
ZAZABELLE (NZ) *BCummings,Australia* 4-7-10 (b) EWilkinson .... 50/1 dh 3
Travelmate *JRFanshawe,GB* 5-8-4 DHarrison .... 9/1 nk 5
The Warrior (NZ) *ROtto,Australia* 6-7-10 GGrylls................................. 50/1 nk 6
Second Coming (NZ) *MMoroney,NewZealand* 5-8-0 GChilds............... 60/1 2 7
The Hind (NZ) *PCHayes,Australia* 5-8-4 (b) JCassidy 11/1 1¼ 8
Bohemiath (AUS) *JDSadler,Australia* 5-7-12 (b) JPatton .... 20/1 sh 9
Brew (NZ) *MMoroney,NewZealand* 5-7-10 (b) LO'Sullivan.................. 40/1 ns 10
Zabuan (NZ) *JEMoloney,Australia* 6-7-10 (b) SHyland 250/1 2¼ 11
64 Yavana's Pace (IRE) *MJohnston,GB* 7-8-6 RHughes .... 30/1 sh 12
Streak (AUS) *RSmerdon,Australia* 5-8-1 GHall.................................. 16/1 2¼ 13
Tie The Knot (AUS) *GWalter,Australia* 5-9-2 (b) RSDye...................... 7/1 ¾ 14
Figurehead (NZ) *MissKLane,Australia* 4-7-12 (b) OBosson .... 160/1 ns 15
Skybeau (NZ) *LJSmith,Australia* 7-8-2 (b) LCassidy .... 66/1 ns 16
Sky Heights (NZ) *CAlderson,Australia* 4-8-12 (b) DOliver.................. 7/2f 2 17
Lady Elsie (AUS) *CIBrown,Australia* 4-7-13 LBeasley 66/1 1½ 18
Laebeel (NZ) *JDSadler,Australia* 5-7-11 SBaster .... 10/1 hd 19
Maridpour (IRE) *MMoroney,NewZealand* 4-8-9 SArnold .... 66/1 sn 20
The Message (NZ) *JBRalph,NewZealand* 6-8-2 ASpiteri.................... 200/1 ns 21
Arena (AUS) *JHawkes,Australia* 4-8-8 DGauci................................. 15/1 22
Rebbor (NZ) *JBCummings,Australia* 4-7-10 (b) CMunce 66/1 23
ur

Able Master (NZ) *BWallace,NewZealand* 4-7-13 GCooksley 50/1
Mrs W. L. Green & J. P. Miller 24ran 3m19.64   TR: 107/123/107/107/112+/103

GULFSTREAM PARK Saturday, Nov 6   Dirt track: FAST, Turf course: GOOD

90 Breeders' Cup Mile (Gr 1) (3yo+) £317,073   1m

68	SILIC (FR) *JCCanani,USA* 4-9-0 CNakatani	72/10	1
	TUZLA (FR) *RBaffert,USA* 5-8-11 DFlores	137/10	nk 2
41	DOCKSIDER (USA) *JWHills,GB* 4-9-0 GaryStevens	84/10	hd 3
82	Lend A Hand *SaeedbinSuroor,GB* 4-9-0 LDettori	134/10	ns 4
68	Hawksley Hill (IRE) *NDrysdale,USA* 4-9-0 (b) PDay	37/10f	½ 5
	Brave Act *RMcAnally,USA* 5-9-0 CMcCarron	139/10	2¾ 6
	Delay of Game (USA) *GRArnoldII,USA* 6-9-0 ASolis	168/10	ns 7
	Kirkwall *RFrankel,USA* 5-9-0 (b) VEspinoza	267/10	hd 8
68	Jim And Tonic (FR) *FDoumen,France* 5-9-0 GMosse	43/10	nk 9
	Middlesex Drive (USA) *PMHauswald,USA* 4-9-0 (b) SSellers	66/10	1 10
	Khumba Mela (IRE) *CClement,USA* 4-8-11 JSantos	362/10	hd 11
82	Susu *SirMichaelStoute,GB* 6-8-11 KFallon	526/10	½ 12
68	Garbu (USA) *WIMott,USA* 5-9-0 JBailey	22/1	4½ 13
68	Quiet Resolve (USA) *MFrostad,Canada* 4-9-0 JChavez	30/1	5 14

J. Terrence Lanni, Et Al 14ran 1m34.26   TR: 125/121/124/124/123/116

91 Breeders' Cup Sprint (Gr 1) (3yo+) £348,780   6f

	ARTAX (USA) *LAlbertrani,USA* JChavez	37/10jf	1
	KONA GOLD (USA) *BHeadley,USA* 5-9-0 ASolis	77/10	½ 2
	BIG JAG (USA) *TPinfield,USA* 6-9-0 JValdivia	101/10	2¾ 3
	Forestry (USA) *RBaffert,USA* 3-8-12 CAntley	37/10jf	½ 4
	Successful Appeal (USA) *JCKimmel,USA* 3-8-12 EPrado	164/10	ns 5
49	Stravinsky (USA) *APO'Brien,Ireland* 3-8-12 (v) MJKinane	48/10	½ 6
	Good And Tough (USA) *FAAlexander,USA* 4-9-0 SSellers	465/10	3 7
	Regal Thunder (USA) *JCCanani,USA* 5-9-0 CNakatani	484/10	1¼ 8
	Lexicon (USA) *RMandella,USA* 4-9-0 (b) KDesormeaux	132/10	1 9
	Furlough (USA) *CMcGaugheyIII,USA* 5-8-11 MESmith	531/10	1¾ 10
	Vicar (USA) *CANafzger,USA* 3-8-12 PDay	162/10	nk 11
	Affirmed Success (USA) *RSchosberg,USA* 5-9-0 JBailey	135/10	½ 12
	Son of a Pistol (USA) *BHeadley,USA* 7-9-0 GGomez	61/10	1¼ 13
	Enjoy The Moment (USA) *WSpawr,USA* 4-8-11 DFlores	20/1	4 14

Paraneck Stable 14ran 1m07.89   TR: 126/125/118+/116/116/115

92 Breeders' Cup Filly & Mare Turf (Gr 1) (3yo+ f+m) £343,897   1m3f

	SOARING SOFTLY (USA) *JJToner,USA* 4-8-11 JBailey	36/10f	1
	CORETTA (IRE) *CClement,USA* 5-8-11 JSantos	162/10	¾ 2
	ZOMARADAH *LMCumani,GB* 4-8-11 LDettori	92/10	hd 3
	Caffe Latte (IRE) *JCCanani,USA* 3-8-7 CNakatani	117/10	hd 4
79	Borgia (GER) *AFabre,France* 5-8-11 KFallon	68/10	ns 5
	Perfect Sting (USA) *JOrseno,USA* 3-8-7 PDay	4/1	1½ 6
	Mossflower (USA) *RSchosberg,USA* 5-8-11 RobbieDavis	198/10	1½ 7
	Pleasant Temper (USA) *WEWalden,USA* 5-8-11 GaryStevens	195/10	3¼ 8
	Gandria (CAN) *JWCheadle,USA* 3-8-7 SSellers	115/1	hd 9
21	Louve (USA) *AFabre,France* 3-8-7 OPeslier	61/1	½ 10
13	Insight (FR) *JEHammond,France* 4-8-11 (b) CAsmussen	232/10	¾ 11
	Natalie Too (USA) *DWLukas,USA* 5-8-11 (b) CAntley	614/10	1½ 12
	Anguilla (USA) *TJSkiffington,USA* 4-8-11 MESmith	44/1	¾ 13
	Spanish Fern (USA) *RFrankel,USA* 4-8-11 (b) CMcCarron	4/1	21 14

Joan & John Phillips 14ran 2m13.89   TR: 120/118/117/118/117+/115+

93 Breeders' Cup Juvenile (Gr 1) (2yo c+g) £343,897   1m110y

	ANEES (USA) *ALHassingerjnr,USA* 2-8-10 (b) GaryStevens	303/10	1
	CHIEF SEATTLE (USA) *JCKimmel,USA* 2-8-10 EPrado	44/10	2½ 2
	HIGH YIELD (USA) *DWLukas,USA* 2-8-10 JBailey	68/10	¾ 3
36	Mull of Kintyre (USA) *APO'Brien,Ireland* 2-8-10 MJKinane	292/10	2¼ 4
	Dixie Union (USA) *RMandella,USA* 2-8-10 ASolis	44/10	4 5
	Forest Camp (USA) *RBaffert,USA* 2-8-10 DFlores	27/10f	½ 6
83	Brahms (USA) *APO'Brien,Ireland* 2-8-10 OPeslier	543/10	1¾ 7
	Personal First (USA) *DEPaulus,USA* 2-8-10 THebert	117/1	hd 8
	Charlie's Beau (USA) *BobbyCBarnett,USA* 2-8-10 EMartinjnr	26/1	½ 9
	Millencolin (USA) *DWLukas,USA* 2-8-10 (b) PDay	22/1	¾ 10
	Captain Steve (USA) *RBaffert,USA* 2-8-10 GGomez	95/10	15 11
	Graeme Hall (USA) *TAPletcher,USA* 2-8-10 (b) JRVelazquez	464/10	3½ 12
	Hugh Hefner (USA) *MFJones,USA* 2-8-10 CNakatani	50/1	2¼ 13

Kiss A Native (USA) *WPWhite,USA* 2-8-10 CVelasquez.................... 82/10　1 14

The Thoroughbred Corporation 14ran 1m42.29　　TR: 120/116/115/112/107/106+

94　Breeders' Cup Turf (Gr 1) (3yo+) £634,146　　　　　　　　　1½m

79	DAYLAMI (IRE) *SaeedbinSuroor,GB* 5-9-0 LDettori........................	16/10f	1
60	ROYAL ANTHEM (USA) *WIMott,USA* 4-9-0 GaryStevens	87/10	2½ 2
	BUCK'S BOY (USA) *PNHickey,USA* 6-9-0 GGomez	64/10	2 3
	Yagli (USA) *WIMott,USA* 6-9-0 JBailey	73/10	1¼ 4
60	Dream Well (FR) *PBary,France* 4-9-0 (b) CAsmussen	119/10	3½ 5
	Bonapartiste (FR) *RMcAnally,USA* 5-9-0 CMcCarron	42/1	nk 6
86	Courteous *PFlCole,GB* 4-9-0 KFallon	105/1	¾ 7
	Honor Glide (USA) *CClement,USA* 5-9-0 JSantos	167/10	2¾ 8
30	Dark Moondancer *RMcAnally,USA* 4-9-0 GMosse	195/10	2½ 9
	Fahris (IRE) *KPMcLaughlin,UAE* 5-9-0 JVelasquez	66/1	1¾ 10
	Val's Prince (USA) *HJBond,USA* 7-9-0 JChavez.............................	52/10	¾ 11
	Unite's Big Red (USA) *RMills,USA* 4-9-0 MESmith	63/1	15 12
86	Thornfield (CAN) *PEngland,Canada* 5-9-0 RDosRamos....................	60/1	1½ 13
63	First Magnitude (IRE) *AFabre,France* 3-8-10 OPeslier	37/1	24 14

Godolphin 14ran 2m24.73　　　　　TR: 135+/131+/127+/125/120/119

95　Breeders' Cup Classic (Gr 1) (3yo+) £1,268,293　　　　　　1¼m

	CAT THIEF (USA) *DWLukas,USA* 4-9-0 PDay	196/10	1
	BUDROYALE (USA) *THWest,USA* 6-9-0 GGomez...........................	265/10	1¼ 2
	GOLDEN MISSILE (USA) *JOrseno,USA* 4-9-0 (b) KDesormeaux	75/1	hd 3
46	Chester House (USA) *RFrankel,USA* 4-9-0 CNakatani	64/1	2 4
65	Almutawakel *SaeedbinSuroor,GB* 4-9-0 JBailey	66/10	½ 5
	Lemon Drop Kid (USA) *FSSchulhofer,USA* 3-8-10 JSantos	63/10	¾ 6
14	Behrens (USA) *HJBond,USA* 5-9-0 (b) JChavez	23/10f	5 7
	Old Trieste (USA) *MPuype,USA* 4-9-0 CMcCarron	273/10	hd 8
	Vision And Verse (USA) *WIMott,USA* 3-8-10 (b) GaryStevens	171/10	1¼ 9
	General Challenge (USA) *RBaffert,USA* 3-8-10 (b) DFlores	53/10	hd 10
65	River Keen (IRE) *RBaffert,USA* 7-9-0 CAntley..............................	13/2	4 11
	Ecton Park (USA) *REWalden,USA* 3-8-10 (b) ASolis	96/10	1½ 12
	Catienus (USA) *RSchosberg,USA* 5-9-0 EPrado..............................	87/1	5 13
	Supreme Sound *MWDickinson,USA* 5-9-0 JRVelazquez......................	126/1	28 14

Overbrook Farm 14ran 1m59.52　　　　TR: 126/123/123/119/118/118

ROME Sunday, Nov 7　SOFT

96　Premio Roma (Gr 1) (3yo+ c+f) £63,763　　　　　　　　　1¼m

18	ELLE DANZIG (GER) *ASchutz,Germany* 4-9-0 AStarke..................	52/10	1
84	HANDSOME RIDGE *JHMGosden,GB* 5-9-3 KDarley.......................	77/10	1½ 2
	SIGNORINA CATTIVA (USA) *JLDunlop,GB* 3-8-12 PatEddery	19/10	5½ 3
62	Fairy Queen (IRE) *SaeedbinSuroor,GB* 3-8-12 LDettori	9/10f	1½ 4
30	Poseidon *LBrogi,Italy* 5-9-3 MPasquale......................................	169/10	2 5
30	Ivan Luis (FR) *LCamici,Italy* 5-9-3 OFancera	119/10	5 6
	Honey Colour (IRE) *ACalchetti,Italy* 5-9-3 MDemuro..........................	32/1	5 7

Gestut Wittekindshof 7ran 2m07.10　　　　TR: 118/118/107/104/100

TOKYO Sunday, Nov 28　FIRM

97　Japan Cup (Gr 1) (3yo+) £1,171,415　　　　　　　　　　1½m

	SPECIAL WEEK (JPN) *TShirai,Japan* 4-9-0 YTake	24/10	1
40	INDIGENOUS (IRE) *IWAllan,HongKong* 6-9-0 DWhyte....................	83/1	1½ 2
84	HIGH-RISE (IRE) *SaeedbinSuroor,GB* 4-9-0 LDettori	19/1	ns 3
79	Montjeu (IRE) *JEHammond,France* 3-8-10 MJKinane	17/10f	¾ 4
	Rascal Suzuka (JPN) *MHashida,Japan* 4-9-0 YShibata	96/10	4 5
	Stay Gold (JPN) *YIkee,Japan* 5-9-0 SKumazawa	13/1	½ 6
	Suehiro Commander (JPN) *SMatsumoto,Japan* 4-9-0 (b) SFujita........	103/1	nk 7
92	Borgia (GER) *AFabre,France* 5-8-10 OPeslier	15/1	nk 8
86	Fruits of Love (USA) *MJohnston,GB* 4-9-0 (v) MRoberts................	197/10	hd 9
79	Tiger Hill (IRE) *PSchiergen,Germany* 4-9-0 THellier	24/10	1½ 10
	Embrasser Moi (JPN) *HSugai,Japan* 5-9-0 (h+b) NSugai....................	43/1	¾ 11
	Umeno Fiber (JPN) *IAizawa,Japan* 3-8-6 MEbina	196/10	6 12
	Osumi Bright (JPN) *TNakao,Japan* 3-8-10 YTake	95/1	3 13
	Stinger (JPN) *KFujisawa,Japan* 3-8-6 NYokoyama	26/1	5 14

Mr Hiroyoshi Usuda 14ran 2m25.50　　　　TR: 124/122/122/122/116/113

SHA TIN Sunday, Dec 12   GOOD to FIRM

98   **Hong Kong Mile (Gr 2) (3yo+) £326,105**   1m

90	DOCKSIDER (USA) *JWHills,GB* 4-9-0 OPeslier	6/5f	1
85	FIELD OF HOPE (IRE) *PBary,France* 4-9-0 SGuillot	10/1	1¾ 2
	RESFA (ARG) *DAHayes,HongKong* 5-9-3 BMarcus	64/10	nk 3
	Muhtathir *SaeedbinSuroor,GB* 4-9-3 LDettori	68/10	nk 4
17	Housemaster (IRE) *IWAllan,HongKong* 3-8-13 KFallon	14/1	1¼ 5
	Danzighill (AUS) *ASCruz,HongKong* 6-9-0 (t) FCoetzee	57/1	sh 6
	Self Feeder (IRE) *PGallagher,USA* 5-9-0 (t) MJKinane	21/1	1¾ 7
	Midnight Bet (USA) *HNagahama,Japan* 5-9-0 (h) MEbina	79/10	sh 8
	Holy Grail (NZ) *IWAllan,HongKong* 5-9-0 DHarrison	28/1	¾ 9
	Kenwood Melody (AUS) *DAHayes,HongKong* 4-9-3 JCassidy	10/1	hd 10
	Che Sara Sara (IRE) *DOughton,HongKong* 7-9-0 DWhyte	61/1	½ 11
52	Wallace *RHannon,GB* 3-8-13 RHughes	43/1	16 12

Mr Gary A. Tanaka 12ran 1m34.70   TR: 123/119/121/120/115/114

99   **Hong Kong Vase (Gr 2) (3yo+) £326,105**   1½m

97	BORGIA (GER) *AFabre,France* 5-9-0 OPeslier	23/1	1
	BIMBOLA (FR) *JBertrandeBalanda,France* 5-8-11 TGillet	49/1	hd 2
35	SEA WAVE (IRE) *SaeedbinSuroor,GB* 4-9-0 (t) LDettori	68/10	½ 3
97	Indigenous (IRE) *IWAllan,HongKong* 6-9-0 (t) DWhyte	31/10	sh 4
89	Rogan Josh (AUS) *BCummings,Australia* 7-9-3 (b) JohnMarshall	9/4f	1¾ 5
	Cronus (NZ) *RJames,NewZealand* 7-9-3 (b) VColgan	41/1	nk 6
	Rosen Kavalier (JPN) *YSuzuki,Japan* 6-9-0 TKikuzawa	11/1	1½ 7
	Hunting Lad (USA) *DAHayes,HongKong* 5-9-0 (b) BMarcus	13/1	¾ 8
	Monza (USA) *LHo,HongKong* 5-9-0 ESaint-Martin	83/1	1¾ 9
	Desert Fox *DOughton,HongKong* 4-9-0 MJKinane	11/1	nk 10
64	Silver Patriarch (IRE) *JLDunlop,GB* 5-9-3 PatEddery	37/10	1¼ 11

Gestut Ammerland 11ran 2m30.10   TR: 120/117/119/119/119/118

100   **Hong Kong Cup (Gr 1) (3yo+) £465,863**   1¼m

90	JIM AND TONIC (FR) *FDoumen,France* 5-9-0 GMosse	7/2	1
65	RUNNING STAG (USA) *PMitchell,GB* 5-9-0 SSellers	25/1	3¾ 2
84	LEAR SPEAR (USA) *DRCElsworth,GB* 4-9-0 TQuinn	13/1	1½ 3
84	Kabool *SaeedbinSuroor,GB* 4-9-0 LDettori	78/10	1¼ 4
	Helene Express (AUS) *DAHayes,HongKong* 4-9-0 BMarcus	51/1	hd 5
	Survey General (IRE) *JMoore,HongKong* 3-8-13 RFradd	15/1	nk 6
	Sunline (NZ) *S&TMcKee,NewZealand* 4-8-11 GChilds	11/10f	hd 7
	Oriental Express (IRE) *IWAllan,HongKong* 6-9-0 ESaint-Martin	11/1	½ 8
	Johan Cruyff *DOughton,HongKong* 5-9-0 (b) FSanchez	11/1	hd 9
	Lord of Warriors (USA) *ASCruz,HongKong* 4-9-0 (t) FCoetzee	60/1	nk 10
60	Dazzling Park (IRE) *JSBolger,Ireland* 3-8-10 KJManning	22/1	hd 11
	Score *STWong,HongKong* 5-9-0 DHarrison	100/1	sh 12

Mr J. D. Martin 12ran 2m01.40   TR: 124/117/114+/111/111/111

1174

INDEX TO SELECTED BIG RACES

Abime (USA) 77
Able Master (NZ) 89
Access All Areas (IRE) 10⁶
Adair (USA) 17, 58³
Afaan (IRE) 49
Affirmed Success (USA) a91
Agnes World (USA) 78*
Air Marshall (IRE) 87⁴
Alabaq (USA) 59⁴
Albaran (GER) 79
Alborada 84*
Alexis (IRE) 8
Aljabr (USA) 24², 41*, 56⁴
All Glory 21⁶
All The Way (IRE) 17⁵, 58⁴
Almaty (IRE) 49⁶
Almushtarak (IRE) 6³, 22³,
    41³, 46⁴, 52³, 69², 84
Almutawakel a1*, 46, a65²,
    a95⁵
Alpha Blues 51⁴
Alrassaam 3, 24⁶
Al Waffi 9⁴
Amethyst (IRE) 54⁴
Amilynx (FR) 88*
Andreyev (IRE) 28
Anees (USA) a93*
Anguilla (USA) 92
Antarctique (IRE) 75⁵
Antinnaz (IRE) 78⁵
Apple of Kent (USA) 21
Arctic Char 25
Arctic (FR) 75⁶
Arctic Owl 35², 74², 88⁶
Arena (AUS) 89
Ares Vallis (IRE) 62
Aretha (IRE) 54
Aristotle (IRE) 87*
Arkadian Hero (USA) 28⁶,
    37⁴, 53³, 78
Artax (USA) a91*
Atalante (GER) 85
Athenry 27
Atlantic Destiny (IRE) 4, 28
Auction House (USA) 3, 82
Averti (IRE) 49, 78

Bachir (IRE) 50³, 66³
Bahamian Bandit 3⁶
Bailey's Whirlwind (USA) 72
Balisada 26*, 41⁴, 69⁴
Barathea Guest 81²
Barbola (USA) 76⁴
Barter Town (USA) a65
Beat All (USA) 17³, 31⁴
Beautiful Dancer (BRZ) 86
Behrens (USA) a14*, a95
Belenus (GER) 55³
Berkoutchi (FR) 7
Bertolini (USA) 7, 25³, 37³,
    43³, 53², 78
Best of The Bests (IRE) 71²
Be The Chief 24
Bethesda 72⁶
Bianconi (USA) 28, 37, 43

Bienamado (USA) 35⁵, 47²,
    63², 86⁵
Big Jag (USA) a91³
Bimbola (FR) 99²
Black Amber (IRE) 70
Black Cash (USA) a65⁶
Blackheath (IRE) 25
Black Rock Desert (USA) 78
Blend of Pace (IRE) 38⁵
Blue Bolivar (IRE) 71⁵
Blueprint (IRE) 44⁴
Blushing Risk (FR) 34
Bohemiath (AUS) 89
Bold Edge 28*, 37², 53⁴, 70*
Bold Fact (USA) 28, 37
Bomfim (USA) 89
Bonapartiste (FR) 94⁶
Boomerang Blade 4
Borgia (GER) 15⁵, 34⁵, 61²,
    79, 92⁵, 97, 99*
Bountiful Lady (USA) 4
Brahms (USA) 73³, 83², a93
Brancaster (USA) 3⁴, 17, 32
Brave Act 90⁶
Brew (NZ) 89
Brushing Up (USA) a14⁴
Buck's Boy (USA) 94³
Budroyale (USA) a95²

Caffe Latte (IRE) 92⁴
Caitano 18*
Calando (USA) 8³, 21, 48
Canon Can (USA) 42⁵
Cape Cross (IRE) 22*, 52*,
    68⁶
Capistrano Day (USA) 4⁴, 12
Capri 35
Captain Steve (USA) a93
Carambola (IRE) 12⁶
Cassandra Go (IRE) 12
Catienus (USA) a95
Cat Thief (USA) a95*
Celeric 27⁴, 42⁶, 74³
Central Park (IRE) a1⁴, 15, 46,
    89²
Cerulean Sky (IRE) 21⁶, 48,
    62³, 79
Charge d'Affaires 68
Charlie's Beau (USA) a93
Che Sara Sara (USA) 98
Chester House (USA) 23⁴, 33⁴,
    46³, a95⁴
Chez Cherie 77⁵
Chief Seattle (USA) a93²
Chinatown (IRE) 71⁴
Choirgirl 26⁶
Churlish Charm 27
Circle of Gold (IRE) 4
Ciro (USA) 81*
City On A Hill (USA) 36*, 50
Claxon 16⁵
Comillas (FR) 8
Commander Collins (IRE) 3
Compton Admiral 3, 17, 33*,
    46⁵

Coretta (IRE) 92²
Cornelius 87⁶
Cortachy Castle (IRE) 49
Courteous 86³, 94
Craigsteel 35*, 44²
Crimplene (IRE) 72³
Croco Rouge (IRE) 5³, 13*,
    33, 61³, 79³
Cronus (NZ) 99⁶
Crystal Downs (USA) 12⁴, 16

Daliapour (IRE) 17², 31², 40
Dancing Place (CHI) 86
Dansili 72, 19⁴, 45³, 56³
Danzigaway (USA) 85⁴
Danzighill (AUS) 98⁶
Darakiyla (IRE) 77⁶
Dark Moondancer 5*, 30*, 94
Daryaba (IRE) 21*, 62*, 79
Dashing Blue 49⁵
Dawson's Legacy (USA) 86
Daylami (IRE) a1⁵, 11², 15*,
    40*, 60*, 79, 94*
Daylight In Dubai (USA) 28
Dazzling Park (IRE) 12³, 60²,
    100
Debbie's Warning 3, 24, 52⁵
Delay of Game (USA) 90
Desaru 3, 25
Desert Fox 99
Desert Magic (IRE) 12
Diamond White 59³
Digital Image 36⁶
Dignify (IRE) 77
Diktat 43*, 53*, 85⁵
Distant Music (USA) 57*, 83*
Divination (FR) 75³
Dixie Union (USA) a93⁵
Docksider (USA) 22², 41²,
    90³, 98*
Dojima Muteki (JPN) 78
Dramatic Quest 57⁵
Dream Well (FR) 5², 15³, 34³,
    60³, 94⁵
Dubai Millennium 17, 39*,
    45*, 69*
Duck Row (USA) 6⁶
Dyhim Diamond (IRE) 37

Easaar 3
Eastern Purple (USA) 28⁵, 53
Easy Dollar 28
Ebisu (GER) 18⁵
Ecton Park (USA) a95
Edabiya (IRE) 12, 62⁵
Ekraar (USA) 57⁴, 87³
Ela Athena 48²
Elaflaak (USA) 72
El Condor Pasa (USA) 13²,
    34*, 61*, 79²
Elle Danzig (GER) 18⁴, 96*
Elmutabaki 47⁵, 58
Embrasser Moi (JPN) 97
Enjoy The Moment (USA) a91
Enrique 3², 10², 25², 41⁵

Enzeli (IRE) 27*, 64[4]
Espionage 63[4]
Etizaaz (USA) 62[2]
Eurolink Raindance (IRE) 54[5]
Evening Promise 4
Exeat (USA) 3, 24

Fa-Eq (IRE) 22[4], 37
Fahris (IRE) 94
Fairlee Mixa (FR) 8[6]
Fairy Gem (IRE) 54[6]
Fairy Queen (IRE) 4, 62[4], 96[4]
Falcon Flight (IRE) 20
Fantastic Light (USA) 23[2], 33[3], 47*, 79
Farfala (FR) 21
Fasliyev (USA) 50*
Fath (USA) 73[2]
Fear And Greed (IRE) 4, 12
Festival Hall (IRE) 31
Field of Hope (IRE) 56[6], 85*, 98[2]
Figurehead (NZ) 89
Fils de Viane (FR) 2[5], 32[6]
First Magnitude (IRE) 2[4], 63[3], 94
Flamingo Road (GER) 55[2], 79
Flaming Quest 47
Flanders (IRE) 49
Fly To The Stars 6*, 22, 56
Forest Camp (USA) a93[6]
Forestry (USA) a91[4]
Forever Midnight (IRE) 72
Fragrant Oasis (USA) 4, 28
Frippet (IRE) 16
Fruits of Love (USA) 15[6], 29*, 40[3], 86[2], 97
Furlough (USA) a91

Gaelic Storm 53
Galloping Gael (USA) a14[5]
Gander (USA) a65[5]
Gandria (CAN) 92
Garbu (USA) 68, 90
General Challenge (USA) a95
Generous Rosi 23
Genghis Khan (IRE) 31, 64[5], 79
Giant's Causeway (USA) 66*
Gifts Galore (IRE) 54
Glamis (USA) 17[6], 47[3]
Gold Academy (IRE) 3[5], 24[3], 41, 69[3], 84[4]
Gold Away (IRE) 13[3], 43[2], 56[2]
Golden Marvel (FR) 32
Golden Missile (USA) a95[3]
Golden Rule 67[4]
Golden Silca 4, 12[2], 26[2]
Golden Snake (USA) 19*, 46[6], 84
Good And Tough (USA) a91
Gorse 70[5]
Gracioso (USA) 2[3], 9*, 20[6], 32[4]
Graeme Hall (USA) a93
Grazalema (USA) 7, 80
Grazia 53

Greek Dance (IRE) 34, 46[2], 79[6], 84[5]
Greensand 4
Grigorovich (USA) 50[4], 66[5]
Gritty Sandie (USA) 86[6]

Halmahera (IRE) 53, 70[6]
Handsome Ridge 13[5], 23[5], 76[6], 84, 96[2]
Happy Woodman (USA) 76
Harbour Island (FR) 50[5]
Hasty Words (IRE) 4
Hawksley Hill (IRE) 68[4], 90[5]
Hawriyah (USA) 26
Helene Express (AUS) 100[5]
High-Rise (IRE) a1, 84[6], 97[3]
High Yield (USA) a93[3]
Holding Court 87
Holy Grail (NZ) 98
Honey Colour (IRE) 96
Honor Glide (USA) 94
Housemaster (IRE) 17[4], 98[5]
Hugh Hefner (USA) a93
Hula Angel (USA) 4[6], 12*, 26
Hunting Lad (USA) 99

Imperial Beauty (USA) 4, 53, 78[2]
Imperialist (IRE) 72[6]
Inchrory 76
Incitatus 68
Indiana Legend (IRE) 7, 25[6]
Indian Danehill (IRE) 7[5], 19[3], 32[2]
Indigenous (IRE) 40[6], 97[2], 99[4]
Inforapenny 54
Insatiable (IRE) 11[4], 33[6], 67*
Insight (FR) 13[6], 92
Intikhab (USA) 6[4]
Invermark 27[2], 51[2], 75[4]
Invincible Spirit (IRE) 73[6]
Iridanos 7
Irish Prize (USA) 7
Iscan (IRE) 58
Island Sands (IRE) 3*, 10[5]
Issey Rose (IRE) 77
Ivan Luis (FR) 30[4], 96[6]

Jalad (IRE) 71[6]
Jaseur (USA) 42[3]
Jemima 72[5]
Jim And Tonic (FR) 6[2], 41[6], 68[3], 90, 100*
Johan Cruyff 100
Josr Algarhoud (IRE) 52[2], 82[3]
Juvenia (USA) 21[5], 62[6]

Kabool 13[4], 59[2], 76[3], 84[3], 100[4]
Kalindi 72
Karmifira (FR) 8[2], 21
Karra Kul (USA) 68
Katun (FR) 27
Kayf Tara 27[3], 42*, 51*, 64*
Kenwood Melody (AUS) 98
Keos (IRE) 28, 43[6], 78[3], 85[2]
Khumba Mela (IRE) 90

Killer Instinct 24[4]
Kilting 16
Kingsalsa (USA) 7[3], 32[5]
King's Best (USA) 83[5]
Kingsclere 71[3]
Kirkwall 90
Kiss A Native (USA) a93
Kissogram 46
Kona Gold (USA) a91[2]
Kuwait Dawn (IRE) 4, 25

Lady Elsie (AUS) 89
Lady In Waiting 48
Lady of Chad 77*
Lady Upstage (IRE) 54
Lady Vettori 77[3]
Laebeel (NZ) 89
Lahar (AUS) 89[3]
Lamzena (IRE) 4
Largesse 51[3], 75
La Sylphide (SWI) 21, 62
Laurentide (USA) 27
Lavery (IRE) 7, 37
Lear Spear (USA) 23*, 33, 59*, 84, 100[3]
Leggera (IRE) 79[4], 88[3dis]
Lemon Drop Kid (USA) a95[6]
Lend A Hand 82[2], 90[4]
Lermontov (USA) 87[2]
Le Roi Chic (FR) 7, 19[6]
Lexicon (USA) a91
Lil's Boy (USA) 11[5]
Limpid 23[6]
Lippe Luigi (IRE) 77
Lisieux Rose (IRE) 67[3]
Littlefeather (IRE) 54[3]
Little Rock 84
Lochangel 37, 49
Lonesome Dude (CAN) 68
Lord of Men 60[6]
Lord of Warriors (USA) 100
Lord Pacal (IRE) 36[5]
Lord Smith 68
Lots of Magic 25*, 82
Loudeac (USA) 13
Louve (USA) 21[4], 92
Lucido (IRE) 17
Lucky Dream (FR) 55[5]
Lucky Legend (IRE) 10

Mahboob (IRE) 80[4], 85
Major Force (USA) 85[6]
Make No Mistake (IRE) 11[3], 30
Malek (CHI) a1[2]
Mall Queen (USA) 72
Mandama (FR) 54
Manndar (IRE) 39[3]
March Groom (USA) 18[3], 30[3]
Maridpour (IRE) 89
Marius Petipa (USA) 10
Mary Stuart (IRE) 48[5]
Master Fay (IRE) 36[4]
Max Tyson (IRE) 2
Mayshiel (IRE) 51[5]
Mensa 25[5]
Middlesex Drive (USA) 90
Midnight Bet (USA) 98

1176

Miletrian (IRE) 77[4]
Millencolin (USA) a93
Miss Amanpuri 16
Mistle Song 48[6]
Mitcham (IRE) 37, 78
Moiava (FR) 4, 8
Monkston Point (IRE) 28
Montjeu (IRE) 2*, 9[2], 20*, 31*, 63*, 79*, 97[4]
Monza (USA) 99
Moon Driver (USA) 72
Mossflower (USA) 92
Mother of Pearl (IRE) 38[4], 62
Mount Abu (IRE) 50[6]
Moutahddee (IRE) 59[6]
Mowbray (USA) 75
Mudaa-Eb 31
Muhtathir 98[4]
Mujahid (USA) 3[3], 75, 24, 82[4]
Mull of Kintyre (USA) 36[2], a93[4]
Munjiz (IRE) 70[2]
Mus-If 10[4]
Mutafaweq (USA) 31[5], 47[4], 58*
Mythical Girl (USA) 12

Nasheed (USA) 21
Natalie Too (USA) 92
Nedawi 27[5], 40[2]
New Story (USA) 77[2]
Night Flight 49
Night Shot 49[4]
Noble Pearl (GER) 8
Northern Quest (FR) 5[5]
Northerntown (USA) 88[3]
Noushkey 16[2], 48, 58[6]
Nowhere To Exit 20[2]

Oath (IRE) 17*, 40
Obviously Fun (IRE) 9[3]
Ocean of Wisdom (USA) 81[3]
Old Trieste (USA) a95
One Won One (USA) 12
On The Ridge (IRE) 22
Optimaite 87
Oriental Express (IRE) 100
Orpen (USA) 3, 10[3], 24, 43
Orso (FR) 80
Osumi Bright (JPN) 97
Our Ambition (IRE) 36

Peace Upholds (IRE) 10
Pegnitz (USA) 46
Perfect Sting (USA) 92[6]
Perfect Vintage 22[5]
Persian Punch (IRE) 27
Personal First (USA) a93
Personal Moon (USA) a14[6]
Perugia (IRE) 77
Pescara (IRE) 4[5], 26[5]
Pink Coral (IRE) 12
Pipalong (IRE) 53
Pleasant Temper (USA) 92
Polaire (IRE) 12, 38[6]
Port Bayou (USA) 31
Port Vila (FR) 83[4]

Poseidon 30[5], 96[5]
Posidonas 29[6]
Poteen (USA) 68
Praslin Island 58
Preseli (IRE) 54*
Presumed (USA) 26, 82
Primo Valentino (IRE) 73*
Proud Native (IRE) 49[3]
Public Purse (USA) 34[6]

Quiet Resolve (USA) 68*, 90

Rabah 29
Race Leader (USA) 66[2]
Rainbow High 27, 74*
Raise A Grand (IRE) 24[5], 41
Rambling Bear 49, 53
Ramruma (USA) 16*, 38*, 48*, 58[2]
Rangoon Ruby (USA) 8
Rascal Suzuka (JPN) 97[5]
Real Quiet (USA) a14[3]
Rebbor (NZ) 89
Red Sea 3
Referendum (IRE) 28
Regal Thunder (USA) a91
Renazig 13
Resfa (ARG) 98[3]
Res Judicata 34
Rhagaas 20[3]
Rivana 12
River Keen (IRE) a65*, a95
Robertico 30[6]
Rob 'n Gin (USA) 68[2]
Rogan Josh (AUS) 89*, 99[5]
Rosen Kavalier (JPN) 99
Rose of Tara (IRE) 38, 67[5]
Rosselli (USA) 49, 53
Rossini (USA) 57[2]
Royal Anthem (USA) 15[2], 29[2], 46*, 60[5], 94[2]
Royal Kingdom (IRE) 71*
Royal Rebel 20
Running Stag (USA) a1, a14[2], 33[5], a65[4], 100[2]
Russian Revival (USA) 28[2]

Sabrinsky (FR) 56
Sadian 29, 44[3]
Saffron Walden (FR) 10*, 17, 46
Sagamix (FR) 5[4], 34[4]
Sainte Marine (IRE) 49[2], 78[6]
Salford Express (IRE) 17, 39[5], 46, 84
Sampower Star 37, 43, 53[5], 70[4], 78[4]
Sand Falcon 80[3]
Sand Partridge (IRE) 54
San Sebastian 75[2]
Sao (IRE) 8
Sardaukar 32[3], 39[4], 76[5]
Saugerties (USA) 34, 55[6]
Scarteen Fox (IRE) 87
Score 100
Sea Wave (IRE) 29[3], 35[4], 99[3]
Seazun (IRE) 72*

Second Coming (NZ) 89
Second Empire (IRE) 11[6]
Secret Saver (USA) 29[5], 35
Seignorial (USA) 42
Self Feeder (IRE) 98
Seltitude (IRE) 85
Sendawar (IRE) 2[2], 7*, 24*, 56*
Seraphina (IRE) 72[4]
Shaya 27
Shebane (USA) 88[4]
Sheer Viking (IRE) 37, 49, 70
Shenck 84[4]
Shiva (JPN) 11*, 23, 84[2]
Showboat 84
Show Me The Money (IRE) 12, 70[3]
Sibling Rival (USA) 27
Sicnee (USA) 25
Side Saddle (IRE) 62
Signorina Cattiva (USA) 96[3]
Silic (FR) 68[5], 90*
Silver Charm (USA) a1[6]
Silver Patriarch (IRE) 15[4], 40[4], 44*, 64[3], 99
Silver Rhapsody (USA) 35[3], 48[3]
Silver Star 8
Sir Nicholas 36[3]
Sister Bella (IRE) 38[3]
Skybeau (NZ) 89
Sky Colony (USA) 68
Sky Heights (NZ) 89
Slickly (FR) 20[4], 32*, 45[2], 56[5]
Slip Stream (USA) 19[2], 80[5]
Soaring Softly (USA) 92*
Sole Che Sorgi (IRE) 80
Solo Mio (IRE) 27
Son of A Pistol (USA) a91
Sorbie Tower (IRE) 22[6]
Spadoun (FR) 2[6]
Spanish Fern (USA) 92
Special Discount (FR) 43
Special Week (JPN) 97*
Spirit of Love (USA) 27
Star of Akkar 21[2]
State Shinto (USA) 39[2], 76*
Stay Gold (JPN) 97[6]
Stephen Got Even (USA) a65[3]
Stinger (JPN) 97
Strategic 76[2]
Stravinsky (USA) 25[4], 37*, 49*, a91[6]
Streak (AUS) 89
Successful Appeal (USA) a91[5]
Suehiro Commander (JPN) 97
Sugarfoot 80[2], 82[5]
Sumitas (GER) 55[4]
Sunday Picnic (JPN) 16[4]
Sunline (NZ) 100
Sunshine Street (USA) 29[4], 40[5], 60[4]
Sunspangled (IRE) 4, 12, 16[6], 38[2], 48, 60
Superior Premium 28[4], 37
Supreme Sound a95
Sure Dancer (USA) 76
Survey General (IRE) 100[6]

Susu 82*, 90
Sweet Opera (FR) 62

Tajoun (FR) 27, 75*, 88²
Ta-Lim 42⁴
Tanaasa (IRE) 86⁴
Tarfaa (IRE) 10
Tchaikovsky (IRE) 20⁵, 31³, 58⁵
Theatreworld (IRE) 67²
The Hind (NZ) 89
The Message (NZ) 89
The Warrior (NZ) 89⁶
Thornfield (CAN) 86*, 94
Three Cheers (IRE) 27⁶, 42²
Through The Rye 17
Tie The Knot (AUS) 89
Tiger Hill (IRE) 18², 34², 55*, 79⁵, 97
Time Zone 47⁶
Timote (IRE) 78
Tioga 57⁶
Tipsy Creek (USA) 28, 37⁶, 49
Tomba 6⁵, 43⁵, 53⁶, 70, 85
Torgau (IRE) 54², 72²
Trans Island 80*, 85³
Travelmate 89⁵

Trinculo (IRE) 73⁵
Triple Dash 7
Tumbleweed Ridge 82
Tuzla (FR) 90²
Tycoon's Dolce (IRE) 8

Umeno Fiber (JPN) 97
Ungaro (GER) 30²
Unite's Big Red (USA) 94
Urban Ocean (FR) 31⁶

Valentine Waltz (IRE) 4³, 8*, 26³
Valentino 66⁴
Val Royal (FR) 17
Val's Prince (USA) 94
Venize (IRE) 8⁵, 45⁵, 80⁶, 85
Vicar (USA) a91
Victory Gallop (CAN) a1³
Vision And Verse (USA) a95
Visionnaire (FR) 21³
Vision of Night 28³, 37⁵, 43⁴, 70
Vita Spericolata (IRE) 72⁶

Wahj (IRE) 28

Wallace 52⁴, 98
Wannabe Grand (IRE) 4², 26³, 37, 53
Warm Heart (USA) 50², 73⁴
Warningford 70, 82⁶
Way of Light (USA) 7⁴, 19⁵, 45⁴, 56
Wince 4*, 12⁵
Win For Us (GER) 88⁵
Winning Venture 57³
Wolf Tooth 59

Xaar 23³, 33²

Yagli (USA) 94⁴
Yakareem (IRE) 25
Yavana's Pace (IRE) 64², 89
Yorkies Boy 53, 78

Zaajer (USA) 17, 35⁶
Zabuan (NZ) 89
Zahrat Dubai 16³, 48⁴
Zazabelle (NZ) 89³
Zenne (IRE) 21
Zentsov Street (USA) 83³, 87⁵
Zindabad (FR) 59⁵
Zomaradah 92³

ERRATA & ADDENDA

'Racehorses of 1996'

Ruby Princess dam should be **Wabarah** and grandsire is **Shirley Heights**

'Racehorses of 1997'

Impish Lady is not related to Chicco di Caffe

'Racehorses of 1998'

Amaranth was not dead
Heart Full of Soul fair **form** at 2 yrs
Running Stag grandam Revada was foaled in **1966**
World Alert dam **stayed 1¼m**

THE TIMEFORM 'TOP HORSES ABROAD'

This review of the year covers the major racing countries outside Britain. It includes Timeform Ratings for the top two-year-olds, three-year-olds and older horses. Horses not rated highly enough to be included in the main lists but which finished in the first three in a European pattern race during the season are included below the cut-off line. Fillies and mares are denoted by (f); * denotes the horse was trained for only a part of the season in the country concerned. Overseas customers wishing to keep in touch with Timeform's coverage of racing through the year can subscribe to Computer Timeform or Timeform Perspective for reports on all the important races. Timeform is also available on the Internet—http://www.timeform.com

IRELAND   No stable in Europe dominated the year's two-year-old racing to the same extent as the Aidan O'Brien yard. Not only was there tremendous strength in depth at Ballydoyle, there was a willingness to deploy that strength not apparent in other leading stables. Already by Royal Ascot, the stable had had twenty-one two-year-old runners yielding seventeen wins; the other four were all placed. **Fasliyev** (Heinz 57 Phoenix Stakes, Prix Morny), **Giant's Causeway** (Prix de la Salamandre), **Aristotle** (Racing Post Trophy) and **Ciro** (awarded Grand Criterium) all won Group 1 events by the end of year, **Brahms**, **Lermontov** and **Zentsov Street** were all placed in Group 1 races in Britain, while **Rossini** (Prix Robert Papin), **Mull of Kintyre** (Gimcrack Stakes) and **Royal Kingdom** (Royal Lodge Stakes) all won good prizes outside Ireland. Railway Stakes winner **Bernstein** was considered at least as good as any of those but his defeat in the National Stakes and the career-ending injury suffered by unbeaten Fasliyev left Giant's Causeway as the stable's main classic contender. The impressive Killavullan Stakes winner **Monashee Mountain** put himself in the Guineas picture late in the year. The O'Brien stable didn't have a complete monopoly on the Irish two-year-old pattern races however; **Sinndar** profited most from Bernstein's faltering in the final furlong to win the National Stakes, while the unbeaten **Preseli** took the Moyglare Stud Stakes to put up one of the best performances by a two-year-old filly in Europe. Other lightly-raced two-year-olds who can be expected to do well are **Broche**, who beat Ciro handily in a Curragh maiden in June on his only start and has now joined Godolphin, the very well-bred filly **Inkling**, who won a similar event impressively in September, and the Leopardstown listed winner Chiang Mai, who looks an interesting middle-distance prospect.

Among the three-year-olds, **Stravinsky** retained his position as the best of his generation trained in Ireland, but only after being returned to sprinting, with a top-class win in the July Cup and a subsequent victory in the Nunthorpe. His stable-companions **Saffron Walden** and **Orpen** took first and third in the Irish Two Thousand Guineas (the only Irish classic kept at home), but neither showed the same form again, and neither did fourth-placed **Mus-If**. Other leading three-year-olds kept their form longer. Leopardstown listed winner **Strategic** went on to show very smart form when runner-up in the Prix Dollar and has since joined Godolphin. There were smart performances too from **Major Force**, who won both the Tetrarch Stakes and the Boland Stakes by wide margins, and Matron Stakes winner **Dazzling Park**, who was placed in both the Irish One Thousand Guineas and the Irish Champion Stakes.

Easily the best effort put up by an Irish-trained older horse came from the Gold Cup winner **Enzeli**, who failed by a long way to repeat the form when fourth on his only subsequent start in an Irish St Leger dominated by British-trained horses. Best of the other older horses were **Burden of Proof**, who won the listed Amethyst Stakes at Leopardstown for a third consecutive year, **Tarry Flynn**, who won three handicaps and the Concorde Stakes at Cork, and **Make No Mistake**, whose best efforts came when winning the Meld Stakes and when third to Shiva and Daylami in the newly-promoted Group 1 Tattersalls Gold Cup. **Sunshine Street** didn't quite reproduce his best three-year-old form, running his best race when fifth in the King George VI and Queen Elizabeth Diamond Stakes at Ascot. Four-year-olds **Bianconi** and Second Empire both had disappointing campaigns and were retired to stud.

Two-Year-Olds

120	Fasliyev	116	Dazzling Park (f)	100	Rainbows Forever
119p	Giant's Causeway	116	Mus-If	100	River Canyon
118	Rossini	116	Orpen	100	*Union Project
115p	Aristotle	115	Tiger Shark		
114	Bernstein	114	*Cupid	99	Moiseyev
114	Brahms	114	*Tchaikovsky	98	Castle Quest (f)
112p	Lermontov	113	Lavery	88	Marius Petipa
112	Mull of Kintyre	113	Rolo Tomasi		
111p	Broche	113	Urban Ocean	**Older Horses**	
111p	Monashee Mountain	112	Black Rock Desert	126	Enzeli
110p	Ciro	111	Antinnaz (f)	118	Burden of Proof
110p	Preseli (f)	111	Show Me The Money (f)	118	Sunshine Street
109	Royal Kingdom	110	Access All Areas	117	Tarry Flynn
109	Zentsov Street	110	Edabiya (f)	116	Make No Mistake
106	Barrier Reef	110	Timote (f)	113	Bianconi
105p	Sinndar	109	High King	113	Free To Speak
104P	Inkling (f)	108	Pharmacist (f)	113	San Sebastian
104?	Murawwi	108	*Polaire (f)	111	Social Harmony
103p	Anzari	108	Sunspangled (f)	111	Theatreworld
103p	Bach	107	Blast of Storm	110	Moving On Up
103+	Warrior Queen (f)	107	Immovable Option	110	One Won One
102p	Jammaal	107	Sister Bella (f)	110	Two-Twenty-Two
102+	Amethyst (f)	107	Yeoman's Point	110	Wray
101p	Fisherman's Creek	106	*Akbar	109	Lil's Boy
101	Sharp Focus	106	Wild Heaven (f)	108	Risk Material
100p	Admiral's Cup	105	Crystal Downs (f)	107	Draft of Vintage
100p	Theoretically (f)	105	Genghis Khan	107	Lisieux Rose (f)
100	Bashkir	105	Namid	106	Campo Catino
100	Galloway Boy	105	Oyster Catcher (f)	105	Golden Fact
100	Poco A Poco (f)	105	Port Bayou	105	Golden Rule
100	Polish Panache	104	Blend of Pace (f)	104	Carhue Lass (f)
		104	Moon Dragon	104	Dane River
99p	Earlene (f)	104	Rubies From Burma (f)	103	Khatani
98	Still Going On	103	Beckon The King	103	Winged Hussar
97	Desert Sky (f)	103	Lucky Legend	102	Landing Slot
95	Aretha (f)	103	Speed Merchant	102	Quinze
95	Yara (f)	103	Tarfaa	101	Sarayan
94	Buffalo Berry (f)	102	Artistic Blue (f)	100+	*Quws
91	Appalachia (f)	102	Peach Out of Reach (f)	100	Dance So Suite
90	Margay (f)	101	Apparatchik (f)	100	Gordi
90	Touch of Innocence (f)	101	Kilkenny Castle	100	Lady Alexander (f)
		101	Scottish Memories	100	Musical Pursuit
Three-Year-Olds		101	The Bomber Liston	100	She's Our Mare (f)
133	Stravinsky	101	Young American	100d	Armilina (f)
123	Saffron Walden	100	Carambola (f)		
120	Strategic	100	Fable	98	Sharp Catch (f)
117	Major Force	100	Hadeb		
		100	Rafayda (f)		

FRANCE   For the third time in four years an outstanding French three-year-old won the Prix de l'Arc de Triomphe. **Montjeu**, rated second-best in France as a juvenile, was bred to shine over longer trips at three and did just that, completing the French/Irish Derby double impressively in the summer before returning in the autumn to defeat the top-class Japanese colt El Condor Pasa in the Arc with a tremendous burst of speed. Although Montjeu's season ended in defeat on firm ground in the

Japan Cup, reports that he'd run his final race were denied by connections and he seems sure to win more top races. Also set to return in 2000 is France's other top three-year-old colt **Sendawar**. After a defeat by Montjeu in the Prix Greffulhe, Sendawar proved high-class at a mile, winning the Poule d'Essai des Poulains, the St James's Palace Stakes and the Prix du Moulin, though heavy ground prevented him taking on Dubai Millennium in either the Prix Jacques le Marois or the Queen Elizabeth II Stakes. **Dansili** was a high-class miler too, gaining places behind Sendawar in the Poulains and Moulin, as well as behind Dubai Millennium in the Jacques le Marois after a clear-cut win in the Prix Messidor. Dansili headed a strong band of Fabre-trained three-year-old colts, which also included Grand Prix de Paris winner and Jacques le Marois runner-up **Slickly**, Prix Dollar winner **State Shinto**, **Gracioso**, who beat a below-par Montjeu in the Prix Lupin (all three are now with Godolphin), Poulains third **Kingsalsa** and Grand Prix de Paris runner-up **Indian Danehill**. Derby also-ran **Val Royal** won the Prix Guillaume d'Ornano before winning a Grade 2 race in America, but two more Fabre three-year-olds who will be around in 2000 are Prix du Conseil de Paris winner **First Magnitude** and Prix Royal-Oak winner **Amilynx**, the latter developing into a very smart stayer on heavy ground in the autumn. Another who did well in the autumn, winning three listed races, was the Criquette Head-trained **Mayaro**, who looks well worth his place in pattern company at four. As in recent years, the latest crop of three-year-old fillies was not strong but it found a clear leader in **Daryaba**, who completed the Prix de Diane/Prix Vermeille double before finishing behind in the Arc. Her Diane win came at the chief expense of **Star of Akkar**, who won three pattern races in all, including the Prix de la Nonette at Deauville. Best three-year-old filly at shorter trips was **Danzigaway**, whose good fourth in the Prix de la Foret was confirmed by her winning the Prix Perth.

Much the best older horse racing in France was the previous season's Japan Cup winner **El Condor Pasa**, who deserved almost as much credit as Montjeu for the part he played in an outstanding Arc. After finishing second to **Croco Rouge** in the Prix d'Ispahan on his European debut, El Condor Pasa beat a strong field in the Grand Prix de Saint-Cloud and won the Prix Foy as well before failing narrowly to make all in the Arc, in which he had Croco Rouge six lengths back in third. Croco Rouge fared best of the three leading French middle-distance three-year-old colts from the previous year. **Sagamix** wasn't at his best in either start and was sold to Godolphin without defending his Arc title, while **Dream Well**, who was placed in several good races, including the Grand Prix de Saint-Cloud, got his head in front only in a Group 3 at Deauville. All three made their reappearance in the Ganay behind British import **Dark Moondancer**, who followed up in the Gran Premio di Milano before ending the year in defeat at the Breeders' Cup, by which time he'd joined an American stable. French-trained runners at Gulfstream fared no better, but it was a different story in Hong Kong the following month when **Jim And Tonic** won the Cup (his second valuable success at Sha Tin in 1999) and **Borgia** narrowly beat Prix de Pomone winner **Bimbola** in the Vase. Injury forced **Gold Away** to miss the Breeders' Cup after he'd shown high-class form in France at a range of distances with places in the Prix d'Ispahan, Maurice de Gheest and Moulin. **Keos** was the best older horse in France to be campaigned regularly at short of a mile, ending the season placed in the Abbaye and the Foret (behind **Field of Hope**), while **Sainte Marine** and the ex-British **Nuclear Debate** were leading sprinters too. **Tajoun** was the top older stayer again, winning the Prix du Cadran before finding only Amilynx too strong in the Royal-Oak.

Expectations in France that Godolphin's Evry-based two-year-olds would dominate the juvenile contests proved wholly unfounded; Godolphin was represented in just five of the French two-year-old pattern races and won only one, the Prix d'Aumale with **Dignify**. **City On A Hill** took the July Stakes, however, and numerous youngsters made promising winning debuts on their only starts. Instead it was the O'Brien stable which carried off four major two-year-old prizes–the Robert Papin,

Morny, Salamandre and Grand Criterium–against, it has to be said, minimal resistance from French stables in those events. Top French two-year-old **Morning Pride** wasn't seen out after early-July (she joined Godolphin at the end of the year) but her form wasn't bettered subsequently. The other leading fillies were Marcel Boussac winner **Lady of Chad** and Criterium de Saint-Cloud winner **Goldamix**, who were both unbeaten in two starts. Behind City On A Hill, the colts were hard to split, the best of them being **Hightori** (Prix Thomas Bryon), **Jokerman** (winner of the Prix des Chenes, and now in the USA), **Lord Flasheart** (Prix de Conde), **Petroselli** (Criterium de Saint-Cloud runner-up) and **Manzor** (Prix du Petit Couvert). Manzor, who beat older horses for his most important win, looks a potentially smart sprinter. Outside the pattern races, two Fabre-trained two-year-olds who won their only starts as though destined for better things were Indian Prospector and **River's Curtain**, the latter another who has joined Godolphin.

Two-Year-Olds		Three-Year-Olds			
114	City On A Hill	137	Montjeu	109p	Daring Miss (f)
113p	Morning Pride (f)	129	Sendawar	109p	Victory Cry (f)
111p	Hightori	125	Dansili	109	All Glory (f)
111	*Jokerman	121	Amilynx	109	Histoire Sainte (f)
110+	Manzor	121	Daryaba (f)	109	Iridanos
110	Lord Flasheart	121	State Shinto	109	Marie de Bayeux (f)
110	Petroselli	119p	Astonished	109	Scottish Glen
109p	Lady of Chad (f)	119	Slickly	109	Seltitude (f)
108p	Goldamix (f)	118	*Caffe Latte (f)	109	Sunday Picnic (f)
107p	Anshaam	118	Gracioso	108	Double Heart
107p	China Visit	117	First Magnitude	108	*Fils de Viane
106	Crystal d'Ass	116	Indian Danehill	108	Franc
106	Ocean of Wisdom	116	Kingsalsa	108	High Hopes
105p	Ejlaal (f)	116	*Val Royal	108	Markale (f)
105	Touch of The Blues	115	Chelsea Manor	108	Nordican Inch (f)
104	Grigorovich	115	Danzigaway (f)	108	Okabango
104	Premier Pas	115	Mayaro	108	Prairie Runner (f)
104	Warjan	115	Star of Akkar (f)	108	Shebane (f)
103	New Story (f)	115	Way of Light	108	Side Saddle (f)
103p	River's Curtain	114	Agol Lack	108	Stella Berine (f)
103p	Texalina (f)	114	Cerulean Sky (f)	108	White Star (f)
103p	Volvoreta (f)	114	Sage Et Jolie (f)	107	Ares Vallis (f)
102p	Cosmographe	114	Shabby Chic (f)	107	Berkoutchi
102p	Lady Vettori (f)	114?	Sardaukar	107	Christophene
102	Loyal Tartare	113	Le Roi Chic	107	Emerald Park
101	Cap Coz (f)	113	Raucous Lad	107	*Imperfect World
101	Dignify (f)	112	Falcon Flight	107	Kansa (f)
101	Vision's Flight	112	Hello Soso (f)	107	Murray River
100p	Bintalreef (f)	112	Irish Prize	107	Restless War
100p	Jaydoom	112	Juvenia (f)	106	Aubergade (f)
100	Blue Moon (f)	112	Louve (f)	106	Blue Cloud (f)
100	Boutron	112	Midnight Foxtrot	106	Casamasa
100	Guthrun (f)	112	Ronda (f)	106	Dream Chief
100	Seattle Bay (f)	112	Spadoun	106	Farfala (f)
		112	Visionnaire (f)	106	Lord Brex
99	Acceleration (f)	111	Grazalema	106	*Palinisa (f)
99	Contexte	111	Hijaz (f)	106	Premiere Chance (f)
99	Legend of Spring (f)	111	Karmifira (f)	106	Prince Powhatan
98p	Moon Driver (f)	111	Northerntown	106	Take Heed
98	Perugina (f)	111	*The Mask	106	Vanishing World
98	Tindari Maria (f)	110	Espionage	105	Choice Spirit (f)
97	Harbour Island (f)	110	La Sylphide (f)	105	Golden Marvel
96	Just A Poser	110	Neptune's Bride (f)	105	Le Rhone
94+	Mall Queen (f)	110	Orso	105	Magic Whisper
93	Mon Pote Le Gitan	110	Spendent	105	Ne Coupez Pas
		110	Venize (f)	105	Raftery
				105	*Rangoon Ruby (f)

105	*Rouen	116	Sainte Marine (f)	109	King Country
105	Sargari	115	Insight (f)	109	Massimo
105	Silver Star (f)	115	*Sestino	109	Quel Senor
105	Sinueuse (f)	115	Ultimately Lucky	109	Trait de Genie
105	Sweet Opera (f)	114	Kashwan	108	Divination (f)
		114	Lone Bid	108	Honorable Money
104	Artistique (f)	114	Mahboob	108	Moteck (f)
104	*Keemoon (f)	114	Milord Fontenaille	108	Slowin
104	Obviously Fun	114	Solo Mio	107	Masalarian
103	Tijiyr	113	Arnaqueur	107	Mulahen
103	*Tycoon's Dolce (f)	113	Blushing Risk	107	*Otavalo
		113	Loudeac	107	Pinmix
Older Horses		113	Lucky Dream	106	Coach
136	*El Condor Pasa	113	Mont Rocher	106	Dressbaby (f)
126	Croco Rouge	113	*Persian Ruler	106	Harlem Snow
125	Gold Away	113	Russian Hope	106	Northern Quest
124	Jim And Tonic	112	Copeland	106	*Pharellia (f)
122	*Dark Moondancer	112	Daymarti	106	Phrygien
122	Dream Well	112	Dyhim Diamond	106	Top Way
122	Sagamix	112	Fragrant Mix	106	Turbotiere (f)
120	Borgia (f)	111	Ben Ewar	105	Battle Green
120	Keos	111	Miss Berbere (f)	105	Diableneyev
119	Field of Hope (f)	111	Perfect Vintage	105	Irish Holmes
119	*Public Purse	111	Tiraaz	105	La Juriste (f)
118	Epistolaire	110	Alliteration	105	Majoune (f)
117	Bimbola (f)	110	Erudite (f)	105	Marrast
117	Sand Falcon	110	Katun	105	Milford Track
117	*Sayarshan	110	Mountjoy	105	Roli Abi
117	Tajoun	110	Native Justice (f)	105	Vissinia (f)
116	Barbola	110	*Sole Che Sorgi		
116	Kadance Ville (f)	110	Terroir	104	Res Judicata
116	Nuclear Debate	109	*Espereo	103	Hoh Chi Min (f)

GERMANY   Only seven of Germany's forty-two pattern races went abroad, the majority of them sprint and mile events in which German horses tend to be less competitive. German runners now compete regularly elsewhere in Europe (with particular success in Italy), even as two-year-olds, and the latest season saw the first win by a German-trained horse in Britain since Star Appeal won the 1975 Eclipse when Chagall took a sales race at Doncaster.

Tiger Hill was Germany's best horse for the second year running, winning three pattern races, including a second Grosser Preis von Baden in which he defeated some of the leading three-year-olds. He did, though, fail to repeat his good effort of the previous year in the Arc but had run a fine race in France earlier in the year when second to El Condor Pasa in the Grand Prix de Saint-Cloud. His old rivals **Caitano** and **Ungaro** took him on again in the latest season, Caitano beating Tiger Hill in a Group 2 at Baden-Baden (receiving weight) and winning a similar event easily at Hamburg before a foot injury kept him off the track for the rest of the year. Ungaro was beaten by Tiger Hill in a Group 2 at Cologne on his reappearance but won the WGZ-Bank Deutschlandpreis (for a second time) and the Grosser Erdgas-Preis, both Group 1 races in the summer. The best older filly was **Elle Danzig**, who won another three pattern races, the most important of them being the Premio Roma in November, and reportedly stays in training at five. Over shorter trips, smart miler **Power Flame** returned as good as ever but was well beaten on his only other start. Sprinter **Auenadler** ran his best race when winning the Benazet-Rennen at Baden-Baden, while **Tertullian** didn't run a bad race all year, his season ending for the second year running with victory in the Premio Chiusura at Milan.

With Tiger Hill retired to stud, top middle-distance races will be up for grabs in 2000 and two of the most likely candidates for those events are three-year-olds **Belenus** and **Hibiscus**. There was only a head between them (in Belenus' favour)

1183

Gerling-Preis, Cologne—
two of Germany's top middle-distance performers, Tiger Hill (far side) and Ungaro

when they met for a third time in the Europa-Preis at Cologne in the autumn. Hibiscus won their first meeting in a listed race in the spring but it was Belenus who came out on top in the Deutsches Derby in which Hibiscus was only sixth. Another to disappoint in the Derby was the leading two-year-old of the previous season **Sumitas**, who took the Mehl-Mulhens Rennen (2000 Guineas) in the spring but didn't make much impact over longer trips except when second to Ungaro in the Deutschlandpreis. The Derby runner-up **Acambaro** was injured and has been retired to stud but the Derby third, filly **Flamingo Road**, subsequently ran very well to split Tiger Hill and Belenus in the Grosser Preis von Baden. Earlier, Flamingo Road had won the Preis der Diana (Oaks) from the Henkel-Rennen (1000 Guineas) winner **Rose of Zollern**. Among other leading three-year-old fillies were **Catella**, who won three pattern races, including a

BMW Deutsches Derby, Hamburg—
Belenus asserts from Acambaro with Preis der Diana winner Flamingo Road in third

Group 2 against older horses at Frankfurt, and St Leger winner **Win For Us**, who was subsequently second in the Long Island Handicap at Aqueduct.

Both the winners of Germany's two-year-old pattern races, the Raab Karcher Baustoffe-Cup winner **Auenklang** (also runner-up in the Prix Robert Papin) and the Preis des Winterfavoriten winner **Glad Master** (first past the post in all four of his starts) made a sufficiently good impression to have been purchased by Godolphin. The placed horses in the Winterfavoriten, **Global Dancer** and **Borsato**, had previously finished second in national listed races to **Lacantun** (a Rainbow Quest half-brother to high-class Lomitas) and **Leopardstown** respectively. The top two-year-old filly was **Well Minded**, who looked unlucky when a close second in the Prix d'Aumale at Chantilly.

Two-Year-Olds					
111	Auenklang	107	Euryanthe (f)	110	Kalatos
108p	Glad Master	106	Banyumanik	110	Key Royal
107	Leopardstown	106	Bela-M (f)	109	El Divino
106	Global Dancer	106	Iora (f)	109	Page's King
103	Well Minded (f)	106	Ituango	108+	Wins Fiction
103	Lacantun	106	Maestoso	108	Wilder Jager
101	Borsato	106	Miss Tobacco (f)	107	Accento
99	Arc Royal (GER)	106	Nagoya (f)	107	Catoki
99	Bear King	106	Nicolaos	107	Loriango
99	Palanca (f)	106	Nightdance (f)	107	Ocasa
		106	Quebra (f)	107	Sambakonig
Three-Year-Olds		105	Ihmegold	107	Starkey
120	Belenus	105	Imperioso	106	Icemoon
119	Hibiscus	105	Monavero	106	Intuition (f)
118	Acambaro	105	Universus	106	Sharp Domino
118	Flamingo Road (f)			105	Alpha Blues
117	Sumitas	102	Fastaghano	105	Azuerro
111	Catella (f)			105	Baleno
111	Gonlargo	**Older Horses**		105	Donna Alicia (f)
111	*Rose of Zollern (f)	127	Tiger Hill	105	Ebisu
110	Montalban	122	Caitano	105	Feenkonig
110	Silvano	119	Ungaro	105	Hamond
110	Welluna (f)	118	Elle Danzig (f)	105	Indian Point
110	Win For Us (f)	116	Power Flame	105	San Suru
109	Recadero	115	Tertullian	105	Up And Away
109	Terek	114	Auenadler		
108	Bernardon	114	Saugerties	103	Margosto
108	Evening Storm	113	Noel	102	Eden Rock
108	Evil Empire (f)	112	Graf Philipp	101	Nashcash
108	Kaldono	112	March Groom	99	El Lute
108	Karakal	111	Laveron	96	Jashin
108	Lekano	111	Robertico	95	Vishnu
		110	Areion		

ITALY   1999 was another year when most of Italy's pattern races went abroad, eight going to British stables, six to Germany and three to France, leaving just eight to be won by home-trained horses. For the first time since 1997, however, a Group 1 event was retained when **Sumati** beat a below-form Silver Patriarch by a nose in the steadily-run Gran Premio del Jockey Club, though the winner's subsequent sale to the USA was a loss Italian racing could ill afford. Italy's best horse was the prolific sprint winner **Late Parade** who was still as good as ever at the age of eight when he won the Gran Premio Citta di Napoli for the second successive year. The other smart older horses were Premio Ellington winner **Ivan Luis** (beating **Apollo Wells** and **Street General**), the ungenuine **Martino Alonso**, miler **Midyan Call** and the Gran Premio di Milano fifth **Poseidon**. **Sole Che Sorgi** also showed smart form at a mile but was moved to France during the summer and subsequently to the USA. Sumati was one of the few three-year-olds who proved better than useful. The Italian equivalents of

Derby Italiano, Rome—a seventh successive win in the race
for a British-based challenger as Mukhalif scores for Godolphin

the Guineas were both kept at home, however, the Premio Regina Elena going to **Shenck** and the Premio Parioli to **Alabama Jacks** narrowly from **Timboroa** and Sumati. Shenck went on to finish a good fourth in the Poule d'Essai des Pouliches before she too was sold to race in America. **Endless Hall** did all his racing in Italy but joined Luca Cumani during the summer and put up a smart effort to beat Timboroa and Sumati in a listed race at Milan. Once again, Italian two-year-olds made no show in the Gran Criterium but there were useful performances by **Blu Air Force**, who

Gran Premio del Jockey-Club, Milan—Sumati provides a rare Group 1 victory for a home-trained horse,
getting home narrowly from the previous year's winner Silver Patriarch

was second in the Criterium de Maisons-Laffitte and by the first two in the Premio Guido Berardelli, **Shibuni's Falcon** and **Dedi Boy**.

	Two-Year-Olds	109	Bagni di Petriolo	111	Ivan Luis
103	Blu Air Force	109	Onice Nero	110	Midyan Call
102	Shibuni's Falcon	109	Su Tirolesu	110	Poseidon
100	Dedi Boy	108	Alabama Jacks	110	*Sole Che Sorgi
100	Makeup A Mystery	108	*Antoniocastiglione	110§	Martino Alonso
97	Sonda (f)	108	London Bank	109	Apollo Wells
96	Xua (f)	108	Timboroa	109	Bardonecchia (f)
94	When You Believe	107	Best Grey	108	*War Declaration
94	Vicinale	106	Award Academy	107	Crisos Il Monaco
93	Golden Indigo	105	Beckmann	106	Blu Carillon
92	Novita Eclatanti	105	My Funny Valentine (f)	106?	Victorian Guide
90	Stella di Re	105	Strawberry Fields	105	Embody
89	Tornado Mitch			105	Rio Napo
89	Toutzi (f)	104	Janestra		
		100	Lady Storm (f)	102	Reinaldo
	Three-Year-Olds	100	Southern House (f)	102	Street General
114	*Sumati				
112	*Endless Hall		**Older Horses**		
110	*Shenck (f)	115	Late Parade		

The following leading horses trained elsewhere in Europe also figured in pattern races:

	Three-Year-Olds	103	Pretty Princ (Hungary)	110	Inchrory (Norway)
109	Valley Chapel (Norway)			110	Jaunty Jack (Norway)
108	Pistachio (Norway)		**Older Horses**	108	Sea Dane (Sweden)
106	Country Club (Poland)	111	Albaran (Norway)	106	Intruder (Denmark)

UNITED ARAB EMIRATES   The highlight of the UAE season, the Dubai World Cup meeting, goes from strength to strength. The 1999 running of the Dubai World Cup was the world's richest race and its purse has been raised by a million dollars to $6m for the 2000 renewal. From an entry of four, Godolphin won its first Dubai World Cup with **Almutawakel**, who held off two of the American challengers, Malek and Victory Gallop, after the main hopes for both Godolphin (High-Rise and Daylami) and the USA (Silver Charm) both disappointed. The supporting card has also been revamped, resulting in a total of $12m on offer in 2000. The Dubai Duty Free, in which Saeed bin Suroor saddled the first four home—**Altibr**, **Spindrift**, **Lord of Men**, and **Rabi**—was the last run in its old format as a consolation event for the World Cup; from 2000, the race will become a nine-furlong contest on turf with prize money boosted to $2m. The existing turf event, the Dubai Turf Classic, which was won narrowly by Fruits of Love from **Nedawi**, will now carry Group 3 status and is to be known as the Dubai Sheema Classic. The card's two listed events also undergo name changes in 2000 to become the Godolphin Mile and the Dubai Golden Shaheen (formerly the Nad Al Sheba Mile and Sprint respectively). Both contests in 1999 were exclusively local affairs. The Mile was dominated by the Godolphin trio **Lend A Hand**, **Muhtathir** and Cape Cross, who all won pattern races in Europe later in the year. The Sprint went to **Ramp And Rave** with the previous year's winner **Mudallel**, successful in his two races beforehand, a below-form sixth. With a million dollars on offer in the latter race, a stronger and more international field can be anticipated in 2000. A new event, the UAE Derby for three-year-olds on dirt, will be added to the card and looks a likely testing ground for Godolphin's Kentucky Derby hopefuls.

The majority of the leading performers in the UAE either began, or are taking a break from, their careers in Europe but the latest season threw up a notable exception in the form of six-year-old mare **Susu**. A 'home-grown' performer in the UAE, she improved considerably to win a seven-furlong listed event on turf at Abu Dhabi in January and developed into the joint highest-rated older filly/mare in Europe later in

Dubai Duty Free, Nad Al Sheba—a smart, front-running performance by Altibr

the season. The Maktoum Challenge series of listed races was dominated by Altibr and Spindrift, the latter winning two of the three rounds before Altibr evened things up in the Duty Free. Other smart performances were put up by **Sibling Rival**, who won a prestige race over a mile and a half at Nad Al Sheba, **Sabadilla**, who was fourth in the Dubai Turf Classic, and the ex-French **Makaruka**, who beat Sabadilla before finishing a place behind him in the Turf Classic. Over shorter trips, smart form was shown by both **Intidab**, who was second to Susu at Abu Dhabi and to Ramp And Rave in the Nad Al Sheba Sprint, and **Kahal**, third and seventh in the same races. Kahal won a seven-furlong conditions race at Nad Al Sheba by eight lengths in between, while Intidab beat subsequent Breeders' Cup Sprint winner Artax in a Grade 2 at Saratoga later in the year.

The performances reviewed here are those that took place in the calendar year 1999. Horses which were trained and raced in the UAE but showed significantly better form elsewhere are not included in the list below.

Older Horses			
126	*Almutawakel	115	*Sabadilla	107	Mashhaer
126	*Nedawi	113	Mudallel	107	*Mountain Song
124	*Lend A Hand	112	*Kahal	107	*Perfect Paradigm
123	*Central Park	111	Makaruka	107	*Song of Freedom
122	*Susu (f)	110	Snow Kid	107	Try Prospect
120	*Muhtathir	109	Get Away With It	106	Keltoi
117	*Altibr	109	*Rabi	106	Kumatour
117	*Sibling Rival	109	Swiss Law	106	*Misbah
116	Ramp And Rave	108	Speedfit Too	105	Bintang
116	*Spindrift	107	Abreeze	105	Designer
115	*Intidab	107	Casino Captive	105	Hattab
115	*Lord of Men	107	Cornish Snow	105	Pearl d'Azur
		107	Mackook	105	Persuasivo Fitz

NORTH AMERICA   In a year that generally lacked an outstanding performer trained in the USA, no clear leader emerged among the three-year-old males on dirt.

Charismatic, **Lemon Drop Kid** and **Cat Thief** all won higher-profile races but it was **General Challenge** who, in our opinion, had marginally the best form, at least when competing in California. Starting a coupled favourite for the Kentucky Derby after winning the Santa Anita Derby, General Challenge didn't get the best of runs at Churchill Downs, finishing in mid-field, but came back to put up two high-class performances in the summer. Firstly he went down by a head to Cat Thief (who received 2 lb) in the Swaps Stakes and then beat older horses in the Pacific Classic, but General Challenge never threatened when only tenth behind Cat Thief in the Breeders' Cup Classic. Those wins in the Swaps Stakes and Breeders' Cup Classic represented Cat Thief's best efforts in a long campaign which he withstood remarkably well. There were excuses for his defeat after the Breeders' Cup when he finished third over an inadequate seven furlongs to **Love That Red** in the Malibu Stakes in December, his twelfth race of the year, all but one of them in Grade 1 company.

Charismatic's season ended a lot sooner in dramatic circumstances but he'd done enough to clinch the Horse of The Year title in the view of the Eclipse award voters. An ex-claimer, he'd been the third colt in succession to win both the Kentucky Derby and the Preakness Stakes but, like Silver Charm and Real Quiet before him, failed in the final leg of the Triple Crown; he finished the Belmont Stakes in third with a fractured near-fore but, dismounted quickly after the line, was fortunately able to be saved for a stud career. The Belmont went instead to Lemon Drop Kid ahead of **Vision And Verse**, the same pair then filling the same places in the Travers Stakes, but neither cut much ice in the Breeders' Cup Classic, finishing sixth and ninth respectively. **Menifee**, who finished second in both the Kentucky Derby and the Preakness, also won two Grade 1 events—the Blue Grass Stakes in April and the Haskell Invitational in August—with the ever-present Cat Thief runner-up on both times. **Vicar** had shown very smart form with wins in the Fountain of Youth Stakes and the Florida Derby (narrowly beating **Wondertross**) but failed to sustain his form. Others who weren't far behind the best three-year-old males were **Badge** (third in the Preakness but then sidelined with an injury), **Prime Timber** (fourth in the Kentucky Derby), **Stephen Got Even** (third against older horses in the Woodward Stakes) and **Ecton Park** who upset stable-mate Menifee in the Super Derby before being another to disappoint in the Breeders' Cup Classic. **Forestry** was the best three-year-old over shorter trips, winning the seven-furlong King's Bishop Stakes before running fourth in the Breeders' Cup Sprint.

Breeders' Cup Classic, Gulfstream—blinkered Cat Thief pulls off a surprise

Whitney Handicap, Saratoga—two top-class performers,
Victory Gallop (nearer camera) just getting the better of Behrens

If the three-year-old colts' pecking order was a little confused, there was no mistaking **Silverbulletday** as the best three-year-old filly. Tremendously tough and consistent, she landed the odds in eight graded events, all against her own age and sex, including the Grade 1 Ashland Stakes, Kentucky Oaks, Alabama Stakes (which she won by nine lengths) and Gazelle Handicap. Her only defeats came when failing to stay against the colts in the Belmont Stakes and when taking on older fillies in the Beldame Stakes and Breeders' Cup Distaff at the end of a long campaign. Her stable-mate **Excellent Meeting** contested the two other legs of the Triple Crown against the colts, doing well to take fifth in the Kentucky Derby before being pulled up in the Preakness. Earlier, she'd won the Las Virgenes Stakes and the Santa Anita Oaks. The other leading fillies on dirt were **On A Soapbox**, successful in the CCA Oaks, **Dreams Gallore**, winner of the Mother Goose, and Acorn Stakes victress **Three Ring**, who was put down after an accident prior to the Mother Goose.

The best performance put up by a three-year-old on turf came from the ex-French colt **Super Quercus** in beating the formerly British-trained **Manndar** in the Early Times Hollywood Derby in November. Filly **Perfect Sting** won the Garden City Breeders' Cup Handicap and the Queen Elizabeth II Challenge Cup before getting a poor run when sixth in the Breeders' Cup Filly & Mare Turf. Two places ahead of her at Gulfstream was the ex-French filly **Caffe Latte**, who'd earlier finished second in the Yellow Ribbon. Santa Anita Oaks runner-up **Tout Charmant** proved as effective on turf as on dirt, winning the Del Mar Oaks before finishing second to Perfect Sting in the Queen Elizabeth II Cup.

Among the older horses on dirt it was a case of 'survival of the fittest'. Of the top performers, only **Behrens**, who had himself missed the second half of his four-year-old season, enjoyed anything like a full campaign as injury took its toll on

1190

Breeders' Cup Sprint, Gulfstream—Artax (No.5) holds off Kona Gold

most of his main rivals. He did, though, fail to make the most of the absentees when a below-form favourite in the Breeders' Cup Classic. Earlier on he'd completed a four-timer in the Gulfstream Park and Oaklawn Handicaps and the Grade 2 Massachusetts and Suburban Handicaps before going down by a nose to **Victory Gallop** in a thrilling Whitney Handicap. Already with the NTRA 'Champions on Fox' series wrapped up by this stage, Behrens' connections decided to miss the series' culminating race, the Pacific Classic (and a potential $230,000 bonus) in favour of a programme geared towards the Breeders' Cup. The Whitney proved to be Victory Gallop's final start, the colt having previously finished third in the Dubai World Cup and broken the track record in a Grade 2 at Churchill Downs. **Silver Charm** also contested those last two races, but bled badly in the first of them and was retired after the second one. He'd earlier finished third to the subsequently disappointing **Puerto Madero** in the Donn Handicap and to **Free House** (with **Event of The Year** second) in the Santa Anita Handicap. Best of the Americans in Dubai was World Cup runner-up **Malek**, who had also finished second beforehand to Silver Charm and Free House in Grade 2s early in the year. Malek went on to finish a good third to **Real Quiet** in the Hollywood Gold Cup but ran poorly when favourite for the Pacific Classic. Real Quiet also won the Pimlico Special Handicap (narrowly when in receipt of weight from Free House) and finished a good third to Behrens in the Massachusetts, but he too was injured after the Hollywood Gold Cup. **Mazel Trick** was a wide-margin winner of Grade 2 and 3 events at Hollywood and Del Mar (from **River Keen**) in the summer but injury prevented him from contesting a Grade 1 later on.

Of the older horses who did make it to the Breeders' Cup Classic, it was River Keen who arrived at Gulfstream in the best form. Formerly a useful all-weather handicapper in Britain, he made into a high-class horse in 1999, finishing second to General Challenge in the Pacific Classic before taking the Woodward Stakes from **Almutawakel** and the Jockey Club Gold Cup from Behrens. River Keen was another leading contender to disappoint in the Breeders' Cup Classic, however, and the places behind Cat Thief went instead to **Budroyale** and **Golden Missile**, who couldn't boast a Grade 1 between them. The tough and consistent Budroyale had earlier finished second in the Hollywood Gold Cup and beat General Challenge, when receiving weight from the three-year-old, in a Grade 2 at Santa Anita. One of Golden Missile's best previous efforts had come when third to **Running Stag** in a Grade 2 at Saratoga. British-trained Running Stag didn't have the Breeders' Cup on his agenda but ran his best races in the USA, winning another Grade 2 impressively at Belmont and finishing second to Behrens in the Massachusetts and fourth to River Keen in the Woodward.

It is rare for a sprinter to have strong claims to being Horse of The Year, but the lack of an outstanding performer over longer trips made Breeders' Cup Sprint winner **Artax** a live candidate, though his overall consistency was open to question. He'd broken long-standing track records in the Carter Handicap at Aqueduct and a Grade 2 at Belmont and had won the Vosburgh Stakes in between, before going on to equal Mr Prospector's track record at Gulfstream, beating **Kona Gold**. Artax was another on the injured list by the end of the year and has been retired. Two of the leading sprinters from the previous season, Breeders' Cup Sprint winner **Reraise** and **Kelly Kip**, both showed they retained their ability with Grade 3 wins in April at Oaklawn and Aqueduct respectively but injuries prevented either of them enjoying a full season.

Most of the leading older fillies on dirt made it to the Breeders' Cup Distaff and the race went largely to form, with front-running **Beautiful Pleasure** beating **Banshee Breeze, Heritage of Gold** and **Keeper Hill**. The consistent Banshee Breeze won the Apple Blossom Handicap and then beat Beautiful Pleasure in the Go For Wand Handicap but Beautiful Pleasure improved in the autumn, reversing places with Banshee Breeze in the Personal Ensign Handicap and then upsetting Silverbulletday in the Beldame before going on to Gulfstream. Distaff third Heritage of Gold enjoyed a successful season on both turf and dirt at Grade 2 level prior to the Breeders' Cup, while fourth-placed Keeper Hill had beaten an out-of-sorts Banshee Breeze in the Spinster Stakes. **Manistique** failed to give her running in the Distaff but had earlier won twice in Grade 1 company in California, the Santa Margarita Handicap and the Vanity Handicap, though neither race was strongly contested. **Catinca** didn't run in the Distaff but had shown very smart form when third to **Furlough** under top weight in the Ballerina Handicap and then beat that filly and Keeper Hill in the Ruffian Handicap.

Breeders' Cup Distaff, Gulfstream—Beautiful Pleasure wins her third Grade 1 race in a row

Breeders' Cup Mile, Gulfstream—Silic holds the late challenges of Tuzla (not on picture) and Docksider (left); Lend A Hand (rails) finishes fourth

Of the older horses on turf, **Buck's Boy** improved on his performance of winning the Breeders' Cup Turf twelve months earlier, despite having a shortened season. In a much stronger renewal he could finish only third to top-class rivals in **Daylami** and **Royal Anthem**, the latter making his US debut for trainer Bill Mott. The same stable's **Yagli**, second the year before, again finished a place behind Buck's Boy in fourth. That was easily Yagli's best effort in the second half of the year, but he'd enjoyed a good run earlier on, taking the Gulfstream Park Breeders' Cup Handicap, the Manhattan Handicap and the United Nations Handicap—only health regulations, criticised in some quarters as being overly stringent, prevented his participation in the King George at Ascot. Seven-year-old **Val's Prince** was another who'd contested the Breeders' Cup Turf before, but as at Belmont two years earlier he finished down the field on the back of a win in the Turf Classic. He'd also run out an easy winner of the Man o'War Stakes earlier in the autumn. Ex-Chilean **Mash One** made his reappearance in the Man o'War and then improved a good deal to win the Oak Tree Turf Championship from **Lazy Lode**. Neither contested the Breeders' Cup Turf but Lazy Lode went on to repeat his win of twelve months earlier in the Hollywood Turf Cup under Laffit Pincay, who six days later broke Bill Shoemaker's world record when riding the 8,834th winner of his career. Other notable performances over middle distances on turf came from Canada's Horse of The Year **Thornfield**, who was a surprise winner of the Canadian International from Fruits of Love and **Courteous**, and **River Bay**, who took the Charlie Whittingham Handicap, a race renamed in honour of the veteran Hall of Fame trainer who died in 1999.

There wasn't a great deal of strength in depth among the older milers, though **Silic** and the mare **Tuzla** both managed to hold off a numerically-strong European challenge for the Breeders' Cup Mile, of which **Docksider** and **Lend A Hand** fared best to fill the frame. That represented improvement from Silic's fifth place in a tight finish to the Atto Mile at Woodbine in which **Hawksley Hill** (fifth at Gulfstream) had passed the post first ahead of **Quiet Resolve** (last in the Breeders' Cup Mile), **Rob 'n Gin** and French-trained **Jim And Tonic**. The last-named, who didn't get the best of runs at Gulfstream either, was hit in the face by Hawksley Hill's rider's whip, causing that horse to be demoted to fourth. Hawksley Hill had an unlucky season, among several narrow defeats being his third place behind **Wild Event** in the Early Times Turf Classic in the spring.

Breeders' Cup Mile runner-up Tuzla was one of the leading older females on turf, though she met a slightly better one afterwards when beaten a neck by the ex-New Zealand filly **Happyanunoit** in the strongly-run Matriarch Stakes. Earlier in the autumn Tuzla had narrowly beaten Happyanunoit and future Yellow Ribbon Stakes winner **Spanish Fern** in the Ramona Handicap giving both weight. The inaugural Breeders' Cup Filly & Mare Turf over eleven furlongs (future runnings will be over ten) was won by **Soaring Softly** from **Coretta**, the same pair having earlier dominated the Flower Bowl Handicap as well. **Tranquility Lake** wasn't at her best in the autumn and didn't contest the Breeders' Cup but had shown very smart form in the summer, winning the Gamely Handicap and finishing second under top weight to the Brazilian Oaks winner **Virginie** in the Beverley Hills Handicap. The previous year's champion turf filly Fiji made a belated return after several set-backs and was well below her best, while Mossflower was another mare who failed to find her form after a lengthy absence.

Both two-year-old events at the Breeders' Cup went to outsiders. **Anees** came from well off the pace to beat the placed horses from the Champagne Stakes, **Chief Seattle** and **High Yield**, in the Breeders' Cup Juvenile and win by two and a half lengths. Chief Seattle was subsequently bought by Godolphin for a US-based campaign. **Greenwood Lake** won by the same margin in similar style from that pair in the Champagne Stakes but missed the Breeders' Cup in favour of the Grade 2 Remsen Stakes, which he won by a head giving the runner-up 9 lb. Greenwood Lake had first come to prominence in the Futurity Stakes at Belmont in September when splitting **Bevo** and the hitherto unbeaten **More Than Ready**, neither of whom ran in the Breeders' Cup. **Captain Steve** improved after finishing eleventh in the latter race, and was an impressive winner of the Hollywood Futurity from High Yield. With none of the leading colts holding outstanding claims in the classics, some less-exposed types may well have come through by the spring, one of the most promising being War Chant (by Danzig out of Breeders' Cup Distaff winner Hollywood Wildcat), who could not have been more impressive in winning a six-furlong maiden at Hollywood on his debut.

Breeders' Cup Juvenile Fillies winner **Cash Run** made virtually all to beat favourite **Chilukki** at Gulfstream but was subsequently beaten at odds on in a Grade 3. However, the best three-year-old prospect from the Juvenile Fillies is third-placed **Surfside**. Out of the champion juvenile filly Flanders, Surfside had earlier beaten **Darling My Darling** in the Frizette Stakes and after the Breeders' Cup (where she wasn't well drawn against speedier rivals) went on to win the Hollywood Starlet Stakes impressively by seven lengths, prompting her trainer to plan a campaign against

Breeders' Cup Filly & Mare Turf, Gulfstream—Soaring Softly is a narrow winner of this new race; Zomaradah (No.6) and the unlucky-in-running Borgia (No.8) do best of the European challengers

the colts in the spring, including the Kentucky Derby. Chilukki, outstayed by Cash Run in the Breeders' Cup, had an unbeaten record previously, having won the Del Mar Debutante Stakes from Juveniles Fillies fourth **Spain** and the Oak Leaf Stakes from **Abby Girl**.

European-trained horses who showed or reproduced their best form in North America are included in this list

† commentary in *Racehorses of 1999*

Two-Year-Olds
120	Anees
119	Bevo
119	Cash Run (f)
119	Greenwood Lake
119	Surfside (f)
118	Chilukki (f)
117	More Than Ready
116	Captain Steve
116	Abby Girl (f)
116	Chief Seattle
115	Darling My Darling (f)
115	Dixie Union
115	High Yield
115	Spain (f)
114	Forest Camp
113	Finders Fee (f)
113	Jostle (f)
113	Mass Market
112	Classic Olympio (f)
112	†Mull of Kintyre
111	Exchange Rate
111	Magicalmysterycat (f)
110	Circle of Life (f)
110	Dance Master
110	Humble Clerk (f)
110	Purely Cozzene
110	Scratch Pad (f)
110	Shawnee Country (f)
109	Crown of Crimson (f)
109	Kiss A Native
109	Scottish Halo
109	Talk Back (f)

DIRT

Three-Year-Olds
128	General Challenge
127	Charismatic
127	Silverbulletday (f)
126	Cat Thief
126	Lemon Drop Kid
125	Vision And Verse
124	Badge
124	Ecton Park
124	Menifee
123	Stephen Got Even
121	Forestry
120	Prime Timber

120	Vicar
120	Wondertross
119	Excellent Meeting (f)
119	Kimberlite Pipe
119	On A Soapbox (f)
119	Stellar Brush
118	Adonis
118	Best of Luck
118	Dreams Gallore (f)
118	Successful Appeal
117	Exploit
117	Love That Red
117	Pineaff
117	Three Ring (f)
117	Worldly Manner
116	Belle Cherie (f)
116	Better Than Honour (f)
116	Certain
116	Desert Hero
116	K One King
116	Marley Vale (f)
116	Positive Gal (f)
116	Smart Guy
116	Temperence Time
116	Yes It's True
115	Cape Canaveral
115	First American
115	Five Star Day
115	Forty One Carats
115	Madison's Charm (f)
115	Straight Man
115	Woodcarver

Older Horses
130	Behrens
130	Victory Gallop
129	Free House
128	Beautiful Pleasure (f)
128	Silver Charm
127	Real Quiet
127	River Keen
126	†Almutawakel
126	Artax
126	Puerto Madero
125	Banshee Breeze (f)
125	Event of The Year
125	Kona Gold
125	Reraise
124	Budroyale
124	Malek
124	Mazel Trick
124	†Running Stag
123	Golden Missile
123	Manistique (f)
123	Catinca (f)
122	Heritage of Gold (f)
122	Old Trieste

121	Affirmed Success
121	Crafty Friend
121	Keeper Hill (f)
120	Archers Bay
120	Kelly Kip
120	Precocity
120	Sir Bear
119	Barter Town
119	Big Jag
119	Bourbon Belle (f)
119	†Chester House
119	Classic Cat
119	Sister Act (f)
119	Stop Traffic (f)
118	Brush With Pride
118	Christmas Boy
118	Furlough (f)
118	Lexicon
118	Magical Allure (f)
117	†Dr Fong
117	Early Warning
117	Good And Tough
117	Gourmet Girl (f)
117	Wild Wonder
116	A Lady From Dixie (f)
116	Dramatic Gold
116	Frisk Me Now
116	Hurricane Bertie (f)
116	India Divina (f)
116	Littlebitlively
116	Mike K
116	Mountain Top
116	Regal Thunder
116	Stormin Fever
116	Victory Stripes (f)
115	Belle's Flag (f)
115	Catienus
115	Dancing Guy
115	Dixie Dot Com
115	Enjoy The Moment (f)
115	Fred Bear Claw
115	Intidab
115	Roza Robata (f)
115	Son of A Pistol
115	Testafly
115	Your Halo

TURF

Three-Year-Olds
120	Super Quercus
119	†Bienamado
119	Mula Gula
119	Perfect Sting (f)
118	†Caffe Latte (f)
118	Tout Charmant (f)
117	Swamp
116	Eagleton

116	Nani Rose (f)	122	Rob 'n Gin	117	Plickk
116	Sweet Ludy (f)	121	Lazy Lode	117	Que Belle (f)
116	†Val Royal	121	Quiet Resolve	117	†Sayarshan
115	†Manndar	121	River Bay	117	See You Soon (f)
115	Marquette	121	Tuzla (f)	117	Virginie (f)
115	Smooth Player (f)	120	†Borgia (f)	116	Brave Act
		120	†Courteous	116	Garbu
Older Horses		120	Soaring Softly (f)	116	Ladies Din
138	†Daylami	120	Tranquility Lake (f)	116	Sonja's Faith (f)
135	†Royal Anthem	120	Wild Event	116	Soviet Line
128	Buck's Boy	119	Bonapartiste	115	Alvo Certo
126	Val's Prince	119	Fahris	115	Anguilla (f)
125	Mash One	119	Honor Glide	115	Bouccaneer
125	Silic	119	†Public Purse	115	Cetewayo
125	Yagli	119	Tanaasa	115	Comic Strip
124	†Docksider	118	Coretta (f)	115	†Insight (f)
124	†Jim And Tonic	118	Kirkwall	115	Isle de France (f)
124	†Lend A Hand	118	Majorien	115	Kessem Power
123	Hawksley Hill	118	Single Empire	115	Middlesex Drive
123	Thornfield	118	Spanish Fern (f)	115	Parade Ground
122	†Dream Well	118	†Zomaradah	115	Poteen
122	Happyanunoit (f)	117	Delay of Game	115	Sapphire Ring (f)

JAPAN   Japanese racing continues to open up on two fronts, internationally and domestically. Group 1 victories in France in 1998 by Seeking The Pearl and Taiki Shuttle showed that Japanese horses could compete successfully at the top level in Europe and further wins for **El Condor Pasa** and **Agnes World** in France in the latest season proved that was no flash in the pan. At home, the Japanese Racing Association announced that the number of races to be opened up to international competition in 2000 would be raised to fourteen (plus a valuable steeplechase), half of them Group 1 contests, including a new event over ten and a half furlongs on dirt on the eve of the Japan Cup to be known as the Japan Cup Dirt. In the longer term, a total of 24 races will be opened to foreign-trained horses by 2004, while foreign-bred horses will be eligible to contest the classics (as long as they have not run outside Japan), beginning with the Derby and St Leger in 2001.

With El Condor Pasa campaigned exclusively in France, the top middle-distance performers in Japan in 1999 were **Grass Wonder** and **Special Week**. Runner-up to El Condor Pasa in the 1998 Japan Cup, Special Week went one better to defeat Hong Kong-based Indigenous, Godolphin's High-Rise and Montjeu in the latest renewal. He also won both Tenno Sho races, the two-mile Spring event (from **Mejiro Bright** and **Seiun Sky**) and the ten-furlong Autumn contest (from **Stay Gold**). Grass Wonder didn't contest the Japan Cup but he'd have been an interesting contender because he

Japan Cup, Tokyo—Special Week keeps the prize at home;
Hong Kong-trained Indigenous (second right) is an excellent second,
with High-Rise and Montjeu (outside) third and fourth

beat Special Week in two Group 1 events, the eleven-furlong Takaruzuka Kinen (with Stay Gold third) and the Arima Kinen (for the second time) over an extended twelve furlongs. Grass Wonder was no slouch over shorter trips either, beating top miler **Air Jihad** in the Group 2 Keio Hai Spring Cup over seven furlongs in May and then finishing runner-up to the same rival in the Yasuda Kinen. Air Jihad's other Group 1 win came in the Mile Championship. Third in that race was **Black Hawk**, who later took the Sprinters Stakes from Agnes World. Following his Prix de l'Abbaye win, Agnes World won a Group 2 event from **Masa Lucky**, who in the spring had won another top sprint, the Takamatsunomiya Kinen, from Seeking The Pearl, the last-named not in the same form as the previous year. The top three-year-olds all met in the Derby, in which **Admire Vega** beat 2000 Guineas winner **T M Opera O** and St Leger winner **Narita Top Road**; none contested the Japan Cup, though T M Opera O subsequently showed the best form of the three when an excellent third in the Arima Kinen. Top three-year-old filly was the 1000 Guineas winner **Primo Ordine**.

El Condor Pasa and Special Week have both been retired to stud, but Grass Wonder, the winner of nine of his twelve starts in Japan, is reportedly to be aimed at the Prix de l'Arc de Triomphe in 2000, while Agnes World could contest the July Cup.

Three-year-olds					
124	T M Opera O	115	Stinger (f)	120	Agnes World
121	Admire Vega			119	King Halo
120	Narita Top Road	**Older Horses**		118	Silk Justice
119	Rascal Suzuka	136	*El Condor Pasa	117	Embrasser Moi
118	Painted Black	126	Grass Wonder	117	Going Suzuka
117	Primo Ordine (f)	125	Special Week	116	Masa Lucky
117	Tayasu Tamotsu	123	Air Jihad	115	Hokkai Rousseau
116	Mejiro Ronzan	121	Black Hawk	115	Matikanefukukitaru
116	Symboli Indy	121	Mejiro Bright	115	Meiner Love
116	To The Victory (f)	121	Seiun Sky	115	Midnight Bet
116	Umeno Fiber (f)	121	Stay Gold	115	Tsukuba Symphony
		121	Tsurumaru Tsuyoshi		

HONG KONG   Five horses trained in Hong Kong were given ratings in the International Classifications, one more than in 1998 when Johan Cruyff was surprisingly awarded champion status ahead of Indigenous. There could be little doubting that **Indigenous** was the best horse in Hong Kong in 1999, even if the 4 lb he was rated clear of **Resfa**, **Johan Cruyff** and the sprinter **Fairy King Prawn** in the International Classifications rather overstates his superiority. Indigenous won only one of his 6 races in Hong Kong, the Hong Kong Gold Cup in March in which he got the better of Johan Cruyff, but he often faced tough international opposition and ran at least as well in defeat behind Jim And Tonic in the Queen Elizabeth II Cup (with Johan Cruyff behind again) in April and Borgia in the Hong Kong Vase, a race he won in 1998, in December. Indigenous also ran outside Hong Kong in two races which comprised part of the Emirates World Series, running creditably when sixth to

Hong Kong Cup, Sha Tin—a third big win in Hong Kong for French-trained Jim And Tonic; Running Stag comes second

Hong Kong Sprint, Sha Tin—a welcome addition to the international circuit for the sprinters; Fairy King Prawn and Crystal Charm hold a strong overseas challenge

Daylami in the King George VI and Queen Elizabeth Diamond Stakes at Ascot in July after his domestic season had finished, then putting up the best performance of his career to finish second to Special Week in the Japan Cup at Tokyo in November.

Entitled to be rated only just inferior to Indigenous is the former South African Derby winner Resfa, who finished third to Docksider in the Hong Kong Mile. Resfa had looked a good prospect early in the year, winning the Classic Trial, but disappointed in the Derby and took a long time to rediscover his form. Johan Cruyff is still a force to be reckoned with but hasn't won since he took the Derby in 1998, the pick of his placed efforts coming in the Gold Cup and the Queen Elizabeth II Cup. He showed signs of deterioration late in the year, as did **Oriental Express**, whose only victory in 1999 came at the expense of a below-par Indigenous in the Champions & Chater Cup in May. Johan Cruyff and Oriental Express looked the pick of the home defence for the upgraded Group 1 Hong Kong Cup, but neither made any impact as overseas-trained horses filled the first four places. The ex-Michael Bell trained **Housemaster** (rated 119 on his form in Britain) burst onto the local scene late in the year and seems sure to take all the beating in the 2000 Hong Kong Derby judged on his fifth place behind Docksider in the Mile. The 1999 Derby winner Holy Grail proved very disappointing later in the year, but the Derby third **Billion Win** subsequently turned in one of the best performances of the year when third in the Gold Cup.

In the less competitive sprinting division, Fairy King Prawn could fairly be regarded as the best in Hong Kong even before he won the inaugural Hong Kong Sprint in December from the ex-English **Crystal Charm**, who was improving in leaps and bounds at the end of the year. Fairy King Prawn won two other races in 1999, notably the Group 1 Chairman's Prize in May. **Best of The Best** made the expected improvement and beat Fairy King Prawn in a valuable handicap in the warm-up for the Sprint, but hasn't yet repeated that form in open competition.

122	†Indigenous	116	Oriental Express	112	Crystal Charm
121	Resfa	115	Best of The Best	111	Hunting Lad
118	Fairy King Prawn	115	Billion Win		
118	Johan Cruyff	115	†Housemaster		

AUSTRALIA AND NEW ZEALAND   With Might And Power side-lined for the entire calendar year, there was a host of contenders for the title of Australasia's best

BMW Cox Plate, Moonee Valley—the Australasian leg of the Emirates World Series is won by New Zealand mare Sunline

thoroughbred, with only a pound between the top five performers, the highest rated of which was the three-year-old colt **Testa Rossa**. In the first of several memorable clashes between the two top colts, Testa Rossa went under to **Redoute's Choice** in the Blue Diamond (towards the end of an arduous two-year-old season), but had been under an injury cloud after pulling up with a sore back on his previous outing.

Redoute's Choice (who had made his debut only seven days prior to the Blue Diamond) was a hot favourite for the Golden Slipper, only to be withdrawn on race day when he came down with a severe bout of travel sickness. Fortunately, both colts returned in sparkling form later in the year, Testa Rossa recording the season's best performance when he won the VicHealth Cup, and Redoute's Choice rallying late after being clearly headed to catch Testa Rossa near the line in the Caulfield Guineas. Both contested the Cox Plate over an extended ten furlongs, and given how they'd shaped at Caulfield, it was a surprise that Redoute's Choice weakened over the longer trip whilst Testa Rossa stayed on gamely from the rear to finish on the heels of the placed horses.

Other three-year-olds to impress were the filly **Pharein**, who beat the older horses at Flemington on Derby day (and followed up five days later), and **Shogun Lodge**, who lost an objection against **Blackfriars** in the Victoria Derby. Queensland-trained sprinter **Falvelon** is now undefeated in seven appearances and it seems that he has not yet been pushed to his limit. The Golden Slipper winner **Catbird** was a flop when he resumed in the spring.

Sky Heights fulfilled the promise he had shown the previous year by taking the Rosehill Guineas and AJC Derby in the first part of the year and his name was always

Foster's Melbourne Cup, Flemington—the blinkered Rogan Josh catches long-time leader Central Park

at the top of the ante-post markets for the big Cup races later on. He landed the major prize at Caulfield (only by a whisker after a fine Damien Oliver ride) and was a creditable third in the Cox Plate before being severely buffeted in the Melbourne Cup and finishing in the ruck. His main adversary was **Dignity Dancer**, who clinched a substantial bonus payment with four straight wins in Melbourne but didn't repeat the form when he returned, perhaps feeling the effects of his earlier exploits.

The high-class, front-running mare **Sunline** was undeniably the leading female. She left her rivals standing when a heavily-backed favourite in the Doncaster, and, although inclined to race too freely on occasions, she performed well when it counted, controlling the pace and then dashing clear in the Cox Plate. She went on to Hong Kong for the Cup but (like so many of the Australasian representatives in recent years) failed to run up to her true form.

Of the older horses **Tie The Knot** was again to the fore, winning three times at Group 1 level, including his second successive Sydney Cup (by five lengths), and, even though he ran on strongly for second in the Cox Plate, he once again finished his Melbourne campaign on a disappointing note when failing dismally in the Melbourne Cup after a lacklustre effort in his final warm-up. **Intergaze** took his Group 1 tally to a remarkable seven wins with three more victories in 1999, upsetting Sky Heights and Sunline in the Queen Elizabeth, though he too trained off in Melbourne after a promising build-up.

The top mare **Bonanova** was sold to prominent administrator and breeder Jim Fleming for $1 million and added to her already considerable value as a broodmare with victory in the Emirates Stakes (with her trademark barnstorming finish), while master trainer Bart Cummings made it an incredible eleven Melbourne Cups with former West Australian horse **Rogan Josh**, whom he transformed from a modest performer into a smart stayer.

There were no real stars among the early-season juveniles, although Danehill filly **Tennessee Midnight** was an impressive debut winner on Oaks day, finishing strongly to win drawing away.

Ratings and text for
Australia and New
Zealand are supplied
courtesy of Larry Young
(AAP Class Racehorses).
More information is
available on the internet
(www.aapracing.com.au).
The ages listed below are
as at 31st December 1999.

Two-Year-Olds
117p Tennessee Midnight (f)
116   King of Danes
115   Happy Giggle
115   Jestarella Boy
115   Little Miss Marnie (f)
115   Phoenix Park
115   Sound The Alarm

Three-Year-Olds
126   Testa Rossa
125   Redoute's Choice
123   Pharein (f)
121   Shogun Lodge
120   Blackfriars
120   Easy Rocking
120d Align
119p Over
119   Diatribe
119d Catbird
119d Charm Scene Land
118   Danglissa (f)
118   My Sienna (f)
118d Fappiano's Son
117p Falvelon
117   Dangerous
117   Fairway
117   Katima (f)
117   Majestically
117   One Under (f)
117   Quorum
117   Real Jester
116   Buzz Lightyear
116   Catamarca (f)
116   Freemason
116   Shalt Not (f)
116d Martree
115   Commands
115   Cullen

115   High Grove (f)
115   Northeast Sheila (f)
115   Oamaru Rhythm
115   Pins
115   Quick Star
115   Shizu (f)
115   Spargo
115   Stella Artois (f)
115d Countess Christie (f)

Four-Year-Olds
125   Sky Heights
125   Sunline (f)
122d Dignity Dancer
121   Isca (f)
120   Mossman
119   Mr Innocent
118   Cent Home
118   Danske
118   Grand Archway (f)
118   Laurie's Lottery
118   Lease
117   Arena
117   Dracula
117   Inaflury (f)
117   Lawyer
117   Theatre
117   Wynciti (f)
116   Black Bean
116   Glamouremus
116   Le Zagaletta
116   Nina Haraka (f)
116   Rose O' War (f)
116   So Casual
116d Shinkansea
115   Allez Suez
115   Bomber Bill
115   Jivago
115   Kenworth
115d Paris Dream

Older Horses
125   Tie The Knot
122   Intergaze
120   Adam
120   Istidaad
120   Referral
119   Bonanova (f)
119   Hero
119   Juggler

119   Magic Music (f)
119   Umrum
118   Catalan Opening
118   Chief De Beers
118   Cronus
118   Dantelah (f)
118   General Nediym
118   Kidman's Cove
118   Northern Drake
118   Paint
118   Rogan Josh
118   Toledo
117   Ab Initio
117   Appoint
117   Banner Headline
117   Bezeal Bay
117   Notoire
117   Rebel
117   Rustic Dream
117   St. Chrisoph
117   Yippyio
117d Thackeray
117d Zuccherino
116   Al Mansour
116   Brave Chief
116   Centre Crest
116   Flavour
116   Integrate (f)
116   Iron Horse
116   Loafer
116   Oliver Twist
116   Return To Go
116   Sir Boom
116   Streak
116   Surface
116   The Hind
116   Vitrinite
116   Zerpour
115   All In Fun
115   Darazari
115   Flak Jacket
115   Guineas
115   Hot As Hell
115   Il Don
115   Joss Sticks
115   Oregon Power
115   Pasta Express
115   Summer Beau

THE 1999 TIMEFORM IRISH HANDICAP

† indicates horse with commentary or essay in *Racehorses of 1999*

Two-Year-Olds

68	Abbeyspring
63	Acorn Blues
81	Additive
89	Adelphi Theatre
–	Adisadel
61p	Adiysha
100p	Admiral's Cup†
76p	Aguinaga
89	Air of Approval
–	Albinona
93p	Albuquerque
–	Alexander Eliott
53	Algarve Sunset
–	Allinthegardenrosy
90	Alluring
?	Alpha Heights†
–	Alvaro
56	Amalita
102+	Amethyst†
61	Amialone
51	An Churach
–	Anns Gamble
103p	Anzari
92p	Apollo Victoria
91	Appalachia
66	Aquanita
70	Archimedes
95	Aretha†
115p	Aristotle†
67	Armenia†
96	Asanovo†
74	Attalicus
–p	Avalanche
84p	Awesome Strike
103p	Bach†
–	Baku
69	Ballyhurry
99	Bally Pride†
54	Banrion
106	Barrier Reef†
65	Barr Na Sraide
100	Bashkir
69?	Basin Street Blues
86	Bayadira
–	Bayruz
87	Beaver Lodge
52	Bellagino
92	Bells Are Ringing
–	Benelli
92	Benovia
74	Bens Secret
94	Berenica
60?	Berige
48	Berkeley Bay
114	Bernstein†
80	Be Seeing You
55	Black Buzz
64p	Blue Satin
–	Blustery
54	Bodakker

114	Brahms†
86p	Brampton
56	Breathonme
71	Bridgeofsighs
111p	Broche†
94	Buffalo Berry
49	Butterfly Morning
62	Buzz Two
–	Byproxy
64	Cakestown Lady
49	Calithea
82	Canadian Girl
67	Captain Lindbergh
63	Carmels Gift
–	Carnickian
56	Carrig Prince
85	Castanetta
–	Castlehannon
33	Castlehaven
98	Castleshane
58p	Casuarina
77	Catz
75p	Caumshinaun
–	Ceo Draiochta
–	Cepangie
–	Chapeau Claque
68	Chateau Lina
98p	Chiang Mai†
53	Christys Pet
110p	Ciro†
74p	Class Charmer
78	Clewbay Charm
66	Cluzot
–	Coach Gent
90p	Cois Cuain
–	Coljac
71	Colourful Cast
75	Colouring
–p	Columbus
89p	Commanche Saddle
95	Conormara
–	Consalvo
91	Contact
63	Contradiction
75	Copper Express
–	Corban
68	Corrib Lady
56	Cosi Island
62	Cotton Grace
53	Crack Dancer†
75p	Creidim
65p	Crest of A Wave
66	Crocus
77	Crusoe
71	Cuigiu†
69p	Cutting The Edge
58p	Dadrala
92	Dance of Love
78	Darbys Bridge
75p	Dark Veil
84	Dashing D

76d	Davide d'Donatello
–	Deemeh
–p	Degree of Charm
70	Desert Anthem
79	Desert Eclipse
65	Desert Safari†
97	Desert Sky
–	Destiny Calling
95p	Determination
61	Diaz
–	Diniesque
86p	Dippers
82	Discreet Option
68	Distinguished Cove
59	Dockside
68	Doctor Manette
76	Dowdstown Guest
47	Dunbrody River
84p	Dunedin Rascal
68	During Lent
99p	Earlene
69	Echo Island
73+	Endymion†
58	Environment
61	Equanimity
76	Essex Street
84	Estival Park
52	Euro Friendly
102	Eurolink Raindance†
79	Evrobi
88	Ezra
95	Fairy Gem†
76	Faithfulbond
120	Fasliyev†
–	Fast Responce
–	February Mountain
51	Fencethegap
66p	Festina Famosa
78	Final Exam
–	Final Image
52	Fine And Allright
94	Finnan
61	First Draw
101p	Fisherman's Creek
66	Flagship Queen
59	Flamme
–	Flushing Flyer
69	Flying Bean†
70	Flying Boat
88	Foe†
65	Forbidden Pleasure
–	Fourstars Lady
59p	Foxtrot
–	Francies Fancy
80	Fureur France
60	Galilee
100	Galloway Boy†
88	Garcia Marquez
84	Gateway
81	Gazelle

61+	Geraldo
119p	Giant's Causeway†
88p	Gifts Galore
–	Ginger Lily
97	Ginola's Magic†
–	Gloating
64	Goldance
76?	Goldenhalo
47	Golden Pamela
67	Golden Spice
83	Golden Storm
–	Golden Times
69	Goldnblues
61	Goldridge
86	Goldstreet
82p	Grand Finale
77	Great Guns
–	Grecian Myth
–	Greco
70	Greengage
84	Gregorian
63?	Guignol
77	Gute
66	Haakool
106	Halland Park Girl†
62	Handsome Anna
79	Harryana†
82	Harry's Game
–	Harvard Wink
65	Headfort Rose
72	Heated Debate
104	Heathyardsblessing†
53p	Heiress
55p	Helenenberg
98	Heritage Hall
–	Hidden Smile
59	Hill Dissident
72	Hill Port
76	Hill Style
84	Holy Orders
99p	Homer
80	Huangdi
–	Imminent
92	Imperialist†
90	Imperial Light
74d	In A Twinkling†
67p	Inchape Rock
84	Indian Desert
80?	Inforapenny
104P	Inkling†
76p	Insenor
86p	Invoque
62	Irish Blessing
–	Irish Voice
49	Ishkasullus
–	Italian Counsel
89	It Happens Now
73	Jalindi
80	Jamieson
102p	Jammaal
69	Janefer John†
75	Jefferson County
71	Jimmy Spot On
81	Jimmy Two Stroke
61?	Jordans Pride
73	Julius

64	Just On The Market
–	Kaftan
–	Kate Lauren
50	Kates Son
86?	Kebabs
–	Kelly's Isle
57	Keltech Swings
81p	Kerry Isle
–	Khairambar
–	Killadoon
88+	King of Connaught
69p	King of Ireland
80	King of Russia
87p	King Street
–	Knock Na Garm Lad
64?	Kudrow
–	La Casa
64p	Ladies View
64§	Lady of Windsor†
90	Lady Upstage†
–	La Eile
–	Lake Innisfree
–	Lake Nyasa
76	Lake Victoria
76p	Lammas
50p	Lar Na Tire
88	La Rosetta
66	La Shalak
60	Lashing Night
?	Late Night Lady†
–p	Lavadores
90p	Legal Jousting
112p	Lermontov†
78	Lets Try Again
82	Lindissima
65?	Lions Den
–	Listen N Learn
103	Littlefeather†
–	Little Surprise
61p	Lorenzino
57p	L'Otage
47	Lovejoy Pet
77	Love Lane†
33	Lucky Fourstars
64	Lys Treasure
63	Macintosh Man
83?	Mac River
–	Maddelina
55	Magical Mick
78p	Majariyya
–	Majestic Wind
95	Mandama
86p	Manhattan
–	Marabeesh
90	Margay
–	Marianella
74	Mary's Joy
–	Masnada
–	Masters of War
79	Maura's Choice
42	Maura's Pet
76p	McDab
87p	Media Puzzle
65	Menchyte
93p	Mercaldo
56	Messrs Maguire

–	Michigann
57	Millennium Peach
72	Minnie Kc
78	Mint Leaf
52	Miskilette
75	Miss Bidder
77	Miss Catwalk
–	Miss Evereddy
63	Miss Pavlova
64	Miss Singer
83d	Misty Peak
–	Mitigate
73	Mitsubishi Trium
–	M N L Duchess
59	M N L Queen
–p	Momento
111p	Monashee Mountain†
50	Montana Lady
54	Montecastillo
69	Montpelier Street
88p	Moon God
56?	Moonridge†
–	Mostovio
–	Moyne Motors
79	Mr Roche T
112	Mull of Kintyre†
104?	Murawwi
61	Murrayfield
–p	Mutahamis
–	My Little Vixen
85	Mythical Nature
85p	Mythological
78	Neutron
83	Newpark Lady
55	Newtown Breeze
52	Newtown Girl
–	Night Brook
65	Noble Frontier
–	Noridge
39	Northern Mill
–p	No Tippling
–	Nyliram
60	Octagonal
–	Okie Dokie
84	On The Batter
63	On Your Marks
55	Orchestral Strings
92	Ostrovsky
89	Our Ambition†
–	Ourbus
73	Owen Roe
74	Pardoned
72p	Patruel
64	Pavla
70	Paws
71	Peak Viewing
58	Pearl Lady
65?	Periwinkle Lad
77	Persian King
–	Peruvian Athlete
88	Peruvian Chief†
65?	Phil's Lady
62p	Pile
74p	Pine Dance
92	Pissaro†
–	Pittsburgh Phil

–	Planet Clare
92p	Plato
87	Plurabelle
100	Poco A Poco
62	Polish Baron
100	Polish Panache
79	Portland†
–	Port Lush
83	Potentille
72	Power Bubble
110p	Preseli†
72+	Prince Among Men†
91p	Promising Lady
–	Purty Dancer
90	Quality Team
68	Rachael's Delight
81	Rainbow Melody†
91	Rainbow Style
92p	Raypour
–	Real Magic
52	Reba
–p	Red Blooded
80	Regal Ash
–	Release Me
61	Reptar
92	Reve de Nuit
85	Reve Russe
–	Ringside View
86	River Sounds
–p	Rody
97p	Romanylei
118	Rossini†
109	Royal Kingdom†
–	Royal Suzy
63	Rozina
–	Run To Jane
52	Sabindy
60	Saintly Sow'n'sow
61	Salab
48	Sally-Ann†
69	Sammagefromtenesse
91	Sand Partridge
–	Sandymount Alice
71p	Sarissa
–	Scopeful
58	Sea Hymn
68	Serpico
99p	Shakespeare†
101	Sharp Focus
84	Shibl
83p	Shoal Creek
77	Silence Beauty
–	Silver Spray
105p	Sinndar†
70	Slaneyside
70?	Slippy Helen
69	Slip Sliding
66	Snowy Owl
76	Social Contract†
57	Society Friend
–	Sockittothem
–	Softly Softly
–	Somegirlsdo
93	Somerset
67	Somesession
95	Soorah

87p	Soviet Blues
56	Spanish Dancer
–	Spoken Word
48	Sportin' Guess
76	Star of Windsor
62p	Stay Cool
89p	Still As Sweet
98	Still Going On
59p	Stonehenge
88	Storm Dream
–	Stormy Frontier
85	Strauss
54	Stubbles
86p	Sugar Baby
82	Summer Break
–	Superblest
43	Supra Star
66	Tammany Hall
95	Tara's Girl†
88	Tarwila
64	Tate Tirol
74	Teach Beaumont
71?	Technocat
99p	Tender Offer
–	Tern
96	Thady Quill†
61	Theatro Danielli
77	The Dark Flasher
–	Theemole
73d	The Gaidd
100p	Theoretically
–	Thepointaboutitis
–	The Rook
104	The Tatling†
–	Three Magpies
66p	Three Wishes
67?	Throw The Deuce
73p	Tobaranama
84p	Topsy Morning
109	Torgau†
90	Touch of Innocence
62	Trimaclana
102	Trinculo†
–	Tristar Lass
67	Trolti
68?	Tropical King
73	Truffle Island
68p	Turn Turtle
–	Turtlena
73	Tushna
–	Twokay
47	Tyrrellspass
96p	Van Dantzig†
86	Via Rodeo
–	Victory Flight
70?	Vida
79p	Viscaria
48	Volpina
79p	Wagner
58	Wanalta
103+	Warrior Queen†
–	Watership Down
79	Waterwing
–	Weownthisonetoo
–	Western Gold
69	White Lavender

94	Windsor Boy†
–	Wisecrack
56	Wonder Bell
67	Xcaret†
95	Yara
–	Yip Jap Stan
57p	Your The Lady
?	Zabarjad
62	Zarasponda
69	Zawoyski
62	Zedekiah
109	Zentsov Street†
60	Zuleika

Three-Year-Olds

75p	Abaiypour
69	Abracadabra
67	Acafan
110	Access All Areas
77	Adari
68d	Adornment†
83	Aeraiocht
–	African Isle
31	African Scene
77	Afsana
70	Aine's Choice
106	Akbar†
48	Akebono
–	Albarakat
62	Alexander Confranc
–	Alexfield
91d	All To Easy
68	Alumna
62	Amberleigh Rainbow
64	Amelesa
67	Amellia
95	American Tabloid
–	Anamara
68	Angelica Tree
59	An Lu Abu†
75	Anna Elise
94	Annieirwin
64	Annunciata
–	Another Justice
94	Ansar
95	Anthem of Love
111	Antinnaz†
73	Apollo Bay
101	Apparatchik
–	Arabian Phoenix
102	Artistic Blue
–	Ash Road
–	Ask Early
92p	Aspen Leaves
73	Aspiration
71	At His Best
–	Athlumney Lady
61	Auntieellensengine
–	Back In Twenty
–	Back On Schedule
–	Back To Bolgers
58	Badiah
85p	Balakar
63	Ballintry Guest
74	Baravelli
83	Bashashah

64p	Bayyana	
120	Beat All†	
87	Beaumont Comfort	
103	Beckon The King	
68	Beech Walk	
40	Bemyhostess	
63	Benfica	
92	Berengarius	
70	Birthday Belle	
108	Black Amber†	
80	Black Paddy	
112	Black Rock Desert†	
–	Black Thunder	
107	Blast of Storm	
104	Blend of Pace	
75	Blind Fiddler	
–	Blue Sirocco	
59	Blue Style	
–	Bold And Bossy	
79	Boley Lass	
–	Bombelaea	
–	Borromini	
–	Boston Girl	
–	Boston Green	
66	Braziliz	
67	Breffni Flyer	
–	Brief Interval	
–	Brighton Lad	
66	Brownsfield	
62?	Cairde Nua	
110	Calando†	
58?	Calico Lady†	
76p	Calladine	
–	Camera Lady	
64	Camillas Estate	
91	Canaletto	
59?	Canary Bird	
110	Capistrano Day†	
100	Carambola†	
82d	Carhue Gold	
50	Carol's Chapel	
104	Cassandra Go†	
98	Castle Quest	
93	Catherina	
67	Catonahottinroof	
67	Celestial Bold	
–	Celtic Lad	
75	Chancery	
94	Chanoud	
–	Chellslittleindian	
71	Chipperchatter	
54d	Chloanna†	
63	Christensen	
61	Ciara Flyer	
78	Ciel d'Or	
43d	Cimeterre	
–	Clanboyo	
–	Claude Greengrass	
51	Clewbay Storm	
90	Cobourg Lodge	
100+	Coliseum	
–	Collon Future	
61	Complex	
–	Correal Princess	
93	Corrientes	
78	Cotopaxi	
84	Creux Noir	
–	Crickstown Lady	
76	Criollo†	
69	Cruagh Express	
–	Crystal Blue	
105	Crystal Downs†	
–	Cuanin Tain	
114	Cupid	
122	Daliapour†	
48d	Dame En Rouge	
–	Dame Portia	
80	Dancing Sea†	
74	Dane's Lady	
78	Dangerousdanmagru	
36	Danny's Roision	
94	Danse Classique	
–	Dans Suggestion	
62d	Daring Imp	
68	Dariole	
–	Dashing Nel	
52p	Dayan	
116	Dazzling Park†	
82d	Deemar	
78	Delphi	
84	Delray	
66d	Delvin Flyer	
97	Desert Magic	
–	Distinctly Swift	
75	Dochas Mor	
63	Doire-Chrinn	
72	Do It	
–	Dolphin Royal	
90	Dolydille	
70	Donostia	
–	Dont Kiss Em	
44	Drum Lady	
70	Dunback	
75d	Dunlea	
–	Eagle Legal	
–	Early Hearing	
110	Edabiya†	
64	Edge Brook	
–	Ejder	
88	El Comendador	
87	Electrum	
–	Elegant	
–	Elegant Scene	
64	Elf Queene	
84+	El Gran Hombre	
57	Elodie Rose	
38	Elven Abbey Side	
73	Emotions High	
71	End of The Day	
121	Enrique†	
–	Erris	
92	Eternal Night	
82	Euro Shift	
90	Evanilda	
76p	Eviyrn	
111	Exeat†	
65	Exquisite Sal	
100	Fable	
86	Faddad	
75	Fadhel†	
97	Father Murphy	
95	Fear And Greed†	
56	Federal Hall	
–	Feminine Mystique	
97	Festival Hall†	
–	Fieldhouse Rose	
55	First Ashore	
64d	First Time Round	
–	Flip The Switch	
88	Floating Agenda	
74	Forest Chief	
–	Fort Shannon	
–	Foyle Way	
94	Franchetti	
–	French Quartet	
76	French Style	
–	Freya	
–	Full Circuit	
87d	Gabby Hayes	
–	Gala Guest	
–	Gallileo Strike	
95	Gaudi	
98	General Cloney	
81	Generous Charmer	
105	Genghis Khan†	
–	George Troy	
80	Gild	
79	Gino Lady	
68	Gin-U-Wine	
73	Glensaul	
89	Go For Grace	
51	Go Girl Go	
110	Golden Silca†	
68	Goodly News	
–	Gorthnacurra	
72	Gothic Theme	
83	Grand Ambition	
99	Granite	
68	Green Geit	
61	Green Magical	
75	Green Pursuit	
–	Grey Sunset	
90	Grianan Realta	
74	Groundswell	
100	Hadeb	
88	Halcyon	
70	Hammering	
54	Harlenog	
71	Hazel Lavery	
73d	Heart of The Ocean	
–	Heather Cove	
64	Helen Bach	
81	Henry Joy	
91d	Hierarchy	
109	High King†	
–	Highland Queen	
–	Highway One Eleven	
–	Hip Pocket	
95p	Hirapour	
72d	Holly's Gold	
61	Hot Bunny	
111	Hula Angel†	
70p	Icydora	
57	Ideal Pursuit	
107	Immovable Option	
–	Inch of River	
–	In Denial	
83	Individual	

85	Inourhearts
72	Institutrice
79p	Intricate Web†
73	Irina
75	Irish Lady
–	Irresistible Force
63	Island Escape
122	Island Sands†
80?	Izmir
57?	Jalouise
58	Jenny Spinner
81	Jewel In The Crown
69	Jordan's Ridge
83	Jovial Lad
–	Joy's Darling
81	Kalahari
64	Kampa Island
63	Kariyadan†
72	Kasota
62	Keltech Star
64	Kevins View
92	Khaysan
101	Kilkenny Castle
54	Killesk Queen
–	Kilpatrick Lill
60	Kimbella
–	Kindred
90	King of The Wire
80d	King's Ego
–	Kissangel
63	Kitmate
–	Knighted
82	Knockanure
–	Kristabelle
83	Lady Belzoni
28	Lady Daville
63	Lady Ellen-M
71	Lady Luck
52	Lady Ursula
–	Lake House
–	La Pipa
72	Larboreus
63	Larifaari
90	La Serina
–p	La Sila
58§	La Tache
48	Laura Aisling
60	Lawnett
54	Lee's Lodge
63	Lefty Fugerri
73	Legend Falls†
65?	Lichen
–	Life Light
58	Lightstorm
63	Little Miss Muffet
–	Little Susie-Q
84	Lookout Point
–	Lucky Bet
75d	Lucky Cat
88	Lucky Gem
61	Lucky In Love
?	Lucky Lech
103	Lucky Legend
–	Lucky Loreley
72	Macabeo
50	Magical Bridge

–	Magical Sandra
97	Maid of Killeen
117	Major Force†
76	Malakal†
–	Mangwana
–	Ma Petite Rouge
–	Maple Grove
74	Maradan
99	Marching Orders
88	Marius Petipa
46	Markellis†
75	Market Mover
57+	Marlene-D
78	Martial Eagle
65	Mary Cassatt
–	Maxime
86	McCracken
–	Me And My Girl
45	Melody's Castle
76	Message Recu
78	Midnight Coup
86	Mighty Pip
63	Mild And Breezy
50	Millbrook Dawn
96	Misniuil
44	Miss Kookaburra
–	Mister Cheer
–	Mister Dolphin
74	Mister Mims
–	Mister Pepper
99	Moiseyev
78	Molly-O
–	Montego
137	Montjeu†
104	Moon Dragon†
78	Moonis
88	Morning Breeze
113	Mother of Pearl†
94	Mrs Evans
98	Mudaa-Eb
116	Mus-If†
87	Musketeer
129	Mutafaweq†
91?	My Lass†
66	Mystic Oak
107	Mythical Girl†
105	Namid
63+	Nashoba
–	Neglected
69	Nick The Butler
–	Noble Messenger
59	Nocturnal
79	Nordic Point
69	Not A Sound
65d	Notional†
68d	Nuit Saint†
82p	Omni Cosmo Touch
–	One For The Money
58d	One O One
55	Onetwothreeoleary
53	Optional
–	Oran
99	Orange Sunset
116	Orpen†
81d	Ostarrichi
68	Outward Bound

78	Ovazione
54§	Oykel Valley
105	Oyster Catcher
–	Padamul
97	Palace Royale
–	Pampita
–	Par Dictio
58	Paris Style
67?	Passionate Pilgrim
69d	Paynestown Lad
79	Peace Upholds
102	Peach Out of Reach
–	Peruge
77	Perugino Diamond
75	Perugino Lady
76	Perugino's Malt†
–	Pewter
108	Pharmacist
–	Pidgeon Bay
–	Piercetown Lad
57	Pilgrim Star
93	Pillar Rock
67	Pinheiros Princess
93	Pink Coral
66d	Pipe Dream†
76	Pip'n Judy
90	Piranesi
82+	Playing Hours
108	Polaire
105	Port Bayou
96	Power And Panache
88	Precedence
42	Pretty Fly Guy†
–	Prime Investor
–	Princess Dream
46	Princess Kali†
91	Prince Valiant
77	Privatize
45	Proper Poser
79	Prospector John
71	Prosperous†
94	Provosky
–	Pure Gin
74	Queen of Art
92	Queen's Love
64	Question of Trust
68	Quick Date
100	Rafayda
100	Rainbows Forever
123	Ramruma†
–	Rashers Dasher
70	Rayelteen
50	Ready To Rock†
–	Red Keane
–	Red Polish
45	Regal Dancer
–	Regality†
–	Remiss
93	Remuria
87	Renvyle Rose
75	Replenish Power
74	Reserved Judgement
43	Returning
90	Rimbaud
79	Rivana
100	River Canyon

–	River Court	82	Spanish Sal	72	Umpqua Eagle
80	River Gorge	37	Sparrow's Trap	100	Union Project
45	River Hopper	103	Speed Merchant	–	Upbeat Leader
–	River Ruler	92	Spokane	74p	Urban Hymn
68?	River Tempest	58p	Sposa	113	Urban Ocean
47	Robergerie	–	Springfield Guest	–	Vadinaxa
81	Robzelda	–	Stanley Wigfield†	58	Valjean
–	Rochambelle	80	Star Trooper	76	Valleria
–	Roisin Rua	–	Steel Dendrobium	68?	Vancouver Isle†
113	Rolo Tomasi	–	Stefanova	–	Vannuccis Daughter
65	Romancia	–	Stephens Street	–	Very Easy
98	Rominten	–	St Fiacre	55	Villa Nova
76	Rooftop	–	Stokkem	–	Violet Blue
76	Rose of Tara	120	Strategic†	–	Wayfarer's Inn
106	Rosselli†	133	Stravinsky†	97	Welsh Wind
77	Royal Barathea	–	Strina	–	Weshouldhav
77	Royal Bart	–	Stylish Brief	–	Western Mariner
98	Royal Command	83	Suddenly	27	West Lake
?	Royal Partnership	81	Sugar Plum Fairy	94	What A Chocolate
109	Royal Rebel†	75	Sukeena	–	What Are Ya-Like
53	Royal Subject	98	Sunday Surprise	74	Whats The News
104	Rubies From Burma	59	Sungazer	106	White Nugget
67	Russian Comrade	59	Sunny Slope†	67	Wild Heaven
?	Ryan's Brief	108	Sunspangled†	117	Wimbledon
123	Saffron Walden†	88	Superiority	98	Wince†
71	Sagar Bay	89	Super Whizz	81	Wish List†
–	Sahara Cheetah	82	Supreme Certainty	81	With A Prayer
83	Sahara Song	72	Surprise Treat	–	Wonder Winnie
75	Sandholes	76	Tacobarry	67	Yattarna
77	San Rocco	75	Taisce	–	Yellow Knife
–	Santissima	96	Taisho	107	Yeoman's Point
104	Santovito	90	Takariya	101	Young American
92d	Sapphire Trio†	62?	Talighta	77	Zaidaan
89	Sarraaf	–	Tallarico	–	Zami
–p	Saxon Prince	103	Tarfaa	67	Zaola
101	Scottish Memories	47	Tashpro	–	Zenana
93	Seasonal Style	114	Tchaikovsky†	76	Zilio
75	Second Nature	–	Tell Nothing		
76	Sellinger's Round	69	Tenalist	**Older Horses**	
70	Senora	101	The Bomber Liston	83	Abaco
55	Sentra	57	The Boxer	–	Abbey Dome
92	Serena	77d	The Moyne Machine	–	Abbeyfeale Con
51	Serrana	–	The Street	52	Abstract View
63	Sesame Heights	88	Tianyi	80+	Abuhail
73	Set The Scene	97	Tiger Royal	–	Act of Defiance
82	Shabob	115	Tiger Shark†	63	Adradee
97	Shallow Ground	87	Tiger Talk†	–	Aerleon Pete
–p	Shandari	110	Timote†	47d	African-Pard
71d	Shannon Arch	51	Tiragon	–	Afrostar
60	Shantonagh	49	To Be Loved	–	Ah Gowan
80	Sharavogue Cookie	57	Touch of Truth	–	Aisling Beag
84	Sharp Gossip	56	Traditional	71?	Ajar
–	Shesasmartlady	–	Traffic Jammer	55	Akasian
80	Shoot The Blues	89	Tragic Lover	–	Albinella
19	Short of A Bob	73	Tramps Ball	73	Aliwaiyn
111	Show Me The Money†	98	Trebizond	39	Aljay
53	Side Winding	54	Tres Chic	65	All Antrim
–	Silent Forest	68	Tribal	–	All Charisma
88	Silverware	–	Tricky Dee	51	Allstars Rocket
–	Simply Hip	–	Tricky Tim	76	All The Colours
84	Sinndiya	–	Trim Star†	–	All The Vowels
107	Sister Bella	112	Triple Dash†	86d	Almerina†
84	Slightly Swift	67	Trojan Bridge	–	Alpine Accentor
63	Snow Petrel	66	True Life	–	Alrahaal
69	Some Steed	53d	Twilight Flatley	66	Althib
96	South of Heaven	34	Two Won Two	117	Altibr†

–	Altitude	32	Bob The Yank	–	Clodagh Valley
52	Amocachi	93	Bob What	54	Clonagam
?	Anabatic	33	Bohemian Belle	63	Clonmel Commercial
47	Annadot	–	Bolero Dancer	52+	Cloone Bridge
44?	Ann's Desire	54?	Breaking The Wave	62	Cnocadrum
–	Another Sally	–	Brief Decline	–	Cockpit Lady
–	Another Word	54	Brief Journey	57?	Cocksure
–	Antrim Coast	?	Brigade Charge	48+	Coillte An Ceoil
96	Archive Footage	–	Britannia	49+	Colins Double
54?	Arctic Weather	–	Brogue Trader	–	Colm's Rock
–	Ardeevin	84	Broken Promise	82+	Commanche Court
52	Ardlea House	–	Broken Right	–	Commin' Up
–	Argideen Vale	–	Bronica	–	Common Currency
100d	Armilina	–	Bubbly Dancer	91	Common Kris
–	Arthurian	–	Bunduff	36	Consider It Done
57	Arts Project†	118	Burden of Proof†	47	Conti
59	Ash Baloo	79	Bushman's River	–	Cool Hand Luke
71	Ashjar	70	By Charlie Allen	6	Copper Faced Jacks
38	Aspen Gem	67	Bypharbeanri	62	Cottage Lord
62	Athas Liath	–	Cabastro	–	Couldn't Say
–	Aughamore	56	Cad A Ra Leat	73	Countessmarkievicz
–	Avalon Accord	65	Calamander	54	Country Flavour
61	Avoid The Rush	–	Call Mary	47	Crazy Falcon
–	Award of Merit	–	Calm Beauty	67?	Crimson Flower
–	Axel Foley	87	Cambodian	35	Crimson Tirol
–	Azura	106	Campo Catino	55	Crown Brief
–	Babe Ruth	–	Canard Valu	72	Crown Point
–	Baby Fresh	54	Cappamore Girl	–	Cryptic Myth
–	Back For Good	–	Captain Bob	–	Cryptic Pattern
–	Back Log	104	Carhue Lass†	78	Crystal Springs
72	Back On Top	63	Carnabrae	65?	Cumas
40	Back To Bavaria	–	Castletubber Lady	–	Curragh Princess
48	Bahao	63	Catarata	–	Cyrano Lory
65	Bailiwick Frontier†	95+	Catch The Dragon	–	Dame Bay
–	Ballalainn	34	Catfoot Lane	–	Danaa Minni
85+	Balla Sola	24	Ceili Kate	100	Dance So Suite
–	Ballygowan Beauty	81	Celtic Lore	49	Dancing Clodagh
72	Ballymote	53	Celtic Minstrel	47	Dancing Venus
90	Bamford Castle	–	Celtic Serenade	104	Dane River
–	Banahoe Boy	55	Celtic Slip	53+	Dante's Battle
92	Barba Papa	77	Challenger Two	86	Daraheen Chief
33	Barnacranny	81	Chaparral Lady	–	Darbela
–	Bawn Duiske	–	Charismatic Jack	88	Darialann
71	Bayling	51	Charlton Spring	40	Dar Zoffer
–	Bb's Perk	36	Cheeky Harry	73	Dawn Project
34	Beal Na Blath	–	Chestnut Falls	138	Daylami†
–	Beaulari	–	Cheviot Indian	?	Deadly Dudley
46	Beebeep	–	Chicago Mae	83	Decisive Action†
–	Beechgrovetreasure	44	Chilling	83	Dee-One-O-One
–	Behy Bridge	72	China Tealeaf	86	Deilginis
63	Bellfan	85	Christiansted†	73	Delirious Tantrum
62	Beneficent	–	Christy Senior	55	Dellsboy
67	Benefits Galore	–	Chuck's Treasure	–	Delray Flyer
22	Berry Sharp	53	Chu Culainn	–	Derravaragh Secret
–	Besiege	85	Cincuenta	–	Desert Kingdom
113	Bianconi†	–	Cirvin	74	Diamond Strike
59d	Biddy Blackhurst	–	City Poser	23	Dicky's Rock
?	Big Tipper	–	Clanfluther	–	Digital Signal
77	Billywill	56	Clangigi	50	Diorama
55	Binneas	38	Clanlucky	–	Dip's Guest
60?	Black Pidgeon	68	Classic Mix	–	Distinctly Right
66	Bless'im	62?	Classic Note	–	Divine Dancer
48?	Blow Wind Blow	79d	Classic Referendum†	50	Donnybrook Fair
47	Blue Jazz	55	Class Society	77+	Dorans Pride
57	Bob Cullen	72	Clever Consul	–	Doso Boy
51	Bobstar Dancer	–	Clodaghs Fancy	–	Double Jig Time

1208

107 Draft of Vintage
95 Dragon Triumph†
55+ Dr Bones
122 Dream Well†
62 Dromhall Lady
74 Dromineer†
– Dual Star
– Duggan Duff
78 Dunrally Fort
? Dusky Lamp
86 Early Fin
113 Eastern Purple†
– Echo Bay
– Eileens Fame
– Electric Isle
58 Eljamil
60 Ella Come Back
– Ellenbrook
51 Eloquent Way
– Embellished
53d Emerald Project
93d En Retard
49? Enterprising
– Entitled Lady
126 Enzeli†
38 Ethbaat
65 Euphoric
– Eurozone
– Eveies Boy
66 Existential
68 Experimental
95d Eymir
– Fairy Rock
36 Fairy Secret
98 Fantastic Quest
– Faraghan
68 Fashion Project
– Fawn Prince
87 Fearsome Factor†
90 Fiddler's Rock
– Fiery Madame
– Final Reminder
? Fionnula's Rainbow
– Fishin Cabin
– Flamenco Fury
41 Flash of Speed
– Flaunt
57? Fleet Lad
37 Flower Hill Lad
– Followthe Allstars
39 Forest Princess
– Forever Relic
46 Forever Young
– Forget Us Not
48d Fort Apache
– Fountain Coin
54 Foxs River
88 Francis Bay
– Francois Laboure
61d Fraser Carey
– Freedom Dancer
113 Free To Speak†
66 Friendly Warning
65 Frisky
59 Frontliner†
57 Furnitureville

116 Gaelic Storm†
– Galkina
92 Ganaway
80 Gan Saru
81 Gates
? Gazalani
– Gentle Mossy
38 Gerrydardis
62 Gers Gold
84d Ger's Royale
82 Gift Token
– Gigi
– Girl In Pearls
– Giveaway
37 Give Her Sally
51+ Glebe Lad
– Glencar Native
– Global Appeal
71 God Forbid
90p Gold Chaser
105 Golden Fact
– Golden Gold
34 Golden Lights
105 Golden Rule
38 Golden Slane
80+ Goldman
62? Gonemoggelease
38 Good Deal
100 Gordi
68? Gorgeous Georgina
116 Gorse†
71 Gossie Madera
99 Graduated
61 Granuale
108 Grazia†
122 Great Dane†
61p Greenflag Princess
– Greenhue
? Greenstead
– Grey Ciseaux
? Grimshaw
– Guivarch
71d Gypsy Melody
114 Haami†
54 Hackler Poitin
60 Halse Copse
– Hang'em High
– Hardtimes
86p Hariymi
– Harry Welsh
75 Hartstown Girl†
79 Have Merci
– Hazarfen
68+ Heart of Armor
78 Heemanela
68+ Heist
27 Helen's Quay
– Hello Again
55 Helorhiwater
57+ Helsingor
48? Hennessy Feeds
– Herb Superb
– Hidden Ability
82+ Hill Society
51 Honeychoice

– Hope She's Lucky
87 Hopping Higgins
– Hoshelaga
– Howies Choice
– Hugo de Perro
46d Hulal
53 Hunan Scholar†
– Huntmore
– Hyde Class Lady
– Ian My Boy
52 Ichi Beau
– Ideal Plan
– If I Only Had Time
63 Iftatah
61 I Have To Go
41 Illusions Tom
62 Impulsif
? Indimaaj
58 Indinolla
72 Inga
§§ In Generosity
45 Innocent Pleasures
40 Inny Lady
124 Insatiable†
70 Irish Charm
– Irish Money
97 Irish Summit
67 Iron County Xmas
68 Irvine
77 Island Doy
? Its Time For A Win
59? Ivor Star
– Jackeen's
91 Jacks Estate
– Jadilian
83 Jay And-A
68 Jeanne d'Arc
42 Jermyn Street
– Jim Dore
68 Jimmy Swift
36 Jina
– Joancha
– Joan's Princess
43 Jodesi
47 Johann Strauss
66p John Magical
57 Joking Rebuff
95 Joleah
38 Jones Lad
– Jumbo Beauty
82 Juneson
87 Just Wondering
– Kabotie
93 Kaldan Khan
– Kamactay
? Kananaskis
64 Karakam
63 Kate Emily
– Katiyar
– Kayaliyna
18 Kay Antoinette
130 Kayf Tara†
76 Keeping The Faith
88 Kenema
40 Kenya
– Kerrier

–	Kerry Again
–	Kerry Belle
79	Khairabar
–	Kharshani
103	Khatani
91	Khatela
55	Kickham's Princess
46	Kickmyhip
–	Kid Vid
65	Kildare Chiller
–	Killucan King
57	Killultagh Breeze
68	King of Peace
67	Kiptanui
–	Knockdoo
57?	Kodabad
37	Kohoutek
100	Lady Alexander†
44	Lady Gullane
113	Lady In Waiting†
63	Lady Jemurco
–	Lady Karam
56	Lady Linzi
–	Lady Native
51	Lady's Heart†
77	Lake Millstatt†
65	Landing Craft
102	Landing Slot
–	Last Battle
107	Late Night Out†
–	Latin
44	Latterly
91	Laurentia
88	Lawz
–	Leader of The Band
–	Leafy Isle
90	Leave Me Alone
55	Leggagh Lady
59	Leixlip Belle
–	Leopard Rock
14	Lesmacadam
87	Lets Clic Together
–	Liamar
47	Libarchie
–	Liffey Ballad
51	Liffeydale
109	Lil's Boy
–	Limited Option
56	Linden's Lotto
–	Lisard River
39	Lisa's Princess
58?	Lisa's Storm
–	Lisieux Lilly
107	Lisieux Rose†
56	Lismeenan
57	Little Bella
–	Little Miss Huff
–	Little Red Bull
63	Little Sean
97d	Lizop
48	Load And Lock
113	Lochangel†
–	London Lights
49	Long Shot John
65	Loquacious
115	Lord of Men†
?	Lorella
61	Love Academy†
57	Love Heart
40	Loyal Deed
39	Ludgrove
59	Luminoso
48	Lunar Lady
–	Mabsoot
–	Madam Lightfoot
55	Maghas
79	Magical Peace
74	Magic Annemarie
63+	Magic Combination
48	Mags Hogan
69	Magua
–	Maid In Blue
–	Major Ballaby
–	Make My Day
116	Make No Mistake†
–	Malacoda
–	Malian Project
75	Maltesse
?	Manhattan Castle
74	Mantles Prince
41	Marchaway
46	Margin Call
117	Maridpour†
–	Marilia†
–	Market Legacy
84	Markskeepingfaith
–	Mary's Manna
?	Masarkal
–	Master Bounce
82	Master Cooper
–	Meet The Press
48	Megabyte
–	Mega Project
–	Melette
?	Menesiah
80	Midnight Lover
64	Mighty Term
74	Millie's Lily
64	Mill Lane Lady
–	Millmount Lady
94	Miltonfield
–	Minister's Cross
–	Mi Picasso
83	Miracle Ridge
31	Miroswaki
65	Mislead
85	Miss Emer
–	Missfortuna
35	Miss Gamble
–	Miss Information
–	Missing Nellie
68	Mission Hills
–	Miss Rich
46?	Mistress Kate
62d	Mobilia
61	Moll Hackabout
–	Moll Mac
39	Molly Coates
?	Monitor
77	Monty's Fancy
69	Moon Masquerade
61	Moon Rose
71	Morristown Dancer
55	Moscow Babe
–	Mountain Rocket
110	Moving On Up
32	Moynoe Princess
69d	Mr McKen
42	Mullawn Dancer
–	Musical Mayhem†
100	Musical Pursuit
65	Mykon Gold
52	My River
68	Mysilverriverfeale
81	Mystic Ridge†
66	My Trivet
97d	Nash House†
79+	Native Dara
–	Nazmi
54	Near Dunleer
–	Nero's Dancer
–	New Chapter
–	Nice-Token
52?	Night In Town
–	Night Scent
107	Nigrasine†
73	No Avail
–	Noble Tom
–	No Grousing
97	Nomore Mr Niceguy†
85	Nordic Isle
–	Northern Brief
–	Often's Girl
–	Ojay
–	Okay
–	Ok John†
–	Oliver's Island
64p	Ollimar
68	Omar
–	Omy Dancer
110	One Won One†
–	Opaque
–	Optional Extra
–	Ortelius
98	Osprey Ridge
–	Other Options
–	Our Valentine
–	Over You Go
93+	Pacon
–	Paddy's View
72	Palace Road
78	Paradable
52	Paris Biv
67	Pas Possible
83	Passing Beauty
65	Passing Danger
68	Patience Lost
89	Patricia's Dream
75d	Peaceful Sarah†
36d	Peace Prevails
80	Perfect Scoundrel
72	Persian Isle
32	Peru Girl
59	Petes Goodun
–	Petite Mews
–	Philly's Dream
–	Pianissimo
–	Pink Daisy

25	Piper Zero	–	Rolling Maul	–	Silver Hope
–	Pipes of Peace	–	Ronette	125	Silver Patriarch†
97	Pirro	–	Rosarium	84	Silvian Bliss
56	Play'ntothegallery	39	Rosie Nell	66	Simpany
–	Playprint	–§	Rossmill Native	76	Simply Monarch
35	Poetic Quest		Rough Magic	51	Sindabezi
65	Polenka	135	Royal Anthem†	63	Sir True Blue
60d	Ponda Rosa	80	Royal Dane	–	Slaney Glow
–	Prairie Road	–	Royal Insignia	–	Slieve Bernagh
58	Pretty Buckskin	87	Royal Midyan	32	Slightly Seedy
–	Pretty Mimosa		Royal Six	71	Slightly Sober
66	Prince de Loir	99	Royal South	25	Smart Guest
–	Prince of Erin	–	Ruano	70	Smart Project
32	Prince Robert	–	Rupert Belle	–	Smiling Away
62?	Private Peace	97	Rush Brook	41?	Smooth Technology
–	Private Placement	35	Rusty Image	–	Snobs Casino
97	Profit Alert	68	Sacrementum	59	Snow Falcon
77	Promalee	76	Saintly Thoughts	111	Social Harmony
62	Prosperous Penny	64	Sally Pledge	70	Society Blue
–	Proud Bishop	–	Sally Rod	72	Society Queen
115	Proud Native†	–	Samapour†	57?	Southern Man
65	Puppet Play†	99d	Sanaka	–	Soviet Beam
72d	Pussy Galore†	113	San Sebastian†	31	Soviet Dreamer
98	Putuna†	–	Santamani	–	Space Trucker
–	Queen of Fibres	–	Sarahs Crusader	–	Spanish Heights
72	Queen Sarabi	49	Saramacca	70d	Sparkling Harmony
–	Quicksand	101	Sarayan	–	Speed Hill
92	Quinstars	43	Sarwani	–	Spirit Dancer
96	Quintus	40	Sauganash Song	82	Spokesman
102	Quinze	85	Saving Bond	40	Spring To Mind
65	Quite Chuffed	46	Savu Sea	55?	Squaw Winter
–	Quits	70	Say Wonderful	61	Star Club
100+	Quws	–	Scary Spice	71	Star Defector
87	Rafting†	–	Schiphol	57?	Stellissima
91	Rahika Rose	–	Schust Madame	59	Sterling High
–	Rainbow Warrior	–	Scotland	59	Stillanall
85d	Rainswept	52	Scottish Song	82	Storm Fromthe East
54	Ramblers Court	70	Sea Fisher	59	Storm Gem
–	Ramike	68	Sea Leopard	–	Strawberry Beds
115	Ramooz†	–	Second Dream	–	Sully Shuffles
72	Rashay	–	Second Empire†	76	Sunless
84	Rathbawn Prince	–	Second Treasure	118	Sunshine Street†
–	Rathclarin	98	Seefinn	116	Superior Premium†
–	Rathcoffey Duchess	92	Seignorial†	74	Support Act
–	Real Guest	70+	Sentosa Star	71	Suzy Street
74	Really Chuffed	–	Shaihar	–	Sweet Cher
–	Real Tempest	62	Shamartini	54	Sweet Rocket
80	Red Robin	–	Shanes Hero	–	Swing West
100	Referendum†	79	Shanko	65	Sycamore Boy
–	Regent Style	–	Shannon Project	32	Symboli Phoenix
79	Reggae Rhythm	–	Shantarini	68	Take Five
98	Remarkable Style	62	Sharazad	61	Takimo
65	Renewed Spirit	–	Sharon Leader	44	Taleca Son†
–	Rewhso	–	Sharon's Magic	–	Tame Deer
–	Richie Rich	74d	Sharpaten	75	Tango Pasion
–	Right Job	98	Sharp Catch	–	Taoibhin
57?	Rilmount	–	Shawalan	61+	Tarakan
108	Risk Material	–	Sherco	–	Tarasi
53	Risky Whisky	66	Shereevagh	117	Tarry Flynn†
104	Risque Lady†	–	She's My Love	–§	Tasik Chini
74	Rite of Spring	100	She's Our Mare†	–	Technohead
89	River Pilot	60	She's Wonderful	115	Tedburrow†
–	River Rock	119	Shiva†	–	Ted Dugal
44	Rizzoli	43	Shoeless Joe	60?	Teknash
	Rock Hard	59	Shvera	–	Teresian Girl
–	Rockholm Boy	59	Silver Eye	–	Texas Friday

98	Thats Logic
71	Thats My Wife
48	Thats Your Opinion
111	Theatreworld†
–	The Barge
78	The Bongo Man
92	The Bower
48+	The Boy King
–	The Cincinnati Kid
68d	The Cushman
–	The Cushroad
–	The Director
–	Theladysnecklace
–	The Magistrate
–	The Realtour
–	The Seventh Sister
54?	The Subbie
84d	The Third Curate†
63	Third Agenda
58d	Three Musketeers
57	Three Rivers
86	Tifosi
86	Tigullio
74	Times O'War
–	Tinerana Law
90d	Tinker Amelia
–§	Too Easy
–	Tootsie Rose
36	Toreero†
63	Total Success
76	To Your Honour
119	Trans Island†
38	Treora
44	True Rock
81	Truscott
99§	Try For Ever
83	Tryphaena
117	Tumbleweed Ridge†
32	Turn To Stone
98	Twickenham
54	Twidledee
51	Twin Pack
110	Two-Twenty-Two†
–	Tyrone's Runner
–	Ultimate Beat
72	Undaunted
62d	Untold Story†
–	Valentine Quin
40	Valerio's Princess
68	Valley Erne
–	Vanilla Man
–	Veritable Gallery
–	Vernon
–	Very Simple
–	Via Bolero
98+	Vivo
–	Wait'n'see†
–	Wait Your Turn
–	Walls Lough
–	War Chief
60?	Watership Dance
39	Wesbest
50	Wesperada
59	Western Seas
61	What A Scene
75	What's The Verdict
–	Wherewilitall End
68	Which Is Which
114	White Heart†
59	Wicklow Way
66	Wild Zing
67	Willyelkra
69	Willyever
69	Windy Project
103	Winged Hussar
–	Winning Saint
–	Winsome Blues
–	Winters Crossing
44	Winton Lass
44	Wire Man
–	Wolver Gal
–	Wolvers Littleure
–	Wolvers Starlet
70	Wonder Will He
–	Wood Leopard
110	Wray
118	Yavana's Pace†
–	Yer Man
97	Yorba Linda
–	Yulara†
39	Yuri The Flyer
80	Zankle
86	Zelden
–	Zenning
94	Zilina
118	Zomaradah†

INDEX TO PHOTOGRAPHS

PORTRAITS & SNAPSHOTS

Horse	Age & Breeding	Copyright	Page
Adair	3 ch.c Theatrical – Amore Cielo	*John Crofts*	30
Alabaq	3 b.f Riverman – Salsabil	*John Crofts*	39
Aljabr	3 gr.c Storm Cat – Sierra Madre	*John Crofts*	48
Almushtarak	6 b.h Fairy King – Exciting	*Clare Williams*	52
Almutawakel	4 b.c. Machiavellian – Elfaslah	*John Crofts*	55
Altibr	4 ch.c Diesis – Love's Reward	*John Crofts*	58
Aristotle	2 b.c Sadler's Wells – Flamenco Wave	*Peter Mooney*	80
Arkadian Hero	4 ch.c Trempolino – Careless Kitten	*John Crofts*	83
Barathea Guest	2 b.c Barathea – Western Heights	*Clare Williams*	107
Beat All	3 b.c Dynaformer – Spirited Missus	*John Crofts*	113
Bernstein	2 b.c Storm Cat – La Affirmed	*Peter Mooney*	122
Bertolini	3 b.c Danzig – Aquilegia	*John Crofts*	124
Best of The Bests	2 ch.c Machiavellian – Sueboog	*John Crofts*	127
Bienamado	3 ch.c Bien Bien –Nakterjal	*John Crofts*	131
Blueprint	4 b.c Generous – Highbrow	*John Crofts*	142
Bold Edge	4 ch.c Beveled – Daring Ditty	*Clare Williams*	149
Borgia	4 ch.f Machiavellian – Cut Ahead	*John Crofts*	157
Brancaster	3 br.c Riverman – Aseltine's Angels	*John Crofts*	161
Cape Cross	5 b.h Green Desert – Park Appeal	*John Crofts*	183
Cape Verdi	4 b.f Caerleon – Afrique Bleu Azur	*John Crofts*	185
Cerulean Sky	3 b.f Darshaan – Solo de Lune	*John Crofts*	201
Ciro	2 ch.c Woodman –Gioconda	*Peter Mooney*	215
Craigsteel	4 b.c Suave Dancer – Applecross	*Laurie Morton*	246
Credit-A-Plenty	3 ch.f Generous – On Credit	*John Crofts*	247
Daliapour	3 b.c Sadler's Wells – Dalara	*John Crofts*	258
Dansili	3 b.c Danehill – Hasili	*John Crofts*	266
Dark Moondancer	4 b.c Anshan – Oh So Well	*John Crofts*	270
Daryaba	3 b.f Night Shift – Darata	*John Crofts*	274
Daylami	5 gr.h Doyoun – Daltawa	*John Crofts*	282
Diamond White	4 b.f Robellino –Diamond Wedding	*Clare Williams*	296
Diktat	4 br.c Warning –Arvola	*John Crofts*	302
Distant Music	2 b.c Distant View – Musicanti	*John Crofts*	309
Docksider	4 ch.c Diesis – Pump	*John Crofts*	313
Dream Well	4 b.c Sadler's Wells – Soul Dream	*John Crofts*	323
Dubai Millennium	3 b.c Seeking The Gold – Colorado Dancer	*John Crofts*	328
Ekraar	2 b.c Red Ransom – Sacahuista	*John Crofts*	340
El Condor Pasa	4 b.c Kingmambo – Saddlers Gal	*John Crofts*	345
Enzeli	4 b.c Kahyasi – Ebaziya	*Caroline Norris*	360
Etizaaz	3 b.f Diesis – Alamosa	*John Crofts*	364
Fairy Queen	3 b.f Fairy King – Dedicated Lady	*John Crofts*	372
Fantastic Light	3 b.c Rahy – Jood	*John Crofts*	377
Fasliyev	2 b.c Nureyev – Mr P'S Princess	*Peter Mooney*	386
Fath	2 b.c Danzig – Desirable	*John Crofts*	389
Field of Hope	4 ch.f Selkirk – Fracci	*John Crofts*	395
Fruits of Love	4 b.c Hansel – Vallee Secrete	*John Crofts*	422
Generous Rosi	4 b.c Generous –Come On Rosi	*John Crofts*	430
Giant's Causeway	2 ch.c Storm Cat – Mariah's Storm	*Peter Mooney*	435
Gold Academy	3 b.c Royal Academy – Soha	*Clare Williams*	442
Golden Snake	3 b.c Danzig – Dubian	*John Crofts*	448
Gorse	4 b.c Sharpo – Pervenche	*Clare Williams*	452
Gracioso	3 ch.c Nureyev – Don't Sulk	*Bertrand*	454
Halland Park Girl	2 b.f Primo Dominie – Katsina	*Clare Williams*	469
Handsome Ridge	5 ch.h Indian Ridge – Red Rose Garden	*John Crofts*	472
Hula Angel	3 b.f Woodman – Jode	*John Crofts*	496

Inkling	2 b.f Seeking The Gold – Number	*Peter Mooney*	513
Innuendo	4 b.f Caerleon – Infamy	*John Crofts*	515
Invermark	5 b.g Machiavellian – Applecross	*John Crofts*	519
Invincible Spirit	2 b.c Green Desert – Rafha	*John Crofts*	520
Island Sands	3 b.c Turtle Island – Tiavanita	*John Crofts*	524
Jim And Tonic	5 ch.g Double Bed – Jimka	*John Crofts*	538
Josr Algarhoud	3 b.c Darshaan – Pont-Aven	*John Crofts*	544
Kabool	4 b.c Groom Dancer – Sheroog	*John Crofts*	549
Kayf Tara	5 b.h Sadler's Wells – Colorspin	*John Crofts*	558
Keos	5 b.h Riverman – Konafa	*John Crofts*	561
Kier Park	2 b.c Foxhound – Merlannah	*Clare Williams*	566
Lady of Chad	2 b.f Last Tycoon – Sahara Breeze	*John Crofts*	587
Lear Spear	4 b.c Lear Fan – Golden Gorse	*John Crofts*	601
Lend A Hand	4 b.c Great Commotion – Janaat	*John Crofts*	605
Lots of Magic	3 b.c Magic Ring – Pounelta	*Clare Williams*	622
Lucido	3 b.c Royal Academy – Lady Ambassador	*John Crofts*	625
Monashee Mountain	2 b.c Danzig – Prospectors Delite	*Peter Mooney*	675
Montjeu	3 b.c Sadler's Wells – Floripedes	*Bertrand*	682
Mujahid	3 b.c Danzig – Elrafa Ah	*John Crofts*	697
Mukhalif	3 ch.c Caerleon – Potri Pe	*John Crofts*	698
Mutafaweq	3 b.c Silver Hawk – The Caretaker	*John Crofts*	706
Nanoushka	4 b.f Taufan – West Chazy	*Clare Williams*	714
Noushkey	3 b.f Polish Precedent – Top of The League	*John Crofts*	736
Nowhere To Exit	3 b.c Exit To Nowhere – Tromond	*John Crofts*	737
Oath	3 b.c Fairy King – Sheer Audacity	*Laurie Morton*	744
Pegnitz	4 b.c Lear Fan – Likely Split	*John Crofts*	771
Persian Punch	6 ch.g Persian Heights – Rum Cay	*John Crofts*	776
Peshtigo	3 b.c Kris S – Fume	*John Crofts*	778
Pipalong	3 b.f Pips Pride – Limpopo	*Alec Russell*	786
Preseli	2 b.f Caerleon – Hill of Snow	*Caroline Norris*	799
Rainbow High	4 b.c Rainbow Quest – Imaginary	*John Crofts*	823
Rambling Bear	6 ch.h Sharrood – Supreme Rose	*Clare Williams*	827
Ramruma	3 ch.f Diesis – Princess of Man	*Laurie Morton*	833
Rhapsodist	3 b.c Affirmed – Secret Rhapsody	*John Crofts*	847
Rossini	2 b.c Miswaki – Touch of Greatness	*Peter Mooney*	864
Royal Anthem	4 b.c Theatrical – In Neon	*Laurie Morton*	868
Royal Kingdom	2 b.c Fairy King – Allicance	*Peter Mooney*	872
Rudi's Pet	5 ch.g Don't Forget Me – Pink Fondant	*Alec Russell*	877
Sadian	4 b.c Shirley Heights – Rafha	*John Crofts*	887
Saffron Walden	3 b.c Sadler's Wells – Or Vision	*Peter Mooney*	890
Sagamix	4 gr.c Linamix – Saganeca	*Bertrand*	892
Sainte Marine	4 b.f Kenmare – Pont-Aven	*John Crofts*	894
Salford Express	3 ch.c Be My Guest – Summer Fashion	*John Crofts*	897
Sampower Star	3 b.c Cyrano de Bergerac – Green Supreme	*Clare Williams*	901
Sea Wave	4 b.c Sadler's Wells – Three Tails	*John Crofts*	913
Sendawar	3 b.c Priolo – Sendana	*John Crofts*	922
Shiva	4 ch.f Hector Protector – Lingerie	*Laurie Morton*	942
Sinndar	2 b.c Grand Lodge – Sinntara	*Caroline Norris*	954
Slickly	3 gr.c Linamix – Slipstream Queen	*John Crofts*	959
Slip Stream	3 b.c Irish River – Sous Entendu	*John Crofts*	961
Stanott	4 b.c Mukaddamah – Seme de Lys	*John Crofts*	977
Star of Akkar	3 b.f Distant Relative – Donna Star	*Bertrand*	978
Stravinsky	3 b.c Nureyev – Fire The Groom	*Peter Mooney*	990
Sugarfoot	5 ch.h Thatching – Norpella	*Alec Russell*	996
Suhaad	3 ch.f Unfuwain – Forest Lair	*Clare Williams*	998
Sunday Picnic	3 b.f Sunday Silence – Atoll	*John Crofts*	1001
Superior Premium	5 br.h Forzando – Devils Dirge	*Alec Russell*	1004
Teggiano	2 b.f Mujtahid – Tegwen	*John Crofts*	1029
Tipsy Creek	5 b.h Dayjur – Copper Creek	*Clare Williams*	1051
Torgau	2 b.f Zieten – Snoozy Time	*Clare Williams*	1059

Touch 'N' Fly	3 b.c Catrail – Menominee	*Laurie Morton*	1062
Trans Island	4 b.c Selkirk – Khubza	*John Crofts*	1066
Tumbleweed Ridge	6 ch.h Indian Ridge – Billie Blue	*John Crofts*	1075
Valentine Waltz	3 b.f Be My Guest – Save Me The Waltz	*John Crofts*	1088
Vicious Circle	5 b.g Lahib – Tight Spin	*John Crofts*	1095
Vision of Night	3 b.c Night Shift – Dreamawhile	*John Crofts*	1098
Wallace	3 b.c Royal Academy – Masskana	*Clare Williams*	1101
Warningford	5 b.h Warning – Barford Lady	*John Crofts*	1105
White Heart	4 b.g Green Desert – Barari	*John Crofts*	1116
Wince	3 b.f Selkirk – Flit	*Laurie Morton*	1122
Xaar	4 b.c Zafonic – Monroe	*John Crofts*	1129
Yavana's Pace	7 ch.g Accordion – Lady In Pace	*John Crofts*	1133
Zahrat Dubai	3 b.f Unfuwain – Walesiana	*John Crofts*	1139
Zomaradah	4 b.f Deploy – Jawaher	*John Crofts*	1144

RACE PHOTOGRAPHS

Race and Meeting	*Copyright*	*Page*
Arthur Guinness Railway Stakes (the Curragh)	*John Crofts*	122
Ascot Stakes (Handicap) (Royal Ascot)	*John Crofts*	483
Aston Upthorpe Yorkshire Oaks (York)	*Alec Russell*	831
Bedford Lodge Hotel Bentinck Stakes (Newmarket)	*John Crofts*	426
Bollinger Champagne Challenge Series Final Handicap (Gentleman Amateurs) (Ascot)	*John Crofts*	235
Bonusprint Stakes (Henry II) (Sandown)	*John Crofts*	76
Bradford & Bingley Rated Stakes (Handicap) (York)	*John Crofts*	994
Breckenbrough Racing Acomb Stakes (York)	*Ed Byrne*	573
Breeders' Cup Turf (Gulfstream Park)	*George Selwyn*	281
Britannia Stakes (Handicap) (Ascot)	*John Crofts*	815
Brook Street Stakes (Handicap) (Goodwood)	*Ed Byrne*	716
Budweiser International Stakes (the Curragh)	*John Crofts*	458
Budweiser Irish Derby (the Curragh)	*John Crofts*	679
Cadogan Silver Salver Handicap (York)	*Alec Russell*	286
Celebration Mile (Goodwood)	*Ed Byrne*	182
Champagne Lanson Sussex Stakes (Goodwood)	*John Crofts*	47
Champions' Gallery Challenge Stakes (Newmarket)	*Ed Byrne*	1009
Charles Heidsieck Champagne Cherry Hinton Stakes (Newmarket)	*Ed Byrne*	1058
Charles Henry Memorial Handicap (York)	*Alec Russell*	462
Charter Design Stakes (Handicap) (York)	*Ed Byrne*	1146
Chester Rated Stakes (Handicap) (Chester)	*Alec Russell*	898
Coldstream Guards Rockingham Stakes (York)	*Alec Russell*	757
Constant Security Handicap (Doncaster)	*Alec Russell*	703
Coral-Eclipse Stakes (Sandown)	*John Crofts*	231
Coral Sprint Trophy (Handicap) (York)	*Alec Russell*	432
Cork And Orrery Stakes (Royal Ascot)	*Alec Russell*	147
Coronation Stakes (Royal Ascot)	*George Selwyn*	101
Coventry Stakes (Royal Ascot)	*George Selwyn*	383
Criterium de Saint-Cloud (Saint-Cloud)	*Ed Byrne*	443
Darley July Cup (Newmarket)	*Ed Byrne*	987
Davenport Hotel Eyrefield Stakes (Leopardstown)	*Peter Mooney*	207
Dewhurst Stakes (Newmarket)	*Ed Byrne*	308
Dubai Arc Trial (Newbury)	*Ed Byrne*	376
Dubai Champion Stakes (Newmarket)	*John Crofts*	42
Dubai City of Gold Shergar Cup Classic (Goodwood)	*Alec Russell*	471
Dubai Poule d'Essai des Poulains (Longchamp)	*John Crofts*	920
Dubai Poule d'Essai des Pouliches (Longchamp)	*Bertrand*	1087
Dubai Sports Shergar Cup Seven (Goodwood)	*George Selwyn*	299
Dubai Turf Classic (Nad Al Sheba)	*Dubai World Cup*	419
Dubai World Cup (Nad Al Sheba)	*Dubai World Cup*	54

Duke of Edinburgh Stakes (Handicap) (Royal Ascot)	*John Crofts*	141
EBF Custom Kitchens Maiden Stakes (Yarmouth)	*Ed Byrne*	114
EBF Galtres Stakes (York)	*Alec Russell*	514
Ed Weetman Haulage And Storage Lincoln Trial Stakes (Handicap) (Wolverhampton)	*Alec Russell*	186
Emirates Airline Prix du Jockey Club (Chantilly)	*Ed Byrne*	678
Emirates Prix du Moulin de Longchamp (Longchamp)	*Bertrand*	921
Entenmann's Irish 1,000 Guineas (the Curragh)	*John Crofts*	495
Entenmann's Irish 2,000 Guineas (the Curragh)	*John Crofts*	889
ESAT Digifone Champion Stakes (Leopardstown)	*Ed Byrne*	280
European Breeders Fund Balaton Lodge Maiden Fillies' Stakes (Newmarket)	*Mary Pitt*	797
Faucets First For Faucets Firth of Clyde Stakes (Ayr)	*Alec Russell*	392
Flying Fillies' Stakes (Pontefract)	*Fotosport*	1103
Foster's Lager Northumberland Plate (Handicap) (Newcastle)	*Alec Russell*	379
Foster's Silver Cup Rated Stakes (Handicap) (York)	*Alec Russell*	825
Frigidaire Champagne Stakes (Doncaster)	*Alec Russell*	307
Gardner Merchant Diadem Stakes (Ascot)	*John Crofts*	148
Geoffrey Freer Stakes (Newbury)	*John Crofts*	950
GNER Park Stakes (Doncaster)	*George Selwyn*	995
Goffs £100,000 Challenge (the Curragh)	*Peter Mooney*	103
Gold Cup (Royal Ascot)	*George Selwyn*	359
Goodwood Cup (Goodwood)	*John Crofts*	556
Grand Criterium (Longchamp)	*Ed Byrne*	214
Grand Prix de Deauville (Deauville)	*John Crofts*	243
Grand Prix de Paris (Longchamp)	*John Crofts*	958
Grand Prix de Saint-Cloud (Saint-Cloud)	*John Crofts*	343
Great North Eastern Railway Doncaster Cup (Doncaster)	*Alec Russell*	380
Greene King Falmouth Stakes (Newmarket)	*John Crofts*	860
Grosvenor Casino Newcastle Sprint (Handicap) (York)	*George Selwyn*	724
Grosvenor Casinos Cup (Handicap) (Goodwood)	*Ed Byrne*	691
Grosvenor Casinos Dante Stakes (York)	*Ed Byrne*	896
H & K Commissions Bookmakers Stakes (Handicap) (Newmarket)	*Ed Byrne*	708
Hardwicke Stakes (Royal Ascot)	*Alec Russell*	420
Hennessy Cognac Blaydon Race (Nursery Handicap) (Newcastle)	*Alec Russell*	571
Hong Kong Jockey Club Trophy (Handicap) (Sandown)	*W. Everitt*	690
Hong Kong Mile (Sha Tin)	*George Selwyn*	312
Hong Kong Vase (Sha Tin)	*George Selwyn*	156
Hopeful Stakes (Newmarket)	*John Crofts*	82
Hungerford Stakes (Newbury)	*Ed Byrne*	604
Jefferson Smurfit Memorial Irish St Leger (the Curragh)	*Peter Mooney*	557
Jersey Stakes (Royal Ascot)	*John Crofts*	621
Jockey Club of Kenya Molecomb Stakes (Goodwood)	*Ed Byrne*	670
Joe Jennings Bookmakers Stakes (Handicap) (Newmarket)	*Ed Byrne*	252
Joel Stakes (Newmarket)	*John Crofts*	509
John Charcol Mortgage Advisers Stakes (Heron) (Kempton)	*Ed Byrne*	551
John Smith's Cup (Handicap) (York)	*Alec Russell*	26
John Smith's Extra Smooth Chipchase Stakes (Newcastle)	*Alec Russell*	470
Joy UK Conditions Stakes (Doncaster)	*Alec Russell*	1047
JRA Nakayama Rous Stakes (Newmarket)	*John Crofts*	895
Juddmonte International Stakes (York)	*Ed Byrne*	866
Juddmonte Lockinge Stakes (Newbury)	*Ed Byrne*	407
Kildangan Stud Irish Oaks (the Curragh)	*Caroline Norris*	830
King George Grosvenor Casinos Stakes (Goodwood)	*Ed Byrne*	876
King George V Stakes (Handicap) (Royal Ascot)	*John Crofts*	350
King George VI And Queen Elizabeth Diamond Stakes (Ascot)	*Ed Byrne*	278
King's Stand Stakes (Royal Ascot)	*John Crofts*	671
Kingston Rated Stakes (Handicap) (Sandown)	*Ed Byrne*	166
Ladbroke (Ayr) Gold Cup (Handicap) (Ayr)	*Alec Russell*	456
Ladbroke (Ayr) Silver Cup (Handicap) (Ayr)	*Alec Russell*	463

Title	Credit	Page
Ladbroke Bunbury Cup (Handicap) (Newmarket)	*Ed Byrne*	456
Ladbrokes Handicap (Newmarket)	*George Selwyn*	775
Ladbrokes Spring Cup (Handicap) (Newbury)	*John Crofts*	152
Letheby & Christopher Old Newton Cup (Handicap) (Haydock)	*Alec Russell*	197
Mail On Sunday Millennium Mile Final (Handicap) (Ascot)	*John Crofts*	511
Marchpole Cup (Handicap) (Goodwood)	*John Crofts*	753
Marriott Hotels Goodwood Stakes (Handicap) (Goodwood)	*Ed Byrne*	484
McArthurglen Designer Outlet City of York Stakes (York)	*John Crofts*	369
Meon Valley Stud Fillies' Mile (Ascot)	*Ed Byrne*	1027
Mercedes Benz Grosser Preis von Baden (Baden-Baden)	*Frank Nolting*	1045
Merewood Homes Yorkshire Cup (York)	*John Crofts*	212
Minstrel Stakes (the Curragh)	*John Crofts*	828
Mitsubishi Shogun Winter Derby (Lingfield)	*W. Everitt*	1006
Moorestyle Convivial Maiden Stakes (York)	*Alec Russell*	388
Motability Rated Stakes (Handicap) (York)	*John Crofts*	46
Moyglare Stud Stakes (the Curragh)	*Caroline Norris*	798
Norfolk Stakes (Royal Ascot)	*Alec Russell*	1104
Northern Rock Gosforth Park Cup (Handicap) (Newcastle)	*Alec Russell*	875
ntl Two-Year-Old Trophy (Redcar)	*Alec Russell*	563
Owen Brown Rockfel Stakes (Newmarket)	*John Crofts*	591
Payne And Gunter Lancashire Oaks (Haydock)	*Alec Russell*	735
Persimmon Homes Nunthorpe Stakes (York)	*Ed Byrne*	988
Petros Rose of Lancaster Stakes (Haydock)	*Alec Russell*	460
Peugeot Gordon Stakes (Goodwood)	*Ed Byrne*	230
Peugeot Lowther Stakes (York)	*John Crofts*	535
Polypipe plc Flying Childers Stakes (Doncaster)	*George Selwyn*	693
Pontefract Apprentice Series (Round 4) Classified Stakes (Pontefract)	*Fotosport*	734
Porcelanosa Sprint Stakes (Sandown)	*John Crofts*	239
Premio Presidente della Repubblica (Rome)	*Perrucci*	199
Premio Vittorio di Capua (Milan)	*Perrucci*	696
Prince of Wales's Stakes (Royal Ascot)	*Alec Russell*	600
Princess Margaret Stakes (Ascot)	*Ed Byrne*	895
Princess of Wales's Greene King Stakes (Newmarket)	*Ed Byrne*	245
Princess Royal Willmott Dixon Stakes (Ascot)	*Ed Byrne*	947
Prix de Blaison (Longchamp)	*Ed Byrne*	330
Prix de Diane Hermes (Chantilly)	*John Crofts*	272
Prix de l'Abbaye de Longchamp Majestic Barriere (Longchamp)	*John Crofts*	35
Prix de la Foret (Longchamp)	*Bertrand*	394
Prix de l'Arc de Triomphe Lucien Barriere (Longchamp)	*Bertrand*	681
Prix de la Salamandre (Longchamp)	*Ed Byrne*	434
Prix de l'Opera Hotel du Lac Barriere (Longchamp)	*John Crofts*	295
Prix de Royallieu Hotel du Golf Barriere (Longchamp)	*Ed Byrne*	371
Prix d'Ispahan (Longchamp)	*Bertrand*	249
Prix Dollar "le Saint Denac" Barriere (Longchamp)	*John Crofts*	981
Prix du Bois (Chantilly)	*John Crofts*	686
Prix du Cadran Casino Croisette Barriere (Longchamp)	*Bertrand*	1018
Prix du Haras de Fresnay-le-Buffard Jacques le Marois (Deauville)	*John Crofts*	326
Prix du Muguet (Saint-Cloud)	*John Crofts*	444
Prix du Palais-Royal (Longchamp)	*Bertrand*	883
Prix du Rond-Point Grand Hotel Barriere (Longchamp)	*Bertrand*	1065
Prix Ganay (Longchamp)	*Bertrand*	269
Prix Kergorlay (Deauville)	*Bertrand*	557
Prix Lupin (Longchamp)	*Ed Byrne*	453
Prix Marcel Boussac Royal Barriere (Longchamp)	*Ed Byrne*	586
Prix Maurice de Gheest (Deauville)	*Bertrand*	300
Prix Morny (Deauville)	*Bertrand*	384
Prix Robert Papin (Maisons-Laffitte)	*Bertrand*	863
Prix Royal-Oak (Longchamp)	*Bertrand*	63
Prix Saint-Alary (Longchamp)	*Bertrand*	201

Prix Vermeille Normandy Barriere (Longchamp)	*John Crofts*	273
Queen Alexandra Stakes (Royal Ascot)	*Alec Russell*	904
Queen Anne Stakes (Royal Ascot)	*George Selwyn*	182
Queen Elizabeth II Stakes (Ascot)	*John Crofts*	327
Queen Mary Stakes (Royal Ascot)	*Alec Russell*	940
Queen Mother's Cup (Ladies) Handicap (York)	*Alec Russell*	404
Queen's Own Yorkshire Dragoons Conditions Stakes (Doncaster)	*Alec Russell*	1063
Queen's Vase (Royal Ascot)	*John Crofts*	355
Racing Post Trophy (Doncaster)	*John Crofts*	79
Reed Printing Beeswing Stakes (Newcastle)	*Alec Russell*	543
Ribblesdale Stakes (Royal Ascot)	*John Crofts*	371
Richmond Stakes (Goodwood)	*John Crofts*	97
Ritz Club Stakes (Handicap) (Ascot)	*John Crofts*	1094
Rothmans Royals Park Hill Stakes (Doncaster)	*John Crofts*	670
Rothmans Royals St Leger Stakes (Doncaster)	*George Selwyn*	705
Royal Hunt Cup (Handicap) (Royal Ascot)	*Caroline Norris*	944
Sagitta 1000 Guineas Stakes (Newmarket)	*Ed Byrne*	1121
Sagitta 2000 Guineas Stakes (Newmarket)	*John Crofts*	523
Saratoga Breeders' Cup Handicap (Saratoga)	*International Racing Bureau*	880
Saudi Arabian Airlines Middle Park Stakes (Newmarket)	*John Crofts*	804
Scarbrough Stakes (Doncaster)	*Alec Russell*	401
Scottish Equitable Gimcrack Stakes (York)	*Ed Byrne*	699
Serpentine Gallery Royal Lodge Stakes (Ascot)	*John Crofts*	871
Shadwell Stud Cheshire Oaks (Chester)	*Alec Russell*	1086
Shadwell Stud Cheveley Park Stakes (Newmarket)	*Ed Byrne*	914
Somerville Tattersall Stakes (Newmarket)	*John Crofts*	908
Stakis Casinos Great Voltigeur Stakes (York)	*John Crofts*	375
Stanley Leisure Sprint Cup (Haydock)	*Alec Russell*	301
Stanley Racing Summer Stakes (York)	*Alec Russell*	503
Stillorgan Park Hotel Flying Five (Leopardstown)	*Ed Byrne*	1026
St James's Palace Stakes (Royal Ascot)	*George Selwyn*	920
£200000 St Leger Yearling Stakes (Doncaster)	*John Crofts*	935
Strensall Stakes (York)	*Alec Russell*	441
Strutt & Parker Maiden Stakes (Newmarket)	*John Crofts*	820
Sun Life of Canada Garrowby Rated Stakes (Handicap) (York)	*Alec Russell*	925
Tattersalls Breeders Stakes (the Curragh)	*Peter Mooney*	468
Tattersalls Gold Cup (the Curragh)	*John Crofts*	941
£300000 Tattersalls Houghton Sales Stakes (Newmarket)	*John Crofts*	506
Tattersalls Musidora Stakes (York)	*John Crofts*	1138
Theo Fennell Glorious Rated Stakes (Handicap) (Goodwood)	*John Crofts*	265
Timeform Futurity (Pontefract)	*Timeform*	1118
Timeform Sprint Rated Stakes (Handicap) (Doncaster)	*Alec Russell*	424
TNT International Aviation July Stakes (Newmarket)	*Ed Byrne*	217
Tom McGee Autumn Stakes (Ascot)	*John Crofts*	417
Tote Bookmakers Silver Tankard Stakes (Pontefract)	*Alec Russell*	476
Tote Cambridgeshire (Handicap) (Newmarket)	*Lesley Sampson*	938
Tote Cesarewitch (Handicap) (Newmarket)	*Ed Byrne*	1056
Tote Chester Cup (Handicap) (Chester)	*Alec Russell*	822
Tote Credit Club Silver Bowl (Handicap) (Haydock)	*Alec Russell*	275
Tote Ebor (Handicap) (York)	*George Selwyn*	1093
Tote Gold Trophy Stakes (Handicap) (Goodwood)	*John Crofts*	647
Tote International Stakes (Handicap) (Ascot)	*W. Everitt*	883
Tote Scoop6 November Stakes (Handicap) (Doncaster)	*Alec Russell*	403
Tote Trifecta Portland (Handicap) (Doncaster)	*George Selwyn*	88
Tripleprint Stakes (Greenham) (Newbury)	*Ed Byrne*	356
UCB Films Cumberland Plate (Handicap) (Carlisle)	*Mary Pitt*	482
Victor Chandler European Free Handicap (Newmarket)	*John Crofts*	124
Victor Chandler September Stakes (Epsom)	*Ed Byrne*	1132
Vodafone Coronation Cup (Epsom)	*John Crofts*	277
Vodafone 'Dash' Rated Stakes (Handicap) (Epsom)	*John Crofts*	1060

Vodafone Derby Stakes (Epsom)	*Ed Byrne*	740
Vodafone Derby Stakes (Epsom)	*Alec Russell*	742
Vodafone Handicap (Epsom)	*John Crofts*	677
Vodafone Horris Hill Stakes (Newbury)	*Ed Byrne*	1081
Vodafone Nassau Stakes (Goodwood)	*Ed Byrne*	1138
Vodafone Network Stakes (Handicap) (Epsom)	*John Crofts*	27
Vodafone Oaks (Epsom)	*John Crofts*	829
Vodafone Stewards' Cup (Handicap) (Goodwood)	*John Crofts*	474
Volvo Contracts Globetrotter Stakes (Handicap) (Goodwood)	*John Crofts*	95
Weatherbys Insurance Lonsdale Stakes (York)	*John Crofts*	196
Weatherbys Ireland Greenlands Stakes (the Curragh)	*Peter Mooney*	335
William Hill Great St Wilfrid Handicap (Ripon)	*Alec Russell*	785
William Hill Mile (Handicap) (Goodwood)	*John Crofts*	617
William Hill Stakes (Handicap) (York)	*Ed Byrne*	1011
William Hill Trophy (York)	*Alec Russell*	773
Willmott Dixon Cornwallis Stakes (Ascot)	*Ed Byrne*	565
Winter Hill Stakes (Windsor)	*Ed Byrne*	1143
Wokingham Stakes (Handicap) (Royal Ascot)	*Alec Russell*	287
Worthington Lincoln (Handicap) (Doncaster)	*Alec Russell*	850

Standing at Whitsbury Manor Stud

COMPTON PLACE

ch 1994 by INDIAN RIDGE - NOSEY by Nebbiolo

Champion European 3yo Sprinter

Rated 125 in Racehorses of 1997

80 mares tested in foal in 1999

First crop Foals 2000

Fee: £3,500 October 1st

C.J. Harper, **Whitsbury Manor Stud**, Fordingbridge, SP6 3QP
Telephone: 01725 - 518254 or 518283. Fax: 01725 - 518503

Enquiries to:
LONDON THOROUGHBRED SERVICES LTD.,
Biddlesgate Farm, Nr Cranborne, Dorset BH21 5RS.
Telephone: 01725 - 517711. Fax: 01725 - 517833.
email: lts@lts-uk.com   Website: www.lts-uk.com

LTS

Standing at Woodland Stud

INCHINOR

chesnut 1990 by AHONOORA - INCHMURRIN by Lomond

HIGHLY SUCCESSFUL YOUNG SIRE

of Multiple **SW GOLDEN SILCA**
Mill Reef Stakes **Gr.2,** 2nd Irish 1000 Guineas **Gr.1**,
Coronation S. **Gr.1**, 3rd Prix Morny **Gr.1**

as well as 1999 two year old
Group Winners UMISTIM & PALANCA

Fee: £6,000 October 1st

Standing at Littleton Stud

KIRKWALL

chesnut 1994 by SELKIRK - KAMKOVA by Northern Dancer

Winner of 5 Group Races in France and USA
21 Starts at 2, 3, 4 and 5 years - His 8 wins include:
Keeneland Turf Mile Stakes, **Gr.2,** Keeneland, 8f **(turf)**
Prix Eugene Adam, **Gr.2,** Saint-Cloud, 10f, (picture above)
Prix de Guiche, **Gr.3,** Longchamp, 9f
Tanforan Handicap, **Gr.3,** Bay Meadows, 8.5f **(turf)**
Bay Meadows Handicap, **Gr.3,** Bay Meadows, 9f **(turf)**
Prix Montenica, **LR,** Saint-Cloud, 8f
3rd Prix Jean Prat, **Gr.1**, Chantilly, 9f
El Rincon Handicap, **Gr.2,** Santa Anita, 9f **(turf)**

Fee: £3,000 October 1st

Standing at Littleton Stud, Winchester, Hants. S022 6QX.
Telephone: 01962 - 880210. Fax: 01962 - 882290.
Enquiries to:
LONDON THOROUGHBRED SERVICES LTD.,
Biddlesgate Farm, Nr Cranborne, Dorset BH21 5RS.
Telephone: 01725 - 517711. Fax: 01725 - 517833.
email: lts@lts-uk.com   Website: www.lts-uk.com

LTS

Standing at Plantation Stud

PURSUIT OF LOVE

bay 1989 by GROOM DANCER - DANCE QUEST by Green Dancer

Champion European 3yo Sprinter

CHAMPION BRITISH FIRST SEASON SIRE

**Sire of Group 1 performers in his first 2 crops inc.
unbeaten Gr.1 winner CATCHASCATCHAN**

CHAMPION BRITISH 2yo SIRE in 1999
(by Individual Winners)

Fee: £5,000 October 1st

Leslie Harrison, Plantation Stud, Exning, Newmarket, Suffolk CB8 7LJ.
Telephone: 01638 - 577341. Fax: 01638 - 578474.
email: plantation.stud@dial.pipex.com

Enquiries to:
LONDON THOROUGHBRED SERVICES LTD.,
Biddlesgate Farm, Nr Cranborne, Dorset BH21 5RS.
Telephone: 01725 - 517711. Fax: 01725 - 517833.
email: lts@lts-uk.com   Website: www.lts-uk.com

LTS

Standing at Littleton Stud

ROBELLINO

bay 1979 by ROBERTO - ISOBELLINE by Pronto
Dual Group Winner, broke course record at Ascot at 2

Proven Sire of Classic Winners

CLASSIC PARK Airlie/Coolmore Irish 1000 Gns **Gr.1**

ROBERTICO German Derby **Gr.1** in 1998

MISTER BAILEYS 2000 Gns **Gr.1**

Fee: £6,000 October 1st

Standing at Littleton Stud, Winchester, Hants. S022 6QX.
Telephone: 01962 - 880210. Fax: 01962 - 882290.
Enquiries to:
LONDON THOROUGHBRED SERVICES LTD.,
Biddlesgate Farm, Nr Cranborne, Dorset BH21 5RS.
Telephone: 01725 - 517711. Fax: 01725 - 517833.
email: lts@lts-uk.com   Website: www.lts-uk.com

LTS

SELKIRK

chesnut 1988 by SHARPEN UP - ANNIE EDGE by Nebbiolo

Champion European Miler 1991 and 1992

A Leading European Sire

FIELD OF HOPE	1st Prix de la Foret **Gr.1** in 1999
SQUEAK	1st Beverly Hills Handicap **Gr.1**
	1st Matriarch Stakes **Gr.1** in 1999
WINCE	1st 1000 Guineas **Gr.1** in 1999
COUNTRY GARDEN	1st Honeymoon Handicap **Gr.2**
KIRKWALL	1st Prix Eugene Adam **Gr.2, 1st** Keeneland Turf Mile **Gr.2,**
	1st Prix de Guiche **Gr.3, 1st** Bay Meadows Handicap **Gr.3**
TRANS ISLAND	1st Prix du Rond Point **Gr.2**
HARBOUR ISLAND	1st Prix de Cabourg **Gr.3**
HIDDEN MEADOW	1st Prix du Palais-Royal **Gr.3**
ORFORD NESS	1st Prix de Sandringham **Gr.3**

Fee: £30,000 October 1st

Kirsten Rausing, Lanwades Stud, Moulton, Newmarket CB8 8QS.
Telephone: 01638 - 750222. Fax: 01638 - 751186.

Enquiries to:
LONDON THOROUGHBRED SERVICES LTD.,
Biddlesgate Farm, Nr Cranborne, Dorset BH21 5RS.
Telephone: 01725 - 517711. Fax: 01725 - 517833.
email: lts@lts-uk.com   Website: www.lts-uk.com

LTS

Standing at Plantation Stud

SLIP ANCHOR

bay 1982 by SHIRLEY HEIGHTS - SAYONARA by Birkhahn

Champion European 3-year-old colt in 1985

Sire of the winners of over £6.1 million

Champion British Based Sire in 1992

Sire of 22 GW/SWs including:
USER FRIENDLY - POSIDONAS - SLICIOUS
STOWAWAY - THIRD WATCH - THREE CHEERS

Fee: £6,000 October 1st

Leslie Harrison, Plantation Stud, Exning, Newmarket, CB8 7LJ.
Telephone: 01638 - 577341. Fax: 01638 - 578474.
email: plantation.stud@dial.pipex.com

Enquiries to:
LONDON THOROUGHBRED SERVICES LTD.,
Biddlesgate Farm, Nr Cranborne, Dorset BH21 5RS.
Telephone: 01725 - 517711. Fax: 01725 - 517833.
email: lts@lts-uk.com   Website: www.lts-uk.com

LTS

AGE, WEIGHT & DISTANCE TABLE
Timeform's scale of weight-for-age for the flat

Dist	Age	July 1-16	July 17-31	Aug 1-16	Aug 17-31	Sept 1-16	Sept 17-30	Oct 1-16	Oct 17-31	Nov 1-16	Nov 17-30	Dec 1-16	Dec 17-31
5f	4	10–0	10–0	10–0	10–0	10–0	10–0	10–0	10–0	10–0	10–0	10–0	10–0
	3	9–11	9–12	9–12	9–12	9–13	9–13	9–13	9–13	10–0	10–0	10–0	10–0
	2	8–8	8–9	8–10	8–11	8–12	8–13	9–0	9–1	9–2	9–2	9–3	9–4
6f	4	10–0	10–0	10–0	10–0	10–0	10–0	10–0	10–0	10–0	10–0	10–0	10–0
	3	9–10	9–10	9–11	9–11	9–12	9–12	9–12	9–13	9–13	9–13	9–13	10–0
	2	8–5	8–6	8–7	8–8	8–9	8–10	8–11	8–12	8–13	9–0	9–1	9–2
7f	4	10–0	10–0	10–0	10–0	10–0	10–0	10–0	10–0	10–0	10–0	10–0	10–0
	3	9–9	9–9	9–10	9–10	9–11	9–11	9–11	9–12	9–12	9–12	9–13	9–13
	2	8–2	8–3	8–4	8–5	8–6	8–7	8–9	8–10	8–11	8–12	8–13	9–0
1m	4	10–0	10–0	10–0	10–0	10–0	10–0	10–0	10–0	10–0	10–0	10–0	10–0
	3	9–7	9–8	9–8	9–9	9–9	9–10	9–10	9–10	9–11	9–12	9–13	9–13
	2			8–2	8–3	8–4	8–5	8–6	8–7	8–8	8–9	8–10	8–11
9f	4	10–0	10–0	10–0	10–0	10–0	10–0	10–0	10–0	10–0	10–0	10–0	10–0
	3	9–6	9–7	9–7	9–8	9–8	9–9	9–9	9–10	9–10	9–11	9–11	9–12
	2					8–1	8–3	8–4	8–5	8–6	8–7	8–8	8–9
1¼m	4	10–0	10–0	10–0	10–0	10–0	10–0	10–0	10–0	10–0	10–0	10–0	10–0
	3	9–5	9–5	9–6	9–7	9–7	9–8	9–8	9–9	9–9	9–10	9–10	9–11
	2					8–0		8–1	8–2	8–4	8–5	8–6	8–7
11f	4	10–0	10–0	10–0	10–0	10–0	10–0	10–0	10–0	10–0	10–0	10–0	10–0
	3	9–3	9–4	9–5	9–5	9–6	9–7	9–7	9–8	9–8	9–9	9–9	9–10
1½m	4	10–0	10–0	10–0	10–0	10–0	10–0	10–0	10–0	10–0	10–0	10–0	10–0
	3	9–2	9–2	9–3	9–4	9–5	9–5	9–6	9–7	9–7	9–8	9–9	9–9
13f	4	9–13	9–13	10–0	10–0	10–0	10–0	10–0	10–0	10–0	10–0	10–0	10–0
	3	9–0	9–1	9–2	9–3	9–4	9–4	9–5	9–6	9–6	9–7	9–8	9–8
1¾m	4	9–13	9–13	9–13	10–0	10–0	10–0	10–0	10–0	10–0	10–0	10–0	10–0
	3	8–13	9–0	9–1	9–2	9–3	9–3	9–4	9–5	9–5	9–6	9–7	9–7
15f	4	9–12	9–13	9–13	9–13	9–13	10–0	10–0	10–0	10–0	10–0	10–0	10–0
	3	8–12	8–13	9–0	9–1	9–1	9–2	9–3	9–4	9–4	9–5	9–6	9–6
2m	4	9–12	9–12	9–13	9–13	9–13	9–13	10–0	10–0	10–0	10–0	10–0	10–0
	3	8–10	8–11	8–12	8–13	9–0	9–1	9–2	9–3	9–3	9–4	9–5	9–5
2¼m	4	9–11	9–12	9–12	9–12	9–13	9–13	9–13	9–13	10–0	10–0	10–0	10–0
	3	8–8	8–9	8–10	8–11	8–12	8–13	9–0	9–1	9–2	9–2	9–3	9–4
2½m	4	9–10	9–11	9–11	9–12	9–12	9–12	9–13	9–13	9–13	9–13	10–0	10–0
	3	8–6	8–7	8–8	8–9	8–10	8–11	8–12	8–13	9–0	9–1	9–2	9–3

For 5-y-o's and older, use 10-0 in all cases.
Race distances in the above tables are shown only at 1 furlong intervals.
For races over odd distances, the nearest distance shown in the table should be used:
thus for races of 1m to 1m 109 yards, use the table weights for 1m;
for 1m 110 yards to 1m 219 yards use the 9f table

**The age, weight and distance table covering January to June
appears on the end paper at the front of the book**